5 cont.	目 109	矛 110	矢 111	石 112	示 113	礻 (113)	礻 [113]	禸 114	禾 115	穴 116	(116)	(116)
立 117	立 (117)	立 (117)	罒 [122]	艮 [138]	衤 [145]	**6**	竹 118	⺮ (118)	米 119	糸 120	缶 121	网 122
罒 [122]	羊 123	⺶ (123)	⺷ (123)	羽 124	羽 (124)	老 125	耂 [125]	而 126	耒 127	耒 (127)	耳 128	耳 (128)
聿 129	⺻ (129)	肉 130	肉 (130)	月 [130]	月 [130]	臣 131	自 132	至 133	臼 134	舌 135	舛 136	舟 137
舟 (137)	艮 138	艮 [138]	色 139	艸 140	艹 [140]	艹 [140]	虍 141	虫 142	血 143	血 (143)	行 144	衣 145
衤 [145]	西 146	覀 (146)	覀 (146)	豕 [152]	𧾷 [157]	**7**	臣 [131]	舛 [136]	見 147	角 148	言 149	谷 150
豆 151	豆 (151)	豕 152	豕 [152]	豸 153	貝 154	赤 155	走 156	走 (156)	足 157	𧾷 (157)	身 158	車 159
辛 160	辛 (160)	辛 (160)	辰 161	辰 (161)	辵 162	辶 [162]	辶 [162]	邑 163	阝 [163]	酉 164	釆 165	里 166
長 [168]	麦 [199]	**8**	金 167	釒 (167)	長 168	镸 [168]	門 169	阜 170	阝 [170]	隶 171	隹 172	雨 173
⻗ (173)	青 174	青 (174)	非 175	食 [184]	斉 [210]	**9**	面 176	革 177	韋 178	韭 179		
音 180	音 (180)	頁 181	風 182	風 (182)	飛 183	食 184	食 (184)	飠 (184)	食 [184]	首 185		
香 186	**10**	韋 [178]	馬 187	骨 188	高 189	髙 [189]	髟 190	鬥 191	鬯 192	鬲 193		
鬼 194	鬼 (194)	竜 [212]	竜 [212]	**11**	髙 [189]	魚 195	鳥 196	鹵 197	鹿 198	鹿 (198)		
麥 199	麦 (199)	麦 [199]	麻 200	麻 (200)	麻 (200)	黄 [201]	黒 [203]	亀 [213]	**12**	黄 201		
黃 [201]	黍 202	黑 203	黒 [203]	黹 204	黽 [205]	鼎 [206]	歯 [211]	**13**	黽 205	鼎 206		
鼓 207	鼓 [207]	鼠 208	鼠 (208)		**14**	鼓 [207]	鼻 209	鼻 (209)	齊 210	斉 [210]		
15	齒 211	歯 [211]	**16/17**	龍 212	竜 [212]	竜 [212]	龜 213	亀 [213]	龜 [213]	龠 214		

THE 12 STEPS

1. All
2. Lone
3. Enclosure
4. Left
5. Right
6. Top
7. Bottom
8. NW
9. NE
10. SE
11. SW
12. High

SEE PAGE 1 FOR EXPLANATORY NOTE

The Modern Reader's Japanese-English Character Dictionary

NOTE CONCERNING CHART INSIDE FRONT COVER. The use of the Radical Chart is explained in the first four appendices. The chart shows all 214 historic radicals arranged by stroke-count, together with their numbers and variants. Here is a key to the chart's make-up: *Large numeral*=the stroke-count of the radicals that follow it. *Small numeral*=the number of the radical. Small numerals having neither parentheses nor brackets indicate the standard forms of the 214 parent radicals. *Small numeral in parentheses*=this radical is a variant form having the same stroke-count as its parent. *Small numeral in brackets*=this radical is a variant form having a different stroke-count from its parent (appearing twice in the chart, once following its parent and once under its correct stroke-count) or a second entry of a radical that seems to have more strokes than traditionally counted.

See Appendix 13 for information as to the many possible positions in which a given radical may be used. The tables given there quickly show whether a given element of a character could be a radical in the position in which it occurs.

"The 12 Steps" inset has been added for ready reference. It gives the key words to the all-important Radical Priority System, explained in Appendix 3.

最新漢英辞典

The Modern Reader's

JAPANESE-ENGLISH CHARACTER DICTIONARY

SECOND REVISED EDITION

by ANDREW NATHANIEL NELSON, PH.D.

CHARLES E. TUTTLE COMPANY : PUBLISHERS

Rutland, Vermont

Tokyo, Japan

Published by the Charles E. Tuttle Co., Inc.
of Rutland, Vermont & Tokyo, Japan
with editorial offices at
Suido 1-chome, 2–6, Bunkyo-ku, Tokyo

LCC Card No. 61–11973
ISBN 0–8048–0408–7
ISBN 4–8053–0529–0 (Japan)

First edition, 1962
First revised edition, 1966
Second revised edition, 1974
Thirty-fifth printing, 1992

Printed in Japan

To my son

Richard Andrew Nelson, M.D.

who as a busy surgeon and against great odds
passed the Japanese National Medical Examinations
given in both oral and written Japanese
thus demonstrating that an American
can master the language

TABLE OF CONTENTS

APPENDICES

END-PAPER CHARTS

FOREWORD

The need for a new Japanese character dictionary is very evident. The language has undergone phenomenal changes since the close of World War II. In 1946 the Japanese Government issued a list of 1,850 "Current Characters" (*Tōyō Kanji*) with the recommendation that publishers and writers confine themselves to these characters in an endeavor to simplify the written language. This was an excellent move, but it multiplies the task of the lexicographer: both the old and the new forms of both the characters and their many compounds must be included, as prewar literature will always remain. Furthermore, the simplification of the writing of many of these Tōyō Kanji has resulted in the actual disappearance of their radicals, those important elements by which they have been arranged in character dictionaries. This calls for an improvement on the traditional radical system in order to provide berths for such characters and, at the same time, make it possible to locate all characters quickly whether their traditional radicals have disappeared or not. Another fact pointing up the need for a new character dictionary is the virtual ending of the former custom of indicating the pronunciation of characters and compounds by the use of the *furigana*, the small syllabary notation along the side of the text.

The present dictionary is both conservative and progressive. It is conservative in preserving the time-honored radicals for arranging the characters. One possible alternative would have been to arrange them by stroke-count; this system has been frequently adopted, particularly since the losing of the radicals, but lacking an accepted order for arranging characters of the same count, it always proves cumbersome and time consuming. The only other alternative would have been to invent an entirely new system; this too has been tried on occasions, with varying degrees of success, but such a system is likely to be even more complicated than that of the traditional radicals, which many students of Japanese have already learned, and to require much additional study, which could be given more profitably to the characters themselves.

The dictionary is also progressive in that it arranges the characters under the traditional radicals in such a way as to make a logical place for lost-radical characters and at the same time to make practically automatic the heretofore difficult task of determining the radical of a given character, thus saving hours of time for the modern reader of the language. This helpful feature, explained in detail in the appendices, carries to a logical conclusion a practice which Rose-Innes adopted to a limited extent in his much-used dictionary.

Students already familiar with characters and radicals may proceed to use the dictionary immediately, as the revision of the traditional radical system results in only about 12 percent of the characters being listed out of their traditional places. Moreover, in each such case a cross-reference has been inserted in the traditional place. And if the user will keep the following rule in mind when deciding between several possible radicals for a given character, in the great majority of cases he will find himself arriving immediately at the main entry of the character without needing the cross references: *Take a* LEFT *radical in preference to a* RIGHT; *take a* TOP *radical in preference to a* BOTTOM.

A study of Appendices 1 to 3 will acquaint the user with the Radical Priority System on which this dictionary is based and, even in the case of the experienced student, will materially speed up the process of locating a character and its compounds. Beginners are urged to read the following preliminary pages and the first six appendices in order to make most efficient use of the dictionary.

The dictionary presents 4,775 characters and 671 variants for a total of 5,446 numbered entries, in addition to many unnumbered insertions of cross references at places where certain characters might be mistakenly looked for. Listed under the main character entries are approximately 5,500 *on* or Chinese readings (these having been limited to readings in current use) and over 6,000 *kun* or Japanese readings, plus almost 70,000 compounds.

The vocabulary covered is that of today's current and common usage, plus such older words as are still encountered in modern literature. The characters and vocabulary of over fifty volumes of carefully selected prewar and postwar material have been carefully checked in an attempt to make the coverage as full and useful as possible within the confines of a portable dictionary. And the addition of cross references to Fuzambō's excellent Japanese-Japanese character dictionary, *Shōkai Kanwa Daijiten*, places many additional vocabulary items, particularly in the historical and classical fields, within quick and convenient reach, thus enormously enlarging the dictionary's usefulness.

Most compound verbs, which are so important in modern Japanese, have been included among the compounds. For brevity, they have been omitted in the case of certain combining verbs that appear so frequently as to be readily understood, such as *hajimaru* and *hajimeru* (to begin), *owaru* and *oeru* (to end), *deru* (to appear), *dasu* (to begin), and *sugiru* (to exceed). (Also for the sake of brevity, and with apologies to the purists, shortened spellings like thru and tho have been used throughout the dictionary.)

Many nouns compounded from two *on* elements become verbs by the addition of the verb *suru*; here either the noun or the verb is included, but usually not both. Nor should the user be surprised if some Japanese words are defined with different parts of speech in English: this is a peculiarity of the language.

No attempt has been made to indicate the era or field to which a word belongs as this is usually quite evident from the context in which the reader finds it. Nor have technical fields been covered beyond the extent required by the general, nonspecialized reader.

In addition to the sources enumerated below, wide reading in the secular and religious fields has furnished much vocabulary. Besides many Shinto and Buddhist words, most of the general terminology of the Protestant and Catholic communions has been included. Not only because of the growing importance of Christianity in Japan today but also because of its being an exellent source of modern colloquial words, practically all of the vocabulary expressed in characters in the Japanese colloquial Bible has been included.

The readings of characters in personal and place names constitute quite a separate problem from ordinary words, one that could never be adequately treated within the scope of a portable dictionary, if indeed a fully satisfactory solution can ever be found. Probably the most thoro study made to date is the Japanese work by Araki Ryōzō, *Nanori Jiten* (Tōkyōdō, Tokyo, 1959), covering both given names and the more difficult family names. As Mr. Araki humorously puts it, this problem of Japanese names is indeed an eighth wonder of the world.

The Japanese Government has made a small approach toward name standardization by decreeing that given names can henceforth be chosen only from the 1,850 Tōyō Kanji plus 92 additional characters authorized for names (see Appendix 12). Such limitation, however, does not apply to family or place names nor, of course, to older given names. Nor has any limit been placed on the readings, however rare, that may be chosen for any authorized character. Fortunately, following the rule that now applies to most formal, public documents, many publishers are making it a practice to show the reading of an author's name in *kana*, usually on the book's colophon; and many Japanese calling cards also give *kana* in more difficult cases. Readings of the names of well-known persons and places can usually be found in Japanese biographical dictionaries and atlases. And many names are so common that, with experience, one can be practically certain of their readings. Lacking any of these aids, in the final analysis it is only the bearer of a name or the resident of a locality who can say definitely how a certain name is to be read.

I wish to express my deep appreciation to the following excellent language teachers, masters of the direct method, for the inspiration to learn spoken Japanese and its intricate but fascinating system of writing: Matsumiya Yahei; William Axling; Takechi-Nozaki Fumiko; Yasui Kensaku; and Ichimura Isao, Head Teacher in the Department of Japanese Language at Japan Missionary College, and his associate teachers, including Hayasaka Fumiko, Kamoda Masukazu, Yamada Yōko, and many others; and to the following persons for their valuable assistance and encouragement in pushing a project of this size thru to completion: my wife, Vera E. Nelson; my son, Dr. Richard A. Nelson; Professor Edwin O. Reischauer, of Harvard University; Leon Picon, of the American Embassy in Tokyo; Professor Yuen Ren Chao, of the University of California; Yoshida Kōjirō, an expert in baseball terminology; Dr. Enoki Ken, of the Nippon Dental College and the Tokyo Medical and Dental University; Ino Takashi, of the Tōkai Regional Fisheries Research Laboratory; Sekine Bunnosuke, of the Tōyō Eiwa Junior College; Hattori Eitarō, of the Japanese Department of Education; President Yamagata Toshio, of Japan Missionary College, and Yanami Hidesada, of his Department of Science; Dr. Ichinose Haruo, Dr. Hayashi Takaharu, and Dr. Takagi Kenzō of the Tokyo Sanitarium-Hospital; Sakonju Tadashi, an experienced translator; Charles E. Tuttle, our publisher, and his efficient Editor-in-Chief, Meredith Weatherby; as well as many others, including Kenkyūsha, our printers, for a completely new typography with large, clear type.

Special thanks must go to the faithful proofreaders—Miss Yamada on the Japanese and Mrs. Nelson on the English—and to Mr. Ichimura, who has read the entire manuscript and rendered most excellent help in the choice of words and in making the definitions accurate and complete. Ralph Friedrich, of the Tuttle Company, has likewise been of great help in the proofreading.

I am indebted to the following works for accurate lexicographical information on the Chinese-Japanese characters:

Chamberlain, Basil Hall: *A Study of Japanese Writing* (*Moji no Shirube*), Kelly and Walsh, Yokohama, 1905

Gillis, I. S., and Pai Ping-ch'i: *Japanese Personal Names*, privately published, Peking, 1940

——: *Japanese Surnames*, privately published, Peking, 1939

Hirota Eitarō: *Yōji no Gijutsu*, Tōkyōdō, Tokyo, 1959

——: *Yōji Yōgo Jiten*, Tōkyōdō, Tokyo, 1960

Hattori Unokichi and Koyanagi Shigeta: *Shōkai Kanwa Daijiten*, Fuzambō, Tokyo, 1955

Matthews, R. H.: *Chinese-English Dictionary*, Harvard Press, Cambridge, 1950

Oyanagi Shigeta: *Shinshū Kanwa Daijiten*, Hakuyūsha, Tokyo, 1953.

Peeke, H. V. S., and Jones, J. Ira: *6000 Chinese Characters*, Kyōbunkan, Tokyo, 1915

Rose-Innes, Arthur: *Beginners' Dictionary of Chinese-Japanese Characters*, 2nd ed., Yoshikawa Shoten, Yokohama, 1937

Sakade, Florence: *A Guide to Reading and Writing Japanese*, Tuttle, Rutland, Vermont, and Tokyo, 1959

Tōyō Kanji Benran, Kyōiku Tosho Kenkyūkai, Tokyo, 1943

Tōyō Kanji Jiten, Chūkyō, Tokyo, Revised 1957

Ueda Bannen: *Daijiten*, Keiseisha, Tokyo, 1934

Wilder, George Durand, and Ingram, J. H.: *Character Analysis*, North China Language School, Peking, 1922.

Further indebtedness is also acknowledged to the following dictionaries and glossaries as well as to countless pamphlets, newspapers, magazines, books, and conversations with Japanese teachers, ministers, priests, and other people in all walks of life for the general vocabulary of the language:

Church Terminology, National Christian Council of Japan, Tokyo, 1958
Cresswell, H.T.; Hiraoka, J.; and Namba, R.: *A Dictionary of Military Terms*, University of Chicago Press, Chicago, 1942
Gendai Yōgo no Kiso Chishiki, Jiyū Kokuminsha, Tokyo, 1958
Ino Takashi: *Systematic List of Economic Aquatic Animals and Plants in Japan*, SCAP, Tokyo, 1951
Ishikawa Mitsuteru: *English-Japanese Medical Dictionary*, Nippon Rinshōsha, Osaka, 1955 ┌Kenkyūsha, Tokyo, 1953
Iwasaki Tamihei and Kawamura Jūjirō: *New English-Japanese Dictionary*,
Jōyaku Yōji Reishū, Japan Foreign Office, Tokyo, 1953 ┌1954
Katsumata Senkichirō: *New Japanese-English Dictionary*, Kenkyūsha, Tokyo,
Kindai-ichi Kyōsuke: *Jikai*, Sanseidō, Tokyo, 1952
Koshōgaku Yōgoshū, Japan Weather Agency, Tokyo, 1949
Kobayashi Uzuo: *Kirisutokyō Yōgo Jiten*, Tōkyōdō, Tokyo, 1954
Kume Takeo: *Hōseki Kikinzoku Jiten*, Kazama Shobō, Tokyo, 1957
Nakayama Fumio: *New Concise Japanese-English Dictionary*, Sanseidō, Tokyo, 1956 ┌Department, Washington, 1946
Nelson, Andrew N.: *Japanese-English Technical Terms Dictionary*, U.S. War
Saitō Hidesaburō: *Japanese-English Dictionary*, Nichieisha, Tokyo, 1931
Sasaki Tachi: *New Concise English-Japanese Dictionary*, Sanseidō, Tokyo, 1955
Satow, Ernest, and Ishibashi Masakata: *English-Japanese Dictionary of the Spoken Language*, 4th ed., Sanseidō, Tokyo, 1919
Seki Kan-ichi and Toyama Tamizō: *Gendai Kokugo Hyōki Jiten*, Tokyo, 1953
Sekine Bunnosuke: *Kiristokyō Yōgo Jiten*, Shingensha, Tokyo, 1958
Shimbun Yōgo no Tebiki, Asahi Newspaper, Tokyo, 1956
Shimbun Yōgoshū, Japan Newspaper Association, Tokyo, 1957 and 1960
Shiraishi Daiji: *Tōyō Kanji*: *Gendai Kanazukai to Sono Tsukaikata*, Ōkurashō Insatsukyoku, Tokyo, 1958 ┌1951
Takahashi Morio: *Romanized Japanese-English Dictionary*, Taiseidō, Tokyo,
Takeda, H.: *Systematic List of Economic Plants in Japan*, SCAP, Tokyo, 1949
Takenobu Yoshitarō: *New Japanese-English Dictionary*, Kenkyūsha, Tokyo, 1944
——: *New Japanese-English Dictionary*, Kenkyūsha, Tokyo, 1949
Tōyō Kanji Jiten, Chūkyō Shuppan Kabushiki Kaisha, Tokyo, Revised 1957

In a sense I have been working on this dictionary ever since I began studying Japanese, some forty-three years ago, and it has occupied me actively during the past five years. Yet no one is more aware than I of how many faults it may still contain. As I now leave Japan to take up new work, I am in no way deserting the dictionary but shall begin preparing for future revisions.

The preceding section of the Foreword was written in February 1961. In response to numerous requests the On-Kun Index was added to the First Revised Edition. The present Second Revised Edition contains additional improvements, including newly added words, expanded or clarified English definitions, and corrections of errors. We wish to thank our many readers who have sent suggestions and corrections, especially Miss Tsuruko Asano, principal of the Tokyo School of the Japanese Language; the Reverend Joseph M. Goedertier, of the Oriens Institute for Religious Research, Tokyo; and Mr. Isao Ichimura, of the Japan Missionary College, Tokyo.

ANDREW N. NELSON

Tokyo

NOTE: Corrections, proposed additions, and other suggestions regarding this dictionary may be sent directly to the publisher's Tokyo office.

TYPOGRAPHICAL EXPLANATIONS

THE PAGE IN GENERAL.

N.B. The first five items below pertain to the first main-character entry on a left-hand page and to the last on a right-hand page.

1. The topmost boldface numeral in the upper, outer corner = the traditional number of the relevant radical.

2. The vertical string of radicals in the outer margin = all the radicals containing the relevant number of strokes, plus their more important variants.

3. The pair of heavy brackets that runs up and down the radical strings as you spin the pages = a quick guide for the eye, such brackets enclosing the relevant radical and, if any, its important variants.

4. The boldface numeral at the head of a radical string = the number of strokes in each parent radical shown in the string.

5. The tiny numeral that follows the heavy brackets up and down the radical strings = the number of strokes in the non-radical part of the relevant main-character entry.

6. Boldface numerals in the lower, outer corner = the inclusive numbers of the characters appearing on that page (i.e., of the upper numerals described in Paragraph 11 below).

7. Numerals centered at the bottom of each page = the page numbers.

8. A column-wide divider consisting of a boldface numeral flanked by horizontal lines = the beginning of a group of characters each of which has the indicated number of strokes in its non-radical part.

9. A page-wide divider consisting of a radical and its number flanked by heavy horizontal lines = the beginning of a new radical division. Also shown are the variants of the radical, its names in Japanese and English, and other pertinent information. The final item, labeled "nickname," gives the term we recommend in an effort to standardize the English nomenclature of the radicals.

THE ENTRIES.

10. Large boldface character at the left of a column = a main-character entry. For the forms of the Tōyō Kanji we follow Chūkyō Shuppan's *Tōyō Kanji Jiten*, edition of 1957. For the other characters we follow Fuzambō.

11. Two numerals, one above the other, immediately after a main-character entry: (a) The upper = the successive number assigned to each main entry in this dictionary and used in all cross references. (b) The lower, preceded by an F = the page in Fuzambō's *Shōkai Kanwa Jiten* where additional information concerning this character and its compounds will be found. Where a variant of the main character appears to the right of the numbers, the F number may refer to the page where the variant is found because the detailed information is given there. Occasionally there are two F numbers, one above the other, the upper one referring to the page where the character to the left is found and the lower one to that of the one to the right. "F-X" means that the character is not found in Fuzambō.

12. Small capital letters immediately to the left of a main character: (a) A =

one of the 881 characters which the Japanese Ministry of Education considers the most essential, having decreed that they shall be mastered during the six years of elementary school (see Appendix 12). (b) B = one of the remaining 969 in the list of 1,850 Tōyō Kanji. (c) P = one of the 28 substitutes that have been made in the Tōyō Kanji by the Newspaper Association. If no small capital letter precedes a main-character entry, it is to be understood that the character, tho outside the 1,850 list, is still sufficiently common in modern literature to be important in a wide mastery of Japanese.

13. Another boldface character (or characters) following a main entry = an alternate form of the character.

14. Reading(s) of a character in capital and small capital letters = the *on* or Chinese pronunciation(s). These are defined only if they have have distinctive meanings; otherwise they partake of the English meanings which follow other readings of the character. (Note that many *on* readings have gone out of use. As a rule, therefore, only those *on* which appear in the compounds given in this dictionary are shown here. For a complete listing of all *on* readings of a character, see the Fuzambō dictionary. See our character 5366 for an example of the great number of *on* readings that have come over from China. See Chūkyō Shuppan's *Tōyō Kanji Jiten* for the officially limited *on* and *kun* readings for the Tōyō Kanji.)

15. Reading(s) of a character in italics = the *kun* or Japanese pronunciation(s), with their English meaning. The excellent Hepburn system of romanization, as exemplified in Kenkyūsha's *Japanese-English Dictionary*, edition of 1949, is followed in this dictionary. In general, the order of listing the *kun* readings is, first, verbs, then other parts of speech, and finally prefixes or suffixes. The punctuation of the *on* and *kun* readings provides information concerning their meaning and uses as indicated by the following examples: (a) "On meaning. ***kun*** meaning." or "On meaning. On meaning. ***kun*** meaning. ***kun*** meaning." = *On* and ***kun*** readings with separate meanings. (b) "On. ***kun*** meaning." = the *on* is not used alone but in compounds partakes of the ***kun*** meaning. (c) "On. On meaning. ***kun*** meaning." = the first *on* is not used alone but in compounds and partakes of the meaning of the other readings; the second *on* has the separate meaning shown. (d) "On ***kun*** meaning." or "On, On ***kun*** meaning." = the *on* (one or more) may be used alone and have the same meaning as the ***kun***.

16. Syllables of a reading enclosed in parentheses = syllables comprising the ***okurigana***, i.e., the inflected part of the word which is written in the cursive ***hiragana*** syllabary. Here we follow the recent Education Ministry recommendations. The auxiliary verbs ***suru***, ***nasu***, and ***naru*** and final particles (***no***, ***na***, ***ni***, ***de***, etc.) are not parts of the preceding words and hence are not enclosed in parentheses; they would, of course, be written in text matter.

17. The characters 国字 (*kokuji*) following a main-character entry = this character was made in Japan and not inherited from China.

18. A radical enclosed in heavy brackets at the end of a main entry = the character's traditional radical, which differs from that under which the character is here entered.

THE COMPOUNDS.

19. Small characters at the left of a column following a main entry = compounds, followed by their readings in italics (parentheses being used as described in Paragraph 16 above) and their English meanings. Note that in listing a compound, since the first character is the same as that of the main entry, it is not repeated but is to be understood.

20. Tiny numerals immediately to the left of a list of compounds = the full number of strokes in the 2nd characters of the compounds (the main-character entry being counted as the 1st character). A new numeral appears whenever the stroke-count changes.

THE CROSS REFERENCES. Our system of cross references can be best explained by a few typical examples, as shown in boxes below.

In Main-Character Entries

| 桟 2193/F-X Nonstandard for 材 2189. | = that 桟 is not authorized by the Government and is not found in standard character dictionaries but is quite widely used for 材 2189.

| 東 See 213. | = that this is the traditional location of this character but our Radical Priority System (see Appendix 3) places it in a different place, under Rad. 4 as entry No. 213.

| 梅 2262/F978 See 梅 2258. | = that the information concerning this character and its compounds is found under the equivalent Tōyō Kanji, our No. 2258.

In Compounds

| (see under 言 4309.0) | = that the word is defined under main-character entry No. 4309.

| =還任 4750.6 | = that the word is also written with these characters and is found under main-character entry No. 4750 in the 6-stroke section.

| =*shui* 趣意 4544.13 | = that the word is equivalent to *shui,* which is found under character 4544 in the 13-stroke section.

| =低回 (see below—12) | = that the word is also written with a different 2nd character and is found immediately below in the 12-stroke section. Similarly with cross references reading "see above."

The Modern Reader's Japanese-English Character Dictionary

1-STROKE RADICALS

RAD. 一 1

Ichi one. Variant: a shorter horizontal. Nickname: One.

一 1/F1 A ICHI one; a. ITSU one. *hi* one. *hito*(*tsu*) one, a unit; the same; just; once. *itsu wa* for one thing, partly. *itsu ni* solely, entirely, only; or. *ichi-* one, a certain; the whole; the same (time); petty, worthless. *hito-* one; a.

[1]一 *ichi-ichi*, *hito*(*tsu*)-*hito*(*tsu*) one by one, separately; everything; in detail
[2]入 *hitoshio* still more, especially
八 *ichi*(*ka*)*bachi*(*ka*) sink or swim
了簡 *ichiryōken* at one's discretion
二及 *ichini*(*ni*)*oyo*(*bazu*) right away, without waiting around
二無 *ichi*(*mo*)*ni*(*mo*)*na*(*ku*) unhesitatingly
丁 *itchō* one block; =一挺 (see below–10)
丁字 *itteiji* a single letter
刀 *ittō* a sword, a blade, a (single) stroke
刀両断 *ittō-ryōdan* cutting in two with one stroke
刀彫 *ittōbo*(*ri*) a one-knife carving
人 *hitori*, *ichinin* one person. *hitori de* alone; by oneself, voluntarily, spontaneously, automatically
人一人 *hitoribitori* one by one
人子 *hitorigo*, *hitorikko* an only child
人芝居 *hitori shibai* a one-man show
人当 *hitoria*(*tari*), *hitoria*(*te*) per person
人歩 *hitoriaru*(*ki*) walking alone
人者 *hitorimono* a single person; someone alone
人物 *ichijimbutsu* a man of some importance, a character
人乗 *ichininno*(*ri*) a single-seater
人前 *hitorimae*, *ichinimmae* full manhood, adult; a plate, one helping
人娘 *hitori musume* an only daughter
人旅 *hitoritabi* traveling alone
人残 *hitori noko*(*razu*) everyone
人称 *ichininshō* first person (in grammar)
人息子 *hitori musuko* an only son
人腹 *hitoribara* taking for granted, rash
人寝 *hitorine* sleeping alone ⌊conclusion
人舞台 *hitori butai* one's unrivaled field
[3]山 *hitoyama* a mountain; the whole mountain; a pile (of something)
己 *ikko* oneself. *ikko no* personal, private
丸 *ichigan* a lump, (into) one
才 *issai* one year old
ケ月 *ikkagetsu* one month
夕 *isseki* one evening, some evening
大 *ichidai* one large . . .
大事 *ichidaiji* a serious matter
子 *hitorigo* an only child. *isshi* a child; an only child
子相伝 *isshi-sōden* transmission of a trade secret from a father to a son
寸 *issun* one *sun*. *chotto* just a minute; a short time; just a little, somewhat; easily, readily, rather ⌈mediate future
寸先 *issunsaki* an inch ahead, the im-
寸逃 *issunnoga*(*re*) quibbling, prevarication
寸法師 *issumbōshi* dwarf, midget
寸遁 *issunnoga*(*re*) quibbling, prevarication
口 *hitokuchi* a mouthful, a bite, a sip, a draft
口同音 *ikku-dōon* reading in unison; saying the same thing
口咄 *hitokuchibanashi* joke, anecdote
口商 *hitokuchi akina*(*i*) an immediate definite deal
口話 *hitokuchibanashi* joke, anecdote
口噺 *hitokuchibanashi* joke, anecdote
[4]戸 *ikko* a house, a household
月 *ichigatsu*, *ichigetsu* January. *hitotsuki*,
木 *ichiboku* one tree ⌊*ichigetsu* one month
水 *issui* a current (of water); a drop
片 *ippen* a piece, a bit
円 *ichien* the whole area; one yen
区 *ikku* a district, a ward, a lot
匹 *ippiki* one animal; two-*tan* bolt of cloth
反 *ittan* one-tenth hectare
双 *issō* a pair (of screens)
介 *ikkai no* mere, only a . . .
辺倒 *ippentō* complete devotion to one side
手 *itte* a move (in a game); one method; a monopoly. *itte ni* single-handed. *hitote* one hand; one's own effort
手販売 *itte hambai* sole agency
毛 *ichimō* one-tenth of a *rin*
毛作 *ichimō saku* a single crop ⌈tion
六勝負 *ichiroku-shōbu* gambling, specula-
六銀行 *ichiroku ginkō* pawnshop
夫一婦 *ippu-ippu* monogamy

夫多妻 *ippu-tasai* polygamy

心 *isshin, hito(tsu)kokoro* one mind, the whole heart, wholeheartedness ⌈tently

心不乱 *isshin-furan ni* wholeheartedly, in-

心同体 *isshin-dōtai* one flesh, union

方 *ippō* a quarter, a side; one direction; one hand; the other hand; one party; the other party; on the other hand; meanwhile; only, simply; in turn. *hito-kata(naranu)* extraordinary; special. *hitokata(narazu)* unusually, greatly

方交通 *ippō kōtsū* one-way traffic

方的 *ippōteki* one-sided, unilateral, arbi-

方通行 *ippō tsūkō* one-way traffic ⌊trary

切 *issai* all, everything, the whole; entirely, absolutely. *hitoki(re)* a slice, a small piece. *hitoki(ri)* a pause, a period, a step; once, some years ago

切合財 *issai-gassai* any and every thing; altogether, without reserve

切経 *Issaikyō* complete Buddhist scriptures

切衆生 *issai-shujō* all creatures

天 *itten* the whole sky, firmament

天万乗 *ittembanjō* the whole realm

天四海 *itten-shikai* the world, the universe

天張 *ittemba(ri)* persistence

元 *ichigen no* unitary

元化 *ichigenka* unification, centralization

元的 *ichigenteki* monistic, unitary, unified,

元論 *ichigenron* monism ⌊centralized

分 *ippun* a minute. *ichibu* one tenth; one hundredth, one percent; one tenth of a *sun*; one quarter *ryō* (an old coin). *ichi-bun* duty, honor

分別 *hitofumbetsu* careful consideration

分金 *ichibu kin* a gold quarter *ryō*

分銀 *ichibu gin* a silver quarter *ryō*

文 *ichimon* one *mon*. one-tenth of a sen; something of insignificant value. *ichibun* a sentence

文字 *ichimonji* a straight line, a beeline

文惜 *ichimon-oshi(mi)* stinginess; miser

文商 *ichimon akina(i)* a penny store; business on a small scale

文無 *ichimonna(shi)* penniless

日 *ichinichi, ichijitsu* one day, a day; the first day (of the month). *hitohi* one day

日一日 *ichinichi-ichinichi* gradually, day by day

日一夜 *ichinichi-ichiya* all day and all night

日千秋 *ichijitsu-senshū* many a weary day

日片時 *ichinichi-henji* a short time

日中 *ichinichijū* all day long

日長 *ichijitsu(no)chō* superiority

日路 *ichinichiji* a day's journey

日増 *ichinichima(shi) ni* day by day

5 矢 *isshi* an arrow; a retort

穴 *hito(tsu)ana* the same hole; one gang

皿 *hitosara* a plate, a dish (of food)

句 *ikku* a phrase, a verse, a line; a *haiku*-poem counter

巡 *hitomegu(ri)* a turn, a round; one full year. *ichijun* a beat, a round

打 *hito-u(chi), ichida* a stroke, a blow. *ichi*

札 *issatsu* a document, a bond ⌊*dāsu* 1 dozen

礼 *ichirei* a bow, a salute, a greeting

旦 *ittan* once; one morning; temporarily

半 *ippan* a half; a part ⌈error

失 *isshitsu* a disadvantage; a defect; an

冊 *issatsu* one copy (of a book)

仕事 *hito shigoto* a task ⌈ple meal

汁一菜 *ichijū-issai* a one-plate meal, a sim-

石 *isseki* one game (of *go*) ⌈one stone

石二鳥 *isseki-nichō* killing two birds with

代 *ichidai* one generation; a lifetime; an age

代記 *ichidaiki* a biography

生 *isse, issei* one existence, a lifetime; a generation, an age; the whole world; the era. *isshō* a lifetime, one's (whole) life; all thru life

生一代 *isshō-ichidai no* the greatest (event) in my life ⌈all thru life

生涯 *isshōgai* a lifetime, one's (whole) life;

生懸命 *isshōkemmei ni* with all one's might

目 *hitome* a glimpse, a glance. *ichimoku* a glance, a look. *hito(tsu)me* a one-eyed monster

目惚 *hitomebo(re)* love at first sight

目散 *ichimokusan ni* at full speed

目瞭然 *ichimoku-ryōzen* very clear

世 *issei* a foreign immigrant to USA; a lifetime; a generation. *isse* a lifetime

世一代 *issei-ichidai* once a lifetime

世紀 *isseiki* a century ⌈of life

世真盛 *isshō (no) massaka(ri)* the noontide

本 *ippon* one (long object); one version; a certain book; a blow; a full-fledged

本立 *ipponda(chi)* independence ⌊geisha

本気 *ippongi* a one-track mind, monotony

本杉 *ipponsugi* a solitary cryptomeria tree

本松 *ippommatsu* a solitary pine tree

本建 *ipponda(te)* a single standard

本道 *ippommichi* a direct unforked road

本釣 *ipponzu(ri)* fishing with a pole

本槍 *ippon-yari* one's sole talent; a guiding principle

本調子 *ipponchōshi, ipponjōshi* monotone

本橋 *ippombashi* a log bridge

6 色 *isshoku, hito-iro* one color. *isshiki* one color; one article

行 *ichigyō, ikkō* a line, a row. *ikkō* a party; a troupe

同 *ichidō* all present, all concerned, all of ⌊us

旬 *ichijun* ten days

団 *ichidan* a body, a group, a party, a gang, ⌊a troupe

因 *ichi-in* a cause

式 *isshiki* a complete set, all, the whole, everything

曲 *ikkyoku* a tune, a melody, a piece of ⌈music

向 *ikkō* (not) at all. *hitasura* earnestly

任 *ichinin suru* entrust (to someone)

件 *ikken* a matter, an item

休 *hitoyasu(mi)* a rest

如 *ichinyo* oneness

列 *ichiretsu* a row, a line

汗 *hitoase* doing a job; riding and sweating ⌈up a horse

再 *issai* once or twice; repeatedly

号 *ichigō* number one

先 *hitomazu* for the present; once; in outline; tentatively

朶 *ichida* a branch (of flowers); a cluster, ⌈a mass (of clouds)

考 *ikkō* consideration, a thought

名 *ichimei* one person; another name

存 *ichizon* one's own discretion; one's own idea; one's own responsibility

安心 *hito anshin* a feeling of relief

合目 *ichigōme* the start of a climb up a mountain

肌脱 *hitohadanu(gu)* pitch in and help

衣帯水 *ichi-i-taisui* a narrow strait

糸 *isshi* a string

糸一毫 *isshi-ichigō* tiny amount

気 *ikki ni* at a breath, at a stroke, at a sit-⌈ting

気呵成 *ikki-kasei ni*=一気 (word above)

字 *ichiji* a character, a letter

字千金 *ichiji-senkin* a word of great value

死 *isshi* one out (in baseball); dying

死後 *isshigo* after one out

死報国 *isshi hōkoku* dying for one's ⌈country

次 *ichiji* the first; a linear (equation)

次電流 *ichiji denryū* primary current

次線輪 *ichiji senrin* primary coil

両 *ichiryō* one vehicle; one *ryō* (an old coin)

両日 *ichiryōjitsu* a day or two

両年 *ichiryōnen* a year or two

年 *ichinen, hitotoshi* one year. *hitotose* one year; some time ago

年中 *ichinenjū* through the year

年生 *ichinensei* first-year student; annual ⌈(plant)

年草 *ichinensō* an annual (plant)

回 *ikkai* once, a time, one time, a round, a game, a bout, a heat, an inning. *hitomawa(ri)* a turn, a round

回分 *ikkaibun* a dose; an installment

回忌 *ikkaiki* first death anniversary

回転 *ikkaiten, ichi kaiten* one revolution; one rotation

回戦 *ikkaisen* first game, first round (of ⌈tennis, etc.)

7 走 *hitohashi(ri), hito(p)pashi(ri)* a spin, a run

図 *ichizu ni* wholeheartedly

応 *ichiō* once; tentatively; in outline. *hitowatari* briefly, in general

位 *ichi-i* first place, first rank; unit's place ⌈(in figures)

吹 *hitofu(ki)* a blast, puff, whiff, gust

役 *hitoyaku* a part to play. *ichiyaku* an office; ⌊an important office

折 *hito-o(ri)* one box

対 *ittsui* a pair (of screens, vases, etc.)

決 *ikketsu suru* be agreed, be settled

別 *ichibetsu* parting

助 *ichijo* a help

更 *ikkō* first watch, 8–10 p.m.

呑 *hitono(mi)* drinking in one gulp

系 *ikkei* a single-family lineage

声 *hitokoe, issei* a voice, a cry, a shout

条 *ichijō* a line, a streak; a matter, a quota-⌊tion

男 *ichinan* a boy; eldest son

芸 *ichigei* an art; one talent

花 *hito hana* a flower; success

束 *issoku, hitotaba* a bundle, a hundred

私人 *isshijin, ichi shijin* a private individual

卵性双生児 *ichiransei sōseiji* identical twins

見 *ikken* a look, a glimpse; first meeting; ⌊apparently

見識 *ichikenshiki* an opinion

角 *ikkaku* corner, section; point; a narwhal; =*hitokado* 一廉 (see below-13)

角獣 *ikkakujū* unicorn

足 *issoku* a pair (footwear). *hitoashi* a step

足飛 *issokuto(bi) ni* at one bound

身 *isshin* thruout the body; oneself, one's own interests. *ichimi* partisans, conspirators, a gang. *hito(tsu)mi* baby clothes

身上 *isshinjō no* personal (affairs)

里 *ichi ri* 2.44 miles

里塚 *ichirizuka* milestone, mileposts (stand-⌈ing one *ri* apart)

局 *ikkyoku* one game (of checkers, etc.)

局部 *ichikyokubu* one part

利 *ichiri* one advantage

利一害 *ichiri-ichigai* advantages and dis-⌈advantages

体 *ittai* one body, one flesh; what on earth, really, in fact, properly speaking; originally. *ittai ni* generally

体化 *ittaika* unification, integration

体全体 *ittai-zentai* whatever (is the matter?); what on earth?

言 *hitokoto, ichigen, ichigon* a word, a single ⌈word

言一行 *ichigen-ikkō* just a word or an act

言二言 *hitokoto-futakoto* a word or two

言半句 *ichigen-hanku, ichigon-hanku* a word, a few words

言居士 *ichigen-koji* a person who always has to have his say

8 門 *ichimon* the family, dependents, the ⌈household

雨 *hito ame* a shower, a rain

1 [一] 丨 丶 ノ 乙 亅

例 *ichirei* one example, an instance
味 *ichimi* an ingredient; a touch, a tinge; conspirators, a gang
帖 *ichijō* a quire (of paper)
往 *ichiō* once, tentatively, in outline
抱 *hitokaka(e)* an armful, one bundle
抹 *ichimatsu* a touch of, a tinge of, a wreath
泡 *hitoawa* a blow, a shock ⌊(of smoke)
版 *ippan* an edition
物 *ichimotsu* an article, a thing; plot, ulterior motive, secret intention. *ichibutsu* a thing ⌈market; short rest
服 *ippuku* a dose; a puff, a smoke; lull, dull
命 *ichimei* a life; a command
念 *ichinen* a determined purpose
宗 *isshū* a sect, a denomination
宛 *hito(tsu)zutsu, hito(tsu)ate* one each
具 *ichigu* one set
昔 *hitomukashi* antiquity
事 *ichiji* one thing. *hitokoto* just a word, a word. *hito(tsu)koto* the same thing
刹那 *issetsuna* a moment, an instant
炊夢 *issui (no) yume* an empty dream
長一短 *itchō-ittan* good points and shortcomings
知半解 *itchi-hankai* superficial knowledge
妻多夫 *issai-tafu* polyandry
泊 *ippaku* stopping one night
泊行軍 *ippaku kōgun* an overnight march
所 *ik(ka)sho, hitotokoro, issho* one place; the same place
所懸命 *isshokemmei ni* with all one's might
杯 *ippai* a cup of; a drink; full; to the utmost; up to (one's income)
杯機嫌 *ippai-kigen* slight intoxication
直 *itchoku* lining out to first base
直線 *itchokusen* a straight line
定 *ittei suru* fix, settle, regularize, define; unify; standardize. *ichijō* something definitely settled. *ittei no* certain, uniform, prescribed, standard, regular, fixed, definite
定不変 *ittei-fuhen* invariable, permanent
刻 *ikkoku* a minute, a moment, an instant. *ikkoku na* stubborn, hot-headed
刻千金 *ikkoku-senkin* an extremely important time
刻早 *ikkoku (mo) haya(ku)* immediately
周 *hitomeguri*＝一巡 (see above-5). *isshū* once around, a revolution, a tour, a lap
周年 *isshūnen* one full year
周忌 *isshūki* first death anniversary
周期 *isshūki* a period (in astronomy)
国 *ikkoku* stubborn, hotheaded; the whole country ⌈system
国一党主義 *ikkoku-ittō shugi* one-party
国一票 *ikkoku-ippyō* one vote per nation
国者 *ikkokumono* a hot-tempered person, a stubborn person
枚 *ichimai* one sheet
枚下 *ichimai shita* one step lower
枚上 *ichimai ue* one step higher
枚貝 *ichimaigai* univalve
枚看板 *ichimai kamban* one's only suit, only coat; leading actor, prima donna; slogan, motto; sole aim
斉 *issei ni* simultaneously, all at once
斉安 *isseiyasu* all-round (market) decline
斉高 *isseidaka* all-round (market) advance
斉射撃 *issei shageki* volley firing, fusillade, a broadside
斉検挙 *issei kenkyo* wholesale arrest, round-up
歩 *ippo* a step
歩一歩 *ippo-ippo* step by step, by degrees
歩金 *ichibu kin* a gold quarter *ryō*
歩前進 *ippo zenshin* a step forward
歩銀 *ichibu gin* a silver quarter *ryō*
夜 *ichiya, hitoyo, hitoya* one night, all night, one evening, overnight
夜大臣 *ichiya daijin* overnight millionaire
夜乞食 *ichiya kojiki* a person made homeless by fire
夜中 *ichiyajū, hitoyajū* all night thru
夜妻 *ichiyazuma, hitoyozuma* temporary consort, prostitute
夜造 *ichiyazuku(ri)* built in a night; stopgap; hastily written ⌈cramming
夜漬 *ichiyazuke* salted just overnight;
9食 *isshoku, ichijiki* one meal (a day)
首 *isshu* a poem
度 *ichido, hitotabi* once, one time, on one occasion
通 *hitotō(ri)* in general, briefly. *ittsū* one copy (of a document). *hitotō(ri) no* ordinary, usual ⌈paper)
連 *ichiren* a series, a chain; a ream (of
途 *ichizu ni* wholeheartedly. *itto* a way, a course; the only way
律 *ichiritsu* evenness, uniformity, equality, monotony. *ichiritsu ni* in the same way
括 *ikkatsu* one lump, one bundle; summing up. *hitokuku(ri)* a bundle. *hitokuru(me)* a bunch, a bundle, a lot
派 *ippa* a school, a sect, a party
級 *ikkyū* one grade; first class
計 *ikkei* a plan
陣 *ichijin* vanguard; a gust of wind
封 *ippū* a sealed letter; a sealed document;
変 *ippen* complete change ⌊an enclosure
軍 *ichigun* an army, the whole army
星 *hito(tsu)boshi* evening star; morning star

思 *hito-omo(i) ni* instantly, resolutely

発 *ippatsu* a shot, a round, a charge

荒 *hitoa(re)* a squall; a burst of anger

巻 *ikkan* one volume. *hitomaki* one roll

昼夜 *itchūya* a whole day and night, 24 hours

院制 *ichi-insei* unicameral system

神教 *isshinkyō* monotheism

音節 *ichionsetsu* monosyllable

姫二太郎 *ichi-hime-ni-tarō* It's good to have a girl first and then a boy.

風呂 *hitofuro* a bath

風変 *ippū kawa(tta)* eccentric, queer; unconventional, original

指 *isshi* a finger

指当 *ichiyubia(tari)* a span

段 *ichidan* more, still more, much more, all the more; a part (of a talk). *ittan* one-tenth hectare

段落 *ichidanraku* a pause

品 *ippin* an item, an article; a dish, a course

品料理 *ippin ryōri* service à la carte

面 *ichimen* one side, one phase; the whole surface; first page (of a newspaper); (on) the other hand; all over

面観 *ichimenkan* one-sided view

面識 *ichimenshiki* a passing acquaintance

重 *hitoe* one layer; single. *hitokosa(ne)* a suit; a set of boxes

重桜 *hitoezakura* a cherry tree bearing single blossoms; single cherry blossoms

重継 *hitoe tsu(gi)* sheep bend (knot)

点 *itten* a speck, dot, point, particle; only one, a very little

点張 *ittemba(ri)* persistence

洗 *issen (suru)* thoroly wash away

昨日 *issakujitsu, ototoi, ototsui* day before yesterday

昨年 *issakunen, ototoshi* year before last

昨夜 *issakuya* night before last

昨昨日 *issakusakujitsu, sakiototoi, sakiototsui* two days before yesterday

昨昨年 *issakusakunen, sakiototoshi* two years before last

昨昨夜 *issakusakuya* two nights before last

昨晩 *issakuban* night before last

10 座 *ichiza* the party; those present; a troupe; the first seat

席 *isseki* a sitting; a speech; a feast

閃 *issen* a flash

俵 *ippyō* one straw-bagful

倍 *ichibai* one share, one amount

挺 *itchō* counter for guns, ink sticks, oars, candles, palanquins, or jinrickshas

桁 *hitoketa* units (in figures)

流 *ichiryū* a school (of art); foremost, first-class, top-notch; unique

将 *isshō* a general

眠 *hitonemu(ri)* a sleep. *ichimin, hitonemu(ri)* the first sleep (of silkworms)

脈 *ichimyaku* a vein, a thread (of connection)

郭 *ikkaku* a city block; an enclosure

員 *ichi-in* a person; a member

案 *ichian* an idea, a plan

差 *hitosa(shi)* a dance

書 *hito(tsu)ga(ki)* an item, itemization. *issho* one letter; one book

息 *hito-iki* a breath, a pause, an effort

荷 *ikka* a load

帯 *ittai* a region, a zone; the whole place

能 *ichinō* one talent; one work

個人 *ikkojin, ichikojin* a private person, an individual

進一退 *isshin-ittai* advance and retreat, ebb and flow, seesawing, fluctuating

紙半銭 *isshi-hansen* a small sum; things of little value

殺多生 *issetsu-tashō* destroying one to save many

致 *itchi* agreement, conformity, consistency; union, co-operation

致点 *itchiten* point of agreement

党 *ittō* a party or clique

党一派 *ittō-ippa* party, faction

笑 *isshō* a laugh, a smile

笑付 *isshō ni fu(su)* laugh (someone) down

隻 *isseki* one boat, one ship

隻眼 *issekigan* a discerning eye; an opinion

週 *isshū* a week

週年 *isshūnen* one full year

週間 *isshūkan* a week

部 *ichibu* a part; a copy (of a publication)

部分 *ichibubun* a part

部始終 *ichibu-shijū* full particulars

家 *ikka, ikke* a house, a home, a family, a household; one's family, one's folks; a style

家団欒 *ikka-danran* a family get-together

家言 *ikkagen* a private opinion, a personal view

軒 *ikken* a house

軒一軒 *ikken-ikken* house to house

軒屋 *ikken-ya* an isolated house

軒家 *ikken-ya* an isolated house

挙 *ikkyo* one effort, one action

挙一動 *ikkyo-ichidō* what little one does

挙手一投足 *ikkyoshu-ittōsoku* a slight effort, the least trouble

挙両得 *ikkyo-ryōtoku* killing two birds with one stone

時 *ichiji* a time; temporarily; at one time. *ittoki* twelfth part of a day. *hitotoki* a little while, a short period. *ichidoki ni* at a time, at one time

時払 *ichijibarai* lump-sum payment

時金 *ichijikin* lump sum

時逃 *ichijinoga(re), ittokinoga(re)* quibbling, temporizing

時的 *ichijiteki* temporary
時凌 *ichiji-shino(gi)* makeshift, temporary expedient
時預 *ichiji-azu(kari)* (baggage) checking, temporary custody. *ichiji-azu(ke)* (baggage) checking, temporary depositing
時賜金 *ichiji shikin* lump-sum grant
般 *ippan no* general, liberal, universal, ordinary, average
般人 *ippanjin, ippannin* an ordinary person
般化 *ippanka* generalization, populariza-
般社会 *ippan shakai* general public ⌊tion
般投票 *ippan tōhyō* referendum, popular
般性 *ippansei* generality ⌊vote, plebiscite
般法 *ippanhō* general law
般的 *ippanteki* general
般概念 *ippan gainen* general idea
般論 *ippanron* general consideration
11 遍 *ippen* once
遇 *ichigū* one meeting
道 *ichidō* one road; a ray (of hope)
頃 *hitokoro* once, some time ago
掃 *issō* a clean sweep
掬 *ikkiku* one scoop (of water)
族 *ichizoku* a family, dependents, relatives, a household ⌈thru
渉 *hitowata(ri)* briefly, in general, glancing
理 *ichiri* a principle, a reason
眸 *ichibō* one sweep, an unbroken view
眼 *ichigan* one eye ⌈one set
組 *hitokumi, ichi kumi* one class. *hitokumi*
敗 *ippai* one defeat ⌈(of soldiers)
隊 *ittai* a party, a gang, a squad, a company
隅 *ichigū, hitosumi* a corner, a nook
階 *ikkai* ground floor, first floor
率 *ichiritsu ni* in the same way
毫 *ichigō* a trifle ⌈shrine; a room
堂 *ichidō* a building, a hall; a temple, a
票 *ippyō* a vote, a ballot
雫 *hitoshizuku* a drop (of water)
盛 *hitosaka(ri)* temporary prosperity. *hitomo(ri)* a pile
絃琴 *ichigenkin* one-stringed instrument
帳羅 *itchōra* one's only (good) suit (or kimono)
陽来復 *ichiyō-raifuku* return of spring
過 *ikka suru* pass away
過性 *ikkasei* transient (pain or fever)
問一答 *ichimon-ittō* answering question by question
張一弛 *itchō-isshi* tension and relaxation
張羅 *itchōra* one's only (good) suit (or ki-
得 *ittoku* one advantage, a merit ⌊mono)
得一失 *ittoku-isshitsu* an advantage and a disadvantage, a merit and a demerit
視同人 *isshi-dōjin* =next word

視同仁 *isshi-dōjin*, impartiality, universal brotherhood, universal benevolence
転 *itten* a turn, complete change
転機 *ittenki* a turning point
宿 *isshuku* staying one night
宿一飯 *isshuku-ippan* just staying for a night and a meal ⌈tion; $8^1/_3$ pounds
貫 *ikkan* consistency, coherence, integra-
貫番号 *ikkan bangō* serial number
望 *ichibō* one sweep, an unbroken view
望千里 *ichibō-senri* the boundless (ocean)
粒 *hitotsubu* a grain ⌈selection
粒選 *hitotsubuyo(ri), hitotsubue(ri)* careful
粒種 *hitotsubudane* an only child
12 間 *ikken* one *ken*, six feet
喝 *ikkatsu* a roar, a thundering cry
場 *ichijō* one time, one place
項 *ikkō* an item
幅 *ippuku* a scroll
握 *ichiaku, hitonigi(ri)* a handful
揃 *hitosoroi, hitosoroe* a set, a suit
揆 *ikki* a riot, an insurrection ⌈overnight
晩 *hito ban* one evening; a night; all night;
棟 *hitomune* one house; the same house
斑 *ippan* a spot; a glimpse, an outline; a part ⌈you)
統 *ittō* a lineage, a line; unification; all (of
飲 *hitono(mi)* a mouthful, a bite; a swallow, a sip; an easy prey
飯 *ippan* a bowl (of rice); a meal
割 *ichiwari* ten percent
散 *issan ni* at top speed
期 *ichigo* one's life, a lifetime. *ikki* a term, a half year, a quarter
策 *issaku* an idea, a plan
畳 *ichijō* one mat ⌈a suit (of a clothes)
着 *itchaku* first arrival; first (in the race);
葦 *ichi-i* one reed; a boat
葉 *ichiyō* a leaf; a page; a copy (of a photo);
報 *ippō* information ⌊a boat
閑張 *ikkamba(ri)* lacquered papier-mâché
堪無 *hitotama(ri) (mo) na(ku)* easily, irresistibly, helplessly
喜一憂 *ikki-ichiyū* mixed blessings, alternation of joys and sorrows
朝 *itchō* temporarily, a short period; once; one morning
朝一夕 *itchō-isseki ni* in a day, in a brief interval ⌈the pen
筆 *hito fude, ippitsu* a few lines, a stroke of
筆書 *hitofudega(ki)* a one-stroke sketch
塁 *ichirui* first base; a fort
塁手 *ichiruishu* first baseman
塁線 *ichiruisen* first-base line
筋 *hitosuji* a line; earnestly, blindly, straightforwardly

筋道 *hitosuji michi* a straight road
筋縄 *hitosuji nawa* a piece of rope; an ordinary method
番 *ichiban* number one, the first; most, best; a game, a round, a bout, a fall, an event (in a meet). *hitotsugai* a pair, a couple, a brace
番手 *ichbante* first player, first worker
番茶 *ichibancha* first-grade tea (first picking) ⌈to arrive
番乗 *ichibanno(ri)* leader of a charge; first
番鶏 *ichibandori* first cockcrowing
等 *ittō* first class, first rank, A1; the most,
等車 *ittōsha* first-class coach ⌊the best
等兵 *ittōhei* private first-class
等卒 *ittōsotsu* private first-class
等国 *ittōkoku* first-class power
等星 *ittōsei* first-magnitude star
等賞 *ittōshō* first prize, blue ribbon
等親 *ittōshin* first-degree relative, member of one's immediate family
18 鼓 *ikko* the first beat of the war drums
廉 *hitokado, ikkado* superiority, something uncommon. *hitokado no* respectable; full-fledged
塩 *hitoshio* slightly salted ⌈lump
塊 *hitokatama(ri)* a group, a lump. *ikkai* a
睡 *issui, hitonemuri* a nap, a short sleep
話 *hito(tsu)banashi* anecdote; common talk
路 *ichiro* one road, one way; straight; earnestly ⌈more, especially
際 *hitokiwa* noticeably, remarkably; still
戦 *issen* a battle, a game, a bout
新 *isshin* complete change, reform, remodeling, renewal, restoration
献 *ikkon* one cup (of saké)
群 *ichigun, hitomu(re)* a group; a flock, a crowd, a herd; a wide expanse (of flow-
歳 *issai* one year old ⌊ers)
置 *hito(tsu)o(ki)* alternate, every other one
夢 *ichimu* a dream; a fleeting thing
寝入 *hitone-i(ri)* a nap ⌈with another
蓮托生 *ichiren-takushō* sharing one's lot
触即発 *isshoku-sokuhatsu* delicate situation, explosive situation
新紀元 *ichi shinkigen* a new era
節 *issetsu* a verse (in the Bible), a stanza, a paragraph, a passage. *hito fushi* a joint, section; a tune, note, strain, measure
節切 *hitoyogi(ri)* one-jointed bamboo musical instrument
義 *ichigi* a reason, a principle, a meaning; the first meaning, the first principle, the first consideration
義的 *ichigiteki* unmistakable (meaning)
幕 *hitomaku* one act
幕物 *hitomakumono* a one-act play
意 *ichi-i* earnestness
意専心 *ichi-i senshin* wholeheartedly
14 層 *issō* more, still more, much more, all the
徳 *ittoku* a virtue ⌊more
摑 *hitotsuka(mi)* a handful, a grasp
旗 *hito hata* a flag; an undertaking
概 *ichigai ni* unconditionally, as a rule
様 *ichiyō* uniformity, evenness, similarity, equality, impartiality
滴 *itteki* a drop
種 *hitokusa* one kind. *isshu* a kind, a species,
端 *ittan* one end; a part ⌊a variety
緒 *issho* meeting, company. *issho ni* together (with); at the same time; in a lump. *issho ni suru* unite; confuse with. *issho(kuta)* medley, heterogeneous mixture
読 *ichidoku* a perusal; one reading
説 *issetsu* another report, another opinion
駄 *ichida* a horse load
管 *ikkan* one flute; one brush
髪 *ippatsu* a hair, a hair's-breadth ⌈arrest
網打尽 *ichimō-dajin* a big haul; wholesale
酸化炭素 *issanka tanso* carbon monoxide
語 *ichigo* one word
語一語 *ichigo-ichigo* word for word
箇 *ikko* one; a piece
箇月 *ikkagetsu* one month
箇年 *ikkanen* one year
15 億 *ichi oku* one hundred million
儀 *ichigi* an incident
撮 *hitotsumami* a pinch (of something), one
稼 *hitokasegi* a job; a gain ⌊piece
線 *issen* a line
諾 *ichidaku* a consent
輛 *ichiryō* one vehicle
駒 *hitokoma* a scene
審 *isshin* first instance, first trial
撃 *ichigeki* a blow, a hit, a poke
徹 *ittetsu na* obstinate, stubborn, inflexible
徹者 *ittetsu mono* stubborn person
諸 *issho*＝一緒 (see above-14)
諸苦茶 *isshokucha* medley, heterogeneous
輪 *ichirin* a flower; a wheel ⌊mixture
輪車 *ichirinsha* monocycle; wheelbarrow
輪挿 *ichirinzashi* a vase for one flower
16 樹 *ichiju* one tree
獲 *ikkaku* one grab
艘 *issō* a ship, a vessel
頻 *hitoshiki(ri)* for a while; at one time
興 *ikkyō* amusement, fun
機軸 *ichi kijiku* a new method
膳 *ichi (no) zen* 1st course at a banquet. *ichizen* a bowl (of rice); a pair (of chopsticks)
膳飯屋 *ichizen meshiya* a chophouse

覧 *ichiran* a look, a glance; a summary; (school) catalog ⌐log
覧表 *ichiranhyō* list, table, schedule, cata-
頭 *ittō* a head (of cattle)
頭立 *ittōda(te)* one-horse (carriage)
頭牽 *ittōbi(ki)* one-horse (carriage)
17 闋 *hitokusari* passage in a discourse, one
擲 *itteki suru* abandon ⌊scene
環 *ikkan* a link
縷 *ichiru* a thin wreath (of smoke); a ray of (hope); a thread; very little
瞥 *ichibetsu* a glance, a look
臂 *ippi* a (helping) hand, one's bit
瞬 *isshun* a moment, an instant
瞬間 *isshunkan* a moment, an instant
18 癖 *hitokuse* trait, peculiarity, idiosyncrasy
儲 *hitomōke* money-making
難 *ichinan* one difficulty, one danger
類 *ichirui* same kind; accomplices, companions
叢 *hitomura* a copse; a crowd; a herd
瀉千里 *issha-senri* one swift effort; fast
騎 *ikki* one horseman ⌊talking; fast writing
騎打 *ikkiu(chi)* personal combat
騎当千 *ikki-tōsen no* matchless (warrior)
騎討 *ikkiu(chi)* personal combat
19 蹴 *isshū, hitoke(ri)* a kick; a rejection
20 議 *ichigi* a word, an opinion, an objection
齣 *hitokusari* a passage in a discourse; one
籌 *itchū* a point, a degree ⌊scene
籌輸 *itchū (o) yu(su)* be a bit inferior
21 躍 *ichiyaku* one bound; at one bound
顧 *ikko* (take no) notice of
22 驚 *ikkyō* surprise, amazement
23 纏 *hitomato(me)* a bunch, a bundle
攫 *ikkaku* one grab
攫千金 *ikkaku-senkin* getting rich quick
24 顰一笑 *ippin-isshō* a mood; a smile or a frown

1

七 See 261.

丁 2/F10 TEI D. 4th. CHŌ counter for guns, tools, leaves, or cakes of something; even number. TŌ. CHIN. *hinoto* 4th calendar sign. *-chō.* leaf (of paper), block, cake (of something).
A
2 丁 *tōtō* ringing of an ax. *chōchō* clashing of swords; felling of trees
5 目 *chōme* city block (of irregular size)
付 *chōzu(ke)* paging, numbering
半 *chōhan* odd and even numbers; dice game; gambling
6 年 *teinen* majority, adulthood, age twenty
年者 *teinensha* adult
字 *teiji* the letter T
字形 *teijikei* T-shaped
字形定規 *teijigata jōgi* T square
7 形 *teikei* T shape
形定規 *teikei jōgi* T square
8 定規 *teijōgi* T square
9 度 *chōdo* exactly, just right
重 *teichō* courtesy
13 数 *chōsū* number of pages; even numbers
稚 *detchi* apprentice, shop boy
稚奉公 *detchibōkō* apprenticeship
14 寧 *teinei* politeness, courtesy; care, conscientiousness

2

干 See 1492. [干]

上 See 798.

丈丈 See 151.

工 3/F-X Nonstandard for **工** 1451.

兀 4/F179 KOTSU high and level; lofty; bald; dangerous. [儿]
24 鷹 *hagetaka* vulture; condor

于 5/F72 U going; from. [二]
20 蘭盆 *urabon*=next word
蘭盆会 *urabon-e*=盂蘭盆会 48.20

与 6/F1566 —**与與** Yo. *ata(eru)* give, award, impart, provide, allot, cause (pain or damage). *azuka(ru)* participate in. *kumi(suru)* take part in. be implicated in; side with; support. *ata(e)* gift, godsend. [臼]
B
2 力 *yoriki* feudal-era police
4 太 *yota* nonsense, idle talk, good-for-nothing fellow. *yota(ru)* live a wicked life
太郎 *yotarō* slow-witted fellow, liar
太者 *yotamono, yotamon* good-for-nothing fellow, hoodlum
太話 *yotabanashi* idle gossip
5 主 *ata(e)nushi* giver
6 件 *yoken* postulate, given conditions, data
8 国 *yokoku* ally
10 党 *yotō* party in power
11 野党 *yoyatō* majority and minority parties
14 奪 *yodatsu* giving and taking
15 論 *yoron* public opinion

A 万 7 F13 F1614 萬 MAN ten thousand; myriad. BAN ten thousand, myriad; fully; if by any chance. *yorozu* ten thousand, myriads, all, everything.

1 一 *man-ichi, man(ga)ichi* if by any chance, 10,000 to 1

2 力 *manriki* vise, jack, capstan

人 *bannin, banjin* all people, everybody

人向 *bannimmu(ki)* all-purpose, suiting everyone 「people

3 口 *bankō* the mouths of many people; many

千 *bansen* a tremendous number

丈 *banjō* full vent

才 *banzai* hurrah; long life; congratulations. *manzai* comic dialogue 「never

万 *bamban* very much, fully; (with neg.)

万一 *bamban-ichi, mamman-ichi* by any chance, ten thousand to one

4 戸 *banko* all houses, many houses

方 *bampō* many lands; many means

化 *banka* many changes

引 *mambiki* shoplifting; shoplifter

天 *banten* the whole world

夫 *bampu* many people

分一 *mambun(no)ichi* one ten-thousandth

止得 *ban-ya(muo)e(zu)* There's no hope. *ban-ya(muo)e(nakereba)* if necessary, when unavoidable

5 目 *bammoku* many eyes 「height

仞 *banjin* 10,000 fathoms; great depth; great

古 *banko* perpetuity, eternity

民 *bammin* all people; the whole nation

代 *bandai* eternity, all ages. *yorozuyo* thousands of years, all generations, eternity

代不易 *bandai fueki* eternity, perpetuity

世 *bansei* all ages, eternity. *yorozuyo* (see under 万代 above–5)

世一系 *bansei ikkei* unbroken imperial line

世不易 *bansei fueki* eternity, perpetuity

6 死 *banshi* certain death

灯 *mandō* Buddhist lantern festival

邦 *bampō* all nations

朶 *banda* many branches

全 *banzen, manzen* perfection

全策 *banzen (no) saku* a safe plan

有 *ban-yū* all things, all creation; universal

有引力 *ban-yū inryōku* universal gravitation

有神教 *ban-yūshinkyō* pantheism 」tion

年 *mannen* ten thousand years; eternity

年床 *mannendoko* leaving a bed unmade

年候補 *mannen kōho* ever unsuccessful candidate, persistent candidate

年雪 *mannen yuki* perpetual snow

年筆 *mannenhitsu* fountain pen 「youth

年新造 *mannen shinzō* woman of perennial

7 言 *mangen* many words

状 *banjō* diversification, multifariousness

別 *bambetsu* various differentiations

劫 *mangō* eternity

芸 *bangei* versatility

来 *banrai* many guests

寿 *banju* longevity

里 *banri* thousands of miles

里長城 *Banri(no) Chōjō* Great Wall of China

8 金 *mankin* ten thousand yen, immense sum

物 *bambutsu, bammotsu* all things, all crea-

卒 *bansotsu* host of soldiers 」tion

宝 *bampō* many treasures

物霊長 *bambutsu (no) reichō* mankind

事 *banji* all, everything 「that can be done.

事休 *banji kyū(suru)* There is nothing more

事窮 *banji kyū(suru)*＝word above

国 *bankoku* all nations

国史 *bankokushi* world history

国民 *bankokumin* the people of all nations

国旗 *bankokki, bankokuki* flags of all nations 「all-trades

9 屋 *yorozuya* general merchant; a Jack-of-

乗 *banjō* sovereignty

軍 *bangun* hosts, all the armies

品 *bampin* (see 万物 above–8)

巻 *mangan* many scrolls; many books

10 骨 *bankotsu* thousands of lives

病 *mambyō* all kinds of sickness

般 *bampan* all things

華鏡 *bankakyō, mangekyō* kaleidoscope

能 *bannō, mannō* all-purpose. *bannō* omnipotence

能薬 *bannōyaku, mannōyaku* cure-all, pan-

11 頃 *bankei* vast expanse 」acea

斛 *bankoku* copious (tears)

貨 *banka* many articles

遍無 *mambenna(ku)* equally, uniformly, without exception, all around

12 尋 *banjin*＝万仞 (see above–5)

策 *bansaku* all means

善 *banzen, manzen* perfection

象 *banshō* all creation, all nature, all the universe

鈞 *mankin* very heavy

葉仮名 *man-yōgana* an early Japanese syllabary composed of Chinese characters used phonetically 「of poems

葉集 *Man-yōshū* Japan's oldest anthology

13 福 *bampuku* all health and happiness

障 *banshō* all obstacles 「dancer

歳 *banzai* hurrah. *manzai* strolling comic

雷 *banrai* heavy thunder

感 *bankan* flood of emotions; many thoughts

愚節 *Bangusetsu* April Fool's Day

14 境 *bankyō* all places; all circumstances

1 [一] 2一 | 、ノ乙 亅

端 *bantan* all, everything
緑 *banryoku* myriad green leaves
態 *bantai* endless variety of forms
16機 *banki* state affairs
17謝 *bansha* many thanks; sincere apologies
18難 *bannan* innumerable difficulties, all obstacles
類 *banrui* all things, all kinds of things
22籟 *banrai* all nature

A 三 8 F14 SAN three. *mi(tsu), mi(ttsu), mi* three.
2又 *mi(tsu)mata* 3-pronged fork
七日 *minanuka, minanoka* 21st day after death; 21st day after birth
人 *sannin* three people
人称 *sanninshō* third person (in grammar)
人殺 *sanninkoro(shi)* triple murder ⌈some
人組 *sanningumi* trio, gang of three, three-
十二分音符 *sanjūnibu ompu* a 32nd note
十八度線 *Sanjūhachido Sen* the Thirty-eighth Parallel ⌈temple Pilgrimage
十三所 *Sanjūsansho* the Thirty-three-
十日 *sanjūnichi* 30th. *misoka* last day of the month ⌈trouble
十六計 *sanjū-rokkei* many plans; avoiding
十年戦争 *Sanjūnen Sensō* the Thirty
十路 *misoji* age thirty ⌊Years' War
3口 *mi(tsu)kuchi* harelip
子 *mi(tsu)go* 3-year old; triplets ⌈man)
才 *sansai* the 3 powers (heaven, earth, and
寸舌 *sanzun (no) shita* eloquent tongue
三九度 *sansan-kudo* exchange of nuptial cups
三五五 *sansan-gogo* by twos and threes
千 *sanzen* 3000; many ⌈universe
千世界 *sanzen sekai* the whole world; the
叉 *sansa* three-pronged fork. *sansa no* three-
叉路 *sansaro* three-forked road ⌊pronged
大国 *Sandaikoku* the Big Three (countries)
大都市 *sandaitoshi* the three largest cities
大節 *sandaisetsu* the three big national holidays ⌈*sampō* three sides
4方 *sambō* three sides; small offering stand.
巴 *mi(tsu)domoe* 3 fat-comma shapes arranged to form a circle
月 *sangatsu* March. *mitsuki* three months
月節句 *Sangatsu (no) Sekku* Girls' Doll Festival (in March)
毛作 *sammōsaku* three crops a year
毛猫 *mikeneko* tricolored cat
分 *sambun suru* trisect; divide by three
分搗 *sambutsuki* 30% polished (rice)
文 *sammon* farthing; cheapness
文小説 *sammon shōsetsu* dime novel
文文士 *sammom-bunshi* hack writer
文判 *sammomban* ready-made seal
尺 *sanjaku* 3 Japanese feet; waistband, belt; cloth girdle ⌈sword
尺秋水 *sanjaku (no) shūsui* a sharpened
尺帯 *sanjaku obi* waistband, belt, cloth girdle
尺童子 *sanjaku (no) dōji* a mere child.
日 *mikka* three days; the third day (of the month)
日三夜 *mikka-miyo* 3 days and 3 nights
日三晩 *mikka-miban* 3 days and 3 nights
日月 *mikazuki* new moon, crescent moon
日天下 *mikka tenka* a brief rule, a brief championship
日坊主 *mikka bōzu* unsteady worker
日路 *mikkaji* three-day journey
5冬 *santō* three winter months ⌈a cane)
本足 *sambon ashi* three legs (two legs and
半 *mi(tsu)ban* 3-stroke alarm
半規管 *sanhankikan* semicircular canals
世 *sanze* past, present, and future existences. *sansei* children of the *nisei*, 3rd generation of Japanese in U.S.
世相 *Sanzesō* the Book of Divination
6死 *sanshi* three outs
曲 *sankyoku* instrumental trio
次元 *sanjigen* three dimensions
羽烏 *sambagarasu* triumvirate, trio; three famous retainers
号雑誌 *sangō zasshi* short-lived magazine
行半 *mikudarihan* letter of divorce. *sangyō-han* 3 lines and a half ⌈advertisement
行広告 *sangyō kōkoku* three-line classified
行広告欄 *sangyō kōkokuran* classified ads
百 *sambyaku* 300; many ⌈yer
百代言 *sambyaku daigen* pettifogging law-
百諸侯 *sambyaku shokō* all the daimyos
色 *sanshoku* three colors ⌈process
色印刷法 *sanshoku insatsuhō* three-color
色版 *sanshokuban* three-color printing (red, yellow, and blue)
色菫 *sanshiki sumire, sanshoku sumire* pansy
色旗 *sanshokki, sanshokuki* tricolor flag
7身 *mi(tsu)mi* baby clothes
体 *santai* the three character styles: square, semicursive, and grass
伸 *sanshin* second postscript
役 *san-yaku* the three highest wrestling ranks; the three highest officials (in labor unions, etc.)
折 *mitsuo(ri)* threefold, folded in three
助 *sansuke* male bathhouse attendant
更 *sankō* midnight, dead of night; the small hours; midnight to 2 a.m., the third of five night watches ⌈and storm)
災 *sansai* the three calamities (fire, flood,

男 *sannan* three men; third son
位 *sammi, san-i* the third rank
位一体 *Sammi-ittai* the Trinity 「gle
角 *mi(tsu)kado* three corners. *sankaku* trian-
角巾 *sankakukin* triangle bandage
角帆 *sankakuho* jib sail
角州 *sankakusu* delta
角形 *sankakukei* triangle
角波 *sankaku nami* choppy sea
角法 *sankakuhō* trigonometry
角定規 *sankaku jōgi* triangles (used in mechanical drawing) 「function
角函数 *sankaku kansū* trigonometrical
角洲 *sankakusu* delta
角帽 *sankakubō* three-cornered hat 「ment)
角琴 *sankakugoto* trigon (a musical instru-
角測量 *sankaku sokuryō* triangulation
角旗 *sankakuki* pennant
角関係 *sankaku kankei* love triangle
角錐 *sankakusui* triangular pyramid
角闘争 *sankaku tōsō* three-cornered fight
8 府 *Sampu* the Three Urban Prefectures
門 *sammon* large triple gate to a temple
弦 *sangen* 3-stringed instrument, samisen
板 *sampan* a sampan
股 *sammata, mi(tsu)mata* forked stick
育 *san-iku* education of the head, hand, and heart
直 *sanchoku* out on a third-base liner
宝 *sampō, sambō* the three treasures of Buddhism (Buddha, the sutras, and the priesthood) 「important requisites
拍子 *sambyōshi* triple time (in music); 3
枚目 *sammaime* comedian
拝 *sampai* worshiping three times
拝九拝 *sampai-kyūhai* kowtowing, bowing repeatedly
国 *sangoku* three countries
国一 *sangoku-ichi* unparalleled in Japan, China, and India
国同盟 *sangoku dōmei* triple alliance
味 *sami* three-stringed guitar
味線 *samisen, shamisen* three-stringed guitar
味線弾 *samisenhiki* samisen player
者凡退 *sansha bontai* out in 1-2-3 order
者会談 *sansha kaidan* three-cornered conversation 「petition
者対立 *sansha tairitsu* three-cornered com-
9 食 *sanshoku* three meals (a day)
昧 *sammai* self-effacement, concentration,
封 *sampū* forced out on third ⌊absorption
軍 *sangun* a great army, a mighty host, the
思 *sanshi* deep reflection ⌊whole army
界 *sangai* past, present, and future exist-
竿 *sankan* broad daylight ⌊ences
春 *sanshun* three spring months

省 *sansei* frequent reflection (meditation)
途川 *Sanzu (no) Kawa* the River Styx
相 *sansō* three phases 「ing current
相交流 *sansō kōryū* three-phase alternat-
秋 *sanshū* three fall months; three years
秋思 *sanshū no omo(i)* longing for loved
乗 *sanjō* cube (in math) ⌊ones
乗根 *sanjōkon* cube root 「newspaper)
面 *sammen* 3 sides, 3 faces; page 3 (of a
面六臂 *sammen-roppi* rush of business; versatility; a man who can do the work of many
面記事 *sammen kiji* page-three news, police news, human-interest stories
段跳 *sandantobi* hop, step, and jump
段構 *sandangama(e)* triple, three-way
段論法 *sandan rompō* syllogism
重 *mie* three-fold, triple, three-ply. *sanjū* triple, treble, threefold, three-ply, triplicate
重宝冠 *sanjū hōkan* (papal) triple tiara
重冠 *sanjūkan* (papal) triple tiara
重奏 *sanjūsō* instrumental trio
重殺 *sanjūsatsu* triple play
重唱 *sanjūshō* vocal trio
重盗 *sanjūtō* triple steal (in baseball)
重結 *sanjū musu(bi)* magnus hitch
重焦点 *sanjū shōten* trifocal
10 倍 *sambai* threefold, three times
振 *sanshin* three strikes, fanning out
時 *(o)sanji* three-o'clock snack
桁 *miketa* hundreds (in figures)
流 *sanryū* third rate
紋 *mi(tsu)mon* triple family crest
夏 *sanka* three summer months
原色 *sangenshoku* three primary colors
校 *sankō* third proof
校終了 *sankō shūryō* third and final proof
部合奏 *sambu gassō* instrumental trio
部合唱 *sambu gasshō* vocal trio
11 唱 *sanshō* three cheers; singing three times
絃 *sangen* 3-stringed instrument; samisen
組 *mi(tsu)gumi, sankumi, mikumi* set of three
教 *Sankyō* Shinto, Buddhism, and Confucianism 「pitches
球三振 *sankyū-sanshin* fanned on three
脚 *sankyaku* tripod; three legs
脚架 *sankyakuga* tripod
12 揃 *mi(tsu)zoroi* 3-piece suit
景 *sankei* three famous beauty spots
筆 *sampitsu* three famous ancient calligraphers: Emperor Saga, Tachibana (no) Hayanari, and Kōbō Daishi
幅対 *sampukutsui* set of three
寒四温 *sankan-shion* alternation of 3 cold and 4 warm days

等 *santō* third class
等分 *santōbun suru* trisect
番鳥 *sambandori* third cockcrowing
番鶏 *sambandori* third cockcrowing
塁 *sanrui* third base
塁手 *sanruishu* third baseman
塁打 *sanruida* three-base hit, triple
塁線 *sanruisen* third-base line 「crying
13 嘆 *santan* praise, admiration; repeatedly
猿 *mizaru, san-en* three monkeys who see, hear, and speak no evil
幕物 *sammakumono* 3-act play
稜鏡 *sanryōkyō* prism
業 *sangyō* a business composed of a restaurant, a house of ill fame, and geisha service
業地 *sangyōchi* licensed red-light quarters
14 選 *sansen* third-term election
徳 *santoku* three primary virtues (valor, wisdom, and benevolence)
箇日 *sanganichi* January one to three
種神器 *Sanshu (no) Jingi* the Three Sacred Treasures (Mirror, Sword, and Jewels)
15 論 *Sanron* Buddhist sect originating in the seventh century
権 *sanken* the three powers of government (legislative, executive, and judicial)
権分立 *sanken bunritsu* separation of powers (executive, legislative, and judicial)
輪 *sanrin* three wheels 「truck
輪車 *sanrinsha* tricycle, three-wheeled
16 頭政治 *santō seiji* triumvirate
17 韓 *Sankan* (old name for) Korea
18 鞭酒 *shampen* champagne 「someone)
21 顧礼 *sanko(no)rei* special confidence (in

A **下** $\frac{9}{F27}$ KA, GE low class; inferiority; lowest, second, or last volume. *kuda(ru)* come down, go down; get down, descend; be given; be less than; have diarrhea; retire; leave the capital. *kuda(saru)* give, confer; oblige, favor with. *kuda(sai)* please give me. *kuda(su)* let down, lower; give, confer; issue (orders); hand down (decisions); have diarrhea; lay (hands) on. *o(riru)* come down, go down, step down, descend; get off; swoop down; land. *o(rosu)* take down, lower, pull down, lift down, let down, drop; launch; let off (passengers); wear (for the first time); cause (abortion); grate; invoke; exercise; borrow (in subtraction); lock. *sa(garu) vi* hang down, dangle; fall, go down, come down; abate; wane; retire; stand back; go behind; be granted. *sa(geru) vt* hang; wear (a decoration); reduce (rank); move back; let go, dismiss; remove; grant; draw (money), withdraw. *shita* lower part, bottom, base, foot; downstairs; subordinate place; below the average; part payment; under, lower; sub-, subordinate; preliminary. *kuda(ranai)* trivial, worthless; absurd, silly; nasty. *kuda(ri)* descent; leaving the capital; diarrhea. *kuda(shi)* purgation, evacuation. *o(roshi)* grating; grater; grated radish. *(o)sa(gari)* former offering; used clothes; leavings (of food). *sa(gari)* decline. *(o)sa(ge)* hair hanging down the neck. *shimo* bottom, lower part, the foot; lower stream; latter; lower part of the body; the masses, the servants; the governed. *shimo ni* below, down, downward. *moto* vicinity. *moto de, moto ni* under (a tree); under (the jurisdiction of). *-ka-, shita no* under, lower, subordinate. *-ka* beneath, below, subordinate; under the direction, command, or influence of.

2 人 *genin* low-rank person, menial
3 山 *gezan, gesan* descent from the mountain
下 *shimojimo, shitajita* the lower classes, the common people
上 *o(ri)-nobo(ri)* going up and down
大根 *oro(shi) daikon* grated radish
士 *kashi* noncommissioned officer
士官 *kashikan* noncommissioned officer
士官兵 *kashikanhei* enlisted men
女 *gejo* maidservant
女下男 *gejo-genan* servants
女中 *shimo jochū* kitchen maid
4 心 *shitagokoro* secret intention, motive
戸 *geko* nondrinker, temperance man
方 *kahō* lower part. *kahō ni* below
火 *shitabi* burning low; decline, waning
刈 *shitaga(ri)* weeding
手 *heta* unskillful, awkward. *shimote* lower part; left part of the stage. *shitade, shitate* the foot; humble position
手人 *geshunin* offender, criminal
手物 *getemono* low-quality products
手屎 *hetakuso* extreme clumsiness 「age
水 *gesui* sewer, drain, ditch, gutter; sewer-
水板 *gesui ita* wooden sewer covers
水道 *gesuidō* drainage system; drain; sewer
水管 *gesuikan* sewer pipe
5 生 *shitaba(e)* underbrush, undergrowth
田 *geden* worn-out rice land
目 *shitame* downward glance; contemptuous look. *saga(ri)me* eyes slanting downward; decline
石 *shita ishi* nether millstone
立 *o(ri)-ta(tsu)* go down and stand
句 *geku, shimo (no) ku* the last part of a poem
札 *sa(ge)fuda* tag, label 「or Bible verse

司 *gesu* menial, churl; petty official. *gesu(baru)* be churlish, be vulgar
民 *kamin, gemin* the masses, the lower classes, the common people
仕事 *shita shigoto* spade work; subcontract
台所 *shimo daidokoro* servants' kitchen
世話 *gesewa* common saying
四半期 *shimo shihanki* last quarter (of the year)
付 *kafu suru* grant, issue
付金 *kafukin* subsidy
半 *kahan* lower half of the body
半身 *shimo hanshin, kahanshin* lower half
半期 *shimo hanki, kahanki* the last half-year
6 臣 *kashin* low-rank retainer
血 *geketsu* bloody bowel discharge
旬 *gejun* last ten days (of a month)
回 *shitamawa(ri)* subordinate part; menial service; subordinate; utility man. *shitamawa(ru)* be less than, be lower than
向 *shitamu(ki)* downward look; business decline. *gekō suru* leave the capital
地 *shitaji* groundwork, foundation; inclination, aptitude; elementary knowledge of, grounding in; prearrangement, spadework; signs, symptoms; first coat of plastering; soy
阪 *gehan* proceeding from Tokyo to Osaka
劣 *geretsu na* base, mean, vulgar
名 *kamei* the undermentioned, the undersigned
吏 *kari* lower official
糸入 *shita-ito-i(re)* shuttle
列車 *kuda(ri) ressha* trains going away from the capital, down train
7 車 *gesha* alighting
図 *shitazu*, rough sketch. *kazu* the lower illustration
作 *gesaku* poor manufacture, poor quality; inferior goods
位 *ka-i* low rank, subordinate position
体 *katai* lower part of the body; lower limbs
坂 *kuda(ri)zaka* downhill; decline; waning
役 *shitayaku* subordinate official; underling
男 *genan* manservant
克上 *gekokujō* a retainer supplanting his lord; juniors dominating seniors
見 *shitami* preliminary inspection, preview; siding (on a house)
見板 *shitami ita* siding (on a house)
町 *shitamachi* downtown section
町風 *shitamachifū* downtown style
足 *gesoku* footgear
足料 *gesokuryō* footwear-checking charge
足番 *gesokuban* footwear doorman
附 *kafu suru* grant, issue
8 金 *shitagane* basic metal (in an art object); old metal. *oro(shi)gane* grater
国 *gekoku suru* leaving for the province

刷 *shitazu(ri)* proof printing
姓 *geshō* person of humble birth
押 *shitao(su)* decline (stock market)
放 *shitabana(re)* slump (on the stock market)
松 *sa(gari) matsu* drooping pine
物 *kabutsu* drinking feast. *o(ri)mono* menstruation; afterbirth
知 *gechi, geji* command, order
肥 *shimogoe* night soil, manure
肢 *kashi* lower extremities, legs
郎 *gerō* servant, valet, menial
垂 *kasui* drooping, hanging down
命 *kamei* order, command
協議 *shita kyōgi* preliminary conference
弦 *kagen* last quarter (of the moon)
弦月 *kagen (no) tsuki* waning moon
9 風 *kafū* subordinate position, lower position
城 *gejō* withdrawing from the castle
拵 *shitagoshira(e)* preparation, spadework
降 *kakō* descent, fall; drop, subsidence
院 *ka-in* the lower (legislative) body
剃 *shitazori* barber's apprentice
段 *gedan, kadan* lower (horizontal) column (of print). *gedan* lowest step, lowest tier, lower berth
乗 *gejō* dismounting
卑 *gebi(ru)* become vulgar, coarsen. *gebi* vulgar, coarse
品 *gehin* vulgarity, coarseness, meanness, indecency. *kahin* inferior article
界 *gekai* this world; hades, the nether world
草 *shitagusa* weeds beneath a tree
巻 *gekan* last volume (in a set of 2 or 3)
剋上 *gekokujō* juniors dominating seniors; a retainer supplanting his lord
屋敷 *shimo yashiki* villa, daimyo's suburban residence
降線 *kakōsen* downward curve
相場 *sa(ge) sōba* bearish market
相談 *shita sōdan* preliminary consultation, arrangements
級 *kakyū* lower grade, low class; junior (officer)
級生 *kakyūsei* underclassmen
級審 *kakyūshin* lower court
級職 *kakyūshoku* subordinate post
10 座 *geza* squatting. *shimoza* lower seat
疳 *gekan* chancre
唇 *shita kuchibiru, kashin* lower lip
値 *shitane* lower price
振 *sa(ge)fu(ri)* plummet, plumb bob
紐 *shita himo* undersash, belt
記 *kaki no* the following
剤 *gezai* laxative
家 *shitaya* small attached annex
穿 *shitabaki* undershorts
書 *shitaga(ki), gesho* rough copy, draft
帯 *shita obi* loin cloth, waist cloth

流 *karyū* downstream, lower reaches of a river; lower classes
流社会 *karyū shakai* lower classes
部 *kabu* lower part, substructure; subordinate (offices)
部機関 *kabu kikan* subordinate offices or
馬 *geba* dismounting ⌊institutions
馬先 *gebasaki* dismounting place
馬評 *gebahyō* irresponsible criticism, hearsay, rumor
11 達 *katatsu suru* command a subordinate
問 *kamon suru* inquire, consult
婢 *kahi* servant girl
張 *shitaba(ri)* undercoat, first coat
情 *kajō* condition of the common people
掛 *shimoga(karu)* talk about indecent things
渋 *shitashibu(ri)* (stock market) steadiness
略 *geryaku* the rest omitted (in quoting)
組 *shitagu(mi)* preliminary typesetting
脚 *kakyaku* legs, lower limbs
船 *gesen* going ashore
野 *geya* retirement from public office
萠 *shitamoe* sprouts, shoots ⌈ing house
宿 *geshuku* board and room, lodging; board-
宿人 *geshukunin* lodger, roomer
宿屋 *geshukuya* lodginghouse
宿料 *geshukuryō* board-and-room charge
12 歯 *shitaba* lower teeth
痢 *geri* diarrhea
場 *o(ri)ba* dismounting place
御 *gegyo suru* dismount (polite)
渡 *sa(ge)-wata(su)* (government) grant; re-
湯 *shimoyu* sitz bath ⌊lease (a criminal)
絵 *shitae* rough sketch, cartoon, design
脹 *shimobukure* abdominal swelling; fat face
貼 *shitabari* undercoat, first coat
期 *shimoki* second half (of the fiscal year)
策 *gesaku* poor plan
着 *shitagi* underwear
落 *geraku* depreciation, decline, fall, slump
葉 *shitaba* lower leaves
衆 *gesu*＝下種 (see below-14)
番 *kaban* going off duty ⌈tion
検分 *shita kembun* preliminary examina-
検査 *shita kensa* preliminary inspection
等 *katō* low grade, lower class; *katō na* inferior, base, vulgar
等動物 *katō dōbutsu* lower animals
等植物 *katō shokubutsu* lower plants
13 殿 *geden* leaving the palace
働 *shitabatara(ki)* subordinate work; as-
僧 *gesō* low-rank priest ⌊sistant, servant
腿 *katai* leg, lower leg
馴 *shitanara(shi)* training
幕 *sa(ge)maku* drop curtain
意 *ka-i* the feelings of the people

塗 *shitanu(ri)* first coat; undercoating
準備 *shita jumbi* preliminary arrangements, spade work
腹 *shitahara, shita(p)para, shitabara* abdomen, stomach, under parts. *geribara*
腹部 *kafukubu* abdomen ⌊diarrhea
14 聞 *shitagi(ki)* inquiring beforehand
僚 *karyō* subordinates, petty officials
僕 *geboku* servant; your humble servant
摺 *shitazu(ri)* proof printing ⌈ple
様 *shimozama* lower classes, common peo-
獄 *gegoku suru* be sent to prison
端 *katan* lower end. *shita(p)pa* lower position; underling
緒 *sageo* sword knot ⌈study
読 *shitayo(mi)* preparatory reading; lesson
髪 *sa(ge)gami* hair hanging down ⌈person
種 *gesu* person of humble rank, humble
種女 *gesu onna* woman of low rank; a term of degradation for a woman
種根性 *gesu konjō* mean feelings
層 *kasō* lower strata; lower classes
層土 *kasōdo* subsoil ⌈ranks of society
層社会 *kasō shakai* the underworld, lower
層階級 *kasō kaikyū* proletariat, lower
駄 *geta* wooden clogs ⌊classes
駄直 *getanao(shi)* repairing clogs; clog re-
駄屋 *getaya* clog shop ⌊pairer
駄掛 *getaga(ke)* wearing wooden clogs
駄番 *getaban* footwear doorman
駄履 *getaba(ki)* wearing clogs ⌈clogs)
駄箱 *getabako* cupboard (for shoes and
15 履 *shitabaki* footgear; underpants
潮 *sa(ge)shio* ebb tide
縫 *shitanu(i)* basting, temporary sewing
調 *shitashira(be)* preliminary investigation;
賜 *kashi* imperial grant ⌊preparation
賤 *gesen* humble birth
敷 *shitaji(ki)* desk pad; mat; something lying underneath; pinned under, crushed beneath
輩 *kahai, gehai* an inferior, a low-class person
請 *shita-uke* subcontract
請負 *shita-ukeoi* subcontract
請業者 *shita-u(ke) gyōsha* subcontractor
16 積 *shitazu(mi)* goods piled underneath; lowest social strata
膨 *shimobuku(re)* round-faced; large at the bottom
薬 *geyaku, kuda(shi)gusuri* laxative. *o(roshi)-gusuri* an abortive
稽古 *shitageiko* rehearsal, preparation
17 瞰 *kakan suru* look down on, get a bird's-
翼 *sa(ge)yoku* wing flap ⌊eye view
18 瞼 *shita mabuta* lower eyelid

顎 *shita ago, kagaku* lower jaw
21 露 *shita tsuyu* dew under the trees; dew dripping from the trees
22 鬚 *shita hige* beard below the mouth
24 齶 *shita ago* lower jaw

— 3 —

戸 See 1817. [戸]

与与 See 6. [臼]

土 10/F-X See 土 1050. [土]

卍卐 See 12 and 79. [十]

丐 11/F39 KAI. *ko(u)* (see under 乞 262.0).

卐 12/F-X BAN. MAN. *manji* the Nazi swastika; the reversed swastika, a variant of 卍 79. [十]
4 巴 *manji-tomoe* falling in whirls; falling thick and fast

丑 13/F39 CHŪ. SHŪ. JŪ. *ushi* 1–3 a.m.; 2nd zodiac sign; cow.

互 14/F73 GO. *tagai ni, katami ni* mutually, reciprocally, together. [二]
B
5 用 *goyō* using together; using in turn
市 *goshi* trade, commerce
同士 *tagaidōshi de* with each other
7 角 *gokaku* equality, evenness, par; good match
助 *gojo* mutual aid, co-operation
助会 *gojokai* a benefit society
助的 *gojoteki* friendly
10 格 *gokaku*=互角 (see above-7)
恵 *gokei* reciprocity, mutual benefits
11 違 *taga(i)chiga(i) ni* alternately
14 選 *gosen* co-optation; mutual election
20 譲 *gojō* conciliation, compromise
譲的 *gojōteki* conciliatory

五 15/F74 GO five. *itsu(tsu), itsu* five; five years old. [二]
A
2 人組 *goningumi* five-family unit; five-man group
人囃子 *gonimbayashi* five court-musician dolls at the Girls' Festival (in March)
十三次 *gojūsan tsugi* the 53 Tōkaidō stages
十年祭 *gojūnensai* jubilee, semicentennial
十歩百歩 *gojippo-hyappo, gojuppo-hyappo* six of one and a half dozen of the other
十音 *gojūon* the Japanese syllabary
十音順 *gojūonjun* the syllabary order
十路 *isoji* fifty years; age fifty
3 寸釘 *gosun kugi* long nail, spike
大国 *Godaikoku* the Five Powers
大洲 *Godaishū* the Five Continents
大洋 *Godaiyō* the Five Oceans
4 日 *itsuka* five days; the fifth day (of the month)
斗米 *gotobei* small salary
辺形 *gohenkei* pentagon
分 *gobu* five percent; fifty percent, half; a tie; evenness
分刈 *gobuga(ri)* close haircut
分五分 *gobugobu* evenly matched; tie
分試 *gobudame(shi)* killing by inches
月 *gogatsu* May. *satsuki* lunar 5th month
月人形 *gogatsu ningyō* Boys' May Festival dolls
月雨 *samidare, satsuki ame* early summer rain
月祭 *gogatsusai* May Day
月晴 *satsukiba(re)* fine weather during the rainy season
月節句 *Gogatsu no Sekku* Boys' Festival
月幟 *gogatsu nobori, satsukinobori* May Boy's Festival paper-carp streamers
月闇 *satsuki yami* dark night in the rainy season
月蝿 *urusa(i)* (see under 煩 2782.0)
月蝿方 *urusagata*=煩方 2782.4
月蝿型 *urusagata*=煩方 2782.4
5 目 *gomoku* a mixture; game of go; gomokumeshi (飯) and gomokuzushi (鮨) (see the next two words
目飯 *gomokumeshi* a rice, fish, and vegetable dish
目鮨 *gomokuzushi* rice mixed with vegetables and delicacies
6 色 *goshiki* the five colors; variegated colors. *goshoku* five colors
行 *gogyō* the five elements (wood, fire, water, earth, and metal)
旬節 *Gojunsetsu* Pentecost
7 戒 *gokai* the five commandments (against murder, lust, theft, lying, and intemperance)
体 *gotai* the whole body; the limbs
更 *gokō* fifth watch, 4–6 a.m.; the five night watches
児 *itsu(tsu)go* quintuplets. *goji* five children
角形 *gokakukei, gokakkei* pentagon
里霧中 *gori-muchū* in a fog, at sea, mystified, bewildered, in a maze, up in the air
8 官 *gokan* the five organs of sense
9 指 *goshi* the five fingers
音音階 *go-on onkai* pentatonic scale
重 *gojū, itsue* fivefold, five-storied, quintuplicate
重塔 *gojū (no) tō* five-storied pagoda
10 桁 *go keta* ten thousands (in figures)
書 *Gosho* Pentateuch
倍子 *fushi, gobaishi, gofushi* gallnut

1 [一] 丨 丶 丿 乙 亅 3

倫 *gorin* the five Confucian filial-piety relationships
倫道 *gorin (no) michi* the five Confucian filial-piety relationships
11 情 *gojō* the five passions (anger, joy, hatred, desire, and grief)
経 *Gokyō* the Five Chinese Classics
絃 *gogen* five strings; a five-stringed instrument
彩 *gosai* the five colors (green, yellow, red, white, and black); five-colored porcelain
悪 *goaku* the five sins in Buddhism (murder, theft, adultery, falsehood, and drink)
常 *gojō* the five cardinal Confucian virtues (justice, politeness, wisdom, fidelity, ⌊and benevolence)
13 感 *gokan* the five senses
節句 *gosekku* the five festivals (Jan. 1, Mar. 3, May 5, July 7, and Sept. 9)
14 徳 *gotoku* the five virtues; tripod; kettle stand
穀 *gokoku* the five grains (wheat, rice, beans, and millet [*awa* and *kibi*])
種競技 *goshu kyōgi* pentathlon
15 畿内 *Gokinai* the Five Home Provinces
線 *gosen* staff (in music)
線紙 *gosenshi* music paper
線譜 *gosenfu* score (in music)
輪 *gorin* the five filial-piety relationships
輪大会 *Gorin Taikai* Olympic Games
輪会議 *Gorin Kaigi* Olympic Congress
輪塔 *gorin (no) tō* five-story pagoda
輪聖火 *Gorin Seika* Olympic Torch
輪旗 *Gorinki* Olympic Flag
18 臓 *gozō* the five viscera (liver, lungs, heart, kidney, and spleen)
臓六腑 *gozō-roppu* the internal organs

A 天 16/F464 TEN sky, air, heavens, celestial sphere, firmament; heaven, Providence, God, Nature; destiny; weather; top; beginning. *ame* sky, heaven. *ama-* heavenly. *amatsu-* heavenly, imperial. [大]

2 人 *tenjin* nature and man; God and man; celestial being. *tennin* heavenly being; celestial maiden
3 女 *tennyo* celestial nymph; goddess
子 *tenshi* the emperor
川 *Ama(no)kawa* Milky Way
工 *tenkō* a work of nature
与 *ten-yo* heaven's gift, a godsend
才 *tensai* genius, prodigy; natural gift
才児 *tensaiji* child prodigy
上 *tenjō* the heavens ⌈surrounding land
上川 *tenjōgawa* a river raised above the
上界 *tenjōkai* the celestial world, heaven
下 *amakuda(ri)* descent from heaven; appointment thru influence. *amakuda(ru)* descend from heaven. *tenka, tenga, ame(ga)shita, ame(no)shita* the whole country; the public; the world; the ruling power; having one's own way
下一 *tenka-ichi* unique thing; best on earth
下一品 *tenka-ippin* best article under heaven
下分目 *tenka-wa(ke)me* fateful, decisive (war)
下晴 *tenka ha(rete)* right and proper, legal
下無双 *tenka-musō* peerless, unequaled
下無比 *tenka-muhi* peerless, unequaled
4 心 *tenshin* zenith; divine will, providence
火 *tempi* oven; (waffle) iron. *tenka* fire caused by lightning
父 *Tempu* Heavenly Father
牛 *kamikirimushi* long-horned beetle
辺 *teppen* top, summit, apex, scalp. *tempen ni* high up in the sky
引 *tembi(ki)* lending money and taking out the interest in advance; deduction
分 *tembun* one's nature, talents, sphere of activity, mission, destiny
手古舞 *tentekomai* whirl of business; humming with activity
水 *tensui* rain water
水桶 *tensui oke* rain barrel
王山 *Tennōzan* Tennozan Hill; strategic ⌊point
王星 *Tennōsei* Uranus
文 *temmon* astronomy
文台 *temmondai* astronomical observatory
文学 *temmongaku* astronomy
文学者 *temmongakusha* astronomer
文家 *temmonka* astronomer
日 *tenjitsu* the sun. *tempi* sun, sunlight
日瓦 *tenjitsugawara* sun-dried brick; adobe
日法 *tempihō* solar-evaporation process (in salt making)
日塩 *tenjitsuen, tempi shio* sun-dried salt
日嗣 *ama(tsu)hitsugi* imperial throne
井 *tenjō* ceiling, ceiling price
井灯 *tenjōtō* ceiling light
井抜 *tenjōnu(ke)* skyrocketing (prices)
井板 *tenjō ita* ceiling boards
井知 *tenjōshi(razu)* skyrocketing (prices)
井桟敷 *tenjō sajiki* gallery
井裏 *tenjō ura* above the ceiling
5 生 *tensei* nature, disposition ⌈gions
外 *tengai* beyond the heavens; farthest re-
平 *tembin*＝天秤 (see below–10)
台 *Tendai* Buddhist sect originating in the eighth century
丼 *tendon* bowl of rice and fried fish
瓜粉 *tenkafun* talcum powder
主 *Tenshu* Lord of Heaven, God

主教 *Tenshukyō* Roman Catholicism
6色 *tenshoku* weather; sky color
后 *tenkō* queen of heaven
衣 *ten-i* heavenly garment
衣無縫 *ten-i-muhō* perfect, flawless
成 *tensei* nature; product of nature. *tensei no* natural, born (musician)
成美 *tensei* (*no*) *bi* natural beauty
刑 *tenkei* divine punishment
刑病 *tenkeibyō* leprosy
年 *tennen* the space of life
守 *tenshu* castle tower
守閣 *tenshukaku* castle tower
地 *tenchi, ametsuchi* heaven and earth, the universe, nature; top and bottom; world, realm, sphere
地人 *tenchijin* heaven, earth, and man
地万物 *tenchi-bambutsu* the whole creation, everything in heaven and earth
地神明 *tenchi-shimmei* the heavenly and earthly gods
地無用 *tenchi-muyō* this side up
地創造 *tenchi sōzō* creation ⌈and earth
地開闢 *tenchi kaibyaku* creation of heaven
気 *tenki* weather; the elements; fine weather. (*o*)*tenki*=*tenki*; temper, mood
気予報 *tenki yohō* weather forecast
気図 *tenkizu* weather map
気具合 *tenki guai* weather conditions
気屋 *tenkiya* moody person
気相談所 *tenki sōdanjo* weather bureau
気都合 *tenki tsugō* weather conditions
気運 *tenkiun* weather conditions
気模様 *tenki moyō* weather conditions
7位 *ten-i* imperial throne
佑 *ten-yū* divine aid
助 *tenjo* divine aid ⌈army
兵 *Tempei* the Imperial Army, heaven-sent
災 *tensai* natural calamity
来 *tenrai no* heavenly, divine, inspired,
寿 *tenju* life span ⌊heaven-sent
邪鬼 *amanojaku* the devil beneath temple guardian deities; a perverse person
花 *tenka* snow
花粉 *tenkafun* talcum powder
体 *tentai* heavenly bodies
体力学 *tentai rikigaku* celestial mechanics
体分光術 *tentai bunkōjutsu* astronomical spectroscopy ⌈raphy
体写真術 *tentai shashinjutsu* astrophotog-
体図 *tentaizu* star map
体学 *tentaigaku* uranography
体物理学 *tentai butsurigaku* astrophysics
体崇拝 *tentai sūhai* star worship, astrolatry
8金 *tenkin* gilt-top (book) ⌈heaven
国 *tengoku* Kingdom of Heaven, paradise,
府 *tempu* fertile land; deep scholarship
底 *tentei* nadir
使 *tenshi, ten* (*no*) *tsuka*(*i*) angel
性 *tensei*=天成 (see above–6)
明 *temmei* dawn, daybreak
杯 *tempai* emperor's gift cup
泣 *tenkyū* rain from a cloudless sky
河 *Ama*(*no*)*gawa, Tenga* the Milky Way
命 *temmei* God's will, Heaven's decree; destiny, karma; one's life
岩戸 *Ama* (*no*) *Iwato* Gate of the Celestial Rock Cave ⌈and earth
長地久 *tenchō-chikyū* coeval with heaven
長節 *Tenchōsetsu* Emperor's Birthday
空 *tenkū* sky, air, ether, firmament ⌈the sea
空海濶 *tenkū-kaikatsu* serene as the sky and
狗 *tengu* long-nosed goblin; boaster
狗風 *tengu kaze* sudden gust
狗話 *tengubanashi* boastful story
竺 *Tenjiku* India
竺牡丹 *tenjiku botan* dahlia ⌈samurai
竺浪人 *tenjiku rōnin* wandering lordless
竺鼠 *tenjiku nezumi* guinea pig
9威 *ten-i* imperial authority, imperial majesty
柱 *tenchū* pillars supporting heaven
祖 *Tenso* the ancestral Sun Goddess
則 *tensoku* natural law, rule of heaven
降 *amakuda*(*ru*) descend from heaven. *amakuda*(*ri*) a command to an inferior
盃 *tempai* emperor's gift cup
帝 *Tentei* Lord, God, Creator, Heavenly
軍 *tengun* heavenly hosts ⌊King
草 *tengusa* agar-agar
為 *ten-i* providential, natural
変 *tempen* striking phenomena in heaven and earth; natural calamity ⌈above–9)
変地異 *tempen-chi-i*=天変 *tempen* (see
神 *tenjin* heavenly gods; Michizane's spirit. *amatsukami* heavenly gods
神地祇 *tenshin chigi* gods of heaven and
神髭 *tenshin hige* goatee ⌊earth
津乙女 *amatsuotome* celestial maiden
津日嗣 *amatsuhitsugi* imperial throne
津神 *amatsukami* heavenly gods
津御子 *amatsumiko* emperor
津御祖 *amatsumioya* imperial ancestor
皇 *Tennō, Sumeragi, Sumerogi* Emperor of
皇杯 *Tennōhai* Emperor's trophy ⌊Japan
皇制 *Tennōsei* Emperor system
皇陛下 *Tennō Heika* His Majesty the Em-
皇家 *Tennōke* the Imperial Family ⌊peror
皇崇拝 *tennō sūhai* emperor worship
皇旗 *Tennōki* Imperial Standard
皇誕生日 *Tennō Tanjōbi* Emperor's Birth-
10原 *ama*(*no*)*hara* the sky, the heavens ⌊day
候 *tenkō* weather

1 [一] 3— 丨丶ノ乙亅

孫 *tenson* descendant of the gods, heavenly grandson
祐 *ten-yū* divine grace, providential help
険 *tenken* natural defenses; a steep place
恵 *tenkei* heaven's blessing; natural advantages; divine rewards
恩 *ten-on* blessings of heaven; blessings of nature; favor of the emperor; divination's luckiest day
宮図 *tenkyūzu* horoscope
狼星 *Tenrōsei* the Dog Star, Sirius
馬 *temba* flying horse, Pegasus ⌈structed
馬空行 *tembakū (o) i(ku)* advance unob-
秤 *tembin* shoulder carrying pole; (balance) scales, steelyard
秤棒 *tembimbō* shoulder carrying pole
蚕 *tensan* wild silkworm
蚕糸 *tegusu* silkworm gut
真 *tenshin* naïveté ⌈ity, innocence
真爛漫 *tenshin-ramman* naïveté, simplic-
11 運 *ten-un* destiny, will of Heaven, luck
授 *tenju* natural gifts ⌈remote region
涯 *tengai* horizon, skyline; heavenly shores;
理 *tenri* rule of heaven, natural laws
堂 *tendō* heaven, paradise
窓 *temmado* skylight
啓 *tenkei* divine revelation; divine oracle
動説 *tendōsetsu* Ptolemaic theory
産 *tensan* natural products
産物 *tensambutsu* natural products
球 *tenkyū* celestial sphere
球図 *tenkyūzu* horoscope
球儀 *tenkyūgi* celestial globe
眼 *tengan* clairvoyant; rolling back the eyes in convulsions
眼通 *tengantsū* clairvoyance
眼鏡 *tengankyō* magnifying glass
頂 *tenchō* zenith
頂点 *tenchōten* zenith
頂儀 *tenchōgi* zenith telescope
道 *tentō* Providence, heaven; the sun. *tendō* the way of heaven; Providence; divine justice; destiny
道干 *tentōbo(shi) no* sun-dried
道虫 *tentōmushi* ladybug
道乾 *tentōboshi no* sun-dried
道様 *tentōsama* the sun; providence; god
12 晴 *appa(re)* splendid, praiseworthy; well
極 *tenkyoku* celestial poles ⌊done
減 *tembiki*＝天引 (see above—4)
測 *tensoku* astronomical observation; shoot-
軸 *tenjiku* celestial axis ⌊ing the sun
朝 *tenchō* imperial court (polite)
童 *tendō* cherub; gods disguised as children; children parading as cherubs
雲 *amagumo* clouds in the sky

象 *tenshō* astronomical phenomenon;
象儀 *tenshōgi* planetarium ⌊weather
然 *tennen* nature; spontaneity. *tennen ni* naturally, spontaneously
然色 *tennenshoku* natural color; technicolor
然色写真 *tennenshoku shashin* color photo
然記念物 *tennen kinembutsu* natural monu-
然港 *tennenkō* natural harbor ⌊ment
然痘 *tennentō* smallpox
然硝子 *tennen garasu* natural glass
然資源 *tennen shigen* natural resources
13 漢 *Tenkan* Milky Way
福 *tempuku* heavenly blessing
誅 *tenchū* Heaven's punishment; well-de-
際 *tensai* horizon ⌊served punishment
稟 *tempin* natural talents
蓋 *tengai* canopy; dome; priestly minstrel's
雷 *tenrai* thunder ⌊reed hood
意 *ten-i* divine will, providence
業 *tengyō* emperor's work
路歴程 *Tenro Rekitei* Pilgrim's Progress
照大神 *Amaterasu Ōmikami* the Sun Goddess ⌈*Daijin* the Sun Goddess
照皇大神 *Amaterasu Ōmikami, Tenshōkō*
資 *tenshi* nature; natural talents
資英邁 *tenshi-eimai* highly gifted
幕 *temmaku* curtain; tent, pavilion
幕造 *temmakuzuku(ri)* tentmaker
幕製造人 *temmaku seizōnin* tentmaker
14 聞 *tembun* emperor's knowledge ⌈ance
網 *temmō* heaven's net, heaven's venge-
領 *tenryō* imperial fief; shogunate control
爾遠波 *te-ni-o-ha* the particles
罰 *tembatsu* divine wrath, divine punishment, visitation ⌈divine punishment
罰覿面 *tembatsu-tekimen* the certainty of
15 摩 *ten (o) ma(suru)* (a building) soars high
賜 *tenshi* heavenly gift, imperial gift
敵 *tenteki* natural enemy
質 *tenshitsu* natural talents
麩羅 *tempura* (Japanese) fritters
賦 *tempu* natural talent, endowment
賦人権 *tempu jinken* natural rights of man
16 壌 *tenjō* heaven and earth
嶮 *tenken* natural defense
機 *tenki* profound secret; emperor's health; the will of heaven
覧 *tenran* imperial inspection
17 聴 *tenchō* emperor's knowledge
爵 *tenshaku* natural nobility; true merit
18 職 *tenshoku* vocation, lifework, calling
顔 *tengan* emperor's countenance
鵞絨 *birōdo* velvet
19 警 *tenkei* heaven-sent warning
20 譴 *tenken* divine punishment
21 魔 *temma* demon, evil spirit

22鷚 *hibari* skylark 「poetry
籟 *tenrai* sound of the wind; beautiful

A 不 17 F31 FU negation; bad; clumsy; ugly. BU clumsy; ugly. *-zu* negation.

1乙 *fuitsu* Very sincerely yours
一 *fuitsu* Very sincerely yours 「sonance
一致 *fuitchi* discord, disagreement, dis-
2二 *fuji* peerless, unparalleled
入 *fui(ri)* small attendance, poor house
十分 *fujūbun* insufficiency, imperfection
人気 *funinki* unpopularity 「heartlessness
人情 *funinjō* unkindness, inhumanity,
3凡 *fubon* uncommon, outstanding
才 *fusai* lack of talent, incompetency
干渉 *fukanshō* nonintervention, noninterference 「early date
4日 *fujitsu, hinarazu* in a few days, at an
仁 *fujin* heartlessness, inhumanity
予 *fuyo* indisposition; emperor's illness; unhappiness 「vention, neutrality
介入 *fukainyū* noninvolvement, noninter-
心得 *fukokoroe* indiscretion, imprudence
手回 *futemawa(shi)* poor preparation, poor arrangements
手際 *futegiwa* clumsiness, ineptitude
毛 *fumō* barren, sour, unproductive (land)
毛地 *fumōchi* unproductive land
公平 *fukōhei* unfairness, injustice, partiality
公正 *fukōsei* injustice, unfairness
分明 *fubummei* indistinct, obscure
分割 *fubunkatsu* indivisibility
文 *fubun* unwritten; illiterate, uneducated
文法 *fubunhō* unwritten law, common law
文律 *fubunritsu* unwritten law, unwritten rule, common law
5払 *fubara(i), fuhara(i)* nonpayment, default
世出 *fuseishutsu* rare, extraordinary, unparalleled 「bungle
出来 *fudeki* poor workmanship, bad job,
必要 *fuhitsuyō* unnecessary
本意 *fuhon-i* reluctance, unwillingness
生産的 *fuseisanteki* unproductive, unfruitful 「worthless
甲斐無 *fugaina(i)* spiritless, cowardly,
仕末 *fushimatsu*＝不始末 (see below–8)
仕合 *fushia(wase)* unhappiness, misfortune, ill luck 「plaint
平 *fuhei* discontent, dissatisfaction, com-
平不満 *fuhei-fuman* discontent and grumbling
平等 *fubyōdō* inequality; unequal (treaties)
用 *fuyō* of no use; waste (products)
用心 *buyōjin, fuyōjin* insecurity; careless-
用品 *fuyōhin* disused article 」ness
用意 *fuyōi* unpreparedness, carelessness
正 *fusei* injustice, iniquity, impropriety, irregularity, dishonesty, illegality
正行為 *fusei kōi* unfair practices, wrongdoing, malpractice, cheating, foul play
正直 *fushōjiki* dishonesty 「graft case
正事件 *fusei jiken* scandal, bribery case,
正乗車 *fusei jōsha* stealing a ride
正視 *fuseishi suru* consider wrong or unjust
正規 *fuseiki* irregularity
正規軍 *fuseikigun* guerrillas
正確 *fuseikaku* inaccuracy, uncertainty
可 *fuka* wrong, bad, improper, unjustifiable, inadvisable
可入性 *fuka-nyūsei* impenetrability
可欠 *fukaketsu na* indispensable, essential
可分 *fukabun* indivisibility
可決 *fukaketsu* indispensable
可抗力 *fukakōryoku* act of God; irresistible force; inevitability
可知 *fukachi na* unknowable, mysterious
可知的 *fukachiteki* agnostic
可知論 *fukachiron* agnosticism
可侵 *fukashin* inviolability, nonaggression
可侵条約 *fukashin jōyaku* nonaggression pact
可思議 *fukashigi* mystery, wonder, miracle
可能 *fukanō* impossibility
可解 *fukakai* mystery
可誤 *fukago* (papal) infallibility 「avoidable
可避 *fukahi* inescapable, inevitable, un-
6臣 *fushin* disloyalty, unfaithfulness
尽 *fujin* Very sincerely yours
印 *fujirushi* poor results
向 *fumu(ki) na* unfit, unsuitable, unmarket-
仲 *funaka* discord 」able
次 *fuji* irregularity
好 *busu(ki)* no liking for, no interest in
朽 *fukyū* immortality
全 *fuzen* partial, incomplete, imperfect
吉 *fukitsu* bad luck, ill omen, inauspiciousness 「perfection, inadequacy
充分 *fujūbun* insufficiency, shortage, im-
似合 *funia(i)* unbecoming, improper, unsuitable, ill-matched, unworthy of
気味 *bukimi na* uncanny, weird, ghastly, ominous. *bukimi* ill feeling
如意 *funyo-i* contrary to one's wishes; short of money
自由 *fujiyū* inconvenience, discomfort; destitution; disability 「strained
自然 *fushizen* unnatural, artificial, affected,
合格 *fugōkaku* failure (in an examination), rejection, disqualification
合理 *fugōri na* unreasonable, irrational, absurd, inconsistent
名数 *fumeisū* abstract number

名誉 *fumeiyo* dishonor, disgrace, shame
老 *furō* perennial youth
老不死 *furō-fushi* perennial youth
老泉 *furōsen* fountain of youth
同 *fudō* difference, diversity, irregularity; disorder
同化 *fudōka* nonassimilation
同意 *fudōi* disagreement, objection
成立 *fuseiritsu* failure, rupture, rejection
成功 *fuseikō* failure
成績 *fuseiseki* poor result, bad record, failure
死 *fushi* immortality, eternal life
死身 *fujimi* invulnerability, immortality, insensibility to pain
死鳥 *fushichō* phoenix bird
行状 *fugyōjō* misconduct, profligacy, immorality
行届 *fuyu(ki)todo(ki)* negligence, carelessness, incompetence, mismanagement
行跡 *fugyōseki* misconduct, profligacy, immorality
行儀 *fugyōgi* bad manners, rudeness
安 *fuan* anxiety, uneasiness; insecurity; suspense
安心 *fuanshin* uneasiness, uncertainty, anxiety, apprehension, restlessness, insecurity, suspense, fear
安気 *fuange na* uneasy
安定 *fuantei* instability; insecurity; crankiness
当 *fua(tari)* failure, unpopularity. *futō na* unjust, unreasonable, undeserved. *futō* injustice, impropriety, unreasonableness
当利得 *futō ritoku* excessive profit
当労働行為 *futō rōdō kōi* unfair labor practices
当廉売 *futō rembai* dumping
在 *fuzai* absence
在地主 *fuzai jinushi* absentee landlord
在投票 *fuzai tōhyō* absentee voting
在証明 *fuzai shōmei* alibi
7 図 *futo* suddenly, casually, accidentally, incidentally, unexpectedly, unintentionally
快 *fukai* displeasure, discomfort
抜 *fubatsu* firm, steadfast, indomitable, invincible, unswerving
肖 *fushō* unworthy, incompetent; I, myself, your humble servant
孝 *fukō* disobedience to parents, lack of filial piety
束 *futsutsuka* a rude, inexperienced, stupid, or incompetent person; ignoramus
完全 *fukanzen na* imperfect, incomplete, faulty, defective
沙汰 *busata* silence, neglect to write, neglect to call
均斉 *fukinsei* asymmetry
身持 *fumimo(chi)* misconduct, profligacy, licentiousness, inconstancy
条理 *fujōri* irrationality, absurdity, inconsistency
体裁 *futeisai* bad form, bad manners, impropriety, indecency
即不離 *fusoku-furi*, neutral, noncommittal
労所得 *furō shotoku* unearned income
作 *fusaku* poor crop, crop failure
作法 *busahō* bad manners, discourtesy
妊 *funin* sterility, barrenness
妊症 *funinshō* sterility, barrenness
決定 *fukettei* pending, unsettled, undecided
決断 *fuketsudan* irresolution, indecision, vacillation
利 *furi* disadvantage, drawback, handicap
利益 *furieki* disadvantage, handicap, drawback, inadvisability, inexpediency
見目 *mijime na* sad, pitiful, wretched
見転芸者 *mizuten geisha* a loose geisha
見識 *fukenshiki na* undignified, compromising, disgraceful
言 *fugen* silence
言不語 *fugen-fugo* silence
言実行 *fugen-jikkō* action before words
足 *fusoku* shortage, lack, deficiency, dearth
足前 *tarazumae* deficit, shortage
足勝 *fusokugachi* needy circumstances
均等 *fukintō*=*fukinkō* 不均衡 (see below–7)
均質 *fukinshitsu no*, of uneven quality; heterogeneous
均衡 *fukinkō* out of balance, imbalance, disparity, inequality
良 *furyō* bad, poor, inferior; wicked, delinquent
良化 *furyōka* degradation, downfall
良少年 *furyō shōnen* juvenile delinquent
良児 *furyōji* juvenile delinquent
良貸付 *furyō ka(shi)tsu(ke)* bad debts
良導体 *furyōdōtai* insulator, nonconductor, poor conductor
承 *fushō*=*fushōchi* 不承知 (see below–7)
承不承 *fushōbushō* reluctantly, unwillingly
承知 *fushōchi* dissent, disagreement, disapproval, objection, refusal
承認 *fushōnin* disapproval, dissent, veto
承諾 *fushōdaku*=*fushōchi* 不承知 (see above–7)
8 斉 *fusei* irregularity, unevenness, asymmetry, lack of uniformity
屈 *fukutsu* fortitude, indomitability
届 *futodo(ki)* rude, insolent, nefarious
例 *furei* indisposition; sickness
味 *mazu(i)* unpalatable, insipid; homely; awkward, bungling; unwise. *fumi* distaste, unsavoriness
拘 *kakawarazu* in spite of, regardless of
況 *fukyō* depression, slump, recession
治 *fuchi, fuji* incurability
服 *fufuku* dissatisfaction, discontent; disagreement, disapproval; objection, protest, complaint

幸 *fukō* unhappiness, sorrow, misfortune: disaster, accident, death

実 *fujitsu* faithlessness, inconstancy, insincerity; falsehood

易 *fueki* immutability, constancy

拡大 *fukakudai* nonexpansion, nonaggravation, localization

始末 *fushimatsu* mismanagement, malpractice, wastefulness, carelessness, misconduct, unthriftiness 「less city

夜城 *fuyajō* nightless gay quarters; night-

退転 *futaiten* determination, conviction

注意 *fuchūi* carelessness, negligence

所存 *fushozon* imprudence, indiscretion

所存者 *fushozommono* thoughtless person

知 *fuchi* ignorance

知火 *shiranuhi, shiranui* phosphorescent light 「agreement

和 *fuwa* discord, trouble, dissension, dis-

和雷同 *fuwa-raidō* blindly following

服 *fufuku* dissatisfaction; disapproval; protest 「ence

服従 *fufukujū* insubordination, disobedi-

参 *fusan* nonattendance, default, nonap-

参加 *fusanka* nonparticipation ⌊pearance

具 *fugu, katawa* deformity; distortion; disability; cripple

具者 *fugusha* cripple, disabled person

忠 *fuchū* disloyalty, infidelity

忠実 *fuchūjitsu* disloyalty, faithlessness

明 *fumei* obscurity, indistinctness, uncertainty, ambiguity; ignorance, lack of

明朗 *fumeirō* unclean, gloomy ⌊wisdom

明瞭 *fumeiryō* indistinctness, dimness, obscurity 「lawfulness

法 *fuhō* lawlessness, injustice, illegality, un-

法入国 *fuhō nyūgoku* illegal entry

法占有 *fuhō sen-yū* unlawful detention (of shipping), unlawful occupation (of a house or land)

法侵入 *fuhō shinnyū* trespassing, intrusion

法集会 *fuhō shūkai* unlawful assembly

定 *futei, fujō* uncertainty, insecurity, incon-

定法 *futeihō* infinitive mood ⌊stancy

定冠詞 *futei kanshi* indefinite article

定詞 *futeishi* infinitive

定期 *futeiki* indeterminate (sentence); irregular (service); tramp (steamer) 「sation

9 通 *futsū* suspension, stoppage, tie-up, ces-

便 *fuben* inconvenience, inexpediency, unhandiness. *fubin* pity, compassion

姙 *funin* sterility, barrenness

軌 *fuki* lawlessness, violation of customs

変 *fuhen* unchangeability, immutability, constancy, permanence; indestructibility

宣 *fusen* Very sincerely yours

要 *fuyō* of no use; unnecessary; waste (products) 「ry

急 *fukyū* nonessential (industry); in no hur-

為 *futame na* disadvantageous, unprofitable, harmful 「grace

面目 *fumemmoku, fumemboku* shame, dis-

品行 *fuhinkō* unchastity, misconduct, dissipation, fornication

恰好 *bukakkō* unshapeliness; clumsiness

相応 *fusōō* unsuited, inappropriate, improper, undeserved 「favor

首尾 *fushubi* failure, fizzle; disgrace, dis-

透明 *futōmei* opacity

風流 *bufūryū* lack of refinement

侵略 *fushinryaku* nonaggression

連続 *furenzoku* discontinuity

祝儀 *bushūgi*=*fukō* 不幸 (see above–8)

軌 *fuki* lawlessness

浄 *fujō* uncleanness, impurity, filthiness, defilement; menses; toilet, latrine

浄場 *fujōba* an unclean place

活発 *fukappatsu na* dull, slow, sluggish, inactive, quiet

活動 *fukatsudō* inaction, lethargy

思儀 *fushigi*=the following word

思議 *fushigi* wonder, mystery, marvel,

発 *fuhatsu* misfire ⌊miracle; curiosity

発弾 *fuhatsudan* dud, unexploded shell; unexploded bomb 「jugal) infidelity

貞 *futei* unchastity, unfaithfulness, (con-

貞寝 *futene* staying in bed out of spite

貞腐 *futekusa(reru)* become sulky, become irresponsible

信 *fushin* unfaithfulness, insincerity; perfidy; mistrust, distrust, discredit

信心 *fushinjin* impiety, unbelief, infidelity

信用 *fushin-yō* distrust, discredit

信任 *fushinnin* nonconfidence 「vote

信任投票 *fushinnin tōhyō* nonconfidence

信任案 *fushinnin an* nonconfidence motion

信仰 *fushinkō* lack of faith, unbelief, impiety, infidelity

信実 *fushinjitsu* insincerity, unfaithfulness

信者 *fushinja*, unbeliever

信義 *fushingi* faithlessness, insincerity

10 逞 *futei* insubordination; outlawry

倫 *furin* impropriety, immorality

埒 *furachi* breach of etiquette, insolence, misconduct 「nation

振 *fushin* dullness, depression, slump, stag-

祥 *fushō* disgraceful, inauspicious, ill-omened, ominous, scandalous

粋 *busui na* inelegant, lacking in polish,

納 *funō* nonpayment, default

敏 *fubin* inability, dullness, unworthiness

党 *futō* nonparticipation

3

能 *funō* incompetency, inefficiency; impossibility; weak point; imbecility
帰 *fuki* returning no more; dying
案内 *fuannai* ignorance, inexperience, unfamiliarity
都合 *futsugō* inconvenience, inexpedience; trouble, harm; impropriety, wrongdoing
流通 *furyūtsū* nonnegotiable 「toy
倒翁 *okiagarikoboshi* tumbler, self-righting
勉強 *fubenkyō* idleness, lack of application, lazy study habits
従順 *fujūjun* disobedience
料簡 *furyōken* indiscretion 「tilled land
耕作地 *fukōsakuchi* nonfarming land; un-
真面目 *fumajime* unsteadiness; lack of sincerity
倶戴天 *fugutaiten* irreconcilable (enemy)
起 *fuki* rising no more (as in illness and death)
起訴 *fukiso* nonprosecution, nonindictment
消化 *fushōka* indigestion
消化物 *fushōkabutsu* indigestible materials
純 *fujun* impurity, adulteration; dishonesty; irregularity
純物 *fujumbutsu* foreign matter, impurities
時 *fuji* emergency, unexpectedness
時着 *fujichaku* emergency landing
時着陸 *fujichakuriku* emergency landing
眠 *fumin* wakefulness, sleeplessness
眠不休 *fumin-fukyū* without sleep or rest, day and night
眠症 *fuminshō* insomnia, sleeplessness
随 *fuzui* paralysis, palsy
随意 *fuzui-i* involuntary
随意筋 *fuzui-ikin* involuntary muscles
凍海 *futōkai* ice-free sea
凍剤 *futōsai* antifreeze
凍液 *futōeki* antifreeze
凍港 *futōkō* ice-free port
11 達 *futatsu* nondelivery
運 *fu-un* misfortune, bad luck, fate
遇 *fugū* misfortune, bad luck, obscurity
猟 *furyō* poor catch
理 *furi*=*fugōri* 不合理 (see above–6) and
敗 *fuhai* invincibility ⌊*muri* 無理 2773.11)
悉 *fushitsu* Very sincerely yours
細工 *busaiku* clumsy work; poor shape; awkward, clumsy; homely, plain
深切 *fushinsetsu* unkindness, unfriendliness
問付 *fumon* (*ni*) *fu*(*su*) ignore, disregard, overlook, connive at 「parity
釣合 *futsuria*(*i*) unbalance, asymmetry, dis-
経済 *fukeizai* poor economy, waste
道理 *fudōri* unreasonableness, absurdity, irrationality
道徳 *fudōtoku* immorality, iniquity

健全 *fukenzen* unhealthful
健康 *fukenkō* poor health; unhealthiness
偏 *fuhen* impartiality, fairness
偏不党 *fuhen-futō* neutrality
断 *fudan* usually, habitually, continually; constantly; indecision, irresolution
断着 *fudangi* ordinary clothes
動 *fudō* immobility, firmness, steadfastness; fixed, motionless, idle
動心 *fudōshin* imperturbability
動産 *fudōsan* real estate
規律 *fukiritsu na* irregular, undisciplined, disorganized, slipshod
規則 *fukisoku* irregularity, unsteadiness
規則動詞 *fukisoku dōshi* irregular verb
得手 *fuete* weak point; unskillfulness
得要領 *futoku-yōryō* vague, ambiguous, irrelevant, noncommittal 「inexpediency
得策 *futokusaku* unwise plan, bad policy,
得意 *futokui* one's weak point
12 間 *buma* clumsiness, stupidity, blunder
備 *fubi* deficiency, imperfection, defect, inadequacy; Yours in haste
順 *fujun* irregularity, unseasonableness
揃 *fuzoroi, fusoroi* unevenness, irregularity, lack of uniformity
渡 *fuwata*(*ri*) nonpayment, dishonoring (a bill); bouncing (check)
測 *fusoku* unexpectedness
期 *fuki* unexpected, accidental
着 *fuchaku* nonarrival, nondelivery
惑 *fuwaku* past forty; following the right course
統一 *futōitsu* disunity, disharmony
勝手 *fukatte* inconvenience; a hard living
裁可 *fusaika* veto, rejection
景気 *fukeiki* hard times, depression; gloom, sullenness, cheerlessness
量見 *furyōken* indiscretion
愉快 *fuyukai* unpleasantness, disagreeableness, unhappiness
検束 *fukensoku* nonrestraint
結果 *fukekka* failure, poor results
然者 *shikarazumba* if not so
換紙幣 *fukan shihei* unconvertible paper money, fiat money 「content
満 *fuman* dissatisfaction, displeasure, dis-
満足 *fumanzoku* dissatisfaction, displeasure, discontent 「popularity
評 *fuhyō* bad reputation, disgrace, un-
評判 *fuhyōban* bad reputation, disgrace, unpopularity
善 *fuzen* evil, sin, vice; mischief
善感 *fuzenkan* negative reaction, unsuccessful vaccination
等 *futō* disparity, inequality

等辺 *futōhen* unequal sides
買 *fubai* not buying
買同盟 *fubai dōmei* boycott, buyer's strike
敬 *fukei* disrespect, irreverence, impiety, blasphemy, profanity
敬虔 *fukeiken* impiety, irreverence
敬罪 *fukeizai* lese majesty
覚 *fukaku* fault, failure, negligence, indiscretion 「ment
覚一投 *fukaku (no) ittō* pitcher's misjudgment
覚者 *fukakumono* shallow thinker; indecisive person; coward 「oneself
覚涙 *fukaku (no) namida* crying in spite of oneself
13 虞 *fugu* emergency
遜 *fuson* arrogance, insolence, disrespect
嗜 *butashinami* poor preparation
滅 *fumetsu* immortality, indestructibility
詳 *fushō* unknown, unidentified
馴 *funare* inexperience, unfamiliarity
戦 *fusen* antiwar, war renunciation
勢 *buzei* few, numerical inferiority
愍 *fubin* pitiful 「perance
摂生 *fusessei* neglect of health, intemperance
節制 *fusessei* intemperance, excesses
寛容 *fukan-yō* intolerance
感症 *fukanshō* sexual frigidity
寝番 *fushimban* night watch; sleepless vigil, vigilance. *nezuban, nezu(no)ban* sleepless vigil 「lenness
愛想 *buaisō* unsociability, brusqueness, sullenness
誠実 *fuseijitsu*=*fusei-i* 不誠意 (the next word)
誠意 *fusei-i* insincerity, dishonesty, untruthfulness, bad faith
廉 *furen* not cheap, high-priced (=高価 see 5248.8)
義 *fugi* immorality; injustice; impropriety, misconduct; adultery; perfidy
義理 *fugiri* dishonesty, injustice; dishonor; ingratitude
適 *futeki* unfitness, inappropriateness, inadequacy, impropriety 「priate
適切 *futekisetsu na* unsuitable, inappropriate
適当 *futekitō* unfitness, inappropriateness, inadequacy, impropriety
適任 *futekinin* unfitness, incompetency
適格 *futekikaku, futekkaku* disqualification, unfitness
意 *fui* suddenness, unexpectedness
意打 *fuiu(chi)* surprise attack
意気 *buiki* vulgarity, lack of refinement
意討 *fuiu(chi)* surprise attack
意試験 *fui shiken* surprise examination
14 慣 *funa(re)* inexperience, unfamiliarity
様 *buzama na* unshapely, unsightly, unpresentable, uncouth, clumsy

漁 *furyō* poor catch
語 *fugo* silence 「ness
徳 *futoku* depravity, immorality, unworthiness
徳漢 *futokukan* a crook, swindler
認可 *funinka* disapproval, rejection
認承 *funinshō* nonrecognition
導体 *fudōtai* nonconductor
導性 *fudōsei* nonconductibility
精 *bushō* laziness, indolence
精不精 *fushō-bushō* grudgingly
精巧 *fuseikō na* clumsy, bungling
精者 *bushōmono* lazybones
精髭 *bushō hige* unshaven face
15 慮 *furyo no* unforeseen, accidental
憫 *fubin* pity, compassion
撓 *futō* unbending; inflexibility, tenacity, indomitableness 「indomitableness
撓不屈 *futō-fukutsu* inflexibility, tenacity, indomitableness
潔 *fuketsu* uncleanness, dirtiness, impurity
縁 *fuen* divorce; unrealized marriage; dim marriage prospects
耦 *fugū* misfortune; obscurity
敵 *futeki na* bold, fearless, daring, tough
熱心 *funesshin* lack of enthusiasm, indifference, inattentiveness
衛生 *fueisei* unsanitary condition
養生 *fuyōjō* intemperance, neglect of health
履行 *furikō* nonperformance, default
賛成 *fusansei* disapproval, disagreement
徹底 *futettei* not thorogoing, unconvincing, inconclusive, inconsistent, illogical, indefinite, half-way
熟練 *fujukuren* unskillfulness
銹鋼 *fushūkō* stainless steel
確 *futashi(ka) na* unreliable, uncertain, indefinite 「unauthentic
確実 *fukakujitsu na* uncertain, unreliable, unauthentic
審 *fushin* incomplete understanding; doubt, question; distrust, suspicion; strangeness; infidelity 「police)
審訊問 *fushin jimmon* questioning (by the police)
調 *fuchō* disagreement, break-off, disorder; slump; out of form
調法 *buchōhō* impoliteness; carelessness; misconduct; clumsiness
調和 *fuchōwa* discord, incongruity
器 *fuki* clumsiness, unskillfulness
器用 *bukiyō* clumsiness, unskillfulness
器用者 *bukiyōsha, bukiyōmono* bungler
器量 *bukiryō, fukiryō* ugliness, homeliness; lack of ability, incompetence
16 磨 *fuma* permanence, immortality
興 *fukyō* displeasure, ill-humor
親切 *fushinsetsu* unkindness, unfriendliness
整脈 *fuseimyaku* irregular pulse 「ness
機嫌 *fukigen* displeasure, ill humor, sullen-

錆鋼 *fuseikō* stainless steel
燃 *funen* incombustibility
燃性 *funensei* incombustibility 「manners
躾 *bushitsuke* ill-breeding, impoliteness, bad
躾者 *bushitsukemono* rude person
穏 *fuon* unrest, turbulence; impropriety
穏分子 *fuon bunshi* disturbing elements
穏文書 *fuom-bunsho* inflammatory pamphlets 「unfairness, unreasonableness
穏当 *fuontō* impropriety, inappropriateness,
17 鮮明 *fusemmei* blurring
謹慎 *fukinshin* indiscretion, imprudence
縹緻 *fukiryō, bukiryō* homeliness, plainness
18 謬性 *fubyūsei* papal infallibility
19 離 *furi* inseparability
23 覊 *fuki* freedom, liberty, independence
25 羈 *fuki* freedom, liberty, independence

4

凹 See 664. [凵]

丏 See 11.

丘 See 174.

凸 See 90. [凵]

世 See 95.

互 18 F-X See 互 31. [二]

巨 19 F604 See 巨 758. [工]

业 20 F-X See 北 751.

丞 21 F43 Jō, Shō help.

B 丙 22 F43 丙 Hei C, 3rd. *hinoe* 3rd calendar sign.

B 且 23 F39 Shō. *katsu* also, furthermore.
2 又 *katsumata* moreover

A 可 24 F324 Koku. Ka good, passable; approval; safe to say, ability to do. *be(karazu)* must not, should not; do not. *i(i)*, *yo(i)*, *yo(shi)* (see under 良 3885.0). *-be(shi)*, *-be(ki)* shall, should, must, ought to, be expected to; perhaps, maybe; can; will; -able -ible. [口]
3 也 *kanari* considerably, fairly, quite
及的 *kakyūteki* as . . . as possible
4 分 *kabun* divisible, separable
分性 *kabunsei* divisibility
5 圧性 *ka-atsusei* compressibility
6 成 *kanari* considerably, fairly, quite
7 決 *kaketsu* approval, adoption
否 *kahi* right or wrong, propriety, advisability, pro and con 「women)
9 祝 *kashiku* Respectfully yours (used by
哀想 *kawaisō na* poor, pitiable, pathetic; pitiless; unjust 「controllable
変 *kahen* variable, changeable, convertible,
変抵抗器 *kahen teikōki* rheostat
10 笑 *oka(shii)* funny, amusing, ridiculous
能 *kanō* possibility
能性 *kanōsei* possibility
能法 *kanōhō* potential mood
能動詞 *kanō dōshi* potential verb
11 惜 *atara, attara* alas; regrettably
動 *kadō* movable, mobile
動性 *kadōsei* mobility
動堰 *kadōzeki* canal gates, river gates
動橋 *kadōkyō* movable bridge
13 溶片 *kayōhen* fuse
溶性 *kayōsei* solubility
愛 *kawai(garu)* love, pet, hold dear; *kawai(rashii)*, *ka-aira(shii)* lovely, sweet. *ka-ai(i)*, *kawai(i)* dear, darling, pet, charm-
愛気 *kawaige* loveliness ⌊ing, lovely, sweet
塑 *kaso* plastic
塑物 *kasobutsu* plastics
塑物質 *kaso busshitsu* plastics
15 憐 *karen na* poor, pitiful; cute, sweet, lovely
撓 *katō* flexible
16 燃性 *kanensei* combustibility, inflammability 「bles
燃物 *kanembutsu* a combustible, inflamma-
17 聴度 *kachōdo* audibility
聴距離 *kachō kyori* audible distance
鍛性 *katansei* malleability
鍛鉄 *katan tetsu* malleable iron
18 鎔片 *kayōhen* fuse
鎔性 *kayōsei* fusibility

A 民 25 F1062 Min. *tami* people, nation, subjects. [氏]
2 人 *minjin* the people, the public
力 *minryoku* national manpower
4 心 *minshin* popular sentiment
戸 *minko* private house
5 本主義 *mimpon shugi* democracy 「fare
生 *minsei* people's livelihood, people's wel-

生委員 *minsei i-in* district welfare officer
主 *minshu* democracy; the head of the na-
主化 *minshuka* democratization ⌊tion
主主義 *minshu shugi* democracy
主国 *minshukoku* democratic state
主的 *minshuteki* democratic 「government
主政体 *minshu seitai* democratic form of
主政治 *minshu seiji* democratic government
主党 *minshutō* democratic party
6 団 *mindan* a foreign-settlement corporation
有 *min-yū* private ownership
7 利 *minri* people's interests
兵 *mimpei* militia; militiaman
芸 *mingei* folk craft, folk art
8 国 *Minkoku* China
法 *mimpō* civil law, civil code
事 *minji* civil affairs; civil case
事上 *minjijō no* civil
事的 *minjiteki* civil
事事件 *minji jiken* civil case
事裁判 *minji saiban* civil trial
事訴訟 *minji soshō* civil suit
9 風 *mimpū* national customs
度 *mindo* cultural standard
草 *tamigusa* people, populace
約説 *min-yakusetsu* social-contract theory
俗 *minzoku* racial customs, folk customs
俗学 *minzokugaku* folklore
政 *minsei* civil government, democracy
政長官 *minsei chōkan* civil governor
10 家 *minka* private house 「ment of the people
11 情 *minjō* condition of the people; the senti-
望 *mimbō* hopes of the people
族 *minzoku* race, people
族史 *minzokushi* history of a people
族主義 *minzoku shugi* nationalism
族自決 *minzoku-jiketsu* self-determination
族的 *minzokuteki* racial ⌊of peoples
族性 *minzokusei* racial trait
族学 *minzokugaku* ethnology
族学者 *minzokugakusha* ethnologist
族宗教 *minzoku shūkyō* ethnic religions
族意識 *minzoku ishiki* national consciousness 「al spirit
族精神 *minzoku seishin* racial spirit, nation-
12 営 *min-ei* private management
間 *minkan no* private, civilian, civil, popular, folk, unofficial
間人 *minkanjin* nongovernment person
間飛行 *minkan hikō* civil aviation
衆 *minshū* people, populace, masses
衆化 *minshūka* popularization
衆駅 *minshū eki* a railway station built with government and popular support
13 福 *mimpuku* national welfare
話 *minwa* folklore

意 *min-i* popular will
業 *mingyō* private enterprise 「Bible)
数記 *Minsūki* the Book of Numbers (in the
14 選 *minsen* popular election
徳 *mintoku* national morality
需 *minju* civilian requirements
需品 *minjuhin* consumer goods
15 権 *minken* civil rights
論 *minron* public opinion
16 謡 *min-yō* popular song, ballad, folk song

A **平** 26/F622 **平** HYŌ. BYŌ. HEI level, peaceful. *tai(rageru)* subjugate; put down (trouble); consume (food), eat up. *tai(ragu)* be suppressed. *hei(tsukubaru)* make a deep bow. *hira ni* earnestly, humbly. *hira(tai)* flat, even, level; simple, plain. *tai(ra)* flat, smooth; calm; a plain; sitting tailor fashion. *tai(rakana)* level; just; peaceful. *hira-* common, ordinary. [干]

3 凡 *heibon na* common, commonplace, ordinary, mediocre 「theater)
土間 *hiradoma* pit, orchestra, parquet (in a
4 日 *heijitsu* weekday, ordinary days
氏 *Heishi* the Tairas 「water
水 *heisui* the usual amount of water; calm
仄 *hyōsoku* meter (in Chinese poetry); consistency
分 *heibun suru* bisect, divide equally
手 *hirate* palm; equality
手打 *hirateu(chi)* a slap, spanking
方 *heihō* square (of a number); square
方形 *heihōkei* square
方根 *heihōkon* square root
5 芝 *hirashiba* sod
台型貨車 *hiradaigata kasha* flatcar
生 *heizei no* usual, ordinary
生着 *heizeigi* usually worn
平 *heihei* level; ordinary 「ocre
平凡凡 *heihei-bombon(taru)* ordinary, medi-
民 *heimin* commoner, plebeian
民主義 *heimin shugi* democracy
6 臼 *hira-usu* horizontal stone hand mill
気 *heiki* composure; unconcern
伏 *hirefu(su)* prostrate oneself before. *heifuku suru* fall prostrate
地 *heichi, hirachi* level ground, plain
仮名 *hiragana* the cursive syllabary
年 *heinen* normal year, civil year
年作 *heinensaku* normal crop
安 *heian* peace, tranquility; Heian era (794–
安京 *Heiankyō* ancient Kyōto ⌊1185)
安朝 *Heianchō* Heian period
行 *heikō* parallelism, parallel
行四辺形 *heikōshihenkei* parallelogram
行棒 *heikōbō* parallel bars

1 【一】丨丶ノ乙亅

行線 *heikōsen* parallel line
[7] 角 *heikaku* straight angle
作 *heisaku* normal crop
身低頭 *heishin teitō suru* prostrate oneself
均 *heikin, narashi* equilibrium, balance, average, mean
均余命 *heikin yomei* life expectancy
均寿命 *heikin jumyō* average life span
均点 *heikinten* average mark, mean point
[8] 坦 *heitan na* even, flat, level
明 *heimei na* clear, simple
泳 *hiraoyo(gi)* breast stroke
版 *heihan* lithography
服 *heifuku* civilian clothes, plain clothes, ordinary clothes
臥 *heiga suru* lie down; be laid up
定 *heitei* suppression, repression, subjugation
底 *hirazoko* flat bottom
底船 *hirasokobune* flat-bottomed boat, scow
価 *heika* normal prices; par; parity
価切下 *heikakirisa(ge)* devaluation
板 *heiban* slab, flat board; monotony; lithography
板測量 *heiban sokuryō* plane-table surveying
炉 *heiro, hiraro* open-hearth furnace
炉法 *heirohō* open-hearth process
易 *hei-i* easiness; simplicity
易化 *hei-ika* simplification
和 *heiwa* peace, harmony
和主義 *heiwa shugi* pacifism
和主義者 *heiwa shugisha* pacifist
和共存 *heiwa kyōzon* peaceful coexistence
和会議 *heiwa kaigi* peace conference
和条約 *heiwa jōyaku* peace treaty
和攻勢 *heiwa kōsei* peace offensive
和的 *heiwateki* peaceful
和国 *heiwakoku* a peaceful country
和国家 *heiwa kokka* peace-loving nation
和産業 *heiwa sangyō* peace-time industries
和論者 *heiwa ronsha* pacifist
[9] 城京 *Heijōkyō* ancient Nara
屋 *hiraya* bungalow, one-story house
屋根 *hirayane* flat roof
信 *heishin* peaceful news
信徒 *hirashinto, heishinto* layman, laity
面 *heimen* level surface, plane
面図 *heimenzu* ground plan; plane figure
面形 *heimenkei* plane figure
面幾何学 *heimen kikagaku* plane geometry
面鏡 *heimenkyō* plane mirror
[10] 原 *heigen* plain, moor, prairie
庭 *hiraniwa* level garden
時 *heiji* normal times, peace time
脈 *heimyaku* normal pulse
袖 *hirasode* wide sleeve
家 *hiraya* bungalow, one-story house. *Heike* the Taira family
素 *heiso* ordinarily, in the past
[11] 淡 *heitan na* simple, quiet
野 *heiya* a plain, open field
常 *heijō* normal; normally, usually
常通 *heijōdō(ri)* as usual
[12] 復 *heifuku* restoration to health
温 *heion* the usual temperature
落 *hiraochi* pancake (landing)
然 *heizen(taru)* calm, composed
等 *byōdō* equality, impartiality
等観 *byōdōkan* considering all people as equals
[13] 滑 *heikatsu na* smooth, even, level, flat
絹 *hiraginu* plain silk
[14] 静 *heisei* tranquility, calm, equanimity
[15] 熱 *heinetsu* normal temperature
[16] 穏 *heion* tranquility, calmness, rest
衡 *heikō* equilibrium, balance; equalization
衡感覚 *heikō kankaku* sense of balance
[17] 謝 *hira-ayama(ri)* earnest apology
鍋 *hiranabe* pan, griddle
[18] 癒 *heiyu* convalescence
織 *hiraori* plain fabrics

A **正** 27/F1034 SEI right, righteousness, justice; original; plus, positive; genuine. SHŌ just; punctual; senior; right, righteousness, justice. *tada(su)* correct; adjust; reform; redress, straighten; amend. *masa(ni)* correctly, surely. *masa(shiku)* surely, no doubt, evidently. *tada(shii)* right, righteous, just; honest, truthful, proper, correct; lawful; healthy; moral; straight; straightforward; perfect. *sei-* regular. [止]

[3] 大 *seidai* (see *kōmei-seidai* 公明正大 579.8)
子 *shōshi* twelve midnight
三角形 *seisankakukei* equilateral triangle
[4] 文 *seibun* the official text
月 *Shōgatsu* the first month; January; the New Year
中 *seichū* the exact middle
切 *seisetsu* tangent (in trigonometry)
午 *shōgo* noon, midday
反対 *seihantai* exactly opposite
比例 *seihirei* direct proportion, direct ratio
中線 *seichūsen* median line
方 *seihō* square
方形 *seihōkei* square
[5] 目 *masame* straight grain
史 *seishi* authentic history
北 *seihoku* due north
正 *seisei to* accurately, exactly; punctually; neatly, nicely
出 *seishutsu no* legitimate (child)
本 *shōhon* book of registration; text of a play. *seihon* text, original, facsimile

甲板 *seikampan* main deck
正堂堂 *seisei-dōdō(taru)* fair and square, open and aboveboard ⌈fender
犯 *seihan* principal offense; principal of-
犯者 *seihansha* principal offender
札 *shōfuda* correct-price tag ⌈ous person
札付 *shōfudazu(ki)* plainly marked; notori-
札値段 *shōfuda nedan* fixed price
6 色 *seishoku* primary colors
西 *seisei* due west
式 *seishiki* proper form, formality
気 *seiki* true heart, true spirit, true character. *shōki* consciousness; sanity, reason;
伝 *seiden* authentic biography ⌊soberness
号 *seigō* plus sign
会員 *seikai-in* regular member
字 *seiji* correct characters
字法 *seijihō* correct orthography
当 *seitō na* just, justifiable, right, due, proper, equitable, reasonable, legitimate,
当化 *seitōka suru* justify, warrant ⌊lawful
当防衛 *seitō bōei* legitimate self-defense.
7 体 *shōtai* natural shape; one's true colors, true character; consciousness; senses
位 *sei-i* correct location, correct position
邪 *seija* right and wrong
否 *seihi* right and wrong
系 *seikei* legitimate line; direct descent
兵 *seihei* regular soldiers
坐 *seiza suru* sit (or squat) straight
投手 *seitōshu* regular pitcher
攻法 *seikōhō* frontal attack ⌈ber
社員 *seisha-in* regular member, staff mem-
角定木 *seikaku jōgi* a try square
8 門 *seimon* main gate, main entrance
価 *seika* net price, regular price
使 *seishi* senior envoy, chief delegate
弦 *seigen* sine (in trigonometry)
物 *shōbutsu* genuine article
服 *seifuku* uniform, regulation dress
宗 *masamune* sword blade by Masamune
妻 *seisai* legal wife
東 *seitō* due east
金 *shōkin* specie, bullion, cash
金銀行 *shōkin ginkō* specie bank
直 *shōjiki* honesty, integrity, frankness
直者 *shōjikimono* honest person
味 *shōmi* net
味重量 *shōmi jūryō* net weight
味値段 *shōmi nedan* net price
9 音 *seion* correct Chinese (*on*) pronunciation
風 *shōfū* right style ⌊of a character
則 *seisoku no* correct, proper, formal regular, systematic, normal
南 *seinan* due south ⌈legal wife; heir
室 *seishitsu* the room for receiving guests;
客 *shōkyaku, seikaku* guest of honor
負 *seifu* positive and negative, plus and minus ⌈frontage, façade
面 *matomo* the front; honesty. *shōmen* front,
面向 *shōmemmu(ki)* front view
面図 *shōmenzu* front elevation
面衝突 *shōmen shōtotsu* head-on collision
10 座 *seiza suru* sit (or squat) straight. *shōza*
格 *seikaku* correct rules ⌊seat of honor
訓 *seikun* correct *kun* reading
朔 *seisaku* beginning of the month or the year; New Year's Day; the calendar
員 *sei-in* regular member
真正銘 *shōshin-shōmei* the genuine article
書 *seisho* square characters, printed style
書法 *seishohō* correct orthography
11 道 *seidō* righteousness; path of righteousness, path of duty, the right track
眼 *seigan* aiming at the eye (with a sword)
経 *seikyō* canon of Scripture ⌈vice-chief
副 *seifuku* original and copy; chief and
貨 *seika* specie, metallic currency
視 *seishi* looking straight ahead; viewing
視眼 *seishigan* correct vision ⌊sincerely
常 *seijō* normalcy, normality; normal
常化 *seijōka* normalization ⌈Church
教 *seikyō* orthodoxy; Greek Orthodox
教会 *Seikyōkai* Greek Orthodox Church
教員 *seikyōin* regular teacher, licensed teacher ⌈teacher
教師 *seikyōshi* ordained minister, regular
規 *seiki no* regular, legal, formal, established, legitimate
規曲線 *seiki kyokusen* probability curve, normal curve
規兵 *seikihei* regulars, regular soldiers
規軍 *seikigun* regular army
12 閏 *seijun* normal and leap (years); legitimate and illegitimate (dynasties)
帽 *seibō* cap of a uniform
割 *seikatsu* secant (in trigonometry)
朝 *seichō* legitimate dynasty
装 *seisō* uniform, full dress
覚 *shōgaku* (Buddhist) perfect enlightenment ⌈drinker
覚坊 *shōgakubō* large sea turtle; heavy
統 *seitō no* legitimate, orthodox, traditional
統派 *seitōha* orthodox school
統信教 *seitō shinkyō* orthodoxy
13 殿 *seiden* main temple; state chamber
絹 *shōken* pure silk ⌈supplement
続 *seizoku* a book or document and its
腹 *seifuku* legitimacy ⌈swer, correct solution
解 *seikai* correct interpretation, correct an-
路 *seiro*=*seidō* 正道 (see above–11)
数 *seisū* positive number

夢 *masayume* a dream that comes true
意 *sei-i* true heart; correct meaning
業 *seigyō* legitimate occupation, honest
電気 *seidenki* positive electricity ⌊business
義 *seigi* righteousness, justice, right, correct
義感 *seigikan* sense of justice ⌊meaning
14嫡 *seiteki, seichaku* legal wife; her child;
main family 「article
銘 *shōmei* genuine autograph; genuine
誤 *seigo* correction
誤表 *seigohyō* errata
15編 *seihen* main part of a book
論 *seiron* sound argument
調 *seichō* traditional tune
賓 *seihin* guest of honor
確 *seikaku* exactness; authenticity, veracity
確爆撃 *seikaku bakugeki* pinpoint bombing
課 *seika* regular curriculum, required sub-
課外 *seikagai* extracurricular ⌊ject
16餐 *seisan* formal dinner, banquet
18鵠 *seikō* the mark, the point, the bull's eye

5

而 See 3689. [而]

死 See 2439. [歹]

石 28/F-X See 石 3176. [石]

丞 See 21.

民 See 25. [氏]

师 29/F-X Nonstandard for 師 113.

亘 30/F80 Sen, Kan request. [二]

亙 31/F80 亙 Kō. *wata*(*ru*) range, reach, extend, last, cover, be spread over. [二]

A 弐 32/F1793 貳 弍 Ji. Ni two; second. *futa*(*tsu*) two. [貝]

4心 *futagokoro, nishin* = 二心 273.4

A 百 33/F1301 佰 Byaku. Hyaku hundred; a great number; all. *momo* hundred; a great number, great amount. [白]

2八鐘 *hyakuhachi* (*no*) *kane* night-watch bells; bells tolling out the old year
人一首 *hyakunin-isshu* 100 poems by 100 famous poets; the poem card game
3万 *hyakuman* million 「millionaire
万長者 *hyakumanchōja* millionaire; multi-
万遍 *hyakumamben* a million times; praying
4方 *hyappō* in every way ⌊a million times
匁 *hyakume* five-sixths of a pound
分比 *hyakubunhi* percentage
分率 *hyakubunritsu* percentage
日咳 *hyakunichizeki* whooping cough
日紅 *sarusuberi* crape myrtle
日草 *hyakunichisō* zinnia
5出 *hyakushutsu suru* arise in great numbers
世 *hyakusei* a long era
6行 *hyakkō* all acts
舌鳥 *mozu* shrike
年祭 *hyakunensai* centennial celebration
色眼鏡 *hyaku-iro megane* kaleidoscope
合 *yuri* lily
合木 *yuri* (*no*) *ki* tulip tree
合根 *yurine* lily bulb
合樹 *yuri* (*no*) *ki* tulip tree
7足 *mukade* centipede
芸 *hyakugei* Jack-of-all-trades 「ers
花 *hyakka* all varieties of flowers; many flow-
花繚乱 *hyakka-ryōran* blooming in profusion; a gathering of many beautiful
8味 *hyakumi* all kinds (of food) ⌊women
官 *hyakkan* all the officials
事 *hyakuji* all, everything
卒長 *hyakusotsuchō* centurion
姓 *hyakushō* farmer, peasant. *hyakusei* the common people
姓一揆 *hyakushō ikki* peasants' revolt
姓家 *hyakushōya* a farmer's home
9計 *hyakkei* all means
点 *hyakuten* hundred points, perfect mark
面相 *hyakumensō* life's many phases
発百中 *hyappatsu-hyakuchū* always hitting the bull's-eye; infallibility
科 *hyakka* many subjects (for study)
科全書 *hyakka zensho* encyclopedia
科事典 *hyakka jiten* encyclopedia
科辞典 *hyakka jiten* encyclopedia
10倍 *hyakubai* a hundredfold
般 *hyappan no* all, every, all kinds of
害 *hyakugai* great damage
鬼夜行 *hyakki-yagyō, hyakki-yakō* pandemonium, scandalous scene
11済 *Kudara* an ancient Korean kingdom
貨 *hyakka* all kinds of goods
貨店 *hyakkaten* department store
12景 *hyakkei* 100 famous views
13雷 *hyakurai* a hundred thunderclaps

戦百勝 *hyakusen-hyakushō* ever-victorious; many successful campaigns; invincibility
14聞 *hyakubun* hearing a hundred times
態 *hyakutai* various phases
15弊 *hyakuhei* all evils
16錬 *hyakuren* well-tempered; well drilled; well trained
獣 *hyakujū* all kinds of animals
薬 *hyakuyaku* sundry remedies
薬長 *hyakuyaku (no) chō* the best medicine, i.e., saké
18難 *hyakunan* all obstacles, all sorts of trouble

A 両 34 F196 兩 RYŌ old Japanese coin; both; two; vehicle counter. *tēru* tael. [入]

2人 *ryōnin* both people
刀 *ryōtō* two swords
刀使 *ryōtōtsuka(i)* = next word
刀遣 *ryōtōtsuka(i)* two-sword fencer; expert in two lines; man of broad tastes
3口 *ryōguchi* both openings; two people; a couple
刃 *ryōba no* double-edged
三日 *ryōsannichi* two or three days
4方 *ryōhō* both
日 *ryōjitsu* both days; two days
氏 *ryōshi* both men
分 *ryōbun suru* bisect, cut in two
天秤 *ryōtembin* two alternatives
切 *ryōgi(ri)* a plain cigarette
切煙草 *ryōgi(ri) tabako* plain cigarette
手 *ryōte* both hands
手利 *ryōtekiki* ambidextrous; ambidextrous person
手花 *ryōte (ni) hana* two blessings at once
5立 *ryōritsu* coexistence, standing together, compatibility
生動物 *ryōsei dōbutsu* amphibious animal
用 *ryōyō* dual use
用機 *ryōyōki* amphibian plane
6舌 *ryōzetsu* double-tongued
両 *ryōryō* both; two each
全 *ryōzen* mutual advantage
名 *ryōmei* both persons
成敗 *ryōseibai* two guilty parties tried and punished together
7足 *ryōashi, ryōsoku* both feet; both legs
肘 *ryōhiji* both elbows
8虎 *ryōko* two tigers; two rivals
岸 *ryōgan* both banks (of a river)
者 *ryōsha* both persons; both things
国 *ryōkoku* both countries
国語 *ryōkokugo* both languages
性 *ryōsei* both sexes
性化 *ryōseika* bisexual flower
性的 *ryōseiteki* bisexual
9度 *ryōdo* both times
便 *ryōben* urination and bowel movement
洋 *ryōyō* Orient and Occident; Atlantic and Pacific
院 *ryōin* = *ryōgi-in* 両議院 (see below–20)
軍 *ryōgun* both armies; both teams
陛下 *Ryōheika* Their Majesties
面 *ryōmen* both faces, both sides
面刷 *ryōmenzu(ri)* printing on both sides
10脇 *ryōwaki* both sides
袖 *ryōsode* both sleeves
家 *ryōke* both families
党 *ryōtō* both political parties
部神道 *Ryōbu Shintō* Shinto-Buddhist amalgamation, dual-aspect Shinto
11側 *ryōgawa, ryōsoku* both sides
得 *ryōtoku* double gain
眼 *ryōgan* both eyes
舷 *ryōgen* both sides of a ship
断 *ryōdan* bisection
脚 *ryōkyaku* both legs
脚器 *ryōkyakuki* a pair of compasses
12開 *ryōbira(ki)* double (two-leaf) door
腕 *ryōude* both arms
雄 *ryōyū* two great men
棲動物 *ryōsei dōbutsu* amphibious animal
極 *ryōkyoku* both extremities; north and south poles, positive and negative poles
極地方 *ryōkyaku chihō* polar areas
極端 *ryōkyokutan* both extremes
替 *ryōgae* money exchange
替人 *ryōgaenin* money changer
替屋 *ryōgaeya* money-exchange shop
替商 *ryōgaeshō* money-exchange business
13損 *ryōzon, ryōson* loss on both sides
義 *ryōgi* double meaning, two meanings
蓋 *ryōbuta* hunting-case watch
蓋時計 *ryōbutadokei* hunting-case watch
14像 *ryōzō* both images
様 *ryōyō* two ways, both ways; two kinds
種 *ryōshu* both kinds
端 *ryōtan, ryōhashi* both ends, either end; both edges; sitting on the fence
15膚 *ryōhada* stripped to the waist
論 *ryōron* both arguments; both theories
輪 *ryōrin* two wheels
16頭 *ryōtō no* double-headed
親 *ryōshin, futaoya* parents, both parents
17翼 *ryōyoku* both wings; both flanks
20議院 *ryōgi-in* both houses (of a legislative assembly)

A 再 35 F211 SAI. *futata(bi)* again, twice. *sai-* re-; second time, again. [冂]

2入学 *sainyūgaku* readmission to a school
入国 *sainyūkoku* re-entry into a country
入国許可書 *sainyūkoku kyokasho* re-entry permit
3下付 *saikafu* reissue, renewal
上映 *saijōei* rerun (of a film)
三 *saisan* again and again, repeatedly

1 [ ] 一 丶 ノ 乙 亅 5

三再四 *saisan-saishi* repeatedly

4 分配 *saibumpai* redistribution

5 刊 *saikan* reprint, republication

犯 *saihan* second offense

犯者 *saihansha* second offender

出 *saishutsu* reappearance, re-emergence

出発 *saishuppatsu* restart, fresh start

生 *saisei* regeneration, resuscitation, return to life; rebirth, reincarnation; narrow escape; reclamation; reproduction

生法 *saiseihō* essay-type (test)

生品 *saiseihin* reclaimed goods

6 任 *sainin* reappointment

再 *saisai* often, frequently

会 *saikai* another meeting; meeting again, reunion

交付 *saikōfu* reissue, regrant

考 *saikō* reconsideration

考慮 *saikōryo* reconsideration

7 告 *saikoku* renotification

吟味 *saigimmi* re-examination, review

投票 *saitōhyō* revoting

来 *sairai* return; second coming; Second Advent; reincarnation

来月 *saraigetsu* month after next

来年 *sarainen* year after next

来週 *saraishū* week after next

8 征 *saisei* second punitive expedition

拝 *saihai* worshipping again; bowing twice; epistolary closing

版 *saihan* reprinting; reprint; second edition

服役 *saifukueki* re-enlistment; second imprisonment

放送 *saihōsō* rebroadcasting

受浸 *saijushin* rebaptism by immersion

武装 *saibusō* rearmament

注 *saichū* repeat order

注文 *saichūmon* repeat order

9 度 *saido* twice, again, second time

訂 *saitei* second revision

変 *saihen* second change, second calamity

思 *saishi* reconsideration

洗礼 *saisenrei* rebaptism by sprinkling

訂版 *saiteihan* second revised edition

保険 *saihoken* reinsurance

軍備 *saigumbi* rearmament

降臨 *Saikōrin* Second Advent

封鎖 *saifūsa suru* reblock, refreeze

建 *seikon* (temple or shrine) rebuilding. *saiken* reconstruction, rebuilding

建築 *seikenchiku* reconstruction, rebuilding

発 *saihatsu* relapse; recurrence

発足 *saihossoku* restart, fresh start

10 起 *saiki* a comeback, recovery, restoration, rally; reflexive (in grammar)

校 *saikō* second proof; reinvestigation

案 *saian* second plan, second draft

挙 *saikyo* another attempt

浸礼 *saishinrei* rebaptism by immersion

帰熱 *saikinetsu* recurrent fever

配分 *saihaibun* redistribution

配置 *saihaichi* reallocation, realignment

従兄 *saijūkei, mata-itoko* elder second cousin

従兄弟 *mata-itoko, saijū keitei, futa-itoko* second cousin

従弟 *saijūtei, mata-itoko* younger second cousin

11 遊 *saiyū* revisit

婚 *saikon* second marriage

現 *saigen* reappearance, return; revival

設 *saisetsu* re-establishment, reorganization

敗 *saihai* second defeat

転 *saiten* changing directions, turning around

許可 *saikyoka* renewal of a permission

教育 *saikyōiku* retraining, re-education

組織 *saisoshiki* reorganization

12 開 *saikai* reopening, resumption

勝 *saishō* another victory

勤 *saikin* reappointment

割引 *saiwaribiki* rediscount

評価 *saihyōka* reassessment, reappraisal

創造 *saisōzō* recreation

尋問 *saijimmon* re-examination

測量 *saisokuryō* resurvey

検査 *saikensa* re-examination

検討 *saikentō* re-examination, review, reappraisal

13 嫁 *saika* remarriage

禁止 *saikinshi* reimposition of an embargo, reprohibition

感染 *saikansen* getting the same sickness again

試合 *saishiai* resumption of a game

試験 *saishiken* re-examination

14 演 *saien* another showing (of a play); recapitulation (in biology)

説 *saisetsu* repeated explanation

読 *saidoku suru* reread

構成 *saikōsei* reconstruction, reorganization, reconstitution

選 *saisen* re-election

選挙 *saisenkyo* re-election

製 *saisei* remanufacture, reconditioning

製品 *saiseihin* reprocessed goods

15 縁 *saien* second marriage

誕 *saitan* resurrection (of a company or school, etc.)

鋳 *saichū* recasting

調査 *saichōsa* re-examination, reinvestigation

確認 *saikakunin* reaffirmation

編 *saihen* reorganization, reshuffle

編成 *saihensei* reorganization, reshuffle

審 *saishin* re-examination, retrial, review

審査 *saishinsa* re-examination

16 燃 *sainen* recurrence, revival, resuscitation, rekindling

興 *saikō* revival, restoration, resuscitation, rehabilitation

輸入 *saiyunyū* reimportation

輸出 *saiyushutsu* re-exportation

17 臨 *Sairin* Second Advent

臨派 *Sairinha* Adventists
20議 *saigi* reconsideration, redeliberation

6

艮 36 F-X See **良** 3885. [艮]

吾 37 F343 Go. *waga* my, our, one's own. *ware* I, oneself, self, ego. [口]
2人 *gojin* we
8妹 *wagimo* my wife
妹子 *wagimoko* my wife
12等 *warera* we
15輩 *wagahai* I

巫 38 F605 Fu sorcerer, sorceress. *miko* medium, shrine maiden. *kannagi, kan, kanko* medium, diviner, shrine maiden. [工]
3子 *miko* medium, sorceress; shrine maiden
山戯 *fuzake(ru)* romp, gambol, frolic; joke, make fun of; flirt
女 *fujo, miko* medium, sorceress; shrine maiden
女寄 *mikoyo(se)*=*kuchiyo(se)* 口寄 868.11
11術 *fujutsu* divination, sorcery, witchcraft

呑 39 F339 **吞** Don. *no(mu)* (see under 飲 5159.0). [口]
3口 *nomiguchi* bung hole: end of a pipe stem
4込 *no(mi)-ko(mu)*=飲込 5159.4
6舟魚 *donshū (no) uo* big fish; great man; notorious man
吐 *donto* drinking and vomiting; coming and going
気 *nonki* optimistic, carefree, careless, heedless
気者 *nonkimono* happy-go-lucky person
7兵衛 *nombē* heavy drinker

A **否** 40 F340 Hi no, noes. *ina(mu)* refuse, decline; deny. *iya(mu)* detest, dislike. *ina* no, nay. *ina(ya)* as soon as, no sooner than, the moment; yes or no; objection; if, whether. *ie, iie* no. *iiya, iya* no, nay; yes, well. [口]
7決 *hiketsu* rejection, voting down
応 *iya(demo)-ō(demo)* willy-nilly, whether willing or not. *iya-ō* an answer re agreement or disagreement
応無 *iyaōna(shi) no* compulsory
否 *iya-iya* reluctantly; by no means
否乍 *iya-iyanaga(ra)* reluctantly
8定 *hitei* denial
定文 *hiteibun* negative sentence
定的 *hiteiteki* negative, contradictory
定語 *hiteigo* negative word
11運 *hiun* bad fortune, misfortune
12程 *iya (to iu) hodo* persistently, bitterly, extremely
14認 *hinin* denial, disapproval, repudiation, veto, nonrecognition

坐 41 F418 See **座** 1515. [土]

B **更** 42 F922 **更** Kō a watch of the night. *fu(kasu)* sit up late. *fu(keru)* (see under 深 2606.0). *arata(maru)* (see under 改 1464.0). *sara ni* again; after all; more and more. *sara(nari)* of course. [曰]
5代 *kōtai suru* exchange (something)
正 *kōsei* correction, revision, rectification
生 *kōsei* rebirth; resuscitation; rehabilitation, reorganization, regeneration
生期 *kōseiki* change of life, menopause
6地 *sarachi* empty lot
年期 *kōnenki* menopause, change of life
衣 *kōi* seasonal changing of clothes; lady court attendant; second lunar month. *koromogae* seasonal changing of clothes
衣室 *kōishitsu* dressing room
7迭 *kōtetsu* change, shake-up, reshuffle, exchanging places
位 *kōi* second accession of the same emperor
改 *kōkai* renewal, renovation, reform
更 *sarasara* (not) at all
8始 *kōshi* renewal, reform
9訂 *kōtei* revision
10紗 *sarasa* cotton print, calico
13新 *kōshin* renewal, innovation, renovation

B **亜** 43 F81 **亞** A. *tsu(gu)* rank next, come after. -A- Asia. *a-* sub-, -ous (in acids). [二]
6成層圏 *asei sōken* substratosphere
米利加 *Amerika* America
米利加合衆国 *Amerika Gasshūkoku* the United States of America
米利加杉 *Amerika sugi* redwood
8欧 *A-ō* Eurasia
9科 *aka* suborder
炭 *atan* lignite, brown coal
砒酸 *ahisan* arsenious acid
10流 *aryū* adherent, follower, imitator
11麻 *ama* flax, hemp, linen
麻仁 *amani* flaxseed, linseed
麻仁油 *amaniyu* linseed oil
麻布 *amanuno* linen
麻製 *amasei no* flaxen, linen
麻織物 *ama orimono* flax fabrics, linen
12属 *azoku* subgroup
温帯 *aontai* subtemperate zone
寒帯 *akantai* subarctic zone

1

1 [一] 7 丨、ノ乙亅

13聖 *asei* a sage of the second order
鉛 *aen* zinc
鉛引 *aembi(ki)* galvanized
鉛末 *aemmatsu* zinc dust
鉛凸版 *aen toppan* photoengraving
鉛版 *aemban* zinc etching
鉛板 *aemban* zinc plate
鉛華 *aenka* zinc white, zinc oxide, flowers of zinc
鉛鉄 *aentetsu* galvanized iron
14種 *ashu* sub-species
15熱帯 *anettai* subtropics

7

房 See 1819. [戸]

肩 See 1820. [肉]

咀 See 907. [口]

岨 See 1411. [山]

並 See 589.

兩 44 / F196 See **両** 34. [入]

亞 45 / F81 See **亜** 43. [二]

忝 46 / F692 See **忝** 209. [心]

兩 47 / F-X Nonstandard for **両** 34.

盂 48 / F1309 U bowl. [皿]

20蘭盆 *Urabon* Feast of Lanterns. *Obon* Festival of the Dead
蘭盆会 *Urabon-e*=word above

函 49 / F228 **凾** KAN. *hako* box. *i(reru)* put into. [凵]
2人 *kanjin* armorer
13数 *kansū* function (in math)
蓋 *kangai* box and cover
17嶺 *Kanrei* the Hakone Mountains

A **画** 50 / F1276 **画 畫 畵** GA, E picture, drawing, painting, sketch. KAKU stroke (in a character). *kaku(suru)* draw, demarcate, mark, divide, map out. *ega(ku)* draw, paint, sketch, describe. [田]
1一 *kakuitsu* uniformity, standardization
一主義 *kakuitsu shugi* standardization
一的 *kakuitsuteki* uniform, standard
2人 *gajin* painter, artist
3工 *gakō, edakumi* painter, artist
才 *gasai* artistic talent
4心 *gashin* artistic instinct
手 *gashu* painter, artist
引 *kakubi(ki)* arranged by strokes
5布 *gafu* canvas for oil painting
本 *gahon* picture copybook
世的 *kakuseiteki* epoch-making
仙紙 *gasenshi* drawing paper
用紙 *gayōshi* drawing paper
6匠 *gashō* painter, artist
因 *ga-in* art motif
会 *gakai* artists' patrons' association
7伯 *gahaku* artist, master painter
8帖 *gajō* picture album
板 *gaban* drawing board, drafting board
法 *gahō* art of drawing and painting
学 *gagaku* drawing
学紙 *gagakushi* drawing paper
9面 *gamen* scene, picture, the field (in TV); photo
風 *gafū* style of painting
室 *gashitsu* art studio
架 *gaka* easel
10師 *gashi* painter, artist
紙 *gashi* drawing paper
家 *gaka* painter, artist
竜点睛 *garyō-tensei* adding the eyes to the dragon; the finishing touch
11廊 *garō* picture gallery
道 *gadō* art of painting
帳 *gachō* picture album
商 *gashō* picture dealer
12幅 *gafuku* picture scroll
筆 *gahitsu* artist's brush
策 *kakusaku suru* plan, scheme, formulate a program, maneuver
然 *kakuzen(taru)* distinct, clear-cut
報 *gahō* illustrated news magazine, pictorial
期的 *kakkiteki* epoch-making
13楼 *garō* picture gallery; high decorated building
障 *gashō* pictured paper doors
意 *ga-i* meaning of a picture
聖 *gasei* master painter
14像 *gazō* portrait, picture
15稿 *gakō* sketch
談 *gadan* discussions on art and painting
鋲 *gabyō* thumb tack, drawing pin
餅 *gabei* rice-cake picture; failure, fiasco, collapse; something of little value
賛 *gasan* legend over a picture

16壇 *gadan* artists' world, painting circles
龍点睛 *garyō-tensei* finishing touches
18題 *gadai* subject of a painting, motif, theme
19譜 *gafū* picture book, picture album
22讃 *gasan* legend over a picture

A 武 51 F1038 Mu. Bu military affairs, military arts, chivalry, military glory, military power, arms. *take(shi)* brave. [止]

2人 *bujin* military man
力 *buryoku* armed might, the sword, force
力外交 *buryoku gaikō* armed diplomacy
力政治 *buryoku seiji* power politics
力戦 *buryokusen* armed conflict
3士 *bushi, mononofu* samurai, warrior
士気質 *bushi katagi, bushi kishitsu* samurai spirit
士道 *bushidō* Bushido, samurai code of chivalry
士階級 *bushi kaikyū* warrior class
4辺 *buhen* military affairs; military people
5功 *bukō* military exploits
弁 *buben* soldier
6臣 *bushin* military retainer
名 *bumei* military fame
7技 *bugi* martial arts
芸 *bugei* martial arts
8門 *bumon* military family, warrior class
官 *bukan* military or naval officer
具 *bugu* arms, armor
学 *bugaku* military science
事 *buji* military affairs; martial arts
者 *musha* warrior
者振 *mushabu(ri)* prowess, gallantry. *mushaburu(i)* shaking with excitement
者振付 *mushabur(i)tsu(ku)* jump into the fray
者修業 *musha shugyō* samurai drill, knight errantry
者絵 *mushae* warrior picture
者慄 *mushaburu(i) suru* shake with excitement
者震 *mushaburu(i)* fighting excitement
9威 *bui* military power
侠 *bukyō* chivalry, gallantry, heroism
神 *bushin* god of military arts
勇 *buyū* bravery, valor, military prowess
勇伝 *buyūden* martial story
10庫 *buko* armory
将 *bushō* military commander
烈 *buretsu* military merit
陵桃源 *Buryōtōgen* Utopia
骨 *bukotsu* uncouth, clumsy, brusque
骨者 *bukotsumono* boor, rustic
家 *buke* samurai; warrior
家物 *bukemono* samurai romance
家政治 *buke seiji* feudal government
家時代 *buke jidai* the feudal period (1185–1867)
11道 *budō* military arts; Bushido
運 *bu-un* the fortunes of war
将 *bushō* military commander
術 *bujutsu* military arts
張 *buba(ru)* be soldierly, be martial
略 *buryaku* strategy, military tactics
教 *bukyō* the teachings of Bushido
断 *budan* militarism
断主義 *budan shugi* militarism
断的 *budanteki* militaristic
断政治 *budan seiji* military government
12備 *bubi* military preparation, armaments, defenses
装 *busō* arms, armament; armed. *busō suru* arm
装中立 *busō chūritsu* armed neutrality
装平和 *busō heiwa* armed peace
装具 *busōgu* accouterments
装都市 *busō toshi* fortified city
装船 *busōsen* armed ship
装解除 *busō kaijo* disarmament
装警官 *busō keikan* armed police
13漢三鎮 *Bukan Sanchin* the Three Wuhan Cities
14徳 *butoku* martial arts
15勲 *bukun* deeds of arms
器 *buki* weapon, arms, ordnance
器倉 *bukigura* armory, arsenal
器庫 *bukiko* armory, ordnance department
器貸与 *bukitaiyo* lend-lease
22鑑 *bukan* book of heraldry

8

並 See 並 589.

盃 52 F1309 F952 See 杯 2206. [皿]

帝 See 帝 305. [巾]

A 昼 53 F907 晝 Chū daytime, midday. *hiru* midday, daytime, noon. [日]

3下 *hirusa(gari)* early afternoon
4日中 *hiruhinaka* daytime; noon
6休 *hiru yasu(mi)* noon recess, noon rest period
行灯 *hiru andon* (useless as) a lantern at noon day
光色電球 *chūkōshoku denkyū* daylight lamp
8夜 *chūya, hiru (mo) yoru (mo)* day and night
夜舎 *chūya (o) o(kazu)* continuing day and night
夜兼行 *chūya-kenkō* working day and night
9食 *chūshoku, chūjiki, hiruge* lunch, midday meal
前 *hirumae* forenoon; just before noon
10時 *hirudoki* noon, lunch time
11過 *hirusu(gi)* afternoon

1 [一]丨、ノ乙亅

頃 *hirugoro* about noon
12 間 *hiruma, chūkan* daytime; during the day
飯 *hirumeshi, chūhan* lunch, midday meal
寐 *hirune* siesta
13 寝 *hirune* siesta
14 鳶 *hiru tombi* sneak thief
15 餉 *hiruge* lunch, midday meal
16 餐 *chūsan* luncheon
興行 *hiru kōgyō* matinee

殂 See 殂 441. [歹]

歪 54/F1039 WAI. E. *hizu(mu)* warp, be crooked, get bent, be strained. *yuga(mu), iga(mu)* warp, swerve, deflect, be crooked, be distorted, be bent, incline, slant; be perverted, be cross-grained. *iga(meru), yuga(meru)* vt bend, curve, warp, distort. *ibitsu no* oval, elliptical; distorted, crooked, irregular, warped. *iga(mi), yuga(mi)* strain, distortion, bend. [止]
2 力 *wairyoku* stress
6 曲 *waikyoku* distortion, falsification, perversion

9

師 See 113. [巾]

扇 See 1823. [戸]

晋 55/F905 晉 SHIN advance. [日]

哥 56/F358 KA. KO. *ani* elder brother. [口]

蚕 A 57/F1678 蠶 蠺 SAN. *kaiko* silkworm. [虫]
6 糸 *sanshi* silk thread, silk yarn
糸業 *sanshigyō* sericulture industry
糸試験所 *sanshi shikenjo* silk experiment station
7 豆 *soramame* broad bean, horse bean
児 *sanji* silkworm
卵 *sanran* silkworm egg
卵紙 *sanranshi* silkworm-egg card
8 具 *sangu* sericultural equipment
9 食 *sanshoku* encroachment, aggression, inroad, invasion
室 *sanshitsu* silkworm-raising room
10 座 *sanza* silkworm basket
紙 *sanshi* silkworm-egg card
13 業 *sangyō* sericulture
14 種 *sanshu* silkworm-egg card

夏 A 58/F449 夏 GE. KA *natsu* summer. [夂]
3 山 *natsuyama* mountains in summer
大根 *natsu daikon* summer daikon
4 日 *kajitsu* summer day
木立 *natsu kodachi* a grove in summer
6 衣 *natsugoromo* summer clothes
向 *natsumu(ki)* for summer
休 *natsuyasu(mi)* summer vacation
羽織 *natsubaori* summer haori (coat)
至 *geshi* summer solstice
至点 *geshiten* summer solstice
至線 *Geshisen* Tropic of Cancer
8 物 *natsumono* summer goods
服 *natsufuku* summer clothes
季 *kaki* summer season
炉冬扇 *karo-tōsen* summer fires and winter fans; useless things
9 枯 *natsuga(re)* summer slump
前 *natsumae ni* before summer
草 *natsugusa* summer grass
負 *natsuma(ke)* suffering from summer heat
10 蚕 *natsugo* summer silkworms
時 *natsudoki, kaji* summertime
時刻 *natsu jikoku* daylight-saving time
時間 *natsu jikan* daylight-saving time
11 野 *natsuno* summer fields
菊 *natsugiku* early chrysanthemums
祭 *natsu matsu(ri)* summer festival
12 越 *natsugo(shi)* keeping over the summer
着 *natsugi* summer clothes
帽子 *natsubōshi* summer hat, straw hat
場 *natsuba* summertime
場所 *natsu basho* summer wrestling tournament
期 *kaki* summer season
期大学 *kaki daigaku* college summer school
期学校 *kaki gakkō* summer school
期時間 *kaki jikan* summer daylight-saving time
14 蜜柑 *natsu mikan* bitter summer orange
15 瘦 *natsuyase* summer loss of weight
18 蟬 *natsuzemi* summer cicadas

10

啇 See 商 321. [口]

噐 Nonstandard for 器 994.

堊 59/F429 A. AKU wall. [土]

焉 60/F1186 EN. *izuku(nzo)* how, why. *koko ni* then. [灬]

戛 61/F761 戞 KATSU halbert. [戈]

9 飛 *katto(basu)* knock out (a homer) ⌈hard
12 然 *katsuzen* the sound of striking something

A 悪 62/F722 悪 O. Aku evil, wrong, vice, wickedness, lawlessness. *a(shikarazu)* do not take offense. *waru(i), a(shii)* bad, evil, wrong; immoral; malicious; blamable; injurious, detrimental, malignant; be indisposed; inferior; homely; poor (memory); inclement; unlucky; out of order; unsavory. *niku(mu)* hate, detest. *niku(i)* hateful, abominable, poor-looking. *waru(bireru)* be timid, be ashamed. *aku(tareru)* be mischievous. *aku(tare)* rowdiness; a rowdy. *waru* rascal, ruffian; wickedness. *niku(shimi)* hatred, enmity. *aku-* bad, wrong, evil, vicious, wicked; unfavorable, false; perverted; treacherous. *-niku(i)* difficult, awkward. [心]

2 人 *akunin* bad man, villain
3 女 *akujo* wicked woman, ugly woman
口 *akkō, warukuchi, aku(tare)guchi* abuse, insult, slander, evil speaking ⌈gossip
口雑言 *akkō-zōgon* all kinds of malicious
4 心 *akushin* evil thought, malicious motive. *oshin* nausea, urge to vomit
文 *akubun* bad style, poor writing
方 *akugata* villain's part
日 *akubi, akunichi* unlucky day
水 *akusui* undrinkable water
化 *akka* worsening, deterioration, aggravation, degeneration, corruption
友 *akuyū* bad companion
太郎 *akutarō* bad boy
天使 *akutenshi* evil angels
天候 *akutenkō* bad weather ⌈villain
5 玉 *akudama* bad character, bad person; the
用 *akuyō* abuse, misuse, perversion
処 *akusho*=悪所 (see below–8)
巧 *warudaku(mi)* wiles, sinister design, trick, conspiracy, intrigue
令 *akurei* a bad decree ⌈be impartial
平等 *akubyōdō* leaning over backwards to
6 舌 *akuzetsu* an evil tongue, gossip
血 *akuchi, oketsu* impure blood
行 *akugyō, akkō* misdeed, wrongdoing, wickedness ⌈distrust
気 *warugi* ill will, evil intent, ill feeling,
因悪果 *akuin-akka* sowing evil and reaping
因縁 *aku-innen* evil destiny ⌊evil
名 *akumei, akumyō* bad reputation, ill repute, bad name
名高 *akumyōdaka(i)* infamous ⌈der
7 言 *akugen* uncomplimentary remarks, slan-
役 *akuyaku* the villain, the villain's part
投 *akutō* wild pitch
阻 *tsuwari, oso* morning sickness
声 *akusei* bad voice; evil speaking
条件 *akujōken* unfavorable conditions ⌈tors
材料 *akuzairyō* adverse stock-market fac-
足掻 *waruagaki* wicked mischief, wicked play ⌈horseplay
巫山戯 *warufuzake* prank, practical joke,
8 例 *akurei* bad example, bad precedent
性 *akusei* virulence; malignant (cancer); pernicious (anemia). *akushō* evil nature; licentiousness, lewdness
所 *akusho* dangerous place; house of ill-
法 *akuhō* a bad law ⌊fame, bad place
念 *akunen* evil thought, malicious motive,
妻 *akusai* bad wife ⌊spite
果 *akka* bad results
者 *warumono* rascal, ruffian, scoundrel
事 *akuji* evil deed, crime, wickedness
知恵 *warujie* cunning, guile
逆 *akugyaku* treason, treachery, atrocity
逆無道 *akugyaku-mudō*=word above
9 風 *akufū* vice, evil manners, bad custom
食 *akujiki suru* eat repulsive things, eat poor food; eat meat. *akushoku suru* eat poor food
疫 *akueki* a plague, pestilence, epidemic
相 *akusō* evil countenance
神 *akujin* evil god
計 *akkei, akukei* plot, trick, evil scheme
政 *akusei* misgovernment
臭 *akushū* bad odor, stench
巷 *aku (no) chimata* skid row, underworld
10 鬼 *akki* evil spirit, demon, devil ⌈horse
馬 *akuba, akume* wild horse, unmanageable
疾 *akushitsu* malignant or virulent disease
症 *akushō* malignant or virulent disease
徒 *akuto* rascal, scoundrel, villain
党 *akutō* rascal, scoundrel, villain
酒 *akushu* cheap liquor
洒落 *warujare* offensive joke
11 道 *akudō* evil course, wrong course
運 *aku-un* bad luck ⌈bling
遊 *waruaso(bi)* prank, evil pleasures, gam-
婦 *akufu* wicked woman
球 *akkyū* hard ball to hit; bad pitch
酔 *waruyo(i)* drunken sickness, drunken
婆 *akuba* a mean old woman ⌊frenzy
貨 *akka* bad money
達者 *warudassha* fast slipshod work
推量 *waruzuiryō* distrust, unjust suspicion
悪戯 *waru-itazura* mischief
習 *akushū* bad habit, vice
習慣 *akushūkan* bad habit, evil practices
12 税 *akuzei* irrational tax
評 *akuhyō* ill repute, bad reputation, unfavorable criticism

1 [一] 丨 、 ノ 乙 亅

寒 *okan* a chill, ague
童 *akudō* bad boy
筆 *akuhitsu* poor handwriting
策 *akusaku* poor policy, poor plan
循環 *akujunkan* vicious circle
13 僧 *akusō* dissolute priest
漢 *akkan* rascal, villain, scoundrel, ruffian, crook
路 *akuro* bad road
夢 *akumu* bad dream, nightmare
意 *akui* ill will, malice, spite, evil intention, bad faith
業 *akugyō* evil, sinful deed. *akugō* evil karma
戦 *akusen* hard fighting, close contest
戦苦闘 *akusen-kutō* hard fighting
感 *akkan* ill feeling, unhappy feeling. *okan* feeling feverish and chilly
感化 *akkanka* evil influence
感情 *akkanjō* ill feeling, ill will, animosity, bad impression
14 様 *a(shi)zama ni* unfavorably, slanderously
辣 *akuratsu* craftiness
銭 *akusen* ill-gotten money; bad coin
態 *akutai* abusive language
徳 *akutoku* vices, corruption, immorality
徳新聞 *akutoku shimbun* irresponsible newspaper
15 縁 *akuen* evil destiny, evil connection, unfortunate love
罵 *akuba* cursing, vilification
霊 *akurei, akuryō* evil spirit
弊 *akuhei* vice, abuse, evil
熱 *onetsu* fever following a chill
賢 *warugashiko(i)* cunning, crafty, wily, sly
質 *akushitsu* poor quality; malignancy; viciousness
質化 *akushitsuka* worsening
戯 *itazura, warusa, waru-itazura* mean mischief. *akugi* practical joke
戯子 *itazurakko* mischievous boy
戯小僧 *itazura kozō* mischievous boy
戯坊主 *itazura bōzu* mischievous boy
戯者 *itazuramono* loose woman; useless fellow, mischief maker
戯書 *itazuraga(ki)* scribbling, doodling
戯盛 *itazurazaka(ri)* mischievous age
戯着 *itazuragi* rompers, play suit
17 擦 *waruzure* oversophistication. *waruzu(reru)* get worse and worse
18 癖 *akuheki, waruguse* bad habit, vice
騒 *warusawa(gi)* disorderly merrymaking
21 魔 *akuma* Satan; devil, demon, evil spirit; fiend
魔払 *akumabara(i)* exorcism

11

雇 See 1826. [隹]

啬 See 279. [口]

惡 63 F722 See 悪 62. [心]

亜 See 留 3003. [田]

戞 64 F761 See 戛 61. [戈]

颪 65 F2074 (国字) *oroshi* wind blowing down from the mountains. [風]

甦 66 F1267 甦 So. Su *yomigae(ru)* (see under 蘇 4097.0). [生]
5 生 *sosei*=*kōsei* 更生 42.5

12

嗇 67 F376 Shoku. *yabusa(ka)* (see under 吝 2066.0). [口]

13

甦 68 F1267 See 甦 66. [生]

爾 69 F1211 尓 尒 Ji. Ni. *nanji* thou, you. *shika* so, in that way. [爻]
7 来 *jirai* since then
9 後 *jigo* thereafter

14

憂 70 F743 B Yū. *ure(u)*, *ure(eru)* grieve, lament, be anxious. *u(ki)*, *u(i)* sad, unhappy, gloomy. *ure(e)*, *ure(i)* distress, sorrow, trouble, anxiety, grief. *usa* gloom, sorrow, melancholy. [心]
4 心 *yūshin* grieving heart
5 目 *ukime* bitter experience, misery, distress, grief, sad thoughts
世 *ukiyo* sad world. *yūsei* worrying about world conditions
6 色 *yūshoku* melancholy air, anxious look, traces of sorrow, gloom
7 身 *ukimi* life of misery
8 国 *yūkoku* patriotism
苦 *yūku* trouble, distress, sorrow
事 *ure(i)goto*, *ukiji*=*ukime* 憂目 (see above–5)
9 思 *yūshi suru* grieve
10 悩 *ure(i)-naya(mu)* be grievously troubled
哭 *ukine* sobbing
11 戚 *yūseki* grief
患 *yūkan* sorrow, worry, distress
12 悶 *yūmon* anguish, mortification
晴 *usabara(shi)* diversion, distraction
13 愁 *yūshū* grief, melancholy, gloom
15 慮 *yūryo* anxiety, dread, cares, solicitude

憤 *yūfun* grief and anger
18顔 *ure(i)gao* anxious look, sad countenance
21懼 *yūku* fear, apprehension, dread
26鬱 *yūutsu* melancholy, dejection, gloom
鬱症 *yūutsushō* melancholia, hypochondria

15

整 See 2436. [攵]

16

壓 壓 See 圧 818. [土]

18

璽 71 F1257 Ji emperor's seal. [玉] B

賾 See 賾 840. [貝]

躄 躄 See 蹶 4587. [足]

畺 72 F1280 Kyō boundary. [田]

21

贗 贗 See 贋 840. [貝]

聽 See 聴 3716. [耳]

22

靨 73 F2043 Yō *ekubo* dimple. [面]

饗 See 饗 841. [食]

靆 See 5071. [雨]

23

魘 See 258. [鬼]

蠶 74 F-X See 蚕 57. [虫]

RAD. 丨 2

Bō rod, stick, line. Variant: a shorter vertical. Nickname: Rod.

2

个 See 個 489.

也 75 F63 Ya. *nari=desu*, to be (classical) [乚]

3

冊 See 丹 163. [丶]

丫 76 F44 A a fork.

丰 77 F49 Bō luxurious growth of grass; fat face.

卅 78 F285 卅 卅 Sō. Zō. *sanjū* thirty. [十]

卍 79 F288 卐 Ban. Man. *manji* gammadion, fylfot, swastika. [十]

4巴 *manji-tomoe* falling in swirls

廿 See 1550. [廾]

弔 80 F653 Chō mourning. *chō(suru)* mourn, condole with. *tomura(u)*, *tobura(u)* mourn for; hold a memorial service for; condole. *tomura(i)*, *tobura(i)* funeral, burial, condolence. [弓] B

4文 *chōbun* funeral address
6合戦 *tomura(i) gassen* battle of revenge
9客 *chōkaku*, *chōkyaku* people attending a funeral or offering condolences
10砲 *chōhō* artillery funeral salute
11問 *chōmon* condolence call
祭 *chōsai* memorial service
祭料 *chōsairyō* gift at a memorial serivce
12詞 *chōshi* message of condolence, memorial address
13辞 *chōji* message of condolence, memorial address
電 *chōden* telegram of condolence
意 *chōi* condolence, sympathy, mourning

14 旗 *chōki* flag at half-mast
銃 *chōjū* volley of rifles at a funeral
歌 *chōka* elegy, dirge
15 慰 *chōi* condolence, sympathy
慰金 *chōikin* condolence money
20 鐘 *chōshō* funeral bell

A **中** 81/F44 CHŪ center, middle; middle (course), (golden) mean; medium, mediocrity, average; second volume (of three). *naka* inside, interior, midst, middle, mean, midway. *uchi* (see under 内 82.0). *chū(suru)* reach the middle; reach the height (of prosperity). *-chū, -jū* thru, thruout, during; all over (town); within, among, in.

2 入 *naka-i(ri)* intermission (during a play)
二階 *chūnikai* mezzanine floor
3 口 *nakaguchi* central entrance; slander
小 *chūshō* medium and small ⌈enterprises
小企業 *chūshō kigyō* medium and smaller
小諸国家 *chūshō shokokka* medium and small nations ⌈vegetables
4 手 *nakate* mid-season rice; mid-season
日 *chūnichi* the middle day, the equinoctial day. *Chū-Nichi* China and Japan. *nakabi* the middle day ⌈tion
止 *chūshi* suspension, stoppage, interrup-
中 *nakanaka* very, considerably; easily, readily; by no means (with neg.)
天 *chūten* mid-air; mid-heaven, zenith
夭 *chūyō* dying young
元 *chūgen* 15th day of the 7th lunar month; last day of Bon Lantern Festival; Bon
分 *chūbun suru* halve ⌊gifts
支 *Chūshi* Central China
支那 *Naka Shina* Central China ⌈balance
心 *chūshin* center, heart; pivot, emphasis;
心人物 *chūshin jimbutsu* central personage
心地 *chūshinchi* center, metropolis
心点 *chūshinten* center
心思想 *chūshin shisō* central idea
5 生 *nakate* mid-season crops
皿 *chūzara* medium-sized dish
句 *chūku* middle part of the verse
外 *chūgai* home and abroad
正 *chūsei* impartiality, fairness
半 *chūhan* middle; half-finished
世 *chūsei* medieval times; Middle Ages
甲板 *chūkampan* main deck
仕 *nakashi* longshoreman, baggageman
仕切 *nakajikiri* partition
立 *chūritsu* neutrality
立地帯 *chūritsu chitai* neutral zone
立国 *chūritsukoku* neutral power
古 *chūko, chūburu* secondhand. *Chūko* Middle Ages
古史 *chūkoshi* medieval history
古車 *chūkosha, chūburusha* secondhand car
古品 *chūkohin* secondhand goods
央 *chūō* center, middle
央突破 *chūō toppa* central breakthru
央政府 *chūō seifu* central government
央集権 *chūō shūken* centralized authoritarian rule ⌈power
央集権化 *chūō shūkenka* centralization of
6 米 *Chūbei* Central America
糸 *chūito* medium-sized thread
老 *chūrō* middle age
旬 *chūjun* middle ten days of a month
気 *chūki* palsy, paralysis
休 *nakayasu(mi)* rest, recess
次 *nakatsugi* (electric) relay; intermediary;
弛 *nakadaru(mi)* a slump ⌊brokerage
近東 *Chūkintō* Near and Middle East
西部 *Chūseibu* Mid-west
衣嚢 *nakagakushi* inside pocket
耳 *chūji* middle ear, tympanum
耳炎 *chūjien* tympanitis ⌈quality
肉 *chūniku* medium build; meat of medium
肉中背 *chūniku-chūzei* medium build
共 *Chūkyō* Chinese Communists; Communist China
共軍 *Chūkyōgun* Chinese Communist Army
年 *chūnen* middle age
年者 *chūnemmono* middle-aged person; a person who changes his line in middle life. *chūnensha* middle-aged person
年増 *chūdoshima* woman approaching mid-
7 身 *nakami*＝中味 (see below–8) ⌊dle age
低 *nakabiku, nakahiku* hollow, concave
佐 *chūsa* lieutenant colonel; commander (navy) ⌈photography)
判 *chūban* medium size; cabinet size (in
形 *chūgata* medium size
更 *chūkō* middle watch, 12–2 a.m.
位 *chūi* medium, mediocrity, average. *chūgurai, chūkurai* about medium
位数 *chūisū* median ⌈felt hat
折 *nakao(ri)* folded in the middle. *nakao(re)*
折帽 *nakaorebō* felt hat
折帽子 *nakaore bōshi* felt hat
8 退 *chūtai* leaving school during a term
味 *nakami* interior, contents, substance, filling; (sword) blade
物 *a(te)mono* guessing; covering
和 *chūwa suru*, neutralize, counteract
取 *naka (o) to(ru)* work out a compromise
欧 *Chūō* Central Europe
京 *Chūkyō* Nagoya
直 *nakanao(ri)* reconciliation
空 *chūkū* mid-air, the air; emptiness. *nakazora* mid-air

毒 *chūdoku* poisoning
東 *Chūtō* Middle East
波 *chūha* medium wave (in broadcasting)
波長 *chūhachō* medium wave
刳 *nakagu(ri)* boring
刳盤 *nakagu(ri)ban* boring machine
国 *Chūgoku* China; middle of a country; the Hiroshima area
国人 *Chūgokujin* a Chinese
国人民共和国 *Chūgoku Jimmin Kyōwakoku* the People's (Communist) Republic of China
性 *chūsei* neuter gender; (chemical) neutrality; sterility; indifference
性子 *chūseishi* neutron
性洗剤 *chūsei senzai* a detergent
枢 *chūsū* center, pivot, nucleus, backbone, central figure, mainstay, pillar, key man
枢性 *chūsūsei* central (nervous system)
枢神経系統 *chūsū shinkei keitō* central nervous system ⌈school
学 *chūgaku* middle school; junior high
学生 *chūgakusei* middle school pupil; junior high school pupil ⌈school
学校 *chūgakkō* middle school; junior high
9風 *chūbu, chūbū, chūfu* palsy, paralysis
速 *chūsoku* intermediate gear
通 *nakadō(ri)* intermediate street. *chūdō(ri)* medium quality
垣 *nakagaki* middle fence
指 *naka yubi, chūshi* middle finger
柄 *chūgara* medium size, medium pattern, medium stature
柱 *nakabashira* middle pillar ⌈mid-autumn
秋 *chūshū* 15th day of the 8th lunar month;
段 *chūdan* half way up a slope or stairway, the landing; center of three (horizontal) columns (of print)
前 *chūzen* front of center field
点 *chūten* middle point, median point
巻 *chūkan* middle volume (of three)
背 *chūzei* average height
南米 *Chūnambei* Central and South Amer-
級品 *chūkyūhin* fair average quality ⌊ica
食 *chūshoku*＝昼食 53.9
食会 *chūshokukai* luncheon meeting
保 *chūho* mediation
保者 *chūhosha* mediator, intercessor
途 *chūto* midway, half way
途半端 *chūto-hampa* half finished, incomplete ⌈a term
途退学 *chūto taigaku* leaving school during
10座 *chūza suru* leave before an affair is over
庭 *nakaniwa* courtyard, quadrangle, middle
核 *chūkaku* kernel, core, nucleus ⌊court
将 *chūjō* lieutenant general; vice-admiral

破 *chūha* half damage
耕機 *chūkōki* cultivator
陰 *chūin* seven-week mourning period
島 *nakajima* island in a pond or river
宮 *chūgū* palace of the empress; empress; emperor's second consort
高 *nakadaka* convex
高音部 *chūkōombu* mezzo-soprano
原 *chūgen* middle of a field; middle of a country; field of contest ⌈paign)
原鹿 *chūgen (no) shika* the aim (in a cam-
流 *chūryū* mid-stream; middle course; middle class
流社会 *chūryū shakai* middle class
部 *chūbu* central part, center, middle, heart
部太平洋 *Chūbu Taiheiyō* Central Pacific
華 *Chūka* Middle Kingdom, China
華人民共和国 *Chūka Jimmin Kyōwakoku* Communist China ⌈(Taiwan)
華民国 *Chūka Minkoku* Chinese Republic
華料理 *Chūka ryōri* Chinese cooking, Chinese dishes
11庸 *chūyō* mean, golden mean, moderation, middle path; Doctrine of the Mean
尉 *chūi* first lieutenant; lieutenant junior
頃 *nakagoro* about the middle ⌊grade
略 *chūryaku* omission of a part (of an article)
脳 *chūnō* midbrain
隊 *chūtai* company (in the army)
断 *chūdan* break, interruption, suspension
堂 *chūdō* main temple building
距離 *chūkyori* middle distance (races)
産階級 *chūsan kaikyū* middle class, bourgeoisie
道 *chūdō* the middle road, middle of the road, mean, moderation ⌈trals
道派 *chūdōha* middle-of-the roaders, neu-
堅 *chūken* main body (of troops); center field; center fielder; nucleus, backbone,
堅手 *chūkenshu* center fielder ⌊mainstay
12越 *chūgoshi* over center field
項 *chūkō* the mean
幅 *chūhaba* medium width
程 *nakahodo* middle, midway
絶 *chūzetsu* interruption, discontinuance, suspension, abeyance ⌈man
軸 *chūjiku* axis, pivot, central figure, key
隔 *chūkaku* septum
飯 *chūhan* the noonday meal
期 *chūki* middle period
尊 *chūzon* middle image (of three)
景 *chūkei* middle distance
買 *nakagai* brokerage
葉 *chūyō* about the middle (of an era)
等 *chūtō* second grade, medium quality, average; middle class; secondary grade

1 一 [丨]3 丶 ノ 乙 亅

等学校 *chūtō gakkō* secondary school
等教育 *chūtō kyōiku* secondary education
等教員 *chūtō kyōin* secondary teachers
間 *chūkan* middle, midway; interim
間子 *chūkanshi* meson, mesotron
間内閣 *chūkan naikaku* interim cabinet
間国 *chūkankoku* buffer state
間派 *chūkanha* middle-of-the-roaders, neutrals, independents
間商人 *chūkan shōnin* middleman, broker
間景気 *chūkan keiki* temporary boom
間搾取 *chūkan sakushu* kickback
間層 *chūskansō* the middle class
間駅 *chūkan eki* way station 「election
間選挙 *chūkan senkyo* by-election, interim
13 傷 *chūshō* slander, libel, defamation
腰 *chūgoshi* half-sitting or half-standing posture
腹 *chūfuku* mountain side, halfway up. *chūppara* irritated, offended
数 *chūsū* arithmetical mean
幕 *nakamaku* middle act
塗 *nakanuri* second (plaster) coat
農 *chūnō* middle-class farmer
継 *chūkei* (radio) relay, hook-up
継所 *chūkeisho* relay station
継放送 *chūkei hōsō* relay broadcasting
継貿易 *chūkei bōeki* transit trade
14 稲 *nakate* mid-season rice
15 編 *chūhen* second part, second volume
篇 *chūhen* second part, second volume
盤戦 *chūbansen* the midst of a campaign
16 積 *nakazu(mi)* loading in the middle
興 *chūkō* restoration, revival, resurgence
興祖 *chūkō(no)so* an ancestor who rejuvenated a dynasty or a family
19 蘇 *Chū-So* China and Soviet Russia

A **内** 82/F192 **内** DAI. NAI inside, interior, within, between, among. *uchi* inside, interior; house, home; within; between, among, out of; mind; myself. *uchi-* inner. *-nai* within, within the scope of. [入]
2 力 *nairyoku* internal stress 「Seal
3 大臣 *Naidaijin* Lord Keeper of the Privy
4 心 *naishin* inmost heart, one's mind, in the
方 *naihō* inside; your wife ⌊heart
内 *uchiuchi* family circle, the inside. *uchiuchi no, nainai* private, informal; secret,
反脚 *naihankyaku* bowlegs ⌊confidential
火艇 *naikatei* launch
分 *naibun* secret, confidential 「tion
分泌 *naibumpi, naibumpitsu* internal secre-
5 示 *naiji, naishi* unofficial announcement
圧 *naiatsu* internal pressure
払 *uchibara(i)* part payment
包 *naihō* connotation, comprehension
出血 *naishukketsu* internal hemorrhage
玄関 *uchi genkan, nai-genkan* side entrance
弁慶 *uchibenkei* braggart
用 *naiyō* internal use; private business
用薬 *naiyōyaku* medicine taken internally
申 *naishin* unofficial report
申書 *naishinsho* pupil's record
外 *naigai* inside and outside; domestic and foreign; approximately. *uchi-soto* inside and out
外人 *naigaijin* nationals and foreigners
外野 *naigaiya* infield and outfield
6 因 *nai-in* the actual reason
気 *uchiki* timidity, shyness, bashfulness
池 *uchi ike* garden pond
旨 *naishi* emperor's secret orders
争 *naisō* internal strife
向性 *naikōsei* introversion
交渉 *uchi kōshō* preliminary negotiations
曲球 *naikyokkyū* an incurve
衣嚢 *uchi kakushi* inside pocket
耳 *naiji* inner ear
耳炎 *naijien* inner-ear inflammation
地 *naichi* homeland; mainland; inland
地人 *naichijin* Japanese in Japan proper
地米 *naichimai* homegrown rice
在 *naizai* immanence, inherence, indwelling
在性 *naizaisei* immanence, inherence, indwelling 「trinsic
在的 *naizaiteki* immanent, internal, in-
7 見 *naiken* preliminary inspection, preview
角 *naikaku* interior angle; inside corner (in baseball)
局 *naikyoku* a bureau in a ministry
応 *naiō* secret understanding, collusion; betrayal 「palace
廷 *naitei* harem; inside the palace; the
住 *naijū* indwelling (life)
攻 *naikō* (disease) settling in internal organs; quarreling among companions
状 *naijō*＝内情 (see below–11)
乱 *nairan* civil war, rebellion
助 *naijo* a wife's help
含 *naigan* implication
弟子 *uchi deshi* private pupil; apprentice
沙汰 *uchizata* secret government business
芸者 *uchi geisha* geisha living in the establishment 「account
8 金 *uchikin* bargain money, money paid on
侍 *naishi* maid of honor
径 *naikei* bore, inside diameter
法 *uchinori* inside measure
治 *naiji, naichi* internal or domestic affairs
命 *naimei* private or secret orders
実 *naijitsu* the facts

定 *naitei* tentative decision
炎 *naien* inner flame
苑 *naien* inner garden, inner park
典 *naiten* sutras, Buddhist literature
妻 *naisai* common-law wife
事 *naiji* personal affairs; internal affairs
国 *naikoku* home country
国産 *naikokusan* domestic product
所 *naisho* kitchen; state of finances
所話 *naishobanashi* secret talk
的 *naiteki* inner, intrinsic, mental, inherited
的生活 *naiteki seikatsu* the inner life
服 *naifuku* internal use
服薬 *naifukuyaku* medicine taken internally
股 *uchimomo, uchimata* inner thigh. *uchimata ni* (walking) pigeon-toed
股膏薬 *uchimata-gōyaku* duplicity, double-dealing; double-dealer, turncoat, fence-sitter
帑 *naido* a ruler's private property
帑金 *naidokin* a ruler's privy purse
9 造 *uchizuku(ri)* inside finishing(of a house)
相 *Naishō* prewar Home Minister
海 *uchi umi, naikai* inlet, bay, inland sea
祝 *uchi iwai* family celebration; small present on such an occasion
約 *naiyaku* (marriage) engagement; secret treaty; tacit understanding; private contract
陣 *naijin* chancel, inner sanctuary
政 *naisei* internal administration; domestic affairs
室 *naishitsu* one's wife
界 *naikai* inner world, inner sphere
奏 *naisō* secret report to the emperor
冑 *uchi kabuto*＝内兜 (see below–11)
省 *naisei* introspection, reflection
祝言 *naishūgen* private wedding
面 *naimen* inside, interior
面的 *naimenteki* inner, internal, inside
通 *naitsū* secret understanding, collusion
通者 *naitsūsha* betrayer
科 *naika* internal medicine
科医 *naika-i* physician, internist
10 庭 *uchiniwa, naitei* inner court, quadrangle
借 *uchiga(ri)* drawing ahead on salary
紛 *naifun* domestic or internal discord
航 *naikō* coastwise service
訌 *naikō* internal or domestic discord
訓 *naikun* private or secret orders
倉 *uchigura* a godown within a building or compound
宴 *naien* private dinner
宮 *Naikū, Naigū* Inner Ise Shrine
陸 *nairiku* inland
陸国 *nairikukoku* landlocked country
陸霧 *nairikumu* inland fog
部 *naibu* interior, inside. *naibu no* internal
部生活 *naibuseikatsu* the inner life
部的 *naibuteki* internal

容 *naiyō* contents, detail, import
容見本 *naiyō mihon* sample pages
容物 *naiyōbutsu* contents (of the stomach)
容証明 *naiyō shōmei* certification of contents
11 達 *naitatsu* unofficial notice
偵 *naitei* scouting
側 *uchigawa* inside, interior, inner part
堀 *uchibori* inner moat, moat within the castle walls
張 *uchiba(ri)* lining, ceiling, wainscoting
情 *naijō* internal conditions; true state of affairs
掛 *uchiga(ke)* throwing down by leg work
接 *naisetsu* inscribed (circle)
探 *naitan* private inquiry, secret investigation
済 *naisai* settlement out of court
訳 *uchiwake* items, breakdown; classification
規 *naiki* private regulations, bylaws, tradition
密 *naimitsu* privacy, secrecy. *naimitsu ni* confidentially, privately, off the record
兜 *uchi kabuto* inside of a helmet; hidden circumstances
患 *naikan* internal or domestic trouble
寄合 *uchi yoria(i)* family council
勘定 *uchi kanjō* secret account
遊星 *naiyūsei* inner planet
斜視 *naishashi* cross-eyed, strabismus
務 *naimu* internal or domestic affairs
務大臣 *Naimu Daijin* prewar Home Minister
務省 *Naimushō* prewar Ministry of Home Affairs
野 *naiya* infield, diamond
野手 *naiyashu* infielder, baseman
野席 *naiyaseki* infield bleachers
12 検 *naiken* preliminary inspection
港 *naikō* inner harbor
湯 *uchiyu* hotsprings water in the home
渡 *uchiwata(shi)* partial delivery; partial payment
腔 *naikō* lumen
診 *naishin* pelvic examination
勤 *naikin* office or indoor work
貸 *uchiga(shi)* advancing part of a salary
報 *naihō* secret information
割引 *uchi waribiki* bank discount
惑星 *naiwakusei* inner planet
証 *naishō* secret, privacy; internal evidence; one's circumstances
証事 *naishōgoto* a secret
証話 *naishōbanashi* confidential talk, whispering
13 殿 *naiden* inner shrine
債 *naisai* domestic loan
福 *naifuku* richer than it appears
隠 *uchikaku(shi)* inside pocket
戦 *naisen* civil war
意 *nai-i* intention, personal opinion

1 一 4〔丨〕丶丿乙亅

裏 *dairi* imperial palace
裏雛 *dairibina* festival dolls representing the emperor and empress
蒙 *Naimō* Inner Mongolia
蒙古 *Uchi Mōko* Inner Mongolia
幕 *uchimaku* inside curtain; inside information. *uchimaku*, *naimaku* the inside; hidden circumstances
幕話 *uchimakubanashi* inside information
14 層 *naisō* inner layers
聞 *naibun no* secret, private (information)
膜 *naimaku* lining membrane
需 *naiju* domestic demand
閣 *naikaku* cabinet, ministry
閣総理大臣 *Naikaku Sōri Daijin* Premier
緒 *naisho ni* secretly
緒話 *naishobanashi* secret talk
15 閲 *naietsu* private perusal
儀 *naigi* one's wife; landlady; something secret or confidential
線 *naisen* indoor wiring; inner line
縁 *naien* common-law marriage
談 *naidan* private conversation
諾 *naidaku* informal consent
謁 *naietsu* private audience
踝 *uchi kurubushi* inner side of the ankle
憂 *naiyū* internal or domestic troubles
輪 *uchiwa* family circle, the inside. *uchiwa no* moderate, conservative; pigeon-toed
輪同志 *uchiwa dōshi* members of the family; insiders
輪揉 *uchiwamome* internal dissention, family trouble
輪喧嘩 *uchiwagenka* family quarrel; quarreling among themselves
16 懐 *uchibutokoro* inside pocket; one's heart, bosom
壁 *naiheki* inner wall
覧 *nairan* private audience
親王 *naishinnō* imperial or royal princess
燃機関 *nainen kikan* internal-combustion engine
17 濠 *uchibori* inner moat
鮮人 *Naisenjin* Japanese and Koreans
18 職 *naishoku* home industry; side line
臓 *naizō* internal organs, intestines, viscera
観 *naikan* introspection
20 議 *naigi*=*mitsugi* 密議 1316.20
鰐 *uchiwani* knock-kneed, pigeon-toed

4

以 See 348. [人]

凹 See 664. [凵]

丗 83/F42 See **世** 95 and **卅** 78. [一]

丗 84/F288/F40 **卋** **世** See 95. [十]

卉 85/F288 **卉** Ki grass. [十]

A **央** 86/F474 Ō middle. [大]

丗 87/F288 **卌** Shū. *shijū* 40. [十]

B **冊** 88/F211 **冊** **冊** **册** Saku. Satsu book counter; volume, book, letter. [冂]

3 子 *sasshi* book, booklet, pamphlet; notebook. *sōshi* copy-book; storybook
5 立 *sakuritsu* imperial investiture
13 数 *sassū* number of books

A **由** 89/F1269 Yū, Yu. *yo(ru)* (see under 依 426.0). *yoshi* reason, cause, significance; means, way; effect; point; intent. *yo(tte)* therefore, consequently. [田]

5 由 *yuyu(shii)* grave, serious, alarming
6 有 *yoshia(ru)* of rank, of noble birth
7 来 *yurai suru* derive from, originate in. *yurai* reason; origin, destiny; history; derivation, source; originally, naturally
来書 *yuraisho* history, memoirs
12 無事 *yoshina(shi)goto* trivial thing, nonsense
14 緒 *yuisho* history, lineage
15 縁 *yuen* acquaintance; relation; affinity; reason

凸 90/F226 Totsu *deko* beetle brow. [凵]

4 円 *totsuen* convexity
円形 *totsuenkei* convexity
5 凹 *dekoboko*, *totsuō* unevenness, ruggedness, roughness
7 角 *tokkaku* convex angle
坊 *dekobō* beetle-browed boy; a mischief
状 *totsujō* protrusion
8 版 *toppan* relief printing
9 面 *totsumen* convex surface
面鏡 *totsumenkyō* convex lens
19 鏡 *tokkyō* convex lens

A **史** 91/F325 **史** Shi history, chronicles; historian; book. [口]

3 上 *shijō no* historical. *shijō ni* in history
6 伝 *shiden* history and biography; historical materials
8 官 *shikan* chronicler
実 *shijitsu* historical fact
的 *shiteki* historic, historical
的現在 *shiteki genzai* historical present
学 *shigaku* (study of) history
学者 *shigakusha* historian

学家 *shigakka* historian
9乗 *shijō* history, annals
10料 *shiryō* historical records
家 *shika* historian
書 *shisho* history book
11略 *shiryaku* outline history
眼 *shigan* historical view; historical insight
12筆 *shihitsu* historical writing
13詩 *shishi* historical poem
跡 *shiseki* historical landmark
15劇 *shigeki* historical drama
談 *shidan* historical story ⌈cussion
論 *shiron* historical treatise, historical dis-
18蹟 *shiseki* historical landmark
観 *shikan* historical view
20籍 *shiseki* historical works, annals

B **甲** 92/F1270 KAN high (voice). KŌ A, 1st class; former; back (of the hand); instep; armor; shell, tortoise shell, carapace. *kōra* shell (of turtle or crab). *yoroi* suit of armor. *kinoe* 1st calendar sign. [田]

1乙 *kō-otsu* A and B, excellent and good; ⌊discrimination
5巡 *kōjun* armored cruiser
6虫 ***kabuto mushi*** a beetle
7走 *kombashi(tta)* shrill, high-pitched
兵 *kōhei* arms; war; armed warrior
声 *kangoe* sharp high voice
状腺 *kōjōsen* thyroid gland
8所 *kandokoro* finger board (of a musical instrument); vital point
卒 *kōsotsu* armored warrior
夜 *kōya* 8 p.m.
板 *kampan, kōhan* deck
板渡 *kampanwata(shi)* free on board, F.O.B.
9冑 *katchū, kōchū* armor and helmet
冑師 *katchūshi* armorer
10高 *kōdaka na* high-backed; high in the instep. *kandaka(i)* shrill, high-pitched
11掛 *kōga(ke)* gauntlet; spats
12鈑 *kōhan* steel plates
殻 *kōkaku* carapace, shell, crust
斐 *kai* effect, result; use, avail, worth
斐甲斐 *kaigai(shii)* gallant, heroic, brave
斐性 *kaishō* resourcefulness, ability
斐無 *kaina(shi)* worthless, useless, hopeless
13鉄 *kōtetsu* armor plate
鉄板 *kōtetsuban* armor plate
鉄艦 *kōtetsukan* armored ship
14種 *kōshu* grade A, first grade
15論乙駁 *kōron-otsubaku* pros and cons
19羅 *kōra* shell, carapace

A **申** 93/F1271 SHIN. *mō(su)* have the honor to; =*iu* (see under 言 4309.0). *saru* 3-5p.m.; 9th zodiac sign; monkey. [田]

2入 *mō(shi)-i(reru)* propose, suggest. *mō(shi)-i(re)* proposal, offer; notice, report
3子 *mō(shi)go* a heaven-sent child (in answer to a Shinto or Buddhist prayer)
上 *mō(shi)-a(geru)* say, tell, state
4分 *mō(shi)bun* objection; shortcomings
込 *mō(shi)-ko(mu)* propose (marriage); offer (mediation); make an overture (of peace); challenge; lodge (objections); request (an interview); apply for (a job); subscribe for; book, reserve. *mōshiko(mi)* proposal, offer, overture; challenge
込書 *mōshikomisho* application blank; written application
込順 *mōshiko(mi)jun* order of applications
5立 *mō(shi)-ta(teru)* declare; plead
付 *mō(shi)-tsu(keru)* order, instruct
出 *mō(shi)-de(ru)* report to, tell; suggest, submit; request. *mō(shi)-i(de), mōshide* proposal; request, claim; report, notice
6合 *mō(shi)-a(waseru)* arrange; appoint; agree upon
7述 *mō(shi)-no(beru)* say, tell, state
告 *shinkoku* report, statement, notification; filing a return
告箱 *shinkokubako* suggestion box
8送 *mō(shi)-oku(ru)* write to; send word to; hand over (official business) ⌈(a price)
受 *mō(shi)-u(keru)* accept; ask for; charge
命記 *Shimmeiki* Deuteronomy ⌈you.
10兼 *mō(shi)-ka(neru)* I'm sorry to trouble
11遅 *mō(shi)-oku(reru)* be slow in saying
添 *mō(shi)-so(eru)* add to what has been said
訳 *mō(shi)wake* excuse, apology
12越 *mō(shi)-ko(su)* send word to, write to
遣 *mō(shi)-tsuka(wasu)*=*mō(shi)-oku(ru)* 申
送 (see above-8)
開 *mō(shi)-hira(ku)* explain, justify ⌈order
渡 *mō(shi)-wata(su)* tell, announce, declare,
14聞 *mō(shi)-ki(kaseru)* tell, talk to
様 *mō(shi)yō* words, expression
15請 *shinsei* application, petition
請書 *shinseisho* written application
18難 *mō(shi)-niku(i)* I'm sorry to trouble you.

A **旧** 94/F1569 **舊** KYŪ old things; old times; old friend; old calendar; former, ex-. *furu-* used article, secondhand. *furu(i)* (see under 古 770.0). [臼]

2人 *furubito*=故人 *kojin* 2044.2
3土 *kyūdo*=*kyūchi* 旧地 (see below-6)
大陸 *Kyūtairiku* the Old World
4友 *kyūyū* an old friend
夫 *kyūfu* former husband
5刊 *kyūkan* back number; old edition
冬 *kyūtō* former winters, the last winter

正月 *Kyūshōgatsu* New Year's Day in the lunar calendar
世界 *Kyūsekai* the Old World
市街 *kyūshigai* the old town
主 *kyūshu* a former lord
主人 *kyūshujin* a former lord
6臣 *kyūshin* an old retainer
衣 *kyūi* worn-out clothes
式 *kyūshiki* old type, old style
地 *kyūchi* former property, former territory
好 *kyūkō* an old friendship
邦 *kyūhō* an old country
交 *kyūkō* an old friendship
号 *kyūgō* old name; back number
宅 *kyūtaku* former residence
名 *kyūmei* old name, maiden name
年 *kyūnen* the old year, last year
年末 *kyūnemmatsu* end of last year
7里 *kyūri, furusato* one's old home
作 *kyūsaku* one's old publication, art work, ⌊etc.
址 *kyūshi* historic ruins
村 *kyūson* an old village
来 *kyūrai* from ancient times, formerly. *kyūrai no* traditional
体制 *kyūtaisei* old regime
8国 *kyūkoku* ancient nation
居 *kyūkyo* former residence
例 *kyūrei* old custom, tradition
姓 *kyūsei* former name, maiden name
法 *kyūhō* an old law; an old method
版 *kyūhan* old edition
物 *kyūbutsu* old things, ancient things
知 *kyūchi* an old friend; an old friendship
官 *kyūkan* former government official
典 *kyūten* tradition; a classic
妻 *kyūsai* a former wife
事 *kyūji, kuji* past events, bygones
制 *kyūsei* old system, old order
制度 *kyūseido* old system, old order
9風 *kyūfū* old customs
俗 *kyūzoku* old customs
恨 *kyūkon* an old grudge ⌈people
派 *kyūha* old school; old style; conservative
封 *kyūhō* a former fief
故 *kyūko* antiquity; an old acquaintance
型 *kyūgata, kyūkei* old style, old type
怨 *kyūen* old grudge
思想 *kyūshisō* old-fashioned idea
約 *kyūyaku* an old promise; the old covenant; the Old Testament
約全書 *Kyūyaku Zensho* Old Testament
約聖書 *Kyūyaku Seisho* Old Testament
10師 *kyūshi* one's old teacher; one's old ⌊master
時 *kyūji* ancient times
株 *kyūkabu* old stock (in a firm)
栖 *kyūsei* old home, former home, old nest
流 *kyūryū* old current; old style
称 *kyūshō* old name, former title
記 *kyūki* an old chronicle, an old record
都 *kyūto* the old capital
套 *kyūtō* conventionalism, old style
家 *kyūka* an old family
恩 *kyūon* old favors
11道 *kyūdō* an old road
婦 *kyūfu* former wife
訳 *kyūyaku* an old translation
趾 *kyūshi* ruins, historic site
規 *kyūki* old regulations
悪 *kyūaku* old crimes, past misdeeds
習 *kyūshū* old customs
章 *kyūshō* ancient laws
遊地 *kyūyū (no) chi* familiar haunts
勘定 *kyūkanjō* old account
教 *Kyūkyō* Roman Catholicism
教徒 *Kyūkyōto* a Roman Catholic
12痾 *kyūa* persistent disease
棲 *kyūsei* old home, former home, old nest
詠 *kyūei* ancient poems; ancient songs
13債 *kyūsai* old debt
跡 *kyūseki* historic ruins ⌈thing
夢 *kyūmu* an ancient dream; a fleeting
幕 *kyūbaku* the old feudal government, shogunate ⌈New Testaments
新約全書 *Kyūshin-yaku Zensho* Old and
新約聖書 *Kyūshin-yaku Seisho* Old and New Testaments
14暦 *kyūreki* the old lunar calendar
聞 *kyūbun* old news
慣 *kyūkan* old customs
説 *kyūsetsu* an old theory; ancient ideas
領 *kyūryō* an old fief
蔵 *kyūzō* one's old possessions
態 *kyūtai* old state of affairs
製 *kyūsei* former manufacture; former make
15劇 *kyūgeki* classical drama
儀 *kyūgi* traditional ceremony
墟 *kyūkyo* ruins, remains
稿 *kyūkō* old manuscript
縁 *kyūen* old relationship; old acquaintance
誼 *kyūgi* old friendship
敵 *kyūteki* old enemy
歓 *kyūkan* an old joy
弊 *kyūhei* standing evil; conservatism; the old school. *kyūhei na* old-fashioned, antiquated, conservative
16懐 *kyūkai* love of antiquity
18蹟 *kyūseki* historic ruins
観 *kyūkan* former state, former appearance
藩 *kyūhan* former clan
藩主 *kyūhanshu* former feudal lord
19臘 *kyūrō* last December, end of last year
識 *kyūshiki* an old friend

A 世 95/F40 丗 卋 廿 SE generation; world.

SEI generation; age, world, counter for kings of the same name. *yo* world, society, public; life, existence, career, lifetime; age, era, generation, times; reign. [一]

2 人 *sejin* people, the public, the world
3 子 *seishi* heir, successor
上 *sejō* the world
才 *sesai* worldly wisdom, practical wisdom, prudence, shrewdness
4 中 *yo* (*no*) *naka* society, the world, the times
5 立 *yo* (*ni*) *ta*(*tsu*) become famous
代 *sedai, seidai* generation; the world; the age
出 *yo* (*ni*) *de*(*ru*) become famous
世 *yoyo* for generations
世限無 *yoyokagi*(*ri*)*na*(*ku*) forever and ever
6 伝 *seiden no* hereditary (estates)
7 局 *seikyoku* world developments
8 的 *yoteki* worldly
直 *yonao*(*shi*) world reformation
事 *seji* worldly affairs
迷言 *yomaigoto* grumbling, muttering, nonsense
知 *sechi* worldly wisdom; stingy person
知辛 *sechigara*(*i*) a hard (life); a tough (world)
9 途 *seito* the world; the path of life
相 *sesō* phase of life; sign of the times; world conditions
柄 *yogara* world conditions, the times
故 *seko, seiko* worldly affairs
変 *seihen* change of times
紀 *seiki* century; era
紀末 *seikimatsu* end of a century
俗 *sezoku* common customs; worldliness; the world, the common people. *sezoku no* common, worldly, vulgar, popular
俗心 *sezokushin* worldliness
俗化 *sezokuka* secularization
俗主義 *sezoku shugi* secularism
俗的 *sezokuteki* wordly
界 *sekai* the world; society; the universe
界一 *sekai ichi* best in the world
界一周 *sekai isshū* round-the-world trip, circumnavigation, globe-trotting
界人 *sekaijin* a cosmopolitan, a world citizen
界大戦 *Sekai Taisen* the World War
界中 *sekaijū* all over the world
界史 *sekaishi* world history
界市民 *sekai shimin* world citizen
界平和 *sekai heiwa* world peace
界主義 *sekai shugi* internationalism, cosmopolitanism
界的 *sekaiteki* world, world-wide, international, universal
界周航 *sekai shūkō* circumnavigation of the earth
界国家 *sekai kokka* world state
界連邦 *sekai rempō* world federation
界政策 *sekai seisaku* global policy
界記録 *sekai kiroku* world record
界経済 *sekai keizai* international economy
界遊歴 *sekai yūreki* globe-trotting, round-the-world tour
界遊歴者 *sekai yūrekisha* globe-trotter
界新記録 *sekai shinkiroku* new world record
界語 *sekaigo* international language, Esperanto
界暦 *sekaireki* world calendar
界選手権 *sekai senshuken* world championship
界銀行 *Sekai Ginkō* the World Bank
界観 *sekaikan* world view
10 帯 *setai, shotai* household, home
帯主 *setainushi* householder
11 過 *yosu*(*gi*) living, livelihood
運 *seiun* course of events
情 *sejō* world conditions; worldly affairs; human nature
務 *seimu* public affairs, worldly affairs
常 *yo* (*no*) *tsune* common occurrence; custom
習 *yonarai* customs of the world
患 *seikan* troubles of this world
道 *sedō* morality
道人心 *sedō jinshin* public morals
捨 *yo* (*o*) *su*(*teru*) depart for a hermit's life
捨人 *yosu*(*te*)*bito* hermit, recluse; monk
12 渡 *yowata*(*ri*) living, subsistency, getting along in the world
統 *seitō* a long family line
評 *sehyō* popular opinion; popularity; rumor
覚 *yo* (*no*) *obo*(*e*) reputation, public esteem
智辛 *sechigara*(*i*) hard (life), tough (world)
間 *seken* world, society, life, people, society, the public; rumor, gossip
間口 *sekenguchi* reputation
間見 *sekemmi*(*zu*)＝*sekenshi*(*razu*) 世間知 (see below–12)
間体 *sekentei* decency, reputation, appearance
間的 *sekenteki* worldly, earthly
間知 *sekenshi*(*razu*) ignorance of the world; a person ignorant of the world
間並 *sekenna*(*mi*) average, ordinary, common. *sekenna*(*mi*) *ni* according to custom
間通 *sekentsū* man of the world
間不見 *sekemmi*(*zu*)＝*sekenshi*(*razu*) 世間知 (see above–12)
間話 *sekembanashi* gossip, chitchat
間擦 *sekenzure no* sophisticated
間離 *sekembana*(*re*) *shita* queer; uncommon; unworldly
13 嗣 *yotsugi, seishi* heir, successor
継 *yotsu*(*gi*) heir, successor
辞 *seji* flattery, compliment
路 *sero, seiro* the path of life
馴 *yona*(*reru*) get used to the world; grow worldly
業 *seigyō* hereditary occupation
話 *sewa* help, aid; good offices, service, recommendation; care, trouble; everyday life

話人 *sewanin* go-between, intermediary; sponsor; caretaker; manager
話女房 *sewa nyōbō* good housekeeper
話好 *sewazu(ki)* obliging person; officious person
話役 *sewayaku*=*sewanin* 世話人 (see above–13)
話掛 *sewa (o) ka(keru)* bother someone about something
話場 *sewaba* low-life scene
話焼 *sewaya(ki)* busybody; arranger. *sewa (ga) ya(keru)* require a lot of care
14 塵 *sejin* the world, earthly affairs
嫡 *seiteki* heir
慣 *yona(reru)* get used to the world; grow worldly
説 *sesetsu* public opinion; popularity; rumor
態 *setai, seitai* social conditions, world conditions; life; the world
15 論 *seron, seiron, yoron* public opinion
論投票 *seron tōhyō* public-opinion poll
論調査 *seron chōsa* public-opinion research
16 諺 *seigen* proverb
18 職 *seishoku* hereditary occupation
22 襲 *seshū* heredity; heritage
襲的 *seshūteki* hereditary
襲権 *seshūken* hereditary right

A 本 $\frac{96}{F940}$ HON book; this, the same, the present, the current; main; true; real; regular, normal; counter for long things. *moto* (see under 元 275.0). [木]

2 人 *honnin* the person himself; the said person; the principal
人次第 *honnin shidai* It depends on him.
3 土 *hondo* mainland; Japan proper
山 *honzan* headquarters temple; this temple
丸 *hommaru* inner citadel
4 心 *honshin* one's right mind, real motive, true sentiment, real intention, conscience
手 *honte* regular way, trump card
日 *honjitsu* today
月 *hongetsu* this month
木 *motoki* original trunk of a tree
元 *hommoto* origin, source; original maker
分 *hombun* one's duty; original position
夫 *hompu* legal husband
文 *hombun, hommon* text (of a treaty); body (of a letter)
文批評 *hommon hihyō* textual criticism
5 田 *honden* old rice field
立 *hontate* bookrack, book ends
庁 *honchō* head government office
代 *hondai* money for books
令 *honrei* this law
本 *motomoto*=元元 275.4
末 *hommatsu* cause and effect; the means and the end; root and branch; substance and shadow; beginning and end
末転倒 *hommatsu-tentō* overturning plans
末顚倒 *hommatsu-tentō* overturning plans
6 色 *honshoku* one's real character; true quality
式 *honshiki* orthodox style. *honshiki no* formal, regular
件 *honken* this case
好 *honzu(ki)* a bookworm; fondness for books
州 *Honshū* Japan proper, Main Island
刑 *honkei* regular penalty
邦 *hompō* this country, our country
旨 *honshi* the main purpose; the true aim; the true reason
号 *hongō* current number
寺 *honji* head temple
宅 *hontaku* principal residence
字 *honji* Chinese characters
当 *hontō, hontō no* true, real, actual, proper, genuine; natural; veritable, substantial. *hontō ni* in earnest; very; really. *hontō(rashii)* probable, plausible, likely
名 *hommyō, hommei* real name
気 *honki* earnestness, seriousness, soberness
気違 *honkichiga(i)* bibliomania; bibliomaniac; raving, madness
会員 *honkai-in* regular member
会議 *honkaigi* plenary session, regular session
年 *honnen* this year
年度 *honnendo* the current year
有 *hon-yū* innate
有観念 *hon-yū kannen* innate idea
7 局 *honkyoku* main office; telephone central
決 *hongima(ri)* final decision
社 *honsha* main shrine; this shrine; main office; our firm
邸 *hontei* principal residence
条 *honjō* this article (of a document)
芸 *hongei* main forte
来 *honrai* originally, primarily, essentially, naturally; properly speaking; just, proper
攻撃 *honkōgeki* main attack
位 *hon-i* standard, basis, principle; system
位貨幣 *hon-i kahei* legal tender
体 *hontai* substance, entity, the thing itself; true form; antitype; object of worship; main part (of a book)
体論 *hontairon* ontology
初 *honsho* origin
初子午線 *honsho shigosen* Greenwich Meridian
8 店 *honten* head office; main store; this store
房 *hombō* main quarters of a temple
姓 *honsei* original surname
性 *honshō, honsei* original nature, real character, oneself
物 *hommono* real article, real thing; expert performance
命 *hommei* prospective winner, favorite in a contest
官 *honkan* former post; permanent appointment; principal assignment; permanent official; the present official; I

妻 *honsai* legal wife
金庫 *honkinko* main depository
国 *hongoku* one's own country
国人 *hongokujin* native, citizen
拠 *honkyo* stronghold, inner citadel; base, headquarters ⌈above)
拠地 *honkyochi*=*honkyo* 本拠 (the word
卦返 *honkegae(ri)* dotage, second childhood
卦帰 *honkegae(ri)* dotage, second childhood
卦還 *honkegae(ri)* dotage, second childhood
9 音 *honne* real intention, motive
屋 *hon-ya* bookstore; publisher; main building. *hon-oku* principal residence
通 *hondō(ri)* main street, boulevard
城 *honjō* this castle; inner citadel
科 *honka* regular course; this lesson
則 *honsoku* rules; original rules
降 *hombu(ri)* regular rainfall ⌈tion
院 *hon-in* this institution, the main institu-
陣 *honjin* troop headquarters; daimyo's inn; stronghold
省 *honshō* this ministry; the home office
食虫 *honku(i)-mushi* bookworm (literal and figurative)
契約 *honkeiyaku* formal contract
建築 *honkenchiku* permanent construction
草 *honzō* plants; medicinal herbs
草学 *honzōgaku* study of medicinal herbs
10 症 *honshō* this sickness
俸 *hompō* regular salary; basic salary; full
校 *honkō* main school; this school ⌊pay
流 *honryū* main current; main current (of
紙 *honshi* this newspaper ⌊thought)
部 *hombu* headquarters
島 *hontō* main island; this island
真 *homma*=*hontō* 本当 (see above–6)
員 *hon-in* this member (of an assembly), I
案 *hon-an* this plan
書 *honsho* the text, the script; this book
能 *honnō* instinct
家 *honke* main family; originator
家本元 *honke-hommoto* original home, birthplace; originator
格 *honkaku* propriety
格化 *honkakuka suru* regularize; get up speed, proceed at full tilt
格的 *honkakuteki* full-dress, regular; genuine, earnest; normal, typical; fundamental
11 道 *hondō* highway, main road; the right
務 *hommu* duty; regular business ⌊road
隊 *hontai* main body (of an army)
堂 *hondō* main temple building; nave
章 *honshō* this chapter ⌈faction
望 *hommō* long-cherished ambition; satis-
盗 *hontō* stealing home (in baseball)

船 *honsen* mother ship; this ship
船渡 *honsenwata(shi)* F.O.B., free on board
12 復 *hompuku* complete recovery
棚 *hondana* bookshelf
極 *hongima(ri)* final decision
給 *honkyū*=*hompō* 本俸 (see above–10)
統 *hontō* true; the main stream in a lineage
結 *hommusu(bi)* square knot
訴 *honso* original (legal) suit ⌈Court
朝 *honchō* this land; our country; Imperial
尊 *honzon* main image, the idol; the main image one worships; object of adoration; the man himself; the master of the house
筋 *honsuji* main thread (of a story)
葬 *honsō* formal funeral
番 *homban* the actual performance
営 *hon-ei* headquarters
然 *honnen* disposition, nature. *honzen no* natural, inborn, inherent
街道 *honkaidō* main road
塁 *honrui* base, stronghold, main fort; home
塁打 *honruida* home run ⌊plate
場 *homba* home, habitat, center
場所 *hombasho* Japanese wrestling pavilion
場物 *hombamono* genuine article
13 殿 *honden* main shrine; inner sanctuary
源 *hongen* origin, root, cause; principle
絹 *honken* pure silk
腹 *hombara, hompuku* legitimate (child)
腰 *hongoshi* earnestness, seriousness
節 *hombushi* top-quality dried bonito
署 *honsho* police headquarters; main office; this office
義 *hongi* true meaning, underlying principle
意 *hon-i* motive, will, real intention, hopes
業 *hongyō* principal occupation
試験 *honshiken* final examination
14 読 *hon-yo(mi)* good reader; scenario reading
誌 *honshi* this magazine
領 *honryō* characteristic; specialty; duty; proper function; original fief
管 *honkan* main pipe
舞台 *hombutai* main stage, public place
15 稿 *honkō* this manuscript
線 *honsen* main (railway) line
縫 *honnu(i)* final stitching
論 *honron* main discourse; this subject;
影 *hon-ei* umbra ⌊body (of a speech)
箱 *hombako* bookcase
舗 *hompo*=*honten* 本店 (see above–8)
調子 *honchōshi* proper key; keynote; normal condition
質 *honshitsu* essence, reality ⌈ally
質的 *honshitsuteki ni* essentially, substanti-
16 懐 *honkai*=*hommō* 本望 (see above–11)
膳 *honzen* regular dinner

館 *honkan* main building; this building
曇 *hongumo*(*ri*) low-cloud overcast
[18]職 *honshoku* principal occupation; an expert; I
題 *hondai* the main question
[19]願 *hongan* Amida Buddha's original vow; long-cherished desire
[20]籍 *honseki* permanent domicile
籍地 *honsekichi* permanent domicile
[23]籤 *honkuji* first prize in a private lottery

A 出 97/F226 SUI. SHUTSU born of; appearing from; going out; sending out. *da*(*su*), *ida*(*su*) put out, take out, pull out, stick out; draw (a gun); stretch out, extend; save (from a fire); expose, bare; exhibit; send, forward, post; publish; hoist (a flag); hang out; present, send in, tender, submit; serve; run (extra trains); produce; pay, contribute; invest, advance (money). *de*(*ru*) appear, come out, emerge; haunt, infest; be found, get back; be served (meals); lead to, enter; find (oneself) at; come out (as a result); leave, go out, get out; attend, appear; work (at); participate; launch (into); run (for an office); be published; sell; depart; graduate; break out, originate; be raised, be produced; issue from, be traced to, be derived from, stem from; protrude, stick out; exceed; interfere, intrude. *de* turnout, attendance, appearance, flow, outflow; pouring; outlay, expenditure, crop, yield, supply; sale, demand; start, outset, origin, birth, stock; one's turn; drawing (of tea). *de*(*shabaru*) intrude, butt in. (*o*)*i*(*de*) being; coming; going; come, come on. (*o*)*i*(*deninaru*) be; come; go. *da*(*shi*) broth, sauce, soup stock; pretext, excuse; cat's-paw, a dupe, a tool. -*da*(*su*) begin to. [凵]

[2]力 *shutsuryoku* output (of a dynamo)
入 *de-i*(*ru*) go in and out; quarrel; have the freedom of the home. *de*(*zu*)-*i*(*razu*) moderation; neither gain nor loss. *da*(*shi*)-*i*(*re*) taking in and out, depositing and withdrawing, receipts and expenditures. *shutsunyū* going in and out; entrance and exit; receipts and payments. *de-ir*(*i*), *dehai*(*ri*) free association, going in and out, entrance and exit; receipts and payments, surplus and deficit; indentation (of a coast)
入口 *de-iriguchi* entrance
入国 *shutsunyūkoku* emigration and immigration
[3]口 *deguchi* exit, gateway, way out; outlet, leak, vent
土 *shutsudo* appearance of an archeological find
土品 *shutsudohin* artifacts
刃 *deba* knife, pointed carver
刃庖丁 *debabōchō* knife, pointed carver
[4]手 *da*(*shi*)*te* one who furnishes the money
方 *dekata* attitude; a move; theater usher
欠 *shukketsu* presence or absence
水 *shussui*, *demizu* flood, freshet, inundation
火 *shukka* fire, outbreak of fire
切 *de-ki*(*ru*) be out of, have no more on hand
分 *da*(*shi*)*bun* one's share (in the expenses)
不精 *debushō* a stay-at-home; homekeeping
[5]立 *i*(*de*)-*ta*(*tsu*) start, leave. *shuttatsu* departure
払 *de-hara*(*i*) be out of
外 *dehazu*(*re*) end, extremity (of a village)
汁 *da*(*shi*)*jiru* broth, stock, sauce
目 *deme* protruding eyes
目金 *demekin* pop-eyed goldfish
処 *shussho*, *dedokoro* birthplace; origin; source, authority; exit
処進退 *shussho-shintai* advancing and retreating; appearance and disappearance; one's daily activities; one's course of action; one's attitude
仕 *shusshi* attendance, serving
仕事 *deshigoto* outside work
札 *shussatsu* issuing tickets
札口 *shussatsuguchi* ticket window
札所 *shussatsujo* ticket office
札係 *shussatsugakari* ticket agent
生 *shusshō* birth
生地 *shusshōchi* birthplace
生年月日 *shusshō nengappi* date of birth
生率 *shusshōritsu* birth rate
生証明書 *shusshō shōmeisho* birth certificate
生数 *shusseisū* number of live births
世 *shusse* successful career, eminence
世作 *shussesaku* a work of art or literature that brings fame
世間 *shusseken* monastic life
世間的 *shussekenteki* unworldly, religious
世頭 *shussegashira* most successful man
[6]色 *shusshoku* prominence; excellence
回 *de-mawa*(*ru*) arrive on the market, be moving
迎 *de-muka*(*eru*) (go to) meet, (come to) meet, greet, receive. *demuka*(*e*) meeting, reception
向 *de-mu*(*ku*), *shukkō suru* go to, proceed to, leave for
任 *demaka*(*se*) random speech
帆 *shuppan* sailing, departure
会 *de-a*(*u*)＝出合 (next word). *shukkai* an encounter
合 *de-a*(*u*) meet, encounter, run across, hold a rendezvous, have a date. *da*(*shi*)-*a*(*u*) contribute jointly
合頭 *dea*(*i*)*gashira ni* as one passes, as one happens to meet

先 *desaki* destination
先機関 *desaki kikan* branch office
血 *shukketsu* hemorrhage, bleeding
血死 *shukketsushi* bleeding to death
血性人 *shukketsusei (no) hito* bleeder, hemophiliac
血症 *shukketsushō* bleeders' affliction
血過多 *shukketsu kata* excessive bleeding
血斑 *shukketsuhan* bloody spots
7 足 *deashi* start; turnout
戻 *de-modo(ri)* divorced woman
抜 *da(shi)-nu(ku)* forestall, anticipate, jump the gun on, outwit, circumvent, steal a march on. *da(shi)nu(ke) ni* suddenly, without notice, unexpectedly ⌈ance
没 *shutsubotsu* appearance and disappear-
社 *shussha* going to the office
兵 *shuppei* dispatch of troops; expedition
花 *debana* first brew of tea
廷 *shuttei* appearance in court
廷日 *shutteibi* court day
初 *dezome* first appearance, debut; firemen's New Year's demonstrations
初式 *dezome shiki* firemen's New Year's demonstrations
身 *shusshin* graduate from; hailing from
身地 *shusshinchi* birthplace, native place
身者 *shusshinsha* alumnus
身校 *shusshinkō* alma mater
来 *deki(ru)* can, be able to; be possible; be done, be finished, be ready; be made of; be established, be set up; be formed; come into being; grow, be produced; break out; be good at; be versed in; become intimate with. *deka(su)* complete, accomplish praiseworthily. *deka(shita)* well done, bravo. *deki(ta)* fully developed, mature, cultured, well-balanced. *deki* make, workmanship; result; crop, harvest. *shuttai, shutsurai* occurrence; completion; fulfillment
来上 *dekia(garu)* be finished, be ready, be made for, be cut out
来丈 *deki(ru)dake* as . . . as possible
来心 *dekigokoro* sudden impulse, passing fancy ⌈brand-new
来立 *dekita(te)* new, newly made, fresh,
来合 *deki-a(u)* be readymade; become intimate with. *dekia(i)* ready-made; com-
来年 *dekidoshi* fruitful year ⌊mon-law (wife)
来次第 *dekishidai* as soon as completed
来物 *dekimono, dekibutsu* able man. *dekimono* tumor, growth, boil, ulcer, abcess,
来事 *dekigoto* incident, affair ⌊rash, pimple
来具合 *dekiguai* result, effect, performance, success

来映 *dekibae* result, effect, performance, success; excellently made; shape and quality of (of an article)
来秋 *dekiaki* autumn at harvest time
来星 *dekiboshi* upstart, mushroom mil-
来値 *dekine* selling price ⌊lionaire
来高 *dekidaka* yield, crop, production
来高払 *dekidakabara(i)* piecework payment
来高仕事 *dekidaka shigoto* piecework
来得限 *de(ki)-u(ru) kagi(ri)* as (much) as possible, as (far) as possible
来損 *deki-sokona(u)* be badly made; fail
8 門 *shutsumon* going out
国 *shukkoku* departure from a country
店 *demise* branch store
府 *shuppu* going to the capital; working in a government office ⌈come in
始 *de-haji(meru)* begin to appear, begin to
物 *demono* rash, boil; secondhand article. *da(shi)mono* performance, program
京 *shukkyō* proceeding to the capital
直 *de-nao(ru)* setting out again. *de-nao(su)* come again, call again, make a fresh start
歩 *de-aru(ku)* go out, take a stroll, go about
芽 *shutsuga* germination, sprouting
典 *shutten* source, authority
放 *da(ship)pana(su), da(shi)-hana(su)* leave on, leave running, leave lying around, leave (a faucet) open
放題 *dehōdai* free flow (of water); random talk, nonsense. *da(shi)hōdai* free flow
奔 *shuppon* abscondence; flight ⌊of water
奔者 *shupponsha* absconder
金 *shukkin* payment, contribution, investment, financing
金者 *shukkinsha* contributor, investor, financier ⌈tributed
金額 *shukkingaku* amount invested or con-
所 *shussho, dedoko, dedokoro* origin, source; authority; exit; point of departure; release from prison
所進退 *shussho shintai* one's daily activities
所勝負 *de(ta)tokoshōbu* leaving a matter to
征 *shussei* departure for the front ⌊chance
征軍 *shusseigun* army in the field
征軍人 *shussei gunjin* soldier at the front
征家族 *shussei kazoku* family of a soldier
版 *shuppan* publication ⌊at the front
版元 *shuppammoto* publisher
版目録 *shuppam-mokuroku* catalog of publications ⌈press
版自由 *shuppan (no) jiyū* freedom of the
版社 *shuppansha* publishing house
版法 *shuppanhō* press law, publication law
版物 *shuppambutsu* publications
版者 *shuppansha* publisher

版屋 *shuppan-ya* publishing house
版界 *shuppankai* the publishing world
版部 *shuppambu* publishing department
版部数 *shuppambusū* circulation, number printed
版許可 *shuppan kyoka* permission to publish
版費 *shuppanhi* publishing costs
版業 *shuppangyō* publishing business
版業者 *shuppan gyōsha* publisher
9 城 *dejiro* branch castle
陣 *shutsujin* departure for the front
軍 *shutsugun* expedition
炭 *shuttan* coal production
度 *shutsudo* frequency
度数 *shutsudosū* frequency
前 *demae* cooked-food delivery. *da(shi)mae* one's share (in the expenses)
前持 *demaemo(chi)* boy who delivers cooked food
発 *shuppatsu* departure
発点 *shuppatsuten* starting point; point of departure
品 *shuppin* exhibit, display
品人 *shuppinnin* exhibitor
品国 *shuppinkoku* exhibiting country
品物 *shuppimbutsu* exhibit
品者 *shuppinsha* exhibitor
10 馬 *shutsuba suru* go on horseback; go in person; run for election
庫 *shukko* delivery from a storehouse; leaving the car barn
師 *suishi* dispatch of troops, expedition
捐 *shutsuen* contribution, subscription
時 *dedoki* time of departure
梅 *tsuyuake* end of the rainy season
航 *shukkō* departure, sailing
郷 *shukkyō* leaving one's home town; a priest going out to teach
荷 *shukka* forwarding, shipping; outgoing freight
這入 *dehai(ri)* going in and out
格子 *degōshi* projecting lattice; latticed bay window
家 *shukke* entering the priesthood; priest, monk
家遁世 *shukke tonsei* monastic seclusion
納 *suitō* receipts and disbursements
納係 *suitōgakari* cashier, treasurer; teller
納簿 *suitōbo* cashbook
席 *shusseki* attendance
席者 *shussekisha* those present, attendance
席率 *shussekiritsu* percent of attendance
席簿 *shussekibo* attendance record
11 違 *de-chiga(u)* miss a visitor. *da(shi)-chiga(u)* miss sending, miss delivering
遅 *da(shi)oku(re)* belated
過 *de-su(giru)* project or protrude too much; be too forward, obtrude
惜 *da(shi)-oshi(mu)* grudge, be stingy, be unwilling to pay

掛 *de-ka(keru)* depart, go out, set out, start, be going out. *degake* about to start out
涸 *degarashi* washed out, insipid
渋 *da(shi)-shibu(ru)* grudge, be stingy, be unwilling to pay. *de-shibu(ru)* be unwilling to go out
猟 *shutsuryō* going hunting
現 *shutsugen* appearance, arrival
船 *debune, defune, idebune* weighing anchor, setting sail; outgoing ship
殼 *da(shi)gara, degara* grounds (of tea and coffee)
商 *deakina(i)* peddling
窓 *demado* bay window
渠 *shukkyo* leaving the (repair) dock
盛 *de-saka(ru)* appear in profusion. *desaka(ri), dezaka(ri)* best time for (corn, etc.), season for
動 *shutsudō* sailing, marching, going out
動命令 *shutsudō meirei* marching orders, sailing orders
産 *shussan* childbirth; production (of goods)
産数 *shussansū* number of births (including stillbirths)
張 *de-ba(ru), de(p)pa(ru)* project, stand out, jut out, set out for. *deba(ri)* projection, ledge. *shutchō* business trip, official trip
張店 *shutchōten* branch store
張所 *shutchōjo* branch office
張員 *shutchōin* agent, representative, dispatched official
12 歯 *deba, de(p)pa* protruding tooth, overbite
超 *shutchō* excess of exports, favorable balance of trade
御 *shutsugyo* emperor's arrival (at his office, etc.)
揃 *de-soro(u)* appear all together, be all present
棺 *shukkan* carrying out a coffin
湯 *ideyu* hot springs
塁 *shutsurui* on base (in baseball)
番 *deban* one's turn
替 *de-kawa(ru) vi* take someone's place. *degawa(ri), dekawa(ri)* periodical relief or replacement of workers
費 *shuppi* expenses, disbursements
場 *shutsujō* stage appearance, performance; participation. *deba* one's turn; place of projection; production center
場者 *shutsujōsha* participants, participating athletes
訴 *shusso* access to courts, bringing an action
訴期限法 *shusso kigenhō* statute of limitations
港 *shukkō* departure; clearance (of a ship)
港船 *shukkōsen* outgoing vessel
港停止 *shukkō teishi* embargo
勤 *shukkin* at work; going to work
勤日 *shukkimbi* employee's work day
勤者 *shukkinsha* workers on the job

勤時間 *shukkin jikan* hour for reporting to work 「cord
勤簿 *shukkimbo* employees' attendance re-
13 嫌 *degira(i)* a stay-at-home
損 *de-sokona(u)* fail to go; fail to come
際 *degiwa* the time of setting out
群 *shutsugun* excellence, pre-eminence
資 *shusshi* investment, financing, contribu-
資金 *shusshikin* capital 「tion
資者 *shusshisha* investor, financier
資額 *shusshigaku* amount invested
14 鼻 *debana, dehana* projecting part (of a headland, etc.); outset, starting out
様 *deyō* attitude; a move, measures (to take)
獄 *shutsugoku* release from prison
端 *deha* chance of going out, opportunity (to succeed). *debana* moment of departure, beginning of work
精 *shussei* diligence, industry
監 *shukkan* leaving prison
演 *shutsuen* stage appearance, performance
演者 *shutsuensha* performer, entertainer,
漁 *shutsugyo, shutsuryō* going fishing 「actor
漁区域 *shutsugyo kuiki* fishing area
漁期 *shutsugyoki* fishing season
漁権 *shutsugyoken* fishing rights
15 潮 *deshio* high tide
稼 *dekasegi* working away from home
撃 *shutsugeki* sortie, sally
駕 *shutsuga* departure (of a noble)
16 廬 *shutsuro suru* come out of retirement
頭 *shuttō* appearance, presence
稽古 *degeiko* giving lessons at pupils' homes
17 講 *shukkō suru* give lectures
藍 *shutsuran* a pupil excelling his master
18 臍 *debeso* protruding navel
額 *debitai* beetle brows, projecting forehead
題 *shutsudai* proposing a question
19 願 *shutsugan* application
願人 *shutsugannin* applicant 「sense
22 鱈目 *detarame* irresponsible utterance, non-

5

民 See 25. [氏]

臾 See **臾** 106. [臼]

卋 $\frac{98}{F288\ F40}$ See **世** 95. [十]

卉 See **卉** 85. [十]

师 Nonstandard for **師** 113.

A **州** $\frac{99}{F600}$ SHŪ province, state; continent. SU sand bar, shallows. [川]
6 州 *shūshū* every state, every province
9 俗 *shūzoku* local customs
11 崎 *susaki* sandspit 「boundary
14 境 *shūkyō* state boundary, provincial

曳 $\frac{100}{F922}$ EI. *hi(ku)* (see under 引 1562.0). [日]
3 子 *hikiko* jinricksha puller
4 火弾 *eikadan* tracer bullet
6 曳 *eiei* heaving, pulling 「bomb
光弾 *eikōdan* tracer bullet, star shell, flare
10 馬 *hikiuma* draft horse
11 船 *hikifune, hikibune, eisen* tugboat; towing
14 網 *hikiami* seine, dragnet

A **向** $\frac{101}{F337}$ KŌ. KYŌ. *mu(kau)* face, be opposite, meet, confront; oppose, defy; proceed to; get, tend toward; approach. *mu(keru)* turn, face; point (a gun); send (a messenger or letter). *mu(ku)* turn towards, (a needle) points to; lean towards; face, front on; suit. *mu(kai)* opposite. *mu(ke), mu(kete)* bound for. *mu(ki)* direction; exposure; aspect; suitability; position (on a proposition). *mu(kō)* the other side; opposite direction; the other party; destination; the next (few years); opposition to. [口]
3 三軒 *mukō sangen* one's next three neighbors 「ment, elevation, rise
上 *kōjō* advancement, progress, improve-
上心 *kōjōshin* ambition, aspiration
4 日性 *kōjitsusei, kōnichisei* disposition (in flowers) to turn toward the sun
日葵 *himawari* sunflower 「presence
5 付 *mu(ki)tsu(ke) ni* to one's face, in one's
6 米 *kō-Bei* pro-American
向 *mu(ki)mu(ki)* suitability
合 *mu(kai)-a(waseru), mu(ki)-a(u), mu(kai)-a(u)* face, confront; be opposite to
地性 *kōchisei* the nature of plants to grow down and root
7 見 *mu(kō)-mi(zu)* recklessness
8 波 *mu(kai)nami* head sea 「change direction
直 *mu(ke)-nao(ru) vi, mu(ke)-nao(su) vt*
岸 *mu(kō)gishi* the opposite bank
学心 *kōgakushin* love of learning
9 風 *mu(kai) kaze* head wind
後 *kōgo* hereafter
背 *kōhai* one's attitude; state of affairs
11 疵 *mu(kō) kizu* frontal wound 「party
側 *mu(kō)gawa* the opposite side; the other
脛 *mu(kō)zune* shin, front of lower leg
12 寒 *kōkan* facing the winter
暑 *kōsho* facing the heat

替 *mu(ke)-kae(ru)* change direction
13 腹 *mu(kap)para* anger, passion ⌈towel
鉢巻 *mu(kō) hachimaki* folded or rolled head

A **印** 102/F296 IN seal, stamp, mark. *in(suru)* print, imprint, impress. *shirushi* sign, mark; symbol, emblem; badge; evidence; souvenir; token; brand, trademark; signs, indications; omen; seal. *-In-* Indian. [冂]

2 刀 *intō* seal-engraving knife
5 本 *impon* printed book
半纏 *shirushibanten* livery coat
6 肉 *inniku* a seal stamp pad
行 *inkō suru* publish
池 *inchi* seal stamp pad
字 *inji* copying
字機 *injiki* typewriter; teletype
7 匣 *imbako* seal stamp box
材 *inzai* seal stock
形 *ingyō* seal, signet
判 *imban, impan* seal, stamp
判師 *imbanshi* seal engraver
8 刻 *inkoku* seal engraving
刻師 *inkokushi* seal engraver
画 *inga* (photographic) print
画紙 *ingashi* (photographic) printing paper
刷 *insatsu* printing
刷人 *insatsunin* printer
刷工 *insatsukō* pressman, printer
刷用 *insatsuyō* for printing
刷所 *insatsujo* press, print shop
刷物 *insatsubutsu* printed matter
刷者 *insatsusha* printer
刷紙 *insatsushi* printing paper
刷術 *insatsujutsu* printing art
刷業 *insatsugyō* printing business
刷機 *insatsuki* printing press
9 度 *Indo* India, Hindustan. *Indo no* Indian,
度人 *Indojin* Indian, Hindu ⌊Hindu
度支那 *Indo-Shina* Indo-China
度洋 *Indoyō* Indian Ocean
度教 *Indokyō* Hinduism
10 紙 *inshi* stamp
書 *insho* typewriting
11 許 *shirushibaka(ri)* only a trifle
章 *inshō* seal, signet
12 棉 *Immen* Indian cotton
税 *inzei* royalty (on a book)
象 *inshō* impression
象付 *inshōzu(keru)* impress (someone)
象主義 *inshō shugi* impressionism
象的 *inshōteki* graphic, impressive
象派 *inshōha* impressionist school
14 綬 *inju* seal ribbon
緜 *Immen* Indian cotton

15 褥 *injoku* small thick desk pad
箱 *imbako* seal box
19 譜 *impu* book of seals
璽 *inji* imperial seal
22 鑑 *inkan* seal impression
籠 *inrō* seal case; pill box, medicine case

A **曲** 103/F921 KYOKU music, tune, melody, composition; interest; pleasure; injustice; fault. *ma(garu) vi* bend, curve, swerve; be crooked; turn; be awry; be perverse; lean; decline. *ma(geru) vt* bend, curve; lean, bow; distort; depart from (principles); pawn. *ma(gari-kuneru)* curve, meander, wind. *kuma* (see under 隈 5008.0). *ma(gatta)* leaning, bent, curved, crooked; winding, meandering, zigzag; perverse, wicked; distorted. *kune(ri)* bend, twist. *ma(garinari) ni* some way or other. [曰]

4 水 *kyokusui* meandering stream
尺 *kanejaku, kyokushaku, maga(ri)jaku, kanezashi* common Japanese foot; carpenter's square ⌈jewels
5 玉 *magatama* (ancient) comma-shaped
目 *maga(ri)me* turn, bend, curve. *kyokumoku* musical selection, program; tunes
6 曲 *kumaguma* nooks, corners
7 角 *maga(ri)kado* street corner, road turn
庇 *kyokuhi* harboring (a criminal)
技 *kyokugi* acrobatic feats
折 *kyokusetsu* winding, meandering; indentations; vicissitudes, complications
芸 *kyokugei* tricks, acrobatic stunts
芸師 *kyokugeishi* acrobat, tumbler
8 物 *ma(ge)mono* circular box ⌈wrong
直 *kyokuchoku* merits (of a case); right or
易 *ma(ge)yasu(i)* pliant, supple, flexible
突 *kudo* flue hole; cooking stove
者 *kusemono* ruffian, villain, knave; thief; suspicious fellow
事 *kyokuji* wickedness, injustice. *kusegoto* crookedness, something not right; something out of the ordinary; something unpleasant, something disgusting; unlawfulness; something unhappy, calam-
学 *kyokugaku* inferior scholarship ⌊ity
学阿世 *kyokugaku-asei* twisting the truth and catering to the public
9 飛 *kyokuto(bi)* fancy diving
度 *kyokudo* curvature
乗 *kyokuno(ri)* trick riding
独楽 *kyokugoma* top-spinning tricks
10 流 *kyokuryū* meandering stream
射 *kyokusha* high-angle fire
射砲 *kyokushahō* howitzer; high-angle gun
馬 *kyokuba* circus; equestrian feats

馬団 *kyokubadan* circus troupe
馬師 *kyokubashi* circus stunt rider
[11]道 *ma(gari)michi* roundabout road; curving road
球 *kyokkyū* curve ball
悪 *kyokuaku* wickedness
率 *kyokuritsu* curvature
[12]弾 *kyokubi(ki)* trick playing (on an instrument)
飲 *kyokuno(mi)* drinking while doing an acrobatic stunt
筆 *kyokuhitsu* misrepresentation, falsification
[13]路 *kyokuro* winding road. *ma(gari)michi* roundabout road; curving road
解 *kyokkai* misconstruction, distortion
節 *kyokusetsu* tune
[14]説 *kyokusetsu* false theory
舞 *kusemai* recitative dance
[15]調 *kyokuchō* melody, tune
論 *kyokuron* biased argument
線 *kyokusen* curve, curved line
線美 *kyokusembi* linear beauty
[19]譜 *kyokufu* musical composition; notes

6

串 104/F50 KAN. KEN. SEN. *kushi* spit, skewer.
[8]刺 *kushiza(shi)* skewering
[9]柿 *kushigaki* persimmons dried on skewers
[12]焼 *kushiya(ki)* broiled food on skewers

7

昌 See 2105. [日]

尚 尙 See 1361. [小]

卑 See 卑 221. [十]

來 See 来 202. [人]

函 105/F229 See 函 49. [凵]

臾 106/F1565 臾 YU, YO, YŌ, a little while; urging. [臼]

A 果 107/F958 KA fruit; reward. *ha(tasu)* carry out, achieve, complete; realize, perform, fufill. *ha(teru)* end, be finished, be exhausted; die, perish. *ōse(ru)* succeed in doing. *hatashite* as was expected; really. *ha(teshi)*, *ha(te)* end, limit, bounds, extremity, result; fate. *-ha(teru)* be tired out; be used up. [木]
[5]皮 *kahi* fruit peeling
汁 *kajū* fruit juice
[6]肉 *kaniku* the flesh of fruit
合 *ha(tashi)a(i)* duel
[7]状 *hata(shi)jō* (fighter's) letter of challenge
[8]取 *hakado(ru)* move right ahead (with the work)
果 *hakabaka(shii)*＝捗捗 1911.10
物 *kudamono* fruit
物屋 *kudamonoya* fruit store
実 *kajitsu* fruit; nut; berry
実店 *kajitsuten* fruit store
実酒 *kajitsushu* cider, wine, plum liquor
[9]食 *kashoku* living on fruit
[11]断 *kadan na* decisive, resolute, drastic
菜 *kasai* fruits and vegetables
[12]敢 *hakana(i)* fleeting, momentary, ephemeral; vain, empty, hopeless; fickle, inconstant, unstable; fragile, frail; pitiful, poor, sad, miserable. *kakan na* resolute, determined, bold
然 *kazen* as was expected
無 *hakana(i)* fleeting, transitory, ephemeral. *ha(teshi)na(ku)* eternally, interminably. *ha(teshi) (ga) na(i)* endless, boundless, fathomless, eternal
報 *kahō* good fortune, luck; happiness
報者 *kahōmono* lucky fellow
[16]糖 *katō* fruit sugar
樹 *kaju* fruit tree
樹園 *kajuen* orchard

A 表 108/F1690 HYŌ table, schedule, diagram, chart, list; memorial to the emperor. *ara(wasu)*, *hyō(suru)* express, show, manifest. *arawa(reru)* (see under 現 2943.0). *omote* surface, right side, face; exterior, outside; front; the street; mat covers; head (of a coin); first half (of an inning). [衣]
[2]二階 *omote nikai* 2nd floor front room
[3]口 *omoteguchi* front door
土 *hyōdo* top soil
[4]日本 *Omote Nihon* Pacific Seaboard of Japan
[5]白 *hyōhaku* expression, confession
皮 *hyōhi* epidermis; bark, rind, peel, husk
立 *omoteda(tsu)* become public, be known. *omoteda(tta)* public, open; formal, official. *omoteda(tte)* publicly, openly; ostensibly; formally
付 *omotetsu(ki)* frontage
札 *hyōsatsu* name plate, door plate
出 *hyōshutsu* expression, presentation
玄関 *omote genkan* front door, vestibule
示 *hyōji* indication, expression
示灯 *hyōjitō* signal light
示物 *hyōjibutsu* something indicative of
示書 *hyōjisho* a written statement
[6]衣 *uwagi* coat, tunic, jacket

向 *omotemu(ki)*=*omoda(tte)* 表立 (see above–5)
号 *hyōgō* symbol, emblem, sign
7芸 *omotegei* main accomplishments
沙汰 *omotezata* publicity, lawsuit
作 *omotesaku* first crop, important crop
決権 *hyōketsuken* voting rights
8門 *omotemon* front gate
明 *hyōmei* indication, manifestation, demonstration, expression, announcement
表紙 *omotebyōshi* front cover
忠塔 *hyōchūtō* war-memorial monument
忠碑 *hyōchūhi* war-memorial monument
具 *hyōgu* mounting (a picture)
具屋 *hyōguya* paperer, picture framer
具師 *hyōgushi* paperer; picture framer
9通 *omotedō(ri)* main street
看板 *omote kamban* sign out in front; a front (for someone)
音文字 *hyōon monji* phonetic symbol
音字母 *hyōon jibo* phonetic alphabet
面 *hyōmen* surface, face, outside; appearance
面上 *hyōmenjō* on the surface
面化 *hyōmenka suru* come to a head, become an issue, break
面的 *hyōmenteki ni* on the surface
面張力 *hyōmen chōryoku* surface tension
10紙 *hyōshi* cover, binding
記 *hyōki suru* publish (information); list (prices); declare (the value); write; address (a package)
座敷 *omote zashiki* front room, parlor, living room
11側 *omotegawa* the front
情 *hyōjō* facial expression
現 *hyōgen* expression, presentation
12着 *uwagi* coat, tunic, jacket
替 *omotega(e)* refacing (*tatami*) mats
装 *hyōsō* mounting
象 *hyōshō* symbol, emblem
13解 *hyōkai* illustration by tables
裏 *hyōri* inside and outside; two sides
意文字 *hyōi monji* hieroglyph, ideograph
14徴 *hyōchō* appearing on the surface; a sign
構 *omotegama(e)* façade, front elevation
彰 *hyōshō* commendation, awarding
15編 *omoteami* plain knitting
18題 *hyōdai* title (of a book or lecture); index

8

胄 See 3747. [肉]

氐 See 292. [氏]

卑 See 221. [十]

帥

109 F614 B Sochi, Sotsu, Shutsu, Sui leading (troops). *sotsu, sochi* (ancient) governor. [巾]
6先 *sossen* taking the initiative

衷

110 F1693 B 衷 Chū heart, mind; inside. *uchi* the inside.
4心 *chūshin* inmost feelings, true heart
11情 *chūjō* inmost feelings, true heart [衣]

甚

111 F1263 Jin exceedingly. *hanaha(da)* very, greatly, exceedingly. *hanaha(dashii)* extreme, excessive, intense, severe, serious, terrible, tremendous, heavy (damage). *ita(ku)* exceedingly. [甘]
3大 *jindai na* very great, enormous; serious
4以 *hanaha(da) mot(te)* exceedingly
六 *jinroku* dunce
5句 *jinku* lively song; lively dance

幽

112 F630 B Yū. *yū(suru)* confine to a room. *kasu(kana)* faint, dim, weak, indistinct, hazy; poor, wretched. [幺]
5玄 *yūgen* mystery, the occult
囚 *yūshū* imprisonment
7谷 *yūkoku* ravine, glen
8門 *yūmon* pyloris
居 *yūkyo* hermitage, retreat; retirement, seclusion
林 *yūrin* deep forest
明 *yūmei* the present and the other world; dark and light
明相隔 *yūmei-aiheda(teru)* die
9香 *yūkō* fragrance
室 *yūshitsu* darkened room; quiet room
客 *yūkaku* a quiet guest; an orchid
界 *yūkai* hades, realm of the dead
契 *yūkei* secret promise
幽 *yūyū(taru)* deep; dark; quiet
10冥 *yūmei* semidarkness; deep and strange; hades
冥界 *yūmeikai* hades, realm of the dead
11鳥 *yūchō* mountain bird
閉 *yūhei* house arrest, confinement, imprisonment; depressed feeling
窓 *yūsō* quiet window
寂 *yūjaku* quiet, sequestered
寂味 *yūjakumi* solitude, quiet
12閑 *yūkan na* quiet and secluded
絶 *yūzetsu* a quiet secluded place
勝 *yūshō* a beautiful and quiet scene
景 *yūkei* a quiet sequestered scene
然 *yūzen na* quiet and secluded
13微 *yūbi na* dim, indistinct
暗 *yūan na* dark and secluded
雅 *yūga* refinement
愁 *yūshū* deep contemplation
14境 *yūkyō* solitude; secluded place
魂 *yūkon* spirits of the dead

15趣 *yūshu* a quiet, natural setting
霊 *yūrei* ghost, apparition, spirit
霊人口 *yūrei jinkō* ghost population
霊会社 *yūreigaisha* bogus company
霊屋敷 *yūrei yashiki* haunted house
霊株 *yūrei kabu* watered stock, bogus shares
霊船 *yūreisen* phantom ship
霊話 *yūreibanashi* ghost story
17邃 *yūsui na* retired and quiet
邃境 *yūsuikyō* secluded place
26欝 *yūutsu* melancholy, dejection, gloom

9

衷 See 110. [衣]

畢 See 3005. [田]

A 師 113 / F615 SHI teacher, master; exemplary person; army; war. [巾]
4父 *shifu* fatherly master
友 *shiyū* master and friends
6匠 *shishō* master, teacher
伝 *shiden* instruction from a master
団 *shidan* army division
団長 *shidanchō* division commander
7走 *shiwasu, shihasu* 12th lunar month
弟 *shitei* teacher and student
承 *shishō* learning from a master
8長 *shichō* teachers, superiors, and men of prominence
門 *shimon* tutelage
事 *shiji suru* study under; look up to; apprentice oneself to teacher
表 *shihyō* model, pattern, paragon, leader, teacher
10訓 *shikun* the instruction of a teacher
家 *shika* the teacher's home
恩 *shion* the kindness of a teacher
11道 *shidō* duty of a teacher
13僧 *shisō* a priestly teacher
14説 *shisetsu* the teacher's theory
15範 *shihan* model; teacher; fencing teacher
範学校 *shihan gakkō* normal school
16儒 *shiju* teacher, scholar

B 剛 114 / F249 GŌ strength. [刂]
2力 *gōriki* herculean strength; mountain carrier-guide
4毛 *gōmō* bristle
6気 *gōki* bravery, stoutheartedness
7体 *gōtai* a rigid body
8性 *gōsei* hardness, rigidity
直 *gōchoku* integrity, moral courage
果 *gōka* valor and decisiveness
者 *gō(no)mono* very strong person, brave warrior, veteran
9胆 *gōtan* boldness, hardihood, courage
勇 *gōyū* bravery, prowess
11健 *gōken* vigor, virility, sturdiness, health
強 *gōkyō* strength, firmness
情 *gōjō* obstinacy, stubbornness
球 *gōkyū* fast ball
13腹 *gōfuku* obstinacy, stubbornness
15毅 *gōki* fortitude, firmness of character, hardihood, manliness
17臆 *gōoku* bravery and cowardice

10

畢 See 3005. [田]

噐 Nonstandard for 器 994. [口]

B 粛 115 / F1530 肅 SHUKU. *shuku toshite* quietly, softly, solemnly. [聿]
5白 *shukuhaku* Respectfully yours
正 *shukusei* regulation, enforcement
8学 *shukugaku* school purge
9軍 *shukugun* army purge
10殺 *shukusatsu suru* wither, blight
党 *shukutō suru* clean up the (political) party
11清 *shukusei* purge, cleanup, liquidation
粛 *shukushuku to* softly, quietly, solemnly
12然 *shukuzen to* softly, quietly, solemnly

11

棗 116 / F985 Sō. *natsume* jujube. [木]
12椰子 *natsume yashi* date (palm)

B 喪 117 / F373 Sō. *mo* mourning. [口]
4心 *sōshin* absent-mindedness; stupor, dejection
中 *mochū* mourning
5主 *moshu* chief mourner
失 *sōshitsu* loss, forfeit, forfeiture
8服 *mofuku* mourning dress
具 *sōgu* funeral accessories
9神 *sōshin*＝喪心 (see above–4)
10家 *sōka* homeless; family in mourning
11章 *moshō* sign of mourning
祭 *sōsai* funerals and festivals

12

嗇 See 67. [口]

肅 118 / F1530 See 粛 115. [聿]

嗣 See 969. [口]

1 一 13 [丨] 丶 ノ 乙 亅

13

暢 119/F914 Chō stretch. [日]
6 気 *nonki* optimistic; carefree; careless, reckless

夥 120/F456 Ka. *obitada(shii)* immense, tremendous. *obitada(shiku)* abundantly; innumerably. [夕]
6 多 *kata* many, plentiful

15

鴨 121/F2142 Ō. *kamo* wild duck; easy mark. [鳥]
5 打 *kamo-u(chi)* duck hunting
8 居 *kamoi* lintel
11 猟 *kamoryō* duck hunting

16

頤 See 5126. [頁]

擧 See 挙 1902.

嚢 122/F-X Nonstandard for 嚢 124.

17

歸 123/F1041 See 帰 1582. [止]

21

嚢 124/F391 Nō pouch, purse. *fukuro* bag, sack, pouch. [口]
4 日 *nōjitsu* some time ago, recently
中 *nōchū* pocket, purse. *nōchū ni* in the bag
7 状 *nōjō* sac shape
8 底 *nōtei* bottom of the bag
10 疱 *nōhō* cyst
剤 *nōzai* capsule
13 腫 *nōshu* cyst

RAD. 丶 3

Ten dot, point (the Japanese comma, like the grave accent). Nickname: Dot.

1

〻 125/F-X Character repetition.

〆 126/F-X 〆 (国字) *shime* adding up; bundle; ream; seal. *kan* 8⅓ pounds. *shime(te)* totaling. *shi(meru)* sum up. [ノ]
4 切 *shimeki(ri)* closing; closing up
10 高 *shimedaka* total
11 粕 *shimekasu* oil cake

2

丸 See 155.

3

丹 See 163.

以 See 348. [人]

才 127/F-X Nonstandard for 第 3385.

尤 128/F573 Yū superb, outstanding. *motto(morashii)* plausible. *yū(naru)* superb, outstanding. *motto(mo)* reasonable, right, just, natural; of course; altho. [尢]
8 物 *yūbutsu* something superior; beautiful woman

4

主 See 285.

丼 See 171.

必 129/F688 A Hitsu certainly. *kanara(zu)* certainly, positively, invariably. *kanara(zushimo)* (not) always, (not) necessarily, (not) all, (not) entirely. [心]
4 中 *hitchū* hitting the target
5 用 *hitsuyō* need, necessity
6 至 *hisshi no* inevitable, necessary
死 *hisshi* inevitable death; desperation. *hisshi no* frantic, desperate
8 定 *hitsujō* certainly, inevitably
治 *hitchi* certain cure
治薬 *hitchiyaku* a necessity guaranteed to cure
9 要 *hitsuyō* need, necessity
要応 *hitsuyō (ni) ō(jite)* as necessary
要条件 *hitsuyō jōken* necessary conditions, requirements
要物 *hitsuyōbutsu* necessities

要事 *hitsuyōji* necessities
要品 *hitsuyōhin* necessities
10 衰 *hissui* bound to decline, decay, or collapse
修 *hisshū* required (subject)
修科目 *hisshū kamoku* required subjects
12 勝 *hisshō* certain victory 「ry
須 *hissu* indispensable, necessary, mandato-
須科目 *hissu kamoku* required subjects
然 *hitsuzen* necessity
然性 *hitsuzensei* necessity, inevitability
然的 *hitsuzenteki ni* inevitably, necessarily
13 携 *hikkei* indispensability; manual, handbook 「to perish
滅 *hitsumetsu* annihilation; death; doomed
14 読 *hitsudoku* required reading
罰 *hitsubatsu* inevitablity of punishment
需 *hitsuju* necessary
需品 *hitsujuhin* necessities, essentials

A 永 130/F1069 EI. *naga*(*i*) long, lengthy. *towa* eternity. *naga*(*raku*) a long time. [水]

3 小作 *eikosaku* perpetual land lease
小作権 *eikosakuken* perpetual land lease
久 *eikyū, tokoshie* eternity, perpetuity, immortality. *eikyū ni, tokoshie ni* everlast-
久性 *eikyūsei* permanency ⌊ingly
久歯 *eikyūshi* permanent tooth
4 日 *eijitsu* a long spring day
5 生 *eisei* eternal life, immortality
永 *eiei* forever. *naganaga to*＝長長 4938.8
代 *eitai* permanence, eternity
代借地 *eitai shakuchi* perpetual lease
世 *eisei* eternity, perpetuity, immortality, permanence
世中立 *eisei chūritsu* permanent neutrality
世中立国 *eisei chūritsukoku* a permanent neutral 「petuity
6 存 *eizon, eison* durability, permanence, per-
年 *einen* many years, a long time
年間 *naganenkan* a long period of time
7 別 *eibetsu* last farewell
劫 *eigō* eternity, perpetuity
牢 *eirō* life imprisonment
寿 *eiju* long life
住 *eijū* permanent residence
住者 *eijūsha* permanent resident, denizen
住権 *eijūken* denizenship; permanent residence
10 眠 *eimin* eternal sleep, death
11 訣 *eiketsu* last farewell
12 遠 *eien* eternity, perpetuity, immortality, permanence
18 続 *eizoku, nagatsuzu*(*ki*) permanence, continuation
続性 *eizokusei* permanence

A 氷 131/F217 冰 HYŌ. *kō*(*ru*) freeze; be frozen over; congeal. *kōri* ice; shaved ice. *hi* ice; hail. [冫]

2 人 *hyōjin* a go-between (in marriage)
3 山 *hyōzan* iceberg
刃 *hyōjin* a sharp, glistening sword
4 水 *kōri mizu, kōrisui* shaved ice, ice water
5 田 *hyōden* a field of eternal snow
7 床 *hyōshō* ice sheet
豆腐 *kōridōfu* frozen tofu
8 枕 *kōri makura* ice pillow
河 *hyōga* glacier
河時代 *hyōga jidai* glacial period
河期 *hyōgaki* glacial period
9 面 *hyōmen* ice surface
屋 *kōriya* ice man, ice shop
柱 *hyōchū* ice pillar. *tsurara* icicle
海 *hyōkai* frozen sea; icy waters
室 *himuro, hyōshitsu, kōri muro* ice house, ice room, cold room
炭 *hyōtan* ice and charcoal; contradiction
砂糖 *kōrizatō* rock candy, sugar candy
削機 *hyōsakuki, hyōsakki* ice-shaving ma-
点 *hyōten* freezing point ⌊chine
点下 *hyōtenka* below zero
10 原 *hyōgen* ice field; ice floe; snow field
挾 *kōribasami* ice tongs 「doubts
11 釈 *hyōshaku* melting like ice; dispelling
雪 *hyōsetsu* ice and snow
袋 *kōribukuro* ice bag
菓 *hyōka* ices
菓子 *kōrigashi* a frozen sweet; sherbert
12 結 *hyōketsu* freezing
期 *hyōki* ice age
晶 *hyōshō* ice crystals
酢酸 *hyōsakusan* glacial acetic acid
13 塊 *hyōkai* lump of ice, block of ice; ice floe
滑 *kōrisube*(*ri*) ice skating
解 *hyōkai* melting, thawing
詰 *kōrizume* packing in ice
14 漬 *kōrizuke* putting down in ice
15 輪 *hyōrin* the moon
蝕 *hyōshoku* glacial scouring
震 *hyōshin* ice quake
醋酸 *hyōsakusan* glacial acetic acid
18 瀑 *hyōbaku* ice fall
19 霧 *hyōmu* ice fog
22 嚢 *hyōnō* ice bag, ice pack

A 半 132/F286 半 HAN half; odd number; semi-, hemi- demi-. *naka*(*ba*) half, semi-, middle, halfway; partly. [十]

2 人前 *hannimmae* half share; half a man
3 口 *hankuchi* half share
弓 *hankyū* small bow

ケ月 *hankagetsu* half a month
ケ年 *hankanen* half a year
4日 *hannichi, hanjitsu* a half day
天 *hanten* half the sky, mid-air
分 *hambun* half. *hampun* half minute
円 *han-en* semicircle
円形 *han-enkei* semicircle
切 *hansetsu* half size. *hanki(re)* half a piece
切符 *hankippu* half-price ticket
月 *hangetsu* half moon, semicircle. *hantsuki* half month
月刊 *hangekkan* a semimonthly
月形 *hangetsugata* semicircle, half-moon
5玉 *hangyoku* child geisha, apprentice entertainer
生 *hansei* half a lifetime. *hanshō* half death
田 *handa* solder; pewter
白 *hampaku* grayish color
句 *hanku* a brief word
半 *hanhan* half and half, fifty-fifty
母音 *hambo-in* semivowel
世紀 *hanseiki* a half century
永久的 *han-eikyūteki* semipermanent
加工品 *hankakōhin* semiprocessed goods
可 *hanka* insufficiency, half ripe
可通 *hankatsū* superficial knowledge; smatterer
6休 *hankyū* half holiday
死 *hanshi* half dead
死半生 *hanshi-hanshō* half dead
年 *hantoshi, hannen* a half year
年毎 *hannengoto ni* semiannually
7里 *hanri* half a *ri* (see Weights and Measures)
作 *hansaku* half crop
折 *hansetsu* half size, half a piece, half length
狂乱 *hankyōran* half-crazed
身 *hanshin* half the body, half length
身不随 *hanshin fuzui* paralyzed on one side
身浴 *hanshin-yoku* sitz bath
身像 *hanshinzō* half-length statue or portrait, bust
8金 *hankin* half the amount
周 *hanshū* semicircle
国 *hangoku* half a *kuni* (province)
価 *hanka* half price
径 *hankei* radius
夜 *han-ya* midnight
季 *hanki* half a quarter, a half period
股引 *hammomohiki* knee underwear
長 *hannaga* fairly high shoes
長靴 *hannagagutsu* fairly high shoes
盲 *hammō* half blind
盲症 *hammōshō* star blindness, half-blindness
官半民 *hankan-hammin* semigovernmental
官的 *hankanteki* semiofficial
官報 *hankampō* semiofficial paper
9音 *han-on* half tone (in music)
途 *hanto* halfway; unfinished
神 *hanshin* demigod
独立 *handokuritsu* semi-independent
透明 *hantōmei* semitransparency
洋袴 *hanzubon* knickerbockers
信半疑 *hanshin-hangi* dubious, incredulous
封建制 *hanhōkensei* semifeudalism
革装釘 *hankawa sōtei* half-leather binding
面 *hammen* half the face; one side, half; the other side, the reverse; the contrary
面識 *hammenshiki* slight acquaintance
10値 *hanne* half price
時 *hantoki* about an hour; a short time
紙 *hanshi* rice paper, thin Japanese writing paper
袖 *hansode* short sleeves
被 *happi* workman's livery coat
殺 *hangoro(shi)* half killed
島 *hantō* peninsula
宵 *hanshō* midnight
病人 *hambyōnin* semi-invalid
部族 *hambuzoku* half tribe
流動体 *hanryūdōtai* semiliquid
陰陽 *han-inyō* bisexualism
陰影 *han-in-ei* penumbra
夏 *hange*＝next word
夏生 *hangeshō* 11th day after the summer solstice, last seed-sowing day
11道 *hammichi* half a *ri* (see Weights and Measures); halfway
張 *hamba(ri)* half sole
球 *hankyū* hemisphere
眼 *hangan de* with a half-opened eye
乾 *hankawa(ki)* half dry
過去 *hankako* imperfect tense
過 *naka(ba)su(gi)* beyond the middle
舷砲 *hangenhō* broadside fire
12間 *hamma*＝*hampa* 半端 (*see below*–14)
焼 *han-ya(ke)* half-burnt; half-done; half-baked; rare
期 *hanki* half term, half year, half period
畳 *hanjō* half mat; hissing, heckling
煮 *hanni(e)* half-boiled, half-done
貴石 *hankiseki* semiprecious stones
開 *hankai* semicivilized. *hambira(ki)* partly open, in half bloom
開国 *hankaikoku* underdeveloped country, half-civilized country
減 *hangen* reduction by half
減期 *hangenki* half life (in physical chemistry)
13解 *hankai* only half understood
靴 *hangutsu, hanka* low shoes; shoes
数 *hansū* half the number
農 *hannō* part-time farming
搗米 *hantsukimai* half-polished rice
艇身 *hanteishin* half a boat length
裸体 *hanratai* seminude, half-naked
意識 *han-ishiki* subconsciousness

14 旗 *hanki* flag at half-mast
端 *hampa* fragment; incomplete set; fraction, odd sum; remnant; incompleteness
導体 *handōtai* semiconductor
製品 *hanseihin* semiprocessed goods
15 潰 *hantsubu(re)* half demolished
輪 *hanrin* semicircle; half-moon
影 *han-ei* penumbra
熟 *hanjuku* half boiled
熟練工 *hanjukurenkō* semiskilled worker
16 壊 *hankai* partial destruction
濁音 *handakuon* semivoiced sound, p-sound
諧音 *hankaion* assonance
18 襟 *han-eri* a quality collar for an under kimono
額 *hangaku* half price, half amount, half fare
20 鐘 *hanshō* fire alarm
鹹水 *hankansui* brackish water
21 纏 *hanten* short coat; workman's livery coat

5

兆 兆 See 637. [儿]

戋 133 / F-X Nonstandard for **銭** 4851.

6

良 134 / F-X See **良** 3885. [艮]

甫 135 / F1268 Ho. Fu. *haji(mete)* for the first time; not until. [用]

尨 136 / F573 Bō shaggy hair; shaggy dog. [尢]

3 大 *bōdai* bulky, enormous, extensive
4 毛 *mukuge* shaggy hair
犬 *mukuinu* shaggy dog

A **求** 137 / F1071 Kyū. Gu. *moto(meru)* want, wish for, request, demand; seek, search for; pursue (pleasure); hunt (a job); buy. [水]

2 人 *kyūjin* help wanted
人口 *kyūjinguchi* job vacancy
人広告 *kyūjin kōkoku* help-wanted ad
人者 *kyūjinsha* employer, someone hunting for workers
4 心力 *kyūshinryoku* centripetal force
6 刑 *kyūkei suru* prosecute
8 法者 *guhōsha* (Buddhist) inquirer
妻広告 *kyūsai kōkoku* ad for a wife
11 道 *kyūdō* seeking for truth
道者 *kyūdōsha* inquirer, truth seeker, catechumen
婚 *kyūkon* proposal, courtship
婚広告 *kyūkon kōkoku* matrimonial ad
婚者 *kyūkonsha* suitor
13 愛 *kyūai* courtship
15 縁 *kyūen* courtship
16 積 *kyūseki* mensuration
17 償 *kyūshō* claim for damages
18 職 *kyūshoku* job hunting, seeking employment
職広告 *kyūshoku kōkoku* situation-wanted ad
職者 *kyūshokusha* job applicant
職係 *kyūshokugakari* applicant interviewer

7

鼡 Nonstandard for **鼠** 5417.

8

叛 Nonstandard for **叛** 220.

B **為** 138 / F1208 **爲** I. *na(ru)* change; be of use; reach to. *na(su)* do. *su(ru)* do; try; play; practice; cost; serve as; pass, elapse. *ni su(ru)* make (something) of (a person); turn into (money). *tame* good, advantage, benefit, welfare, sake; to, in order to; because of, as a result of. *tame ni* for, for the sake of, to one's advantage, in favor of, on behalf of. [爪]

2 人 *hitotonari* temperament
4 手 *narite* candidate; suitable person
5 出来 *shi-deka(su)* finish up
6 尽 *shi-tsuku(su)* do everything possible
合 *shi-a(u)* do together
7 体 *teitaraku* state of affairs, predicament. *etai* nature, character
初 *shi-so(meru)* begin to do. *shiso(me)* outset, beginning
来 *shikita(ri)* customs
8 果 *shi-ō(seru)* accomplish
放題 *shihōdai* having one's own way
9 政者 *iseisha* statesman
政家 *iseika* politician
10 残 *shi-noko(su)* leave unfinished
納 *shiosa(me)* finishing up
11 遂 *na(shi)-to(geru), shi-to(geru)* accomplish, finish, fulfill
過 *shi-su(giru)* overdo, do too much
術 *se(n)sube* proper methods
終 *na(shi)-o(eru) vt* accomplish, finish. *na(shi)-o(waru) vi* finish
悪 *shiniku(i)* hard to do
12 遣 *shi(te) ya(ru)* do for (someone); deceive, hoodwink
筋 *tamesuji* patron; effective means
落 *shio(chi), shioto(shi)* omission, oversight. *shi-oto(su)* fail to do; make light of, neglect
替 *kawase* money order; exchange
替手形 *kawase tegata* draft
替尻 *kawasejiri* balance of exchange

替相場 *kawase sōba* exchange rates
替銀行 *kawase ginkō* exchange bank
替管理 *kawase kanri* exchange control
[13]損 *shi-sokona(u), shi-son(jiru)* fail, blunder, make a mistake 「doing
続 *shi-tsuzu(keru)* continue to do, persist in
[14]種 *shigusa*＝仕草 362.9

A **単** $\frac{139}{F374}$ **單** TAN one, single, simple, singular, individual. *tan(naru)* mere, simple, sheer. *tan ni* simply, merely, only, solely. *hitoe* one layer, single. 〔口〕

[1]一 *tan-itsu na* single, simple, sole, in- ⌊dividual
一化 *tan-itsuka* simplification
一性 *tan-itsusei* unitary
一神教 *tan-itsu shinkyō* monotheism
[2]刀直入 *tantō-chokunyū* getting right into the subject, frankness
[3]子葉 *tanshiyō* monocotyledon
[4]文 *tambun* simple sentence
元 *tangen* a teaching unit
比 *tampi* simple ratio
比例 *tampirei* simple proportion
[5]句 *tanku* simple phrase
打 *tanda* one-base hit 「lism
本位 *tanhon-i* single standard, monometal-
本位制 *tanhon-isei* single standard, mono- ⌊metallism
弁 *tamben* univalve
弁花 *tambenka* single-petaled flower
[6]行本 *tankōbon* separate volume
衣 *tan-i, hitoe* unlined kimono
衣物 *hitoemono* unlined kimono
色 *tanshoku* single color
色光 *tanshokkō* monochromatic light
色画 *tanshokuga* a monochrome
式 *tanshiki* simple system; single-entry (bookkeeping)
式火山 *tanshiki kazan* simple volcano
式学級 *tanshiki gakkyū* single-grade (classroom)
式簿記 *tanshiki boki* single-entry bookkeeping
[7]角 *tankaku no* one-horned
作 *tansaku* single crop
身 *tanshin* alone; unaided; away from home
身銃 *tanshinjū* single-barreled gun
坐式 *tanzashiki no* single-seated
坐機 *tanzaki* single-seater
利 *tanri* simple interest
利表 *tanrihyō* simple-interest table
利法 *tanrihō* simple-interest method
位 *tan-i* unit, denomination; credit (in school)
位労働組合 *tan-i rōdō kumiai* local (labor) union
位制度 *tan-i seido* point system, credit system
位組合 *tan-i kumiai* local labor union
[8]価 *tanka* unit cost, unit price
性 *tansei* unisexual
物 *hitoemono* unlined kimono
[9]相 *tansō* single phase
級 *tankyū* single-grade (classroom)
軌 *tanki* monorail; single track
音 *tan-on* monosyllable; monotony
音節 *tan-onsetsu no* monosyllabic
音節語 *tan-onsetsugo* monosyllable
発 *tampatsu* single engine
発銃 *tampatsujū* single-barreled gun
発機 *tampatsuki* single-engined plane
独 *tandoku* solo (flight); independence; singleness. *tandoku no* single, sole, lone. *tandoku de* independently, individually, separately, alone, singlehanded, unassisted
独内閣 *tandoku naikaku* one-party cabinet
独会見 *tandoku kaiken* exclusive interview
独行為 *tandoku kōi* individual action, unilateral act
独行動 *tandoku kōdō* independent action
独飛行 *tandoku hikō* solo flight
独講和 *tandoku kōwa* separate peace
[10]帯 *hitoe obi* unlined sash
従陣 *tanjūjin* single column (in marching)
峰駱駝 *tampō rakuda* Arabian camel, dromedary, a one-hump camel
記 *tanki* single-entry (bookkeeping); voting for one person only
記投票 *tanki tōhyō* voting for one person ⌊only
純 *tanjun* simplicity
純化 *tanjunka* simplification
純性 *tanjunsei* simplicity
[11]細胞 *tansaibō* single cell
眼 *tangan* one eye
眼鏡 *tangankyō* monocle
[12]葉 *tan-yō* simple leaf; monoplane
葉飛行機 *tan-yō hikōki* monoplane
葉機 *tan-yōki* monoplane
[13]試合 *tanshiai* singles (in tennis)
数 *tansū* singular number
数型 *tansūkei* singular form
[14]複 *tanfuku* simplicity and complexity; singular and plural; single and double; singles and doubles (in tennis)
語 *tango* word; vocabulary; single-character ⌊word
語集 *tangoshū* word book
語篇 *tangohen* glossary, vocabulary 「track
[15]線 *tansen* single line; solid wire; single
調 *tanchō* monotone, monotony, dullness
[16]機 *tanki* a lone plane 「single column
縦列 *tanjūretsu* Indian file, single file,

[18]騎 *tanki* a single horseman
簡 *tankan* brevity, simplicity

10

梵 140 F983 BON Sanskrit; purity; Buddhist believer. [木]
[4]天王 *Bonten-ō* Brahma, the Creator
[6]字 *Bonji* Sanskrit characters
[8]刹 *bonsetsu, bonsatsu* temple
妻 *bonsai* a Buddhist priest's wife
[14]語 *Bongo* Sanskrit
[20]鐘 *bonshō* temple bell

B **巣** 141 F601 **巢** Sō. *su* nest, rookery, breeding place, beehive, cobweb; den, haunt. *suku(u)* build (a nest). [巛]
[4]引 *subi(ki)* setting (of a hen)
[8]立 *suda(chi)* leaving the nest; becoming independent; leaving one's confinement; graduation
[13]隠 *sugaku(re)* hiding in the nest
窟 *sōkutsu* den, haunt, hangout, home
[15]箱 *subako* nest box, hive
[18]雛 *suhina* nestling
[19]鶏 *sudori* setting hen
[22]籠 *sugomo(ru)* to nest

11

弑 See 1558. [弋]

12

尠 142 F573 **尟** SEN. *sukuna(kumo), sukuna(kutomo)* at least. *sukuna(karazu)* not a little, in no small numbers. *sukuna(i)* (see under 少 166.0). [小]

A **業** 143 F994 GYŌ vocation, occupation, business, trade, profession; industry; undertaking; studies; arts; conduct, act; service; achievement. GŌ karma. *waza* deed, act, work, art, performance, trick. [木]
[4]火 *gōka* hell fire
[6]因 *gōin* karma
[8]物 *wazamono* sharp sword
果 *gōka* effects of karma
者 *gyōsha* the trade, businessmen concerned
突張 *gōtsukuba(ri)* boasting, pride
[9]界 *gyōkai* the business world, industry, the trade
界紙 *gyōkaishi* trade journal
[10]病 *gōbyō* incurable disease
[11]務 *gyōmu* business, affairs, duties, work, service, operations
[12]報 *gōhō* karma effects, fate, inevitable retribution
[13]腹 *gōhara* spite, resentment
[14]種 *gyōshu* business category
態 *gyōtai* business conditions
[17]績 *gyōseki* achievement, performance, results, work, contribution
[19]曝 *gōzara(shi)* disgrace, shame

14

舗 See 552. [金]

16

厳 See 253. [口]

17

叢 144 F317 Sō plexus. *kusamura* clump of bushes, grassy place, thicket, jungle, the bush. *mura-, muraga(ru)* (see under 群 3667.0). [又]
[5]生 *sōsei* dense growth; healthy growth
立 *murada(chi)* standing in a group
氷 *sōhyō* pack ice
[8]雨 *murasame* passing shower
林 *sōrin* Zen monastery
[10]祠 *hokora, sōshi* small shrine
書 *sōsho* series (of publications); a library (of literature)
時雨 *murashigure* autumn shower
[12]雲 *murakumo* cloud masses
[15]談 *sōdan* collection of stories

RAD. ノ 4

No (the katakana). At top: 一 *no kammuri*. Variants: of varying lengths.

Nickname: *Kana No.*

1

乃 145 F54 DAI. NAI. *sunawa(chi)* whereupon, accordingly. *no* possessive particle. *soko(de)*=其処 590.5.
[4]父 *daifu* father
公 *daikō* a boastful first-person pronoun
[6]至 *naishi* from . . . to; or

メ Nonstandard for 〆 126.

1 一丨丶[ノ]乙亅

A 九 146/F59 KYŪ, KU *kokono(tsu)*, *ko* nine. [乙]

2 九表 *kuku (no) hyō* multiplication table
十 *kujū*, *kyūjū* ninety
十九折 *tsuzura-o(ri)* winding road
3 寸五分 *kusun-gobu* a dagger
4 日 *kokonoka* nine days; the ninth day (of the month)
月 *kugatsu* September
牛一毛 *kyūgyū (no) ichimō* a mere fraction, a drop in the bucket
天 *kyūten* sky; heavens; palace
天直下 *kyūten-chokka* falling headlong, plummeting; sudden crash
分 *kubu* nine parts; nine percent; almost
分九厘 *kubu-kurin* ten to one, nine cases out of ten
5 仭功 *kyūjin(no)kō* spectacular success
6 地 *kyūchi* very low land
回戦 *kyūkaisen* regulation game; 9th inning
死一生 *kyūshi-isshō* narrow escape from death
7 折 *kyūsetsu* many turns (in a road)
8 拝 *kyūhai* bowing many times (in apology)
9 泉 *kyūsen* hades, nether regions
重 *kokonoe* ninefold; imperial palace, the Court
重天 *kyūchō no ten* the palace
星 *kyūsei* astrology, horoscope
星家 *kyūseika* astrology, star reader
星術 *kyūseijutsu* astrology, horoscopy
10 夏 *kyūka* summer
11 族 *kyūzoku* the nine nearest generations of relatives
13 腸 *kuchū*=*harawata* (see under 腸 3798.0)
14 穀 *kyūkoku* the nine grains
15 輪 *kurin* pagoda finial

— 2 —

乞 See 262. [乙]

ケ 147/F44 = 个 = 個 See 489. [丨]

九 148/F224 = 凡 See 654. [几]

々 149/F-X Character repetition.

B 乏 150/F56 BŌ. *tobo(shii)*, *tomo(shii)* meager, scarce, limited; destitute, hard up.

B 丈 151/F13 = 丈 JŌ 10 feet; length, measure; Mr. or Mrs. (re artists). *take* height, stature; length, measure; all (one has). *dake* only; alone; no more; merely. [一]

4 比 *takekura(be)* comparison of statures
夫 *masurao*, *jōfu* hero; gentleman; warrior. *jōbu na* healthy, strong, robust; solid, durable
7 余 *jōyo* over ten feet
8 長 *takenaga* tall

B 刃 152/F230 = 刅 = 刄 JIN blade, sword, cutting tool. NIN. *ha* blade, edge. *yaiba* blade, sword. [刀]

6 向 *hamu(kau)* strike at; bite back; turn on, rise against, oppose, defy
先 *hasaki* edge of a blade
8 物 *hamono* edged tool, cutlery
10 針 *habari* lancet
12 渡 *hawata(ri)* sword length, walking on a sword
13 傷 *ninjō* bloodshed
傷沙汰 *ninjōzata* bloodshed

A 久 153/F55 KYŪ. KU. *hisa(shii)* long, long-continued, an old (story). *hisa(shiku)* for a long time.

3 久 *hisabisa* a long time, many days
4 方 *hisakata* sky, moon
方振 *hisakataburi* a long time, many days
10 振 *hisa(shi)buri* a long time, many days
12 遠 *kuon*, *kyūen* eternity
16 懐 *kyūkai* a long-cherished hope
17 闊 *kyūkatsu* neglect of friends
濶 *kyūkatsu* neglect of friends
濶序=next word
濶叙 *kyūkatsu (o) jo(su)* apologize for a long neglect of friends

B 及 154/F311 = 及 KYŪ. *oyo(bosu)* exert, exercise, cause. *oyo(bu)* reach, come up to, amount to; befall, happen to; extend; match, equal. *oyo(banai)* unnecessary; unattainable. *oyo(bi)* and, as well as. [又]

5 乍 *oyo(bazu)naga(ra)* to the best of my ability, poor tho it be
11 第 *kyūdai* passing an examination
第者 *kyūdaisha* successful examinee
第点 *kyūdaiten* passing grade
12 落 *kyūraku* success or failure (in exams)
13 腰 *oyo(bi)goshi* a bent back
18 難 *oyo(bi)gata(i)* hard to attain to

B 丸 155/F50 GAN. *maru* full (month); perfection; purity; the ship-name suffix anciently used after the name of a sword or a child. *maru(meru)* make round, round off, roll up, curl up; seduce; cajole; explain away. *tama* pills. *maru de* quite, completely, absolutely; just like; as it were.

maru(i), *maru(kkoi)* round, circular, spherical. [丶]
1一 *maruichi* bisected-circle seal
2十 *marujū* cross in a circle ⌈plump
3丸 *marumaru* completely. *marumaru to*
4込 *maru(me)-ko(mu)* coax, seduce
刈 *maruga(ri)* close clipping
切 *maruki(ri)*, *maru(k)ki(ri)*=*maru de* (see
公 *marukō* official price ⌊under 丸 155.0)
天井 *maru tenjō* arched ceiling
太 *maruta* log
太小屋 *marutagoya* log cabin, blockhouse
太材 *marutazai* round timber
太足場 *maruta ashiba* scaffolding
木 *maruki* log
木舟 *marukibune* dugout canoe
木造 *marukizuku(ri)* rustic work
木船 *marukibune* dugout canoe
木橋 *marukibashi* log bridge
5瓦 *marugawara* concave roof tile
石 *maruishi* boulder, cobble
出 *maruda(shi)* bare, exposed, undisguised; broad (provincial accent)
本 *marubon* reciter's book
6行灯 *maru andon* round paper lantern
7見 *marumi(e)* completely visible
形 *marugata* round shape, circle
呑 *maruno(mi)* swallowing whole
禿 *maruhage* complete baldness ⌈hill
坊主 *marubōzu* close-cropped head; bald
8味 *marumi* roundness, rotundity
取 *marudo(ri) suru* monopolize
事 *marugoto* in its entirety, whole
9首 *marukubi* round-necked (T shirt)
持 *marumo(chi)* moneyed man
洗 *maruara(i)* washing kimonos without taking them apart
除 *tamayoke*=弾除 1575.9
負 *maruma(ke)* complete defeat
括孤 *marugakko* parentheses
10帯 *maruobi* one-piece sash
砥石 *maru toishi* grindstone
11彫 *marubo(ri)* three-dimensional sculpture
窓 *marumado* circular window
12焼 *maruya(ke)* total fire loss; completely burned. *maruya(ki)* barbecue ⌈record
勝 *maruga(chi)* complete victory; clean
提灯 *marujōchin* round lantern
13傷 *tama kizu* bullet wound
損 *maruzon* total loss
腰 *marugoshi* unarmed
裸 *maru hadaka* nude
14鼻蜂 *maruhanabachi* bumblebee
15潰 *marutsubu(re)* complete ruin, collapse
16鋼 *marukō* round steel bar
鋸 *marunoko* circular saw
薬 *gan-yaku* pill
髷 *marumage* married woman's hairdo
諳記 *maru anki* indiscriminate memorizing
18儲 *marumōke* clear gain
28鑿 *marunomi* a gouge

A 千 156/F283 仟 SEN *chi* thousand; many. [十]

1一夜 *Sen-ichiya* Thousand and One Nights
2人力 *senninriki* strength of a thousand men
人針 *sennimbari* a 1000-stitch belt (a soldier's charm)
3千 *sensen*, *chiji* thousands. *chiji* a great number of; variety. *chiji ni* in pieces
三屋 *semmitsuya* broker, land agent; great liar, unreliable person
万 *chiyorozu* a great many. *semman* ten million; myriad. *semban* exceedingly, very many, very much, indeed
万長者 *semmanchōja* multimillionaire, billionaire ⌈fathomable; unutterable
万無量 *semmam-muryō* innumerable; un-
4日 *sennichi* one thousand days
木 *chigi* ornamental crossed rafter ends on shrine gables
切 *chigi(ru)* cut up fine; pick (fruit). *sengiri* short small pieces of vegetables
分 *sembun* division by 1000; $\frac{1}{1000}$ ⌈sand
分率 *sembunritsu* permillage, rate per thou-
5生 *sennari* a great collection (of things)
古 *senko* all ages; great antiquity; eternity
石船 *sengokubune* large junk
仭 *senjin* great depth; great height
仭谷 *senjin (no) tani* bottomless ravine
代 *chiyo*, *sendai* a thousand years; a very long period
代紙 *chiyogami* gaily colored paper
6両 *senryō* 1000 *ryō* (an old Japanese coin)
両役者 *senryō yakusha* star (actor), prima donna; leading figure
両箱 *senryōbako* box of 1000 *ryō*
年 *sennen* millennium, one thousand years
年期 *sennenki* millennium
年間 *sennenkan* a thousand-year period
7辛万苦 *senshin-banku* many hardships
言万語 *sengen-bango* many words
状万態 *senjō-bantai* various forms; various circumstances
里 *senri* 1000 *ri*; a long distance
里眼 *senrigan* clairvoyance; clairvoyant
8金 *senkin* 1000 yen; 1000 pieces of gold; pricelessness
夜 *chiya*, *sen-ya* many nights
卒長 *sensotsuchō* captain of a thousand
枚通 *semmaidō(shi)* an awl ⌈ing waves
波万波 *sempa-bampa* many waves, onrush-

1 一 丨 丶 ³[丿] 乙 亅

⁹度 *chitabi, sendo* a thousand times
草 *chigusa* great variety of flowering plants
変万化 *sempembanka* innumerable changes, infinite variety
思万考 *senshi-bankō* deep meditation, mature consideration
客万来 *senkaku-banrai, senkyaku-banrai* flood of customers
軍万馬 *sengumbamba* series of battles
姿万態 *senshi-bantai* endless variety
秋 *senshū* a thousand years; many years
秋楽 *senshūraku* the last day of wrestling; the concluding program
¹⁰倍 *sembai* a thousand-fold
般 *sempan* variety
島 *Chishima* the Kurile Islands
差万別 *sensa-bambetsu* infinite variety
¹¹遍一律 *sempen-ichiritsu* no change
鳥 *chidori* plover
鳥足 *chidori ashi* tottering steps
¹²鈞 *senkin* 1000 pounds; 1000 *kan*; great weight
尋 *chihiro* thousand fathoms; great depth
紫万紅 *senshi-bankō* variegated colors (of flowers)
¹³歳 *chitose* a thousand years
載 *senzai* a thousand years; a long time; a millenium; perpetuity
載一遇 *senzai-ichigū* experienced once in a thousand times; the best day of one's life
¹⁴態万様 *sentai-ban-yō* great diversity of form
¹⁵慮 *senryo* much thought
慮一失 *senryo (no) isshitsu* the mistake of a wise man
篇 *sempen* many volumes
篇一律 *sempen-ichiritsu* monotony, lack of variety

3

勿 See 743. [勹]

乏 See 150.

壬 See 2921. [士]

之 See 280.

卅 See 丗 78. [十]

及 157/F-X See 及 154. [又]

尹 158/F574 In an official rank. [尸]

B **匁** 159/F271 (国字) *momme, me* $\frac{1}{100}$ *hyakume* (see Weights and Measures). [勹]

B **升** 160/F285 Shō 1.8 liter. *masu* a measuring box. [十]

夭 161/F473 Yō early death; calamity. [大]

⁶死 *yōshi* premature death
⁷折 *yōsetsu* premature death
¹⁰逝 *yōsei* premature death

A **午** 162/F285 Go *uma* 11 a.m.–1 p.m.; 7th zodiac sign. *uma* horse; south. [十]

⁶后 *gogo* afternoon, p.m.
⁸刻 *gokoku* noon
⁹後 *gogo* afternoon, p.m.
後中 *gogojū* thruout the afternoon
前 *gozen* forenoon, a.m.
前中 *gozenchū* thruout the morning
¹⁰砲 *gohō* noon gun
¹¹過 *hirusu(gi)* after noon
¹³睡 *gosui* nap, siesta
¹⁶餐 *gosan* lunch, dinner
餐会 *gosankai* luncheon party

B **丹** 163/F50 = 冄 Tan red; red lead; pills. *ni* red; red earth. [丶]

⁴心 *tanshin* sincerity, faithfulness
⁶色 *ni-iro* red
朱 *tanshu* cinnabar, vermilion
⁸青 *tansei* red and blue; painting
念 *tannen* application, diligence
毒 *tandoku* erysipelas
⁹砂 *tansha* cinnabar
前 *tanzen* large padded kimono
¹³誠 *tansei* sincerity; efforts, diligence
塗 *ninu(ri) no* red painted, vermilion lacquered
¹⁴精 *tansei suru* work earnestly
碧 *tampeki* red and green

A **夫** 164/F472 Fū, Fu husband; man. *otto, tsuma* husband, spouse. *se* a woman's familiar call for her husband or elder brother. *so(re)* that. [大]

²人 *fujin* wife, married lady, Mrs.
³子 *fūshi* term of address for a teacher; Confucius
⁴夫 *soresore* each, severally, respectively
⁷役 *buyaku* forced labor; exacted service
君 *fukun, se(no)kimi* one's husband
⁸妻 *fusai* man and wife; Mr. and Mrs.
¹¹婦 *fūfu, meoto, myōto* husband and wife; couple; pair
婦生活 *fūfu seikatsu* married life

婦仲 *fūfu naka* conjugal relations, conjugal affection
婦共稼 *fūfu tomokasegi* dual income, husband and wife both working
婦別 *fūfu waka(re)* divorce, separation
婦連 *myōtozu(re)* husband and wife traveling together ⌈trothal, marriage contract
婦約束 *fūfu yakusoku* engagement, be-
婦道 *fūfu (no) michi* marital virtues
婦喧嘩 *fūfugenka* matrimonial quarrel
15 権 *fuken* husband's marital rights

B **井** 165/F79 Shō. Sei *i* well. [二]
4 戸 *ido* well
戸水 *ido mizu* well water
戸車 *idoguruma* well pulley
戸屋形 *ido yakata* well roof
戸浚 *idosarae* well cleaning
戸側 *idogawa* well curb
戸掘 *idoho(ri)* well digging; well digger
戸替 *idoga(e)* well cleaning
戸綱 *idozuna* well rope
戸端 *idobata* well side
戸端会議 *idobata kaigi* well-side gossip
8 底 *seitei* well bottom; narrow place
底蛙 *seitei (no) kawazu* a frog in a well;
9 泉 *seisen* well ⌊narrow-minded man
10 桁 *igeta* well crib; parallel crosses
12 堰 *iseki* sluice, dam ⌈person
蛙 *seia* a frog in a well; narrow-minded
筒 *izutsu* well crib
然 *seizen*＝整然 2436.12
14 綱 *izuna* well rope

A **少** 166/F570 Shō small; few; young. *suko(shi)* a small quantity, a little; a few; something; a little while; a short distance. *suko(shimo)* (not) at all. *suku(nai)*, *suke(nai)* few, a little, scarce, insufficient, seldom. *suku(nakarazu)* not a little, in no small numbers. *suku(nage)* scarcity. *suku(nakutomo)*, *suku(nakumo)* at least. [小]
3 女 *shōjo*, *otome* daughter, young lady,
4 少 *shōshō* a little, a few, slightly ⌊virgin
6 安 *shōan*＝小安 1355.6
壮 *shōsō* youth
壮士官 *shōsō shikan* young officer
壮有為 *shōsō-yūi no* young and able
年 *shōnen* boy, juvenile
年少女 *shōnen-shōjo* boys and girls
年文学 *shōnembungaku* juvenile literature
年犯罪 *shōnen hanzai* juvenile delinquency
年団 *Shōnendan* Boy Scouts
年会 *shōnenkai* junior society
年労働 *shōnen rōdō* child labor
年法 *shōnenhō* juvenile law
年院 *shōnen-in* reform school
年感化院 *shōnen kanka-in* reform school
年審判所 *shōnen shimpanjo* juvenile court
7 佐 *shōsa* major; lieutenant commander; wing commander
弟 *shōtei* young brother
8 者 *shōsha* young person
国民 *shōkokumin* the rising generation, children
9 食 *shōshoku* light eating, spare diet
食家 *shōshokuka* light eater
10 時 *shōji* one's early days, a little while
将 *shōshō* major general; rear admiral; air commodore
恩 *shōon* small favors
11 康 *shōkō* some improvement (in a patient)
欲 *shōyoku* a little covetousness
尉 *shōi* second lieutenant; ensign
12 閑 *shōkan* short interval of leisure
量 *shōryō* small quantity, small dose
13 資本 *shōshihon* small capital
数 *shōsū* few; minority
数民族 *shōsū minzoku* minority peoples
数者 *shōsūsha* the minority
数党 *shōsūtō* minority party
15 敵 *shōteki* weak opponent, weak enemy
16 憩 *shōkei* short rest, recess
18 額 *shōgaku* small amount

4

史 See 91. [口]

央 See 86. [大]

必 See 129. [心]

冊 See **冊** 87. [十]

本 See 96. [木]

牛 167/F286 See **半** 132. [十]

尓 168/F571/F1211 **介** See **爾** 69. [小]

册 169/F211 **冊** See **冊** 88. [冂]

乎 170/F56 Ko. *ya, ka* question mark.

1 一 | 、 4 ノ 乙 亅

5 古止点 *okototen* marks to aid in reading Chinese classics

丼 171/F54 TON. TAN. *domburi* bowl; bowl of food. [丶]
8 物 *domburimono* food served in a large bowl
13 鉢 *domburibachi* bowl

乍 172/F56 SA. *-naga(ra)* tho, notwithstanding; while, during; both, all. *tachima(chi)* (see under 忽 1652.0).
12 然 *sarinagara* however, but

弗 173/F654 FUTSU. *doru* dollar. [弓]
9 相場 *doru sōba* dollar exchange
10 素 *fusso* fluorine
素酸 *fussosan* fluoric acid
15 箱 *dorubako* cashbox; backer, patron

B **丘** 174/F42 KYŪ. KU. *oka* hill, knoll, rising ground. [一]
3 上 *kyūjō* hilltop
4 辺 *okabe* vicinity of a hill
10 疹 *kyūshin* pimple, papule
陵 *kyūryō* hill, hillock

B **斥** 175/F871 **斥** SEKI. *shirizo(ku) vi* retreat, recede, withdraw. *shirizo(keru) vt* repel, repulse; reject. [斤]
2 力 *sekiryoku* repulsion, repulsive force
10 候 *sekkō* scout, patrol, spy
候兵 *sekkōhei* reconnoitering party
候隊 *sekkōtai* reconnoitering party

A **包** 176/F271 **包** HŌ. *tsutsu(mu)* wrap, pack up; cover with; dress in; conceal. *kuru(mu)* wrap up, tuck in. *kuru(meru)* lump together, include, sum up; quibble. *tsutsu(mi)* bundle, package, parcel, bale. *tsutsu(minaku)* without concealment, without reserve, frankly. [勹]
2 丁 *hōchō* kitchen knife; cooking
4 込 *tsutsu(mi)-ko(mu)* wrap up
5 皮 *hōhi* foreskin
皮切断 *hōhi setsudan* circumcision
7 囲 *hōi* siege, encirclement
含 *hōgan suru* include, comprise, comprehend, cover, imply ⌈paper
8 金 *tsutsu(mi)gane* a money tip wrapped in
物 *tsutsu(mi)mono* bundle, package
直 *tsutsu(mi)-nao(su)* rewrap
9 括 *hōkatsu*＝*hōgan* 包含 (see above–7)
括的 *hōkatsuteki* inclusive, comprehensive
10 紙 *tsutsu(mi)gami* wrapping paper
容 *hōyō suru* comprehend, embrace, imply, tolerate
茎 *hokei* phimosis
帯 *hōtai* bandage, dressing
11 釦 *tsutsu(mi) botan* covered button
12 装 *hōsō* packing, wrapping
13 摂 *hōsetsu* connotation
隠 *tsutsu(mi)-kaku(su)* conceal, keep secret, cover up. *tsutsu(mi)kaku(shi)* concealment ⌈show
飾 *tsutsu(mi)-kaza(ru)* cover up and make a
14 蔵 *hōzō suru* contain, keep, comprehend, imply, entertain (an idea)

A **末** 177/F942 BATSU. MATSU end; powder. *sue* end, close; tip, top; trivialities; the future; posterity; youngest child. *sue ni* finally. *ura* top end, tip. *ure* new shoots, new growth (of a tree). *-matsu* the end of; powder. [木]
3 女 *matsujo* youngest daughter ⌈child
子 *basshi, masshi, sueko, sue(k)ko* youngest
4 方 *sue(tsu)kata* end of a period; end of the
日 *matsujitsu* last day (of a month) ⌊world
5 生 *suenari* fruit near the end of the vine; weak-looking fellow
広 *suehiro* folding fan. *suehiro(gari)* spreading out like an open fan
代 *matsudai* eternity
末 *suezue* distant future; descendants; lower classes. *sue(no)sue* the last
世 *sue(no)yo, masse* last days
6 成 *uranari*＝*suenari* 末生 (see above–5)
寺 *matsuji* branch temple
年 *matsunen* the last years, the final years, the last generation
7 尾 *matsubi* end, close
技 *matsugi* poor workmanship ⌈jester
社 *massha* subordinate shrine; professional
弟 *mattei, battei* youngest brother; last dis-
男 *batsunan* youngest son ⌊ciple
8 長 *suenaga(ku)* long, forever
季 *makki* closing years, last stage
若 *urawaka(i)* youthful
始終 *sueshijū* forever, for life
法 *mappō* latter days (in Buddhism), age of decadence ⌈cadent-age theory
法思想 *mappō shisō* pessimism due to de-
9 香 *makkō* incense, incense powder
枯 *uraga(re)* dying of the little twigs and
派 *mappa* sect; underling ⌊branches
茶 *matcha* powdered tea
10 座 *matsuza* lowest seat
流 *matsuryū, batsuryū* descendants
恐 *sueoso(roshii)* ominous, likely to grow worse
席 *masseki, basseki* lowest seat ⌈(humble)
席汚 *masseki (o) kega(su)* attend a meeting

11梢 *masshō* tree top, tip; periphery; minor details, nonessentials
梢的 *masshōteki* trivial, minor, insignificant
梢神経 *masshō shinkei* peripheral nerves
12項 *makkō* the last paragraph
期 *makki* closing years, last stage. *matsugo* deathbed, hour of death
葉 *batsuyō* the last descendant; the last days of any age. *matsuyō* end, close. *uraba, ureba* end leaves, top leaves, last leaves
筆乍 *mappitsunaga(ra)* a letter-closing phrase expressing regret for a delay
13路 *matsuro, batsuro* last days, end, fate
節 *massetsu* minor details, nonessentials
裔 *matsuei, batsuei* descendants
14僚 *batsuryō* low-ranking official
端 *mattan* end, tip, extremities
15輩 *mappai* underling, rank and file
16頼 *suetano(moshii)* promising (future)

A **失** 178/F474 SHITSU error; fault; disadvantage; loss; demerit. *na(kunaru)* (see under 無 2773.0). *na(ku) nasu, na(ku) suru, na(kusu) vt* lose; run out of; remove; absorb. *shis(suru)* lose, miss; forget; be excessive. *u(seru)* disappear, vanish. *ushina(u)* lose, miss (a chance). [大]
4心 *shisshin* trance, stupefaction, faint
火 *shikka* accidental fire ⌈rudeness
5礼 *shitsurei* discourtesy, impoliteness,
去 *u(se)-sa(ru)* disappear, be gone
6血 *shikketsu* loss of blood
地 *shitchi* lost territory ⌈bleness
当 *shittō* injustice; impropriety; unreasona-
考 *shikkō* misunderstanding
名 *shitsumei* name unknown
名氏 *shitsumeishi* unknown person
7言 *shitsugen* improper language, a slip
体 *shittai*＝失態 (see below–14)
8物 *u(se)mono* lost article
効 *shikkō* lapse, abatement, invalidation
命 *shitsumei* losing one's life, dying
念 *shitsunen* lapse of memory, forgetting;
明 *shitsumei* loss of eyesight ⌊oblivion
明者 *shitsumeisha* blind person
9速 *shissoku* a stall (in flying)
透 *shittō suru* devitrify
神 *shisshin* trance, stupefaction, faint
陥 *shikkan* surrender, fall
政 *shissei* misgovernment
点 *shitten* a run charged to the pitcher
10恋 *shitsuren* unrequited love
笑 *shisshō* spontaneous laughter
格 *shikkaku* disqualification, elimination; incapacity (legal)
格者 *shikkakusha* disqualified person
11脚 *shikkyaku suru* lose one's standing, fall, be overthrown, stumble
敗 *shippai* failure, mistake, blunder
望 *shitsubō* disappointment, despair
12敬 *shikkei suru* say goodbye; act impolitely; steal. *shikkei* rudeness, impoliteness, dis-
策 *shissaku* blunder, slip, error ⌊respect
着 *shitchaku* mistake, negligence
費 *shippi* expenses
13跡 *shisseki* abscondence, disappearance ⌈sity
意 *shitsui* despair, disappointment; adver-
禁 *shikkin* incontinence (of urine or feces)
業 *shitsugyō* unemployment ⌈lowance
業手当 *shitsugyō teate* unemployment al-
業者 *shitsugyōsha* unemployed person
業保険 *shitsugyō hoken* unemployment insurance ⌈men's estimation)
14墜 *shittsui suru* lose, forfeit, fall, sink (in
態 *shittai* mismanagement, fault, error, failure; disgrace, discredit
語 *shitsugo* forgetting the words, inability to pronounce a word correctly
語症 *shitsugoshō* loss of speech, agnosia
15権 *shikken* loss of rights, disenfranchise-
調 *shitchō* lack of harmony ⌊ment
踪 *shissō* abscondence, disappearance
16錯 *shissaku* blunder, slip, error
18職 *shisshoku* unemployment
職者 *shisshokusha* unemployed person

A **未** 179/F943 MI not yet. *ima(da)* as yet, hitherto; not yet (with neg.). *ima(dani)* still, even now, until this very day. *mada* not yet; still; so far; more, besides; only. *ima(dashi)* something to be desired. *hitsuji* 1–3 p.m.; 8th zodiac sign; sheep. *mi-* un-, not yet. [木]
2了 *miryō no* unfinished, unfilled (order), unexecuted
丁年 *miteinen* minority, under age
3亡人 *mibōjin* widow
4公表 *mikōhyō* not yet officially announced
5刊 *mikan no* unpublished
未 *madamada* still, still more, much more
処分 *mishobun* unsettled, unfinished, un-
処置 *mishochi* untreated ⌊divided (profits)
払 *mihara(i)* unpaid
払込 *miharaiko(mi)* not paid up (capital)
収 *mishū* accrued, outstanding
収入金 *mishūnyūkin* accounts receivable
6成 *misei* uncompleted, unfinished, crude
成年 *miseinen* minority, not of age
成年者 *miseinensha* a minor ⌈not grown up
成品 *miseihin* unfinished goods; a person
7見 *miken no* unacquainted, unknown

改心者 *mikaishinsha* unconverted person
完 *mikan no* incomplete, unfinished
完成 *mikansei no* incomplete
来 *mirai* future; future life; future tense
来完了 *mirai kanryō* future perfect
来派 *miraiha* futurism
決 *miketsu* pending, unsettled
決囚 *miketsushū* unconvicted prisoner
決済 *mikessai* outstanding (account)
決算 *mikessan* outstanding (account)
決監 *miketsukan* detention prison
8 届 *mitodo(ke)* failing to report
明 *mimei* early dawn
到 *mitō* untrodden, unexplored
青年 *miseinen* minority, not of age
知 *michi* unknown, strange
知数 *michisū* unknown number
定 *mitei* undecided, pending
定稿 *miteikō* unfinished manuscript
9 信者 *mishinja* unbeliever; inquirer
発 *mihatsu ni* before anything happens, previously
発行 *mihakkō* unissued
発見 *mihakken* undiscovered, unexplored
発表 *mihappyō* not yet announced
発達 *mihattatsu* undeveloped
10 進 *mishin* nonpayment of tribute
納 *minō* payment default
記入 *mikinyū* blank (book)
消化 *mishōka* unfulfilled (orders)
耕地 *mikōchi* uncultivated land
配当 *mihaitō* undivided (profits)
帰還者 *mikikansha* unrepatriated person
11 済 *misai no* unpaid
設 *misetsu* uninstalled, projected
教育 *mikyōiku no* untrained
組織 *misoshiki* unorganized
遂 *misui* attempted (crime)
遂罪 *misuizai* attempted crime
婚 *mikon* unmarried
婚者 *mikonsha* unmarried person
経過 *mikeika* unexpired
経験 *mikeiken no* inexperienced
経験者 *mikeikensha* inexperienced person
12 満 *miman* less than, below
然 *mizen ni* before anything happens, previously
曾有 *mizou, misou* unprecedented, unheard of
復員 *mifukuin no* undemobilized
登記 *mitōki* unregistered
就学児童 *mishūgaku jidō* preschool child
着 *michaku* nonarrival
着手 *michakushu* (work) not yet started
開 *mikai* uncivilized, barbarous; not blooming
開拓 *mikaitaku* undeveloped, wild (areas)
開拓地 *mikaitakuchi* undeveloped area
開発 *mikaihatsu* undeveloped (countries), backward, unentered
開墾 *mikaikon* uncultivated
開墾地 *mikaikonchi* virgin soil, uncultivated land
13 詳 *mishō no* unknown, unidentified
解決 *mikaiketsu no* unsettled, pending
14 聞 *mimon* having not yet heard
練 *miren* unskilled; lingering affection
製品 *miseihin* unfinished article
15 確定 *mikakutei* unsettled, pending
踏 *mitō* untrodden, unexplored
踏査 *mitōsa* unexplored
熟 *mijuku na* unripe, raw; unskilled, immature, inexperienced
熟者 *mijukumono* a green hand, a novice
16 墾 *mikon* uncultivated
墾地 *mikonchi* uncultivated land

5

向 See 101. [口]

毎 See 2467. [毋]

曳 See 曳 106. [曰]

耒 See 来 202. [人]

乑 180/F-X SHŪ assemble.

A 后 181/F336 KŌ. Go after; behind; back; later. *kisaki* empress, queen. [口]
6 妃 *kōhi* queen
10 宮 *kōkyū* harem; imperial consort; palace

夷 182/F475 I barbarian. *ebisu* barbarian, savage; Ainu. [大]
7 狄 *iteki* barbarians, aliens
8 国 *ikoku* land of the barbarians
9 俗 *izoku* customs of the barbarians

B 吏 183/F336 吏 RI an official. [口]
2 人 *rijin* officials
9 臭 *rishū* officialism, red tape
10 員 *ri-in* officials
党 *ritō* party of officials
11 道 *ridō* official ethics
務 *rimu* the work of the officials

B 朱 184/F944 SHU cinnabar; vermilion. *aka* scarlet, red, bloody. [木]
3 子学 *Shushigaku* Neo-Confucianism

6 肉 *shuniku* red ink pad
印 *shuin* red seal
印状 *shuinjō* license with a red seal; shogunate license to trade
印船 *shuinsen* shogunate-licensed trading ship
8 門 *shumon* red-lacquered gate
泥 *shudei* red pottery
9 点 *shuten* red mark
10 唇 *shushin* red lips
書 *shusho, shuga(ki)* writing in red
12 筆 *shuhitsu* red-ink brush
13 塗 *shunu(ri)* red (lacquer) red and black
14 墨 *shuboku, shuzumi* red-ink stick. *shuboku*
16 鞘 *shuzaya* red-lacquered sword sheath
18 顔 *shugan* flushed face

劣 185 F259 RETSU. *oto(ru)* be inferior to, be worse than. [力]
B
3 才 *ressai* inferior talents
8 者 *ressha* an inferior
10 弱 *retsujaku* inferiority
弱意識 *retsujaku ishiki* inferiority complex
11 情 *retsujō* animal passions, carnal desire, lust
敗 *reppai* defeat of the weaker
悪 *retsuaku na* inferior, coarse
12 等 *rettō* inferiority, low grade
等感 *rettōkan* inferiority complex
等複合 *rettō fukugō* inferiority complex
等観念 *rettō kannen* inferiority complex
13 勢 *ressei* numerical inferiority; weakness
勢感 *resseikan* inferiority complex

争 186 F1208 **爭** Sō. *araso(u)* dispute, argue; be at variance; compete. *araso(i)* dispute, strife, quarrel, dissension, conflict; rivalry, contest. *araso(warenai)* indisputable, undeniable, unmistakable. *ika(de)* how. [爪]
A
6 好 *araso(i)zu(ki) na* quarrelsome, contentious
7 乱 *sōran* rioting, disturbances
8 事 *araso(i)goto* dispute
9 点 *sōten* point at issue
怒 *araso(i)-ika(ru)* be angry and quarrelsome
11 訟 *sōshō* dispute. *sōshō no* contentious
12 訴 *araso(i)-utta(eru)* accuse, rise up in judgment against
13 戦 *araso(i)-tataka(u)* fight with, contend with
14 端 *sōtan* beginning of a dispute
奪 *sōdatsu*=next word
奪戦 *sōdatsusen* contest, competition, struggle, challenge
15 論 *sōron* argument, dispute, controversy
18 闘 *sōtō* strife, struggle
19 覇 *sōha* contending for victory, struggling for supremacy championship game
覇戦 *sōhasen* struggle for supremacy,
20 議 *sōgi* dispute, conflict

危 187 F297 KI. *abu(nagaru)* be afraid of, feel uneasy about, shrink from. *aya(bumu)* fear, have misgivings, be doubtful, mistrust. *aya(meru)* wound; murder. *abu(nai), abu(nakkashii), ayau(i)* dangerous; critical, grave; uncertain, unreliable; limping; narrow, close; watch out. [卩]
B
6 気 *abu(na)ge* possibility of danger
地 *kichi* dangerous position, peril
7 局 *kikyoku* crisis
坐 *kiza suru* sit up straight
9 殆 *kitai* danger, jeopardy, distress
急 *kikyū* emergency, crisis
急存亡 *kikyū-sombō* a life-and-death matter
10 峰 *kihō* a high, steep peak
害 *kigai* injury, harm; danger
険 *kiken* danger, risk
険人物 *kiken jimbutsu* dangerous character
険地帯 *kiken chitai* danger zone
険角度 *kiken kakudo* critical angle
険性 *kikensei* riskiness, danger
険物 *kikembutsu* dangerous goods, explosives, combustibles
険信号 *kiken shingō* danger signal, red light
険思想 *kiken shisō* dangerous thoughts
険視 *kikenshi suru* regard as dangerous
11 惧 *kigu* fear, misgivings
12 極 *kikyoku* crisis; grave danger; serious depression
絵 *abu(na)e* suggestive or indecent picture
13 虞 *kigu* fear, misgivings
14 疑 *kigi* fear, misgivings
16 篤 *kitoku* on the verge of death
機 *kiki* crisis, emergency
機一髪 *kiki-ippatsu* critical moment
機打者 *kiki dasha* pinch hitter
機突破 *kiki toppa* crisis relief
18 難 *kinan* danger, hazard, distress
21 懼 *kiku* fear, misgivings

年 188 F626 NEN year; term of service. *toshi* year; age, time of life. [干]
A
3 子 *toshigo* second child born within a year
下 *toshishita* younger, junior
上 *toshiue* older, senior
久 *toshihisa(shiku)* for many years, anciently
4 内 *nennai* within the year
分 *nembun* yearly amount
月 *nengetsu, toshitsuki* months and years, time
月日 *nengappi* date
中 *nenjū* thruout the year
中行事 *nenjū gyōji* annual functions or events
少 *nenshō* youth
少者 *nenshōsha* youth, minor, young people

1 一丨丶【ノ】乙亅

5 玉 *toshidama* New Year's gift
礼 *nenrei* New Year's greetings
収 *nenshū* annual income
市 *toshi* (*no*) *ichi* year-end fair
令 *nenrei* age
末 *nemmatsu* year end
甲斐無 *toshigai* (*mo*) *na*(*i*) unbecoming, unsuitable; disgraceful
功 *nenkō* long service, long experience
功制度 *nenkō seido* seniority rule
代 *nendai* age, era, period; date
代記 *nendaiki* chronicle, chronology
代順 *nendaijun* chronological order
6 老 *toshio*(*iru*) grow old. *toshioi* old person
回 *toshimawa*(*ri*) age relationship, luck attending age. *nenkai* anniversary service (in Buddhism)
次 *nenji* annual; dates
号 *nengō* era name
毎 *toshigoto*(*ni*) annually, every year
百年中 *nembyaku-nenjū* all year round; year after year
会 *nenkai* conference; annual convention
会費 *nenkaihi* annual fee
年 *toshidoshi*, *nennen* years, year by year, annually. *toshi* (*ga*) *toshi* considering his age
年中 *nen*(*gara*)-*nenjū*, *nen*(*ga*)-*nenjū* all year round, year after year
年歳歳 *nennen-saisai* annually, every year
7 豆 *toshi* (*no*) *mame* beans of the bean-scattering ceremony
改 *toshiarata*(*maru*) the New Year dawns
利 *nenri* annual interest rate
初 *nensho* beginning of the year; New Year's greetings
別 *nembetsu* by years
忘 *toshiwasu*(*re*) year-end drinking party
忌 *nenki* death anniversary; Buddhist anniversary service
男 *toshiotoko* bean scatterer
甫 *nempo* beginning of the year
来 *nenrai* for some years
8 金 *nenkin* annuity, pension
延 *toshibae* approximate age
明 *nen-a*(*ke*) expiration of a term of service. *toshia*(*keru*) the New Year dawns
波 *toshinami* old age, oncoming age
取 *toshito*(*ru*), *toshi*(*o*)*to*(*ru*) grow old, age
限 *nengen* length of time, term
若 *toshiwaka*(*i*), *toshiwaka no* young, youthful
表 *nempyō* chronological tables, chronology
長 *nenchō* seniority
長者 *nenchōsha* a senior, elderly people
始 *nenshi* beginning of the year; New Year's greetings, New Year's calls
始状 *nenshijō* New Year's card
季 *nenki*＝年期 (see below–12)
季奉公＝年期奉公 (see below–12)

9 度 *nendo* year; fiscal year; school year; term
拾 *toshi* (*o*) *hiro*(*u*) grow old
恰好 *toshi kakkō*, *toshigakkō* approximate age
10 俸 *nempō* annual salary
租 *nenso* annual tax
益 *nen-eki* annual profit
差 *nensa* annual variation
弱 *toshiyowa* child born in last half of the year
配 *nempai* age
配者 *nempaisha* elderly person
貢 *nengu* land tax (in kind); tribute; ground rent
貢米 *nengumai* annual rice tax
11 強 *toshizuyo* child born in first half of the year
掛 *toshiga*(*ke*) yearly payment
盛 *toshizaka*(*ri*) prime of life
祭 *toshi matsu*(*ri*) annual festival. -*nensai* anniversary
頃 *toshigoro* age; marriageable age; age of puberty; adolescence; for some years
頃日頃 *toshigoro-higoro* these days
産 *nensan* annual production
産額 *nensangaku* annual production
寄 *toshiyo*(*ru*), *toshi*(*ga*)*yo*(*ru*) grow old. *toshiyo*(*ri*) old person, an elder; older councillor
寄子 *toshiyo*(*ri*)*go* child of one's old age
寄役 *toshiyo*(*ri*)*yaku* a senior's role
寄臭 *toshiyo*(*ri*)*kusa*(*i*) slovenly like an old man
寄染 *toshiyo*(*ri*)*ji*(*mita*) characteristic of the aging
12 歯 *nenshi* age
越 *toshiko*(*shi*) year end, New Year's Eve. *toshi* (*o*) *ko*(*su*) the year ends
間 *nenkan* era, period of a year; for the year...
税 *nenzei* annual tax
給 *nenkyū* annual salary
割 *nenwa*(*ri*) annual rate
報 *nempō* annual report
期 *nenki* term of service; apprenticeship
期明 *nenkia*(*ke*) expiration of a term of service
期者 *nenkimono* apprentice
期奉公 *nenki bōkō* apprenticeship, indenture
賀 *nenga* New Year's greetings; New Year's call
賀状 *nengajō* New Year's card
賀郵便 *nenga yūbin* New Year's mail
賀葉書 *nenga hagaki* New Year's postcard
13 数 *nensū* number of years
嵩 *toshikasa* senior, older, elderly
14 増 *toshima* mature woman, middle-aged woman
端 *toshiha* age; years
暮 *toshi* (*no*) *ku*(*re*) year end. *toshiku*(*reru*) the year ends
15 賦 *nempu* annual installment
輪 *nenrin* annual tree ring
輪史学 *nenrin shigaku* dendrochronology
輩 *nempai* age, age of experience
輩者 *nempaisha* elderly person

16頭 *toshigashira* the oldest person; beginning of the year. *nentō* beginning of the year
17齢 *nenrei* age
18額 *nengaku* yearly amount
19瀬 *toshi(no)se* New Year's Eve, the year end
譜 *nempu* personal chronological history
22鑑 *nenkan* yearbook

6

局 See 局 1384. [尸]

免 189 F-X See 免 573. [儿]

良 190 F-X See 良 3885. [艮]

呑 191 F-X See 呑 39. [口]

夾 192 F477 Kyō insert between. [大]
14雑物 *kyōzatsubutsu* foreign element, impurity, admixture

B 励 193 F269 勵 REI. *hage(mu)* be diligent. *hage(masu)* encourage, inspire; raise (the voice). *hage(mi)* encouragement, stimulation; incentive. [力]
6行 *reikō suru* enforce strictly, carry out (regulations)
合 *hage(mi)-a(u)* vie with one another. *hage(mi)a(i)* encouragement, emulation
7声 *reisei* shouts of encouragement
14精 *reisei* diligence

B 寿 194 F448 壽 SU. JU age; one's natural life; longevity; congratulations. *kotobu(ku)* congratulate; wish one well. *kotoho(gu)* congratulate. *kotobuki* long life; congratulations. [士]
5司 *sushi* rice mixed with other foods
6老人 *Jurōjin* a god of longevity
8命 *jumyō* life, life span
9盃 *juhai* toasting, drinking to someone's health
12詞 *yogoto* congratulating an emperor for a long prosperous reign
賀 *juga* long-life celebrations, particularly the 61st, 77th, and 88th birthdays
14像 *juzō* statue (of a living person)
17齢 *jurei* long life; age; life

A 系 195 F1437 KEI system; lineage; faction, group; zone; corollary; connection. [糸]
6列 *keiretsu* order, succession
列化 *keiretsuka suru* put in order, systematize
7図 *keizu* genealogy, pedigree
図学 *keizugaku* genealogy (the study)
12統 *keitō* system; geological formation; lineage, ancestry
統的 *keitōteki* systematic
統神学 *keitō shingaku* systematic theology
統樹 *keitōju* geneological tree
19譜 *keifu* genealogy, lineage

B 束 196 F951 SOKU bundle, sheaf, ream (of paper). *taba(neru)* bundle, tie in a bundle; govern, manage, control. *tsuka(neru)* tie in bundles; fold (one's arms); administer. *taba* bundle, bunch, sheaf, coil. *tabane* bundle; control, management. *tsuka* handbreadth; bundle. [木]
10帯 *sokutai* old ceremonial court dress
11脩 *sokushū* bundle of dried meat; present to a teacher; registration fee
12間 *tsuka(no)ma* brief time, a moment
14髪 *sokuhatsu* Western hairdo
16積 *taba(ne)-tsu(mu)* shock (grain)
縛 *sokubaku* restraint, restriction, shackles

A 承 197 F775 JŌ. SHŌ. *u(keru)* (see under 受 2826.0). *uketamawa(ru)* hear, listen to, be informed. [手]
4引 *shōin* consent, acceptance, agreement
允 *shōin* consent, acceptance, agreement
6伏 *shōfuku* compliance, consent, submission
8服 *shōfuku* compliance, consent, submission
知 *shōchi* consent, assent, admitting, acknowledgment, compliance, agreement
知助 *shōchi(no)suke* agreement
9前 *shōzen* continued (from)
13継 *shōkei* succession, accession, inheritance
14認 *shōnin* approval, consent, agreement, recognition, acknowledgment
認状 *shōninjō* certificate of approval
15諾 *shōdaku* acquiescence, consent, agreement

兎 198 F188 兔 兎 To. *usagi* rabbit, hare, cony. [儿]
3口 *mitsukuchi* harelip
4欠 *iguchi, toketsu* harelip
毛 *u(no)ke* just a hair
6耳 *usagi mimi* long ears; a gossiper
肉 *toniku* rabbit meat
有 *to(mo)a(re)* anyhow, in any case
7角 *to(nimo)kaku(nimo), to(ni)kaku, to(ya)kaku, to(mo)kaku(mo), to(mo)kaku, tokaku* anyhow, anyway, somehow or other, generally speaking, in any case. *tokaku* this and that; many; be apt to
9狩 *usagiga(ri)* rabbit hunting
10馬 *usagiuma* donkey

11 脣 *iguchi, mitsukuchi, toshin* harelip
12 結 *usagi musu(bi)* loop knot
斯 *to(ya)kō* this or that
14 網 *usagi ami* rabbit-catching net

B **卵** 199/F298 Ran ovum. *tamago* egg; spawn, roe; (an expert) in the making. [卩]

3 子 *ranshi* ovum, ovule, egg cell
5 生 *ransei* oviparity; produced from eggs
白 *rampaku* white of an egg, albumin
6 色 *tamago iro* yellowish color
7 状 *ranjō* egg-shaped
形 *tamagogata, rankei* egg-shaped, oval
8 泡立器 *tamago-awada(te)ki* egg beater
9 胞 *ranhō* egg sac
11 黄 *ran-ō* yolk of an egg
殻 *rankaku* eggshell
細胞 *ransaibō* ovum, egg cell
巣 *ransō* ovary
巣炎 *ransōen* ovaritis
12 焼 *tamagoyaki* fried eggs; omelet
塔 *rantō* oval tombstone
塔場 *rantōba* cemetery
14 管 *rankan* fallopian tube, oviduct
22 嚢 *rannō* egg case

A **我** 200/F759 Ga ego, self, selfishness, egotism. *waga* my, our, one's own. *ware* I, oneself, self, ego. [戈]

2 人 *ware-hito* myself and others
4 心 *waga kokoro* my heart
方 *wagahō* our side, we
5 立 *ga (o) ta(teru)* insist on one's own ideas
出 *ga (o) da(su)* insist on one's own ideas
乍 *ware naga(ra)* for me (to do such a thing)
田引水 *gaden insui* drawing water for one's own field, promoting one's own interests
6 先 *waresaki ni* self first
7 身 *wagami* myself, oneself
折 *ga (o) o(ru)* defer to another
我 *wareware* we. *ware(mo)-ware(mo)* vying with one another
君 *waga kimi* my lord
利 *gari* self-interest
利我利 *garigari* selfishness, selfish person
8 国 *wa(ga) kuni* our country
知 *wareshi(razu)* involuntarily, instinctively
事 *wagakoto* personal affair
武者羅 *gamushara na* reckless, daredevil
物 *wagamono* one's own property
物顔 *wagamonogao* like one's own. *wagamonogao ni* in a lordly manner
9 通 *ga (o) tō(su)* insist on one's own ideas
10 流 *garyū* self-taught; one's own way
家 *wagaya* our home, our house
党 *wa(ga)tō* our party
11 張 *ga (o) ha(ru)* insist on one's own ideas
情 *gajō* selfishness; bias; personal feelings
欲 *gayoku* selfishness
執 *gashū* egotism; obstinacy
12 勝 *warega(chi)* everybody for himself
等 *warera* we
13 意 *ga-i* self-will, obstinacy
意得 *waga-i (o) e(ru)* approve of
14 慢 *gaman* patience, perseverance, endurance, tolerance, self-control, self-denial
15 褒 *warebome* self-praise
輩 *wagahai* I
16 儘 *wagamama* selfishness, egoism; wilfulness, disobedience; whim

A **兵** 201/F206 Hei, Hyō soldier, private; troops, army; warfare; arms; strategy, tactics. *tsuwamono* soldier, warrior. [八]

2 力 *heiryoku* military force; force of arms; strength of an army
3 士 *heishi* soldier
刃 *heijin* sword blade
4 戈 *heika* swords; arms; warfare
火 *heika* fire caused by war
5 仗 *heijō* arms; armed soldier
6 団 *heidan* army corps
式体操 *heishiki taisō* military drill
7 車 *heisha* war chariot
乱 *heiran* war, disturbance
児帯 *heko-obi* waist band
役 *heieki* military service
役忌避 *heieki-kihi* evading the draft
役免除 *heieki menjo* draft exemption
8 長 *heichō* lance corporal
制 *heisei* military system
卒 *heisotsu* soldier, private
舎 *heisha* barracks
事 *heiji* military affairs
法 *heihō* art of war, strategy, tactics
法家 *heihōka* tactician, strategist
学 *heigaku* military science, strategy, tactics
学者 *heigakusha* tactician, strategist
学校 *heigakkō* naval academy
9 革 *heikaku* arms; war
食 *heishoku* food for soldiers and noncommissioned officers
威 *hei-i* military power
科 *heika* branch of the army
変 *heihen* military disturbance
10 馬 *heiba* arms and cavalry; troops; war; military affairs
匪 *heihi* bandits
員 *hei-in* military strength, military personnel
家 *heika* soldier; tactician, strategist
書 *heisho* book on military science
站 *heitan* supply train, communications
站学 *heitangaku* logistics
站部 *heitambu* commissariat

站基地 *heitan kichi* supply base
站線 *heitansen* supply line, line of communications
11略 *heiryaku* strategy
船 *heisen* warship
隊 *heitai* soldier; sailor
曹 *heisō* warrant officer
曹長 *heisōchō* chief warrant officer
12備 *heibi* war preparations
営 *heiei* barracks
13禍 *heika* ravages of war
粮 *hyōrō* (army) provisions, food
数 *heisū* number of soldiers
14種 *heishu* branch of an army
端 *heitan* hostilities; beginning of hostilities
語 *heigo* military term
15権 *heiken* military authority
鋒 *heihō* the point of a sword; the advance of an army
器 *heiki* arms, ordnance
器工 *heikikō* armorer
器工場 *heiki kōjō* arsenal, ordnance factory, armory
器庫 *heikiko* armory
器廠 *heikishō* armory, arsenal, ordnance department
18難 *heinan* distress of war
燹 *heisen* fire caused by war
糧 *hyōrō* (army) provisions; food
糧米 *heiryōmai* army rice
糧攻 *hyōrōze(me)* starvation tactics
20籍 *heiseki* military register

A **来** 202/F123 **來徠耒** RAI coming. *ki(taru)* come, arrive; be due to; next, forthcoming. *ki(tasu)* cause, bring about, produce. *ku(ru)* come, come to hand, arrive, approach; call on; come on (rain); set in, be due; become, grow, get; come from; be caused by; derive from. *-rai* since (last month); for (10 days). *rai-* next (year). [人]

4方 *kikata* your coming. *ki(shi)kata, ko(shi)kata* the past
月 *raigetsu* next month
日 *rainichi* arrival in Japan; coming to Japan. *ku(ru)hi* the coming days
日来日 *ku(ru)hi(mo)-ku(ru)hi(mo)* every day
5立 *kita(te)* new arrival
由 *raiyū*=*yurai* 由来 89.7
付 *kitsu(keru)* call frequently
可 *ki(taru)be(ki)* the coming, the next
世 *raisei* the future, posterity. *raise* the next world
6迎 *raigō* the coming of Amida Buddha to welcome the spirits of the dead; mountaintop sunrise
向 *ki-mu(kau)* come facing (us)
任 *rainin* arrival at one's post
阪 *raihan* coming to Osaka
合 *ki-a(waseru)* happen to come along
宅 *raitaku* coming of a visitor to one's home
年 *rainen, ku(ru)toshi* the coming year
会 *raikai* attendance
会者 *raikaisha* attendance, those present
7車 *raisha* your coming, your visiting me
攻 *raikō* invasion
状 *raijō* letter received
社 *raisha* visit to a company
邸 *raitei* visiting someone's residence
来週 *rairaishū* week after next
8店 *raiten* coming to the store
往 *raiō* going and coming, next year
9信 *raishin* letter received
院 *rai-in* coming to the hospital
春 *raishun, raiharu* next spring
客 *raikyaku, raikaku* visitor, caller
客攻会 *raikyakuzeme (ni) a(u)* be besieged with visitors
客筋 *raikyaku suji* customers, clients
10週 *raishū* next week
航 *raikō* arrival of ships; arrival by ship
貢 *raikō suru* come to pay tribute
書 *raisho* letter received
11掛 *ki-ka(karu)* happen to come. *kiga(ke) ni* on the way here
寇 *raikō* invasion, raid
遊 *raiyū* visit
遊者 *raiyūsha* visitor, tourist
訪 *raihō* visit, call
訪者 *raihōsha* visitor, caller
12復 *raifuku* return, coming back
援 *raien* assistance, support
診 *raishin* doctor's visit
朝 *raichō* arrival in Japan, visiting Japan
着 *raichaku* arrival
賀 *raiga* your coming; coming with happy news
場 *raijō* attendance
場者 *raijōsha* those attending
13電 *raiden* incoming telegram
意 *rai-i* purpose of a visit
14歴 *raireki* history, career
15談 *raidan* interview
駕 *raiga* your coming, your presence
賓 *raihin* guest, visitor; visitor's arrival
賓席 *raihinseki* visitors' seats
17聴 *raichō* attendance
臨 *rairin* attendance, presence; visit, coming, advent
鮮 *raisen* coming to Korea
18難 *kiniku(i)* difficult to come
観 *raikan* inspection visit
観者 *raikansha* visitor (to an exhibit)
22襲 *raishū* raid, attack, invasion

7

肩 肩 See 1820. [肉]

1 一 丨 丶 【丿】 7 乙 亅

皁 See 4977. [阜]

臾 See 106. [臼]

果 See 107. [木]

承 See 197. [手]

卯 See 199. [卩]

戾 See 戻 1818. [戸]

卑 See 卑 221. [十]

兔 See 兎 198. [儿]

幷 203 / F627 See 并 580. [干]

來 204 / F123 See 来 202. [人]

鼡 Nonstandard for 鼠 5417.

炙 205 / F1181 SHA. *abu(ru)* (see under 焙 2768.0). [火]

乖 206 / F57 KAI oppose, disobey.
19 離 *kairi* estrangement, separation

毟 207 / F1060 (国字) *mushi(ru)* pluck, pick, tear. [毛]
8 取 *mushi(ri)-to(ru)* tear off, pluck off

B **岳** 208 / F598 嶽 GAKU. *take* peak, mountain. [山]
4 父 *gakufu* father-in-law

忝 209 / F692 忝 TEN. *katajikena(i)* grateful, indebted. *katajikena(kumo)* graciously. [小]
10 涙 *katajike namida* tears of gratitude

A **刷** 210 / F242 SATSU. *su(ru)* print. [刂]
8 子 *sasshi, hake* brush; commutator brush
上 *su(ri)-a(agaru)* be off the press. *su(ri)-a(geru)* finish printing, print off
4 込 *su(ri)-ko(mu)* insert (an illustration); stencil (a pattern)
毛 *hake* paint brush
毛目 *hakeme* brush marks
毛先 *hake saki* brush tip
5 立 *su(ri)ta(te)* just off the press
出 *su(ri)-da(su)* print, publish; begin to print
本 *su(ri)hon* printed book
8 物 *su(ri)mono* printed matter
直 *su(ri)-nao(su)* reprint
11 違 *su(ri)chiga(i)* misprint
13 損 *su(ri)-sokona(u)* misprint, spoil in printing
新 *sasshin* reform, renovation, innovation

B **垂** 211 / F421 SUI. *ta(rasu)* suspend, hang down; slouch. *ta(reru), shida(reru) vt* and *vi* hang, droop, drop, lower, pull down; dangle; sag; drip, ooze, trickle; leave behind (at death); give, confer. *tare* hanging; straw curtain; lapel; pocket flap; skirts of a coat; gravy; soy sauce. *nannan to suru* be on the verge of (doing), be close to. [土]
3 下 *suika suru* be pendent, hang down. *ta(re)-sa(garu) vi* hang, dangle. *ta(re)-sa(geru) vt* hang (a curtain); droop (a tail); lower (a blind)
4 込 *ta(rashi)-ko(mu) vt* drop into drop by drop
木 *taruki* rafter
5 示 *suishi* instruction
6 耳 *taremimi* lop-eared
8 直 *suichoku* vertical, perpendicular
直線 *suichokusen* perpendicular line
9 迹 *suijaku* appearances of Buddha to save men
10 涎 *suizen* watering at the mouth
11 教 *suikyō* information, instruction
13 楊 *suiyō* weeping willow
飾 *tarekaza(ri)* pendant
幕 *taremaku* hanging screen, curtain
準 *suijun* plummet, plumb line
14 髪 *suberakashi* hair tied in back and hanging down. *taregami* long flowing hair
15 穂 *ta(ri)ho* drooping ears (of grain)
線 *suisen* perpendicular line
範 *suihan suru* set an example
22 籠 *ta(re)-ko(meru)* lie over, hang over; stay indoors

B **奉** 212 / F479 HŌ. BU. *hō(zuru)* present, dedicate; obey, follow, believe in, serve. *matsu(ru), tatematsu(ru)* offer, present; revere; do respectfully. [大]
4 公 *hōkō* public service; apprenticeship
公人 *hōkōnin* servant, employee
公口 *hōkōguchi* place of employment
公先 *hōkōsaki* place of employment
5 加 *hōga* donation
加帳 *hōgachō* subscription list

仕 *hōshi* service, serving
仕女 *hōshime* deaconess
仕者 *hōshisha* servant (of the people)
6行 *bugyō* shogunate administrator
灯 *hōtō* votive lantern
安 *hōan suru* enshrine
迎 *hōgei* welcome
迎門 *hōgeimon* welcome arch
7伺 *hōshi suru* inquire about (one's health)
体 *hōtai suru* carry out the will of one's lord
呈 *hōtei* dedication, presentation
8送 *hōsō suru* see an emperor off
拝 *hōhai* worship
祀 *hōshi suru* enshrine
9持 *hōji* bear, present, hold up (the emper-
祝 *hōshuku* celebration ⌊or's picture)
10書 *hōsho* high-quality paper
納 *hōnō* dedication, offering, oblation
納物 *hōnōbutsu* votive offering
納額 *hōnōgaku* votive tablet
11唱 *hōshō* singing
12答 *hōtō* reply to the throne
賀 *hōga* respectful congratulations
賀帳 *hōgachō* subscription list
13献 *hōken suru* offer (to a shrine)
献式 *hōkenshiki* dedicatory ceremony
献物 *hōkembutsu* votive offering
献頌 *hōkenshō* offertory; offertory music
14読 *hōdoku* respectful reading
15還 *hōkan suru* restore to the emperor
弊 *hōhei* offering
弊使 *hōheishi* imperial messenger to a shrine, envoy returning courtesies
17戴 *hōtai suru* have (a prince for a president); be the recipient of (an imperial favor); reverently accept
18職 *hōshoku suru* be in the service of

A **東** 213/F952 Tō *higashi* east. *azuma* east; Eastern Japan. [木]

3上 *tōjō* going to Tokyo; going east 「Orient
4方 *tōhō, tōbō* east, eastward; eastern; the
方教会 *Tōhō Kyōkai* The Eastern Church
天 *tōten* the eastern sky
天紅 *tōtenkō* crowing in the morning
5北 *tōhoku, higashikita* northeast. *Tōhoku* the
北人 *Tōhokujin* Northeasterner ⌊Northeast
半 *tōhan* the eastern half
半球 *Higashi Hankyū* Eastern Hemisphere
6行 *tōkō* eastbound
向 *higashimu(ki)* facing east
邦 *Tōhō* Oriental country, the Orient
夷 *tōi* eastern barbarians
印度 *Higashi Indo* East Indies
印度会社 *Higashi Indo Gaisha* East India Company

西 *tōzai* east and west; Orient and Occident; Your attention please.
西屋 *tōzaiya* town crier 「north
西南北 *tōzainamboku* east, west, south, and
7男 *azuma otoko* a man from East Japan
亜 *Tōa* East Asia, the Orient 「ples
亜諸民族 *Tōa shominzoku* East-Asian peo-
亜諸国 *Tōa shokoku* East-Asian countries
8門 *tōmon* eastern gate
国 *tōgoku* eastern country; eastern provinces; Kanto Provinces
径 *tōkei* east longitude
征 *tōsei* eastern expedition
欧 *Tōō* Eastern Europe
郊 *tōkō* eastern suburbs
京都 *Tōkyōto* Tokyo Metropolis
奔西走 *tōhon-seisō suru* busy oneself, bestir oneself, be on the go, take an active
岸 *tōgan* eastern coast; east bank ⌊interest
岸沿 *tōganzo(i) ni* along the east coast; along the eastern seashore 「the east
9面 *tōmen* facing the east; east face, east side;
風 *tōfū, kochi, kochi kaze* east wind; spring wind
屋 *azumaya* arbor, bower, summer house
独 *Tōdoku* East Germany
軍 *tōgun* the eastern army
南 *tōnan, higashiminami,* southeast
南亜 *Tōnan-a* Southeast Asia
海 *tōkai* eastern sea
海地方 *Tōkai Chihō* Eastern-Sea Area
海道 *Tōkaidō* Eastern Sea Road
洋 *Tōyō* Orient
洋人 *Tōyōjin* Orientals
洋主義 *Tōyō shugi* the Orient for the
洋風 *tōyōfū no* Oriental ⌊Orientals
洋通 *Tōyōtsū* Orientalist
洋段通 *Tōyō dantsū* Oriental rug
10進 *tōshin suru* proceed east
航 *tōkō* sailing east, eastbound
部 *tōbu* eastern part
都 *Tōto* the Eastern Capital, Yedo; Tokyo
宮 *tōgū, haru(no)miya* crown prince
11側 *higashigawa* east side, east bank. *tōsoku*
清 *Tōshin* Eastern China ⌊east side
経 *tōkei* east longitude
寄 *higashiyo(ri)* easterly (wind)
12雲 *shinonome* daybreak, dawn
14遷 *tōsen suru* move (the capital) east
漸 *tōzen* eastward advance
端 *tōtan* east end, eastern tip
歌 *tōka* the old Kanto-area folk songs

— 8 —

扁扁 See 1822. [戸]

1 一 丨 丶 B 丿 乙 亅

帥 See 109. [巾]

奏 See 1178. [大]

彥 彦 See 3347. [彡]

勉 214 F262 See 勉 228. [力]

B 盾 215 F1320 JUN. *tate* shield, buckler, escutcheon; pretext. [目]

咫 216 F353 SHI short; span. [口]
4尺 *shiseki* a very short distance

胤 217 F1540 IN descendant. *tane* issue, offspring; paternal blood. [肉]
11違 *tanechiga(i)* half-brother; half-sister

A 省 218 F1320 SEI. SHŌ ministry, department; province (in China). *habu(ku)* omit, eliminate; curtail, economize. *kaeri(miru)* (see under 顧 5141.0). *tsukasa* (see under 司 877.0). [目]
5令 *shōrei* ministerial ordinance
11略 *shōryaku* abbreviation, abridgment, omission
12筆 *shōhitsu* abbreviation; simplified form of a character. *seihitsu* cutting out some strokes in a character; omitting some passages
営 *shōei* operated by the government
14察 *seisatsu* reflection, consideration
15線 *Shōsen* Government Railway Line

眉 219 F1321 BI. MI. *mayu* eyebrow. [目]
4毛 *mayuge* eyebrows
5目 *bimoku* face, looks, features
尻 *mayujiri* end of an eyebrow
6宇 *biu* brow(s)
尖刀 *naginata* halberd
7庇 *mabisashi* visor; eyeshade
11雪 *bisetsu* snow-white eyebrows
唾物 *mayutsubamono* fake
12間 *miken* brow, middle forehead
14墨 *mayuzumi* blackened eyebrows; eyebrow pencil

叛 220 F317 HON. HAN rebellion. *somu(ku)* (see under 背 3754.0). [又]
4心 *hanshin* rebellious spirit
6臣 *hanshin* rebellious retainer
7乱 *hanran* rebellion
8逆 *hangyaku* treason, treachery, rebellion, insurrection, mutiny
9軍 *hangun* rebel army, mutinous troops
10徒 *hanto* rebels, insurgents
将 *hanshō* rebel leader
13賊 *hanzoku* rebel
跡 *hanseki* results of rebellion
意 *han-i* spirit of rebellion
14旗 *hanki* standard of revolt

B 卑 221 F288 卑 HI. *iya(shii)* humble; base, mean, vile, vulgar; greedy. *iya(shimu)*, *iyashi(meru)* despise. [十]
3小 *hishō* petty, trifling
下 *hige* humility, self-depreciation
6近 *hikin* common, simple
劣 *hiretsu* meanness, foul play
劣漢 *hiretsukan* a despicable person
7見 *hiken* my humble opinion
言 *higen* slang expression
8屈 *hikutsu* meanness, servility
怯 *hikyō* cowardice; meanness; unfairness
陋 *hirō* low rank; wickedness; vulgarity
金属 *hikinzoku* base metals
9俗 *hizoku na* vulgar, coarse
10称 *hishō* this wretch (oneself); you wretch
12属 *hizoku* lineal descendants (beyond grandchildren)
猥 *hiwai* indecency, obscenity
14語 *higo* slang
15賤 *hisen* low class

B 看 222 F1322 看 KAN. *mi(ru)* see. [目]
6守 *kanshu* jailer
守者 *kanshusha* jailer
8取 *mi-to(ru)* care for the sick. *kanshu suru* see thru, perceive, notice, get wind of
板 *kamban* sign, signboard, doorplate; poster, billboard; appearance; figurehead; policy; attraction; closing time
板屋 *kamban-ya* sign maker
板倒 *kambandao(re)* ostentatious
板娘 *kambam-musume* show girl
板描 *kambanka(ki)* sign painter
9点 *kanten* viewpoint
客 *kankaku* spectators, visitors, audience
10破 *miyabu(ru)*, *kampa suru* see thru, penetrate, fathom
病 *kambyō* nursing (a patient)
病人 *kambyōnin* nurse
病疲 *kambyōzuka(re)* nursing fatigue
11過 *kanka* connivance, shutting one's eyes to
做 *mina(su)* consider as
経 *kankin* silent sutra reading
貫 *kankan* weighing; platform scales
20護 *kango* nursing
護兵 *kangohei* army nurse, medic
護長 *kangochō* chief nurse (in the army)

護法 *kangohō* nursing art
護卒 *kangosotsu* army nurse, medic
護学 *kangogaku* nursing science
護疲 *kangotsuka(re)* nursing fatigue
護婦 *kangofu* (female) nurse
護婦長 *kangofuchō* head nurse
護婦学院 *kangofu gakuin* nurses' training school
護婦養成所 *kangofu yōseijo* nurses' training school

A **乗** 223/F57 **乘** Jō power (in math); multiplication; record; vehicle; vehicle counter. *no(ru), no(kkaru)* ride, board, mount; get up on; spread (paints); be taken in; share in, join; be found in (a dictionary); feel like doing; be mentioned in; be in harmony with. *no(seru)* place, put, lay, set; let (one) take part; impose on; record, mention. *no(ri-konasu)* manage (a horse). *jō(jiru), jō(zuru)* take advantage of; multiply (in math); follow blindly. *no(ri)* riding, ride; (two)-seater; spread (of paints).

2 入 *no(ri)-i(reru) vi* and *vt* ride or drive into (a place); extend (a line into a city). *no(ri)-i(ru)* ride or drive into (a place). *nori-i(re)* driving into
3 上 *no(ri)-a(geru)* run aground, be stranded
4 手 *no(ri)te* passenger; rider, good rider
反 *no(ruka)-so(ruka)* win or lose, sink or swim
込 *no(ri)-ko(mu) vt* and *vi* board, embark on, get into (a car); ship (passengers); man (a ship); help (someone) into; march into, enter
切 *no(ri)-ki(ru), nokki(ru)* overcome, get thru. *no(ri)-ki(ru)* ride or sail across; weather, tide over
心地 *no(ri)gokochi* one's feeling while riding
5 付 *no(ri)-tsu(keru)* ride up to; get used to riding. *no(ri)tsu(ke)* one's regular (taxi)
出 *no(ri)-da(su)* set out, set sail; embark on; lean forward; begin to ride
用自動車 *jōyō jidōsha* passenger auto
用車 *jōyōsha* passenger auto
6 回 *no(ri)-ma(waru)* ride around. *no(ri)-ma(wasu) vt* drive (a car) around, ride (a bicycle) around
気 *no(ri)ki* interest, eagerness
号 *jōgō* sign of multiplication
合 *no(ri)-a(wasu), no(ri)-a(waseru)* happen to ride together, share a vehicle. *noriai* bus, stagecoach; riding together; fellow passenger; joint partnership
合自動車 *noriai jidōsha* bus
合馬車 *noriai basha* stagecoach
合船 *noriaibune* ferryboat
7 戻 *no(ri)-modo(su)* ride (a horse) back, drive (a car) back
良 *no(ri)yo(i)* easy to ride, riding well
車 *jōsha* entraining
車口 *jōshaguchi* entrance to a station
車券 *jōshaken* passenger ticket
車賃 *jōshachin* railway fare
車駅 *jōsha eki* entraining point
8 逃 *no(ri)ni(ge)* stealing a ride; stolen ride
法 *jōhō* multiplication
物 *no(ri)mono* vehicle
取 *no(t)to(ru), no(ri)-to(ru)* capture, occupy, usurp
取策 *no(t)to(ri)saku* a plot against (someone)
9 飛 *no(ri)-to(basu)* tear along (the road)
通 *no(ri)-tō(ru)* ride thru, ride along
除 *jōjo* multiplication and division
客 *jōkyaku, jōkaku* passenger
降 *jōkō, no(ri)o(ri)* getting on and off
降者優先 *jōkōsha yūsen* priority to pedestrians
降場 *jōkōjō* (station) platform
10 進 *no(ri)-susu(meru)* ride forth
逸 *no(ri)-hagu(reru)* miss a train
員 *jōin* crew
馬 *jōba, no(ri)uma* riding horse; saddle horse
馬服 *jōbafuku* riding habit
馬隊 *jōbatai* mounted corps, cavalcade
馬靴 *jōbagutsu* riding boots
11 遅 *no(ri)-oku(reru)* miss (a train)
過 *no(ri)-su(gosu)* ride past
捨 *no(ri)-su(teru)* get off, abandon (a ship)
掛 *no(ri)-ka(keru), no(ri)-ka(karu)* be about to board; be riding on; get on top of; lean over; set about; collide with
移 *no(ri)-utsu(su)* transfer (a stowaway). *no(ri)-utsu(ru)* change (cars or horses), transfer; possess; inspire
船 *jōsen suru* embark; be on board
悪 *no(ri)niku(i)* hard to ride
務員 *jōmuin* trainman, train crew
組 *no(ri)-ku(mu)* get on aboard; join a ship. *noriku(mi)* crew
組員 *norikumi-in* crew
12 越 *no(ri)-ko(eru)* climb over; ride across; surmount. *no(ri)-ko(su)* ride past; pass; outdistance. *noriko(shi)* riding past (one's station)
場 *no(ri)ba* car stop, platform
替 *no(ri)-ka(eru)* transfer
換 *no(ri)-ka(eru)* transfer. *norika(e)* transfer
換券 *norikaeken* ticket for transfer
換場 *norika(e)ba* platform for transfer
換駅 *norikae eki* transfer point
13 損 *no(ri)-sokona(u)* miss (a train)
溢 *no(ri)-kobo(reru)* be crowded with passengers
馴 *no(ri)-na(rasu)* break in (a horse)
14 算 *jōzan* multiplication
15 潰 *no(ri)-tsubu(su)* ride (a horse) to death

1 一 | 、 [ノ] 乙 亅 8

16積 *jōseki* product (in math)
18冪 *jōbeki* power (in math)
20艦 *jōkan* joining one's warship

A 重 224/F1930 CHŌ. JŪ, nest of boxes. *kasa(neru)* pile up, heap up, add, repeat. *kasa(naru)* pile up, be piled up; lie on one another. *omo(ru)* get heavy; grow serious. *omo(njiru)*, *omo(nzuru)* honor, respect, esteem, prize. *omo(i)*, *omo(tai)* heavy; massive; serious; important; severe; oppressed. *omo(mi)* importance, weight, dignity. *omo(sa)* weight. *kasa(ne)* pile, heap, layer; suits; set; course (of stones). *kasa(nete)* repeatedly, again. *omo(na)*, *omo(naru)* main, principal, important. *jū-* heavy; double. *-e* -fold, ply. *-jū* -fold. [里]

2力 *jūryoku* gravity
3工業 *jūkōgyō* heavy industry
大 *jūdai na* important, serious
大化 *jūdaika* aggravation
大性 *jūdaisei* importance, seriousness
大視 *jūdaishi* taking (something) seriously
4心 *jūshin* center of gravity
火器 *jūkaki* heavy weapons
手 *omode* serious wound or injury
手代 *omotedai* head steward (of an estate)
水 *jūsui* heavy water
水素 *jūsuiso* heavy hydrogen
5用 *jūyō suru* appoint to a responsible post
目 *omome* a little heavy ⌈pickle-tub covers
石 *omoshi*, *omo(shi) ishi* stone weights on
立 *omoda(tsu)*, *omoda(tta)* main, principal, important, conspicuous, prominent
圧 *jūatsu* pressure
代 *jūdai* successive generations
犯 *jūhan*, *chōhan* felony; felon; old offender
出 *jūshutsu suru* cite again
母音 *jūbo-in* diphthong
6臣 *jūshin* chief vassal; senior statesman
任 *jūnin* heavy responsibility, important post; re-election, reappointment
刑 *jūkei* heavy sentence ⌈overlap; pile up
合 *kasa(nari)-a(u)* lie on top of each other,
7言 *jūgon* a succession of words of similar
囲 *jūi*, *chōi* close siege ⌊meaning
体 *jūtai* seriously ill
吹 *shibu(ku)* splash, spray
役 *omoyaku* heavy responsibilities; director. *jūyaku* director, directorate
利 *jūri* compound interest ⌈prison)
労働 *jūrōdō* heavy labor; hard labor (in
8味 *omomi* weight; importance; emphasis;
油 *jūyu* crude oil; fuel oil ⌊dignity
版 *jūhan* additional printing, literary piracy
刻 *jūkoku* reprinting

宝 *chōhō(garu)* find useful; think highly of. *chōhō* convenience, usefulness. *chōhō*, *jūhō* priceless treasure
苦 *omokuru(shii)* heavy, cumbrous; gloomy, oppressive, leaden; awkward (ex-
金属 *jūkinzoku* heavy metals ⌊pression)
9厚 *jūkō* thickness; composure and dignity. *chōkō* composure and dignity
科 *jūka* serious crime; heavy punishment
重 *kasa(ne)-gasa(ne)* frequently; sincerely; exceedingly. *omo-omo(shii)* serious, grave, dignified. *jūjū no* repeated, manifold. *jūjū ni* extremely. *jūjū nimo* re-
星 *jūsei* multiple star ⌊peatedly
奏 *jūsō* instrumental duet
軌条 *jūkijō* heavy rail ⌈bonate; baking soda
炭酸曹達 *jūtansan sōda* sodium bicar-
点 *jūten* colon; emphasis, importance
点主義 *jūten shugi* priority system
要 *jūyō na* important, momentous; essential; principal, major
要性 *jūyōsei* importance, gravity
要視 *jūyōshi suru* regard highly
要産業 *jūyō sangyō* key industry
10病 *jūbyō* serious illness
砲 *jūhō* heavy artillery
祚 *jūso*, *chōso* second accession to the throne
殺 *jūsatsu* double play
荷 *jūka* heavy freight; heavy responsibility. *omoni* load, heavy burden, encumbrance ⌈tion
恩 *chōon* special blessing. *jūon* heavy obliga-
書用羊皮紙 *kasa(ne)ga(ki)yō yōhishi* pal-
症 *jūshō* serious illness ⌊impsest
症者 *jūshōsha* the seriously ill
症例 *jūshōrei* serious cases (of illness)
11過 *omosu(giru)* be too heavy
掛 *kasa(ne)-ka(keru)* lap, overlap
液 *jūeki* heavy liquids
視 *jūshi* serious consideration
訳 *jūyaku* retranslation
陽 *chōyō* Chrysanthemum Festival (the 9th day of the 9th lunar month)
患 *jūkan* serious illness
曹 *jūsō* sodium bicarbonate, baking soda
責 *jūseki* heavy responsibility
商主義 *jūshō shugi* mercantilism
婚 *jūkon* bigamy
婚者 *jūkonsha* bigamist
12復 *chōfuku*, *jūfuku*＝重複 (see below–14)
湯 *omoyu* thin rice gruel, rice water
税 *jūzei* heavy taxation
詞 *kasa(ne) kotoba* repeated word or phrase
創 *omode* serious wound or injury
畳 *chōjō* piled one upon another; excellent, splendid

着 *kasa(ne)gi* wearing one garment over another
量 *jūryō* weight; heavyweight boxer
量挙 *jūryōa(ge)* weight lifting
量拳闘選手 *jūryō kentō senshu* heavyweight champion
量感 *jūryōkan* thick and heavy
量感覚 *jūryō kankaku* sense of weight
量選手 *jūryōsenshu* heavyweight champion
量噸 *jūryōton* dead-weight tonnage
量噸数 *jūryō tonsū* dead-weight tonnage
13 詰 *jūzume* food packed in nest of a lacquered boxes
愛 *jūai* endearment
罪 *jūzai* felony, serious crime
戦車 *jūsensha* heavy tank
禁錮 *jūkinko* imprisonment with hard labor
農主義 *jūnō shugi* emphasizing agriculture
傷 *jūshō, omode* serious wound or injury
傷者 *jūshōsha* severely wounded person
14 説 *jūsetsu* re-explanation
罰 *jūbatsu* heavy punishment
態 *jūtai* seriously ill
酸素 *jūsanso* heavy oxygen
複 *chōfuku, jūfuku* duplication, overlapping, repetition, redundancy
複保険 *jūfuku hoken* double insurance
15 縁 *jūen* double marriage (in the same family); intermarriage
器 *jūki* a treasure; an invaluable person
箱 *jūbako* nest of boxes
箱読 *jūbakoyo(mi)* corrupt pronunciation (*on-kun* mixture)
16 噸 *jūton* long ton
積 *jūseki suru* pile up
篤 *jūtoku na* serious (illness)
機 *jūki* heavy machine gun
機関銃 *jūkikanjū* heavy machine gun
17 聴 *jūchō* hard of hearing
謹慎 *jūkinshin* close confinement (in one's barracks)
18 職 *jūshoku* responsible position
鎮 *jūchin* leader, authority, mainstay
騎兵 *jūkihei* heavy cavalry
19 爆 *jūbaku* heavy bomber
爆撃機 *jūbakugekiki* heavy bomber

9

師 See 113. [巾]

泰 See 2526. [氺]

扇 扇 See 1823. [戸]

看 看 See 222. [目]

乘 225 F57 乗 See 223.

芻 226 F1589 Sū grass cutting; hay. [艸]

殷 227 F1051 In flourishing. [殳]
10 殷 *in-in(taru)* roaring, booming, bellowing, pealing, reverberating
11 盛 *insei* prosperity
12 富 *impu* wealth, prosperity
14 賑 *inshin* prosperity

A 勉 228 F262 勉 勈 BEN. *tsuto(meru)* (see under 勤 732.0). *tsuto(mete)* as much as possible; diligently. [力]
7 励 *benrei* diligence
8 学 *bengaku* study
11 強 *benkyō* study; diligence; discount, reduction
強中 *benkyōchū* while studying
強家 *benkyōka* scholar, diligent student

烏 229 F1183 U. O. *karasu* crow, raven. [灬]
3 口 *karasuguchi* ruling pen
4 木 *kokutan* ebony
6 行水 *karasu (no) gyōzui* a quick bath
合衆 *ugō(no)shū* disorderly crowd, mob
羽玉 *ubatama no* jet black; pitch dark
羽色 *karasuba iro* glossy black
有先生 *uyū sensei* fictitious person
有帰 *uyū (ni) ki(suru)* be reduced to ashes
7 貝 *karasugai* fresh-water mussel
8 金 *karasugane* money lent at daily interest
10 竜茶 *ūroncha* oolong tea
紙 *karasugami* coarse dark-brown paper
11 蛇 *karasu hebi* a black snake
野豌豆 *karasuno endō* vetch, tare
12 帽子 *eboshi* noble's court headgear
犀角 *usaikaku* black rhinoceros horn
13 賊 *ika* squid, cuttlefish
14 鳴 *karasuna(ki)* cry of the crow
滸 *oko(gamashii)* presumptuous, impertinent; ridiculous, absurd
滸沙汰 *oko(no)sata* stupidity, absurdity, presumption, impertinence
17 濡羽色 *karasu no nureba iro* glossy black (hair)

A 島 230 F592 嶋 嶌 Tō *shima* island. [山]
2 人 *tōjin* islanders
3 山 *shimayama* island mountain
4 中 *tōchū* all over the island
内 *tōnai* on the island

5田 *shimada* a hairdo
庁 *tōchō* island government office
巡 *shimamegu(ri)* island tour
主 *tōshu* island chief ⌈of Eternal Youth
台 *shimadai* ornament representing the Isle
司 *tōshi* island governor
民 *tōmin* islanders
6伝 *shimazuta(i)* island-hopping
守 *tōshu, shimamori* island chief
8育 *shimasoda(chi)* brought up on an island
国 *shimaguni, tōgoku* island country
国根性 *shimaguni konjō* insularism
9風 *shimakaze* island wind
帝国 *tōteikoku* island empire
10根 *shimane* island country
流 *shimanaga(shi)* exile, banishment ⌈exile
破 *shimayabu(ri)* escaping from an island
陰 *shimakage* the other side of the island
島 *shimajima* islands
16嶼 *tōsho* islands

10

扈 See 1824. [戸]

巣 See 141. [巛]

悤 See 怱 1660. [心]

尉 231 F564 I. *jō* jailer; old man; rank; B company officer. [寸]
8官 *ikan* company officer

兜 232 F190 Tō. To. *kabuto* helmet, headpiece. [儿]
6虫 *kabuto mushi* beetle

雀 233 F2010 Jaku. *suzume* sparrow. [隹]
12斑 *sobakasu* freckles
13蜂 *suzumebachi* wasp, hornet
21躍 *jakuyaku suru* leap for joy, exult

爽 234 F1210 Sō. *sawa(yakana)* refreshing, bracing; clear, resonant, sweet (voice); fluent. [爻]
7快 *sōkai na* refreshing, exhilarating
10凉 *sōryō na* cool and refreshing
11爽 *sawasawa toshite* refreshingly

梟 235 F981 Kyō. *fukurō* owl. *kyō(suru)* expose (a severed head). [木]
9首 *kyōshu* exposure of a severed head
10将 *kyōshō* brave general
11猛 *kyōmō* fierce
悪 *kyōaku* great treachery; very atrocious person
12雄 *kyōyū* ringleader, accomplished villain
13罪 *kyōzai* crime of exposing a severed head
15敵 *kyōteki* treacherous enemy

彫 236 F665 Chō carving. *ho(ru)* carve, engrave, chisel, sculpture, in- B scribe. [彡]
3工 *chōkō* carver, engraver, sculptor
上 *ho(ri)-a(geru)* emboss, carve in relief; finish carving or engraving
上細工 *ho(ri)a(ge)zaiku* relief work, embossing
4心鏤骨 *chōshin-rukotsu* excellent literary
5付 *ho(ri)-tsu(keru)* carve (designs) ⌊work
8金 *chōkin* metal carving ⌈tattooing
物 *ho(ri)mono* carving; engraving; sculpture;
刻 *ho(ri)-kiza(mu)* engrave, carve. *chōkoku* carving, engraving, sculpture
刻刀 *chōkokutō* graver, chisel
刻版 *chōkokuban* an engraving ⌈a statue
刻物 *chōkokubutsu* an engraving; a carving;
刻界 *chōkokukai* sculpture circles
刻師 *chōkokushi* engraver; carver
刻家 *chōkokuka* engraver; carver
刻術 *chōkokujutsu* sculpture; engraving; the plastic art
12琢 *chōtaku* carving and polishing
13塑 *chōso* carving and modeling
塑術 *chōsojutsu* the plastic art
14像 *chōzō* sculpture; carved statue, graven image

11

扉 See 1825. [戸]

雇 雇 See 1826. [隹]

兜 See 232. [儿]

粤 237 F1430 Etsu alas. [米]

棗 See 116. [木]

棘 238 F985 Kyoku thorn. *toge* thorn, splinter; spine; biting words. *odoro* briers, thicket, the bush. [木]

喬 239 F374 Kyō high; boasting. [口]
4木 *kyōboku* tall tree, forest tree, arbor

奥 240/F484 **奥** Ō. OKU heart, interior. *oku(maru)* lie deep in,
B extend far back. *oku(matte)* secluded, innermost. [大] ⌈recesses
3山 *okuyama* remote mountain, mountain
4手 *okute* late crops. *oku(no)te* left hand; upper hand; secret skills; secret, mystery; last resort, trump card
方 *okugata* lady, nobleman's wife
5付 *okuzuke* colophon
6行 *okuyuki* depth, length, in depth
印 *okuin* official seal
向 *okumu(ki)* inner part of the house
地 *okuchi, ōchi* interior, backwoods, hinterland ⌈northern part of Japan
州 *ōshū* interior province; the interior;
旨 *ōshi* deep truth; deep knowledge
7床 *okuyuka(shii)* refined, graceful, modest
妙 *ōmyō* secret
8底 *okusoko, okuzoko* depth, bottom (of one's
9院 *oku(no)in* inner sanctuary ⌊heart)
津城 *okutsuki* tomb, grave
津城所 *okutsukidokoro* tomb, grave
10庭 *oku niwa* inner garden, back yard
書 *okugaki* postscript (to a book); verification; publication data (in a book)
座敷 *oku zashiki* inner parlor
11深 *okubuka(i), okufuka(i)* deep, profound
許 *okuyuru(shi)* secret; initiation; diploma
12歯 *okuba* molars, back teeth
間 *oku(no)ma* inner room
勤 *okuzuto(me)* working as a lady's maid
御殿 *okugoten* noble's private quarters
13義 *okugi, ōgi* mystery, secret, hidden pur-
意 *okui* true intention ⌊pose
14様 *okusama, okusan* your or his wife; married lady; madam
様孝行 *okusan kōkō* devoted to one's wife

12

楽 See 2324. [木]

蜃 See 4657. [辰]

彙 See 1586. [彑]

奥 See **奥** 240. [大]

肅 See **粛** 115. [聿]

辟 241/F1853 HEKI false; punish; crime; law; ruler. [辛]

8易 *hekieki suru* wince; shrink back; succumb to; be frightened; be disconcerted

殿 242/F1053 TEN. DEN hall, mansion,
B palace, temple, rear guard. *dono* mister. *shingari* rear. *tono* lord; mansion, palace. *dono* Mr. [殳]
3下 *Denka* Highness
上 *tenjō, denjō* the court; palace circles; palace floor ⌈official
上人 *tenjōbito, denjōbito* courtier, court
上間 *tenjō(no)ma* palace floor
4方 *tonogata* men, gentlemen
中 *denchū* in the palace
6宇 *den-u* a shrine building
8舎 *densha* a palace
9軍 *dengun* rear guard
10原 *tonobara* the nobility; (polite for) man
11達 *tonotachi* the nobility; (polite for) visitors
堂 *dendō* palatial building
12御 *tonogo* gentlemen
14閣 *denkaku* palace
様 *tonosama* feudal lord
様仕事 *tonosama shigoto* dilettante work, amateur work (in art) ⌈(in art)
様芸 *tonosamagei* dilettantism; amateurism
様育 *tonosamasoda(chi)* brought up in
様風 *tonosamafū* lordly air ⌊luxury
様蛙 *tonosamagaeru* bullfrog, edible frog

13

睾 See 4211. [目]

熏 See **燻** 2817. [灬]

劂 243/F253 KETSU carve. [刂]
2人 *ketsujin* sculptor; carver; seal engraver

孵 244/F524 FU. *kae(su)* hatch, incubate. [子]
4化 *fuka* incubation, hatching
化器 *fukaki* incubator
7卵 *furan* incubation, hatching
卵器 *furanki* incubator

14

舗 See 552. [舌]

翩 245/F1509 **翩** HEN fluttering (of a flag); wave; turn; soar. [羽]
15翩 *hempen(taru)* fluttering; frivolous
18翻 *hempon(taru)* fluttering; frivolous

4

1 一 丨 丶 [丿] 乙 亅

14

B 戲 246/F763 戯 戯 GI. GE. *tawamu(reru)* play, sport, frolic; joke; flirt with. *tawa(keru)* fool, play the fool; act indecently; be silly over; talk foolishly, *ja(reru)*, *za(reru)* be playful, gambol. *jara(kasu)* calling for jokes. *odo(keru)* joke. *soba(eru)* play pranks, be spoiled. [戈]

3 口 *odo(ke)guchi* joke
4 文 *gibun* humorous writing
5 芝居 *odoke shibai* comedy, burlesque
6 曲 *gikyoku* drama, play
交 *zarekawa(su)* exchange jokes
7 言 *zaregoto, gigen* joke
作 *gesaku, gisaku* cheap literature, fiction; writing for amusement
作者 *gesakusha* fiction writer, dime novelist
8 画 *giga* cartoon, comics 「humorist
者 *tawa(ke)mono* fool. *odo(ke)mono* joker,
事 *zaregoto, tawamu(re)goto* wanton sporting
10 笑 *gishō* playful laughter
書 *gisho* rambling writings
12 絵 *zare-e* a picture drawn in fun
13 話 *odo(ke)banashi* funny story
14 語 *tawakoto*＝*uwagoto* 譫言 4444.7
歌 *zareuta* limerick, funny song, comic song

B 劇 247/F254 GEKI drama, play. *hage(shii)* (see 烈 2761.0). [刂]

4 化 *gekika* dramatization
文学 *geki bungaku* dramatic literature
6 団 *gekidan* troupe, theatrical company
7 作 *gekisaku* play writing
作家 *gekisakuka* playwright, dramatist
8 的 *gekiteki* dramatic
毒 *gekidoku* deadly poison
9 通 *gekitsū* dramatic expert
変 *gekihen*＝激変 2712.9
界 *gekikai* the stage, theatrical world
臭 *gekishū* strong odor
甚 *gekijin* intenseness, violence, severity, vehemence, keenness
映画 *geki eiga* film drama 「son
10 剤 *gekizai* powerful medicine; violent poi-
烈 *gekiretsu* violence, severity, intenseness,
11 道 *gekidō* drama, dramatic art ⌊fierceness
務 *gekimu* exhausting work
12 痛 *gekitsū* intense pain, sharp pain
評 *gekihyō* drama criticism
暑 *gekisho* severe heat
場 *gekijō* theater
場通 *gekijōkayo(i)* attending shows
13 詩 *gekishi* dramatic poetry
戦 *gekisen* severe fight
15 談 *gekidan* talk on drama
論 *gekiron* heated discussion
震 *gekishin* severe earthquake

16 壇 *gekidan* the stage, the theatrical world
薬 *gekiyaku* powerful medicine; violent
18 職 *gekishoku* exhausting work ⌊poison

15

戯 See 戯 246. [戈]

壁 See 1148. [土]

勵 See 励 193. [力]

頤 See 頤 5126. [頁]

舘 舘 See 館 5174. [舌]

劒 劔 See 剣 696. [刀]

縣 See 県 1362. [糸]

歔 248/F1032 KYO cry. [欠]

11 欷 *kyoki, susurina(ki)* sobbing, weeping

燄 249/F1200 燄 焔 焰 EN. *honoo, homura* flame, blaze. [火]

6 色 *enshoku* flame color, flame scarlet, bright
12 硝 *enshō* gunpowder, niter ⌊reddish orange
16 燄 *en-en(taru)* blazing, fiery

16

壓 250/F443 壓 See 圧 818. [土]

戲 251/F763 See 戯 246.

擧 See 挙 1902. [臼]

虧 252/F1657 KI wane. *ka(keru)* (the moon) wanes. [虍]

4 月 *kigetsu* waning moon
18 損 *kison suru* break

A 嚴 253/F389 嚴 GON. GEN strictness, severity. *gen(ni)* strictly, severely, rigidly. *gen (ni) suru* fortify, strengthen, secure. *gen(taru)* strict, severe, stern. *ikame(shii)* solemn, majestic; dreadful, stern, ostentatious. *kibi(shii)* severe, strict, stern; intense (cold). *ogoso(kana)* austere, majestic, dignified, stately, awful, impressive. *ikatsu(i)* grim, stern. [口]

⁴父 *gempu* your honored father
⁵冬 *gentō* severe winter 「rigidness
正 *gensei* strictness, impartiality, exactness,
正中立 *gensei chūritsu* strict neutrality
正科学 *gensei kagaku* exact science
⁶刑 *genkei* severe punishment
旨 *genshi* strict order; your order
守 *genshu* strict observance
存 *genson* real existence
⁷戒 *genkai* strict guard
君 *genkun* your honored father 「mand
⁸命 *gemmei* strict order, peremptory com-
⁹律 *genritsu* strict law 「measures
科 *genka* severe punishment, rigorous
封 *gempū suru* seal hermetically
重 *genjū* strictness, rigor, severity. *genjū na* firm, strong, secure 「verity
¹⁰格 *genkaku* strictness, rigor, austerity, se-
秘 *gempi* strict secrecy, top-secret
訓 *genkun* strict instruction
容 *gen-yō* stern expression
¹¹達 *gentatsu* strict order
探 *gentan* strict search, sharp lookout
密 *gemmitsu* strictness
粛 *genshuku* gravity, solemnity, seriousness, dignity, rigor, austerity
¹²寒 *genkan* intense cold
暑 *gensho* extreme heat 「authoritatively
然 *genzen to* solemnly, gravely, majestically,
¹³誅 *genchū suru* punish severely
禁 *genkin* ban, interdict, strict prohibition
¹⁴選 *gensen* careful selection
酷 *genkoku* severity, rigor 「measures
罰 *gembatsu* severe punishment, rigorous
¹⁵談 *gendan* strong protest, demand for an explanation, serious talk

17

歸 See 帰 1582. [止]

蹙 254/F1826 蹴 SHUKU a tight place; scowling; approaching, shrinking. [足]

18

贋 See 贋 840. [貝]

蹷 蹷 See 蹶 4587. [足]

A願 255/F2065 GAN prayer, petition, vow. *nega(u)* desire, wish, hope; beg, implore. *nega(i)* desire, wish, request, prayer; petition, application. *nega(wakuwa)* I pray. *nega(washii)* desirable. [頁] 「Buddhism)

²力 *ganriki* the power of prayer (in
³下 *nega(i)-sa(geru)* withdraw a request
⁴文 *gammon* Shinto or Buddhist prayer (read)
⁵立 *ganda(te)* Shinto or Buddhist prayer
叶 *nega(ttari)-kana(ttari)* everything working out as desired
主 *ganshu* a temple petitioner
出 *nega(i)-de(ru)* apply for. *nega(i)de* appli-
⁷状 *ganjō* written request ⌊cation, petition
求 *nega(i)-moto(meru)* entreat
⁸事 *nega(i)goto* prayer, one's desire 「blank
⁹面 *gammen* the front page of an application
¹⁰酒 *ganshu* praying at a temple or shrine for help to stop drinking
書 *gansho* written application or petition
¹¹掛 *ganga(ke)* Shinto or Buddhist prayer
望 *gambō, gammō* desire, wish, aspiration
¹³解 *ganhodo(ki)* release from a vow
意 *gan-i* object of an application

19

巖 See 1442. [山]

獻 See 献 2901.

嚴 256/F389 See 厳 253. [口]

20

顧 顧 See 5141. [頁]

21

贗 贗 See 贋 840. [貝]

22

巖 See 巌 1442. [山]

饜 257/F2090 See 饜 841. [食]

靨 See 73. [面]

23

魘 258/F2126 EN, YŌ. *una(sareru)* have a nightmare. [鬼]

24

顱 259/F2069 RO head, skull. [頁]

RAD. 乙 5

Otsu second (in order). Variants: 乚, ⺃ *tsuribari* fishhook.
Nickname: Fishhook.

B 乙 260 F58 ITSU. OTSU B, 2nd; the latter; duplicate. *otsu na* strange, queer, quaint; witty; stylish, spicy, chic; tasty; romantic. *kinoto* 2nd calendar sign.
[3]子 *otogo* last child
女 *otome* virgin, maiden
女心 *otomegokoro* a girl's feeling, a maiden's mind
[5]巡 *otsujun* second-class cruiser
[8]夜 *otsuya, itsuya* about 10 p.m.
[9]姫 *otohime* youngest princess

1

九 See 146.

A 七 261 F11 SHICHI *nana(tsu), na, nana* seven. [一]
[2]七日 *shichishichinichi* 49th day after death
十 *shichijū, nanajū* seventy
十人訳 *Shichijūninyaku* Septuagint
十路 *nanasoji* age seventy
[3]夕 *tanabata, shichiseki* July 7 Festival of the Weaver; prayer ceremony for children's artistic development
[4]日 *nanuka, nanoka* seven days; the seventh
月 *Shichigatsu* July ⌊day (of the month)
辺形 *shichihenkei* heptagon
不思議 *nanafushigi* the seven wonders
五三 *shichi-go-san* the lucky numbers 7, 5, and 3; shrine visit by children aged 7, 5, and 3
五三縄 *shimenawa* sacred shrine rope
五調 *shichigochō* seven-and-five-syllable meter ⌈(chances)
分三分 *shichibu-sambu* seven to three
分袖 *shichibusode* three-quarter sleeves
分搗 *shichibuzu(ki)* seventy percent polished (rice)
[5]生 *shichishō* seven lives ⌈colors
[6]色 *nana-iro, shichishoku* the seven prismatic
曲 *nanamaga(ri)* tortuous or spiral (path)
回忌 *shichikaiki* seventh anniversary of a death ⌈death
年忌 *shichinenki* seventh anniversary of a
[7]角形 *shichikakkei* heptagon ⌈day
[8]夜 *shichiya* celebration of a child's seventh
宝 *shippō* the seven treasures (gold, silver, pearls, agate, crystal, coral, and lapis lazuli); cloisonné
宝焼 *shippōyaki* cloisonné
[9]厘 *shichirin* earthen charcoal brazier (for
屋 *nana(tsu)ya* pawnshop ⌊cooking)
海 *nanatsu no umi* the seven seas
重 *nanae* sevenfold, seven-ply
星 *shichisei* the Big Dipper, Ursa Major
草 *nanakusa* the seven spring flowers; the
面鳥 *shichimenchō* turkey ⌊seven fall flowers
面倒 *shichimendō* great trouble, difficulty
[10]週祭 *Nanashū (no) Matsu(ri), Nanamawari (no) Iwai* the Feast of Weeks, Pentecost
[11]道 *shichidō* the seven districts of ancient Japan
絃琴 *shichigenkin* seven-stringed koto
堂伽藍 *shichidō garan* complete seven-structure temple compound
転八起 *nanakoro(bi)-yao(ki)* the vicissitudes of life; always rising after a fall
転八倒 *shittembattō* writhing in agony
[13]福神 *Shichifukujin* the Seven Gods of Luck
[14]種 *nanakusa* the seven spring flowers; the seven fall flowers ⌈cooking)
[15]輪 *shichirin* earthen charcoal brazier (for
賢 *shichiken* the seven wise men
[18]曜 *shichiyō* the seven luminaries (sun, moon, and five planets); the seven days of the week
[19]顚八起 *shichiten-hakki* always rising in spite of repeated failures; the vicissitudes of life
顚八倒 *shittembattō* writhing in agony

2

也 See 75.

巳 See 1460. [已]

已 See 1461. [巳]

乞 262 F63 KITSU. KOTSU. *ko(u)* (see under 請 4390.0).
[4]丐 *kotsugai* beggar
[8]取 *ko(i)-to(ru)* ask for and receive
[9]食 *kojiki* beggar; begging
[10]高評 *kōkōhyō* with the author's compliments ⌈his bride
[12]婿 *koi muko* bridgegroom who is loved by

3

巴 263 F607 HA. *tomoe* huge comma design. [巳]
5瓦 *tomoegawara* comma-pattern tile
旦杏 *hadankyō* plum

屯 264 F585 TON ton. CHUN. *tamuro* police station; camp, barracks. [屮]
5田 *tonden* colonization
田兵 *tondenhei* agricultural soldiers, colonizers 「police station
8所 *tonsho* post, quarters, military station;
12営 *ton-ei* military camp, barracks, camping

5

㐂 265 F-X Nonstandard for 喜 1115.

6

乱 See 3856.

7

乳 266 F64 NYŪ. *chi, chichi* milk; the breasts; B loop.
4牛 *chichi ushi, nyūgyū* milk cow, dairy cattle
化 *nyūka* emulsification
5汁 *nyūjū* milky juice; latex; milk
用牛 *nyūyōgyū* milk cow
兄弟 *chikyōdai* foster brother or sister
幼児 *nyūyōji* infant
石英 *nyūsekiei* milky quartz 「mother
母 *uba, nyūbo, omba* wet nurse, nursing
母車 *ubaguruma* baby buggy
白 *nyūhaku* milky white, lactescent
白色 *nyūhakushoku* milky white, lactescent
6色 *nyūshoku* milk white
7呑子 *chinomigo* baby, suckling child
状 *nyūjō* milky
状液 *nyūjō eki* milky juice, latex
児 *nyūji* suckling, infant, baby
児死亡率 *nyūji shibōritsu* infant mortality
児脚気 *nyūji kakke* infantile beriberi
8房 *chibusa, nyūbō* breast, nipple, udder
9首 *chikubi, chichi kubi* teat, nipple
香 *nyūkō* frankincense, olibanum
臭 *nyūshū* boyishness, inexperience. *chichikusa(i)* smelling of milk; immature
臭児 *nyūshūji* greenhorn, fledgling
10剤 *nyūzai* emulsion
11液 *nyūeki* latex
菓 *nyūka* emulsion
12歯 *nyūshi* first set of teeth
棒 *nyūbō* pestle
飲児 *chino(mi)go* baby, suckling child
13搾 *chichishibo(ri)* milking; milker
腺 *nyūsen* mammary gland
酪 *nyūraku* butter
鉢 *nyūbachi, nyūhachi* mortar
業 *nyūgyō* the dairy business
14製品 *nyūseihin* dairy products
様突起 *nyūyō-tokki* mastoid
酸 *nyūsan* lactic acid
酸菌 *nyūsankin* lactic-acid bacilli
16濁 *nyūdaku* emulsion
糖 *nyūtō* milk sugar, lactose
頭 *nyūtō* nipple, teat
17癌 *nyūgan* breast cancer
19繰 *chichiku(ru)* have illicit sex relations
離 *chibana(re), chichibana(re)* weaning

8

胤 See 217. [肉]

10

乾 See 784.

13

亂 267 F66 亂 See 乱 3856.

RAD. 亅 6

Hane bō feathered stick or *kagi* hook, barb. Nickname: Barb.

1

亍 See 2. [一]

了 268 F67 RYŌ. *ryō(suru)* finish, complete; B understand. *ryō to suru* acknowledge. *shima(u)* get thru with
7見 *ryōken*＝了簡 (see below–18)
承 *ryōshō* acknowledgment
8知 *ryōchi suru* know, understand, appreciate
12覚 *ryōkaku suru* come to understand
13解 *ryōkai* understanding, comprehension
18簡 *ryōken* idea, thought, intention, inclination, motive, decision; discretion; forgiveness; toleration

簡違 *ryōkenchiga(i)* wrong idea; delusion; indiscretion, false step

2

孑 269/F518 KETSU mosquito larva. [子]

³孑 *bōfura, bōfuri* mosquito larva

A 才 270/F771 SAI ability, talent, aptitude, genius, acumen, intelligence, wit; cubic foot; =歳 (see under 2434.0) *zae* intelligence, ability, talent. [手]

²人 *saijin* talented person, clever person
力 *sairyoku* abilty, talent
³女 *saijo* talented woman
子 *saishi* talented man, clever man
⁴分 *saibun* disposition
⁶色 *saishoku* wit and beauty
名 *saimei* fame; reputation for ability
気 *saiki* wisdom
気煥発 *saiki-kampatsu* great wisdom
気縦横 *saiki-jūō* great wisdom
⁷走 *saibashi(ru)* be clever, be quick-witted, be precocious
芸 *saigei* talent and accomplishments; wisdom and works
⁸物 *saibutsu=saijin* 才人 (see above–2)
知 *saichi* wit and intelligence
学 *saigaku* talent and education
¹⁰能 *sainō* talent, ability
¹¹略 *sairyaku* wise planning.
略有 *sairyaku (no) a(ru)* resourceful
¹²媛 *saien* literary woman; talented woman
弾 *saihaji(keru)* be presumptuous, be clever and forward
腕 *saiwan* skill, ability
量 *sairyō* measurement
筆 *saihitsu* literary talent, clever style
智 *saichi* wit and intelligence
覚 *saikaku* ready wit; raising (money); plan, device
¹³幹 *saikan* ability
槌 *saizuchi* small wooden mallet
槌頭 *saizuchi atama* head like a hammer head
¹⁴徳 *saitoku* intelligence and virtue
¹⁵器 *saiki* talent
¹⁶噸 *saiton* measured ton
¹⁹藻 *saisō* poetic talent

3

A 予 271/F1783 豫 YO I, myself, the writer. *arakaji(me)* previously. *kane(te)* previously, already, lately. [豕]

⁴予 *kanegane* often, lately, already
⁵示 *yoji suru* show signs of, foreshadow
令 *yorei* preparatory command
⁶行 *yokō* rehearsal
行演習 *yokō enshū* rehearsal
防 *yobō* prevention, protection against
防医学 *yobō igaku* preventive medicine; a prophylactic
防法 *yobōhō* precautionary measures
防注射 *yobō chūsha* immunization, shots
防接種 *yobō sesshu* immunization, vaccination
防策 *yobōsaku* precautionary measures
防戦争 *yobō sensō* preventive war
防線 *yobōsen* guard (against attack)
防薬 *yobōyaku* prophylactic medicine
⁷見 *yoken suru* foresee, foreknow. *yoken* divination
告 *yokoku* previous notice, preliminary announcement
言 *yogen* prediction, prognostication. *kanegoto* prediction; promise
言者 *yogensha* predictor, prognosticator
⁸波 *yoha*=余波 408.8
知 *yochi* intimation, premonition, foreknowledge, prediction
表 *yohyō suru* prefigure, foreshadow
定 *yotei* prearrangement; program, plan; expectation; estimate
定日 *yoteibi* scheduled date, expected date
定案 *yoteian* program, prospectus
定期日 *yotei kijitsu* prearranged date
定期限 *yotei kigen* target date
定説 *yoteisetsu* predestination
⁹後 *yogo* prognosis, aftereffects, recuperation, convalescence
科 *yoka* preparatory course; preparatory department
科生 *yokasei* preparatory-department student
約 *yoyaku* contract, subscription, booking, reservation, pledge, advance order
約出版 *yoyaku shuppan* publication after securing subscriptions
約名簿 *yoyaku meibo* subscription list
約者 *yoyakusha* subscriber
約済 *yoyakuzu(mi)* reserved, engaged
¹⁰納 *yonō* advance payment
¹¹習 *yoshū* lesson preparation; rehearsal
断 *yodan suru* guess, predict, conclude
¹²測 *yosoku* forecast, estimate
期 *yoki* expectation, anticipation, hope, foresight, forecast
覚 *yokaku* hunch, foreboding, premonition
報 *yohō* forecasting, prediction, previous notification
報音 *yohōon* telephone time-warning sound
備 *yobi* preparation; preliminaries; reserve; spare
備工作 *yobi kōsaku* spade work, preliminaries
備士官学校 *yobi shikan gakkō* reserve officers' cadet school
備交渉 *yobi kōshō* preliminary negotiations
備会議 *yobi kaigi* preliminary conference

備兵 *yobihei* reservists
備役 *yobieki* service in the first reserve
備判事 *yobi hanji* supernumerary judge
備金 *yobikin* reserve fund, emergency fund
備知識 *yobi chishiki* background knowledge
備協約 *yobi kyōyaku* preliminary agreement
備科 *yobika* preparatory course
備品 *yobihin* spares, reserve supply
備室 *yobishitsu* spare room
備馬 *yobiba* spare horse
備校 *yobikō* preparatory school
備員 *yobi-in* reserve men
備部品 *yobi buhin* spare parts
備座席 *yobi zaseki* rumble seat
備将校 *yobi shōkō* reserve officers
備隊 *yobitai* reserve corps
備運動 *yobi undō* limbering up
備費 *yobihi* reserve fund, emergency fund preliminary expenses
備試験 *yobi shiken* preliminary exam
備選手 *yobi senshu* reserve player
備錨 *yobi ikari* spare anchor
備艦隊 *yobi kantai* reserve fleet
13 鈴 *yorei* first bell
感 *yokan* premonition, hunch
想 *yosō* anticipation, forecast, conjecture, imagination; estimate
想外 *yosōgai* unexpected, unforeseen, strange
想収穫高 *yosō shūkakudaka* crop estimate
想利益 *yosō rieki* estimated profits
想通 *yosōdō*(*ri*) as expected
想屋 *yosōya* crystal gazer, dopester
想高 *yosōdaka* estimate
14 選 *yosen* nomination, primary election, elimination match
選会 *yosenkai* primary caucus
算 *yosan* estimate, appropriation, budget
算上 *yosanjō no* budgetary
算外 *yosangai* outside the budget
算案 *yosan-an* budget proposal
算措置 *yosan sochi* budgetary provision
15 震 *yoshin* preliminary tremor
審 *yoshin* preliminary examination, pretrial hearing
審廷 *yoshintei* court of first instance
16 謀 *yobō* premeditation, aforethought
21 餞会 *yosenkai* farewell meeting, send-off

7

承 See 197. [手]

A 事 272/F68 Ji thing, matter. *koto* thing, matter, fact, circumstances, business, reason, experience. *tsuka*(*eru*) serve, work for. *koto* (*ni yoru to*) possibly, probably. *koto to suru* deal in; take pleasure in; make it your business. *-ji* fact, matter. *-koto* alias.

3 大 *jidai* subserviency to the stronger
大主義 *jidai shugi* worship of the powerful
大思想 *jidai shisō* admiration of the powerful
4 欠 *kotoka*(*ku*) lack, be in need of
切 *kotoki*(*reru*) expire, die
勿主義 *kotonaka*(*re*) *shugi* pacifism, peace-at-any-price principle
5 立 *kotoda*(*teru*) do something different; make a big thing of
由 *jiyū* reason, cause
犯 *jihan* crime
6 好 *koto* (*o*) *kono*(*mu*) revel in trouble and discord
共 *kotodomo* things, matters
毎 *kotogoto ni* in everything; always
件 *jiken* event, incident, affair, case, plot, trouble, scandal
件表 *jikenhyō* docket
7 足 *kotota*(*ru*), *kotota*(*riru*) suffice, serve the purpose, be satisfied
局 *jikyoku* circumstances
体 *jitai* situation, state of affairs
8 例 *jirei* example; precedent
物 *jibutsu* things, affairs
宜 *jigi* a fitting thing
典 *jiten* encyclopedia
事 *kotogoto* everything. *kotogoto*(*shii*) bombastic, pretentious, exaggerated
事物物 *jiji-butsubutsu* everything
実 *jijitsu* fact; reality; as a matter of fact
実上 *jijitsujō* actually, in fact
実無根 *jijitsu-mukon* contrary to fact
実調査 *jijitsu chōsa* fact-finding
9 迹 *jiseki* evidence, trace
相 *jisō* aspect, phase, phenomenon
柄 *kotogara* matter, affair, circumstance
珍 *koto-mezura*(*shiku*) like something strange
故 *jiko* accident, incident, trouble; circumstances, reasons
変 *jihen* accident, disaster; incident, uprising, emergency
後 *jigo-* after, post-, ex post facto
後承諾 *jigo shōdaku* ex-post-facto approval
前 *jizen no* prior, before the fact
前日付 *jizen hizuke* antedating
前同意 *jizen* (*no*) *dōi* prior consent
前割当 *jizen waria*(*te*) prearranged quota
前検閲 *jizen ken-etsu* prepublication censorship
11 情 *jijō* circumstances, reasons
理 *jiri* reason, facts, propriety, sense
細 *koto-koma*(*kani*), *koto-koma*(*yakani*) minutely, in detail
寄 *kotoyo*(*su*) find an excuse. *kotoyo*(*seru*) pretend. *kotoyo*(*sete*) on the plea of, under the pretext of
務 *jimu* business, clerical work
務引継 *jimuhikitsu*(*gi*) taking over an office
務会 *jimukai* business meeting

務当局 *jimu tōkyoku* officials in charge
務次官 *jimu jikan* permanent vice-minister, undersecretary
務局 *jimukyōku* secretariat, executive office
務所 *jimusho* office
務的 *jimuteki* businesslike, practical
務服 *jimufuku* work clothes
務官 *jimukan* administrative official, secretary, commissioner
務長 *jimuchō* manager; purser
務長官 *jimu chōkan* chief secretary
務取扱 *jimutoriatsukai* acting director
務室 *jimushitsu* office
務員 *jimuin* clerk
務家 *jimuka* man of affairs
務量 *jimuryō* amount of business
務総局 *jimu sōkyoku* secretariat-general
務総長 *jimu sōchō* secretary-general, director
務器 *jimuki* business machines
12 項 *jikō* matters, facts, items
無 *koto(mo)na(ge) na* careless. *kotona(shi)* nothing; nothing to be done; safe; easy. *kotona(ku)* without accident, uneventfully
象 *jishō* phenomenon, a matter
13 跡 *jiseki* evidence, trace, vestige
新 *koto-atara(shiku)* anew; again, specially, formally
業 *jigyō* enterprise, business, industry; operations
業化 *jigyōka* industrialization
業年度 *jigyō nendo* fiscal year
業界 *jigyōkai* industrial or business world
業部 *jigyōbu* operations department
業家 *jigyōka* enterprising man; businessman; industrialist
業税 *jigyōzei* business tax
14 誤 *koto-ayama(ri)* mistake in speaking
態 *jitai* situation, state of affairs
17 績 *jiseki* achievement, exploit; merits
18 蹟 *jiseki* evidence, trace, vestige

2-STROKE RADICALS

二

RAD. 二 7

Ni two. Variant: shorter horizontals. Nickname: Two.

二 273 二 F69 NI two; second. JI. *futa(tsu), fu, fū, futa* two. A 二

2 八 *nihachi* sixteen
七日 *futananuka* second week's memorial services
人 *futari, ninin* two persons, pair, couple
人三脚 *ninin-sankyaku* three-legged race
人連 *futarizu(re)* a party of two
人前 *futarimae, ninimmae* the (work) of two; (meals) for two
人称 *nininshō* second person (in grammar)
人殺 *futarigoro(shi)* double murder
人組 *niningumi* twosome
十日 *hatsuka* twenty days; twentieth (day of the month)
十日大根 *hatsuka daikon* the small garden radish
十日鼠 *hatsuka nezumi* mouse
十代 *nijūdai* one's twenties
十世紀 *nijisseiki* twentieth century
十四時間制 *nijūyojikansei* around-the-clock system
十重 *hatae* many-fold
十歳 *hatachi* age twenty
3 子 *futago* twins; a twin
三 *nisan* two or three
丸 *ni (no) maru* outer citadel
口目 *futakuchime* a pet expression
大政党主義 *nidaiseitō shugi* two-party system
4 心 *futagokoro, nishin* duplicity, treachery, double-dealing
手 *futate* two groups, two bands
方 *futakata* both people
月 *nigatsu* February. *futatsuki* two months
毛作 *nimōsaku* two crops a year
六時中 *nirokujichū* night and day, all the time
日 *futsuka* two days; the second (day of the month)
日酔 *futsukayoi* a hangover
王 *Niō* Guardian Deva Kings
王門 *Niōmon* the temple gate of the *Nio*
分 *nibun suru* halve, bisect
分音符 *nibu ompu* half note
元的 *nigenteki* dual
元放送 *nigen hōsō* a broadcast in which participants speak from different stations
元論 *nigenron* dualism
5 目 *futame to* for a second time
矢 *ni (no) ya* second arrow
乍 *futa(tsu)naga(ra)* both
句 *ni (no) ku* another word, answer
句出 *ni(no)ku (ga) de(nu)* be at a loss for words
世 *nise* two existences, the present and the future. *nisei* junior; the second (king of the same name); American-born Japanese; second generation; a foreigner of Japanese parentage
世固 *nise (no) kata(me)* marriage vows
世契 *nise (no) chigi(ri)* marriage vows

世約束 *nise (no) yakusoku* marriage vows
本立 *nihonda(te)* double feature (movie)
本建 *nihonda(te)* dual system; double standard
本差 *nihonza(shi)* two-sworded (samurai)
本棒 *nihombō* simpleton; henpecked husband; sniveler
6列 *niretsu* two rows; double file
字 *niji* two characters; name
共 *futa(tsu) tomo* both
返事 *futa(tsu)-henji* an immediate (happy) reply
交替制労働 *nikōtaisei rōdō* two-shift work ⌈program
色 *nishoku* two-color, dichromatic
色刷 *nishokuzu(ri)* two-color printing
死 *nishi* two out
死後 *nishigo* after two outs
百二十日 *nihyaku hatsuka* 220th day, end of the storm period
百十日 *nihyaku tōka* 210th day from the beginning, the storm day
号 *nigō* number two; concubine
号宅 *nigōtaku* concubine's house
次 *niji* second, secondary. *ni (no) tsugi* secondary, subordinate
次元 *nijigen* two dimensions
次方程式 *niji hōteishiki* quadratic equation
次会 *nijikai* a second feast the same night
次的 *nijiteki* secondary
7伸 *nishin* postscript
位 *ni-i* second place
役 *futayaku* double role
町 *ni (no) machi* inferior, second-rate
形 *futanari* hermaphrodite
更 *nikō* second watch, 10 p.m. to midnight
君 *nikun* two masters
束三文 *nisoku-sammon* cheap
言 *futakoto* two words; repetition. *nigon* double dealing, double tongue
言目 *futakotome* the constant burden of
足 *ni (no) ashi* hesitation ⌊some people's talk
足三文 *nisoku-sammon* dirt cheap
足草鞋 *nisoku (no) waraji* many irons in
足動物 *nisoku dōbutsu* bipeds ⌊the fire
8念 *ninen* two ideas
拍子 *nibyōshi* double time
国間 *nikokukan no* bilateral
股 *futamata* bifurcation, fork, parting of the way ⌈timeserver
股膏薬 *futamata gōyaku* double-dealing;
直 *nichoku* lining out to second base
直角 *nichokkaku* a straight angle
者 *nisha* two things; two persons
者選一 *nisha-sen-itsu* an alternative
者選一法 *nisha-sen-itsuhō* completion test (one out of two choices)

枚目 *nimaime* actor in a love scene
枚舌 *nimaijita* double tongue, double deal-
枚貝 *nimaigai* bivalve ⌊ing
枚折 *nimaio(ri)* a folio
9食 *nishoku, nijiki* two meals (a day)
通 *nitsū* two copies. *futatō(ri)* duplicate pair; two kinds, two ways, twofold
俣 *futamata*＝二股 (see above–8)
相 *nisō* two-phase
封 *nifū* forced out on second
段見出 *nidan mida(shi)* a two-line heading
院 *ni-in* the two houses of a legislature
院制 *ni-insei* bicameral system
院制度 *ni-inseido* bicameral system
乗 *nijō suru* square, multiply (a number) by
乗根 *nijōkon* square root ⌊itself
連式 *nirenshiki* duplex
連発 *nirempatsu* double-barreled gun
連銃 *nirenjū* double-barreled gun
度 *nido* two times
度三度 *nido-sando* again and again
度刈 *nidoga(ri)* getting two crops a year
度手間 *nido tema, nidodema* double effort
度咲 *nidoza(ki)* second blooming
度添 *nidozo(i)* second wife
重 *futae, nijū* double, twofold
重人格 *nijū jinkaku* double personality
重写 *nijū utsu(shi)* double exposure
重外交 *nijū gaikō* dual diplomacy
重母音 *nijū boin* diphthong
重生活 *nijū seikatsu* double life
重否定 *nijū hitei* double negative
重底 *nijūzoko* double bottom; double sole
重抵当 *nijū teitō* second mortgage
重国籍 *nijū kokuseki* dual nationality
重星 *nijūsei* double star
重奏 *nijūsō* instrumental duet
重釜 *nijūgama* jacketed kettle, double boiler
重唱 *nijūshō* vocal duet
重窓 *nijū mado* storm window ⌈morality
重道徳 *nijū dōtoku* double standard of
重税 *nijūzei* double duty
重焼付 *nijū yakitsu(ke)* double printing
重焦点 *nijū shōten* bifocal
重結婚 *nijū kekkon* bigamy
重橋 *Nijūbashi* Double Bridge at the Palace
重撮影 *nijū satsuei* double exposure
重織 *nijūo(ri)* double-weight cloth
重顎 *nijū ago* double chin
重露出 *nijū roshutsu* double exposure
10倍 *nibai* double, twice, twofold
桁 *futaketa* tens (in figures)
核 *nikaku* binuclear
流 *niryū* second-rate, inferior
宮 *Nigū* the Two Ise Shrines
軒建 *nikenda(te)* duplex (house)

週間 *nishūkan* fortnight, two weeks
進三進 *nichi(mo)sachi(mo)* in a dilemma
部 *nibu* two parts, two copies; the second
部合奏 *nibu gassō* instrumental duet ⌊part
部合唱 *nibu gasshō* vocal duet
部教授 *nibu kyōju* two-session system
11 道 *futamichi* branch roads, forked roads, crossroads, two ways (of proceeding)
階 *nikai* second floor, upstairs
階建 *nikaidate* two-storied building
12 結 *futamusu(bi)* two half hitches
割 *futa(tsu)wa(ri)* half; cutting in two. *niwari* 20%
着 *nichaku* runner-up, second (in a race)
葉 *niyō* two flat things. *futaba* bud, sprout
筋道 *futasuji michi* branch roads, crossroads
塁 *nirui* second base
塁手 *niruishu* second baseman
塁打 *niruida* two-base hit, double
等 *nitō* second class; second
等辺三角形 *nitōhen sankakukei* isosceles
等分 *nitōbun* bisection ⌊triangle
等分線 *nitōbunsen* bisector
等賞 *nitōshō* second prize
等親 *nitōshin* second-degree relative
番 *niban* second, number two, runner-up
番刈 *nibanka(ri)* second crop; aftermath
番作 *nibansaku* second crop
番抵当 *niban teitō* second mortgage
番星 *nibamboshi* second star of the evening
番煎 *nibansen(ji)* a rehash
13 置 *futa(tsu)o(ki)* every third ⌈and geisha)
業地 *nigyōchi* entertainment quarters (food
義的 *nigiteki ni* secondarily
14 様 *niyō* two methods
種 *nishu* second-class (mail)
舞 *ni(no)mai* repeating the same failure
15 輪 *nirin* two wheels, two flowers
輪車 *nirinsha* child's bicycle; two-wheeled
16 膳 *ni (no) zen* side dish ⌊vehicle
親 *futaoya* parents, both parents
頭立 *nitōda(te)* two-horse cart
頭建 *nitōda(te)* two-horse cart
頭筋 *nitōkin* biceps
頭膊筋 *nitōhakkin* (arm) biceps
18 繭 *futa(tsu) mayu* double cocoon

1

于 See 5.

三 See 8. [一]

[illegible] Nonstandard for 工 1451.

2

互 See 14.

井 See 165.

五 See 15.

云 274/F73 UN. *yu(u), i(u)* (see under 言 4309.0).

4 云 *shikajika, unnun* and so forth, and so on,
9 為 *un-i* words and deeds ⌊and the like

A 元 275/F180 GAN, GEN *yuan*; origin; New Year's Day; first year of an era. GEN Mongol (dynasty). *moto* beginning, origin; foundation, basis, source; cause; root (of a tree); (raw) material, base; capital; principal; cost; forebears; formerly. *moto(yori)* originally; of course. [儿]
3 三 *ganzan* New Year's Day; January 1 to 3
4 手 *motode* funds, capital, stock
方 *motokata* capitalist, wholesaler
日 *Ganjitsu* New Year's Day
凶 *genkyō* ringleader ⌈nature, naturally
元 *motomoto* from the first, originally; by
込 *motogo(me)* breech-loading
込銃 *motogo(me)jū* breechloader
5 払 *motobara(i)* prepayment ⌈Year's Day
旦 *gantan* New Year's morning; New
本 *gampon* principal, capital
6 任 *gennin*＝還任 4750.6
号 *gengō* era name
兇 *genkyō* ringleader
年 *gannen* first year (of a reign)
老 *genrō* elder statesman, veteran, authority
老院 *genrōin* (Roman) senate
気 *genki* vigor, energy, vitality, vim, stamina, spirit, courage, pep
気付 *genkizu(keru)* vt pep up, cheer up
気者 *genkimono* a live wire (a person)
7 利 *ganri* principal and interest
来 *ganrai* originally, primarily, logically, naturally, essentially
8 金 *motokin, gankin* capital, principal
価 *genka* cost price
肥 *motogoe* first fertilizing ⌈manhood
服 *gempuku, gembuku* ceremony of attaining
直 *motone* cost
始 *genshi* origin ⌈Jan. 3
始祭 *Genshisai* Shinto Festival of Origins
9 首 *genshu* ruler, sovereign
通 *motodō(ri)* as ever, as before ⌈ventor
祖 *ganso* originator, founder, pioneer, in-

軍 *Gengun* the Mongol forces
帥 *gensui* (field) marshal, fleet admiral, general of the army
帥府 *Gensuifu* Supreme Military Council
10値 *motone* cost
冦 *Genkō* the Mongol Invasion
素 *genso* element
11帳 *motochō* ledger
悪 *gen-aku* head gangster
寇 *Genkō* the Mongol Invasion ⌈the hair
12結 *motoyu(i), motoi* paper cord for tying
朝 *ganchō* New Year's morning
15標 *gempyō* zero milestone
締 *motoji(me)* manager, boss, promoter
勲 *genkun* elder statesman
請人 *moto-u(ke)nin* master contractor
請負人 *moto-ukeoinin* master contractor

3

亙 See 亙 31.

4

亙 亙 See 31.

亘 See 30.

5

亜 See 43.

6

亞 See 亜 43.

些 276 / F80 SA. *chi(to), chit(to), isasaka* a little, a bit, sometimes.
4少 *sashō no* trifling, little, few, slight
8些 *sasa(taru)* trifling, trivial
事 *saji* something small or petty
11細 *sasai na* trivial, small, petty

7

帝 277 / F613 See 帝 305. [巾]

竜 See 5440. [竜]

9

商 278 / F363 See 商 321. [口]

10

啻 279 / F367 SHI. *tada(naranu)* incomparable. *tada ni* merely, only, simply. [口]

亠 RAD. 8

Nabebuta kettle lid, *ten-ichi* (Rad. 3 *ten* plus Rad. 1 *ichi*), or *keisan kammuri* (crown shaped like a Japanese paperweight). Variant: ⼇.
Nickname: Lid.

1

之 280 / F55 SHI. *kore* this. *ko(no)* this. [丿]
18繞掛 *shinnyū (o) ka(keru)* exaggerate

亡 281 / F82 B 亡 BU. MU. MŌ. Bō my late, the late; dying; being destroyed. *na(ku)naru* (see under 無 2773.0). *na(ku) suru* lose. *horo(biru)* perish, be ruined. *horo(bosu)* ruin, destroy, overthrow. *na(ki)* the late, the deceased. *na(shi) ni, na(shi) de* without.
2人 *na(ki)hito* the deceased
3子 *bōshi* dead child
4父 *bōfu* my late father
友 *bōyū* deceased friend
夫 *bōfu* my late husband
5母 *bōbo* my late mother
兄 *bōkei* one's deceased elder brother
失 *bōshitsu* loss
7状 *bōjō* discourtesy; lawlessness
児 *bōji* one's dead child
君 *bōkun* one's deceased lord
8国 *bōkoku* ruined country
姉 *bōshi* one's late elder sister
物 *na(ki)mono ni suru* do away with
妻 *bōsai* one's late wife
者 *mōja* the dead. *na(ki)mono ni suru* kill
命 *bōmei* exile

2 二[亠]人亻𠆢儿入八丷冂冖冫几凵刀刂力勹匕匚匸十卜卩厂厶又

命者 *bōmeisha* displaced persons, (political) refugees
9後 *na(ki)ato* after one's death
11婦 *bōfu* deceased wife; deceased lady
14魂 *bōkon, na(ki)tama* departed soul, spirit
15霊 *bōrei* the dead, departed spirits, apparition, ghost
16骸 *nakigara* remains, corpse
親 *bōshin, na(ki)oya* deceased parent
18軀 *nakigara* remains, corpse

2

亢 282 / F83 Kō high spirits.
10進 *kōshin* rise, acceleration, exasperation
16奮 *kōfun*=興奮 615.16

A **六** 283 / F202 Riku. Roku *mu(tsu), mu(ttsu), mu* six. *mu(zukashii)* (see under 難 5038. 0). [八]
2十四分音符 *rokujūshibu ompu* 64th note
十余州 *rokujūyoshū* the 66-odd provinces of old Japan
十路 *musoji* age sixty
3大州 *Roku Daishū* the Six Continents
三制 *roku-sansei* 6-3 system of education
ケ敷 *muzuka(shii)* (see under 難 5038.0)
4方 *roppō* the six directions (north, south, east, west, up, and down)
日 *muika* six days; the sixth (day of the month)
月 *Rokugatsu* June
辺形 *rokuhenkei* hexagon
分儀 *rokubungi* sextant
6合 *rikugō* the universe, the cosmos
百六号 *roppyakurokugō* 606, salvarsan
7花 *rikka* snow
角 *rokkaku* hexagon
角形 *rokkakkei* hexagon
角堂 *rokkakudō* hexagonal building
8法 *roppō* six law codes
法全書 *Roppō Zensho* the Statute Books
9連発 *roku rempatsu* six-chambered (revolver)
重奏 *rokujūsō* instrumental sextette
重唱 *rokujūshō* vocal sextette
10部 *rokubu* Buddhist pilgrim; six copies
書 *Rokusho* Hexateuch. *rikisho* six classes of characters
根清浄 *rokkon-shōjō* purification of the six roots of perception
11情 *rokujō* the six emotions (joy, anger, sorrow, pleasure, love, and hatred)
12腑 *roppu* the six internal organs
13感 *rokkan* the six senses
16親 *rokushin* the six blood relationships

3

A **市** 284 / F609 Shi city, town; market. *ichi* market; fair. [巾]
2人 *shijin* resident, townfolk; merchant. *ichibito* market people
3子 *ichiko* sorceress, medium, female fortuneteller
上 *shijō* in the town, in the street
4日 *ichibi* market day
区 *shiku* municipal district; streets
中 *shichū* in the city
内 *shinai* the city, within the city limits
井 *shisei* the street; the town
井人 *shisei (no) hito* townspeople
5庁 *shichō* municipal office
立 *shiritsu* municipal, city
立学校 *shiritsu gakkō* municipal school
外 *shigai* outside the city limits; suburbs
外電話 *shigai denwa* long distance
民 *shimin* citizen, townspeople
民法 *shiminhō* civil law
民権 *shiminken* citizenship
6吏員 *shiri-in* city employee, city official
会 *shikai* city council
会議員 *shikai gi-in* city councilman
有 *shiyū* owned by the city
有地 *shiyūchi* city land
有物 *shiyūbutsu* municipal property
有財産 *shiyū zaisan* municipal property
7役所 *shiyakusho* city hall
町 *shichō* cities and towns
町村 *shichōson* cities, towns, and villages; municipalities
8門 *shimon* city gate
長 *shichō* mayor
価 *shika* market price, current price
松 *ichimatsu* checked (pattern)
況 *shikyō* market conditions
制 *shisei* municipal organization, municipality
参事会 *shisanjikai* city council
9政 *shisei* municipal government
10部 *shibu* urban areas
11販 *shihan* marketing
12場 *ichiba, shijō* market
税 *shizei* city tax
葬 *shisō* municipal funeral
費 *shihi* municipal expenditure
営 *shiei* municipal operation
営住宅 *shiei jūtaku* municipal housing
街 *shigai* the streets; town, city
街地 *shigaichi* town areas
街戦 *shigaisen* street fighting
13債 *shisai* municipal bond
肆 *shishi* store; market storehouse
電 *shiden* municipal railway, city streetcar
勢 *shisei* city conditions; municipal census
勢調査 *shisei chōsa* municipal census
14塵 *shijin* city dust; city confusion
20議 *shigi* city assemblyman

A **主** 285 / F51 **主** Su. Shū. Shu Lord; lord, master, employer; aim; main thing. *aruji* head of the house, master, mistress, husband. *nushi* owner; master, husband; lover; a god; you. *omo(na)*, *omo(naru)* main, principal, important. *omo(ni)* chiefly, principally, mostly. *shu(taru)* main, principal, major. *shu toshite* mainly, chiefly. *omo-* main. [丶]

2 人 *shujin, aruji* master, head (of a household), landlord; one's husband; employer; host
人公 *shujinkō* master, head (of a household); hero or heroine (of a story)
人役 *shujin-yaku* host, toastmaster
人持 *shujimmo(chi)* a samurai attached to a ⌊daimyo
人顔 *shujingao* proprietary air
力 *shuryoku* main force, main strength
力株 *shuryoku kabu* leading shares
力艦 *shuryokukan* capital ship
力艦隊 *shuryoku kantai* main fleet
3 上 *shujō* emperor
4 文 *shubun* the text; the main clause (in grammar); the main part of a document
日 *Shujitsu, Shu (no) Hi* the Sabbath, the Lord's Day
5 用 *shuyō* the master's business; necessary business ⌈fender
犯 *shuhan* principal offense; principal of-
犯者 *shuhansha* principal offender
6 色 *shushoku* predominant color
因 *shuin* primary cause, prime factor
帆 *shuhan* main sail
刑 *shukei* principal penalty
旨 *shushi*=*shui* 趣意 4544.13
成分 *shuseibun* main ingredient
任 *shunin* person in charge ⌈chief, head
任者 *shuninsha* person in charge, manager,
7 位 *shui* first place, leading position
役 *shuyaku* a major role; a big part; a star
君 *shukun* lord, master
我 *shuga* ego, self
我主義 *shuga shugi* egoism, love of self
体 *shutai* the subject; constituency, con-
体的 *shutaiteki* subjective ⌊stituents
体性 *shutaisei* independence, autonomy
8 長 *shuchō* head, chief
法 *shuhō* main laws
物 *shubutsu* the main thing
祈 *Shu (no) Ino(ri)* the Lord's Prayer
取 *shūdo(ri) suru* enter the service of a daimyo ⌈orders
命 *shūmei, shumei* ruler's orders, master's
事 *shuji* manager, director, secretary
治医 *shuji-i* attending physician
治効能 *shuji kōnō* chief virtue (of a medi-
知主義 *shuchi shugi* intellectualism ⌊cine)
知的 *shuchiteki* intellectual
9 音 *shuon* tonic, keynote

持 *shumo(chi), shūmo(chi)* serving a master;
虹 *shuniji* primary rainbow ⌊employee
査 *shusa* chief investigator
思 *shūomo(i)* worrying about one's master's affairs; one who so worries
食 *shushoku* staple food; main article of diet
食物 *shushokubutsu* staple food; main article
計 *shukei* paymaster, accountant ⌊of diet
計局 *shukeikyoku* budget bureau
客 *shukaku, shukyaku* host and guest; principal and auxiliary ⌈order
客転倒 *shukaku-tentō* opposites; reverse
客顛倒 *shukaku-tentō* opposites; reverse order ⌈staple
要 *shuyō na* main, principal, chief, essential,
要人物 *shuyō jimbutsu* key people
要工業 *shuyō kōgyō* key industries
要国 *shuyōkoku* principal countries
要物価 *shuyō bukka* prices of staple commodities
要点 *shuyōten* main point, keynote
要駅 *shuyōeki* principal stations
10 馬 *shume* equerry
従 *shujū, shūjū* master and servant, lord and retainer, employer and employee
根 *omone, shukon* main root, taproot
将 *shushō* commander-in-chief; captain (of
班 *shuhan* head position ⌊a team)
砲 *shuhō* main battery, main armament
脈 *shumyaku* main mountain range
殺 *shūkoro(shi)* murder of one's master
部 *shubu* main part; complete subject
家 *shuka* employer's house
恩 *shuon* the favor of one's master
格 *shukaku* nominative case
格補語 *shukaku hogo* subject complement
流 *shuryū* main current
流派 *shuryūha* main faction
宰 *shusai* supervision; chairmanship
宰者 *shusaisha* chairman, president
席 *shuseki* head seat, head, chief, president, governor, chairman ⌈diplomatic corps
席外交官 *shuseki gaikōkan* doyen of the
席全権 *shuseki zenken* chief delegate
席判事 *shuseki hanji* chief judge
11 唱 *shushō* advocacy, promotion
婦 *shufu* housewife, mistress
張 *shuchō* assertion, claim, advocacy; emphasis, contention, insistence; opinion,
情的 *shujōteki* emotional ⌊tenet
情論 *shujōron* emotionalism
眼 *shugan* chief aim; main point
眼点 *shuganten* main point
務 *shumu* competent (authorities)
務大臣 *shumu daijin* the cabinet minister
動 *shudō* leadership ⌊in charge

動的 *shudōteki* autonomous
産地 *shusanchi* chief producing center
産物 *shusambutsu* main product
脳 *shunō* head, leading spirit
脳者 *shunōsha* head, leading spirit
脳部 *shunōbu* governing body, the executives
教 *shukyō* bishop, prelate, primate
教室 *shukyōshitsu* home room (in a school)
教冠 *shukyōkan* miter
12 訴 *shuso* main complaint
軸 *shujiku* main shaft
筆 *shuhitsu* editor in chief
筋 *shūsuji* people close to the head man
晩餐 *Shu (no) Bansan* the Lord's Supper
13 意 *shui* main meaning; opinion, idea; aim, motive
幹 *shukan* chief editor, managing editor; manager
義 *shugi* principle, policy, basis; -ism
義者 *shugisha* advocate (of a theory or principle); man of principle, ideologist
催 *shusai* sponsorship, promotion
催者 *shusaisha* sponsor, promoter, organizer
催国 *shusaikoku* sponsoring nation
戦 *shusen* advocacy of war
戦投手 *shusen tōshu* top pitcher
戦論 *shusenron* war advocacy, jingoism, bellicose argument
14 語 *shugo* subject (of a sentence)
領 *shuryō* chief, leader
管 *shukan* supervision, management; supervisor, manager
監 *shukan*＝主幹 (see above–13)
製品 *shuseihin* main products
演 *shuen* starring, playing the leading part
演者 *shuensha* star, leading actor
導 *shudō* main leadership
導権 *shudōken* leadership, initiative
15 潮 *shuchō* main current
調 *shuchō* keynote; main melody
審 *shushin* chief umpire
賓 *shuhin* main guest, guest of honor
箱 *Shu (no) Hako* Ark of the Lord
権 *shuken* sovereignty, dominion
権在民 *shuken-zaimin* the sovereignty of the people
権国 *shukenkoku* sovereign nation
権者 *shukensha* sovereign, ruler
権侵犯 *shuken shimpan* infringement of sovereignty
16 薬 *shuyaku* principal agent (in a medicine)
謀 *shubō* chief, leader
謀者 *shubōsha* leader
17 翼 *shuyoku* main planes (of an airplane)
18 題 *shudai* subject, theme, motif
題歌 *shudaika* theme song
観 *shukan* subjectivity; subject, ego
観主義 *shukan shugi* subjectivism
観性 *shukansei* subjectivity
観的 *shukanteki* subjective
観論 *shukanron* subjectivism
19 禱文 *Shutōbun* the Lord's Prayer (Catholic)

4

亦 286/F85 Eki. Yaku. *mata* also, again.

亥 287/F85 Gai. *inoshishi*, *i* 9–11p.m.; 12th zodiac sign; hog.

妄 288/F491 Bō. Mō. *mida(ri) ni* without authority, without reason, arbitrarily, unnecessarily, indiscriminately, recklessly. *mida(rigamashii)* morally corrupt. [女]
5 用 *bōyō* misuse, abuse
弁 *bōben* incoherent talk
7 言 *bōgen* reckless remark, abusive language
8 念 *mōnen* distracting ideas, irrelevant thoughts
9 信 *mōshin, bōshin* blind belief, credulity
10 挙 *bōkyo* unreasonable actions, lack of discrimination
11 動 *mōdō suru, bōdō suru* act blindly
執 *mōshū* deep-rooted delusion
12 評 *bōhyō, mōhyō* unfair criticism, abusive remarks
13 想 *mōsō, bōsō* wild idea, delusion
14 説 *bōsetsu, mōsetsu* fallacy, false report
語 *mōgo, bōgo*＝*bōgen*妄言 (see above–7)
15 誕 *bōtan* falsehood

B **充** 289/F182 Jū fill. *a(teru)* (see under 当 1359.0). *mi(chiru)*, *mi(tasu)* (see under 満 2636.0). [儿]
4 分 *jūbun* enough; satisfactory, adequate; perfect; thoro
5 用 *jūyō suru* appropriate to, earmark for
6 血 *jūketsu* congestion (medical)
行 *atega(u)*＝宛行 1292.6
当 *jūtō suru* allot, appropriate
当金 *jūtōkin* appropriation
7 足 *jūsoku* sufficiency
8 実 *jūjitsu* substantiality; fullness, completion, perfection. *jūjitsu shita* full, complete; replete with; substantial (meal), solid (reading)
10 員 *jūin* reserves, recruits, draftees
12 備 *jūbi* completion, perfection
満 *jūman suru, michimichi(te) iru* be filled with, be pregnant with, team with
13 塡 *jūten suru* fill (up), plug; replenish. *jūten* filling (in a tooth)
溢 *jūitsu* overflow, abundance, exuberance
塞 *jūsoku suru vt* plug, fill up, block. *vi* be filled, be stopped up

電 *jūden* charging (batteries)

電器 *jūdenki* charger

A 交 290 F83 Kō coming and going; association; change of seasons. *maji(waru)*, *maji(ru)* associate with, mingle with; interest; join. *maji(eru)* mix; converse with, cross (swords). *ma(zeru)*, *ma(jiru)* (see under 混 2604.0). *kawa(su)* exchange (messages); dodge, parry, avoid, turn aside. *komogomo* alternately.

[3]叉 *kōsa* crossing, intersection

叉点 *kōsaten* crossing, intersection

[4]互 *kōgo no* mutual, reciprocal, alternate

友 *kōyū* friend, companion

友関係 *kōyū kankei* one's associate

[5]付 *kōfu suru* deliver, furnish with (copies)

付金 *kōfukin* grant, subsidy, bounty

付者 *kōfusha* deliverer, donor

代 *kōtai* alternation, change, relief, relay, shift

代投手 *kōtai tōshu* relief pitcher

代作業 *kōtai sagyō* working in shifts

代制 *kōtaisei* shift system

代員 *kōtai-in* a shift (of workmen)

代操業 *kōtai sōgyō* working in shifts

[6]交 *komogomo* alternately, in succession

合 *kōgō* sexual union

[7]尾 *kōbi* copulation (in animals)

[8]易 *kōeki* trade, commerce

[9]信 *kōshin* correspondence, communication

点 *kōten* point of intersection

通 *kōtsū* traffic; communication; transport; navigation

通公社 *kōtsū kōsha* travel bureau

通巡査 *kōtsū junsa* traffic officer

通安全 *kōtsū anzen* traffic safety

通妨害 *kōtsū bōgai* traffic obstruction

通事故 *kōtsū jiko* traffic accident

通信号 *kōtsū shingō* traffic signal

通違反 *kōtsū ihan* traffic violation

通規則 *kōtsū kisoku* traffic rules

通道徳 *kōtsū dōtoku* traffic ethics

通運輸業 *kōtsū-un-yugyō* transportation business

通量 *kōtsūryō* traffic, traffic volume

通費 *kōtsūhi* traveling expenses, carfare

通路 *kōtsūro* traffic route

通網 *kōtsūmō* traffic network

通遮断 *kōtsū shadan* blockade, quarantine

通整理 *kōtsū seiri* traffic control

通機関 *kōtsū kikan* transportation facilities

[10]配 *kōhai* mating, crossbreeding, crossfertilization

流 *kōryū* alternating current; (cultural) exchange; intermingling

流人事 *kōryū jinji* personnel shuffle

差 *kōsa suru* to cross

差点 *kōsaten* crossing, intersection

[11]遊 *kōyū* friend; friendship

情 *kōjō* intimacy, friendship

接 *kōsetsu* sexual intercourse

渉 *kōshō* negotiation, discussion; connection

渉委員 *kōshō i-in* negotiating committeemen

渉員 *kōshōin* negotiators

[12]番 *kawa(ri)ban(ko) ni*, *kawa(ri)ban ni* alternately. *kōban* police box

替 *kōtai*＝交代 (see above–5)

換 *kōkan* exchange, reciprocity, barter; substitution; clearing (of checks)

換手 *kōkanshu* switchboard operator

換円 *kōkan-en* convertible yen

換台 *kōkandai* (telephone) switchboard

換局 *kōkankyoku* (telephone) exchange

換所 *kōkanjo* clearing house

換学生 *kōkan gakusei* exchange student

換品 *kōkanhin* thing bartered, trade-in

換船 *kōkansen* repatriation ship

換教授 *kōkan kyōju* exchange professor

換貿易制 *kōkan-bōekisei* barter system

換器 *kōkanki* (telephone) switchboard

[13]詢 *kōjun* promotion of social intercourse

感 *kōkan* rapport, mutual sympathy

感神経 *kōkan shinkei* sympathetic nerves

戦 *kōsen* war, battle, hostilities

戦国 *kōsenkoku* belligerents

戦権 *kōsenken* right of belligerency

際 *kōsai* association, intercourse, comradeship, acquaintance

際上 *kōsaijō* as a matter of social courtesy

際好 *kōsaizu(ki) na* sociable

際社会 *kōsai shakai* society, social circles

際国 *kōsaikoku* friendly powers, treaty powers

際法 *kōsaihō* etiquette, social code

際家 *kōsaika* sociable person

際費 *kōsaihi* entertainment expenses

際場裡 *kōsaijōri* society

際嫌 *kōsaigira(i)* unsociable

際範囲 *kōsai han-i* circle of acquaintance

[14]雑 *kōzatsu*＝*kōhai* 交配 (see above–10)

読 *kōdoku suru* read responsively

読文 *kōdokubun* responsive readings

[15]誼 *kōgi* friendship

霊術 *kōreijutsu* spiritism, spiritualism

歓 *kōkan*＝交驩 (see below–27)

歓会 *kōkankai* reception

[16]錯 *kōsaku* mixture, blending, complication

[18]織 *kōshoku*, *ma(ze)o(ri)* mixed weave

[19]響曲 *kōkyōkyoku* symphony

響楽 *kōkyōgaku* symphony (orchestra)

響楽団 *kōkyōgakudan* symphony (orchestra)

[20]譲 *kōjō* mutual concession, compromise

2 二[亠]人亻𠆢儿入八丷冂冖冫几凵刀刂力勹匕匚匸十卜卩厂厶又

27驩 *kōkan* exchange of courtesies, fraternization

5

忘 291 F691 忘 B Bō. *wasu(reru)* forget; be forgetful of; forget about; forget (an article). *wasu(reppoi)* forgetful. [心]

6年 *bōnen* forgetting the hardships of the old year
年会 *bōnenkai* year-end party
7却 *bōkyaku* memory lapse, forgetfulness
我 *bōga* selflessness, trance, ecstasy; enthusiasm
形見 *wasu(re)gatami* memento, souvenir, keepsake; posthumous child
8物 *wasu(re)mono* something forgotten
10恩 *bōon* ingratitude
12勝 *wasu(re)ga(chi) no* forgetful, oblivious of, negligent

6

斉 See 5423. [斉]

氓 292 F1063 Bō people. [氏]

享 293 F86 B Kyō. *u(keru)* (see under 受 2826.0).

6年 *kyōnen* age at death
有 *kyōyū* possession, enjoyment
8受 *kyōju suru* receive, accept, enjoy, be given
受者 *kyōjusha* recipient
9持 *kyōji* securing rights and profits
13楽 *kyōraku* enjoyment, pleasure
楽生活 *kyōraku seikatsu* gay life
楽主義 *kyōraku shugi* epicureanism
楽的 *kyōrakuteki* pleasure-seeking

卒 294 F289 卆 A Sotsu soldier, private. *sos(suru)* die, pass away. [十]

4中 *sotchū* apoplexy, cerebral stroke
5去 *sokkyo, shukkyo* death
6伍 *sotsugo* rank and file, the ranks
先 *sossen* taking the initiative
8直 *sotchoku* frankness, openheartedness
10倒 *sottō* fainting, swooning
12然 *sotsuzen* suddenly, unexpectedly
塔婆 *sotoba* wooden grave tablet; stupa
13業 *sotsugyō* graduation
業生 *sotsugyōsei* graduate, alumnus
業式 *sotsugyōshiki* graduation exercises
業後 *sotsugyōgo* after graduation
業証書 *sotsugyō shōsho* graduation certificate
14爾 *sotsuji na* abrupt, sudden

京 295 F86 亰 A Kei ten quadrillion. Kyō capital, metropolis; ten quadrillion; Kyoto. *miyako* capital, metropolis.

2人 *keijin* citizen of the capital
人形 *kyōningyō* Kyoto doll
3女 *kyōonna* Kyoto woman
4方 *kyōgata* the direction of Kyoto; Kansai area; citizens of Kyoto; nobles
6地 *kyōchi* the capital; Kyoto and its environs
阪 *Kei-Han* Kyoto and Osaka
阪神 *Kei-Han-Shin* Kyoto-Osaka-Kobe
7形 *kyōgata* style current in the capital
8物 *kyōmono* Kyoto products
表 *Kyō-omote* vicinity of Kyoto
9風 *kyōfū* Kyoto style; urbanity, refinement
洛 *keiraku, kyōraku* capital; Kyoto
10師 *keishi* capital, metropolis; old Kyoto
浜 *Kei-Hin* Tokyo and Yokohama
華 *keika* capital; flower capital
12葉 *Kei-Yō* Tokyo and Chiba

育 296 F1536 A Iku. *soda(tsu)* be raised, be brought up, grow, grow up. *soda(teru), haguku(mu)* raise, rear, bring up. *soda(te)* bringing up, raising. *soda(chi)* breeding, growth. [肉]

3上 *soda(te)-a(geru)* raise, rear, bring up, train, educate
4方 *soda(te)kata* method of bringing up, method of raising
5生 *ikusei* rearing, training
6行 *soda(chi)-yu(ku)* grow up
成 *ikusei* rearing, training
成栽培 *ikusei saibai* vegetable and fruit growing
7児 *ikuji* care of children
児法 *ikujihō* the rearing of children
児食 *ikujishoku* baby food
児院 *ikuji-in* orphanage, nursery school
児室 *ikujishitsu* nursery
児時間 *ikuji jikan* nursing time
8苗 *ikubyō* raising seedlings
英 *ikuei* education
英会 *ikueikai* scholarship society; educational society
14種 *ikushu* (plant) breeding
種所 *ikushujo* (plant) nursery
種家 *ikushuka* (plant) breeder
16親 *soda(te) oya* foster parent
18雛器 *ikusūki* breeder

盲 297 F1317 盲 B Bō. Mō blindness. *mekura, meshii* blindness; blind man; ignorance, ignoramus. [目]

2人 *mōjin* blind person
5打 *mekura-u(chi)* hitting blindly; random firing
目 *mōmoku* blindness
目的 *mōmokuteki* blind (devotion)

目飛行 *mōmoku hikō* instrument flying
7判 *mekuraban* blindly stamping one's seal
8学校 *mōgakkō* school for the blind
9信 *mōshin* blind belief, credulity
点 *mōten* blind spot
10進 *mōshin* rushing recklessly; presumption
従 *mōjū* blind obedience
射 *mōsha* shooting wildly
11亀 *mōki* blind turtle
探 *mekurasagu(ri)* blindly groping
動 *mōdō, bōdō* acting blindly
断 *mōdan* hasty conclusion
窓 *mekura mado* blind window
執 *mōshū* deep-rooted conviction
貫銃創 *mōkan jūsō* lodged-bullet wound
唖 *mōa* blind and dumb ⌈dumb
唖学校 *mōa gakkō* school for the blind and
12買 *mekuraga(i)* buying blindly
13愛 *mōai* blind love
想 *mōsō, bōsō* wild idea, delusion
滅法 *mekura meppō* recklessness
腸 *mōchō* appendix; caecum
腸炎 *mōchōen* appendicitis ⌈literates
14暦 *mekuragoyomi* picture calendar for il-
導犬 *mōdōken* seeing-eye dog
管銃創 *mōkan jūsō* lodged-bullet wound
15撃 *mekura-u(chi)* random shooting
16壁 *mekura kabe* windowless wall
19爆 *mōbaku* indiscriminate bombing

A **夜** 298 / F454 YA night. *yo* evening, night. *yoru* night, nighttime, evening; at night. *yo(nabe)* night work. *yo(mosugara)* all night. [夕]
3上 *yoa(gari)* weather clearing at night
叉 *yasha* female demon
4中 *yachū, yojū* all night, the whole night. *yonaka* midnight, dead of night
分 *yabun* evening, night, nighttime
5立 *yoda(chi)* setting out at night
市 *yo-ichi* night market
半 *yowa, yahan* midnight, dead of night
目明 *yome (nimo) aka(rui)* luminous in the
仕事 *yoshigoto* night work ⌊dark
6色 *yashoku* shades of night; night scene
行 *yakō* night travel, night train. *yagyō* walking around at night
凪 *yonagi* evening calm ⌈man
回 *yomawa(ri)* night watch; night watch-
気 *yaki* night air, stillness of night, cool
曲 *yakyoku* a nocturne ⌊evening
毎 *yogoto* every night
会 *yakai* evening party, ball
会服 *yakaifuku* evening dress
会結 *yakai musu(bi)* evening hairdo
光 *yakō* nocturnal luminescence
光虫 *yakōchū* phosphorescent animalcule
光時計 *yakōdokei* luminous watch
光塗料 *yakō toryō* luminous paint
7伽 *yotogi* watching, vigil; watcher
攻 *yoze(me)* night attack
更 *yofuka(shi)* staying up late, nighthawk. *yofuke ni, yofuke(te)* late at night
来 *yarai* overnight; since last night
汽車 *yogisha* night train
尿症 *yanyōshō* bed-wetting
見世 *yomise* night shop, night fair
見国 *yomi (no) kuni* hades, the next world
8長 *yonaga* long night
雨 *ya-u* night rain
店 *yomise* night shop, night fair
逃 *yoni(ge)* night flight
泊 *yahaku* night mooring
歩 *yoaru(ki)* walking around at night
具 *yagu* bedding
空 *yozora* the night sky
盲症 *yamōshō* night blindness
明 *yoa(kashi)* staying up all night, all-night vigil. *yoa(ke)* dawn, daybreak
明明星 *yoake (no) myōjō* morning star
夜 *yoyo, yo(na)yo(na)* every evening, night
夜中 *yoru-yonaka* midnight ⌊after night
学 *yagaku* night classes, night school
学校 *yagakkō* night school
9風 *yokaze* night wind
食 *yashoku* supper, night meal
通 *yodō(shi)* all night
前 *yazen* last night
昼 *yoru-hiru* day and night ⌈side all night
10晒 *yozara(shi)* leaving things exposed out-
桜 *yozakura* cherry trees at evening
航 *yakō* night travel
討 *yo-u(chi)* night attack
陰 *ya-in* shades of evening, dead of night
烏 *yogarasu* night crow
宮 *yomiya* eve of a festival vigil
11鳥 *yachō* nocturnal bird ⌈road at night
道 *yomichi* going out at night, night trip,
遊 *yoaso(bi)* night amusements
深 *yobuka(i)* (staying) up late at night. *yofuke ni, yofu(ke), yofu(kete)* late at night
船 *yofune* night boat
釣 *yozu(ri)* night angling
著 *yogi*＝夜着 (see below–12)
商 *yoakina(i)* night trading
商人 *yoakindo* night shopkeeper
盗 *yatō* night burglar
盗虫 *yatōmushi* cutworm, army worm
12啼 *yonaki* crying at night
勤 *yakin* night duty, night shift
寒 *yosamu, yozamu* night cold; cold night
嵐 *yoarashi* night storm

2 二[亠]人亻ヘ儿入八ソ冂冖冫几凵刀刂力勹匕匚匸十卜卩厂ム又

景 *yakei* night view 「quilt
着 *yogi* nightclothes; heavy kimono-like
番 *yoban, yaban* night watch, night sentry
営 *yaei* encamping at night
間 *yakan* night, nighttime 「school
間中学 *yakan chūgaku* evening middle
間部 *yakambu* night-school session
間勤務 *yakan kimmu* night work
間営業 *yakan eigyō* open at night
間預金金庫 *yakan yokin kinko* night-de-
13 働 *yobatara(ki)* night work 」posit safe
暗 *ya-an* dead of night, shades of night
詰 *yozu(me)* night watch 「parties
話 *yawa, yobanashi* night talks; evening tea
戦 *yasen* night warfare
業 *yagyō* night work, night shift
想曲 *yasōkyoku* a nocturne
14 鳴 *yona(ki)* crying at night
15 稼 *yokasegi* night work; burglary
19 霧 *yogiri* night fog
警 *yakei* night watchman
21 露 *yotsuyu* evening dew, night dew
22 籠 *yogomo(ri)* night of prayer in a temple
襲 *yashū* night attack
24 鷹 *yotaka* nighthawk, street walker

7

氐 See 292. [氏]

彦 See **彥** 3347. [彡]

京 299/F86 See **京** 295.

虽 300/F-X See **虹** 4117. [虫]

弯 Nonstandard for **彎** 1579.

奕 301/F483 EKI large. [大]
5 世 *ekisei* many generations

亮 302/F87 RYŌ clear; help.
10 陰 *ryōan*＝諒闇 4387.17

P **亭** 303/F87 TEI restaurant; mansion; arbor; cottage; vaudeville, music hall, stage name. CHIN arbor, pavilion, summer house.
4 午 *teigo* noon 「husband
5 主 *teishu* master, host; landlord, innkeeper;
主関白 *teishu kampaku* autocratic husband
9 亭 *teitei(taru)* lofty, towering

B **哀** 304/F355 AI. *awa(remu)* pity, have mercy on, sympathize with. *awa(re)* grief, sorrow; misery; compassion, pathos. *awa(reppoi)* plaintive, piteous, doleful. [口]
4 切 *aisetsu na* pathetic
弔 *aichō* sympathetic condolences
5 史 *aishi* sad story, sad history
6 気 *awa(re)ge na* sad, sorrowful, pensive
号 *aigō* moan, wailing
7 別 *aibetsu* sad parting
9 音 *aion* sad voices; sad sounds
10 哭 *aikoku* grief, mourning, lamentation
11 悼 *aitō* condolence, regret, sympathy, sor-
惜 *aiseki* grief, sorrow 」row, lament
情 *aijō* sadness
12 痛 *aitsū* sorrowing with the bereaved
訴 *aiso* appeal, complaint
詞 *aishi* message of condolence
13 傷 *aishō* sorrow, grief
詩 *aishi* elegy
話 *aiwa* sad tale
愁 *aishū* sorrow, grief
感 *aikan* pathos
愍 *aibin* pity
楽 *airaku* grief and pleasure
14 歌 *aika* elegy, dirge, sad song, lamentation
慕 *aibo* cherish the memory of, yearn for
15 憫 *aibin* pity
憐 *airen* pity, compassion
調 *aichō* mournful melody; minor key
歓 *aikan* sadness and joy
19 願 *aigan* appeal, entreaty, petition

B **帝** 305/F613 **帝** TEI emperor; the god of heaven; the creator. *mikado* emperor (of Japan). [巾]
3 土 *teido* imperial domain
4 日 *teijitsu* lucky day
王 *teiō* sovereign, emperor
王切開術 *teiō sekkaijutsu* Caesarian section
王神権説 *teiō shinken setsu* theory of the divine right of kings
7 位 *tei-i* the throne, the crown
8 制 *teisei* imperial government, imperialism
京 *teikyō* the capital
命 *teimei* imperial order
国 *teikoku* empire; imperial
国主義 *teikoku shugi* imperialism
国主義的 *teikokushugiteki* imperalistic
9 威 *tei-i* imperial majesty
城 *teijō* palace 「monarchical rule
政 *teisei* imperial government; imperialism;
冠 *teikan* imperial crown, diadem

室 *teishitsu* Imperial Family; Imperial ⌊Household
10 座 *teiza* imperial throne
陵 *teiryō* imperial mausoleum
都 *teito* imperial capital
11 道 *teidō* the imperial way, principles of ⌊imperial rule
13 業 *teigyō* imperial task
14 徳 *teitoku* emperor's virtue
15 廟 *teibyō* imperial mausoleum ⌈palace
18 闕 *teiketsu* imperial palace gate; imperial

A 変 306/F1772 變 變 HEN change; accident, calamity; uprising; something strange. *hen(jiru)*, *hen(zuru)* *vi* change into, be transformed, be transfigured. *vt* transform, alter, convert. *ka(waru)* change, vary; be revised; be different; be queer; move; be transferred. *ka(eru)* change, vary, convert; revise, amend. *kawa(ri)* change, alteration; difference. *kawa(tta)* another, different; various; particular; unusual, novel; peculiar. *kawa(ranu)* constant, unchangeable. *kawa(rinaku)* unchangeably, constantly; eternally; uneventfully. *hen na* strange, suspicious-looking; queer, eccentric, funny. *hen ni* curiously, strangely. [言]

2 人 *henjin* eccentric person ⌈apostasy
4 心 *henshin* change of mind, inconstancy,
化 *henka* change, variation, alteration, mutation, transition; transformation, transfiguration, metamorphosis; variety, diversity; inflection, declension, conjugation. *henge* goblin, ghost, apparition, bugbear
化球 *henkakyū* ball with a change of speed
幻 *hengen* transformation
幻自在 *hengen-jizai* ever-changing
5 目 *kawa(ri)me* change, turning point, transition, new program
圧 *hen-atsu* transformation (of a current)
圧所 *hen-atsujo* transformer substation
圧器 *hen-atsuki* transformer ⌈coloration
6 色 *henshoku* change of color; fading, dis-
名 *hemmei* assumed name, alias
光星 *henkōsei* variable star
成 *hensei* metamorphosis
成岩 *henseigan* metamorphic rock
死 *henshi* accidental death
死者 *henshisha* person accidentally killed
7 身 *henshin* disguise
位 *hen-i* change of position
改 *henkai suru* revise (rules)
乱 *henran* disturbance, uprising, war
災 *hensai* accident, disaster ⌈voice
声期 *henseiki* puberty in boys, change in
体 *hentai* abnormality ⌈syllabary
体仮名 *hentaigana* anomalous cursive
形 *henkei* transformation, metamorphosis, modification, variation, deformation; variety, deformity, monster
形虫類 *henkeichūrui* the amoeba
更 *henkō* change, modification, alteration
更不能 *henkō funō* unchangeable
8 性 *hensei suru vt* and *vi* denature; degen- ⌊erate
法 *hempō* law revision; revised law
物 *hembutsu* eccentric person
易 *kawa(ri)yasu(i)* changeable, unsettled; inconstant
果 *kawa(ri)-ha(teru)* be completely changed
者 *kawa(ri)mono* an eccentric
事 *henji* accident, emergency, calamity
9 革 *henkaku* change, reform
造 *henzō* alteration, defacement, debasement, falsification, forgery
通 *hentsū* resourcefulness, adaptability
則 *hensoku* irregularity
奏曲 *hensōkyoku* variation (in music)
速 *hensoku* shifting gears
速機 *hensokuki* transmission
10 症 *henshō suru* take a turn, develop into
格 *henkaku* irregularity, irregular conjuga- ⌊tion
容 *hen-yō* changed appearance
哲無 *hentetsu (mo) na(i)* usual, mediocre, monotonous
流器 *henryūki* transformer ⌈mutation
11 移 *hen-i* change, alteration; transmutation,
転 *henten* mutation, change, vicissitude
動 *hendō* change, fluctuation
異 *hen-i* accident; variation, mutation
12 換 *henkan* change, conversion, diversion, transformation
装 *hensō*, disguise, masquerade
13 数 *hensū* variable (in math)
節 *hensetsu* apostasy, betrayal
電所 *hendensho* transformer substation
14 遷 *hensen* transition, vicissitudes, change
種 *henshu*, *kawa(ri)dane* novelty, exception; hybrid, mutation, variety, freak; eccentric personality
貌 *hembō* transfiguration
模様 *kawa(ri) moyō* fancy pattern
態 *hentai* transformation, metamorphosis; abnormality
態心理 *hentai shinri* abnormal mentality
態心理学 *hentai shinrigaku* abnormal psychology
態的 *hentaiteki* abnormal
態性欲 *hentai seiyoku* abnormal sexuality
15 調 *henchō* change of tone, variation (in music); irregularity, anomaly, abnormality; modulation (in radio)
質 *henshitsu* deterioration, degeneration
質者 *henshitsusha* a degenerate

8

衷 307/F1693 See 衷 110. [衣]

斎 See 齋 5425. [文]

孪 Nonstandard for 孿 2035.

袞 308/F1691 See 衮 317. [衣]

烹 309/F1185 Hō. *ni(ru) vt* boil, cook. [灬]

旁 310/F880 Bō. *tsukuri* the right half of a character when the left half is its radical. *katawa(ra)* (see under 傍 520.0). *katagata* at the same time. [方]

[10]旁 *katagata* incidentally, at the same time

B 畝 311/F1274 Bō. Ho ridge, furrow, rib (in cloth). *se* thirty tsubo. *une* (see under 畦 3004.0). *u(neru)* undulate, meander, surge, swell, roll. [田]

[5]立 *uneda(te)* building rice-field ridges

[13]溝 *unemizo* furrow ridges

B 衰 312/F1692 衰 Sui. *otoro(eru)* decline, wane, weaken, abate, decay, wither, waste away. [衣]

[3]亡 *suibō* ruin, downfall, collapse

[5]世 *suisei* this decadent world

[6]色 *suishoku* fading color; fading beauty

死 *suishi suru* become emaciated and die; wither away

兆 *suichō* signs of decline

[8]退 *suitai*=*suibi* 衰微 (see below–13)

果 *otoro(e)-ha(teru)* be utterly spent or crushed

[10]残 *suizan na* emaciated, worn out

耗 *suimō suru* weaken and decline

弱 *suijaku* weakness, debility, prostration, breakdown

[11]運 *suiun* declining fortunes, decadence

[12]替 *suitai suru* decline, weaken

[13]微 *suibi* decline, decadence, waning; ebb tide

滅 *suimetsu* decline and fall

勢 *suisei* downward tendency, decay, decline

[14]態 *suitai* weakening, decline

[15]弊 *suihei* decline

[16]頽 *suitai*=*suibi* 衰微 (see above–13)

[18]軀 *suiku* emaciated body

B 恋 313/F755 戀 Ren. *ko(u)* be in love. *koi(suru)* love, fall in love with. *koi(shigaru)* yearn for, miss. *koi* love, tender sentiment. *koi(shii)* dear, beloved, darling. [心]

[2]人 *koibito* lover, sweetheart

[4]心 *koigokoro* love, love's awakening

文 *koibumi* love letter

水 *koi mizu* tears of love

仇 *koigataki* one's rival in love

[6]死 *koijini* dying of love

仲 *koinaka* love, love relationship

[7]佗 *ko(i)-wa(biru)* be lovesick

乱 *ko(i)-mida(ru)* be lovesick

初 *ko(i)-so(meru)* begin to love

忍 *ko(i)-shino(bu)* live on love

[8]河 *koi kawa* oceans of love

妻 *koizuma* loving wife

[9]風 *koikaze* love's zephyr

草 *koigusa* lovesickness

[10]疲 *koizuka(re)* haggard from love

病 *koi yami, koi yamai* lovesickness

恋 *renren toshite* fondly, longingly

[11]情 *renjō* love, attachment. *koinasake* lovesickness

猫 *koi neko* cats in season

盛 *koizaka(ri)* lovesick period

[12]着 *renchaku* attachment, love

焦 *ko(i)-ko(gareru)* yearn for, be deeply in love with

[13]煩 *koiwazura(i)* lovesickness

路 *koiji* romance, love's pathway

愛 *ren-ai* love, love-making, passion, emotion, affections

愛至上主義 *ren-aishijō shugi* love for love's sake

愛遊戯 *ren-ai yūgi* trifling with love

愛結婚 *ren-ai kekkon* love marriage

愛関係 *ren-ai kankei* love affair, love relationship

愛観 *ren-aikan* philosophy of love

[14]歌 *koiuta, koika, renka* love song, love poem

暮 *ko(i)-kura(su)* live deeply in love

慕 *ko(i)-shita(u)* miss, yearn for. *rembo suru* love, fall in love with

[15]敵 *koigataki* love rival

慰 *koinagusa(me)* comforting the lovelorn

[22]籠 *ko(i)-komo(ru)* be deeply in love

9

烹 See 309. [灬]

斎 See 5425. [斉]

産 314/F1267 See 産 3354. [生]

衷 See 衷 110. [衣]

袤 315 / F1695 Bō length. [衣]

孰 316 / F524 JUKU. *izu(re)* where, which, who. [子]

衮 317 / F1691 **袞** KON imperial robes. [衣]

16龍 *konryō* imperial robes

毫 318 / F1060 Gō a fine hair; brush. *gō(mo)* (not) in the least, (not) at all. [毛]

5末 *gōmatsu*=*suko(shi)* (see under 少 166.0) and *gō(mo)* (see under 毫 318.0)

18釐 *gōri* very small quantity

A **率** 319 / F1239 **率** SOTSU. RITSU rate, percentage; proportion; coefficient, factor; constant; index. *hiki(iru)* lead, spearhead (a group), command (troops). [亠]

8土 *sotto* face of the earth

6先 *sossen* taking the initiative

8直 *sotchoku* frankness, openheartedness

10倒 *sottō* fainting, swooning

12然 *sotsuzen* suddenly, unexpectedly

14爾 *sotsuji na* abrupt, sudden

牽 320 / F1220 KEN. *hi(ku)* (see under 引 1562.0). [牛]

4引 *ken-in suru* haul, tow, pull, drag

引力 *ken-inryoku* pulling power

引車 *ken-insha* tractor

7束 *kensoku* restraint; being exclusively absorbed in something

8制 *kensei* check, restraint, constraint; diversion, feint, screen

制球 *kenseikyū* a throw to check a runner

9連 *kenren suru* be related to

11強 *kenkyō* distortion of facts

強付会 *kenkyō-fukai no* farfetched, distorted

A **商** 321 / F363 **商** SHŌ trade; merchant; quotient. *akina(u)* sell, handle, trade in. *akina(i)* trade, business. [口]

2人 *shōnin, akindo, akyūdo, akiudo* trader, shopkeeper, merchant

3大 *shōdai* commercial college

才 *shōsai* business ability

工 *shōkō* commerce and industry

工会議所 *Shōkō Kaigisho* Chamber of Commerce and Industry

工業 *shōkōgyō* commerce and industry

工業者 *shōkōgyōsha* commercial and industrial men

5用 *shōyō* business

用文 *shōyōbun* business correspondence

用語 *shōyōgo* commercial term

6会 *shōkai* company, firm

号 *shōgō* firm name, trade name

行為 *shōkōi* commercial transaction

7状 *shōjō* market conditions

社 *shōsha* company, firm

利 *shōri* commercial profit

売 *shōbai* trade, business, commerce; transaction, occupation, trade

売人 *shōbainin* merchant; professional, expert

売気 *shōbaigi* commercial spirit, profit motive

売気質 *shōbai katagi* mercenary spirit

売柄 *shōbaigara* nature of one's business; business instinct

売道具 *shōbai dōgu* stock-in-trade

売筋 *shōbai suji* business connections

売替 *shōbaiga(e)* change of occupation

売敵 *shōbaigataki* professional jealousy; business rivalry

8況 *shōkyō* business conditions

法 *shōhō* trade, business, commerce; commercial law

取引 *shōtorihiki* business transaction

店 *shōten* shop, store

店街 *shōtengai* shopping district; shopping street

学士 *Shōgakushi* Bachelor of Commercial Science

学博士 *Shōgaku Hakushi* Doctor of Commercial Science

事 *shōji* commercial affairs

事会社 *shōjigaisha* commercial company

9科 *shōka* commercial course

科大学 *shōka daigaku* commercial college

品 *shōhin* goods, stock, merchandise

品目録 *shōhin mokuroku* inventory, catalog

品在高 *shōhin zaidaka* amount of inventory

品券 *shōhinken* merchandise certificate

品学 *shōhingaku* (study of) merchandising

10家 *shōka* mercantile house, store; merchant

11運 *shōun* fortunes of business

略 *shōryaku* business policy

経 *shōkei* commerce and economics

務 *shōmu* commercial affairs

務官 *shōmukan* commercial attaché

船 *shōsen* merchant ship

船大学 *shōsen daigaku* merchantile-marine college

船学校 *shōsen gakkō* merchant-marine school

船隊 *shōsentai* merchant fleet

船旗 *shōsenki* merchant flag

12港 *shōkō* commercial port

量 *shōryō* consideration, deliberation, discussion

策 *shōsaku* business policy

13業 *shōgyō* commerce, trade, business

業文 *shōgyōbun* commercial correspondence

業化 *shōgyōka* commercialization
業史 *shōgyōshi* history of commerce
業主義 *shōgyō shugi* commercialism
業地 *shōgyōchi* business district
業学 *shōgyōgaku* commercial science
業学校 *shōgyō gakkō* commercial school
業放送 *shōgyō hōsō* commercial broadcast
業界 *shōgyōkai* commercial world
業美術 *shōgyō bijutsu* commercial art
業都市 *shōgyō toshi* commercial city
業組合 *shōgyō kumiai* guild, trade association
業道徳 *shōgyō dōtoku* business morality
業街 *shōgyōgai* shopping street
業港 *shōgyōkō* commercial port
業数学 *shōgyō sūgaku* commercial mathematics
業算術 *shōgyō sanjutsu* commercial arithmetic
14魂 *shōkon* commercial spirit
慣習 *shōkanshū* commercial practice
慣習法 *shōkanshūhō* commercial law
15権 *shōken* commercial supremacy, commercial rights
談 *shōdan* business transaction
舗 *shōho* shop, store
標 *shōhyō* trademark
標権 *shōhyōken* trademark rights
16機 *shōki* business opportunity
館 *shōkan* firm, trading company
20議 *shōgi* conference, consultation
議員 *shōgi-in* counselor, trustee

10

啻 See 279. [口]

B **蛮** 322 F1679 **蠻** BAN barbarian. [虫]
2人 *banjin* savage, barbarian
力 *banryoku* brute force
5民 *bammin* savage people
6行 *bankō* barbarism, brutality
地 *banchi* barbaric region
7声 *bansei* rough voice
8的 *banteki* savage, barbarous, rustic
9風 *bampū* barbarian customs
勇 *ban-yū* brute courage, reckless valor, foolhardiness
10骨 *bankotsu* brute courage, recklessness
11族 *banzoku* savage tribe
習 *banshū* barbarous custom
14境 *bankyō* land of the barbarians
語 *bango* language of the barbarians
16隷 *banrei* slaves of the barbarians
18襟 *bankara* uncouthness; rough person

A **就** 323 F573 SHŪ. JU. *tsu(ku)* settle in (place); take (a seat); take (a position); depart; study (under a teacher). *(ni) tsu(ite)* concerning; along; under; per. *tsu(ite) wa, tsu(kimashite) wa* concerning. *-zu(ku)* to become. [尢]
4中 *nakanzuku* especially, above all, among other things
6任 *shūnin* assumption of office, inauguration
任式 *shūninshiki* inauguration ceremony, installation
7床 *shūshō* bedridden
役 *shūeki suru* be placed in commission; enter servitude
労 *shūrō* actual work
8学 *shūgaku* entering school; school attendance
学年齢 *shūgaku nenrei* school age
学児童 *shūgaku jidō* school child
学義務 *shūgaku gimu* compulsory school attendance
10眠 *shūmin* retiring, going to sleep
航 *shūkō* commissioning a ship
13寝 *shūshin suru* go to bed, retire
寝前 *shūshinzen* before retiring
業 *shūgyō* employment, starting work
業日数 *shūgyō nissū* days worked
業地 *shūgyōchi* place of work
業時間 *shūgyō jikan* work hours
業率 *shūgyōritsu* percentage of employment
業規則 *shūgyō kisoku* work regulations
15褥 *shūjoku suru* retire, go to bed
16縛 *shūbaku* arrest
18職 *shūshoku* finding employment
職口 *shūshokuguchi* position, opening, employment
職先 *shūshokusaki* place of employment
職時 *shūshokuji* time of employment
職運動 *shūshoku undō* job hunting
職斡旋 *shūshoku assen* placement
職難 *shūshokunan* scarcity of employment

11

雍 324 F2014 YŌ. *yawa(ragu), yawa(rageru)* (see under 和 3268.0). [隹]

稟 325 F1381 **禀** HIN, RIN salary in rice. [禾]
7告 *rinkoku* notice, notification
8性 *hinsei, rinsei* nature, character
15質 *hinshitsu* natural disposition
請 *rinsei* petition
請書 *rinseisho* petition
20議 *ringi* reaching a decision by using a circular letter

B **棄** 326 F984 **弃** KI. *su(teru)* (see under 捨 1944.0). [木]
3子 *sutego* foundling
5石 *sute-ishi*＝捨石 1944.5
世 *kisei* death
6老 *kirō* an old person thrown away in the mountains
死 *kishi* exposing a corpse in the city

7 却 *kikyaku suru* reject, dismiss; abandon,
児 *kiji* abandoned child ⌊renounce, waive
言葉 *sutekotoba* a sharp parting remark
9 約 *kiyaku* breaking a promise
背 *kihai* giving up and turning back
10 捐 *kien* donation; abandonment
15 権 *kiken suru* abstain from voting; renounce
権者 *kikensha* nonvoter ⌊one's rights

裏 327/F1698 **裡** B Ri inside. *uchi ni* amidst, in. *ura* reverse, wrong side; undersurface, inside; palm, sole; opposite; back, rear; lining, last half (of an inning). [衣]

3 山 *urayama* the hill back of one's home; a hill back from the seashore
口 *uraguchi* back door, rear entrance
口営業 *uraguchi eigyō* illegal business
4 手 *urate* back of the house
方 *urakata* lady consort (to a high person-
毛 *urake* fleece lining ⌊age); scene shifter
反 *uragae(ru)*, *uragae(su)*, *uragae(shi)*＝裏
木戸 *urakido* back door ⌊返 (see below–6)
日本 *Ura-Nippon* Japan Sea coast areas
切 *uragi(ri)* treachery, betrayal, perfidy. *uragi(ru)* betray ⌈informer
切者 *uragirimono* betrayer, traitor, turncoat,
5 付 *urazu(keru)* support; endorse; substantiate. *urazu(ke)* backing, security; proof, foundation; lining (something); something lined. *urazu(ki)* lined; something lined
付物資 *urazu(ke)busshi* collateral goods
打 *ura-u(chi)* lining, backing; vouching for
打紙 *ura-u(chi)gami* end leaves (of a book), lining paper
6 返 *uragae(su)* turn inside out; turn the other way, turn (something) over. *uragae(ru)* be turned inside out. *uragae(shi)*
地 *uraji* lining ⌊inside out; upside down
合 *ura-a(wase)* fitting things back to back; agreement of minds
名 *urana* secret name, alias
7 囲 *uragako(i)* back fence
作 *urasaku* second crop, interim crop
町 *uramachi* back street, back alley, slums
声 *uragoe* falsetto
8 門 *uramon* back gate ⌈ment, slums
店 *uradana* house in an alley, rear tene-
板 *ura-ita* roof boards; ceiling
長屋 *uranagaya* rear tenement
表 *ura-omote* wrong side out; both sides; reverse, opposite; double-dealing
表紙 *urabyōshi* back cover
9 屋 *uraya* alley house, rear tenement, slum
通 *uradō(ri)* back street, side street, alley
背戸 *urasedo* back door
面 *rimen* back, reverse, other side, inside, tails (of coins), background
面史 *rimenshi* hidden historical background
10 庭 *ura niwa* rear garden, back yard
紋 *uramon* informal crest
釘 *urakugi* nails sticking thru
鬼門 *urakimon* unlucky quarter (southwest)
書 *uragaki* endorsement; proof; note on back of the scroll
書人 *uragakinin* endorser
書譲渡 *uragaki jōto* endorsing over to
11 道 *ura michi* back street; secret path
問 *urado(u)* ascertain a person's innermost feelings
側 *uragawa* the reverse, the lining
情 *ura nasake* inner affection
12 貸屋 *uragashiya* house in back for rent
13 腹 *urahara* opposite, reverse, contrary
話 *urabanashi* a story not generally known
14 漉 *uragoshi* strainer, colander
18 襟 *uraeri* neckband lining

12

齊 See 5423. [齊]

裹 328/F1701 Ka. *tsutsu(mu)* (see under 包 176.0). [衣]

豪 329/F1781 B Gō great, powerful, excelling. [豕]

6 気 *gōki* sturdy spirit
壮 *gōsō* splendor, magnificence, grandeur
7 快 *gōkai na* exciting, stirring, lively; heroic; largehearted; splendid
8 放 *gōhō na* largehearted, frank, unaffected
物 *erabutsu, eramono* great man
者 *gō(no)mono* past master, veteran
雨 *gōu* heavy rain, downpour, cloudburst
雨禍 *gōuka* flood devastation
9 胆 *gōtan* boldness, hardihood
勇 *gōyū* bravery, prowess
10 家 *gōka* wealthy and powerful family
華 *gōka* splendor, pomp, extravagance
華版 *gōkaban* de luxe edition
11 遊 *gōyū* wild merrymaking
族 *gōzoku* powerful family or clan
盛 *gōsei*＝*gōsha* 豪奢 (see below–12)
爽 *gōsō* fine disposition
商 *gōshō* wealthy merchant
商層 *gōshōsō* wealthy merchant class
12 傑 *gōketsu* hero, great man
猪 *yama-arashi* porcupine
飲 *gōin* heavy drinking, carousing
奢 *gōsha* luxury, magnificence, extravagance

13 腹 *gōfuku* obstinacy, stubbornness
勢 *gōsei*=*gōsha* 豪奢 (see above–12)
農 *gōnō* wealthy farmer
14 語 *gōgo* bombast, boasting, big talk
15 邁 *gōmai* intrepidity, indomitableness

13

齊 See 5423. [齊]

齎 See 5426. [齊]

蝱 330 F1669 See 虻 4117. [虫]

褒 331 F1705 褒 Hō. *ho(mechigiru)*, *ho(mesoyasu)* praise, extol. *ho(meru)* praise, commend. [衣]
3 上 *ho(me)-a(geru)* praise, extol
5 立 *ho(me)-ta(teru)* praise, extol
6 合 *ho(me)a(i)* logrolling tactics
7 状 *hōjō* certificate of merit, honorable mention
言葉 *homekotoba* eulogy, compliment
8 奉 *ho(me)-matsu(ru)* praise; render homage to
9 美 *hōbi* prize, reward
10 称 *ho(me)-tata(eru)* admire, praise, applaud
貶 *hōhen* praise and censure, criticism
11 章 *hōshō* medal
12 詞 *ho(me) kotoba* words of praise
13 辞 *hōji* praise, eulogy
奨 *hōshō* compensation
14 歌 *ho(me)-uta(u)* sing praises to
15 賞 *hōshō* prize, reward

14

壅 332 F442 Yō. *fusa(gu)* *vt* plug up, shut up. *fusa(garu)* *vi* be plugged up, be shut up. [土]

15

齋 See 5425. [齊]

褒 333 F1705 See 褒 331. [衣]

褻 334 F1705 Setsu filthy. [衣]

16

甕 335 F1262 Ō. *kame*, *mika* jar, jug, vat, urn, vase. [瓦]

17

齏 336 F-X See 齏 5427. [齊]

18

贏 337 F1807 Ei victory; surplus; wrap. [貝]
7 余 *eiyo* remainder

19

齎 See 5426. [齊]

羸 338 F1504 Rui weak; thin. [羊]
10 弱 *ruijaku* weakness, feebleness, imbecility

21

齏 See 5427. [齊]

RAD. 人 9

Hito man. At left: イ *nimben*. At top: 𠆢 *yane* roof, *hito-yane* or *hitogashira*. Nickname: Man.

A **人** 339 F88 Jin man, person, people. Nin man, person. *hito* man, human being, mankind, person, people; character, personality; a true man; man of talent; adult; other people; messenger; visitor. *hito(rashii)* like a decent person, human. *hito-(tonari)* hereditary disposition. *-jin* man; expert. *-nin* man, person. *-to* person.
1 一倍 *hito-ichibai* unusual; more than all others
2 人 *hitobito* men, people, everybody. *ninnin* each person
力 *jinriki* human power. *jinryoku* human strength, human effort, human agency
力車 *jinrikisha* jinricksha
3 士 *jinshi* well-bred man; people
子 *Hito (no) Ko* the Son of Man, Christ. *hito(k)ko* (not) a soul
山 *hitoyama* crowd of people
才 *jinzai* man of talent

才登用 *jinzai-tōyō* selection for high office
口 *jinkō* population; common talk
口密度 *jinkō mitsudo* population density
口調査 *jinkō chōsa* census
口膾炙 *jinkō* (*ni*) *kaisha suru* become famous ⌈ficial; artificiality
工 *jinkō* human work, human skill; arti-
工池 *jinkō ike* artificial pool ⌈respiration
工気胸療法 *jinkō-kikyō-ryōhō* artificial
工地震 *jinkō jishin* artificial earthquake
工林 *jinkōrin* planted forest
工的 *jinkōteki* artificial, unnatural
工雨 *jinkōu* artificial rain
工呼吸 *jinkō kokyū* artificial respiration
工呼吸法 *jinkō kokyūhō* artificial respiration
工受胎 *jinkō jutai* artificial insemination
工受粉 *jinkō jufun* artificial fertilization (of plants)
工受精 *jinkō jusei* artificial insemination
工降雨 *jinkō kōu* artificial rain
工栄養 *jinkō eiyō* bottle feeding
工栄養児 *jinkō eiyōji* bottle-fed child
工真珠 *jinkō shinju* artificial pearls
工流産 *jinkō ryūzan* abortion
工雪 *jinkō yuki* artifical snow
工港 *jinkōkō* artificial harbor
工雷 *jinkōrai* artificial lightning
工孵化法 *jinkō fukahō* artificial incubation
工避妊法 *jinkō hininhō* contraception
工衛星 *jinkō eisei* man-made satellite
4 手 *hitode* a worker, a hand
込 *hitogo*(*mi*) a crowd of people ⌈the world
中 *hitonaka* society, company, the public,
夫 *nimpu, nimbu* coolie, laborer, carrier
心 *jinshin, hitogokoro* human nature; senti-
心地 *hitogokochi* consciousness ⌊ment
文 *jimmon, jimbun* humanity; civilization
文史 *jimbunshi* history of civilization
文主義 *jimbun shugi* humanism
文地理 *jimbun chiri* descriptive geography
文学派 *jimbungakuha* humanists
文科学 *jimbun kagaku* social sciences
5 立 *hitoda*(*chi*) a crowd of people
外 *jingai* breech of morals; inhuman treatment; absence of human habitation. *ningai* outcast, outlaw
払 *hitobara*(*i*) clearing out the people
出 *hitode* crowd, turnout
世 *jinsei* this world; life
本主義 *jimpon shugi, jimbon shugi* humanism, humanitarianism
代名詞 *jindaimeishi* personal pronoun
目 *hitome, jimmoku* a glimpse; public gaze
目余 *hitome ni ama*(*ru*) be too prominent
付 *hitozuki* reputation

付合 *hitozu*(*ki*)*a*(*i*) social disposition
民 *jimmin* people, subjects, the public
民投票 *jimmin tōhyō* plebiscite, referendum
民戦線 *jimmin sensen* popular front
生 *jinsei* human life
生派 *jinseiha* humanists ⌈tion column
生案内欄 *jinsei-annai ran* personal-ques-
生哲学 *jinsei tetsugaku* philosophy of life
生記録 *jinsei kiroku* human document
生観 *jinseikan* view of life
6 肉 *jinniku* human flesh
臣 *jinshin* subjects; retainers
死 *hitoji*(*ni*) death, casualty
任 *hitomaka*(*se*) leaving (it) to others
伝 *hitozute* hearsay; message ⌈charm
好 *hitozu*(*ki*) attractiveness, amiability,
肌 *hitohada* the skin; body warmth
交 *hitomajiwa*(*ri*) association with people
当 *hitoa*(*tari*) influence of one's manners
件費 *jinkenhi* personnel expenses
名 *jimmei* a person's given name
名辞典 *jimmei jiten* biographical dictionary
名辞書 *jimmei jisho* biographical dictionary
名録 *jimmeiroku* directory, name list
名簿 *jimmeibo* directory, name list
気 *ninki* popularity; business conditions; popular feeling. *hitoke* signs of life (in a place)
気役者 *ninki yakusha* stage favorite, star
気投票 *ninki tōhyō* popularity contest
気者 *ninkimono* popular person, favorite
気取 *ninkito*(*ri*) bid for popularity, publicity stunt ⌈on public favor
気商売 *ninki shōbai* occupations dependent
7 足 *ninsoku* coolie, laborer, carrier. *hitoashi*
車 *jinsha* jinricksha ⌊pedestrian traffic
位 *jin-i* a person's rank
材 *jinsai, jinzai* man of talent
別 *nimbetsu* census taking
助 *hitodasu*(*ke*) act of mercy
形 *ningyō* doll, puppet, figure
声 *hitogoe* a human voice, a cry
良 *hito* (*no*) *i*(*i*) of good character
君 *jinkun* sovereign, ruler
寿 *jinju* man's life span
見知 *hitomishi*(*ri*) shyness
応待 *hitoashirai* treatment of people
里 *hitozato* human habitation
里離 *hitozato-hana*(*reta*) lonely (place)
体 *jintai* human body. *nintei* personal appearance
体学 *jintaigaku* somatology ⌈person
体実験 *jintai jikken* testing on a living
体模型 *jintai mokei* anatomical model of the human body
形芝居 *ningyō shibai* puppet show

2 二亠人イ𠆢儿入八ソ冂冖冫几凵刀刂力勹匕匚匸十卜卩厂厶又

形回 *ningyōmawa*(*shi*) puppet operator
形使 *ningyōtsuka*(*i*) puppet operator
形師 *ningyōshi* doll maker ⌈person
身 *jinshin, hitomi* the human body, one's
身売買 *jinshin baibai* slave trade; white-slave trade
身攻撃 *jinshin kōgeki* personal attack
身保護 *jinshin-hogo* habeas corpus
身保護令状 *jinshin-hogo reijō* writ of habeas corpus ⌈tim
身御供 *hitomi gokū* human sacrifice; vic-
8使 *hitozuka*(*i*) handling one's workmen
怖 *hito-oji* a child's fear of a stranger
性 *jinsei* human nature, instinct, humanity, humanism
波 *hitonami* wave of humanity; stampede
泣 *hitona*(*kase*) annoyance, nuisance
知 *jinchi* human intellect, knowledge. *hitoshi*(*renu*), *hitoshi*(*rezu*) secret, hidden, unseen, inward
取 *hitoto*(*ri*) prisoner's base (a game)
並 *hitona*(*mi*) *no* ordinary
参 *ninjin* carrot; ginseng
受 *hito-u*(*ke*) popularity
苛 *hito-iji*(*me*) bullying, teasing
妻 *hitozuma* a married woman
非人 *nimpinin* a brute of a man
的 *jinteki* human; personal
的資源 *jinteki shigen* man-power resources
命 *jimmei* (human) life
命救助 *jimmei kyūjo* lifesaving
物 *jimbutsu* person, man; character, personage; talented man
物寸描 *jimbutsu-sumbyō* thumb-nail sketch
物画 *jimbutsuga* portrait painting
物経済 *jimbutsu keizai* human engineering
物評 *jimbutsuhyō* personal criticism; character sketch ⌈revealing character
物像 *jimbutsuzō* statue; picture; a picture
事 *hitogoto* others' affairs. *jinji* personal affairs; personnel affairs
事不省 *jinji-fusei* unconsciousness ⌈tion
事行政 *jinji gyōsei* personnel administra-
事院 *Jinji-in* National Personnel Authority
事異動 *jinji idō* personnel changes
事欄 *jinji ran* personal column
9屋 *hitoya* prison, jail
通 *hitodō*(*ri*), *hitotō*(*ri*) pedestrian traffic
垣 *hitogaki* a crowd of people
後 *jingo* behind others, losing out to others
柱 *hitobashira* human pillar, human sacrifice
柄 *hitogara* character; personality; personal
相 *ninsō* physiognomy ⌊appearance; gentility
前 *hitomae* the public, company. *hitomae de* in public, in company ⌈personality
品 *jimpin* personal appearance; character,
皇 *ninnō* emperor
待顔 *hitoma*(*chi*)*gao* a look of expectation
海戦術 *jinkai senjutsu* infiltration tactics, human-wave tactics
食 *hitoku*(*i*) cannibalism; biting (someone)
食人種 *hitoku*(*i*) *jinshu* cannibals
面 *jimmen* human face
面獣心 *nimmen-jūshin, jimmen-jūshin* a beast in human form ⌈form
面獣身 *jimmen-jūshin* a beast in human
為 *jin-i* human work; human agency; art; artificiality
為的 *jin-iteki* artificial, unnatural ⌈biology)
為淘汰 *jin-i tōta* artificial selection (in
相 *ninsō* physiognomy, looks, countenance
相占 *ninsō urana*(*i*) divination by facial
相見 *ninsōmi* physiognomist ⌊features
相書 *ninsōga*(*ki*) personal description
造 *jinzō* artificial, synthetic; imitation
造人間 *jinzō ningen* robot
造氷 *jinzōgōri* artificial ice
造石油 *jinzō sekiyu* synthetic oil
造米 *jinzōmai* imitation rice
造宝石 *jinzō hōseki* artificial jewels
造真珠 *jinzō shinju* artificial pearls
10馬 *jimba* men and horses
骨 *jinkotsu* human bones
倫 *jinrin* human relations; morality
時 *ninji* man-hour
称 *ninshō* person; personal (in grammar)
殺 *hitogoro*(*shi*) murder; murderer
家 *jinka* house, human habitation
畜 *jinchiku* men and animals
笑 *hitowara*(*ware*) laughingstock. *hitowara*(*wase*) *na* ridiculous, laughable. *hitowara*(*i*), *hitowara*(*e*) something people would laugh at
真似 *hitomane* mimicry, imitation
差 *hitosa*(*shi*) index finger
差指 *hitosa*(*shi*) *yubi* index finger ⌈ality
格 *jinkaku* character, personality, individu-
格化 *jinkakuka* impersonation; personification
格者 *jinkakusha* man of character; person
格権 *jinkakuken* personal rights
員 *jin-in* staff, personnel, crew; the number of persons
員淘汰 *jin-in tōta* personnel reduction
員整理 *jin-in seiri* personnel cut
員縮少 *jin-in shukushō* personnel reduction
11魚 *ningyo* mermaid, merman
達 *hitotachi* people
違 *hitochiga*(*i*), *hitochiga*(*e*) mistaken identity; a person so changed that it's hard to recognize him
探 *hitosaga*(*shi*) searching for someone

欲 *jin-yoku* human desires, human passions
寄 *hitoyo(se)* a gathering of people
雪崩 *hitonadare* a surging crowd
望 *jimbō* popularity
望家 *jimbōka* popular character
道 *jindō* humanity; sidewalk
道主義 *jindō shugi* humanism; humanitarianism
道的 *jindōteki* humane
情 *ninjō* humanity, sympathy, kindness; human nature; common sense; customs and manners
情本 *ninjōbon* a novel
情味 *ninjōmi* human interest, kindness
情負 *ninjōma(ke)* overcome by sympathy
情劇 *ninjōgeki* human-interest play
情噺 *ninjōbanashi* love story, real-life story
12 傑 *jinketsu* great man, hero
証 *jinshō, ninshō* testimony of a witness
買 *hitoka(i)* slave traffic; slave dealer
蒸 *hito-iki(re)* stuffiness
集 *hitodaka(ri)* a crowd
智 *jinchi* human intellect; knowledge
無 *hitona(shi), hito(de)na(shi)* brute, miscreant, ungrateful fellow
喰 *hitokui* cannibalism; biting (someone)
喰人種 *hitokui jinshu* cannibals
間 *ningen* man, person, human being
間以上 *ningen ijō no* superhuman
間以前 *ningen izen no* prehuman
間手作 *ningen-tezuku(ri) no* man-made
間社会 *ningen shakai* human society
間味 *ningemmi* human kindness; human weakness
間性 *ningensei* human nature, humanity
間的 *ningenteki* human
間並 *ningenna(mi)* the common run of people
間苦 *ningenku* human suffering
間学 *ningengaku* anthropology
間界 *ningenkai* the world of humans
間嫌 *ningengira(i)* misanthropy; misanthropist
間愛 *ningen ai* human love
間業 *ningen waza* the work of man
間堕落 *ningen (no) daraku* the fall of man
間爆弾 *ningen bakudan* human bomb
間離 *ningembana(re)* unworldly; superhuman
13 嫌 *hitogira(i)* one who dislikes people; dislike of people
煙 *jin-en* smoke from human habitations
絹 *jinken* rayon, artificial silk
馴 *hitona(re)* used to people; tame
数 *ninzu, ninzū, hitokazu* the number of people
意 *jin-i* public sentiment
猿同祖説 *jin-en dōsosetsu* monkey-ancestry theory
跡 *jinseki, hitoato* signs of human habitation
跡未到 *jinseki-mitō* unexplored
跡未踏 *jinseki-mitō* unexplored
14 選 *jinsen* personnel selection
聞 *hitogi(ki)* reputation, respectability
境 *jinkyō* human habitation
徳 *jintoku, nintoku* personal virtue; natural virtue
様 *hitosama* (polite) other people, another
熅 *hito-iki(re)* stuffiness, lack of ventilation
語 *jingo* human speech
魂 *hitodama* will-o'-the-wisp; spirit of a dead person
蔘 *ninjin* carrot; ginseng
種 *jinshu* race of people
種改良 *jinshu kairyō* racial eugenics
種的 *jinshuteki* racial
種学 *jinshugaku* ethnology
15 膚 *hitohada* the skin; body warmth
影 *hitokage, jin-ei* a person's shadow; a form
質 *hitojichi* hostage, prisoner
権 *jinken* human rights
権蹂躙 *jinken-jūrin* trampling on human rights
16 懐 *hitonatsu(koi)* friendly, amiable. *hitonatsu(kashii)* lonesome for
頼 *hitodayo(ri), hitodano(mi)* reliance on others
頭 *jintō* the number of people, population
頭税 *nintōzei, jintōzei* poll tax
17 擦 *hitozure* sophistication
爵 *jinshaku* worldly honors
糞 *jimpun* night soil
18 騒 *hitosawa(gase)* false alarm
類 *jinrui* man, mankind, humanity
類史 *jinruishi* human history
類学 *jinruigaku* anthropology, ethnology
類学者 *jinruigakusha* anthropologist; ethnologist
類猿 *jinruien* anthropoid ape
類愛 *jinruiai* love for humanity
22 籟 *jinrai* instrumental music
23 攫 *hitosarai* kidnapping; kidnapper

1

个 340 F44 See 個 489. [丨]

2

分 See 578. [刀]

仄 See 815.

内 See 82. [入]

仐 341 F-X Nonstandard for 傘 518.

仂 342 F-X Nonstandard for 働 532.

仆 343 F94 Fu fall; lie down; bend.

仍 344 F96 Jō. *yo(tte)* therefore, consequently.

什 345 F92 Jū ten; utensil, thing.

1 一 *jūichi* tithe
8 物 *jūmotsu* furniture, fixtures; utensil;
宝 *jūhō* treasured article ⌊treasure
15 器 *jūki* utensil, appliance, furniture

仇 346 F94 Kyū. *ada, ata, kataki* foe, enemy; revenge; enmity, grudge, feud; harm, evil; ruin; invasion.

6 同士 *katakidōshi* enemy
10 討 *ada-uchi* vengeance, retaliation
15 敵 *kyūteki* bitter enemy
23 讐 *kyūshū* revenge; bitter enemy

B **介** 347 F95 Kai shell, shellfish. *kai(suru)* be in between; mediate; concern oneself with. *kai(shite)* thru the medium of.

2 入 *kainyū* intervention
5 甲 *kaikō* crust-like shell
6 在 *kaizai* intervention
8 抱 *kaihō suru* nurse; look after
10 病 *kaibyō suru* nurse a patient
11 添 *kaizo(e)* helper, assistant, second
殻 *kaikaku* sea shell
13 意 *kai-i suru* worry about, care about
16 錯 *kaishaku suru* assist at harakiri
錯人 *kaishakunin* a second at harakiri; attendant; attendance, assistance
23 鱗 *kairin* fish and shellfish

A **以** 348 F102 I. *mot(te)* with, by, by means of; because; in view of.

3 下 *ika* less than, under, below; and downward; not exceeding; the following; the rest
上 *ijō* more than, over, above; and up; beyond; the above-mentioned; since, as
4 内 *inai* within, less than ⌊long as; the end
心伝心 *ishin-denshin* telepathy; sympathy, quiet understanding
5 外 *igai ni* with the exception of; excepting. *mot(te) (no) hoka* absurd, unreasonable
北 *ihoku* north of; and northward
6 西 *isei* west of; and westward
7 来 *irai* since ⌈merly; in ancient times
8 往 *iō* hereafter; thereafter; the future; for-
東 *itō* east of; and eastward
9 後 *igo* hereafter; thereafter
降 *ikō* on and after; hereafter; thereafter
前 *izen ni* ago, since, before, previously
南 *inan* south of; and south
12 遠 *ien* and beyond

A **仁** 349 F93 Jin virtue, benevolence, humanity, charity; man. Nin kernel.

2 人 *jinnin* man of virtue, humanitarian
4 心 *jinshin* benevolence, humanity
王 *Niō* Guardian Deva Kings
王力 *Niōriki* Herulean strength
王門 *Niōmon* temple gate guarded by fierce Deva Kings
5 兄 *jinkei* term of address for a friend
7 君 *jinkun* benevolent ruler
8 者 *jinsha* man of virtue; humanitarian
9 侠 *jinkyō* chivalrous spirit
政 *jinsei* benevolent rule
10 恕 *jinjo* benevolence, magnanimity
恵 *jinkei* graciousness, mercy, charity
11 術 *jinjutsu* benevolent act; healing art
12 智 *jinchi* benevolence and wisdom
13 慈 *jinji* benevolence, mercy
愛 *jin-ai* benevolence, charity, love
義 *jingi* humanity and justice; duty; moral code (of a gang)
義礼智信 *jin-gi-rei-chi-shin* the 5 Confucian virtues (benevolence, justice, courtesy, wisdom, and sincerity)
14 徳 *jintoku* benevolence, goodness ⌈ganza
15 輪加狂言 *niwaka kyōgen* farce, extrava-

A **化** 350 F273 **化** Ka influence. Ke. *ba(kasu)* bewitch, enchant, confuse, delude. *ba(keru)* appear in disguise. *ka(suru), ka(su), ke(suru)* change into, convert into, transform, be reduced; influence, improve (someone). *fu(keru)* steam (rice); change with age; spoil from weathering. *(o)ba(ke)* goblin, apparition. *-ka* -ize (a verbal ending meaning "to change"). [匕]

5 生 *kasei* growth, metamorphosis. *keshō* goblin ⌈acter, disguise
皮 *bake (no) kawa* masking one's true char-
石 *kaseki* petrifaction, fossilization; fossil
石学 *kasekigaku* paleontology
石層 *kasekisō* fossil bed
6 合 *kagō* compounding (in chemistry)
合物 *kagōbutsu* chemical compound
成 *kasei* change, transformation
成工業 *kasei kōgyō* chemical industry
成肥料 *kasei hiryō* chemical fertilizer
7 身 *keshin* (Buddhist) incarnation; personification; impersonation
8 物 *ba(ke)mono* goblin, apparition
育 *ka-iku* evolution, growth
学 *kagaku* chemistry ⌈ing
学工学 *kagaku kōgaku* chemical engineer-
学工業 *kagaku kōgyō* chemical industry
学反応 *kagaku hannō* chemical reaction
学式 *kagaku shiki* chemical formula

学兵器 *kagaku heiki* chemical weapons
学者 *kagakusha* chemist
学肥料 *kagaku hiryō* chemical fertilizer
学変化 *kagaku henka* chemical change
学記号 *kagaku kigō* chemical symbols (for the elements)
学線 *kagakusen* actinic rays
学療法 *kagaku ryōhō* medical treatment
学繊維 *kagaku sen-i* synthetic fibers
10 骨 *kakotsu* ossification
12 粧 *keshō* make-up
粧下 *keshō shita* make-up base
粧水 *keshōsui, keshō mizu* face lotion
粧代 *keshōdai* lady's pin money; cosmetics expense
粧台 *keshōdai* dressing table, dresser
粧石鹸 *keshō sekken* toilet soap
粧品 *keshōhin* toilet articles
粧室 *keshōshitsu* powder room, lavatory
粧料 *keshōryō* lady's pin money
粧部屋 *keshōbeya* lavatory; dressing room
粧道具 *keshō dōgu* toilet set
粧着 *keshōgi* dressing gown ⌈bricks
粧煉瓦 *keshō renga* ornamental tile; facing
粧箱 *keshōbako* vanity case; fancy box
14 導 *kadō* influencing (a person) for good
17 繊 *kasen* synthetic fibers ⌈head
膿 *kanō suru* suppurate, fester, come to a
膿菌 *kanōkin* suppurative germ

A 仏 351/F116 佛 BUTSU Buddha, Buddhism. FUTSU French. *hotoke* Buddha; merciful person; Buddhist image; the dead.

2 力 *butsuriki* the power of Buddha
3 工 *bukkō* maker of Buddhist images and altar fittings ⌈the Buddha mind
4 心 *busshin, hotokegokoro* the Buddha heart,
文 *Futsubun* French, French writing, French literature
5 生会 *busshōe* Buddha's birthday celebration
6 式 *busshiki* Buddhist ritual
気 *hotokegi* a compassionate heart
印 *Futsu-In* French Indo-China
会 *butsue* Buddhist memorial service
寺 *butsuji* Buddhist temple
名 *butsumyō* a Buddha's name
7 作 *hotokezuku(ru)* become haggard
陀 *Budda, Butsuda* Buddha
8 門 *Butsumon* Buddhism; priesthood
国 *Fukkoku* France
性 *hotokeshō, busshō* the Buddha nature
刹 *bussetsu, bussatsu* Buddhist temple
画 *butsuga* Buddhist picture
参 *bussan suru* visit a Buddhist temple
具 *butsugu* Buddhist altar equipment
典 *butten* Buddhist scriptures, sutras
学 *butsugaku* Buddhist learning
果 *bukka* Buddhahood, Nirvana
者 *bussha* a Buddhist; a Buddhist priest
事 *butsuji* Buddhist memorial service
舎利 *busshari* Buddha's ashes
法 *Buppō* Buddhism
法僧 *buppōsō* the Buddha, the doctrine, and the priesthood
9 祖 *Busso* Founder of Buddhism
前 *butsuzen* before the Buddha or a mortuary tablet ⌈nious
臭 *hotokekusa(i)* otherworldly, sanctimo-
10 座 *butsuza* Buddhist image seat; temple
師 *busshi* Buddhist image maker ⌊pulpit
徒 *butto* a Buddhist
家 *bukke* Buddhist priest
書 *bussho* Buddhist scriptures ⌈to Buddha
恩 *butsuon* grace of Buddha; indebtedness
11 道 *butsudō* Buddhism, Buddhist teachings
経 *bukkyō* Buddhist sutras
教 *Bukkyō* Buddhism
堂 *butsudō* Buddhist temple
貨 *fukka* francs
頂面 *butchōzura* sour look
12 間 *butsuma* Buddhist family chapel
葬 *bussō* Buddhist funeral
13 殿 *butsuden* Buddhist temple
僧 *bussō* Buddhist priest
滅 *butsumetsu* Buddha's death; unlucky day
跡 *busseki* a place sacred to Buddhism
14 閣 *bukkaku* Buddhist temple
像 *butsuzō* Buddhist image
様 *hotoke sama* a Buddha; a deceased per-
説 *bussetsu* Buddha's teaching ⌊son
語 *Futsugo* French language. *butsugo* Buddhist term ⌈territory
領 *Futsuryō* French possession, French
15 縁 *butsuen* Buddha's providence
器 *bukki* Buddhist altar fittings
16 噸 *futsuton* metric ton
壇 *butsudan* Buddhist household altar
18 顔 *hotokegao* a gentle face
20 艦 *Futsukan* French warship
蘭西 *Furansu* France

A 今 352/F94 KIN. KON now, the present; the coming; this. *ima* now, the present time; just now, soon, immediately; (one) more. *ima demo* even now, still, as yet. *ima dewa* now, nowadays. *ima ni* before long; even now, still. *ima nimo* at any time, soon. *ima ya* now. *ima(mekashii)* fashionable. *ima(mekasu)* modernize. *ima(motte)* until now. *ima-* modern.

1 一 *ima hito(tsu)* one more

一度 *ima ichido* once more

2人 *konjin* present-day people; people of this world

3夕 *konseki, kon-yū* this evening, tonight

上 *Kinjō* the reigning emperor

上陛下 *Kinjō Heika* the reigning emperor

4方 *ima(shi)gata, imagata* a moment ago

以 *ima mot(te)* still, yet, (not) yet

少 *ima suko(shi)* a little more

月 *kongetsu* this month

月分 *kongetsubun* (charge) for this month

今 *ima-ima* right now. *ima(ka)ima(ka)* eagerly waiting. *ima(ga)ima* just now

今迄 *ima (ga) ima made* till just now

日 *kyō, konnichi* today, this day. *Konnichi wa* How do you do.

日日 *kyōbi* nowadays

日迄 *kyō made, konnichi made* until today

日的 *konnichiteki* modern, up-to-date

日明日 *kyō-asu* today and tomorrow; today or tomorrow; in a day or two

日様 *konnichisama* sun god

5生 *konjō* this life, this world

古 *kinko* now and anciently

冬 *kontō* this winter; next winter; last winter

出来 *imadeki* something new

世界 *konsekai* this world

世紀 *konseiki* this century

6回 *konkai* lately; this time

迄 *ima made* till now

次 *konji* the present time. *konji no* new, recent

年 *konnen, kotoshi* this year

7更 *imasara* now, at this late hour

8夜 *kon-ya* this evening, tonight

尚 *ima nao* still, even now

昔 *konjaku, konseki* past and present

明日 *kommyōnichi* today and (or) tomorrow

9風 *imafū* modern style

度 *kondo* this time, now; next time; another time

後 *kongo* after this, hereafter

秋 *konshū* this fall; next fall; last fall

春 *konshun* this spring; next spring; last spring

10週 *konshū* this week

般 *kompan* now, recently; this time

夏 *konka* this summer; next summer; last summer

宵 *koyoi* this evening, tonight

時 *imadoki,* recently, these days; at this hour

時分 *ima jibun* about this time

11遅 *ima(ya)oso(shi) to* impatiently, eagerly

頃 *imagoro* about this time

道心 *ima dōshin* neophyte, novice

12晩 *komban* tonight, this evening. *Komban wa* Good evening.

暁 *kongyō* this morning; this morning at dawn

程 *imahodo* recently; a moment before

期 *konki* the present term

朝 *kesa, konchō* this morning

朝方 *kesagata* this morning

13際 *imawa* one's dying hour

14様 *imayō* modern style

様歌 *imayō uta* a Heian poetry style

3

仟 353/F100 See 千 156.

以 See 348.

尒 354/F195/F1211 See 爾 69. [入]

仝 355/F195/F330 See 同 619 and 全 384. [入]

仞 356/F100 仞 JIN fathom.

仗 357/F98 JŌ. *tsue* cane; whipping rod.

仔 358/F97 SHI (animal) offspring.

4牛 *ko-ushi* calf

犬 *ko-inu* puppy

6羊 *kohitsuji* lamb

虫 *shichū* larva

11細 *shisai* reasons, circumstances; significance; particulars; hindrance, obstruction, interference

仙 359/F99 SEN hermit; wizard. *sento* cent.

2人 *sennin* hermit; wizard; fairy; otherworldly person

人掌 *saboten, shaboten* cactus

3女 *sennyo, senjo* fairy, nymph

4丹 *sentan* the elixir (of life)

7花紙 *senkashi* reclaimed paper

9界 *senkai* dwelling place of hermits; a pure land away from the world

10骨 *senkotsu* unusual physique, outstanding appearance; philosophic turn of mind; the sacrum, sacral bone

郷 *senkyō* fairyland, enchanted land

11術 *senjutsu* wizardry; the secret of immortality

13窟 *senkutsu* enchanted cave

14境 *senkyō* fairyland, enchanted land

16薬 *sen-yaku* panacea; elixir (of life)

令 360/F101 A RYŌ ancient laws. REI order, command; ordinance, law, decree. *rei(suru)* command, order, dictate. *-shi(mu)* old causative verbal ending.

4夫人 *reifujin* Mrs., Lady, Madam; your wife

5兄 *reikei* your elder brother
6色 *reishoku* servile looks
旨 *reishi, ryōji* a prince's message; command of a prince
名 *reimei* good reputation, fame
7状 *reijō* warrant, summons; written order
弟 *reitei* your younger brother
8姉 *reishi* your elder sister
妹 *reimai* your younger sister
9姪 *reitetsu* your niece
室 *reishitsu* your wife
10娘 *reijō* your daughter, young lady
孫 *reison* your grandchild
息 *reisoku* your son
11堂 *reidō* (polite) home; mother
望 *reibō* good reputation
12婿 *reisei* your son-in-law
13嗣 *reishi* heir
14聞 *reibun* good reputation, fame
閨 *reikei* your wife, his wife, Mrs.
16嬢 *reijō* your daughter, your lady

A **他** 361 F97 TA. another, the other, others, another thing; the rest; another place. *ta-* another, other. *hoka* (see under 外 1168.0).

2力 *tariki* outside help; salvation by faith
力本願 *tariki-hongan* salvation by faith in Amida Buddha; reliance upon others
人 *tanin, adabito* another person, unrelated person, outsider, stranger
人扱 *tanin-atsuka(i)* treating like a stranger
人行儀 *tanin gyōgi* reserved manners
人空似 *tanin (no) sorani* accidental resemblance
3山 *tazan* another mountain; another temple
山石 *tazan (no) ishi* object lesson, food for thought
4心 *tashin*=*ta-i* 他意 (see below–13)
方 *tahō* another side; different direction; (on) the other hand
日 *tajitsu* some day; hereafter, at some future time
5出 *tashutsu* going out
世界 *tasekai* other worlds
生 *tashō* previous existence; future existence; transmigration
生縁 *tashō (no) en* karma from a previous existence
6行 *tagyō* absence from home. *takō* going out
年 *tanen* some other year; some day
7見 *taken* viewing by others; showing others
言 *tagen, tagon* telling others; revealing to others
村 *tason* another village
作農 *tasakunō* tenant farming
8店 *taten* another shop, store, or firm
姓 *tasei* another surname
所 *yoso, tasho* another place
物 *tabutsu, ta(no)mono* the other thing, the other man's property
宗 *tashū* another sect
事 *taji* other matters, other people's affairs
念 *tanen* thinking about something else
念無 *tanenna(ku)* eagerly, intently
国 *takoku* foreign country; another province
国人 *takokujin* foreigner, alien, stranger
国民 *takokumin* other nations, other peoples
国者 *takoku mono* stranger, a person from another place
9面 *tamen* the other side; another direction; (on) the other hand
律 *taritsu* heteronomy, subjection, subordination
派 *taha* the other group
界 *takai suru* die. *takai* the next world; death
県 *taken* another prefecture
10称 *tashō* third person (in grammar)
殺 *tasatsu* murder
郷 *takyō* another place; a foreign country
家 *take* another family
流 *taryū* another style; another school (of thought); different blood
流試合 *taryūjiai* contest between different schools (of fencing, etc.)
11動詞 *tadōshi* transitive verb
12覚的 *takakuteki* objective (symptoms)
覚症 *takakushō*=the following word
覚症状 *takaku shōjō* objective symptoms, symptoms observed by the doctor
郷 *takyō* foreign country
13愛 *ta-ai* altruism
意 *ta-i* other intention, secret purpose, ulterior motive, ill will, fickleness, double-mindedness
14聞 *tabun* publicity, reaching other ears
領 *taryō* another fief
16薦 *tasen* recommendation

A **仕** 362 F97 SHI official; civil service. *tsuka(eru)*, serve, work for. *tsukamatsu(ru)* serve; do (polite).

2入 *shi-i(reru)* laying in stock
入物 *shi-i(re)mono* stock of goods received
3口 *shikuchi* method, way
女 *tsuka(e)me* maidservant
上 *shi-a(garu) vi* be finished. *shi-a(geru) vt* finish
上工 *shiagekō* finishing workman
上払 *shia(ge)bara(i)* piecework pay
4手 *shite* protagonist; hero; leading part
切 *shi-ki(ru)* partition, divide; mark off; settle accounts; toe the mark. *shiki(ri)* partition, division, boundary; compartment; settlement of accounts; toeing the mark. *shi-ki(renai)* impossible to do
分 *shi-wa(keru)* assort, classify; journalize (in accounting)

込 *shi-ko(mu)* train, bring up, educate; fit into, stock up on. *shikom(i)* training; stocking up; preparation
込杖 *shiko(mi)zue* a sword cane 「means
方 *shikata* way, method, resource, course,
方無 *shikata (no) na(i), shikata (ga) na(i), shikatana(i)* it can't be helped, it's inevitable; it's no use; can't stand it; be impatient; be annoyed. *shikatana(ku), shikatana(shi) ni* helplessly, reluctantly
方話 *shikatabanashi* talking with gestures
5 打 *shiu(chi)* treatment; behavior, conduct
払 *shi-hara(u)* pay
末 *shimatsu*＝始末 1208.5
付 *shi-tsu(keru)* be used to a job; begin to do; make; baste, tack; plant. *shitsu(ke)* rice planting; tacking, basting
付糸 *shitsu(ke) ito* tacking; basting (thread)
出 *shida(shi)* catering; shipment. *shi-da(su)* begin to do; cater
出来 *shi-deka(su)* finish up
出屋 *shida(shi)ya* caterer
立 *shi-ta(teru)* tailor; make; prepare; train; send (a messenger). *shita(te)* tailoring, dressmaking, sewing; making; preparation
立下 *shita(te)oro(shi)* brand-new (clothes)
立方 *shita(te)kata* style of clothes; method of tailoring; method of training
立券 *shitateken* free dressmaking ticket (with a purchase of cloth)
立物 *shitatemono* sewing, tailoring; newly-tailored clothes 「ing)
立直 *shita(te)nao(shi)* making over (cloth-
立屋 *shita(te)ya* tailor; dressmaker
6 返 *shikae(shi)* doing over; tit for tat; retaliation, revenge 「(men); send, forward to
向 *shi-mu(keru)* treat, act toward, handle
合 *shiai*＝試合 4361.6. *shia(wase)* fortune, luck; happiness, blessing
合者 *shia(wase)mono* fortunate person
7 形 *shikata*＝仕方 (see above–4)
来 *shikita(ri)* custom, conventional practice
8 送 *shioku(ri)* allowance, remittance
始 *shi-haji(meru)* begin, start
直 *shi-nao(su)*＝*ya(ri)-nao(su)* 遣直 4732.8
官 *shikan* government service; samurai's service 「as commanded
奉 *tsuka(e)-matsu(ru)* serve (polite); build
放題 *shihōdai* having one's own way
事 *shigoto* work, employment, occupation
事日 *shigotobi* work day
事台 *shigotodai* workbench, work table
事師 *shigotoshi* workman; enterpriser; schemer
事部屋 *shigotobeya* workroom
事場 *shigotoba* place where one works; construction site
事着 *shigotogi* work clothes; business suit
事箱 *shigotobako* workbox
9 度 *shitaku*＝支度 2039.9
拵 *shikoshira(e)* preparation 「gestures
草 *shigusa* treatment; behavior, action;
10 納 *shiosa(me)* finishing up
致 *shi (o) ita(su)* resign
兼 *shi-ka(neru)* be unable to do; hesitate, be reluctant. *shi-ka(nenai)* be capable of anything
留 *shi-to(meru)* bring down (a bird), kill
11 遂 *shi-to(geru)* accomplish, finish, fulfill
済 *shi-su(masu)* succeed as planned
組 *shi-ku(mu)* devise, arrange, plan, plot. *shiku(mi)* construction; contrivance, arrangement; plan, plot
訳 *shi-wa(keru)*＝仕分 (see above–4)
掛 *shi-ka(keru)* commence; lay (mines); set (traps); wage (war); challenge. *shikaka(ri)* commencement. *shika(ke)* mechanism, gadget; (small) scale; half finished
掛花火 *shikake hanabi* a fireworks piece
訳書 *shiwakesho* specifications
訳帳 *shiwakechō* bookkeeping journal
12 着 *shiki(se)* livery, servant's clothes provided by employers
替 *shi-ka(eru)* do over, start anew
13 損 *shi-sokona(u), shi-son(jiru)* blunder, fail, make a mistake 「perienced in
馴 *shi-na(reru)* be used to doing, be ex-
業 *shiwaza* act, action, deed
置 *shio(ki)* execution; punishment
置者 *shio(ki)mono* a criminal
置場 *shio(ki)ba* execution ground
14 種 *shigusa* method; attitude; actor's expressions; actions. 「help
様 *shiyō* way, method; resource; remedy,
様書 *shiyōga(ki)* specifications
様無 *shiyō (ga) na(i)* It can't be helped. It is inevitable. *shiyō (no) na(i)* hopeless, good-for-nothing, incorrigible
舞 *shima(u)* finish, conclude; put away; save; close, wind up. *shimai* end, termination; informal noh play 「hoard up
舞込 *shima(i)-ko(mu)* lay away, stow away,
舞物 *shima(i)mono* goods left unsold
舞屋 *shimotaya* a store that has gone out of business; a household that lives without carrying on a business
15 儀 *shigi* situation, developments, outcome

A **付** 363/F98 FU. *fu(suru)* give to, submit to, refer to; affix, attach, append. *tsu(keru)* vt attach, join, stick, glue, fasten;

sew on; furnish (a house with); wear, put on; make an entry; appraise, set (a price); apply (ointment); bring alongside; place (under guard or a doctor); follow, shadow; add, append, affix; load; give (courage to); keep (an eye on); establish (relations or understanding). *tsu(ku) vi* be connected with; be dyed; be stained; be scarred; be recorded; be attached to; (fires) start; follow; become allied to; accompany; study with; increase, be added to. *(o)tsu(ki)* attendant, escort. *tsu(ke)* bill, bill of sale. *(ni) tsu(ki)* per, apiece; because of; regarding. *tsu(ki)* (printing) impression; sociability; appearance. *tsu(katari)* addition, accessory, appendage, supplement, appendix; complement; an excuse. *(ni) tsu(ite)* (see under 就 323.0). *-zu(ke)* dated. *-zu(ki)* attached to, furnished with. *tsu(ke)-* fixed, external. *-tsu(ke)* date. *-tsu(ki)* attached to, under, to.

2 人 *tsu(ke)bito* assistant, attendant; chaperon; suite

入 *tsu(ke)-i(ru)* take advantage of, impose on

3 上 *tsu(ke)-a(garu)* be elated; be spoiled; take advantage of

与 *fuyo* grant, allowance, endowment

4 文 *tsu(ke)bumi* love letter

火 *tsu(ke)bi* incendiarism

込 *tsu(ke)-ko(mu)* take advantage of, impose on; make an entry. *tsu(ke)ko(mi)* entry, booking

切 *tsu(ki)ki(ri)*, *tsu(k)ki(ri)* constant attendance (by a doctor)

元気 *tsu(ke) genki* show of courage

不足 *tsu(ke)busoku* undercharge

5 目 *tsu(ke)me* aim; (to aim at) a weak point

札 *tsu(ke) fuda* tag, label

出 *tsu(ke)-da(su)* charge. *tsu(ke)da(shi)* bill, account

加 *tsu(ke)-kuwa(eru)* add to. *fuka* addition, annexation, supplement, appendage

加税 *fukazei* additional tax

6 回 *tsu(ke)-mawa(su)*, *tsu(ke)-mawa(ru)* follow, shadow, hanker after, hover around

近 *fukin* neighborhood, environs, vicinity

会 *fukai* add to; twist the meaning

合 *tsu(ke)-a(waseru)* add to. *tsu(ki)-a(u)* keep company with, associate with, get along with. *tsu(ki)a(i)* association, fellowship, acquaintance, friendship. *tsu(ki)a(wase)* perfect occlusion; vegetable relish with meat

7 言 *fugen* postscript, additional remarks

足 *tsu(ke)-ta(su)* add to. *tsu(ke)ta(shi)* addition, appendix, supplement, postscript

図 *fuzu* attached map or plan

8 届 *tsu(ke)todo(ke)* tip, present

所 *tsu(ke)dokoro* viewpoint

注 *fuchū* annotation, comment

物 *tsu(ki)mono* accessory, appendage

狙 *tsu(ke)-nera(u)* prowl after, shadow, keep watch on

直 *tsu(ke)-nao(su)* repair again, join again

者 *tsu(ki)mono* attendant; curse; devil possession

表 *fuhyō* attached list

事 *tsu(kanu) koto* something sudden

具合 *tsu(ki) guai*=*tsu(ki)* (see under 363.0)

和 *fuwa* blindly following others

知恵 *tsu(ke)jie* hint, suggestion

和雷同 *fuwa-raidō* following blindly

9 則 *fusoku* additional rules, by-laws, supplementary provisions

10 馬 *tsu(ki)uma*, *tsu(ke)uma* bill collector for the night's entertainment; followers

値 *tsu(ke)ne* the bid, the offer

従 *tsu(ki)-shitaga(u)* follow, accompany, join up with; obey implicitly; flatter

根 *tsu(ke)ne* root, joint, base, crotch

紙 *tsu(ke)gami* tag, slip, label

紐 *tsu(ke) himo* child's sash

記 *fuki* appendix, addition, note

託 *futaku suru* commit to, refer to, submit to

随 *tsu(ki)-shitaga(u)* follow, accompany, cleave to. *fuzui* incidental, attendant, annexed, accompanying

帯 *futai* incidental, accessory, secondary, collateral

帯犯 *futaihan* accessory offense

帯事項 *futai jikō* supplementary item

帯費用 *futai hiyō* incidental expenses

11 掛 *tsu(ke)ka(ke)* overcharge

著 *fuchaku*=付着 (see below–12)

黒子 *tsu(ke)bokuro* artificial facial beauty spot

添 *tsu(ki)-so(u)* escort and wait on, accompany, chaperon. *tsukiso(i)* attendance on; attendant, escort, chaperon, retinue

添人 *tsukisoinin* attendant

添婦 *tsukisoifu* practical nurse

12 換 *tsu(ke)-ka(eru)* renew, replace, change for, attach anew

着 *fuchaku* adhesion, cohesion, agglutination

落 *tsu(ke)o(chi)*, *tsu(ke)o(toshi)* omission in a bill

替 *tsu(ke)ka(e)* replacement

景気 *tsu(ke)geiki* borrowed prosperity

焼 *tsu(ke)ya(ki)* broiling with soy

焼刃 *tsu(ke)yakiba* pretension, affectation

属 *fuzoku* attached, annexed; affiliated, associated; subordinate, incidental, dependent, auxiliary, accessory

属物 *fuzokubutsu* belongings, appendage, appurtenances

属品 *fuzokuhin* accessory, fittings, appurtenances

属書 *fuzokusho* appendix, supplementary notes

属節 *fuzoku setsu* subordinate clause

2 二亠人イ𠆢儿入八丷冂冖冫几凵刀刂力勹匕匚匸十卜卩厂厶又

14 鼻 *tsu(ke)bana* false nose, artificial nose
箋 *fusen* tag, slip, label
髪 *tsu(ke)gami* false hair
16 録 *furoku* supplement, appendix
薬 *tsu(ke)gusuri* ointment, lotion
髭 *tsu(ke)hige* false moustache
髷 *tsu(ke)mage* false coiffure
19 離 *tsu(kazu)-hana(rezu)* indecision ⌈debate
20 議 *fugi suru* bring up a matter, discuss,
23 纏 *tsu(ki)-mato(u), tsu(ki)-matsu(waru), tsu-(ke)-mato(u)* follow around, shadow, hang around (a woman)

A **代** 364 / F100 DAI period, age, generation; charge, rate, fee, cost, price. *yo* (see under 世 95.0). *ka(eru)* change, turn, convert, exchange, renew, substitute, replace. *ka(waru)* replace, relieve. *kawa(ri)* substitute, deputy, proxy, alternate, relief; compensation; second helping. *shiro* price; substitution; materials. *kawa(ri) ni* instead of. *(sono) kawa(ri) ni* on the other hand.

2 人 *dainin* substitute, deputy, proxy, repre-
4 父 *daifu* godfather ⌊sentative, agent
5 母 *daibo* godmother
代 *daidai, yoyo* for generations; hereditary. *kawa(ru)gawa(ru), kawa(ri)gawa(ri)* al-
打 *daida* pinch-hitting ⌊ternately
打者 *daidasha* pinch hitter
弁 *daiben suru* pay by proxy; act for another; speak for another
弁者 *daibensha* spokesman, mouthpiece
用 *daiyō* substitution
用肉 *daiyō niku* meat substitute
用食 *daiyōshoku* substitute food
用品 *daiyōhin* a substitute
6 返 *daihen suru* answer a roll call for another
印 *dai-in* signing by proxy
任 *dainin* agency, acting official
休 *daikyū* compensatory holiday
地 *daichi* substitute land
合 *kawa(ri)-a(u)* relieve each other, take
名詞 *daimeishi* pronoun ⌊turns
行 *daikō* acting as an agent
行者 *daikōsha* agent, proxy
行機関 *daikō kikan* agency
7 走 *daisō* substitute runner
位 *dai-i* substitution
作 *daisaku* ghostwriting ⌈stand-in, a double
役 *daiyaku, kawa(ri) yaku* substitute actor, a
言 *daigen* speaking for another; attorney
言人 *daigennin* attorney
8 価 *daika* price, cost, charge
拝 *daihai* vicarious worship
物 *daibutsu* substitute. *shiromono* thing, article, goods; fellow; affair

参 *daisan* visiting a temple for another
官 *daikan* chief magistrate, governor, bailiff (Tokugawa era) ⌈the bill
金 *daikin* price, cost, charge, the money,
金引換 *daikin hikikae* C.O.D.
表 *daihyō* representation, type, example, model; delegate
表団 *daihyōdan* delegation ⌈tive work
表作 *daihyōsaku* masterpiece, a representa-
表者 *daihyōsha* representative, delegate
表的 *daihyōteki* representative, exemplary,
表部 *daihyōbu* diplomatic mission ⌊model
9 待 *daima(chi)* waiting in place of someone
品 *daihin* substitute article ⌊else
栄 *kawa(ri)ba(e)* successful substitution
10 将 *daishō* brigadier general; commodore
納 *dainō* payment for another
員 *dai-in* proxy
案 *daian* alternate plan
書 *daisho* scribe, amanuensis
書人 *daishonin* scribe, amanuensis
11 務 *daimu* vicarious management
執行 *daishikkō* carrying out by proxy
理 *dairi* representation, agency, proxy, deputy, agent, attorney; substitute, alternate; acting (principal, etc.)
理人 *dairinin* proxy, agent, substitute, deputy, alternate, representative, attorney ⌈embassy
理大使 *dairi taishi* chargé d'affaires of an
理公使 *dairi kōshi* chargé d'affaires of a legation
理投票 *dairi tōhyō* voting by proxy
理店 *dairiten* agency ⌈bove-11)
理者 *dairisha*=*dairinin* 代理人 (see a-
理委任状 *dairi ininjō* power of attorney
理牧師 *dairi bokushi* vicar
理部 *dairibu* mail-order department;
理業 *dairigyō* agency ⌊branch store
理領事 *dairi ryōji* acting consul
理権 *dairiken* agency; (attorney's) right of representation ⌈sistant; locum tenens
12 診 *daishin* doctor's assistance; doctor's as-
筆 *daihitsu* amanuensis ⌈nately
番 *kawa(ri)ban(ko) ni, kawa(ri)ban ni* alter-
替 *daiga(wari)* subrogation, change of
替物 *daitaibutsu* substitute ⌊ownership
替品 *daiga(e)hin* substitute article
13 僧 *daisō* substitute priest
署 *daisho suru* sign for another
置 *daichi suru* replace
数 *daisū* algebra
数式 *daisū shiki* algebraic expression
数学 *daisūgaku* algebra
14 演 *daien suru* substitute for an actor
読 *daidoku* reading for another

16稽古 *daigeiko* substitute teaching
燃車 *dainensha* car running on substitute ⌊fuel
赭 *taisha* red ocher
赭色 *taisha iro* yellowish brown
17償 *daishō* compensation, indemnification, reparation; consideration
講 *daikō* substitute lecturing ⌈2080.10
謝 *taisha*=*shinchin-taisha* 新陳代謝
19願 *daigan* praying by proxy; applying by proxy ⌈place of another
願人 *daigannin* one who offers prayer in
20艦 *daikan* replacement warship
議 *daigi* representing others in a conference
議士 *daigishi* member of a congress
議制度 *daigi seido* parliamentary system
議政体 *daigi seitai* representative government ⌈ment
議政治 *daigi seiji* representative govern-
議員 *daigi-in* representative, delegate
議員団 *daigi-indan* delegation

4

仿 365/F106 Bō, Hō stand still; wander.

倅 366/F142 **倅** Sai. Sotsu. Sochi. *segare* son, my son.

伉 367/F106 Kō same kind; compare with.
10配 *kōhai* spouse, married couple

A **件** 368/F105 Ken matter, case, item. *kudan* example, precedent. *kudan no* the usual; the said; the above-mentioned. *kudari* the above-mentioned.
13数 *kensū* number of cases or items

伍 369/F107 Go five; five-man squad; file, line. *go(suru)* rank with, associ- ⌊ate with. *itsu(tsu)* five.
8長 *gochō* corporal

B **伐** 370/F108 Batsu. *u(tsu)* strike, attack; punish. *ki(ru)* (see under 切 ⌊667.0).
4木 *batsuboku* felling, logging
5出 *ki(ri)-da(su)*=切出 667.5
10倒 *battō* felling
11採 *bassai* felling, deforestation, lumbering

伎 371/F107 Gi, Ki deed; skill.
3女 *gijo* woman entertainer
工 *gikō* artisan
7芸 *gigei* arts, handicrafts, accomplishments
10倆 *giryō* ability, talent, skill, capacity
能 *ginō* skill, ability, capacity
13楽 *gigaku* ancient music

伊 372/F106 I that one. *I-*, *-I* Italy.
4太利 *Itaria, Itarii* Italy
7呂波 *i-ro-ha* the first three *kana* of the syllabary
11達 *date na* vainglorious, showy
達女 *date onna* a flapper
達男 *date otoko*=next word
達者 *datesha* dandy, dude
達姿 *date sugata* flashy appearance
達巻 *datemaki* under sash; omelet wrapper
達着 *dategi* showy clothes
達衆 *dateshū* a dandy, a gallant; chivalrous person ⌈of Ise
13勢大神宮 *Ise Daijingū* the Grand Shrines
勢大廟 *Ise Taibyō* the Grand Shrines of Ise
勢参 *Ise-mai(ri)* Ise pilgrimage
勢蝦 *ise ebi* spiny lobster
14語 *Igo* Italian language
20艦 *Ikan* Italian warship

B **企** 373/F106 Ki. *kuwada(teru)* plan, plot, propose, design, intend, contemplate; attempt, undertake. *taku(ramu)* scheme, plan, play a trick, invent, conspire, frame up. *takura(mi)* plan, design, artifice; trick, intrigue. *kuwada(te)* plan, attempt, undertaking.
3及 *kikyū* attempt
7図 *kito* plan, project, scheme
8画 *kikaku* plan; planning
13業 *kigyō* an enterprise
業心 *kigyōshin* enterprising spirit
業化 *kigyōka* commercialization
業合同 *kigyō gōdō* a trust
業者 *kigyōsha* industrialist
業連合 *kigyō rengō* a cartel
業家 *kigyōka* industrialist
業整備 *kigyō seibi* curtailment of business operations
14劃 *kikaku* plan; planning

A **任** 374/F105 Jin. Nin duty, responsibility; office; mission; term. *maka(su)*, *maka(seru)* entrust to, leave to. *nin(jiru)*, *nin(zuru)* appoint, nominate; assume (responsibility); pose as. *mama* (see under 儘 558.0).
5用 *nin-yō* appointment, employment
6地 *ninchi* one's post, appointment
8官 *ninkan* appointment, investiture
免 *nimmen* appointments and dismissals
命 *nimmei* appointment, nomination, ordination, commission, designation
命式 *nimmeishiki* investiture
命状 *nimmeijō* written appointment

2 二亠人亻𠆢儿入八丷冂冖冫几凵刀刂力勹匕匚匸十卜卩厂厶又

2 二 亠 人 イ 𠆢 儿 入 八 丷 冂 冖 冫 几 凵 刀 刂 力 勹 匕 匚 匸 十 卜 卩 厂 厶 又

9 侠 *ninkyō* chivalry, generosity, heroism chivalrous spirit
11 務 *nimmu* duty, function, office, mission
12 期 *ninki* term of office
期中 *ninkichū* during one's tenure ⌈will
13 意 *nin-i* option, pleasure, discretion, free
意出頭 *nin-i shuttō* voluntarily appearing for police questioning
18 職 *ninshoku* ordination

B **仰** 375/F103 GYŌ. KŌ. *ao(gu)* look up; look up to; ask for, depend on; seek; respect, revere; drink, take. *ao(muku)*, *ao(noku)* look up. *ao(nokeru)* turn up (one's face or a card). *os(sharu)* say, speak, tell, talk (polite). *ō(serareru)* say, state (polite). *ō(se)* statement, command, wishes (of a superior).
3 山 *gyōsan* large quantity, plenty, abundance, a great many ⌈back
4 反 *nokezo(ru)* bend back; throw (the head)
天 *gyōten suru* be amazed, be horrified
5 付 *ō(se)-tsu(keru)* command; request; appoint. *ō(se)-tsu(karu)* receive a command
出 *ō(se)-da(su)* announce, proclaim
6 仰 *gyōgyō(shii)* exaggerated, bombastic, highly colored
向 *aomu(keru)* turn up (one's face or a card). *aomu(ku)* look up, lie face up
向様 *aomu(ke)zama* on one's back
7 見 *ao(gi)-mi(ru)* look up to, look up at;
角 *gyōkaku* angle of elevation ⌊revere
附 *ō(se)-tsu(keru)* command; request; appoint. *ō(se)-tsu(karu)* receive a command
8 奉 *ao(gi)-tatematsu(ru)* polite for *ao(gu)* (see under 375.0)
臥 *gyōga* sleeping face up
臥位 *gyōgai* lying face up
11 視 *gyōshi suru* look up to, revere
望 *gyōbō suru*, *ao(gi)-nozo(mu)* look to (for help); look up to, revere
14 様 *nokezama ni* on one's back

A **似** 376/F112 JI. *ni(ru)* resemble. *ni(seru)* copy, imitate; counterfeit, forge. *ni(tsukawashii)* suitable, appropriate, becoming. *-ni* takes after (his mother).
5 付 *ni-tsu(ku)*=*ni-a(u)* 似合 (see below–6). *ni-tsu(kawashii)* suitable, becoming
6 合 *ni-a(u)* become, suit, be like, match well. *nia(i)* well-matched; suitable, becoming. *nia(washii)* well-matched, suitable, becoming
而非 *ese-* (see under 似非–below 8)
気無 *nigena(i)* unlike, unbecoming, unworthy of, out of keeping with
8 者 *ni(ta)mono* similar people
非 *ni(te)hi(naru)* falsely similar, counterfeit. *ese-* false, would-be, sham, pretended, mock, spurious, pseudo-, quasi-
非者 *esemono* sham, fraud, counterfeit; impostor, pretender
非事 *esegoto* laughable affair, unlaudable affair, something unreliable
非笑 *esewara(i)* smirk, affected smile
非理窟 *eserikutsu* sophistry
非親 *ese oya* distant disinterested parent
9 通 *nikayo(u)* resemble closely
11 寄 *ni-yo(ru)* resemble. *niyo(ri)* similarity. *ni(tari)-yo(ttari)* much the same
18 顔 *nigao* likeness, portrait
顔書 *nigaoka(ki)* portrait painter; drawing
顔絵 *nigaoe* likeness, portrait ⌊portraits

B **伏** 377/F107 FUKU. *fu(su) vi* bend down, bow down, iie prostrate. *fu(seru) vt* turn over, lay face down; cover; lay (pipes), lay (an ambush); hide. *fuku(suru)* stoop, bend down, crouch; lie down, prostrate oneself, fall prostrate; hide; yield to, submit to. *fu(shite)* bowing down; humbly, respectfully.
5 目 *fu(shi)me* downcast look ⌈etc.)
6 字 *fu(se)ji* asterisk, blank type (dots, circles,
在 *fukuzai suru* lie concealed, be hidden
7 兵 *fukuhei* ambush, troops in ambush
8 拝 *fu(shi)-oga(mu)* kneel and worship
9 屋 *fu(se)ya* humble cottage, hut
奏 *fukusō* report to the throne
10 倒 *fu(shi)-tao(reru)* fall down
射 *fukusha suru* to shoot lying prone
射濠 *fukushagō* sheltered trench
11 転 *fu(shi)-maro(bu)* fall and roll over; wrig-
13 罪 *fukuzai* pleading guilty ⌊gle about
勢 *fu(se)zei*, *fukuzei* ambush
14 樋 *fu(se)doi* covered drain
15 縫 *fu(se)nu(i)* hemming ⌈tionary measures
線 *fukusen* underplot (in a novel); precau-
21 魔殿 *fukumaden* abode of demons; hotbed (of graft); pandemonium
22 籠 *fu(se)kago* coop, hen coop

B **仲** 378/F104 CHŪ. *naka* relation; relationship.
2 人 *nakōdo*, *chūnin* go-between; matchmaking
人口 *nakōdoguchi* matchmaker's story; saying nice things about a person
4 介 *chūkai* agency, intermediation
介物 *chūkaibutsu* intermediary, medium, channel ⌈dleman
介者 *chūkaisha* mediator, go-between, mid-
5 仕 *nakashi* longshoreman; baggageman

兄 *chūkei* the younger of two elder brothers
冬 *chūtō* mid-winter
立 *nakada(chi)* mediation, agency; agent, mediator, middleman, go-between
立人 *nakadachinin* middleman, mediator, go-between
6好 *nakayoshi* see following entry
7良 *nakayo(ku)* on cordial terms. *nakayo(shi)* intimacy; chum
8居 *nakai* waitress
直 *nakanao(ri)* reconciliation. *nakane* average price
9春 *chūshun* mid-spring
保 *chūho* mediation, intercession
保者 *chūhosha* mediator, intercessor
秋 *chūshū* 8th lunar month; mid-autumn
秋明月 *chūshū (no) meigetsu* harvest moon
10値 *nakane* average price
核 *chūkaku* nucleus, core, kernel
夏 *chūka* midsummer
11違 *nakataga(i)* discord, estrangement
断 *chūdan* break, interruption, suspension
12買 *nakagai* brokerage
買人 *nakagainin* broker, jobber
裁 *chūsai* arbitration, mediation, peacemaking, intercession
裁人 *chūsainin* arbitrator, mediator
裁者 *chūsaisha* arbitrator, mediator
裁裁判 *chūsai saiban* arbitration
裁裁判所 *chūsai saibansho* court of arbitration
間 *nakama* company, circle, party; associate, confederate, accomplice. *chūgen* samurai's attendant, footman
間入 *nakama-i(ri)* joining a group
間外 *nakamahazu(re)* being left out
間同士 *nakamadōshi* comrades
間値段 *nakama nedan* trade price
間割 *nakamawa(re)* split among friends, internal discord
間喧嘩 *nakamagenka* quarrel among friends
間褒 *nakamabome* logrolling, mutual admiration
13働 *nakabatara(ki)* maid, servant
継 *chūkei* (radio) relay, hook-up

A 伝 379/F161 傳 TEN. DEN legend, tradition; life, biography; commentary; communicating. *tsuta(u)* go along, walk along, follow. *tsuta(waru)* be transmitted, be circulated, be introduced into; go along, walk along. *tsuta(eru)* report, tell, impart, transmit, propagate, teach, bequeath. *tsuta(e)* legend, tradition. *tsute* intermediary, good offices, connections; someone to trust. *-zuta(i) ni* along (the wall).

5世 *densei suru* transmit from generation to generation
令 *denrei* messenger, orderly, runner
令者 *denreisha* herald, orderly, messenger
7来 *denrai suru* be transmitted, be handed down; be imported. *denrai no* ancestral, hereditary; imported
声器 *denseiki* speaking tube
言 *dengon* verbal message, word. *tsutegoto* verbal message; rumor
言板 *dengomban* message board
承 *denshō* transmission, legend, tradition, folklore
承文学 *denshō bungaku* oral literature
8送 *densō* dissemination, circulation, diffusion, propagation; transmission, communication, delivery
法 *dembō* teaching Buddhism; rough person; bullying; ostentatious bravado
法肌 *dembō-hada* rough-and-tumble; a bullying disposition
奇 *denki* romance (fiction)
奇小説 *denki shōsetsu* romance (fiction)
奇的 *denkiteki* legendary
9奏 *densō suru*, deliver a message to the emperor
単 *dentan* leaflet
音器 *den-onki* megaphone, speaking tube; sound box
染 *densen* contagion
染毒 *densendoku* virus, germ
染病 *densembyō* contagious disease, infectious disease, epidemic
10家 *denka* heirloom; trump card; last resort; family tradition
書鳩 *denshobato* carrier pigeon, homing pigeon
馬 *temma* post horse
馬船 *temmasen* large sculling boat
記 *denki* biography
記文学 *denki bungaku* biographical literature
記作者 *denki sakusha* biographer
記物 *denkimono* biographical writings
11達 *dentatsu* transmission, communication, delivery
唱 *denshō* tradition
授 *denju* initiation, instruction
習 *denshū* learning
票 *dempyō* chit, sales slip, voucher
道 *dendō suru* evangelize. *dendō* evangelism, missionary work
道者 *dendōsha* evangelist, evangelistic worker
道師 *dendōshi* evangelist
道船 *dendōsen* missionary boat
道集会 *dendō shūkai* evangelistic meeting
12統 *dentō* tradition, convention
統的 *dentōteki* traditional, conventional
13話 *tsuta(e)banashi* legend
14聞 *dembun suru*, *tsuta(e)-ki(ku)* learn by hearsay. *dembun* hearsay, rumor, report
説 *densetsu* legend, tradition
誦 *denshō* tradition
導 *dendō* conduction, transmission
導性 *dendōsei* conductivity
導度 *dendōdo* conductivity

15播 *dempa* propagation, circulation, diffusion, dissemination
18騎 *denki* mounted orderly

A **休** 380/F109 KYŪ. *yasu(mu)*, *kyū(suru)* *vi* rest; take a day off; be finished; be absent; retire, sleep. *yasu(meru)* *vt* rest (oneself); let idle; suspend; have (someone) rest; set at ease, give relief to; fallow (land). *yasu(maru)* be rested, feel at ease, repose, be relieved. *yasu(maseru)* excuse (someone); give a holiday to; make (someone) rest. *yasura(u)* rest, relax. *yasu(mi)* rest, recess, respite, suspension; vacation, holiday; absence; moulting.

4心 *kyūshin*＝*anshin* 安心 1283.4
火山 *kyūkazan* dormant volcano
日 *kyūjitsu* holiday, rest day
日明 *kyūjitsua(ke)* the day after a holiday
止 *kyūshi* pause, cessation, rest
止符 *kyūshifu* rest (in music); period, full stop
5刊 *kyūkan* suspension of publication
6休 *yasu(mi)-yasu(mi)* resting at times; thinking carefully
地 *yasu(me)chi* fallow land
会 *kyūkai* adjournment, recess
会明 *kyūkaia(ke)* reassembling of a legislature
7足 *kyūsoku* resting
廷 *kyūtei* court recess
廷日 *kyūteibi* no-court day
8所 *yasu(mi)dokoro* resting place, haven of rest
学 *kyūgaku* temporary absence from school; suspension
泊所 *kyūhakujo* temporary quarters
9神 *kyūshin*＝*anshin* 安心 1283.4
怠 *kyūtai* laziness, neglect
茶屋 *yasu(mi)jaya* wayside teahouse
10校 *kyūkō* closing school (temporarily); dropping one's studies
祥 *kyūshō* good omen
航 *kyūkō* suspension of sailings
眠 *kyūmin* idle (facility); dormant
眠期 *kyūminki* dormant season
息 *kyūsoku* rest, relief, relaxation
息所 *kyūsokujo* restroom, lobby, lounge
息時間 *kyūsoku jikan* recess
11戚 *kyūseki* weal and woe, welfare
転 *kyūten* (elevator) not running
12場 *yasu(mi)ba* resting place. *kyūjō* theater closure; stage absence
閑 *kyūkan* fallowing
閑地 *kyūkanchi* fallow land
診 *kyūshin* no medical examinations (today)
診日 *kyūshimbi* doctor's no-consultation day
13意 *kyūi* peace, tranquility
載 *kyūsai* nonappearance in print
暇 *kyūka* holiday, vacation, furlough
暇願 *kyūka nega(i)* application for leave
電 *kyūden* electricity cut-off
電日 *kyūdembi* no-electricity day
業 *kyūgyō* shop closed, business suspended, shutdown, holiday
業日 *kyūgyōbi* business holiday
戦 *kyūsen* truce, armistice
戦会談 *kyūsen kaidan* armistice conference
戦条約 *kyūsen jōyaku* armistice treaty
戦協定 *kyūsen kyōtei* cease-fire agreement
戦記念日 *Kyūsen Kinembi* Armistice Day
14演 *kyūen suru* suspend performance
15養 *kyūyō* rest, recreation
養室 *kyūyōshitsu* rest or recreation room
16錘 *kyūsui* idle spindles
憩 *kyūkei* rest, recess, intermission
憩所 *kyūkeijo* restroom, lounge
憩室 *kyūkeishitsu* restroom, lounge
17講 *kyūkō* lecture cancelled
18職 *kyūshoku* temporary retirement; suspension from office

A **会** 381/F927 **會** E Buddhist ceremony; understanding. KAI meeting, assembly; party; association, club. *a(u)* meet, interview. *a(waseru)* causative of *a(u)*; expose to, subject to. *kai(suru)* meet, assemble; join. *e(suru)* understand. *tamatama* casually, unexpectedly; few. [曰]

4心 *kaishin* congeniality, satisfaction
5主 *kaishu* sponsor of a meeting
6同 *kaidō* an assembly, a meeting
式 *eshiki* a temple service
合 *kaigō* meeting, assembly
7社 *kaisha* company, corporation
社員 *kaisha-in* company employee
見 *kaiken* interview, audience
見者 *kaikensha* interviewer
見記 *kaikenki* record of an interview
8長 *kaichō* chairman, president (of a society)
所 *kaisho* meetingplace; club
9食 *kaishoku* dining together; mess
則 *kaisoku* society regulations, constitution
計 *kaikei* account; finance; accountant; treasurer; paymaster; a reckoning; bill
計士 *kaikeishi* certified public accountant
計年度 *kaikei nendo* fiscal year
計官 *kaikeikan* accountant, treasurer
計学 *kaikeigaku* accountancy
計検査 *kaikei kensa* audit, auditing
10陰 *e-in* the perineum
員 *kai-in* member; the membership
員証 *kai-inshō* membership certificate
席 *kaiseki* meeting place; restaurant dinner; seats for the public
席料理 *kaiseki ryōri* banquet

席膳 *kaisekizen* elaborate dinner tray
11得 *etoku* understanding, comprehension, grasp, perception, appreciation
釈 *eshaku* salutation, greeting, recognition, bow
規 *kaiki* society by-laws
商 *kaishō* negotiation, talks
堂 *kaidō* church, chapel, tabernacle, synagogue
堂司 *kaidōzukasa* ruler of a synagogue
12場 *kaijō* meeting place, the grounds
飲 *kai-in suru* drinking and carousing together
衆 *kaishū* audience, congregation
集 *kaishū* audience, assembly, meeting
費 *kaihi* membership fee
報 *kaihō* bulletin, report
期 *kaiki* session (of a legislature)
期中 *kaikichū* during a session
葬 *kaisō* attendance at a funeral
葬者 *kaisōsha* attendants at a funeral, mourners
13話 *kaiwa* conversation
戦 *kaisen* engagement, battle
意 *kai-i* a type of characters made up of meaningful parts (e.g., 東 and 休)
意文字 *kai-i moji* ideograph
14読 *kaidoku* a reading-and-discussion meeting
厭 *e-en* epiglottis
厭軟骨 *e-en nankotsu* epiglottis
15談 *kaidan* conversation, discussion, interview
16頭 *kaitō* society president
館 *kaikan* assembly hall
20議 *kaigi* conference, assembly, council, convention, congress, meeting
議日程 *kaigi nittei* conference program
議所 *kaigisho* place of assembly
議事項 *kaigi jikō* agenda
議室 *kaigishitsu* council room
議場 *kaigijō* place of assembly
議録 *kaigiroku* minutes, proceedings

A **仮** 382/F149 **假** KA. KE (Buddhist) vanity. *kari no* temporary, provisional; informal, unauthorized; fleeting; assumed (name); interim; acting. *kari ni* temporarily, provisionally; for example; for argument's sake. *kari nimo* even for an instant, even as a joke.

2入学 *kari nyūgaku* provisional enrollment
3小屋 *karigoya* booth, shack, hut, temporary shed
5令 *tatoe, tatoi* if, even if, tho, altho
世 *kari (no) yo* this transient world
処分 *kari shobun* temporary measures
払 *karibara(i)* temporary advance (of money)
払金 *karibara(i)kin* temporary advance (of money)
出所 *kari shussho* parole; release on bail
出獄 *kari shutsugoku* parole; release on bail
6死 *kashi* apparent death; asphyxiation
宅 *karitaku* temporary dwelling
字 *kana* Japanese syllabaries
名 *kana* Japanese syllabaries. *kamei, kemyō, karina* pseudonym, alias, pen name
名文 *kanabumi* publication in *kana* alone
名文字 *kana moji* the Japanese syllabary symbols
名手本 *kanadehon* Japanese *kana* copybook
名本 *kanabon* publication in *kana* alone
名交 *kanama(jiri)* mixed writing (characters and *kana*)
名交文 *kanama(jiri)bun* mixed writing (characters and *kana*)
名草紙 *kanazōshi* a story in the *kana*
名書 *kanaga(ki)* writing in the *kana*
名遣 *kanazuka(i)* syllabary spelling
名勝 *kanaga(chi)* using more *kana* than characters
7役 *kariyaku* temporary post
決 *kaketsu* conditional approval
初 *karisome* temporariness, transience; trifle; negligence. *karisome nimo* for a moment; even as a joke; even in the slightest degree
声 *kasei* falsetto
条約 *kari jōyaku* provisional treaty
住 *karizuma(i)* temporary residence
住居 *karizumai* temporary residence
8刷 *karizur(i)* proof printing
性 *kasei* false (symptoms)
枕 *kari makura* a nap
泊 *kahaku* emergency anchoring
臥 *karibushi* nap
命 *kari (no) inochi* this transient life
舎 *kariya* temporary dwellings
免状 *kari menjō* temporary certificate
定 *katei* assumption, supposition, hypothesis
定法 *kateihō* subjunctive mood
定款 *kari teikan* provisional articles
受金 *kariu(ke)kin* money temporarily receipted
受取 *kari uketori* temporary receipt
受取証 *kari uketorishō* temporary receipt
9屋 *kariya* temporary residence; temporary shelter building
拵 *karigoshira(e)* makeshift; temporary
相 *kasō* appearance, phenomenon
政府 *kari seifu* provisional government
面 *kamen* mask, disguise
面舞踏会 *kamen butōkai* masquerade ball
10病 *kebyō* feigned illness
借 *kashaku* borrowing; pardon, extenuation; a type of characters substituted for others of the same sound (e.g., 燕 for 宴)
埋 *kariu(me)* temporary burial
眠 *kamin* nap
称 *kashō* temporary name
託 *kataku* pretense, pretext
家 *kari ie* temporary house

宮 *kari miya* temporary shrine
記入 *kari kinyū* suspense account
差押 *kari sashio(sae)* provisional seizure
進級 *kari shinkyū* conditional promotion
埋葬 *kari maisō* temporary burial
納 *kanō* deposit
納金 *kanōkin* deposit
納税 *kari nōzei* tax payment under protest
11 設 *kasetsu* temporary, provisional; hypothesis, supposition; fiction
宿 *kari (no) yado(ri)* temporary dwelling; this transient world
釈放 *kari shakuhō* release on parole
勘定 *kari kanjō* suspense account
庵 *kari-io, kario, kariho* booth, tabernacle, temporary dwelling
庵祭 *Kari-io (no) Matsu(ri)* Feast of Booths, Feast of Tabernacles
12 歯 *kashi* false tooth
痘 *katō* light case of smallpox
植 *kariu(e), kashoku* temporary planting
渡 *kariwata(shi)* temporary approximate payment
粧 *keshō* make-up
貼 *kariba(ri)* temporary pasting
寓 *kagū* temporary residence
葺 *karibuki* temporary roofing
普請 *karibushin* temporary building
装 *kasō* masquerade, disguise, fancy dress; converted (cruiser)
装巡洋艦 *kasō jun-yōkan* merchant cruiser
装舞踏会 *kasō butōkai* masquerade ball
13 殿 *karidono* temporary shrine
睡 *kasui, utatane* nap, siesta
寝 *karine* nap, siesta; stopping at an inn
想 *kasō* imagination, supposition; potential (enemy)
14 漆 *kashitsu* varnish
説 *kasetsu* hypothesis, supposition
綴 *karitoji* temporary binding; paper binding
綴本 *karitojihon* paper-bound book
15 縫 *karinu(i)* temporary sewing, basting
調印 *kari chōin* initialing (a pact)
16 橋 *karibashi* temporary bridge
親 *kari oya* adopted parents; temporarily assumed parents
17 繃帯 *kari hōtai* first-aid dressing
20 議長 *kari gichō* acting chairman, acting president

A **合** 383/F328 Gō one-tenth *shō* (see Weights and Measures); one of ten stations up a mountain. *a(u)* fit, suit; agree with, match, be correct; pay, be profitable. *a(wasu), a(waseru)* join together; be opposite, face; unite, combine, connect; add up; mix; match; overlap; compare, check with. *a(wasaru)* get together, unite. *gas(suru) vi* and *vt* join together; sum up; combine, unite, mix; agree with. *a(i)-* joint; associate, accomplice. *a(wase)-* joined together; opposite, facing. [口]

1 一 *gōitsu* unification, union, oneness
2 力 *gōryoku* resultant force; co-operation. *gōriki* alms, assistance, contribution, Buddhist almsgiving
3 口 *a(i)kuchi* chum, pal
子 *a(ino)ko* Eurasian, mulatto; crossbreed; hybrid
4 手 *a(ino)te* interlude; accompaniment; side-show; strain of music
方 *a(i)kata* accompaniment
切 *gassai* all; altogether
切袋 *gassaibukuro* traveling bag
5 目 *a(wase)me* joint, seam
札 *a(i)fuda* check
弁 *gōben* joint management; pool
本 *gappon* a collection in one volume
冊 *gassatsu, gōsatsu* a collection in one volume
6 羽 *kappa* raincoat
行 *a(wase)-okona(u)* carry on together; do at the same time
式 *gōshiki* formal, regular; valid; categorical
印 *a(i)jirushi* comradeship badge. *ai-in* verification seal
名会社 *gōmeigaisha* unlimited partnership
同 *gōdō* union, combination, amalgamation, fusion; congruence
同会議 *gōdō kaigi* joint session
同軍 *gōdōgun* combined armies
同慰霊祭 *gōdō ireisai* joint service for the war dead
成 *gōsei* synthesis, composition; synthetic; composite, mixed, combined, compound
成力 *gōseiryoku* resultant force
成物 *gōseibutsu* a compound
成宝石 *gōsei hōseki* synthetic gems
成酒 *gōseishu* synthetic saké
成語 *gōseigo* compound word
成樹脂 *gōsei jushi* plastics, synthetic resins
成繊維 *gōsei sen-i* synthetic fiber
7 図 *aizu* sign, signal
体 *gattai* union, combination, alliance, annexation
作 *gassaku* joint work, collaboration
判 *a(i)ban* medium-sized paper; medium-sized book
言葉 *a(i)kotoba* password, watchword
8 金 *gōkin* alloy
性 *a(i)shō* affinity, compatibility
抱 *gōhō* an armful
板 *gōhan, gōban, a(wase)ita* veneer board, plywood
版 *gōhan* joint publication
物 *a(wase)mono* something joined together
祀 *gōshi suru* enshrine together
服 *aifuku* spring or fall wear

併 *gappei, gōhei* combination, union, amalgamation, consolidation, merger, coalition, fusion, annexation, affiliation, incorporation ⌈ness)
併症 *gappeishō* complications (in an ill-
法 *gōhō* legality, legitimacy, lawfulness
法化 *gōhōka* legalization ⌈abiding, in order
法的 *gōhōteki* legal, lawful, legitimate, law-
法性 *gōhōsei* lawfulness, validity
9計 *gōkei* total
乗 *a(i)no(ri)* riding together
点 *gaten, gatten* understanding, comprehension, grasp; consent
奏 *gassō* concert, ensemble
奏調 *gassōchō* concert pitch
10流 *gōryū* confluence; union, linking up
砥 *a(wase)do* double whetstone
致 *gatchi* agreement, concurrence, con-
釘 *a(i)kugi* double-pointed nail ⌊forming to
剤 *gōzai* medical compound
衾 *gōkin suru* sleep together
格 *gōkaku* passing an examination; eligibility
格者 *gōkakusha* successful applicant
格者名 *gōkakushamei* names of successful candidates
11符 *a(i)jirushi* comradeship badge
著 *gōcho, gatcho* joint authorship
祭 *gōsai suru* enshrine together
宿 *gasshuku* lodging together
宿所 *gasshukujo* boardinghouse
唱 *gasshō* chorus
唱団 *gasshōdan* chorus, choir
唱隊 *gasshōtai* chorus, choir
唱隊長 *gasshōtaichō* choir leader
唱隊員 *gasshōtai-in* choir member
理 *gōri* rationality
理化 *gōrika* rationalization
理主義 *gōri shugi* rationalism
理性 *gōrisei* rationality, reasonableness
理的 *gōriteki* reasonable, rational, logical
12間 *aima* interval
棒 *a(i)bō* companion
評 *gappyō* joint review, joint criticism
詞 *a(i)kotoba* password
掌 *gasshō* pressing palms together (in prayer)
着 *aigi* between-season wear
衆国 *Gasshūkoku* United States of America; a federal state
13戦 *kassen* battle, engagement ⌈nership
資 *gōshi suru* joint stocks, enter into part-
資会社 *gōshigaisha* limited partnership
意 *gōi* agreement, consent, mutual under-
意心中 *gōi shinjū* double suicide ⌊standing
意情死 *gōi jōshi* double suicide
14憎 *ainiku* unfortunately
算 *gassan* totaling
15調 *gōchō* tuning (in music)
歓 *gōkan* enjoying pleasure together
16薬 *a(i)gusuri* specific remedy ⌈between
壁 *gappeki* a neighbor with just a wall
憲性 *gōkensei* constitutionality ⌈key
17鍵 *a(i)kagi* pass key, duplicate key, master
19鏡 *a(wase) kagami* opposite mirrors
20議 *gōgi* consultation, conference
議制 *gōgisei* parliamentary system
議制度 *gōgi seido* parliamentary system

A 全 384/F195 全 仝 ZEN all. *mattō-(suru)* accomplish, fulfill, complete, preserve (life). *matta(ki)* perfect, complete, whole, sound, intact. *matta(ku)* entirely, completely, wholly, perfectly; truly, indeed. *zen-* all, whole, entire, all, complete, overall; pan-. [入]

2力 *zenryoku* all one's energy, full capacity
人 *zenjin* a saint; a person well-balanced morally and intellectually
人生 *zenjinsei* the whole life
人格 *zenjinkaku* one's whole personality
3土 *zendo* the whole land, the whole country
山 *zenzan* the whole mountain
4心 *zenshin* one's whole heart
戸 *zenko* all the houses (in town) ⌈full text
文 *zembun* whole sentence; full paragraph;
以 *matta(ku) mo(tte)* as a matter of fact
天 *zenten* all heaven
日制 *zennichisei* the full-day (school system)
反射 *zenhansha* total reflection
5甲 *zenkō* an all-A (student)
史 *zenshi* complete history
世界 *zensekai* the whole world
生涯 *zenshōgai* one's whole life
民衆 *zemminshū* all the peoples
市 *zenshi* the whole city
市民 *zenshimin* all the citizens of the city
6米 *zem-Bei* all-America, pan-American
休止符 *zenkyūshifu* a whole rest (in music)
地 *zenchi* the whole world, all lands
地方 *zenchihō* the whole area
会一致 *zenkai-itchi* unanimous
会衆 *zenkaishū* the whole assembly, the whole congregation
7角 *zenkaku* em, em quad (in printing)
図 *zenzu* complete map, whole view
局 *zenkyoku* general situation, whole aspect
快 *zenkai* complete recovery of health
形 *zenkei* the whole form; a perfect form
住民 *zenjūmin* all the inhabitants
体 *zentai* the whole; whatever (is the matter). *zentai de* in all
体主義 *zentai shugi* totalitarianism
体主義国 *zentaishugikoku* totalitarian state

身 *zenshin* the whole body; full-length (portrait)
身不髄 *zenshin fuzui* total paralysis
身浴 *zenshin-yoku* full bath ⌈illness
身病 *zenshimbyō* general constitutional
身衰弱 *zenshin suijaku* general prostration
身麻酔 *zenshin masui* general anesthesia
身像 *zenshinzō* full-length portrait or statue
身黴毒 *zenshimbaidoku* syphilis of the whole system
8長 *zenchō* over-all length, span
所 *matta(ku) (no) tokoro* entirely
治 *zenchi, zenji* complete recovery
乳 *zennyū* whole milk
欧 *zen-Ō* all Europe
岸 *zengan* all the banks (of a river)
免 *zemmen* complete exemption
波受信機 *zempa jushinki* all-wave receiver
店 *zenten* the whole store
店中 *zentenchū* thruout the store
知 *zenchi* omniscience ⌈omnipotence
知全能 *zenchi-zennō* omniscience and
国 *zenkoku, zengoku* the whole country; nation-wide, national
国大会 *zenkoku taikai* national convention; national athletic meet
国区 *zenkokuku* national constituency
国中継 *zenkoku chūkei* nation-wide hookup
国民 *zenkokumin* the whole nation
国的 *zenkokuteki* nation-wide ⌈broadcast
国放送 *zenkoku hōsō* national network
9通 *zentsū* opening of the whole (railway
科 *zenka* complete course ⌊line)
級 *zenkyū* the whole class
段 *zendan* the whole page
軍 *zengun* the whole army; the whole team
巻 *zenkan* the whole reel; the whole volume
封地 *zenhōchi* the whole fief
音 *zen-on* whole tone (in music)
音符 *zen-ompu* whole note
速 *zensoku* full speed
速力 *zensokuryoku* full speed
面 *zemmen* the whole surface
面的 *zemmenteki* all-out, general, over-all, complete, extensive, full-scale
面戦争 *zemmen sensō* total war, all-out war
10校 *zenkō* the whole school
納 *zennō* full payment
紙 *zenshi* the whole sheet; the whole news-
豹 *zempyō* the whole, all the rest ⌊paper
都 *zento* the whole metropolis
島 *zentō* the whole island ⌈crew
員 *zen-in* all members; all hands, the whole
家 *zenka* the whole family, the whole house
容 *zen-yō*＝*zembō* 全貌 (see below–14)
書 *zensho* complete book; complete set

荷重 *zenkajū* full load
般 *zempan* the whole. *zempan no* universal, general, whole ⌈wholly
般的 *zempanteki ni* generally, universally,
部 *zembu* all, the whole; entirely, altogether
部保険 *zembu hoken* full insurance
能 *zennō* omnipotence ⌈ability
能力 *zennōryoku* full capacity, all one's
能者 *zennōsha* the Almighty, The Omnip-
11道 *zendō* all Hokkaido ⌊otent One
域 *zen-iki* the whole area
船 *zensen* the whole ship
訳 *zen-yaku* complete translation
敗 *zempai* complete defeat
隊 *zentai* the entire force (of soldiers)
責任 *zensekinin* full responsibility
強風 *zenkyōfū* whole gale
盛 *zensei* height of prosperity
盛時代 *zensei jidai* golden age
盛期 *zenseiki* golden age
12開 *zenkai suru* open fully. *zenkai* full throttle ⌈summation
備 *zembi* completeness, perfection, con-
焼 *zenshō* total destruction by fire
量 *zenryō* the whole quantity
集 *zenshū* complete works
智 *zenchi* omniscience ⌈absolutely
然 *zenzen* wholly, entirely, completely,
幅 *zempuku* overall width; wing span. *zempuku no* all, every, utmost
幅的 *zempukuteki ni* fully
勝 *zenshō* complete victory
勝軍 *zenshōgun* ever-victorious army
景 *zenkei* panoramic view, bird's-eye view
景写真 *zenkei shashin* panoramic photo
廃 *zempai* total abolition
廃論 *zempairon* abolitionism
廃論者 *zempaironsha* abolitionist
13損 *zenson* total loss ⌈struction
滅 *zemmetsu* annihilation, complete de-
数 *zensū* the whole number, all
勢力 *zenseiryoku* full force
裸 *zenra* nude
裸体 *zenratai* stark naked body ⌈story
14貌 *zembō* full portrait; whole aspect; full
製品 *zenseihin* manufactured article
15潰 *zenkai* complete destruction
線 *zensen* the whole line; all lines
編 *zempen* whole book, whole volume
篇 *zempen* whole book, whole volume
霊 *zenrei* one's whole soul
質化 *zenshitsuka* transubstantiation
論点 *zenronten* the whole point ⌈authority
権 *zenken* plenipotentiary powers; full
権大使 *zenken taishi* ambassador plenipotentiary

権公使 *zenken kōshi* minister plenipotentiary
権委員 *zenken i-in* plenipotentiaries
16 壊 *zenkai* complete destruction
17 優 *zen-yū* straight A's
翼飛行機 *zen-yoku hikōki* a flying wing
18 癒 *zen-yu* complete healing
軀 *zenku* the whole body
額 *zengaku* total, full amount

5

仰 See 375.

似 See 376.

佛 385 / F116 See **仏** 351.

佗 386 / F116 See **侘** 415.

坐 See **座** 1515. [土]

夾 See 192. [大]

估 387 / F111 Ko price; business; selling.

伶 388 / F111 Rei actor.
2 人 *reijin* court musician, minstrel

佑 389 / F115 U, Yū help.
7 助 *yūjo* assistance

佃 390 / F112 Ten. *tsukuda* cultivated rice field.
12 煮 *tsukudani* food preserved by boiling down in soy

佇 391 / F113 Cho. *tatazu(mu)* stop, linger, loiter. *tatazumai* appearance, shape, figure, bearing.
5 立 *choritsu suru* stand still

佐 B 392 / F114 Sa help.
8 官 *sakan* field officer
9 保姫 *saohime* goddess of spring
13 幕 *sabaku* adherence to the shogunate
14 様 *sayō* yes, indeed; well... *sayō na* such, of that kind, like that

佚 393 / F116 Itsu, Tetsu be lost; peace; hide; mistake; beautiful; in turn.
10 書 *issho* a lost book
13 楽 *itsuraku* pleasure

但 B 394 / F112 Tan. Dan. *tadashi* but, however, excepting that.
5 付 *tadashizu(ki) no* conditional
10 書 *tadashiga(ki)* proviso

伺 B 395 / F111 Shi. *ukaga(u) vt* and *vi* visit; ask, inquire, question; hear, be told; implore (a god for an oracle).
8 事 *ukaga(i)goto* inquiry
10 候 *shikō suru* wait upon (someone)
11 探 *ukaga(i)-sagu(ru)* spy out
済 *ukaga(i)zu(mi)* instructions received

伴 B 396 / F111 Han. Ban. *tomona(u)* accompany, bring with; be accompanied by; be involved in. *tomo* companion, follower.
4 天連 *Bateren* Portuguese missionaries; Christianity
9 食 *banshoku* eating with a guest; nominal official (a slighting term)
侶 *hanryo* companion
奏 *bansō* accompaniment
奏部 *bansōbu* accompaniment
13 僧 *bansō* priests assisting at a Buddhist service

伯 B 397 / F110 Haku count; earl; eldest brother; uncle; chief official.
4 父 *oji, hakufu* uncle
5 母 *oba, hakubo* aunt
兄 *hakkei* the eldest son
6 仲 *hakuchū suru* be evenly matched
8 叔 *hakushuku* brothers; one's father's brothers
13 楽 *bakurō* horse trader
17 爵 *hakushaku* count; earl

伽 398 / F112 Ga. Ka. Kya. *togi* nursing; nurse; attending; attendant; entertainer.
5 芝居 *(o)togi shibai* fairy play, pantomime
9 草子 *(o)togizōshi* fairy-tale book
13 話 *(o)togibanashi* fairy tale, nursery tale
17 藍 *garan* temple, monastery
藍洞 *garandō* hollowness, emptiness, void
藍鳥 *garanchō* pelican
19 羅 *kyara* aloes wood; aloes-wood perfume

侘 399 / F116 Ta. *wabi(ru)* be worried, be grieved, pine for. *wabi* subdued taste. *wabi(shii)* wretched, comfortless, lonesome.
2 人 *wabibito* lonesome person; unwanted person; poverty-stricken person

7言 *wabigoto* sad words, anxious words
声 *wabigoe* sad voice
住 *wabizuma(i)* wretched abode; solitary life
住居 *wabizumai* wretched abode; solitary ⌊life
13寝 *wabine* lonesome sleep
14歌 *wabiuta* a sad song; singing in a lonesome tone

佞 400/F119 佞

NEI flattery; insincerity.

2人 *neijin* flatterer, smooth talker, crafty person
5弁 *neiben* flattery, cajolery, adulation
6臣 *neishin* crafty courtier; traitor
奸 *neikan na* treacherous, wicked, perverse
8者 *neisha* smooth talker, crafty person
9姦 *neikan na* treacherous, wicked, perverse
11悪 *neiaku* perverseness; perverse person
12智 *neichi* craftiness

A 位 401/F113

I rank, place, grade. *kurai* grade, rank; court order, dignity, nobility; situation; throne, crown. *kurai suru* occupy a position. *-kurai* about, almost, as; rather; at least; enough to. *-i* rank, place.

6次 *iji* order of rank; order of seating
地 *ichi* situation, position, location, place
8取 *kuraido(ri)* grade, class, quality; unit; ⌊digit
官 *ikan* rank and official position
9相 *isō* phase (in science)
冠 *ikan* ancient headgear showing rank
負 *kuraima(ke)* being unworthy of one's rank; being outranked ⌈rank
10倒 *kuraidao(re)* inability to live up to one's
記 *iki* court-rank diploma ⌈mous rank
記追贈 *iki-tsuisō* conferment of posthu-
11階 *ikai* court rank
階勲等 *ikai-kuntō* court rank and honors
12牌 *ihai* Buddhist mortuary tablet
牌堂 *ihaidō* mortuary chapel
13置 *ichi* situation, position, location, place
15勲 *ikun* rank and order of merit

B 含 402/F340

GAN. *fuku(mu)* hold in the mouth; bear in mind, understand; cherish, harbor; contain, comprise, have, hold, include, embrace; be charged or loaded with, be dripping with, be full of, be suffused with. *fuku(maseru)*, *fuku(masu)* soak, saturate; suckle, make one hold something in the mouth; include; instruct, make one understand. *fuku(meru)* include, instruct, make one understand. *fuku(mi)* implication, hidden meaning; latitude; atmosphere, tone, sentiment; inclusion. [口]

4水化合物 *gansui-kagōbutsu* hydrate
水炭素 *gansuitanso* carbohydrate
6有 *gan-yū suru* contain, have, hold, include
有量 *gan-yūryō* content (of a mineral, etc.)
7声 *fuku(mi)goe* muffled voice
8味 *gammi suru* taste; think over carefully
油層 *gan-yusō* oil strata
金 *gankin* containing gold
10笑 *fuku(mi)wara(i)* suppressed laugh, smile, giggle, chuckle
11羞草 *ojigisō* sensitive plant, mimosa
13蓄 *ganchiku* implication, significance
14嗽 *gansō, ugai* gargling, rinsing
塵率 *ganjinritsu* dust content
16糖 *gantō* sugar content
糖量 *gantōryō* sugar content

B 伸 403/F111

SHIN stretching. *no(biru)* extend, lengthen, stretch, spread; be postponed; increase; grow; progress, develop; be straightened, be flattened, be smoothed; be exhausted. *no(basu)*, *no(beru)* (see under 延 1547.0). *no(su)* stretch, spread, smooth out; roll out; iron; stretch, extend; gain influence; knock out. *no(bi)* stretching (the body); excess, surplus; postponement; growth; spread. *no(biyakana)* comfortable, carefree. *noshi* an iron.

3上 *no(shi)-a(geru)* promote; make richer. *no(shi)-a(garu)* stand on tiptoe; rise in the world; become arrogant. *no(bi)-a-(garu)* stretch, reach to, stand on tiptoe
4反 *no(ruka)-so(ruka)* win or lose, sink or ⌊swim
5広 *no(be)-hiro(geru) vt* stretch out
7伸 *no(bi)no(bi) suru* feel at ease, feel carefree
8長 *shinchō* expansion, extension, elongation
9度 *shindo* elasticity
10展 *shinten* expansion, extension
悩 *no(bi)-naya(mu)* be sluggish (business)
11張 *shinchō* expansion, extension, elongation
掛 *no(shi)-ka(karu)* lean on; bend over; ⌊come upon
12筋 *shinkin* protractor muscle
14暢 *shinchō*＝伸張 above (see above–11)
15餅 *noshimochi* flattened rice cakes
17縮 *shinshuku, no(bi)chiji(mi)* expansion and contraction; elasticity, flexibility
縮自在 *shinshuku jizai na* elastic, flexible, telescoping, expandable
縮性 *shinshukusei* elasticity
縮法 *shinshukuhō* sliding scale
縮税率 *shinshuku zeiritsu* flexible tariff

A 住 404/F114 住

JŪ dwelling, living. *su(mu)*, *su(mau)*, *jū(suru)* live, reside, inhabit. *su(mai)* residence.

2人 *jūnin* resident, inhabitant

4 込 *su(mi)-ko(mu)* live in, live with
心地良 *su(mi)gokochi (no) yo(i)* comfortable to live in
5 処 *su(mi)ka* dwelling; den (of robbers); nest
生活 *jūseikatsu* manner of housing
民 *jūmin* inhabitants, residents, population
民税 *jūminzei* municipal tax
民登録 *jūmin tōroku* resident registration
6 宅 *jūtaku* residence, house
宅地 *jūtakuchi* residential district
宅難 *jūtakunan* housing shortage
8 居 *jūkyo, sumai* dwelling, residence, address
居手当 *jūkyo teate* rent allowance
所 *jūsho, su(mi)dokoro* residence, address, domicile
所録 *jūshoroku* address book
9 持 *jūji* chief priest of a temple
荒 *su(mi)-a(rasu)* leave a house in bad shape
10 家 *sumika, jūka* dwelling, residence
11 著 *su(mi)-tsu(ku)* settle down
12 着 *su(mi)-tsu(ku)* settle down
替 *su(mi)-kae(ru)* change one's residence
13 僧 *jūsō*=*jūshoku* 住職 (see below–18)
14 慣 *su(mi)-na(reru)* get used to living in
18 職 *jūshoku* chief priest (of a Buddhist temple)
難 *su(mi)niku(i)* inconvenient (residence), unpleasant (surroundings)

A **体** $\frac{405}{F2111}$ **體 躰** TAI the body; substance, object; reality; style, form; image counter. TEI appearance, air; condition, state, form. *tai(suru)* obey, comply with; keep in mind. *karada* body; health. [骨]

2 力 *tairyoku* physical strength
4 内 *tainai* interior of the body
中 *karadajū* thruout the body
5 付 *karadatsu(ki)* body build, figure
6 刑 *taikei* corporal punishment; jail sentence
当 *taiata(ri)* body blow, ramming attack, sacrifice attack
7 言 *taigen* uninflected word
位 *tai-i* physical standard; physique
技 *taigi* boxing and jujitsu
形 *taikei* form, figure
良 *teiyo(ku)* decently, gracefully; plausibly; politely; tactfully
系 *taikei* system, organization
系化 *taikeika* organization, systematization
系的 *taikeiteki* systematic
8 長 *taichō* length of an animal
制 *taisei* structure, system, set-up, organization
育 *tai-iku* physical education, gymnastics, athletics
育家 *tai-ikuka* physical culturist, athlete
育館 *tai-ikukan* gymnasium
9 面 *taimen* honor, reputation; dignity; prestige; appearances
重 *taijū* body weight
臭 *taishū* body odor; a characteristic (of someone)
要 *taiyō* important point
10 粉 *karada (o) ko ni suru* work assiduously
格 *taikaku* physique, constitution
格検査 *taikaku kensa* physical examination
11 得 *taitoku* realization, experience; comprehension; mastery
惜 *karada (o) o(shimu)* be lazy
液 *taieki* body fluids
現 *taigen suru* personify, impersonate, embody
12 腔 *taikō, taikū* body cavity
腔壁 *taikōheki, taikūheki* body wall
量 *tairyō* body weight
量器 *tairyōki* scales for weighing
温 *taion* body temperature
温計 *taionkei* clinical thermometer
温器 *taionki* clinical thermometer
裁 *teisai* form, style; appearance, show; get-up, format; decency
裁上 *teisaijō* for appearance' sake
裁良 *teisaiyo(ku)* tastefully, respectfully, decently
裁振 *teisaibu(ru)* put on airs
13 感 *taikan* bodily sensation
14 様 *taiyō* situation; terms
認 *tainin* an understanding based on experience
貌 *taibō* appearance
罰 *taibatsu* corporal punishment
15 熱 *tainetsu* body heat
質 *taishitsu* physical constitution
16 積 *taiseki* volume, capacity
操 *taisō* gymnastics, calisthenics
操場 *taisōjō* gymnasium; drill ground
18 軀 *taiku* the body, stature, physique, constitution
験 *taiken* experience
験談 *taikendan* story of one's experience

A **低** $\frac{406}{F113}$ **彽** TEI low. *hiku(i)* low, short; humble; low (voice).

3 下 *teika* fall, decline, lowering, deterioration
4 木 *teiboku* shrub, shrubbery
5 目 *hikume* low ball (in baseball)
圧 *teiatsu* low pressure; low voltage
丘陵 *teikyūryō* low hills
6 回 *teikai* loitering, lingering, reluctance to leave
地 *teichi* low ground, bottom land, plain
当 *teitō* mortgage, hypothec, security
劣 *teiretsu* low grade, inferiority; coarseness, vulgarity
気圧 *teikiatsu* low atmospheric pressure, cyclone; bad temper, tense situation
7 吟 *teigin suru* hum, sing in a low voice
声 *teisei* low voice, whisper
利 *teiri* low interest
利金 *teirikin* low-interest money

利金融 *teiri kin-yū* low-interest credit
利資金 *teiri shikin* low-interest funds
8 迷 *teimei* low-hanging (clouds)
佪 *teikai*＝低回 (see above–6)
学年 *teigakunen* lower grades in school
金利 *teikinri* low interest
物価 *teibukka* low prices
周波 *teishūha* low frequency
性能 *teiseinō* low efficiency
空 *teikū* low ceiling; low altitude
空飛行 *teikū hikō* low-altitude flying
9 度 *teido* low degree, low grade, low class
速 *teisoku* low (gear), slow speed
俗 *teizoku* vulgar
徊 *teikai*＝低回 (see above–6)
級 *teikyū* low grade; vulgar
音 *teion* bass (in music); low voice
音部記号 *teiombu kigō* base clef
10 能 *teinō* low intelligence, feeble-mindedness, imbecility
能児 *teinōji* feeble-minded child; poor scholar
能者 *teinōsha* imbecile, moron
11 唱 *teishō suru* hum, sing softly
率 *teiritsu* low rate
教会 *Teikyōkai* the Low Church
12 温 *teion* low temperature
減 *teigen* decrease, reduction, fall, depreciation, mitigation
湿 *teishitsu* low and damp
落 *teiraku* fall, decline, slump
雲 *teiun* low-hanging clouds
開発国 *teikaihatsukoku* backward nations
13 廉 *teiren* cheap, inexpensive
触 *teishoku*＝抵触 (see 1878.13)
置 *teichi* low (toilet tank)
資 *teishi* low-interest funds
賃金 *teichingin* low wages
障碍 *teishōgai* low hurdles
14 語 *teigo suru* whisper, murmur, talk in a low voice
15 潮 *teichō* low tide
調 *teichō* low tone, undertone, dullness, (market) weakness
16 頭 *teitō suru* bow low
頭平身 *teitō-heishin suru* prostrate oneself
17 翼 *teiyoku no* low-wing
18 額 *teigaku* small amount

A **作** 407 / F118 — SA. SAKU a work, a production; tillage; harvest; ridge (in a field). *tsuku(ru)* make, create, manufacture, prepare, draw up, write, compose; build; coin; cultivate; organize, establish; make up (a face), trim (a tree); fabricate; prepare food; commit (sin). *(o)tsuku(ri)* make-up; sliced raw fish. *tsuku(ri)* (see under 造 4701.0).
3 土 *sakudo* surface soil
上 *tsuku(ri)-a(geru)* build up; complete
4 手 *tsuku(ri)te* maker, builder, creator; tenant farmer
文 *sakubun* composition, writing
方 *tsuku(ri)kata* way of making; recipe, how to grow (something); style of building; construction; workmanship
木 *tsuku(ri)gi* a well-trimmed tree
5 用 *sayō* action, operation, function, effect
立 *tsuku(ri)-ta(teru)* adorn, decorate, dress up; build up
付 *sakuzuke* planting. *tsuku(ri)tsu(ke)* fixed
出 *tsuku(ri)-da(su)* manufacture, raise (crops), turn out, create, make; invent; dream up
6 成 *sakusei* framing, drawing up, making; writing
返 *tsuku(ri)-kae(su)* remake
合 *tsuku(ri)-a(waseru)*＝造合 4701.6
当 *sakua(tari)* good crop
名 *tsuku(ri)na* pseudonym, alias
曲 *sakkyoku* musical composition
曲者 *sakkyokusha* composer
曲家 *sakkyokuka* composer
7 言 *tsuku(ri)goto* fabrication, lie
身 *tsuku(ri)mi* sliced raw fish
図 *sakuzu suru* draw figures; construct (in geometry). *sakuzu* drawing
声 *tsuku(ri)goe* feigned voice; unnatural voice
男 *saku otoko* farm hand; tenant
8 例 *sakurei* model of writing
法 *sahō* manners, etiquette, propriety
泣 *tsuku(ri)na(ki)* make-believe crying
物 *sakumotsu* crops. *tsuku(ri)mono* artificial product; decoration; fake; crop. *sakubutsu* literary work
盲 *tsuku(ri) mekura* feigned blindness
直 *tsuku(ri)-nao(su)* remake, rebuild
事 *tsuku(ri)goto* fabrication, lie, fiction
者 *sakusha* author
者不知 *sakusha shirazu* anonymous
者未詳 *sakusha mishō* anonymous, author unknown
9 風 *sakufū* literary style
眉 *tsuku(ri) mayu* painted eyebrows
柄 *sakugara* crop conditions; quality (of art)
品 *sakuhin* work, performance, production, opus
為 *sakui* artificiality; act; commission (of a crime)
10 病 *tsuku(ri) yamai, sakubyō* feigned illness
家 *sakka* writer, novelist; artist
笑 *tsuku(ri)wara(i)* forced laugh
酒屋 *tsuku(ri)zakaya* saké brewer; saké brewery
12 場 *sakuba* farm; workshop.
替 *tsuku(ri)-ka(eru)* remake, remold, convert, reconstruct, adapt; parody
13 損 *tsuku(ri)-sokona(u), tsuku(ri)-zokona(u), tsuku(ri)-son(jiru)* fail in making
話 *tsuku(ri)banashi* fable, fabrication, fiction, myth

意 *sakui* design, motif, idea, conception, intention
詩 *sakushi* writing poetry; poem
詩法 *sakushihō* versification
戦 *sakusen* military or naval operations
戦上 *sakusenjō no* operational, strategic
戦計画 *sakusen keikaku* campaign plan
業 *sagyō* work, operations, manufacturing; fatigue duty
業用 *sagyōyō* for work, for manufacturing
業衣 *sagyō-i* work clothes
業服 *sagyōfuku* work clothes
業場 *sagyōba, sagyōjō* works; workshop
業費 *sagyōhi* operational expense
業療法 *sagyō ryōhō* occupational therapy
14 歌 *sakka* writing songs or poems; poem
製 *sakusei* manufacture
16 興 *sakkō suru* promote, arouse
機嫌 *tsuku(ri) kigen* feigning good feeling
18 顔 *tsuku(ri)gao* affected look, made-up face

A **余** 408 / F116 / F2085 **餘** Yo I, myself, the writer; surplus, other; remainder. *ama(ri)* rest, remainder, remnant; surplus, balance; excess; remains, scraps, residue; fullness. *ama(ru)* remain, be in excess, be too many. *ama(su)* leave, spare, save. *-yo* over, more than. *ama(ri) ni* too much, excessively, too. *yo no* other, the rest. *-yo* over, more than. *-ama(ri)* upward of, over, more than.

2 人 *yonin, yojin* others, other people
力 *yoryoku* remaining strength; reserve power; money to spare
4 日 *yojitsu* remaining time, days left
切 *yosetsu* cotangent (in trigonometry)
分 *yobun* extra, excess, surplus
水吐 *yosuihaki* spillway
水路 *yosuiro* spillway
5 生 *yosei* one's remaining years
世 *yosei* one's remaining years
白 *yohaku* blank space, margin
白注 *yohakuchū* marginal notes, glosses
6 色 *yoshoku* complementary color
地 *yochi* place, room, margin; scope
光 *yokō* afterglow, lingering light
7 角 *yokaku* complementary angle
技 *yogi* avocation, hobby
沢 *yotaku* blessings, benefits (of modern civilization)
芳 *yohō* lingering fragrance; continuing fame (after death)
8 弦 *yogen* cosine (in trigonometry)
波 *yoha* secondary effect, aftermath; trail (of a storm), sequel, consequence. *nagori*=名残 1170.10
物 *ama(ri)mono* remains, leavings, remnant; surplus. *ama(shi)mono* something not needed; a person who is in the way
命 *yomei* one's remaining days
炎 *yoen* burning embers
事 *yoji* other things, the rest; leisure tasks
念 *yonen* another idea
念無 *yonenna(ku)* earnestly, intently
所 *yoso* another place
所目 *yosome* another's eyes, casual observer
所乍 *yosonaga(ra)* while at a distance, indirectly, casually
所行 *yosoyu(ki), yoso-i(ki)* going out; company manners, one's best (clothes)
所見 *yosomi* looking away
所余所 *yosoyoso(shii)* distant, cold, formal
所者 *yosomono* stranger
所事 *yosogoto* another's affair
所無 *ama(su) tokoro na(ku)* fully, thoroly
所聞 *yosogi(ki)* reputation, respectability
9 音 *yo-in*=余韻 (see below-19)
風 *yofū* surviving custom, holdover influence
香 *yokō* lingering odor
後 *yogo*=予後 271.9
殃 *yoō* trouble brought on by sins of forebears
計 *yokei* abundance, surplus, excess, superfluity
臭 *yoshū* lingering odor
栄 *yoei* posthumous honors
10 病 *yobyō* secondary disease, complications
財 *yozai* spare cash, available funds, remaining fortune
党 *yotō* remnants of a party or a gang
烈 *yoretsu* ancestors' meritorious deeds; the evil effects of the lives of our predecessors
11 得 *yotoku* emoluments, additional profits
情 *yojō* suggestiveness (of a poem), lingering charm, lasting impression
剰 *yojō* surplus, balance, residue
習 *yoshū* old remaining customs
12 喘 *yozen* lingering life, feeble existence, brink of ruin
禄 *yoroku* additional gain
程 *yohodo, yo(p)podo* very, greatly, much, to a large extent
割 *yokatsu* cosecant (in trigonometry)
寒 *yokan* lingering winter
裕 *yoyū* surplus, margin, room, time, allowance, scope, rope
裕綽綽 *yoyū-shakushaku(taru)* composed, calm and broadminded
13 暇 *yoka* spare time, leisure
煙 *yoen* lingering smoke
賊 *yozoku* the remaining bandits
罪 *yozai* other crimes, further offenses
意 *yo-i* implied meaning
勢 *yosei* surplus power, force, momentum, impetus, inertia

業 *yogyō* side line, avocation
義無 *yogina(ku)*=余儀無 (see below–15)
14 塵 *yojin* trailing dust; aftereffects
聞 *yobun* gossip, rumor
徳 *yotoku* influence of great virtue; influence of ancestors
滴 *yoteki* drippings
15 慶 *yokei* fortunate heredity; blessings, the reward of virtue; something bequeathed to posterity
憤 *yofun* pent-up anger, rage
談 *yodan* sequel (of a story); digression
震 *yoshin* aftershock
弊 *yohei* resulting evil, a holdover
熱 *yonetsu* waste heat; remaining heat
儀 *yogi, yo(no)gi* another method; another problem
儀無 *yogina(ku)* unavoidably, necessarily, inevitably
16 薫 *yokun* lingering odor
興 *yokyō* side show, entertainment
17 齢 *yorei* life expectancy
18 燼 *yojin* smouldering fire, embers
類 *yorui* remnants of a party or a gang
19 瀝 *yoreki* lingering raindrops; remaining portion of a drink; favors
韻 *yo-in* reverberation; swelling (of a hymn); trailing note; lingering memory
蘊 *youn* inexhaustible supply

A **何** 409/F115 KA. *nan, nani* what. *dore* which; who. *nan da* What! Why! Well! What do you mean! *nan da ka* some way or other. *nan dattara* if you like. *nan de* why, what for. *nan demo* anything; by all means; probably. *nani* oh! what! why, well. *nani ka* something, anything. *nanikashira* something or other; I don't know what it is but . . . *nani kato* one way or another. *nanni(mo), nani(mo)* nothing, no (with neg.). *nan ni seyo, nani(shiro), nani(se)* at any rate, anyhow. *nani yori no* most, best. *nani yori mo* first of all. *nan nara* if you wish, if you can, if desirable. *nan no* what, what kind of. *nam, nan to, nan te* what, whatever; What! How! Look here! *nan toka* some way or other; so and so. *nan tomo* nothing; quite. *nan to nareba* for, because. *nan(zo)* something, anything; why, how, what. *izu(re)* where, which, who. *izu(re) mo* both; (neg.) neither. *izu(re) ni seyo, izu(re) ni shitemo* either way, in any case. *nan da ga, nan da kedo* to speak frankly. *nani(ka), nani(yara)* some, any, something, anything. *nan(narito)* anything, whatever. *nan(taru)* How! What! (beautiful, etc.). *dō(shite)* how; why; absurd, on the contrary. *dō(shitemo)* by all means, surely; no matter what you do; by no means; willy-nilly; after all; all things considered. *dō(se)* anyway, at all events, after all, naturally, at all. *nani(kanitsuke)* concerning many things. *nani(kuso)* an interjection of determination. *nani(watomoare)* nevertheless, anyway. *nan-* some (thousands).

1 一 *nani hito(tsu)* (not) one
2 人 *nannin* how many (people). *nampito mo, nambito mo* everyone, all
3 千 *nanzen* many thousands. *nanzen . . . ka* how many thousands
4 方 *donata* who. *dotchi, dochira* where, what place; which; who. *dochira demo, dochira ka* either
日 *nannichi* how many days, what day
月 *nangatsu* what month
分 *nanibun* anyway, please. *nanibun no* some, something or other, as much as possible
心無 *nanigokorona(ku)* without any special thought
5 用 *naniyō de* on what business
付 *nani(ka) (ni) tsu(kete)* one way or another
奴 *doitsu, doyatsu* who
代目 *nandaime* what ordinal number (of a president)
処 *izuko, izuku, doko, doko-ira* where. *doko ka* somewhere, anywhere, in some respects
処迄 *doko made* how far; to what extent. *doko made mo* anywhere; thru thick and thin, to the utmost; persistently, stubbornly; in all respects; thoroly
処其処 *dokosoko* such and such a place
処無 *doko(tomo)na(ku)* aimlessly; somehow. *doko(to)na(ku)* somehow, for some reason; vaguely
6 回 *nankai* how many times. *nankai mo* time and time again
共 *nan tomo* (neg.) nothing; quite
年 *nannen* how many years; what year
気無 *nanigena(i)* casual, unconcerned. *nanigena(ku)* unintentionally, calmly, innocently, inadvertently
色摺 *nanshokuzu(ri)* multicolored printing
7 言 *nan(to)i(u)* how (beautiful, etc.)
何 *dore-dore* which (emphatic). *nani(ga)nan(daka)* what's what. *naninani* what are the items?
条 *nanjō* how
呉 *nanikure to* in various ways
呉無 *nanikure (to) na(ku)* in various ways
8 彼 *nani(yara)-ka(niyara), nani(ka)-ka(nika), nani(ya)-ka(ya)* this and that. *nan(toka)-kan(toka), nan(da)-kan(da)* something or other. *nani(mo)ka(mo)* anything and everything
物 *nanimono* something; nothing (neg.)
卒 *nanitozo, dōzo* please

者 *nanimono* who, what kind of a person. *nanimono ka* someone
事 *nanigoto* what; something, everything, nothing (neg.)
[9]屋 *nan(demo)ya* Jack-of-all-trades
度 *nando* how many times, how often. *nando mo* many times, often. *nando demo* any number of times. *nando ka* many times
故 *naze, naniyue* why, how
某 *nanigashi, nanibō, nan (no) nanigashi* a certain person; a certain amount
食顔 *naniku(wanu) kao* innocent look
[10]個 *nanko* how many pieces
時 *itsu* when, how soon. *nanji, nandoki* what time. *itsu demo* any time; always; never (with neg.). *itsu ka* some time, some day; at one time, one day, the other day, before we know it. *itsu kara* since when, how long. *itsu mo* always, usually; never (with neg.); every time. *itsumo no* usual, habitual. *itsu demo, nandoki demo* whenever, at any time. *itsu shika* unawares, before you know it. *itsu zoya* once, some time ago
時迄 *itsu made* till when, how soon, how long. *itsu made mo* indefinitely
時何時 *itsu-itsu* when (emphatic). *itsu nandoki* at any time; every moment
時何時迄 *itsuitsumade mo* indefinitely; for a long time
時時分 *itsu jibun* about what time
時頃 *itsugoro* about when, how soon
時間 *nan jikan* how many hours. *itsu(no)ma(nika), itsu(no)ma(niyara)* unawares, unnoticed; before you know it
時無 *itsu(ni)na(i)* unusual
[11]遍 *namben* how many times, how often. *nambem mo* repeatedly
[12]程 *dorehodo* how much, how long, how far. *nanihodo* how much, how many
期 *nanki mo* many periods
等 *nanra, nanira* what, whatever, what sort of, any kind of, nothing whatever (with neg.). *nanra(ka) no* some . . . or other
番 *namban* what number
無 *nan(demo) na(i)* easy, trifling, harmless. *nani(ka)na(shi) ni* casually. *nan(towa)-na(shi) ni, nan(to)na(ku), nani(to)na-(ku)* somehow or other
[13]歳 *nansai* how old (is he)
[14]様 *nanisama* what kind; how; indeed, truly; extremely; to be sure
箇 *nanko* how many pieces
箇月 *nankagetsu* how many months
[18]曜日 *naniyōbi, nanyōbi* what day of the week

6

忿 See 587. [心]

來 See 来 202.

侭 Nonstandard for 儘 558.

倰 Nonstandard for 佞 400.

佰 $\frac{410}{F120}$ See 百 33.

侑 $\frac{411}{F126}$ Yū gift.

佻 $\frac{412}{F121}$ Chō frivolity.

佪 $\frac{413}{F120}$ Kai go around.

侈 $\frac{414}{F124}$ Shi luxury; pride; extravagance; arbitrariness, selfishness.

侘 $\frac{415}{F126}$ Ta be proud; be lonely. *wabi(shii)* lonely.

侃 $\frac{416}{F123}$ Kan strong; just, right; love of peace.
[8]侃諤諤 *kankan-gakugaku no* outspoken

侏 $\frac{417}{F126}$ Shu actor; supporting post (in a roof truss).
[16]儒 *shuju* dwarf

佶 $\frac{418}{F121}$ Kitsu, Kichi healthy; correct.
[8]屈 *kikkutsu*＝詰屈 4359.8

佯 $\frac{419}{F120}$ Yō. *itsuwa(ru)* (see under 偽 510.0).
[7]狂 *yōkyō* feigned madness

佩 $\frac{420}{F120}$ Hai. *ha(ku), o(biru)* wear, put on (a sword).
[2]刀 *haitō suru* carry a sword
[5]用 *haiyō* wearing
[10]剣 *haiken suru* wear a sword

侮 $\frac{421}{F128}$ 侮 Bu. *anado(ru), anazu(ru)* B despise, make light of. *anado(ri)* contempt, scorn.
[7]言 *bugen* insult

10辱 ***bujoku*** insult, contempt; slight
14慢 ***buman*** contempt, insult, offense
蔑 ***bubetsu*** contempt, scorn, slight

A 価 422/F170 價 KA. *atai* price, cost, value, worth. *atai suru* be worth, merit; cost, be valued at.

10値 ***kachi*** value, merit
値有 ***kachi-a(ru)*** valuable
値高 ***kachitaka(i)*** valuable
格 ***kakaku*** price, cost, value
格表 ***kakakuhyō*** price list
格差 ***kakakusa*** price margin
18額 ***kagaku*** valuation, amount

A 舎 423/F1571 舍 舎 SEKI. SHA inn; hut, house, mansion. [舌]

5兄 ***shakei*** my elder brother
6宅 ***shataku*** residence
7弟 ***shatei*** my younger brother
利 ***shari*** bones of the Buddha or a saint
利別 ***sharibetsu*** syrup
利塩 ***sharien*** Epsom salts, magnesium sulfate
12営 ***shaei*** billeting, quarters
14監 ***shakan*** dormitory dean

A 念 424/F694 NEN sense, idea, thought; feeling; desire; concern, attention, care. *nen(jiru), nen(zuru)* pray silently; have in mind, be anxious about. *omo(u)* (see under 思 3001.0). [心]

2力 ***nenriki, nenryoku*** will power; faith
入 ***nen-i(ri), nen-i(re)*** care, scrupulousness, conscientiousness
入方 ***nen (no) i(re)kata*** caution
4仏 ***nembutsu*** the Buddhist prayer formula; Hail Amida
5写 ***nensha*** spirit photography
8念 ***nennen*** continually thinking about something
9為 ***nen (no) tame*** just to be sure
10校 ***nenkō*** the very final proof (printing)
珠 ***nenju*** rosary
書 ***nensho*** memorandum
14誦 ***nenju*** Buddhist invocation
15慮 ***nenryo=nen*** 念 (see under 424.0)
16頭 ***nentō*** mind
19願 ***nengan*** one's heart's desire; an earnest petition

B 併 425/F141 倂 HEI. *awa(saru) vi* get together, unite. *awa(seru) vt* put together, unite. *awa(sete)* collectively, altogether; in addition, besides; at the same time. *shika(shi)* however, but. *shika(mo)* moreover, furthermore, nevertheless, and yet.

5用 ***heiyō suru, awa(se)-mochi(iru)*** use jointly, use at the same time
乍 ***shika(shi)naga(ra)*** however
6合 ***heigō*** annexation, merger, absorption
考 ***awa(se)-kanga(eru)*** consider together
有 ***heiyū suru*** own together; combine
行 ***heikō*** parallel
行線 ***heikōsen*** parallel railways
7呑 ***heidon*** annexation, merger, swallowing up
9発 ***heihatsu*** complications (in illness)
発症 ***heihatsushō*** complications (in illness)
10起 ***heiki suru*** occur simultaneously
進 ***heishin suru*** advance together
称 ***heishō suru*** classify together
記 ***heiki suru*** line up together (in writing)
殺 ***heisatsu*** double play (in baseball)
13置 ***heichi*** juxtapostion, placing side by side

B 依 426/F127 I. E. *yo(ru)* depend on. *yo(tte)* therefore, consequently. *(ni) yo(ri)* due to, depending on.

6存 ***izon, ison*** dependence, reliance
7估 ***eko*** favoritism, partiality, prejudice, bias
估地 ***ikoji*** obstinacy, stubbornness
估贔屓 ***ekohiiki=eko*** 依估 (see above–7)
8拠 ***ikyo*** dependence
10託 ***itaku*** dependence (on someone)
託射撃 ***itaku shageki*** firing from elbow rests
12然 ***izen toshite*** still, as yet, as of old
15嘱 ***ishoku suru*** entrust with
16頼 ***irai*** request; trust; dependence
頼心 ***iraishin*** spirit of dependence
頼状 ***iraijō*** written request
19願 ***igan*** in accordance with one's request
願免官 ***igan menkan*** retirement at one's own request

B 侍 427/F125 JI. *habe(ru), ji(suru)* wait upon, serve. *samurai* warrior, samurai.

3女 ***jijo*** lady attendant, maid
5立 ***jiritsu suru*** assist (a dignitary)
史 ***jishi*** private secretary; respectfully
6臣 ***jishin*** courtier, attendant
気質 ***samurai katagi*** samurai spirit
7医 ***ji-i*** court physician
8者 ***jisha*** attendant, valet; altar boy
10従 ***jijū*** chamberlain
従長 ***jijūchō*** grand chamberlain
従官 ***jijūkan*** chamberlain
従武官 ***jijū bukan*** emperor's aide-de-camp
従職 ***jijūshoku*** board of chamberlains
11婢 ***jihi*** lady in waiting
13僧 ***jisō*** acolyte
14読 ***jidoku*** imperial tutor
15衛 ***jiei*** bodyguard
衛長 ***jieichō*** captain of the guard
17講 ***jikō*** imperial tutor

A **例** 428 F125 REI custom, usage, precedent; case, example, parallel, illustration. *tato(eru)* compare to, speak figuratively, illustrate. *tatoe* (see under 譬 4445.0). *tato(eba)* for example. *tameshi* instance, example, case, precedent, an experience.

4 文 *reibun* model sentence
日 *reijitsu* week day, ordinary day; appointed day
月 *reigetsu* every month
5 示 *reishi* illustration
外 *reigai* exception. *reigai na* exceptional
外無 *reigai na(ku)* without exception
6 式 *reishiki* regular ceremony, established form
会 *reikai* regular meeting
年 *reinen* normal year, average year; every year, annually
年祭 *reinensai* annual festival
7 言 *reigen* preface, foreword
8 刻 *reikoku* the regular time
10 時 *reiji* the usual time
11 規 *reiki* established rule
祭 *reisai* regular festival, annual festival
12 証 *reishō* illustration, example
13 解 *reikai* illustration, example
話 *reiwa* illustration
数 *reisū* number of cases
18 題 *reidai* example, exercises (in a textbook)

B **佳** 429 F120 KA beautiful; good; excellent. *i(i), yo(i), yo(shi)* (see under 良 3885.0).

2 人 *kajin* a beautiful woman
4 月 *kagetsu* a good month; bright moon
木 *kaboku* beautiful trees
什 *kajū* excellent poem
5 句 *kaku* beautiful passage of literature
7 言 *kagen* good words
辰 *kashin* lucky day, happy day, auspicious occasion
作 *kasaku* a good piece of work
良 *karyō na* good, favorable, successful
8 例 *karei* a good example
味 *kami* delicious taste
肴 *kakō* delicacy, rare treat; good-eating fish
9 品 *kahin* choice article
客 *kakyaku* a good visitor
10 酒 *kashu* good wine; a good drink
宴 *kaen* congratulatory banquet
容 *kayō* comely face
12 景 *kakei* beautiful view
13 話 *kawa* good story
節 *kasetsu* auspicious occasion
14 境 *kakyō* climax (of a story)
15 趣 *kashu* good taste; a good impression
編 *kahen* an outstanding poem
調 *kachō* good tune
賓 *kahin* good guest, interesting guest
篇 *kahen* an outstanding poem
19 麗 *karei* beauty
20 醸 *kajō* sweet saké; good wine

A **命** 430 F348 MYŌ. MEI command, decree; life; destiny. *mei(jiru), mei(zuru)* command; appoint. *inochi* life. *mikoto* words of a ruler; lord, prince. [口]

3 乞 *inochigoi* pleading for one's life
4 日 *meinichi* death anniversary
中 *meichū* a hit
中弾 *meichūdan* (direct) hit; straight shot
中数 *meichūsū* number of hits
5 令 *meirei* command, decree, directive, order
令一下 *meirei-ikka* immediately, as soon as the order is given
令文 *meireibun* imperative sentence
令形 *meireikei* imperative mood
令法 *meireihō* imperative mood
令書 *meireisho* decree, directive
6 名 *meimei* naming, christening
7 辛辛 *inochikaragaru* for dear life; barely escaping alive
8 取 *inochito(ri) no* fatal
知 *inochishi(razu)* recklessness; daredevil. *inochishi(razu) no* long-lasting
9 拾 *inochibiro(i)* narrow escape from death
10 根 *meikon* life
脈 *meimyaku* life, thread of life
冥加 *inochi-myōga* providential protection
11 運 *meiun* fate, doom
掛 *inochiga(ke) de* at the risk of life
終 *mei(ji)-o(waru)* finish giving orders
13 数 *meisū* span of life; destiny
14 綱 *inochi (no) tsuna* the thread of life
18 題 *meidai* thesis, proposition
20 懸 *inochigake no* risky, desperate. *inochigake de* at the risk of life

A **供** 431 F126 KYŌ. KU. GU. *kyō(suru)* offer, present, submit; serve (a meal) supply. *sona(eru)* offer, sacrifice, dedicate. *(o)tomo suru* accompany. *(o)sona(e)* offering. *tomo* attendant, companion, retinue.

2 人 *tomobito* companion
3 与 *kyōyo suru* give, furnish, provide
5 出 *kyōshutsu* delivery
出米 *kyōshutsumai* (farmers') rice deliveries
6 米 *kumai* rice offered to a god. *kyōmai* rice delivered to the government
回 *tomomawa(ri)* retinue, suite
7 応 *kyōō* treat, feast, banquet
述 *kyōjutsu* affidavit, deposition, testimony
述者 *kyōjutsusha* deponent, testifier
述書 *kyōjutsusho* affidavit, deposition, testimony
8 奉 *gubu suru* accompany, be in attendance on
物 *kumotsu, sona(e)mono* an offering

2 二亠[人 6イ𠆢]儿入八ソ冂冖冫几凵刀刂力勹匕匚匸十卜卩厂厶又

物台 *kumotsudai* altar
9 待 *tomoma(chi)* attendant's waiting room
10 進 *gushin* giving offerings
料 *kyōryō* an offering
宴 *kyōen* banquet, dinner
託 *kyōtaku* deposit
託金 *kyōtakukin* deposit of money
託物 *kyōtakubutsu* something deposited
託者 *kyōtakusha* depositor
11 祭 *gusai* offerings; offerings and worship
12 御 *kugo, gugo* emperor's meal
揃 *tomozoroi* attendants, retinue
給 *kyōkyū* supply
給地 *kyōkyūchi* supply center
給者 *kyōkyūsha* supplier
給源 *kyōkyūgen* source of supply
給路 *kyōkyūro* supply route
13 勢 *tomozei* attendants, retinue
15 養 *kuyō* memorial service
養塔 *kuyōtō* memorial tower
養塚 *kuyōzuka* unknown person's grave
16 覧 *kyōran* display, show ⌊mound

A 使 432/F122 使 SHI use; messenger. *tsuka(u)* use; handle, manipulate; employ; need, want; spend, consume; speak (English); practise (fencing); take (one's lunch); circulate (bad money). *tsuka(i) suru* go as an envoy. *tsuka(eru)* useful, serviceable. *tsuka(wasu)* (see under 遣 4732.0). *tsuka(i-konasu)* handle (men); master (a tool); acquire a command of (a language). *-shi(mu)* old causative verbal ending. *tsuka(i)* mission, errand, message; messenger, bearer; trainer, tamer; familiar spirit.

2 丁 *shitei* servant, janitor, messenger
4 手 *tsuka(i)te* user, consumer; employer; prodigal, spendthrift; (fencing) master
方 *tsuka(i)kata* how to use, treatment, management (of help) ⌈self to using
込 *tsuka(i)-ko(mu)* embezzle; accustom one-
切 *tsuka(i)-ki(ru)* use up, exhaust, wear out
分 *tsuka(i)wa(ke)* proper use. *tsuka(i)-wa-(keru)* use properly
5 立 *tsuka(i)da(te)* causing you trouble
処 *tsuka(i)dokoro* use
旧 *tsuka(i)-furu(su)* wear out (something)
古 *tsuka(i)-furu(su)* wear out (something)
出 *tsukaide* lasting quality, good wearing
用 *shiyō suru* employ, use, utilize
用人 *shiyōnin* employee, servant
用例 *shiyōrei* examples showing the use (of
用法 *shiyōhō* use, directions ⌊a word)
用者 *shiyōsha* user, consumer
用価値 *shiyō kachi* utility value
用料 *shiyōryō* rent, hire
用量 *shiyōryō* amount used
用権 *shiyōken* use, right to use
6 臣 *shishin* envoy
尽 *tsuka(i)-tsuku(su)* use up, squander
先 *tsuka(i)saki* the place where one is sent on an errand ⌈enslave
7 役 *shieki suru* employ, use, set to work;
役動詞 *shieki dōshi* causative verb
8 所 *tsuka(i)dokoro* use
物 *tsuka(i)mono* gift; bribe; usable article
歩 *tsuka(i)aru(ki)* running errands
果 *tsuka(i)-hata(su)* use up, squander
者 *shisha* messenger; envoy
命 *shimei* mission, errand; message
命者 *shimeisha* messenger
9 途 *shito* purpose for which money is spent; the way money is spent
10 残 *tsuka(i)noko(ri), tsuka(i)noko(shi)* remnant, remainder, odds and ends, leavings
料 *tsuka(i)ryō* use
徒 *shito* apostle, disciple
徒行伝 *Shitogyōden* Acts of the Apostles
徒承伝 *shito shōden* apostolic succession
徒信条 *Shito Shinjō* Apostle's Creed
徒信経 *Shito Shinkyō* Apostles' Creed
徒書 *Shitosho* the Epistles (of the New Testament) ⌈New Testament)
徒書簡 *Shito Shokan* the Epistles (of the
徒達 *Shitotachi* the Apostles
徒継承 *shito keishō* apostolic succession
11 過 *tsuka(i)-su(giru)* use excessively, use too much; spend too much; overwork
道 *tsuka(i)michi* use ⌊someone
頃 *tsuka(i)goro* handy ⌈atives
13 聘 *shihei* exchange of diplomatic represent-
賃 *tsuka(i)chin* messenger tip or charge
節 *shisetsu* envoy; embassy, mission; delegate
節団 *shisetsudan* mission, delegation
14 嗾 *shisō* instigation
慣 *tsuka(i)-na(rasu)* accustom oneself to using; train; break in (horses). *tsuka(i)-na(reru)* get accustomed to using
様 *tsuka(i)yō* how to use

7

盆 See 594. [皿]

俐 433/F132 俐 RI clever.
5 巧 *rikō* cleverness, wisdom, intelligence
9 発 *rihatsu*=word above

侮 434/F128 See 侮 421.

俤 435 F138 (国字) *omokage* = 面影 5087.15.

俥 436 F138 (国字) *kuruma* jinricksha.

俣 437 F-X (国字) *mata* crotch, thigh, groin.

俟 438 F136 SHI. *ma(tsu)* (see under 待 1609.0).

俏 439 F-X SHŌ. *yatsu(su)* disguise oneself as; adorn oneself; pine away; act shamefully; abbreviate (a character).

侶 440 F129 RYO. RO. *tomo* companion, follower.

7 伴 *ryohan* companion

俎 441 F132 俎 So altar of sacrifice. *mana-ita* chopping board.

3 上 *sojō* on the chopping board
8 板 *mana-ita* chopping board

俘 442 F134 FU. *toriko* captive.

13 虜 *furyo* captive, prisoner of war
虜収容所 *furyo shūyōjo* concentration camp

侯 443 F128 B Kō marquis; lord, daimyo.

7 伯 *kōhaku* nobles; feudal lords
8 国 *kōkoku* principality
17 爵 *kōshaku* marquis, marquess
爵夫人 *kōshaku fujin* marchioness

促 444 F131 B SOKU. SAKU. *unaga(su)* urge, press, demand; stimulate; quicken; incite; invite (attention to).

6 成 *sokusei* growth promotion
成栽培 *sokusei saibai* raising out-of-season crops with artificial heat
9 音 *sokuon* assimilated sound (represented by つ [*tsu*] in Japanese)
10 進 *sokushin suru* promote, encourage, facilitate, accelerate, spur on
進剤 *sokushinzai* accelerant, stimulant

俠 445 F136 KYŌ chivalry. *kyan* tomboy, bobby soxer, flapper.

3 女 *kyōjo* gallant woman
6 気 *kyōki, otokogi,* chivalrous spirit
9 客 *kyōkaku, otokodate*=男立 (see under 2996.5)
勇 *kyōyū* gallantry, chivalry
10 骨 *kyōkotsu* chivalrous spirit

俚 446 F134 RI rustic, ill-mannered.

6 耳 *riji* the ears of the public
7 言 *rigen* slang, dialect
9 俗 *rizoku* vulgarity; rural customs
14 語 *rigo* slang, dialect
16 謡 *riyō* ballad, folk song, popular song
諺 *rigen* proverb, saying

俄 447 F131 GA. *niwaka* sudden, abrupt, unexpected; improvised, offhand.

4 分限 *niwaka bugen* mushroom millionaire
5 仕込 *niwakajiko(mi)* hasty preparation
仕立 *niwakajita(te)* extemporary, improvised
6 成金 *niwaka narikin* overnight millionaire
8 雨 *niwaka ame* shower
盲 *niwaka mekura* sudden blindness; one suddenly blinded
9 造 *niwakazuku(ri)* makeshift, improvised
10 勉強 *niwaka benkyō* cramming
12 然 *gazen* suddenly, abruptly
景気 *niwakageiki* temporary boom

俊 448 F131 B SHUN excellence, genius.

3 士 *shunshi* a genius
才 *shunsai* genius; talented person, prodigy
7 足 *shunsoku* swift horse, talented person
抜 *shumbatsu* uncommon, above average
秀 *shunshū* genius; talented man, prodigy
8 英 *shun-ei* excellence; genius
10 馬 *shumme, shumba* swift horse
逸 *shun-itsu* excellence, genius
敏 *shumbin na* keen, quick-witted
11 偉 *shun-i* large and excellent
12 傑 *shunketsu* a genius, hero
童 *shundō* precocious child
14 徳 *shuntoku* great virtue
豪 *shungō* talent; a man of outstanding learning and virtue
15 賢 *shunken* excellent wisdom

係 449 F130 A KEI. *kakari* duty; person in charge. *kaka(waru)* concern oneself in, have to do with; affect, influence; stick to (opinions). *kaka(ru)* is the work of. *kaka(wari)* relation, connection. *ka(karu)* (see under 掛 1952.0); concern, affect, involve.

6 合 *kaka(ri)a(i)* unfortunate relationship
争 *keisō* dispute, contention
争物 *keisōbutsu* the legal point of contention
8 長 *kakarichō* chief clerk
官 *kaka(ri)kan* official in charge
10 員 *kaka(ri)-in* clerk in charge
留 *keiryū* mooring, anchorage

11船 *keisen* mooring a ship
累 *keirui* encumbrances, dependents; implication, complicity
12属 *keizoku* relationship
13数 *keisū* coefficient (in math)

便 450/F129 A BEN excreta, stools; evacuation. (See also 451.)
8所 *benjo* lavatory, latrine, comfort station, ⌊toilet
9通 *bentsū* bowel movement
10秘 *bempi* constipation
12壺 *ben tsubo* night-soil vault
13意 *ben-i* call of nature, bowel-movement ⌊inclination
14管 *benkan* sewer pipe
15器 *benki* bedpan, chamber pot, urinal

便 451/F129 A BEN convenience, facility. BIN chance; mail, letter. *ben(jiru)*, *ben(zuru)* will do, answer the purpose, make convenient. *tayo(ru)* rely on, have recourse to. *tayo(ri)* news, tidings; connection. *yosuga* way, means. (See also 450.) ⌈clothes
6衣 *ben-i* convenient clothes, ordinary
衣隊 *ben-itai* plain-clothes soldiers, mufti corps
7利 *benri na* convenient, handy, useful
利屋 *benriya* expressman, utility man
8佞 *bennei* flattery, adulation
法 *bempō* handy method, shortcut, ex- ⌊pedient
服 *bempuku* civilian clothes
宜 *bengi* convenience, accommodation, advantage, expedience
宜上 *bengijō* for convenience' sake
宜主義 *bengi shugi* opportunism, expediency ⌈*bemben to* idly
9便 *bemben(taru)* protuberant, paunchy.
乗 *binjō* taking advantage of a ride or an opportunity, taking a ship
乗主義者 *binjō shugisha* opportunist
乗者 *binjōsha* hitchhiker; one who catches a ride (with a friend)
10益 *ben-eki* convenience; benefit, profit
11船 *binsen* available steamer ⌈of sojourn
13殿 *binden, benden* emperor's temporary place
14箋 *binsen* stationery, writing paper
16覧 *benran* manual, handbook, compendium

侵 452/F128 B SHIN. *oka(su)* invade, raid; violate, trespass, intrude on.
2入 *shinnyū* invasion, raid, aggression, trespass
入者 *shinnyūsha* invader, trespasser, raider
入軍 *shinnyūgun* invading army
4水 *shinsui*=浸水 2572.4 ⌈ment
5犯 *shimpan* invasion, violation, infringe-
9食 *shinshoku* erosion; corrosion
10害 *shingai* infringement, violation, trespass, impairment
11掠 *shinryaku* aggression, invasion, raid
寇 *shinkō* invasion
略 *shinryaku* aggression, invasion, raid
略国 *shinryakukoku* aggressor nation
略的 *shinryakuteki* aggressive
略者 *shinryakusha* aggressor, invader
略軍 *shinryakugun* invading army
略戦争 *shinryaku sensō* aggressive war
15蝕 *shinshoku* erosion; corrosion
撃 *shingeki suru* invade and attack

俗 453/F132 A ZOKU customs, manners; the world; worldliness; vulgarity; mundane things; the laity. *zoku(ppoi)* cheap (reading); vulgar, worldly-minded.
2人 *zokujin* layman; worldling ⌈wisdom
3才 *zokusai* worldly wisdom; practical
4化 *zokka suru* vulgarize, secularize, popu- ⌊larize
文 *zokubun* colloquial style
文学 *zokubungaku* popular literature
5用 *zokuyō* worldly matters
世 *zokusei* this world, earthly life
世界 *zokusekai* everyday world
世間 *zokuseken* the workaday world
6耳 *zokuji* vulgar ears, attention of the masses
気 *zokki, zokke* vulgarity, worldliness, worldly ambition
向 *zokumu(ki)* popular (literature)
曲 *zokkyoku* folk song, ballad ⌈characters
字 *zokuji* popular characters; nonstandard
名 *zokumei* popular name; common name; secular name; bad reputation. *zokumyō*
吏 *zokuri* petty official ⌊secular name
7見 *zokken* popular view, laymen's opinion
言 *zokugen* colloquial language
体 *zokutai* condition of the (Buddhist) laity
形 *zokugyō* the figure of the common man
8姓 *zokusei* (a priest's) secular surname
物 *zokubutsu* worldly-minded person, vulgar person ⌈unholy desires
念 *zokunen* worldliness, worldly ambition,
受 *zoku-u(ke)* popular appeal
学 *zokugaku* popular music
事 *zokuji* worldly affairs; daily routine
9界 *zokkai* secular life, workaday world
臭 *zokushū* vulgarity, worldly-mindedness
10流 *zokuryū* populace, common run of men; worldly customs
称 *zokushō* popular name, common name
書 *zokusho* cheap fiction
11情 *zokujō* worldly-mindedness; worldly ⌊affairs
眼 *zokugan* popular opninion
務 *zokumu* secular affairs, worldly cares, daily routine

悪 *zokuaku* worldliness, vulgarity, coarseness
累 *zokurui* worldly troubles; worldliness
習 *zokushū* custom, usage
12 間 *zokkan* the world; the public
衆 *zokushū* people, crowd, masses, the public
13 僧 *zokusō* a worldly priest
解 *zokkai* explanation in common language
話 *zokuwa* worldly story; gossip
楽 *zokugaku* worldly music
14 塵 *zokujin* the world, earthly affairs
語 *zokugo* colloquial language; colloquialism
説 *zokusetsu* common saying, popular version; folklore, tradition
歌 *zokka* popular song, folk song, ditty, ballad
15 縁 *zokuen* worldly connection
調 *zokuchō* popular music, vulgar music
論 *zokuron* popular opinion
談 *zokudan* common talk, worldly conversation
輩 *zokuhai* worldlings, the crowd
趣味 *zokushumi* vulgar taste
16 儒 *zokuju* mediocre scholar
諦 *zokutai* simplified (Buddhist) teaching
謡 *zokuyō* popular song, folk song, ballad, ditty
諺 *zokugen* proverb, popular saying
20 議 *zokugi* popular opinion

A 信 454/F137 SHIN truth; faith, fidelity, sincerity; trust, confidence, reliance. *shin(jiru)*, *shin(zuru)* believe; believe in; place trust in, confide in, have faith in. *makoto* sincerity, fidelity, devotion.

4 込 *shin(ji)-ko(mu)* believe implicitly. *shin(ji)-ko(masu)* lead to believe
天翁 *shinten-ō, ahōdori* albatross
心 *shinjin* faith, belief, devotion, godliness
心家 *shinjinka* pious man, religionist
心深 *shinjimbuka(i)* deeply religious, devout, godly, faithful
5 玄袋 *shingembukuro* cloth bag
用 *shin-yō* confidence, trust, faith; dependence, reliance; belief, credence; credit
用状 *shin-yōjō* letter of credit
用状態 *shin-yō jōtai* credit standing
用取引 *shin-yō torihiki* credit transaction
用取引先 *shin-yō torihikisaki* charge customer
用協同組合 *shin-yō kyōdō kumiai* co-operative credit association
用借 *shin-yōga(ri)* debt of honor
用組合 *shin-yō kumiai* credit association
用貸 *shin-yōga(shi)* loans without collateral
用詐欺 *shin-yō sagi* confidence game
6 伏 *shimpuku suru* be convinced
任 *shinnin* trust, confidence, credence
任状 *shinninjō* credentials
任投票 *shinnin tōhyō* vote of confidence
任統治制度 *shinnin tōchi seido* trusteeship system
仰 *shinkō* belief, creed; religious faith
仰生活 *shinkō seikatsu* a life of faith; religious life
仰告白 *shinkō kokuhaku* profession of faith
仰的 *shinkōteki* religious, spiritual
仰者 *shinkōsha* believer, devotee
仰深 *shinkōbuka(i)* devout
仰箇条 *shinkō kajō* articles of faith
号 *shingō* signal, semaphore; signaling
号手 *shingōshu* flag man
号灯 *shingōtō* signal light
号所 *shingōjo* signal station
号塔 *shingōtō* signal tower
号電波 *shingō dempa* beam (signal)
号旗 *shingōki* signal flag
号機 *shingōki* signal, semaphore
7 条 *shinjō* article of faith, creed, belief
8 服 *shimpuku suru* be convinced
念 *shinnen* belief, faith, conviction
実 *shinjitsu* sincerity, honesty, truth, faithfulness
受 *shinju suru* believe, accept (truths)
者 *shinja* believer, devotee, adherent; Christian
奉 *shimpō* belief, faith
奉者 *shimpōsha* adherent, devotee, believer
9 約 *shin-yaku* vow, promise
10 倚 *shinki* reliance, trust, confidence
書 *shinsho* letter, personal correspondence
徒 *shinto* layman, believer, adherent, follower, laity
徒伝道 *shinto dendō* lay evangelism
徒伝道者 *shinto dendōsha* lay missionary
託 *shintaku* trust; entrusting
託会社 *shintakugaisha* trust company
託投資 *shintaku tōshi* trust investment
託契約 *shintaku keiyaku* trust agreement
託統治 *shintaku tōshi* trusteeship
託業 *shintakugyō* trust business
託資金 *shintaku shikin* trust fund
11 経 *shinkyō* creed
望 *shimbō* confidence, popularity
教 *shinkyō* religion, faith, belief
教自由 *shinkyō (no) jiyū* religious liberty, liberty of conscience
13 愛 *shin-ai suru* love and believe in
義 *shingi* faith, fidelity, loyalty
14 認 *shinnin* acknowledge, acceptance, admission
管 *shinkan* fuse
疑 *shingi* belief or doubt
15 賞必罰 *shinshō-hitsubatsu* sure penalty and certain rewards
16 憑 *shimpyō* trust, credit, credence
憑性 *shimpyōsei* authenticity, credibility
頼 *shinrai* reliance, trust, confidence
頼性 *shinraisei* credibility, authenticity

頼為合 *shinraishi-a(u)* enjoy each other's confidence
頼感 *shinraikan* feeling of trust

A 保 455 / F135 Ho. Hō. *ho(suru)* guarantee. *tamo(tsu)* keep, preserve, hold, retain, maintain; support, sustain; last, endure, keep well (food), wear well, be durable.

5 母 *hobo* kindergarten teacher
母養成所 *hoboyōseijo* kindergarten teacher institute
6 合 *mo(chi)-a(u)* maintain equilibrium; share expenses. *tamo(chi)a(i)* interdependence, steadiness. *mo(chi)a(i)* interdependence
存 *hozon* preservation, conservation, storage, maintenance
全 *hozen* integrity; preservation, conservation
全会 *hozenkai* (family) corporation
全会社 *hozen kaisha* (family) corporation
安 *hoan* peace preservation; security
安林 *hoanrin* forest reserve
安要員 *hoan yōin* mine guards (during a strike)
有 *hoyū* possession, retention, maintenance
有米 *hoyūmai* rice holdings
有者 *hoyūsha* owner
守 *hoshu* conservatism
守主義 *hoshu shugi* conservatism
守的 *hoshuteki* conservative
守党 *hoshutō* conservative party, the Right, Tories
7 身 *hoshin* self-protection
身術 *hoshinjutsu* art of self-protection
8 姆 *hobo* kindergarten teacher
育 *ho-iku suru* nurse, nurture, rear
育所 *ho-ikujo* nursery school, nursery
育園 *ho-ikuen* nursery school, day nursery
9 持 *hoji* maintainence, preservation
持者 *hojisha* holder (of a record)
10 留 *horyū suru* reserve, defer
険 *hoken* insurance, guarantee
険付 *hokenzu(ki)* guaranteed; insured
険会社 *hokengaisha* insurance company
険医 *hoken-i* insurance doctor
険金 *hokenkin* insurance money
険金受取人 *hokenkin uketorinin* beneficiary
険料 *hokenryō* insurance premium
11 菌者 *hokinsha* germ carrier
釈 *hoshaku* bail
釈金 *hoshakukin* bail
健 *hoken* health preservation, hygiene, sanitation
健医 *hoken-i* public-health doctor
健所 *hokenjo* health center
健婦 *hokenfu* public-health nurse
12 温 *ho-on* keeping warm; heat insulation
税 *hozei* customs bond
税倉庫 *hozei sōko* bonded warehouse
証 *hoshō* guarantee, security, pledge
証人 *hoshōnin* guarantor, bondsman
証牛乳 *hoshō gyūnyū* certified milk
証付 *hoshōtsu(ki)* guaranteed, certified
証金 *hoshōkin* security money, bond, deposit
13 障 *hoshō* guarantee, security
障占領 *hoshō senryō* protective occupation (of a country)
14 管 *hokan* custody, deposit, storage
管人 *hokannin* custodian, trustee
管会社 *hokangaisha* safety-deposit company
管物 *hokambutsu* goods in custody, property in trust
管金 *hokankin* money on deposit
管林 *hokanrin* managed forest
管料 *hokanryō* custody fee, storage charge
管証 *hokanshō* certificate of custody
15 線 *hosen* track maintenance
養 *hoyō* health preservation; recuperation; recreation
養地 *hoyōchi* health resort
養所 *hoyōsho* sanatorium
養院 *hoyōin* sanatorium
20 護 *hogo* care, shelter, protection; favor, patronage
護色 *hogoshoku* protective coloration
護金 *hogokin* subsidy
護国 *hogokoku* protectorate
護者 *hogosha* protector, guardian, patron
護委員 *hogo i-in* rehabilitation worker
護鳥 *hogochō* protected bird
護税 *hogozei* protective duty
護検束 *hogo kensoku* protective arrest
護貿易 *hogo bōeki* protective trade
護聖人 *hogo (no) seijin* patron saint
護領 *hogoryō* protectorate
護関税 *hogo kanzei* protective tariff
護関税率 *hogo kanzeiritsu* protective tariff
護観察 *hogo kansatsu* probation

8

偖 See 498.

俸 456 / F142 See 伜 366.

倡 457 / F146 See 娼 1235.

倂 458 / F141 See 併 425.

倣 459 / F159 See 倣 513.

倪 460 / F147 Gei stare.

倢 461 / F146 Shō fast, speedy.

倖 462 / F144 Kō happiness, luck.

倆 463 / F142 Ryō skill.

倩 464 / F147 Sen. *tsuratsura* carefully, attentively, profoundly.

衾 465 / F1693 Kin. *fusuma* quilt, bedding. [衣]

B **倣** 466 / F146 Hō. *nara(u)* imitate, follow, emulate.

A **俵** 467 / F140 Hyō bag, bale, sack; bag counter. *tawara* straw bag.
[8]物 *tawaramono* goods in straw bags
[13]数 *hyōsū* number of straw bags

倘 468 / F144 Shō if; dullness.
[8]佯 *shōyō* wandering

倥 469 / F147 Kō boorish; urgent.
[11]偬 *kōsō* hurrying

倔 470 / F144 Kutsu stubborn.
[11]強 *kukkyō* strong health

拿 471 / F794 Da arrest, capture. [手]
[10]捕 *daho* capture, seizure

俺 472 / F141 En. *ore* I.
[12]等 *oira, orera* we

倨 473 / F147 Kyo pride; squatting with legs outstretched. *ogo(ru)* be proud.
[13]傲 *kyogō* pride, arrogance

B **倫** 474 / F147 Rin companion.
[11]理 *rinri* ethics, morals
理的 *rinriteki* ethical
理学 *rinrigaku* ethics, moral philosophy

倭 475 / F148 Wa *Yamato* ancient Japan.
[2]人 *wajin* (an old word for) a Japanese
[11]寇 *wakō* Japanese pirates

倚 476 / F145 I. Ki. *yo(ru)* lean on, rest against.
[3]子 *isu* chair, couch, seat; office, position
[20]懸 *yo(ri)-ka(karu)* lean on, recline on; rely on

倶 477 / F140 Gu. Ku. *tomo ni* (see under 共 581.0).
[8]舎 *Kusha* Buddhist sect originating in the seventh century
[9]発 *guhatsu* concurrence
[13]楽部 *kurabu* club, fraternity, sorority; clubhouse

倡 478 / F146 Shō actor.
[8]佯 *shōyō* wandering
和 *shōwa* cheering in chorus
[11]婦 *shōfu* prostitute, harlot

B **倹** 479 / F173 **儉** Ken economy. *tsuma(shii)* thrifty, economical.
[9]約 *ken-yaku* economy, frugality
約家 *ken-yakuka* thrifty person; economist
[10]素 *kenso* economical and simple

P **俸** 480 / F141 Hō salary.
[12]給 *hōkyū* salary, pay
給日 *hōkyūbi* pay day
給生活者 *hōkyū-seikatsusha* salaried man
給袋 *hōkyūbukuro* pay envelope
[13]禄 *hōroku* retainer's stipend, pay, salary
禄米 *hōrokumai* rice allowance

A **候** 481 / F144 Kō season, weather. *sōrō* classical verbal ending equivalent to colloquial *-masu.*
[4]文 *sōrōbun* epistolary style
[11]鳥 *kōchō* bird of passage, migratory bird
[12]補 *kōho* candidacy
補生 *kōhosei* cadet
補地 *kōhochi* proposed site; site chosen
補者 *kōhosha* candidate, applicant

倦 482 / F147 Ken. *u(mu), aki(ru), agu(mu)* get tired of, lose interest in.
[9]怠 *kentai* fatigue, weariness, boredom
怠期 *kentaiki* the stage of fatigue
怠感 *kentaikan* a washed-out feeling
[10]疲 *u(mi)-tsuka(reru)* grow weary, get tired of
[14]厭 *ken-en* weariness
[15]撓 *u(mazu)-tayu(mazu)* untiringly, assiduously
[16]憊 *kempai* extreme fatigue

A **倍** 483 / F142 **倍** Bai double, twice; times, -fold. *bai(suru) vi* and *vt* double; be doubled; increase.
[3]大 *baidai* double size
[5]旧 *baikyū no* redoubled, increased

加 *baika* doubling
9 音 *baion* overtone, harmonic
11 率 *bairitsu* magnification, magnifying power
13 数 *baisū* multiple
14 増 *baima(shi)*, *baizō* doubling
18 額 *baigaku* double amount

俯 484 / F139 Fu. *fu(su)* bend down, bow down, lie prostrate. *utsumu(ku)*, *utsumu(keru)*＝俯向 (see below–6).
6 向 *utsumu(keru)* turn upside down; turn (face) downward. *utsumu(ku)* look downward, stoop. *utsumu(ke)*, *utsumu(ki)* lying face down; upside down
伏 *utsubu(su)* lie on one's face. *fufuku* prostration
仰 *fugyō* looking up and down; actions; being obliging
仰角 *fugyōkaku* angle of elevation
7 角 *fukaku* angle of dip
17 瞰 *fukan suru* command a view of
瞰図 *fukanzu* bird's-eye view

B **俳** 485 / F140 Hai actor.
2 人 *haijin* a haiku poet
4 文 *haibun* prose with a poetic haiku flavor
友 *haiyū* (haiku) poetry pals
5 句 *haiku* 17-syllable poem in 3 lines of 5, 7, and 5 syllables; hokku
6 号 *haigō* pseudonym of a haiku poet
名 *haimei*, *haimyō* a haiku poet's pen name
8 味 *haimi* subdued taste, refined taste; a haiku (poetic) flavor
画 *haiga* briefly drawn picture, haiku picture
9 徊 *haikai* loitering, sauntering. *motō(ru)* wander around
13 聖 *haisei* famous haiku poet; the poet Basho
16 壇 *haidan* the world of the haiku
諧 *haikai* 17-syllable poem, haiku; humorous haiku
諧師 *haikaishi* writer of haikai poems
17 優 *haiyū* actor, actress, player

A **倉** 486 / F142 Sō storehouse. *kura* warehouse, godown; cellar; depository, treasury; granary, elevator.
2 入 *kura-i(re)* warehousing
5 主 *kuranushi* warehouse owner
出 *kurada(shi)* releasing stored goods
7 作 *kurazuku(ri)* warehouse style
8 卒 *sōsotsu* being very busy
9 皇 *sōkō* hurry, bustle
10 荷 *kurani* warehouse goods
庫 *sōko* storehouse, godown; magazine
庫会社 *sōkogaisha* warehousing company
庫業 *sōkogyō* warehousing business
12 渡 *kurawata(shi)* ex-warehouse
15 敷 *kurashiki* storage charges
敷料 *kurashikiryō* storage charges
16 廩 *sōrin* rice granary

B **倒** 487 / F143 Tō. *tao(reru)*, *ko(keru)* fall, collapse, drop; break down, die, succumb to; fall senseless; be ruined; have a bad debt. *tao(su)* bring down, throw down, blow down, fell, knock down, trip up; defeat; ruin, overthrow; kill; leave unpaid; cheat. *tao(re)* bad debt. *saka(sa)*, *saka(sama)*, *saka(shima)* reverse, inversion, upside down.
5 句 *tōku* reading Chinese in the Japanese order
6 死 *tōshi* dying by the wayside
伏 *tao(re)-fu(su)* fall down
8 事 *sakasamagoto* wrong order
11 産 *tōsan* insolvency, bankruptcy
13 睫 *sakasa matsuge*, turned-in eyelashes
幕 *tōbaku suru* overthrow the shogunate
置 *tōchi* turning things upside down; placing nonessentials before essentials
置法 *tōchihō* inversion of the word order in a sentence
14 閣 *tōkaku suru* overthrow the cabinet
像 *tōzō* inverted image
15 潰 *tōkai suru* collapse, be destroyed
影 *tōei* reflection
16 壊 *tōkai suru* collapse, be destroyed
錯 *tōsaku* perversion
20 懸 *tōken* hanging (someone) upside down

B **値** 488 / F146 Chi *atai*, *ne* price, cost, value. *atai suru* value.
3 巾 *nehaba* price range, price fluctuation
下 *nesa(gari)* price decline. *nesa(ge)* price reduction
上 *nea(gari)* price advance, increase in value. *nea(ge)* price hike, mark-up
4 引 *nebiki* price reduction, discount
切 *negi(ru)* haggle, bargain
5 打 *neuchi* value, worth, price; dignity
6 安 *neyasu* cheapness
9 段 *nedan* price, cost
段付 *nedanzu(ke) suru* price at
段表 *nedanhyō* price list
段書 *nedanga(ki)* price list
11 遇 *chigū* meeting (someone)
頃 *negoro* reasonable price
動 *neugo(ki)* price fluctuation
12 幅 *nehaba* price range or fluctuation
14 増 *nema(shi)*＝*nea(ge)* 値上 (see above–3)
15 踏 *nebu(mi)* appraisal, estimation, evaluation
16 積 *nezumo(ri)* estimation, valuation
鞘 *nezaya* margin, spread (in prices)

A 個 489 F142 个 ケ KA article counter. KO individual; article counter.

2 人 *kojin* private person, individual. *kojin no* personal, private, individual
人用 *kojin-yō* for personal use
人主義 *kojin shugi* individualism
人名 *kojimmei* personal name
人性 *kojinsei* individuality, personality, idiosyncrasy ⌈centered
人的 *kojinteki* individual, personal, self-
人指導 *kojin shidō* personal guidance, tutoring ⌈sonal equation
人差 *kojinsa* individual differences; per-
人個人 *kojin-kojin* individual, one by one
人展 *kojinten* one-man exhibition, one-man show
人教授 *kojin kyōju* private instruction
人経営 *kojin keiei* private management
人誤差 *kojin gosa* personal equation
7 体 *kotai* an individual
別 *kobetsu* a particular case
別的 *kobetsuteki ni* individually
条 *kajō* article, clause, item
条書 *kajōgaki* itemization ⌈crasy
8 性 *kosei* personality; individuality, idiosyn-
性的 *koseiteki* personal, individual
10 展 *koten* personal exhibition
個 *koko* one by one; individuals. *koko ni* individually, separately
個別別 *koko-betsubetsu* each one separately
13 数 *kosū* number of articles

A 借 490 F145 SHA, SHAKU borrowing. *ka(riru)*, *ka(ru)* borrow; have a loan; hire, rent; buy on credit. *ka(ri)* borrowing; debt; loan.

2 人 *karinin* borrower ⌈*kari-i(re)* debt
入 *ka(ri)-i(reru)* borrow, rent, lease, charter.
入金 *kari-irekin* loan, debt ⌈charter
3 上 *ka(ri)-a(geru)* hire, lease, requisition,
4 手 *ka(ri)te* borrower, debtor; tenant ⌈ing
方 *ka(ri)kata* debtor; debit; way of borrow-
火 *ka(ri)bi* borrowing fire; borrowed fire
込 *ka(ri)-ko(mu)* borrow ⌈(car)
切 *ka(ri)-ki(ru)* reserve. *ka(ri)ki(ri)* reserved
5 主 *karinushi* borrower, debtor; tenant
出 *ka(ri)-da(su)* borrow, take out
用 *shakuyō* borrowing, loan
用者 *shakuyōsha* borrower
用証書 *shakuyō shōsho* promissory note
6 字 *ka(ri)ji* characters borrowed (to represent
宅 *ka(ri)taku* rented house ⌊the meaning)
名 *ka(ri)na* borrowed name
衣裳 *ka(ri)-ishō* borrowed clothes
地 *ka(ri)chi, shakuchi* leased land
地権 *shakuchiken* lease, leasehold
7 住 *ka(ri)zuma(i)* living in rented quarters
8 店 *ka(ri)dana* rented shop
逃 *ka(ri)ni(ge)* running away from a debt
放 *ka(rip)pana(shi)* borrowing without returning
物 *ka(ri)mono* something borrowed
取 *ka(ri)do(ri)* borrowing without returning
金 *shakkin* loan, debt, liabilities ⌈lector
金取 *shakkinto(ri)* bill collection; bill col-
受 *ka(ri)-u(keru)*=*ka(riru)* (see under 借 490.0)
受人 *ka(ri)u(ke)nin* borrower, debtor; tenant
受金 *ka(ri)u(ke)kin* borrowed money
9 屋 *shakuya* rented house
10 倒 *ka(ri)-tao(su)* evade payment
料 *shakuryō* rent money
財 *shakuzai* loan, debt, liability
家 *shakuya, shakka, ka(ri)-ie, ka(ri)ya* house for rent, rented house, renting a house
家人 *shakkanin, shakuyanin* tenant, renter
家争議 *shakka sōgi* tenancy troubles
家住居 *shakuyazumai* living in rented quarters
11 問 *shamon suru, shakumon suru* inquire
12 間 *ka(ri)ma* rented room
換 *ka(ri)-ka(eru)* convert (a loan). *ka(ri)-ka(e)* conversion, refunding, renewal
款 *shakkan* loan
着 *ka(ri)gi* borrowed clothes ⌈loans
集 *ka(ri)-atsu(meru)* borrow money, call for
貸 *ka(ri)ka(shi), shakutai* loan; lending and borrowing ⌈standing debt; overdraft
越 *ka(ri)-ko(su)* overdraw. *ka(ri)ko(shi)* out-
越金 *karikoshikin* overdraft; outstanding
13 賃 *ka(ri)chin* rent, hire ⌊debt
14 銭 *shakusen* debt
16 覧 *shakuran suru* borrow and read

A 修 491 F138 SHŪ. SHU. *osa(maru)* govern oneself, conduct oneself well. *osa(meru)* study, complete (a course); cultivate; master; order (one's life); repair.

2 了 *shūryō* completion (of a course)
3 士 *Shūshi* Master of Arts
5 史 *shūshi* compilation of a history
正 *shūsei* amendment, revision, modification, alteration, correction, retouching
正者 *shūseisha* amender
正案 *shūseian* proposed amendment
6 好 *shūkō* amity, friendship
交 *shūkō* amity, friendship
行 *shugyō* training, practice, ascetic practices, discipline; pursuit of knowledge
行者 *shugyōsha* practitioner of (Buddhist) austerities

7身 *shūshin* morals, ethics, moral training
改 *shūkai* personal reformation
8法 *shūhō* (Buddhist) prayer and austerities
学 *shūgaku* learning
学旅行 *shūgaku ryokō* field trip
9造 *shūzō, shuzō* repairing
訂 *shūtei* correction, revision
院 *shūin* friary
院長 *shūinchō* prelate, prior, abbot
11得 *shūtoku* learning, acquirement
理 *shūri, shuri* repair, mending
理工 *shūrikō* repair man
理中 *shūrichū* under repair
道 *shūdō* learning; studying the fine arts
道士 *shūdōshi* monk, friar
道女 *shūdōjo* (Catholic) nun 「nastic life
道生活 *shūdō seikatsu* monasticism, mo-
道会 *shūdōkai* (Catholic) order
道院 *shūdōin* monastery, convent, cloister
道院制度 *shūdōin seido* monasticism
道誓願 *shūdō seigan* vows of religious
12復 *shūfuku* repair, mending ⌊orders
補 *shūho* repairing
営 *shūei* building work
13煉 *shūren* culture, training
飾 *shūshoku suru* decorate, adorn; polish up (writing); modify (in grammar)
飾語 *shūshokugo* modifier
業 *shūgyō, shugyō* pursuit of knowledge
業年限 *shūgyō nengen* length of the course of study
辞 *shūji* figure of speech; rhetorical flourish
辞法 *shūjihō* rhetoric
辞学 *shūjigaku* rhetoric
14練 *shūren* drill, practice, training, culture
練者 *shūrensha* (Catholic) neophyte
15撰 *shūsen* editing, compiling
養 *shūyō* culture, (mental) training, self-
熟 *shūjuku* developing skill ⌊discipline
16錬 *shūren* culture, training
築 *shūchiku* repair, renovation, restoration
整 *shūsei* adjustment; retouching (in photography)
18験者 *shugenja* mountaineering ascetic
繕 *shūzen* repairs, mending
繕工 *shūzenkō* repair man
繕工場 *shūzen kōjō* repair shop
繕費 *shūzenhi* repair expense
19羅 *shura* fighting; scene of carnage
羅巷 *shura (no) chimata* scene of carnage
羅道 *shuradō* scene of carnage 「of carnage
羅場 *shuraba* fighting scene. *shurajō* scene

9

貧 See 600. [貝]

條 492 / F980 See 条 1164. [木]

假 493 / F149 See 仮 382.

偬 494 / F-X Sō feel pain, suffer.

做 495 / F153 SA. *-na(su)* make.

盒 496 / F1311 Kō. covered utensil. [皿]

脩 497 / F1544 SHŪ dried meat; study; dry up. [肉]

偖 498 / F153 F830 撦 SHA. *sate* well, now.

偲 499 / F154 SHI. SAI. *shino(bu)* recollect, remember.

偓 500 / F152 AKU fuss.
9促 *akuseku to* fussily, sedulously, busily

偕 501 / F152 KAI together.
6老 *kairō* growing old together 「ship
老同穴 *kairō-dōketsu* a happy life partner-
13楽 *kairaku* enjoying oneself with others

偵 502 / F155 TEI spy.
P
8知 *teichi* spying, investigating
14察 *teisatsu* scouting, reconnaissance
察隊 *teisatsutai* scouting party, patrol

偃 503 / F148 EN dam, weir.
4月 *engetsu* crescent moon
月刀 *engetsutō* scimitar
8臥 *enga suru* lie face down

偸 504 / F156 偷 TSU, TŌ steal.
6安 *tōan suru* snatch a moment of rest; dicker
11視 *tōshi* stealthy glance ⌊for time
盗 *chūtō* robber; theft

貪 505 / F1791 TAN, DON coveting. *musabo(ru)* covet, indulge in. [貝]
6汚 *tan-o* greed, corruption
9食 *donshoku* voracity, ravenousness. *musabo(ri)-ku(u), musabo(ri)-kura(u)* greedily devour

11 婪 *donran, tanran* covetousness, greed
15 慾 *don-yoku* covetousness, greed

偉 B 506 / F150 I greatness. *era(garu)* be conceited. *era(i)* great, famous, remarkable, excellent.

2 人 *ijin* great man
力 *iryoku* power, might, authority, influence
3 大 *idai* greatness, grandeur
才 *isai* remarkable man
丈夫 *ijōfu* a hero, a great man, a big man
5 功 *ikō* great deed
8 物 *eramono, erabutsu* great man
効 *ikō* great effect
10 容 *iyō* majestic appearance, dignity
挙 *ikyo* excellent deeds
烈 *iretsu* great achievement
13 跡 *iseki* remaining works, results of a man's labor
業 *igyō* great enterprise, exploits
14 徳 *itoku* outstanding virtue
15 勲 *ikun* great achievement
17 績 *iseki* glorious achievements
18 蹟 *iseki*＝偉跡 (see above–13)
観 *ikan* grand sight

停 A 507 / F153 TEI stopping. *todo(maru), todo(meru), to(maru)* (see under 止 2429.0).

4 止 *teishi* suspension, ban; stop, standstill; deadlock, stalemate; interruption; abeyance
止価格 *teishi kakaku* pegged price
止線 *teishisen* stop line
6 会 *teikai* adjournment, suspension of a meeting; recess of a legislature
年 *teinen* retiring age, age limit
7 車 *teisha* stopping a vehicle
車場 *teishajō, teishaba* railway station; taxi stand
8 泊 *teihaku* anchorage, moorings
学 *teigaku* suspension from school
9 音 *teion* rest (in music)
音符 *teiompu* rest (in music)
10 留 *teiryū suru* stop, halt
留所 *teiryūjo* car stop
11 船 *teisen* stopping a ship, detention, quarantine
船場 *teisenjō* ferry landing
13 滞 *teitai* stagnation, tie-up; retention, accumulation, congestion; falling into arrears
戦 *teisen* armistice, cease fire
頓 *teiton* standstill, stalemate, set-back, abeyance
電 *teiden*, electricity failure
電日 *teidembi* no-electricity day
18 職 *teishoku* suspension from office

偶 B 508 / F156 GŪ even number; couple, man and wife; friend; same kind; doll. *tama no* occasional, rare. *tamasaka* occasionally. *tamatama* casually, unexpectedly; accidentally

2 人 *gūjin* puppet; doll
6 因 *gūin* contingent cause
成 *gūsei no* impromptu
有 *gūyū suru* have an accident
7 作 *gūsaku* something accidentally accomplished; two working together
吟 *gūkin* impromptu poem (humble)
9 発 *gūhatsu* sudden outbreak; accidental, incidental
発的 *gūhatsuteki* accidental, incidental, occasional, casual
11 偶 *tamatama* casually, unexpectedly, accidentally
12 詠 *gūei* impromptu poem (humble)
然 *gūzen* chance, accident, fortuity
13 数 *gūsū* even number
感 *gūkan* random thoughts
14 語 *gūgo* conversation
像 *gūzō* image, idol, statue
像化 *gūzōka* idolization
像礼拝 *gūzō reihai* idolatry
像破壊 *gūzō hakai* iconoclasm, image breaking
像視 *gūzōshi* idolization
像教 *gūzōkyō* idolatry
像教徒的 *gūzōkyōtoteki* idolatrous
像崇拝 *gūzō sūhai* idol worship, idolatry

側 A 509 / F154 SOKU. *soba(mu) vi* lean to one side, oppose, look aside, regret. *soba(meru)* shove to one side, look at out of the corner of one's eyes. *gawa* a side; surroundings; (watch) case. *hata* side, edge; a third person. *kawa* side; row. *soba* side, vicinity. *katawara* (see under 傍 520.0). *hono(kana)* faint, indistinct; stupid; few.

3 女 *sobame* concubine
4 辺 *sokuhen* corner
火山 *sokkazan* parasite volcano
5 圧 *sokuatsu* lateral pressure
仕 *sobazuka(e)* personal attendant, valet, maid
6 近 *sobachika(ku)*, nearby. *sokkin* close associate, braintruster
近者 *sokkinsha* close associate
7 役 *sobayaku* personal attendant
杖 *sobazue* blow received by a bystander
8 泳 *sokuei* side stroke
9 室 *sokushitsu* a noble's concubine
背 *sokuhai* flank
面 *sokumen* side, flank; sidelight; lateral
面図 *sokumenzu* side view
面観 *sokumenkan* side view
10 根 *sokkon* lateral root
射 *sokusha* flanking fire
部 *sokubu* the side
14 聞 *sokubun suru* hear casually

2 二亠人亻9 𠆢儿入八ソ冂冖冫几凵刀刂力勹匕匚匸十卜卩厂厶又

15 線 *sokusen* sidetrack, siding; side line (at a game)
16 壁 *sokuheki* side wall

偽 510 / F168 **僞** B

GI. *itsuwa(ru)* lie, falsify; deceive; pretend; deceive, cheat. *nise* (see under 贋 840.0).

5 札 *nise satsu, gisatsu* forged document, counterfeit money
史 *gishi* falsified history
本 *gihon* spurious book, a forgery
6 印 *gi-in* forged seal
名 *gimei* false name, assumed name
似症 *gijishō* suspected case
7 言 *gigen* falsehood
作 *gisaku* apocryphal work, forgery, spurious article
兵 *gihei* dummy soldiers
君子 *nise kunshi, gikunshi* hypocrite, snob
8 物 *gibutsu, nisemono* spurious article, a forgery, counterfeit
版 *gihan* pirated edition
学 *gigaku* false science; science out of line with the world of thought
者 *itsuwa(ri)mono* impostor, liar
9 計 *gikei* deceptive plan
造 *gizō* forgery, falsification, fabrication, counterfeiting
造罪 *gizōzai* forgery
10 称 *gishō suru* assume a false name
書 *gisho* spurious letter, apocryphal book, a forgery
11 悪 *giaku* pretense of evil
12 筆 *gihitsu* forged handwriting; plagiarism
装 *gisō* camouflage
報 *gihō* false report
善 *gizen* hypocrisy
善者 *gizensha* hypocrite
証 *gishō* perjury, false testimony
証者 *gishōsha* perjurer, false witness
証罪 *gishōzai* crime of perjury
13 電 *giden* false telegram
14 語 *itsuwa(ri)-kata(ru)* speak falsely
誓 *itsuwa(ri)-chika(u)* swear falsely. *gisei* perjury, false oath

偏 511 / F151 **偏** B

HEN side; left radical of a character; inclining. *hen(suru)* incline toward, be biased. *katayo(ru)* lean, incline; be biased. *katayo(ri)* inclination; offset; polarization. *hitoe ni* earnestly; humbly; solely.

2 人 *henjin* eccentric person
3 土 *hendo* rural areas
4 心 *henshin* eccentricity (in mechanics)
片 *katahera* one of a pair; one side
辺 *katahoto(ri)* corner, remote country place
5 平 *hempei na* flat
6 向 *henkō* propensity, inclination; deflection
好 *henkō* partiality
光 *henkō* polarized light; polarization
在 *henzai* maldistribution
7 見 *katayo(ri)-mi(ru)* show partiality. *henken* prejudice, narrow view
狂 *henkyō* monomania; monomaniac
8 屈 *henkutsu* eccentricity, bigotry, obstinacy
性 *hensei* eccentric personality
9 食 *henshoku* unbalanced diet
狭 *henkyō* narrow-mindedness; narrowness
降 *katabu(ri)* rainy spell
重 *henchō suru* make too much of. *henchō, henjū* preponderance
10 流 *henryū* drift
針 *henshin* deflection
差 *hensa* declination, deflection, variation, deviation, drift
11 斜 *hensha* declination, deviation
執 *henshū* bias, eccentricity, obstinacy
13 愛 *hen-ai* partiality, favoritism
窟 *henkutsu* eccentricity, bigotry, obstinacy
照 *katade(ri)* a stretch of sunshine (after rain)
14 歴 *henreki* travels, pilgrimage
頗 *hempa* favoritism, discrimination
16 頭痛 *henzutsū, hentōtsū* headache on one side; migraine
18 癖 *hempeki* eccentricity, crankiness

健 512 / F154 A

KEN health, strength; stick-to-itiveness. *suko(yakana)* vigorous healthy, sound. *shitataka ni* heartily; severely.

6 気 *kenage* courage. *kenage na* manly, heroic, brave; praiseworthy; industrious
全 *kenzen* health, soundness. *kenzen na* healthy, sound, wholesome
在 *kenzai* good health
7 投 *kentō* good pitching
否 *kempi* condition of health
児 *kenji* stalwart youth
忘 *kembō* forgetfulness
忘症 *kembōshō* amnesia, loss of memory
8 実 *kenjitsu na* steady, sound, reliable
歩 *kempo* good walker
者 *shitatakamono* desperate character, scoundrel; strong-willed person
9 胃剤 *ken-izai* stomach medicine
胃錠 *ken-ijō* stomach tablets
10 祥 *kenshō* spirit, pep, energy
11 脳剤 *kennōzai* brain tonic
啖 *kentan* gluttony, voracity
啖家 *kentanka* glutton, gormandizer
脚 *kenkyaku* good walker
脚家 *kenkyakuka* good walker
康 *kenkō* health. *kenkō na* sound; wholesome
康地 *kenkōchi* healthy place, health resort
康体 *kenkōtai* healthy body
康児 *kenkōji* healthy child
康者 *kenkōsha* a healthy person

康法 *kenkōhō* hygiene
康的 *kenkōteki* hygienic, healthful, sanitary
康美 *kenkōbi* physical beauty
康保険 *kenkō hoken* health insurance
康保険医 *kenkō hoken-i* health insurance doctor
康証明書 *kenkō shōmeisho* health certificate
康診断 *kenkō shindan* physical examination
12棒 *kembō* good batting
勝 *kenshō* good health
筆 *kempitsu* powerful pen
筆家 *kempitsuka* ready writer
18闘 *kentō* good fight, strenuous efforts

10

禽 See 528. [内]

傲 See 529.

倣 513/F159 **倣** Kō. *nara(u)* imitate, follow, emulate.

翕 514/F1507 Kyū gather. [羽]
12然 *kyūzen* spontaneously, with one accord

傅 515/F157 Fu instructor, tutor (to a prince). *kashizu(ku)* wait upon, serve.
8育 *fuiku* bringing up, tuition

傀 516/F157 Kai large.
17儡 *kairai, kugutsu* puppet; dummy
儡政府 *kairai seifu* puppet government
儡師 *kairaishi* puppet player; wirepuller

B **傑** 517/F158 Ketsu excellence. *sugu(reru)* excel.
2人 *ketsujin* an outstanding person
3士 *kesshi* hero, great man
5出 *kesshutsu suru* excel, be foremost
7作 *kessaku* masterpiece; boner, blunder
8物 *ketsubutsu* remarkable character, great man

傘 518/F158 San. *kasa* umbrella, parasol. *karakasa* paper umbrella.
3下 *sanka* affiliated with; under the jurisdiction of
5立 *kasata(te)* umbrella stand
6地 *kasaji* umbrella cloth
7形碍子 *kasagata gaishi* umbrella insulator
9屋 *kasaya* umbrella shop
持 *kasamo(chi)* umbrella carrier
10紙 *kasagami* oiled umbrella paper
12歯車 *kasahaguruma* bevel gear

A **備** 519/F158 Bi. *sona(waru)* be furnished with, be endowed with, possess; be among, be one of. *sona(eru)* furnish, provide, equip, install; have ready; prepare; possess, have; be endowed with; be armed with. *sona(e)* preparation, provision, guarding. *tsubu(sa) ni* in detail, with great care; completely; again and again.
5付 *sona(e)tsu(ke)* equipment, provision. *sona(e)-tsu(keru)* provide, furnish, equip, install
6考 *bikō* note, remarks, N.B.
7忘 *bibō* reminder
忘録 *bibōroku* memorandum, notebook
9品 *bihin* fixtures, furnishings, equipment
後表 *bingo omote* a quality *tatami* covering
荒 *bikō* provision for famine
荒食 *bikōshoku* emergency food
荒貯蓄 *bikō chochiku* famine-relief fund
10砲 *bihō* armament
13蓄 *bichiku* stored, reserved
蓄米 *bichikumai* reserved rice

B **傍** 520/F157 Hō. Bō *katawa(ra), waki, soba* side; besides; while. *katawa(ra) no* nearby. *katawa(ra) ni* beside, nearby. *hata* side; edge; a third person.
2人 *bōjin* bystander
5目 *okame, hatame* looking on by an outsider
目八目 *okame-hachimoku* superior observation by an outsider
6耳 *katamimi* things overheard
7見 *okami*=*okame* 傍目 (see above–5)
杖 *sobazue* blow received by a bystander
系 *bōkei* collateral family; subsidiary; affiliated
8受 *bōju* interception, tapping
迷惑 *hata meiwaku* inconvenience to those nearby
若無人 *bōjaku-bujin* arrogance, audacity, insolence, defiance
9点 *bōten* marks to facilitate reading of Chinese
10訓 *bōkun* marginal notes; *fu(ri)gana* (振仮名 1920.6)
11惚 *okabore* unrequited love, secret affections
視 *bōshi suru* look on from the side
12註 *bōchū* marginal notes
15線 *bōsen* side line, underline
輩 *hōbai* term of address among retainers of the same lord; people working in the same office; students of the same teacher; companions
17聴 *bōchō* hearing, attendance, auditing
聴人 *bōchōnin* hearer, auditor, audience
聴券 *bōchōken* admission ticket
聴席 *bōchōseki* visitor's gallery, seats for the public
聴料 *bōchōryō* admission fee
聴随意 *bōchō zui-i* admission free

聴無料 *bōchō muryō* admission free
18 観 *bōkan suru* look on, remain a spectator
観者 *bōkansha* bystander, onlooker
観的 *bōkanteki ni* as a spectator

11

傳 521 F161 See **伝** 379.

會 522 F927 See **会** 381. [曰]

僂 523 F165 Rō, Ru bend over.

僊 524 F166 Sen hermit.
2 人 *sennin* = 仙人 359.2

傴 525 F163 U, Ku bend over.
13 僂 *kuru, semushi* hunchback; rickets

愈 526 F727 **愈 愈 愈** Yu. *iyo-iyo* = 愈愈 (next word). [心]
13 愈 *iyo-iyo* more and more, increasingly; at last; beyond doubt

僅 527 F166 Kin. *wazu(ka)* a little, a small quantity.
4 少 *kinshō* few, little, insignificant
少差 *kinshōsa* narrow majority; a shade of difference
13 僅 *kinkin* merely, no more than

禽 528 F1370 Kin bird; captive; capture. *tori* bird. [内]
8 舎 *kinsha* poultry shed
11 鳥 *kinchō* birds
16 獣 *kinjū* birds and animals

傲 529 F160 Gō. *ogo(ru)* be proud.
8 岸 *gōgan* haughtiness, pride
10 倨 *gōkyo* arrogance
12 然 *gōzen(taru)* proud, haughty
14 慢 *gōman* pride, haughtiness, insolence, arrogance
慢不遜 *gōman-fuson na* haughty, arrogant, overbearing

傭 530 F160 Yō. *yato(u)* employ, hire.
2 人 *yōnin* employee
7 兵 *yōhei, yato(i)hei* mercenary soldier
11 船 *yōsen* chartered ship
船契約 *yōsen keiyaku* chartering ships
13 聘 *yōhei suru* employ

債 531 F163 B Sai debt; loan.
5 主 *saishu* creditor
8 券 *saiken* bond, debenture
10 鬼 *saiki* cruel creditor; bill collector
11 務 *saimu* debt, liabilities
務者 *saimusha* debtor
15 権 *saiken* credit; claim
権者 *saikensha* creditor

働 532 F166 A (国字) Dō. *hatara(ku)* work, labor; do, act, commit, practise; work on; come into play; be conjugated; reduce the price. *hatara(ki)* work, labor; action, function, operation; movement, motion; conjugation, inflection; talent; achievement.
2 人 *hatara(ki)bito, hatara(ki)te* a worker; a good worker
3 口 *hatara(ki)guchi* position, opening
4 手 *hatara(ki)te, hatara(ki)de* a worker; a good worker, a breadwinner, an able man
8 者 *hatara(ki)mono* hard worker
9 通 *hatara(ki)tō(shi) de* working right on thru
10 振 *hatara(ki)bu(ri)* way of working, discharge of duty
11 掛 *hatara(ki)-ka(keru)* work on someone, influence, appeal to; begin to work
盛 *hatara(ki)zaka(ri)* prime of life
13 蜂 *hatara(ki)bachi* worker bee

催 533 F159 B Sai. *moyō(su)* hold (a meeting); give (a dinner); feel; show signs of, develop symptoms of, feel (sick). *moyō(shi)* meeting, gathering; (bodily) urge.
6 合 *moya(u)* co-operate (in enterprises)
7 告 *saikoku* notification
8 物 *moyō(shi)mono* points of interest; tourist attraction; an exhibit; events
9 促 *saisoku suru* demand, request, urge (action), press for
促状 *saisokujō* dun, letter requesting money, etc.
10 涙瓦斯 *sairui gasu* tear gas
涙弾 *sairuidan* tear-gas bomb
涙銃 *sairuijū* tear-gas gun
眠 *saimin* hypnotism
眠剤 *saiminzai* sleeping medicine
眠術 *saiminjutsu* hypnotism
眠薬 *saimin-yaku* sleeping medicine
11 淫剤 *sai-inzai* an aphrodisiac

傾 534 F164 B Kei. *kashi(gu) vi* lean, incline, tilt, list, tip, careen, lurch. *kashi(geru) vt* lean, incline, tilt. *katamu(ku), katabu(ku), kata(gu)* incline toward, tilt, slant, slope, lurch, heel over; be disposed to; trend toward, be prone to; go down (sun); wane, sink, decline. *katamu(keru) vt* incline, list, bend, lean, tip, tilt, slant; concentrate on; devote to; ruin; squander; empty. *kata(geru) vt* incline, tilt, slant. *nada(reru)* slope, descend, slide (snow, etc.). *katamu(ki)* slope, inclination, list; tendency, trend; bent; disposition, bias. *nada(re)* (see under 頽 5130.0).

4 込 *nada(re)-ko(mu)* rush or crowd into
6 向 *keikō* tendency, trend; disposition
7 角 *keikaku* inclination
8 国 *keikoku* a beauty, a siren, a courtesan, a prostitute
注 *keichū* devotion, concentration
9 度 *keido* inclination
城 *keisei*=*keikoku* 傾国 (see above–8)
10 倒 *katamu(ke)-tao(su)* cast down, lay low. *keitō suru* devote oneself to, concentrate on; admire, idolize
差 *keisa* dip (of the compass)
11 斜 *keisha* inclination, bevel, slope, list, dip
斜角 *keishakaku* angle of inclination
斜面 *keishamen* inclined plane, slope
斜度 *keishado* gradient
12 落 *nada(re)-o(chiru)* slide down (snow, etc.)
17 聴 *keichō* listening closely
18 瀉 *keisha* decanting
覆 *keifuku suru* turn upside down

B **傷** 535 F163 SHŌ wound, injury. *ita(mu)* (see under 痛 3054.0). *ita(meru)* hurt, injure, impair, spoil, worry, bother, afflict, cause pain. *kizu* wound, injury, hurt; cut, gash, bruise, scratch; scar; weak point. *ita(mi)* pain, ache.

3 口 *kizuguchi* wound
4 心 *shōshin* heartbreak, grief
5 付 *kizutsu(keru)* wound, injure; damage, mar; disgrace. *kizutsu(ku)* get injured, be wounded
7 悴 *shōsui* great grief
兵 *shōhei* wounded soldier
8 物 *kizumono* defective article; unvirtuous girl
咎 *kizutogame* inflamed wound
者 *shōsha* wounded or injured person
9 神 *shōshin* heartbreak, grief
10 害 *shōgai* wound, injury, accident, casualty
害保険 *shōgai hoken* accident insurance
病 *shōbyō* injuries and sickness
病兵 *shōbyōhei* sick and wounded soldiers
病捕虜 *shōbyō horyo* sick and wounded prisoners
11 痕 *kizuato, shōkon* scar
悴 *shōsui* great grief
痍 *shōi* wound, injury
痍軍人 *shōi gunjin* wounded soldier, disabled veteran
12 創 *shōsō* wound, injury
13 傷 *ita-ita(shii)* pitiful, pathetic
嘆 *shōtan* crying in pain
跡 *kizuato* scar
15 歎 *shōtan* crying in pain
16 薬 *kizugusuri* salve, ointment

B **僧** 536 F168 **僧** Sō monk, priest.

5 尼 *sōni* monks and nuns
正 *sōjō* high priest of a Buddhist sect
6 衣 *sōi* priest's garb
号 *sōgō* priest's religious name
寺 *sōji* Buddhist priest; a temple with a resident priest
7 位 *sōi* priestly rank
体 *sōtai* the form of a Buddhist priest; priestly attire
坊 *sōbō* priests' quarters
形 *sōgyō* the form of a Buddhist priest; priestly attire
兵 *sōhei* priest soldier
8 門 *sōmon* priesthood; Buddhism
房 *sōbō* priests' temple quarters
服 *sōfuku* priest's garb
9 俗 *sōzoku* priests and laymen
侶 *sōryo* (Buddhist) priest, monk
院 *sōin* monastery, temple
10 徒 *sōto* (Buddhist) priests, monks
家 *sōka* Buddhist temple
11 堂 *sōdō* temple meditation hall or certain other temple structures
庵 *sōan* priest's hermitage
庵生活 *sōan seikatsu* hermit life
18 職 *sōshoku* (Buddhist) priesthood
20 籍 *sōseki* (Buddhist) priesthood

12

僞 537 F168 See **偽** 510.

僧 538 F168 See **僧** 536.

僑 539 F166 KYŌ temporary home.

A **像** 540 F166 **像** ZŌ image, statue, figure, picture, portrait.

僮 541 F170 TŌ, DŌ child; servant; foolishness.

僥 542 F168 GYŌ luck; seek; desire.

10 倖 *gyōkō* windfall, godsend, good fortune

儁 543 F172 SHUN excellence; talented person.

7 秀 *shunshū* genius, prodigy, talented man

僕 544/F167 Boku manservant, I. *shimobe* manservant; servant (of God).
P
6 仲間 *shimobe nakama* fellow servant
11 婢 *bokuhi* male and female servants

僚 545/F167 Ryō official; companion.
B
4 友 *ryōyū* comrade, coworker
11 船 *tomobune* consort ship
16 機 *ryōki* consort plane
20 艦 *ryōkan* consort ship

僣 546/F168 See 僭 560.

13

儉 547/F173 See 倹 479.

價 548/F170 See 価 422.

儈 549/F173 Kai middleman.

儚 550/F175 Bō. *hakana(i)*＝果敢 107.12.

億 551/F172 億 Oku 100,000,000.
A
3 万長者 *okumanchōja* billionaire
6 兆 *okuchō* people, multitude, masses
7 劫 *okkū na* troublesome, annoying

舖 552/F1953/F1572 舖 舗 鋪 Ho shop, store. [舌]
B
11 道 *hodō* pavement; paved street
12 装 *hosō* pavement; paving
装煉瓦 *hosō renga* paving brick

僻 553/F171 Heki prejudice, bias; rural area. *heki(suru)* be biased, be warped. *higa(mu)* be prejudiced, be soured. *higami* prejudice, bias; inferiority complex. *higa-* evil, untrue, erroneous.
4 心 *higamigokoro* warped mind
5 目 *higame* squint; sight error; bias; misunderstanding, misjudgment
6 地 *hekichi* remote place
在 *hekizai* being off to one side; being away off in the country
7 見 *hekiken* prejudice
言 *hekigen* unreasonable talk
邑 *hekiyū* remote village
村 *hekison* remote village
8 事 *higagoto* immoral act; mistake
10 陬 *hekisū* remote place
根性 *higami konjō* prejudiced mind
11 隅 *hekigū* corner, nook
12 遠 *hekien no* remote, outlying
14 境 *hekikyō* deep rural areas
説 *hekisetsu* prejudiced opinion
15 論 *hekiron* prejudiced opinion

儀 554/F171 Gi rule; ceremony; affair, case, a matter.
B
2 刀 *gitō* ceremonial sword
5 仗 *gijō* cortege, guard
仗兵 *gijōhei* guard of honor
礼 *girei* courtesy, etiquette
礼兵 *gireihei* guard of honor
礼的 *gireiteki* formal
6 刑 *gikei* model, pattern, copy
式 *gishiki* ceremony, rite, ritual, service
式用 *gishikiyō no* ceremonial
式主義 *gishiki shugi* ritualism, ceremonialism
式張 *gishikiba(ru)* formalize, stick to formality, be ceremonious, be punctilious
8 典 *giten* ceremony, rite, ritual, service
表 *gihyō* a model
9 型 *gikei* model, pattern, copy
10 宸 *gishin* empress dowager's home
容 *giyō* bearing, manners
12 装 *gisō* ceremonial equipment
装馬車 *gisō basha* state carriage
15 範 *gihan* precedent, model

14

舘 555/F1572/F2087 舘 See 館 館 5174. [舌]

劔 556/F255 劒 See 剣 696. [刀]

儔 557/F174 Chū companion; similar kinds.

儘 558/F175 Jin. *mama* as it is; as one likes; because.

儕 559/F175 Sei, Sai companion.
15 輩 *saihai* colleagues, fellows

僭 560/F169 僭 Sen. *sen(suru)* boastfully usurp.
3 上 *senjō* audacity, forwardness
4 王 *sen-ō* usurper king
5 用 *sen-yō* using something belonging exclusively to someone else
主 *senshu* usurper, tyrant
7 位 *sen-i* usurpation of a throne
8 取 *senshu* usurpation
10 称 *senshō* pretension, assumption (of a title)
12 越 *sen-etsu* audacity, forwardness
14 奪 *sendatsu* usurpation

儒 561 / F174 Ju Confucianism; Confucianist; Chinese scholar.
B
4 仏 *Ju-Butsu* Confucianism and Buddhism
5 生 *Jusei* Confucian scholar
6 艮 *jugon* dugong, sea pig
8 官 *jukan* official Confucian teacher
者 *Jusha* a Confucianist
学 *Jugaku* Confucianism
学者 *Jugakusha* Confucian scholar
学界 *Jugakkai* Confucian circles
10 家 *Juka* Confucianist
11 道 *Judō* Confucianism
教 *Jukyō* Confucianism
教主義 *Jukyō shugi* Confucianism
教的 *Jukyōteki* Confucian

15

儲 See 565.

儡 562 / F176 Rai defeat.

償 563 / F175 Shō. *tsuguna(u)* make up for, recompense, redeem (one's faults), compensate for, indemnify, atone for.
B
7 却 *shōkyaku* repayment, redemption, amortization
8 金 *shōkin* reparation, redemption
15 還 *shōkan* repayment, redemption, amortization

優 564 / F176 Yū actor; superiority; gentleness. *sugu(reru)* (see under 勝 3787.0). *masa(ru)* excel, surpass, outrival. *yasa(shii)* gentle, tender, graceful, affectionate, kindly, amiable, suave. *yasa-*, gentle affectionate. *yasa(shige) na* gentle, kind, sweet-looking. *yū ni* easily, amply, sufficiently, well, skillfully.
B
3 女 *yasa-onna* gentle woman, affectionate woman
5 生学 *yūseigaku* eugenics
生結婚 *yūsei kekkon* eugenic marriage
6 劣 *yūretsu* superiority or inferiority, quality
先 *yūsen* preference, priority
先外貨 *yūsen gaika* preferred foreign currency
先的 *yūsenteki* preferential
先株 *yūsen kabu* preferred stock
先権 *yūsenken* priority, preference, preferential right
7 位 *yūi* predominance, ascendancy, superiority
利 *yūri na* advantageous, better, profitable
形 *yasagata* slender figure
男 *yasa-otoko* man of gentle manners; man of delicate features
秀 *yūshū* excellence, superiority
秀品 *yūshūhin* high-grade merchandise
良 *yūryō* excellence, superiority
良児 *yūryōji* superior child
良品 *yūryōhin* superior articles
良馬 *yūryōba* thorobred horse
良株 *yūryō kabu* gilt-edged stock
8 長 *yūchō na* slow, tedious, deliberate, leisurely
退 *yūtai suru* retire voluntarily, bow out
性 *yūsei* dominance
者 *yūsha* superior individual
9 美 *yūbi* grace, refinement, elegance
姿 *yasasugata* graceful figure
待 *yūtai suru* treat kindly, receive hospitably, welcome
待券 *yūtaiken* complimentary ticket
柔 *yūjū* indecisiveness
柔不断 *yūjū-fudan* indecisiveness
11 遇 *yūgū* hearty welcome, hospitality, good treatment
婉 *yūen na* elegant, grand
12 渥 *yūaku na* gracious
越 *yūetsu* supremacy, predominance
越性 *yūetsusei* supremacy, predominance
越感 *yūetsukan* superiority complex
越複合 *yūetsu fukugō* superiority complex
越権 *yūetsuken* special rights, predominant rights
等 *yūtō* excellency, superiority
等生 *yūtōsei* honor student
等卒業生 *yūtō sotsugyōsei* honors graduate
等賞 *yūtōshō* honor prize
等賞状 *yūtō shōjō* grand-prize diploma
勝 *yūshō* victory, championship
勝劣敗 *yūshō reppai* survival of the fittest
勝杯 *yūshōhai* championship cup
勝者 *yūshōsha* prize winner, pennant winner, victor
勝馬 *yūshōba* winning horse
勝旗 *yūshōki* championship pennant
13 雅 *yūga* elegance, refinement
勢 *yūsei* superiority, superior power, preponderance, predominance
15 諚 *yūjō* gracious imperial message
19 艶 *yūen na* charming, fascinating

16

儲 565 / F177 Cho. *mō(karu)* be profitable, yield a profit. *mō(keru)* get, earn, gain. *mōke* profits, earnings.
3 口 *mōkeguchi* profitable job
6 尽 *mōkezu(ku) de* for investment, to make money
7 位 *cho-i* heirship
役 *mōkeyaku* lucrative position
8 物 *mōkemono* good bargain; a find
13 蓄 *chochiku* savings

19

儷 566 / F178 Rei companion.

二亠[人イ𠆢]儿入八ソ冂冖冫几凵刀刂力勹匕匚匸十卜卩厂厶又

儺 567 / F178 NA, DA exorcism.

20

龕 568 / F2180 GAN niche or alcove for an image. [龍]

[6]灯 *gandō* Buddhist altar light

儼 569 / F179 GEN serious; not to be touched. *gen* (*to shite*) solemnly, gravely, majestically, authoritatively.

[12]然 *genzen to* solemnly, gravely, majestically, authoritatively

RAD. 儿 10

Hito-ashi man's legs. Nickname: Legs.

1

兀 See 4.

2

元 See 275.

允 See 843.

3

兄 See 875.

4

光 See 1358.

充 See 289.

兆兆 See 637.

兇 570 / F183 KYŌ wickedness.

[3]刃 *kyōjin* assassin's dagger
[4]手 *kyōshu* assassin
[6]行 *kyōkō* violence, murder, crime
[7]状 *kyōjō* crime, offense
状持 *kyōjōmo*(*chi*) a criminal
[8]具 *kyōgu* dangerous weapon
[9]変 *kyōhen* catastrophe; assassination
[10]徒 *kyōto* outlaw, rebel, rioter
悍 *kyōkan* heinousness, ferocity
[11]猛 *kyōmō* fierce
悪 *kyōaku na* atrocious, fiendish, brutal
[13]漢 *kyōkan* villain, outlaw, assassin
賊 *kyōzoku* villain
[15]暴 *kyōbō* brutality, ferocity, atrocity
器 *kyōki* dangerous weapon
[18]類 *kyōrui* wicked gang

A **先** 571 / F183 SEN the future; priority, precedence. *saki*(*njiru*), *saki*(*nzuru*) precede; forestall, anticipate. *saki* point, tip, end; nozzle; head (of a line); the first priority; the future; objective, destination; sequel, remainder; the other party; future. *saki no* previous, prior. *saki ni* before, earlier than; ahead, beyond, away; previously; recently. *ma*(*zu*) first (of all); about, almost, hardly (with neg.); anyway; well, now. *sen ni* formerly. *sen no* former, previous, old, late.

[2]人 *senjin* predecessor, pioneer, ancestor
入 *sennyū* preconception, prejudice
入主 *sennyūshu* preconception, prejudice
入感 *sennyūkan*＝next word
入観 *sennyūkan* preconception, prejudice, preoccupation ⌈engagement
[3]口 *senkuchi* previous application; previous
山 *sakiyama* skilled miner
[4]手 *sente* the first move; initiative, forestalling. *sakite* front lines, vanguard
方 *sempō* the other party, he, they; destination. *sakikata* the person in front; companion ⌈days ago
日 *saki*(*no*)*hi*, *senjitsu* the other day, a few
月 *sengetsu* last month
父 *sempu* deceased father
王 *sen-ō*, *sennō* the late king, the preceding king; good ancient kings
以 *ma*(*zu*)*mo*(*tte*) first of all, in the first place ⌈shaped
太 *sakibuto* thicker toward the end, club-
夫 *sempu* former husband; late husband
日付 *sakihizuke* dating forward
込銃 *sakigo*(*me*)*jū* muzzle loader
天性 *sentensei* hereditary
天的 *sententeki* inborn, innate, inherent, congenital, hereditary

天病 *sentembyō* hereditary disease

天梅毒 *sentem-baidoku* congenital syphilis

5 生 *sensei* teacher, master, doctor

立 *sakida(tsu)* go before, precede; die before; take precedence. *sakida(teru)* have (someone) go ahead

付 *sakizu(ke)* dating forward

代 *sendai* family predecessor; previous age; previous generation

払 *sakibara(i)* advance payment; payment on delivery; forerunner

主 *senshu* former master; late master

古 *senko* ancient times

世 *saki (no) yo* previous existence

史学 *senshigaku* prehistory

6 行 *sakiyu(ki), saki-i(ki)* the future. *senkō* preceding, going first

回 *sakimawa(ri)* going on ahead; forestalling; anticipating; arrival before another

安 *sakiyasu* lower future quotations

年 *sennen* former years, formerly, a few years ago

考 *senkō* one's late father

先 *ma(zu)ma(zu)* tolerable. *sakizaki* the distant future; places one visits. *mama* well, well

先月 *sensengetsu* month before last

在 *senzai* pre-existence

在性 *senzaisei* priority

任 *sennin* seniority, predecessor

任者 *senninsha* senior official, senior members

任将校 *sennin shōkō* senior officer

任順 *senninjun* order of seniority

7 走 *sakibashi(ru)* be forward, be impertinent

攻 *senkō* batting first

役 *sen-yaku* former post; former occupant of the post

投 *sentō* starting pitcher

売 *sakiu(ri)* advance sale

君 *senkun* previous ruler; ancestors

見 *senken* foresight, anticipation

見明 *senken (no) mei* foresight, anticipation

見者 *senkensha* seer

住民族 *senjū minzoku* aborigines

住者 *senjūsha* former occupant

決 *senketsu* previous decision

決問題 *senketsu mondai* question to be settled first

8 金 *sakigane* advance payment

非 *sempi* past sin, past folly

例 *senrei* precedent

知 *senchi* foresight; speedy comprehension

制 *sensei* headstart (of several runs)

刻 *senkoku* already, a while ago

夜 *sen-ya* a few nights ago

妻 *sensai* former wife; late wife

物 *sakimono* futures

物売買 *sakimono baibai* dealing in futures

物買 *sakimonoga(i)* buying futures; speculation

取 *senshu suru* earn the first (runs); preoccupy. *sakido(ri)* taking before others

取特権 *senshu tokken* prior right

取得点 *senshu tokuten* first runs scored

9 度 *sendo* recently

途 *sendo* crisis in a battle; death

便 *sembin* previous letter

約 *sen-yaku* previous engagement; prior contract

陣 *senjin* vanguard, advance guard

帝 *sentei* the late emperor

客 *senkyaku* the preceding visitor

皇 *sennō* the previous emperor

祖 *saki(no)oya, saki(tsu)oya, senzo* ancestor

祖伝来 *senzo-denrai no* inherited

発 *sempatsu* forerunner, advance party. *sempatsu suru* go on ahead

発投手 *sempatsu tōshu* starting pitcher

発隊 *sempatsutai* advance party

10 高 *sakidaka* higher future quotations

週 *senshū* last week

師 *senshi* former teacher

借 *sakiga(ri)* borrowing in advance

哲 *sentetsu* ancient wise men

進 *senshin* seniority; advance; leadership

進国 *senshinkoku* advanced nations

般 *sempan* the other day, some time ago

般来 *sempanrai* for some time

11 達 *sendatsu* guide, leader, pioneer. *senda(tte)* recently, the other day

頃 *senkoro, sakigoro* recently, the other day

婦 *sempu* former wife; late wife

務 *semmu* the most important task

細 *sakiboso* tapering toward the end

著 *senchaku* first arrival

12 塔 *sentō* spire, steeple

棒 *sakibō* front palanquin carrier; cat's-paw

渡 *sakiwata(shi)* future delivery

程 *sakihodo* some time ago

勝 *senshō* scoring the first point; winning the first game

登 *sentō*＝先頭 (see below–16)

着 *senchaku* first arrival

番 *semban* precedence; first move (in games)

貸 *sakiga(shi)* payment in advance

遣 *senken suru* send ahead

遣部隊 *senkembutai* advance troops, vanguard

覚 *senkaku* learned man, pioneer

覚者 *senkakusha* seer, pioneer, leading spirit, enlightened person

13 触 *sakibu(re)* previous or preliminary announcement

聖 *sensei* ancient sage; Confucius

14 様 *sakisama* the other party

端 *sentan* pointed end, tip; fine point; cusp; spearhead, vanguard

2 二亠人イ𠆢【儿】入八丷冂冖冫几凵刀刂力勹匕匚匸十卜卩厂厶又
5

隣 *sakidonari* next door but one
導 *sendō* guidance, leadership
駆 *sakiga(keru)* be the first. *sakiga(ke)* charging ahead of others; the first to charge; the initiative, the lead; pioneer, forerunner, harbinger. *senku* outrider, forerunner; pilot car; pioneer, herald, precursor
駆者 *senkusha* forerunner, herald, pioneer
15潜 *sakikugu(ri)* forestalling, anticipating
鋒 *sempō* advance guard
鋭 *sen-ei* radical; acute
輩 *sempai* senior, superior, elder, older graduate; progenitor; old-timer
賢 *senken* ancient sage ⌈first; advance guard
16頭 *sentō* the head, the lead, the van, the
頭打者 *sentō dasha* lead-off man (in base-
18蹤 *senchō* precedent ⌊ball)
鞭 *semben* initiative; pioneering
験的 *senkenteki* transcendental
験論 *senkenron* transcendentalism
19繰 *sengu(ri) ni* in order, in turn
蹴 *senshū* the kick-off
20議 *sengi* initiative, prior consideration
議権 *sengiken* right to prior consideration

5

兎 See 198.

克 See 772.

兌 See 582.

A 児 572 F189 = 兒 JI, NI child. *ko* child; the young of animals.
chigo=稚児 3292.7
8女 *jijo* boys and girls; children ⌈scendants
10孫 *jison* children and grandchildren, de-
11曹 *jisō* children
12童 *jidō* child, juvenile
童文学 *jidō bungaku* juvenile literature
童心理学 *jidō shinrigaku* child psychology
童画 *jidōga* pictures drawn by a child
童福祉 *jidō fukushi* child welfare
童劇 *jidōgeki* juvenile play
15戯 *jigi* mere child's play

6

兔 See 兎 198.

兒 See 児 572.

B 免 573 F187 = 免 免 MEN dismissal. *manuga(reru)*, *manuka(reru)* escape from, be rescued from, avoid, evade, avert, elude, be exempted, be relieved from pain, get rid of. *men(jiru)*, *men(zuru)* dismiss; exempt. *(ni) men(jite)* in deference to.
5囚 *menshū* discharged prisoner
7役 *men-eki* release from office, military service, or prison
状 *menjō* diploma; license
8官 *menkan* dismissal, discharge
9除 *menjo* exemption, discharge, exoneration
疫 *men-eki* immunity; immunization
疫血清 *men-eki kessei* serum
疫性 *men-ekisei* immunity
10租 *menso* tax exemption
租地 *mensochi* tax-exempt land
11責 *menseki* exemption from responsibility
許 *menkyo* license, certificate, permit
許状 *menkyojō* license, certificate, permit
許証 *menkyoshō* license, permit
12訴 *menso* acquittal, dismissal (of a case)
税 *menzei* tax exemption; duty exemption
税表 *menzeihyō* duty-free list
税品 *menzeihin* duty-free articles
13罪 *menzai* acquittal, pardon; papal indul-
罪符 *menzaifu* an indulgence ⌊gence
17黜 *menchutsu* dismissal
18職 *menshoku* dismissal, discharge

10

兜 See 232.

RAD. 入 11

Iru enter. At top: 𠆢 *iri-yane* "entering" roof or *iri-gashira* "entering" top.
Nickname: Entering.

Note that it is often very difficult to distinguish between Rads. 9 and 11 when these occur at the top as *hito-yane* and *iri-yane*; therefore we have treated all such cases as Rad. 9.

A 入 574/F190 NYŪ. JU. *i(ru)* go in, come in; flow into; set; set in. *hai(ru)* enter; break into; join; enroll; contain, hold; accommodate; have (an income of). *i(reru)* put in, take in, bring in, let in, admit, introduce, commit (to prison), usher in; insert; set (jewels); employ; listen to; tolerate, comprehend; include; pay (interest); cast (votes). *i(ri)* entering, setting (of the sun); audience; capacity; income; beginning. *-i(re)* container, receptacle.

3 口 *irikuchi, iriguchi, hai(ri)guchi* entrance, gate, approach, mouth
子 *i(re)ko* nest (of boxes)
4 込 *i(re)-ko(mu)* put forth (effort). *i(ri)-ko(mu)* go into, come into, penetrate; become complicated. *i(ri)go(mi)* coming in together; unreserved seats for the public
日 *i(ri)hi* setting sun
木 *i(re)ki* wood inlay. *nyūboku* calligraphy
毛 *i(re)ge* false hair, switch
水 *jusui, nyūsui* suicide by drowning, drowning oneself
内 *judai* imperial bridal party's entry into the court
仏 *nyūbutsu* enshrining a Buddhist image
切 *i(ri)-ki(reru)* (all) are able to get in
夫 *nyūfu suru* marry into the wife's family
手 *nyūshu* receipt, procurement
手難 *nyūshunan* difficulty of obtaining
5 用 *i(ri)yō, nyūyō* need, demand, necessity
目 *i(ri)me* expenses. *i(re)me* artificial eye
立 *i(ri)-ta(tsu)* = *ta(chi)-i(ru)* 立入 3343.2
代 *i(ri)-ka(waru), i(re)-ka(waru), i(re)-ka(eru)* = 入替 (see below–12)
母屋 *irimoya* hip-gable roof
札 *nyūsatsu* bid, bidding
札者 *nyūsatsusha* bidder
6 舟 *i(ri)bune, i(ri)fune* incoming ship; ship's arrival
江 *i(ri)e* inlet, cove, creek, bay
交 *i(ri)-ma(jiru)* mix with, be mixed. *i(re)-ma(zeru)* (vt) mix
合 *i(re)-a(waseru)* make up for
会 *nyūkai* admission, joining, enrollment
会式 *nyūkaishiki* initiation ceremony
会金 *nyūkaikin* admission fee, initiation fee
会者 *nyūkaisha* entrant, new member
7 廷 *nyūtei* admission to the courtroom
乱 *i(ri)-mida(reru)* be jumbled together
牢 *nyūrō* imprisonment
来 *nyūrai* an august visit, arrival
社 *nyūsha* joining a company
社試験 *nyūsha shiken* test for a position in a company
8 金 *nyūkin* payment, money received; money due
門 *nyūmon* entering an institute; primer; manual; introduction to
門者 *nyūmonsha* beginner
所 *nyūsho* entrance, admission; imprisonment, internment
波 *i(ri)nami* incoming wave
物 *i(re)mono* receptacle, container
京 *nyūkyō* entering the capital
念 *nyūnen ni* with scrupulous care
舎 *nyūsha* entering a dormitory
定 *nyūjō* Zen contemplation = *nyūjaku* 入寂 (see below–11)
知恵 *i(re)jie* suggestion, hint
国 *nyūkoku, nyūgoku* entering a country
国税 *nyūkokuzei* alien tax, landing tax
苑 *nyūen* entering the garden
苑券 *nyūenken* ticket to the garden
学 *nyūgaku* matriculation
学生 *nyūgakusei* new student
学式 *nyūgakushiki* entrance ceremony
学考査 *nyūgaku kōsa* entrance examination
学志願者 *nyūgaku shigansha* applicants for admission
学金 *nyūgakukin* matriculation fee
学者 *nyūgakusha* new student
学試験 *nyūgaku shiken* entrance examinations
学難 *nyūgakunan* difficulty of getting into a college
学願書 *nyūgaku gansho* application for admittance to a school
9 信 *nyūshin* entering the faith
城 *nyūjō* triumphant entry into a castle
相 *i(ri)ai* sunset
海 *iriumi* bay, gulf, inlet, creek
洛 *juraku* proceeding to Kyoto
津 *nyūshin* entering a port
神 *nyūshin* inspiration; superhuman skill, genius
室 *nyūshitsu* entering a room; studying under a Buddhist teacher
院 *nyūin* hospitalization
院患者 *nyūin kanja* in-patients

[10]庫 *nyūko* warehousing, storing; entering the car barn
梅 *nyūbai* entering the rainy season
校 *nyūkō* matriculation
浸 *i(ri)-bita(ru)* seep in; stay long
浜 *i(ri)hama* salt farm
浴 *nyūyoku* bath, bathing
党 *nyūtō* joining a political party
貢 *nyūkō suru* pay tribute
荷 *nyūka, i(ri)ni* arrival of goods; goods received
射 *nyūsha* incidence
射角 *nyūshakaku* angle of incidence
[11]違 *i(re)-chiga(eru)* misplace. *i(re)chiga(i)* passing each other
掛 *i(ri)-ka(keru)* be about to enter (a bath etc.). *irekake* called off
混 *i(ri)-maji(ru) vi* mix with, be mixed. *i(re)-ma(zeru) vt* mix
眼 *i(re)me* artificial eye
組 *i(ri)-ku(mu)* be or become complicated
船 *nyūsen, i(ri)fune* ship's arrival
隊 *nyūtai* enlistment
寇 *nyūkō* invasion, encroachment
寂 *nyūjaku* death of a priest; nirvana; spiritual liberty
道 *nyūdō* entering the priesthood; priest
道雲 *nyūdōgumo* great columns of clouds; cumulo-nimbus
[12]歯 *i(re)ba* artificial tooth
超 *nyūchō* excess of imports
婿 *i(ri)muko* man who takes his wife's name
御 *nyūgo* emperor's return to the inner palace
換 *i(re)-ka(eru)* replace, substitute, shift
揚 *i(ri)-a(geru), i(re)-a(geru)* lavish money on
棺 *nyūkan* placing in the coffin
植 *nyūshoku* settlement, immigration
殖 *nyūshoku* settlement, immigration
朝 *nyūchō* visiting Japan; arrival in Japan
営 *nyūei* entering the barracks; enlistment
渠 *nyūkyo* entering a dock
費 *nyūhi* expenses
智慧 *i(re)jie, i(re)chie* suggestion, hint
港 *nyūkō* entering a port
港料 *nyūkōryō* ship's harbor charges
湯 *nyūtō* taking a hot bath; bathing at hot springs
湯客 *nyūtōkyaku* a bathing guest at a hot spring
替 *i(re)-ka(waru), i(ri)-ka(waru) vi* change places, relieve (one another). *i(re)-ka(eru) vt* replace, substitute
替部品 *ireka(e) buhin* replacement parts
場 *nyūjō* admission; entrance, entering
場門 *nyūjōmon* admission gate
場券 *nyūjōken* admission ticket; platform ticket
場者 *nyūjōsha* visitors, attendance
場料 *nyūjōryō* admission fee, gate receipts
場断 *nyūjō (o) kotowa(ri)* No Admittance
場税 *nyūjōzei* admission tax
場権 *nyūjōken* liberty of entrance
[13]滅 *nyūmetsu* dying, entering nirvana; death (of a Buddhist saint)
試 *nyūshi* entrance examinations
電 *nyūden* telegram received
[14]閣 *nyūkaku* joining the cabinet
獄 *nyūgoku* imprisonment
綿 *irewata* cotton padding
雑 *i(ri)-maji(ru) vi* mix with, be mixed. *i-(re)-ma(zeru) vt* mix
魂 *jukon, jikkon, jukkon* intimacy
墨 *i(re)zumi* tattooing
監 *nyūkan* imprisonment
選 *nyūsen* chosen (in a competition)
選者 *nyūsensha* winner, winning candidate
漁者 *nyūgyosha* fishing-lot fisherman
漁料 *nyūgyoryō* fishing-lot charge
漁権 *nyūgyoken* fishing-lot rights
[15]質 *i(re)jichi, nyūshichi* pawning
賞 *nyūshō* winning a prize
賞者 *nyūshōsha* prizewinner
[20]籍 *nyūseki* entrance in the family register

2

内 See 内 82.

3

全 See 全 384.

尒 575/F195/F1211 See 爾 69.

4

仝 576/F195 See 全 384.

6

兩 See 両 34.

RAD. 八 12

Hachi eight. At top: 八 or *hachigashira*. Variants: 𠆢 and 丷.
Nickname: Eight.

A 八 577/F197 八 HATSU, HACHI *ya*(*tsu*), *ya*(*ttsu*), *ya* eight. (*o*)*ya*(*tsu*) between-meal snack.
2 丁 *hatchō* skillfulness
九分 *hakkubu* nearly, almost
十路 *yasoji* eighty years of age 「opening
3 口 *ya*(*tsu*)*kuchi* kimono underarm sleeve
千代 *yachiyo* eternity, thousands of years
千年 *yachitose, hassennen* 8000 years; thousands of years; eternity 「herbs
千草 *yachigusa* variety of plants, various
千歳 *yachitose* thousands of years; eternity
4 日 *yōka* eight days; the eighth (day of the
月 *Hachigatsu* August ⌊month)
切 *ya*(*tsu*)*gi*(*ri*) cutting into 8 parts; octavo
辺形 *hachihenkei* octagon
手 *ya*(*tsu*)*de* 8-fingered-leaf shrub
手網 *ya*(*tsu*)*de ami* 8-armed scoop net
分目 *hachibumme, hachibume* eight-tenths; moderation
分音符 *hachibu ompu* an 8th note 「corners
方 *happō* all sides, directions, quarters, or
方美人 *happō-bijin* a person beautiful from all angles; everybody's friend
方塞 *happō fusaga*(*ri*) all doors closed, blocked in every direction
5 目鰻 *ya*(*tsu*)*me unagi* lamprey eel
6 州 *Yashima* (an old name for) Japan
当 *ya*(*tsu*)*ata*(*ri*) outburst of anger. *ya*(*tsu*)*ata*(*ri*) *ni* indiscriminately, recklessly
字 *hachi* (*no*) *ji* figure eight
字髭 *hachiji hige* finely-trimmed moustache
百万 *yaoyorozu* myriads 「logrolling
百長 *yaochō* put-up job, prearranged affair,
百屋 *yaoya* vegetable store; Jack-of-all-trades; dabbling in all lines of knowledge
7 角形 *hakkakkei* octagon
折判 *ya*(*tsu*)*o*(*ri*)*ban* octavo
8 卦 *hakke* eight divination signs; divination
苦 *hakku* the eight pains (of Buddhism)
9 荒 *hakkō* the national boundaries
咫鏡 *Yata* (*no*) *Kagami* the Sacred Mirror (one of the Three Imperial Treasures)
面 *hachimen* eight faces; all sides
面六臂 *hachimen-roppi* 8 faces and 6 arms; versatile, all-round, many-sided
面玲瓏 *hachimen-reirō* beautiful from all sides; perfect serenity, affability
重 *yae* double (blossom); eightfold
重咲 *yaeza*(*ki*) double blossom
重垣 *yaegaki* fences within fences
重桜 *yaezakura* double cherry blossoms
重歯 *yaeba* double tooth; oblique tooth
重雲 *yaegumo* layers of clouds
重潮路 *yae* (*no*) *shioji* distant seas
10 挺 *hatchō* skillfulness
釜 *yakama*(*shii*)＝喧 (see under 962.0)
紘 *hakkō* the eight directions; the whole land; the whole world
紘一宇 *hakkō-ichiu* universal brotherhood, all eight corners of the world under one roof
11 達 *hattatsu* (roads) running in all directions; convenient transportation; ability in any line
道 *hachidō* the 8 districts of feudal Japan
掛 *hachiga*(*ke*) twenty percent discount. *hakke* divination
12 裂 *ya*(*tsu*)*za*(*ki*) tearing limb from limb, tearing apart, cutting (a person) to pieces
13 福 *Hachifuku* the Beatitudes
14 端 *hattan* twilled fabric
15 潮路 *yashioji* long sea voyage 「God of War
幡 *Hachiman* God of War; shrine of the
幡知 *yawatashi*(*razu*) labyrinth, maze
幡宮 *Hachimangū* Shrine of the God of War 「rinth, maze
幡藪知 *yawata* (*no*) *yabu shi*(*razu*) laby-
16 橋 *ya*(*tsu*)*hashi* zigzag bridge 「network
24 衢 *yachimata* multiple road crossing; road

2

六 See 283.

A 分 578/F230 分 BUN dividing; part, segment; share; ration; rate; degree; one's lot, one's status; relation; duty; kind, lot. FUN a minute of time; one-sixtieth of a degree; one-tenth of a momme (see Weights and Measures). BU rate, part, percentage; one percent; thickness; odds; chance of winning; one-tenth of a *shaku* (see Weights and Measures); one quarter of a *ryō*. *wa*(*karu*) understand, comprehend; know, be known, be identified; be open to reason, be sensible; can tell (what will happen); appreciate; be announced; be discovered; recognize. *wa*(*keru*) divide, split, separate; isolate; distribute, share;

distinguish; spare. *wa(katsu)* divide, separate; share with; distinguish between. *wa(kazu)* without differentiation. *waka(re)*, *wa(kareru)* (see under 別 674.0). *wa(kari)* understanding, comprehension. *wa(ke)* sharing, division; draw, tie. *wa(kachi)* distinction, differentiation, discrimination. *bun-* branch, detached. [刀]

2 入 *wa(ke)-i(ru)* force one's way, push thru
力 *bunryoku* component force
3 工場 *bunkōjō* branch factory
子 *bunshi* numerator; molecule; (bad) elements
子量 *bunshiryō* molecular weight
子説 *bunshi setsu* molecular theory
与 *wa(ke)-ata(eru)*, *waka(chi)-ata(eru)* apportion to, share. *bun-yo suru* distribute. *bun-yo* distribution, allocation; dispensation; impartation
与税 *bun-yozei* tax allotment (to local government)
4 区 *bunku* subdistrict
化 *bunka* specialization, differentiation
切 *wa(kari)-ki(ru)* understand completely. *wa(kari)-ki(tta)* obvious, undeniable
分 *wa(kare)-waka(re) ni*＝別別 674.7
水山脈 *bunsui sammyaku* watershed, divide
水界 *bunsuikai* watershed, divide
水線 *bunsuisen* watershed, divide
水嶺 *bunsuirei* watershed, divide
5 母 *bumbo* denominator
目 *wa(ke)me* dividing line; parting (of the hair); partition; crisis
立 *bunritsu* segregation, separation, independence
外 *bungai* not within proper limits, excessive; unmerited; special
出 *wa(kare)-de(ru)* branch out, diverge, radiate
布 *bumpu* distribution
冊 *bunsatsu* separate volume, installment
6 団 *bundan* branch, chapter
地 *bunchi* parceling out an estate
合 *wa(kachi)-a(u)*, *wa(ke)-a(u)* share
会 *bunkai* branch, chapter
争 *wa(kare)-araso(u)* quarrel and separate
列 *bunretsu* filing off (in a parade)
列式 *bunretsushiki* military review
光 *bunkō* spectrum
光学 *bunkōgaku* spectroscopy
光器 *bunkōki* spectroscope
7 身 *bunshin* parturition, delivery; one's child; branch, offshoot; one's other self
局 *bunkyoku* branch office
体 *buntai* fission
社 *bunsha* branch shrine
利 *bunri* crisis (in an illness)
売 *bumbai*, *wa(ke)u(ri)* selling separately
良 *wa(kari)yo(i)* easy to understand. *wa(ke)-yo(i)* easy to divide
析学 *bunsekigaku* analytics
別 *fumbetsu* discernment, judgment, wisdom. *bumbetsu* discrimination; separation, division; classification; distinction
別心 *fumbetsushin* prudence, distinction, discrimination
別盛 *fumbetsuzaka(ri)* the age of wisdom, around forty
岐 *bunki* divergence, ramification, forking
岐点 *bunkiten* diverging point; turning point; fork, crossroads; junction; parting of the ways
岐駅 *bunki eki* junction
岐線 *bunkisen* branch line, spur
8 店 *bunten* branch store, branch of a firm
明 *bummei*, *bummyō* clearness; clear understanding
取 *wa(kachi)-to(ru)* divide the spoils, receive a share. *wa(ke)-to(ru)* apportion, share. *wa(ke)do(ri)* sharing, division
易 *wa(kari)yasu(i)* easy to understand. *wa(ke)yasu(i)* easy to divide
泌 *bumpitsu*, *bumpi* secretion
泌液 *bumpitsu eki* a secretion
限 *bungen* social standing. *bugen* social standing; wealth
限者 *bugenja* a rich man
担 *buntan* apportionment
担金 *buntankin* share of expenses; contribution
担額 *buntangaku* amount allotted; contribution
析 *bunseki* analysis, assaying
析化学 *bunseki kagaku* analytical chemistry
析表 *bunsekihyō* analysis table
析試験 *bunseki shiken* assaying
9 厚 *buatsu na*, *buatsu(i)* thick, bulky, massive
厘 *funrin* (not) in the least, (not) a bit
屋 *wa(karazu)ya* obstinate person; blockhead
秒 *fumbyō* a moment
袂 *bumbei* parting (from someone)
院 *bun-in* branch (of an institution); branch temple; detached building
封 *bumpō* hiving off, swarming; dividing a fief
乗 *bunjō* riding separately
前 *wa(ke)mae* share, quota
点 *bunten* equinox; fork, junction
室 *bunshitsu* isolated room, detached office, annex
巻 *bumma(ki)* alternating-current winding
度器 *bundoki* protractor
県地図 *bunken chizu* prefecture maps
派 *bumpa* denomination, sect, branch, faction. *bumpa suru* separate from
派主義 *bumpa shugi* sectarianism; sectionalism
科 *bunka* department, section, branch; course; school
科会 *bunkakai* subcommittee meeting
界 *bunkai* delimitation, demarcation; border, boundary
界線 *bunkaisen* line of demarcation
10 骨 *bunkotsu* part of a person's ashes

進 *bunshin suru* divide and advance
校 *bunkō* branch school
流 *bunryū* tributary
納 *bunnō* installment payment or delivery
針 *funshin* minute hand
家 *bunke* branch family
党 *buntō* secession from a party
書 *wa(kachi)ga(ki)* leaving spaces between words in *kana* script
配 *bumpai* division, sharing; distribution, allotment
配金 *bumpaikin* dividend (on shares)
捕 *bundo(ru)* capture, seize, plunder
捕物 *bundo(ri)mono* loot, booty, plunder
捕品 *bundo(ri)hin* loot, booty, plunder
娩 *bumben* delivery, confinement, childbirth
娩作用 *bumben sayō* delivery, parturition
娩臥床 *bumben gashō* lying-in bed
娩時 *bumbenji* time of delivery (of a child)
娩期 *bumbenki* time of delivery (of a child)
11 野 *bun-ya* field, sphere, division, branch
隊 *buntai* squad; division (in the navy); small unit
悪 *wa(kari)niku(i)* hard to understand
宿 *bunshuku* billeting
教場 *bunkyōjō* detached classroom
12 遣 *bunken* detachment, detail
疏 *bunso*=*benkai* 弁解 847.13
詞 *bunshi* participle
散 *bunsan* break-up, dispersion, decentralization, divergence; bankruptcy
掌 *bunshō* division of duties
量 *bunryō* quantity, amount, dose
営 *bun-ei* outpost, detached garrison
極 *bunkyoku* polarization; lining up with
極化 *bunkyokuka* polarization; lining up with
割 *bunkatsu* partition, division, dismemberment
割払 *bunkatsubara(i)* installment paying
裂 *bunretsu* dissolution, dismemberment, break-up, disintegration, segmentation, fission, split, schism, separation
裂性 *bunretsusei* fissionable
裂物質 *bunretsu busshitsu* fissionable materials
13 溜 *bunryū* cracking, fractional distillation (of gasoline)
際 *bunzai* social standing
数 *bunsū* fraction
署 *bunsho* substation, branch office
業 *bungyō* division of labor, specialization, assembly-line production
解 *bunkai* analysis; parsing; decomposition; dismantling; disintegration; dissolution; reduction (in chemistry)
解的 *bunkaiteki* analytical
解能 *bunkainō* power (of an optical instrument)
解蒸溜法 *bunkai jōryūhō* cracking (in chemistry)
14 銅 *fundō* weight, counterweight
領 *bunryō*=*ryōbun* 領分 5124.4
15 権 *bunken* decentralization of authority
課 *bunka* subdivision, section, branch
賦 *bumpu* assignment, allocation
蝕 *bunshoku* partial eclipse
16 館 *bunkan* annex
餐 *bunsan suru* distribute (the emblems in Communion)
17 轄 *bunkatsu* separate jurisdiction
18 類 *bunrui* classification, group
類法 *bunruihō* classification system
類学 *bunruigaku* science of classification
類表 *bunruihyō* classified table
19 離 *bunri* division, separation. *bunri suru*, *wa(ke)-hana(su)* separate from, detach
離主義者 *bunri shugisha* separatists, schismatics
離機 *bunriki* separator
20 蘖 *bunketsu, bungetsu* sprouting profusely from one plant
譲 *bunjō* selling (real-estate) lots
譲地 *bunjōchi* lots for sale

A 公 $\frac{579}{F200}$ 公

Kō prince, duke, lord; public. KU. *ōyake* public, open; official, governmental; formal. *kimi* prince, lord. *-kō* lord, daimyo; companion; a subordinate.

2 人 *kōjin* public character
3 子 *kōshi* young nobleman
4 方 *kubō* public affairs; the court; the shogun; the shogunate
辺 *kōhen* public ceremonies; public affairs
分母 *kōbumbo* common denominator
公然 *kōkōzen to* publicly
文 *kōbun* official document; archives
文書 *kōbunsho* official document; archives
5 示 *kōji* public announcement. *kōshi* edict
布 *kōfu* proclamation, announcement
司 *kōshi, konsu* company, firm (in China)
生活 *kōseikatsu* public life
生涯 *kōshōgai* public career, public life
立 *kōritsu* public (institution)
立学校 *kōritsu gakkō* public school
正 *kōsei* justice, fairness, impartiality
正証書 *kōsei shōsho* notarized document
用 *kōyō* government business; public use; public expense
用文 *kōyōbun* official terminology
用車 *kōyōsha* official vehicle
平 *kōhei* justice, fairness
平政策 *Kōhei Seisaku* Fair Deal
平無私 *kōhei-mushi* impartiality, fair play
民 *kōmin* citizens, freemen
民生活 *kōmin seikatsu* national life
民学校 *kōmin gakkō* citizenship training school

民科 *kōminka* civics
民権 *kōminken* civil rights, citizenship, franchise
民館 *kōminkan* public hall, community center
6 団 *kōdan* public corporation
吏 *kōri* public official
休 *kōkyū* legal holiday
休日 *kōkyūbi* legal holiday
安 *kōan* public welfare, public safety
安官 *kōankan* railway police
式 *kōshiki* formula; formality
式主義 *kōshiki shugi* formalism
式試合 *kōshiki shiai* championship match
会 *kōkai* public meeting
会堂 *kōkaidō* public hall; town hall
会問答 *kōkai mondō* catechism
有 *kōyū* public ownership
有地 *kōyūchi* public land
有林 *kōyūrin* public forest
有物 *kōyūbutsu* public property
共 *kōkyō* society, the community. *kōkyō no* public, communal
共心 *kōkyōshin* public spirit
共団体 *kōkyō dantai* public organization
共図書館 *kōkyō toshokan* public library
共物 *kōkyōbutsu* public property
共事業 *kōkyō jigyō* public utilities
7 言 *kōgen* declaration, profession
役 *kōeki* public service
私 *kōshi* government and people; public and personal affairs. *kōshi no* public and private
邸 *kōtei* official residence
売 *kōbai* public sale, public auction
告 *kōkoku* public notice
沙汰 *ōyakezata* public question
社 *kōsha* public corporation
社債 *kōshasai* public bonds
判 *kōhan* public hearing, trial
判廷 *kōhantei* court, courtroom
判調査 *kōhan chōsa* trial record
8 金 *kōkin* public funds
国 *kōkoku* dukedom, duchy, principality
的 *kōteki* public, official
表 *kōhyō* official proclamation
事 *kōji* government business
使 *kōshi* minister (of a legation)
使館 *kōshikan* legation
明 *kōmei* fairness, justice
明正大 *kōmei-seidai* fairness, justice
法 *kōhō* public law
法人 *kōhōjin* juridical person, public corporation
武 *kōbu* nobles and soldiers; imperial court and the shogunate
武合体 *kōbu-gattai* shogunate marital union with the Imperial Family
定 *kōtei* official (rate)
定価 *kōteika* ceiling or fixed price
定価格 *kōtei kakaku* ceiling or fixed price
定相場 *kōtei sōba* ceiling price, official quotation
9 侯 *kōkō* princes and marquises; great feudal lords
約 *kōyaku* public commitment or promise
海 *kōkai* high seas
海上 *kōkaijō* on the high seas
10 庫 *kōko* finance corporation
庭 *kōtei* place of ceremony; public place
租 *kōso* public tax
家 *kuge* Imperial Court; court noble
害 *kōgai* pollution
差 *kōsa* common difference (in math); allowance, margin, tolerance
孫樹 *ichō* gingko or maidenhair tree
称 *kōshō* public name, announcing publicly
称資本 *kōshō shihon* authorized capital
益 *kōeki* public good
益法人 *kōeki hōjin* legal person working for the public weal
益事業 *kōeki jigyō* public utilities
益質屋 *kōeki shichiya* public pawn shop
益優先 *kōeki-yūsen* public interest first
11 道 *kōdō* public highway; justice
達 *kindachi* kings, children of nobles, young nobleman. *kōtatsu* official announcement
理 *kōri* axiom, maxim, self-evident truth
許 *kōkyo* official government permission
転 *kōten* revolution (around the sun)
娼 *kōshō* licensed prostitution; registered prostitute
娼全廃 *kōshō zempai* abolition of licensed prostitution
設 *kōsetsu* public (institution)
設市場 *kōsetsu ichiba* public market
教 *kōkyō* Roman Catholicism
教会 *Kōkyōkai* Roman Catholic Church
教要理 *Kōkyō yōri* Catholic catechism
務 *kōmu* public service, official business
務災害 *kōmu saigai* accidents in line of duty
務員 *kōmuin* government worker
務疾病 *kōmu shippei* sickness incurred in line of duty
12 評 *kōhyō* popular opinion
訴 *kōso* accusation, prosecution
卿 *kugyō, kuge*=*kuge* 公家 (see above–10)
葬 *kōsō* public funeral
募 *kōbo* public appeal, public contribution
営 *kōei* public management
費 *kōhi* public expenditure
報 *kōhō* official bulletin, communiqué
裁 *kōsai* judicial decision
然 *kōzen no* open, avowed, public, official
然秘密 *kōzen (no) himitsu* an open secret
証 *kōshō* authentication, notarization
証人 *kōshōnin* notary public
証役場 *kōshō yakuba* notary public's office
開 *kōkai suru* present to the public
開外交 *kōkai gaikō* open diplomacy

開状 *kōkaijō* open letter
開図書館 *kōkai toshokan* public library
開講座 *kōkai kōza* extension lectures
衆 *kōshū* the public
衆伝道 *kōshū dendō* public evangelism
衆便所 *kōshū benjo* public lavatory
衆浴場 *kōshū yokujō* public bathhouse
衆道徳 *kōshū dōtoku* public morals
衆電話 *kōshū denwa* public telephone
衆衛生 *kōshū eisei* public health and sani- ⌊tation
13園 *kōen* park
傷 *kōshō* occupational accident
債 *kōsai* public debt, public bond or securi- ⌊ties
暇 *kōka* leave of absence, furlough
試 *kōshi* national examinations
路 *kōro* public road; highway
署 *kōsho* government office
義 *kōgi* justice, equity
電 *kōden* official telegram
準 *kōjun* postulate (in math)
14選 *kōsen* public election
僕 *kōboku* public servant
演 *kōen* public performance
領 *kōryō* duchy, dukedom, principality
算 *kōsan* probability
徳 *kōtoku* civic virtues
徳心 *kōtokushin* public spirit
認 *kōnin* official authorization, recognition, license, accreditation ⌈accountant
認会計士 *kōnin kaikeishi* certified public
認候補 *kōnin kōho* official candidate
認候補者 *kōnin kōhosha* official candidate
15儀 *kōgi* imperial court; shogunate government; authorities; public affairs. *kōgi no* official, government
憤 *kōfun* public indignation
論 *kōron* public opinion, unbiased criticism
課 *kōka* public imposts, taxes
器 *kōki* public institution
敵 *kōteki* public enemy
敵一号 *kōteki ichigō* public enemy No. 1
16館 *kōkan* official residence
17聴会 *kōchōkai* public hearing
爵 *kōshaku* prince, duke
爵夫人 *kōshaku fujin* princess, duchess
18職 *kōshoku* public office ⌈officials
職追放 *kōshoku tsuihō* purge of public
20議 *kōgi* just view; public opinion

4

兊 See 兌 582. [儿]

并 $\frac{580}{F627}$ 幷 Hei put together. [干]

7呑 *heidon*＝併呑 425.7

A共 $\frac{581}{F206}$ Kyō. *tomo* both; neither (with neg.); all; and, as well as; including; with, together with; plural ending. *tomo ni suru* share with, participate in. *tomo ni* both; alike; together, along with, with; including. (*to*) *tomo ni* together with.
2力 *kyōryoku* co-operation
4切 *tomogi(re)* same cloth (for patching)
5用 *kyōyō* common use
立 *kyōritsu* joint, common
布 *tomogire* same cloth (for patching)
白髪 *tomoshiraga* growing old together ⌊(a couple)
犯 *kyōhan* complicity
犯者 *kyōhansha* accomplice
6共 *tomodomo ni* together, in company
存 *kyōson, kyōzon* coexistence
存共栄 *kyōson-kyōei* coexistence and co- ⌊prosperity
有 *kyōyū* joint ownership
有地 *kyōyūchi* public land; a common
有物 *kyōyūbutsu* common property
有者 *kyōyūsha* joint owners, part owners
有財産 *kyōyū zaisan* community property
同 *kyōdō* co-operation, collaboration, association; joint (defense)
同一致 *kyōdō itchi* unanimous co-oper- ⌊ation
同井戸 *kyōdō ido* common well
同水栓 *kyōdō suisen* common faucet
同生活 *kyōdō seikatsu* community life; cohabitation
同会見 *kyōdō kaiken* news conference
同防衛 *kyōdō bōei* joint defense
同体 *kyōdōtai* a co-operative body; co-operative system
同社会 *kyōdō shakai* communal society, community ⌈apartment house
同住宅 *kyōdō jūtaku* a settlement; an
同声明 *kyōdō seimei* joint declaration
同性 *kyōdōsei* co-operation
同者 *kyōdōsha* coworker ⌈en
同炊事場 *kyōdō suijiba* community kitch-
同便所 *kyōdō benjo* comfort station
同相続人 *kyōdō sōzokunin* joint heir
同計算 *kyōdō keisan* pooling; joint account
同租界 *kyōdō sokai* international settlement ⌈solidarity
同責任 *kyōdō sekinin* joint responsibility;
同組合 *kyōdō kumiai* a co-operative; a partnership ⌈ty chest
同救済基金 *kyōdō kyūsai kikin* communi-
同経営 *kyōdō keiei* joint management
同募金 *kyōdō bokin* community chest
同疎開 *kyōdō sokai* community evacuation
同墓地 *kyōdō bochi* public cemetery
同農場 *kyōdō nōjō* collective farm
同戦線 *kyōdō sensen* united front
同管理 *kyōdō kanri* joint control

2 二亠人イヘ儿入八ソ冂冖冫几凵刀リカ勹匕匚匸十卜卩厂ム又 5

同線 *kyōdōsen* party line
[7]助 *kyōjo* co-operation
労者 *kyōrōsha* coworker
[8]学 *kyōgaku* coeducation
学制 *kyōgakusei* coeducational plan
和主義 *kyōwa shugi* republicanism
和国 *kyōwakoku* republic
和制 *kyōwasei* republicanism
和制度 *kyōwa seido* republicanism
和政体 *kyōwa seitai* republican form of government
和政治 *kyōwa seiji* republican government
和党 *kyōwatō* Republican Party
[9]食 *tomogu(i)* cannibalism (in animals), mutual destruction, internecine struggle, eating each other; damaging each other
栄 *kyōei* mutual prosperity
栄圏 *kyōeiken* coprosperity sphere
通 *kyōtsū no* common
通点 *kyōtsūten* common feature 「language
通語 *kyōtsūgo* common term, common
[10]倒 *tomodao(re)* falling together, mutual destruction, joint bankruptcy
振 *kyōshin* resonance
益 *kyōeki* common profit 「prize show
進会 *kyōshinkai* competitive exhibition,
[11]訳 *kyōyaku* joint translation
著 *kyōcho* coauthorship
済 *kyōsai* mutual aid
済組合 *kyōsai kumiai* a co-operative society, a mutual-benefit association
販 *kyōhan* co-operative selling 「company
販会社 *kyōhangaisha* co-operative sales
産化 *kyōsanka* communization
産分子 *kyōsan bunshi* communist elements
産中国 *Kyōsan Chūgoku* Communist China
産主義 *kyōsan shugi* communism, collectivism 「country
産主義国 *kyōsan shugikoku* communist
産主義者 *kyōsan shugisha* a communist
産地区 *kyōsan chiku* communist area
産系 *kyōsankei* communist controlled
産国家群 *kyōsan kokkagun* Communist
産軍 *kyōsangun* communist army ⌊bloc
産陣営 *kyōsan jin-ei* the Communist camp
産党 *Kyōsantō* Communist Party
産党政治局 *Kyōsantō Seijikyoku* Politburo
産党細胞 *kyōsantō saibō* communist cell
産圏 *kyōsanken* communist sphere
[12]営 *kyōei* joint management
[13]催 *kyōsai* two or more organizations sponsoring a meeting together
裏 *tomo-ura* lining a kimono with the same material as the kimono itself
寝 *tomone* sleeping together
感 *kyōkan* sympathy, response
[14]鳴 *kyōmei, tomona(ri)* resonance, sympathy
鳴者 *kyōmeisha* sympathizer, fellow trav-
演 *kyōen* coacting, costarring ⌊eler
演者 *kyōensha* costar, coactor
[15]稼 *tomokase(gi)* (husband and wife) earning a living together
編 *kyōhen* joint editorship
編者 *kyōhensha* coeditor
[16]謀 *kyōbō* conspiracy, complicity
謀者 *kyōbōsha* conspirator, accomplice
[18]襟 *tomoeri* same-colored neckband
観福音書 *kyōkan fukuinsho* diatessaron

5

兵 See 201.

谷 See 4458. [谷]

兌 582/F187 **兊** Da exchange. [儿]
[12]換 *dakan* conversion (of paper money)
換券 *dakanken* convertible banknotes
換銀行 *dakan ginkō* bank of issue

呉 583/F342 **吳** B Go. *ku(reru)* give; do (something) for. [口]
[4]手 *ku(re)te* donor; one who does something for you 「nestly
[7]呉 *kuregure mo* repeatedly, sincerely, ear-
[8]服 *gofuku* piece goods, dry goods, draperies
服店 *gofukuten* dry-goods store
服物 *gofukumono* piece goods, dry goods,
服屋 *gofukuya* dry-goods store ⌊draperies
服商 *gofukushō* dry-goods dealer
[9]音 *go-on* Wu-dynasty pronunciation
某 *kuregashi* so-and-so 「boat
[12]越同舟 *goetsu-dōshū* enemies in the same
遣 *kure(te) ya(ru)* give, do (something) for

弟 584/F655 A Dai. Tei younger brother, faithful service to those older; brotherly affection. *otōto, ototo, oto* younger brother. [弓]
[3]小父 *oto-oji* parent's younger brother, uncle
子 *deshi, teishi* pupil, disciple, adherent, follower; apprentice. *teishi* young person; teacher's student-helper
子入 *deshi-i(ri)* apprenticeship; enrolling
[4]分 *otōtobun* a friend treated as a younger brother
[7]弟子 *otōto deshi* new pupil; new disciple
[8]妹 *teimai* younger brothers and sisters
[9]姫 *otohime* youngest princess 「daughters
[10]娘 *otomusume, otōto musume* younger

息子 *otomusuko, otōto musuko* younger sons
12御 *otōtogo* your young brother
13嫁 *otōto yome, otoyome* younger brother's wife
17優 *otomasa(ri)* a younger brother who excels an older brother

6

具 585/F208 **具** See 3128.

忩 586/F-X See **忽** 1660. [心]

忿 587/F696 FUN. *ika(ru)* be angry. [心]
9怒 *fundo*＝憤怒 1773.9
12然 *funzen to* indignantly, in a rage
18懣 *fumman* anger, resentment, indignation, chagrin, irritation

A **典** 588/F209 **典** TEN ceremony, celebration; law code. *nori* rule, law.
5礼 *tenrei* ceremony; etiquette, courtesy; (Catholic) liturgy
8侍 *tenji* maid of honor, lady in waiting
拠 *tenkyo* authority
物 *tembutsu* pawned article
9則 *tensoku* regulations
故 *tenko* authentic precedent
型 *tenkei* type, pattern
型的 *tenkeiteki* typical, model, ideal
13雅 *tenga na* refined, graceful, elegant, classic
14獄 *tengoku* warden of a prison
15範 *tempan* model, standard, law
16薬 *ten-yaku* court physician
19麗 *tenrei na* graceful
20籍 *tenseki* books

B **並** 589/F43/F1398 **並 竝** HEI. *nara(bu)* line up, be in a row; rank with, rival, equal. *nara(beru)* arrange, place in order, marshall, put side by side, display, serve (food); enumerate; compare with. *na(mi)* common, ordinary, average. *nara(bi) ni* and, besides, as well as. *nara(bi)* row, line, side. *na(mete)* all. [一]
3大抵 *na(mi)-taitei no* ordinary
4方 *nara(be)kata* arrangement
木 *namiki* roadside tree; row of trees
木路 *namiki michi* avenue of trees
5立 *nara(be)-ta(teru)* enumerate. *heiritsu* standing abreast
外 *na(mi)hazu(re)* above the average, extraordinary; abnormal; unreasonable
6行 *heikō* parallel
列 *heiretsu* arrangement; row, parallel
存 *heizon* coexistence
7足 *na(mi)ashi* walking pace, slow march
8居 *na(mi)-i(ru)* sit in a row
並 *na(mi)na(mi)* ordinary; *na(mi)na(minaranu)* extraordinary
歩 *na(mi)ashi* walking pace, slow march
9型 *na(mi)gata* ordinary or regulation size
10進 *heishin suru* keep pace with, keep abreast of
12幅 *na(mi)haba* ordinary-width cloth (about 28 cm.)
無 *nara(bi)na(i), nara(bi)na(ki)* unparalleled, unequaled, unique
13置 *heichi* juxtaposition, placing side by side
14製 *namisei* ordinary make

其 590/F208 KI. *so(no)* that (adj.). *sore* that, it. *sore da kara* therefore. *sore da noni* nevertheless. *sore datte* but. *sore de* thereupon, therefore. *sore de koso* all the more. *sore da noni, sore na noni* nevertheless. *sore wa sō toshite* be that as it may. *sore tomo* or. *sore ja, sore dewa* then, in that case; well. *sore demo* nevertheless. *sore kara* after that; since; and then, and; from then on. *sore koso* the very thing, *sore nara* if so. *sore ni* besides, moreover, what is more. *sore ni shite mo* even so, nevertheless. *sore ni shite wa* considering that. *sore wa sō to* but now, to change the subject.
8上 *so(no)ue* on top of that, over and above, in addition, besides
丈 *sore dake* that much; only that; only that much. *soredake ni* all the more because
4辺 *so(no) hen* thereabouts, in the neighborhood
手 *so(no) te* that trick, that move, that way
内 *so(no) uchi* soon, before long; some day; meanwhile; among the number
日暮 *so(no)higura(shi)* hand-to-mouth existence
日稼 *so(no)hi kasegi* day labor
方 *sochira, sonata, sochi, so(no)hō* over there, your place; you, your family; the other one. *sotchi, so(no)hō, sonata* that direction, that way, that one, that
方此方 *sochikochi* here and there; this and that; probably
方達 *sochitachi, so(no)hōtachi* you (plural)
方等 *sochitora, sochira, so(no)hōra* you (plural)
5付 *sore(ni)tsu(kete)mo, sore(ni)tsu(ki), sore(ni)tsu(ite)* concerning that
他 *so(no)ta* the others, the rest
奴 *soitsu* that guy; that one, that, it
外 *so(no) hoka* the rest, the others

処 *soko* that place, there; to that extent; when, at this juncture. *soredokoro ka* on the contrary, out of the question (too busy). *soko(ra), soko(ira)* about there, around there. *soko de* then, thereupon, accordingly

処当 *soko(ra) ata(ri)* about there, around there

処迄 *soko made* that far

処此処 *soko-koko ni* here and there, in places; sporadically

[6]式 *soreshiki* only that much

成 *sorenari ni* in its own way; as it is

迄 *sore made* till then; so long, so far, so much, to that extent; the end

向 *so(no) mu(ki)* that direction; the person concerned

[7]位 *sore kurai, soregurai, so(no) kurai, so(no)-gurai* about that many, about so much

身其儘 *so(no)mi-so(no)mama* just as it is

[8]居 *sore (de) i(te)* and yet

物 *so(no) mono* the thing itself

限 *sorekiri, sore(k)kiri, sore kagi(ri)* no more than that

実 *so(no)jitsu* really, in reality

其 *sore(wa) sore(wa)* exceedingly, terrific. *sorezore* each, respectively. *sore(wa) sore toshite* be that as it may

昔 *so(no) mukashi* old times, antiquity

者 *so(no) mono* the person himself. *soresha* specialist, a professional; geisha, prostitute

[9]通 *so(no) tō(ri)* That's right; exactly, just like that

後 *so(no)go* thereafter, later, since then

除 *so(tchi)no(ke) ni suru* neglect, lay aside, slight, ignore

故 *soreyue* therefore

相応 *sore sōō ni* in a corresponding degree

[11]道 *so(no) michi* line of business, profession, trade, art

頃 *so(no) koro* about that time

許 *sore bakari* only that, about that much

[12]程 *sore hodo* so, so far, to that extent; (not) very

筋 *so(no) suji* the authorities concerned

筈 *so(no) hazu* proper, just, reasonable

無 *sore (to) na(ku)* indirectly, by implication

場 *so(no)ba* the place, the spot, the occasion, the situation

場逃 *so(no)banoga(re)* temporizing, stopgap

場限 *so(no)bakagi(ri)* on the spur of the moment. *so(no)bakagi(ri) no* temporary, makeshift

[13]節 *so(no) setsu* at that time

[14]様 *sonna, so(no)yō na* that kind of. *so(no)yō ni* in that way

[15]儀 *so(no)gi* such is the case

[16]儘 *so(no)mama* as it is, in that condition

積 *so(no) tsumo(ri) de* with that in mind

[18]癖 *so(no) kuse* nevertheless, still

— 7 —

並 See 並 589. [一]

荊 591/F1601 See 荆 689. [艹]

茲 592/F1239 See 玆 2919. [玄]

酋 593/F1916 酋 SHŪ chieftain. [酉]

[8]長 *shūchō* chief, chieftain

盆 594/F1309 盆 B BON Lantern Festival, Festival of the Dead; tray. [皿]

[5]石 *bonseki* tray-landscape foundation stone

[6]地 *bonchi* round valley, hollow, basin

灯籠 *Bondōrō, Bon tōrō* a *Bon*-Festival lantern

[8]画 *bonga* tray landscape

[10]栽 *bonsai* miniature tray landscape

[11]祭 *Bon Matsu(ri)* the *Bon* Festival

[12]景 *bonkei* tray landscape

提灯 *bonjōchin* the *Bon* Festival lantern

[14]踊 *Bon Odo(ri)* the *Bon* Festival Dance

暮 *Bon-ku(re)* *Bon* and year-end seasons

前 595/F246 前 A SEN. ZEN before. *mae* front, fore part; head (of a line); presence; ago, before; previously; (five minutes) to. *mae ni* ahead, before. *(o)-mae(san)* you; my dear; hey. *-mae* a helping, portion; lady (So-and-so). *-zen* ago, before. *zen-* former, previous, one-time; the above. *saki ni* (see under 先 571.0). [刂]

[2]人 *zenjin* predecessor, former people

人未到 *zenjin-mitō* unexplored

人未踏 *zenjin-mitō* unexplored

[3]山 *zenzan* foothills, first range of mountains

下 *maesa(gari)* front part low

口上 *mae kōjō* introductory remarks

[4]文 *zembun* the above statement; preamble

方 *maekata* previously, some time ago. *zempō* front

日 *zenjitsu, maebi* the day before

厄 *maeyaku* the year before a critical age

以 *mae mot(te)* previously

夫 *zempu* former husband

[5]生 *zenshō* previous existence

払 *maebara(i)* advance payment

古 *zenko* old times, ancient days

立 *maeda(te)* plume, crest

立腺 *zenritsusen* prostate gland

史 *zenshi* prehistory

史時代 *zenshi jidai* prehistoric period

代 *zendai* previous generation; former ages
代未聞 *zendai-mimon* unparalleled, unheard of, record-breaking
半 *zempan* first half
半期 *zempanki* first half period
半戦 *zempansen* first half of the game
世 *zense, mae (no) yo, saki (no) yo* previous existence. *zensei* antiquity; the previous
世生存 *zense seizon* pre-existence ⌊era
世紀 *zenseiki* last century; ancient times
世界 *zensekai* prehistoric age
6 行 *zenkō* former conduct
回 *zenkai* last time; last session
向 *maemu(ki)* facing forward
兆 *zenchō* omen, portent, sign, premonition,
列 *zenretsu* front row ⌊harbinger
号 *zengō* preceding issue
名 *zemmei* one's previous name
年 *zennen* the preceding year, last year
年度 *zennendo* preceding fiscal year
任 *zennin no* former (official)
任地 *zenninchi* former post
任者 *zenninsha* predecessor
7 言 *zengen* previous remarks
足 *mae ashi* forefeet
身 *zenshin* antecedents, ancestor; previous position; previous existence; predecessor organization
述 *zenjutsu no* the above-mentioned
坊 *zembō* former crown prince; the late crown prince
条 *zenjō* preceding article, preceding entry
車 *zensha* the car ahead; front wheel
車軸 *zenshajiku* front axle
売 *maeu(ri)* advance sale, booking
売券 *maeu(ri) ken, zembaiken* ticket sold in
8 門 *zemmon* front gate ⌊advance
非 *zempi* past folly, past sin
屈 *zenkutsu suru* bend forward. *maekaga-*
例 *zenrei* precedent ⌊*(mi)* slouch
板 *maeita* dashboard; frontlet
知 *maeji(rase)* previous notice; omen, signs;
肢 *mae ashi, zenshi* forefeet ⌊premonition
垂 *maedare* apron
官 *zenkan* one's former post
者 *zensha* the former
表 *zempyō*＝*zenchō* 前兆 (see above–6)
金 *maekin, zenkin* advance payment
金払 *zenkimbara(i)* payment in advance
夜 *zen-ya* last night, the previous night
夜祭 *zen-yasai* Christmas Eve
9 面 *zemmen* front part, frontage, façade
便 *zembin* one's last letter
祝 *mae iwa(i)* celebration in anticipation
約 *zen-yaku* previous engagement, previous promise

段 *zendan* preceding paragraph; first part
軍 *zengun* front-line troops
途 *zento* one's future prospects; outlook; the journey ahead
途有望 *zento yūbō* promising future
科 *zenka* criminal record, previous offense
科者 *zenkamono* person with a criminal record
前 *maemae* beforehand; for a long time
前回 *zenzenkai* the time before last, last
奏 *zensō* prelude (in music) ⌊time but one
奏曲 *zensōkyoku* prelude, overture
後 *zengo, mae-ushi(ro)* front and back, before and behind, before and after. *zengo* about that (time); longitudinal; context, order, sequence. *-zengo* nearly, approximately
後不覚 *zengo-fukaku* unconsciousness
後左右 *zengo-sayū* in all directions
後策 *zengosaku* means of settling a problem
後撞着 *zengo-dōchaku* self-contradiction
10 庭 *zentei* front yard ⌈performer
座 *zenza* opening performance; minor
週 *zenshū* last week; the week before
納 *zennō* prepayment, advance payment
記 *zenki no* the above-mentioned
陳 *zenchin no* the above-mentioned
部 *zembu* front part, fore, front
書 *maega(ki)* preface, preamble. *zensho* first of two books; previous writing; previous letter
哲 *zentetsu* former men of wisdom and virtue ⌈a loan
借 *maega(ri), zenshaku* getting an advance;
借金 *zenshakukin, zenshakkin* loan, advance
栽 *senzai* garden; trees and flowers in a
栽物 *senzaimono* greens, vegetables ⌊garden
進 *zenshin* advance, drive, progress
進力 *zenshinryoku* driving power
進部隊 *zenshimbutai* advance troops
進基地 *zenshin kichi* advance base
進運動 *zenshin undō* forward motion
哨 *zenshō* outpost
哨地 *zenshōchi* outpost
哨勤務 *zenshō kimmu* outpost duty
哨戦 *zenshōsen* skirmish; prefinals (in
哨線 *zenshōsen* scouting line ⌊games)
哨騎兵 *zenshō kihei* outpost cavalry
11 婦 *zempu* previous wife
掛 *maeka(ke)* apron ⌈a brief letter
略 *zenryaku* first part omitted; salutation of
脚 *mae ashi, zenkyaku* forelegs
脳 *zennō* forebrain
著 *zencho* ibid.; the above-mentioned publication ⌈bord
菜 *zensai* relishes, hors d'œuvres, smörgås-

章 *zenshō* preceding chapter
勘定 *mae kanjō* paying in advance
掲 *zenkei no* the above-named
掲書 *zenkeisho* op. cit.
12 歯 *maeba, zenshi* front tooth
開 *maebira(ki)* open in front
場 *zemba* morning market session
項 *zenkō* the preceding paragraph
提 *zentei* preamble, premise, reason, prerequisite
渡 *maewata(shi)* advance payment; advance delivery
腕 *maeude, zenwan* forearm
期 *zenki* first term, first half year, preceding period, early period
葉 *zen-yō* preceding page
貸 *maega(shi)* advance payment
景 *zenkei* foreground, front view
景気 *maegeiki* prospect, promise, outlook
装 *zensō* muzzle loading
装砲 *zensōhō* muzzle loader
13 触 *maebu(re)* previous notice; herald; harbinger, portent
節 *zensetsu* preceding paragraph, section, or verse
電 *zenden* the last telegram
照灯 *zenshōtō* headlights
置 *zenchi, maeo(ki)* preface, introduction
置詞 *zenchishi* preposition
14 歴 *zenreki* personal history
徴 *zenchō*＝前兆 (see above–6)
膊 *zempaku* forearm
説 *zensetsu* former opinion
髪 *maegami* forelock
舞台 *maebutai* apron stage
鼻緒 *maehanao* sandal or clog strap
駆 *zenku* vanguard, precursor, forerunner, leader
駆戦 *zenkusen* skirmish; prefinals (in games)
15 線 *zensen* front line; (weather) front
輪 *zenrin, maewa* front wheel
審 *zenshin* preliminary trials
篇 *zempen* first part, first volume
賢 *zenken* wise men of the past
衛 *zen-ei* advance guard, vanguard
衛戦 *zen-eisen* skirmish; prefinals (in games)
16 頭部 *zentōbu* the front, the forehead
17 輿 *sakigoshi* front palanquin carrier
18 蹤 *zenshō* precedent
額 *zengaku* forehead
額部 *zengakubu* forehead. *zengakubu no* frontal
19 禱 *zentō* invocation

8

釜 釜 See 2834. [金]

B **翁** 596 F1505 **翁** Ō old man; venerable. *okina* old man. [羽]

A **益** 597 F1310 **益** EKI, YAKU gain, benefit, profit, use, advantage. *eki(suru)* be beneficial, useful, profitable, or valuable. *ma(su)* (see under 増 1137.0). [皿]
4 友 *ekiyū* good friend, useful friend
6 虫 *ekichū* beneficial insect
8 金 *ekikin* profit
9 荒男 *masurao* warrior; manly person
荒猛男 *masurao-takeo* warrior; manly person
10 益 *masumasu* increasingly, more and more
11 鳥 *ekichō* beneficial bird

A **兼** 598 F210 **兼** KEN and, in addition, concurrently. *ken(su), ka(neru)* combine with, serve as both; hold an additional post; use with. *ka(nete)* simultaneously. *-ka(neru)* cannot; hesitate to; be impatient.
5 用 *ken-yō* combined use, combination, serving two purposes
仕 *ka(ne)-tsuka(eru)* serve at the same time
6 行 *kenkō* doing simultaneously
任 *kennin* concurrent post
合 *ka(ne)a(i)* equilibrium, poise. *ka(ne)-a(u)* to balance, to poise
7 役 *ka(ne)yaku* carrying on a second line of work
8 併 *kempei suru* unite
官 *kenkan* additional post
10 修 *kenshū* studying two lines together (as a major and a minor)
兼 *ka(ne)ga(ne)* often, lately, already
帯 *kentai* combined use, combination, filling two positions; serving two purposes
11 務 *kemmu* additional post
12 備 *kembi suru* be proficient in both, combining both. *ka(ne)-sona(eru)* have both, combine with
補 *kempo* carrying on a second line of work
勤 *kenkin* additional post
営 *ken-ei suru* operate or carry on simultaneously
13 摂 *kensetsu* concurrent post
業 *kengyō* side line
業農家 *kengyō nōka* part-time farmer
18 職 *kenshoku* concurrent post
題 *kendai* subject for a poem

9

曽 Nonstandard for **曾** 604.

剪 599 F251 F1509 **翦** SEN. *hasa(mu)* clip, snip. *ki(ru)* cut. [刀]
2 刀 *sentō* scissors; punch
4 毛 *semmō* wool shearing
切 *hasa(mi)-ki(ru)* nip off, snip, clip, trim off
8 枝 *senshi* pruning

定 *sentei* pruning
定鋏 *senteibasami* pruning shears
9 除 *senjo suru* cut off, cut out
12 裁 *sensai suru* cut,trim, shear, prune
裁機 *sensaiki* shearing machine

A 貧 600/F1789 **貧** HIN, BIN poverty. *hin(suru)* become poor, live in poverty. *mazu(shii)* poor, destitute; meager. [貝]

3 土 *hindo* poor soil; a poor country
乏 *bimbō* poverty
乏人 *bimbōnin* poor man, the poor
乏性 *bimbōshō* destined to poverty
乏所帯 *bimbōjotai* poor household
乏神 *bimbōgami* god of poverty
乏揺 *bimbōyusu(ri)*, *bimbōyuru(gi)* nervous mannerism
乏暮 *bimbōgura(shi)* needy circumstances
乏鬮 *bimbō kuji* unlucky number, a blank; bad bargain
5 民 *himmin* poor people
民街 *himmingai* slums
民窟 *himminkutsu* slums
6 血 *hinketsu* anemia
血症 *hinketsushō* anemia
7 困 *hinkon* poverty; lack
8 苦 *hinku* hardship, serious poverty
者 *hinja* poor person
9 相 *hinsō na* poor looking
10 家 *hinka* poor home
弱 *hinjaku na* poor, meager, scanty
12 棒 *bimbō* poverty
寒 *hinkan* destitution
富 *himpu* rich and poor; wealth and poverty
13 鉱 *hinkō* low-grade ore
農 *hinnō* needy peasant
15 賤 *hinsen na* poor and lowly
窮 *hinkyū* great poverty
窮化 *hinkyūka suru* impoverish

10

巽 601/F608 SON. *tatsumi* southeast. [巳]

奠 602/F484 TEN decision. [大]

10 都 *tento suru* transfer the capital

孳 603/F524 **孳** JI. SHI increase; bear children. [子]

12 孳 *shishi toshite* untiringly, diligently

曾 604/F926 SŌ. SO. *katsu(te)*, *kat(te)* once, before, formerly; ever, never (neg.); former, ex-. [日]

9 祖父 *sōsofu*, *hiijiji*, *hiōji* great-grandfather
祖母 *sōsobo*, *hiibaba*, *hiōba* great-grandmother
10 孫 *hiimago*, *sōson*, *hiko*, *himago* great-grandchild
11 遊 *sōyū* former visit

B 普 605/F908 **普** FU. *amane(ku)* widely, generally. [日]

3 及 *fukyū* diffusion, dissemination
及版 *fukyūban* cheap popular edition
4 辺 *fuhen*=*fuhensei* 普遍性 (see below–11)
辺性 *fuhensei*=普遍性 (see below–11)
9 段 *fudan*=不断 17.11
段着 *fudangi* ordinary clothes
通 *futsū* ordinary, common, usual, mediocre
通人 *futsūjin* ordinary person
通名詞 *futsū meishi* common noun
通法 *futsūhō* common law
通科 *futsūka* regular or general course
通株 *futsū kabu* common stock
通選挙 *futsū senkyo* universal suffrage
11 偏 *fuhen*=*fuhensei* 普遍性 (see below–11)
偏性 *fuhensei*=普遍性 (see below–11)
遍 *fuhen*=*fuhensei* 普遍性 (see below–11)
遍妥当性 *fuhen-datōsei* ability to fit into any situation
遍性 *fuhensei* universality, ubiquity, omnipresence
遍的 *fuhenteki* universal, omnipresent
14 選 *fusen* universal suffrage
15 請 *fushin* building, construction
請場 *fushimba* building plot

A 善 606/F368 ZEN good, goodness, right, virtue. *i(i)*, *yo(i)* (see under 良 3885.0). *yo(ku) suru* be skilled in. *yo(shi)* good, all right, well, so. *yō(koso)* Well, good for you; Well, that's a rude thing to do. [口]

2 人 *zennin* good people
4 心 *zenshin* virtue, moral sense, conscience
5 玉 *zendama* good person
用 *zen-yō* good use
処 *zensho suru* tide over, make the best of, use discretion
6 行 *zenkō* good deed, good conduct; benevolence
因善果 *zen-in-zenka* good actions lead to good rewards
7 良 *zenryō* goodness, virtue, excellence
男善女 *zennan-zennyo* pious men and women
8 性 *zensei* innate goodness of man
果 *zenka* good results
事 *zenji* good thing, good deed
知識 *zenchishiki* Buddhist evangelist
9 政 *zensei* good government
美 *zembi* the good and the beautiful
哉 *zenzai* Well done!; soft bean-jam
後 *zengo* giving careful thought to the future; finishing up carefully

後策 *zengosaku* relief measure, remedy, countermeasure, means of settling a problem

[10]根 *zenkon* good deeds, charity

書 *zensho* beautiful calligraphy; a calligrapher; a good book

[11]道 *zendō* path of virtue, righteousness

悪 *zen-aku, zennaku* good and evil. *yo(shi)-waru(shi), yo(shi)-a(shi), yo(i)-waru(i)* good or bad; merits or demerits; quality; suitability. *yo(kare)-a(shikare)* good or bad, right or wrong

[13]戦 *zensen suru* fight a good fight

意 *zen-i* good faith; good will, good intentions; favorable sense

感 *zenkan* successful vaccination, positive reaction

業 *zengō* good deeds

[14]徳 *zentoku* virtues

隣 *zenrin* good neighbor

導 *zendō* proper guidance

[15]霊 *zenrei* spirit of goodness

尊 607/F564 **尊** A SON. *tatto(bu), tōto(bu), tatto(mu), tōto(mu)* (see under 貴 4504.0). *tatto(i), tōto(i)* precious, valuable, priceless; noble, exalted, sacred. *mikoto* lord, prince. [寸]

[3]大 *sondai* haughtiness, pomposity, self-sufficiency

下 *sonka* Obediently yours

上 *sonjō* one's superior

[4]父 *sompu* your father

公 *sonkō* you (polite); your father

王 *sonnō* reverence for the emperor, advocate of imperial rule

王家 *Sonnōka* Royalists

王党 *Sonnōtō* Imperialists

王討幕 *sonnō-tōbaku* reverence for the emperor and the overthrow of the shogunate

王攘夷 *sonnō-jōi* reverence for the emperor and expulsion of the barbarians

[5]台 *sondai* you (ancient or literary)

兄 *sonkei* (polite) an elder brother; an elderly person

[6]号 *songō* honorary title

宅 *sontaku* your house

名 *sommei* your name

[7]体 *sontai* your health; (Buddhist) image

君 *sonkun* (polite) someone's father; one's companion

来 *sonrai* your visit

[8]長 *sonchō* one's superiors, one's seniors

命 *sommei* your order

者 *sonja* Buddhist saint; man of high repute; guest of honor

[9]信 *sonshin suru* revere

重 *sonchō* respect, esteem, regard

卑 *sompi* high and low, aristocrat and plebeian

皇 *sonnō*＝尊王 (see above–4)

[10]称 *sonshō* honorary title

家 *sonka* your house

容 *son-yō* your countenance

書 *sonsho* (polite) someone's letter

[11]族 *sonzoku* direct ancestors

堂 *sondō* your family; your mother

崇 *sonsū* reverence, veneration

[12]属 *sonzoku* direct ancestors; noble ancestors

敬 *sonkei* respect, esteem, honor, reverence

貴 *sonki* noble (person)

[13]意 *son-i* your idea

[14]像 *sonzō* statue of a noble character; your picture

[15]慮 *sonryo* your will, your idea

影 *son-ei* portrait (polite)

[17]厳 *songen* dignity, majesty, sanctity

[18]顔 *songan* your countenance

簡 *sonkan* (polite) someone's letter

11

愈 See **愈** 526. [心]

巽 608/F210 See **巽** 614.

普 609/F908 See **普** 605. [日]

與 610/F1566 See **与** 6. [臼]

煎 611/F1192 SEN. *i(ru)* broil, parch, roast, fire (tea), boil down (in oil). *sen(jiru)* boil, decoct, infuse. [灬]

[5]立 *i(ri)ta(te)* freshly parched. *sen(ji)ta(te) no* freshly drawn (tea)

付 *i(ri)-tsu(keru)* parch, roast, broil, scorch. *i(ri)-tsu(ku)* be scorched; boil down

汁 *senji* broth

出 *sen(ji)-da(su)* extract by boiling, prepare an infusion of, decoct

玉子 *iritamago* scrambled eggs

[7]豆腐 *iridōfu* dry seasoned tofu

[9]茶 *sencha* green tea

[10]剤 *senzai* decoction

[13]詰 *sen(ji)-tsu(meru)* boil down, condense

[15]餅 *sembei* Japanese cracker; wafer

餅蒲団 *sembeibuton* thin bedding; hard bed

[16]薬 *sen(ji)gusuri, sen-yaku* (medical) decoction, infusion

[17]鍋 *irinabe* roasting pan

慈 612/F736 **慈** B JI. *itsuku(shimu)* love, be affectionate to; pity. *itsuku(shimi)* affection, love. [心]

[4]心 *jishin* benevolence, mercy

父 *jifu* affectionate father

5 母 *jibo* affectionate mother
兄 *jikei* affectionate elder brother
8 雨 *jiu* beneficial or welcome rain
10 訓 *jikun* kind counsel; mother's advice
恵 *jikei* mercy and love
11 眼 *jigen* merciful eye
12 悲 *jihi* compassion, benevolence, charity, mercy
悲心 *jihishin* benevolence
善 *jizen* charity, philanthropy
善心 *jizenshin* benevolence, liberality
善市 *jizen ichi* charity bazaar
善会 *jizenkai* philanthropic society
善事業 *jizen jigyō* philanthropic work
善家 *jizenka* charitable person, philanthropist
善箱 *jizembako* charity box
善鍋 *jizennabe* charity pot
13 愛 *jiai* affection, kindness, love, benevolence

13

翦 613/F1509 See 剪 599. [羽]

14

冀 614/F210 兾 KI. *koinega(u)* (see under 希 1470.0).
7 図 *kito* hopefully planning
8 念 *kinen*=*kibō* 希望 1470.11
11 望 *kibō*=希望 1470.11

A 興 615/F1567 KŌ. KYŌ interest, entertainment, pleasure. *kyō(garu)* be amused or interested in. *kyō(jiru)*, *kyō(zuru)* amuse oneself, make merry. *oko(ru)* rise, flourish. *oko(su)* revive, retrieve (fortunes), raise up. [臼]
3 亡 *kōbō* rise and fall, ups and downs
6 行 *kōgyō* entertainment industry
行化 *kōgyōka suru* stage or film a story
行主 *kōgyō nushi* showman, promoter, producer
行師 *kōgyōshi* showman, show manager
7 亜 *kōa* Asia development
8 国 *kōkoku* making a country prosperous; prosperous country
味 *kyōmi* interest
味本位 *kyōmi hon-i no* popular (literature, etc.)
味津津 *kyōmi-shinshin(taru)* of great interest
味深 *kyōmibuka(i)*, *kyōmifukai* very interesting
9 信所 *kōshinjo* detective agency
信録 *kōshinroku* directory
10 起 *kōki* rise, ascendency; aroused energy; high-spirited action
隆 *kōryū* rise, prosperity
11 敗 *kōhai* rise and fall (of nations)
12 廃 *kōhai* rise and fall; destiny
替 *kōtai* rise and fall (of nations)
13 業 *kōgyō* industrial enterprise
業銀行 *kōgyō ginkō* industrial bank
15 趣 *kyōshu* interest (in something)
16 醒 *kyōza(meru)* lose interest. *kyōza(mashi)*, *kyōza(me)* a kill-joy, a wet blanket
奮 *kōfun* excitement, agitation, stimulation
奮剤 *kōfunzai* stimulant

15

輿 616/F1848 YO. *kago*, *koshi* palanquin; bier. [車]
2 入 *koshi-i(re)* wedding; bridal procession; bride's entry to groom's home
6 地 *yochi* earth, world
11 望 *yobō* popularity, esteem, reputation; confidence
15 論 *yoron* public opinion
論調査 *yoron chōsa* public-opinion survey

RAD. 冂 13

Dōgamae (enclosure like that of *dō* "same"), *makigamae*, or *keigamae*.
Variants: 冂, 月, 刂. Nickname: Upside-down Box.

2

丹 丹 See 163. [丶]

A 円 617/F211/F407 圓 EN circle; yen. *mado(ka) na* round; tranquil. *maru(i)*, *maro(yaka) na* round, circular, spherical. *tsubura na* round, rotund. *maru* circle; money.
4 心 *enshin* center of a circle
内 *ennai* within the circle
5 丘 *enkyū* knoll, hummock
本 *empon* a one-yen book
6 曲 *enkyoku* roundabout way (of speaking or working)
安 *enyasu* cheap yen
光 *enkō* halo
虫類 *enchūrui* round worms
7 形 *enkei*, *marugata* circle, round shape
8 居 *madoi* small gathering, happy circle
価 *enka* value of the yen
味 *marumi* roundness, rotundity

2 二亠人イ𠆢儿入八ソ 3[冂]冖冫几凵刀刂力勹匕匚匸十卜卩厂厶又

弧 *enko* arc
周 *enshū* circumference
周率 *enshūritsu* circular constant, pi
卓 *entaku* round table
卓会議 *entaku kaigi* round-table conference
9建 *enda(te)* yen base
柱 *enchū* column, shaft, cylinder. *marubashira* cylindrical column
陣 *enjin* circle, ring
盆 *marubon* round tray
型 *marugata* circle, circular form
屋根 *maru yane* dome, cupola
為替 *engawase* yen exchange
10高 *endaka* exchange in favor of the yen
座 *enza* sitting in a circle; round straw mat
11域 *en-iki* yen bloc, yen area
規 *enki* a pair of compasses
頂 *enchō* dome, cupola
寂 *enjaku* nirvana; death of the Buddha or a priest
窓 *marumado* round window
貨 *enka* yen currency
運動 *en-undō* circular motion
転 *enten(taru)* orotund, spherical; smoothly rolling
転滑脱 *enten-katsudatsu* versatility, adaptability, tact
12弾 *endan* round shot
満 *emman* perfection, harmony, peace, satisfaction, smoothness, integrity, completeness
筒 *entō* cylinder
13滑 *enkatsu, enkotsu* smoothness, harmony
鉋 *maruganna* round carpenter's plane
蓋 *engai* cupola, dome, vault
14舞 *embu* waltz
15墳 *enfun* burial mound
熟 *enjuku* ripeness, mellowness, maturity, perfection
盤 *emban* disk; discus
盤投 *embanna(ge)* discus throw
16錐 *marugiri* round gimlet. *ensui* cone
錐形 *ensuikei* cone
17壔 *entō* cylinder
18顔 *marugao* round face
19鏡 *enkyō, maru kagami* round mirror
28罐 *marugama* cylindrical boiler
25顱 *enro* tonsure, shaven head

3

冊 冊 冊 冊 See 88.

冋 618/F397 冋 冋 See 1028. [冂]

4

再 See 35.

A **同** 619/F330 **仝 仝** Dō the same, the said, ibid. *dō(jiru), dō(zuru)* agree. *ona(ji), onna(ji)* same, identical, equal; uniform; equivalent; similar; common (origin); changeless. *ona(jiku) suru* make similar; have the same (idea). *ona(jiku)* the same (name). [口]

1一 *dōitsu* sameness, similarity, identity, equality; fairness
一人 *dōitsunin* the same person
一視 *dōitsushi suru* class with, put on a par with, regard in the same light
2人 *dōjin, dōnin* same person, said person; clique; fraternity; kindred spirits; comrade, colleague
人種 *dōjinshu* racial identity, same race
人雑誌 *dōjin zasshi* a magazine of a society
3上 *dōjō* same as above, ditto, ibid.
工異曲 *dōkō-ikyoku* equal workmanship but differing style
士 *dōshi* fellow, companion
士打 *dōshiu(chi)* killing each other by mistake
士討 *dōshiu(chi)* killing each other by mistake
4日 *dōjitsu* the same day
月 *dōgetsu* the same month
氏 *dōshi* the same person, the said person
父母 *dōfubo* the same parents
分母 *dōbumbo* common denominator
心 *dōshin* same mind, unanimity; concentricity; policeman. *dōshin no* concentric
心円 *dōshin-en* concentric circles
仁 *dōjin* universal benevolence
仁教会 *Dōjin Kyōkai* Universalist Church
化 *dōka* assimilation, adaptation, absorption
化作用 *dōka sayō* assimilation, metabolism, anabolism
文 *dōbun* same script; same language
文同種 *dōbun-dōshu* same race and same script
文通達 *dōbun tsūtatsu* (Papal) encyclical
5処 *dōsho* the same place
穴 *dōketsu* being buried in the same grave
巧異曲 *dōkō-ikyoku* practically the same
6舟 *dōshū* shipmates, fellow passengers
色 *dōshoku* the same color
気 *dōki* same temperament, same turn of mind
地 *dōchi* the same place; that place
列 *dōretsu* same rank, same file; company; attendance
邦 *dōhō* the same country
字 *dōji* the same character
行 *dōkō* travelling together. *dōgyō* fellow pilgrim, fellow practicer of austerities
行者 *dōkōsha* fellow travellers
年 *ona(ji)doshi* same age. *dōnen* that year, same year; same age
年輩 *dōnempai* persons of the same age

名 *dōmei, dōmyō* the same name
名異人 *dōmei-ijin* namesake; person with the same name
好 *dōkō* similar tastes
好会 *dōkōkai* association of like-minded people
好者 *dōkōsha* people of similar tastes
7 車 *dōsha suru* taking the same car or train
局 *dōkyoku* the said bureau, the same bureau
体 *dōtai ni* as one, together
役 *dōyaku* colleague
村 *dōson* the same village; that village
町 *dōchō* the same town; that town
社 *dōsha* the same firm
形 *dōkei* the same shape
系 *dōkei* affiliated, akin
坐 *dōza*=同座 (see below–10)
伴 *dōhan suru* accompany, go with
伴者 *dōhansha* companion
位 *dōi* the same rank; the same digit
位元素 *dōi genso* isotope
労 *dōrō* working together
労者 *dōrōsha* fellow worker
志 *dōshi* same mind; kindred soul, comrade
志打 *doshiu(chi)* internal strife, fighting among themselves
志会 *dōshikai* an association of kindred spirits
志的 *dōshiteki* companionable
8 門 *dōmon* fellow student
店 *dōten* the same store, the same shop
房 *dōbō* the same room; sharing a room; sharers of a room
価 *dōka* equivalent
姓 *dōsei* the same surname
所 *dōsho* the same place, the same address, the said place
朋 *dōbō* companions
夜 *dōya* the same night; that night
宗 *dōshū* the same sect
学 *dōgaku* the same school
事 *dōji* the same event; no change (on the stock market)
国 *dōkoku* the same country, the same province, the said country
国民 *dōkokumin* fellow countrymen
居 *dōkyo* living with (someone)
居人 *dōkyonin* a person living with the family
性 *dōsei* the same sex; homosexuality; homogeneity; congeniality
性愛 *dōseiai* homosexual infatuation
9 信 *dōshin* the same faith
侶 *dōryō, dōryo* companion
相 *dōsō* the said (cabinet) minister
派 *dōha* the same sect
祖 *dōso* common ancestor
封 *dōfū* enclosure. *dōfū suru* enclose
乗 *dōjō* riding together
前 *dōzen* same as above, ditto, ibid.
点 *dōten* tie, draw
室 *dōshitsu* the same room
型 *dōkei* the same type, the same pattern
県 *dōken* the same prefecture
省 *dōshō* the said ministry, the same ministry
音 *dōon* the same sound; one voice
音語 *dōongo* homonym
級 *dōkyū* the same grade, same class
級生 *dōkyūsei* classmates
胞 *dōhō, harakara, dōbō* brothers, brethren, fellow countrymen, fellowmen
胞愛 *dōhōai* brotherly love
10 座 *dōza* sitting together; the same theater; involvement, entanglement, implication
席 *dōseki* sitting together, being present together
病 *dōbyō* the same sickness
格 *dōkaku* the same rank, equality; apposition
流 *dōryū* the same style; same school; common origin
紙 *dōshi* the same newspaper
郷 *dōkyō* same village, town, or province
衾 *dōkin* sharing the bed
家 *dōke* the said family; the same family
党 *dōtō* the same political party
書 *dōsho* the same book, the said book
時 *dōji* the same time. *dōji no* synchronous, simultaneous. *dōji ni* coincident with; on the other hand; while
時代 *dōjidai* the same age, same period
11 道 *dōdō suru* go with, accompany
視 *dōshi suru* treat alike
断 *dōdan* the same, ditto
宿 *dōshuku* lodging in the same hotel
異 *dōi* similarities and differences
船 *dōsen* the same ship; taking the same ship
船人 *dōsen (no) hito* fellow voyager
情 *dōjō* sympathy
情心 *dōjōshin* sympathy, compassion
情者 *dōjōsha* sympathizer
族 *dōzoku* the same family, same tribe, same race
族会 *dōzokukai* family council, family company
族会社 *dōzokugaisha* family corporation, affiliated concern
窓 *dōsō* the same school
窓生 *dōsōsei* schoolmate, fellow student, alumnus
窓会 *dōsōkai* alumni meeting
12 棲 *dōsei suru* cohabit with, live together
筆 *dōhitsu* the same handwriting
等 *dōtō* equality, same rights; same rank
然 *dōzen* the same
期 *dōki* the same period; same class; synchronism
期生 *dōkisei* classmate
13 腹 *dōfuku* born of the same mother; kindred spirits
数 *dōsū* same number
罪 *dōzai* the same offense
勢 *dōzei* party, company
感 *dōkan* the same feeling, sympathy; concurrence
義 *dōgi* the same meaning

2 二亠人亻𠆢儿入八丷 [冂] 冖冫几凵刀刂力勹匕匚匸十卜卩厂厶又

義語 *dōgigo* synonym
業 *dōgyō* the same trade, same business
業者 *dōgyōsha* person in the same business; the profession, the trade ⌈craft, guild
業組合 *dōgyō kumiai* trade association,
意 *dōi* the same meaning; same opinion; agreement, consent, approval
意見 *dōiken* the same opinion
意義 *dōigi* the same meaning
意語 *dōigo* synonym
盟 *dōmei* alliance, league, union
盟休校 *dōmei kyūkō* student strike
盟条約 *dōmei jōyaku* treaty of alliance
盟国 *dōmeikoku* ally (of another nation)
盟軍 *dōmeigun* allied armies
盟怠業 *dōmei taigyō* go-slow strike
盟罷業 *dōmei higyō* strike
14 僚 *dōryō* associate, colleague
様 *dōyō* same, same kind, identical, like, equal. *ona(ji) yō ni* similarly
説 *dōsetsu* the same opinion
誌 *dōshi* the same magazine
語反復 *dōgo-hampuku* tautology
種 *dōshu* the same kind; homogeneousness; the same race ⌈language
種同文 *dōshu-dōbun* same race and same
種類 *dōshurui* the same kind
15 慶 *dōkei* a matter for mutual congratulation
権 *dōken* the same rights, equal rights
輩 *dōhai* comrade, colleague, one's equal
趣味 *dōshumi* the same interests
調 *dōchō* alignment; tuning
調者 *dōchōsha* fellow traveler, sympathizer
質 *dōshitsu* the same quality, same nature, homogeneity
質的 *dōshitsuteki* homogeneous
18 職 *dōshoku* the same occupation; the said occupation
類 *dōrui* the same kind; accomplice
額 *dōgaku* the same amount
藩 *dōhan* the same clan

5

冑 See 3747. [肉]

6

冐 See **冒** 2117.

罔 620/F1491 Mō, Bō net. *ami* net. [网]

岡 621/F589 Kō. *oka* hill, knoll, rising ground. [山]
4 辺 *okabe* vicinity of a hill

引 *okahiki, okappiki* detective, plain-clothes-⌊man
5 目 *okame* onlooker, bystander
9 持 *okamo(chi)* wooden carrying box
11 惚 *okabore* unrequited love, secret affections
12 湯 *okayu* tank of clean water (in a bath ⌊house)
焼 *okaya(ki)* jealousy, envy
場所 *okabasho* red-light district

周 622/F345 A **周** Shū circuit, lap, circumference, vicinity; Chou (dynasty). *mawari* (see under 回 1028.0). *gururi* surroundings. [口]
4 辺 *shūhen* circumference, perimeter; environs, outskirts ⌈ings
6 回 *shūkai* circumference, girth, surround-
年 *shūnen* whole year; anniversary
7 囲 *shūi* circumference, girth; surroundings
忌 *shūki* death anniversary
8 到 *shūtō na* scrupulous, careful, meticulous, ⌊complete
易 *shūeki* divination
知 *shūchi* common knowledge
知徹底 *shūchi-tettei* (something) known to ⌊all
波 *shūha* cycle, wave, frequency
波変調 *shūha henchō* frequency modula- ⌊tion, FM
波帯 *shūhatai* frequency band
波数 *shūhasū* frequency (in electricity)
10 流 *shūryū* flowing around ⌈ship
航 *shūkō* circumnavigation; a circle tour by
11 密 *shūmitsu na* = *shūtō na* 周到 (see ⌊above-8)
遊 *shūyū* tour, round trip
遊券 *shūyūken* excursion ticket
章 *awa(teru)* (see under 慌 1725.0). *shūshō* agitation, frustration ⌈consternation
章狼狽 *shūshō-rōbai* dismay, discomfiture,
旋 *shūsen* good offices, recommendation, mediation; (Tokugawa-era) employment ⌊office
旋人 *shūsennin* agent, middleman
旋屋 *shūsen-ya* broker, employment agency
旋料 *shūsenryō* brokerage, commission
旋業 *shūsengyō* brokerage, commission agency ⌈employment agency
旋業者 *shūsengyōsha* broker, middleman;
12 智 *shūchi* common knowledge
極星 *shūkyokusei* circumpolar star
期 *shūki* period, cycle
期性 *shūkisei* cyclic, periodic
16 覧 *shūran* looking all around

7

冐 623/F212 See **冒** 2117.

9

冕 624/F213 Ben crown.
9 冠 *benkan* crown

RAD. 冖 14

Wa kammuri (crown shaped like the katakana *wa*) or *beki kammuri* "covering" crown. Nickname: *Kana Wa.*

2

B 冗 625 F213 F527 冗 宂 Jō uselessness.

4文 *jōbun* redundancy
5用 *jōyō* unnecessary work, unnecessary expense
句 *jōku* redundant phrase
6多 *jōta* superabundance
8長 *jōchō* verbosity, tediousness
物 *jōbutsu* redundancy, superfluity
官 *jōkan* supernumerary official
10員 *jōin* supernumerary
12筆 *jōhitsu* worthless painting and writing
費 *jōhi* unnecessary expenses
14漫 *jōman* verbosity
語 *jōgo* redundancy
15談 *jōdan* joke
談口 *jōdanguchi* joke
談事 *jōdangoto* joking matter

3

A 写 626 F556 寫 写 SHA. *utsu(ru)* be photographed; be projected (on a screen); (light or shadows) fall on. *utsu(su)* copy, transcribe, duplicate, reproduce, trace; describe, picture, photograph. *utsu(shi)* copy, duplicate, facsimile, transcript. [宀]

5出 *utsu(shi)-da(su)* reveal, show
本 *shahon* manuscript, written copy, codex
生 *shasei* sketching; drawing from nature; portrayal, description
生文 *shaseibun* word picture
生帖 *shaseichō* sketchbook
生画 *shaseiga* picture drawn from life
6字 *shaji* copying, transcription
8実 *shajitsu* a real picture; realism
実主義 *shajitsu shugi* realism, literalism
実的 *shajitsuteki* realistic, graphic, true to life
10真 *shashin* photograph
真石版 *shashin sekiban* photolithography
真凸版 *shashin toppan* phototype
真判定 *shashin hantei* deciding the winner from a photo
真判定決勝 *shashin hantei kesshō* photo finish
真版 *shashimban* photostat; photographic plate; photogravure
真屋 *shashin-ya* photographer, photo studio
真師 *shashinshi* photographer
真班 *shashinhan* (newspaper) cameramen
真嫌 *shashingira(i)* camera shy
真帳 *shashinchō* photograph album
真術 *shashinjutsu* photography
真望遠鏡 *shashimbōenkyō* photographic telescope
真植字 *shashin-shokuji* photosetting (in printing)
真測量 *shashin sokuryō* photographic surveying
真結婚 *shashin kekkon* picture marriage
真電送 *shashin densō* phototelegraphy
真器 *shashinki* camera
真館 *shashinkan* photo studio
真機 *shashinki* camera
真機店 *shashinkiten* camera shop
真顔 *shashingao* one's looks in a photo
12植 *shashoku* photosetting (in printing)
絵 *utsu(shi)e* magic-lantern picture; child's copying pictures, shadowgraph
象 *shashō* image

7

B 冠 627 F213 KAN crown, diadem; first, best, peerless. *kamu(ru)* (see *kaburu* 被 4225.0). *kan(suru)* crown, cap; name, designate; entitle; initiate on coming of age. *kammuri* crown, diadem; a top character radical.

4毛 *kammō* thistledown
水 *kansui* flooding, submergence
木 *kabuki* lintel, crossbar; gate with a crossbar; roofed gate
木門 *kabukimon* gate with a crossbar
7位 *kan-i* system indicating court ranks by headgear colors
状 *kanjō no* coronary
8枉 *kammuri (o) ma(geru)* become displeased; get stubborn
者 *kanja, kaja* young person; young servant; a young man come of age (at 16)
9省 *kanshō* a letter salutation
11動脈 *kandōmyaku* coronary artery
婚葬祭 *kankonsōsai* ceremonial occasion
12絶 *kanzetsu suru* be unique, be unsurpassed
詞 *kanshi* article (in grammar)
13辞 *kanji* stereotyped epithet

A 軍 628 F1835 GUN army, force, troops. *ikusa* war; battle; campaign; army. [軍]

2刀 *guntō* saber, side arms, service sword
人 *gunjin* soldier, military man
人生活 *gunjin seikatsu* military life

3士 *gunshi* soldiers
4手 *gunte* army cotton gloves
犬 *gunken* war dog
夫 *gumpu* military porter
5功 *gunkō* meritorious war service
礼 *gunrei* military honors
民 *gummin* the military and civilians
令 *gunrei* military command
令部 *Gunreibu* Naval General Staff
司令官 *gunshireikan* army commander
司令部 *gunshireibu* military headquarters
用 *gun-yō* military use
用犬 *gun-yōken* war dog
用地図 *gun-yō chizu* army (topographic) map
用金 *gun-yō-kin* war funds, war chest; campaign fund
用品 *gun-yōhin* military stores, munitions of war
用鳩 *gun-yōbato* carrier pigeon
用機 *gun-yōki* warplane
6衣 *gun-i* military clothes
団 *gundan* army corps
団長 *gundanchō* corps commander
7役 *gun-eki, gun-yaku* military service
兵 *gumbyō, gumpyō, gumpei* armed forces; battle troops
医 *gun-i* military surgeon
医学校 *gun-i gakkō* military medical college
医監 *gun-ikan* surgeon major general
医総監 *gun-i sōkan* surgeon general
8長 *gunchō* combat commander
門 *gummon* camp gate; a general (polite)
使 *gunshi* truce bearer
服 *gumpuku* military or naval uniform
制 *gunsei* military system, military organization
卒 *gunsotsu* soldier
学 *gungaku* military science, strategy, tactics
官憲 *gunkanken* military authorities
拡 *gunkaku* expansion of armaments
拡競争 *gunkaku kyōsō* armaments race
法 *gumpō* military law; martial law; tactics, strategy
法会議 *gumpō kaigi* court-martial
国 *gunkoku* nation at war, militant nation
国主義 *gunkoku shugi* militarism
国色 *gunkokushoku* military character
事 *gunji* naval and military affairs; military
事力 *gunjiryoku* military force, military strength
事上 *gunjijō no* military, strategic
事工場 *gunji kōjō* war plant
事公債 *gunji kōsai* war bond, war loan
事犯 *gunjihan* military offense
事行動 *gunji kōdō* military movements
事同盟 *gunji dōmei* military alliance
事会議 *gunji kaigi* council of war
事的 *gunjiteki* military
事協定 *gunji kyōtei* military pact
事面 *gunjimen* military aspect
事通 *gunjitsū* man versed in military affairs
事通信員 *gunji tsūshin-in* war correspondent
事施設 *gunji shisetsu* military installations
事秘密 *gunji himitsu* military secret
事基地 *gunji kichi* military base
事教練 *gunji kyōren* military training
事費 *gunjihi* war funds, war expenditures
事裁判 *gunji saiban* court martial
事裁判所 *gunji saibansho* military court
事輸送 *gunji yusō* military transport
事諜報 *gunji chōhō* military intelligence
事警察 *gunji keisatsu* military police
事顧問 *gunji komon* military adviser
9律 *gunritsu* martial law; articles of war; military discipline; military law
神 *gunshin* god of war; war hero
紀 *gunki* military discipline
陣 *gunjin* camp, battlefield
陣医学 *gunjin igaku* military medicine
政 *gunsei* military government
政府 *gunseifu* military government
政部 *gunseibu* military government
10馬 *gumba* army horse
扇 *gunsen* ancient commander's fan
師 *gunshi* strategist, tactician; schemer
旅 *gunryo* army; soldiers; war
将 *gunshō* army commander
容 *gun-yō* military accouterments; troop formation
書 *gunsho* military book, war history
記 *gunki* war chronicle
記物語 *gunki monogatari* war chronicle
配 *gumbai* strategem, tactics; (ancient) military leader's fan; wrestling umpire's fan
配団扇 *gumbai uchiwa* (ancient) military leader's fan
部 *gumbu* military authorities, army circles
部独裁 *gumbu dokusai* military dictatorship
11道 *gundō* military road
情 *gunjō* military situation
略 *gunryaku* strategy, tactics
務 *gummu* military and naval affairs; military service
船 *gunsen* warship
規 *gunki* military regulations
票 *gumpyō* military scrip
曹 *gunsō* sergeant
隊 *guntai* army, troops, corps
隊化 *guntaika* militarization
隊生活 *guntai seikatsu* army life
隊式 *guntaishiki* military style, army style
隊行進曲 *guntai kōshinkyoku* military march
隊葬 *guntaisō* military funeral
12属 *gunzoku* civilian in military employ
帽 *gumbō* military cap

港 *gunkō* naval port, naval station
営 *gun-ei* military camp
装 *gunsō* soldier's equipment
費 *gumpi* war funds, war expenditures
備 *gumbi* armaments, military preparations
備制限 *gumbi seigen* limitation of armaments
備拡張 *gumbi kakuchō* expansion of armaments
備撤廃 *gumbi teppai* complete disarmament
備縮小 *gumbi shukushō* reduction of armaments
[13]鼓 *gunko* war drum
路 *gunro* military road
靴 *gunka* military shoes
勢 *gunzei* military forces, host, troops
資 *gunshi* war materiel; military expenses; war fund; campaign funds
資金 *gunshikin* war funds; campaign funds
楽 *gungaku* military music
楽手 *gungakushu* military bandsman
楽長 *gungakuchō* military band master
楽隊 *gungakutai* military or naval band
[14]閥 *gumbatsu* army clique, militarist party
旗 *gunki* battle flag, colors, ensign
歌 *gunka* war song
管区 *gunkanku* military district
需 *gunju* munitions, military stores
需工場 *gunju kōjō* war plant
需工業 *gunju kōgyō* munitions industry
需品 *gunjuhin* munitions of war, military stores
需景気 *gunju keiki* war prosperity
[15]談 *gundan* war story
器 *gunki* implements of war
[16]機 *gunki* military secret
[17]縮 *gunshuku* disarmament, limitation of arms
縮協定 *gunshuku kyōtei* disarmament agreement
[18]職 *gunshoku* military profession, military post
[19]警 *gunkei* military police
[20]議 *gungi* war council
籍 *gunseki* military or naval register, muster roll
艦 *gunkan* warship, battleship
艦鳥 *gunkanchō, gunkandori* frigate bird

— 8 —

冤 See 冤 631.

冦 See 寇 1313. [宀]

冢 629/F214 See 塚 1120.

冥 630/F215 MEI, MYŌ dark.
[8]土 *meido* hades, realm of the dead
[4]王星 *Meiōsei* (planet) Pluto
[5]加 *myōga* divine protection
加金 *myōgakin* votive offering; forced contributions (Edo era)
[7]利 *myōri* providence, luck, favor, advantage
[8]府 *meifu* hades, realm of the dead, sheol
[9]途 *yomi, meido* hades, realm of the dead, sheol
界 *meikai* hades, realm of the dead
[10]冥 *meimei no* dark; invisible; divine
[13]暗 *meian* gloom, shade
福 *meifuku* happiness in the next world
想 *meisō* meditation, contemplation
[14]境 *meikyō* shades of the dead
罰 *meibatsu* retribution, divine punishment
[17]闇 *meian* gloom, shade

— 9 —

冨 See 富 1321. [宀]

冤 631/F215 冤 冤 EN false charge; hatred.
[8]枉 *en-ō* false charge
[13]罪 *enzai* false charge

— 13 —

冪 632/F216 See 羃 3651.

RAD. 冫 15

Ni-sui (two-stroke "water," as distinguished from Rad. 85). Also known as the "ice" radical because of its use in the early form of the character for *kōri* "ice."
Nickname: Ice.

— 3 —

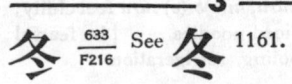

冬 633/F216 See 冬 1161.

— 4 —

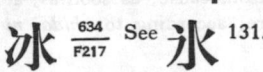

冰 634/F217 See 氷 131.

冴 635 / F218 **冴** Go. *sa(eru)* be clear; be serene; be cold, be skillful.

[6]行 *sa(e)-yu(ku)* gradually clear, gradually get cold
返 *sa(e)-kae(ru)* be very clear; be keenly cold
[7]冴 *sa(e)za(e) shita* cheerful (look), healthy (complexion)
[12]渡 *sa(e)-wata(ru)* get cold; freeze over
[15]輝 *sa(e)-kagaya(ku)* shine clearly

冲 636 / F218 F1081 See **冲** 2505.

B **兆** 637 / F182 **兆** Chō sign, omen, indication, portent; trillion. *kiza(su)* show signs or symptoms of. *kizashi* signs, omen, symptoms. [儿]

[5]民 *chōmin* the whole nation, all the people
[10]候 *chōkō* sign, indication, omen, symptom

A **次** 638 / F1026 Shi. Ji order, sequence; times; next; below. *tsu(gu)* rank next to, come after. *tsugi* next; stage station, stage. *tsugi ni* then, subsequently. *tsu(ide)* next, secondly, subsequently. *-ji* order. [欠]

[3]女 *jijo* second daughter
子 *jishi* the next child
[4]元 *jigen* dimension (in math)
[5]代 *jidai* the next era
兄 *jikei* second elder brother
打者 *jidasha* the batter on deck
[6]回 *jikai* next time
次 *tsugitsugi ni* one by one, one after another, successively
会 *jikai* the next meeting
号 *jigō* next issue
年 *jinen* the next year
[7]序 *jijo* order, system
位 *ji-i* second rank, second place
亜 *jia-* hypo- (in chemicals)
条 *jijō* the next article, the next entry
男 *jinan* second son
男坊 *jinambō* second son
[8]長 *jichō* vice- or assistant executive
官 *jikan* vice-minister, under-secretary, assistant secretary
表 *jihyō* the following table
[9]便 *jibin* the next mail
点 *jiten* runner-up
点者 *jitensha* runner-up
[10]席 *jiseki* associate, junior, assistant; runner-up
将 *jishō* second in command
[11]第 *shidai* order, precedence; circumstances, occasion; reason, cause; as soon as; at one's pleasure; according to. *shidai ni* gradually
第書 *shidaiga(ki)* printed program
[12]間 *tsugi(no)ma* antechamber; next room
期 *jiki* next term
善 *jizen no* second best
[13]数 *jisū* degree (in math)

5

状 See 2839. [犬]

況 639 / F218 F1087 See **況** 2516.

冶 640 / F218 Ya melting.

[3]工 *yakō* metallurgical worker
[8]金 *yakin* metallurgy
金学 *yakingaku* metallurgy (the science)
金学者 *yakingakusha* metallurgist

冴 641 / F218 See **冴** 635.

A **冷** 642 / F219 Rei cold, cool. *hi(eru)* cool down, grow cold; feel chilly. *hiya(su)* cool, refrigerate. *hi(yakasu)* cool, refrigerate; banter, make fun. *same(ru) vi* cool, get cold; abate, subside; dampen, cool down (interest); come down (a fever). *sama(su) vt* cool, let cool; dampen, throw a damper on, spoil. *hi(e)* chilling, exposure. *hiya* cold drinking water. *hi(yayakana)* cold; chilly; indifferent, coldhearted; surly, curt, cool, composed. *(o)hi(ya)* cold water; cold boiled rice. *tsume(tai)* cold, chilly, icy, freezing; coldhearted. *hi(yari) toshita* cool, chilly, cold.

[2]入 *hi(e)-i(ru)* become completely chilled
[3]上 *hi(e)-a(garu)* get completely chilled
[4]込 *hi(e)-ko(mu)* get colder; get chilled
切 *hi(e)-ki(ru)* become completely chilled
水 *hi(ya)mizu, reisui* cold water
水浴 *reisuiyoku* cold bath, cold shower
水摩擦 *reisui masatsu* cold rub
[5]奴 *hi(ya)yakko* iced tofu
[6]肉 *reiniku* cold meat
気 *reiki* cold, chill; cold weather; cold wave; cold air
汗 *hi(ya)-ase, reikan* cold sweat
光 *reikō* cold light, luminescence
血 *reiketsu* cold-bloodedness; coldheartedness
血動物 *reiketsu dōbutsu* cold-blooded animal
血漢 *reiketsukan* cold-blooded person
[7]冷 *hi(ya)hiya suru, hi(e)bi(e) suru* feel chilly; be fearful
麦 *hi(ya)mugi* iced noodles
却 *reikyaku* cooling, refrigeration

却期間 *reikyaku kikan* cooling-off period
却器 *reikyakuki* refrigerator, cooler, freezer; radiator (of a car)
8雨 *reiu* chilly rain
性 *hi(e)shō* sensitivity to cold
房 *reibō* air conditioning, aircooling
房完備 *reibō kambi* air-conditioned
房車 *reibōsha* air-conditioned car
房装置 *reibō sōchi* air-conditioning; air-cooling apparatus
9泉 *reisen* cold mineral springs
10剛 *reigō* chilling (steel)
酒 *hi(ya)zake, reishu* cold saké
害 *reigai* cold-weather damage
笑 *reishō* derisive smile, scornful laugh, sneer, cynicism
笑的 *reishōteki* sarcastic, derisive
凍 *reitō* refrigeration, freezing, cold storage
凍車 *reitōsha* refrigerator car
凍剤 *reitōzai* refrigerant
凍魚 *reitōgyo* refrigerated fish
凍船 *reitōsen* refrigerator ship
凍業 *reitōgyō* cold-storage business
凍器 *reitōki* deep freeze; freezer; refrigerating machine
11遇 *reigū* frigid reception, cold treatment
淡 *reitan* indifference, coolness, lukewarmness; cold-heartedness
眼 *reigan* cold look
12評 *reihyō* sarcasm, sneer, jeer
飯 *hi(ya)meshi* cold rice
募 *hi(e)-tsuno(ru)* get colder, get chilled
然 *reizen=reitan* 冷淡 (see above–11)
覚 *reikaku* sensation of cold
湿布 *reishippu* cold compress
13腹 *hi(e)bara* abdominal chills, diarrhea
戦 *reisen* cold war
罨法 *reiampō* cold compress, cold pack
14語 *reigo* hard words
酷 *reikoku* cruelty; heartlessness; bitterness
静 *reisei* calmness, coolness, composure, serenity
蔵 *reizō* cold storage, refrigeration
蔵車 *reizōsha* refrigerator car
蔵法 *reizōhō* refrigeration
蔵庫 *reizōko* refrigerator, icebox
蔵船 *reizōsen* refrigerator ship
15嘲 *reichō* cooling (something)
罵 *reiba* sneer, scoffing, abuse
熱 *reimetsu* heat and cold, temperature
17厳 *reigen na* grim, stern, stark, heartless

— 6 —

冽 643/F220 Retsu cold.
8冽 *retsuretsu* extremely cold

— 8 —

凉 644/F220 F1117 See **涼** 2598.

凋 645/F220 Chō. *shibo(mu)* (see under 萎 3973.0).
6尽 *chōjin* withering, decay, decline
10残 *chōzan* ruined blossoms
11悴 *chōsui* becoming emaciated
12落 *chōraku* decline, decay, fall, withering

凌 646/F221 Ryō. *shino(gu)* endure; keep out (rain); stave off; tide over, pull thru; defy; slight; surpass, excel, eclipse. *shinogi* tiding over.
8波性 *ryōhasei* seaworthiness
10辱 *ryōjoku* insult; outrage, rape
12場 *shino(gi)ba* shelter
雲 *ryōun no* skyscraping, very high
15駕 *ryōga suru* excel, surpass, outdo

凄 647/F220 Sei. *sugo(mu)* threaten. *sugo(i)* uncanny, weird; ghastly, horrible; intimidating; enormous; amazing. *susama(jii)* terrible; amazing; absurd.
4文句 *sugomonku* intimidating language
8味 *sugomi* weirdness, ghastliness, dreadfulness
11惨 *seisan* ghostliness, gruesomeness
12絶 *seizetsu na* weird, gruesome, lurid
13愴 *seisō na* desolate, dreary
19艶 *seien na* weirdly beautiful

B **准** 648/F220 F1143 **準** Jun quasi-, semi-, associate. *jun(jiru), jun(zuru)* (see under 準 791.0). *nazora(eru)* pattern after, liken to, imitate. *(ni) jun(jite)* in proportion (to).
3士官 *junshikan* warrant officer
6州 *junshū* a territory
7決勝 *junkesshō* semifinals
10将 *junshō* brigadier general; commodore
11尉 *jun-i* warrant officer
許 *junkyo* approval, sanction

B **凍** 649/F221 Tō. *kō(ru), shi(miru), i(teru)* freeze; be frozen over; congeal. *kō(rasu) vt* freeze, refrigerate. *kogo(ru) vi* congeal, freeze. *kogo(eru)* freeze, be chilled, be frozen. *kogo(raseru) vt* freeze, congeal, condense.
3土 *tōdo* frozen soil
5石 *tōseki* soapstone
付 *shi(mi)-tsu(ku), kō(ri)-tsu(ku), kogo(e)-tsu(ku)* freeze to, be frozen to
氷 *shi(mi)-kō(ru)* freeze hard, feel gloomy
6肉 *tōniku* frozen meat

死 *kogo(e)ji(nu), kogo(e)-shi(nu), tōshi suru* freeze to death, die of cold
死者 *tōshisha* person frozen to death
7 豆腐 *shimidōfu, kogo(ri)dōfu* frozen tofu
8 雨 *tōu* winter rain; freezing rain
10 原 *tōgen* tundra
害 *tōgai* frost damage
12 寒 *tōkan* frost, bitter cold
結 *tōketsu* freezing
結資産 *tōketsu shisan* frozen assets
結器 *tōketsuki* freezer
13 傷 *shimoyake, tōshō* frostbite, chilblains
傷者 *tōshōsha* a case of frostbite
15 瘡 *tōsō* chilblains, frostbite
16 餒 *tōtai, tōdai* privation

A 弱 650/F657 弱 JAKU weakness; the weak. *yowa(maru), yowa(ru) vi* weaken, be emaciated; be dejected; be perplexed. *yowa(meru) vt* weaken. *yowa-(ru) vt* impair, weaken, enfeeble. *yowa(i)* weak, feeble, frail, tender; unskilled; weak (wine). *(ka)yowa(i)* frail, feeble. *(hi)yowa(i)* weak, sickly. *-jaku* a little less than. [弓]

3 小 *jakushō* puniness; youth
小国 *jakushōkoku* minor power
4 込 *yowa(ri)-ko(mu)* weaken, be at wits' end
切 *yowa(ri)-ki(ru)* faint, be exhausted
少 *jakushō* puniness; youth
5 目 *yowa(ri)me* a time of weakness
目祟目 *yowa(ri)me (ni) tata(ri)me* misfortunes never come singly
6 虫 *yowamushi* weakling, coward
行 *jakkō* weakness in execution
気 *yowaki* faintheartedness; bearish sentiment
肉強食 *jakuniku-kyōshoku* survival of the fittest
年 *jakunen* youth
年者 *jakunemmono, jakunensha* youngster
7 身 *yowami* weakness
弟 *jakutei* young brother
志 *jakushi* weak will
材料 *yowazairyō* bearish factor
体 *jakutai* weak (organization)
体化 *jakutaika* weakening
8 国 *jakkoku* weak country
卒 *jakusotsu* cowardly soldier
者 *yowa(i)mono, yowa(ki)mono* weak person, the weak. *jakusha* the weak, the underdog
味 *yowami* weakness
味噌 *yowamiso* weakling, coward
9 冠 *jakkan* aged 20; youth
点 *jakuten* weak point
保合 *yowamochia(i)* (stock market) barely holding steady
音 *yowane* complaints. *jakuon* soft sound
音器 *jakuonki* damper, mute (on musical instruments)
10 衰 *yowa(ri)-otoro(eru)* languish
弱 *yowayowa(shii)* frail, slender, feminine
11 視 *jakushi* weak sight
13 腰 *yowagoshi* weak attitude
15 敵 *jakuteki* weak enemy
震 *jakushin* weak earthquake shock
輩 *jakuhai* young person; inexperienced person, a novice
17 齢 *jakurei* youth

13

凜 651/F222 凛 RIN cold.

8 冽 *rinretsu na* biting, severe, intense, rigorous
10 烈 *rinretsu*=word above
12 然 *rinzen(taru)* commanding, awe-inspiring
15 凜 *rinrin(taru)* severe, intense, biting. *riri-(shii)* gallant, chivalrous, manly, imposing, dignified, awe-inspiring

14

B 凝 652/F222 GYŌ. *kogo(rasu), kogo(raseru) vt* freeze, congeal. *ko(ru)* feel stiff, get stiff; be absorbed in, be devoted to, be a fanatic; to elaborate. *kogo(ru)* congeal, freeze. *ko(rasu)* concentrate, devote, apply, strain, rack. *shiko(ru)* stiffen, harden. *kori* stiffness, swelling, hardening. *ko(tta)* elaborate, exquisite, tasty, refined, artistic. *shiko-(ri)* muscle stiffness.

5 立 *gyōritsu* standing absolutely still
6 血 *gyōketsu suru* curdle. *gyōketsu* blood clot
8 性 *ko(ri)shō* enthusiasm for one thing; fastidiousness
乳 *gyōnyū* curd, curdled milk, rennet
念 *gyōnen* concentration of thought
固 *ko(ri)-kata(maru)* coagulate, curdle, clot; be fanatical. *korikata(mari)* coagulation, clot; enthusiast, fanatic. *gyōko* solidification, congealing, coagulation, condensation
固点 *gyōkoten* freezing point
10 脂 *gyōshi* solidified oil
11 視 *gyōshi* stare, steady gaze, fixation. *mitsu-(meru)* stare at, gaze at, fix the eyes on
望 *gyōbō suru* look intently
12 結 *gyōketsu* coagulation, curdling, setting, congealing, freezing, refrigeration, condensation, solidification
然 *gyokuzen toshite* quietly
集 *gyōshū* cohesion; condensation
集力 *gyōshūryoku* cohesive power
着 *gyōchaku* adhesion
着力 *gyōchakuryoku* adhesion
13 塊 *gyōkai* clot
滞 *gyōtai* delay
17 縮 *gyōshuku* condensation
20 議 *gyōgi* deliberation, consultation

RAD. 几 16

Tsukue table or *ki-nyō* "table" enclosure. Variant: 𠘨 *kazegamae* (enclosure like that of *kaze* "wind"). Nickname: Windy (cf. Rad. 182).

几 653/F223 KI table.

11 帳 *kichō* a screen
帳面 *kichōmen na* methodical, punctual, steady

凡 B 654/F223 凡 凢 HAN. BON mediocrity. *oyo(so)*, *ōyo(so)* as a rule; approximately. *sube(te)* all, the whole; entirely; in general. *a(rayuru)* all, every.

2 人 *bonjin, bonnin* ordinary person, mediocre
3 小 *bonshō* small and of mediocre talent
凡 *bombon(taru)* ordinary, usual
才 *bonsai* mediocrity, ordinary ability
4 手 *bonshu* mediocre ability, a person of ordinary skills
夫 *bompu, bombu* ordinary man
5 打 *bonda* poor batting
失 *bonshitsu* a common mistake
6 百 *bompyaku, bombyaku* many, many kinds
7 作 *bonsaku* poor piece of writing
8 退 *bontai* out in 1-2-3 order
例 *hanrei* introductory remarks, explanatory notes
9 俗 *bonzoku* mediocrity; the masses, ordinary run of men
10 骨 *bonkotsu* ordinary person
流 *bonryū* ordinary style
書 *bonsho* ordinary book; ordinary handwriting
11 庸 *bon-yō* mediocrity; commonplace
庶 *bonsho* common people
眼 *bongan* (thru) a layman's eyes
常 *bonjō na* ordinary, common
12 策 *bonsaku* commonplace policy
13 僧 *bonsō* unranked priest, ordinary priest
戦 *bonsen* dull game
愚 *bongu* common person; foolish commoner
15 慮 *bonryo* ordinary minds, ordinary men
器 *bonki* ordinary talent

3

凧 655/F224 (国字) *ikanobori, tako* kite.

12 揚 *takoa(ge)* kite flying

4

凩 656/F224 (国字) *kogarashi* wintry wind.

凪 657/F224 (国字) *nagi* lull, calm. *na(gu)* become calm, die down.

夙 658/F452 SHUKU. *tsuto ni* bright and early; early in life; long ago; for a long time. *madoki ni* earlier, already, beforehand. [夕]

6 成 *shukusei* precocity
7 志 *shukushi* long-cherished desire
8 夜 *shukuya* from morning till night; day and night; always

6

凭 659/F224 HYŌ. HEI. *mota(reru)* lean on, recline on; lie heavy (on the stomach). *yo(ru)* lean on, rest against.

11 掛 *mota(se)-ka(keru) vt* lean against, set against. *mota(re)-ka(karu)*, *yo(ri)-ka(karu) vi* lean on, recline on; rely on
12 椅子 *mota(re) isu* reclining chair

9

凰 660/F224 Ō. KŌ female phoenix bird.

10

凱 661/F224 GAI victory song.

11 旋 *gaisen* triumphal return
旋門 *gaisemmon* arch of triumph
旋軍 *gaisengun* returning victorious army
14 歌 *gaika* victory song; victory

12

鳳 662/F2138 HŌ male phoenix bird. [鳥]

5 仙花 *hōsenka* balsam
7 声 *hōsei* verbal message
11 凰 *hōō* mythical phoenix bird
15 輦 *hōren* imperial carriage
駕 *hōga* imperial carriage

RAD. 凵 17

Ukebako open box or *kangamae* "open box" enclosure. Nickname: Open Box.

2

B 凶 **663/F225** Kyō evil; bad luck; disaster; bad harvest.

3 刃 *kyōjin* assassin's dagger
4 手 *kyōshu* assassin
日 *kyōjitsu, kyōnichi* unlucky day
6 行 *kyōkō* violence, murder, crime
兆 *kyōchō* evil omen
宅 *kyōtaku* unlucky house
年 *kyōnen* bad year, bad harvest
7 作 *kyōsaku* bad harvest, poor crop
状 *kyōjō* crime, offense
状持 *kyōjōmo(chi)* a criminal
8 具 *kyōgu* dangerous weapon
事 *kyōji* calamity, misfortune
9 音 *kyōin* bad news; news of a death
変 *kyōhen* catastrophe; assassination
荒 *kyōkō* poor crops; famine
10 徒 *kyōto* rioter, outlaw, rebel
党 *kyōtō* gang, gangsters
11 猛 *kyōmō* fierce
悪 *kyōaku na* atrocious, fiendish, brutal
12 報 *kyōhō* bad news
13 漢 *kyōkan* villain, outlaw, assassin
賊 *kyōzoku* villain
歳 *kyōsai* poor-crop year
夢 *kyōmu* bad dream, inauspicious dream
14 聞 *kyōbun* bad news
15 暴 *kyōbō* brutality, ferocity, atrocity
器 *kyōki* dangerous weapon
18 類 *kyōrui* wicked gang

3

出 See 97.

凸 See 90.

凹 **664/F226** Ō hollow, sunken. *heko(mu)* be dented, be indented, yield to, give, sink, collapse, cave in; be snubbed; be defeated. *heko(maseru)*, *heko(masu)* *vt* dent, indent, depress; humiliate. *kubo(maru)* be low (as a hollow). *kubo(meru)*, hollow out. *kubo, boko* hollow, depression. *heko(mi)* dent, hollow, depression.

5 田 *kubota* rice field in a low place
凸 *ōtotsu* unevenness, roughness, ruggedness
6 地 *ōchi* depression, hollow, pit, basin
7 形 *ōkei* intaglio; concavity
8 所 *ōsho* concavity, cavity, hollow, depression
版 *ōhan, ōban* intaglio (printing)
9 面 *ōmen* concavity
面鏡 *ōmenkyō* concave lens or mirror
11 眼 *ōgan* cavernous eyes
眼鏡 *ōgankyō* concave glasses
18 溜 *kubotama(ri)* a hollow; a pond in a hollow

6

函 凾 See 49.

画 See 50. [田]

7

幽 See 112. [幺]

RAD. 刀 18

Katana sword. At right: 刂 *rittō* standing "sword." Nickname: Sword.

A 刀 **665/F229** Tō sword, saber, knife, engraving tool. *katana* sword, blade.

3 工 *tōkō* swordsmith
下 *tōka ni* under the sword
刃 *tōjin* sword blade
4 手前 *katana (no) temae* a samurai's face
5 礼 *tōrei* sword salute
6 自 *tōji* lady, matron, mistress, housekeeper
匠 *tōshō* swordsmith
圭 *tōkei* doctor
圭家 *tōkeika* doctor
7 身 *tōshin* sword blade
9 持 *katanamo(chi)* swordbearer
架 *tōka* sword rack
背 *tōhai, mine* back of a sword

背打 *mineu(chi)* striking with the back of the sword
10 剣 *tōken* sword
剣商 *tōkenshō* sword dealer
11 痕 *tōkon* sword scar
疵 *katana kizu* sword wound
掛 *katanaka(ke)* sword rack
12 筆吏 *tōhitsu (no) ri* minor official
13 傷 *tōshō* sword cut
14 鋩 *tōbō* point of a sword
17 鍛冶 *katana kaji* swordsmith
20 懸 *katanakake* sword rack

1

刈 刃 刄 See 152.

2

分 分 See 578.

刈 666 / F234 B KAI. *ka(ru)* cut, clip; shear; reap; trim, prune.
2 入 *ka(ri)-i(reru)* harvest, reap
入人 *kari-i(re)bito* reapers
3 干 *ka(ri)-ho(su)* cut and dry (in the sun)
上 *ka(ri)-a(geru)* reap completely; trim up (the hair); dress up
4 手 *ka(ri)te* mower, reaper
込 *ka(ri)-ko(mu)* cut, trim, clip; dress, prune. *kariko(mi)* haircut, pruning
5 田 *ka(ri)ta* harvested rice field
立 *karita(te)* new-mown; newly cut (hair)
8 取 *ka(ri)-to(ru)* mow, reap, harvest
取機 *karito(ri)ki* reaping machine
9 除 *kaijo suru* remove, cut off
10 株 *ka(ri)kabu* stubble
根 *ka(ri)ne* stubble
12 葺 *ka(ri)-fu(ku)* thatch (a roof)
13 跡 *ka(ri)ato* cut-over land
15 穂 *ka(ri)ho* harvested grain

切 667 / F233 A SETSU. SAI. *ki(ru)* cut, chop, hash; carve; saw; clip, shear; slice, strip; fell, cut down; punch; sever (connections); pause, break off; disconnect, turn off; hang up; cross (a street); discount, sell below cost; shake (water) off. *ki(reru)* cut well, be sharp; break, snap; wear out; be injured; burst, collapse; break off, be disconnected; be out of; expire; sever (connections) with; sharp, shrewd; less than. *ki(rasu)* *vt* be out of, be short of. *ki(re)* cloth; piece, cut, chop, strip, slice, scrap; counter for such. *ki(ri)* limits, end, bounds; period, place to leave off, closing sentence. *setsu na* earnest, eager; kind; keen, acute. *setsu(nai)* oppressive, suffocating; painful, trying. *-kitte no* the most . . . of all. *-ki(ru)* finish, be thru, complete; be able to. *-ki(ri)* all there is; only; since.
2 入 *ki(ri)-i(ru)* cut into, raid. *ki(ri)-(reru)* cut and insert
3 子 *ki(ri)ko* facet
干 *kiribo(shi)* dried daikon strips
下 *ki(ri)-o(rosu)* slash downward. *ki(ri)-sa(geru)* cut down, prune; cut and hang down; reduce, cut shorter
上 *ki(ri)-a(geru)* close, finish. *kiria(ge)* end, conclusion
口 *ki(ri)kuchi* cut end, section; opening, slit
口上 *ki(ri)kōjō* stiff formality, set terms
4 戸 *ki(ri)do* low gate, side gate
方 *ki(ri)kata* how to cut, how to slice
火 *ki(ri)bi* Shinto fire-purification ceremony; flint sparks
片 *seppen* cut-off scraps
切 *ki(re)gi(re)* pieces, scraps. *setsusetsu* politeness; feeling of loneliness
支丹 *Kirishitan* (early) Japanese Christianity
手 *ki(re)te* man of ability. *kitte* postage stamp; merchandise certificate. *ki(ri)te* cutter, certificate
手蒐集 *kitte shūshū* philately
込 *ki(ri)-ko(mu)* cut into; raid, attack; cut up. *ki(re)-ko(mu)* cut into. *ki(re)ko(mi)* cut, notch, incision
込炭 *ki(ri)ko(mi)tan* run-of-the-mine coal
分 *ki(ri)-waka(tsu)*, *ki(ri)-wa(keru)* cut up
分法 *setsubunhō* syncopation
5 目 *ki(re)me* rift, gap, break; pause, interruption. *ki(ri)me* cut, section, notch, incision; end (of a task)
石 *ki(ri)-ishi* hewn stone, quarried stone
立 *ki(ri)-ta(teru)* cut, slash, slay all. *ki(ri)-ta(tsu)* rise perpendicularly. *ki(ri)ta(te)* freshly cut. *ki(ri)ta(tta)* steep, precipitous
付 *ki(ri)-tsu(keru)* slash at a person
外 *ki(ri)-hazu(su)* miss in attempting to kill
払 *ki(ri)-hara(u)* clear away; clear land; prune, lop off
札 *ki(ri)fuda* trump card
去 *ki(ri)-sa(ru)* cut off
出 *ki(ri)-da(su)*, *ki(ri)-ida(su)* quarry; cut (timber); cut and carry off; begin to talk, break the ice. *ki(ri)da(shi)* pointed knife; logging; (beef) scraps; starting to speak
6 回 *ki(ri)-mawa(su)* run around killing; manage everything, control; cut carelessly (a cook or a surgeon)
死 *ki(ri)ji(ni)* fighting to the death (with swords)
返 *ki(ri)kae(shi)* railway switchback
伏 *ki(ri)-fu(seru)* slay, cut down (a foe)
地 *ki(re)ji* cloth
合 *ki(ri)a(i)* crossing swords, fighting with swords, cutting each other (in fighting)

2 二亠人亻𠆢儿入八丷冂冖冫几凵[刀 2刂]力勹匕匚匸十卜卩厂厶又

先 *ki(s)saki* point of a sword; =*hokosaki* 矛先 3164.6
羽 *kiriha* coal face, working face
羽詰 *seppatsu(maru)* be at one's wit's end, be cornered
7言 *setsugen* urging, persuasion; declaration
身 *ki(ri)mi* slice, chop
迫 *seppaku* pressure, urgency; imminence; acuteness, tenseness
形 *ki(ri)kata* a way to cut, a way to slice
花 *ki(ri)bana* cut flowers
狂言 *ki(ri)kyōgen* last act
抜 *ki(ri)-nu(keru)* cut one's way thru, tide over, struggle thru. *ki(ri)-nu(ku)* cut out, clip from, extract. *kirinu(ki)* scraps
抜帖 *kirinu(ki)chō* scrapbook
売 *kiriu(ri)* selling by the piece
売主義 *kiriu(ri) shugi* prostitution
8味 *ki(re)aji* sharpness (of a sword), the feel of a cutting edge
拡 *ki(ri)-hiro(geru)* cut and enlarge
放 *ki(ri)-hana(su)*, *ki(ri)-hana(tsu)* cut loose, let loose, cut off, detach, dismember,
枝 *ki(ri)eda* slips (to plant) ⌊cut in two
杭 *ki(ri)kui* stump ⌈businessman
物 *ki(re)mono* edged tool; cutlery; shrewd
刻 *ki(ri)-kiza(mu)* hew, chop up, mangle, mince ⌈sincerely, urgently
実 *setsujitsu ni* strongly, keenly, vividly,
岸 *ki(ri)gishi* steep bank, cliff
妻 *ki(ri)zuma* gable
取 *ki(ri)-to(ru)* cut off, cut out; whittle down; tear out; cut down; amputate. *kirito(ri)* cutting; tearing off, cutting off; robbery with assault, burglary; robber, burglar
取強盗 *kirito(ri) gōtō* violent robbery, burglary; robber, burglar
取線 *kirito(ri) sen* perforated line
9屋 *ki(re)ya* dry-goods store
通 *ki(ri)-tō(su)* cut thru (with a road, tunnel, or canal). *kiridō(shi)* (railway) cut
枯 *ki(ri)-ka(rasu)* destroy, kill off (trees)
畑 *ki(ri)hata*, *ki(ri)batake* hillside farm; fallow ground
除 *ki(ri)-no(keru)*, *setsujo suru* cut off, cut
炭 *ki(ri)zumi* cut-up charcoal ⌊out
10屑 *ki(ri)kuzu* scraps, chips. *ki(re)kuzu* cloth scraps ⌈cultivation
起 *ki(ri)-oko(su)* open up waste land for
倒 *ki(ri)-tao(su)* cut down, chop down, fell
株 *ki(ri)kabu* stump, stubble
破 *ki(ri)-yabu(ru)* cut to pieces ⌈paper scrap
紙 *ki(ri)kami* cut paper, paper cut in half,
釘 *ki(ri)kugi* brad; double-pointed nail
殺 *ki(ri)-koro(su)* slay

11痔 *ki(re)ji* anal fistula
疵 *ki(ri)kizu* a cut, a gash
張 *kiriba(ri)* patching ⌈killing a commoner
得 *ki(ri)doku* no retribution for a samurai
情 *setsujō* ardent love
接 *ki(ri)tsu(gi)* grafting ⌈discard
捨 *ki(ri)-su(teru)* cut down, slay; omit,
掛 *ki(k)ka(ke)* chance; start; clue; excuse
捲 *ki(ri)-maku(ru)* slash about, attack and
据 *ki(ri)-su(eru)* cut down an enemy ⌊scatter
組 *ki(ri)-ku(mu)* piece together; mortise; miter; dovetail
崩 *ki(ri)-kuzu(su)* level (a hill); cut thru (a mountain); break (a strike); split (the opposition)
窓 *ki(ri)mado* windows cut out of a wall
笥 *ki(ri)-saina(mu)* hack to pieces
望 *setsubō* earnest desire, longing
盛 *kirimo(ri)* management, administration; preparing food
乾 *ki(ri)boshi* dried strips of daikon
細裂 *ki(ri)-komaza(ku)* cut up small
符 *kippu* ticket ⌈puncher
符切 *kippuki(ri)* ticket punch; ticket
符売 *kippu-u(ri)* ticket seller
符売場 *kippu uriba* ticket window; box office, ticket ⌈amputation
断 *setsudan* section; cutting, severance,
断図 *setsudanzu* sectional drawing
断面 *setsudammen* section (in drawing)
断患者 *setsudan kanja* amputee
断機 *setsudanki* cutter, cutting machine
12開 *sekkai suru*, *ki(ri)-hira(ku)* clear (land), open up; cut thru. *sekkai* incision, operation, section. *ki(ri)hira(ki)* clearing (land); excavating
間 *ki(re)ma* interval, break, rift (in clouds)
場 *ki(ri)ba* coal face, working face
揃 *ki(ri)-soro(eru)* cut and even up, cut several pieces to the same size
結 *ki(ri)-musu(bu)* cross swords with
貼 *kiriba(ri)* patching
創 *ki(ri)kizu* cut, gash; incision
割 *ki(ri)-wa(ru)* cut in two ⌈miscuously
散 *ki(ri)-chi(rasu)* cut down all, slash pro-
落 *ki(ri)-oto(su)* cut down, lop off, prune
無 *ki(ri) (no) na(i)* endless, boundless. *ki(ri)na(shi)* always, continuously. *-ki(re)na(i)* cannot, be unable to. *-ki(ra)na(i)* not thru, not finished
裂 *ki(ri)-sa(ku)* cut off, cut up; cut to pieces
歯 *sesshi* gnashing of teeth
歯扼腕 *sesshi-yakuwan suru* be enraged, be indignant, be impatient, gnashing the teeth and clenching the arms on the breast (in anger or regret)

換 *ki(ri)-ka(eru)* change, exchange, convert, renew; throw a switch; replace; switch over ⌈time to renew (a license)
換時 *kirika(e)doki* time to switch over;
替 *ki(ri)-kawa(ru)* change completely. *ki(ri)-ka(eru)* change, exchange, convert, renew, throw a switch, replace; switch over ⌈12)
替時 *kirika(e)doki*＝切換時 (see above-
13 傷 *ki(ri)kizu* cut, gash
継 *ki(ri)tsu(gi) suru* cut and patch
腹 *seppuku* disembowelment, harakiri
解 *ki(ri)-hodo(ku)* cut open a tied bundle; releasing prisoners
詰 *ki(ri)-tsu(meru)* shorten; reduce, economize. *ki(ri)tsu(me)* retrenchment, curtailment
毀 *ki(ri)-kowa(su)* cut to pieces
愛 *setsuai* deep love ⌈sion
賃 *ki(ri)chin* brokerage, exchange commis-
暖簾 *ki(ri)noren* a short split entrance cur-
14 嘖 *ki(ri)-saina(mu)* hack to pieces ⌊tain
端 *ki(re)hashi, ki(rep)pashi, ki(ri)hashi* scraps, cut end, cut-off piece
髪 *ki(ri)gami* bobbed hair
15 線 *sessen* tangent (in trigonometry)
論 *setsuron* persistent argument
調 *ki(ri)-totono(eru)* trim (hedges)
幣 *ki(ri)nusa* paper and sacred *sakaki* branches cut and mixed with rice to scatter before the gods ⌈(character)
磋 *sessa* polishing (stones); polishing
磋琢磨 *sessa-takuma* diligent application
16 諫 *sekkan* admonition, expostulation
整 *ki(ri)-totono(eru)* cut and prepare (stones)
17 縮 *ki(ri)-chiji(meru)* cut smaller; economize
19 願 *setsugan* entreaty, supplication
縄 *ki(ri)nawa* piece of rope cut for a certain purpose
離 *ki(ri)-hana(reru)* cut off and separate
22 籠 *ki(ri)ko* facet

3

刊 See 1493.

召 668/F323 SHŌ. *me(su)* call, send for; wear, put on; take (a bath); ride in; buy; eat, drink; catch (a cold). *me(shi)* summons, a call. *(o)me(shi)* summons, a call; dressing; clothing; striped crepe. [口] B
2 入 *me(shi)-i(reru)* call in
3 上 *me(shi)-a(garu)* eat (polite). *me(shi)-a(geru)* forfeit, confiscate; call out
上物 *me(shi)a(gari)mono* food
5 出 *me(shi)-da(su)* call out, summon
7 状 *shōjō* letter of invitation ⌈employ
8 使 *me(shi)tsuka(i)* servant. *me(shi)-tsuka(u)*
抱 *me(shi)-kaka(eru)* employ, engage. *meshikaka(e)* mercenary troops
物 *me(shi)mono* clothing (polite)
命 *shōmei* call; divine call
9 連 *me(shi)-tsu(reru)* bring along, accompany
10 捕 *me(shi)-to(ru)* arrest, apprehend
致 *shōchi suru* call together
11 寄 *me(shi)-yo(seru)* call (someone) to you, call together, call to come
12 換 *me(shi)ka(e)* change of clothes
募 *shōbo* levy, enlistment
替 *me(shi)ka(e)* change of clothes
喚 *shōkan* summons
喚状 *shōkanjō* call, summons, subpoena
集 *shōshū suru, me(shi)-atsu(meru)* call together
集令 *shōshūrei* mustering-out order
15 還 *shōkan* recall
請 *shōsei suru* call together

4

列 See 2438.

刕 Nonstandard for 州 99.

师 Nonstandard for 師 113.

刎 669/F234 FUN. *ha(neru)* decapitate.
3 上 *ha(ne)-a(garu)* jump up, spring up
6 死 *funshi* decapitating oneself
16 頸 *funkei* decapitation

刑 670/F234 KEI penalty, sentence, punishment. *kei(suru)* sentence. B
6 死 *keishi* execution
名 *keimei* penalty designations
吏 *keiri* executioner
7 余 *keiyo* previous conviction
余者 *keiyosha* ex-convict
8 法 *keihō* criminal law
具 *keigu* instruments of punishment
典 *keiten* criminal law books
事 *keiji* criminal case; detective
事上 *keijijō no* penal, criminal
事犯 *keijihan* criminal offense ⌈criminal
事処分 *keiji shobun* punishment of a
事事件 *keiji jiken* criminal case
事被告 *keiji hikoku* the accused
事被告人 *keiji hikokunin* the accused

事裁判 *keiji saiban* criminal trial
事訴訟 *keiji soshō* criminal action
9律 *keiritsu* criminal law
10徒 *keito* condemned person, prisoner
11務作業 *keimu sagyō* prison industry
務官 *keimukan* prison guard
務所 *keimusho* prison, penitentiary
務所長 *keimushochō* warden
12場 *keijō* place of execution
期 *keiki* prison term
14獄 *keigoku* jail; punishment
罰 *keibatsu* judgment, penalty, punishment
15戮 *keiriku* punishment, penalty; execution

5

利 See 3264.

初 See 4215.

免 See 免 573. [儿]

刦 671/F239/F260 刧 See 劫 718.

删 672/F237 SAN cut down.

8定 *santei* revision of a passage
10修 *sanshū* revision, reform

A **判** 673/F237 判 HAN stamp, seal; a monogram signature; judgment. *han(jiru)* judge, decide; guess; solve, decipher, interpret; divine. *waka(ru)* (see under 分 578.0). *-ban* size (of paper or books).

3士 *hanshi* judge advocate
子 *hanko* personal seal
6任官 *hanninkan* junior official
7決 *hanketsu* judgment, decision, decree, sentence
別 *hambetsu* distinction, discrimination
8例 *hanrei* judicial precedent
明 *hammei suru* become clear, be confirmed
物 *han(ji)mono* puzzle, riddle
官 *hangan* judge, magistrate
者 *hanja* judge (of literary contests)
事 *hanji* judge
取 *hanto(ri)* traveling around getting seal stamps
取帳 *hanto(ri)chō* chit book, delivery book
定 *hantei* judgment, decision, award, verdict
定勝 *hanteiga(chi)* winning on a decision
11断 *handan* judgment, decision, adjudication, conclusion; decipherment; divination
断力 *handanryoku* judgment, discernment
12絵 *han(ji)e* picture puzzle
然 *hanzen(taru)* clear, distinct, evident, definite
検事 *hankenji* judges and prosecutors
14読 *handoku* decipherment, interpretation, making out
読難 *handoku(shi)gata(i)* illegible

A **別** 674/F238 別 BETSU. *wa(keru)*, *waka(tsu)* (see under 分 578.0). *waka(reru)* branch off, diverge from, fork; split; be divided; part with; be divorced; bid farewell; break up, disperse, scatter. *betsu* another, different, particular, separate; extra; exception; difference, distinction. *betsu ni* specially, particularly. *bes(shite)* especially, particularly. *waka(chi)* distinction, discrimination, differentiation. *waka(re)* branch, fork; division, section; farewell. *wake(te)* above all, especially, all the more. *-betsu* classified by.

2人 *betsujin*, *betsunin* different person, changed man
3口 *betsukuchi* different item, different lot, different kind
与 *waka(chi)-ata(eru)* divide and pass around
4戸 *bekko* separate house
切 *waka(ri)-ki(ru)* understand completely
天地 *bettenchi* another world
5目 *waka(re)me* turning point, junction, parting of the ways
冊 *bessatsu* separate volume, extra issue, supplement
仕立 *betsushita(te)* tailormade
世界 *bessekai* another world
6行 *betsugyō* another line
号 *betsugō* another name
宅 *bettaku* secondary residence
当 *bettō* groom, footman, stableman, equerry; intendant, steward
争 *waka(re)-araso(u)* quarrel and separate
名 *betsumei*, *betsumyō* another name, alias, pseudonym
7言 *betsugen sureba* in other words. *betsugen* other words
状 *betsujō* a different situation
別 *betsubetsu ni*, *waka(re)-waka(re) ni* separately, apart, severally, individually
形 *bekkei* another form (of a character)
邸 *bettei* villa, detached residence
条 *betsujō* something unusual
8居 *bekkyo* separation, limited divorce
送 *bessō* separate mail, separate shipment
使 *besshi* special messenger; another messenger
杯 *beppai* farewell cup, farewell dinner
法 *beppō* different method
物 *betsumono* another thing, exception, special case
表 *beppyō* an annexed (statistical) table
事 *betsuji* another affair; mishap

9途 *betto* special, special reserve (account)
便 *betsubin de* by separate post
後 *betsugo* since we parted
派 *beppa* different sect, party, or school
珍 *betchin* velveteen
科 *bekka* special course; another course
院 *betsuin* branch temple
封 *beppū de* under separate cover
段 *betsudan* special, particular
盃 *beppai* farewell cup; farewell dinner
前 *wa(ke)mae* share, quota
品 *beppin* a beautiful woman (vulgar)
室 *besshitsu* separate room, special room
荘 *bessō* villa
染 *betsuzo(me)* special dyeing
除権 *betsujoken* right of exclusion
10席 *besseki* different seat, special seat, separate room ⌈another
個 *bekko no* several, separate, different,
時 *betsuji* another time; time of separation
格 *bekkaku* special, extraordinary
称 *besshō* another name, alias, pseudonym
紙 *besshi* enclosure
納 *betsunō* another method of payment
記 *bekki* separate paragraph; separate
家 *bekke* branch family ⌊volume
宴 *betsuen* farewell dinner
書 *waka(chi)gaki*＝分書 578.10
配達 *betsu haitatsu* special delivery
11道 *waka(re)michi* forked road, crossroads, branch road, parting of the ways
堂 *betsudō* separate building
勘定 *betsu kanjō* separate account ⌈force
動隊 *betsu dōtai* flying column, detached
問題 *betsu mondai* a different thing, another question, a different case
12間 *betsuma* separate room, special room
項 *bekkō* separate paragraph; special heading ⌈ing
棟 *betsumune* outbuilding, detached build-
隔 *wa(ke)heda(te)* distinction, favoritism
無 *betsuna(ku)* without distinction
報 *beppō* another report
13殿 *betsuden* palace annex, shrine annex
辞 *betsuji* farewell address, parting words
誂 *betsu atsura(e)* special order
路 *betsuro* different road. *waka(re)michi* forked road. *waka(re)ji* parting of the ways; the way to hades; one's way after the parting
意 *betsui* different opinion, ill will; intention to part
業 *betsugyō* villa; another line of work
働隊 *betsu dōtai* flying column, detached force ⌈variety
14種 *besshu* another kind, distinct species,
箇 *bekko*＝別個 (see above–10)
製 *bessei* special make
15趣 *besshu* deep interest
儀 *betsugi* other affair, special matter
16館 *bekkan* annex
17嬪 *beppin* beauty, beautiful woman, pretty
懇 *bekkon* intimacy ⌊girl
19離 *betsuri* parting, separation

6

刮 See 3857.

到 See 3846.

兔 675/F188 See **兎** 198. [儿]

刲 676/F241 KEI pierce.

刮 677/F-X KATSU tear off.

A **券** 678/F243 **劵** KEN ticket, coupon, bond, certificate.
9面 *kemmen* the face of a bond, draft, or certificate

刹 679/F243 SECHI. SETSU. SATSU temple.
6那 *setsuna* moment, instant, juncture
那的 *setsunateki* ephemeral, transitory

刳 680/F241 **刳** KO. *egu(ru)* gouge, hollow out, bore, excavate. *ku(ru)* bore; gouge; scoop out, hollow out; excavate.
6舟 *kuribune* dugout canoe ⌈drill
7抜 *ku(ri)-nu(ku)* gouge out; excavate; bore,
形 *kurikata* molding
11貫 *ku(ri)-nu(ku)*＝刳抜 (see above–7)

刷 See 210.

B **刻** 681/F244 KOKU time; carving, engraving, cutting. *kiza(mu)* cut fine, chop up; mince, hash; carve (images); engrave (seals); chisel, cut, notch. *ho(ru)* (see under 彫 236.0). *kiza(mi)* shredded tobacco; notch, nick. *kiza* scratch.
1一刻 *koku-ikkoku* moment by moment;
3下 *kokka* the present ⌊hour by hour
5目 *kiza(mi)me* notch, nick, marks on a ruler
付 *kiza(mi)-tsu(keru)* engrave, carve out

出 *kiza(mi)-da(su)* carve out
本 *kokuhon* wood-block book
6 印 *kokuin* carved seal ⌈acters
字 *kokuji* carving characters; carved char-
7 足 *kiza(mi)ta(shi)* mincing steps
8 限 *kokugen* time, appointed time
刻 *kokukoku, kokkoku ni* moment by mo-
苦 *kokku* hard work ⌊ment; hour by hour
13 煙草 *kiza(mi) tabako* shredded tobacco
16 薄 *kokuhaku* cruelty

B **刺** 682 F243 SHI calling card. *sa(su)* pierce, thrust, stab, prick; bite, sting; pin down; sew, stitch; put (a runner) out; pole (a boat); catch (with a line); stick. *sa(saru)* stick, be stuck. *ira, toge* thorn, splinter; spine; biting words. *sashi* sharpened tube for testing rice in bags.
3 子 *sashiko* a lined garment with over-all
7 抜 *togenu(ki)* tweezers, forceps ⌊stitching
身 *sashimi* sliced raw fish
身庖丁 *sashimibōchō* fish-slicing knife
8 青 *irezumi, shisei* tattooing
股 *sasumata* two-pronged weapon for catching a criminal
刺 *ira-ira suru* get nervous, fret, get irritated. *togetoge(shii)* sharp, harsh, stinging
9 通 *sa(shi)-tō(su)* stab, pierce, run (a sword)
客 *shikaku, sekkaku* assassin ⌊thru
草 *irakusa* nettle
10 殺 *sa(shi)-koro(su)* stab to death. *shisatsu suru* put out (in baseball); stab to death
11 違 *sa(shi)-chiga(eru)* stab at each other
貫 *sa(shi)-tsuranu(ku)* pierce
12 絡 *shiraku* bloodletting
戟 *shigeki* stimulus, impetus, incentive, excitement, irritation, encouragement
戟性 *shigekisei* stimulative, incentive, irritative
戟物 *shigekibutsu* stimulus, incentive
戟的 *shigekiteki* stimulating
戟剤 *shigekizai* stimulant
13 傷 *shishō, sa(shi)kizu* stab; puncture wound
14 網 *sa(shi)ami* gill net
15 衝 *shishō* stabbing; stimulation
16 激 *shigeki*＝刺戟 (see above–12)
激的 *shigekiteki* stimulating ⌈sewing
19 繡 *shishū* embroidery. *nui* embroidery,

A **制** 683 F241 SEI system, organization; imperial command; laws, regulation. *sei(suru)* control, govern, suppress, restrain, hold back; establish.
4 止 *seishi* control, check, restraint, inhibition ⌈ascendancy, supremacy
5 圧 *seiatsu* oppression, control, mastery,
札 *seisatsu* roadside prohibition-edict boards
令 *seirei* regulations
7 肘 *seichū*＝掣肘 1923.7 ⌈etc.)
作 *seisaku* production (of a painting, book,
作室 *seisakushitsu* studio, workshop
8 定 *seitei* enactment, establishment, creation
服 *seifuku* uniform
服制帽 *seifuku-seibō* cap and uniform
空 *seikū* mastery of the air
空権 *seikūken* mastery of the air
限 *seigen* limit, limitation, restriction
限速度 *seigen sokudo* speed limit
限漢字 *seigen kanji* restricted Chinese characters
9 度 *seido* system, organization, institution
約 *seiyaku* condition, limitation, restriction
海権 *seikaiken* control of the seas
11 欲 *seiyoku* control of passions, control of
規 *seiki*＝正規 27.11 ⌊appetite
球 *seikyū* (pitcher's) control
球力 *seikyūryoku* (pitcher's) control
動 *seidō* breaking (mechanism)
動手 *seidōshu* brakeman
動機 *seidōki* brake
12 帽 *seibō* regulation cap; school cap
勝 *seishō* victory, championship
馭 *seigyo*＝制御 (see below–12)
裁 *seisai* restraint, punishment, sanctions
御 *seigyo* control, governing; checking, suppression; repression; restraint; mastery; management
御盤 *seigyoban* switchbox
御器 *seigyoki* controller, regulator
御機 *seigyoki* controller, regulator
14 酸剤 *seisanzai* anti-acid preparation
17 禦 *seigyo*＝制御 (see above–12)
19 覇 *seiha* conquest, domination, supremacy, mastery; championship

7

勉 684 F262 See **勉** 228. [力]

則 See 4487.

前 See 595.

負 685 F1787 See **負** 4488. [貝]

剋 686 F246 See **剋** 776.

剄 687 F245 KEI beheading.

剌 688/F246 RATSU oppose; be biased.

荆 689/F1601 **荊 荊** KEI thorn; whip. *ibara* thorn, brier. [艹]

8妻 *keisai* my wife
9冠 *keikan* crown of thorns
12棘 *bara, keikyoku* brambles, thorns

B **削** 690/F245 **削** SAKU. *kezu(ru)* plane, sharpen, whittle, pare, shave (leather); scrape off; cross out; reduce, curtail. *so(gu), so(geru)* (see under 殺 2454.0). *hatsu(ru)* cutting down little by little; taking a percentage.

4片 *sakuhen* splinter, chip
5氷機 *sakuhyōki* ice-shaving machine
8取 *kezu(ri)-to(ru)* shave off, scrape off
9除 *sakujo* elimination, cancellation, deletion, erasure
10屑 *kezu(ri)kuzu* shavings
12減 *sakugen* reduction, curtailment
落 *kezu(ri)-oto(su)* scrape off, plane off
13節 *kezu(ri)bushi* flaked bonito
15摩 *sakuma* denudation

剃 691/F245 TEI. *so(ru), su(ru)* shave.

2刀 *kamisori* razor
刀気触 *kamisori kabure* razor rash
刀研 *kamisoritogi* one who sharpens razors
刀負 *kamisorima(ke)* razor rash
刀砥 *kamisorido* razor strop; hone
3上額 *suria(ge)bitai* high and broad forehead
5立 *surita(te), sorita(te) no* clean shaven, freshly shaven
11捨 *so(ri)-su(teru)* cut off the hair; take the tonsure
12落 *so(ri)-oto(su), su(ri-oto(su)* shave off the hair
14髪 *teihatsu* tonsure, cutting off the hair

8

剛 See 114.

剤 See 5424.

帰 See 1582. [止]

[illegible] 692/F-X Nonstandard for **魚** 5281.

B **剖** 693/F248 **剖** HŌ. BŌ divide.

剔 694/F248 TEKI cutting.

5出 *tekishutsu* extraction, removal, excision
7抉 *tekketsu suru* gouge, gouge out; expose
9除 *tekijo* removal (in surgery)

剝 695/F250 HAKU. *ha(geru)* come off, peel off, be worn off; fade, discolor. *ha(gu), ha(gasu), he(gu)* tear off, peel off, rip off, strip off; skin, flay; disrobe; deprive of. *mu(keru)* peel off, come off, be taken off. *mu(ku)* peel, pare, hull. *hezu(ru)* pilfer, steal a portion. *muku(reru)* be tangled up with, be connected with.

5出 *mu(ki)-da(su)* show, bare (the teeth). *mu(ki)da(shi)* nakedness; frankness
7身 *sukimi* a meat or fish slicer. *mukimi* shellfish removed from the shell
8取 *ha(gi)-to(ru)* tear off; strip; rob. *hagito(ri)* pad (of paper)
11脱 *hakudatsu suru* come off, peel off
12焼 *sukiyaki* Japanese beef meal, sukiyaki
落 *hakuraku suru, ha(ge)-o(chiru)* peel off
14暦 *haga(shi)goyomi* calendar pad
奪 *hakudatsu suru* deprive of, divest of
製 *hakusei* stuffing
製術 *hakuseijutsu* taxidermy
19離 *hakuri suru vt* and *vi* peel off

B **剣** 696/F255 **劍 劒 劔** KEN sword, saber, blade, bayonet; sting; clock hand. *tsurugi* sword.

3士 *kenshi* fencer
5玉 *kendama* ball-and-cup toy
付食 *kentsu(ku) (o) ku(wasu)* burst out in anger. *kentsu(ku) (o) ku(u)* be the victim of a burst of anger
付鉄砲 *kentsu(ki)deppō* fixed bayonet
6先 *kensaki* point of a sword
7状 *kenjō* sword-shaped
形 *kengata* sword shape
呑 *kennon na* risky, dangerous, insecure
8法 *kempō* fencing
突 *kentsuku* rough scolding
9客 *kenkaku* fencer, swordsman
10帯 *kentai* sword belt
11道 *kendō* fencing, swordmanship
術 *kenjutsu* fencing
12戟 *kengeki* weapons, arms
13幕 *kemmaku* threatening attitude
14豪 *kengō* master fencer
舞 *kembu* sword dance
15劇 *kengeki* sword play
18難 *kennan* the calamity of being killed by the sword
19璽 *kenji* sacred sword and jewels

9

剪 See 599.

剳 697 F252 Tō sickle. Satsu stay, remain
8 青 *irezumi* tattooing

B 剰 698 F251 剩 Jō. *amatsusa(e)* besides.
7 余 *jōyo* surplus, balance
余金 *jōyokin* surplus, balance
10 員 *jōin* surplus people
12 費 *jōhi* unnecessary expenses
14 語 *jōgo* redundancy

A 副 699 F251 Fuku duplicate, copy; assistant, associate. *so(u) vi* suit, meet, satisfy; marry; accompany; be added to; be adjusted to. *so(eru) vt* add to, attach, append; accompany; garnish; imitate. *fuku-* vice-, sub-, deputy, assistant, substitute; auxiliary, supplementary, additional; collateral.
8 大統領 *fukudaitōryō* vice-president
4 手 *fukushu* assistant, associate
木 *fukuboku* splint
尺 *fukushaku* vernier scale
5 本 *fukuhon* duplicate, copy
収入 *fukushūnyū* additional income
司令 *fukushirei* deputy commander
6 因 *fukuin* secondary cause
次的 *fukujiteki* secondary
会長 *fukukaichō* vice-president (of a society)
7 見出 *fukumida(shi)* subtitle
作用 *fukusayō* reaction, secondary effect
社長 *fukushachō* firm vice-president
8 使 *fukushi* vice-envoy, deputy delegate
官 *fukukan, fukkan* adjutant, aide, aide-de-camp
抵当 *fukuteitō* collateral security
牧師 *fukubokushi* associate pastor, curate
9 虹 *fukuniji* secondary rainbow
食 *fukushoku* side dish; supplementary food
食物 *fukushokubutsu* side dish; supplementary food
10 将 *fukushō* second in command
書 *fukusho* copy, duplicate
11 産物 *fukusambutsu* by-product, side line
12 詞 *fukushi* adverb
葬品 *fukusōhin* articles buried with the dead
13 署 *fukusho* countersignature
業 *fukugyō* subsidiary business, side line
14 読本 *fukutokuhon* supplementary reader
領事 *fukuryōji* vice-consul
15 審 *fukushin* sub-umpire, sub-referee
賞 *fukushō* extra prize
18 題 *fukudai* subtitle, subheading
20 議長 *fukugichō* vice-chairman

10

剩 700 F251 See 剰 698.

剴 701 F252 Gai scythe; suitability.
4 切 *gaisetsu* appropriateness, adequacy, aptness

A 創 702 F252 Sō. *kizu* (see under 傷 535.0). *haji(meru)* start, originate.
5 立 *sōritsu* establishment, founding, organization
立者 *sōritsusha* founder, organizer
刊 *sōkan* launching a magazine; first issue
刊号 *sōkangō* first issue
世 *sōsei* creation of the world
世記 *Sōseiki* Genesis
7 見 *sōken* originality, creation, invention
作 *sōsaku* production, literary creation; work
作力 *sōsakuryoku* creative power, genius, creative originality
作的 *sōsakuteki* creative
作家 *sōsakuka* writer, novelist
作権 *sōsakuken* rights of authorship
8 始 *sōshi* creation, founding, initiating
始者 *sōshisha* originator
9 面 *sōmen* surface of a wound
建 *sōken* establishment, foundation
建者 *sōkensha* founder
造 *sōzō* creation
造力 *sōzōryoku* creative power
造主 *Sōzōshu, Sōzōnushi* Creator
造物 *sōzōbutsu* creature, creation
造的 *sōzōteki* creative
造者 *sōzōsha* creator; Creator
造説 *sōzōsetsu* creationism
10 案 *sōan* original idea
案者 *sōansha* originator, inventor
11 痍 *sōi* wound, scar
痕 *sōkon* scar
設 *sōsetsu*=*sōritsu* 創立 (see above–5)
設者 *sōsetsusha* founder
13 傷 *sōshō* wound
意 *sōi* original idea; originality
業 *sōgyō* establishment
業者 *sōgyōsha* founder, promoter
業費 *sōgyōhi* initial expenses
14 製 *sōsei* invention, origination, discovery

B 割 703 F252 割 Katsu. *wa(ru)* divide, cut, halve; separate; split, rip; break, crack, smash; dilute. *wa(reru)* break, split, cleave, fissure, be smashed. *sa(ku)* cut up, cleave; sever, separate, divide; spare (time); cede, alienate. *wa(re)* broken piece. *wa(ri)* rate, ratio, proportion, percentage, profit, assignment. *wa(ri) ni* comparatively. *wari* 10%.

4 方 *wa(ri)kata* comparatively
木 *wa(ri)ki* split firewood
込 *wa(ri)-ko(mu)* wedge oneself in, cut in, muscle in on. *wa(ri)ko(mi)* sharing a theater box; muscling in on; wedging oneself in
切 *wa(ri)-ki(reru)* be divisible by. *wa(ri)-ki(ru)* divide; give a clear explanation. *wa(ri)ki(renai)* indivisible; unconvincing; incomprehensible; unaccounted for
引 *wa(ri)-bi(ku)* discount. *waribiki* discount, reduction, rebate
引券 *waribikiken* a discount coupon
5 目 *wa(re)me* crevice, crack, split, rift, chasm, fissure
付 *wa(ri)-tsu(keru)* allot, assign, distribute, divide among. *waritsu(ke)* allotment, assignment, distribution; layout, editing
出 *wa(ri)-da(su)* calculate, compute; infer
礼 *katsurei* circumcision
礼無 *katsureina(ki)* uncircumcised
6 竹 *wa(ri)dake* split bamboo
返 *warikae(shi)* rebate ⌈adjacent sheets
印 *wa(ri)-in* a seal over the edges of
合 *wariai* rate, ratio, proportion, percentage. *wariai ni* comparatively; contrary to expectations
安 *wariyasu na* comparatively cheap
当 *wa(ri)-a(teru)* assign, allot, divide among, distribute, prorate, assess. *waria(te)* assignment, allotment, quota,
当額 *wariategaku* allotment ⌊rationing
7 材 *wa(ri)zai* split log, split timber
判 *wa(ri)ban* a seal over the edges of adjacent sheets
麦 *wa(ri)mugi* ground barley
戻 *wa(ri)-modo(su)* rebate
戻金 *wa(ri)modo(shi)kin* rebate money
8 拠 *kakkyo suru* hold one's ground; defend
注 *wa(ri)chū* inserted note ⌊local authority
物 *wa(re)mono* broken article; fragile article
易 *wa(re)yasu(i)* brittle, fragile, easily cracked, perishable
9 前 *wa(ri)mae* share, quota
前勘定 *wa(ri)mae kanjō* Dutch treat
10 高 *waridaka na* comparatively high
振 *wa(ri)-fu(ru)*=*wa(ri)-a(teru)* 割当 (see above–6). *wa(ri)fu(ri)*=*waria(te)* 割当 (see above–6)
書 *wa(ri)ga(ki)* interlinear notes
栗 *wa(ri)guri* rubble, broken stone
栗石 *wa(ri)guri ishi* crushed rock, macadam
烹 *kappō* cooking, cuisine
烹店 *kappōten* restaurant
烹着 *kappōgi* coverall apron, cook's apron
11 勘 *wa(ri)kan* Dutch treat
符 *wa(ri)fu* tally, check ⌈several contractors
12 普請 *wa(ri)bushin* dividing work among
13 楔 *wa(ri) kusabi* split wedge
腹 *kappuku* disembowelment, harakiri
愛 *katsuai suru* share, spare, part with reluctantly
14 算 *wa(ri)zan* division (in math) ⌈bonus
増 *warima(shi)* extra wages, premium,
増金 *warima(shi)kin* premium, bonus
15 線 *kassen* secant (in trigonometry)
賦 *wappu* allotment, quota
箸 *wa(ri)bashi* split chopsticks
19 鏨 *wa(ri) tagane* ripping chisel
20 譲 *katsujō* cession of territory

11

剿 704 F-X **勦** Shō. Sō destroy.
13 滅 *sōmetsu* clean sweep, annihilation

剽 705 F253 Hyō threat.
9 窃 *hyōsetsu* piracy; plagiarism
10 悍 *hyōkan* fierceness; daring
11 盗 *hyōtō* highwayman
12 軽 *hyōkin* facetious, droll, funny
軽者 *hyōkimmono* a comical person

12

劂 See 243.

劄 706 F-X See **箚** 3405.

劃 707 F253 Kaku divide.
1 一 *kakuitsu* uniformity, standardization
10 時代的 *kakujidaiteki* epoch-making
12 然 *kakuzen(taru)* distinct, clear-cut
期 *kakki* epoch
期的 *kakkiteki* epoch-making

13

劇 See 247.

劍 708 F255 See **剣** 696.

劉 709 F254 Ryū axe; kill.

2 二亠人亻𠆢儿入八丷冂冖冫几凵[刀刂]勹勺匕匚匸十卜卩厂厶又 13

劈 710 F254 HEKI. *tsunza(ku)* break, tear, pierce, split, burst.
[12]開 *hekikai* cleavage (in gems)
[16]頭 *hekitō* outset

14

劉 See 709.

劑 See 剤 5424.

劒 711 F255 劔 See 剣 696.

燚 712 F-X See 燚 249. [火]

頼 713 F1804 See 頼 5129. [貝]

23

釁 714 F1928 KIN sprinkling blood on the altar. [酉]
[14]端 *kintan* beginning of a war; basis of a misunderstanding

RAD. 力 19

Chikara strength. Nickname: Strong

A 力 715 F256 RIKI. RYOKU. *riki(mu)* strain, bear up, exert one's strength; swagger, bluff, boast. *tsuto(meru)* (see under 勤 732.0). *chikara* strength, energy, force, might, power; agency; authority, influence; vigor; stress, emphasis; exertions, endeavors; efficacy; help, support, good offices; ability, faculty, capability, attainment; means, resources. *-riki* strength. *-ryoku* strength, power.
[1]一杯 *chikara-ippai ni* with all one's strength
[2]入 *chikara (o) i(reru)* put forth effort
[3]士 *rikishi* Japanese wrestler; a strong man
及 *chikara oyo(bazu)* be unable to accomplish
[5]石 *chikara ishi* a lifting stone
付 *chikarazu(ku) vi* be strengthened, revive, be invigorated, be encouraged. *chikarazu(keru) vt* strengthen (someone)
仕事 *chikara shigoto* physical work
[6]行 *rikkō* strenuous efforts, exertion
尽 *chikarazu(ku) de* by sheer strength
任 *chikaramaka(se) ni* with all one's might
合 *chikara-a(wase)* test of strength
自慢 *chikara jiman* boasting of one's strength
[7]走 *rikisō* hard running
足 *chikara ashi* strong legs
作 *rikisaku* literary masterpiece
役 *rikieki* physical labor
抜 *chikaranu(ke)* discouragement, disappointment
投 *rikitō* powerful pitching
[8]泳 *rikiei* powerful swimming
学 *rikigaku* dynamics, mechanics
[9]革 *chikaragawa* leather stirrup
持 *chikaramo(chi)* strong man
点 *rikiten* leverage; emphasis, importance
負 *chikarama(ke)* misdirection of one's strength
[10]倆 *rikiryō* talent, skill
帯 *chikara obi* abdominal-support belt
弱 *chikarayowa(i)* weak
[11]強 *chikarazuyo(i)* reassuring, emboldened
添 *chikarazo(e)* assistance
動的 *rikidōteki* dynamic
[12]量 *rikiryō* physical strength; capacity, ability; tact
落 *chikara-o(toshi)* loss of energy, fatigue, discouragement, disappointment
無 *chikarana(ge) ni* feebly, dejectedly
[13]試 *chikaradame(shi)* trial of strength, quiz
戦 *rikisen* hard fighting
業 *chikara waza* heavy work
[14]漕 *rikisō suru* row hard
説 *rikisetsu* emphasis, stress
[15]瘤 *chikara kobu* large biceps
瘤入 *chikarakobu (o) i(reru)* work earnestly; render aid
[18]闘 *rikitō* hard fight
織機 *rikishokki* power loom
[20]競 *chikara kurabe* trial of strength

3

功 See 1454.

A 加 716 F258 KA addition, increase. *kuwa(waru)* join in; accede to; gain in (influence); increase. *kuwa(eru)* add, sum up; append; include; increase; inflict. *kuwa(uru) ni* besides, furthermore.
[2]入 *kanyū* joining, entry, admission, affiliation, adherence, signing, subscription
入金 *kanyūkin* admission fee

入者 *kanyūsha* member, entrant, participant; (telephone) subscriber
8 工 *kakō* processing, manufacturing, treatment ⌈goods
工品 *kakōhin* processed goods, finished
工紙 *kakōshi* processed paper, coated paper
工歯 *kakōshi* dental bridge
工税 *kakōzei* processing tax
工費 *kakōhi* processing cost
工貿易 *kakō bōeki* processing trade
工賃 *kakōchin* processing fees
工業 *kakōgyō* processing industries
4 水分解 *kasui bunkai* hydrolysis
5 圧 *ka-atsu* increasing pressure
6 号 *kagō* plus sign; sign of addition
年 *kanen* adding years
7 里 *kari* potassium, potash
役 *kayaku* temporary extra work
判 *kahan suru* affix a seal
判人 *kahannin* signatory
8 味 *kami* seasoning, flavoring
法 *kahō* addition
担 *katan* support; conspiracy, complicity
担者 *katansha* accomplice
9 持 *kaji* incantation, faith-healing
重 *kajū, kachō* weighting (in averaging); aggravation
冠 *kakan* a man's coming-of-age ceremony
虐愛 *kagyakuai* sadism
速度 *kasokudo* acceleration
速運動 *kasoku undō* accelerated motion
除 *kajo* insertion and deletion
除式 *kajoshiki* looseleaf
10 俸 *kahō* extra allowance
留多 *karuta* playing cards
配 *kahai* additional ration
配米 *kahaimai* extra rice ration
害 *kagai* assault, violence, damaging (some-
害者 *kagaisha* assailant ⌊one)
11 階 *kakai* promotion
12 湿 *kashitsu* humidification
禄 *karoku* increase in a samurai's stipend
給 *kakyū* raising salaries
筆 *kahitsu* correction, revision
硫 *karyū* vulcanizing
硫法 *karyūhō* vulcanization
減 *kagen* addition and subtraction; allowance for; degree; condition; seasoning, flavor; moderation; adjustment; influence (of the weather); state of health;
減抵抗器 *kagen teikōki* rheostat ⌊chance
減乗除 *kagenjōjo* the four arithmetical operations ⌈assistant
13 勢 *kasei* assistance, backing, reinforcements;
農砲 *kannonhō* cannon
盟 *kamei* participation, affiliation
盟者 *kameisha* participants
盟国 *kameikoku* member nation, signatory
14 増 *kazō* increase, addition
算 *kasan, kuwa(e)zan* addition
15 養 *kayō* caring for the sick. *kayō suru* take
熱 *kanetsu* heating ⌊care of oneself
16 薬 *kayaku* spices, seasoning; adding ingredients (in medicine)
餐 *kasan* caring for one's health
糖粉乳 *katō funnyū* sweetened powdered
17 療 *karyō* medical treatment ⌊milk
齢 *karei* adding to one's years
20 護 *kago* divine protection

4

劣 See 185.

5

努 717/F260 A Do *tsuto(meru)* (see under 勤 732.0). *tsuto(mete)* as much as possible; diligently.
2 力 *doryoku* endeavor, exertion, effort, labor, strain, industry
力家 *doryokuka* hard worker

劫 718/F260 **刧 刦** Kō, Gō, Kyō threat; long ages. *obiya(kasu)* threaten.
4 火 *gōka* world-destroying conflagration
11 掠 *kyōryaku, gōryaku* pillage, plunder
略 *kyōryaku, gōryaku* pillage, plunder
盗 *gōtō* highway robber
14 罰 *gōbatsu* eternal punishment

励 See 193.

助 719/F259 A Jo help, rescue. *tasu(karu)* be saved, be rescued, survive; be helpful. *tasu(keru)* help; save, rescue; give relief to; spare (life); reinforce; promote; abet. *su(keru)* help. *tasu(ke), suke* assistance. *jo-* assistant.
2 力 *joryoku* assistance, support
3 上 *tasu(ke)-a(geru)* help up; pick up, bring safely to land
4 手 *tasu(ke)te, sukete* helper, helpmeet. *joshu* helper, assistant, tutor; interne
太刀 *sukedachi* assistance (in a fight), seconds (in a fight)
5 平 *sukebei* lewdness; lewd person
出 *tasu(ke)-da(su)* help out of (trouble),
6 舟 *tasukebune* timely help ⌊extricate
合 *tasu(ke)-a(u)* help each other, co-operate
守 *tasu(ke)-mamo(ru)* protect, preserve, keep

成 *josei* fostering, aiding
成金 *joseikin* subsidy, grant-in-aid
7役 *joyaku* assistant official
言 *jogon, jogen* advice, suggestion
言者 *jogensha, jogonsha* adviser, counsellor
8長 *jochō* promotion, fostering
命 *jomei* sparing a life, clemency, reconsidering a dismissal
10起 *tasu(ke)-oko(su)* help up
11船 *tasu(ke)bune* lifeboat; a friend in need, ⌊help
祭 *josai* (Catholic) deacon
動詞 *jodōshi* auxiliary verb
教 *jokyō* assistant teacher
教授 *jokyōju* assistant instructor
教諭 *jokyōyu* assistant or associate professor
産 *josan* midwifery
産所 *josanjo* maternity home
産院 *josan-in* maternity hospital
産婦 *josampu* midwife
12詞 *joshi* a particle (in grammar)
13辞 *joji* particle (in grammar); auxiliary word
勢 *josei* encouragement, backing. *sukezei*, reinforcements ⌈of objects
数詞 *josūshi* counters for various categories
14監督 *jokantoku* assistant director (in taking
演 *joen* co-star ⌊professional movies)
演者 *joensha* co-star

A **労** 720/F266 **勞** Rō labor, toil, trouble. *rō(suru)* labor, toil, strive; put (someone) to work; thank (someone) for their efforts; comfort. *itawa(ru)* pity, sympathize with, console, care for, be kind to. *negira(u)* thank for, reward for. *itawa(ri)* trouble, service, labor; sympathy; illness; carefulness, attention. *itazuki* pain, trouble.

2力 *rōryoku* labor; toil; trouble
5功 *rōkō* meritorious deed
7労 *rōrō(taru)* tired out ⌈surance
災保険 *rōsai hoken* worker's accident in-
作 *rōsaku* toil, labor; laborious task
作教育 *rōsaku kyōiku* manual training
役 *rōeki* work, labor, toil
役場 *rōekijō* prison labor camp
8使 *rōshi* laborers and employers
苦 *rōku* labor, toil, hardship
11務 *rōmu* labor, work, service
務者 *rōmusha* laborer, workman
動 *rōdō* manual labor, work, toil
動者 *rōdōsha* laborer, worker
13賃 *rōchin* wages ⌈laborers
資 *rōshi* capital and labor; capitalists and
農 *rōnō* workers and farmers
農政府 *Rōnō Seifu* Soviet Government
農党 *rōnōtō* labor-farmer party
働 *rōdō* manual labor, work, toil
働力 *rōdōryoku* labor, manpower, working
働大臣 *Rōdō Daijin* Labor Minister ⌊force
働収容所 *rōdō shūyōsho* labor camp
働市場 *rōdō shijō* labor market
働同盟 *rōdō dōmei* labor federation
働争議 *rōdō sōgi* labor trouble, strike
働条件 *rōdō jōken* working conditions
働攻勢 *rōdō kōsei* labor offensive
働者 *rōdōsha* laborer, worker
働委員会 *rōdō iinkai* labor-relations board
働省 *Rōdōshō* Labor Ministry
働党 *rōdōtō* labor party ⌈hours
働時間 *rōdō jikan* working hours; man
働祭 *Rōdōsai* Labor Day, May Day
働組合 *rōdō kumiai* labor union
働階級 *rōdō kaikyū* working classes
働運動 *rōdō undō* labor movement
働運動者 *rōdō undōsha* labor agitator
働歌 *rōdōka* songs of labor
14銀 *rōgin* wages, labor wages

6

B **劾** 721/F261 Gai criminal investigation.

9奏 *gaisō suru* report an official's offense to the emperor

A **効** 722/F261/F851 **效** Kō efficacy, benefit; efficiency; effect, result; success. *ki(ku)* be effective.

2力 *kōryoku* effect, efficacy; validity
5用 *kōyō* use, utility, effect, benefit
目 *kikime* effect, efficacy, impression
8果 *kōka* effect, efficacy, result
果的 *kōkateki* effective, successful
10能 *kōnō* effect, efficacy, virtue, benefit
能書 *kōnōga(ki)* statement of the efficacy of
11率 *kōritsu* efficiency ⌊a medicine
18験 *kōken* efficacy, effect

7

勉 勉 See **勉** 228.

勁 723/F261 Kei strong.

8卒 *keisotsu* excellent soldier
10悍 *keikan* strong and fierce
11捷 *keishō* strong and nimble
15敵 *keiteki* formidable foe

勃 724/F261 Botsu suddenness; rise.

9勃 *botsubotsu(taru)* spirited, rising, energetic
発 *boppatsu* outbreak, outburst, sudden oc-
10起 *bokki suru* stand erect, stiffen ⌊currence

12 然 *botsuzen to* suddenly; in a fit of anger
16 興 *bokkō* sudden rise to power

B **勅** 725 F262 F854 **敕** CHOKU *mikotonori* imperial decree.

5 令 *chokurei* imperial edict
6 旨 *chokushi* imperial order, imperial will
任 *chokunin* imperial appointment
任官 *chokuninkan* imperial appointee
8 使 *chokushi* imperial messenger
命 *chokumei* imperial command
9 宣 *chokusen* imperial decree
10 書 *chokusho* imperial rescript
11 問 *chokumon* imperial question
許 *chokkyo* imperial sanction
勘 *chokkan* the emperor's censure
12 筆 *chokuhitsu* imperial autograph ⌈peror
答 *chokutō* emperor's reply; reply to the em-
裁 *chokusai* imperial decision or sanction
13 意 *chokui* meaning or gist of a decree
14 語 *chokugo* imperial rescript
選 *chokusen* imperial nomination ⌈thology
選集 *chokusenshū* emperor-sponsored an-
15 撰 *chokusen* compilation for the emperor; emperor's literary production
諚 *chokujō* imperial message
16 諭 *chokuyu* imperial instructions
18 額 *chokugaku* imperial scroll
題 *chokudai* theme of the Imperial Poetry
19 願 *chokugan* imperial prayer ⌊Contest

A **勇** 726 F262 YŪ bravery, courage, heroism. *isa(mu)* cheer up, be in high spirits. *isa(mashii)* courageous, valiant.

2 力 *yūryoku* courage
3 士 *yūshi* brave man, hero
4 夫 *yūfu* valiant man
5 立 *isa(mi)-ta(tsu)* cheer up, be encouraged
6 壮 *yūsō* bravery, heroism ⌊(by)
肌 *isa(mi)hada* gallantry
名 *yūmei* fame, great renown ⌈boldness
気 *yūki* courage, bravery, valor, nerve,
気付 *yūkizu(ke)* have a burst of courage
7 図 *yūto* ambitious undertaking
決 *yūketsu* decisiveness
8 退 *yūtai suru* retire voluntarily, bow out
武 *yūbu* bravery, valor, military prowess
者 *yūsha* hero, man of valor ⌈forward
往 *yūō* spirited advance, energetically going
往邁進 *yūō-maishin suru* dash ahead, push forward
9 飛 *yūhi* flying jump, great achievement
姿 *yūshi* gallant figure
10 進 *yūshin suru* dash forward bravely
将 *yūshō* brave general, great soldier
烈 *yūretsu* bravery, valor, courage
11 健 *yūken* sound health
婦 *yūfu* heroine, brave woman
断 *yūdan* resolute decision
猛 *yūmō* daring, bravery, valor
猛心 *yūmōshin* intrepid spirit
12 敢 *yūkan* heroism, gallantry, bravery
13 戦 *yūsen* brave fight, desperate fight
15 邁 *yūmai na* heroic, courageous
21 躍 *yūyaku suru* take heart, be in high spirits

8

勉 See 228.

B **脅** 727 F1542 KYŌ. *obiya(kasu)* threaten; coerce. [肉]

7 迫 *kyōhaku* threat, menace, terrorism, coer-
迫状 *kyōhakujō* intimidating letter ⌊cion
迫的 *kyōhakuteki* menacing, threatening
迫者 *kyōhakusha* intimidator
迫罪 *kyōhakuzai* intimidation
9 威 *kyōi* threat, menace ⌈menace
12 喝 *kyōkatsu suru* threaten, intimidate,

9

勒 See 5089.

務 See 3167.

勢 728 F265 See **務** 3167.

B **勘** 729 F264 KAN perception, intuition; the sixth sense.

5 付 *kanzu(ku)* suspect, sense, scent
弁 *kamben* pardon, forgiveness, forbearance
6 気 *kanki* disfavor, disinheritance
当 *kandō* disinheritance
考 *kankō* consideration, deliberation
合 *kangō* checking and verifying
合貿易 *kangō bōeki* licensed trade
7 決 *kanketsu suru* investigate and decide
忍 *kannin* patient endurance
8 例 *kanrei* considering old precedents
所 *kandokoro* finger board (of an instrument); vital point
定 *kanjō* calculation; account; settlement of an account; consideration, allowance
定日 *kanjōbi* settlement day
定尻 *kanjōjiri* balance of an account
定尽 *kanjōzu(ku) de* in a mercenary spirit
定取 *kanjōto(ri)* bill collector ⌈treasurer
定係 *kanjōgakari* cashier, accountant,
定書 *kanjōga(ki)* bill, one's account

定高 *kanjōdaka(i)* calculating, mercenary, closefisted
定違 *kanjōchiga(i)* miscalculation
定場 *kanjōba* cashier's counter
9 査 *kansa* investigation ⌈tion
10 進 *kanshin* reporting after careful investiga-
校 *kankō suru* examine and correct
案 *kan-an suru* think ⌈guess
11 違 *kanchiga(i)* misunderstanding, wrong
責 *kanseki* reproving for a fault
12 検 *kanken suru* investigate
15 審 *kanshin* careful investigation
19 繰 *kangu(ru)* be suspicious of

A **動** 730/F263 Dō motion; change; confusion. *dō(jiru), dō(zuru)* be perturbed, be agitated. *ugo(ku) vi* move, stir, shift, shake, swing; operate, run, go, work; be touched, be influenced, waver, fluctuate, vary, change, be transferred. *ugo(kasu) vt* move, shift; set in motion, operate; inspire, rouse, influence; mobilize; deny; change. *ugo(ki)* movement, activity, trend, development, change. *yaya(mosureba), yaya(tomosureba)* be apt to, be liable to, be inclined to.

2 力 *dōryoku* power, motive power, dynamic
力学 *dōrikigaku* kinetics, dynamics ⌊force
力降下 *dōryoku kōka* power dive
力源 *dōryokugen* source of power
力資源 *dōryoku shigen* sources of power
4 天 *dōten* heaven-shaking event
6 回 *ugo(ki)-mawa(ru)* move around
因 *dōin*＝導因 1354.6
気 *dōki* palpitation, pulsation, throbbing
向 *dōkō* trend, tendency, movement, at-
名詞 *dōmeishi* gerund ⌊titude
7 体 *dōtai* moving body
作 *dōsa* action, movements, motions; bearing, behavior, manners
乱 *dōran* agitation, commotion, riot
8 的 *dōteki* dynamic, kinetic
物 *dōbutsu* animal
物化 *dōbutsuka* animalization
物学 *dōbutsugaku* zoology
物相 *dōbutsusō* fauna
物界 *dōbutsukai* animal kingdom
物崇拝 *dōbutsu sūhai* zoolatry
物園 *dōbutsuen* zoo
物愛 *dōbutsu ai* love for animals
物誌 *dōbutsushi* fauna
物質 *dōbutsushitsu* animal matter
10 員 *dōin* mobilization
員令 *dōinrei* mobilization order
脈 *dōmyaku* artery
脈血 *dōmyakuketsu* arterial blood
脈硬化 *domyaku kōka* arteriosclerosis
脈硬化症 *dōmyaku kōkashō* arteriosclerosis, hardening of the arteries
11 悸 *dōki* palpitation, pulsation, throbbing
転 *dōten* being surprised and stunned; transition, change
産 *dōsan* personal property, personal effects
12 揺 *dōyō* shaking, trembling, pitching, rolling, oscillation; agitation, excitement;
軸 *dōjiku* driving axle ⌊unrest, commotion
量 *dōryō* momentum
植物 *dōshokubutsu* plants and animals, flora
詞 *dōshi* verb ⌊and fauna
詞状名詞 *dōshijō meishi* gerund
13 勢 *dōsei* state, condition, movements
滑車 *dōkassha* movable pulley
14 静 *dōsei* state, condition, movements
態 *dōtai* movement; vital (statistics)
15 輪 *dōrin* driving wheel
16 機 *dōki* motive, incentive
20 議 *dōgi* a motion

10

勝 See 3787.

募 See 3996.

勞 731/F266 See **労** 720.

A **勤** 732/F268 **勤** Kin. Gon. *tsuto(maru)* be fit for, be equal to, function properly. *tsuto(meru)* serve, fill a post, serve under; exert oneself, endeavor, work, be diligent; play (the part of). *tsuto(me)* service, duty, business; Buddhist religious services.

2 人 *tsuto(me)nin* office worker, salaried man, white-collar worker ⌈ment
3 口 *tsuto(me)guchi* position, place of employ-
上 *tsuto(me)-a(geru)* serve out one's apprenticeship, serve out one's time
4 王 *kinnō* imperialism, loyalism
王家 *kinnōka* a loyalist
王攘夷 *kinnō-jōi* loyalty to the emperor and expulsion of the foreigners
6 行 *tsuto(me)-okona(u)* carry on (work). *gongyō* Buddhist religious service
気 *tsuto(me)gi* mercenary spirit
向 *tsuto(me)mu(ki)* one's business, one's
先 *tsuto(me)saki* place of work ⌊duties
7 求 *gongu* inquiring re the Buddha way
労 *kinrō* labor, exertion
労大衆 *kinrō taishū* working people
労者 *kinrōsha* working man

労奉仕 *kinrō hōshi* labor service
労所得 *kinrō shotoku* earned income
労階級 *kinrō kaikyū* salaried class, working class 「giving Day, November 23
労感謝日 *Kinrō Kansha (no) Hi* Thanks-
8 苦 *kinku* toil and hardship
奉公 *tsuto(me)bōkō* apprenticeship
9 恪 *kinkaku* faithful service
怠 *kintai*=*kinda* 勤惰 (see below–12)
皇 *kinnō* imperialism
皇家 *kinnōka* a loyalist
皇攘夷=勤王攘夷 (see above–4)
10 倹 *kinken* industry, diligence, frugality
振 *tsuto(me)bu(ri)* assiduity; conduct
勉 *kimben* industry, diligence
11 盛 *tsuto(me)zaka(ri)* the prime of one's
務 *kimmu* service, duty, work ⌊career
務先 *kimmusaki* place of employment
務地手当 *kimmuchi teate* area allowance
務交代 *kimmu kōtai* change of shifts
務年限 *kimmu nengen* term of service
務者 *kimmusha* workers, men on duty
務実績 *kimmu jisseki* service record
務員 *kimmuin* worker, employee
務評定 *kimmu hyōtei* evaluation of workers
12 惰 *kinda* diligence and indolence; diligence;
番 *kimban* on duty in Edo ⌊attendance
13 働 *tsuto(me)-hatara(ku)* work diligently
続 *kinzoku* continuous service
続者 *kinzokusha* a man of long service

— 11 —

勤 733/F268 See 勤 732.

勦 734/F268 Shō. Sō destroy.
10 討 *sōtō* complete annihilation
13 滅 *sōmetsu* eradication, annihilation

勢 735/F267 A Se. Sei. energy; military strength. *ikio(izuku)* gather strength. *ikio(i)* force, vigor, energy, spirit, life; authority, influence, power, might; impetus; course (of events), tendency; necessarily. *hazumi* spring, bound, rebound; inertia, momentum; impetus, stimulus, impulse; instant; chance.
2 力 *seiryoku* influence, power, might, strength; force, energy 「power of
力下 *seiryokuka ni* under the influence or
力家 *seiryokuka, seiryokka* man of influence
力圏 *seiryokuken* sphere of influence
力範囲 *seiryōku han-i* sphere of influence
3 子 *seko* beater (on a hunt)
4 込 *ikio(i)ko(mu)* brace oneself
7 車 *hazumiguruma* flywheel
良 *ikio(i)yo(ku)* vigorously 「power
8 門 *seimon* influential family, the man in
9 威 *seii*=*isei* 威勢 1803.13
10 家 *seika* influential family; the man in power
11 運 *seiun* trend, tendency
望 *seibō* power and popularity
12 揃 *seizoro(i)* array, muster, line-up; full force

勧 736/F269 勸 A Kan. *susu(meru)* recommend, advise, encourage; offer (wine). *susu(me)* recommendation, advice, encouragement.
3 工 *kankō* encouragement of industry
工場 *kankōba* fair, bazaar
4 化 *kange* religious-fund soliciting; Buddhist preaching 「per string
5 世縒 *kanzeyori* twisted paper, twisted-pa-
7 告 *kankoku* advice, counsel, recommenda-
告状 *kankokujō* letter of advice ⌊tion
告者 *kankokusha* adviser, counselor
告案 *kankokuan* recommendation
8 学 *kangaku* encouragement of learning
9 降 *kankō* call to surrender
10 進 *kanjin* temple solicitation
進元 *kanjimmoto* backer, promoter
進帳 *kanjinchō* temple solicitation book
12 善懲悪 *kanzen-chōaku* rewarding good and punishing evil; political justice; moral purpose
善懲悪劇 *kanzen-chōaku geki* morality play
13 奨 *kanshō* encouragement, stimulation
農 *kannō* encouragement of agriculture
業 *kangyō* encouragement of industry; in-
14 説 *kanzei suru* urge, persuade ⌊dustry
誘 *kan-yū* invitation, inducement, solicitation, canvassing; persuasion, encouragement 「man
誘員 *kan-yūin* canvasser, traveling sales-
15 賞 *kanshō* praise and encouragement

— 13 —

勲 See 2794.

— 14 —

勵 737/F269 See 励 193.

勳 738/F269 See 勲 2794.

— 17 —

勸 739/F269 See 勧 736.

2 二亠人亻𠆢儿入八丷冂冖冫几凵刀刂力【勹】匕匚匸十卜卩厂厶又

RAD. 勹 20

Tsutsumigamae "wrapping" enclosure. Nickname: Wrapping.

1

B 勺 740/F270 勺 SHAKU one-tenth of a *go* (see Weights and Measures); dip, ladle.

2

匁 See 159.

勾 741/F271 Kō be bent.

4 引 *kadowaka(su)* kidnap. *kōin suru* arrest, seduce, abduct. *kadowaka(shi)* kidnapper. *kōin* arrest, custody

引状 *kōinjō* summons, warrant of arrest

5 玉 *magatama* comma-shaped jewels

10 配 *kōbai* slope, incline, gradient, grade, pitch

留 *kōryū* detention, confinement

匂 742/F271 (国字) *nio(u)* be fragrant, smell; stink; glow, be bright. *nio(wasu)*, *nio(waseru)* *vt* give out an odor, scent, or perfume; suggest, insinuate. *nioi* smell, odor, scent; stench; fragrance, aroma, perfume.

8 油 *nioi abura* perfumed hair oil

11 袋 *nioibukuro* sachet

菖蒲 *nioi shōbu* aromatic cane, orris

勿 743/F271 MOCHI. BUTSU. *naka(re)* must not, do not, be not.

7 忘草 *wasurenagusa* forget-me-not.

体 *mottai* overemphasis. *mottai(buru)* assume airs.

体無 *mottaina(i)* sacrilegious; unworthy of; wasteful

8 怪 *mokke* something unexpected

怪幸 *mokke (no) saiwa(i)* stroke of luck, godsend, windfall

15 論 *mochiron* naturally, of course

3

包包 See 176.

匆 744/F715 See 怱 1660. [心]

A 句 745/F322 Kō. KU phrase, clause, sentence, passage, paragraph; expression; line, verse, stanza; 17-syllable poem. [口]

4 切 *kugi(ru)* *vt* punctuate; cut off; mark off, stop. *kugi(ri)* stopping place, punctuation, pause

5 句 *kuku* every clause

6 会 *kukai* a gathering of *haiku* poets

7 作 *kusaku* composing *haiku* poems

8 法 *kuhō* phraseology, diction

9 点 *kuten* period (in punctuation)

12 集 *kushū* collection of *haiku* poems

13 節 *kusetsu* phrases and clauses

義 *kugi* meaning of a phrase

意 *kui* meaning of a phrase

14 読 *kutō* punctuation, pause

読点 *kutōten* punctuation marks

4

匈 746/F272 Kyō turmoil; Hungary.

5 奴 *Kyōdo* Huns

牙利 *Hangari* Hungary

B 旬 747/F890 JUN ten-day period. *shun* season (for specific products). [日]

4 日 *junjitsu* ten-day period

月 *jungetsu* a month and ten days; ten months; a short time

5 外 *junhazu(re)* off-season

刊 *junkan* published every ten days

7 余 *jun-yo* over ten days

12 報 *jumpō* ten-day report

7

匍 748/F272 Ho crawl, creep.

11 匐 *hofuku* creeping, crawling, sneaking

球 *hokyū, goro* grounder

8

芻 See 226. [艸]

9

匐 749/F273 FUKU, HOKU crawl.

6 行疹 *fukkōshin* ringworm

2 二亠人亻𠆢儿入八冫冂冖冫几凵刀刂力勹[匕]8 匚匸十卜卩厂厶又

RAD. 匕 21

Saji spoon or *hi* (the katakana). Variant: 匕. Nickname: *Kana Hi*.

匕 750 F273 Hi. *saji* spoon.

9 首 *aikuchi, hishu* dagger, dirk

2

化 See 350.

3

A **北** 751 F274 **业** Hoku. *kita* north.

3 山 *kitayama* a northern hill
下 *kitaoro(shi)* cold wind from the northern uplands
上 *hokujō* going north
大西洋 *Kita Taiseiyō* North Atlantic
大西洋条約 *Kita Taiseiyō Jōyaku* North Atlantic Treaty
4 辺 *hokuhen* northern extremity
方 *hoppō* north, northward; northern. *kita (no) kata* nobleman's true wife; facing the north
天 *hokuten* northern sky
支 *Hokushi* North China
支事変 *Hokushi Jihen* the Marco Polo Bridge Incident
斗七星 *Hokuto Shichisei* Big Dipper
斗星 *Hokutosei* Big Dipper
5 氷洋 *Hokuhyōyō, Hoppyōyō* Arctic Ocean
北西 *hokuhokusei* north-northwest
北東 *hokuhokutō* north-northeast
半 *hokuhan* northern half
半球 *Kita Hankyū* Northern Hemisphere
6 行 *hokkō* northbound; sailing north
向 *kitamu(ki)* facing north, northern exposure
光 *hokkō* northern lights
回帰線 *Kita Kaikisen* Tropic of Cancer
西 *hokusei, kitanishi* northwest
西航路 *Hokusei Kōro* Northwest Passage
米 *Hokubei* North America
米土人 *Hokubei dojin* American Indian
米合衆国 *Hokubei Gasshūkoku* the United States of America
7 辰 *Hokushin* North Star
8 門 *kitamon* north gate
枕 *kita makura* turning the head to the north in sleeping
郊 *hokkō* northern suburbs
受 *kita-u(ke)* facing the north
東 *hokutō, kitahigashi* northeast
国 *hokkoku, kitaguni* northern provinces, northern countries
国人 *hokkokujin* northerner
欧 *Hokuō* Northern Europe; land of the Norsemen, Scandinavia
欧人 *Hokuōjin* Northern European, Norsemen, a Scandinavian
岸 *hokugan* north coast; north bank
岸沿 *hokuganzo(i) ni* along the north coast; along the northern seashore
9 面 *hokumen* north face, north side; the north; facing north
風 *hokufū, kita kaze* north wind
海 *hokkai* northern sea. *Hokkai* North Sea
洋 *hokuyō* northern waters
10 進 *hokushin suru* proceed north
航 *hokkō* sailing north
部 *hokubu* north, northern part
叟笑 *hokusoe(mu)* chuckle, gloat over. *hokusowara(i)* smile of success
11 側 *kitagawa* north side, north bank. *hokusoku* north side
寄 *kitayo(ri)* northerly (wind)
清事変 *Hokushin Jihen* North China Incident; Boxer Uprising
12 満 *Hokuman* North Manchuria
朝 *Hokuchō* Northern Dynasty
極 *Hokkyoku* North Pole
極光 *hokkyokukō* northern lights, aurora borealis
極洋 *Hokkyokuyō* Arctic Ocean
極海 *Hokkyokukai* Arctic Ocean
極星 *Hokkyokusei* North Star
極圏 *Hokkyokuken* Arctic Circle
極熊 *hokkyokuguma* polar bear
14 境 *hokkyō* northern boundary
端 *hokutan* northern extremity
15 緯 *hokui* north latitude
17 鮮 *Hokusen* North Korea
嶺 *Hokurei* northern mountain; Mt. Hiei

4

B **旨** 752 F889 Shi. *uma(garu)* relish, show a liking for. *mune* purport; principle; instructions; will, thinking. *uma(i)* delicious, appetizing; skillful, clever, expert; wise; successful; fortunate; splendid; promising. [日]

5 汁 *uma(i) shiru* the lion's share, the cream
6 旨 *uma-uma to* successfully, nicely
15 趣 *shishu*=*shui* 趣意 4544.13

8

能 See 853. [肉]

眞 753 F1323 See **真** 783. [目]

2 二亠人亻𠆢儿入八丷冂冖冫几凵刀刂力勹[匕]匚匸十卜卩厂厶又

9

辵 See 2131.

頃 754/F2055 KEI. *koro* time; about, toward. *koro(shimo)* just at that time. *-goro* about (re time). [頁]
[6]合 *koroa(i)* suitable time; propriety; moderation
[8]刻 *keikoku* a short period

12

A **疑** 755/F1283 GI. *utaga(u)*, *utagu(ru)* doubt; distrust; be suspicious of. *utaga(i)*, *utagu(ri)* doubt, question, uncertainty, skepticism; suspicion; distrust. *utaga(washii)* doubtful, questionable, uncertain, disputable; suspicious. [疋]
[4]心 *gishin* doubt, suspicion, fear, apprehension
[6]似 *giji-* suspected, quasi-, pseudo-, sham
似症 *gijishō* suspected case
字 *giji* a character of questionable form
[8]念 *ginen* doubt, suspicion, misgivings, scruples
[9]点 *giten* doubtful point
[11]惧 *gigu* apprehension, uneasiness
深 *utaga(i)buka(i)* doubting, distrustful, incredulous; suspicious
問 *gimon* question, problem, doubt
問文 *gimombun* interrogative sentence
問代名詞 *gimon daimeishi* interrogative pronoun
問符 *gimonfu* question mark
問詞 *gimonshi* interrogative word
[12]雲 *giun* cloud of suspicion
惑 *giwaku* doubt, misgivings, distrust, suspicion
[13]辞 *giji* a questionable word
義 *gigi* doubt
[14]獄 *gigoku* scandal, graft case
[21]懼 *giku* apprehension, uneasiness

RAD. 匚 22

Hakogamae (box-on-side enclosure). Variant: 匸. This variant is actually Rad. 23 but is treated herein as Rad. 22. Nickname: Box on Side.

2

B **匹** 756/F278 HITSU. HIKI head, (animal) counter; roll of cloth. [匸]
[4]夫 *hippu* a man; a coarse man; a rustic
夫匹婦 *hippuhippu* coarse men and women
夫勇 *hippu(no)yū* rash courage
[11]婦 *hippu* coarse woman; country woman
[15]敵 *hitteki suru* compare with, match, rival, be equal to
[16]儔 *hitchū* an equal, a match

A **区** 757/F279 **區** KU ward, district, section. [匸]
[4]区 *kuku(taru)*, *machimachi no* several, various, divergent, conflicting
内 *kunai* in the ward or borough
切 *kugi(ru)* punctuate; cut off; mark off. *kugi(ri)* punctuation
分 *kuwa(ke)*, *kubun* division, section, demarcation; (traffic) lane; compartment; classification, sorting
[5]処 *kusho* dividing for administrative purposes; partition; division
民 *kumin* ward residents
[6]会 *kukai* ward assembly
会議員 *kukai gi-in* ward assemblyman
[7]別 *kubetsu* distinction, difference; classification
役所 *kuyakusho* ward office
[8]長 *kuchō* ward headman
画 *kukaku* division, section; compartment; boundary; area; block
画整理 *kukaku seiri* land readjustment, town planning
[11]域 *kuiki* limits, boundary; domain, zone, sphere, territory
[12]検 *kuken* local prosecutor
費 *kuhi* ward expenses
裁判所 *ku saibansho* local court
間 *kukan* section (of track, etc.)
間列車 *kukan ressha* local train
[14]劃 *kukaku*=区画 (see above–8)
劃整理 *kukaku seiri*=区画整理 (see above–8)
[20]議 *kugi* ward assemblyman

B **巨** 758/F604 **巨** KYO. KO. *ōki(i)*, *ōi(naru)* big, large, great. [工]
[2]人 *kyojin* giant; great man
人国 *kyojinkoku* land of giants
[3]口 *kyokō* big mouth
万 *kyoman* huge fortune, millions
大 *kyodai na* huge, enormous
大症 *kyodaishō* gigantism
[5]石 *kyoseki* megalith
石記念物 *kyoseki kinembutsu* megalith
[6]匠 *kyoshō* master, masterhand, maestro
[7]体 *kyotai* large build
材 *kyozai* big timber; big caliber (man)
利 *kyori* huge profit
[8]波 *kyoha* billow, large wave
刹 *kyosatsu* large temple

岩 *kyogan* huge rock, crag
歩 *kyoho* long strides
9星 *kyosei* giant sun; great man, big shot
10峰 *kyohō* gigantic peak
砲 *kyohō* huge gun
財 *kyozai* huge fortune
11細 *kyosai* large and small matters; particulars, details. *kosai* greatness and smallness; details, particulars, circumstances
船 *kyosen* ocean liner
舶 *kyohaku* ocean liner
商 *kyoshō* wealthy merchant
盗 *kyotō* big-time robber
視的 *kyoshiteki* macroscopic
12弾 *kyodan* huge projectile
富 *kyofu* great riches
費 *kyohi* great cost
13漢 *kyokan* giant
賊 *kyozoku* big-time bandit, big-time pirate
資 *kyoshi* large capital, enormous fund
14魁 *kyokai* ringleader, chief
像 *kyozō* huge image
16頭 *kyotō* leader, magnate, big name
17擘 *kyohaku* an authority, a big shot, a star
18軀 *kyoku* big frame
額 *kyogaku* enormous sum
20艦 *kyokan* large warship
鐘 *ōgane* large hanging bell

3

匝 759/F276 Sō go around.

4

匡 760/F276 Kyō correct; save; assist.
5正 *kyōsei* reform, correction, training

B **匠** 761/F276 Shō workman, artisan; means; idea. *takumi* artisan, mechanic; carpenter.
6気 *shōki* affectation, desire to be impressive

5

匣 762/F276 Kō. *hako* box.

A **医** 763/F1926 **醫** I medicine, the healing art; doctor. *i(suru)*, *iya(su)* cure, heal; quench (thirst). [酉]
3大 *idai* medical university
4化学 *ikagaku* medical chemistry
6会 *ikai* medical society
7局 *ikyoku* medical office, dispensary
伯 *ihaku* doctor (polite)
8長 *ichō* head doctor
官 *ikan* medical officer
者 *isha* doctor
事伝道 *iji dendō* medical missionary work
学 *igaku* medical science, medicine
学士 *igakushi* Bachelor of Medicine, M.B.
学史 *igakushi* history of medicine
学生 *igakusei* medical student
学技術士 *igaku gijutsushi* medical technician
学界 *igakukai* medical world
学博士 *Igaku Hakushi, Igaku Hakase* M.D., Doctor of Medicine
9界 *ikai* medical world
科 *ika* medical science; medical department
科大学 *ika daigaku* medical school
院 *i-in* doctor's office, dispensary
院長 *i-inchō* head doctor
10員 *i-in* medical staff; doctor
家 *ika* doctor
書 *isho* medical book
師 *ishi* doctor
師会 *ishikai* medical association
師法 *ishihō* medical practitioner's law
11術 *ijutsu* medicine, healing art
務 *imu* medical affairs
務室 *imushitsu* medical office
12博 *ihaku* doctor of medicine
13業 *igyō* medical practice
16薬 *iyaku* medicine
薬分業 *iyaku-bungyō* separation of medical and dispensary practice
薬品 *iyakuhin* medical supplies
17療 *iryō* medical care; medical
療伝道 *iryō dendō* medical missionary work
療車 *iryōsha* clinic car, traveling clinic
療材料 *iryō zairyō* medical supplies
療法人 *iryō hōjin* medical corporation
療品 *iryōhin* medical supplies
療保険 *iryō hoken* medical-care insurance
療施設 *iryō shisetsu* medical facilities
療報酬 *iryō hōshū* medical fee
療器械 *iryō kikai* medical appliances, surgical instruments
療機関 *iryō kikan* medical institution
20籍 *iseki* register of physicians

8

B **匿** 764/F279 Toku. *kakuma(u)* shelter, shield, hide. [匸]
6名 *tokumei* anonymity; pseudonym

匪 765/F277 Hi negation; wicked person.
6団 *hidan* bandit gang
10徒 *hito* bandit
躬 *hikyū* self-sacrificing service
13賊 *hizoku* bandit, rebel

—— 9 ——

區 766/F279 See 区 757. [匸]

—— 12 ——

匱 767/F277 Kɪ. *hitsu* chest, coffer; rice tub.

RAD. 匸 23

Kakushi-gamae "hiding" enclosure. This radical is treated herein as a variant of Rad. 22. Nickname: Hiding.

RAD. 十 24

Jū ten. Variants: 𠂇, 𠂉. The enclosure 𠂇 is sometimes included as a variant of this, but not herein. Nickname: Cross.

A 十 768/F279 Jū *tō, to* ten.

1 一月 *jūichigatsu* November

一面観世音 *Jūichimen Kanzeon* 11-faced Goddess of Mercy

一面観音 *Jūichimen Kannon* 11-faced Goddess of Mercy

一献金 *jūichi kenkin* tithes

2 八番 *jūhachiban* No. 18; one's favorite stunt; one's hobby. *ohako* one's favorite stunt; one's hobby

人力 *jūninriki* the strength of ten

人十色 *jūnin-to-iro* Everyone has his own interests and ideas.

人並 *jūninna(mi)* average, mediocrity

二支 *jūnishi* the 12 signs of the zodiac

二月 *jūnigatsu* December

二分 *jūnibun* more than enough

二折 *jūnio(ri)* duodecimo (folding)

二使徒 *Jūni Shito* Twelve Apostles

二単衣 *jūnihitoe* lady's ceremonial court dress

二指腸 *jūnishichō* duodenum

二指腸虫 *jūnishichōchū* hookworm

二時 *jūniji* twelve oclock; noon; midnight

二宮 *jūnikyū* the constellations of the zodiac

3 干 *jikkan* the 10 calendar signs

三夜 *jūsan-ya* 13th day (of the moon); the night of the 13th day of the 9th lunar month

万 *jūman* a hundred thousand

万億土 *jūman-okudo* eternity, paradise

4 手 *jitte* short metal truncheon

文字 *jūmonji* cross. *jūmonji no* cruciform. *jūmonji ni* crosswise

中八九 *jitchū-hakku* 8 or 9 cases out of ten

日 *tōka* ten days; the tenth (day of the month)

日菊 *tōka (no) kiku* coming too late

月 *jūgatsu* October

月革命 *Jūgatsu Kakumei* the October Revolution

五 *jūgo* fifteen

五夜 *jūgoya* night of the full moon; the night of the 15th day of the 8th lunar month

六分音符 *jūrokubu ompu* a 16th note

六夜 *izayoi* 16-day-old moon

分 *jūbun* enough, satisfactory; perfect; thoro. *jūbun suru* divide into ten

分一 *jūbun (no) ichi* the tithe; a tenth

5 目 *jūmoku* all eyes

代 *jūdai* the teens; the tenth generation

台 *jūdai* teens

6 全 *jūzen* perfection, consummation; absolute safety

字 *jūji* cross. *jūji ni* crosswise. *jūji no* crossed, cruciform

字火 *jūjika* crossfire

字形 *jūjikei* cross. *jūjikei no* cruciform

字架 *jūjika* cross; the Cross (of Christ)

字架状 *jūjikajō no* cruciform

字架像 *jūjikazō* crucifix

字軍 *Jūjigun* Crusades; Crusaders

字軍騎士 *Jūjigun Kishi* the Crusaders

字砲火 *jūji hōka* cross fire

字街 *jūjigai* crossroads, street crossing

字路 *jūjiro* crossroads

字線 *jūjisen* cross hairs

字鍬 *jūjishū* a pick; a pickax

7 戒 *jikkai* the ten Buddhist precepts

把一紮 *jippa-hitokara(ge)* sweeping (criticism)

8 雨 *jūu* a refreshing rain once in ten days

9 指 *jisshi, jusshi* the ten fingers

重 *toe* tenfold

10 倍 *jūbai* ten times, tenfold

哲 *jittetsu, juttetsu* Basho's Ten Disciples; Confucius' Ten Disciples

能 *jūnō* fire shovel, fire pan

部門分類法 *Jūbumon Bunruihō* Dewey Decimal System

進 *jisshin no* decimal. *jisshin* decimal system
進分類法 *jisshin bunruihō* decimal classification
進法 *jisshinhō* decimal system
進制 *jisshinsei* decimal system
13 数 *jūsū-* ten-odd
14 誡 *Jikkai* the Ten Commandments, the Decalog
種競技 *jisshu kyōgi* decathlon
15 億 *jū oku* a billion
21 露盤 *soroban* abacus

1

千 See 156.

2

午 See 162.

升 See 160.

卅 卅 See 78.

卆 769/F289 See 卒 294.

3

丗 See 世 95 and 卅 78. [一]

卌 卌 See 87.

卉 See 85.

半 半 See 132.

卋 See 世 95.

A 古 770/F320 Ko old. *furu(i)* old, aged, ancient, antiquated; stale, threadbare; outmoded, obsolete article. *furu(biru)* look old, get old. *furu(bokeru)* look old; become musty; wear out. *furu, furu-* used, secondhand. *furu(ku)* anciently, formerly. *inishie* antiquity, ancient times. *(o)furu* used article. *furu(mekashii)* old and familiar. [口]

2 人 *kojin* ancient people
刀 *kotō* an old sword
3 川 *furukawa* an old river
4 手 *furute* disused article; ex-soldier; retired official
方 *kohō* an old method
木 *koboku* an old tree
切 *furugi(re)* old cloth; old rags
井戸 *furu-ido* an old unused well
文 *kobun, komon* ancient writing
文学 *kobungaku* paleography, the study of ancient writings
文書 *kobunsho, komonjo* ancient documents
今 *kokon* ancient and modern times, all ages, past and present
今東西 *kokon-tōzai* all times and places
今無類 *kokon-murui* best ever
5 句 *koku* an ancient expression; an old poem
史 *koshi* ancient history
写本 *koshahon* an old manuscript; a codex
生物 *koseibutsu* extinct plants and animals
生物学 *koseibutsugaku* paleontology
本 *furubon, furuhon* old book, secondhand book. *kohon* secondhand book; ancient book
本屋 *furuhon-ya* secondhand book store
代 *kodai* ancient times
代人 *kodaijin* the ancients
代史 *kodaishi* ancient history
代語 *kodaigo* ancient language
6 米 *komai* old rice
老 *korō* old people, seniors, elders
血 *furuchi* impure blood
式 *koshiki* old style; ancient rites
曲 *kokyoku* old music
池 *furu-ike* an old pool, an old pond
寺 *furudera, koji* an old temple
字 *koji* ancient writing
印紙 *ko-inshi, furu-inshi* used stamps
自動車 *furujidōsha* used car
色 *koshoku* faded color, antique look
色蒼然 *koshoku-sōzen(taru)* antique-looking
伝 *koden* legend, tradition
伝説 *kodensetsu* old tradition
7 言 *kogen* obsolete word; old proverb
里 *furusato* home town, birthplace; an old village; a historic village
体 *kotai* old custom, old style
址 *koshi* historic ruins
兵 *kohei* old soldier, veteran. *furutsuwamono* an old veteran; an old hand
希 *koki* aged seventy
来 *korai* from time immemorial. *korai no* ancient, time-honored
社寺 *koshaji* old shrines and temples
8 金 *furugane* scrap iron, scrap metal
例 *korei* old precedent, tradition, custom
法 *kohō* old method, old law
注 *kochū* commentaries of the ancients
河 *furukawa* an old river
狐 *furugitsune* old fox, old-timer, schemer
服 *furufuku* old clothes, old suit
制 *kosei* ancient establishment; ancient laws

剎 *kosatsu* ancient temple
画 *koga* ancient painting
学 *kogaku* classical studies
昔 *koseki* ancient times
武士 *kobushi* feudal warrior, samurai. *furu-tsuwamono* an old veteran; an old hand
往今来 *koō-konrai* in all ages, since antiquity
版 *kohan* old edition
版本 *kohambon* old edition
物 *furumono, kobutsu* antique, old article, secondhand goods
物商 *kobutsushō* curio or secondhand dealer
参 *kosan* seniority, long service
参者 *kosansha* senior, oldtimer
事 *koji* ancient events
事来歴 *koji raireki* origin and history; particulars
事記 *Kojiki* Japan's Ancient Chronicle
典 *koten* old book; classics; classic
典文学 *koten bungaku* classical literature
典主義 *koten shugi* classicism
典的 *kotenteki* classical
典学 *kotengaku* the classics
典派 *kotenha* classical school
典語 *kotengo* classical or dead languages
9 音 *ko-on* old character pronunciation
風 *kofū* old customs, old style
俗 *kozoku* old custom
城 *kojō* old castle
柯 *koka* coca (source of cocaine)
臭 *furukusa(i)* stale, old fashioned; hackneyed, trite
茶 *kocha* last year's tea
草 *furukusa* last year's grass, dead grass
美術品 *kobijitsuhin* old art object
10 格 *kokaku* convention, usage; old customs, old etiquette
株 *furukabu* old-timer, veteran, senior
酒 *furuzake* last year's saké; old saké. *koshu* well-cured saké
流 *koryū* old manners, old style; old school (of art)
狸 *furudanuki* old badger, veteran, old-timer, schemer, old fox
祠 *koshi* an old small shrine
称 *koshō* old name
訓 *kokun* ancient instruction; an old reading of a character
記 *koki* ancient records
都 *koto* ancient city; former capital
衰 *furu(bi)-otoro(eru)* waste away
家 *furuie* old house, deserted house
書 *kosho* old book, rare book
11 疵 *furukizu* an old wound
趾 *koshi* historic ruins
巣 *furusu* old home, former haunt
強者 *furutsuwamono* old soldier, veteran
道 *kodō* old road; ancient methods; ancient moral teachings; the way of learning
道具 *furudōgu, kodōgu* old furniture; curios; secondhand goods
道具屋 *furudōguya* secondhand store
12 渡 *kowatar(i)* an old imported article
稀 *koki* age seventy
註 *kochū* commentaries of the ancients
創 *furukizu* an old wound
着 *furugi* old clothes, secondhand clothing
筆 *kohitsu* old writing
筆家 *kohitsuka* an expert in old writing
13 傷 *furukizu* scar, old wound; old unpleasant incident
雅 *koga* classical elegance, antiquity
詩 *koshi* ancient poems
跡 *koseki, furuato* historic spot, ruins
鉄 *furugane, furutetsu* scrap iron, scrap metal
靴 *furugutsu* old shoes
義 *kogi* old meaning, old interpretation
意 *ko-i* ancient ways; the feelings of the ancients
楽 *kogaku* ancient music
聖 *kosei* ancient sage
戦場 *kosenjō* ancient battlefield
14 語 *kogo* obsolete word; old proverb
説 *kosetsu* ancient belief
歌 *furu-uta, koka* old song, old poem
豪 *kogō* veteran, old-timer, a man of experience
墨 *koboku* old ink stick
銭 *kosen* old coin
銭学 *kosengaku* numismatics
15 廟 *kobyō* old shrine
儀 *kogi* ancient rites
墳 *kofun* old mound, old grave, ancient tomb
賢 *koken* ancient sage
器 *koki* an antique
16 諺 *kogen* old proverb
18 蹟 *koseki* historic spot, ruins
顔 *furugao* familiar face, old-timer

4

卋 See 世 95. [一]

老 See 3683. [老]

考 See 3684. [老]

出 丘 See 79 and 12.

卉 771/F288 See 卉 85.

5

B 克 772/F187 Koku. *ka(tsu)* (see under 勝 3787.0). *yo(ku)* kindly; skillfully. [丿儿]

3 己 *kokki* self-denial, self-control
己心 *kokkishin* spirit of self-denial
8 明 *kokumei* faithfulness, diligence, conscientiousness
服 *kokufuku* subjugation, conquest
12 復 *kokufuku* restoration

A **孝** 773/F520 Kō filial piety. [子]

3 女 *kōjo* filial daughter
子 *kōshi* filial child
4 心 *kōshin* filial devotion
6 行 *kōkō* filial piety
7 弟 *kōtei* filial piety
10 悌 *kōtei* filial piety
11 道 *kōdō* filial piety
経 *Kōkyō* the Book of Filial Piety
12 順 *kōjun* obedience, filial piety
敬 *kōkei* filial piety
15 養 *kōyō* discharge of filial duties

—— 6 ——

老 See 3686. [耂]

叀 See 叀 221.

卓 See 802.

卒 See 294.

阜 See 4977. [阜]

者 See 3685. [耂]

A **協** 774/F290 Kyō co-operation.

2 力 *kyōryoku* co-operation
力者 *kyōryokusha* co-worker; co-operator
力鋼 *kyōryokukō* high-tension steel
4 心 *kyōshin* unison, accord
6 会 *kyōkai* association, society
同 *kyōdō* co-operation, collaboration, association
同組合 *kyōdō kumiai* a co-operative; a partnership
同動作 *kyōdō dōsa* concerted action
7 技者 *kyōgisha* contestant, athlete
8 和 *kyōwa* concord, harmony, concert
定 *kyōtei* pact, agreement
定案 *kyōteian* agreement, proposal
定書 *kyōteisho* agreement, protocol
9 奏曲 *kyōsōkyoku* concerto
約 *kyōyaku* pact, convention, agreement
約国 *kyōyakukoku* high contracting powers, signatories
約書 *kyōyakusho* written agreement
11 商 *kyōshō* negotiation; agreement
商国 *kyōshōkoku* allies
13 業 *kyōgyō* co-operative industry
15 賛 *kyōsan* mutual aid, co-operation; approval, authorization
調 *kyōchō* co-operation, conciliation, harmony; firm (market) tone
調主義 *kyōchō shugi* collaboration
20 議 *kyōgi* conference, deliberation
議会 *kyōgikai* council, conference, convention
議会員 *kyōgikai-in* conferees
議所 *kyōgisho* conference site
議官 *kyōgikan* conferees
議事項 *kyōgi jikō* agenda
議員 *kyōgi-in* delegate

A **直** 775/F1317 Jiki, Choku honesty, frankness; simplicity; cheerfulness; correctness; being straight; night duty. *nao(ru)* be mended; get well; be restored; return to normal; be installed (as a legal wife); change (from third to second class). *nao(su)* mend, repair, put in order, reform, correct; revise, amend; re-do, alter; cure; restore; adjust, regulate; convert (money). *jika ni* directly, firsthand, in person. *jiki* direct, in person; soon; at once; just; near by. *jiki ni* soon; immediately; easily. *ne* price, cost, value. *su(gu)* immediately; easily; right (near). *su(gu) na* honest, upright. *tada(chi) ni* immediately, directly, in person. *hita to* close to. *nao(ki)* straight, upright. *nao(shi)* correction; repair; repairman. *tada* direct; close; straight; immediately. *nao* straight; mischief; ordinary, common. *hita* earnestly; immediately; exactly. [目]

2 刀 *chokutō* straight sword
3 下 *chokka suru* fall perpendicularly. *chokka* directly under. *nesa(ge)* a cut in price. *nesa(gari)* a fall in price
上 *chokujō* directly above; going steadily upward. *nea(gari)* price advance; increase in value. *nea(ge)* price hike, mark-up
4 中 *tadanaka* middle
引 *nebi(ki)* price reduction, discount
切 *negi(ru)* haggle, bargain
方体 *chokuhōtai* right-angled parallelepiped
5 打 *neu(chi)* value, worth, price; dignity
払 *jikibara(i)* cash payment
出 *chokushutsu suru* shoot straight out; grow straight down

2 二亠人イ𠆢儿入八丷冂冖冫几凵刀刂力勹匕匚匸 7[十]卜卩厂ム又

立 *chokuritsu* vertical, perpendicular, upright, erect. *chokuritsu suru* stand erect, rise perpendicularly
立不動 *chokuritsu-fudō* standing at atten-
立茎 *chokuritsukei* erect stem └tion
6 行 *chokkō* thru, non-stop
伝 *jikiden* direct transmission (of mysteries or skill); initiation
列 *chokuretsu* series wiring
7 角 *chokkaku* right angle
言 *chokugen* plain speaking
走 *hitabashi(ri)* running swiftly
系 *chokkei* lineal descendant, direct line
売 *chokubai suru* sell directly
弟子 *jiki deshi* personal pupil
足袋 *jika tabi* work tabi
8 送 *chokusō* direct delivery
往 *chokuō suru* go unhesitatingly forward
径 *chokkei* diameter
披 *jikihi, chokuhi* personal, confidential
押 *hitao(shi) ni* steadily └(letter)
物 *nao(shi)mono* mending
垂 *hitatare* ancient ceremonial court robe
直 *jikijiki no* personal, direct ┌gun)
参 *jikisan* immediate follower (of the sho-
取引 *jiki torihiki* spot transaction, cash transaction
9 面 *chokumen suru* face, confront, be confronted by ┌service
通 *chokutsū* direct communication, thru
後 *chokugo* immediately after, right behind
段 *nedan* price, cost
前 *chokuzen* just before
奏 *jikisō* direct report to the throne
巻 *chokuma(ki)* series-wound
映館 *chokueikan* chain movie theaters
10 進 *chokushin suru* go right on, go straight
流 *chokuryū* direct current └ahead
航 *chokkō* direct voyage, direct service
射 *chokusha* direct fire, frontal fire; direct
11 達 *jikitatsu* direct delivery └rays
頃 *negoro* reasonable price
球 *chokkyū* straight ball
視 *chokushi suru* look straight at, face
経 *chokkei* diameter └squarely
訳 *chokuyaku* literal translation
情 *chokujō* frankness, impulsiveness
情径行 *chokujō-keikō* frankness; impulsiveness ┌firsthand
接 *chokusetsu* direct, immediate, personal,
接伝染 *chokusetsu densen* direct infection
接行動 *chokusetsu kōdō* direct action
接法 *chokusetsuhō* direct method; indicative mood
接的 *chokusetsuteki* direct
接教授法 *chokusetsu kyōjuhō* direct method
接税 *chokusetsuzei* direct tax
接費 *chokusetsuhi* direct cost
接話法 *chokusetsu wahō* direct quotation
12 属 *chokuzoku* direct control
喩 *chokuyu* simile
渡 *jikawata(shi)* direct delivery
焼 *jikaya(ki)* broiling over an open fire
税 *chokuzei* direct tax
結 *chokketsu* direct connection
訴 *jikiso* direct appeal
筆 *jikihitsu* one's own handwriting. *chokuhitsu* writing with an upright brush; frank writing ┌personal answer
答 *chokutō, jikitō* prompt answer, direct
営 *chokuei* direct management
覚 *chokkaku* intuition, insight
覚的 *chokkokuteki ni* intuitively
13 腸 *chokuchō* rectum
話 *jikiwa* one's own account (of something)
路 *chokuro, sugumichi* straight road, short
感 *chokkan* intuition └cut
感的 *chokkanteki* intuitive
14 様 *su(gu)sama* immediately
説法 *chokusetsuhō* indicative mood
截 *chokusetsu na* frank, straightforward
截簡明 *chokusetsu-kammei* simple and plain
15 踏 *nebu(mi)* appraisal, setting prices, estimation, evaluation
線 *chokusen* straight line, air line, beeline
線形 *chokusenkei* rectangular figures
談 *jikidan, jikadan* personal account (of);
談判 *jika dampan* direct talks └direct talks
撃 *chokugeki* direct hit
撃弾 *chokugekidan* direct hit
16 諫 *chokkan* personal admonition
鞘 *nezaya* margin, spread (in prices)
覧 *jikiran* respectfully looking at (something)
積出 *jiki tsumidashi* immediate shipment
輸入 *chokuyunyū, jiki yunyū* direct import
輸出 *chokuyushutsu, jiki yushutsu* direct export
17 謝 *hita-ayama(ru)* earnestly apologize
轄 *chokkatsu* direct control
轄地 *chokkatsuchi* area under direct control (of the shogun)
轄植民地 *chokkatsu shokuminchi* crown
18 観 *chokkan* intuition, insight └colony
観的 *chokkanteki* intuitive

7

卑 See 221.

者 See 者 3685. [耂]

剋 776 F246 **尅 剋** Koku victory. [刂]

哉 777 F358 Sai. *kana* how! what! alas! *ya* question mark. [口]

A **南** 778 F291 Nan. *minami, minnami* south. *minami suru* proceed southward.

2 十字星 *Minami Jūjisei* Southern Cross
3 下 *nanka suru* go south
山 *nanzan* southern mountain; Mt. Kōya
山寿 *nanzan(no)ju* longevity
4 中 *nanchū suru* crossing the meridian
天 *nanten* the southern sky
太平洋 *Minami Taiheiyō* South Pacific
支 *Nanshi* South China
支那海 *Minami Shinakai* South China Sea
方 *nampō* south; southern, southward
方産 *nampōsan* products of the south seas
5 瓜 *kabocha, nanka, tōnasu* squash, pumpkin
氷洋 *Nanhyōyō, Nampyōyō* Antarctic Ocean
半 *nanhan* southern half
半球 *Minami Hankyū* Southern Hemisphere
北 *namboku* north and south
北朝 *Nambokuchō* Northern and Southern Dynasties (1336–1392)
北戦争 *Namboku Sensō* (U.S.) Civil War
6 米 *Nambei* South America
行 *nankō* southbound
西 *nansei, minaminishi* southwest
向 *minamimu(ki)* southern exposure, facing south
光 *nankō* southern lights
回帰線 *Minami Kaikisen* Tropic of Capricorn
7 宋 *Nansō* the Southern Sungs
阿 *Nan-a* South Africa
阿連邦 *Nan-a Rempō* Union of South Africa
阿戦争 *Nan-a Sensō* Boer War
8 門 *nammon* south gate
国 *nangoku* southern countries
欧 *Nan-ō* Southern Europe
郊 *nankō* southern suburbs
東 *nantō, minamihigashi* southeast
征北伐 *nansei-hokubatsu* attacking in all directions
岸 *nangan* south coast; south bank
岸沿 *nanganzo(i) ni* along the southern coast; along the southern seashore
京 *Nankin* Nanking
京木綿 *nankimmomen* nankeen (cloth)
京玉 *nankindama* glass beads
京米 *nankimmai* Chinese rice, foreign rice
京虫 *nankimmushi* bedbug
京豆 *nankimmame* peanut
京町 *Nankimmachi* Chinatown
京花火 *nankin hanabi* firecracker
京袋 *nankimbukuro* gunny sack
京焼 *Nankin-ya(ki)* Nanking porcelain, chinaware
京錠 *nankinjō* padlock, hasp
京繻子 *nankin jusu* nankeen satin
9 面 *nammen* south face, south side; the south. *nammen suru* face the south; ascend the throne; rule
風 *nampū, minami kaze* south wind
海 *nankai* southern sea
洋 *Nan-yō* South Seas
洋諸島 *Nan-yō Shotō* South Sea Islands
南西 *nannansei* south-southwest
南東 *nannantō* south-southeast
10 進 *nanshin suru* proceed south
航 *nankō* sailing south, southbound
部 *nambu* southern part
都 *nanto* southern capital, Nara
11 側 *minamigawa, nansoku* south side
隅 *nangū* southern corner
寄 *minamiyo(ri)* southerly (wind)
船北馬 *nansen-hokuba* constant traveling, restless wandering
12 満 *Namman* South Manchuria
朝 *Nanchō* Southern Dynasty
蛮 *namban* southern barbarians; red pepper
蛮人 *nambanjin* the southern barbarians, the early Europeans
蛮船 *nambansen* the early European ships
無 *namu* hail (in Buddhist prayers)
無阿弥陀仏 *Namu Amida Butsu* Hail Amida
無妙法蓮華経 *Namu Myōhō Rengekyō* Hail Lotus Sutra
極 *Nankyoku* South Pole
極大陸 *Nankyoku Tairiku* Antarctica
極光 *nankyokukō* aurora australis, southern lights
極星 *nankyokusei* the southern polar stars
極洋 *Nankyokuyō* Antarctic Ocean
極海 *Nankyokukai* Antarctic Ocean
極帯 *Nankyokutai* Antarctic Zone
極圏 *Nankyokuken* Antarctic Circle
13 溟 *nammei* the southern ocean
14 端 *nantan* southern tip
15 緯 *nan-i* south latitude

— 8 —

尅 779 F562 F246 See **剋** 776. [寸]

恊 780 F-X Nonstandard for **協** 774.

B **栽** 781 F973 Sai planting. [木]

11 培 *saibai* cultivation (of plants)
培所 *saibaijo* plantation
培種 *saibaishu* agricultural species

B 索 782/F1446 SAKU rope, cord. *tsuna* (see under 綱 3561.0). *moto(meru)* search for. [糸]

4 引 *sakuin* index
7 条 *sakujō* cable, rope
条鉄道 *sakujō tetsudō* cable railway
8 具 *sakugu* rigging, gear, tackle
10 莫 *sakubaku(taru)* desolate, bleak, dreary
11 道 *sakudō* overhead freight-carrying cable
12 然 *sakuzen(taru)* dry, desolate
15 敵 *sakuteki* searching for the enemy

A 真 783/F1323 **眞** SHIN truth; reality; genuineness; Buddhist sect originating in the thirteenth century. *makoto* (see under 誠 4352.0). *shin ni, hon ni* truly, actually, really. *ma-* just, right, due (east); pure, genuine, true. [目]

1 一文字 *ma-ichimonji* straight, as the crow flies
2 二 *ma(p)puta(tsu) ni, mafuta(tsu) ni* right in half
人 *shinjin* true man
人間 *maningen* an honest man, a good citizen
3 下 *mashita* right under, directly below
上 *ma-ue* right above
丸 *ma(m)maru* perfect circle. *ma(m)maru(i)* perfectly round
4 心 *magokoro* sincerity, devotion
水 *mamizu* fresh water
中 *manaka, ma(n)naka* center, middle, midway
円 *ma(m)maru* perfect circle. *ma(m)maru(i)* perfectly round
円真珠 *shin-en shinju* cultured pearls
5 打 *shin-u(chi)* star performer
北 *makita* due north
平 *ma(t)taira na* perfectly level. *ma(p)pira* (not) by any means; humbly, sincerely
冬 *mafuyu* dead of winter
只中 *ma(t)tadanaka* right in the midst of, right at the height of
四角 *mashikaku, ma(s)shikaku* square
白 *ma(s)shiro, mashiro* pure white
白斑 *mashirafu* white spots
正 *shinsei* genuine, authentic, true, pure
正直 *mashōjiki, ma(s)shōjiki* perfectly honest
正面 *mashōmen, ma(s)shōmen* directly opposite, right in front
田 *sanada* plait; braid
田虫 *sanada mushi* tapeworm
田紐 *sanada himo* braid
田編 *sanada a(mi)* plait
6 竹 *madake* a long-jointed bamboo
西 *manishi* due west
因 *shin-in* true reason, true motive
近 *maji(ka) ni* nearness, proximity. *majika(i)* near at hand
向 *ma(k)kō* brow; front; helmet front. *mamuka(i), mamu(ki)* face to face, straight ahead, just in front of. *hitamu(ki) na* earnest; singlehanded
如 *shinnyo* the absolute, absolute reality
帆 *maho* full sail
先 *ma(s)saki* the head, the foremost; beginning
似 *mane(ru)* imitate, mimic, mock, follow suit. *mane* mimicry, imitation; behavior, pretense
似事 *manegoto* sham, make-believe, mere form
7 言 *Shingon* Buddhist sect originating in the eighth century
赤 *ma(k)ka* deep red, crimson
否 *shimpi* true or false
8 青 *ma(s)sao na* deep blue; ghastly pale
底 *shintei*＝心底 1645.8
価 *shinka* true value
味 *shimmi* true meaning
性 *shinsei* inborn nature, genuine
物 *shimbutsu* genuine article
直 *ma(s)sugu na* straight, direct, upright, erect; honest; frank
東 *mahigashi* due east
夜中 *mayonaka* dead of night, midnight
逆 *masaka* by no means
逆様 *ma(s)sakasama ni* headlong, head over heels
実 *shinjitsu* truth, reality, fact; in reality, truly
実一路 *shinjitsu-ichiro* path of sincerity
実性 *shinjitsusei* fidelity, truth, authenticity, credibility
空 *shinkū* vacuum. *shinkū no* hollow, empty
空帯 *shinkūtai* air pocket
空掃除器 *shinkū sōjiki* vacuum cleaner
空電球 *shinkū denkyū* vacuum bulb
空管 *shinkūkan* vacuum tube
9 迹 *shinseki* true autograph
後 *ma-ushi(ro)* right behind
砂 *masago* sand
紅 *shinku* crimson
前 *ma(m)mae ni* right in front of, just opposite
南 *maminami* due south
美 *shimbi* true beauty
勇 *shin-yū* true courage, true heroism
海豚 *ma-iruka* porpoise, dolphin
面目 *majime* serious, earnest, honest. *shimmemmoku* one's true character, oneself; seriousness, earnestness
面目腐 *majimekusa(ru)* pretend to be serious
相 *shinsō* the truth, the facts, the real situation
相調査 *shinsō chōsa* fact finding
昼 *mahiru* broad daylight, midday
昼間 *ma(p)piruma* broad daylight
10 症 *shinshō* genuine case (of a disease)
個 *shinko no* real, true
夏 *manatsu* midsummer

剣 *shinken* real sword; earnestness
剣勝負 *shinken-shōbu* fighting with real swords; game played in real earnest
珠 *shinju* pearl
珠母 *shinjubo* mother-of-pearl
珠色 *shinju iro* pearl gray
珠光 *shinjukō* pearl iridescence
珠貝 *shinjugai* pearl oyster
珠取 *shinjuto(ri)* pearl fishing; pearl diver
珠細工 *shinjuzaiku* pearl work
珠湾 *Shinju Wan* Pearl Harbor
珠層 *shinjusō* mother-of-pearl
珠質 *shinjushitsu* mother-of-pearl
珠養殖 *shinju yōshoku* pearl culture
珠養殖場 *shinju yōshokujō* pearl-oyster beds
珠擬 *shinjumaga(i)* imitation pearl
11 黒 *ma(k)kuro na* jet black
偽 *shingi* truth or error, authenticity
情 *shinjō* true feeling
深 *mabuka ni* down over the eyes
理 *shinri* truth
率 *shinsotsu* honesty, sincerity, frankness
盛 *ma(s)saka(ri), masaka(ri)* height of, middle of; full bloom
清水 *mashimizu* pure water, clear water
唯中 *ma(t)tadanaka* right in the midst of
魚板 *mana-ita* chopping board
12 筆 *shimpitsu* autograph; one's own handwriting; personal note
最中 *ma(s)saichū* midst; height
善美 *shin-zem-bi* the true, the good, and the beautiful
13 裸 *ma(p)padaka* nudity
跡 *shinseki* true autograph
際 *magiwa ni*＝間際 4949.13
新 *ma-atara(shii)* brand new
義 *shingi* true meaning
蒼 *massao* very pale
暗 *makkura* total darkness; shortsightedness
暗闇 *makkurayami* total darkness
意 *shin-i* real intention, true motive; true meaning
意義 *shin-igi* true meaning
14 綿 *mawata* silk floss, silk wadding
箇 *shinko no* real, true
疑 *shingi* truth or error, authenticity
15 影 *shin-ei* portrait, photograph
摯 *shinshi* sincerity, earnestness
16 鴨 *magamo* mallard duck
諦 *shintei, shintai* ultimate truth, essence (in Buddhism)
17 鍮 *shinchū* brass
18 蹟 *shinseki* true autograph
髄 *shinzui* essence, pith, spirit, soul, essentials, core, kernel, the life blood
鯉 *magoi* black carp
顔 *magao* serious look
19 贋 *shingan* the genuine and the spurious
鯛 *madai* red sea bream

9

乾 784 F65 B KAN. KEN heaven; emperor. *ho(su)* vt dry; desiccate; drain (off); drink up; dry up. *ka(seru)* dry up, scab, slough; be poisoned (with lacquer). *kawa(ku)* dry, dry up; be dry. *kawa(kasu)* vt dry, desiccate. *kara(biru)* dry up, shrivel. *kawa(ki)* drying; dryness. *hoshi-* dried, cured. [乙]
3 干 *karabo(shi)* sun-dried fish or vegetables
上 *hiaga(ru)* dry up, parch; ebb away
5 田 *kanden* dry rice field
皮 *kampi* dried hides
世帯 *kasejotai* poverty-stricken household
生姜 *kanshōga* powdered ginger
生植物 *kansei shokubutsu* desert plants
生薑 *kanshōga* powdered ginger
6 肉 *hoshiniku* dried meat, pemmican
地農法 *kanchi nōhō* dry farming
7 材 *kanzai* dry lumber
8 固 *hi-kata(maru), kanko suru* dry and harden
杯 *kampai* a toast
板 *kampan, kamban* dry plate
季 *kanki* dry season
果 *kanka* dried fruit
坤 *kenkon* heaven and earth; universe
坤一擲 *kenkon-itteki* throwing all into a task
性 *kansei* dryness, dry (pleurisy)
性油 *kanseiyu* drying oil, linseed oil
物 *kambutsu* groceries. *hoshimono* laundry on the line. *karamono* dried fish
物屋 *kambutsuya* grocery store
9 風 *kara(k)kaze, karakaze* dry wind
咳 *karazeki, kara seki* dry cough, hacking cough
拭 *karabuki* polishing with a dry cloth
枯 *kanko suru, hika(rabiru)* completely dry up
草 *kansō, hoshigusa, hoshi kusa* hay, dry grass
海苔 *hoshinori* dried edible seaweed
10 留 *kanryū* dry distillation
芻 *kansū* hay
11 魚 *hoshiuo, hizakana, hiuo, kangyo* dried fish
舷 *kangen* freeboard
菜 *kansai* dried vegetables
菓子 *higashi* candy; cookies
船渠 *kansenkyo, kandokku* dry dock
12 飯 *karei, kareii, hoshi-ii* dried boiled rice
期 *kanki* dry season
裂 *kanretsu* cracks in drying lumber
葡萄 *hoshibudō* raisins
湿 *kanshitsu* degree of humidity
湿計 *kanshitsukei* humidity meter
13 溜 *kanryū* dry distillation
煎 *kara-i(ri)* roasting, broiling
電池 *kandenchi* dry cell
酪 *kanraku* cheese
酪素 *kanrakuso* casein

14 徳 *kentoku* emperor's virtue
15 蝕 *kanshoku* the rotting of lumber stored with poor air circulation
16 瓢 *kampyō* dried gourd strings ⌈dehydrated
17 燥 *kansō* drying; dryness, aridity; insipid;
燥牛乳 *kansō gyūnyū* powdered milk
燥地 *kansōchi* dry land
燥地農業 *kansōchi nōgyō* dry farming
燥材 *kansōzai* seasoned lumber
燥卵 *kansō tamago* dehydrated eggs
燥炉 *kansōro* drying furnace
燥季 *kansōki* dry season
燥果 *kansōka* dried fruit
燥室 *kansōshitsu* drying room
燥洗濯 *kansō sentaku* dry cleaning
燥剤 *kansōzai* a drying agent
燥野菜 *kansō yasai* dehydrated vegetables
燥期 *kansōki* dry spell, dry period
燥無味 *kansō-mumi* dryness, dullness
燥腐朽 *kansō fukyū* dry rot
燥器 *kansōki* drier
燥機 *kansōki* drier

10

貢 See 4495. [貝]

10 準 785/F1143 See 準 791. [水]

辜 786/F1853 Ko sin, fault. *tsumi* crime. [辛]

A 博 787/F293 HAKU. BAKU. *haku*(*suru*) command esteem, win acclaim; gain, receive. *-haku* doctor, Ph.D.; exposition, fair, exhibition.
3 大 *hakudai* large and wide
士 *Hakase, Hakushi* Ph.D.
士号 *hakasegō* doctor's degree, Ph.D.
4 引旁証 *hakuin-bōshō* citing copious refer-
5 打 *bakuchi* gambling ⌊ences
打打 *bakuchiu*(*chi*) gambling
7 労 *bakurō* horse trader
8 学 *hakugaku* erudition ⌈energetic activity
学力行 *hakugaku-ryokkō* wide learning and
物 *hakubutsu* wide learning; natural history
物学 *hakubutsugaku* natural history
物館 *hakubutsukan* museum
9 奕 *bakuchi, bakueki* gambling
奕打 *bakuchiu*(*chi*) gambler
奕宿 *bakuchi yado* gambling den
10 徒 *bakuto* gambler
13 雅 *bakuga no* well-informed, accomplished
愛 *hakuai* charity, benevolence, philanthropy, humanity
愛家 *hakuaika* philanthropist
14 聞 *hakubun no* well-informed, erudite
16 覧 *hakuran* extensive reading, wide knowledge
覧会 *hakurankai* fair, exhibition, exposition
覧強記 *hakuran-kyōki* reading and record-
19 識 *hakushiki* extensive knowledge ⌊ing

B 裁 788/F1697 SAI. *saba*(*ku*) judge. *ta*(*tsu*) cut out (a suit); (see also under 絶 3539.0). *saba*(*ki*) judgment, decision, verdict. *ta*(*chi*) cutting, cut. [衣]
3 上 *ta*(*chi*)*a*(*gari*) (tailor's) cutting; styling
4 方 *ta*(*chi*)*kata* cutting, cut
5 可 *saika* sanction, approval
7 決 *saiketsu* decision, judgment, ruling
決書 *saiketsusho* written verdict
判 *saiban* trial; adjudication
判人 *saibannin* judge
判上 *saibanjō no* judicial
判沙汰 *saibanzata* law suit, litigation
判長 *saibanchō* presiding judge
判所 *saibansho* a court; courthouse
判官 *saibankan* the judge
判権 *saibanken* jurisdiction
8 板 *ta*(*chi*)*-ita* tailor's cutting board
物 *ta*(*chi*)*mono* cutting (cloth or paper)
定 *seitei* decision, ruling, award, arbitration
庖丁 *ta*(*chi*)*bōchō* tailor's knife
10 屑 *ta*(*chi*)*kuzu* cuttings, scraps
庭 *saba*(*ki*) (*no*) *niwa* law court
11 掛 *ta*(*chi*)*-ka*(*keru*) begin to cut
許 *saikyo* sanction, approval ⌈decide, judge
断 *saidan suru* cut off; cut out (clothes);
断師 *saidanshi* (tailor's) cutter
12 割 *ta*(*chi*)*-wa*(*ru*) cut open, cut apart; divide
量 *sairyō* discretion
15 縫 *saihō* sewing. *ta*(*chi*)*-nu*(*u*) cut and sew
縫師 *saihōshi* tailor, seamstress

11

B 載 789/F1840 SAI. *no*(*ru*), *no*(*seru*) (see under 乗 223.0). [車]
9 炭 *saitan* coaling
11 貨屯数 *saika tonsū* deadweight tonnage
貨吃水 *saika kissui* ship's draft
貨吃水線 *saika kissuisen* Plimsoll mark,
16 積 *saiseki* carrying; loading ⌊the draft line
録 *sairoku suru* record

A 幹 790/F628 KAN. *miki* (tree) trunk. [干]
6 竹割 *karatakewa*(*ri*) cutting straight down; cleaving (a person) in two
8 事 *kanji* manager, secretary
事長 *kanjichō* chief secretary (of a party)

10 流 *kanryū* main current
部 *kambu* management, the executives, the
部会 *kambukai* board of directors ⌊leaders
15 線 *kansen* main line, trunk line

A 準 791/F1143 準 JUN. *jun*(*jiru*), *jun*(*zuru*) apply correspondingly, correspond to, be proportionate to, conform to. *nazora*(*eru*) pattern after, liken to, imitate. *jun-* semi-, quasi-, associate; standard; rule; level; aim. (*ni*) *jun*(*jite*) in proportion to. [氵]

4 尺 *junshaku* surveyor's leveling pole
5 用 *jun-yō suru* apply
6 会員 *junkai-in* associate member
7 社員 *junsha-in* associate member; junior employee
決勝 *junkesshō* semifinals
決勝戦 *junkesshōsen* semifinals
8 拠 *junkyo* conformity; authority (of); standard
9 則 *junsoku* regulations; standard ⌊ard
急 *junkyū* local express
11 教員 *junkyōin* assistant teacher
12 備 *jumbi* preparation; provision, reserve
備日 *jumbi* (*no*) *hi* preparation day
備金 *jumbikin* reserve fund
備資金 *jumbi shikin* reserve funds
備銀行 *jumbi ginkō* reserve bank
備管制 *jumbi kansei* preliminary control of lights ⌈(in law)
13 禁治産 *junkinchisan* quasi-incompetence
19 縄 *junjō* a level and an inked string; norm, rule, standard

— 12 —

斡 792/F870 ATSU go around; rule, administer. [斗]

11 旋 *assen* kind offices, mediation
旋人 *assennin* mediator, agent, go-between
旋料 *assenryō* agent's charge

截 793/F761 SETSU. *ta*(*tsu*) (see under 絶 3539.0).) *ki*(*ru*) (see under 切 667.0). [戈]

4 切 *ta*(*chi*)-*ki*(*ru*) cut off, block, disconnect
11 断 *setsudan* cutting off
断面 *setsudammen* transverse section
断機 *setsudanki* cutting machine; guillotine
12 然 *setsuzen*(*taru*) clear, sharp, distinct

— 14 —

翰 794/F1510 KAN letter; writing brush. [羽]

8 長 *Kanchō* Cabinet (Chief) Secretary
林 *kanrin* literary circles
林院 *kanrin-in* academy, institute
14 墨 *kamboku* brush and ink; writing; drawing

— 15 —

韓 See 5107. [韋]

戴 795/F764 TAI. *itada*(*ku*) *vi* and *vt* be crowned with, wear; live under (a ruler); install (a president); receive, accept; buy; take, eat, drink. [戈]

8 物 *itada*(*ki*)*mono* gift
9 冠式 *taikanshiki* coronation

— 20 —

聽 See 聴 3716. [耳]

— 22 —

矗 796/F1333 CHOKU luxuriance. [目]

顰 See 2437. [頁]

RAD. 卜 25

Uranai divination or *to* (the katakana). Variants: ⺊, ⺊. Nickname: *Kana To*.

卜 797/F295 BOKU divining. *boku suru*, *urana*(*u*) tell a fortune, predict; choose, settle, fix. *uranai*, *ura* divination.

8 居 *bokkyo suru* choosing a homesite by divination
者 *bokusha* fortuneteller, soothsayer, diviner
10 書 *urabumi* diviner's book
13 筮 *bokuzei* fortunetelling, divination

— 1 —

A 上 798/F22 JŌ top; best; first volume. SHŌ upper part; government. *ue* up, upper part, top, summit; surface; far better; higher; (in) authority; as far as . . . is concerned; besides; after; emperor, sovereign; upon (examination); influence of (liquor);

lord, shogun; superior. *a*(*garu*) rise, go up; climb up; advance, appreciate; be promoted; improve; enter, call on; be offered; accrue; be finished; (expenses) come to; go bankrupt; begin spinning (cocoons); be caught; get ruffled; eat, drink; die; weaken (as a battery); let up (rain). *a*(*geru*) raise, elevate; fly (kites); praise; increase, advance; promote, elevate; vomit; usher in, admit; send (to school); offer; present, leave with; finish; arrange (expenses); observe, perform; quote, mention, give (examples); bear (a child); improve (talents); do up (the hair); arrest; engage; fry; (rains) stop. *a*(*gattari*) poor business. *a*(*gari*) ascent, rise, advance; yield; death; spinning; completion; stop; finish. *nobo*(*ru*) rise, ascend, go up, climb; go to (the capital); add up to; be promoted; advance (in price); sail up; come up (on the agenda). *nobo*(*su*), *nobo*(*seru*) raise; record; bring up (a matter); serve (food); send some one out (from Kyoto). *nobo*(*ri*) ascent; up train (toward the capital). *kami* top; head; upper part; upper stream; emperor; a superior; upper part of the body; the above. *-ue* my dear (father). *-jō* aboard a ship or vehicle; from the standpoint of; as a matter of (fact). *jō-* governmental; imperial; best; high class; going up; presenting; showing. *uwa-*, upper, upward, outer, surface, top. *-a*(*gezu*) every (two days, etc.). *-a*(*gari*) after (rain); ex-(official, etc.). **[—]**

2 人 *shōnin* Buddhist saint, priest

3 口 *nobo*(*ri*)*guchi* starting point for a mountain ascent. *a*(*gari*)*guchi*, a(*gari*)*kuchi* entrance

上 *jōjō* the best

女中 *kami jochū* head servant

下 *shōka*, *jōge* high and low; the government and the people; going up and down. *a*(*ge*)*oro*(*shi*) raising and lowering; loading and unloading. *a*(*ge*)*sa*(*ge*) raising and lowering; praising and blaming; modulation. *nobo*(*ri*)*-kuda*(*ri*) going up and down. *a*(*gari*)*sa*(*gari*) rise and fall, fluctuation. *kamishimo* samurai garb; an old ceremonial garb; the government and the people; the upper and lower parts of the body

下水道 *jōgesuidō* water and sewer services

下動 *jōgedō* vertical motion (in earthquakes)

下線 *jōgesen* both (railway) tracks

4 戸 *jōgo* drinker; drinker's habits

文 *jōbun* the foregoing

辺 *uwabe* exterior, surface, outside; outward appearance. *jōhen* the upper side

込 *a*(*gari*)*-ko*(*mu*) enter, step in

中下 *jō-chū-ge* excellent-good-poor; first-second-third (class)

分別 *jōfumbetsu* good idea, wise policy

手 *uwate*, *kamite* upper part; upper stream; left side (of a stage). *jōzu* skill, dexterity

手者 *jōzumono* flatterer

方 *jōhō* upper part. *ue*(*tsu*)*gata* nobles, the upper class. *kamigata* Kyoto and vicinity

方贅六 *kamigata-zeiroku* people of the Kyoto area

水 *jōsui* water supply

水道 *jōsuidō* waterworks

天 *jōten* heaven; God, Providence, the Supreme Being, the Absolute

天気 *jōtenki* fair weather

5 玉 *jōdama* fine jewel; best article; pretty woman

田 *jōden* high rice field; very fertile rice field

白 *jōhaku* first-class rice

皮 *jōhi*, *uwakawa* outer skin, cuticle, epidermis

目 *uwame* upward glance, upturned eyes. *a*(*gari*)*me* eyes slanting upward; rising tendency

石 *uwa-ishi* upper millstone

句 *kami* (*no*) *ku*, *jōku* the first part of a poem or verse

代 *jōdai* ancient times

付 *uwatsu*(*ku*) be fickle, be flippant, be restless

包 *uwazutsu*(*mi*) cover, wrapper, envelope

司 *jōshi* superior authorities

世 *jōsei*, *kamitsuyo* antiquity; ancient times

出来 *jōdeki* good performance

甲板 *jōkampan* upper deck

申 *jōshin* report to a superior

申書 *jōshinsho* written report

古 *jōko* ancient times

古史 *jōkoshi* ancient history

半 *jōhan* first half, upper half

半身 *jōhanshin* bust, upper half of the body

半期 *kami hanki* first half of a year

6 米 *jōmai* first-class rice

臼 *uwa-usu* upper millstone

衣 *uwagi*, *jōi* coat, tunic, jacket, outer garment

旬 *jōjun* first ten days of a month

回 *uwamawa*(*ru*) exceed

気 *jōki* dizziness; rush of blood to the head

汲 *uwagu*(*mu*) draw off the top liquid

旨 *jōshi* the emperor's thoughts

列車 *nobo*(*ri*) *ressha* up train, trains going toward the capital

向 *uwamu*(*ku*), *uemu*(*ku*) look upward, turn upward, rise. *uwamu*(*ki*), *uemu*(*ki*) upturn; upward tendency; looking upward

向線 *jōkōsen* upswing

7 足 *jōsoku* high retainer

図 *jōzu* the upper illustration

述 *jōjutsu* the above-mentioned

位 *jōi* high rank, precedence
体 *jōtai* upper part of the body
作 *jōsaku* good crop; masterpiece
坂 *nobo(ri)zaka* ascent, upgrade
役 *uwayaku* senior official, one's superior
告 *jōkoku* appeal (of a case)
8 長 *jōchō* one's superior, a senior, an elder
底 *a(ge)zoko* false bottom
使 *jōshi* shogun's envoy ⌈moon
弦 *jōgen* first quarter (of a moon); a crescent
板 *a(ge)ita* movable floor boards; trap door
物 *a(gari)mono* food offering; yield; waste. *jōmono* quality goods
服 *uwafuku* outer garment
肢 *jōshi* upper limbs, arms
限 *jōgen* maximum (in math)
直 *uwane* higher price; price rise
官 *jōkan* superior officer
空 *uwa(no)sora* inattention, absent-mindedness. *jōkū* high-altitude sky, upper air
京 *jōkyō* proceeding to the capital
京中 *jōkyōchū* in the capital
表 *jōhyō* memorial to the emperor
表紙 *uwabyōshi* cover, front cover, wrapper, jacket
昇 *jōshō suru* rise, ascend, climb
昇気流 *jōshō kiryū* ascending air current
昇限度 *jōshō gendo* ceiling (in aviation)
昇線 *jōshōsen* rising curve
9 面 *jōmen* surface, top, exterior. *uwatsura, uwa(t)tsura* surface, appearances
廻 *uwamawa(ru)* be more than
映 *jōei* screen projection
枯 *uwaga(reru)* die at the top
洛 *jōraku* proceeding to the capital
計 *jōkei* best policy
降 *a(gari)o(ri)* ascent and descent
段 *jōdan* dais, raised part of the floor; seats of honor, upper row of seats; upper berth; upper (horizontal) column (of print). *a(gari)dan* staircase, doorsteps
乗 *jōjō* the best. *uwano(ri)* supercargo
帝 *jōtei* Shangti, God, Lord, Creator, the Supreme Being ⌈mission
前 *uwamae* outer skirt; percentage, com-
品 *jōhin* refinement, decency; first-class article. *jōbon* Buddhism's highest paradise
客 *jōkyaku* guest of honor; good customer
界 *jōkai* upper world, heaven
皇 *jōkō* retired emperor
巻 *jōkan* volume one
背 *uwazei* stature, height
首尾 *jōshubi* success, happy result
相場 *a(ge)sōba* bullish market
草履 *uwazōri* indoor sandals, slippers

屋 *uwaya* a shed ⌈mansion
屋敷 *kami yashiki* a daimyo's main Tokyo
級 *jōkyū* higher grade, advanced class, high
級生 *jōkyūsei* upper classman ⌊class
院 *jōin* Upper House, Senate, Lords
院議員 *jōin gi-in* senator, member of the
奏 *jōsō* report to the Throne ⌊upper house
奏文 *jōsōbun* report to the Throne
10 馬 *jōba* excellent horse ⌈yield
高 *a(gari)daka* revenue, income, receipts,
席 *jōseki* seniority, precedence; upper seat
座 *jōza, kamiza* chief seat, seat of honor
唇 *uwakuchibiru, jōshin* upper lip
値 *uwane* good price
酒 *jōshu* high-class saké ⌈paper
紙 *uwagami* paper cover, wrapper, wrapping
紐 *uwahimo* outside string (on a package)
航 *jōkō* going upstream
記 *jōki no* the above-mentioned
陸 *jōriku* landing, disembarkation
荷 *uwani* top cargo; top of the load
書 *uwaga(ki)*, address; superscription. *jōsho* memorial to the throne
帯 *uwaobi* outer sash
流 *jōryū* upper stream; upper classes
流社会 *jōryū shakai* upper classes
部 *jōbu* upper part, top, upper side, surface
部構造 *jōbu kōzō* superstructure
納 *jōnō* payment to the government
納米 *jōnōmai* rice-tax delivery ⌈ment
納金 *jōnōkin* money paid to the govern-
11 道 *nobo(ri) michi* uphill road
達 *jōtatsu* progress, proficiency
側 *uwa(k)kawa, uwakawa, uwagawa* upper side, surface
張 *uwaba(ri)* face, coat, veneer. *uwa(p)pa(ri)* overalls, wrapper, duster, smock
掲 *jōkei no* the above-mentioned
梓 *jōshi* publication; wood-block printing
略 *jōryaku* first paragraphs omitted
宿 *jōyado* first-class inn ⌈placed on top
盛 *uwamo(ri)* adding to the top; what's
菓子 *jōgashi* quality cakes
掛水車 *uwaga(ke) suisha* overshot water
12 歯 *uwaba* upper teeth ⌊wheel
場 *a(gari)ba* landing, landing place
提 *jōtei* introducing (a bill)
湯 *a(gari)yu* clean hot bath water for rinsing
疏 *jōso suru* report to the emperor ⌈(a bill)
程 *jōtei* departure on a journey; introducing
絵 *uwae* printed figures (on cloth or pot-
腕 *jōwan* upper arm ⌊tery)
訴 *jōso* appeal (in court)
貼 *uwabari* finishing coat of paper
畳 *a(ge)datami* a *tatami* finished on both
策 *jōsaku* excellent plan; best policy ⌊sides

二亠人イ𠆢儿入八ソ冂冖冫几凵刀刂力勹匕匚匸十[卜]卩厂厶又

着 *uwagi* coat, tunic, jacket, outer garment
番 *jōban* being on duty
智 *jōchi* Sophia University; supreme wisdom
裁 *jōsai* imperial decision
景気 *jōkeiki* boom, prosperity
御一人 *kami go-ichinin* the emperor
棟 *jōtō* raising the ridgepole
棟式 *jōtōshiki* ridgepole-raising ceremony
等 *jōtō* superiority, first class, very good
等兵 *jōtōhei* superior private
等兵曹 *jōtō heisō* chief petty officer
等品 *jōtōhin* first-class article
13 傭 *uwabatara(ki)* housemaid
滑 *uwasube(ri)* superficial, careless, inattentive
腿 *jōtai* thigh
詰 *nobo(ri)-tsu(meru)* go to the top; be engrossed in
靴 *uwagutsu* overshoes, rubbers, galoshes
筵 *uwamushiro*＝next word
蓆 *uwamushiro* thin padded mat laid on the *tatami*
蓋 *a(ge)buta* trap door; removable floor boards
意 *jōi* the emperor's wishes
塗 *uwanu(ri)* last plaster coat, last painting, finish
14 聞 *jōbun* an imperial hearing
様 *uesama* emperor, shogun, honored person. *uezama* up. *(o)nobo(ri)san* visitor from the country
演 *jōen* stage performance
端 *jōtan* top, tip, upper end
膊 *jōhaku* upper arm
蔟 *jōzoku* spinning of cocoons; the silkworm's last sleep
製 *jōsei* superior make; superior binding
製本 *jōseibon* best binding
層 *jōsō* upper layer; upper air; upper story; higher class
層土 *jōsōdo* topsoil
層気流 *jōsō kiryū* upper air currents
層風 *jōsōfū* winds aloft
層建築 *jōsō kenchiku* superstructure; upper stories
層階級 *jōsō kaikyū* upper classes, high society
層雲 *jōsōun* upper clouds
15 履 *uwabaki* hallway slippers
潮 *a(ge)shio* incoming tide
澄 *uwazu(mi)* the clear top of a liquid
謁 *jōetsu* interview with an important person
敷 *uwashi(ki), uwaji(ki)* bordered matting
箱 *uwabako* outer box, outer casing
質 *jōshitsu* fine quality
調子 *uwachōshi* high pitch, higher tone. *uwa(t)chōshi na* flippant, frivolous, shallow
16 燗 *jōkan* top quality hot saké
積 *uwazu(mi)* deck cargo; upper layer of goods
臈 *jōrō* court lady, noblewoman
諭 *jōyu* imperial edict
覧 *jōran* imperial inspection
機嫌 *jōkigen* good humor
17 擦 *uwazu(ru)* sound shallow, sound hollow (in speaking)
翼 *jōyoku* upper wing of a plane
18 瞼 *uwamabuta* upper eyelid
顎 *jōgaku, uwa-ago* upper jaw; palate
覆 *uwaōi* cover, covering
噛合 *uwakamia(wase)* overbite
19 離 *a(ge)-hana(su)* cut off (the head)
20 騰 *jōtō* advance, rise, jump
議 *jōgi suru* place on the agenda
21 欄 *jōran* top or preceding horizontal column

3

占 B $\frac{799}{F295}$ SEN. *shi(meru)* occupy, hold, have, get, take (a seat). *urana(u)* divine, forecast, augur. *uranai* divination, fortunetelling, soothsaying. *shi(meta)* I've got it; all right, fine.

2 卜 *semboku* divination, fortunetelling, soothsaying
5 用 *sen-yō* exclusive use
6 当 *urana(i)-a(teru)* divine
有 *sen-yū* exclusive possession, occupancy
有権 *sen-yūken* right of exclusive possession
7 住 *senjū suru* occupy
8 居 *senkyo suru* occupy a certain place
法 *sempō* divination
者 *uranaisha* diviner, fortuneteller, soothsayer, palmist
拠 *senkyo* occupation
拠地 *senkyochi* occupied territory
取 *senshu* preoccupation
取権 *senshuken* right of preoccupancy
9 星術 *senseijutsu* astrology
10 師 *uranaishi*＝*uranaisha* 占者 (see above–8)
書 *urabumi* diviner's book
14 算 *urayasan* a diviner
領 *senryō* capture, possession, occupation. *senryō suru* have a room to oneself
領下 *senryōka no* occupied (by an army)
領地 *senryōchi* occupied territory
領地帯 *senryō chitai* occupied zone
領軍 *senryō gun* army of occupation

6

点 $\frac{800}{F\text{-}X}$ Nonstandard for 点 804.

卦 $\frac{801}{F296}$ KA. KE a divination sign.

14 算 *keisan* paperweight

卓 B $\frac{802}{F290}$ TAKU table, desk; high. [十]

3 子 *takushi, teiburu* table
上 *takujō* after-dinner (speech); on the table, on the desk
上電話 *takujō denwa* desk phone

5 用 *takuyō* desk (equipment); table use
出 *takushutsu*=*takuetsu* 卓越 (see below–12)
7 見 *takken* clearsightedness, penetration, farsightedness; excellent idea
抜 *takubatsu*=*takuetsu* 卓越 (see below–12)
8 効 *takkō* great efficiency
11 球 *takkyū* pingpong, table tennis
袱台 *chabudai* tea table
12 絶 *takuzetsu*=*takuetsu* 卓越 (see below–12)
筆 *takuhitsu* excellent literary work
越 *takuetsu* excellence, superiority, preeminence; prevalence
越風 *takuetsufū* prevailing wind
14 説 *takusetsu* excellent opinion
15 論 *takuron* sound argument, clever presentation
19 識 *takushiki*=*takken* 卓見 (see above–7)

7

貞 803 / F1787 B Jō. TEI chastity; constancy; righteousness. [貝]

8 女 *teijo* virtuous woman, faithful wife
6 臣 *teishin* a faithful retainer
8 実 *teijitsu* fidelity, faithfulness
10 純 *teijun* rectitude
烈 *teiretsu na* very virtuous (woman)
11 婦 *teifu* virtuous woman, faithful wife
淑 *teishuku* chastity, feminine modesty
13 節 *teisetsu* fidelity, constancy, chastity, virginity
15 潔 *teiketsu* chastity, purity
16 操 *teisō* chastity, virginity
操蹂躪 *teisō jūrin* violation of chastity, rape
操観念 *teisō kannen* sense of virtue

点 804 / F2164 A **點 點** TEN point; mark; score, run; speck; stain; defect; a detail; standpoint; items, pieces; decimal point; vote. *ten*(*jiru*), *ten*(*zuru*) drop; light, kindle; make tea. *tobo*(*ru*), *tomo*(*ru*) burn, be lighted. *tomo*(*su*), *tobo*(*su*) light, turn on. *tsu*(*ku*) (electricity) comes on. *sa*(*su*) light (a fire); apply moxa cautery. [黒]

4 心 *tenshin, tenjin* Zen monk's snack; refreshment, cakes; Chinese dessert
水 *tensui* water jug, pitcher
火 *tenka* lighting, ignition
火栓 *tenkasen* spark plug
火薬 *tenkayaku* priming powders
5 示 *tenji* pointing out
付 *tentsu*(*ke*)=*saiten* 採点 1947.9
6 灯 *tentō* lighting
字 *tenji* Braille
光 *tenkō* spotlight
在 *tenzai suru* be dotted with
8 呼 *tenko* roll call, muster
画 *tenga* stippling. *tenkaku* the strokes of a character
者 *tenja* critic of *haiku* poetry
取 *tento*(*ri*) competition for school marks; keeping score; score
取虫 *tento*(*ri*)*mushi* derisive term for a diligent student
9 点 *tenten* here and there, sporadically, scattered; in drops; little by little; dot, spot
茶 *tencha* boiling tea (for a tea ceremony)
11 描 *tembyō* sketch
眼 *tengan suru* drop medicine in the eyes
眼水 *tengansui* eye lotion
眼器 *tenganki* eye dropper
12 検 *tenken* inspection, examination; roll calling
景 *tenkei* the incidental details of a picture
13 睛 *tensei* adding eyes and other finishing touches to an animal painting
滅 *temmetsu* turning a light on and off
滅器 *temmetsuki* electric switch
数 *tensū* marks, credits, points; score, runs; number of items
数切符 *tensū kippu* ration-point coupon
数制 *tensūsei* point rationing system
14 綴 *tentei, tentetsu* a line (of mountains, islands, houses, etc.)
滴 *tenteki* falling drops, raindrops
滴器 *tentekiki* dropper
15 播 *tempa* sowing spaced seeds
線 *tensen* dotted line; perforated line
16 頭 *tentō suru* nod

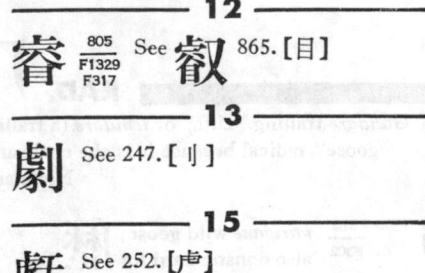

12

睿 805 / F1329 / F317 See **叡** 865. [目]

13

劇 See 247. [刂]

15

虧 See 252. [虍]

RAD. 卩 26

Warifu seal or *fushizukuri* right-side "joint." Variant: 㔾 *mage warifu* crooked seal.
Nickname: Seal.

3

卯 806 / F296 Bō. *u* 5-7 a.m.; 4th zodiac sign; rabbit; east.

[4]月 *uzuki* 4th lunar month

[7]花 *u(no)hana* refuse from tofu

4

印 See 102.

危 See 187.

5

卵 See 199.

即 See 3886.

卺 807 / F300 Kin cup.

却 808 / F300 **卻** B Kyaku. *kae(tte)* instead, on the contrary; rather, all the more.

[3]下 *kyakka suru* reject, dismiss, ignore

[14]説 *sate* well, now

6

巻 809 / F-X Nonstandard for **巻** 1465.

卷 810 / F299 See **巻** 1466.

7

卻 See **却** 808.

卽 811 / F300 **卽** See **即** 3886.

卸 812 / F300 B Sha. *oro(su)* sell at wholesale; grated (vegetables). *oroshi* wholesale.

[3]大根 *oro(shi) daikon* grated daikon

[7]売 *oroshiuri* wholesale

[8]金 *oro(shi)gane* grater

[10]値 *oroshine* wholesale price

[11]商 *oro(shi)shō* wholesaler

問屋 *oro(shi) ton-ya* wholesaler

10

卿 813 / F301 **卿** Kei, Kyō you; lord; secretary; state minister.

[12]等 *keira* you (daimyos)

RAD. 厂 27

Gandare trailing "cliff" or *ichidare* (a trailing *ichi* "one"). Also known as the "trailing goose" radical because it is the enclosure in the character for *gan* "wild goose."
Nickname: Cliff.

厂 814 / F302 *karigane* wild goose; also nonstandard for **歷** 835.

2

仄 815 / F93 Soku. *hono(meku)* be seen dimly; glimmer. *hono(mekasu)* hint at, intimate, suggest, allude to. *hono(kana)* faint, indistinct; stupid; few. *hono(mekashi)* hint, intimation. [人]

[4]仄 *honobono to* dimly, faintly

[5]白 *honojiro(i)* dimly white

[13]暗 *honogura(i)* gloomy; obscure

[14]聞 *sokubun suru* casually hear

厄 816 / F302 P Yaku misfortune, bad luck, evil, disaster.

[4]日 *yakubi* critical day, unlucky day

介 *yakkai* trouble, bother, worry; dependence, support; kindness; obligation

介払 *yakkaibara(i)* good riddance

介物 *yakkaimono* nuisance, encumbrance
介者 *yakkaimono* dependent, hanger-on
介事 *yakkaigoto* trouble, difficulty, burden
[5]払 *yakubara(i)* good riddance; exorcism. *yakuhara(i)* exorcism
[6]年 *yakudoshi* critical age, unlucky year
[7]災 *yakusai* calamity, disaster, accident
[9]除 *yakuyo(ke)* warding off evil
前 *yakumae* the year before the unlucky year ⌈year
負 *yakuma(ke)* victimized by the unlucky
[12]落 *yakuoto(shi)* escape from evil, exorcism
[18]難 *yakunan* calamity, evil, misfortune

A **反** 817/F312 HON. *tan* roll of cloth (c. 10 yds.); .245 acres, 300 tsubo. HAN antithesis, opposite, antagonism; anti-. *so(ru) vi* warp; curve; lean backward. *so(rasu), so(raseru) vt* bend, warp. *han(suru)* be inconsistent with, oppose; contradict; transgress; rebel. *kae(ru) vi* change, turn over, turn upside down. *kae(su) vt* change, turn over, turn upside down. *sori* warp, curvature, curve. arch. *kae(tte)* (see under 却 808.0). [又]

[4]日 *hannichi* anti-Japanese
毛 *hammō* reclaimed wool
比 *hampi* inverse ratio
比例 *hampirei* inverse proportion
[5]目 *hammoku* antagonism, hostility
収 *tanshū* production per *tan* (see Weights
古 *hogu, hogo* wastepaper ⌊and Measures)
古籠 *hogukago* wastebasket
[6]米 *hambei* anti-American
返 *so(ri)-ka(eru)* warp; bend backward; throw the head (or shoulders) back,
吐 *hedo* vomiting ⌊throw out the chest
合 *sori ga a(wanai)* be unable to co-operate
共 *hankyō* anticommunist
[7]身 *hanshin* bending backward, strutting. *so(ri)mi* strutting, sticking out the chest
応 *hannō* reaction, response
攻 *hankō* counteroffensive
抗 *hankō* resistance, insubordination, defiance, opposition, hostility, rebellion
別 *tambetsu* acreage, land area
形 *so(ri)kata* warped shape
作用 *hansayō* reaction
社会的 *hanshakaiteki* antisocial
乱 *hanran* rebellion
乱者 *hanransha* rebel, insurgent
乱軍 *hanran gun* rebel army
対 *hantai* opposition, resistance, antagonism, hostility, contrast, objection, dissension; reverse, opposite, vice versa
対色 *hantaishoku* clashing colors
対者 *hantaisha* opposer, adversary, dissenter ⌈jaw protruding)
対咬合 *hantai kōgō* cross bite (with lower
対党 *hantaitō* opposition party
対訊問 *hantai jimmon* cross-examination
対側 *hantaigawa* the opposite side
対貿易風 *hantai bōekifū* antitrade winds
対語 *hantaigo* antonym
対論 *hantairon* opposing argument
[8]逆 *hangyaku*＝叛逆 220.8 ⌈and Measures)
歩 *tambu* one-tenth hectare (see Weights
英 *han-ei* anti-British ⌈Reformation
宗教改革 *Hanshūkyō Kaikaku* Counter-
物 *tammono* cloth; textiles, drapery; dry goods, piece goods
物屋 *tammonoya* dry-goods store
[9]面 *hammen ni* on the other hand
映 *han-ei* reflection, influence
独 *handoku* anti-German
則 *hansoku* transgression; default; foul; balk; irregularity
故 *hogu, hogo* wastepaper
省 *hansei* reflection, introspection; reconsideration; meditation, contemplation
革命 *hankakumei* counterrevolution
政府 *hanseifu* antigovernment
政府党 *hanseifutō* opposition party
軍 *hangun* antimilitary
軍的 *hangunteki* antimilitary
発 *hampatsu suru* repel, repulse; rebound; recover; resist ⌈siliency, elasticity
発力 *hampatsuryoku* repellent force; re-
[10]哺 *hampo* caring for one's parents in return
徒 *hanto* rebels, insurgents
芻 *hansū* chewing the cud, rumination
射 *hansha* reflection, reverberation
射作用 *hansha sayō* reflex action
射的 *hanshateki* reflective; reflecting; reflexive. *hanshateki ni* reminiscingly
射運動 *hansha undō* reflex action ⌈scope
射望遠鏡 *hansha bōenkyō* reflecting tele-
射鏡 *hanshakyō* reflector ⌈in return
[11]問 *hammon suru* cross-examine; retort; ask
側 *hansoku suru* turn over in bed
転 *hanten suru* turn around, roll over, turn from side to side
動 *handō* reaction; recoil, kick
動主義 *handō shugi* reactionism
動的 *handōteki* reactionary
動派 *handōha* the reactionaries
動革命 *handō kakumei* counterrevolution
動思想 *handō shisō* reactionary ideas
動家 *handōka* a reactionary
[12]歯 *soppa* projecting teeth
間 *hankan* counterintelligence
復 *hampuku* repetition

証 *hanshō* counterevidence
訴 *hanso* counteraction, counterclaim
落 *hanraku* reaction
植民主義 *hanshokumin shugi* anticolonialism
13 賊 *hanzoku* rebel
戦 *hansen* antiwar
数 *hansū* reciprocal number
感 *hankan* antipathy, animosity
照 *hanshō* reflection, influence
意語 *han-igo* antonym
14 旗 *hanki* standard of revolt
様 *kaisama* upside down; inside out
語 *hango* irony; rhetorical question; antonym; word in reverse
駁 *hambaku, hampaku* refutation, rebuttal
歌 *hanka* tanka appendage to a long poem
15 撥 *hampatsu*＝反発 (see above–9)
論 *hanron* refutation; rebuttal
影 *han-ei* reflection, influence
撃 *hangeki* counterattack
16 噬 *hanzei* turning against one's master; returning evil for good
橋 *so(ri)hashi, so(ri)bashi* arched bridge
18 覆 *hampuku suru* reverse; repeat
19 響 *hankyō* echo, reverberation; repercussion, reaction, influence
繰返 *so(k)ku(ri)-ka(eru)* throw one's head back (boastfully)
20 騰 *hantō* reactionary price rise

3

斥斥 See 175. [斤]

圧 818 / F443 **壓 壓** EN. ATSU. *as(su-ru)* press, oppress, dominate, overwhelm. *he(su)* push, press. *o(su), o(shi)* (see under 押 1885.0). [土] A

2 力 *atsuryoku* pressure, stress
力団体 *atsuryoku dantai* pressure groups
力計 *atsuryokukei* pressure gauge
4 込 *he(shi)-ko(mu)* push into
5 石 *o(shi)ishi* stone weight
出 *asshutsu* pressing out
6 死 *asshi* crushing to death
伏 *appuku suru* overpower, subdue
合 *he(shi)-a(u)* jostle, push
舌器 *atsuzetsuki* tongue depressor
7 折 *he(shi)-o(ru)* smash, break
迫 *appaku* pressure, coercion, oppression
迫感 *appakukan* feeling of oppression
8 拉 *o(shi)-hishi(gu)* smash, suppress
服 *appuku suru* overpower, overwhelm, subdue, keep down
制 *assei* oppression, tyranny, despotism
制的 *asseiteki* oppressive, despotic
制者 *asseisha* oppressor, tyrant
延 *atsuen* rolling
延工場 *atsuen kōjō* rolling mill
延機 *atsuenki* rolling machine
延鋼 *atsuenkō* rolled steel
9 砕 *assai* crushing
神 *asshin* pressure sensation
巻 *akkan* best part (of a book); masterpiece; highlight; best in the lot
10 殺 *o(shi)-koro(su)* crush, stifle, or squeeze to death. *assatsu* crushing to death
倒 *attō suru* overwhelm, overpower, crush; outdo, surpass
倒的 *attōteki* overwhelming
12 勝 *asshō* complete victory
覚 *akkaku* sense of pressure
13 搾 *assaku* pressure, compressing
搾空気 *assaku kūki* compressed air
搾器 *assakuki* press, compressor
17 縮 *asshuku* compression, pressing, constriction, condensation
縮性 *asshukusei* compressibility
縮空気 *asshuku kūki* compressed air
縮率 *asshukuritsu* compressibility
縮器 *asshukuki* compressor
19 濾器 *atsuroki* filter press

4

后 See 181. [口]

厓 819 / F-X Nonstandard for **歴** 835.

灰 820 / F1178 **灰** KAI. *hai* ashes. *aku* puckery juice. *hai ni suru* burn up; cremate. *hai ni naru* be reduced to ashes; be cremated. [火] B

3 土 *haitsuchi* ashes and earth; poor volcanic soil
5 皿 *haizara* ash tray
白 *kaihaku* ash color, light gray
白質 *kaihakushitsu* gray matter
汁 *aku* lye; harsh taste
汁抜 *akunu(ki)* removal of the harsh taste in vegetables. *akunu(ke)* refined, elegant, urbane
6 色 *hai iro* ashen, ash color, gray
成 *hai ni na(ru)* be reduced to ashes; be cremated
7 吹 *haifu(ki)* bamboo (tobacco) ash receptacle
均 *hainarashi* ash leveler
8 押 *haiosa(e), haio(shi)* ash leveler (use in a brazier)
受 *haiu(ke)* ash pan, ash tray
青色 *kaiseishoku* grayish blue
9 洗 *akuara(i)* scour, washing vegetables in lye
神楽 *haikagura* raising a cloud of ashes
12 殼 *haigara* ashes

落 *haioto(shi)* ash tray, ash pit
18 掻 *haikaki* poker, ash rake ⌈stroyed
滅 *kaimetsu suru vt* burn up. *vi* be de-
塗 *haimami(re)* covered with ashes
14 塵 *kaijin* ashes and dust
緑色 *kairyokushoku* greenish gray
16 篩 *haifurui* ash strainer
18 燼 *kaijin* complete destruction

6

厓 821/F302 See **崖** 1428.

7

盾 See 215.【目】

厖 822/F302 Bō large; mix.
3 大 *bōdai* swelling; expansion

B **厘** 823/F303 Rin one-tenth of a *sen*; one-tenth of a *bu* (see Weights and Measures).
4 毛 *rimmō* a farthing, a trifle

A **厚** 824/F303 Kō. *atsu(bottai)* very thick; heavy. *atsu(i)* thick; rich; kind, cordial. *atsu(kamashii)* impudent, shameless, brazen. *atsu(sa)* thickness.
4 手 *atsude no* thick (paper, etc.)
切 *atsugi(ri)* thick slice
化粧 *atsugeshō* heavy make-up
5 皮 *atsukawa* thick hide; shamelessness
礼 *kōrei* heartfelt thanks
氷 *atsugōri* thick ice
生 *kōsei* public welfare, health promotion
生大臣 *Kōsei Daijin* Minister of Welfare
生年金 *kōsei nenkin* welfare pension
生省 *Kōseishō* Welfare Ministry
6 臼 *atsu-usu* stone hand mill
地 *atsuji* thick cloth
7 利 *kōri* large profits
志 *kōshi* kindness, kind intention
8 味 *atsumi* thickness
板 *atsu-ita* plank, thick board; plate glass; heavy metal sheet; heavy brocaded obi
9 相 *Kōshō* Welfare Minister
10 紙 *atsugami* thick paper, cardboard
恩 *kōon* great favor; obligation
11 遇 *kōgū* cordial welcome, kind treatment
情 *kōjō* kindness, favor, hospitality
12 着 *atsugi* wearing thick clothes
13 意 *kōi* kindness, favor
15 誼 *kōgi* your kindness
16 薄 *kōhaku* thickness, partiality
18 顔 *kōgan* impudence, audacity

8

A **原** 825/F304 Gen original, primitive. *hara* field, plain, prairie, tundra, moor, wilderness. *hara(ppa)* plain. *gen-* original, primitive, primary, fundamental; raw.
2 人 *genjin* primitive man
3 寸 *gensun* actual size, full size
寸大 *gensundai* actual size, full size
子 *genshi* atom
子力 *genshiryoku* atomic energy
子力学 *genshi rikigaku* atomic mechanics
子兵器 *genshi heiki* atomic weapons
子価 *genshika* valence, atomic value
子物理学 *genshi butsurigaku* atomic physics, nuclear physics
子症 *genshishō* symptoms of atomic illness
子病 *genshibyō* radiation sickness
子核 *genshikaku* nucleus of an atom
子砲 *genshihō* atomic cannon
子時代 *genshi jidai* atomic age
子破壊機 *genshi hakaiki* cyclotron
子量 *genshiryō* atomic weight
子雲 *genshiun* atomic cloud
子弾頭 *genshi dantō* atomic warhead
子戦 *genshisen* atomic war
子戦争 *genshi sensō* atomic war
子説 *genshi setsu* atomic theory
子爆発 *genshi bakuhatsu* atomic explosion
子爆弾 *genshi bakudan* atom bomb
4 文 *gembun* the text, the original
木 *gemboku* pulpwood
毛 *gemmō* raw wool
水爆 *gensuibaku* atom and hydrogen bombs
5 句 *genku* the original passage (in a document)
由 *gen-yū* reason, cause
本 *gempon* the original, original copy, script
民 *gemmin* aborigines ⌈primitive
生 *gensei* spontaneous generation; primeval,
生林 *genseirin* primeval forest, virgin forest
生動物 *gensei dōbutsu* protozoa
6 糸 *genshi* thread for weaving
虫 *genchū* a protozoan
成岩 *genseigan* primary rocks
成岩石 *gensei ganseki* primary rocks
色 *genshoku* primary color ⌈printing
色写真版 *genshoku shashimban* tricolor
色版 *genshokuban* tricolor printing
因 *gen-in* root cause, factor, occasion, origin, source
因不明 *gen-in fumei* cause unknown
因結果 *gen-in kekka* cause and effect, causality
7 図 *genzu* original drawing
状 *genjō* original state
告 *genkoku* plaintiff, accuser, prosecutor
住民 *genjūmin* natives, aborigines
判決 *genhanketsu* original decision

2 二亠人イ𠆢儿入八ソ冂冖冫几凵刀刂力勹匕匚匸十卜卩【厂】8 ム又

2 二亠人イ入儿入八ソ冂冖冫几凵刀刂力勹匕匚匸十卜卩 9 [厂] 厶又

材料 *genzairyō* raw material
作 *gensaku* original work
作者 *gensakusha* the original author (of a translated work)
形 *genkei* original form
形質 *genkeishitsu* protoplasm, plasma
[8]油 *gen-yu* crude oil
注 *genchū* the original notes
版 *gemban* original edition
物 *gembutsu* the original
画 *genga* original picture
典 *genten* original document
価 *genka* cost price
価計算 *genka keisan* cost accounting
始 *genshi* origin; primitive, primeval
始人 *genshijin* primitive man
始林 *genshirin* primeval forest, virgin forest
始的 *genshiteki* primitive, original, primeval
始時代 *genshi jidai* primitive times
始教会 *genshi kyōkai* the early church; the primitive church
始動物 *genshi dōbutsu* protozoa
[9]音 *gen-on* fundamental tone
点 *genten* starting point
品 *gempin* the original article
泉 *gensen*＝源泉 2656.9
茸 *haratake* common mushroom
型 *genkei* prototype, antitype; model, pattern
則 *gensoku* principle, general rule
則的 *gensokuteki* general
[10]料 *genryō* raw materials
紙 *genshi* stencil; silkworm egg sheet
被 *gempi* plaintiff and defendant
案 *gen-an* original bill, motion, draft, or plan
書 *gensho* the original document
素 *genso* chemical element
振動 *genshindō* fundamental vibration
[11]理 *genri* principle, theory, basic truth
野 *gen-ya* waste land, wilderness, moor, field, plain. *harano*＝*nohara* 野原 4814.10
隊 *gentai* one's home unit
票 *gempyō* stub (of a checkbook)
動 *gendō* motive
動力 *gendōryoku* motive power
著 *gencho* the original work
著者 *genchosha* author
産地 *gensanchi* place of origin; home, habitat
産物 *gensambutsu* primary product
[12]註 *genchū* the original notes
裁判 *gensaiban* original judgment
裁判所 *gensaibansho* original court, court of first instance
[13]詩 *genshi* original poem
鉱 *genkō* ore, raw ore
罪 *genzai* original sin
義 *gengi* original meaning
意 *gen-i* original meaning
[14]像 *genzō* original statue
種 *genshu* pure breed
綿 *gemmen* raw cotton
語 *gengo* original word or language
[15]論 *genron* theory, principles
審 *genshin* original sentence
器 *genki* standard (for weights and measures)
稿 *genkō* manuscript
稿用紙 *genkō yōshi* manuscript paper
稿料 *genkōryō* payment for a manuscript
稿稼 *genkō kasegi* living on one's writing
稿紙 *genkōshi* manuscript paper
[16]糖 *gentō* unrefined sugar
頭 *gentō* the field, the parade ground
[17]繊維 *gensen-i* raw fibers, minute fibers
[19]簿 *gembo* ledger, original record
爆 *gembaku* atom bomb
爆症 *gembakushō* symptoms of atomic illness
[20]籍 *genseki* original domicile, permanent address

9

厠 826 F305 F640 **廁** SHI. *kawaya* privy, toilet.

10

厦 827 F306 KA. SA. *ie* house.

厥 828 F305 KETSU that.
[7]冷 *ketsurei* clamminess, coldness of body

厨 829 F306 F643 **廚 廚** CHŪ. ZU. *kuriya* kitchen.
[3]子 *zushi* miniature shrine in a temple
[7]芥 *chūkai* garbage
芥箱 *chūkaibako* garbage box
[8]房 *chūbō* kitchen, galley

雁 830 F2010 **鴈** GAN *kari, karigane* wild goose. [隹]
[4]文 *kari (no) fumi* a letter
爪 *ganzume* a Japanese rake
木 *gangi* stepped pier; toothing gear; escapement; hooked stick; zigzag
木車 *gangiguruma* escape wheel; pulley
木鑢 *gangi yasuri* rasp
[5]皮紙 *gampishi* rice paper, tissue paper
玉章 *kari (no) tamazusa* a letter
[6]行 *gankō* the flight formation of geese; lining up shoulder to shoulder like flying geese; leading out
字搦 *ganjigarami ni, ganjigarame ni* (bind) firmly
[8]金 *karigane* wild goose
使 *kari (no) tsuka(i)* a letter
[9]音 *karigane* wild goose

首 *gankubi* pipe bowl. *karikubi* goose neck
便 *kari (no) tayori* a letter
[10]骨 *kariganebone* scapula, shoulder blade
[10]書 *gansho* letter

— 11 —

厩 See 832.

— 12 —

厲 831/F307 REI whetstone; encourage.
[6]行 *reikō* encouragement

厩 832/F306 F642 **厩 廏 廐** KYŪ. *umaya* barn, stable.
[8]肥 *kyūhi* manure, compost
舎 *kyūsha* barn

B **暦** 833/F917 **曆** RYAKU. REKI. *koyomi* calendar, almanac. [日]
[4]日 *rekijitsu* calendar day; time
月 *rekigetsu* calendar month
[6]年 *rekinen* calendar year, civil year; time
年度 *rekinendo* calendar year
[7]改正 *koyomi kaisei* calendar reform
[8]学 *rekigaku* the study of the calendar
法 *rekihō* calendar making
法改正 *rekihō no kaisei* calendar reform
[11]術 *rekijutsu* calendar-construction rules
[13]数 *rekisū* calendar making; number of years; one's fate; the year

厭 834/F306 EN. YŌ. YŪ. *a(kiru)* get tired of, lose interest in, have enough. *a(kasu)* satiate, surfeit; bore, tire, weary. *ito(u)* dislike, hate; grudge (doing), spare (oneself); be weary of; take (good) care of. *agu(mu)* be tired of doing. *i(yarashii)*, *ito(washii)*, *i(yana)* detestable, disagreeable.
[2]人 *enjin* misanthropy
人者 *enjinsha* misanthrope
[5]世 *ensei* pessimism, weariness with life
世主義 *ensei shugi* pessimism
世的 *enseiteki* pessimistic
世家 *enseika* pessimist
世悲観者 *ensei-hikansha* pessimist
世観 *enseikan* pessimistic view of life, pessimism
[8]味 *iyami*＝嫌味 1250.8
性 *a(ki)shō* fickle nature, flighty temperament
[11]悪 *en-o suru* dislike, detest
[13]戦 *ensen* war weariness

A **歴** 835/F1041 **歷** REKI continuation; passing (of time). *rekki to shita* clear, plain, unmistakable. [止]
[4]日 *rekijitsu* the passing of time
[5]世 *rekisei*＝*rekidai* 歴代 (see below–5)
仕 *rekishi* (successive lords) using the same retainers
代 *rekidai* successive generations, successive emperors
代史 *rekidaishi* chronicles, annals
史 *rekishi* history
史上 *rekishijō* historically
史地図 *rekishi chizu* historical map; atlas
史地理 *rekishi chiri* historical geography
史的 *rekishiteki* historic, historical, traditional
史画 *rekishiga* historical picture
史学 *rekishigaku* history
史学派 *rekishigakuha* historical school
史家 *rekishika* historian
史哲学 *rekishi tetsugaku* historical philosophy
史劇 *rekishigeki* historical drama
史観 *rekishikan* historical viewpoint
[6]伝 *rekiden* tradition
任 *rekinin suru* successively fill several posts
年 *rekinen* year after year
年齢 *rekinenrei* chronological age
[11]遊 *rekiyū suru* tour, itinerate
訪 *rekihō* round of calls; tour of visitation
[12]朝 *rekichō* successive reigns; successive emperors; successive dynasties
然 *rekizen(taru)* plain, distinct, clear
[13]戦 *rekisen* long military service
[14]歴 *rekireki* notables, dignitaries; illustrious families. *rekireki(taru)* clear
[16]覧 *rekiran* looking around

— 13 —

鴈 836/F2140 F2010 See **雁** 830. [鳥]

— 14 —

歷 837/F1041 See **歴** 835. [止]

曆 838/F917 See **暦** 833. [日]

— 15 —

壓 839/F443 **壓** See **圧** 818. [土]

— 17 —

贋 840/F1808 **贗 贗 贗** GAN counterfeit. *nise* sham, counterfeit, forgery, imitation, false (prophet). *ni(seru)* (see under 似 376.0). [貝]

2 二亠人亻𠆢儿入八丷冂冖冫几凵刀刂力勹匕匚匸十卜卩[厂]厶又 17

4 手紙 *nise tegami* forged letter
5 札 *nise satsu, nise fuda, gansatsu* counterfeit paper money
6 印 *nise-in* forged seal
7 作 *gansaku* sham, counterfeit
8 金 *nisegane* counterfeit money
物 *gambutsu, nisemono* imitation, counterfeit, forgery, sham
9 首 *nisekubi* falsified severed head
造 *ganzō* counterfeiting, forgery, fabrication
造紙幣 *ganzō shihei* counterfeit paper money

蹷 See 蹶 4587.

20

贗 贋 See 贋 840.

21

饜 841/F2090 饜 En. *a*(*kiru*) be surfeited; be fed up with. [食]

RAD. 厶 28

Mu (the katakana). Nickname: *Kana Mu.*

厶 842/F308 Shi. *watakushi* I.

2

允 843/F179 In sincerity; permit. [儿]
11 許 *inkyo* permission, license

3

去 See 1051.

弁 844/F1484 辮 Ben braid. (See also 845, 846, and 847). [糸]
14 髪 *bempatsu* pigtail, queue

A 弁 845/F1259 瓣 Ben petal; valve. (See also 844, 846, and 847). [瓜]
14 膜 *bemmaku* valve (in internal organs)
20 鰓類 *bensairui* bivalves

A 弁 846/F1854 辨 Ben discrimination. *ben*(*jiru*), *ben*(*zuru*) manage, dispose of, carry thru; distinguish, discriminate. *wakima*(*eru*) discern, discriminate, know, understand, bear in mind. (See also 844, 845, and 847). [辛]
4 天 *Benten* god of wealth, music, eloquence, and water
6 当 *bentō* lunch
当屋 *bentōya* lunch vendor
当箱 *bentōbako* lunch box
7 別 *bembetsu* discrimination
10 財天 *Benzaiten*=Benten 弁天 (see above-4)
11 済 *bensai* settlement, payment
理 *benri* management
理士 *benrishi* patent attorney
18 解 *benkai*=弁解 847.13

15 慶格子 *benkeigōshi* checked pattern, plaid
慶縞 *benkeijima* plaid, checked pattern
17 償 *benshō*=next word
償金 *benshōkin* reparation, indemnity, compensation, reimbursement

A 弁 847/F1856 辯 Ben speech, dialect. oratory. *ben*(*jiru*) speak, talk, argue. (See also 844, 845 and 846). [辛]
3 口 *benkō* speech, manner of speaking
士 *benshi* speaker, orator
才 *bensai* eloquence, oratorical talent
5 立 *ben*(*ji*)-*ta*(*teru*) speak eloquently, talk volubly
6 舌 *benzetsu* speech
8 明 *bemmei* explanation, defense, justification
者 *bensha* speaker, orator
11 務官 *bemmukan* commissioner
12 疏 *benso* excuse, plea, defense
証 *benshō* demonstration, proof
証法 *benshōhō* dialectic, dialectics
証論 *benshōron* apologetics; dialectics
13 解 *benkai* explanation, justification, defense, excuse, apology
14 駁 *bembaku, bempaku* refutation, contradiction, rebuttal, disproof, disputation
15 論 *benron* discussion, argument, debate; oral proceedings, pleading
論大会 *benron taikai* oratorical contest
18 難 *bennan* denunciation, criticism
20 護 *bengo* defense, vindication, explanation, pleading
護人 *bengonin* counsel, defender, advocate
護士 *bengoshi* lawyer, attorney
護士会 *bengoshikai* bar association
護団 *bengodan* defense counsel
護者 *bengosha* defender, advocate
護依頼人 *bengo irainin* client
護料 *bengoryō* lawyer's fee

A 台 848/F1564 臺 TAI. DAI stand, pedestal, rack, table, dais, bench, block; holder, support; mounting, setting. *utena* calyx; tower; platform. *tsukasa* (see under 司 877.0). *-dai* level, mark; the decade of one's age; plateau, height, eminence; counter for vehicles, machines, tables, benches, etc. [至]

3 下 *daika* your honor; his honor
4 木 *daigi* (gun) stock, unworked block of wood; parent-tree stock (in grafting)
5 石 *dai-ishi* stone pedestal
尻 *daijiri* butt of a gun
本 *daihon* script, scenario
6 地 *daichi* plateau, tableland, eminence
7 車 *daisha* push car; flatcar
形 *daikei*＝*teikei* 梯形 2283.7
8 命 *taimei* command of a shogun or high official
所 *daidokoro* kitchen
所用品 *daidokoro yōhin* kitchenware
9 風 *taifū* typhoon
風眼 *taifūgan* eye of a typhoon
10 座 *daiza* pedestal
秤 *daibakari* platform scales
紙 *daishi* cardboard; mat, mount
11 帳 *daichō* ledger, register
12 場 *daiba* fort, battery
無 *daina(shi) ni suru* spoil, mar, ruin, destroy, make a mess of
湾 *Taiwan* Formosa
湾人 *Taiwanjin* a Formosan
詞 *serifu* speech, words, lines, remarks
詞回 *serifu-mawa(shi)* theatrical elocution
14 閣 *taikaku, daikaku* tall building, castle; the cabinet
16 頭 *taitō*＝擡頭 2021.16
覧 *tairan* inspection by the empress or the crown prince
17 臨 *tairin* visit by the empress or the crown prince
18 顔 *taigan* your face

—— 4 ——

牟 849/F1216 BŌ. MU pupil of the eye; mooing of a cow. [牛]

—— 6 ——

A 参 850/F309 參 SHIN. SAN three; going; coming; visiting. *mai(ru)* go; come; call, visit; visit a shrine; be defeated; be nonplussed; be madly in love; die. *mai(raseru)* beat, floor (someone), bring (someone) to his knees. *san(jiru)*, *san(zuru)* go; visit; come. *(o)mai(ri)* visits to shrines or temples.

2 入 *sannyū suru* come, visit, go
3 上 *sanjō suru* call on, visit
与 *san-yo* participation (in public affairs); counselor, consultant
与者 *san-yosha* participant
与官 *san-yokan* parliamentary councilor
4 内 *sandai* palace visit
5 加 *sanka* participation, joining, intervention
加者 *sankasha* participant, entrant
6 向 *sankō suru* proceed to
列 *sanretsu* attendance, presence, participation
列者 *sanretsusha* attendant
会 *sankai* attendance (at a meeting)
会者 *sankaisha* attendance
考 *sankō* reference, consultation
考人 *sankōnin* a person given as a reference
考図書館 *sankō toshokan* reference library
考品 *sankōhin* reference materials
考書 *sankōsho* reference book
考書目 *sankō shomoku* bibliography
考資料 *sankō shiryō* reference data
8 拝 *sampai* worship, visits to shrines or tombs
画 *sankaku suru* take part in planning
事 *sanji* secretary, councilor
事会 *sanjikai* a council
事官 *sanjikan* counselor
9 洛 *sanraku* going to the capital
院 *San-in* House of Councilors
政 *sansei* participation in government
政官 *sanseikan* parliamentary under-secretary
政権 *sanseiken* suffrage, franchise
10 酌 *sanshaku suru* compare and choose the good; consult, refer to
宮 *sangū* visit to the Ise Shrine
差 *shinshi(taru)* uneven, of different lengths or heights
11 道 *sandō* road approaching a shrine
堂 *sandō* visiting a home or temple
12 朝 *sanchō* visiting the palace
着 *sanchaku* arrival; payment on sight
集 *sanshū* assembling (of people)
勤交代 *sankin kōtai* daimyos' alternating Edo residence
賀 *sanga* congratulatory palace visit
賀者 *sangasha* congratulatory visitors
賀帳 *sangachō* congratulatory visitors' book
13 殿 *sanden* palace visit
禅 *sanzen* Zen meditation
詣 *sankei* temple or shrine visit, pilgrimage, homage
戦 *sansen* participation in a war
照 *sanshō* reference, comparison
16 謀 *sambō* staff officer; participation in planning
謀本部 *Sambō Hombu* General Staff Headquarters
謀長 *sambōchō* chief of staff
18 観 *sankan* visit, inspection
観人 *sankannin* visitor
20 議 *sangi* councilor; participation in government
議院 *Sangi-in* House of Councilors, Upper House
議院議員 *Sangi-in gi-in* member of the House of Councilors

2 二亠人イ𠆢儿入八丷冂冖冫几凵刀刂力勹匕匚匸十卜卩厂[厶]6 又

22 籠 *sanrō suru* retiring (to a temple or shrine) for prayer

7

貟 Nonstandard for 員 928.

怠 851/F699 TAI laziness, neglect. *okota(ru)* neglect; be off guard; be feeling better. *nama(keru)* be lazy, be idle; neglect. *okota(rinaku)* diligently, *okota(razu) ni* carefully. [心] (B)

8 屈 *taikutsu* tedium, boredom
者 *nama(ke)mono* a lazy person
10 納 *tainō*＝滞納 2661.10
12 惰 *taida* laziness, idleness
勝 *okota(ri)ga(chi)* neglectful
13 業 *taigyō* slow-down tactics, sabotage
14 慢 *taiman* negligence; procrastination; carelessness

8

畚 852/F483 畚 HON. *mokko* earth-carrying basket. *fugo* hamper, bamboo basket. [大]

能 853/F1541 NŌ ability, talent, skill, capacity; noh play, classical drama. *ato(u)* = *deki(ru)* 出来 97.7. *yoku(suru)* be skilled in. *yo(ku)* skillfully, thoroly. [肉] (A)

2 力 *nōryoku* ability, faculty, capacity
4 文 *nōbun* skilled in writing
文家 *nōbunka* skilled writer
5 弁 *nōben* eloquence, oratory
弁家 *nōbenka* orator
6 吏 *nōri* able official
7 狂言 *nō kyōgen* noh farce, noh interlude
役者 *nō yakusha* noh actor
8 事 *nōji* one's work
9 面 *nōmen* noh mask
10 書 *nōsho* excellent calligraphy; calligraphy. *nōga(ki)* advertising the excellence of ones's wares; boasting
11 動 *nōdō* activity, actual work
動的 *nōdōteki* active
動免疫 *nōdō men-eki* active immunity
動態 *nōdōtai* active voice
率 *nōritsu* efficiency
率的 *nōritsuteki* efficient
率給 *nōritsukyū* efficiency wages
率賃金 *nōritsu chingin* efficiency wages
12 筆 *nōhitsu* skilled penmanship; skilled calligrapher
無 *nōna(shi)* incompetence; ne'er-do-well
13 楽 *nōgaku* noh drama
楽堂 *nōgakudō* noh theater
14 舞台 *nō butai* noh stage

9

叄 854/F309 See 参 850.

19

囔 See 1021.

RAD. 又 29

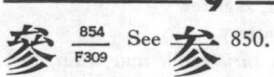

Mata again. Variant: 㕚. Nickname: Again.

又 855/F311 又 YŪ. *mata* again, and, furthermore; on the other hand. *mata moya* again. *mata shitemo* again. *mata wa* or. *mata to* in addition, besides this; twice. (B)

2 又 *matamata* again and again
3 小作 *mata kosaku* subtenancy, sublease
4 日 *mata(no)hi* another day; the next day
木 *matagi* forked tree, forked branch
5 写 *mata-utsu(shi)* copying again
6 名 *mata(no)na* alias, another name
7 弟子 *mata deshi* indirect pupil
10 借 *mataga(ri)* subtenancy
候 *matazoro* again
家来 *matagerai* secondary retainer
12 買 *mataga(i)* buying thru an agent
無 *mata na(i)*, *mata (to) na(i)* unique, matchless, unparalleled, never again
貸 *mataga(shi)* sublease
14 聞 *matagi(ki)* hearsay
隣 *matadonari* second door from here
15 請 *mata-uk(e)* subcontract
請負 *mata-ukeoi* subcontract
16 頼 *matadano(mi)* indirect request

1

叉 856/F311 SA. SHA. *mata* fork (of a road); crotch (of a tree).

4 手網 *sadeami* dip net, scoop net
10 庫 *azekura* ancient log cabin
14 銃 *sajū* stacked arms

2

反 See 817.

及 See **及** 154.

収 857/F315 See **収** 860.

A **友** 858/F312 Yū. *tomo* friend, companion, pal.
2 人 *yūjin* friend
6 邦 *yūhō* friendly nation, ally
交 *yūkō* friendship, amity, companionship
好 *yūkō* friendship, amity, companionship
好条約 *yūkō jōyaku* treaty of friendship
好国 *yūkōkoku* friendly nation
好的 *yūkōteki* friendly, amicable
好通商航海 *yūkō tsūshō kōkai* (treaty of) friendship, commerce, and navigation
8 朋 *yūhō* friend
宜 *yūgi* friendship, friendly relations
9 垣 *tomogaki* friend
軍 *yūgun* allied army, friendly troops
10 討 *tomo-u(chi)* friends shooting one another
党 *yūtō* allied political party
11 情 *yūjō* friendship, fellowship
釣 *tomozuri* fishing with decoys
達 *tomodachi* friend, companion
達付合 *tomodachizu(ki)a(i)* friendly relations
達甲斐 *tomodachigai* true friendship
13 義 *yūgi* friendship's responsibilities
愛 *yūai* friendship
愛結婚 *yūai kekkon* companionate marriage
15 誼 *yūgi* friendship, friendly relations
誼国家 *yūgi kokka* friendly nation

B **双** 859/F 312/F2015 **雙** Sō a pair; a set; comparison; counter for pairs.
2 十節 *Sōjūsetsu* the Double Tenth, October 10, the Chinese national holiday
3 子 *futago* twins, twin
子葉 *sōshiyō* dicotyledon
子葉植物 *sōshiyō shokubutsu* dicotyledon
4 手 *sōshu* both hands
方 *sōhō* both sides, both parties. *sōhō no* mutual, both
互 *sōgo* mutual, reciprocal
六 *sugoroku* a child's dice game
5 生 *sōsei* bearing twins; twins
生児 *sōseiji* twins
6 成 *futana(ri)* hermaphrodite
曲線 *sōkyokusen* hyperbola
7 対 *sōtai* relativity, reciprocity, symmetry
8 肩 *sōken* shoulders
9 発 *sōhatsu* two-motored
発機 *sōhatsuki* two-motored plane
10 紙 *sōshi* copybook; notebook; storybook; fiction; books
胴機 *sōdōki* twin-fuselage plane
峰駱駝 *sōhō rakuda* two-humped camel, Bactrian camel
11 眸 *sōbō* the pupils of both eyes; both eyes
脚 *sōkyaku* both feet
務契約 *sōmu keiyaku* bilateral agreement
眼 *sōgan* both eyes; binocular
眼鏡 *sōgankyō* field glasses, binoculars
12 幅 *sōfuku* pair of hanging scrolls
葉 *futaba* bud, sprout
殻類 *sōkakurui* bivalves
13 暗車 *sōansha* twin propellers
15 輪 *sōrin* two wheels
16 頭 *sōtō no* double-headed
蹄 *sōtei* cloven foot
蹄獣 *sōteijū* cloven-hoofed animal
17 翼 *sōyoku* both wings
18 璧 *sōheki* pair of bright jewels; matchless things; matchless people

3

A **収** 860/F315/F844 **收収収收收**
Shū income. *osa(maru)*, *osa(meru)* (see 納 3508.0). [攵]
2 入 *shūnyū* receipts, income, revenue, proceeds, earnings
入印紙 *shūnyū inshi* revenue stamp
入役 *shūnyūyaku* government treasurer
入源 *shūnyūgen* source of income
4 支 *shūshi* income and expenditure
5 用 *shūyō* expropriation
7 没 *shūbotsu* confiscation of possessions
束 *shūsoku suru* tie up
8 金 *shūkin* collecting; collections
受 *shūju suru* receive
9 拾 *shūshū suru* get under control, save (the situation)
10 益 *shūeki* earnings, proceeds, returns
差 *shūsa* aberration
納 *shūnō* crop, harvest, receipts
納係 *shūnōgakari* receiving teller
納額 *shūnōgaku* amount received
容 *shūyō* accommodation, seating, housing custody, admission; entering (in a dictionary)
容力 *shūyōryoku* capacity, accommodation
容所 *shūyōjo* home, asylum, camp
容者 *shūyōsha* inmates
容能力 *shūyō nōryoku* capacity, accommodation
容患者 *shūyō kanja* in-patients
容設備 *shūyō setsubi* accommodations
11 得 *shūtoku suru* receive
12 着 *shūchaku* sorption (in physical chemistry)

集 *shūshū* gathering up; collection; accumulation
税 *shūzei* tax collection, taxation
税人 *shūzeinin* tax collector
税吏 *shūzeiri* tax collector
税所 *shūzeisho* tax-collection office
税官 *shūzeikan* revenue officer
13 賄 *shūwai* accepting bribes, corruption, graft
14 奪 *shūdatsu suru* rob
蔵 *shūzō* garnering, collection
監 *shūkan* imprisonment
監力 *shūkanryoku* cell capacity
監状 *shūkanjō* commitment warrant
16 縛 *shūbaku suru* arrest and tie up
輯 *shūshū* gathering up
録 *shūroku suru* collect, record
覧 *shūran suru* grasp; win over
獲 *shūkaku*＝収穫 (see below–18)
獲感謝祭 *Shūkaku Kanshasai* Thanksgiving Day; harvest festival
17 斂 *shūren* exaction (of taxes); convergence, contraction, astriction
縮 *shūshuku* contraction, shrinking, constriction
縮期血圧 *shūshukuki ketsuatsu* systolic blood pressure
18 繭 *shūken* cocoon crop
穫 *shūkaku* harvest, harvesting, ingathering, crop
穫予想 *shūkaku yosō* crop estimate
穫物 *shūkakubutsu* the harvest, the yield
穫高 *shūkakudaka* the income, the crop, the yield
穫時 *shūkakuji* time of harvest
穫期 *shūkakuki* harvest time
24 攬 *shūran* grasping, winning over

6

受 See 2826.

取 取 See 3699.

叔 $\frac{861}{F315}$ Shuku uncle; youth.
B
4 父 *oji, shukufu* uncle
5 母 *oba, shukubo* aunt

7

叟 See 863.

叛 See 220.

叙 $\frac{862}{F317\ F851}$ 敍 敘 Jo. *jo(suru)* relate, narrate, describe, write; confer (a rank); write a preface.
B
4 文 *jobun* preface, introduction
6 任 *jonin* investiture
7 述 *jojutsu* description, narration
位 *joi* investiture
8 事 *joji* narration, description
事文 *jojibun* narration, description
事詩 *jojishi* descriptive poetry, epic poem
11 情 *jojō* description of feelings; lyricism
情詩 *jojōshi* lyric poetry; lyric poem
12 景 *jokei* scenery description
14 説 *josetsu* explanation, interpretation
15 賜 *joshi* distributing ranks, rewards, and pensions
勲 *jokun* conferring of decorations
17 爵 *joshaku* conferring a peerage

8

叟 $\frac{863}{F317}$ Sō. Shū old person.

桑 $\frac{864}{F975}$ Sō. *kuwa* mulberry. [木]
B
5 田 *sōden* mulberry plantation
6 色 *kuwa iro* light yellow
8 門 *sōmon* priesthood; Buddhism
苗 *sōbyō* mulberry seedling
苺 *kuwa ichigo* fruit of the mulberry
9 海 *sōkai* this world's sudden changes
畑 *kuwabatake* mulberry field
13 園 *sōen* mulberry plantation
14 摘 *kuwatsu(mi)* picking mulberry leaves; mulberry-leaf pickers

14

叡 $\frac{865}{F317\ F1329}$ 睿 Ei intelligence; imperial.
6 旨 *eishi* the emperor's instructions
8 知 *eichi* wisdom, intelligence; intellect
12 智 *eichi* wisdom, intelligence; intellect
13 感 *eikan* the emperor's approval
14 聞 *eibun ni* in the emperor's hearing
15 慮 *eiryo* the emperor's pleasure
16 覧 *eiran* the emperor's personal inspection

16

叢 See 144.

雙 $\frac{866}{F2015}$ See 双 859. [隹]

18

矍 $\frac{867}{F1332}$ Kaku surprise and confusion. [目]
28 鑠 *kakushaku* vigorous old age. *kakushaku(taru)* hale and hearty

3-STROKE RADICALS

口 RAD. 30

Kuchi mouth. At left: *kuchi hen*. Nickname: Mouth.

A **口** 868 / F318 KU. KŌ mouth. *kuchi* mouth, lips; speech, words; one's taste, stopper, plug; nozzle, orifice, slit, aperture; door, gate, entrance; route, ascent; employment, job; call (for a doctor); share; kind, lot, brand; beginning; rumor, opening (of a boil). *kuchi ni suru* taste, eat; speak of, refer to. *kuchi(zukara)* personally. *kuchi(anguri)* dumfounded, open-mouthed. *kuchi(saganai)* gossipy, critical, jabbering.

2 八丁 **kuchihatchō** voluble, eloquent

入 **kuchi-i(re)** acting as go-between; good offices. **kuchi (o) i(reru)** throw in a suggestion

入屋 **kuchi-i(re)ya** employment agency

3 口 **kuchiguchi** each entrance, every mouth. **kuchiguchi ni** severally, unanimously

巾 **kuchihaba(ttai)** acting smart, bragging

才 **kōsai** clever speech

下手 **kuchibeta** defective speech, slowness of speech; poor talker

小言 **kuchi kogoto** scolding, faultfinding

三味線 **kuchijamisen, kuchizamisen** humming a samisen tune ⌈duction

上 **kōjō** verbal message, statement; intro-

上手 **kuchijōzu na** smooth-speaking

上書 **kōjōga(ki)** a written statement

4 中 **kōchū** interior of the mouth

切 **kuchiki(ri)** start broaching (a subject)

元 **kuchimoto** the mouth; shape of the mouth; near an entrance

分 **kuchiwa(ke)** assortment

不調法 **kuchi buchōhō** poor talker

止 **kuchido(me) suru** forbid to speak, muzzle (a person)

止料 **kuchido(me)ryō** hush money

火 **kuchibi** fuse; spark plug; cause (of war); origin (of a quarrel)

火切 **kuchibi (o) ki(ru)** start a conversation

辺 **kōhen ni** around the mouth

辺単純疱疹 **kōhen tanjun hōshin** cold sore

内 **kōnai** in the mouth

内炎 **kōnaien** stomatitis

5 外 **kōgai suru** tell, divulge

占 **kuchiura** gathering from another's words

弁 **kōben** eloquence

出 **kuchida(shi)** interference, meddling. **kuchi (o) da(su)** interrupt a conversation

巧者 **kuchigōsha (na)** smooth-spoken

可笑 **kuchiokashi** witty talking, joking

付 **kuchizu(keru)** kiss. **kuchitsu(ki)** the mouth; manner of speech; mouthpiece (of a cigarette) ⌈a mouthpiece

付煙草 **kuchitsu(ki) tabako** cigarette with

6 舌 **kōzetsu** words, tongue. **kōzetsu, kuzetsu** talking recklessly; quarreling; curtain lecture

回 **kuchimawa(shi)** an expression; phrase-

気 **kōki** bad breath; intimation ⌊ology

伝 **kōden, kuchizuta(e), kuchizute** oral tradition; tradition

任 **kuchimaka(se)** random talk

汚 **kuchigitana(i)** foul-mouthed, abusive. **kuchiyogo(shi)** tantalizing sample (of food)

号 **kuchizusa(mu)**＝口遊 (see below–11)

当 **kuchia(tari)** taste; reception, hospitality

早 **kuchibaya** rapid talking

先 **kuchisaki** lips, mouth; snout; proboscis; professions, lip service, mere words

争 **kuchiaraso(i)** quarreling

返答 **kuchihentō** talking back, retort

耳 **kōji** mouth and ear

耳学 **kōji (no) gaku** shallow learning

7 走 **kuchibashi(ru)** speak, tell, blurt out

車 **kuchiguruma** cajolery ⌈(mu) hum

吟 **kōgin** humming to oneself. **kuchizusa-**

吻 **kōfun** way of speaking; intimation

抜 **kuchinu(ki)** corkscrew

利 **kuchikiki** eloquent person; mouthpiece; man of influence; mediator, middleman ⌈tradition

承 **kōshō** passing on by word of mouth, oral

言葉 **kuchi kotoba** words in common use

角 **kōkaku** corners of the mouth

角力 **kuchizumō** war of words

述 **kōjutsu** oral statement, dictation, lecture

述書 **kōjutsusho** affidavit

述試験 **kōjutsu shiken** oral examination

8 金 **kuchigane** bottle cap; clasp, base (of a light globe)

固 **kuchigata(me)** verbal promise

味 *kōmi* taste, flavor, deliciousness
径 *kōkei* aperture, bore, caliber
明 *kuchia(ke)* start, beginning
取 *kuchito(ri)* groom, horse boy; side dish
直 *kuchinao(shi)* removing a bad taste
実 *kōjitsu* excuse, pretext
受 *kuju* listening to someone talking
拍子 *kuchibyōshi* counting time orally
忠実 *kuchimame na* talkative, voluble
性無 *kuchisagana(i)* gossipy; abusive
奇麗 *kuchigirei* ＝口綺麗 (see below–14)
供 *kōkyō* affidavit, deposition
供書 *kōkyōsho* affidavit, deposition 「ology
9 廻 *kuchimawa(shi)* an expression; phrase-
拭 *kuchifu(ki)* napkin
紅 *kuchibeni* lipstick; red-rimmed 「prudent
重 *kuchiomo na, kuchiomo(i)* slow of speech;
前 *kuchimae* way of speaking; profession
宣 *kōsen* oral statement
臭 *kōshū* bad breath, halitosis
茶 *kuchija* adding more tea
荒 *kuchiara* rough speaking
約 *kōyaku* verbal promise
約束 *kuchi yakusoku* verbal promise
10 座 *kōza* account
唇 *kōshin* lips, labia
凌 *kuchishino(gi)* hand-to-mouth living
振 *kuchiburi* way of speaking; intimation
脇 *kuchiwaki* edges of the mouth
書 *kuchiga(ki) suru* write with the brush in the mouth. *kōsho, kuchiga(ki)* affidavit, written confession
恐 *kuchioso(roshi)* terrible talker
真似 *kuchimane* mimicry
祥無 *kuchisagana(i)* gossipy, abusive
11 過 *kuchisu(gi) suru* make a living
遅 *kuchioso* slow of speech
遊 *kuchizusa(mu), kuchizusa(bu)* hum; sing to oneself; compose impromptu (poems)
惜 *kuya(shii), kuya(shigaru)* (see under 悔 1682.0). *kuchio(shii)* regrettable, mortifying 「tain)
掛 *kuchi (ga) ka(karu)* be called (to enter-
授 *kōju, kuju* oral instruction, dictation
添 *kuchizo(e)* advice, support, good offices
移 *kuchiutsu(shi)* mouth-to-mouth feeding; oral transmission, tradition
許 *kuchimoto*＝口元 (see above–4)
悪 *kuchi (no) waru(i)* evil-mouthed. *kuchiwaru* reviling; abuser
寄 *kuchiyo(se)* spiritism, necromancy, telepathy; medium, sorceress
笛 *kuchibue* whistling
堅 *kuchigata(i)* close-mouthed, discreet
達 *kōtatsu, kōdatsu* verbal message, oral
達者 *kuchidassha na* talkative ⌊instructions
12 開 *kuchia(ke)* beginning
幅 *kuchihaba(ttai)* acting smart, bragging
減 *kuchibe(rashi)* cutting down personnel
絵 *kuchie* frontispiece
証 *kōshō* oral testimony
軽 *kuchi (ga) karu(i)* careless (talker). *kuchigaru* glibness, volubility
飲 *kuchino(mi)* drinking from a bottle
割 *kuchi (o) wa(ru)* confess to a crime
喧 *kuchiyakama(shii)* nagging, faultfinding, scolding; talkative, gossipy
喧嘩 *kuchigenka* quarreling
腔 *kōkō, kōkū* oral cavity
腔外科 *kōkō geka, kōkū geka* oral surgery
答 *kuchigota(e)* talking back, retort, oral answer. *kōtō* oral answer
答試問 *kōtō shimon* oral examination
13 煩 *kuchiurusa(i)* nagging
腹 *kōfuku* mouth and stomach
触 *kuchizawari* taste
試 *kōshi* oral examination
跡 *kōseki* manner of speaking
際 *kuchigiwa* around the mouth
馴 *kuchina(rashi)* vocal or oral drill. *kuchina(reru)* develop vocal or oral skill
数 *kuchikazu* number of dependents; words, speech; number of shares. *kōsū* number of accounts; number of times
塞 *kuchifusa(gi)* stopping someone from
話術 *kōwajutsu* lip reading ⌊talking
蓋 *kōgai* palate
蓋垂 *kōgaisui* uvula
14 慣 *kuchina(reru)* develop vocal or oral skill
演 *kōen* oral narration 「the mouth
滌 *kuchisusu(gu), kuchisoso(gu)* gargle; rinse
碑 *kōhi* legend, folklore, tradition
端 *kuchi(no)ha* rumor, gossip. *kōtan* mouth
網 *kuchiami* (dog) muzzle
誦 *kōshō* humming; reading aloud
酸 *kuchi (ga) suppa(ku) naru, kuchi (o) suppa(ku) suru* repeat tediously
銭 *kōsen* commission, brokerage; net profit
綺麗 *kuchigirei* speaking elegantly; speaking clearly; not coveting food. *kuchigirei ni* speaking like an innocent person
説 *kudo(ku)* persuade, entreat, woo, seduce. *kuzetsu* quarrel; curtain lecture; jabbering
説立 *kudo(ki)-ta(teru)* entreat, urge strongly
説掛 *kudo(ki)-ka(keru)* persuade
説落 *kudo(ki)-o(tosu)* persuade, talk (someone) into (something), seduce
語 *kōgo* colloquial language
語文 *kōgobun* colloquial language
語体 *kōgotai* colloquial style; colloquialism
語訳 *kōgoyaku* colloquial translation
語詩 *kōgotai* colloquial style; colloquialism

15 論 *kōron* dispute, argument
輪 *kuchiwa* muzzle
慰 *kuchinagusa(mi)* relieving tension by reading poetry or munching food
賢 *kuchisaka(shii), kuchigashiko(i)* clever in talking
調 *kuchō* tone, expression
調法 *kuchi chōhō* clever speaking
16 頼 *kuchidano(mi)* oral requirement
髭 *kuchi hige* moustache
頭 *kōtō* oral
頭弁論 *kōtō benron* oral argument
頭投票 *kōtō tōhyō* voice vote
頭試問 *kōtō shimon* oral examination
頭試験 *kōtō shiken* oral examination
頭審問 *kōtō shimmon* court hearing
18 癖 *kuchiguse* way of saying, favorite phrase
穢 *kuchigitana(i)* foulmouthed
糧 *kōryō* rations
覆 *kuchiō(i)* mask
19 鏡 *kōkyō* mouth speculum
22 籠 *kuchigomo(ru)* stammer, mumble, falter. *kugomo(ru)* mumbling

2

台 See 848.

召 See 668.

古 See 770.

可 See 24.

句 See 745.

史 史 See 91.

号 See **号** 882. [虎]

叱 Nonstandard for **叱** 873.

叭 869/F324 Hatsu open.

叺 870/F327 (国字) *kamasu* straw bag; tobacco pouch.

叶 871/F327 Kyō. *kana(eru)* grant, answer, hear (a prayer). *kana(u)* (see under 適 4738.0).

叮 872/F324 Tei courtesy.
17 嚀 *teinei*＝丁寧 2.14.

叱 873/F325 Shitsu. *shika(ru)* scold, reprove.
5 付 *shika(ri)-tsu(keru)* scold severely
正 *shissei* correction, improvement
7 声 *shissei* hiss
8 呼 *shikko suru* shout up at
9 飛 *shika(ri)-to(basu)* scold severely, blow
咤 *shitta* scolding
11 責 *shisseki* rebuke, reprimand

叫 叫 See **叫** 881.

只 874/F323 Shi. *tada* free. *tada sae* in addition to, to add to.
4 中 *tadanaka ni* in the midst of
今 *tada-ima*＝唯今 942.4
切符 *tadagippu* free ticket, pass
5 只 *tadatada* only by
8 物 *tadamono* ordinary person
取 *tadato(ri)* getting something for nothing
者 *tadamono* ordinary person
奉公 *tadabōkō* serving without pay
9 独 *tada hito(ri)* only one
乗 *tadano(ri)* stolen ride, free ride
13 働 *tadabatara(ki)* working for nothing
14 管 *hitasura* earnestly

A **兄** 875/F181 Kei brother; you. Kyō. *ani, nii(san)* elder brother. *se* a woman's familiar call for her husband or elder brother. [儿]
3 上 *aniue* elder brother
4 分 *anibun* one regarded as an elder brother
7 君 *senokimi, anigimi* endearing term for elder brother
弟 *kyōdai, keitei, ani-oto, ani otōto* brother, brethren
弟子 *anideshi* senior schoolmate, senior apprentice
弟分 *kyōdaibun* buddy, pal, sworn brother
弟会社 *kyōdaigaisha* affiliated companies
弟姉妹 *kyōdai-shimai* brothers and sisters, brethren
弟愛 *kyōdai-ai* brotherly love
8 妹 *keimai* older brother and younger sister
事 *keiji suru* regard as one's senior
9 姫 *ehime* eldest daughter
10 息子 *ani musuko* my eldest son
12 御 *anigo* elder brother (polite)
貴 *aniki* elder brother, one's senior
13 嫁 *aniyome* elder brother's wife
14 様 *niisama, niisan* elder brother

3 [口] 2 口 土 士 夂 夊 夕 大 女 子 宀 寸 小 ⺌ 尢 尸 屮 山 川 巛 工 己 巾 干 幺 广 廴 廾 弋 弓 彐 彑 彡 彳

叩 876 F322 Kō. *tata*(*ku*) strike, beat, hit, knock, thrash, slap, rap, pat, pound, maul, clap (hands); sound out (views); criticize. *tata*(*ki-nomesu*) knock down, beat up. *tata*(*ki*) dusting; duster.

3 上 *tata*(*ki*)-*a*(*geru*) work up; improve by training
大工 *tata*(*ki*) *daiku* clumsy carpenter
4 込 *tata*(*ki*)-*ko*(*mu*) drive into; throw into (prison); hammer in, inculcate
切 *tata*(*ki*)-*ki*(*ru*) hack down, chop down, mangle
5 立 *tata*(*ki*)-*ta*(*teru*) beat severely
付 *tata*(*ki*)-*tsu*(*keru*) beat, thrash; throw at
出 *tata*(*ki*)-*da*(*su*) begin to beat (a drum); beat and drive out; dismiss, send away
6 肉 *tata*(*ki*)*niku* meat loaf; meat ball
伏 *tata*(*ki*)-*fu*(*seru*) knock down; utterly defeat
合 *tata*(*ki*)-*a*(*u*) fight, exchange blows. *tata*-(*ki*)-*a*(*waseru*) strike (things) together
8 直 *tata*(*ki*)-*nao*(*su*) beat back into shape; correct by discipline
10 起 *tata*(*ki*)-*oko*(*su*) rouse, shake, awake
倒 *tata*(*ki*)-*tao*(*su*) knock down, beat down
消 *tata*(*ki*)-*ke*(*su*) beat out (a fire)
破 *tata*(*ki*)-*yabu*(*ru*) smash in, smash down
殺 *tata*(*ki*)-*koro*(*su*) beat to death
12 割 *tata*(*ki*)-*wa*(*ru*) break to pieces, smash
落 *tata*(*ki*)-*o*(*tosu*) knock down, knock off
13 鉦 *tata*(*ki*)*gane* temple ceremonial gong
毀 *tata*(*ki*)-*kowa*(*su*) knock to pieces; smash up, wreck
15 潰 *tata*(*ki*)-*tsubu*(*su*) smash up, crushingly defeat
16 頭 *nukazu*(*ku*) bow, kowtow, prostrate oneself. *kōtō* kowtow, bow
頭戦術 *kōtō senjitsu* kowtowing strategy

A **司** 877 F327 Shi official; government office. *tsukasado*(*ru*) rule, administer, conduct. *tsukasa* office, government office; director, head official.

5 令 *shirei* command, control; commander
令官 *shireikan* commanding officer
令長官 *shirei chōkan* commander-in-chief
令部 *shireibu* headquarters, the command
令塔 *shireitō* conning tower
6 会 *shikai* chairmanship; chairman
会者 *shikaisha* chairman, toastmaster, moderator
式 *shishiki* directing a ceremony; celebrant
式者 *shishikisha* leader, presiding minister, master of ceremonies
式聖職 *shishiki seishoku* celebrant
8 直 *shichoku* judicial authorities, the court, the bench, a judge
法 *shihō* administration of justice
法大臣 *Shihō Daijin* Minister of Justice
法官 *shihōkan* judicial official
法省 *Shihōshō* Justice Ministry
法保護 *shihō hogo* judicial protection
法部 *shihōbu* the judicature
法権 *shihōken* judicial powers, powers of jurisdiction
法警察 *shihō keisatsu* judicial police
9 政官 *shiseikan* civil administrator
政長官 *shisei chōkan* civil administrator
10 書 *shisho* librarian
11 教 *shikyō* (Catholic) bishop
教区 *shikyōku* diocese
祭 *shisai* (Catholic) priest
祭職 *shisaishoku* (Catholic) priesthood
12 税官 *shizeikan* assessor, tax officer

A **右** 878 F326 Yū. U. *migi*, *migiri* right, right hand. *migi suru* turn to the right.

3 大臣 *Udaijin* Minister of the Right
4 手 *migite*, *mete* right hand
方 *uhō* the right
辺 *uhen* right side
中間 *uchūkan* between right field and center
心房 *ushimbō* right auricle
心室 *ushinshitsu* right ventricle
5 左 *migi-hidari* right and left
打者 *migi dasha* right-handed batter
6 回 *migimawa*(*ri*) righthanded rotation, clockwise
7 足 *usoku*, *migi ashi* right foot
折 *usetsu suru* turn to the right
社 *usha* right wing socialist party
利 *migiki*(*ki*) righthandedness; righthander
邪飛 *ujahi* foul off to the right
8 枕 *migimakura ni* (lying) on the right side
岸 *ugan*, *migi kishi* right bank, right shore (as you go down a river)
表 *uhyō* the chart at the right
往左往 *uō-saō suru* go right and left, go this way and that
9 派 *uha* rightists, the Right
前 *uzen*, *migimae* folding the left side of a kimono over the right. *uzen* in front of the right fielder
巻 *migima*(*ki*) clockwise
10 党 *utō* rightists, the Right
書 *migiga*(*ki*) written from right to left
11 眼 *ugan* right eye
舷 *ugen* starboard
寄 *migiyo*(*ri*) leaning toward the right; rightist
側 *usoku*, *migigawa* right hand, right side
側通行 *Migigawa Tsūkō* Keep to the Right
12 越 *ugo*(*shi*) over right field
腕 *migi ude*, *uwan* right arm
筆 *uhitsu* amanuensis, secretary
13 傾 *ukei* leaning to the right, rightist
14 端 *utan* right edge; right end; right lane
17 犠飛 *ugihi* right-field sacrifice fly

3 [口] 口土士夂夊夕大女子宀寸小⺌尢尸屮山川巛工己巾干幺广廴廾弋弓彐彑彡彳

翼 *uyoku* right wing, rightists; right field; right flank
翼手 *uyokushu* right fielder
翼団体 *uyoku dantai* right-wing groups
21 顧左眄 *uko-saben suru* look right and left; vacillate, waver

3

各 See 1163.

名 See 1170.

后 See 181.

同 See 619.

吉 See 1053.

向 See 101.

合 See 383.

吏 吏 See 183.

吋 879/F330 Tō. *inchi* inch.

吃 880/F327 Kitsu. *domo(ru)* stammer, stutter.
4 水 *kissui* draft (of a ship)
水線 *kissuisen* (loaded) water line
6 逆 *shakkuri, kitsugyaku* hiccups
9 音 *kitsuon* stammering, stuttering
14 緊 *kikkin* urgent
22 驚 *bikkuri suru* be surprised
驚仰天 *bikkuri-gyōten suru* be startled, be shocked, be stunned
驚箱 *bikkuribako* jack-in-the-box

B **叫** 881/F323 **叫 吽** Kyō. *sake(bu)* shout, exclaim, cry, yell, roar, howl; cry for, clamor for, advocate. *wame(ku)* shout, cry, yell, clamor.
5 出 *sake(bi)-da(su)* cry out
6 号 *kyōgō suru* cry aloud ⌈roar, howl
7 声 *sake(bi)goe* shout, cry, yell, scream, wail,
求 *sake(bi)-moto(meru)* cry for
8 呼 *sake(bi)-yo(bawaru)* wail
泣 *sake(bi)-na(ku)* wail
12 喚 *kyōkan* shout, scream
訴 *sake(bi)-utta(eru)* cry out against

A **号** 882/F1656 **號** Gō number; item, title, pseudonym; Buddhist name. *gō(suru)* assume the name of; name, call, style; declare, announce. *-gō* suffix after a foreign ship name. [虎]
4 火 *gōka* signal fire
5 外 *gōgai* newspaper extra
令 *gōrei* order, command
6 叫 *gōkyō* calling in a loud voice
8 泣 *gōkyū* lamentation, wailing
9 音 *gōon* reverberating sound; audible signal, ⌊a call
10 砲 *gōhō* signal gun
哭 *gōkoku* lamentation, wailing
11 笛 *gōteki* whistle
14 旗 *gōki* signal flag; flag emblem
20 鐘 *gōshō* signal bell

B **吐** 883/F336 Tō. *ha(ku)* disgorge, vomit; belch, emit; give vent to; confess; tell (lies), speak. *tsu(ku)* breathe; disgorge; tell (lies).
3 口 *ha(ki)guchi* spillway; marketing. *ha(ke)-guchi* outlet, vent
下 *ha(ki)-kuda(shi)* vomiting and purging
5 出 *ha(ki)-da(su)* vomit, disgorge, spit out; breathe out; send out (smoke); belch (fire and smoke); say (angrily)
6 血 *toketsu* vomiting blood
気 *ha(ki)ke* nausea
8 物 *tobutsu suru* vomit
乳 *tonyū suru* throw up milk
10 剤 *tozai* emetic
息 *to-iki* sigh, a long breath
11 捨 *ha(ki)su(te)* exhaust, discharge
掛 *ha(ki)-ka(keru)* spit at, spit on
12 散 *ha(ki)-chi(rasu)* pour out (evil words)
16 薬 *ha(ki)gusuri* emetic
18 瀉 *tosha* vomiting and diarrhea
瀉物 *toshabutsu* vomit and bowel discharge
21 露 *toro suru* express one's mind, give vent to, open (one's heart)

吊 884/F-X Chō. *tsuru(su), tsu(ru)* hang, suspend; wear (a sword).
3 下 *tsu(ri)-sa(garu) vi* dangle, be suspended, be hung down from. *tsuri-sa(geru) vt* dangle, be suspended, be hung down
上 *tsu(ri)-a(geru)* hang up, haul up, suspend, raise, hoist, weigh (an anchor). *tsuru(shi)a(ge)* kangaroo court; impeach- ⌊ment
4 天井 *tsuri-tenjo* suspended ceiling
太鼓 *tsuridaiko* suspended drum

[5]出 *tsuri-da(su)* pull out (a fish); decoy, lure
[9]革 *tsurikawa* (hanging) strap. *tsu(ri)-oro(su)* hang, suspend, let down
柿 *tsuru(shi)gaki* dried persimmons
[10]紐 *tsurihimo* supporting cord
索 *tsurinawa* rope for hanging things up
[11]眼 *tsurime* slant eyes
窓 *tsuru(shi) mado* vertically sliding windows
梯子 *tsuribashigo* rope ladder
[12]棚 *tsuridana* hanging shelf
[16]橋 *tsuribashi* suspension bridge
[17]環 *tsuriwa* flying ring (in a gym); watch fob
繃帯 *tsuri hōtai* (arm) sling
[18]鎖 *tsurigusari* supporting chain
[19]縄 *tsuri nawa* rope for hanging things up
[20]籃 *tsuri kago* hanging basket; nacelle, gondola

B **吸** 885 F342 吸 KYŪ. *su(u)* inhale; imbibe, sip; suck, suck out.

[2]入 *kyūnyū* inhalation. *su(i)-i(reru)* suck in
入剤 *kyūnyūzai* inhalant
入液 *kyūnyūeki* spray, vapor
入器 *kyūnyūki* inhaler
[3]口 *su(i)kuchi* cigarette holder, mouthpiece (on a pipe)
上 *su(i)-a(geru)* suck up, pump up. *suia(ge)* suction; sucking
[4]込 *su(i)-ko(mu)* inhale, imbibe; suck in; absorb, engulf, swallow up; suck down
引 *kyūin* absorption, suction, attraction
水 *kyūsui* suction
水管 *kyūsuikan* water pipe
[5]付 *su(i)-tsu(keru)* attract; light (a cigarette). *su(i)-tsu(ku)* adhere to, stick to
出 *su(i)-da(su)* suck out, draw out, pump out
出膏薬 *su(i)da(shi) kōyaku* poultice, an antiphlogistic
収 *kyūshū* absorption; suction; attraction; extinction (of light)
収力 *kyūshūryoku* absorptive power
収性 *kyūshūsei* absorptiveness
収剤 *kyūshūzai* an absorbent
収薬 *kyūshūyaku* an absorbent
[6]気 *kyūki* breathing in
血 *kyūketsu* sucking blood
血鬼 *kyūketsuki* an extortioner, a vampire
血動物 *kyūketsu dōbutsu* bloodsucker
[7]角 *kyūkaku* cupping glass
角子 *kyūkakushi* cupping glass
[8]物 *su(i)mono* soup
物椀 *su(i)mono wan* soup bowl
取 *su(i)-to(ru)* suck up, soak up, suck out; extort, squeeze out (money)
取紙 *suitorigami* blotting paper, blotter
[10]差 *su(i)sa(shi)* cigarette butt
[12]殻 *su(i)gara* tobacco ashes
飲 *kyūin* (opium) smoking. *suino(mi)* feeding cup (for a patient)
飲器 *kyūinki* feeding cup (for a patient)
着 *kyūchaku suru* adhere, stick fast
着剤 *kyūchakuzai* an absorbent
[14]管 *kyūkan* suction pipe, siphon
塵器 *kyūjinki* vacuum cleaner
[15]盤 *kyūban* sucker (on an octopus)
[16]瓢 *su(i)fukube* cupping glass

4

吾 See 37.

否 See 40.

吝 See 2066.

合 See 402.

邑 See 4756. [邑]

吞 呑 See 39.

局 886 F-X See 局 1384. [尸]

呉 887 F342 See 呉 583.

吸 888 F342 See 吸 885.

品 889 F-X Nonstandard for 品 923.

呎 890 F345 SHAKU. *fuiito* foot.

呂 891 F345 RYO, RO backbone.

[9]律 *roretsu* articulation, pronunciation

吻 892 F343 FUN proboscis. *kuchiwaki* sides of the mouth.

[6]合 *fungō* coincidence, conformity, concurrence; union; junction

吼 893 F343 KŌ. KU. *ho(eru)* bark, bay, howl, bellow, roar; cry.

[7]声 *ho(e)goe* bark, bellow, howl, roar

吶 894 F342 Totsu stutter.
[12]喊 *tokkan* war cry
[13]嗟 *tossa* moment, instant. *tossa ni* at once

B **呈** 895 F341 **呈** Tei *tei(suru)* offer, present; send (a letter); exhibit; develop (symptoms); assume (airs).
[3]上 *teijō* presentation
[5]出 *teishutsu* presentation
示 *teishi, teiji* presentation
示払 *teijibara(i)* payment on demand
[6]色 *teishoku* color, coloring

呆 896 F345 Hō. Bō. *aki(reru)* be amazed, be aghast, be disgusted, be shocked. *hoke* dullheadedness.
[6]返 *aki(re)-ka(eru)* be amazed at, be disgusted with
気 *akke* blank amazement. *ukke* stupid fellow
気者 *ukkemono* stupid fellow
気無 *akkena(i)* disappointing
[8]果 *aki(re)-hat(eru)* be amazed at, be disgusted with
[12]然 *bōzen to* in blank amazement
[18]顔 *aki(re)gao* amazed look

吠 897 F339 Hai. Bei. *ho(eru)* bark, bay, howl, bellow, roar; cry.
[5]付 *ho(e)-tsu(ku)* bark at
[6]回 *ho(e)-mawa(ru)* run around barking; run around yelling
叫 *ho(e)-sake(bu)* howl, roar, cry out
[7]声 *ho(e)goe* bark, howl, roar, bellow, baying
陀 *Bēda* the Vedas
陀文学 *Bēda bungaku* Vedic literature
[9]面 *hoezura* tearful face
[11]掛 *ho(e)-ka(keru)* bark at
猛 *ho(e)-ta(keru)* roar

B **吟** 898 F339 Gin singing; recital; song; poem. *gin(jiru), gin(zuru)* sing, chant, recite.
[6]行 *ginkō* traveling minstrel
[7]社 *ginsha* poetry club
声 *ginsei* reciting voice
[8]味 *gimmi* testing, scrutinizing, careful inquiry
[9]客 *ginkaku* poet
[11]唱 *ginshō* recite, chant
遊詩人 *gin-yū shijin* troubadour, minnesinger, minstrel
[12]詠 *gin-ei* singing, recital; song, poem
[14]誦 *ginshō suru* recite, chant
[16]嘯 *ginshō suru* recite, chant

A **君** 899 F337 Kun mister (familiar). *kimi* you (familiar); ruler.
[3]子 *kunshi* true gentleman, wise man; an official
子人 *kunshijin* true gentleman, wise man
[4]父 *kumpu* one's lord and father
王 *kunnō* king
辺 *kumpen* (at) the ruler's side
公 *kunkō* lord, master, ruler
[5]代 *Kimi(ga)yo* Japan's national anthem
民 *kummin* the king and his people
主 *kunshu* ruler
主国 *kunshukoku* monarchy
主専制 *kunshu sensei* autocratic monarchy
主政 *kunshusei* monarchy
主政体 *kunshu seitai* monarchy
[6]臣 *kunshin* ruler and ruled; master and servant
[7]位 *kun-i* throne, crown
[8]国 *kunkoku* king and country
命 *kummei* imperial command, one's lord's orders
[9]侯 *kunkō* daimyo (polite)
[10]家 *kunka* ruler's residence
恩 *kun-on* imperial benevolence
[11]側 *kunsoku* the (palace) court
[12]等 *kimira* you folks
[17]臨 *kunrin suru* reign; control, dictate
[19]寵 *kunchō* a lord's favor

A **告** 900 F344 **告** Koku. *tsu(geru)* tell, inform, announce, proclaim; bid, order. *tsu(ge)* oracle, revelation, inspiration.
[3]口 *tsu(ge)guchi* talebearing
[4]文 *kokubun* written appeal of a case
天子 *hibari* skylark
[5]白 *kokuhaku* confession, acknowledgment
示 *tsu(ge)-shime(su)* tell, proclaim. *kokuji* notification, bulletin
示板 *kokujiban* bulletin board
[6]回 *tsu(ge)-mawa(su)* noise abroad
[7]別 *kokubetsu* leave-taking, farewell
別式 *kokubetsushiki* funeral service
[8]知 *tsu(ge)-shi(raseru), tsu(ge)-shi(rasu), kokuchi suru* tell, notify, reveal. *kokuchi* notice, announcement
知板 *kokuchiban* bulletin board
知書 *kokuchisho* notice
[9]発 *kokuhatsu* prosecution; indictment; accusation, complaint, denunciation
発状 *kokuhatsujō* bill of indictment
発者 *kokuhatsusha* prosecutor; accuser, informant
[11]達 *kokutatsu* notification
[12]訴 *kokuso* accusation, complaint
訴人 *kokusonin* one who brings suit
[13]辞 *kokuji* address, farewell address
解 *kokkai* penance
[16]諭 *kokuyu* official notice, proclamation

B **吹** 901 F343 Sui. *fu(ku) vi* and *vt* breathe, blow; play (a wind instrument);

emit; smelt; mint; brag. *fu(kasu)* *vt* smoke, puff.

2 入 *fu(ki)-i(reru)* breathe into; blow into; (winds) blow in

3 口 *fu(ki)guchi* nozzle ⌈tain)

下 *fu(ki)-o(rosu)* blow down (from a moun-

上 *fu(ki)-a(garu)* be blown up high (as dust, or water in geysers). *fuki-a(geru)* spout (water), blow up; wash ashore. *fu(ki)a(ge)* fountain, spouting, spray

4 手 *fu(ki)te* blower ⌈subside

止 *fu(ki)-ya(mu)* blow over, die down,

分 *fu(ki)-wa(keru)* winnow; smelt; assay; blow apart

井戸 *fu(ki)-ido* artesian well, drilled well

込 *fu(ki)-ko(mu)* blow into, breathe into; record; inspire, instill. *fukiko(mi)* record-

込所 *fukiko(mi)sho* recording studio ⌊ing

5 矢 *fu(ki)ya* blowgun ⌈trumpet); brag

立 *fu(ki)-ta(teru)* blow up (a fire); blow (a

代 *fu(ki)ka(e)*＝吹替 (see below–12)

付 *fu(ki)-tsu(keru)* blow against (a house), blow (sparks) upon; blow ashore. *fu(ki)-tsu(ku)* (winds) blow against (something), blow (something) along; blow up (a fire in a brazier). *fu(ki)tsu(ke)* spraying; air

払 *fu(ki)-hara(u)* drive away (clouds) ⌊blast

去 *fu(ki)-sa(ru)* *vt* blow away

出 *fu(ki)-da(su)* begin to blow; breathe out; burst out laughing. *fu(ki)-de(ru)* begin to blow; break out (in sores)

出物 *fu(ki)demono* skin eruption, rash, pimple, eczema, boil, ulcer ⌈coal fire)

6 竹 *fu(ki)dake* bamboo blowpipe (for a char-

回 *fu(ki)-mawa(su)* blow around. *fu(ki)-mawa(shi)* blowing; stroke of fortune

返 *fu(ki)-kae(su)* blow and overturn; resuscitate

当 *fu(ki)-a(taru)* *vi* blow against, strike. *fu(ki)-a(teru)* *vt* (winds) blow against, hit (something) with a blow gun

7 伸 *fu(ki)-no(basu)* blow (glass)

抜 *fu(ki)-nu(ku)* blow thru, blow over, blow itself out. *fukinu(ki)* ventilation, draft; streamer, pennant

折 *fu(ki)-o(ru)* break by blowing

8 送 *fu(ki)-oku(ru)* *vt* waft, blow over to

直 *fu(ki)nao(shi)* recasting, recoinage

9 飛 *fu(t)to(bu)* *vi* be blown off, blow off. *fu(ki)-to(basu)* *vt* blow away, blow off

通 *fu(ki)-tō(su)* blow thru, penetrate; keep blowing. *fukitō(shi)* windy place

降 *fu(ki)bu(ri)* driving rain

荒 *fu(ki)-susa(mu)*, *fu(ki)-susa(bu)*, *fu(ki)-a(reru)*, *fu(ki)-a(rasu)* blow violently, sweep over, devastate

奏 *suisō* playing wind instruments

奏者 *suisōsha* wind-instrument player

奏楽 *suisōgaku* wind-instrument music

奏楽団 *suisō gakudan* wind-instrument or-

奏楽隊 *suisō gakutai* brass band ⌊chestra

奏楽器 *suisō gakki* wind instruments

10 起 *fu(ki)-oko(su)* blow up (a wind); fan up (a wind); fan up (a fire)

倒 *fu(ki)-tao(su)* blow down

値 *fukine* jump in prices, boom

晒 *fu(ki)-sara(su)*＝吹曝 (see below–19)

消 *fu(ki)-ke(su)* blow out (a fire)

流 *fu(ki)-naga(su)* blow away, drive out of course. *fukinaga(shi)* streamer, pennant

破 *fu(ki)-yabu(ru)* blow to pieces

挙 *suikyo suru* propose (for office)

11 過 *fu(ki)-su(giru)* blow past, sweep past

捲 *fu(ki)-maku(ru)* *vi* (the wind) sweeps along; brag, boast. *fu(ki)-meku(ru)* *vt* blow off (a roof)

掛 *fu(ki)-ka(keru)* blow on, breathe on, spray. *fu(k)ka(keru)*＝*fu(ki)-ka(keru)*; challenge, pick (a quarrel); make an unreasonable demand

寄 *fu(ki)-yo(seru)* drift, blow together. *fu(ki)yo(se)* collection; drift (of sand or snow)

雪 *fubuki* snowstorm, blizzard. *fubu(ku)* (winds) blow hard; (snow) is driven

12 渡 *fu(ki)-wata(ru)* blow over (an area)

散 *fu(ki)-chi(rasu)* scatter, blow about

募 *fu(ki)-tsuno(ru)* blow with growing in-

落 *fu(ki)-oto(su)* blow down (fruit) ⌊tensity

替 *fukika(e)* substitute actor; dummy; stand-in; recasting, reminting

13 溜 *fu(ki)damari* snowdrift

零 *fu(ki)-kobo(reru)* boil over

14 鳴 *suimei suru* blow (a whistle). *fu(ki)-na(rasu)* blow a blast

舞 *fu(ki)-mawa(su)* (winds) blow erratically

16 頻 *fu(ki)-shiki(ru)* blow hard

17 聴 *fuichō* announcement, publicity, advertisement, notification, recommendation

19 曝 *fu(ki)-sara(su)* blow with unhindered sweep. *fu(ki)sara(shi) no*, *fu(ki)zara(shi) no* exposed to the wind, weather-beaten, wind-blown, wind-swept, bleak, bare

離 *fu(ki)-hana(su)* blow off, blow apart; blow darts

— 5 —

和 咊 See 3268.

命 See 430.

周周 See 622.

咏 902/F352 See **詠** 4336.

咤 See **咤** 916.

呟 903/F-X GEN. *tsubuya(ku)* mutter, grumble, murmur.

咆 904/F350 Hō bark, roar; get angry.
[10]哮 *hōkō* yell, roar, howl

呶 905/F348 Do noisy.
[8]呶 *dodo* harping on the same point

呱 906/F347 Ko cry.
[8]呱 *koko* baby's birth cry
呱声 *koko (no) koe* baby's birth cry

咀 907/F349 So bite; eat.
[21]嚼 *soshaku* chewing, mastication
嚼面 *soshakumen* chewing surface

咎 908/F352 **咎** KYŪ. *toga(meru)* blame, censure, reprimand, find fault with, rebuke; challenge; get inflamed. *toga* fault, blame; charge, offense, sin.
[2]人 *toganin* criminal, offender
[5]立 *togameda(te)* blame, censure, faultfinding, rebuke

咄 909/F349 TOTSU pshaw, God forbid, Shame on you, exclamation of surprise. *hanashi* (see under 話 4358.0).
[8]咄 *totsutotsu* (tongue) clicking; groaning; exclamation of surprise
[10]家 *hanashika* storyteller
[13]嗟 *tossa* moment, instant. *tossa ni* at once
嗟間 *tossa (no) ma* the twinkling of an eye

呻 910/F348 SHIN. *ume(ku)* groan, moan. *umeki* groan, moan, moaning.
[6]叫 *ume(ki)-sake(bu)* groan
[7]吟 *shingin suru, ume(ku)* groan. *shingin* moaning, groaning; pining
声 *umekigoe* groan, moan, moaning

呵 911/F347 KA. *ka(su)* scold; blow on. *shika(ru)* scold, reprove.
[5]付 *shika(ri)-tsu(keru)* scold severely
[8]呵 *kaka* ha ha (laughing)
[11]責 *kashaku* torture, maltreatment

呪 912/F346 JU spell, curse, incantation. *majina(u)* charm, cast a spell over. *noro(u)* curse. *noroi* curse, anathema, malediction. *majinai* spell, charm, enchantment.
[4]文 *jumon* magic formula, incantation, curse,
[8]咀 *juso* curse, anathema ⌊spell, charm
法 *juhō* enchanter's formula
物 *jubutsu* fetish
物神 *jubutsushin* fetish
物崇拝 *jubutsu sūhai* fetishism
[11]符 *jufu* charm, amulet, talisman
術 *jujutsu* magic, incantation, sorcery
術的 *jujutsuteki* magical
[12]詛 *juso* curse, anathema
[16]縛 *jubaku* a spell

A **味** 913/F347 MI taste, flavor, dash; touch, tinge; counter for foods and drinks. *aji(wau)* taste; appreciate, experience. *aji, aji(wai)* taste, flavor, aroma; zest; experience; tinge. *aji na* clever, witty, smart.
[4]方 *mikata* friend, ally, supporter. *ajiwa(i)-*
[5]付 *ajitsu(ke)* seasoning ⌊*kata* way to taste
加減 *aji kagen* seasoning
[6]気無 *ajikina(i)* irksome, insipid, wretched,
[7]見 *ajimi* sampling, foretaste ⌊vain
利 *ajikiki* taster
[8]知 *ajiwa(i)-shi(ru)* taste and know
到 *mitō suru* taste thoroly
[11]得 *mitoku suru* taste thoroly
淋 *mirin* sweet saké
[12]覚 *mikaku* sense of taste
[13]感 *mikan* sense of taste
楽 *aji(wai)-tano(shimu)* enjoy (art, etc.)
[14]読 *midoku suru* appreciate a book
[15]醂 *mirin* sweet saké
噌 *miso* fermented bean paste; flattery
噌付 *miso (o) tsu(keru)* make a mess of, fizzle
噌汁 *miso shiru, misojiru* bean-paste soup
噌豆 *miso mame* soy beans ⌈black teeth
噌歯 *miso(p)pa* decayed baby tooth; dirty
噌煮 *misoni* boiling with bean paste
噌漬 *misozuke* pickled in bean paste
噌漉 *misokoshi* bean-paste strainer
噌擂 *misosu(ri)* grinding bean paste; flattery

B **呼** 914/F348 Ko. *yo(bu)* call, call out to; invoke; summon; invite; attract; send for; name, designate; bring about. *yo(bawaru)=sake(bu)* (see under 叫 881.0). *-yo(bawari) suru* treat as, denounce as, call (someone something).

2 入 *yo(bi)-i(reru)* call in, restore (a disowned son)
3 下 *yo(bi)-o(rosu)* call down (from above)
上 *yo(bi)-a(geru)* call out, call up, call the roll
子 *yo(bu)ko, yo(bi)ko* police whistle
子鳥 *yobukodori* cuckoo
4 止 *yo(bi)-to(meru)*＝呼留 (see below–10)
水 *yo(bi)mizu* priming water
込 *yo(bi)-ko(mu)* call in; restore a disowned son
5 立 *yo(bi)-ta(teru)* call out, call (someone to) come, summon
付 *yo(bi)-tsu(keru)* call (to someone), send for, summon
出 *yo(bi)-da(su)* call out, call before, call up; summon, subpoena; decoy; conjure up, involve
出状 *yobida(shi)jō* subpoena, summons
出符号 *yobida(shi) fugō* call letters
出電話 *yobida(shi) denwa* a trunk call
6 回 *yo(bi)-mawa(ru)* go around calling out (for someone)
気 *koki* exhalation
返 *yo(bi)-kae(su)* recall, call back
迎 *yo(bi)-muka(eru)* send for
叫 *yo(bawari)-sake(bu)* cry out to
合 *yo(bi)-a(u)* call each other (brethren); call to each other
号 *kogō suru* cry out, proclaim; appeal to; exaggerate
名 *yo(bi)na* given name, popular name, alias
吸 *kokyū* breath, respiration; knack, secret; tone, time. *kokyū suru* breathe
吸運動 *kokyū undō* breathing exercises
吸器 *kokyūki* respiratory organs
吸器病 *kokyūkibyō* respiratory disease
7 応 *koō suru* hail each other; act in concert; respond to
戻 *yo(bi)-modo(su)* call back, call home; resuscitate, recall
声 *yo(bi)goe* call, yell, hail; street huckster's call; rumor
売 *yo(bi)u(ri)* hawking, peddling
求 *yo(bi)-moto(meru)* call upon, call for (help)
8 物 *yo(bi)mono* attraction, feature, main event
奉 *yo(bi)-matsu(ru)* call upon (a god or rulers)
10 起 *yo(bi)-oko(su)* *vt* wake, rouse, call; call up; recall
値 *yo(bi)ne* nominal price, price asked, bidding
格 *kokaku* vocative case
称 *koshō suru* call out, call (someone by name or title)
留 *yo(bi)-to(meru)* call (to someone) to stop, challenge; call back
11 違 *yo(bi)chiga(e)* calling by the wrong name
掛 *yo(bi)-ka(keru)* call out to, accost; address (a crowd). *yo(bi)ka(ke)* a call (to prayer)
捨 *yobisu(te)* calling to someone disrespectfully
寄 *yo(bi)-yo(seru)* send for, summon, call together
12 集 *yo(bi)-atsu(meru)* assemble, *yo(bawari)-atsu(meru)* call together. *yo(bawari)-atsu(maru)* be called together
覚 *yo(bi)-sa(masu)* *vt* wake up
13 鈴 *yo(bi)rin* buzzer, door bell, call bell
馴 *yo(bi)-na(reru)*＝next word
14 慣 *yo(bi)-na(reru)* be used to calling (someone by a certain name)
誤 *yo(bi)-ayama(ru)* call by the wrong name
16 醒 *yo(bi)-sa(masu)* *vt* wake up

6

咫 See 216.

哀 See 304.

哉 See 777.

咨 915/F353 SHI investigate, inquire; weep.

咤 916/F353 **咜** TA clicking (with the tongue).

咯 917/F354 KAKU quarrel.
6 血 *kakketsu* lung hemorrhage

哄 918/F357 KŌ resound, reverberate.
10 笑 *kōshō* loud laughter
12 然 *kōzen to* (laugh) broadly, loudly

咬 919/F354 KŌ. *ka(mu)* (see under 噛 1012.0).
6 合 *kōgō, kamiawa(se)* occlusion (in dentistry)
12 痙 *kōkei* lockjaw
13 傷 *kōshō* bite (injury)

咽 920/F355 IN. EN. ETSU. *muse(ru), muse(bu)* be choked, be smothered. *muse(ppoi)* stuffy, suffocating. *nodo* throat, gullet, windpipe; voice.
6 返 *mu(se)-kae(ru)* be severely choked
8 泣 *muse(bi)-na(ku)* sob
12 喉 *inkō* throat
喉炎 *inkōen* pharyngitis
16 頭 *intō* pharynx
頭炎 *intōen* pharyngitis

咳 921/F354 **欬** GAI cough. *se(ku)* cough. *shiwabu(ku)* cough, clear one's throat. *seki* cough. *shiwabuki* cough; clearing the throat.

²入 *se(ki)-i(ru)* cough persistently
³上 *se(ki)-a(geru)* have a coughing spell; sob convulsively
⁴止 *sekido(me)* cough medicine; throat tablet
込 *se(ki)-ko(mu)* have a fit of coughing
⁵払 *sekibara(i)* clearing the throat, coughing
⁶気 *gaike* severe coughing
返 *se(ki)-kae(su)* cough to relieve discomfort
¹⁰病 *gaibyō, shiwabuki yamai* illness accompanied by coughing
¹¹唾 *gaida* cough and spittle
¹⁴嗽 *gaisō* cough, coughing

B 咲 922 F354 咲 SHŌ. *sa(ku)* bloom, blossom. *-sa(ki)* blooming.
⁴匂 *sa(ki)-nio(u)* bloom beautifully and fragrantly
分 *sa(ki)-wa(keru)* bloom in many colors. *sa(ki)wa(ke)* variegated flowering
⁵出 *sa(ki)-de(ru), sa(ki)-da(su)* begin to bloom, come out
⁷乱 *sa(ki)-mida(reru)* bloom in profusion
初 *sa(ki)-so(meru)* begin to bloom
¹⁰残 *sa(ki)-noko(ru)* be still in bud; be still blooming
¹²揃 *sa(ki)-soro(u)* be in full bloom
渡 *sa(ki)-wata(ru)* bloom over a wide area, continue to bloom
勝 *sa(ki)-masa(ru)* bloom first; bloom beautifully
散 *sa(ki)-chi(ru)* (the blossoms) fall
¹³溢 *sa(ki)-kobo(reru)* bloom in profusion
誇 *sa(ki)-hoko(ru)* bloom in glory

A 品 923 F356 HIN refinement, dignity; article. HON item, course (in a meal). *shina* article, goods, thing; quality; brand; kind, type; ways, conditions; character.
⁴切 *shinagi(re)* out of stock, sold out
分 *shinawa(ke)* assortment
⁵目 *himmoku* list of articles
⁶行 *hinkō* conduct, behavior; moral character, respectability
行方正 *hinkō-hōsei* respectability
⁷位 *hin-i* dignity, nobility; grade, quality, fineness; character
作 *shina (o) tsuku(ru)* pretend to be someone; attract attention to oneself
形 *shinakatachi* countenance, personal appearance
⁸物 *shinamono* goods, stock, articles
定 *shinasada(me)* estimation, judgment, criticism (of goods)
性 *hinsei* character
性発達 *hinsei hattatsu* character development
性鍛錬 *hinsei tanren* character building
⁹柄 *shinagara* quality, brand
枯 *shinaga(re)* shortage of goods
品 *shinajina* various articles
¹⁰格 *hinkaku* grace, dignity
致 *hinchi* quality
書 *shinaga(ki)* catalog, inventory, itemization; bill of fare
¹²詞 *hinshi* part of speech
等 *hintō* grade, quality
評 *himpyō* criticism, comment
評会 *himpyōkai* competitive exhibition, a fair
¹³数 *shinakazu, hinsū* number of articles, amount of stock
彙 *hin-i* quality, kind
¹⁴種 *hinshu* kind, description, grade, variety, breed
¹⁵調 *shinashira(be)* stock taking
質 *hinshitsu* quality
¹⁶薄 *shina-usu* shortage of goods
¹⁸類 *hinrui* kinds of articles

7

哭 See 2880.

哥 See 56.

唇 See 4654.

唐 唐 See 1516.

唄 924 F360 BAI. *uta* songs accompanied by the samisen.

B 唆 925 F360 SA. *sosono(kasu)* tempt, seduce; instigate; promote.

哮 926 F359 KŌ. *ta(keru)* roar, howl, growl, bellow.

哩 927 F358 RI. *mairu* mile.
¹³数 *mairusū* mileage

A 員 928 F358 EN. IN *-in* member; number; the one in charge.
⁴内 *innai* within the membership
⁵外 *ingai* nonmembership
¹³数 *inzū, inzu, insū* number of members, things, or people

哺 929 F359 HO taking in the mouth. *kuku(meru) vt* feed from mouth to mouth; tell simply. *kuku(mu) vi* hold in the mouth; keep in mind.
⁸育 *ho-iku suru* suckle, nurse, nurture; rear
育所 *ho-ikusho* nursery school; nursery

3 口 口 土 士 夂 夊 夕 大 女 子 宀 寸 小 ⺌ 尢 尸 屮 山 川 巛 工 己 巾 干 幺 广 廴 廾 弋 弓 彐 彑 彡 彳

乳 *honyū* lactation, suckling
乳児 *honyūji* suckling child
乳瓶 *honyūbin* nursing bottle
乳動物 *honyū dōbutsu* mammal

哨 930 F358 Shō scout, sentinel.

7戒 *shōkai* patrol, patroling
兵 *shōhei* sentry, sentinel
8舎 *shōsha* sentry box
9海艇 *shōkaitei* patrol vessel
20艦 *shōkan* patrol ship

哲 931 F359 B Tetsu clear.

2人 *tetsujin* wise man, sage, philosopher
8学 *tetsugaku* philosophy
学史 *tetsugakushi* history of philosophy
学的 *tetsugakuteki* philosophical
学者 *tetsugakusha* philosopher
学博士 *Tetsugaku Hakushi, Tetsugaku Hakase* Doctor of Philosophy
11理 *tetsuri* the philosophy (of something)

8

問 See 4944.

商 商 See 321.

喝 Nonstandard for 喝 953.

啗 932 F366 Tan. *ku(rawasu)* allure, entice.

啖 933 F366 Tan eat.

8呵 *tanka* caustic words

啀 934 F363 Gai. *iga(mu)* wrangle; growl at.

6合 *iga(mi)-a(u)* wrangle, growl at each other

啄 935 F363 Taku. *tsuiba(mu)* peck, pick up.

4木鳥 *kitsutsuki* woodpecker

啜 936 F366 Setsu. *susu(ru)* sip, suck up.

3上 *susu(ri)-a(geru)* suck up
8泣 *susu(ri)-na(ku)* sob

唸 937 F362 Ten. *una(ru)* groan, moan; roar, howl, snarl, growl, bellow, trumpet, snort; hum, buzz; sough.

7声 *una(ri)goe* groan, moan
9独楽 *una(ri)goma* a humming top

唾 938 F363 Da. *tsuba, tsubaki* sputum; saliva.

11液 *daeki* saliva
液腺 *daekisen* salivary glands
13腺 *dasen* salivary gland
棄 *daki subeki* detestable, disgusting, revolting. *daki suru* spit; detest, hate, abhor, reject

唖 939 F367 A. *oshi* deaf-mute.

8者 *asha* deaf-mute
12然 *azen to* in mute amazement
13鈴 *arei* dumbbell
18蟬 *oshizemi* silent female cicada

啓 940 F365 **啓** B Kei open; say.

3上 *keijō suru* speak respectfully
5白 *keihaku* informing
示 *keiji* revelation
9発 *keihatsu* enlightenment, development, improvement, education, edification
13蒙 *keimō* enlightenment, instruction
14慕 *keibo suru* revere and long for

唱 941 F362 A Shō. *tona(eru)* recite, chant; call upon; cry, yell (*banzai*); advocate, preach; quote (prices).

6名 *shōmyō* reciting Buddha's name
8和 *shōwa* cheering in chorus
11道 *shōdō* advocacy
道者 *shōdōsha* proponent
14導 *shōdō* advocacy
歌 *shōka* song; singing
歌隊 *shōkatai* choir
歌集 *shōkashū* collection of songs

唯 942 F361 B Yui. I. *tatta* only, merely, solely, simply. *tada* only, merely, solely, simply; earnestly; perfectly, generally.

1一 *yui-itsu, yuitsu* sole, unique, the one and only. *tada hitotsu* sole, only one
一神道 *Yui-ichi Shintō* Pure Shinto
4今 *tadaima* now, at present; right now; soon; Here I am; I just got back.
心論 *yuishinron* idealism
6名論 *yuimeiron* nominalism
7我的 *yuigateki* egoistic
我独尊 *yuiga-dokuson* feeling of supremacy
我論 *yuigaron* egoism
8物主義 *yuibutsu shugi* materialism

物史観 *yuibutsu shikan* materialistic conception of history
物的 *yuibutsuteki* materialistic
物論 *yuibutsuron* materialism
物論的 *yuibutsuronteki* materialistic
9 美主義 *yuibi shugi* estheticism
美的 *yuibiteki* esthetic
美派 *yuibiha* esthetes
11 理論 *yuiriron* rationalism
唯 *i-i toshite* willingly, meekly
唯諾諾 *i-idakudaku toshite* quite willing; readily; submissively; meekly; at one's beck

9

喬 See 239.

嗇 See 279.

喜 See 1115.

善 See 606.

喪 See 117.

單 943 F374 See 单 139.

喨 944 F373 Ryō, Rō clear voice.

啼 945 F367 啼 Tei. *na(ku)* (animals and birds) cry, bark, chirp, etc.

喙 946 F370 Kai. *kuchibashi* (bird) bill.

喩 947 F373 Yu. *tato(eru), tatoi, tatoe* (see under 譬 4445.0).

喟 948 F372 Ki moan.
12 然 *kizen* dejection

喊 949 F370 Kan cry, call.
7 声 *kansei* war cry, battle cry

喞 950 F372 唧 Shoku. Soku. *kako(tsu)* speak resentfully.
18 顔 *kako(chi)gao* sorrowful countenance

喃 951 F368 Nan chatter, rattle on.
12 喃 *nannan to* volubly, glibly, chatteringly. *nōnō* a word used in calling someone
14 語 *nango* love talk

喀 952 F367 Kaku vomit.
6 血 *kakketsu* lung hemorrhage
13 痰 *kakutan* expectoration, sputum

喝 953 F371 Katsu scold; get hoarse.
8 采 *kassai* applause, cheers
10 破 *kappa suru* declare, proclaim

喘 954 F370 Zen. *ae(gu)* pant, gasp, breathe hard.
7 求 *ae(gi)-moto(meru)* long after
10 息 *zensoku* asthma; broken wind (in a horse)

喰 955 F375 (国字) *kura(u), ku(u)* eat, drink; receive (a blow). *ku(u)* (see under 食 5154.0).
4 込 *kura(i)-ko(mu)*＝食込 5154.4
5 付 *kura(i)-tsu(ku)* bite

啣 956 F-X Kan. Gan. *kuwa(eru)* take or hold in the mouth or between the teeth.
4 込 *kuwa(e)-ko(mu)* (a prostitute) brings in a victim
13 煙草 *kuwa(e) tabako de* with a cigarette in the mouth
煙管 *kuwa(e)giseru de* with a pipe in the mouth

喇 957 F369 Ratsu, Ra chatter, rattle on.
5 叭 *rappa* trumpet, horn, bugle
叭手 *rappashu* bugler, trumpeter
叭飲 *rappano(mi)* drinking from a bottle
14 嘛 *rama* lama
嘛教 *Ramakyō* Lamaism

喚 958 F371 B Kan. *ome(ku), wame(ku)* cry, scream, yell, shout, clamor. *yo(bu)* (see under 呼 914.0).
5 立 *wame(ki)-ta(teru)* bawl, squall, yell, cry out, clamor
7 声 *kansei, wame(ki)goe* shout, yell, scream,
8 呼 *kanko suru* cry out
10 起 *kanki suru* arouse, evoke
11 問 *kammon* summons

喋 959 F370 Chō. *shabe(ru), shabe(kuru)* talk, chat, chatter.
5 立 *shabe(ri)-ta(teru)* talk volubly

3 9 [口] 口 土 士 夂 夊 夕 大 女 子 宀 寸 小 ⺌ 尢 尸 屮 山 川 巛 工 己 巾 干 幺 广 廴 廾 弋 弓 彐 彑 彡 彳

11捲 *shabe(ri)-maku(ru)* talk volubly
12喋 *chōchō suru* chatter, be long-winded
散 *shabe(ri)-chi(rasu)* spread gossip, talk carelessly

喉 960/F369 Kō. *nodo* throat, voice.

4仏 *nodobotoke* Adam's apple
元 *nodomoto* throat
6自慢 *nodojiman* pride of voice
9音 *kōon* guttural sound
首 *nodokubi* throat
彦 *nodobiko* uvula
16頭 *kōtō* larnyx
頭炎 *kōtōen* laryngitis
頭痛 *kōtōtsū* sore throat
頭蓋 *kōtōgai* epiglottis
頭癌 *kōtō gan* cancer of the larnyx

B **喫** 961/F373 Kitsu. Keki. *kis(suru)* eat, drink, smoke; receive (a blow, etc.).

4水 *kissui* draft (of a ship)
水線 *kissuisen* water line (of loaded ship)
9茶 *kissa, kitcha* tea drinking, tea house
茶店 *kissaten* tea house, coffee shop
12飯 *kippan* eating
13煙 *kitsuen* smoking (tobacco)
煙車 *kitsuensha* smoking car
煙者 *kitsuensha* smoker
煙室 *kitsuenshitsu* smoking room
煙家 *kitsuenka* smoker
14緊 *kikkin* very urgent
緊事 *kikkinji* a very urgent matter
22驚 *bikkuri suru* be surprised. *kikkyō* surprise, astonishment

喧 962/F372 Ken. *kamabisu(shii)* noisy, boisterous. *yakama(shii)* noisy, boisterous; critical; troublesome; much-discussed; fastidious.

6伝 *kenden suru* noise abroad, circulate
7狂 *kenkyō na* noisy and apparently crazy
9屋 *yakama(shi)ya* exacting person, faultfinder
12喧囂囂 *kenken-gōgō* pandemonium
13嘩 *kenka* quarrel, dispute
嘩好 *kenkazu(ki)* quarrelsome
嘩早 *kenkabaya(i), kenka(p)paya(i)* combative, pugnacious
嘩買 *kenka (o) ka(u)* stir up a quarrel
嘩腰 *kenkagoshi* defiant attitude
16噪 *kensō* noisy, uproarious; nuisance
18擾 *kenjō* noise, uproar
騒 *kensō* noise, uproar, a nuisance
21轟 *kengō* noise, uproar
囂 *kengō* noise, uproar

A **営** 963/F1203 營 Ei camp; performing. *itona(mu)* perform (ceremonies); build; conduct (business); follow (a profession), operate (a store); build. *itona(mi)* business, occupation, operation. [火]

4内 *einai* inside the barracks
中 *eichū* within the barracks
5外 *eigai* outside the barracks
6団 *eidan* corporation, foundation
7利 *eiri* gain, money-making
利会社 *eirigaisha* commercial concern
利法人 *eiri hōjin* profit-making corporation
利事業 *eiri jigyō* business enterprise
8門 *eimon* barracks gate
所 *eisho* barracks, camp
林 *eirin* forestry
舎 *eisha* barracks
9造 *eizō* building, construction
造物 *eizōbutsu* building, structure, public works
10庭 *eitei* barracks' parade ground
倉 *eisō* guardhouse, detention barracks
11巣 *eisō* building a nest
12営 *eiei to* strenuously, eagerly, diligently
13業 *eigyō* business, trade
業区域 *eigyō kuiki* business district
業用 *eigyōyō* business purposes
業主 *eigyōshu, eigyōnushi* proprietor
業所 *eigyōsho* place of business
業者 *eigyōsha* trader
業費 *eigyōhi* operating expenses
18繕 *eizen* upkeep (of equipment)

10

嗇 See 67.

喪 See 117.

號 See 号 882. [虍]

嘩 964/F381/F1765 譁 Ka noisy.

嗛 965/F377 Ken insufficient; put in the mouth.

嗉 966/F-X So bird's craw.

22嚢 *sonō* bird's craw, crop

嗤 967/F378 嗤 Shi. *wara(u)* (see under 笑 3374.0). *azawara(u)* ridicule.

10笑 *shishō* smile, ridicule

嗚 968 F376 U, O weep. *ā* ah, alas, an interjection of surprise or sadness.
⁹咽 *oetsu* sobbing, weeping

嗣 969 F378 B SHI heir. *tsu(gu)* succeed to, inherit; follow; patch. [口]
³子 *shishi* heir, successor
⁷君 *shikun* heir of a ruler
¹³業 *shigyō* inheritance

嗟 970 F377 SA be satisfied; grieve. *a* ah.
⁹哉 *awaya* an instant ⌈praise
¹³嘆 *satan suru* lament, deplore; admire,
¹⁵歎 *satan suru*=word above

嗄 971 F376 SA. *ka(rasu)* make one's throat hoarse. *ka(reru)*, *shaga(reru)*, *shiwaga(reru)* get hoarse. *kare(bamu)* get slightly hoarse.
⁷声 *ka(re)goe*, *shaga(re)goe*, *shiwaga(re)goe*
¹³嗄 *ka(re)ga(re)* hoarse ⌊hoarse voice

嗜 972 F377 SHI. *tashina(mu)* like, have a taste for; be prudent, be modest, be temperate. *tashina(mi)* taste; prudence; modesty; etiquette; accomplishment; attention to appearance.
⁶好 *shikō* taste, liking, preference
好品 *shikōhin* luxury articles
¹⁰眠 *shimin* lethargy ⌈for
¹¹欲 *shiyoku* fondness for, appetite, weakness

嗅 973 F376 KYŪ. *ka(gu)* smell, sniff, scent.
²入薬 *kyūnyūyaku* medicine inhaled thru the
⁴手 *kagite* a smeller ⌊nose
込 *ka(gi)-ko(mu)* smell deeply; investigate by smelling
分 *ka(gi)-wa(keru)* tell by scent
⁵付 *ka(gi)-tsu(keru) vt* scent, sniff, smell; detect, sense
出 *ka(gi)-da(su)* sniff out, get wind of
⁶当 *ka(gi)-a(teru)* smell out, investigate by
⁸官 *kyūkan* the olfactory organ ⌊smelling
⁹神経 *kyūshinkei* olfactory nerve
¹⁰剤 *kyūzai* smelling medicine
¹²覚 *kyūkaku* sense of smell
¹³感 *kyūkan* sense of smell
煙草 *kagitabako* snuff
¹⁶薬 *kagigusuri* smelling medicine; snuff

嘆 974 F378 B 嘆 TAN sigh. *nage(ku)* sigh, lament, moan, grieve; regret, deplore, sorrow. *tan(jiru)*, *tan(zuru)* deplore, mourn, regret, be indignant. *nage(kashii)*, *nage(kawashii)* sad, wretched, deplorable.
²入 *nage(ki)-i(ru)* be weeping inconsolately
⁶叫 *nage(ki)-sake(bu)* wail ⌈tion
⁷声 *tansei* sigh, lamentation; sigh of admira-
⁸明 *nage(ki)-a(kasu)* cry all night; weep for a long period of time
⁹美 *tambi* admiration, adoration
美者 *tambisha* admirer, adorer
¹⁰称 *tanshō* praise, admiration, applause
衰 *nage(ki)-otoro(eru)* mourn and languish
息 *tansoku* sigh, grief, deploring
¹²訴 *nage(ki)-utta(eru)* complain
悲 *nage(ki)-kana(shimu)* lament, mourn
¹³辞 *tanji* interjection; admiration
¹⁵賞 *tanshō* praise, admiration, applause
賞者 *tanshōsha* admirer
¹⁹願 *tangan* entreaty, appeal, petition, suit

11

嘉 See 1136.

嘗 See 1369.

號 See 号 882.

嘆 975 F378 See 嘆 974.

噓 Nonstandard for 噓 993.

噌 Nonstandard for 噌 984.

嘛 976 F381 MA what.

嗾 977 F378 ZOKU. SOKU. SŌ. *keshika(keru)* sick on, egg on, instigate.

嘈 978 F379 SŌ noisy.
²¹囃 *munayake*, *sōzatsu* heartburn, sour stomach

嗷 979 F378 嗸 GŌ noisy.
¹²訴 *gōso* direct petition

嘖 980 F381 SAKU. *saina(mu)* scold, torment, chastise.
¹⁴嘖 *sakusaku toshite* noisily, loudly

3 【口】 口土士夂夊夕大女子宀寸小⺌尢尸屮山川巛工己巾干幺广廴廾弋弓彐彑彡彳

11

嗽 981/F378 Sō. *susu(gu)*, *yusu(gu)* rinse, wash, pour on. *kuchisusu(gu)*, *kuchisoso(gu)* rinse the mouth, gargle. *ugai* gargling.
9咳 *sōgai* coughing

嘔 982/F380 Ō. *mukatsu(ku)* feel nauseated; be angry. *ha(ku)* vomit.
6気 *ōki*, *hakike* nausea
吐 *ezu(ku)* vomit. *ōto* vomiting.

A 鳴 983/F2139 MEI. *na(ku)* (animals and birds) cry, bark, chirp, etc. *na(ru)* sound, ring, roar; (thunder) rumbles; (clocks) strike; boom; resound, echo; be famous; (fingers) itch for; sonorous, ringing, squeaky. *na(rasu)* *vt* ring, sound, blow (a whistle), beat (drums), clank, clink, clap, crack (a whip), smack (lips), cluck (one's tongue), honk; air (grievances); attain (celebrity). *na(ri)* sound, ringing. [鳥]
3子 *naruko* clapper
4戸 *naruto* whirlpool, maelstrom
5出 *na(ki)-da(su)* begin to sing or chirp
6合 *na(ki)-a(wase)* birds' singing contest
7声 *na(ki)goe* sound of a bird or animal
8門 *naruto* whirlpool, maelstrom
物 *na(ri)mono* music; musical instruments
物入 *na(ri)mono-i(ri)* loud proclamation, bombastic announcement
9飛 *na(kazu)-to(bazu)* inactive, obscure
神 *na(ru)kami* thunder
11動 *meidō* rumbling
笛 *meiteki* playing the flute
12渡 *na(ri)-wata(ru)* resound, re-echo
散 *na(ki)-chi(rasu)* (birds) cry and scatter blossoms with the breeze caused by their wings
13禽 *meikin* songbird
19響 *na(ri)-hibi(ku)* reverberate, echo, resound, be sonorous
20鐘 *meishō* hour bell
21轟 *na(ri)-todoro(ku)* rage, roar

12

噌 984/F384 Sō, Zō, Shō throat.

噚 985/F-X *Ei-biro* fathom.

噀 986/F383 SON blow out water (elephants and whales).

嘶 987/F382 SEI. *inana(ku)* neigh, whinny, bray.

嘸 988/F383 BU. *sazo*, *sazo ya*, *sazokashi* how, indeed, no doubt, I dare say.
15嘸 *sazosazo* emphatic for *sazo* (see under 嘸 988.0).

B 嘱 989/F392 囑 SHOKU requesting. *shoku suru* request; send a message.
5目 *shokumoku suru* pay attention to, notice, observe, watch
10託 *shokutaku suru* commission, charge (a person) with, give (a person) charge of. *shokutaku* part-time employment
11望 *shokubō* expectation

噎 990/F384 ITSU. *mu(seru)*, *muse(bu)* be choked, be smothered.
2入 *muse(bi)-i(ru)* sob convulsively
6返 *mu(se)-kae(ru)* cough up (something)
8泣 *musebina(ki)* sobbing

噂 991/F383 SON. *uwasa* rumor, gossip, hearsay.
5主 *uwasa (no) nushi* the man talked about
13話 *uwasabanashi* rumor, gossip, hearsay
14種 *uwasa (no) tane* source of rumor, subject of gossip

嘲 992/F382 CHŌ. *azake(ru)* ridicule, insult.
7弄 *chōrō* ridicule
10笑 *azawara(u)* jeer at. *chōshō* derisive smile, ridicule, sneer. *seserawara(u)*, *azake(ri)-wara(u)* laugh to scorn
15罵 *chōba* taunt, insult

嘘 993/F381 KYO. *uso* lie, falsehood, fib, fabrication.
2八百 *usohappyaku* full of lies
5皮 *uso(no)kawa* a pure fabrication
6吐 *usotsuki* liar, fibber
字 *usoji* miswritten character
7言 *usogoto* lie, falsehood
9発見器 *uso hakkenki* lie detector
発見機 *uso hakkenki* lie detector
13話 *usobanashi* fable, untruth

A 器 994/F385 器 噐 KI container; utensil, instrument, tool, apparatus; set; ability. *utsuwa* vessel, receptacle, utensil, implement, instrument; capacity, ability.
5用 *kiyō* cleverness, ingenuity; shrewdness; versatility
用人 *kiyōjin* a clever person
用貧乏 *kiyō-bimbō* Jack-of-all-trades and master of none
7材 *kizai* machine parts

8物 *utsuwamono, kibutsu* container, receptacle; utensil; tool; furnishings
官 *kikan* organ (of the body)
具 *kigu* utensil, appliance; apparatus; tool; fixtures
10財 *kizai* tools
11械 *kikai* appliance; apparatus; instrument
械体操 *kikai taisō* calisthenics using equipment
12量 *kiryō* looks, features, personal beauty; ability; dignity
量人 *kiryōjin* talented person
量負 *kiryōma(ke)* good looks but poor luck; too smart for success
13楽 *kigaku* instrumental music

噴 995 / F387 FUN. *fu(ku)* spout, emit, flush out.
B
4井 *fuki-i* artesian well, drilled well
井戸 *fuki-ido* artesian well, drilled well
水 *funsui* jet of water, squirt, fountain
水孔 *funsuikō* jet, spout
水井戸 *funsui ido* artesian well
火 *funka* eruption, volcanic activity
火口 *funkakō* crater
火山 *funkazan* volcano
5出 *fu(ki)-da(su)* spout out, gush out, spurt out, shoot out, send out, discharge, exude. *funshutsu* gushing, spouting, eruption
6気 *funki suru* flutter, puff (as a locomotive)
8沫 *fummatsu* splash, spray
9泉 *funsen* fountain, spring, geyser
10射 *funsha* jet, jet propulsion
射推進 *funsha suishin* jet propulsion
11貫井戸 *fukinuki ido* artesian well, drilled well
12飯 *fumpan suru* burst out laughing
13煙 *fun-en* smoke (out of a chimney)
19霧 *fummu* spray
霧器 *fummuki* atomizer, sprayer

13

噐 996 / F385 See 器 994.

噬 997 / F386 ZEI bite.

噺 998 / F387 (国字) *hanashi* (see under 話 4358.0).

嘯 999 / F381 SHŌ. *usobu(ku)* roar, howl; feign indifference; recite emotionally.

嘴 1000 / F382 / F1722 觜 SHI beak, bill. *kuchibashi, hashi* (bird) bill.

噪 1001 / F385 SŌ be noisy.
9音 *sōon* noise, cacophony

噯 1002 / F386 AI breathe.
6気 *aiki, okubi* belching

嚆 1003 / F387 KŌ call.
5矢 *kōshi* the first, the pioneer

噤 1004 / F384 KIN. *tsugu(mu)* shut (one's mouth).
3口 *kinkō* saying nothing, silence

噸 1005 / F387 (国字) TON ton.
12税 *tonzei* tonnage dues
13数 *tonsū* tonnage

14

嚳 1006 / F1203 See 営 963. [火]

嚀 1007 / F387 NEI kindness.

嚇 1008 / F387 KAKU. *odo(su), odo(kasu)* (see under 威 1803.0).
B
9怒 *kakudo* fierce anger
17嚇 *kakukaku(taru)* brilliant, glorious

噦 1009 / F384 KAI. *mukatsu(ku)* feel nauseated; be angry. *shaku(ru)* to scoop; to hiccup. *shakkuri* hiccups.
3上 *shaku(ri)-a(geru)* sob convulsively
8泣 *shaku(ri)-no(ku)* sob
13溝 *shakuri mizo* groove
鉋 *shakuriganna* rabbet plane

15

嚏 1010 / F388 TEI. *kushami, kusame, kusami* sneeze.

嚠 1011 / F-X RYŪ, RU a clear sound.
9亮 *ryūryō(taru)* clear, sonorous
12喨 *ryūryō(taru)* clear, sonorous

嚙 1012 / F388 GŌ. *ka(mu)* bite, gnaw, chew; gear with; (waves) dash against.
4反 *ka(mi)-kae(su)* chew the cud
切 *ka(mi)-ki(ru)* bite off, gnaw off
分 *ka(mi)-wa(keru)* chew, tell by tasting; understand, appreciate
5付 *ka(mi)-tsu(ku)* bite at
6合 *ka(mi)-a(u) vi* fight or bite each other; engage (gears); occlude (teeth). *ka(mi)-a(waseru) vt* clench (teeth); engage (gears); set (animals fighting)

3 15【口】口土士夂夊夕大女子宀寸小⺌尢尸屮山川巛工己巾干幺广廴廾弋弓彐彑彡彳

合 *ka(nde) fuku(meru)* teach very carefully
9碎 *ka(mi)-kuda(ku)* crunch, crush with the
10破 *ka(mi)-yabu(ru)* bite to pieces ⌊teeth
殺 *ka(mi)-koro(su)* bite to death; keep back, suppress
12裂 *ka(mi)-sa(ku)* tear by biting
13傷 *kamikizu* bite mark
煙草 *kamitabako* chewing tobacco
14鳴 *ka(mi)-na(rasu)* gnash the teeth
緊 *ka(mi)-shi(meru)* chew well; meditate on; digest (ideas); appreciate (kindness)
15潰 *ka(mi)-tsubu(su)* crunch with the teeth

嚮 1013 F388 嚮 Kyō. *saki ni* (see under 先 571.0).
4日 *kyōjitsu* the other day; the day before
14導 *kyōdō* leadership, guidance; leader, guide

16

嚠 See 1011.

嚬 1014 F388 Hin scowl.

嚥 1015 F388 En swallow.
3下 *enka, enge* swallowing
下痛 *engetsū* difficulty in swallowing

17

嚴 See 厳 253.

18

嚼 1016 F390 Shaku. *ka(mu)* (see under 噛 1012.0).

囀 1017 F391 Ten. *saezu(ru)* sing, chirp, twitter, warble; prattle, chatter.
14歌 *saezu(ri)-uta(u)* (birds) sing

囁 1018 F391 Shō. *sasaya(ku)* whisper, murmur.
6合 *sasaya(ki)-a(u)* whisper together

囃 1019 F391 Satsu. Sō. *haya(su)* play (on an instrument); accompany; beat time; banter, jeer; applaud.
3子 *hayashi* Japanese orchestra; band, accompaniment ⌈a song (for rythm)
子詞 *hayashi kotoba* meaningless words in

囂 1020 F391 Gō. *kashima(shii), kamabisu(shii), kashigama(shii)* noisy, boisterous.
12然 *gōzen(taru)* noisy, uproarious, vociferous
21囂 *gōgō(taru)* noisy, uproarious, vociferous

囈 1021 F391 Gei foolish talk.
7言 *uwagoto* delirious utterances
14語 *tawagoto, tawakoto, geigo* nonsense, jargon, talking in one's sleep

19

囊 See 124.

轡 1022 F1852 Hi. *kutsuwa* (horse's) bit. [車]
6虫 *kutsuwa mushi* a noisy cricket

21

囑 1023 F392 See 嘱 989.

RAD. 囗 31

Kunigamae (enclosure as in *kuni* "country"). Nickname: Box.

2

B 囚 1024 F392 Shū criminal, arrest. *tora(eru), torawa(reru)* (see under 捕 1919.0).
2人 *meshiudo, shūjin, torawa(re)bito* prisoner,
6衣 *shūi* a convict's clothes ⌊convict
7役 *shūeki* prison work
8者 *torawa(re)mono* prisoner, convict,
10徒 *shūto* prisoner, convict ⌊criminal
13虜 *shūryo* arrest; arrested person; captive
14獄 *hitoya, shūgoku* prison house
16縛 *shūbaku suru* arrest and tie up

A 四 1025 F393 Shi four. *yo(tsu), yo(ttsu), yo, yon* four.
2十 *yonjū, shijū* forty
十雀雁 *shijūkaragan* Canada goose
十路 *yosoji* age forty
人 *yonin, yottari* four people
人乗 *yoninno(ri)* four-seater ⌈of four
人組 *yoningumi* foursome, quartette, group

[3]女 *yonjo, shijo* fourth daughter

子 *yo(tsu)go* quadruplets

大節 *Shidaisetsu, Yondaisetsu* four main prewar Shinto festivals (New Year's, Empire Day, the Emperor's Birthday, and Emperor Meiji's Birthday ⌈month)

[4]日 *yokka* four days; the fourth day (of the

切 *yo(tsu)gi(ri)* quartering; quarter

天王 *shitennō* four heavenly kings; the Tokugawa Big Four

手網 *yo(tsu)de ami* four-armed scoop net

斗樽 *shitodaru* a 4-*to* (about 20 gal.) barrel

爪錨 *yotsume ikari* grapnel

月 *shigatsu* April. *yotsuki* four months

月馬鹿 *shigatsu baka* April fool

辺 *shihen* neighborhood; frontiers, four sides (of a quadrilateral)

辺形 *shihenkei* quadrilateral, quadrangle

六判 *shirokuban* duodecimo

六時中 *shirokujichū* twenty-four hours, day and night; constantly, always

方 *shihō, yomo* four directions; all directions; four sides ⌈directions

方八方 *shihō-happō* far and wide, in all

方山 *yomoyama no* various, sundry

方拝 *Shihōhai* Shinto New Year's Cere-

分円 *shibun-en* quadrant ⌊mony

分六 *shiburoku* six-to-four ratio

分五裂 *shibun-goretsu* disruption

分板 *shibu ita* thin board, half-inch board

分音符 *shibu ompu* quarter note

分儀 *shibungi* quadrant (the instrument)

[5]辻 *yo(tsu)tsuji* street crossing, four corners

民 *shimin* the 4 classes; the whole nation

半分 *shihambun* quarter, fourth

半世紀 *shihanseiki* a quarter of a century

半期 *shihanki* quarter (of a year)

目 *yo(tsu)me* crest of four squares; four eyes

目垣 *yo(tsu)megaki* trellis, rough bamboo fence ⌈window

目格子 *yo(tsu)megōshi* lattice work; lattice

目錐 *yo(tsu)megiri* square drill

[6]夷 *shi-i* barbarians, foreigner

次元 *shijigen, yojigen, yonjigen* fourth

旬節 *Shijunsetsu* Lent ⌊dimension

百四病 *shihyakushibyō* all human sickness-

百余州 *shihyakuyoshū* all China ⌊es

[7]足 *shisoku, yo(tsu) ashi* four legs. *yo(tsu)ashi*

身 *yo(tsu)mi* a child's kimono ⌊beast, animal

囲 *shi-i* circumference, girth; surroundings

折 *yo(tsu)o(ri)* quarto (a page or book size about 9½×12½ inches)

阿 *azumaya* arbor, summer house

更 *shikō, yonkō* fourth watch of the night, two to four a.m.

声 *shisei* the four (mandarin) tones

児 *yo(tsu)go* quadruplets

君子 *shikunshi* the four princely plants (plum, orchid, bamboo, and chrysan-

足獣 *shisokujū* quadruped ⌊themum)

角 *yosumi* all the corners, four corners. *yotsukado* four corners; intersection, street crossing. *shikaku* square; quadrilateral ⌈prim

角四面 *shikaku-shimen na* methodical,

角形 *shikakkei* quadrilateral, square

角張 *shikakuba(ru)* be formal

角錐 *yonkakusui* quadrilateral pyramid

[8]周 *shishū* surroundings ⌈arms and legs

肢 *shishi* the limbs, the extremities, the

苦八苦 *shiku-hakku* much agony

季 *shiki* the four seasons

季払 *shikibara(i)* quarterly payments

季咲 *shikiza(ki)* blooming all seasons; such a flower

[9]則 *shisoku* the four arithmetical operations

発 *shihatsu* four-engined

重奏 *shijūsō* instrumental quartette

通八達 *shitsū-hattatsu* accessible from all

面 *shimen* four sides, all sides ⌊directions

面楚歌 *shimen-soka* completely surrounded (by the enemy) ⌈whole world

海 *shikai* the four seas, the seven seas; the

海同胞 *shikai-dōhō* universal brotherhood

[10]這 *yo(tsu)bai* crawling. *yo(tsum)bai* on all fours, falling flat, sprawling

時 *shiji* the four seasons; all year round. *yoji* four o'clock

桁 *yoketa* thousands (in figures)

部合奏 *shibu gassō* instrumental quartette

部合唱 *shibu gasshō* vocal quartette

書 *Shisho* the Four Chinese Classics

書五経 *Shisho-Gokyō* the Nine Chinese

[11]球 *shikyū* four balls, base on balls ⌊Classics

組 *yo(tsu)gumi* foursome. *yo(tsu)gumi no*

絃 *shigen* four-stringed lute ⌊quadruple

隅 *yosumi* four corners

望 *shibō* wide view all around

捨五入 *shisha-gonyū* counting .5 and over as 1 and discarding .4 and less

[12]幅 *yono* four-unit width (cloth) ⌈*wari* 40%

割 *yo(tsu)wa(ri)* quartering. *yonwari, shi-*

散 *shisan suru* disperse, scatter

[13]聖 *shisei* the world's four great sages (Gautama, Confucius, Socrates, and Christ)

福音書 *Shifukuinsho* the Four Gospels

[14]選 *shisen* fourth-term election

境 *shikyō* boundaries

隣 *shirin* whole neighborhood, surrounding countries ⌈wheeled vehicle

[15]輪車 *yonrinsha, shirinsha, yorinsha* four-

[21]顧 *shiko suru* look around

A **因** 1026 / F399 IN cause, factor. *china(mu)* be associated with. *yo(ru)* depend on, be limited to. *yo(tte)* therefore, consequently. *chinami ni* by the way, in this connection.

[3] 子 *inshi* factor, element (in math)
[5] 由 *in-yu* cause
[8] 果 *inga* cause and effect; retribution, karma; fate, destiny; misfortune
果応報 *inga-ōhō* reward according to deeds, retribution
果者 *ingamono* unlucky person
果律 *ingaritsu* law of causality
[9] 盾 *injun* indecision, vacillation
[11] 習 *inshū* custom, convention, tradition
[12] 循 *injun* indecision, vacillation
循姑息 *injun-kosoku na* temporizing, tardy, time-serving
[13] 業 *ingō* causes and actions, results of one's actions in a former existence. *ingō na* heartless, cruel
数 *insū* factor (in math)
数分解 *insū-bunkai* factoring (in math)
[15] 縁 *innen* cause and effect; karma; fate; affinity, connection; origin, history; pretext
[22] 襲 *inshū* custom, convention, tradition

A **団** 1027 / F409 **團** TON. DON. DAN body, group, corps, gang, party, company, troupe; circle.

[3] 子 *dango* dumpling
子鼻 *dangobana* flat nose
[4] 円 *dan-en* roundness; peacefulness in the home; conclusion
[6] 交 *dankō* collective bargaining
[7] 体 *dantai* corporation, party, body, organization, group, association, entity
体行動 *dantai kōdō* collective action
体交渉 *dantai kōshō* collective bargaining
[8] 長 *danchō* leader of a group
服 *dampuku* association uniform
[10] 員 *dan-in* member of a group
匪 *dampi* bandits; Boxers
匪乱 *Dampi (no) Ran* Boxer Rebellion
扇 *uchiwa* round fan; referee's fan
扇太鼓 *uchiwa taiko* fan-shaped drum
栗 *donguri* acorn
栗眼 *donguri manako* goggle-eyed
[12] 結 *danketsu* unity, union, combination
結力 *danketsuryoku* cohesion; capacity for united action
結心 *danketsushin* feeling of unity, esprit de corps
[14] 旗 *danki* association flag
歌 *danka* association song
[23] 欒 *danran* family circle; harmony

A **回** 1028 / F397 **囘 囬 囘** E. KAI time; round, game, bout, heat, inning, innings; go around. *megu(ru)*, *mawa(ru)* *vi* and *vt* turn, go around; revolve, rotate, spin, gyrate; patrol, tour; take effect (medicine); be distributed; be past (time); be transferred. *mawa(rasu)*, *mawa(su)* turn, revolve, rotate; circularize; pass around; forward, transmit; refer to; transfer; lend money. *motō(ru)* wander around. *mawa(ri)* rotation; circumference, girth; surroundings, border; detour; tour; efficacy or effect (of something taken); spread (of flames). *mawa(shi)* loin cloth; cape, mantle. *megu(rasu)* enclose, surround; turn, turn around; ponder; devise. *mawa(rikudoi)* circuitous. *-mawa(ri)* via; a round, a turn; a size; a cycle (12 years). (See under 廻 1548 for other related compounds.)

[4] 文 *kaibun, kaimon, mawa(shi)bumi* circular letter
天 *kaiten no* epoch-making, stupendous
心 *kaishin* conversion
心者 *kaishinsha* a convert
[5] 生 *kaisei* resurrection, resuscitation
旧 *kaikyū* longing for the old days
付 *kaifu suru* transmit, refer to, send to, pass on to (of something)
収 *kaishū* collection (of materials); recovery
右 *mawa(re) migi* right about face
礼 *kairei* round of complimentary calls
礼客 *kaireikyaku* New Year's callers
[6] 米 *kaimai* rice transportation; rice deliveries
虫 *kaichū* round intestinal worm
気 *mawa(ri)gi* distrust
向 *ekō* Buddhist memorial service
合 *mawa(ri)a(wase)*, *megu(ri)a(wase)* turn of fortune, chance, fate. *kaigō* chance meeting
回 *mawa(ri)-mawa(tte)* after many vicissitudes
回教 *Fuifuikyō, Uiuikyō* Mohammedanism, Islam
[7] 折 *kaisetsu* diffraction
状 *kaijō* circular letter
忌 *kaiki* death anniversary
[8] 金 *mawa(ri)gane* money to invest
国 *kaikoku* pilgrimage, tour
歩 *mawa(ri)-aru(ku)* walk around
者 *mawa(shi)mono* spy, secret agent
送 *kaisō* forwarding, transportation
送車 *kaisōsha* streetcar returning to the barn
[9] 持 *mawa(ri)mo(chi)* doing by turns
勅 *kaichoku* (papal) encyclical
春 *kaishun* return of spring; recovery (from illness); rejuvenation
[10] 流 *kairyū* flowing around; a stream flowing
航 *kaikō* navigation, cruise

訓 *kaikun* the requested instructions
書 *kaisho* answer to a letter
根性 *mawa(ri) konjō* distrust
帰 *kaiki* revolution, recurrence. *kaiki suru* revolve, return, recur
帰年 *kaikinen* equinoctial year ⌈Capricorn)
帰線 *kaikisen* the tropics (of Cancer and
帰熱 *kaikinetsu* recurrent fever
11廊 *kairō* corridor
道 *mawa(ri)michi* detour, roundabout way
旋 *kaisen* rotation, revolution, convolution,
章 *kaishō* circular letter ⌊coiling, spiraling
梯子 *mawa(ri)bashigo* winding stairway
階段 *mawa(ri) kaidan* winding stairway
運業 *kaiungyō* marine transportation busi-
遊 *kaiyū* excursion, circular tour ⌊ness
遊船 *kaiyūsen* excursion steamer
船 *kaisen* barge; cargo vessel
船問屋 *kaisendon-ya* shipping agency
船業 *kaisengyō* marine transportation busi-
教 *Kaikyō* Mohammedanism; Islam ⌊ness
教国 *Kaikyōkoku* Mohammedan country
教徒 *Kaikyōto* a Mohammedan, a Moslem
転 *kaiten* revolution, rotation; revolving, swivel; turnover
転戸 *kaitendo* revolving door
転木馬 *kaiten mokuba* merry-go-round
転灯 *kaitentō* revolving light ⌈furnace
転炉 *kaitenro* rotary oven, revolving
転計 *kaitenkei* revolution counter
転盆 *kaitembon* Lazy Susan, revolving tray
転砲 *kaitenhō* swivel gun
転砲塔 *kaiten hōtō* revolving turret
転率 *kaitenritsu* rate of turnover
転窓 *kaitem-mado* transom window
転椅子 *kaiten isu* swivel chair
転資金 *kaiten shikin* revolving fund
転儀 *kaitengi* gyroscope
転翼 *kaiten-yoku* rotor
転羅針儀 *kaiten rashingi* gyrocompass
12遠 *mawa(ri)dō(i)* roundabout, long-winded
游 *kaiyū* a run of fish; traveling around for pleasure
診 *kaishin* doctor's hospital rounds
飲 *mawa(shi)no(mi)* drink in turn from one
答 *kaitō* reply ⌊cup
番 *mawa(ri)ban ni* alternately
報 *kaihō* circular; reply ⌈tion
復 *kaifuku* recovery, restoration, rehabilita-
復中 *kaifukuchū* convalescing period
復期 *kaifukuki* convalescence
13祿 *kairoku* god of fire
路 *kairo* (electric) circuit
想 *kaisō* reflection, reminiscence
想録 *kaisōroku* memoirs
数 *kaisū* frequency, number of times
数券 *kaisūken* railway ticket book
数乗車券 *kaisū jōshaken* book of railway
14暦 *kaireki* arrival of the New Year ⌊tickets
歴 *kaireki* round, patrol, tour
読 *kaidoku suru* read (a book in turn)
舞台 *mawa(ri)butai* revolving stage
漕 *kaisō* marine transportation
漕店 *kaisōten* shipping agency
漕問屋 *kaisōdon-ya* shipping agency
15線 *kaisen* (electric) circuit
縁 *mawa(ri)en* veranda around two sides
避 *kaihi* evasion, shirking, dodging, circumvention, avoiding
避所 *kaihisho* place to pass (on a narrow
16錐 *mawa(shi)giri* auger (tool) ⌊road)
燈籠 *mawa(ri)dōrō* revolving lantern
覧 *kairan* circulation
覧文庫 *kairam-bunko* circulating library
覧板 *kairamban* circular letter
21顧 *kaiko* recollection, retrospect
顧的 *kaikoteki* retrospective
顧録 *kaikoroku* memoirs, reminiscences

4

囬 1029 F397 See **回** 1028.

囯 1030 F403 See **国** 1037.

囮 1031 F399 KA. GA *otori* decoy, lure, stool pigeon.

A **囲** 1032 F406 **圍** I enclosure. *kako(mu)*, *kako(u)* enclose, surround, encircle; besiege; preserve, store; keep. *kako(mi)*, *kako(i)* enclosure, paling; tea arbor; storage.
2入 *kako(mi)-i(reru)* gather in
8者 *kako(i)mono* concubine
炉裏 *irori* sunken hearth
12堰 *kako(i)zeki* cofferdam
13障 *ishō* fence
碁 *igo*, Japanese checkers, *go*
18繞 *inyō suru*, *ijō suru* surround

B **困** 1033 F400 KON. *koma(ru)* be distressed be in trouble, be destitute, be embarrassed, be perplexed, be annoyed. *koma(raseru)*, *koma(rasu)* embarrass, annoy.
4厄 *kon-yaku* trouble, misfortune, hardship
切 *koma(ri)-ki(ru)*=*koma(ri)-ha(teru)* 困果 (see below–8) ⌈果 (see below–8)
7抜 *koma(ri)-nu(ku)*=*koma(ri)-ha(teru)* 困
却 *konkyaku* embarrassment, perplexity, trouble

[8]果 *koma(ri)-ha(teru)* be greatly perplexed; be greatly embarrassed
者 *koma(ri)mono* good-for-nothing person; source of trouble
苦 *konku* hardships, privation
苦欠乏 *konku-ketsubō* hardships, privation
[10]悩 *koma(ri)-naya(mu)* be in deep trouble
[12]惑 *konwaku*=*tōwaku* 当惑 1359.12
[15]窮 *konkyū* poverty, distress
窮者 *konkyūsha* the poor, the needy
[16]憊 *kompai* exhaustion, fatigue
[18]難 *konnan* trouble, distress, perplexity

A 図 1034/F408 圖 To plan. ZU drawing, plan, figure, cut, chart, diagram, illustration, graph. *haka(ru)* (see 計 4312.0). *haka(razaru)* unexpected. *haka(razu) mo* unexpectedly, unintentionally, accidentally.

[2]入 *zu-i(ri)* illustrated (book)
[3]工 *zukō* draftsman
上 *zujō* on the map
[4]引 *zuhi(ki)* drafting, drawing; draftsman
太 *zubuto(i)* bold, audacious, impudent
[5]示 *zushi* explanatory diagram, illustration
[6]式 *zushiki* diagram, graph
当 *zu (ni) ata(ru)* hit the mark; work well
[7]図 *zūzū(shii)* impudent, audacious, bold, brazenfaced
体 *zūtai* body
抜 *zunu(keru)* tower above, be outstanding
形 *zukei* figure, diagram
形幾何学 *zukei kikagaku* descriptive geometry
[8]法 *zuhō* drawing, draftsmanship
版 *zuhan* plate, figure, illustration
取 *zudo(ri)* sketching; sketch, plan
画 *zuga* drawing (the study); a drawing, a picture
表 *zuhyō* chart, diagram, graph
[9]面 *zumen* drawing, plan, map, sketch
柄 *zugara* a design
星 *zuboshi* the bull's-eye, the mark
[10]案 *zuan* design, plan, sketch, drawing
案家 *zuanka* designer
書 *tosho, zusho* books
書出版会社 *tosho shuppangaisha* publishing company
書出版者 *tosho shuppansha* publisher
書出納台 *tosho shutsunōdai* library charging desk
書目録 *tosho mokuroku* catalog of publications
書受入 *tosho u(ke)-i(re)* library accessioning
書受入原簿 *tosho u(ke)-i(re) gembo* accession book
書室 *toshoshitsu* library room
書票 *toshohyō* book label
書解題 *tosho kaidai* bibliography
書請求票 *tosho seikyūhyō* library call slip
書閲覧人 *tosho etsurannin* library reader
書閲覧用紙 *tosho etsuran yōshi* library call slip
書閲覧室 *tosho etsuranshitsu* reading room
書閲覧料 *tosho etsuranryō* library admission charge
書館 *toshokan* library
書館長 *toshokanchō* head librarian
書館学 *toshokangaku* library science
書館員 *toshokan-in* library clerk, librarian
[12]葉 *zuyō* a map
[13]解 *zukai* illustration, explanatory diagram
[14]様 *zuyō* illustration; map; style
説 *zusetsu* explanatory diagram; illustrated book
像学 *zuzōgaku* iconology, iconography
[18]題 *zudai* caption for an illustration
[19]譜 *zufu* chart, picture, figure
[22]鑑 *zukan* picture book

5

囹 1035/F401 REI prison.

[10]圄 *reigo* prison

A 固 1036/F401 Ko. *kata(maru)* *vi* harden, stiffen, solidify, set, settle, congeal, clot, curdle, conglomerate; get together; be devoted to; settle down (weather). *kata(meru)* *vt* harden; tighten; freeze; curdle; strengthen; stabilize; defend, fortify; collect, amass; settle down, locate. *kata(me)* defense, fortification; guard; pledge, engagement. *kata(mari)* (see under 塊 1122.0). *kata(i)* (see under 堅 1096.0). *moto(yori)* from the beginning; of course.

[4]太 *katabuto(ri)* of firm build
[6]守 *koshu* persistence, tenacity, adhering
有 *koyū no* personal, characteristic, peculiar to, inherent
有名詞 *koyū meishi* proper noun
有財産 *koyū zaisan* personal property
有語 *koyūgo* idiomatic expression
[7]体 *kotai* a solid (body)
体化 *kotaika* solidification
体燃料 *kotai nenryō* solid fuel
形 *kokei* a solid (body)
形分 *kokeibun* solids
形体 *kokeitai* a solid (body)
形物 *kokeibutsu* a solid; solid food
形便 *kokeiben* firm (ordinary) feces
形食物 *kokei shokumotsu* solid food
形燃料 *kokei nenryō* solid fuel
[8]陋 *korō* perversity, bigotry, conservatism
苦 *katakuru(shii)* formal, ceremonious; awkward; punctilious; strict
定 *kotei* fixing, fixation, fixed; identification (of biological specimens)
定化 *koteika* fixation, freezing (credits)

定給 *koteikyū* fixed salary
定費 *koteihi* fixed charge
定資本 *kotei shihon* fixed capital
定資産 *kotei shisan* fixed assets ⌈cause)
9 持 *koji suru* persist in (a belief), adhere to (a
10 疾 *koshitsu* chronic illness
11 執 *koshū, koshitsu* adherence; persistence
唾飲 *katazu (o) no(mu)* be intensely anxious
12 着 *kochaku suru* adhere to
13 塩 *katashio* rock salt
辞 *koji suru* positively decline
14 飴 *kata-ame* hard candy

A 国 1037/F403 國 囯 圀 KOKU country.
kuni country, land, realm; province; native land. (*o*)*kuni* your country.
2 人 *kunibito, kokujin* a people, natives
力 *kokuryoku* national strength, national resources
3 士 *kokushi* patriot, distinguished citizen
土 *kokudo* country, territory, domain
土防衛 *kokudo bōei* national defense
土計画 *kokudo keikaku* land planning
4 手 *kokushu* skilled doctor
父 *kokufu* father of his country
王 *kokuō* king, monarch
中 *kunijū* thruout the country
分寺 *kokubunji* ancient provincial temples
内 *kokunai* domestic; the interior of a country ⌈tion
内消費 *kokunai shōhi* domestic consump-
内産業 *kokunai sangyō* domestic industries
内戦 *kokunaisen* civil war
文 *kokubun* national literature; national language
文法 *kokubumpō* Japanese grammar
文学 *kokubungaku* Japanese literature
文学史 *kokubungakushi* history of Japanese literature
文科 *kokubunka* Japanese literature course
5 母 *kokubo* empress, empress dowager
用 *kokuyō* national expenses, national resources, national use
巡 *kunimegu(ri)* touring countries
史 *kokushi* national history
払 *kunibara(i)* exile, deportation
主 *kokushu* feudal lord, governor of a medieval province (*kuni*)
司 *kunizukasa, kokushi* governor of a medieval province (*kuni*)
本 *kokuhon* foundation of the nation
外 *kokugai* overseas, outside the country
外追放 *kokugai tsuihō* deportation
立 *kokuritsu* national (institution)
立公園 *kokuritsu kōen* national park
立図書館 *kokuritsu toshokan* national library
立墓地 *kokuritsu bochi* national cemetery
民 *kokumin, kunitami* the people, a national; national
民化 *kokuminka* nationalization ⌈ture
民文学 *kokumim-bungaku* national litera-
民生活 *kokumin seikatsu* national life
民主義 *kokumin shugi* nationalism
民投票 *kokumin tōhyō* plebiscite
民性 *kokuminsei* national character
民服 *kokuminfuku* national civilian uniform
民的 *kokuminteki* national ⌈school
民学校 *kokumin gakkō* national elementary
民所得 *kokumin shotoku* national income
民軍 *kokumin gun* national army ⌈tion
民皆兵 *kokumin kaihei* universal conscrip-
民思想 *kokumin shisō* national sentiment
民党 *kokumintō* Chinese Nationalist Party
民経済 *kokumin keizai* national economy
民道徳 *kokumin dōtoku* national morality, civic virtues ⌈tion
民登録 *kokumin tōroku* national registra-
民感情 *kokumin kanjō* national sentiment
民精神 *kokumin seishin* national spirit
民精神総動員 *kokumin seishin sōdōin* national spiritual mobilization
6 交 *kokkō* diplomatic relations
号 *kokugō* name of a country
安 *kokuan* national peace ⌈officer
守 *kokushu* medieval governor's executive
光 *kokkō* national glory, national prestige
名 *kokumei* name of a country
自慢 *kuni jiman* provincial pride
字 *kokuji* native script; the *kana* syllabary; characters made in Japan ⌈writing
字改良 *kokuji kairyō* reform of Japanese
防 *kokubō* national defense
防色 *kokubōshoku* khaki color
防服 *kokubōfuku* civilian wartime uniform
防軍 *kokubōgun* national defense forces
防費 *kokubōhi* defense expenditures
会 *kokkai* national assembly, diet, congress, parliament ⌈Congress
会図書館 *Kokkai Toshokan* Library of
会衛視 *kokkai eishi* sergeant-at-arms
会議事堂 *Kokkai Gijidō* Diet Building; House of Parliament; U. S. Capitol
会議員 *kokkai gi-in* national assemblyman
有 *kokuyū* national ownership
有化 *kokuyūka* nationalization
有地 *kokuyūchi* national land
有林 *kokuyūrin* national forest
有財産 *kokuyū zaisan* national resources
有鉄道 *kokuyū tetsudō* national railways
7 体 *kokutai* national structure, national polity

5 技 *kokugi* national skills; national sport
状 *kokujō* condition of the country
乱 *kokuran* civil strife
別 *kunibetsu* classification by nations
花 *kokka* national flower
君 *kokkun* sovereign ⌈dialect
言葉 *kuni kotoba* national language; local
利 *kokuri* national interests; profit to the country
利民福 *kokuri-mimpuku* the prosperity of the country and the happiness of the
8 国 *kuniguni* nations ⌊people
府 *kokufu* provincial capital; Nationalist Government of China. *kokubu* (ancient)
使 *kokushi* envoy ⌊local government office
法 *kokuhō* national law, public law
育 *kunisodachi* brought up in the country
宝 *kokuhō* national treasure; national hero
歩 *kokuho* fortunes of state
典 *kokuten* state ceremony; national literature; Japanese book
帑 *kokudo* national treasury
武士 *kunibushi* provincial samurai
定 *kokutei* stipulated by law, compiled by the state
定公園 *kokutei kōen* national park
学 *kokugaku* study of Japanese literature
学者 *kokugakusha* Japanese classical scholar
事 *kokuji* national affairs
事犯 *kokujihan* political offense, treason
9 音 *kokuon* local pronunciation; Japanese pronunciation of characters
風 *kokufū, kuniburi* national customs; popular songs, folk songs
廻 *kunimegu(ri)* touring the countries (*kuni*)
威 *kokui* national prestige
造 *kunizuku(ri)* founding a nation
俗 *kokuzoku* national customs
持 *kunimo(chi)* feudal lord
柄 *kunigara* national character. *kokuhei* reins of government ⌈tration
政 *kokusei* government, national adminis-
軍 *kokugun* Japanese armed forces
是 *kokuze* national policy
連 *Kokuren* United Nations
連安全保障理事会 *Kokuren Anzen Hoshō Rijikai* UN Security Council
連事務総長 *Kokuren Jimu Sōchō* UN Secretary General
連軍 *Kokurengun* UN Forces
連教育科学文化機構 *Kokuren Kyōiku Kagaku Bunka Kikō* UNESCO
連旗 *Kokurenki* UN flag ⌈sembly
連総会 *Kokuren Sōkai* UN General As-
10 原 *kunibara* spacious country
庫 *kokko* national treasury
辱 *kokujoku* national dishonor
師 *kokushi* Buddhist priest
恥 *kokuchi* national humiliation
訓 *kokkun* Japanese reading of a Chinese character which is used without reference to the real meaning of the character
都 *kokuto* national capital ⌊in China
益 *kokueki* national prosperity
書 *kokusho* credentials (to a ruler); a ruler's message; national record; national liter-
華 *kokka* national pride or glory ⌊ature
恩 *kokuon* blessings received from one's
粋 *kokusui* national characteristics ⌊country
粋主義 *kokusui shugi* ultranationalism
家 *kokka* nation, country
家公務員 *kokka kōmuin* government of-
家主義 *kokka shugi* nationalism ⌊ficials
家地方警察 *kokka chihō keisatsu* national rural police ⌈government
家扶助 *kokka fujo* assistance from the
家的 *kokkateki* national, state
家宗教 *kokka shūkyō* national religion
家神道 *Kokka Shintō* State Shinto
家経済 *kokka keizai* national economy
家群 *kokkagun* family of nations, group of nations ⌈tions
家試験 *kokka shiken* government examina-
家管理 *kokka kanri* state control
家総動員 *kokka sōdōin* national general mobilization
家憲章 *kokka kenshō* national charter
家警察 *kokka keisatsu* national police
11 道 *kokudō* national highway ⌈fortunes
運 *koku-un* national destiny, national
情 *kokujō* condition of the country
設 *kokusetsu* provided by the government
訛 *kuni nama(ri)* provincial accent
許 *kunimoto* birthplace, one's country, one's home province
教 *kokkyō* state religion, state church
章 *kokushō* national emblem
基 *kokki* foundation of a nation
患 *kokkan* national disaster
務 *kokumu* state affairs
務大臣 *kokumu daijin* minister of state; minister without portfolio
務長官 *Kokumu Chōkan* Secretary of State
産 *kokusan* domestic products
産品 *kokusanhin* domestic products
祭 *kokusai* national festival
祭日 *kokusaibi* national holiday
12 税 *kokuzei* national tax
朝 *kokuchō* imperial court
富 *kokufu* national wealth
策 *kokusaku* national policy
葬 *kokusō* state funeral

替 *kuniga(e)* transfer of a daimyo
費 *kokuhi* national expenditures
喪 *kokusō* national mourning
営 *kokuei* government-operated
営化 *kokueika* nationalization
営墓地 *kokuei bochi* national cemetery
13債 *kokusai* national debt; national bonds, national securities
漢 *kokkan* Japanese and Chinese literature
賊 *kokuzoku* traitor, rebel
鉄 *kokutetsu* national railways
電 *kokuden* government electric line
禁 *kokkin* a national prohibition
勢 *kunizei* local armed forces. *kokusei* national strength; condition of the country
勢調査 *kokusei chōsa* national census
際 *kokusai* international (intercourse)
際人 *kokusaijin* citizen of the world
際化 *kokusaika* internationalization
際公法 *kokusai kōhō* international public law
際友誼 *kokusai yūgi* international friendship, comity of nations
際司法裁判所 *Kokusai Shihō Saibansho* International Court of Justice
際主義 *kokusai shugi* internationalism
際共産主義 *Kokusai Kyōsan Shugi* International Communism
際共産党 *Kokusai Kyōsantō* Comintern, International Communism
際地球観測年 *Kokusai Chikyū Kansokunen* International Geophysical Year
際仲裁裁判所 *Kokusai Chūsai Saibansho* International Court of Arbitration, the Hague Court
際赤十字 *Kokusai Sekijūji* International Red Cross
際社会 *kokusai shakai* community of nations
際私法 *kokusai shihō* international private law
際法 *kokusaihō* international law
際的 *kokusaiteki* international
際連合 *Kokusai Rengō* United Nations
際連合軍 *Kokusai Rengōgun* United Nations Army
際連盟 *Kokusai Remmei* League of Nations
際通 *kokusaitsū* authority on international affairs
際通信社 *Kokusai Tsūshinsha* International News Service
際通貨基金 *Kokusai Tsūka Kikin* International Monetary Fund
際都市 *kokusai toshi* cosmopolitan city
際麻薬輸入団 *kokusai mayaku yunyūdan* international narcotics ring
際間 *kokusaikan no* international
際結婚 *kokusai kekkon* interracial marriage
際場裡 *kokusai jōri* international arena
際語 *kokusaigo* an international language
際管理 *kokusai kanri* international control
際警察軍 *kokusai keisatsu gun* international police force
14旗 *kokki* national flag
構 *kunigama(e)* national structure; the closed-box radical (of a character)
歌 *kokka* national anthem
製品 *kokuseihin* Japanese product
選弁護人 *kokusen bengonin* counsel assigned by the court
語 *kokugo* national language; Japanese
語改良 *kokugo kairyō* reform of the Japanese language
語学 *kokugogaku* study of languages
境 *kokkyō, kunizakai* frontier, national boundary
境刺戟 *kokkyō shigeki* border raid
境線 *kokkyōsen* boundary line
境警備 *kokkyō keibi* border guards
15儀 *kokugi* state function
権 *kokken* sovereign rights; national prestige
論 *kokuron* public opinion, public discussion
賓 *kokuhin* national guest
勲 *kokkun* meritorious service for the state
器 *kokki* statesman
幣社 *kokuheisha* national shrine
16憲 *kokken* national constitution
18儲 *kokucho* imperial heir
難 *kokunan* national crisis, national disaster
19璽 *kokuji* the seal of state
警 *kokkei* national police
20籍 *kokuseki* nationality, citizenship

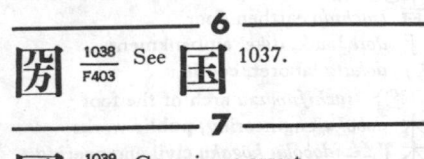

6

圀 1038/F403 See 国 1037.

7

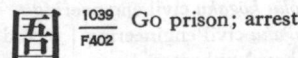

圄 1039/F402 Go prison; arrest.

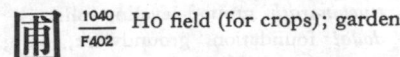

圃 1040/F402 Ho field (for crops); garden.

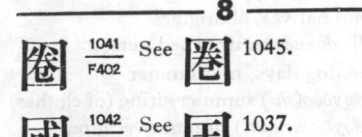

8

圈 1041/F402 See 圏 1045.

國 1042/F403 See 国 1037.

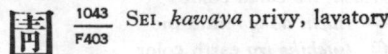

圊 1043/F403 SEI. *kawaya* privy, lavatory.

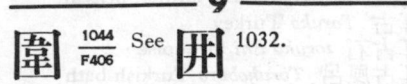

9

圍 1044/F406 See 囲 1032.

圏 1045/F402 **圏** KEN sphere, circle, range, radius. B

4 内 *kennai* within the range or orbit
5 外 *kengai* outside the range or orbit
9 点 *kenten* a circle (for emphasis)

10

圓 1046/F407 See **円** 617.

園 1047/F407 EN garden, yard, plantation, farm. *sono* garden, park. A

2 丁 *entei* gardener
5 生 *sono-o* garden
主 *enshu* garden or orchard owner
6 地 *enchi* park
7 児 *enji* kindergarten pupil
芸 *engei* horticulture, floriculture, gardening
芸家 *engeika* gardener, horticulturist
8 長 *enchō* kindergarten principal
9 亭 *entei* arbor, bower, summer house
10 圃 *empo* fields and gardens; truck farm, vegetable garden
11 遊会 *en-yūkai* garden party

11

圖 1048/F408 See **図** 1034.

團 1049/F409 See **団** 1027.

RAD. 士 32

Tsuchi earth. At left: 𡈽 *tsuchi-hen*. Variant: 士. This variant is actually Rad. 33 but, except for the radical character itself, is herein treated as a variant of Rad. 32. Nickname: Earth.

土 1050/F410 **土** To. Do earth, ground; Saturday; Turkey. *tsuchi* earth, soil, ground. A

2 人 *dojin* natives, aborigines
人形 *tsuchi ningyō* clay doll
3 工 *dokō* earthwork; coolie, laborer
下座 *dogeza suru* prostrate oneself
4 戸 *tsuchido* earthen door
手 *dote* bank, dike, embankment
方 *dokata* laborer, coolie
不踏 *tsuchifumazu* arch of the foot
木 *doboku* engineering, public works
木工学 *doboku kōgaku* civil engineering
木学 *dobokugaku* civil engineering
5 付 *tsuchitsu(kazu)* unbeaten, having a clean record
平 *tsuchinarashi* ground-leveling roller
台 *dodai* foundation, groundwork, base; fundamentally, entirely
民 *domin* natives, aborigines
左衛門 *dozaemon* drowned person
用 *doyō* dog days, midsummer
用干 *doyōbo(shi)* summer airing (of clothes)
用休 *doyō yasu(mi)* summer vacation
用波 *doyō nami* high waves in the dog days
6 色 *tsuchi iro* earth color
団子 *tsuchi dango* mud pie
気色 *tsuchike iro* earth color
百姓 *dobyakushō* dirt farmer, peasant
耳古 *Toruko* Turkey
耳古石 *toruko ishi* turquoise
耳古風呂 *Torukoburo* Turkish bath
耳古帽 *torukobō* fez
耳其 *Toruko* Turkey
地 *tochi* land, tract, lot; estate; soil; locality; territory; the neighborhood
地付 *tochitsu(ki)* land attached, with land
地収用 *tochi shūyō* expropriation of land
地台帳 *tochi daichō* land register
地会社 *tochigaisha* real-estate company
地私有 *tochi shiyū* private ownership of land
地改良 *tochi kairyō* land improvement
地言葉 *tochi kotoba* dialect
地国有 *tochi-kokuyū* state ownership of land
地柄 *tochigara* nature of the locality
地家屋 *tochi-kaoku* real estate; land and buildings
地訛 *tochi namari* colloquial expression
7 足 *dosoku de* with footgear on
均 *tochinara(shi)* ground-leveling roller
兵 *dohei* local soldiers; native soldiers
牢 *tsuchirō* underground cell, dungeon
芥 *dokai* rubbish, dirt
8 国 *Dokoku* Turkey
肥 *tsuchiko(eta)* fertile
金属 *dokinzoku* earth metals
性骨 *doshōbone* (derisive for) disposition, nature
性根 *doshōne* disposition, nature
9 室 *tsuchimuro* mud house
星 *Dosei* Saturn
臭 *tsuchikusa(i)* earth-smelling; rustic, boorish
俗 *dozoku* local customs

俗学 *dozokugaku* folklore, ethnography
建 *dōken* civil engineering and construction
建屋 *doken-ya* contractor
建業 *dokengyō* civil engineering and construction
砂 *dosha* earth and sand
砂降 *doshabu(ri)* downpour
砂崩壊 *dosha hōkai* landslide
10 匪 *dohi* rebellious natives
埃 *tsuchibokori, tsuchihokori* dust
倉 *tsuchigura, dosō* underground storehouse
釜 *dogama* earthen pot
留 *tsuchido(me)* sand guard
俵 *dohyō* sandbag; ring, wrestling arena
俵場 *dohyōba* ring, arena
俵際 *dohyōgiwa* scaffold, place of execution
11 黒 *tsuchiguro(i)* dark dirt color
偶 *dogū* earthen figure, wooden image, dummy, puppet
瓶 *dobin* earthen teapot
寄 *tsuchiyo(se)* covering the roots
袋 *dotai* sandbag
断場 *dotamba* place of execution, scaffold
崩 *dohō* collapse
崩瓦解 *dohō-gakai* collapse, downfall
産 *miyage* souvenir, present
産物 *miyagemono* souvenir, present
産法案 *miyage hōan* pork barrel
産話 *miyagebanashi* story of one's travels
12 間 *doma* unfloored room; dirt floor
塀 *dobei* mud wall
焼 *tsuchiya(ki)* unglazed earthenware
塁 *dorui* earthwork, breastwork
筆 *tsukushi, tsukushimbo* horsetail
葬 *dosō* burial, interment
着 *dochaku no* aboriginal, indigenous, native
着民 *dochakumin* natives, aborigines
13 塊 *dokai, tsuchikure* clod, lump of earth
煙 *tsuchi kemuri* cloud of dust
賊 *dozoku* bandit, rebel, insurgent
窟 *dokutsu* cave
14 語 *dogo* native tongue, dialect
管 *dokan* earthen pipe, drainpipe
蔵 *dozō* warehouse, storehouse, godown
製 *dosei, tsuchisei* earthen, terra cotta
豪 *dogō* (ancient) powerful provincial family
豪劣神 *dogō-resshin* oppressive landowner
15 墳 *dofun* grave mound
踏 *tsuchifu(mazu)* arch of the foot
蕃 *doban* natives, aborigines
質 *doshitsu* nature of the soil
器 *doki, kawarake* unglazed earthenware, earthenware, crockery, pottery
16 壌 *dojō* soil, earth
橋 *dobashi* earthen bridge
篩 *tsuchifurui* earth strainer
壁 *tsuchi kabe* mud wall
螢 *tsuchibotaru* glowworm
壇場 *dotamba* place of execution, scaffold
龍 *mogura, mugura* mole
龍色 *mogura iro* taupe
龍塚 *mogurazuka* molehill
龍戦術 *mogura senjutsu* underground campaign
17 鍋 *donabe, tsuchi nabe* earthen pot
18 類金属 *dorui kinzoku* earth metals
曜 *Doyō* Saturday
曜日 *Doyōbi* Saturday
19 瀝青 *dorekisei, asufuaruto* asphalt
20 饅頭 *domanjū, tsuchi manjū* grave mound
21 竈 *dogama* soft-charcoal furnace; soft charcoal
22 嚢 *donō* sandbag

——— 1 ———

壬 See 2921. [士]

圡 See **土** 1050.

——— 2 ———

圧 See 818.

A **去** $\frac{1051}{F308}$ Kyo. Ko. *sa(ru) vi* leave, move away, quit; pass, elapse, be gone, be over; be distant from., *vt* remove, eliminate, get rid of; divorce. *sa(ru)*- used in specifying a certain day in the past, last (June). [厶]

4 文 *sa(ri)bumi=sa(ri)jō* 去状 (see below–7)
月 *kyogetsu* last month
6 行 *sa(ri)-yu(ku)* go away
年 *kyonen, kozo* last year
7 状 *sa(ri)jō* bill of sale (for land); bill of divorcement
来 *kyorai* coming and going; past and future
11 頃 *sa(ru)koro* formerly, some years ago, a few days ago
12 就 *kyoshū* course of action; attitude
13 勢 *kyosei* castration; enervation; emasculation
勢牛 *kyōseigyū* bullock, ox, steer
18 難 *sa(ri)gata(i)* hard to part with

——— 3 ———

壮 See 2837. [士]

圭 $\frac{1052}{F413}$ Kei corner, angle, edge; jewel.

7 角 *keikaku* angle, corner
14 算 *keisan* paperweight

B **吉** $\frac{1053}{F329}$ Kichi, Kitsu *yoshi* good luck; joy, congratulations. [口]

方 *kippō, ehō* lucky direction

日 *kichinichi, kitsujitsu* lucky day
凶 *kikkyō* fortune, sunshine and shadow
5 礼 *kichirei, kitsurei* auspicious ceremony; festival
旦 *kittan* lucky day
左右 *kissō* good news; good or bad news
6 兆 *kitchō* lucky omen
7 辰 *kisshin* lucky day
8 例 *kichirei, kitsurei* time-honored custom
事 *kichiji, kitsuji* auspicious event
9 相 *kissō* good omen
10 祥 *kisshō* lucky omen
11 野紙 *yoshinogami* tissue paper
野桜 *yoshinozakura* a common kind of cherry tree
12 報 *kippō* good news
13 瑞 *kichizui, kitsuzui* lucky omen
夢 *kichimu, kitsumu* good dream
14 徴 *kitchō* lucky omen
15 慶 *kikkei* congratulatory event, rejoicing

A 寺 1054/F560 JI *-ji, tera* temple. [寸]

2 入 *tera-i(ri)* admission to a temple school
3 上 *tera-a(gari)* admission to a temple school
子 *terako* temple-school pupil
子屋 *terakoya* temple primary school
小姓 *teragoshō* temple boy servant
小屋 *terakoya* temple primary school
4 内 *jinai* in the temple compound
5 巡 *teramegu(ri)* temple-pilgrimage journey
6 回 *teramegu(ri)* temple-pilgrimage journey
号 *jigō* Buddhist temple name
守 *teramori* temple sexton
7 社 *jisha* temples and shrines
兵 *jihei* monk-soldiers
男 *tera otoko* temple sexton
8 門 *jimon* temple gate; temple
参 *teramai(ri)* temple visit
9 廻 *teramegu(ri)* temple-pilgrimage journey
院 *ji-in* temple
10 格 *jikaku* temple rank
11 務 *jimu* temple affairs
務所 *jimusho* temple office
12 塔 *jitō* a temple pagoda
13 僧 *jisō* temple priest
禄 *jiroku* benefice
詣 *teramō(de), teramai(ri)* visiting a temple
預 *tera-azuke* confinement in a temple
14 様 *(o)terasama* temple priest
銭 *terasen* charge for the temporary use of land or buildings
領 *jiryō* temple estate, glebe
15 請 *tera-u(ke)* Buddhist conversion certificate
請状 *tera-u(ke)jō* Buddhist conversion ⌈certificate

A 在 1055/F412 ZAI outskirts, suburbs, country *a(ru)* (see 有 3727.0). *i(masu), owa(su)* to be (polite). *a(ri) to arayuru* all, every. *zai-* located in.

4 方 *a(ri)kata* way something should be. *zaikata* rural district
天 *zaiten no* in heaven, heavenly
中 *zaichū* within
中物 *zaichūbutsu* contents
日 *zai-Nichi* in Japan. *ari(shi)hi* bygone days; during one's lifetime
日中 *zai-Nichichū* while resident in Japan
日本 *zai-Nihon* resident in Japan
5 処 *arika* one's whereabouts, retreat, refuge, hiding place; location (of something)
世 *zaisei* on the earth. *ari(shi)yo* on the earth; past days
世中 *zaiseichū* during one's lifetime
外 *zaigai* abroad
外邦人 *zaigai hōjin* Japanese residents ⌈abroad
外事務所 *zaigai jimusho* overseas agency
外研究員 *zaigai kenkyūin* overseas research personnel
6 合 *a(ri)-a(u)* happen to have
宅 *zaitaku suru* be in, be at home
在 *a(ri)a(ri) to* distinctly, vividly
米 *arimai* rice on hand. *zai-Bei* staying in America
米中 *zai-Beichū* while resident in America
任 *zainin suru* hold office
任中 *zaininchū* while in office
7 廷 *zaitei* serving in the imperial court; appearing in court
役 *zaieki* being employed; serving in the army; (ships) being commissioned
社 *zaisha suru* be in office
来 *zairai, a(ri)ki(tari)* usage, tradition
村地主 *zaison jinushi* resident landlord
位 *zai-i* reigning
位中 *zai-ichū* during the reign of
住 *zaijū suru* live, reside, dwell
住者 *zaijūsha* resident
8 国 *zaikoku* living in one's province
所 *zaisho* the country; one's residence; one's home town. *a(ri)dokoro*=*arika* 在処 (see above–5)
英中 *zai-Eichū* while resident in England
京 *zaikyō* resident in the capital
京中 *zaikyōchū* while in the capital
官 *zaikan* tenure of office
官中 *zaikanchū* while in office
官者 *zaikansha* officeholder
学 *zaigaku* enrolled in school
学生 *zaigakusei* student; undergraduate
学年限 *zaigaku nengen* the time limit for completing a curriculum

[9]室 *zaishitsu suru* be in the room
[10]家 *zaika* farmhouse; the country. *zaike*
華 *zai-Ka* in China ⌊a formal Buddhist
荷 *arini, zaika* goods on hand, inventory
庫 *zaiko* stock, stockpile
庫品 *zaikohin* goods on hand, inventory
校 *zaikō suru* be in school
校生 *zaikōsei* present students ⌈country
郷 *zaigō, zaigo* rural districts. *zaikyō* in the
郷者 *zaigōsha* person from the country
郷軍人 *zaigō gunjin* veteran, reservist
留 *zairyū suru* reside temporarily
留民 *zairyūmin* residents
留外人 *zairyū gaijin* foreign residents
留邦人 *zairyū hōjin* Japanese in foreign
[11]宿 *zaishuku suru* be in, be at home ⌊lands
貨 *zaika* goods on hand, inventory
野 *zaiya* out of office; the party out of power
野党 *zaiyatō* the party out of power
[12]勤 *zaikin suru* serve, hold office
無 *a(riya)-na(shiya)* to be living or not to be living; be true or not true. *a(ruka)-na(ika)* too small; existing or not existing; to be held or not to be held
番中 *zaibanchū* on duty
場所 *aribasho*=*arika* 在処 (see above–5)
[14]銘 *zaimei* maker's signature
獄 *zaigoku* in prison
獄中 *zaigokuchū* while in prison
監 *zaikan* in prison
監者 *zaikansha* prisoner; prison population
[17]韓 *zai-Kan* stationed in Korea
[18]職 *zaishoku suru* hold office, remain in office
職年限 *zaishoku nengen* tenure of office
職期間 *zaishoku kikan* tenure of office
[20]籍 *zaiseki* be enrolled ⌈ment
籍学生数 *zaiseki gakuseisū* school enroll-

A **地** 1056 / F413 CHI earth, land, ground, the surface of the earth; soil; place, region; territory; room, space; position; site; foundation. JI ground, land, earth; the surface of the earth; foundation, soil; texture, weave, fabric; field (of a flag); region; disposition; respectability; accompaniment; narrative part; fact. *ji(beta)* the ground, the earth. *tsuchi* earth, soil, ground.

[2]力 *chiryoku* fertility
[3]口 *jiguchi* play on words
久節 *Chikyūsetsu* Empress' Birthday
上 *chijō no* terrestrial, earthly, mundane, temporal. *chijō ni* on the ground, on earth, in this world
上力 *chijō (no) chikara* temporal power
上水 *chijōsui* surface water
上軍 *chijō gun* ground forces
上権 *chijōken* lease
下 *jige* ordinary officials; common people. *chika* underground, subterranean; base-
下水 *chikasui* subterranean water ⌊ment
下牢 *chikarō* underground dungeon
下足袋 *jika tabi* heavy-soled work tabi
下茎 *chikakei* rhizome
下室 *chikashitsu* basement, cellar ⌈ment
下政府 *chika seifu* underground govern-
下道 *chikadō* underground passage
下細胞 *chika saibō* underground elements
下運動 *chika undō* underground move-
下街 *chikagai* underground market ⌊ment
下鉄 *chikatetsu* subway
下鉄道 *chikatetsudō* subway
下資源 *chika shigen* underground resources
下権 *chikaken* subsurface rights
下線 *chikasen* underground cable or wire
[4]心 *chishin* earth's center, earth's core
区 *chiku* area, region, lot
辷 *jisube(ri)* landslide
中 *chichū* underground, subterranean
元 *jimoto no* local. *jimoto* that country
太 *jibuto no* coarse (texture)
中海 *Chichūkai* Mediterranean Sea
文 *chimon, chibun* physiographical features
文学 *chimongaku, chibungaku* physiography
水 *chisui* subterranean water
水火風 *chi-sui-ka-fū* the four elements: earth, water, fire, and wind
引 *jibiki* seine fishing
引網 *jibikiami*=地曳網 (see below–6)
方 *chihō* locality, region, area, section; the country; vicinity, neighborhood. *jikata* rural locality; coastal waters
方区 *chihōku* prefectural or local con-
方化 *chihōka* localization ⌊stituencies
方主義 *chihō shugi* provincialism
方色 *chihōshoku* local color
方回 *chihō mawa(ri)* provincial tour
方性 *chihōsei* local color
方版 *chihōban* provincial edition
方的 *chihōteki* local
方官 *chihōkan* local authorities
方制度 *chihō seido* local government
方風 *chihōfū* local wind ⌊system
方病 *chihōbyō* endemic disease; animal
方時 *chihōji* local time ⌊disease
方訛 *chihō namari* provincialism, local dialect, local accent
方税 *chihōzei* local taxes
方債 *chihōsai* local bonds
方新聞 *chihō shimbun* local newspaper
方闘争 *chihō tōsō* local strike
[5]目 *chimoku* land category
代 *jidai, chidai* land rent

玉 *jitama* home-grown eggs; local eggs
玉子 *jitamago* home-grown eggs; local eggs
主 *jinushi* landlord
主層 *jinushisō* the landowners
平 *chihei* ground level
平面 *chiheimen* horizontal plane
平線 *chiheisen* horizon, skyline
6 米 *jimai* locally produced rice
糸 *ji-ito* homespun thread
色 *ji-iro* ground color
虫 *jimushi* grub, ground beetle
衣 *chi-i* lichen
気 *chiki* earth vapors
肌 *jihada* texture, grain
合 *jia(i)* texture, weave, fabric
先 *jisaki* frontage
名 *chimei* place name
団駄 *jidanda* stamping with vexation
回 *jimawa(ri)* neighborhood, neighboring districts; provincial, local; a street tough
回船 *jimawa(ri)sen* coastwise steamer
曳 *jibiki* seine fishing
曳網 *jibiki ami* dragnet, seine (for inshore fishing)
7 車 *jiguruma* a wagon
図 *chizu* map, chart, plan
位 *chi-i* position, status, place, office, post
利 *chiri* excellent topography. *chi(no)ri* geographical advantage
声 *jigoe* natural voice
牢 *jirō* dungeon
卵 *jitamago* home-grown eggs; local eggs
吹雪 *jifubuki* drifting snow
役権 *chiekiken* easement, servitude
均 *jinarashi* ground leveling
均機 *jinarashiki* bulldozer
形 *chikei* topography. *jigyō* ground leveling; groundwork
形図 *chikeizu* topographical map
形学 *chikeigaku* physiography, geomorphology
8 金 *jigane* metal, ore, ground metal; true character
固 *jigata(me)* ground leveling; ground tamping
底 *chitei* the bowels of the earth; underground
価 *chika* land value
味 *chimi* nature of the soil. *jimi na* plain, simple, quiet, sober, modest, conservative
坪 *jitsubo* ground area
板 *ji-ita* flooring, planking
炉 *jiro* fireplace in the ground
物 *chibutsu* natural objects, landmarks, places to hide. *jimono* local product
取 *jido(ri)* ground plan, layout
歩 *chiho* one's ground, one's stand, standing, position, footing
券 *chiken* title deed
学 *chigaku* physiography
表 *chihyō* surface of the earth
所 *jisho* land, ground, tract, plot
所持 *jishomo(chi)* landowner
所熱 *jisho netsu* land fever, land hunger
9 廻 *jimawa(ri)*＝地回 (see above–6)
峡 *chikyō* isthmus
持 *jimo(chi)* landowner
相 *chisō* divination by the lay of the land; topography
狭 *chikyō* isthmus
神 *chijin* earthly deities
変 *chihen* natural calamity
点 *chiten* spot, point, place, position
界 *chikai* boundary
政学 *chiseigaku* geopolitics
面 *jimen* surface (of land), ground, land, lot
面持 *jimemmo(chi)* landowner
10 唄 *jiuta* ballad, folk song
核 *chikaku* earth's nucleus
酒 *jizake* locally brewed saké
祇 *chigi* earthly deities
租 *chiso* land tax
紋 *jimon* pattern
帯 *chitai* zone, belt, region, area
紙 *jigami* fan paper
紙形 *jigamigata* fan shape
11 道 *chidō* tunnel; slow but sure method. *jimichi* leisurely walk. *jimichi na* fair, honest
階 *chikai* basement
殻 *chikaku* the earth's crust
異 *chi-i* physiographical changes
袋 *jibukuro* cupboard near the floor
動 *chidō* earth tremors; earth's rotation
動説 *chidōsetsu* heliocentric or Copernican theory
域 *chi-iki* region, area, zone
域的 *chi-ikiteki* local, regional
域差 *chi-ikisa* regional differences
理 *chiri* geography, topography
理学 *chirigaku* geography
理学者 *chirigakusha* geographer
理書 *chirisho* geography book
球 *chikyū* earth, globe
球人 *chikyūjin* earthdwellers
球物理学 *chikyū butsurigaku* geophysics
球照 *chikyūshō* earthshine
球儀 *chikyūgi* terrestial globe
12 温 *chion* underground temperature
税 *chizei* land tax
軸 *chijiku* earth's axis
割 *jiwa(re)* earth fissure or crack. *jiwa(ri)* land allotment
13 続 *jitsuzu(ki)* land contiguity
腫 *jibare* swelling around a wound
蜂 *jibachi* digger wasp
隙 *chigeki* chasm, cleft, fissure
勢 *chisei* topography
塗 *jinu(ri)* first coat. *chi (ni) mami(reru)* be defeated; fail (in business)

雷 *jirai* land mine
雷火 *jiraika* land mine
雷弾 *jiraidan* high-explosive shell
14 歴 *chireki* geography and history
鳴 *jina(ri), chimei* earth tremor
境 *jizakai* landmark, boundary
誌 *chishi* topography
磁気 *chijiki* terrestial magnetism
模様 *ji-moyō* background pattern (woven into cloth)
層 *chisō* stratum, layer
層学 *chisōgaku* stratigraphy
獄 *jigoku* hell
獄耳 *jigoku mimi* sharp ears
獄行 *jigokuyu(ki)* going to hell
蔵 *Jizō* a Buddhist guardian deity of children
蔵眉 *jizō mayu* arched eyebrows
蔵菩薩 *Jizō Bosatsu* a Buddhist guardian deity of children
蔵顔 *jizōgao* round cheerful face
15 線 *shisen* ground wire
熱 *chinetsu, jinetsu* subterranean heat
盤 *jiban* base, foundation, the ground; footing, foothold; sphere of influence; constituency
質 *chishitsu* geology, geological features; nature of the soil. *jishitsu* texture
質分析 *chishitsu bunseki* soil analysis
質図 *chishitsuzu* geological map
質学 *chishitsugaku* geology
震 *jishin* earthquake
震図 *jishinzu* seismogram
震国 *jishinkoku* an earthquake-ridden country
震学 *jishingaku* seismology
震計 *jishinkei* seismograph
震帯 *jishintai* earthquake belt
震観測 *jishin kansoku* seismometry
16 積 *chiseki* acreage
頭 *jitō* lord of a manor
錦 *tsuta* ivy
18 類 *chirui* land category
鎮祭 *jichinsai* ground-breaking ceremony
19 霧 *chimu* ground fog
響 *jihibi(ki)* earth tremor
瀝青 *jirekisei, chirekisei* asphalt
20 籍 *chiseki* land register

4

坐 See **座** 1515.

壮 See **壯** 2837. [士]

坚 1057/F-X Nonstandard for **堅** 1096.

址 1058/F416 SHI ruins.

A **壱** 1059/F447 **壹** ICHI, ITSU one. [士]

坏 1060/F418 HAI. *tsuki* bowl.

A **坂** 1061/F417 HAN. *saka* incline, slope, hill.
3 下 *sakamoto* bottom of the hill
11 道 *sakamichi* hill road
13 路 *hanro* hill road

B **坊** 1062/F417 BŌ priest's residence; (Buddhist) priest; boy. *bō(ya)* boy. *bo(tchan)* your, his, or her boy. *tsukasa* (see under 司 877.0).
4 中 *bōchū* inside a temple; in the streets
5 本 *bōhon* books published unofficially
主 *bōzu* Buddhist priest, monk; shaven head; boy; rascal
主山 *bōzuyama* bare mountain
主刈 *bōzuga(ri)* closely cropped hair
主臭 *bōzukusa(i)* smacking of Buddhism
主読 *bōzuyo(mi)* singsong reading
主頭 *bōzu atama* tonsure, shaven head
6 守 *bōmori* sexton; low-rank priest; priest's wife
8 門 *bōmon* town gate, street
舎 *bōsha* priests' quarters
12 間 *bōkan* all over town
14 様 *bōsan* priest

B **坑** 1063/F419 KŌ pit, hole.
3 口 *kōkō* mine entrance
4 区 *kōku* mine area
木 *kōboku* mine pillars
水 *kōsui* mine-pit water
夫 *kōfu* miner
内 *kōnai* mine pit, shaft
内夫 *kōnaifu* underground miner
5 外 *kōgai* surface, out of the pit
外夫 *kōgaifu* surface (mine) worker
8 底 *kōtei* mine-pit bottom
11 道 *kōdō* (mine) level; tunnel

A **志** 1064/F690 SHI record; shilling; =*kokorozashi*. *kokoroza(su)* plan, intend, aim at, aspire to, resolve, determine. *kokorozashi* will, intention, motive; determination; aim; ambition, hopes; gift; kindness; offering (Buddhist). *shiringu* shilling. [心]
3 士 *shishi* patriot, public-spirited man
6 気 *shiki* spirit, sentiment, morale
向 *shikō* intention, aim

8 尚 *shishō* will, intention
11 望 *shibō* desire, ambition, choice
望者 *shibōsha* aspirant; applicant
13 節 *shisetsu* constant fidelity
15 趣 *shishu* heart, mind
16 操 *shisō* constancy, purpose, integrity
19 願 *shigan* desire, aspiration; application, volunteering
願兵 *shiganhei* volunteer soldier
願者 *shigansha* applicant, volunteer, aspirant, candidate
願書 *shigansho* written application

A **均** 1065 / F417 KIN. *nara(su)* to level, to average. *hito(shii)* equal, similar, alike, equivalent.

1 一 *kin-itsu, kin-ichi* uniformity, equality
一説 *kin-ichisetsu, kin-itsusetsu* uniformitarianism
4 分 *kimbun* equal division
5 圧 *kin-atsu* equal pressure
8 斉 *kinsei* symmetry, balance
並 *hitona(mi)* same, ordinary
12 等 *kintō* equality, uniformity, evenness, identity
等待遇 *kintō taigū* equal treatment
等割 *kintōwa(ri)* per-capita rate
13 勢 *kinsei* balance of power, uniformity
15 質 *kinshitsu* homogeneity
16 衡 *kinkō* equilibrium, balance
霑 *kinten suru* share equally
整 *kinsei* symmetry, balance

A **声** 1066 / F447 **聲** F1527 SHŌ. SEI *koe* voice; tone; alarm, cry; (bird) song, chirp. [耳]

5 立 *koe (o) ta(teru)* speak
6 合 *koea(wase)* singing or talking in unison
名 *seimei* fame, popularity
自慢 *koe jiman* pride of voice
色 *seishoku* voice and countenance; songs and women. *kowa-iro* tone of voice
色遣 *kowa-iro (o) tsuka(u)* imitate someone's speech
7 呑 *koe (o) no(mu)* keep quiet, say nothing
8 価 *seika* good reputation, fame, popularity
並 *koena(mi)* voice quality
明 *seimei* declaration, statement, proclamation
明書 *seimeisho* public statement
9 音 *kowane* tone of voice, timber of the voice. *seion* voice quality, vocal sound
柄 *koegara* voice quality
変 *koegawa(ri)* change of voice. *seihen* a break in one's voice
10 高 *kowadaka ni, koetaka(rakani), koedaka(ku), koetaka(ku)* with a loud voice
涙 *seirui* tears in the voice
息 *seisoku* news, message
帯 *seitai* vocal chords
帯模写 *seitai mosha* vocal mimicry
11 問 *seimon* news, message
掛 *koe (o) ka(keru)* call to (someone). *koegaka(ri)* influence, recommendation
望 *seibō* popularity, fame
12 援 *seien* encouragement, support, rooting, cheering
量 *seiryō* voice volume
13 誉 *seiyo* fame, honor, glory
楽 *seigaku* vocal music
楽家 *seigakuka* vocalist
14 聞 *seibun* fame, honor, glory
様 *koezama* voice quality
15 調 *seichō* tone of voice
17 優 *seiyū* radio actor

A **売** 1067 / F1801 **賣 賣** MAI. BAI selling. *u(ru)* sell, deal in, betray, deceive, impose on, tell on, pick (a quarrel). *u(reru)* sell, be in demand, enjoy a large sale; be well known. *u(ri)* sale, selling. *u(re)* sale, demand. [貝]

2 人気 *u(ri) ninki* bearish sentiment, selling support
卜 *baiboku* divination, divining for money, fortunetelling
卜者 *baibokusha* diviner, fortuneteller
3 口 *u(re)kuchi, u(ri)guchi* outlet, market, demand
女 *baita, baijo* harlot, prostitute
子 *u(rek)ko* popular person. *u(ri)ko* salesman, saleswoman, salesboy, salesgirl
下 *u(ri)-sa(geru)* sell, dispose of. *u(ri)sa(ge)* official sale by the government
上 *u(ri)-a(geru)* sell out. *uria(ge)* sales, proceeds; sale, closing sale
上元帳 *uria(ge)-motochō* sales ledger
上金 *uriage-kin* amount sold, sales
上高 *uria(ge)daka* amount sold, sales
上帳 *uria(ge)chō* sales book
上証 *uria(ge)shō* bill of sale
4 方 *u(ri)kata* salesmanship; seller
止 *urido(me)* suspension of sale
切 *u(ri)-ki(reru)* be sold out. *u(ri)-ki(ru)* sell out, clear out. *uriki(re)* sold out, a sellout
手 *urite* seller
手形 *u(ri) tegata* bill of sale
文 *baibun* hack writing
文業 *baibungyō* hack writing
込 *u(ri)-ko(mu)* sell, find a market for
込戦 *uriko(mi)sen* competitive selling to limited customers
5 立 *urita(te)* selling off, an auction
広 *u(ri)-hiro(geru), u(ri)-hiro(meru)* extend the sale of, find a market for
代 *u(ri)shiro=uria(ge)* 売上 (see above–3)
付 *u(ri)-tsu(keru)* palm off, force a sale
叩 *u(ri)-tata(ku)* make a bear drive, undersell

弘 *u(ri)-hiro(meru)*=売広 (see above–5)
払 *u(ri)-hara(u)* sell off, close out
主 *urinushi* seller, vendor
出 *u(ri)-ida(su), u(ri)-da(su)* offer for sale; gain a reputation. *urida(shi)* sale
6 舟 *u(ri)bune* boats for sale
色 *baishoku* prostitution
行 *ureyu(ki), ure-i(ki)* sale, demand, a run
回 *u(ri)-mawa(ru)* go around selling
尽 *u(ri)-tsuku(su)* sell off, clear out
気 *u(ri)ki* bearish sentiment, selling support
先 *u(ri)saki, u(re)saki* market, outlet, demand, buyer
名 *baimei* self-advertisement
7 足 *u(re)ashi* selling; a sale
戻 *u(ri)modo(shi)* resale (on the stock market)
位 *bai-i* buying a rank
初 *u(ri)zome* placing on sale for the first time; first New Year's sale
却 *baikyaku* sale
余 *u(ri)-ama(su)* reserve some (not selling all)
声 *u(ri)goe* peddler's cry
見本 *u(ri)mihon* sample
言葉 *u(ri)kotoba* tit-for-tat; exchange of compliments
8 店 *baiten* booth, stand, store
退 *u(ri)-no(ku)* realize, liquidate
価 *baika* selling price
放 *u(ri)-hana(su)* sell off, close out
物 *urimono* article for sale, offerings, for sale
官 *baikan* selling appointments
歩 *u(ri)-aru(ku)* peddle
国 *baikoku* treason
国奴 *baikokudo* traitor
9 飛 *u(ri)-toba(su)* sell off
食 *urigu(i)* live by selling one's property
屋 *u(ri)ya* seller
約 *baiyaku* sales contract
品 *baihin* article for sale
急 *u(ri)-iso(gu)* push the sale, be anxious to sell
相場 *u(ri) sōba* bear market; selling rate (of exchange)
為替 *u(ri)gawase* selling exchange
春 *baishun* prostitution
春婦 *baishunfu* prostitute
10 高 *u(re)daka, u(ri)daka* amount of sales
値 *urine* selling price
残 *u(re)-noko(ru)* remain unsold, remain unmarried. *u(re)noko(ri)* goods left unsold; unmarried woman
流 *u(ri)-naga(su)* sell to a distant customer
家 *u(ri)ya, u(ri)-ie* house for sale
留 *u(ri)da(me)* banking the sales money; sales receipts
捌 *u(ri)sabaki* sale; selling. *u(ri)-saba(ku)* sell, deal in, dispose of; sell widely
捌人 *u(ri)sabakinin* agent, dealer
笑 *baishō* prostitution
笑婦 *baishōfu* prostitute, streetwalker
11 過 *u(ri)su(gi)* overselling
惜 *u(ri)-oshi(mu)* be indisposed to sell, hoard, restrict sales
控 *u(ri)-hika(eru)* refrain from selling
掛 *u(ri)ka(ke)* credit sales
渋 *u(ri)-shibu(ru)* be indisposed to sell, hoard, restrict sales
得金 *baitokukin* proceeds of a sale
淫 *bai-in* social evil, prostitution
淫婦 *bai-impu* prostitute
12 越 *u(ri)ko(shi)* selling more than you own
渡 *u(ri)-wata(su)* sell, negotiate, sign away. *uriwata(shi)* sale and delivery
減 *u(ri)-he(rasu)* sell off inventories
勝 *u(ri)-ka(tsu)* sell higher than anyone else
買 *baibai, u(ri)ka(i)* trading, buying and selling; sale
焦 *u(ri)-a(seru)* push the sale, be anxious to sell
場 *uriba* counter, salesroom, shop, store
場係 *uribagakari* sales clerk
場監督 *uriba kantoku* floorwalker
13 僧 *maisu* miscreant priest
損 *u(ri)-sokona(u)* lose a sale, fail to find a market
溜 *u(ri)dame* proceeds; cash on hand
15 勲 *baikun* selling decorations
16 薬 *baiyaku, u(ri)gusuri* patent medicine, drugs

5

垂 See 211.

坡 1068 / F419 HA dike; dam; slope; bank.

坩 1069 / F420 KAN jar, pot.
12 堝 *rutsubo, kanka* crucible, melting pot

坤 1070 / F419 KON divination sign; land, earth.
14 徳 *kontoku* virtues of the empress

坦 1071 / F419 TAN level; wide.
8 坦 *tantan(taru)* level, even; peaceful
16 懐 *tankai* frankness

B **坪** 1072 / F420 坪 HEI. HYŌ. *tsubo* area about thirty-six square feet.
4 刈 *tsuboga(ri)* crop estimate per *tsubo*
6 当 *tsubo a(tari)* per *tsubo* (see Weights and Measures)
10 庭 *tsubo niwa* a small court garden
13 数 *tsubosū* area in *tsubo*, floor space

A **幸** 1073 / F628 Kō happiness, fortune. *sachi*, *saiwa(i)* happiness; blessing; good fortune. *shiawase* good fortune, happiness, blessing, mercy. *kō(su)* (the emperor) travels. [干]

4不幸 *kōfukō* weal or woe, good or evil, sunshine and shadow
6先 *saisaki* good omen; good beginning
9便 *kōbin* favorable opportunity
甚 *kōjin* a favor; supreme happiness
11運 *kōun* good fortune
運児 *kōunji* child of fortune
12無 *sachinashi* no luck, bad luck
13福 *kōfuku* happiness, welfare
15慶 *kōkei* joy; blessing

6

垜 1074 / F422 **垛** Ta, Da firing mound.

垣 1075 / F422 En. *kaki* fence, hedge, wall.
3下 *kakimoto* at the bottom of the fence
5本 *kakimoto* at the bottom of the fence
10根 *kakine* fence, hedge
12越 *kakigo(shi)* over or thru the fence
間見 *kaimami(ru)* peep at, glimpse

垢 1076 / F422 Kō. Ku. *aka* dirt, grime, scale, wax (in ears).
5付 *akazu(ku)* be soiled, get dirty
7抜 *akanu(ke)* refined, elegant, urbane
9染 *akaji(miru)* become grimy
17擦 *akasuri* washcloth
19離 *kori* purification, lustration

A **型** 1077 / F422 Kei *kata* model, mold, matrix, impression; style, type, pattern, make; set form; usage.
5打機 *kata-u(chi)ki* stamping machine
8板 *kata ita* die plate
9砂 *kata suna* sand for casting
削盤 *katakezu(ri)ban* shaper
10破 *katayabu(ri) no* unusual, queer, novel
紙 *katagami* sewing pattern
16録 *katarogu* catalog

B **城** 1078 / F423 **城** Jō castle. Sei. *shiro* castle, citadel.
3下 *jōka* castle town; feudal capital; the area around a castle
下町 *jōkamachi* castle town, the town ⌈around a castle
下盟 *jōka (no) chikai* surrender, capitulation
4戸 *kido* outer castle gate
内 *jōnai* inside the castle
中 *jōchū* within the castle
5代 *jōdai* castle warden
外 *jōgai* outside the castle
市 *jōshi* castle town, fortified town
主 *jōshu* lord of a castle
6池 *jōchi* castle and moat; castle moat
守 *jōshu* lord of a castle
7址 *jōshi* castle ruins
兵 *jōhei* castle garrison
邑 *jōyū* castle town
8門 *jōmon* castle gate
府 *jōfu* town wall; town; capital; barrier
9柵 *jōsaku* castle, fort
10将 *jōshō* castle commander
郭 *jōkaku* castle, citadel
11砦 *jōsai* fort, stronghold, citadel
12塁 *jōrui* fort
13楼 *jōrō* castle tower, watchtower
跡 *shiro ato* castle ruins, castle site
塞 *jōsai* fort, stronghold, castle
16壁 *jōheki* castle wall, rampart
壁伝 *jōhekizuta(i) ni* along the castle wall

7

城 1079 / F423 See **城** 1078.

恚 1080 / F706 I anger. [心]

埃 1081 / F422 Ai. *hokori* dust. *hokori(ppoi)* dusty.

袁 1082 / F1694 En long kimono. [衣]
9彦道 *engendō* gambling

埓 1083 / F424 **埒** Retsu. Ratsu. Rachi pale, picket; picket fence; limits. *rachi(ga aku)* be settled, come to an end.
5外 *rachigai* beyond bounds, beyond the pale
12無 *rachi (mo) na(i)* absurd, foolish

B **埋** 1084 / F423 Mai. *uzu(maru)*, *u(maru)* be filled up, be buried, be imbedded in. *uzu(meru)*, *u(meru)* bury, inter, fill up, pour in, plug up, inlay; make up for. *i(keru)* bury (in the ground); bank (a fire). *uzu(moreru)*, *u(moreru)* be buried, be covered; live in obscurity.
4火 *uzu(mi)bi* banked fire
込 *i(ke)-ko(mu)* bury in the ground
木 *u(me)ki* wood inlay; wooden plug; filling crack or hole with wood. *u(more)gi* lignite, bogwood, fossil wood
木細工 *u(me)kizaiku* mosaic in wood

5穴 *u(me)ana* hole for burying things; a loss to be made up
立 *u(me)-ta(teru)* reclaim, fill in, fill up. *ume-ta(te)* reclamation, filling in
立地 *umetatechi* reclaimed land
6地 *u(me)chi* reclaimed land
合 *u(me)-a(waseru)* make amends, compensate for
伏 *maifuku suru* lie concealed, lie in ambuscade
伏歯 *maifukushi* impacted tooth
7没 *maibotsu suru, maimotsu suru* be buried, be entombed; remain obscure
9炭 *ikezumi* banked charcoal fire
草 *u(me)kusa* padding, stuffing, filler
10骨 *maikotsu* interring the bones
11設 *maisetsu suru vt* lay underground
12湯 *u(me)yu* bath which has been cooled down
葬 *maisō* burial, interment
替 *u(me)-ka(eru)* rebury, reinter
13溝 *u(me)mizo* underground sewer
14樋 *uzu(mi)doi* underground drain
蔵 *maizō suru* burying or hiding underground
蔵地帯 *maizō chitai* mine field
蔵物 *maizōbutsu* buried treasure
蔵量 *maizōryō* amount of underground deposits
15線 *maisen* underground cable

8

塔 See 1110.

堊 See 59.

堂 See 1365.

域 1085/F424 IKI region; limits; stage, level.
B
4内 *ikinai* inside the area
5外 *ikigai* outside the area

埦 1086/F-X WAN bowl.

埵 1087/F425 TA hard soil.

埼 1088/F427 KI. *saki* cape, spit, promontory.

埠 1089/F425 FU wharf.
16頭 *futō* wharf, pier, quay

埴 1090/F425 SHOKU. *hani, hena* clay.
8土 *henatsuchi, hanatsuchi* clay
5生宿 *ha-nyū (no) yado* a humble house
15輪 *haniwa* ancient clay images buried with the dead

培 1091/F426 BAI. Hō. *tsuchika(u)* cultivate, foster.
B
6地 *baichi* bacteria culture medium
11強 *tsuchika(i)-tsuyo(meru)* foster, develop and strengthen
15養 *baiyō* cultivation, nurture, culture

堕 1092/F440 **墮** DA. *da(suru)* descend to, lapse into, degenerate.
B
2力 *daryoku* inertia, momentum, force of habit
9胎 *datai* miscarriage, abortion
12落 *daraku* depravity, corruption, degradation, delinquency, apostasy, degeneration
落的 *darakuteki* depraved, corrupt, degenerate, apostatized
13罪 *dazai* the fall of man

壷 1093/F447 **壺** Ko. *tsubo* jar, pot; hinge knuckle; one's aim. [士]
3口 *tsuboguchi* jar mouth
8金 *tsubogane* hinge knuckle
11瓶 *tsubogame* night-soil receptacle
12焼 *tsuboyaki* shellfish cooked in the shell
28鑿 *tsubo nomi* hollow chisel

堆 1094/F428 TAI. *uzutaka(i)* piled high.
3土 *taido* mound
5石 *taiseki* moraine
8肥 *taihi, tsumigoe* compost, barnyard manure
11雪 *taisetsu* snowdrift
16積 *taiseki* accumulation, pile, heap

堀 1095/F427 KUTSU. *hori* moat, canal, ditch.
P
3川 *horikawa* canal
4井戸 *hori ido* bored well
5出物 *horida(shi)mono* a rare find; a bargain; a treasue trove
6江 *horie* canal
10留 *horido(me)* ditch end
12割 *horiwa(ri)* canal, dock, ditch
14端 *horibata* edge of the moat

堅 1096/F428 KEN. *kata(i)* hard, solid; tough, rigid; tight; steady, firm; strict; safe, reliable, upright; chaste, constant; stiff; bookish; classical; stubborn. *tate no* longitudinal; lengthwise; vertical, perpendicular.
B
2人 *katajin* steady person, honest man
4木 *katagi* hardwood, oak
太 *katabuto(ri)* solidly built (person)
5田 *katada* hard dry rice field

3 口囗[土士]8 夂夊夕大女子宀寸小⺌尢尸屮山川巛工己巾干幺广廴廾弋弓彐彑彡彳

穴 *tateana* pit; mine shaft; mine pit; ancient dwelling site
甲利兵 *kenkō-rihei* strong armor and sharp weapons
6 気 *katagi na* honest, upright, steady
守 *kenshu* strong defense; strict observation (of rules)
7 志 *kenshi* iron purpose
牢 *kenrō* solidity, stability, durability
忍 *kennin* perseverance, fortitude
忍不抜 *kennin fubatsu* perseverance, fortitude
忍持久 *kennin-jikyū* untiring perseverance
8 固 *kengo na* strong, solid, secure, firm
肥 *katabuto(ri) no* solidly built (person)
実 *kenjitsu na* steady, sound, reliable
岩 *kengan* solid rock
苦 *katakuru(shii)* formal; punctilious; awkward
果 *kenka* nut
果油 *kenkayu* nut oil
9 造 *katazō* honest man, steady person
城 *kenjō* strong fortress
持 *kenji suru* hold on to, stick to
陣 *kenjin* stronghold
炭 *katazumi* hard charcoal
信礼 *kenshinrei* (Christian) confirmation
10 框 *tate-gamachi* vertical door frame
11 魚 *katsuo* bonito
12 棧 *tatesan* vertical framework
塁 *kenrui* stronghold
13 塩 *katashio* rock salt
塞 *kensai* strong fort
14 樋 *tate-doi* vertical drainpipe
20 艦 *kenkan* powerful battleship
23 罐 *tatekama* vertical cylindrical boiler

B **執** 1097/F425 SHITSU. SHŪ. *to(ru)* (See under 取 3699.0). *shis(suru)* take, hold, grasp; take to heart; form an attachment; persist in.

2 刀 *shittō* operating (in a hospital)
刀者 *shittōsha* operating surgeon
4 心 *shūshin* devotion, attachment, infatuation
6 成 *to(ri)-na(su)* mediate, intervene, intercede for, recommend. *to(ri)na(shi)* arrangement; influence; mediation, intercession; good offices
成人 *to(ri)na(shi)bito* intercessor, mediator
成手 *to(ri)na(shi)te* intercessor, mediator
行 *to(ri)-okona(u)*＝*okona(u)* (see under 行 4213.0). *shikkō* performance
行吏 *shikkōri* bailiff, process server
行委員 *shikkō i-in* executive committee; executive officer
行委員会 *shikkō i-inkai* executive committee
行停止 *shikkō teishi* stay of execution; stopping operations
行猶予 *shikkō yūyo* stay of execution, suspended sentence
行権 *shikkōken* executive authority
行機関 *shikkō kikan* executive organ
8 拗 *shitsuyō* obstinacy, persistence
念 *shūnen* tenacity; implacability
念深 *shūnembuka(i)* unforgiving, revengeful, vindictive; tenacious
事 *shitsuji* steward, deacon
事職 *shitsujishoku* office of deacon
9 政 *shissei* government, ruler, minister of state
奏 *shissō suru* transmit to the emperor
11 著 *shūchaku*＝執着 (see below–12)
達 *shittatsu* relaying a superior's words
達吏 *shittatsuri* bailiff, process server
務 *shitsumu* discharging one's office duties
務心得 *shitsumu kokoroe* office rules
務時間 *shitsumu jikan* office hours
12 着 *shūchaku, shūjaku* attachment, adhesion, tenacity
着心 *shūchakushin* persistence
筆 *shippitsu* writing
筆中 *shippitsuchū* now being written
筆者 *shippitsusha* writer, author
筆料 *shippitsuryō* writing fee
13 意 *shitsui* obstinacy, persistence in opinions
15 権 *shikken* regent
権職 *shikkenshoku* regency

A **基** 1098/F426 KI radical (in chemistry); counter for lanterns, wreaths, motors, silos, and heavy machines; foundation; fundamentals; basis. *motoi, moto* basis, foundation, origin. *motozu(ku)* be based on, be founded on.

5 石 *kiseki* cornerstone, foundation stone
本 *kihon* basis, standard
本代謝 *kihon taisha* basic metabolism
本金 *kihonkin* foundation, endowment fund
本的 *kihonteki* basic, fundamental, standard
本的人権 *kihonteki jinken* basic human rights
本協定 *kihon kyōtei* basic agreement, a formula
本英語 *Kihon Eigo* Basic English
本科目 *kihon kamoku* basic subjects
本単位 *kihon tan-i* official standards for weights and measurements
本原理 *kihon genri* basic principles
本財産 *kihon zaisan* endowment, permanent property
本産業 *kihon sangyō* basic industries
本給 *kihonkyū* basic salary or wages
本賃金 *kihon chingin* basic wage
6 色 *kishoku* ground color
因 *ki-in* cause
地 *kichi* base
7 形 *kikei* basic type
8 金 *kikin* fund, endowment, foundation

底 *kitei* base, basis, foundation
肥 *kihi, motogoe* initial fertilizing
岩 *kigan* bedrock
性岩 *kiseigan* basic rocks
9音 *kion* fundamental tone
点 *kiten* cardinal point
型 *kikei* basic type
10部 *kibu* base, pedestal, foundation
11脚 *kikyaku* base
13数 *kisū* cardinal number
幹 *kikan* mainstay, nucleus
準 *kijun* standard, basis, norm, criterion
準化 *kijunka* normalization, standardization
督 *Kirisuto* Christ, Messiah
督者 *Kirisutosha* a Christian
督教 *Kirisutokyō* Christianity
督教化 *Kirisutokyōka suru* Christianize, evangelize
督教国 *Kirisutokyōkoku* a Christian country
15線 *kisen* base line; base of a triangle
盤 *kiban* base, foundation, basis
調 *kichō* keynote, basis
調演説 *kichō enzetsu* keynote address
18礎 *kiso* foundation, base, basis
礎工事 *kiso kōji* foundation work
礎代謝 *kiso taisha* basic metabolism
礎杭 *kisogui* foundation piling
礎的 *kisoteki* fundamental, basic
礎音 *kiso-on* fundamental tone
礎科学 *kiso kagaku* basic science
礎原価 *kiso genka* first cost
礎控除 *kiso kōjo* basic deduction
礎産業 *kiso sangyō* basic industry

9

埊 See 3009.

壺 1099 / F447 See 壷 1093. [士]

壹 1100 / F447 See 壱 1059. [士]

堺 1101 / F432 / F1272 See 界 2998.

壻 1102 / F447 See 婿 1239. [士]

塀 1103 / F-X See 塀 1131.

塚 1104 / F-X See 塚 1120.

堝 1105 / F429 Ka crucible, melting pot.

堙 1106 / F429 In close up, stop up.
13滅 *immetsu* extinction, destruction, suppression

堡 1107 / F429 Ho, Hō fort.
12塁 *hōrui, horui* fort, stronghold

堤 B 1108 / F430 Tei *tsutsumi* dike, bank, embankment.
3上 *teijō* on the bank
6防 *teibō* bank, dike, levee
防伝 *teibōzuta(i)* along the dike

塔 B 1109 / F433 Tō tower, pagoda, steeple, obelisk, monument.
9型 *tōgata* tower or steeple type
11婆 *tōba* wooden grave tablet; stupa; pagoda

堵 1110 / F432 To fence, railing, enclosure; dwelling.
6列 *toretsu* line (of men)
列兵 *toretsuhei* soldiers drawn up

堰 1111 / F430 En. *se(ku)* dam up; check, stop, prevent. *seki* dam, embankment
4止 *se(ki)-to(meru)* intercept, check; dam up
止湖 *sekito(me)ko* dammed-up lake
12堤 *entai* dike, weir

堪 B 1112 / F430 Kan. *ta(eru)* endure; support; withstand, resist, brave, weather; be fit for, be equal to. *ko(raeru)* endure; tolerate; control, stifle; pardon. *kota(eru)* endure. *tama(ranai)* be unbearable; be "dying" to (do something).
4切 *ta(e)-ki(reru), kora(e)-ki(reru)* endure to the end, bear up. *kora(e)-ki(renai), ta(e)-ki(renai)* be unable to stand it any longer
7忍 *kannin* pardon; patience, patient endurance. *ta(e)-shino(bu)* endure, bear patiently
忍袋 *kannimbukuro* patience
8性 *kora(e)shō* patience
10兼 *tama(ri)-ka(neru), ta(e)-ka(neru), kora(e)-ka(neru)* be unable to endure, lose one's patience; give way
能 *tannō, kannō* skill, mastery; sufficiency
航能力 *tankō nōryoku* navigability
18難 *ta(e)gata(i), kora(e)gata(i)* unbearable, intolerable

場 A 1113 / F431 **塲** Jō place, grounds, links, range, course, track, ring. *ba* place, site; space; seat; scene; occasion, situation.
4内 *jōnai* within the grounds or hall

5 代 *badai* admission fee
末 *basue* outskirts, suburbs
外 *jōgai* outside the premises; outside the market, on the curb; over the fence
外本塁打 *jōgai honruida* home run over the fence
外取引所 *jōgai torihikisho* curb market
6 合 *ba-ai* occasion, circumstances, case
当 *ba-a(tari)* applause-seeking, sensational (speech)
8 所 *basho* place, area, locality, quarter; position, location; seat, site; scene; room, space; experiences; wrestling match
所柄 *bashogara* character of a place, location, situation; occasion
所塞 *bashofusa(gi)* an obstacle
所踏 *basho (o) fu(mu)* gain experience
9 面 *bamen* place, scene, spectacle
後 *baoku(re)* stage fright; nervousness
10 席 *baseki* room, space; seat, place
11 違 *bachiga(i)* wrong place, different place
12 裡 *-jōri* arena (of competition)
13 馴 *banare* experience
数 *bakazu* experience; many places
塞 *bafusa(gi)* stopgap, space filler; useless
14 磁石 *bajishaku* field magnet ⌊thing

報 1114 / F430 A Hō news, report; reward, retribution. *hō(jiru)*, *hō(zuru)* repay, requite; report, inform, disseminate. *muku(iru)* reward, compensate; repay; revenge. *muku(i)* reward; retribution. *shirase* (see under 知 3169.0).

5 本反始 *hōhon-hanshi* repaying our debt of gratitude to our ancestors
6 返 *muku(i)-kae(su)* requite ⌈statement
7 告 *hōkoku* report, information, returns,
告者 *hōkokusha* reporter, informer
告書 *hōkokusho* written statement, written
告簿 *hōkokubo* report book ⌊report
8 国 *hōkoku* patriotism, national service
知 *hōchi* news, report, intelligence, infor-
知機 *hōchiki* alarm, communicator ⌊mation
10 恩 *hōon* repaying kindness, gratitude
11 捨 *hōsha* recompense, requital of a favor
道 *hōdō*=*hōchi* 報知 (see above–8)
道陣 *hōdōjin* a camp of reporters waiting for news; the news front
12 復 *hōfuku* retaliation, revenge
答 *hōtō* answer, reply ⌈fee, pay, salary
13 酬 *hōshū* remuneration, reward, honorarium,
酬目当 *hōshū mea(te)* desire for gain
奨 *hōshō* compensation
奨金 *hōshōkin* cash bonus, reward, bounty
奨物質 *hōshō busshi* grant to encourage production
14 徳 *hōtoku* requital of kindness
15 賞 *hōshō* prize, reward
17 謝 *hōsha* recompense, requital of a favor
償 *hōshō* reward, compensation, remuneration ⌈production
償物資 *hōshō busshi* grant to encourage

喜 1115 / F371 A Ki. *yoroko(bu)* rejoice, be glad, be pleased. *yoroko(basu)* gladden, please, make happy. *yoroko(bi)* joy, delight, pleasure. *yoroko(bashii)* joyful, glad, pleasant. [口]

6 色 *kishoku* joyful countenance ⌈with joy
迎 *yoroko(bi)-muka(eru)* welcome, receive
叫 *yoroko(bi)-sa(kebu)* shout for joy
字祝 *ki(no)ji (no) iwai* 77th birthday cele-
7 走 *yoroko(bi)-hashi(ru)* run for joy ⌊bration
寿 *kiju* 77th birthday
寿祝 *kiju (no) iwai* 77th birthday celebra-
8 雨 *kiu* good rain ⌊tion
呼 *yoroko(bi)-yo(bawaru)* shout for joy
受 *yoroko(bi)-u(keru)* gladly accept ⌈affair
事 *yoroko(bi)goto* happy event, pleasant
9 祝 *yoroko(bi)-iwa(u)* joyously celebrate
勇 *yoroko(bi)-isa(mu)* be in high spirits, be
怒 *kido* joy and anger ⌊cheerful
怒哀楽 *kido-airaku* joy and anger, feelings
10 悦 *kietsu* gladness, delight
11 捨 *kisha* charity, donation
12 喜 *kiki(taru)* gleeful, joyful ⌈meet with joy
集 *yoroko(bi)-tsudo(u)*, *yoroko(bi)-atsu(maru)*
13 楽 *yoroko(bi)-tano(shimu)* rejoice and be happy. *kiraku* joy, pleasure
誇 *yoroko(bi)-hoko(ru)* exult
14 踊 *yoroko(bi)-odo(ru)* dance for joy
歌 *yoroko(bi)-uta(u)* rejoice and sing
歌劇 *kikageki* comic opera
15 劇 *kigeki* comedy
憂 *kiyū* joy and sorrow, weal and woe

— 10 —

墓 See 4027.

塞 See 1324.

塙 1116 / F434 Kaku. Kō. *hanawa* projecting tableland, projecting mountain.

塒 1117 / F432 Shi. Ji. *negura* roost. *toya* hen coop; roost; actor's rest room *toguro* coil, spiral.

塋 1118 / F432 Ei cemetery.

11 域 *ei-iki* cemetery

塘 1119 F434 Tō dike, embankment.
11 鳥 *garanchō* pelican

塚 1120 F434 F214 冢塜 Chō. *tsuka* mound, hillock, tumulus.
5 穴 *tsuka ana* grave

B 塑 1121 F432 So modeling, molding.
9 造 *sozō* modeling, molding
造芸術 *sozō geijutsu* plastic arts
14 像 *sozō* plaster image, clay figure, plastic image

B 塊 1122 F432 Kai lump, chunk, clod, mass, clot, ingot. *katamari* lump, chunk, clod, mass; clump, cluster, group; flock; bigotry; personification (of). *-kure* lump, clod.
3 土 *kaido* lump of earth
7 状 *kaijō no* massive
8 茎 *kaikei* tuber
9 炭 *kaitan* lump coal
10 根 *kaikon* tuberous root
13 鉱 *kaikō* lump ore
16 鋼 *kaikō* steel ingot

塡 1123 F434 Ten. *ha(maru)*, *ha(meru)* (see under 嵌 1432.0.).
4 込 *ha(me)-ko(mu)*=*ha(meru)* (see under 嵌 1432.0). *hama(ri)-ko(mu)* telescope, fall into, get into (trouble), be infatuated with; be addicted to
6 充 *tenjū suru* fill up, plug, stuff, tamp, calk
材 *tenzai* filler, filling matter
12 湯 *umeyu* bath which has been cooled down
補 *tempo suru* fill up; compensate for, make good; replenish, complete
13 隙 *tengeki* calking, filling
塞 *tensoku suru* fill up, stop up

B 塗 1124 F433 To. *nu(ru)* paint; plaster; daub, lacquer. *mabu(su)* smear, sprinkle or cover with. *mabu(reru)*, *mami(reru)* be covered or smeared with. *nu(ri)* coating, lacquering, varnishing, painting; lacquered.
3 工 *tokō* painter, plasterer
上 *nu(ri)-a(geru)* finish painting or lacquering
4 方 *nu(ri)kata* way to paint
5 立 *nu(ri)-ta(teru)* put on thick make-up. *nu(ri)ta(te) no* newly painted or plastered
付 *nu(ri)-tsu(keru)* daub, smear
布 *tofu suru* apply (ointment)
6 机 *nu(ri)zukue* lacquered table
8 板 *nu(ri)-ita* blackboard
油 *toyu* unction, act of anointing
物 *nurimono* lacquerware
抹 *tomatsu suru* paint over, smear, paint out
抹剤 *tomatsuzai* liniment, ointment
9 屋 *nu(ri)ya* lacquerer
柄 *nu(ri)e* lacquered handle
盆 *nu(ri)bon* lacquered tray
炭 *totan* misery, distress
炭苦 *totan no kuru(shimi)* very sad situation
10 師 *nu(ri)shi* lacquerer
消 *nu(ri)-ke(su)* paint out
料 *toryō* paints
12 椀 *nu(ri)wan* lacquered bowl
絵 *nu(ri)e* a picture-card for coloring
散 *nu(ri)-chi(rasu)* besmear, daub all over
替 *nu(ri)-ka(eru)* repaint
装 *tosō* painting, coating
装店 *tosōten* painter's shop
装屋 *tosōya* painter
13 隠 *nu(ri)-kaku(su)* cover up
15 潰 *nu(ri)-tsubu(su)* paint out
箸 *nu(ri)bashi* lacquered chopsticks
16 薬 *nu(ri)gusuri* liniment, ointment
壁 *nu(ri)kabe* plastered wall
17 擦 *tosatsu* rubbing and smearing
擦剤 *tosatsuzai* liniment
22 籠 *nu(ri)-ko(meru)* hide and plaster over

A 塩 1125 F435 F2153 塩鹽 En salt. *shio* salt; seasoning.
2 入 *shio-i(re)* salt shaker
4 引 *shiobi(ki)* salt-cured; salted fish
分 *embun* salt, salinity
水 *ensui, shio mizu* brine, salt water
水風呂 *shiomizuburo* salt-water bath
5 田 *enden* salt field, salt farm
圧 *shio-o(shi)* pickling salted vegetables under a weight
汁 *shiojiru* salt water, brine
出 *shioda(shi) suru* steep out the salt
加減 *shio kagen* seasoning
6 米 *embei* salt and rice; the necessities of life
気 *shioke* saltiness
地 *shiochi, shioji*, salty wasteland
7 豆 *shio mame* salted beans
辛 *shiokara* salted fish; salted fish entrails. *shiokara(i)* salty, brackish
辛声 *shiokaragoe* hoarse voice
8 味 *shio aji* seasoning
性 *ensei* salinity, saltiness
物 *shiomono* salted fish
9 海 *Shio (no) Umi* the Salt Sea, the Dead Sea
泉 *ensen* salt spring
10 梅 *ambai* seasoning; conditon; manner; state of health
浜 *shiohama* salt farm
釜 *shiogama* salt pan

害 *engai* salt-air damage
素 *enso* chlorine
素酸 *ensosan* chloric acid
11魚 *shiozakana* salted fish
豚 *shio buta* salt pork
断 *shioda(chi)* salt-free diet
基 *enki* base (in chemistry)
乾 *shioboshi, enkan* salted and dried
12揉 *shiomomi* squeezing vegetables limp in salt
湯 *shioyu* hot salt water; hot salt-water bath
焼 *shioyaki* fish broiled with salt; boiling off sea water to make salt
税 *enzei* salt tax
蒸 *shiomu(shi)* salting and steaming
煮 *shioni* boiled salted fish
13煙 *shio kemuri* smoke from the salt furnaces
鉱 *enkō* salt mine
塩梅 *shio ambai* seasoning
14漬 *shiozuke* pickling in salt
酸 *ensan* hydrochloric acid
蔵 *enzō suru* preserve in salt
17餡 *shio an* salty bean jam
鮭 *shiozake, shiojake* salted salmon
18類 *enrui* salts

11

塵 See 5376.

墨 See 5404.

塲 1126 / F431 See 場 1113.

臺 1127 / F1564 See 台 848. [至]

壽 1128 / F448 See 寿 194. [士]

墮 1129 / F440 See 堕 1092.

墟 1130 / F439 墟 Kyo, Ko ruins.

塀 1131 / F437 塀 (国字) Hei wall, fence.
12越 *heigo(shi) ni* over the fence
13際 *heigiwa de* by the fence

墜 1132 / F437 Tsui fall.
B
3下 *tsuika* fall
6死 *tsuishi suru* fall to one's death
12落 *tsuiraku suru*, fall, crash

塾 1133 / F436 Juku private school; boarding school; gate house.
5生 *jukusei* private-school student
8長 *jukuchō* private-school principal
16頭 *jukutō* private-school principal; private-school student leader

塹 1134 / F436 Zan moat, ditch.
17壕 *zangō* trench, dugout
壕工事 *zangō kōji* trench building
壕生活 *zangō seikatsu* trench warfare
壕戦 *zangōsen* trench warfare
壕熱 *zangō netsu* trench fever

A **境** 1135 / F436 境 Kyō, Kei boundary; region; condition; stage.
sakai boundary, border, frontier; place.
3土 *kyōdo* national boundaries, national territory
4内 *keidai* compound, grounds, precincts
5目 *sakaime* border, boundary line; crisis
6地 *kyōchi* feelings; sphere; place; viewpoint
9界 *kyōkai* boundary, limits, frontier; environment determined by karma; environment; rank. *keikai* border
界標 *kyōkaihyō* landmark, boundary stone
界線 *kyōkaisen* boundary line
10致 *keichi* scenery of the area
11遇 *kyōgū* environment, circumstances
域 *kyōiki* boundary; precincts
涯 *kyōgai* environment, circumstances, one's lot, in life

嘉 1136 / F379 Ka. *yomi(suru)* applaud, praise, esteem, appreciate, approve of. [口]
4手 *kashu* skilled calligrapher
日 *kajitsu* auspicious day, good day
月 *kagetsu* auspicious month; beautiful moonlight; lunar 3rd month
木 *kaboku* beautiful trees
5礼 *karei* congratulatory ceremony
卉 *kaki* beautiful trees and plants
6兆 *kachō* auspicious omen
7言 *kagen* wise saying
辰 *kashin* lucky day, auspicious occasion
8例 *karei* happy precedent
味 *kami* fine taste
尚 *kashō* friendship; respect
典 *katen* congratulatory ceremony
事 *kaji* happy event
10祥 *kashō* good omen
納 *kanō suru* approve, appreciate, accept (a gift)
13瑞 *kazui* good omen
節 *kasetsu* auspicious occasion

15 儀 *kagi* auspicious occasion
調 *kachō* good tune
賞 *kashō* approval
17 齢 *karei* a long happy life

A **増** 1137 / F438 **增** Zō increase. *masa(ru)*, *ma(su)* *vt* increase, add to, augment, gain; promote (health); enlarge, extend. *vi* increase. *fuga(su)* *vt* increase. *fue(ru)* *vi* increase. *ma(shi)* increase, extra; every (day). *ma(shi) na* better.

3 上慢 *zōjōman* bragging about one's strength
大 *zōdai suru* increase, enlarge, enhance
大号 *zōdaigō* enlarged issue (of a magazine)
4 水 *ma(shi)mizu* increase in the volume of water. *zōsui suru* rise, swell, flood
5 加 *zōka suru*, *ma(shi)-kuwa(waru)* *vi* increase, multiply. *ma(shi)-kuwa(eru)* *vt* increase, add, multiply. *zōka* increase, addition
収 *zōshū* increased yield, increased income
刊 *zōkan* special number
刊号 *zōkangō* special number (of a magazine)
6 血 *zōketsu suru* make blood
7 兵 *zōhei* reinforcements
8 長 *zōchō suru* grow presumptuous, get puffed up
刷 *zōsatsu* additional printing
注 *zōchū* additional notes
版 *zōhan* enlarged edition
9 派 *zōha* reinforcements
音 *zōon* sound amplification
音器 *zōonki* sound amplifier
発 *zōhatsu suru* increase (a bond) issue; put on an extra train
発列車 *zōhatsu ressha* extra train
10 進 *zōshin suru* promote, increase, advance
俸 *zōhō* salary increase
配 *zōhai* increased ration; bonus; increased dividends
員 *zōin* personnel increase
11 強 *zōkyō suru* augment, reinforce, increase
設 *zōsetsu* building enlargement, additional installations
産 *zōsan* production increase
12 殖 *zōshoku suru* increase, multiply, propagate
減 *zōgen* increase and decrease, rise and fall
税 *zōzei* tax increase
結 *zōketsu* adding extra (coaches)
給 *zōkyū* wage increase
補 *zōho* enlargement, supplement
量 *zōryō* quantity increase
援 *zōen* reinforcement
援部隊 *zōem-butai* reinforcements
幅 *zōfuku* amplification (in electricity)
幅装置 *zōfuku sōchi* amplifier
幅器 *zōfukuki* amplifier
13 置 *zōchi suru* establish more (offices)
資 *zōshi* capital increase
14 徴 *zōchō* imposition of extra taxes
16 築 *zōchiku suru* extend (a building)
18 額 *zōgaku* increased amount

12

墨 See **墨** 5404.

增 1138 / F438 See **増** 1137.

墟 1139 / F439 See **墟** 1130.

賣 1140 / F1801 **賣** See **売** 1067. [貝]

B **墳** 1141 / F440 Fun mound; tomb.
18 墓 *fumbo* grave, tomb
墓地 *fumbo (no) chi* native country

13

壅 See 332.

隷 See 5026. [隶]

B **墾** 1142 / F441 Kon *ha(ru)* open up farmland.
5 田 *konden, harita* new rice fields

P **壌** 1143 / F445 **壤** Jō earth, soil.
3 土 *jōdo* soil

墻 1144 / F441 / F1212 **牆** Shō. *kaki* fence, hedge, wall.
16 壁 *shōheki* fence and wall; fence; wall

墺 1145 / F441 Ō land, shore; Austria.
4 太利 *Ōstoria* Austria
6 匈国 *Ōkyōkoku* Austria-Hungary
8 国 *Ōkoku* Austria

B **壇** 1146 / F442 **壇** Dan stage, rostrum, dais; terrace; altar; world (of literature, etc.)
3 上 *danjō* on the platform; on the stage; on the altar
10 家 *danka* families which are temple supporters
12 場 *danjō* stage

3 ロ 口 [土 士] 夂 夊 夕 大 女 子 宀 寸 小 ⺍ 尢 尸 屮 山 川 巛 工 己 巾 干 幺 广 廴 廾 弋 弓 彐 彑 彡 彳
13

B 壊 1147/F444 壞 E. Kai break. *kowa(su)* break; destroy; tear up; crack; smack; mar. *kowa(reru)* be broken; be demolished; fall into ruin.

6血病 *kaiketsubyō* scurvy
7乱 *kairan* corruption, demoralization, subversion, disturbance, destruction
9変 *kaihen* disintegration (of elements)
10疽 *eso* gangrene
残 *kaizan* being broken up and ruined
12廃 *kaihai* ruin, decay
13滅 *kaimetsu* destruction, annihilation

B 壁 1148/F441 Heki wall; lining (of the stomach); fence; partition. *kabe* wall.

1一重 *kabehitoe=kabedonari* 壁隣 (see below–14)
3土 *kabetsuchi* wall mud, plaster, stucco
5立 *hekiritsu* precipitous; nothing but four empty walls
7床 *kabedoko* ornamental alcove
8板 *kabe ita* wainscoting
画 *hekiga* fresco, wall painting; picture hanging on a wall
10紙 *kabegami* wallpaper
書 *kabega(ki), hekisho* ancient laws posted on walls
11掛 *kabeka(ke)* tapestry
寄 *kabeyo(ri) ni* by the wall
12間 *hekikan* between the walls; on the wall
越 *kabego(shi) ni* with a wall between
訴訟 *kabe soshō* grumbling to oneself
13際 *kabegiwa ni* near the wall
塗 *kabenu(ri)* plastering
新聞 *kabe shimbun* wall newssheet (often handwritten)
14隣 *kabedonari* neighbor with just a wall between
22龕 *hekigan* niche, recess

14

壓 壓 See 圧 818.

壔 1149/F443 Tō cylinder; fort.

壑 1150/F442 Gaku, Kaku valley.

壕 1151/F443 Kō. Gō trench, dugout, air-raid shelter. *hori* moat; ditch; canal.

15

壘 See 塁 3009.

壙 1152/F444 Kō hole.

5穴 *kōketsu* grave, tomb

翹 1153/F1511 Gyō excellence. [羽]

11望 *gyōbō* hope, expectancy

16

壞 1154/F-X See 壊 1147.

壠 1155/F445 F444 See 壟 5441.

壜 1156/F444 罎 Don. *bin* bottle, vial, jar.

2入 *bin-i(ri) no* bottled
5代 *bindai* charge for the bottle
13詰 *binzume no* bottled

17

壤 1157/F445 See 壌 1143.

19

蠹 1158/F1679 蠧 To worm-eaten; damage; wicked person. [虫]

8毒 *todoku suru* demoralize
11魚 *shimi* clothes moth, silverfish, bookworm
13賊 *tozoku suru* smash up

25

豔 1159/F1779 F1581 See 艶 3890. [豆]

RAD. 士 33

Samurai warrior. Except for the radical character itself, entered below, this radical is treated herein as a variant of Rad. 32. Nickname: Samurai.

A 士 1160/F445 Shi samurai; man, gentleman; scholar. *samurai* samurai, knight. *-shi* suffix for academic degrees

2人 *shijin* samurai
3女 *shijo* men and women
4分 *shibun* samurai status, samurai class

5 民 *shimin* all classes of people; the people
6 気 *shiki* morale; martial spirit
7 君子 *shikunshi* gentleman, man of honor
8 卒 *shisotsu* private, soldier
官 *shikan* (military or naval) officer
官学校 *Shikan Gakkō* Military Academy
9 風 *shifū* samurai discipline; samurai customs
10 師 *shishi* (ancient) judge
師記 *Shishiki* the Book of Judges
11 道 *shidō* chivalry, knighthood, samurai code
族 *shizoku* descendants of samurai
規 *shiki* rules for samurai
13 農工商 *shi-nō-kō-shō* warriors-farmers-artisans-tradesmen; class distinction
14 魂商才 *shikon-shōsai* gentlemanly spirit and business acumen

RAD. 夂 34

At top: *fuyugashira* (like crown of *fuyu* "winter"). At bottom: *natsu-ashi* (like legs of *natsu* "summer"). As enclosure: 夂 *sui-nyō*. This variant and some of the foregoing terms are actually Rad. 35 but are treated herein as Rad. 34. Nickname: Winter.

2

A **冬** 1161 / F216 冬 Tō *fuyu* winter. *fuyu(meku)* become wintry. [丫]

4 月 *tōgetsu* winter season; winter moon
天 *tōten* wintry sky, wintry weather
日和 *fuyubiyori* a fine winter day
支度 *fuyujitaku* winter preparations
木 *fuyuki, fuyugi, tōboku* deciduous trees in winter
木立 *fuyukodachi* deciduous trees in winter
6 向 *fuyumu(ki) no* for winter
休 *fuyu yasu(mi)* winter vacation, winter holidays
至 *tōji* winter solstice
至点 *tōjiten* winter solstice
至線 *Tōjisen* Tropic of Capricorn
8 物 *fuyumono* winter clothing
服 *fuyufuku* winter clothing
季 *tōki* winter season
空 *fuyuzora* winter sky
芽 *tōga* winter buds
9 枯 *fuyuga(re)* winter decay, winter withering, winter business slump
10 眠 *tōmin* hibernation
宮 *tōkyū* winter palace
将軍 *Fuyu Shōgun* Jack Frost
12 越 *fuyugo(shi)* wintering
場 *fuyuba* winter season
着 *fuyugi* winter clothing
営 *tōei* winter quarters; wintering
期 *tōki* winter season
期間 *tōkikan* winter season
14 構 *fuyugama(e)* preparations for winter
22 籠 *fuyugomori* hibernation, wintering

A **処** 1162 / F1653 處 SHO. *sho(suru)* manage, deal with; sentence, condemn; act, behave; conduct oneself(well). *tokoro* (see under 所 1821.0). *-ka* place. [虍]

3 女 *shojo, otome* virgin, maiden
女地 *shojochi* virgin soil
女作 *shojosaku* one's first published work
女性 *shojosei* virginity, maidenhood
女林 *shojorin* virgin forest
女峰 *shojohō* an unclimbed mountain
女航海 *shojo kōkai* maiden voyage
女期 *shojoki* virginity, maidenhood
女膜 *shojo maku* hymen
4 分 *shobun* disposition of, disposal, management; measure, action; punishment
方 *shohō* prescription, formula
方書 *shohōsho* (doctor's) prescription
方箋 *shohōsen* (doctor's) prescription
5 弁 *shoben*＝*shochi* 処置 (see below–13)
生法 *shoseihō* secret of success
生術 *shoseijutsu* secret of success
処 *shosho* various places. *tokorodokoro* here and there
処方方 *shosho-hōbō* here and there
世 *shosei* conduct of life, getting on
世訓 *shoseikun* rules for living a good life
6 刑 *shokei* (infliction of) punishment, execution
刑台 *shokeidai* gallows
刑法 *shokeihō* means of execution
7 決 *shoketsu* decision, resolution, settlement, determination; resignation
8 法 *shohō* prescription, formula
11 違 *tokorochiga(i)* mistaking the place
遇 *shogū* treatment
理 *shori* procedure, management, treatment. *shori suru* manage, dispose of, settle, adjust
務 *shomu* management of affairs
断 *shodan* judgment, decision
13 置 *shochi* disposal, management; action, measure; treatment
14 罰 *shobatsu* penalty, punishment
罰令 *shobatsurei* penal regulations

— 3 —

A **各** 1163/F328 KAKU each. *ono-ono* each, every, either, respectively. [口]

²人 *kakujin* each individual
⁴戸 *kakko* every door
月 *kakugetsu* every month
方面 *kaku hōmen* every direction; all quarters
⁵処 *kakusho* each place, various places
⁶自 *kakuji* each individual
回 *kakukai* each time
地 *kakuchi* each place; various areas
州 *kakushū* all the provinces, all the states
各 *ono-ono* each, every, either, respectively
各方 *ono-onogata* all of you
⁷位 *kakui* gentlemen, sirs
別 *kakubetsu ni* individually, separately
条 *kakujō* each item
町村 *kakuchōson* each town and village
⁸国 *kakkoku* all countries, various nations, each nation
例 *kakurei* each illustration
所 *kakusho* each place, various places
宗 *kakushū* all sects
⁹面 *kakumen* all phases
通 *kakutsū* each document; each letter
派 *kakuha* each party, all sects, each faction
科 *kakka* each subject, each department
点 *kakuten* each point
界 *kakukai* each field, various circles
巻 *kakkan* each volume
省 *kakushō* each ministry
¹⁰般 *kakuhan no* all, every, various
部 *kakubu* every part; various parts; every department
員 *kakuin* each one
書 *kakusho* each book
個 *kakko* every one, each. *kakko ni* individually, respectively, each
個撃破 *kakko-gekiha* divide and rule
¹¹階 *kakukai* each floor
階止 *kakukaidoma(ri)* stopping at each floor
¹²項 *kakkō, kakukō* each item, each clause
¹⁴層 *kakusō* each stratum; each class
様 *kakuyō* various
種 *kakushu* each kind, all kinds
種学校 *kakushu gakkō* miscellaneous schools
駅 *kakueki* every station
駅停車 *kakueki teisha* local train
¹⁵論 *kakuron* detailed exposition
¹⁸藩 *kakuhan* each clan

— 4 —

麦 See 5385. [麦]

A **条** 1164/F980 **條** Jō article, clause, item; line, stripe, streak; column (of smoke); ray (of light). *kudari* article, clause, paragraph. *-jō* since, because, altho, tho; article (of a document). [木]

⁴文 *jōbun* text, provisions
⁵目 *jōmoku* articles, stipulations
令 *jōrei* law, ordinance, bylaw, rule, regulation
⁶件 *jōken* proviso, stipulation, condition
件付 *jōkentsu(ki)* conditional
⁷条 *jōjō* every item
⁸例 *jōrei* law, ordinance, bylaw, rule
法 *jōhō* itemized regulations
⁹約 *jōyaku* treaty, pact
約国 *jōyakukoku* treaty signatory
約港 *jōyakukō* treaty port
¹¹痕 *jōkon* streak
理 *jōri* logic, reason
規 *jōki* provisions, rules
章 *jōshō* provisions, clauses
¹²項 *jōkō* clause, article, stipulations
款 *jōkan* stipulation, provision, article, clause
¹³鉄 *jōtetsu* bar iron, rod iron
蒔 *sujimaki* drilling, sowing in rows

— 7 —

夏 See 58.

— 12 —

憂 See 70. [心]

— 14 —

螽 1165/F1672 SHŪ grasshopper. [虫]

¹⁸蟖 *kirigirisu* grasshopper, katydid

— 19 —

變 1166/F1772 See 変 306. [言]

夊 RAD. 35

Sui or *yuku* to go. This radical is treated herein as a variant of Rad. 34.
Nickname: Winter Variant.

RAD. 夕 36

Yūbe evening or *ta* (the katakana). Nickname: *Kana Ta.*

A 夕 1167 / F449 SEKI. *yū, yū(be)* evening.

3 山 *yūyama* mountains at evening
4 方 *yūgata, yūkata* evening
日 *yūhi* setting sun
化粧 *yūgeshō* one's evening toilet
月 *yūzuki* evening moon
月夜 *yūzukiyo* moonlit evening
5 立 *yūdachi* sudden shower, evening shower, squall
立雲 *yūdachigumo* a shower cloud
刊 *yūkan* evening paper
刊紙 *yukanshi* evening paper
6 凪 *yūnagi* evening calm
8 拝 *yūhai* vespers, evening worship
泊 *yūdoma(ri)* stopping for the night
波 *yūnami* evening waves
刻 *yūkoku* evening
空 *yūzora* evening sky
河岸 *yūgashi* evening fish market
9 風 *yūkaze* evening breeze
映 *yūbae* sunset glow
虹 *yūniji* evening rainbow
星 *yūzutsu* evening star, Venus
栄 *yūba(e)* sunset glow
食 *yūge, yūshoku* supper, evening meal
食会 *yūshokukai* supper party
食後 *yūshokugo* after supper
10 時雨 *yūshigure* evening shower
11 涼 *yūsuzu(mi)* enjoying the evening cool
陽 *sekiyō* setting sun
12 晴 *yūba(re)* clearing up in the evening
焼 *yūya(ke)* sunset colors
嵐 *yūarashi* evening storm
雲 *yūgumo* evening clouds
間暮 *yūmagu(re)* evening
景 *yūkei* evening
景色 *yūgeshiki* evening scene
飯 *yūhan, yūmeshi* evening meal
飯後 *yūhango* after supper
飯時 *yūhandoki* supper time
13 煙 *yūkemuri, yūkeburi* evening hearth smoke
照 *yūshō* evening glow, afterglow
14 暮 *yūgu(re)* evening
15 餉 *yūge* evening meal
影 *yūkage* evening light; evening shadows
16 曇 *yūgumori* evening cloudiness
17 闇 *yūyami* dusk, twilight
顔 *yūgao* moonflower; bottle gourd
霞 *yūgasumi* evening mist
19 禱 *yūtō* vespers, evening prayers
霧 *yūgiri* evening mist
21 轟 *yūtodoroki* evening noise
24 靄 *yūmoya* evening haze

2

A 外 1168 / F450 GE. GAI outside, without, beside, beyond the scope of. *hazu(su)* take off, remove, unfasten, undo, detach, disconnect, put out of gear; miss, fail; avoid, evade, dodge. *hazu(reru)* be off, come off, be or get out of place, be out of gear, run off the track, slip out or off, be dislocated, be disconnected, be off the hook (a phone), be unbuttoned, be unzipped. *soto* outside, exterior, open air. *hazu(re)* end, verge, extremity, tip; outskirts; miss, failure. *hoka* some other place; outside; the rest. *hoka no* other, another, different. *no hoka ni* with the exception of. *hoka naranu* none other than, nothing but.

2 力 *gairyoku* external force
人 *gaijin* foreigner, alien
人社会 *gaijin shakai* foreign community
人部隊 *gaijimbutai* foreign legion
3 土 *gaido* foreign country, rural area
山 *toyama* the last mountain in a chain; foothills
4 心 *gaishin* double-mindedness
方 *gaihō* outward. *soppo, soppō* the other way, outside, another direction, off to the side
辺 *gaihen* environs, outskirts
5 皮 *gaihi* outer cover, crust, shell, husk, shuck, hull, cuticle, skin
圧 *gaiatsu* external pressure, outside pressure
史 *gaishi* unofficial history
用 *gaiyō* external use
用薬 *gaiyōyaku* external medicine
出 *gaishutsu, sotode* going out, outing, airing
出日 *gaishutsubi* leave day, day off
出中 *gaishutsuchū* while away, while out; out of the office
出好 *gaishutsuzu(ki)* gadabout
出時間 *gaishutsu jikan* leave time
出着 *gaishutsugi* street wear
出嫌 *gaishutsugira(i)* a stay-at-home
出禁止令 *gaishutsu kinshirei* curfew
6 米 *gaimai* foreign rice
衣 *gai-i* outer garment
因 *gai-in* the surface reason
回 *sotomawa(ri)* circumference, perimeter; outside work; circumferential line
気 *gaiki* the air, the open air
伝 *gaiden* a traditional biography

3 口囗土士夂夊【2 夕】大女子宀寸小⺌尢尸屮山川巛工己巾干幺广廴廾弋弓彐彑彡彳

地 *gaichi* overseas territory, outlying territory
灯 *gaitō* outside light
邦 *gaihō* foreign country
夷 *gai-i* foreign barbarians
向性 *gaikōsei* extroversion
曲球 *gaikyokkyū* outcurve (baseball)
耳 *gaiji* external ear
耳炎 *gaiji-en* external otitis
字 *gaiji* characters not among the *Tōyō Kanji*; foreign letters, foreign language
字紙 *gaijishi* foreign-language newspaper
字新聞 *gaiji shimbun* foreign-language newspaper
交 *gaikō* diplomacy, foreign relations
交上 *gaikōjō* diplomatic
交手段 *gaikō shudan* diplomatic measures
交方針 *gaikō hōshin* diplomatic policy
交文書 *gaikō bunsho* diplomatic document
交白書 *gaikō hakusho* diplomatic white paper
交用語 *gaikō yōgo* diplomatic language
交団 *gaikōdan* diplomatic corps
交交渉 *gaikō kōshō* diplomatic negotiations
交攻勢 *gaikō kōsei* diplomatic offensive
交的 *gaikōteki* diplomatic
交官 *gaikōkan* diplomat, diplomatic official
交使節団 *gaikō shisetsudan* diplomatic mission
交界 *gaikōkai* diplomatic circles
交政策 *gaikō seisaku* diplomatic policy, diplomacy
交員 *gaikōin* canvasser, traveling salesman
交家 *gaikōka* diplomat
交術 *gaikōjutsu* diplomacy
交筋 *gaikō suji* foreign-office sources
交辞令 *gaikō jirei* diplomacy, flattery
交関係 *gaikō kankei* foreign relations
交談判 *gaikō dampan* diplomatic negotiations
交機関 *gaikō kikan* diplomatic channels
7 見 *gaiken, sotomi* external appearance
車 *gaisha* foreign automobile
囲 *sotogako(i)* outer fence
局 *gaikyoku* external bureau
廷 *gaitei* emperor's offices; foreign royal court
役 *gaieki* overseas military service
形 *gaikei* external form, externals, appearance
角 *gaikaku* external angle; outside corner (in baseball)
角高目 *gaikaku takame* high on the outside corner of the plate (baseball)
来 *gairai no* foreign, imported
来者 *gairaisha* person from abroad
来患者 *gairai kanja* outpatient
来語 *gairaigo* word of foreign origin
8 侮 *gaibu* ridicule by foreign countries; outside ridicule
使 *gaishi* foreign envoy
姓 *gaisei* mother's family name
姉 *gaishi* wife's elder sister
征 *gaisei* foreign campaign
板 *gaihan* outer shell, outer plate
泊 *gaihaku* overnight stay
法 *sotonori* outside measurements
物 *gaibutsu* the externals, material things; external object, foreign matter
的 *gaiteki* external, exterior, outside
歩 *sotoaru(ki)* going out for a walk
炎 *gaien* outer flame
苑 *gaien* outer garden, outer park
典 *Gaiten* Apocrypha
事 *gaiji* foreign affairs
国 *gaikoku, totsukuni* foreign country; foreign
国人 *gaikokujin* foreigner, alien
国行 *gaikokuyu(ki), gaikokui(ki)* going abroad
国伝道 *gaikoku dendō* foreign missions
国使臣 *gaikoku shishin* foreign envoy
国風 *gaikokufū* foreign style
国為替 *gaikoku kawase* foreign exchange
国租界 *gaikoku sokai* foreign concession
国船 *gaikokusen* foreign ship
国債 *gaikokusai* foreign loan
国語 *gaikokugo* foreign language
9 面 *gaimen* exterior, surface, outside, outward appearance. *tonomo* outside the house
為 *gaitame* foreign exchange
相 *Gaishō* the Foreign Minister
海 *gaikai, soto umi* open sea, the high seas
洋 *gaiyō* ocean, open sea
陣 *gejin, gaijin* transept, room just outside the inner sanctuary of a shrine or temple
政 *gaisei* diplomatic affairs, foreign policies
客 *gaikaku, gaikyaku* tourist, foreign visitor
界 *gaikai* outside world; physical world; the externals
食 *gaishoku* eating out
食券 *gaishokuken* (post-war) rationed meal ticket
祖 *gaiso* mother's parents
祖父 *gaisofu* maternal grandfather
祖母 *gaisobo* maternal grandmother
科 *geka* surgery
科医 *geka-i* surgeon
科的 *gekateki* surgical
科学 *gekagaku* surgery
科結 *geka musu(bi)* surgeon's knot
10 庭 *gaitei, soto niwa* outer court
孫 *gaison* child of a daughter who enters another home
紙 *gaishi* foreign-language newspaper
部 *gaibu* exterior, outside world
套 *gaitō* overcoat, cloak
宮 *Gekū, Gegū* Outer Shrine of Ise
郭 *gaikaku* outer wall; outline; contour
郭団体 *gaikaku dantai* auxiliary organization
11 戚 *gaiseki* maternal relative

道 *gedō* heresy, paganism; heretic, pagan (from the Buddhist standpoint); wicked person
側 *gaisoku, sotogawa* exterior, outside
族 *gaizoku* mother's or wife's relatives
経 *gaikei* outside diameter
船 *gaisen* foreign ship ⌈Buddhist religions
教 *gaikyō* Confucianism and other non-
殻 *gaikaku* shell, crust
商 *gaishō* foreign merchant
寇 *gaikō* foreign invasion
患 *gaikan* foreign troubles, outside troubles
斜視 *gaishashi* walleyed, strabismus
遊 *gaiyū* foreign travel
遊星 *gaiyūsei* outer planet ⌈etry)
接 *gaisetsu suru* be circumscribed (in geom-
接円 *gaisetsuen* circumscribed circle
貨 *gaika* imported goods; foreign money
貨予算 *gaika yosan* foreign-currency con-
貨債 *gaikasai* foreign-currency bond ⌊trol
務 *gaimu* foreign affairs
務大臣 *Gaimu Daijin* the Foreign Minister
務省 *Gaimushō* Foreign Affairs Ministry
務員 *gaimuin* canvasser, commercial travel-
野 *gaiya* outfield ⌊er
野手 *gaiyashu* outfielder
野席 *gaiyaseki* outfield bleachers
野飛球 *gaiya hikyū* fly ball to the outfield
12塀 *sotobei* outer wall
港 *gaikō* outer port
焔 *gaien* outer flame
甥 *gaisei* the wife's brothers
勤 *gaikin* outside duty, canvassing
殼 *gaikaku* shell, crust
塁 *gairui* an outwork (in castle fortifications)
惑星 *gaiwakusei* major planet, outer planet
13廓 *gaikaku* outer wall; outline, contour
債 *gaisai* foreign loan, foreign bond, foreign
傷 *gaishō* external wound ⌊debt
電 *gaiden* foreign cable
業 *gaigyō* field work (in surveying)
蒙 *Gaimō* Outer Mongolia
蒙古 *Soto Mōko* Outer Mongolia
資 *gaishi* foreign capital, foreign money
資導入 *gaishi dōnyū* introduction of
14層 *gaisō* outer layers ⌊foreign capital
聞 *gaibun* reputation, honor; respectability
構 *sotogama(e)* outward structure, external
語 *gaigo* foreign language ⌊appearance
貌 *gaibō* one's looks, external appearance, externals, exterior ⌈gawa daimyo
様 *tozama* outside the group; non-Toku-
様大名 *tozama daimyō* non-Tokugawa daimyo ⌈cle; outside wire
15線 *gaisen* outside telephone line; outer cir-
敵 *gaiteki* foreign enemy
賓 *gaihin* foreign visitor
篇 *gaihen* introductory part of a book
輪 *gairin* paddlewheel
輪山 *gairinzan* the outer crater
輪船 *gairinsen* paddle-wheel steamer
16壁 *gaiheki* outer wall
17濠 *sotobori* outer moat
18観 *gaikan* external appearance, outside view
題 *gedai* title (of a play or book); a play, a piece
20艦 *gaikan* foreign warship ⌈pointed out
鰐 *sotowa, sotowani* walking with the feet

3

夙 See 658.

多 $\frac{1169}{F453}$ 夛 A TA much. *ō(i)* many; copious, abundant; much; frequent. *ta-* many-(sided); multi-; poly-. *ta to suru* appreciate, thank.

2人数 *taninzu* multitude
3大 *tadai* great quantity, great number
小 *tashō*＝多少 (see below–4)
才 *tasai na* talented
士 *tashi* many talented men
士済済 *tashi-seisei* galaxy of able men
4毛 *tamō* hairiness
孔 *takō no* porous; cavernous; open (weave)
分 *tabun* probably, maybe; very likely, presumably; a great deal, a great many
方面 *tahōmen no* various, different, many-
辺形 *tahenkei* polygon ⌊sided, versatile
辺的 *tahenteki* multilateral
孔性 *takōsei* porosity
孔管 *takōkan* perforated pipe
少 *tashō* a little, somewhat, any, some, slightly, more or less. *ō(kare)-sukuna-(kare)* more or less
少縁 *tashō (no) en* some karma from a
元 *tagen* pluralism ⌊previous existence
元描写 *tagembyōsha* descriptions from different viewpoints
元論 *tagenron* pluralism
5用 *tayō* pressure of business
弁 *taben* talkativeness, verbosity
収穫 *tashūkaku* abundant harvest
生 *tashō* transmigration of souls
生縁 *tashō (no) en* karma from a previous
6伐 *tabatsu* overcutting (forests) ⌊existence
忙 *tabō* pressure of work
多 *tata* very many, very much; more and
汗症 *takanshō* excessive sweating ⌊more
血 *taketsu na* hasty
血質 *taketsushitsu no* hasty
年 *tanen* many years

年生 *tanensei* perennial
肉 *taniku* fleshy
肉性 *tanikusei* fleshy, pulpy, succulent
肉果 *tanikuka* pulpy fruit
肉質 *tanikushitsu* fleshy, pulpy, succulent
7 言 *tagen, tagon* loquacity, verbosity; many words
足 *tasoku* multiped
岐 *taki* digression; many branches (of a road); many divergences
技 *tagi* many skills
売 *tabai* large sale, large turnover
芸 *tagei* versatility
作 *tasaku* being prolific in writing
作家 *tasakuka* voluminous writer
形 *takei* multiformity
形性 *takeisei no* multiform
角 *takaku* many-sided, multiple, multilateral, diversified
角形 *takakkei* polygon
角的 *takakuteki* many-sided, versatile, diversified, multilateral
角経営 *takaku keiei* many-sided enterprise
角農業 *takaku nōgyō* diversified farming
8 雨 *ta-u* a heavy rain
幸 *takō* great happiness, good fortune
妻 *tasai* plurality of wives
肢選択法 *tashi-sentakuhō* multiple-choice (test)
事 *taji* eventfulness; storm and stress; press of business
事多端 *taji-tatan no* busy, eventful (life)
9 恨 *takon* many regrets; great discontent
相 *tasō* multiphase
段式 *tadanshiki* multistage (rocket)
型性 *takeisei no* multiform
連装 *tarensō* multibarreled (gun)
面 *tamen* many sides, many phases
面体 *tamentai* polyhedron
音節 *taonsetsu* polysyllable
音節語 *taonsetsugo* polysyllable
重 *tajū* multiplex, multiple
重星 *tajūsei* multiple star
重電信法 *tajū denshinhō* multiplex telegraphy
発式 *tahatsushiki* multiengined
発性 *tahatsusei* multiple (sclerosis)
発機 *tahatsuki* multiengined plane
神教 *tashinkyō* polytheism
神教国 *tashinkyōkoku* pagan countries
神教的 *tashinkyōteki* polytheistic
神教徒 *tashinkyōto* polytheist
神論 *tashinron* polytheism
10 病 *tabyō* frail health
能 *tanō* versatility
座機 *tazaki* multiseated plane
11 過 *ōsu(giru)* be too many, be too much
淫 *ta-in* lasciviousness, lust
彩 *tasai no* colorful, varicolored
望 *tabō* great promise, bright prospects
産 *tasan* fecundity, bearing more than one offspring at a time; productivity
産系 *tasankei* prolific woman
情 *tajō* inconstancy, licentiousness; sentimentalism
情仏心 *tajō-busshin* tenderheartedness
情多恨 *tajō-takon* sentimentality; ardent loves and deep sorrows
情多感 *tajō-takan na* passionate, sentimental
12 量 *taryō* large quantity, a great deal
衆 *tashū* a crowd
項式 *takōshiki* polynomial expression
項選択 *takō-sentaku* multiple-choice (test)
葉飛行機 *tayō hikōki* multiplane
葉機 *tayōki* a multiplane
13 勢 *tazei* a crowd of people, numerical superiority
感 *takan* sensibility, susceptibility, sentimentality
義 *tagi* various meanings
義選択法 *tagi-sentakuhō* multiple-choice (test)
福 *(o)tafuku* plain woman, homely woman
福豆 *(o)tafuku mame* a big broad bean
福風 *(o)tafuku kaze* mumps
数 *tasū* a large number, multitude; majority
数人 *tasūnin* many persons
数決 *tasūketsu* decision by the majority
数国間 *tasūkokukan no* multilateral
数党 *tasūtō* majority party
数票 *tasūhyō* majority vote, plurality
14 聞 *tabun* much information. *tabun no* well-informed
端 *tatan* many items; pressure of business
寡 *taka* quantity, number, amount
様 *tayō* diversity, variety
様性 *tayōsei* diversity, variety
種 *tashu* various kinds, many kinds
種多様 *tashu-tayō na* various, multifarious, diversified
読 *tadoku* extensive reading
読家 *tadokuka* wide reader, well-read man
15 慾 *tayoku* greed, covetousness
趣 *tashu* wide interests (in art, etc.)
趣味 *tashumi* many-sided interests
16 頭 *tatō no* many-headed
17 謝 *tasha* many thanks; a thousand apologies
18 難 *tanan na* full of difficulties, thorny, tumultuous
額 *tagaku* large sum
19 識 *tashiki* extensive knowledge

A **名** 1170* / F333 Myō. Mei distinguished, noted; wise; name. *na* name; fame, reputation; pretext. *na(zukeru)* name, call. *na(ute) no* notorious, famous. *-mei* counter for persons. [口]
2 刀 *meitō* noted sword, fine blade
人 *meijin* master, expert
人肌 *meijinhada* the eccentric spirit of artists
人芸 *meijingei* expert skill

人戦 *meijinsen* chess championship
3 士 *meishi* a celebrity
山 *meizan* famous mountain
工 *meikō* expert artisan
4 手 *meishu* expert
月 *meigetsu* moon of the 15th day of the 8th lunar month and the 13th day of the 9th month ⌈choice wood
木 *meiboku* historic tree; fine incense wood;
分 *meibun* moral duty; justice
文 *meibun* fine prose; beautiful passage
文句 *meimonku* a fine expression; famous
文家 *meibunka* fine writer ⌊words
5 立 *nada(taru)* famous, notorious
句 *meiku* happy expression; famous phrase; wise saying; excellent haiku poem
代 *myōdai* proxy, deputy, representative. *nadai* star (actor), famous, notorious
札 *nafuda* name plate; name card; place card; identification tag
主 *nanushi* (ancient) village head
付 *nazu(keru)* name, call, entitle, christen
付親 *nazu(ke) oya* godparent ⌈nominal
目 *meimoku, myōmoku* title, name; pretext;
目的 *meimokuteki ni* nominally
目論 *meimokuron* nominalism
6 臣 *meishin* illustrious retainer
匠 *meishō* master artisan
成 *na (o) na(su)* become famous
曲 *meikyoku* famous music
号 *myōgō* name of a Buddha or Bodhisattva.
字 *myōji* surname ⌊*meigō* fame
有 *na-a(ru), na(no)a(ru)* famous, notorious
7 医 *mei-i* famous doctor
吟 *meigin* excellent haiku poem
妓 *meigi* famous geisha
折 *na-o(re)* disgrace
状 *meijō suru* describe
売 *na (o) u(ru)* become famous
灸 *meikyū* famous moxa cautery
花 *meika* famous flower
君 *meikun* wise ruler
言 *meigen* beautiful words, famous words
言集 *meigenshū* analects
作 *meisaku* literary masterpiece
作選 *meisakusen* selection of masterpieces
利 *meiri, myōri* wealth and honor
利心 *meirishin* worldly spirit
声 *meisei* fame, reputation
声嘖嘖 *meisei-sakusaku* renowned
告 *nano(ri)*＝名乗 (see below–9)
告出 *nano(ri)-de(ru)* give one's name
告合 *nano(ri)-a(u)* introduce each other
8 門 *meimon* noble or illustrious family
取 *natori* a professional name (in the arts) received from one's teacher
刹 *meisatsu* famous temple
宝 *meihō* rare treasure
所 *meisho* place of interest, beauty spot. *nadokoro* name and address; beauty spot
所旧跡 *meisho-kyūseki* scenic and historic
物 *meibutsu* specialty, noted product ⌊places
物男 *meibutsu otoko* popular figure
画 *meiga* famous picture, masterpiece
画伯 *meigahaku* famous artist
宛 *na-ate* address (on a letter)
宛人 *na-atenin* addressee
実 *meijitsu* name and reality
実共 *meijitsu tomo ni* both in name and in
刺 *meishi* (calling) card ⌊fact
刺入 *meishi-i(re)* card case
刺受 *meishi-u(ke)* card tray
9 香 *meikō* fine incense
城 *meijō* famous castle; sturdy castle
相 *meishō* famous premier; famous minister
前 *namae* name; given name
品 *meihin* perfect article, a gem
茶 *meicha* fine tea
負 *na(ni)o(u), na(nishi)o(u)* (reputation) agrees with facts; be famous
指 *naza(shi)* naming, designation. *naza(su)* name, mention by name
指選 *naza(shi)-era(bu)* designate by name
乗 *nano(ru)* profess to be, introduce oneself as. *nano(ri)* announcing one's candidacy; self-introduction
乗出 *nano(ri)-de(ru)* give one's name
乗合 *nano(ri)-a(u)* introduce each other
10 馬 *meiba* fine horse
高 *nadaka(i)* famous, notorious
酒 *meishu* superior saké ⌈become famous
流 *meiryū* famous people. *na (o) naga(su)*
将 *meishō* famous commander
称 *meishō* name, title, term
剣 *meiken* famous sword; excellent sword
家 *meika* good family; a celebrity, an au-
案 *meian* splendid idea, good plan ⌊thority
辱 *na (o) hazukashi(meru)* lose one's rep- utation ⌈remains, relics
残 *nagori* farewell; keepsake, remembrance;
残惜 *nagori-o(shii)* reluctant to part
11 遂 *nato(geru)* become successful; become famous ⌈one's reputation
惜 *na (o) oshi(mu)* be careful to preserve
訳 *meiyaku* excellent translation
産 *meisan* noted product, specialty
著 *meicho* famous work, masterpiece
望 *meibō* reputation, popularity
望家 *meibōka* popular person, a man highly
12 揚 *na (o) a(geru)* become famous ⌊esteemed
勝 *meishō* scenic spot
詞 *meishi* noun

答 *meitō* right answer, excellent answer
筆 *meihitsu* excellent calligraphy, excellent calligrapher
無 *nana(shi)* nameless, anonymous, un-
13 園 *meien* famous garden ⌊known
僧 *meisō* famous priest
辞 *meiji* term, name
跡 *myōseki* family name
数 *meisū* number of items, articles, etc.; a compound which includes a number
節 *meisetsu* fame and fidelity
義 *meigi* name; justice, moral duty
義人 *meiginin* nominal person
義上 *meigijō no* nominal ⌈tige; honorary
誉 *meiyo* honor, credit, glory; dignity; pres-
誉心 *meiyoshin* desire for fame
誉欲 *meiyoyoku* desire for fame
誉章 *meiyoshō* medal of honor
誉教授 *meiyo kyōju* professor emeritus
誉毀損 *meiyo kison* libel, defamation, slander
誉棄損 *meiyo kison* libel, defamation, ⌈slander
誉慾 *meiyo yoku* desire for fame
誉職 *meiyoshoku* honorary position
14 聞 *meibun, myōmon* fame, honor
説 *meisetsu* excellent idea
歌 *meika* famous poem
歌集 *meikashū* anthology
15 儀 *meigi* name; justice; moral duty
編 *meihen* literary masterpiece
論 *meiron* sound argument, excellent opinion
篇 *meihen* literary masterpiece
器 *meiki* rare utensil, curio
調子 *meichōshi* eloquence
16 親 *naoya, na(zuke)oya* godparent
薬 *meiyaku* famous medicine
17 優 *meiyū* great actor, star ⌈title of a play
18 題 *nadai* star (actor), famous, notorious;
19 簿 *meibo* register of names
22 鑑 *meikan* directory

5

夜 See 298.

10

夢 See 4028.

11

夥 See 120.

RAD. 大 37

Dai large. At top: *dai kashira*. Variant: 大. Nickname: Big.

A 大 1171 / F456 Tai, Dai large, huge, grand; the greater; size; very; inveterate (smoker); severe (damage); success. *ō(kii)* large, great, grand, mighty, immense; severe; heavy. *ō(inaru)* big, large, great. *ō(i)ni* very, much, greatly, exceedingly. *ō(zappana)* rough (estimate); loose (talk); generous. *ō(makana)* rough, (estimate); general, generous. *tai-* big, huge, grand, major. *tai(shita)* many, much, enormous; great, grand; important; serious; severe, intense; very; what a lot of. *ō(ki)ni* greatly, very much. *ō(isa)*, *ō(kisa)* size, dimensions, volume. *tai(shite)* very, much, greatly, seriously. *ō(bira) ni* openly, publicly. *dai(soreta)* ambitious; daring; outrageous, atrocious. *-dai* the size of .... *dai-* great, prominent, large-scale, serious, severe, gross. *ō-* large, great; heavy (rain); loud (voice); full-size, life-size.

1 一座 *ōichiza* large troupe
2 刀 *daitō, tachi, taitō* long sword
力 *dairiki, tairiki* great strength
〆 *ōshime* grand total
八車 *daihachiguruma* large wagon, dray
八洲 *Ōyashima* the Eight Great Islands (of
八島 = preceding word ⌊Japan)
入 *ōi(ri)* full house
入道 *ōnyūdo* giant, monster, specter
入袋 *ōiribukuro* full-house bonus
人 *otona(buru)* act like a man. *otona(biru)* look grown up; become precocious. *otona* adult. *taijin* giant; adult; man of virtue. *taijin, ushi* polite term used in addressing an important person. *otona(shii)* gentle, quiet, good-tempered ⌈mean
人気無 *otonagena(i)* childish; unmanly;
人物 *daijimbutsu* great man, man of great character ⌈fledged
人並 *otonana(mi) no* like a man; full-
人染 *otonaji(miru)* become manly
人振 *otonabu(ru)* act like a man
3 巾 *ōhaba* = full width; big scale
弓 *ōyumi, taikyū* crossbow, longbow. *daikyū* longbow; archery

凡 *ōyoso* approximately
丈夫 *daijōbu* safe, secure, all right; sure; infallible. *daijōfu* a man, a great man, a brave man
大的 *daidaiteki* great, grand, immense; sweeping (victory); wholesale, large-scale
上段 *daijōdan* raising a sword (to kill)
下馬 *ōgeba* large dismounting signs
三角帆 *daisankakuho* lateen sail
川 *ōkawa, taisen* large river
川端 *ōkawabata* Sumida riverside
工 *daiku* carpenter
工店 *daikuten* carpenter shop
山 *ōyama, taizan* large mountain
山猫 *ōyama neko* lynx
山鳴動 *taisan-meidō* great trouble
口 *ōguchi* large mouth; bragging; exaggeration; large amount. *ōkuchi* large mouth; large amount, large opening
口物 *ōguchimono* big lot (of goods)
口径砲 *daikōkeihō* large cannon
口需要者 *ōkuchi juyōsha* large user
小 *daishō* great and small (people); size; large and small sizes; long sword and short sword. *dai(nare)-shō (nare)* whether large or small
小便 *daishōben* urination and defecation
小問 *daishō (o) to(wazu)* whether large or small 「small
小論 *daishō (o) ron(zezu)* whether large or
4 戸 *ōdo* large main gate
方 *ōkata* probably; almost, mostly; the public. *taihō* in general; broadmindedness; the public
月 *dai (no) tsuki* the long months
水 *ōmizu* flood, inundation
王 *daiō* the great king
円 *daien* large circle; a great circle
凶 *daikyō* very bad luck; atrocity, brutality
厄 *taiyaku* great calamity, great misfortune
切 *taisetsu* important, momentous, significant. *ōgi(ri)* large cut; last scene of a drama; catastrophe; end
分 *daibu, daibun* greatly, considerably
少 *daishō* great and small (people); size, large and small sizes 「steward
夫 *tayū, taifu* main actor. *taifu, daifu* high
日本 *Dai Nippon, Dai Nihon, Ōyamato* Japan 「ter 大. *ōmoji* capital letters
文字 *daimonji* large characters; the charac-
反対 *daihantai* intense opposition
元帥 *daigensui* generalissimo
太鼓 *ōdaiko* bass drum, large drum
木 *taiboku, ōki* large tree
木戸 *ōkido* big wooden gate; big town gate
欠 *ōakubi* big yawn
欠伸 *ōakubi* big yawn
火 *taika* big fire, conflagration, holocaust
火傷 *ōyakedo* bad burn
内 *ōuchi* the court, the palace
内山 *ōuchiyama* the palace
仏 *daibutsu* huge image of a Buddha
仏殿 *daibutsuden* temple of a huge Buddha
手 *ōte* front castle gate; unit attacking the front castle gate. *ōde* both arms; arms spread out
手門 *ōtemon* front castle gate
手柄 *ōtegara* great exploit
手筋 *ōtesuji* large operators, big traders
公 *taikō* ruler
公国 *daikōkoku* grand duchy
公使 *taikōshi* ambassadors and ministers
公望 *taikōbō* sports fisherman
5 白 *taihaku* large cup
皿 *ōzara* large plate, platter, charger
矢 *ōya* large arrow
石 *ōishi, taiseki* big stone
穴 *ōana* big hole; huge deficit; (make) a killing; a big upset (at the races)
尼 *ōama* an old nun
外 *ōhazu(re)* utter failure; big mistake; wild
巧 *taikō* great skill, dexterity ⌊guess
功 *taikō* great merit, distinguished services
正 *Taishō* Taisho era (1912–1925)
写 *ōutsu(shi)* a close-up
古 *taiko* ancient times
兄 *ōani* eldest brother. *taikei* polite word for elder brother or someone a little older
半 *taihan* majority, greater part; mostly, nearly all, generally
冊 *taisatsu* bulky volume
旦那 *ōdanna* proprietor, man of the house
出来 *ōdeki* huge success; brilliant move
芝居 *ōshibai* a great drama
打物 *ōu(chi)mono* long weapons
主教 *daishukyō* archibishop (Protestant)
司教 *daishikyō* archibishop (Catholic)
広間 *ōhiroma* grand hall; rotunda
代裏 *daidairi* (ancient) imperial palace
立回 *ōta(chi)mawa(ri)* serious quarrel
立物 *ōda(te)mono* principal actor; promi-
仕事 *ōshigoto* big business ⌊nent figure
仕掛 *ōjika(ke)* large scale
礼 *tairei* state ceremony, enthronement
礼服 *taireifuku* court dress, full-dress uniform
平 *taihei* peace, tranquility
平洋 *Taiheiyō* Pacific Ocean
目 *ōme* generous supervision; winking at, conniving with
目玉 *ōmedama* the big eyes; scolding 「at
目見 *ōme(ni)mi(ru)* overlook, let go, connive

本 *ōmoto* foundation, base, source, fountainhead; fundamentals. *taihon* cardinal principles, great foundation
本山 *daihonzan* important sectarian-headquarters temple
本営 *Daihon-ei* Imperial Headquarters
6 老 *tairō* senior minister
耳 *ōmimi* large ears; being slow of hearing; carelessness
臣 *daijin* cabinet member; high government official
凪 *ōnagi* flat calm
回 *ōmawa(ri)* circuitous route
成 *taisei* completion, accomplishment; compilation; attainment of greatness, success
向 *ōmuko(u)* standing section, the gallery; the masses
曲 *ōma(gari)* large bend in the road. *ōwada* inlet, creek
任 *tainin* great task, important position, important mission
仰 *ōgyō* exaggeration
奸 *daikan* great wickedness
汗 *ōase* copious sweating
邦 *taihō* great country
全 *taizen* encyclopedia, complete works
旨 *ōmune, taishi* the main idea
吉 *daikichi* excellent luck
字 *ōaza* major section of a village. *taiji* large characters. *dai (no) ji* spread-eagle form like the character 大
当 *ōata(ri)* good luck; great success; a killing; bumper crop
兇 *daikyō* notorious scoundrel
江戸 *Ōedo* the great city of Edo
休止 *daikyūshi* (soldier's) long rest period
団円 *daidan-en* end, grand finale; catastrophe
宇宙 *daiuchū* the great universe
西洋 *Taiseiyō* Atlantic Ocean
肌脱 *ōhadanu(gi)* stripping to the waist
臼歯 *daikyūshi* molar
自然 *daishizen* Mother Nature
多数 *daitasū* the great majority
地 *daichi* ground, earth, the solid earth
地主 *ōjinushi* large landowner
好 *daisu(ki)* very fond of
好物 *daikōbutsu* favorite dish
会 *taikai* large meeting, mass meeting, rally, general meeting, conference, convention; tournament, meet
会堂 *daikaidō* cathedral
寺 *ōdera* large temple
寺院 *daiji-in* large temple
年 *ōtoshi* last day of the year
年増 *ōtoshima* a beautiful mature woman
行 *taikō* great deeds
行天皇 *taikō tennō* the late emperor
行李 *daikōri* heavy baggage; field train
同 *daidō* general resemblance; combination, union
同小異 *daidō-shōi* substantial identity
同団結 *daidō danketsu* merger, combination
尽 *daijin* rich man, millionaire, magnate
尽風 *daijinkaze* air of a millionaire
尽遊 *daijin aso(bi)* riotous pleasures
気 *taiki* atmosphere, the air
気圧 *taikiatsu* atmospheric pressure
気圏 *taikiken* the atmosphere
安 *taian* lucky day
安日 *daiannichi, taiannichi* lucky day
安売 *ōyasu-u(ri)* big bargain sale
名 *daimyō* feudal lord, daimyo. *taimei* great honor
名旅行 *daimyō ryokō* junket, spendthrift tour
名領 *daimyōryō* fief
7 豆 *daizu, ōmame* soy bean; long stride
足 *ōashi* large feet; long stride
医 *tai-i* great physician
尾 *taibi* end
序 *daijo* prologue, opening act
佐 *taisa* colonel; (navy) captain
作 *taisaku* masterpiece, monumental work
体 *daitai* outline, summary; generally, on the whole; in substance; originally
役 *taiyaku* important task, important role
把 *ōtaba* large bundle; exaggeration; in general
村 *ōmura, taison* large village
社 *taisha* grand shrine; Izumo Shrine
利 *tairi* huge profit
乱 *tairan* great disturbance, rebellion
別 *taibetsu* general classification
判 *ōban* large old Japanese gold coin; large size (paper or book), folio
助 *ōtasu(kari), ōdasu(kari)* a big help
形 *ōgata* large size, large pattern. *ōgyō* exaggeration, bombast
系 *taikei* outline (of a subject)
兵 *taihei* large army. *taihyō* great stature, large body
志 *taishi* great ambition, aspiration
牢 *tairō*＝太牢 1172.7
旱 *taikan* serious drought
男 *ōotoko* giant. *dai (no) otoko* a real man, a big man
我 *daiga, taiga* the absolute ego, the higher self
君 *ōkimi, ōgimi* sovereign. *taikun* tycoon
束 *ōtaba* large bundle
花火 *ōhanabi* grand fireworks display
売出 *ōurida(shi)* large sale
角豆 *sasage* cowpea
伽藍 *daigaran* huge temple; cathedral
見出 *ōmida(shi)* big headline
見得 *ōmie* magnificent gesture
言 *taigen* grand words; excellent ideas; exaggeration; words of boasting
言壮語 *taigen-sōgo* bragging, exaggeration
身 *taishin* man of rank; man of wealth
身槍 *ōmi (no) yari* long-handled spear
車 *ōguruma* wagon, truck

車輪 *daisharin* large wheel; giant swing; feverishly at work
伯父 *ōoji* great-uncle, granduncle
伯母 *ōoba* great-aunt, grandaunt
声 *ōgoe* loud voice. *taisei* stentorian voice, sonorous tone
声疾呼 *taisei-shikko suru* harangue
麦 *ōmugi* barley
麦刈 *ōmugika(ri)* barley harvest
局 *taikyoku* the general situation; the issue
局的 *taikyokuteki* general, the whole (situation)
局論 *taikyokuron* a broad view (of the 「situation)
8金 *taikin, ōgane* enormous sum, great cost
門 *daimon* large outer gate of a Buddhist temple. *ōmon* front gate
雨 *ōame, taiu* heavy rainfall, downpour
国 *taikoku* large country; major powers
店 *ōmise* large store
供 *ōdomo* young grownups
呼 *taiko* loud cry, shout
味 *ōaji no* tasteless, insipid
姉 *ōane, taishi* eldest sister 「house
所 *ōdokoro, ōdoko* powerful family, great
抵 *taitei* generally, usually, probably; nearly,
杯 *taihai* large cup 「almost
枚 *taimai* large sum
波 *ōnami* big wave, billow, swell
河 *taiga, ōkawa* large river
知 *daichi* supreme wisdom; sage, a Solomon
股 *ōmata* straddle; long stride
刹 *taisetsu, taisatsu* large temple
効 *taikō* great efficacy
命 *taimei* a ruler's command
参 *ōmai(ri)* large crowds of worshippers
官 *taikan* high official, dignitary
宗 *taisō* foundation; fundamentals
受 *ōu(ke)* great popularity, a hit
空 *ōzora, taikū* sky, firmament, space
典 *taiten* state ceremony; important law; excellent publication
昔 *ōmukashi* great antiquity
往生 *daiōjō* peaceful death; the death of a priest; euthanasia 「Shepherd
牧者 *Daibokusha* Christ, the Great
明神 *daimyōjin* title of a Shinto god
金持 *ōganemochi* very rich man
金儲 *ōganemōke* making a fortune
使 *taishi* ambassador
使館 *taishikan* embassy
物 *ōmono* big thing; big shot; big game
物食 *ōmonogu(i)* defeating one's superior
叔父 *ōoji* great-uncle, granduncle
叔母 *ōoba* great-aunt, grandaunt
事 *daiji, taiji* great thing, great undertaking; serious affair, emergency; importance, significance. *daiji ni suru* value, prize, esteem; be careful of. *daiji(nai)* It matters little. *ōgoto* serious matter
事取 *daiji (o) to(ru)* act carefully 「patricide
逆 *taigyaku* hideous wickedness; treason;
逆無道 *daigyaku-mudō* high treason
逆罪 *taigyakuzai* treason; patricide
法 *taihō* fundamental law
法会 *taihōe* high Buddhist memorial service
法輪 *daihōrin* great wheel of (the Buddhist) law
英国 *Dai Eikoku* British Commonwealth
英帝国 *Dai-Ei Teikoku* British Empire
英断 *daieidan* resolute step
東亜 *Daitōa* Greater East Asia
東亜共栄圏 *Daitōa Kyōeiken* Greater East Asia Coprosperity Sphere
東亜省 *Daitōashō* Ministry for Greater East Asia Affairs
東亜戦争 *Daitōa Sensō* the Greater East Asia War
学 *daigaku* college, university 「dent
学生 *daigakusei* university or college stu-
学出 *daigakude* college graduate 「uate
学出身者 *daigaku shusshinsha* college grad-
学自由 *daigaku (no) jiyū* academic freedom
学町 *daigaku machi* college town
学者 *daigakusha* great scholar
学院 *daigakuin* postgraduate school
学帽 *daigakubō* college cap
学総長 *daigaku sōchō* university president
和 *Yamato* ancient Japan
和心 *Yamatogokoro* Japanese spirit
和火燵 *Yamatogotatsu* foot warmer
和民族 *Yamato minzoku* Japanese race
和言葉 *Yamato kotoba* classical Japanese
和島根 *Yamato shimane* Japanese islands
和絵 *Yamatoe* pictures of ancient Japanese
和琴 *Yamatogoto* ancient koto 「life
和綴 *Yamato toji* Japanese-style bookbinding 「tanka
和歌 *Yamato uta* thirty-one syllable poem,
和魂 *Yamatodamashii* Japanese spirit
和撫子 *Yamato nadeshiko* women of Japan
9食 *taishoku, ōgu(i)* gluttony, voracity; glut-
度 *taido* magnanimity, generosity 「ton
廻 *ōmawari* circuitous route 「ment
虐 *taigyaku* great cruelty; very bad govern-
通 *ōdō(ri)* main street, highway, thorofare. *daitsū* man of accomplishment
盾 *ōdate* large shield
便 *daiben* feces, excrement
垣 *ōgaki* large enclosing fence
指 *ōyubi* thumb
括 *ōguku(ri)* wrapping up in one bundle
持 *ōmo(te)* big welcome

3 ロ口土士夂夊夕【大】女子宀寸小⺌尢尸屮山川巛工己巾干幺广廴廾弋弓彐彑彡彳

柄 *ōhei* arrogance. *ōgara* large build; large pattern (in kimonos)
約 *taiyaku*=*tairyaku* 大略 (see below–11)
計 *taikei* far-reaching policy, long-range plan, great plan
郡 *taigun* a great county
盃 *taihai, ōsakazuki* a large cup
帝 *taitei* a great emperor
軍 *taigun* large army, large force, mighty host. *ōikusa* a big battle; a great war
姦 *taikan* great villainy
荒 *ōa*(*re*) severe storm; great violence
要 *taiyō* summary, outline
型 *ōgata* large size, large pattern
急 *ōiso*(*gi*) great haste
負 *ōma*(*ke*) crushing defeat; big bargain
為 *ō*(*i*)*na*(*rashimeru*) magnify (in the sight of)
速力 *daisokuryoku* high speed
洪水 *Daikōzui* the Flood
胡坐 *ōagura* careless cross-legged squatting
威張 *ōiba*(*ri*) great bragging; great braggart
飛球 *daihikyū* long fly
活躍 *daikatsuyaku* vigorous personal activity
屋 *ōya* landlord
屋根 *ōyane* main roof
相 *taisō*=大層 (see below–14)
相撲 *ōzumo* annual wrestling matches; exciting wrestling match
海 *taikai, daikai, ōumi* the ocean, the open sea
海原 *ōunabara* ocean, the mighty deep
祖父 *daisofu* great-grandfather
祖母 *daisobo* great-grandmother
胆 *daitan* boldness, intrepidity, hardihood; audacity
胆不敵 *daitan-futeki na* bold and wilful; daredevil; audacious, undaunted
降 *ōbu*(*ri*) heavy precipitation
降霜 *daikōsō* heavy frost
政 *taisei* administration of a country, imperial rule
政奉還 *taisei-hōkan* restoration of imperial rule
乗的 *daijōteki* broad-minded
乗仏教 *Daijō Bukkyō* Mahayana Buddhism, Greater-Vehicle Buddhism
変 *taihen* serious, terrible; innumerable; immense; What!; a great change
変安上 *taihen yasua*(*gari*) very cheap
前 *ōmae* the presence of a god or ruler
前提 *daizentei* major premise
勇 *taiyū* great courage
勇士 *daiyūshi* great warrior
音 *daion* loud noise, loud voice
音声 *daionjō* stentorian voice
音響 *daionkyō* a great noise
風 *ōkaze, taifū* strong wind, storm, hurricane, typhoon. *ōbu*(*ri*) big things; large size. *ōfū* arrogance
風子油 *daifūshiyu* chaulmoogra oil
風呂敷 *ōburoshiki* big cloth wrapper; bragging
風雨 *daifūu* big rainstorm
神 *ōkami* god
神酒 *omiki* Shinto saké offering; saké
神宮 *Daijingū* the Ise Shrine
神楽 *daikagura* street dance and jugglery performance; sacred shrine music and dancing
洋 *taiyō* ocean
洋州 *Taiyōshū* Oceania
洋性 *taiyōsei* oceanic (climate)
洋学 *taiyōgaku* oceanography
洋島 *taiyōtō* oceanic islands
洋航路船 *taiyō-kōrosen* ocean liner
10 庭 *ōniwa* the great court
病 *taibyō* serious illness
師 *daishi* a great Buddhist teacher
剛 *daigō* great strength; very strong man
倭 *Ōyamato* Japan
振 *ōbu*(*ri*) big things; large size
旆 *taihai* standard, banner; imperial standard
浪 *tairō, ōnami* surge (of waves)
砲 *taihō* gun, cannon, artillery
破 *taiha* dilapidation, ruin, havoc, serious damage
蚊 *gagambo* daddy longlegs
袖 *ōsode* wide sleeves
釘 *ōkugi* big nail, spike
島 *ōshima* large island
宮 *ōmiya* grand shrine
害 *taigai* great harm, big damage
釜 *ōgama* large kettle, cauldron
笑 *ōwara*(*i*), *taishō* loud laughter
差 *taisa* wide difference, great discrepancy, striking contrast
書 *taisho suru* write in large letters
息 *ōiki, taisoku* sigh, long breath
恩 *daion, taion* great kindness; great obligation
挙 *taikyo* great enterprise; united effort
秦 *Taishin* the Great Roman Empire
時代 *ōjidai* great antiquity. *ōjidai na* old-fashioned
株主 *ōkabunushi* large stockholder
流行 *dairyūkō, ōhayari* the fashion, the rage
殉教 *Daijunkyō* the Great Martyrdom
馬鹿 *ōbaka* big fool
恐慌 *daikyōkō* great panic
陰暦 *tai-inreki* lunar calendar
真面目 *ōmajime* great earnestness
修道院 *daishūdōin* abbey
原 *taigen* origin, foundation
原則 *daigensoku* broad principle
悟 *taigo, daigo* great wisdom; (Buddhist) enlightenment. *daigo*=next word
悟徹底 *daigo-tettei, taigo-tettei* spiritual awakening, dawn of truth, attainment of a philosophy of life
酒 *ōzake, taishu* heavy drinking
酒飲 *ōzakeno*(*mi*) heavy drinker

将 *taishō* general; admiral; head, leader, boss
将軍 *taishōgun* generalissimo; boss, head
祓 *ōharai, ōbarai* Shinto purification ceremony (June 30 and Dec. 31); exorcism
祓詞 *ōharai (no) kotoba* Shinto purification prayer
都 *taito* great city
都会 *daitokai* big city
家 *taika* mansion, large building; rich or illustrious family; great master, authority. *taike* wealthy family, aristocratic family; an authority, a scholar. *ōya* main building, main house; landlord
家族 *daikazoku* a big family; a big circle of relatives
能 *tainō* power, great might
能者 *Tainōsha* the Omnipotent God
部 *taibu, daibu* the larger part; a many-volume set. *taibu no, daibu no* voluminous, copious, bulky
部分 *daibubun* greater part, majority; mostly, largely
部屋 *ōbeya* large room; actors' room; utility man; lesser stars
宮司 *daigūji* chief priest of the Ise Shrine
宮御所 *Ōmiyagosho* Empress Dowager's Palace
宮様 *Omiyasama* Empress Dowager
根 *daikon* the huge white radish, daikon
根役 *daikon-yaku* poor actor, ham (actor)
根卸 *daikon-oro(shi)* grated daikon; daikon grater
根漬 *daikonzuke* pickled daikon
陸 *tairiku* continent; the Continent (of Asia)
陸系 *tairikukei no* continental
陸性 *tairikusei* continental (climate)
陸的 *tairikuteki* continental
陸島 *tairikutō* continental island
陸棚 *tairikubō, tairikuhō, tairikudana* continental shelf
11 魚 *taigyo* large fish; large catch
鳥 *ōtori* large bird
鹿 *ōjika, ōshika* elk; moose
麻 *ōasa* hemp. *asa* hemp; flax; ramie; jute; linen. *taima* Shinto paper offerings
虚 *taikyo* the sky, the great void
違 *ōchiga(i)* great difference
尉 *tai-i* captain; lieutenant junior grade
婚 *taikon* imperial wedding
掛 *ōgaka(ri)* large-scale
捷 *taishō* a great victory
晦 *ōtsugumori* last day of the year
猟 *tairyō, dairyō* a large catch
略 *tairyaku* summary, outline; great plan; approximately
粒 *ōtsubu* a large drop; a large grain
組 *ōgu(mi)* making up (a newspaper)
脳 *dainō* brain, cerebrum
船 *ōbune, taisen* big ship, ocean liner
蛇 *daija, orochi* monster serpent, boa; large snake
欲 *daiyoku, taiyoku*＝大慾 (see below–15)
敗 *taihai* crushing defeat, complete rout
赦 *taisha* amnesty; plenary indulgence
野 *ōno* big field
釣 *ōzuri* big catch (of fish)
陽 *taiyō* sun
隊 *daitai* battalion
瓶 *ōbin* magnum, two-quart wine bottle
著 *taicho* great work, voluminous work
雪 *ōyuki, taisetsu* heavy snow; heavy snow season
患 *taikan, ōwazura(i)* serious illness; disaster; great trial
梁 *ōhari, ōbari* large beam, crossbeam
望 *taibō, taimō* aspiration, ambition
盗 *taitō* notorious robber
盛 *ōmo(ri)* heaping measure, large serving
匙 *ōsaji* tablespoon
晦日 *Ōmisoka* December 31; New Year's Eve
理石 *dairiseki* marble
兜虫 *ōkabuto mushi* Atlas beetle
野貝 *ōnogai* soft-shelled clam
執事 *daishitsuji* archdeacon
強風 *daikyōfū* strong gale
旋風 *daisempū* tornado
掃除 *ōsōji* semiannual house cleaning
遊星 *daiyūsei* major planet
経師 *daikyōji* (ancient) paperhanger
動脈 *daidōmyaku* aorta, main artery
袈裟 *ōgesa* exaggeration; grandiosity; large-scale
規模 *daikibo no* large-scale
過 *taika* serious error, grave fault
過去 *daikako* past-perfect tense
酔 *taisui* drunken stupor
酔者 *taisuisha* drunkard
商店 *daishōten* emporium
商人 *daishōnin, ōakindo* a great merchant
斎 *Taisai* Lent
斎節 *Taisaisetsu* Lent
黒 *Daikoku* a god of wealth
黒柱 *daikokubashira* central pillar, king post; pillar, mainstay; family head
黒頭巾 *daikoku zukin* tam-o'-shanter, round Scotch cap, beret
悪 *daiaku* atrocity, outrage
悪人 *daiakunin* consummate villain, thoroughgoing rascal
悪者 *ōwarumono* notorious scoundrel
祭 *taisai, ōmatsu(ri)* grand festival
祭日 *taisaibi, taisaijitsu* national holiday
祭司 *daisaishi* high priest
道 *daidō, taidō* highway, street; great moral principle. *ōdo(ri)* main street
道具 *ōdōgu* stage setting, scene; large stage equipment
道商 *daidō akina(i)* hawking, street sale

道商人 *daidō shōnin* street vendor
12 喝 *daikatsu suru, taikatsu suru* thunder, roar, yell at
慌 *ōawate* great excitement
淵 *ōfuchi* the great deep
絎 *ōguke* large stitch; long needle
勝 *taishō* great victory
詔 *taishō* imperial rescript
飯 *ōmeshi* hearty meal
傘 *ōgasa* large umbrella
喜 *ōyoroko(bi)* great joy
寒 *daikan, taikan* midwinter, coldest period
嵐 *ōarashi* severe storm
暑 *taisho* midsummer day (about July 23)
童 *ōwarawa ni* with all one's might
筋 *ōsuji* outline, summary
筒 *ōzutsu* cannon
葬 *taisō* imperial funeral
智 *taichi* great wisdom; sage
覚 *daikaku* great wisdom; (Buddhist) enlightenment
喪 *taimo, taisō* imperial mourning, national mourning
痛手 *ōitade* severe wound; hard blow; great loss
割引 *ōwaribiki* big discount
勝利 *daishōri* great victory
評判 *daihyōban, ōhyōban* sensation
場所 *ōbasho* (regular) wrestling tournament; wide place
惑星 *daiwakusei* major planet
間違 *ōmachiga(i)* big mistake
募集 *daiboshū* wholesale call (for workers)
喧嘩 *ōgenka* big quarrel
廈高楼 *taika-kōrō* large and imposing buildings
圏 *taiken* great circle
圏航路 *taiken kōro* great-circle route
幅 *ōhaba* full width; big scale
幅物 *ōhabamono* broadcloth, wide goods
極 *Taikyoku* the Absolute, the First Cause, the Imperial Throne; the maximum
極殿 *Daigokuden* (ancient) Palace Council Hall
奥 *ōoku* inner palace; harem
奥様 *ōokusama* your grandmother
量 *tairyō, dairyō* large quantity
量生産 *tairyō seisan* mass production
量点 *tairyōten* large score
量虐殺 *tairyō gyakusatsu* mass murder, genocide
量得点 *tairyō tokuten* large score
統 *taitō* imperial line
統領 *daitōryō* president
統領夫人 *daitōryō fujin* the first lady
統領令 *daitōryōrei* presidential decree
統領官邸 *Daitōryō Kantei* Executive Mansion
統領教書 *daitōryō kyōsho* president's message
御 *ōmi-, omi-* honorific prefix
御心 *ōmikokoro* imperial heart or will
御世 *ōmiyo* imperial reign
御足 *omiashi* your foot

御位 *ōmikurai* imperial throne
御国 *ōmikuni* great august country
御所 *ōgosho* retired shogun; boss
御神 *ōmikami* the Sun Goddess
御酒 *omiki* Shinto saké offering; saké
御稜威 *ōmi-itsu* imperial prestige
御鬮 *omikuji* a written temple or shrine oracle
衆 *taishū* a crowd, the masses; general public
衆文学 *taishū bungaku* popular literature
衆化 *taishūka* popularization
衆向 *taishūmu(ki)* for everybody, popular
衆伝道 *taishū dendō* public evangelist
衆作家 *taishū sakka* popular writer
衆性 *taishūsei* popularity
衆物 *taishūmono* popular story
衆食堂 *taishū shokudō* (cheap) restaurant, eating place
衆政策 *taishū seisaku* policy toward the masses
衆娯楽 *taishū goraku* mass entertainment
衆教育 *taishū kyōiku* popular education
衆課税 *taishū kazei* taxing the public
衆獲得運動 *taishū kakutoku undō* public-sympathy drive
18 廈 *taika* large house, grand building, skyscraper
痴 *taichi* a great fool
傷 *ōkizu* serious injury, deep gash
塊 *taikai* great mass, hunk, chunk
嫌 *daikira(i)* abhorrence, great aversion
損 *ōzon* heavy loss
滝 *ōdaki* large waterfall
禍 *taika* great disaster
祿 *tairoku* large fief
話 *ōbanashi* indecent talk
詰 *ōzume* finale, final scene
賊 *taizoku* notorious robber
路 *ōji* highway, main street, thorofare
跨 *ōmatagi* large strides
鉈 *ōnata* ax
隠 *tai-in* great hermit
数 *taisū* great number; round numbers
盞 *taisan* a large cup
節 *taisetsu* great principle; higher law
蒜 *ninniku* garlic
零 *ōkoboshi* loud complaining
意 *tai-i* gist, outline, summary
勢 *taizei, ōzei* crowd, multitude. *taisei* general trend, current thought
愚 *taigu* a great fool
禁 *taikin* strict prohibition
農 *dainō* large-scale farming; wealthy farmer
僧正 *daisōjō* high priest, cardinal
椿事 *daichinji* tragic or disastrous accident
楓子油 *taifūshiyu* chaulmoogra oil
慈大悲 *daiji-daihi* great mercy and compassion

預言者 *Daiyogensha* the Major Prophets
殿 *ōtono, otono* (polite) palace; daimyo
殿様 *ōtonosama* senior feudal lord
福 *daifuku* great fortune, good luck ⌈book
福帳 *daifukuchō* old-fashioned account
腿 *daitai* thigh, femur
腿部 *daitaibu* thigh
腸 *daichō* colon, large intestine
腸炎 *daichōen* colitis
群 *taigun* large crowd, large herd, large flock, large school (of fish)
群衆 *daigunshū* a great multitude
罪 *daizai* terrible crime, grave sin
罪人 *daizainin* desperate criminal
聖 *taisei* a great sage
聖堂 *daiseidō* cathedral
業 *taigyō* great undertaking, noble work, great achievement
業物 *ōwazamono* a sharp sword
戦 *taisen* great war, world war
戦車 *daisensha* super tank ⌈war
戦前 *taisenzen, taisemmae* before the great
義 *taigi* law of justice; moral obligation; righteousness; loyalty and patriotism; a great cause ⌈relations; justice
義名分 *taigi-meibun* true sovereign-subject
義明文 *taigi-meibun* true sovereign-subject
鼓 *taiko, ōtsuzumi* large drum ⌊relationship
鼓判 *taikoban* oversized personal seal
鼓持 *taikomo(chi)* male restaurant entertainer; flatterer
鼓腹 *taikobara* fat stomach
鼓橋 *taikobashi* arched bridge
14 層 *taisō* very, very much. *taisō na* a great deal, plenty; exaggerated, extravagant
閤 *taikō* father of the *kampaku* (ancient chief adviser to the emperor)
関 *ōzeki* champion wrestler ⌈wealth
徳 *daitoku* virtuous priest; priest; man of
摑 *ōzukami* big handful; the whole (of a problem), outline; summary
概 *taigai* in general; mostly, principally, almost; probably; about, roughly. *taigai ni* moderately, reasonably
様 *ōyō na* easygoing, generous; haughty
獄 *taigoku, daigoku* roundup, wholesale arrest
綱 *ōzuna* hawser, cable. *taikō* general rules, fundamental principles; outline, general
豪 *daigō* great man; rich man ⌊features
算 *taisaku* fundamental policy, long-range
暮 *ōgu(re)* end of the year ⌊plan
雑把 *ōzappa* rough (estimate); loose (talk); generous
熊星 *Daiyūsei* the Dipper, Ursa Major
静脈 *daijōmyaku* the main vein, vena cava

演習 *daienshū* grand maneuvers
綬章 *daijushō* grand cordon
嘗祭 *Daijōsai* the Great Thanksgiving Festival following an enthronement ceremony
監督 *daikantoku* archbishop, primate
歌劇 *daikageki* grand opera
漁 *tairyō, dairyō* large catch
漁旗 *tairyōbata* flag signalling a big catch
蔵 *ōkura* big storehouse ⌊of fish
蔵大臣 *Ōkura Daijin* Finance Minister
蔵省 *Ōkurashō* Finance Ministry ⌈tures
蔵経 *Daizōkyō* complete Buddhist scrip-
15 廟 *taibyō* imperial mausoleum; Ise Shrines
慶 *taikei* great happiness
儀 *taigi* national ceremony. *taigi na* laborious; troublesome; wearisome; languid
嘘 *ōuso* big lie
権 *taiken* supreme power, sovereignty
潮 *ōshio* spring tide, flood tide
編 *taihen* a masterpiece, a great work
輪 *tairin* large wheel; large flower
鋲 *taibyō* spike ⌈enemy
敵 *taiteki, daiteki* great rival, powerful
篇 *taihen* masterpiece, a great work
慾 *daiyoku, taiyoku* greed, covetousness; greedy person; great desire
賢 *taiken* sage, man of great wisdom
磐石 *daibanjaku* large stone, huge crag
熱熱 *ōatsuatsu* keenly enthusiastic; infatu-
震 *taishin* big earthquake ⌊ated with
震災 *daishinsai* a great earthquake; the 1923 Tokyo earthquake
器 *taiki* large receptacle; great genius
器晩成 *taiki-bansei* Great talents mature late. ⌈fucian scholar
16 儒 *daiju, taiju* great scholar; great Con-
橋 *ōhashi* large bridge
樹 *taiju* large tree
積 *ōzu(mori)* rough estimate
頭 *ōatama* large head; leader, boss
錐 *ōgiri* auger
鮃 *ohyō* northern halibut
憲章 *Daikenshō* Magna Carta, Great Char-
鋸 *ōnokogiri, ōga* felling saw, pit saw ⌊ter
鋸屑 *ogakuzu* sawdust
17 闇 *ōyami* wholesale blackmarketing
鼾 *ōibiki* loud snoring
霜 *ōshimo* heavy frost
檀那 *ōdanna* proprietor, man of the house
韓民国 *Daikamminkoku, Taikaminkoku*
檣 *taishō* mainmast ⌊Republic of Korea
檣帆 *taishōhan* mainsail
18 儲 *ōmōke* large profit
鎌 *ōgama* scythe
騒 *ōsawa(gi)* clamor, uproar, tumult

観 *taikan* general view, general survey; philosophical view
難 *tainan, dainan* great disaster, great misfortune, dire distress
顔 *ō(kina) kao* arrogant countenance
繭 *ōmayu* large cocoon
藩 *taihan* clan of the 1st degree
19 願 *daigan, taigan* ambition, aspiration; earnest prayer; the heart's desire
鯛 *ōdai* large seabream
蟻 *ōari* army ant
蟻喰 *ōarikui* ant bear, great anteater
20 艦 *taikan* big warship

1

天 See 16.

夭 See 161.

夫 See 164.

A 太 1172/F470 TAI. TA. *futo(ru)* get fat, gain, fill out. *futo(rasu), futora(seru)* fatten, feed up; enrich. *futo(i)* big, thick, burly, fat; deep, sonorous (voice); shameless, audacious, insolent. *futo-* big, fat, noble. *hanaha(da)* (see under 甚 111.0).

2 刀 *tachi* long sword ⌈tion, contention
刀打 *tachiu(chi)* crossing swords; opposi-
刀先 *tachisaki* sword tip; force of the tongue ⌈cutter
刀取 *tachito(ri)* harakiri assistant; head
刀音 *tachioto* clash of swords
刀風 *tachikaze* sword swish; brave fight
刀持 *tachimo(chi)* swordbearer
刀捌 *tachisabaki* wielding the sword
刀筋 *tachisuji* swordsmanship
刀影 *tachikage* sword flash
刀懸 *tachikake* sword rack
3 子 *taishi* crown prince; prince
山 *taizan* large mountain
4 夫 *tayū, taifu* chief actor in a noh play; entertainer; courtesan; kabuki female-role actor; main actor
公 *taikō* grand duke, prince
公望 *taikōbō* sports fisherman
5 古 *taiko* ancient times
白 *taihaku* refined sugar; thick silk thread; a sweet potato; Venus
白星 *yūzutsu, taihakusei* evening star; ⌊Venus
平 *taihei* peace, tranquility
平洋 *Taiheiyō* Pacific Ocean
平洋戦争 *Taiheiyō Sensō* the Pacific War
平楽 *taiheiraku* irresponsible talk
6 糸 *futo-ito* coarse thread, low-count yarn
后 *taikō* empress dowager, queen dowager
守 *taishu* governor, viceroy, governor-⌊general
字 *futoji* bold-faced type
早計 *taisōkei* making mistakes by hurrying ⌊too much
西洋 *Taiseiyō* Atlantic Ocean
7 初 *taisho* the beginning of the world
牢 *tairō* emperor's sacrifice to the gods; splendid feast; Edo jail
8 物 *futomono* dry goods, piece goods
股 *futomomo* thigh
宗 *taisō* dynasty, founder, progenitor, imperial ancestor; origin (of all things)
9 祖 *taiso* founder, progenitor, first emperor (of a dynasty)
巻 *futoma(ki)* thick cigarette
神宮 *Daijingū* the Ise Shrine
皇太后 *taikō taikō* the empress dowager
10 書 *futoga(ki)* bold stroke
宰府 *Dazaifu* (ancient) Kyūshū government headquarters
陰 *tai-in* moon
陰暦 *tai-inreki* lunar calendar
11 虚 *taikyo* the sky; the origin of the universe
脛 *futohagi* calf of the leg
陽 *taiyō* sun
陽日 *taiyōjitsu* solar day
陽月 *taiyōgetsu* solar month
陽灯 *taiyōtō* artificial sunlight
陽年 *taiyōnen* solar year
陽系 *taiyōkei* solar system
陽神 *taiyōshin* sun god
陽神経叢 *taiyō shinkeisō* solar plexus
陽神話 *taiyō shinwa* sun myths
陽時 *taiyōji* solar time
陽崇拝 *taiyō sūhai* sun worship
陽黒点 *taiyō kokuten* sunspot
陽暦 *taiyōreki* solar calendar, Julian calen-⌊dar
陽熱 *taiyō netsu* solar heat
12 傅 *taifu* tutor to the imperial family
軸 *futojiku* thick-bodied (pen)
筋 *futosuji* thick line, bar
13 腹 *futo(p)para no* generous, magnanimous
鼓 *taiko* a big drum; professional jester; flatterer; big obi bow
鼓判 *taikoban* large seal
鼓形 *taikokei* barrel shape ⌈flatterer
鼓持 *taikomo(chi)* professional jester;
鼓結 *taikomusu(bi)* big obi bow ⌈child
鼓腹 *taikobara* paunch, potbelly, big with
鼓橋 *taikobashi* arched bridge
14 閤 *taikō* the father of an imperial adviser; Toyotomi Hideyoshi
綱 *futozuna* cable, hawser
18 織 *futo-o(ri)* coarse silk

— 2 —

失 See 178.

央 See 86.

— 3 —

夷 See 182.

— 4 —

夾 See 192.

— 5 —

奉 See 212.

奄 1173 / F477 En cover.

[8]奄 *en-en* breath; breathing

奈 1174 / F479 **柰** Na what?

[7]何 *ikan* what, how
良朝 *Narachō* Nara period (710–794)
良漬 *narazuke* pickles seasoned in saké lees
[12]落 *naraku* hell, hades; eternity; theater basement

奔 1175 / F482 **奔** Hon *hashi(ru)* run.
B
[7]走 *honsō* bustle; activity, good offices
[8]放 *hompō na* wild, incorrigible, extravagant
命 *hommei*=*honsō* 奔走 (see above–7)
[10]馬 *homba* galloping horse; runaway horse
逸 *hon-itsu suru* run away, scamper off
流 *honryū* torrent, rapids
[20]騰 *hontō* price jump, boom

奇 1176 / F477 Ki strangeness, curiosity, eccentricity. *kusu(shiki)*, *ku(shiki)* strange, mysterious. *kusu(shiku) mo*, *ku(shiku) mo* strangely, mysteriously, ironically. *ki (to) suru* regard as wonderful.
B
[2]人 *kijin* eccentric person
[3]才 *kisai* genius, wizard, prodigy
[5]功 *kikō* signal success; remarkable effect
[6]行 *kikō* eccentric conduct
[7]言 *kigen* paradox
妙 *kimyō na* strange, queer, wonderful
抜 *kibatsu na* novel, original, striking, extraordinary, strange
形 *kikei* deformity, abnormality
兵 *kihei* storm troops, flying corps, commandos
声 *kisei* queer voice
[8]物 *kibutsu*, *kimotsu* curio; curiosity; eccentric person
知 *kichi* genius
効 *kikō*=奇功 (see above–5)
岩 *kigan* fantastic crag
怪 *kikai na*, *ki(k)kai na* strange, wonderful; weird; outrageous, scandalous, insolent
怪千万 *kikai-semban* very strange
奇 *kiki* something very strange
奇妙妙 *kiki-myōmyō* something very strange
奇怪怪 *kiki-kaikai* something very strange
[9]計 *kikei* ingenuity, clever plan
[10]骨 *kikotsu na* eccentric; outstanding (person)
病 *kibyō* strange disease
特 *kitoku* miracle. *kitoku na*, *kidoku na* commendable; charitable
書 *kisho* strange book
[11]遇 *kigū* chance meeting
道 *kidō* strange plan; unusual plan
偶 *kigū* odd and even numbers
異 *ki-i na* odd, strange, wonderful
習 *kishū* strange custom
貨 *kika* curiosity; good opportunity (to make a profit)
術 *kijutsu* jugglery; magic
術師 *kijutsushi* juggler; magician
[12]傑 *kiketsu* remarkable man
絶 *kizetsu* very strange
勝 *kishō* surprise victory; successful execution; beauty spot
童 *kidō* prodigy, remarkable child
智 *kichi* genius
策 *kisaku* clever plan
策縦横 *kisaku-jūō* clever planning
[13]瑞 *kizui* good omen
禍 *kika* accident, disaster, misfortune
話 *kiwa* strange talk
跡 *kiseki* miracle, wonder, mystery
数 *kisū* odd number; masculine number
想 *kisō* original idea; strange notion
想天外 *kiso-tengai* original idea
[14]聞 *kibun* strange news, revelation; anecdote
算 *kisan* strange resources; expedient
態 *kitai* queer, strange, fantastic
[15]縁 *kien* irony of fate, strange coincidence
談 *kidan* strange story, adventure story
論 *kiron* strange argument; different idea
[16]謀 *kibō* clever stratagem
獣 *kijū* strange animal
薬 *kiyaku* very effective medicine
[17]矯 *kikyō* eccentric conduct
[18]癖 *kiheki* eccentric habit
観 *kikan* strange sight
蹟 *kiseki* miracle, wonder, mystery
蹟的 *kisekiteki* miraculous
[19]警 *kikei na* witty, original, smart
麗 *kirei*=綺麗 3558.19

麗好 *kireizu(ki)* love of cleanliness
麗所 *kireidoko* beautiful women; geisha
麗事 *kireigoto* fine skill; simplicity
[22]襲 *kishū* surprise attack
襲攻撃 *kishū kōgeki* surprise attack
襲部隊 *kishū butai* shock troops
襲戦 *kishūsen* surprise attack; guerrilla warfare

6

奕 See 301.

契 1177/F481 B Kei. *chigi(ru)* pledge, vow, swear, promise.
[6]印 *kei-in* a seal over the edges of two sheets
合 *keigō* coincidence, agreement
[9]約 *keiyaku* contract, agreement, covenant, testament
約者 *keiyakusha* contracting parties
約書 *keiyakusho* contract
約箱 *Keiyaku (no) Hako* Ark of the Covenant
[16]機 *keiki* opportunity, chance

奏 1178/F481 B Sō. *kana(deru)* play (an instrument). *sō(suru)* play on; speak to a ruler; report to (the emperor); complete.
[3]上 *sōjō* report to the emperor
[5]功 *sōkō* fruition, success, efficacy
[6]任 *sōnin* emperor-approved appointment
任官 *sōninkan* official whose appointment is emperor-approved
[8]法 *sōhō* playing (an instrument); touch
効 *sōkō* fruition, success, efficacy
[12]弾 *sōdan* reporting (a miscreant official) to the emperor
[13]楽 *sōgaku* instrumental music
楽者 *sōgakusha* instrumentalist
楽席 *sōgakuseki* orchestra seats
楽堂 *sōgakudō* concert hall
[14]聞 *sōmon* report to the emperor
鳴曲 *sōmeikyoku* sonata (in music)
[15]請 *sōsei* petitioning the emperor
[16]覧 *sōran* submitting (a document) to the emperor; imperial inspection

7

畚 畚 See 852.

奐 Nonstandard for 魚 5281.

套 1179/F483 Tō hackneyed.

8

爽 See 234. [爻]

奢 See 1180.

器 Nonstandard for 器 994.

9

奥 See 240.

奠 See 602.

奢 1180/F484 Sha. *ogo(ru)* be extravagant; treat. *ogo(ri)* luxury, extravagance; (my) treat.
[8]侈 *shashi* luxury, extravagance
[10]恣 *shashi* pride and self-will
[13]肆 *shashi* pride and self-will

10

奧 See 奥 240.

奨 1181/F485 B 獎 Shō *susu(meru)* urge, encourage.
[7]励 *shōrei* encouragement, promotion, exhortation; message, address
励金 *shōreikin* incentive pay, subsidy
励者 *shōreisha* promoter, supporter
[8]学 *shōgaku* encouragement of learning
学金 *shōgakukin* scholarship (grant)
学資金 *shōgaku shikin* scholarship fund
[14]導 *shōdō suru* encourage and lead

11

奬 1182/F485 See 奨 1181.

奪 1183/F485 B Datsu. *uba(u)* take by force, snatch away, oust, dispossess, deprive of, plunder, usurp; absorb (attention); fascinate.
[5]去 *uba(i)-sa(ru)* take away
[6]回 *dakkai* recovery, recapture, rescue
返 *uba(i)-kae(su)* take back, recapture
合 *uba(i)-a(u)* scramble for, struggle for
[8]取 *uba(i)-to(ru)*, *dasshu suru* plunder. *dasshu* capture, seizure, occupation
[9]胎 *dattai* plagiarism
[11]掠 *datsuryaku*=*ryakudatsu* 掠奪 1931.14

略 *datsuryaku=ryakudatsu* 掠奪 1931.14
15 還 *dakkan* recovery, recapture, rescue

13

奮 1184 F485 A FUN. *furu(u)* be invigorated, be spirited, flourish. *furu(tte)* energetically, heartily.
5 立 *furu(i)-ta(tsu)* rouse oneself, be inspired. *furu(i)-ta(taseru)* stir up, arouse
迅 *funjin* dashing forward impetuously
7 励 *funrei* strenuous efforts, push, hustle
9 発 *fumpatsu* strenuous effort, spurt
10 起 *furu(i)-oki(ru), funki suru* rouse oneself, be stirred up. *furu(i)-oko(su), funki saseru* stir up
進 *funshin=funjin* 奮迅 (see above–5)
12 然 *funzen* resolutely, courageously
13 戦 *funsen* hard fighting
15 撃 *fungeki* fierce attack
16 激 *fungeki* animation, inspiration, excitement
18 闘 *funtō* hard struggle, desperate fight, strenuous effort

RAD. 女 38

Onna woman. At left: *onna hen*. Nickname: Woman.

女 1185 F486 A JO, NYO, NYŌ woman, girl, daughter. *onna, omina* woman, female, sweetheart, girl. *onna(rashii)* womanly, ladylike; effeminate. *onna(datera) ni* unladylike. *me-* female.
2 人 *nyonin, jojin* woman
人禁制 *nyonin-kinsei* no admittance to women
3 女 *meme(shii)* effeminate, unmanly
工 *jokō* factory woman worker
丈夫 *jojōfu* heroine; outstanding woman
大学 *onna daigaku* cultural books for women
三昧 *onnazammai* indulging in lewdness
子 *joshi, nyoshi* woman, female, girl. *onna(no)ko* girl; daughter; baby girl. *onago* girl, woman, maid
子大学 *joshi daigaku* women's college
子供 *onna kodomo* a woman and her child; a nonentity; a man of straw; an encumbrance
子青年会 *joshi seinenkai* young women's association
子青年団 *joshi seinendan* young women's association
子部 *joshibu* girls' section
4 心 *onnagokoro* a woman's heart
手 *onnade* the cursive (*hiragana*) syllabary; a woman's handwriting; the work of women
夫 *myōto* husband and wife, couple, pair
天下 *onnadenka* a woman who rules the home
戸主 *onna koshu* female head of a house
文字 *onna moji* the cursive syllabary (*hiragana*); a woman's handwriting
王 *joō, nyoō* queen; belle; princess
王蜂 *joōbachi* queen bee
中 *jochū* servant, maid; waitress, barmaid
中入用 *jochū iriyō* servant wanted
中奉公 *jochū bōkō* domestic service
中部屋 *jochūbeya* maid's room
中難 *jochūnan* scarcity of servants
5 囚 *joshū* female prisoner
史 *joshi* Mrs., Miss
付 *onnatsu(ki)* a woman's countenance
犯 *nyobon* (priest's) clandestine romance
礼 *jorei* etiquette for ladies
主 *onna aruji* mistress, hostess, landlady
出入 *onna-de-i(ri)* troubles concerning women
正月 *Onna Shōgatsu* January 15, the ladies' New Year
芝居 *onna shibai* a play by actresses only
白波 *onna shiranami* woman robber
世帯 *onnajotai* household of women
生 *josei* schoolgirl; coed
生徒 *joseito* schoolgirl, coed
6 色 *joshoku* feminine charms; sensuality
気 *onnagi* a woman's heart. *onnake, onnakke* signs of a woman around
伊達 *onnadate* a woman who champions the underdog (a female Robin Hood)
任 *onnama(kase)* committing one's work to a woman
好 *onnazu(ki)* woman admirer; one admired by women; a lustful man
仮名 *onnagana* the *hiragana*
7 医 *joi* woman doctor
戒 *jokai* (Buddhist) commandment against lewdness
体 *nyotai, jotai* a woman's body
坂 *onnazaka* the gentler of two slopes
狂 *onnaguru(i)* philandering
形 *onnagata, oyama* female impersonator
兵 *johei* woman soldier (WAC, WAVE, etc.)
系 *jokei* female line
声 *josei* female voice
旱 *onna hideri* shortage of women
児 *joji* baby girl, primary schoolgirl
8 松 *609memmatsu* red pine
波 *menami* receding wave, backwash
官 *jokan, nyokan* court lady, maid of honor

店員 *joten-in* salesgirl
郎 *jorō* prostitute, geisha
郎屋 *jorōya* brothel
郎買 *jorōka(i)* patronizing prostitutes
郎衆 *jorōshu* prostitute
房 *nyōbo, nyōbō* court lady; wife
房役 *nyōbōyaku* righthand man ⌈ladies
房言葉 *nyōbō kotoba* court language of
房持 *nyōbōmo(chi)* a married man
学 *jogaku* women's lessons
学生 *jogakusei* girl student
学院 *jogakuin* girls' school
学校 *jogakkō* girls' school ⌈gender
性 *josei* woman; womanhood; feminine
性化 *joseika* feminization, feminism
性的 *joseiteki* feminine, effeminate
性美 *joseibi* womanly beauty
性解放論 *josei kaihōron* feminism
9 食 *onnaku(i)* philanderer, lady-killer
持 *onnamo(chi)* for ladies
神 *megami, joshin, nyoshin* goddess
院 *nyōin, nyo-in* a (Buddhist) nun from the
帝 *jotei* empress ⌊Imperial Family
客 *onna kyaku* lady visitor
皇 *jokō* empress, queen ⌈womanish pose
姿 *onna sugata* the guise of a woman;
10 振 *onnabu(ri)* a woman's charms; a wom-
訓 *jokun* women's lessons ⌊an's looks
殺 *onnagoro(shi)* the killing of a woman; a
帯 *onna obi* a woman's obi ⌊handsome man
冥利 *onna myōri* advantage of being a woman
部屋 *onnabeya* maids' quarters, women's apartment ⌈taurant)
将 *okami, joshō* landlady, hostess (of a res-
将軍 *joshōgun* an Amazon ⌈female
流 *joryū* accomplished woman; fair sex;
流文学 *joryū bungaku* feminine literature
流作家 *joryū sakka* woman novelist
流歌手 *joryū kashu* woman singer
11 達 *onnatachi* women. *onnadate* woman outlaw who champions the underdog
盛 *onnazaka(ri)* the prime of womanhood
執事 *onna shitsuji* deaconess ⌈bauchery
道楽 *onna dōraku* sensual pleasures, de-
教員 *jokyōin* lady teacher
教師 *jokyōshi* lady teacher
12 傑 *joketsu* heroine; outstanding woman
婿 *josei* son-in-law
御 *nyōgo* court lady; the concubine of an
湯 *onnayu* ladies' bath ⌊emperor
装 *josō* female attire; dressing in female
給 *jokyū* waitress ⌊attire
給仕 *onna kyūji* waitress
尊 *joson* respect for women ⌈men
尊男卑 *joson-dampi* putting women above
13 僧 *nyōsō* Buddhist nun
嫌 *onnagira(i)* woman-hater
業 *onna waza* the work of women
14 誑 *onnatarashi* philanderer, lady-killer
誡 *jokai* instructions for women
監 *jokan* female-prisoners' ward
15 権 *joken* women's rights; woman suffrage
16 親 *onna oya* mother
17 優 *joyū* actress
優劇 *joyūgeki* a play whose female parts are played by women and not men
優髷 *joyūmage* an actress' coiffure
18 難 *jonan* trouble with women
20 護島 *nyōgo(ga)shima* isle of women
22 鑑 *jokan* model for women

2

B 奴 1186 / F488 DO manservant, slave; fellow. NU manservant. *yakko* servant, valet, footman; clown; the fellow, the guy. *yatsu* fellow, guy. *me-* prefix indicating ridicule or despite.

5 凧 *yakkodako* kites shaped like ancient foot-
7 豆腐 *yakkodōfu* tofu cut in cubes ⌊men
9 姿 *yakko sugata* disguised footman
10 原 *yatsubara* fellows, guys
11 婢 *dohi, nuhi* servant; male or female slaves
12 等 *yatsura* fellows, guys
14 僕 *doboku* manservant; slave
様 *yakko san* that guy
鳴 *dona(ru)* roar, shout, yell, growl
鳴込 *dona(ri)-ko(mu)* storm into
鳴立 *dona(ri)-ta(teru)* roar, rave, rage
鳴附 *dona(ri)-tsu(keru)* scold, call down
鳴散 *dona(ri)-chi(rasu)* rant right and left
15 輩 *dohai* we; servants; those fellows
16 隷 *dorei* slave, servant
隷化 *doreika* enslaving
隷所有者 *dorei shoyūsha* slaveholder
隷制 *doreisei* slavery
隷制度 *dorei seido* slavery ⌈on
隷視 *doreishi suru* treat as slaves, look down
隷略奪者 *dorei ryakudatsusha* slave raider
隷廃止主義 *dorei haishi shugi* abolitionism
隷廃止論 *dorei haishiron* abolitionism
隷解放 *dorei kaihō* emancipation of slaves

3

妄 See 288.

妁 1187 / F490 SHAKU go-between.

B 妃 1188 / F491 HI queen; princess. *kisaki* queen.

13 殿下 *Hidenka* Her Imperial Highness (a princess or consort)

如 1189 F490 B Jo. Nyo. *goto(ki)* like, such as, as if. *shi(kazu)* be better, be best. *shi(ku)* be equal to, be like. *goto(ku)* like, as, as if. *goto(shi)* seem to be, be like.

8 上 *jojō* the above-mentioned
才無 *josaina(i), josai (no) na(i)* clever, shrewd, smart, adroit, tactful; sociable
4 月 *kisaragi* 2nd lunar month
7 来 *nyorai* Buddha
何 *ikaga, dō* How (about it)? How (are you)? *ikan* what, how. *ikaga(washi)* unreliable; questionable. *ika(na), ika(naru)* what (kind), anybody, everybody; nobody (with neg.). *ika ni* how. *ika ni mo* indeed, really, certainly; apparently, as if. *ika nimo shite* by all means
何物 *ikamono* spurious article
何許 *ikabaka(ri)* about how much
何程 *ikahodo* how much, how many, no matter how much
何様 *ikayō* how; what kind. *ikasama* how; what kind; fraud, swindle; I see; to be sure
何様師 *ikasamashi* cheater, deceiver
8 法 *nyohō* pious, faithful, honest
実 *nyojitsu ni* truly, realistically
雨露 *jōro* watering can
13 意 *nyo-i* priest's staff; ease, comfort
21 露 *jōro, joro* watering can

奸 1190 F488 Kan wickedness, mischief, rudeness.

2 人 *kanjin* knave, scoundrel
3 才 *kansai* craftiness, cunning
4 凶 *kankyō* wickedness, wicked people
手段 *kanshudan* underhanded trick
6 臣 *kanshin* traitor
曲 *kankyoku* wickedness; wicked scheming
吏 *kanri* corrupt official
7 佞 *kannei* craftiness, wickedness
邪 *kanja* wicked person; wickedness
8 物 *kambutsu* rascal, villain, crook
9 計 *kankei* trick, evil design, sharp practice
10 徒 *kanto* wicked people
11 婦 *kampu* wicked woman
悪 *kan-aku* wickedness, treachery
商 *kanshō* dishonest merchant
12 詐 *kansa* craft, guile, deceit
策 *kansaku* sinister scheme
智 *kanchi* cunning, subtlety
13 賊 *kanzoku* villain, traitor, ruffian
16 謀 *kambō* wicked scheming
16 黠 *kankatsu* craftiness; crafty person
19 譎 *kanketsu* perverseness and prevarication

好 1191 F489 B Kō. *kono(mu)* like, be fond of. *su(ku)* like, love, be fond of. *kono(mi)* taste, fondness, bent, choice, wish; fashion, mode. *kono(mashii)* desirable, pleasant, enviable. *kono(nde)* by choice, willingly; often. *suki* liking, love, taste, bent. *yo(shi)* good, all right, well, so. *yo(shimi)* friendship, intimacy, good will. *su(kanai)* odious, disagreeable. *i(i), yo(i)* (see under 良 3885.0). *su(itarashii)* lovable, charming, nice. *-zu(ki)* lover of, fan, enthusiast, maniac. good; favorable.

1 一対 *kōittsui* well-matched couple
2 人物 *kōjimbutsu* good-natured man
3 士 *kōshi* fine man, gentleman
子 *i(i) ko, yo(i) ko* good child, nice boy, nice girl
下物 *kōkabutsu* favorite dish, relish
4 手 *kōshu* good move (in a game)
化 *kōka* getting better
天気 *kōtenki* fine weather
不好 *su(ki)-busu(ki)* taste, likes and dislikes
5 加減 *i(i) kagen no, yo(i) kagen no* moderate, temperate, proper; haphazard; unconvincing, halfhearted. *i(i) kagen* quite, rather (old)
古 *kōko* love of antiquities
古癖 *kōkoheki* antiquarianism, love of antiquities
打 *kōda* a good hit
打者 *kōdasha* (baseball) slugger
打順 *kōdajun* good batting order
6 仲 *i(i) naka, yo(i) naka* intimacy; being in love
在 *kōzai* a good living
地位 *kōchi-i* advantageous position
印象 *kōinshō* good impression
成績 *kōseiseki* good results
気 *i(i)ki na* easygoing, optimistic; conceited
気味 *i(i)kimi, i(i)kibi, yo(i)kimi* serves you right
好 *su(ki)-kono(mu)* like, be fond of. *su(ki)-zu(ki)* a matter of taste
好翁 *kōkōō* an old man of character
好爺 *kōkōya* a good-natured old man
色 *kōshoku* sensuality, lewdness, lust
色文学 *kōshoku bungaku* pornographic literature
色本 *kōshokubon* suggestive story
色家 *kōshokuka* sensual person
色漢 *koshokukan* sensual person
7 技 *kōgi* fine play, fine game, good acting
投 *kōtō* nice pitching
男子 *kōdanshi* handsome man
角家 *kōkakuka* wrestling fan
材料 *kōzairyō* good data, good news
位置 *kōichi* good location
8 例 *kōrei* good illustration
味 *kōmi* sweet taste; delicacies
況 *kōkyō* prosperity, boom
物 *i(i) mono, yo(i) mono* a good thing. *kōbutsu* something good; a favorite dish

尚 *kōshō* taste, fashion
者 *su(ki)mono* lover of, person with a taste for; lecherous person
取組 *kōtorikumi* good game, good match
放題 *su(ki)hōdai* doing just as one pleases
奇 *kōki* curiosity, inquisitiveness
奇心 *kōkishin* curiosity, inquisitiveness
学 *kōgaku* love of learning
学心 *kōgakushin* love of learning
事 *kōji* happy event; good act; curiosity. *kōzu* curiosity, amateurism, dilettantism
事者 *kōjisha* amateur, dilettante
事家 *kōzuka* dilettante, amateur
9 音 *kōin* good news
発 *kōhatsu* frequent occurrence
10 個 *kōko* propriety. *kōko no* ideal, excellent
都合 *kōtsugō na* favorable, fortunate
時季 *kōjiki* good season for
時期 *kōjiki* good season for
時節 *kōjisetsu* good season for
時機 *kōjiki* opportune moment, nick of time
11 運 *kōun* good fortune, lucky break
情 *kōjō* good feeling, friendliness
転 *kōten* favorable turn, improvement
悪 *kōo* likes and dislikes; fancy; partiality
望 *kōbō* promising future
球 *kōkyū* a fine pitch (to hit)
球家 *kōkyūka* baseball fan
12 順 *kōjun na* favorable
晴 *kōsei* fine weather
期 *kōki* right time
景気 *kōkeiki* boom, good times
結果 *kōkekka* good results, success
評 *kōhyō* public favor, favorable criticism
評嘖嘖 *kōhyō-sakusaku* very popular
13 適 *kōteki* very suitable, ideal
嫌 *su(ki)-kira(i)* likes and dislikes, taste
漢 *kōkan* fine fellow
愛 *kōai suru* love, care for, be fond of
感 *kōkan* good feeling, good impression
楽家 *kōgakuka* music lover
意 *kōi* good will, friendliness, favor, kindness, courtesy, good offices
意上 *kōijō* as a favor
意的 *kōiteki* friendly, sympathetic
戦 *kōsen* pro-war; bellicosity, belligerency
戦的 *kōsenteki* warlike
戦国 *kōsenkoku* warlike nation
戦国民 *kōsen kokumin* warlike nation
14 演 *kōen* good acting
箇 *kōko* propriety. *kōko no* ideal, excellent
15 誼 *kōgi* friendship, intimacy, your kindness
調 *kōchō no* favorable, promising, satisfactory
餌 *kōji* bait, decoy; lure, temptation
劇家 *kōgekika* theatergoer
影響 *kōeikyō* favorable influence

敵 *kōteki*=next word
敵手 *kōtekishu* worthy opponent
16 機 *kōki* good chance, psychological moment
機会 *kōkikai* good chance, psychological moment
18 顔 *i(i) kao, yo(i) kao* good looks; good humor; smiling face; influential person
題目 *kōdaimoku* good topic

4

妥 See 2823.

姊 See 姉 1207.

妒 1192 F492 See 妬 1205.

妣 1193 F495 HI mother.

妓 1194 F492 GI singing girl, geisha, courtesan, prostitute.
13 楼 *girō* brothel
16 館 *gikan* brothel

姸 1195 F501 妍 KEN beauty, splendor, grace.
19 艶 *ken-en* charm, beauty
19 麗 *kenrei* beauty of facial features
23 豔 *ken-en* charm, beauty

B **妨** 1196 F495 BŌ. HŌ. *samata(geru)* disturb, prevent, hamper, hinder, obstruct. *samata(ge)*=*jama* 邪魔 2849.21.
10 害 *bōgai* interference, obstruction, disturbance
害物 *bōgaibutsu* obstacle, impediment
害放送 *bōgai hōsō* radio jamming
13 碍 *bōgai*=妨害 (see above–10)
19 礙 *bōgai*=妨害 (see above–10)

B **妊** 1197 F492 姙 NIN. *hara(mu), migomo(ru)* become pregnant; be pregnant; be filled with.
3 女 *hara(mi) onna* pregnant woman
10 娠 *ninshin* pregnancy, conception
娠中 *ninshinchū* during pregnancy
娠中絶 *ninshin chūzetsu* artificial abortion
娠調節 *ninshin chōsetsu* birth control
11 産婦 *ninsampu* expectant and nursing mothers
婦 *nimpu* pregnant woman
婦服 *nimpufuku* maternity dress

妖 1198 F493 YŌ attractive, bewitching; calamity.

3女 *yōjo* fairy, witch, enchantress, vampire
6気 *yōki* ghostly, spooky
8怪 *yōkai* ghost, apparition
怪談 *yōkaidan* ghost story
9星 *yōsei* unlucky star; comet
美 *yōbi* bewitching beauty
11婦 *yōfu* enchantress, a Jezebel
術 *yōjutsu* magic, sorcery, witchcraft
婆 *yōba* witch, hag
12雲 *yōun* ominous cloud
14精 *yōsei* elf, sprite, fairy
19艶 *yōen* voluptuous charm
21魔 *yōma* ghost, apparition

B 妙 1199/F494 Myō strange, queer; mystery, miracle; cleverness. *tae(naru)* exquisite, excellent; melodious; delicate; charming; marvelous. *myō(chikirin)* strange, queer.
4手 *myōshu* excellent skill; expert; good move
5用 *myōyō* wonderful effect
句 *myōku* clever expression; fine verse
6曲 *myōkyoku* sweet melody, fine piece of music
7技 *myōgi* outstanding skill, splendid feat, stunt
8味 *myōmi* charms, exquisite beauty
所 *myōsho* point of beauty, beauty
法 *myōhō* clever method; marvelous law of Buddha; mystery
法蓮華経 *Myōhōrengekyō* the Lotus Sutra
8典 *myōten* sacred book
9音 *myōon* beautiful sound
計 *myōkei* wise plan, clever trick
10致 *myōchi*=*myōmi* 妙味 (see above–8)
案 *myōan* bright idea, excellent plan
11理 *myōri* wonderful truths
12絶 *myōzetsu no* superb, exquisite
策 *myōsaku* clever plan
筆 *myōhitsu* excellent calligraphy or painting
13適 *myōteki* strange; natural
14境 *myōkyō* wonderful place
算 *myōsan* clever plan
15趣 *myōshu* beauties, charms
16機 *myōki* delicate shift in trends
薬 *myōyaku* miracle drug
17齢 *myōrei* youth
19麗 *myōrei* beautiful face

5

妥 See 3346.

委 See 3267.

姆 1200/F496 Bo wet nurse.

姑 1201/F497 Ko. *shūtome, shūto* mother-in-law.
10息 *kosoku* makeshift

姐 1202/F497 So girl; elder sister; maidservant.
12御 *anego* elder sister (polite)

B 姓 1203/F498 Shō. Sei surname, family name. *kabane* new name conferred by the emperor.
4氏 *seishi* surname
6名 *seimei* name

A 妹 1204/F496 Mai. *imōto, imoto, imo* younger sister.
4分 *imōtobun* sworn sister
8姑 *imoshūtome* sisters of a wife
9背 *imose*=妹脊 (see below–10)
10娘 *imōto musume* younger daughter
脊 *imose* man and wife; elder brother and younger sister; elder sister and younger brother
12婿 *imōto muko* husband of a younger sister
御 *imōtogo* your sister

妬=妒 1205/F495 To. *neta(mu)* be jealous of, be envious of. *neta(mi)* jealousy. *neta(mashii)* jealous of, envious of; enviable.
4心 *toshin* jealousy
7見 *neta(mi)-mi(ru)* look upon with envy

A 妻 1206/F496 Sai (my) wife. *tsuma* wife, spouse.
3女 *saijo* wife; wife and daughters
子 *saishi, tsumako* wife and children, one's family
4戸 *tsumado* side door; paneled door
6合 *mea(waseru)* arrange a marriage (for a girl)
7君 *saikun* wife
8妾 *saishō* wife and concubines
9室 *saishitsu* wife
10恋 *tsumagoi* love for one's spouse
格子 *tsumagōshi* latticework
帯 *saitai* marriage, matrimony
帯者 *saitaisha* married man
12鈍 *sainoro* being henpecked

A 姉=姊 1207/F496 Shi. *ane* elder sister. *nē(san)* elder sister; waitress; girl. *nē(ya)* maid. *-shi* Miss, Mrs.
3上 *aneue* elder sister
女房 *ane nyōbō* a wife who is older
4分 *anebun* elder sister
7君 *anegimi* elder sister
8妹 *shimai, ane-imōto* sisters
妹会社 *shimaigaisha* affiliated companies

3 口口土士夂夊夕大[女]5子宀寸小⺌尢尸屮山川巛工己巾干幺广廴廾弋弓彐彑彡彳

妹品 *shimaihin* companion product
妹船 *shimaisen* sister ship
10 娘 *ane musume* elder daughter
12 婿 *ane muko* elder sister's husband
御 *anego* elder sister (polite)
貴 *aneki* elder sister
14 様 *nēsan, nēsama* elder sister
様冠 *anesankabu(ri)* female workers' head towels

A 始 1208/F497 SHI beginning. *haji(maru) vi* begin, start, open; date from; (season) sets in; arise, break out; originate in. *haji(maranai)* be of no avail, accomplish nothing. *haji(meru) vt* begin, open, start, originate, inaugurate, initiate. *haji(mari)* beginning, inception, opening, start, origin. *haji(me)* beginning, origin. *haji(mete)* (for) the first time; not until. *haji(memashite)*, *haji(mete)* for the first time (I greet you).

5 末 *shimatsu* circumstances; management; disposal, settlement; control
末屋 *shimatsuya* thrifty person
末書 *shimatsusho* written explanation, written apology
9 祖 *shiso* founder, originator, pioneer, progenitor
発 *shihatsu* first train, first bus; starting (station)
発駅 *shihatsu eki* starting station
10 原 *shigen* origin, inception
11 終 *shijū, shotchū* all the time, always, constantly. *shijū no* the whole, all
球 *shikyū* the firstball, opening of the ball game
球式 *shikyūshiki* throwing the first ball, opening of the ball game
動 *shidō* starting (in machines)
動機 *shidōki* starter
12 期 *shiki* beginning date; initial stage
13 業 *shigyō* commencement of work; beginning of a class
業式 *shigyōshiki* opening ceremony
15 審 *shishin* first trial

— 6 —

姜 See 3657.

威 See 1803.

姙 1209/F499 See 妊 1197.

姸 1210/F501 See 妍 1195.

娜 1211/F504 DA graceful.

姪 1212/F501 TETSU. *mei* niece.

姥 1213/F500 BO. MO. *uba* aged woman.
10 桜 *ubazakura* a faded beauty

B 姻 1214/F502 IN marry.
10 家 *inka* a family related by marriage
11 戚 *inseki* in-laws
族 *inzoku* relative by remarriage
族閥 *inzokubatsu* nepotism

B 姿 1215/F502 SHI. *sugata* figure, form, shape; appearance, attire; posture; oneself; portrait; aspect.
7 見 *sugatami* dresser, full-length mirror
10 容 *shiyō* form, appearance, countenance
11 盛 *sugatazaka(ri)* the charming beauty of young womanhood
12 絵 *sugatae* portrait
13 勢 *shisei* posture, pose
14 態 *shitai* figure, form, style

B 姫 1216/F501 姬 KI. *hime* princess; young lady of birth. *hime-* little, pretty.
8 小松 *hime komatsu* a small pine
7 君 *himegimi* princess, young lady of birth
9 垣 *himegaki* low fence
10 宮 *himemiya* princess
12 御前 *himegoze, himegozen* princess; young lady of birth; a sweet little girl
14 様 *hiisama* daughter of a noble
15 糊 *himenori* rice paste, rice starch
22 鑑 *hime kagami* a model woman; a model for young women

姦 1217/F500 KAN wickedness, mischief. *kan(suru)* seduce, assault, rape. *kashima(shii)* noisy, boisterous.
2 人 *kanjin* villain, scoundrel
3 才 *kansai* craftiness, cunning
4 凶 *kankyō* wickedness, wicked person
夫 *kampu* adulterer, paramour
6 曲 *kankyoku* wickedness; wicked scheming
吏 *kanri* corrupt official
7 佞 *kannei* wickedness
邪 *kanja* wickedness; wicked person
8 物 *kambutsu* rascal, villain, crook
9 計 *kankei* trick, evil design, sharp practice
通 *kantsū* adultery
通者 *kantsūsha* adulterer, adulteress
通罪 *kantsūzai* crime of adultery
10 徒 *kanto* wicked people
11 婦 *kampu* adultress

淫 *kan-in* adultery
悪 *kan-aku* wickedness, treachery
12 詐 *kansa* craft, guile, deceit
雄 *kan-yū* great traitor, great villain
富 *kampu* ill-gotten gain
13 賊 *kanzoku* traitor, villain, ruffian
16 謀 *kambō* wicked scheming
18 黠 *kankatsu* craftiness; crafty person
19 譎 *kanketsu* perverseness and prevarication

7

姫 1218 F501 See **姬** 1216.

娩 1219 F505 BEN bear (children).

B **娠** 1220 F505 SHIN pregnancy.

娟 1221 F504 EN, KEN beauty of face.

娣 1222 F505 TEI. *imoto, imōto* younger sister.

婀 1223 F505 **娿** A. *ada, ada(ppoi)*＝阿娜 4985.9.
9 娜 *ada(meku)* (women) charm, bewitch

娑 1224 F504 SHA old woman.
11 婆 *shaba* this corrupt world
婆気 *shabaki, shabake* worldly desires or ambitions

B **娘** 1225 F504 JŌ. *musume* daughter, girl, young woman.
3 子 *jōshi* girl, woman
子軍 *jōshigun* Amazonian troops
4 心 *musumegokoro* girlish innocence「woman
6 気質 *musume katagi* the nature of a young
10 師 *musumeshi* burglarizing a storehouse
11 盛 *musumezaka(ri)* the prime of young womanhood
12 婿 *musume-muko* adopted son-in-law

B **娯** 1226 F504 **娛** Go pleasure.
13 楽 *goraku* pleasure, amusement, recreation, entertainment
楽用 *gorakuyō* for amusement
楽品 *gorakuhin* plaything
楽室 *gorakushitsu* recreation room
楽場 *gorakujō* amusement place
楽街 *gorakugai* amusement quarter
楽機関 *goraku kikan* recreational facilities

8

娩 See 1219.

娯 **娛** See 1226.

婬 1227 F508 See **淫** 2603.

婪 1228 F508 RAN covet.

婁 1229 F505 RU, RŌ frequently; tie.

娶 1230 F505 SHU. *meto(ru)* marry (a woman). *meawa(seru)* arrange a marriage (for a girl).

娵 1231 F505 SHU. SHŪ. SU. *yome* (see under 嫁 1249.0).
2 入 *yome-i(ri)* marriage, wedding

婢 1232 F507 HI maidservant. *hashitame* maidservant.
14 僕 *hiboku* servants, menials

婉 1233 F506 EN graceful.
6 曲 *enkyoku na* euphemistic, circumlocutatory, roundabout, indirect, insinuating
9 美 *embi* beauty, charm

B **婆** 1234 F506 BA. *baba* old woman; grandmother. *baba, babā* old woman; wet nurse. *bā(ya)* wet nurse; old maid; old housekeeper.
4 心 *bashin* grandmotherly solicitude
14 様 *bāsan* old woman; grandmother
19 羅門 *Baramon* Brahman

娼 1235 F505 **倡** SHŌ prostitute.
7 妓 *shōgi* prostitute, harlot
10 家 *shōka* brothel
11 婦 *shōfu* prostitute, harlot
13 楼 *shōrō* brothel

B **婚** 1236 F506 KON marriage.
5 礼 *konrei* wedding ceremony
9 姻 *kon-in* marriage
姻届 *kon-in todoke* marriage registration
約 *kon-yaku* engagement, betrothal
約者 *kon-yakusha* fiancé, fiancée
10 家 *konka* one's husband's family

宴 *kon-en* wedding feast
12 期 *konki* marriageable age
13 嫁 *konka* marriage
15 儀 *kongi* wedding ceremony

A **婦** 1237/F507 **婦** FU woman; wife; bride.
2 人 *fujin* lady, woman, female
人用 *fujin-yō* for ladies
人会 *fujinkai* ladies' society
人参政権 *fujin sanseiken* woman suffrage
人科 *fujinka* gynecology
人科学 *fujinkagaku* gynecology
人病 *fujimbyō* women's diseases
人解放 *fujin kaihō* emancipation of women
人警官 *fujin keikan* policewoman
3 女 *fujo* woman, womankind
女子 *fujoshi* woman and child
8 長 *fuchō* head nurse
10 容 *fuyō* etiquette for women
11 道 *fudō* womanhood, duties of women
14 選 *fusen* woman suffrage
徳 *futoku* womanly virtues
15 権 *fuken* woman's rights
19 警 *fukei* policewoman

9

㛐 See 1245.

婢 See 1232.

媛 1238/F509 EN. *hime* princess; young lady of noble birth.

B **婿** 1239/F508/F447 **壻 聟** SEI. *muko* son-in-law.
2 入 *muko-i(ri) suru* become the heir of one's wife's family
8 取 *mukoto(ri)* adopting a son-in-law
取娘 *mukoto(ri) musume* a daughter whose husband is adopted into her family
11 探 *mukosaga(shi)* hunting a husband for one's daughter
15 養子 *muko-yōshi* son-in-law adopted as an heir

媚 1240/F509 BI. *ko(biru)* flatter, humor, flirt (by a woman), curry favor. *kobi* flattery, cajolery, flirtation.
14 態 *bitai* coquetry
16 薬 *biyaku* an aphrodisiac
17 諂 *ko(bi)-hetsura(i)* adulation, flattery

B **媒** 1241/F508 BAI. *nakadachi* go-between.
4 介 *baikai* mediation, intervention, agency
介物 *baikaibutsu* medium, agency; carrier (of germs), vehicle
6 妁 *baishaku* matchmaking
妁人 *baishakunin* matchmaker, go-between
7 体 *baitai* medium (in biology)
材 *baizai* a catalytic agent
9 染 *baisen* color fixing
10 酌 *baishaku* matchmaking
酌人 *baishakunin* matchmaker, go-between
11 鳥 *otori* a lure, decoy, stool pigeon. *baichō* decoy bird
15 質 *baishitsu* medium (of transmission)

10

媽 1242/F510 BO mother; mare.

嫗 1243/F510 Ō mother; grandmother; woman. *ōna* old woman.

媳 1244/F510 SEKI. *yome* (see under 嫁 1249.0).

嫂 1245/F511 SŌ. *aniyome* elder brother's wife.

媾 1246/F510 KŌ association, intimacy.
6 曳 *aibiki* date, rendezvous, clandestine courting
8 和 *kōwa suru* make peace

嫋 1247/F511 JŌ. *nayo(yakana)* supple, pliant delicate, slender. *shina(yakana)* (see under 撓 1994.0). *tao(yakana)* graceful.
6 竹 *nayotake* pliant bamboo
13 嫋 *nayonayo to* feebly, languidly. *nayonayo toshita* feeble, delicate, slender. *jōjō* blowing (of a wind); soft, pliant; resounding

嫉 1248/F511 SHITSU. *sone(mu)* be jealous, envy. *neta(mu)* (see under 妬 1205.0). *sone(mi)*, *neta(mi)* jealousy, envy.
8 妬 *shitto* jealousy, envy
妬心 *shittoshin* jealousy, envy
11 深 *sone(mi)buka(i)*, *neta(mi)buka(i)* envious, jealous
視 *shisshi* jealousy; glaring at; envy

B **嫁** 1249/F510 KA. *ka(suru)*, *ka(su)* marry (a man); be married to; blame. *totsu(gu)* marry off; get married. *yome* bride, young wife, daughter-in-law.
2 入 *yome-i(ri)* marriage, wedding
入支度 *yome-i(ri)-jitaku* trousseau
入衣裳 *yome-i(ri) ishō* trousseau
3 女 *yomejo* bride
8 取 *yometo(ri)* taking a wife

11 笠 *yome(ga)kasa* limpet, tent shell
12 期 *kaki* marriageable age
御 *yomego* bride (polite)
御寮 *yomegoryō* bride (polite)
13 資 *kashi* dowry

嫌 1250/F511 **嫌** KEN. *iya(garu)* dislike, hate; be unwilling (to do something). *kira(u)* hate, detest, dislike. *kira(i)* dislike, disinclination, abhorrence, prejudice; tinge, touch, suspicion. *kira(i) na* distasteful, disagreeable, repugnant. *iya na* disagreeable. *iya(garase)* a disagreeable thing. *iya(rashii)* unpleasant, offensive *iya ni* disagreeably, offensively.

6 気 *iyaki* aversion, repugnance
7 忌 *kenki* dislike, aversion
8 味 *iyami* disagreeableness; gaudiness; mannerism; sarcasm
11 悪 *ken-o* dislike, hatred, abhorrence
悪感 *ken-okan* dislike, hatred
13 嫌 *iya-iya* reluctantly
嫌乍 *iya-iyanagara* reluctantly
14 厭 *ken-en* dislike, hate, loathing
疑 *kengi* suspicion; accusation
疑者 *kengisha* suspected person

11

嫣 1251/F512 EN beauty.

12 然 *enzen(taru)* graceful, smiling, polite

嫩 1252/F513 DON young; weak.

9 草 *don-yō, wakaba* young foliage
12 葉 *wakakusa* young grass

嫡 1253/F512 **嫡** B CHAKU, TEKI legitimacy; legitimate child; legitimate wife; direct descent.

3 子 *chakushi* legitimate child
5 出 *chakushutsu* legitimacy (of birth)
出子 *chakushutsushi* legitimate child
7 男 *chakunan* heir, eldest son
8 妻 *chakusai* legitimate wife
9 室 *chakushitsu* legitimate wife
10 孫 *chakuson* eldest son of one's son and heir; eldest son's descendants
流 *chakuryū* lineage of the eldest son
14 嫡 *chakuchaku* direct succession

12

嬋 1254/F514 SEN beautiful.

10 娟 *senken(taru)* graceful, charming, beautiful

嬉 1255/F513 KI. *ure(shigaru)* be glad, be pleased, rejoice. *ure(shigaraseru)* please, delight, flatter. *ure(shisōna), ure(shigena)* delightful, joyful, happy. *ure(shii)* glad, happy, delightful, pleasant.

8 泣 *ure(shi)na(ki)* crying for joy
10 涙 *ure(shi)namida* tears of joy
笑 *kishō* happy laughter
11 遊 *kiyū* playing happily
15 戯 *kigi suru* frolic
嬉 *kiki(taru)* gleeful, joyful

嬌 1256/F514 KYŌ attractive.

6 名 *kyōmei* reputation for beauty
7 声 *kyōsei* lovely voice
9 姿 *kyōshi* lovely figure
10 笑 *kyōshō* charming smile
11 羞 *kyōshū* charming and coy
14 態 *kyōtai, shina* coquetry
19 艶 *kyōen* fascinating beauty

13

嬢 B 1257/F516 **孃** JŌ girl, daughter, young lady; Miss.

3 子 *jōshi* a young woman
14 様 *jōsan, (o)jōsan* young lady; your daughter

嬖 1258/F514 HEI agreeable person.

6 臣 *heishin* favorite retainer

14

嬲 See 3014.

嬪 1259/F515 HIN bride; marriage.

嬰 1260/F515 EI sharp (in music;) baby.

7 児 *eiji, midorigo* infant, baby

嬶 1261/F-X (国字) *kakā, kaka* wife (vulgar).

4 天下 *kakā denka* government by women, petticoat government

17

孃 1262/F516 See **嬢** 1257.

孀 1263/F516 SŌ. *yamome* widow.

子 RAD. 39

Ko child. At left: *ko hen.* Nickname: Child.

子 See 269.

A 子 1264 / F516 SHI viscount, master; child; male; fruit; seed. SU. *ko* child, offspring; the young (of animals). *ne* 11 p.m. to 1 a.m.; 1st zodiac sign, rat; north. *ko-* small.

[3]女 *shijo* children
山羊 *koyagi* kid
子孫孫 *shishi-sonson* descendants, posterity
[4]牛 *ko-ushi* calf
犬 *ko-inu* puppy
分 *kobun* follower, protégé, apprentice; adopted son; bad elements
午線 *shigosen* the meridian
午線経過 *shigosen keika* crossing the meridian
午環 *shigokan* meridian circle
[6]羊 *kohitsuji* lamb
早 *kobaya(i)* easily becoming pregnant
芋 *ko-imo* young taro tubers
会社 *kogaisha* subsidiary company
安貝 *koyasugai* cowrie
守 *komori* amah; baby tending; baby sitter
守歌 *komori uta* lullaby, nursery rhyme
[7]役 *koyaku* child actor, child actress; child's role
弟 *shitei* children
沢山 *kodakusan* many children (in the family)
[8]宝 *kodakara* treasure of children
供 *kodomo* child. *kodomo(rashii)* childlike
供心 *kodomogokoro* childish mind
供日 *Kodomo (no) Hi* Children's Day, May 5
供気 *kodomogi* the feelings of a child
供好 *kodomozu(ki)* love of children
供向 *kodomomu(ki)* for children
供扱 *kodomoatsuka(i)* treating like a child
供臭 *kodomokusa(i)* childish
供染 *kodomo(jimita)* childish
供時代 *kodomo jidai* childhood
供部屋 *kodomobeya* nursery, children's room
供銀行 *kodomo ginkō* children's bank (in schools)
供騙 *kodomodama(shi)* fooling a child; childish trick
[9]音 *shi-in, shion* consonant
星 *koboshi* minor star in a binary or multiple star
持 *komo(chi)* a mother; maternity; pregnancy
持甘藍 *komo(chi) kanran* Brussels sprouts
持石 *komo(chi) ishi* conglomerate
持魚 *komo(chi) uo* seed fish
[10]孫 *shison* posterity, descendants
株 *kokabu* new shares of stock
殺 *kogoro(shi)* infanticide
息 *shisoku* son
宮 *shikyū* womb
宮口 *shikyūkō* cervix of the uterus
宮炎 *shikyūen* uteritis
宮病 *shikyūbyō* uterine disease
宮癌 *shikyūgan* uterine cancer
[11]鹿 *kojika* fawn, young deer
猫 *koneko* kitten
細 *shisai*＝仔細 358.11
豚 *kobuta* young pig, shoat
規 *hototogisu* cuckoo
[12]等 *kora* children
葉 *shiyō* the first leaves of a sprouting seed
[13]僧 *kozō*＝小僧 1355.13
獅子 *kojishi* lion cub
煩悩 *kobonnō* fondness for children
福 *kobuku* many children (in the family)
福者 *kobukusha, kofukusha* a person blessed with a large family
飼 *koga(i)* raising from infancy; raising animals from birth
飼者 *kogaimono* an apprentice
[14]種 *kodane* issue, offspring, descendants
[17]癇 *shikan* eclampsia, puerperal convulsions
爵 *shishaku* viscount
爵夫人 *shishaku fujin* viscountess
[22]嚢 *shinō* seed bag

1

B 孔 1265 / F518 KŌ. KU. *ana* (see under 穴 3313.0). *hanaha(da)* (see under 甚 111.0).

[3]子 *Kōshi* Confucius
子廟 *Kōshibyō* Confucian shrine
[4]夫子 *Kōfūshi* Confucius
[5]穴 *kōketsu* hole, crack, space
[8]門 *Kōmon* Confucian School
性 *kōsei* porosity
孟 *Kō-Mō* Confucius and Mencius
孟学 *Kōmōgaku* Confucianism
[11]教 *Kōkyō* Confucianism
雀 *kujaku* peacock
雀石 *kujakuseki* malachite
雀草 *kujakusō* maidenhair fern
雀歯朶 *kujaku shida* maidenhair fern
[13]聖 *Kōsei* Confucius; a talented man

孕 1266 / F518 YŌ. *hara(mu)* become pregnant; be pregnant; be filled with.

[3]女 *hara(mi) onna* pregnant woman
子 *hara(mi)go* fetus

3

字 See 1281.

A 存 1267/F519 SON. ZON. *zon(jiru), zon(zuru)* know, be aware of, be acquainted with; think, believe, feel. *son(suru)* exist, be extant, remain, live; retain, maintain, preserve; consist of; depend on. *nagara(eru)* live on, live long.
[3]亡 *sombō* life or death, existence, fate
上 *zon(ji)-a(geru)* know, be aware of, be acquainted with
[4]分 *zombun ni* to one's heart's content, freely, without reserve
[5]立 *sonritsu* existence, subsistence
外 *zongai* contrary to expectations; beyond expectations
生 *zonjō suru* live
生中 *zonjōchū* during life
[6]在 *sonzai* existence, subsistence, being
在論 *sonzairon* ontology
[7]否 *sompi* existence, life or death
[8]知 *zonchi* knowledge of
念 *zonnen* thought, idea, concept
命 *zommei* alive, living; existence
命中 *zommeichū* during life, while living
[11]寄 *zon(ji)-yo(ru)* remember, recall. *zon(ji)-yo(ri)* one's views; one's acquaintances
掛無 *zonjigakena(i)* unexpected
[12]廃 *sompai* continuance or abolition; existence
[13]置 *sonchi suru* maintain, retain, continue
意 *zon-i* thought; idea
続 *sonzoku* continuance, continued existence, duration
続期間 *sonzoku kikan* the duration

4

孝 See 773.

孜 1268/F520 SHI industriousness.
[7]孜 *shishi to shite* untiringly, diligently

5

季 See 3266.

孟 1269/F521 Mō chief; beginning.
[3]子 *Mōshi* Mencius
[10]夏 *mōka* early summer

B 孤 1270/F522 Ko orphan. *minashigo* orphan. *hitori de* alone
[3]山 *kozan* a lone mountain
[5]立 *koritsu* isolation; helplessness
立主義 *koritsu shugi* isolationism
立政策 *koritsu seisaku* isolationist policy
[6]舟 *koshū* a lone boat
帆 *kohan* solitary sailboat
灯 *kotō* solitary light
[7]身 *koshin* lonely person
村 *koson* isolated village
児 *koji, minashigo* orphan
児院 *koji-in* orphanage
[8]松 *koshō* a lone pine tree
忠 *kochū* undying devotion
[9]城 *kojō* an isolated castle
独 *kodoku* solitude, isolation, loneliness
軍 *kogun* isolated force
客 *kokaku* a lone traveler
[10]高 *kokō* splendid isolation, proud loneliness; nobility of character
剣 *koken* a sword; only a sword
島 *kotō* a solitary island
[12]雁 *kogan* a solitary wild goose
[13]愁 *koshū* lonely contemplation
[15]蝶 *kochō* a lone butterfly
影 *koei* a lone figure; lonesome person
影悄然 *koei shōzen toshite* forlorn and crestfallen

A 学 學 1271/F524 GAKU learning, study, science, scholarship, erudition. *mana(bu)* learn, study. *mana(bi)* learning, knowledge; study.
[2]力 *gakuryoku* scholarship, knowledge, literary ability
力考査 *gakuryoku kōsa* achievement test
[3]才 *gakusai* scholastic ability
士 *Gakushi* Bachelor of Arts; college graduate
士院 *Gakushi-in* the Academy
[4]区 *gakku* school district
方 *mana(bi)kata* way to study
内 *gakunai* within the campus
友 *gakuyū* schoolmate, classmate, alumnus
友会 *gakuyūkai* alumni association
[5]外 *gakugai* off-campus, outside the school
兄 *gakkei* older student
用品 *gakuyōhin* school supplies
生 *gakusei* student
生主事 *gakusei shuji* dean of students
生用語 *gakusei yōgo* schoolboy slang
生帽 *gakuseibō* school cap
生監 *gakuseikan* dean of students
[6]会 *gakkai* institute, academy, learned society, literary society
年 *gakunen* school year
名 *gakumei* technical name
[7]位 *gakui* academic degree

究 *gakkyū* scholar, student

究的 *gakkyūteki* scholastic, academic

芸 *gakugei* art and science, literary attainments, culture

芸会 *gakugeikai* a student literary program

8長 *gakuchō* college president, rector

府 *gakufu* educational institution, seat of learning

取 *mana(bi)-to(ru)* apply a lesson to oneself

制 *gakusei* educational system

舎 *gakusha* school building

事 *gakuji* educational affairs; learning, studies

者 *gakusha* scholar, learned man, scribe

者間 *gakushakan* among scholars

9風 *gakufū* academic traditions, school character, method of study, a school (of thought)

海 *gakkai* the world of knowledge

派 *gakuha* school, sect

級 *gakkyū* school class, grade, form, standard

則 *gakusoku* school regulations

院 *gakuin* school, academy, seminary

政 *gakusei* government educational administration

界 *gakkai* academic or scientific world

科 *gakka* curriculum, course

科目 *gakkamoku* school subjects

10修 *gakushū* learning, study

徒 *gakuto* scholar, student, disciple, follower

部 *gakubu* faculty, department, college, school

部長 *gakubuchō* dean of a university department

校 *gakkō* school, educational institution

校一覧 *gakkō ichiran* school catalog

校区 *gakkōku* school district

校出 *gakkōde* educated person, college graduate

校用品 *gakkō yōhin* school supplies

校医 *gakkōi* school doctor

校長 *gakkōchō* school principal

校法人 *gakkō hōjin* educational foundation

校差 *gakkōsa* scholastic disparity among schools

校給食 *gakkō kyūshoku* school feeding

校園 *gakkōen* school garden

校構内 *gakkō kōnai* campus

11務 *gakumu* educational affairs

堂 *gakudō* educational institution, academy

窓 *gakusō* school

問 *gakumon* learning, studies, scholarship, knowledge, education, culture, science

問的 *gakumonteki* scholarly

理 *gakuri* scientific principle, a theory

理的 *gakuriteki* theoretical

習 *gakushū* learning, study

習法 *gakushūhō* study methods

習場 *gakushūjō* a school

術 *gakujutsu* science, learning, scholarship, art and science

術用語 *gakujutsu yōgo* technical term

術的 *gakujutsuteki* scientific

術語 *gakujutsugo* technical term

12帽 *gakubō* school cap

殖 *gakushoku* scholarship, learning

童 *gakudō* school child, pupil

費 *gakuhi* school expenses

期 *gakki* school term

期末 *gakkimatsu* end of a school term

期試験 *gakki shiken* term examinations

13園 *gakuen* school, educational institution; campus

僧 *gakusō* a learned priest pursuing his studies

資 *gakushi* school expenses, educational fund, endowment

業 *gakugyō* studies, schoolwork, classwork, scholarship

14歴 *gakureki* school career, academic record

閥 *gakubatsu* academic clique, school fraternity

僕 *gakuboku* a teacher's student helper

徳 *gakutoku* learning and virtue

説 *gakusetsu* theory

監 *gakkan* college dean

15課 *gakka* lesson, schoolwork, classwork, subject

寮 *gakuryō* school dormitory

16館 *gakkan* academy, school

17積 *gakuseki* student's record

齢 *gakurei* school age

19識 *gakushiki* scholarship, learning, scientific attainments

20籍 *gakuseki* school register

籍簿 *gakusekibo* school register

6

孩 1272 / F523 GAI baby; infancy.

7児 *gaiji* baby, infant

8所 *gaisho* (Catholic) limbo of infants

7

A 孫 1273 / F523 SON descendants. *mago, hiko* grandchild.

3子 *magoko* children and grandchildren, descendants

4手 *mago(no)te* back scratcher

引 *magobi(ki)* reference to secondary sources

7弟子 *mago deshi* disciples of one's disciples

10娘 *mago musume* granddaughter

株 *mago kabu* second issue of new shares

8

孰 See 316.

9

孳 See 603.

10

孶 1274/F524 See 孳 603.

11

孵 See 244.

13

學 1275/F524 See 学 1271.

14

孺 1276/F526 Ju child.

8子 *jushi* child, lad, youngster

RAD. 宀 40

U kammuri (crown like the katakana *u*). Note that the crown 穴 is Rad. 116. Nickname: *Kana U*.

2

宂 宂 冗 See 3313.

宄 1277/F527 See 宄 625.

3

写 1278/F-X See 写 626.

B 宅 1279/F527 Taku home, house, residence; our home; my husband.

6地 *takuchi* building lot, residential land; homestead
扱 *takuatsuka(i)* delivery to the house
8送 *takusō* delivery
送品 *takusōhin* consignment
12診 *takushin* home consultation
診時間 *takushin jikan* home office hours

B 宇 1280/F527 U eaves; roof; house; heaven.

4内 *udai* the whole world. *udai ni* in the whole world, under the sun
8宙 *uchū* universe, cosmos
宙万物 *uchū-bambutsu* all the universe
宙引力 *uchū inryoku* universal gravitation
宙的 *uchūteki* universal
宙服 *uchūfuku* space suit
宙学 *uchūgaku* cosmology
宙発生論 *uchūhasseiron* cosmogony
宙飛行機 *uchū hikōki* space ship
宙時代 *uchū jidai* space age
宙旅行 *uchū ryokō* space travel
宙船 *uchūsen* space ship
宙雲 *uchūun* cosmic clouds
宙塵 *uchūjin* cosmic dust
宙線 *uchūsen* cosmic rays
宙論 *uchūron* cosmology
11頂天 *uchōten* exaltation, rapture, ecstasy

A 字 1281/F519 Ji character, letter, word, handwriting. *aza* section of a village. *azana* nickname, alias, pseudonym. [子]

4引 *jibiki* dictionary
5母 *jibo* letter, alphabet, syllabic character; matrix; type
句 *jiku* terms, wording
6号 *jigō* name; nickname; size of type
7体 *jitai* form or style of a character
余 *jiama(ri)* too many characters (for the meter)
8画 *jikaku* character strokes
突 *jitsu(ki)* a pointer
典 *jiten* character dictionary
9面 *jimen, jizura* the appearance of the writing
音 *jion* Chinese (*on*) pronunciation of a character
音語 *jiongo* words formed from Chinese (*on*) sounds
10消 *jike(shi)* eraser
訓 *jikun* the Japanese (*kun*) reading of a character
書 *jisho* character dictionary
11探 *jisaga(shi)* word puzzle
13源 *jigen* construction of a character
解 *jikai* explanation of a passage
数 *jisū* number of characters
彙 *ji-i* glossary, dictionary
幕 *jimaku* title, caption
義 *jigi* meaning of a word
義的 *jigiteki* literal
義通 *jigidō(ri)* literally

A 守 1282/F528 Shu. Su. *mamo(ru)* defend, protect; keep, observe, obey; abide by; stick to; be true to. *mo(ru)* observe. *mamo(ri)* defense; guarding. *mori* nursemaid, baby sitter; baby sitting; (lighthouse) keeper. (*o*)*mamo(ri)* charm, amulet. *kami* feudal lord.

2刀 *mamo(ri)gatana* self-defense sword

[5]立 *mo(ri)-ta(teru)* bring up; support, rally around
旧 *shukyū* conservatism
札 *mamo(ri)fuda* paper charm
本尊 *mamo(ri) honzon* guardian deity, patron deity
[6]行 *mamo(ri)-okona(u)* keep, obey
成 *shusei* preservation, maintenance
[7]役 *moriyaku* guardian
抜 *mamo(ri)-nu(ku)* hold fast, protect to the end
兵 *shuhei* guards
[8]卒 *shusotsu* soldiers on guard
[9]神 *mamo(ri)gami, shushin* guardian deity
[10]唄 *moriuta* lullaby; nursery rhyme
宮 *yamori* gecko, wall lizard
[11]袋 *mamo(ri)bukuro* amulet case
[12]備 *shubi* garrison, defense; fielding (baseball)
備兵 *shubihei* garrison, guard
備隊 *shubitai* garrison
備率 *shubiritsu* fielding average (baseball)
[13]節 *shusetsu* constancy, integrity
勢 *shusei* the defensive; defensive attitude; passive attitude
戦 *shusen* defensive war, defensive fight
戦同盟 *shusen dōmei* defensive alliance
[14]歌 *moriuta* lullaby, nursery rhyme
銭奴 *shusendo* a miser, a niggard
[15]衛 *shuei* a guard, a watchman, a doorkeeper
衛長 *shueichō* captain of the guard
[20]護 *shugo* protection; guard; safeguard
護天使 *shugo tenshi* guardian angel
護役 *shugoyaku* guardian
護神 *shugoshin* guardian deity

A 安 1283 / F529 AN. *yasu(maru)* be rested, feel at ease, be relieved, repose. *yasu(njiru), yasu(nzuru)* be contented, be at ease. *yasura(u)* rest, relax. *yasu(i)* cheap, inexpensive; peaceful, quiet; gossipy, thoughtless. *yasu* cheap, low; drop (in prices). *yasu(ppoi)* cheap-looking, tawdry, insignificant. *yasu(rakana)* peaceful, tranquil, calm, restful. *yasu(pika)* knickknack, cheap finery.

[3]上 *yasua(gari)* economy. *yasu(gari) no* cheap, economical
小説 *yasushōsetsu* cheap fiction
[4]手 *yasude* cheap kind
月給 *yasugekkyū* meager salary
月給取 *yasugekkyūto(ri)* low-salaried man
心 *anshin* peace of mind, freedom from care; (sense of) relief or security; reassurance
心立命 *anshin-ritsumei* spiritual peace, enlightenment; calm resignation to fate; philosophy
心感 *anshinkan* sense of security
[5]打 *anda* safe hit
本丹 *ampontan* simpleton, dunce
芝居 *yasushibai* cheap theater
石榴 *zakuro* pomegranate
[6]安 *yasuyasu* very peaceful. *yasuyasu to* very easily, without trouble
危 *anki* fate, safety, welfare
死術 *anshijutsu* euthanasia
気 *anki* ease, comfort, feeling at home
気配 *yasukihai* bearish tone, weak tone (on the stock market)
全 *anzen* safety, security
全弁 *anzemben* safety valve
全灯 *anzentō* safety lamp
全地帯 *anzen chitai* safety zone, safety island
全系数 *anzen keisū* safety coefficient
全剃刀 *anzen kamisori* safety razor
全保障 *anzen hoshō* security
全保障理事会 *Anzen Hoshō Rijikai* Security Council
全帯 *anzentai* safety belt
全率 *anzenritsu* safety factor
全第一 *Anzen Dai Ichi* Safety First
全策 *anzensaku* safe plan
全硝子 *anzen garasu* safety glass
全装置 *anzen sōchi* safety device
全感 *anzenkan* sense of security
全器 *anzenki* safety device
[7]住 *anjū suru* live peaceably
佚 *an-itsu* ease, idleness
利 *yasuri* low interest
否 *ampi* safety, welfare, well-being
売 *yasu-u(ri)* selling cheap
条 *an(no)jō* as expected
坐 *anza* sitting at ease; leisure
材料 *yasuzairyō* bearish factor
身立命 *anshin-ritsumei*＝安心立命 (see above–4)
[8]国 *yasukuni, ankoku* a peacefully ruled country
固 *anko* security, firmness, stability
居 *ankyo, angyo* an easy life
価 *anka* low price
泊 *yasudoma(ri)* cheap inn
物 *yasumono* cheap article, bargain
臥 *anga* quiet rest
直 *anchoku* cheapness, low price
易 *an-i* ease
定 *antei* stability, equilibrium, stabilization, composure. *an(no)jō* as expected
定性 *anteisei* inclined to be stable or composed
定板 *anteiban* stabilizing fin
定度 *anteido* stability
定感 *anteikan* sense of security
[9]保 *ampo* security
神立命 *anshin-ritsumei*＝安心立命 (see above–4)
[10]逸 *an-itsu* ease, idleness
値 *yasune* low price
眠 *amnin* quiet sleep
泰 *antai* peace, security, tranquility

料理屋 *yasuryōriya* cheap restaurant
酒 *yasuzake* cheap saké
酒場 *yasusakaba* cheap saloon
息 *ansoku* rest, repose
息日 *ansokubi, ansokunichi, ansokujitsu* the Sabbath; a sabbath; a day of rest
息日学校 *Ansokunichi Gakkō* Sabbath School
息所 *ansokujo* resting place
息香酸 *ansokukōsan* benzoic acid
11悪 *yasu(karō)-waru(karō)* You get what you pay for.
宿 *yasuyado* cheap hotel
産 *anzan* easy delivery
12閑 *ankan to* idly, indolently
堵 *ando* relief, reassurance
惰 *anda* shiftlessness; laziness
着 *anchaku* safe arrival
普請 *yasubushin* cheap structure
13寝 *yasu-i* quiet sleep
置 *anchi* enshrinement, installation (of an image)
意 *an-i*=*anshin* 安心 (see above–4)
楽 *anraku* ease, comfort
楽死 *anrakushi* euthanasia, mercy killing
楽椅子 *anraku isu* easy chair
14銭 *yasuzeni* small amount of money
雑誌 *yasuzasshi* cheap magazine
静 *ansei* rest, quiet, tranquility
静度 *anseido* degree of quiet (required in a patient)
寧 *annei* public peace, tranquility
寧秩序 *annei-chitsujo* peace and order
15慮 *anryo*=*anshin* 安心 (see above–4)
請合 *yasu-u(ke)a(i)* rash promise, lightly undertaking (something)
16穏 *annon, an-on* peace, quiet, tranquility

—— 4 ——

宍 1284 F531 See 肉 3724.

宋 1285 F530 Sō Sung (dynasty); dwell.
8学 *Sōgaku* the learning of the Sungs
9音 *Sōon* Sung-dynasty pronunciation
12朝 *Sōchō* Sung dynasty
14銭 *Sōsen* Sung currency

宏 1286 F531 Kō wide, large.
3大 *kōdai na* vast, extensive, magnificent
6壮 *kōsō na* grand, imposing
7図 *kōto* large plans
9荘 *kōsō* splendor, grandeur
12遠 *kōen na* vast and far-reaching
量 *kōryō* generosity, broadmindedness
13業 *kōgyō* a large extensive enterprise
17謨 *kōbo* broad national-development plan

牢 1287 F1217 Rō prison, jail; hardness. [牛]
2人 *rōnin*=浪人 2570.2
入 *rōi(ri)* entering prison
5乎 *rōko(taru)* firm, strong, inflexible, steadfast
6死 *rōshi* death in prison
7囲 *rōgako(i)* prison wall
役人 *rōyakunin* jailer
8固 *rōko(taru)*=牢乎 (see above–5)
9屋 *rōya* prison, jail
10破 *rōyabu(ri)* jailbreak
記 *rōki suru* fix in the memory
12番 *rōban* jailer
14獄 *rōgoku* prison, jail

A **完** 1288 F531 Kan completion, end. *mattō(suru)*, *matta(ku)* (see under 全 384.0).
2了 *kanryō* completion, conclusion
了形 *kanryōkei* perfect tense
了時制 *kanryō jisei* perfect tense
3工 *kankō* completion
5本 *kampon* complete works
6成 *kansei suru* finish; be finished
成法 *kanseihō* completion (test)
成者 *kanseisha* one who completes
成品 *kanseihin* finished goods
全 *kanzen* perfection, completeness
全主義 *kanzen shugi* perfectionism
全性 *kanzensei* state of perfection
全無欠 *kanzen-muketsu* absolute perfection
全雇用 *kanzen koyō* full employment
全雇傭 *kanzen koyō* full employment
全数 *kanzensū* integer, whole number
7投 *kantō* full-game pitcher
9封 *kampū* complete blockade
10納 *kannō* full payment; full delivery
11遂 *kansui* completion
済 *kansai* full payment, liquidation
訳 *kan-yaku* complete translation
敗 *kampai* complete defeat
12備 *kambi* perfection, completion
結 *kanketsu* conclusion, completion
勝 *kanshō* complete victory
13数 *kansū* integer, whole number
15徹 *kantetsu*=貫徹 2469.15
膚 *kampu* whole skin, uninjured skin
膚無迄 *kampuna(ki) made* thoroly, completely; scathingly
18璧 *kampeki* perfect gem, flawlessness; perfection, completeness

—— 5 ——

宕 1289 F532 Tō cave.

B **宜** 1290 F536 GI. *yo(i)*, *i(i)* (see under 良 3885.0). *yoro(shii)* all right. *yoro(shiku)* regards, greetings; well, properly, at your own discretion. *yo(shi)* good, all right, well, so. *mube*, *ube* truly.
[10]候 *yōsōrō*, *yōsoro* Hold her steady (a ship).
[15]敷 *yoroshiku* (see under 宜 1290.0)

B **宙** 1291 F534 CHŪ air, space, mid-air, sky, heaven; memorization; interval of time.
[6]返 *chūgae(ri)* somersault; looping the loop
[9]乗 *chūno(ri)* aerial stunts

宛 1292 F536 EN. *a(teru)* address (a letter). *sanaga(ra)* just like. *-zutsu* apiece; each. *ataka(mo)* just as; as it were; fortunately. *-ate* addressed to.
[6]行 *atega(u)* allot, fasten to, supply with, choose (a wife for); match with; patch; cover; apply to
先 *atesaki* address
名 *atena* address
名印刷機 *atena insatsuki* addressing machine
[7]扶持 *a(tegai)buchi* discretionary allowance
[8]金 *ategane* metal patch
[11]転 *enten(taru)* smoothly rolling
[12]然 *enzen*＝*atakamo* 恰 1675.0

B **宝** 1293 F558 **寳 寶** HŌ treasure. *takara* treasure, valuables; wealth; jewels; mammon.
[2]刀 *hōtō* sacred sword; treasured sword
[5]玉 *hōgyoku* gem, jewel, precious stone
石 *hōseki* gem, jewel
[6]舟 *takarabune* treasure-ship picture
[7]貝 *takaragai* cowrie, porcelain shell
[8]典 *hōten* thesaurus, treasury of words; manual; precious book
物 *hōmotsu*, *takaramono* a treasure
物殿 *hōmotsuden* museum, treasury
物館 *hōmotsukan* treasure house
[9]冠 *hōkan* crown, diadem
持腐 *takara (no) mo(chi)gusa(ri)* wasting talents
[10]庫 *hōko* treasure house, treasury
珠 *hōshu* gem, jewel
祚 *hōso* imperial throne; imperial reign
剣 *hōken* sacred sword
島 *takarajima* treasure island
[11]探 *takarasaga(shi)* treasure hunt
船 *takarabune* a picture of a treasure ship
[14]算 *hōsan* emperor's age
蔵 *hōzō* the treasury; treasure house
[15]箱 *takarabako* strongbox
器 *hōki* treasured article
[21]籤 *takara kuji* raffle, lottery
[22]鑑 *hōkan* handbook, thesaurus, dictionary

A **宗** 1294 F532 SŌ. SHŪ religion, sect, denomination. *mune* main point, essence; origin.
[5]主 *sōshu* suzerain
[6]匠 *sōshō* master (in an art), teacher
旨 *shūshi* doctrine, creed; sect, religion, a faith; one's line, one's taste
旨変 *shūshiga(e)* conversion; proselytism
[7]社 *sōsha* the state; the world
[8]国 *sōkoku* the home country (in contrast to colonies)
法 *shūhō* (Buddhist) sectarian regulations
制 *shūsei* religious institutions
典 *shūten* scriptures of a Buddhist sect
門 *shūmon*＝*shūshi* 宗旨 (see above–6)
門改 *shūmon-arata(me)* religious investigation
[9]風 *shūfū* customs of a religious sect
祖 *shūso* sect founder
派 *shūha* sect, denomination
派的 *shūhateki* sectarian, denominational
派学校 *shūha gakkō* denominational school
派神道 *Shūha Shintō* Sectarian Shinto
[10]徒 *shūto* believer, devotee, follower. *muneto* principal vassal; important people
家 *sōka*, *sōke* head family, main stock; originator
[11]族 *sōzoku* relative; one's whole family
規 *shūki* religious rules
務 *shūmu* (Buddhist) sectarian affairs
務所 *shūmusho* temple office
務総長 *shūmu sōchō* head of a Buddhist sect
教 *shūkyō* religion, a faith, creed, cult
教上 *shūkyōjō* from the standpoint of religion
教心 *shūkyōshin* religious sentiment, piety
教史 *shūkyōshi* history of religion
教史家 *shūkyōshika* a historian of religions
教自由 *shūkyō (no) jiyū* religious liberty
教団体 *shūkyō dantai* religious organization
教狂 *shūkyōkyō* religious fanaticism; fanatic
教改革 *Shūkyō Kaikaku* Protestant Reformation
教改革者 *shūkyō kaikakusha* reformer
教的 *shūkyōteki* religious
教画 *shūkyōga* religious picture
教学 *shūkyōgaku* the study of religion
教性 *shūkyōsei* religious character
教法人 *shūkyō hōjin* registered religious organization
教界 *shūkyōkai* the religious world
教家 *shūkyōka* religious teacher, minister; religious man
教哲学 *shūkyō tetsugaku* philosophy of religion
教教育 *shūkyō kyōiku* religious education
教裁判 *Shūkyō Saiban* the Inquisition
教戦争 *shūkyō sensō* religious war

教暦 *shūkyōreki* religious calendar
教劇 *shūkyōgeki* religious drama, passion play, mystery play, miracle play
教観 *shūkyōkan* religious view
14 閥 *shūbatsu* sectarianism
15 廟 *sōbyō* ancestral mausoleum
論 *shūron* sectarian arguments

A **官** 1295/F533 KAN the Government, the authorities; the Court. *tsukasa* (see under 司 877.0).
2 人 *kanjin* officials
3 女 *kanjo* court lady. *kannyo* women workers in the palace of the shogun or emperor
4 氏名 *kanshimei* official title and name
辺 *kampen* government circles, officialdom
辺筋 *kampen suji* government circles, officialdom ⌈agencies
公庁 *kankōchō* government and public
公吏 *kankōri* public officials ⌈(schools)
公私立 *kankōshiritsu* public and private
公署 *kankōsho* public offices
5 用 *kan-yō* government business; official use
立 *kanritsu* government-operated
仕 *kanshi* government service
本 *kampon* government publication; book belonging to the government ⌈office
司 *kanshi* government official; government
民 *kammin* government and people
庁 *kanchō* government office; authorities
庁用語 *kanchō yōgo* official terminology
庁前 *kanchōmae* in front of the government
6 印 *kan-in* government seal ⌊office
地 *kanchi* government land
宅 *kantaku* official residence
名 *kammei, kammyō* official title
吏 *kanri* government official or clerk
有 *kan-yū* government ownership
有地 *kan-yūchi* government land
有林 *kan-yūrin* national forest
7 位 *kan-i* office and rank; official rank
社 *kansha* central-government shrine
私 *kanshi* public and private; government
邸 *kantei* official residence ⌊and citizenry
兵 *kampei* government forces
8 金 *kankin* government funds
長 *kanchō* chief of a government office
林 *kanrin* government forest
治 *kanchi* nonrepresentative government
物 *kambutsu, kammotsu* government prop-
服 *kampuku* official uniform ⌊erty
制 *kansei* government organization
命 *kammei* official orders, official business
舎 *kansha* official residence
学 *kangaku* government school; official
事 *kanji* government business ⌊teaching

房 *kambō* secretariat ⌈the Cabinet
房長官 *Kambō Chōkan* Chief Secretary of
9 食 *kanshoku* meals furnished by the govern-
威 *kan-i* authority of the office ⌊ment
途 *kanto* government service
海 *kankai* officialdom
紀 *kanki* official discipline ⌈army
軍 *kangun* government forces, imperial
品 *kampin* government property
界 *kankai* officialdom
臭 *kanshū* bureaucratic trend, red-tapism
省 *kanshō* government office, department
10 庫 *kanko* government storehouse
修 *kanshū* government editing
記 *kanki* written appointment (to an office)
員 *kan-in* officials
能 *kannō* body functions; carnal desire
能小説 *kannō shōsetsu* sex novel
能主義 *kannō shugi* sensualism
能的 *kannōteki* sensual
11 道 *kandō* government road
務 *kammu* official business
船 *kansen* government ship
許 *kankyo* government license
設 *kansetsu* established by the government
12 等 *kantō* official rank, civil-service grade
営 *kan-ei* government operation
報 *kampō* official telegram; official gazette
尊民卑 *kanson-mimpi* overemphasis on government at the expense of the people
給 *kankyū* government supply
給品 *kankyūhin* government issues
費 *kampi* government expense
費生 *kampisei* government student
13 衙 *kanga* government office
話 *Kanwa* the Mandarin language
署 *kansho* government office
業 *kangyō* government enterprise
14 歴 *kanreki* one's official career
選 *kansen* government-appointed (official)
緑 *kanroku* salary
銀 *kangin* government funds
製 *kansei* government manufacture
僚 *kanryō* bureaucracy, officialdom
僚化 *kanryōka* bureaucratization
僚主義 *kanryo shugi* bureaucracy
僚的 *kanryōteki* bureaucratic
僚制 *kanryōsei* bureaucracy ⌈ment
僚政治 *kanryō seiji* bureaucratic govern-
15 撰 *kansen* government compilation
権 *kanken* government authority
線 *kansen* government railway line
幣 *kampei* government offerings to certain shrines ⌈prewar shrines
幣社 *kampeisha* second highest class of
16 録 *kanroku* government salary

憲 *kanken* officials, authorities
17 爵 *kanshaku* office and title
18 職 *kanshoku* government service

A **定** 1296 / F534 TEI deciding. JŌ. *sada(maru)* be decided, be settled, quiet down. *sada(meru)* establish, lay down, stipulate; decide, determine; appoint, set (a date); pacify. *kima(ru)* be decided, be settled, be arranged; be certain to, be doomed to. *sada(me)* law, rule, regulation, provision; decision; appointment, arrangements; destiny, fate, karma. *sada(mari)* usage, custom, routine, rule; tranquility. *sada(kana)*＝*tashi(kana)* (see under 確 3217.0). *sada(mete)*, *sada(meshi)* presumably, surely. *ki(matte)* usually, always, invariably. *jō-* regular, permanent.

4 日 *teijitsu* fixed date, appointed date; ordinary times
木 *jōgi* ruler, square; standard
文句 *kima(ri) monku* stereotyped expression
5 石 *jōseki* formula, rules
立 *teiritsu* thesis
圧 *teiatsu* constant pressure
本 *teihon* authentic book or manuscript
収 *teishū* fixed income
収入 *teishūnyū* fixed income
6 式 *jōshiki, teishiki* prescribed form; formula, formality. *teishiki no* regular, formal
年 *teinen* age limit, retiring age
休 *teikyū* regular holiday
休日 *teikyūbi* regular holiday
7 見 *teiken* definite opinion
位 *tei-i* orientation; fixed position
役 *teieki* prescribed (prison) labor
形 *teikei* fixed form, regular shape
足数 *teisokusu* quorum
角軌道 *teikaku kidō* trajectory
住 *teijū suru* settle down
住地 *teijūchi* permanent abode
住者 *teijūsha* permanent resident
8 店 *jōmise* permanent store
例 *jōrei*, *teirei* usage, precedent; standing orders; regular (meeting)
法 *jōhō* fixed rule, formula
限 *teigen suru* limit, confine, restrict
刻 *teikoku* regular time, appointed time
性分析 *teisei bunseki* qualitative analysis
価 *teika* fixed price
価表 *teikahyō* price list
命 *jōmyō* normal life span. *teimei* fate; predetermined length of life
命論 *teimeiron* fatalism
命論者 *teimeironsha* fatalist
9 食 *teishoku* regular meal; table d'hôte
連 *jōren* regular customers, frequenters, patrons
律 *teiritsu* fixed law, fixed rhythm
則 *teisoku* established rule, law
点 *teiten* fixed point
客 *jōkyaku* regular customer, frequent visitor
省 *teisei* kindness to parents
冠詞 *teikanshi* definite article
型 *teikei* definite form, type
型化 *teikeika* standardization
型的 *teikeiteki* typical
型詩 *teikeishi* rhymed verse or poems with fixed forms (such as tanka, *haiku*, sonnets, etc.)
10 席 *jōseki* variety hall; regular seats
紋 *jōmon* family crest
案 *teian* proposal, suggestion, plan
員 *tei-in* regular staff, full number; seating capacity; quorum; full complement
員外 *tei-ingai* supernumerary
時 *teiji* regular time, stated period. *jōtoki* ancient gun or drum time signal; the signaler
時外 *teijigai* overtime
時制 *teijisei* part-time (school system)
11 道 *teidō* natural way, destiny
理 *teiri* theorem, proposition. *jōri* accepted truth
規 *teiki* prescribed, regular. *jōgi* a ruler; a (carpenter's) square; a standard
率 *teiritsu* fixed rate
宿 *jōyado* regular hotel
常 *teijō no* regular; stationary
得意 *jōtokui* regular patron
12 植 *teishoku* the transplantation of seedlings
給 *teikyū* fixed allowance, fixed salary
評 *teihyō* public acknowledgment, general opinion
款 *teikan* articles of incorporation
無 *sada(me)na(ki)* fickle, uncertain, changeable, transient
温 *teion* fixed temperature
温器 *teionki* thermostat
量 *teiryō* fixed quantity; calculation; dose
量分析 *teiryō bunseki* quantitative analysis
着 *teichaku* fixing, fastening, fixation; stationed (at)
着物 *teichakubutsu* fixtures
着液 *teichaku eki* fixing solution
着網 *teichaku ami* fixed offshore fish trap
期 *teiki* stated period; season (train) ticket; rice sold on time; time transaction; time deposit; regular
期払 *teikibara(i)* payment on terms
期刊行物 *teiki kankōbutsu* periodicals
期米 *teikimai* rice sold on time
期列車 *teiki ressha* regular train
期的 *teikiteki* periodic
期券 *teikiken* season (train) ticket, commutation ticket
期取引 *teiki torihiki* time transaction
期風 *teikifū* periodic wind, monsoon
期乗車券 *teiki jōshaken* season (train) ticket
期航空路 *teikikōkūro* air route
期航空機 *teiki kōkūki* commercial plane, airliner

期航路 *teiki kōro* regular air service
期旅客機 *teiki ryokakuki* regular plane
期船 *teikisen* regular ship
期預金 *teiki yokin* time deposit
期調査 *teiki chōsa* routine checkup
13数 *teisū* fixed number, full number, quorum; constant; destiny
置 *teichi* stationary, fixed
業 *teigyō* regular occupation. *jōgō* fixed fate, karma
滑車 *teikassha* fixed pulley
詰 *jōzu(me)* permanent staff
詰員 *jōzu(me)-in* permanent man
義 *teigi* definition
義論 *teigiron* dogmatics
14説 *teisetsu* definite opinion, established theory
15論 *teiron* fixed opinion, established theory
質分析 *teishitsu bunseki* quantitative analysis
16積 *teiseki* fixed area
18礎式 *teisoshiki* cornerstone ceremony
職 *teishoku* regular occupation, steady job
職者 *teishokusha* regular worker
額 *teigaku* fixed amount, flat sum
額税 *teigakuzei* fixed-amount tax
額量 *teigakuryō* ration
額預金 *teigaku yokin* fixed deposit
19繋場 *teikeijō* anchorage area

A **実** 1297 F554 **實** JITSU truth, reality; sincerity, fidelity; kindness; faith; substance, essence. *mino(ru)* ripen; bear fruit. *jitsu ni, ge ni* truly, really, in truth, surely, in fact. *jitsu wa* really, in fact. *mi* seed, berry, nut, fruit; substance, contents; ingredients; (soup) stock. *makoto* (see under 誠 4352.0). *sane* fruit stone, kernel; nucleus.

2入 *mi-i(ri)* crop; earnings, gains
力 *jitsuryoku* real ability, merit, efficiency; arms, force
力行使 *jitsuryoku kōshi* use of force, wildcat strike
力者 *jitsuryokusha* powerful person
力派 *jitsuryokuha* powerful group
3子 *jisshi* one's own child
4父 *jippu* one's real father
尺 *jisshaku* true measure
5母 *jitsubo* one's real mother
写 *jissha* on-the-spot photograph
兄 *jikkei* one's own elder brother
包 *jippō* real cartridge
生 *miba(e), mishō* seedling
生活 *jisseikatsu* real life
収 *jisshū* actual income, take-home pay
収入 *jisshūnyū* actual income, take-home pay
世界 *jissekai* the outside world
世間 *jisseken* the everyday world
用 *jitsuyō* utility; practical use
用主義 *jitsuyō shugi* pragmatism
用向 *jitsuyōmuki* for practical use
用的 *jitsuyōteki* practical
用品 *jitsuyōhin* utility article
用新案 *jitsuyō shin-an* utility model; practical design
6印 *jitsuin* registered seal
刑 *jikkei* prompt corporal punishment
名 *jitsumei, jitsumyō* real name
有 *jitsu-u* reality
存 *jitsuzon* existence
存主義 *jitsuzon shugi, jisson shugi* existentialism
在 *jitsuzai* real existence, reality
在論 *jitsuzairon* realism
地 *jitchi* practice; the actual site
地教育 *jitchi kyōiku* workshop
地経験 *jitchi keiken* practical experience
地試験 *jitchi shiken* practical examination, driving test
行 *jikkō* practice, performance, action, execution, realization
行力 *jikkōryoku* executive ability
行予算 *jikkō yosan* operating budget
行委員 *jikkōi-in* executive committee; action committee
行者 *jikkōsha* executor, performer, a man of action, one who carries out (plans or principles)
行家 *jikkōka* man of action, practical man
行難 *jikkōnan* impracticability
7見 *jikken* actual observation
状 *jitsujō* actual state of affairs
形 *jikkei* actual size
否 *jippi* fact and falsehood, accuracy, the truth
弟 *jittei* one's real younger brother
兵力 *jitsuheiryoku* effective strength
社会 *jisshakai* the real world, actual society
労働 *jitsurōdō* actual labor
芭蕉 *mibashō* banana tree
利 *jitsuri* utility, benefit, profit
利主義 *jitsuri shugi* materialism, utilitarianism
体 *jittai* substance, entity; antitype
体化 *jittaika suru* substantiate
体的 *jittaiteki* antitypical
体画 *jittaiga* stereograph
体変化 *jittai henka* transubstantiation
体論 *jittairon* substantialism, ontology, noumenalism
体鏡 *jittaikyō* stereoscope
8例 *jitsurei* example, illustration
価 *jikka* true value; sterling worth; actual price; cost; market value
妹 *jitsumai* one's real younger sister
姉 *jisshi* one's real elder sister
効 *jikkō* efficacy, efficiency
直 *jitchoku* steadfastness; seriousness
学 *jitsugaku* practical learning, realism
念論 *jitsunenron* realism
況 *jikkyō* real condition

況放送 *jikkyō hōsō* on-the-spot broadcast
物 *jitsubutsu* substance; the real thing, genuine article, the original
物大 *jitsubutsudai* life-size
物教訓 *jitsubutsu kyōkun* object lesson
物教授 *jitsubutsu kyōju* object-lesson teaching
9 施 *jisshi* execution, enforcement
相 *jissō* actual facts; reality
科 *jikka* practical course
10 株 *jitsukabu* real stocks
記 *jikki* authentic record
益 *jitsueki* net profit
員 *jitsuin* effectives
家 *jikka* one's original family
11 現 *jitsugen* realization, fruition, materialization
理 *jitsuri* principles actually practiced
情 *jitsujō* actual state of affairs
情調査 *jitsujō chōsa* fact-finding
動 *jitsudō* actual work hours
動時間 *jitsudō jikan* actual work hours
習 *jisshū* practice
習生 *jisshūsei* student apprentice, student assistant
務 *jitsumu* business affairs, business practice
務委員 *jitsumu i-in* executive committee
務家 *jitsumuka* businessman
12 検 *jikken* inspection, identification
景 *jikkei* actual view
量 *jitsuryō* real quantity
費 *jippi* actual expense; cost price
弾 *jitsudan* real cartridge, live shell; solid shot; money
弾射撃 *jitsudan shageki* live-ammunition practice
測 *jissoku* actual survey
測図 *jissokuzu* accurate ordnance map
証 *jisshō* actual proof
証主義 *jisshō shugi* positivism
証哲学 *jisshō tetsugaku* positivism, positive philosophy
証論 *jisshōron* positivism
13 話 *jitsuwa* true story
跡 *jisseki* actual traces, evidence
戦 *jissen* actual fighting
数 *jissū* actual number
意 *jitsui* sincerity, faithfulness, kindness; true heart
感 *jikkan* actual sensation, realization, low passions
豊 *mino(ri)yuta(kana)* fruitful
勢力 *jisseiryoku* actual power; effectives
働 *jitsudō* actual work hours
働時間 *jitsudō jikan* actual work hours
践 *jissen* practice
践的 *jissenteki* practical
践躬行 *jissen-kyūkō* practicing what you preach
業 *jitsugyō* industry, business
業学校 *jitsugyō gakkō* vocational school
業界 *jitsugyōkai* industrial circles, business world
業家 *jitsugyōka* industrialist, businessman
際 *jissai* truth, fact, practice, reality, actual situation; actually; indeed. *jissai no* real, actual
際上 *jissaijō no* effective, real, actual, substantial. *jissaijō* as a matter of fact
際化 *jissaika* making practical
際生活 *jissai seikatsu* real life, practical life
際的 *jissaiteki* practical
際家 *jissaika* practical man, expert
際教育 *jissai kyōiku* practical education
際感 *jissaikan* sense of reality
14 歴 *jitsureki* career; actual experiences
聞 *jitsubun* something one has heard directly; hearing directly
像 *jitsuzō* real image
演 *jitsuen* stage show; exhibition, demonstration
説 *jissetsu* true account, real fact
態 *jittai* actual condition, realities
15 権 *jikken* real power
線 *jissen* solid line
質 *jisshitsu* substance, essence, quality; material, contents
質上 *jisshitsujō* in substance, substantially
質的 *jisshitsuteki* substantial, essential, material, real
質賃金 *jisshitsu chingin* real wages, take-home pay
16 積 *jisseki* capacity, actual size
録 *jitsuroku* authentic account
録物 *jitsurokumono* historical novel
17 績 *jisseki* actual results
18 蹟 *jisseki* actual traces, evidence
験 *jikken* experimentation; experience
験心理学 *jikken shinrigaku* experimental psychology
験所 *jikkenjo* experiment station
験的 *jikkenteki* experimental, empirical
験室 *jikkenshitsu* laboratory
験場 *jikkenjō* proving ground
19 爆弾 *jitsubakudan* live bomb

6

宦 1298 / F539 KAN official.

8 官 *kangan* eunuch
者 *kanja* eunuch

宥 1299 / F539 YŪ. *nada(meru)* soothe, calm, pacify. *nada(me)* expiation, atonement, reconciliation.

8 免 *yūmen* forgiveness, pardon
和 *yūwa* appeasement
和政策 *yūwa seisaku* appeasement policy
和論者 *yūwaronsha* appeaser
10 恕 *yūjo suru* forgive, excuse
17 賺 *nada(me)-suka(su)* coax, soothe and humor

A **室** 1300 F538 SHITSU room, apartment, compartment, chamber. *muro* greenhouse; (ice) house; cellar.

4 内 *shitsunai* indoor, indoors, interior of a room
内灯 *shitsunaitō* inside lights (of a train)
内音楽 *shitsunai ongaku* chamber music
内遊戯 *shitsunai yūgi* indoor games
内場面 *shitsunai bamen* interior scene
内装飾 *shitsunai sōshoku* interior decorating; upholstering
内装飾師 *shitsunai sōsokushi* interior decorator; upholsterer
内楽 *shitsunaigaku* chamber music
内電話 *shitsunai denwa* interphone
内劇 *shitsunaigeki* a play suitable for a small room
5 外 *shitsugai* outdoors
7 町 *Muromachi* Muromachi era
8 長 *shitsuchō* room monitor
9 咲 *muroza(ki)* blooming under glass
12 温 *shitsuon* room temperature

A **宣** 1301 F537 SEN. *notama(u)* be pleased to say, say. *sen(suru)*, *no(ru)* proclaim, announce. *nobe(ru)* (see under 述 4675.0).

3 下 *senge* imperial proclamation
5 布 *sempu* proclamation, promulgation
旨 *senji* imperial command
伝 *no(be)-tsuta(eru)* proclaim, preach. *senden* propaganda, publicity
伝者 *sendensha* herald, propagandist
伝屋 *senden-ya* propangandist, publicity man
伝係 *sendengakari* publicity man
伝部 *sendembu* publicity department
伝隊 *sendentai* propaganda squad
伝費 *sendenhi* publicity expense; advertising expense
伝戦 *sendensen* propaganda war; advertising campaign
伝業 *sendengyō* publicity business
伝業者 *senden gyōsha* publicity agent
伝機関 *senden kikan* propaganda machinery
7 告 *senkoku* sentence, verdict, pronouncement
言 *sengen* declaration, proclamation, profession, statement
言書 *sengensho* (written) declaration, manifesto, statement
8 明 *semmei* enunciation
命 *semmyō* (ancient) imperial proclamation (re-enthronement, succession, marriages, new era names, etc.)
10 託 *sentaku* oracle
11 教 *senkyō* missionary work; preaching; evangelism
教者 *senkyōsha* evangelist, preacher
教師 *senkyōshi* missionary
12 揚 *sen-yō suru* enhance, increase, exalt
13 義 *sengi* justification
戦 *sensen* declaration of war
戦布告 *sensen-fukoku* declaration of war
14 誓 *sensei* vowing, swearing
誓式 *senseishiki* administering an oath
誓書 *senseisho* written oath, deposit
15 撫 *sembu* placation, pacification

A **客** 1302 F536 KAKU, KYAKU visitor; guest, customer, client; passenger. *kaku-* last (month).

2 人 *kyakujin*, *marōdo* visitor, guest
3 土 *kyakudo*, *kakudo* bringing in topsoil; journey; destination
4 月 *kakugetsu* last month
止 *kyakudo(me)* turning away customers; full house
引 *kyakuhi(ki)* soliciting patronage; hotel runner; procurer
分 *kyakubun* guest, honorary member
5 用 *kyakuyō* for guests
礼 *kyakurei* courtesies toward guests
冬 *kakutō* last winter
布団 *kyakubuton* guest bedding
6 死 *kakushi*, *kyakushi* dying abroad
気 *kakki* youthful ardor; rashness
地 *kakuchi* foreign country
好 *kyakuzu(ki)*, *kyakugono(mi)* choosy (in accepting guests or taxi passengers)
扱 *kyakuatsuka(i)* entertainment of guests
年 *kakunen* last year
7 足 *kyakuashi* customers, clientele
車 *kyakusha*, *kakusha* railway passenger coach
体 *kakutai*, *kyakutai* object (in law and philosophy)
位 *kakui* secondary place
択 *kyakuera(mi)* choosy in accepting guests
兵 *kyakuhei* mercenary soldier, volunteer
来 *kyakurai* visitor, caller
8 取 *kyakuto(ri)* men who guide visitors to a hotel; prostitutes' hunting for patrons
舎 *kakusha* hotel, inn
受 *kyaku-u(ke)* reception of guests
9 待 *kyakuma(chi)* waiting for passengers
亭 *kyakutei* inn
室 *kyakushitsu*, *kakushitsu* stateroom; guest room; parlor
室係 *kyakushitsugakari* room clerk
10 座 *kyakuza* seats for the guests
席 *kyakuseki* seats for guests
旅 *kakuryo* traveler; travel
員 *kakuin*, *kyakuin* associate or honorary member; guest (editor)
11 遊 *kakuyū* traveling abroad
情 *kakujō* feelings of a stranger or traveler
船 *kyakusen*, *kakusen* passenger boat
商売 *kyaku shōbai* hotel, restaurant, or entertainment business
12 間 *kyakuma* parlor, guest room
勤 *kyakuzutome* travelers' guide
寓 *kakugū suru* sojourn, reside temporarily

筋 *kyaku suji* character of a customer
13 殿 *kyakuden* guest's reception room in a temple or a noble's home
僧 *kyakusō* traveling priest 「country
戦 *kyakusen* fighting in a foreign or enemy
歳 *kakusai* last year
意 *kakui* traveler's homesickness
14 種 *kyakudane* character of customers
語 *kakugo, kyakugo* object (in grammar)
16 膳 *kyakuzen* guest's dinner tray 「world
18 観 *kyakkan, kakkan* the object; the material
観性 *kyakkansei, kakkansei* objectivity
観法 *kyakkanhō, kakkanhō* objective method
観的 *kyakkanteki, kakkanteki* objective
観視 *kyakkanshi suru* look at objectively
観描写 *kakkan byōsha* objective description
19 臘 *kakurō* last December

— 7 —

宰 1303 / F540 B SAI manager; rule.
9 相 *saishō* prime minister; councilor
12 卿 *saikei* minister; prime minister
14 領 *sairyō* management, supervision; manager, supervisor

宴 1304 / F541 B EN feast, banquet, party, entertainment. *utage* party, banquet.
6 会 *enkai* feast, banquet, party, entertainment
会場 *enkaijō* banquet hall
10 席 *enseki* banquet, dinner party; banquet
11 遊 *en-yū* drinking party hall; banquet seat
12 飲 *en-in* drinking bout
13 楽 *enraku* revelry, festivities, merrymaking

宸 1305 / F543 SHIN eaves; palace; imperial courtesy.
12 筆 *shimpitsu* emperor's autograph
15 慮 *shinryo* emperor's heart
憂 *shin-yū* emperor's anxiety
16 翰 *shinkan* imperial letter
18 襟 *shinkin* emperor's heart

害 1306 / F540 **害** A GAI injury, harm, damage, mischief, interference. *gai(suru), sokona(u)* injure, harm, mar, spoil, damage, impair.
4 心 *gaishin* evil intention, malice, ill will
6 虫 *gaichū* harmful insect, blight, vermin
8 物 *gaibutsu* evil; pest, plague; nuisance
毒 *gaidoku* evil, harm; mischief; virus; poison; evil influence; blight
11 鳥 *gaichō* injurious bird 「influence
悪 *gaiaku* harm, injury, evil, mischief, evil
13 意 *gai-i* malice, ill will, murderous intent

宵 1307 / F541 **宵** P SHŌ. *yoi* evening, early night hours.
3 口 *yoi (no) kuchi* nightfall, early evening
4 月 *yoizuki* evening moon
月夜 *yoizukiyo* moonlit evening
8 明星 *yoi (no) myōjō* evening star, Venus
10 宵 *yoiyoi* every evening
11 張 *yoi(p)pa(ri)* sitting up late; nighthawk
祭 *yoimatsu(ri)* eve of a festival, vigil
12 越 *yoigo(shi)* (kept) overnight
13 寝朝起 *yoine-asa-o(ki)* early to bed and early to rise
14 鳴 *yoina(ki)* cockcrowing in the evening
17 闇 *yoiyami* moonless night, dark evening

案 1308 / F975 A AN proposition, suggestion, plan, idea; opinion; expectation; bill, draft, measure; table. *an(jiru), an(zuru)* worry, be anxious, be afraid, ponder, fear. *an(zuru) ni* it seems to me that. [木]
3 上 *anjō* on the table
山子 *kakashi, kagashi* scarecrow; figurehead
4 文 *ambun* draft
分 *ambun* proportional division
内 *annai* guidance; guide; announcement, invitation, notice; familiarity (with)
内広告 *annai kōkoku* classified advertisements
内図 *annaizu* information map
内状 *annaijō* letter of invitation
内所 *annaijo* information office
内者 *annaisha* guide
内記 *annaiki* guidebook
内書 *annaisho* guidebook
内業者 *annai gyōsha* guide
内標 *annaihyō* direction sign
内嬢 *annaijō* girl guide
5 外 *angai* surprisingly; disappointingly; unexpectedly
出 *anshutsu* contrivance, invention, studying out (something)
6 件 *anken* item, case, matter
8 定 *an(no)jō* as feared, as expected
18 顔 *an(ji)gao* worried look

容 1309 / F544 A YŌ form; looks. *i(reru)* put into; permit; accept (advice). *katachi* form, shape; personal appearance.
3 子 *yōsu*＝様子 2341.3
6 色 *yōshoku* looks, personal appearance
気 *katagi* spirit, character, trait
共 *yōkyō* pro-Communist
共派 *yōkyōha* pro-Communist faction, fellow travelers
7 体 *yōtai, yōdai* state of health, condition (of a patient). *yōdai(buru)* put on airs, act important

体書 *yōdaiga(ki), yōdaisho* diagnosis, medical bulletin, medical certificate
8物 *iremono* receptacle, container
易 *tayasu(i)* easy, simple, light. *yōi na* easy, simple. *yōi(narazu), yōi(naranu)* serious, dangerous, important
9相 *yōsō* features, looks, physiognomy
姿 *yōshi* form, figure, appearance
11赦 *yōsha* pardon, forgiveness, mercy
赦無 *yōshana(ku)* mercilessly
12喙 *yōkai* meddling, interference, interrupting a conversation
量 *yōryō* capacity, content, volume
14認 *yōnin suru* tolerate, approve of, admit
貌 *yōbō* looks, personal appearance
態 *yōtai, yōdai*＝容体 (see above–7)
疑 *yōgi* suspicion
疑者 *yōgisha* suspected person
15儀 *yōgi* deportment, demeanor
器 *yōki* container, receptacle, capsule
16積 *yōseki* capacity, volume, bulk, measure-
積量 *yōsekiryō* volume ⌊ment, content
積噸数 *yōseki tonsū* displacement tonnage

宮 1310 / F539 A — KU, KYŪ, GŪ constellations (of the zodiac); palace. *miya* Shinto shrine; Imperial Palace; prince, princess.
2人 *miyabito* courtier
3女 *kyūjo* court lady
4内庁 *Kunaichō* Imperial Household Agency
内官 *kunaikan* imperial household official
内省 *Kunaishō* the former Imperial Household Department ⌈minister
内卿 *kunaikyō* (ancient) imperial household
中 *kyūchū, kujū* imperial court ⌈Shrines
中三殿 *Kyūchū Sanden* the Three Palace
中礼服 *kyūchū reifuku* court dress
中席次 *kyūchū sekiji* order of court pre-
中喪 *kyūchūmo* court mourning ⌊cedence
5巡 *miyamegu(ri)* pilgrimage to shrines
仕 *miyazuka(e)* court or temple service
司 *gūji* chief priest of a Shinto shrine
6刑 *kyūkei* castration (of men)
守 *miyamori* guarding a shrine; the watcher
守頭 *miyamorigashira* captain of the temple
7作 *miyazuku(ri)*＝宮造 (see below–9)
廷 *kyūtei* the Court, the Palace
廷列車 *kyūtei ressha* imperial or royal train
8居 *miyai* shrine compound; imperial palace
門 *kyūmon* palace gate
参 *miyamai(ri)* shrine visit ⌈construction
9造 *miyazuku(ri)* palace construction; shrine
相 *Kyūshō* Imperial Household Minister
柱 *miyabashira* palace pillars; shrine pillars
室 *kyūshitsu* palace
城 *Kyūjō* the Imperial Palace
城前広場 *Kyūjōmae Hiroba* Imperial Palace Plaza
10師 *miyashi* miniature-shrine maker
家 *miyake* imperial prince's home or family
11道 *miyaji* road to a palace; road to a shrine
域 *kyūiki* shrine grounds; palace area
13殿 *kyūden* palace
路 *miyaji* road to a palace; road to a shrine
14様 *miyasama* prince, princess
18闕 *kyūketsu* imperial palace

家 1311 / F541 A — KA, KE house. *ie* house, home, residence; housing; family, household; family name; fortune. *-ya* house, shop, store, seller; dealer. *-ke* family. *-ka*, person, profession.
2人 *iebito* people living in the house. *kajin* the family, one's folks. *kenin* retainer, follower
3女 *kajo* heiress, daughter of the home
子 *ie(no)ko* retainer
子郎党 *ie(no)ko rōtō* family followers, clansmen, adherents
4中 *uchijū, kachū, iejū* the whole family; all over the house. *kachū* retainer
什 *kajū* furniture, fixtures
元 *iemoto* main family; wife's home
父 *kafu* my father
父長権 *kafuchōken* patriarchal authority
内 *kanai* family, household; one's wife. *ya-uchi* family; inside the house
内工業 *kanai kōgyō* home industry
内手工業 *kanai shukōgyō* home handicrafts ⌈a husband as joint heir
5付 *ietsu(ki)* heiress; daughter who brings in
奴 *kado* male servant
主 *yanushi, ienushi, ie aruji* head of the house, houseowner, landlord
令 *karei* steward, butler
兄 *kakei* my elder brother
出 *iede* leaving home; abscondence
6老 *karō* chief retainer, daimyo's minister
臣 *kashin* vassal, retainer
号 *yagō*＝屋号 1392.6
守 *iemori, yamori* caretaker, houseowner
毎 *iegoto ni* at every door
名 *iena, kamei* the name of the house, the family name. *kamei, kamyō, kemyō* family name, family honor
伝 *kaden* family history; family (secret) formula; family tradition
伝宝物 *kaden hōmotsu* family heirloom
宅 *kataku* domicile; premises
宅侵入 *kataku shinnyū* trespassing
宅捜索 *kataku sōsaku* domiciliary search
7見 *iemi* coming to see a house

作 ***kasaku*** house for rent; building. ***ietsuku-(ri)*** style of house. ***iezuku(ri)*** house ⌊building
扶 ***kafu*** steward
兎 ***kato*** tame rabbit
声 ***kasei*** honor of the family
君 ***kakun, iegimi*** head of the house
来 ***kerai*** retainer, retinue, servant
系 ***kakei*** family lineage
系図 ***kakeizu*** family tree
8 長 ***kachō*** family head, patriarch
門 ***kamon*** one's family or clan
居 ***kakyo suru*** stay at home
例 ***karei*** family custom
法 ***kahō*** family code
並 ***iena(mi), yana(mi)*** row of houses, every
宝 ***kahō*** heirloom ⌊door
苞 ***iezuto*** a souvenir brought home
学 ***kagaku*** hereditary learning
具 ***kagu*** furniture, fixtures
具屋 ***kaguya*** furniture shop
具師 ***kagushi*** furniture man
事 ***kaji*** household affairs; housework; household economy ⌈household
事向 ***kajimu(ki)*** household affairs; for the
事科 ***kajika*** domestic-science course
事経済 ***kaji keizai*** household economy
事費 ***kajihi*** household expenses
9 風 ***kafū*** family tradition
信 ***kashin*** word from home
持 ***iemo(chi)*** home-owner; owner of houses; housekeeping ⌈portance in divination)
相 ***kasō*** the construction of a house (of im-
柄 ***iegara*** parentage, pedigree; a good family
乗 ***kajō*** family history ⌈nances; livelihood
計 ***kakei*** household economy, family fi-
計費 ***kakeihi*** household expenses
計簿 ***kakeibo*** household account book
屋 ***kaoku*** house; building
屋台帳 ***kaoku daichō*** house register
屋税 ***kaokuzei*** house tax ⌈homestead
屋敷 ***ieyashiki*** houses and lands, estate,
政 ***kasei*** household economy
政学 ***kaseigaku*** domestic science
政科 ***kaseika*** domestic-science course
政婦 ***kaseifu*** housekeeper
10 借 ***kashaku, ieka(ri)*** renting a house
従 ***kajū*** steward, butler, attendant
根 ***yane*** roof, roofing, housetop
桜 ***iezakura*** cherry tree in the garden
格 ***kakaku*** family status
紋 ***kamon*** family crest
訓 ***kakun*** family precepts ⌈one's birthplace
郷 ***kakyō*** one's old home; one's homeland,
家 ***ieie*** every house or family ⌈household
宰 ***ietsukasa, iezukasa, kasai*** steward of a
畜 ***kachiku*** domestic animals

書 ***kasho*** letter from home
財 ***kazai*** household goods; family wealth
財道具 ***kazai dōgu*** household goods
庭 ***katei*** home; family
庭工業 ***katei kōgyō*** family industry
庭用 ***kateiyō*** for home use
庭用品 ***kateiyōhin*** household goods
庭礼拝 ***katei reihai*** family worship
庭向 ***kateimu(ki)*** for the home
庭的 ***kateiteki*** domestic or family (affairs)
庭経済 ***katei keizai*** household economy
庭訪問 ***katei hōmon*** visit to a home, home visitation
庭教育 ***katei kyōiku*** home education ⌈ess
庭教師 ***katei kyōshi*** private tutor; govern-
庭常備薬 ***katei jōbiyaku*** household medi-
庭着 ***kateigi*** clothing worn at home ⌊cines
庭裁判所 ***katei saibansho*** domestic-affairs
庭欄 ***katei ran*** family column ⌊court
11 運 ***ka-un*** family fortunes
婦 ***kafu*** housewife
探 ***iesaga(shi), yasaga(shi)*** searching a house (for something); domiciliary search;
移 ***ya-utsu(ri)*** moving ⌊house hunting
常 ***kajō*** family custom
累 ***karui*** family troubles
産 ***kasan*** family property
族 ***kazoku*** family, household
族手当 ***kazoku teate*** family allowance
族向 ***kazokumu(ki)*** family style
族会議 ***kazoku kaigi*** family council
族扶養義務 ***kazoku fuyō gimu*** family responsibility
族法 ***kazokuhō*** family-rights law ⌈family
族的 ***kazokuteki ni*** like a member of the
族制度 ***kazoku seido*** family system
族連 ***kazokuzure*** taking the family along
族風呂 ***kazokuburo*** family bath (in a hotel)
族席 ***kazoku·seki*** family box seats
族員 ***kazokuin*** members of the family
族数 ***kazokusū*** size of a family
族歴 ***kazokureki*** family history
12 筋 ***iesuji*** lineage, pedigree, family line
集 ***kashū*** a poet's poetical works
無 ***iena(shi)*** homeless
普請 ***yabushin*** house building
13 禄 ***karoku*** hereditary stipend
続 ***ietsuzu(ki)*** row of houses
路 ***ieji*** the road home
跡 ***ieato*** remains of a home; family name
数 ***yakazu, ie kazu*** number of houses
鳩 ***iebato*** dove, domestic pigeon
裏 ***iezuto*** a souvenir brought home
賃 ***yachin*** house rent
業 ***kagyō*** one's occupation or business
禽 ***kakin*** poultry, fowls

禽商 *kakinshō* poultryman
資 *kashi* family estate
資分散 *kashi bunsan* bankruptcy
督 *katoku* family headship; inheritance; family estate 「ly headship
督相続 *katoku sōzoku* succession to a fami-
督権 *katoku (no) ken* birthright
14 僮 *kadō* house servant
僕 *kaboku* house boy, manservant
鳴 *yana(ri)* rattling of a house 「pearance
構 *iegama(e)* house structure, style, or ap-
蔵 *iekura* house and storeroom; storeroom within the house. *kazō* household pos-
塾 *kajuku* private school ⌊sessions
15 敷 *yashiki*＝屋敷 1392.15
16 鴨 *ahiru* domestic duck
親 *kashin* one's parents
憲 *kaken* family constitution
18 職 *kashoku* one's trade or profession
難 *kanan* family misfortune
19 蠅 *iebae* housefly
蟻 *ieari* house ant
譜 *kafu* genealogy, pedigree
鶏 *kakei* chickens
20 醸 *kajō* home brew

— 8 —

寃 1312 F215 See **冤** 631.

寇 1313 F548 = **寇 寇** Kō. *ada* (see under 仇346.0).

寅 1314 F547 In. *tora* 3–5 a.m.; 3rd zodiac sign; tiger.

B **寂** 1315 F546 Jaku death of a priest; quietly. Seki quietly. *sa(biru)* mellow, mature. *sabi(shigaru)* feel lonely, miss someone. *sabi* patina, antique look; elegant simplicity; trained reciter's voice. *sami(shii)*, *sabi(shii)* lonely, lonesome; solitary, deserted, desolate. *seki to shita* hushed, still, silent.
6 光浄土 *jakkō-jōdo* Buddhist paradise
7 声 *sa(bi)goe* quiet and impressive voice
12 然 *sekizen(taru)* lonely, lonesome, desolate
13 寞 *sekibaku(taru)* lonely, lonesome, desolate
滅 *jakumetsu* Nirvana, death, annihilation
滅為楽 *jakumetsu-iraku* the joy of entering
14 寥 *sekiryō* loneliness, desolateness ⌊Nirvana

B **密** 1316 F547 Mitsu secrecy; denseness (of population); minuteness; carefulness; fineness. *hiso(kana)*, *hiso(yakana)* secret, private, stealthy, hushed, still. *misoka* secret.
2 入国 *mitsunyūgoku* smuggling oneself into a country
入国団 *mitsunyūgokudan* smuggling ring
4 夫 *maotoko, mippu* adulterer
5 生 *missei suru* grow luxuriantly
令 *mitsurei* secret orders
6 会 *mikkai* clandestine meeting
旨 *misshi* secret orders
行 *mikkō suru* prowl about
行巡査 *mikkō junsa* plain-clothes man
7 告 *mikkoku* secret information
告者 *mikkokusha* informer, betrayer 「sale
売 *mitsubai* smuggling, bootlegging, illicit
売者 *mitsubaisha* smuggler, bootlegger
売淫 *mitsubai-in* unlicensed prostitution
8 送 *missō suru* send secretly
使 *misshi* secret messenger, secret agent
林 *mitsurin* thicket, jungle, dense forest
法 *mippō* Buddhist mystery
画 *mitsuga* detailed drawing, carefully finished picture
事 *mitsuji* secret
9 度 *mitsudo* density
造 *mitsuzō* illicit manufacture, moonshining
約 *mitsuyaku* secret agreement
計 *mikkei* secret plan
勅 *mitchoku* secret decree
封 *mippū suru* seal tight
室 *misshitsu* secret room
通 *mittsū* misconduct, adultery; intrigue; criminal connection
通者 *mittsūsha* adulterer
10 書 *missho* secret message
航 *mikkō* stowing away (on a ship)
航団 *mikkōdan* smuggling ring
航者 *mikkōsha* stowaway
11 閉 *mippei suru* seal tight
偵 *mittei* spy
婦 *mippu* adulteress
接 *missetsu na* close, intimate. *missetsu suru* stand close together; stick together
猟 *mitsuryō* poaching (in hunting)
教 *mikkyō* esoteric Buddhism; mysterious religion; the mysteries
密 *mitsumitsu ni* privately, secretly. *hisohiso* secretly, in confidence
12 着 *mitchaku suru* adhere to, be glued to
葬 *missō* private funeral
雲 *mitsu-un* thick clouds
集 *misshū suru* swarm, crowd together
集部隊 *misshū butai* massed troops 「trade
貿易 *mitsubōeki* smuggling, contraband
貿易者 *mitsubōekisha* smuggler 「fishing
14 漁 *mitsuryō, mitsugyo* secret unlicensed
語 *mitsugo* whispers, confidential talk
15 談 *mitsudan* secret or confidential talk

儀 *mitsugi* secrets held within a certain group; initiation to such a group
儀教 *mitsugikyō* mystery religions
16 謀 *mitsubō* plot, intrigue, conspiracy
輸 *mitsuyu* smuggling; contraband
輸入 *mitsuyunyū* smuggling; contraband
輸入品 *mitsuyunyūhin* smuggled goods
輸入船 *mitsuyunyūsen* smuggling vessel
輸出 *mitsuyushutsu suru* smuggle abroad
輸出入 *mitsu yushutsunyū* smuggling
輸団 *mitsuyudan* smuggling ring
輸船 *mitsuyusen* smuggling vessel
20 議 *mitsugi* secret conference; private consultation
醸 *mitsujō* bootlegging

8 **宿** 1317 / F545 SHUKU lodging; inn; post town, relay station, stage. *yado(ru)* lodge, dwell, live in; roost, be pregnant. *yado(su)* keep (a guest); carry (a virus); conceive (a child). *yado* house, home, dwelling; address; inn, lodgings, shelter. *yado(ri)* shelter, taking shelter, lodging.

3 下 *yadosa(gari)* short leave from work
4 引 *yadohi(ki)* hotel runner
六 *yadoroku* my hubby, my old man (the husband)
5 外 *shukuhazu(re)* edge of a stage town
主 *yadonushi* landlord, host. *shukushu* host (in biology)
世 *shukuse* previous existence; karma; fate
世因縁 *shukuse innen* karma
6 老 *shukurō* old men, elders, seniors
年 *shukunen* many years
7 坊 *shukubō* temple lodgings
志 *shukushi* long-cherished desire
8 雨 *shuku-u* long rain (spell)
舎 *shukusha* lodging, quarters, billet
直 *shukuchoku, tonoi* night duty, night watch
所 *shukusho* address, quarters, lodgings
所氏名 *shukusho-shimei* name and address
泊 *shukuhaku* lodging
泊人 *shukuhakunin* lodger, boarder, guest
泊所 *shukuhakujo* lodgings
泊料 *shukuhakuryō* board-and-room charge
命 *shukumei* fate, destiny, predestination
命的 *shukumeiteki* fatal
命論 *shukumeiron* fatalism
命論者 *shukumeironsha* fatalist
命観 *shukumeikan* fatalism
9 恨 *shukkon* long-standing hatred
陣 *shukujin* encampment
怨 *shukuen* old grudge
屋 *yadoya* inn, hotel, lodginghouse
屋業 *yadoyagyō* hotel business
屋業者 *yadoya gyōsha* hotel man
10 病 *shukubyō* chronic illness
借 *yadoka(ri)* renting a house
将 *shukushō* veteran general
料 *shukuryō* board-and-room charge
根草 *shukkonsō* perennial plant
11 運 *shuku-un* fate, destiny
帳 *yadochō* hotel register
許 *yadomoto* one's lodgings, one's residence
酔 *shukusui, futsukayo(i)* a hangover
悪 *shukuaku* past sins, old crimes
患 *shukukan, shukkan* chronic illness; a long-standing grief
望 *shukubō* a long-cherished desire
12 痾 *shukua* chronic disease
割 *yadowa(ri)* billeting, quartering
善 *shukuzen* virtues of a previous arrangement
営 *shukuei* billeting; camp
替 *yadoga(e)* change of quarters
場 *shukuba* post town, relay station, stage
場町 *shukuba machi* hotel town (on the old post roads)
無 *yadona(shi)* homeless person, tramp
無子 *yadona(shi)go* homeless child
13 継 *shukutsu(gi)* (relayed) from post station to post station
罪 *shukuzai* sins of previous existence; original sin
意 *shukui* cherished opinion
賃 *shukuchin, yadochin* hotel charges, lodging expenses
業 *shukugyō* karma's reward
14 銭 *yadosen* hotel charges
駅 *shukueki* post town, relay station; stage
15 縁 *shukuen* karma; destiny, fate
敵 *shukuteki* old enemy
弊 *shukuhei* deep-rooted evil
16 謀 *shukubō* premeditated plan
18 題 *shukudai* homework, lessons; pending question
題帳 *shukudaichō* workbook
19 願 *shukugan* long-cherished desire

A **寄** 1318 / F546 KI. *yo(seru)* let approach, bring near; gather, collect, summon, muster; add up; push aside; attack; send a letter; contribute to; become dependent on, take refuge with. *yo(kosu)* send, forward, deliver. *yori* attendance, gathering; collection (of money). *yo(ru)* approach; assemble; call at; come; lean toward; obey; lean on, depend on; conclude; be possessed (by devils); present (offerings). *yo(tte-takatte)* in a crowd. *-yori* from (the north).

3 与 *kiyo* contribution; service
与過失 *kiyo kashitsu* contributory negligence
4 辺 *yo(ru)be* friend, protector, helper
手 *yo(se)te* enemy, attacking force, onset
木 *yo(ri)ki* driftwood. *yo(se)gi* wooden mosaic
切 *yo(se)gi(re)* remnants, scraps of cloth

切細工 *yo(se)ki(re)zaiku* patchwork
5出 *yo(ri)-da(su)* pick out, sort out, single out
付 *yo(se)-tsu(keru)* let come near. *yo(ri)-tsu(ku)* approach; open (the stock market). *yo(ri)tsu(ki)* opening session (of a stock market). *kifu* donation, endowment
付行為 *kifu kōi* act of endowment, donation
付金 *kifukin* donation, endowment
付者 *kifusha* donor
付財産 *kifu zaisan* endowment
生 *kisei* parasitism
生木 *yadorigi* mistletoe; parasite
生火山 *kisei kazan* parasite volcano
生虫 *kiseichū* parasite, parasitic insects
生虫学 *keiseichūgaku* parasitology
生体学 *kiseitaigaku* parasitology
生物 *kiseibutsu* parasite
6返 *yo(se)-kae(ru)* approach and return
年波 *yo(ru) toshinami* oncoming age, old age
合 *yo(ri)-a(u) vi* assemble, meet, grow together. *yo(ri)-a(waseru) vt* intertwine. *yoriai* meeting, assembly, party. *yo(se)-a(waseru)* get (people or things) together
合世帯 *yoria(i)jotai* heterogeneous group (of people)
7住 *kijū* temporary residence
8泊 *kihaku* anchoring
波 *yosenami*, surf
居 *kikyo* temporary dwelling; staying with someone else
居蟹 *yadokari* hermit crab
9食 *kishoku* parasitism, dependency, sponging
10席 *yose* variety hall, storytellers' hall, music hall, vaudeville
起 *yoko(su)* send, forward; deliver
進 *kishin* contribution, donation
値 *yorine* opening price
航 *kikō suru* call at a port, anchor
託 *kitaku* deposition
書 *yosega(ki)* collection of autographs. *kisho* contributed article
留 *kiryū* temporary residence, sojourn
留地 *kiryūchi* place of sojourn
留届 *kiryū todoke* registry of a temporary residence
留者 *kiryūsha* temporary resident, sojourner
11道 *yo(ri)michi suru* call on the way; detour; stop over
捨 *kisha* charity, donation
掛 *yo(ri)-ka(karu) vi*, *yo(se)-ka(keru) vt* lean against. *yosekake* leaning; lean-to
添 *yo(ri)-so(u)* draw near; snuggle against
寄 *yo(ri)yo(ri)* occasionally
宿 *kishuku* lodging, board
宿人 *kishukunin* boarder
宿生 *kishukusei* dormitory student
宿舎 *kishukusha* boarding house; school dormitory
宿舎生 *kishukushasei* dormitory student
宿料 *kishukuryō* boarding expenses
12場 *yo(ri)ba* rendezvous, meeting place
港 *kikō suru* call at a port
寓 *kigū* lodger, paying guest
棟造 *yo(se)munezuku(ri)* hip roof
集 *yo(se)-atsu(meru)* gather, collect, glean, scrape together; rally (soldiers). *yo(ri)-atsu(maru)* assemble, meet
集人 *yo(ri)-atsu(mari)bito* rabble
14語 *kigo suru* send word by
算 *yo(se)zan* addition (in math)
15縋 *yo(ri)-suga(ru)* cling to, rely on
稿 *kikō suru* contribute (to a newspaper)
稿者 *kikōsha* contributor of articles
稿家 *kikōka* contributor of articles
16頼 *yo(ri)-tano(mu)* depend on, take refuge in
17鍋 *yo(se)nabe* chowder
18贈 *kizō, kisō* donation, presentation
贈本 *kizōbon, kisōbon* complimentary copy
贈者 *kizōsha, kisōsha* donor, contributor
贈品 *kizōhin, kisōhin* present, donation
贈書 *kizōsho* books received

9

寐 1319 / F549 Bɪ. *ne(ru)* sleep.

寓 1320 / F551 Gū temporary abode. *gū(suru)* reside temporarily; keep; imply, suggest.

7言 *gūgen* allegory, parable
8居 *gūkyo* temporary residence
所 *gūsho* temporary residence
舎 *gūsha* inn, temporary lodging place
13話 *gūwa* allegory, fable, parable
意 *gūi* hidden meaning; symbolism; implication; moral

富 1321 / F549 **冨** A Fu. Fū. *to(masu)* enrich. *to(meru)* wealthy; abundant. *to(mu)* be rich, become wealthy; teem with, abound in; be fruitful; be rife; be replete. *tomi* wealth, mammon, fortune; resources; lottery.

2力 *furyoku* wealth, resources
3士山形 *fujisangata* shape of Mt. Fuji
士形 *fujigata* shape of Mt. Fuji
士絹 *fujiginu* fuji silk
士額 *fujibitai* a Mt. Fuji brow
5札 *tomi fuda* lottery ticket
6有 *fuyū* wealth, affluence
8岳 *Fugaku* Mt. Fuji
者 *fūsha, fusha* rich person, millionaire
国 *fukoku* rich country, national resources, national enrichment
国強兵 *fukoku-kyōhei* national wealth and military strength

9 祐 *fuyū* wealth, affluence
栄 *to(mi)-saka(eru)* prosper
10 家 *fūka* wealthy family
11 強 *fukyō* wealth and power
商 *fushō* rich merchant
12 裕 *fuyū* wealth, affluence
裕化 *fuyūka suru* enrich, make wealthy
貴 *fuki, fūki, fukki,* wealth and honor
貴利達 *fūki-ritatsu* wealth and success
13 源 *fugen* source of wealth, natural resources
鉱 *fukō* rich ore
農 *funō* rich farmer
14 豪 *fugō* wealthy man, millionaire
16 興業 *tomi kōgyō* lottery enterprise
17 嶽 *Fugaku* Mount Fuji
23 籤 *tomikuji* lottery, lottery ticket

A 寒 1322/F550 寒 KAN midwinter, coldest season. *samu(garu)* be sensitive to cold. *samu(gari)* a person sensitive to cold. *samu(i)* cold, chilly.

3 土 *kando* lonesome place; poor place
士 *kanshi* a poverty-stricken and helpless person

4 心 *kanshin suru* shudder at, be alarmed
月 *kangetsu* wintry moon
水 *kansui* cold water
中 *kanchū* midwinter, cold season
天 *kanten* agar-agar, vegetable gelatin; freezing weather; wintry sky
天版 *kantemban* hectograph
5 生 *kansei* poverty-stricken student; this (humble) student
玉子 *kantamago* winter eggs
6 竹 *kanchiku* solid bamboo
色 *kanshoku* cold color
行 *kangyō* midwinter religious austerities
衣 *kan-i* winter clothing
地 *kanchi* cold region
灯 *kantō* a light on a cold night; the light of a flame
光 *kankō* solitary light
気 *kanki, samuke* cold, cold weather
気立 *samukeda(tsu)* feel cold, have a chill; feel afraid
7 村 *kanson* deserted village, poor village, out-of-the-way village
声 *kansei* a cold voice. *kangoe* midwinter voice training
花 *kanka* winter flowers; the snow
卵 *kantamago* winter eggs
冷 *kanrei* cold, chilliness
冷地 *kanreichi* cold district
冷前線 *kanrei zensen* cold front
冷紗 *kanreisha* cheesecloth
8 雨 *kan-u* cold rain
国 *kankoku* cold country, cold region
明 *kan-a(ke)* end of the cold season
波 *kampa* cold wave
肥 *kangoe, kangoyashi* winter fertilizing, midwinter manuring
夜 *kan-ya* cold night, winter night
参 *kammai(ri)* midwinter pilgrimage
空 *samuzora* wintry sky, cold weather
苦 *kanku* suffering from the cold
9 風 *kampū, samukaze* cold wind, winter wind
屋 *samu(gari)ya* cold-sensitive person
威 *kan-i* intense cold
点 *kanten* points on the skin sensitive to temperature
室 *kanshitsu* cold house for raising frigid-zone plants
草 *kansō* winter grass
負 *samu(sa)make, kammake* fearful of the cold, weakening in cold weather
紅梅 *kankōbai* winter red-blossom plum tree
垢離 *kangori* midwinter cold-water ablutions
10 庭 *kantei* winter garden
疾 *kanshitsu* a cold
凌 *samu(sa)-shino(gi)* getting thru the winter; means of weathering the winter
晒 *kanzara(shi)* exposure to cold weather
梅 *kambai* early plum blossoms
流 *kanryū* cold current
剤 *kanzai* freezing mixture
郷 *kankyō* poor isolated village
烏 *kangarasu* winter crows
害 *kangai* damage from cold
帯 *kantai* frigid zone
烈 *kanretsu* severe cold weather
素 *kanso* poor and simple
修行 *kanshugyō* (Buddhist) winter austerities
11 鳥 *kanchō* winter bird
菊 *kangiku* winter chrysanthemums
貧 *kampin* very poor, indigent
雀 *kansuzume* winter sparrow
12 極 *kankyoku* polar regions
湿 *kanshitsu* cold and moisture
暑 *kansho* hot and cold; temperature; summer and winter
雲 *kan-un* wintry clouds
13 椿 *kantsubaki* winter camellia
詣 *kammai(ri), kammōde* midwinter pilgrimage
暖 *kandan* heat and cold, temperature
暖計 *kandankei* thermometer
14 酸 *kansan* poverty and weakness; loneliness
製 *kansei* made in the cold season
15 餅 *kammochi* midwinter rice cake
熱 *kannetsu* heat and cold; chills and fever
16 稽古 *kangeiko* winter exercises

10

寞 1323/F552 BAKU lonely, quiet.

塞 1324/F434 SOKU. SAI. *fusa(gu), fusa(geru)* *vt* close, shut, cover, block, wall up obstruct, fill; occupy. *fusa(garu)* be

closed, be blocked, be obstructed, be clogged, be shut; be occupied. *se*(*ku*) dam up; check, stop, prevent. [土]
2 入 *se*(*ki*)-*i*(*reru*) stop, check
7 余 *se*(*ki*)-*ama*(*ru*) be unable to hold back
10 栓 *sokusen* an embolism

B **寛** 1325/F557 **寬** KAN leniency, generosity. *kutsuro*(*gu*) relax, feel at home. *kutsuro*(*geru*) loosen, ease, relax. *yutta*(*ri*) *suru* make oneself at home. *yutta*(*ri*) *toshite* at ease, composed. *yutta*(*ri*) *shita* quiet, calm, leisurely, composed. *kutsuro*(*gi*) ease; room, space. *hiro*(*i*) broadminded. *yuru*(*yakana*) (see under 緩 3584.0).
3 大 *kandai* magnanimity, liberality; tolerance, leniency
4 仁 *kanjin* magnanimity, generosity
6 衣 *kan-i* lounging clothes
仮 *kanka suru* forgive; tolerate
刑 *kankei* lenient sentence
8 典 *kanten* leniency, clemency
9 厚 *kankō* kindness and largeheartedness
宥 *kan-yū* forgiveness
10 恕 *kanjo* generosity; forgiveness, mercy, leniency
容 *kan-yō* forbearance, tolerance, generosity. *kan-yō no* generous, lenient, long-suffering, broadminded, tolerant, liberal
容主義 *kan-yō shugi* (religious) toleration
容性 *kan-yōsei* generosity, magnanimity, lenience, tolerance, forbearance
12 裕 *kan-yū* generosity, leniency
17 濶 *kankatsu na* loose (garments); generous
厳 *kangen* lenity and severity

B **寝** 1326/F553 **寢** SHIN sleeping; resting; bed. *ne*(*ru*) sleep; retire; be bedridden; lie down; lie idle; remain unsold. *ne*(*kasu*), *ne*(*kaseru*), *ne*(*seru*) put to sleep; send to bed; lay down, let lie idle. *ne*(*soberu*) sprawl, lie sprawled. *ne*(*sobireru*) be wakeful, fail to sleep. *i*(*nu*) sleep. *ne* sleep. *ne*(*shina*) *ni* on retiring. *ne*(*zu*) *ni* sleeplessly.
2 入 *ne-i*(*ru*) fall asleep; be dull (the stock market)
入込 *ne-i*(*ri*)-*ko*(*mu*) sleep in, sleep soundly
入端 *ne-i*(*ri*)*bana* first part of a night's sleep
3 刃 *netaba* dull blade, blunt sword
小便 *neshōben* bedwetting
4 込 *neko*(*mi*), *nego*(*mi*) asleep; in bed. *neko*(*mu*) fall asleep; oversleep; be sick in bed
仏 *nebotoke* recumbent Buddha
不足 *nebusoku* lack of sleep
化粧 *negeshō* removal of make-up before retiring
心 *negokoro* sleeping comfort
心地 *negokochi* sleeping comfort
心地心 *negokochigokoro* sleeping comfort
5 圧 *neo*(*shi*) pressing clothes under bedding
付 *shin* (*ni*) *tsu*(*ku*) retire, go to bed. *ne-tsu*(*ku*) fall asleep, be confined to bed. *ne-tsu*(*kaseru*) put to sleep. *ne*(*kashi*)-*tsu*(*keru*) put to sleep, send to bed
白粉 *neshiroi* make-up before retiring
台 *shindai*, *nedai* bed, bedstead, bunk, berth, couch, crib, cot
台虫 *shindai mushi* bedbug
台車 *shindaisha* sleeping car
台券 *shindaiken* sleeping-car ticket
6 衣 *shin-i* night clothes
返 *negaeri* tossing or turning in bed; changing sides; betrayal. *negae*(*ru*) change sides; betray
汗 *nease* night sweat
耳水 *nemimi* (*ni*) *mizu* great surprise, thunderbolt
耳聞 *nemimi* (*ni*) *ki*(*ku*) hear while asleep
7 言 *negoto* talking in sleep, nonsense
床 *nedoko* bed, cot, berth
冷 *nebi*(*e*) catching cold while sleeping
坊 *nebō* oversleeping, late rising
抉 *ne-koji*(*reru*) be unable to sleep
忘 *ne-wasu*(*reru*) oversleep
乱髪 *nemida*(*re*)*gami* hair mussed up in sleep
8 房 *shimbō* bedroom
所 *nedoko*, *shinjo* bedroom
泊 *ne-toma*(*ri*) *suru* stay with, lodge
取 *ne-to*(*ru*) steal another's lover
直 *ne-nao*(*su*) go back to bed
具 *shingu* bedding
苦 *neguru*(*shii*) unable to sleep well
物 *ne*(*kashi*)*mono* unsold goods
物語 *nemonogatari* bedtime story
9 首 *nekubi* head of a sleeping person
食 *shinshoku* food and sleep. *negu*(*i*) living in idleness
相 *nezō* sleeping posture
室 *shinshitsu* bedroom
臭 *negusa*(*i*) smelling as if someone slept here
姿 *nesugata* sleeping form
巻 *nemaki* night clothes
10 起 *neoki* lying down and arising; waking; daily living
酒 *nezake* a nightcap, a drink at bedtime
息 *ne-iki* a sleeper's breathing
莫蓙 *negoza* sleeping mat
11 鳥 *nedori*, *netori* birds at roost
過 *ne-su*(*giru*), *ne-su*(*gosu*) oversleep
違 *ne-chiga*(*eru*) strain (the back) in sleep
惚 *ne-bo*(*keru*), *ne-tobo*(*keru*) be half asleep
寂 *nesabi*(*shii*) missing a sleeping companion
道具 *nedōgu* bedding
転 *ne-koro*(*bu*) lie down, throw oneself down
転椅子 *nekoro*(*bi*) *isu* deck chair
12 棺 *negan* coffin
覚 *ne-za*(*meru*) awake. *nezato*(*i*) light sleeper

椅子 *ne-isu* couch, lounge
間 *nema* bedroom
間着 *nemaki* night clothes
[18]損 *ne-sokona(u)* miss a chance to sleep; be wakeful
際 *negiwa ni* just before retiring
飽 *ne-a(kiru)* be tired of sleeping
殿 *shinden* Heian noble's residence
殿造 *shindenzuku(ri)* Heian residential architecture
[14]厭 *ne-a(kiru)* be tired of sleeping
腐 *nekusa(ru)* oversleep
様 *nezama* sleeping posture
静 *ne-shizu(maru)* fall asleep
[17]藁 *newara* (stable) litter, straw
[18]穢 *igitana(i)* always sleepy; oversleeping
顔 *negao* sleeping face

11

寢 1327 F553 See 寝 1326.

寬 1328 F557 See 寛 1325.

實 1329 F554 See 実 1297.

賓 1330 F1799 See 賓 1339. [貝]

寨 1331 F556 SAI fort.

寤 1332 F553 GO awake; understand.

[12]寐 *gobi nimo* whether awake or asleep

寥 1333 F554 RYŌ lonely.

[14]寥 *ryōryō(taru)* few, rare; lonely, lonesome

A **察** 1334 F552 SATSU. *sas(suru)*, *sas(shiru)* presume, surmise; judge; realize, understand; imagine, suppose; sympathize with. *sas(shi)* conjecture; judgment; understanding, consideration, sympathy.

[8]知 *satchi* inference

B **寧** 1335 F555 寧 NEI. *mushi(ro)* rather, preferably.

[4]日 *neijitsu* peaceful day, quiet day
[20]馨児 *neikeiji* child prodigy

蜜 1336 F1666 MITSU honey, nectar, molasses, honeydew. [虫]

[4]月 *mitsugetsu* honeymoon
[7]豆 *mitsumame* boiled beans with treacle
[8]房 *mitsubō* honeycomb
[9]柑 *mikan* tangerine, mandarin orange
[13]蜂 *mitsubachi* honeybee
[21]蠟 *mitsurō* beeswax

B **寡** 1337 F552 KA minority, few, minimum; widow. *yamome* widow. *sukuna(i)* (see under 少 166.0).

[2]人 *kajin* my humble self (used by royalty)
[4]少 *kashō no* little, few, scanty
夫 *yamome* widower
[7]言 *kagen* taciturnity, reticence
作 *kasaku* low production
兵 *kahei* small army force
男 *yamome, yamome otoko, yamo-o* widower
[8]居 *kakyo* widowhood
[11]婦 *kafu, yamome* widow
欲 *kayoku* unselfishness
[13]勢 *kazei* small military force
[14]聞 *kabun* limited information
[15]慾 *kayoku* unselfishness
黙 *kamoku* taciturnity, reticence
[16]頭政治 *katō seiji* oligarchy

12

寫 1338 F556 See 写 626.

B **賓** 1339 F1799 賓 HIN guest. [貝]

[9]待 *hintai suru* treating as an honored guest
客 *hinkyaku* guest, guest of honor
[10]格 *hinkaku* objective case
[13]辞 *hinji* object of a verb

B **寮** 1340 F557 RYŌ hostel, dormitory; villa; tea pavilion. *tsukasa* (see under 司 877.0).

[5]母 *ryōbo* matron (of a dormitory)
生 *ryōsei* boarding student
[8]長 *ryōchō* one in charge of a dormitory
[14]歌 *ryōka* dormitory song

B **審** 1341 F556 SHIN hearing, trial, investigation. *saba(ku)* judge. *saba(ki)* judgment. *tsumabira(ka)* (see under 詳 4357.0).

[7]判 *shimpan, shimban* refereeing, umpireship; trial, judgment
判役 *shimpan-yaku* umpire, referee, judge
判官 *shimpankan* umpire, referee, judge
判者 *shimpansha* umpire, referee, judge
[9]査 *shinsa* judgment, examination, inspection, investigation, screening, auditing (of salaries)
査員 *shinsa-in* judges, examiners
美 *shimbi* appreciation of the beautiful

美学 *shimbigaku* aesthetics
美眼 *shimbigan* aesthetic sense
11問 *shimmon* interrogation, hearing, trial
理 *shinri* trial, hearing, examination
20議 *shingi* deliberation, discussion, review
議会 *shingikai* deliberative assembly; inquiry commission

—— 13 ——

館 館 See 館 5174. [舌]

憲 1342 F747 憲 KEN law. [心]
A
7兵 *kempei* military police
8法 *kempō* constitution; constitutional law
法記念日 *Kempō Kinembi* Constitution Day (May 3)
法違反 *kempō-ihan* unconstitutionality
9政 *kensei* constitutional government
政国 *kenseikoku* a country with a constitutional government
11章 *kenshō* constitution, charter

—— 14 ——

蹇 1343 F1824 KEN. *iza(ru)* crawl along. *izari* a cripple. *ashinae* lame person, a cripple. [足]
11脚 *kenkyaku* cripple

賽 1344 F1805 SAI dice; temple visit. [貝]
5目 *sai (no) me, saime* dots on dice
14銭 *saisen* offering
銭箱 *saisembako* offering box

—— 16 ——

實 1345 F558 See 実 1293.

寵 1346 F558 CHŌ favor, affection, love, patronage.
5用 *chōyō suru* show favor to
6臣 *chōshin* favorite retainer; court favorite
7児 *chōji* favorite child, pet
9姫 *chōki* favorite imperial concubine
10恩 *chōon* great favor
11遇 *chōgū* patronage, special favor
13愛 *chōai* favor, affection, love, patronage

—— 17 ——

寶 1347 F558 See 宝 1293.

RAD. 寸 41

Sun (the Japanese inch). At right: *sunzukuri*. Nickname: Inch.

寸 1348 F559 SUN one-tenth of a foot; measure.
B
3土 *sundo* an inch of land
4切 *sungi(ri)* a straight cut
分 *sumbun* a bit, a little
不足 *suntarazu* short person
6地 *sunchi* an inch of land
7言 *sungen* short but significant words
足 *sunta(razu)* short person
余 *sun-yo* a small amount remaining, a small remnant
志 *sunshi* small token of appreciation
8忠 *sunchū* my loyalty (humble)
法 *sumpō* measure, dimension; plan, program, arrangement
法通 *sumpōdō(ri)* to measure; as specified
9前 *sunzen* just before
衷 *sunchū* somewhat of a desire; my desire
10進 *sunshin* inching along
時 *sunji* a moment, a minute
陰 *sun-in* a moment, a minute
書 *sunsho* note, short letter
11描 *sumbyō* thumbnail sketch
断 *sundan suru* cut to pieces, tear to pieces
毫 *sungō* (not) a bit
12評 *sumpyō* brief review, thumbnail sketch
13暇 *sunka* a moment's leisure
楮 *suncho* note, short letter
鉄 *suntetsu* small weapon; pithy saying
隙 *sungeki* moment of leisure
15劇 *sungeki* dramatic sketch
18簡 *sunkan* brief note, short letter

—— 3 ——

寺 See 1054.

—— 4 ——

対 See 2067.

3 口口土士夂夊夕大女子宀 4【寸】小⺌尢尸屮山川巛工己巾干幺广廴廾弋弓彐彑彡彳

寿 See 194. [士]

6

耐 See 3690. [而]

封 1349 / F560 B Fū seal; sealing; closing. Hō fief. *fū(jiru)*, *fū(zuru)* seal, close up, confine, blockade. *hō(zuru)* appoint; invest with a fief; erect a mound.

2入 *fūnyū* enclosure (in a letter)
3土 *hōdo* feudal estate; mound of worship
4込 *fū(ji)-ko(meru)*, *fū(ji)-ko(mu)* enclose, confine, contain, seal up
切 *fūkiri* release of the first run (of a film); beginning
切館 *fūkirikan* a first-run theater
5目 *fū(ji)me* sealed edge
冊 *hōsaku* imperial order to invest with a fief
6印 *fūin* seal
地 *hōchi* fief, daimiate
9建 *hōken* feudalism
建社会 *hōken shakai* feudal society
建体制 *hōken taisei* feudal system
建的 *hōkenteki* feudal
建制 *hōkensei* feudalism
建制度 *hōken seido* feudalism
建思想 *hōken shisō* feudal ideas
建時代 *hōken jidai* the feudal period (1185–1867)
建道徳 *hōken dōtoku* feudal morality
建領主 *hōken ryōshu* feudal lord
10殺 *fūsatsu* forced out (baseball)
書 *fūsho* sealed letter, sealed document
12筒 *fūtō* envelope
15糊 *fū(ji) nori* sealing paste
緘 *fūkan* seal
緘葉書 *fūkan hagaki* letter card
18鎖 *fūsa* blockade; freezing (funds)
21蠟 *fūrō, fū(ji)rō* sealing wax

専 1350 / F563 A 專 Sen. *moppa(ra)* mainly, solely.

1一 *sen-itsu, sen-ichi* concentration; best care; primary importance. *sen-itsu no* special, exclusive, principal
4心 *senshin* undivided attention, concentration; singleness of purpose
5用 *sen-yō* private use, personal use, exclusive use
用車 *sen-yōsha* personal car
用機 *sen-yōki* personal plane
6行 *senkō* arbitrary action
任 *sennin* full-time service
有 *sen-yū* exclusive possession
有物 *sen-yūbutsu* exclusive possession
有権 *sen-yūken* monopoly, exclusive right
7攻 *senkō* special research
決 *senketsu* arbitrariness
売 *sembai* monopoly
売公社 *Sembai Kōsha* Monopoly Corporation
売局 *Sembaikyoku* Monopoly Bureau
売制 *sembaisei* trade monopoly
売品 *sembaihin* monopoly goods, specialty
売特許 *sembai tokkyo* patent
売権 *sembaiken* monopoly
8念 *sennen* close attention
制 *sensei* despotism, autocracy
制主義 *sensei shugi* despotism, autocracy
制君主 *sensei kunshu* autocrat, tyrant
制君主政体 *sensei kunshu seitai* absolute monarchy
制国 *senseikoku* absolute monarchy
制的 *senseiteki* despotic, autocratic, arbitrary
制政体 *sensei seitai* autocratic government
制政治 *sensei seiji* absolute government
門 *semmon* specialty, line, profession
門化 *semmonka* specialization
門外 *semmongai* layman, outsider
門用語 *semmon yōgo* technical term
門団体 *semmon dantai* professional organization
門医 *semmon-i* medical specialty
門店 *semmonten* specialty store
門的 *semmonteki* professional, technical
門委員 *semmon i-in* technical expert
門学校 *semmon gakkō* professional school
門家 *semmonka* specialist, professional, expert
門書 *semmonsho* books in special fields
門教育 *semmon kyōiku* technical or professional education
門語 *semmongo* technical term
9科 *senka* special course
政 *sensei* despotism, autocracy
10恣 *senshi* arbitrariness; despotism, tyranny
修 *senshū* specialization
修科 *senshūka* special course
従 *senjū suru* specialize
従者 *senjūsha* full-time worker
従員 *senjūin* full-time union officer
11断 *sendan* arbitrary action
務 *semmu* special duty; main business; (train) conductor; managing director
務取締役 *semmu torishimariyaku* managing director
12属 *senzoku* attached to; exclusive; specialization; specialist
13意 *sen-i*=*senshin* 専心 (see above–4)
業 *sengyō* specialty, monopoly, main occupation
業者 *sengyōsha* specialist
15権 *senken* exclusive right; despotism, arbitrary power
横 *sen-ō* arbitrariness; despotism, tyranny
横的 *sen-ōteki* arbitrary

— 7 —

射 See 4603.

将 See 2840.

尅 See 剋 776.

— 8 —

將 See 将 2840.

尋 See 尋 1585.

專 1351 F-X 専 See 専 1350.

尉 See 231.

— 9 —

尋 See 1585.

尊 尊 See 607.

尌 1352 F-X JU standing (something) up.

— 11 —

對 1353 F566 See 対 2067.

A 導 1354 F567 DŌ leading. *michibi(ku)* guide, lead, conduct, usher. *michibi(ki)* guidance. *shirube* guide; guiding; road sign.

2 入 *michibi(ki)-i(reru), dōnyū suru* lead into, bring into; induce; invite; import; introduce

3 下 *michibi(ki)-kuda(ru)* bring down

上 *michibi(ki)-nobo(ru)* bring up, lead up

4 手 *michibi(ki)te* a guide

水 *dōsui* conducting water; hydraulic

水圧力 *dōsui atsuryoku* hydraulic pressure

水学 *dōsuigaku* hydraulics, hydrodynamics

水路 *dosuiro* raceway, canal

火 *michibi* fuse, powder train

火索 *dōkasaku* fuse, powder hose

火管 *dōkakan* fuse

火線 *dōkasen* fuse; cause, agency, incentive, impetus, occasion

火縄 *michibi-nawa* powder hose

5 出 *michibi(ki)-da(su)* bring out, bring forth, lead out

6 因 *dōin* inducement, incentive, motive, cause, contributing factor

返 *michibi(ki)-kae(su)* bring back, win back, restore

7 体 *dōtai* conductor; medium

尿 *dō-nyō suru* catheterize

尿管 *dō-nyōkan* ureter

8 者 *dōsha* guide

9 通 *michibi(ki)-tō(ru)* lead thru

10 師 *dōshi* officiating (Buddhist) priest

帰 *michibi(ki)-kae(ru)* bring back, lead back

11 教 *michibi(ki)-oshi(eru)* instruct

13 電体 *dōdentai* conductor of electricity

電性 *dōdensei* conductivity

電度 *dōdendo* conductivity

電率 *dōdenritsu* conductivity

14 管 *dōkan* conduit, pipe, aqueduct; standpipe; duct

15 線 *dōsen* leading wire

RAD. 小 42

Shō small. Variant: ⺌. Nickname: Little.

A 小 1355 F567 SHŌ smallness; minor; small. *chii(sai), chii(sana), chi(sai)* small, little, diminutive, minute, fine, trivial. *isasa* small. *ko-* small; short; pretty; petty; nearly. *o-* little; nice, pretty. *shō-* humility prefix; small. *sa-* honorary prefix.

2 力 *kojikara* a little strength

刀 *shōtō* the shorter sword. *kogatana* knife, pocket knife

刀細工 *kogatanazaiku* wood carving; makeshift; cheap trick

人 *shōjin* small person, dwarf; child; mean person; person of small caliber. *shōnin* child. *kobito* dwarf, Lilliputian, pygmy, manikin

人国 *shōjinkoku* land of pygmies, Lilliput

人物 *shōjimbutsu* ungenerous person; low-charactered person

人数 *koninzū* small number of people

3 女 *shōjo* girl, little daughter. *ko-onna* a young servant; a little girl

川 *ogawa, kogawa* brook, creek

巾 *kohaba* single or narrow width

弓 *koyumi* toy bow

口 *koguchi* end, edge; clue; beginning; small lots; small sum

口扱 *koguchiatsuka(i)* small railway-express shipments

小 *shōshō* a little, a few, slightly

小姓 *kogoshō* young page to a noble

山 *koyama* hill, mound

山羊 *koyagi* kid

才 *kosai, shōsai* quite clever

才子 *kozaishi* clever man

才覚 *kosaikaku* cleverness

4 月 *shō (no) tsuki* short months

止 *koyami* lull, break, let-up

水 *shōsui* urine, urination

爪 *kozume* root of a fingernail

片 *shōhen* piece, fragment

牛 *ko-ushi* calf

犬 *ko-inu* puppy

円 *shōen* small circle

仏 *kobotoke* small image of Buddha

孔 *shōkō, koana* small hole

引 *shōin* short introduction

分 *shōbun, kowa(ke)* subdivision, breakdown

文字 *komoji* small letters, lower-case letters

火 *boya, shōka* blaze, small fire

火器 *shōkaki* light weapons

天地 *shōtenchi* a small world

天狗 *kotengu* a small but skillful man (in the military arts)

六 *komuzuka(shii)*＝小難 (see below 18)

六ケ敷 *komuzuka(shii)*＝小難 (see below 18)

心 *shōshin* timidity, cowardice; prudence

心者 *shōshimmono* coward, timid person

心翼翼 *shōshin-yokuyoku* infinite care; trembling

手 *kote* fencing gloves, gauntlet; forearm

手先 *kotesaki* (a good) hand (at)

手調 *koteshira(be)* tryout, rehearsal, work-out, preliminary examination

切 *kogi(re)* pieces of cloth, rags. *kogi(ru)* cut up small; haggle, bargain

切手 *kogitte* check

切手帳 *kogittechō* checkbook

太 *kobuto(ri)* plump, buxom; pudgy

太刀 *kodachi* small short sword

太鼓 *kodaiko* small drum; side drum

5 用 *shōyō, koyō* small matter; urination

皿 *kozara* saucer, small plate

石 *sazare-ishi* small stone. *ko-ishi* pebble, gravel, small stone

穴 *koana* little hole; small groove

尻 *kojiri* end of the sheath of a sword

史 *shōshi* short history

払 *kobara(i)* paying in small installments; small installments

札 *kofuda* a one-act ticket; a small tag

丘 *shōkyū* hillock

出 *koda(shi)* passing out a small quantity; frugal use; choosing some out of many; articles so chosen

本 *kohon* small-sized book

正月 *koshōgatsu* Little New Year's, 15th and 16th days of 1st lunar month

市民 *shōshimin* lower middle class

旦那 *kodanna* young master

世界 *shōsekai* small world

主観 *shōshukan* narrow personal views

母 *oba* aunt (honorary)

母様 *obasan, obasama* aunt; lady

生 *shōsei* I

生意気 *konama-iki* impertinence, conceit, impudence

包 *kozutsumi* parcel, package

包郵便 *kozutsumi yūbin* parcel post

冊 *shōsatsu* booklet

冊子 *shōsasshi* booklet, pamphlet, tract, brochure

半日 *kohannichi* almost a half day

半年 *kohannen* nearly half a year

半時 *kohantoki* quarter hour; nearly half an hour

田 *oda* rice field

田原提灯 *odawarajōchin* collapsible cylindrical paper lantern

田原評定 *odawara hyōjō* endless talk, fruitless debate

田原評議 *odawara hyōgi* endless talk, fruitless debate

6 米 *kogome* broken rice

羊 *kohitsuji* lamb

耳 *komimi* little ears (that happen to overhear)

臣 *shōshin* lower-rank retainer; this humble retainer

舟 *obune, kobune* boat, lighter, small craft

回 *komawa(ri)* sharp turn

成 *shōsei* small success

曲 *shōkyoku* short musical piece

伝 *shōden* short biography

弛 *odayu(mu), odaya(mu)* let up briefly (rain, etc.)

安 *shōan* somewhat at ease; satisfaction with minor accomplishments

字 *shōji* small characters, small type; one's baby name. *koaza* small village subsection

当 *koata(ri)* a feeler

早 *kobaya(ku)* somewhat in a hurry; earlier than usual

名 *shōmyō* lesser feudal lord

吏 *shōri* petty official

地主 *shōjinushi* small landowner

臼歯 *shōkyūshi* bicuspid

企業 *shōkigyō* small industries

気 *shōki* timidity, cowardice, prudence

気味 *kokimi, kokibi* sentiment, feeling

休 *koyasu(mi)* short rest, breather

休止 *shōkyūshi* short rest

百合 *sayuri* lily

百姓 *kobyakushō* petty farmer, tenant, peasant

会 *shōkai* small gathering

会派 *shōkaiha* the minor parties

会堂 *shōkaidō* chapel

7 言 *kogoto* scolding, faultfinding

谷 *shōkoku* ravine
豆 *azuki* red bean
貝 *kogai* little shell
走 *kobashi(ri)* hurrying along with small steps
足 *koashi* mincing steps
車 *oguruma* little cart; wheel
序 *shōjo* short introduction
忰 *kosegare* one's little son, little fellow, kid
村 *shōson* hamlet, small village
社 *shōsha* little shrine; low-rank shrine; my company
別 *kowake* subdivision
形 *kogata* small size, small design
兵 *kohyō* small stature; weak soldier
弟 *shōtei* the younger of two younger brothers; (humble) my younger brother
声 *kogoe* low voice, whisper
男 *ko-otoko* young man; short man
我 *shōga* the ego, one's private self
束 *kotaba* small bundle
役人 *koyakunin* minor official
沢山 *kodakusan* quite a few; not too many
坊主 *kobōzu* young priest, acolyte, novice
見出 *komida(shi)* subtitle, subheading
角材 *shōkakuzai* scantling
亜細亜 *Shōajiya* Asia Minor
身 *shōshin* humble position; person of low rank. *komi* tang (of a sword)
身者 *shōshimmono* person of low rank
町 *komachi* beauty, belle, queen
町娘 *komachi musume* beauty, belle, queen
判 *koban* small size (in printing); small Edo gold coin
判形 *kobangata* oval, elliptical
利 *shōri* small profit
利口 *korikō* somewhat talented, cleverness
利巧 *korikō* somewhat talented, cleverness
売 *ko-uri* retail sale
売店 *ko-uriten* retail store
売商 *ko-urishō* retail trade
麦 *komugi* wheat
麦色 *komugi iro* cocoa brown
麦刈 *komugika(ri)* wheat harvest
麦粉 *komugiko* wheat flour
児 *shōni* little child, infant
児科 *shōnika* pediatrics
児科医 *shōnika-i* pediatrician
児科学 *shōni kagaku* pediatrics
児病 *shōnibyō* children's diseases
児時代 *shōni jidai* infancy, childhood
児麻痺 *shōni mahi* infantile paralysis
作 *kosaku* (firm) tenancy. *kozuku(ri)* small size; small stature; small physique
作人 *kosakunin* tenant farmer
作米 *kosakumai* rent paid in rice
作地 *kosakuchi* tenant farm land
作争議 *kosaku sōgi* tenant uprising
作料 *kosakuryō* farm rent
作農 *kosakunō* tenant farming
作農民 *kosaku nōmin* tenant farmers
作権 *kosakuken* tenant rights
8 金 *kogane* small fortune; small sum
門 *komon* small gate
雨 *kosame, koame* light rain, drizzle
供 *kodomo* child
使 *kozukai* janitor; errand boy, servant; spending money
咄 *kobanashi* short story
姓 *koshō* child, youth; page to a noble
姑 *kojūto, kojūtome* sister-in-law
径 *shōkei* lane, path
性 *koshō* child, youth; page to a noble
林 *obayashi*, forest. *kobayashi, shōrin* small forest
枝 *koeda* twig; spray
板 *ko-ita* slat
波 *sazanami, sasanami, konami* ripples
知 *shōchi* shallow brains, little knowledge
股 *komata* short steps; crotch, thigh, groin
肥 *kobuto(ri)* somewhat fat
刻 *kokiza(mi)* mincing, chopping fine
舎 *koya* ＝小屋 (see below–9)
官 *shōkan* petty official
者 *komono* menial, servant; small fry
事 *shōji* small matter
奇麗 *kogirei na* trim, neat, snug
委員会 *shōiinkai* subcommittee
国 *shōkoku* small country, weak nation
国民 *shōkokumin* small nation; rising generation
店 *shōten* my little shop. *komise* little store
店員 *shōten-in* shop boy
松 *komatsu* young pine tree
松原 *komatsubara* young pine grove
物 *komono* small articles, a little thing
物印刷 *komono insatsu* job printing
突 *kozu(ku)* prod, poke, thrust, push, shake; swing; irritate; thrash
突回 *kozu(ki)-mawa(su)* manhandle, shake; tease; find fault with
学 *shōgaku* elementary education
学生 *shōgakusei* elementary pupil
学校 *shōgakkō* elementary school
夜 *sayo* night
夜中 *sayonaka* midnight
夜曲 *sayokyoku* serenade
夜更 *sayofu(keru)* The night deepens.
夜時雨 *sayo shigure* rain at night, night drizzle
夜嵐 *sayo arashi* night wind, night storm
9 風 *kokaze* light breeze
食 *shōshoku, kogu(i)* light eating, spare diet
盾 *kodate* small shield; screen; cover
柱 *kobashira* small pillar
柄 *kogara* short stature. *kozuka* knife attached to a sword sheath

派 *shōha* a small faction, a small party
胞 *shōhō* vesicle
胆 *shōtan* timidity; cowardice; prudence
計 *shōki* subtotal
降 *koburi* light snow, light rain, drizzle
変 *shōhen* a slight change
亭 *shōtei* small pavilion, arbor
泉 *ko-izumi* a little spring
草 *ogusa* small grasses, small weeds
昼 *kohiru* a little before noon; mid-morning
勇 *shōyū* a little courage ⌊snack
急 *koiso(gi) ni* somewhat in a hurry
冠者 *kokanja* youth
海峡 *shōkaikyō* narrow channel
飛球 *shōhikyū* pop fly
前提 *shōzentei* minor premise
為替 *kogawase* small money order
要塞 *shōyōsai* blockhouse
首 *kokubi* neck; head ⌈in curiosity
首傾 *kokubi (o) katamu(keru)* tilt the head
便 *shōben* urine, urination
便所 *shōbenjo* urinal
指 *koyubi, shōshi* little finger
指頭大 *shōshitōdai* the size of the end of the little finger
乗仏教 *Shōjō Bukkyō* Hinayana or Lesser-Vehicle Buddhism
乗的 *shōjōteki* narrow-minded
品 *shōhin* something very small; an essay, a literary sketch
品文 *shōhimbun* essay, literary sketch
型 *kogata* small size, small design
型映画 *kogata eiga* small-size movie
面 *kozura* face (impolite)
面倒 *komendō na* annoying, troublesome
面憎 *kozuraniku(i)* impudent; disgusting
春 *koharu* 10th lunar month; Indian sum-
春日 *koharubi*=next word ⌊mer
春日和 *koharubiyori* Indian-summer day, balmy autumn day
屋 *shōoku, koya* cottage, hut, booth, cabin, shed. *koya* theater
屋代 *koyadai* theater rent
屋掛 *koyaga(ke) suru* pitch camp. *koyaga(ke)* building a temporary hut; temporary
屋組 *koyagu(mi)* framework ⌊hut, shack
10高 *kodaka(i)* slightly elevated
鬼 *ko-oni* imp, little devil
庭 *koniwa* small garden
逕 *shōkei* path, lane
俵 *kohyō* small sack; small bag
哨 *shōshō* picket
唄 *ko-uta* ditty, ballad
娘 *komusume* early-teen-age girl, bobby-
振 *kobu(ri)* small size ⌊soxer
破 *shōha* slight damage

紋 *komon* fine pattern ⌈shy
恥 *kohazu(kashii)* ashamed, embarrassed,
脇 *kowaki* side (of the body)
袖 *kosode* padded silk garment
針 *kobari* short needle, short stitches
家 *shōka, ko-ie, oya* little house; poor home
宴 *shōen* small dinner party
差 *shōsa* small difference, narrow margin
書 *koga(ki)* writing in details; adding mar-
息 *ko-iki* short breaths ⌊ginal notes
株主 *shōkabunushi* small stockholder
浮動 *shōfudō* moderate (stock-market) fluc-
陪審 *shōbaishin* petty jury ⌊tuations
馬 *ko-uma* pony, colt
馬鹿 *kobaka* somewhat of a fool. *kobaka ni suru* treat with contempt
骨 *kobone* small bones
骨折 *koboneo(ru)* make a little effort. *shōkossetsu* minor bone fracture
料理店 *koryōriten* small restaurant
料理屋 *koryōriya* small restaurant
都市 *shōtoshi* small town
都会 *shōtokai* small town
島 *kojima, shōtō* small island, islet
島田 *ojimada* rice field on a small island
倉 *kokura* duck (cloth)
倉服 *kokurafuku* schoolboy's school uni-
党 *shōtō* minor political party ⌊form
党分立 *shōtō bunritsu* division into small political parties
荷物 *konimotsu* parcel, package
荷駄馬 *konida uma* pack horse
11魚 *kozakana, kouo* small fish, fingerling
康 *shōkō* lull, respite, some improvement
過 *shōka* minor error ⌊(in a patient)
桶 *ko-oke* pail, small tub
猫 *koneko* kitten
球 *shōkyū* small ball, small globe
脳 *shōnō* cerebellum
船 *kobune* boat, lighter, small craft
欲 *shōyoku* a slight covetousness
敗 *shōhai* a minor defeat
野 *ono* field
隊 *shōtai* platoon, troop
瓶 *kobin* small bottle
悪 *shōaku* a little sin, a minor crime
宿 *koyado* simple lodging
異 *shōi* minor differences
窓 *komado* small window
雪 *koyuki* light snowfall
運送 *ko-unsō* parcel transportation
遊星 *shōyūsei* asteroid
規模 *shōkibo* small scale
鳥 *kotori* small bird
鳥屋 *kotoriya* bird shop
道 *komichi* path, lane, alley, byway

道具 *kodōgu* small pieces of equipment; small tools; small stage properties
細工 *kozaiku* handiwork; tricks; tinkering
細工師 *kozaikushi* a man with a handicraft; a tricky person
商 *koakina(i)* retail business, small trade
商人 *koakindo, koshōnin, koakyūdo* small businessman
盗 *shōtō* petty thief. *konusu(mi)* petty theft
盗人 *konusubito* petty thief
粒 *kotsubu, shōryū* small grain, fine particle
粒金 *kotsubukin* one-fourth *ryō*
粒真珠 *kotsubu shinju* seed pearl
12 喧 *koyakama(shii)* fastidious, faultfinding, fussy about everything
揚 *koa(ge)* unloading (ships) ⌈of skill
腕 *ko-ude, kokaina* forearm; weak arm; lack
飲 *shōin* small dinner party
善 *shōzen* a small kindness
寒 *shōkan* winter's milder period
景 *shōkei* a beautiful scene; a small picture of a landscape
量 *shōryō* small quantity, small dose; narrowmindedness ⌈ster, stripling
童 *kowarabe, kowarawa, kowappa* young-
策 *shōsaku* petty trick
筒 *kozutsu* rifle; small arms
買 *koga(i) suru* buy in small quantities
落 *shōraku* slight (stock-market) decline
葉 *shōyō* lobule, appendage
雲 *shōun* small cloud
智 *shōchi*＝小知 (see above–8)
琴 *ogoto* harp, koto
景気 *shōkeiki* a little boom
集会 *shōshūkai* small gathering
惑星 *shōwakusei* asteroid
幅 *kohaba* single-width (cloth)
幅物 *kohabamono* single-width cloth
蒸気 *kojōki* steam launch
蒸気船 *kojōkisen* steam launch
割 *kowa(ri)* slat, piece of wood
割材 *kowa(ri)zai* scantling
割板 *kowa(ri)ita* slat, piece of wood
遣 *kozukai* spending money, incidental expenses
遣取 *kozukaito(ri)* side job, odd jobs
遣帳 *kozukaichō* petty cashbook
遣銭 *kozukaisen, kozukai zeni* spending money, incidental expenses
間 *koma* small room; brief interval
間切 *komagi(re)*＝細切 3522.4
間使 *komazukai* maid ⌈wares
間物 *komamono* notions, knicknacks, sundry
間物屋 *komamonoya* haberdashery
間結 *koma musu(bi)* square knot
13 鼓 *kotsuzumi* hand drum

鼠 *konezumi* small rat
僧 *kozō* young Buddhist priest; errand boy, shop boy; youngster
暗 *kogura(i), ogura(i)* dusky; shady
暇 *shōka* a brief leisure
楯 *kodate* small shield; screen; cover
槌 *kozuchi* small mallet; gavel; wand
禄 *shōroku* small stipend
腸 *shōchō* small intestines
腰 *kogoshi* hips; a slight genuflexion, a
艇 *shōtei* small boat ⌊slight bow
話 *shōwa, kobanashi* anecdote, yarn, small talk ⌈narrow street
路 *komichi, kōji* path, lane, alley, byway,
鉢 *kobachi* small bowl
鈴 *osuzu, kosuzu* a little bell
隙 *shōgeki* crevice, small gap; minor discord
歇 *koyami* discontinuance for a short time
禽 *shōkin* small birds
節 *shōsetsu* a small knot (in wood); bar (in music); faithfulness in small matters
罪 *shōzai* minor sin, minor crime
舅 *kojūto* brother-in-law
勢 *kozei* small force, small family
楊子 *koyōji* toothpick
資本 *shōshihon* small capital
意気 *ko-iki na* stylish, chic, neat, tasteful
預言書 *Shōyogensho* Minor Prophets
腹 *kobara* abdomen
腹立 *koharada(tsu)* become irritated
数 *shōsū* a fraction; a comparatively small
数点 *shōsūten* decimal point ⌊number
農 *shōnō* small farmer, peasant, landowner
農民 *shōnōmin* the small farmers
農地 *shōnōchi* small farm holdings
農階級 *shōnō kaikyū* peasantry
14 鼻 *kobana* wings of the nose
像 *shōzō* figurine, statuette
鳴 *sasana(ki)* low twittering
憎 *koniku(rashii)* hateful, horrible, provok-
旗 *kobata* little flag ⌊ing
碑 *shōhi* this (humble) monument
踊 *ko-odori* dancing for joy
酷 *ko(p)pido(ku)* severely, harshly
銭 *kozeni* small change, loose coins
歌 *ko-uta* ballad, ditty, little song
管 *shōkan* small pipe
綺麗 *kogirei na* trim, neat, snug
熊星 *Shōyūsei* Ursa Minor
熊座 *Kogumaza* Little Bear, Ursa Minor
説 *shōsetsu* novel, romance, story, fiction
説体 *shōsetsutai* the fictional form
説家 *shōsetsuka* novelist, fiction writer
銃 *shōjū* rifle, small arms
銃射程 *shōjū shatei* rifle range
銃弾 *shōjūdan* bullet

15潮 *koshio* neap tide
編 *shōhen* short article
縁 *koen* small veranda
膝 *kohiza* the knee
影 *shōei* a small-size photograph
敵 *shōteki* weak opponent, weak enemy
皺 *kojiwa* little wrinkles, crow's feet
箱 *kobako* small box
篇 *shōhen* short article
蕪 *kokabu* small turnip
慧 *kozaka(shii)*=next word
賢 *kozaka(shii)*, *kogashiko(i)* smart, conceited; tricky, shrewd
劇場 *shōgekijō* little theater
器 *shōki* small receptacle; man of small caliber
器用 *kogiyō na* smart, clever
衝 *kozu(ku)* prod, shake, swing; irritate
衝回 *kozu(ki)-mawa(su)* grab by the chest and shake
衝突 *shōshōtotsu* skirmish
16鴨 *kogamo* duckling
樽 *kodaru* keg
頭 *kogashira* foreman
鮑 *tokobushi* abalone, ear shell
頸 *kokubi* neck of a garment
憩 *shōkei* short rest, recess
機転 *kokiten* being smart; being tricky
17糠 *konuka* rice bran
糠雨 *konuka ame* drizzling rain
18難 *komuzuka(shii)* bothersome, troublesome, finicky, peevish. *shōnan* small misfortune; minor fault
額 *shōgaku* small amount
題 *shōdai* subtitle, subhead; trivial subject
藩 *shōhan* the smaller clans
19鯨 *kokujira* gray whale
20騰 *shōtō* slight (stock-market) advances
競合 *kozeria(i)* skirmish, bickering; wrangle
艦隊 *shōkantai* flotilla, small fleet
21癪 *koshaku na* impertinent, impudent
躍 *ko-odo(ri)* dancing or jumping for joy
22嚢 *shōnō* small bag, vesicle
24鬢 *kobin* side lock (of hair)

1

少 See 166.

2

尓 1356 / F571 / F1211 尒 See 爾 69.

3

劣 See 185. [力]

尖 1357 / F572 SEN. *toga(ru)*, *tonga(ru)* be pointed, be sharp, taper off; be displeased, get angry. *toga(rasu)*, *tonga(rasu)*, *toga(rakasu)* sharpen, point; raise (one's voice); put (one's nerves) on edge. *tonga(ru)*, *tonga(rakaru)* get cross. *toga(ri)*, *tongar(i)* point, tip, peak.
7兵 *sempei* advance guard
12塔 *sentō* pinnacle, spire, steeple
13端行 *sentan (o) i(ku)* be in style
14鼻 *toga(ri)bana* hawk nose
端 *sentan*=先端 571.14
15鋒 *sempō* point
鋭 *sen-ei* radical; acute
鋭化 *sen-eika suru* become acute, be aggravated
鋭分子 *sen-ei bunshi* radical elements
16頭 *sentō* pinnacle, spire, steeple

A **光** 1358 / F186 KŌ light. *hika(ru)* shine, glitter, sparkle, twinkle, flash. *hika(rakasu)*, *hika(rasu)* show one's authority, strut around; shine (a light) on. *hikari* light, beam, flash, glare, gleam, twinkle, sparkle, glimmer, glow, brightness, radiance, glitter, luster; influence (of parents). [儿]
2力 *kōryoku* intensity of light
4化学 *kōkagaku* photochemistry
6芒 *kōbō* shaft of light, flash of lightning
年 *kōnen* light year
合成 *kōgōsei* photosynthesis
行差 *kōkōsa* aberration (in astronomy)
7体 *kōtai* luminous body
来 *kōrai* your visit, your company
束 *kōsoku* a beam of light
沢 *kōtaku* brilliance, polish, luster
沢紙 *kōtakushi* glossy paper
沢綿糸 *kōtaku menshi* mercerized cotton thread
8波 *kōha* light wave
物 *hika(ri)mono* shooting star; luminous body; metal scraps; gold and silver coins
炎 *kōen* light and flames; energy
明 *kōmyō* light, hope, bright future; glory; halo
明度 *kōmeido* power (of binoculars)
学 *kōgaku* optics
学硝子 *kōgaku garasu* optical glass
9速 *kōsoku* speed of light
神 *hikari (no) kami* Mazda (the sun god)
冠 *kōkan* corona
点 *kōten* luminous point
栄 *kōei* honor, glory; privilege
背 *kōhai* halo
風 *kōfū* a pleasant wind after a rain
風霽月 *kōfū-seigetsu* a bright moon after a storm; serenity of mind
度 *kōdo* brightness, luminosity

度計 *kōdokei* photometer
10 流 *kōryū* stream of light
被 *kōhi* permeating all
陰 *kōin* time
11 球 *kōkyū* photosphere
鹵石 *kōroseki* carnalite
彩 *kōsai* brilliance, splendor
彩陸離 *kōsai rikuri* splendor, brilliancy
12 焔 *kōen* flame
景 *kōkei* scene, spectacle; aspect
量 *kōryō* radiation intensity
覚 *kōkaku* optic sense, sensation of light
13 源 *kōgen* light source
暈 *kōun* halation, ghost (in photography)
照 *kōshō* shining
電 *kōden* photoelectricity
電池 *kōdenchi* photoelectric cell
電管 *kōdenkan* photoelectric cell
15 線 *kōsen* light; light ray, beam
輪 *kōrin* halo
輝 *hika(ri)-kagaya(ku)* shine, glitter. *kōki* brightness, splendor
熱 *kōnetsu* light and heat
熱費 *kōnetsuhi* fuel-and-light expense
16 頭 *kōtō* bald head
17 環 *kōkan* corona
臨 *kōrin* our visit, your company

A **当** 1359 / F1279 **當** Tō right; appropriateness, fairness; himself; itself; at the time. *a(taru) vi* and *vt* hit, strike, dash into; touch; shine on; guess right, be fulfilled; succeed; confront; lie (to the south); treat; feel out; undertake; be worth; correspond to; be related to; apply to; draw (a prize); be assigned to; be affected by; be spoiling; be exposed to; warm oneself; shave; grind; this coming (15th); turn out well; take well; be punished (by heaven); stand to reason; deal with; engage (the enemy); need not to (with negative); have (one's turn); be charged with. *a(teru)* apply, place, put; hit (the mark); guess; succeed; expose to; sit (on a cushion); assign, allocate; call on (a pupil). *a(terareru)* be affected (by), suffer (from); be bored, be annoyed. *masa ni* properly, naturally. *a(taranai)* do not deserve, be not justifiable, be not proper. *a(tari)* bruise; bite; exposure (to wind); success, hit; clue, trail, scent; batting average; on this (occasion); in the direction (of). *a(te)* aim; hopes, reckoning; dependence, confidence; clue; pad; blow, stroke. *a(tezuppō)* guesswork, haphazard work. *a(tekko)* guesswork, guessing game. *tō no* the said (person or thing). *-a(tari)* per. *tō-* this (city, etc.). 【田】

2 人 *tōnin* the one concerned, the said person, the man himself
3 口 *a(te)kuchi* insinuation
山 *tōzan* this mountain, this temple
千 *tōsen* a matchless warrior
4 手 *tōte* we; our group
日 *tōjitsu* the appointed day, the occasion
月 *tōgetsu* this month
木 *a(te)gi* batten, scantling
込 *a(te)-ko(mu)* count on, anticipate, expect
切 *a(te)gi(re)* patch
今 *tōkon* the present, these days
分 *tōbun* for the present, temporarily
方 *tōhō* I; our part
方側 *tōhōgawa* we
5 石 *a(te)-ishi* touchstone
処 *a(te)do* aim
付 *a(te)-tsu(keru)* insinuate
代 *tōdai* the present generation; those days; the present family head
外 *a(tari)-hazu(re)* success or failure, risk. *a(te)-hazu(re)* disappointment
札 *a(tari)-fuda* the winning ticket
主 *tōshu* the present head of the family
用 *tōyō* current use; the business in hand
用日記 *tōyō nikki* diary
用漢字 *Tōyō Kanji* the official 1850 "Current Characters"
世 *tōsei* the present time
世向 *tōseimu(ki)* the latest fashion
世風 *tōseifū* the latest fashion, the fashionable style
6 地 *tōchi* this locality
寺 *tōji* this temple
字 *a(te)ji* a phonetic-equivalent character; a substitute character
年 *tōnen* the current year; that year. *a(tari)-doshi* bumper year
7 言 *a(te)koto* insinuation
身 *a(te)mi* body blow, knockout punch
住 *tōjū* the present chief priest of a temple
役 *a(tari)yaku* successful role. *tōyaku* this role; this officer
社 *tōsha* this shrine, this firm
初 *tōsho* original; at the beginning
否 *tōhi* right or wrong; justice; propriety, suitability
芸 *a(tari)gei* successful role
狂言 *a(tari) kyōgen* successful play, a hit
局 *tōkyoku* = next word
局者 *tōkyokusha* the authorities concerned, the powers that be, the one in authority; an insider
8 金 *tōkin* cash; paying in cash
国 *tōkoku* our country
店 *tōten* this shop, this store, we
所 *tōsho* this place. *a(te)do* aim
物 *a(te)mono* riddle, guessing; covering

3 口 口 土 士 夂 夊 夕 大 女 子 宀 寸 [小 4 ⺌] 尢 尸 屮 山 川 巛 工 己 巾 干 幺 广 廴 廾 弋 弓 彐 彑 彡 彳

夜 *tōya* that night
季 *tōki* present period, this term
直 *tōchoku* on duty
直室 *tōchokushitsu* night-duty room
事 *tōji* related matters. *a*(*te*)*goto* hopes, reckoning; inference, guessing
事国 *tōjikoku* the country concerned
事者 *tōjisha* the person concerned
9面 *tōmen suru* face, confront. *tōmen no* immediate, urgent
風 *tōfū* the present fashion
屋 *a*(*tari*)*ya* a lucky person; a good hitter
度 *tōdo* now, this time
前 *a*(*tari*)*mae* proper, just, fair, reasonable, natural, ordinary, normal, usual
為 *tōi* what should be
10馬 *a*(*te*)*uma* confronting a mare with a stallion to test readiness to mate; preparatory move
時 *tōji* in these days; in those days; time
流 *tōryū* the style
家 *tōke* this house, this family
座 *tōza* the present; for some time; current; temporary; immediate; current checking account
座逃 *tōzanoga*(*re*) an excuse; an elusion; makeshift 「measure
座凌 *tōza shino*(*gi*) *ni* as a temporary
座預金 *tōza yokin* current checking ac-
11得 *tō* (*o*) *e*(*ta*) accurate, correct 」count
推量 *a*(*te*)*zuiryō*, *a*(*te*)*suiryō* guess, guesswork, conjecture
12散 *a*(*tari*)*-chi*(*rasu*) find fault with every-
朝 *tōchō* the present imperial court 」body
期 *tōki* the present period, this term
嵌 *a*(*te*)*-ha*(*meru*) apply to; assign to. *a*(*te*)*-ha*(*maru*) apply to; be true of; conform
落 *tōraku* election result 」to
然 *tōzen* justly, properly, naturally, necessarily, of course
番 *tōban* being on duty or on guard; man on
番号 *a*(*tari*) *bangō* winning number 」duty
惑 *tōwaku* perplexity, embarrassment; doubt; confusion
惑顔 *tōwakugao* puzzled look
13該 *tōgai* the appropriate (authorities)
鉢 *a*(*tari*)*bachi* earthenware mortar
節 *tōsetsu* these times
障無 *a*(*tari*)*sawa*(*ri*) *ga na*(*i*) be harmless; be noncommittal, be neutral
意即妙 *tōi-sokumyō* ready wit
路 *tōro* the authorities, the authorities con-
路者 *tōrosha* the authorities 」cerned
歳 *tōsai* this year; a yearling
歳児 *tōsaiji* a yearling 「lottery)
14選 *tōsen* election to office; winning (a
選者 *tōsensha* successful candidate 「dig at
17擦 *a*(*te*)*-kosu*(*ru*) *vt* insinuate, satirize, take a
18職 *tōshoku* this occupation; the present occupation; present duties 「drawing lots
20競 *a*(*te*)*kura*(*be*) guess; guessing game;
21籤 *tōsen*, *a*(*tari*) *kuji* the winning ticket
籤者 *tōsensha* prizewinner

4

肖 1360 F1533 B — Shō resemble. *ayaka*(*ru*) resemble. [肉]

8者 *ayaka*(*ri*)*mono* lucky fellow; similar person, one who resembles someone
14像 *shōzō* portrait, picture
像画 *shōzōga* portrait; portrait painting

5

毟 See 207. [毛]

尚＝尙 1361 F572 P — Shō. *nao* further, furthermore, still, still more, yet; just like. *tatto*(*bu*) (see under 貴 4504.0). *hisa*(*shii*) long, long-continued, an
2又 *naomata* further, besides 」old (story).
4以 *naomo*(*tte*) still more, all the more
友 *shōyū* becoming intimate with the ancients (by reading their works)
5且 *naokatsu* and yet
古 *shōko* worship of ancient civilizations
古主義 *shōko shugi* worship of ancient
6早 *shōsō* prematurity 」civilizations
7更 *naosara* still, still more, all the more
8尚 *naonao* still more, all the more
武 *shōbu* militarism, warlike spirit

6

省 See 218. [目]

県＝縣 1362 F1475 A — Ken prefecture; district (in China). *agata* ancient demarcated cultivated areas. [糸]

2人 *kenjin* native of a prefecture
人会 *kenjinkai* an association of people from the same province
3下 *kenka* in or under the prefecture, thruout the prefecture
5立 *kenritsu* prefectural (institution)
庁 *kenchō* prefectural office
外 *kengai* outside the prefecture
令 *kenrei* prefectural ordinance
6会 *kenkai* prefectural assembly
有 *ken-yū* owned by the prefecture
7社 *kensha* prefectural shrine
8治 *kenchi* prefectural administration

知事 *ken chiji* prefectural governor
11 道 *kendō* prefectural road
視学 *kenshigaku* prefectural school inspector
12 税 *kenzei* prefectural tax
営 *ken-ei* prefectural operation
13 債 *kensai* prefectural loan
勢調査 *kensei chōsa* prefectural census
20 議 *kengi* prefectural assemblyman
議会 *kengikai* prefectural assembly
議会議員 *kengikai gi-in* prefectural assembly man

7

A **党** 1363 F2165 **黨** Tō party, faction, clique; companions. *tō(suru)* side with, make common cause with. [黑]

2 人 *tōjin* party member, partisan
3 与 *tōyo* companions; conspirators
4 内 *tōnai* intra-party
6 色 *tōshoku* partisan coloring
争 *tōsō* party rivalry
同伐異 *tōdō-batsui* partisanship, cliquism
7 利 *tōri* party interests
利党略 *tōri-tōryaku* (thinking of) party interests and policies
9 首 *tōshu* party leader
紀 *tōki* party discipline
則 *tōsoku* party rules
是 *tōze* party platform
派 *tōha* party, faction, clique
派心 *tōhashin* factiousness
派秘密会 *tōha himitsukai* party caucus
10 員 *tōin* party member, partisan
11 情 *tōjō* condition of the political party
略 *tōryaku* party policy, party platform
務 *tōmu* party affairs
規 *tōki* party regulations
12 費 *tōhi* party expenses; party dues
13 勢 *tōsei* party strength
14 閥 *tōbatsu* faction; cliquism
15 論 *tōron* party platform, party opinion
輩 *tōhai* associates, companions
弊 *tōhei* party evils
18 類 *tōrui* faction, partisans, gang
20 議 *tōgi* party policy, platform, party conference
籍 *tōseki* party registration, membership (in a party)

8

A **常** 1364 F617 Jō. Shō. *tsune* normal conditions, regular course of events; one's habit. *tsune no* ordinary, normal, continual. *tsune ni* always, continually. *towa* eternity. *tada* ordinarily. *tsune(naranu)* in vain. *toko-* ever-, endless. [巾]

1 乙女 *toko-otome* ever-youthful maiden
2 人 *tadabito, tsunebito, jōjin* common man, ordinary person, plain individual
4 心 *jōshin* a sincere heart
日頃 *tsunehigoro* always, usually
5 世国 *tokoyo (no) kuni* distant country; heaven; hades
平倉 *jōheisō* grain reserve
用 *jōyō* common use; addition
用手段 *jōyō shudan* regular means
用者 *jōyōsha* constant user; addict
用漢字 *jōyō kanji* commonly used characters
6 灯 *jōtō* an all-night light
会 *jōkai* regular meeting
任 *jōnin* permanent (post)
任委員 *jōnin i-in* standing committee
任委員会 *jōnin i-inkai* standing committee
7 住 *jōjū* constancy, continuity; always; usually
住座臥 *jōjūzaga ni* always
8 供 *jōku* continual offering
例 *jōrei* custom, usual practice
法 *jōhō* usual method
服 *jōfuku* ordinary clothes
事 *jōji* everyday affair
夜 *tokoyo* endless night
夜灯 *jōyatō* all-night light
9 食 *jōshoku* daily diet, staple food
連 *jōren* regular companions
軌 *jōki* proper course; beaten track
客 *jōkyaku* regular customer; frequent visitor
春 *tokoharu* eternal spring
10 員 *jōin* regular personnel
素祭 *jōsosai* continual meal offering
時 *jōji* usually, habitually, ordinarily
時運転 *jōji unten* regular service
夏 *tokonatsu* perennial summer; a wild pink (flower)
夏国 *tokonatsu no kuni* land of perpetual summer
套 *jōtō no* commonplace, conventional
套手段 *jōtō shudan* old trick, usual practice, regular means
套句 *jōtōku* stock phrase
套語 *jōtōgo* hackneyed expression, household word
11 道 *jōdō* ordinary way, universal practice
経 *jōkei* unchanging moral principles
規 *jōki* established usage; common standard
宿 *jōyado* regular hotel
常 *tsunezune* always, usually
得意 *jōtoku-i* regular customer
務 *jōmu* regular business; executive director
務委員会 *jōmu i-inkai* executive committee
務取締役 *jōmu torishimariyaku* executive director
設 *jōsetsu* permanent; standing (committee)
設小売店舗 *jōsetsu ko-uri tempo* permanent retail store
設館 *jōsetsukan* cinema
習 *jōshū* usage, custom, common practice

習犯 *jōshūhan* habitual crime; habitual criminal
習的 *jōshūteki* habitual, regular
習者 *jōshūsha* habitual offender
習飲酒者 *jōshū inshusha* habitual drunkard
12 雇 *jōyatoi* regular employee
温 *jōon* normal temperature
勤 *jōkin no* full-time (official)
勝 *jōshō* ever-victorious
勝軍 *jōshōgun* ever-victorious army
備 *jōbi no* standing, permanent, regular
備兵 *jōbihei* regular army
備金 *jōbikin* reserve fund
備軍 *jōbigun* standing army
備薬 *jōbiyaku* household remedy
13 数 *jōsū* constant (in math); fate
節 *tokobushi* abalone, ear shell
置 *jōchi* permanent, standing (committee)
置委員 *jōchi i-in* standing committee
14 態 *jōtai* normalcy
緑 *jōryoku* evergreen
緑樹 *jōryokuju* evergreen tree
15 駐 *jōchū* staying permanently
磐 *tokiwa, towa* eternity
磐木 *tokiwagi* evergreen tree
磐津 *tokiwazu* a type of ballad
16 衡 *jōkō* avoirdupois
燔祭 *jōhansai* continual burnt offering
17 闇 *tokoyami* perpetual darkness
19 識 *jōshiki* common sense
識的 *jōshikiteki* sensible, practical
20 議委員会 *jōgi i-inkai* executive board
議員 *jōgi-in* standing committee

雀 See 233. [隹]

A **堂** 1365/F427 Dō temple; shrine; hall; reception room; firm; state chamber. *-dō* temple, shrine; shop, store. [土]
3 上 *dōjō* on the roof; court nobles
上人 *tōshōnin, dōjōbito* court noble
4 内 *dōnai* in the temple
6 守 *dōmori* building guard
宇 *dōu* temple, hall, building
8 房 *dōbō* the inside of a house
11 堂 *dōdō(taru)* imposing, majestic, grand, magnificent, stately; fair, square
堂巡 *dōdōmegu(ri)* roll-call vote; vicious circle; going round and round (in an argument); circling a shrine or temple in worship
堂回 *dōdōmegu(ri)* = word above
12 塔 *dōtō* temple buildings; temple
奥 *dōō* interior of a hall or temple; secret knowledge

9

B **掌** 1366/F806 Shō. *tsukasado(ru)* rule, administer, conduct. *tanagokoro* palm, hollow of the hand. [手]
3 大 *shōdai* palm size, small patch (of land)
4 中 *shōchū* in the hand; (something) very small; (something) easily manipulated
中玉 *shōchū (no) tama* the apple of one's eye
中本 *shōchūbon* pocket edition
7 状 *shōjō* palmate, hand-shaped
8 典 *shōten* ritualist
12 握 *shōaku suru* grasp, seize, hold, command
14 管 *shōkan* handling, managing, manipulating

10

尠 尟 See 142.

當 1367/F1279 See 当 1359. [田]

甞 1368/F1263/F381 See 嘗 1369. [甘]

11

嘗 1369/F381/F1263 **甞** Shō. *na(meru)* lick; lap up; burn up; taste; undergo; underrate, despise. *katsu(te)* (see under 曾 604.0). [口]

裳 1370/F1701 Shō. *mo* ancient skirt. [衣]
7 束 *shōzoku* costume, dress
13 裾 *mosuso* = *suso* (see under 裾 4247.0)

12

B **輝** 1371/F1844 Ki. *kagaya(ku)* shine, sparkle, gleam, twinkle; brilliant, radiant, bright. *kagaya(kasu)* *vt* light up, brighten, illumine. *kagaya(ki)* brilliancy, radiance, splendor, glitter. *kagaya(kashii)* bright (future); brilliant (achievement). [車]
5 石 *kiseki* pyroxene; augite
出 *kagaya(ki)-de(ru)* shine out from
12 渡 *kagaya(ki)-wata(ru)* shine out far and wide
15 輝 *kiki* brilliance

A **賞** 1372/F1800 Shō prize, reward; praise. *shō(suru), home(ru)* praise, commend, admire, enjoy (beauty). *me(deru)* love; appreciate. [貝]
3 与 *shōyo* reward, prize, bonus
与金 *shōyokin* a bonus
7 状 *shōjō* honorable mention, certificate of merit
8 金 *shōkin* prize, monetary reward
味 *shōmi* relish, gusto, appreciation

杯 *shōhai* trophy, prize cup
玩 *shōgan* admiration, appreciation, enjoyment
9盃 *shōhai* trophy, prize cup
品 *shōhin* (nonmonetary) prize
美 *shōbi* praise, admiration
12揚 *shōyō* praise, admiration
牌 *shōhai* medal
詞 *shōshi* commendation, eulogy
13嘆 *shōtan suru* admire and praise
14罰 *shōbatsu* rewards and punishments; praise and blame; justice
15賜 *shōshi* offering a prize; the prize
歎 *shōtan suru* admire and praise
賛 *shōsan* praise, admiration, commendation
翫 *shōgan*＝賞玩 (see above-8)

22讃 *shōsan* praise, admiration, commendation
鑑 *shōkan suru* admire and praise

15

斃 1373/F863 HEI. *tao(reru), tao(su)* (see under 倒 487.0). [攵]
6死 *heishi suru* fall dead, die

17

黨 1374/F2165 See 党 1363. [黑]

耀 1375/F1512 YŌ. *kagaya(ku), kagaya(kasu), kagaya(kashii)* (see under 輝 1371.0). [羽]

RAD. 尢 43

Dai no mageashi crooked-leg *dai* (large). *Mottomo* just, right, reasonable, natural. Nickname: Crooked Big (cf. Rad. 37).

1

尤 See 128.

4

尨 See 136.

9

就 See 323.

RAD. 尸 44

Shikabane or *kabane* corpse. Nickname: Flag.

尸 1376/F574 SHI corpse. *shikabane, kabane* corpse, the remains.
16諫 *shikan* protest by suicide
骸 *shigai* corpse, remains

1

尹 See 158.

尺 1377/F574 B SEKI. SHAKU Japanese foot (see Weights and Measures); rule; measure, scale; length. *sashi* measure, rule.
2八 *shakuhachi* bamboo flute
〆 *shakujime* a unit of timber measurement (1×1×12 feet)
3寸 *shakusun, sekisun* a bit, a little; a strip (of land); short length
6地 *shakuchi, sekichi* a single square foot of land; a small strip of land
7余 *shakuyo* over a foot
8取 *shakuto(ri)* measuring worm
取虫 *shakuto(ri)mushi* measuring worm
9度 *shakudo* linear measure, scale, gauge, standard
10骨 *shakkotsu* ulna
11貫法 *shakkanhō* Japanese system of weights and measures

2

尼 1378/F575 B 尼 JI. NI *ama* nun.
6寺 *amadera* convent
7君 *amagimi* a lady who becomes a nun
8法師 *ama hōshi* (Buddhist) nun
10将軍 *ama shōgun* female shogun
13僧 *nisō* (Buddhist) priestess
僧院 *nisōin* convent
18顔 *amagao* a face with no make-up

尻 1379/F575 Kō. *shiri* buttocks, hips; rear or back of a person; bottom (of a kettle); tail end, tag end.

[8]下 *shirisa(gari)* a drop in the back part of anything; lowering the voice at the end of a sentence ⌈heels; rising market
上 *shiria(gari)* rising intonation; head over
[4]込 *shirigo(mu)* flinch, shrink back, hesitate
切 *shiriki(re)* half-finished
切蜻蛉 *shiriki(re) tombo* something half-finished
[5]目 *shirime ni* looking askance
[6]当 *shiria(te)* trouser-seat lining
[7]尾 *shippo, shiri(p)po* tail; end
抜 *shirinu(ke)* forgetfulness
[8]長 *shiri (ga) naga(i)* overstaying (guest)
押 *shirio(shi)* boosting, pushing; incitement; instigator; wirepuller
[9]拭 *shirinugu(i)* taking the blame or loss for another
重 *shiriomo, shiri (ga) omo(i)* slow-moving
[10]馬 *shiriuma* blindly following, indiscriminate imitation
窄 *shirisubo(mari), shirisubo(ri)* tapering; anticlimax, weak ending
[11]紮 *shirikara(ge)* tucking up the kimono behind ⌈behind
[12]絡 *shirikara(ge)* tucking up the kimono
軽 *shirigaru ni* lightly. *shirigaru na* wanton, loose
割 *shiri (ga) wa(reru)* (a secret) is exposed
[14]端折 *shiri(p)pasho(ri), shirihasho(ri)* tucking up the kimono behind
[15]餅 *shirimochi* falling on one's buttocks

— 3 —

B **尽** 1380/F1313 **盡** Jin. *tsu(kusu)* use up, run out of, exhaust; serve, befriend, work for, endeavor, do (one's duty). *tsu(kiru)* become exhausted, be consumed, spend, end. *kotogoto(ku)* all, entirely, completely. *-zu(ku) de* for the sake of, by means of, by force of. *-zu(kushi)* a full enumeration of. *-jin* last day of the month. [皿]

[2]力 *jinryoku* efforts; assistance
[4]日 *jinjitsu* the whole day
[5]未来 *jimmirai* forever, eternity
[8]果 *tsu(ki)-ha(teru)* be exhausted
忠 *jinchū* loyalty ⌈ism
忠報国 *jinchū-hōkoku* loyalty and patriot-
[13]瘁 *jinsui* strenuous efforts; assistance

— 4 —

屁 1381/F577 Hi. *he, onara* breaking wind, passing gas.

[11]理窟 *herikutsu* quibbling
理窟屋 *herikutsuya* quibbler

B **尿** 1382/F576 Nyō *shito, yubari, ibari* urine.

[5]石 *nyōseki* urinary calculus
[8]毒症 *nyōdokushō* uremia
[9]砂 *nyōsa* urinary sand
[10]素 *nyōso* urea
[11]道 *nyōdō* urethra
瓶 *shibin* urinal, pot
[12]量 *nyōryō* amount of urination
検査 *nyō kensa* urinalysis
[13]意 *nyōi* the urge to urinate
[14]酸 *nyōsan* uric acid
管 *nyōkan* ureter
[15]器 *nyōki* bed pan, urinal

B **尾** 1383/F576 Bi tail; end; counter for fish. *o* tail; trail (of a meteor); lower slope (of a mountain).

[3]上 *onoe* mountain ridge
[6]羽 *oha* tail feather
行 *bikō* following, trailing, shadowing
灯 *bitō* taillight; stop light
[7]花 *obana* Japanese pampas grass
[8]使 *ozuka(i)* tail wagging
長猿 *onagazaru* long-tailed monkey
[9]風 *bifū* tail wind
[10]骨 *bikotsu* coccyx
根 *one* a mountain ridge
部 *bibu* tail
[12]無猿 *ona(shi)zaru* ape
[14]端 *bitan* tail tip
[15]骶骨 *biteikotsu* coccyx
[16]橇 *bisori* tail skid
頭付 *okashiratsu(ki)* whole fish
錠 *bijō* buckle, clasp
錠金 *bijōgane* buckle, clasp
[17]翼 *biyoku* tail, tail plane
[21]鰭 *obire* caudal fin. *ohire* tail and fin; exaggeration ⌈guage)
[22]籠 *birō* indelicate, indecent, vulgar (lan-

A **局** 1384/F576 **局** Kyoku bureau, board, office; central; post office; affair; duty; situation; conclusion. *tsubone* court lady; her apartment; lady-in-waiting.

[4]区 *kyokku* postal-zone number
[5]外 *kyokugai* the outside; an independent position; irrelevance
外中立 *kyokugai chūritsu* neutrality, in-
外者 *kyokugaisha* outsider ⌊difference
[6]名 *kyokumei* call sign, station name ⌈rence)
地 *kyokuchi* locality, the site (of the occur-

地化 *kyokuchika* localization
地風 *kyokuchifū* local wind
地戦争 *kyokuchi sensō* limited war
8長 *kyokuchō* bureau chief, director, post-
限 *kyokugen suru* limit, localize ⌊master
所 *kyokusho* part, section; local
所時 *kyokushoji* local time
所麻酔 *kyokusho masui* local anesthetic
9面 *kyokumen* checkerboard; aspect, situation
待 *kyokuma(chi)* to be called for, waiting at the (telegraph) office
10紙 *kyokushi* Japanese vellum ⌈staff
員 *kyokuin* clerk; bureau staff; post-office
留 *kyokudo(me)* general delivery ⌈privates
部 *kyokubu* part, section; affected region;
部麻酔 *kyokubu masui* local anesthetic
部麻痺 *kyokubu mahi* partial paralysis
部露出 *kyokubu roshutsu* indecent exposure
11務 *kyokumu* departmental business
12渡 *kyokuwata(shi)* telegrams to be called for at the post office
番 *kyokuban* telephone-exchange number
報 *kyokuhō* service telegram; official bulletin

5

A 届 $\frac{1385}{F578}$ 屆 KAI. *todo(ku)* reach, arrive, be received; be attentive, be realized. *todo(keru)* report, notify; forward. *todoke* report, notice; forwarding, delivery.

5出 *todo(ke)-de(ru)* report. *todoke-ide*, *todokede*=*todoke* (see under 届 1385.0).
6先 *todo(ke)saki* destination, address, consignee ⌈ten report
10書 *todo(ke)sho*, *todo(ke)ga(ki)* notice, writ-
11済 *todo(ke)zu(mi)* filed

B 屈 $\frac{1386}{F578}$ KUTSU. *kus(suru)* bend, bend over; give in, submit to, yield to; flinch. *kaga(mu)*, *kaga(maru)*, *kogo(meru)* stop, lean over, crouch. *kago(mu)* bow, stoop, bend over. *kaga(meru)* bow (the knee); bend (the legs).

4込 *kaga(mi)-ko(mu)* bend over
6曲 *kukkyoku suru* be crooked, bend, wind; be indented; be refracted
伏 *kuppuku* surrender, submission
托 *kuttaku* anxiety; trouble; boredom
7伸 *kusshin* extension and contraction; bending and stretching; flexibility
折 *kussetsu* bending; indentation; refraction
折望遠鏡 *kussetsu bōenkyō* refracting telescope
8服 *kuppuku* surrender, submission
9指 *kusshi* counting on the fingers; promi-
10従 *kutsujū* submission, servitude ⌊nence
託 *kuttaku* worry, trouble; preoccupation; boredom, ennui
辱 *kutsujoku* humiliation, insult; defeat
辱的 *kutsujokuteki* disgraceful, humiliating
11強 *kukkyō* robust health; obstinacy
12筋 *kukkin* flexor muscle
15撓 *kuttō* bending
撓性 *kuttōsei* flexibility

A 居 $\frac{1387}{F577}$ KO. KYO residence. *i(ru)*, *o(ru)* be, exist; be found in, stay in; inhabit; live with, reside; be present; remain (sitting).

3士 *koji* active (Buddhist) layman
丈 *itake* one's sitting height ⌈ingly
丈高 *itakedaka ni*, *idakedaka ni* domineer-
4心地 *igokochi* relaxation (at home)
心地良 *igokochiyo(i)* feeling at home, being comfortable. *igokochi (no) yo(i)* cozy, comfortable
中 *kyochū* standing between two people; usual situation ⌈tion
中調停 *kyochū-chōtei* mediation, arbitra-
5立 *i(temo)-ta(ttemo)* restless, impatient, itching (to tell)
乍 *inaga(ra)* at home, as one sits
民 *kyomin* residents, inhabitants
6回 *imawa(ri)* vicinity, neighborhood
宅 *kyotaku* a residence ⌈ent
合 *i-a(wasu)*, *i-a(waseru)* happen to be pres-
合抜 *ia(i)nu(ki)* sword player, sword play
7抜 *inu(ki)* a going concern
邸 *kyotei* dwelling place
坐 *i-suwa(ru)* stay on, settle down, remain (in office). *isuwa(ri) no* stationary, permanent
住 *kyojū suru* reside. *izuma(i)* sitting position. *kyojū* residence; address
住地 *kyojūchi* residence; address
住者 *kyojūsha* resident, inhabitant
住費 *kyojūhi* housing expenses
住証明書 *kyojū shōmeisho* residence cer-
住権 *kyojūken* right of residence ⌊tificate
8所 *idokoro*, *kyosho* residence, whereabouts, address. *o(ri)dokoro* the place where one is
並 *i-nara(bu)* sit in a row, be arrayed
直 *i-nao(ru)* sit straight; change one's attitude; come out strong; turn into a robber; resort to threat
直強盗 *inao(ri) gōtō* burglar who becomes violent when detected
9食 *igu(i)* living in idleness
廻 *imawa(ri)* vicinity, neighborhood
城 *kyojō* daimyo's residential castle
室 *kyoshitsu* living room; private room, den

相撲 *izumō* wrestling in a sitting posture
待 *ima(chi)* sitting and waiting
待月 *ima(chi)zuki* 18-day-old moon
10 候 *isōrō* hanger-on, dependent, parasite
残 *i-noko(ru)* work overtime; remain behind
浸 *ibita(ru)* move in to stay, camp (in a bar)
眠 *inemu(ri)* doze, nap
酒屋 *izakaya* saloon, pub
留 *kyoryū* residence
留民 *kyoryūmin* residents
留地 *kyoryūchi* settlement, concession
留守 *irusu* "not at home" (said when one doesn't want to see callers)
11 据 *i-su(waru)*=居坐 (see above–7)
12 間 *ima* living room, private room
堪 *i(ta)tama(ranai)* too warm; unable to remain
竦 *i-suku(mu), i-suku(maru)* cower, crouch
着 *i-tsu(ku)* settle down
集 *i-atsu(maru)* be gathered together
然 *kyozen* standing firm, steadiness; tranquility; status quo
場 *o(ri)ba* the place where one is
場所 *ibasho* residence; whereabouts
13 睡 *inemu(ri)* nap, doze
続 *i-tsuzu(keru)* stay on
催促 *izaisoku suru* hang on till paid
15 敷当 *ishikia(te)* kimono seat lining
18 職 *ijoku* sedentary occupation
職人 *ijokunin* sedentary artisan

6

昼 See 53.

屏 1388/F580 See **屛** 1398.

屆 1389/F-X Nonstandard for **届** 1400.

屎 1390/F579 SHI. KI. *kuso* excrement, droppings.
7 尿 *shinyō* excreta

屍 1391/F579 SHI corpse. *shikabane* corpse, remains.
7 体 *shitai* corpse
体遺棄罪 *shitai ikizai* crime of abandoning a corpse
9 姦 *shikan* violating a corpse
臭 *shishū* smell of death, putrid smell
10 諫 *shikan* warning a ruler with one's corpse
骸 *shigai* corpse, remains

A **屋** 1392/F579 OKU roof; house. *-ya* shop, store; seller, dealer; business.
3 上 *okujō* housetop, roof
上庭園 *okujō teien* roof garden
4 内 *okunai* indoors
5 外 *okugai* open air, outdoors
台 *yatai* a float; a stall
台店 *yatai mise* street stall, stand, booth
台骨 *yataibone* framework, foundation; means, property
6 号 *yagō* store name, house name, hereditary family name, a stage-family name
7 体 *yatai*=屋台 (see above–5)
形 *yakata* house, mansion, boat cabin
形船 *yakatabune* houseboat, barge, pleasure boat
8 舎 *okusha* house, building
並 *yana(mi)* row of houses
10 根 *yane* roof, roofing, housetop
根伝 *yanezuta(i)* running from roof to roof
根屋 *yaneya* roofer, thatcher
根葺 *yanefuki* thatching a roof; roof thatcher
根裏 *yaneura* attic; loft
15 敷 *yashiki* mansion, residence, premises; residential site
敷町 *yashiki machi* exclusive residential section

7

屐 1393/F579 GEKI clog.

屓 1394/F584 = **屭** KI exerting strength.

屑 1395/F580 SETSU. *kuzu* rubbish, junk, trash, waste, scraps, rags, crumbs, waste paper; the scum of society.
2 入 *kuzu-i(re)* garbage can
6 米 *kuzugome, kuzumai* broken rice
糸 *kuzu ito* waste silk
肉 *kuzu niku* meat scraps, dog meat
羊毛 *kuzu yōmō* shoddy, reclaimed wool
8 物 *kuzumono* trash, junk
9 屋 *kuzuya* junk man
拾 *kuzuhiro(i)* ragpicking; ragpicker
10 値 *kuzune* scrap value
13 鉄 *kuzu tetsu* scrap iron
14 綿 *kuzu wata* waste cotton
18 繭 *kuzu mayu* waste cocoon
22 籠 *kuzu kago* wastebasket

A **展** 1396/F580 TEN expand.
5 示 *tenji* exhibition, display
示会 *tenjikai* exhibition
示場 *tenjijō* (place of) an exhibition
8 性 *tensei* malleability
11 転 *tenten* rolling
転反側 *tenten-hansoku* tossing in bed, sleeplessness
望 *tembō* view, outlook, prospect
望台 *tembōdai* observatory; observation platform

望車 *tembōsha* observation car
望哨 *tembōshō* observation post, lookout
望鏡 *tembōkyō* periscope; field glass
12開 *tenkai suru* unfold, develop, evolve; deploy
13墓 *tembo* visiting a grave
16覧 *tenran* exhibition
覧会 *tenrankai* exhibition, exhibit
覧物 *tenrambutsu* exhibit
覧室 *tenranshitsu* showroom
18観 *tenkan* exhibition

— 8 —

屠 See 1399.

展 See 1396.

犀 1397 F1221 SAI rhinoceros. [牛]
7角 *saikaku* a rhinoceros horn
利 *sairi na* keen, acute, penetrating

屏 1398 F580 屛 HEI, BYŌ wall, fence, screen.
8居 *heikyo suru* live in retirement
9風 *byōbu* folding screen
風岩 *byōbu iwa* sheer cliff
10息 *heisoku suru* bate one's breath; be cowed into silence

— 9 —

犀 See 1397. [牛]

屢 Nonstandard for 屡 1401.

屠 1399 F581 TO. *hofu(ru)* slaughter, butcher, massacre, slay.
4牛 *togyū* slaughtering, butchering
牛場 *togyūjō* slaughterhouse
6肉 *toniku* butcher's meat
8所 *tosho* slaughterhouse
10畜 *tochiku* butchering, slaughtering
殺 *tosatsu* slaughter, butchering; massacre
殺夫 *tosatsufu* butcher, slaughterer
殺場 *tosatsujō* slaughterhouse
殺業 *tosatsugyō* butchering business
12場 *tojō* slaughter house
13腹 *tofuku* disembowelment
19蘇 *toso* spiced saké
蘇機嫌 *toso kigen* drunk with New Year's saké

A 属 1400 F583 屬 ZOKU genus; subordinate official. SHOKU. *zoku(suru), zoku(su)* belong to, be among; fall under; be affiliated with; be subject to; be vested in, be inherent in
5目 *shokumoku* attention, observation
6地 *zokuchi* dependency, territory
州 *zokushū* province
邦 *zokuhō* vassal state, dependency
名 *zokumei* generic name
吏 *zokuri* subordinate official
8国 *zokkoku* vassal state, dependency
性 *zokusei* attribute
官 *zokkan* government clerk, subordinate official
具 *zokugu* accessories, equipment, appliances
11望 *shokubō* expectation
14僚 *zokuryō* subordinate
領 *zokuryō* possession, dependency, dominion

— 11 —

屡 1401 F582 RU. *shibashiba* often, frequently.
6次 *ruji ni* successively, repeatedly
14屡 *shibashiba* often, frequently
鳴 *shibana(ku)* sing unceasingly

B 層 1402 F582 層 SŌ (social) class; stratum, layer, seam, bed, formation; story, floor; course (of stones).
7位学 *sōigaku* stratigraphy
状 *sōjō* stratified
状岩 *sōjōgan* stratified rock
12雲 *sōun* stratus clouds
13楼 *sōrō* tall building
14閣 *sōkaku* many-storied building
16積雲 *sōsekiun* strato-cumulus clouds

— 12 —

層 1403 F582 See 層 1402.

B 履 1404 F582 RI. *fu(mu)* (see 踏 4571.0). *ha(ku)* put on (the feet). *kutsu* shoes, boots.
6行 *rikō* performance, fulfillment, execution, observance
8物 *hakimono* footwear
物店 *hakimonoten* footwear store
10修 *rishū suru* study, complete (a course)
11違 *ha(ki)-chiga(eru)* to put on someone else's footwear; be mistaken
14歴 *rireki* personal history, career
歴書 *rirekisho* personal history, vita

— 18 —

屬 1405 F583 See 属 1400.

— 21 —

屭 1406 F584 See 屓 1394.

RAD. 屮 45

Furukusa old "grass" (i.e., the less complicated "grass," as distinguished from Rad. 140). Variants: 艸, 屮. Nickname: Old Grass.

1

屯 See 264.

RAD. 山 46

Yama mountain. At left: *yamahen*. Nickname: Mountain.

A **山** 1407 F585 SAN mount, mountain. *yama* mountain, hill, height, knoll; heap, pile; crown (of a hat); seam (of an obi); speculation, adventure; climax, acme, crisis; forest; mine.

2 刀 *yamagatana* woodman's hatchet
又山 *yama-mata-yama* mountain upon mountain
人 *yamabito* mountain people; hermit
人蔘 *yama ninjin* wild carrot
3 口 *yamaguchi* start of a climb
女 *yamame* trout, young salmon
山 *yamayama* mountains; very much
川 *yamagawa* mountain stream. *sansen* mountains and rivers
下 *yamashita, yamamoto, sanka* foot of a mountain
小屋 *yamagoya* mountain hut
上 *sanjō* mountain top
上垂訓 *Sanjō (no) Suikun* Sermon on the Mount
4 手 *yamate, yama(no)te* hilly section of Tokyo; bluff; uptown
方 *yamakata* mountainous area
月 *sangetsu* the moon above a mountain
木 *yamagi* mountain trees
犬 *yama inu* wild dog, wolf, coyote, jackal
辺 *yamabe* the vicinity of a mountain
中 *yamanaka, sanchū* in the mountains
内 *sannai* in the mountains; in a temple compound
元 *yamamoto* colliery, mine; base of a mountain; owner of a mountain
分 *yamawa(ke)* halving, equal division
火事 *yamakaji* forest fire
毛欅 *buna* beech tree
水 *yama mizu* mountain spring water. *sansui* hills and water; landscape, scenery; landscape painting; landscape garden
水画 *sansuiga* landscape painting; a landscape
水画家 *sansui gaka* landscape painter
5 田 *yamada* rice fields in the hills
巡 *yamamegu(ri)* mountain trip; mountain pilgrimage; drizzling rain
主 *yamanushi* owner of a mountain area, mountain watchman
出 *yamada(shi)* a rustic
6 色 *sanshoku* mountain scenery; color of the mountains
行 *sankō, yamayu(ki), yama-i(ki)* trip into the mountains
気 *sanki* mountain air. *yamaki, yamake, yamagi* speculative spirit; enterprise; pretension
向 *yamamu(kō)* across the mountain
伏 *yamabushi* mountain priest, itinerant priest, hermit
伝 *yamazuta(i)* along the mountains, following a mountain road
地 *yamachi, sanchi* hilly country, mountain area
肌 *yamahada* mountain surface
号 *sangō* temple name
寺 *yamadera* mountain temple
守 *yamamori* forest ranger
光 *sankō* mountain scenery
羊 *yagi* goat
羊肉 *yagi niku* goat meat
羊鬚 *yagi hige* goatee
7 里 *yamazato* mountain village, hilly district
住 *yamazuma(i)* living in the mountains
抜 *yamanu(ke)* landslide
村 *sanson* mountain village
系 *sankei* mountain system
男 *yama otoko* wild man; woodsman; hillbilly; mountaineer
吹 *yamabuki* yellow rose
吹色 *yamabuki iro* bright yellow, golden; gold
形 *yamagata* chevron
形歯車 *yamagata haguruma* herringbone gears

8門 *sammon* main (two-story) temple gate

雨 *san-u* rain from the mountains

国 *yamaguni* mountainous province

房 *sambō* a mountain villa; a home in the mountains

径 *sankei* mountain path

河 *sanga, sanka* mountains and rivers; stronghold

育 *yamasoda(chi)* bred in the mountains

幸 *yama (no) sachi, yama sachi* mountain food products

苞 *yamazuto* mountain souvenirs

岳 *sangaku* mountains

岳病 *sangakubyō* altitude sickness

林 *sanrin* mountains and forests; mountain forest

林官 *sanrinkan* forester

林学 *sanringaku* forestry

林保護 *sanrin hogo* forest conservation

林開拓 *sanrin kaitaku* deforestation

林業 *sanringyō* forestry industry

林檎 *yama ringo* crab apple

林濫伐 *sanrin rambatsu* reckless deforestation

9面 *yamazura* mountain surface

風 *sampū, yama kaze* mountain wind

廻 *yamamegu(ri)*＝山巡 (see above-5)

途 *santo* mountain road

城 *yamashiro* a mountain castle

姫 *yamahime* mountain goddess

姥 *yama uba* mountain witch

峡 *yamagai, yamakai, sankyō* gorge, ravine, gap, vale

相 *sansō* the form of a mountain

海 *sankai* mountains and seas; land and sea

狩 *yamaga(ri)* hunting in the mountains

神 *yama (no) kami* god of the mountain; a wife

亭 *santei* mountain villa; mountain inn

彦 *yamabiko* mountain echo; mountain god

荒 *yama-ara(shi)* porcupine

茶 *tsubaki* camellia

荘 *sansō* mountain villa, mountain retreat

草 *yamakusa* mountain grass

津浪 *yama tsunami* landslide

背 *sampai* mountain ridge; the back side of the mountain. *yamase* mountain ridge; wind blowing from mountains to the sea

背風 *yamase kaze* wind blowing from mountains to the sea

10骨 *sankotsu* a large rock

師 *yamashi* speculator; adventurer; impostor, swindler; miner; lumber dealer

桜 *yamazakura* a wild cherry tree, prunus serrulata

砲 *sampō* mountain gun, mountain artillery

祇 *yamatsumi* mountain god

脈 *sammyaku* mountain range

陰 *yama kage, san-in* shelter of the mountains; northern slopes

陵 *sanryō* mountains and hills; imperial tomb

容 *san-yō* the form of a mountain

高 *yamataka* derby hat

高帽 *yamatakabō* derby hat

家 *sanka, yamaga* mountain home, chalet. *yama (no) ie* mountaineers' hut

家住 *yamagazuma(i)* mountain life

家育 *yamagasoda(chi)* country-bred

11鳥 *yamadori* pheasant; mountain bird

疵 *yama kizu* pottery firing flaw

道 *sandō* mountain pass, mountain path. *yama michi* mountain path

側 *sansoku* mountainside, hillside

掛 *yamaka(ke)* piled high

梔 *kuchinashi* gardenia

添 *yamazo(i)* along the foot of a mountain

脚 *sankyaku* the foot of a mountain

野 *san-ya* fields and mountains

陽 *san-yō* the southern face of a mountain; the sunny slopes

勘 *yamakan* speculation in business

頂 *sanchō* mountain top

崩 *yamakuzure* landslide

窓 *sansō* window in a mountain villa; mountain villa

梨 *yama nashi* wild pear

盛 *yamamo(ri)* heap, pile, full measure

砦 *sansai* mountain fortifications; bandit den

猫 *yamaneko* wildcat, lynx

猫争議 *yamaneko sōgi* wildcat strike

12越 *yamago(e), yamago(shi)* crossing a mountain

開 *yamabira(ki)* opening of the mountain-climbing season

湯 *yama(no)yu* mountain hot springs

焼 *yamaya(ki)* burning of dead grass

勝 *yamaga(chi) no* hilly, mountainous

蛙 *yamagaeru* brown frog

蛭 *yamabiru* land leech

颪 *yama oroshi* a wind blowing down off the mountains

奥 *yamaoku* mountain recesses

嵐 *yama arashi* mountain storm

登 *yamanobo(ri)* mountain climbing

番 *yamaban* forest ranger

葡萄 *yama budō* wild grapes

紫水明 *sanshi-suimei* scenic beauty

間 *sankan* in the mountains. *yama-ai* glen, ravine, gorge

間僻地 *sankan-hekichi* deep mountain recesses

椒 *sanshō* black pepper

椒魚 *sanshō uo* salamander

葵 *wasabi* Japanese horse-radish

葵大根 *wasabi daikon* foreign horse-radish

葵目鑢 *wasabime yasuri* rasp

葵卸 *wasabioro(shi)* grater

葵漬 *wasabizuke* pickled horse-radish

13鼠 *yama nezumi* woodchuck; groundhog

僧 *sansō* (Buddhist) priest
塊 *sankai* isolated mountains; mountain range
楼 *sanrō* high mountain building
猿 *yamazaru* wild monkey; a rustic
稜 *sanryō* mountain ridge
続 *yamatsuzu(ki)* mountain chain
腹 *sampuku* hillside, mountainside
蜂 *yamabachi* hornet
裾 *yama suso, yamazuso* foot of a mountain
賊 *sanzoku* mountain bandit
路 *yamaji, sanro* mountain road
際 *yamagiwa* mountain ridge, skyline, base of a mountain
群 *sangun* mountain range
塞 *sansai* mountain fortress; den of bandits
勢 *sansei* condition in the mountains; shape of the mountains
鳩 *yamabato* turtledove
鳩色 *yamabato iro* yellowish blue
14 鳴 *yamana(ri)* rumbling in the mountains.
yamana(rashi) poplar
端 *yama(no)ha* mountain ridge
駅 *san-eki* a stage town in the mountains
寨 *sansai* mountain fortification; bandit den
窩 *sanka* roving mountainous tribes; nomads; outcast tribe; ancient hermit people
15 膚 *yamahada* the face of a mountain
稼 *yamakasegi* work in the mountains
賤 *yamagatsu, yamashizu* mountain dwellers
霊 *sanrei* mountain deity
駕籠 *yama kago* mountain palanquin
16 懐 *yamabutokoro* mountain valley, heart of the mountains
積 *yamazu(mi), sanseki* mountainous pile, big pile
17 嶽 *sangaku* mountains
18 鼬 *yama itachi* ermine
繭 *yama mayu* wild cocoon
19 鯨 *yama kujira* wild-boar meat
霧 *yamagiri* fog in the mountains
麓 *sanroku* the foot of a mountain
21 籐 *tō* rattan, cane
躑躅 *yama tsutsuji* rhododendron
22 巓 *santen* mountain top
籟 *sanrai* the sound of a mountain breeze in the trees
籠 *yamagomo(ri)* retiring in the mountains; retiring to a mountain temple

3

屶 1408/F-X Nonstandard for **出** 97.

屹 1409/F588 KITSU towering (mountains).
5 立 *kitsuritsu suru* tower, rise, soar
9 度 *kitto* surely
12 然 *kitsuzen(taru)* towering

4

岐 B 1410/F589 KI. *chimata* (see under 巷 1465.0).
5 出 *waka(re)-de(ru)* branch out, diverge, radiate
13 路 *kiro* forked road, branch road, crossroad

5

岳 See 208.

岡 See 621.

岨 1411/F590 So a rocky mountain.

岬 1412/F590 Kō. *misaki, saki* cape, spit, promontory.
12 湾 *kōwan* indentations, capes

岸 A 1413/F590 GAN. *kishi* bank, shore, coast, brink.
4 辺 *kishibe* shore
6 向 *kishimu(kō)* opposite bank
10 根 *kishine* base of the river bank
11 道 *kishi michi* river-bank road, cliff road
16 頭 *gantō* top of a riverbank
壁 *gampeki* wharf, breakwater; steep coastal cliff

岩 A 1414/F590 GAN. *iwa* rock, crag; reef.
3 山 *iwayama* rocky mountain (large or small)
4 戸 *iwato* cave door; grotto; cave home
水 *iwamizu* water flowing from the rocks
5 石 *ganseki* rock, crag
穴 *iwa ana* rocky cave
本 *iwamoto* base of a rock
7 床 *ganshō* bedrock
8 波 *iwanami* waves breaking against the rocks
苔 *iwagoke* rock moss
9 飛 *iwato(bi)* diving from a high rock; such a diver
屋 *iwaya* cavern, grotto, rocky cave
峡 *iwa hazama* cleft in the rocks
洞 *gantō* rocky grotto
乗 *ganjō na* solid, firm, stout. *ganjō* excellent horse; 5-to-15-year-old horse
室 *iwamuro* stone hut
10 根 *iwane, iwagane* rock, crag; base of a rock
11 魚 *iwana* bull trout
道 *iwamichi* road along the top of a rocky cliff
組 *iwagu(mi)* arrangement of garden rocks
清水 *iwa shimizu* spring water among rocks
12 間 *iwama* cleft in the rocks; among the rocks or crags
棚 *iwatana* ledge

淵 *iwabuchi* deep water at the foot of a
壺 *iwatsubo* rocky cave ⌊rocky cliff
13塩 *gan-en, iwashio* rock salt
隠 *iwagaku(re)* the shadow of a rock
窟 *gankutsu* rocky cave
14層 *gansō* rock formation
16橋 *iwabashi* natural rock bridge; stones forming a crossing over rapids
17礁 *ganshō* reef
19瀬 *iwase* rocky rapids

6

峙 1415/F591 JI. *sobada(tsu)* tower, soar.

B **峠** 1416/F591 (国字) *tōge* mountain pass; crisis, crest, climax.
11道 *tōge michi* a road over a mountain pass

B **峡** 1417/F593 **峽** KYŌ gorge, ravine. *hazama*=*hazama* 狭間 2882.12.
7谷 *kyōkoku* glen, ravine, gorge, canyon
12間 *kyōkan* between the mountains; ravine,
湾 *kyōwan* fjord ⌊defile

A **炭** 1418/F1181 **炭** TAN charcoal; coal. *sumi* charcoal. [火]
2入 *sumi-i(re)* charcoal container
3山 *tanzan* coal mine
4木 *sumigi* charcoal wood
火 *sumibi, tanka* charcoal fire; coals of fire
化 *tanka* carbonization
化水素 *tanka suiso* hydrocarbon
化物 *tankabutsu* carbide ⌈gen
水 *tansui* coal and water; carbon and hydro-
水化物 *tansuikabutsu* carbohydrates
水車 *tansuisha* engine tender
水船 *tansuisen* supply ship
5田 *tanden* coal field
6団 *tadon* charcoal ball
7車 *tansha* coal wagon, coal truck, coal car
坑 *tankō* coal mine ⌊(of a locomotive)
坑夫 *tankōfu* coal miner
8取 *sumito(ri)* charcoal scuttle
9屋 *sumiya* charcoal dealer
10庫 *tanko* coal bin, coal bunker
俵 *sumidawara* charcoal sack
挾 *sumibasa(mi)* charcoal tongs
消 *sumike(shi)* covered jar for putting out
脈 *tammyaku* coal vein ⌊burning coals
疽病 *tansobyō* anthrax
素 *tanso* carbon
素紙 *tansoshi* carbon paper
素棒 *tansobō* carbon rod; carbon points
素線 *tansosen* carbon filament

12焼 *sumiya(ki)* charcoal making; charcoal
焼竈 *sumiya(ki)gama* charcoal kiln ⌊maker
13継 *sumitsu(gi)* replenishing charcoal
鉱 *tankō* coal mine
鉱業 *tankōgyō* coal-mining industry
14層 *tansō* coal seam
塵 *tanjin* coal dust
酸 *tansan* carbonic acid
酸水 *tansansui* carbonated water
酸孔 *tansankō* a mofette
酸瓦斯 *tansan gasu* carbon dioxide
酸泉 *tansansen* carbonated spring
酸紙 *tansanshi* carbon paper
酸曹達 *tansan sōda* sodium carbonate
15窯 *sumigama* charcoal kiln
質 *tanshitsu* coal quality
20礦 *tankō* coal mine
21竈 *sumigama* charcoal kiln

7

島 See 230.

峽 1419/F593 See 峡 1417.

豈 1420/F1777 KAI. GAI. *ani* an interjection of surprise. [豆]

峭 1421/F591 SHŌ high and steep.
5立 *shōritsu* steep and soaring (mountains)

峨 1422/F591 **峩** GA high mountain.
10峨 *gaga(taru)* rugged, craggy

B **峰** 1423/F592 **峯** HŌ. *mine, ne* peak, summit, top; back (of a sword).
5打 *mineu(chi)* striking with the back of a
10峰 *minemine* peaks ⌊sword
13続 *minetsuzu(ki)* succession of peaks
16頭 *hōtō* the summit of a peak
22巒 *hōran* mountain range

峻 1424/F592 SHUN high; steep.
3下剤 *shungezai* strong purgative
7坂 *shumpan* steep slope
拒 *shunkyo* positive refusal
別 *shumbetsu* sharp distinction
8刻 *shunkoku* heartlessness
命 *shummei* strict order; your orders
10峰 *shumpō* steep peak
烈 *shunretsu na* unrelenting, severity, stern-
13路 *shunro* steep road ⌊ness

14 酷 *shunkoku* heartlessness
17 厳 *shungen na* strict, harsh, severe
嶺 *shunrei* steep peak

8

崗 1425 / F594 Kō hill.

崎 1426 / F593 Ki steep. *misaki, saki* cape, spit, promontory.
14 嶇 *kiku* steepness of a road; life's trials

崛 1427 / F595 崫 Kutsu high and lofty (mountains).
10 起 *kukki suru* rise abruptly, tower high

崖 1428 / F594 崕 厓 Gai. *gake* cliff, bluff, precipice.
11 崩 *gakekuzu(re)* landslide
13 路 *gakeji, gake michi* narrow cliff road; steep stony road
14 端 *gakebata* edge of a cliff

崇 B 1429 / F593 Sū, Shū high. *aga(meru)* respect, revere, adore, worship.
4 仏 *sūbutsu* revering the Buddhas
仏派 *sūbutsuha* (ancient) pro-Buddhist faction
8 拝 *sūhai* worship; admiration, adoration; cult
拝者 *sūhaisha* worshiper, admirer, idolater, devotee
10 高 *sūkō na* lofty, noble, sublime
高美 *sūkōbi* sublime beauty, the sublime
12 敬 *sūkei* reverence, adoration, veneration

崩 B 1430 / F595 崩 Hō. *hō(jiru), hō(zuru)* die. *kuzu(su)* demolish, destroy; level (a hill); crumble (bread); change (money); simplify; put in disorder; cut (prices). *kuzu(reru)* crumble, collapse, cave in, be destroyed, get out of shape; be routed; worsen (weather). *kuzu(shi)* simplified form. *-kuzu(re)* delinquent, degenerate.
5 去 *kuzu(re)-sa(ru)* collapse, crumble away
6 字 *kuzu(shi)ji* abbreviated character
7 売 *kuzu(shi)u(ri)* selling separately
10 書 *kuzu(shi)ga(ki)* grass-hand penmanship
12 御 *hōgyo* demise, death of an emperor
落 *kuzu(re)-o(chiru)* fall down flat; dissolve. *hōraku* collapse, cave-in; slump, crash, heavy decline
13 滅 *kuzu(re)-horo(biru)* crumble to ruins
15 潰 *hōkai* collapse, cave-in
16 壊 *hōkai* collapse, cave-in

9

嵐 1431 / F596 Ran. *arashi* storm, tempest.
6 気 *ranki* mountain air

嵌 1432 / F596 Kan. *ha(maru)* go into, fit into; fall into, plunge into; be deceived. *ha(meru)* put on, pull on; inlay, set in; fit in; fill in; throw into; ensnare, cheat.
2 入 *kannyū suru, ha(me)-i(reru)* inlay, insert, fit in, dovetail, telescope
4 込 *ha(me)-ko(mu)* = *ha(meru)* (see under 嵌 1432.0)
木細工 *hamekizaiku* inlaid woodwork
7 役 *hama(ri)yaku* fitting role
11 細工 *hamezaiku* inlaid work; inlay worker
12 替 *ha(me)-kae(ru)* change (buttons or the cords of wooden clogs, etc.)
18 頓 *kanton* strangulation (as in hernia)

10

嵩 1433 / F596 Sū. *kō(zuru), kō(jiru)* be aggravated, grow worse. *kasa(mu)* grow bulky, rise, swell, increase in volume; mount up. *kasa* bulk, volume, quantity, size.
10 高 *kasadaka na* bulky, voluminous; high-handed
11 張 *kasaba(ru)* be bulky
掛 *kasa (ni) ka(karu)* take a highhanded attitude

11

嶋 1434 / F597 / F592 嶌 島 See 島 230.

嶇 1435 / F597 Ku steep.

嶄 1436 / F597 嶃 Zan steep (mountain), high.
12 然 *zanzen(taru)* prominent, conspicuous, unrivaled

13

嶮 1437 / F598 See 険 5000.

嶼 1438 / F598 Sho island.

14

嶽 1439 / F598 See 岳 208.

嶺 1440 / F598 Rei. Ryō. *mine, ne* (see under 峰 1423.0).

嶷 1441 / F598 Gyoku wise.
5 立 *gyokuritsu* rising, towering

— 17 —

巌 1442/F599 **巖** GAN. *iwa* rock, crag, reef. *iwao* (massive) rock.
9 洞 *gantō* cave
乗 *ganjō*=岩乗 1414.9
12 棲 *gansei* cave dwelling; living in the mountains; hermit
13 窟 *gankutsu* cave, cavern, grotto
15 質 *ganshitsu* properties of stone
16 頭 *gantō* top of a rock
壁 *gampeki* cliff

巇 1443/F599 KI, GI steep.

— 18 —

巖 Nonstandard for **巌** 1442.

巍 1444/F599 GI high.
10 峨 *giga(taru)* lofty, towering
12 然 *gizen(taru)* lofty, towering
21 巍 *gigi(taru)* lofty, towering

— 19 —

巒 1445/F599 RAN small peak.

巓 1446/F599 TEN. *itadaki* summit.

— 20 —

巖 See **巌** 1442.

川 RAD. 47

Kawa river or *sambon kawa* 3-stroke "river" (to distinguish it from the 8-stroke river 河). Variant: 巛 *magari kawa* curving "river." Nickname: River.

A **川** 1447/F600 SEN. *kawa* river, stream, brook.
3 口 *kawaguchi* mouth of a river
川 *kawagawa* rivers
下 *kawashimo* downstream. *kawakuda(ri)* going down a river
上 *kawakami* upper stream; upstream. *kawanobo(ri)* going up a river
4 心 *senshin* the middle of the river
手 *kawate* riverside; tax on travelers crossing a river
止 *kawado(me)* no ferry service
辺 *kawabe* riverside
5 尻 *kawajiri* river mouth; lower stream
付 *kawatsu(ki)* along the river
6 竹 *kawatake* river bamboo
向 *kawamuka(i)*, *kawamu(kō)* the opposite side of the river
伝 *kawazuta(i) ni* along the river
州 *kawasu* sand bank in a river
合 *kawa-a(i)* confluence
守 *kawamori* guard at the ford
7 床 *kawadoko*, *kawatoko* river bed
8 沿 *kawazo(i) ni* along the river
波 *kawa nami* waves on a stream
股 *kawamata* river fork
岸 *kawagishi* riverbank
9 面 *kawazura*, *kawamo*, *kawa(no)omo* river surface
音 *kawa oto* sound of a flowing river
風 *kawa kaze* river breeze
柱 *kawabashira* bridge pillar
柳 *kawa yanagi* purple willow, river willow. *senryū* comic *haiku* poem
洲 *kawasu* river sand bar
狩 *kawaga(ri)* river fishing
施餓鬼 *kawa segaki* memorial service for the drowned
10 原 *kawara*, *kawahara* dry river bed; river beach
流 *kawanaga(re)* river drowning
11 魚 *kawa-uo*, *kawazakana* river fish
遊 *kawa-aso(bi)* boating, rowing
淀 *kawa yodo* river pool
猟 *kawaryō* river fishing
船 *kawabune*, *kawa fune* river boat, barge, ferry
釣 *kawatsuri* river fishing
12 遠 *kawaochi* opposite river bank
開 *kawabira(ki)* river festival
幅 *kawa haba* river width
揚 *kawa-a(ge)* unloading (a ship) at the riverside; raising water out of a river
渡 *kawawata(shi)* crossing a river
颪 *kawa oroshi* wind blowing down the river
筋 *kawa suji* river course
越 *kawago(e)*, *kawago(shi)* crossing a river
越人足 *kawago(shi) ninsoku* coolies that carry people across a river
蒸汽 *kawa jōki* river steamer
蒸汽船 *kawa jōkisen* river steamer
13 路 *kawaji* watercourses
14 端 *kawabata* riverside
15 縁 *kawabuchi*, *kawaberi* riverside

蝦 *kawa ebi* crayfish
論 *kawa ron* struggle over water rights
19 瀬 *kawase* rapids, shallows
獺 *kawa uso, kawa oso* otter
藻 *kawamo* plants of the river shallows
霧 *kawagiri* river mist
28 鑿 *kawaseseri* river fishing

— 2 —

巡 See 4667.

— 3 —

巡 See 4667.

州 See 99.

— 4 —

A **災** 1448/F1179 SAI. *wazawai* calamity, misfortune, woe, evil, curse. [火]
4 厄 *saiyaku* calamity, disaster, accident
5 民 *saimin* calamity sufferers
10 害 *saigai* disaster, calamity, accident
害地 *saigaichi* stricken area
害保険 *saigai hoken* accident-and-sickness insurance
害救助 *saigai kyūjo* disaster relief
11 異 *sai-i* natural calamity
患 *saikan* misfortune, calamity
13 禍 *saika* accident, calamity, disaster, misfortune
18 難 *sainan* calamity, disaster, accident, misfortune

— 8 —

巣 1449/F601 See **巢** 141.

— 9 —

A **順** 1450/F2055 JUN order; turn; right; docility, obedience; occasion. [頁]
4 化 *junka suru* acclimate
天 *junten* following the way of heaven
5 正 *junsei na* correct and reasonable
礼 *junrei* pilgrimage; pilgrim
礼歌 *junrei uta* pilgrim's song
6 行 *junkō* progressing in order
次 *junji* gradually. *junji ni* in order, successively
当 *juntō na* proper, right, regular, normal
7 位 *jun-i* order, rank, precedence
良 *junryō na* gentle, peaceful, obedient
応 *junnō* adaptation; sympathy
応性 *junnōsei* adaptability
序 *junjo* order; system; procedure
序不同 *junjo-fudō* random order
序正 *junjotadashi(ku)* in exact order
序書 *junjoga(ki)* program
序数詞 *junjo sūshi* ordinal number
8 延 *jun-en* postponement
逆 *jungyaku* obedience and disobedience, right and wrong
送 *jun-oku(ri)* passing on from person to person
拝 *jumpai* circuit pilgrimage
9 風 *jumpū* favorable wind, tail wind
盃 *jumpai* passing the cups
11 道 *jundō* the right road; following the path of truth
転 *junten* normal winds
12 順 *junjun ni* in order, in turn
番 *jumban* order, turn
13 路 *junro* regular route; itinerary
14 境 *junkyō* favorable circumstances, prosperity
15 調 *junchō* smoothness, favorable condition
養子 *jun-yōshi* younger brother adopted as a son
19 繰 *jungu(ri) ni* in turn, in order

RAD. 工 48

E (the katakana). At left: エ *takumi hen* (left-side "carpenter's square"). Nickname: *Kana E.*

A **工** 1451/F602 KU. KŌ artisan, mechanic; manufacture; work. *takumi* artisan, mechanic; carpenter. *taku(mu)* plan; scheme.
2 人 *kōjin* workman, craftsman
3 女 *kōjo* factory girl
大 *kōdai* engineering college
4 夫 *kufū* device, invention, scheme, means. *kōfu* coolie, workman, laborer
手 *kōshu* workman, trackman
手学校 *kōshu gakkō* trade school
6 匠 *kōshō* mechanic, artisan, craftsman
合 *guai, guwai* fitness, order, condition; way, style; convenience; decency, propriety; state of health; situation; arrangements
7 兵 *kōhei* army engineers
作 *kōsaku* building, engineering; handicraft; maneuvering (in politics)
作物 *kōsakubutsu* building; manufactured articles
作品 *kōsakuhin* handicrafts
作船 *kōsakusen* factory ship
作機械 *kōsaku kikai* machine tools
芸 *kōgei* industrial arts, technology

芸学 *kōgeigaku* technology
芸学校 *kōgei gakkō* technological school
芸品 *kōgeihin* industrial-art objects
芸美術 *kōgei bijutsu* mechanical art
8房 *kōbō* (artisan's) studio
具 *kōgu* tool, implement
学 *kōgaku* engineering
学士 *Kōgakushi* Bachelor of Engineering
学博士 *Kōgaku Hakase, Kōgaku Hakushi*
事 *kōji* construction ⌊Doctor of Engineering
事中 *kōjichū* under construction
事場 *kōjiba* construction site
9面 *kumen* contriving, managing, raising (funds); circumstances, pecuniary status
科 *kōka* engineering course
科大学 *kōka daigaku* engineering college
10員 *kōin* factory worker, artisan
11率 *kōritsu* rate of production
商 *kōshō* industry and commerce; workmen
務 *kōmu* engineering ⌊and businessmen
務店 *kōmuten* engineering firm
務所 *kōmusho* engineering office
12程 *kōtei* process; work progress
費 *kōhi* construction costs
場 *kōjō, kōba* factory, workshop, mill
場主 *kōjōshu* factory owner
場生産 *kōjō seisan* prefabrication
場地 *kōjōchi* factory district
場長 *kōjōchō* factory manager
場制 *kōbasei* factory system
場街 *kōjōgai* factory town
場渡 *kōjōwata(shi)* factory delivery
場疎開 *kōjō sokai* factory dispersion
13賃 *kōchin* wages, pay, labor cost
業 *kōgyō* industry
業大学 *kōgyō daigaku* technical college
業化 *kōgyōka* industrialization
業化学 *kōgyō kagaku* industrial chemistry
業用 *kōgyōyō* for industrial use
業史 *kōgyōshi* history of industry
業地 *kōgyōchi* industrial area
業地帯 *kōgyō chitai* industrial area
業国 *kōgyōkoku* industrial nation
業界 *kōgyōkai* industrial circles
業家 *kōgyōka* manufacturer
業塩 *kōgyōen* industrial salt
14銀 *kōgin* wages, pay
銭 *kōsen* wages, pay
15廠 *kōshō* arsenal

2

巨 1452/F604 See **巨** 758.

B **巧** 1453/F604 Kō. *taku(mi) na* skilled. *taku(manai), taku(manu)* artless, natural, unintentional. *taku(mi)* skill, ingenuity.
4手 *kōshu* a skillful workman
5弁 *kōben* quibbling
6舌 *kōzetsu* a clever speaker
匠 *kōshō* skilled carpenter; skilled workman
7妙 *kōmyō* skill, cleverness, ingenuity
技 *kōgi* skilled workmanship
言 *kōgen* flattery ⌈ity
言令色 *kōgen-reishoku* ingratiating genial-
8拙 *kōsetsu* tact, skill, performance, work-
知 *kōchi* cleverness, tact ⌊manship
者 *kōsha* cleverness, skill, tact
11遅 *kōchi* slow but sure
12智 *kōchi* cleverness, tact
16緻 *kōchi na* elaborate, finely wrought

A **功** 1454/F257 Kō merits, meritorious deeds; success; credit, honor; effect; class (in court orders). Ku merits. *isao, isaoshi* merit; meritorious deed. [力]
5田 *kōden* (ancient) rice-field reward
6臣 *kōshin* meritorious retainer
伐 *kōbatsu* many exploits
名 *kōmyō* great achievement
名心 *kōmyōshin* ambition, love of fame
7利 *kōri* utility; utilitarian
利主義 *kōri shugi* utilitarianism
利的 *kōriteki* utilitarian, businesslike
利説 *kōrisetsu* utilitarianism
労 *kōrō* meritorious deed; services
労金 *kōrōkin* reward for meritorious services
労者 *kōrōsha* man of distinguished service
労章 *kōrōshō* distinguished-service medal (police and railways)
10能 *kōnō* work; efficiency
11過 *kōka* merits and demerits
13罪 *kōzai* merits and demerits
業 *kōgyō* exploit, achievement
14徳 *kōtoku, kudoku* charity, virtue, merit
15勲 *kōkun* meritorious service to ruler and country
17績 *kōseki* meritorious service, merit

A **左** 1455/F602 Sa left; the following. *hidari* left; the left; leftist. *hidari suru* turn to the left.
3大臣 *Sadaijin* (ancient) Minister of the
4手 *hidarite* left hand; the left ⌊Left
方 *sahō* the left
辺 *sahen* left side
分 *hidariwa(ke)* parting (the hair) at the left
中間 *sachūkan* between left field and center
心房 *sashimbō* left auricle (of the heart)
心室 *sashinshitsu* left ventricle (of the heart)

5右 *sayū suru* command, dominate, control, sway. *sayū* left and right; one's side; one's attendants. *tokō* this or that. *sa-u* left and right; news; condition; criticism; command. *to(ni)kaku(ni)* anyway. *to(mo)kaku(mo), to(mo)kaku* anyhow, in any case. *hidari migi* left and right
打者 *hidari dasha* left-handed batter
6回 *hidarimawa(ri)* counterclockwise
向 *hidarimu(ki)* turning to left
団扇 *hidari uchiwa* living in comfort
7折 *sasetsu suru* turn to the left
社 *sasha* left-wing socialist party
利 *hidarikiki*, left-handedness; left-hander; saké drinker. *hidarigitcho* left-handedness; left-hander
邪飛 *sajahi* foul to the left ⌈tions
見右見 *tomikōmi* viewing from all direc-
8注 *sachū* left marginal notes
岸 *sagan* left bank (of a river)
表 *sahyō* chart at the left
官 *sakan, shakan* plasterer
官職 *sakanshoku, shakanshoku* plasterer
9廻 *hidarimawa(ri)*=左回 (see above–6)
派 *saha* left wing; left faction; leftist
歪 *hidariyuga(mi)* inclining to the left
前 *hidarimae* the wrong way, folding left-side of a kinomo under the right; adversity. *sazen* front of left field
室 *sashitsu* left ventricle (of the heart)
巻 *hidarima(ki)* counterclockwise; perverse;
10記 *saki* the following ⌊mentally off
党 *satō* opposition party, the Opposition; leftists, the left; drinker, wine lover
書 *hidariga(ki)* writing from the left
袒 *satan* support, alliance
袒者 *satansha* supporter
11眼 *sagan* left eye
舷 *sagen* port, port side ⌈ist
寄 *hidariyo(ri)* leaning toward the left; left-
側 *hidarigawa, sasoku* left side; the left
側通行 *Hidarigawa Tsūkō* Keep to the
12越 *sago(shi)* over left field ⌊Left
程 *sahodo* so much, much, very
証 *sashō* proof
勝手 *hidari katte=hidarikiki* 左利 (see
腕 *hidari ude* left arm ⌊above–7)
腕投手 *sawan tōshu* left-handed pitcher
13傾 *sakei* leftist, radical, inclination to the
褄 *hidarizuma* geisha ⌊left
14遷 *sasen* demotion, degradation
様 *sayō* such, like that; yes, indeed; well, let me see. *sayo(nara), sayō(nara)* goodbye. *sonna* that kind of. *hidarizama* wicked way
端 *satan* left edge; left end; left lane

15器用 *hidarigitcho* left-handedness; left-
17犠飛 *sagihi* left-field sacrifice fly ⌊hander
翼 *sayoku* left flank; left wing, leftist, radical movement; left field
翼手 *sayokushu* left fielder
19縄 *hidarinawa* the wrong way; adversity
21顧 *sako* turning toward the left
顧右見 *sako-uken* indecision
顧右眄 *sako-uben* irresolution, vacillation

4

巫 See 38.

汞 1456 / F1073 Kō mercury. [水]

攻 1457 / F846 Kō. *se(meru)* attack, assault.
B *se(me)* attack, offensive. [攵]
2入 *se(me)-i(ru)* invade, raid, rush in to attack, penetrate into
3口 *se(me)guchi* point of attack
下 *se(me)-kuda(ru)* go down and attack
上 *se(me)-nobo(ru)* go up against, attack
4手 *se(me)te* assailant, assaulter; attacking force; offensive
込 *se(me)-ko(mu)* attack and invade
太鼓 *se(me)daiko* drum signal for a charge
5立 *se(me)-ta(teru)* attack incessantly
付 *se(me)-tsu(keru)* fiercely attack
6伐 *kōbatsu* punitive expedition
伏 *se(me)-fu(seru)* subdue
防 *kōbō* offense and defense
合 *se(me)-a(u)* attack each other ⌈fielding
守 *kōshu* offense and defense; batting and
守同盟 *kōshu dōmei* defensive and offensive alliance
7囲 *se(me)-kako(mu)* besiege. *kōi* siege
抜 *se(me)-nu(ku)* successfully storm a castle; attack fiercely
究 *kōkyū* investigation, research
8取 *se(me)-to(ru), kōshu suru* take by storm, capture
具 *semegu* siege engines
9城 *kōjō* siege
城砲 *kōjōhō* siege gun, siege artillery
10倦 *se(me)-agu(mu)* become disheartened in conducting a siege
悩 *se(me)-naya(mu)* afflict
11略 *kōryaku* capture, occupation, invasion
寄 *se(me)-yo(ru), se(me)-yo(seru)* overtake and attack
道具 *se(me) dōgu* weapons of attack, military engines, instrument of warfare
12落 *se(me)-oto(su)* take by storm. *kōraku* capturing (a castle)

18滅 *se(me)-horo(bosu)* attack and overthrow; utterly destroy; subdue
戦 *se(me)-tataka(u)* assault
勢 *kōsei* offensive, aggression
15撃 *kōgeki suru, se(me)-u(tsu)* attack and crush, cut down. *kōgeki* attack, assault, raid; criticism, denunciation
撃力 *kōgekiryoku* striking power
撃的 *kōgekiteki* aggressive, offensive
撃者 *kōgekisha* invader, aggressor, assailant
撃軍 *kōgekigun* attacking army
撃開始時間 *kōgeki kaishi jikan* zero hour
撃戦 *kōgekisen* aggressive war
撃機 *kōgekiki* attack plane
20懸 *se(me)-ka(keru), se(me)-ka(karu)* approach to attack

7

差 See 3662.

貢 1458 / F1789 B Kō. Ku. *mitsugi* tribute. *mitsu(gu)* support, finance. *kō(suru)* bear tribute. [貝]
6米 *kōbei, kōmai* tribute rice, tax paid in rice
8使 *kōshi* tribute bearers
物 *mitsugimono, kōbutsu, kōmotsu* tribute
10進 *kōshin* bearing tribute
租 *kōso* tribute, annual tax
租米 *kōsomai* tax rice, tribute rice
13献 *kōken* contribution, service
15調 *kōchō* offering tribute; tribute
賦 *kōfu* tribute; paying tribute

9

項 1459 / F2055 B Kō clause, paragraph; item; term (in math). *unaji* nape of the neck. [頁]
5目 *kōmoku* head, item, provision, clause
8垂 *unada(reru)* bow the head

RAD. 己 49

Onore self. Variants: 巳 *sude ni* already, 巳 *mi* snake. Nickname: Snake.

巳 1460 / F607 Shi. *mi* 9-11 a.m.; 6th zodiac sign; serpent.

已 1461 / F607 I. *sude ni* (see under 既 3887.0). *ya(mu), ya(meru)* (see under 止 2429.0).
3下 *ika*＝以下 348.3

己 1462 / F606 A Ko. Ki F, 6th. *onore, ono* oneself, myself, yourself. *ono(gajishi)* as one pleases. *tsuchinoto* 6th calendar sign.
5奴 *unu* you rascal
12等 *oira, onorera* we

1

巴 See 263.

4

忌 忌 1463 / F689 B Ki mourning; death anniversary; something detestable. *i(mu)* abhor, have an aversion for, avoid, shun; taboo; abstain from. *ima(washii)* objectionable, abominable, offensive; ominous, unlucky. *i(mi)* mourning; taboo. [心]
4日 *i(mi)bi* unlucky day; death anniversary; purification and fast day. *kijitsu, kinichi* death anniversary
月 *kigetsu* month of mourning
中 *kichū* in mourning
引 *kibi(ki)* absence from work due to mourning
5可 *i(mu)be(ki)* detestable, abominable
6名 *i(mi)na* posthumous name, real name
7忌 *i(ma)-i(mashii)* annoying, provoking
言葉 *i(mi) kotoba* tabooed word
8明 *kimei, i(mi)-a(ke), i(mi)-a(ki), kia(ke)* end of mourning; end of childbirth-purification period
物 *i(mi)mono* tabooed thing; thing abstained from
服 *kibuku* mourning clothes
10部 *Imbe, Imibe* ancient (Shinto) priestly family
12詞 *i(mi) kotoba* tabooed word
13嫌 *i(mi)-kira(u)* detest, hate
15避 *kihi* evasion, shirking; challenge (in law)
憚 *kitan* reserve, scruples
憚無 *kitanna(ku)* frankly, without reserve
16諱 *ki-i, kiki* offense, displeasure

改 1464 / F845 A Kai. *arata(meru)* change, modify, convert; renew, renovate; reform, mend, rectify; amend, revise, improve; examine, inspect, search. *arata(maru)* be renewed, be renovated; change, be modified, be revised; be improved, be reformed; be ceremonious. *arata(mete)* again, anew, formally. [攵]
4元 *kaigen* change of the era

3 口口土士夂夊夕大女子宀寸小⺌尢尸屮山川巛工 6 己巾干幺广廴廾弋弓彐彑彡彳

心 *kaishin* conversion; reform
心者 *kaishinsha* convert
5 令 *kairei suru* countermand an order
札 *kaisatsu* ticket examination
札口 *kaisatsuguchi* ticket gate
正 *arata(me)-tada(su)* revise. *kaisei* revision, amendment; improvement, amelioration ⌈Standard Version
正標準訳 *Kaisei Hyōjun-yaku* Revised
6 行 *kaigyō suru* indent
印 *kai-in* changing seals
任 *kainin* replacement
号 *kaigō* changing a title; changing an era
名 *kaimei* changing a name ⌊name
7 作 *kaisaku* adaptation (of a story)
良 *kairyō* improvement, reform
良服 *kairyōfuku* utility suit
良者 *kairyōsha* reformer
8 姓 *kaisei* changing a family name
版 *kaihan* revised edition
定 *kaitei* reform
易 *kaieki* renewing ⌈proselytism
宗 *kaishū* conversion (to another faith);
宗者 *kaishūsha* convert; proselyte
9 変 *kaihen* change, innovation, reformation, transformation
革 *kaikaku* reform, reformation
革案 *kaikaku an* reform measure
造 *kaizō* remodeling, reconstruction
造説 *kaizōsetsu* cataclysm theory
訂 *kaitei* revision
訂版 *kaiteiban* revised edition
訂訳 *Kaiteiyaku* Revised Version ⌈ment
訂増補 *kaitei-zōho* revision and enlarge-
10 修 *kaishū* repair, improvement, (riparian) ⌊works
悛 *kaishun* penitence, repentance
悟 *kaigo* repentance
称 *kaishō suru* rename, retitle
党 *kaitō* changing sides (in politics)
進 *kaishin* reform; progress
進的 *kaishinteki* progressive
進党 *kaishingō* progressive party
11 組 *kaiso* reorganization
悪 *kaiaku* change for the worse, deteriora-
過 *kaika* apologizing for a mistake ⌊tion
過遷善 *kaika-senzen* apologizing for a mistake and doing good
訳 *kaiyaku* retranslation, revision
訳者 *kaiyakusha* revisers
12 廃 *kaihai* reorganization, change ⌈tion
善 *kaizen* reform, improvement, ameliora-
葬 *kaisō* reburial
装 *kaisō* remodeling, modernization
13 新 *kaishin* renovation, innovation, reforma-
14 選 *kaisen* re-election ⌊tion
暦 *kaireki* new year; calendar reform
15 編 *kaihen* reorganization
鋳 *kaichū* reminting; recasting
16 築 *kaichiku* rebuilding, remodeling
18 竄 *kaizan* falsification, mutilation, alteration; correction, amendment, revision
題 *kaidai* retitling

6

巷 1465 F608 Kō. *chimata* forking road; street; scene; quarters; arena, theater.
12 間 *kōkan* the world
14 説 *kōsetsu* rumor, talk of the town

巻 1466 F299 B 巻 Ken. Kan volume, book, part; reel. *ma(ku)* roll up; wind, coil; tie around; wind up. *maki* roll (of silk); volume, book; winding (of a clock). [己]
3 土重来 *kendo-jūrai* making a success after failure
上 *ma(ki)-a(geru) vt* roll up; hoist, heave up; take away, rob; blow up (dust). *ma(ki)-a(garu) vi* curl up into the air (smoke); roll up. *ma(ki)a(ge)* lifting, hoisting
4 毛 *ma(ki)ge* curl, ringlet
尺 *makijaku* measuring tape
込 *ma(ki)-ko(mu) vt* roll up, enfold; engulf, swallow up, drag into, involve in
内 *kannai* in this volume
5 付 *ma(ki)-tsu(keru)* wind or tie around, coil. *ma(ki)-tsu(ku)* coil or wind around; twist about
末 *kammatsu* end of a book
6 舌 *ma(ki)jita* trill, rolling the tongue
返 *makikae(shi)* bickering; give and take; fighting back and forth
7 尾 *kambi* end of a book
8 帙 *kanchitsu* a book and its case; books; number of volumes
枠 *ma(ki)waku* spool, bobbin, reel
物 *makimono* a (horizontal) scroll ⌈winding
直 *ma(ki)nao(shi)* rebinding (a scroll); re-
取紙 *ma(ki)to(ri)shi* roll of paper
9 首 *kanshu* first page of a book
狩 *ma(ki)ga(ri)* grand hunt
10 起 *ma(ki)-oko(su)* stir up
紙 *makigami* rolled paper
11 添 *makizo(e)* involvement, entanglement
12 結 *ma(ki) musu(bi)* clove hitch
雲 *ma(ki)gumo, ken-un* cirrus clouds
軸 *ma(ki)jiku* scroll
軸帯 *kanjikutai* roller bandage
揚 *ma(ki)-a(geru), ma(ki)a(ge), ma(ki)-a(garu)*＝巻上 (see above–3)

揚機 *ma(ki)a(ge)ki* hoist, winch, windlass
揚轆轤 *ma(ki)a(ge) rokuro* capstan
13 煙草 *ma(ki)tabako* cigarette
14 管 *ma(ki)kan* coiled pipe
髪 *ma(ki)gami* tress, curl
層雲 *kensōun* cirro-stratus clouds
15 線 *ma(ki)sen* winding (in electricity)
16 頭 *kantō* beginning of a book
積雲 *kensekiun* cirro-cumulus clouds
17 鮨 *ma(ki)zushi* sushi wrapped in seaweed or egg-omelet strips
藁 *ma(ki)wara* bundle of straw (used as an archery target)
22 鬚 *kenshu* tendril

— 9 —

巽 See 601.

RAD. 巾 50

Haba width or *kin, kire* cloth. At left: *haba hen* or *kimben*. Nickname: Cloth.

巾 1467/F609 KIN towel. *haba* (see 幅 under 1484.0).
4 木 *habaki* baseboard
5 広 *hababiro no* wider than usual
7 車 *kinsha* decorated vehicle
12 着 *kinchaku* purse, money bag
着切 *kinchakuki(ri)* pickpocket

— 2 —

市 See 284.

A 布 1468/F610 HO. FU. *nuno* cloth.
3 子 *nunoko* padded cotton clothes
巾 *fukin* dish cloth; napkin
4 片 *fuhen* piece of cloth
引 *nunobi(ki)* stretched cloth; cloth lining
切 *nunogi(re)* piece of cloth
5 目 *nunome* texture
石 *fuseki suru* arrange stones (in a *go* game); place party members in strategic government positions
令 *furei* official notice, proclamation, announcement
6 衣 *fu-i, ho-i* common people; ordinary dress, cotton clothing
団 *futon* bedding, mattress
地 *nunoji* cloth
7 局 *fukyoku* arrangement, composition
告 *fukoku* proclamation, declaration, notification, decree, edict
告書 *fukokusho*=word above
8 表紙 *nunobyōshi* cloth binding
9 施 *fuse* alms, charity; temple offering
陣 *fujin* line-up. *fujin suru* take up a position
染 *nunozo(me), nunoso(me)* piece dyeing
海苔 *funori* laundry starch
10 晒 *nunozara(shi)* bleaching cloth; fuller
11 達 *futatsu* proclamation, notification
設 *fusetsu*=敷設 2059.11
袋 *Hotei* a god of fortune
袋腹 *hoteibara* protuberant abdomen
教 *fukyō* missionary work, propaganda, propagation, proselytism
教所 *fukyōjo* small chapel
教師 *fukyōshi* missionary, chaplain, propagandist
13 置 *fuchi* arrangement, composition, design

— 3 —

师 Nonstandard for 師 113.

B 帆 1469/F611 HAN. *ho* sail.
4 木綿 *homomen* sailcloth, canvas
5 布 *honuno, hampu* sailcloth, canvas
立貝 *hotategai* scallop (shell)
7 走 *hobashi(ru)* sail, be under sail. *hansō* sailing; gliding
9 柱 *hobashira* mast
前船 *homaesen* sailing vessel
10 桁 *hogeta* (sail) boom, yard
莚 *homushiro* sail matting
11 船 *hansen, hobune* sailing vessel
掛 *hoka(keru)* sail, set sail
掛船 *hoka(ke)bune* sailboat
15 影 *hokage* a sail
17 檣 *hanshō* mast

— 4 —

A 希 1470/F612 KI. KE. *-Gi-* Greece. *koinega(u)* beg, request, pray, beseech; hope, desire. *mare na* rare, few, phenomenal. *ki-* dilute (acid).
4 少 *kishō* scarcity
元素 *kigenso* rare element
5 代 *kidai, kitai* uncommon, remarkable, matchless
世 *kisei* rare
6 有 *ke-u* rare, extraordinary
有金属 *ke-u kinzoku* rare metals
7 求 *kikyū suru* aspire to, seek, demand, ask for

3 口口土士夂夊夕大女子宀寸小⺌尢尸屮山川巛工已【巾】干幺广廴廾弋弓彐彑彡彳

10書 *kisho* rare book
11釈 *kishaku* dilution
望 *kibō* hope, desire, aspiration, anticipation; request
望者 *kibōsha* candidate, applicant, aspirant, one who desires
望的観測 *kibōteki kansoku* wishful thinking
望配給 *kibō haikyū* optional extra ration
16薄 *kihaku na* thin, dilute, sparse, weak

5

帚 See 1581.

帛 See 3096.

帙 1471/F613 CHITSU Japanese book cover.
2入 *chitsu-i(ri)* a book kept in a Japanese book cover

帑 1472/F612 TŌ. DO money depository

帖 1473/F612 CHŌ. JŌ quire (of paper); bundle of seaweed; screen counter; notebook.
9面 *chōmen* notebook
面面 *chōmenzura* accounts; appearance
19簿 *chōbo* account book

6

帝 帝 See 305.

帥 See 109.

7

師 See 113.

席 See 1513.

帯 1474/F616 A 帶 TAI belt; zone. *obi* obi, belt, sash, girdle, band; belting. *o(biru)*, *tai(suru)* wear (at the belt), carry, be armed with; be entrusted with; assume, take on (the character of), be tinged with; gird up (one's loins). *-tai* zone, region.
2刀 *taitō* the sword at one's side
4止 *obidome* sash clip, sash band
5皮 *obikawa* leather belt
6同 *taidō suru* be accompanied by
式 *obishiki* belt (conveyor)
地 *obiji* sash material, obi cloth
7芯 *obishin* sash padding
状 *obijō* long narrow strip
状地 *taijōchi* strip of land
8金 *obigane* banding iron
9革 *obikawa* leather belt
封 *obifū* a half-wrapper (used in mailing)
10紙 *obigami* wrapper
剣 *taiken* sword at one's side
11側 *obikawa* obi cloth
12揚 *obia(ge)* sash to hold obi in place
13解 *obito(ki)* untying an obi
鉄 *obitetsu* band iron
電 *taiden* electric charge
電体 *taidentai* charged body
14緑 *tairyoku* greenish
緑色 *tairyokushoku* greenish
15締 *obiji(me)* band for an obi
線 *taisen* tie (in music)
勲 *taikun* wearing a decoration
16鋼 *obikō* band steel, hoop
鋸 *obi nokogiri, obi noko* band saw
18鎖 *obigusari* chain belt

8

常 See 1364.

帶 1475/F616 See 帯 1474.

帽 1476/F618 See 帽 1483.

帷 1477/F617 I curtain, screen.
3子 *katabira* thin morning kimono
11帳 *ichō* curtain
12幄 *iaku* headquarters, general staff
幄上奏 *iaku jōsō* direct appeal to the throne by the military
幄臣 *iaku(no)shin* close adviser
13幕 *ibaku* curtain; field staff headquarters; secret meeting place

帳 1478/F616 A CHŌ notebook; account book; register; album; curtain dividing a room. *tobari* curtain.
4元 *chōmoto* manager, promoter, bookmaker
5尻 *chōjiri* footings, account balance
付 *chōtsu(ke)* bookkeeping; bookkeeper
6合 *chōa(i)* balance of accounts; keeping accounts; comparison
9面 *chōmen* notebook, account book, register
面面 *chōmenzura* accounts; appearance
10消 *chōke(shi)* cancellation, writing off

12 場 *chōba* counter, desk; office; jinricksha pool
19 簿 *chōbo* account book, register

9

幃 1479 / F619 Ki, I bag

幀 1480 / F619 Tei making books or scrolls.

幄 1481 / F619 Aku curtain. *tobari* curtain.
8 舎 *akusha* pavilion

幇 1482 / F619 Hō help.
7 助 *hōjo* assistance, backing
12 間 *hōkan*. *taikomochi* professional jester; flatterer

B 帽 1483 / F619 = 帽 帽 帽 帽 Bō cap, headgear.
3 子 *bōshi* cap, hat, headgear
子屋 *bōshiya* hat shop
11 章 *bōshō* cap badge

B 幅 1484 / F619 Fuku hanging scroll, picture; width; counter for scrolls. *haba* width, breadth, range; difference (in price); power, influence.
5 広 *hababiro* wide width; wide obi
7 利 *habakiki* man of influence
9 飛 *habato(bi)* broad jump
10 員 *fukuin* width, beam, breadth, extent
13 跳 *habatobi* broad jump

10

幕 See 4026.

幌 1485 / F619 Kō. *horo* awning, hood, (folding) top. *tobari* curtain.
9 型自動車 *horogata jidōsha* sedan
10 馬車 *horo basha* covered wagon, covered carriage
蚊帳 *horogaya* mosquito net

11

幔 1486 / F620 Man. curtain.
13 幕 *mammaku* curtain, drapery

12

幮 1487 / F-X See 幮 1491.

幟 1488 / F621 Shi. *nobori* flag, banner, streamer.

幡 1489 / F621 Han. Hon. *hata* flag.

B 幣 1490 / F621 幣 Hei Shinto zigzag paper offerings; bad habit; humble prefix; gift. *nusa* Shinto offerings of cloth, rope, or cut paper.
7 束 *heisoku* Shinto offerings of cloth, rope, or cut paper
8 物 *heimotsu*, *heibutsu* offering to a god; a present
制 *heisei* monetary system
帛 *heihaku* Shinto offerings of cloth or cut paper
13 殿 *heiden* the room between the hall of worship and the inner sanctuary of a shrine

15

幮 1491 / F621 幮 Ju, Chu, Chū curtain.

干 RAD. 51

Kan dry or *ichi-jū* (*ichi* "one" plus *jū* "ten"). Nickname: One Ten.

B 干 1492 / F622 Kan. *hi(ru)* parch, get dry; ebb, recede. *ho(su)* (see under 乾 784.0). *tate* shield. *hidaru(i)* hungry.
3 上 *hiaga(ru)* dry up, parch; ebb away
与 *kan-yo* participation
大根 *ho(shi)daikon* dried daikon
4 戈 *kanka* shield and spear; weapons; war
支 *kanshi* sexagenary cycle
天 *kanten* drought, dry weather
5 付 *hi-tsu(ku)* dry up
犯 *kampan* infringement, violation
6 肉 *ho(shi)niku* dried meat, pemmican
8 固 *ho(shi)-kata(meru)* vt, *ho(shi)-kata(maru)* vi dry up, harden by drying. *hikata(maru)* vi dry and harden
物 *himono*, *karamono* dried fish. *ho(shi)mono* laundry on the line
拓 *kantaku suru* reclaim by drainage
拓地 *kantakuchi* reclaimed land
9 城 *kanjō* bulwark, defender, safeguard

柿 *ho(shi)gaki* dried persimmons
草 *ho(shi)gusa, ho(shi)kusa, kansō* hay, dry grass
海苔 *ho(shi)-nori* dried laver, edible seaweed sheets
10殺 *ho(shi)-koro(su)* starve (an animal) to death
害 *kangai* drought damage
11魚 *hi-uo, kangyo, hizakana, ho(shi) uo, ho(shi)zakana* dried fish
涸 *hikara(biru) vi* completely dry up. *ho(shi)-ka(rasu) vt* dry up (a river)
渉 *kanshō* interference, intervention
菜 *ho(shi)na* dried rape, dried greens
乾 *hiboshi ni suru vt* starve to death. *hiboshi ni na(ru) vi* starve to death
菓子 *higashi* candy; cookies
12場 *ho(shi)ba* drying ground
満 *kamman* ebb and flow, tide
飯 *hoshi-i* cooked and dried (for preservation) rice
割 *hiwa(re)* cracking due to drying
葉 *hiba* dried daikon leaves
葡萄 *ho(shi) budō* raisins
13預 *kan-yo* participation
15魃 *kambatsu* drought
潮 *kanchō, hikishio, hishio* ebb tide
潟 *higata, hikata* tideland; dry beach
16瓢 *kampyō* dried gourd strings
21鰯 *hoshika, hi-iwashi, ho(shi) iwashi* dried sardines
22鱈 *hidara* dried codfish

— 1 —

午 See 162. [十]

— 2 —

平 See 26.

A 刊 1493/F234 KAN publishing; carve, engrave. [刂]
5本 *kampon* printed book
6行 *kankō* publication
行物 *kankōbutsu* a publication

— 3 —

年 See 188.

并 See 580.

— 5 —

幸 See 1073.

幷 See 并 580.

— 10 —

幹 See 790.

RAD. 幺 52

At top: *itogashira* "thread" top. At left: *yō hen* left-side "young."
Nickname: Short Thread (cf. Rad. 120).

— 1 —

B 幻 1494/F629 GEN. *maboroshi* vision, dream; illusion, apparition.
4日 *genjitsu* mock sun
月 *gengetsu* mock moon
5世 *gensei* this fleeting world
出 *genshutsu suru* appear as a phantom, appear dimly
6灯 *gentō* stereopticon, magic lantern
灯会 *gentōkai* stereopticon meetings
灯器 *gentōki* stereopticon projector
灯機械 *gentō kikai* stereopticon projector
8怪 *genkai* strange, mysterious
11術 *genjutsu* magic, witchcraft, sorcery
視 *genshi* visual hallucination
12惑 *genwaku* fascination, glamor, bewitching
覚 *genkaku* illusion, hallucination
13滅 *gemmetsu* disillusionment
夢 *gemmu* dreams, visions
想 *gensō* illusions
想曲 *gensōkyoku* fantasy
14像 *genzō* phantom, vision, illusion
15影 *gen-ei* phantom, vision, illusion
影的 *gen-eiteki* illusionary
17聴 *genchō* auditory hallucination

— 2 —

B 幼 1495/F629 YŌ infancy, childhood; infants, children. *osana(i), itokena(i)* infant. *ito-* very young.
3女 *yōjo* baby girl, little girl
子 *osanago, yōshi* baby, infant, child
4心 *osanagokoro* child's mind; innocent heart

木 *yōboku* young tree
友達 *osanatomodachi* childhood friend
少 *yōshō* infancy, childhood
少児 *yōshōji* infant, child
5 生 *yōsei* larva
主 *yōshu* young master
6 虫 *yōchū* larva
名 *yōmei, yōmyō* one's infant name
年 *yōnen* infancy, childhood
年工 *yōnenkō* child laborer
年労働 *yōnen rōdō* child labor
年学校 *yōnen gakkō* military preparatory school
年時代 *yōnen jidai* childhood
年期 *yōnenki* childhood
7 君 *yōkun* young master
児 *yōji* infant, baby, little child
児死亡率 *yōji shibōritsu* infant mortality rate
児食 *yōjishoku* baby food
児洗礼 *yōji senrei* infant baptism
児預所 *yōji azu(kari)jo* nursery
8 芽 *yōga* germ (in grains)
者 *yōsha* infant, child
9 帝 *yōtei* child emperor
10 時 *yōji* infancy, childhood
恋 *osanagoi* puppy love
宮 *itomiya* infant prince
弱 *yōjaku* young and weak
11 魚 *yōgyo* young fish
鳥 *yōchō* young bird, fledgling
12 童 *yōdō* a small child
13 禽 *yōkin* chick, young bird
愚 *yōgu* childish innocence
馴染 *osananajimi* childhood playmate
稚 *yōchi* infancy, babyhood; crudeness
稚園 *yōchien* kindergarten, preschool
16 樹 *yōju* young tree
17 齢 *yōrei* tender age
齢児 *yōreiji* young child
18 顔 *osanagao* one's baby features

6

幽 See 112.

9

B 幾 1496/F632 幾 Ki. *iku(ra)* how many, how much; how far, how long; so much per; however (difficult). *iku(ra)ka* some, something, anything; somewhat, a little, to some extent, partly; in a way. *iku(ra) mo* any amount, any number; (neg.) not many, not much. *iku(tsu)* how many; how old. *hotohoto* almost, quite, really. *iku-* some, several, many; how many, how much.

2 人 *ikunin, ikutari* how many people. *ikunin ka* several people. *ikunin demo* any number of people
3 久 *ikuhisa(shiku)* eternally, forever
万 *ikuman* many tens of thousands
千 *ikusen* thousands (of people)
才 *ikusai* how old, what age
4 月 *ikutsuki* how many months
分 *ikubun* some, something, a part. *ikubun ka* somewhat, partly
日 *ikunichi, ikka* how many days; what day (of the month). *ikunichi ni* what day. *ikunichi demo* for any number of days
日後 *ikunichi(ka) (no) nochi* after some days
日幾日 *ikunichi (mo) ikunichi (mo)* for many days
5 目 *ikume* what weight
代 *ikuyo* many generations
世 *ikuyo* many generations
6 年 *ikutose, ikunen* how many years. *ikunen mo* for many years
多 *ikuta no* many
7 何 *ikubaku* how much, how many. *kika* geometry
何学 *kikagaku* geometry
何学的 *kikagakuteki* geometric
何画法 *kika gahō* descriptive geometry
何級数 *kika kyūsū* geometrical series, geometrical progression
8 夜 *ikuyo* how many nights; night after night
昔 *ikumukashi* how ancient
9 度 *ikudo, ikutabi* how often, how many times. *ikudo mo* frequently, many times,
通 *ikutō(ri)* how many kinds. *ikutsū* how many copies; how many letters
秋 *ikuaki* many autumns; many years
重 *ikue nimo* again and again; earnestly
10 時 *ikuji* what time
11 許 *ikubaku* how much, how many
望 *kibō* 14th night of the lunar month
12 程 *ikuhodo* about how much
程無 *ikuhodo (mo) na(ku)* not much

12

畿 1497/F1280 Ki capital; capital suburbs. [田]

4 内 *Kinai* the Five Home Provinces around Kyoto

3 口囗土士夂夊夕大女子宀寸小⺌尢尸屮山川巛工己巾干幺[广]2 廴廾弋弓彐彑彡彳

RAD. 广 53

Madare trailing *ma* (i.e., the enclosure of Rad. 200 *ma* "hemp"). Also called *ten-ichi-dare* (i.e., a trailing Rad. 8). Nickname: Dotted Cliff (cf. Rad. 27).

2

B 庁 1498/F647 廳 Chō government office.
5 令 *chōrei* government order
8 舎 *chōsha* government office building

A 広 1499/F645 廣 Kō. *hiro(garu)* *vi* spread out, extend, reach to. *hiro(geru)* *vt* expand, enlarge, widen; unfurl; open (arms or a package), stretch, spread. *hiro(maru)* spread, be diffused, prevail, be propagated, pervade, be circulated, become popular. *hiro(meru)* extend, widen, enlarge; spread, disseminate; popularize; advertise, introduce, announce. *hiro(me)* announcement, advertisement. *hiro(i)*, *hiro(yakana)* wide, broad, extensive, spacious.
3 口 *hirokuchi* broad mouth; large-mouthed bottle
小路 *hirokōji* thorofare
大 *kōdai na* vast, extensive, magnificent
大無辺 *kōdai-muhen na* boundless, immeasurable, infinite
5 広 *hirobiro toshita* extensive, spacious, roomy
目見 *hiro(i) me (de) mi(ru)* treat magnanimously
6 汎 *kōhan na* wide, extensive, widespread, comprehensive
壮 *kōsō na* grand, imposing
7 角 *kōkaku* wide angle
言 *kōgen* boastful speech
告 *kōkoku* advertisement; public notice; poster, handbill; publicity
告主 *kōkokunushi* (radio) sponsor
告灯 *kōkokutō* advertising lights
告気球 *kōkoku kikyū* advertising balloon
告社 *kōkokusha* advertising agency; publicity bureau
告取 *kōkokuto(ri)* advertising solicitor
告取次店 *kōkoku toritsugiten* advertising agency
告放送 *kōkoku hōsō* commercial radio
告屋 *kōkokuya* advertising agency; sandwich man
告料 *kōkokuryō* advertising rates
告部 *kōkokubu* publicity department
告書 *kōkokuka(ki)* ad writer
告税 *kōkokuzei* advertising tax
告業 *kōkokugyō* advertising business
告欄 *kōkokuran* advertising columns
8 居 *kōkyo* spacious residence
9 屋 *hiro(me)ya* town crier, sandwich (advertising) man
狭 *kōkyō* width; area
軌 *kōki* wide gauge
10 原 *kōgen* wide plain, open country
袖 *hirosode* wide sleeve
11 野 *kōya, hirono* open field, open country
域 *kōiki* wide area
袤 *kōbō* extent, area, expanse
12 遠 *kōen na* vast and far-reaching
間 *hiroma* hall, saloon (on a ship)
場 *hiroba* open field, public square, plaza
幅 *hirohaba* double width
量 *kōryō* largeheartedness, generosity
葉樹 *kōyōju* broad-leafed tree
報 *kōhō* publicity
報部 *kōhōbu* public relations department
13 漠 *kōbaku(taru)* vast, wide, boundless
義 *kōgi* broad sense, broader application
蓋 *hirobuta* large tray; cover for a kimono chest
15 縁 *hiroen* broad veranda; eaves
範 *kōhan*＝広汎 (see above–6)
範囲 *kōhan-i* wide scope, vast range
17 闊 *kōkatsu na* spacious, wide, extensive
濶 *kōkatsu na* spacious, wide, extensive

3

庄 1500/F633 Shō level.
9 屋 *shōya* village headman
13 園 *shōen* manor

4

庇 1501/F633 Hi. *kaba(u)* protect, shield; defend, plead for; harbor (criminals). *hisashi* eaves; canopy; penthouse; visor.
5 立 *kaba(i)-ta(te) suru*＝*kaba(u)* (see under 庇 1501.0)
14 髪 *hisashigami* low pompadour
20 護 *higo* protection, patronage
護物 *higobutsu* a shelter
護者 *higosha* patron, guardian

A 序 1502/F633 Jo beginning; preface; order, precedence; farewell address; curtain raiser. *tsuide* order; occasion, chance. *tsuide ni* while, on the way, incidentally, while you're about it.
4 文 *jobun* preface, foreword, introduction

6 曲 *jokyoku* prelude, overture
次 *joji* order, sequence
列 *joretsu* rank, grade, order
7 言 *jogen* preface, foreword
9 奏 *josō* introduction (in music)
12 開 *jobira(ki)* beginning (of a celebration)
詞 *joshi* preface
13 数 *josū* ordinal number; numbering
幕 *jomaku* curtain raiser
楽 *jogaku* prelude, overture
14 説 *josetsu* introduction
15 論 *joron* introduction, preface
盤 *joban* opening a game of chess or checkers
盤戦 *jobansen* the beginning of a campaign

B 床 1503 F 633 F1212 **牀** Shō floor; bed. *toko* bed; sickbed; floor; alcove; padding. *tatami* body; (river) bed. *yuka* floor. *yuka(shii)* admirable, respectable; sweet, charming; interesting; tasteful, mysterious. *-shō* counter for beds.

2 入 *toko-i(ri)* consummation of marriage
几 *shōgi* camp stool, folding stool
3 山 *tokoyama* wrestler's hairdresser; wig maker; a theatrical coiffeur
下 *yukashita* under the floor
上 *tokoa(ge)* recovery from a long illness. *shōjō* on the bed. *yukaue* on the floor, above the floor, floor (lamp)
5 払 *tokobara(i)* recovery from illness
6 机 *shōgi* camp stool, folding stool
8 店 *tokomise* booth, stall
板 *toko ita* alcove floor board. *yuka ita* floor boards
虱 *tokojirami* bedbug
9 屋 *tokoya* barber; barber shop
柱 *tokobashira* ornamental alcove post
11 張 *tokoba(ri)* flooring
12 間 *toko(no)ma* large ornamental living-room alcove
換 *tokoga(e)* transplanting saplings
就 *toko (ni) tsu(ku)* go to bed
13 置 *toko-o(ki)* alcove ornament
置物 *toko okimono* alcove ornament
15 蝨 *tokojirami* bedbug
17 擦 *tokozure* bedsore
19 離 *tokobana(re)* getting out of bed

A 応 1504 F749 **應** Ō yes, all right. *ō(jiru)*, *ō(zuru)* answer, reply to; respond to, accept, obey, comply with, accede to, agree to; subscribe for; apply for (admission); meet, supply; fulfill, satisfy. *kota(eru)* respond; answer; be affected by (pain or stimulation); be effective. *(ni) ō(jite)* in proportion to, in answer to, in obedience to. *irae* answer. *masa(ni)* in the act of, on the point of. [心]

2 力 *ōryoku* stress
4 分 *ōbun* appropriate, reasonable
5 召 *ōshō suru* be drafted
召兵 *ōshōhei* draftee
召者 *ōshōsha* draftee
用 *ōyō* practical application; practice; adaptation; improvement; applied (physics)
用化学 *ōyō kagaku* applied chemistry
用科学 *ōyō kagaku* applied science
用問題 *ōyō mondai* supplementary question
7 対 *ōtai suru* receive, deal with, grant an interview
対振 *ōtaibu(ri)* manner of meeting people
9 信 *ōshin* answer signal
待 *ōtai*＝応対 (see above–7)
変 *ōhen* expediency
急 *ōkyū* temporary, emergency
急手当 *ōkyū teate* first aid
急手段 *ōkyū shudan* emergency measures
急策 *ōkyūsaku* emergency measures
10 砲 *ōhō* return fire
射 *ōsha suru* return the fire
11 問 *ōmon* responding to the question
接 *ōsetsu* reception
接室 *ōsetsushitsu* drawing room, reception room
接間 *ōsetsuma* drawing room, parlor
12 訴 *ōso* countersuit
答 *ōtō* answer, reply, response
報 *ōhō* retribution
募 *ōbo* subscription; application; enlistment, enrollment, entry; response
募者 *ōbosha* subscriber, applicant, entrant, volunteer; buyer (of bonds)
援 *ōen* aid; reinforcement; rescue; backing; cheering
援団 *ōendan* rooting section, rooting group
援歌 *ōenka* rooters' song
13 酬 *ōshū* reply
戦 *ōsen suru* accept a challenge, return the fire
15 諾 *ōdaku* consent; compliance

5

庚 1505 F635 Kō G, 7th. *kanoe* 7th calendar sign.

5 申塚 *kōshinzuka* stone image of travelers' guardian deity

庖 1506 F634 Hō kitchen.

2 丁 *hōchō* kitchen knife; cooking; cook
丁人 *hōchōnin* cook
丁師 *hōchōshi* cook
12 厨 *hōchū* kitchen

A 府 1507 F635 Fu urban prefecture; government office; representative body; storehouse. *tsukasa* (see under 司 877.0).

3 下 *fuka* metropolitan suburban districts
5 立 *furitsu* managed by an urban prefecture
庁 *fuchō* urban prefectural office
令 *furei* urban prefectural ordinance
6 会 *fukai* urban prefectural assembly
会議員 *fukai gi-in* urban prefectural assemblyman
8 知事 *fu chiji* urban prefectural governor
9 県 *fuken* prefectures
12 税 *fuzei* urban prefectural tax
営 *fuei* urban prefectural enterprise
20 議会 *fugikai* urban prefectural assembly
議会議員 *fugikai gi-in* urban prefectural assemblyman

A **底** 1508 / F634 TEI bottom, base; kind, sort. *soko* bottom; sole; depth, bowels (of the earth); bottom price.

2 入 *soko-i(re)* touching bottom (stock market)
力 *sokojikara* latent energy, reserve strength
3 土 *sokotsuchi* subsoil
4 辺 *teihen* base (in geometry)
止 *teishi suru* stop
引網 *sokobi(ki)ami* dragnet; dragnet fishing
5 石 *soko ishi* hard core
叩 *soko (o) tata(ku)* empty completely
払 *soko (o) hara(u)* empty completely
本 *teihon* original text
6 光 *sokobika(ri)* lurking luster, latent light
気味悪 *sokokimiwaru(i)* uncanny, ominous
7 角 *teikaku* base angle
豆 *sokomame* blister
冷 *sokobi(e)* chilling to the bone
抜 *sokonu(ke)* bottomless; unbounded; extreme; self-indulgent; indiscreet
抜上戸 *sokonu(ke) jōgo* heavy drinker
抜騒 *sokonu(ke) sawa(gi)* boisterous merrymaking
8 波 *sokonami* ground swell (the wave)
知 *sokoshi(ranu), sokoshi(renu)* bottomless
9 革 *sokogawa* sole; sole leather
10 値 *sokone* bottom price
流 *teiryū* bottom current, undercurrent
荷 *sokoni* ballast
11 釣 *sokozuri* bottom fishing
12 開 *sokobira(ki)* hopper (car)
無 *sokona(shi)* bottomless
13 意 *soko-i* inmost thoughts; secret intention; ulterior motive; undertone (in stock market)
意地 *soko-iji* bottom of one's heart
16 積 *sokozu(mi)* goods stowed at the bottom, (ship's) ballast

A **店** 1509 / F634 TEN shop, store. *mise, tana* shop, store, booth. *tana* shop, store; house (for rent).

3 子 *tanako* tenant
5 立 *tanada(te)* eviction notice
主 *tenshu* storekeeper, shopkeeper
古 *tamburu(shi)* shopworn goods
台 *misedai* counter in a store
仕舞 *misejimai* closing a business
6 先 *misesaki* shop front
7 売 *miseu(ri)* sale at a store
8 者 *tanamono, mise (no) mono* shop clerks
9 則 *tensoku* store rules
卸 *tana-oro(shi)* inventory taking; faultfinding; comments
前 *tanasaki* shop front
屋 *ten-ya* store, cooked-food store
屋物 *ten-yamono* caterer's dishes
10 借 *tanaga(ri)* renting a house (from someone), tenancy
晒 *tanazara(shi)* shopworn goods
浚 *tanazarae* clearance (sale)
員 *ten-in* clerk
振舞 *tanaburumai* shop celebration
11 商 *tana akina(i)* storekeeping
12 開 *misebira(ki)* opening a store
番 *miseban* tending a shop, salesman
貸 *tanaga(shi)* renting a house (to someone)
13 飾 *misekaza(ri)* window dressing
賃 *tanachin* house rent
15 舗 *tempo* shop, store
請 *tana-u(ke)* security for a tenant
請人 *tana-u(ke)nin* guarantor for a tenant
16 頭 *tentō* shop front, shop window; counter; store

6

廍 1510 / F-X Nonstandard for 鹿 5375.

A **度** 1511 / F636 DO degree; extent, measure, limit; a time; graduation, scale; composure. TAKU. TO. *do(suru)* save, redeem, reclaim. *wata(su)* (see under 渡 2635.0). *tabi* time, occasion; repetition. *-tai* desiderative verbal suffix.

5 失 *do (o) ushina(u)* wander aimlessly
外 *dohazu(re), dogai* out of one's consideration, extraordinary, excessive
外視 *dogaishi suru* disregard, neglect, overlook
6 合 *doa(i)* degree, extent, rate
7 忘 *dowasu(re)* memory slip, forgetting for the moment
9 度 *tabitabi, dodo* often, frequently
重 *tabikasa(naru)* occur repeatedly; repeated
胆 *dogimo* heart, spirit
胆抜 *dogimo (o) nu(ku)* startle (someone)
10 胸 *dokyō* courage, pluck, nerve, bravery
11 盛 *domo(ri)* graduation, scale
12 量 *doryō* magnanimity, generosity
量法 *doryōhō* measurement

量原器 *doryō genki* standard of measurement (in a bureau of standards)
量衡 *doryōkō* weights and measures
13数 *dosū* frequency, number of times
18難 *do(shi)gata(i)* incorrigible, inveterate, hopeless, beyond saving

7

A 庫 1512 F637 Ku. Ko storehouse. *kura* (see under 倉 486.0).
2入 *kura-i(re)* warehousing
5出 *kurada(shi)* releasing stored goods
8官 *kokan* treasurer 「storehouse
11移 *kura-utsushi* transporting to another
13裏 *kuri* priests' quarters; monastery kitchen

A 席 1513 F616 Seki seat; mat; a place, room, occasion. *mushiro* straw mat, matting. [巾]
3上 *sekijō* in the seat, in the assembly. *sekijō de* at the meeting, on the occasion
上演説 *sekijō enzetsu* impromptu speech
5代 *sekidai*=*sekiryō* 席料 (see below–10)
6次 *sekiji* seating order, precedence
次札 *sekiji fuda* place card
8画 *sekiga* offhand drawing
9亭 *sekitei*=*yose* 寄席 1318.10
巻 *sekken suru* conquer everything
10借 *sekiga(ri)* renting a room or hall
料 *sekiryō* room charge; cover charge; admission fee, price of a seat
書 *sekiga(ki)* offhand writing
11捲 *sekken suru* sweep over and completely subdue
12順 *sekijun* seating order, precedence
貸 *sekiga(shi)* renting seats

A 庭 1514 F637 Tei. *niwa* yard, courtyard, garden.
3口 *niwaguchi* garden entrance
上 *teijō* in the garden
下駄 *niwa geta* garden clogs
4火 *niwabi* bonfire
中 *teichū* in the garden
内 *teinai* in the garden
木 *niwaki* garden tree, shrub, shrubbery
木戸 *niwa kido* garden gate
5石 *niwa ishi* decorative garden stones; steppingstones; flagstones
6回 *niwamawa(ri)* around the garden; things concerning the garden
伝 *niwazuta(i)* passing through the yard
先 *niwasaki de* in the garden
7作 *niwatsuku(ri)* gardening
9前 *teizen, niwasaki de* in the garden
10師 *niwashi* landscape gardener
訓 *teikin* home precepts, parental discipline, home education
11掃 *niwaha(ki)* sweeping the garden
雀 *niwa suzume* garden sparrow
球 *teikyū* tennis
球界 *teikyūkai* tennis world
球選手 *teikyū senshu* tennis player
12番 *niwaban* guard of the inner garden
13園 *teien* garden, park
園地 *teienchi* garden plot
園師 *teienshi* gardener, landscape architect
園術 *teienjutsu* landscape gardening
16樹 *teiju* shrubbery, shrub
燎 *niwabi, teiryō* bonfire

B 座 1515 F637 坐 Za seat, cushion; throne; a gathering; stand, pedestal, platform; (metal) washer; theater; troupe; constellation. *suwa(ru)* squat down, sit down, (eyes) are fixed on. *za(suru)* be involved in; squat; sit down. *i(masu)* be, go, come (polite). *suwa(ri)* stability. *-za* (ancient) guild.
3下 *zaka* polite letter ending 「troupe
4中 *zachū* in the room; member of the
元 *zamoto* theater manager, producer
込 *suwa(ri)-ko(mu)* sit down, plant oneself down 「strike
込罷業 *suwa(ri)ko(mi) higyō,* sit-down
5白 *za (ga) shira(keru)* A chill falls over the gathering. 「theater
付 *zatsu(ki)* regular actor attached to a
礼 *zarei* courtesy while squatting
主 *zasu, zashu* head priest of a temple. *zashu* theater owner
右 *zayū ni* at one's right; at one's side
右銘 *zayū (no) mei* desk motto
6州 *zasu suru* run aground
7位 *za-i* seating order, precedence
8金 *zagane* metal washer
長 *zachō* chairman, president, moderator; troupe owner-leader 「or's residence
所 *zasho* one's seat; one's location; emper-
臥 *zaga* sitting and lying down
9食 *zashoku suru* live in idleness
持 *za (o) mo(tsu)* act as hostess or master of ceremonies
洲 *zasu suru* run aground
乗 *zajō suru* be on board
10高 *zakō* sitting height
浴 *zayoku* sitz bath
剤 *zazai* suppository
員 *za-in* troupe personnel
胼胝 *suwa(ri)dako* foot callous due to sedentary habits
席 *zaseki* seat, pew; cockpit
席満員 *zaseki man-in* standing room only

3 口口土士夂夊夕大女子屮寸小尣尢尸屮山川巛工己巾干幺[广]廴廾弋弓彐彑彡彳

骨 *zakotsu* hip bone
骨神経 *zakotsu shinkei* sciatic nerve
骨神経痛 *zakotsu shinkeitsū* sciatic neuralgia
11 視 *zashi suru* look on indifferently, be a mere spectator
13 禅 *zazen* meditation (in Zen Buddhism)
蒲団 *zabuton* cushion
業 *zagyō* sedentary work
業者 *zagyōsha* sedentary work
14 像 *zazō* seated image
15 標 *zahyō* co-ordinates (in math)
談 *zadan* discussion, talking things over
談会 *zadankai* round-table talk, discussion group
敷 *zashiki* room, apartment, drawing room; giving a banquet; entertainer's evening engagement
敷牢 *zashikirō* room for confining people
敷着 *zashikigi* geisha's costume worn while entertaining
16 薬 *zayaku* suppository
興 *zakyō* amusement, entertainment, fun, party games
頭 *zagashira* theater-troupe leader; leading man. *zatō* ancient blind official; blind masseur; blind man; blind musician
頭鯨 *zatō kujira* humpback whale
17 礁 *zashō* running aground
18 職 *zashoku* sedentary work
職者 *zashokusha* sedentary worker
19 繰 *zagu(ri)* hand reeling

唐 1516 / F360 **唐** B Tō Tang (dynasty); China; foreign countries. *Kara* China; Cathay; Korea; foreign countries. *Kara-*, *Tō-* Chinese; Korean; foreign. *kara(meku)* look like something Chinese. [口]

2 人 *Tōjin, karabito* a Chinese; a foreigner
3 土 *Tōdo, Morokoshi* China, Cathay
丸籠 *tōmaru kago* basket for transporting criminals
4 戸 *karado* Chinese-style gate
手 *karate* a weaponless defense system
木 *karaki* rare foreign wood
犬 *kara-inu* foreign dog, lion-dog (statues in shrine gardens). *tōken* foreign dog
天 *tōten* velveteen
天竺 *Kara-Tenjiku* China and India
5 本 *tōhon* books from China
6 糸 *tōito* foreign thread, foreign yarn
臼 *kara usu* mortar for hulling grain
衣 *kara koromo, karagoromo* ancient Chinese clothes; strange clothes
7 作 *karazuku(ri)* Chinese building style
辛子 *tōgarashi* red pepper
8 金 *karakane* bronze
門 *karamon* arched Chinese-style gate
国 *Karakuni* China
松 *karamatsu* larch
物 *karamono* goods from China or Korea
画 *tōga* Chinese painting; Chinese-style painting
突 *tōtotsu* suddenly, unexpectedly
物 *tōbutsu* imported goods
物屋 *tōbutsuya* foreign-goods store
物商 *tōbutsushō* foreign-goods store
9 音 *tōon* Tang-dynasty pronunciation
風 *karafū* Chinese style
紅 *karakurenai* deep crimson
竿 *karasao* flail
変木 *tōhemboku* a blockhead
津物 *karatsumono* earthenware, chinaware
胡麻 *tōgoma* castor-bean plant; castor beans
草 *karakusa* arabesque
草模様 *karakusa moyō* arabesque design
10 馬 *kara uma* (ancient) foreign horse
桃 *karamomo* apricot
紙 *karakami* thick door paper; opaque sliding paper door
紙障子 *karakami shōji* opaque sliding paper door; Tang-dynasty yellow drawing paper
11 船 *karafune, tōsen* Chinese ship; foreign ship
12 硯 *tōken* Chinese ink slab
朝 *Tōchō* the Tang dynasty
傘 *karakasa* paper umbrella
黍 *tōkibi* maize, Indian corn
筆 *tōhitsu* writing brush made in China
13 詩 *tōshi* Tang-dynasty poem
獅子 *kara shishi* lion
14 様 *karayō* Chinese style
語 *kara kotoba* ancient Chinese words; foreign language
歌 *kara uta* Chinese poem
箕 *tōmi* winnowing fan, fanning machine
墨 *kara sumi, tōboku* Chinese quality ink stick
15 鋤 *karasuki* Chinese plow
16 錦 *karanishiki* Chinese brocade
17 鍬 *tōguwa* a heavy-duty hoe
薯 *kara-imo* sweet potato
縮緬 *tōchirimen* muslin
18 櫃 *karabitsu* Chinese chest
20 繻子 *tōjusu* Korean silk satin

8

坐 1517 / F-X Nonstandard for **座** 1515.

康 1518 / F639 A Kō peace.

14 寧 *kōnei* a peaceful world

廊 1519 / F641 **廊廊** B Rō corridor, hall, lobby; tower; watchtower.

3 下 *rōka* corridor, hall, lobby, vestibule

B **庸** 1520 F639 Yō tax paid in labor; ordinary; employment.

2人 *yōjin* ordinary people. *yōnin* employee
3才 *yōsai* mediocre talent
6劣 *yōretsu na* mediocre, commonplace; stupid
7君 *yōkun* stupid ruler
13愚 *yōgu* mediocrity; imbecility
14徳 *yōtoku* common morality
15器 *yōki* an ordinary individual
16儒 *yōju* an ordinary Confucianist; an ordinary scholar

庵 1521 F638 **菴** An hermitage, retreat. *io, iori* hermitage; living in a hermitage.

5主 *anshu* owner of a hermitage
6守 *iomori* guard of a hermitage
7住 *anju, anjū* owner of a hermitage; living in a hermitage
9室 *anshitsu* hermit's cell, sylvan retreat

B **庶** 1522 F638 **庶** Sho all; illegitimate child.

2人 *shonin, shojin* masses, (common) people
3子 *shoshi* illegitimate child
5兄 *shokei* illegitimate elder brother
出 *shoshutsu* illegitimate birth
民 *shomin* masses, the common people
7系 *shokei* illegitimate line
8事 *shoji* various matters, everything
9政 *shosei* all phases of government
10流 *shoryū* illegitimate family branch
11務 *shomu* general affairs, miscellaneous affairs
12幾 *shoki suru* desire, hope. *koinega(u)* (see under 希 1470.0)

9

廁 1523 F640 See **厠** 826.

廊 1524 F641 **廊** See **廊** 1519.

廂 1525 F640 Shō. Sō. *hisashi* eaves; canopy; penthouse; vizor.

B **廃** 1526 F644 **廢** Hai obsolescence; cessation; discarding. *hai(suru)* abolish, abandon; repeal, annul; depose; discontinue. *suta(reru), suta(ru)* become useless, get out of date, die out; be abolished; decline (in prosperity). *ya(meru)* (see under 止 2429.0). *suta(ri)* waste. *ya(me)* end, discontinuance, stop.

2人 *haijin* invalid, cripple; useless person; abandoned person
刀 *haitō suru* abolish the wearing of swords
4止 *haishi* abolition, discontinuance, abrogation
5立 *hairitsu* enthronement and dethronement
刊 *haikan* discontinuance of publication
6気 *haiki* exhaust, ventilation
寺 *haiji* ruined temple
字 *haiji* obsolete character
宅 *haitaku* deserted house
合 *haigō* abolition and amalgamation
合整理 *haigō seiri* reorganization, rearrangement
7位 *hai-i* dethronement
坑 *haikō* abandoned mine
址 *haishi* ruins
材 *haizai* scrap wood
兵 *haihei* disabled soldier
8官 *haikan* abolition of a post
苑 *haien* superannuated plantation
典 *haiten* a discarded organization
学 *haigaku* leave school, stop one's studies
物 *haibutsu* scrap, waste, refuse. *suta(ri)mono* useless thing, obsolete thing
物利用 *haibutsu riyō* the utilization of waste products
9屋 *haioku* deserted house
除 *haijo suru* remove, take away
帝 *haitei* deposed emperor
品 *haihin* scrap, waste
10馬 *haiba* superannuated horse
疾 *haishitsu* disablement, deformity
校 *haikō* discontinuing a school
残 *haizan*＝敗残 4494.10
家 *haike* ending a family line; an extinct family. *haika* an extinct or abandoned family
案 *haian* rejected measure, discarded draft
11虚 *haikyo* ruins of a castle
娼 *haishō* abolition of prostitution
船 *haisen* scrapped vessel, superannuated ship
12税 *haizei* abolition of a tax
絶 *haizetsu* extinction
朝 *haichō suru* depose (a ruler)
13園 *haien* superannuated plantation
滅 *haimetsu* ruin, decay
鉱 *haikō* abandoned mine
毀 *haiki*＝next word
棄 *haiki* abandonment, repeal, annulment, abrogation
置 *haichi* abolition and establishment
業 *haigyō* closing up shop, quitting the business
14嫡 *haichaku* disinheritance
語 *haigo* obsolete word
15墟 *haikyo* ruins
16頽 *haitai* decay, deterioration, decadence
18藩 *haihan* abolition of clans
藩置県 *haihan-chiken* the abolition of the clans and the setting up of prefectures
20艦 *haikan* superannuated warship

— 10 —

厨 1527/F642 See 厨 829.

廈 1528/F641 KA. *ie* house.

廓 1529/F642 KAKU enclosure; quarter. *kuruwa* enclosure, quarter; red-light district

3大 *kakudai suru* enlarge
11清 *kakusei* purification, purge, clean-up

B 廉 1530/F641 廉 REN purity; honesty; low price; corner. *yasu(i)* (see under 安 1283.0). *kado* reason, charge, suspicion; point, account.

3士 *renshi* a pure uncovetous person
6吏 *renri* an honest official
7売 *rembai* bargain sale, dumping
8直 *renchoku* integrity, honor, uprightness
価 *renka* low price
価版 *renkaban* popular edition
価品 *renkahin* low-priced goods
10恥 *renchi* honor, integrity
恥心 *renchishin* sense of shame; sense of honor
13際 *kado(aru)sai* special occasion
15潔 *renketsu* honesty, integrity, uprightness

— 11 —

塵 See 5376. [土]

廄 1531/F642 廐 See 厩 832.

B 腐 1532/F1546 FU. *kusa(ru)*, *kusa(reru)* rot, decay; turn sour; fester; corrode; be corrupted; feel gloomy. *kusa(rasu)*, *kusa(raseru)*, *kusa(rakasu)* *vt* let spoil, rot, corrode, addle. *kuta(su)* let rot, spoil; slander. *kusa(su)* ridicule. *kusare-* spoiled, decayed, rotten. [肉]

4心 *fushin* pains, trouble, hard work, diligence, intense application
6肉 *funiku* tainted meat, putrid flesh; carrion; gangrene
朽 *fukyū* decay, decomposition, putrefaction
合 *kusa(re)-a(u)* enter into illicit intimacy. *kusa(re)a(i)* illicit relations; shady connections
7乱 *furan* inflammation, festering, decomposition
卵 *furan* bad egg
8刻 *fukoku* etching
果 *kusa(ri)-ha(teru)* be corrupt
9食 *fushoku* corrosion, erosion, rot, rust
11敗 *fuhai* decay, decomposition, rottenness, putrefaction; necrosis; corruption, degeneration, depravity
12葉土 *fuyōdo* leaf mold
植 *fushoku* humus, leaf mold
植土 *fushokudo* humus, leaf mold
植質 *fushokushitsu* humus
15穂 *kusa(ri)ho* mildew
縁 *kusa(re)en* mismated marriage; unpleasant relationships
蝕 *fushoku* corrosion, erosion, rot, rust
16儒 *fuju* pedant, worthless scholar
21爛 *furan* putrefaction

— 12 —

廏 See 厩 832.

廚 1533/F643 See 厨 829.

廢 1534/F644 See 廃 1526.

廣 1535/F645 See 広 1499.

廠 1536/F644 SHŌ workshop.

8舎 *shōsha* barracks

廛 1537/F643 TEN fine residence; shop, store.

15鋪 *tempo* shop

廟 1538/F643 BYŌ mausoleum; shrine; palace.

6宇 *byōu* mausoleum, shrine
11堂 *byōdō* the court, cabinet, ministry
20議 *byōgi* Cabinet Council; Cabinet decision

B 慶 1539/F742 KYŌ. KEI. *kei(suru)* congratulate. *yoroko(bu)* rejoice, be happy over. [心]

4弔 *keichō* congratulations and condolences
弔電報 *keichō dempō* special telegram for congratulations or condolences
6兆 *keichō* herald of happiness
8事 *keiji* auspicious event
9祝 *keishuku* congratulation, celebration
12賀 *keiga* congratulation
13福 *keifuku* happiness, well-being

— 13 —

廩 1540/F646 RIN rice storehouse.

— 14 —

應 1541/F749 See **応** 1504. [心]

膺 1542/F1553 Yō breast; strike. [肉]

18懲 *yōchō* punishment, chastisement

— 16 —

鏖 See 5379. [金]

麃 See 5378. [鹿]

廬 1543/F647 Ro. *io, iori* hermitage; living in a hermitage.

— 18 —

麝 See 5382. [鹿]

— 21 —

鷹 1544/F2150 Yō. Ō. *taka* hawk. [鳥]

6匠 *takajō* falconer, hawker
9狩 *takaga(ri)* hawking, falconry
12揚 *ōyō* generosity, largeheartedness; easy-going

— 22 —

廳 1545/F647 See **庁** 1498.

RAD. 廴 54

Ennyō (enclosure for 延 *en, nobiru* "stretch, lengthen"). Also *innyō* or *innyū*, the "long stride" radical. Nickname: Stretching.

— 4 —

延 See **延** 1547.

廷 1546/F648 Tei imperial court; government office.
B

2丁 *teitei* court attendant
4内 *teinai* in the court
6臣 *teishin* courtier, court official
吏 *teiri* lesser court official

— 5 —

A **延** 1547/F647 **延** En stretching. *no(biru), no(bi)* (see under 伸 403.0). *no(basu)* lengthen, stretch, extend; let (nails) grow; straighten; uncoil; spread out; reach out; postpone; dilute; smooth out; develop (talents); amass (riches). *no(beru)* make (a bed); stretch, widen, lengthen. *no(be)* futures, credit (buying); stretching; total.

2人員 *no(be) jin-in* total personnel
4引 *en-in, ennin* delay, postponement, procrastination
日数 *no(be) nissū* total days
5広 *no(bi)-hiro(garu)* stretch, extend
払 *no(be)bara(i)* deferred payment
6会 *enkai* postponement or adjournment (of a meeting)
年 *ennen* longevity
7寿 *enju* prolongation of life
8金 *no(be)gane* sheet metal; hammered-out sheets; sword, dagger
延 *no(bi)no(bi)* stretching. *no(bi)no(bi) ni naru* be delayed. *en-en(taru)* meandering, serpentine
坪 *no(be)tsubo* total floor space
性 *ensei* malleability
板 *no(be)ita* hammered-out plates
命 *emmei* prolongation of life; long life, longevity
取引 *no(be) torihiki* dealing in futures
長 *enchō* extension, elongation, prolongation, continuation; extent, length
長戦 *enchōsen* extra-inning game
9音 *en-on* long vowel sound
10紙 *no(be)gami* paper handkerchief
納 *ennō* deferred payment
時間 *no(be)jikan* total hours
11袤 *embō* size (of the land)
12棒 *no(be)bō* (metal) bar
渡 *no(be)wata(shi)* forward delivery
焼 *enshō* spread of a fire
期 *enki* postponement, adjournment, deferment, respite
着 *enchaku* delayed arrival
13滞 *entai* delay, procrastination, arrearage
17齢 *enrei* prolongation of life
18髄 *enzui* afterbrain

— 6 —

廻 1548/F649 **廻** Kai. *mawa(su), mawa(ru)* (see under 回 1028.0). *megu(ru), megu(ri)* (see under 巡 4667.0). (See under 回 1028 for other related compounds.)

4 文 *kaibun, kaimon* circular letter
天 *kaiten no* epoch-making, stupendous
6 米 *kaimai* rice arrivals
合 *megu(ri)-a(u)* meet by chance
7 折 *keisetsu* diffraction
状 *kaijō* circular letter
8 国 *kaikoku* pilgrimage, tour
送 *kaisō* forwarding, transportation
10 航 *kaikō* navigation, cruise
11 廊 *kairō* corridor
旋 *kaisen* rotation, revolution
章 *kaishō* a circular
転 *kaiten* revolution, rotation
転椅子 *kaiten isu* swivel chair
14 漕 *kaisō* marine transportation
漕業 *kaisōgyō* marine-transportation business
16 覧 *kairan* circulation of letter or document

A **建** 1549 / F648 KON, KEN build, raise. *ta(tsu)*, *ta(teru)* (see under 立 3343.0).

4 方 *ta(te)kata* architectural style; how to build
込 *ta(te)-ko(mu)* be closely built up
5 立 *konryū* building, erection
白 *kempaku* memorial, petition
白書 *kempakusho* memorial, petition
6 回 *ta(te)-megu(rasu)* build around
地 *ta(te)chi* building plot
7 言 *kengen* memorial, petition, proposal
材 *kenzai* building materials
売 *ta(te)ur(i)* ready-built (house)
8 国 *kenkoku, kengoku* establishing a nation
坪 *tatetsubo* floor space
物 *tatemono* building; architecture
直 *ta(te)-nao(ru)* be rebuilt. *ta(te)-nao(su)* rebuild
具 *tategu* house fittings (doors and windows)
具屋 *tateguya* cabinetmaker
9 連 *ta(te)-tsura(neru)* build house after house
前 *tatemae* framework-erection ceremony; framing a house; fundamental principles
造 *kenzō* building, construction
造物 *kenzōbutsu* building, edifice
10 値 *tatene* official quotations; exchange rates; prices
株 *ta(te)kabu* listed stocks
11 掛 *ta(te)ka(ke)* under construction
設 *kensetsu* building, establishment
設工事 *kensetsu kōji* construction work
設的 *kensetsuteki* constructive
設者 *kensetsusha* builder, founder
設省 *Kensetsushō* Construction Ministry
12 策 *kensaku* recommendation, suggestion
替 *ta(te)-ka(eru)* rebuild
13 業 *kengyō* starting an enterprise
14 増 *ta(te)-ma(su)* build on. *tatema(shi)* extension, annex
網 *ta(te)ami* dragnet, set net, seine
碑式 *kempishiki* dedication of a monument
16 築 *kenchiku* building, architecture
築用材 *kenchiku yōzai* building materials
築技師 *kenchiku gishi* architect
築材料 *kenchiku zairyō* building materials
築物 *kenchikubutsu* building, edifice
築学 *kenchikugaku* architecture
築者 *kenchikusha* builder
築師 *kenchikushi* builder
築家 *kenchikuka* architect
築術 *kenchikujutsu* architecture
築許可 *kenchiku kyoka* building permit
築税 *kenchikuzei* tax on construction
築費 *kenchikuhi* construction costs
築資材 *kenchiku shizai* building materials
築業 *kenchikugyō* building industry
築業者 *kenchikugyōsha* builder
築線 *kenchikusen* building line
築請負 *kenchiku ukeoi* building contract
築請負業者 *kenchiku ukeoi gyōsha* contractor
20 艦 *kenkan* naval construction
議 *kengi* proposal, petition, recommendation
議者 *kengisha* mover, proposer
議案 *kengian* motion, proposition

RAD. 廾 55

Nijū-ashi "twenty" legs (i.e., legs resembling *ni-jū* "twenty"). Variant: 廾.
Nickname: Letter H.

1

廿 1550 / F649 JŪ. *nijū* twenty

4 日 *hatsuka* twenty days; twentieth day (of the month)

2

弁 See 844, 845, 846, 847.

3

共 See 581. [八]

4

弄 See 2924.

— 5 —

昔 See 2108.[日]

— 6 —

巷 See 1465.[巳]

— 7 —

恭 See 1680.[心]

— 12 —

B 弊 1551/F650 獘 HEI evil, abuse, vice, bad custom; breakage; our (humble); Shinto zigzag paper offering; tribute. *tsuie* expenses. *hei-* our (humble).

[6]宅 *heitaku* shack; my humble home
衣 *hei-i* shabby clothes
衣破帽 *hei-i-habō* shabby clothes and an old hat
[7]村 *heison* impoverished village; my poor village
社 *heisha* our firm
[8]店 *heiten* our shop
制 *heisei* a poor system, a poor organization
[9]風 *heifū* evil habit, bad custom, abuse
政 *heisei* maladministration
[10]家 *heika* my humble home
害 *heigai* evil, vice, abuse; harmful influence; bad effect
[11]習 *heishū* corrupt custom, bad habit
[15]履 *heiri* worn-out sandals; worn-out shoes

— 13 —

彝 See 1587.[彑]

— 15 —

彝 See 彝 1587.[彑]

弋 RAD. 56

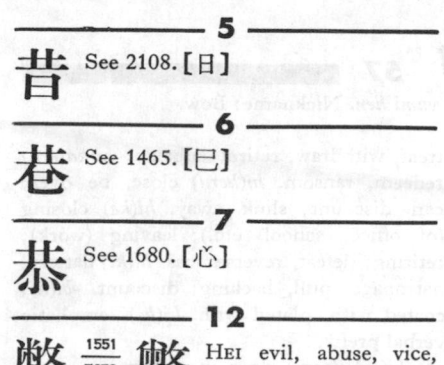

Shikigamae (enclosure for 式 *shiki* "ceremony"). Nickname: Ceremony.

弋 1552/F651 YOKU piling.

— 1 —

弌 1553/F651 *ichi* one.

— 2 —

弍 1554/F651 See 弐 32.

— 3 —

弐 See 32.

弎 1555/F651 *san* three.

A 式 1556/F651 SHIKI ceremony, rite, function; method, system; style, form, type, plan; formula, expression (in math); model; law; standard. *-shiki* style, type.

[4]文 *shikibun* liturgy, ritual, worship manual
日 *shikijitsu* ceremonial occasion
[5]目 *shikimoku* feudal law code
台 *shikidai* step or platform in an entranceway; slatted removable floor in an entrance hall
[6]次 *shikiji* the order of a ceremony
年 *shikinen* year of special festivals
[8]服 *shikifuku* ceremonial dress
典 *shikiten* ceremony, celebration, rites
[9]後 *shikigo* after the ceremony
[10]部長 *Shikibuchō* Grand Master of Court Ceremonies
部官 *shikibukan* master of court ceremonies
[12]場 *shikijō* place of the ceremony; ceremonial hall
[13]微 *shikibi* decline (in royal fortunes)
辞 *shikiji* address, speech

— 9 —

貳 1557/F1793 See 弐 32.[貝]

弑 1558/F652 SHI. *shii(suru)* murder one's lord, assassinate, kill (one's father).

[8]逆 *shiigyaku*, *shigyaku* regicide, murder of one's lord

— 11 —

鳶 1559/F2140 EN. *tobi* black kite; fireman; hook. *tombi* black kite; cloak; pilferer.[鳥]

[2]人足 *tobi ninsoku* fireman
[3]口 *tobiguchi* fire ax, fire hook
[6]色 *tobi iro* brown, auburn
[8]者 *tobi(no)mono* fireman
[12]衆 *tobi(no)shū* fireman
[16]頭 *tobigashira* chief fireman
[18]職 *tobishoku* casual laborer, construction laborer

RAD. 弓 57

Yumi bow (for arrows). At left: *yumi hen.* Nickname: Bow.

B 弓 1560 F652 KYŪ bow; violin bow. *yumi* bow; archery; violin bow; bow shape.

2人 *kyūjin* maker of archery bows
4手 *yunde* archer's hand; the left hand
引 *yumi (o) hi(ku)* draw the bow; rebel
5矢 *yumiya* bow and arrow
矢八幡 *yumiya hachiman* god of war
7状 *kyūjō* arch. *kyūjō no* arched, crescent-shaped
形 *kyūkei* crescent form, circle segment. *yuminari, yumigata* arch, arc, curve
8弦 *yumizuru, yunzuru, kyūgen* bowstring
取 *yumito(ri)* archer, warrior, samurai; famous archer; archery
10師 *yumishi* bow maker
馬 *kyūba* bow and horse; archery and horsemanship
馬家 *kyūba (no) ie* a samurai family
馬道 *kyūba (no) michi* the way of the samurai
11道 *kyūdō* archery
術 *kyūjutsu* archery
術師 *kyūjutsushi* archer
張 *yumiha(ri)* bow-handled paper lantern
張月 *yumiha(ri)zuki* crescent moon; waxing moon; waning moon
張提灯 *yumiha(ri)jōchin* bow-handled paper lantern
12場 *yumiba* archery ground, archery gallery. *yuba*=*yaba* 矢場 3168.12
13勢 *yunzei* the power of a bow; the archer's strength
15箭 *kyūsen* bows and arrows; arms; war
箭家 *kyūsen (no) ie* a samurai family
箭道 *kyūsen (no) michi* samurai spirit; the way of the samurai
20懸 *yugake* archer's glove

1

弔 See 80.

弖 1561 F654 TE (used phonetically).

14爾乎波 *te-ni-o-ha* the particles
爾遠波 *te-ni-o-ha* the particles

A 引 1562 F653 IN. *hi(ku)* *vt* draw, pull, haul, tug, jerk, drag, trail, bend, attract; lead (horses or captives); draw (lines); admit; install (utilities); quote, refer to; look up (words); subtract, reduce; apply, daub on; blunt (a sword); patronize; choose; draw (a line); catch (a cold). *vi* retreat, withdraw, retire; subside. *hi(kaseru)* redeem, ransom. *hi(keru)* close, be over; can discount; slink away. *hi(ke)* closing (of office, school, etc.); leaving (work); retiring; defeat, reverse; loss. *hi(ki)* flattery, patronage, pull, backing; discount. *-bi(ki)* coated with, plated with. *hi(ki)-* emphatic verbal prefix.

2入 *hi(ki)-i(reru)* drag in, bring into; win over, interest, entice; pull in, pull back
力 *inryoku* gravitation, attraction
3下 *hi(ki)-sa(garu)* *vi* retire, withdraw. *hi(ki)-sa(geru)* pull down, lower, reduce. *hi(ki)-oro(su)* pull down; drag off (the rocks), refloat
上 *hi(ki)-a(geru)* *vi* withdraw, retire, leave; be repatriated. *vt* pull up; increase (fares); evacuate; refloat, salvage; recover (a body); promote
上作業 *hikia(ge) sagyō* salvage operations
4戸 *hi(ki)do* sliding door
比 *hi(ki)-kura(beru)* compare
水 *hi(ki)mizu* irrigation
分 *hi(ki)-wa(keru)* pull apart, separate. *hikiwake* a drawn game
手 *hi(ki)te* knob, handle, catch; patron, admirer. *hi(ku)te* admirer; inducer
手繰 *hi(t)taku(ru)* snatch away, wrest from
止 *hi(ki)-to(meru)*=引留 (see below–10)
止策 *hikito(me) saku* measures to induce a person to desist
切 *hi(ki)-ki(ru)* pull and cut; saw off. *hi(kimo)-ki(ranu), hi(kimo)-ki(razu)* uninterrupted. *hi(kimo)-ki(razu) ni* uninterruptedly
切無 *hi(k)ki(ri)na(shi) ni* incessantly, continuously, in rapid succession
火 *inka suru* ignite, catch fire
火性 *inkasei* inflammability
火点 *inkaten* ignition point
込 *hi(ki)-ko(mu)*=*hi(ki)-i(reru)* 引入 (see above–2). *hi(k)ko(mu)* draw back, retire; sink, cave in; keep behind; disappear. *hi(k)ko(masu), hi(k)ko(meru), hi(k)ko(mu)* *vt* draw in, take in; withdraw, retract, pull inside. *hikko(mi), hikiko(mi)* retreat, withdrawal; retirement; depression (a hole)
込車輪 *hikiko(mi) sharin* retractable wheel
込性 *hikko(mi)shō* retiring disposition; conservatism

込思案 *hikko(mi)jian* conservatism
込勝 *hikko(mi)ga(chi) no* retiring (disposition)
込管 *hikiko(mi)kan, hi(k)ko(mi)kan* service pipe
込線 *hikikomisen* service wire. *hi(k)komisen* railway siding
5目 *hi(ke)me* weakness; drawing back
付 *hi(t)tsu(keru), hi(ki)-tsu(keru)* fascinate; pull up (at a gate;) have a convulsion. *hi(t)tsu(ku)* stick to, cling to. *hi(ki)tsu(ke)* fit, convulsion
叩 *hi(p)pata(ku)* thrash, box, slap, strike
外 *hi(ki)-hazu(su), hi(p)pazu(su)* pull down, take off, unfasten. *hi(p)pazu(su)* dodge, parry off
払 *hi(ki)-hara(u)* evacuate, vacate
札 *hi(ki)fuda* handbill; lottery ticket
写 *hi(ki)utsu(shi)* copy, tracing
去 *hi(ki)-sa(ru)* retreat, withdraw; subside; deduct
立 *hi(t)ta(teru), hi(ki)-ta(teru)* favor; patronize; support; promote; rouse; enhance; emphasize; shut; escort (a prisoner), march (a person) off. *hi(ki)-ta(tsu)* become active; be inspired; become brisk; set off (to advantage), look better
立役 *hikita(te)yaku* a front; supporter, a friend (in court)
出 *hi(ki)-da(su)* take out, extract; drag out; draw out, lead out, entice out, bring out. *hikida(shi)* (desk) drawer; withdrawal
出物 *hi(ki)demono* gift, souvenir
用 *in-yō* a quotation
用文 *in-yōbun* a quotation
用句 *in-yōku* a quotation
用符 *in-yōfu* quotation marks
6回 *hi(ki)-mawa(su)* draw (a curtain); parade about; guide
返 *hi(ki)-kae(su)* repeat; send back, reverse; bring back; turn back, retrace (steps)
汐 *hi(ki)shio* ebb tide
合 *hi(ki)-a(u)* be profitable, pay; pull against each other. *hi(ki)-a(waseru)* introduce; compare, collate, check. *hi(ki)-a(waseru)* compare, contrast; introduce. *hi(ki)a(i)* reference, comparison; witness; a deal
当 *hi(ki)-a(teru)* apply, compare. *hi(ki)a(te)* mortgage, security
7見 *inken* audience, interview
戻 *hi(ki)-modo(su)* bring back, restore; improve (business); turn back, retrace (steps)
伸 *hi(ki)-noba(su), hi(ki)-no(beru)*＝引延 (see below–8). *hikinoba(shi)* photographic enlargement
抜 *hi(ki)-nu(ku), hi(kko)nu(ku)* extract; uproot; select, pull out
8金 *hi(ki)gane* trigger
延 *hi(ki)-no(beru), hi(ki)-noba(su)* stretch out, prolong; elongate; extend; beat out; spin out; enlarge; postpone; filibuster
退 *intai suru, hi(ki)-shirizo(ku)* draw back, retreat. *hi(ki)-no(keru)* drag out of the way. *intai* retirement
例 *inrei* quotation, referring to precedent
放 *hi(ki)-hana(tsu), hi(ki)-hana(su)* pull apart
明 *hi(ki)a(ke)* daybreak
波 *hi(ki)nami* backwash
物 *hi(ki)mono* gift, souvenir
直 *hi(ki)-nao(su)* restore, bring back, redraw (lines, etc.)
雀 *hi(ki)-mush(iru)*＝*mushiru* (see under 雀 207.0)
者 *hi(kare)mono* man under arrest
取 *hi(ki)-to(ru)* take charge of, respond to; take delivery of; claim (a body); retire; die
取人 *hikitorinin* claimer, caretaker, guarantor (of a parolee)
取手 *hikitorite* = *hikitorinin* 引取人 (see preceding word)
受 *hi(ki)-u(keru)* be responsible for; take charge of, undertake; consent to; accept, guarantee; contract (a disease). *hikiu(ke)* undertaking; acceptance, underwriting; guarantee, guarantor
受人 *hikiukenin* guarantor; acceptor (of a draft); underwriter
受手 *hikiukete* = *hikiukenin* 引受人 (see word above)
9連 *hi(ki)-tsu(reru)* bring along
眉 *hi(ki)mayu* painted eyebrows
括 *hi(k)kuru(meru), hi(ki)-kuru(meru)* bring to a conclusion
降 *hi(ki)-o(rosu)* pull down, bring down
10起 *hi(ki)-oko(su)* raise up, pull up; cause, bring about; raise (questions); create (trouble), provoke, stir up
値 *hi(ki)ne* reduced price
倒 *hi(ki)-tao(su)* pull down, drag down
捕 *hi(ki)-tora(eru), hi(t)tora(eru)* capture, seize, arrest
時 *hi(ke)doki* closing time
渫 *hi(s)sara(u)* snatch, grab, take away
破 *hi(ki)-yabu(ru)* tear, tear up, tear away
致 *inchi* arrest, custody
被 *hi(k)kabu(ru)* pull (bedclothes) over the head
剝 *hi(ki)-ha(gu), hi(ki)-ha(gasu)* = *ha(gu)* (see under 剝 695.0). *hi(ki)-mu(ku)* = *mu(ku)* (see under 剝 695.0)
殺 *hi(ki)-koro(su)* run over and kill
留 *hi(ki)-to(meru)* restrain, check; detain, keep back, hold, stop

口口土士夊夂夕大女子宀寸小⺌尢尸屮山川巛工己巾干幺广廴廾弋[弓]彐彑彡彳

11掛 *hi(k)ka(karu)* be caught in, get stuck; be involved; be cheated. *hi(k)ka(keru)* hang on, hook, throw on; ensnare; defraud, evade (payment); drink (saké). *hi(ki)-ka-(keru)* hang up (something); pull (something) over one; request; make connections with. *hi(k)ka(kari)* a hold; connection, complicity, involvement; affair; unsettled account. *hi(k)ka(ke)* hook

据 *hi(ki)-su(eru)*=*su(eru)* (see under 据 1935.0)

移 *hi(ki)-utsu(ru)* move to. *hi(ki)-utsu(su)* =*utsu(su)* (see under 移 3282.0)

船 *hi(ki)bune* tugboat

釣 *hi(t)tsuri* scar, mark of a burn

動 *hi(ki)-ugo(kasu)* pull and move around; tempt and lead around

寄 *hi(ki)-yo(seru)* draw nearer, drag in; ⌊attract

窓 *hi(ki)mado* skylight, trap door

責 *inseki suru* take the responsibility

菓子 *hi(ki)gashi* ornamental gift cakes

率 *insotsu suru* lead, command

率者 *insotsusha* leader

張 *hi(p)pa(ru)* pull, draw, jerk, drag, tug at; stretch over; take (someone) to; entice, invite; delay (payment)

張上 *hi(p)pa(ri)-a(geru)*=*hiki-a(geru)* 引上 (see above–3)

張込 *hi(p)pa(ri)-ko(mu)* pull in, drag into

張凧 *hi(p)pa(ri)dako* socialite

張出 *hi(p)pa(ri)-da(su)* take out, drag out, bring out, lead out, pull out

張回 *hi(p)pa(ri)-mawa(su)* pull around

12喩 *in-yu* allusion

換 *hi(ki)-ka(eru)* exchange, change, convert. *hikika(ete)*, *hikika(e)* on the contrary, on the other hand; while, when

渡 *hi(ki)-wata(su)* deliver, transfer, hand over; extradite; stretch across. *hikiwata-(shi)* delivery, turning over to, extradition

絞 *hi(ki)-shibo(ru)*=*shibo(ru)* (see under 絞 3535.0); draw a bow to the limit; draw aside (curtains); tuck up; strain (the ⌊voice)

証 *inshō* quotation, citation

着 *hi(ki)-tsu(keru)*, *hi(t)tsu(keru)*=引付 (see above–5)

落 *hi(ki)-oto(su)* pull down

裂 *hi(s)sa(ku)*, *hi(ki)-sa(ku)* tear off, tear up, rip open; split; separate ⌈oats

割燕麦 *hikiwa(ri) embaku* oatmeal, rolled

越 *hi(k)ko(su)*, *hi(ki)-ko(su)* move, change quarters

越先 *hikko(shi) saki* destination in moving

揚 *hi(ki)-a(geru)*=引上 (see above–3)

揚者 *hikiagesha* returnee

替 *hi(ki)-kae(ru)*, *hi(k)kae(ru)* exchange (things); change from; reverse

替券 *hikikaeken* cloakroom check

13継 *hi(ki)-tsu(gu)* take over or hand over (duties); inherit

続 *hi(ki)-tsuzu(ku)* continue, occur in succession. *hi(ki)tsuzu(ki)* continually

詰 *hi(ki)-tsu(meru)* shorten; tighten; econo-⌊mize

置 *inchi* arrest

幕 *hi(ki)maku* a draw curtain

照 *inshō* reference

掻 *hi(k)ka(ku)* scratch, claw, maul

掻回 *hi(k)ka(ki)-mawa(su)* ransack, mess up, carry on highhandedly

14摑 *hi(t)tsuka(mu)* grab at

綱 *hi(ki)zuna* tow rope; bell rope

算 *hi(ki)zan* subtraction ⌈soul

導 *indō* guidance; address to the departed

摺 *hi(ki)-zu(ru)* drag along; seduce; prolong. *hi(ki)zuri* train (of a dress); a low ⌊woman

摺込 *hi(ki)-zu(ri)-ko(mu)* drag in

摺出 *hi(ki)-zu(ri)-da(su)* drag out

摺回 *hi(ki)-zu(ri)-mawa(su)* drag around

15潮 *hi(ki)shio* ebb tide

緩 *hi(ki)-yuru(mu)* weaken the stock market

締 *hi(ki)-shi(maru)* become tense; be tightened. *hiki-shi(meru)* tighten; stiffen; strain, brace ⌈(after a burn)

17縮 *hi(ki)tsuri* cramp; convulsion; drawn skin

19離 *hi(ki)-hana(su)*, *hi(p)pana(su)* pull apart, separate; outdistance

繰返 *hi(k)ku(ri)-kae(ru)* capsize; collapse; lie on one's back; be reversed; betray. *hi(k)ku(ri)-kae(su)* capsize; knock down; turn over; turn inside out; turn up (a card). *hi(k)ku(ri)kae(shi)* topsy-turvy, upside down, inside out ⌈knot)

縄結 *hi(ki)nawa musu(bi)* carrick bend (a

20懸 *hi(k)kake*, *hi(k)ka(kari)*, *hi(k)ka(karu)*, *hi(k)ka(keru)*=引掛 (see above–11)

21纏 *hi(ki)-mato(meru)*=*matomeru* (see under 纏 3627.0) ⌈doors; be confined indoors

22籠 *hi(ki)-komo(ru)*, *hi(k)komo(ru)* stay in-

23攫 *hi(s)sara(u)* snatch, grab, take away

攣 *hi(ki)-tsu(ru)* have a cramp or spasm; twitch; strain (a ligament); have a convulsion. *hikitsuri* scar; spasm, cramp, twitch, convulsion

2

弗 See 173.

弘 $\frac{1563}{F655}$ Kᴜ. Kō. *hiro(i)* broad, wide.

11済会 *kōsaikai* benefit association

[12]報 *kōhō* publicity
報部 *kōhōbu* public relations department

3

弛 1564 / F655 CHI. SHI. *taru(mu) vi* slacken, loosen, relax. *tayu(mu)* slacken one's efforts. *taru(meru) vt* loosen, slack up on. *tayu(i)* tired and weak, listless; without any ambition. *yuru(i), yuru(meru), yuru(mu)* (see under 緩 3583.0)
[11]張 *shichō* stretching and releasing; alternation of firmness and laxity
張熱 *shichōnetsu, chichōnetsu* remittent fever
[12]廃 *chihai suru, shihai suru* relax, slacken
[15]緩 *chikan, shikan* relaxation; getting careless

4

弟 See 584.

5

弥 1565 / F661 **彌** BI. MI. *iya* all the more, increasingly.
[3]久 *bikyū suru* stretch out, lengthen (said of time)
上 *iya(ga)ue nimo* all the more, to cap it all
[5]生 *yayoi* spring; third lunar month
立 *yoda(tsu)* quiver with horror
[6]次 *yaji(ru)* cheer, support, root for; hoot at, obstruct; jeer at. *yaji* cheering, rooting; heckling, jeering; rooters, hecklers, mob; spectators; busybody; intruder
次馬 *yajiuma* rabble, mob; spectators; busybody; intruder
[8]弥 *iyoiyo* more and more
果 *iyaha(te)* away off in the distance
[9]栄 *iyasaka(eru)* prosper more and more. *iyasaka* increasing prosperity
[11]猛 *yatake ni* impetuously, courageously
猛心 *yatakegokoro* brave heart
[14]増 *iyamashi ni* more and more; *iyama(su)* go on increasing
[15]撒 *misa* Catholic mass
縫 *bihō* stopgap, temporizing, patching up, glossing over
縫策 *bihōsaku* makeshift, stopgap policy

弩 1566 / F656 DO. *ōyumi* crossbow, long bow.
[3]弓 *dokyū* catapult
[9]級艦 *dokyūkan* dreadnaught

B **弧** 1567 / F656 Ko arc; arch; bow.
[6]灯 *kotō* arc light
光 *kokō* arc light
[7]状 *kojō no* arc-shaped
形 *kokei* an arc
[15]線 *kosen* an arc

B **弦** 1568 / F656 GEN bowstring; chord (in geometry); hypotenuse; crescent (moon); bowstring; string (of an instrument). *tsuru* bowstring; teakettle handle made of bamboo or vines.
[4]月 *gengetsu* crescent moon
[7]声 *gensei* sound of the strings
[9]音 *tsuru oto* sound of a vibrating bowstring
[13]楽 *gengaku* singing accompanied by stringed instruments
楽隊 *gengakutai* string band
楽器 *gengakki* stringed instruments
[14]歌 *genka* singing
管 *genkan* wind and string instruments
[15]線 *gensen* catgut

6

弯 Nonstandard for **彎** 1579.

7

弱 1569 / F657 **弱** See 650.

8

A **張** 1570 / F658 CHŌ counter for bows and stringed instruments. *ha(ru) vt* put up (a tent); stretch, spread, string, tighten; cover, line; strain; square (elbows); give (a banquet); run (a store); stake (money); display; slap, box, spank; lay (flooring); insist on (one's own way); guard; run after (a girl); fill (with water). *vi* swell, be full; form (ice); be expensive; increase; be heavy; grow stiff; brace up. *ha(ri)* tension; will power, pluck, pride; expansion steadiness. *-ba(ri)* fashion.
[2]力 *chōryoku* tension, tensile strength
[3]子 *ha(ri)ko* papier-mâché
上 *ha(ri)-a(geru)* raise or strain (the voice)
上綱 *ha(ri)a(ge)zuna* halyard
[4]手 *ha(ri)te* slapping (someone)
込 *ha(ri)-ko(mu)* keep watch; be eager for; invest in
切 *ha(ri)-ki(reru)* burst out. *ha(ri)-ki(ru)* string up, stretch tight; be tense, be enthusiastic
[5]目 *ha(ri)me* the edge of a piece pasted on to another
巡 *ha(ri)-megu(rasu)* ramify
付 *ha(ri)-tsu(keru)* stick on, paste up (a notice), affix (stamps)
札 *ha(ri)fuda* placard, bill, poster; tag
札無用 *ha(ri)fuda muyō* Post No Bills
出 *ha(ri)-da(su)* put up a notice, project, jut out. *harida(shi)* bill, poster, notice; overhang
出窓 *harida(shi) mado* bay window

本 *chōhon* cause; originator; ringleader, perpetrator

本人 *chōhonnin, chōbonnin* originator, ringleader, perpetrator

6合 *ha*(*ri*)-*a*(*u*) vie with, emulate, compete with. *haria*(*i*) rivalry, competition; responsiveness; inducement

7抜 *ha*(*ri*)*nu*(*ki*) papier-mâché

8板 *ha*(*ri*)-*ita* fulling board; kimono drying board

物 *ha*(*ri*)*mono* cloth-fulling

10倒 *ha*(*ri*)-*tao*(*su*) knock down, floor (a man)

紋 *ha*(*ri*)*mon* pasted crest

紙 *ha*(*ri*)*gami* sticker, bills, label, tag

紙禁止 *ha*(*ri*)*gami kinshi* Post No Bills

12間 *ha*(*ri*)*ma* span (in building)

番 *ha*(*ri*)*ban* watch, guard; watchman, sentinel

替 *ha*(*ri*)-*ka*(*eru*) repaper, replaster, re-upholster, recover

裂 *ha*(*ri*)-*sa*(*keru*) burst open; split, break, splinter

13詰 *ha*(*ri*)-*tsu*(*meru*) strain, stretch, string up, make tense, cover over, freeze over

14網 *ha*(*ri*)*ami* stretched net, set net

綱 *ha*(*ri*)*zuna* guy rope

A **強** 1571 / F658 **强** Kyō, Gō strength, might; strong person. *tsuyo*(*i*) strong, powerful, mighty, robust, vigorous, healthy; brave, courageous; severe, intense; durable, solid. *tsuyo*(*maru*) get strong. *tsuyo*(*meru*) *vt* strengthen, intensify. invigorate; confirm; emphasize, increase, redouble. *tsuyo*(*garu*) show one's toughness. *tsuyo*(*gari*) bluff, show of strength. *shi*(*iru*) force, coerce, constrain, compel. *shi*(*ite*) forcibly, against one's will. *anaga*(*chi*) necessarily, wholly. *kowa*(*i*) tough, hard, stiff. *-kyō* a little over, and a fraction. *-zuyo*(*i*) very.

2力 *kyōryoku* power, might. *gōriki* Herculean strength; mountain carrier-guide

力犯 *gōrikihan* crime of violence

3大 *kyōdai na* mighty, powerful

弓 *gōkyū* strong bow

4火 *tsuyobi* a good (cooking) fire

化米 *kyōkamai* enriched rice

引 *gōin ni* by main force, forcibly

心剤 *kyōshinzai* heart stimulant

5圧 *kyōatsu* pressure, oppression, coertion

弁 *kyōben suru* quibble, sophisticate

半 *kyōhan* more than half, the greater part

打 *kyōda* hard blow; heavy hit (in baseball); drive (in tennis)

打者 *kyōdasha* heavy hitter

6気 *tsuyoki* strong spirit. *gōgi na* great, powerful, grand

壮 *kyōsō na* robust, sturdy, strong, vigorous

壮剤 *kyōsōzai* tonic

行 *kyōkō* forcing; enforcement

行軍 *kyōkōgun* forced march

行偵察 *kyōkō teisatsu* reconnaisance in force

7言 *shiigoto* forcefully dominating the conversation

兵 *kyōhei* good soldier; powerful army

迫 *kyōhaku suru* compel, use duress

迫観念 *kyōhaku kannen* persecution complex

8雨 *kyōu* heavy rain

固 *kyōko* firmness, stability, security, strength

国 *kyōkoku* strong nation, powerful country

肩 *kyōken* strong-armed (player)

味 *tsuyomi* strength, strong point

直 *kyōchoku, gōchoku* integrity; rigidity

弩 *kyōdo* strong bow

者 *kyōsha* strong person. *gō*(*no*)*mono* very strong person; brave warrior

突張 *gōtsu*(*ku*)*ba*(*ri*) hardheartedness; headstrong person

歩 *kyōho* forced walk; walking race

歩競走 *kyōho kyōsō* walking race

制 *kyōsei* coercion, compulsion, enforcement

制力 *kyōseiryoku* authority, legal power

制天引 *kyōsei tembi*(*ki*) compulsory check-off

制処分 *kyōsei shobun* legal disposition

制労動 *kyōsei rōdō* forced labor, slave labor, hard labor (in prison)

制作業 *kyōsei sagyō* reform work

制的 *kyōseiteki* compulsory, forced

制結婚 *kyōsei kekkon* forced marriage

制疎開 *kyōsei sokai* forced evacuation, eviction, dismantling, demolishing

制徴募 *kyōsei chōbo* forced enlistment, labor levy

制調停 *kyōsei chōtei* compulsory mediation

制競売 *kyōsei kyōbai* forced auction sale

9音 *kyōon* accent, stress

風 *kyōfū* moderate gale, strong wind

度 *kyōdo* intensity, strength

持 *kowamo*(*te*) fear-motivated respect

胆 *gōtan* boldness, hardihood

姦 *gōkan* rape, violation, assault

要 *kyōyō* coercion, enforcement, extortion, persistent demand. *shi*(*i*)-*sema*(*ru*) coerce

10剛 *kyōgō* strong man

振 *kyōshin* strong swing (on a ball)

酒 *kōshu* heavy drinking

将 *kyōshō* strong general, brave general

記 *kyōki* excellent memory, good memory

烈 *kyōretsu na* strong, intense; gaudy

弱 *kyōjaku* strength, power

11健 *kyōken* robust health

強 *kowagowa* sound of stiff materials rustling

張 *kowaba*(*ru*) *vi* stiffen; become fearful. *kowaba*(*raseru*), *kowaba*(*rasu*) *vt* starch

情 *gōjō* obstinacy, stubbornness

球 *gōkyū* fast ball
悪 *gōaku* wickedness
盗 *gōtō* burglar, robber; burglary, robbery
欲 *gōyoku* greed, avarice
欲非道 *gōyoku-hidō na* insatiable, relentless, rapacious
12 訴 *gōso* direct petition
靭 *kyōjin na* tough, tenacious, stiff
飲 *gōin* heavy drinking, carousing
飯 *kowameshi* rice cooked with red beans
硬 *kyōkō na* firm, vigorous, unbending
硬派 *kyōkōha* diehards, tough elements
13 腰 *tsuyogoshi* firm attitude
腹 *gōfuku* obstinacy, stubbornness
勢 *gōsei na* splendid, great, magnificent
意見 *kowa-iken* warning, severe reproof; positive ideas
14 豪 *kyōgō* strong man; champion 「lence
奪 *gōdatsu* pillage, plunder, extortion; vio-
奪物 *gōdatsubutsu* plunder, loot
奪者 *gōdatsusha* plunderer, robber
15 劇 *kyōgeki na* strong and violent
談 *gōdan* vigorous negotiations, peremptory
調 *kyōchō* emphasis ⌊demands
敵 *gōteki, kyōteki* formidable enemy
暴 *kyōbō* strong and rough, violent
震 *kyōshin* severe earthquake
慾 *gōyoku* greed, avarice
請 *sega(mu), sebi(ru)* tease, press for, tap for (money). *yusu(ru)* extort, blackmail. *neda(ru)* tease, coax, solicit, demand. *gōsei* blackmail, extortion; importunity
請取 *neda(ri)-to(ru), sebi(ri)-to(ru)* tease for and take. *yusu(ri)-to(ru)* wring money out of person
権 *kyōken* the power of the state
権主義 *kyōken shugi* authoritarianism
権政治 *kyōken seiji* power politics 「tion
権発動 *kyōken-hatsudō* invoking legal ac-
16 激 *kyōgeki na* strong and violent
諫 *kyōkan* strong argument (against)
19 識 *kyōshiki* excellent memory
22 襲 *kyōshū* assault, storming; terrific hitting
襲隊 *kyōshūtai* assault unit

9

强 1572 / F660 See **強** 1571.

弼 1573 / F660 **弻** Hitsu help.

粥 1574 / F1430 Iku. Juku. *kayu, kai* rice gruel. [米]
9 食 *kayushoku* a meal of rice gruel
13 腹 *kayubara* living on rice gruel

B **弾** 1575 / F660 **彈** Dan bullet. *dan(jiru), dan(zuru), tan(zuru)* play or twang on a stringed instrument. *hi(ku)* play on. *haji(ku)* fillip, flip, snap; repel, shed (water); use (an abacus). *haji(keru)* split open; spring off. *hazu(mu)* spring, bound, rebound; be inspired, be spurred on; invest in; be generous (in tipping); breathe with difficulty. *hajiki* (metal) spring; marbles. *tama* bullet, shot, shell.
2 力 *danryoku* elasticity, flexibility
力性 *danryokusei* elasticity, resilience, flexibility; adaptability
3 子 *danshi* shot, bullet 「ball, projectile
丸 *dangan, tama* bullet, shot, shell, cannon
丸切手 *dangan kitte* postal-savings coupons
丸列車 *dangan ressha* super-express, flier
丸除 *dangan-yo(ke)* protection against bullets
丸黒子 *dangan-kokushi* tiny piece (of land)
丸衝撃 *dangan shōgeki* shell shock
4 手 *hi(ki)te* player, performer
片 *dampen* shell splinter
込 *tamago(me)* loading a gun
5 玉 *haji(ki)dama* marbles 「sion
圧 *dan-atsu* pressure, oppression, suppres-
出 *haji(ki)-da(su)* snap out; expel; calculate; squeeze out (the money needed)
6 返 *haji(ki)-kae(ru)* spring back, rebound, boomerang
7 豆 *haji(ke)mame* pop beans; parched peas
初 *hi(ki)zome* first New Year's playing of an
条 *bane* metal spring ⌊instrument
8 金 *haji(ki)gane* spring; hammer (of a gun)
雨 *dan-u* hail of bullets
性 *dansei* elasticity 「sure, criticism
劾 *dangai* impeachment, accusation, cen-
9 指 *danshi* fillip, a snap; a moment
除 *tamayoke* protection against bullets, bulletproof
奏 *dansō* playing on stringed instruments
奏法 *dansōhō* touch (on a stringed instrument)
奏者 *dansōsha* stringed-instrument player
11 痕 *dankon* bullet hole, bullet mark
道 *dandō* trajectory, line of fire
道学 *dandōgaku* ballistics
12 程 *dantei* range, gunshot
着 *danchaku* hit, impact
着距離 *danchaku kyori* range, gunshot
13 傷 *tama kizu* bullet wound
幕 *dammaku* barrage
鉄砲 *haji(ki)deppō* air gun
14 語 *hi(ki)gata(ri)* reciting with one's own stringed accompaniment
16 機 *bane, danki* (metal) spring

頭 *dantō* warhead
薬 *dan-yaku* ammunition
薬車 *dan-yakusha* ammunition car or cart
薬匣 *dan-yakukō* ammunition box
薬庫 *dan-yakuko* powder magazine
薬帯 *dan-yakutai* ammunition belt
薬盒 *dan-yakugō* ammunition pouch
薬筒 *dan-yakutō* cartridge, rounds

— 12 —

彈 1576/F660 See 弾 1575.

— 13 —

彊 1577/F661 Kyō, Gō strong.
8国 *kyōkoku* a strong country
弩 *kyōdo* strong bow
15敵 *kyōteki* strong enemy

— 14 —

彌 1578/F661 See 弥 1565.

— 19 —

鬻 See 5275. [鬲]

彎 1579/F662 Wan curve; stretching a bow.
2入 *wannyū* gulf
4月 *wangetsu* crescent
月状 *wangetsujō* crescent shape
6曲 *wankyoku* curve, crook, bend

RAD. 彐 58

Kei-gashira or *i-no-kashira* pig's head. Also called *yo* (the katakana).
Variants: ⺕, ⺔, 彑. Nickname: Pig's Head.

— 3 —

夛 1580/F-X See 多 1169. [夕]

— 5 —

帚 1581/F613 Shū. Sō. *hōki* broom. [巾]

— 7 —

帰 1582/F1041 歸 皈 A Ki. *kae(ru)* return; take one's leave; come again; come around (time). *kae(su)* send (someone) back. *ki(suru)* come to, arrive at, result in, end in, lead to; belong to, ascribe to; put down to; impute; be due to; fall into (one's power); (his blood) be upon (him). *kae(ri)* return; return trip. *kae(rigake) ni, kae(rishina) ni, kae(rusa) ni* on returning. *(o)kae(ri) nasai* welcome home, welcome back. [止]
1一 *ki-itsu* unity, unification. *ki-itsu suru* be united into one, be reduced to one
2人 *kae(ranu) hito* dead person
4心 *kishin* longing for home
支度 *kae(ri)jitaku* preparations to return
化 *kika* naturalization
化人 *kikajin* naturalized person
5田 *kiden* (an official) returning to the farm
立 *kae(ri)ta(te)* returnee
去 *kae(shi)-sa(ru)* send away
6米 *kibei* nisei who spend their childhood in Japan; returning to America
向 *kikō suru* proceed to
伏 *kifuku* surrender, submission
任 *kinin* returning to one's post
帆 *kihan* returning sailing ship
宅 *kitaku* homecoming, returning home
休 *kikyū* soldier's early release
休兵 *kikyūhei* soldier on leave
7足 *kae(ri) ashi ni* on the return journey
車 *kae(ri)guruma* returning conveyance
村 *kison* returning to one's village
邸 *kitei* returning home
来 *kirai* coming back
8国 *kikoku* returning to one's country
府 *kifu* returning to one's government post
依 *kie* conversion. *kie suru* believe (in Buddhism)
服 *kifuku* surrender, submission
臥 *kiga* retirement from public service
京 *kikyō, kikei* returning to the capital
参 *kisan* returning to a former service
空 *kae(ru) sora* an inclination to return
昔 *kae(ranu) mukashi* the past
9途 *kito* homeward journey
洛 *kiraku* returning to Kyoto
陣 *kijin* returning from the war
降 *kikō* surrender, submission
品 *kae(ri)hin* returned goods
省 *kisei* homecoming
10従 *kijū* surrender
旅 *kae(ranu) tabi* the journey to the next world

校 *kikō suru* return to school
耕 *kikō suru* return to the soil
航 *kikō* homeward passage
郷 *kikyō* returning home
荷 *kae(ri)ni* return cargo
家本能 *kika honnō* homing instinct
納 *kinō* induction (in argumentation)
納的 *kinōteki* inductive
納法 *kinōhō* inductive method
11 道 *kae(ri)michi* the way back, return trip
掛 *kaeriga(ke) ni* on the return journey
船 *kisen* returning to one's ship; a ship that has returned
隊 *kitai* returning to one's unit
巣性 *kisōsei* homing instinct
12 雁 *kigan* returning wild geese ⌈restored to
属 *kizoku suru* revert to, be returned to, be
順 *kijun* submission, return to allegiance
港 *kikō suru* return to port
程 *kitei* distance back, the road back
結 *kiketsu* conclusion, end, result
期 *kiki* time of return
着 *kichaku* return, conclusion
営 *kiei* returning to barracks
朝 *kichō* returning from abroad
朝後 *kichōgo* after returning from abroad
13 路 *kiro* homeward journey; return circuit. *kae(ri)michi* the way back, return trip
農 *kinō* going back to the soil ⌈back
新参 *kae(ri) shinzan* a person who has come
15 趣 *kishu* conclusion
還 *kikan* return, repatriation; feedback
還兵 *kikanhei* returned soldiers
還者 *kikansha* a repatriate ⌈direction
17 嚮 *kishu* conclusion. *kisū* trend, tendency;
20 艦 *kikan* returning to one's warship

8

尋 1583/F564 See 尋 1585. [寸]

彗 1584/F662 SUI comet.
9 星 *suisei, hōkiboshi* comet

9

尋 1585/F566 尋 尋 B JIN fathom. *tazu(neru)* look for, inquire for, ask (someone) a question. *hiro* fathom. *tsu(ide)* next, secondly, subsequently. [寸]
2 人 *tazu(ne)bito* missing person, wanted person
5 出 *tazu(ne)-ida(su), tazu(ne)-da(su)* search out; hunt up, hunt down
6 合 *tazu(ne)-a(waseru)* question one another
7 求 *tazu(ne)-moto(meru)* inquire of; seek for
8 物 *tazu(ne)mono* lost article
者 *tazu(ne)mono* fugitive from justice, man wanted by the police
11 問 *jimmon* questioning
常 *jinjō no* common, usual
常一様 *jinjō-ichiyō* mediocrity; ordinary type
常小学校 *jinjō shōgakkō* elementary school
常科 *jinjōka* elementary course
12 極 *tazu(ne)-kiwa(meru)* search out, inquire in detail
15 窮 *tazu(ne)-kiwa(meru)* search out, inquire in detail

10

彙 1586/F663 I same kind.
12 報 *ihō* bulletin, collection of reports

13

彝 1587/F663 彝 I moral principle.
10 訓 *ikun* moral principles

15

歸 See 帰 1582. [止]

彝 1588/F663 See 彝 1587.

RAD. 彡 59

Kami kazari hair ornament. On right: *sanzukuri* right-hand "hair ornament" or right-hand "three." Nickname: Short Hair (cf. Rad. 190).

4

A 形 1589/F663 GYŌ. KEI shape. *kata* shape, form, make, size, format, mark; pattern, design. *katachi* form, shape; personal appearance. *nari* form, figure, appearance, dress.

4 木 *katagi* wooden model; woodcut printing block
5 代 *katashiro* paper image used in a purification ceremony
付 *katatsu(ki)* a print (cloth)
6 成 *keisei* formation
気 *katagi* spirit, character, trait
似 *keiji* similarity in form
而下 *keijika no* physical, material
而下学 *keijikagaku* the physical sciences
而上 *keijijō no* metaphysical
而上学 *keijijōgaku* metaphysics
式 *keishiki* form; formality
式化 *keshikika* formalization
式主義 *keishiki shugi* formalism, red-tapism
式的 *keishikiteki* formal
式美 *keishikibi* beauty of form
式論 *keishikiron* formalism
7 体 *keitai* shape, form. *narikatachi* appearance
作 *katachizuku(ru)* form, shape, make, mold; build-up
状 *keijō* shape, form
声 *keisei* a type of character one part of which suggests the meaning and one the pronunciation (e.g. 河 and 悶)
見 *katami* memento, souvenir
見分 *katamiwa(ke)* distribution of mementos
9 造 *katachizuku(ru)* form, shape, make, mold; build-up
相 *gyōsō* features, expression; aspect. *keisō* phase, form
姿 *nari sugata* appearance, form, costume
10 振 *narifu(ri)* appearance, costume
容 *keiyō* form, figure, appearance; qualification, description; modifying; figure of speech
容詞 *keiyōshi* adjective
11 許 *katabaka(ri)* only a formality, just a small token
12 勝 *keishō* picturesque scenery; advantageous position
無 *katana(shi)* all knocked out of shape, worthless
象 *keishō* shape, figure; appearance; phenomenon
13 跡 *keiseki* traces, evidences, indications
勢 *keisei* condition, situation, prospects
14 貌 *keibō* form, figure, looks
態 *keitai* shape, form, structure
態学 *keitaigaku* morphology
15 影 *keiei* the form and its shadow; things inseparable
16 鋼 *katakō* shaped steel
骸 *keigai* framework; wreck

6

彥 彦 See 3347.

8

彫 See 236.

B 彩 1590/F665 彩 SAI. *irodo(ru)* color, paint, make up.

6 色 *saishiki* coloring, painting
色画 *saishikiga* colored painting
8 画 *saiga* painting, colored picture
12 雲 *saiun* cloudscape; glowing clouds
14 層 *saisō* chromosphere (of the sun)
管 *saikan* artist's brush
管振 *saikan (o) furu(u)* paint or draw

9

彭 1591/F666 HŌ swelling; sound of a drum; vigorous; prosperous.

12 湃 *hōhai(taru)* surging

須 1592/F2056 SU. SHU. *subeka(raku)* by all means, necessarily. [頁]

8 臾 *shuyu* moment, instant
17 彌壇 *shumidan* Buddhist image dais

11

B 彰 1593/F666 彰 SHŌ. *aki(rakana)* clear.

14 徳 *shōtoku suru* publicly praise

12

B 影 1594/F667 EI shadow. *kage* light; shadow; silhouette; phantom; reflection; figure; trace.

7 身 *kagemi ni* (in) a person's shadow
8 画 *kage-e* silhouette
武者 *kagemusha* general's double; wire-puller; man behind the scenes
法師 *kagebōshi* shadow, shadowy figure, silhouette
12 絵 *kage-e* silhouette
富士 *kage Fuji* Mt. Fuji's reflection; a cloud over Fuji's summit

14像 *eizō* shadow, image, phantom
像崇拝 *eizō sūhai* image worship; iconolatry
16薄 *kage* (*ga*) *usu*(*i*) emaciated

19響 *eikyō* influence, effect, consequences
響力 *eikyōryoku* influence, effect, consequences
響下 *eikyōka ni* under the influence of

RAD. 彳 60

Gyōnimben (a left-hand element like the first part of Rad. 144 *gyō*, the "going" radical, but used only at the left like Rad. 9 *nimben* left-hand "man"; hence, the "going man" radical). All characters historically treated under Rad. 144 行 are, with the exception of the radical character itself, treated herein as Rad. 60. Nickname: Going Man.

彳 1595/F667 TEKI. *tatazu*(*mu*) stop, linger, loiter.

— 3 —

行 See 4213. [行]

⿰彳卫 1596/F-X Nonstandard for 衛 1639.

— 4 —

彷 1597/F667 HŌ. *samayo*(*u*) wander around, stray, loiter.
8彿 *hōfutsu suru* closely resemble
12徨 *hōkō* wandering, fluctuation, variation. *urotsu*(*ku*) loiter, putter, prowl, knock around. *uro-uro* loiteringly, in confusion

A **役** 1598/F668 EKI war, campaign, battle, expedition; exacted unpaid labor. YAKU office, post, position, appointment, duty; role; use, service, help. *eki*(*suru*) employ, enlist the services of, press into service.
2人 *yakunin* official, officer, office holder
人風 *yakunin kaze* official bearing, official dignity
人根性 *yakunin konjō* official bearing
4牛 *ekigyū* work cattle
夫 *ekifu* laborer, coolie ⌈lot
不足 *yakubusoku* dissatisfaction with one's
5立 *yakuda*(*teru*), *yakuda*(*tsu*), *yaku*(*ni*)*ta*(*tsu*) be useful, be helpful, serve the purpose
付 *yakuzu*(*ke*) allotment of duties; role. *yakuzu*(*ki*) responsible person; assuming office
目 *yakume* duty, office, business, role
目柄 *yakumegara de* by virtue of office
6回 *yakumawa*(*ri*) part, burden, responsibility ⌈low–9)
向 *yakumu*(*ki*)=*yakugara* 役柄 (see be-
宅 *yakutaku* official residence
名 *yakumei* official title
8者 *ekisha* servant, emissary; church worker, minister. *yakusha* actor, actress, perform-
所 *yakusho* government office ⌊er, official
所仕事 *yakusho shigoto* bureaucracy, red tape ⌈ism
所式 *yakushoshiki* red tape, departmental-
所風 *yakushofū* red tape, departmentalism
9柄 *yakugara* nature of one's office, one's position ⌈board; staff
10員 *yakuin* officer, official, person in charge;
員会 *yakuinkai* board meeting
11得 *yakutoku* the extra emoluments of office
務 *ekimu* labor, service
12場 *yakuba* city hall, a public office
割 *yakuwa*(*ri*) allotment of duties; role
替 *yakuga*(*e*) change of post ⌈assistant priest
13僧 *yakusō* temple sexton; officiating priest;
14徳 *yakutoku* emolument, excess remuneration, privileges incidental to an office
15儀 *yakugi* duty, office, business, role

— 5 —

彽 1599/F669 See 低 406.

徂 1600/F670 So go.

彿 1601/F669 髴 FUTSU dimly.

B **径** 1602/F675 徑 KEI path; diameter; method. *michi* (see under 道 4724.0.).
6行 *keikō* going around; developments
10庭 *keitei* the great difference between indi-
13路 *keiro* course, route, channel ⌊viduals

B **征** 1603/F670 SEI. *sei*(*suru*) attack the rebellious; collect taxes.

5 圧 *seiatsu* control, conquest
6 衣 *sei-i* military uniform; traveling garb
伏 *seifuku*＝征服 (see below–8)
伐 *seibatsu* subjection, conquest; chastisement, punishment, extermination
夷 *sei-i* pacifying the barbarians
夷大将軍 *Sei-i Taishōgun* Commander-in-Chief of the Expeditionary Force Against the Barbarians
8 服 *seifuku* conquest, subjugation; mastery, overcoming
服者 *seifukusha* conqueror, overcomer
服欲 *seifukuyoku* an ambition to have others carry out one's ideas
9 途 *seito* military expedition; journey, travel
客 *seikaku* traveler
10 馬 *seiba* steed; war horse; traveler's horse
討 *seitō*＝*seibatsu* 征伐 (see above–6)
討軍 *seitōgun* expeditionary force
11 略 *seiryaku* conquest, subjugation
13 戦 *seisen* going off to war
14 塵 *seijin* cavalry dust; road dust; travel
17 韓 *seikan* invasion of Korea

彼 1604 / F668 B HI he; that. *kare* he. *ka(no)*, *a(no)* that, the. *are* that, that time. *are(demo)* in a way, in spite of appearances, as it is.
3 女 *kanojo* she; girl friend
丈 *aredake* that much
4 氏 *kareshi* he; beau, lover
切 *are(k)ki(ri)*, *aregi(ri)*, *areki(ri)* since that time; only that much
方 *anata*, *kanata*, *achi*, *atchi*, *achira* that; the other; the other side; there, yonder; foreign country. *atchi* Get out of here.
方任 *anatamaka(se)* letting things slide
方此方 *anata-konata*, *achikochi*, *achira-kochira* here and there, to and fro, fore and aft
5 処 *asuko*, *asoko*, *kashiko* yonder, over there, that place
奴 *aitsu*, *kyatsu*, *kayatsu* that fellow, that guy
世 *a(no)yo* the next world
6 地 *ka(no)chi* that land
此 *are kore*, *kare kore*, *are(ya)-kore(ya)* this and that, one thing or another
7 我 *higa* oneself and others, each other
8 者誰時 *kawataredoki* dawn
岸 *higan* equinoctial week; Buddhist services during that week; the other shore; goal
岸桜 *higanzakura* early-flowering cherry
9 是 *are-kore* this or that
12 程 *arehodo* so much, to that extent
等 *karera* they

往 1605 / F669 往 A Ō. *ina(su)* let go; chase away. *yuki* going; travel. *yu(ku)* (see under 行 4213.0).
4 日 *ōjitsu* ancient times
5 古 *ōko* ancient times
生 *ōjō* death, submission. *ōjō suru* be at one's wit's end
生際 *ōjōgiwa* the point of death
6 返 *yu(ki)kae(ri)* round trip
交 *yukikai*＝行交 4213.6
年 *ōnen* years ago, formerly, the years past
7 来 *yukiki*, *ōrai* coming and going; street traffic; road, street, highway, boulevard; fluctuations; correspondence, association; occurring to the mind
来止 *ōraido(me)* No Thorofare, Road Closed
8 往 *ōō* sometimes, occasionally, often
券 *ōken* the going half of a round-trip ticket
昔 *ōseki* ancient times
者 *ōsha* the past
事 *ōji* the past, past events
9 信 *ōshin* first half of a reply card
10 時 *ōji* ancient times
航 *ōkō* outward voyage
帰 *yu(ki)-kae(ri)* round trip
11 訪 *ōhō* visit, interview
12 診 *ōshin* doctor's visit, house call
復 *ōfuku* round trip; correspondence; association
復切符 *ōfuku kippu* return ticket
復運動 *ōfuku undō* reciprocating motion
復葉書 *ōfuku hagaki* return postcard
復爆撃 *ōfuku bakugeki* shuttle raid
13 路 *ōro* outward journey
15 還 *yu(ki)-kae(ri)*, *ōkan* traffic, coming and going, round trip; highway

6

徊 1606 / F671 KAI wandering.

衍 1607 / F1685 EN overflowing. [行]
4 文 *embun* pleonasm, redundancy
6 字 *enji* superfluous character
13 義 *engi* expansion, amplification; commentary, adaptation

律 1608 / F671 A RICHI, RITSU law, regulation; rhythm. *ris(suru)* judge, settle, gauge, control. *Ritsu* Buddhist sect originating in the eighth century.
4 文 *ritsubun* the provisions of law; poetry
5 令 *ritsuryō* ancient laws. *ritsurei* national laws
8 例 *ritsurei* ordinance, criminal law
法 *rippō* law, rule, legislation; Law of God
法主義 *rippō shugi* legalism
法学者 *rippō gakusha* scribe, lawyer

10格 *ritsukaku* a rule, versification, metrical scheme ⌈periodic motion
11動 *ritsudō* rhythm, rhythmic movement,
13義 *richigi* honesty, integrity, simplicity, sincerity, loyalty ⌈man
義者 *richigimono* honest and industrious
14語 *ritsugo* poetic verse ⌈man
15儀者 *richigimono* honest and industrious

A 待 1609/F671 TAI waiting. *ma(tsu) vi* and *vt* wait, wait for; expect, watch for; depend on; treat, deal with. *ma(chi-agumu)* be tired of waiting. *ma(tta)* hold on, not ready. *ma(taseru)* detain, keep waiting.

2人 *ma(chi)bito* expected visitor
6伏 *ma(chi)bu(seru)* lie in wait for. *ma(chi)bu(se)* ambush, lying in wait
合 *ma(chi)-a(u)* wait for each other. *ma(chi)-a(waseru)* waiting at a set time. *machiai* tea-ceremony waiting room; geisha entertainment place
合所 *machiaijo* rendezvous; waiting booth
合室 *machiaishitsu* waiting room
7侘 *ma(chi)-wa(biru)* be tired of waiting
8明 *ma(chi)-a(kasu)* wait all night
命 *taimei* awaiting orders; being put on the waiting list
受 *ma(chi)-u(keru)* await, expect ⌈ing
9草臥 *ma(chi)-kutabi(reru)* be tired of wait-
10倦 *ma(chi)-agu(mu), ma(chi)-aki(ru)* be tired
針 *ma(chi)bari* marking pin ⌊of waiting
兼 *ma(chi)-ka(neru)* wait impatiently for
時間 *ma(chi) jikan* waiting time
11遇 *taigū* treatment, reception, entertainment, (hotel) service; salary, remuneration; rank
偶 *taigū*=word above ⌈in vain
惚 *ma(chi)-bo(keru), ma(chi)-bō(keru)* wait
設 *ma(chi)-mō(keru)* expect, wait expectantly for
望 *ma(chi)-nozo(mu)* look for, wait eagerly for. *taibō* expectant waiting
12遠 *ma(chi)dō(shii), ma(chi)dō(i)* being long in coming; waiting anxiously for
期 *taiki*=待機 (see below–16)
焦 *ma(chi)-ko(gareru)* wait eagerly for
無 *ma(tta)na(shi)de* without waiting
14厭 *ma(chi)-agu(mu)* be tired of waiting
構 *ma(chi)-kama(eru)* watch for, wait eagerly for, be prepared for
網 *ma(chi)ami* set net
暮 *ma(chi)-ku(rasu)* wait all day for
15避 *taihi* shunting (in railroading); taking shelter; escaping
避線 *taihisen* siding, sidetrack
避壕 *taihigō* dugout, shelter, trench

16機 *taiki suru* watch and wait, stand by, wait for a chance

A 後 1610/F672 Go, Kō back, rear, behind. *ato* back, rear; results; remainder, sequel; posterity; successor; survivor; effect, influence; estate. *ato no* back, rear, posterior; previous, last; later, subsequent; next, following; future. *ato ni* after, behind, back, backward; ago; next. *oku(rasu), oku(raseru)* retard, delay, defer. *oku(re)* failure, defeat; backwardness, shyness, fear. *oku(reru)* be late, be delayed, be overdue; lag behind; (clocks) lose. *ushi(ro)* back, rear, behind. *ushiro(metai)* underhanded, suspicious. *nochi* after, since then; future; after one's death. *-go* after, afterwards, later on, since, hence.

2人 *kōjin* posterity, future generations
3口 *atokuchi* aftertaste; remainder; a later turn, engagement, or appointment
山 *atoyama* miner's helper
千両 *ushi(ro) senryō* the beauty of a woman seen from the back ⌈back. *gote* passivity
4手 *ushi(ro)de* (tied with) hands behind the
毛 *oku(re)ge* tresses, stray locks ⌈year
厄 *atoyaku* year following one's critical
片付 *atokatazu(ke)* clearing up, putting things in order ⌈later on
日 *gojitsu, gonichi* later on, some other day
日談 *gojitsudan* reminiscences, recollections
方 *kōhō, shirie, atokata* rear, back. *nochikata*
方部隊 *kōhō butai* rear guards ⌊later
方勤務 *kōhō kimmu* the home front
天 *kōten* results of environment
天性 *kōtensei* characteristics acquired from one's environment
天的 *kōtenteki* acquired, cultivated
5代 *kōdai* future generations, posterity
払 *atobara(i)* deferred payment
半 *kōhan* latter half
世 *kōsei, nochi (no) yo* coming age; last days, posterity. *gose, nochi (no) yo* the next world, the future life
弁天 *ushiro benten* the beauty of a woman seen from the back ⌈selling out
仕舞 *atojimai* clearing up, winding up,
生 *kōsei* being born later; younger people. *goshō* the future life ⌈carefully
生大事 *goshō daiji ni* religiously, earnestly,
半生 *kōhansei* latter half of life
半期 *kōhanki* latter half year
半戦 *kōhansen* latter half of a game
6回 *atomawa(shi)* postponement
向 *ushi(ro)mu(ki)* looking backward
列 *kōretsu* rear, back row
灯 *kōtō* taillight

合 *ushi(ro)a(wase) ni* back to back
光 *gokō* halo, corona
先 *atosaki* front and rear; first and last; both ends; context; circumstances, consequences. *atosaki ni suru* reverse, invert
年 *kōnen* in later years, afterward
任 *kōnin* successor
任難 *kōninnan* difficulty in finding a successor
7 足 *atoashi, ushi(ro) ashi* hind leg
身 *kōshin* one's future rebirth; a successor organization
図 *kōto* plans for the future
序 *kōjo* postscript to a book
戻 *atomodo(ri)* going backward, retrogression
述 *kōjutsu suru* state hereafter
作 *atosaku* second crop
役 *atoyaku* successor
来 *kōrai* the future
見 *kōken, ushi(ro)mi* guardianship; assistance
見人 *kōkennin* guardian, tutor, assistant
車 *kōsha* rear car; rear wheel; gun carriage
車軸 *kōshajiku* back axle
尾 *kōbi* rear, tail
尾灯 *kōbitō* taillight
8 金 *atokin, atogane* balance of payment
門 *kōmon* back gate; back door
送 *kōsō suru* send to the rear; send later
退 *atozusa(ri), atoshiza(ri), atojisa(ri)* falling back, drawing back. *kōtai* retreat, retrogression
味 *atoaji* aftertaste
押 *ato-o(shi)* pushing, backing, boosting
明 *ushi(ro) aka(ri)* a light from the back
板 *ushi(ro) ita* backboard (of a wagon)
肢 *kōshi* hind legs
刻 *gokoku* later on, afterward
夜 *goya* from midnight to morning
命 *kōmei* further instructions
昆 *kōkon* descendants, posterity
妻 *gosai* second wife
学 *kōgaku* younger scholars; younger generation; knowledge to be available in the future
者 *kōsha* the latter
始末 *ato shimatsu* settlement, liquidation, clearing up
知恵 *atojie* hindsight
事 *kōji* future affairs; affairs after one's death
事託 *kōji (o) taku(su)* entrust all to someone when dying
9 面 *kōmen* back side (of something)
首 *ushiro kubi* the back of the head
胤 *kōin* descendant, scion
便 *kōbin* next mail
後 *atoato* distant future. *nochinochi* distant future; future life
咲 *oku(re)za(ki)* late blossoms
悔 *kōkai* repentance, remorse
指 *ushi(ro) yubi* bird's hind toe; finger of scorn
陣 *gojin, kōjin* rear guard
段 *kōdan* latter part (of the story)

前 *ushi(ro)-mae* with front side back
軍 *kōgun* rear guard
室 *kōshitsu* widow; widow of a noble
姿 *ushi(ro) sugata* retreating figure, appearance from the back
架 *kōka* toilet
思案 *atojian* afterthought
奏 *kōsō* postlude
奏曲 *kōsōkyoku* postlude
10 庭 *kōtei* back yard or garden
逸 *kōitsu suru* fumble (a ball)
流 *kōryū* slip stream
祓 *atobarai* cleansing a room after the coffin has left
記 *kōki* postscript
宮 *kōkyū* imperial consort; harem; palace
家 *goke* the bereaved family, widow, widowhood
害 *kōgai* later damage
釜 *atogama* successor
窄 *atosuboma(ri)* narrower and smaller at the end
書 *atoga(ki)* postscript. *kōsho* sequel to a book
部 *kōbu* rear, stern, back part
部灯 *kōbutō* taillight
進 *kōshin* retreat, moving backward; younger generation
進地域 *kōshin chi-iki* underdeveloped areas
進性 *kōshinsei no* backward
進国 *kōshinkoku* backward country
進諸国 *kōshin shokoku* backward nations
11 清 *atogiyo(me)*=*atobarai* 後祓 (see above—10)
添 *nochizo(i)* second wife
略 *kōryaku* omitting the last part of an article
脚 *ato ashi* hind legs
産 *kōsan, atozan, nochizan* afterbirth, placenta
患 *kōkan* seeds of trouble; a future worry
祭 *ato (no) matsu(ri)* too late for the fair, too late for the doctor
12 場 *goba* afternoon market session
項 *kōkō* following clause
棒 *atobō* rear palanquin bearer
程 *nochihodo* later on
期 *kōki* latter period; late (Nara); latter half year; second semester
景 *kōkei* setting, background
葉 *kōyō* posterity, future generations; the latter days of an era
替 *atogawa(ri)* successor
装 *kōsō* breech-loading
報 *kōhō* later report, further information
援 *kōen* assistance, support, backing
援会 *kōenkai* supporters' association
援者 *kōensha* backer, supporter, patron, sponsor
13 園 *kōen* back yard
暗 *ushi(ro)gura(i)* shady, underhanded, suspicious, secretive
楯 *ushi(ro)date* backing, support, protection; backer, supporter
腹 *atobara* afterpains; child by second wife

詰 *gozu(me)* rear guard
馳 *oku(re)base* eleventh hour, last minute
幕 *atomaku* next; next job
裔 *kōei* descendants
嗣 *kōshi* heir, successor
鉢巻 *ushi(ro) hachimaki* head band tied behind
置詞 *kōchishi* postposition
続 *kōzoku no* succeeding, following
続年度 *kōzoku nendo* the following fiscal year
継 *kōkei* succession; successor, heir
継内閣 *kōkei naikaku* incoming cabinet
継者 *kōkeisha* successor, heir
14 腐 *atogusa(ri)* trouble afterward
聞 *kōbun* later information
塵 *kōjin* second best; subordination; second fiddle; dust raised after vehicles
髪 *ushi(ro)gami* the hair at the back of the head
15 衛 *kōei* rear guard
編 *kōhen* later volume
輪 *atowa, kōrin* back wheel
影 *ushi(ro) kage* retreating figure, appearance from the back
憂 *kōyū* future worry
篇 *kōhen* last volume, later volumes, last part of the book; sequel
輩 *kōhai* younger men; younger generation; one's juniors
賢 *kōken* wise men of the future
16 頭 *kōtō* back of the head
頭部 *kōtōbu* back of the head
頸部 *kōkeibu* nape of the neck
17 輿 *atogoshi* rear palanquin bearer
療法 *kōryōhō* after treatment
18 難 *gōnan, kōnan* future trouble, consequences
21 顧 *kōko* looking back; anxiety

7

徑 1611 / F675 See **径** 1602.

B **徐** 1612 / F674 Jo. *omomu(ro) ni* slowly, deliberately, gently.
6 行 *jokō suru* go slowly
8 歩 *joho* walking slowly
10 徐 *jojo ni, sorosoro* gradually, steadily, slowly; quietly
14 漕 *josō suru* paddle, row slowly

A **従** 1613 / F677 **從** Shō. Ju. Jū secondary, incidental, subordinate accessory, junior; retainer; follow. *shitaga(u)* obey, submit to, comply with, observe (a law); follow; accompany. *shitaga(eru)* be accompanied by, take (someone) with you; subjugate, subdue. *shitaga(tte)* consequently, therefore; in accordance with, in proportion to, as. *ju-* junior or second (in court ranks).
3 士 *jūshi* attendant, retainer
5 犯 *jūhan* accomplice; complicity
兄 *jūkei* elder cousin
兄弟 *itoko, jūkeitei* male cousin
6 行 *shitaga(i)-yu(ku)* go after, follow after
因 *jūin* secondary cause
7 兵 *jūhei* guards
弟 *jūtei* younger cousin
来 *jūrai* heretofore; existing
8 妹 *jūmai* younger female cousin
物 *jūbutsu* accessory (in law)
卒 *jūsotsu* servant of a soldier
者 *jūsha* follower, attendant, valet, retinue, servant
事 *jūji suru* engage in, carry on, practice medicine
姉 *jūshi* older female cousin
姉妹 *jūshimai, itoko* female cousin
9 前 *jūzen ni* heretofore. *jūzen no* previous, former
軍 *jūgun suru* follow the army; join the colors
軍記者 *jūgun kisha* war correspondent
軍記章 *jūgun kishō* war medal
10 容 *shōyō(taru)* composed, calm, tranquil
11 婢 *jūhi* servant woman
12 順 *jūjun na* submissive, obedient, docile, gentle, meek, tame, pliant, amenable
量税 *jūryōzei* specific duty
属 *jūzoku* subordination; dependency
属文 *jūzokubun* subordinate clause
属的 *jūzokuteki* subordinate, dependent
属節 *jūzoku setsu* subordinate clause
13 業 *jūgyō suru* be employed; resume work
業者 *jūgyōsha* employee
業員 *jūgyōin* employee, working force
14 僕 *jūboku* attendant male servant
15 横 *jūō*=縦横 3597.15
18 騎 *jūki* followers on horseback

A **徒** 1614 / F675 To party, set, gang, companions; people. *ada* emptiness, vanity, futility, uselessness, faithlessness, ephemeral thing. *itazura* vanity; uselessness. *itazu(ra) ni* in vain, uselessly, aimlessly. *tada, tada no* free, gratis. *tada(naranu)* unusual, extraordinary, serious. *tada* ordinarily. *ada(shi)* fickle, vain; another. *kachi* walking. *muda* futility, uselessness, waste. *kachi de* on foot.
2 人 *tadabito* common man. *adabito* fickle person. *kachibito* foot traveler
3 口 *adaguchi* unnecessary words. *mudaguchi* idle talk, nonsense
士 *kachi* foot soldier
4 心 *adagokoro* fickle heart
手 *toshu* empty-handed, penniless
手体操 *toshu taisō* calisthenics
手空拳 *toshu-kūken de* empty-handed; without capital
5 矢 *adaya* futile arrow shot
立 *kachida(chi)* setting out on foot
広 *dada(p)piro(i), dadabiro(i)* tremendously broad

[6]行 *tokō* going afoot
死 *toshi suru* die in vain. *toshi* a dog's death
刑 *tokei* penal servitude, prison term
名 *adana* rumor about a romance
[7]言 *mudagoto* useless words
走 *kachibashi(ri)* running on foot
足 *muda-ashi suru* go on a fruitless errand
身 *tada(naranu) mi* pregnant woman
花 *adabana* an abortive flower
労 *torō* wasted effort, lost labor
弟 *totei* apprenticeship; apprentice; errand boy
弟制度 *totei seido* apprentice system
弟学校 *totei gakkō* apprentice school
弟教育 *totei kyōiku* education of apprentices
弟期間 *totei kikan* apprenticeship term
弟養成 *totei yōsei* apprenticeship training
[8]波 *adanami* noisy wave
物 *adamono* useless thing, fleeting thing
者 *tadamono* ordinary person
事 *tadagoto, adagoto* useless thing, fleeting thing, trivial matter
武者 *kachimusha* foot soldier
歩 *toho, kachi* walking
歩兵 *tohohei* foot soldier
歩者 *tohosha* pedestrian
歩連絡 *toho renraku* a transfer involving a walk
歩旅行 *toho ryokō* hike, hiking, walking tour
歩旅行者 *toho ryokōsha* foot traveler
歩競走 *toho kyōsō* walking race
[9]食 *toshoku* life of idleness
[10]骨 *mudabone* fruitless effort, useless endeavor
桜 *adazakura* ephemeral cherry flowers
党 *totō* conspirators; conspiracy; faction, junta
荷 *kachini* foot traveler's baggage
[11]渉 *kachiwata(ri), toshō* fording
[12]疎 *adaorosoka ni* (think) light (of). *adaorosoka na* careless
雲 *adagumo* fleeting cloud
然 *tsurezure, tozen* tedium, leisure hours
費 *tohi* waste
[13]路 *kachiji* going afoot; the road one travels afoot
跣 *kachihadashi* going barefooted
夢 *adayume* idle dream
業 *adawaza* some other thing; useless thing
[14]爾 *toji* something worthless or meaningless
[15]論 *toron* worthless argument
輩 *tohai* group, set, fellows

8

従 1615 / F677 See **従** 1613.

徠 1616 / F678 F123 See **来** 202.

徛 1617 / F-X KI cross over.

徜 1618 / F677 SHŌ wander.
[9]徉 *shōyō* wandering

徘 1619 / F677 HAI wander.
[9]徊 *haikai*＝俳徊 485.9

衒 1620 / F1686 GEN. *tera(u)* show off, parade, display; pretend, feign. [行]
[6]気 *genki* affectation, ostentation, vanity
[8]学 *gengaku* pedantry, display of learning

A **術** 1621 / F1686 **術** JUTSU art, technique, skill; means; artifice, trick, stratagem; resources; magic, conjury. *sube* way, means, resource. [行]
[4]中 *jutchū* trick, trap
[8]知 *jutchi* wisdom and accomplishments
者 *jutsusha* witch, magician, conjuror
[9]計 *jukkei* stratagem, ruse, trick, policy
[12]策 *jussaku* artifice, stratagem, trick, intrigue, policy
無 *subena(shi), jutsuna(i)* nothing can be done
[13]数 *jussū*＝*jussaku* 術策 (see above–12)
[14]語 *jutsugo* technical term, terminology

A **得** 1622 / F676 TOKU profit, advantage, benefit. *e(ru), u(ru)* get, acquire, find, earn, win, gain, receive; can, be able to, may; commit (sin). *e(tagaru)* covet, have a desire for. *toku(suru)* gain, save; benefit. *e(tari)* fine, excellent. *e(te)* being apt to.
[4]分 *tokubun* profits, winnings, one's share
心 *tokushin* consent; conviction; satisfaction
心尽 *tokushinzu(ku)* mutual consent
手 *ete* strong point, specialty, forte
手物 *etemono* one's specialty
手勝手 *etegatte, etekatte* selfishness, wilfulness
[5]失 *tokushitsu* pros and cons, gains and losses, desirability
[6]安 *eyasu(i)* easily obtainable
[7]言 *e(mo)-i(warenu)* indescribable, unspeakable, indefinable, exquisite
体 *etai* nature, character
[8]物 *emono* weapon
易 *eyasu(i)* easily obtainable
[9]度 *tokudo suru* enter the (Buddhist) priesthood
点 *tokuten* marks, score, runs
点掲示板 *tokuten keijiban* scoreboard
[11]道 *tokudō* attainment of (Buddhist) salvation
得 *tokutoku toshite* proudly, triumphantly
票 *tokuhyō* votes obtained

票数 *tokuhyōsū* votes obtained
12策 *tokusaku* profitable plan, good plan. *tokusaku na* advisable, wise, expedient
喪 *tokusō* gaining and losing
13業士 *tokugyōshi* special-school graduate
意 *tokui(garu)* be elated. *tokui* prosperity; triumph, elation; strong point; customer, client
意回 *tokuimawa(ri)* calling on customers; traveling salesman
意気 *tokuige na* proud, elated ⌈customer
意先 *tokuisaki* customer, client; credit
意顔 *tokuigao* triumphant air
意満面 *tokui-mammen* pride
15賢 *e(tari) kashiko(shi)* That's it! Wonderful! Just what I had hoped for. I was just waiting for this
18難 *egata(i)* rare, hard to get
顔 *e(tari)gao* look of triumph, proud face

9

徨 1623 F680 Kō wandering.

徧 1624 F680 HEN revolve; everywhere.

B 循 1625 F681 JUN follow.

6吏 *junri* faithful official
15還 *junkan* circulation, rotation, cycle
17環 *junkan* circulation, rotation, cycle
環期 *junkanki* cycle
環線 *junkansen* loop line
環論 *junkanron*＝next word
環論証 *junkan ronshō* circular reasoning, begging the question, vicious circle

B 街 1626 F1686 KAI. GAI street, avenue; town. *machi* town; quarters; street. [行]

3上 *gaijō* street
6灯 *gaitō* street light, road lamp
7角 *machi kado* street corner
10郭 *gaikaku* area between streets, a block
11道 *kaidō, gaidō* highway
13路 *gairo* road, street, avenue, arcade
路樹 *gairoju* shade tree, roadside tree
16録 *gairoku* recorded street interview
頭 *gaitō* street ⌈tographer
頭写真師 *gaitō shashinshi* pavement pho-
頭募金 *gaitō bokin* street solicitation
頭演説 *gaitō enzetsu* street speech ⌈view
頭録音 *gaitō rokuon* recorded street inter-

A 復 1627 F680 FUKU. *fuku(suru)* return to. revert to, be restored to, resume (one's duties); revenge; reward. *mata, mata to* again.

3小作 *mata kosaku* subtenancy, sublease
4文 *fukubun* translating classical Japanese back into classical Chinese
氏 *fukushi* resumption of former name
円 *fukuen* end of an eclipse
仇 *fukkyū, fukukyū* revenge, reprisal
元 *fukugen* restoration to original state
5旧 *fukkyū, fukukyū* recovery, restoration, restitution, rehabilitation
申 *fukushin* report
刊 *fukkan* reissue, revived publication
写 *mata-utsu(shi), fukusha* a recopy; copying again ⌈regime), reaction
古 *fukko* restoration, revival (of a former
古調 *fukkochō* trend toward old styles
6任 *fukunin* reappointment, reinstatement
交 *fukkō* restoration of diplomatic relations
7位 *fukui* restoration, rehabilitation, reinstatement, reinstallment
役 *fukueki* rejoining the colors
弟子 *mata deshi* disciple of one's disciple
8刻 *fukkoku* reproducing a book from identi-
命 *fukumei* report ⌊cal plates
券 *fukuken* ticket's return portion
9故 *fukko*＝復古 (see above–5)
奏 *fukusō suru* reinvestigate and report to the throne
活 *fukkatsu* revival, rebirth, resuscitation, regeneration, resurrection
活祭 *Fukkatsusai* Easter
10原 *fukugen* restoration (to original state)
借 *fukushaku, mataga(ri)* subtenancy
校 *fukkō, fukukō* return to school, readmit-
祚 *fukuso* restoration to the throne ⌊tance
航 *fukkō* return voyage
配 *fukuhai* resumption of dividends
党 *fukutō* reinstatement in a party
書 *fukusho* a written answer ⌈reversion
帰 *fukki* return, comeback, reinstatement,
従兄弟 *mata itoko* second cousin
員 *fukuin* demobilization
員兵 *fukuinhei* demobilized soldier
員者 *fukuinsha* demobilized persons
11唱 *fukushō*＝復誦 (see below–14)
習 *fukushū* review. *sarai* review; rehearsal
12復 *matamata* again, repeatedly
答 *fukutō* reply, response
貸 *mataga(shi)* sublease
13辟 *fukuheki* restoration of a ruler
路 *fukuro* return trip
業 *fukugyō suru* return to work
14聞 *matagi(ki)* hearing over again
読 *fukudoku* review ⌈command)
誦 *fukushō suru* recite, rehearse; repeat (a

15 権 *fukken, fukkuken* reinstatement, rehabilitation, restoration of rights
縁 *fukuen* restoring marital or other relations
調 *fukuchō* a comeback
請 *mata-u(ke)* subcontract
請負 *mata ukeoi* subcontract
16 興 *fukkō* revival, resuscitation, resurgence, restoration, rehabilitation, a comeback, renaissance
18 職 *fukushoku* reinstatement, resumption of office, reappointment
20 籍 *fukuseki* reinstating as a member; returning to original domicile
23 讎 *fukushū* revenge, reprisal, retaliation
讐 *fukushū* revenge, reprisal, retaliation

B **御** 1628 / F678 Go honorific prefix. Gyo imperial honorary prefix. *gyo-(suru)* control, manage, manipulate, govern; handle; drive (a cart). *o-, on-, mi-* honorific prefixes.

1 一新 *go-isshin* Meiji restoration
2 八 *oyatsu* eating between meals
力 *michikara* power of God
人好 *ohitoyo(shi)* easily duped
七夜 *oshichiya* seventh day after birth
3 子 *miko* children of the king; Son of God, Christ
三家 *Gosanke* the Three Tokugawa Branches
大 *ontai* boss, governor, general
大葬 *gotaisō* imperial funeral
下 *osa(ge)* hair hanging down the back
下問 *gokamon* emperor's question
上 *okami* emperor, government, authorities; a noble; hostess at a restaurant
上様 *okamisan* wife, madame. *onobo(ri)san* visitor from the country
4 心 *mikokoro* God's will, God's purpose
方 *mikata* friend, ally, supporter. *onkata* person (polite)
水 *omizu* water; holy water
中 *onchū* and Company; Messrs.
互 *otagai ni* mutually, together
尤 *gomotto(mo)* quite right, reasonable
不浄 *gofujō* lavatory, toilet, latrine, comfort station
切匙 *osekkai* meddling; officious person
太鼓 *otaiko* professional jester; drum; the puffed-out bow (of an obi); flattery
日様 *ohisama* the sun
月様 *otsukisama* the moon
父様 *otōsama, otōsan* father
引摺 *ohikizuri* trailing skirt; immoral woman
手 *mite* the hand of God
手玉 *otedama* jackstones; bean bags
手打 *oteu(chi)* a lord killing his retainer
手洗 *mitarashi* holy water at a shrine. *ote-ara(i)* toilet, lavatory; washstand
手許金 *otemotokin* privy purse
5 代 *miyo* reign, period
札 *ofuda* Shinto talisman
汁 *otsuke* the broth of cooked dishes
礼 *orei*＝*rei* (see under 礼 3229.0)
包 *okuru(mi), otsutsu(mi)* child's quilt
民 *mitami* people of the king
世 *miyo* reign, period
台所 *midaidokoro* nobleman's wife
付武官 *otsuki bukan* aide, military attaché
玉 *otama* egg; tadpole
玉杓子 *otamajakushi* tadpole; wooden tablespoon
生大事 *goshō-daiji ni* zealously
生憎様 *oainikusama* I am sorry.
出 *oide* (polite) coming; going; being
出来 *odeki* rash, eruption
出座 *odemashi* going out, visiting; presence
出御出 *oide-oide* said beckoning to a person to come
召 *ome(shi) ni naru* ride; call (someone); wear
召列車 *ome(shi) ressha* train for royalty
召物 *ome(shi)mono* clothes
召替 *ome(shi)ka(e)* changing cars; changing clothes
召縮緬 *ome(shi) chirimen* striped crepe
召艦 *ome(shi)kan* imperial flagship
目文字 *omemoji* meeting someone
目玉 *omedama* scolding, reprimand
目目 *omeme* the eye (child's word)
目出度 *omedeta(i)* happy, auspicious. *omedetō* congratulations
目通 *omedō(ri)* an audience (with), interview; presence
目掛 *ome(ni)ka(karu)* meet (someone). *ome-(ni)ka(keru)* show someone (something)
用 *goyō* your order; your business; official business; king's business
用地 *goyōchi* imperial estate
用邸 *goyōtei* detached palace, imperial villa
用始 *goyō haji(me)* reopening of offices after New Year's
用納 *goyō-osa(me)* year-end office closing
用達 *goyōtashi* purveyors to the government
用掛 *goyōgakari* Imperial Household official
用商人 *goyō shōnin* purveyor to the government
用組合 *goyō kumiai* company union
用新聞 *goyō shimbun* government newspaper
用聞 *goyōki(ki)* taking orders
6 血 *onchi* blood (polite); the blood of Christ
衣 *gyo-i* imperial clothes
好 *okono(mi) no* favorite, requested
旨 *mimune* nobleman's will; God's will
字 *on(no)ji* enough
守 *omamori* a charm,
宇 *gyo-u* imperial reign

先 *osaki* the future. *osaki e, osaki ni* (go) ahead of me; first. *onsaki* one who walked before a noble
存 *gozon(ji)* your acknowledgement; your knowledge; your acquaintance, your
自身 *gojishin* himself, herself ⌊awareness
百度 *ohyakudo* circling a shrine 100 times
当家 *gotōke* your house, your family
気色 *mikeshiki* view (polite)
気毒様 *oki(no)dokusama* I am sorry.
朱印 *goshuin* shogun's sealed letter
朱印船 *goshuinsen* shogunate-licensed ship
多分 *gotabun* friend of the majority
多忙中 *gotabōchū* while you were so busy
名 *mina* God's name. *gyomei* emperor's name, imperial signature ⌈seal
名御璽 *gyomei-gyoji* imperial seal, privy
7 言 *mikotoba* God's Word, the Bible. *mikoto* words of a ruler
身 *omi, ommi* you (familiar)
位 *mikurai* the throne
決 *okima(ri)* usage, custom, routine
社 *miyashiro* shrine
告 *mitsuge, otsuge* oracle, message
忍 *oshino(bi)* traveling incognito
陀仏 *odabutsu* dead man
来光 *goraikō* mountain-top sunrise viewing; mountain-top sunrise
沙汰 *gosata* words of a ruler
杓文字 *oshamoji* ladle, dipper, scoop
足労様 *Gosokurōsama* You have gone to much trouble
見外 *omiso(re)* failure to recognize
見知置 *omishi(ri)o(ki)* meeting you
伽 *otogi* keeping (a person) company; nursing (a patient)
伽国 *otogi (no) kuni* fairyland
声 *mikoe* your voice; the voice of God
声掛 *okoega(kari)* command, recommenda-
8 金 *okane* money ⌊tion
門 *mikado* emperor, palace gate
使 *mitsuka(i)* angel; messenger
抱 *okaka(e)* one's personal attendant (chauffeur, doctor, etc.)
杯 *gyohai* cup (polite); emperor's cup
物 *gyobutsu* imperial property
参 *omai(ri)* visiting a shrine or temple
幸 *miyuki, gokō* visit or attendance of an
苑 *gyoen* imperial garden ⌊emperor
免 *gomen* your pardon; declining (something); dismissal; permission; licensed, chartered. *gomen nasai* Pardon me.
者 *gyosha* driver, coachman, bus driver
事 *onkoto* thing (honorific); you (famiilar)
虎子 *omaru* bedpan, pot
乳母 *omba* wet nurse

法度 *gohatto* law, ordinance; prohibition
国 *mikuni* heavenly kingdom; our country
国風 *mikuniburi* Japanese manners; Japanese literature ⌈*goku* an offering
供 *otomo suru* accompany. *osona(e), gokū,*
供料 *gokūryō* votive offering
所 *gosho* an old imperial palace
所車 *goshoguruma* (ancient) ox carriage
9 拾 *ohiro(i)* walking, hiking
柳 *gyoryū* tamarisk
冠 *okammuri* displeasure
負 *oma(ke)* something extra, embellishment, exaggeration. *oma(ke) ni* further-
通夜 *otsuya, otsūya* a wake ⌊more
為転 *otamegoka(shi)* cheating under pretense of kindness
星様 *ohoshisama* the stars
持 *omo(tase)* gift
持物 *omota(se)mono* gift ⌈volcanoes)
神火 *goshinka* the fires of the gods (in
神酒 *omiki* sacred wine, wine offering
前 *mimae* before (God). *omae* you; Hey there you. *gozen* before a noble; you (polite); (an ancient) term of address for a titled lady
前会議 *gozen kaigi* imperial conference
10 悩 *gonō* your illness; the emperor's illness
株 *okabu* one's position; favorite trick; forte; characteristic
酒 *miki* sacred wine, wine offering. *goshu,*
酌 *oshaku* serving saké ⌊*osake* saké
陵 *goryō* imperial tomb
剣 *gyoken* emperor's sword
宴 *gyoen* court banquet ⌈palanquin
旅所 *otabisho* resting place for the sacred
宸筆 *goshimpitsu* imperial autograph
破算 *gohasan* recalculation; fresh start
真影 *goshin-ei* imperial portrait
蚕纏 *okaikoguru(mi)* silk attire
託 *gotaku* tedious talk; impertinent talk; =next word
託宣 *gotakusen* oracle; stating something trivial as if important
都合 *gotsugō* your convenience ⌈serving
都合主義 *gotsugō shugi* opportunism, time-
座 *mikura, mikurai, miza* imperial throne, God's throne. *goza(ru), owa(shimasu)* polite for *a(ru)* (see under 有 3727.0)
座形 *ozanari* mere formality; a commonplace. *ozanari ni* in a perfunctory manner
座所 *gozasho* throne, imperial chamber,
料 *goryō* imperial property ⌊imperial seat
料地 *goryōchi* imperial estate
料林 *goryōrin* imperial forest
家人 *gokenin* a lower-grade retainer
家芸 *o-iegei* specialty, monopoly

家騒動 *o-ie sōdō* family quarrel
11 厠 *okawa* bedchamber
捻 *ohine(ri)* wrapped coin offering
経 *okyō* sutras
堂 *midō* main temple of a monastery
菜 *okazu* side dish
袋 *ofukuro* mama
偉方 *oeragata* dignitary
曹司 *onzōshi* son of noble
転婆 *otemba* tomboy, flapper
猟場 *goryōba* imperial forest
遍路 *ohenro* pilgrimage
眼鏡 *omegane* (your) glasses; (your) judgment, discernment
12 裁可 *gosaika* imperial sanction
筆先 *ofudesaki* oracle
勤品 *otsuto(me)hin* bargain goods
無沙汰 *gobusata* neglect to visit (someone)
開 *ohira(ki)* adjournment, close
開山 *gokaisan* temple founder
詠 *gyoei* imperial poem
詠歌 *goeika* Buddhist pilgrimage hymn
飯 *gohan, omamma* boiled rice; a meal
飯炊 *gohantaki* rice cooking
飯時 *gohandoki* mealtime
飯蒸 *gohammu(shi)* warming up rice; rice steamer
13 飾 *okaza(ri)* divine ornaments; New Year's decorations; figurehead
数 *okazu* side dish
預 *oazu(ke)* wait (command to a dog); postponement
寝 *oyo(ru)* sleep. *gyoshin* the emperor's going to bed, going to sleep, or sleeping
感 *gyokan* imperial approval
業 *miwaza* the works of God
福分 *ofukuwa(ke)* share of a gift
裾分 *osusowa(ke)* sharing a gift
馳走 *gochisō* entertainment, treat, feast, dinner, banquet, hospitality
新造 *goshinzo, goshinzō* wife of a prominent person; wife
稜威 *mi-itsu* virtue of the emperor, glory of the throne
愛想 *oaisō* hospitality; cuteness; (restaurant) bill; attachment
殿 *goten* palace; court; mansion, home of a noble
殿医 *goten-i* shogunate doctor
辞儀 *ojigi* bow, greeting; refusal, hesitation
辞儀戦術 *ojigi senjutsu* kowtowing strategy
跳 *oha(ne)* tomboy, flapper
跳様 *oha(ne)san* tomboy, flapper
蔭 *okage* indebtedness, favor, help, support
蔭様 *okagesama de* thanks to you
意 *gyo-i* your will, your pleasure
意入 *gyo-i (ni) i(ru)* to please
意得 *gyo-i (o) e(tai)* want to meet; want someone's opinion
14 製 *gyosei* an emperor's poem or song
誓 *michika(i)* God's promises
歌会 *O-utakai* Imperial Poetry Party
歌所 *O-utadokoro* Imperial Poetry Bureau
髪 *ogushi* the hair (polite)
髪上 *ogushia(ge)* hairdressing (polite)
15 調 *mitsugi* tribute
諚 *gojō* command of a noble; emperor's message
慶 *gyokei* greetings, congratulations; joy
慶事 *gokeiji* imperial wedding, imperial birth
影 *gyoei* portrait of a noble
影石 *mikage ishi* granite
幣 *gohei* Shinto offerings of cloth, rope, or cut paper
幣担 *gohei-katsugi* superstitious person
霊 *mitama* departed spirit; Holy Spirit
霊代 *mitamashiro* symbol of the spirit of the deceased
霊屋 *mitamaya, otamaya* ancestral tomb, mausoleum
16 膳 *gozen* meal, rice, tray, low table
薦 *okomo* beggar
薩 *osatsu* sweet potato
覧 *goran ni naru* see, look, inspect; try (to do). *gorō(jiru)* see (polite)
親父 *goshimpu* your father
嬢様 *ojōsama, ojōsan* young lady, (your) daughter
17 講 *okō* Buddhist service
輿 *mikoshi* palanquin of a Shinto god
18 難 *gonan* calamity, misfortune
雛様 *ohinasama* festival dolls
題 *gyodai* theme of Imperial Poetry Contest
題目 *odaimoku* Nichiren prayer
19 鏡 *mikagami* sacred mirror (in a shrine)
璽 *gyoji* imperial seal, privy seal
簾 *misu* bamboo screen
21 饌 *gyosen, mike* offering to a god; food present to an emperor
22 籠 *okomo(ri)* praying all night in a shrine or temple
27 鬮 *mikuji* sacred lot, written oracle, divination

10

術 1629/F-X Nonstandard for 術 1621.

衙 1630/F1687 GA government office. [行]

B 微 1631/F682 微 BI, MI minuteness; insignificance; vagueness; fewness. *kasu(kana)* (see under 幽 112.0).
2 力 *biryoku* poor ability; the little one can do; slender means; little influence
3 才 *bisai* minor talent; my talents (humble)
小 *bishō* minuteness
小体 *bishōtai* granule, minute particle
4 少 *bishō* minute quantity
分 *bibun* differential calculus

分子 *bibunshi* atom; molecule; tiny particle
分学 *bibungaku* differential calculus
分積分学 *bibun-sekibungaku* differential and integral calculus
5功 *bikō* minor achievement
生物 *biseibutsu* microscopic organism, microbe, germ
生物学 *biseibutsugaku* microbiology
6行 *bikō* traveling incognito
光 *bikō* faint light, shimmer
7吟 *bigin suru* hum
妙 *bimyō* delicacy, subtlety, nicety
志 *bishi* small ambition, my ambition
8雨 *biu* light rain
服 *bifuku* incognito
苦笑 *bikushō* wry smile, faint forced smile
9音 *bion* a faint sound
風 *bifū* breeze, zephyr
衷 *bichū* true heart, inmost thoughts, sincerity
10笑 *bishō, hohoe(mi)* smile. *hohoe(mu)* smile; begin to bloom
恙 *biyō* indisposition, slight illness
弱 *bijaku* feebleness
粉炭 *bifuntan* pulverized coal
11細 *bisai* minuteness, fineness; details
酔 *bisui, horoyo(i)* slight intoxication
粒子 *biryūshi* a very tiny particle
視的 *bishiteki* microscopic
動 *bidō* tremor, quiver
動計 *bidōkei* microseismograph
12量 *biryō* very small amount
測計 *bisokukei* micrometer
温 *bion* lukewarmness, low temperature
温的 *bionteki* indifferent, lukewarm
温浴 *bion-yoku* tepid bath
温湯 *biontō, nurumayu* lukewarm water
13傷 *bishō* slight wound, minor injury, scratch
微 *bibi(taru)* slight, small tiny, petty, feeble, insignificant
睡 *madoro(mu)* drowse, doze off, nap. *bisui* short sleep
禄 *biroku* small stipend, pittance
罪 *bizai* minor offense
意 *bi-i* small token (of gratitude), my (humble) feelings
14塵 *mijin* particle, bit, atom
塵計 *mijinkei* micrometer
15賤 *bisen* low rank, humble station, obscurity
熱 *binetsu* slight fever
震 *bishin* slight earthquake
震計 *bishinkei* microseismograph
16積分 *bisekibun* differential and integral calculus
穏的 *bionteki* indifferent, lukewarm
20騰 *bitō* fractional advance (in prices)
21醺 *bikun* slight intoxication

— 11 —

銜 1632 / F1950 KAN. *kutsuwa* horse's bit. *kuwa(eru)* (see under 啣 956.0). [金]

A **徳** 1633 / F684 **德** TOKU virtue, goodness; good; gain; power to command respect.
4化 *tokka* moral influence, moral reform
分 *tokubun* profits, winnings, one's share
5目 *tokumoku* virtues
用 *tokuyō na* economical
用品 *tokuyōhin* bargain goods
6行 *tokkō* virtuous deeds, goodness
7沢 *tokutaku* grace, blessing
利 *tokkuri, tokuri* bottle
8性 *tokusei* morality, moral nature
育 *tokuiku* spiritual education, moral training
9風 *tokufū* nobility of character
政 *tokusei* benevolent government; moratorium
11教 *tokkyō* moral teachings
望 *tokubō* moral influence
望家 *tokubōka* man of high repute
13義 *tokugi* morality, integrity, sincerity
義上 *tokugijō* morally, in honor
義心 *tokugishin* sense of honor, moral sense
15器 *tokki* talent and virtue; virtuous person
16操 *tokusō* morality, chastity, virtue

B **徴** 1634 / F683 **徵** CHŌ sign, symptom, omen. *chō(suru)* collect, solicit, seek; judge by; question; refer to; call for (someone); demand. *shirushi* sign, indication, omen.
5用 *chōyō* commandeering, drafting, requisitioning, expropriating
収 *chōshū* collection, levy, assessment
収料 *chōshūryō* collection fee
7兵 *chōhei* conscription, recruitment, enlistment
兵令 *chōheirei* conscription decree
兵忌避 *chōhei kihi* draft evasion
兵免除 *chōhei menjo* draft exemption
兵制 *chōheisei* conscription system
兵制度 *chōhei seido* conscription system
兵猶予 *chōhei yūyo* temporary draft exemption
兵検査 *chōhei kensa* physical exam for conscription
兵適齢 *chōhei tekirei* draft age
9発 *chōhatsu* levy, forage, requisition, commandeering
発令 *chōhatsurei* requisition order
発船 *chōhatsusen* requisitioned ship
発隊 *chōhatsutai* foraging party
発権 *chōhatsuken* right of requisition
10候 *chōkō*＝兆候 637.10
12証 *chōshō* token, sign

3 口口土士夂夊夕大女子宀寸小⺌尢尸屮山川巛工己巾干幺广廴廾弋弓彐彑彡【彳】 12

税 *chōzei* tax collection, taxation
税令書 *chōzei reisho* tax bill
募 *chōbo* enlistment, recruitment
募人 *chōbonin* labor service; forced labor
集 *chōshū* levy, enlistment, recruiting
集令 *chōshūrei* order calling up draftees

12

徵 1635/F683 See 徴 1634.

德 1636/F684 See 徳 1633.

B 徹 1637/F685 TETSU clear. *tes(suru)* pierce, penetrate, strike home; go thru, sit up (all night). *tō(ru)* penetrate, permeate. *tō(su)* (see under 通 4703.0).
5 収 *tesshū* withdrawal
6 回 *tekkai*=撤回 1999.6
8 退 *tettai* withdrawal, evacuation
夜 *tetsuya* all night; all-night vigil; sleepless night
底 *tettei* thoroness, completion
底的 *tetteiteki* thoro, exhaustive, complete
底爆撃 *tettei bakugeki* saturation bombing
10 宵 *tesshō* all night, without sleep
12 廃 *teppai* abolition, removal
16 頭徹尾 *tettō-tetsubi* thoroly, thru and thru, completely, from start to finish

B 衝 1638/F1687 SHŌ brunt; opposition (in astronomy); highway; collision; important point. *tsu(ku)* (see under 突 3316.0). [行]
3 丈 *tsuitake* body length
4 心 *shōshin* heart failure
天 *shōten* high spirits
5 立 *tsuita(te)* single-leaf screen
6 当 *shō(ni)a(taru)* be appointed to a most important position
8 突 *shōtotsu* collision, bump, impact; conflict, discord, quarrel; encounter, clash
9 風 *shōfū* air blast
11 動 *shōdō* shock; impulse, impetus
動的 *shōdōteki* impulsive
15 撃 *shōgeki* shock, crash, impact; bombardment (in physics); (emotional) shock; trauma
撃療法 *shōgeki ryōhō* shock treatment

A 衛 1639/F1688 衞 EI protection. [行]
3 士 *eji, eishi* ancient imperial guards; soldiers on guard
5 生 *eisei* health, hygiene, sanitation
生上 *eiseijō no* hygienic, sanitary
生兵 *eiseihei* medic, medical corpsman
生材料 *eisei zairyō* medical supplies
生法 *eiseihō* hygiene, hygienics
生的 *eiseiteki* hygienic, sanitary
生官 *eiseikan* health officer
生学 *eiseigaku* hygiene, hygienics
生係 *eiseigakari* health officer
生院 *eisei-in* sanitarium
生施設 *eisei shisetsu* sanitary facilities
生思想 *eisei shisō* sanitary knowledge
生班 *eiseihan* a sanitation detail
生家 *eiseika* one who cautiously watches his health
生病院 *eisei-byōin* sanitarium-hospital
生隊 *eiseitai* medical corps
6 戍 *eiju* garrisoning
戍地 *eijuchi* garrison town
7 兵 *eihei* palace guards; guard, sentinel; garrison
兵勤務 *eisei kimmu* guard duty
8 所 *eisho* place guarded by soldiers; torpedo room (of a battleship)
9 星 *eisei* satellite
星国 *eiseikoku* satellite country
星都市 *eisei toshi* satellite towns
11 視 *eishi* guards at a parliament

13

衞 1640/F1688 See 衛 1639. [行]

B 衡 1641/F1688 KŌ measuring rod; scales. *kubiki* yoke. [行]
5 平 *kōhei na* equitable
9 度 *kōdo* weights and measures
15 器 *kōki* scales; weighing

14

徽 1642/F686 KI good; beautiful; badge.
6 号 *kigō* flag emblem, banner, crest
11 章 *kishō* badge, emblem, ensign

20

黴 1643/F2167 BAI. *kabi* mold, mildew, must, fungus. *kabi(ru)* get moldy, get musty, mildew. [黑]
4 止 *kabido(me)* fungicide
8 雨 *tsuyu, baiu*, rainy season
毒 *baidoku* syphilis
毒性 *baidokusei* syphilitic
9 臭 *kabikusa(i)* musty, moldy; hackneyed
11 菌 *baikin* bacillus, bacteria, germ
菌学 *baikingaku* bacteriology, microbiology
菌説 *baikin setsu* germ theory

21

衢 1644/F1688 KU crossroads. [行]

4-STROKE RADICALS

RAD. 心 61

Kokoro heart. At left 忄 (3 strokes) *risshimben* left-side standing "heart." At bottom: ⺗ or ⺗ *shita-gokoro* bottom "heart." Nickname: Heart.

A **心** 1645 F686 SHIN heart, mind, spirit; motive, sense (of duty); padding; wick; core; marrow; vitality. *kokoro* mind spirit; mentality; idea, thought; heart, feeling; wholeheartedness, sincerity, sympathy; attention; interest, care; will; intention; taste, mood; true meaning (of a poem); thought. *kokoro kara, shin kara* wholeheartedly, sincerely, cordially. *kokoro(narazumo)* unwillingly, reluctantly. *kokoro suru* attend to, care for, mind, notice, pay attention to; take heed.

2 入 *kokoro-i(re), kokoro-i(ri)* preparation, concern, anxiety
力 *shinryoku* mental power
3 土 *shindo* subsoil
上 *kokoroa(gari)* arrogance
丈 *kokoro (no) take* one's mind, inner thoughts
丈夫 *kokorojōbu na* courageous, secure
4 木 *shingi* axletree
火 *shinka* fire of anger or jealousy
支度 *kokorojitaku* mental attitude
中 *shinjū* double suicide, lover's suicide. *shinchū* heart, mind, inmost thoughts, true motive; at heart
中立 *shinjūda(te)* fidelity
切 *shinki(ri)* snuffers
切鋏 *shinki(ri)basami* snuffer
5 立 *kokoroda(te)* disposition, personality, temperament
付 *kokorozu(ku)* notice, realize, sense; exercise care. *kokorozu(ke)* tip, gratuity; suggestion
外 *shingai* unexpected, regrettable, mortifying
幼 *kokoro-osana(i)* childish
失 *kokoro-use(ru)* faint away
6 耳 *shinji* mind and ears
血 *shinketsu* sincerity
尽 *kokorozu(kushi)* earnest work, kindness, solicitude, efforts
休 *kokoroyasu(me)* consolation
伏 *shimpuku*=心服 (see below–8)
任 *kokoromaka(se)* one's own way, as one desires
好 *kokoroyo(i)* happy, feeling good
忙 *kokorozewashi(i)* rushed (feeling)
扱 *kokoroatsuka(i)* consideration (for others); worry; care; anxiety; solicitude
汲 *kokoro (o) ku(mu)* guess
当 *kokoroa(tari)* knowledge, idea, clue; guess. *kokoroa(te)* hope, expectation, reliance; guess
早 *kokorobaya na* quick-tempered
有気 *kokoroa(ri)ge na* significant, meaningful
次第 *kokoro shidai* depending on how one feels
気 *shinki* mind
気一転 *shinki-itten* changing one's mind
安 *kokoroyasu(i)* intimate, friendly, feeling at ease
安立 *kokoroyasuda(te) ni* out of familiarity; as a mark of friendship
行 *kokoroyu(ku)* be satisfied, be lighthearted
行迄 *kokoroyu(ku) made* to one's heart's content
行許 *kokoroyu(ku) baka(ri)* to your heart's content, as much as you please
地 *kokochi, shinchi* feeling, sensation, mood; idea; mental attitude, mental state
地好 *kokochiyo(ku)* pleasantly; willingly
地良 *kokochiyo(ku)* pleasantly; willingly, agreeably
7 足 *kokorota(ru)* be satisfied
床 *kokoroyuka(shii)* refined
材 *shinzai* heartwood
利 *kokoroki(ku), kokoro (ga) ki(ku)* have good sense; be clever
肝 *shinkan, kokorogimo* heart
乱 *kokoromida(re)* lack of prudence
附 *kokorozu(ke)* tip, gratuity; suggestion
忘 *kokorowasu(re)* sudden failure of memory
余 *kokoro ni ama(ru)* be at one's wit's end
労 *shinrō*=*shimpai* 心配 (see below–10)
身 *shinshin* mind and body
身喪失 *shinshin sōshitsu* mental derangement
8 底 *kokoro (no) soko, shinsoko, shintei* bottom of one's heart, real intention, motive
延 *kokorobae* mind, heart
房 *shimbō* auricle
易 *kokoroyasu(i)*=心安 (see above–6)
疚 *kokoroyama(shii)* conscience-stricken
迷 *kokoro (no) mayo(i)* illusion
性 *shinsei* mind, mentality; nature, disposition
泣 *urana(ku)* weeping within
的 *shinteki* mental, psychological, psychical
服 *shimpuku* admiration and devotion, hearty submission

命 *shimmei* the heart and life
苦 *kokoroguru(shii)* regrettable, sorry, conscience-stricken, unfortunate
学 *shingaku* ethics, moral philosophy
事 *shinji* one's thoughts
取皿 *shinto(ri)zara* fire pan
苛立 *kokoro-irada(tsu)* be irritated
長閑 *kokoronodoka na* peaceful, calm in ⌊heart, at ease
9 音 *shin-on* heart tone
通 *shintsū* understanding the deeper meaning. *kokoro (ga) kayo(u)* be understood by
便 *kokorodayori* dependence
待 *kokoroma(chi)* anticipation, expectation
後 *kokoro-okure* timidity
持 *kokoromo(chi)* feeling, sensation, mood; somewhat, a little
柄 *kokorogara* frame of mind
浅 *kokoroasa(i)* (person) with little sympathy; shallow
砕 *kokoro (o) kuda(ku)* worry ⌈lations
祝 *kokoro-iwa(i)* wholehearted congratu-
胆 *shintan* one's heart
重 *kokoro-omo(i)* distressing ⌈stancy
変 *kokorogawa(ri)* change of mind; incon-
室 *shinshitsu* ventricle of the heart ⌈ing
急 *kokoro-iso(gi), koko, ose(ku)* rushed feel-
染 *kokoro (ni) soma(nu)* uncongenial (work)
神 *shinshin* mind ⌈ment
神喪失 *shinshin sōshitsu* mental derange-
10 鬼 *kokoro (no) oni* alarmed conscience. *kokoro (o) oni ni suru* determine not to give in ⌈tion; character
根 *kokorone* inner feelings; motive; disposi-
残 *kokoronoko(ri)* regret, reluctance
浮 *kokoro (ni) uka(bu)* think about
粉 *kokoro (o) ko ni suru* apply oneself to
恥 *kokorohazu(kashii)* shameful
致 *kokoro (o) ita(su)* apply one's mind to
留 *kokoro (o) to(meru)* pay attention to
弱 *kokoroyowa(i)* weak-willed, fickle
配 *shimpai, kokorokuba(ri)* anxiety, worry, fear, suspense; trouble, care; good offices
配性 *shimpaishō* worry habit
配事 *shimpaigoto* cares, worries, troubles
11 遊 *kokorosusa(bi)* comfort
強 *kokorozuyo(i)* feeling reassured, confident; heartening (news). *kokorogowa(i)* stout-hearted; headstrong
情 *shinjō* one's heart, feelings. *kokoronasake* ⌊kind heart
惜 *kokoro-oshi(i)* regrettable
掛 *kokoroga(keru), kokoro (ni) ka(keru)* intend, lean, aim; look forward to; bear in mind; be careful to provide for. *kokoroga(kari)* worry, anxiety. *kokoroga(ke)* readiness, intention, aim; study, effort; attention, care

清 *kokorogiyo(i)* pure in heart
添 *kokorozo(e)* advice, suggestion
淋 *kokorosabi(shii)* somewhat lonely. *urasabi(shii)* lonely, lonesome
深 *kokorobuka(i)* thoughtful, prudent
眼 *shingan* mind's eye, mental vision
移 *kokoro-utsu(ri)* inconstancy, change of heart ⌈ening, helpless, forlorn
細 *kokoroboso(i)* lonely, depressed, disheart-
組 *kokorogu(mi)* intention
動 *kokoro (o) ugo(kasu)* be stirred up; apply one's mind to. *kokoro ga ugo(ku)* worry
悪 *kokorowaru(i), kokoro-a(shii)* evil-hearted; feeling bad
密 *kokorohiso(kani)* inwardly, secretly
寂 *kokorosabi(shii)* somewhat lonely
羞 *kokorohazuka(shii)* shameful
黒 *kokoroguro(i)* evil-hearted ⌈heart
悸亢進 *shinki kōshin* palpitation of the
悸昂進 *shinki kōshin* heart acceleration
許 *kokorobaka(ri)* just a little, mere token
許無 *kokoromoto-na(i)* uneasy, apprehensive; insecure; unreliable
酔 *shinsui* fascination, admiration, devotion
酔者 *shinsuisha* enthusiast, admirer, fan
得 *kokoroe(ru)* know, understand, be aware of; regard as; give consent. *kokoroe* rules, instructions, information; acting (principal); understanding
得違 *kokoroechiga(i)* mistake, misunderstanding; indiscretion
得難 *kokoroegata(i)* strange, inexplicable, hard to understand
得顔 *kokoroegao* proud face
理 *shinri* mentality, psychology
理的 *shinriteki* mental, psychological, psychical ⌈ophy
理学 *shinrigaku* psychology, mental philos-
理学上 *shinrigakujō* psychologically
理学的 *shinrigakuteki* psychological
理戦争 *shinri sensō* psychological warfare
12 痛 *shintsū*=*shimpai* 心配 (see above–10)
遣 *kokoroya(ri)* relaxation, recreation; sympathy; comfort. *kokorozuka(i)* solicitude, anxiety, regard for
晴 *kokoroba(rashi)* diversion; recreation
棒 *shimbō* axle, shaft, mandrel, piston rod
短 *kokoromijika(i)* short-tempered, restless
程 *kokoro (no) hodo* true heart, true feeling
粧 *kokoroyosoi* preparation
勝 *kokoromasa(ri)* firm character
裡 *shinri* mind, heart
証 *shinshō* a judge's conviction of a prisoner's guilt or innocence; one's impression ⌊of a person
軽 *kokorogaru(i)* rash; hasty
隔 *kokoroheda(te)* closing one's heart

寒 *kokorosamu(i)* deeply impressed
悲 *uragana(shii)*, *kokorogana(shii)* sad, sorrowful ⌈be confused
惑 *kokoro-mado(i)* delusion. *kokoro-mado(u)*
覚 *kokoro-obo(e)* remembrance; memo
象 *shinshō* mental image
筋 *shinkin* heart muscle
筋炎 *shinkin-en* myocarditis
無 *kokoro (nimo) na(i)* insincere; unintentional. *kokorona(i)* without ideas, unsympathetic; unrefined; heartless, thoughtless, indiscreet; cruel
無気 *kokoronage* heartlessness ⌈retainer
13腹 *shimpuku* sincerity; the heart; most loyal
障 *kokorozawa(ri)* anxiety, solicitude, worry
裏 *shinri* mind, heart
楽 *kokorodano(shii)* happy
豊 *kokoroyuta(kani)* without fear
置 *kokoro-o(ku)* be careful; hesitate
置無 *kokoro-o(ki)na(ku)* frankly; confidentially; without anxiety; heartily; without hesitation
電図 *shindenzu* electrocardiogram
電計 *shindenkei* electrocardiograph
意 *shin-i*, *kokorobae* mind, heart. *kokorobase* mind, heart; thoughtfulness
意気 *kokoro-iki* disposition, spirit, feeling
意地 *kokoro-iji* stubbornness ⌊toward
14像 *shinzō* mental image
境 *shinkyō* mental state; mental attitude
憎 *kokoroniku(i)* detestable; refined, graceful, excellent; reticent
構 *kokorogama(e)* mental attitude, prepara-
緒 *shincho* the mind, emotion ⌊tion
読 *shindoku* reading between the lines
静 *kokoroshizu(kani)* calmly, serenely. *kokoroshizu(ka)* at peace ⌈heart
魂 *shinkon* heart, soul; the bottom of one's
算 *shinsan*, *tsumori*＝*tsumori* (see under 積 ⌊3306.0)
15憂 *kokoro-u(i)* heartless
慰 *kokoronagusa(me)* a comfort
賢 *kokorokashiko(i)* wise in heart
器用 *kokorokiyō na* wise
霊 *shinrei* the spirit, soul
霊学 *shinreigaku* occultism, spiritism
霊術 *shinreijutsu* spiritualism
霊教 *shinreikyō* occult science, spiritualism
霊現象 *shinrei genshō* spiritualistic phenomena
霊論 *shinreiron* occult science, spiritualism
16儘 *kokoro (no) mama* as one pleases
懐 *kokoroyukashi(i)* refined
積 *kokorozumo(ri)* expectation
頭 *shintō* mind, heart
頼 *kokorodano(mi)* dependence, hope, expectation

覧 *kokoro-obo(e)* remembrance; reminder;
機 *shinki* mind, mental attitude ⌊notes
機一転 *shinki-itten* changing one's mind
17闇 *kokoro (no) yami* darkness of the heart
優 *kokoroyasa(shii)* kindhearted
18穢 *kokorogitana(i)* foul-minded, evil-minded
糧 *kokoro (no) kate* food for thought
騒 *kokorosawa(gi)* uneasiness. *kokoro (ga) sawa(gu)* be stirred up
髄 *shinzui*＝真髄 783.18
臓 *shinzō* heart; nerve, cheek
臓弁膜症 *shinzō bemmakushō* valvular disease of the heart
臓炎 *shinzōen* inflammation of the heart
臓病 *shinzōbyō* heart disease
臓部 *shinzōbu* the heart of, the core of
臓麻痺 *shinzō mahi* heart failure, heart
19願 *shingan* heart's desire; prayer ⌊attack
鏡 *shinkyō* the heart; a heart clearly differentiating between good and evil; pure heart
20懸 *kokoroga(ke)*＝心掛 (see above–11)
22驕 *kokoro-ogo(ru)* become proud

— 1 —

必 See 129.

— 3 —

応 See 1504.

志 See 1064.

忘 See 291.

忌 忌 See 1463.

忖 1646 F690 SON conjecture.

9度 *sontaku* conjecture, surmise, judgment

忙 1647 F692 B Bō. *isoga(shii)*, *sewa(shii)* busy, occupied. *sewa(shinai)* restless, fidgety, in a hurry.

4中 *bōchū* during pressure of business
10殺 *bōsatsu* being worked to death, being pressed with work

忍 1648 F690 B 忍 NIN. *shino(bu)* bear, endure, put up with; hide (oneself). *shino(baseru)*, *shino(basu)* conceal, secrete. *shino(bi)* stealing (into); spy; sneak thief; surreptitious visit to a house of ill fame. *shino(biyakani)* stealthily, secretly.

2 入 *shino(bi)-i(ru)* slip in, sneak in, steal into
4 込 *shino(bi)-ko(mu)* slip in, sneak in, steal into
5 冬 *nindō, suikazura* honeysuckle
出 *shino(bi)-de(ru)* slip out, sneak out
6 返 *shino(bi)gae(shi)* sharp-pointed wooden or metal prongs atop fences or walls
7 足 *shino(bi) ashi* tiptoeing, stealthy steps
声 *shino(bi)goe* whisper, suppressed voice
8 泣 *shino(bi)na(ki)* subdued sobbing
歩 *shino(bi)-aru(ku)* sneak around. *shino(bi)-aru(ki)* traveling incognito
苦 *ninku* endurance, stoicism
者 *ninja* (ancient) spy. *shino(bi)mono* spy, scout
9 音 *shino(bi) ne* weak voice; tearful voice
姿 *shino(bi)sugata* disguise, incognito
耐 *nintai* patience, perseverance, fortitude
耐強 *nintaizuyo(i)* persevering, patient, stoical
10 逢 *shino(bi)ai* secret meeting. *shino(bi)-a(u)* meet clandestinely
従 *ninjū* submission, resignation, meekness
笑 *shinobiwara(i)* stifled laugh, giggle, chuckle
辱 *ninjoku* forbearance, fortitude, resignation, forgiveness
11 術 *ninjutsu* occult art
寄 *shino(bi)-yo(ru)* steal up to, steal upon
13 寝 *shino(bi)ne* slipping away to sleep
傷沙汰 *ninjōzata* a bloody affair
18 難 *shino(bi)gata(i)* unbearable, intolerable, insupportable

4

忿 See 587.

念 See 424.

忝 忝 See 209.

忩 See 忽 1660.

怦 1649/F716 See 悴 1704.

惱 1650/F706 See 恼 1669.

忸 1651/F695 JIKU shame.
8 怩 *jikuji(taru)* bashful, shameful

忽 1652/F695 KOTSU. *tachima(chi)* in a moment, instantly, immediately, all of a sudden. *yuruga(se)* neglect, disregard.
5 布 *hoppu* hops
11 焉 *kotsuen* suddenly
12 然 *kotsuzen, kotsunen* suddenly
15 諸 *kossho* neglect, disregard; sudden destruction

忠 1653/F692 A CHŪ loyalty, devotion, fidelity, faithfulness.
4 犬 *chūken* faithful dog
6 臣 *chūshin* loyal subject, faithful retainer
7 言 *chūgen* good advice
告 *chūkoku* advice, warning
良 *chūryō* loyalty
孝 *chūkō* loyalty and filial piety
君 *chūkun* loyalty to the ruler
君愛国 *chūkun-aikoku* loyalty and patriotism
8 実 *chūjitsu, mame, mame(yaka)* faithfulness, devotion, honesty, fidelity
実忠実 *mamemame(shii)* honest and devoted, energetic, assiduous
実度 *chūjitsudo* fidelity (in radio)
9 信 *chūshin* faithfulness, devotion, loyalty
貞 *chūtei* constant loyalty
勇 *chūyū* loyalty and bravery
10 純 *chūjun* loyalty, obedience
恕 *chūjo* sincerity and sympathy
烈 *chūretsu* unswerving loyalty
11 婢 *chūhi* faithful maidservant
12 順 *chūjun* allegiance, loyalty, obedience
勤 *chūkin* faithful service, devotion
13 愛 *chūai* loyalty, devotion
節 *chūsetsu* loyalty, devotion
誠 *chūsei* loyalty, sincerity, integrity
誠心 *chūseishin* loyalty, sincerity, devotion
義 *chūgi* loyalty, devotion
義立 *chūgida(te)* act of loyalty
義顔 *chūgigao* loyal-appearing
14 僕 *chūboku* faithful manservant
魂 *chūkon* the loyal dead, faithful spirit
魂碑 *chūkonhi* monument to the war dead
15 霊塔 *chūreitō* monument to the war dead
16 諫 *chūkan* loyal remonstrance

快 1654/F693 A KAI pleasure, enjoyment. *kokoroyo(i)* pleasant, agreeable, comfortable, refreshing, delightful; well (from illness). *kokoroyo(ku)* cheerfully, comfortably, gladly. *kokoroyo(shi)* willing, happy. *kokoroyo(ge) na* cheerful, pleasant, comfortable.
2 刀 *kaitō* sharp sword
4 心 *kaishin no* agreeable, congenial
方 *kaihō* convalescence
5 打 *kaida* clean hit; good drive (baseball)
弁 *kaiben* fluency, eloquence
7 技 *kaigi* superb skill
足調 *kaisokuchō* allegro
男子 *kaidanshi* an agreeable man
男児 *kaidanji* a fine fellow

走 *kaisō* fast sailing, fast running
走船 *kaisōsen* yacht, clipper
走艇 *kaisōtei* yacht, clipper
8 雨 *kaiu* refreshing rain
味 *kaimi* pleasure, delight
的 *kaiteki*＝快適 (see below–13)
事 *kaiji* pleasure, joyful event
9 活 *kaikatsu na* cheery, jovial
哉 *kaisai* shout of joy
美 *kaibi* good feeling
美感 *kaibikan* good feeling
速 *kaisoku* high speed; celerity; mobility
速船 *kaisokusen* high-speed ship
速調 *kaisokuchō* allegro
10 眠 *kaimin* pleasant sleep
挙 *kaikyō* brilliant achievement
記録 *kaikiroku* fine record
12 傑 *kaiketsu* a handsome man
晴 *kaisei* fine weather
絶 *kaizetsu no* exceedingly pleasant
勝 *kaishō* easy victory
腕 *kaiwan* shrewdness, remarkable ability
報 *kaihō* good news
13 適 *kaiteki na* comfortable, pleasant, agreeable
漢 *kaikan* jolly fellow
艇 *kaitei* speed boat
感 *kaikan* agreeable sensation, comfort
楽 *kairaku, keraku* pleasure, enjoyment
楽主義 *kairaku shugi* Epicureanism
楽説 *kairakusetsu* Epicureanism
15 談 *kaidan* pleasant chat
諾 *kaidaku* ready consent
調 *kaichō* harmony; excellent condition
17 闊 *kaikatsu na* fine (spirit), frank
18 癒 *kaiyu* recovery from illness

5

怠 See 851.

思 See 3001.

怩 1655/F702 Jɪ shame.

怺 1656/F704 (国字) *kora*(*eru*) (see under 堪 1112.0).

怏 1657/F696 Ō dissatisfaction; have a grudge.
8 怏 *ōō toshite* despondently, moodily

怜 1658/F698 Rᴇɪ wise.
10 悧 *reiri* cleverness, sagacity

怫 1659/F703 Fᴜᴛsᴜ anger.
12 然 *futsuzen to* indignantly, in a rage

怱 1660/F715 **悤 匆 忩** Sō rush, be flustered.
6 忙 *sōbō* hurry, being busy
8 卒 *sōsotsu na* sudden, abrupt; precipitous; hurrying
9 怱 *sōsō* hurry, bustle

怯 1661/F703 Kʏō cowardice. *hiru*(*mu*) wince, flinch, hesitate, waver, fear. *obi*(*eru*) get frightened; be intimidated; feel shy; have a nightmare.
10 恐 *obi*(*e*)-*oso*(*reru*) fear and tremble
弱 *kyōjaku* cowardice
17 懦 *kyōda* cowardice, timidity
臆 *o*(*mezu*)-*oku*(*sezu*) fearlessly, boldly, courageously

B **怖** 1662/F697 Fᴜ. *o*(*jiru*), *oji*(*keru*) fear, be frightened; be timid; get nervous. *oso*(*reru*) fear, be overawed, be apprehensive. *kowa*(*garu*) fear, be afraid of. *kowa*(*i*) fearful, frightful, terrible, weird. *kowa*(*garaseru*) frighten, terrorize. *kowa*(*gari*) timidity, cowardice.
6 気 *ojike, ozoke* fear; awe; timidity; nervousness
8 怖 *ozu-ozu, odo-odo, oji-oji, kowagowa* timidly; nervously, gingerly
10 恐 *o*(*ji*)-*oso*(*reru*) fear
12 惑 *o*(*ji*)-*mado*(*u*) be terrified
18 顔 *kowa*(*i*) *kao* angry look, grim face

怨 1663/F701 Eɴ. Oɴ. *ura*(*mu*), *en*(*zuru*) bear a grudge, show resentment; be jealous. *ura*(*meshii*), *ura*(*migamashii*) hateful, bitter. *urami* grudge, hatred, malice, bitterness.
6 色 *enshoku* a hostile look
7 言 *engen, uramigoto* grudge, complaint, murmuring
声 *ensei* complaint, murmur
8 府 *empu* object of hatred
念 *onnen* grudge, malice, hatred
9 恨 *enkon* enmity, grudge
13 嗟 *ensa* grudge, resentment
15 敵 *onteki* sworn enemy
霊 *onryō* revengeful ghost; apparition
23 讐 *enshū, onshū* grudge, revenge

B **怒** 1664/F697 Dᴏ. Nᴜ. *ika*(*ru*), *oko*(*ru*) become angry, be offended, become excited. *ika*(*ri*) anger, indignation, rage, wrath. *ika*(*raseru*), *oko*(*raseru*) offend, anger, irritate. *oko*(*rippoi*) touchy, excitable, hot-tempered.

4 [心小⺗] 戈戸手扌支攴攵文斗斤方无日曰月木欠止歹殳毋比毛氏气水氵氺火灬爪爫父爻爿丬片牙牛犬犭

3上戸 *oko(ri) jōgo* quarrelsome drinker
5付 *oko(ri)-tsu(keru)* scold, storm at
出 *oko(ri)-da(su)* fly into a rage
6色 *doshoku* anger, angry countenance
気 *doki* anger; indignation, resentment
叫 *ika(ri)-sake(bu)* rage
号 *dogō* roar, outcry, howl
争 *ika(ri)-araso(u)* quarrel
7坊 *oko(rim)bō* hotheaded person
狂 *ika(ri)-kuru(u)* be terribly angry
声 *dosei* harsh words; angry voice; excited voice
8肩 *ika(ri)kata* square shoulders
易 *ika(ri)yasu(i)* easily angered
11唸 *ika(ri)-una(ru)* growl
14鳴 *dona(ru)* shout at
髪 *dohatsu* anger; hair standing on end
17濤 *dotō* raging billows, high waves

B **怪** 1665 F702 KE, KAI mystery; apparition. *aya(shimu)* doubt; be suspicious of; wonder at. *aya(shigena), aya(shii)* undependable, strange, mysterious. *ke(shikaran), ke(shikaranu)* rude, disgraceful, indecent, unpardonable, outrageous, absurd.

2力 *kairiki, kairyoku* superhuman strength
人物 *kaijimbutsu* mystery man
4火 *kaika* mysterious fire, will-o'-the wisp
文書 *kaibunsho* objectionable literature
6死 *kaishi* mysterious death
気 *aya(shi)ge na* questionable, shady, suspicious; unsteady; threatening (rain); broken (English)
光 *kaikō* weird light, will-o'-the-wisp
7我 *kega* wound, injury; accident, error; casualty
我人 *keganin* injured or wounded person
我負 *kegama(ke)* accidental defeat
我勝 *kegaga(chi)* accidental victory
8怪 *kaikai* great danger
物 *kaibutsu* monster, apparition
奇 *kaiki na*=*kikai na* 奇怪 1176.8
奇小説 *kaiki shōsetsu* mystery story
事 *kaiji* mystery, wonder, scandal
事件 *kaijiken* mystery case
11魚 *kaigyo* a strange fish
鳥 *kechō, kaichō* ominous bird
偉 *kai-i na* unusually large and muscular
捷 *kaishō* agility, promptness, shrewdness
異 *kai-i* monster. *kai-i na* mysterious; marvelous; grotesque
盗 *kaitō* mysterious thief
12傑 *kaiketsu* prodigy, extraordinary man
腕 *kaiwan* unusual ability, shrewdness
訝 *kegen na, kaiga na* suspicious, puzzled, dubious
童 *kaidō* problem child; prodigy
13漢 *kaikan* suspicious-looking person
14聞 *kaibun* strange rumor; scandal
暢 *kaichō* exhilaration, carefree feeling
説 *kaisetsu* strange rumor
15談 *kaidan* ghost story
16獣 *kaijū* monster

A **性** 1666 F701 SEI sex, gender; nature, attribute. SHŌ nature, disposition; quality; purity. *saga* one's nature; custom.

4分 *shōbun* nature, disposition
5生活 *sei seikatsu* sex life
犯罪 *sei hanzai* sex crime
6向 *seikō* inclination, disposition
行 *seikō* character and conduct
行為 *sei kōi* sexual act
交 *seikō* sexual intercourse
交不能 *seikō funō* sexual impotency
7状 *seijō* characteristics
別 *seibetsu* distinction by sex
来 *seirai*=生来 2991.7
8知識 *sei chishiki* sex information
的 *seiteki* sexual
的犯罪 *seiteki hanzai* sex crime
9急 *seikyū* quick temper, impatience
10骨 *seikotsu* one's natural constitution; one's natural skills
病 *seibyō* venereal disease
根 *shōne* nature, disposition, spirit, mind
能 *seinō* performance, efficiency
格 *seikaku* character, personality
格破綻者 *seikaku hatansha* abnormal character
格俳優 *seikaku haiyū* actor expert in character portrayal
格描写 *seikaku byōsha* character portrayal
格異常 *seikaku ijō* abnormal personality
格劇 *seikakugeki* character drama
11情 *seijō* character, disposition, nature
理 *seiri* inherent characteristics, natural endowments
教育 *sei kyōiku* sex education, sex information
道徳 *sei dōtoku* sexual morality
問題 *sei mondai* sex problem
悪 *seiaku, shōwaru* evil disposition
悪説 *seiakusetsu* doctrine of original sin
欲 *seiyoku* sexual desire
欲倒錯 *seiyoku tōsaku* sexual perversion
欲倒錯者 *seiyoku tōsakusha* sexual pervert
12善説 *seizensetsu* doctrine of man's innate goodness
13愛 *seiai* sexual love
感 *seikan* sexual emotion, sexual sensibility
15慾 *seiyoku* sexual desire
質 *seishitsu* nature, disposition, temperament; qualities, properties; nature (of an undertaking)
衛生 *sei eisei* sexual hygiene, social hygiene
器 *seiki* reproductive organs

器崇拝 *seiki sūhai* phallicism

18 癖 *seiheki* disposition, inclination, characteristic, idiosyncrasy

懲無 *shōko(ri) (mo) na(i)* unrepentant, untaught by experience, incorrigible

A **急** 1667/F700 **急** Kyū emergency; suddenness; danger; haste; steep. *iso(gu)* hurry, hasten. *se(kasu)* rush, hurry, expedite. *se(ku) vi* and *vt* hurry, make haste; be impatient; press, urge, hurry up. *a(seru)* be hasty, be in a hurry, be impatient. *kyū na* urgent, sudden; precipitous; sharp (turn); swift. *kyū ni* in a hurry, promptly; suddenly; at a moment's notice.

4 火 *kyūka* a nearby fire, a sudden fire

込 *se(ki)-ko(mu), se(k)ko(mu)* become excited, be agitated, be in a hurry, become impatient

勾配 *kyūkōbai* steep slope

5 用 *kyūyō* urgent business

立 *se(ki)-ta(teru)* hurry, urge, speed up, urge on

6 死 *kyūshi* sudden death

先峰 *kyūsempō* leader, champion, forerunner, vanguard

行 *kyūkō* express train; going in a hurry

行券 *kyūkōken* express ticket

行便 *kyūkōbin* express mail

行軍 *kyūkōgun* quick march, double-quick

7 走 *iso(gi)-hashi(ru)* run quickly

足 *iso(gi)ashi* fast pace

迫 *kyūhaku* urgency; imminence

告 *kyūkoku* urgent notice

坂 *kyūhan* steep hill

坂道 *kyūsakamichi* steep road

8 雨 *kyūu* sudden shower

送 *kyūsō suru* rush (something), dispatch

追 *kyūtsui* hot pursuit

使 *kyūshi* courier, express messenger

所 *kyūsho* vital point, vitals, tender spot, vulnerable spot; secret, key (to)

物 *iso(gi)mono* a rush order; urgent business

命 *kyūmei* urgent orders

昇 *kyūshō* sudden rise (in temperature)

歩 *kyūho* fast walking. *iso(gi)-aru(ku)* hurry along

事 *kyūji* urgent matter, sudden development

性 *kyūsei* acute (illness)

性灰白髄炎 *kyūsei kaihakuzuien* poliomyelitis

性病 *kyūseibyō* acute illness

9 風 *kyūfū* squall

信 *kyūshin* urgent message

派 *kyūha suru* dispatch, expedite

変 *kyūhen* sudden turn; emergency, accident

造 *kyūzō* hurried construction

造家屋 *kyūzō kaoku* prefabricated house; quonset

降 *kyūkō suru* drop rapidly; dive

降下 *kyūkōka* swoop, nose dive

降下爆撃 *kyūkōka bakugeki* dive bombing

速 *kyūsoku na* swift, prompt

速冷凍 *kyūsoku reitō* quick freeze

速度 *kyūsokudo* high speed

速潜航 *kyūsoku senkō* crash dive (of a submarine)

10 症 *kyūshō* sudden illness; emergency case

逝 *kyūsei* sudden death

峻 *kyūshun na* steep

流 *kyūryū* swift current; rapids

配 *kyūhai* special delivery

書 *kyūsho* urgent letter

病 *kyūbyō* sudden illness

病人 *kyūbyōnin* emergency case

進 *kyūshin* rapid progress; going to extremes; radicalism

進化 *kyūshinka suru* become radical

進主義 *kyūshin shugi* radicalism

進的 *kyūshinteki* radical, extreme

進派 *kyūshinha* radicals

進党 *kyūshintō* radical party

11 務 *kyūmu* urgent business, pressing need

設 *kyūsetsu* speedy installation

患 *kyūkan* emergency patient

停車 *kyūteisha* sudden stop

斜面 *kyūshamen* steep slope

転 *kyūten* sudden change

転回 *kyūtenkai* sudden turn, doubling back

転直下 *kyūten-chokka suru* fall headlong; take a sudden turn

転換 *kyūtenkan* sudden change

12 場 *kyūba* emergency, crisis

須 *kyūsu, kibisho* teapot

勝 *sekkachi* hot-tempered person. *sekkachi na* restless, impatient, quick-tempered

募 *kyūbo* recruiting (workers) in a hurry

落 *kyūraku* slump (in prices)

報 *kyūhō* urgent message, alarm

13 雷 *kyūrai* thunder, thunderclap

電 *kyūden* urgent telegram

傾斜 *kyūkeisha* steep slope; heavy list

14 増 *kyūzō* surge, sudden increase

15 劇 *kyūgeki na* sudden, precipitous; radical

談 *kyūdan* fast talking, urgent conversation

撃 *kyūgeki* surprise attack

16 遽 *kyūkyo* hastily, hurriedly

激 *kyūgeki na* sudden, precipitous; radical

18 騎 *kyūki* fast horse

難 *kyūnan* imminent danger; sudden calamity

20 騰 *kyūtō* sudden jump in prices

霰 *kyūsan* sudden hailstorm

22 襲 *kyūshū* surprise attack; raid

— **6** —

恙 See 3660.

恚 See 1080.

恋 See 313.

息 See 3844.

恥 See 3704.

恃 1668 / F704 Ji *tano(mu)* depend on.

恟 1669 / F706 **忷** Kyō fear.

恕 1670 / F706 Jo. *jo(suru)* excuse, tolerate, forgive.

恍 1671 / F705 Kō unclear. *tobo(keru)* grow senile; be stupid; joke; pretend not to know. *ho(reru)* (see under 惚 1711.0).

[9]面 *tobo(ke)zura* a stupid look
[11]惚 *kōkotsu* rapture, ecstasy, trance
[18]顔 *tobo(ke)gao* a stupid look

恪 1672 / F709 Kaku carefulness.

[6]守 *kakushu suru* adhere to, cling to, be loyal to
[12]勤 *kakugon, kakkin* working earnestly

恫 1673 / F709 Dō, Tō painful; fearful.

[12]喝 *dōkatsu* intimidation, threat, bluster
愒 *dōkatsu* intimidation, threat, bluster

恣 1674 / F707 Shi. *hoshiimama* self-indulgent, wayward, selfish, arbitrary.

[13]肆 *shishi*=*hoshiimama* (see under 恣 1674.0)
意 *shi-i* selfishness, arbitrariness
意的 *shi-iteki* selfish

恰 1675 / F711 Kō. *ataka(mo), adaka(mo)* just as, as tho; fortunately.

[6]好 *kakkō* shape, form, appearance; pose, posture; manner; approximately. *kakkō na* suitable, reasonable
[12]幅 *kappuku* build, physique

恤 1676 / F707 Jutsu relieve. *megu(mu)* (see under 恵 1681.0). *awa(remu)* have mercy on.

[7]兵 *juppei* soldiers' relief
兵資金 *juppei shikin* war-relief fund

恨 1677 / F707 B Kon. *ura(mu)* bear a grudge, show resentment. *ura(mi)* grudge, hatred, malice. *ura(meshii)* hateful, bitter.

[7]言 *ura(mi)goto* grudge, grievance, complaint
[8]事 *konji* regrettable matter
[10]殺 *konsatsu* intense bitterness

恢 1678 / F706 Kai wide; large; enlarge.

[7]宏 *kaikō suru* amplify, spread, extend
[9]恢 *kaikai* expansiveness, extensiveness, wideness
[12]復 *kaifuku* recovery, restoration, rehabilitation
復期 *kaifukuki* convalescence

恬 1679 / F709 Ten composure. *ten toshite* coolly, nonchalantly, indifferently.

[11]淡 *tentan na* unselfish, disinterested
[12]然 *tenzen toshite* coolly, indifferently
[16]澹 *tentan* unselfish, disinterested

恭 1680 / F709 B Kyō. *uya-uya(shii)* respectful, reverent.

[10]倹 *kyōken* modesty, humility; courtesy, respect
[12]順 *kyōjun* allegiance
敬 *kyōkei* respect, reverence, veneration
賀 *kyōga* respectful congratulations
賀新年 *Kyōga Shinnen* Happy New Year
[17]謙 *kyōken* modesty, humility

恵 1681 / F721 B **惠 惠** Kei. E. *megu(mi)* blessing, grace, favor; kindness, mercy, benevolence, charity. *megu(mu)* bless; show mercy to, render benevolence to.

[3]与 *keiyo suru* present, give, bestow
[4]方 *ehō* lucky direction
方参 *ehōmai(ri)* New Year's visit to a shrine or temple in a lucky direction
比須 *Ebisu* a god of wealth
比須顔 *ebisugao* smiling face
[7]投 *keitō* presentation
沢 *keitaku* blessing; pity; favor; benefit
[18]贈 *keizō* presentation

悔 1682 / F713 B **悔** Kai. Ge. *ku(iru)* repent, regret. *ku(yamu)* regret, repent of; mourn for, condole with. *ku(i)* regret, repentance. *ku(yami)* condolence visit; regret, repentance. *ku(yashigaru)* be chagrined (at one's failure); regret (a circumstance); resent (an insult). *kuya(shii)* vexing, regrettable, mortifying.

[7]言 *kuya(mi)goto* words of condolence

坊 *ku(yashim)bō* person who quickly regrets (something)
改 *ku(i)-arata(meru)* repent of. *ku(i)arata-(me)* repentance, penitence
状 *ku(yami)jō* condolence letter
8泣 *ku(yashi)naki* cry of remorse
9恨 *kaikon* remorse; regret; contrition, repentance
10悛 *kaishun* penitence, repentance (Catholic)
涙 *ku(yashi) namida* tears of regret or re-
紛 *ku(yashi)magi(re) ni* out of spite ⌊morse
悟 *kaigo* repentance, penitence, contrition, remorse
悟者 *kaigosha* a penitent, a contrite sinner
16頽 *ku(i)-kuzuo(reru)* be discouraged and remorseful

B **恒** 1683/F704 **恆** Kō always. *tsune ni* always.

3久 *kōkyū* perpetuity, permanency
久化 *kōkyūka* perpetuation
久性 *kōkyūsei* permanency
久的 *kōkyūteki* permanent
4心 *kōshin* steadiness, constancy
5圧 *kōatsu* constant pressure
6存 *kōzon* conservation (of energy)
8例 *kōrei* regular ceremony; established custom, common usage
性 *kōsei* permanency, constancy
9風 *kōfū* constant wind, trade wind
星 *kōsei* fixed star
11産 *kōsan* fixed property
常 *kōjō* constancy
常的 *kōjōteki* constant
12温線 *kōonsen* isotherm
13数 *kōsū* constant (in science)
15儀 *kōgi* traditional rites

A **恩** 1684/F708 ON kindness, goodness, favor, mercy, blessing, benefit.

2人 *onjin* benefactor, patron
5主 *onshu* benefactor, patron
6返 *ongae(shi)* requital of a favor
6光 *onkō* the blessing of sunlight; the favor
7沢 *ontaku* favor, benefit ⌊of one's lord
8知 *onshi(razu)* ingratitude; ungrateful person
命 *ommei* gracious words; gracious command
典 *onten* favor, act of grace, special privilege
9威 *on-i* justice and mercy; kindness and
恤 *onjutsu* pity, mercy, charity ⌊dignity
宥 *on-yū* forgiveness
10師 *onshi* one's honored teacher
借 *onshaku* loan, borrowing
恵 *onkei* grace, favor, benefit, blessings
恵日 *onkeibi* days of grace
恵期間 *onkei kikan* period of probation, probationary time
11情 *onjō* compassion; affection
赦 *onsha* amnesty, general pardon
12給 *onkyū* pension
13愛 *on-ai* kindness and affection, love
義 *ongi* favor, obligation, debt of gratitude
14徳 *ontoku* sympathy, mercy, grace
15誼 *ongi*＝恩義 (see above–13)
賜 *onshi* imperial gift; gracious gift
賞 *onshō* reward
18顔 *ongan* compassionate face
簡 *onkan* your letter
19寵 *onchō* grace, favor
21顧 *onko* favor, patronage
23讐 *onshū* love and hate

B **恐** 1685/F705 **恐** KYō. *oso(reru)*, *oso-(roshigaru)* fear, dread, be afraid; be overawed; be apprehensive. *oso(raku)* perhaps, possibly. *oso(re)* fear, dread; consternation; anxiety; reverence, awe; danger, risk; chance, signs. *oso(renaga-ra)* most respectfully. *oso(roshii)* terrible, awful, fierce; tremendous, marvelous. *kowa(i)* fearful, dreadful.

2入 *oso(re)-i(ru)* be awestruck; be overwhelmed; be humiliated; be astonished, be sorry to trouble, beg pardon; be disconcerted; plead guilty, stand cor-
4日病 *kyō-Nichibyō* Japanophobia ⌊rected
水病 *kyōsuibyō* rabies ⌈spectfully
5乍 *oso(re)naga(ra)* most humbly, most re-
6気 *osoro(shi)ge na* frightening, awful
多 *oso(re)-ō(i)* august, gracious, awe-inspiring, awful
米病 *kyō-Beibyō* fear of America
7迫 *kyōhaku suru* threaten
8英病 *kyō-Eibyō* Anglophobia
妻病 *kyōsaibyō* fear of one's wife
怖 *kyōfu* fear, terror, panic
怖心 *kyōfushin* feeling of terror
怖症 *kyōfushō* morbid fear
怖時代 *Kyōfu Jidai* the Reign of Terror
怖感 *kyōfukan* sense of fear
怖観念 *kyōfu kannen* fear complex
9独病 *kyō-Dokubyō* Germanophobia
10従 *oso(re)-shitaga(u)* cringe and follow
悦 *kyōetsu* delight, pleasure
悚 *kyōshō* crouching in fear
恐 *oso(ru)-oso(ru)* nervously, timidly, cautiously, reverently. *kowagowa* fearfully. *kyōkyō* respect (in letters)
12慌 *kyōkō* panic, scare, consternation
惑 *oso(re)-mado(u)* be terrified
喝 *kyōkatsu* threat, blackmail

喝取材 *kyōkatsu-shuzai* blackmail, extortion, shakedown
喝罪 *kyōkatsuzai* blackmail
惶 *kyōkō* fear and trembling; your humble servant
惶敬白 *kyōkō keihaku* respectfully yours
惶謹言 *kyōkō kingen* respectfully yours
13 慎 *oso(re)-tsutsu(shimu)* fear and respect
戦 *oso(re)-onono(ku)* tremble, shudder
14 察 *kyōsatsu suru* respectfully appreciate another's feelings
16 龍 *kyōryū* dinosaur
17 縮 *kyōshuku* obligation, appreciation; regret; shame
謹 *oso(re)-tsutsu(shimu)* fear and respect
21 懼 *kyōku* fear, awe, dread
露病 *kyō-Robyō* Russophobia

— 7 —

悉 See 4808.

悪 See 62.

怱 See 忽 1660.

悔 1686/F713 See 悔 1682.

悛 1687/F713 SHUN amend.

悒 1688/F712 YŪ. *fusa(gu)* be depressed, have the blues.

悚 1689/F713 SHŌ fear.
12 然 *shōzen* horror; shuddering

悌 1690/F712 TEI serving our elders.
12 順 *teijun* obedience

悍 1691/F712 KAN rough, clumsy; violent.
10 馬 *kamba* unruly horse

悋 1692/F712 RIN stingy.
6 気 *rinki* jealousy, envy
13 嗇家 *rinshokuka* miserly person

悃 1693/F711 KON sincerity.
16 篤 *kontoku* kindness, cordiality

悧 1694/F132 See 俐 433.

悄 1695/F711 SHŌ anxiety.
10 悄 *shioshio, sugosugo* all alone, despondent, crestfallen, heavy-hearted, weak
12 然 *shōzen(taru)* despondent, crestfallen

悦 1696/F711 悅 B ETSU joy, rapture, ecstasy, amusement. *yoroko(bashii), yoroko(bi), yoroko(bu)* (see under 喜 1115.0).
8 服 *eppuku* willing submission
13 楽 *etsuraku* enjoyment, pleasure

患 1697/F715 B GEN. KAN disease. *wazura(u)* be ill, suffer from; be afflicted. *ure(e), ure(i)* (see under 憂 70.0).
8 泣 *wazura(i)-na(ku)* weep
者 *kanja* patient, victim (of a disease)
10 部 *kambu* diseased part, the affected area
家 *kanka* (doctor's) patient
13 禍 *kanka* disaster, misfortune, sorrow
18 難 *kannan* tribulation

悩 1698/F724 惱 B NŌ distress, illness. *naya(mu)* worry, be troubled, be afflicted, be in pain. *naya(masu)* annoy, embarrass, afflict, worry, oppress, torment. *naya(mi)* anguish, worry, distress, pain. *naya(mashii)* painful, distressing; melancholy; teasing.
8 苦 *naya(mi)-kuru(shimu)* be sorely troubled
10 殺 *nōsatsu suru* captivate, charm, fascinate

悖 1699/F713 HAI. *moto(ru)* be contrary (to), go against, deviate from.
4 反 *haihan suru* be contrary to, go against, violate
8 逆 *haigyaku* unlawfulness, criminality
11 理 *hairi* absurdity
14 徳 *haitoku* immorality, corruption

悟 1700/F714 B GO. *sato(ru)* perceive, discern, realize, understand, comprehend; attain enlightenment, find one's philosophy. *sato(ri)* understanding, comprehension; Buddhist enlightenment; philosophy.
2 入 *gonyū suru* enter (Buddhist) enlightenment
了 *goryō* complete comprehension
4 方 *sato(ri)kata* way of understanding
8 性 *gosei* wisdom, reason
11 道 *godō* (Buddhist) enlightenment
18 難 *sato(ri)gata(i)* hard to understand

悠 1701/F714 YU. YŪ distant, longtime; leisure.
3 久 *yūkyū* eternity, permanence

8長 *yūchō na* slow, tedious, deliberate, leisurely
10容 *yūyō* repose, composure, serenity
11悠 *yūyū(taru)* quiet, calm, composed, leisurely, deliberate; eternal, boundless, vast
悠自適 *yūyū-jiteki* easy comfortable retirement
12遠 *yūen* remoteness; eternity; repose
揚 *yūyō* repose, composure, serenity; easy climbing (in a plane)
然 *yūzen(taru)*=*yūyū(taru)* 悠悠 (see above–11)

8

惹 See 3991.

悲 See 5082.

悶 See 4947.

惡 See 悪 62.

惠 1702 F721 惠 See 恵 1681.

惧 1703 F724 F754 惧 See 懼 1792.

悴 1704 F716 悴 Sui becoming emaciated. *segare,* son

悸 1705 F717 Ki pulsate; shudder.

悼 B 1706 F717 Tō. *ita(mu)* grieve over.
11惜 *tōseki* lamentation
12詞 *tōshi* grieving over a bereavement
13辞 *tōji* message of condolence, funeral oration
14歌 *tōka* an elegy

悵 1707 F716 Chō be sad.
9恨 *chōkon* deep regret; bitter resentment
12然 *chōzen to* sadly, sorrowfully

惣 1708 F724 Sō all.
7社 *sōsha* a shrine enshrining several gods
11菜 *sōzai* side dish

惟 1709 F721 I. *omom(miru)* consider, reflect. *omo(u)* (see under 思 3001.0).
9神 *kannagara* as of old
神道 *Kannagara (no) Michi* Shinto

惑 B 1710 F719 Waku. *mado(u)*=*mayo(u)* (see under 迷 4681.0). *mado(wasu), mado(wakasu)*=*mayo(wasu)* (see under 迷 4681.0). *mado(i)* delusion; perplexity.
7乱 *wakuran* bewilderment, confusion
8者 *mado(i)mono* wanderer
9星 *wakusei* planet
星間 *wakuseikan no* interplanetary
18溺 *wakudeki* indulgence, addiction; infatuation

惚 1711 F720 Kotsu. *ho(reru)* fall in love with, admire, be entranced with. *boke(ru)* grow senile; become mentally weak; fade, discolor. *hoke(ru)* grow senile; become mentally weak; become enthusiastic; be beside oneself. *hoke, boke* dull; dullheadedness.
4込 *ho(re)-ko(mu)* fall deeply in love
6色 *boke iro* dull color
気 *noroke(ru)* boast of love conquests. *noroke* love affair
気話 *norokebanashi* talking about romance
11惚 *horebore to* fondly. *horebore suru* be charmed
16薬 *ho(re)gusuri* love charm, love potion

惜 B 1712 F721 Seki. Shaku. *o(shimu), o(shigaru)* be sparing of; be frugal with; be stingy with; regret; value, prize; be reluctant. *o(shii)* regrettable, pitiful, disappointing; precious; wasteful. *o(shimazu)* without regret, ungrudgingly; generously. *o(shiminaku)* freely, regardless of expenses. *o(shisō) ni* grudgingly, reluctantly.
6気 *o(shi)ge* regret grudgingly; generously
気無 *o(shi)ge(mo)na(ku)* without regret, ungrudgingly; generously
7別 *sekibetsu* parting regrets
10陰 *seki-in* extremely careful use of time
11敗 *sekihai* regrettable defeat; defeat by a narrow margin
13歳 *sekisai* lamenting the departing of the old year

慘 B 1713 F738 慘 San. Zan disaster; cruelty; wretchedness. *mugo(i)* cruel, merciless, harsh. *mugo(tarashii)* cruel; horrible; tragic. *san(taru)* disastrous, appalling. *mijime na* sad, pitiful, wretched.
6死 *zanshi, sanshi* tragic death, violent death
死体 *zanshitai* mangled body
死者 *zanshisha* mangled body
7状 *sanjō* pitiful situation
8事 *sanji* disaster, tragedy, terrible accident
9胆 *santan(taru)* pitiable, wretched
10害 *sangai* ravages, havoc, heavy damage
殺 *zansatsu* slaughter, massacre, murder
殺死体 *zansatsu shitai* mangled body
殺者 *zansatsusha* murderer, slayer

殺事件 *zansatsu jiken* murder case
11敗 *zampai, sampai* overwhelming defeat, crushing defeat
12絶 *sanzetsu* great cruelty
落 *sanraku* slump, sudden fall
13禍 *sanka* terrible disaster, calamity, horrors (of war)
14酷 *zankoku* cruelty, atrocity, brutality
15劇 *sangeki* tragedy, tragic event
16憺 *santan(taru)* pitiable, wretched, tragic
澹 *santan(taru)* pitiable, wretched, tragic

A **情** 1714/F718 **情** SEI. JŌ feeling, emotion; passion; affection; heart; human nature; sympathy; sincerity; circumstances, facts; obstinacy. *nasake* sympathy, compassion.

2人 *jōnin, jōjin* sweetheart, lover
4心 *nasakegokoro* sympathy, compassion
火 *jōka* flame of love
夫 *jōfu* adulterer, paramour
5史 *jōshi* love story
6死 *jōshi* double love suicide
交 *jōkō* intimacy; illicit relations. *nasake (o) kawa(su)* have illicit relations with
合 *jōa(i)* unity of sentiment, sympathy
7状 *jōjō* circumstances, conditions
状酌量 *jōjō shakuryō* sentence reduction due to commiserative circumstances
8味 *jōmi* charm, glamor, attraction; warm-heartedness
知 *nasakeshi(razu)* pitiless
念 *jōnen* sentiment
実 *jōjitsu* personal considerations; favoritism; actual circumstances
炎 *jōen* fierce passion
事 *jōji* love affair, liaison
況 *jōkyō* circumstances
況証拠 *jōkyō shōko* circumstancial evidence
10致 *jōchi* mood, sentiment, artistic effect
11婦 *jōfu* adulteress
張 *jō (o) ha(ru)* be stubborn
深 *nasakebuka(i)* tenderhearted, compassionate
理 *jōri* heart and mind; reason and sentiment
移 *jō (ga) utsu(ru)* become fond of
欲 *jōyoku* passions, carnal desire
12景 *jōkei* scene; nature and sentiment
無 *nasakena(i)* heartless, cruel; pitiful, shameful, regrettable
報 *jōhō* information, news, intelligence report
報屋 *jōhōya* sports dopester
報部 *jōhōbu* information bureau
報経路 *jōhō keiro* pipeline, information channel
報機関 *jōhō kikan* counterintelligence corps
13痴 *jōchi* illicit love-making
話 *jōwa* lover's talk; love story
愛 *jōai* affection, love
義 *jōgi* friendship
勢 *jōsei* state of affairs, condition, indication, appearance
感 *jōkan* emotion, feeling
意 *jōi* emotion and will; sentiment
意投合 *jōi-tōgō* mutual understanding
14歌 *jōka* love song
態 *jōtai* situation, state of affairs
緒 *jōcho, jōsho* emotion, feeling
緒主義 *jōsho shugi* emotionalism
15趣 *jōshu* mood, sentiment; artistic effect
縁 *jōen* love affair
誼 *jōgi* friendship
調 *jōchō* atmosphere, tone, mood, spirit
弊 *jōhei* abuses, favoritism
慾 *jōyoku* passions, carnal desire
熱 *jōnetsu* passion; enthusiasm
16懐 *jōkai* heart, thoughts, feelings
操 *jōsō* sentiment

9

慨 See 1741.

意 See 5113.

愈 See 526.

愛 See 2829.

慈 See **慈** 612.

愒 1715/F730 KATSU, KEI, KETSU, KAI covet; threaten.

慍 1716/F734 **慍** UN. ON. *ika(ru)* be angry, get excited, be offended.

惱 1717/F724 See **悩** 1698.

惼 1718/F726 HEN narrow-minded.

愆 1719/F727 KEN mistake, fault, offense.

11祭 *kensai* guilt offering, trespass offering

惶 1720/F725 KŌ fear.

21懼 *kōku* reverence; epistolary closing

愀 1721/F726 SHŪ respect.

12然 *shūzen* change in the color of the face; grief

惻 1722 F726 SOKU be sad.
[12]惻 *sokusoku* pitiful condition
[13]隠 *sokuin* pity, sympathy

愕 1723 F730 GAKU. *odoro(ku)* be surprised; be frightened.
[12]然 *gakuzen to* in terror, in amazement

愍 1724 F728 BIN. MIN. *awa(remu)* pity, have mercy on, sympathize with. *awa(remi)* pity, compassion.
[12]然 *binzen(taru)* pitiable

B 慌 1725 F738 慌 慌 KŌ. *awa(teru)* be confused, lose one's head, be hurried, be hasty. *awa(te-futameku)* be confused, be disconcerted, be panicked. *awatada(shii)* busy, bustling, hurried, confused.
[8]者 *awa(te)mono* absent-minded person, blunderer, scatterbrain, careless person
[12]惑 *awa(te)-mado(u)* be flurried and perplexed

B 愉 1726 F727 愉 YU rejoice. *tano(shimu)*, *tano(shii)* (see under 楽 2324.0).
[7]快 *yukai na* happy, pleasant, delightful; cheerful
[10]悦 *yuetsu* joy
[13]楽 *yuraku* pleasure, joy

B 惰 1727 F724 DA laziness. *okota(ru)* (See under 怠 851.0).
[2]力 *daryoku* inertia, momentum, force of habit
[6]気 *daki* indolence, listlessness
[8]性 *dasei* inertia, momentum, force of habit
[10]眠 *damin* indolence, inactivity, idle slumber
弱 *dajaku*＝懦弱 1784.10.
[13]勢 *dasei*＝惰性 (see above–8)

A 想 1728 F724 SŌ idea, conception, thought. *omo(u)* (see under 思 3001.0).
[8]到 *sōtō suru* think of, consider, hit upon
念 *sōnen* idea, conception
定 *sōtei* hypothesis, assumption
[9]思 *sōshi* mutual love
[10]起 *sōki* recollection, remembrances
[11]望 *sōbō* admiration; yearning; anticipation
[14]像 *sōzō* imagination, supposition, conjecture
像力 *sōzōryoku* imagination, imaginative power
像上 *sōzōjō no* imaginary
像化 *sōzōka* idealization
像境 *sōzōkyō* dream world, Utopia
像説 *sōzōsetsu* hypothesis

B 愁 1729 F726 SHŪ. *ure(u)*, *ure(eru)* grieve, lament, be anxious. *ure(i)*, *ure(e)* sad, unhappy, gloomy.
[4]心 *shūshin* a sad heart, distress of mind
[6]色 *shūshoku*＝*yūshoku* 憂色 70.6
[7]吟 *shūgin* grieving and worrying
[9]思 *shūshi* a sad heart, distress of mind
眉 *shūbi* worried look, knitted brows, anxiety
眉開 *shūbi (o) hira(ku)* be relieved of worry
[12]悶 *shūmon* sadness and agony
訴 *shūso* appeal, petition, supplication
雲 *shūun* clouds of sorrow; gloom
然 *shūzen toshite* sorrowfully
[13]嘆 *shūtan* lamentation, sorrow
腸 *shūchō* grieving
傷 *shūshō* grief, lamentation; condolence
傷様 *(o)shūshōsama* an expression of condolence
[15]歎 *shūtan* grief, lamentation
歎場 *shūtamba* tragic scene
歎話 *shūtambanashi* tale of woe

B 愚 1730 F730 GU folly, foolishness, absurdity; fool. *oro(kana)*, *oro(kashii)* foolish, stupid, dull. *gu-* my humble (opinion).
[2]人 *gujin* fool, dunce
[3]女 *gujo* my daughter
才 *gusai* poor ability, my poor intelligence
[4]父 *gufu* my (foolish) father (humble)
夫 *gufu* foolish man
[5]母 *gubo* one's (foolish) mother (humble)
生 *gusei* I (humble)
付 *gu(nimo)-tsu(kanu)* ridiculous, absurd
札 *gusatsu* my letter
兄 *gukei* my (foolish) elder brother (humble)
民 *gumin* ignorant people
[6]老 *gurō* my old self
臣 *gushin* foolish retainer
行 *gukō* folly, foolish move
劣 *guretsu* foolishness, stupidity, absurdity
考 *gukō* my humble opinion
[7]見 *guken* my humble opinion
言 *gugen* my (foolish) words (humble)
作 *gusaku* poor piece of writing
弟 *gutei* my (foolish) younger brother (humble)
弄 *gurō* mockery, ridicule
図 *guzu(ru)* grumble, criticize; tease; charge falsely; be cloudy. *guzu* dullard
図付 *guzutsu(ku)* dally, loiter, loaf, dawdle, hesitate, be irresolute
図愚図 *guzuguzu* slowly, lazily, leisurely, hesitatingly
[8]妹 *gumai* my (foolish) younger sister (humble)
姉 *gushi* my (foolish) elder sister (humble)
拙 *gusetsu* foolish and clumsy; I (humble)
物 *gubutsu* fool, bonehead

4 心 小 9 小 戈 戸 手 扌 支 攴 攵 文 斗 斤 方 无 日 曰 月 木 欠 止 歹 殳 毋 比 毛 氏 气 水 氵 氺 火 灬 爪 爫 父 爻 爿 丬 片 牙 牛 犬 犭

陋 *gurō* foolish and mean
直 *guchoku* simple honesty; tactless frank- ⌊ness
妻 *gusai* my (foolish) wife (humble)
忠 *guchū* my loyalty
者 *gusha, oro(ka)mono* fool, dunce
[9]昧 *gumai* stupidity, ignorance
計 *gukei* a foolish plan; my (foolish) plan
衷 *guchū* my feelings ⌊(humble)
連隊 *gurentai* gang of young toughs
[10]将 *gushō* foolish general; stupid commander
案 *guan* my humble opinion, my (foolish) plan (humble); a foolish plan
書 *gusho* trashy book; my humble work
息 *gusoku* my (foolish) son (humble)
挙 *gukyo* foolish undertaking
[11]問 *gumon* foolish question
婦 *gufu* foolish woman; my wife
[12]鈍 *gudon* stupidity, silliness
策 *gusaku* my (foolish) plan (humble); foolish plan, poor policy
[13]僧 *gusō* foolish priest; I (humble, used by ⌊a priest)
蒙 *gumō* stupidity
意 *gui* my humble idea
痴 *guchi* grumbling; folly, foolishness. *guchi(ru)* complain
痴言 *guchigoto* foolish talk
痴話 *guchibanashi* tedious grumbling
[14]説 *gusetsu* foolish view; my humble opinion
察 *gusatsu* my guess, my observation
[15]慮 *guryo* my (foolish) idea
稿 *gukō* my poem, my manuscript
論 *guron* foolish argument, absurd opinion; my humble opinion
[19]癡 *guchi* grumbling, complaining. *guchi(ru)* complain

A **感** 1731/F732 **感** **KAN** feeling, sensation, sentiment; sense; emotion; impression; intuition. *kan(jiru), kan(zuru)* feel, experience, be conscious of; be impressed by; respond to. *kan(ji)* feeling, sense, sensation; perception; sensibility; impression; sentiment; effect, influence; touch, the feel.

[2]入 *kan(ji)-i(ru)* be deeply impressed
[4]心 *kanshin* admiration, wonder
方 *kan(ji)kata* way of feeling (about something) ⌈correction
化 *kanka* influence, inspiration; reform,
化事業 *kanka jigyō* reformatory work
化院 *kanka-in* reformatory
[5]付 *kanzu(ku)* suspect, sense, scent
[6]光 *kankō* exposure to light; sensitization
光板 *kankōban* sensitized plate, dry plate
光度 *kankōdo* photosensitivity
光紙 *kankōshi* photographic printing paper
[7]応 *kannō* inspiration; divine response; sympathy; effect, efficacy; influence; induction (in electricity)
吟 *kankin* reciting with emotion
状 *kanjō* letter of commendation
声 *kansei* voice of admiration
[8]佩 *kampai* deep impression
性 *kansei* sensitivity, sensitiveness, sense
所 *kandokoro* finger board; vital point
泣 *kankyū suru* be deeply affected, be touched. *kankyū* crying for joy
知 *kanchi* perception ⌈poem)
取 *kan(ji)-to(ru)* take in; appreciate (a
服 *kampuku* admiration, wonder
官 *kankan* sense organ
易 *kan(ji)yasu(i)* sensitive to, excitable, nervous, emotional; impressionable
受 *kanju* impression; (radio) reception
受性 *kanjusei* receptivity, sensitivity, susceptibility; irritability
[9]度 *kando* sensitivity; severity (of a quake)
冒 *kambō, kaze* a cold, influenza
染 *kansen* infection
[10]悟 *kango* feeling and understanding
恩 *kan-on* gratitude
涙 *kanrui* tears of gratitude ⌈of, realize
[11]得 *kantoku suru* get wind of, become aware
動 *kandō* impression, inspiration, emotion, ⌊excitement
動詞 *kandōshi* interjection
情 *kanjō* feelings; emotion; sentiment; impulse; passion
情的 *kanjōteki* emotional, impulsive
情家 *kanjōka* emotional person
情論 *kanjōron* heated argument
[12]喜 *kanki* joy, delight, ecstasy
覚 *kankaku* feeling, sensation; senses
覚主義 *kankaku shugi* sensualism
覚神経 *kankaku shinkei* sensory nerves
覚論 *kankakuron* sensationalism; sensualism; esthetics
覚器官 *kankaku kikan* sensory organs
[13]嘆 *kantan* admiration, wonder
嘆詞 *kantanshi* interjection
触 *kanshoku* sense of touch, feeling, sensa- ⌊tion
電 *kanden* electric shock
傷 *kanshō* sentimentality
傷的 *kanshōteki* sentimental
慨 *kangai* deep emotion
慨無量 *kangai-muryō* full of deep emotion
話 *kanwa* testimony (in church)
話会 *kanwakai* testimony meeting ⌈feelings
想 *kansō* thoughts, impressions, sentiments,
想文 *kansōbun* description of impressions
[14]銘 *kammei* deep impression
銘的 *kammeiteki* impressive
銘深 *kammeifuka(i)* impressive

15歎 *kantan* admiration; wonder
歎文 *kantambun* exclamatory sentence
歎符 *kantanfu* exclamation point
歎詞 *kantanshi* interjection
憤 *kampun suru* be inspired to action
賞 *kanshō* appreciation and praise; reward ⌊for merit
潮河川 *kanchō kasen* tidal river
16懐 *kankai* deep impression
激 *kangeki* deep emotion, inspiration, im- ⌊pression
興 *kankyō* interest; fun
奮 *kampun* deep emotion, impression, inspiration
奮興起 *kampun-kōki* inspired and aroused to action ⌈ing; grace
17謝 *kansha* thanks; appreciation; thanksgiv-
謝状 *kanshajō* letter of thanks, testimonial, citation ⌈offering
謝祭 *kanshasai* Thanksgiving Day; thank

10

慕 See 4040.

愍 See 1724.

慈 See 慈 612.

慍 1732/F734 See 慍 1716.

慂 1733/F736 Yō direct (someone), advise.

愾 1734/F735 Gai, Ki, Ke breathlessness; anger.

慥 1735/F741 Zō. *tashi(kani)* certainly, doubtless.

慊 1736/F737 慊 Ken satisfaction.
11焉 *ken-en(taru)* discontented, dissatisfied

慇 1737/F736 In courtesy.
17懃 *ingin* courtesy; intimacy, friendship
懃無礼 *ingin-burei* hypocritical courtesy

慄 1738/F736 Ritsu fear; shudder.
12然 *ritsuzen* horror, shudder, trembling

愧 1739/F734 Ki. *haji(ru)* feel ashamed. *haji(rau)* feel shy, be coy, be bashful, blush.
6死 *kishi suru* die of shame, be mortally ashamed

愴 1740/F734 Sō be sad. *itama(shii)* pathetic, sad.
12然 *sōzen* deep sorrow
13愴 *sōsō* sadness

B 慨 1741/F741 慨 慨 慨 Gai be sad. *nage(ku)* sigh, lament.
5世 *gaisei* concern for the public welfare
12然 *gaizen to* indignantly, with deep regret
13嘆 *gaitan* deploring, regret

B 愼 1742/F735 慎 Shin. *tsutsu(shimu)* be discreet, be careful, be prudent, be cautious; restrain oneself, be moderate. *tsutsu(mashige) ni* reverently, respectfully, humbly, modestly. *tsutsu(mashii)*, *tsutsu(mashiyaka) na* modest, reserved, humble, bashful. *tsutsu(shimi)* prudence, modesty, discretion, self-control.
9重 *shinchō* caution, prudence, discretion
11深 *tsutsu(shimi)buka(i)* discreet, prudent, cautious, modest, self-denying
15慮 *shinryo* courteously careful

A 態 1743/F737 Tai condition, figure, appearance; voice (of verbs). *waza to* intentionally, deliberately, knowingly. *zama* plight, state, appearance, spectacle.
7見 *Zama (o) mi(ro).* Just look at your blunder.
9度 *taido* attitude; posture, bearing, manner
12裁 *teisai*＝体裁 405.12
13勢 *taisei* attitude; arrangements
14様 *taiyō* situation, terms
態 *wazawaza* purposely

11

慮 See 4112.

憂 See 70.

慶 See 1539.

慨 See 慨 1741.

慘 1744/F738 See 惨 1713.

憩 1745/F746 See 憩 1765.

慾 1746 / F743 See 欲 4461.

慼 1747 / F743 慼 慽 SEKI grieve.

慷 1748 / F742 KŌ weep, grieve.

13 慨 *kōgai* resentment, indignation
慨家 *kōgaika* deplorer of existing evils

慫 1749 / F741 SHŌ advise; persuade.

14 慂 *shōyō* suggestion, persuasion, advice, inducement

慟 1750 / F739 DŌ be sad, grieve.

10 哭 *dōkoku* wailing, lamentation

慳 1751 / F742 KEN regret; stinginess.

11 貪 *kendon na* hardhearted, blunt, greedy

慴 1752 / F742 SHŪ, SHŌ fear; threaten.

6 伏 *shūfuku suru* crouch in fear; be overpowered

慧 1753 / F740 KEI wise.

10 悟 *keigo* cleverness
眼 *keigan* keen eye
敏 *keibin na* clever, astute

慚 1754 / F739 慙 ZAN. *haji(ru)* feel ashamed.

6 色 *zanshoku* blushing with shame
死 *zanshi suru* die of shame; feel very much ashamed
13 愧 *zanki* compunction, shame, humiliation

B **慢** 1755 / F740 MAN laziness; ridicule.

4 心 *manshin* self-conceit, pride
7 言 *mangen* boasting
8 性 *mansei* chronic
性化 *manseika* become chronic
性病 *manseibyō* chronic disease
14 語 *mango* boasting
15 罵 *mamba* scorn, derision

A **慣** 1756 / F740 KAN. *nara(u)*, *na(rasu)*, *na(reru)*, *na(re)* (see under 馴 5194.0).

5 用 *kan-yō no* common, customary, conventional; colloquial
用上 *kan-yōjō* by usage
用手段 *kan-yō shudan* favorite trick; usual practice
用句 *kan-yōku* an idiom; a common expression
用的 *kan-yōteki* common, colloquial, customary
用音 *kan-yōon* popular pronunciation of a character
用語 *kan-yōgo* idiom; colloquial expression
6 行 *kankō* usual practice, routine
行犯 *kankōhan* habitual criminal
8 性 *kansei* inertia
例 *kanrei* custom, usage, precedent
例上 *kanreijō* traditionally, conventionally
11 習 *kanshū* custom, common practice
習法 *kanshūhō* common law
16 親 *na(re)-shita(shimu)* get used to

B **憎** 1757 / F744 憎 ZŌ. *niku(mu)* hate, detest. *niku(garu)* hate. *niku(i)* hateful, abominable; poor-looking. *niku(rashii)* hateful, horrible, provoking. *niku(shimi)* hatred, enmity. *niku(rashige) ni* hatefully, maliciously.

3 口 *niku(mare)guchi* abusive language
子 *niku(mare)ko*, *niku(marek)ko* bad boy
6 合 *niku(mi)-a(u)* hate one another
気 *nikuge* hate
気無 *nikuge (no) na(i)* innocent, artless, harmless
7 体 *nikutei na* impudent, insolent, hateful
役 *niku(mare)yaku* unpopular role
8 物 *niku(mare)mono* object of hatred
9 思 *niku(karazu) omo(u)* care for, have a fancy for
11 悪 *zōo* malice, hatred, abhorrence
悪心 *zōoshin* malice, hatred, abhorrence
13 嫌 *niku(mi)-kira(u)* detest
14 憎 *nikuniku(shii)* hateful, detestable, loathsome

B **慰** 1758 / F741 I. *nagusa(mu) vt* and *vi* amuse oneself; make sport of; seduce. *nagusa(meru)*, *i(suru)* comfort, console, cheer. *nagusa(me)* comfort, consolation, diversion. *nagusa(mi)* amusement, pleasure.

5 主 *Nagusa(me)nushi* the Comforter, the Holy Spirit
半分 *nagusa(mi)-hambun* partly for pleasure
6 合 *nagusa(me-a(u)* comfort one another
安 *ian* solace, comfort; relaxation, recreation
安会 *iankai* recreational get-together
安所 *ianjo* army brothel
安婦 *ianfu* army prostitute
7 労 *irō suru* recognize (a person's) services
労会 *irōkai* banquet in honor of someone's services
労金 *irōkin* bonus for special services
8 物 *nagusa(mi)mono* object of pleasure; plaything, laughingstock

[10]留 *iryū suru* dissuade from resigning
[11]問 *imon* condolences; a sympathy call
問状 *imonjō* condolence letter
問使 *imonshi* condolence bearer
問品 *imonhin* comfort articles
問旅行 *imon ryokō* goodwill tour
問婦 *imonfu* army comfort girl ⌈soldiers
問船 *imonsen* ship sent to comfort the
問袋 *imombukuro* soldiers' comfort bags
[13]楽 *iraku* comfort, pleasure
[15]撫 *ibu* pacification, soothing
霊祭 *ireisai* memorial service
霊塔 *ireitō* memorial tower
[17]謝 *isha* consolation
謝料 *isharyō* consolation money
藉 *isha, iseki* consolation
藉料 *isharyō* consolation money

12

憲 See 1342.

憎 1759/F744 See 憎 1757.

橤 1760/F1015 See 蕊 4045. [木]

慨 1761/F-X 慨 See 慨 1741.

憊 1762/F744 HAI fatigue.

憬 1763/F747 KEI. *akoga(reru)* long for.

憖 1764/F745 GIN. *namaji, namaji(i) ni, namaji(kka)* thoughtlessly, rashly, halfheartedly, imperfectly, unsatisfactorily.

B 憩 1765/F746 憇 KEI. KATSU. *iko(u)* rest, relax, repose.

憮 1766/F747 BU disappointment.
[12]然 *buzen* discouraged, disappointed, astonished

憧 1767/F746 SHŌ. TŌ. DŌ. *akoga(reru)* yearn after, long for; thirst for; aspire to; admire, adore.
[15]憬 *dōkei, shōkei, akoga(re)* longing, aspiration

憔 1768/F745 SHŌ get thin.
[7]忰 *shōsui* emaciation, haggardness
[11]悴 *shōsui* emaciation, haggardness

憑 1769/F745 HYŌ be possessed. *tsu(ku)* possess, obsess, haunt. *tsuka(reru)* be devil-possessed, be haunted by.
[8]拠 *hyōkyo* authority
物 *tsukimono* devil possession; curse

憚 1770/F745 TAN. *habaka(ru)* be afraid of; hesitate; have scruples about, shrink from; pay deference to, stand in awe of; spread (clouds). *habaka(ri)* fear, awe; hesitation; compunction, scruple; reserve, deference; comfort station.
[5]乍 *habaka(ri)naga(ra)* with deference, with hesitancy, I'm sorry but . . .
[14]様 *habaka(ri)sama* Thanks for your trouble

憫 1771/F746 BIN anxiety. *aware(mu)* have mercy on.
[10]笑 *binshō suru* smile with pity
[12]然 *binzen(taru)* pitiable
[14]察 *binsatsu* compassion, sympathy

憐 1772/F744 REN. *awa(remu)* pity, have mercy on, sympathize with. *awa(remi)* pity, compassion.
[11]情 *renjō* pity, compassion
深 *awa(remi)buka(i)* compassionate
[13]愍 *remmin* compassion, pity, mercy
[15]憫 *rembin* compassion, pity, mercy

B 憤 1773/F746 FUN. *ikidō(ru)* resent, be indignant, become angry. *mutsuka(ru)* be angry (because of being unhappy); be always crying. *ikidōri* resentment, indignation.
[6]死 *funshi suru* die in a fit of anger; be unfortunately put out (in baseball)
[9]怒 *fundo, funnu* anger, rage, resentment, indignation, exasperation
[10]起 *funki suru* rouse oneself, be stirred up
[12]然 *funzen to* indignantly, in a rage
[13]慨 *fungai* resentment, indignation
[14]概 *fungai* resentment, indignation
[16]激 *fungeki* resentment; indignation

[18]懣 *fumman*＝忿懣 587.18

13

應 See 応 1504.

懃 1774/F748 KIN courtesy.

懌 1775 / F750 Eki rejoice.

憺 1776 / F748 Tan calm, quiet; move.

懊 1777 / F750 Ō sorrow, be in distress. *jirettа(i)* provoking, irritating; impatient, vexed.
10悩 *ōnō* agony, worry, trouble

B **憾** 1778 / F748 Kan. *ura(mu)* regret, be sorry for. *ura(mi)* regret. *ura(murakuwa)* regrettably.
7言 *ura(mi)goto* grudge, grievance, complaint

懈 1779 / F748 Kai, Ke laziness. *tayu(i)* (see under 弛 1564.0).
9怠 *ketai, kaitai* laziness; negligence
15緩 *kekan* laziness, negligence

B **憶** 1780 / F747 **憶** Oku think, remember. *omo(u)* think.
8念 *okunen* something one always remembers
10病 *okubyō* cowardice, timidity
11断 *okudan* deciding without the facts
12測 *okusoku* guess, speculation, supposition
14説 *okusetsu* hypothesis, speculation, surmise

B **懇** 1781 / F748 Kon. *nengo(ro) na* kind, courteous, hospitable, cordial.
4切 *konsetsu* kindness, cordiality, exhaustiveness
7求 *konkyū* earnest desire
8命 *kommei* kind words, kind advice
10書 *konsho* your kind letter
11情 *konjō* kindliness
望 *kombō, kommō* entreaty
13意 *kon-i* kindness, intimacy, friendship
話 *konwa* friendly chat
話会 *konwakai* social gathering
15請 *konsei* entreaty, request
談 *kondan* chat; consultation
談会 *kondankai* social gathering; round-table discussion
16篤 *kontoku* kindness, cordiality
親 *konshin* friendship, intimacy
親会 *konshinkai* social gathering
17懇 *konkon to* earnestly, repeatedly
19願 *kongan* entreaty, supplication, petition
願的 *konganteki ni* appealingly, imploringly
願者 *kongansha* petitioner, suppliant

B **懐** 1782 / F752 **懷** Kai heart, feeling. *natsu(kashimu), natsu(kashigaru)* yearn for, miss someone. *natsu(keru)* win over, win another's heart. *natsu(ku)* become attached to. *omo(u)* (see under 思 3001.0). *futokoro* bosom, breast, heart; pocket, purse. *natsu(kkoi)* affectionate, affable, tame. *natsu(kashii)* dear, longed-for; yearning for. *natsu(kashimi)* yearning, nostalgia, kindly feeling.
2刀 *futokorogatana* dagger; confidant
4手 *futokorode* hands in pockets, folded arms
中 *kaichū* one's pocket
中物 *kaichūmono* pocketbook; contents of the pocket
中時計 *kaichūdokei* watch
中電燈 *kaichū dentō* flashlight
中鏡 *kaichū kagami* pocket mirror
5旧 *kaikyū* longing for the old days
古 *kaiko* recalling the old days
古談 *kaikodan* reminiscences
7妊 *kainin* conception, pregnancy
8抱 *kaihō suru* entertain, harbor. *da(ki)-kaka(reru)* embrace; hold in the arms
具合 *futokoro-guai* one's financial situation
炉 *kairo* pocket heater
炉灰 *kairobai* pocket-heater fuel
9胎 *kaitai* conception, becoming pregnant
柔 *kaijū* conciliation, pacification, appeasement
春 *kaishun* arrival at puberty
10紙 *futokorogami, kaishi* handkerchief paper
都合 *futokoro-tsugō* one's financial situation
剣 *kaiken* dagger (for self-defense)
郷 *kaikyō* nostalgic reminiscence
郷病 *kaikyōbyō* nostalgia, homesickness
11勘定 *futokoro-kanjō* counting one's pocket money; one's financial position
14銭 *futokoro zeni* pocket money
慕 *kaibo suru* yearn for
疑 *kaigi* unbelief, skepticism, doubt
疑心 *kaigishin* unbelief, skepticism, doubt
疑主義者 *kaigi shugisha* atheist, skeptic, freethinker
疑説 *kaigisetsu* skepticism
疑論 *kaigiron* skepticism

14

懣 1783 / F750 Man worry, agony, anger.

懦 1784 / F750 Da weakness, cowardice.
4夫 *dafu* coward, weakling
10弱 *dajaku* effeminacy, emasculation, laziness

B **懲** 1785 / F751 **懲** Chō. *ko(rasu), ko(rashimeru), chō(zuru)* chastise, punish, discipline. *ko(riru)* learn by experience; be disgusted with.
7役 *chōeki* penal servitude
戒 *chōkai* disciplinary punishment, official reprimand
戒処分 *chōkai shobun* disciplinary action
8果 *ko(ri)-ha(teru)* = *koriru* (see 懲 1785)

治 *chōji* chastisement, punishment
治監 *chōjikan* reformatory, penitentiary
11悪 *chōaku* chastisement, punishment
14罰 *chōbatsu* discipline, punishment
罰的 *chōbatsuteki* punitive, disciplinary
17膺 *chōyō* discipline, punishment
18懲 *korigori suru, korikori suru* learn from experience; have had enough

— 15 —

懲 1786/F751 See 懲 1785.

懴 1787/F754 = 懺 ZAN, SAN remorse.
9悔 *zange, sange* repentance, confession, penitence

— 16 —

懷 1788/F752 See 懐 1782.

懶 1789/F752 RAI. *monou(i)* languid, weary, lazy; melancholy, gloomy, dull. *nama(keru)* be lazy, be idle; neglect. *monogusa(i)* lazy.
8者 *nama(ke)mono* lazy fellow, idle fellow
12惰 *randa, raida* laziness, idleness

懸 1790/F753 KEN. KE. *ka(keru), ka(karu)* (see under 掛 1952.0). B
4引 *kakehi(ki)* bargaining, maneuvering
5氷 *kempyō* icicle
6吊式 *kakezurishiki* underslung
7車 *kensha* retiring from public office on account of age; age 70
8念 *kenen* fear, anxiety, concern
命 *kemmei* eagerness, earnestness; risking one's life
河 *kenga* rushing stream
河弁 *kenga (no) ben* eloquence, eloquent speech
垂 *kensui* chinning
垂運動 *kensui undō* chinning exercises
9造 *kakezuku(ri)* hut built out over a valley or river
軍 *kengun* flying corps column; expeditionary army
10釘 *kakekugi* peg
案 *ken-an* pending question or problem
11崖 *kengai* overhanging cliff, precipice
章 *kenshō* military sash
12絶 *kenzetsu* great difference
隔 *ka(ke)-heda(taru)* be remote from; be different from. *ka(ke)-heda(teru)* estrange (people). *kenkaku* difference, discrepancy, gap
替 *kakeka(e)*=掛替 1952.12
腕直筆 *kenwan-chokuhitsu* holding the brush vertically and the arm above the table (in writing large characters)
13想 *kesō* falling in love, attachment
想文 *kesōbun, kesōbumi* love letter
14樋 *kakehi* water pipe, conduit, flume
15賞 *kenshō* offering prizes; prize winning; prize, reward
賞当選者 *kenshō tōsensha* prizewinner
賞金 *kenshōkin* prize money, reward
賞募集 *kenshō boshū* prize contest
賞論文 *kenshō rombun* prize essay
16橋 *kakehashi* viaduct; suspension bridge; intermediary
壅垂 *ken-yōsui* uvula
19離 *ka(ke)-hana(reru)* be far from; be different from

— 17 —

懺 1791/F754 See 懴 1787.

— 18 —

懼 1792/F754 = 惧 惧 KU. *oso(reru)* fear, be overawed, be apprehensive.

— 19 —

戀 1793/F755 See 恋 313.

RAD. 戈 62

Hoko tasseled spear. At right: *hokozukuri* or *hokogamae*. Variant, at right: 戈. Nickname: Tasseled Spear (cf. Rads. 56 and 110).

戈 1794/F755 KA. *hoko* halbert; arms; festival car, float.

— 1 —

戊 1795/F756 BO E, 5th. *tsuchinoe* 5th calendar sign.

— 2 —

戌 1796/F756 JUTSU. *inu* 7–9 p.m.; 11th zodiac sign; dog.

戍 1797/F756 JU protection.
8卒 *jusotsu* border guard

戎 1798/F756 Jū warrior; arms. *ebisu* barbarian, savage; Ainu.

3 士 *jūshi* warrior, soldier
6 衣 *jūi* armor; military uniform
夷 *jūi* barbarians
7 兵 *jūhei* soldiers
15 器 *jūki* arms, weapons of war

A **成** 1799/F757 **成** Sei. Jō. *na(ru)* become, get or grow (old), form (a part of); set in, come (time or seasons); turn into; be reduced to; consist of; be accomplished; result in; prove (fatal); amount to; play the part of; elapse; reach (a certain age); bear, stand; be promoted; be pleased to. *na(su)* do, perform, accomplish; form, make, accomplish. *(o)na(ri)* departure of a high personage; visit of a high personage.

2 人 *seijin* adult. *seijin suru* come of age
人日 *Seijin (no) Hi* Adult's Day (January 15)
人学校 *seijin gakkō* school for adults
人教育 *seijin kyōiku* adult education
3 下 *na(ri)-sa(garu)* stoop to, be reduced to
丈 *na(ru)take* as . . . as possible; whenever practicable
上 *na(ri)-a(garu)* rise from the ranks, rise suddenly. *na(ri)a(gari)* upstart
上者 *na(ri)a(gari)mono* upstart; one suddenly rich
4 心 *seishin* nature, disposition
仏 *jōbutsu* attaining Buddhahood, entering Nirvana; death
分 *seibun* ingredient; component; contents
文 *seibun* writing a document; a document
文化 *seibunka* legalization, codification
文法 *seibunhō* statute law, written law
文律 *seibunritsu* statute law, written law
文契約 *seibun keiyaku* written contract
5 立 *na(ri)-ta(tsu)* consist of; materialize; be concluded. *seiritsu* materialization, realization, formation, organization, completion. *na(ri)ta(chi)* origin, history
句 *seiku* set phrase, idiomatic phrase
代 *na(ri)-ka(waru)* replace (someone)
可 *na(ru)be(ku)* as . . . as possible, whenever possible
功 *seikō* success, achievement, prosperity
功者 *seikōsha* successful man
6 竹 *seichiku* liquidation, settlement
虫 *seichū* adult insect; adult invertebrate animal
行 *na(ri)-yu(ku)* turn out, become of (a person). *nariyu(ki)* developments, course of events; outcome, consequences, destiny
因 *sei-in* origin, cause
合 *na(ri)-a(u)* be nicely finished, be perfected, be completed; go together; become one; become intimate
年 *seinen* majority, adult age, legal age, man's estate
年式 *seinenshiki* coming-of-age ceremony
年期 *seinenki* adulthood
7 体 *seitai* adult form. *na(ri)katachi* appearance, costume
形 *seikei* plastic surgery
否 *seihi* success or failure
余 *na(ri)-ama(ru)* to make more than enough
8 金 *narikin* the newly rich
長 *seichō* growth
育 *sei-iku*=生育 2991.8
実 *Jōjitsu* Buddhist sect originating in the seventh century
典 *seiten* code of laws; established rites
果 *na(ri)-ha(teru)* be reduced to, become. *seika* results, outcome. *na(re) (no) ha(te)* shadow of one's former self
事 *na(rō) koto (nara), na(ru) koto (nara)* if possible
9 約 *seiyaku* promise
10 員 *sei-in* charter members
案 *seian* definite plan
11 道 *jōdō suru* attain Buddhahood
婚 *seikon* marriage
掛 *na(ri)-ka(keru), na(ri)-ka(karu)* be coming down with (an illness)
済 *na(ri)-su(masu)* (completely) become
敗 *seibai suru* punish, judge, bring to justice, deal with (a culprit). *seihai* success or failure
規 *seiki no* regular, formal, official, prescribed
12 歯 *seishi* permanent teeth
程 *na(ru)hodo* I see, well, really, to be sure
策 *seisaku* previous strategy; prospects of success
就 *jōju* fulfillment; completion, realization, consummation
13 損 *na(ri)-sokona(u)* fail to become, be unsuccessful in
義 *seigi* justification (Catholic)
業 *seigyō* completion of one's work or study
14 語 *seigo* a set phrase
算 *seisan* prospects of success
層 *seisō* stratification
層岩 *seisōgan* sedimentary rock
層圏 *seisōken* stratosphere
層圏飛行 *seisōken hikō* stratosphere flight
層圏飛行機 *seisōken hikōki* stratoplane
15 熟 *seijuku* ripeness; maturity, maturation, attainment of skill
熟児 *seijukuji* fully-developed baby
熟期 *seijukuki* puberty; adolescence; maturity
17 績 *seiseki* results, marks, rating, score
績順 *seisekijun* student rank

— 3 —

我 See 200.

成 1800/F757 See **成** 1799.

B **戒** 1801/F759 Kai commandment; admonition. *imashi(meru)* admonish, warn, prohibit. *imashi(me)* precept, exhortation, instruction, commandment.

4 心 *kaishin* caution, vigilance, discretion
6 行 *kaigyō* penance, austerities
名 *kaimyō, kaimei* Buddhist initiation name; posthumous name
7 告 *kaikoku* warning, caution
9 律 *kairitsu* precepts, commandments
10 師 *kaishi* Buddhist teacher
13 慎 *kaishin suru* be discreet, take care, be cautious
飭 *kaichoku* caution, reprimand
16 壇 *kaidan* temple ordination platform
17 厳 *kaigen* guarding against danger
厳令 *kaigenrei* martial law
20 護 *kaigo* safe custody

— 4 —

或 1802/F760 Waku. Koku. *a(ru)* some, one, a certain, a. *arui(wa)* or; possibly.

— 5 —

B **威** 1803/F502 I dignity, majesty, authority. *odo(su)* threaten; frighten; intimidate. *odoshi* menace, threat; scarecrow. [女]

2 力 *iryoku* power, might, authority, influence
力半径 *iryoku hankei* destructive range
力偵察 *iryoku teisatsu* reconnaissance in force
3 丈高 *itakedaka ni* angrily
4 文句 *odoshi monku* bluff, threatening language
5 付 *odo(shi)-tsu(keru)* to be threatening
令 *irei* authority
圧 *iatsu* coercion
圧的 *iatsuteki* domineering, coercive
6 光 *ikō* power, authority, influence
名 *imei* fame, prestige
7 迫 *ihaku* menace, threat
8 服 *ifuku suru* awe into submission
武 *ibu* authority and force
9 風 *ifū* majesty, dignity
信 *ishin* prestige, authority, honor
10 容 *iyō* dignity, majestic appearance
烈 *iretsu* majesty
11 望 *ibō* influence and popularity
張 *iba(ru), eba(ru)* be proud, swagger
張屋 *iba(ri)ya* braggart, boaster
13 勢 *isei* power, might, authority, influence; high spirits
14 徳 *itoku* virtue and influence
15 儀 *igi* dignity, majesty; dignified manner
権 *iken* authority, power
17 厳 *igen* dignity, majesty
嚇 *ikaku* menace, threat
嚇的 *ikakuteki* threatening, menacing

— 7 —

戛 See 61.

戚 1804/F760 Soku. Seki relative; sadness.

— 8 —

戛 1805/F761 See **戛** 61.

戟 1806/F761 Geki. *hoko* halbert; arms.

— 9 —

感 1807/F732 See **感** 1731. [心]

盞 1808/F1312 San wine cup. *sakazuki* wine glass, saké cup. [皿]

戡 1809/F761 Kan victory.

8 定 *kantei* military suppression of disorder

A **戦** 1810/F762 **戰** Sen war; battle; game, match. *tataka(u)* wage war; fight; engage in a contest; struggle against. *onono(ku)* tremble, shudder. *wanana(ku)* tremble. *tataka(wasu)* cause a quarrel; bring about a war between other nations; argue hotly; compete. *soyo(gu)* rustle, tremble, quiver, sway, stir. *tataka(i)* war, fight; battle, encounter, strife, conflict; contest (in athletics). *ikusa* war, fight, battle, encounter.

2 力 *senryoku* war potential
3 士 *senshi* soldier, combatant, warrior
4 斗 *sentō* battle, combat, action
火 *senka* war conflagration; war disasters; sword and fire
中 *senchū* during the war
友 *sen-yū* comrade-in-arms
5 史 *senshi* military history; history of the war
功 *senkō* distinguished war service, military merit
犯 *sempan* war crime; war criminal
犯者 *sempansha* war criminal
6 地 *senchi* battlefield, war front
好 *tataka(i)zu(ki)* warlike, bellicose
列 *senretsu* line of battle; line (of ships)
死 *senshi* death in action
死者 *senshisha* men killed in action

4 心忄小【9戈】戸手扌支攴攵文斗斤方无日曰月木欠止歹殳毋比毛氏气水氵氺火灬爪爫父爻爿丬片牙牛犬犭

争 *sensō* war, warfare, campaign; battle
争中 *sensōchū* during the war
争未亡人 *sensō mibōjin* war widow
争犯罪 *sensō hanzai* war crime
争犯罪人 *sensō hanzainin* war criminal
争行為 *sensō kōi* act of war
争呆 *sensōboke* combat fatigue
争状態 *sensō jōtai* belligerency, state of war
争法規 *sensō hōki* the rules of war
争放棄 *sensō hōki* war renunciation
争能力 *sensō nōryoku* war potential
争景気 *sensō keiki* war prosperity
争裁判 *sensō saiban* war-crimes trial
争裁判所 *sensō saibansho* war-crimes court
争犠牲者 *sensō giseisha* war victim
7 局 *senkyoku* war situation
役 *sen-eki* war, battle, campaign
抜 *tataka(i)-nu(ku)* fight to a finish
乱 *senran* wars, disturbances
利品 *senrihin* war spoils, trophies
没 *sembotsu* death in battle, killed in action
没者 *sembotsusha* the war dead
車 *sensha* tank; chariot
車長 *senshachō* tank commander
車砲 *senshahō* tank gun
車隊 *senshatai* tank corps
車戦 *senshasen* tank battle, tank warfare
車壕 *senshagō* tank trap
災 *sensai* war damage
災地 *sensaichi* war-stricken area
災者 *sensaisha* war victim
災孤児 *sensai koji* war orphan
災後 *sensaigo* after the war
災流民 *sensai ryūmin* displaced persons
災家族 *sensai kazoku* bombed-out family
8 法 *sempō* strategy, tactics, campaign plan
況 *senkyō* war situation
果 *senka* war results 「civil war
国 *sengoku* belligerent country; country in
国時代 *sengoku jidai* era of civil wars; turbulent period
歿 *sembotsu* death in battle; killed in action
歿者 *sembotsusha* the war dead
歿勇士 *sembotsu yūshi* the war dead
9 陣 *senjin* war preparations; battlefield
後 *sengo* after the war
後派 *sengoha* postwar generation
前 *senzen* prewar days, before the war
前派 *senzenha* prewar generation
10 記 *senki* military history
病死 *sembyōshi* death from war-contracted
時 *senji* wartime, war period ⌊disease
時工場 *senji kōjō* munitions plant
時中 *senjichū* during the war, in wartime
時手当 *senji teate* war bonus
時公債 *senji kōsai* war loan
時功労章 *senji kōrōshō* distinguished-service medal
時色 *senjishoku* wartime look 「footing
時体制 *senji taisei* war organization, war
時利得税 *senji ritokuzei* war-profits tax
時状態 *senji jōtai* state of war, belligerency, war conditions 「suit
時服 *senjifuku* field-service uniform; utility
時定員 *senji tei-in*=*senji hensei* 戦時編成 (see below–10)
時国債 *senji kokusai* war bonds
時保険 *senji hoken* war-risk insurance
時産業 *senji sangyō* war industry
時景気 *senji keiki* war boom 「band
時禁制品 *senji kinseihin* wartime contra-
時補償 *senji hoshō* war indemnity 「footing
時編成 *senji hensei* war establishment, war
11 域 *sen-iku* war area, theater of war
捷 *senshō* victory, triumph
隊 *sentai* corps; squadron
敗 *sempai* defeat in war
敗国 *sempaikoku* defeated nation
術 *senjutsu* tactics, strategy, art of war,
術家 *senjutsuka* tactician ⌊campaign plan
術用 *senjutsuyō no* tactical
略 *senryaku* strategy, tactics
略上 *senryakujō* strategically, from the viewpoint of strategy
略的 *senryakuteki* strategic
略物資 *senryaku busshi* strategic goods
略家 *senryakuka* strategist 「ing
略爆撃 *senryaku bakugeki* strategic bomb-
12 備 *sembi* war preparations; war preparedness
場 *senjō* battlefield, the front, war theater
渦 *senka* the confusion of war
評 *sempyō* criticism of the game
雲 *sen-un* war clouds
費 *sempi* war expenditures
報 *sempō* war news, war intelligence
勝 *senshō* victory, triumph
勝国 *senshōkoku* victor nation
勝者 *senshōsha* victor
13 債 *sensai* war debts, war bonds 「ering
慄 *senritsu* shuddering; frightfulness; shiv-
禍 *senka* war damage, ravages of war
跡 *senseki* old battlefield; aftermath of war
意 *sen-i* fighting spirit, hostile intention
戦恐恐 *sensen-kyōkyō toshite* nervously, gingerly 「gingerly
戦兢兢 *sensen-kyōkyō toshite* nervously,
傷 *senshō* war wound
傷病 *senshōbyō* war injury or illness
傷病者 *senshōbyōsha* war invalid
14 歴 *senreki* war experience, war service
塵 *senjin* dust of battle

端 *sentan* hostilities
[15]線 *sensen* battle line, front
[16]機 *senki* time to strike; military secret
[17]績 *senseki* war record; score
[18]闘 *sentō* battle, action, combat
闘力 *sentōryoku* combat strength
闘的 *sentōteki* active; fighting
闘服 *sentōfuku* combat uniform
闘員 *sentōin* fighter, combatant
闘教会 *sentō (no) kyōkai* the church militant
闘隊形 *sentō taikei* line of battle, battle array
闘帽 *sentōbō* army field cap
闘靴 *sentōgutsu* combat shoes
闘旗 *sentōki* battle flag
闘機 *sentōki* fighter plane
闘艦 *sentōkan* battleship
[20]艦 *senkan* battleship

10

截 See 793.

戠 1811/F761 SEN be destroyed.

11

慼 1812/F743 See 慼 1747.

戮 1813/F762 RIKU kill.
[2]力 *rikuryoku* co-operation

戲 See 246.

12

戰 1814/F762 See 戦 1810.

戯 1815/F763 See 戯 246.

13

戴 See 795.

戲 See 戯 246.

14

蹙 See 254.【足】

18

戳 1816/F-X GU halbert.

RAD. 戸 63

To door. Also called *togashira, to kammuri*, or *todare*. Variant: 戶.
Nickname: Door.

A 戸 1817/F764 戶 户 Ko house; door; family; counter for houses. *to* door.
[3]口 *toguchi* door, doorway. *kokō* number of houses; population
[4]戸 *koko* houses; *koko ni* at each door, from door to door
[5]外 *kogai* open-air, outdoors
付警報器 *totsu(ke)-keihōki* door alarm
主 *koshu* head of a family
主権 *koshuken* family headship
[6]毎 *kogoto ni* at every door; from door to door
[7]別 *kobetsu* each house, house to house
別訪問 *kobetsu hōmon* house-to-house visit
別割 *kobetsuwa(ri)* house taxation rate
[8]迷 *tomayo(i)* being lost, losing one's bearings
板 *to-ita* rain shutter (when used for carrying)
枠 *towaku* door frame
[9]前 *tomae* warehouse door; warehouse front
[10]框 *togamachi* door frame
[11]袋 *tobukuro* built-in box for shutters
[12]棚 *todana* locker, cabinet, closet, sideboard, cupboard
惑 *tomado(i) suru* be at sea, lose one's bearings
[13]障子 *toshōji* wooden and translucent doors
数 *kosū* number of houses
数割 *kosūwa(ri)* household tax
[15]締 *tojima(ri)* fastening the doors, closing up. *tojime* shutting a door
[18]襖 *tobusuma* a door with paper on one side and wood on the other
[20]籍 *koseki* census; family register
籍抄本 *koseki shōhon* extract of a family register
籍役場 *koseki yakuba* family-registration office
籍法 *kosekihō* family-registration law
籍証明書 *koseki shōmeisho* family-registry certificate
籍調 *koseki shirabe* census taking
籍謄本 *koseki tōhon* copy of a family register
籍簿 *kosekibo* family register

3

P **戻** 1818 / F765 **戾** REI. *modo(ru)* return, turn back; revert to, resume, return to; be returned; go backward. *modo(su)* return, restore; turn back (a clock); reject; vomit. *moto(ru)* (see under 悖 1699.0).

2 入 *modo(shi)-i(re)* reimbursement
8 金 *modo(shi)kin* refund
9 品 *modo(ri)hin* returned goods
10 荷 *modo(shi)ni* return cargo
11 道 *modo(ri)michi* the way back, return journey

4

戾 See **戻** 1818.

B **房** 1819 / F765 **房** Bō house, room; tassel. *fusa* tuft, tassel, fringe; lock (of hair); cluster, bunch, segment (of an orange).

4 毛 *fusage* lock, tuft, tassel
中 *bōchū* in the room; in the bedroom
8 房 *fusafusa* tufty, fringy, bushy (tail), fleecy
事 *bōji* sexual intercourse
事過度 *bōji kado* sexual excess
9 室 *bōshitsu* a room

B **肩** 1820 / F1535 **肩** KEN. *kata* shoulder. [肉]

2 入 *kata-i(re)* assistance. *kata (o) i(reru)* assist, sponsor, participate
3 口 *katakuchi* (top of) the shoulder
下 *katasaga(ri)* uneven (hem); wrong slant (in writing)
4 引 *kembi(ki)* stiff shoulders
5 代 *katagawa(ri)* relief palanquin bearer; one who shoulders another's debt or business proposition
甲 *kenkō* shoulder
甲骨 *kenkōkotsu* shoulder blade
甲部 *kenkōbu* shoulder
6 当 *kata-a(te)* shoulder pad
先 *katasaki* (top of) the shoulder
7 身 *katami* shoulder and body; face (that one loses), honor
車 *kataguruma* (riding) on the shoulders
8 押 *kata-o(shi)* shoulder-pushing game; support, assistance
並 *kata (o) nara(beru)* stand or walk in a row; run neck and neck
9 透 *katasuka(shi)* dodging
持 *kata (o) mo(tsu)* assist, flatter
怒 *kata (o) ika(rasu)* strut along
風切 *kata (de) kaze (o) ki(ru)* strut along
胛骨 *kenkōkotsu* shoulder blade
10 骨 *katabone* shoulder blade
部 *kembu* shoulders
息 *kata (de) iki suru* pant
書 *kataga(ki)* title, degree; address (on a letter); criminal record
書付 *kataga(ki)zu(ki)* titled (person); notorious (person)
11 張 *kata (ga) ha(ru)* feel shoulder pains
掛 *kataka(ke)* shawl
脱 *katanu(gu)* partially remove outer garment; strip to the waist
章 *kenshō* shoulder strap, epaulette
袋 *katabukuro* shoulder bag
12 越 *katago(shi)* over the shoulder
幅 *katahaba* breadth of one's shoulders
揚 *kata-a(ge)* shoulder tuck
替 *katagawa(ri)*＝肩代 (see above–5)
貸 *kata (o) ka(su)* assist, sponsor, participate
13 馴 *katanara(shi)* light training, warming up, workout
15 摩 *kemma* rubbing shoulders with the crowd
摩轂撃 *kemma-kokugeki* jostling and bustling
18 癖 *kempeki* stiff shoulders; massage

A **所** 1821 / F766 **所** So. SHO place. *tokoro* place, spot, scene, site, seat; locality, district; room; distance; address; point, feature; passage (in a book), part; thing; time, moment; extent; matter of course. *tokoro ga* but, however, on the contrary. *toko* place. *tokoro de* well. *-sho, -jo* place, office, bureau.

4 化 *shoke* acolyte, priestling
以 *yuen* reason, the reason why
5 生 *shosei* one's child; one's parents; one's birthplace
用 *shoyō* errand, business, appointment
由 *shoyū* reason
払 *tokorobara(i)* exile to the country
6 行 *shogyō* acts, works
存 *shozon* thought, opinion
自慢 *tokoro jiman* boasting of one's place
在 *shozai* whereabouts, site, position, location, place where something is kept
在地 *shozaichi* seat, location
在無 *shozaina(i)* be bored, have nothing to do
有 *shoyū* possession, ownership; property
有主 *shoyūnushi* owner, proprietor
有地 *shoyūchi* the land one owns
有物 *shoyūbutsu* one's possessions
有者 *shoyūsha* owner, proprietor
有格 *shoyūkaku* possessive case
有権 *shoyūken* ownership
7 見 *shoken* view, opinion, impressions, findings
労 *shorō* illness, indisposition
作 *shosa* conduct; gesture
作事 *shosagoto* dance drama, posture dance
8 長 *shochō* office head, factory head, institute head
念 *shonen* thought, deep thought

定 *shotei no* fixed, prescribed
所 *shosho, tokorodokoro* here and there, several places
所方方 *shosho-hōbō* here and there
9 信 *shoshin* belief, conviction, opinion
柄 *tokorogara* locality, neighborhood, situation; the place being what it is
狭 *tokorosema(i)* crowded; littered up; small (quarters)
思 *shoshi* thought, idea, opinion
要 *shoyō* need
為 *sho-i* results; influence, effect; fault. *se-i, sho-i* act, action, deed, results, results of one's actions
持 *shoji suru* possess, have, own; carry
持人 *shojinin* bearer, holder
持金 *shojikin* funds, money in hand
持者 *shojisha* bearer, holder, possessor
持品 *shojihin* one's personal effects
10 員 *shoin* staff, personnel; staff member
書 *tokoroga(ki)* address
帯 *shotai* household, home
帯主 *shotainushi* head of a household, householder
帯持 *shotaimo(chi)* housekeeping; householder
帯染 *shotaiji(miru)* be domesticated
帯道具 *shotai dōgu* household goods
帯数 *shotaisū* number of households
11 違 *tokorochiga(i)* mistaking the place
産 *shosan* result, outcome
望 *shomō* desire, request, wish
得 *shotoku* income, earnings; possessions. *tokoro (o) e(ru)* secure a position exactly to one's liking
得者 *shotokusha* income earner
得税 *shotokuzei* income tax
得層 *shotokusō* income group
得顔 *tokoroegao ni* triumphantly
得額 *shotokugaku* amount of income
12 属 *shozoku* attached to; one's post
期 *shoki* anticipation, expectation
替 *tokoroga(e)* moving to a new address
番地 *tokorobanchi* address
13 嫌 *tokorokira(wazu)* anywhere, everywhere; indiscriminately
詮 *shosen* after all
置 *shochi*＝処置 1162.13
感 *shokan* impressions
業 *shogyō* acts, works
載 *shosai no* printed, published, reported
14 説 *shosetsu* statement, assertion
領 *shoryō*＝*ryōchi* 領地 5124.6
罰 *shobatsu* penalty, punishment
蔵 *shozō* possession
管 *shokan* jurisdiction
管庁 *shokanchō* the authorities concerned
15 論 *shoron* argument
16 懐 *shokai* impressions, opinions

謂 *iwayuru* the so-called
17 轄 *shokatsu* jurisdiction
19 願 *shogan* desire, wish, request

5

扁 1822 / F767 **扁 扁** HEN level, small. *hira(tai)* (see under 平 26.0).

5 平 *hempei* flatness
平足 *hempeisoku* flatfoot
6 舟 *henshū* skiff, little boat
8 青石 *henseiseki* lapis lazuli
10 桃 *hentō* almond
桃油 *hentōyu* almond oil
桃腺 *hentōsen* tonsils
桃腺炎 *hentōsen-en* tonsillitis; quinsy
18 額 *hengaku* framed picture or motto

6

B **扇** 1823 / F768 **扇** SEN. *ao(gu)* fan. *ōgi* folding fan.

3 子 *sensu* folding fan
4 分 *ao(gi)-wa(keru)* winnow
7 形 *senkei, ōgigata* fan shape
状 *senjō* fan-shaped
状地 *senjōchi* alluvial delta
9 面 *semmen* fan paper; folding fan
屋 *ōgiya* fan maker
風機 *sempūki* electric fan
11 情 *senjō* lasciviousness
情的 *senjōteki* lascivious, sensational, suggestive
動 *sendō* instigation, agitation
動者 *sendōsha* instigator, agitator

7

扈 1824 / F768 KO follow.

10 従 *kojū suru* be in attendance on. *koshō, kojū* follower

8

扉 1825 / F769 HI. *tobira* door; title page, front page.

B **雇** 1826 / F2013 **雇** KO. *yato(u)* employ, hire. *yatoi* employee. [傭]

2 人 *yatoinin* employee
入 *yato(i)-i(reru)* employ, hire; charter (a boat).
3 口 *yato(i)guchi* employment, job
5 主 *yatoinushi* employer
用 *koyō* employment
用主 *koyōnushi* employer
用者 *koyōsha* employer
7 役 *koeki* employing

兵 *yato(i)hei* mercenary soldier
10 員 *koin* employee
11 庸 *koyō* employment, employing
13 傭 *koyō* employment
聘 *kohei suru* employ
賃 *yato(i)chin* wages

RAD. 手 64

Te hand. At left: 手, 手, and 扌 (3 strokes) *tehen*. Nickname: Hand.

扌 See 270.

A 手 1827 / F769 SHU. *te* hand, arm; help; handwriting; handle, means; trick, snare; skill; kind; direction, side; trouble, care; control, management; possession; connection; injury. *te ni suru* carry. *te(bura) de* empty-handed. *te(zukara)* personally, with one's own hands. *te(gusune)* prepared and waiting. *-te* person; kind; direction; money.

1 一束 *te-issoku* length of a hand
一杯 *te-ippai* hands full; barely making ends meet; full operation
2 入 *te (o) i(reru)* reach into; correct, retouch, repair; raid; interfere. *te-i(razu)* requiring little trouble; untouched, virgin (forest). *te-i(re)* repair, remodeling; care, trimming; raid, round-up
力 *shuryoku* hand power
八丁口八丁 *tehatchō-kuchihatchō no* very skilled (person)
3 口 *teguchi* style of work; method employed
下 *te (o) kuda(su)* set to work; do in person; participate; murder. *teshita* subordinate, follower
丈夫 *tejōbu na* strong
土産 *temiyage* visitor's present
小荷物 *tekonimotsu* luggage, hand baggage
工 *shukō* manual work, handicraft
工芸 *shukōgei* handicraft
工教育 *shukō kyōiku* manual training
工業 *shukōgyō* manual labor, handicrafts
4 心 *tegokoro* discretion, consideration, allowance
手 *tete* hands (child's word). *te(ni)te(ni)* in everyone's hands
爪 *tezuma* work at hand; =*tejina* 手品 (see below–9)
込 *tego(me)* rape, violation, outrage. *te(no) ko(nda)* complicated, laborious, elaborate
中 *shuchū ni* in the hand
元 *temoto*=手許 (see below–11)
分 *tewa(ke)* division of work. *te (o) wa(katsu)* break off relations with
文庫 *tebunko* small bookcase
内 *te(no)uchi* palm; skill, capacity; gift, alms; scope of one's ability
内職 *tenaishoku* piecework at home
引 *te (o) hi(ku)* lead by the hand; sever connections with. *tebi(ki)* guidance; introduction, primer; good offices, pull; introducer, backer; guide; spinning (silk) by hand
引書 *tebi(ki)sho* guidebook
不入 *te-irazu* requiring little work; untouched, virgin (forest)
不足 *tebusoku* shorthanded
水 *temizu, chōzu* water for washing the hands
水場 *chōzuba* toilet, lavatory
水鉢 *chōzubachi* washbasin
切 *te (o) ki(ru)* cut the hand; sever connections with. *tegi(re)* severance of connections
切金 *tegirekin* alimony, heart balm
切話 *tegi(re)banashi* talk of separation
5 玉 *tedama* jackstones; bean bags. *tedama ni* (leading) by the nose
立 *teda(te)* method, means
広 *te (o) hiro(geru)* extend operations. *tebiro(i)* roomy, spacious; large (practice); extensive (trade)
甲 *te(no)kō, tekkō* covering for the back of the hand. *tekkō* old-style Japanese glove
代 *tedai* clerk, salesman (in a store)
外 *te (no) hoka* beyond expectation
打 *te (o) u(tsu)* clap hands; adopt (a measure); strike a bargain. *teu(chi)* striking a bargain; reconciliation, handmade; killing by one's own hands
払 *tebara(i) suru* have nothing left
平 *te (no) hira* palm
写 *shusha* copying by hand
占 *teura* palmistry
出 *teda(shi)* interference; striking the first blow
本 *tehon* model, pattern, copy, standard
加減 *tekagen* allowance, discretion; tact; skill; measuring in the hand
古摺 *tekozu(ru)* be at wit's end, have a hard time with
付 *te (o) tsu(keru)* touch, lay hands on; attempt, have carnal connections with. *te (ni) tsu(kanai)* unable to settle down (to anything). *tetsu(ke)* way of doing; earnest money, deposit. *tetsu(ki)* way of using the hand

付金 *tezukekin, tetsukekin* earnest money, deposit
弁 *teben de* furnishing one's own lunch
弁当 *tebentō de* furnishing one's own lunch
仕事 *teshigoto* manual labor, hand work
仕舞 *tejimai* clearance (of goods); covering (of shorts) or liquidation (of longs) (stock market)
仕舞売 *tejimai u(ri)* clearance sale ⌈ing)
札 *tefuda* name card; a hand (in card play-
札形 *tefudagata* card-size photo, quarter plate ⌈plate
札判 *tefudaban* card-size photo, quarter
6 尽 *te (o) tsu(kusu)* take pains, do everything possible
返 *tegae(shi)* working on something over and over, resewing a kimono; resistance
近 *tejika na, tejika(i)* near, handy, familiar
休 *teyasu(mi), teyasu(me)* rest, pause
交 *shukō suru* hand over, deliver
合 *tea(i)* fellow, chap; party, company, set (of people). *tea(wase)* game, contest, sale, transaction
早 *tebaya(i)* quick, nimble, agile
先 *tesaki* fingers; cat's-paw, tool, agent
向 *tamu(keru)* offer, pay tribute (to the dead). *temu(kau)* resist, oppose, lift one's hand against. *tamu(ke)* offering, parting gift, tribute (to the dead)
向草 *tamu(ke)gusa* Shinto offering; tribute (to the dead) ⌈help; helper, assistant
伝 *tetsuda(u)* help, take part in. *tetsuda(i)*
伝手 *tetsuda(i)te* helper, assistant
当 *tea(tari)* the feel; within reach. *tea(tari-battari)* hit-and-miss manner. *teate* allowance, compensation, tip, bonus. *tea(te)* (police) search; treatment, dressing, medical care ⌈hazardly
当次第 *tea(tari) shidai ni* at random, hap-
回 *temawa(shi)* preparation. *te (o) mawa(su)* send out agents, use spies. *temawa(ri)* personal effects; personal surroundings; bodyguard. *te (ga) mawa(ru)* be attentive to, attend to everything ⌈prepare
回兼 *temawa(shi)-ka(neru)* be unable to
回品 *temawa(ri)hin* personal effects
7 車 *teguruma* handcart, gocart, wheelbarrow; personal jinricksha
序 *tetsuide ni* as opportunity presents itself
応 *tegotae* resistance, response; effect, result
作 *tezuku(ri) no* handmade, homemade, homegrown. *tesaku* land cultivated for oneself
走 *tabashi(ru)* fly about, scatter
折 *tao(ru)* break off, pluck; deflower
技 *shugi* technique, procedure

抜 *te (o) nu(ku)* eliminate steps, save labor; drop out (of a project); do slipshod work. *tenu(kari)* omission, oversight, error, slip. *tenu(ki)* omission; intentional negligence
利 *tekiki* expert, master hand, one clever with the hands
助 *tedasu(ke)* help, assistance
兵 *shuhei* soldiers under direct command
弄 *temasaguri* searching with the fingers;
投弾 *tena(ge)dan* hand grenade ⌊fumbling
足 *teashi* hands and feet, limbs. *shusoku* hands and feet; subordinates
足纏 *teashimato(i)* encumbrance
沢 *shutaku* soil from handling
沢本 *shutakubon* one's favorite books; books from the library of . . .
余 *teama(su), te (ni) ama(ru)* be beyond one's power; incorrigible ⌈handle
余者 *teama(shi)mono* someone difficult to
芸 *shugei* handicrafts, manual arts, useful
芸品 *shugeihin* handicrafts ⌊arts
形 *tegata* draft, promissory note
形交換所 *tegata kōkanjo* clearinghouse
形振出 *tegata furida(shi)* bank draft
形割引 *tegata waribiki* discounting a note
8 金 *tekin* key money, earnest money, deposit. *tegane* ready money
届 *te (ga) todo(ku)* reach (a goal)
底 *tanasoko* palm (of the hand)
刷 *tezu(ri)* hand printing
始 *tehajime* beginning, outset
帖 *techō* notebook
性 *teshō* skill
招 *temane(ku)* beckon
放 *tebana(su)* let go, release; part with, dispose of, send away; leave uncared for; leave off work. *tebana(shi)* hands off (in driving); leaving alone. *tebana(shi) de* freely, uncritically
明 *tea(ki)* leisure, spare time
枕 *temakura suru* use the arm for a pillow
法 *shuhō* technique, technical skill; execution
物 *te(no)mono* specialty, strong point, forte; something in the hand
並 *tena(mi)* skill, performance
斧 *chōna, teono* adze
直 *tenao(shi)* later adjustment
実 *temame na* diligent; skillful ⌈below–9)
妻 *tezuma* finger tips; =*tejina* 手品 (see
者 *te(no)mono* one's men. *tesha* skilled person ⌈row
押車 *teo(shi)guruma* handcart; wheelbar-
忠実 *temame na* faithful in one's work
長 *tenaga* long-armed person; kleptomaniac
長猿 *tenagazaru* gibbon

4 心 小 小 戈 戸 [手 扌] 支 支 攵 文 斗 方 斤 无 日 日 月 木 欠 止 歹 殳 毋 比 毛 氏 气 水 氵 氺 火 灬 爪 爫 父 爻 爿 丬 片 牙 牛 犬 犭

0

拍 *tebata(ki)* hand clapping
拍手 *tebyōshi* beating time; careless move
取 *teto(ri)* skillful wrestler, good manager. *tedo(ri)* net profit; net income; take-home pay 「ready
取早 *te(t)to(ri)baya(i)* quick; rough and
取足取 *teto(ri)-ashito(ri), te(o)to(ri)-ashi(o)to(ri)* by main force, by the hands and feet, bodily
取金 *tedorikin* take-home pay
9 首 *tekubi* wrist 「liberal (gift)
厚 *teatsu(i)* cordial, courteous, hospitable;
透 *tesu(ki)* leisure, spare time
垢 *teaka* soil from handling
後 *teoku(re)* too late, belated treatment
拱 *te (o) komanu(ku)* fold the arms; do nothing to help; meditate
拭 *tenugui, tefuki* towel
拵 *tegoshira(e) no* handmade
枷 *tekase* handcuffs, manacles 「small
狭 *tezema na, tezema(i)* narrow, cramped,
段 *shudan, tedate* resources, way, means, device, expedient, measures 「liberal
重 *teomo(i)* serious; cordial, hospitable,
柔 *teyawa(rakani)* gently, kindly, leniently
荒 *teara(i), teara na* rough, rude, harsh; violent; outrageous. *teara(ku), teara ni* roughly, violently, rudely
巻 *tema(ki)* hand-rolled cigarette
染 *tezo(me)* hand dyed
背 *shuhai* back of the hand
変品変 *te(o)ka(e)-shina(o)ka(ete)* by all pos-
風 *teburi* manners ⌊sible means
風琴 *tefūkin* accordion, hand organ
活 *te-ike* personal flower arrangement; personal attendant; redemption of a geisha or prostitute and providing a home for her
活花 *teike (no) hana* a redeemed geisha
品 *tejina* sleight of hand, tricks, juggling
品師 *tejinashi* magician, juggler
洗 *teara(i)* washing the hands; washbasin; washstand; lavatory, toilet
洗所 *tearaijo* lavatory
洗鉢 *teara(i)bachi* washbowl
前 *temae* I; you; this side of; this way, toward you; living, livelihood; due to; for the sake of, tea-ceremony procedures; self, ones' own. *(o)temae* tea-serving skill
前味噌 *temae miso* self-praise; bean paste of one's own making
前勝手 *temaegatte* selfishness
負 *te (o) o(u)* hurt yourself. *te(ni)o(enai)* unmanageable, incorrigible. *teo(i)* wound; wounded person
負猪 *teo(i)jishi* wounded boar; desperado
負獅子 *teo(i)jishi* wounded lion; desperado

持 *temo(chi)* holdings, goods on hand
持不沙汰 *temo(chi)busata* idleness, suspense; ennui
持品 *temochihin* holdings, goods on hand
持商品 *temo(chi) shōhin* goods on hand
柄 *tegara* merit, feat, exploit
柄者 *tegaramono* meritorious person
柄話 *tegarabanashi* bragging about exploits
柄顔 *tegaragao* triumphant look
相 *tesō* lines of the palm
相占 *tesō uranai* palmistry
相見 *tesōmi* palmist, palm reader
相学 *tesōgaku* palmistry
相術 *tesōjutsu* palmistry
10 振 *te (o) fu(ru)* shake one's hand. *tebu(ri)*
捕 *tedo(ri)* capturing ⌊gesture
捌 *tesaba(ki)* processing, maneuvering
挾 *tabasa(mu)* carry under the arm; wear,
酒 *tezake* homemade saké ⌊gird on
紋 *shumon* lines in the palm
紙 *tegami* letter, note, epistle
記 *shuki* taking notes; memo
討 *teu(chi)* killing with one's own sword
配 *tekuba(ri), tehai* arrangements; disposition (of men); preparations
酌 *tejaku* drinking alone
部 *shubu* the hand
書 *shusho* autograph; autographed letter. *teka(ki)* good penman 「hand; give up
挙 *te (o) a(geru)* raise a hand; show one's
弱女 *tawayame, taoyame* graceful maiden
真似 *temane* gesture, signs; dumb show, pantomime
都合 *tetsugō*=*tsugō* 都合 4769.6
荷物 *tenimotsu* luggage, baggage, personal
料理 *teryōri* home cooking ⌊effects
紡績 *tebōseki* hand spinning
11 疵 *tekizu* wound (on the battlefield)
違 *techiga(i)* hitch, something wrong
遊 *teaso(bi)* playing; plaything; gambling. *tesusabi* patting to comfort; play with
遅 *teoku(re)* too late, belated treatment
彫 *tebo(ri)* hand carving
頃 *tegoro na* handy, suitable, moderate
帳 *techō* notebook
強 *tezuyo(i)* strong, firm; severe. *tegowa(i)* stiff, unyielding, stubborn 「hand-glued
張 *teba(ru)* be beyond one's power. *teba(ri)*
掛 *tega(keru)* handle, manage, work with; rear, look after; have experience with. *te (o) ka(keru)* touch, handle. *te (ni) ka(karu)* fall into another's hand. *te (ga) ka(karu)* require a lot of care. *te (ni) ka(keru)* kill by one's hand; take care of, bring up. *tega(kari)* contact, trail, scent; on hand; hand hold; clue, key

控 *tebika(eru)* hold back, hold off, refrain from. *tebika(e)* note, memorandum; holding back
捷 *tebashiko(i)* quick, nimble, agile
掘 *tebori* digging by hand
探 *tesagu(ri)* fumbling, groping
械 *tegase, tekase* manacles, handcuffs
桶 *teoke* wooden bucket
淫 *shuin* masturbation
理 *shuri* lines in the palms
球 *tedama* cue ball
組 *tegu(mi)* hand composition (in printing); folding one's arms
脱 *tenu(kari)* a slip (in procedure), oversight
船 *tebune* one's own ship
釣 *tezu(ri)* line fishing (with no pole)
堅 *tegata(i)* steady, firm; solid, secure
盛 *temo(ri)* helping oneself, self-service; managing for one's own convenience; trap, trick; self-approved
袋 *tebukuro* gloves, mittens; gauntlet; mitt
細工 *tezaiku* handiwork, handicraft, handmade goods
許 *temoto* money on hand, one's purse; usual skill. *temoto ni* at hand, under one's care
許金 *temotokin* money on hand
毬 *temari* handball
毬唄 *temari uta* a handball song
毬歌 *temari uta* a handball song
習 *tenara(i)* penmanship; practice; learning
習草紙 *tenara(i)zōshi* copybook
習師匠 *tenara(i) shishō* writing master
動 *shudō* hand-operated
動式 *shudōshiki* hand-operated
動車 *shudōsha* handcar
動具 *tedōgu* hand tool; utensil; one's things
術 *shujutsu* surgical operation
術台 *shujutsudai* operating table
術衣 *shujutsu-i* operating gown
術的 *shujutsuteki* surgical
術室 *shujutsushitsu* surgery, operating room
術料 *shujutsuryō* operating fee
12 痛 *te-ita(i)* severe, serious, hard (blow)
遣 *tezukai* arrangements; dispositions (of men); subordinate
順 *tejun* process, routine, procedure
幅 *tehaba* handbreadth
揃 *tezoroi* full number
握 *te (o) nigi(ru)* shake hands; clasp hands (in fear); make up with
植 *teu(e)* personal planting
棒 *tembō* man whose arms are useless; armless man
渡 *tewata(shi)* personal delivery
焼 *te (o) ya(ku)* burn one's fingers, have a bitter experience with. *teya(ki) no* home baked

焙 *teaburi* hand warmer, small brazier
短 *temiji(kana)* short, brief
絡 *tegara* hair decoration
証 *teshō* evidence
創 *tekizu* wound (on the battlefield)
掌 *shushō, te(no)hira* the palm of the hand
筋 *tesuji, te (no) suji* palm lines; skill (in writing, painting, etc.); means, method; connections. *te (no) suji* veins on the hand
筈 *tehazu* program, plan
答 *tegota(e)* resistance; response; effect; result
筆 *shuhitsu* one's own handwriting
筒 *tezutsu* pistol
着 *te (o) tsu(keru)* begin, start work on
落 *teo(chi)* omission, slip, oversight, neglect
惑 *temadoi* fluster, confusion
替 *tega(wari)* substitute worker
無 *te(mo)na(ku)* easily
覚 *teobo(e)* memory of skills
貸 *te (o) ka(su)* lend a hand
軽 *tegaru na* easy, ready; simple, informal, offhand; cheap. *tegaru(i)* easy (to do)
軽料理 *tegaru ryōri* refreshments, light lunch
腕 *shuwan* ability, skill
勝手 *tegatte* allowance; discretion; tact; skill
腕家 *shuwanka* man of ability
提 *tesage* handbag
提灯 *tejōchin* hand lantern
提金庫 *tesage kinko* cash box, portable safe
提袋 *tesagebukuro* handbag
提鞄 *tesage kaban* briefcase, grip
提籠 *tesage kago* hand basket
間 *tema* time; labor; trouble; wages
間代 *temadai* labor charge
間仕事 *tema shigoto* piecework, odd jobs
間取 *temado(ru)* take time, be delayed
間損 *temazon* wasted labor
間隙 *temahima* labor and time
間賃 *temachin* wages
間潰 *tematsubu(shi)* waste of time
13 鼓 *tetsuzumi* tambourine
傷 *tekizu* wound (on the battlefield)
煩 *te (o) wazura(wasu)* trouble someone
触 *te (o) fu(reru)* touch, lay hands on. *tezawa(ri)* feel, touch
解 *tehodo(ki)* introduction, primer, rudiments
話 *shuwa* finger language
詰 *tezu(maru)* be hard up, be driven to the wall. *tezu(me)* forced liquidation. *tezu(mari)* hard up; stalemate
跡 *shuseki* handwriting (specimen)
鉤 *tekagi* hook
隙 *tesuki* leisure, spare time
障 *tezawari* the feel
飼 *tega(i)* rearing (animals)

馴 *tena*(*rasu*) tame; train (a person). *tena*(*reru*) get used to; become skilled in
勢 *tezei* troops under one's command
業 *tewaza* manual work; skill; art
続 *tetsuzu*(*ki*) procedure, process (of laws),
続上 *tetsuzu*(*ki*)*jō* procedurally ⌊formalities
際 *tegiwa* performance, execution; skill; tact ⌈erly, tactfully
際良 *tegiwayo*(*ku*) skillfully, neatly, clev-
数 *tekazu* trouble; number of moves (in a game). *tesū* trouble, pains, care
数料 *tesūryō* handling charge, commission
裏 *shuri* in the hand. *te* (*no*) *ura* palm
裏剣 *shuriken* dart, dirk, throwing knife
塩 *teshio* table salt; small dish
塩皿 *teshiozara* small dish, saucer
塩掛 *teshio* (*ni*) *ka*(*keru*) rear, raise, tame; train (flower)
14選 *tesen* handpicking (in mining)
鳴 *te* (*o*) *na*(*rasu*) call by clapping
慣 *tena*(*reru*)＝手馴 (see above–13)
摑 *tezukami* talking with the fingers
摺 *tesuri* railing, balustrade
槍 *teyari* javelin
種 *tegusa* fingering; gambling; plaything
綱 *tazuna* bridle, reins
踊 *teodo*(*ri*) posture dancing
酷 *tehido*(*i*) severe, cruel, merciless
銃 *tezutsu* pistol
窪 *te*(*no*)*kubo* hollow of the hand
箒 *tebōki* small broom
管 *tekuda* art, technique; guile, wiles, coquetry; deceit
蔓 *tezuru* interest, influence, connections, good offices, medium
製 *tesei* handmade, homespun
榴弾 *shuryūdan*, *teryūdan* hand grenade
綺麗 *tegirei na* neat, clean, dexterous
爾尾葉 *te-ni-o-ha* the particles (in grammar) ⌈gers
鼻 *tebana* blowing the nose with the fin-
鼻擤 *tebana* (*o*) *ka*(*mu*) blow the nose with ⌊the fingers
旗 *tebata* hand flag
旗信号 *tebata shingō* flag signalling
漉 *tesuki* handmade paper
漉紙 *tesukigami* handmade paper
練 *shuren* manual skill. *teren* methods of deception
練手管 *teren-tekuda* methods of deception
15編 *tea*(*mi*) hand knitting
縫 *tenu*(*i*) *no* hand-sewn, hand-tailored
緩 *tenuru*(*i*) mild, lenient; relaxed; lukewarm; slow, dilatory
駒 *tegoma* person kept in reserve
箱 *tebako* hand box, toilet case
慰 *tenagusa*(*mi*) fingering; gambling
16懐 *tenazu*(*keru*) tame, domesticate; win
機 *tebata* hand loom ⌊over; win one's heart
積 *tezumo*(*ri*) rough measurement
錠 *tejō* handcuffs, manacles
録 *shuroku* personal record
鋸 *tenoko* hand saw
頸 *tekubi* wrist
薄 *teusu* weakness, shortage; inadequate preparations. *teusu*(*i*) scarce, short of;
翰 *shukan* letter ⌊slender (means)
17厳 *tekibi*(*shii*) severe, scathing, cruel
濡 *te* (*o*) *nu*(*rasazu*) *ni* without getting wet; without lifting a finger
燭 *teshoku* portable candlestick
鍋 *tenabe* pan ⌈the hand
翳 *te* (*o*) *kaza*(*su*) shading (the eyes) with
療治 *teryōji* self-treatment, home treatment
邇乎波 *te-ni-o-ha* the particles (in gram-
鞠 *temari* handball ⌊mar)
鞠唄 *temari uta* handball song
18癖 *tekuse* kleptomania; hand mannerisms
織 *teo*(*ri*) hand weaving
職 *teshoku* handicraft
蹟 *shuseki* handwriting (specimen)
簡 *shukan* letter
簞笥 *tedansu* chest of drawers
19縄 *tenawa* curtain rope; rope binding a criminal; halter rope
鏡 *tekagami* hand mirror; copybook; model
鞴 *tefuigo* a hand bellows
離 *tebana*(*reru*) to not need constant care; be finished and ready to deliver
繰 *tagu*(*ru*) haul in, reel in; trace; unravel. *teguri* spinning by hand; dragnet; arrangement; management ⌈(*geru*) haul in
繰上 *taku*(*shi*)-*a*(*geru*) tuck up. *tagu*(*shi*)-*a*-
繰込 *tagu*(*ri*)-*ko*(*mu*) haul in ⌈(a clue)
繰出 *tagu*(*ri*)-*da*(*su*) pay out (a line); trace
繰揚 *tagu*(*ri*)-*a*(*geru*) haul in
繰網 *tegu*(*ri*) *ami* dragnet
20懸 *tekake* handling something; concubine. *tega*(*kari*)＝手掛 (see above–11)
21纏 *temadoi*, *tematoi* foot clogs on one's hands; encumbrance, hindrance to work
22鑑 *tekagami* model; copy; paragon
籠 *tekago* hand basket. *tegome* rape, violation; outrage

2

B **払** 1828 / F785 **拂** FUTSU. *hara*(*u*) clear out, sweep away, wipe off, brush off, drive away, banish; prune; parry; pay; dispose of; wield (a sword) sideways; show interest in. (*o*)*hara*(*i*) payment; unneeded things for sale.
3下 *hara*(*i*)-*sa*(*geru*) sell, dispose of

下品 *haraisagehin* articles sold by the government

4手 *hara(i)te* payer

込 *hara(i)-ko(mu)* pay in, pay up, pay an installment. *haraiko(mi)* payment, installment, subscription

込資本 *haraiko(mi) shihon* paid-up capital

5出 *hara(i)-da(su)* disburse, pay out; drive away

6返 *hara(i)-kae(su)* pay back

7戻 *hara(i)-modo(su)* refund, reimburse

8底 *futtei* shortage, scarcity, famine

退 *hara(i)-no(keru)* brush aside, ward off, drive away

物 *hara(i)mono* discarded article; article to be disposed of

9拭 *fusshoku suru* wipe out, sweep away

除 *hara(i)-nozo(ku)* remove, sweep away

10残 *hara(i)noko(ri)* arrears, balance due

11過 *hara(i)-su(giru)* overpay

捨 *hara(i)-su(teru)* cast off

済 *hara(i)zu(mi)* paid up, settled

12暁 *futsugyō* dawn

渡 *hara(i)-wata(su)* pay, pay out, pay over; cash (a check)

落 *hara(i)-oto(su)* shake off, brush off

15箱 *(o)hara(i)bako* dismissal

A **打** 1829 F772 CHŌ, DA striking. *u(tsu)* strike, hit, beat, knock, slap, punch, thrash, smite; clap (one's hands); beat (a drum); ring (a bell); (clocks) strike; impress, touch; shoot; pound in (a nail); water, sprinkle; braid; play (checkers); till (the soil); temper (a sword); prepare (buckwheat noodles); present (a play); cast (a net); pay (earnest money). *bu(tsu)* strike, beat; tell, speak; address (an audience). *dāsu* dozen. *u(chi-nomesu)* knock down, beat up. *u(chi)-* emphatic verbal prefix.

2力 *daryoku* batting power

3下 *u(chi)-o(rosu)* strike on the head, strike down on, bring an ax down on

上 *u(chi)-a(geru)* shoot up, send up, set off (fireworks); dash against; cast up on shore, wash ashore; finish, end (a performance)

上花火 *uchiage hanabi* skyrocket

4手 *dashu* (cricket) bowler. *u(chi)te, u(t)te*＝討手 4316.4

方 *u(chi)kata* how to shoot; batting, stroking (in tennis); how to punctuate

止 *u(chi)-ya(mu)*＝*ya(mu)* (see under 止 2429.0). *u(chi-to(meru)* kill, bring down (a bird). *u(chi)do(me)* end of an entertainment or match

水 *u(chi)mizu* watering, sprinkling

火 *u(chi)bi* flintstone fire

込 *u(chi)-ko(mu)* drive in, pound in, shoot into, fall deeply in love, be thrown into, be absorbed in

切 *bu(t)tagi(ru)* cut off, chop off. *u(chi)-ki(ru) vt* end, close, discontinue. *bu(k)ki(ru)* chop, mangle

切棒 *bukkirabō* abruptness, brusqueness

5立 *u(chi)-ta(teru)* establish

付 *u(chi)-tsu(keru)* strike, knock; pound in (a nail); throw at. *u(chi)tsu(ke) ni* bluntly, directly, flatly. *u(tte)-tsu(ke)* appropriateness of work

叩 *u(chi)-tata(ku), bu(t)tata(ku)* pound, strike bruise,

払 *u(chi)-hara(u)* beat off, shake off, sweep off, brush off, drive off, repel, rout

打 *chōchō*＝丁丁 2.2

出 *u(chi)-da(su)* begin to beat; open fire; emboss; end, be over. *u(chi)-de(ru), u(tte)-de(ru)* sally out, come forward, be a candidate; fire. *u(chi)da(shi)* close of a performance; embossing; delivery (of a ball)

出小槌 *u(chi)de (no) kozuchi* mallet of luck (Aladdin's lamp)

出後 *u(chi)da(shi)go* after the show

6回 *u(chi)-mawa(su)* beat about

尽 *u(chi)-tsuku(su)* shoot up all (ammunition)

返 *u(chi)-kae(su)* strike back; return (the ball); rally; repeat; plow up; renovate (old cotton). *u(chi)kae(shi)* striking back; change of scene

向 *u(chi)-mu(kau)*＝*mu(kau)* (see under 向 101.0)

伏 *u(chi)-fu(seru)* overpower, have power over. *u(chi)-fu(su)* humble oneself

当 *u(chi)-a(teru)* dash against

合 *u(chi)-a(u)* fight, exchange blows. *u(chi)-a(waseru)* strike (a thing) against (another). *uchi-a(wase)* previous arrangement; preliminaries, appointment

合会 *uchiawa(se)kai* caucus, consultation, preliminary meeting

7身 *u(chi)mi* bruise, contusion

抜 *u(chi)-nu(ku)* punch, perforate; stamp out (coins); penetrate, pierce; shoot thru

沈 *u(chi)-shizu(mu)* be completely discouraged

克 *u(chi)-ka(tsu)*＝打勝 (see below–12)

見所 *u(chi)mi(taru) tokoro* to all appearances

8金 *u(chi)gane* (gun) hammer, cock. *u(chi)kin* extra money paid in a trade

固 *u(chi)-kata(meru)* harden by tamping

延 *u(chi)-no(basu), u(chi)-no(beru)* hammer out

退 *u(chi)-shirizo(ku)* repulse

拉 *u(chi)-hishi(gu)* batter, smite

取 *u(chi)-to(ru)* catch, arrest; take possession of; kill

殴 *bu(n)nagu(ru)* (emphatic) strike, beat

者 *dasha* batter, hitter

垂髪 *u(chi)taregami* letting the hair hang down

明 *u(chi)-a(keru), u(chi)-a(kasu)* reveal, confide in

明話 *u(chi)a(ke)banashi* confidential talk, confession, revealing a secret

物 *u(chi)mono* forged work; sword, weapon; molded cake

物造 *u(chi)monozuku(ri)* hammered work

物師 *u(chi)monoshi* toolmaker, swordsmith

9 飛 *bu(t)to(basu)* (emphatic), beat, strike knock; let go off. *bu(t)to(bu)* (emphatic)

首 *u(chi)kubi* decapitation ⌊jump

建 *u(chi)-ta(teru)* erect, build

廻 *u(chi)-mawa(su)* build an enclosure

連 *u(chi)-tsu(reru)*=*tsu(reru)* (see under 連 4702.0)

砕 *u(chi)-kuda(ku), bu(chi)-kuda(ku)* smash,

乗 *u(chi)-no(ru)* ride (a horse) ⌊crush

変 *u(tte)-kawa(ru)* change completely

点 *daten* runs batted in ⌈4488.0)

負 *u(chi)-ma(kasu)*=*ma(kasu)* (see under 負

10 倒 *bu(t)tao(su)* knock down. *bu(t)tao(reru)* fall down, be knocked down. *u(chi)-tao(reru)*=*tao(reru)* (see under 倒 487.0). *u(chi)-tao(su)* knock down; overthrow. *datō* knockout; overthrowing

従 *u(chi)-shitaga(eru)* subjugate

悩 *u(chi)-naya(masu)* harass. *u(chi)-naya(mu)* be troubled with

振 *u(chi)-fu(ru)*=*furu* (see under 振 1920.0)

残 *u(chi)-noko(su)* leave unhurt

消 *u(chi)-ke(su)* deny, contradict. *uchike(shi)* denial, negation; negative (in grammar)

破 *u(chi)-yabu(ru)*=*yabu(ru)* (see under 破 3186.0). *daha* breaking, destruction, defeat, conquest, overthrow

粉 *u(chi)ko* blade-sharpening powder

紐 *u(chi)himo* braid, braided cord

殺 *bu(chi)-koro(su)* club to death. *u(chi)-koro(su)* club to death, stone to death, shoot to death, slay

笑 *u(chi)-e(mu)* smile slightly

荷 *u(chi)ni* jetsam, jettisoned cargo

留 *u(chi)-to(meru)* kill, bring down (a bird). *u(chi)do(me)* end of a match or an enter-

11 毬 *dakyū* (ancient) Japanese polo ⌊tainment

過 *u(chi)-su(giru)* pass by (time)

掛 *u(tte)-kaka(ru)* attack a person. *u(chi)-ka(karu), bu(chi)-ka(karu)* strike at (someone). *u(chi)ka(ke)* long outer robe

据 *u(chi)-su(eru)* whip (a horse) ⌈1944.0)

捨 *u(chi)-su(teru)*=*suteru* (see under 捨

捲 *u(chi)-maku(ru)* pound a pitcher (in

球 *dakyū* batting; batted ball ⌊baseball)

眺 *u(chi)-naga(meru)* = *naga(meru)* (see under 眺 3138.0)

敗 *u(chi)-yabu(ru)* defeat, crush

率 *daritsu* batting average ⌈beat upon

寄 *u(chi)-yo(seru)* break upon (the shore),

貫 *u(chi)-nu(ku), u(chi)-tsuranu(ku)* pierce

萎 *u(chi)-shio(reru)*=*shio(reru)* (see under 萎 3973.0)

菓子 *u(chi)gashi* molded confectionery

12 遣 *utcha(ru), utcha(rakasu)* throw away, throw down, abandon, neglect, leave alone, leave a (person) out

開 *u(chi)-bira(ku)*=*hiraku* (see under 開 4950.0). *dakai* break, development, new

場 *u(chi)ba* threshing floor ⌊turn, solution

順 *dajun* batting order

棒 *dabō* batting; bat

勝 *u(chi)-ka(tsu)* defeat, conquer, overcome, surmount, recover from (illnesses)

診 *dashin* percussion, tapping (in medicine)

割 *u(chi)-wa(ru)*=*wa(ru)* (see under 割

散 *u(chi)-chi(rasu)* scatter violently ⌊703.0)

落 *u(chi)-o(tosu)* knock down; shoot down; knock out (a tooth); thresh out; lop off (branches) ⌈5031.0)

集 *u(chi)-tsudo(u)*=*tsudo(u)* (see under 集

13 傷 *u(chi)kizu* bruise, contusion

損 *u(chi)-sokona(u)* miss, fail to hit

続 *u(chi)-tsuzu(keru)* give repeated blows; fire in succession; batter; continue. *u(chi)-tsuzu(ku)* long, long-continued

数 *dasū* times at bat

毀 *u(chi)-kowa(su), bu(chi)-kowa(su)*=*kowa(su)* (see under 毀 2460.0)

寛 *u(chi)-kutsu(rogu)*=*kutsu(rogu)* (see under 寛 1325.0)

置 *u(chi)-o(ku)* place (emphatic)

電 *daden suru* send a telegram

楽器 *dagakki* percussion instrument

解 *u(chi)-to(keru)* open one's heart, be frank, throw aside reserve

解話 *u(chi)to(ke)banashi* friendly chat, heart-to-heart talk

14 鳴 *u(chi)-na(rasu)*=*na(rasu)* (see under 鳴

網 *u(chi)ami* casting net ⌊983.0)

魂消 *bu(t)tamage(ru)* be terribly startled

綿機 *u(chi)wataki* cotton gin

穀 *dakoku* flailing ⌈ing machine

穀機 *dakokki* threshing instrument, thresh-

算 *dasan* calculation, self-interest, selfishness ⌈centered

算的 *dasanteki* calculating, mercenary, self-

15 線 *dasen* batting line-up

敷 *u(chi)shi(ki)* a spread, an altar cloth

撲 *daboku* contusion, blow

撲傷 *dabokushō* bruise, contusion

撃 *dageki* blow. hit, shock; batting,

撃王 *dagekiō* king of " swat " ⌊hitting

撃率 *dagekiritsu* batting average
撃賞 *dagekishō* batting award
16 壊 *bu(chi)-kowa(su)* break, shatter, smash; upset (a plan), ruin, spoil, frustrate; bungle
17 擲 *bu(n)nagu(ru)* strike, beat, hit. *chōchaku* thrashing, spanking, slapping, striking, beating
18 懲 *u(chi)-ko(rasu)* discipline, chasten, punish by whipping ⌈noise
21 囃 *u(chi)-haya(su)* make a loud (musical)

3

扛 1830 F773 Kō raise.
10 秤 *chikiri* large beam balance

扨 1831 F-X **扨** *sate* well, now.

扞 1832 F773 Kan restrain.
10 格 *kankaku* incompatibility, divergence (of views), inconsistency, antagonism

扣 1833 F773 Kō. *hika(e)*, *hika(eru)* (see under 控 1941.0).
? 除 *kōjo* subtraction, deduction

扠 1834 F773 Sa. *sate* well, now.
3 叉 *sate mata* and again
13 置 *sateo(ku)* leave as is

托 1835 F773 Taku. *taku(suru)* (see under 託 4315.0).
7 身 *takushin* (Catholic) incarnation ⌈priest
13 鉢 *takuhatsu* religious mendicancy; begging

B **扱** 1836 F774 **扱** Sō. Kyū. *atsuka(u)* treat; entertain; manage, deal with, conduct, work on; handle; manipulate. *shigo(ku)* squeeze thru the hand, strip off. *ko(ku)* thresh, strip. *shigoki* woman's undergirdle, waistband; squeezing thru.
2 人 *atsuka(i)nin* person in charge ⌈meanly
3 下 *ko(ki)-oro(su)* thresh; strip off; criticize
8 使 *ko(ki)-tsuka(u)* work (a person) hard
11 混 *ko(ki)-ma(zeru)* mix together
寄 *ko(ki)-yo(seru)* rake together
12 落 *ko(ki)-o(tosu)* thresh, strip off

4

承 See 197.

扱 See 1836.

抛 1837 F-X See **抛** 1875.

抔 1838 F779 Hō. *nado* and so forth.

抃 1839 F777 **抃** Ben strike with the hand.
14 舞 *bembu* dancing for joy

抉 1840 F777 Ketsu. *egu(ru)* gouge, hollow out, bore, excavate. *koji(ru)* gouge; wrench, pry. *kuji(ru)* pick, scoop.
8 取 *egu(ri)-to(ru)* gouge out

抒 1841 F779 Cho, Sho, Jo tell.
11 情 *jojō* expression of one's feelings; lyricism
情的 *jojōteki* lyrical
情詩 *jojōshi* lyric poetry; lyric poem
情詩人 *jojō shijin* lyric poet
情詩風 *jojōshifū* lyricism
情歌 *jojōka* lyric poetry; lyric poem

扼 1842 F775 Yaku. *yaku(suru)* command, dominate; prevent, obstruct; hold, grip; crush, defeat.
10 殺 *yakusatsu suru* choke to death
12 腕 *yakuwan suru* clinch the fists, roll up the sleeves in anger

抓 1843 F779 Sō. *tsu(neru)*, *tsu(meru)*, *tsu(mu)*, *tsuma(mu)* pick, pinch; hold in the fingers; summarize.
5 出 *tsuma(mi)-da(su)* pick up and throw out
8 物 *tsuma(mi)mono* crackers, etc., to munch on while drinking ⌈stealthily
9 食 *tsumamigu(i)* picking and eating; eating
洗 *tsumamiara(i)* washing out spots

扮 1844 F773 Fun. *fun(suru)*, *yatsu(su)* impersonate, dress up (as), disguise oneself (as). *sogi* thin shingles.
8 板 *sogi ita* thin shingles ⌈of dress
12 装 *funsō suru* impersonate. *funsō* garb, style
13 飾 *funshoku*＝粉飾 3469.13

B **択** 1845 F833 **擇** Taku. *yo(ru)*, *era(bu)*, *e(ru)* (see under 選 4744.0).
1 一 *taku-itsu* choosing an alternative
一的 *taku-itsuteki* alternative
4 分 *yo(ri)-wa(keru)* (see under 選分 4744.4)

7拔 *takubatsu* choosing from among many
10屑 *yorikuzu* waste, trash, refuse

把 1846 / F777 HA bundle, bunch, sheaf, coil. *to(ru)* (see under 取 3699.0). *wa* bundle, faggot, sheaf.

4手 *totte, torite, hashu* handle, knob, grip. *hashu* grasping the hand
7住 *hajū suru* retain, keep in mind
住力 *hajūryoku* retentive power
9持 *haji suru* grasp, hold, clasp
12握 *ha-aku* grasp, hold, grip

B **拒** 1847 / F787 **拒** KYO *koba(mu)* refuse, reject, decline; repudiate; resist, oppose, prevent; deny. *fuse(gu)* (see under 防 4980.0).

4止 *kyoshi suru* refuse, decline, check
7否 *kyohi* denial, veto, rejection
否権 *kyohiken* veto right
12絶 *kyozetsu* refusal, rejection, rebuff
絶品 *kyozetsuhin* rejected articles

B **批** 1848 / F775 HI strike.

5正 *hisei suru* criticize and correct
7判 *hihan* criticism, comment
判的 *hihanteki* critical
9点 *hiten* correction marks (in a manuscript); emphasis marks; points to be criticized
10准 *hijun* ratification
准書 *hijunsho* instrument of ratification
12評 *hihyō* criticism, comment
評家 *hihyōka* critic, reviewer
評眼 *hihyōgan* critical eye
18難 *hinan* criticism, denunciation
20議 *higi suru* blame, criticize

B **抄** 1849 / F777 SHŌ selection, summary; one-tenth of a *shaku* (勺). *shō(suru)* copy; copy out. *su(ku)* spread out thin; manufacture (paper).

3上 *suku(i)-a(geru)* scoop up, dip up
5写 *shōsha* excerpt, quotation
出 *shōshutsu suru* take excerpts
本 *shōhon* excerpt, abridgment, book of selections
8物 *shōmono* a printed digest of a book; a copied book; (ancient) Japanese commentary on a Chinese book
10書 *shōsho*=*shōhon* 抄本 (see above–5)
紙 *shōshi* paper making
紙機 *shōshiki* paper-making machine
11掠 *shōryaku* robbery
略 *shōryaku* robbery
訳 *shōyaku* abridged translation
16録 *shōroku* quotation, selection; summary

B **扶** 1850 / F774 FU. *tasu(keru)* (see under 助 719.0).

6合 *tasu(ke)-a(u)* co-operate, help each other
7助 *fujo* aid, help, support, relief
助料 *fujoryō* pension
8育 *fuiku* bringing up (children)
育料 *fuikuryō* charge for rearing others' children
9持 *fuchi* stipend, allowance, sustenance
持米 *fuchimai* rice allowance
10桑 *Fusō* Japan
11掖 *fueki* help, support
12植 *fushoku* implantation; establishment, extension
15養 *fuyō* support, maintenance
養家族 *fuyō kazoku* family dependents
17翼 *fuyoku suru* aid, support

B **抑** 1851 / F778 YOKU *osa(eru), osa(e)* (see under 押 1885.0). *somosomo* well, now; in the first place.

4止 *yokushi suru* check, checkmate, stave off
切 *osa(e)ki(renai)*=*osa(e)gata(i)* 抑難 (see below–18)
5圧 *yokuatsu* oppression, repression, pressure, suppression, restraint
付 *osa(e)-tsu(keru)* hold down, curb, control
7抑 *yokuyoku* discreet, careful, cautious
8物 *osa(e)mono* the last (special) course (of a banquet)
制 *yokusei suru* control, restrain, suppress
制力 *yokuseiryoku* restraining power
制均衡 *yokusei (to) kinkō* system of checks and balances
10留 *yokuryū* internment
留国 *yokuryūkoku* detaining country
留所 *yokuryūjo* internment camp
留者 *yokuryūsha* internee
留船 *yokuryūsen* interned ship
12揚 *yokuyō* modulation, intonation, accent, rhythm, cadence
18難 *osa(e)gata(i)* uncontrollable, irresistible, irrepressible
26鬱 *yoku-utsu* depression (in psychiatry)

B **抗** 1852 / F780 KŌ. *kō(suru)* resist, defy, oppose, antagonize.

4日 *kōnichi* anti-Japanese
5弁 *kōben* plea, defense, protest, refutation, contradiction, answer
生 *kōsei no* antibiotic
生物質 *kōsei busshitsu* an antibiotic
生物質学 *kōsei busshitsugaku* science of antibiotics
6争 *kōsō* dispute; resistance
7言 *kōgen* protest, retort
拒 *kōkyo* resistance
告 *kōkoku* protest, appeal
8毒素 *kōdokuso* antitoxin, antivenom
命 *kōmei* disobedience
命罪 *kōmeizai* the crime of military disobedience
10病力 *kōbyōryoku* resistance to disease

11 張力 *kōchōryoku* tensile strength
13 戦 *kōsen* resistance
15 敵 *kōteki* resistance to the enemy
20 議 *kōgi* protest, objection
議文 *kōgibun* written protest

A **技** 1853/F776 GI art, craft; ability, skill, feat, performance. *waza* (see under 業 143.0).

8 工 *gikō* artisan, craftsman
4 手 *gishu, gite* assistant engineer; (telegraph) operator
5 巧 *gikō* art, craftmanship, skill, technique; trick
巧的 *gikōteki* skillful, clever; ornate
7 芸 *gigei* arts, crafts, accomplishments
8 法 *gihō* technique
官 *gikan* technical official
10 師 *gishi* engineer, technician
倒 *gitō* technical knockout
倆 *giryō* skill
能 *ginō* ability, capacity, skill, talent
11 術 *gijutsu* art, technique, skill
術士 *gijutsushi* engineer, technician
術官 *gijutsukan* technical official
術者 *gijutsusha* technician, engineer
術家 *gijutsuka* technician, specialist, expert
術賠償 *gijutsu baishō* reparations in technical help
12 量 *giryō* skill
14 監 *gikan* chief engineer

B **抜** 1854/F787 **拔** BATSU. *nu(ku)* extract, uncork, pull out; root up; unsheathe; pilfer; quote; remove; omit; capture; outrun; shoot thru. *nu(keru)* come off, fall out, slip out; be omitted; be missing; be rid of; pass thru; escape; be captured; withdraw; be less than. *nu(kasu)* omit, skip over. *nuki(nderu)* excel in, surpass. *nu(karu)* be careless; slip, make a mistake. *nu(kari)* negligence; carelessness. *nu(ki)* omission, removal; defeating. *nu(karanu)* shrewd, on one's guard.

2 入 *nu(ke)-i(ru)* crawl into
刀 *battō* drawing a sword; drawn sword
3 上 *nu(ke)-a(garu)* be bald in front
小路 *nu(ke) kōji* a thru passage
4 毛 *nu(ki)te, nu(ki)de* overhand stroke
毛 *nu(ke)ge* falling hair, combings, molt
切 *nu(ke)-ki(ru)* get rid of, get free from
5 目 *nu(ke)me* imprudence. *nu(ke)me(nai)* shrewd, alert, careful, tactful, clever
穴 *nu(ke)ana* secret passage, underground exit; loophole; way of escape
代 *nu(ke)-kowa(ru)* shed, molt
写 *nu(ki)utsu(shi)* selection, excerpt
去 *nu(ke)-sa(ru)* lose all (strength). *nu(ki)-sa(ru)* pull out. *bakkyo* extraction (of teeth)
出 *nu(ki)-da(su), nu(ki)-ida(su)* select, extract, pull out. *nu(ke)-da(su), nu(ke)-de(ru)* slip out, sneak away, break out, get loose; excel, surpass, choose the best. *nu(ki)-de(ru)* be outstanding
本 *bappon* eradication
打 *nukiu(chi)* sudden attack
打的 *nukiu(chi)teki ni* without notice
6 糸 *basshi* removal of stitches. *nu(ki)ito* drawn thread
合 *nu(ki)-a(waseru)* unsheathe together
衣紋 *nu(ki)emon de* with kimono collar pulled back
7 身 *nu(ki)mi* drawn sword
作 *nu(ke)saku* dunce, simpleton
抜 *nu(ke)nu(ke) to* unashamedly
足 *nu(ki)ashi de* stealthily, gingerly
足差足 *nu(ki)ashi-sa(shi)ashi de* stealthily, gingerly
8 刷 *nu(ki)zu(ri)* a publication of the important parts of a book
放 *nu(ki)-hana(su), nu(ki)-hana(tsu)* unsheathe, draw out, take out
参 *nu(ke)mair(i)* secret pilgrimage
取 *nu(ki)-to(ru)* pilfer, steal; pull out, extract, take out, tear off
取検査 *nukito(ri) kensa* inspection of (grain) samples
9 首 *nu(ke)kubi* long-necked monster
連 *nu(ki)-tsu(reru), nu(ki)-tsura(neru)* draw swords together
砕 *nu(ki)-kuda(ku)* break (teeth)
10 粋 *bassui*=抜萃 (see below–11)
剣 *bakken* drawing a sword
差 *nu(ki)sa(shi)* slipping off and on; taking on and off. *nu(ki)sa(shinaranu)* impossible; being in a dilemma
書 *nukiga(ki)* selection, excerpt
荷 *nu(ki)ni* pilfered goods. *nokeni* smuggled goods
11 道 *nu(ke)michi* bypass; secret path; way of escape, loophole; last resources; excuse
捨 *nu(ki)-su(teru)* cut off from, uproot and throw away
殻 *nu(ke)gara* the shed skin (of a snake or cicada); a person whose mind is elsewhere
商 *nu(ke)akina(i)* smuggling
萃 *bassui* quotation, selection, excerpt; abstract, summary
帳萃 *bassuichō* scrapbook
12 歯 *basshi* extraction of teeth
殼 *nu(ke)gara* a cicada's shell; a cast-off snake skin; a mere shadow of oneself
落 *nu(ke)-o(chiru)* fall out. *nu(ki)-oto(su)* let fall
集 *nu(ki)-atsu(meru)* pull out and gather up. *nukiatsu(me)* quotation; summary

4 心 小 ⺌ 戈 戸 【手 扌】 支 攴 攵 文 斗 斤 方 无 日 曰 月 木 欠 止 歹 殳 毋 比 毛 氏 气 水 氵 氺 火 灬 爪 ⺤ 父 爻 爿 丬 片 牙 牛 犬 犭

替 *nu*(*ke*)-*ka*(*waru*) shed, molt
13 路 *nu*(*ke*)*michi*＝抜道 (see above–11)
群 *batsugun, bakkun* pre-eminence
裏 *nu*(*ke*)*ura* bypass; way of escape ⌈story
14 読 *nukiyo*(*mi*) *suru* read or tell part of a
駆 *nu*(*ke*)*ga*(*ke*) stealing a march on; fore-
15 撃 *nukiu*(*chi*) sudden attack ⌊stalling; scoop
16 錨 *batsubyō* weighing anchor
17 擢 *batteki* selection, choice
翳 *nu*(*ki*)-*kaza*(*su*) draw a sword and hold it up over one's forehead
18 襟 *nu*(*ki*)*eri* pulled-back collar
顔 *nu*(*karanu*) *kao* a watchful eye

A **折** 1855 / F780 Setsu. *o*(*ru*) *vt* break, snap, fracture, knock out (teeth); fold, turn down; bend; make (a paper toy); yield (oneself), give in. *o*(*reru*) snap, break; be folded; give in, submit; turn (to the left or right). *o*(*re*) fragment, broken piece. *o*(*ri*) breaking; small food box; time, occasion, juncture; opportunity. *ori*(*shimo*) just then. *o*(*ri*) *kara* just at that time. -*ori*- folding; signature (of a book)

2 入 *o*(*ri*)-*i*(*reru*) fold and insert; tuck in; turn in; read into. *o*(*ri*)-*i*(*tte*) earnestly
3 口 *o*(*re*)*kuchi* a split, a break
子 *o*(*ri*)*ko* folder (the person)
山 *o*(*ri*)*yama* the outside edge of a fold
4 戸 *o*(*ri*)*do* folding doors
方 *o*(*ri*)*kata* how to fold
木 *o*(*re*)*gi* broken tree
尺 *o*(*ri*)*jaku* folded ruler
込 *o*(*ri*)-*ko*(*mu*) tuck, turn in; insert. *o*(*re*)-*ko*(*mu*) fold and insert. *o*(*ri*)*ko*(*mi*) insert
中 *setchū*＝折衷 (see below–9)
木戸 *o*(*ri*) *kido* folding wooden doors
手本 *o*(*ri*)*dehon* folding copybook
5 句 *o*(*ri*)*ku* acrostic verse
半 *seppan* halving
本 *o*(*ri*)*bon, o*(*ri*)*hon* a folding book, a folder
目 *o*(*re*)*me, o*(*ri*)*me* fold, crease, dog-ear
目切目 *o*(*ri*)*me-ki*(*ri*)*me*＝*kichōmen* 几帳面 653.11 ⌈monious
目正 *o*(*ri*)*metada*(*shii*) well-mannered; cere-
6 曲 *o*(*ri*)-*ma*(*geru*) bend, turn up, turn down
好 *o*(*ri*)*yo*(*ki*) timely, opportune; lucky. *o*(*ri*)*yo*(*ku*) fortunately, just in time
合 *o*(*ri*)-*a*(*u*), *o*(*re*)-*a*(*u*) come to an agreement. *o*(*ri*)*a*(*i*), *o*(*re*)*a*(*i*) mutual relations; compromise, agreement, understanding
地図 *o*(*ri*) *chizu* folding map
返 *o*(*re*)-*kae*(*ru*) tell again and again. *o*(*ri*)-*kae*(*su*) turn up, turn down, fold back; repeat. *o*(*ri*)*kae*(*shi*) lapel, cuffs, flap; chorus, refrain; repetition
返点 *o*(*ri*)*kae*(*shi*)*ten* turn-back point
返運転 *o*(*ri*)*kae*(*shi*) *unten* shuttle service
7 角 *sekkaku* at great pains; on purpose, expressly; kindly. *sekkaku no* valuable,
折 *o*(*ri*)*o*(*ri*) occasionally ⌊long-awaited
助 *o*(*ri*)*suke* footman, flunkey ⌈curtsy
8 屈 *o*(*re*)-*kaga*(*mu*) bend. *o*(*ri*)*kaga*(*mi*) bend,
取 *o*(*ri*)-*to*(*ru*) break and take, pick (flowers)
9 柄 *o*(*ri*) *kara* just then, at that time. *orie* broken handle
砕 *o*(*ri*)-*kuda*(*ku*) strike down, break down. *o*(*re*)-*kuda*(*keru*) be broken
重 *o*(*ri*)-*kasa*(*naru*) *vi* overlap; telescope. *o*(*ri*)-*kasa*(*neru*) *vt* fold back, turn down
衷 *setchū* compromise; cross, blending, eclecticism
衷主義 *setchū shugi* syncretism
10 紙 *o*(*ri*)*gami* folded paper; colored folding paper; affidavit, testimonial ⌈notorious
紙付 *o*(*ri*)*gamizu*(*ki*) certified, guaranteed;
釘 *o*(*re*)*kugi, o*(*ri*)*kugi* hooked nail; broken
釘流 *o*(*re*)*kugiryū* scrawl ⌊nail
11 掛 *o*(*ri*)-*ka*(*keru*) bend and hang up
脚 *o*(*ri*)*ashi* folding table
悪 *o*(*ri*)*a*(*shiku*) inopportunely, unfortunate-
崩 *o*(*ri*)-*kuzu*(*reru*) collapse ⌊ly
12 椅子 *o*(*ri*)-*isu* folding chair
畳 *o*(*ri*)-*tata*(*mu*) fold up
畳式 *o*(*ri*)*tatamishiki* collapsible, folding
畳自在 *o*(*ri*)*tatamijizai* collapsible, folding
畳椅子 *o*(*ri*)*tatami isu* folding chair
畳機 *o*(*ri*)*tatamiki* folding machine
13 詰 *orizume* food packed in a small box
節 *o*(*ri*)*fushi* chance, occasion; just then; occasionally; opportunity, time
電 *setsuden* zigzag lightning
14 鞄 *o*(*ri*) *kaban* folding brief case
15 衝 *sesshō* negotiation ⌈(position)
敷 *o*(*ri*)-*shi*(*ku*) kneel. *o*(*ri*)*shi*(*ki*) kneeling
箱 *o*(*ri*)*bako* small box made of cardboard or thin wood ⌈ping, spanking
18 檻 *sekkan* chastisement, correction; whip-
襟 *o*(*r*)*ieri* turned-down collar; sack coat

A **投** 1856 / F779 Tō throw. *to*(*jiru*), *tō*(*zuru*) throw, throw away, throw into; abandon; launch into, embark on; join (a party); invest in; seize (an opportunity); agree with; catch (the public eye). *na*(*geru*) throw, hurl; give up; sell at a loss. *na*(*ge*) a throw, a spill, a fall.

2 入 *na*(*ge*)-*i*(*reru*) throw into; dump in together. *tōnyū suru* throw into; invest. *nage-i*(*re*) free-style flower arrangement
3 下 *tōka suru* throw down, drop; invest
上 *na*(*ge*)-*a*(*geru*) throw up (in the air)

与 *tōyo suru, na(ge)-ata(eru)* throw to (the dogs)
4 込 *na(ge)-ko(mu)* throw into, dump into. *na(ge)ko(mi)* free-style flower arrangement
手 *tōshu* pitcher, bowler (in cricket)
手力 *tōshuryoku* pitching power
手団 *tōshudan* pitching staff
手位置 *tōshu ichi* pitcher's box
手板 *tōshuban* pitcher's box
手陣 *tōshujin* pitching staff
手戦 *tōshusen* pitching duel
5 付 *na(ge)-tsu(keru)* throw at; throw (someone) down
出 *na(ge)-da(su)* throw out, throw down; stretch out (legs); give up, renounce
仕事 *na(ge) shigoto* slipshod work
石 *tōseki* throwing stones
石機 *tōsekiki* stone catapult
6 返 *na(ge)-kae(su)* throw back
合 *tōgō* agreement, coincidence
光器 *tōkōki* floodlight projector
7 足 *na(ge)ashi* sitting with legs stretched out
身 *tōshin* suicide by drowning
売 *nageu(ri)* bargain sale
売品 *nageurihin* articles on special sale
8 物 *na(ge)mono* sacrifice goods
函 *tōkan suru* mail (a letter). *tōkan* throwing into a box
9 飛 *na(ge)-to(basu)* throw away
首 *na(ge)kubi* dropping the head (in thought)
砕 *na(ge)-kuda(ku)* dash to pieces
降 *tōkō* surrender
係蹄 *na(ge)wana* a lasso
10 倒 *na(ge)-tao(su)* throw (someone) down
射 *tōsha* projection (in math); incidence (in physics); throwing (spears)
殺 *na(ge)-koro(su)* throw and kill
索 *na(ge)nawa* a lasso
罠 *na(ge)wana* a lasso
荷 *na(ge)ni* jetsam, jettisoned cargo
捕手 *tōhoshu* the battery (in baseball)
書 *tōsho* correspondence, contribution
書家 *tōshoka* correspondent, contributor
11 掛 *na(ge)-ka(keru)* throw at; cast over, throw around
捨 *na(ge)-su(teru)* throw away
球 *tōkyū* throwing a ball, pitching, bowling (in cricket); a pitched ball
宿 *tōshuku suru* put up at a hotel
宿者 *tōshukusha* hotel guest
票 *tōhyō* vote, voting, ballot, suffrage
票日 *tōhyōbi* voting day
票区 *tōhyōku* voting precinct
票用紙 *tōhyō yōshi* ballot
票所 *tōhyōjo* polling place, the polls
票函 *tōhyōkan* ballot box
票者 *tōhyōsha* voter
票偽造 *tōhyō gizō* vote forgery
票集 *tōhyō-atsu(me)* gathering votes
票数 *tōhyōsū* the number of votes
票棄権 *tōhyō kiken* nonvoting
票棄権者 *tōhyō kikensha* nonvoter
票権 *tōhyōken* right to vote, suffrage, voice
票箱 *tōhyōbako* ballot box
票締切 *tōhyō shimeki(ri)* closing of the polls
票録 *tōhyōroku* voting record
12 遣 *na(ge)-ya(ru)* throw away, leave to chance. *na(ge)yari* negligence, irresponsibility
弾 *tōdan* dropping a bomb
落 *na(ge)-oto(su)* throw down, drop
13 棄 *na(ge)-su(teru)* throw away. *tōki suru* abandon, give up
業 *na(ge)waza* throwing trick
資 *tōshi* investment
資信託 *tōshi shintaku* investment trust
14 槍 *na(ge)yari* dart, javelin, lance; javelin throw
網 *na(ge)ami, toami* casting net
獄 *tōgoku* imprisonment
獄者 *tōgokusha* prisoner
15 影 *tōei suru* reflect, project (an image)
影図法 *tōei zuhō* projection in drawing
稿 *tōkō* contribution (to a magazine)
稿者 *tōkōsha* contributor (to a magazine)
稿欄 *tōkōran* readers' column
16 錨 *tōbyō* anchoring, anchorage
薬 *tōyaku* medication, prescription, dosage
機 *tōki* speculation
機心 *tōkishin* spirit of speculation
機的 *tōkiteki* speculative, risky, adventurous
機熱 *tōki netsu* speculation fever
17 環 *na(ge)wa* quoits
擲 *tōteki suru* throw
擲競技 *tōteki kyōgi* weight-throwing competition
19 縄 *na(ge)nawa* a lasso
離 *na(ge)-hana(su)* throw away

— 5 —

抑 See 1851.

拂 1857 / F785 See **払** 1828.

拒 1858 / F787 See **拒** 1847.

拔 1859 / F787 See **抜** 1854.

抬 Nonstandard for **擡** 2021.

拆 1860 / F785 TAKU open.

拌 1861/F786 HAN stir and mix.

拏 1862/F787 DA catch, arrest.

拊 1863/F786 FU. *ha*(*ru*) slap, strike.

拯 1864/F792 SHŌ, JŌ help. *suku*(*u*) (see under 救 2051.0).

拐 1865/F787 **拐** KAI falsify; kidnap.

[10]帯 *kaitai* absconding with money
帯者 *kaitaisha* absconder

拈 1866/F786 NEN. *hine*(*ru*) twirl, twist, twiddle; wring, wrench; bend (the body); incline (the head); pinch; defeat. *hine*(*ri*) pinch (of salt); small gift of money; a twist.

[5]出 *nenshutsu suru, hine*(*ri*)-*da*(*su*), *hine*(*ri*)-*ida*(*su*) think up, propose

拉 1867/F786 RATSU. *ras*(*suru*) drag along; kidnap. *Ra* Latin. *hishi*(*geru*) be flattened, be crushed, collapse, give way; be discouraged. *hishi*(*gu*) crush, smash, overpower.

[2]丁 *Raten* Latin
丁語 *Ratengo* Latin
[10]致 *ratchi suru* carry away, take captive, kidnap

拇 1868/F785 BO thumb.

[6]印 *boin* thumb print
[9]指 *boshi* thumb
指大 *boshidai* thumb size
指頭大 *boshitōdai* the size of the end of the thumb
[11]趾 *boshi* big toe

拗 1869/F788 Ō. YŌ. *ne*(*jiru*), *neji*(*reru*) (see under 捩 1942.0). *kune*(*ru*), *neji*(*keru*) be crooked, be twisted, be distorted; perverse, cross. *neji*(*kureru*) = *neji*(*reru*) (see under 捩 1942.0). *koji*(*rasu*) aggravate (a cold). *koji*(*reru*) be twisted; go wrong, get out of order; become complicated; become cross; become aggravated; mark time. *su*(*neru*) pout.

[7]言葉 *su*(*ne*) *kotoba* grumbling
[8]者 *neji*(*ke*)*mono, su*(*ne*)*mono* perverse person
[9]音 *yōon* diphthong

抹 1870/F784 MATSU paint, erase, rub.

[8]油 *matsuyu* extreme unction
[9]茶 *matcha* powdered quality tea
香 *makkō* incense; incense powder
香鯨 *makkō kujira* sperm whale
[10]消 *masshō* = *massatsu* 抹殺 (see next word)
殺 *massatsu* erasure, obliteration; denial; ignoring (an opinion); execution, liquidation

B **拠** 1871/F836 **據 㩀** KYO. KO. *yo*(*ru*) be based on, follow. *yo*(*tte*) therefore, consequently.

[5]可 *yo*(*ru*)*be*(*ki*) authoritative
[6]有 *kyoyū suru* appropriate as one's own
[8]所 *yo*(*ri*)*dokoro* source, authority
所無 *yondokorona*(*i*) unavoidable, urgent, necessary
[9]城 *kyojō* one's own entrenched castle
点 *kyoten* position, point, base

B **拍** 1872/F786 **拍** HYŌ, HAKU beat (in music). *u*(*tsu*) (see under 打 1829.0).

[3]子 *hyōshi* time, rhythm, beat, measure, number; tact; chance, the moment
子木 *hyōshigi* wooden clappers, bones
子抜 *hyōshinu*(*ke*) disappointment
[4]手 *hakushu* applause, handclapping. *kashiwade* handclapping (at a shrine)
[7]車 *hakusha* spur (on boots)
車加 *hakusha* (*o*) *kuwa*(*eru*) spur on a horse; encourage fast action

B **拓** 1873/F787 TAKU *hira*(*ku*) open, clear, break up (land).

[3]士 *takushi* settler, colonizer
[5]本 *takuhon* rubbed copy; folio of rubbings
[6]地 *takuchi* opening up land
[12]植 *takushoku* colonization, exploitation
殖 *takushoku* colonization, exploitation
殖者 *takushokusha* colonist

P **披** 1874/F782 HI open.

[7]見 *hiken suru* peruse (a letter)
[14]歴 *hireki suru* express (opinions)
[17]講 *hikō suru* recite poems
[19]瀝 *hireki suru* express (opinions)
[21]露 *hirō* announcement
露目 *hirome* announcement, advertisement
露会 *hirōkai* reception (wedding, etc.)
露宴 *hiroen* reception (wedding, etc.)

抛 1875/F786 **拋** HŌ. *hō*(*ru*) hurl. *nageu*(*tsu*) (see under 擲 2023.0).

[8]上 *hō*(*ri*)-*a*(*geru*) hurl up

4込 *hō(ri)-ko(mu)* throw into
5出 *hō(ri)-da(su)* throw out; dismiss, fire; throw up (a job)
7投 *hō(ri)-na(geru)* throw, heave, toss
8物線 *hōbutsusen* parabola
10射 *hōsha suru* shoot
射線 *hōshasen* parabola
13棄 *hōki suru, na(ge)-su(teru)* waive, resign, abandon, renounce ⌈way; neglect
17擲 *hōteki suru* abandon, give up; throw a-

A **拡** 1876 / F838 **擴** KAKU. *hiro(geru), hiro(garu)* (see under 広 1499.0).
3大 *kakudai* magnification, enlargement
大率 *kakudairitsu* magnifying power
大鏡 *kakudaikyō* magnifying glass, magnifier ⌈alization
6充 *kakujū* expansion; amplification; gener-
7声器 *kakuseiki* loud-speaker
声装置 *kakusei sōchi* public address system
声機 *kakuseiki* loud-speaker
11張 *kakuchō* extension, expansion, increase, enlargement, aggrandizement, increase, ⌊dilation
張力 *kōchōryoku* tensile strength
12散 *kakusan* scattering, diffusion

B **抽** 1877 / F784 CHŪ pull; extract; excel. *nuki(nderu)* excel in, surpass; choose the best. *nu(ku)* (see under 抜 1854.0). *hi(ku)* pull.
4斗 *hikidashi* (desk) drawer
5出 *chūshutsu suru* educe, abstract, extract. *hikidashi* (desk) drawer; withdrawal
12象 *chūshō* abstraction
象名詞 *chūshō meishi* abstract noun
象的 *chūshōteki* abstract
象論 *chūshōron* abstract argument, gener- ⌊alities
14選 *chūsen* lottery, raffle, drawing
21籤 *chūsen* lottery, raffle, drawing
籤券 *chūsenken* lottery ticket
籤器 *chūsenki* lottery wheel

B **抵** 1878 / F783 TEI touch, reach, resist.
6当 *teitō* mortgage, hypothec, security
当物 *teitōbutsu* security, pawn, collateral
当流 *teitōnaga(re)* foreclosure
当権 *teitōken* mortgage
7抗 *teikō* resistance, opposition, defiance; (electrical) resistance
抗力 *teikōryoku* power of resistance; re- ⌊sisting force
抗罪 *teikōzai* mutiny
抗箱 *teikōbako* resistance box
抗器 *teikōki* resistor, rheostat ⌈ment
13触 *teishoku* conflict, contradiction, infringe-

B **担** 1879 / F835 **擔** TAN carry; raise. *katsu(gu)* shoulder (a load). *kata(geru)* shoulder, carry on the shoulder. *nina(u)* carry on the shoulder; bear a burden. *katsugi* carrier, coolie.
2入 *katsu(gi)-i(reru)* carry in
入足 *katsugi ninsoku* carrier, coolie
3上 *katsu(gi)-a(geru), katsu(gi)-nobo(ru)* ⌊carry up
4手 *ninaite* bearer, carrier
夫 *tampu* porter
6任 *tannin* charge (of something)
当 *tantō* charge (of something)
当者 *tantōsha* the one in charge
9屋 *katsugiya* superstitious person; black-market peddler
保 *tampo* mortgage, security, guarantee
保付 *tampozu(ki)* secured (loan)
架 *tanka* stretcher, litter
架卒 *tankasotsu* stretcher bearer
10荷 *tanka* stretcher, litter
11商 *katsugiakina(i)* peddling; peddler

B **拙** 1880 / F789 SETSU clumsy, unskillful. *tsutana(i), mazu(i)* clumsy, bungling, unskillful.
3工 *sekkō* poor workman
4文 *setsubun* poor writing, my writing
6宅 *settaku* my humble home
劣 *setsuretsu na* clumsy, unskillful
7作 *sessaku* poor work; my humble work
技 *setsugi* clumsy work; my humble efforts
8者 *sessha* I (humble); an untalented person; an ignorant person
9速 *sessoku* rough-and-ready, hasty
10家 *sekka* my humble home
11訳 *setsuyaku* (my) poor translation
悪 *setsuaku* clumsiness, lack of skill
著 *setcho* my (humble) production
12策 *sessaku* poor policy, poor plan
筆 *seppitsu* bad handwriting
13僧 *sessō* your humble priest; a foolish priest
15稿 *sekkō* poor manuscript; my manuscript

B **拘** 1881 / F788 KŌ seize, arrest. *kakawa(ru)* be concerned with; adhere to; be wedded to one's opinion. *kakawa(razu)* in spite of, regardless of.
4引 *kōin* arrest, custody
引状 *kōinjō* summons, warrant of arrest
7束 *kōsoku* restriction, binding, duress
束力 *kōsokuryoku* binding power (of rules)
束者 *kōsokusha* restrainer
束時間 *kōsoku jikan* actual working hours; portal-to-portal time
束時間払賃金 *kōsoku jikambara(i) chingin* portal-to-portal pay

4 心 忄 小 戈 戸 [手 扌] 支 攴 攵 文 斗 斤 方 无 日 曰 月 木 欠 止 歹 殳 毋 比 毛 氏 气 水 氵 氺 火 灬 爪 爫 父 爻 爿 丬 片 牙 牛 犬 犭

8泥 *kōdei suru* adhere to, be a stickler for
10留 *kōryū* detention, arrest, custody
留状 *kōryūjō* arrest warrant
留所 *kōryūjo* detention room
13禁 *kōkin* confinement, detention, imprisonment
置 *kōchi* detention, confinement, arrest
置所 *kōchisho* detention house, prison

5 A **招** 1882/F790 SHŌ. *mane(ku)* beckon to, invite, summon; engage (someone), call (a doctor); incur, cause. *mane(ki)* invitation.

4引 *shōin suru* call someone to come
7声 *shōsei* call (of God)
来 *shōrai suru* lead to, invite, incur, cause
8命 *shōmei* call (of God)
9降 *shōkō* urging surrender
客 *shōkyaku* invitation; invited guest
待 *shōtai, shōdai* invitation
待日 *shōtaibi* preview date; invitation date
待会 *shōtaikai* reception
待状 *shōtaijō* letter of invitation
待券 *shōtaiken* complimentary ticket
待客 *shōtai kyaku* invited guest
待席 *shōtaiseki* reserved seat for a guest
10致 *shōchi* summons, invitation
宴 *shōen* giving an invitation to a banquet
11寄 *mane(ki)-yo(seru)* call from, bring from
12雇 *shōko suru* call and employ
集 *shōshū suru, mane(ki)-atsu(meru)* call together
13聘 *shōhei* engagement, employment
電 *shōden* summons by wire
14魂 *shōkon* invocation of spirits of the dead
魂社 *shōkonsha* shrine to the war dead
魂祭 *Shōkonsai* Memorial Day
15請 *shōsei* invitation, call
請国 *shōseikoku* inviting power, host nation

B **抱** 1883/F783 **抱** HŌ. *da(ku)* hug, embrace, hold in the arms; sit (on eggs). *ida(ku)* hug, embrace, hold in the arms; entertain (hope); cherish (a desire); harbor (malice); hold, have. *da(kasu)* set a hen. *da(kko) suru* hug, embrace, hold in the arms. *kaka(eru)* hold or carry under or in the arms. *kaka(e)* armful; employee.

2入 *kaka(e)-i(reru)*=*kakaeru* (see under 抱 1883.0)
3上 *da(ki)-a(geru)* take up in one's arms
4止 *da(ki)-to(meru)* hold (a person) back, restrain, catch
込 *da(ki)-ko(mu)* win over, carry in the arms. *kaka(e)-ko(mu)*=*kakae(ru)* (see under 抱 1883.0)
5付 *da(ki)-tsu(ku)* embrace; hold forcibly
主 *kaka(e)nushi* employer
6合 *da(ki)-a(u)* hug, embrace. *da(ki)-a(waseru)* cause to embrace; pawn off poor articles. *hōgō* combination; embrace
合心中 *da(ki)a(i) shinjū* double suicide
合売 *dakiawa(se) u(ri)* combination sale
合法 *dakia(wase)hō* contact printing (in photography)
合物 *hōgōbutsu* compound
7車 *kaka(e)guruma* private jinricksha
卵 *hōran* incubation
卵期 *hōranki* incubation period
8抱 *da(ki)-kaka(eru)* hold, carry, or embrace (in one's arms)
9括 *hōkatsu* inclusion, comprehension
負 *hōfu* aspiration, ambition, pretension
10起 *da(ki)-oko(su)* lift (a person) up, help (a person) to his feet or to sit up (in bed)
留 *da(ki)-to(meru)* hug to restrain
11寄 *da(ki)-yo(seru)* embrace
著 *da(ki)-tsu(ku)* embrace; hold forcibly
12竦 *da(ki)-suku(meru)* hug tight
着 *da(ki)-tsu(ku)* embrace; hold forcibly
13寝 *da(ki)ne* sleeping with a baby
腹 *hōfuku* convulsed with laughter
腹絶倒 *hōfuku-zettō* convulsed with laughter
14緊 *da(ki)-shi(meru), ida(ki)-shi(meru)* embrace closely, cuddle, hug
15締 *da(ki)-shi(meru), ida(ki)-shi(meru)* embrace closely, cuddle, hug
16懐 *hōkai* harboring, cherishing, entertaining
擁 *hōyō* a hug, an embrace

A **拝** 1884/F790 **拜** HAI worship. *hai(suru)* worship, bow in veneration, pay respects to; receive (an imperial command); see (the emperor). *oga(mu), oroga(mu)* worship, pray to, adore, reverence; look at (with reverence).

1一神教 *hai-itsushinkyō* henotheism
4火教 *Haikakyō* Zoroastrianism
5礼 *hairei* worship
6伏 *haifuku* bowing; bowing and worshiping
7見 *haiken suru* see, look at, inspect
呈 *haitei* presentation; Dear Sir
承 *haishō suru* I hear that . . .
8送 *haisō* (humble) seeing someone off
披 *haihi* (humble) opening (a letter)
命 *haimei* receiving an official appointment
受 *haiju suru* receive, accept
具 *haigu* Faithfully yours
物教 *haibutsukyō* fetishism
金 *haikin* worship of mammon
金主義 *haikin shugi* mammonism
金宗 *haikinshū* mammonism
9屋 *oga(mi)ya* medicine man, charmer
眉 *haibi* personal meeting

星教 *haiseikyō* star worship
10借 *haishaku* loan, borrowing
倒 *oga(mi)-tao(su)* entreat into consenting
11啓 *haikei* Dear Sir, Dear Madam
12復 *haifuku* in reply to your esteemed letter; Dear Sir, Dear Madam
診 *haishin* medical examination (polite)
賀 *haiga* greetings, congratulations
13殿 *haiden* outer shrine, hall of worship; holy place; nave
辞 *haiji suru* resign, decline
跪 *haiki suru* kneel reverently
14聞 *haibun* (humble) listening, hearing
塵 *haijin* flattering a superior
誦 *haishō suru* read, note
読 *haidoku suru* read, note. *haidoku* reverent reading
察 *haisatsu* guess
領 *hairyō suru* receive (from a superior)
領物 *hairyōbutsu* a gift (from a superior)
15謁 *haietsu* an audience (with the emperor)
16覧 *hairan* (humble) looking at, examining
17趨 *haisū suru* call on, visit
聴 *haichō suru* listen attentively
謝 *haisha suru* thank
戴 *haitai* (humble) receiving (something)
18顔 *haigan* personal meeting
観 *haikan* inspection, visit
観料 *haikanryō* (museum) admission charge

B 押 1885/F784 Ō. *o(su)* push, shove; press, squash, compress; stamp, seal; do in spite of. *osa(eru)* stop, check, restrain, pin down; suppress, subdue, control; catch, arrest; govern; stop (the ears); withhold; attach, seize; secure (evidence), estimate conservatively. *oshi* weight; authority, influence; self-confidence; a fall (in the stock market). *osa(e)* weight, paperweight; rear guard; defense; pressure, suppression; control. *o(shite)* forcibly; importunately; in spite of. *o(shi)-* emphatic verbal prefix.
2入 *o(shi)-i(reru)* push in, force in, squeeze in. *o(shi)-i(ru)* break into. *oshi-i(re)* clothes closet. *o(shi)-i(ri)* burglar, robber
3下 *o(shi)-sa(geru)* depress, force down. *o(shi)-o(rosu)*=*orosu* (see under 下 9.0)
上 *o(shi)-a(geru)* force up, push up, boost
4止 *o(shi)-to(meru)*, *o(shi)-todo(meru)* stop, prevent, restrain
引 *o(shi)hi(ki)* pushing and pulling
切 *os(shi)-ki(ru)* have one's own way, push thru, push and cut. *osa(e)-ki(ru)* shutout (in baseball). *o(shi)ki(tte)* boldly, daringly. *o(shi)ki(ri)* straw cutter; short mane
分 *o(shi)-wa(keru)* push apart, elbow thru
込 *o(shi)-ko(mu)* vi push in, crowd into, herd into. *o(shi)-ko(meru)* vt shut up, imprison. *o(shi)ko(mi)* clothes closet; burglar
込強盗 *o(shi)ko(mi) gōtō* burglar
5立 *o(shi)-ta(teru)*, *o(t)ta(teru)* raise, set up, erect; hoist
広 *o(shi)-hiro(geru)*, *(op)piro(geru)*=*hiro(geru)* (see under 広 1499.0)
付 *o(shi)-tsu(keru)*, *o(t)tsu(keru)* push against, press down, thrust on; compel, urge; force on, intrude on, impose on. *o(shi)tsu(kegamashii)* unreasonable
弘 *o(shi)-hiro(meru)* extend, spread, amplify; propagate
収 *ōshū* seizure, confiscation
出 *oshida(shi)* presence, appearance; forced (run); pushing out of. *o(shi)-da(su)*, *o(shi)-ida(su)* push out; squeeze out; crowd out; set out all together. *o(shi)-de(ru)* force one's way out
出絵具 *oshida(shi) enogu* tube paint
6返 *o(shi)-kae(su)* force back, jostle
印 *ōin* affixing one's seal
伏 *o(shi)-fu(saseru)* force to lie down
当 *o(shi)-a(teru)* push (something) against
気味 *o(shi)gimi* the upper hand, the ascendancy
合 *o(shi)-a(u)*, *o(shi)a(i) suru* jostle, crowd; haggle
合圧合 *o(shi)a(i)-he(shi)a(i)* pushing and jostling
7走 *o(p)pashi(ru)* run (emphatic)
戻 *o(shi)-modo(su)* force back; reject, turn down
迫 *o(shi)-sema(ru)* press hard, crowd against
均 *o(shi)-nara(su)* average, generalize
折 *o(shi)-o(ru)* break by pushing
売 *oshi-uri* high-pressure salesmanship
花 *o(shi)bana* pressed flowers
抜機 *o(shi)nu(ki)ki* punch press
8固 *o(shi)-kata(meru)* press together
退 *o(shi)-no(keru)* push away, brush aside, elbow thru, crowd out
送 *ōsō* escort
拡 *o(shi)-hiro(geru)*, *o(p)piro(geru)*=*hiro(geru)* (see under 広 1499.0)
押 *o(shimo)-o(saremo)-shinai* (a man) of established reputation
板 *o(shi)-ita* pressing board
並 *o(shi)na(bete)* generally
直 *o(shi)-nao(su)* restore, correct. *o(shi)-nao(ru)* sit correctly
取 *o(t)to(ru)* seize, snatch
取巻 *o(t)to(ri)ma(ku)* surround, encircle, enclose
9通 *o(shi)-tō(ru)* force one's way thru. *o(shi)-tō(su)* carry thru, accomplish, persevere; insist on
型 *o(shi)gata* impression taken by pressing
10進 *o(shi)-susu(meru)* push, push thru, expedite. *o(shi)-susu(mu)* push on, press onward

借 *o(shi)ga(ri)* out of money or supplies, having to borrow
倒 *o(shi)-tao(su)* push down; overwhelm
流 *o(shi)-naga(su)* wash away, sweep away; (waves) drive on
破 *o(shi)-yabu(ru)* break thru
11 捺 *ōnatsu* sealing (a document)
捲 *o(shi)-maku(ru)* press on to the end
頂 *o(shi)-itada(ku)* raise reverently to one's head
寄 *o(shi)-yo(seru)* push aside; advance on; besiege (an office); bear down upon; make for the door. *o(shi)-yo(ru)* press together, come close
問答 *o(shi)mondō* heated questioning and answering, dispute
掛 *o(shi)-ka(karu)* lean on, rely on. *o(shi)-ka(keru)* intrude on, throng into
掛客 *o(shi)ka(ke) kyaku* uninvited guest
12 遣 *o(shi)-ya(ru)* push away
開 *o(shi)-hira(ku), o(shi)-a(keru)* force open, push open
渡 *o(shi)-wata(su)* cross over; force one's way across
絵 *o(shi)e* raised cloth pictures
隔 *o(shi)-heda(teru)*=*heda(teru)* (see under 隔 5016.0)
葉 *o(shi)ba* pressed leaves
割麦 *o(shi)wa(ri) mugi* rolled barley
13 詰 *o(shi)-tsu(maru)* approach the year end; be jammed, be tight. *o(shi)-tsu(meru)* pack (in a box); drive to the wall
15 潰 *o(shi)-tsubu(su)* smash, crush
縁 *o(shi)buchi* strips to hold something down
黙 *o(shi)-dama(ru)* keep silent
16 錠 *o(shi)jō* thumb latch
17 戴 *o(shi)-itada(ku)* raise reverently to one's head
18 鎮 *o(shi)-shizu(meru)* quiet (someone)
19 離 *o(p)pana(su)* emphatic for *hana(su)* (see under 離 5040.0)
韻 *ōin* rhyme, rhyming
韻詩 *ōinshi* rhymed verse

6

拿 See 471.

挀 1886 / F793 See 拍 1872.

挟 Nonstandard for 挾 1915.

挛 Nonstandard for 攣 2035.

挈 1887 / F796 KEI carry by hand.

挱 1888 / F793 SATSU be imminent.

挌 1889 / F797 KAKU strike, hit, fight.
18 闘 *kakutō* scuffle; wrestling; first fight

挂 1890 / F795 KEI, KAI hang.
9 冠 *keikan, kaikan* resignation

挘 1891 / F797 (国字) *mushi(ru)* pluck, pick, tear.
8 取 *mushi(ri)-to(ru)* tear off, pluck off

拱 1892 / F792 KYŌ arch. *kyō(suru), komanu(ku), komane(ku)* fold (the arms).
4 手 *kyōshu* folding the arms
手傍観 *kyōshu-bōkan suru* look on with folded arms, let things go

拵 1893 / F793 SON. *koshira(eru)* make, prepare, manufacture. *koshira(e)* make, workmanship; mounting; arrangement; attire; make-up. *koshira(etate)* newly made.
8 物 *koshira(e)mono* counterfeit, imitation
直 *koshira(e)-nao(su)* remake, remodel
事 *koshira(e)goto* fabrication

拮 1894 / F792 KATSU, KETSU, KITSU be imminent.
7 抗 *kikkō* rivalry, competition, antagonism
屈聱牙 *kikkutsu-gōga* bookish, stiff (style)
11 据 *kikkyo* diligence

拷 1895 / F793 B KŌ, GŌ beat, torture.
10 訊 *gōjin* torture
11 問 *gōmon* torture, the rack, third degree
問台 *gōmondai* the rack, instrument of torture
15 器 *gōki* instruments of torture

括 1896 / F792 B KATSU. *kuku(ru)* tie up, hang (someone); arrest; fasten. *kuru(mu)* wrap up, tuck in. *kuru(meru)* (see under 包 176.0). *kubi(ru)* constrict. *kubi(reru)* be constricted, contracted, or compressed. *ko(ru)* pack, tie up. *kuku(ri)* tying; bundle; knot; management; conclusion; trap. *kubi(re)* constriction, compression.
5 付 *kuku(ri)-tsu(keru)*=*kuku(ru)* (see under 括 1896.0)
8 弧 *kakko* parentheses; brackets
枕 *kuku(ri) makura* stuffed pillow

拭 1897 / F792 SHOKU. *fu(ku)* wipe, mop, swab. *nugu(u)* wipe, mop.
4 込 *fu(ki)-ko(mu)* polish, shine, wipe thoroly

⁵去 *nugu(i)-sa(ru)* put off, wipe off, wipe away
⁸取 *fu(ki)-to(ru)* wipe off, wipe out, mop up. *nugu(i)-to(ru)* wipe away
¹⁰消 *fu(ki)-ke(su)* wipe out, wipe off, erase
¹¹掃除 *fuki sōji* cleaning, housework
¹²落 *nugu(i)-oto(su)* wipe off, wipe away. *fu(ki)-oto(su)* rub out (a stain)

P 挑 1898/F797 CHŌ. *ido(mu)* challenge; contend for; make love to.
⁹発 *chōhatsu* provocation, excitement, encouragement, suggestion
発的 *chōhatsuteki* provocative, suggestive, lascivious, seditious
¹³戦 *chōsen* challenge, defiance
戦状 *chōsenjō* written challenge
戦的 *chōsenteki* defiant, aggressive, provocative, challenging
戦者 *chōsensha* challenger
¹⁵撥 *chōhatsu*＝挑発 (see above–9)

按 1899/F796 AN. *an(zuru)* hold; consider, investigate.
⁴分 *ambun* proportional division
分比例 *ambun hirei* proportional allotment
手 *anshu* ordination, laying on of hands
手礼 *anshurei* ordination
手礼式 *anshureishiki* ordination ceremony
¹⁰配 *ambai* arrangement, assignment; adjustment, modification, tempering
¹¹排 *ambai*＝the word above
¹³腹 *ampuku* abdominal massage
¹⁴察 *ansatsu* scrutiny
¹⁵摩 *amma* massage; masseur

拳 1900/F792 GEN. KEN *kobushi* fist.
⁵玉 *kendama* cup-and-ball toy
⁸固 *genko* fists and knuckles
¹⁰骨 *genkotsu* fists and knuckles
拳 *kenken* respectful attitude
匪 *Kempi* Boxers
匪乱 *Kempi (no) Ran* Boxer Rebellion
¹⁴銃 *kenjū* pistol, revolver
¹⁸闘 *kentō* boxing, prizefighting
闘界 *kentōkai* boxing circles
闘家 *kentōka* pugilist
闘場 *kentōjō* boxing ring
闘選手 *kentō senshu* pugilist

A 拾 1901/F793 SHŪ. JŪ ten. *hiro(u)* pick up, gather; find; set (type); go on foot.
³上 *hiro(i)-a(geru)* pick up, pick out ⌈thing)
⁴方 *hiro(i)kata* way of picking up (some-
⁵収 *shūshū suru* get under control, save
主 *hiro(i)nushi* finder
出 *hiro(i)-da(su)* pick out, select
⁸取 *shūshu suru* pick up, gather
物 *hiro(i)mono* something picked up, a find; a bargain; a windfall
歩 *hiro(i)-aru(ku)* picking one's way
¹¹得 *shūtoku suru* pick up, find
得物 *shūtokubutsu* found article
得者 *shūtokusha* finder
¹²集 *hiro(i)-atsu(meru), shūshū suru* gather up, collect; glean
¹⁴遺 *shūi* gleanings
読 *hiro(i)yo(mi)* skimming (a book)
¹⁶録 *shūroku suru* select and record

A 挙 1902/F1567 擧 舉 KYO plan, project; behavior; actions; step. *a(geru)* celebrate (a ceremony); join (hands in an effort); have (a child); arrest. *a(garu)* become prosperous; be captured. *kozo(ru)* meet all together. *a(gete)* all, whole, in a body. *kozo(tte)* all, all together. [日]
⁴手 *kyoshu* show of hands, raising the hand; salute, touching the cap
止 *kyoshi* bearing, deportment
⁵用 *kyoyō suru* appoint, promote
示 *kyoshi suru* cite
句 *ageku* in the end, finally
世 *kyosei* all the people of the world
⁶行 *kyokō* performance, celebration, solemnization
式 *kyoshiki* holding a ceremony
⁷足 *ageashi* faultfinding
兵 *kyohei* raising an army
⁸国 *kyokoku* the whole nation
国一致 *kyokoku-itchi* national unity
国皆兵制度 *kyokoku-kaihei seido* universal conscription
¹⁰家 *kyoka* the whole family
¹¹族 *kyozoku* the whole family
動 *kyodō* deportment, conduct
祭 *kyosai* presentation of offerings
措 *kyoso* deportment, conduct
措失 *kyoso (o) ushina(u)* lose one's composure
¹²証 *kyoshō* presentation of proof

A 持 1903/F794 JI. *ji(suru)* hold, entertain, maintain; observe (principles). *mo(tsu) vi* and *vt* hold, take, have, possess; carry; maintain; have charge of; wear, last long; pay; bear (a grudge). *mo(teru)* be warmly welcomed; can hold, can carry; propertied, wealthy. *mo(taseru)* let (a person) have, give; get (a wife) for; give to carry; send by; keep, preserve; lean or set against; make (someone) pay. *mo(tanu), mo(tanai)* propertyless, have-not. *mo(chi)* wear, durability; (my) charge; (ladies') wear.

[3]上 *mo(chi)-a(geru)* raise, lift, jack up; flatter, praise. *mo(chi)-a(garu)* be raised, be lifted; happen; be promoted with one's class; teaching the same group thru the ⌊years
久 *jikyū* endurance, persistence
久力 *jikyūryoku* endurance, persistence
久策 *jikyūsaku* dilatory tactics ⌈action
久戦 *jikyūsen* delaying action, holding
[4]方 *mo(chi)kata* way to hold; attitude
込 *mo(chi)-ko(mu)* bring in; lodge (a protest); bring to (a decision)
切 *mo(chi)-ki(ru)* keep, continue to hold; hold all; maintain; talk of nothing else. *mo(chi)ki(ri)* sole topic (of conversation)
分 *mochibun* share (of costs); interest in (a business)
[5]主 *mochinushi* proprietor, owner, possessor
古 *mo(chi)-furu(su)* be long in use
去 *mo(chi)-sa(ru)* carry away; make off with
出 *mo(chi)-da(su)* take out; rescue; embezzle; offer (a plan)
[6]舟 *mo(chi)fune* one's own ship
行 *mo(tte)-yu(ku)* take along
回 *mot(te)-mawa(ru), mo(chi)-mawa(ru). mo(chi)-mawa(su)* carry around. *mo(tte)-mawa(tta)* circuitous. *mochimawa(ri)* securing decisions by circularizing members
成 *mo(te)na(shi)* treatment, service, reception, hospitality, entertainment. *mo(te)-na(su)* welcome, entertain, treat
扱 *mo(chi)-atsuka(u)* handle
合 *mo(chi)-a(waseru)* have on hand. *mo(chi)-a(u)* maintain equilibrium; share expenses. *mo(chi)-a(wase)* things on hand; money on hand. *mo(chi)-a(i)* interdependence; steadiness (of the market)
合品 *mo(chi)a(wase)hin* goods on hand
[7]戒 *jikai* observance of the Buddhist commandments
役 *mo(chi)yaku* one's role
来 *mo(tte)-ku(ru)* bring, fetch. *mo(chi)-ki(tasu)* take, bring; bring about. *mo(tte)-ko(i)* ideal, excellent, just right
余 *mo(te)ama(su)* be embarrassed with; find unmanageable; have too much of
余者 *mo(te)ama(shi)mono* scamp; nuisance, white elephant
[8]送 *mo(chi)oku(ri)* bracket, truss
逃 *mochini(ge) suru* make off with, abscond with ⌈quality
味 *mo(chi)aji* natural flavor, characteristic
物 *mochimono* property, belongings
直 *mo(chi)-nao(su) vi* and *vt* change one's hold; improve, rally, recover
歩 *mo(chi)-aru(ku)* carry about
参 *jisan suru* bring, take along. *jisan* (by the) kindness of
参人 *jisannin* bearer
参金 *jisankin* dowry
[9]持 *mo(chitsu)-mo(taretsu)* helping one another
映 *mo(te)ha(yasu)* praise, extol ⌊other
前 *mo(chi)mae* nature, property; share
[10]病 *jibyō* chronic illness
料 *mo(chi)ryō* private use
家 *mo(chi)-ie* one's own house
荷 *mo(chi)ni* stock, holdings; load ⌈back
帰 *mo(chi)-kae(ru), mo(tte)-kae(ru)* carry
株 *mo(chi)kabu* one's stock holdings ⌈pany
株会社 *mo(chi)kabugaisha* holding com-
[11]過 *mo(chi)-su(giru)* have too much of
運 *mo(chi)-hako(bu)* carry, transport. *mo(chi)hako(bi)* portable, carrying
掛 *mo(chi)-ka(keru)* offer, propose. *mo(tase)-ka(keru)* lean against
寄 *mo(chi)-yo(ru)* (each) contributes ⌈tion
崩 *mo(chi)-kuzu(su)* ruin oneself by dissipa-
[12]越 *mo(chi)-ko(su)* defer; carry forward; hold over
場 *mo(chi)ba* place of duty, one's post, one's beat; jurisdiction
堪 *mo(chi)-kota(eru)* maintain, keep; hold out (longer)
替 *mo(chi)-ka(eru)* shift from one hand to the other; marry again
[13]続 *mo(chi)-tsuzu(keru)* persist in. *jizoku* continuation
続的 *jizokuteki* continuous, lasting
[14]厭 *mo(chi)-agu(mu)* be tired of holding
腐 *mo(chi)gusa(re)* useless possession
説 *jisetsu* pet theory
[15]論 *jiron* pet theory
[16]薬 *jiyaku* favorite medicine

A **指** 1904 / F795 SHI finger. *sa(su)* point to, indicate; name, designate; insert, put into; fill, pour into, drop into (eyes); hold up (an umbrella); wear (a sword); offer (a cup); play; move (in games); rise, flow; be tinged with; point to; proceed to; fix (a day); measure (with a ruler); measure and make (a box); play (chess or checkers). *yubi* finger. *sa(shite)* for, to, toward.
[2]人形 *yubi ningyō* fingertip doll
[3]小辞 *shishōji* a diminutive (in grammar)
[4]手 *sashite* a move; a hand (in playing)
孔 *yubi ana* finger hole (on an instrument)
切 *yubiki(ri)* a pledge by hooking each other's little finger
[5]令 *shirei* order, notice, instructions, directive ⌈ment
圧療法 *shiatsu ryōhō* finger-pressure treat-

示 *sa(shi)-shime(su), shishi suru* indicate, point out. *shiji, shishi* indication, instructions, directions. *shiji* a type of character depicting numerals or directions 「pronoun
示代名詞 *shiji daimeishi* demonstrative
示灯 *shijitō* pilot light, indicator light
示板 *shijiban* notice board
示器 *shijiki* indicator
6 印 *shi-in* fingerprint
先 *yubisaki* fingertip
先仕事 *yubisaki shigoto* finger work
名 *shimei suru* name, mention, designate, nominate
名者 *shimeisha* nominator, designator
向 *shikō* directional (antenna)
向性 *shikōsei* directional (antenna)
向電波 *shikō dempa* directional beam
7 折 *yubio(ri)*＝*kusshi* 屈指 1386.9
折数 *yubio(ri)-kazo(eru)* count on one's
図 *sashizu* instructions, orders ⌊fingers
図人 *sashizunin* director, instructor; designated person
図書 *sashizusho* (written) orders, directions
8 担 *sa(shi)-nina(u)* shouldering (a load) between carriers
板 *yubi ita* finger board (on a stringed instrument); (door) finger plate
命 *shimei suru* issue specific orders 「ization
定 *shitei* appointment, designation, author-
事 *shiji* numeral characters or characters indicating direction (e.g. 三 and 上)
呼 *shiko* beckoning, hailing
呼間 *shiko (no) aida, shiko (no) kan* hailing distance 「ornament
物 *sashimono* cabinet work, joinery; armor
物屋 *sashimonoya* cabinet maker
物師 *sashimonoshi* cabinet maker
9 相撲 *yubizumō* thumb wrestling
南 *shinan* instruction, guidance
南役 *shinan-yaku* instructor, teacher, master
南所 *shinansho* school, institute
南番 *shinamban* instructor, teacher, master
10 値 *sashine* buying-price limits
紋 *shimon* fingerprint, thumb print
差 *yubisa(shi)* pointing with the finger; index tabs. *yubisa(su)* point to 「carriers
荷 *sa(shi)ni* a load shouldered between two
針 *shishin* compass needle; guide, manual
針面 *shishimmen* dial (of an instrument)
11 痕 *shikon* fingerprints. *yubi ato* finger mark
宿 *sa(shi)yado* recommending a traveler's next hotel; the recommended hotel
貫 *yubinuki* thimble
12 弾 *yubihaji(ki)* flip, fillip. *shidan, shitan* flip, fillip; rejection; disdain
嵌 *yubihame* thimble, ring thimble
揮 *shiki* command, supervision, instructions, direction, leading
揮刀 *shikitō* saber, parade sword
揮下 *shikika* under one's command
揮官 *shikikan* commander
揮者 *shikisha* commander, director; conductor (of a band), leader
揮棒 *shikibō* baton
13 話 *shiwa* finger language
触 *yubizawa(ri)* fingering, touching
数 *shisū* index, index number; exponent
14 銜 *yubi (o) kuwa(eru)* hold the finger in the mouth; be unable to participate
摘 *shiteki* pointing out, indication
導 *shidō* guidance, leadership, coaching
導主事 *shidō shuji* supervisor
導性 *shidōsei* leadership
導法 *shidōhō* guidance plan
導者 *shidōsha* leader
導委員 *shidō i-in* steering committee
導要録 *shidō yōroku* cumulative guidance record
導員 *shidōin* instructor, advisor, supervisor
導案 *shidōan* teaching plan
導原理 *shidō genri* guiding principle
導精神 *shidō seishin* guiding spirit
導権 *shidōken* leadership
15 麾 *shiki*＝指揮 (see above–12)
標 *shihyō* indication, index
輪 *yubiwa* finger ring
16 頭 *shitō* fingertip 「finger
頭大 *shitōdai* the size of the end of the little
17 環 *yubiwa* finger ring
18 覆 *yubiō(i)* finger shield
21 顧 *shiko* pointing to, taking notice of

7

捏 1905 F801 **揑** NETSU falsify. *ko(neru)* knead, mix; argue. *ne(ru)* (see under 練 3565.0). *tsuku(neru)* knead, mold.
8 上 *de(tchi)-a(geru)* invent, fabricate, frame up
6 回 *ko(ne)-mawa(su)* knead, mix; be muddy
返 *ko(ne)-kae(su)* knead, mix; be muddy
合機 *konea(wase)ki* kneading machine
9 造 *netsuzō* fabrication, forgery, falsehood
10 粉 *koneko* dough
13 鉢 *konebachi* kneading trough

捐 1906 F802 EN throw away.

捋 1907 F801 RATSU. RACHI exercise field (for horses).

挵 1908 / F-X RŌ. *moteaso(bu)* play with, handle things.

捉 1909 / F801 SOKU. SAKU. *tora(eru)* (see under 捕 1919.0). *tsukama(eru)*, *tsura(maeru)*, *torama(eru)* catch, seize, arrest, capture. *tsuka(maru)*, *tsura(maru)* be caught, be arrested; cling to.

挨 1910 / F798 AI push open.

9 拶 *aisatsu* greeting, salutation; address, reply, response; notice

捗 1911 / F802 CHOKU. HO. *hakado(ru)* make progress.

8 取 *hakado(ru)* advance, make headway
10 捗 *hakabaka(shii)* rapid, expeditious, active; favorable

捌 1912 / F801 HACHI, HATSU. *saba(ku)* sell; dispose of, deal with; handle, manipulate; loosen (the hair). *saba(keru)* sell, be in demand; be worldly wise; be disentangled; tear, break. *ha(keru)* drain, flow off, run out; sell, be in demand. *ha(ke)* drainage; draining; sale, demand. *saba(keta)* sociable, frank.

3 口 *hakeguchi*, *sabakiguchi* outlet, market; vent
方 *saba(ki)kata* marketing
14 髪 *saba(ki)gami* loosened hair

挫 1913 / F798 ZA. *kuji(ku)* crush, break, sprain, dislocate; frustrate; unnerve; dampen (spirits). *kuji(keru)* be broken, crushed, or sprained; be discouraged.

7 折 *zasetsu* frustration, collapse, setback, reverses, discouragement
12 創 *zasō*=next word
13 傷 *zashō* bruise, sprain, strain, contusion

挺 1914 / F799 TEI. CHŌ counter for guns, tools, ink sticks, oars, candles, palanquins, and jinrickshas. *tei(suru)* bravely volunteer.

3 子 *teko* lever
子台 *tekodai* fulcrum
7 身 *teishin* volunteer
身隊 *teishintai* volunteer corps
10 進 *teishin suru* go ahead of, dash forward
進隊 *teishintai* advance corps

挟 1915 / F800 KYŌ. *hasa(mu)*, *sashihasa(mu)* put between, hold between; insert, jam into; nip; interpose. *hasa(maru)* get between, be caught in, be jammed in, be hemmed in, be sandwiched between, be pinned under, lie between.

4 込 *hasa(mi)-ko(mu)* insert
5 出 *hasa(mi)-da(su)* clamp onto and take away
6 虫 *hasami mushi* earwig
10 討 *hasamiu(chi)* pincer operation; squeeze
殺 *kyōsatsu suru* run down (a runner in baseball)
将棋 *hasami shōgi* Japanese checkers
15 箱 *hasamibako* carrying-pole boxes
撃 *kyōgeki* pincer operation *hasamiuchi* pincer attack

挿 1916 / F816 **插 揷** SŌ. *sa(su)* insert, put in; graft (a branch); wear (a sword); carry (in the belt). *hasa(mu)*, *hasa(maru)*, *sashihasa(mu)* (see under 挟 1915.0).

2 入 *sōnyū* insertion, incorporation, interpolation
4 木 *sashiki* a cutting; planting
5 句 *sōku* parenthetical expression
旧 *sa(shi)-furu(su)* wear out (a comb or sword)
7 図 *sōzu* illustration (in a book)
花 *sōka*, *sashibana* flower arrangement
8 画 *sashie*, *sōga* illustration (in a book)
12 絵 *sashie* illustration (in a book)
弾子 *sōdanshi* cartridge clip
13 話 *sōwa* episode

B **捜** 1917 / F822 **搜** SŌ. *saga(su)* search, look for, locate; glean.

5 出 *saga(shi)-da(su)*=*saga(shi)-a(teru)* 捜当 (see below-6)
6 回 *saga(shi)-mawa(ru)* hunt around
当 *saga(shi)-a(teru)* find out, discover, detect, locate, search out, hunt up
7 求 *saga(shi)-moto(meru)* seek for
8 物 *saga(shi)mono* something one is looking for
9 査 *sōsa* investigation, search
10 射 *sōsha* searching gunfire
索 *sōsaku* search, investigation; dragging (a river)
索令状 *sōsaku reijō* search warrant
索兵 *sōsakuhei* scout
索隊 *sōsakutai* search party
索権 *sōsakuken* right of search
索機 *sōsakuki* search plane
12 絵 *saga(shi)e* picture puzzle

挽 1918 / F800 BAN. *hi(ku)* saw; turn (on a lathe); pull (a cart); grind (in a mill).

4 切 *hi(ki)-ki(ru)* saw off
5 台 *hikidai* sawhorse
6 肉 *hikiniku* ground meat, minced meat
回 *bankai* recovery, restoration, retrieval
7 材 *hikizai* lumber
材工場 *hikizai kōjō* lumber mill
8 物 *hikimono* lathe work

物師 *hikimonoshi* a turner
9茶 *hikicha* powdered tea
10馬 *bamba* work horse
屑 *hikikuzu* sawdust
12割 *hi(ki)-wa(ru)* saw. *hikiwa(ri)* lumber
割材 *hikiwa(ri)zai* lumber
14歌 *banka* elegy, dirge

B **捕** 1919 F802 Bu. Ho. *tora(eru)*, *torama(eru)*, *tsukama(eru)*, *to(ru)* catch, arrest, capture. *tsukama(ru)* be caught, be captured. *to(reru)* (see under 取 3699.0). *tora(wareru)* be caught, be captured, be arrested; be a slave to; be seized with.

2人 *tora(ware)bito* captives, exiles
4手 *hoshu* catcher. *torite* (ancient) policeman
5囚 *hoshū* prisoner, captive, captivity
去 *tora(e)-sa(ru)* take away, carry away
6行 *tora(e)-yu(ku)* carry into captivity, lead away
伏 *to(ri)-fu(seru)* bring down (a thief)
吏 *hori* (ancient) policeman
7身 *torawa(re) (no) mi* a captive
8物 *torimono* a capture, an arrest
者 *torimono* a capture, an arrest
所 *tora(e)dokoro* the point, meaning. *tsuka(mae)dokoro* grip, hold
所無 *tsuka(mae)dokoro (no) na(i)* slippery; sly; vague
9食 *hoshoku suru* prey upon
10逸 *ho-itsu* catcher's letting a ball go thru
捉 *hosoku* capture, seizure
殺 *hosatsu suru* catch and kill; assist (in baseball)
拿 *hoda* capture, seizure
11球 *hokyū* a catch (in baseball)
移 *tora(e)-utsu(su)* carry away captive
13虜 *horyo* prisoner, captive; captivity
16獲 *hokaku* capture, seizure
縛 *hobaku* arrest, seizure
19縄 *torinawa*, *hojō* rope for tying criminals
鯨 *hogei* whaling
鯨船 *hogeisen* whaling ship

B **振** 1920 F798 Shin *fu(ru)* wave, wag, swing, shake; sprinkle; brandish; jilt, reject; attach, allot. *fu(reru)* lean toward, deflect, tend; shake, swing, oscillate. *furu(u)* shake, wield, brandish; be invigorated, be spirited, flourish. *fu(rareru)* be jilted, be rejected. *fu(ri)* appearance, manners, air, dress, form, posture; pretense, affectation; discipline; custom; swing, shaking; (dance) postures; slant, inclination, deviation, deflection; casual customer; sword counter. *fu(re)* deflection, deviation. *fu(rutta)* splendid, extraordinary, striking, original. *-bu(ri)* lapse of-, after (two years, etc.); for (three days, etc.); manner, style.

3子 *fu(ri)ko*, *shinshi* pendulum, bob
上 *fu(ri)-a(geru)* fling up, swing up, whip out, brandish, toss (the head)
4方 *fu(ri)kata* (my) plans
込 *fu(ri)-ko(mu)* pay in, pay up, pay an installment
切 *fu(ri)-ki(ru)* sever, shake off, free oneself
分 *fu(ri)-wa(keru)* divide in half, distribute. *furiwa(ke)* hair parted and hanging down; carrying packages on a strap over the shoulders
分荷物 *furiwa(ke) nimotsu* a joined pair of bundles slung over the shoulder
分髪 *furiwa(ke)gami* hair parted and hanging down
5立 *fu(ri)-ta(teru)* shake up; toss (one's head); dishevel; raise (one's voice). *fu(ri)-ta(tsu)* rouse oneself, be inspired
付 *furitsu(ke)* Japanese dance composition; dance coaching
払 *fu(ri)-hara(u)* shake off, whisk off
出 *fu(ri)-da(su)* shake out; infuse, decoct; write (a check). *furida(shi)* start; drawing or issuing (a draft)
出人 *furidashinin* remitter, writer (of a check)
出局 *furidashikyoku* the post office issuing a money order
6回 *fu(ri)-mawa(su)* brandish, wave, flourish, wave about, swing; display, show off
返 *fu(ri)-ka(eru)* turn the head, look over one's shoulder, turn around, look back
向 *fu(ri)-mu(keru)* turn toward; apply toward, appropriate to. *fu(ri)-mu(ku)* turn toward, look back
合 *fu(ri)a(i)* consideration, comparison, balancing; usage, practice, custom
当 *fu(ri)-a(teru)* assign (work)
仮名 *fu(ri)gana* side *kana* (to show the pronunciation of characters)
7作 *shinsaku* prosperity
乱 *fu(ri)-mida(su)* shake (one's hair) loose, dishevel
売 *fu(ri)u(ri)* hawking, peddling
8放 *fu(ri)-hana(su)*＝振離 (see below–19)
受人 *fu(ri)u(ke)nin* drawee
9飛 *fu(ri)-to(basu)* swing and throw
客 *fu(ri) (no) kyaku* chance customer
10袖 *fu(ri) sode* long sleeves, long-sleeved kimono
10被 *fu(ri)-kabu(ru)* hold aloft, brandish
起 *furu(i)-oko(su)* arouse, awaken, promote. *shinki* encouragement, stimulation
起日 *shinkibi* rally day
11捨 *fu(ri)-su(teru)* shake off; discard, forsake, abandon, desert, leave off
掛 *fu(ri)-ka(keru)* sprinkle over, splash on. *fu(ri)-ka(karu)* be splashed. *furika(ke)* fish flour

動 *fu(ri)-ugo(kasu) vt* swing, shake, wag. *fu(ri)-ugo(ku) vi* swing, shake, oscillate. *shindō* oscillation, swing, vibration

粛 *shinshuku* strict enforcement

12幅 *shimpuku* amplitude (of vibrations); the swing of a pendulum

落 *fu(ri)-oto(su), furu(i)-oto(su)* shake off, throw off, spill, sift out, eliminate

替 *fu(ri)-ka(eru)* transfer (funds). *furikae* change, transfer, postal-transfer account

替貯金 *furikae chokin* postal-transfer account

13解 *fu(ri)-hodo(ku)* shake and untangle

鈴 *shinrei* ringing a bell; hand bell

14舞 *furuma(u)* behave oneself, entertain, treat. *furumai* behavior, deportment, demeanor, conduct, manners; entertainment, feast

舞酒 *furumaizake* a saké treat

15撒 *fu(ri)-ma(ku)* sprinkle, scatter, diffuse, disperse; lavish

16興 *shinkō* promotion, encouragement, arousing

17盪 *shintō* concussion, shock, impact

翳 *fu(ri)-kaza(su)=fu(ri)-a(geru)* 振上 (see above–3)

19離 *fu(ri)-hana(su)* shake oneself loose, tear away from

22顫 *shinsen* tremor

顫譫妄症 *shinsen semmōshō* delirium tremens

8

掌 See 1366.

挩 Nonstandard for 挽 1918.

掴 Nonstandard for 摑 1985.

捗 Nonstandard for 捗 1911.

掟 1921 / F809 Tō. Chō. Jō *okite* law, **commandments, regulations.**

捫 1922 / F803 Mon to stroke.

11著 *monchaku* trouble; dispute

掣 1923 / F810 Sei pull; pull back; restrain.

7肘 *seichū* restraint, check, restriction, control, interference

揶 1924 / F819 Ya tease, play with.

12揄 *yayu suru, karaka(u)* ridicule, tease, banter with

掖 1925 / F808 Eki side (of the body); carry under the arm.

8門 *ekimon* small gate at the side of a large one

掉 1926 / F806 Tō, Chō shake and move.

7尾 *tōbi no, chōbi no* crowning, final finishing

掏 1927 / F807 Tō. *su(ru)* pick a pocket.

13摸 *suri* pickpocket; pickpocketing

捥 1928 / F802 Wan arm. *mogi(ru), mo(gu)=mo(gi)-to(ru)* 捥取 (see below–8). *mo(geru)* come off, be broken off. *ude* arm; talent, ability.

8取 *mo(gi)-to(ru)* wrest from, snatch from; tear off, break off

捺 1929 / F804 Natsu press, print. *o(su), sa(su)* affix a seal, stamp.

6印 *natsuin* sealing (a document)

9染 *nassen, oshizome, nasen* (textile) printing

B **措** 1930 / F814 So. *o(ku)* give up, suspend, discontinue, lay aside, set apart; except.

13置 *sochi* measure, step, move, action

辞 *soji* phraseology, wording, diction

辞法 *sojihō* syntax

掠 1931 / F809 Ryaku. *kasu(meru)* rob, pillage; graze (in passing), skim, sweep over; cheat; hint, suggest. *kasu(ru)* graze (one's leg); squeeze, exploit. *kasu(reru)* be grazed, touch, chip; become hoarse. *kasuri* grazing (something); squeeze, percentage, kickback.

8取 *kasu(me)-to(ru), ryakushu suru* rob, cheat, despoil; seize, capture

13傷 *kasu(ri) kizu* scratch, bruise; slight damage; slight (business) failure

14奪 *kasu(me)-uba(u)* plunder. *ryakudatsu* pillage, plunder, looting

掩 1932 / F813 En *ō(u)* cover, shade, conceal, shelter

13蓋 *engai* cover, covering, blanketing

15蔽 *empei* cover, obscuration, occultation,

撃 *engeki* surprise attack, relief

20護 *engo* covering, protection, aegis, backing, relief

捲 1933 / F803 Ken. *ma(ku)* roll, wind, coil; tie around, wind up. *maku(ru), meku(ru)* turn over (pages); turn up (a card); tear off, take up, rip off; tuck up, bare (one's arm), roll up (one's sleeves).

maku(reru) *vi* turn over, turn up; tear off, rip; be rolled up. *makure* burr, snag, catch.
3 上 *maku(ri)-a(geru)*, *maku(shi)-a(geru)*, *ma(ki)a(geru)* = *ma(ki)a(geru)* 巻上 1466.3
土重来 *kendo-jūrai* making a success after failure
5 立 *maku(shi)-ta(teru)* talk volubly, rattle on
12 落 *maku(re)-o(chiru)* tear off and fall

揭 1934/F818 **揭** Kei. Ketsu. *kaka(geru)* B put up, hang out, hoist, display; publish, insert; describe; mention.
5 示 *keiji* bulletin, notice
示板 *keijiban* bulletin board
示場 *keijiba* notice wall
11 揚 *keiyō suru* hoist, fly, display
13 載 *keisai* publication, insertion

据 1935/F803 Kyo. *su(eru)* set (a table); lay (a P foundation); place (a gun); install, equip; appoint (to a position). ***su(waru)*** squat down, sit down, (eyes) are fixed on.
5 石 *sue-ishi* garden flagstones
付 *su(e)-tsu(keru)* install, equip; set up; mount, place in position; set (a charge)
8 物 *suemono* alcove ornament
9 風呂 *suefuro* wooden bath tub
13 置 *su(e)-o(ku)* leave as it is, defer; leave (a loan) unredeemed; establish
16 膳 *suezen* an individually served meal

描 1936/F815 Byō. *ka(ku)* write, compose; B draw, paint. *ega(ku)* paint, sketch, draw, describe.
4 切 *ega(ki)-ki(ru)* draw exactly
5 写 *byōsha* description; portrayal; drawing, painting, picture
出 *ega(ki)-da(su)* portray, delineate, depict. *byōshutsu*=*byōsha* 描写 (see above–5)
8 画 *byōga* drawing, painting ⌈line
15 線 *byōsen* a drawn line. *byōsen suru* draw a

掬 1937/F814 Kiku. *kiku(su)*, *musu(bu)* scoop up water with the hand. *suku(u)* scoop, dip, ladle.
3 上 *suku(i)-a(geru)* dip up, scoop up
5 出 *suku(i)-da(su)* bail out
7 投 *suku(i)na(ge)* tripping up (someone)
8 取 *suku(i)-to(ru)* dip up, scoop up
14 網 *suku(i)ami* scoop net, dip net

捷 1938/F804 Shō victory; fast.
7 利 *shōri* victory
8 径 *shōkei* short cut; expedient
9 勁 *shōkei* nimble and strong

急 *shōkyū* speed, urgency
12 報 *shōhō* news of victory
13 戦 *kachi-ikusa* victory

捧 1939/F802 Hō. *sasa(geru)* lift up; give; offer, consecrate, devote, sacrifice, dedicate.
2 刀 *hōtō* sword salute. *hōtō suru* present (credentials), submit, offer
7 呈 *hōtei* dedication, presentation; gift
8 物 *sasa(ge)mono* offering, sacrifice
9 持 *hōji suru* bear, present, hold up (the emperor's picture)
13 腹 *hōfuku* convulsed with laughter
腹絶倒 *hōfuku-zettō* convulsed with laugh-
14 読 *hōdoku suru* read reverently ⌊ter
銃 *sasa(ge)tsutsu* presenting arms

捻 1940/F804 Nen. *hine(ri)*, *hine(ru)* (see under 拈 1866.0). *ne(jiru)*, *neji(reru)* (see under 捩 1942.0). *hineku(ru)* twirl, twist, play with; twist (the truth in reasoning).
3 子 *neji* screw, faucet, watch spring
4 込栓 *nejiko(mi)sen* plug, attachment
5 出 *hine(ri)-da(su)* squeeze out; work out a plan. *nenshutsu suru* contrive, devise (means), raise (money)
6 回 *hineku(ri)-mawa(su)*, *hine(ri)-mawa(su)* tinker with, twist up, twirl
8 取 *hine(ri)-to(ru)* pinch (something) from
9 廻 *hineku(ri)-mawa(su)* twist up, tinker with
10 挫 *nenza* sprain
11 転 *nenten* twisting, torsion
15 潰 *hine(ri)-tsubu(su)* crush between fingers
16 錐 *neji(re)kiri* a twist drill

控 1941/F811 **控** Kō. *hika(eru)* draw in; B hold back, suspend (judgment); refrain from; be moderate; write, make notes; wait; have; moderate (a report). *hika(e)* memo; duplicate; waiting; prop; reserve.
5 目 *hika(e)me no* moderate, temperate, reserved, conservative
7 邸 *hika(e)tei* villa, retreat
8 所 *hika(e)jo* waiting room
制 *kōsei* checking, controlling
9 除 *kōjo* subtraction, deduction
室 *hika(e)shitsu* waiting room
屋敷 *hika(e) yashiki* villa, retreat
10 書 *hika(e)ga(ki)* notes, memo
11 帳 *hika(e)chō* notebook
12 訴 *kōso* (legal) appeal
訴状 *kōsojō* petition of appeal
訴院 *kōso-in* court of appeal

訴裁判所 *kōso saibansho* appellate court
訴権 *kōsoken* right of appeal
訴審 *kōsoshin* appeal trial

捩 1942 / F803 REI. RETSU. *yoji(ru)*, *ne(jiru)* screw, twist, wrench, distort, wring, turn (a faucet); make capital out of someone's slip of the tongue. *yoji(reru)*, *neji(reru)* be twisted, be distorted, kink, twist, be awry; be perverse. *moji(ru)* twist. distort; parody. *mojiri* Japanese overcoat; parody. *nejiri*, *nejire* torsion.

3 上 *ne(ji)-a(geru)* screw up
子 *neji* screw, faucet, watch spring
子錐 *nejigiri* gimlet, drill ⌈test to
4 込 *ne(ji)-ko(mu)* screw in; thrust into; pro-
切 *ne(ji)-ki(ru)* wrench off, twist off
6 向 *ne(ji)-mu(keru)* twist, toward
曲 *ne(ji)-ma(geru)* bend by twisting
伏 *ne(ji)-fu(seru)* overpower, get (someone)
合 *ne(ji)-a(u)* struggle with ⌊down
7 折 *ne(ji)-o(ru)* twist off
折釘 *nejio(re) kugi* screw hook
8 取 *ne(ji)-to(ru)*, *neji(ri)-to(ru)* wring off, wrest from
11 寄 *ne(ji)-yo(ru)* twist one's way along
12 開 *ne(ji)-a(keru)* wrench open, pry open
13 鉢巻 *neji(ri) hachimaki*, *neji hachimaki* twisted towel worn around the head
14 網 *moji ami* minnow net

B 掘 1943 / F806 KUTSU. *ho(ru)* dig, delve; core; excavate; sink (wells); dig up; scoop out; pick (the ear); probe.

3 下 *ho(ri)-sa(geru)* dig down; delve, investi-
上 *ho(ri)-a(geru)* dig up, dig out ⌊gate
4 込 *ho(ri)-ko(mu)* dig in, dig into
井戸 *ho(ri)-ido* artesian well, bored well
5 出 *ho(ri)-da(su)* dig out, unearth, exhume, extricate, excavate; pick up (a rare book)
出物 *horida(shi)mono* treasure trove; lucky find; bargain
6 返 *ho(ri)-kae(su)* turn up (the soil); tear up (a road)
池 *ho(ri)-ike* an artificial pool
当 *ho(ri)-a(teru)* find, dig up, strike (oil)
7 抜 *ho(ri)-nu(ku)* bore thru, bore into
抜井戸 *horinuki ido* bored well
9 削 *kussaku* excavation
建小屋 *ho(t)ta(te)goya* hut, shack, cabin
10 起 *ho(ri)-o(kosu)* dig up; plow up
進 *kusshin suru* excavate, tunnel
11 崩 *ho(ri)-kuzu(su)* demolish
12 開 *ho(ri)-hira(ku)* excavate
割 *horiwa(ri)* canal
28 鑿 *kussaku* excavation

B 捨 1944 / F803 捨 SHA. *su(teru)* throw away, discard, abandon, desert, discard, give up, abandon; renounce, relinquish; resign; lay down (one's life); part with; sacrifice; reject, condemn.

3 子 *su(te)go* foundling
小舟 *su(te) obune* drifting boat; deserted
4 犬 *su(te) inu* stray dog ⌊person
切 *su(te)-ki(ru)* renounce, give up
5 石 *su(te)-ishi* ornamental garden rocks; road ballast; preparatory work ⌈away
去 *su(te)-sa(ru)* forsake; send away; throw
台詞 *su(te)zerifu* sharp parting remark
6 仮名 *su(te)gana* connective *kana* to assist in reading or to indicate inflection (in Chinese classics)
7 身 *su(te)mi* self-abandonment. *shashin* becoming a priest
売 *su(te)u(ri)* sacrifice sale
児 *su(te)go* foundling
8 金 *su(te)gane* wasted money
所 *su(te)dokoro* dumping ground
10 値 *su(te)ne* sacrifice price
書 *su(te)ga(ki)* rambling writing
11 猫 *su(te) neko* stray cat
12 場 *su(te)ba* dumping ground, dump
詞 *su(te)-kotoba* sharp parting remark
13 鉢 *su(te)bachi* despair, desperation
置 *su(te)-o(ku)* let alone, let pass, overlook

B 掃 1945 / F805 掃 SŌ. *ha(ku)* sweep; brush; gather up.

5 立 *hakita(te)* newly swept
出 *ha(ki)-da(su)* sweep out
7 初 *ha(ki)zome* first sweeping of the year
8 取 *ha(ki)-to(ru)* sweep away, sweep off
9 海 *sōkai* mine sweeping
海船 *sōkaisen* mine sweeper
海艇 *sōkaitei* mine sweeper
除 *sōji* cleaning, sweeping; clean-up, purge
除人 *sōjinin* cleaner, janitor
除屋 *sōjiya* night-soil man
除婦 *sōjifu* cleaning woman
除器 *sōjiki* vacuum cleaner
除機 *sōjiki* vacuum cleaner
10 討 *sōtō* cleaning up, sweeping, mopping up
射 *sōsha* sweeping fire
留 *ha(ki)da(me)* dust heap, rubbish heap
11 捨 *ha(ki)-su(teru)* sweep away, sweep out
寄 *ha(ki)-yo(seru)* sweep up
掃除 *ha(ki)-sōji* sweeping and cleaning
12 集 *ha(ki)-atsu(meru)* sweep up
13 滅 *sōmetsu* clean sweep, annihilation
溜 *ha(ki)da(me)* sweepings, rubbish heap, dump
15 蕩 *sōtō* clearing up, sweeping, mopping up

A **授** 1946 / F805 JU give, grant. *sazu(keru)* grant, confer, award, invest (with authority); impart, teach. *sazu(karu)*, *sazu(keraru)* be gifted with, be granted, be awarded, be accorded, be blessed with; be taught.

3 与 *juyo* awarding, conferring
与式 *juyoshiki* presentation ceremony
7 戒 *jukai* Buddhist initiation ceremony
8 物 *sazu(kari)mono* godsend, windfall, gift, boon, blessing
受 *juju suru* give and receive, deliver and receive
乳 *junyū* lactation, suckling
乳婦 *junyūfu* wet nurse
乳期 *junyūki* lactation period
9 洗 *jusen suru* baptize (by sprinkling)
洗者 *jusensha* baptizer (by sprinkling)
10 粉 *jufun* pollinization, fertilization
浸 *jushin suru* baptize by immersion
浸者 *jushinsha* baptizer (by immersion)
11 経 *jukyō* teaching the sutras
産 *jusan* placement, employment
産所 *jusanjo* vocational institute (to help the unemployed)
産施設 *jusan shisetsu* vocational-aid center
産場 *jusanjō* employment office
13 業 *jugyō* teaching, instruction, classwork
業料 *jugyōryō* tuition fees
業時間 *jugyō jikan* school hours
14 精 *jusei* fertilization, pollination
15 権 *juken* authorization
賞 *jushō* awarding a prize
17 爵 *jushaku suru* elevate to the peerage

A **採** 1947 / F809 **採** SAI. *to(ru)*, *to(reru)* (see under 取 3699.0).

2 入 *to(ri)-i(reru)*=取入 3699.2
3 上 *to(ri)-a(geru)*=取上 3699.3
4 方 *to(ri)kata* way of taking (a photo)
5 用 *saiyō suru* use, adopt, employ. *saiyō* introduction, adoption, acceptance; appointment, employment
石 *saiseki* quarrying
出 *saishutsu suru, to(ri)-da(su)* take out
6 血 *saiketsu suru* take a blood sample
伐 *saibatsu* felling (trees)
光 *saikō* lighting
7 択 *saitaku suru* adopt, select
決 *saiketsu* vote, roll call, ballot taking
否 *saihi* adoption or rejection; employment or rejection
8 金 *saikin* gold mining; gold extraction
取 *saishu* picking, gathering, collecting, harvesting; extracting (alcohol)
油 *saiyu* oil drilling
油権 *saiyuken* oil concession
9 点 *saiten* marking, grading
点者 *saitensha* marker, scorer
炭 *saitan* coal mining
炭所 *saitanjo* coal mine, colliery
10 残 *to(ri)noko(ri)* gleaning
11 掘 *saikutsu* mining
12 量 *sairyō* discretion
集 *saishū* collecting, gathering
13 鉱 *saikō* mining
14 綿器 *saimenki* cotton picker
種圃 *saishuho* seed garden
種園 *saishuen* seed garden
算 *saisan* profit
算制 *saisansei* (institutional) financial independence
16 録 *sairoku suru* transcribe, record

B **排** 1948 / F807 HAI *hai(suru)* exclude, expel, reject; push aside, push open; defy; disregard; anti-(Japanese, etc.).

4 日 *hai-Nichi* anti-Japanese
仏派 *haibutsuha* (ancient) anti-Buddhist faction
水 *haisui* drainage; draining; bailing; displacement
水渠 *haisuikyo* drain, culvert
水量 *haisuiryō* displacement
水路 *haisuiro* sewer system
水管 *haisuikan* drainpipe
水噸数 *haisui tonsū* displacement tonnage
5 斥 *haiseki* rejection, exclusion, ostracism, expulsion
外 *haigai* antiforeign
他 *haita* exclusion
他的 *haitateki* exclusive
出 *haishutsu* discharge, exhaust, evacuation
出物 *haishutsubutsu* excreta
6 米 *hai-Bei* anti-American
列 *hairetsu* arrangement, grouping, disposition
気 *haiki* exhaust, ventilation
気坑 *haikikō* ventilation
気鐘 *haikishō* air pump, bell jar
7 尿 *hainyū* urination
卵 *hairan* ovulation
8 英 *hai-Ei* anti-British
泄 *haisetsu* evacuation, discharge, exhaust
泄物 *haisetsubutsu* excrement, excretion
9 便 *haiben* evacuation, bowel movement
除 *haijo* exclusion, removal
臭管 *haishūkan* stench pipe
11 液 *haieki* drainage (in surgery)
球 *haikyū* volley ball
雪 *haisetsu* snow removal
貨 *haika* boycott
13 置 *haichi* arrangement, disposition (of troops)
15 撃 *haigeki* denouncement, rejection
17 擠 *haisei suru* exclude, reject, expel
膿 *hainō* drainage of pus

B **探** 1949 / F809 TAN. *sagu(ru)* search, look for; explore; spy upon, sound out;

probe (a wound). *saga(su)* search. *sagu(ri)* sounding out; spy; probe.

3 下 *sagu(ri)-sa(geru)* dig for

上 *sagu(ri)-a(geru)* examine by touch

5 出 *sagu(ri)-da(su)* spy out, worm out, smell out, search out

6 回 *sagu(ri)-mawa(su)*, *sagu(ri)-mawa(ru)* grope for, fumble for

合 *sagu(ri)a(i)* testing each other's feelings

当 *sagu(ri)-a(teru)* grope and find, discover, locate

7 足 *sagu(ri)ashi* groping (one's way)

求 *saga(shi)-moto(meru)* search for. *tankyū* quest, pursuit, research

究 *tankyū* search, research, inquiry

究心 *tankyūshin* spirit of inquiry

究物 *tankyūbutsu* quest

究者 *tankyūsha* investigator

8 知 *tanchi* detection

知器 *tanchiki* detector

9 査 *tansa* inquiry, investigation

海灯 *tankaitō* searchlight

10 梅 *tambai* plum-blossom viewing

険 *tanken* exploration, expedition

索 *tansaku* search; inquiry, investigation

索的 *tansakuteki* searching (inquiry)

11 訪 *tambō* searching; hunting a news story; journalist

訪記者 *tambō kisha* reporter, interviewer

偵 *tantei* detective work; espionage; detective; spy, investigator, agent

偵小説 *tantei shōsetsu* detective story

偵犬 *tanteiken* police dog

偵物 *tanteimono* detective story

12 測 *tansoku* exploring; spying

湯 *kagatachi* hot-water ordeal

勝 *tanshō* sightseeing

検 *tanken* exploration, expedition

検記 *tankenki* exploration record

検家 *tankenka* explorer

検船 *tankensen* explorers' vessel

検隊 *tankentai* exploration party

13 照灯 *tanshōtō* searchlight

鉱 *tankō* prospecting

鉱者 *tankōsha* prospector

14 聞 *tambun* detection

15 賞 *tanshō* sightseeing

18 題 *tandai* (ancient) army headquarters

推 1950 / F812 A 推 SUI conjecture. *o(su)* infer, conclude; guess, suppose; recommend, support. *o(shite)* by conjecture, by deduction.

2 力 *suiryoku* thrust, driving power

5 弘 *o(shi)-hiro(meru)*＝押弘 1885.5

6 当 *o(shi)-a(teru)* guess

考 *suikō* inference, deduction, deliberation

7 究 *suikyū* inference

8 知 *suichi* inference, deduction, conjecture

服 *suifuku suru* admire and respect

参 *suisan* visiting; discourtesy

定 *suitei* presumption, conclusion, estimation

9 計 *suikei* estimate

10 称 *suishō* praise; admiration

挙 *suikyo suru* propose (for office)

挙式 *suikyoshiki* installation ceremony

進 *suishin* propulsion, drive, promotion

進力 *suishinryoku* impulse, propulsion

進機 *suishinki* propeller

11 問 *suimon* questioning; investigating (a crime)

移 *sui-i* transition, change. *o(shi)-utsu(ru)* (times) change, (months) pass

断 *suidan* inference, deduction, conclusion

理 *suiri* reasoning, inference, presumption

理小説 *suiri shōsetsu* detective story

12 測 *suisoku* conjecture, supposition. *o(shi)-haka(ru)* enter into another's feelings

量 *suiryō*＝*suisatsu* 推察 (see below–14)

13 奨 *suishō* recommendation, commendation

14 選 *suisen* recommendation

輓 *suiban* recommendation

敲 *suikō* polish, elaboration, choice of diction

察 *suisatsu* guess, inference, imagination; consideration, sympathy

算 *suisan* calculation, reckoning

15 賞 *suishō* recommendation, commendation

論 *suiron* reasoning, inference, deduction

論式 *suironshiki* syllogism

16 薦 *suisen* recommendation, nomination

薦状 *suisenjō* letter of recommendation

薦者 *suisensha* recommender, proposer

薦委員会 *suisen i-inkai* nominating committee

17 戴式 *suitaishiki* installation ceremony

接 1951 / F810 A 接 SETSU. *ses(suru)* touch, contact; adjoin; receive (visitors); be in receipt of; encounter, experience; draw near. *tsu(gu)* join, piece together, splice, cement, set (broken bones); graft (trees). *ha(gu)* patch. *hagi* patch, patches; patching; seam, joint.

4 手 *tsugite* joint, pipe coupling

木 *tsugiki* grafting; grafted tree

木法 *tsugikihō* grafting

5 目 *tsugime*, *hagime* joint, seam, suture

収 *sesshū* seizure, requisition

6 近 *sekkin* proximity, approach; intimate relations

地 *setchi* ground (connection)

合 *ha(gi)-a(waseru)* sew together; join. *setsugō*, *tsugō* union, joining

合剤 *setsugōzai* glue

7 角 *sekkaku* adjacent angle

迫 *seppaku*＝切迫 667.7

伴 *seppan*＝*settai* 接待 (see below–9)

吻 *seppun* kiss, kissing
見 *sekken* interview, reception
見日 *sekkembi* reception day, at-home day
尾辞 *setsubiji* suffix
尾語 *setsubigo* suffix
8 受 *setsuju suru* receive, intercept
9 待 *settai* reception, welcome; serving (food)
待室 *settaishitsu* reception room
客 *sekkyaku* receiving visitors
客用 *sekkyakuyō* for customers
客係 *sekkyakugakari* receptionist ⌈ress
客婦 *sekkyakufu* (restaurant) hostess; wait-
客業 *sekkyakugyō* hotel and restaurant ⌊business
10 骨 *sekkotsu* bonesetting
骨医 *sekkotsui* bonesetter
骨術 *sekkotsujutsu* bonesetting
11 眼鏡 *setsugankyō* eyepiece
12 着剤 *setchakuzai* binding agent, glue
13 辞 *setsuji* prefixes and suffixes
戦 *sessen* hand-to-hand fighting; close game
続 *setsuzoku* connection, junction, joining
続詞 *setsuzokushi* conjunction
触 *sesshoku* contact, touch, tangency
触反応 *sesshoku hannō* catalysis
触作用 *sesshoku sayō* catalytic action
触面 *sesshokumen* contact surface, contacts (with people) ⌈tangency
触点 *sesshokuten* point of contact; point of
触感染 *sesshoku kansen* contagion
14 種 *sesshu* inoculation, vaccination
15 穂 *tsugiho* graft, slip; scion
16 頭辞 *settōji* prefix
頭語 *settōgo* prefix
20 攘 *setsujō* contiguity

B **掛** 1952/F608 KAI. KEI. *ka(karu) vi* hang on, be suspended from, be caught, be trapped; be built; begin; arrive at; require, cost; play against, oppose; be splashed; weigh (a pound); be levied; (the instrument or tool) works; attack, fall on; is now showing at; consult; depend (on a son). *ka(keru) vt* hang; set up (a ladder); cover; construct, install; sit down; sprinkle, pour on; put on; ring up; weigh; multiply; levy; pay (in installments); anchor; start (a machine); wind; turn on (radio); spend on; offer (prizes); put (under treatment); set (on fire). *kakari* duty; person in charge; expenses, charges; tax; dependence (on someone); scale; outward appearance; construction; beginning; bite (of a tool). *ka(ke)* buckwheat noodles in soup; credit; overcharge; installment. *-ka(keru)* begin, start to. *-ka(ketewa)* (in) the matter of, in. *-ga(ke)* wearing; on (the way); ten percent; times (as large). *-ka(ke)* half finished; (clothes) hook; (table) cover.

2 人 *ka(kari)bito, ka(kari)udo* dependent, hanger-on
3 子 *ka(kari)go* one's support in old age
小屋 *ka(ke)goya* lean-to, temporary hut
4 込 *ka(ke)-ko(mu)* lock with a key
引 *ka(ke)hi(ki)* bargaining; maneuvering
心地 *ka(ke)gokochi* the feel (of a chair)
5 目 *ka(ke)me* weight
矢 *ka(ke)ya* mallet ⌈cian)
付 *ka(kari)tsu(ke) no* one's regular (physi-
外 *ka(ke)hazu(shi)* putting on and off; disengaging (gear) ⌈notices; nameplate
札 *ka(ke) fuda* small hanging plaque for
払 *ka(ke)bara(i)* settlement of accounts
汁 *ka(ke) shiru, ka(ke)jiru* dressing (on food)
出 *ka(ke)da(shi)* penthouse
代金 *ka(ke) daikin* bill, amount to pay
布 *ka(ke)fu* cloth cover
布団 *ka(ke)buton* covering quilt
6 回 *ka(ke)-megu(rasu)* surround, enclose
字 *ka(ke)ji* hanging scroll
先 *ka(ke)saki* credit customers ⌈trance
行灯 *ka(ke) andon* paper lantern at the en-
合 *ka(ke)-a(u)* negotiate with, bargain with. *ka(ke)-a(wasu) vt* multiply; cross, interbreed. *ka(kari)-a(u)* have dealings with; be involved in. *ka(kari)a(i)* implication, involvement. *kakea(i)* negotiations; dialogue ⌈logue
合話 *kakea(i)banashi* storytelling in dia-
合漫才 *ka(ke)a(i) manzai* comic dialogue
7 図 *kakezu* wall map, wall picture
声 *ka(ke)goe* shouting encouragement; shouting in unison to aid effort
売 *kakeu(ri)* selling on credit
8 金 *kakekin* installment payments; credit sales. *ka(ke)gane* hatch, hasp, latch
物 *ka(ke)mono* hanging picture or scroll; (food) dressing; coverlet
肥 *ka(ke)goe* liquid manure
直 *ka(ke)-nao(su)* reweigh; rehang
取 *kaketo(ri)* bill collection; collector
取引 *ka(ke)torihiki* doing business on credit ⌈rently
9 持 *kake-mo(chi)* holding positions concur-
衿 *ka(ke) eri* changeable kimono collar
冠 *keikan* resignation
竿 *ka(ke)zao* clothes-drying pole
負 *ka(kari)ma(ke)* earnings not covering ex-
看板 *ka(ke) kamban* hanging sign ⌊penses
茶屋 *ka(ke) chaya* wayside teahouse
10 倒 *ka(ke)dao(re)* bad debt; earnings not covering expenses
値 *ka(ke)ne* overcharge; exaggeration

紙 *ka(ke)gami* wrapper, (book) jacket
時計 *ka(ke)dokei* wall clock
11 違 *ka(ke)-chiga(u)* cross (on the way)
帳 *ka(ke)chō* charge-account book
捨 *kakezu(te)* abandoning an installment
商 *ka(ke)akina(i)* selling on credit ⌊contract
12 減 *ka(ke)be(ri)* weight loss
湯 *ka(kari)yu* clean hot bath water for rins-
絵 *ka(ke)-e* hanging picture ⌊ing off
詞 *ka(ke) kotoba* play on words
軸 *kakejiku* hanging scroll
買 *ka(ke)ga(i)* credit purchase
集 *ka(ke)atsu(me)* bill collecting
替 *ka(ke)-ka(eru)* replace, rebuild, substitute. *kakeka(e)* rebuilding (a bridge); rehanging (a scroll). *kakega(e)* substitute
13 鉤 *ka(ke) kagi, ka(ke)bari* long hook
筵 *ka(ke) mushiro* mat curtain
幕 *ka(ke) maku* hangings
蒲団 *ka(ke)buton* covering quilt
14 暦 *ka(ke)goyomi* wall calendar
樋 *ka(ke)doi* water pipe, conduit, flume
銭 *ka(ke)sen* stakes, bet
算 *ka(ke)zan* multiplication
15 蕎麦 *ka(ke) soba* buckwheat noodles in seasoned broth
16 橋 *ka(ke) hashi* viaduct, suspension bridge
18 額 *ka(ke)gaku* hanging framed picture ⌈ing
醬油 *ka(ke)jōyu* diluted *shōyu* for season-
22 籠 *ka(ke)-komo(ru)* lock oneself in

9

揭 See 1934.

搜 See 捜 1917.

挠 Nonstandard for 撓 2002.

插 1953 / F816 揷 See 挿 1916.

揩 1954 / F818 KAI wipe.

揄 1955 / F814 YŌ. YU pull; tease, play with.

揆 1956 / F815 KI category; principle; plot; way of doing; plan; road; uprising. *bachi* drumstick.

揃 1957 / F814 SEN. *soro(u)* be complete; be equal; be even, be uniform; be all present. *soro(eru)* arrange; make even; complete, get ready. *soroi* all, both, together, uniform. uniformity; attendance. *soro(tte)* in a body, en masse; all alike. *-soroi* set; suit.

揣 1958 / F818 SHI. SUI. *haka(ru)* conjecture.
15 摩 *shima* guess, conjecture ⌈tion
摩臆測 *shima-okusoku* conjecture, specula-

搭 1959 / F823 TŌ load (a vehicle); ride.
9 乗 *tōjō suru* board, get on
乗者 *tōjōsha* passenger, occupant
13 載 *tōsai suru* load; entrain; embark

揮 1960 / F818 B KI. *furu(u)* (see under 振 1920.0).
9 発 *kihatsu* volatilization
発油 *kihatsuyu* gasoline
発油税 *kihatsuyuzei* gasoline tax
11 毫 *kigō* writing, painting, drawing

揑 Nonstandard for 捏 1905.

援 1961 / F819 援 B EN *tasu(keru)* help, save.
4 引 *en-in* reference
5 用 *en-yō suru* claim, quote, invoke
7 兵 *empei* relief, reinforcements
助 *enjo* assistance, help, pay, support
助額 *enjogaku* amount of aid
8 例 *enrei* illustration
9 軍 *engun* relief, reinforcements
11 隊 *entai* reinforcements ⌈relief
20 護 *engo* covering, protection, aegis, backing,

揉 1962 / F815 JŪ. *mo(mu)* rub; massage, shampoo; debate vigorously; train, coach; worry; shove and carry (a portable shrine). *mo(meru)* get into trouble, trouble arises; be rumpled, get out of shape. *mo(mareru)* be tried, be buffeted. *mo(me)* trouble.
8 下 *mo(mi)-o(rosu)* to massage
上 *mo(mi)-a(geru)* massage. *momia(ge)* tuft of hair under the temples
4 手 *momide* rubbing one's hands
5 立 *mo(mi)-ta(teru)* rub vigorously; stir up,
出 *mo(mi)-da(su)* squeeze out ⌊exasperate
6 合 *mo(mi)-a(u)* jostle, shove and push, have
8 事 *momegoto* trouble ⌊friction
9 革 *momigawa* buff, polisher
10 消 *mo(mi)-ke(su)* hush up, suppress; smother (a fire); rub out; crush out; stifle
17 療治 *momiryōji* shampoo, massage

B **握** 1963/F818 AKU. *nigi(ru)* grasp, hold; make (sushi balls); assume (power); make (money); get (proof). *nigi(rasu)* let (someone) take hold of your hand; slip money to, bribe. *nigi(ri)* grasp, grip; handful; handle; rice ball, sushi ball.

2 力 *akuryoku* grasping power
4 手 *akushu* handshaking; reconciliation; harmony
9 屋 *nigi(ri)ya* miser, grasping fellow
10 索 *nigi(ri)zuna* grab line
拳 *nigi(ri) kobushi* clenched fist
12 飯 *nigi(ri)meshi, musubi* rice ball
13 詰 *nigi(ri)-tsu(meru)* grasp and squeeze together
15 潰 *nigi(ri)-tsubu(su)* crush, crumple; shelve, table
締 *nigi(ri)-shi(meru)* squeeze, wring, clasp, hold tightly
17 鮨 *nigi(ri)zushi* sushi ball

B **换** 1964/F817 **換** KAN. *ka(eru)*, *ka(waru)* (see under 代 364.0).

3 刃 *ka(e)ba* extra blades
5 玉 *ka(e)dama* a substitute, a double
6 衣 *kan-i* changing clothes
地 *ka(e)chi* substitute land
刑 *kankei* change of a sentence from a fine to hard labor
気 *kanki* ventilation
気筒 *kankitō* ventilator
7 言 *kangen (sureba)* in other words
8 金 *kankin suru* realize, turn into money
価 *kanka suru* convert into money
物 *ka(e)mono* exchanging; something exchanged
10 骨奪胎 *kankotsu-dattai* adaptation, modification; plagiarism
11 乾 *ka(e)-ho(su)* drain, empty (a well)
12 喩 *kan-yu* metonymy
着 *ka(e)gi* spare suit
14 算 *kansan* conversion, change, exchange
算表 *kansanhyō* conversion table

B **揺** 1965/F821 **搖** YŌ. *yu(reru)*, *yu(rameku)*, *yu(ratsuku)*, *yu(ragu)*, *yu(rugu)* *vi* shake, sway, rock, roll, pitch, tremble, quake, flicker, vibrate, jolt. *yu(suru)*, *yu(suburu)*, *yu(saburu)* *vt* swing, shake, rock. *yu(rugasu)*=*yu(ri)-ugo(kasu)* 揺動 (see below–11). *yu(re)* vibration; shock; variety.

3 下 *yu(ri)-sa(geru)* shake down
上 *yu(ri)-a(geru)* swing up, jiggle (a baby on one's back)
5 立 *yu(rugi)-ta(tsu)* stand shaking
6 返 *yu(ri)kae(shi)* an after-quake
曳 *yōei suru* flutter, tremble; trail, linger
10 起 *yu(ri)-oko(su)*, *yu(suri)-oko(su)* wake (someone) up
11 動 *yu(ri)-ugo(ku)* *vi* quake; swing. *yu(ri)-ugo(kasu)* *vt* shake, wave, swing, sway. *yu(re)-ugo(ku)* tremble
祭 *yōsai* wave offering
12 揺 *yu(ra)yu(ra)*, *yōyō* wavering, unsettled
落 *yu(ri)-oto(su)* shake off, shake down
無 *yu(rugi)na(i)* firm, steady, secure
椅子 *yu(ri)-isu* rocking chair
15 震 *yu(rugi)-furu(eru)* quake and tremble
20 籃 *yōran, yu(ri)kago* cradle
籃地 *yōran (no) chi* the home of, the cradle of, birthplace
籃時代 *yōran jidai* infancy, babyhood
籃期 *yōranki* infancy, babyhood
22 籠 *yu(ri)kago* cradle

B **揚** 1966/F817 YŌ praise. *a(garu)*, *a(geru)* (see 上 under 798.0); fry in deep fat. *a(ge)* tuck; fried tofu; fried food.

2 力 *yōryoku* lifting power
3 子江 *Yōsukō* Yangtze River
4 戸 *a(ge)do* push-up door
水 *yōsui* pumping water
水所 *yōsuijo* pumping plant
水装置 *yōsui sōchi* pumping equipment
5 句 *a(ge)ku* in the end, finally
7 言 *yōgen suru* declare, assert, profess
足 *a(ge)ashi* faultfinding
8 板 *a(ge)-ita* removable floor boards, trap door
物 *a(ge)mono* fried food
油 *a(ge)abura* frying oil
9 屋 *a(ge)ya* brothel
10 荷 *a(ge)ni* cargo being unloaded
陸 *yōriku* disembarkation; unloading
陸料 *yōrikuryō* landing charge
11 窓 *a(ge)mado* push-up window
12 場 *a(ge)ba* wharf, landing (place)
揚 *yōyō(taru)* triumphant, exultant
雲雀 *a(ge)hibari* skylark
13 幕 *a(ge)maku* Noh theater-entrance curtain
15 餅 *a(ge) mochi* fried rice-cake
16 錨機 *yōbyōki* anchor windlass
17 鍋 *a(ge)nabe* frying pan
20 饅頭 *a(ge) manjū* fried bean-jam bun

A **提** 1967/F815 TEI. CHŌ. *sa(geru)* take along, carry in the hand. *hissa(geru)* carry.

5 示 *teiji suru*, *teishi suru* present; exhibit; suggest
出 *teishutsu suru* present, introduce (a bill), tender (a resignation), lodge (a petition)
出者 *teishutsusha* proposer, mover
6 灯 *chōchin* paper lantern
灯行列 *chōchin gyōretsu* lantern procession
灯屋 *chōchin-ya* lantern maker

灯持 *chōchimmo(chi)* lantern carrier; exaggerated propaganda
7言 *teigen* proposal, motion
8供 *teikyō* offer, tender
9要 *teiyō* summary
香炉 *teikōro, sa(ge) kōro* censer
10起 *teiki suru* bring suit; raise a question; file a claim
案 *teian* proposition, suggestion, overture, proposal
案者 *teiansha*, proposer, proponent
案家 *teianka* proposer, proponent
11唱 *teishō* (Buddhist) lecture; advocacy
婆 *Daiba* Deva
12訴 *teiso suru* sue
琴 *teikin* violin
琴家 *teikinka* violinist
13携 *teikei* concert, co-operation
督 *teitoku* admiral, commodore
15論 *teiron* premise
20議 *teigi* proposal, motion

10

摹 See 4035.

搜 1968/F822 See **捜** 1917.

搖 1969/F821 See **揺** 1965.

搏 1970/F820 HAKU. *u(tsu)* (see under 打 1829.0).

搢 1971/F822 SHIN put between, insert.
11紳 *shinshin* rank; high-ranking person, nobles

搦 1972/F822 JAKU. JOKU. DAKU. *kara(meru)* bind, tie up, arrest. *-gara(mi)* the whole (basket); around (thirty years old).
4手 *karamete* rear; back entrance; one who arrests; force attacking the rear of a castle
8取 *kara(me)-to(ru)* arrest, capture

B **搬** 1973/F823 HAN carry, transport.
2入 *hannyū suru* carry in
5出 *hanshutsu suru* carry out
8送 *hansō suru* convey
送帯 *hansōtai* conveyor belt

摸 1974/F826 MO. search. *mo(suru)* imitate; copy.
5写 *mosha* copying; copy, replica
10倣 *mohō* copy, imitation
索 *mosaku* groping
17擬 *mogi* imitation
擬投票 *mogi tōhyō* straw vote
擬店 *mogiten* refreshment booths (at a party)
擬戦 *mogisen* sham fight
擬試験 *mogi shiken* trial examination

B **搾** 1975/F823 SAKU. *shibo(ru), shi(meru)* (see under 絞 3535.0).
4木 *shimegi* oil press
5汁 *shibo(ri)jiru* juices
出 *shiborida(shi)* (toothpaste) tube
8油 *sakuyu* oil expression (from seeds or nuts)
取 *shibo(ri)-to(ru)=shiboru* (see under 絞 3535.0). *sakushu* exploitation; squeezing; sweating
乳 *sakunyū* milking
11粕 *shibo(ri) kasu, shimekasu* strained lees; oil cake
13滓 *shibo(ri) kasu, shimekasu* strained lees
17糟 *shimekasu* oil cake, strained lees

B **摂** 1976/F841 **攝** SETSU. *ses(suru)* act in place of; carry on in addition to. *to(ru)* (see under 取 3699.0).
4氏 *sesshi* centigrade
5生 *sessei* health preservation, hygiene
6行 *sekkō* performing for another; performing simultaneously
8取 *sesshu* intake, absorption; adoption
9政 *sesshō, sessei* regency; regent
政皇后 *sesshō kōgō* empress regent, queen regent
政宮 *sesshō (no) miya* prince regent
10家 *sekke* the line of regents
11理 *setsuri* providence
理的 *setsuriteki* providential
14関 *sekkan* (ancient) regents
関家 *sekkanke* the line of regents
15養 *setsuyō* care of health, recuperation
20護腺 *setsugosen* prostate gland
護腺炎 *setsugosen-en* prostatitis

B **携** 1977/F840 **攜 擕** KEI. *tazusa(eru)* carry (in the hand); be armed with; carry along, bring (someone) along. *tazusa(waru)* participate in, be concerned in.
2入 *tazusa(e)-i(ru), tazusa(e)-i(reru)* carry into, bring into
3下 *tazusa(e)-kuda(ru)* carry down, take down
上 *tazusa(e)-nobo(ru), tazusa(e)-a(geru)* carry up out of, bring up
5出 *tazusa(e)-da(su)* carry out
6行 *keikō suru* carry along, bring. *tazusa(e)-yu(ku)* carry to, bring to, carry away
10帰 *tazusa(e)-kae(ru)* bring back

帯 *keitai* portable. *keitai suru* carry along
帯口糧 *keitai kōryō* field rations
帯兇器 *keitai kyōki* concealed weapons; a criminal's weapons
帯兵器 *keitai heiki* small arms ⌈hold effects
帯物件 *keitai bukken* personal and house-
帯品 *keitaihin* personal effects, luggage
帯食糧 *keitai shokuryō* portable army rations

搗 1978 / F822 Tō. *tsu(ku), ka(tsu)* pound, hull, husk; stamp (ore).
3 上 *tsu(ki)-a(geru)* finish pounding (rice)
4 手 *tsukite* pounder (of grain) ⌈tinous rice)
5 立 *tsukita(te)* freshly pounded *mochi* (glu-
加 *ka(tete)-kuwa(ete)* besides, moreover
6 臼 *tsuki usu* grain mortar ⌈gloss)
衣 *tōi* pounding cloth (to bring out the
合 *ka(chi)-a(u)* clash, collide, conflict, interfere with; fall on (a certain day), coincide
米 *tsukigome* polished rice ⌊with
米屋 *tsukigomeya* rice-polishing mill
9 砕 *tsu(ki)-kuda(ku)* smash, grind
10 栗 *kachiguri* dried chestnut
11 混 *tsu(ki)-ma(zeru)* mix together, pound together, roll into one
12 減 *tsukibe(ri)* grain-pounding loss
14 精 *tsu(ki)-shira(geru)* polish by pounding
15 潰 *tsu(ki)-tsubu(su)* pound to a jelly

A **損** 1979 / F820 SON loss; disadvantage, handicap. *son(suru)* lose, suffer loss. *sokona(u), sokone(ru), son(zuru), son(jiru)* harm, hurt, injure, damage, mar; lose, oppress. *-son(jiru), -sokona(u)* fail in (doing), fail to (do), miss, err in. *-son(ji), -sokona(i)* slip, error, failure.
3 亡 *sombō, sommō* loss
4 毛 *sommō* loss
友 *son-yū* unprofitable friend
5 失 *sonshitsu* loss
8 金 *sonkin* money loss
所 *sonsho* damaged place
10 耗 *sommō* loss ⌈disadvantage
益 *son-eki* loss and gain; advantage and
料 *sonryō* charge for the use of certain arti-
料貸 *sonryōga(shi)* letting out for hire ⌊cles
害 *songai* damage, injury, loss; casualties; prejudice
害保険 *songai hoken* insurance against loss
害高 *songaidaka* damages
害賠償 *songai baishō* restitution, compensation for damages or injuries
11 得 *sontoku* loss and gain; advantages and
12 量 *sonryō* ullage ⌊disadvantages
13 傷 *sonshō* damage, injury, casualty

搔 1980 / F821 Sō. *ka(ku)* scratch; clear away; rake; comb; paddle; cut off (a head). *ka(ki)-* emphatic suffix.
2 入 *ka(ki)-ire(ru)* rake in, gather in
3 干 *ka(i)-ho(su)* drain dry
上 *ka(ki)-a(geru)* comb upward
口説 *ka(ki)-kudo(ku)* complain of
4 込 *ka(ki)-ko(mu)* carry under the arm, rake in. *kakko(mu)* eat fast
切 *ka(ki)-ki(ru)* cut; cut off; cut and take
分 *ka(ki)-wa(keru)* push or shove aside
5 玉 *kakitama* egg soup
立 *ka(ki)-ta(teru)* stir; rake (the fire); beat, whip; turn up (a wick); arouse (interest), stir up (trouble) ⌈thief; shoplifter
払 *kappara(u)* pilfer, filch. *kappara(i)* sneak
出 *ka(i)-da(su)* bail out (a boat); drain out. *ka(ki)-da(su)* scrape out, rake out
6 回 *ka(ki)-mawa(su)* stir, churn, beat, whip; ransack; have one's own way
灯 *ka(i)-tomo(su)* trim lamps
合 *ka(ki)-a(waseru)* adjust, arrange
7 均 *ka(ki)-nara(su)* rake smooth, level out
乱 *ka(ki)-mida(su)* disturb, ruffle, disarrange
卵 *kaki tamago* egg soup
8 爬 *sōha* curetting, scraping, scooping out
退 *ka(ki)-no(keru)* push or thrust aside
抱 *ka(ki)-ida(ku)* emphatic for *ida(ku)* (see under 抱 1883.0)
取 *ka(i)-do(ru)* take; tuck up. *ka(ki)-to(ru)* scrape off, scrape out
毟 *ka(ki)-mushi(ru)* rend, tear, scratch off
9 巻 *kaima(ki)* sleeved quilt
10 挟 *ka(ki)-hasa(mu)* carry under the arm
消 *ka(ki)-ke(su)* wipe out, efface
流 *ka(ki)-naga(su)*=*naga(su)* (see under 流 2576.0)
破 *ka(i)-ya(ru), ka(ki)-ka(buru)* tear up
11 疵 *kaki kizu* scratch
痒 *sōyō* scratching an itchy place
掘 *kaibo(ri) suru* drain (a pond)
掃 *ka(ki)-ha(ku)* sweep, brush, gather up
探 *ka(ki)-sagu(ru)* scratch around (for something). *ka(ki)-saga(su), ka(ki)-sagu(ru), ka(i)-sagu(ru)* forage; ransack
細 *ka(i)-hoso(ru)* become thin (people)
寄 *ka(ki)-yo(seru)* rake up, gather up
崩 *ka(ki)-kuzu(su)* scratch raw; scratch out
混 *ka(ki)-ma(zeru)* mix, mix up
混機 *kakima(ze)ki* mixer
12 揚 *kakia(ge)* fritters; combing upward
創 *kaki kizu* scratch ⌈(a head)
落 *ka(ki)-oto(su)* scrape off (mud); cut off
集 *ka(ki)-atsu(meru)* rake up, gather up
裂 *ka(ki)-sa(ku)* rend, tear up, scratch and
14 鳴 *ka(ki)-na(rasu)* thrum, strum ⌊tear up

4 心小⺗戈戸【手扌】支攴攵文斗斤方无日曰月木欠止歹殳毋比毛氏气水氵氺火灬爪爫父爻爿丬片牙牛犬犭 11

摑 *ka(i)-tsuka(mu)* grasp firmly
摘 *ka(i)-tsuma(mu)* summarize
暮 *kaikure* (not) at all
雑 *ka(ki)-ma(zeru)* mix by stirring, mix up
雑機 *kakimazeki* mixer
15 撫 *ka(ki)-na(deru)* comb, smooth down. *kainade no* poor, indifferent
潜 *ka(i)-kugu(ru)* pass thru, pass under
16 壊 *ka(ki)-kowa(su)* scratch and ruin
操 *ka(i)-gu(ru)* haul in (a rope); handle ⌊(reins)
曇 *ka(ki)-kumo(ru)* be overcast
18 繕 *ka(i)-tsukuro(u)* adjust; put in order; ⌊gloss over
23 攫 *kassara(u)* pilfer, filch

11

擠 儕 See 498.

摩 摩 See 5392.

據 1981 F-X See 拠 1871.

摯 1982 F826 Shi gift; seriousness.

摧 1983 F825 Sai. *kuda(keru)*, *kuda(ku)* (see under 砕 3179.0).

摺 1984 F827 Shō, Shū fold; rub. *su(ru)* rub; print (on cloth).
4 込 *su(ri)-ko(mu)* rub in
5 本 *surihon* printed book ⌈etc.)
付 *su(ri)-tsu(keru)* print colors (on cloth,
付木 *suritsu(ke)gi* (early word for) matches
7 足 *suri-ashi* shuffling feet, dragging feet
13 鉢 *suribachi* mixing bowl

摑 1985 F824 Kaku. *tsuka(mu)* catch, seize, grasp, hold, lay hands on. *tsuka(maru)* hang onto, grab onto. *tsuka(maeru)* catch, seize, arrest, capture. *tsuka(maseru)* make (a person) catch hold of, let (a person) grasp; bribe; palm off; impose upon. *tsuka(mi)* handful; grip.
5 出 *tsuka(mi)-da(su)* take out by handfuls
6 合 *tsuka(mi)-a(u)* tussle, grapple
8 取 *tsuka(mi)-to(ru)*, snatch off, grasp
拉 *tsuka(mi)-hishi(gu)* crush
所 *tsuka(mi)dokoro* hold, grip
所無 *tsuka(mi)dokoro (no) na(i)* vague, evasive
10 殺 *tsuka(mi)-koro(su)* squeeze to death
11 掛 *tsuka(mi)-ka(karu)* grab at
15 潰 *tsuka(mi)-tsubu(su)* grasp and crush

B **撃** 1986 F833 撃 Geki. *u(tsu)* attack, defeat, destroy, conquer. *uchi-*, *u(tsu)*, *bu(tsu)* (see under 打 1829.0).
4 方 *u(chi)kata* how to fire (a gun)
止 *u(chi)-to(meru)* kill, bring down (a bird)
7 沈 *gekichin suru* sink a ship ⌈refuse, rebuff
8 退 *gekitai suru* repulse, dislodge, reject,
取 *u(chi)-to(ru)*＝打取 1829.8
9 柝 *gekitaku* stroke of the clappers
砕 *gekisai suru* defeat (the enemy)
発 *gekihatsu* percussion
10 破 *gekiha suru*, *u(chi)-yabu(ru)* defeat, crush, ⌊rout, overthrow; refute
剣 *gekken* fencing
殺 *gekisatsu suru* kill (a person) by shooting
留 *u(chi)-to(meru)* kill, bring down (a bird)
13 滅 *gekimetsu* destruction, annihilation, extermination
鉄 *gekitetsu*, *u(chi)gane* gun hammer
14 摧 *gekisai* crushing, destruction
墜 *gekitsui suru* shoot down
18 懲 *u(chi)-ko(rasu)* punish by whipping
20 攘 *gekijō*＝*gekitai* 撃退 (see above–8). *u(chi)-hara(u)*＝打払 (see 1829.5)

B **摘** 1987 F824 摘 Teki. *tsuma(mu)* (see under 抓 1843.0). *tsu(mu)* pick, pluck, pull out; trim, clip, nip; gather.
4 切 *tsu(mi)-ki(ru)* pick off; pick all, strip
5 示 *tekishi suru*, *tekiji suru* point out, give the gist ⌈tract; expose, point out
出 *tekishutsu suru* pick out, take out, ex-
7 花 *tekika* thinning out fruit blossoms
8 芽 *tekiga* thinning out buds
果 *tekika* thinning fruit ⌈picking
取 *tsu(mi)-to(ru)* pick, pluck. *tsu(mi)to(ri)*
取人 *tsu(mi)to(ri)nin* picker
取期 *tsu(mi)tori(ki)* picking season
9 食 *tsumamigu(i)*＝抓食 1843.9
洗 *tsumamiara(i)* washing out spots
草 *tsu(mi)kusa* gathering wild greens
要 *tekiyō* summary, outline ⌈point out
発 *tekihatsu suru* expose, unmask, lay bare,
発者 *tekihatsusha* informer, exposer, denunciator
10 破 *tsu(mi)-yabu(ru)* wring off (its head)
記 *tekki suru* sum up, summarize
13 載 *tekisai suru* summarize, print an extract
16 録 *tekiroku* summary

12

擒 See 2008.

擡 1988 F830 See 儕 498.

撈 1989 F827 Rō catch fish.

撻 1990 F832 TATSU whip (someone), strike.

撩 1991 F830 RYŌ disorder.
7乱 *ryōran* profuse blooming

播 1992 F831 HA. BAN. HAN. *ma(ku)* plant, sow.
14種 *hashu* sowing, planting
種期 *hashuki* planting time

撲 1993 F831 BOKU. *u(tsu)* (see under 打 B 1829.0). *bu(tsu)* strike, beat; tell, speak; address (an audience). *ha(ru)* slap, strike.
10倒 *ha(ri)-tao(su)* knock down, floor (a man)
殺 *bokusatsu* clubbing to death
13滅 *bokumetsu* eradication, destruction, extermination

撓 1994 F828 TŌ. *tawa(mu) vi* be bent, bend. *tawa(meru) vt* curb, bend. *shina(u)* bend, be pliant, be flexible, be supple, sag. *shiwa(ru)* bend, be pliant. *shio(ru) vt* bend. *ta(meru)* bend, train (branches). *tayu(mu)* slacken one's efforts. *shina(yakana)* pliant, flexible, limber, lithe, graceful. *tawa(wa) ni* heavily. *tawa(yakana)* pliable, flexible, limber.
8垂 *shinada(reru)* droop; snuggle up to
垂掛 *shinada(re)-ka(karu)* snuggle up to
15撓 *tawatawa* bending low

撞 1995 F829 撞 DŌ. TŌ. *tsu(ku)* (see under 突 3316.0).
4木 *shumoku* wooden bell hammer
木杖 *shumokuzue* crutch; T-headed staff
木形 *shumokugata* T-shape
木鮫 *shumokuzame* hammerhead shark
11球 *tamatsuki, dōkyū* billiards
12着 *dōchaku* conflict, inconsistency, contradiction

撰 1996 F831 SAN. SEN composing, editing, compiling, selecting. *sen(suru)* write, compose. *era(bu), era(mu)* (see under 選 4744.0).
7述 *senjutsu* editing, compilation
8定 *sentei* choice
者 *senja* author
9食 *e(ri)gu(i)* being choosy in eating
10修 *senshū* writing, editing
12集 *senshū* compiling writings; compilation

撚 1997 F829 NEN. *yo(ru) vt* twist, twine. *yo(reru)* get twisted, be kinky. *yori* twist, strand. *hine(ru)* (see under 拈 1866.0).
6糸 *yori-ito* twisted thread, twine, yarn
7戻 *yori (o) modo(su)* untwist, untwine; reunite, be reconciled
10索 *yorisaku* stranded cable
11掛 *yori (o) ka(keru)* twist, twine; brace oneself
15線 *yorisen* stranded wire

撒 1998 F828 SATSU. *ma(ku)* scatter; sprinkle; give (someone) the slip.
4水 *ma(ki) mizu, sassui, sansui* watering, sprinkling
水夫 *sassuifu* one who sprinkles the streets
水自動車 *sassui jidōsha, sansui jidōsha* tank-truck sprinkler
水車 *sassuisha, sansuisha* water cart, street sprinkler
5布 *sappu suru* spread, scatter, sprinkle. *sampu* scattering; sprinking; dispersion
布剤 *sappuzai* disinfecting powder
布薬 *sappuyaku* disinfecting powder
12散 *ma(ki)-chi(rasu)* scatter about; squander
15餌 *makie* scattered food; ground bait

撤 1999 F829 TETSU. *tes(suru)* withdraw; disarm (a ship); dismantle (a B fort); remove, reject, exclude.
5収 *tesshū* withdrawal
去 *tekkyo* withdrawal, evacuation, removal
6回 *tekkai suru* withdraw, revoke, retract, relinquish, forgo, repeal
7却 *tekkyaku* withdrawal, evacuation, removal
兵 *teppei suru* evacuate troops
8底 *tettei* thoroughness, completion
退 *tettai* withdrawal, evacuation
12廃 *teppai* abolition, removal

撫 2000 F830 BU. *na(deru)* stroke, pat, smooth down.
3子 *nadeshiko* a pink
下 *na(de)-o(rosu)* stroke down
上 *na(de)-a(geru)* comb back
4切 *nadegi(ri)* killing several with one sweep of the sword; a clean sweep
5付 *na(de)-tsu(keru)* comb down, smooth down. *nadetsu(ke)* smooth hair, flowing hair
付髪 *nadetsu(ke)gami* smooth hair, flowing hair
8肩 *nadegata* sloping shoulders
育 *buiku* care, tending
9恤 *bujutsu* relief, aid
11斬 *nadegi(ri)*＝撫切 (see above–4)
15養 *buyō* care, tending

4 心 忄 小 戈 戸 【手 扌】 12 支 攴 攵 文 斗 斤 方 旡 日 曰 月 木 欠 止 歹 殳 毋 比 毛 氏 气 水 氵 氺 火 灬 爪 爫 父 爻 爿 丬 片 牙 牛 犬 犭

B **撮** 2001/F831 SATSU. *tsuma(mu)* (see under 抓 1843.0). *to(ru)* take (pictures). *tsuma(mi)* knob, (bell) button; pinch (of salt).
- 4 方 *torikata* way of taking (a photo)
- 5 出 *tsuma(mi)-da(su)* pick out, drag out, throw out
- 8 物 *tsumamimono* a relish
- 取 *tsuma(mi)-to(ru)* pick (apples), pinch off
- 直 *to(ri)-nao(su)* retake (in photography)
- 9 食 *tsumamigu(i)* eating with the fingers; eating stealthily; corruption, graft
- 洗 *tsumamiara(i)* washing out spots
- 要 *satsuyō* summary, outline, compendium
- 15 影 *satsuei* photographing
- 影所 *satsueijo* studio; movie lot

撥 2002/F830 HATSU. BACHI bone plectrum. *hane(ru)* brush up; reject, exclude, eliminate, skip over; jettison. *hane(kasu)* splash, bespatter.
- 5 付 *hane-tsu(keru)* refuse, reject, repel, rebuff, turn down
- 出 *hane-da(su)* eliminate, reject, strike out
- 6 返 *hane-kae(su)* repulse
- 7 条 *bane* metal spring
- 8 物 *hanemono* rejected goods
- 9 音 *hatsuon* the sound of the *kana* "*n*"
- 飛 *hane-to(basu)* send (something) flying; spatter, splash
- 除 *hane-no(keru)* push aside, brush aside
- 10 荷 *haneni* jetsam; jettisoned cargo; eliminated cargo
- 11 掛 *hane-ka(keru)* splash, bespatter
- 釣瓶 *hanetsurube* a well sweep
- 12 散 *hane-chi(rasu)* splash, spatter
- 14 銭 *hanesen* commission, squeeze

13

據 2003/F836 See 拠 1871.

擇 2004/F833 See 択 1845.

擔 2005/F835 See 担 1879.

擊 2006/F833 See 撃 1986.

擧 2007/F837 舉 See 挙 1902.

擒 2008/F835 KIN *toriko* captive.

擘 2009/F836 HAKU tear up.

撼 2010/F832 KAN move.

撿 2011/F832 KEN inspect, check, bind, consider.

擅 2012/F833 SEN. *hoshiimama* self-indulgent, wayward, selfish, arbitrary.
- 11 断 *sendan* arbitrary action
- 15 権 *senken* exclusive right; despotism

B **擁** 2013/F832 YŌ. *yō(suru)* embrace, hug; possess; protect; lead.
- 5 立 *yōritsu suru* back, support [by fire]dication
- 20 護 *yōgo* protection, defense, assistance; indication
- 護者 *yōgosha* defender, supporter, advocate

擂 2014/F833 RAI. *su(ru)* grind, mash, grate.
- 5 半 *suriban* fire gong warning of a nearby fire
- 半鐘 *suribanshō* fire gong warning of a nearby fire
- 7 身 *surimi* minced meat or fish
- 9 砕 *su(ri)-kuda(ku)* grind fine, pulverize
- 10 粉木 *suri kogi* pestle
- 13 鉢 *suribachi* mixing bowl
- 15 餌 *surie* ground food

B **操** 2015/F834 SŌ. *ayatsu(ru)* manipulate, operate, steer; pull strings. *ayado(ru)* tie across (the back). *misao* chastity, virginity, constancy, fidelity, honor.
- 2 人形 *ayatsu(ri) ningyō* puppet, marionette
- 6 守 *sōshu* constancy, fidelity
- 行 *sōkō* conduct, deportment
- 行点 *sōkōten* conduct, deportment
- 7 作 *sōsa* operation, handling, managing
- 車 *sōsha* operation (of trains)
- 車係 *sōshagakari* train dispatcher
- 車場 *sōshajō* switchyard
- 8 典 *sōten* drill manual
- 10 砲 *sōhō* handling of a gun
- 11 船余地 *sōsen yochi* sea room
- 舵 *sōda* steering (of a ship)
- 舵手 *sōdashu* quartermaster
- 舵室 *sōdashitsu* pilothouse
- 12 短 *sōtan* curtailed operation
- 短罷業 *sōtan higyō* slow-down strike
- 觚 *sōko* literary pursuits
- 觚会 *sōkokai* literary world
- 觚者 *sōkosha* journalist, writer
- 觚界 *sōkokai* literary world
- 13 業 *sōgyō* operation, work

業率 *sōgyōritsu* percentage of capacity pro-
業費 *sōgyōhi* operating expenses ⌊duction
業短縮 *sōgyō tanshuku* curtailment of op-
14練 *sōren* military exercises, drill ⌊erations
16縦 *sōjū* management, manipulation, piloting, operation, control, maneuvering, driving, steering ⌈manager
縦士 *sōjūshi* pilot; manipulator; wirepuller;
縦法 *sōjūhō* manipulation, control ⌈16)
縦者 *sōjūsha*=*sōjūshi* 操縦士 (see above-

14

擠 2016/F836 SEI push aside.

擤 2017/F-X KŌ. KYŌ. *ka(mu)* blow the nose.

擿 2018/F839 TEKI expose, reveal.
9発 *tekihatsu*=摘発 1987.9

擯 2019/F837 HIN push (people) back, reject.
5斥 *hinseki* rejection, exclusion, ostracism; contempt

擣 2020/F837 TŌ. *u(tsu)* pound.
6衣 *tōi* pounding cloth to bring out the gloss

擡 2021/F836 TAI. *mota(geru)* lift, raise.
16頭 *taitō suru* raise one's head, come to the fore, become infuential, gain power, become famous

擢 2022/F836 TEKI. TAKU. *nuki(nderu)* excel in, surpass. *nu(ku)* pull out, select.
5用 *tekiyō suru, takuyō suru* select, choose

擲 2023/F838 TEKI. CHAKU. *nagu(ru)* hit, beat, thrash. *nageu(tsu)* give up, abandon; relinquish; resign, renounce; lay aside; lay down.
10書 *nagu(ri)ga(ki)* scribble
12弾 *tekidan* grenade

擱 2024/F838 KAKU lay down, put down.
7坐 *kakuza* running aground
8岸 *kakugan suru* run aground ⌈aground
岩 *kakugan suru* run on a sunken rock, run
12筆 *kakuhitsu suru* finish (a letter, article, or book)

B **擦** 2025/F837 SATSU. *kosu(ru)* rub, scour, scrub, scratch, scrape, brush. *kosu(reru)* be rubbed. *su(ru)* rub, chafe; strike (a match); frost (glass). *su(reru)* rub, chafe, wear; become sophisticated. *nasu(ru)* rub on, smear; blame another. *kasu(reru)*, *kasu(ru)* graze; squeeze; exploit. *suri* frosted, ground. *-zure* bedsores; sophistication.
4火 *suribi* flintstone fire; match
込 *su(ri)-ko(mu)* rub in, grind and mix
切 *su(ri)-ki(reru)* wear out. *su(ri)-ki(ru)* cut by rubbing; spend all
5付 *kosu(ri)-tsu(keru)*, *su(ri)-tsu(keru)* rub on, rub against; strike (a match), rub hard. *nasu(ri)-tsu(keru)* blame another;
半 *suriban* gong fire alarm ⌊rub on, smear
6合 *su(re)-a(u)* rub against, chafe, jostle with, be at variance with, quarrel
8者 *suremono* sophisticated person
9枯 *sure(k)ka(rashi)*, *sureka(rashi)* sophisti-
10消 *su(ri)-ke(su)* erase, efface ⌊cated person
剤 *satsuzai* liniment
剝 *su(ri)-mu(keru) vi* be grazed, be abraded; be chafed. *su(ri)-mu(ku) vt* graze, abrade, chafe
11疵 *surikizu* marring caused by rubbing
違 *su(ri)-chiga(u)*, *su(re)-chiga(u)* pass each
過傷 *sakkashō* abrasion, scratch ⌊other
12揉 *su(tta)mo(nda)* quarrel
減 *su(ri)-he(rasu)* wear down, rub off, abrade
落 *su(ri)-oto(su)* rub off, scrape off, file off
13傷 *suri kizu* scratch, graze, abrasion. *surekizu* marring caused by rubbing
17擦 *suresure ni* close by; by a shave; barely. *suresure* unfriendly

B **擬** 2026/F837 GI. *gi(suru)* aim (a gun) at; nominate for office; imitate, mimic; compare. *nazora(eru)* pattern after, imitate, liken to. *ni(seru)*, *nise* (see under 贋 840.0). *magai* imitation, sham.
2人 *gijin* personification
人化 *gijinka* personification
人法 *gijinhō* personification
4毛 *gimō* imitation wool
5古 *giko suru* imitate the classical styles
古文 *gikobun* classical style
古主義 *giko shugi* classicism
古的 *gikoteki* classical
6色 *gishoku* protective coloring
死 *gishi* feigning death
似 *giji-*=疑似 755.6
羊皮紙 *giyōhishi* parchment paper
7作 *gisaku* copying; a copy
兵 *gihei* dummy troops
声 *gisei* onomatopoeia

4 心 小 ⺗ 戈 戸 15【手 扌】 支 攴 攵 文 斗 斤 方 无 日 曰 月 木 欠 止 歹 殳 毋 比 毛 氏 气 水 氵 氺 火 灬 爪 爫 父 爻 爿 丬 片 牙 牛 犬 犭

声法 *giseihō* onomatopoeia
声語 *giseigo* onomatopoetic word
[8]物 *magaimono* imitation
宝珠 *gibōshu* stone-leek flower, bridge railing-post knob
制 *gisei* legal fiction
制的 *giseiteki* fictitious
制資本 *gisei shihon* fictitious capital
[9]革紙 *gikakushi* imitation leather
音 *gion* sound effects, imitation sound, background
音効果 *gion-kōka*=preceding word
[10]砲 *gihō* dummy gun
[12]装 *gisō* camouflage, disguise
[13]戦 *gisen* sham battle
勢 *gisei* bluff, (enemy) deception
[14]態 *gitai suru* simulate, imitate
製 *gisei* imitation, forgery, a copy; copying
製弾 *giseidan* blank cartridge
[17]壕 *gigō* dummy trench
[19]爆弾 *gibakudan* dummy bomb

15

擕 See 携 1977.

擴 2027 / F838 See 拡 1876.

擽 2028 / F838 Ryaku. Raku. Reki. *kusu(guru)* tickle. *kusugu(ttai)* ticklish; funny.

擺 2029 / F838 Hai push open.
[11]動 *haidō* oscillation

擾 2030 / F838 Jō disturb, throw into confusion.
[7]乱 *jōran* riot, commotion

攀 2031 / F839 Han. *yo(jiru)* climb, scale.
[11]梯 *hantei* scaling ladder
[12]登 *yo(ji)-nobo(ru), hanto suru* climb, scale

17

攘 2032 / F840 Jō chase away; reject; steal.
[6]夷 *jōi* expulsion of the foreigners
夷論 *jōiron* exclusion policy

18

攘 See 2032.

攝 2033 / F841 See 摂 1976.

攜 2034 / F840 See 携 1977.

19

攣 2035 / F841 Ren crooked, bent.

20

攫 2036 / F842 Kaku. *sara(u)* carry off, snatch; sweep away, wash away; abduct. *tsuka(mu)* (see under 摑 1985.0).
[8]取 *kakushu suru* grasp

攪 2037 / F842 Kaku, Kō disturb, throw into confusion.
[7]乱 *kōran, kakuran* disturbance, agitation
[8]拌 *kōhan suru, kakuhan suru* agitate, stir, whip, beat, churn, mix
拌器 *kakuhanki* agitator, beater, shaker
乳 *kakunyū* churning
乳棒 *kakunyūbō* churn dasher
乳器 *kakunyūki* churn

攬 2038 / F842 Ran hold (in the hand).

RAD. 支 65

Shi or *eda* branch. Also called *jū-mata* (*jū* "ten" plus *mata* "also"). As enclosure: 攴 *shinyō* or *edanyō*. Nickname: Branch.

A **支** 2039 / F842 支 Shi branch. *sasa(eru)* support, maintain, sustain, hold; prop, bolster; check, stem. *tsuka(eru)* be obstructed, be blocked, be stopped up, break down, be choked. *ka(u)* prop up. *sasae* prop, fulcrum. *-Shi-* China.
[3]口 *sasaeguchi* mean criticism of friends
[5]庁 *shichō* government branch office
弁 *shiben* payment, disbursement
出 *shishutsu* expenditure, disbursement

出額 *shishutsugaku* expenditure, disbursement
払 *shi-hara(u)* pay. *shiharai* payment
払人 *shiharainin* payer
払日 *shiharaibi* pay day
払地 *shiraraichi* place of payment
払猶予 *shiharai yūyo* payment postponement
6那 *Shina* China
那人 *Shinajin* a Chinese
那服 *Shinafuku* Chinese dress
那学 *Shinagaku* Sinology
那事変 *Shina Jihen* the China Incident
那海 *Shinakai* China Sea
那酒 *Shinashu* Chinese wines
那料理 *Shina ryōri* Chinese food
那語 *Shinago* Chinese language
7言 *sasaegoto* mean criticism
材 *shizai* support, stay, prop
社 *shisha* branch office
局 *shikyoku* branch office
局長 *shikyokuchō* branch manager
8店 *shiten* branch store, branch office
所 *shisho* branch office, substation
9度 *shitaku* preparation, arrangements; costume, dress; trousseau
途 *shito* branch road
柱 *shichū* prop, brace, support, fulcrum, underpinning
点 *shiten* fulcrum, bearing
持 *shiji* support, maintenance
持層 *shijisō* supporters
10流 *shiryū* tributary, branch
脈 *shimyaku* spur, branch, feeder
索 *shisaku* a stay (supporting a mast)
部 *shibu* branch office
部長 *shibuchō* branch manager
配 *shihai* management, control, rule, guidance
配人 *shihainin* manager
配力 *shihairyoku* controlling power, ruling power
配下 *shihaika* under subjection
配民族 *shihai minzoku* master race
配的 *shihaiteki* controlling, dominant
配者 *shihaisha* ruler, administrator
配階級 *shihai kaikyū* ruling class
配層 *shihaisō* the ruling class
配権 *shihaiken* control, supremacy
11族 *shizoku* branch family; tribe
12援 *shien* aid, support
給 *shikyū* supply, allowance, payment
13障 *shishō* obstacle, hindrance; trouble
署 *shisho* branch office, substation
15廠 *shishō* government branch office
線 *shisen* branch line, spur
19離滅裂 *shiri-metsuretsu* incoherence, inconsistency, disruption

— 6 —

翅 2040 F1505 SHI *hane* (insect) wings. [羽]
7状 *shijō* wing shape

— 8 —

攲 2041 F844 KI. *sobada(teru)* prick up (one's ears).

— 9 —

鼓 See 5415. [鼓]

RAD. 攴 66

Boku strike. Generally called *to-mata* (the katakana *to* plus *mata* "again"). At right: 攵 *bokunyō, bokuzukuri,* or *no-bun* (like Rad. 67 *bun* but with first stroke changed to katakana *no*). Nickname: Folding Chair.

— 2 —

收 2042 F844 **收** See **収** 860.

— 3 —

攻 See 1457.

改 See 1464.

收 2043 F844 **收** See **収** 860.

— 4 —

放 See 2084.

— 5 —

A **故** 2044 F849 KO. *yue* reason, cause; circumstances. *yue ni* therefore, consequently. *kotosara ni* especially, intentionally. *furu(i)* (see under 古 770.0). *ko-* the late.
2人 *kojin* the deceased; an old friend. *furubito* the ancients; elderly persons; longtime residents

3 山 *kozan* birthplace, one's old home
5 旧 *kokyū* old acquaintance
主 *koshu* former master
6 老 *korō* old people, seniors
宅 *kotaku* old home, former home
7 里 *furusato, kori* home town, birthplace
8 国 *kokoku* one's native land; an old country
物 *kobutsu* old article, secondhand article; old tradition
知 *kochi* an old acquaintance; an old intimacy
制 *kosei* former laws; the old system
京 *kokyō* old capital
実 *kojitsu* ancient customs
事 *koji* origin; historical fact; tradition
事来歴 *koji-raireki* origin and history; particulars
9 俗 *kozoku* old customs
10 株 *furukabu* old-timer, veteran, senior
紙 *koshi* wastepaper
殺 *kosatsu* premeditated murder
郷 *kokyō* birthplace, homeland, home town
家 *koka* an old family
11 道 *kodō* the old morality; an old road
習 *koshū* old custom
12 買 *kobai* buying stolen goods
智 *kochi* predecessors' wisdom
13 意 *koi* intention, purpose; bad faith
障 *koshō* hindrance, obstacle; difficulty; breakdown; accident; objection
障車 *koshōsha* disabled car
15 縁 *koen* old relationships, old acquaintances
16 親 *koshin* deceased parent; old friend

A **政** 2045 / F848 SHŌ. SEI. *matsurigoto* government, rule.

4 友 *seiyū* political friend
5 庁 *seichō* government office
令 *seirei* government ordinance, cabinet order
6 争 *seisō* political controversy
7 見 *seiken* political views
局 *seikyoku* political situation
体 *seitai* form of government, polity
社 *seisha* political association
8 所 *Mandokoro* shogunate offices
況 *seikyō* political situation
事 *seiji* political affairs; administrative business
事結社 *seiji kessha* political party
府 *seifu* the government, the administration
府当局 *seifu tōkyoku* government authorities
府案 *seifuan* administration measure
府党 *seifutō* government party
府側 *seifugawa* the administration
府間 *seifukan no* intergovernmental
府筋 *seifu suji* government circles
治 *seiji* government, administration, politics
治力 *seijiryoku* political power, political influence
治上 *seijijō no* political
治史 *seijishi* political history
治犯 *seijihan* political offense; political offender
治犯人 *seiji hannin* political offender
治地理 *seiji chiri* political geography
治休戦 *seiji kyūsen* political truce
治的 *seijiteki* political
治学 *seijigaku* political science, politics
治屋 *seijiya* professional politician, small politician
治革命 *seiji kakumei* political revolution
治家 *seijika* politician, statesman
治哲学 *seiji tetsugaku* political philosophy
治運動 *seiji undō* political campaign, political agitation
治道徳 *seiji dōtoku* political morality
治結社 *seiji kessha* political organization
治熱 *seiji netsu* political excitement
治警察 *seiji keisatsu* political police
9 派 *seiha* political faction, political party
変 *seihen* political change, change of government
客 *seikyaku, seikaku* politician
界 *seikai* political world, political circles
10 党 *seitō* political party
党内閣 *seitō naikaku* party cabinet
党史 *seitōshi* history of political parties
党政治 *seitō seiji* party government
党員 *seitōin* members of a political party
11 道 *seidō* administration, government, rule
情 *seijō* political conditions
商 *seishō* businessman with political ties
経学 *seikeigaku* politics and economics
経科 *seikeika* department of economics and political science
務 *seimu* political affairs, affairs of state
務次官 *seimu jikan* parliamentary vice-minister
務官 *seimukan* parliamentary official
教 *seikyō* government and education; Church and State
教分離 *seikyō bunri* separation of Church and State, disestablishment of a church
教条約 *seikyō jōyaku* concordat, treaty between Church and State
略 *seiryaku* statecraft, political strategy; expedient
略家 *seiryakuka* political tactician
略婚 *seiryakukon* marriage of expedience
略結婚 *seiryaku kekkon* marriage of expedience
12 策 *seisaku* policy; political measures
13 戦 *seisen* political campaign
14 綱 *seikō* political creed; political platform
15 論 *seiron* politics, political discussion
敵 *seiteki* political opponent
弊 *seihei* political evils
権 *seiken* political power; reins of government, administration

権欲 *seiken-yoku* ambition for political power
談 *seidan* a talk on politics or a law case
談演説 *seidan enzetsu* political speech, campaign speech

6

效 2046 F851 F261 See 効 722.

B 敏 2047 F853 敏 BIN agility; alertness. *hashiko(i), hashi(k)ko(i)* clever; agile.
8 才 *binsai* outstanding talent
9 速 *binsoku* quickness, agility, activity
活 *binkatsu* quickness, agility, activity
11 達 *bintatsu* wisdom
捷 *binshō* agility, promptness, shrewdness
12 腕 *binwan* ability, capacity
腕家 *binwanka* able person
13 感 *binkan* sensitivity, susceptibility
感性 *binkansei* sensitivity, susceptibility

7

敗 See 4494.

赦 See 4536. [赤]

敕 2048 F854 See 勅 725.

敏 2049 F853 See 敏 2047.

敍 2050 F851 敘 See 叙 862.

A 救 2051 F853 KYŪ. *suku(u)* save, help, rescue, relieve (suffering), redeem, reclaim. *suku(i)* salvation, help, rescue, relief.
3 上 *suku(i)-a(geru)* pick up and rescue, save from
与 *kyūyo* granting salvation
4 手 *suku(i) (no) te* helping hand
5 主 *suku(i)nushi* rescuer; Saviour
民 *kyūmin* helping and saving the people
出 *suku(i)-da(su)* help out of (trouble), extricate, rescue from, reclaim (from a life of sin). *kyūshutsu* deliverance, rescue
出者 *kyūshutsusha* deliverer
世 *kyūsei* salvation of the world
世主 *Kyūseishu* the Saviour, the Messiah
世軍 *Kyūseigun* Salvation Army
6 米 *kyūmai, suku(i)mai* relief rice
7 助 *kyūjo* rescue, relief, aid
助米 *kyūjomai* relief rice
助法 *kyūjohō* lifesaving
助者 *kyūjosha* rescuer, deliverer, saviour
助信号 *kyūjo shingō* S O S, distress signal
助船 *kyūjosen* lifeboat, rescue boat, salvage boat
助隊 *kyūjotai* rescue party
助網 *kyūjo ami* streetcar fender; safety net
8 国 *kyūkoku* national salvation
拯論 *kyūjōron* soteriology
治 *kyūji* cure, remedy
治策 *kyūjisaku* a cure
命 *kyūmei* lifesaving
命服 *kyūmeifuku* life preserver
命具 *kyūmeigu* life preserver
命帯 *kyūmeitai* life belt
命浮標 *kyūmei fuhyō* life buoy
命索 *kyūmeisaku* lifeline
命袋 *kyūmeibukuro* life buoy
命艇 *kyūmeitei* lifeboat
命網 *kyūmeimō* life net
9 神 *suku(i) (no) kami* a special providence
荒 *kyūkō* famine relief
恤 *kyūjutsu* relief, aid
恤金 *kyūjutsukin* relief fund
急 *kyūkyū* deliverance in an emergency
急処置 *kyūkyū shochi* applying first aid
急車 *kyūkyūsha* ambulance
急法 *kyūkyūhō* first aid
急策 *kyūkyūsaku* emergency measures
急箱 *kyūkyūbako* first-aid kit
急薬 *kyūkyūyaku* first-aid medicines
11 船 *suku(i)bune* rescue vessel; lifeboat
貧 *kyūhin* poor relief
貧院 *kyūhin-in* poorhouse
済 *kyūsai* relief, aid; emancipation; salvation; rescue
済金 *kyūsaikin* relief fund
済者 *kyūsaisha* deliverer, savior
済事業 *kyūsai jigyō* relief work
済策 *kyūsaisaku* relief measure
済資金 *kyūsai shikin* relief fund
済論 *kyūsairon* soteriology
12 援 *kyūen* relief, rescue, reinforcement
援米 *kyūemmai* relief rice
援投手 *kyūen tōshu* relief pitcher
援金 *kyūenkin* contribution
15 霊 *kyūrei* salvation, soulwinning
霊者 *kyūreisha* soulwinner
18 難 *kyūnan* rescue, salvage
難作業 *kyūnan sagyō* relief or salvage work
20 護 *kyūgo* relief, rescue
護米 *kyūgomai* relief rice
護所 *kyūgosho* first-aid station
護事業 *kyūgo jigyō* relief work
護班 *kyūgohan* relief squad, rescue party

A 教 2052 F852 敎 KYŌ faith. *oshi(eru)* teach, give lessons; in-

form; coach. *oso(waru)* learn, be taught take lessons in. *oshi(e)* teaching; lesson, precept; doctrine, tenet; creed, faith; religion; philosophy.
3子 *oshi(e)go* pupil, disciple
4方 *oshi(e)kata* method of teaching
父 *kyōfu* godfather, sponsor; church fathers
込 *oshi(e)-ko(mu)* inculcate, implant
区 *kyōku* parish, district, diocese
区民 *kyōkumin* parishioner ⌈evangelization
化 *kyōka* culture, education; civilization;
化団体 *kyōka dantai* social service or religious organization ⌈work
化事業 *kyōka jigyō* cultural or educational
5母 *kyōbo* godmother, sponsor
生 *kyōsei* student teacher
示 *kyōji* instruction, teaching
主 *kyōshu* founder of a religion; spiritual
本 *kyōhon* textbook ⌊head
外別伝 *kyōge betsuden* Buddhist esoteric teaching ⌈ing; rules
令 *kyōrei* teaching and commanding; teach-
令集 *kyōreishū* papal decretals
6団 *kyōdan* religious body, a religious order
旨 *kyōshi* tenets, doctrine
会 *kyōkai* church; church building
会外 *kyōkaigai* outside the church
会史 *kyōkaishi* church history
会合同 *kyōkai gōdō* church union
会法 *kyōkaihō* canon law
会員 *kyōkai-in* church member
会堂 *kyōkaidō* church, chapel, cathedral, tabernacle
会暦 *kyōkaireki* church calendar
7材 *kyōzai* teaching materials
戒 *kyōkai* exhortation, preaching
戒師 *kyōkaishi* prison chaplain, prison missionary
役者 *kyōekisha* clergy, pastor, minister
役者会 *kyōekishakai* ministers' meeting
8知 *oshi(e)-shi(raseru)* inform, teach
官 *kyōkan* educational official; public-school teacher
具 *kyōgu* teaching tools, teaching aids
典 *kyōten* canon, sacred scriptures of a religion; teaching guide
学 *kyōgaku* education, educational affairs
法 *kyōhō* religion, cult
法師 *kyōhōshi* religious teacher, scribe,
育 *kyōiku* education ⌊rabbi
育上 *kyōikujō* educationally speaking
育会 *kyōikukai* educational association
育年齢 *kyōiku nenrei* educational age
育法 *kyōikuhō* teaching methods
育的 *kyōikuteki* educational, cultural
育学 *kyōikugaku* pedagogy, education
育者 *kyōikusha* educator
育制度 *kyōiku seido* educational system
育委員 *kyōiku i-in* school-board member
育委員会 *kyōiku i-inkai* school board; board of education ⌈mission
育使節団 *kyōiku shisetsudan* educational
育界 *kyōikukai* educational circles
育映画 *kyōiku eiga* educational film
育勅語 *Kyōiku Chokugo* Imperial Rescript
育家 *kyōikuka* educator ⌊on Education
育費 *kyōikuhi* school expenses; educational fund ⌈ments
育測定 *kyōiku sokutei* educational measure-
育程度 *kyōiku teido* educational standards
育漢字 *kyōiku kanji* the characters required to be learned by elementary-school students ⌈of Military Education
育総監 *Kyōiku Sōkan* Inspector-General
育課程 *kyōiku katei* course, curriculum
育機関 *kyōiku kikan* educational institu-
9祖 *kyōso* founder or head of a sect ⌊tions
室 *kyōshitsu* classroom
草 *oshi(e)gusa* lesson, moral
派 *kyōha* sect, denomination
派神道 *Kyōha Shintō* Sectarian Shinto
則 *kyōsoku* teaching rules; school rules
則本 *kyōsokubon* music practice book, technical textbook
科 *kyōka* lesson; course, curriculum
科目 *kyōkamoku* studies in school
科用図書 *kyōkayō tosho* textbooks, school-
科書 *kyōkasho* textbook ⌊books
皇 *kyōō, kyōkō* pope
皇大使 *kyōkō taishi* papal nuncio
皇公使 *kyōkō kōshi* papal nuncio
皇庁 *Kyōkōchō* Vatican
皇令 *kyōkōrei* papal decretals
皇制度 *Kyōkō Seido* Papacy
皇冠 *kyōkōkan* the Pope's tiara
皇無謬説 *kyōkō mubyūsetsu* papal infalli-
皇領 *Kyōkōryō* the Papal States ⌊bility
皇職位 *kyōkō shokui* the Papacy
10徒 *kyōto* believer, adherent
案 *kyōan* teaching program, teaching plan
書 *kyōsho* (presidential) message
師 *kyōshi* teacher, minister, rabbi, mission-
師用 *kyōshiyō* for the teacher ⌊ary
唆 *kyōsa* instigation
唆者 *kyōsasha* instigator
唆罪 *kyōsazai* crime of instigation
訓 *kyōkun* lesson, precept, moral, instruc-
訓的 *kyōkunteki* instructive, edifying ⌊tion
訓書 *kyōkunsho* books of instruction
員 *kyōin* teacher; faculty ⌈cate
員免許状 *kyōin menkyojō* teacher's certifi-
員検定 *kyōin kentei* teacher certification

員養成所 *kyōin yōseijo* teacher training school
[pline
11規 *kyōki* church regulations, church disci-
務 *kyōmu* school affairs, religious affairs
務係 *kyōmugakari* registrar
習 *kyōshū* training, instruction
習所 *kyōshūjo* training institute
授 *kyōju* teaching; professor
授団 *kyōjudan* faculty
授会 *kyōjukai* faculty meeting
授法 *kyōjuhō* teaching methods
理 *kyōri* doctrine, tenet, creed, dogma
理上 *kyōrijō no* doctrinal
理学 *kyōrigaku* dogmatics
理要綱 *kyōri yōkō* catechism
理問答 *kyōri mondō* catechism
理問答書 *kyōri mondōsho* catechism
理論 *kyōriron* dogmatics
12場 *kyōjō* classroom
程 *kyōtei* teaching method
13義 *kyōgi* doctrine, tenet, creed; dogma
義的 *kyōgiteki* doctrinal
義学 *kyōgigaku* dogmatics
14練 *kyōren* military drill
説 *kyōsetsu* dogma
導 *oshi(e)-michibi(ku)* instruct and guide. *kyōdō* instruction, training
誨 *kyōkai* exhortation, preaching
誨師 *kyōkaishi* prison chaplain, prison
15儀 *kyōgi* religious doctrine [missionary
権 *kyōken* educational authority; ecclesiastical authority; the church
課 *kyōka* a course; a textbook
範 *kyōhan* teaching methods; model teaching; textbooks
養 *kyōyō* culture, education, refinement
養学科 *kyōyō gakka* liberal arts
養学部 *kyōyōgakubu* liberal-arts school
養費 *kyōyōhi* cultural expense
16壇 *kyōdan* rostrum, platform
諭 *oshi(e)-sato(su)* instruct. *kyōyu* instruction; instructor, teacher
頭 *kyōtō* head teacher
憲 *kyōken* church constitution
18鞭 *kyōben* a teacher's whip; teaching school
職 *kyōshoku* teaching; ministry, priesthood, clergy
職者 *kyōshokusha* minister, clergyman,
職員 *kyōshokuin* faculty, teachers [teacher
20籍 *kyōseki* church membership

8

敦 2053/F859 TON industry; kindliness.

6朴 *tomboku na* honest and homely
9厚 *tonkō* simplicity, naïveté
16樸 *tomboku na* honest and homely

敢 2054/F857 KAN. *ae(nai)* sad, tragic, piti- B ful; frail, feeble; fleeting; unkind. *ae(te)* positively, daringly.

6行 *kankō* execution, decisive action
死 *kanshi* determination to die
争 *kansō* courageous fight
9為 *kan-i* daring, bravery
12然 *kanzen to* boldly, fearlessly, bravely
13戦 *kansen suru* fight to the death
18闘 *kantō suru* fight bravely. *kantō* determined fighting

敬 2055/F859 KEI. KYŌ. *kei(suru)* respect, A honor, revere. *uyama(u)* respect, revere, honor, venerate.

4天 *keiten* reverence of heaven
弔 *keichō* condolence
5白 *Keihaku* Sincerely yours
礼 *keirei* bow, salutation, salute
6仰 *keigyō suru* respect, revere
老 *keirō* respect for the aged
7承 *keishō suru* hear, listen reverently
8拝 *keihai* reverent worship
服 *keifuku suru* admire and respect
具 *keigu* Sincerely yours
忠 *keichū* loyal service
事 *keiji* respectful service
9昵 *keijitsu* respect and intimacy
神 *keishin* godliness, reverence, piety
重 *keichō suru* respect, revere
10称 *keishō* title of honor
虔 *keiken* piety, devotion, reverence
虔主義 *keiken shugi* pietism
12遠 *keien suru* keep (a person) at a distance; give (a batter) a walk; "kick upstairs"
13愛 *keiai* respect and affection
意 *kei-i* respect, honor
14語 *keigo* honorific word
慕 *keibo* love and respect
17謙 *keiken* piety, devotion
20譲 *keijō suru* respect; take a humble attitude

散 2056/F857 SAN. *san(jiru)*, *san(zuru)* scat- A ter, disperse; spend, squander; dispel, dissipate, chase away. *bara(su)* pull down; take apart; sell (to get rid off); liquidate; defeat; expose. *chi(ru)* fall, scatter, be scattered, be shed; disperse; (rumor) spreads; run, spread, blur. *chi(rasu)* scatter; disperse; dissipate (fog); dispel; take down or loosen (the hair); rout; distribute (handbills); distract (attention); splash on (a pattern). *chi(rakasu)* scatter (around), disarrange, leave untidy. *chi(rakaru)* lie scat-

4 心 小 ⺌ 戈 戸 手 扌 支 [攴 攵]8 文 斗 斤 方 旡 日 曰 月 木 欠 止 歹 殳 毋 比 毛 氏 气 水 氵 氺 火 灬 爪 爫 父 爻 爿 丬 片 牙 牛 犬 犭

tered around, be in disorder. *chi(rabaru)* scatter, be scattered (about), lie around. *chi(rashi)* handbill. *bara* bulk. *-san* (medicinal) powder.

[8]大 *sandai* dilation ⌈the end of a play
[4]太鼓 *chi(rashi)daiko* the drum signalling
水 *sansui* water sprinkling
水車 *sansuisha* street sprinkler
切 *zangiri* regular haircut (in contrast to the topknot style)
切頭 *zangiri atama* cropped head
文 *sambun* prose
文的 *sambunteki* prosaic
文詩 *sambunshi* poetry in prose
[5]去 *chi(ri)-sa(ru)* scatter, be scattered
失 *sanshitsu suru* be scattered and lost
布 *sampu* scattering; sprinkling; dispersion
広告 *chi(rashi) kōkoku* handbill
[6]会 *sankai* adjournment
光 *sankō* diffused light ⌈dotted with
在 *sanzai suru* be scattered, straggle, be
[7]見 *sanken suru* be seen here and there
佚 *san-itsu suru* get scattered and lost
乱 *chi(ri)-mida(reru)* disperse in all directions, be scattered around. *sanran* dis-
兵 *sampei* skirmisher ⌊persion, scattering
兵壕 *sampeigō* trench (in warfare)
[8]歩 *sampo* walk, stroll
[9]発 *sampatsu* scattered shots; scattered hits
発的 *sampatsuteki* sporadic
[10]逸 *san-itsu suru* get scattered and lost
紛 *chi(ri)-mayo(u)* scatter around
財 *sanzai* expense, waste of money, extrava-
剤 *sanzai* powdered medicine ⌊gance, spree
書 *chi(rashi)ga(ki)* irregular writing; writing on alternate lines; writing on odds and
荷 *barani* bulk cargo ⌊ends of paper
華 *sange* Buddhist flower-scattering ceremony. *sange suru* die a heroic death
[11]娼 *sanshō* scattered prostitution
掛 *chi(ri)-ka(karu)* begin to fall; fall on
票 *sampyō* scattered votes ⌊(something)
[12]開 *sankai* deployment (of skimishers)
弾 *baradama* shot, case shot
散 *sanzan, sanza(ppara)* severely, harshly, terribly; thoroughly, utterly. *chi(ri)chi(ri), chi(ri)ji(ri)* sporadically, separately
策 *sansaku* walk, stroll ⌈disappear
落 *sanraku suru* fall and scatter, fall and
[13]蓮華 *chi(ri) renge* porcelain spoon
[14]漫 *samman na* vague, desultory, distracted
銭 *barasen* small change ⌈splash
模様 *chi(rashi) moyō* scattered pattern,
髪 *chi(rashi)gami* hair dishevelled or let down. *sampatsu* disheveled hair; haircutting
髪屋 *sampatsuya* barber
[15]敷 *chi(ri)-shi(ku)* lie scattered
[16]積 *barazu(mi)* bulk shipment
薬 *san-yaku* powdered medicine. *chi(rashi)-gusuri* a cure-all medicine

9

A 数 $\frac{2057}{F861}$ 數 SAKU. SOKU. SU. SŪ strength; fate; law; numbers, figures; numerical. *kazo(eru)* count, calculate, enumerate. *kazu* number, figure. *kazu(naranu)* insignificant, humble. *shibashiba* often, frequently. *sū-* several.

[2]人 *sūnin* several people
十 *sūjū* scores (of people)
丁 *sūchō* several blocks
[3]子 *kazu(no)ko* herring roe
万 *sūman* tens of thousands
千 *sūsen* thousands
上 *kazo(e)-a(geru)* count up, enumerate
ケ所 *sūkasho* several places
[4]込 *kazo(e)-ko(mu)* number among
切 *kazo(e)-ki(renai), kazo(e)-ki(renu)* countless, incalculable
分間 *sūfunkan* a few minutes
日 *sūjitsu* a few days, several days
日中 *sūjitsuchū* within a few days
日来 *sūjitsurai* for the last few days
日後 *sūjitsugo* after several days
日間 *sūnichikan* several days
[5]立 *kazo(e)-ta(teru)* count up, enumerate
犯 *sūhan* several offenses
占 *kazu urana(i)* divining with numbers
台 *sūdai* several vehicles
[6]行 *sūgyō, sūkō* several lines
回 *sūkai* several times
次 *sūji* again and again
列 *sūretsu* progression, series (in math)
百 *sūhyaku* several hundred
年 *sūnen* several years. *kazo(e)doshi* Japan-
名 *sūmei* several people ⌊ese age
多 *amata, sūta* many, multitude. *kazu-ō(ku)* in great numbers
地点 *sūchiten* several places
字 *sūji* figure, numeral; tabular matter
字上 *sujijō* numerically, arithmetically
[8]知 *kazushi(renu)* numberless
取 *kazuto(ri)* counting game; tally; scorer
刻 *sūkoku* several hours
直 *kazo(e)-nao(su)* recount
限無 *kazu-kagi(ri)na(ku)* numberless
奇 *sūki na* unlucky
奇屋 *sukiya* tea-ceremony arbor
学 *sūgaku* mathematics
学上 *sūgakujō* mathematically
学的 *sūgakuteki* mathematical

学者 *sūgakusha* mathematician
学家 *sūgakuka* mathematician
9度 *sūdo* several times
秒 *sūbyō* several seconds
10個 *sūko* several (objects)
倍 *sūbai* several times as (large)
値 *sūchi* numerical value ⌈dhist) rosary
珠 *juzu, zuzu* a string of beads; a (Bud-
11違 *kazo(e)-chiga(eru)* count wrong, miscal-
章 *sūshō* several chapters ⌊culate
寄 *suki* fancy, artistic taste; refined arts. *sūki* colorfulness; varied fortunes. *suki na* refined. ⌈for; lecherous person
寄者 *sukisha* lover of, person with a taste
寄屋 *sukiya* tea-ceremony parlor; detached tea-ceremony house
理 *sūri* mathematical principle; mathe-
理上 *sūrijō* mathematically ⌊matics
理的 *sūriteki* mathematical ⌈cal economics
理派経済学 *sūriha keizaigaku* mathemati-
12渡 *kazo(e)-wata(su)* count out (things)
詞 *sūshi* numeral
量 *sūryō* quantity, volume
等 *sūtō* very, much, exceedingly
葉 *sūyō* several (sheets, photos, etc.)
13損 *kazo(e)-sokona(u)* count wrong
数 *kazukazu* many
14滴 *sūteki* a few drops
語 *sūgo* a few words
歌 *kazo(e) uta* a number song
箇 *sūko* several (objects)
種 *sūshu* several kinds
種類 *sūshurui* several kinds
15億 *sūoku* hundreds of millions
16頭 *sūtō* several head (of cattle)
18難 *kazo(e)gata(i)* countless

10

敲 敲 See 5249.

11

數 2058/F861 See 数 2057.

B 敷 2059/F861 敷 Fu. *shi(ku)* spread; pave; sit (on a cushion); lay (a railway); gravel (a road); promulgate; draw up. *shi(ki)* (flower) stand; deposit money.
5瓦 *shi(ki)gawara* floor tile
皮 *shi(ki)gawa* fur cushion, bearskin, etc.
石 *shiki-ishi* paving stone, flagstone, pave-
写 *shi(ki)utsu(shi)* tracing ⌊ment
台 *shi(ki)dai*=式台 1556.5
布 *shikifu* (bed) sheet, sheeting
6地 *shikichi* site
8金 *shikikin* deposit money
居 *shiki-i* threshold, doorsill
延 *fuen*=敷衍 (see below–9)
板 *shi(ki)-ita* floor boards
物 *shikimono* carpet, rug, matting, cushion
9革 *shi(ki)gawa* inner sole ⌈ment
衍 *fuen* amplification, development, enlarge-
砂 *shi(ki)zuna* sand for spreading (on the
10島 *Shikishima* (ancient) Japan ⌊yard)
島道 *Shikishima (no) michi* the art of Japanese poetry ⌈mine, etc.)
11設 *fusetsu* construction, laying (a railroad,
設水雷 *fusetsu suirai* submarine mine
設権 *fusetsuken* construction rights
設機雷 *fusetsu kirai* submarine mine
13詰 *shi(ki)-tsu(meru)* cover over, spread all
煉瓦 *shi(ki) renga* paving bricks ⌊over
蒲団 *shi(ki)buton* the lower *futon*
14網 *shi(ki)ami* a square fish net lowered on a pivoted pole
銀 *shi(ki)gin* deposit money
17藁 *shi(ki)wara* litter, stall straw

A 敵 2060/F860 敵 Teki enemy, foe, opponent. *teki(suru)* turn against, fight against, antagonize, be a match for. *kataki* enemy; competitor; revenge.
4手 *tekishu* opponent, adversary; the hand of the enemy
中 *tekichū* midst of the enemy
5本主義 *tekihon shugi* make-believe, feint,
6地 *tekichi* enemy territory ⌊pretense
同士 *katakidōshi* mutual enemies
7役 *katakiyaku, tekiyaku* villain's role
状 *tekijō* the condition of the enemy
兵 *tekihei* enemy troops
対 *tekitai* hostility, antagonism, contention
対心 *tekitaishin* hostility, enmity, animosity
対行為 *tekitai kōi* hostilities, hostile act
対行動 *tekitai kōdō* hostilities, hostile act
対的 *tekitaiteki* hostile ⌈forces
8味方 *teki-mikata* friend or foe; opposing
国 *tekikoku, tekkoku* enemy country
国語 *tekikokugo* the enemy's language
性 *tekisei* enemy character
性国 *tekiseikoku* hostile country
性者 *tekiseisha* person of enemy character
性貨物 *tekisei kamotsu* goods destined for
9城 *tekijō* enemy castle ⌊the enemy
陣 *tekijin* enemy camp, enemy position
持 *katakimo(chi)* a person subject to revenge
軍 *tekigun* enemy army
背 *tekihai* the enemy rear
前 *tekizen* before the enemy ⌈enemy
前上陸 *tekizen jōriku* landing in face of the

10匪 *tekihi* enemy bandit
将 *tekishō* enemy general
討 *katakiu(chi)* vengeance, revenge
11側 *tekigawa* enemy side
情 *tekijō* enemy movements
視 *tekishi suru* regard with hostility; show enmity toward. *tekishi* hostility, enmity
船 *tekisen* enemy ship
産 *tekisan* enemy property
貨 *tekika* enemy goods
12弾 *tekidan* enemy bullets
塁 *tekirui* enemy fort
営 *tekiei* enemy camp
13意 *teki-i* hostility, enmity, animosity
勢 *tekizei* enemy strength
愾 *tekigai* hostility, enmity, animosity
愾心 *tekigaishin* hostility, enmity, animosity
14旗 *tekiki, tekki* enemy flag
15影 *tekiei* signs of the enemy
16機 *tekiki, tekki* enemy plane
18騎 *tekiki, tekki* enemy cavalry
20艦 *tekikan, tekkan* enemy ship
艦隊 *teki kantai* enemy fleet
22襲 *tekishū* enemy attack

12

整 See 2436.

13

厳 See 253. [口]

斂 2061/F863 REN tighten, stiffen.

14

斃 See 1373.

釐 2062/F1935 RI few; one-tenth of a *bu*. [里]
8金税 *rikinzei* likin, local Chinese customs charges

19

變 2063/F1772 See 変 306. [言]

RAD. 文 67

Bun literature. Nickname: Literary.

A文 2064/F863 文 MON 1/100 of a *hyakume*; crest; figures; = BUN. BUN literary text, production, composition; sentence; style; literature, art; the pen; civil affairs; decoration; characters; elegance. *aya* design; figure of speech; plan, plot. *fumi* letter, note. *-mon* size (of tabi).
2人 *bunjin* literary man
3才 *bunsai* literary talent
士 *bunshi* literary man
士連 *bunshiren* men of letters
4月 *fuzuki, fumizuki* 7th lunar month
中 *bunchū* in the document
化 *bunka* culture, civilization
化人 *bunkajin* man of culture
化日 *Bunka (no) Hi* Culture Day, November 3
化史 *bunkashi* cultural history
化生活 *bunka seikatsu* cultural life
化会館 *bunka kaikan* cultural center
化村 *bunka mura* modern village
化住宅 *bunka jūtaku* modern dwelling
化的 *bunkateki* cultural
化国 *bunkakoku* civilized country
化国家 *bunka kokka* cultured nation
化映画 *bunka eiga* cultural film
化財 *bunkazai* cultural assets
化祭 *bunkasai* cultural festival
化遺産 *bunka isan* cultural inheritance
化勲章 *bunka kunshō* culture medal
5目 *ayame* designs, patterns; distinction
民 *bummin* civilian
句 *monku* phrase, expression; complaint; objection; excuse
句無 *monkuna(shi)* perfect, satisfactory
6臣 *bunshin* civil official
机 *fuzukue* book table
名 *bummei* literary fame
字 *moji, monji* letter, ideograph, character; writings
字板 *mojiban* dial, clock face
字通 *mojidō(ri) no* literal
字盤 *mojiban* dial, clock face
7言 *bungen, mongon* phrase, expression
身 *irezumi, bunshin* tattooing
体 *buntai* literary style
芸 *bungei* liberal arts, literary arts, learning
芸批評 *bungei hihyō* literary criticism
芸的 *bungeiteki* literary
芸界 *bungeikai* art and literary circles
芸家 *bungeika* literary man
芸復興 *Bungei Fukkō* Renaissance, Revival of Learning
芸欄 *bungeiran* literary column

[8]例 *bunrei* model sentence; model for writing ⌈ary works
林 *bunrin* literary circle; collection of liter-
物 *bumbutsu* civilization
盲 *mommō* ignorance, illiteracy ⌈coloring
采 *bunsai* rhetorical flourishes; beautiful
具 *bungu* writing materials, stationery
苑 *bun-en* literary world; anthology
典 *bunten* grammar book
事 *bunji* civil affairs, literary matters
房具 *bumbōgu* writing materials, stationery
房具屋 *bumbōguya* stationer
治 *bunji* civilian administration
治的 *bunjiteki* civilian
官 *bunkan* civil official ⌈military) service
官優位 *bunkan-yūi* superiority of civil (to
武 *bumbu* literary and military arts, the sword and the pen
武百官 *bumbu hyakkan* civil and military
法 *bumpō* grammar ⌊officials
法上 *bumpōjō* grammatically
法家 *bumpōka* grammarian
明 *bummei* civilization, culture
明人 *bummeijin* civilized people
明史 *bummeishi* history of civilization
明国 *bummeikoku* civilized country
明病 *bummeibyō* diseases of civilization, venereal disease
明開化 *bummei kaika* civilization and en-
学 *bungaku* literature ⌊lightenment
学士 *Bungakushi* Bachelor of Arts
学上 *bungakujō no* literary
学史 *bungakushi* history of literature
学会 *bungakukai* literary society
学作品 *bungaku sakuhin* literary pro-
学的 *bungakuteki* literary ⌊duction
学者 *bungakusha* literary man, scholar
学界 *bungakukai* literary world
学書 *bungakusho* a literary work
学博士 *Bungaku Hakushi* Doctor of Liter-
学賞 *bungakushō* literary award ⌊ature
[9]面 *bummen* contents of a letter
通 *buntsū* correspondence, communication
相 *Bunshō* Education Minister ⌈course
科 *bunka* department of literature; literary
政 *bunsei* cultural administration
段 *bundan* paragraph ⌈archives
[10]庫 *bunko* hand box, bookcase; library,
脈 *bummyaku* context
案 *bun-an* draft ⌈prose
華 *bunka* glory of civilization; beauty in
弱 *bunjaku* frivolity, effeminacy
書 *bunsho, monjo* document, writing, letter, note, archives, literature, correspondence, records
書伝道 *bunsho dendō* literature evangelism

部 *mombu* education
部大臣 *Mombu Daijin* Education Minister
部省 *Mombushō* Education Ministry
[11]鳥 *bunchō* Java sparrow, paddy bird
道 *bundō* learning
運 *bun-un* cultural progress, enlightenment
彩 *bunsai* rhetorical flourishes
責 *bunseki* responsibility for the wording of an article ⌈and literature
理 *bunri* context, line of thought; science
理学 *bunrigaku* liberal arts and science
教 *bunkyō* education, culture
教府 *bunkyō (no) fu* office of education
章 *bunshō* sentence; article, composition;
章体 *bunshōtai* literary style ⌊style
章家 *bunshōka* good writer
章道 *bunshōdō* art of writing
章語 *bunshōgo* literary language
[12]博 *Bunhaku* Doctor of Literature
棚 *fudana* bookshelf
詞 *bunshi* the words of a sentence
集 *bunshū* anthology, prose collection
無 *monna(shi) no* penniless
筆 *bumpitsu* writing, literary art
筆家 *bumpitsuka* literary man
筆業 *bumpitsugyō* literary profession
[13]雅 *bunga* elegance, grace (in literature)
辞 *bunji* the words of a sentence
飾 *bunshoku* rhetorical flourishes
義 *bungi* meaning (of a passage)
意 *bun-i* meaning (of a passage)
勢 *bunsei* force (in writing)
楽 *bunraku* puppet show
献 *bunken* literature; records, documents; bibliography
献学 *bunkengaku* bibliography
[14]様 *aya* (see under 文 2064.0)
豪 *bungō* literary master ⌈characters
墨 *bumboku* literature; documents; (written)
選 *bunsen* anthology; typesetting
選工 *bunsenkō* typesetter
語 *bungo* literary language
語文 *bungobun* literary language
語体 *bungotai* literary style
[15]談 *bundan* literary talk
箱 *fubako* letter box, dispatch box
範 *bumpan* model composition
勲 *bunkun* distinguished civil services
[16]壇 *bundan* literary circles; literary column
[18]鎮 *bunchin* paperweight
題 *bundai* theme, subject
[19]藻 *bunsō* rhetorical flourishes; literary talent

— 3 —

斈 **2065** F-X Nonstandard for **学** 1271.

吝 2066/F338 RIN. *shiwa(i)*, *yabusa(kana)* miserly, stingy, unwilling, sparing (of praise). **kechi** stinginess. [口]

7坊 **shiwambō** miser, stingy fellow
13嗇 *rinshoku*, **kechi** stinginess, miserliness
嗇坊 **kechimbō** miser, stingy fellow
嗇臭 **kechikusa(i)** stingy; shabby
嗇家 *rinshokuka* miser, stingy person
嗇漢 *rinshokukan* miser, stingy person

A **対 對** 2067/F566 TAI the opposite; antonym; even, equal; versus; (score of 3) to (1); counter-, anti-, versus. *tai(suru)* face, confront, be opposite; receive (visitors); subtend. *(ni) tai(suru)* toward, to, in, by, against, in answer to; in contrast to; compared with. *tai(shi)*, *tai(shite)* against, opposite, face to face; before; at; contrary to; in preparation for; toward; in return for; as compared with, in contrast to. *tsui* pair, couple, set. [寸]

2人 *taijin* personal, personnel (affairs)
4支 *tai-Shi* toward China, with China
比 *taihi* contrast, comparison, opposition, dissimilitude, analogy
辺 *taihen* opposite side (in geometry)
手 *aite, taishu* opponent, adversary; the other party ⌈enemy country
手国 *aitekoku, taishukoku* rival country;
内 *tainai* internal or domestic (affairs)
内的 *tainaiteki* internal, domestic
中 *tai-Chū* toward China, with China
中共 *tai-Chūkyō* toward Red China, with Red China
日 *tai-Nichi* toward Japan, with Japan
日援助 *tai-Nichi enjo* aid to Japan
日感情 *tai-Nichi kanjō* feeling toward
5生 *taisei* opposition, symmetry ⌊Japan
句 *tsuiku* couplet, distich; antithesis
処 *taisho suru* deal with, cope with
立 *tairitsu* opposition, antagonism; correlation, co-ordination
立者 *tairitsusha* opponent
外 *taigai* international (problems), foreign (relations), overseas
外的 *taigaiteki* external (affairs)
外援助 *taigai enjo* foreign aid
外貿易 *taigai bōeki* overseas trade
外硬派 *taigai kōha* vigorous foreign policy
外関係 *taigai kankei* foreign relations
6米 *tai-Bei* with America, toward America
地速度 *taichi sokudo* ground speed
当 *taitō no* corresponding, equivalent, homologous
当額 *taitōgaku* corresponding amount
7局 *taikyoku* facing a situation
対 *taitai* evenness, equality, a tie
決 *taiketsu* showdown, confrontation
別 *taibetsu* contradistinction
坐 *taiza suru* sit facing each other, sit
位法 *tai-ihō* counterpoint ⌊opposite to
角 *taikaku* opposite angle
角線 *taikakusen* diagonal line
応 *taiō* correspondence, equivalence, op-
応策 *taiōsaku* countermeasure ⌊position
抗 *taikō* opposition, antagonism, rivalry; counteraction
抗攻撃 *taikō kōgeki* counterattack
抗馬 *taikō uma, taikōba* rival horse; rival
抗策 *taikōsaku* countermeasure ⌊candidate
8価 *taika* compensation; equivalent; consideration; prices
欧 *tai-Ō* with Europe, toward Europe
岸 *taigan* opposite shore
英 *tai-Ei* toward England, with England
者 *taisha* opponent, rival
物鏡 *taibutsukyō* objective lens
空 *taikū* antiaircraft
空砲火 *taikū hōka* antiaircraft fire, flak
9連 *tairen* couplet
峙 *taiji suru* confront each other, keep up rivalry, hold one's own against
持 *taiji suru* stand one's ground ⌈many
独 *tai-Doku* toward Germany, with Ger-
陣 *taijin suru* encamp opposite the enemy, confront each other ⌈one)
面 *taimen* interview, meeting, facing (some-
面交通 *taimen kōtsū* facing traffic, walking on the right side
面的 *taimenteki* face to face ⌈together
10席 *taiseki suru* sit facing each other; attend
座 *taiza suru* sit facing each other, sit op-
流 *tairyū* convection current ⌊posite to
酌 *taishaku* two drinking together
案 *taian* counterproposal
華 *tai-Ka* toward China, with China
称 *taishō* symmetry (in math); second
称的 *taishōteki* symmetrical ⌊person
症 *taishō* specific (treatment)
症剤 *taishōzai*=next word
症薬 *taishōyaku* allopathic or specific medi-
校 *taikō* interschool, intercollegiate ⌊cine
校試合 *taikōjiai* interschool match
校競技 *taikō kyōgi* interschool match
11偶 *taigū* spouse; pair; antithesis
眼 *taigan (renzu)* eyepiece
訳 *taiyaku* parallel versions
12幅 *tsuifuku* pair of hanging pictures
策 *taisaku* countermeasure
等 *taitō* equality, par, parity, equivalent
象 *taishō* object (of worship); subject (of taxation); concern

象物 *taishōbutsu* subject, object (of worship)
13置 *taichi suru* set opposite or against
戦 *taisen* waging war, competition
戦車砲 *taisenshahō* antitank gun
数 *taisū* logarithms
数表 *taisūhyō* logarithm tables
照 *taishō* contrast, antithesis, comparison
照的 *taishōteki* diametrically opposite
話 *taiwa* conversation, dialogue
話体 *taiwatai* conversational style
話者 *taiwasha* interviewer, interlocutor
15論 *tairon* arguing face to face; arguing against a proposition
敵 *taiteki* hostile; (trade) with the enemy
質 *taishitsu suru* confront; confront with another witness
談 *taidan* conversation, interview, dialogue
談者 *taidansha* interviewer
16顔 *taigan*=*taimen* 対面 (see above–9)
蹠 *taiseki, taisho* diametrical opposition
蹠地 *taisekichi, taishochi* the antipodes
蹠的 *taisekiteki, taishoteki* diametrically opposite
蹠点 *taisekiten, taishoten* nadir
19蘇 *tai-So* toward Soviet Russia, with Soviet Russia
21露 *tai-Ro* toward Russia, with Russia

— 4 —

斉 See 5423. [斉]

— 5 —

彦 2068/F665 See 彥 3347. [彡]

— 6 —

斊 2069/F1658 See 蚊 4123. [虫]

斎 2070/F867/F2175 See 斎 5425.

紊 2071/F1440 BIN, BUN disturb, throw into confusion. [糸]
7乱 *bunran, binran* disorder, confusion

— 7 —

斎 See 5425. [斉]

産 2072/F1267 See 産 3354. [生]

— 8 —

斑 See 2950.

斐 See 5081.

— 11 —

齋 See 5426. [斉]

RAD. 斗 68

To or *to masu* (a unit of measure). Also, at right, *tozukuri*. Nickname: Dots and Cross.

斗 2073/F868 B To ten *shō* (see Weights and Measures); a one-*to* measure; saké ladle; the Big Dipper. *-bakari* (see under 許 4324.0) (Also nonstandard for 鬪 and pronounced Tō.)
9南 *tonan* south of the Big Dipper; the whole world
10酒 *toshu* a *to* of saké; a big supply of saké

— 6 —

料 See 3468.

— 7 —

斛 See 4302.

斜 2074/F869 B SHA slanting, oblique. *hasu, hasukai* slanting, diagonal, oblique. *nana(me)* slanting, diagonal, oblique, askew; unpleasant, disagreeable. *nana(menarazu)* exceedingly.
4日 *shajitsu* westering sun
辺 *shahen* oblique side, leg (of a triangle), hypotenuse
方形 *shahōkei* rhombus
5平面 *shaheimen* oblique plane
6向 *nana(me)-mu(kō) ni* diagonally across
交 *hasukai* diagonal, oblique
列駐車 *sharetsu chūsha* angle parking
7角 *shakaku* oblique angle, bevel
9面 *shamen* slope, inclined plane
前 *nana(me)-mae* advancing obliquely

巷 *shakō* red-light district
11 眼 *shagan*=*shashi* 斜視 the next word
視 *shashi, yabunira(mi)* strabismus, squint (cross-eye or walleye)
視眼 *shashigan* squint eye (cross-eye or walleye)
陽 *shayō* setting sun
陽族 *shayōzoku* declining upper class
陽階級 *shayō kaikyū* declining upper class
12 塔 *shatō* Leaning Tower (of Pisa)
堤 *shatei* sloping bank
歯車 *nana(me) haguruma* bevel gear
13 照 *shashō* rays of the setting sun
14 構 *sha(ni)kama(eru)* take one's stance

15 線 *shasen* oblique line
影 *shaei* slanting shadow
16 頸 *shakei* wryneck

— 9 —

斟 2075 / F870 SHIN dip (water); estimate.
10 酌 *shinshaku suru* consider, allow for, guess; dip (water); add some and cut out some
12 量 *shinryō* conjecture

— 10 —

斡 See 792.

RAD. 斤 69

Kin (a Japanese pound) or *ono* ax. On right: *onozukuri*. Nickname: Ax.

B 斤 2076 / F870 KIN *kin* $1\frac{1}{3}$ pounds (see Weights and Measures), catty; axe.
5 目 *kimme* weight in *kin* or catties
12 量 *kinryō* weight

— 1 —

斥 See 175.

丘 See 174. [一]

— 3 —

兵 See 201. [八]

— 4 —

斧 See 2833.

岳 See 208. [山]

欣 2077 / F1026 KIN rejoice. *yoroko(bu), yoroko(bashii)* (see under 喜 1115.0). [欠]
7 快 *kinkai na* pleasant, delightful
8 欣 *kinkin* joy, delight
10 悦 *kin-etsu* joy, gladness
12 喜 *kinki* joy, delight
然 *kinzen(taru)* joyful, cheerful
14 慕 *kimbo* admiration, adoration
舞 *kimbu* dancing with joy
16 懐 *kinkai suru* think happily of

— 7 —

斬 See 4613.

A 断 2078 / F875 斷 DAN decision, judgment; cutting. *dan(jiru), dan(zuru)* conclude, judge. *ta(tsu)* (see under 絶 3539.0). *kotowa(ru)* decline, refuse; apologize; give notice; warn; dismiss; prohibit. *dan(jite)* positively, decidedly; by no means. *kotowa(ri)* refusal; excuse, apology; notice, warning; permission; prohibition. *(o)kotowa(ri)* not allowed.
3 口 *dankō* fracture (in gems)
4 日 *ta(chi)bi* fast day; Lent ⌈water
水 *dansui* suspension of water supply, no
切 *ta(chi)-ki(ru)* cut off; disconnect; block
片 *dampen* fragment, piece, bit, crumb, odds and ends, shred, scrap
片的 *dampenteki* fragmentary, piecemeal
5 乎 *danko* firm, decisive, resolute, determined, drastic, conclusive
去 *ta(chi)-sa(ru)* cut off, do away with
末魔 *dammatsuma* the hour of death
6 行 *dankō* decisive action, resolute enforce-
交 *dankō* rupture of relations ⌊ment
7 言 *dangen* (positive) assertion, declaration, affirmation ⌈osition
状 *kotowa(ri)jō* a letter turning down a prop-
8 金 *dankin* warm friendship
固 *danko*=断乎 (see above–5)
物 *ta(chi)mono* food abstained from, forbidden food ⌈despairing of
念 *dannen* abandonment, relinquishment,

定 *dantei* decision, conclusion
岸 *dangan* rugged beach, sea cliff
郊競走 *dankō kyōsō* cross-country race
9 食 *danjiki* fast, fasting
除 *ta(chi)-nozo(ku)* cut off, do away with
面 *dammen* section; cross section
面図 *dammenzu* cross-section drawing
10 案 *dan-an* decision, conclusion
書 *kotowa(ri)ga(ki)* proviso, explanatory
酒 *danshu* giving up alcohol ⌊note
酒友会 *Danshu Tomo (no) Kai* Alcoholics
11 崖 *dangai* precipice, cliff ⌊Anonymous
章 *danshō* literary fragment
断乎 *dandanko*=*danko* 断乎 (see above–5)
12 絶 *danzetsu* extinction, rupture, severance
割 *ta(chi)-wa(ru)* cut open, cut apart
落 *ta(chi)-oto(su)* snap off
雲 *dan-un* scattered clouds ⌈absolutely
然 *danzen* resolutely, decisively, positively,
裁 *dansai* cutting (paper, etc.)
裁機 *dansaiki* printer's paper cutter
13 滅 *ta(chi)-horo(bosu)* put to death, cut off,
腸 *danchō* heartbreak ⌊consume
罪 *danzai* conviction, condemnation; de-
想 *dansō* random thoughts ⌊capitation
続 *danzoku* stopping and starting ⌈and on
続的 *danzokuteki* intermittent, fitful, off
続器 *danzokuki* a make-and-break device
14 層 *dansō* (geological) fault, shift, slip
種 *danshu* castration, sterilization
髪 *dampatsu* haircutting; bobbed hair
截 *dansetsu suru* cut
15 線 *dansen* disconnection, broken wire
篇 *dampen* short piece of writing, unfin-
16 頭 *dantō* decapitation ⌊ished book
頭台 *dantōdai* guillotine
18 簡 *dankan* fragmentary documents

8

斯 2079 / F872 SHI this. *ka(karu)* such. *ka(ku)*, *ka(kute)*, *ka(kushite)* thus, in this way. *kō* thus, so, like this, in this way. ***kō to*** a word filling in awkward spaces in conversation. *ka(no)* that.

6 如 *ka(ku) no goto(ku)* thus. *ka(ku)* ***no goto-(ki)*** such (a)
7 言 *kō i(u)* this kind of, such
9 界 *shikai* this field (of medicine), this circle (of experts), this society
11 道 *shidō* profession, line, craft; field
許 *kakubaka(ri)*, *kabaka(ri)*=*korehodo* 是程 2120.12
12 程 *kahodo*=*korehodo* 是程 2120.12
斯 *kōkō*, *kakukaku*, *kakkaku* so and so, such
14 様 *kayō na* such ⌊and such
様斯様 *kayōkayō no* such and such

9

A **新** 2080 / F873 **新** SHIN newness, novelty. *atara(shii)* new, novel, fresh, recent, modern. *atara(shigaru)* be fond of. *ara(ta) ni suru* make new. *ara-*, *ara(tana)* new, fresh, novel. *ara* newness; something new. *sara* newness; something new. *nii-* new. *shin-* new, modern, novel, fresh, neo-.

2 人 *shinjin* new face; new star; man of advanced ideas
刀 *shintō* new sword; modern sword
入 *shinnyū* new, incoming, entering
入生 *shinnyūsei* new student
入者 *shinnyūsha* newcomer
3 工夫 *shinkufū* new device, new gadget
大陸 *shintairiku* new continent; New World
4 手 *arate* new move, new form, new trick; reinforcements
月 *shingetsu* new moon, crescent
毛 *shimmō* virgin wool
円 *shin-en* the new yen
天地 *shintenchi* the new world
中間層 *shinchūkansō* the new middle class
仏 *arabotoke*, *shimbotoke* recently buried person
仏教 *Shim-Bukkyō* the New Buddhism
5 田 *arata*, *shinden* new rice field
札 *shinsatsu* new paper money
主 *shinshu* new ruler
令 *shinrei* new decree
古 *shinko* new and old
出 *shinshutsu* new appearance ⌈book
本 *shimpon* a new publication; a brand-new
平民 *shinheimin* the former eta class
市街 *shinshigai* the new town ⌈going
旧 *shinkyū* new and old; incoming and out-
旧両約聖書 *Shinkyū Ryōyaku Seisho* the Old and New Testaments, the full Bible
刊 *shinkan* new publication
刊書 *shinkansho* new publication
刊紹介 *shinkan shōkai* book review
世代 *shinsedai* new era
世界 *shinsekai* new world; the New World
世帯 *shinjotai*, *arajotai* a new home
生 *shinsei* new life; new birth, rebirth, regeneration; reincarnation
生児 *shinseiji* newborn baby
生命 *shinseimei* new life
生面 *shinseimen* new phase
生活 *shinseikatsu* new life
生運動 *shinsei undō* new-life movement
生涯 *shinshōgai* new life, new career
6 米 *shimmai* new rice; novice, beginner, newcomer

式 *shinshiki* a new form; a new formula

曲 *shinkyoku* new tune, new musical composition

任 *shinnin* new appointment

地 *shinchi* reclaimed land; newly-laid-out land; red-light district

宅 *shintaku* new residence; a new branch family

安値 *shin-yasune* new low, all-time low (in prices)

仮名遣 *shinkanazukai* the new *kana* spelling

字 *shinji* characters made in Japan

字体 *shinjitai* a new form of a character

年 *shinnen* New Year

年御歌会 *Shinnen O-utakai* New Year's Imperial Poetry Party

7 車 *shinsha* new car

作 *shinsaku* a new production, a new book

役 *shin-yaku* new post

村 *shinson* new village

形 *shingata* new style

邸 *shintei* new residence

兵 *shimpei* raw recruit, new conscript

声 *shinsei* a new note

来 *shinrai* newcomer

局面 *shinkyokumen* new aspect

体 *shintai* new style

体制 *shintaisei* new system, new structure

体詩 *shintaishi* new poetic style; new-style poem

8 居 *shinkyo* new residence, new home

店 *shimmise* new store

例 *shinrei* new example, new precedent

味 *shimmi* fresh taste, freshness; novelty

枕 *niimakura* the bridal bed

法 *shimpō* new method; new law

注 *shinchū* new commentary

服 *shimpuku* new clothes

奇 *shinki* novelty, originality

芽 *shimme* sprout, bud, shoot

妻 *niizuma* bride, young wife

学期 *shingakki* new school term

知識 *shinchishiki* up-to-date knowledge, advanced ideas

版 *shimpan* new publication

版物 *shimpammono* new publication

郎 *shinrō* bridegroom

郎新婦 *shinro-shimpu* the bride and groom

参 *shinzan* newcomer, novice

参者 *shinzammono* newcomer, novice

事実 *shinjijitsu* new facts

事業 *shinjigyō* new enterprise

制 *shinsei* new system

制大学 *shinsei daigaku* new-system university

制中学校 *shinsei chūgakkō* new-system junior high school

制高等学校 *shinsei kōtō gakkō* new-system senior high school

9 風 *shimpū* new style

香 *shinko, shinkō* picked vegetables, pickles

柄 *shingara* new pattern

派 *shimpa* new school (of thought); new-style *kabuki*

秋 *shinshū* early autumn

院 *shin-in* a newly abdicated emperor

盆 *niibon* first lantern festival after death

前 *shimmae, shimmai* novice, beginner, newcomer

客 *shinkyaku* new visitor; new customer

星 *shinsei* a nova, a new star; a new movie star

茶 *shincha* first tea of the season

草 *niikusa* new grass growth

型 *shingata* new style

紀元 *shinkigen* new era, new stage

面目 *shimmemmoku* new phase, new aspect

思想 *shinshisō* new idea

造 *shinzō* new construction; new wife; single young lady

造語 *shinzōgo* newly coined word

約 *Shin-yaku* New Testament

約聖書 *Shin-yaku Seisho* the New Testament

訂 *shintei* new revision

訂版 *shinteiban* newly revised edition

政 *shinsei* new government regime

政権 *shinseiken* the new administration

春 *shinshun* the New Year

春早早 *Shinshun sōsō* early in the New Year

品 *shimpin* new article

品同様 *shimpin dōyō* looking like new

品種 *shinhinshu* new kinds

発見 *shinhakken* new discovery

発足 *shinhossoku* new start

発明 *shinhatsumei* recent invention

発意 *shimbochi* novice, neophyte

10 馬 *shimba* new horse, unbroken horse

進 *shinshin no* a rising (scholar); an up-and-coming (leader)

値 *shinne* new price

修 *shinshū* new compilation

涼 *shinryō* beginning of the cool season

株 *shinkabu* new stock, new shares

酒 *shinshu* new saké, new brew

都 *shinto* new capital

家 *shinke* newly established family

案 *shin-an* new idea, new design, novelty, new departure

党 *shintō* new political party

書 *shinsho* new book

荷 *shinni* new supply, fresh goods

時代 *shinjidai* new era

秩序 *shinchitsujo* new order

高値 *shintakane* new high, all-time high

記録 *shinkiroku* new record

陳代謝 *shinchin-taisha* renewal, replacement, regeneration; metabolism

帰朝者 *shinkichōsha* Japanese just returned from abroad

11 道 *shindō* new road

婦 *shimpu* bride

粧 *shinshō*=*shinsō* 新装 (see below–12)

訳 *shin-yaku* new translation, new version
設 *shinsetsu* new organization
釈 *shinshaku* new interpretation
著 *shincho* new book
雪 *shinsetsu* fresh snow
患者 *shinkanja* a new case, a new patient
規 *shinki* novelty, originality
規蒔直 *shinki-makinao(shi)* starting afresh
教 *Shinkyō* Protestantism
教国 *Shinkyōkoku* Protestant countries
教徒 *Shinkyōto* a Protestant
婚 *shinkon* new marriage; newly married
婚夫婦 *shinkon fūfu* newlyweds
婚生活 *shinkon seikatsu* early married life
婚旅行 *shinkon ryokō* honeymoon
12 装 *shinsō* new garb; new equipment; new binding; new finish
報 *shimpō* new information, news
開 *shinkai* newly opened, reclaimed
開地 *shinkaichi* reclaimed land, newly
着 *shinchaku* new arrivals ⌊opened land
着荷 *shinchakuni* newly arrived goods
13 殿 *shinden* new palace; new mansion
解 *shinkai* new interpretation
路 *shinro* new road
義 *shingi* new meaning
傾向 *shinkeikō* new trend
14 暦 *shinreki* new calendar; solar calendar
選 *shinsen* newly elected; newly compiled
種 *shinshu* new species
緑 *shinryoku* fresh verdure
説 *shinsetsu* new theory
語 *shingo* new word
穀 *shinkoku* new rice, new grain ⌈endeavor
境地 *shinkyōchi* a new area; a new field of
嘗祭 *Niinamesai* Shinto Harvest Festival
製 *shinsei* new, newfangled ⌊(Nov. 23)
製品 *shinseihin* new products
聞 *shimbun* newspaper
聞口調 *shimbun kuchō* newspaper style
聞代 *shimbundai* newspaper monthly subscription charge ⌈vertising
聞広告 *shimbun kōkoku* newspaper ad-
聞用紙 *shimbun yōshi* newsprint
聞体 *shimbuntai* newspaper style
聞社 *shimbunsha* newspaper company
聞売 *shimbun-u(ri)* news dealer
聞売店 *shimbum-baiten* newsstand
聞条例 *shimbun jōrei* press law
聞屋 *shimbun-ya* newspaper delivery center; newspaperman; newsboy
聞科 *shimbunka* journalism (course)
聞界 *shimbunkai* the newspaper world
聞通信社 *shimbun tsūshinsha* news agency
聞班 *shimbunhan* press section
聞紙 *shimbunshi* newspapers
聞紙上 *shimbunshijō ni* in a newspaper
聞記者 *shimbun kisha* journalist, reporter
聞記事 *shimbun kiji* newspaper article
聞配達 *shimbun haitatsu* newspaper delivery boy ⌈delivery boy
聞配達夫 *shimbun haitatsufu* newspaper
聞倫理規程 *shimbun rinri kitei* newspaper
聞業 *shimbungyō* journalism ⌊code of ethics
聞種 *shimbundane* news; news source
聞購読者 *shimbun kōdokusha* newspaper subscriber
15 劇 *shingeki* new drama; new school of acting
編 *shimpen* new edition
調 *shinchō suru* have (some clothes) made
鋳 *shinchū* new minting ⌈newly built
鋭 *shin-ei* freshly picked, newly produced;
趣向 *shinshukō* new idea; novel device; novelty; originality
16 艘 *shinzō, shinzo*＝新造 (see above–9)
館 *shinkan* new building, annex
薬 *shin-yaku* new medicine ⌈1946)
憲法 *Shinkempō* the New Constitution (of
機軸 *shinkijiku* new device; new departure; new idea ⌈tion
築 *shinchiku* new building, new construc-
築祝 *shinchiku iwa(i)* housewarming
興 *shinkō* new, rising, newly established, newly awakened
興国 *shinkōkoku* rising nation
興宗教 *shinkō shūkyō* new religions
興勢力 *shinkō seiryoku* resurgence of power
17 講 *shinkō* new lecture
鮮 *shinsen* freshness
鮮味 *shinsemmi* freshness
18 顔 *shingao* newcomer, new face
19 羅 *Shiragi* an ancient Korean Kingdom

— 14 —

斷 $\frac{2081}{F875}$ See 断 2078.

RAD. 方 70

Hō direction or *kata* side, person. On left: *hōhen* or *katahen*. Nickname: Direction.

A 方 $\frac{2082}{F877}$ Hō direction, way; side; part; square; also=方法 (see below–8). *kata* direction; settlement; person. *masa ni* right now. *-gata* type, style. *-kata* manner, method, fashion; side, party; toward (evening); person in charge; care of. *-e* direction; location; time. (*ni*) *ata*(*ri*) at the time of.

3 土 *hōdo* country
寸 *hōsun* square *sun*; one's idea; one's object
4 方 *katagata* people, persons; everywhere; this and that; any way. *hōbō* every direction, everywhere
円 *hōen* squares and circles
今 *hōkon* the present time
丈 *hōjō* ten feet square; superior priest's quarters; chief priest of a temple
5 処 *hōsho* location
正 *hōsei* contract, behavior, moral character
6 舟 *hakobune* an ark; (Noah's) ark; the ark (of the covenant)
式 *hōshiki* formula; form; method, system; formalities, usage
尖碑 *hōsenhi* obelisk
向 *hōkō* direction, bearings, course, line, destination, aim
向板 *hōkōban* destination sign
向舵 *hōkōda* rudder
向探知機 *hōkō tanchiki* radar
向転換 *hōkō tenkan* change of direction; change of one's aim in life
7 角 *hōgaku* direction, quarter
言 *hōgen* dialect; provincialism
里 *hōri* a square *ri* (see Weights and Measures)
形 *hōkei* square
図無 *hōzu* (*no*) *na*(*i*) endless, limitless
位 *hōi* direction, course
位基点 *hōi kiten* cardinal points of the compass
8 所 *hōsho* location
法 *hōhō* way, method, means, scheme, process
法論 *hōhōron* methodology
9 面 *hōmen* direction, way; side; district; sphere; line; phase
途 *hōto* means, way
便 *hōben* expedient, means, instrument
陣 *hōjin* square formation, phalanx
10 針 *hōshin* magnetic needle; course, policy, plan, principle, purpose
剤 *hōzai* prescription
案 *hōan* plan, program
11 術 *hōjutsu* art, method, magic
略 *hōryaku* plan, scheme, program
眼紙 *hōganshi* graph paper
12 策 *hōsaku* plan, policy
程式 *hōteishiki* equation
16 錐 *hōsui* square drill; square pyramid
錐形 *hōsuikei* square pyramid

4

於 $\frac{2083}{F879}$ O. (*ni*) *oi*(*te*) at, in, on, as for, as to. (*ni*) *o*(*keru*) at, in.

A 放 $\frac{2084}{F846}$ Hō. *hana*(*tsu*) set free, release, fire, shoot; circulate (rumors); emit, give out; set fire to; banish. *hana*(*su*) let go, release, disengage; liberate. *hana*(*reru*) free oneself from. *hō*(*ru*) throw, hurl, toss; give up; neglect; let alone. *ho*(*ttarakasu*) neglect, leave undone, lay aside. [攵]

2 入 *hana*(*shi*)-*i*(*reru*) let loose in, turn loose in
3 下 *hōka* throwing down; juggling
上 *hō*(*ri*)-*a*(*geru*) hurl up
4 心 *hōshin* absentmindedness; peace of mind
水 *hōsui* drainage, discharge
水路 *hōsuiro* drainage canal; tailrace
水管 *hōsuikan* drainpipe
火 *hōka* arson, incendiarism
火犯 *hōkahan* arson, incendiarism
火狂 *hōkakyō* pyromaniac
5 生 *hōjō* setting (birds) free
付 *hō*(*ri*)-*tsu*(*keru*) hurl against
去 *hana*(*chi*)-*sa*(*ru*) set free
出 *hō*(*ri*)-*da*(*su*)=抛出 1875.5. *hōshutsu* release, discharge, exhaust
6 血 *hōketsu* bloodletting
任 *hōnin* nonintervention
光 *hōkō* emission of light
7 言 *hōgen* irresponsible talk
尿 *hōnyō* urination
屁 *hōhi* breaking wind, passing gas
佚 *hōitsu* self-indulgence, debauchery
吟 *hōgin suru* sing loudly
技 *hana*(*re*)*waza* a grand work
8 念 *hōnen* relaxation, ease
免 *hōmen* release, acquittal
物線 *hōbutsusen* parabola
牧 *hōboku* grazing, pasturage
牧地 *hōbokuchi* pasture, grazing land
送 *hōsō* broadcasting
送伝道 *hōsō dendō* radio evangelism
送局 *hōsōkyoku* broadcasting station
送員 *hōsōin* radio announcer
送記者 *hōsō kisha* radio newsman
9 逐 *hōchiku suru* expel, banish, deport; dismiss

神 *hōshin* freedom from care. *hōshin suru* be dumbfounded
胆 *hōtan* fearlessness
10 馬 *hana(re)-uma* runaway horse
逸 *hōitsu* self-indulgence, debauchery
埓 *hōratsu* dissipation, debauchery
校 *hōkō* school expulsion
恣 *hōshi* self-indulgence
帰 *hana(shi)-kae(raseru)* release and send back
流 *hōryū suru* stock (with fish), let loose
流瓶 *hōryūbin* drift bottle
浪 *hōrō* wandering
浪者 *hōrōsha* wanderer
浪罪 *hōrōzai* vagrancy
浪癖 *hōrōheki* wanderlust
射 *hōsha* emanation, radiation, emission, discharge
射学 *hōshagaku* radiology
射性 *hōshasei* radioactive
射性同位元素 *hōshasei dōi genso* radioisotope
射性物質 *hōshasei busshitsu* radioactive materials
射能 *hōshanō* radioactivity, radiation
射道路 *hōsha dōro* radial roads
射雲 *hōsha-un* radioactive cloud
射線 *hōshasen* radiation
11 鳥 *hōchō* setting birds free; birds to be set free
眼 *hōgan* squares on a map or graph paper
眼紙 *hōganshi* graph paper
12 遣 *hana(chi)-ya(ru)* let loose; banish, purge
散 *hōsan* radiation; emanation; diffusion; evaporation
13 痰 *hōtan* spitting around
肆 *hōshi* self-indulgence
飼 *hana(chi)ga(i), hana(shi)ga(i)* grazing, pasturage
棄 *hōki* abandonment, resignation, renunciation, waiving
置 *hōchi suru* leave alone, neglect, let lie
電 *hōden* electric discharge
資 *hōshi* investment
14 慢 *hōman*=the next word
漫 *hōman* recklessness, laxity, indiscretion
歌 *hōka* loud singing
歌高吟 *hōka-kōgin* loud singing
15 論 *hōron* harangue
談 *hōdan* irresponsible talk; chat
養 *hōyō* outdoor feeding, turning loose
課 *hōka* class dismissal
課後 *hōkago* after school
熱 *hōnetsu* radiation; radiant heat
熱器 *hōnetsuki* radiator
蕩 *hōtō* dissipation, prodigality
蕩者 *hōtōsha* a prodigal, a profligate
蕩家 *hōtōka* a prodigal, a profligate
蕩息子 *hōtō musuko* prodigal son
16 縦 *hōjū, hōshō* self-indulgence, debauchery
17 擲 *hōteki suru* abandon, give up, neglect
18 題 *-hōdai* at will, to one's heart's content
24 鷹 *hōyō* falconry, hawking

5

B 施 $\frac{2085}{F880}$ SHI. SE. *hodoko(su)* give alms; conduct (educational work); carry out; administer (first aid); apply (bandages); perform (an operation). *hodoko(shi)* alms, almsgiving.

3 工 *shikō suru, sekō suru* carry out, execute, operate
与 *hodoko(shi)-ata(eru)* give alms. *seyo* charity
5 主 *seshu* chief mourner; donor, benefactor
6 米 *semai* relief rice
行 *shikō suru* execute, carry out. *segyō suru* give alms
7 条 *shijō* making lines; rifling a gun barrel
8 物 *hodoko(shi)mono* alms, almsgiving
肥 *sehi* fertilization, manuring
9 政 *shisei* government, administration, statesmanship
政方針 *shisei hōshin* party line; the administration program
11 術 *shijutsu* surgical operation
設 *shisetsu* institution, establishment; equipment, facilities
12 散 *hodoko(shi)-chi(rasu)* give alms freely
策 *shisaku* a policy, a measure
13 業 *shigyō, segyō* management, operation
業林 *segyōrin* commercial forest
15 餓鬼 *segaki* service for the unmourned dead
16 薬 *seyaku* free medicine
17 療 *seryō* free medical treatment
療病院 *seryō byōin* charity hospital
療患者 *seryō kanja* charity patient

6

旁 See 310.

旆 $\frac{2086}{F882}$ HAI flag.

旃 $\frac{2087}{F881}$ SEN woolen cloth.

6 那 *senna* senna

A 旅 $\frac{2088}{F881}$ 旅 RYO journey; go around. *tabi* journey. *tabi suru* make a trip.

2 人 *tabibito, ryojin* traveler, wayfarer
人宿 *ryojin yado* inn
4 心 *tabigokoro* the tedium of a journey
中 *ryochū* on a journey
支度 *tabijitaku* journey preparation; traveling outfit
日記 *tabi nikki* travel diary
5 用 *ryoyō* traveling expenses
立 *tabida(tsu)* set out on a trip. *tabida(chi)* departure
出 *tabide* departure

芝居 *tabi shibai* performance by traveling troupe
[6]衣 *tabigoromo* traveling clothes
回 *tabimawa(ri)* touring
団 *ryodan* brigade
先 *tabisaki* destination; place of sojourn. *tabisaki de* while traveling
行 *ryokō* travel, trip, journey
行先 *ryokōsaki* destination
行券 *ryokōken* passport
行者 *ryokōsha* traveler, tourist
行免状 *ryokō menjō* passport
行記 *ryokōki* travelog, itinerary
行家 *ryokōka* traveler, tourist
行案内 *ryokō annai* guidebook; itinerary
行傷害保険 *ryokō-shōgai hoken* travel-accident insurance
[7]戻 *tabimodo(ri)* return from a trip
住 *tabizuma(i)* one's stopping place on a trip
役者 *tabi yakusha* traveling player
芸人 *tabi geinin* itinerant player
芸者 *tabi geisha* itinerant geisha
[8]所 *tabisho* resting place for a *mikoshi*
枕 *tabi makura* sleeping away from home; journey
舎 *ryosha* hotel, inn
歩 *tabiaru(ki)* traveling
空 *tabi (no) sora* strange land
券 *ryoken* passport
者 *tabi (no) mono* traveler
[9]連 *tabizu(re)* traveling companion
亭 *ryotei* inn, hotel
姿 *tabi sugata* traveling outfit
客 *ryokaku, ryokyaku* traveler, passenger, tourist
客列車 *ryokaku ressha* passenger train
客運輸 *ryokaku un-yu* passenger traffic
客業 *ryokakugyō* tourist trade
客機 *ryokakki* passenger plane
[10]疲 *tabitsuka(re)* travel fatigue
烏 *tabigarasu* one who is always traveling
[11]情 *ryojō* travel weariness
宿 *tabi yado, ryoshuku* hotel
商 *ryoshō* commercial salesman
商人 *tabi shōnin* peddler, commercial traveler
[12]順 *Ryojun* Port Arthur
程 *ryotei* distance, journey
費 *ryohi* traveling expenses
装 *ryosō* traveling outfit
装束 *tabi shōzoku* traveling outfit
[13]僧 *tabisō* itinerant priest
路 *tabiji* journey
寝 *tabine* staying at an inn
愁 *ryoshū* lonesomeness on a journey
[15]痩 *tabiyase* losing weight from traveling
稼 *tabikase(gi)* itinerant work
[16]窶 *tabiyatsure* travel fatigue
興行 *tabi kōgyō* traveling show
館 *ryokan* hotel
館業 *ryokangyō* hotel business
[22]嚢 *ryonō* traveling bag
籠 *hatago* inn
籠屋 *hatagoya* inn

7

旆 See 2086.

旅 See **旅** 2088.

旌 2089/F883 Sᴇɪ flag; praise.
[14]旗 *seiki* flag, banner

旅 2090/F883 A Zᴏᴋᴜ family, relatives, clan, tribe, race. *yakara* family, relatives; party, colleagues, gang.
[5]生 *zokusei suru*=簇生 3441.5
[8]長 *zokuchō* patriarch, chief, family head
制 *zokusei* patriarchal family system
制政治 *zokusei seiji* patriarchal government
[10]称 *zokushō* family-rank designation
党 *zokutō* companions
[14]閥主義 *zokubatsu shugi* nepotism
[15]縁 *zokuen* family ties
[20]籍 *zokuseki* social status and domicile

旋 2091/F882 B Sᴇɴ go around.
[4]毛 *tsumuji, semmō* a whirl of hair on the head; a cowlick
毛曲 *tsumujima(gari)* cranky person
[6]回 *senkai* revolution, rotation, turning, circling
回砲 *senkaihō* swivel gun
[7]条銃 *senjōjū* rifle
[9]風 *sempū, tsumuji kaze* whirlwind
律 *senritsu* melody
[11]転 *senten* turning, rotation
[15]盤 *semban* lathe
盤工 *sembankō* turner, lathe man

9

旒 2092/F884 Rʏū counter for flags.

10

旗 2093/F884 A Kɪ. *hata* flag, banner, standard, ensign, pennant, streamer.
[3]下 *kika, hatamoto* beneath the banner. *hatamoto* a vassal directly under the shogun
[4]手 *kishu* standard bearer
日 *hatabi* national holiday
元 *hatamoto* a vassal directly under the shogun
[5]本 *hatamoto*=preceding word

6色 *hata-iro* tide of war; outlook. *kishoku*=*kishi* 旗幟 (see below–15)
印 *hatajirushi*=*kishi* 旗幟 (see below–15)
号 *kigō* flag emblem
行列 *hata gyōretsu* flag parade
8取 *hatato(ri)* flag race
9持 *hatamo(chi)* standard bearer
亭 *kitei* inn, restaurant
竿 *hatazao* flagstaff, flagpole
巻 *hata (o) ma(ku)* surrender, give up
10振 *hatafu(ri)* flagman; starter; flag wagging
挙 *hata-age*=旗揚 (see below–12)
11章 *hatajirushi, kishō* flag mark, ensign; slogan
魚 *kajiki* marlin, swordfish
魚鮪 *kajiki maguro* mole
12揚 *hata-a(ge)* raising an army; launching a business
13鼓 *kiko* colors and drums; army
鼓堂堂 *kiko-dōdō to* triumphantly, with colors flying
15幟 *kishi* flag, banner; one's attitude, one's stand
標 *hatajirushi* flag mark, ensign; slogan
16頭 *hatagashira* top of the flagpole; chief
20艦 *kikan* flagship

14

旛 2094/F885 HEN flag.

RAD. 无 71

Mu or *nashi* nothing. Also *munyō*. Variants: 旡 and 无 or 旡 (5 strokes). Do not confuse with Rad. 92. Nickname: Crooked Heaven (cf. 天 *ten* heaven)

5

既 See 3887.

7

旣 2095/F885 旣 See 既 3887.

21

蠶 2096/F1678 See 蚕 57. [虫]

RAD. 日 72

Hi or *nichi* day. At left: *hi hen* or *nichi hen*. Variant: 曰. This variant is actually Rad. 73 but, with the exception of the radical character itself, is treated herein as a variant of Rad. 72. Nickname: Sun.

A 日 2097/F886 JITSU, NICHI, NITSU day; Sunday. *hi* sun; time; day, date. *hi(narazu)* before long, in a few days. *hi niwa* if, in case. *hi(mosugara)* all day long. *-ka* day. *-Nichi-* Japanese.
1一日 *hi-hitohi, hi-ichinichi, hi(gana)-ichi nichi* all day long, day by day
2入 *hi(no)-i(ri)* sunset
入方 *hi (no) i(ru) hō* west
3夕 *nisseki* day and night
子 *nisshi* number of days, time
干 *hibo(shi)* sun-dried, sun-baked
久 *hihisa(shiku)* for a long time, for some time
下 *hi (no) shita ni* under the sun, in the whole world
丸 *hi(no)maru* the Japanese flag, sun disk, sun flag
4日 *hi(ni)hi(ni)* daily. *hibi* daily; days. *nichinichi* daily, every day
比 *Nippi* Japan and the Philippines
込 *Hi (ga) ko(mu)* The day is fast approaching.
中 *nitchū* during the day. *hinaka* broad daylight, daytime. *Nitchū* Japan and Red China
仏 *Nichi-Futsu* Japan and France
切 *higi(ri)* fixed day; setting the day
支 *Nisshi* Japan and China
支事変 *Nisshi Jihen* Sino-Japanese War (1937–41)
月 *jitsugetsu* sun and moon; time, days, years
月星辰 *jitsugetsu-seishin* heavenly bodies
5目 *hi(no)me* sun, sunlight
立 *hida(tsu), hida(chi)*=肥立 3740.5

加 *Nichi-Ka* Japan and Canada
外 *itsuzoya* When was it?; recently, once,
収 *nisshū* one day's income ⌊some time ago
永 *hinaga* long spring days
用 *nichiyō* daily use, of daily necessity
用品 *nichiyōhin* daily necessities
付 *hizuke* date, dating ⌈date line
付変更線 *hizuke henkōsen* the international
刊 *nikkan* daily publication, a daily
刊新聞 *nikkan shimbun* daily newspaper
出 *hi(no)de, nisshutsu* sunrise
出方 *hi (no) de(ru) hō* east
出国 *hi-i(zuru) kuni, hi(no)deguni* Japan, Land of the Rising Sun
本 *Nihon, Nippon* Japan. *Hi(no)moto* Land of the Rising Sun
本一 *Nihon-ichi, Nippon-ichi* Japan's best
本人 *Nihonjin, Nipponjin* Japanese
本刀 *Nihontō* Japanese sword
本三景 *Nihon Sankei* Japan's 3 noted scenic sights (Matsushima, Miyajima, and Amanohashidate)
本犬 *Nihonken, Nihon inu* Japanese dog
本史 *Nihonshi* Japanese history
本化 *Nihonka* Japanization
本主義 *Nihon shugi* Japanism
本交通公社 *Nihon Kōtsū Kōsha* Japan Travel Bureau
本男子 *Nihon danshi* sons of Japan
本的 *Nihonteki* Japanese (art)
本画 *Nihonga* Japanese painting or drawing
本画界 *Nihongakai* Japanese art circles
本国有鉄道 *Nihon Kokuyū Tetsudō* Japanese National Railways
本風 *Nihonfū* Japanese style
本海 *Nihonkai* the Japan Sea
本海流 *Nihon Kairyū* Japan Current
本専売公社 *Nippon Sembai Kōsha* Japan Monopoly Corporation
本酒 *Nihonshu* saké
本紙 *Nihonshi* Japanese paper
本書紀 *Nihonshoki* an ancient Japan chronicle
本訳 *Nihon yaku* Japanese translation
本脳炎 *Nihon nōen* Japanese encephalitis, sleeping sickness
本間 *Nihomma* Japanese-style room
本晴 *Nihomba(re)* ideal weather, clear sky, glorious weather
本電信電話公社 *Nippon Denshin Denwa Kōsha* Japan Telegraph and Telephone Corporation
本語 *Nihongo, Nippongo* Japanese language
本髪 *Nihongami* Japanese hairdo
本製 *Nihonsei* Japanese make
本銀行 *Nihon Ginkō* Bank of Japan
本贔屓 *Nippombiiki* pro-Japanese
6 米 *Nichi-Bei* Japan and America
印 *Nichi-In* Japan and India
伊 *Nichi-I* Japan and Italy
次 *nichiji* the date
当 *hiata(ri)* sunny place; exposure to the sun. *nittō* daily allowance, a day's pay
共 *Nikkyō* Japan Communist Party
毎 *higoto ni* daily
向 *hinata* sunny place, sunshine. *hinata-(bokko)* basking in the sun
向水 *hinata mizu* sun-warmed water
向臭 *hinatakusa(i)* the fresh smell of sunning; countrified
光 *nikkō* sunshine, sunlight, sun
光石 *nikkōseki* sunstone
光信号 *nikkō shingō* heliogram
光浴 *nikkōyoku* sun-bath ⌈ning
光消毒 *nikkō shōdoku* disinfection by sun-
光療法 *nikkō ryōhō* heliotherapy, sun cure
7 赤 *Nisseki* Japan Red Cross
足 *hiashi* daytime; sun's position
決 *higi(me) de* by the day
宋 *Nissō* Sino(Sung)-Japanese
系 *Nikkei* Japanese descent
系米人 *Nikkei Beijin* Japanese-American
没 *nichibotsu* sunset
没後 *nichibotsugo* after sunset
没前 *nichibotsuzen* before sunset
没時 *nichibotsuji* time of sunset
没頃 *nichibotsugoro* about sunset
8 延 *hino(be)* postponement
送 *hioku(ri)* passing the time (days)
明 *Nichi-Min* Sino(Ming)-Japanese
取 *hido(ri)* setting a date; the date
限 *nichigen* time limit, date, term
夜 *nichiya* day and night; always
直 *nitchoku* a day shift; the day's work
参 *nissan* daily visits (to a shrine, etc.)
歩 *hibu* daily interest
英 *Nichi-Ei* Japan and England
東 *Nittō* Japan, Land of the Rising Sun
長 *hinaga* a long day
長石 *nitchōseki* sunstone ⌈situation
和 *hiyori* weather conditions; fair weather;
和下駄 *hiyori geta* fair-weather clogs
和見 *hiyorimi* weather forecasting; weather vane; opportunism; marking time; wait-and-see (policy)
9 食 *nisshoku* solar eclipse
逐 *hi (o) o(tte)* day by day
柄 *higara* kind of day (lucky or unlucky)
計 *nikkei* daily account, daily expenses; the day's total
除 *hiyoke* sunshade, awning, blind
独 *Nichi-Doku* Japan and Germany

独伊防共協定 *Nichi-Doku-I Bōkyō Kyōtei* the Tripartite Agreement between Japan, Germany, and Italy
10差 *hiza(shi)* sunlight; sun's height
華 *Nikka* Japan and Nationalist China
帰 *higae(ri)* a one-day (trip)
週運動 *nisshū undō* diurnal motion
進 *nisshin* advancing daily
進月歩 *nisshin-geppo* steady advance
時 *nichiji* date, time, date and hour
時計 *hidokei* sundial
記 *nikki* diary, journal
記帳 *nikkichō* a diary
射 *hizashi* sunlight; height of the sun
射病 *nisshabyō* heatstroke; sunstroke
陰 *hikage* shade
陰者 *hikagemono* one who stays out of the public eye, an obscure person; a concubine
11頃 *higoro* normally, habitually, always; for a long time
捲 *himekuri* calendar pad
掛 *higake* daily installment
済 *hinashi* daily installment
脚 *hiashi* daytime; sun's position
産 *nissan* daily output
盛 *hizaka(ri)* high noon
貨 *nikka* Japanese goods; Japanese money
乾 *hiboshi* sun-dried, sun-baked
章旗 *Nisshōki* Rising Sun Flag
清 *Nisshin* Sino (Manchu)-Japanese
清戦争 *Nisshin Sensō* Sino-Japanese War
清戦役 *Nisshin Sen-eki* Sino-Japanese War
常 *nichijō* everyday, usually, always; daily; ordinary
常用品 *nichijō yōhin* daily necessities
常茶飯事 *nichijō sahanji* an everyday occurrence
12雇 *hiyatoi* day-to-day employment
間 *hiai* time; daily interest rate
満 *Nichi-Man* Japan and Manchuria
焼 *hiya(ke)* sunburn
短 *himijika* shortening of the days
程 *nittei* day's schedule
給 *nikkyū* day wages, daily wage
割 *hiwa(ri)* daily rate; daily quota. *hiwarihide* by the day
勤 *nikkin* daily work
傘 *higasa* parasol
貸 *higa(shi)* lending by the day
報 *nippō* daily news, daily report
13蓮 *Nichiren* Buddhist sect originating in the thirteenth century
溜 *hidama(ri)* sunny place; exposure to the sun
数 *nissū* number of days, time. *hikazu* number of days; the kind of a day (lucky or unlucky)
暈 *nichiun* halo, ring around the sun

新 *nisshin* starting each day anew
新月歩 *nisshin-geppo* steadily advancing
蔭 *hikage* shade
蔭者 *hikagemono* one who stays out of the public eye
照 *hide(ri), nisshō* sunshine, drought, dry weather
照計 *nisshōkei* heliograph, sunshine recorder
嗣 *hitsugi* imperial throne
嗣御子 *hitsugi (no) miko* crown prince
傭 *hiyō, hiyatoi* day-to-day employment
傭取 *hiyōto(ri)* day laborer
傭稼 *hiyōkasegi* working by the day; day laborer
14読 *hiyo(mi)* day-by-day calendar
誌 *nisshi* diary, journal
語 *Nichigo* Japanese language
銀 *Nichigin* Bank of Japan
銭 *hizeni* daily receipts; a loan to be repaid in daily installments
増 *hima(shi) ni* daily, day by day, gradually
増物 *hima(shi)mono* things left over
暮 *higu(re), hi(no)ku(re)* twilight; sunset, dusk, evening. *higur(ashi)* a day's living
暮方 *higu(re)gata* sunset, twilight, dusk, evening
15稼 *hikasegi* day labor
課 *nikka* daily lesson; one's regular work
賦 *hibu* daily installments
輪 *nichirin* sun, orb of day
蝕 *nisshoku* solar eclipse
影 *hikage* sunlight; sun's shadow
16録 *nichiroku* journal
17濠 *Nichi-Gō* Japan and Australia
鮮 *Nissen* Japan and Korea
韓 *Nikkan* Japan and Korea
18曝 *hizarashi* bleaching; exposure to the sun
覆 *hiōi, hioi* sunshade, awning, curtain, blind
曜 *Nichiyō* Sunday
曜日 *Nichiyōbi* Sunday
曜日休業令 *Nichiyōbi Kyūgyōrei* Sunday laws
曜版 *Nichiyōban* Sunday Edition
曜学校 *Nichiyō Gakkō* Sunday School
19蘇 *Nisso* Japan and the Soviet
蘭 *Nichi-Ran* Japan and Holland
21露 *Nichi-Ro* Japan and Russia
露戦役 *Nichi-Ro Sen-eki* Russo-Japanese War

1

旦 2098 F888 TAN dawn, morning.

8夕 *tanseki* morning and evening, day and night
6那 *danna* master; husband; gentleman
那方 *dannagata* the gentlemen, Messrs.
那様 *dannasan, dannasama* master; husband; gentleman
14暮 *tambo* morning and evening

4 心忄小戈戸手扌支攴夊文斗斤方旡[日] 2 曰 月木欠止歹殳毋比毛氏气水氵氺火灬爪爫父爻爿丬片牙牛犬犭

2

旨 See 752.

旬 See 747.

曳 See 100. [曰]

曲 See 103. [曰]

旭 2099 / F890 KYOKU. *asahi* the morning sun, the rising sun.
4 日 *kyokujitsu* the rising sun
日昇天 *kyokujitsu-shōten* = preceding word
日旗 *Kyokujitsuki* Rising Sun Flag
6 光 *kyokkō* rays of the rising sun
13 暉 *kyokki* rays of the rising sun
14 旗 *Kyokki* Rising Sun Flag

A 早 2100 / F889 SA. SŌ. SATSU. *haya(i)* quick, fast, speedy; brisk; prompt; early; premature. *haya(meru)* *vt* hasten, precipitate, accelerate, expedite; advance (the date). *haya(maru)* be hasty, be rash. *haya(ru)* be hasty, be rash. *(o)ha(yō)* good morning. *haya(sa)* swiftness; being early; speed. *ha(ya)* already, now, so soon.
3 川 *hayakawa* swift river
口 *hayakuchi, hayaguchi* fast talking; tongue twister
口言葉 *hayakuchi kotoba* tongue twister
4 引 *hayabi(ki)* leaving early
天 *sōten* dawn, early morning
分 *hayawa(kari)* quick understanding; easy guide
少女 *saotome* rice-planting girl
手 *hayate* squall
手回 *hayatemawa(shi)* early preparations
手雲 *hayategumo* hurricane clouds
5 目 *hayame ni* early, ahead of time
立 *hayada(chi)* early morning departure
打 *haya-u(chi)* dispatch by horse
出 *hayade* early arrival at the office
世 *sōsei* early death
仕舞 *hayajimai* early closing
生 *haya-uma(re)* born between Jan. 1 and March 31. *hayana(ri)* early crop, early fruit. *wase* early ripening; a precocious child
生児 *sōseiji* premature baby
生種 *waseshu* an early variety
6 老 *sōrō* premature old age
耳 *hayamimi* insider; keen of hearing
回 *hayamawa(ri)* a dash around (the world)
成 *sōsei* early maturity
死 *hayaji(ni), sōshi* premature death
早 *sōsō, hayahaya* Hurry up. *hayabaya* early, immediately. *sōsō* Hurriedly yours
年 *sōnen* youth, early years
合点 *hayaga(t)ten, hayagaten* hasty conclusion, premature judgment
7 足 *haya-ashi* quick pace, quick march, trot, fast walking
技 *hayawaza* quick work; sleight of hand
呑込 *hayanomiko(mi)* hasty conclusion
見表 *hayamihyō* chart, table
言葉 *hayakotoba* fast speaking
8 退 *sōtai, hayabi(ki), hayabi(ke)* leaving early
所 *haya(i) tokoro* promptly
参 *sōsan* early arrival (at a meeting); early morning visit (to a shrine or temple)
事 *haya(i) koto* promptness
者勝 *haya(i)monoga(chi)* first-come-first-served
取 *hayato(ri)* snapshot
取写真 *hayato(ri) shashin* snapshot
苗 *sanae* rice seedlings
苗取 *sanaeto(ru)* transplant rice
苗歌 *sanae uta* rice-planting song
9 速 *sassoku* immediately, speedily
咲 *hayaza(ki)* early blooming; precocious
秋 *sōshū* early fall
計 *sōkei na* rash, premature, hasty
変 *hayagawa(ri)* quick change of costume, sudden transformation
春 *sōshun* early spring
急 *sōkyū, sakkyū* urgent, pressing; great speed
飛脚 *hayabikyaku* courier, running messenger
発性痴呆症 *sōhatsusei chihōshō* dementia praecox
10 馬 *haya-uma* post horse, steed
起 *hayao(ki), sōki* early rising
逝 *sōsei* early death
書 *hayaga(ki)* writing in a hurry
11 道 *hayamichi* shortcut
婚 *sōkon* early marriage
掘 *hayabo(ri)* early crop
桶 *hayaoke* (cheap) coffin
船 *hayafune* clipper, fast boat
雪 *sōsetsu* early snow
教育 *sōkyōiku* early education
産 *sōzan* premature birth
産児 *sōzanji* premature baby
12 間 *hayama ni* early
晩 *sōban* early and late; sometime or other; finally, after all
暁 *sōgyō* daybreak, dawn
飯 *hayameshi* early meal; fast eating
朝 *sōchō* early morning
場米 *hayabamai* early rice
期 *sōki* early stage
期診断 *sōki shindan* early diagnosis
13 業 *hayawaza* quick work; sleight of hand
寝 *hayane* retiring early

14稲 *wase* an early rice. *wase no* early ripening;
15蕨 *sawarabi* early bracken ⌊precocious
熟 *sōjuku* precocity; premature develop-
駕籠 *hayakago* express palanquin ⌊ment
19瀬 *hayase* swift current, rapids
禱 *sōtō* morning prayers, matins
20鐘 *hayagane* fire bell

3

更 See 42. [日]

旱 2101/F891 KAN. *hideri* drought, dry weather; shortage.
4水 *kansui* drought and floods
天 *kanten* drought, dry weather
7災 *kansai* drought disaster
9荒 *kankō* land ruined by drought
10害 *kangai* drought damage
12雲 *kan-un* dry cloud
13損 *kanson* drought damage to fields
15魃 *kambatsu* drought

4

東 See 213. [木]

昏 See 2479.

冐 2102/F212 See 冒 2117. [冂]

昂 2103/F891 See 昻 2116.

旺 2104/F891 Ō. *sakan* flourishing, successful; beautiful; vigorous.
11盛 *ōsei na* excellent, flourishing, prosperous

昌 2105/F892 SHŌ prosperous; bright, clear.
5平 *shōhei* peace, tranquility

昆 2106/F891 KON descendants; elder brother.
5布 *kombu, kobu* tangle, kelp, sea tang, devil's
布茶 *kobucha, kombucha* kelp tea ⌊apron
6虫 *konchū* insect, bug
虫学 *konchūgaku* entomology

A **易** 2107/F896 EKI divination, augury, fortunetelling. I easiness. *yasu(i)* easy, simple, light; habitual. *-yasu(i)* be liable to, be ready to, be easy to.
6行 *igyō* easy way of salvation, Buddhist salvation by faith
8易 *i-i(taru)* simple, easy. *yasuyasu* very easy
学 *ekigaku* study of divination
者 *ekisha* fortuneteller, diviner
事 *kaegoto* swapping, exchanging
11道 *ekidō* divination, fortunetelling
術 *ekijutsu* art of divination
経 *Ekikyō* the Book of Divination
断 *ekidan* divination, fortunetelling
17簀 *ekisaku* death, demise of sages

B **昔** 2108/F897 SHAKU. SEKI. *mukashi* antiquity, old times.
4日 *sekijitsu* old times
5乍 *mukashinaga(ra)* as of yore
6年 *sekinen* antiquity; formerly; years ago
気質 *mukashi-katagi* old-time spirit
8昔 *mukashi-mukashi* long ago
者 *mukashimono* old folks
9風 *mukashifū no* old-fashioned
10時 *sekiji* old times ⌈niscences
13話 *mukashibanashi* folklore, legend; remi-
馴染 *mukashinajimi* old friend, crony
14様 *mukashiyō* old-fashioned
語 *mukashigata(ri)* an ancient tale

B **昇** 2109/F892 SHŌ. *nobo(ru), nobori* (see under 上 798.0).
3口 *nobo(ri) kuchi, nobo(ri)guchi* way up (to trains)
4天 *shōten* ascension; the Ascension (of ⌊Christ)
6任 *shōnin* promotion
9級 *shōkyū* promotion, advancement
叙 *shōjo* promotion (of officials), advance-
段 *shōdan* promotion ⌊ment
降 *shōkō* rise and fall; ascent and descent; fluctuations ⌈(ship) entrance
降口 *shōkōguchi* companionway, hatchway,
降場 *shōkōjō* (station) platform
降機 *shōkōki* elevator, hoist, dumb-waiter
10進 *shōshin* promotion, advancement
格 *shōkaku* raising of status
華 *shōka* sublimation (in chemistry)
12給 *shōkyū* salary raise ⌈imperial court
13殿 *shōden* the privilege of attending the
16龍 *nobo(ri)ryū* rising dragon
20騰 *shōtō suru* rise, go up, soar

A **明** 2110/F893 MEI clearness, shining; eyesight; discernment. MYŌ next (week), tomorrow (morning). MIN Ming (Dynasty). *a(keru)* open; empty, vacate; leave (a space); clear (the table); make (a hole); reserve (a seat). stay away from; dawn; end, expire, be over; open, begin. *a(ku)* open, be opened; start, begin, commence; become vacant, become empty, be

4 心 忄 ⺗ 戈 戸 手 扌 支 攴 攵 文 斗 斤 方 无 【日 曰】 月 木 欠 止 歹 殳 毋 比 毛 氏 气 水 氵 氺 火 灬 爪 爫 父 爻 爿 丬 片 牙 牛 犬 犭

disengaged, be free; expire, be over. *a(kasu)* spend, pass the time; reveal, divulge. *a(ke)* expiration, end; dawn. *akashi* proof. *aka(ri)* light, lamp; vindication. *aka(rui)* bright, light; cheerful, sunny; clear, clean; conversant with. *aki(raka)* bright: clear, plain, distinct, definite, obvious, indisputable, evident. *a(kuru)* next, following. *saya(keshi)* clear; refreshing; pure. *a(ke)* dawn. *a(ki)*- empty, vacant, unoccupied, spare (time).

4 方 *a(ke)gata* dawn
月 *meigetsu* bright moon, bright moonlight
分 *meibun* moral duty; justice
天子 *meitenshi* wise ruler
文 *meibun* express provision
文化 *meibunka suru* stipulate
日 *myōnichi, ashita, asu* tomorrow. *a(keno)hi* the next day; tomorrow
日明後日 *asu-asatte* tomorrow or next day
5 白 *meihaku na* clear, unmistakable
示 *meiji, meishi* clear statement
払 *a(ke)-hara(u)* leave open (a house or window); throw open
主 *meishu* wise ruler
弁 *meiben* clear understanding
6 色 *meishoku* bright color
地 *a(ki)chi* vacant lot, vacant land
先 *aka(ri)saki ni* in (a person's) light
年 *myōnen* next year
7 言 *meigen* declaration, assertion
快 *meikai* clear, explicit
君 *meikun* wise ruler
8 国 *Minkoku* China of the Mings
店 *a(ki)dana, a(ki)mise* vacant store
放 *a(ke)-hana(su)* throw open, open wide; leave open. *a(ke)-hana(reru)* grow light, dawn. *a(kep)pana(shi)* leaving (a door) open; blunt, frank, openhearted
取 *aka(ri)to(ri)* skylight, dormer
盲 *a(ki)mekura* illiterate
治神宮 *Meiji Jingū* Meiji Shrine
治節 *Meiji Setsu* Emperor Meiji's birthday anniversary
治維新 *Meiji Ishin* Meiji Restoration
明 *aka-aka to* brightly. *meimei* very clear
明白白 *meimei-hakuhaku* very clear
明星 *a(ke) (no) myōjō* morning star, Venus
明後日 *myōmyōgonichi, shiasatte, yanoasatte, yana-asatte* two days after tomorrow
9 屋 *a(ki)ya* vacant house
度 *meido* brightness
城 *a(ki)jiro* vacant castle
神 *myōjin* gracious deity
星 *myōjō* morning star; Venus; Lucifer; (literary) star
春 *myōshun* next spring
後日 *myōgonichi, asatte* day after tomorrow
後年 *myōgonen* year after next
10 倫 *meirin* making clear the moral obligations of man
残 *a(ke)-noko(ru)* lingering (night)
記 *meiki suru* specify
敏 *meibin* intelligence, discernment
烏 *a(ke)garasu* crows cawing at dawn
家 *a(ki)ya, a(ki)-ie* vacant house, empty house
哲 *meitetsu* wise man, sage
部屋 *a(ki)beya* vacant room
朗 *meirō na* clear, bright, cheerful
朗化 *meirōka suru* cheer up, brighten
11 達 *meitatsu* wisdom, intelligence
視 *meishi* clear vision
断 *meidan* wise judgment
窓 *aka(ri) mado* window
笛 *meiteki* a good flute
巣 *a(ki)su* empty nest; vacant house; pilferer
細 *meisai* details, particulars. *meisai na* obvious
細書 *meisaisho* detailed statement, specifications
眸 *meibō* bright eyes
眸皓歯 *meibō-kōshi* beautiful face
眸禍 *meibōka* ruin brought about by one's beauty
12 間 *a(ki)ma* vacant room. *a(kezuno)ma, a(kazuno)ma* forbidden or haunted room
媚 *meibi na* picturesque, beautiful
晩 *myōban* tomorrow night
晰 *meiseki na* clear, distinct
渡 *a(ke)-wata(ru)* dawn, become light. *a(ke)-wata(su)* vacate; evacuate; surrender
答 *meitō* definite answer
番 *a(ke)ban* off duty
智 *meichi* wisdom, intelligence
御目出 *a(kemashite) omede(tō) (gozaimasu)* Happy New Year
朝 *myōchō, myōasa* tomorrow morning. *Minchō* Ming dynasty; Ming style
朝活字 *Min-chō katsuji* Ming-dynasty-style characters
13 解 *meikai* clear understanding
障子 *a(kari) shōji* translucent paper doors
滅 *meimetsu suru* appear and disappear, flicker, glimmer
滅灯 *meimetsutō* occulting light
暗 *meian* light and darkness
暗灯 *meiantō* occulting light
暗度 *meiando* brightness
14 徳 *meitoku* illustrious virtue
徴 *meichō* clarification
察 *meisatsu* discernment, insight
暮 *aka(shi)-ku(rasu), a(ke)-ku(rasu)* live. *a(ketemo)-ku(retemo)* always. *a(ke)-ku(re)* day and night, morning and evening; day in and day out, all the time, early and late
15 澈 *meitetsu* the clearness of water

澄 *meichō na* clear
確 *meikaku na* clear, distinctive, definite
17 瞭 *meiryō* clearness
19 離 *a(ke)-hana(reru)* become light, dawn
鏡 *meikyō* clear mirror
鏡止水 *meikyō shisui* serene frame of mind
20 鐘 *a(ke) (no) kane* a bell at dawn
礬 *myōban* alum

5

昼 See 53.

昞 2111/F903 **昺 炳** See 2754.

旺 2112/F-X Nonstandard for **曜** 2162.

昧 2113/F900 MAI dark; foolish.
11 爽 *maisō* daybreak, dawn

A **昭** 2114/F901 SHŌ clear, bright.
5 示 *shōshi suru* show clearly
代 *shōdai* enlightened era, glorious reign
6 和 *Shōwa* the name of the era beginning in 1926
9 昭 *shōshō* clearness

昵 2115/F902 JITSU reconcile, approach; become intimate.
6 近 *jikkin* intimacy
17 懇 *jikkon* intimacy

昂 2116/F891 **昻** KŌ rise.
10 進 *kōshin* rise; acceleration; exasperation
12 揚 *kōyō suru* exalt, promote, enhance
然 *kōzen(taru)* elated, triumphant
16 奮 *kōfun*=興奮 615.16
20 騰 *kōtō* sudden price jump

B **冒** 2117/F212 **冐 冐** BŌ. *oka(su)* risk, face, defy, dare; (diseases) attack; damage; desecrate; assume (a name). [冂]
10 険 *bōken* risk, venture, adventure
険的 *bōkenteki* adventurous, risky
険談 *bōkendan* adventure story
16 頭 *bōtō* opening paragraph or statement
18 瀆 *bōtoku, bōdoku* blasphemy, profanity, desecration, sacrilege

B **映** 2118/F898 EI reflecting; projection. *ei(jiru), ei(zuru)* be reflected in, shine on; impress, appear to. *ha(eru)* shine, be brilliant; look attractive. *utsu(ru)* be reflected; match, harmonize, be becoming; be taken (a photo). *utsu(su)* (see under 写 626.0). *ha(yasu)* applaud, cheer. *utsu(ri)* reflection, print, impression; match, harmony, effect. *hae* glory.
5 写 *eisha* projection
写幕 *eisha maku* screen (for pictures)
写機 *eishaki* projector
8 画 *eiga* cinema, movie, moving picture, film
画化 *eigaka* filming, making a film version
画界 *eigakai* screen world, filmdom
画劇 *eigageki* screen play
画館 *eigakan* movie theater
12 渡 *ha(e)-wata(ru)* shine all over
14 像 *eizō* reflection, image, silhouette

A **昨** 2119/F900 SAKU the past; yesterday, last (year). *saku-* last (year); yesterday.
3 夕 *sakuyū* last evening
4 今 *sakkon* nowadays, recently
日 *sakujitsu, kinō* yesterday
日今日 *kinō (no) kyō* just now
5 冬 *sakutō* last winter
6 年 *sakunen* last year
年末 *sakunemmatsu* end of last year
8 夜 *sakuya, yūbe* last night, last evening
非今是 *sakuhi-konze* vacillation, fickleness
9 秋 *sakushū* last fall
春 *sakushun* last spring
10 紙 *sakushi* yesterday's paper
夏 *sakka* last summer
12 晩 *sakuban* last night, last evening
暁 *sakugyō* at daybreak yesterday
朝 *sakuchō* yesterday morning

A **是** 2120/F901 ZE right, justice. *kore* this. *kore de* with this. *kore demo* such as I am. *koko ni* here. *kore kara* now, from now on, from here.
3 丈 *kore dake* only this much, this much, so much
4 切 *koregi(ri), koreki(ri), kore(k)ki(ri)* just this time, never again, This is all.
以 *kore (o) motte* with this
以上 *kore ijō* better than this
5 正 *zesei* correction, revision
6 式 *koreshiki* such a trifle; just this much
迄 *kore made* until now; before now; no more hope
先 *kore (yori) saki* previously, meanwhile; farther on
7 見 *kore-mi(yogashi) ni* ostentatiously
位 *koregurai*=*kore dake* 是丈 (see above–3)
8 於 *koko (ni) oi(te)* then
限 *kore kagi(ri)*=*koregi(ri)* 是切 (see above–4)

非 *zehi* right or wrong, pro and con; surely, by all means. *zehi suru* comment on, criticize
非共 *zehitomo* surely; please
非曲直 *zehi-kyokuchoku* good and bad; right and wrong
非無 *zehina(i)* inevitable; necessary, unavoidable
9 是 *kore kore* this and that; etc. *kore(wa)-kore(wa)* an exclamation of surprise
是非非 *zeze-hihi* fair and just, clear-cut (policy)
11 許 *korebaka(ri)* only this, so little
12 程 *korehodo* this much, so much, (not) more
等 *korera* these
14 認 *zenin* approval

A 星 2121 F897 SEI, SHŌ star. *hoshi* star; spot, dot, mark; bull's eye; one's fortune; point, score.

4 斗 *seito* stars
月夜 *hoshizukiyo* starlit night
5 占 *hoshi urana(i), seisen* astrology, horoscope
6 行 *seikō* great speed
回 *hoshimawa(ri)* one's fortune
団 *seidan* star cluster
合 *hoshia(i)* July 7th meeting of two lover stars
7 図 *seizu* star map
形 *hoshigata* star shape
条旗 *Seijōki* the Stars and Stripes
辰 *seishin* stars, heavenly bodies
辰崇拝 *seishin sūhai* astrolatry, star worship
8 雨 *seiu* meteoric shower
明 *hoshi aka(ri)* starlight
河 *Seika* the Milky Way
夜 *seiya* starry night
学 *seigaku* astronomy
学家 *seigakuka* astronomer; astrologer
9 食 *seishoku=empei* 掩蔽 1932.15
型 *hoshigata* star shape
珊瑚 *hoshi sango* bloodstone
10 座 *seiza* constellation
座早見図 *seiza hayamizu* planisphere
11 宿 *seishuku* constellation
章 *seishō* badge, star
祭 *Hoshi Matsu(ri)* Tanabata Weaver Star Festival (July 7)
12 雲 *seiun* nebula
雲説 *seiunsetsu* nebular hypothesis
13 群 *seigun* star cluster
15 標 *seihyō* asterisk, star
影 *hoshikage* starlight
17 霜 *seisō* years, time

A 春 2122 F899 SHUN spring. *haru* spring, Springtime. *haru(meku)* become springlike.

2 七草 *haru (no) nanakusa* the seven herbs of spring
3 山 *haruyama* mountains in spring
4 心 *shunshin* thoughts of spring; air of spring; sexual passion
方 *harube* springtime
日 *haruhi, shunjitsu* spring day
分 *shumbun* vernal equinox
分日 *Shumbun (no) Hi* the Vernal Equinox (holiday, March 21)
分点 *shumbunten* the vernal equinoctial point
5 立 *haruta(tsu)* Spring is coming on.
本 *shumpon* pornographic book
6 色 *shunshoku* spring scenery
気 *shunki* atmosphere of spring, spring fever, spring landscape
帆 *shumpan* a boat floating on the water in spring, spring sailing
光 *shunkō* spring scenery
先 *harusaki* early spring
7 売 *haru (o) u(ru)* sell one's virtue
告鳥 *harutsu(ge)dori* nightingale
8 雨 *harusame, shun-u* spring rain; bean-jelly sticks
物 *harumono* spring goods
郊 *shunkō* spring countryside
画 *shunga* indecent picture; pornography
季 *shunki* spring, springtime
季皇霊祭 *Shunki Kōreisai* Shinto Festival of the Vernal Equinox
9 風 *haru kaze, shumpū* spring breeze
信 *shunshin* signs of spring, tidings of flowers
思 *shunshi* thoughts of spring
草 *haru kusa* new spring grass
秋 *haru-aki, shunjū* spring and fall; months and years
秋富 *shunjū (ni) to(mu)* be young
10 時 *shunji* springtime
眠 *shummin* morning sleep in spring
蚕 *haruko, harugo, shunsan* spring silkworms
宵 *shunshō* spring evening, spring night
宮 *tōgū, haru (no) miya* the crown prince. *shunkyū* palace of the crown prince
容 *shun-yō* spring scene
夏秋冬 *shun-ka-shū-tō* the four seasons; the year round
11 情 *shunjō* sexual passion
野 *haruno* fields in spring
陽 *shun-yō* springtime; spring sunshine
雪 *shunsetsu* spring snow
12 暁 *shungyō* spring dawn
寒 *shunkan* late cold spell
嵐 *shunran* spring storm; spring mists
着 *harugi* spring wear, New Year's clothes
場所 *haru basho* spring wrestling tournament
景 *shunkei* spring scene
景色 *harugeshiki* spring scenery
13 暖 *shundan* warm spring weather
蒔 *harumaki* spring sowing
夢 *shummu* a dream of a spring evening; something fleeting
雷 *shunrai* spring thunder

愁 *shunshū* gloom in spring
15 駒 *harugoma* spring colt; pony dance; pep
16 機発動期 *shunki hatsudōki* age of puberty
17 霞 *harugasumi* spring haze
18 蝉 *haruzemi* spring cicada

— 6 —

晋 晉 See 55.

書 See 3719. [曰]

晦 Nonstandard for **晦** 2135.

晃 2123/F905 **晄** Kō clear.
10 晃 *kōkō(taru)* brilliant, light

晏 2124/F905 An late; (the sun) sets; quiet.
6 如 *anjo* being at ease, comfort, peace
12 然 *anzen to* peacefully

晒 2125/F906/F920 **曬** Sai. *sara(su)* bleach, refine; expose, air. *sarashi* bleaching; bleached cotton.
4 木綿 *sarashi momen* bleached cotton cloth
5 台 *sarashidai* pillory, stocks
8 者 *sarashimono* exposed criminal
9 首 *sarashi kubi* unburied severed head
10 粉 *sarashiko* bleaching powder, chloride of lime
14 飴 *sarashi ame* thick rice syrup

A **時** 2126/F903 Ji hour, o'clock, time; Buddhist sect originating in the thirteenth century. *toki* time, hour, moment; occasion; season; opportunity; the times; tense. *toki(meku)* prosper, flourish, be influential; prosperous, influential. *toki ni* now, by the way, in passing. *toki(naranu)* unseasonable, untimely, inopportune; sudden, unexpected. *toki ni totte* on the occasion, for the occasion. *toki niwa, toki(tama), toki toshite* occasionally. *toki(shimo), toki(shimoare)* just then. *toki to shite* sometimes, in some cases. *-ji* time, period.
2 人 *jijin* contemporaries. *toki (no) hito* a person in the public eye
3 下 *jika* at present
4 文 *jibun* modern writing
日 *jijitsu* the date, the time; days
化 *shike(ru)* be stormy; be gloomy. *shike* stormy weather, heavy sea; scarcity of fish; business depression
分 *jibun* time, hour, season, time of year; (proper) time, opportunity; those days
分時 *jibundoki* mealtime
5 外 *tokihazu(re)* unseasonable, untimely, inopportune
世 *jisei* the times, the era. *tokiyo* era, age; current trends
世時節 *tokiyo-jisetsu* the times and seasons; this world's constant changes
代 *jidai* period, age, stage, antiquity
代色 *jidaishoku* era color
代行列 *jidai gyōretsu* historic pageant
代性 *jidaisei* characteristic of the age
代物 *jidaimono* an antique, historical object; historical play
代後 *jidai-oku(re)* out-of-date
代相 *jidaisō* trend of the times
代思相 *jidai shisō* current thinking
代思潮 *jidai shichō* trend of the times
代病 *jidaibyō* morbid idea of the times
代遅 *jidai-oku(re)* out-of-date
代精神 *jidai seishin* spirit of the times
代劇 *jidaigeki* historic costume play
代錯誤 *jidai sakugo* anachronism; being behind the times
代寵児 *jidai (no) chōji* a man of the times
6 至 *toki-ita(ranu)* unappreciated. *toki-ita(tte)* timely
好 *jikō* fashion, fad, vogue
7 局 *jikyoku* situation
折 *tokio(ri)* at times, occasionally
余 *jiyo* over an hour
辰儀 *jishingi* chronometer
8 雨 *shigu(reru)* the late rains fall; tears fall. *shigure, jiu* late fall or early winter rain; shedding tears
価 *jika* current price
服 *jifuku* appropriate clothing
制 *jisei* tense (in grammar)
効 *jikō* statute of limitations
宜 *jigi* the right time; season's greetings; bowing
宗 *Jishū* a Buddhist sect
刻 *jikoku* time, hour, the time
刻表 *jikokuhyō* time table, schedule
事 *jiji* current events
事問題 *jiji mondai* current topics
事解説 *jiji kaisetsu* comment on current events
限 *jigen* time limit; period; limited
限装置 *jigen sōchi* timing mechanism
限錠 *jigenjō* time lock
限爆弾 *jigem-bakudan* time bomb
9 風 *jifū* fashion of the day
疫 *jieki* epidemic, pestilence, plague
速 *jisoku* speed per hour
俗 *jizoku* ways of the age; current trends; conventionality
相 *jisō* tense (in grammar)
点 *jiten* occasion
計 *tokei* clock, watch, timepiece

計工 *tokeikō* watchmaker
計台 *tokeidai* clock stand, clock tower
計仕掛 *tokeijika(ke)* clockwork
計仕掛爆弾 *tokeijika(ke) bakudan* time bomb
計回 *tokeimawa(ri)* clockwise
計店 *tokeiten* watchmaker, jewelry store
計屋 *tokeiya* watchmaker, jeweler
計信管 *tokei shinkan* clockwork fuse
計師 *tokeishi* watchmaker, jeweler
計番 *tokeiban* clock master
計爆弾 *toke(i) bakudan* time bomb
10 借 *tokiga(ri)* temporary loan
流 *jiryū* trend of the times
砲 *jihō* time gun
時 *tokidoki* sometimes, occasionally, frequently; each time, each season. *tokidoki no* seasonal, occasional, recurrent. *jiji* from time to time
時刻刻 *jiji-kokkoku* hourly, momentarily
差 *jisa* time difference
差出勤 *jisa shukkin* staggered office hours
候 *jikō* season, time of year; climate
候中 *jikōata(ri)* under the weather
候外 *jikōhazu(re)* unseasonable
11 鳥 *hototogisu* cuckoo
運 *jiun* tide of fortune
偶 *tokitama* at times, infrequently, occasionally
球 *jikyū* time ball
務 *jimu* current affairs
移 *toki (o) utsu(sazu)* immediately
習 *jishū* periodic reviewing
得 *toki (o) e(ru)* be prosperous
得顔 *toki(o)egao ni* proudly, triumphantly
12 給 *jikyū* payment by the hour
評 *jihyō* editorial comment
期 *jiki* time, the times, season
無 *tokina(shi)* no settled time; atmosphere of failure
貸 *tokiga(shi)* temporary loan, call money, trust credit
報 *jihō* review; time siren
場合 *toki (to) baai de* according to time and place
間 *jikan* an hour; time; period
間外 *jikangai* late; overtime; outside of hours
間表 *jikanhyō* timetable, schedule
間制賃金 *jikansei chingin* hour-pay system
間記録器 *jikan kirokuki* time clock
間割 *jikanwari* timetable, schedule
間給 *jikankyū* payment by the hour
間給水 *jikan-kyūsui* hour-restricted water supply
間塞 *jikanfusagi* stopgap
間厲行 *jikan reikō* promptness in appointments
13 勢 *jisei* spirit of the age, trend of the times, conditions
節 *jisetsu* season; the times; opportunity
節柄 *jisetsugara* in these times
14 様 *jiyō* latest fashion
15 儀 *jigi* season's greetings; bowing
論 *jiron* contemporary opinion, comment on current events
弊 *jihei* evils of the times
16 機 *jiki* opportunity, time, occasion
20 鐘 *jishō* hour bells, (ship's) time bells

7

書 2127 F907 See 昼 53.

晣 晢 See 晰 2136.

晩 2128 F906 晚 See 晚 2145.

晤 2129 F907 Go clear.

晃 2130 F213 Nonstandard for 晃 624.

匙 2131 F275 SHI. JI. *saji* spoon. [匕]
5 加減 *saji kagen* about a spoonful; dosage, prescription; discretion, consideration, allowance
7 投 *saji (o) na(geru)* withdraw, give up as hopeless

曼 2132 F925 MAN wide; beautiful. [曰]
7 陀羅 *mandara* mandala, picture of Buddhas
10 荼羅 *mandara* mandala, picture of Buddhas

晨 2133 F908 SHIN morning, early.
8 明 *shimmei* morning star
9 星 *shinsei* morning star

曹 2134 F925 SŌ, ZŌ friend. [曰]
5 司 *zōshi* cadet, young son
8 長 *sōchō* sergeant-major
11 達 *sōda* soda
達水 *sōdasui* soda water

晦 2135 F908 KAI dark. *kura(masu)* give the slip to, disappear. *tsugomori* month end, last day of the month; the dark of the moon.
4 日 *misoka* the last day of the month
8 明 *kaimei* day and night, night and darkness
10 朔 *kaisaku* last and first days of successive months
冥 *kaimei* darkness
11 渋 *kaijū* ambiguity, obscurity

8

昏 See 604. [日]

普 See 605.

晰 2136 F910 **晳 晣** SHAKU. SEKI clear.

B **晶** 2137 F910 SHŌ clear; crystal.
4 化 *shōka* crystallization

A **暑** 2138 F912 **暑** SHO summer heat. *atsu(garu)* feel the heat, swelter. *atsu(gari)* sensitivity to heat; a person sensitive to hot weather. *atsu(i)* hot, warm, sultry. *atsu(sa)* heat, hot weather.
4 中 *shochū* midsummer, hot season. *atsusa-ata(ri)* heatstroke, sunstroke
中見舞 *shochū mima(i)* summer health inquiry
中休暇 *shochū kyūka* summer vacation
6 気 *atsuke, shoki* hot weather; heatstroke, sunstroke
気中 *shokiata(ri)* heatstroke, sunstroke
8 苦 *atsuguru(shii), atsukuru(shii)* sultry, sweltering weather
9 屋 *atsu(gari)ya* person sensitive to hot weather
10 凌 *atsu(sa)shino(gi)* relief from the heat
12 寒 *shokan* heat and cold; a year
15 熱 *shonetsu* summer heat

B **暁** 2139 F917 **曉 暁** GYŌ. *akatsuki* dawn, daybreak; in the event (of).
4 天 *gyōten* dawn
天星 *gyōten (no) hoshi* morning star; a few
5 旦 *gyōtan* dawn, daybreak
6 色 *gyōshoku* scene at dawn
7 更 *akatsuki (no) kō* early morning, 4–6 a.m.
8 明星 *ake (no) myōjō* morning star, Venus; Lucifer
9 通 *gyōtsū* thoro knowledge
紅 *gyōkō* rosy dawn
星 *gyōsei* morning star, Venus; rarity
10 起 *gyōki* arising early
11 達 *gyōtatsu* thoro knowledge
12 智 *gyōchi* great wisdom
20 鐘 *gyōshō* a bell at daybreak

B **替** 2140 F926 TAI. TEI. *ka(eru), kawa(ru), kawa(ri)* (see under 代 364.0). *ka(e)-* spare, substitute, exchange. *kae de* at, for, per. [曰]
3 刃 *ka(e)ba* extra blades
5 玉 *ka(e)dama* substitute, a double
6 地 *ka(e)chi* substitute land
字 *ka(e)ji* a substitute character of the same pronunciation
名 *ka(e)na* alias
7 狂言 *kawa(ri) kyōgen* new play, new program
8 肩 *ka(e)gata* spare palanquin carrier
事 *ka(e)goto* swapping, exchanging
10 馬 *ka(e)uma* spare horse
11 得 *ka(e)doku* gain in exchanging (something)
12 着 *ka(e)gi* a change of clothing
13 損 *ka(e)zon* loss in exchanging (something)
蓋 *ka(e)buta* extra lid
14 歌 *ka(e)uta* parody in song

A **量** 2141 F1935 RYŌ quantity, amount, volume; magnanimity; a measure. *haka(ri)* measure, weight. *haka(ru)* (see under 計 4312.0). [里]
2 入 *haka(ri)-i(reru)* measure into
3 子論 *ryōshiron* quantum theory
4 込 *haka(ri)-ko(mu)* measure liberally
水器 *ryōsuiki* water meter
5 目 *ryōme* weight
6 刑 *ryōkei* weighing an offense
7 見 *ryōken*＝了簡 268.18
売 *haka(ri)u(ri)* selling by measure
8 的 *ryōteki* quantitative
知 *haka(ri)-shi(ru), ryōchi suru* to measure, to fathom
直 *haka(ri)-nao(su)* reweigh; measure again
11 産 *ryōsan* mass production
13 感 *ryōkan* volume (in a painting)
15 器 *ryōki* a measure for volume

A **景** 2142 F909 KEI view, scene.
6 色 *keshiki, keishoku* scenery, landscape
仰 *keikō* love of virtue. *keigyō* adoration, admiration; a love of virtue
気 *keiki* the times, business conditions; liveliness
気付 *keikizu(ku)* boom, become active. *keikizu(ke)* promotion stunt
気良 *keikiyo(ku)* briskly, prosperously
8 況 *keikyō* situation; outlook
物 *keibutsu* (seasonal) scenery; premium, present
9 品 *keihin* premium, present, bonus
品券 *keihinken* premium lottery ticket
10 致 *keichi* beauty of nature
11 教 *Keikyō* Nestorianism
教徒 *Keikyōto* a Nestorian
12 勝 *keishō*＝形勝 1589.12
雲 *keiun* an auspicious cloud
13 福 *keifuku* great happiness
14 慕 *keibo suru* honor, worship
15 趣 *keishu* scenery, landscape
18 観 *keikan* spectacle, view

A **晴** 2143/F910 **晴** SEI. *ha(reru)* clear up; (doubts) vanish; be refreshed. *ha(rasu)* dispel, clear away (gloom); refresh (oneself). *ha(re)* fine weather. *ha(reyakana)* clear, bright; radiant, cheerful. *ha(rete)* openly, publicly. *ha(regamashii)* openhearted, frank.

3 上 *ha(re)-a(garu)* clear up
4 天 *seiten* fine weather, clear sky
天白日 *seiten-hakujitsu* innocence; clear ⌊weather
6 好 *seikō* beautiful clear skies
衣 *haregi, hareginu* one's best clothes
衣裳 *hare-ishō* one's best clothes
8 雨 *seiu* rain or shine; weather conditions
雨計 *seiukei* barometer
9 姿 *ha(re)sugata* wearing one's best clothes
10 陰 *sei-in* sunlight and shadow
朗 *seirō* clear, fair, fine, bright
耕雨読 *seikō-udoku* working in fair weather and reading in wet
11 着 *ha(re)gi* one's best clothes
12 間 *ha(re)ma* clear interval
晴 *ha(re)ba(reshii), harebare(shita)* clear, cloudless; cheerful, refreshing; splendid
渡 *ha(re)-wata(ru)* clear up
着 *ha(re)gi* one's best clothes
場所 *ha(re) (no) basho* a large gathering
勝負 *ha(re) shōbu* public contests
14 模様 *ha(re) moyō* clearing weather
16 曇 *seidon* fine weather and cloudy

智 2144/F910 CHI wisdom, intellect; intelligence, reason; strategem.

2 力 *chiryoku*＝知力 3169.2 ⌈courage
4 仁勇 *chi-jin-yū* wisdom, benevolence, and
8 育 *chi-iku* mental education
者 *chisa* wise man, sage ⌈courageous men
9 勇 *chiyū* intelligence and courage; wise and
10 将 *chishō* resourceful general
能 *chinō* knowledge and ability ⌈deception
能犯 *chinōhan* intellectual crime, crime of
能指数 *chinō shisū* IQ, intelligence quotient
能商 *chinōshō* IQ, intelligence quotient
能検査 *chinō kensa* mental test
恵 *chie* wisdom, sense, sagacity, intelligence,
恵者 *chiesha* wise man ⌊resourcefulness
恵袋 *chiebukuro* one's close adviser; brain
恵歯 *chieba* wisdom tooth ⌊trust
恵輪 *chie (no) wa* puzzle ring
恵熱 *chie netsu* fever accompanying denti-
恵競 *chiekurabe* quiz contest ⌊tion
11 略 *chiryaku* ingenuity, talents
12 歯 *chishi* wisdom tooth ⌈and fools
13 愚 *chigu* wisdom and foolishness; wise men
15 慮 *chiryo* wise idea; planning ability
慧 *chie*＝智恵 (see above–10)
16 謀 *chibō* ingenuity, resourcefulness
19 識 *chishiki* wisdom
22 嚢 *chinō* brains, wits

B **晩** 2145/F906 **晩 晩** BAN evening, night; the end of all things; late.

4 方 *bangata* toward evening
5 生 *okute* late rice; late crops
冬 *bantō* late winter
6 成 *bansei* late success; late development
年 *bannen* late in life
7 花 *banka* late-blooming flowers
8 刻 *bankoku* toward evening
学 *bangaku* late education
9 秋 *banshū* late fall
春 *banshun* late spring
10 酌 *banshaku* an evening drink of saké
夏 *banka* late summer
蚕 *bansan* late cocoons
11 遅 *ban oso(ku)* late at night
婚 *bankon* late marriage
涼 *banryō* the cool of the evening
12 飯 *bammeshi* evening meal, supper
景 *bankei* evening; an evening scene
13 節 *bansetsu* life's closing years
照 *banshō* setting sun
14 稲 *bantō, okute* late rice
16 餐 *bansan* supper, dinner
餐式 *Bansanshiki* the Lord's Supper, Eucharist, Holy Communion
餐会 *bansankai* dinner party, banquet
17 霜 *bansō* late frost
霞 *banka* evening afterglow
19 禱 *bantō* evening prayer
20 鐘 *banshō* curfew; evening bell

A **最** 2146/F926 SAI. *motto(mo)* most. *sai-* ultra, most, maximum, extreme. *ito-* extremely, greatly. [日]

3 小 *saishō* the smallest, the minimum
小限 *saishōgen* minimum
小限度 *saishō gendo* minimum
上 *saijō* the best; the highest
上級 *saijōkyū* superlative degree; highest
上等 *saijōtō* top quality, super ⌊class
上権 *saijōken* supreme power, supremacy
大 *saidai* maximum, greatest, largest
大限 *saidaigen* maximum
大限度 *saidai gendo* maximum ⌈above–3)
大級 *saidaikyū*＝*saijōkyū* 最上級 (see
大速力 *saidai sokuryoku* maximum speed
下 *saika* lowest; worst
下位 *saika-i* lowest position, lowest rank
下級 *saikakyū* lowest class, lowest grade
下等 *saikatō* lowest grade

下層 *saikasō* the lowest class (of people)
4中 *saichū ni. sanaka ni* in the midst of, at the height of. *monaka* middle; bean-jam wafer
4少 *saishō* the fewest, the least, the minimum; the youngest
5北 *saihoku* northernmost
古 *saiko* the oldest
右翼 *saiuyoku* extreme right wing
左翼 *saisayoku* extreme left wing
6西 *saisei* westernmost
合 *moyai* doing co-operatively
早 *mohaya* now, soon, already, by now
多数 *saitasū* the largest number
尖端 *saisentan* the lead, forefront
好調 *saikōchō* perfect (pitching) form
近 *saikin* recently; latest, newest
近親 *saikinshin* nearest relative
近親者 *saikinshinsha* nearest relative
7尾 *saibi* the end, the very last
初 *saisho* the first, the beginning
良 *sairyō* the best, the ideal
良種 *sairyōshu* best variety
低 *saitei* lowest, minimum
低温度計 *saitei ondokei* minimum thermometer
低寒暖計 *saitei kandankei* minimum thermometer
8長 *saichō no* longest
底 *saitei* lowest, minimum
果 *saiha(te)* farthest limit; farthest land
東 *saitō* easternmost
9南 *sainan* southernmost
前 *saizen* foremost; short time ago; just now
前列 *saizenretsu* forefront, very front line
前線 *saizensen* spearhead, front, first line
後 *saigo, iyahate* the last, the end. *saigo no* last, final. *saigo ni* in conclusion; in the long run
後的 *saigoteki* final
後通告 *saigo tsūkoku* ultimatum
後通牒 *saigo tsūchō* ultimatum
10徐行 *saijokō* dead slow, very slow
恵国 *saikeikoku* most-favored nation
恵国条款 *saikeikoku jōkan* most-favored-nation clause
恵国待遇 *saikeikoku taigū* most-favored-nation treatment
高 *saikō* maximum, supreme, highest, best
高司令官 *saikō shireikan* commander-in-chief
高司令部 *saikō shireibu* supreme command
高位 *saikōi* highest place
高学府 *saikō gakufu* highest seat of learning
高価格 *saikō kakaku* ceiling price
高法規 *saikō hōki* supreme law
高点 *saikōten* highest point; highest mark
高品 *saikōhin* articles of highest quality
高峰 *saikōhō* highest peak; highest point reached
高善 *saikōzen* the highest good
高裁 *Saikōsai* Supreme Court
高裁判所 *Saikō Saibansho* Supreme Court
高最低寒暖計 *saikō-saitei kandankei* maximum-and-minimum thermometer
高温度計 *saikō ondokei* maximum thermometer
高寒暖計 *saikō kandankei* maximum thermometer
高権 *saikōken* supreme power, absolute supremacy
高潮 *saikōchō* highwater mark; high tide; climax, peak, acme
11深 *saishin* greatest depth
悪 *saiaku* the worst
寄 *moyo(ri) no* neighboring, nearest
盛期 *saiseiki* golden age, height of prosperity; the season, the best time (for)
強 *saikyō* strongest
強調 *saikyōchō* re-emphasis
終 *saishū* the last, the end; final
終日 *saishūbi* the last day
終回 *saishūkai* the last inning
終的 *saishūteki* ultimate
終段階 *saishū dankai* the final step
終案 *saishū an* the final plan
12勝 *saishō* the supreme thing, the best
期 *saigo* one's last moments; death; fate
善 *saizen* the very best
最 *itodo* more and more
敬礼 *saikeirei* profound obeisance, deep respect
短 *saitan* shortest
短距離 *saitan kyori* shortest distance
13愛 *saiai no* dearest, beloved
適 *saiteki* optimum
適地 *saitekichi* the most suitable site
適任者 *saitekininsha* the best qualified person
新 *saishin* newest, latest, up-to-date
新式 *saishinshiki* latest style
新版 *saishimpan* latest edition
新流行 *saishin ryūkō* latest fashion

9

普 See 普 605.

尠 2147/F573 See 尠 142. [小]

會 See 会 381. [曰]

暁 2148/F917 See 暁 2139.

暑 2149/F912 See 暑 2138.

暉 2150/F912 Kɪ shine, light.

13暉 *kiki* brilliance

4 心小⺌戈戸手扌支攴攵文斗斤方无[日 9 日]月木欠止歹殳毋比毛氏气水氵氺火灬爪爫父爻爿丬片牙牛犬犭

暈 2151 / F911 UN halo, ring, corona. *boka(su) vt* shade off; obscure. *bo(keru) vi* fade, become dim. *kasa* halo, ring, corona.

6色 *unshoku* iridescence
8取 *kumado(ri)* shading; make-up
17翳 *un-ei* halation (in photography)

B **暇** 2152 / F911 KA rest, leisure. *hima* time; leisure; poor business; leave of absence; dismissal; divorce. *itoma* leisure, spare time; dismissal; divorce; leave; leave-taking.

3乞 *itomagoi* farewell visit
4日 *kajitsu* holiday, day off
8取 *himado(ru)* take time; be delayed
15潰 *himatsubu(shi)* waste of time

B **暖** 2153 / F912 **煖** DAN warmth. *atata(meru), atta(meru) vt* warm, heat. *atata(maru), atta(maru)* warm oneself, sun oneself, get warm. *atataka(i), attaka(i)* warm, mild, genial, cordial.

5冬 *dantō* mild winter
冬異変 *dantō-ihen* an unusually mild winter
6色 *danshoku* warm-looking (clothes)
気 *danki* heat, warmth, warm weather
地 *danchi* warm region
衣 *dan-i* warm clothes; dressing warmly
衣飽食 *dan-i-hōshoku* warm clothing and plenty to eat, luxury
8国 *dankoku, dangoku* warm country
房 *dambō* heating
波 *dampa* warm wave
炉 *danro* fireplace, hearth, stove
9室 *danshitsu* heated room, greenhouse, hothouse
10流 *danryū* warm current
帯 *dantai* subtropics
13戦争 *atataka(i) sensō* warm war
19簾 *noren* shop curtain, sign curtain; reputation, goodwill
簾師 *norenshi* swindler, crook

A **暗** 2154 / F912 **闇** AN dark. *kura(mu)* grow dark; be dazzled; be blinded. *kura(masu)* disappear, give (a person) the slip. *kura(ku) suru* darken, shade, make dim. *kura(gari)* darkness, gloom. *kura(i)*, dark, gloomy, somber; dim, faint; ignorant. *yami* (see under 闇 4969.0). *kura(me)* gathering darkness. *an (ni)* tacitly, implicity, informally, indirectly, obscurely.

4中 *anchū* in the dark
中飛躍 *anchū hiyaku* secret maneuvers
中摸索 *anchū mosaku* groping in the dark
5示 *anji* hint, suggestion
6色 *anshoku* dark color
合 *angō* coincidence
灰色 *ankaishoku* dark gray, taupe
号 *angō* code, password
号文 *angōbun* coded message
7車 *ansha* propeller, screw
町 *kura(i) machi* the underworld
君 *ankun* foolish ruler
赤色 *ansekishoku* dark red
8所 *ansho* dark place
夜 *an-ya* dark night
事 *kuragoto* secret acts
9香 *ankō* a fragrance from somewhere; the fragrance of flowers at night
室 *anshitsu* dark room
紅 *ankō* dark red
紅色 *ankōshoku* dark red
10流 *anryū* undercurrent
涙 *anrui* silent tears
紛 *kuramagi(re) ni* under cover of darkness
弱 *anjaku* weak-mindedness
記 *anki* memorization
記物 *ankimono* something to be memorized
殺 *ansatsu* assassination
殺者 *ansatsusha* assassin
11唱 *anshō* memorization, recitation
転 *anten* sudden darkening of the stage (to change scenery)
渠 *ankyo* drain, culvert
黒 *ankoku* darkness
黒日 *Ankokubi* the Dark Day
黒面 *ankokumen* seamy side, gloomy side
黒界 *ankokukai* the underworld
黒時代 *Ankoku Jidai* the Dark Ages
黒街 *ankokugai* the underworld
12喩 *an-yu* metaphor
雲 *an-un* dark clouds
惑 *ku(re)-mado(u)* be nonplussed
然 *anzen* discouraged, disappointed, astonished
紫色 *anshishoku* dark purple
13溝 *ankō* buried drain-tile sewer
路 *anro* dark road; underground passage
愚 *angu* weak-mindedness, stupidity
暗 *an-an* darkness; stillness in the depths
暗裏 *an-anri ni* tacitly, implicitly, obscurely, by implication, secretly
14誦 *anshō* memorization, recitation
算 *anzan* mental arithmetic
緑色 *anryokushoku* dark green
褐色 *ankasshoku* dark brown
15潮 *anchō* undercurrent
影 *an-ei* shadow, gloom
黙 *ammoku* silence
黙了解 *ammoku (no) ryōkai* tacit understanding
16澹 *antan* darkness, gloom
17闇 *kurayami, kureyami* darkness; dark place; privacy; lawlessness

礁 *anshō* reef, sunken rock
翳 *an-ei* shadow, gloom
18 闘 *antō* secret feud
21 躍 *an-yaku* secret maneuvers
26 鬱 *an-utsu* gloom, melancholy

10

暢 See 119.

暮 See 4041.

暦 See 833.

暝 2155 F914 MEI dark.

11

暫 2156 F914 ZAN *shibara(ku)* for a while, a moment; for a long time.
B
8 定 *zantei* provisional, tentative
定条約 *zantei jōyaku* provisional treaty
定的 *zanteiteki* provisional, tentative
定案 *zanteian* tentative plan
10 時 *zanji, shibashi* a short while, for some time. *zanji no* transient, momentary

暴 2157 F915 BAKU, BŌ violence, force, outrage, cruelty. *aba(reru)* rage, rave, fret; buck. *aba(ku)* (see under 発 3092.0).
A
2 力 *bōryoku* violence, force, terrorism
力団 *bōryokudan* terrorist organization, gangster group
力沙汰 *bōryokuzata* acts of violence
3 子 *aba(rek)ko* unruly child
4 込 *aba(re)-ko(mu)* storm into, burst into
5 令 *bōrei* wicked decree
出 *aba(re)-da(su)* grow restive, begin to act violently; begin to buck
民 *bōmin* mob, insurgents
6 行 *bōkō* act of violence, assault, outrage
回 *aba(re)-mawa(ru)* rampage, tear around, run riot
吏 *bōri* dishonest official
7 言 *bōgen* harsh or abusive language
走 *bōsō* running wildly
戻 *bōrei* tyranny, atrocity
投 *bōtō* wild pitch; wild throw
状 *bōjō* atrocity, violence
狂 *aba(re)-kuru(u)* rage, run amuck, tear around
利 *bōri* excessive profits, usury
君 *bōkun* tyrant
8 逆 *bōgyaku* violence, lawlessness
者 *aba(re)mono* rowdy
若無人 *bōjaku-bujin* arrogance, defiance
虎馮河 *bōko hyōka* perilous venture, risky attempt
9 廻 *aba(re)-mawa(ru)*＝暴回 (see above–6)
威 *bōi* tyranny, great violence, havoc
虐 *bōgyaku* tyranny, atrocity
政 *bōsei* tyrannical government
発 *bōhatsu* accidental gun discharge
勇 *bōyū* brute strength
食 *bōshoku* gluttony, intemperance in eating
食家 *bōshokuka* glutton, excessive eater
風 *bōfū* storm
風雨 *bōfūu* rainstorm
風信号 *bōfū shingō* storm warning
風進路 *bōfū shinro* storm path
風雪 *bōfūsetsu* blizzard, snowstorm
風圏 *bōfūken* storm area
風警報 *bōfū keihō* storm warning
10 馬 *aba(re) uma* restive horse, runaway
進 *bōshin* rushing recklessly; presumption
徒 *bōto* mob, rioters, insurgents, mutineers
挙 *bōkyo* violence, outrage; riot
11 悪 *bōaku* violence, tyranny, atrocity
動 *bōdō* riot, uprising
動者 *bōdōsha* rioter, insurgent, rebel, mutineer
動罪 *bōdōzai* rioting charge
12 評 *bōhyō* fierce criticism
落 *bōraku* slump, sharp break, crash, heavy decline (in prices)
飲 *bōin* heavy drinking, carousing
飲家 *bōinka* wild drinker
13 漢 *bōkan* ruffian, desperado
14 慢 *bōman* insolence, arrogance
説 *bōsetsu* preposterous theory
15 論 *bōron* irrational argument
20 騰 *bōtō* sudden (price) rise
21 露 *bakuro* exposure, disclosure

12

曆 See 暦 833.

曉 2158 F917 See 暁 2139.

暸 2159 F916 RYŌ clear.

曇 2160 F917 DON. *kumo(ru) vi* cloud up; fog up, become dim, be blurred; be gloomy. *kumo(rasu) vt* cloud up, dim, blur, fog, dull (the color); tarnish; shade (one's face); darken. *kumo(ri)* cloudiness, shadow; blur, dimness; gloom; suspicion; slur, stain; frosted (glass).
B
4 日 *kumo(ri)bi* cloudy day; the sun covered with clouds

天 *donten* cloudy weather, overcast sky
12勝 *kumo(ri)ga(chi) na* cloudy

13

曙 See 2163.

曖 2161 / F918 AI dark; not clear.
9昧 *aimai* vagueness, ambiguity, obscurity

14

曜 2162 / F919 **曜** Yō day of the week; light; shining. A
4日 *yōbi* weekday

曙 2163 / F918 SHO. *akebono* dawn, daybreak.
6光 *shokō* dawn; prospects

題 2164 / F2063 DAI subject, theme, topic; title, caption, heading; question, problem. *dai(suru)* give a title to. [頁] A
5目 *daimoku* title (of a book); heading
句 *daiku* prefatory motto
6号 *daigō* book title
字 *daiji* preface of a book or title
名 *daimei* title
7言 *daigen* preface; title (of a monument)
材 *daizai* subject matter, theme
8画 *daiga* title of a picture
12詠 *daiei* writing a poem on a given theme
詞 *daishi*=*daigen* 題言 (see above–7)
13辞 *daiji* prefatory motto
意 *dai-i* meaning of the subject
19簽 *daisen* book title

15

響 See 5114. [音]

曝 2165 / F919 BAKU. *sara(su)* bleach; refine; expose, air.
9首 *sharekōbe, sarekōbe* skull
10書 *bakusho* airing of books
21露 *bakuro* exposure, disclosure

曠 2166 / F919 Kō wide; worthless.
3久 *kōkyū* wasting time
4日 *kōjitsu* wasting time
日弥久 *kōjitsu-bikyū* procrastination
5古 *kōko no* historic, unprecedented
世 *kōsei no* unparalleled, epoch-making
10原 *kōgen* wide plain, open country
11野 *kōya, hirono* wilderness, moorland, prairie
18職 *kōshoku* neglect of official duty

16

馨 See 5190. [香]

17

嚮 嚮 See 響 5114. [音]

曩 2167 / F920 Nō *saki ni* (see under 先 571.0).

19

曬 See 晒 2125.

RAD. 曰 73

Iwaku to speak or *hirabi* (a flattened Rad. 72 *hi*). With the exception of the radical itself, which follows, this radical is treated herein as a variant of Rad. 72. Nickname: Flat Sun.

曰 2168 / F921 ETSU. OCHI. *iwa(ku)* say; reason; pretext; a history, a past, a story. *notama(u)* say, be pleased to say
5付 *iwa(ku)tsu(ki) no* (someone) with a history

RAD. 月 74

Tsuki **moon. At left:** ***tsuki-hen.*** **With the exception of the radical character itself, which character follows, this radical is herein treated as a variant of Rad. 130. Nickname: Moon.**

A 月 2169 / F928 GETSU moon; month; Monday. GATSU month (of the year). *tsuki* moon; month.

3 下 *gekka ni* on a moonlight night, in the moonlight
下氷人 *gekka hyōjin* go-between, matchmaker, Cupid ⌈and tide; one's star
4 日 *gappi* date. *tsukihi* months and days, time
月 *tsukizuki* every month
水 *gessui* menstruation
5 石 *gesseki* moonstone
立 *tsuita(chi)* first day of the month
代 *sakayaki* shaven part of the head
刊 *gekkan* monthly publication
払 *tsukibarai* monthly installments
収 *gesshū* monthly income ⌈comment
旦 *gettan* first day of the month; criticism,
末 *getsumatsu, tsukizue* end of the month
世界 *gessekai* lunar world, the moon
仕舞 *tsukijimai* month end
6 色 *gesshoku* moonlight
回 *tsukimawa(ri)* one's luck for the month
毎 *tsukigoto ni* monthly ⌈common
次 *getsuji* monthly. *tsukinami* every month;
次的 *tsukinamiteki* formal, conventional
光 *gekkō* moonlight, moonbeam
光冠 *gekkōkan* lunar corona ⌈birth
7 足 *tsukita(razu), tsukita(ranu)* premature
迫 *geppaku* month end; end of December
役 *tsukiyaku* menstruation ⌈*no* monthly
決 *tsukigi(me)* monthly contract. *tsukigi(me)*
利 *getsuri* monthly interest
別 *tsukibetsu* by months
形 *gekkei, tsukigata* half-moon shape
余 *getsuyo* over a month
来 *getsurai* a few months ago
見 *tsukimi* viewing the moon; moonlight
見玉子 *tsukimi tamago* fried egg ⌊party
見団子 *tsukimi dango* dumplings offered to the moon
見卵 *tsukimi tamago* fried egg
見草 *tsukimisō* moon flower
見宴 *tsukimi (no) en* moon-viewing party
8 送 *tsukioku(ri)* putting off from month to
例 *getsurei* monthly ⌊month
始 *tsukihaji(me)* beginning of the month
明 *getsumei, tsukiaka(ri)* moonlight
物 *tsuki (no) mono* menstruation
並 *tsukina(mi)* every month; common

参 *tsukimair(i)* monthly visit (to a shrine or
表 *geppō* monthly list ⌊temple)
事 *getsuji* menstruation
長石 *getchōseki* moonstone
夜 *tsukiyo, getsuya* moonlight night
夜見 *tsukiyomi, tsukuyomi* the moon
9 面 *getsumen* the moon's surface
食 *gesshoku* eclipse of the moon
眉 *tsuki (no) mayu* pretty arched eyebrows
待 *tsukima(chi)* waiting for the moonrise
後 *tsukioku(re)* back numbers (of a monthly)
10 俸 *geppō* monthly salary
都 *tsuki (no) miyako* city in the moon
華 *gekka* moonlight
桂 *gekkei* laurel; moon; moonlight
桂冠 *gekkeikan* crown of laurel
桂樹 *gekkeiju* laurel tree, bay tree
11 遅 *tsukioku(re)* a month or more older
頃 *tsukigoro* these past months
掛 *tsukigake* monthly installments
産 *gessan* monthly output
雫 *tsuki (no) shizuku* dewdrops
雪花 *tsuki-yuki-hana* moon, snow, and flowers; the beauty of the four seasons;
経 *gekkei* menstruation ⌊elegance
経帯 *gekkeitai* hygienic band, sanitary nap-
12 雇 *tsukiyato(i)* hiring by the month ⌊kin
越 *tsukigo(shi) no* (bill) hanging over from last month
極 *tsukigime* monthly contract. *tsukigime no*
評 *geppyō* monthly review ⌊monthly
割 *tsukiwari* monthly allocation
番 *tsukiban* monthly duty, monthly shift
替 *tsukiga(e)* every other month
報 *geppō* monthly report, monthly review
卿雲客 *gekkei unkaku* court nobles
評 *geppyō* monthly review
評子 *geppyōshi* monthly reviewer
給 *gekkyū* monthly salary
給日 *gekkyūbi* pay day
給取 *gekkyūto(ri)* salaried man
給袋 *gekkyūbukuro* pay envelope ⌈temple)
13 詣 *tsukimōde* monthly visit (to a shrine or
跨 *tsuki (o) mata(gu)* extend into the next
障 *tsuki (no) sawari* menstruation ⌊month
暈 *getsu-un, tsukigasa* a halo, a ring
14 読 *tsukiyomi* the moon
15 輪 *tsuki (no) wa* ring around the moon. *getsurin, gatsurin* moon

蝕 *gesshoku* eclipse of the moon
影 *tsukikage, getsuei* moonlight, moonbeams
賦 *geppu* monthly installment
賦払 *geppubara(i)* monthly payments
17 謝 *gessha* monthly tuition
齢 *getsurei* age of the moon
18 額 *getsugaku* monthly amount
曜 *Getsuyō* Monday
曜日 *Getsuyōbi* Monday
21 露 *getsuro* the moon and dew; moonlight reflected from the dew

RAD. 木 75

Ki tree. At left: *ki hen.* Nickname: Tree.

A 木 2170/F938 BOKU tree. MOKU tree; Thursday. *ki, ko* tree; wood; timber. lumber; wooden clappers.

2 刀 *bokutō, kodachi* wooden sword
3 口 *koguchi* cut end, butt end. *kiguchi* cross section of wood; lumber quality
下 *ki (no) shita, ko (no) shita* under a tree
工 *mokkō* woodworking; woodworker
工所 *mokkōjo* woodworking shop; sawmill
工場 *mokkōjō* woodworking shop; sawmill
4 木 *kigi* every tree; many trees; all kinds of ⌊trees
毛 *mokumō, mokuge* excelsior
片 *mokuhen* block; chip; splinter
仏 *kibotoke, kibutsu* wooden Buddha; insensible person
切 *kigi(re)* piece of wood, chip, chunk, ⌊splinter
太刀 *kidachi* wooden sword
戸 *kido* gate, wicket, wooden door, wooden gate; entrance; castle gate
戸札 *kido fuda* wooden admission ticket
戸番 *kidoban* doorman, gatekeeper
戸御免 *kido gomen* admission free
戸銭 *kidosen* admission fee
5 瓦 *kigawara, kogawara* wooden roof tiles
皮 *mokuhi* bark
皿 *kizara* wooden dish 「texture
目 *mokume* wood grain. *kime* wood grain;
立 *kodachi* clump of trees, thicket, grove, standing trees
札 *kifuda* wooden tag or ticket
末 *konure* twig, tree top 「objects
石 *bokuseki* trees and stones, inanimate
石漢 *bokusekikan* unsusceptible person
6 羽 *koba* shingles
舟 *kibune* wooden ship
匠 *mokushō* carpenter
灰 *kibai* wood ashes
印 *kijirushi* woodcutter's mark
地 *kiji* grain of wood; plain wood
肌 *kohada, kihada* bark of a tree
伊乃 *miira* mummy
竹継 *ki (ni) take (o) tsu(gu)* lack harmony
7 材 *mokuzai* wood, timber, lumber
杓 *kisaku* wooden ladle
8 杯 *mokuhai* wooden cup
枕 *kimakura* wooden pillow
取 *kido(ri)* lumber dressing
実 *ko(no)mi, ki(no)mi* fruit, nut, berry
沓 *kigutsu* wooden shoes 「leaves
芽 *ko(no)me, ki(no)me* leaf buds; roasted tea
苺 *ki-ichigo* raspberry 「block print
版 *mokuhan* wood-block printing; wood-
版画 *mokuhanga* wood-block print
版摺 *mokuhanzuri* wood engraving
9 食 *mokujiki* fruit diet
香 *kiga, ki(no)ka* smell of fresh wood
屋 *kiya* lumber shed, lumber merchant
拾 *kihiro(i)* gathering wood; wood gatherer
枯 *koga(rashi)* wintry wind
柵 *mokusaku* wooden barricade, fence
盃 *mokuhai* wooden cup
星 *Mokusei* Jupiter
型 *kigata* wooden pattern
造 *mokuzō, kizuku(ri)* sawmilling. *mokuzō* ⌊wooden
造船 *mokuzōsen* wooden ship
炭 *mokutan, kizumi* charcoal
炭画 *mokutanga* charcoal drawing
10 骨 *mokkotsu* wooden frame (of a building)
屑 *kikuzu* shavings, chips
晒 *kizarashi* tree-ripened persimmons
振 *kibu(ri)* tree shape
栓 *mokusen* wooden plug
釘 *kikugi* wooden peg
陰 *kokage* tree shade, bower
剣 *bokken* wooden sword
莓 *ki-ichigo* raspberry
納屋 *kinaya* woodshed
馬 *mokuba* rocking horse 「gym)
馬飛 *mokubato(bi)* horse vaulting (in a
挽 *kobiki* sawyer
挽小屋 *kobikigoya* small sawmill
挽所 *kobikisho* sawmill
11 魚 *mokugyo* wooden temple drum
彫 *kibo(ri), mokuchō* wood carving
深 *kobuka(i)* deep in the forest
理 *mokuri* tree rings; the grain of wood

船 *mokusen* wooden ship
訥 *bokutotsu* rugged honesty
菟 *mimizuku, zuku* horned owl
細工 *kizaiku* woodwork
蛋白石 *mokutampakuseki* wood opal
偶 *deku, mokugū, bokugū* wooden figure, dummy, puppet
偶坊 *dekunobō* puppet (doll); blockhead
[12]間 *ko*(*no*)*ma* thru the trees; among the ⌊trees
場 *kiba* lumberyard
割 *kiwa*(*ri*) allotment of lumber
登 *kinobo*(*ri*) tree climbing
琴 *mokkin* marimba, xylophone
喰虫 *kikui mushi* wood borer
椎 *saizuchi* small wooden mallet ⌈head
椎頭 *saizuchi atama* head like a hammer
遣 *kiyari* workmen's chant; carrying a big load together
遣音頭 *kiyari ondo* workmen's chant
遣唄 *kiyari uta* workmen's chant
葉 *ko*(*no*)*ha, ki*(*no*)*ha* foliage of trees
葉石 *ko*(*no*)*ha ishi* fossil leaf
葉微塵 *ko*(*p*)*pa-mijin* to fragments, into
[13]鼠 *kinezumi* squirrel ⌊atoms
蓮 *mokuren* magnolia ⌈darkness of a forest
暗 *kogura*(*i*) dark (in a forest). *kogu*(*re*)
槌 *kizuchi* mallet, gavel
鉢 *kibachi* wooden bowl
隠 *kogaku*(*re*) hiding behind the trees
靴 *kigutsu* wooden shoes
煉瓦 *kirenga, mokurenga* wooden bricks
賃宿 *kichin-yado* cheap lodging house
賊 *tokusa* horsetail
賊色 *tokusa iro* blackish green
[14]像 *mokuzō* wooden image; figurehead
摺 *kizuri* lath
精 *mokusei* wood alcohol, methyl alcohol;
銃 *mokujū* wooden gun ⌊an echo
蔦 *kizuta* ivy ⌈forest
暮 *kogu*(*re*), *ko*(*no*)*ku*(*re*) darkness of a
瑪瑙 *mokumenō* wood agate
端 *ki*(*no*)*hashi, koppa* block, chip (of wood); worthless thing; worthless person
端微塵 *koppa-mijin* smithereens
管 *mokkan* wooden pipe; bobbin
管楽器 *mokkan gakki* wind instruments
舞 *komai* laths ⌊of wood
舞掻 *komaikaki* lathing; lather
製 *mokusei no* wooden, made of wood
製品 *mokuseihin* woodenware ⌈ton plant
綿 *momen* cotton, cotton cloth. *kiwata* cot-
綿糸 *momen ito* cotton thread ⌈clothes
綿物 *momemmono* cotton goods; cotton
綿織物 *momen orimono* cotton fabrics
[15]履 *pokkuri, bokkuri, bokuri* girls' flat clogs
瘤 *kikobu* knot (on a tree)
膚 *kihada* bark of a tree
槿 *mukuge* rose of Sharon
醂 *kizuwa*(*shi*) ripe persimmon
鋏 *kibasami* pruning shears
箱 *kibako* wooden box ⌈*suru* echo, resound
霊 *kodama* spirit of a tree; echo. *kodama*
質 *mokushitsu* lignum, woody tissue, woody
[17]螺旋 *mokuneji* wood screw ⌊fiber
[18]髄 *mokuzui* pith
叢 *komura* clump of trees; shade of dense
曜 *Mokuyō* Thursday ⌊trees
曜日 *Mokuyōbi* Thursday
[19]蘭 *mokuran* magnolia
[21]蠟 *mokurō* vegetable wax
鐸 *bokutaku* bell with a wooden clapper; a leader; a great teacher

1

本 See 96.

末 See 177.

未 See 179.

B 札 2171 / F940 SATSU paper money; counter for bonds, etc. *fuda* tag, placard; name plate; check; charm, (playing) card; tender, bid.
[2]入 *satsu-i*(*re*) billfold, wallet
[4]止 *fudado*(*me*) full house
[5]付 *fudatsu*(*ki*) branded, marked (with prices); notorious; ex-convict
[7]束 *satsu taba* bundle of paper money
[8]所 *fudasho* amulet issuing office

2

朱 See 184.

权 2172 / F-X Nonstandard for 權 2360.

朶 2173 / F946 DA branch.

B 机 2174 / F946 KI. *tsukue* desk, table.
[3]下 *kika* under the desk
上 *kijō* top of a desk. *kijō no* academic, theoretical, impractical
[4]辺 *kihen* around the table

B 朽 2175 / F946 KYŪ. *ku*(*chiru*) decay, rot; remain in seclusion.

4木 *kuchiki* decayed wood. *kyūboku* decayed wood; an old person ⌈completely decay
8果 *ku(chi)-ha(teru)* rust away, rot away,
10残 *ku(chi)-noko(ru)* decay and remain
12廃 *kyūhai* decay
葉 *kuchiba* dead leaves
16壊 *kyūkai* rotten and easily broken

朴 2176/F945 Boku simple, plain; docile. *hō* P tree used for the legs of clogs.
8直 *bokuchoku* simplicity, naïveté, honesty
念仁 *bokunenjin* a quiet unsociable person;
11訥 *bokutotsu* rugged honesty ⌊blockhead
12歯 *hōba* heavy clogs
16樹 *enoki* nettle tree

3

朽 杇 See 2175.

束 See 196.

条 See 1164.

杢 2177/F951 (国字) Moku woodworker.

杆 2178/F947 **桿** Kan shield; pole.
7状 *kanjō* rodlike
状菌 *kanjōkin* bacillus
11菌 *kankin* bacillus

李 2179/F947 Ri. *sumomo* plum.

杌 2180/F947 Gotsu. Kotsu. *kirikui* stump, stubble.

杠 2181/F951 Kō carry on the shoulder.

杞 2182/F951 **杞** Ko, Ki river willow.
15憂 *kiyū* absurd fear, needless anxiety

杖 2183/F949 Jō. *tsue* staff, cane.
6曳 *tsue (o) hi(ku)* take a walk; travel
9柱 *tsue-hashira* a cane and a pillar; a person one banks on

杙 2184/F950 Yoku. *kui* stake, post, picket, piling.
5打 *kuiu(chi)* driving a pile

杏 2185/F948 Kyō. *anzu* apricot.
3子 *anzu* apricot

杣 2186/F952 (国字) *soma* timber forest; timber, lumber; woodcutter.
2人 *somabito* woodsman, woodcutter
3山 *somayama* timber forest

杓 2187/F949 Shaku ladle, scoop.
3子 *shakushi* dipper, ladle, scoop
子定規 *shakushi-jōgi* hard-and-fast rule, formalism, officialism
4文字 *shamoji* dipper, ladle, scoop

杜 2188/F950 To. Zu. *mori* woods, grove.
4氏 *tōji* saké brewer
8松 *toshō* juniper tree
12絶 *tozetsu* suspension, interruption
14漏 *zurō na* careless, negligent
15撰 *zusan na* slovenly, careless, inaccurate
18鵑 *token, hototogisu* cuckoo
鵑花 *tokenka, satsuki* an early small azalea

材 2189/F948 Zai log; timber, lumber, wood; A material; talent.
4木 *zaimoku* logs, timber, lumber
木屋 *zaimokuya* lumberyard, lumber dealer
木商 *zaimokushō* lumber business; lumber dealer
木問屋 *zaimokudon-ya* lumber wholesaler
木結 *zaimoku musu(bi)* timber hitch
木置場 *zaimoku o(ki)ba* lumberyard
10料 *zairyō* materials; factor; data
13幹 *zaikan* ability
15質 *zaishitsu* lumber quality
器 *zaiki* talent, ability

杉 2190/F947 San. *sugi* cryptomeria, sugi, P Japan cedar.
3下駄 *sugi geta* clogs of cryptomeria wood
4戸 *sugido* cryptomeria door
5生 *sugifu* cryptomeria forest
皮 *sugikawa* cryptomeria bark
7形 *suginari no* cone-shaped
8板 *sugi ita* cryptomeria boards
並木 *sugi namiki* an avenue of cryptomerias
9垣 *sugigaki* a cryptomeria hedge
柱 *sugibashira* cryptomeria posts
11菜 *sugina* horsetail (plant)
12葉 *sugiba* cryptomeria leaves
15箸 *sugibashi* cryptomeria chopsticks

A 村 2191/F948 SON *mura* village, hamlet.
2人 *murabito* villager
八分 *murahachibu* ostracism
4内 *sonnai* within the village
夫子 *sompūshi* village schoolmaster; an educated person in the country
5立 *sonritsu* established by the village
民 *sommin* villagers
芝居 *mura shibai* village show
6老 *sonrō* old people of the village
会 *sonkai* village assembly
名 *sommei* village name
吏 *sonri* village official
有 *son-yū* village ownership
有林 *son-yūrin* village forest
7邑 *son-yū* village
里 *murazato* villages
村 *muramura* villages
社 *sonsha* village shrine
役場 *mura yakuba* village office
8長 *sonchō* village mayor
雨 *murasame* passing shower
制 *sonsei* village organization
舎 *sonsha* a village home
学究 *son gakkyū* village schoolmaster
9政 *sonsei* village government
10翁 *son-ō* an old villager
時雨 *murashigure* autumn shower
11道 *sondō* village road
祭 *mura matsuri* village festival
12税 *sonzei* village tax
童 *sondō* village child
落 *sonraku* village, hamlet
営 *son-ei* operated by the village
費 *sompi* village expenses
14境 *murazakai* edge of the village

4

東 See 213.

果 See 107.

柯 2192/F-X See 柯 2217.

杙 2193/F-X Nonstandard for 材 2189.

B 析 2194/F956 SEKI divide; tear; analyze.

杷 2195/F954 HA a kind of rake.

杼 2196/F954 CHO. *hi* shuttle.

杳 2197/F953 YŌ darkness, indistinctness. *yō to shite* dimly; (not) in the least.

杪 2198/F952 BYŌ. *kozue* twig; treetop.

枘 2199/F958 ZEI. NEI. *hozo* tenon, cog.

枇 2200/F955 BI spoon.
8杷 *biwa* loquat

杵 2201/F954 SHO. SO. *kine* wooden pestle, pounder.
9柄 *kinezuka* long-handled pestle
14歌 *kine uta* grain pounders' song

B 枚 2202/F958 BAI. MAI counter for thin flat things. *-mai* page, leaf (of a book), sheet.
10挙 *maikyo suru* enumerate, mention
13数 *maisū* the number of flat things

杭 2203/F952 KŌ. GŌ. *kui* stake, post, picket, piling.
5打 *kuiu(chi)* driving a pile
打機 *kuiu(chi)ki* pile driver

枉 2204/F955 Ō. *ma(geru)* (see under 曲 103.0). *ma(gete)* forcibly, against one's will.
8易 *ma(ge)-yasu(i)* pliant, supple, flexible
15駕 *ōga* your visit

枠 2205/F959 (国字) *waku* frame, framework; reel, spindle, spool; rim; box (in printing); limit.
4内 *wakunai* within the limits
5外 *wakigai* beyond the limits
7形空中線 *wakugata kūchūsen* loop antenna, frame aerial
11組 *wakugu(mi)* frame, framework, framing

B 杯 2206/F952 盃 HAI cup, glass; toast, congratulatory cup; counter for cupfuls. *sakazuki* wine glass, saké cup; chalice, cup.
8事 *sakazukigoto* drinking feast; exchange of nuptial cups; pledging over winecups
9洗 *haisen* a sink
15盤 *haiban* glasses and plates
盤狼藉 *haiban-rōzeki* disorderly drinking party

枡 2207/F959 **桝** (国字) *masu* measuring box.

5目 *masume* measure
7形 *masugata* square shape
売 *masu-u(ri)* sale by measure
11組 *masugu(mi)* temple bracket assemblies
12落 *masuoto(shi)* rattrap
13掻 *masukaki* stick for leveling the contents of a measuring box

B **枢** 2208/F1008 **樞** Sū. *toboso* pivot; door.

8府 *Sūfu* Privy Council
9要 *sūyō* importance
11務 *sūmu* important business; secret business
密 *sūmitsu* secret government affairs
密院 *Sūmitsuin* Privy Council
密顧問官 *Sūmitsu Komonkan* Privy Counselor
12軸 *sūjiku* pivot; axle; center
軸国 *Sūjikukoku* the Axis Powers
16機 *sūki* important state affairs
機卿 *sūkikyō* (Catholic) cardinal

枕 2209/F956 Chin. *makura* pillow.

2刀 *makuragatana* bedside sword
3上 *chinjō* bedside
4木 *makuragi* railroad tie
辺 *makurabe, chimpen* bedside
元 *makuramoto* bedside
6当 *makura-a(te)* pillow slip
合戦 *makura kassen* pillow fight
10席 *chinseki* pillow and rug; bed; bedroom; night entertainer
捜 *makurasaga(shi)* bedroom theft; bedroom thief
紙 *makuragami* toilet paper
時計 *makuradokei* alarm clock
11探 *makurasaga(shi)*＝枕捜 (see above–10)
掛 *makuraka(ke)* pillow slip
許 *makuramoto* bedside
屏風 *makura byōbu* bed screen
12詞 *makura kotoba* stereotyped epithet
16頭 *chintō* bedside
18覆 *makuraōi* pillow slip

A **林** 2210/F957 Rin. *hayashi* forest.

4木 *rimboku* forest tree
5立 *rinritsu* forest (of chimneys)
8学 *ringaku* forestry
学士 *Ringakushi* Bachelor of Forestry
学者 *ringakusha* forestry expert
学博士 *Ringaku Hakase* a Doctor of Forestry
9政 *rinsei* forestry management
泉 *rinsen* landscape garden
11道 *rindō* forest road
務官 *rimmukan* (government) forester
産 *rinsan* forestry products
産物 *rinsambutsu* forest products
野 *rin-ya* woodland, forests
野庁 *rin-yachō* forestry agency
野局 *rin-yakyoku* forestry bureau
12間 *rinkan* in the forest
間学校 *rinkan gakkō* outdoor school, camping school
13業 *ringyō* forestry
15縁 *rin-en* forest edge
17檎 *ringo* apple
檎酒 *ringoshu* cider
檎酸 *ringosan* malic acid

B **枝** 2211/F959 Shi. Ki. *eda, e* branch, bow, twig, limb.

3川 *edagawa* branch of a river
4切 *edaki(ri)* pruning
5付 *edatsu(ki)*＝*edabu(ri)* 枝振 (see below–10)
7角 *edazuno* antlers
豆 *edamame* green soybeans
折 *edao(ri)* breaking branches (to mark a mountain trail). *shio(ri)* guide book
折戸 *shio(ri)do* garden gate, gate of branches
8垂柳 *shidare yanagi* weeping willow
垂桜 *shidarezakura* weeping cherry
9城 *edajiro* branch castle
柿 *edagaki* persimmons on the branch; persimmons drying on a skewer
枯病 *edaga(re)byō* twig blight
10振 *edabu(ri)* ramifications; shape (of a tree)
11道 *edamichi* branch road
族 *shizoku* tribe; branch family
移 *eda-utsu(ri)* moving from branch to branch
隊 *shitai* detachment (of troops)
接 *edatsugi* cleft grafting
接法 *edatsugihō* cleft grafting
12結 *eda musu(bi)* rolling hitch
葉 *edaha, shiyō* leaves and branches, foliage; ramifications; side issues; digression; minor details
葉末節 *shiyō-massetsu* branches and leaves; unimportant details
13話 *edabanashi* digression
幹 *shikan* trunk and branches
継 *edatsu(gi)* cleft grafting
継法 *edatsu(gi)hō* cleft grafting

B **松** 2212/F954 **枩** Shō. *matsu* pine.

3山 *matsuyama* pine-covered hill
4木 *matsu(no)ki* pine tree
内 *matsu(no)uchi* New Year's season
6虫 *matsumushi* a cricket
竹 *matsutake* New Year's pine-and-bamboo decorations
竹梅 *shō-chiku-bai* pine-bamboo-plum; congratulatory tree decorations

[8]明 *taimatsu* pine torch, torchlight, firebrand
林 *matsubayashi* pine forest
板 *matsuita* pine board
並木 *matsu namiki* an avenue or row of pines
[9]風 *matsukaze, shōfū* wind thru the pines
柏 *shōhaku* pines and oaks; faithfulness
茸 *matsutake, matsudake* a kind of edible mushroom
[10]原 *matsubara* pine grove
脂 *matsuyani, shōshi* rosin, pine resin
根油 *shōkon-yu* turpentine
[11]魚 *katsuo, shōgyo* bonito
毬 *matsukasa* pine cone
[12]傘 *matsukasa* pine cone
葉 *matsuba* pine needles
葉杖 *matsubazue* crutches
[13]飾 *matsukaza(ri)* New Year's pine decorations
[19]韻 *shōin* music of the pines
[21]露 *shōro* a kind of edible mushroom
[22]籟 *shōrai* sighing of the pine trees

A 板 2213/F955 HAN. BAN. *ita* board, plank; planking; plate, sheet; the stage.

[3]子 *itago* a board on which to practice swimming strokes (in water); floor planks in a small Japanese boat
[4]戸 *itado* wooden door
木 *hangi*＝版木 2843.4
切 *itaki(re)* piece of wood, scrap lumber
元 *hammoto* publisher
[5]石 *ita-ishi* slate; slab; flagstone
本 *hampon* a book printed from wood blocks; a printed book
仕切 *itajikiri* wooden partition
付草履 *itazu(ki) zōri* wooden-soled sandals
目 *itame* grain (in wood)
目紙 *itamegami* paper made of several pasted sheets
[6]行 *hankō* wood-block printing
[7]囲 *itagako(i)* board fence, wooden fence
庇 *itabisashi* eaves
床 *itadoko* wooden-floored *tokonoma* alcove
材 *itazai* boards
車輪 *ita sharin* disk wheel
[8]金 *itagane* metal plate, sheet metal; sheet gold or sheet silver. *bankin* sheet gold; sheet silver
画 *hanga* woodcut print
表紙 *itabyōshi* wooden book covers
[9]垣 *itagaki* wooden fence
前 *itamae* a cook
屋 *itaya* a board roof; a house roofed with boards
屋貝 *itayagai* scallop (shell)
屋根 *ita yane* wooden roof
[10]扇 *ita ōgi* fan made of wooden strips
挟 *itabasami* dilemma, predicament
挽 *itahiki* sawing lumber
紙 *itagami* cardboard
書 *bansho* writing on a blackboard
[11]張 *itaba(ri)* boarding; planking; boarded-up place
[12]場 *itaba* a cook (in a restaurant)
塀 *itabei* wooden wall, board fence
割 *itawa(ri)* splitting into boards; boards so formed
葺 *itabuki* roofing of boards
硝子 *ita garasu* plate glass
間 *ita(no)ma* wooden floor
間稼 *ita(no)ma kase(gi)* bathhouse thief
[14]摺 *hansuri* wood-block printing
[15]縁 *itaen* floored veranda
敷 *itaji(ki)* wooden floor; removable slatted floor
[16]橋 *itabashi* wooden bridge
壁 *ita kabe* wooden wall
[19]簾 *itasudare* Venetian blind

5

某 See 2989.

枇 See 2200.

柔 See 3166.

柁 2214/F962 See 舵 3871.

柮 2215/F966 TOTSU to cut; a stump.

柝 2216/F965 TAKU sounding sticks.

柯 2217/F966 柯 KA handle.

柰 2218/F966 See 奈 1174.

柢 2219/F965 TEI root; be founded on.

栃 2220/F968 (国字) *tochi* horse chestnut.

柊 2221/F962 SHU. SHŪ. *hiiragi* holly.

枷 2222/F961 KA. *kase* shackles, irons, handcuffs, bonds.

柚 2223/F965 YU. YŪ. JIKU. *yuzu* citron.

[3]子 *yuzu* citron
子湯 *yuzuyu* hot citron bath
[12]湯 *yuzuyu* hot citron bath

枸 2224 F961 Ku quince tree.
19 櫞酸 *kuensan* citric acid

柑 2225 F963 Kon. Kan citrus fruit; orange.
3 子類 *kōjirui* citrus fruits
16 橘類 *kankitsurui* citrus fruits

柩 2226 F966 Kyū bier. *hitsugi* coffin, hearse, casket.
7 車 *kyūsha* hearse

栂 2227 F968 (国字) *tsuga* hemlock, hemlock-spruce.
8 松 *tsuga-matsu* hemlock-spruce

柾 2228 F968 (国字) *masa*, *masame* straight grain. *masaki* spindle tree.
5 目 *masame* straight grain

柵 2229 F968 = **栅** Saku stockade, fence, palisade. *shigara(mu)* entwine around; check (a current) with a weir. *shigarami* weir.
9 垣 *sakugaki* fence

柏 2230 F963 Haku. Hyaku. *kashiwa* oak.
4 手 *kashiwade* handclapping at a shrine
14 槙 *byakushin* juniper tree
15 餅 *kashiwa mochi* rice cake wrapped in oak leaf

柿 2231 F962 = **杮** Shi. Ji *kaki* persimmon. *kokera* shingle.
6 色 *kaki iro* yellowish brown
8 板 *kokera ita* thin shingles
11 渋 *kakishibu* persimmon juice

柘 2232 F965 Sha, So wild mulberry.
14 榴 *zakuro* pomegranate
榴子 *zakuroshi* garnet
榴石 *zakuro ishi* garnet
榴珠 *zakuroshu* garnet

B **柳** 2233 F967 Ryū. *yanagi* willow.
6 糸 *ryūshi* graceful willow branches
行李 *yanagigōri* wicker trunk
7 条 *ryūjō* willow branches
9 眉 *ryūbi* beautiful eyebrows
13 腰 *yanagigoshi* slender figure, slim waist; ⌈willowy
暗花明 *ryūan-kamei* bright flowers under dark willows; rural springtime; red-light district

B **柄** 2234 F962 = **柄** Hei. *e* handle, crank, grip, hilt, shaft, knob, spoke (of steering wheel on a ship). *gara* pattern, design; build; character, nature. *tsuka* hilt, grip, handle (of a knife).
7 杓 *hishaku* dipper, ladle, scoop
9 染 *garazo(me)* dyeing in designs
11 袋 *tsukabukuro* sword-hilt cover
16 樽 *edaru* fancy 2-handled (saké) barrel

A **査** 2235 F966 Sa investigate.
5 収 *sashū suru* investigate and confiscate
8 定 *satei* assessment; revision; audit (of salaries); investigation and decision
11 問 *samon* inquiry, hearing
問会 *samonkai* court of inquiry
12 証 *sashō* visa; investigation and attestation
13 照 *sashō* a check-up
14 察 *sasatsu* inspection, investigation
15 閲 *saetsu* inspection, examination

A **柱** 2236 F966 = **柱** Chū cylinder, supports for strings on a lute; pillar, post. *hashira* pillar, column, post, pole; support, prop, stay; sole support; counter for Shinto gods. *ji* bridge (of a stringed instrument).
5 石 *chūseki* pillar, mainstay, cornerstone
6 式 *chūshiki* column type
7 体 *chūtai* column shaft
状 *chūjō* columnar, pillar-like
10 時計 *hashiradokei* wall clock
11 廊 *chūrō* colonnade, portico
掛 *hashiraka(ke)* a motto or picture hanging on a post
14 暦 *hashiragoyomi* wall calendar
16 頭 *chūtō* capital of a column

B **架** 2237 F961 Ka frame, mount, stand, support; hang up; shelf. *ka(suru)* build (a bridge), construct. *ka(keru) vt* hang.
3 上 *kajō* on the shelf
工歯 *kakōshi* dental bridge
工義歯 *kakō gishi* dental bridge
5 台 *kadai* abutment; stand, frame, holder
8 空 *kakū* aerial, overhead, trolley; fiction. *kakū no* fanciful, fictitious, Utopian
空索道 *kakū sakudō* aerial cableway
空線 *kakūsen* aerial cable, overhead wire, trolley wire
11 設 *kasetsu* construction, building
道橋 *kadōkyō* road overpass
15 線 *kasen* aerial wiring
16 橋 *kakyō* bridge building ⌈work
橋工事 *kakyō-kōji* bridge-construction

B **枯** 2238 F959 KO. *ka(reru)* wither, die, be dead; age; be seasoned; fog up. *ka(rasu)* kill (vegetation); let dry; season (lumber). *ka(rebamu)* wither. *ka(re)-, ka(ra)-* dead.

3 山 *ka(re)yama* a hill covered with dead vegetation
4 方 *ka(re)gata* time for the leaves to fall
木 *ka(re)ki, ka(ra)ki, koboku* dead tree
5 生 *ka(re)fu* area of dead grass
芝 *ka(re) shiba* dry lawn, dry grass
6 色 *ka(re) iro* dead color
死 *koshi* withering, dying
亙 *ka(re)-wata(ru)* die completely, die all over the area
7 花 *ka(re)bana* faded flowers
8 枝 *ka(re)eda, ka(ra)eda, ka(re)-e* dead branch
林 *korin* the bare woods in winter
果 *ka(re)-ha(teru)* waste away
9 枯 *ka(re)ga(re)* the dying of the leaves, beginning to wither
草 *ka(re)gusa, ka(re)kusa* dry grass, hay
10 骨 *kokotsu* decomposed bones; buried person; deceased person
凋 *kochō suru* wither, decay
11 淡 *kotan* elegant simplicity
渇 *kokatsu suru* dry up; be exhausted; become poverty-stricken
野 *ka(re)no* desolate field
12 葉 *ka(re)ha, ka(re)ba, koyō* dead leaf
14 増 *ka(re)-masa(ru)* go on withering
竭 *koketsu suru* dry up
15 槁 *kokō* withering, emaciation
20 礬 *kohan* burnt alum
21 露柿 *korogaki* dried persimmons

A **栄 榮** 2239 F998 EI prosperity, glory, splendor, honor. *saka(eru)* prosper, flourish, thrive. *ha(eru)* shine, be brilliant; look attractive. *saka(e)* glory, prosperity. *hae* glory. *hae(aru)* glorious.

4 化 *eika suru* glorify
6 行 *saka(e)-yu(ku)* become more and more prosperous or glorious
光 *eikō* glory
7 位 *ei-i* exalted position
利 *eiri* wealth and fame
8 典 *eiten* honors; ceremony, exercises
9 冠 *eikan* laurels, garland
枯 *eiko* ups and downs, rise and fall, vicissitudes
枯盛衰 *eiko seisui* prosperity and decline, vicissitudes of fortune
10 進 *eishin* promotion, advancement
称 *eishō* honorable title
華 *eiga* glory, splendor, prosperity; luxury; majesty
辱 *eijoku* honor and disgrace; prestige, dignity, honor, reputation
11 達 *eitatsu* fame, distinction, rise, advancement
転 *eiten* promotion
12 落 *eiraku* flourishing and declining
13 誉 *eiyo* honor, fame, glory
15 養 *eiyō* nutrition, nourishment, sustenance
養士 *eiyōshi* nutritionist
養分 *eiyōbun* nutrient
養不足 *eiyō fusoku* undernourishment, malnutrition
養不良 *eiyō furyō* undernourishment, malnutrition
養生理学 *eiyō seirigaku* nutritional physiology
養失調 *eiyō shitchō* undernourishment, malnutrition
養価 *eiyōka* food value
養物 *eiyōbutsu* nutriment, nourishing food
養学 *eiyōgaku* dietetics
養素 *eiyōso* nutrient
養障害 *eiyō shōgai* nutritional disorder
17 爵 *eishaku* peerage, title
18 曜 *eyō, eiyō* luxury, splendor, prosperity
20 耀 *eyō, eiyō* luxury, splendor, prosperity

B **染** 2240 F963 SEN. *so(mu), so(maru)* be dyed, be imbued with, be tainted with. *so(meru)* dye, color, paint. *shi(miru)* soak in, permeate, infiltrate; pierce (as a wind); be imbued with, be influenced by; smart; be sensitive to pain. *shi(mi)* stain, blot, spot, smudge. *so(me)* dyeing, printing. *-zo(me)* dyed.

2 入 *shi(mi)-i(ru)=shi(mi)-ko(mu)* 染込 (see below–4)
3 工 *senkō* dyer
上 *so(me)-a(garu)* be completely dyed. *so(me)-a(geru)* finish dyeing
4 方 *so(me)kata* dyeing process
込 *so(me)-ko(mu)* dye in designs. *shi(mi)-ko(mu)* soak into, permeate, infiltrate; be impressed with
分 *so(me)-wa(keru)* dye in different colors
毛 *semmō* dyeing the hair
毛剤 *semmōzai* hair dye
5 付 *shi(mi)-tsu(ku)* be dyed in deeply, be stained. *so(me)-tsu(keru)* dye in (patterns)
出 *so(me)-da(su)* dye (patterns)
6 糸 *so(me) ito* dyed thread
返 *so(me)-kae(su)* redye. *shi(mi)-kae(ru)=shi(mi)-ko(mu)* 染込 (see above–4)
地 *so(me)ji* dyed cloth
色 *senshoku* dyeing
色体 *senshokutai* chromosome
7 抜 *so(me)-nu(ku)* dye in the grain. *shi(mi)-nu(ki)* removal of stains
更 *so(me)-kae(ru)* redye
8 直 *so(me)-nao(su)* redye
物 *somemono* dyeing; dyed goods
物屋 *somemonoya* dyer
物師 *somemonoshi* dyer

⁹革 *so(me)kawa* dyed leather
通 *shi(mi)-tō(ru)* soak thru, penetrate, permeate, infiltrate
柄 *so(me)gara* dyed designs
型 *so(me)gata* dyed pattern
染 *shimijimi*＝泌泌 2522.8
飛白 *so(me)gasuri* a cotton cloth with printed patterns
10料 *senryō* dyes, dyestuffs
粉 *so(me)ko* dyestuff
12渡 *shi(mi)-wata(ru)* penetrate, spread, pervade
着 *shi(mi)-tsu(ku)* be deeply dyed
替 *so(me)ka(e)* redyeing
筆 *sempitsu* writing; painting
筆料 *sempitsuryō* writing fee
14髪剤 *sempatsuzai* hair dye
模様 *so(me) moyō* printed pattern
16薬 *so(me)gusuri* dye, dyestuff
18織 *senshoku* dyeing and weaving

A **相** 2241/F1319 Sō aspect, phase, physiognomy. SHŌ minister of state, councilor. *ai-* together, each other; mutually, reciprocally; fellow-; emphatic verbal prefix. 【目】

⁴方 *sōhō*＝双方 859.4
反 *aihan suru* be contrary to, disagree with
引 *aibi(ki) suru* pull apart, pull against each other
手 *aite* companion, mate, date, partner; the other party, opponent, adversary; object
手方 *aitekata* the other party, opponent
手役 *aiteyaku* partner, opposite player or actor, companion
手国 *aitekoku* the country we are dealing with
手取 *aitedo(ru)* take on (opponents); sue
互 *sōgo* mutual, reciprocal. *aitagai ni* mutually, each other, one another
互安全保障 *sōgo anzen hoshō* mutual security
互会社 *sōgogaisha* mutual insurance company
互作用 *sōgo sayō* reciprocal action, interaction
互扶助 *sōgo fujo* mutual aid
互条約 *sōgo jōyaku* bilateral treaty, treaty of reciprocity
互依存 *sōgo ison* interdependence
互保険会社 *sōgo hokengaisha* mutual insurance company
互組合 *sōgo kumiai* co-operative society, mutual-aid association
互援助 *sōgo enjo* mutual assistance
互援助条約 *sōgo enjo jōyaku* mutual-assistance treaty
互貿易 *sōgo bōeki* mutual trade
互貯蓄銀行 *sōgo chochiku ginkō* mutual savings bank
互銀行 *sōgo ginkō* mutual-financing bank
互関係 *sōgo kankei* reciprocity, interrelationship
⁵仕 *aishi* companion, associate
打 *aiu(chi)* striking each other simultaneously
加平均 *sōka heikin* arithmetical mean
生 *aioi* growing up together
生松 *aioi (no) matsu* twin pines; double pine
⁶老 *aio(i)* a couple growing older together
成 *aina(ru)* emphatic for *na(ru)* 成 (see under 1799.0)
曳 *aibiki* lovers' secret meeting, a date
次 *aitsu(gu)* follow in succession. *aitsu(ide)* in succession
好 *sōkō, sōgō* looks, features, countenance
交 *ai-maji(waru)* associate with. *tsuru(mu)* mate, copulate
会 *aikai suru* assemble
共 *aitomo ni* together
年 *aidoshi* the same age
争 *aiaraso(u)* quarrel, dispute
合傘 *aia(i)gasa de* under the same umbrella
似 *sōji* resemblance, similarity, analogy
似形 *sōjikei* similar figures (in math)
似点 *sōjiten* points of agreement
伝 *sōden* inheritance, heirship; conferring of priestly orders
伝不動産 *sōden fudōsan* family estate
伝動産 *sōden dōsan* heirloom
当 *sōtō na* suitable, proper, corresponding, reasonable; respectable; sufficient, adequate, passable. *sōtō suru* befit, be worthy of; deserve, merit; correspond to; be proportionate to
当品 *sōtōhin* articles of similar value
当数 *sōtōsū* quite a number
当欄 *sōtōran* corresponding column
⁷見 *sōmi* physiognomist
図 *aihaka(ru)* counsel together. *aizu* sign, signal
床 *aidoko* sleeping in the same room
応 *fusawa(shii)* suitable, becoming, fitting, worthy of, proper, adequate. appropriate. *sōō* suitability, fitness
励 *aihage(mu)* encourage each other
伴 *aitomona(u)* accompany. *shōban* participation
作 *aisaku* intercrop
住 *aizu(mi)* living together
役 *aiyaku* colleague
扶 *aitasu(keru)* help each other
克 *sōkoku* rivalry
弟子 *aideshi* fellow pupil, fellow apprentice
身互 *aimitaga(i)* mutual assistance
対 *aitai suru* face each other, lie opposite. *sōtai* relativity, reciprocity, symmetry. *aitai de* personally, directly
対立 *aitairitsu suru* oppose; face each other
対尽 *aitaizu(ku) de* by common consent

対的 *sōtaiteki* relative, reciprocal
対性 *sōtaisei* relativity
対性原理 *sōtaisei genri* theory of relativity
対原理 *sōtai genri* theory of relativity
対湿度 *sōtai shitsudo* relative humidity
対義務 *sōtai gimu* reciprocal obligations
8 退 *aibiki suru* mutually retreat
性 *aishō* affinity, compatibility
並 *ainara(bu)* line up with
定 *aisada(meru)* ordain, decide on
9 連 *aitsurana(ru)* be joined
俟 *aima(tte)* coupled with, in co-operation with
持 *aimo(chi)* co-operation, interdependence, mutual help; common possession; sharing (expenses)
計 *aihaka(ru)* plan together
客 *aikyaku* roommate; fellow passenger; one sharing a seat
乗 *aino(ri)* riding together. *sōjō* multiplication
変 *aikawa(razu)* as usual
剋 *sōkoku* rivalry
前後 *aizengo* about the same time
相傘 *aiaigasa de* under the same umbrella
思 *sōshi* mutual love
思仲 *sōshi (no) naka* courtship
思相愛 *sōshi-sōai* mutual love
10 孫 *aimago* persons with same grandparents
称 *sōshō* symmetry
討 *aiu(chi)* two or more pouncing on one enemy
殺 *sōsatsu, sōsai* offset, cancellation (of obligations)
容 *ai-i(renai)* contrary, incompatible
11 惚 *aibore* mutual love
接 *aises(suru)* meet, get together
済 *aisu(mimasen)* I'm sorry.
添 *aiso(u)* marry and live together
宿 *aiyado(ri), aiyado* lodging together
異 *sōi*＝相違 (see below–11)
異点 *sōiten* point of difference
違 *sōi* difference, disparity, gap, discrepancy, disagreement, variation, contrast
違点 *sōiten* point of difference
違無 *sōinai* no doubt that. *sōina(ku)* without fail, surely
12 間 *aima* interval; leisure. *ai(no)ma* a room between; low central room in certain shrines
婿 *aimuko* husbands of sisters
棒 *aibō* pal, partner, accomplice
結 *aimusu(bu)* join together with
傘 *aigasa de* under the same umbrella
喜 *aiyoroko(bu)* rejoice together
等 *sōtō* equality
集 *aiatsu(maru), aitsudo(u) vi* gather together
場 *sōba* market price; speculation; estimation
場師 *sōbashi* speculator, operator, plunger
13 嫁 *aiyome* women whose husbands are brothers
携 *aitazusa(ete)* together with, hand-in-hand, in couples
煌 *aikira(meku)* flash together
継 *aitsu(gu)* continue
触 *aifu(reru)* touch each other
戦 *aitataka(u)* fight
愛 *sōai* mutual love
槌 *aizuchi, ai(no)tsuchi* chiming in with another's conversation
槌打 *aizuchi (o) u(tsu)* chime in with, echo (someone)
続 *sōzoku* succession, inheritance, descent
続人 *sōzokunin* heir
続争 *sōzoku araso(i)* succession quarrels
続者 *sōzokusha* heir
続財産 *sōzoku zaisan* inheritance
続税 *sōzokuzei* inheritance tax
続権 *sōzokuken* heirship, right of inheritance
14 構 *aikama(ete)* certainly, beyond doubt
貌 *sōbō* features, looks, physiognomy
関 *sōkan* mutual relationship, interdependence
関的 *sōkanteki* correlative
関係数 *sōkan keisū* coefficient of correlation
関関係 *sōkan kankei* reciprocity, interrelation, correlation
15 輪 *sōrin* pagoda finial
撃 *aiu(chi)* striking each other simultaneously
器 *shōki* capacity for premiership
撲 *sumō* wrestling; wrestling match; wrestler
撲取 *sumōto(ri)* wrestler
談 *sōdan* consultation, conversation, talk; bargain; offer, proposal; agreement, arrangement. *sōdan(zuku)* mutual agreement
談会 *sōdankai* consultation, conference
談役 *sōdan-yaku* counselor, consultant
談所 *sōdanjo* information bureau, consultation bureau
談相手 *sōdan aite* adviser, confidant
16 謀 *aihaka(ru)* plan together; plot together
整 *aitotono(u)* be prepared, be arranged. *aitotono(eru)* prepare, arrange
17 償 *aitsuguna(u)* recompense each other
19 識 *sōshiki* acquaintance

— 6 —

柳 See 2233.
栗 See 4275.
桑 See 864.
案 See 1308.

栽 See 781.

桝 2242/F-X See **枡** 2207.

桧 Nonstandard for **檜** 2388.

栞 2243/F969 KAN. *shiori* bookmark; guidebook.

框 2244/F975 KYŌ. *kamachi* frame, framework.

桎 2245/F975 SHITSU fetters.
11梏 *shikkoku* fetters, bonds, yoke

桛 2246/F977 (国字) *kase* reel, hank, skein.
6糸 *kase ito* reeled thread

栓 2247/F968 SEN bolt, stopper, cork, plug, ear plug, bung, faucet, peg.
7抜 *sennu(ki)* corkscrew

栖 2248/F968 SEI. *su* (see under 巣 141.0).
10息 *seisoku suru* inhabit, live in, lodge in

桐 2249/F975 TŌ. *kiri* the paulownia tree.
3下駄 *kiri geta* clogs of paulownia wood
8油 *kiriyu, kiri abura, tōyu* wood oil, tung oil, nut oil, China wood oil
18簞笥 *kiri tansu* chest of drawers of paulownia wood

桁 2250/F973 KŌ. *keta* beam, girder; spar, yard; unit or column (in figures).
5外 *ketahazu(re)* wide difference; extraordinary ⌈wide difference
11違 *ketachiga(i)* off on the decimal point;
16橋 *ketahashi* girder bridge

柴 2251/F967 SHI. SAI. *shiba* brushwood, firewood.
4木 *shibaki* brushwood ⌈gatherer
刈 *shibaka(ri)* gathering firewood; firewood
8門 *saimon* brushwood gate, humble cottage
10栗 *shibaguri* small chestnut
11笛 *shibabue* leaf flute

P **桟** 2252/F986 **棧** SAN crosspiece, cleat, frame, door bolt; shelf; jetty; suspension bridge.
5瓦 *sangawara* pantile, common roof tile
10俵 *sandawara* round straw cover
俵法師 *sandawarabōshi* round straw cover
11道 *sandō* plank road
15敷 *sajiki* reviewing stand, box, gallery
16橋 *sambashi* wharf, jetty. *sankyō* wharf; bridge

桂 2253/F973 KEI. *katsura* Judas tree, katsura tree, cinnamon tree.
5皮 *keihi* cassia bark, cinnamon
皮油 *keihiyu* cinnamon oil
7男 *katsurao, katsura otoko* man in the moon
9冠 *keikan* crown of laurel
冠詩人 *keikan shijin* poet laureate
11庵 *keian* servants' registry

B **核** 2254/F971 **核** KAKU nucleus, core, seed, kernel. *kaku no* nuclear. *sane* fruit stone, kernel, nucleus.
4心 *kakushin* core, kernel
反応 *kaku hannō* nuclear reaction
分裂 *kaku bunretsu* nuclear fission ⌈terials
分裂質 *kaku bunretsushitsu* fissionable ma-
7兵器 *kaku heiki* nuclear weapons
8武装 *kaku busō* nuclear arms
実験 *kaku jikken* nuclear experiments
物理学 *kaku butsurigaku* nuclear physics
12弾頭 *kaku dantō* nuclear warhead

B **桃** 2255/F974 TŌ. *momo* peach.
3山 *Momoyama* era (1576–1598)
6色 *momo iro* rose, pink
色遊戯 *momo-iro yūgi* love affair
色雑誌 *momo-iro zasshi* yellow journal
7花 *tōka* peach blossom
13園 *momozono* peach orchard
節句 *Momo (no) Sekku* the Doll Festival
源 *tōgen*＝*tōgenkyō* 桃源境 (see below–13)
源郷 *tōgenkyō*＝桃源境 (see below–13)
源境 *tōgenkyō* quiet country garden; heaven on earth; Shangri-La

B **桜** 2256/F1023 **櫻** Ō. *sakura* flowering cherry; cherry blossoms; pink color; horse meat.
4月 *sakurazuki* 3rd lunar month
木 *sakuragi* cherry tree
6肉 *sakura niku* horse meat
色 *sakura iro* the color of cherry blossoms; pink, cerise
7坊 *sakurambō* edible cherry
花 *ōka, sakurabana* cherry-blossom season
9狩 *sakuraga(ri)* looking for cherry blossoms
草 *sakurasō* primrose
10時 *sakuradoki* cherry-blossom season

桃 ***sakurambō, ōtō*** edible cherry
紙 ***sakuragami*** handkerchief paper, toilet
12 湯 ***sakurayu*** cherry-blossom drink ⌊paper
雲 ***ōun*** clouds of cherry blossoms
14 漬 ***sakurazuke*** pickled cherry blossoms
16 樹 ***ōju*** cherry tree

A **株** 2257 / F970 SHU. ***kabu*** stump; shares, stocks; connections; business; counter for small plants.

4 分 ***kabuwa(ke)*** dividing roots
5 主 ***kabunushi*** shareholder ⌈general meeting
主総会 ***kabunushi sōkai*** stockholders'
6 式 ***kabushiki*** shares, stocks
式市場 ***kabushiki shijō*** stock market
式会社 ***kabushiki gaisha*** joint-stock corporation
式仲買 ***kabushiki nakagai*** stock brokerage
式仲買人 ***kabushiki nakagainin*** stockbroker
式合資会社 ***kabushiki gōshi gaisha*** joint-stock limited partnership ⌈change
式取引所 ***kabushiki torihikijo*** stock ex-
式相場 ***kabushiki sōba*** stock quotations
8 金 ***kabukin*** a share, stock
価 ***kabuka*** price of stocks
券 ***kabuken*** stock certificate
9 屋 ***kabuya*** stockbroker
11 張 ***kabuha(ri)*** a root sprouting profusely

B **梅** 2258 / F978 **梅** BAI. ***ume*** plum, plum tree.

3 干 ***umeboshi*** pickled plums
7 見 ***umemi*** plum-blossom viewing
花 ***baika*** plum blossoms
8 枝 ***ume(ga)e*** plum branch
林 ***bairin*** plum orchard
毒 ***baidoku*** syphilis
毒性 ***baidokusei*** syphilitic
雨 ***baiu, tsuyu*** rainy season ⌈season
雨明 ***tsuyua(ke), baiua(ke)*** end of the rainy
雨型 ***tsuyugata*** rainy-season meteorological
雨時 ***tsuyudoki*** rainy season ⌊conditions
雨晴 ***tsuyuba(re)*** end of the rainy season
9 香 ***ume(ga)ka*** plum-blossom fragrance
畑 ***umebatake*** plum orchard
10 酒 ***umeshu, baishu*** plum brandy
12 酢 ***umezu*** plum juice, plum vinegar
13 園 ***baien*** plum orchard
14 暦 ***umegoyomi*** harbingers of spring (plum
漬 ***umezuke*** pickled plums ⌊blossoms)

A **格** 2259 / F972 KŌ. KAKU status, rank; capacity, character; standard; a rule; a case (in law); case (in grammar).

3 下 ***kakusa(ge)*** demotion, downgrading
上 ***kakua(ge)*** status elevation
子 ***kōshi*** lattice, coffer, grating, fretwork
子戸 ***kōshido*** lattice door
子窓 ***kōshi mado*** latticed window
子細工 ***kōshizaiku*** latticework
子縞 ***kōshijima*** checkered pattern
子織 ***kōshio(ri)*** checkered-patterned cloth
4 天井 ***gōtenjō*** coffered ceiling
5 付 ***kakuzu(ke), kakutsu(ke)*** rating, classification, allocation, conditioning
外 ***kakuhazu(re)*** inferior, ungraded (goods). ***kakugai*** special, exceptional
外品 ***kakugaihin*** inferior goods
6 好 ***kakkō*** = 恰好 1675.6 ⌈rules of etiquette
式 ***kakushiki*** status, rank, social standing;
式張 ***kakushikiba(ru)*** be overly formal
安 ***kakuyasu na*** cheap, reasonable
安品 ***kakuyasuhin*** bargain goods
7 言 ***kakugen*** maxim, proverb
別 ***kakubetsu ni*** especially, exceptionally
8 例 ***kakurei*** precedent; ruling
9 段 ***kakudan no*** special, exceptional, remarkable, appreciable
10 差 ***kakusa*** difference in quality
納 ***kakunō*** housing for equipment or ma-
納庫 ***kakunōko*** hangar ⌊chines
12 幅 ***kappuku*** build, physique
筆 ***kakuhitsu suru*** conclude writing
15 調 ***kakuchō*** the style and meter of a poem
18 闘 ***kakutō*** fist fight; scuffle; wrestling

A **校** 2260 / F969 **校** KYŌ. KŌ school; (printing) proof; comparison; correction; investigation. ***kō(su)*** test, correct, proofread. ***-kō*** school; proof.

2 了 ***kōryō, kyōryō*** proofreading completed
4 内 ***kōnai*** school grounds
友 ***kōyū*** schoolmate, alumnus
友会 ***kōyūkai*** alumni association
5 主 ***kōshu*** school owner
本 ***kōhon*** perfected text
外 ***kōgai*** outside the school; extension
外生 ***kōgaisei*** extension student ⌈ing
外教授 ***kōgai kyōju*** extra-curricular teach-
正 ***kōsei*** proofreading
正刷 ***kōseizu(ri)*** galley proofs
正係 ***kōseigakari*** proofreader
正済 ***kōseizu(mi)*** proof OK
6 合 ***kyōgō*** proofreading
7 医 ***kōi*** school doctor
8 長 ***kōchō*** principal, schoolmaster, rector
門 ***kōmon*** school gate
服 ***kōfuku*** school uniform
舎 ***kōsha*** school building
定 ***kōtei*** revision
具 ***kōgu*** school equipment

9 風 *kōfū* school spirit; school customs
紀 *kōki* school rules
則 *kōsoku* school regulations
訂 *kōtei* revision
訂版 *kōteiban* revised edition
10 庭 *kōtei* campus, school playground
訓 *kōkun* school rules; school mottos
倉 *azekura* ancient log cabin
書 *kōsho* correcting the characters in books; ⌊collating old books
11 務 *kōmu* school affairs
勘 *kōkan suru* compare and consider, compare with the original and correct
章 *kōshō* school pin
12 葬 *kōsō* school funeral
14 僕 *kōboku* school janitor
旗 *kōki* school flag
歌 *kōka* school song
15 閲 *kōetsu* revision

A 根 2261/F971 KON root (of a plant); root, radical (in science and math.); stamina. *ne* root; base (of a hill); head (of a boil); origin; foundation; peak. *ne(kosogi)*, *ne(kosoge)* all, completely, thoroly. *ne(kkara)* (not) at all, (not) in the least.

3 子 *nekko* root, stump, stub
上 *nea(gari)* roots above ground
4 方 *nekata* the lower part; the root
比 *konkura(be)* endurance contest
引 *nebi(ki)* uprooting; redemption, ransom
元 *kongen* root, origin, cause, source. *nemoto* part near the root; base, bottom
分 *newa(ke)* dividing plants (roots)
太 *neda* joints, sills. *nebuto* (skin) boil
切 *negi(ri)* radical cure; excavation
切虫 *neki(ri)mushi* cutworm
切葉切 *neki(ri)-haki(ri)* everything; completely
5 生 *konjō* disposition, nature
付 *nezu(ku)*, *netsu(ku)* take root. *netsu(ke)* toggle for suspending a pouch from belt
本 *kompon* root, origin, cause; basis. *nemoto* = *kongen* 根元 (see above–4)
本主義 *kompon shugi* fundamentalism
本主義者 *kompon shugisha* fundamentalist
本法 *komponhō* fundamental law ⌈drastic
本的 *komponteki na* fundamental, basic,
6 回 *nemawa(ri)* circumference of the root. *nemawa(shi)* digging around the root
扱 *neko(gi)* uprooting
号 *kongō* radical sign (in math)
気 *konki* patience, perseverance, energy
気負 *konkima(ke)* being overcome in perseverance
8 底 *kontei* root; basis, foundation
治 *konchi*, *konji* complete cure
肥 *negoe* initial fertilizer, root fertilizer
限 *konkagi(ri)* with all one's might
茎 *konkei* root stalk, rhizome
性 *konjō* disposition, nature
性骨 *konjōbone* disposition, nature
拠 *konkyo* basis, foundation; authority
拠地 *konkyochi* base, headquarters
9 城 *nejiro* stronghold, citadel; headquarters, base of operations
持 *ne (ni) mo(tsu)* resent, bear a grudge
柢 *kontei* root; basis, foundation
負 *komma(ke)* losing stamina; losing in a test of strength; losing patience
10 原 *kongen* root, origin, cause
庭 *kontei* root, basis, foundation
差 *ne-za(su)* take root; originate in; show signs of. *neza(shi)* taking root; breeding, birth
11 問 *nedo(i) suru* be inquisitive
強 *nezuyo(i)* firmly rooted; deep-seated. *nezuyo(ku)* firmly, steadfastly, tenaciously
張 *neba(ri)* deep spreading roots
接 *netsugi* root grafting
深 *nebuka(i)* deep-rooted, ingrained
雪 *neyuki* lingering snow
基 *konki* origin, cause
菜類 *konsairui* root crops ⌈completely
掘葉掘 *neho(ri)-haho(ri)* inquisitively;
12 絶 *konzetsu*, *nedaya(shi)* eradication
柢 *kontei* = 根底 (see above–8)
葉 *kon-yō* leaves near the base of a plant
葉無 *ne (mo) ha (mo) na(i)* without foundation ⌈an arrowhead; groundless
無 *nena(shi)* without root; an arrow without
無言 *nena(shi)goto* unfounded report
無草 *nena(shi)gusa* duckweed; something unsettled
13 源 *kongen* root, origin, cause, source
継 *netsu(gi)* splicing rotten underpinning
際 *negiwa* root of a tree
幹 *konkan* root and trunk; basis; nucleus; keynote
14 精 *konjō* disposition, nature
15 瘤 *konryū* root tubercles
締 *neji(me)* tamping down the soil around the roots
18 覆 *neōi* mulch
20 競 *konkura(be)* endurance contest

7

梵 See 140.

梟 See 235.

梻 See 枡 2207.

梅 2262/F978 See 梅 2258.

條 See 条 1164.

梠 Nonstandard for 椆 2394.

梏 2263/F979 KOKU manacles.

械 2264/F982 KAI fetters; machine; instrument. A

桷 2265/F977 KAKU rafter.

梃 2266/F978 CHŌ. TEI. *teko* lever.

梻 2267/F983 (国字) *shikimi* (see under 樒 2354.0).

梓 2268/F979 SHI. *azusa* catalpa tree.

梮 2269/F982 KIKU. *kanjiki* snowshoes.

桴 2270/F977 FU. *bachi* drumstick. *ikada* raft.

渠 2271/F1134 KYO ditch, canal, dock. [水]

14魁 *kyokai* ringleader, chief, boss

梔 2272/F979 SHI gardenia

3子 *kuchinashi* gardenia

梭 2273/F982 SA. *hi* shuttle.

11魚 *kamasu* barracuda

桶 2274/F977 YŌ, TŌ. *oke* tub, bucket.

9屋 *okeya* cooper

梨 2275/F981 RI. *nashi* pear; pear tree.

13園 *rien* theatrical world; pear orchard

20礫 *nashi (no) tsubute* no communication

梢 2276/F981 SHŌ. *kozue* twig; treetop.

12葉 *ureba* the end leaves

梱 2277/F982 梱 KON. *kō(ru)* pack, tie up. *kōri* bale (of silk or thread). *kori* bale, pack, package.

5包 *kompō* packing, crating; package

梗 2278/F979 KŌ, KYŌ for the most part; close up.

13塞 *kōso(ku)* stoppage, blocking; infarction; (money) stringency

14概 *kōgai* outline, summary

梶 2279/F983 BI. *kaji* oar, sculling oar, shaft.

4木 *kaji(no)ki* paper mulberry

12棒 *kajibō* (wagon) shafts

桿 2280/F977/F947 See 杆 2178.

梁 2281/F977 RYŌ bridge beams. *hari, utsubari, uchibari* beam, girder. *yana* weir, fish trap, fish pond.

3山泊 *ryōzampaku* center of operations; gathering of kindred spirits

上君子 *ryōjō (no) kunshi* robber; rat

4木 *ryōboku* beam

7材 *harizai* beam, girder

12間 *harima* a span (in construction)

梳 2282/F982 SO. *su(ku)* comb (the hair); card (wool). *kushikezu(ru)* comb.

3子 *sukiko* hairdresser's assistant

4手 *sukite* hairdresser's assistant

毛 *sukige* combings

8油 *sukiabura* pomade

取 *su(ki)-to(ru)* comb (the hair) out clean

14綿 *sukimen* cotton carding

19櫛 *sukigushi* fine-toothed comb

梯 2283/F982 TEI. *hashigo* ladder, stairs; insatiable drinking.

3子 *hashigo, teishi* ladder, stairs; insatiable drinking

子形 *hashigogata* ladder shape

子段 *hashigodan* step, stair, stairway

子乗 *hashigono(ri)* ladder stunts

子酒 *hashigozake* insatiable drinking; heavy drinker

子飲 *hashigono(mi)* insatiable drinking; heavy drinker

子登 *hashigonobo(ri)* ladder climbing; by leaps and bounds

4尺 *teishaku* map scale

7状 *teijō* echelon formation; trapezoid

形 *hashigogata, teikei* echelon formation; trapezoid

9陣 *teijin* echelon

11隊 *teitai* echelon

—— 8 ——

棘 See 238.

4 心忄⺌戈戸手扌支攴攵文斗斤方无日曰月[木]8 欠止歹殳毋比毛氏气水氵氺火灬爪爫父爻爿丬片牙牛犬犭

棗 See 116.

楮 See 2311.

棧 2284 / F986 See **栈** 2252.

棱 2285 / F987 RYŌ, RŌ sharp place.

椒 2286 / F989 SHŌ mountain ash.

椀 2287 / F988 WAN wooden bowl, lacquered bowl.

椚 2288 / F990 (国字) *kunugi* a kind of oak used for charcoal.

棍 2289 / F984 KON a cane.

12 棒 *kombō* club, nightstick; lever

椅 2290 / F988 I chair.

3 子 *isu* chair, seat, couch; office, position

棹 2291 / F988 TŌ. *sao* (see under 竿 3369.0). *saosa(su)* pole (a boat).

14 歌 *tōka* boat song, boatmen's song

椰 2292 / F990 YA coconut tree.

3 子 *yashi* palm tree, coconut tree
子油 *yashiyu* palm oil, coconut oil

棕 2293 / F985 / F990 **椶** SHU the hemp palm.

19 櫚 *shuro* the hemp palm
櫚油 *shuroyu* palm oil

棋 2294 / F984 **碁** KI, GI Japanese chess.
B
3 士 *kishi* a chess player
7 局 *kikyoku* chess game; chessboard
9 客 *kikyaku, kikaku* chess player
15 敵 *kiteki* one's opponent in a chess game

棉 2295 / F984 MEN *wata* cotton.

7 花 *menka* raw cotton
18 織機 *men-o(ri)ki* cotton loom

椎 2296 / F989 TSUI. *tsuchi* hammer, mallet. *shii* an oak.

9 茸 *shiitake* a kind of edible mushroom
10 骨 *tsuikotsu* vertebra

棲 2297 / F987 SEI. *su(mu)* live, dwell.

5 処 *sumika* dwelling; nest; den (of robbers)
10 息 *seisoku suru* inhabit, live in, lodge in
息地 *seisokuchi* habitat

棺 2298 / F988 KAN *hitsugi* casket, coffin.
B
7 車 *kansha* hearse
9 舁 *kankaki* pallbearer
11 側 *kansoku ni* beside the coffin
掛 *kanka(ke)* coffin drape, pall
桶 *kan oke* casket, coffin

棟 2299 / F986 TŌ. *mune* ridge, ridgepole.

3 上 *munea(ge)* ridgepole raising
上式 *munea(ge) shiki* ridgepole-raising ceremony
4 木 *munagi* ridgepole
5 瓦 *munegawara* ridge tile
11 梁 *tōryō* chief support, pillar (in a nation); chief, leader, foreman
12 割長屋 *munewa(ri) nagaya* duplex; a long partitioned house

棚 2300 / F985 HŌ. BYŌ. *tana* shelf, ledge, rack, mount, mantelpiece; trellis, lattice.

3 上 *tana-a(ge) suru* shelve, pigeonhole, table (a motion), sidetrack
4 引 *tanabi(ku)* trail, hang over (fog or smoke)
7 状 *hōjō* shelf formation
承 *tana-u(ke)* shelf bracket
牡丹 *tanabota* windfall
10 晒 *tanazarashi* shopworn stock

森 2301 / F987 SHIN. *mori* woods, grove.
A
8 林 *shinrin* forest, wood
林学 *shinringaku* forestry
林限界 *shinrin genkai* timber line
林帯 *shinrintai* forest zone
林開墾 *shinrin kaikon* clearing a forest
林愛護 *shinrin aigo* forest conservation
12 閑 *shinkan to shita* silent, hushed, deserted
森 *shinshin* deeply forested; towering
17 厳 *shingen na* solemn, grave, awe-inspiring
19 羅 *shinra* luxurious growth; crowds of people
羅万象 *shinra-banshō* all creation, the universe

棒 2302 / F985 BŌ stick, cane, rod, pole, stake, pile, club, bar; line, dash.
B
3 口紅 *bō kuchibeni* lipstick

4引 bōbi(ki) cancellation, writing off
切 bōki(re) a piece of wood; a piece of a broken pole
手振 bōtefu(ri) peddler ⌈of surprise)
5立 bōda(chi) standing up straight (because
7杙 bōgui stake, pile
状 bōjō cylindrical shape
8使 bōtsuka(i) cudgel play; cudgel player
押 bōo(shi) pole-pushing (game)
杭 bōgui pile, stake
乳切 bōchigi(ri), bōchigi(re) broken stick
9紅 bō beni lipstick
10倒 bōtao(shi) pole-fighting game
振 bō (ni) fu(ru) fail, come to naught
高飛 bō takato(bi) pole vault
高跳 bō takatobi pole vault
11術 bōjutsu cudgel play
組 bōgu(mi) setting type in a galley; one's
13鉄 bō tetsu bar iron ⌊pal
14鼻 bōbana tip of a pole
読 bōyo(mi) accentless reading; reading Chinese in the Chinese order
銀 bō gin bar silver
磁石 bō jishaku bar magnet
16縞 bōjima stripes
鋼 bōkō bar steel
諳記 bō anki rote memorization
22鱈 bōdara dried cod

A **植** 2303/F988 SHOKU planting. u(eru) plant, set out, raise, sow; set type. u(waru) be planted.

2人 u(e)bito planters
4込 u(e)-ko(mu) plant (trees). u(e)ko(mi) shrubbery, thick growth of plants
木 ueki garden plant, shrub, tree
木屋 uekiya gardener, nurseryman
木鉢 uekibachi flowerpot ⌈implant
5付 u(e)-tsu(keru) plant, set out, transplant;
付機 uetsu(ke)ki seed-planting machine
皮 shokuhi skin grafting
皮法 shokuhihō skin grafting
皮術 shokuhijutsu skin grafting ⌈nist, settler
民 shokumin colonization, settlement; colo-
民地 shokuminchi colony, settlement
民地化 shokuminchika colonization
民政策 shokumin seisaku colonialism
民時代 shokumin jidai colonial period
民都市 shokumin toshi (Roman) colony
6字 shokuji typesetting, composition
字機 shokujiki linotype
8林 shokurin afforestation
物 shokubutsu plant, vegetation, flora
物性 shokubutsusei vegetable property
物学 shokubutsugaku botany
物界 shokubutsukai vegetable kingdom
物病 shokubutsubyō plant disease
物崇拝 shokubutsu sūhai plant worship
物採集 shokubutsu saishū plant collecting
物園 shokubutsuen botanical garden
物誌 shokubutsushi flora
物質 shokubutsushitsu vegetable matter
10疱瘡 u(e)bōsō vaccination, inoculation
12替 u(e)-ka(eru) transplant, replant
16樹 shokuju tree planting
樹祭 Shokujusai Arbor Day

A **検** 2304/F1018 **檢** KEN investigation. ken(suru) investigate.

4水 kensui examination of water
尺 kenjaku suru scale timber
分 kembun inspection, examination
5札 kensatsu examination of tickets
出 kenshutsu search; (chemical) detection
圧 ken-atsu measuring pressure
圧器 ken-atsuki pressure gauge
6死 kenshi investigating a death; autopsy
印 ken-in stamp of approval
地 kenchi land survey
字 kenji list of characters (by total strokes) whose radicals are obscure
糸器 kenshiki yarn-testing machine
7車 kensha vehicle inspection
尿 kennyō urine examination ⌈custody
束 kensoku restraint, restriction; arrest,
8使 kenshi official who verifies the facts
波 kempa detection (in electricity)
乳 kennyū milk examination
事 kenji prosecuting attorney
事局 kenjikyoku prosecutor's office
定 kentei official certification, approval, authorization; examination, inspection;
定料 kenteiryō examination fee ⌊license
定済 kenteizu(mi) inspected (by the government) ⌈aminations
定試験 kentei shiken teachers' licensing ex-
9便 kemben stool examination
音器 ken-onki sonometer
屍 kenshi investigating a death; autopsy
屍官 kenshikan coroner
疫 ken-eki quarantine
疫所 ken-ekisho quarantine station
疫官 ken-ekikan quarantine doctor
査 kensa inspection, examination
査役 kensayaku inspector, auditor
査所 kensajo inspection station
査官 kensakan inspector, auditor
査済 kensazu(mi) examined, passed
10校 kengyō blind court musician
梅 kembai syphilis test ⌈test
討 kentō investigation, examination, study,
針 kenshin inspection of a meter or a gauge

索 *kensaku suru* refer to, look up (a word); make a laboratory test
案 *ken-an* post-mortem examination
挙 *kenkyo* arrest, roundup
流計 *kenryūkei* galvanometer, ammeter
流器 *kenryūki* galvanometer, ammeter
11 視 *kenshi* investigation of the facts
問 *kemmon* inspection, examination
問所 *kemmonjo* checkpoint
眼 *kengan* optometry, eye examination
眼医 *kengan-i* optometrist
12 証 *kenshō* verification, inspection
番 *kemban* geisha exchange
湿器 *kenshitsuki* hygrometer
温 *ken-on* thermometry
温器 *ken-onki* clinical thermometer
診 *kenshin* medical examination
診日 *kenshimbi* medical-examination day
14 算 *kenzan* verification of accounts, checking figures
察 *kensatsu* investigation and prosecution
察庁 *kensatsuchō* prosecuting attorney's office
察官 *kensatsukan* prosecuting attorney
15 震器 *kenshinki* seismograph
閲 *ken-etsu* inspection, censorship
閲官 *ken-etsukan* inspector, censor
潮 *kenchō* tidal observation
潮器 *kenchōki* tide gauge
16 糖計 *kentōkei* saccharimeter
19 鏡 *kenkyō* microscopic examination
覈 *kenkaku* strict investigation
23 黴 *kembai* syphilis test

極 2305 / F995 A KYOKU end; highest rank; the poles; (electric) poles. GOKU very, extremely, highly, most, quite. *kiwa(maru)* terminate; reach an extreme; be in a dilemma. *kiwa(meru)* investigate thoroly, master; carry to extremes. *ki(meru)* (see under 決 2509.0). *ki(maru)* (see under 定 1296.0). *kime* agreement, contract. *kima(ri)* settlement, conclusion, agreement; system, regularity; rule; habit. *kiwa(marinai)* endless, eternal. *kiwa(mete)* very, exceedingly. *kiwa(mi)* height, acme, extremity. *-gime* by (the month).

2 力 *kyokuryoku* with all one's might
3 大 *kyokudai* the greatest, maximum
上 *gokujō* first-rate, finest quality, the best
小 *kyokushō* the smallest, minimum
小型写真機 *gokukogata shashinki, gokushōgata shashinki* miniature camera
4 手 *kimete* winning move, deciding factor
月 *gokugetsu* December; the last month of the year
内 *gokunai* top-secret, confidential
切 *kima(ri)ki(tta)* fixed, definite, stereotyped; self-evident, clear
文句 *kima(ri) monku* stereotyped phrase
込 *ki(me)-ko(mu)* take for granted, assume, pretend
込人形 *kimeko(mi) ningyō* kimono-dressed doll pasted on wood
5 玉 *ki(me)dama* winning pitch
付 *ki(me)-tsu(keru)* scold, reprimand. *kiwa(me)tsu(ki)* guaranteed
北 *kyokuhoku* extreme north, North Pole
右 *kyoku-u* extreme right
左 *kyokusa* extreme left
6 尽 *kiwa(me)-tsuku(su)* know thoroly; measure the full extent
印 *gokuin* seal, stamp die, hallmark, impression; proof of genuineness
地 *kyokuchi* the pole, polar regions
刑 *kyokkei* capital punishment; extreme penalty
光 *kyokkō* northern lights, aurora borealis; southern lights, aurora australis
7 言 *kyokugen* extreme criticism
位 *kyokui* highest position (of a retainer)
8 所 *kyokusho* end, conclusion
限 *kyokugen* limit, extremity
東 *Kyokutō* Far East
9 度 *kyokudo* highest degree, the extreme, maximum
洋 *kyokuyō* polar seas
点 *kyokuten* highest point, climax, summit, zenith; nadir, bottom
美 *kyokubi* surpassing beauty
前線 *kyoku zensen* polar front
10 流 *kyokuryū* polar current
秘 *gokuhi* top-secret, confidential
致 *kyokuchi* culmination, perfection
11 球 *ki(me)dama* forte; mainstay; winning shot (in sports)
貧 *gokuhin* destitution
彩色 *gokusaishiki* brilliant coloring, full color (illustrations)
道 *gokudō na* wicked, villainous, brutal, dissipated
道者 *gokudōmono* scoundrel, villain, profligate
悪 *gokuaku* brutality, atrocity. *kima(ri)waru(i)* awkward, embarrassed
悪人 *gokuakunin* confirmed criminal, very wicked person
12 圏 *kyokken, kyokuken* polar circle
極 *gokugoku* very, severely
寒 *gokkan* intense cold, midwinter
量 *kyokuryō* maximum dose
暑 *gokusho* severe heat
13 微 *kyokubi, gokubi* infinitesmal, microscopic
意 *gokui* mystery; the secrets (of the art)
楽 *gokuraku* paradise
楽往生 *gokurakuōjō* easy death; euthanasia
楽浄土 *gokuraku jōdo* (Buddhist) paradise

楽鳥 *gokurakuchō* bird of paradise
14製 *gokusei* the best make
端 *kyokutan* an extreme, extremity
端主義 *kyokutan shugi* radicalism, extremism
端家 *kyokutanka* extremist, radical
端論 *kyokutanron* extreme view, radical view
端論者 *kyokutan ronsha* extremist
15論 *kyokuron* extreme argument; extreme criticism
熱 *gokunetsu* high fever; intense heat

9

概 See 2344.

楚 See 3022.

業 See 143.

棄 棄 See 326.

椶 2306/F990 See 棕 2293.

樋 Nonstandard for 樋 2338.

榊 Nonstandard for 榊 2330.

榔 2307/F997 Rō.

槌 2308/F1001 Tsui. *tsuchi* hammer, mallet.

楡 2309/F993 Yu. *nire* elm.

楢 2310/F993 Shū. Yū. *nara* oak.

楮 2311/F994 Cho. *kōzo* paper mulberry.

椴 2312/F990 Tan fir.
8松 *todomatsu* fir, white fir

楕 2313/F1015 橢 Da ellipse.
4円 *daen* oval, ellipse
円形 *daenkei* oval, ellipse

楯 2314/F995 Jun. *tate* shield, buckler, escutcheon; pretext.
8突 *tatetsu(ku)* oppose, defy

楓 2315/F992 Fū. Fu. *kaede* maple tree.
3子香 *fūshikō* galbanum

椽 2316/F990 Ten. *en* veranda, porch, balcony, margin, edge. *taruki* rafter.
3大 *tendai* rafter size; powerful writing

楠 2317/F993 Nan. *kusu, kusunoki* camphor tree.
4木 *kusunoki* camphor tree

楷 2318/F996 Kai square-character style; straight tree; correctness, rule, model.
6行草 *kai-gyō-sō* square, cursive, and grass characters
10書 *kaisho* square character, printed style

椿 2319/F991 Chin. *tsubaki* camellia.
8油 *tsubaki abura* camellia oil
事 *chinji* accident; sudden occurrence

楫 2320/F993 Shū. *kai, kaji* oar, sculling oar, rudder.
8取 *kajito(ri)* helmsman
9音 *kaji oto* the sound of oars

楊 2321/F991 Yō *kawa yanagi* willow.
3子江 *Yōsukō* Yangtze River
8枝 *yōji* toothpick; toothbrush
9柳 *yanagi, kawa yanagi, yōryū* riverside willows

B 楼 2322/F1006 樓 Rō tower, turret, lookout, high building. *takadono* stately mansion.
3上 *rōjō* upper story; balcony; roof garden
5主 *rōshu* brothel proprietor
8門 *rōmon* tower gate, two-story gate
14閣 *rōkaku* many-storied building

楔 2323/F992 Ketsu. Setsu. *kusabi* wedge; arrowhead; cleat; chock; tie, pledge; dovetail.
5石 *kusabi-ishi* keystone
7状文字 *ketsujō moji* cuneiform writing
形 *kusabigata, kekkei* wedge-shaped, V-shaped; cuneiform
形文字 *kusabigata moji* cuneiform writing
10栓 *kusabisen* cotter pin, key

A 楽 2324/F1004 樂 RAKU comfort, ease, relief; pleasure; concluding program. GAKU music. *tanoshi(mu)*, *tano(shibu)* enjoy; amuse oneself; anticipate. *tano(shimi)*, *tanoshi(bi)* pleasure, enjoyment, happiness; amusement; anticipation. *tano(shii)* merry, pleasant, cheerful, joyful. *tano(shige) na* merry, pleasant, happy, gay. *raku na* easy.

2 人 *gakujin* musician, minstrel. *rakujin* person living at ease
3 土 *rakudo* paradise, a pleasant land
士 *gakushi* bandsman, musician
弓 *gakkyū* bow (of a violin)
才 *gakusai* musical talent
4 手 *gakushu* musician, bandsman
天 *rakuten* optimism
天主義 *rakuten shugi* optimism
天主義者 *rakuten shugisha* optimist
天地 *rakutenchi* paradise; amusement park
天的 *rakutenteki* optimistic, cheerful, happy-go-lucky
天家 *rakutenka* optimist, easygoing person
5 台 *gakudai* music stand
6 団 *gakudan* band, orchestra
曲 *gakkyoku* musical composition, tune
地 *rakuchi* pleasant circumstances
8 長 *gakuchō* bandmaster, conductor, musical director
典 *gakuten* musical grammar
9 音 *gakuon* musical tone
界 *gakkai* music circles, the world of music
屋 *gakuya* dressing room, greenroom; behind the scenes
屋落 *gakuya-o(chi)* a matter not understood by the outside, inside information; shoptalk
屋話 *gakuyabanashi* backstage talk
10 員 *gakuin* bandsman
書 *rakuga(ki)* scribbling in public places
11 隊 *gakutai* band, orchestra
章 *gakushō* a movement (in music)
12 焼 *rakuya(ki)* hand-molded pottery
勝 *rakushō* easy victory
13 園 *rakuen* pleasure garden, paradise
殿 *gakuden* hall of music
寝 *rakune* nap, rest
楽 *rakuraku to* comfortably; very easily. *rakuraku suru* feel relieved
聖 *gakusei* celebrated musician
隠居 *rakuinkyo* comfortable retirement
15 劇 *gakugeki* opera, musical drama
調 *gakuchō* musical tone
器 *gakki* musical instrument
器伴奏 *gakki bansō* instrumental accompaniment
器店 *gakkiten* music shop
16 壇 *gakudan* music circles
18 観 *rakkan* optimism
観主義 *rakkan shugi* optimism
観的 *rakkanteki* optimistic, hopeful
19 譜 *gakufu* sheet music, music book, musical notation, the score

10

槿 See 2356.

滎 2325/F998 See 栄 2239.

樅 Nonstandard for 樅 2353.

榜 2326/F997 Bō rudder; oar; name plate

槃 2327/F1000 HAN tub.

槁 2328/F1000 Kō die (vegetation).

榻 2329/F1000 榻 Tō chair.

榊 2330/F1002 (国字) *sakaki* sacred Shinto tree.

榾 2331/F1000 KOTSU. *hota* chip, piece of wood.
9 柮 *hota* piece of wood
柮火 *hotabi* a wood fire

榎 2332/F996 KA. *enoki* hackberry; nettle tree; lotus tree.

榛 2333/F997 SHIN. *hashibami* hazel, filbert. *han* black alder.
4 木 *han(no)ki* black alder

槊 2334/F1001 槊 SAKU halberd.
7 杖 *sakujō* ramrod, cleaning rod

槓 2335/F1002 Kō lever.
7 杆 *kōkan* lever

榕 2336/F997 Yō. *akō* an evergreen mulberry.
16 樹 *yōju* banyan

樺 2337/F1011 KA. *kaba*, *kamba* birch.

4太 *Karafuto* Sakhalin
6色 *kaba iro* reddish yellow

樋 2338 / F1006 Tō. *hi*, *toi* water pipe, gutter, downspout; aqueduct, flume; conduit; trough.
8門 *himon* sluice

槙 2339 / F1001 Shin twig. *maki* an ornamental evergreen.
5皮 *maihada*, *makihada* oakum, calking
6肌 *maihada*, *makihada* oakum, calking

榴 2340 / F1000 F1012 **榴** Ru, Ryū pomegranate.
12散弾 *ryūsandan* shrapnel shell
弾 *ryūdan* shell
弾砲 *ryūdampō* howitzer
20霰弾 *ryūsandan* shrapnel shell

A**様** 2341 / F1009 **様 樣 様 槎**
Yō way, manner, method; kind, class; (to that) effect. *sama* situation, circumstances, condition. *sama* Mr., Mrs., Messrs., Mme., Miss, Master. *yō na* like, such as. *yō ni* in order to. *zama* plight, state, appearance, spectacle.
3子 *yōsu* situation, aspect, circumstances, movements; appearance; behavior, signs
子振 *yōsubu(ru)* put on airs, pose for effect
5付 *samazu(ke) suru* address everyone with "Mr."
6式 *yōshiki* style, form, pattern
7見 *Zama (o) mi(ro).* Just look at your blunder.
体 *yōtai* form, situation; condition of the patient
9相 *yōsō* aspect, phase, condition
14様 *samazama na* various, varied, sundry
態 *yōtai* form; situation, condition

槍 2342 / F1001 Sō. *yari* spear, lance, javelin.
5玉 *yaridama* victim, sacrifice
6先 *yarisaki* spearhead
7投 *yarina(ge)* javelin throwing, javelin contest
兵 *sōhei* spearman, lanceman
8法 *sōhō* drilling with spears
9持 *yarimo(chi)* spearman; spear carrier
10衾 *yaribusuma* ring of steel
11術 *sōjutsu* drilling with spears
術家 *sōjutsuka* spearman
18騎兵 *sōkihei* lancer

A**構** 2343 / F1001 **構** Kō. *kama(eru)* build; keep house; take a posture; assume an attitude; pose as; be ready for; feign, pretend; set up (camp). *kama(u)* mind, care about; pay attention to; interfere with; be hospitable; tease, molest; expel, banish. *ku(u)* build (a nest). *kama(e)* construction, architecture, style, appearance; posture; attitude; enclosure radical. *kama(i)* meddling, concern; entertainment, hospitality; banishment. *(o)kama(i nashi ni)* regardless of.
4手 *kama(i)te* companion, protector
文 *kōbun* sentence construction, syntax
内 *kōnai*, *kama(e)uchi* compound, grounds, premises
5外 *kōgai* outside the premises
6成 *kōsei suru* comprise. *kōsei* composition, organization, construction, line-up
成分子 *kōsei bunshi* components
成団体 *kōsei dantai* affiliated organizations
成員 *kōsei-in* member
7図 *kōzu* plot (of a novel); plan (of a life); composition (of a painting); design; sketch
材 *kōzai* construction materials
9造 *kōzō* construction, framework, structure; set-up, organization
造上 *kōzōjō* structurally
造鋼 *kōzōkō* structural steel
13想 *kōsō* plan, idea, conception, plot
16築 *kōchiku suru* build, construct
築物 *kōchikubutsu* a structure

B**概** 2344 / F1003 **槪 槩** Gai condition, situation; approximation. *gai(shite)* generally, as a rule, on the whole. *ōmu(ne)*=*taigai* 大概 1171.14.
7見 *gaiken* general view, outline
言 *gaigen* summary, general remarks
8況 *gaikyō* outlook, over-all condition, general situation
念 *gainen* general idea, concept
念化 *gainenka* generalization
念的 *gainenteki ni* roughly, generally
9括 *gaikatsu* summary, generalization
計 *gaikei* rough estimate
則 *gaisoku* general rules, general principles
要 *gaiyō* summary, outline, synopsis, résumé
11略 *gairyaku* outline, summary, gist, résumé; roughly, approximately, in brief
12報 *gaihō* summary
13数 *gaisū* round numbers
14説 *gaisetsu* general statement, outline
貌 *gaibō* outline (of an event)
算 *gaisan* approximation, rough estimate
15論 *gairon* introduction, outline, general remarks
18観 *gaikan* general view, outline

B **模** 2345 F1009 Mo. Bo. *mo(suru)* copy, imitate, mock. *katado(ru)* pattern after, imitate, symbolize.
5 写 *mosha* copying; copy, replica
写器 *moshaki* mimeograph
7 形 *mokei* model, pattern
9 型 *mokei* model, pattern 「counterfeit
造 *mozō* imitation, copy, reproduction;
造宝石 *mozō hōseki* imitation gem
造品 *mozōhin* imitation
造紙 *mozōshi* vellum paper
造真珠 *mozō shinju* imitation pearls
10 倣 *mohō* copy, imitation
索 *mosaku* groping 「cumstances
14 様 *moyō* pattern, design; appearance; cir-
様入 *moyōi(ri) no* figured 「change
様替 *moyōga(e)* remodeling, alteration,
15 糊 *moko* dimness, vagueness, stupidity
範 *mohan* model, pattern, example
範生 *mohansei* model student
範的 *mohanteki* exemplary
範試合 *mohan jiai* exhibition game
17 擬 *mogi* imitation 「a party)
擬店 *mogiten* buffet, refreshment booth (at
擬戦 *mogisen* sham fight
擬試験 *mogi shiken* trial examination

11

榴 See 2340.

樞 2346 F1008 See 枢 2208.

橢 2347 F1015 See 楕 2313.

樓 2348 F1006 See 楼 2322.

樣 2349 F1009 樣 See 様 2341.

樂 2350 F1004 See 楽 2324.

概 槪 See 概 2344.

槽 2351 F1004 Sō tub, tank, vat.

槻 2352 F1004 Ki. *tsuki* Zelkova tree.

樅 2353 F1005 Shō. *momi* fir, white fir, silver fir.

樒 2354 F1006 Mitsu. *shikimi* a tree whose branches are placed on Buddhist graves.

樏 2355 F1006 Rui. *kanjiki* snowshoes.

槿 2356 F1004 Kin rose of Sharon.
1 花 *kinka* rose of Sharon

樫 2357 F1017 (国字) *kashi* evergreen oak.
12 棒 *kashibō* oak club, oak stick

樟 2358 F1008 Shō. *kusu* camphor tree; camphor.
4 木 *kusu(no)ki* camphor tree
11 脳 *shōnō* camphor
脳油 *shōnōyu* camphor oil
脳精 *shōnōsei* spirits of camphor

A **標** 2359 F1007 Hyō signpost; mark; target; designate. *shirushi* (see under 印 102.0).
4 木 *hyōboku* signpost, grave post
5 石 *hyōseki* boundary stone; milestone
示 *hyōji* indication, expression; marking
札 *hyōsatsu* name plate, door plate
本 *hyōhon* specimen
6 灯 *hyōtō* signal light, pilot light
号 *hyōgō* symbol, emblem, sign
8 柱 *hyōchū* top marginal notes
的 *hyōteki* mark, target
定 *hyōtei suru* orientate; range (a telescope)
9 柱 *hyōchū* pylon, guidepost
10 高 *hyōkō* height above sea level
記 *hyōki* a mark; marking
11 章 *hyōshō* ensign, emblem, badge, mark
12 註 *hyōchū* top marginal notes
13 準 *hyōjun* standard, norm, level, criterion, canon, measure
準化 *hyōjunka* standardization
準米 *hyōjummai* standard rice
準型 *hyōjungata* standard type
準軌間 *hyōjun kikan* standard railway gauge 「time
準時 *hyōjunji* standard time, Greenwich
準時計 *hyōjundokei* chronometer
準液 *hyōjun-eki* standard solution (liquid)
準語 *hyōjungo* standard language
14 旗 *hyōki* flag marker 「*kamban* 看板 222.8
榜 *hyōbō suru* profess, advocate. *hyōbō*=
語 *hyōgo* slogan, motto
18 題 *hyōdai* title (of a book)
19 縄 *shimenawa* sacred shrine rope

識 *hyōshiki* landmark; sign, signal, beacon; criterion

A **權** 2360/F1023 **權** GON, KEN authority, power; rights, concession. *gon-* assistant (in the Shinto hierarchy).

2力 *kenryoku* power, authority, influence
力争 *kenryoku araso(i)* struggle for supremacy
力者 *kenryokusha* man of power
力政治 *kenryoku seiji* power politics
4内 *kennai* within one's authority
化 *gonge* (Buddhist) incarnation, avatar, embodiment, personification
5外 *kengai* outside the jurisdiction (of)
6臣 *kenshin* influential retainer
7助 *gonsuke* manservant
利 *kenri* rights, claim, privilege, title; authority, powers; goodwill; franchise; ⌊agency.
利付 *kenrizu(ki)* rights attached
利金 *kenrikin* key money
8門 *kemmon* man of influence
限 *kengen* power, authority, jurisdiction
官 *kenkan* influential official
妻 *gonsai* concubine
9変 *kempen* expediency ⌈tion or person)
要 *ken-yō* important and influential (posi-
柄 *kempei* authority, power
柄尽 *kempeizu(ku)* authoritative, dictatorial
威 *ken-i* authority, power, dignity, prestige
威的 *ken-iteki* authoritative
威者 *ken-isha* an authority
威筋 *ken-i suji* authoritative sources
威誌 *ken-ishi* authoritative magazine
10原 *kengen* title (to territory)
益 *ken-eki* rights, interests
家 *kenka* influential house
能 *kennō* authority, power; function, faculty
11道 *kendō* policy, expediency, trick, makeshift ⌈Tokugawa Ieyasu
現 *gongen* incarnation of Buddha, avatar;
眼 *kengan* testing vision
12詐 *kensa* deceptive plan
貴 *kenki* rank and influence; a man of rank ⌊and influence
13勢 *kensei* power, influence
勢家 *kenseika* a powerful man
16衡 *kenkō* balance, equilibrium
謀 *kembō* scheme, stratagem, plot
謀家 *kembōka* schemer ⌈Machiavellism
謀術数 *kembō-jussū* trickery, diplomacy,
17輿 *ken-yo* origin, beginning

A **横** 2361/F1015 **橫** Ō horizontal. *yoko* side, flank; horizontal direction; width, breadth, beam; woof. *yoko(taeru)* lay (oneself) down, lie down; place across. *yoko(tawaru)* lie down, stretch out

2丁 *yokochō* lane, alley, side street ⌊on.
4手 *yokode* hand clapping. *yokote ni* at one side, at one's side
木 *yokogi* crosspiece, bar, crossbar, crosstree, singletree, rail
辷 *yokosuberi* skid, slip, sideslip
切 *yokogi(ru)* intersect, cross
太 *yokobuto(ri)* plumpness, pudginess
文 *ōbun* horizontal writing, Western writing
文字 *yoko moji* European writing., cross- ⌊wise writing
引 *yokobi(ki)* crosscut
引鋸 *yokobi(ki) nokogiri* crosscut saw
5目 *yokome* side glance; amorous glance;
穴 *yoko ana* cave, tunnel ⌊crosscut saw
付 *yokozu(ke)* coming alongside
6糸 *yoko ito* woof
死 *ōshi* violent, tragic, accidental, or unnatural death; a dog's death
向 *yokomu(ki)* turning sidewise
好 *yokozu(ki)* immoderately fond of
帆 *ōhan* square sail
合 *yokoa(i)* side, flank
行 *ōkō suru* walk sideways; swagger; stride
行闊歩 *ōkō-kappo* swaggering around
7見 *yokomi* side glance
谷 *ōkoku* transverse valley
位 *ōi* transverse position of the fetus
投 *yokona(ge)* throwing sideways, side throw
町 *yokochō* lane, alley, side street
車 *yokoguruma* perverseness
車押 *yokoguruma (o) o(su)* be perverse
8長 *yokonaga* oblong
雨 *yoko ame* driving rain
逆 *ōgyaku* boisterous, wild, unreasonable
抱 *yokoda(ki)* carrying (a child) under the
泳 *yoko-oyogi* side stroke ⌊arm
波 *yokonami* side wave, broadside sea, transverse wave
取 *yokodo(ri)* usurpation; seizure; snatching; intercepting
肥 *yokobuto(ri)* fat
臥 *ōga* lying on the side
殴 *yokonagu(ri)* side blow, sideswipe
歩 *yokoaru(ki) suru* walk sideways
9面 *yokotsura, yoko(t)tsura, yokozura* side of ⌊the face
風 *yoko kaze, ōfū* cross wind
飛 *yokoto(bi)* scurrying away
柄 *ōhei* arrogance
降 *yokobu(ri)* driving rain
乗 *yokono(ri)* riding sideways ⌈velope
封筒 *yokobūtō, yoko fūtō* Western-style en-
10這 *yokobai suru* crawl sideways
倒 *yokodao(re)* lying sideways along (the track). *yokotao(shi), yokodao(shi)* skidding and tumbling

4 心 小 ⺌ 戈 戸 手 扌 支 攴 攵 文 斗 斤 方 无 日 曰 月 【木】11 欠 止 歹 殳 毋 比 毛 氏 气 水 氵 氺 火 灬 爪 爫 父 爻 爿 丬 片 牙 牛 犬 犭

桁 *yokogeta* crossbeam
流 *yokonaga(re)* flowing into blackmarket channels. *yokonaga(shi)* diversion into illegal channels
書 *yokoga(ki)* writing horizontally
紙破 *yokogamiyabu(ri)* perverseness, waywardness
恋慕 *yoko rembo* illicit love
座標 *ōzahyō* abscissa
11 道 *yokomichi* side street; crossroad; wrong way; side issue; evil course. *ōdō* wickedness, wrong, injustice; crossroad
舵 *ōda* diving rudder
転 *ōten* lateral turn; barrel roll (of a plane)
隊 *ōtai* rank, line
貫 *ōkan* running across: east and west
笛 *yokobue, ōteki* flute, fife
笛吹 *yokobuefu(ki)* flutist
断 *ōdan* crossing, intersection
断者 *ōdansha* street-crossing pedestrians
断歩道 *ōdan hodō* pedestrian crossing
断面 *ōdammen* cross section
断路 *ōdanro* crossroad
断線 *ōdansen* transverse line
著 *ōchaku*＝横着 (see below–12)
12 幅 *yokohaba* breadth, width
揺 *yokoyu(re)* rolling, a roll
棒 *yokobō* bar, horizontal bar; dash; horizontal line
軸 *yoko jiku* horizontal shaft, cross axle
筋 *yoko suji* transversal; lateral stripes
着 *ōchaku* dishonesty; cunning; impudence; laziness; selfishness
雲 *yokogumo* bank of clouds
裂 *yokoza(ki), yokoza(ke)* a horizontal tear
隔膜 *ōkakumaku* the diaphragm
13 溢 *ōitsu* overflowing, inundation
睨 *yokonira(mi)* a sharp sidelong glance
腹 *yoko(p)para, yokohara, yokobara* side, flank
路 *yokomichi*＝横道 (see above–11)
罫 *yokokei* horizontal lines
意地 *yoko-iji* perverseness, obstinacy
14 槍 *yokoyari* interruption
様 *yokosama* wickedness. *yokosama ni* sideways, laterally, askance
綱 *yokozuna* champion wrestler; tops in his class
綴 *yokotoji* side stitch
隣 *yokodonari* next door
領 *ōryō* usurpation, seizure, dispossession; embezzlement, misappropriation
奪 *ōdatsu*＝the word above
15 暴 *ōbō* violence, oppression, highhandedness
震 *ōshin* horizontal shock (quake)
線 *ōsen* horizontal line, abscissa
線小切手 *ōsen kogitte* crossed check
16 縞 *yokojima* lateral stripes
縦 *yokotate* length and breadth
薙 *yokonagi* side sweep; sweeping from side to side
18 額 *yokogaku* framed horizontal scroll
顔 *yokogao* profile, side view, silhouette
19 櫛 *yokogushi* side comb
20 議 *ōgi* arguing persistently
25 鬢 *yokobin* side locks; cheek

12

橋 See 2382.

橤 See 蕊 4045.

橫 2362 / F1015 See 横 2361.

樣 2363 / F-X See 様 2341.

橊 2364 / F1012 See 榴 2340.

槪 2365 / F-X 槪 See 概 2344.

橡 2366 / F1015 橡 Shō. *tochi* horse chestnut.

橅 2367 / F1012 Bo. Mo. *buna* beech tree.

橘 2368 / F1013 Kitsu. *tachibana* mandarin orange; orange crest.

橦 2369 / F1015 Shu pole.

樵 2370 / F1010 Shō. *kiko(ru), ko(ru)* cut wood. *kikori* woodcutting; woodcutter, lumberjack.
4 夫 *kikori, shōfu* woodcutter, lumberjack

橈 2371 / F1012 Dō. *kai* oar, scull, paddle.
8 受 *kaiu(ke)* oarlock
10 座 *kaiza* oarlock

樸 2372 / F1010 Boku. *kohada* bark of a tree.
4 仁人 *bokunenjin* a quiet unsociable person; one not too bright
8 直 *bokuchoku* simplicity, naïveté, honesty

橇 2373 / F1012 Kyō. Zei. *sori* sled, sleigh, sledge, skid. *kanjiki* snowshoes.
4 犬 *sori inu* sled dog
13 滑 *sorisuberi* sleighing

欖 2374 / F1012 KAN.

25欖 *kanran* olive
欖山 *Kanranzan* Mount of Olives
欖石 *kanranseki* chrysolite, olivine
欖油 *kanran-yu* olive oil

樽 2375 / F1011 SON. *taru* barrel, cask, keg, tub.

2入 *taru-i(ri)* barreled (liquor)
9柿 *tarugaki* persimmons seasoned in saké barrels (to remove astringency)
13詰 *taruzume* barreled, casked

橙 2376 / F1013 TŌ. *daidai* bitter orange.

5皮 *tōhi* orange peeling
6色 *daidai iro* orange color
7花 *tōka* orange blossom
花油 *tōkayu* neroli oil
12酢 *daidaizu* bitter-orange juice

B **樹** 2377 / F1011 JU *ki* tree, wood. *ta(teru)* (see under 立 3343.0).

3下 *juka ni* under a tree
上 *jujō no, jujō ni* on a tree
4木 *jumoku* trees and shrubs, arbor
木学 *jumokugaku* dendrology
木限界線 *jumoku genkaisen* timber line
5皮 *juhi* bark
立 *juritsu* establishment, setting (a record)
氷 *juhyō* silver frost (on trees)
7身 *jushin* tree trunk
8林 *jurin* forest
9海 *jukai* a sea of foliage, a sea of forests
10脂 *jushi* resin, rosin
陰 *kokage, juin* shade of a tree
11液 *jueki* sap
頂 *juchō* top of a tree
12間 *jukan* among the trees; between the trees
葉 *juyō* leaves of a tree
13蔭 *kokage, juin* shade of a tree
幹 *jukan* trunk of a tree
17齢 *jurei* a tree's age

A **橋** 2378 / F1012 KYŌ. *hashi* bridge.

4爪 *hashizume* bridge approach
5台 *hashidai, kyōdai* bridge abutment
6守 *hashimori* bridge watchman
8杭 *hashigui* bridge pile
桟 *hashigui* bridge pile
9架 *kyōka* bridge girder
10桁 *hashigeta* bridge girder
畔 *kyōhan* bridge approach
11脚 *kyōkyaku* bridge pier
梁 *kyōryō* bridge
12渡 *hashiwata(shi)* building a bridge; mediation, good offices
普請 *hashi bushin* bridge construction
13詰 *hashizume* bridge approach
14銭 *hashisen* bridge toll
16頭 *kyōtō* vicinity of a bridge
頭陣地 *kyōtō jinchi* bridgehead
頭堡 *kyōtōhō* bridgehead, beachhead
20懸 *hashigaka(ri)* bridge-type passageway

A **機** 2379 / F1014 **機** KI opportunity; occasion, time; machine, airplane. *hata* loom.

3女 *kijo* female weaver
才 *kisai* promptness, quick wit, superior talent
上 *kijō* aboard a plane
上掃射 *kijō sōsha* strafing
4内 *kinai* within the plane
内通信 *kinai tsūshin* intercom
5巧 *kikō* contrivance; means; clever thinking
失 *ki (o) ushina(u)* lose a chance
甲 *kikō* armored
甲車両 *kikō sharyō* armored vehicles
甲部隊 *kikō butai* armored corps
6先 *kisen* before the occurrence
帆船 *kihansen* steam-and-sail ships
会 *kikai* opportunity, chance
会主義 *kikai shugi* opportunism
会均等 *kikai kintō* equal opportunity
7見 *ki (o) mi(ru)* watch for an opportunity
尾 *kibi* airplane tail
体 *kitai* fuselage
材 *kizai* machine parts, machinery, equipment
8知 *kichi* wit, resources, tact
宜 *kigi* opportunity, occasion
9首 *kishu* nose of a plane
屋 *hataya* weaver
乗 *ki (ni) no(ru)* take advantage of an opportunity
変 *kihen* opportunism; deceptive power
要 *kiyō* important considerations
10根 *kikon* talent, gift
敏 *kibin* shrewdness, alertness, astuteness
能 *kinō* faculty, function, process
能的 *kinōteki* functional
11運 *kiun* luck; tendency; opportunity
略 *kiryaku* resources; expedient; tact
務 *kimu* important state affairs
船 *kisen* motorboat
転 *kiten* tact, ready wit
密 *kimitsu* secrecy, secret
密費 *kimitsuhi* secret fund
動 *kidō* mobile
動力 *kidōryoku* mobile power, motive force; maneuverability
動化 *kidōka* mechanization
動部隊 *kidō butai* mechanized unit

動演習 *kidō enshū* maneuvers
械 *kikai* machine, mechanism, gear
械工 *kikaikō* mechanic, machinist
械工具 *kikai kōgu* machine tools
械工学 *kikai kōgaku* mechanical engineer-ing
械工場 *kikai kōjō* machine shop, engineer-⌈ing works
械工業 *kikai kōgyō* machine industry
械化 *kikaika* mechanization; mechanized
械刈 *kikaiga(ri)* haircutting with clippers
械文明 *kikai bummei* machine civilization
械仕掛 *kikai jika(ke)* mechanism, machin-⌊ery
械糸 *kikai ito* filatures
械体操 *kikai taisō* calisthenics using equip-ment
械油 *kikai abura, kikaiyu* machine oil, ⌈lubricating oil
械的 *kikaiteki* mechanical
械学 *kikaigaku* mechanics
械屋 *kikaiya* machinist
械製 *kikaisei no* machine-made
械製作所 *kikai seisakujo* machine shop
械編 *kikaia(mi)* machine knitting
械縫 *kikainu(i)* machine sewed
械機 *kikaibata* power loom
12 軸 *kijiku* axis; axle; plan; contrivance
智 *kichi* wit, resources, tact
13 微 *kibi* secrets, inner workings, delicate turn
雷 *kirai* (sea) mine
雷原 *kiraigen* mine field
業 *kigyō* the textile industry
業界 *kigyōkai* textile world
業家 *kigyōka* weaver, textile manufacturer
嫌 *kigen* health; cheer; temper, mood
嫌気褄 *kigen kizuma* another's whim
嫌伺 *kigen-ukaga(i)* inquiry about some-one's health
嫌良 *kigen-yo(ku)* cheerfully, with good ⌈grace
嫌取 *kigento(ri)* humoring; flatterer
嫌買 *kigenka(i)* a man of moods
嫌顔 *kigengao* joyful face
14 構 *kikō* mechanism, structure, organization, ⌈set-up
種 *kishu* the type of plane
銃 *kijū* machine gun
銃掃射 *kijū sōsha* machine-gunning
関 *kikan* engine, machine; means, instru-ment; agency, organization; facilities; ⌊institution; organ
関士 *kikanshi* engineer
関手 *kikanshu* locomotive engineer
関車 *kikansha* locomotive
関兵 *kikanhei* fireman, stoker; machinist
関助手 *kikan joshu* railway fireman
関長 *kikanchō* chief engineer
関室 *kikanshitsu* engine room
関庫 *kikanko* roundhouse
関砲 *kikanhō* machine gun
関紙 *kikanshi* bulletin, organ
関部 *kikambu* ship's engineers
関誌 *kikanshi* bulletin, regular publication ⌊of a society
関銃 *kikanjū* machine gun
関雑誌 *kikan zasshi*=*kikanshi* 機関誌 (see ⌊above–14)
15 縁 *kien* opportunity
鋒 *kihō* point, brunt (of an attack)
影 *kiei* (sight of) a plane
器 *kiki* machinery and tools
16 謀 *kibō* plan, scheme, plot
17 翼 *kiyoku* airplane wings
18 織 *hatao(ri)* weaving; weaver; grasshopper
織虫 *hatao(ri) mushi* grasshopper

13

隸 See **隸** 5026. [隶]

檥 2380/F1020 See **艤** 3880.

檢 2381/F1018 See **検** 2304.

檎 2382/F1018 KIN, GON pear; apple; Pyrus.

橿 2383/F1017 KYŌ a kind of oak.

槲 2384/F1018 KAI. *kashiwa* oak.

檄 2385/F1017 GEKI written appeal, manifesto, declaration, summons. *geki(su-ru)* appeal to, send a manifesto.
4 文 *gekibun* written appeal, manifesto

檀 2386/F1017 **檀** DAN, TAN a kind of cedar, sandalwood. *ma-yumi* spindletree.
6 那 *danna* master; husband; gentleman
那寺 *dannadera* one's family's temple
10 徒 *danto* temple supporter
紙 *danshi* fine crepe paper
家 *danka* families supporting a temple

檣 2387/F1019 SHŌ. *hobashira* mast.
3 上 *shōjō* top of the mast
6 灯 *shōtō* front-mast light
9 竿 *shōkan* mast
16 頭 *shōtō* masthead

檜 2388/F1018 KAI. *hinoki, hi* Japanese cy-press.
5 皮 *hiwada* cypress bark

皮葺 *hiwadabuki* cypress-bark roof
[12]葉 *hiba* cedar-like shrub
[14]舞台 *hinoki butai* cypress-floored stage, high-class stage

14

櫃 2389/F1021 KI. *hitsu* chest, coffer; rice tub.

檳 2390/F1020 BIN the betel-nut palm.
[13]榔 *binrō* betel nut, betel-nut palm
榔子 *binrōji* betel nut

櫂 2391/F1021 TŌ. *kai* oar, scull, paddle.
[8]拍子 *kaibyōshi* rowing stroke

檻 2392/F1020 KAN. *ori* cage, pen, corral, fold; cell, jail.
[8]房 *kambō* cell, ward
[9]穽 *kansei* corrals and traps

15

櫧 See 2400.

麓 See 5377. [鹿]

櫞 2393/F1022 EN a kind of lemon tree.

櫚 2394/F1021 RO, RYO a kind of quince.

櫟 2395/F1022 REKI. *kunugi* a kind of oak used for charcoal.

櫝 2396/F1022 TOKU. *hitsu* chest, coffer; rice tub.

櫓 2397/F1021 艪 RO sculling oar; oar; tower. *yagura* tower, turret; scaffolding.
[18]櫂 *rokai* oars
臍 *robeso* sculling-oar pivot; oarlock

櫛 2398/F1021 SHITSU. *kushi* comb.
[4]比 *shippi suru* stand in a long row
[5]払 *kushihara(i)* comb-cleaning brush
[7]形 *kushigata* comb-like; arch-shaped; arched window
[9]風沐雨 *shippū moku-u* hard toil, hardships
[10]挽 *kushibiki* comb making

16

欖 2399/F1025 欖 RAN the Chinese olive tree.

櫧 2400/F1022 SHO. So. *kashi* oak.

欄 2401/F1023 B 欄 RAN column (in a newspaper); blank; space; railing. *obashima* handrail.
[3]干 *rankan* railing, balustrade
[5]外 *rangai* margin (of a page)
[12]間 *ramma* transom; transom work

17

欄 2402/F1023 See 欄 2401.

權 2403/F1023 See 権 2360.

櫻 2404/F1023 See 桜 2256.

欅 2405/F1023 KYO. *keyaki* Zelkova tree.

19

欛 2406/F1025 See 欛 2409.

欒 2407/F1025 RAN chinaberry tree; round; harmonious

21

欖 2408/F1025 See 欖 2399.

欛 2409/F1025 欛 HA. *tsuka* hilt, grip, handle (of a knife).

22

鬱 2410/F2121 鬱 UTSU gloom, depression, melancholy. *us(suru)*, *fusa(gu)* be depressed, have the blues.
[4]込 *fusa(gi)-ko(mu)* be depressed, have the blues
[6]血 *ukketsu* blood congestion
気 *ukki* close air; gloom, melancholy
[8]林 *utsurin* dense forest
金色 *ukon iro* saffron color
金香 *ukkonkō* tulip
[9]勃 *utsubotsu(taru)* pent up, stored; energetic, irresistible
[10]陶 *uttō* sultriness, stuffiness; unpleasantness; bother. *uttō(shii)* gloomy, depressing; dull, cloudy
[12]散 *ussan* recreation, diversion, distraction

4 心小⺌戈戸手扌支攴攵文斗斤方无日曰月【木[22]】欠止歹殳毋比毛氏气水氵氺火灬爪爫父爻爿丬片牙牛犬犭

4 心小忄戈戸手扌支攴攵文斗斤方无日曰月 25[木]欠止歹殳毋比毛氏气水氵氺火灬爪爫父爻爿丬片牙牛犬犭

葱 *ussō* luxurious foliage; energetic spirits
13 蒼 *ussō(taru)* thick, dense, luxuriant
15 憤 *uppun* resentment, grudge, anger
16 積 *usseki* congestion, stagnation
26 欝 *utsu-utsu to* gloomily, cheerlessly

— 25 —

鬱 2411/F2121 See 欝 2410.

RAD. 欠 76

Akubi yawn; also *ken, ketsu,* or *kakeru* lacking. Nickname: Yawning.

A 欠 2412/F1026/F1489 缺 KETSU lack, gap. *ka(ku)* lack; break, crack, chip; neglect; fail in; omit. *ka(keru)* be broken (off), be chipped; lack, be missing; wane; be vacant (a position). *ka(kasu)* miss (a meeting). *ka(ke)* broken piece (of glass, etc.). *akubi* yawn (欠 only).
3 乏 *ketsubō* want; dearth, famine; scarcity, shortage
乏症 *ketsubōshō* deficiency disease
4 文 *ketsubun* missing part (of a manuscript)
片 *kakera* fragment, splinter, chunk
5 目 *ka(ke)me* break; rupture; short weight
礼 *ketsurei* neglect of courtesies
可 *ka(ku)beka(razaru)* indispensable
本 *keppon* missing volume
6 如 *ketsujo* lack, privation, deficiency
号 *ketsugō* missing number (of a magazine)
字 *ketsuji* omitted word; courtesy spaces left above famous names
7 伸 *akubi* yawn
9 除 *ketsujo* removal, omission
点 *ketten* faults, defect, weakness
盈 *ketsuei* lack and plenty
食 *kesshoku* going without a meal
食児童 *kesshoku jidō* pupils going to school without lunch
陥 *kekkan* defect, fault, deficiency
陥児 *kekkanji* defective child
10 唇 *iguchi, kesshin* harelip
航 *kekkō* steamship-service suspension
配 *keppai* curtailment of rations
員 *ketsuin* vacant position
格 *kekkaku* lack of qualifications
格者 *kekkakusha* unqualified person
席 *kesseki* absence; default
席届 *kesseki todoke* report of a school absence
席者 *kessekisha* absentee
席裁判 *kesseki saiban* court sentence of an absent criminal
12 場 *ketsujō* not in the line-up
量 *ketsuryō* ullage
番 *ketsuban* missing number
勤 *kekkin* absence
勤届 *kekkin todoke* report of an absence
勤者 *kekkinsha* absentee
勤率 *kekkinritsu* absenteeism rate
13 損 *kesson* deficit, shortage, loss; damage
14 漏 *ketsurō* omission
16 壊 *kekkai suru* collapse

— 2 —

次 See 638.

— 4 —

欣 See 2077.

欧 2413/F1032 歐 Ō Europe.
B
2 人 *Ōjin* a European
4 文 *ōbun* European language, foreign text
化 *ōka* Europeanization, Westernization
氏管 *ōshikan* eustachian tube
6 米 *Ō-Bei* Europe and America
州 *Ōshū* Europe
州共同市場 *Ōshū Kyōdō Shijō* European Common Market
7 亜 *Ō-A* Europe and Asia
9 風 *Ōfū* European style, Occidental
洲 *Ōshū* Europe
19 羅巴 *Yōroppa* Europe
21 露 *Ō-Ro* European Russia

— 6 —

欬 2414/F1027 See 咳 921.

— 7 —

欲 See 4461.

欵 2415/F1027 See 款 2418.

欷 2416/F1027 KI cry.
8 泣 *kikyū* sobbing
16 歔 *kikyo* sobbing

8

欽 See 4829.

欹 2417/F1027 I. *sobada(teru)* prick up (one's ears).

B **款** 2418/F1028 款 欵 KAN article, section; goodwill, friendship; collusion.

9 通 *kan (o) tsū(jiru)* collusion with the enemy
待 *kantai* entertainment, hospitality
14 語 *kango* pleasant chat

B **欺** 2419/F1028 KI. GI *azamu(ku)*, *dama(su)* deceive, cheat, delude.

8 取 *azamu(ki)-to(ru)* take by deceit, defraud
12 惑 *azamu(ki)-mado(wasu)* deceive and lead astray
16 瞞 *giman* deception, imposition
瞞的 *gimanteki* deceptive, false
瞞者 *gimansha* deceiver

9

款 2420/F-X See 款 2418.

歇 2421/F1030 KETSU out of (food, etc.), be exhausted; stop; rest.

10

歎 See 2424.

A **歌** 2422/F1030 KA. *uta(u)* sing, recite, chant, carol. *uta* poem, tanka, ballad, poetry; singing.

2 人 *kajin, utabito* poet
3 口 *utaguchi* mouthpiece (of a flute); poetic style; poetic skill
女 *utame* singer, songstress
上 *uta(i)-a(geru)* write poetry
4 心 *utagokoro* poetic sentiment
手 *kashu, uta(i)te* singer, vocal soloist
5 仙 *kasen* great poet
出 *uta(i)-da(su)* break out in song
6 曲 *kakyoku* melody, tune, song
交 *uta(i)-ka(wasu)* sing responsively
合 *uta(i)-a(u)* sing responsively. *uta-awa(se)* poetry contest
会 *kakai, utakai* poetry party, poetry competition
会始 *utakaihaji(me)* Imperial Poetry Contest
7 吹 *kasui* singing and playing the flute
妓 *kagi* geisha, singing girl
沢 *utazawa* popular ballad
声 *utagoe* singing; singing voice. *uta(i)goe* singing voice. *kasei* singing
言葉 *uta kotoba* poetic diction
8 枕 *utamakura* oft-repeated descriptive epithets in poetry
学 *kagaku* poetry, versification
9 風 *kafū* poetic style
垣 *utagaki* (ancient) dancing-and-singing party
姫 *utahime* songstress
神 *kashin* muse, goddess of poetry
10 屑 *utakuzu* doggerel, trivial poetry
格 *kakaku* poetry style; poetry rules
書 *kasho* book of poems
留多 *karuta* playing cards
11 道 *kadō* versification; tanka poetry
唱 *kashō* song; singing. *uta-uta(i)* singer; prostitute
崇 *uta(i)-aga(meru)* extol in song
12 詞 *uta kotoba* poetic diction. *kashi* the words of a song
詠 *utayo(mi)* poet, tanka composer
集 *kashū* anthology; a book of poetry
13 話 *kawa* poetry talk
聖 *kasei* a great poet
14 碑 *kahi* a tanka inscription
誦 *kashō* singing loudly
歌者 *uta-uta(u) mono* singer
舞 *kabu* singing and dancing, entertainment
舞伎 *kabuki* popular drama, kabuki
舞妓 *kabuki* popular drama, kabuki
15 劇 *kageki* opera
稿 *kakō* manuscript of a poem
調 *kachō* tune, melody, air, aria
論 *karon* poetry review
16 壇 *kadan* poetry circles
謡 *kayō* song, ballad
謡曲 *kayōkyoku* popular song
18 題 *kadai* name of a poem
20 競 *utakura(be)* poetry contest

11

歐 2423/F1032 See 欧 2413.

歎 2424/F1031 TAN grief, lamentation. *nage(ku)*, *nageka(shii)*, *negekawa(shii)* (see under 嘆 974.0).

7 声 *tansei* sign, lamentation; sigh of admiration
9 美 *tambi* admiration, adoration
10 称 *tanshō* praise, admiration, applause
息 *tansoku* sigh, grief, deploring
13 嗟 *tansa* groan, sigh of despair
15 賞 *tanshō* praise, admiration, applause
19 願 *tangan* entreaty, petition, appeal, suit
願書 *tangansho* written petition

A **歡** 2425/F1032 歓 KAN joy, pleasure. *yoroko(bi)*, *yoroko(bu)* (see under 喜 1115.0).

4 心 *kanshin* favor
6 会 *kankai* a happy party
迎 *kangei* welcome
迎会 *kangeikai* welcome meeting, reception
迎攻 *kangeize(me)* lionization
迎門 *kangeimon* welcome arch
迎辞 *kangei (no) ji* welcome address
7 声 *kansei* cheers, shout of joy
8 送 *kansō* hearty send-off
送会 *kansōkai* farewell meeting
呼 *kanko* ovation, a cheer
呼声 *kanko (no) koe* shout of joy, a cheer
9 待 *kantai* entertainment, hospitality, warm reception
12 喜 *kanki, kangi* joy, gladness
13 楽 *kanraku* pleasure, enjoyment
楽街 *kanrakugai* amusement center; red-light district
楽郷 *kanrakukyō* amusement district
15 談 *kandan* pleasant chat

— 12 —

歔 See 248.

— 13 —

歛 2426 / F-X Nonstandard for 斂 2061.

歟 2427 / F1032 Yo *ya, ka* an interrogative particle.

— 17 —

歡 2428 / F1032 See 歓 2425.

RAD. 止 77

Tomeru to stop. At left: 𣥂 *tome hen.* Nickname: Stopping.

A 止 2429 / F1033 SHI. *to(maru)* stop, halt, stand still, pull up; cease, be interrupted, be discontinued; be choked; alight on, perch, roost; be held in position. *to(meru)* stop; check; allay (pain); fasten; turn off; detain; forbid to do; dissuade. *todo(maru)* stop, halt, stay, remain, stay behind; be limited to. *todo(meru)* stop, cease, detain, put an end to; leave; fix; remain in (a certain condition); content oneself with. *ya(mu) vi* end, stop, cease; subside, calm down, pass; die out, be extinguished; leave, go off; be abandoned. *ya(meru) vt* end, discontinue; give up, abandon; abolish; resign, retire. *yo(su)* stop, discontinue, give up. *sa(su)* stop; leave something unfinished. *to(me)* stopping; prohibition; end; a stop. *to(mare)* halt, stop. *ya(mi), ya(me)* end, discontinuance, stop. *yoshi* stop, discontinue. *todo(me)* finishing blow. *to(mari)* stop, stoppage; end, termination. *-sa(shi)* stopping.

4 木 *to(mari)gi* roost, perch
水 *shisui* still water
手 *to(me)te* peacemaker (in a quarrel)
手綱 *to(me) tazuna* checkrein
5 立 *to(me)da(te) suru* check, stop, prevent; dissuade
処 *to(me)do* termination, end
6 血 *shiketsu* stopping of bleeding, stanching
血法 *shiketsuhō* stanching blood
血剤 *shiketsuzai* a hemostatic drug
7 役 *to(me)yaku* peacemaker (in a quarrel)
男 *to(me)otoko* peacemaker
9 音器 *shionki* (piano) damper; damping
10 息 *shisoku* stopping to rest
11 得 *ya(mu) (o) e(zu)* unavoidably, inevitably, necessarily. *ya(mu) (o) e(nai)* unavoidable, necessary, inevitable, obligatory
宿 *shishuku* lodging
宿人 *shishukunin* lodger, boarder
宿所 *shishukusho* lodgings
12 間 *ya(mi)ma* lull (in a storm)
結 *to(me) musu(bi)* overhand knot
痛剤 *shitsūzai* painkiller
13 置 *todo(me)-o(ku)* keep here
17 螺旋 *to(me) neji* lock nut
18 難 *ya(mi)gata(i)* compelling

— 1 —

正 See 27.

— 2 —

此 2430 / F1037 SHI. *ko(no)* this, current; next, coming; last, past. *kore* this.

2 人 *ko(no) hito* this person
3 上 *ko(no)ue* furthermore, besides; any longer. *ko(no)ue wa* now. *ko(no)ue(monai)* best, greatest, matchless. *ko(no)ue tomo* furthermore
丈 *kore dake* only this much, this little
4 月 *ko(no) tsuki* this month
辺 *ko(no) hen, ko(no) atari, kokora* in this area, around here

分 *ko(no) bun dewa* at this rate
方 *ko(no)hō* this one; I, we. *kochira, konata, kotchi* here, this side. *ko(no) kata* since; this person ⌈(of activity)
方面 *ko(no) hōmen* this direction; this field
[5]外 *ko(no) hoka* besides this; moreover;
奴 *koitsu* this guy, this fellow ⌊except this
世 *ko(no)yo* this world, this life ⌈here
処 *koko* here, this place. *koko(ira)* around
処迄 *koko made* to this point; up till now
処先途 *koko (o) sendo to* making a last stand
処彼処 *koko-kashiko* here and there, far and wide, everywhere
処暫 *koko shiba(raku)* recently
[6]次 *ko(no) tsugi* next ⌈such and such
此 *kore-kore* this and that; etc.; so and so,
先 *ko(no) saki* hereafter, farther on
年 *ko(no) toshi* this year ⌈years
年頃 *ko(no) toshigoro* for years, in recent
[7]位 *ko(no) kurai* about so much, so many, so large, so wide, etc.
[8]所 *ko(no) tokoro* now, lately. *koko* here
限 *kore kagi(ri)* only this much
[9]度 *ko(no) tabi* at this time
通 *ko(no) tō(ri)* like this; as you see
後 *ko(no)go, ko(no) nochi* hereafter
故 *ko(no) yue ni* for this reason
段 *ko(no) dan* at this time
前 *ko(no) mae* last time, previously
点 *ko(no) ten* this point of view, this angel
[10]時 *ko(no) toki* at this time, then
[11]道 *ko(no) michi* the art, the line, the trade, the profession ⌈recently
頃 *ko(no)goro, ko(no)koro* these days, now,
許 *kore baka(ri), kore(p)paka(ri), kore(p)paka(shi)* only this, only this much ⌈cently
[12]間 *ko(no) aida, konaida* the other day, re-
程 *ko(no)hodo* the other day, recently
等 *korera* these
[13]際 *ko(no)sai* now, on this occasion
節 *ko(no) setsu* now, at present
[14]様 *ko(no)yō na* such, this kind of. *ko(no) yō*
種 *ko(no)shu* this kind ⌊*ni* in this way
[16]儘 *ko(no) mama* as it is

3

歩 2431/F1037 See 歩 2433.

4

武 See 51.

B 肯 2432/F1536 Kō. *ukega(u), gae(njiru), gae(nzuru)* agree to, consent, comply with, undertake. [肉]

[8]定 *kōtei suru* affirm, acknowledge
定文 *kōteibun* affirmative sentence
定的 *kōteiteki* affirmative
[14]綮 *kōkei* the point, the mark

A 歩 2433/F1037 歩 Ho step, pace; foot soldier. Bu rate; six feet square, *tsubo*; chance of winning. *aru(ku)* walk, hike, step. *ayu(mu)* walk, step. *fu* pawn (in chess).

[1]一歩 *ho-ippo* step by step
[4]方 *aru(ki)kata* pace, gait, way of walking
引 *bubi(ki)* discount, reduction, rebate
[5]付 *aru(ki)tsu(ki)* manner of walking
[6]回 *aru(ki)-mawa(ru)* walk around, gad about
行 *hokō* walking
行可能 *hokō-kanō na* ambulalory (patient)
行者 *hokōsha* pedestrian
合 *ayu(mi)-a(u)* step up to, compromise. *buai* rate, ratio, percentage; commission
合高 *buaidaka* percentage
合算 *buaizan* percentage calculation
[7]初 *aru(ki)zome* a baby's first steps
兵 *hohei* infantry, foot soldier
[8]板 *ayu(mi)-ita* footboard; running board;
卒 *hosotsu* infantryman ⌊gangplank
歩 *hoko* step by step, one step at a time. *aru(ki)-aru(ki)* while walking along
武 *hobu* a short distance; walking
[9]度 *hodo* pace, cadence
度計 *hodokei* pedometer
[10]哨 *hoshō* sentinel, sentry
振 *aru(ki)bu(ri)* pace, gait, way of walking
[11]廊 *horō* connecting corridor
道 *hodō* footpath, sidewalk ⌈compromise
寄 *ayu(mi)-yo(ru)* step up to, approach;
[12]測 *hosoku* pacing (a distance)
割 *buwa(ri)* proportion; commission
程記録計 *hotei kirokukei* pedometer
[13]数 *hosū* number of steps
数計 *hosūkei* pedometer
[15]調 *hochō* pace, step, cadence, acting in
[16]橋 *hokyō* footbridge ⌊unison
[20]競 *aru(ki)kura* walking race

5

歪 See 54.

9

B 歳 2434/F1040 歳 Sei, Sai year, age; time; occasion; opportunity; limit; vicinity. *toshi* age. *-sai* years old, age, year.

[2]入 *sainyū* annual revenue
[4]月 *saigetsu* time

5 市 *toshi* (*no*) *ichi* year-end market
旦 *saitan* the New Year
出 *saishutsu* annual expenditures
末 *saimatsu* year end
6 次 *saiji* year
7 余 *saiyo* over a year
8 事 *saiji* the year's events
9 首 *saishu* beginning of the year
10 時記 *saijiki* almanac
12 晩 *saiban* year end
費 *saihi* annual expenditure
13 歳 *saisai* yearly, every year
14 暮 *seibo* year-end; year-end present
徳神 *toshitokujin* goddess of lucky directions
19 瀬 *toshi*(*no*)*se* New Year's Eve

10

歴 See 835.

B **雌** 2435 / F2014 SHI female. *mesu, men-, me-* female. [隹]
3 山羊 *meyagi* she-goat, nanny goat
4 牛 *me-ushi* cow, heifer
4 犬 *mesu inu* female dog, bitch
6 伏 *shifuku suru* remain in obscurity
7 花 *mebana* female flower
8 虎 *metora* tigress
10 馬 *meuma* mare
11 鳥 *mendori* hen; female bird
鹿 *mejika* doe, hind
豚 *mebuta* sow
12 雄 *shiyū, mesu-osu* male and female
象 *mezō* cow elephant
13 蜂 *mebachi* queen bee
獅子 *mejishi* lioness
14 熊 *meguma* she-bear
15 蕊 *meshibe, shizui* pistil
19 蘂 *shizui* pistil

12

歷 See 歷 835.

A **整** 2436 / F862 整 SEI arranging. *totono*(*e-ru*), *totono*(*u*) (see under 調 4392.0). [攵]
6 地 *seichi* land readjustment; soil preparation
列 *seiretsu* array, line-up, parade
合 *seigō* adjustment, co-ordination; integration; consolidation; conformity (in geology)
7 形 *seikei* plastic surgery
形手術 *seikei shujutsu* plastic operation
形外科 *seikei geka* plastic surgery
8 枝 *seishi* pruning
版 *seihan* composing type
直 *totono*(*e*)-*nao*(*su*) rearrange, prepare again
9 除 *seijo* divisibility
10 骨 *seikotsu* osteopathy, bone-setting
流 *seiryū* rectification, commutation; detection
流子 *seiryūshi* commutator
流器 *seiryūki* rectifier (in electricity)
11 理 *seiri* arrangement, adjustment, regulation, consolidation; liquidation, reorganization; retrenchment, curtailment, shake-up, abridgement
理部 *seiribu* (newspaper) make-up department
理箱 *seiribako* filing cabinet; card file
理簞笥 *seiridansu* filing cabinet
12 備 *seibi* complete equipment; consolidation
然 *seizen*(*taru*) orderly, regular, systematic, trim, accurate, well-organized
13 数 *seisū* integer, whole number
頓 *seiton* (good) order, arrangement, regulation
15 調 *seichō* head oarsman, stroke

14

歸 See 帰 1582.

20

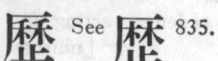

顰 2437 / F2069 HIN scowl. *hiso*(*meru*), *shika*(*meru*) raise (the eyebrows), knit (the brows), scowl. *hiso*(*mi*) scowling. [頁]
9 面 *shikamezura, shikame*(*t*)*tsura* grimace, sullen face
10 笑 *hinshō* forced laugh; laughing while scowling
18 蹙 *hinshuku suru* frown on; be shocked at

RAD. 歹 78

Ichi-ta (*ichi* "one" plus the katakana *ta*) or *gatsu* dried bones. At left: *ichi-ta hen* or *gatsu hen*. As enclosure: 歹 *shinigamae* (enclosure like that of *shinu* "die") or *ichi-ta*.
Nickname: Death.

2

A 列 2438 F235 Retsu row, rank, tier, file, column, line; procession; queue. *res(suru) vi* attend, rank with. *vt* line up. *tsura(neru)*, *tsura(naru)* (see under 連 4702.0). [刂]

4 氏 *resshi* Reaumur (thermometer)
王 *retsuō* chronicles of the kings
王紀 *Retsuōki* the Book of Kings
6 次 *retsuji* order, sequence, precedence
伝 *retsuden* series of biographies
伝体 *retsudentai* biographical style
7 車 *ressha* train
8 国 *rekkoku* the powers, all nations
9 侯 *rekkō* many feudal lords
10 座 *retsuza* presence, attendance, sitting in a row
記 *rekki* enumeration, listing
島 *rettō* archipelago, chain of islands
挙 *rekkyō* enumeration
席 *resseki* attendance, presence
席者 *ressekisha* those present, the guests, the attendance
11 強 *rekkyō* the great powers
13 福 *reppuku* beatification
福式 *reppukushiki* beatification ceremony
聖 *ressei* successive emperors; canonization
聖式 *resseishiki* canonization
18 藩 *reppan* the various clans

A 死 2439 F1043 Shi death. *shi(nu)*, *shi(suru)* die. *shi(nareru)* be bereaved, have (someone) die.

2 人 *shinin, shibito, shi(ni)bito* dead person, the killed
力 *shiryoku* desperate effort
3 亡 *shibō* death
亡広告 *shibō kōkoku* obituary notice
亡届 *shibō todoke* report of death
亡表 *shibōhyō* mortality tables
亡者 *shibōsha* the deceased; persons killed, deaths
亡者欄 *shibōsharan* obituary column
亡率 *shibōritsu* mortality, death rate
亡診断書 *shibō shindansho* death certificate
亡数 *shibōsū* number of deaths
亡欄 *shibōran* obituary column
4 文 *shibun* a document no longer of any value
方 *shi(ni)kata* manner of death; way to commit suicide
水 *shi(ni)mizu* water given to the dying
中 *shichū* fatal situation
切 *shi(ni)-ki(ru)* die
分 *shi(ni)-waka(reru)* be separated by death
火山 *shikazan* extinct volcano
支度 *shi(ni)jitaku* preparation for death
5 生 *shishō, shisei* life and death
目 *shi(ni)me* the moment of death
囚 *shishū* condemned criminal
処 *shi(ni)dokoro, shisho* place to die; place of death
去 *shikyo* death
出 *shide* dying and proceeding to the next world
出山 *shide (no) yama* the next world
出旅 *shide (no) tabi* journey to the next world
6 肉 *shiniku* dead flesh, carrion
色 *shishoku* pallor of death
灰 *shikai* cinders, ashes
地 *shichi* jaws of death, fatal situation; battlefield
守 *shishu* stubborn defense
行進 *shi (no) kōshin* death march
因 *shi-in* cause of death
因統計 *shi-in tōkei* statistics on death; causes of death
刑 *shikei* capital punishment
刑囚 *shikeishū* criminals condemned to death
刑執行 *shikei shikkō* execution of a criminal
刑場 *shikeijō* place of execution
刑罪 *shikeizai* capital offense
7 角 *shikaku* dead space (in firing)
決 *shi (o) kes(suru)* resign to die
没 *shibotsu* death
別 *shibetsu* bereavement
花 *shi(ni)bana* a glorious death
児 *shiji* dead child; stillborn child
体 *shitai* corpse, remains
体検案 *shitai ken-an* autopsy
体解剖 *shitai kaibō* autopsy
体置場 *shitai o(ki)ba* morgue
体遺棄罪 *shitai ikizai* crime of abandoning a corpse
8 金 *shi(ni)gane* wasted money; idle capital; money saved for death
所 *shisho, shi(ni)dokoro* place of death; place to die
歿 *shibotsu* death
法 *shihō* a dead law
命 *shimei* life and death; fate
苦 *shiku* death pangs, agony of death
果 *shi(ni)-ha(teru)* die (out), become extinct
学問 *shi(ni) gakumon* unprofitable knowledge
物 *shibutsu* dead thing, inanimate object

物狂 *shi(ni)monoguru(i)* death struggle; desperation, frantic efforts
者 *shisha* dead person
者狂 *shi(ni)monoguru(i)*＝死物狂 (see above–8)
者達 *shishatachi* the dead
9 面 *shimen* death mask
屍 *shishi* corpse
相 *shisō* shadow of death
神 *shi(ni)gami* god of death; death
胎 *shitai* dead fetus
重 *shi(ni)-kasa(naru)* die in swift succession. *shijū* dead weight
変 *shi(ni)-ka(waru)* be reborn in another existence
軍 *shi(ni)-ikusa* a fight to the death; soldiers who so fight
後 *shi(ni)-oku(reru)* outlive, survive. *shigo* after death, posthumously
後強直 *shigo kyōchoku* rigor mortis
海 *Shikai* Dead Sea
海写本 *Shikai Shahon* Dead Sea Scrolls
活 *shikatsu* life and death
活問題 *shikatsu mondai* a matter of life and death
10 馬 *shiba* dead horse
病 *shibyō* fatal disease
時 *shinidoki* the time to die; the time of death
恥 *shi(ni) haji* shameful death
脈 *shimyaku* fatal pulse; exhausted ore vein
致 *shi (o) ita(su)* die
11 掛 *shi(ni)-ka(karu)* be dying. *shi(ni)-ka(keru)* be dying
球 *shikyū* dead ball
許 *shi(nu) bakari* about to die
産 *shizan, shisan* stillbirth
産児 *shisanji* stillborn baby
12 絶 *shi(ni)-ta(eru)* die out, become extinct. *shizetsu* extinction, destruction
期 *shiki, shigo* time of death, the last hour
装束 *shi(ni) sōzoku* burial clothes
覚悟 *shi(ni) kakugo* readiness to die
場 *shi(ni)ba* place of death
場所 *shi(ni)basho* place of death
13 損 *shi(ni)-sokona(u)* fail in suicide attempt; outlive one's time
滅 *shimetsu* extinction, destruction
際 *shi(ni)giwa* dying hour
戦 *shisen* death struggle
節 *shisetsu* fidelity in the face of death
罪 *shizai* capital punishment
傷 *shishō* casualties, killed and wounded
傷者 *shishōsha* casualties, killed and wounded
14 様 *shi(ni)zama* manner of death
語 *shigo* dead language; obsolete word
蔵 *shizō* hoarding
15 線 *shisen* the death line; dead wire (in electricity); crisis; the brink of death
賜 *shi (o) tama(u)* permit one to commit harakiri
霊 *shiryō* departed spirits
16 骸 *shigai* corpse, remains
18 闘 *shitō* life-and-death struggle
顔 *shi(ni)gao* the face of a dead person
20 懸 *shi(ni)-kaka(ru)* to be dying. *shi(ni)kake* on the verge of death

4

殁 2440 F1045 See 没 2506.

5

殆 2441 F1046 TAI. DAI. *hoton(do), hotohoto* almost, quite, really.

殃 2442 F1045 Ō. *wazawai* (see under 禍 3254.0).
7 災 *ōsai* calamity
13 禍 *ōka* calamity

6

殊 2443 F1046 B SHU. *koto ni* especially, exceptionally, above all.
5 外 *koto(no)hoka* exceedingly, unusually; unexpectedly
功 *shukō* meritorious deeds
7 更 *kotosara ni* especially, intentionally
9 珍 *shuchin* something very strange
10 恩 *shuon* a special kindness
11 遇 *shugū* cordial treatment, special favor
12 勝 *shushō na* laudable, admirable, commendable
15 勲 *shukun* meritorious deeds
19 寵 *shuchō* special favor

殉 2444 F1046 B JUN. *jun(jiru), jun(zuru)* die a martyr, follow (someone) by committing suicide; follow in resigning.
6 死 *junshi suru*＝*jun(jiru)* (see under 殉 2444.0)
8 国 *junkoku* dying for one's country
11 教 *junkyō* martyrdom
教者 *junkyōsha* martyr
18 職 *junshoku* dying at one's post
難 *junnan* martyrdom
難者 *junnansha* martyr, victim

残 2445 F1047 A ＝殘 ZAN remainder; balance. *noko(ru)* remain, be left over; stay, linger; survive. *noko(su)* leave behind; keep back; leave undone; reserve; save, amass; bequeath. *sokona(u)* (see under 損 1979.0). *noko(razu)* all, entirely, without exception. *noko(ri)* remainder, remnant, residue.
3 亡 *zambō* defeat and flight
4 日 *zanjitsu* the setting sun; the remaining days
月 *zangetsu* waning moon, morning moon
火 *zanka* embers, remaining fire
片 *zampen* remaining piece

[5]生 *zansei* one's remaining years
冬 *zantō* the remaining days of winter
本 *zampon* books in stock, books unsold
[6]灯 *zantō* the lights still burning
光 *zankō* afterglow
多 *noko(ri)ō(i)* regrettable; reluctant to part
年 *zannen* one's remaining years
存 *zanzon suru, zanson suru* survive, remain
存物 *zanzombutsu* things remaining
存者 *zansonsha* survivor, holdover
存器官 *zanson kikan* rudimentary organ
[7]兵 *zampei* remnant troops, survivors
花 *zanka* the remaining flowers
忍 *zannin* cruelty, atrocity, brutality
忍性 *zanninsei* brutal nature, bloodthirstiness
余 *zan-yo* remainder, residue, remnant, balance
余財産 *zan-yo zaisan* remaining assets
余額 *zan-yogaku* balance
[8]金 *zankin* balance, surplus
物 *zambutsu, noko(ri)mono* remnants; scraps, leftovers, remains
刻 *zankoku* cruelty, atrocity, brutality
夜 *zan-ya* daybreak
肴 *zankō* the fish uneaten
念 *zannen* regret, disappointment, chagrin
念乍 *zannennaga(ra)* altho regrettable
念賞 *zannenshō* consolation prize
[9]香 *zankō* lingering scent
虐 *zangyaku* cruelty, atrocity, brutality
秋 *zanshū* the last days of autumn
紅 *zankō* the scattered flowers remaining
星 *zansei* the morning star
春 *zanshun* the last days of spring
品 *zampin* remnant sale
品整理 *zampin seiri* clearance sale
[10]高 *zandaka, noko(ri) daka* balance, remainder
涙 *zanrui* traces of tears
殺 *zansatsu* slaughter, massacre, murder
部 *zambu* remainder, remnant
夏 *zanka* the last days of summer
党 *zantō* remnants of a defeated party
留 *zanryū suru* remain behind
[11]惜 *noko(ri)o(shii)* regrettable; reluctant to part
陽 *zan-yō* the setting sun
限 *noko(ru)-kuma(naku)* thruout; thoroly; everywhere
菊 *zangiku* chrysanthemums blooming on to early winter
雪 *zansetsu* lingering snow
盗 *zantō* the bandits still at large
務 *zammu* unfinished business
務整理 *zammu seiri* winding up the business
[12]渣 *zansa* residue, dregs, leavings
飯 *zampan* left-over rice; leavings from a meal
殽 *zankō* the fish left over from a meal
期 *zanki* unexpired period

寒 *zankan* cold spell in spring
暑 *zansho* lingering summer heat
塁 *zanrui* runners left on bases; remaining forts
[13]滓 *zanshi* residue, dregs, leavings
煙 *zan-en* lingering smoke
賊 *zanzoku* inflicting damage; one who does so; bandits still at large
夢 *zammu* a lingering dream
照 *zanshō* afterglow
業 *zangyō* overtime
業手当 *zangyō teate* overtime pay
[14]像 *zanzō* afterimage
酷 *zankoku* cruelty, atrocity, brutality
[15]編 *zampen* the books still in existence; the books on the shelves
影 *zan-ei* traces, relics
敵 *zanteki* enemy stragglers
熱 *zannetsu* lingering summer heat
[16]骸 *zangai* corpse, carcass; ruins, debris, wreck, remains of
[18]額 *zangaku* balance (of an account)
類 *zanrui* those who remain; those not killed
簡 *zankan* fragmentary copy of a book

8

殘 2446/F1047 See 残 2445.

殛 2447/F1049 KYOKU punish.
[6]刑 *kyokkei* capital punishment; extreme penalty

殖 B 2448/F1047 SHOKU increasing. *fu(eru)* increase, multiply, accrue; (water) rises. *fu(yasu)* increase, add to, raise, multiply, augment.
[5]広 *fu(e)-hiro(garu)* increase and spread abroad, multiply
民 *shokumin*=植民 2303.5
[10]高 *fuedaka* increase, increment
財 *shokuzai* saving money; money-making; increasing one's wealth
[11]産 *shokusan* increase in production; industry; production
[14]増 *fu(e)-ma(su)* multiply

14

殯 2449/F1050 HIN lying in state, unburied coffin.
[10]宮 *hinkyū* temporary imperial mortuary

17

殲 2450/F1051 SEN massacre.
[18]滅 *semmetsu* annihilation

RAD. 殳 79

Ru-mata (the katakana *ru* plus *mata* "again"). Nickname: Windy Again (cf. Rads. 16 and 29).

4

B **殴** 2451/F1055 **毆** Ō. *nagu(ru)* hit, beat, thrash.

4 込 *nagu(ri)-ko(mu)* attack, assault, break into
5 付 *nagu(ri)-tsu(keru)* strike, beat, thrash
打 *ōda* blow, assault (and battery)
6 返 *nagu(ri)-kae(su)* strike back
合 *nagu(ri)-a(u)* fight, exchange blows
9 飛 *nagu(ri)-to(basu)* knock over, strike (someone) hard
10 倒 *nagu(ri)-tao(su)* knock down
殺 *nagu(ri)-koro(su)*, *ōsatsu suru* strike dead, beat to death
13 傷 *ōshō* striking and injuring; a bruise

5

B **段** 2452/F1051 DAN steps, stair, flight of stairs; column; paragraph; act, scene; case, question; grade, class, rank, level; degree, extent. TAN a measure of land. *kiza* scratches, mutilation (of furniture).

5 平 *dambira* broadsword, sword
丘 *dankyū* terrace, bench
7 別 *tambetsu* acreage, land area
8 物 *dammono* many-act musical drama. *tammono*＝反物 817.8
取 *dando(ri)* program, plan, arrangements
歩 *tambu* one-tenth hectare
9 通 *dantsū* rug, carpet
畑 *dambata* terraced farm
段 *dandan* steps, staircase, terrace; gradually, increasingly, one after another. *giza-giza* notches, indentation; ruggedness; fringes
段畑 *dandambatake* terraced fields
11 違 *danchiga(i)* different class, different level
階 *dankai* grade, rank, step, phase, stage. *kizahashi* steps; arrangments
袋 *dambukuro* large sack; baggy trousers
梯子 *dambashigo* staircase
12 落 *danraku* period, stop, section, end of a paragraph; conclusion, settlement
14 鼻 *dambana* aquiline nose

6

殷 See 227.

殻 2453/F-X KAI laughing voice.

A **殺** 2454/F1052 **殺** SATSU. SAI. SETSU. *koro(su)* kill, murder, butcher; waste (money); suppress (anger); hold (breath); put out, strike out. *so(gu)* *vt* chip, slice off, cut aslant, split off; diminish, reduce; dampen, spoil, mar. *so(geru)* *vi* split, splinter; be sunken; be sharpened; miss the mark.

2 人 *satsujin* murder, homicide, manslaughter
人犯 *satsujinhan* the crime of murder
人光 *satsujinkō* death ray
人光線 *satsujin kōsen* death ray
人的 *satsujinteki* murderous; deadly (heat); hectic (situation); cutthroat (competition)
人鬼 *satsujinki* cutthroat, bloodthirsty felon
人罪 *satsujinzai* murder, competition
4 文句 *koro(shi) monku* a "killing" expression; cooing words
5 生 *sesshō suru* destroy life, kill animals. *sesshō na* cruel
生戒 *sesshōkai* Buddhist precept against killing
生禁断 *sesshō kindan* hunting and fishing prohibited
6 竹 *so(gi)dake* sharp bamboo sticks
伐 *satsubatsu na* bloodthirsty, brutal, savage, warlike, fierce
合 *koro(shi)-a(u)* kill one another
虫剤 *satchūzai* insecticide
気 *sakki* bloodthirstiness; fury; wild excitement
気立 *sakkida(tsu)* get excited; be bloodthirsty
8 到 *sattō suru* rush in, pour in, throng to; descend on, storm, swoop down on
9 屋 *koro(shi)ya* a hired assassin
風景 *sappūkei* inelegance, vulgarity, lack of taste; dreariness
10 倒 *sattō*＝殺到 (see above–8)
害 *satsugai*, *setsugai* murder, killing, manslaughter, assassination
害人 *satsugainin* murderer, slayer
害者 *satsugaisha* murderer, slayer
11 掠 *satsuryaku* killing and robbing
略 *satsuryaku* killing and robbing
菌 *sakkin* sterilization, disinfection, pasteurization
菌力 *sakkinryoku* germicidal effect
菌剤 *sakkinzai* germicide, disinfectant
13 傷 *sasshō* bloodshed; casualties
意 *satsui* murderous intent
鼠剤 *sassozai* rat poison
15 戮 *satsuriku* massacre, slaughter

7

殺 2455 F1052 ＝ See 殺 2454.

P 殼 2456 F1053 ＝ 殼 KAKU. *kara* husk, hull, nutshell; cast-off skin; tofu refuse; corpse; earth's crust; eggshell

7 麦 *karamugi* unhulled wheat or barley

9 竿 *karazao, karasao* flail

8

殻 2457 F1053 ＝ See 殼 2456.

殽 2458 F1053 — Kō mix.

殷 2459 F-X — KYŪ surrender.

9

毀 2460 F1054 — KI. *kobo(tsu)* break, destroy, demolish. *kobo(reru)* be nicked, be broken, go to pieces. *kowa(su)* break, smash, destroy; take to pieces; frustrate. *kowa(reru)* break, be broken, be wrecked, be ruined, go to pieces, be damaged, be destroyed; break down; miscarry, be broken off. *kowa(re)* breakage, wreckage, fragment.

8 物 *kowa(re)mono* fragile article

11 敗 *kihai suru* destroy

13 傷 *kishō* injury, damage

損 *kison* injury, damage

棄 *kiki* damage, destruction

誉 *kiyo* praise and censure, criticism

誉褒貶 *kiyo-hōhen* praise and censure, criticism

殿 See 242.

10

A 穀 2461 F1384 ＝ 穀 穀 KOKU cereals, grain. [禾]

8 物 *kokumotsu* cereals, grain

9 食 *kokushoku* cereal diet; grain-eating

10 粉 *kokufun* grain or rice flour

倉 *kokugura, kokusō* granary, grain elevator

11 粒 *kokuryū* kernel, a grain

断 *kokuda(chi)* abstinence from grains

12 減 *kokube(ri)* volume loss in stored grain

象虫 *kokuzō mushi* grain weevil

15 潰 *gokutsubu(shi)* idler, drone

18 類 *kokurui* grains

11

毆 See 殴 2451.

穀 2462 F1384 ＝ See 穀 2461. [禾]

毅 2463 F1055 — KI strong.

12 然 *kizen(taru)* dauntless, firm, resolute

12

穀 2464 F1434 F1384 ＝ See 穀 2461. [米]

轂 2465 F1848 — KOKU hub. *koshiki* hub (of a wheel). [車]

毋 RAD. 80

Haha mother, *kan no haha* (like the top element of *kan*, a unit of weight), or *nakare* not. Variant: 母 (5 strokes) *haha*. Nickname: Mother.

A 母 2466 F1055 — BO. *haha* mother; cause; motive. *(o)kā(san)* mother, mama.

3 上 *haha-ue* my dear mother

子 *boshi, hahako* mother and child. *boshi* principal and interest

子家庭 *boshi katei* fatherless home

子寮 *boshiryō* mothers' home; home for mothers and children

4 方 *hahakata* the mother's side (of the family)

日 *Haha (no) Hi* Mother's Day

6 后 *bokō* empress dowager

7 体 *botai* mother's body; parent organization

系 *bokei* maternal line

系制度 *bokei seido* matriarchal system

系家族 *bokei kazoku* matriarchal family

8 乳 *bonyū* mother's milk

国 *bokoku* mother country

国語 *bokokugo* mother tongue

性 *bosei* motherhood

性愛 *boseiai* a mother's love

9 音 *bo-in, bo-on* vowel

屋 *omoya, moya* main building (of a noble's home)

指 *boshi* thumb
胎 *botai* mother's womb
型 *bokei* matrix (in printing)
10 校 *bokō* one's alma mater
殺 *hahakoro*(*shi*), *hahagoro*(*shi*) matricide
11 鳥 *hahadori* mother bird
違 *hahachiga*(*i*) stepbrother, stepsister
船 *bosen* mother ship
堂 *bodō* your mother
教会 *bokyōkai* mother church
12 港 *bokō* home port
斑 *bohan* pigmentation
御 *hahago* (polite for) mother
御前 *hahagozen* (polite for) mother
14 様 *kāsama, kāsan* mother, mama
語 *bogo* mother tongue
15 権 *boken* maternal authority
権制度 *boken seido* matriarchal system
16 親 *hahaoya* mother
親似 *hahaoyani* taking after one's mother
20 艦 *bokan* mother ship, tender, carrier

—— 2 ——

A 毎 2467 / F1056 MAI. *-goto ni* each, every, at an interval of, whenever. *mai-* every, each, apiece.

3 夕 *maiyū* every evening
4 日 *mainichi* every day, daily
月 *maigetsu, maitsuki* monthly, every month
6 回 *maikai* every time
次 *maiji* every time
号 *maigō* each issue
年 *mainen, maitoshi* every year, annually
毎 *maimai* each time; frequently; always
8 夜 *maiyo* every evening, every night
9 度 *maido* each time; frequently; always
10 週 *maishū* every week, weekly
時 *maiji* every hour, per hour
12 晩 *maiban* every evening, every night
朝 *maiasa, maichō* every morning
期 *maiki* every term, every quarter

—— 4 ——

A 毒 2468 / F1056 毒 DOKU poison; virus, venom, germ, toxin; harm, injury; malice, spite. *doku*(*suru*) poison, harm, corrupt, spoil. *doku*(*zuku*) curse, revile, abuse.

2 人参 *doku ninjin* poison hemlock
3 口 *dokuguchi* abuse, foul tongue
刃 *dokujin* assassin's dagger
4 心 *dokushin* malice, spite
手 *dokushu* the clutches (of a usurer, a villain, etc.)
中 *dokuata*(*ri*) poisoning
5 牙 *dokuga* poison fang
矢 *dokuya* poisoned arrow
汁 *dokujū* poisonous juices
6 舌 *dokuzetsu* wicked tongue; abusive language
虫 *doku mushi, dokuchū* poisonous insect
気 *dokuke, dokki* noxious air, poisonous air, virulence, poisonous breath; malice, spite
気抜 *dokki* (*o*) *nu*(*ku*) startle someone
7 言 *dokugen* abusive language
麦 *dokumugi* darnel, tares
見 *dokumi* tasting for poison
見役 *dokumiyaku* taster for poison
8 性 *dokusei* virulence, poisonous character
物 *dokubutsu* poisonous substance, toxicant
炎 *dokuen* poisonous flame
突 *dokuzu*(*ku*) gossip, spread rumors
毒 *dokudoku*(*shii*) poisonous; venomous, malicious, acrimonious; heavy, gross, disagreeable
味 *dokumi* tasting for poison
味役 *dokumiyaku* taster for poison
9 除 *dokuyoke* protection against poisoning
草 *dokusō* poisonous plant
10 消 *dokuke*(*shi*) antidote
酒 *dokushu* poisoned saké
殺 *dokusatsu* poisoning
害 *dokugai* poisoning
素 *dokuso* toxin, ptomaine poison
11 婦 *dokufu* wicked woman, vampire
液 *dokueki* poisonous liquid
蛇 *dokuja, doku hebi* venomous serpent
断 *dokuda*(*chi*) abstaining from certain food
悪 *dokuaku* great wickedness
12 焰 *dokuen* poisonous flame
筆 *dokuhitsu* stinging pen
13 腺 *dokusen* poison gland
蛾 *dokuga* poisonous moth
14 説 *dokusetsu*＝*dokuzetsu* 毒舌 (see above–6)
蜥蜴 *doku tokage* venomous lizard
15 質 *dokushitsu* poisonous element, poisonous nature
16 薬 *dokuyaku* poison, poisonous drug

—— 7 ——

B 貫 2469 / F1792 KAN $8\frac{1}{3}$ pounds (see Weights and Measures). *tsuranu*(*ku*) pierce, penetrate, perforate; shoot thru; attain (one's object). *nuki* brace. [貝]

2 入 *kannyū suru* penetrate
4 木 *kannuki, kan*(*no*)*ki* gate bar
5 目 *kamme* $8\frac{1}{3}$ pounds; weight
主 *kanju, kanzu* (Buddhist) head priest
8 長 *kanchō* superintendent priest
9 首 *kanshu* head priest
通 *kantsū suru* pierce, penetrate, perforate, tunnel thru
10 流 *kanryū suru* flow thru
11 頂 *kanchō* superintendent priest
13 禄 *kanroku* weight, dignity

15徹 *kantetsu* accomplishment, realization, fulfillment; penetration
16録 *kanroku* weight, dignity
20籍 *kanseki* census

比 RAD. 81

Kuraberu to compare. Nickname: Comparing.

A 比 2470 / F1057 Hɪ ratio; comparison; an equal, a match. *hi(suru)* compare. *kura(beru)* compare, balance, contrast. *tagu(eru)* compare with. *kura(bekko)* race. *tagui* kind, sort, class. *koro* time; about, toward. -*Hi*- Philippines. -*kura(be)* contest, trial (of strength).
4比 *hihi* all, one and all
5目魚 *hirame* flounder, flatfish, halibut
丘 *biku* Buddhist priest
丘尼 *bikuni* Buddhist priestess
6年 *hinen* every year, year by year
色計 *hishokukei* colorimeter
8肩 *hiken suru* rank with
価 *hika* parity
況 *hikyō* comparison
物 *kura(be)mono* comparison, match
例 *hirei* proportion; ratio
例代表 *hirei daihyō* proportional representation
例代表制 *hirei daihyōsei* proportional representation
例配分 *hirei haibun* proportional allotment
9重 *hijū* specific gravity; density; priority, relative importance
10倫 *hirin* a peer, an equal
島 *Hitō* Philippines
11率 *hiritsu* ratio; percentage
12喩 *hiyu* simile, metaphor; allegory, parable, fable
喩的 *hiyuteki* figurative, allegorical
13適 *hiteki*=*hitteki* 匹敵 756.15
較 *hikaku* comparison; comparative (anatomy)
較史 *hikakushi* comparative history
較言語学 *hikaku gengogaku* comparative philology
較的 *hikakuteki* relative, comparative
較宗教学 *hikaku shūkyōgaku* comparative religions
較級 *hikakukyū* comparative degree
14隣 *hirin* vicinity
15論 *hiron* analogy; comparative study
敵 *hiteki*=*hitteki* 匹敵 756.15
熱 *hinetsu* specific heat
17翼 *hiyoku* wings abreast; congenial couple; single garment made to look double
翼塚 *hiyokuzuka* lover's double grave
18類 *hirui* a parallel, an equal
類無 *hiruina(i)* unparalleled, incomparable

5

毗 毘 See 2997.

B 皆 2471 / F1304 Kᴀɪ. *mina*, *minna* all, everybody, everything. [白]
5目 *kaimoku* altogether; (not) at all
6伝 *kaiden* initiation
伐 *kaibatsu* clearing (land)
伐地 *kaibatsuchi* cleared land
9皆 *minamina* all (people)
皆様 *minaminasama* all the people, all of you
10納 *kainō* full (tax) payment
殺 *minagoro(shi)* massacre, annihilation
既 *kaiki* total eclipse, totality
既日食 *kaiki nisshoku* complete solar eclipse
既月食 *kaiki gesshoku* complete lunar eclipse
既日蝕 *kaiki nisshoku* complete solar eclipse
既月蝕 *kaiki gesshoku* complete lunar eclipse
既食 *kaikishoku* total eclipse, totality
既蝕 *kaikishoku* total eclipse, totality
11済 *kaisai* full payment, settlement
12無 *kaimu* nothing
勤 *kaikin* perfect attendance
勤賞 *kaikinshō* reward for perfect attendance
14様 *minasama*, *minasan* all of you, all the people

8

琵 2472 / F1252 Bɪ glissando on strings; a lute. [王]
12琶 *biwa* lute
琶法師 *biwa hōshi* lute-playing itinerant priest
琶湖 *Biwako* Lake Biwa

4 心小⺌戈戸手扌支攴攵文斗斤方无日曰月木欠止歹殳毋比[毛]氏气水氵氺火灬爪爫父爻爿丬片牙牛犬犭

RAD. 毛 82

Ke hair (of animals). Variant, as enclosure: 毛⻌. Nickname: Fur.

A 毛 2473/F1059 Mō hair, tenth of a *rin*. *ke* hair, fur, feather, down. *ke(darake)* hairy.

4 孔 *keana* pores
切 *kegi(re)* abrasion from wearing wool
5 穴 *keana* pores
叩 *kebataki* feather duster
布 *mōfu* blanket, steamer rug
生液 *mōseieki* hair grower
生薬 *kehaegusuri* hair restorer
皮 *kegawa, mōhi* fur, skin, pelt
皮商 *kegawashō* furrier
皮製品 *kegawa seihin* fur products
6 糸 *ke-ito* wool yarn, worsted
羽 *keba* nap, fuzz, pile
色 *ke-iro* color of the hair; disposition
虫 *kemushi* caterpillar
衣 *kegoromo* fur coat
7 抜 *kenu(ki)* hair tweezers
更 *kegawari* shedding, molting
8 並 *kena(mi)* the lie of the hair; color of the hair; disposition; lineage
9 染 *kezo(me)* dyeing the hair
染薬 *kezo(me)gusuri* hair dye
10 根 *mōkon* hair root
莨 *kimpōge* buttercup
留 *kedo(me)* the nut of a violin bow
唐 *ketō* foreigner
唐人 *ketōjin* foreigner
11 彫 *kebo(ri)* engraving lines
深 *kebuka(i)* hairy
脛 *kezune* hairy legs
細血管 *mōsai kekkan* capillaries
細管 *mōsaikan* capillaries
12 焼 *keya(ki)* singeing
程 *kehodo mo* (not) a bit
筋 *kesuji* a hair
筆 *mōhitsu* writing or painting brush
替 *kega(wari)* shedding, molting
無山 *kena(shi)yama* bald hill
13 嫌 *kegira(i)* antipathy, prejudice
鉤 *kebari* (fishing) fly
際 *kegiwa* the hairline
裏 *keura* fur lining
14 箒 *kebōki* feather brush
管 *mōkan* capillaries
髪 *mōhatsu* hair
製品 *mōseihin* woolen goods
15 編 *keami* knitting; knitted
16 頭 *mōtō* (not) at all
17 氈 *mōsen* rug, carpet
18 織 *keo(ri)* woolen goods
織物 *keorimono* woolen goods
22 嚢 *mōnō* hair follicle

4

毟 See 207.

耄 See 耄 3686. [耂]

6

毦 See 3686. [老]

7

毫 See 318.

毬 2474/F1061 Kyū. *iga* burr. *mari* ball.

7 投 *marina(ge)* playing catch
8 果 *kyūka* tree cone
果植物 *kyūka shokubutsu* conifer
10 栗 *igaguri* chestnuts in burrs; close-cropped head

8

毯 2475/F-X Tan wool rug.

毳 2476/F1061 Zei. *keba* nap, fuzz, pile. *mukuge* down, fluff.

5 立 *kebada(tsu)* be fluffy, be plushy

13

氈 2477/F1061 氈 Sen woolen cloth, rug.

RAD. 氏 83

Uji surname, clan. Nickname: Clan.

A 氏 2478/F1062 SHI Mr.; family, clan. *uji* clan; lineage, birth; surname.
2 人 *ujibito* clansman
3 子 *ujiko* shrine parishioner
6 寺 *ujidera* clan temple
名 *shimei*, *ujina* surname
名点呼 *shimei tenko* roll call
9 神 *ujigami* Shinto clan god, patron deity. *uji (no) kami* clan chieftain
11 族 *shizoku* family, clan
族制度 *shizoku seido* family system, clan system
19 譜 *shifu* genealogy

1

民 See 25.

4

呉 See 292.

昏 2479/F895 KON dark; evening, dusk. [日]
7 乱 *konran* derangement, muddle, bewilderment
8 迷 *kommei* confusion, bewilderment; stupor, unconsciousness
昏 *konkon to* unconsciously
10 倒 *kontō* swoon, faint
冥 *kommei* complete darkness
11 酔 *konsui* dead drunk
12 惑 *konwaku* ignorance of truth and lack of judgment
13 睡 *konsui* coma, stupor, dead sleep
睡病 *konsuibyō* sleeping sickness

5

呉 See 292.

RAD. 气 84

Kigamae "vapor" enclosure. Nickname: Steam.

2

A 気 2480/F1064 氣 炁 気 KI, KE spirit, mind, soul, heart; intention; bent, interest; mood, feeling; temper, disposition, nature; care, attention; air, atmosphere; flavor; odor; energy, essence. air, indications, symptoms; taste; touch, dash, shade, trace; spark, flash; suspicion. *ki(ni)suru* mind, care, take to heart, be nervous about. *ki(ni)naru* weigh on the mind, get on one's nerves; take a fancy to; feel inclined to. *ki (ga) suru* think, feel. *ki(ga) aru* have the intention (of doing something). *-ke*, *-ge* feeling; taste.
2 入 *ki (ni) i(ru)* be pleased with, be satisfactory. *ki(ni)i(ri)* favorite, pet
力 *kiryoku* energy, vigor, vitality, mettle, push
3 丈 *kijō na* stouthearted
丈夫 *kijōbu* reassurance
丈者 *kijōmono* stouthearted person
4 心 *kigokoro* temper, disposition
込 *kigo(mi)* ardor, enthusiasm, ambition
孔 *kikō* pore; (whale's) blowhole
引 *ki (o) hi(ku)* analyze a person's thinking
化 *kika* evaporation; vaporization
化器 *kikaki* carburetor
分 *kibun* feeling, mood, spirit
分転換 *kibun tenkan* mental diversion; change of environment
5 立 *ki (ga) ta(tsu)* get excited, be aroused. *kida(te)* disposition, temperament
弁 *kiben* air valve
失 *ki (o) ushina(u)* faint
付 *ki (ga) tsu(ku)* be aware of, notice, realize. *ki (o) tsu(keru)* take care of, be careful, be attentive to, take note of; be on the lookout. *kizu(ku)* notice, perceive, find out, think of, get wind of. *kitsu(ke)* encouragement; restorative, stimulant, smelling salts; reviving. *ki(o)tsu(ke)* Attention! *-kitsuke*, *-kizuke* in care of
付薬 *kizukegusuri* a stimulant
圧 *keo(sareru)* be overpowered, be overawed. *kiatsu* atmospheric pressure
圧計 *kiatsukei* barometer
圧配置 *kiatsu haichi* the weather picture

心 小 小 戈 戸 手 扌 支 攴 攵 文 斗 斤 方 无 日 曰 月 木 欠 止 歹 殳 毋 比 毛 氏 气 2 水 氵 氺 火 灬 爪 爫 父 爻 爿 丬 片 牙 牛 犬 犭

6 色 *keshiki*(*bamu*) look hurt; get excited; get angry. *kishoku* mood, feeling; expression. *kewai*, *kehai* sign, indication. *keshiki* signs, indications; feelings; popularity; your will, your pleasure; reason; getting excited, getting angry. *kishoku* countenance; feelings

回 *ki* (*o*) *ma*(*wasu*), *ki* (*ga*) *mawa*(*ru*) give play to imagination; make a suspicious conjecture

団 *kidan* air mass

尽 *kizu*(*kushi*) earnest exertion

気 *ki* (*ga*) *ki* (*denai*) be always worrying

向 *ki*(*ga*) *mu*(*ku*), *ki*(*ni*) *mu*(*ku*) feel inclined

任 *kimaka*(*se*) one's pleasure, free will

休 *kiyasu*(*me*) *ni* for peace of mind

忙 *kizewa*(*shii*) restless, bustling, fidgety

扱 *kiatsuka*(*i*) solicitude, anxiety, worry

早 *kibaya na*, *ki* (*no*) *haya*(*i*) quick-tempered

多 *ki* (*ga*) *ō*(*i*) wavering, vacillating

宇 *kiu* magnanimity; feeling

宇快濶 *kiu-kaikatsu na* magnanimous

合 *kia*(*i*) feeling, temper, disposition; a puff of breath; yell

合入 *kia*(*i*) (*o*) *i*(*reru*) encourage

合負 *kia*(*i*)*ma*(*ke*) *suru* be outdone by another's will power

合術 *kia*(*i*)*jutsu* hypnotism

7 迫 *kihaku* soul; great energy, great mental power

抜 *ki* (*ga*) *nu*(*keru*) be discouraged. *ki*(*ga*)-*nu*(*keta*), *ki*(*no*)*nu*(*keta*) insipid, stale. *kinu*(*ke*) absentmindedness, dejection

折 *kio*(*re*) depression, dejection

沈 *ki* (*ga*) *shizu*(*mu*) be discouraged

状 *kijō na* gaseous

狂 *ki* (*ga*) *kuru*(*u*) = *kuru*(*u*) (see under 狂 2872.0). *kiguru*(*i*) out of one's senses; out of season (flowering)

利 *ki* (*ga*) *ki*(*ku*) have good judgment, be clever. *ki* (*o*) *ki*(*kasu*) use one's head, be sensible. *ki* (*no*) *ki*(*ita*) sensible, intelligent, clever, respectable, in good taste. *ki* (*no*) *ki*(*kanai*) dull, awkward, unrefined

位 *kigurai* feelings

位高 *kigurai* (*no*) *taka*(*i*) noble, proud, dignified

体 *kitai* gas, vapor, gaseous body

体力学 *kitai rikigaku* aerodynamics, aeromechanics

体化 *kitaika* vaporization

体動力学 *kitai dōrikigaku* aerodynamics

8 長 *kinaga na* leisurely, patient

送 *kisō* pneumatic-tube dispatch

迷 *kimayo*(*i*) hesitation, uneasiness

性 *kishō* disposition, temperament

拙 *kimazu*(*i*) disagreeable, unpleasant

直 *kinao*(*ri*) improvement (in stock market)

易 *kiyasu*(*ku*) freely, with a light heart

受 *kiu*(*ke*) popularity, favor, reception, reputation

苦労 *kigurō* worry, anxiety

所為 *ki* (*no*) *se-i* fancy, imagination

泡 *kihō* air bubble

泡水準器 *kihō suijunki* spirit level

取 *kedo*(*ru*) suspect, sense. *kido*(*ru*) be affected, assume airs, pose as. *kido*(*ri*) affectation

取屋 *kido*(*ri*)*ya* affected person, dandy, dude

炎 *kien* flame; bombast, tall talk

炎万丈 *kiem-banjō* high spirits

毒 *ki*(*no*)*doku* pitiable, miserable; regrettable; too bad

毒様 (*o*)*ki*(*no*)*dokusan*, (*o*)*ki*(*no*)*dokusama* That's too bad.

味 *kimi*, *kibi* feeling; touch, dash, shade, tinge; taste and savor; suspicion. *-kimi*, *-gimi* tendency. *kiaji* market tone

味好 *kimiyo*(*i*) good feeling

味合 *kimia*(*i*) touch, dash, shade, tinge; suspicion

味悪 *kimiwaru*(*i*), *kibiwaru*(*i*) uncanny, weird, lurid, gruesome, ominous, repulsive, eerie, creepy

9 音 *kion* aspirate

風 *kippu*, *kifū* character, disposition, temper; morale, spirit

食 *ki* (*ni*) *ku*(*wanu*) go against the grain, be unsatisfactory, be disagreeable, dislike

後 *kioku*(*re*) timidity

持 *kimochi* feeling, mood. *kimochi*(*yoku*) agreeably, cheerfully

相 *kissō* look, expression

海 *kikai* atmosphere

重 *kiomo*(*i*) heavyhearted, depressed

乗 *kino*(*ri*) *suru*, *ki* (*ga*) *noru* be interested in

変 *kigawa*(*ri*) change of mind; fickleness

前 *kimae* temperament; generosity

品 *kihin* (moral) tone, dignity, grace, nobility, refinement

室 *kishitsu* air chamber

荒 *kiara na* hot-tempered

急 *kizewa*(*shii*) restless, bustling, fidgety

保養 *kihoyō* recreation, relaxation

負 *kio*(*u*) brace oneself; stir up one's fighting spirit

負立 *kio*(*i*)-*ta*(*tsu*), rouse against, nerve (for a struggle), brace up; be enthusiastic

10 高 *kedaka*(*i*) noble, exalted, graceful

疲 *kizuka*(*re*) mental fatigue, worry, boredom

病 *ki* (*ni*) *ya*(*mu*) worry about, be sensitive about. *kiya*(*mi*), *kibyō* blues, depression. *ki* (*no*) *yamai* anxiety illness; nervous breakdown

進 *ki* (*ga*) *susu*(*mu*) feel inclined

振 *kebu*(*ri*) air, appearance; behavior; bearing; indications

根 *kikon* aerial root; energy, perseverance

格 *kikaku* grace, dignity

流 *kiryū* air current

紛 *kimagure* caprice, whim, uneven temper

恥 *kihazu(kashii)* ashamed, bashful, shy, embarrassed

胸 *kikyō* pneumothorax

脈 *kimyaku* connection; collusion; communication

配 *kehai, kewai* sign, indication. *kikuba(ri)* vigilance; worry. *kihai* market trend

兼 *kiga(ne)* constraint, deference, scruple, hesitation

差 *ki (ga) sa(su)* be concerned

留 *ki (ni) to(meru)* give heed to, take notice of

弱 *kiyowa(i)* timid, fainthearted

骨 *kikotsu* spirit, soul, mettle, backbone. *kibone* mental effort

骨折 *kibone (ga) o(reru)* be ever worrying

随 *kizui* wilfulness, selfishness, self-indulgence

随気儘 *kizui-kimama na* willful

息 *kisoku, iki* breathing; breath

息奄奄 *kisoku-en-en* gasping for breath, dying

候 *kikō* climate; weather; season

候学 *kikōgaku* climatology

候風 *kikōfū* seasonal wind, monsoon

候順応 *kikō junnō* acclimatization

候療法 *kikō ryōhō* climatotherapy

11 運 *kiun* luck; tendency, opportunity

遅 *kioku(re) no* afraid

強 *kizuyo(i)* brave, resolute; reassuring; hardhearted. *kizuyo(ku)* resolutely, cheerily, confidently

掛 *kiga(kari)* anxiety

済 *ki (ga) su(mu)* be satisfied, be appeased

移 *kiutsu(ri)* fickleness; sympathy

組 *kigu(mi)* attitude, ardor, preparation

細 *ki (ga) hoso(i)* cowardly

転 *kiten* tact; ready wit

悪 *ki (o) waru(ku) suru* hurt one's feelings

崩 *kikuzu(re) suru* be worn out of shape. *kikuzu(re)* slump, depression

動車 *kidōsha* diesel train

張 *kiba(ru)* exert oneself, make an effort; be extravagant, make a show. *kiba(ri)* exertion, effort. *ki (ga) ha(ru)* be under tension

張屋 *kiba(ri)ya* one who shows off

密 *kimitsu* airtight

密室 *kimitsushitsu* airtight chamber

球 *kikyū* balloon

球庫 *kikyūko* balloon hangar

球隊 *kikyūtai* balloon corps

違 *kichiga(i)* insanity; mania, fanaticism; lunatic; fanatic, enthusiast, fan

違日和 *kichiga(i)biyori* unsettled weather

違水 *kichiga(i) mizu* alcoholic liquor

違花 *kichiga(i)bana* flower blooming out of season

違雨 *kichiga(i) ame* fitful rain

違染 *kichiga(i)ji(miru)* resemble a lunatic

違病院 *kichiga(i) byōin* mental hospital

12 圏 *kiken* atmosphere

遣 *kizuka(u)* be anxious about, worry about. *kizuka(i)* fear, worry, solicitude. *kizuka(washii)* anxious

遠 *ki (ga) tō(ku) naru* feel dizzy

揉 *ki (o) mo(mu)* worry, be anxious

晴 *kiba(rashi)* diversion, recreation, relaxation, amusement. *ki (o) ha(rasu)* clear one's mind

温 *kion* air temperature

短 *kimijika na* hot-tempered, touchy, impatient

絶 *kizetsu* fainting

散 *kisan(ji)* relaxation, diversion, amusement, recreation

筒 *kitō* steam cylinder

落 *kio(chi)* discouragement, despondency. *ki (o) oto(su)* be discouraged

換 *ki (o) kae(ru)* change one's mind

焔 *kien* flame; bombast, tall talk

焔家 *kienka* big talker

軽 *kigaru na* cheerful; buoyant, lighthearted

軽者 *kigarumono* jolly fellow

無 *ki(no)na(i)* indifferent, lukewarm, uninterested

無性 *kibushō* laziness

無精 *kibushō* laziness

象 *kishō* climate, weather, weather conditions; meteorology (of a place); disposition, temperament; characteristics

象庁 *Kishōchō* Weather Bureau

象台 *kishōdai* weather observatory

象学 *kishōgaku* meteorology

象注意報 *kishō chūihō* weather warning

象特報 *kishō tokuhō* storm warning

象観測 *kishō kansoku* meteorological observations

象観測船 *kishō kansokusen* weather-observation ship

13 働 *kibatara(ki)* quick wit, tact; quick-witted person

嫌 *kigen* health; cheer; temper, mood

慨 *kigai* spirit, pep, pluck; backbone; self-respect; courage

褄 *kizuma* feelings

触 *kabu(reru)* have a skin eruption; be influenced by, become infected with (communism). *kabure* skin eruption, boils from poisonous plants; students influenced by socialism or communism

詰 *kizuma(ri)* constraint, embarrassment

障 *ki (ni) sawa(ru)* offend; get offended. *kiza* affectation. *kizawa(ri)* disagreeable feeling

稟 *kihin* hereditary traits

塞 *kifusa(gi)* gloom, depression

嵩 *kigasa* determination to win

節 *kisetsu* courage and integrity; weather

置 *ki (ga) o(kenai)* feel at home

勢 *kisei* energy, enthusiasm, spirit

楽 *kiraku* feeling at home, ease, comfort

14 構 *kigama(e)* anticipation, readiness

概 *kigai*＝気慨 (see above–13)

魂 *kikon* spirits of the dead

4 心⺗⺌戈戸手扌支攴攵文斗斤方无日曰月木欠止歹殳毋比毛氏【气】水氵氺火灬爪爫父爻爿丬片牙牛犬犭

管 *kikan* windpipe, trachea
管支 *kikanshi* bronchial tube
管支炎 *kikanshien* bronchitis
管支肺炎 *kikanshi haien* bronchial pneumonia
管炎 *kikan-en* tracheitis
15 魄 *kihaku*＝気迫 (see above–7)
鋭 *kiei* spirit, impetuosity, energy
慰 *kinagusa(mi)*＝*kiba(rashi)* 気晴 (see above–12)
熱 *kinetsu* steam heat
質 *kishitsu* temperament, disposition. *katagi* spirit, character, trait
16 縺 *kimotsu(re)* confused feelings
儘 *kimama, ki(no)mama* willfulness, selfishness, self-indulgence
儘放題 *kimama-hōdai* behaving as one pleases
18 難 *kimuzuka(shii)* hard to please, moody
難屋 *kimuzuka(shi)ya* a person hard to please, moody person
19 韻 *ki-in* refinement, taste, tone
20 懸 *ki (ni) ka(karu)* be anxious about. *ki (ni) ka(kenai)* take no notice of; take it easy. *kigaka(ri)* anxiety
22 嚢 *kinō* air sac, air bladder, gas bag
26 欝 *kiutsu* gloom, melancholy

4

気 See **気** 2480.

6

氣 2481/F1064 See **気** 2480.

RAD. 水 85

Sui or *mizu* water. At left: 氵 (3 strokes) *sanzui* (3-stroke "water," as distinguished from Rad. 15). At bottom: 氺 (5 strokes) *shita mizu*. Nickname: Water.

A **水** 2482/F1065 SUI water; ice water; Wednesday. *mizu* water. *mizu(ppoi)* watery.

2 入 *mizu-i(razu) de* privately, among ourselves. *mizu-i(re)* water jug, pitcher
入話 *mizu-i(razu) no hanashi* heart-to-heart talk
力 *suiryoku* water power
力工学 *suiryoku kōgaku* hydraulic engineering
力学 *suirikigaku, suiryokugaku* hydraulics
力発電所 *suiryoku hatsudensho* hydroelectric plant
力電気 *suiryoku denki* hydroelectricity
3 口 *mizukuchi* faucet; dam inlet, dam outlet. *minakuchi* irrigation water gate
上 *suijō* water (transportation); aquatic; floating. *minakami* headwater, source
上小学校 *suijō shōgakkō* primary schools for children living on the water
上水車 *mizua(ge) suisha* scoop water wheel
上生活 *suijō seikatsu* life on the water
上生活者 *suijō seikatsusha* seafarer
上飛行機 *suijō hikōki* hydroplane, seaplane
上機 *suijōki* hydroplane, seaplane
上警察 *suijō keisatsu* water police
上競技 *suijō kyōgi* water sports
4 心 *mizugokoro* advice on swimming; readiness to follow
手 *kako* pilot, sailor. *mizu (no) te* castle water supply
月 *suigetsu* water and a moon; reflection of the moon; jellyfish
火 *suika* fire and water
牛 *suigyū* water buffalo
辺 *suihen* water's edge, beach
引 *mizuhiki* two-color strings for tying gifts
切 *mizugi(re)* water shortage
天 *suiten* sea and sky
分 *suibun* moisture, water, humidity; juice; water content
不入 *mizu-i(razu) de* privately, among ourselves
化物 *suikabutsu* hydrate
夫 *suifu, kako* sailor, mariner, seaman
夫仲間 *suifu nakama* shipmate
夫長 *suifuchō* boatswain
中 *suichū* submarine, aquatic, underwater; in water. *mizuata(ri)* illness from water
中速力 *suichū sokuryoku* submerged speed
中爆弾 *suichū bakudan* depth bomb
中爆雷 *suichū bakurai* depth charge
5 母 *kurage* jellyfish
玉 *mizutama* a drop of water; a drop of dew
生 *suisei* aquatic (plant)
仙 *suisen* daffodil; narcissus
仕事 *mizu shigoto* washing and scrubbing
白粉 *mizu oshiroi* liquid face paint
加減 *mizu kagen* amount of water
石鹸 *mizu sekken* soft soap
田 *suiden, mizuta* paddy field
田作 *suidensaku* working the rice fields
圧 *suiatsu* hydraulic pressure
圧計 *suiatsukei* water-pressure gauge
圧管 *suiatsukan* penstock
圧機 *suiatsuki* hydraulic press

平 *suihei* water level; horizontal
平社 *Suiheisha* an organization to restore the eta class to full social privileges
平面 *suiheimen* water level, level surface
平動 *suiheidō* horizontal earthquake vibration ⌈ment
平運動 *suihei undō* social-equality move-
平距離 *suihei kyori* horizontal distance
平棒 *suihei bō* horizontal bar
平線 *suiheisen* horizon
平器 *suiheiki* a level
6 色 *mizuiro* light blue, water green
虫 *mizumushi* water insect; athlete's foot
気 *mizuke* dampness, moisture, juice. *suiki* dropsy; moisture, humidity, vapor
汲 *mizuku(mi)* drawing water
防 *suibō* flood prevention
争 *mizu araso(i)* irrigation dispute
成岩 *suiseigan* sedimentary rock
死 *suishi* drowning
死人 *suishinin* drowned person
先 *mizusaki* course; current direction; pilot;
先人 *mizusakinin* ship's pilot ⌊piloting
先案内 *mizusaki-annai* pilot; piloting
7 車 *suisha, mizuguruma* water wheel
攻 *mizuze(me)* cutting off the water supply from a castle; flooding a castle compound (in warfare); flooding thru broken dikes
利 *suiri* water utilization; water supply; irrigation
系 *suikei* water system
声 *suisei* sound of flowing water
牢 *mizurō* dungeon using water torment
災 *suisai* flood
芸 *mizugei* water stunts
冷式 *suireishiki* water-cooled
吹雪 *mizu fubuki* spray
見舞 *mizu mima(i)* visit to flood victims
位 *sui-i* water level
位標 *sui-ihyō* watermark
兵 *suihei* (navy) sailor ⌈sailor suit
兵服 *suiheifuku* naval sailor's suit; girl's
呑 *mizunomi* drinking glass
呑百姓 *mizunomibyakushō* poor farmer
呑場所 *mizunomibasho* drinking fountain
呑器 *mizunomiki* drinking fountain
8 門 *suimon* floodgate, penstock, sluice
明 *suimei* shimmering of clear water
枕 *mizu makura* water pillow
杯 *mizu sakazuki* farewell cups of water
沫 *suimatsu* spray, splash
泡 *minawa* foam, bubbles. *suihō* foam, bubble; nothing; failure
油 *mizu abura* hair oil; lamp oil
炊 *mizutaki* boiling without seasoning ⌈fruit
物 *mizumono* matter of chance; liquid;

肥 *suihi* liquid manure
苔 *mizugoke* bog moss; incrustation
取舟 *mizuto(ri)bune* water-carrying boat
治療法 *suichiryōhō* hydrotherapy
底 *minasoko, suitei* sea bottom, river bottom
底荷 *mizu sokoni* water ballast
性 *mizushō* light, flirtatious, wanton
性塗料 *suisei toryō* water colors; distemper
茎 *mizuguki* writing brush
茎跡 *mizuguki (no) ato* beautiful calligra-
泳 *suiei, mizu-oyo(gi)* swimming ⌊phy
泳大会 *suiei taikai* swimming meet
泳場 *suieijō* swimming place; swimming
泳帽 *suieibō* bathing cap ⌊pool
泳着 *suieigi* swimming suit
9 面 *suimen, minomo* surface of the water
音 *mizuoto, mizu (no) oto* the sound of water
屋 *mizuya* water carrier; holy-water font at a shrine or temple; dish cupboard
指 *mizusashi* water jug, pitcher
柱 *mizubashira* column of water; waterspout. *suichū* column of water
枯 *mizuga(re)* drought ⌈discharge
洟 *mizu(p)pana, mizubana* watery nasal
洩 *mizumori* leaking
神 *suijin* water god, water nymph
盃 *mizu sakazuki* farewell cups of water
軍 *suigun* (old word for) navy
星 *Suisei* Mercury ⌈distant
臭 *mizukusa(i)* watery; reserved, formal,
草 *suisō, mizukusa* aquatic plant
風呂 *mizuburo* cold bath
飛沫 *mizu shibuki* water spray
茶屋 *mizuchaya* a busy shop selling tea and
浅黄 *mizuasagi* light blue ⌊drinks
垢 *mizuaka* incrustation, slime
垢離 *mizugori* cold-water ablutions
洗 *mizuara(i), suisen* washing
洗式 *suisenshiki* flush type
洗式便所 *suisenshiki benjo* flush toilet
洗便所 *suisembenjo* flush toilet
10 馬 *suiba* fording a river on horseback
師 *suishi* (old word for) navy
捌 *mizuhake* drainage
流 *suiryū* current, stream, watercourse
浴 *suiyoku* bathing, cold bath. *mizua(bi)* bathing
浸 *mizubita(shi)* flooded out, submersion
紋 *suimon* wavelet, water rings
脈 *suimyaku* water vein
陸 *suiriku* land and water
郷 *suikyō, suigō* riverside district
都 *suito* town on the water's edge
差 *mizusa(shi)* water jug, pitcher. *mizu (o) sa(su)* cause trouble between people
時計 *mizudokei* water clock

心小⺌戈戸手扌支攴攵文斗斤方旡日曰月木欠止歹殳毋比毛氏气【水氵氺】火灬爪爫父爻爿丬片牙牛犬犭

疱 *suihō* blister
疱瘡 *mizubōsō* chicken pox
耕 *suikō* hydroponics
耕法 *suikōhō* hydroponics
素 *suiso* hydrogen
素爆弾 *suiso bakudan* hydrogen bomb
害 *suigai* flood damage, inundation
害地 *suigaichi* flooded area
害防止 *suigai bōshi* flood control ⌈ures
害対策 *suigai taisaku* flood-control meas-
害保険 *suigai hoken* flood insurance
害家屋 *suigai kaoku* flooded homes
害救済 *suigai kyūsai* flood relief
害罹災民 *suigai risaimin* flood victims
11 鳥 *mizudori, mizutori, suichō* waterfowl
運 *suiun* water transportation
遊 *mizuaso(bi)* wading, playing in water
域 *sui-iki* river basin; an area of the ocean
張 *mizuba(ri)* fulling
桶 *mizuoke* pail, bucket, cistern
深 *suishin* water depth
球 *suikyū* water polo
船 *mizubune* cistern, water trough; water boat; water-logged boat
瓶 *mizugame* water jar
密 *suimitsu* watertight
萍 *suihyō* floating waterweed ⌈leaves
菜 *mizuna* a variety of greens with slender
盛 *mizumo(ri)* a carpenter's level ⌈fessions)
責 *mizuze(me)* water torture (to secure con-
菓子 *mizugashi* fruit ⌈ness
商売 *mizu shōbai* the entertainment busi-
理学 *suirigaku* hydrography
悪戯 *mizu itazura* playing in water
掛論 *mizuka(ke)ron* futile argument
眼鏡 *mizu megane* diver's goggles
魚 *suigyo* fish and water ⌈ship
魚交 *suigyo (no) majiwa(ri)* intimate friend-
族 *suizoku* aquatic animals
族館 *suizokukan* aquarium
彩画 *suisaiga* water-color painting
彩画家 *suisai gaka* water-color painter
彩絵具 *suisai enogu* water colors
道 *suidō* waterworks; water pipes; city water; aqueduct; waterway, channel
道工事 *suidō kōji* water works
道局 *suidōkyoku* water bureau
道栓 *suidōsen* hydrant, faucet
道料 *suidōryō* water charge
道部 *suidōbu* water department
道橋 *suidōkyō* aqueduct bridge
産 *suisan* marine products
産大学 *suisan daigaku* fisheries college
産技師 *suisan gishi* marine-products expert
産物 *suisambutsu* marine products
産学 *suisangaku* fishery science
産学校 *suisan gakkō* fisheries school
産業 *suisangyō* fisheries, marine products
12 圏 *suiken* the hydrosphere ⌊industry
痘 *suitō* chicken pox
棲 *suisei* aquatic (animal)
温 *suion* water temperature
程 *suitei* water route
絵 *mizue* water-color painting
脹 *mizubukure* water blister
筒 *suitō* water bottle, canteen
着 *mizugi* swimming suit
落 *mizuo(chi)* solar plexus, pit of the stom-
葬 *suisō* burial at sea ⌊ach
番 *mizuban* irrigation-water watchman
煮 *mizuni* boiled in unsalted water
無月 *minazuki* 6th lunar month
蒸気 *suijōki* water vapor
疏通 *mizuhake* drainage
揚 *mizua(ge)* landing (goods); earnings; defloration; preservation (of cut flowers)
揚機 *mizua(ge)ki* irrigation wheel
割 *mizuwa(ri)* diluting with water; packing inferior goods beneath a high-quality
割株 *mizuwa(ri)kabu* watered stock ⌊layer
晶 *suishō* quartz
晶体 *suishōtai* crystalline lens
量 *suiryō* water volume
量計 *suiryōkei* water meter
飲 *mizuno(mi)* drinking glass ⌈farmers
飲百姓 *mizuno(mi) byakushō* poor tenant
飲器 *mizuno(mi)ki* drinking fountain
13 閘 *suikō* canal lock
掻 *mizukaki* webfoot, web
楊 *kawa yanagi* riverside willows
楢 *mizu nara* an oak ⌈cistern, reservoir
溜 *mizutamari* pool, puddle. *mizutame*
煙 *mizu kemuri, suien* spray, splashes
腫 *suishu* dropsy
路 *suiro* waterway, channel; aqueduct
飼 *mizuka(u)* to water (a horse)
禽 *suikin* waterfowl
嵩 *mizu kasa* water volume
勢 *suisei* force of water
鉄砲 *mizudeppō* squirt gun
溶性 *suiyōsei* water-soluble
溶液 *suiyōeki* a solution
源 *suigen* river source, fountainhead
源地 *suigenchi* catchment basin, reservoir
際 *mizugiwa, migiwa* water's edge, beach
際立 *mizugiwada(tte)* splendid (performance); neat (job); clean (hit)
準 *suijun* water level; standard
準器 *suijunki* a level (the tool)
雷 *suirai* torpedo ⌈ship
雷母艦 *suirai bokan* torpedo-boat depot
雷防禦網 *suirai bōgyomō* torpedo net

雷艇 *suiraitei* torpedo boat
雷敷設 *suirai shisetsu* mine laying
雷敷設艦 *suirai shisetsukan* mine layer
14 増 *mizuma(shi)* dilution, watering
漉 *mizuko(shi)* filter, strainer, percolator
滴 *suiteki* drop of water
漬 *mizuzu(ku)* soak or stand in water
稲 *suitō* wet-land rice
精 *suishō* quartz
練 *suiren* swimming practice; art of swimming
飴 *mizuame* rice honey
管 *suikan* water pipe, hose
酸化物 *suisan kabutsu* hydroxide
様便 *suiyōben* watery stools
様液 *suiyōeki* aqueous humor
蜜 *suimitsu* (a quality) peach
蜜桃 *suimitsutō* (a quality) peach
墨 *suiboku* India-ink painting; India ink for painting
墨画 *suibokuga* India-ink painting
銀 *suigin* mercury
銀灯 *suigintō* mercury-vapor lamp
銀柱 *suiginchū* column of mercury
銀寒暖計 *suigin kandankei* mercury thermometer
15 撒 *mizumaki* street sprinkling
槽 *suisō* water tank, water trough, cistern
澄 *mizusu(mashi)* water spider
線 *suisen* water line
論 *suiron* water dispute
蝕 *suishoku* erosion
盤 *suiban* flower basin
16 樽 *mizudaru* (ship's) water tub
膨 *mizubukure* water blister
頭 *suitō* near the water
薬 *mizugusuri, suiyaku* liquid medicine
18 翻 *mizukobo(shi)* slop bucket
甕 *mizugame* water jar
曜 *Suiyō* Wednesday
曜日 *Suiyōbi* Wednesday
難 *suinan* sea disaster; flood
難除 *suinan-yoke* charm against drowning
難救助 *suinan kyūjo* sea rescue
難救済 *suinan kyūsai* sea rescue
19 瀬 *mizuse* swift current; a fording place
爆 *suibaku* hydrogen bomb
獺 *kawa uso* otter
鏡 *mizu kagami* reflecting water
20 蘚 *mizugoke* bog moss; incrustation
礬土鉱 *suibandokō* bauxite
礬鉱 *suibankō* bauxite
22 嚢 *suinō* water bag, filter, percolator

1

氷 See 131.

永 See 130.

2

求 See 137.

氾 2483 F1070 HAN spread out; wide.
17 濫 *hanran* flooding

汀 2484 F1070 TEI. *migiwa* water's edge, shore.
15 線 *teisen* beach line

汁 2485 F1071 P JŪ, SHŪ juice. *shiru* juice; sap; soup, broth; gravy; pus. *tsuyu* juice; sap; soup, broth; gravy.
8 物 *shirumono* soups
11 液 *jūeki* juice
12 椀 *shiru wan* bowl of soup; soup bowl

3

汞 See 1456.

汎 2486 F1091 HAN. *uka(bu)* (see under 浮 2575.0).

汝 2487 F1073 JO. *nanji, nare* you, thou.
12 等 *nanjira* you (classical plural)

汐 2488 F1071 SEKI. SHAKU. *shio* tide; salt water; opportunity.
3 干狩 *shiohiga(ri)* low-tide shell gathering
12 焼 *shioya(ke)* tanned by salt air

池 2489 F1074 A CHI. *ike* pond, pool, cistern, basin, reservoir.
4 心 *chishin* center of a pond, bottom of a pond
辺 *chihen* edge of a pond
8 沼 *chishō* ponds and swamps
9 神 *ikegami* god of the pond
10 畔 *chihan* edge of a pond
11 魚 *chigyo* pond fish
16 頭 *chitō* edge of a pond

汎 汎 2490 F1071 HAN pan-.
4 太平洋 *hantaiheiyō* Pan-Pacific
6 米 *ham-Bei* Pan-American
9 独 *han-Doku* Pan-German
神教 *hanshinkyō* pantheism
神論 *hanshinron* pantheism
13 愛 *han-ai* philanthropy, humanity
意語 *han-igo* ambiguous term
15 論 *hanron* outline, summary

江 2491 / F1073 Kō. *e* inlet, bay.

B

3 口 *kōkō* large estuary
山 *kōzan* rivers and mountains
上 *kōjō* riverside; the banks of the Yangtze
4 心 *kōshin* the middle of the river
月 *kōgetsu* the moon over a river; the moon reflected in a river
水 *kōsui* river water; the Yangtze
戸 *Edo* Edo, Tokyo, Edo era (1603–1867)
戸子 *Edo(k)ko* true Tokyoite
戸前 *Edomae* Edo-style (cooking)
5 北 *kōhoku* north of the Yangtze
6 西 *kōsei* the western part of the lower Yangtze area
7 村 *kōson* river village
8 河 *kōga* the Yangtze and Yellow rivers
東 *kōtō* east of a river
9 風 *kōfū* river wind
海 *kōkai* rivers and seas; a place separated from the mundane world
9 南 *kōnan* south of the Yangtze
10 畔 *kōhan* riverside, river bank
12 湖 *kōko* the public, the world

汲 2492 / F1075 Kyū. *ku(mu)* draw (water), ladle, dip, scoop, pump; consider; sympathize with; drink; think.

2 入 *ku(mi)-i(reru)* draw in
3 干 *ku(mi)-ho(su)* pump out, bail out
上 *ku(mi)-a(geru)* pump up; scoop up
4 水 *ku(mi)mizu, kyūsui* pumping water
込 *ku(mi)-ko(mu)* fill with water
5 立 *kumita(te) no* fresh from the well
出 *ku(mi)-da(su)* pump out, bail out, dip out
6 汲 *kyūkyū toshite* diligently, industriously
8 取 *ku(mi)-to(ru)* draw (water), dip, ladle, drain, bail out; take into consideration, make allowance for
取屋 *kumito(ri)ya* night-soil man
11 乾 *ku(mi)-ho(su)* pump out, bail out
12 替 *ku(mi)-ka(eru)* pumping out a well

汗 2493 / F1071 Kan. *ase(bamu), ase suru* be sweaty. *ase* perspiration. *ase(daku)* dripping with sweat. *ase(mizuku)* dripping with sweat.

B

4 水 *asemizu* copious sweating
不知 *aseshirazu* prickly-heat powder
牛充棟 *kangyū-jūtō* a superabundance of books
6 血 *kanketsu* sweat and blood
衣 *kan-i* undershorts; clothes wet with perspiration
7 含 *asegu(mu)* perspire
8 性 *aseshō* tendency to perspire
知 *aseshi(razu)* prickly-heat powder
取 *aseto(ri)* underwear
9 疣 *asemo, asebo* prickly heat, heat rash
拭 *asefuki* cloth for wiping off the sweat
臭 *asekusa(i)* smelling of sweat
染 *aseji(miru)* be stained with sweat
10 馬 *kamba* perspiring horse
疹 *asemo, asebo* prickly heat, heat rash
流 *asenaga(shi)* washing off the sweat
13 搔 *ase(k)kaki, asekaki* heavy perspirer
腺 *kansen* sweat gland
塗 *asemidoro* dripping with sweat
18 顔 *kangan* sweating from shame
顔至 *kangan (no) ita(ri)* deeply ashamed, feeling awkward
19 襦袢 *asejiban* underwear

汚 2494 / F1072 **汙** O. *kega(su)* make dirty, stain, pollute, defile, contaminate; disgrace, dishonor; rape. *kega(reru)* get dirty; be defiled; be contaminated. *yogo(su) vt* stain, soil, pollute; defile, debauch. *yogo(reru) vi* get dirty, be stained, be contaminated, tarnish. *yogo(reta)* loathsome; obscene. *kega(re)* uncleanness, impurity, disgrace. *yogo(re)* dirt, spot, stain, filth. *kitana(i)* dirty, filthy, unclean, soiled; shabby; indecent, obscene; base, sordid; stingy; foul, *kega(rawashii)* filthy; unfair.

B

4 水 *osui* filthy water, sewage
6 行 *okō=shūkō* 醜行 4798.6
名 *omei* stigma, dishonor, disgrace, slur, infamy
吏 *ori* corrupt official
8 物 *obutsu* dust, dirt, filth, garbage, ashes; impurities; sewage. *yogo(re)mono* the washing, laundry
事 *kega(shi)goto* blasphemy
9 俗 *ozoku* bad custom, evil habit
垢 *okō* dirt, uncleanness
臭 *oshū* evil odor
染 *osen* stain, blot, spot, smudge, disgrace
点 *oten* stain, blot, spot, smudge, blur; flaw; disgrace
点抜 *shimi-nu(ki)* removal of stains
10 辱 *ojoku* disgrace, humiliation, insult
11 習 *oshū* evil habit
13 損 *oson* stain
14 塵 *ojin* filthy dust, rubbish
16 濁 *odaku* corruption, graft
18 穢 *owai, oai* night soil, muck, filth, uncleanness, squalor. *oe* filth, dirt
穢屋 *owaiya* night-soil man
職 *oshoku* graft, bribery
職罪 *oshokuzai* graft, bribery

— 4 —

沌 2495 / F1079 Ton primeval chaos.

汰 2496 F1075 DA. TA luxury; select.

沁 2497 F1076 SHIN. *shi(miru)* penetrate, soak in.

汪 2498 F1074 Ō flowing full; expanse of water; wide; deep; large.
9洋 *ōyō* great expanse of water; leisure

沍 2499 F1079 Go close up; freeze, freeze over; congeal.
12寒 *gokan* intense cold

沐 2500 F1079 MOKU. *moku(suru)* wash; bathe; moisten.
8雨 *moku-u* getting soaked in the rain
10浴 *mokuyoku* washing the hair and bathing; cleansing the body, ablutions
12猴 *mokkō* monkey

沓 2501 F1080 Tō. *kutsu* shoes, boots.
3下 *kutsushita* socks, stockings
5石 *kutsu ishi* pillar or post foundation ⌊stones
10師 *kutsushi* shoemaker
11脱 *kutsunu(gi)* bootjack

沃 2502 F1076 YOKU pour; fertility.
3土 *yokudo* fertile soil, mold
6地 *yokuchi* fertile land
9度 *yōdo* iodine
10素 *yōso* iodine
11野 *yokuya* fertile field
21饒 *yokujō na* fertile, rich, fruitful

B **沢** 2503 F1165 **澤** TAKU swamp; blessing. *sawa* swamp, marsh, dale, valley.
3山 *takusan* a great many, a large quantity, abundance, plenty
4水 *sawa mizu* swamp water
辺 *sawabe* edge of a swamp
5田 *sawada* flooded rice fields; rice fields
6地 *sawachi* marshy land ⌊near a swamp
11庵 *takuan* pickled daikon ⌈radish)
庵漬 *takuanzuke* pickled daikon (the huge

沙 2504 F1081 SA. SHA. *isago, suna* sand.
3土 *sado* sandy soil
7汰 *sata* instructions, directions, orders; notice, information, message; report, rumor; affair
汰止 *sataya(mi)* calling off; dropping
汰限 *sata (no) kagi(ri)* absurd, preposterous
汰書 *satasho* written instructions; written ⌊message
8門 *shamon* Buddhist priest
9洲 *sasu* sand bar, sandbank, reef
10蚕 *gokai* lugworm
13漠 *sabaku* desert
15噀 *namako* sea cucumber
16嘴 *shashi, sashi* sand bar, sandspit
17彌 *shami* Buddhist acolyte, novice

B **沖** 2505 F1081 **冲** CHŪ. *okitsu, oki* offing, open sea. *chū(suru)* rise high in the sky.
4辺 *okibe* the offing
天 *chūten* rising into the heavens
5出 *okida(shi)* bearing off the coast
白波 *oki(tsu) shiranami* white waves at sea
6合 *okia(i)* offshore, offing
仲仕 *okinakashi* longshoreman
8取 *okito(ri)* offshore fishing
取値段 *okito(ri) nedan* cost including
10値 *okine* free-overside price ⌊freight, C.I.F.
島 *oki(tsu) shima* an offshore island
11釣 *okizuri* offshore fishing
12渡 *okiwata(shi)* free overside
14漁 *okiryō* offshore fishing
16積土 *chūsekido* alluvial soil
19繫 *okigakari* anchoring in the offing

B **没** 2506 F1080 **沒 歿** BOTSU. MOTSU. *bos(suru)* sink, set, go down; hide, be hidden, fall into; disappear; die. *botsu* rejection of manuscript; deceased. (Some scholars limit the meaning of 歿 to dying.).
2入 *botsunyū suru* be absorbed in ⌈cal
入格的 *botsujinkakuteki* formal, mechani-
4分暁漢 *wakarazuya* a fool, a person who doesn't understand anything
5収 *bosshū* confiscation
6年 *botsunen* year of death
交渉 *bokkōshō, botsukōshō* no connection (with), no relation to
7却 *bokkyaku suru* discard and ignore
我 *botsuga* selflessness
9後 *botsugo* after death, posthumously
食子 *mosshokushi, bosshokushi* gallnut
食子酸 *mosshokushisan* gallic acid
10書 *bossho* rejected manuscript ⌈literature)
11理想 *botsurisō* lack of ideals; realism (in
常識 *botsujōshiki* lack of common sense
12落 *botsuraku* ruin, downfall, bankruptcy
落者 *botsurakusha* a bankrupt; ruined people
13義道 *mogidō na* cruel, brutal, heartless
15趣味 *bosshumi na* insipid, prosaic, dull
16頭 *bottō suru* be absorbed in, be devoted to

汽 2507/F1076 **滊** Ki vapor; steam.
A
5 圧 *kiatsu* steam pressure
圧計 *kiatsukei* steam gauge
7 車 *kisha* train; steam train
車弁 *kishaben* railway lunch
車弁当 *kisha bentō* railway lunch
車便 *kishabin de* by rail, by express, by
車道 *kishamichi* railway line ⌊freight
車賃 *kishachin* railway fare
11 笛 *kiteki* steam whistle, siren
船 *kisen* steamship
船会社 *kisengaisha* steamship company
13 艇 *kitei* steam launch
14 関 *kikan* boiler, steam generator
管 *kikan* steam pipe
16 嘴 *kishi* steam nozzle
23 罐 *kikan* boiler, steam generator
罐夫 *kikanfu* boilerman
罐室 *kikanshitsu* boiler room
罐管 *kikankan* boiler tube

沈 2508/F1078 Chin. Shin. Jin aloes. *shizu-(mu) vi* sink, be submerged;
B
subside, cave in; feel depressed, be overcome with. *shizu(meru) vt* sink, submerge, immerse. *shizu(me)* immersion.
2 丁花 *jinchōge, chinchōge* sweet-smelling daphne ⌈dip
3 下 *chinka* sinking, subsidence, settlement,
7 吟 *chingin suru* meditate, muse
沈 *chinchin, shinshin* = *shinshin* 深深 2606.11 ⌈sion
没 *chimbotsu* sinking, foundering, submer-
没船 *chimbotsusen* sunken vessel
8 泥 *chindei* silt ⌈gold
金彫 *chinkimbo(ri)* lacquer ware inlaid with
金塗 *chinkinnu(ri)*=the word above
9 重 *chinchō* composure and dignity
思 *chinshi* contemplation, meditation
勇 *chin-yū* self-possession, cool courage
香 *chinkō, jinkō* aloes
香樹 *chinkōju* aloes ⌈dence, sinking
降 *chinkō* sedimentation, settling, subsi-
降速度 *chinkō sokudo* (blood) sedimentation
10 荷 *shizu(me)ni* jetsam, jettison ⌊rate
11 淪 *chinrin suru* sink into obscurity, lose caste, be ruined
球 *shizu(mu) tama* sinker (in baseball)
船 *chinsen* sunken ship
設 *chinsetsu suru* lay (mines)
12 痛 *chintsū* pathetic, sad
渣 *chinsa* sediment, dregs
着 *chinchaku* composure, calmness
13 澱 *chinden*=沈澱 (see below–16) ⌈tion
溺 *chindeki* indulgence, addiction, dissipa-
滞 *chintai* stagnation, inactivity
14 静 *chinsei* stillness, tranquility, placidity; slackness, dullness, stagnation, inactivity
15 潜 *chinsen suru* be engrossed in
毅 *chinki* composure
黙 *chimmoku* silence, reticence ⌈person
黙家 *chimmokuka* man of silence, reticent
16 積 *chinseki* sedimentation, deposition
澱 *odo(mu)* precipitate, settle. *chinden* precipitation, sedimentation, subsidence
澱池 *chindenchi* settling reservoir
澱物 *chindembutsu* deposit, precipitate
澱槽 *chindensō* settling tank
26 鬱 *chin-utsu* melancholy, gloom

決 2509/F1075 Ketsu decision, vote. *kes(suru) vt* settle, vote on, judge, decide.
A
vi be settled, be decided; collapse, give way. *ki(maru)* (see under 定 1296.0). *ki(meru)* fix, decide, agree upon; appoint, choose; resolve. *ki(me)* arrangement, contract. *(o)ki(mari)* usage, custom, routine; fixed charge. *kes(shite)* (with neg.) never, by no means.
4 心 *kesshin* determination, resolution
手 *ki(me)te* deciding factor, winning move
水 *kessui* water breaking thru a dike or water gate ⌈pretend
込 *ki(me)-ko(mu)* take for granted, assume,
文句 *ki(mari) monku* favorite phrase, cliché
5 付 *ki(me)-tsu(keru)* scold, reprimand
6 行 *kekkō* decisive action ⌈spirit
死 *kesshi* preparedness for death, do-or-die
死隊 *kesshitai* suicide corps
7 別 *ketsubetsu* separation, farewell
8 所 *ki(me)dokoro, ki(me)doko* the time to decide; important time
河 *kekka* river flooding thru broken dikes
定 *kettei* decision, determination, conclusion, settlement
定投票 *kettei tōhyō* deciding vote
定版 *ketteiban* final edition (of a book)
定的 *ketteiteki* definite, final, decisive, conclusive, peremptory
定書 *ketteisho* written decision or findings
定権 *ketteiken* right of decision, decisive
定論 *ketteiron* determinism ⌊power
10 起 *kekki suru* rise, spring to one's feet
11 済 *kessai* settlement, liquidation
断 *ketsudan* decision, determination
断力 *ketsudanryoku* resolution, determina-
12 答 *kettō* definite answer ⌊tion, decision
着 *ketchaku* conclusion, settlement
然 *ketsuzen(taru)* firm, decisive, determined
裂 *ketsuretsu* breakdown, rupture
裁 *kessai* sanction, approval

勝 *kesshō* decision (in a contest)
勝者 *kesshōsha* finalist
勝点 *kesshōten* goal, finishing line
勝戦 *kesshōsen* finals
勝線 *kesshōsen* goal line, finishing line
13 意 *ketsui* resolution, determination
戦 *kessen* decisive battle; deciding match, finals
戦投票 *kessen tōhyō* final election
14 疑論 *ketsugiron* casuistry
選 *kessen* final election
選投票 *kessen tōhyō* final vote, run-off primary
算 *kessan* settlement, liquidation
算日 *kessambi* settlement day
算期 *kessanki* financial settlement period
算報告 *kessan hōkoku* balance sheet
15 潰 *kekkai* rip, break
16 壊 *kekkai* rip, break
18 闘 *kettō* duel
20 議 *ketsugi* resolution, decision, vote
議文 *ketsugibun* written resolution
議事項 *ketsugi jikō* actions taken, resolutions
議案 *ketsugian* resolution, proposal
議権 *ketsugiken* right of voting
議録 *ketsugiroku* minutes of a meeting
議機関 *ketsugi kikan* party machine, caucus, voting organ

5

泉 See 3099.

泪 2510 F1095 F1120 See 淚 2569.

沾 2511 F1087 See 霑 5058.

沱 2512 F1083 Ta, Da flowing of tears.

泄 2513 F1087 Setsu, Ei leak.

泔 2514 F1089 Kan. *yusu(ru)* rinse and comb (the hair).

沫 2515 F1083 Matsu. *awa* (see under 泡 2523.0). *shibuki* spray, splash.

B **況** 2516 F1087 況 Kyō. *ma(shite)* still more, still less (neg.). *iwa(n-ya)* still more; (neg.) much less.

沽 2517 F1087 Ko buying and selling; price.
8 券 *koken* bill of sale; a person's character; face
13 聖 *kosei* simony

沛 2518 F1082 Hai big rain; swamp.
8 雨 *haiu* downpour, cloudburst
12 然 *hazen* downpour, cloudburst

沮 2519 F1083 So. *haba(mu)* (see under 阻 4984.0).
4 止 *soshi*=阻止 4984.4
12 喪 *sosō* loss of power, loss of energy, dejection

A **泳** 2520 F1096 Ei. *oyo(gu)* swim; totter; keep afloat, get along. *oyo(gi)* swim, swimming.
4 手 *oyo(gi)te* swimmer
5 出 *oyo(gi)-da(su)* set out swimming
6 回 *oyo(gi)-mawa(ru)* swim around
8 法 *eihō* swimming style
者 *eisha* swimmer

B **沼** 2521 F1086 Shō swamp, lake. *numa* swamp, bog, pond, lake.
5 田 *numata* marshy rice field
6 気 *shōki* marsh gas, methane
地 *numachi, shōchi* marsh land
7 沢 *shōtaku* marsh, swamp
12 湖 *shōko* swamps and lakes

B **泌** 2522 F1088 Hitsu, Hi flow; soak in; penetrate; secrete.
7 尿 *hinyō* urinary
尿科学 *hinyōkagaku* urology
尿器 *hinyōki, hitsunyōki* urinary organs
尿器科学 *hitsunyōki kagaku* urology
8 泌 *shimijimi* keenly, seriously, heartily, thoroly

泡 2523 F1092 Hō. *awa, abuku* bubble, foam, froth, scum, suds.
5 立 *awada(teru)* bubble, foam, lather
立器 *awada(te)ki* eggbeater
立機 *awada(te)ki* eggbeater
8 沫 *hōmatsu, utakata* bubble, foam, froth
沫会社 *hōmatsugaisha* industrial bubble
11 粒 *awatsubu* a bubble
雪 *awayuki* light snow
14 銭 *abukuzeni* easy money, ill-gotten money

B **沸** 2524 F1085 Futsu. *wa(ku) vi* boil, get hot; ferment; seethe; be in an uproar; gush out; grow, breed, be hatched. *wa(kasu) vt* boil; heat up (the bath); melt.
3 上 *wa(ki)-a(garu)* boil up; well up
5 立 *wa(ki)-ta(tsu)* boil up, seethe, ferment, stir
6 返 *wa(ki)-kae(ru)* seethe, boil up; be in an uproar
9 点 *futten* boiling point
12 湯 *futtō* boiling water

[20]騰 *futtō* boiling, seething, bubbling; agitation
騰点 *futtōten* boiling point

沿 2525 / F1087 **㳂** B
EN following along. *so(u)* run along; lie along; be situated on.

[8]岸 *engan* coast, shore
岸国 *engankoku* coastal nation
岸漁業 *engan gyogyō* offshore fishing
[9]革 *enkaku* history, development
海 *enkai* coast, shore, sea, inshore, coastal waters
海州 *Enkaishū* Maritime Provinces
[11]道 *endō* route, course; roadside
[13]路 *enro* route
[15]線 *ensen no* along the railway line

泰 2526 / F1095 B
TAI calm, peace; easy; large, wide. *Tai* Thai, Siam.

[3]山 *taizan* high mountain; Mt. Taishan (in China)
山鳴動 *taizan-meidō* great trouble
[4]斗 *taito* an authority
[5]平 *taihei* peace, tranquility
平期 *taiheiki* a period of peace
[6]西 *Taisei* the Occident
安 *taian* peace, tranquility
[8]国 *Taikoku* Thailand, Siam
[12]然 *taizen(taru)* calm, composed; firm
然自若 *taizen-jijaku* imperturbability, presence of mind

泊 2527 / F1088 B
HAKU (3-day) stay. *to(maru)* stay at, put up at; ride at anchor. *to(meru)* lodge a person. *toma(ri)* anchorage; stopping (for the night); night duty.

[4]込 *toma(ri)-ko(mu)* stop at, live in, stay overnight
[6]地 *hakuchi* anchorage, berth
合 *toma(ri)-a(waseru)* stop at the same inn
[9]客 *toma(ri) kyaku* overnight guest
[11]掛 *toma(ri)ga(ke)* visiting over night
渠 *hakkyo* wet dock, a dock where water is held when the tide ebbs
船 *hakusen* anchoring
船渠 *hakusenkyo* wet dock
[12]番 *toma(ri)ban* night duty
[13]賃 *toma(ri)-chin* hotel charges

治 2528 / F1085 A
JI. CHI peace; government. *ji(suru)* cure, heal; rule; conserve (resources). *osa(meru), chi(suru)* govern, manage, regulate; quell, subdue; patch up; heal. *osa(maru)* be at peace; calm down; be settled, be ruled. *nao(su), nao(ru)* (see under 直 775.0).

[3]山 *chisan* flood-control tree planting on a watershed
下 *chika no* under the rule of
[4]水 *chisui* riparian works, flood control
水工学 *chisui kōgaku* hydraulic engineering
水工事 *chisui kōji* riparian works
[5]平 *chihei* peace and tranquility
世 *chisei, jisei* reign, rule, regime, dynasty
外法権 *chigai-hōken* extraterritoriality
[6]安 *chian* public peace and order
安条例 *chian jōrei* peace regulations
安維持 *chian iji* maintenance of public peace
安維持法 *chian-ijihō* peace-preservation law
安警察 *chian keisatsu* peace-preservation police
[7]乱 *chiran* war and peace
[8]国 *chikoku* government
者 *chisha* ruler, governor
[9]要 *chiyō* principles of government
[11]略 *chiryaku* statesmanship
産 *chisan* property management
[13]跡 *chiseki* administration's record
罪 *chizai* criminal procedure
[17]績 *chiseki* administration's record
療 *chiryō* medical treatment
療代 *chiryōdai* doctor's fee
療所 *chiryōsho* infirmary, treatment rooms
療法 *chiryōhō* therapeutics, cure, remedy
療学 *chiryōgaku* therapeutics
療師 *chiryōshi* one who gives treatments
[18]癒 *chiyu* healing, cure, recovery
癒力 *chiyuryoku* healing power

波 2529 / F1092 A
HA wave. *nami* wave, billows.

[3]及 *hakyū suru* be propagated; extend, spread; affect, influence
[4]止場 *hatoba* wharf, quay, jetty, pier
[5]立 *namida(tsu)* be choppy, be wavy, be rolling (with billows); boil up; ripple
打 *namiu(tsu)* dash against; undulate
打際 *namiu(chi)giwa* beach
打髪 *namiu(tsu)kami* wavy hair
布 *habu* a poisonous Okinawa snake
布茶 *habucha* stinkweed-seed tea
布草 *habusō* stinkweed
[7]状 *hajō* wave, undulation
乱 *haran*＝波瀾 (see below–20)
形 *namigata* ripple mark
花 *nami (no) hana* salt
[8]長 *hachō* wave length
枕 *nami makura* sea voyage
沫 *nami shibuki* spray, spindrift
[9]面 *hamen* wave surface; wave front
風 *namikaze* wind and waves; discord, trouble
除 *namiyoke* breakwater, sea wall
乗 *namino(ri)* surf riding. *nami (ni) no(ru)* ride on a wave (of success)
[10]高 *hakō* wave height

浪 *harō* waves, billows
紋 *hamon* ripple, wave ring
11 動 *hadō* wave motion, undulatory motion
頂 *hachō* wave crest
寄 *namiyo(ru)* be wavy
12 間 *namima ni* on the waves
颪 *namioroshi* a strong wind at sea
13 路 *namiji* sea route; sea voyage
跡 *namiato* ripple marks
際 *namigiwa* the ocean beach
15 穂 *nami(no)ho, namiho* whitecaps
線 *hasen* wavy line
16 頭 *hatō* on the waves; wave crest; on the sea; whitecaps. *namigashira* whitecaps
17 濤 *hatō* billows, rough seas, large waves
磯際 *nami-isogiwa* the water's edge (on a beach) ⌈fluctuations
20 瀾 *haran* waves, billows; commotion; wide
瀾万丈 *haram-banjō* great changes

河 2530 F1083 A

Ka. *kawa* river, stream.

3 上 *kajō* on the river; by the river; upper
口 *kakō* river mouth, estuary ⌊reaches
口港 *kakōkō* estuary harbor
川 *kasen* rivers
川工学 *kasen kōgaku* riparian engineering
川工事 *kasen kōji* riparian works
4 心 *kashin* middle of the river
水 *kasui* river water, river; stream
公 *kakō* water god
5 北 *kahoku* north of the Yellow River
7 身 *kashin* current of the river
床 *kashō, kawatoko* river bed
系 *kakei* river system ⌈channel
8 底 *kawazoko, katei* river bed, river bottom;
東 *katō* east of the river
岸 *kashi* riverside, waterfront; fish market; scene, place; one's trade or field. *kawagishi, kagan* riverside, river bank
岸通 *kashidō(ri)* river road
岸揚 *kashia(ge)* riverfront unloading
岸端 *kashibata* riverside
9 峡 *kakyō* swift-river canyon
津 *kashin* ford; river port
神 *kashin* river god
南 *kanan* south of the Yellow River
10 馬 *kaba* hippopotamus
流 *karyū* stream
畔 *kahan* riverside ⌈bed
原 *kawara, kawahara* river beach, dry river
原乞食 *kawara kojiki* Edo actors (a term of opprobrium)
原物 *kawaramono* beggar, outcast; actor
11 魚 *kagyo, kawa uo* river fish
鹿 *kajika* singing frog
豚 *fugu, katon* puffer, globefish
12 港 *kakō* river port
湾 *kawan* estuary
童 *kappa, kawa(p)pa* fabulous amphibian, mermaid; expert swimmer
13 楊 *kawayanagi* riverside willows
戦 *kasen* fighting in a river (not in boats)
跡湖 *kasekiko* river-bed lake
19 獺 *kawa uso* otter
23 鱒 *kawa masu* brook trout

注 注 2531 F1094 A

Chū notes, comment; N.B. *chū(suru)* comment on; annotate. *soso(gu) vt* pour into, pour on, irrigate, sprinkle; shed (tears). *vi* (rain) falls; flow into; pay attention to, concentrate on. *tsu(gu)* pour in, fill, put in (more coal). *sa(su)* pour (a drink), serve (drinks); mix into.

2 入 *chūnyū suru* pour into, put into, inject, impregnate, infuse, instill, implant, im- ⌊bue
4 水 *chūsui* flooding; douche
込 *soso(gi)-ko(mu)* pour into, flow into. *tsu(gi)-ko(mu)* pour into; invest, sink (money) into
文 *chūmon* an order
文用紙 *chūmon yōshi* order blank
文先 *chūmonsaki* where you place your order
文帖 *chūmonchō* order book
文取 *chūmonto(ri)* taking orders
文品 *chūmonhin* goods ordered
文流 *chūmonnaga(re)* canceled order
文書 *chūmonsho, chūmonga(ki)* order form
文帳 *chūmonchō* order book
文聞 *chūmonki(ki)* taking orders
5 目 *chūmoku* attention, observation, notice
出 *soso(gi)-da(su)* pour out
7 足 *tsu(gi)-ta(su)* pour more into
告 *chūkoku* advice, warning ⌈anointing oil
8 油 *chūyu* oiling, lubrication. *soso(gi) abura*
油器 *chūyuki* oiler, lubricator
9 連 *shime* sacred Shinto rope
連飾 *shimekaza(ri)* sacred Shinto rope
連縄 *shimenawa* sacred Shinto rope
10 進 *chūshin* information, warning
記 *chūki suru* make entries, write down
射 *chūsha* injection, shot
射針 *chūshabari* hypodermic needle
射液 *chūsha eki* injection (the liquid)
射器 *chūshaki* hypodermic syringe
11 掛 *soso(gi)-ka(karu)* flow into, flow against. *soso(gi)-ka(keru)* pour out upon
視 *chūshi* close observation, attention, scrutiny
釈 *chūshaku* notes, comment, exegesis
13 解 *chūkai* notes; comment; commentary
解者 *chūkaisha* commentator
解書 *chūkaisho* commentary

意 *chūi* attention, care, heed; warning, advice, hint; interest
意力 *chūiryoku* power of attention
意人物 *chūi jimbutsu* suspicious character
意事項 *chūi jikō* N.B.; suggestions; matters requiring attention
意書 *chūiga(ki)* notes, instructions
意報 *chūihō* storm warning

泣 2532 F1093 B Kyū. *na(ku)* cry, weep, wail, moan. *na(kasu)*, *na(kaseru)* let cry, make cry; grieve, worry. *na(keru)* shed tears, be moved to tears.

2 入 *na(ki)-i(ru)* weep silently or bitterly
3 上戸 *na(ki)jōgo* drunkard
4 止 *na(ki)-ya(mu)* stop crying
5 付 *na(ki)-tsu(ku)* implore, entreat
出 *na(ki)-da(su)* burst into tears, begin to cry
6 虫 *na(ki)mushi* crybaby
血 *kyūketsu* shedding tears of blood
伏 *na(ki)-fu(su)* throw oneself down crying; break down
叫 *na(ki)-sake(bu)* cry, yell, scream, wail
7 言 *na(ki)goto* complaint, grievance
沈 *na(ki)-shizu(mu)* break down and cry
別 *na(ki)waka(re)* tearful parting
声 *na(ki)goe* a cry, a crying voice
男 *na(ki)otoko* men hired as mourners; a man who often cries
8 明 *na(ki)-a(kasu)* cry all night
泣 *na(ki)na(ki)* between sobs, with an aching heart; barely. *na(ku)na(ku)* tearfully, with an aching heart
味噌 *na(ki)miso* crybaby, one who cries easily
9 面 *na(ki)tsura, na(kit)tsura* tear-stained face
10 倒 *na(ki)-tao(reru)* fall down crying
涙 *na(ki) (no) namida (de)* in tears
涕 *kyūtei* crying in tears
笑 *na(ki)wara(i)* tearful smile, tragi-comedy
真似 *na(ki)mane* crocodile tears, weeping in mimicry
11 寄 *na(ki)yo(ri)* getting together to comfort one another
崩 *na(ki)-kuzu(reru)* break down and cry
12 喚 *na(ki)-sake(bu)* cry, yell, scream, wail
場 *na(kase)ba* pathetic scene
訴 *kyūso* appeal (to authorities)
落 *na(ki)-o(tosu)* persuade in tears
悲 *na(ki)-kana(shimu)* cry and grieve
13 嗄 *na(ki)-ka(rasu)* cry oneself hoarse
腫 *na(ki)-ha(rasu)* cry one's eyes out
寝入 *na(ki)ne-i(ri)* crying oneself to sleep
14 暮 *na(ki)-ku(rasu)* live in sorrow
16 曦 *na(ki)-jaku(ru)* sob
頻 *na(ki)-shiki(ru)* wail, sob bitterly
17 濡 *na(ki)-nu(reru)* be tearstained
18 顔 *na(ki)gao* tear-stained face

泥 2533 F1093 P Dei mud, mire. *nazu(mu)* adhere to, be attached to. *doro, hiji* mud, mire, dirt, slush; disgrace.

3 土 *deido* mud, mire
4 中 *deichū* in the mire
火山 *deikazan* mud volcano
水 *deisui, doromizu* muddy road
水生活 *doromizu seikatsu* life of shame
水社会 *doromizu shakai* red-light districts
水稼業 *doromizu kagyō* life of vice
5 玉 *dorodama* dead pearl, a dark and imperfect pearl
田 *dorota* muddy rice field
仕合 *dorojiai* corrupt campaign mudslinging
6 地 *deichi* swamp, marsh, bog, morass
7 足 *doro ashi* muddy feet
坊 *dorobō* thief, burglar, robber
状 *deijō no* muddy, pasty
弄 *doro-ijiri* playing in the mud
8 金 *deikin* alluvial gold
泥 *dorodoro* all muddied up
沼 *doronuma* bog, slough, quagmire
板岩 *deibangan* shale
9 海 *doro umi* muddy ocean
臭 *dorokusa(i)* smelling of mud
炭 *deitan, sukumo* peat
炭地 *deitanchi* peat bog, peat moss
炭沼 *deitanshō* peat bog
炭苔 *deitangoke* peat moss
10 浚 *dorosarai* mud dredging
浚機 *dorosaraiki* dredger
11 道 *doromichi* muddy road
掬 *dorosukui* mud scoop
酔 *deisui* dead drunk
12 棒 *dorobō* thief, burglar, robber
落 *doro-oto(shi)* mud scraper
絵具 *doro enogu* distemper (in painting)
13 滓 *deisai* sludge
鉱 *deikō* slime ore
靴 *dorogutsu* muddy shoes
塗 *doromami(re)* covered with mud
試合 *dorojiai* mudslinging, corrupt campaign
搔 *dorokaki* door scraper
搔器 *dorokakiki* door scraper
17 濘 *nuka(ru), nukaru(mu)* get muddy, be muddy, be slushy. *nukarumi, nukari, deinei* mud, slush, mire; muddy road
19 縄 *doro nawa* unpreparedness, last-minute preparations; locking the barn after the horse is gone

油 2534 F1085 A Yu. Yū. *abura* oil. *abura(giru)* be excessively fat.

2 入 *abura-i(ri)* oiled
4 手 *aburade, aburatte* greasy hands
井 *yusei* oil well
井戸 *abura ido* oil well; oil spring

5 田 *yuden* oil field, oil well, oil land
圧 *yuatsu* oil pressure; hydraulic
布 *yufu* oilcloth, oiled cloth
母頁岩 *yuboketsugan* oil shale
6 虫 *aburamushi* cockroach; plant louse; hanger-on
団 *yuton* waxed cloth; oiled-paper cushion
気 *aburake, abura(k)ke* greasiness, oiliness
汗 *abura-ase* perspiration from pain
7 足 *abura ashi* sweaty feet
身 *aburami* fat (of meat)
冷 *yurei* oil cooling
状 *yujō no* oily
8 性 *yusei no* oily
性塗料 *yusei toryō* oil paint
注 *aburasoso(gu)* anoint with oil
注者 *aburasoso(gareta) mono* anointed one
送船 *yusōsen* oil tanker
送管路 *yusōkanro* pipeline
送管線 *yusōkansen* pipeline
9 染 *aburaji(miru)* become oily or oil stained
単 *yutan* oilcloth, tarpaulin
10 庫 *yuko* oil bunker
桃 *aburamomo* nectarine
紙 *aburagami, yushi* oil paper, oiled paper
脂 *yushi* fat, fats and oils
差 *aburasa(shi)* oiler, oil cup, oil can
砥石 *abura to-ishi* oil stone
11 断 *yudan* negligence, unpreparedness, carelessness
12 揚 *abura-a(ge), aburage* fried tofu
壺 *aburatsubo* oil cup, oil can, oil bottle
然 *yūzen toshite* freely, copiously, abundantly
量計 *yuryōkei* oil gauge
絵 *aburae* oil painting
絵具 *abura enogu* oil paints
13 煙 *yuen* lampblack, carbon black
煠 *abura-itame* frying
照 *aburade(ri)* sultry sun
障子 *abura shōji* translucent oiled-paper doors
搾 *aburashibo(ri)* oil press
搾具 *abura shiborigu* oil press
搾器 *abura shiboriki* oil press
14 層 *yusō* oil strata
管 *yukan* oil pipe
墨 *aburazumi* marking ink
15 締木 *aburashi(me)gi* oil press
槽 *yusō* oil tank
槽車 *yusōsha* tank car
槽船 *yusōsen* oil tanker
16 濃 *abura(k)ko(i), aburako(i)* greasy, fatty, oily
薬 *aburagusuri* ointment, liniment, salve
17 糟 *aburakasu* oil cake, the soy-bean waste after the oil is expressed
18 蟬 *aburazemi* common locust
20 灌 *aburasoso(gu)* anoint with oil
灌者 *aburasoso(gareta) mono* anointed one

A 法 2535 / F1089 Hō law, rule, principle; legislation, regulation; code; method, way, model, manner, system, process, art, technique; rites, religion, doctrine; reason; mood (of verbs). *nori* law, rule; model; doctrine.

2 力 *hōriki* the merits of Buddhism
人 *hōjin* legal person, corporation
人税 *hōjinzei* corporation tax
4 文 *hōbun* the law; letter of the law; law and literature
文化 *hōbunka suru* legalize, enact into a law
王 *Hōō* Pope; Gautama; famous priest
王庁 *Hōōchō* Vatican
王令 *Hōōrei* Papal decretals
王制度 *Hōō seido* Papal system, the Papacy
王使節 *Hōō shisetsu* Papal delegate
王政治 *Hōō seiji* Papacy
王無謬説 *Hōō mubyūsetsu* Papal infallibility
王権 *Hōōken* Papacy
王職 *Hōōshoku* Papacy
5 外 *hōgai* exorbitant, unreasonable; extraordinary
主 *hossu, hosshu* high priest (of a Buddhist sect)
令 *hōrei* laws and ordinances
6 衣 *hōi, hōe* robes of (Buddhist) priests
式 *hōshiki*＝方式 2082.6
印 *hōin* the highest rank in the Buddhist priesthood; (Edo) scholar; (Edo) artist
灯 *hōtō* the light of Buddhism; religious tradition
会 *hōe* (Buddhist) memorial service
号 *hōgō* (Buddhist) posthumous name
名 *hōmyō* (Buddhist) priest's name; posthumous name
7 身 *hosshin* immortal soul (in Buddhism)
医学 *hōigaku* medical jurisprudence
廷 *hōtei* law court, courtroom
廷侮辱 *hōtei bujoku* contempt of court
廷侮辱罪 *hōtei-bujokuzai* contempt of court
8 例 *hōrei* regulations for carrying out laws
帖 *hōjō* folding copybook
的 *hōteki* legal, legalistic
服 *hōfuku* judge's robe, barrister's robe, clerical robe
官 *hōkan* judge; judiciary
典 *hōten* code of laws, statute
事 *hōji* (Buddhist) memorial service
治 *hōchi* constitutional government
治国 *hōchikoku* constitutional state
制 *hōsei* laws, legislation
制局 *Hōseikyoku* Legislative Bureau
制経済 *hōsei keizai* law and economics
定 *hōtei* legal, designated by law
定貨幣 *hōtei kahei* legal tender
定猶予期間 *hōtei yūyo kikan* days of grace

学 *hōgaku* law, jurisprudence
学士 *Hōgakushi* LL.B., Bachelor of Laws
学博士 *Hōgaku Hakushi* LL.D., Doctor of Laws
9度 *hotto, hatto* law, ordinance; prohibition
相 *Hōshō* Minister of Justice. *Hossō* Buddhist sect originating in the seventh century
科 *hōka* law course, law department
則 *hōsoku* law, rule
政 *hōsei* law and government
界 *hōkai* (Buddhism's) universe
皇 *hōō* tonsured emperor; Pope
要 *hōyō* (Buddhist) memorial service
律 *hōritsu* law
律上 *hōritsujō* legally
律学 *hōritsugaku* jurisprudence
律学者 *hōritsu gakusha* lawyer
律屋 *hōritsuya* lawyer
律家 *hōritsuka* lawyer, jurist
律案 *hōritsuan* proposed law
律書 *hōritsusho* law book
律語 *hōritsugo* legal term
10師 *hōshi* (Buddhist) priest
悦 *hōetsu* religious exaltation, ecstasy, rapture
被 *happi* workman's livery coat
案 *hōan* bill, measure
華経 *Hokekyō* the Lotus Sutra
益剝奪 *hōeki hakudatsu* outlawry
11眼 *hōgen* next to the highest priestly rank in Buddhism
経 *hōkei* law and economics
貨 *hōka* legal tender
術師 *hōjutsushi* magician
理 *hōri* principle of law
理学 *hōrigaku* jurisprudence
曹 *hōsō* judge, judiciary
曹界 *hōsōkai* legal circles
規 *hōki* regulations, laws; legislation
規典令 *hōki-tenrei* laws and regulations
規典例 *hōki-tenrei* laws and regulations
務 *hōmu* judicial affairs
務大臣 *Hōmu Daijin* Minister of Justice
務官 *hōmukan* judiciary, judge advocate
務省 *Hōmushō* Ministry of Justice
12博 *Hōhaku* Doctor of Laws
塔 *hōtō* (Shinto) votive lantern
統 *hōtō* the succession of (Buddhist) teachings
13話 *hōwa* (Buddhist) sermon
楽 *hōraku* pleasure of a virtuous (Buddhist) life; entertainment; entertainment for the gods
14網 *hōmō* justice, meshes of the law
語 *hōgo* (Buddhist) sermon
15権 *hōken* legal right
談 *hōdan* (Buddhist) sermon
論 *hōron* (Buddhist) doctrinal discussion
養 *hōyō* (Buddhist) memorial service
幣 *hōhei* fapi, Chinese legal tender
17螺 *hora* trumpet shell; boast
螺吹 *horafu(ki)* boaster
螺貝 *horagai* conch, trumpet shell; boast
18難 *hōnan* (Buddhist) religious persecution

6

浊 Nonstandard for 濁 2710.

洌 2536/F1097 Retsu pure.

洄 2537/F1096 Kai flowing water.

12游 *kaiyū* run of fish

洵 2538/F1101 Jun alike. *makoto* truth.

洲 2539/F1101 Shū continent. Su sand bar, shallows. *shima* island. *kuni* country.

4内 *shūnai* inside the state; inside the country
5外 *shūgai* outside the state; outside the country
11崎 *susaki* sandspit

洩 2540/F1100 Ei. Setsu. *mo(ru)*, *mo(reru)*, *mo(rasu)* (see under 漏 2682.0).

14聞 *mo(re)-ki(ku)* overhear

洛 2541/F1098 Raku Kyoto, the capital.

4中 *rakuchū* in Kyoto
5外 *rakugai* suburbs of Kyoto; metropolitan suburbs

涕 2542/F1099 I. Tei tear; nasal discharge. *hana, hanashiru* nasal discharge.

4水 *hanamizu* watery nasal discharge
8垂 *hanatare*, *hanatara(shi)*, *hana(t)tare*, *hana(t)tara(shi)* dirty nose; sniveler
垂小僧 *hanatare kozō* dirty-nosed youngster; urchin

津 2543/F1099 B Shin. *tsu* port, harbor; ferry. *tsuyu* (see under 汁 2485.0).

8波 *tsunami* tidal wave
9津 *shinshin* brim full of
津浦浦 *tsutsu-ura-ura ni* thruout the land, in every nook and corner
10浪 *tsunami* tidal wave
11液 *tsubaki* sputum, saliva

洪 2544/F1100 P Kō flood; vast.

3大 *kōdai* great size
4水 *kōzui, ōmizu* inundation, flood, deluge

7図 *kōto* ambitious scheme
10恩 *kōon* great blessings, great benevolence
11基 *kōki* foundation of a great enterprise
13業 *kōgyō* great achievement

洒 2545/F1097 Sha. Son. Sai. Sen wash, rinse, sprinkle. *susu(gu)* wash, pour on, rinse.
9洒落落 *shasha-rakuraku na*=*sharaku na* 洒落 (see below–12)
11掃 *saisō* cleaning
脱 *shadatsu na* unconventional, unconstrained
12落 *share(ru)* joke, play on words, dress stylishly, try to look smart. *sharaku na* unconventional, frank, unconstrained. *share* sense of humor; witticism, joke, pun, play on words; personal adornment. *(o)share* personal adornment
落気 *shareke, share(k)ke* a bent for joking; sense of humor; vanity in dress
落臭 *sharakusa(i)* knowing, smart, impudent

洞 2546/F1099 Dō cavity. Tō cave. *hora* cave, den, excavation.
5穴 *hora-ana, dōketsu* cave, den, excavation
7見 *dōken* insight, penetration
8門 *dōmon* tunnel
9峠 *hora(ga)tōge* sitting on the fence
11視 *dōshi* insight, discernment
13窟 *dōkutsu* cave
14察 *dōsatsu, tōsatsu* insight, discernment
察力 *dōsatsuryoku* insight
察眼 *dōsatsugan* insight
18観 *dōkan* insight, penetration

A **派** 2547/F1103 **派** Ha group, party, clique; faction, sect; school (of art, etc.). *ha(suru)* dispatch, send.
4手 *hade* flashiness, gaudiness, gaiety. *hade(yakana)* flashy, gaudy
手好 *hadezu(ki) na* fond of display
手者 *hadesha* man of fashion, a dandy
手姿 *hade sugata* flashy appearance
5生 *hasei* derivation; dividing and growing
生的 *haseiteki* derivative, secondary
生語 *haseigo* a derivative
出 *hashutsu suru vt* and *vi* send out, dispatch; be derived from
出所 *hashutsujo* branch office; police box
出婦 *hashutsufu* housekeeper working by the day
7別 *habetsu* division (by sects, etc.)
兵 *hahei* dispatch of troops
12遣 *haken suru* send, dispatch
遣軍 *hakengun* expeditionary army
遣隊 *hakentai* detachment (of troops)
14閥 *habatsu* clique, faction

B **浄** 2548/F1121 **淨** Jō. *kiyo(i), kiyo(meru), kiyo(maru)* (see under 清 2605.0).
3土 *jōdo* pure land, (Buddhist) paradise
土宗 *Jōdoshū* a Buddhist sect originating in the 12th century
土真宗 *Jōdo Shinshū* a Buddhist sect originating in *Jōdōshū*
土教 *Jōdokyō* Buddhist teaching concerning paradise
4火 *jōka* sacred fire
化 *jōka* purification, clean-up
水 *jōsui* clean water
水池 *jōsuichi* filter bed
5写 *jōsha* clean copy
6衣 *jōi, jōe* pure white robe; Shinto priest's robe
地 *jōchi* sacred area, temple area, temple food storehouse
7戒 *jōkai* (Buddhist) commandments
9界 *jōkai* sacred place, (Buddhist) paradise
玻璃 *jōhari* clear crystal
10財 *jōzai* money offering, votive offering, collection
書 *jōsho* clean copy
11域 *jōiki* sacred precincts
菌槽 *jōkinsō* septic tank
13罪 *jōzai* purgation (from sins)
14瑠璃 *jōruri* a ballad-drama
18穢 *jōe* pure things and sordid; the world of the Buddhas and that of ordinary men

A **浅** 2549/F1131 **淺** Sen. *asa(i)* shallow; superficial; short (time); slight (connection); pale, light (color). *asa(hakana)* frivolous, shallow, rash, foolish. *asa(mashii)* wretched, miserable, pitiable; despicable, base, shameful. *asa-* light (color); slight (wound).
3才 *sensai* lack of ability, incompetence
4手 *asade* slight wound
5田 *asada* shallow rice field
6吃水 *senkissui* shallow draft
7見 *senken* superficial idea, shallow view
8学 *sengaku* superficial knowledge, superficiality
知恵 *asajie* shallow wit
9紅 *senkō* light red
海 *senkai* shallow sea
海魚 *senkaigyo* shallow-sea fish
草海苔 *asakusa nori* laver, sheets of dried seaweed
草紙 *asakusagami* coarse toilet paper
10浮彫 *ukibo(ri)* bas-relief
11黄 *asagi* light blue, pale blue
黒 *asaguro(i)* dark, dusky, swarthy, brunet, dark-complexioned, dark-skinned
12葱 *asagi* light blue, pale blue
13蜊 *asari* short-necked clam
墓 *asahaka na* frivolous, shallow, rash, foolish
14聞 *sembun* a narrow view

4 心小⺌戈戸手扌支攴攵文斗斤方无日曰月木欠止歹殳毋比毛氏气【水氵氺】6 火灬爪⺤父爻爿丬片牙牛犬犭

緑 *asamidori* light green
5 慮 *senryo* indiscretion, thoughtlessness
16 薄 *sempaku* shallowness; superficiality, flimsiness, frivolity
17 鍋 *asanabe* shallow pan
19 瀬 *asase* shoal, shallows, sand bar, ford

洋 2550 / F1096 A — Yō ocean, sea, channel. *yō-* foreign, Western, European.

2 刀 *yōtō* saber
3 上 *yōjō* on the ocean, in mid-ocean
4 犬 *yōken* Western dog
5 本 *yōhon* a Western book; a book bound in Western style
6 行 *yōkō* foreign travel; company, firm
灰 *yōkai* cement
式 *yōshiki* Western style
灯 *yōtō* lamp
8 服 *yōfuku* Western clothes
服屋 *yōfukuya* clothing store, tailor shop; tailor
学 *yōgaku* Western learning
学者 *yōgakusha* students of Western learning
画 *yōga* Western painting; Western film
画界 *yōgakai* Western-art circles (in Japan)
画家 *yōgaka* painter of Western pictures
9 風 *yōfū* Western style
洋 *yōyō(taru)* vast, broad, wide
紅 *yōkō* carmine, crimson
盃 *koppu* tumbler, glass
室 *yōshitsu* Western-style room
食 *yōshoku* Western food
食屋 *yōshokuya* Western-style restaurant
食器 *yōshokuki* Western dishes
品 *yōhin* haberdashery
品店 *yōhinten* foreign-goods shop
品屋 *yōhin-ya* foreign-goods shop
10 酒 *yōshu* Western liquor
紙 *yōshi* Western paper
書 *yōsho* Western book
家具 *yōkagu* Western furniture
11 梨 *yōnashi* Western pear
貨 *yōka* Western money
菓子 *yōgashi* Western confectionery
12 間 *yōma* Western-style room
傘 *yōgasa* Western umbrella
装 *yōsō* Western dress
琴 *yōkin* piano
裁 *yōsai* Western dressmaking
裁学校 *yōsai gakkō* Western dressmaking school
裁師 *yōsaishi* Western-style dressmaker
13 楽 *yōgaku* Western music
楽器 *yōgakki* Western musical instruments
14 種 *yōshu* foreign breed
綴 *yōtoji* Western-style binding
銀 *yōgin* nickel silver, German silver
算 *yōzan* Western arithmetic
髪 *yōhatsu* Western hairdo
16 館 *yōkan* Western-style building

洗 2551 / F1097 B — Sen. *ara(u)* wash; inquire into, probe. *ara(i)* wash; washing.

3 上 *ara(i)-a(geru)* finish washing; wash well
4 分 *ara(i)-wa(keru)* separate by washing
5 立 *ara(i)da(teru), ara(i)-ta(teru)* examine closely, ferret out, check up on. *ara(i)ta(te)* just washed
去 *ara(i)-sa(ru)* wash away
礼 *senrei* baptism by sprinkling
礼式 *senreishiki* baptism by sprinkling
礼名 *senrei na* name given at baptism
礼室 *senreishitsu* baptistry
礼場 *senreijō* baptistry
礼盤 *senreiban* baptism font
6 米 *semmai* cleaned rice
7 足 *sensoku* washing the feet; foot bath
足式 *sensokushiki* foot-washing ceremony
車 *sensha* car wash
車場 *senshajō* car-washing place
8 物 *ara(i)mono* the washing, laundry
9 砂利 *ara(i)jari* washed gravel
浄 *senjō* washing, cleaning, rinsing; ablution
浄式 *senjōshiki* ablutions
面 *semmen* washing the face
面台 *semmendai* washstand
面所 *semmenjo* washroom, lavatory
面器 *semmenki* washbasin, washbowl
10 晒 *ara(i)zara(shi)* laundry-worn garment
浚 *ara(i)zara(i)* everything, the whole thing; completely
流 *ara(i)-naga(su)* wash away
粉 *ara(i)ko* powdered soap
剤 *senzai* cleansing agent
11 張 *ara(i)ha(ri)* fulling; washing and stretching
清 *ara(i)-kiyo(meru)* wash clean, cleanse
眼 *sengan* eye washing
脳 *sennō* brainwashing
12 場 *ara(i)ba* place to do laundry
湯 *sentō* bathhouse, public bath
落 *ara(i)-oto(su)* wash off, wash out (stain), rinse out (soap)
13 煉 *senren* refining; polishing
鉱 *senkō* ore washing
鉱夫 *senkōfu* ore washer (the workman)
14 滌 *sendeki, senjō* washing, rinsing
練 *senren* refining, polishing
髪 *sempatsu* washing the hair, shampoo. *ara(i)gami* washed hair
15 盤 *semban* washbasin, laver
16 薬 *ara(i)gusuri* lotion
17 濯 *ara(i)susu(gi)* washing, laundry. *sentaku* laundering. *susugi* rinsing, washing; water for washing the feet
濯石鹼 *sentaku sekken* laundry soap
濯板 *sentaku ita* washboard
濯物 *sentakumono* the washing
濯屋 *sentakuya* laundry; laundryman

濯挟 *sentakubasami* clothes pin

濯機 *sentakuki* washing machine

濯盥 *sentakudarai* wash tub

A **活** 2552 / F1101 KATSU resuscitation; living; being helped. *i(kiru), i(kasu)* (see under 生 2991.0). *hatara(ku)* (see under 働 532.0). *i(keru)* keep alive; arrange flowers (in a vase). *iki* freshness; stet.

2 力 *katsuryoku* vitality

人 *katsujin* a living person

人形 *ikiningyō* living doll; lifelike doll

人画 *katsujinga* picture formed of living people

4 仏 *katsubutsu, ikibotoke* living Buddha; Grand Lama

火山 *kakkazan* active volcano

5 目 *katsumoku suru* watch with keen interest

写 *kassha* candid photography

弁 *katsuben* silent-film interpreter

用 *katsuyō* practical use; declension, conjugation, inflexion

用形 *katsuyōkei* conjugation

用例 *katsuyōrei* paradigm

用語 *katsuyōgo* inflected words

6 気 *kakki* liveliness, vigor, activity

気付 *kakkizu(keru)* invigorate, animate. *kakkizu(ku)* become active, become animated

字 *katsuji* type

字引 *ikijibiki* a walking dictionary

字本 *katsujibon* books printed from movable type

字地金 *katsuji jigane* type metal

字合金 *katsuji gōkin* type metal

字盤 *katsujiban* type case

字鋳造 *katsuji chūzō* type casting

字鋳造所 *katsuji chūzōsho* type foundry

字鋳造機 *katsuji chūzōki* type caster

7 作 *ikezuku(ri)* slicing live fish

花 *ikebana* flower arrangement

8 例 *katsurei* living example

性 *kassei* activated, active (oxygen)

法 *kappō* practical plan

況 *kakkyō* vigor, activity, liveliness

物 *katsubutsu* living being

版 *kappan* type, printing

版本 *kappambon* printed book

版所 *kappanjo* print shop

版刷 *kappanzuri* type printing; printed matter

版屋 *kappan-ya* print shop; printer

9 活 *iki-iki* lively

胆 *ikigimo* liver from a living animal

計 *kakkei* livelihood, living

炭 *ikezumi* banked charcoal fire

発 *kappatsu* vigor, vivacity, activity

10 栓 *kassen* faucet

索 *zukkoke* noose, slipknot

殺 *kassatsu* life and death

殺自在 *katsusatsu-jizai* power of life and death

11 魚 *ikeuo* fish kept in a tank for food

眼 *katsugan* open eyes, penetrating eye; insight

船 *ikebune* live-fish tank

動 *katsudō* activity, action, operations; energy; service; function; movies

動力 *katsudōryoku* activity, vitality

動的 *katsudōteki* active, dynamic

動写真 *katsudō shashin* moving picture

動家 *katsudōka* energetic person

12 喩 *katsuyu* personification

13 路 *katsuro* way of escape, last resort

塞 *kassoku* piston

塞桿 *kassokukan* piston rod

14 歴 *katsureki* historical drama

語 *katsugo* living words

舞台 *katsubutai* living stage, arena, sphere of activity

15 劇 *katsugeki* action picture; riotous scene

潑 *kappatsu* vigor, vivacity, activity

線 *kassen* live wire

16 嘴 *kasshi* faucet

21 躍 *katsuyaku suru* be active in, jump into action

A **海** 2553 / F1110 **海** KAI *umi* sea, ocean.

2 人 *ama, kaijin* fisherman; salt maker

人小舟 *ama obune* fisherman's boat

3 口 *kaikō* harbor entrance

士 *ama* fisherman, salt maker

女 *ama* woman shell diver

山 *umiyama* sea and mountains; height and depth

千山千 *umisen-yamasen* an old codger

上 *kaijō* maritime, seafaring, seaborne, overseas

上自衛隊 *Kaijō Jieitai* Maritime Self-defense Force

上保安 *kaijō hoan* maritime safety

上保安官 *Kaijo Hoankan* Marine Police

上保安部 *Kaijo Hoambu* Marine Police headquarters

上保険 *kaijō hoken* maritime insurance

上権 *kaijōken* sea power

4 手 *umite* near the sea

月 *kurage* jellyfish. *kaigetsu* a clear moon over the ocean

牛 *kaigyū, umi-ushi* sea cow, dugong

辺 *kaihen, umibe, unabata, umibeta* seashore, beach, coast, seaside

内 *kaidai* the whole (island) country

中 *kaichū* in the sea; marine. *watanaka* in the ocean; on the ocean

王星 *Kaiōsei* Neptune

水 *kaisui* sea water

水浴 *kaisuiyoku* sea bathing

水浴場 *kaisuiyokujō*, bathing beach

水帽 *kaisuibō* bathing cap

水着 *kaisuigi* bathing suit

5 氷 *kaihyō* coastal sea ice

外 *kaigai* overseas, foreign; abroad
外版 *kaigaiban* overseas edition
外放送 *kaigai hōsō* overseas broadcasting
外事情 *kaigai jijō* overseas news
外派兵 *kaigai hahei* sending troops overseas
外発展 *kaigai hatten* overseas expansion
外進出 *kaigai shinshutsu* overseas expansion
外渡航 *kaigai tokō* foreign voyage
外電報 *kaigai dempō* overseas cable
6 気 *kaiki* sea air, sea breeze
防 *kaibō* coast defense
防艦 *kaibōkan* coast-defense ship
老 *ebi* lobster; shrimp, prawn
老色 *ebi-iro* reddish brown
老茶 *ebicha* maroon
老錠 *ebijō* padlock
7 角 *kaikaku* headland, cape
里 *kairi* knot, nautical mile
図 *kaizu* marine chart
技 *kaigi* seamanship
抜 *kaibatsu* height above sea level
坊主 *umibōzu* sea monster
兵 *kaihei* (U.S.) marines
兵隊 *kaiheitai* (U.S.) marines
8 門 *kaimon* straits, channel, sound
国 *kaikoku* maritime nation, sea-girt country
味 *kaimi* marine food products
松 *umimatsu* seacoast pines
法 *kaihō* maritime law
沿 *umizo(i)* coastlands
苔 *nori* laver (an edible seaweed)
苔巻 *norima(ki)* rice wrapped in seaweed
事 *kaiji* maritime affairs
事思想 *kaiji shisō* knowledge of the sea
事裁判所 *kaiji saibansho* maritime court
底 *kaitei* ocean floor; submarine
底火山 *kaitei kazan* submarine volcano
底地震 *kaitei jishin* submarine earthquake
底電信 *kaitei denshin* submarine telegram
底電線 *kaitei densen* submarine cable
岸 *kaigan* seashore, coast, beach, waterfront. *umigishi* beach, seaside
岸防備 *kaigam-bōbi* coast defense
岸沿 *kaiganzo(i) ni* along the coast; along the seashore
岸通 *kaigandō(ri)* bund
岸線 *kaigansen* coastline; coastal railway
9 面 *kaimen* (surface of) the sea, sea level. *umizura* surface of the sea
風 *kaifū, umi kaze* sea breeze
相 *Kaishō* Navy Minister
神 *kaijin, kaishin, watatsumi* sea god, Neptune
胆 *uni* sea urchin
南 *kainan* southern coasts
星 *hitode* starfish
峡 *kaikyō* straits, channel, sound
峡植民地 *Kaikyō Shokuminchi* Straits Settlements
草 *kaisō, umikusa* seaweeds, marine plants
草麺 *kaisōmen* seaweed noodles
洋 *kaiyō* ocean
洋気候 *kaiyō kikō* marine climate
洋学 *kaiyōgaku* oceanography
軍 *kaigun* navy
軍力 *kaigunryoku* naval strength
軍大臣 *Kaigun Daijin* Navy Minister
軍工廠 *kaigun kōshō* naval dockyard
軍兵学校 *Kaigunhei Gakkō* Naval Academy
軍国 *kaigunkoku* a naval power
軍省 *Kaigunshō* Admiralty, Navy Department
軍葬 *kaigunsō* navy funeral
軍旗 *kaigunki* navy flag
軍機 *kaigunki* navy plane
10 馬 *kaiba, seiuchi* walrus. *todo* sea lion
原 *unabara, wata(no)hara* ocean, sea, the deep
浜 *kaihin* seashore, beach, coast
流 *kairyū* ocean current
狸 *kairi* beaver
豹 *azarashi, kaihyō* seal
家 *umi (no) ie* beach pavilion
容 *kaiyō* magnanimous forgiveness
員 *kai-in* sailor, seaman, crew
員審判所 *kai-in shimpanjo* marine court
陸 *kairiku* land and sea
陸空 *kairikukū* land, sea, and air
陸風 *kairikufū* land and sea breezes
11 魚 *kaigyo* sea fish
鳥 *kaichō, umidori* sea bird
亀 *umigame* sea turtle
道 *kaidō* coastal highway
域 *kai-iki* an area of the ocean
深 *kaishin* ocean depth
猫 *umi neko* sea gull
豚 *iruka* dolphin, porpoise
船 *umibune* seagoing vessel
蛇 *kaida, umi hebi* sea serpent
商 *kaishō* marine commerce
運 *kaiun* marine transportation; maritime
運業 *kaiungyō* shipping business; merchant marine
産 *kaisan* marine products
産物 *kaisambutsu* marine products
産業 *kaisangyō* marine-products industry
12 湾 *kaiwan* gulf, bay
港 *kaikō* ocean port
淵 *kaien* ocean depths, ocean deep
程 *kaitei* distance by sea, nautical mileage
葬 *kaisō* burial at sea
堡 *kaihō* coastal battery
象 *seiuchi, kaizō* walrus
13 鼠 *namako* sea cucumber
塩 *kaien* salt made from sea water
損 *kaison* sea damage
溝 *kaikō* an ocean deep
路 *kairo, umiji* ocean route, sea paths

際 *umigiwa* seaside, beach
戦 *kaisen* naval battle
跡湖 *kaisekiko* inland salt lake
賊 *kaizoku* pirate
賊船 *kaizokusen* pirate ship
14 鳴 *umina(ri), kaimei* roar of the ocean
端 *umibata* beach, seashore, coast
精 *umi(no)sei* mermaid
綿 *kaimen* sponge
関 *kaikan* maritime customs
関税 *kaikanzei* import duties
15 蝕 *kaishoku* sea erosion
盤車 *hitode* starfish
潮 *kaichō* tide, current
潮音 *kaichōon* sound of the tide
16 鴨 *umigamo* sea duck
嘯 *kaishō* tidal bore
錨 *kaibyō* drag anchor
獣 *kaijū* marine animal
燕 *umi tsubame* stormy petrel
壁 *kaiheki* sea wall, break water
龍王 *kairyūō* dragon king, dragon god
18 難 *kainan* sea disaster
難救護所 *kainan kyūgosho* life-saving station
19 獺 *rakko* sea otter
藻 *kaisō* seaweeds, marine plants
霧 *kaimu* sea fog
20 鯽 *umi tanago* surf perch
21 魔 *Kaima* Davy Jones
22 鰻 *anago, umi unagi* sea eel
鷗 *umi kamome* sea gull
23 鱒 *umi masu* sea trout
26 驢 *ashika* sea lion, hair seal

7

派 See 2547.

溲 2554 F1146 See 溲 2646.

涉 2555 F1115 See 渉 2591.

海 2556 F1110 See 海 2553.

涛 Nonstandard for 濤 2719.

浬 2557 F1108 Ri nautical mile, knot. *kairi* knot, nautical mile.

涵 2558 F1117 涵 KAN steep (in water), dip; put into.
15 養 *kan-yō* cultivation, training, fostering

涕 2559 F1116 TEI. *namida* tears; sympathy.
8 泣 *teikyū* weeping

涎 2560 F1115 SEN. EN. *yodare* slobber, saliva.
11 掛 *yodareka(ke)* bib

涓 2561 F1115 KEN a drop; pure.
10 埃 *ken-ai* something very small
14 滴 *kenteki* a drop of water

浣 2562 F1107 KAN wash.
6 衣 *kan-i* washing clothes; laundered clothes
13 腸 *kanchō* enema
14 熊 *araiguma* raccoon

浩 2563 F1107 浩 澔 Kō wide expanse; abundance; vigorous.
12 然 *kōzen na* great and prosperous; broad-minded
然気 *kōzen (no) ki* energy, vigor
19 瀚 *kōkan na* bulky, voluminous

涅 2564 F1113 湼 NETSU black soil.
6 色 *kuri iro* black
14 槃 *nehan* nirvana
槃会 *nehan-e* anniversary of the Buddha's death

涌 2565 F1115 湧 Yō. Yu. *wa(ku)* (see under 沸 2524.0).
5 立 *wa(ki)-tat(su)* bubble up, well up
出 *wa(ki)-de(ru), yōshutsu suru* gush forth or out, spout, flow out, well up, bubble up. *wa(ki)-da(su)* cause to gush out
10 起 *wa(ki)-oko(ru)* arise

浚 2566 F1106 SHUN. *sara(eru), sara(u)* clean, dredge, drag.
8 泥機 *shundeiki* mud dredge
12 渫 *shunsetsu* dredging
渫船 *shunsetsusen* dredger
渫機 *shunsetsuki* dredger

浜 B 2567 F1172 濱 HIN. *hama* beach, seashore; fishing village.
4 手 *hamate* near the beach
辺 *hamabe* beach, seashore
9 面 *hamazura* the open beach
風 *hama kaze* beach wind
12 焼 *hamayaki* sea bream broiled whole
街道 *hama kaidō* beach road
13 路 *hamaji* beach road

A **浴** 2568 / F1110 **浴** YOKU. *yoku(suru)* bathe, be favored with; bask in. *a(biru)* bathe in, pour on oneself, bask in, be flooded with, be under (fire); be accused of, be charged with, expose oneself to, be subjected to, receive (applause). *a(biseru)* pour on; subject to, impute to, deluge with.

[5] 用 *yokuyō* for the bath
用石鹼 *yokuyō sekken* bath soap
[6] 衣 *yokui, yukata* unlined cotton kimono, bathrobe, dressing gown
衣掛 *yukataga(ke) de* wearing an unlined summer kimono
[9] 後 *yokugo* after the bath
客 *yokkaku, yokkyaku* bathing guest
室 *yokushitsu* bathroom
[11] 掛 *a(bise)-ka(keru)* = *a(biseru)* (see under 浴 2568.0)
[12] 場 *yokujō* bathroom, bathhouse
場主 *yokujōshu* bathhouse keeper
[15] 槽 *yokusō* bathtub

B **涙** 2569 / F1120 **淚 泪** RUI. *namida* tear; sympathy. *namida(ppoi)* easily shedding hears
[5] 乍 *namidanaga(ra) ni* in tears
[7] 含 *namidagu(mu)* be moved to tears. *namidagu(mashii)* tearful, sad, pathetic
声 *namidagoe* tearful voice
[8] 金 *namidakin* consolation money
雨 *namida ame* a light rain
[10] 脆 *namidamoro(i)* given to weeping
[11] 眼 *ruigan* eyes welling with tears
[13] 腺 *ruisen* tear gland
[14] 管 *ruikan* tear duct
[18] 顔 *namidagao* tearful face
[22] 嚢 *ruinō* tear sac

B **浪** 2570 / F1108 **浪** RŌ. *nami* waves, billows.
[2] 人 *rōnin* lordless samurai, adventurer; unsuccessful examinee; jobless person
人組 *rōningumi* the student group who failed in entrance examinations
[3] 士 *rōshi* = *rōnin* 浪人 (see above–2)
[6] 宅 *rōtaku* home of a lordless samurai
曲 *rōkyoku* musical recital of ancient tales
曲師 *rōkyokushi* minstrels
[7] 花節 *naniwabushi* minstrels; musical recital of ancient tales
花節語 *naniwabushi-kata(ri)* minstrels
[9] 速 *Naniwa* ancient Osaka
[10] 浪 *rōrō* wandering
華 *Naniwa* ancient Osaka
[12] 費 *rōhi* waste, extravagance
費癖 *rōhiheki* spendthrift habits
[14] 漫主義 *rōman shugi* romanticism
漫的 *rōmanteki* romantic (school)
漫派 *rōmanha* romantic school, romanticism

B **浦** 2571 / F1107 Ho. *ura* creek, inlet; bay, gulf; beach, seacoast.
[2] 人 *urabito* seaside dweller
[4] 辺 *urabe* seacoast
[6] 舟 *urabune, urafune* ships at anchor in the bay
凪 *uranagi* calm on the bay
回 *urawa* coastal indentations
曲 *urawa* coastal indentations
伝 *urazuta(i)* following the seacoast
州 *urasu* sandspit
安国 *Urayasu (no) Kuni* (ancient name for) Japan
[7] 里 *urazato* seaside village
[8] 波 *uranami* breakers
和 *uranagi* calm on the bay
[9] 風 *urakaze* sea breeze
洲 *urasu* sandspit
[12] 越 *urako(shi)* crossing the bay; sea breeze
[13] 路 *uraji* road leading to the beach
[15] 潮 *urashio* bay tides
[17] 磯 *ura-iso* sea beach

B **浸** 2572 / F1113 **浸** SHIN. *hita(su)* soak, dip, steep, immerse, moisten, wet, dunk, drench. *hita(ru)* be soaked in, be immersed in, be flooded, be submerged; be bathed in; be addicted to. *tsuka(ru)* be soaked in; be submerged; be flooded; take a dip; be seasoned. *(o)hita(shi)* boiled greens with dressing.
[2] 入 *shinnyū suru* seep in, flow in
[4] 水 *shinsui* inundation, flood, submersion; leaking
水家屋 *shinsui kaoku* houses under water
[5] 出 *shinshutsu* = 滲出 2677.5
礼 *shinrei* baptism by immersion
礼水槽 *shinrei (no) suisō* baptistry
礼式 *shinreishiki* an immersion baptism
礼派 *Shinreiha* Baptists
礼教会 *Shinrei Kyōkai* Baptist Church
礼場 *shinreijō* baptistry
[9] 食 *shinshoku* erosion; corrosion
染 *shinsen* = *shinjun* 浸潤 (see below–15)
透 *shintō* permeation, infiltration, osmosis
透作戦 *shintō sakusen* infiltration operations
[10] 害 *shingai* = 侵害 452.10
[15] 潤 *shinjun* permeation, infiltration, saturation
蝕 *shinshoku* erosion; corrosion

A **酒** 2573 / F1917 SHU *sake* saké, rice wine; alcoholic liquor. [酉]
[4] 手 *sakate* drink money, tip
太 *sakebuto(ri)* getting fat from drinking
[5] 母 *shubo* yeast, ferment
仙 *shusen* heavy drinker

代 *sakadai, sakashiro* price of saké; saké gift to workmen; workmen's bonus, tip
石酸 *shusekisan* tartaric acid
6肉 *shuniku* saké and meat
色 *shushoku* wine and women, debauchery
好 *sakezu(ki)* drinker
池肉林 *shuchi-nikurin* sumptuous feast
気 *sakake, shuki* smell of liquor
気違 *sake kichiga(i)* crazed with drink; such a drunk; heavy drinking; heavy drinker
7狂 *shukyō* drunken frenzy
乱 *shuran* drunken frenzy; vicious drinker
呑 *sakenomi* drinker
男 *sake otoko* brewer
8店 *saketen, sakamise* saké shop
杯 *shuhai* wine glass
毒 *shudoku* alcoholism
肴 *shukō, sake-sakana* food and drink
肴料 *shukōryō* monetary gift for food
9屋 *sakaya* wine shop; wine merchant
保 *shuho* canteen, post exchange, PX
後 *shugo* after drinking saké
客 *shukaku* drinker
臭 *sakekusa(i)* reeking of liquor
食 *shushoku, shushi* revelry; saké and food
食料 *shushokuryō* monetary gift for food
造 *shuzō, sakezuku(ri), sakazuku(ri)* saké brewing
造米 *shuzōmai* rice for saké brewing
造家 *shuzōka* brewer
造税 *shuzōzei* tax on alcoholic liquor
造場 *shuzōjō* brewery, distillery
造業 *shuzōgyō* brewery business
10席 *shuseki* banquet, feast
徒 *shuto* drinking companion
浸 *sakabita(ri), sakebita(ri)* steeped in liquor; drinking daily. *sakabita(shi)* steeped in liquor
家 *shuka* wine shop; drinker
宴 *shuen* banquet, drinking bout
息 *saka-iki* alcoholic breath
振舞 *sakaburumai* drinking bout
11淫 *shuin* wine and women
粕 *sake kasu* saké lees
脱 *shadatsu na* unconventional; unconstrained; (mentally) detached
船 *sakabune* wine press, vat
販 *shuhan* sale of liquor
断 *sakada(chi)* swearing off from drinking
盛 *sakamo(ri)* carousal, revelry
12場 *sakaba* bar, barroom
税 *shuzei* liquor tax
飲 *sakeno(mi)* drinker
壺 *sakatsubo* saké jar
量 *shuryō* drinking capacity
落 *sharaku na* frank; open-hearted. *share* witticism; joke
落者 *sharemono* a dandy, a fop
落臭 *sharakusa(i)* forward, impertinent
13塩 *sakashio* saké seasoning
肆 *shushi* liquor store
戦 *shusen* drinking bout
14豪 *shugō* heavy drinker
蔵 *sakagura* wine cellar, wineshop
精 *shusei* alcohol, spirits, hard liquor
精飲料 *shusei inryō* alcoholic liquor
15幟 *shushi* saloon banner
槽 *sakabune* wine press, vat
器 *shuki* saké cup
16樽 *sakadaru* wine barrel
興 *shukyō* conviviality, merrymaking
機嫌 *sasakigen* tipsiness
17糟 *sake kasu* saké lees
18癖 *sakekuse, sakaguse, shuheki* drinking habits
類 *shurui* alcoholic liquors
21饌 *shusen* food and drink

A **消** 2574/F1114 **消** Shō, *ke(su)* extinguish, blow out; turn off, erase, cross out; neutralize (odors or poisons); deaden (noise); cancel (in fractions). *ki(eru), ki(yuru)* be extinguished; melt away; disappear, die out; wear away; burst (as a bubble).

2入 *ki(e)-i(ru)* vanish
3口 *ke(shi)guchi* fire-fighting front
4方 *ki(e)gata* about to go out or disappear
止 *ke(shi)-to(meru)* extinguish, get under control
火 *shōka* fire fighting
火水管 *shōka suikan* fire hose
火用 *shōkayō* for fire
火用水 *shōka yōsui* water for fires
火栓 *shōkasen* fire hydrant
火器 *shōkaki* fire extinguisher
化 *shōka* digestion, assimilation
化力 *shōkaryoku* digestive power
化不良 *shōka furyō* indigestion
化作用 *shōka sayō* digestive process
化剤 *shōkazai* aid to digestion
化液 *shōka eki* digestive fluid
化管 *shōkakan* digestive tract
化器 *shōkaki* digestive organs
5去 *ke(shi)-sa(ru)* erase, blot out. *ki(e)-sa(ru)* disappear, die out, melt away. *shōkyo* elimination
失 *ki(e)-u(seru)* die out, disappear, fail. *shōshitsu* disappearance, vanishing
石灰 *shōsekkai* slacked lime, calcium hydroxide
6印 *keshi-in* postmark, cancellation stamp
灯 *shōtō* putting out the lights
光 *shōkō* passing time, getting along
防 *shōbō* fire fighting

防手 *shōbōshu* fireman
防夫 *shōbōfu* fireman
防自動車 *shōbō jidōsha* fire engine
防官 *shōbōkan* fire-department officer
防栓 *shōbōsen* fire hydrant
防部 *shōbōbu* fire department
防組 *shōbōgumi* company of firemen
防隊 *shōbōtai* fire brigade
防署 *shōbōsho* fire station
7 沈 *shōchin* dejection, depression
却 *shōkyaku* erasure, effacement; expenditure; repayment, redemption, amortization
8 長 *shōchō* ebb and flow, prosperity and decay
果 *ki(e)-ha(teru)* disappear, vanish
炎剤 *shōenzai* an antiphlogistic
毒 *shōdoku* disinfection, sterilization, fumigation, pasteurization
毒衣 *shōdokui* disinfected garment
毒液 *shōdoku eki* antiseptic solution
毒済 *shōdokuzu(mi)* disinfected
毒器 *shōdokuki* sterilizer
毒薬 *shōdokuyaku* disinfectant
9 飛 *ke(shi)-to(bu)* fly off
除 *shōjo* deletion
炭 *ke(shi)zumi* extinguished charcoal
音 *shōon* silencing (a machine) ⌈damper
音器 *shōonki* silencer, muffler, mute,
10 残 *ki(e)-noko(ru)*, *kenoko(ru)* remain unmelted; linger (snow)
消 *ki(e)gi(e)* (a fire) just about out; absent-mindedness ⌈summer
夏 *shōka* summering, going away for the
耗 *shōkō suru*, *shōmō suru* consume, exhaust, dissipate, use up
耗品 *shōmōhin* supplies, consumer goods
耗症 *shōmōshō* atrophy, a wasting disease
耗戦 *shōmōsen* war of attrition
息 *shōsoku* news, letter, circumstances
息子 *shōsokushi* doctor's probe
息文 *shōsokubun* personal letter
息通 *shōsokutsū* informed person
息筋 *shōsoku suji* informed circles
11 掛 *ki(e)-ka(karu)* about to go out, about to
12 閑 *shōkan* killing time ⌊disappear
散 *shōsan* dissipation, dispersion, disappearance
壺 *ke(shi)tsubo* charcoal extinguishing jar
寒 *shōkan* getting thru the winter
然 *shōzen(taru)* despondent, crestfallen
極 *shōkyoku* negative pole; conservatism
極主義 *shōkyoku shugi* negativism
極性 *shōkyokusei* passiveness
極的 *shōkyokuteki* passive, negative, conservative, destructive
費 *shōhi* consumption; expenditure
費力 *shōhiryoku* consumer buying power
費市場 *shōhi ichiba* consumers' market
費地 *shōhichi* consumer area
費材 *shohizai* consumer goods
費者 *shōhisha* consumer
費物資 *shōhi busshi* consumer goods
費高 *shōhidaka* (amount of) consumption
費財 *shōhizai* consumer goods
費組合 *shōhi kumiai* co-operative society
費税 *shōhizei* excise tax, consumption tax
13 滅 *ke(shi)-horo(bosu)* destroy, consume. *shōmetsu suru* be destroyed. *shōmetsu* extinction, disappearance, nullification
煙機 *shōenki* smoke consumer
14 磁 *shōji* demagnetization
15 憂 *shōyū* dispelling grief
16 磨 *shōma* abrasion, wearing down
18 難 *ki(e)ga(te) no* lingering (snow)
20 護謨 *keshigomu* rubber eraser

浮 2575 / F1108 **浮** B FU. *u(ku)* float, be floated, rise to the surface; be cheered up; be set on edge, feel loose (teeth); be left over, be saved. *u(kasu)*, *u(kaberu)* *vt* float, launch, sail (a toy ship), refloat; waft; express (feelings in the face); recall. *u(kabu)* *vi* float, refloat, surface; flit across (the face), occur to; play (about the lips, as a smile); rise in the world; rest in peace. *u(kareru)* be in high spirits, go on a spree. *u(kasareru)* be carried off, be captivated, be exhilarated. *u(kanu)* gloomy. *u(ki)* cork, float, buoy, lifebuoy, life belt. *u(ita)* gay, cheerful, frivolous. *u(ki)-* floating.

2 力 *furyoku* buoyancy, lift
3 土 *u(ki)tsuchi* light "floating" soil
女 *u(kare)me* prostitute
上 *u(ki)-a(geru)* come to the surface, surface, float, refloat, be refloated; be lifted out of the water; come out in relief. *fujō suru*, *u(ki)-a(garu)*, *u(kabi)-a(garu)* float, refloat, surface
上彫 *u(ki)a(ge)bo(ri)* relief, embossed carving
4 心 *fushin* center of buoyancy
木 *fuboku* driftwood ⌈be exhilarated
5 立 *u(ki)-ta(tsu)* be buoyant, be cheered up,
付 *u(wa)tsu(ku)* be fickle, be flippant, be restless
氷 *fuhyō* ice floe, drift ice
出 *u(ki)-de(ru)* come to the surface; loom. *u(ki)da(shi)* embossed
石 *fuseki*, *karuishi*, *u(ki)-ishi* pumice stone
石鹸 *u(ki)sekken* floating soap
世 *ukiyo* this transitory world, the earth
世波 *ukiyo (no) nami* this world's troubles
世風 *ukiyo (no) kaze* this world's troubles
世草子 *ukiyozōshi* realistic Edo novel

世絵 *ukiyoe* genre picture, ukiyoe
世絵派 *ukiyoeha* the ukiyoe school
世絵師 *ukiyoeshi* an ukiyoe artist
6 舟 *u(ki)bune* pontoon ⌈affair
名 *u(ki)na* romance, scandal, rumor, love
灯台 *u(ki) tōdai* lightship ⌈tonness
気 *u(wa)ki* inconstancy, faithless love, wan-
気分 *u(kare) kibun* sportive spirit, mirth, gaiety ⌈tious person
気者 *u(wa)kimono* inconstant lover, licen-
7 言 *fugen* wild rumor, unfounded report
身 *u(ki)mi* floating on one's back
体 *futai* floating body
沈 *fuchin, u(ki)shizu(mi)* rise and fall, ebb and flow, ups and downs, vicissitudes
男 *u(kare) otoko* dissolute man
足 *u(ki)ashi* wavering
足立 *u(ki)ashita(tte)* ready to run away
足場 *u(ki)ashiba* floating work platform
8 沼 *u(ki)numa, u(ki)nu* muddy swamp
歩 *u(kare)-aru(ku)* gad around. *u(ki)ayu(mi)* walking lightly, tiptoeing
具 *u(ki)gu* water wings
9 垢 *u(ki)aka* scum ⌈battleship
城 *fujō, u(ki)shiro* floating castle, giant
洲 *u(ki)su* floating grass plot (in a muddy lake) ⌈precarious business
草 *u(ki)kusa* floating weed, duckweed;
10 根 *u(ki)ne* roots of water plants
浮 *u(ki)u(ki) to* buoyantly, cheerfully, jaun-
秤 *u(ki)bakari* hydrometer ⌊tily
脂 *u(ki) abura* floating oil
烏 *u(kare)garasu* crow crying by moonlight
島 *u(ki) shima* floating island
荷 *u(ki)ni* flotsam, flotage
華 *fuka* display, ostentation, vanity, frivolity
起重機 *u(ki) kijūki* floating crane
流 *furyū* floating, drifting
流水雷 *furyū suirai* floating mine
流機雷 *furyū kirai* floating mine, drifting
浪 *furō* vagrancy, wandering ⌊mine
浪人 *furōnin* a vagrant
浪児 *furōji* juvenile vagrant, waif
浪者 *furōsha* hobo, tramp, vagabond
11 魚 *u(ki)uo* surface fish
彫 *ukibori* relief, embossed carving
萍 *u(ki) kusa* floating plants
袋 *u(ki)bukuro* air bladder; water wings, life preserver, float, tire
巣 *u(ki)su* floating nest
船渠 *u(ki)dokku* floating dock
遊 *fuyū* floating, suspension
遊生物 *fuyū seibutsu* plankton ⌈unsettled
動 *fudō suru* float; be wafted; fluctuate; be
動人口 *fudō jinkō* floating population
12 揚 *fuyō* floating, flotage, flotation
渣 *u(ki)kasu* scum
游 *fuyū* floating, suspension
葉 *fuyō, u(ki)ha* floating leaf
雲 *fu-un, u(ki)gumo* floating cloud; some-
貸 *u(ki)ga(shi)* illegal loan ⌊thing unsettled
桟橋 *u(ki)sambashi* floating pier ⌈ing
13 腰 *u(ki)goshi no* wavering, unsteady, falter-
腫 *muku(mu)* swell, bloat. *fushu, mukumi* edema, dropsy ⌈sleeping adulterously
寝 *u(ki)ne* sleeping in a ship; uneasy sleep;
14 漂 *fuhyō* floating, flotage
説 *fusetsu* wild rumor, speculation
塵子 *unka* leaf hopper, a rice insect
15 標 *fuhyō* buoy
潮 *u(ki)shio* tidal current
輪 *u(ki)wa* buoyant water ring ⌈bridge
16 橋 *fukyō, u(ki)hashi* floating bridge, pontoon
錨 *fubyō* floating anchor, drift anchor
薄 *fuhaku* frivolity, levity
18 織 *u(ke)o(ri), u(ki)o(ri)* weaving with raised figures; brocade ⌈party
騒 *u(kare)sawa(gi)* merrymaking; noisy
19 瀬 *u(kabu)se* chances in life
22 嚢 *u(ki)bukuro*＝浮袋 (see above–11)

A **流** 2576/F1103 Ru. Ryū current; counter for flags. *naga(reru)* flow, trickle, ooze, drain, run down; be washed away; float, drift; wander; be forfeited, be foreclosed; lapse; incline to; be swayed by; (years) pass. *naga(su)* dash, pour, sluice, let run out, flush; float, set adrift; spill; shed (tears); wash away, wash off; forfeit, foreclose; exile; cruise (taxis). *naga(re)* flow, stream, waters, current; passage (of time); descent; school; abandonment; foreclosure; tendency. *naga(shi)* sink; bath-attendant service; cruising (taxi); strolling musician. *(o)naga(re)* suspension, adjournment, calling off. *-ryū* style, fashion, type, form, manner; school, system; class, order, rate, rank, grade.

2 人 *runin* exile
入 *ryūnyū suru, naga(re)-i(ru)* flow into
3 川 *naga(re)gawa* running stream
下 *naga(re)-kuda(ru)* flow down; drink down; descend
亡 *ryūbō* having no settled abode
丸 *naga(re)dama* stray bullet
4 木 *ryūboku, naga(re)gi* driftwood
水 *naga(re) mizu, ryūsui* running water
元 *naga(shi)moto* kitchen sink and work area
込 *naga(re)-ko(mu)* flow into, run into; drift into. *naga(shi)-ko(mu)* wash down; pour into
込担保 *naga(re)ko(mi) tampo* foreclosure

5 用 *ryūyō* diversion, misappropriation
目 *naga(shi)me* sidelong glance
矢 *naga(re)ya* stray arrow
石 *sasuga ni* as might be expected
去 *naga(re)-sa(ru)* flow past
氷 *ryūhyō* drift ice, ice drift
失 *ryūshitsu suru* be washed away
出 *naga(re)-de(ru), naga(re)-da(su)* flow out, flow on, gush forth; drain out; drift away; shed water. *ryūshutsu* discharge, outward flow, drain (of gold)
民 *ryūmin* drifting people, displaced persons
布 *rufu* circulation, diffusing, dissemination
布本 *rufubon* popular edition
6 血 *ryūketsu* bloodshed
返 *naga(re)-kae(ru)* flow back
汗 *ryūkan* perspiration ⌈drifting lantern
灯 *ryūtō* setting paper lanterns adrift; a
合 *naga(re)-a(waseru)* flow together
会 *ryūkai* adjournment for lack of a quorum
年 *ryūnen* the stream of time
刑 *ryūkei, rukei* deportation, banishment, exile; transportation of a criminal
刑地 *ryūkeichi* penal colony
刑者 *ryūkeisha* an exile
行 *naga(re)-yu(ku)* flow along. *haya(ru)* be fashionable, be popular, be prevalent; flourish, prosper, have a large practice. *ryūkō, hayari* fashion, popularity, prev-
行文句 *hayari monku* cant phrase ⌊alence
行地 *ryūkōchi* infected area
行児 *ryūkōji, hayari(k)ko* popular person; popular geisha
行言葉 *hayari kotoba* popular expression
行性感冒 *ryūkōsei kambō* flu, influenza
行風 *hayari kaze* influenza
行後 *ryūkō-oku(re)* going out of fashion
行病 *ryūkōbyō, hayari yamai* epidemic,
行眼 *hayarime* conjunctivitis ⌊pestilence
行感冒 *ryūkō kambō* flu, influenza
行語 *ryūkōgo* a word on everybody's lips
行歌 *hayari uta, ryūkōka* popular song
7 作 *naga(re)zuku(ri)* wave style of shrine roof
作業 *naga(re) sagyō* assembly-line operation
体 *ryūtai* fluid
体力学 *ryūtai rikigaku* hydrodynamics
言 *ryūgen, rugen* false rumor
言飛語 *ryūgen-higo* rumor, gossip
言蜚語 *ryūgen-higo* rumor, gossip
8 歩 *naga(re)-aru(ku)* wander around
者 *naga(re)mono* vagrant; stranger; bird of
9 連 *ryūren* staying on ⌊passage
通 *ryūtsū* circulation of money; flow of water; ventilation
速 *ryūsoku* speed of a current
俗 *ryūzoku* convention, the beaten track
派 *ryūha* a school of thought; a system
眄 *ryūben, naga(shi)me* sidelong glance, looking askance
砂 *ryūsha* river sand; sandy area, desert
星 *ryūsei, naga(re)boshi* falling star, meteor;
星雨 *ryūseiu* meteoric shower ⌊skyrocket
10 涎 *ryūzen suru* (the mouth) waters for something; greatly desire
浪 *rurō* vagrancy, wandering, exile
涕 *ryūtei suru* shed tears, weep
11 過 *naga(re)-su(giru)* flow past, flow over
域 *ryūiki* river basin
捨 *naga(shi)-su(teru)* throw out (a liquid)
転 *ruten* perpetual motion; vicissitudes; wandering, vagrancy; transmigration
寄 *naga(re)-yo(ru)* drift in
産 *ryūzan* abortion; miscarriage, failure
動 *ryūdō* flow, flowing, floating, circulation, fluidity, mobility; liquid (assets); current
動体 *ryūdōtai* a fluid ⌊(liabilities)
動物 *ryūdōbutsu* fluid, liquid, liquid food
動食 *ryūdōshoku* liquid diet, liquid food
動資本 *ryūdō shihon* liquid capital
12 弾 *ryūdan, naga(re)dama* stray bullet
渡 *naga(re)-wata(ru)* wander about
寓 *ryūgū* a roaming life
筋 *naga(re) suji* course (of a river)
着 *naga(re)-tsu(ku)* drift to, be washed
落 *ryūraku* drift, driftage ⌊ashore
量 *ryūryō* amount of flow
量計 *ryūryōkei* flow meter
13 罪 *ruzai* exile, banishment; transportation (of a criminal)
感 *ryūkan* flu, influenza
14 暢 *ryūchō* fluency, facility
網 *naga(shi) ami* drift net
説 *ryūsetsu* false rumor
15 儀 *ryūgi* a school of thought; style; system; method, form, way
弊 *ryūhei* current evil, abuse
質 *ryūshichi, naga(re)jichi* forfeited pawned article
線型 *ryūsenkei* streamlined
18 謫 *ryūteki* exile, banishment
竄 *ryūzan* deportation, banishment, exile
19 離 *ryūri suru, sasura(u)* wander, roam
麗 *ryūrei na* fluent, flowing, smooth
鏑馬 *yabusame* horseback archery
21 露 *ryūro suru* disclose, reveal, express

8

渚 See 2617.

渠 See 2271.

涎 See 2560.

涵 2577 F1117 See 涵 2558.

涙 2578 F1120 See 涙 2569.

淺 2579 F1131 See 浅 2549.

淨 2580 F1121 See 浄 2548.

渗 Nonstandard for 滲 2677.

渊 Nonstandard for 淵 2625.

渕 Nonstandard for 淵 2625.

P 渓 2581 F-X 溪 KEI valley. *tani* valley.
4水 *keisui* mountain stream
7谷 *keikoku* valley, ravine, canyon
声 *keisei* sound of a valley stream
9泉 *keisen* valley spring
10流 *keiryū* mountain stream
12間 *keikan* ravine

港 2582 F1137 See 港 2630.

淆 2583 F1118 KŌ turbidity; mixing.

P 涯 2584 F1116 GAI shore.

淀 2585 F1118 TEN. DEN. *yodo*(*mu*) (see under 澱 2709.0). *yodo* pool (in a river), eddy.

淼 2586 F1132 BYŌ wide expanse of water.
12淼 *byōbyō* endless expanse of water

淪 2587 F1122 RIN sink; ripple.
12落 *rinraku* ruin, misery, fall

淘 2588 F1120 TŌ select.
7汰 *tōta* selection; weeding out, reducing, retrenchment; dismissal, shake-up

淙 2589 F1120 SŌ sound of flowing water.
11淙 *sōsō*(*taru*) murmuring, babbling

淳 2590 F1126 JUN pure.
6朴 *jumboku* simplicity and honesty
7良 *junryō* simple goodness

B 渉 2591 F1115 涉 SHŌ. *wata*(*ru*) (see under 渡 2635.0).
5外 *shōgai* public relations, liaison
11猟 *shōryō* extensive reading

B 淑 2592 F1119 SHUKU. *shito*(*yakana*) graceful, polite, gentle; pure.
3女 *shukujo* lady
14徳 *shukutoku* womanly virtues

涸 2593 F1117 KO. *ka*(*reru*) *vi* dry up, go dry; be exhausted; mature, mellow. *ka*(*rasu*) *vt* dry up, exhaust.
11渇 *kokatsu suru* dry up; be exhausted; become poverty-stricken
14竭 *koketsu suru vi* dry up

淦 2594 F-X KAN. KON. *aka* bilge water.
4水 *kansui* bilge water
6汲 *akakumi* bailing equipment
8取 *akato*(*ri*) bailing equipment

淋 2595 F1118 RIN lonely. *sabi*(*reru*) become deserted, decline in prosperity. *sabi*(*shii*), *sami*(*shii*), *samu*(*shii*) lonely, lonesome, solitary, deserted, desolate.
4巴液 *rimpa eki* lymph
巴腺 *rimpasen* lymph gland
10疾性 *rinshitsusei* gonorrheal
14漓 *rinri*(*taru*) profuse

B 渇 2596 F1137 渴 KATSU thirst. *kas*(*suru*) be thirsty; dry (up); long for. *kawa*(*ku*) be thirsty; feel dry; dry up, be parched. *kawa*(*ki*) thirst.
4水 *kassui* water shortage
水期 *kassuiki* water-shortage period
6仰 *katsugō, katsugyō* adoration, admiration
10衰 *kawa*(*ki*)-*otoro*(*eru*) be dry and dreary
11望 *kawa*(*ki*)-*nozo*(*mu*) long for. *katsubō* craving, longing, thirsting for

A 済 2597 F1169 濟 SAI. SEI. *su*(*mu*) end; do without; avoid; be excusable; need not. *su*(*masu*), *su*(*maseru*) finish up; settle (one's account); make do. *na*(*su*) pay back. *suku*(*u*) (see under 救

2051.0). *su(manai)* inexcusable, unjustifiable, regrettable, repentant. *su(mimasen)* Excuse me; I'm sorry. *su(mi)* settled, O.K. *-zu(mi)* finished.

3 口 *su(mi)guchi* the end of an incident
5 生 *saisei* life saving
民 *saimin* relieving the sufferings of the people
世 *saisei* social reform
世事業 *saisei jigyō* public-welfare work
9 度 *saido* (Buddhist) redemption, salvation (from pain)
11 済 *seisei, saisai* many
崩 *na(shi)-kuzu(su)* pay little by little; finish little by little. *na(shi)kuzu(shi)* payment by installments

B **涼** 2598/F1117 **凉** RYŌ cool. *suzu(mu)* cool oneself, enjoy the evening air. *suzu(shii), suzu(yaka) na* cool, refreshing.

5 台 *suzu(mi)dai* bench for enjoying the evening cool
6 舟 *suzu(mi)bune* barge for enjoying the evening cool
気 *ryōki* the cool air
8 雨 *ryōu* cooling rain
味 *ryōmi* coolness, cool
夜 *ryōya* cool evening
9 風 *suzukaze, ryōfū* cool breeze
秋 *ryōshū* cool fall; 9th lunar month
客 *suzu(mi)kyaku* people enjoying the cool evening

A **液** 2599/F1117 EKI liquid, fluid, juice, sap, secretion. *tsuyu* (see under 汁 2485.0).

4 化 *ekika* liquefaction
5 圧 *ekiatsu* fluid pressure
汁 *ekijū* juice; sap
7 冷 *ekirei* liquid-cooling
状 *ekijō* liquid state
体 *ekitai* liquid, fluid
体比重計 *ekitai hijūkei* hydrometer
体圧力 *ekitai atsuryoku* fluid pressure
体空気 *ekitai kūki* liquid air
8 肥 *ekihi* liquid fertilizer
9 面 *ekimen* surface of a liquid
10 浸 *ekishin* immersion
剤 *ekizai* liquid medicine
12 量 *ekiryō* liquid measure

B **渋** 2600/F1164 **澁** JŪ. SHŪ. *shibu(ru)* hesitate, be reluctant; have loose painful bowel movements. *shibu* puckery taste (of persimmons); sobriety, quietness. *shibu(i)* puckery, astringent; sullen; quiet, sober; tasty (in dress).

5 皮 *shibukawa* astringent skin (of a chestnut); discolored skin
6 色 *shibu iro* tan color
7 抜 *shibunu(ki)* removing puckery taste
8 味 *shibumi* puckery taste, astringency; good taste, sobriety, refinement
苦 *shūku* bitter puckery taste; disharmony
9 面 *jūmen, shibuzura, shibutsura* sullen face, grimace
柿 *shibugaki* puckery persimmon
茶 *shibucha* coarse tea
10 紙 *shibukami, shibugami* paper treated with astringent persimmon juice
11 渋 *shibushibu, shibujibu, shibu(ri)-shibu(ri)* reluctantly, grudgingly
13 滞 *shūtai, jūtai* stagnation, retardation
腹 *shibu(ri)bara* painful loose bowels

B **添** 2601/F1132 TEN. *so(u) vi* accompany; marry; be added to; suit, meet, satisfy, be adjusted to. *so(eru) vt* add to, attach, append; accompany; garnish; imitate.

4 文 *so(e)bumi* accompanying letter
木 *so(e)gi* splint, splice, brace
手紙 *so(e)tegami* accompanying letter
5 付 *tempu suru* append, accompany
加 *tenka suru* annex, append, add
7 役 *so(e)yaku* secondary post, assistant
状 *so(e)jō* accompanying letter
言葉 *so(e)kotoba* advice, support, good offices
8 物 *so(e)mono* addition, supplement, premium
臥 *so(i)bushi* (mother and child) sleeping together
乳 *so(e)ji suru* suckle (a child)
9 削 *tensaku* correction
10 書 *tensho, so(e)ga(ki)* postscript, additional writing, letter of introduction; accompanying letter
11 遂 *so(i)-to(geru)* be faithful till death
12 景 *tenkei* human interest (in pictures)
13 寝 *so(i)ne* sleeping with one's child

B **淡** 2602/F1121 TAN. *awa(i)* light, faint, pale, fleeting; a little.

4 水 *tansui* fresh water
水魚 *tansuigyo* fresh-water fish
水湖 *tansuiko* fresh-water lake
5 白 *tampaku na*＝淡泊 (see below–8)
6 色 *tanshoku* light color
7 赤色 *tansekishoku* rose color
8 泊 *tampaku na* light; frank; indifferent to
9 紅 *tankō* pink, rose pink
紅色 *tankōshoku* pink, rose pink
11 淡 *tantan(taru)* unconcerned, disinterested; plain, light
彩 *tansai* light coloring
菜 *igai* sea mussel
雪 *awayuki* a light snowfall
黒色 *tankokushoku* gray

黄 *tankō* lemon yellow, buff, straw color
黄色 *tankōshoku* lemon yellow, buff, straw ⌊color
12紫色 *tanshishoku* light purple
13緑色 *tanryokushoku* light green
14墨 *tamboku* pale India ink
褐色 *tankasshoku* light brown
15影 *tan-ei* adumbration
17藍色 *tanranshoku* light blue

淫 2603 / F1122 **婬** IN lewdness, licentiousness. *in*(*suru*) indulge in, go to excess. *mida*(*rana*), *mida*(*rigawashii*) licentious, indecent, lewd.

4心 *inshin* sexual passion
6行 *inkō* obscenity, harlotry
7佚 *in-itsu* profligacy
乱 *inran* debauchery, lewdness, lascivious⌊ness
声 *insei* cheap music
売 *imbai* prostitution
売婦 *imbaifu* prostitute
売宿 *imbai yado* brothel
8雨 *in-u* prolonged rain, long damaging rain
奔 *impon* lewdness, lasciviousness
事 *inji* lascivious act
9風 *impū* lewd manners, immorality
10祠 *inshi* shrine of an evil deity
書 *insho* pornographic book
11婦 *impu* harlot
欲 *in-yoku* lust
12猥 *inwai* indecency, obscenity
13楽 *inraku* carnal pleasure
15蕩 *intō* dissipation, lewdness
慾 *in-yoku* lust
19靡 *imbi* impurity, obscenity

A **混** 2604 / F1127 KON. *kon*(*jiru*), *kon*(*zuru*) *vi* and *vt* mix; blend; adulterate; confound, confuse. *ma*(*zeru*) mix, blend, mingle; include, let in on. *ma*(*zaru*), *ma*(*jiru*) *vi* be mixed, be blended; mingle with.

2入 *konnyū suru vi* and *vt* mingle, adulterate; get mixed
5用 *kon-yō suru vt* mix, mingle
6色 *konshoku* compound color, hue
同 *kondō* confusion; mixing; merger
気 *ma*(*jiri*)*ke* mixture, impurities
返 *ma*(*ze*)-*kae*(*su*), *ma*(*zek*)*kae*(*su*) stir up; interrupt, interfere with
交 *konkō* confusion, jumble, mixture
在 *konzai* mixture
合物 *kongōbutsu* mixture, compound, amal⌈gam
血 *konketsu* racial mixture
血児 *konketsuji* half-breed, mulatto, Eur⌈asian
成 *konsei* mixture, composition
成酒 *konseishu* mixed liquor
合 *ma*(*ze*)-*a*(*waseru*) *vt* mix, blend, compound. *maji*(*ri*)-*a*(*u*) *vi* mix. *kongō* mixing; mixture
合列車 *kongō ressha* mixed freight-and-pas⌈senger train
合体 *kongōtai* a mixture
合酒 *kongōshu* mixed liquors
合機 *kongōki* mixing machine
7作 *konsaku* mixed crops
沌 *konton* chaos, nebulosity, confusion
乱 *konran* disorder, chaos, confusion
声 *konsei* mixed voices
声合唱 *konsei gasshō* mixed chorus
8迷 *kommei* ＝昏迷 2479.8
物 *ma*(*jiri*)*mono* mixture, something impure. *ma*(*ze*)*mono* adulteration, mixture
和 *konwa* mixture, mingling
和物 *konwabutsu* mixture
和機 *konwaki* mixing machine
9信 *konshin* jamming, interference
10浴 *kon-yoku* mixed bathing (in a bath house)
流 *konryū* cross currents
紡 *kombō* mixed spinning; mixed yarn
11淆 *konkō* mixture, confusion, jumble
混 *konkon toshite* copious (flow); confused
12然 *konzen*(*taru*) whole, entire, harmonious
13戦 *konsen* free-for-all fight
載 *konsai* mixed loading; mixed freight
14雑 *konzatsu* confusion, disorder, congestion
雑時 *konzatsuji* rush hour
15線 *konsen* entanglement of wires; confusion
16濁 *kondaku* turbidity, muddiness

A **清** 2605 / F1128 **淸** SHŌ, SEI, SHIN China, Manchu (dynasty). *kiyo*(*meru*) purify, cleanse; consecrate; exorcise. *kiyo*(*maru*), *kiyo*(*mawaru*) be purified, be cleansed. *su*(*masu*) (see under 澄 2699.0). *kiyo*(*i*) clean, clear; pure, innocent; noble. *kiyo*(*me*) purification, sanctification; cleansing, purgation; exorcism; ablution. *kiyo*(*rakana*) clear.

1一票 *kiyo*(*ki*) *ippyō* honest vote
3子音 *seishi-in* voiceless sound
4水 *shimizu, seisui* clear water, pure water
元 *kiyomoto* a ballad-drama
友 *seiyū* refined friend
8冽 *seiretsu na* clear, limpid
所 *kiyodokoro* kitchen in a noble's home
明 *seimei* pure and clear
事 *kiyo*(*me*)*goto* purification
国 *Shinkoku* China under the Manchus
国人 *Shinkokujin* the Chinese people (under ⌊the Manchus)
9音 *seion* unvoiced sound
香 *seikō* fragrance, perfume
洌 *seiretsu na* clear (water)
秋 *seishū* clear fall (weather)

剃 *kiyozori* second time over in shaving
泉 *seisen* crystal spring
栄 *seiei* your health and prosperity
風 *seifū* a cool refreshing breeze
風明月 *seifū-meigetsu* pure as the wind and clear as the moon; purity of heart
浄 *seijō, shōjō* purity, spotlessness
浄無垢 *shōjō-muki* perfect purity, innocence
10 流 *seiryū* clear stream
酒 *seishu, sumizake* refined saké
祥 *seishō* spirit, energy
純 *seijun* purity
陰 *sei-in* cool shadows
党 *seitō* clearing a political party (of undesirable elements)
書 *seisho, kiyoga(ki)* clean copy
素 *seiso* neatness
11 遊 *seiyū* excursion, outing
清 *seisei suru* feel refreshed, feel relieved. *sugasuga(shii)* refreshing, soothing
貧 *seihin* honorable poverty
掃 *seisō* cleaning
掃夫 *seisōfu* garbage man
教 *Seikyō* Puritanism
教徒 *Seikyōto* Puritans
涼 *seiryō na* cool, refreshing
涼剤 *seiryōzai* refrigerant
涼飲料水 *seiryō inryōsui* cooling drink
12 閑 *seikan* quiet, tranquility
朝 *Shinchō* Manchu dynasty. *seichō, shinchō* square character with thin horizontal strokes
朝活字 *seichō katsuji* square character with thin horizontal strokes
13 適 *seiteki* health, prosperity, comfort
福 *seifuku* happiness, welfare
節 *seisetsu* integrity
楚 *seiso* neatness
廉 *seiren* purity and unselfishness, honesty, integrity
廉潔白 *seiren-keppaku* uprightness
新 *seishin na* fresh, new
新味 *seishimmi* freshness
14 算 *seisan* liquidation, settlement
15 澄 *seichō na* clear; serene
談 *seidan* elevated conversation
潔 *seiketsu* cleanliness, neatness, purity
潔法 *seiketsuhō* general housecleaning
16 濁 *seidaku* purity and impurity; good and evil
興 *seikyō* innocent amusement
17 聴 *seichō* your kind attention (to my talk)

A 深 **2606** F1124 SHIN deep. *fuka(meru) vt, fuka(maru) vi* deepen, heighten, intensify, strengthen. *fuka(mi)* a depth, deep place; profundity. *fuka(su)* sit up late. *fuke(ru)* get late; grow old; reach the height of the season. *fuka(i)* deep; thick, dense; profound, intense; intimate.

2 入 *fuka-i(ri) suru* be engrossed in, be taken up with, go too far into
3 山 *miyama, shinzan* mountain recesses, remote mountains
山木 *miyamagi* deep-forest trees
山幽谷 *shinzan-yūkoku* distant mountains and solitary valleys
山桜 *miyamazakura* wild flowering cherry
山鴉 *miyamagarasu* mountain crow
山躑躅 *miyama tsutsuji* wild azalea
4 手 *fukade* deep wound, severe injury, mortal wound
爪 *fukazume* the quick of a fingernail
化 *shinka* deepening
切 *shinsetsu* kindness
5 玄 *shingen* mystery
6 仲 *fuka(i) naka* intimacy
交 *shinkō* close friendship
7 谷 *shinkoku* deep valley, ravine
更 *shinkō* midnight, dead of night
8 長 *shinchō na* profound, deep
追 *fukao(i)* chasing (the enemy) too far
味 *fukami* depth; deep place
夜 *shin-ya* dead of night, midnight
沓 *fukagutsu* long boots or shoes
呼吸 *shinkokyū* deep breathing, deep breath
刻 *shinkoku na* serious, keen, acute, significant
刻化 *shinkokuka* intensification, aggravation
9 厚 *shinkō na* deep (sympathy), close (relations)
度 *shindo* depth
浅 *shinsen* depth
重 *shinchō na* relaxed and dignified
思 *shinshi* deep thinking
怨 *shin-en* deep resentment
甚 *shinjin no* profound, deep
紅 *shinku* deep crimson
紅色 *shinkōshoku* deep ruby red
海 *shinkai* deep sea. *shinkai no* abysmal
海作業 *shinkai sagyō* deep-sea salvage
海波 *shinkaiha* deep-sea wave
海魚 *shinkaigyo* deep-sea fish
海漁業 *shinkai gyogyō* deep-sea fisheries
海線 *shinkaisen* deep-sea cable
海爆弾 *shinkai bakudan* depth charge
10 酒 *fukazake* heavy drinking
耕 *shinkō* deep plowing
11 彫 *fukabo(ri)* deep carving
情 *fukanasake* inordinate show of affection
深 *fukabuka to* very deeply. *shinshin* getting later; getting quiet; deep interior; feeling (the cold)
酔 *fukayo(i)* deep drunkenness
窓 *shinsō* a secluded inner room. *shinsō ni* very carefully
雪 *shinsetsu, miyuki* deep snow
12 痛 *shintsū* deep sorrow
遠 *shin-en na* profound, deep, unfathomable

間 *fukama* depth, deep place; intimacy
閑 *shinkan toshita* silent, hushed, deserted
淵 *shin-en* abyss, ravine
奥 *shin-ō*＝*unnō* 蘊奥 4095.12
13 傷 *fukade* deep wound, severe injury
靴 *fukagutsu* long boots
意 *shin-i* deep meaning
14 閨 *shinkei* inner bedroom
緑 *shinryoku* dark green. *fukamidori* dark green; verdure
酷 *shinkoku na* serious, keen, acute
15 履 *fukagutsu* long boots; high shoes
慮 *shinryo* thoughtfulness, foresight, prudence
潭 *shintan* abyss, ravine
憂 *shin-yū* deep anxiety, great fear; deep grief
16 謀 *shimbō* deeply laid plan
謀遠慮 *shimbō-enryo* careful plans for the future
17 邃 *shinsui na* profound, abstruse
謝 *shinsha* deep gratitude, sincere apology
鍋 *fukanabe* deep pan, pot

9

溲 See 2646.

湧 2607 F1141 See 涌 2565.

渴 2608 F1137 See 渇 2596.

澆 Nonstandard for 澆 2690.

湲 2609 F1143 KAN the sound of running water.

渟 2610 F1133 TEI stop.

湃 2611 F1140 HAI sound of waves.

渣 2612 F1134 SA dregs.

渥 2613 F1134 AKU kindness.

渫 2614 F1136 SETSU dredging; cleaning out.

湊 2615 F1140 SŌ. *minato* harbor, port.

湑 2616 F1140 SHO. *shitami* dregs, lees.

渚 2617 F1133 SHO. *nagisa* beach, shore, strand.

湍 2618 F1140 TAN rapids; rushing stream; seething. *se* (see under 瀬 2735.0).

渙 2619 F1132 KAN scatter.

9 発 *kampatsu* proclamation

游 2620 F1138 YŪ float. *oyo(gu)* swim.

9 侠 *yūkyō* chivalrous man; gangster

湮 2621 F1142 IN sink; plug up.

7 没 *imbotsu suru* fall into ruins; sink into oblivion, disappear
13 滅 *immetsu* destruction, suppression

湛 2622 F1141 TAN. *tata(eru)* fill; wear (a smile).

12 湛 *tantan(taru)* overflowing; deep, abysmal
然 *tanzen(taru)*＝the word above

渺 2623 F1139 BYŌ minuteness; boundless, far, wide. *byō(taru)* little, tiny, insignificant.

9 茫 *byōbō(taru)* boundless, vast
12 渺 *byōbyō(taru)* boundless, vast
然 *byōzen(taru)* boundless, vast
13 漠 *byōbaku(taru)* boundless, vast

渾 2624 F1139 KON large; all; turbidity. *sube(te)* (see under 凡 654.0).

4 天儀 *kontengi* celestial globe
7 身 *konshin* the whole body
沌 *konton* chaos, confusion, nebulosity
12 渾 *konkon*＝混混 2604.11
然 *konzen(taru)* whole, entire; harmonious

淵 2625 F1126 EN edge. *fuchi* deep pool, deep water, abyss, the depths.

8 底 *entei* bottom of the abyss
12 淵 *fuchibuchi* depths (of the sea)
13 源 *engen* origin, source, fountainhead
18 藪 *ensō* center, seat, home, cradle of
叢 *ensō* center, seat, home, cradle of
19 瀬 *fuchise* pools and shoals; vicissitudes

B 滋 2626 F1148 滋 JI more and more; be luxuriant; planting; turbidity.

8 雨 *jiu* beneficial rain, welcome rain
味 *jimi no* dainty, delicious, nourishing
11 強飲料 *jikyō inryō* tonic drink

15 養 *jiyō* nourishment
養分 *jiyōbun* nutritious element, nutrient
養物 *jiyōbutsu* nourishing food
養剤 *jiyōzai* nutrient medicine (as vitamins)
養過多 *jiyōkata* hypertrophy
養灌腸 *jiyō kanchō* rectal feeding

B **湾** 2627 / F1176 **灣** WAN gulf, bay, inlet.

2 入 *wannyū* inlet, gulf
3 口 *wankō* bay entrance
4 内 *wannai* inside the bay
6 曲 *wankyoku* curve, crook, bend
7 形 *wankei* bay formation
8 屈 *wankutsu* curve, crook, bend
10 流 *Wanryū* Gulf Stream
12 奥 *wan-ō* bay bottom
16 頭 *wantō* head of a bay

A **湖** 2628 / F1141 Ko *mizu-umi* lake.

3 上 *kojō* on the lake
4 心 *koshin* center of a lake
水 *kosui* lake
辺 *kohen* the vicinity of a lake
8 底 *kotei* lake bottom
岸 *kogan* lake shore
沼 *koshō* lakes and marshes
沼学 *koshōgaku* limnology
9 面 *komen* lake surface
風 *kofū* lake breeze
10 畔 *kohan* lake shore, lakeside
12 港 *kokō* lake harbor

P **渦** 2629 / F1135 KA. *uzumaki, uzu* eddy, whirlpool, vortex.

4 中 *kachū* in the whirlpool
7 状星雲 *kajō seiun* spiral nebula
状星雲説 *kajō seiunsetsu* nebular hypothesis
9 巻 *uzumaki* eddy, whirlpool, vortex; coil. *uzuma(ku)* eddy, whirl, swirl, curl (smoke)
巻発条 *uzumaki hatsujō* coiled spring
10 流 *karyū* eddy, whirlpool, maelstrom
紋 *kamon* whirlpool design
11 動 *kadō* vortex
12 雲説 *ka-unsetsu* nebular hypothesis
15 潮 *uzushio* whirling tides
線 *uzusen* spiral line
輪 *uzuwa* whirlpool form

A **港** 2630 / F1137 **港港** Kō *minato, -kō* port, harbor.

3 口 *kōkō, minatoguchi* harbor entrance
4 内 *kōnai* inside the harbor
5 外 *kōgai* outside the harbor
市 *kōshi* port city
7 図 *kōzu* harbor map
町 *minatomachi* harbor town
8 門 *kōmon* harbor entrance
10 都 *kōto* port city
11 務 *kōmu* harbor service
務部 *kōmubu* harbor office
務部長 *kōmu buchō* harbormaster
12 税 *kōzei* harbor dues
湾 *kōwan* harbors
湾労働者 *kōwan rōdōsha* longshoreman
16 頭 *kōtō* waterfront

B **湿** 2631 / F1169 **濕** SHITSU dampness, moisture; itch. *shime(ru)* get damp, get moist, get wet. *shime(su), shime(rasu)* wet, moisten, dampen. *shito(ru)* get damp, become moist. *shime(ppoi)* damp, moist, humid, wet; gloomy, depressing. *shime(ri)* dampness, humidity, moisture; a sprinkle. *shime(yakana)* quiet, gentle; gloomy, dismal.

5 田 *shitsuden* rice fields that always have standing water
布 *shippu* compress, fomentation
6 気 *shike(ru), shikke(ru)* get damp, be moist, be wet. *shikke, shikki, shime(ri)ke* moisture, humidity, dampness. *shike* moisture
地 *shitchi* swampy land, damp ground
7 声 *shime(ri)goe* tearful voice
8 板 *shitsuban* wet plate (photography)
性 *shissei* wet (pleurisy)
性肋膜炎 *shissei rokumakuen* wet pleurisy
9 度 *shitsudo* humidity
度計 *shitsudokei* hygrometer
10 疹 *shisshin* eczema, rash
11 船渠 *shitsusenkyo, shitsudokku* wet dock
12 量 *shitsuryō* wet weight
15 潤 *shitsujun* moisture, humidity, dampness
潤気候 *shitsujun kikō* humid climate
潤空気 *shitsujun kūki* moist air, humid air
19 霧 *shitsumu* wet fog

A **測** 2632 / F1136 SOKU. *haka(ru)* (see under 計 4312.0).

6 地 *sokuchi* land survey, geodetic survey
地学 *sokuchigaku* geodesy
8 知 *haka(ri)-shi(ru), sokuchi suru* infer, understand, fathom, determine
定 *sokutei* measurement, survey, sounding, calibration, determination, test
定法 *sokuteihō* mensuration
9 度 *sokudo* measurement
音器 *sokuonki* sonometer
10 候 *sokkō* meteorological observation

候所 *sokkōjo* weather station
11深 *sokushin* sounding
距儀 *sokkyogi* range finder
12程器 *sokuteiki* (ship's) log
量 *sokuryō* survey; surveying; sounding; measurement
量士 *sokuryōshi* surveyor
量術 *sokuryōjutsu* the science of surveying
量船 *sokuryōsen* surveying ship
13鉛 *sokuen* plummet, sounding lead
微尺 *sokubishaku* micrometer
微計 *sokubikei* micrometer
15線 *sokusen* measuring line
熱 *sokunetsu* calorimetry
12遠機 *sokuenki* range finder
15熱器 *sokunetsuki* calorimeter
16錘 *sokusui* sounding lead
18難 *haka(ri)gata(i)* immeasurable, inestimable, unfathomable, inscrutable, hard to foresee
19縄 *haka(ri)nawa* measuring line

A 湯 2633/F1142 Tō hot water. *yu* hot water, hot bath, hot spring.
3口 *yuguchi* source of a hot spring
女 *yuna* hot-springs prostitute
上 *yua(gari)* just after the bath; bathrobe
4水 *yumizu* hot and cold water; plenty of everything
中 *yuata(ri) suru* be affected by hot springs
引 *yubi(ku)* parboil
元 *yumoto* the source of a hot spring
文字 *yumoji* loin cloth
5玉 *yudama* boiling-water bubbles
札 *yufuda* bath ticket
加減 *yukagen* bath temperature
6気 *yuge* steam, vapor
7冷 *yuza(mashi)* boiled water, cooled hot water; water cooler. *yuza(me)* after-bath chill
呑 *yunomi* teacup
花 *yu (no) hana, yubana* hot-springs incrustations
豆腐 *yudōfu* boiled tofu
8沸 *yuwa(kashi)* teakettle
治 *tōji suru* take healing baths
治場 *tōjiba* health resort
9屋 *yuya* public bathhouse
通 *yudō(shi)* steaming
垢 *yuaka* incrustation, boiler scale
巻 *yuma(ki)* loin cloth
10釜 *yugama* kettle, cauldron
浴 *yuami* bath
浴海綿 *yuami kaimen* bath sponge
11船 *yubune* bathtub
責 *yuze(me)* boiling-water ordeal
桶 *yuoke* bathtub
桶読 *yutōyo(mi)* mixing an *on* and a *kun* reading in the same word
12場 *yuba* hot-springs bathroom, home bathroom
葉 *yuba* dried tofu
煮 *yuni* boiling, seething
湯婆 *yutampo* hot-water bottle
13殿 *yudono* bathroom
滝 *yudaki* hot falls, hot shower
煎 *yusen* decoction, boiling (in a double boiler)
14銭 *yusen* bath charge
15槽 *yubune* bath tub
熨斗 *yunoshi* steam ironing
16薬 *tōyaku* infusion
20灌 *yukan* washing a body for burial

A 温 2634/F1135 = 溫 On. *atata(meru), atta(meru)* warm, heat. *atata(maru), atta(maru), nuku(maru)* warm oneself, sun oneself, get warm. *nukumo(ru)* warm oneself, get warm. *nuku(meru)* warm slightly. *nukumo(ri), nuku(mi)* (slight) warmth. *nukuto(i), nuku(i)* warm, mild, genial. *atataka(i), attaka(i)* warm, mild, genial, cordial.
4水 *onsui* warm water
5石 *onjaku* heated warming stone; pocket warmer
布 *ompu* hot compress
6色 *onshoku* warm color; angry countenance
気 *onki* warmth, sultriness, heat
存 *onzon suru, onson suru* preserve, retain
血動物 *onketsu dōbutsu* warm-blooded animal
7言 *ongen* kind word
床 *onshō, ondoko* hotbed
良 *onryō na* gentle, amiable
灸 *onkyū* moxa cautery
8和 *onwa na* gentle, mild, temperate
突 *ondoru* Korean floor heater, hypocaust
9厚 *onkō na* gentle
室 *onshitsu* greenhouse
故 *onko* looking into the past; checking into history
故知新 *onko-chishin* learning from the past
度 *ondo* temperature
度計 *ondokei* thermometer
度感覚 *ondo kankaku* sense of temperature
泉 *onsen, ideyu* hot spring
泉郷 *onsenkyō* hot-springs town
泉場 *onsemba, onsenjō* spa, hot-springs resort
10座 *onza* sitting peacefully
容 *on-yō* kindly face
帯 *ontai* temperate zone
浴 *on-yoku* hot bath, warm bath
浴療法 *on-yoku ryōhō* hot-water treatments
11健 *onken na* quiet, dependable, uniform
情 *onjō* warm heart; kindliness
情主義 *onjō shugi* kind treatment (of employees)
習 *sara(eru), sara(u)* review, rehearse, practice. *onshū, sarai* review, rehearsal
習会 *onshūkai* (Japanese) music-and-dance recital

12 順 *onjun* gentleness, docility, obedience
湯 *ontō* comfortably hot bath; hot spring
温 *nukunuku* comfortably warm
湿布 *onshippu* hot fomentations
13 雅 *onga na* graceful, affable
感 *onkan* sense of heat
罨法 *on-ampō* hot fomentations
暖 *ondan* warmth
暖前線 *ondan zensen* warm front
15 顔 *ongan* kindly face

B 渡 2635/F1134 To. *wata(ru)* cross, ford, ferry; be imported; change hands; make one's way thru life; sweep across; migrate; be provided. *wata(su)* carry across, ferry over, bring over; hand over, deliver; deal (cards); transfer (a business); pay (wages); bridge; stretch (something) across; lay across. *wata(ri)* passage, transit; gangplank; length, diameter; negotiations; migration (of birds); payable at. *wata(shi)* ferry; delivery; transfer; ford. *watarai* one's occupation.

2 人 *wata(ri)bito, wata(ri)nin* migratory worker; hobo; stranger
3 川 *Wata(ri)gawa* River Styx
4 仏 *to-Futsu* going to France
5 台 *to-Dai* going to Taiwan
世 *tosei* living, livelihood, subsistence; business, trade, profession
世人 *toseinin* chivalrous man; gangster
6 舟 *wata(shi)bune, wata(ri)bune* ferryboat
合 *wata(ri)-a(u)* cross swords, exchange
守 *wata(shi)mori* ferryman ⌊blows; argue
会宮 *Watarai (no) Miya* the Ise Shrines
米 *to-Bei* going to the States
米中 *to-Beichū* while in America
7 初 *wata(ri)zo(me)* bridge dedication
来 *torai suru* visit; come across the sea. *torai* importation, influx, entrance (of a new religion)
8 板 *wata(ri)-ita* gangplank, board crosswalk
物 *wata(ri)mono* imported goods; heirloom;
欧 *to-Ō* going to Europe ⌊wages
歩 *wata(ri)-aru(ku)* wander from place to place, walk across. *toho* walking
英 *to-Ei* going to England ⌈stranger
者 *wata(ri)mono* migratory worker; hobo;
奉公 *wata(ri)bōkō* working here and there
河 *toga, toka* river crossing ⌊as a servant
河地帯 *toka chitai* bridgehead
9 海 *tokai* crossing the ocean; passage
津見 *wadatsumi, watatsumi* Neptune, the
洋 *toyō* transoceanic ⌊ocean, the sea
洋爆撃 *toyō bakugeki* overseas bombing
10 唐 *to-Tō* going to the China of the Tangs
航 *tokō* voyage, tour; a sailing, a crossing
航地 *tokōchi* the land of one's sojourn
航者 *tokōsha* foreign traveler, passenger
航免状 *tokō menjō* passport
航費 *tokōhi* traveling expenses
11 鳥 *wata(ri)dori* migratory bird, bird of pas-
過 *toka* crossing a strait ⌊sage
廊 *wata(ri)rō* covered passageway
廊下 *wata(ri) rōka* covered passageway
船 *wata(shi)bune, wata(ri)bune, tosen* ferry
船場 *tosemba, tosenjō* ferrying place
船賃 *tosenchin* ferry charge
12 場 *wata(shi)ba* ferrying place, ford
御 *togyo suru* proceed to, repair to
13 賃 *wata(shi)chin* ferrying charge
14 銭 *wata(shi)sen* ferry charge
15 稼 *wata(ri) kase(gi)* migratory work
16 鴉 *wata(ri)garasu* a large Hokkaido crow
頭 *totō* ferry
橋式 *tokyōshiki* bridge-opening ceremony
17 鮮 *to-Sen* going to Korea

A 満 2636/F1151 滿 Man fullness, enough; pride. *mi(tsuru), mi(chiru)* be full; rise (tides); mature, expire. *mi(tasu)* fill; supply, make good; satisfy, appease, answer (the need), meet (the demand). *man-* full, fully, fulfillment; a full (year); a full (5 years).

2 人 *Manjin* a Manchurian
了 *manryō* expiration ⌈mountain
3 山 *manzan* the whole hill, the whole
干 *michihi, mankan* ebb and flow
4 月 *mangetsu* full moon
水 *mansui* full to the brim
天 *manten* the whole sky
天下 *mantenka* the whole world ⌈can see
5 目 *mammoku* whole view; as far as the eye
目蕭条 *mammoku-shōjō(taru)* bleak, dreary
6 州 *Manshū* Manchuria
州国 *Manshūkoku* Manchukuo
州事変 *Manshū Jihen* The Manchurian Incident ⌈language
州語 *Manshūgo* the Manchurian Chinese
7 足 *manzoku* satisfaction, contentment. *manzoku na* satisfactory, complete, proper, sound (health). *mi(chi)-ta(riru)* fulfill,
身 *manshin* the whole body ⌊fill up
作 *mansaku* bumper crop
更 *manzara* (not) wholly, (not) altogether
9 面 *mammen* the whole face
洲 *Manshū* Manchuria
点 *manten* perfect, perfect score
10 座 *manza* the whole assembly
悦 *man-etsu* great joy, rapture
株 *mankabu* full subscription (for shares)

配 *mampai* full delivery of rationed goods
員 *man-in* no vacancy, full house
11 堂 *mandō* the whole audience
遍無 *mambenna(ku)*＝万遍無 7.11
12 開 *mankai* full bloom
喫 *mankitsu suru* have enough of; fully enjoy
幅 *mampuku* full width; full area
満 *mi(chi)-mi(chiru)* fill up. *mamman(taru)* full of (vigor, etc.)
渡 *mi(chi)-wata(ru)* be prevalent
腔 *mankō no* wholehearted
期 *manki* expiration (of a period)
塁 *manrui* full bases
場 *manjō* the whole assembly
場一致 *manjō-itchi de* unanimously
13 溢 *mi(chi)-afu(reru)* be full of
腹 *mampuku* satiety
鉄 *Mantetsu* South Manchurian Railway
蒙 *Mammō* Manchuria and Mongolia
載 *mansai* full load
15 潮 *manchō, michishio* high tide
17 鮮 *Man-Sen* Manchuria and Korea
18 額 *mangaku* full amount
19 願 *mangan* fulfillment of a vow
20 艦飾 *mankanshoku* dressed-up (ship); dolled-up (person)

A **減** 2637 / F1133 GEN decrease, decline. *gen(ji-ru), gen(zuru)* decrease; mitigate, appease; dwindle; subtract, deduct. *he(ru), me(ru)* decrease, dwindle, subside; wear and tear; get hungry. *he(su), he(rasu)* reduce, decrease, shorten, curtail; be hungry. *me(ri), he(ri)* decrease, wear, loss, waste.

3 口 *he(razu)guchi* the last word, talking back to
4 水 *gensui* low water; subsiding water; reduced water supply
反 *gentan* acreage reduction
込 *me(ri)-ko(mu)* sink into, stick into
少 *genshō* decrease, reduction, decline
5 圧 *gen-atsu* lowering the pressure
収 *genshū* decrease in income or production
6 刑 *genkei* reduction of penalty
号 *gengō* sign of subtraction
光 *genkō suru* extinguish; dim
7 車 *gensha* reduction in transportation service
作 *gensaku* short crop, diminished yield
身法 *genshinhō* weight-reducing program
8 退 *gentai* decline, ebb, waning, subsiding; loss (of appetite); failing (eyesight)
価 *genka* discount, price reduction
法 *gempō* subtraction
物 *he(razu)mono* worthless person
免 *gemmen* reduction and exemption; mitigation and remission
9 食 *genshoku* cutting down on food; reduced rations
度 *gendo* reduction
封 *gempō* cutting down the size of a fief
段 *gentan* acreage reduction
点 *genten* demerit mark
速 *gensoku* speed reduction
速度 *gensokudo* speed reduction
10 高 *he(ri)daka* ullage, loss in weight
俸 *gempō* salary reduction
租 *genso* tax reduction
耗 *gemmō, genkō* decrease
配 *gempai* dividend reduction
殺 *gensatsu suru, gensai suru* diminish, reduce, attenuate, deaden, impair, detract from
衰 *gensui* decrease
員 *gen-in* personnel reduction
11 張 *meriha(ri)* loosening and tightening
産 *gensan* decreased production
12 税 *genzei* reduction of taxes
給 *genkyū* wage cut, salary reduction
軽 *genkei* reduction (of a penalty)
量 *genryō* loss in quantity
筆 *gempitsu* writing briefly
等 *gentō* reduction, mitigation, commutation; lowering the class
13 債 *gensai* partial payment of a debt
損 *genson* decrease; loss, wear, depreciation
資 *genshi* reduction of capital
14 磁 *genji* demagnetization
算 *genzan* subtraction
15 摩 *gemma* lubrication
16 磨 *gemma* lubrication
磨性 *gemmasei* antifriction, lubricating
17 縮 *genshuku* reduction, retrenchment
18 額 *gengaku* reduction, cut

10

滋 See 2626.

漓 See 2668.

準 See 791.

溫 2638 / F1145 F1135 See 温 2634.

滊 2639 / F1148 F1076 See 汽 2507.

溟 2640 / F1144 MEI dark; ocean.

漣 2641 / F1156 REN. *sazanami* ripples.

滓 2642 / F1149 SHI. *ori* dregs, sediment, grounds. *kasu* dregs, grounds, refuse, sediment, scum, dross.

滲 2643 / F1143 SHIN water.

[9]神 *shinshin* court nobles

溷 2644 / F1146 KON get muddy.

[16]濁 *kondaku* turbidity, muddiness

滂 2645 / F1147 BŌ, HŌ flow.

[8]沱 *bōda to* copiously, abundantly

溲 2646 / F1146 **溲** SHU, SHŪ urine.

[11]瓶 *shubin* chamber pot

滄 2647 / F1147 SŌ ocean.

[9]海 *sōkai* blue sea

[13]溟 *sōmei* blue sky

黎 2648 / F2162 REI dark, black; many. [黍]

[5]民 *reimin* the common people

[8]明 *reimei* daybreak, dawn

[11]黒 *reikoku* dark complexion

漠 2649 / F1156 BAKU vague, obscure; desert; wide.

[12]然 *bakuzen* vague, obscure

[13]漠 *bakubaku* vague, obscure; vast, boundless

滔 2650 / F1149 TŌ overflowing.

[4]天 *tōten* spreading all over the sky

天勢 *tōten (no) ikioi* irresistible power

[13]滔 *tōtō(taru)* rushing, swift; eloquent; universal

溢 2651 / F1144 ITSU. *afu(reru)* overflow, flow over, inundate. *kobo(reru) vi* spill, overflow, be scattered. *kobo(su) vt* spill; grumble over.

[4]水 *issui* inundation, overflow

[5]出 *isshutsu* overflowing, effusion, gushing out

[6]血 *ikketsu* effusion of blood, internal hemorrhage

溺 2652 / F1146 DEKI. *obo(reru)* drown, indulge in. *obo(rasu), obo(rakasu)*, drown (a person); cause to indulge in.

[6]死 *dekishi, obo(re)ji(ni), obo(re)shi(ni)* drowning

死体 *dekishitai* drowned body

死者 *dekishisha* drowned person

[13]愛 *dekiai* dotage, infatuation

溯 2653 / F1145 **遡** SAKU. SO. *sakanobo(ru)* go upstream; retrace the past.

[3]上 *sojō suru* go up stream

及 *sakkyū, sokyū* tracing back

及的 *sokyūteki* retrospective

[6]行 *sokō* going upstream

[9]洄 *sokai* going upstream

[10]航 *sokō* going up against a stream

溪 2654 / F1145 See **渓** 2581.

B **滝** 2655 / F1174 **瀧** RŌ. SŌ. *taki* waterfall; rapids, cascade.

[3]口 *takiguchi* top of a waterfall

川 *takigawa* rapids

[12]飲 *takino(mi)* gulping down a drink

壺 *takitsubo* pool below a waterfall

登 *takinobo(ri)* (fish) climbing a waterfall

[19]瀬 *taki(tsu)se* rapids; waterfall

B **源** 2656 / F1143 GEN *gen-, minamoto* source, origin. *Minamoto* Genji family, the Minamotos.

[4]氏 *Genji* Genji, the Minamoto family

[5]平 *Gempei* Genji and Heike, the Minamoto and Taira clans

[9]泉 *gensen* fountainhead, wellspring, source, origin

泉所得税 *gensen shotokuzei* withholding income tax

泉徴収 *gensen chōshū* collecting (taxes) at the source

泉課税 *gensen kazei* taxation at source

[10]流 *genryū* source, origin

溝 2657 / F1144 KŌ. *dobu* ditch, gutter, sewer, drain. *mizo* ditch, gutter, drain; groove, slot; gulf, gap.

[3]川 *mizogawa* a moat of running water

[4]水 *dobu mizu* ditch water

切 *mizoki(ri)* grooving, fluting

[8]板 *dobu ita* boards covering a ditch

泥 *dobu doro* silt, muck

[10]浚 *mizosara(i)* ditch cleaning

[11]渠 *kōkyo* ditch, sewer, canal, aqueduct; rift, gulf

[17]壑 *kōgaku* ditches and valleys

溜 2658 / F1144 RYŪ. *tama(ru) vi* collect, gather, accumulate; be saved (money); be in arrears. *ta(meru) vt* accumulate, pile up, store, save, collect. *tama(ri)* waiting room, rendezvous, taxi stand, parking place; (stair) landing; (baseball) dugout; soy sauce. *tame* sink, sump, manure vat.

[4]水 *tama(ri) mizu* standing water, stagnant water
込 *ta(me)-ko(mu)* save up; hoard, amass; store up
[6]池 *tame-ike* reservoir, irrigation pond, tank, cistern
[9]食 *tamegu(i) suru* eat enough to last a long time
[10]涙 *tame namida* pent-up tears
息 *tame-iki* sigh, deep breath
[11]桶 *tameoke* tub; manure bucket
[12]飲 *ryūin* gastric disturbance
飲下 *ryūin (ga) sa(garu)* feel at ease again
[13]置 *ta(me)-o(ku)* store, lay by

溶 2659 F1146 **溶** B Yō. *to(keru) vi* melt, dissolve, thaw. *to(kasu) vt* melt, dissolve, liquefy. *to(ku) vt* dissolve, melt.
[4]化 *yōka* melting
[5]去 *to(ke)-sa(ru) vt* melt away. *to(kashi)-saru vt* melt (something) away
[6]合 *to(ke)-a(u)* melt into, fade into
[8]性 *yōsei* soluble
明 *yōmei* fade-in (in movies)
岩 *yōgan* lava
[10]剤 *yōzai* solvent, solution; flux (in metallurgy)
[11]接 *yōsetsu* welding
液 *yōeki* solution, solvent
[12]媒 *yōbai* a solvent
[13]暗 *yōan* fade-out, dissolving (in movies)
鉱炉 *yōkōro* blast furnace
解 *yōkai* melting; solution; liquefaction
解力 *yōkairyoku* solvency
解状態 *yōkai jōtai* in solution
解性 *yōkaisei* solubility
解度 *yōkaido* solubility
解点 *yōkaiten* melting point

滅 2660 F1147 B METSU. *horo(biru)* be ruined; perish. *horo(bosu)* ruin, destroy, overthrow. *mes(suru) vi* die, be destroyed, be extinguished. *vt* destroy, exterminate; extinguish. *meri* loss, waste, leakage.
[2]入 *me-i(ru)* feel depressed
[3]亡 *metsubō* downfall, destruction
[5]去 *horo(boshi)-sa(ru)* destroy and obliterate. *horo(bi)-sa(ru)* perish from
失 *horo(bi)-u(seru)* perish
[6]尽 *horo(boshi)-tsuku(su)* completely destroy
多 *metta na* reckless, careless. *metta ni* seldom, rarely
多打 *metta-u(chi)* random shooting
多矢鱈 *mettayatara ni* recklessly, frantically, indiscriminately
多斬 *mettagiri* hacking to pieces
[7]却 *mekkyaku* destruction, extinction
私奉公 *messhi-hōkō* selfless patriotic service
[8]金 *mekki* gilt; gilding, plating
法 *meppō na* absurd, unreasonable, exorbitant; extraordinary; awful, horrible
[9]度 *metsudo* nirvana, final emancipation, complete annihilation of self
相 *messō na* extraordinary, unreasonable
茶 *mecha na* absurd, unreasonable, unjust
茶苦茶 *mechakucha* confusion; absurdity, mess, wreck, ruin
茶滅茶 *mechamecha* mess, wreck, ruin, confusion
[11]菌 *mekkin*=*sakkin* 殺菌 2454.11
[12]絶 *horo(boshi)-ta(yasu)* destroy. *horo(bi)-ta(eru)* be destroyed
散 *horobo(shi)-chi(rasu)* scatter and destroy
裂 *metsuretsu* incoherence, inconsistency; disruption

滞 2661 F1150 **滯** B TAI stopping. *todokō(ru)* stagnate; be delayed, be left undone; be overdue, fall into arrears. *nazu(mu)* lose heart; be in pain; be in earnest, adhere to, be attached to. *todokō(ri)* stagnation; hitch, hindrance, delay; arrearage, indebtedness. *tai-* staying in (a certain country).
[4]支 *tai-Shi* staying in China
日 *tai-Nichi* staying in Japan
仏 *tai-Futsu* staying in France
[6]米 *tai-Bei* staying in America
伊 *tai-I* staying in Italy
在 *taizai* stay, sojourn
在中 *taizaichū* during one's stay
在地 *taizaichi* place of sojourn
在者 *taizaisha* visitor, sojourner
在客 *taizaikyaku* guest, sojourner
在費 *taizaihi* hotel expenses
[8]欧 *tai-Ō* staying in Europe
英 *tai-Ei* staying in England
京 *taikyō* staying in the capital
京中 *taikyōchū* while in Tokyo
空 *taikū* staying in the air
空飛行 *taikū hikō* endurance flight
空時間 *taikū jikan* flight duration
[9]独 *tai-Doku* staying in Germany
陣 *taijin* encampment
[10]郷 *taikyō* living in one's native place
荷 *taika*=滞貨 (see below–11)
留 *tairyū* stay, sojourn
納 *tainō* nonpayment, default, delinquency; back taxes
納処分 *tainō shobun* coercive collection
納者 *tainōsha* defaulter; delinquent taxpayer
[11]貨 *taika* freight congestion; accumulation of stocks
[12]勝 *todokō(ri)ga(chi)* tendency to leave undone; tendency to stagnate
[21]露 *tai-Ro* staying in Russia

A **漢** 2662 / F1156 **漢** KAN Han (Dynasty); (old name for) China; masculine suffix.

2 人 *Kanjin* a Chinese
3 口 *Kankō* Hankow
土 *Kando* China
才 *Kanzai, Kansai* mastery of Chinese literature
4 文 *kambun* Chinese writing, Chinese composition
文学 *kambungaku* Chinese literature
方 *kampō* Chinese medicinal art
方医 *kampō-i* Chinese herb doctor
方医学 *kampō igaku* Chinese medicinal art
方薬 *kampōyaku* Chinese medicine
5 民族 *Kamminzoku* Chinese people
6 竹 *kanchiku* solid bamboo
奸 *kankan* traitor, betrayer
字 *kanji* the Chinese characters
名 *kammei* Chinese name
8 学 *kangaku* Chinese literature
学者 *kangakusha* Sinologue
法 *kampō* Chinese medicinal art
法医 *kampō-i* Chinese herb doctor
法薬 *kampōyaku* Chinese medicine
和 *Kan-Wa* China and Japan, Chinese and Japanese (languages)
和字典＝next word
和辞典 *Kan-Wa jiten* Chinese-Japanese character dictionary
9 音 *kan-on* Han-dynasty pronunciation
10 家 *kanka* Han dynasty; Chinese herb doctor
書 *kansho, karabumi* Chinese book, Chinese classics
11 族 *Kanzoku* Han (Chinese) race
訳 *kan-yaku* translation into Chinese
12 朝 *kanchō* Han dynasty
13 詩 *kanshi* Chinese poetry
詩文 *kanshibun* Chinese poetry and literature
14 語 *kango* Chinese word
16 儒 *kanju* Chinese Confucian scholar
薬 *kan-yaku* Chinese medicine
20 籍 *kanseki* Chinese book, Chinese classics

B **滑** 2663 / F1149 KATSU. KOTSU. *sube*(*ru*) slide, glide, skate; be slippery; slip; fail in exams. *nume*(*rakasu*). *sube*(*rasu*), *sube*(*rakasu*) let slip, make slip. *nume*(*ru*) be lazy, play all the time. *sube*(*ri*) sliding, slipping; slippage; slide; slip; skid. *sube*(*rakana*) smooth. *name*(*rakana*) smooth. *nume*(*ri*) slime, slipperiness. *sube*(*kkoi*) smooth, slippery, velvety, slick.

2 入 *sube*(*ri*)-*i*(*ru*) slide into
3 下 *sube*(*ri*)-*kuda*(*ru*) slide down
4 止 *suberido*(*me*) tire chains; nonskid heels
尺 *suberijaku* slide rule
込 *sube*(*ri*)-*ko*(*mu*) slide into (a base); slip into (a ditch)
5 皮 *suberikawa, suberigawa* sweatband
弁 *katsuben, sube*(*ri*)*ben* slide valve
台 *suberidai* launching platform, ways; (children's) slide; sliding bed
出 *sube*(*ri*)-*de*(*ru*) slide out of. *sube*(*ri*)*da*(*shi*) start, beginning. *sube*(*ri*)-*da*(*su*) start sliding; start out
石 *kasseki* talc
石粉 *kassekiko* talcum powder
7 車 *kassha, semi* pulley, block, tackle
走 *kassō* gliding, planing, sliding, skating, coasting, taxiing
走路 *kassōro* runway
走輪 *kassōrin* landing gear
8 板 *suberi-ita* runner (on a sled)
易 *sube*(*ri*)*yasu*(*i*) greasy, slimy, slippery
歩 *nume*(*ri*)-*aru*(*ku*) saunter around
空 *kakkū suru* glide, volplane
空士 *kakkūshi* glider pilot
空機 *kakkūki* glider, sailplane
9 降 *kakkō* descent (by ski, glider, etc.)
10 席 *kasseki* sliding seat
剤 *katsuzai* lubricant
11 脱 *katsudatsu* slipperiness
寄 *sube*(*ri*)-*yo*(*ru*) slide up to
12 結 *suberimusu*(*bi*) slip knot
落 *sube*(*ri*)-*o*(*chiru*) slip off
16 稽 *kokkei* joke, pleasantry, humor. *odoke* joke
稽口 *odokeguchi* joke
稽本 *kokkeibon* comic books
稽芝居 *odoke shibai* comedy, burlesque
稽者 *odokemono* joker, humorist
稽家 *kokkeika* humorist, joker
稽話 *odokebanashi* funny story

11

溜 See 2658.

漑 See 2689.

満 2664 / F1151 See **滿** 2636.

漢 2665 / F1156 See **漢** 2662.

滞 2666 / F1150 See **滯** 2661.

潅 Nonstandard for **灌** 2739.

潟 Nonstandard for **瀉** 2695.

滸 2667 / F1151 Ko vicinity.

漓 2668 / F1155 Ri dropping; soak in.

漱 2669 / F1158 Sō. *kuchisusu(gu), kuchisoso(gu)* gargle, rinse the mouth.

漲 2670 / F1158 Chō. *minagi(ru)* overflow, be swollen; overflow (with sympathy.)

滌 2671 / F1150 Teki. Deki. *susu(gu)* rinse, pour on. *ara(u)* wash.

滾 2672 / F1151 Kon flow. *tagi(ru) vi* boil, seethe, foam. *tagi(rakasu) vt* boil up.

14 滾 *konkon to* copiously (flowing)

漿 2673 / F1159 Shō a drink.

8 果 *shōka* berry
11 液 *shōeki* juice, sap; blood serum

B **滴** 2674 / F1151 **渹** Teki *shizuku* drop. *shitata(ru)* drip, drop; trickle. *shitatari* drop; trickle.

3 下 *tekika suru* drop, drip, distill, trickle
4 水 *tekisui* water dripping
16 薬 *tekiyaku* (medicine) drops

漉 2675 / F1154 Roku. *su(ku)* manufacture paper; spread out thin. *ko(su)* strain, filter, percolate.

2 入 *suki-i(re)* watermarking
6 返 *su(ki)gae(su)* remanufacture, remake (paper)
10 紙 *koshigami* filter paper
14 網 *koshiami* strainer

漬 2676 / F1157 Shi. *tsu(keru)* soak, moisten, steep; pickle, preserve, add (salt) to. *tsuka(ru), hita(su), hita(ru)* (see under 浸 2572.0).

1 込 *tsu(ke)-ko(mu)* pickling a large amount
8 物 *tsukemono* Japanese pickles
10 梅 *tsukeume* pickling plums
11 菜 *tsukena* greens for pickling

滲 2677 / F1150 Shin. *shi(miru)* (see under 染 2240.0). *niji(mu)* blot, spread, run, blur, ooze.

2 入 *shinnyū* permeation, infiltration, percolation
5 出 *shi(mi)-de(ru)* ooze, exude, percolate, soak thru. *shinshutsu* exudation, percolation, effusion; extraction (in chemistry)
出性 *shinshutsusei* wet (pleurisy)
出性体質 *shinshutsusei taishitsu* allergic constitution
9 通 *shi(mi)-tō(ru)*＝染通 2240.9
透 *shintō* permeation, infiltration, osmosis
12 渡 *shi(mi)-wata(ru)*＝染渡 2240.12

B **漂** 2678 / F1153 Hyō. *tadayo(u)* float (on the water).

5 白 *hyōhaku* bleaching
失 *hyōshitsu suru* drift away
8 泊 *hyōhaku* wandering, vagabondage; drifting
9 砂 *hyōsa* drift sand
10 浪 *hyōrō* wandering, vagabondage
流 *hyōryū* drifting
流木 *hyōryūboku* driftwood
流民 *hyōryūmin* persons adrift; castaways
流者 *hyōryūsha* a person adrift; a castaway
流物 *hyōryūbutsu* flotsam
流船 *hyōryūsen* a drifting ship; a derelict
11 著 *hyōchaku* drifting ashore
12 着 *hyōchaku* drifting ashore
然 *hyōzen to* aimlessly, unexpectedly

B **漆** 2679 / F1154 Shitsu. *urushi* lacquer, varnish.

3 工 *shikkō* lacquer work; lacquer worker
6 気触 *urushikabure* lacquer poisoning
9 革 *urushi kawa* enameled leather
屋 *urushiya* lacquer shop
食 *shikkui* plaster, mortar, stucco, whitewash
食塗 *shikkuinu(ri)* plastering
11 黒 *shikkoku* jet black
細工 *urushizaiku* lacquer ware
12 喰 *shikkui*＝漆食 (see above–9)
絵 *urushie* lacquer painting
13 塗 *urushinu(ri)* lacquering; lacquer ware
14 蔦 *urushizuta* poison ivy
15 器 *shikki* lacquer ware

B **漸** 2680 / F1158 Zen gradually advancing. *yōya(ku), yōyō* gradually; finally; barely.

5 加 *zenka* gradual increase
6 次 *zenji* gradually
8 追 *zen (o) ō(te)* gradually
9 持 *zen (o) mo(tte)* gradually
降 *zenkō* gradual decrease
10 時 *zenji* gradually
進 *zenshin* gradual progress, steady advance
進主義 *zenshin shugi* moderatism
進的 *zenshinteki* gradual, moderate
12 減 *zengen* gradual decrease
落 *zenraku* gradual decline
13 滅 *zemmetsu* gradual destruction
14 漸 *yaya-yaya* gradually

増 *zenzō* gradual increase
増的 *zenzōteki* increasingly
[20]騰 *zentō* gradual rise (in prices)

漕 2681/F1155 Sō. *ko(gu)* row, scull, paddle.

[2]入 *ko(gi)-i(ru)* row in. *ko(gi)-i(reru)* row (a boat) in
[4]手 *kogite, sōshu* rower, oarsman
[5]付 *ko(gi)-tsu(keru)* row up to, reach
出 *ko(gi)-da(su), ko(gi)-ida(su)* begin to row
[6]回 *ko(gi)-mawa(ru)* row around
[7]戻 *ko(gi)-modo(su)* row back
別 *ko(gi)-waka(reru)* row away
[9]通 *ko(gi)-kayo(u)* travel by rowboat
[11]船 *kogibune* rowboat
寄 *ko(gi)-yo(ru), ko(gi)-yo(seru)* row up to
[12]渡 *ko(gi)-wata(ru)* row across
程 *sōtei* boat-race distance
着 *ko(gi)-tsu(keru), ko(gi)-tsu(ku)* row up to, reach
[13]損 *ko(gi)-sokona(u)* run into a boat; strike the shore
艇 *sōtei* rowing, boating
[14]暮 *ko(gi)-kura(su)* row all day long

漏 2682/F1154 B Rō leaking; water clock; time. *mo(ru), mo(reru)* leak, escape; shine thru; find expression; be disclosed; be omitted, be excluded. *mo(rasu)* spill, let leak; omit, miss, leave out; divulge; betray; give vent to, express; let go. *mo(ri)* leak, leakage.

[3]口 *rōkō* vent, leak
[4]水 *rōsui* water leakage
斗 *jōgo, rōto* funnel
斗状 *rōtojō* funnel-shaped
斗雲 *rōto-un* funnel cloud
[5]出 *rōshutsu* leak, leakage, seepage
[7]告 *rōkoku* letting secrets leak out
[8]泄 *rōei, rōsetsu* leakage; disclosure
刻 *rōkoku* water clock
[9]屋 *rōoku* leaky house
洩 *rōei, rōsetsu* leakage; disclosure
[12]無 *mo(re)na(ku)* without exception
[13]損 *rōson* leakage, ullage
電 *rōden* short circuit, leakage of electricity
[14]聞 *rōbun suru* overhear

漫 2683/F1157 B Man. *suzu(ro), sozo(ro)* involuntarily, in spite of oneself. *mida(ri) ni* (see under 妄 288.0). *midari-(gamashii)* morally corrupt.

[3]才 *manzai* comic dialogue
[4]文 *mambun* random notes
[7]言 *mangen, sozo(ro)goto* rambling talk
[8]雨 *sozo(ro) ame* a drizzle
歩 *mampo, sozo(ro)aru(ki), susu(ro)aru(ki)* a ramble, a stroll, a walk
性 *mansei* chronic
性病 *manseibyō* chronic disease
画 *manga* comics, cartoon, caricature
画家 *mangaka* cartoonist
[10]涙 *sozo(ro) namida* involuntary tears
[11]遊 *man-yū* trip, tour, travel
遊客 *man-yū kyaku* tourist, sight-seer
[12]評 *mampyō* literary gossip, rambling criticism
寒 *sozo(ro) samu(i)* rather cold
筆 *mampitsu* random notes
然 *manzen(taru)* random, rambling, desultory
[14]読 *mandoku* desultory reading
漫 *mamman(taru)* vast, boundless
漫的 *mammande* slow, slow-going
[15]罵 *mamba* abuse, irresponsible criticism
談 *mandan* idle talk, comic chat
談家 *mandanka* humorist
[16]録 *manroku* random comments

漁 2684/F1152 A Gyo, Ryō fishing; fishery; catch, haul. *sunado(ru), isa(ru)* to fish. *asa(ru)* fish, forage, browse, hunt for; gather (news).

[4]戸 *gyoko* fisherman's hut
火 *gyoka, isaribi* fisherman's fire lure
父利 *gyofu(no)ri*＝漁夫利 (see below-4)
区 *gyoku* fishing area
夫 *gyofu* fisherman
夫利 *gyofu(no)ri* running off with a prize while others are fighting for it
[5]民 *gyomin* fishermen
[6]舟 *gyoshū, isaribune* fishing boat
色 *gyoshoku* debauchery
回 *asa(ri)-mawa(ru)* forage around, hunt around
[7]村 *gyoson* fishing village
利 *gyori* fishing interests
労 *gyorō* fishing
[8]法 *gyohō* fishing method
具 *gyogu* fishing tackle
者 *gyosha* fisherman
[10]師 *ryōshi* fisherman
翁 *gyoō* old fisherman
家 *gyoka* fisherman's home
書 *gyosho* book hunting
[11]猟 *gyoryō* fishing and hunting
船 *gyosen, ryōsen* fishing boat
[12]場 *gyojō, ryōba* fishing grounds
港 *gyokō* fishing port
期 *gyoki, ryōki* fishing season
[13]業 *gyogyō* fishing industry
業権 *gyogyōken* fishing rights
[14]網 *gyomō* fishing net
歌 *gyoka* fisherman's song
[15]撈 *gyorō* fishing
[16]獲 *gyokaku* fishing; catch, haul
獲物 *gyokakubutsu* a catch of fish

A 演 2685/F1155 EN. *en(jiru), en(zuru)* perform, play, act, enact, render, stage, put on.

5出 *enshutsu* production, performance, rendition, presentation; a play
出者 *enshutsusha* producer, director
出家 *enshutsuka* producer, director
7技 *engi* acting, performance
技場 *engijō* entertainment hall
芸 *engei* entertainment, performance
芸会 *engeikai* an entertainment
芸者 *engeisha* performer, artiste
8武 *embu* military exercises, fencing and judo
9奏 *ensō* (musical) performance, recital
奏会 *ensōkai* concert, recital
奏曲目 *ensō kyokumoku* musical program
奏法 *ensōhō* execution, technique, interpretation 「sham battle; seminar
11習 *enshū* practice, exercises; maneuvers,
習林 *enshūrin* experimental forest
習場 *enshūjō* parade ground 「ry, adaptation
13義 *engi* expansion, amplification; commenta-
14舞場 *embujō* theater, playhouse
説 *enzetsu* speech, lecture, address, oration
説法 *enzetsuhō* eloquence, oratory
説家 *enzetsuka* speaker, orator
15劇 *engeki* drama, play
劇的 *engekiteki* dramatic, theatrical
劇界 *engekikai* the theatrical world
劇術 *engekijutsu* dramatics
劇場 *engekijō* the stage, the theater
16壇 *endan* rostrum, platform
17戯 *engi* play, theatricals; drama; dramatics
18題 *endai* subject of an address
19繹 *en-eki* deductive reasoning
繹法 *en-ekihō* deductive method

12

澁 2686/F1164 See 渋 2600.

澔 2687/F1165/F1107 See 浩 2563.

澈 2688/F1164 TETSU become clear.

漑 2689/F1155 GAI pour.

潑 2690/F1159 HATSU leap; pour on.

9剌 *hatsuratsu(taru)* lively, animated

濆 2691/F1168 濆 FUN gush forth.

潭 2692/F1162 TAN pool; abyss; deep. *fuchi* (see under 淵 2625.0).

潺 2693/F1163 SEN sound of flowing water.

12湲 *senkan(taru)* babbling (brook)

澆 2694/F1164 GYŌ frivolity.

8季 *gyōki* decadence, degeneration

潟 2695/F1161 SEKI. *kata* lagoon.

12湖 *sekiko* salt-water lagoon

澗 2696/F1161 = 澗 KAN valley river.

4水 *kansui* water of a valley stream
7声 *kansei* the sound of a valley stream

澎 2697/F1165 HŌ, HYŌ sound of flowing water.

12湃 *hōhai(taru)* surging
湖島 *Bōkotō* Pescadores 「sion, or bloating
満感 *bōmankan* a feeling of fullness, disten-

A 潔 2698/F1159 潔 KETSU. *isagiyo(i)* pure, clean, righteous; manly, gallant, sportsmanlike.

5白 *keppaku* purity, innocence, integrity
11斎 *kessai* abstinence, purification
18癖 *keppeki* fastidiousness

B 澄 2699/F1164 CHŌ. *su(mu)* be clear, become clear, clarify. *su(masu)* clear, clarify, settle; strain (one's ears); look grave.

5汁 *suma(shi)jiru* clear broth or stock (seasoned with shaved dried bonito, certain seaweeds, etc.)
6亙 *su(mi)-wata(ru)* be perfectly clear
8明 *chōmei* lucidity, serenity, clearness, clarity 「looking girl
9屋 *su(mashi)ya* self-composed person, prim-
12渡 *su(mi)-wata(ru)* be perfectly clear
15徹 *chōtetsu na* transparent

B 潤 2700/F1161 JUN. *uruo(u) vi* be watered; profit by, receive benefits, become rich. *uruo(wasu), uruo(su) vt* moisten, water, irrigate, dip; enrich, profit. *uru(mu)* be dimmed, be clouded, get muddy; be wet. *fuya(kasu)* steep, soak. *fuya(keru)* swell up, become soaked. *uruo(i)* dampness, rain; gain; favor; charm. *uru(mi)* dimness, cloudiness, opacity, blur; moisture.

6色 *junshoku* rhetorical flourishes

7沢 *juntaku* gloss, luster; moisture, abundance; profit, favor
12筆 *jumpitsu* painting and writing
筆料 *jumpitsuryō* writing fee, painting fee
13飾 *junshoku* rhetorical flourishes
滑 *junkatsu* lubrication
滑油 *junkatsuyu* lubricating oil

潰 2701 F1163 KAI. *tsubu(su)* crush, smash, break; dissipate; waste (time); kill, butcher; demolish; melt down. *tsubu(reru)* be smashed, break, be destroyed, collapse; be defaced (type); be ruined; be worn down. *tsui(eru)* be routed, collapse.
7走 *kaisō* rout, stampede
決 *kaiketsu* rip, break, cleavage, crevasse
利 *tsubushi (ga) ki(ku)* be clever at any task
乱 *kairan* rout
10値 *tsubu(shi)ne* scrap value
家 *tsubu(re)ie* demolished house; tumble-down house
11敗 *kaihai* complete defeat
12散 *kaisan* being broken up and scattered
落 *tsubu(re)-o(chiru)* collapse
13滅 *kaimetsu* destruction, annihilation
14瘍 *kaiyō* ulcer

B **潮** 2702 F1162 CHŌ. *shio* tide; salt water; opportunity. *ushio* tide, sea water.
2入 *shio-i(ri)* coming in of the tide
3干 *shiohi* low tide
干狩 *shiohiga(ri)* shell gathering at low tide
4水 *chōsui* tidewater. *shio mizu* sea water
6気 *shioke* salt air
汲 *shiokumi* flooding salt beds
合 *shioa(i)* between tides
先 *shiosaki* rising of the tide; time to begin
汐 *chōseki* ebb and flow, tide
汐風 *chōsekifū* tidal wind
8門 *chōmon* tide gate
9音 *chōon* sound of waves
風 *shio kaze* sea breeze, salt air
待 *shioma(chi)* waiting for the tide
海 *shio umi* the sea
紅 *chōkō suru* redden, flush, color up
津波 *shio tsunami* tidal bore
10候 *chōkō* tide period
時 *shiodoki* tidal hour; favorable opportunity, psychological moment
流 *chōryū* tide, tidal current; trend
害 *chōgai* tidewater damage
差 *chōsa* tide range
12湯 *shioyu* sea-water bath
焼 *shioya(ke)* tanned by salt air. *shioya(ki)* broiling fish with salt
嵐 *shio arashi* strong sea breeze
13閘 *chōkō* tide lock
煙 *shio kemuri* salt spray
解 *chōkai* diliquescence
路 *shioji* the sea, the deep
15標 *chōhyō* tide mark
18騒 *shiosai* roar of the sea

B **潜** 2703 F1160 **潛** SEN. *hiso(meru)* conceal, hide; lower (the voice). *hiso(maru)* be hushed. *hiso(mu)* lurk, lie dormant, be hidden. *kazu(ku)* dive, submerge. *kugu(ru)* pass thru, pass under. *mogu(ru)* dive; get into, crawl into. *kugu(ri)* wicket gate, side gate. *hisoka ni* secretly.
2入 *sennyū* infiltration, sneaking in
4心 *senshin* meditation
戸 *kugu(ri)do* side door, side gate, wicket gate, private door
込 *mogu(ri)-ko(mu)* get in, crawl in, slip in; hide
水 *sensui* diving
水夫 *sensuifu* diver
水母艦 *sensui bokan* submarine tender
水服 *sensuifuku* diving suit
水病 *sensuibyō* submarine sickness, bends
水業 *sensuigyō* diving business
水業者 *sensuigyōsha* diver, diving contractor
水器 *sensuiki* diving bell, diving apparatus
水艦 *sensuikan* submarine
6行 *senkō* traveling in disguise; submarine voyage
行運動 *senkō undō* underground movement
伏 *sempuku* concealment, hiding, ambush; incubation
伏性 *sempukusei no* latent (disease)
伏期 *sempukuki* incubation period
在 *senzai* potentiality, latency, dormancy
在失業 *senzai shitsugyō* potential unemployment
在意識 *senzai ishiki* subconsciousness, subliminal self
7没 *sembotsu suru* be submerged, dive
8幸 *senkō* emperor's secret visit
函 *senkan* construction caisson
函病 *senkambyō* bends, caisson sickness
9待 *hiso(mi)-ma(tsu)* lie in ambush, lurk around
10流 *senryū* undercurrent
航 *senkō* submarine voyage
航水雷 *senkō suirai* submarine torpedo
航艇 *senkōtei* submarine, U-boat
11望鏡 *sembōkyō* periscope
13隠 *hiso(mi)-kaku(reru)* lie in wait
勢力 *senseiryoku* potential energy, latent power
15潸 *samezame* bitterly (crying)

13

澤 2704 F1165 See 沢 2503.

瀆 2705 F1168 See 涜 2691.

澳 2706 / F1166 IKU, Ō curving shoreline; bend in a river; offing.

8 門 *Makao* Macao

濛 2707 / F1169 MŌ dark.

6 気 *mōki* fog, mist, vapor

16 濛 *mōmō(taru)* dense, thick, dim, vague

澹 2708 / F1167 TAN frankly, simply.

8 泊 *tampaku*＝淡泊 2602.8

16 澹 *tantan*＝淡淡 2602.11

澱 2709 / F1166 DEN. *ori* dregs, sediment, grounds. *yodo(mu)* stagnate, be stagnant; settle, deposit; be sluggish; hesitate; stammer. *yodo* pool (of a river).

10 粉 *dempun* starch

粉質 *dempunshitsu* starchiness

B **濁** 2710 / F1167 JOKU, DAKU *nigo(ri)* uncleanness; wrong; voiced sound. *nigo(ri)* muddiness, impurity; voiced marks; voiced consonant; unrefined saké. *nigo(ru)* be muddy, be impure; be voiced; be vague. *nigo(su)*, *nigo(rasu)* make muddy, make cloudy; quibble; prevaricate.

3 子音 *dakushi-in* voiced consonant

4 水 *dakusui* muddy water

5 世 *dakusei, jokuse* corrupt world

6 江 *nigo(ri)e* muddy stream

7 声 *nigo(ri)goe, damigoe, dakusei* hoarse voice, thick voice

9 音 *dakuon* voiced sound

点 *dakuten, nigo(ri) ten* voiced consonant marks

10 流 *dakuryū* muddy stream

酒 *dakushu, nigo(ri)zake, doburoku* unrefined saké, raw saké

B **濃** 2711 / F1168 NŌ dark, thick, undiluted. *ko(i)* dark, deep; saturated; strong (drink); intimate; thick. *koma(yakana)* ardent.

4 化 *nōka* thickening, concentration

化粧 *ko(i)geshō* heavy make-up

8 青色 *nōseishoku* deep blue

9 厚 *nōkō* thickness, density, concentration; richness; elaborateness; ardency; tenseness

度 *nōdo* density, thickness, consistency, concentration

茶 *ko(i) cha* dark brown, umber color

紅色 *nōkōshoku* crimson

11 淡 *nōtan* light and shade

紺 *nōkon* dark blue, navy blue

密 *nōmitsu na* thick; crowded

黄土 *nōkōdo* sienna

12 紫 *komurasaki* dark purple

紫色 *nōshishoku* deep purple

13 溶液 *nōyōeki* concentrated solution

14 褐色 *nōkasshoku* dark brown

緑 *nōryoku* dark green

緑色 *nōryokushoku* dark green

17 縮 *nōshuku* concentration

19 艶 *nōen na* charming, bewitching

霧 *nōmu* dense fog

B **激** 2712 / F1167 GEKI. *geki(suru)* get excited, be agitated, be enraged, be exasperated, chafe; urge, encourage, incite. *hage(shii)* (see under 烈 2761.0).

4 化 *gekka, gekika* intensification, aggravation

6 成 *gekisei suru* aggravate, intensify, accelerate, precipitate

7 励 *gekirei* urging, encouragement, incitement

声 *gekisei* gruff voice

8 突 *gekitotsu* crash, collision

9 変 *gekihen* sudden change, upheaval, convulsion, cataclysm

昂 *gekkō, gekikō* excitement, exasperation, indignation, resentment

発 *gekihatsu* fit, spasm; outburst, explosion of anger

臭 *gekishū* strong odor

怒 *gekido* rage, indignation, exasperation

甚 *gekijin* violence, severity

10 高 *gekikō, gekkō* excitement, agitation

浪 *gekirō* high waves, high seas

流 *gekiryū* swift current, raging stream, rapids

烈 *gekiretsu* violence, severity, vehemence, fierceness

11 情 *gekijō* violent emotion, passion, fury, outburst

務 *gekimu* exhausting work

動 *gekidō* terrible shock, concussion, upheaval; agitation

12 痛 *gekitsū* sharp pain

越 *gekietsu na* violent, vehement, fiery

減 *gekigen* marked decrease, sharp decline

湍 *gekitan* rapids, torrent

暑 *gekisho* severe heat

落 *gekiraku* slump, crash, heavy decline

13 戦 *gekisen* severe fight

14 増 *gekizō* sudden increase; heavy swell

語 *gekigo* harsh language

15 憤 *gekifun* terrible anger; resentment

論 *gekiron* heated argument

賞 *gekishō* high praise

震 *gekishin* severe earthquake

賛 *gekisan* great praise

18 闘 *gekitō* fierce fighting

職 *gekishoku* exhausting work

14

濳 2713 / F1160 潜 See 潜 2703.

濕 2714 / F1169 See 湿 2631.

濟 2715 / F1169 See 済 2597.

濱 2716 / F1172 See 浜 2567.

濘 2717 / F1169 NEI muddiness. *nuka(ru)* be muddy.

濯 2718 / F1171 TAKU. *soso(gu), susu(gu), yusu(gu), isu(gu)* wash, pour on, rinse.

濤 2719 / F1170 TŌ. *nami* waves, billows.

7 声 *tōsei* sound of the waves

濠 2720 / F1170 GŌ. *hori* moat, ditch, canal. *Gō-* Australia.

6 州 *Gōshū* Australia

濶 2721 / F1983 **闊** KATSU wide.

8 歩 *kappo suru* stride, strut, swagger

11 達 *kattatsu* magnanimity, generosity

12 葉樹 *katsuyōju* deciduous or broad-leafed tree

鴻 2722 / F2142 KŌ large, great; large bird. *ōtori* large wild goose. [鳥]

3 大 *kōdai na* vast, immense, tremendous

4 毛 *kōmō* goose feathers; something very light

7 図 *kōto* ambitious scheme

8 学 *kōgaku* learning; learned man

10 益 *kōeki* great benefit

恩 *kōon* great blessings, great benevolence

11 基 *kōki* foundation of a great enterprise

13 業 *kōgyō* great achievement

16 儒 *kōju* great scholar

18 鵠 *kōkoku* great man

濡 2723 / F1170 JU. *nure(ru)* be wet, get wet, be damp, be soaked; make love. *nura(su)* wet, soak, dip, dampen.

4 手 *nurete* wet hand

文 *nurebumi* love letter

仏 *nurebotoke* Buddhist image out in the open

6 米 *nuregome* water-damaged rice

色 *nure iro* (glossy) wet color

衣 *nureginu, nuregoromo* wet clothes; false charge

衣着 *nureginu (o) ki(ru)* accept the guilt of another

8 事 *nuregoto* love affair

10 紙 *nuregami* damp paper

荷 *nureni* sea-damaged goods

11 雪 *nureyuki* damp snow

12 場 *nureba* love scene

渡 *nu(re)-wata(ru)* get wet all over

13 鼠 *nure nezumi* drowned rat; a person soaked to the skin

14 髪 *nuregami* newly-washed hair; glossy hair

15 縁 *nure-en* open veranda

濫 2724 / F1171 B **濫** RAN overflow; spread over. *mida(ri) ni* (see under 妄 288.0). *midari(gamashii)* morally corrupt.

2 入 *ran-nyū* discourteous running in and out

5 用 *ran-yō* abuse, misuse, misappropriation

立 *ranritsu* standing in disorder; (candidates) coming forward in great numbers; confusion, turmoil

出 *ranshutsu suru* publish (in great quantity), flood the market

6 伐 *rambatsu* indiscriminate deforestation

7 作 *ransaku* overproduction; excessive writing

9 造 *ranzō* overproduction, careless manufacture

発 *rampatsu* excessive money issue

11 設 *ransetsu suru* establish too many (schools)

12 飲 *ran-in* drinking excessively

費 *rampi* waste, extravagance

14 読 *randoku* indiscriminate reading

製 *ransei* overproduction; careless manufacture

15 賞 *ranshō suru* lavish honors and rewards upon

16 獲 *rankaku* indiscriminate fishing or hunting

靛 *ranjō* indigo

18 觴 *ranshō* origin, source, beginning

15

濾 2725 / F1172 RO. *ko(su)* filter.

10 紙 *roshi* filter paper

11 過 *roka* filtering

瀑 2726 / F1173 BAKU. *taki* waterfall; rapids, cascade.

5 布 *bakufu* waterfall

瀆 2727 / F1172 TOKU, DOKU blaspheme. *kega(su) vt* defile, pollute, stain. *kega(reru) vi* be defiled, be polluted, be soiled.

9 神 *tokushin* blasphemy, sacrilege, profanity

神罪 *tokushinzai* blasphemy, sacrilege, profanity

18 職 *tokushoku* bribery, graft

職罪 *tokushokuzai* bribery, graft

瀉 2728 / F1172 SHA. *kuda(shi)* purgation, evacuation.

3 下剤 *shagezai* a cathartic

6血 *shaketsu* bloodletting
7利塩 *sharien* Epsom salts, magnesium sulfate
12痢 *shari* diarrhea
13腹 *geribara* diarrhea

16

瀧 2729/F1174 See **滝** 2655.

瀚 2730/F1173 KAN wide and large.

瀞 2731/F1174 SEI. SHŌ. *toro* pool (in a river).

瀕 2732/F1173 HIN shore, brink; near. *hin(suru)* be on the verge of.
6死 *hinshi* on the verge of death

瀝 2733/F1173 REKI dropping.
8青 *rekisei, chan* asphalt, bitumen, (mineral) pitch
青炭 *rekiseitan* bituminous coal

瀟 2734/F1174 SHŌ pure, clean.
9洒 *shōsha na* elegant, trim, neat, refined
19瀟 *shōshō* heavy rain and wind
22灑 *shōsha*＝瀟洒 (see above–9)

瀬 2735/F1174 **瀨** RAI. *se* current, torrent, rapids, shallows, shoal.
B
4戸 *seto* strait, channel
戸口 *setoguchi* the entrance to a strait
戸欠 *setoka(ke)* potsherd
戸引 *setobi(ki), setohi(ki)* enameled
戸内海 *Setonaikai* Inland Sea
戸物 *setomono* porcelain; pottery
戸物屋 *setomonoya* dish store
戸際 *setogiwa* crucial moment, crisis, threshold, brink, eleventh hour
15踏 *sebu(mi)* wading to test depth; first trial, trial balloon, making inquiries

濾 2736/F1173 RO. *ko(su)* strain, filter, percolate.
4水機 *rosuiki* filter
5布 *koshi nuno* filter cloth
7床 *roshō* filter bed
10紙 *roshi, koshigami* filter paper
11液 *roeki* filtrate
過 *roka* filtering, percolation
過池 *rokachi* filter bed
過紙 *rokashi* filter paper
過器 *rokaki* filter, strainer, percolator

17

瀾 2737/F1175 RAN large waves.

瀰 2738/F1174 BI wide.
14漫 *biman* diffusion, permeation

灌 2739/F1175 KAN. *soso(gu)* (see under 注 2531.0).
4木 *kamboku* shrub, shrubbery
水 *kansui* sprinkling, irrigation
仏 *kambutsu* Buddha's birthday celebration
仏会 *kambutsue* Buddha's birthday celebration
10流 *kanryū suru* irrigate
11域 *kan-iki* drainage basin
祭 *kansai* drink offering, libation
13腸 *kanchō* enema
15漑 *kangai* irrigation, watering
漑地 *kangaichi* irrigated land

19

灑 2740/F1175 SHA, SAI pour.
12落 *sharaku* clear-cut personality

灘 2741/F1176 TAN. *nada* open sea.
8波 *Naniwa, Namba* ancient Osaka

22

灣 2742/F1176 See **湾** 2627.

4 心小⺌戈戸手扌支攴攵文斗斤方无日曰月木欠止歹殳毋比毛氏气【水氵氺】22 火灬爪爫父爻爿丬片牙牛犬犭

RAD. 火 86

Hi or *ka* fire. At left: *hi hen.* At bottom: 灬 *yotsu ten* four dots or *renga* or *rekka* (*ka* "fire" in a *retsu* "row"). Nickname: Fire.

A 火 2743 F1176 Ko. Ka fire; Tuesday. *hi* fire, flame, blaze. (*toro*)*bi* low fire. *ho* fire.

2 入 *hi-i*(*re*) fire pan; first lighting (of a furnace); heating
力 *karyoku* steam power; heating power; force of the flames
力電気 *karyoku denki* steam-generated electricity
3 干 *hibo*(*shi*)＝火乾 (see below–11)
口 *hokuchi* tinder. *kakō* crater. *higuchi* burner; muzzle (of a gun); origin of a fire
口石 *higuchi ishi* flint stone
口丘 *kakōkyū* volcanic cone
口金 *hoguchigane* metal fire-striking rod
口原 *kakōgen* crater basin
口原湖 *kakōgenko* crater lake
口湖 *kakōko* crater lake
口箱 *hokuchibako* tinderbox
口壁 *kakōheki* crater wall
山 *kazan* volcano
山口 *kazankō* crater
山灰 *kazambai* volcanic ash
山国 *kazankoku* volcanic country
山泥 *kazandei* volcanic mud
山岩 *kazangan* lava, igneous rock
山学 *kazangaku* volcanology
山活動 *kazan katsudō* volcanic activity
山脈 *kazammyaku* volcanic range
山島 *kazantō* volcanic island
山帯 *kazantai* volcanic zone
山弾 *kazandan* volcanic boulders
山錐 *kazansui* volcanic cone
山礫 *kazanreki* volcanic ash
4 手 *hi*(*no*)*te* flames, blaze, fire
水 *himizu* fire and water; discord
片 *kahen* sparks
中 *kachū* in the fire
元 *himoto, hi* (*no*) *moto* origin of a fire
夫 *kafu* fireman, stoker
切 *hiki*(*ri*) rubbing sticks to make a fire
切臼 *hiki*(*ri*) *usu* fire stone
5 玉 *hidama, hi* (*no*) *tama* fireball, falling star
皿 *hizara* chafing dish; fire grate; bowl of a pipe
矢 *hiya* fire arrow
付 *hitsu*(*ke*) arson; an incendiary. *hitsu*(*ki*) kindling
失 *kashitsu* accidental fire
加減 *hikagen* condition of the fire
打 *hiu*(*chi*) striking fire with steel on stone; or the equipment used
打石 *hiuchi-ishi* flint stone
打金 *hiu*(*chi*)*gane* the steel (of a flint-and-steel set)
打道具 *hiu*(*chi*) *dōgu* flint and steel
打箱 *hiu*(*chi*)*bako* tinderbox
6 色 *hi iro* color of red-hot metal; dark crimson
刑 *kakei* burning at the stake
宅 *kataku* burning house; this world of suffering
先 *hisaki* flames; forefront of the fire. *hosaki* flame tips
成岩 *kaseigan* igneous rocks
気 *kaki* fire. *hi*(*no*)*ke* heat of fire
気厳禁 *Kaki—Genkin* Inflammable—Keep Out
7 車 *hi* (*no*) *kuruma* fiery chariot; extreme poverty
床 *kashō, hidoko* fire bed, fire grate
攻 *hize*(*me*) fire attack
吹竹 *hifu*(*ki*)*dake* bamboo blowpipe for charcoal fires
見 *hi*(*no*)*mi* fire tower
見櫓 *hi*(*no*)*mi yagura* fire tower
花 *hibana* spark
花散 *hibana* (*o*) *chi*(*rasu*) quarrel incessantly
災 *kasai* conflagration, fire
災保険 *kasai hoken* fire insurance
災報知器 *kasai hōchiki* fire-alarm box
災警報 *kasai keihō* fire alarm
8 門 *kamon* cannon mouth
明 *hiaka*(*ri*) firelight
炉 *karo* hearth; furnace; stove
炙 *hiaburi* burning to death; the stake
炎 *kaen* flames, blazes
炎放射器 *kaen hōshaki* flame thrower
炎瓶 *kaembin* Molotov cocktail
事 *kaji* conflagration, fire
事見舞 *kaji mima*(*i*) sympathy call after a fire
事泥 *kajidoro* thief at a fire
事場 *kajiba* scene of the fire
事場泥棒 *kajiba dorobō* thief at a fire
9 風 *kafū* fire and wind
食 *kashoku* eating cooked food
屋 *hoya* lamp chimney
持 *himo*(*chi*) fire-holding qualities
柱 *hibashira* pillar of fire; blazing column
海 *hi* (*no*) *umi* a lake of fire; the Lake of Fire
除 *hiyoke* protection from fire
室 *kashitsu* firebox
急 *kakyū* urgency, emergency
点頃 *hitobo*(*shi*) *koro* evening
星 *Kasei* Mars
星人 *Kaseijin* Martian
10 酒 *kashu* strong drink

粉 *hi*(*no*)*ko* sparks
砲 *kahō* gun, cannon
砲攻撃 *kahō kōgeki* gunfire ⌈tinguisher
消 *hike*(*shi*) fireman; fire brigade; fire ex-
消役 *hike*(*shi*)*yaku* trouble shooter
消壺 *hike*(*shi*) *tsubo* charcoal extinguisher
11 遊 *hiaso*(*bi*) playing with fire; playing with
桶 *hioke* round wooden brazier ⌊love
移 *hiutsu*(*ri*) catching fire, igniting
脚 *hiashi* spreading of a fire
祭 *kasai* offering by fire
責 *hize*(*me*) ordeal by fire
乾 *hiboshi* fire-dried; drying by the fire
悪戯 *hi itazura* playing with fire
達磨 *hidaruma* mass of flames
12 渡 *hiwata*(*ri*) fire walking
焚 *hitaki* building a fire
焙 *hiaburi* burning to death, the stake
脹 *hibukure* burn blister
筒 *hozutsu* gun barrel
番 *hi*(*no*)*ban* night watch, fire watchman
焚 *hitaki* building a fire
無焜炉 *hina*(*shi*) *konro* fireless cooker
焰 *kaen* flame, blaze
焰放射器 *kaen-hōshaki* flame thrower
葬 *kasō* cremation
葬炉 *kasōro* crematory
葬場 *kasōba* crematory
13 傷 *yakedo, kashō* burn, scald
搔 *hikaki* poker, fire rake
煙 *kaen* fire and smoke
鉢 *hibachi* brazier
戦 *kasen* shooting battle
勢 *kasei* force of the flames
照 *hote*(*ru*) feel hot, flush, burn. *hote*(*ri*) glow, heat; burning sensation
蓋 *hibuta* cover for a gun barrel
蓋切 *hibuta* (*o*) *ki*(*ru*) open fire
14 種 *hidane* live coals (for starting a fire); remains of a fire
綿 *kamen* gun cotton
15 線 *kasen* firing line
影 *hokage* firelight; fire; shadows of the firelight; forms moving in the firelight
箸 *hibashi* tongs
箭 *kasen* fire arrow
熱 *kanetsu* heat
器 *kaki* firearms
熨斗 *hinoshi* flatiron
16 燵 *kotatsu* charcoal brazier in a floor well
薬 *kayaku* gunpowder
薬庫 *kayakuko* powder magazine
燄 *kaen* flame, blaze
燄放射器 *kaen-hōshaki* flame thrower
18 曜 *Kayō* Tuesday
曜日 *Kayōbi* Tuesday

難 *kanan* fire calamity
難除 *kanan-yoke* charm against fire
19 縄 *hinawa* fuse cord
縄銃 *hinawajū, hinawazutsu* matchlock, harquebus
23 鑽 *hikiri* rubbing sticks to make a fire
鑽臼 *hikiri usu* fire stone

2

灰 2744 F1178 See 灰 820.

P **灯** 2745 F1178 F1201A **燈** TEI. CHŌ. Tō lamp, light. counter for lights. *akari, akashi, tomoshibi, hi* a light.

3 下 *tōka* beneath the lamp
下親 *tōka shitashi*(*mu*) study earnestly
4 心 *tōshin* wick
心油 *tōshin-yu* kerosene ⌈light
火 *tōka* a light, lamplight. *tōka ni* by lamp-
火管制 *tōka kansei* light control, brownout, blackout
火親 *tōka shitashi*(*mu*) study earnestly
5 用 *tōyō* for illumination
用石油 *tōyō sekiyu* kerosene
台 *tōdai* lighthouse, beacon; lampstand
台守 *tōdaimori* lighthouse keeper
6 光 *tōkō* light, lamplight
光信号 *tōkō shingō* flashlight signaling
7 芯 *tōshin* wick
8 油 *tōyū, toboshi abura* lamp oil
明 *tōmyō* light offered to a god
明台 *tōmyōdai* stand for an offering of a light
11 船 *tōsen* lightship
15 標 *tōhyō* light buoy
影 *hokage, tōei* flicker of light
22 籠 *tōrō* garden lantern, votive lantern
籠流 *tōrō-naga*(*shi*) setting afloat the *Bon* Festival lanterns

3

災 See 1448.

灼 2746 F1179 **灼** SHAKU. *arata*(*kana*) miraculous.

15 熱 *shakunetsu* incandescence, red heat, scorching heat

灸 2747 F1179 KYŪ moxa cautery, chastisement. *yaito* moxa cautery.

8 所 *kyūsho* moxa-treatment points (scars)
治 *kyūji* moxa cautery
9 点 *kyūten* moxa-treatment points (scars)
11 術 *kyūjutsu* moxa cautery

4

炙 See 205.

炬 2748 / F1181 Ko. Kyo torch, signal fire.
4火 *kyoka* pine torch, torchlight, firebrand
8岩 *kyogan* penetrating eye
16燵 *kotatsu* charcoal brazier in a floor well

炒 2749 / F1180 Sō. Shō. *i(ru)* broil; parch; roast (in a pan); fire (tea); fry.
iri parching, roasting, popping.
5玉子 *iritamago* scrambled eggs
6米 *irigome* parched rice
7豆 *irimame* parched beans
8物 *irimono* parched grains or beans
13塩 *irijio* parched salt

炉 B 2750 / F1206 **爐** Ro furnace, kiln, hearth; (nuclear) reactor.
4火 *roka* hearth fire
辺 *robata, rohen* fireside, hearth
7床 *roshō* hearth
10格子 *rogōshi* furnace grate
12棚 *rodana* mantlepiece
13滓 *rokasu* slag, refuse metals
14端 *robata* fireside, hearth
16頭 *rotō* around the hearth

炎 B 2751 / F1180 En inflammation. *honō, honoho, homura* flame, blaze.
3上 *enjō* blazing up; destruction (of a large building) by fire
4天 *enten* blazing heat, scorching sun
8炎 *en-en(taru)* blazing, fiery
9威 *en-i* extreme heat, sultriness
10症 *enshō* inflammation
12暑 *ensho* intense heat, heat wave
15熱 *ennetsu* sweltering heat

炊 B 2752 / F1180 Sui. *ta(ku), kashi(gu)* cook, boil.
4夫 *suifu* a male cook
5出 *takida(shi)* emergency rice feeding
8具 *suigu* cooking utensils
事 *suiji* cooking, culinary affairs
事係 *suijigakari* cook, chef
事場 *suijiba* kitchen, cookhouse, field kitchen, galley
11婦 *suifu* cook, kitchen maid
13飯器 *suihanki* electric rice cooker
29爨 *suisan* cooking

5

為 See 138.

炭 See 1418.

炮 2753 / F1182 Hō burn; roast.

炳 2754 / F1182 **昞 昺** Hei clear and bright.
5平 *heiko* very clear

炯 2755 / F1182 **烱** Kei light; clear.
9炯 *keikei(taru)* glaring, penetrating
11眼 *keigan* keen eye

炸 2756 / F1182 Saku frying; explosion.
9発 *sakuhatsu* explosion
12裂 *sakuretsu* explosion
裂弾 *sakuretsudan* explosive
16薬 *sakuyaku* explosives

畑 A 2757 / F1273 (国字) *hata, hatake* field, farm, plantation, garden; one's specialty. [田]
4水練 *hatake suiren* book learning
5打 *hata-u(chi)* plowing up ground
6地 *hatachi* farmland
7作 *hatasaku* upland farming
8物 *hatakemono* products of the field
11違 *hatakechiga(i)* out of one's line
13鼠 *hata nezumi* field mouse

6

烏 See 229.

烟 2758 / F1185 See **煙** 2784.

烛 Nonstandard for **燭** 2811.

烘 2759 / F1184 Kō. *abu(ru)* (see under 焙 2768.0).

烙 2760 / F1184 Raku burn.
6印 *rakuin* mark, brand, stigma, branding iron

烈 B 2761 / F1182 Retsu. *hage(shii)* violent, vehement, furious, severe, acute, intense, extreme, passionate, heated, stormy (applause); tempestuous (temperament); mighty.
3士 *resshi* patriot, hero

女 *retsujo* heroine
4日 *retsujitsu* a hot day
火 *rekka* raging fire
夫 *reppu* patriot; hero
9風 *reppū* violent wind, hurricane, gale
10烈 *retsuretsu(taru)* ardent, intense, vehement
11婦 *reppu* a virtuous woman; heroine
15震 *resshin* violent earthquake

7

烹 See 309.

焉 See 60.

烱 2762/F1185 See 炯 2755.

烽 2763/F1185 Hō signal fire.
4火 *hōka, noroshi* signal fire, rocket, beacon

8

焦 See 5029.

煉 Nonstandard for 煉 2783.

焠 2764/F1187 SAI. *nama(su)* anneal.

焱 2765/F1191 EN. *honō* flame, blaze.

焜 2766/F1187 KON shine.
8炉 *konro* portable cooking stove. *shichirin* small charcoal stove

焔 2767/F1191 See 燄 249.

焙 2768/F1186 HŌ. HAI. *hō(jiru)* fire, heat, roast. *abu(ru)* roast, toast, broil, grill; warm; dry.
5出 *aburida(shi)* invisible (ink)
9茶 *hōjicha* roasted tea
10烙 *hōroku* baking pan ⌈fire.
22籠 *aburiko* grill; basket for drying over a

焚 2769/F1186 FUN. *ta(ku)* burn, kindle, build (a fire); boil, cook. *ya(ku)* (see under 焼 2772.0).
3口 *takiguchi* fuel-feed hole
4火 *takibi* blazing fire, bonfire
5付 *ta(ki)-tsu(keru)* light, kindle, build (a fire); instigate, stir up. *takitsu(ke)* kindling, fire lighter
出 *takida(shi)* emergency rice feeding
6尽 *ta(ki)-tsu(kusu)* burn up; run out of fuel
8物 *takimono* firewood, kindling, fuel
10書 *funsho* burning of books
11捨 *ta(ki)-su(teru)* leave a fire to burn out
12落 *takioto(shi)* embers, charred firewood

A然 2770/F1191 ZEN. NEN. *sō, sa* so. *shika(rashimeru)* to decree. *sō(shite), so(shite)* and. *sa(ri) towa* if so, well. *sa(ru)* a certain, such. *shika(raba)* if so, in that case. *shika(razu)* no, it is not so. *shika(redomo)* but. *shika(ri)* yes, you are right. *shika(rubeki)* due, proper, reasonable, respectable, justifiable. *shika(ru) ni* however, nevertheless, on the contrary. *shika(shi), sare(do)* but, however. *shika(mo)* moreover, nevertheless. *shikashi* however, but. *shika* so, in that way. *-zen* resembling.
5可 *shika(ru)be(ku)* as you think best, appropriately, reasonably ⌈as if; just like
乍 *shikashinagara* but, however. *sanaga(ra)*
6迄 *samade* to that extent, so much
有 *shikarashi(meru)* make (someone) do so
気無 *sarigena(i)* unconcerned, nonchalant
7体 *sa(aranu)tei* an unconcerned air
8者 *shikaraba* if so. *sarumono* a certain person; a man of no common order
12程 *sahodo* very much, much, very. *saruhodo ni* well, now
斯 *sōkō* this and that; hesitatingly
然 *shikajika* and so on. *so(u)so(u)* again and
14様 *sayō na*＝佐様 392.14 ⌊again
15諾 *zendaku* word of honor

B煮 2771/F1193 煮 煑 SHA. *ni(eru)* boil, cook, be cooked, be boiled. *ni(ru) vt* boil, cook. *ni* cooking.
2〆 *ni-shi(meru)* boil up thoroly
3干 *nibo(shi)* small dried sardines
上 *ni(e)-a(garu)* be thoroly boiled. *ni-a(geru)*
4方 *nikata* cookery; cook ⌊boil thoroly
込 *ni-ko(mu)* cook together. *niko(mi)* meat and vegetable stew
切 *ni(e)-ki(ranai)* be half-cooked; vague, halfhearted, vacillating
5立 *ni-ta(teru)* boil up, bring to a boil. *nita(tsu)* boil up, bring to a boil; begin to
付 *ni-tsu(keru)* boil hard ⌊boil
汁 *nitsuyu, nishiru* gravy, stock, broth
加減 *niekagen* amount of boiling
出 *nida(su) vt* boil down, decoct, extract. *nida(shi)* stock, broth

4 心小⺌戈戸手扌支攴攵文斗斤方旡日曰月木欠止歹殳毋比毛氏气水氵氺[火灬]爪爫父爻爿犭片牙牛犬犭

出汁 *nida(shi)jiru* soup stock, broth
[6]色 *ni-iro* color of well-cooked food; broth
返 *ni(e)-kae(ru), ni(ekuri)-kae(ru)* boil over, seethe, ferment, come to a boil
合 *ni-a(waseru)* boil together
[7]豆 *nimame* boiled beans
冷 *ni-sa(masu)* let cool after boiling
花 *nibana* fresh tea
抜 *ninu(ki)* paste made from boiled rice flour
抜玉子 *ninu(ki) tamago* boiled egg
売 *niu(ri)* selling cooked food
売屋 *niu(ri)ya* eating house
[8]炊 *nitaki* boiling
物 *nimono* cooking; cooked food
直 *ni-nao(su)* boil again, recook
沸 *shafutsu suru, ni(e)-ta(giru)* boil up
沸消毒 *shafutsu shōdoku* sterilization by boiling
[9]染 *ni-shi(meru)* boil hard
[10]凍 *nikogo(ri)* boiled-down food
殺 *nikoro(shi)* death by boiling
[11]魚 *nizakana* boiled fish
過 *ni-su(giru), ni-su(gosu)* overdo, overboil
頃 *nigoro* the time the cooking is done
崩 *ni(e)-kuzu(reru)* be cooked to pieces
[12]湯 *ni(e)yu* boiling water
焼 *niya(ki)* cooking
焚 *nitaki* cooking
[13]溢 *ni(e)-kobo(reru)* boil over
詰 *ni-tsu(maru)* be boiled down. *ni-tsu(meru) vt* boil down
[14]滾 *ni(e)-ta(giru) vi* boil up, seethe, ferment
[15]蕩 *ni-toro(kasu)* simmer until dissolved
[16]凝 *nikogori* boiled-down food; jelly
[19]繰返 *ni(e)-ku(ri)-kae(ru)* boil up
[20]麵 *nyūmen* boiled vermicelli

8 A **焼** 2772 / F1202 **燒焼** SHŌ burning. *ya(ku) vt* set fire to, burn, fire; bake, roast (over a fire), toast, broil, parch; char, scorch, singe; cremate; print (photos); be envious of. *ya(keru) vi* be burnt, be burnt down; be roasted, be toasted, be grilled, be broiled; be scorched; be sunburnt; warm up, heat up (as a motor); be tarnished, fade; have heartburn; be jealous of; glow, be illuminated. *ya(ki)* baking, toasting, roasting, broiling; roast; porcelain; tempering; discipline.

[2]入 *ya(ki)-i(re)* hardening, tempering. *ya(ki) (o) i(reru)* torture
[3]土 *shōdo, ya(ke)tsuchi* baked clay, parched ground
山 *ya(ke)yama* burning mountain; burnt-over mountain
刃 *ya(ki)ba* tempered blade
[4]切 *ya(ke)-ki(ru)* burn itself out
太 *ya(ke)buto(ri)* getting richer after a fire
木杭 *ya(ke)bokkui* charred posts; firebrand
火箸 *ya(ke)hibashi* hot tongs
[5]瓦 *ya(ke)gawara* burnt tile
穴 *ya(ke)ana* hole made by burning
立 *ya(ki)-ta(teru)* burn fiercely. *ya(ki)ta(te)* piping hot, freshly baked; freshly roasted, freshly broiled
処 *ya(ke)do* burn; scald
付 *ya(ki)-tsu(keru)* join by baking; bake (porcelain); enamel; glaze; plate; stain (glass); fuse together; print (pictures). *ya(ki)-tsu(ku)* scorch. *yakitsu(ke)* baking; enamelling; plating; annealing; (photographic) printing
払 *ya(ki)-hara(u)* burn up, consume. *ya(ki)-hara(i)* violent burning of unwanted goods
打 *yakiu(chi)* setting on fire, attacking and burning
失 *ya(ke)-u(seru), shōshitsu suru* destroy by fire
出 *ya(ke)-da(sareru)* be burnt out. *ya(ke)-da(sare)* people burnt out
玉機関 *ya(ki)dama kikan* semi-diesel engine
石 *ya(ke)-ishi* hot stone; pumice stone, lava
石膏 *ya(ki)sekkō* plaster of Paris
[6]米 *ya(ki)gome* parched rice, burnt rice
肉 *ya(ki)niku* roast meat, roast fowl
回 *ya(ki) (ga) mawa(ru)* lose one's energy
尽 *ya(ki)-tsuku(su)* burn up, consume, reduce to ashes. *ya(ke)-tsu(kiru)* burn out
成 *yakina(su)* bake (pottery)
印 *ya(ki)-in* brand, branding iron; stigma
芋 *ya(ki)-imo* baked or roasted sweet potato
団子 *ya(ki)dango* toasted dumpling
夷 *shōi* burning up
夷弾 *shōidan* incendiary bomb, incendiary shell
死 *shōshi, ya(ke)ji(ni)* death by fire
死体 *shōshitai* charred body
死者 *shōshisha* person burnt to death
[7]足 *ya(ke)ta(ranai)* rare, underdone
灼 *shōshaku suru* cauterize
判 *ya(ki)han, ya(ki)ban* branding iron, brand; stigma
却 *shōkyaku* destruction by fire, incineration
麦 *ya(ki)mugi* parched barley
串 *ya(ki)gushi* skewer, spit
豆腐 *ya(ki)dōfu* broiled bean curd
戻 *ya(ki)-modo(su)* anneal, temper
戻鋼 *ya(ki)modo(shi)kō* tempered steel
[8]金 *ya(ki)gane* branding iron, marking iron
板 *ya(ki)-ita* hot plate
枠 *ya(ki)waku* photographic printing frame
物 *ya(ki)mono* pottery, porcelain
直 *ya(ki)-nao(su)* rebake; warm over; overbake; rehash; adapt; imitate; overprint (in photography)
林檎 *ya(ki)ringo* baked apple

9香 shōkō incense offering
畑 ya(ki)bata, ya(ke)bata, ya(ki)batake, ya(ke)batake burnt-over fields
砂 ya(ke)zuna hot sandbag (for treatments)
型 ya(ki)gata dry-sand mold
海苔 ya(ki)nori toasted seaweed
10残 ya(ke)-noko(ru) remain unburnt, escape a fire. ya(ke)noko(ri) articles saved from a fire; remains after a fire
酒 ya(ke)zake drowning one's cares in saké
討 ya(ki)u(chi) an attack with fire
酎 shōchū a low-grade alcoholic drink
殺 ya(ki)-koro(su) vt burn to death, burn alive
畠 ya(ki)bata, ya(ke)bata, ya(ki)batake, ya(ke)batake burnt-over fields
栗 ya(ki)guri roasted chestnut
11魚 ya(ki)zakana broiled fish
鳥 ya(ki)tori fried chicken, roast fowl
痕 shōkon scar from a burn
過 ya(ki)-su(giru) overcook; overprint (photography)
捨 ya(ki)-su(teru) burn up, incinerate
接 ya(ki)tsu(gi) suru cement broken porcelain together by baking
豚 ya(ki)buta roast pork
野 ya(ke)no burnt field, burnt prairie
野原 ya(ke)nohara, ya(ke)no(ga)hara burnt-out area
12場 ya(ki)ba crematory
渣 ya(ke)kasu cinders
絵 ya(ki)e pyrography; pyrograph
蛤 ya(ki)hamaguri baked clams
鈍 ya(ki)-nama(su) anneal
飯 ya(ki)meshi fried rice
落 ya(ke)-o(chiru) be burnt down
焦 ya(ke)ko(ge), ya(ke)koga(shi) hole made by burning
13傷 ya(ki)kizu a burn
塊 shōkai clinker
塩 ya(ki)shio baked salt, table salt
滅 shōmetsu sasu, ya(ki)-horobo(su) vt destroy by fire. shōmetsu suru vi be destroyed by fire
腹 ya(ke)bara despair, desperation
跡 ya(ke)ato fire ruins
棄 ya(ki)-su(teru) destroy by fire. shōki destruction by fire
14増 ya(ki)ma(shi) an extra print
網 ya(ki)ami toasting grill, broiling grill
15餅 ya(ki)mochi toasted rice cake
麩 ya(ki)fu baked wheat-gluten bread
窯 ya(ki)gama kiln, oven
蕎麦 ya(ki)soba chow mein
17鍋 ya(ki)nabe frying pan
19鏝 ya(ki)gote hot iron; flatiron; soldering iron, cautering iron; pyrographic iron

無 A 2773 F1187 Mu, Bu nothing, nil, negation. na(i), na(shi) none. na(kattara) if there were none; were it not for; unless. mu ni suru make worthless. na(ku) naru be lost; run short, be used up; disappear; die. naku(su), na(ku) suru lose; run out of; remove; absorb. na(kute) without; for want of; in the absence of. na(sasōna) unlikely, improbable. na(kumogana) needless, useless. na(shi) ni, na(shi) de without.
一文 muichimon penniless
一物 muichibutsu, muichimotsu penniless
2二 muni matchless, unparalleled
二無三 muni-musan＝遮二無二 4737.2
力 muryoku helpless, incompetent; lack of funds
力化 muryokka suru become powerless
人 bunin, mujin shortage of help; unmanned. mujin, munin uninhabited
人地帯 mujin chitai no-man's land
人飛行機 mujin hikōki pilotless plane
人島 mujintō uninhabited island
人電車 mujin densha runaway tram
人境 mujin(no)kyō uninhabited region
3口 mukuchi reticence
下 muge ni flatly, squarely, point-blank
才 musai incompetence, lack of ability
干渉 mukanshō nonintervention
上 mujō no supreme, best, greatest
上光栄 mujō (no) kōei great fame
上権 mujōken supremacy
4心 mushin request. mushin no innocent; insentient; involuntary
手 mute de empty-handed; with bare hands; unarmed; without funds
比 muhi no peerless, unparalleled
毛 mumō hairless
水 musui anhydrous
日付 muhizuke undated
分別 mufumbetsu rashness, indiscretion
方針 muhōshin without a plan
月謝 mugessha free tuition
欠 muketsu perfection
欠席 mukesseki perfect attendance
辺 muhen na limitless, boundless, infinite
辺際 muhensai infinity
双 musō peerless, unparalleled
双側 musōgawa hunting case (of a watch)
5代 mudai free, no charge
功 mukō void, invalid; ineffective
生 musei lifeless
生物 museibutsu inanimate object; lifeless thing
札 musatsu without tickets
札乗車 musatsu jōsha riding without tickets
主 mushu ownerless
主義 mushugi unprincipled, lacking a fixed purpose
用 muyō useless; unwanted; unnecessary; prohibited; without business
用心 buyōjin insecurity, carelessness

用心配 *muyō (no) shimpai* needless worry
用長物 *muyō (no) chōbutsu* useless thing
礼 *burei* discourtesy, rudeness
礼者 *bureimono, bureisha* rude person
礼講 *bureikō* informal party, unrestrained revelry
6 色 *mushoku* colorless, achromatic
休 *mukyū* no holiday
地 *muji* solid color
灯 *mutō* no light (at night)
考 *mukanga(e)* thoughtlessness
自覚 *mujikaku na* apathetic, blind to, unconscious of
任所大臣 *muninsho daijin* minister of state without portfolio
字幕映画 *mujimaku eiga* film without subtitles
血 *muketsu* bloodless
血革命 *muketsu kakumei* bloodless revolution
尽 *mujin* infinity, endless, unfathomable; lottery savings system
尽蔵 *mujinzō* inexhaustible supply
死 *mushi* no outs
死満塁 *mushi-manrui* no outs and bases full
気力 *mukiryoku* lethargy, enervation
気味 *bukimi* ill-feeling
防備 *mubōbi* unfortified, open, defenseless
防備都市 *mubōbi toshi* open city
安打 *muanda* no hits
安打無得点 *muanda-mutokuten* a no-hit and no-run (game)
名 *mumei* unnamed, anonymity, obscurity; unjustifiable
名氏 *mumeishi* anonymous person
名兵士 *mumei heishi* the unknown soldier
名指 *mumeishi* ring finger
名骨 *mumeikotsu* hipbone
名戦士 *mumei senshi* the unknown soldier
7 住 *mujū* (temple) without a resident priest
位 *mui* without rank
私 *mushi* unselfishness, impartiality
芸 *mugei no* uncultured, unaccomplished
邪気 *mujaki* innocence, artlessness
沙汰 *busata* silence, neglect to write or call
作法 *busahō* bad manners, discourtesy, rudeness
花果 *ichijiku, ichijuku* fig
材料 *muzairyō* no new factors (on the stock market)
投票 *mutōhyō* elected without opposition
批判的 *muhihanteki* uncritical
医地域 *mui-chi-iki* doctorless area
医村 *muison* doctorless village
尾 *mubi* tailless
尾翼機 *mubiyokuki* flying wing, tailless plane
体 *mutai* forcibly
体財産 *mutai zaisan* intangible assets
技巧 *mugikō* artless
技能 *muginō no* unskilled (job)
利子 *murishi* non-interest-bearing
利息 *murisoku* non-interest-bearing
形 *mukei no* abstract, incorporeal, immaterial; moral, spiritual; invisible, intangible
形文化財 *mukei-bunkazai* intangible cultural asset
言 *mugon* silence
言行 *mugon (no) gyō* silent austerities
言劇 *mugongeki* pantomime
我 *muga* selflessness; ecstasy
我夢中 *muga-muchū* unconsciousness; ecstasy
我境 *muga(no)kyō* self-effacement
条件 *mujōken* unconditional
条件降伏 *mujōken kōfuku* unconditional surrender
条件降服 *mujōken kōfuku* unconditional surrender
条約 *mujōyaku* treatyless
声 *musei* voiceless, noiseless, silent
声子音 *musei shi-in* voiceless sound
声音 *museion* voiceless sound
声映画 *musei eiga* silent film
声銃 *museijū* noiseless gun
8 届 *mutodo(ke)* without permission; without notice
性 *musei* asexual. *bushō* laziness, indolence. *mushō*＝無暗 *muyami* (see below–13)
明 *mumyō* darkness, illusion
効 *mukō* void, invalid; ineffective
官 *mukan* without office
毒 *mudoku* nonpoisonous
拘束 *mukōsoku* nonrestraint
制限 *museigen* unlimited, unrestricted
担保 *mutampo* unsecured, without collateral
表情 *muhyōjō na* expressionless
免許 *mumenkyo* unlicensed
価 *muka* priceless; valueless
価値 *mukachi no* worthless
味 *mumi* tasteless, flat, insipid
味乾燥 *mumi-kansō na* dry as dust, uninteresting
抵当 *muteitō* (borrowing) without security
抵抗 *muteikō* nonresistance, passive resistance
法 *muhō* injustice; wrong; unlawfulness; outrage; violence
法者 *muhōmono* outlaw, outrageous fellow
知 *muchi* ignorance, illiteracy, stupidity
知蒙昧 *muchi-mōmai* unenlightenment
念 *munen* regret; resentment; chagrin; impassive state of mind
念無想 *munen-musō* impassive state of mind
定見 *muteiken* lack of principle, inconstant
定形 *muteikei* amorphous
実 *mujitsu* falsehood; innocence
実罪 *mujitsu (no) tsumi* false charge
学 *mugaku* ignorance; illiteracy
学者 *mugakusha* an ignorant person
事 *buji* safety, security; peace, tranquility; good health; boredom
事故 *mujiko* no accident, no trouble; safety (week)
所得 *mushotoku* without income
所属 *mushozoku* free, independent, nonaffiliated, nonpartisan

所属地帯 *mushozoku chitai* no-man's land
妻 *musai* celibacy
妻主義 *musai shugi* celibacy
妻者 *musaisha* single person
限 *mugen* infinite, endless, unfathomable; infinity, eternity ⌈finitely great
限大 *mugendai* infinity. *mugendai no* in-
限小 *mugenshō* the infinitesimal
限地獄 *mugen jigoku* a Buddhist hell ⌈lar
限軌道 *mugen kidō* endless track, caterpil-
限責任 *mugen sekinin* unlimited liability
9 音 *buin* long silence, neglect (to write)
垢 *muku* purity, innocence; plain-colored suit; an all-white garb
冠 *mukan* uncrowned
臭 *mushū* odorless
要 *muyō*＝無用 (see above–5)
信心 *mushinjin* impiety, unbelief, infidelity
恰好 *bukakkō* unshapeliness, clumsiness
造作 *muzōsa* easiness; simplicity; artlessness
計画 *mukeikaku na* haphazard, unplanned
思慮 *mushiryo* thoughtlessness, indiscretion
封書状 *mufū shojō* unsealed letter
神経 *mushinkei* callousness, apathy, stolidity
神論 *mushinron* atheism
茶 *mucha na* absurd, unreasonable; reckless, wanton; excessive, immoderate
茶苦茶 *muchakucha* confused; absurd, unreasonable; reckless, mad
為 *bui, mui* idleness, inaction
為替 *mukawase, mugawase* no draft, no ex-
風 *mufū* dead calm ⌊change involved
風帯 *mufūtai* doldrums
風流 *mūfūryū* lack of refinement
軌道 *mukidō* trackless
軌道生活 *mukidō seikatsu* dissipated life
軌道電車 *mukidō densha* trolley bus
政府 *museifu* anarchy
政府主義 *museifu shugi* anarchism
政府主義者 *museifu shugisha* anarchist
10 骨 *bukotsu* uncouth, clumsy, brusque
根 *mukon* groundless, unfounded, false
残 *muzan* cruel, merciless, pitiful
粋 *busui na* inelegant, unromantic, lacking in polish
恥 *muchi* shamelessness, impudence
益 *mueki* futility, uselessness, carelessness
害 *mugai* harmless, innocent, inoffensive
記名 *mukimei* blank (endorsement), unregistered, uninscribed (shares)
症状 *mushōjō* no symptoms
格社 *mukakusha* an ungraded shrine
秩序 *muchitsujo* disorder, confusion, chaos
差別 *musabetsu, mushabetsu* indifference; making no discrimination

骨者 *bukotsumono* uncouth person
挨拶 *buaisatsu* impoliteness, incivility
酒精 *mushusei* nonalcoholic ⌈animal
脊椎動物 *musekizui dōbutsu* invertebrate
原罪御孕 *mugenzai* (*no*) *onyado*(*ri*) im-
病 *mubyō* no illness ⌊maculate conception
病息災 *mubyō-sokusai* perfect health
配 *muhai* nondividend
配当 *muhaitō* nondividend
料 *muryō* no charge, free
料図書館 *muryō toshokan* free library
料貸出図書館 *muryō kashidashi toshokan* free circulating library
能 *munō* inefficiency, incompetence
能力 *munōryoku* incompetence, impotence
能力者 *munōryokusha* incompetent or inefficient person ⌈person
能者 *munōsha* incompetent or inefficient
11 疵 *mukizu* flawless, faultless, sound, without blemish
道 *budō, mudō* tyranny; atrocity; wickedness
偏 *muhen* justice, impartiality
惨 *muzan* cruel, merciless; pitiful
情 *mujō* heartlessness, cruelty ⌈ignore
視 *mushi suru* disregard, defy, set aside,
聊 *buryō, muryō* boredom, tediousness
欲 *muyoku* not covetous
常 *mujō no* uncertain, evanescent, transient
異 *bui*＝*buji* 無事 (see above–8)
菌 *mukin* pasteurized, sterilized, aseptic,
責任 *musekinin* irresponsibility ⌊germfree
停車 *muteisha* nonstop
得点 *mutokuten* scoreless (game)
規律 *mukiritsu* disorderliness, negligence
経験 *mukeiken* inexperience ⌈tionalism
教会主義 *mukyōkai shugi* nondenomina-
教育 *mukyōiku na* uneducated, uncultured
断 *mudan* unannounced; unauthorized
断欠勤 *mudan kekkin* absent without per-
宿 *mushuku* homeless ⌊mission, AWOL
宿者 *mushukusha* vagrant, homeless person
産 *musan* without property
産者 *musansha* proletarian, have-nots
産政党 *musan seitō* proletarian party
産党 *musantō* proletarian party
産階級 *musan kaikyū* proletarians, property-less class
理 *muri* unreasonable, unjustifiable, unnatural; impossible, beyond one's strength; overwork; extravagance. *muri*(*karanu*), reasonable, natural. *muri ni* forcibly, against one's will ⌈will
理矢理 *muriyari ni* forcibly, against one's
理心中 *muri shinjū* forced double suicide
理押 *murio*(*shi*) pushing things too far
理取 *murido*(*ri*) exaction, extortion

理往生 *muri-ōjō* forced obedience
理強 *muriji-i* coercion
理無体 *muri-mutai* forcibly 「sympathy
理解 *murikai* lack of understanding or
理遣 *muriyari ni* forcibly, against one's will
理算段 *muri-sandan* proceeding in spite of difficulties; straining to raise money
理難題 *muri-nandai* unreasonable demand
12 帽 *mubō de* hatless
税 *muzei* duty-free, tax-free
給 *mukyū* unpaid, nonsalaried
辜 *muko no* innocent, harmless
筆 *muhitsu* illiteracy
筋 *mukin* nonreinforced
策 *musaku* resourcelessness
智 *muchi* ignorance, illiteracy, stupidity
無 *na(ke)na(shi)* the little one has. *na(i)na(i) suru* hide
割礼 *mukatsurei* uncircumcision
証拠 *mushōko* lack of evidence
統制 *mutōsei* uncontrolled
結果 *mukekka* negative result
勝負 *mushōbu* a tie, a draw
着陸 *muchakuriku* nonstop (flight)
報酬 *muhōshū no* nonsalaried
遠慮 *buenryo* forwardness, impertinence, audacity, boldness, frankness
痛 *mutsū* painless
痛分娩 *mutsū bumben* painless childbirth
間 *buma* clumsiness, stupidity; blunder
間地獄 *muken jigoku* a Buddhist hell
量 *muryō* infinite, immeasurable
量寿 *muryōju* immeasurable bliss
期 *muki* unlimited, perpetual, indefinite
期刑 *mukikei* life imprisonment
期限 *mukigen* unlimited, perpetual, indefinite 「ting another date
期延期 *muki enki* postponed without set-
期懲役 *muki chōeki* life imprisonment
13 傷 *mukizu*＝無疵 (see above-11)
嗜 *butashinami* poor preparation
碍 *muge* freedom from obstacles
数 *musū* innumerable
鉄砲 *muteppō na* reckless, thoughtless
義道 *mogidō na* cruel, brutal, heartless
頓着 *mutonjaku* nonchalance, indifference
慈悲 *mujihi na* cruel, merciless
感覚 *mukankaku* insensibility, numbness, apathy, callousness
試験 *mushiken de* without examination
鉛白粉 *muen-oshiroi* non-lead face paint
想無念 *musō-munen* Zen meditation
暗 *muyami na, muyami(yatarana)* thoughtless, rash, indiscreet; immoderate; unnecessary
暗矢鱈 *muyami-yatara na*＝word above
節制 *musessei* intemperance, profligacy
節操 *musessō* unchastity, inconstancy
電 *muden* wireless, radio
電放送 *muden hōsō* radio broadcast
勢 *buzei, muzei* shortage of men, numerical inferiority
勢力 *museiryoku* powerless, without in-
賃 *muchin* no charge 」fluence
賃乗車 *muchin jōsha* free ride, stolen ride
煙 *muen* smokeless
煙火薬 *muen kayaku* smokeless powder
煙炭 *muentan* anthracite coal
愛敬 *buaikyō* rudeness; unsociability
愛想 *buaisō* rudeness; unsociability
愛嬌 *buaikyō* unsociability, rudeness
罪 *muzai* innocent, not guilty
罪判決 *muzai hanketsu* acquittal
罪放免 *muzai-hōmen* innocent and acquit-
蓋 *mugai no* open, uncovered 」ted
蓋車 *mugaisha* open freight car
蓋貨車 *mugai kasha* open freight car
意味 *muimi* meaningless, nonsensical, to no purpose 「purpose
意義 *muigi* meaningless, nonsensical, to no
意識 *muishiki* unconsciousness; involuntariness 「tary
意識的 *muishikiteki* unconscious; involun-
資力 *mushiryoku* lack of funds
資本 *mushihon* without funds
資格 *mushikaku* disqualification; incapacity
資格者 *mushikakusha* disqualified person
14 慚 *muzan* cruel, merciless; pitiful
様 *buzama na* unshapely, unsightly, unpresentable; uncouth, clumsy
精 *bushō* sloth, laziness
銘 *mumei* unsigned, no signature
雑作 *muzōsa* easiness; simplicity; artlessness 「apathy
関心 *mukanshin* unconcern, indifference,
関係 *mukankei no* unconcerned, unrelated
銭 *musen* without money; no need for
銭旅行 *musen ryokō* hitchhiking 」money
銭遊興 *musen-yūkyō* merrymaking without paying 「bill
銭飲食 *musen-inshoku* jumping a restaurant
駄 *muda* futility, uselessness, waste
駄口 *mudaguchi* idle talk, nonsense
駄死 *mudaji(ni)* useless death
駄言 *mudagoto* useless words
駄足 *muda-ashi suru* make a fruitless call
駄骨 *mudabone* fruitless effort
駄書 *mudaga(ki)* idle scribbling
駄遣 *mudazukai* squandering
駄話 *mudabanashi* idle talk, gossip
15 慮 *muryo* approximately

論 *muron* of course, naturally
敵 *muteki* invincible, unrivaled
暴 *mubō* recklessness, thoughtlessness
窮 *mukyū* eternity, immortality
慾 *muyoku* not covetous
慙 *muzan* cruel, merciless; pitiful
器用 *bukiyō* clumsiness, unskillfulness
趣味 *mushumi* lack of taste, vulgarity; prosaic
調法 *buchōhō* discourtesy
賞行為 *mushō (no) kōi* volunteer service
縁 *muen* no surviving relatives
縁仏 *muembotoke* a deceased without relatives
縁墓地 *muembochi* cemetery for the unclaimed
線 *musen* wireless; no electricity service; no need for electricity
線工学 *musen kōgaku* radio engineering
線灯台 *musen tōdai* radio beacon
線通信 *musen tsūshin* radio communication
線航路標識 *musen kōro hyōshiki* radio beacon
線電信 *musen denshin* wireless telegraphy
線電報 *musen dempō* radiogram
線電話 *musen denwa* radio telephone
線標識 *musen hyōshiki* radio beacon
線操縦 *musen sōjū* radio-controlled (plane)
16 稽 *mukei* absurdity, nonsense
糖 *mutō* unsweetened
謀 *mubō na* reckless, thoughtless
頭 *mutō* headless
頼 *burai* villainy
頼漢 *buraikan* villain, scoundrel, outlaw
機 *muki* inorganic, mineral
機化学 *muki kagaku* inorganic chemistry
機物 *mukibutsu* inorganic substance; minerals (in food)
17 償 *mushō* free, no charge
爵 *mushaku* untitled
18 難 *bunan* safety, security; faultlessness; no difficulty
類 *murui* choicest, finest
題 *mudai* no title
謬性 *mubyūsei* infallibility
職 *mushoku* unemployed; no occupation
職者 *mushokusha* unemployed person
職業 *mushokugyō* unemployed; no occupation
19 礙 *muge* freedom from obstacles
識 *mushiki* ignorance, illiteracy
韻詩 *muinshi* blank verse, unrhymed poem
警告 *mukeikoku de* without warning
警察 *mukeisatsu* anarchy, lawlessness
20 競争 *mukyōsō* without a rival
籍者 *musekimono* person without registered domicile; vagrant; outlaw
22 鑑札 *mukansatsu* without a license

— **9** —

煎 See 611.

焼 2774 F1202 See **焼** 2772.

煮 2775 F1193 **煑** See **煮** 2771.

熖 Nonstandard for **焰** 2787.

煨 2776 F1195 WAI banked fire.

煥 2777 F1194 KAN shine.
9 発 *kampatsu suru* glitter, brighten

煌 2778 F1192 KŌ. *kirame(ku)* glitter, gleam, twinkle. *kira(rakana), kirabi(yakana)* glittering, bright and beautiful; clear speech.
9 星 *kiraboshi* glittering stars
13 煌 *kōkō(taru)* bright, brilliant

煠 2779 F1194 YŌ. CHŌ. SŌ. SHŌ. *ita(meru)* to sauté. *yu(deru) vt* boil, seethe. *yu(daru) vi* boil, seethe.
3 上 *yu(de)-a(geru)* finish boiling
5 汁 *yudejiru* broth
7 卵 *yudetamago* boiled eggs
13 溢 *yu(de)-kobo(su)* scald, parboil

煖 2780 F1193 DAN warm.
6 衣 *dan-i* warm clothes; dress warmly
8 炉 *danro* fireplace, hearth, stove
房 *dambō* heating
房車 *dambōsha* heated automobile
房装置 *dambō sōchi* heating system

煤 2781 F1194 BAI. *susu* soot. *susu(keru), susuba(mu), susu(buru)* get sooty, be sooty, get smoked up; be smoke-dried.
5 田 *baiden* coal field
払 *susuhara(i)* housecleaning
6 竹 *susudake* smoked bamboo
色 *susu iro* sooty color, grayish black
10 埃 *susu-hokori* soot and dust
11 掃 *susuhaki* housecleaning
13 煙 *baien* soot and smoke, smoke

B **煩** 2782 F1195 BON. HAN trouble, worry. *wazura(u)* be ill; worry, be afflicted, be in pain, be troubled. *wazura(wasu), wazura(waseru)* trouble, keep (someone) busy, disturb, annoy. *uru(sagaru)* feel annoyed by, regard as a nuisance. *uru(sai)* annoying, troublesome, irksome, in-

4 心 忄 ⺗ 戈 戸 手 扌 支 攴 攵 文 斗 斤 方 旡 日 曰 月 木 欠 止 歹 殳 毋 比 毛 氏 气 水 氵 氺 【火 9 灬】 爪 ⺤ 父 爻 爿 丬 片 牙 牛 犬 犭

quisitive, importunate. *wazura(i)* agony, anxiety; illness; involvement, trouble. *wazura(washii)* troublesome, complicated, confused.

4 方 *urusagata* disagreeable disposition; disagreeable person

6 忙 *hambō* pressure of business

多 *hanta* so many as to be a nuisance

7 労 *hanrō* worry, annoyance

9 型 *urusagata*＝煩方 (see above–4)

10 悩 *bonnō* evil passions, carnal desire

11 務 *hammu* troublesome work

累 *hanrui* cares, annoyances

12 悶 *hammon* anguish, worry, trouble

14 瑣 *hansa na* troublesome; complicated; minute; subtle; delicate

語 *hango* tedious language

雑 *hanzatsu* complexity, trouble, complication, intricacy

15 熱 *iki(ru)* be hot and sultry

18 簡 *hankan* rush and leisure; complication and simplicity

煉

2783/F1192 REN. *ne(ru)* refine (metals). *neri* kneading over fire.

5 白粉 *nerioshiroi* liquid face-powder

瓦 *renga* brick

瓦屋 *rengaya* brickmaker

瓦師 *rengashi* bricklayer

瓦粘土 *renga nendo* brick clay

瓦場 *rengajō* brickyard

瓦塀 *rengahei* brick wall

瓦製造所 *renga seizōjo* brickyard

瓦鋪道 *renga hodō* brick pavement

瓦職 *rengashoku* bricklayer

6 合 *ne(ri)-a(waseru)* knead together; compound

羊羹 *neriyōkan* bean jelly

8 固 *ne(ri)-kata(meru)* harden by kneading

物 *nerimono* paste, bean jelly, pastry

乳 *rennyū* condensed milk

9 炭 *rentan* briquette

10 粉 *neriko* dough

12 歯磨 *nerihamigaki* tooth paste

14 獄 *rengoku* purgatory

15 餌 *nerie* moist feed for birds

16 薬 *nerigusuri, neriyaku* ointment

17 鍛 *ne(ri)-kita(eru)* temper; drill, train

B 煙 烟

2784/F1193 EN smoke. *kemu(ru), kebu(ru)* smoke, smolder, be smoky, appear dim. *kemu(rasu)* smoke up, fumigate. *kemu(i), kebu(i)* smoky. *kemuri, kemu, kebu, keburi* smoke; fumes; spray. *kemu(tagaru)* be sensitive to smoke; feel awkward. *kebu(tai), kemu(tai)* smoky; feeling awkward.

4 火 *enka* rocket, beacon. *hanabi* fireworks, firecrackers

水晶 *kemuri suishō* smoky quartz

5 出 *kemurida(shi), kemuda(shi)* chimney, funnel

8 雨 *en-u* misty, fine, or drizzling rain

波 *empa* hazy sea, spray

毒 *endoku* smoke pollution

突 *entotsu* chimney, smokestack, funnel, stovepipe

突男 *entotsu otoko* chimney sitter

9 草 *tabako* tobacco

草入 *tabako-i(re)* cigarette case; tobacco pouch; cigar box

草盆 *tabako bon* tobacco brazier

草飲 *tabakono(mi)* a smoker

草銭 *tabako zeni* spending money

10 害 *engai* smoke pollution

11 道 *endō* flue

12 弾 *endan* smoke bomb

筒 *entō* chimney, smokestack, funnel, stovepipe

13 路 *enro* flue

幕 *emmaku* smoke screen

14 塵 *engin* cloud of dust; worldly affairs

管 *enkan* chimney. *kiseru* (tobacco) pipe; stolen train ride

管乗 *kiseruno(ri)* stolen train ride

17 霞 *enka* smoke and mist; a view

19 霧 *emmu* haze, mist, smog

A 照

2785/F1195 SHŌ. *te(ru)* shine. *te(rasu)* shine on, shed light on, illuminate; compare with. *te(reru)* be bashful. *te(ri)* sunshine; dry weather, drought; gloss, luster.

3 上 *te(ri)-a(garu)* clear up after a rain

4 尺 *shōshaku* backsight (of a gun)

込 *te(ri)-ko(mu)* shine into; shine for a long period. *te(ri)ko(mi)* sunshine, long dry spell

5 付 *te(ri)-tsu(keru)* shine down on, beat down on

出 *te(rashi)-da(su)* shed light on

6 返 *te(ri)-kae(su)* reflect

合 *te(ri)-a(waseru), te(rashi)-a(waseru), te(rashi)-a(wasu), shōgō suru* verify, check, compare

会 *shōkai* inquiry

会中 *shōkaichū* in communication (with)

7 応 *shōō* balance (in writing); accordance

8 明 *shōmei* illumination, lighting, flare

明弾 *shōmeidan* flare, star shell

9 度 *shōdo* (intensity of) illumination

降 *te(ri)fu(ri)* sunshine and rain; changing moods

星 *shōsei* muzzle sight

査 *shōsa* verification

10 射 *shōsha* shining

12 渡 *te(ri)-wata(ru)* shine all over

葉 *te(ri)ha* glossy leaves

13 隠 *te(re)kaku(shi)* covering up one's shame

照坊主 *te(ru)te(ru)bōzu* paper doll used in praying for good weather
準 *shōjun* aim, aiming, sight
準爆撃 *shōjum-bakugeki* precision bombing
15 影 *shōei* portrait
輝 *te(ri)-kagaya(ku)* shine brightly
16 覧 *shōran suru* see clearly
17 臨 *shōrin suru* rule; come (polite)

10

熏 See **燻** 2817.

熔 2786 F1197 F1961 See **鎔** 4904.

熖 2787 F1200 See **燄** 249.

熄 2788 F1197 SOKU cessation.

熙 2789 F1193 KI shine.

熅 2790 F1197 UN. ON. *iki(re)* sultriness, stuffiness.

熊 2791 F1197 YŪ. *kuma* bear.
4 手 *kumade* rake, fork
9 狩 *kumaga(ri)* bear hunting
11 祭 *kuma matsu(ri)* bear-sacrifice festival
13 蜂 *kumabachi* hornet
22 襲 *Kumaso* (ancient) Kyushu tribe

煽 2792 F1196 SEN. *ao(ru)* fan, flap; instigate, agitate; bolster up; gulp down, quaff. *ao(gu)* fan; instigate. *oda(teru)* stir up, instigate; flatter.
4 止 *ao(ri)do(me)* door stop
5 石 *senseki* natural coke
立 *ao(ri)-ta(teru), ao(gi)-ta(teru)* instigate, stir up
11 動 *sendō* instigation, agitation
情 *senjō* lasciviousness
情的 *senjōteki* lascivious, sensational, suggestive

11

熨 2793 F1199 I. UTSU. *noshi* flatiron. *no(su)* smooth out, straighten out.
4 斗 *noshi* label attached to gifts; a paper imitation of *noshi awabi*, the next word
斗鮑 *noshiawabi* strip of dried abalone marking a present

B **勳** 2794 F269 **勲** KUN merit, order of merit. *isao, isaoshi* meritorious deed; merit. [力]
5 功 *kunkō* merits, distinguished services
6 臣 *kunshin* meritorious retainer
7 位 *kun-i* order of merit
状 *kunjō* letter of commendation with an award
労 *kunrō* merit, meritorious deed
10 記 *kunki* decoration diploma
11 章 *kunshō* decoration, order, medal
12 等 *kuntō* order of merit
17 爵 *kunshaku* peerage and order of merit

B **熟** 2795 F1198 JUKU. *u(reru), juku(suru), juku(su)* ripen, mellow, mature; acquire skill; be ripe for; become popular (as a word). *u(mu)* ripen. *kona(reru)* be digested; combine; be skilled; be pulverized. *na(reru)* (see under 馴 5194.0). *jit(to)* firmly, intently, patiently.
6 成 *jukusei suru* ripen, mature; cure; ferment
字 *jukuji=jukugo* 熟語 (see below-14)
考 *jukukō, jukkō* due consideration, deliberation, mature reflection
8 知 *jukuchi* thoro knowledge
9 音 *jukuon* the syllabary syllables
思 *jukushi* careful consideration
柿 *jukushi* ripe persimmon
柿主義 *jukushi shugi* waiting quietly for things to develop
柿臭 *jukushikusa(i)* drunk
10 眠 *jukumin* sound sleep
蚕 *jukusan* mature silkworm
11 達 *jukutatsu* mastery, proficiency
視 *jukushi* steady gaze, scrutiny
酔 *jukusui* dead drunk
13 睡 *jukusui* sound sleep
路 *jukuro* familiar road
14 語 *jukugo* a word of two or more characters; a set phrase
読 *jukudoku* careful reading
練 *jukuren* skill, mastery, practice
練工 *jukurenkō* skilled workman
練者 *jukurensha* skilled individual
15 談 *jukudan=jukugi* 熟議 (see below-20)
蕃 *jukuban* friendly tribesmen
熟 *tsukuzuku to* thoroly, entirely, really, wistfully, earnestly, attentively, greatly, profoundly, keenly. *tsuratsura* attentively, carefully, deeply
慮 *jukuryo* mature deliberation
慮断行 *jukuryo-dankō* deliberate and decisive
16 覧 *jukuran* scrutiny
20 議 *jukugi* due deliberation, careful consultation

B **默** 2796 F2163 **黙** MOKU keeping silence. *moku(suru)* be silent.

moda(*su*) be silent; leave as it is. *dama*(*ru*), *moda*(*su*) become silent, stop speaking, say nothing. *damma*(*ri*) silence, reticence. [黒]

4 止 *mokushi suru* keep silent. *moda*(*su*) be silent; leave as it is
込 *dama*(*ri*)-*ko*(*mu*) say no more, sink into silence
5 礼 *mokurei suru* bow silently
示 *mokushi* revelation; implication
示文学 *mokushi bungaku* apocalyptic literature
示録 *Mokushiroku* Revelation
6 考 *mokkō* contemplation, meditation
7 坐 *mokuza suru* sit in silence
否権 *mokuhiken* the right to keep silent
8 念 *mokunen* remaining silent
9 屋 *dama*(*ri*)*ya* silent person
約 *mokuyaku* tacit understanding
思 *mokushi* contemplation
契 *mokkei* secret understanding without speaking
省 *mokusei* quiet reflection
10 殺 *mokusatsu suru* ignore
秘 *mokuhi* secrecy, silence
秘権 *mokuhiken* the right to keep silent
11 過 *mokka* overlooking, connivance
視 *mokushi suru* wink at, overlook, tolerate
許 *mokkyo* tacit permission, connivance
12 然 *mokuzen*(*taru*) silent, tacit, mute
13 想 *mokusō* meditation, reverie
14 読 *mokudoku* silent reading
認 *mokunin* tacit approval, admission, connivance
15 劇 *mokugeki* pantomime
諾 *mokudaku* tacit consent
黙 *mokumoku*(*taru*) silent, tacit, mute
18 難 *moda*(*shi*)*gata*(*i*) hard to refuse
19 禱 *mokutō* silent prayer; silent tribute

11 A 熱 2797 / F1199 熱 NETSU heat, warmth; temperature; fever; mania, fad; enthusiasm; passion. *nes*(*suru*) *vt* heat, make hot; burn, boil. *vi* become warm; become excited; become earnest. *atsu*(*garu*) feel the heat, swelter. *iki*(*ru*) be hot and sultry. *hotō*(*ru*), *hotobo*(*ru*) get heated; get angry. *atsu*(*i*) hot. *hotobo*(*ri*) warmth, heat; sensation, furore; enthusiasm, energy, momentum; reputation. *atsu*(*gari*) person sensitive to heat.

2 力学 *netsurikigaku* thermodynamics
3 上 *netsu* (*o*) *a*(*geru*) become earnest
4 火 *nekka* intense heat. *atsubi* hot fire
中 *netchū* enthusiasm, zeal, mania
心 *nesshin* earnestness, enthusiasm
心家 *nesshinka* enthusiast, devotee, fan
心党 *nesshintō* zealots
5 弁 *netsuben* fervent speech
6 灰 *atsubai* hot ashes
気 *netsuke* feverishness. *nekki* heat, hot air; enthusiasm
気消毒 *nekki shōdoku* heat (hot-air) sterilization
血 *nekketsu* hot blood, fiery spirit, zeal
血児 *nekketsuji* a hot-blooded man
血漢 *nekketsukan* a hot-blooded man
7 位 *netsui* thermal unit
冷 *netsusa*(*mashi*) antipyretic
狂 *nekkyō* enthusiasm, frenzy, rage, mania, excitement
8 国 *nekkoku* hot country
性 *nessei* earnestness; accompanied by high fever
波 *neppa* heat wave
苦 *atsukuru*(*shii*) sultry, sweltering
9 風 *neppū* fiery-hot wind
屋 *atsu*(*gari*)*ya* person sensitive to heat
度 *netsudo* degree of temperature or enthusiasm
発 *neppatsu*＝発熱 3092.15
単位 *netsu tan-i* heat unit
10 核 *netsukaku* thermonuclear
涙 *netsurui* hot tears
烈 *netsuretsu na* ardent, passionate, vehement
射病 *nesshabyō* sunstroke, heat prostration
病 *netsubyō* fever
病的 *netsubyōteki* feverish
帯 *nettai* torrid zone, tropics
帯性 *nettaisei* tropical
帯林 *nettairin* tropical forest
帯魚 *nettaigyo* tropical fish
11 情 *netsujō* fervor, warmth, ardent love, passion
球 *nekkyū* hot pitch (baseball)
望 *netsubō* fervent hope, longing
12 湯 *nettō* boiling water
量 *netsuryō* heat value, caloric value
13 鬧 *nettō* din, hustle and bustle
源 *netsugen* heat source
誠 *nessei* earnestness, warmth, enthusiasm, devotion, sincerity
愛 *netsuai* ardent love, devotion
意 *netsui* zeal, enthusiasm
感 *nekkan* feverish feeling
戦 *nessen* hot fight, close game
戦争 *atsu*(*i*) *sensō* hot war
14 演 *netsuen* enthusiastic performance
15 線 *netsusen*, *nessen* heat rays; hot wire, infrared (rays)
罵 *netsuba* vehement reproach
16 燗 *atsukan* hot saké
17 療法 *netsu ryōhō* heat therapy
19 願 *netsugan* earnest entreaty
禱 *nettō* fervent prayer

12

燕 See 4070.

谿 谿 See 249.

燒 2798/F1202 See 焼 2772.

燵 2799/F1205 (国字) TATSU a foot-warmer.

A 燈 2800/F1201/F1178 See P 灯 2745.

熾 2801/F1200 SHI burning; flourishing. *oko(ru)* be kindled. *oko(su)* build a fire.
10 烈 *shiretsu* violence, severity, fierceness

燔 2802/F1202 HAN burn.
6 刑 *hankei* burning to death, the stake
11 祭 *hansai* burnt offering

燋 2803/F1201 SHŌ scorch; bonfire.
15 熱 *shōnetsu* scorching heat; scorching
熱地獄 *shōnetsu jigoku* burning hell

燎 2804/F1201 RYŌ burn, bonfire.
4 火 *ryōka* signal fire, bonfire
10 原火 *ryōgen (no) hi* prairie fire, wildfire

燧 2805/F1204 SUI signal fire. *hiuchi* tinder, making a fire (with flint and iron). *hikiri* making a fire (with wood).
5 石 *suiseki, hiuchi ishi* flint
6 臼 *hikiri usu* fire stone
8 杵 *hikirigine* rubbing stick (for making a fire)

燗 2806/F1203 燗 RAN. KAN warming saké. *kan(suru)* heat saké.
7 冷 *kanza(mashi)* leftover warmed saké
10 酒 *kanzake, kanshu* warmed saké
14 徳利 *kandokuri* saké-warming bottle
17 鍋 *kannabe* saké-warming pan

燐 2807/F1201 RIN phosphorus.
3 寸 *matchi* match
4 火 *rinka* phosphorescence
6 光 *rinkō* phosphorescence
9 肥 *rimpi* phosphate manure
14 酸 *rinsan* phosphoric acid

A 燃 2808/F1200 NEN. *mo(su), mo(yasu)* burn. *mo(yuru), mo(eru)* burn, blaze, glow.
3 上 *mo(e)-a(garu)* blaze up, burn up
4 木 *mo(e)gi* firebrand
切 *mo(e)-ki(ru)* burn out, burn up
5 立 *mo(e)-ta(tsu)* blaze up, burn up
付 *mo(e)-tsu(ku)* ignite
出 *mo(e)-da(su)* ignite, begin to burn. *mo(e)-de(ru)* blaze out
6 行 *mo(e)-yu(ku)* burn along, burn up to
8 拡 *mo(e)-hiro(garu)* (fires) spread
杭 *mo(e)gui* half-burnt post
易 *mo(e)yasu(i)* inflammable
9 思 *mo(eru) omo(i)* burning passion
10 残 *mo(e)noko(ri)* embers, something half-burnt
差 *mo(e)sa(shi)* embers, something half-burnt
料 *nenryō* fuel
料廠 *nenryōshō* fuel depot
11 移 *mo(e)-utsu(ru)* catch fire, ignite
崩 *mo(e)-kuzu(reru)* burn up
盛 *mo(e)-saka(ru)* burn fiercely
12 焼 *nenshō* combustion
殻 *mo(e)gara* embers, cinders
焦 *mo(e)-koge(ru)* be charred in a fire
13 滓 *mo(e)kasu* cinders
15 質 *nenshitsu* combustibility
18 難 *mo(e)niku(i)* noninflammable

13

營 See 営 963.

點 2809/F2164 See 点 804. [黑]

B 燥 2810/F1204 SŌ dry up. *kawa(ku), hasha(gu)* vi dry up, parch.

燭 2811/F1205 SOKU, SHOKU light; candle power.
5 台 *shokudai* candlestick, candlestand
6 光 *shokkō* candle power; candlelight

燠 2812/F1204 U. IKU. Ō. *oki* embers, live coals.
4 火 *okibi* blazing fire
13 搔 *okikaki* poker, fire shovel

燦 2813/F1204 SAN brilliance. *san(taru)* brilliant.
12 然 *sanzen* brilliance, radiance
17 燦 *sansan(taru)* brilliant, bright
21 爛 *sanran(taru)* brilliant, bright, radiant

14

燿 2814/F1205 YŌ shine.

燹 2815/F1205 SEN prairie fire; signal fire.

4 心 忄 小 戈 戸 手 扌 支 攴 攵 文 斗 斤 方 无 日 曰 月 木 欠 止 歹 殳 毋 比 毛 氏 气 水 氵 氺 【火 灬】 爪 爫 父 爻 爿 丬 片 牙 牛 犬 犭 14

燼 2816/F1205 Jɪɴ embers.

7 余 *jin-yo* embers; survival

燻 2817/F1197 **熏** Kᴜɴ. *ibu*(*ru*) smolder, fume, smoke. *ibu*(*su*) fumigate; oxidize; smoke (meat). *kusu*(*beru*), *fusu*(*boru*), *kusu*(*boru*), *kuyu*(*ru*) smoke, smolder; get sooty; stay indoors; remain in obscurity. *kusu*(*beru*), *fusu*(*beru*), *kuyu*(*raseru*) smoke, smoke out, fumigate. *ibu*(*shi*) fumigation; oxidation; smoking (meat).

5 出 *ibu*(*shi*)-*da*(*su*) smoke out
6 肉 *kunniku* smoked meat
12 蒸 *kunjō* fumigation
蒸剤 *kunjōzai* fumigant
14 銀 *ibu*(*shi*)*gin* oxidized silver
製 *kunsei* smoking (fish or pork)
製品 *kunseihin* smoked products

— 15 —

爆 2818/F1205 Bᴀᴋᴜ. *ha*(*zeru*) burst open, pop, split.

B
4 心 *bakushin* center of the explosion, epicenter
心地 *bakushinchi* center of the explosion
6 竹 *bakuchiku* firecracker
死 *bakushi* death from bombing
7 沈 *bakuchin* blowing up and sinking
9 音 *bakuon* buzzing, whirr; explosion, detonation
風 *bakufū* bomb blast, shell blast, explosion blast
砕 *bakusai* blasting
発 *bakuhatsu* explosion, blasting
発力 *bakuhatsuryoku* explosive power
発物 *bakuhatsubutsu* explosives
発的 *bakuhatsuteki* explosive
発室 *bakuhatsushitsu* combustion chamber
発信管 *bakuhatsu shinkan* detonating fuse
発管 *bakuhatsukan* detonator
発薬 *bakuhatsuyaku* blasting powder, explosive compound
10 粉 *bakufun* explosive powder
笑 *bakushō* roar of laughter
破 *bakuha* explosion, blasting
破薬 *bakuhayaku* blasting charge
12 弾 *bakudan* bomb
弾投下 *bakudan tōka* bombing
裂 *bakuretsu* explosion, blasting
裂弾 *bakuretsudan* bomb, explosive shell
13 傷 *bakushō* damage from explosion
煙 *bakuen* the smoke of an explosion
雷 *bakurai* depth bomb
14 鳴 *bakumei* detonation
15 撃 *bakugeki* bombing
撃手 *bakugekishu* bombardier
撃行 *bakugekikō* bombing mission
撃照準器 *bakugeki shōjunki* bombsight
撃機 *bakugekiki* bombing plane
16 薬 *bakuyaku* blasting powder, explosive compound

— 16 —

爐 2819/F1206 See **炉** 2750.

— 17 —

爛 2820/F1206 Rᴀɴ. *tada*(*reru*) be sore, be inflamed, be bleary; fester. *tada*(*rakasu*) cause to be inflamed.

5 目 *tada*(*re*)*me* sore eyes, bleary eyes
6 死 *ranshi* burning to death
14 漫 *ramman*(*taru*) glorious, luxuriant, splendid
15 熟 *ranjuku* overripeness; overmaturity; full maturity; mellow ripeness
17 糜 *rambi*=*biran* 糜爛 5395.21
21 爛 *ranran*(*taru*) fiery, glaring, piercing; blazing, flaming; glittering

— 25 —

爨 2821/F1207 Sᴀɴ. *kashi*(*gu*) cook, boil.

RAD. 爪 87

Tsume, nail, claw. At top: 爫 or ⺤ *tsume kammuri* or *no-tsu* (the katakana *no* plus the katakana *tsu*). Nickname: Claw.

爪 2822/F1207 Sō. *tsume* nail, claw, talon, hoof; hook, catch; plectrum.

4 木 *tsumagi* twigs for fuel, brushwood
切 *tsumeki*(*ri*) nail clipper
5 牙 *sōga* teeth and claws; clutches; cat's-paw, tool
立 *tsumada*(*teru*) stand on tiptoe; stretch
6 印 *tsume-in* thumbprint
先 *tsumasaki* tiptoe, tip of the toe
9 革 *tsumakawa* leather toe covers on clogs
音 *tsuma-oto* sound of drumming fingers; sound of a koto; sound of hoofs
紅 *tsumabeni* fingernail polish

11 痕 *tsume ato* scratch; pinch mark
掛 *tsumaga(ke)* toe covers on clogs
12 弾 *tsumebi(ki), tsumabi(ki)* playing a stringed instrument with fingers. *tsumahajiki* flip, fillip; elbowing; ostracism; black sheep
13 跡 *tsume ato* scratch; pinch mark
楊子 *tsumayōji* toothpick
楊枝 *tsumayōji* toothpick
16 磨 *tsumemigaki* nail file; manicure
19 繰 *tsumagu(ru)* to finger

3

B 妥 2823 F495 妥 DA peace; depravity. [女]
6 当 *datō* appropriateness, propriety
当性 *datōsei* propriety, adequacy, pertinence, soundness
8 協 *dakyō* compromise, understanding, agreement
協的 *dakyōteki* compromising
協案 *dakyōan* compromise plan
協策 *dakyōsaku* compromise plan
12 結 *daketsu* an agreement

4

争 See 争 186.

爬 2824 F1208 HA scratch.
6 虫 *hachū* reptile
行 *hakō* creeping, crawling

采 2825 F1928 采 SAI dice; form, appearance. *to(ru)* take. *irodori* coloring. [釆]
5 目 *saime, sai(no)me* dots on dice
6 地 *saichi* fief, domain
7 邑 *saiyū* fief; vassalage
10 配 *saihai* baton of command; duster

A 受 2826 F316 JU receive. *u(keru)* receive, accept, take, get, obtain; catch (a ball); stop (a blow), parry; answer (the phone); undergo (an operation); take (an exam); sustain (a loss); be exposed to (ridicule); face, front on; inherit; catch the public fancy. ***uka(ru)*** pass (an examination). ***u(ke)*** receiving; receptacle; support, prop; (pot) holder; popularity; agreement. [又]
2 入 *u(ke)-i(reru)* accept, receive; assent to, grant
入体制 *u(k)e-i(re) taisei* preparedness (for new personnel), reception set-up (for immigrants)
入態勢 *u(ke)-i(re) taisei*=word above
3 口 *u(ke)guchi, u(ke)kuchi* mouth with protruding lower lip
4 木 *u(ke)gi* a support
止 *u(ke)-to(meru)* stop, catch; parry, ward off
太刀 *u(ke)dachi* defensive position
5 皿 *u(ke)zara* saucer
払 *u(ke)hara(i)* receipts and payments
出 *u(ke)-da(su)* redeem, ransom, buy out, pay off, take out of pawn
付 *u(ke)-tsu(keru)* receive, accept (an application). ***uketsuke*** receipt, acceptance; receptionist; information desk
付係 *uketsukegakari* receptionist, usher
6 肉 *juniku* incarnation
任 *junin suru* be nominated, accept an appointment
合 *u(ke)a(i)* guarantee, assurance
血者 *juketsusha* blood recipient
刑 *jukei suru* serve time
刑者 *jukeisha* convict, convicted person
7 身 *ukemi* being acted upon, passivity, defensive position; passive voice; safe ways to fall
戒 *jukai* Buddhist confirmation, becoming a Buddhist
戻 *u(ke)-modo(su)*=*u(ke)-da(su)* 受出 (see above–5)
売 *ukeu(ri)* retailing; second-hand (knowledge)
8 命 *jumei* commission (of an official)
直 *u(ke)-nao(su)* receive (baptism) again
苦 *Juku* the Passion (of Christ)
苦日 *Jukubi* Good Friday
取 *u(ke)-to(ru)* receive, take delivery, accept; believe; understand, interpret. ***uketori*** receipt, acknowledgement
取人 *uketorinin* recipient, payee
取帳 *uketorichō* receipt book
取済 *uketorizu(mi)* payment received
取証 *uketorishō* receipt, voucher
9 胎 *jutai* conception, fertilization
持 *u(ke)mo(tsu)* take charge of, be in charge of. ***ukemo(chi)*** charge (of something); matter in one's charge
持時間 *ukemo(chi) jikan* teaching hours
信 *jushin* receipt of a message; radio reception
信人 *jushinnin* addressee
信機 *jushinki* receiver
洗 *jusen* baptism (by sprinkling). ***jusen suru*** be baptized
洗者 *jusensha* a person baptized by sprinkling
洗数 *jusensū* number baptized (by sprinkling)
負 *u(ke)-o(u)* contract for, undertake. ***ukeoi*** a contract
負人 *ukeoinin* contractor
負仕事 *ukeoi shigoto* job work, contract work
負師 *ukeoishi* contractor
負賃金 *ukeoi chingin* piecework pay
10 流 *u(ke)-naga(su)* ward off, parry, turn aside
粉 *jufun* pollinization, fertilization
納 *junō* receipt, acceptance

4 心忄⺗戈戸手扌支攴攵文斗斤方无日曰月木欠止歹殳毋比毛氏气水氵氺火灬[爪爫]4 父爻爿丬片牙牛犬犭

託 *jutaku* trust, custody, charge
容 *u(ke)-i(reru), juyō suru* accept
配者 *juhaisha* recipient of rations
益 *jueki suru* benefit by
益者 *juekisha* beneficiary
浸 *jushin suru* be baptized (by immersion)
浸者 *jushinsha* a person baptized by immersion
浸数 *jushinsū* number baptized (by immersion)
11 授 *juju* receiving and giving
理 *juri suru* entertain (an action against), accept, take up (a report)
動 *judō* passiveness, passivity
動的 *judōteki* passive
動態 *judōtai* passive voice
12 検 *juken suru* be subjected to an investigation
訴 *juso* acceptance of a legal suit
診 *jushin* getting a physical examination
答 *u(ke)kota(e)* reply, response
給者 *jukyūsha* pensioner
註 *juchū suru* accept an order
註額 *juchūgaku* volume of orders
渡 *ukewata(shi)* delivery, transfer, payment; give-and-take
渡日 *ukewata(shi)bi* settlement day, delivery day
渡期日 *ukewata(shi) kijitsu* delivery date
13 傷 *jushō suru* get hurt; get wounded
損 *u(ke)-sokona(u)* fail to parry; fail to catch, miss
継 *u(ke)-tsu(gu)* inherit, succeed to, take over
働免疫 *judō men-eki* passive immunity
話器 *juwaki* receiver, headphones
話機 *juwaki* receiver, headphones
14 精 *jusei* fertilization, pollination
膏者 *jukōsha* anointed one
像 *juzō suru* receive TV broadcasts
像機 *juzōki* TV set
領 *juryō* receipt, acceptance
領者 *juryōsha* receiver, recipient
領高 *juryōdaka* amount received, receipts
領書 *juryōsho* receipt
領証 *juryōshō* receipt
15 諾 *judaku* acceptance
賞 *jushō* receiving a prize
賞者 *jushōsha* prize winner
17 講生 *jukōsei* trainee
18 贈 *jusō suru, juzō suru* receive a present
難 *junan* ordeal, trouble, sufferings; the crucifixion
難日 *Junambi* Good Friday
難曲 *junankyoku* passion (a musical composition)
難者 *junansha* sufferer
難週 *Junanshū* Passion Week
難節 *Junansetsu* Lent
難劇 *junangeki* passion play
験 *juken suru* take an examination
験生活 *juken seikatsu* life while preparing for examinations
験者 *jukensha* examinee
験学校 *juken gakkō* preparatory school, a school preparing students for examinations
験科 *jukenka* examination-coaching course
験料 *jukenryō* examination fee
験票 *jukenhyō* examination admission ticket
験資格 *juken shikaku* qualifications for taking an examination
験準備 *juken jumbi* preparing for exams

5

爰 2827 F1208 En. *koko ni* here.

8

爲 2828 F1208 See 138. **為**

9

A **愛** 2829 F731 AI love, affection, favorite. *ai(suru), me(zuru), me(deru)* love; admire, appreciate. *ai(rashii)* lovely, pretty, sweet. *ito(shii)* beloved, dear, loving, pitiable. *mana-* love. [心]

2 人 *aijin* lover; lover of mankind
3 子 *ito(shi)go, aishi* favorite child; beloved child
4 犬 *aiken* pet dog
犬家 *aikenka* dog lover
5 用 *aiyō* habitual use; favorite
他 *aita* altruism
他主義 *aitashugi* altruism
6 好 *aikō* love for, liking for
好者 *aikōsha* lover of
好家 *aikōka* lover of
7 吟 *aigin* favorite poem or song; lover of poetry and song
児 *aiji* beloved child
弟子 *aideshi, manadeshi* favorite pupil
8 育 *ai-iku* tender nurture
妾 *aishō* prostitute
苦 *aikuru(shii)* charming, sweet, cute
妻 *aisai* beloved wife
妻家 *aisaika* devoted husband
国 *aikoku* patriotism
国心 *aikokushin* patriotism
国主義 *aikokushugi* patriotism
国者 *aikokusha* patriot
玩 *aigan suru* be fond of
玩物 *aigambutsu* prized article; pet
玩者 *aigansha* lover, admirer, fancier
玩動物 *aigan dōbutsu* animal pet
10 娘 *manamusume* favorite daughter
孫 *aison* beloved grandchild
称 *aishō* pet name, term of endearment
息 *aisoku* cute boy, beloved son; your son

校心 *aikōshin* love of one's school
党心 *aitōshin* party loyalty; party spirit
書家 *aishoka* booklover
馬 *aiba* favorite horse
馬家 *aibaka* horse lover
郷 *aikyō* local patriotism
郷心 *aikyōshin* local patriotism
11 唱 *aishō suru* love to read
情 *aijō* love, affection
惜 *aiseki suru* miss (someone); be loathe to part
猫 *aibyō* pet cat
欲 *aiyoku* passion, love and lust
執 *aishū* attachment, covetous affection
鳥家 *aichōka* bird lover
球家 *aikyūka* baseball fan
12 婿 *aisei* favorite son-in-law
着 *aichaku, aijaku* attachment, covetous affection
飲家 *ai-inka* habitual drinker
敬 *aikei, aikyō* love and respect; = *aikyō* 愛嬌 (see below–15)
敬笑 *aikyōwara(i)* flattering smile
13 煙家 *aienka* habitual smoker
禽 *aikin* pet bird
禽家 *aikinka* bird lover
想 *aiso, aisō* civility, amiability, courtesy, compliments, entertainment, hospitality, sociability
想尽 *aisozu(kashi), aisōzu(kashi)* alienating (someone)
14 徳 *aitoku* (Christian) charity
憎 *aizō* likes and dislikes, love and hatred, partiality
誦 *aishō suru* love to read
慕 *aibo* love, attachment, adoration
読 *aidoku* reading with pleasure
読者 *aidokusha* reader, subscriber, admirer
読書 *aidokusho* favorite book (of a writer)
15 憫 *aibin* pity, compassion
撫 *aibu suru* love dearly. *aibu* caress
慾 *aiyoku* passion; love; lust
嬌 *aikyō* charm, winsomeness, attractiveness, courtesy
嬌者 *aikyōmono* amicable fellow, funny little fellow
16 嬢 *aijō* beloved daughter
機 *aiki* one's personal plane; one's own camera
餐 *aisan* (Christian) love feast, communion
餐会 *aisankai* (Christian) love feast
20 護 *aigo* protection, tender care
21 顧 *aiko* patronage, favor

— 10 —

孵 See 244. [子]

— 13 —

B 爵 2830 F1209 爵 SHAKU peerage, court rank.
7 位 *shakui* peerage, court rank

— 14 —

爵 2831 F1209 See 爵 2830.

RAD. 父 88

Chichi father. Nickname: Father.

A 父 2832 F1209 父 FU. *chichi* father. *(o)tō(chan)* papa, daddy (juvenile).
3 子 *fushi* father and child
上様 *chichiue sama* your father; my dear father
4 方 *chichikata, tetekata* father's side, male line
日 *Chichi (no) Hi* Father's Day
5 母 *chichihaha, fubo, tete-haha* father and mother
兄 *fukei* parents and older brothers; guardians
兄会 *fukeikai* parents' association
6 老 *furō* elders, the aged
7 君 *chichigimi, fukun* father (polite)
系 *fukei* male line, father's side
系家族 *fukei kazoku* paternal family
9 音 *fuin, fuon* consonant
祖 *fuso* ancestors, forefathers
10 殺 *chichigoro(shi)* patricide
12 御 *tetego, chichigo* your father
無子 *chichina(shi)go* fatherless child
無児 *tetena(shi)go* illegitimate child
14 様 *tōsan, tōsama* papa, daddy, father
15 権 *fuken* paternal rights, paternity
16 親 *chichi oya, tete oya* father
親似 *chichioyani* taking after one's father

— 4 —

斧 2833 F871 FU. *ono* ax, hatchet. [斤]
5 正 *fusei* correction, revision
7 足類 *fusokurui* bivalves
13 鉞 *fuetsu* ax; battle-ax; curtailment

— 6 —

釜 2834 F1941 釜 FU. *kama* kettle, caldron, iron pot; boiler. *kanae* three-legged kettle. [金]
6 糸 *kama ito* floss silk

4 心 小 ⺌ 戈 戸 手 扌 支 攴 攵 文 斗 斤 方 无 日 曰 月 木 欠 止 歹 殳 毋 比 毛 氏 气 水 氵 氺 火 灬 爪 爫 8 [父] 爻 爿 丬 片 牙 牛 犬 犭

9 屋 *kamaya* large-kettle installer
茹 *kama-ude, kamayude* boiling or roasting in a kettle
12 飯 *kamameshi* rice served in the kettle
焚 *kamataki* stoker, fireman
13 煎 *kama-iri* boiling in a kettle; boiling (a criminal) to death
14 鳴 *kamana(ri)* sound of a boiling kettle
15 敷 *kamashi(ki)* kettle rest

— 8 —

爺 2835 / F1210 Yᴀ. *jii, jii(ya)* old man. *jijii* old man, grandpa.
9 臭 *jijikusa(i)* old-mannish

RAD. 爻 89

Majiwaru to mix. Variant: 㸚. Nickname: Double X.

— 5 —

爼 2836 / F1210 / F132 See 俎 441.

— 7 —

爽 See 234.

— 10 —

爾 See 69.

RAD. 爿 90

Hidari kata (a left-hand *kata* "side," to distinguish it from Rad. 91).
Variant: 丬 (3 strokes) *shō hen.* Nickname: Left Side.

— 3 —

B **壯** 2837 / F446 **壮** Sō manhood; prosperity. *saka(n)* prosperous. [士]

2 丁 *sōtei* a young man, an able-bodied youth
3 士 *sōshi* henchman, political bully
大 *sōdai* grandeur, splendor
4 夫 *sōfu* able-bodied man
6 年 *sōnen* the prime of life
行 *sōkō* a grand farewell
行会 *sōkōkai* farewell party
7 言 *sōgen* spirited words
図 *sōto*＝*sōkyo* 壮挙 (see below–10)
快 *sōkai na* stirring, thrilling, exciting
志 *sōshi* ambition, aspiration
8 者 *sōsha* man in his prime
9 途 *sōto* ambitious course
重 *sōchō*＝荘重 3938.9
美 *sōbi* magnificence, grandeur
10 挙 *sōkyo* great undertaking; heroic attempt
烈 *sōretsu na* heroic, brave
11 健 *sōken na* healthy, robust
12 絶 *sōzetsu na* sublime, heroic, magnificent
14 語 *sōgo* bragging, exaggeration
17 厳 *sōgon* solemnity, sublimity, impressiveness, magnificence, majesty
齢 *sōrei* prime of life, around thirty
18 観 *sōkan* grandeur, grand spectacle
19 麗 *sōrei* splendor, grandeur

— 4 —

牀 2838 / F1212 See 床 1503.

A **狀** 2839 / F1223 **状** Jō condition, circumstances; form, appearances; letter. [犬]

8 況 *jōkyō* circumstances
10 挟 *jōbasami* letter file
挿 *jōsa(shi)*＝next word
差 *jōsa(shi)* simple letter file, letter rack
11 袋 *jōbukuro* envelope
12 景 *jōkei* scene; nature and sentiment
13 勢 *jōsei*＝情勢 1714.13
14 態 *jōtai* state of affairs, situation
15 箱 *jōbako* message case

— 7 —

B **將** 2840 / F562 **将** Shō commander, general, admiral. *hata* or, and again. *masa ni* soon, from now on; just about. [寸]

2 几 *shōgi* camp stool, folding stool

3 士 *shōshi* officers and men
7 兵 *shōhei* officers and men
来 *shōrai* future, prospects
来有望 *shōrai-yūbō na* promising
来性 *shōraisei* future, possibilities, prospects
8 卒 *shōsotsu* officers and men
官 *shōkan* general, admiral
9 帥 *shōsui* commander
星 *shōsei* a general
軍 *shōgun* general, commander, shogun
軍家 *shōgunke* the shogunate family
軍職 *shōgunshoku* shogunate, office of the shogun
10 校 *shōkō* commissioned officer
11 略 *shōryaku* generalship
12 棋 *shōgi* chess
棋指 *shōgisashi* chess player
棋倒 *shōgidao(re)* falling one after another in a row
棋盤 *shōgiban* chessboard
15 器 *shōki* capacity for generalship

—— 13 ——

牆 2841/F1212 See 墻 1144.

片 RAD. 91

Migi kata (a right-hand *kata* "side," to distinguish it from Rad. 90) or *kata hen.* Nickname: Right Side.

片 2842/F1212 B HEN *hira* leaf, sheet, petal, flake. *kata-* one (eye, etc.); single (shift, etc.); one-way; one-sided.

1 一方 *kata-ippō*＝*kattahō* 片方 (see below–4)
3 口 *katakuchi* lipped bowl; one side of a story
下 *katasa(gari)*＝肩下 1820.3
刃 *kataha* single-edged (sword)
4 戸 *katado* one-leaf door
方 *katappō, katahō, katakata* one side; one party; the other side; the other party; mate to (a shoe)
片 *hempen* pieces, scraps
辺 *katahoto(ri)* corner, remote rural location
引 *katahi(ki)* flattering some people only
手 *katate* one hand. *katate no* single-handed, one-handed
手仕事 *katate shigoto* side job
手桶 *katate oke* pail
手間 *katadema, katatema* spare time
手落 *katateo(chi)* partiality, unfairness
手業 *katate waza* side job
5 目 *katame* one eye. *mekkachi* one-eyed person
付 *katazu(keru)* put in order; put away; dispose of, solve, finish; marry off, get married. *katazu(ku)* be put in order; be settled, be disposed of; marry (a man)
丘 *kataoka* a hill steeper on one side
田舎 *kata-inaka* backwoods
6 糸 *kata ito* single-strand thread
耳 *katamimi* one ear
帆 *katahō* close-hauled sail
仮名 *katakana, katakanna* the square syllabary
合掌 *kata gasshō* a one-handed gesture of respect
肌 *katahada* one shoulder bared
肌脱 *katahada nu(gu)* bare one shoulder; assist
7 角 *katakado* one corner
貝 *katagai* univalve
足 *kata ashi* one leg; one foot
身 *katami* one side of the body or dress; sliver; slice (of bonito); half (a beef carcass)
里 *katazato* out-of-the-way village
町 *katamachi* town on one side of a road only
言 *hengen* a word, a few words. *katakoto* lisp, babble; one side of a story
言交 *katakotoma(jiri)* lisping, babbling; broken (English)
言隻句 *hengen-sekku* just a word
8 岡 *kataoka* a hill steeper on one side
孤 *kataminashigo* child who has lost one parent
押 *katao(shi)* shoulder-pushing game; pushing from one side only
枝 *kata eda, katae* branches on one side
泣 *katana(ki)* weeping alone
盲 *katameshii* one-eyed person
岩 *hengan* schist
岸 *katagishi* one bank (of a river)
空 *katazora* one part of the sky
9 便 *katadayori, katabin* one-way correspondence
恨 *kata-ura(mi)* hated by one group only
思 *kata-omo(i)* unrequited love
為替 *katagawase* unbalanced exchange
面 *katamen, katatsura, kata-omote* one side, one face
面物 *katamemmono* cloth with pattern on only one side; single-faced phonograph record
10 時 *henji, katatoki* moment, instant. *katatoki mo* even for a moment
流 *katanaga(re)* a shed roof
眠 *katanemu(ri)* nap; light sleeping

脇 *katawaki* the side of the chest; one side, the side; aside
陰 *katakage* shade (of a tree or building); shelter
恋 *katakoi* unrequited love
荷 *katani* one-sided load
息 *kata-iki* gasping for breath
栗粉 *katakuriko* an edible starch (from dog-tooth violet)
11道 *katamichi* one way
掛 *kataka(ke)* hanging on one side; sailing with one sail
眼 *katame* one eye
脚 *kata-ashi* one leg; one foot
隅 *katasumi* nook, corner
務的 *hemmuteki* unilateral
務契約 *hemmu keiyaku* one-sided or unilateral contract
脳 *hennō* (refined) camphor
脳油 *hennōyu* camphor oil
寄 *katayo(ri), katayo(ru)* (see under 偏 511.0)
寄見 *katayo(ri)-mi(ru)* show partiality
側 *katagawa, katakawa* one side
側町 *katakawa machi* one-sided street, one-way street
側通行 *katagawa tsūkō* one-way traffic
側街 *katagawa machi* a road with houses on one side only
12廂 *katabisashi, kata hisashi* single-sloped roof
結 *katamusu(bi)* overhand knot
腕 *kata-ude* one arm; right-hand man
跛 *katachimaba*=*katahō* 片方 (see above–4)
落 *kataoto(shi)* pushing down one side; partiality. *katao(chi)* heavy on one side; preponderance; partiality; one part cut off
番 *kataban* single shift
雲 *hen-un, katagumo* scattered clouds
貿易 *katabōeki* one-way trade, unbalanced trade
割 *katawa(ri)* half. *katawa(re)* fragment; one of the group; the other half; the accomplice
割月 *katawa(re)zuki* crescent moon, half-moon
13寝 *katane* sleeping on the side
意地 *kata-iji na* narrow-minded, uncompromising, stubborn
腹 *katahara* one side (of the body)
腹痛 *katahara-ita(i)* absurd, ridiculous, contemptible
14聞 *katagi(ki)* one-sided information
端 *kata(p)pashi, katahashi* an end, an edge, a side; smattering; fag end; petty official
端者 *katawamono* a cripple, a disabled person
15膝 *katahiza* one knee
輪 *katawa* deformity
影 *hen-ei* glimpse; shadow, sign, speck (of cloud)
膚 *katahada* one side of the body bared
膚脱 *katahada nu(gu)* bare one shoulder; assist
16親 *kata-oya* one parent
頬 *katahō, kataho-o, katahoho* one cheek
17蹇 *kata-izari* crippled in one knee
臂 *katahiji* one elbow
18顔 *katagao* one side of the face, one face
19靡 *katanabi(ki)* being swayed by one side only
21贔屓 *katahiiki* flattering some people only
22聾 *katatsumbo* deaf in one ear
23鱗 *henrin* a (fish) scale; a part, a particle; a glimpse

4

A 版 2843 F1213 HAN printing block or plate; printing; edition, impression; board; label.

4木 *hangi* (printing) block, woodcut, engraving block
元 *hammoto* publisher
5本 *hampon* wood-block book; printed book
6行 *hankō* printing block; publication; stamp
7図 *hanto* dominion, territory
8画 *hanga* woodcut print
9屋 *han-ya* block cutter, stamp or seal engraver
14摺 *hansuri* printing from plates
15権 *hanken* copyright
権法 *hankenhō* copyright law
権侵害 *hanken shingai* copyright infringement
20籍 *hanseki* register of land and people; land and people

8

牋 2844 F1213 See 箋 3404.

牌 2845 F1213 HAI label, signboard; medal. *pai* mahjong playing tiles.

9

牌 See 2845.

牒 2846 F1214 CHŌ label; genealogy; circular. *chō(zu)* circularize, notify.

15

牘 2847 F1214 TOKU letter.

牙 RAD. 92

Kiba tusk or *kiba hen*. Variant: 牙 (5 strokes). Do not confuse with Rad. 71.
Nickname: Tusk.

牙 2848/F1214 **牙** GA. GE. *kiba* tusk, fang, canine tooth, eyetooth.

9保 *gaho* brokerage
城 *gajō* stronghold, inner citadel
12営 *gaei* headquarters camp
15儈 *gakai* broker, agent

2

B **邪** 2849/F1905 **邪** SA. JA injustice, unrighteousness, wickedness. *yokoshima* wickedness, wrong, injustice. [阝]

4心 *jashin* sinister design
5正 *jasei* right and wrong, truth and error
6行 *jakō* going diagonally; wickedness
気 *jaki* miasma, poison, pestilential vapor; malice, evil; a cold
曲 *jakyoku* wickedness, injustice
7見 *jaken* cruelty, hardheartedness; wrong view
8佞 *janei* wickedness and flattery; wicked flatterer
法 *jahō* sorcery, witchcraft; heresy
知 *jachi* perverted talent, cunning, guile
念 *janen* sinister design, evil intention
宗 *jashū* heretical sect, heresy, evil (foreign) religion
宗門 *jashūmon* heretical religion
9神 *jashin* evil deity, false god; demon
飛球 *jahikyū* foul ball
10鬼 *jaki* a devil, imp, evil spirit
険 *jaken* cruelty, hardheartedness
11道 *jadō* evil course; heresy
婬 *ja-in* adultery
推 *jasui* unjust suspicion, distrust
淫 *ja-in* lewdness, immorality
視 *jashi* an evil eye
球 *jakyū* foul ball
欲 *jayoku* carnal desire
教 *jakyō* heresy, paganism, heathenism
悪 *ja-aku* wickedness, viciousness, vice
12揄 *jayu suru* ridicule, tease
雲 *ja-un* ominous clouds
13想 *jasō* wicked person
14説 *jasetsu* heresy
慳 *jaken* cruelty, hardheartedness
慳者 *jakemmono* heartless person
15慾 *jayoku* carnal desire, evil passion
21魔 *jama* hindrance, obstacle, barrier, inconvenience, encumbrance, interference, disturbance
魔立 *jamada(te)* hindrance, interference, disturbance
魔物 *jamamono* obstacle, hindrance, burden; nuisance, a bore
魔者 *jamamono* a person who is in the way

8

B **雅** 2850/F2012 **雅** GA elegance, refined taste. *miya(bita)*, *miya(biyakana)* graceful, refined. [隹]

2人 *gajin* writer, man of taste, dilettante
4文 *gabun* elegant style, classic style
5兄 *gakei* polite word used in addressing a friend in a letter
6号 *gagō* pen name, pseudonym
名 *gamei* ornate name
7言 *gagen* polite expression, refined diction
8味 *gami*=*gachi* 雅致 (see below–10)
9俗 *gazoku* the refined and the vulgar; the classical and the colloquial
客 *gakaku* writer, man of taste, dilettante
10称 *gashō* correct name; elegant name; name of a poem
致 *gachi* artistry, good taste, elegance, grace, artistic effect; gusto
12量 *garyō* magnanimity, generosity, tolerance, liberality, broad-mindedness, capacity
13楽 *gagaku* ceremonial court music
14語 *gago* polite expression, refined diction
歌 *Gaka* Song of Solomon
15趣 *gashu* artistry, elegance, taste
談 *gadan* elite conversation
16懐 *gakai* esthetic sentiment

11

鴉 2851/F2140 A. *karasu* crow, raven. [鳥]

4片 *ahen* opium

RAD. 牛 93

Ushi cow. At left: 牜 *ushi hen.* Nickname: Cow.

牛 2852 / F1215 Go. Gyū beef, cow. *ushi* cattle, cow, bull, ox.
A
2 刀 *gyūtō* butcher knife
3 小屋 *ushigoya* cattle barn
4 方 *ushikata* cattle herder
5 皮 *gyūhi* cowhide
6 羊 *gyūyō* cattle and sheep
耳 *gyūji(ru)* control, lead, command; direct.
肉 *gyūniku* beef ⌊*gyūji* ox ears
肉屋 *gyūnikuya* butcher; butcher shop
7 車 *gyūsha, ushiguruma* oxcart. *gissha* (ancient) cow carriage
8 追 *ushio(i)* cattle herder
使 *ushitsuka(i)* cattle herder
舎 *gyūsha* cow barn, cow shed
歩 *gyūho, ushi (no) ayumi* snail's pace
乳 *gyūnyū* (cow's) milk
乳屋 *gyūnyūya* milkman, milk dealer
9 屋 *gyūya* butcher shop, beef restaurant
疫 *gyūeki* rinderpest, cattle plague
10 馬 *gyūba* horses and cattle
脂 *gyūshi* beef tallow, beef suet
殺 *ushikoro(shi)* slaughterer
部屋 *ushibeya* cow stall
12 痘 *gyūtō* cowpox, vaccine
蛙 *ushigaeru* bullfrog
飯 *gyūmeshi* beef bowl
飲 *gyūin* drinking like a cow
飲馬食 *gyūim-bashoku* gluttony
13 酪 *gyūraku* butter ⌈herd; cattleman
飼 *ushika(i)* raising cattle; cowboy, cow-
蒡 *gobō* burdock ⌈etable dish, sukiyaki
17 鍋 *gyūnabe* popular Japanese beef-and-veg-
糞 *gyūfun* cow manure
19 蠅 *ushibae* warble fly
23 罐 *gyūkan* canned beef

2

牟 See 849.

牝 2853 / F1216 Hin *mesu, men, me-* female.
4 牛 *meushi* cow
犬 *mesu inu, me-inu* female dog, bitch
6 羊 *mehitsuji* ewe
7 牡 *mesu-osu* male and female
8 狐 *megitsune* female fox
11 鹿 *mejika* doe, hind
13 獅子 *mejishi* lioness
19 鶏 *hinkei* hen

3

牢 See 1287.

告 2854 / F344 See 告 900. [口]

牡 2855 / F1217 Bo. *osu, on-, o-* male.
3 山羊 *oyagi* billy goat, he-goat
4 牛 *o-ushi* bull, ox, steer
丹 *botan* tree peony
丹杏 *botankyō* plum
丹刷毛 *botambake* powder puff
丹雪 *botan yuki* large snowflakes
丹餅 *botamochi* glutenous rice cake enclosed ⌊in bean jam
6 羊 *ohitsuji* ram
10 馬 *o-uma* stallion, horse
11 鹿 *ojika* stag, buck
猫 *oneko* tomcat
20 蠣 *kaki* edible oyster
蠣田 *kakida* oyster bed
蠣床 *kakidoko* oyster bed, oyster farm
蠣船 *kakibune* oyster boat
蠣殻 *kakigara* oyster shell

4

牧 2856 / F1217 Boku. *boku(suru)* care for, shepherd, feed. *maki* pasture.
A
2 人 *bokujin* shepherd, herdsman
4 牛 *bokugyū* grazing cattle; pasturing cattle
夫 *bokufu* ranch hand
5 民 *bokumin* governing the people
民官 *bokuminkan* governor of the people
6 地 *bokuchi* pasture land, grazing land
羊 *bokuyō* sheep raising
羊地 *bokuyōchi* pastoral land
羊者 *bokuyōsha* shepherd
羊歌 *bokuyōka* pastoral poem
会 *bokkai* pastoral care
会学 *bokkaigaku* pastoral theology
会祈禱 *bokkai kitō* pastoral prayer
会書簡 *Bokkai Shokan* the Pastoral Epistles
8 者 *bokusha* shepherd, herdsman
9 草 *bokusō, makigusa* grass, pasture
草類 *bokusōrui* pasture grasses
10 馬 *bokuba* grazing horse
畜 *bokuchiku* cattle raising
畜業 *bokuchikugyō* cattle raising
師 *bokushi* pastor, minister, priest

師補 *bokushiho* assistant pastor
師管轄区 *bokushi kankatsuku* parish
師館 *bokushikan* parsonage ⌈pastorate
師職 *bokushishoku* the ministry; orders;
11 野 *bokuya* pasture land, ranch
笛 *bokuteki* shepherd's flute
12 場 *bokujō* stock farm, pasture. *makiba* pasture, grazing land
童 *bokudō* cowboy, shepherd
14 歌 *bokka* pastoral song

A **物** 2857 / F1218 BUTSU. MOTSU. *mono* thing, object, matter; somebody, something, success; reason. *mono no* about, nearly, a matter of. *mono(suru)* do, perform; write (poetry).
2 入 *mono-i(ri)* expenses
力 *butsuryoku* the power of material things; the power of wealth
3 乞 *monogoi* begging
上担保 *butsujō tampo* secured mortgage
干 *monoho(shi)* a frame for drying clothes
干竿 *monoho(shi)zao* clothes-drying pole
干場 *monoho(shi)ba* drying place
4 心 *monogokoro* judgment, discretion. *busshin* matter and mind
分 *monowaka(ri)* understanding
5 申 *monomō(su)* I say; Hello
6 色 *busshoku suru* look for; select
件 *bukken* thing, article
好 *monogono(mi)* fastidiousness. *monozu(ki)* curiosity, eccentricity, whim
交 *bukkō, butsukō* barter
争 *monoaraso(i)* quarreling, rivalry
7 足 *monota(razu), monota(rinai)* unsatisfying; unsatisfactory; something missing
侘 *monowabi(shii)* lonely, comfortless
体 *buttai* body, solid, object, substance. *mottai*＝勿体 743.7
狂 *monoguru(i)* insanity; mad person (in plays). *monoguru(oshii), monoguru(shii), monoguru(washii)* crazy, wild, desperate
別 *monowaka(re)* rupture (of relations)
忘 *monowasu(re)* forgetfulness
売 *mono-u(ri)* peddler, vendor; peddling
忌 *mono-imi* fast, abstinence
言 *mono-i(u)* speak; talk. *mono-i(wazu)* saying nothing; a quiet person; a dumb person. *mono-i(i)* way of speaking; speech, language; dispute; objection
言事 *mono-i(u) koto* speaking ⌈patrol
見 *monomi* sight-seeing; watchtower; scout;
見事 *mono(no)migoto ni* splendidly
見高 *monomidaka(i)* burning with curiosity
見遊山 *monomi yūsan* pleasure-seeking
見櫓 *monomi yagura* watchtower
8 取 *monoto(ri)* thief
怪 *mokke* something unexpected. *mono(no)-ke* specter, evil spirit
性 *bussei* property of matter
怖 *mono-oji* timidity
知 *monoshi(razu)* ignorant person. *monoshi-(ri)*＝物識 (see below–19)
具 *mono(no)gu* weapons, armor
学 *monomana(bi)* learning
事 *monogoto* things, matters ⌈tentious
物 *monomono(shii)* showy, pompous, pre-
物交換 *butsubutsu-kōkan* barter
的 *butteki* material, physical
的損害 *butteki songai* property damage
的資原 *butteki shigen* material resources
的資源 *butteki shigen* material resources
価 *bukka* prices
価水準 *bukka suijun* price level
価安定 *bukka antei* price stabilization
価表 *bukkahyō* price list
価指数 *bukka shisū* price index
価釘付 *bukka kugizu(ke)* pegging of prices
価騰貴 *bukka tōki* rise in prices
9 音 *mono-oto* sound, noise
持 *monomo(chi)* wealthy person
指 *monosashi* ruler, measure, yardstick
珍 *monomezu(rashii)* curious
故 *bukko suru* die; be dead
哀 *mono (no) awa(re)* pathos; esthetic sense. *monoawa(re)* a pity
思 *mono-omo(u)* worry; be buried in grief. *mono-omo(i)* reverie, meditation; anxiety. *mono-omo(washige) na* pensive, medita- ⌊tive
柔 *monoyawa(rakana)* mild, gentle
臭 *monogusa* laziness; idler. *monogusa(na), monogusa(i)* lazy
相飯 *mossōmeshi* prison rations
活論 *bukkatsuron* animism
品 *buppin* goods, article, commodity
品保険 *buppin hoken* property insurance
品税 *buppinzei* commodity tax
10 凄 *monosugo(i)* ghastly, lurid, weird; terrible, tremendous. *monosusama(jii)* dreadful, alarming
恥 *monohazuka(shii)* shy, bashful
陰 *monokage* cover, hiding
案 *monoan(ji)* worry, anxiety
笑 *monowara(i)* laughingstock, joke
差 *monosa(shi)* ruler, measure, yardstick
真似 *monomane, monomanebi* imitating (sounds or gestures)
納 *butsunō* payment in kind
納税 *butsunōzei* tax payment in kind
11 情 *butsujō* public feeling; state of affairs
惜 *mono-o(shimi)* stinginess
淋 *monosabi(shii)* lonely, lonesome, dreary

欲 *butsuyoku* worldly desire
断 *monoda(chi)* fast, abstinence
堅 *monogata(i)* firm, honest, faithful
貨 *bukka* commodities
捨場 *monosuteba* garbage dump
産 *bussan* produce, product
産地 *bussanchi* place of production
産取引所 *bussan torihikijo* commodity exchange
理 *butsuri* natural law; physics
理化学 *butsuri kagaku* physical chemistry; physics and chemistry
理的 *butsuriteki* physical (properties, etc.)
理学 *butsurigaku* physics
理学者 *butsurigakusha* physicist
理論 *butsuriron* materialism
理療法 *butsuri ryōhō* physiotherapy
12越 *monogo(shi) ni* indirectly
税 *butsuzei* tax on goods and possessions
量 *butsuryō* material resources
悲 *monogana(shii)* sad, plaintive, melancholy
覚 *mono-obo(e)* memory
象 *busshō* an object; material phenomena
貰 *monomora(i)* beggar; sty (on the eyelid)
13暗 *monogura(i)* fairly dark
腰 *monogoshi* manner, bearing, demeanor
馴 *monona(reru)* be used to; be skilled; be sophisticated
数 *mono (no) kazu* something of value
新 *monoatara(shii)* something new
置 *mono-oki* storeroom
羨 *mono-uraya(mi)* envy, jealousy
資 *busshi* commodities, resources
14慣 *monona(reru)* be used to; be skilled; be sophisticated
種 *monodane* the fundamental thing
静 *monoshizu(kana)* quiet, still; serene
語 *monogatari* story, legend, romance, narrative. *monogata(ru)* tell, narrate
語劇 *monogatarigeki* melodrama
15論 *butsuron* public discussion, public criticism
憂 *mono-u(i)* (see under 懶 1789.0)
慾 *butsuyoku* worldly desire
質 *busshitsu* matter, substance
質文明 *busshitsu bummei* material civilization
質主義 *busshitsu shugi* materialism
質主義的 *busshitsushugiteki* materialistic
質的 *busshitsuteki* material (things)
質偏重 *busshitsu henchō* materialism
18騒 *bussō na* disturbed, troublous, unsettled, dangerous. *monosawaga(shii)* noisy, boisterous
19識 *monoshi(ri)* extensive knowledge; well-informed person, scholar
20議 *butsugi* public discussion, public criticism

5

B **牲** 2858 F1219 SEI. *ikenie, nie* sacrifice, offering, gift.

牴 2859 F1219 TEI touch.

13触 *teishoku*＝抵触 1878.13

6

A **特** 2860 F1219 TOKU special. *toku ni* especially, particularly.

8大 *tokudai* oversize
上 *tokujō no* finest, highest grade
4火点 *tokkaten* pillbox
5示 *tokuji suru* be distinguished by
功 *tokkō* special efficacy
6色 *tokushoku* characteristic, peculiarity, idiosyncrasy
旨 *tokushi* special consideration
有 *tokuyū* characteristic of, peculiar to
有性 *tokuyūsei* peculiarity
有財産 *tokuyū zaisan* one's separate property
7車 *tokusha* (army) tank
技 *tokugi* special skill, specialty
志 *tokushi* volunteering; zeal; benevolence
志家 *tokushika* volunteer, self-sacrificing person
売 *tokubai* special sale
売日 *tokubaibi* bargain day
別 *tokubetsu* special, extraordinary
別号 *tokubetsugō* special number
別扱 *tokubetsu atsuka(i)* special handling
別列車 *tokubetsu ressha* special train
別急行 *tokubetsu kyūkō* limited express
別席 *tokubetsu seki* reserved seat
8例 *tokurei* special case, exception
使 *tokushi* special envoy, special messenger
性 *tokusei* characteristic, peculiarity
典 *tokuten* special favor, privilege
長 *tokuchō* distinctive feature; stong point, forte, merit
長的 *tokuchōteki* characteristic
効 *tokkō* special efficacy
効薬 *tokkōyaku* specific remedy
命 *tokumei* special appointment
命全権大使 *tokumei zenken taishi* envoy extraordinary and ambassador plenipotentiary
命全権公使 *tokumei zenken kōshi* envoy extraordinary and minister plenipotentiary
定 *tokutei suru* specify
定局 *tokuteikyoku* privately-owned post office
定税 *tokuteizei* differential tax
価 *tokka* special price
価品 *tokkahin* bargain goods
価品売場 *tokkahin uriba* bargain counter
価販売 *tokka hambai* bargain sale

9 級 *tokkyū* extra-special class or grade
点 *tokuten* special favor, privilege
発 *tokuhatsu* special (train)
急 *tokkyū* limited express
科兵 *tokkahei* technical soldier
科隊 *tokkatai* technical corps
約 *tokuyaku* special contract
約店 *tokuyakuten* special agent, chain store
待 *tokutai* special treatment, distinction
待生 *tokutaisei* scholarship student
待券 *tokutaiken* complimentary ticket
派 *tokuha suru* dispatch
派大使 *tokuha taishi* ambassador extraordinary
派使節 *tokuha shisetsu* special envoy, special mission
派員 *tokuha-in* delegate; special correspondent
10 進 *tokushin* special promotion in rank
記 *tokki* special mention
配 *tokuhai* special ration, special dividend, bonus
高 *tokkō* thought-control police
高課 *tokkōka* thought-control police
恵 *tokukei, tokkei* special favor, privilege
恵待遇 *tokkei taigū* preferential treatment
恵税率 *tokkei zeiritsu* preferential tariff
恵関税 *tokkei kanzei* preferential duties
殊 *tokushu na* special, characteristic, typical, individual, unique
殊性 *tokushusei* peculiarity, characteristic
殊学校 *tokushu gakkō* special school
殊飛行 *tokushu hikō* acrobatic flight
殊病 *tokushubyō* peculiar disease
殊部落 *tokushu buraku* an eta community
殊教育 *tokushu kyōiku* education for the handicapped
殊喫茶 *tokushu kissa* cabaret, night club
殊銀行 *tokushu ginkō* chartered bank
殊鋼 *tokushukō* special steel
11 設 *tokusetsu* special installation
務 *tokumu* special duty
務兵 *tokumuhei* special-service soldier
務機関 *tokumu kikan* spying organization
務艦 *tokumukan* special-service vessel
赦 *tokusha* amnesty, special pardon
赦令 *tokusharei* act of amnesty
産 *tokusan* specialty, special product
産地 *tokusanchi* special-product area
産物 *tokusambutsu* special products
産品 *tokusanhin* specialties, special products
異 *tokui* peculiar, unique
異体質 *tokui taishitsu* allergy, idiosyncrasy
異性 *tokuisei* singularity, special characteristics
異質 *tokuishitsu* idiosyncrasy
許 *tokkyo* patent, (company) charter, concession, license, special permission
許庁 *Tokkyochō* Patent Agency
許状 *tokkyojō* charter, special license
許品 *tokkyohin* patented article
許証 *tokkyoshō* letters patent
許権 *tokkyoken* patent
許権使用料 *tokkyoken shiyōryō* royalty
12 等 *tokutō* special grade
報 *tokuhō* news flash
飲街 *tokuingai* red-light district
筆 *tokuhitsu* special mention
筆大書 *tokuhitsu-taisho suru* write in large or red letters
集 *tokushū* special edition; special collection
集号 *tokushūgō* special issue
13 電 *tokuden* special telegram
14 選 *tokusen* special selection; recognition; special make
徴 *tokuchō* distinctive feature
種 *tokudane* exclusive news, scoop. *tokushu* special kind
需 *tokuju* emergency demand
製 *tokusei* special make
15 賞 *tokushō* special commendation; special reward
質 *tokushitsu* characteristic, special quality
権 *tokken* privilege, special rights, prerogative; (civil) liberties; chartered rights
権者 *tokkensha* privileged person
権階級 *tokken kaikyū* privileged classes
16 輯 *tokushū* special edition
薦 *tokusen* specially recommended

7

犀 See 1397.

牽 See 320.

犁 2861 F1221 See 犂 2863.

8

犇 2862 F1221 Hon. *hishi(meku)* clamor; jostle; squeak. *hishi to* firmly, tightly.
12 犇 *hishihishi* tightly, firmly; thick and fast; crowded

犂 2863 F1221 犁 Ri. Rei. Ryū. *suki* plow.
4 牛 *yaku, rigyū* yak
6 先 *sukizaki* plowshare
16 篦 *sukibera* plowshare

10

犒 2864 F1221 Kō. *negira(u)* thank for, reward for.

13

犠 2865 F1222 犧 Gi sacrifice.
B
5 打 *gida* sacrifice hit

9 牲 *gisei* (animal) sacrifice, offering; self-sacrifice
牲打 *giseida* sacrifice hit
牲的 *giseiteki* self-sacrificing
牲者 *giseisha* victim, prey
牲制度 *gisei seido* sacrificial system

15

犢 2866 F1222 Toku. *ko-ushi* calf.

RAD. 犬 94

Inu dog. At left: 犭 (3 strokes) *kemono hen* left-hand "animal." Nickname: Dog.

A **犬** 2868 F1222 Ken dog. *inu* dog; spy. *inu-(koro)* puppy.
3 小屋 *inugoya* kennel
6 死 *inuji(ni) suru* die a dog's death; die in vain
合 *inua(wase)* dog fight; sicking dogs on each other
7 芸 *inugei* dog trick
8 侍 *inuzamurai* depraved samurai
泳 *inuoyogi* dog paddle
舎 *kensha* kennel, doghouse
9 狩 *inuga(ri)* mad-dog hunt; wild-dog hunt
10 馬 *kemba* dog and horse; my humble self
釘 *inukugi* spike
殺 *inukoro(shi)* dog catcher
骨折 *inuboneo(ri)* fruitless effort
11 猫 *inu-neko* dogs and cats
啇 *inushō* dog fancier
12 歯 *kenshi* cuspid, eyetooth, canine tooth
13 掻 *inukaki* dog paddle
猿 *ken-en* dog and monkey; loggerheads
15 潜 *inukuguri* dog's hole in a fence
16 儒 *kenju* a highbrow scholar
儒学派 *kenjugakuha* the Cynics
23 鷲 *inuwashi* golden eagle

2

A **犯** 2869 F1223 Bon. Han offense, crime; counter for criminal offenses. *oka(su)* commit, sin against; violate, break; defy, disregard; attack, assault; seduce, rape.
2 人 *hannin* criminal, offender
6 行 *hankō* crime, offense
8 逆 *hangyaku* defiance of law and morality
9 則 *hansoku* transgression; default
則者 *hansokusha* transgressor; defaulter
13 跡 *hanseki* evidences of a crime
意 *han-i* criminal intent; malice
罪 *hanzai* crime, offense
罪人 *hanzainin* offender, criminal, convict
罪心理 *hanzai shinri* criminal psychology
罪心理学 *hanzai shinrigaku* criminal psychology
罪学 *hanzaigaku* criminology
罪者 *hanzaisha* offender, criminal, convict
罪型 *hanzaigata* criminal type
罪容疑者 *hanzai yōgisha* suspected criminal
罪捜査 *hanzai sōsa* criminal investigation
罪嫌疑者 *hanzai kengisha* suspected criminal

14 鼻褌 *fundoshi* loincloth

16

犧 2867 F1222 See **犠** 2865.

3

状 See 2839.

4

狀 See **状** 2839.

狄 2870 F1225 Teki barbarian.

狆 2871 F1225 Chū. *chin* Pekinese dog, lap dog, Japanese pug, Japanese spaniel. *chin(koro)* puppy.

B **狂** 2872 F1224 Kyō lunatic. *kyō(suru)* go insane; be beside oneself with. *kuru(u)* go insane; lose one's head; run amuck, rave; be madly in love; go haywire, break down; be upset; warp; fluctuate; miss the mark; (winds) howl. *kuru(waseru)*, *kuru-(wakasu)*, *kuru(wasu)* derange, dislocate; drive mad; upset, discomfit, disturb. *fu(reru)* go mad, be crazy. *kuru(i)* madness, insanity; confusion; warp; going wide of the mark; fluctuations. *kuruo(shi)* about crazy. *kuru(washii)* appearing to be crazy. *-kyō* maniac, enthusiast, fan.
2 人 *kyōjin* lunatic, maniac
3 女 *kyōjo* madwoman
4 文 *kyōbun* humorous composition

犬 *kyōken* mad dog
犬病 *kyōkembyō* rabies
5句 *kyōku* comic 17-syllable haiku poem
6回 *kuru(i)-mawa(ru)* rave, run amuck
死 *kyōshi, kuru(i)ji(ni)* death from madness
気 *kyōki* madness, insanity
妄 *kyōbō, kyōmō* crazy
7乱 *kyōran* fury, frenzy, madness
言 *kyōgen* play, drama; program; noh comedy; trick, make-believe
言自殺 *kyōgen jisatsu* faked suicide
言作者 *kyōgen sakusha* dramatist, playwright
言師 *kyōgenshi* noh comedian
8的 *kyōteki* insane; frantic; fanatic
奔 *kyōhon suru* rush around, run wild; bestir oneself
炎 *kyōen* fierce flames
者 *kyōsha* lunatic, maniac
9風 *kyōfū* fierce wind
咲 *kuru(i)za(ki)* off-season flowering
信 *kyōshin* fanaticism
信性 *kyōshinsei* fanaticism
信的 *kyōshinteki* fanatical
信者 *kyōshinsha* fanatic, faddist
12喚 *kuru(i)-wame(ku)* rave
焔 *kyōen* fierce flames
喜 *kyōki* wild joy, ecstasy
13痴 *kyōchi* madness and foolishness
漢 *kyōkan* madman
詩 *kyōshi* humorous Edo poems
夢 *kyōmu* a crazy dream
愚 *kyōgu* madness and foolishness
想 *kyōsō* fantasy, daydream
想曲 *kyōsōkyoku* rhapsody
14歌 *kyōka* comic tanka poem
態 *kyōtai* disgraceful conduct
15暴 *kyōbō* rage, frenzy
17濤 *kyōtō* raging billows
20瀾 *kyōran* raging billows
騰 *kyōtō* sudden jump in stock-market prices
躁 *kyōsō* fury, frenzy; clamor

5

狎 2873 / F1225 Ō. *na(reru)* (see under 馴 5194.0).

狒 2874 / F1226 Hɪ baboon.
8狒 *hihi* baboon

狗 2875 / F1226 Ku pup, dog.
6肉 *kuniku* dog flesh

狛 2876 / F1226 Haku lion-dog shrine guardians. *koma* part of ancient Korea.
4犬 *koma inu* lion-dog (stone) shrine guardians

狙 2877 / F1226 So. *nera(u)* aim at, sight; watch for, shadow, stalk. *nera(i)* aim.
8所 *nera(i)dokoro* target; objective
15澄 *nera(i)-su(masu)* take careful aim
撃 *neraiu(chi), sogeki* shooting, sniping
撃兵 *sogekihei* sniper; marksman

狐 2878 / F1225 Ko. *kitsune* fox.
4火 *kitsunebi* St. Elmo's fire, will-o'-the-wisp
5付 *kitsunetsu(ki)* spirit possession; one possessed by spirits
6色 *kitsune iro* tan, light brown
8狗狸 *kokkuri* Ouija board; table tapping, table tipping
9臭 *wakiga* abnormal underarm odor
10狸 *kori* foxes and badgers, sly fellow; enchantment
格子 *kitsunegōshi* lattice work
12提灯 *kitsune (no) chōchin* St. Elmo's Fire, will-o'-the-wisp; Jack-o'-lantern
13嫁入 *kitsune (no) yome-i(ri)* a line of will-o'-the-wisps; sudden shower during sunshine
14疑 *kogi* doubt, hesitation, indecision

6

狢 2879 / F1227 See **貉** 4480.

哭 2880 / F359 Koku. *nage(ku), na(ku)* cry, weep, wail, moan. *koku(suru)* weep, wail, mourn for. [口]

狡 2881 / F1227 Kō. *zuru(i), kosu(i)* cunning, sly, crafty; niggardly.
6吏 *kōri* crafty official
7兎 *kōto* sly rabbit; swift rabbit
12智 *kōchi* craft, cunning
13猾 *kōkatsu* cunning
15賢 *zurugashiko(i)* crafty, cunning
16獪 *kōkai* cunning, craftiness; sophistication

狭 2882 / F1228 B **狹** Kyō. *seba(meru)* *vt* narrow, contract, reduce. *seba(maru)* *vi* narrow, become narrow, contract. *sema(i)* narrow, small (area), limited, tight. *sa-* honorary prefix.
3小 *kyōshō na* narrow, cramped, limited
山 *sayama* a small mountain
4心症 *kyōshinshō* heart attack, angina pectoris
8門 *sema(ki) mon* narrow gate
苦 *semakuru(shii)* cramped

9 軌 *kyōki* narrow gauge
巷 *kyōkō* narrow streets ⌈baseball)
10 殺 *kyōsatsu suru* run down and put out (in
窄 *kyōsaku* constriction, strangulation
11 過 *semasu(giru)* be too narrow
斜 *kyōsha* red-light district
斜巷 *kyōsha (no) chimata* red-light district
12 間 *hazama* interval; interstice; ravine, glen; loophole (in a castle) ⌈minded
隘 *kyōai na* narrow, cramped; narrow-
量 *kyōryō* narrow-mindedness
13 義 *kyōgi* narrow sense
19 霧 *sagiri* light fog, mist, haze

B **狩** 2883/F1227 SHU. *ka(ru)* hunt. *ka(ri)* hunting; raiding; gathering (mushrooms); viewing (maples).
2 人 *kariudo, karyūdo,* hunter
3 小屋 *ka(ri)goya* hunting lodge
4 犬 *ka(ri) inu* hunting dog
込 *ka(ri)ko(mi)* round-up, arrest
5 矢 *ka(ri)ya* hunter's arrow
立 *ka(ri)-ta(teru)* chase away, hunt out
出 *ka(ri)-da(su)* hunt out, round up
6 衣 *ka(ri)ginu* hunting suit; (ancient) official garb
7 声 *ka(ri)goe* hunters' shouts
11 猟 *shuryō* hunting
猟小屋 *shuryō koya* shooting lodge
猟地 *shuryōchi* hunting grounds
猟会 *shuryōkai* hunting party
猟法 *shuryōhō* game laws
猟免状 *shuryō menjō* hunting license
猟家 *shuryōka* hunter
猟期 *shuryōki* hunting season
猟場 *shuryōjō* game preserve
12 場 *ka(ri)ba* hunting preserve ⌈ing
14 暮 *ka(ri)-kura(su)* spend (one's days) hunt-
20 競 *ka(ri)kura(be), ka(ri)kura* hunting chase

A **独** 2884/F1234 **獨** DOKU alone. *hitori, hitori(botchi)* alone, on one's own. *hitori(deni)* of itself, spontaneously, automatically. *-Doku-* Germany.
1 乙 *Doitsu* Germany
2 力 *dokuryoku* one's own effort
3 口 *hito(ri)guchi* monologue, soliloquy
4 仏 *Doku-Futsu* Germany and France
天下 *hitoritenka, hitoridenka* sole figure, boss of the show, without a rival
天狗 *hitori tengu* conceited person
5 白 *dokuhaku* monologue, soliloquy
占 *dokusen, hitoriji(me)* exclusive possession; monopoly; brushing everyone else aside ⌈prise, a trust
占企業 *dokusen kigyō* monopolistic enter-
占的 *dokusenteki* monopolistic
占事業 *dokusen jigyō* monopolistic enterprise, a trust
占禁止法 *dokusen-kinshihō* antitrust law
立 *dokuritsu* independence, freedom; self-support; separation, isolation. *hitorida(chi)* standing alone, independence
立心 *dokuritsushin* spirit of independence
立主義 *dokuritsu shugi* secessionism, separatism ⌈self-respect
立自尊 *dokuritsu-jison* independence and
立自営 *dokuritsu-jiei* independence and self-support
立国 *dokuritsukoku* independent country
立性 *dokuritsusei* inclination toward independence
立独行 *dokuritsu-dokkō* independence, self-reliance ⌈reliance
立独歩 *dokuritsu-doppo* independence, self-
立祭 *Dokuritsusai* Independence Day
立戦争 *Dokuritsu Sensō* Revolutionary War
立語 *dokuritsugo* an independent word (in
立権 *dokuritsuken* autonomy ⌊a sentence)
6 自 *dokuji no* original, peculiar, characteristic; personal, individual
行 *dokkō* self-reliance; traveling alone
伊 *Doku-I* Germany and Italy
合点 *hitorigatten, hitorigaten* hasty conclu-
7 見 *dokken* private views ⌊sion
言 *dokugen, hitorigoto* soliloquy; monologue
走 *dokusō* running alone; sailing alone
住居 *hitorizumai* living alone ⌊(ships)
吟 *dokugin* solo poem-recitation
決 *hitorigi(me)* on one's own authority
坐 *dokuza* sitting alone
身 *dokushin, hitorimi* single life, celibacy
身者 *dokushinsha* single person
身寮 *dokushinryō* bachelor's quarters
8 居 *dokkyo* solitude, solitary life
往 *dokuō* going one's own way
歩 *hitori-aru(ki)* walking alone; going it alone. *doppo* ambulatory
英 *Doku-Ei* Germany and England
学 *dokugaku* self study
房 *dokubō* solitary cell
房監禁 *dokubō kankin* solitary confinement
9 活 *udo* edible-stem vegetable plant resembling rhubarb
相撲 *hitori zumō* just beating the air
奏 *dokusō* instrumental solo
奏会 *dokusōkai* instrumental recital
10 逸 *Doitsu* Germany
修 *dokushū* studying by oneself
特 *dokutoku* peculiarity, uniqueness
酌 *dokushaku* drinking alone ⌈tion book, key
案内 *hitori annai, dokuannai* self-instruc-

11 得 *dokutoku* peculiarity, uniqueness
唱 *dokushō* vocal solo
唱会 *dokushōkai* vocal recital
眼 *dokugan no* one-eyed
眼龍 *dokuganryū* one-eyed hero
断 *dokudan* arbitrary decision; dogmatism
断専行 *dokudan-senkō* arbitrary action
習 *dokushū* studying by oneself
習書 *dokushūsho* crib, pony
12 善 *hitoriyo(gari), dokuzen,* self-importance, self-conceit, self-complacency, self-gratification ⌈oneself is right
善主義 *dokuzen shugi* a feeling that only
善的 *dokuzenteki* self-righteous, self-com-
創 *dokusō* originality, invention ⌊placent
創力 *dokusōryoku* creative talent, inventive power, originality, initiative
創性 *dokusōsei* originality
創的 *dokusōteki* original, creative
裁 *dokusai* autocracy, dictatorship
裁者 *dokusaisha* autocrat, dictator
裁的 *dokusaiteki* autocratic, dictatorial
裁制 *dokusaisei* dictatorship, autocracy
裁政治 *dokusai seiji* autocracy, dictatorship
13 寝 *hitorine* sleeping alone
禁法 *dokkinhō* antitrust law
楽 *koma* top
楽鼠 *koma nezumi* dancing mouse ⌈alone
14 漕 *dokusō* running alone; (ship) sailing
語 *dokugo* talking to oneself, monologue, soliloquy. *Dokugo* German language
領 *Dokuryō* German possessions
暮 *hitorigu(rashi)* single life, celibacy
舞台 *hitoributai* alone on the stage; monopolizing the stage; one-man show
演 *dokuen* solo recital; solo performance
演会 *dokuenkai* solo recital. solo perfor-
16 稽古 *hitorigeiko* self-education ⌊mance
壇場 *dokudanjō* one's unrivaled field, unchallenged position
擅 *dokusen* doing as one pleases
擅場 *dokusenjō*=*dokudanjō* 独壇場 (see
20 艦 *Dokukan* German warship ⌊above-16)

—— 7 ——

狹 See 狭 2882.

狽 2885/F1229 BAI wolf; be flurried.

狷 2886/F1227 KEN short-tempered.

4 介 *kenkai na* narrow-minded, uncompromising ⌈mising
10 狹 *kenkyō na* narrow-minded, uncompro-

狸 2887/F1228 貍 RI. *tanuki* badger; cunning person.

10 眠 *tanuki nemu(ri)* feigned sleep
11 婆 *tanuki baba* witch, cunning hag
13 寝 *tanukine* feigned sleep
寝入 *tanuki ne-i(ri)* feigned sleep
16 親父 *tanuki oyaji* cunning old man

狼 2888/F1228 RŌ. *ōkami* wolf.

4 火 *rōka* beacon fire
9 星 *Rōsei* Sirius, Dog Star
10 狽 *urota(eru)* get confused, lose one's head. *rōbai* consternation, dismay, panic
狽者 *urotaemono* one easily flustered
13 煙 *rōen, noroshi* signal fire, beacon, rocket
16 燧 *rōsui* beacon fire
17 藉 *rōzeki* confusion, disorder, violence, riot
藉者 *rōzekimono* rioter, ruffian

—— 8 ——

猪 2889/F1231 猪 CHO. *i, inoshishi, shishi* wild boar.

8 口 *choko, choku* saké cup ⌈impudent
口才 *chokozai na, chokusai na* impertinent,
5 牙 *choki* light flat-bottomed rowboat
牙船 *chokibune* light flat-bottomed boat
8 突 *chototsu* recklessness ⌈warrior
武者 *inoshishi musha* daredevil, foolhardly
9 首 *ikubi* bull neck (short and thick)
勇 *choyū* foolhardiness, desperate courage
13 飼 *inoshishika(i)* keeper of wild boars
16 頸 *ikubi* bull neck (short and thick)

猊 2890/F1229 GEI lion; the seat of a famous priest.

3 下 *geika* your highness, your grace, your eminence

猖 2891/F1229 SHŌ storm around; be insane; severe; violence.

15 獗 *shōketsu* rage, violence, fury

猜 2892/F1230 SAI jealousy; doubt.

7 忌 *saiki* envy, jealousy
忌心 *saikishin* envy, jealousy
14 疑 *saigi* suspicion, jealousy and doubt
疑心 *saigishin* suspicion, jealousy and doubt

猫 2893/F1231 BYŌ. *neko* cat.

2 入 *neko-i(razu)* rat poison
5 可愛 *nekokawai(garu)* dote on (children)
6 舌 *nekojita* aversion to hot food
7 車 *nekoguruma* wheelbarrow

足結 *nekoashi musu(bi)* cat's-paw knot
9 背 *nekoze* stoop, round shoulders
10 被 *nekokaburi* hypocrisy, false modesty, feigned innocence; hypocrite; wolf in sheep's clothing
11 族 *byōzoku* cat family
脚 *nekoashi* carved table leg
15 撫声 *nekonadegoe* coaxing voice, insinuating voice
17 糞 *nekobaba* embezzlement, misappropriation

猟 2894 / F1236 = 獵 獵 Ryō shooting, hunting; game, take, bag. *kari* hunting; raiding.
B
2 人 *kariudo, karyūdo, ryōjin* hunter, sportsman
刀 *ryōtō* hunting knife
4 犬 *ryōken, kari inu* hunting dog
6 色 *ryōshoku* lewdness, debauchery
色家 *ryōshokuka* philanderer, lewd person
8 虎 *rakko* sea otter
狗 *ryōku* hunting dog
具 *ryōgu* hunting equipment
季 *ryōki* hunting season
官 *ryōkan* office-seeking
官運動 *ryōkan undō* office-seeking
奇 *ryōki* hunting for the bizarre
奇文学 *ryōki bungaku* bizarre literature
10 師 *ryōshi* hunter
12 場 *ryōba, ryōjō* game preserve, hunting grounds
期 *ryōki* hunting season
14 銃 *ryōjū* shotgun, hunting gun

猛 2895 / F1230 Mō wildness, fierceness; strength. *take(ru)* become furious, rush, rage, rave. *take(ku), mō ni* valiantly, bravely, fiercely.
B
4 火 *mōka* raging flames; heavy gunfire
犬 *mōken* fierce dog
反撃 *mōhangeki* fierce counterattack
5 打 *mōda* slugging (in baseball)
打者 *mōdasha* slugger (in baseball)
打球 *mōdakyū* a hard-hit ball
7 攻 *mōkō* fierce attack
攻撃 *mōkōgeki* fierce attack
8 雨 *mōu* heavy rain, downpour, cloudburst
虎 *mōko* fierce tiger
毒 *mōdoku* deadly poison
者 *mosa* veteran; man of valor
9 威 *mōi* violence, fierceness
勇 *mōyū* bravery
省 *mōsei* serious reflection
10 進 *mōshin suru* dash forward, drive on
将 *mōshō* brave general, brave warrior
射 *mōsha* heavy fire; severe fighting
烈 *mōretsu na* violent, furious, fierce, keen (competition), intense, awful
訓練 *mōkunren* hard training
11 鳥 *mōchō* bird of prey
猛 *takedake(shii)* fierce, ferocious; audacious
悪 *mōaku na* savage, ferocious
運動 *mōundō* frantic efforts; strong lobby
12 然 *mōzen to* fiercely, resolutely, savagely
13 禽 *mōkin* bird of prey
勢 *mōsei* great strength; military strength
14 練習 *mōrenshū* intensive practice
15 撃 *mōgeki* severe blow, fierce attack
16 獣 *mōjū* fierce animal
獣使 *mōjūzuka(i)* wild-animal trainer
獣狩 *mōjūga(ri)* big-game hunting
19 爆 *mōbaku* heavy bombing
22 襲 *mōshū* fierce attack

— 9 —

猴 2896 / F1231 Kō monkey.

猶 2897 / F1232 = 猶 Yū. Yu. *nao* (see under 尚 1361.0).
B
8 子 *yūshi* nephew; another's child considered as one's own
4 予 *yūyo* postponement, grace, extension (of time); reprieve, stay; delay; slackness
予期間 *yūyo kikan* renewal period, period of grace, legal delay, cooling-off period
7 余 *yūyo*＝猶予 (see above–4)

猥 2898 / F1230 Wai obscene. *mida(ra) na* licentious, indecent, lewd. *mida(ri) ni* (see under 妄 288.0). *midari(gamashii)* morally corrupt.
5 本 *waibon* pornographic book
14 雑 *waizatsu* confusion, disorder
15 談 *waidan* indecent talk
17 褻 *waisetsu* obscenity, indecency, licentiousness

猩 2899 / F1231 Shō orangutan.
9 紅熱 *shōkōnetsu* scarlet fever
12 猩 *shōjō* orangutan; heavy drinker
猩木 *shōjōboku* poinsettia
猩草 *shōjōsō* poinsettia
猩緋 *shōjōhi* scarlet

猪 2900 / F1231 See 猪 2889.

献 2901 / F1237 = 獻 Ken, Kon counter for drinks. *sasa(geru), ken(jiru), ken(zuru), tatematsu(ru)* present, dedicate, offer.
B
3 上 *kenjō suru* present to
4 木 *kemboku* donating lumber to a shrine or temple; such donated lumber

5本 *kempon* presentation (copy)
立 *kondate* menu, program, schedule
立表 *kondatehyō* menu
6灯 *kentō* votive light or lantern
7言 *kengen* memorial, petition, proposal
呈 *kentei* presentation
身 *kenshin* devotion, dedication
身的 *kenshinteki* self-sacrificing, devoted
身者 *kenshinsha* dedicated person
8杯 *kempai suru* drink to someone's health
物 *kemmotsu* a present. *sasagemono* offering
金 *kenkin* offering, donation, collection
金者 *kenkinsha* donor
金袋 *kenkimbukuro* offering bags
金箱 *kenkimbako* offertory box
9盃 *kempai suru* drink to someone's health
茶 *kencha* powdered-tea offering
10酌 *kenshaku* offering a drink
貢 *kenkō* paying tribute
納 *kennō* presentation, donation
納地 *kennōchi* dedicated land
納者 *kennōsha* donor
納品 *kennōhin* gift
11堂 *kendō* dedication of a temple or church
堂式 *kendōshiki* dedication ceremony
12詠 *ken-ei* dedication of a poem
策 *kensaku* suggestion, recommendation
替 *kentai suru* assisting a ruler in suppressing evil and upholding good
13酬 *kenshū* exchange of wine-cups
21饌 *kensen* offering to a god

10

獏 2902 / F1786 **貘** BAKU tapir.

猾 2903 / F1232 KATSU crafty.

獅 2904 / F1233 SHI lion. *shishi* lion.

3子 *shishi* lion
子王 *shishiō* king of beasts
子吼 *shishiku* lion's roar; a denouncing speech; oratorical skill
子使 *shishizuka(i)* lion tamer
子鼻 *shishibana, shishi(p)pana* pug nose
子舞 *shishimai* lion-mask dance
子奮迅 *shishi funjin* rushing ahead full tilt

猿 2905 / F1232 EN monkey. *mashira* monkey. *saru* monkey, ape; mimic; sly person; door bolt; fastener.

2人 *enjin* ape man
5芝居 *saru shibai* monkey show
6回 *sarumawa(shi)* monkey trainer
似 *saruni* accidental personal resemblance
8股 *sarumata* undershorts
知恵 *sarujie* shallow cleverness
9面 *sarumen* monkey face
廻 *sarumawa(shi)* monkey trainer
10真似 *sarumane* indiscriminate imitation
11眼 *saru manako* large sunken eyes
12猴 *enkō* long-armed monkey
13楽 *sarugaku* noh-drama prototype
15賢 *sarugashiko(i)* cunning
17臂 *empi* a long arm
18類 *enrui* the apes
22轡 *sarugutsuwa* (mouth) gag

11

B **獄** 2906 / F1233 GOKU prison, jail. *hitoya* prison, jail.

4内 *gokunai* prison interior
中 *gokuchū* in prison, imprisoned
5囚 *gokushū* prisoner
6衣 *gokui* prison uniform
死 *gokushi* death in prison
吏 *gokuri* jailer
8門 *gokumon* prison gates
房 *gokubō* prison cell
卒 *gokusotsu* prison guards; hell's tormenting devils
舎 *gokusha* prison house, jail
9屋 *gokuya* prison, jail
則 *gokusoku* prison regulations
11窓 *gokusō* prison window; prison
道 *gokudō na* brutal, villainous, wicked, dissipated
道者 *gokudōmono* scoundrel, villain, profligate
13裏 *gokuri* inside the prison

12

𤢖 See **猶** 2897.

默 See **黙** 2796. [黑]

獠 2907 / F1234 RYŌ hunting; night hunting.

獗 2908 / F1234 KETSU storm around, be crazy.

B **獸** 2909 / F1237 **獣** JŪ. *kedamono, kemono* animal, beast.

4心 *jūshin* brutal heart
毛 *jūmō* animal hair
5皮 *jūhi* animal skin, hide
6肉 *jūniku* meat, flesh of animals
行 *jūkō* bestiality, assault (on a woman)
7医 *jūi* veterinarian
医学 *jūigaku* veterinary science

医学校 *jūi gakkō* veterinary college
医業 *jūigyō* veterinary practice
[8]性 *jūsei* animal nature, bestiality, brutality
的 *jūteki* brutal, beastly
[9]疫 *jūeki* cattle disease
姦 *jūkan* bestiality
炭 *jūtan* animal charcoal
[10]脂 *jūshi* animal fat, tallow
帯 *jūtai* zodiac
[11]欲 *jūyoku* carnal desire, lust, bestiality
[15]慾 *jūyoku* carnal desire, lust, bestiality
[18]類 *jūrui* beasts, animals

13

獨 2910 F1234 See 独 2884.

獪 2911 F1235 KAI crafty.

獲 2912 F1236 KAKU. *e(ru)*, *u(ru)* (see under 得 1622.0).
B
[8]物 *emono* game, bag, catch, spoils, prize, trophy, booty, prey
[11]得 *kakutoku* acquisition, possession

14

獵 See 猟 2894.

獰 2913 F1236 DŌ, NEI bad.
[11]悪 *dōaku* wickedness, perverseness
猛 *dōmō*, *neimō* ferocity

15

獸 2914 F1237 See 獣 2909.

獵 2915 F1236 See 猟 2894.

16

獵 See 猟 2894.

獻 2916 F1237 See 献 2901.

獺 2917 F1237 DATSU. *uso*, *kawa uso* otter.

5-STROKE RADICALS

RAD. 玄 95

Gen blackness. Nickname: Dark (cf. Rad. 203).

玄 2918 F1238 GEN occultness, mystery, black.
B
[2]人 *kurōto* professional, expert; geisha, prostitute
人筋 *kurōto suji* professionals, the initiated
[5]玄 *gengen* profundity
冬 *gentō* winter
[6]米 *gemmai* unpolished rice, whole-grained rice
米食 *gemmaishoku* unpolished-rice diet
[7]妙 *gemmyō na* abstruse, occult, mysterious, miraculous
[9]風 *gempū* impressiveness, deep feeling, solemnity
[10]孫 *yashago, genson* great-great-grandchild
翁 *gennō* large hammer
[11]黄 *genkō* black and yellow; heaven and earth
理 *genri* abstruse theory, profound mystery
[12]雲 *gen-un* black clouds; India ink
[13]義 *gengi* (Catholic) mystery
[14]徳 *gentoku* mysterious virtue, profound virtue
関 *genkan* porch, entranceway, vestibule, front door
関払 *genkambara(i)* a "not-at-home" dismissal of a guest
関先 *genkansaki* front door, entrance
関番 *genkamban* doorkeeper, janitor

5

玆 2919 F1239 兹 茲 SHI. *koko ni* here.

畜 2920 F1274 CHIKU domesticated fowl and animals. [田]
B
[4]犬 *chikken* keeping a dog
[5]生 *chikushō* beast, brute
生道 *chikushōdō* incest
[8]肥 *chikuhi* animal fertilizer
舎 *chikusha* barns and poultry sheds
[10]殺 *chikusatsu* slaughtering
[11]産 *chikusan* animal husbandry
産業 *chikusangyō* animal husbandry
産業者 *chikusangyōsha* rancher, stock-raiser
[18]類 *chikurui* domestic animals, livestock

— 6 —

率率 See 319.

RAD. 玉 96

Tama jewel. Variant: 王 (4 strokes) ō king. At left: 𤣩 (4 strokes) *tama hen* or *ō hen*. At bottom: 壬 (4 strokes). Nickname: Jewel.

壬 2921 F446 NIN. JIN I, 9th. *mizunoe* 9th calendar sign. [士]

A **王** 2922 F1243 Ō *kimi* king, rule, magnate, baron.

3 土 *ōdo* royal or imperial domain
女 *ōjo* princess
子 *ōji* prince
4 手 *ōte* check, checkmate
水 *ōsui* aqua regia
化 *ōka* imperial influence; assimilation (of new territory)
公 *ōkō* king and princes; noble rank
5 母 *ōbo* king's mother, queen mother; grandmother (polite)
立 *ōritsu* royal
民 *ōmin* king's subject
6 衣 *ōi* royal robes
后 *ōkō* queen
妃 *ōhi* queen
7 佐 *ōsa* helping the king
位 *ōi* the throne, the crown
位回復 *ōi kaifuku* restoration of a ruler
位継承 *ōi keishō* succession to the throne
位継承者 *ōi keishōsha* successor to the throne
8 国 *ōkoku* kingdom, monarchy
法 *ōhō* king's decree
制 *ōsei* monarchical system
命 *ōmei* king's command
者 *ōja, ōsha* king, ruler, monarch, sovereign; royalty
事 *ōji* imperial or royal cause
9 威 *ōi* royal majesty
侯 *ōkō* princes, royalty, crowned heads
城 *ōjō* royal castle
冠 *ōkan* crown, diadem; bottle cap
室 *ōshitsu* ruling family
政 *ōsei* imperial rule, monarchy
政復古 *Ōsei Fukko* Imperial Restoration
政維新 *Ōsei Ishin* Imperial Restoration
10 座 *ōza* throne; God's throne; championship
師 *ōshi* emperor's teacher; imperial army
孫 *ōson* royal grandchild
旅 *ōryo* troops under the emperor's command
都 *ōto* royal capital
家 *ōke* royal family
宮 *ōkyū* royal palace
党 *ōtō* Tories, Royalists
11 道 *ōdō* rule of right; principles of royalty
族 *ōzoku* royalty; royal (family); member of a royal family
12 統 *ōtō* royal line, royal descendants
朝 *ōchō* dynasty
13 業 *ōgyō* rule, rulership
14 旗 *ōki* royal standard
15 権 *ōken* ruling authority, the State
19 覇 *ōha* rulers and usurpers

A **玉** 2923 F1240 GYOKU gem, jewel, precious stone; jade. *tama* ball, bowl, sphere, bulb; lens; gem, jewel; bullet, shot, shell; billiards; tool, cat's-paw; pretty girl; person; margin (in stocks); testicles. *tama-* beautiful; round.

3 子 *tamago* egg; spawn, roe; (an expert) in the making
子泡立器 *tamago-awada(te)ki* eggbeater
子巻 *tamagomaki* meat rolled in thin omelet
子焼 *tamagoyaki* fried eggs; omelet
4 戸 *tamado* a beautiful door; the door of a shrine
什 *gyokujū* your poem
手箱 *tamatebako* Pandora's box; treasured casket
5 目 *tamamoku* pretty (wood) grain
台 *tamadai* billiard table
石 *gyokuseki* gems and stones; wheat and tares. *tama ishi* pebble, boulder
石混交 *gyokuseki-konkō* a mixture of good and bad
石混淆 *gyokuseki-konkō* a mixture of good and bad
6 成 *gyokusei suru* attain perfection
印 *gyokuin* jewel seal
汗 *tama (no) ase* beads of perspiration
虫 *tamamushi* an insect with iridescent wings
虫甲斐絹 *tamamushi kaiki* iridescent silk cloth
虫色 *tamamushi iro* iridescence
7 体 *gyokutai* imperial presence, emperor's person
声 *tama (no) koe* sweet voice, silvery voice; beautiful words
条 *gyokujō* beautiful branches; important rules

串 *tamagushi, tamakushi* Shinto sacred paper-decked *sakaki*-branch offering
[8]杯 *gyokuhai* jade cup
垂 *tamadare* bamboo curtain; palace
歩 *gyokuho* walking (polite)
突 *tamatsu(ki)* billiards
苗 *tamanae* rice sprouts
[9]屋 *tamaya* jeweler, lapidary
垣 *tamagaki* shrine fence
砕 *gyokusai* honorable death, honorable defeat
冠 *gyokkan* jeweled crown; beautiful crown, ceremonial crown
姿 *gyokushi* beautiful figure
砂利 *tama jari* pebbles, gravel
音 *gyokuon* emperor's voice. *gyokuin* voice or sound as clear as a bell
音放送 *gyokuon hōsō* the emperor's broadcast
[10]屑 *gyokusetsu* pulverized jewels; snow; beautiful literature
座 *gyokuza* imperial throne, throne
容 *gyokuyō* beautiful features
[11]疵 *tama (ni) kizu* a flaw in the jewel
転 *tamakoroga(shi)* bowling; roulette; pinball
章 *gyokushō* excellent composition; your letter. *tamazusa* your letter
細工 *tamazaiku* jewelry
[12]詠 *gyokuei* your poem
散 *tamachi(ru)* scatter (like balls); glisten (like light on a sword blade)
筆 *gyokuhitsu* your handwriting
葱 *tamanegi* onion
葉 *gyokuyō* beautiful leaf; the Imperial Family
無 *tamana(shi)* total loss, spoiling
[13]殿 *gyokuden* jeweled palace; beautiful mansion
楼 *gyokurō* a magnificent structure
飾 *tamakaza(ri)* jewelry
蜀黍 *tōmorokoshi* corn, maize
[14]摧 *gyokusai* brave death
緒 *tama(no)o* bead string; thread of life
[15]稿 *gyokkō* your manuscript
盤 *gyokuban* jade dish, beautiful dish
質 *gyokushitsu* beautiful disposition
輦 *gyokuren* imperial carriage
器 *gyokki* jeweled utensil
[17]輿 *tama (no) koshi* jeweled palanquin
[18]髄 *gyokuzui* chalcedony
繭 *tama mayu* dupion cocoon
顔 *gyokugan* beautiful face; emperor's face
顔容 *tama (no) kambase* beautiful face
[19]韻 *gyokuin* your poem
璽 *gyokuji* the seal of a sovereign
簾 *gyokuren* beautiful jeweled blind; blind (polite). *tama sudare* a blind decorated with beads
藻 *tamamo* seaweed
[20]霰 *tama arare* hail
[21]露 *gyokuro* refined green tea

3

弄 2924 / F650 Rō. *ijiku(ru), rō(suru)* play with, trifle with. *iji(ru)* touch, tamper with, play with. *moteaso(bu)* (see under 玩 2925.0). *hineku(ru)* twirl, twist, play with. [廾]

[4]火 *rōka* playing with fire
[6]舌 *rōzetsu* tongue wagging
回 *iji(ri)-mawa(su), hineku(ri)-mawa(su)* twist up, tinker with
[7]言 *rōgen* tongue wagging
[9]廻 *hineku(ri)-mawa(su)* twist up, tinker with
[12]筆 *rōhitsu* writing and twisting the truth

4

玩 2925 / F1244 Gan. *mochiaso(bu), moteaso(bu)* play; take pleasure in; play (on an instrument); play with; make sport of; trifle with (affections).

[7]弄 *ganrō suru* make sport of, toy with, play with
弄物 *ganrōbutsu* plaything, toy
[8]味 *gammi suru* taste, enjoy, appreciate
物 *gambutsu, moteaso(bi)mono* toy, plaything
具 *gangu, omocha* toy
具屋 *omochaya* toy shop
具商 *gangushō* toy shop

5

珀 2926 / F1245 Haku amber.

珂 2927 / F1245 Ka jewel.

玲 2928 / F1245 Rei sound of jewels.

玳 2929 / F1245 / F1252 **瑇** Tai tortoise shell.

[12]瑁 *taimai* tortoise shell

珈 2930 / F1245 Ka ornamental hairpin.

[12]琲 *kōhii* coffee
琲沸 *kohiiwaka(shi)* coffeepot
琲挽 *kōhiihiki* coffee grinder; coffee grinding

玻 2931 / F1245 Ha glass.

[15]璃 *hari* crystal, glass

珊 2932 / F1245 **珊** San stagger; loneliness. *senchi* centimeter.

[13]瑚 *sango* coral
瑚虫 *sangochū* coral insect
瑚海 *Sangokai* Coral Sea

瑚島 *sangotō* coral island
瑚礁 *sangoshō* coral reef

B **珍** 2933 F1246 CHIN rare, curious, strange. *mezura(shigaru)* think (something is) strange. *mezu(rashigatte)* out of curiosity. *mezura(shii)* new, novel, rare, strange, curious, unusual; nice (gift).

4 什 *chinjū* rare article, rare utensil
5 本 *chimpon* rare book
6 気 *mezu(rashi)ge ni* with curiosity
7 妙 *chimmyō* queerness, oddity
8 味 *chimmi* delicacy
物 *chimbutsu* curiosity
奇 *chinki* novelty, curiosity
宝 *chimpō* valuables, treasure
果 *chinka* rare fruit
肴 *chinkō* rare dish
事 *chinji* marvel, rare event
9 柄 *chingara* rare pattern
重 *chinchō suru* prize, value highly
品 *chimpin* curio, rare article
客 *chinkyaku, chinkaku* welcome visitor
10 書 *chinsho* rare book
11 菓 *chinka* rare sweets
現象 *chingenshō* strange phenomenon
12 稀 *chinki* something strange, something rare
貴 *chinki na* curious, valuable
無類 *chimmurui no* queer, singular, unique; phenomenal
14 聞 *chimbun* news, revelation
説 *chinsetsu* novel idea, strange theory
蔵 *chinzō no* treasured (book, etc.)
15 談 *chindan* funny story, anecdote, news, episode, gossip
器 *chinki* rare article
17 糞漢 *chimpunkan* gibberish, jargon, nonsense

6

珞 2934 F1247 RAKU necklace.

B **班** 2935 F1247 HAN corps, unit, squad; party, companions, group; order.

5 田 *handen* ancient farmland allotment
田収授 *handen-shūju* (ancient) government distribution of land
8 長 *hanchō* group leader
9 点 *hanten* spot, speck

B **珠** 2936 F1247 SHU. JU. *tama* gem, jewel.

5 玉 *shugyoku* gem, jewel, jewelry
13 数 *juzu, zuzu* a string of beads; a (Buddhist) rosary
数玉 *juzudama* rosary bead
数繋 *juzutsuna(gi)* tying in a row
数繋囚人 *juzutsuna(gi) (no) shūjin* chain gang
14 算 *shuzan* abacus calculation

珪 2937 F1247 **硅** KEI jade tablet or sceptre (as symbol of authority); silicon.

3 土 *keido* silica, silicon dioxide
4 化木 *keikaboku* petrified wood
木石 *keibokuseki* petrified wood
5 石 *keiseki* silica
8 岩 *keigan* quartzite
9 砂 *keisha* silica; quartz
肺症 *keihaishō* silicosis of the lungs
10 素 *keiso* silicon
14 酸 *keisan* silicic acid

7

琅 2938 F1249 **瑯** RŌ a precious stone.

琉 2939 F1250 RYŪ, RU lapis lazuli.

11 球 *Ryūkyū* the Loochoos
15 璃 *ruri* emerald; lapis lazuli

A **望** 2940 F934 MŌ. BŌ full moon; hope. *nozo(mu)* desire; aspire to; expect, hope for; like, choose; see, command (a view of). *nozo(mashii)* desirable, welcome, advisable. *nozo(mi)* desire, hope, expectation; ambition; prospects; preference. *mochi* full moon. [月]

4 手 *nozo(mi)te* applicant; candidate, aspirant; buyer
月 *mochizuki, bōgetsu* full moon
5 外 *bōgai no* unexpected
6 次第 *nozo(mi) shidai* as desired
7 見 *nozo(mi)-mi(ru)* scan (the scene); look into (the future). *bōken* watching from afar
9 通 *nozo(mi)dō(ri)* as desired
10 郷 *bōkyō* homesickness, nostalgia
12 遠 *bōen-* telescopic
遠写真 *bōenshashin* telephoto
遠鏡 *bōenkyō* telescope, binoculars
13 楼 *bōrō* watchtower
蜀 *bōshoku* insatiability
16 薄 *nozo(mi)usu* little hope

A **球** 2941 F1248 KYŪ globe, sphere, ball; bulb; (radio) tube. *tama* ball, bowl, sphere, bulb.

2 入軸承 *tama-i(re) juku-u(ke)* ball bearing
4 心 *kyūshin* center of a sphere
孔 *kyūkō* golf-green cup
6 団 *kyūdan* baseball team
7 体 *kyūtai* sphere, globe
技 *kyūgi* any game where a ball is used
投 *tamana(ge)* playing ball, playing catch

状 *kyūjō* globular shape
形 *kyūkei* globular form
8 茎 *kyūkei* (plant) bulb
9 速 *kyūsoku* speed of the ball
拾 *tamahiro(i)* caddy; poor ball player
乗 *tamano(ri)* balancing or running on a ball
界 *kyūkai* baseball world
面 *kyūmen* spherical surface
面三角 *kyūmen sankaku* spherical triangle
面三角形 *kyūmen sankakukei* spherical triangle
面三角法 *kyūmen sankakuhō* spherical trigonometry
面幾何学 *kyūmen kikagaku* spherical geometry
10 根 *kyūkon* tuber, bulb, rhizome
11 菜 *tamana* cabbage
12 場 *kyūjō* baseball diamond
13 電 *kyūden* ball lightning
碍子 *tamagaishi* globe insulator
14 算 *tamazan* abacus calculation
窩関節 *kyūka kansetsu* ball-and-socket joint
15 戯 *kyūgi* billiards
審 *kyūshin* baseball umpire

理 2942 F1249 A Ri reason, justice, truth, principle. *kotowari* reason.

4 不尽 *rifujin na* unreasonable, unfair, absurd
化学 *rikagaku* physics and chemistry
5 由 *riyū* reason, cause; pretext, excuse; consideration, motive
外 *rigai no* supernatural; transcendental
6 合 *ria(i)* reason
会 *rikai* understanding
8 非 *rihi* relative merits. *ri(ga)hi(demo)* no matter what happens
屈 *rikutsu*＝理窟 (see below–13)
法 *rihō* law
念 *rinen* idea, ideology
性 *risei* reason, reasoning power
性的 *riseiteki* reasonable
知 *richi* intellect, intelligence
知的 *richiteki* intellectual
事 *riji* director, trustee
事会 *rijikai* board of directors; UN Security Council
事長 *rijichō* board chairman
事国 *rijikoku* member nation (of the United Nations Security Council)
学 *rigaku* physics, physical sciences
学士 *Rigakushi* Bachelor of Science
学者 *rigakusha* physicist, scientist
学界 *rigakukai, rigakkai* scientific world
学博士 *Rigaku Hakushi* Doctor of Science
9 科 *rika* science
神論 *rishinron* deism
10 財 *rizai* economy, finance
財学 *rizaigaku* political economy
財家 *rizaika* financier, economist
容 *riyō* tonsorial art
容学校 *riyō gakkō* barber school
容師 *riyōshi* barber, hairdresser
容業 *riyōgyō* barber and beauty parlor business
12 博 *rihaku* Doctor of Science
無 *warina(i)* no reason for it, nothing can be done about it, terrific
智 *richi* intellect, intelligence
智的 *richiteki na* intellectual
13 詰 *rizu(me)* persuasion, reasoning. *ri (ni) tsu(maru)* be pushed to the wall in an argument
義 *rigi* truth
解 *rikai* understanding, comprehension; appreciation
解力 *rikairyoku* comprehension, understanding
路 *riro* reason, argument
路整然 *riro-seizen toshita* logical
窟 *rikutsu* theory; reason, logic; argument; pretext. *rikutsu(ppoi)* argumentative
窟屋 *rikutsuya* argumentative person
窟責 *rikutsuze(me)* stern and unsympathetic criticism
想 *risō* ideal
想化 *risōka* idealization
想主義 *risō shugi* idealism
想的 *risōteki* ideal
想型 *risōgata* ideal type
想郷 *risōkyō* earthly paradise, utopia
想家 *risōka* idealist
14 髪 *rihatsu* haircutting
髪店 *rihatsuten* barbershop
髪師 *rihatsushi* barber, hairdresser
15 論 *riron* theory
論的 *rironteki* theoretical; argumentative
論家 *rironka* theorist
論闘争 *riron tōsō* public debate

現 2943 F1248 A Gen present, existing, actual. *gen(zu)* reveal; be revealed. *ara(wasu)* show, indicate, display, prove, disclose, express; represent; distinguish oneself. *ara(wareru)* appear, emerge, come in sight, show up; be revealed, be discovered; be mentioned; become famous. *gen ni* actually, really. *utsutsu* reality; reverie; ecstasy, absent-mindedness; vision. *ara(ware)* manifestation, expression. *ara(wa)* (see under 露 5069.0).

2 人神 *arahitogami* the divine present emperor
3 下 *genka* the present time
4 尺 *genshaku* full size
今 *genkon* the present time, today
5 生 *gennama* hard cash
出 *ara(ware)-de(ru)* appear. *genshutsu* appearance, revelation, emergence
用語 *gen-yōgo* living language

世 *gensei, gense, genze, utsu(shi)yo* this present world, this life, this transient world
世的 *genseiteki, genseteki* worldly, secular
世紀 *genseiki* this century
代 *gendai* present age, today, modern times
代人 *gendaijin* moderns
代文 *gendaibun* current style
代化 *gendaika* modernization
代主義 *gendai shugi* modernism
代主義者 *gendai shugisha* modernist
代式 *gendai shiki* modern style
代版 *gendaiban* modern edition
代風 *gendaifū* modern style
代臭 *gendaishū* modernity
代語 *gendaigo* living language, present-day language
代劇 *gendaigeki* modern play
6 米 *gemmai* rice on hand
任 *gennin* present post; incumbent
存 *genson, genzon* living, existing, extant; the Real Presence
有 *gen-yū* existing, present, in actual possession
年度 *gennendo* the present fiscal year
地 *genchi* the actual place. *genchi no* local
地調査 *genchi chōsa* on-the-spot investigation
行 *genkō no* present, existing, current, in force, in operation
行犯 *genkōhan* flagrant crime, crime seen by a policeman
行犯人 *genkō hannin* criminal taken in the act
行法 *genkōhō* existing legislation, present law
行訳 *genkōyaku* the translation now in use
在 *genzai* the present time, now; present tense; actually; the Real Presence
在地 *genzaichi* place where one is now located
在完了 *genzai kanryō* present-perfect tense
在品 *genzaihin* stock on hand
在高 *genzaidaka* amount on hand
在員 *genzai-in* present members
7 身 *genshin, utsu(shi)mi* this mortal body; this present existence. *utsusemi* this mortal body
利 *genri* present profits
兵 *gempei* soldiers at hand
状 *genjō* existing state of affairs, present situation, status quo
状維持 *genjō-iji* preserving the status quo
住 *genjū* present residence; present head priest of a temple
住地 *genjūchi* present address
住所 *genjūsho* present address
役 *gen-eki* active service; commissioned (battleship)
役兵 *gen-ekihei* soldier on active duty
役選手 *gen-eki senshu* active player
8 送 *gensō* sending cash, shipping gold
価 *genka* current price
板 *gemban* the negative
況 *genkyō* present condition
物 *gembutsu, gemmotsu* the actual article
制 *gensei* present system
官 *genkan* present post
金 *genkin* cash, specie, money in hand, down payment. *genkin na* mercenary
金化 *genkinka* cashing (in), converting to cash, liquidating assets
金出納帳 *genkin suitōchō* cashbook
金出納簿 *genkin suitōbo* cashbook
金主義 *genkin shugi* cash policy, mercenariness
金売買 *genkim-baibai* cash sale
実 *genjitsu* actuality, reality
実化 *genjitsuka* realization, materialization
実主義 *genjitsu shugi* realism
実性 *genjitsusei* possibility of being realized
実的 *genjitsuteki* realistic, materialistic, pragmatic, actual, real
実派 *genjitsuha* realists
実界 *genjitsukai* the real world
実暴露 *genjitsu bakuro* disillusionment
9 神 *aragami* present living deity, the present emperor
前 *genzen* before one's eyes
政府 *genseifu* the present government
品 *gempin* the actual articles, stock on hand
品給与 *gempin kyūyo* wages in kind
10 高 *gendaka* present amount
症 *genshō* present symptoms
俸 *gempō* present salary
員 *gen-in* present members
時 *genji* the present time
時代 *genjidai* the present time
11 務 *gemmu* present business
12 然 *genzen to* plainly, distinctly
象 *genshō* phenomenon, occurrence, appearance
場 *gemba, genjō* the scene, the spot. *gemba* the construction site
場不在 *genjō fuzai* absence
場不在証明 *genjō fuzai shōmei* alibi
13 数 *gensū* actual number, effectives
勢 *gensei* present state; present strength
業 *gengyō* outdoor service, field work
業員 *gengyōin* outdoor worker, field worker, operative
14 像 *genzō* developing (a film)
像液 *genzō eki* developing solution
18 職 *genshoku* present position

— 8 —

琵 See 2472.

瑯 See 琅 2938.

琲 2944 / F1251 Hai string of many pearls.

琶 2945 / F1252 Ha, Be lute.

琢 2946 / F1250 Taku polish.

16 磨 *takuma* diligent application

琥 2947 / F1250 Ko jeweled utensil.

9 珀 *kohaku* amber

琺 2948 / F1252 Hō enamel.

13 瑯 *hōrō* enameled ware

瑯質 *hōrōshitsu* (tooth) enamel

琴 2949 / F1251 B Gon. Kin harp. *koto* long horizontal Japanese harp, a koto; lyre. *kinnokoto* a seven-stringed koto.

4 爪 *kotozume* plectrum

6 曲 *kinkyoku* playing on the koto

9 柱 *kotoji* stop, bridge (on musical instruments)

13 瑟 *kinshitsu, kinhitsu* large and small Japanese harps

瑟相和 *kinshitsu aiwa(su)* be happily married

15 線 *kinsen* heartstrings

斑 2950 / F867 Han spot. *buchi, madara, hadare* spots, specks, patches. *fu* spot, speck, speckle, stripe, streak. *mura* unevenness, inequality; blemishes; capriciousness. [文]

2 入 *fui(ri)* spotted, mottled, variegated

4 犬 *madara inu, buchi inu* a spotted dog

5 白 *hampaku* grayish color

6 気 *muraki* uneven temper; whim

7 条 *hanjō* mottled streaks

8 岩 *hangan* porphyry

9 点 *hanten* spot, speck

10 馬 *shima uma* zebra

消 *muragi(e)* snow remaining in spots

紋 *hammon* spot, speck

11 雪 *madara yuki, hadare yuki* snow remaining in spots

15 蝶 *madarachō* monarch butterfly

9

瑇 2951 / F1252 See 玳 2929.

瑙 2952 / F1253 Nō agate, onyx.

瑟 2953 / F1254 Shitsu large koto.

瑯 琅 2954 / F1249 Rō a jewel.

瑁 瑁 2955 / F1252 Mai ancient Chinese imperial jewels.

瑚 瑚 2956 / F1253 Ko, Go ancestral-offering receptacle.

瑜 2957 / F1253 Yu a jewel.

7 伽 *Yuga* Yoga

伽行者 *Yuga gyōsha* a Yogi

瑕 2958 / F1253 Ka. *kizu* flaw; weak point. *ara* defect, flaw, blemish.

11 疵 *kashi* flaw, defect, blemish

15 瑾 *kakin* flaw, defect, blemish, stain

瑞 2959 / F1253 Zui congratulations.

6 気 *zuiki* good omen

兆 *zuichō* good omen

9 相 *zuisō* good omen

10 祥 *zuishō* good omen

11 鳥 *zuichō* a bird of good omen

12 雲 *zuiun* auspicious clouds

13 瑞 *mizumizu(shii)* young and vivacious

夢 *zuimu* auspicious dream

15 穂 *mizuho* new heads of rice

穂国 *Mizuho(no)kuni* Japan, the Land of Abundant Rice

聖 聖 2960 / F1522 A Shō, Sei saint; sage; great master; holiness, sacredness, holy. *hijiri* high-ranking priest; emperor; sage; saint; a master. *sei(naru)* holy, sacred. *sei (to) suru* keep holy. *sei-* holy. [耳]

2 人 *shōnin, seijin* sage, saint, holy man, great religious leader

3 土 *seido* sacred place

山 *seizan* sacred mountain, holy mountain

上 *seijō* the emperor

4 日 *seijitsu* the sacred sun; a holy day; the Sabbath, the Lord's Day

水 *seisui* holy water

火 *seika* sacred fire, sacred torch

王 *seiō* the emperor (polite); a wise and virtuous emperor

化 *seika* sanctification

天子 *seitenshi* wise and virtuous emperor

公会 *Seikōkai* Anglican Church, Episcopalian Church

5 母 *Seibo* the emperor's mother; a sage's mother; the Virgin Mary

句 *seiku* Bible verse

史 *seishi* sacred history

代 *seidai* glorious reign

主 *seishu*=*seiō* 聖王 (see above–4)
世 *seisei* glorious reign
礼典 *seireiten* sacraments
6伝 *seiden* (Catholic) tradition
地 *seichi* Holy Land; sacred ground
会 *seikai* sacred assembly, church
旨 *seishi* the imperial will
年 *seinen* holy year
名 *Seimei* (God's) Holy Name
7体 *seitai* eucharist, host
沢 *seitaku* imperial favor
別 *seibetsu* consecration; sanctification
君 *seikun* a virtuous emperor
寿 *seiju* the emperor's age
8性 *seisei* sanctity, sacredness
所 *seijo* sanctuary, temple; holy place
明 *seimei* a polite word used in addressing the emperor
油 *seiyu* holy oil
河 *seiga* sacred river
夜 *seiya* the holy night; the night Christ was born
典 *seiten* a sage's writings, the sacred books of a religion; the Bible, the Scriptures; rites, sacraments
学 *seigaku* learning of the sages; Confucianism
者 *shōja, seija* saint, holy man; Holy One
画像 *seigazō* icon
金曜日 *Seikin-yōbi* Good Friday
9約 *seiyaku* covenant
勅 *seichoku* imperial rescript
帝 *seitei* a virtuous emperor
10週 *Seishū* Holy Week
峰 *seihō* sacred peak
徒 *seito* saint, disciple
訓 *seikun* sacred teachings
都 *Seito* the Holy City, Jerusalem
哲 *seitetsu* sage, wise man
恩 *seion* imperial favor
座宣言 *seiza sengen* ex-cathedra
骨 *seikotsu* sacred bones
骨匣 *seikotsukō* reliquary
書 *Seisho* Bible, Scriptures
書上 *Seishojō no* Biblical
書朗読 *Seisho rōdoku* Scripture reading
11運 *seiun* fortunes of the emperor
域 *sei-iki* sacred precincts
経 *seikei* canon of scripture; a sage's writing
教 *seikyō* sacred teachings; Christianity; the teachings of the saints
断 *seidan* imperial decision
堂 *seidō* Confucian temple; temple; sanctuary
道 *shōdō* the holy path (of Buddhism)
道門 *shōdōmon* (Buddhist) doctrine of salvation by works
12湖 *seiko* sacred lake
詔 *seishō* imperial command
雄 *seiyū* holy man, hero saint
遺物 *sei-ibutsu* religious relic
晩餐 *Seibansan* the Lord's Supper, Holy Communion
13跡 *seiseki*=聖蹟 (see below–18)
戦 *seisen* holy war, crusade
意 *sei-i* the imperial will; the will of a sage; the will of God
楽 *seigaku* sacred music
業 *seigyō* sacred work; imperial achievements
14聞 *seibun* imperial knowledge
像 *seizō* sacred image; icon; the image of a saint; an image of Confucius
徳 *seitoku* virtues; the emperor's virtues
算 *seisan* the emperor's age
歌 *seika* sacred song, hymn, chant
歌隊 *Seikatai* choir
歌隊長 *seikataichō* choirmaster
歌集 *seikashū* hymnal
15廟 *seibyō* Confucian temple
慮 *seiryo* imperial wishes
潔 *seiketsu* holiness, sacredness; purification; sanctification
霊 *Seirei* Holy Spirit
賢 *seiken* the sages and saints
駕 *seiga* imperial carriage
器 *seiki* consecrated utensil, sacred vessel
誕祭 *Seitansai* Christmas
誕節 *Seitansetsu* Christmas
16壇 *seidan* altar, pulpit
諭 *seiyu* the emperor's wisdom
覧 *seiran suru* (the emperor) observes
餐 *Seisan* Holy Communion; Eucharist
餐式 *Seisanshiki* Holy Communion, Lord's Supper, the Sacrament, Eucharist
17聴 *seichō* (the emperor) listens
18蹟 *seiseki* a spot honored by the imperial presence
職 *seishoku* ministry, clergy, holy orders
職者 *seishokusha* minister, clergyman
職席 *seishokuseki* chancel
職授与 *seishoku juyo* investiture
19寵 *seihō* grace
譚曲 *seitankyoku* oratorio

— 10 —

璃 See 2967.

瑳 2961 / F1255 SA polish.

瑱 2962 / F1255 TEN ear decoration.

瑪 2963 / F1254 ME agate, onyx.

13瑙 *menō* agate

瑰 2964 F1254 KAI strange.
11偉 *kai-i*＝魁偉 5277.11

瑠 2965 F1254 RU lapis lazuli.
15璃 *ruri* lapis lazuli
璃色 *ruri iro* ultramarine, bright blue

瑣 2966 F1254 SA small; chain.
5末 *samatsu na* trivial, trifling
8事 *saji* a trifle; something petty
11細 *sasai na* trivial, small, petty
14瑣 *sasa(taru)* trivial, insignificant; tedious

11

瑠 See 2965.

璃 2967 F1255 RI lapis lazuli.

瑾 2968 F1255 KIN a jewel.

13

璧 2969 F1256 HEKI. *tama* (see under 球 2941.0).

B **環** 2970 F1256 **環** KAN ring. *wa* circle, ring, link, wheel, hoop, loop. *tamaki* circle, ring.
7状 *kanjō* ring, loop, circle
状線 *kanjōsen* loop line, belt line
9指 *kanshi* ring finger
海 *kankai* surrounding seas. *kankai no* sea-girt
11視 *kanshi* concentrated attention
13節 *kansetsu* segment (of a worm)
14境 *kankyō* environment, circumstances
境悪 *kankyōaku* unfavorable external developments
17礁 *kanshō* atoll

14

璽 See 71.

環 See **環** 2970.

16

瓏 2971 F1257 RŌ clarity; sound of jewels.

17

瓔 2972 F1257 YŌ, EI jeweled necklace.
10珞 *yōraku* necklace, hanging temple decorations

RAD. 瓜 97

Uri melon. Nickname: Melon.

瓜 2973 F1258 KA. *uri* melon.
5田 *kaden* melon patch
6虫 *tentōmushi* ladybug
8実顔 *urizanegao* oval face; classic face
10核顔 *urizanegao* oval face, classic face
18箪 *hyōtan* gourd, bottle gourd
箪鯰 *hyōtan namazu* slippery fellow

6

瓠 2974 F1258 KO. *hisago* gourd.

11

瓢 2975 F1259 BYŌ. HYŌ *hisago* gourd.

14

瓣 2976 F1259 See 弁 845.

RAD. 瓦 98

Kawara tile. As enclosure: 瓦. Nickname: Tile.

瓦 2977 F1259 GA. *kawara* tile. *guramu* gram.
[5]石 *gaseki* tiles and stones; worthless things; rubble; rubbish
[6]全 *gazen* mediocre life
[8]版 *kawaraban* printing from impressions on baked tiles
[9]屋 *kawaraya* tiler; tilemaker
屋根 *kawara yane* tiled roof
[10]家 *kawaraya* tile-roofed house
[12]焼 *kawaraya(ki)* tilemaking; tilemaker
斯 *gasu* gas
葺 *kawarabuki* tile roofing
落 *gara* stock-market slump
落落 *garao(chi)* stock-market slump, crash
[13]解 *gakai* collapse, overthrow, fall, breakdown
[18]職 *kawarashoku* tiler; tile maker
[20]礫 *gareki* rubble; rubbish

2

瓧 2978 F1260 (国字) *dekaguramu* decagram, 10 grams.

3

瓩 2979 F1260 (国字) *kiroguramu* kilogram, 1000 grams.

4

瓰 2980 F1260 (国字) *deshiguramu* decigram, $\frac{1}{10}$ gram.

瓱 2981 F1260 (国字) *miriguramu* milligram, $\frac{1}{1000}$ gram.

6

瓷 2982 F1260 SHI high-quality porcelain.

瓸 2983 F1260 (国字) *hekutoguramu* hectogram, 100 grams.

瓶 2984 F1260 =甁 HEI, BIN bottle, vial, jar, flask. *kame* jar, jug, vat, urn, vase.
[13]詰 *binzume* bottling; canning in jars

8

甁 See 瓶 2984.

9

甅 2985 F1261 (国字) *senchiguramu* centigram, $\frac{1}{100}$ gram.

甃 2986 F1260 SHŪ. *shikigawara* floor tile.
[5]石 *shiki-ishi*=敷石 2059.5

10

甍 See 4046.

11

甎 2987 F1261 F1350 See 磚 3219.

13

甕 See 335.

RAD. 甘 99

Amai sweet. Nickname: Sweet.

B 甘 2988 F1262 KAN. *ama(eru)*, *ama(ttareru)* presume upon, take advantage of; coax. *ama(nzuru)*, *ama(njiru)* be content with, be resigned to. *ama(yakasu)* pamper, be indulgent, coddle. *ama(i)* sweet; honeyed (words); lenient; half-witted; easy-going; soft, mild; loose; trashy, sentimental. *ama(ttarui)* sugary, sentimental. *uma(i)* (see under 旨 752.0). *ama-* sugared, sweet; slightly salted.
[3]口 *amakuchi* sweet flavor; mildness; sweet tooth; flattery; stupidity. *umakuchi* clever talking
子 *ama(ttarek)ko* spoiled child
[4]心 *kanshin* satisfaction
井 *kansei* excellent well

6死 *kanshi suru* die happily
7言 *kangen* flattery, blarney
汞 *kankō* calomel, mercurous chloride
8雨 *kan-u* refreshing rain
受 *kanju suru* submit to, put up with
苦 *kanku* joys and sorrows, ups and downs
味 *kammi, amami* sweetness, lusciousness
味料 *kammiryō* sweetening ingredients
9泉 *kansen* spring of excellent water
美 *kambi* sweetness
草 *kanzō* licorice
茶 *amacha* hydrangea tea
海苔 *amanori* purple laver, an edible sea-weed
10酒 *amazake* sweet saké
党 *amatō* person with a sweet tooth
栗 *amaguri* broiled sweet chestnuts
納豆 *amanattō* sweet red-bean candy
12煮 *amani* sweet cooking
13塩 *amajio* slightly salted
辞 *kanji* clever speech; flattery
夢 *kammu* pleasant dreams
14酸 *kansan* sweets and bitters, pains and pleasures
蔗 *kansho, kansha, satōkibi* sugar cane
蔗糖 *kanshotō* cane sugar, sucrose
17藍 *kanran* cabbage
薯 *kansho* sweet potato
19藷 *satsuma imo, kansho* sweet potato
21露 *kanro* nectar, sweetness
露水 *kanrosui* syrup, nectar, sweetened water

— 4 —

甚 See 111.

B 某 2989/F963 Bō one, a certain; that person; that thing. *nanigashi* somebody, a certain person; a certain amount. *soregashi* somebody, a certain person; I. [木]
4月 *bōgetsu* a certain month
氏 *bōshi* a certain person
6地 *bōchi* a certain piece of land
8所 *bōsho* a certain place

— 6 —

甛 2990/F1263 See 甜 3859.

— 8 —

甞 See 嘗 1369.

RAD. 生 100

Umareru to be born. Nickname: Birth.

A 生 2991/F1263 Shō, Sei birth; life, existence, living; subsistence; student. *ha(eru)* grow, spring up; cut (teeth). *ha(yasu)* grow, cultivate, wear (a beard). *i(kasu)* revive, resuscitate; restore to life; let live, spare a life; make the most of; give life to; stet. *i(keru)* keep alive; arrange flowers (in a vase); living (adj.). *i(kiru)* live, subsist, exist; be enlivened; stet; be safe (on first). *na(rasu)* cause to bear (fruit). *na(ru)* grow (on a plant), bear (fruit). *na(su)* bear (a child). *shō(jiru), shō(zuru)* produce, yield, create, give rise to, bear, breed; happen, result from. *uma(reru)* be born. *u(mu)* (see under 産 3354.0). *nama* raw, uncooked, fresh; unripe; half-boiled; rare; hard cash; impertinent, conceited; inexperienced; (beer) on tap; crude (rubber), unprocessed. *i(ki)* living; freshness; stetting. *u(mare)* birth, origin, lineage; birthplace. *u(mi)* childbirth, bearing a child. *-fu* grassy place; woods. *ki-* pure, undiluted, genuine; raw, crude.
1一本 *ki-ippon no* pure, unadulterated; simple, honest
2人形 *i(ki) ningyō* lifelike doll, living doll
3子 *namako* ore, bullion, pig, corrugated sheet iron. *u(mino)ko* a mother's own child. *na(sanu)ko* stepchild; adopted child
干 *namabi, namabo(shi)* half-dried
上 *o(i)-nobo(ru), ha(e)-a(garu), o(i)-a(garu)* grow
4方 *i(ki)kata* way of life, how to live
水 *nama mizu* unboiled water
火 *i(ke)bi* banked fire
爪 *namazume* the quick (of fingernails)
仏 *i(ki)botoke* a living Buddha; an incarnation of Buddha; a virtuous priest
分 *shōbun* nature, disposition
欠伸 *nama akubi* slight yawn
化学 *seikagaku* biochemistry
木 *namaki* a living tree; unseasoned wood
木綿 *kimomen* unbleached cotton cloth
5母 *seibo* one's real mother
瓜 *kyūri* cucumber
生 *sei-sei* lively, vividly. *namanama(shii)* green, fresh, raw; unripe; still warm (game birds, etc.); reeking (of blood). *i(ki)-i(ki) toshita* lively, vivid, graphic
白 *namajiro(i), namatchiro(i)* pale, wan

皮 *kigawa, namakawa* raw hides, pelts
目 *i(ki)me* hope of living
付 *u(mare)-tsu(ku)* be endowed with. *u(mi)-tsu(keru)* give birth to, lay, deposit, spawn *u(maremo)tsu(kanu)* not congenital. *u(mare)tsu(ki)* nature, character, disposition; by nature, naturally
写 *i(ki)utsu(shi), shōutsu(shi)* close resem-
台 *u(mi)dai* birthstool ⌊blance
乍 *i(ki)naga(ra)* alive. *u(mare)naga(ra)* by nature, naturally
出 *u(mi)-da(su)* bring forth, yield, produce; give birth to. *u(mi)-de(ru)* be born. *ha-(e)-de(ru)* sprout, come up. *u(mare)-de(ru)* be born. *o(i)-ide(ru)* grow up
民 *seimin* the people, subjects
半可 *namahanka na* superficial, half-baked
石灰 *ki-ishibai, kisekkai, seisekkai* quicklime
甲斐 *i(ki)gai* (something) worth living (for)
立 *u(mi)ta(te)* newly laid, fresh (eggs). *uma(re)-ta(te)* newborn. *oita(chi)* early days, childhood; antecedents; personal history, growing up
立地 *oita(chi) (no) chi* birthplace
6 米 *namagome* uncooked rice
糸 *ki-ito* raw silk thread
肉 *seiniku* fresh meat
色 *seishoku* animated look, energetic ap-
血 *ikichi* lifeblood ⌊pearance
行 *o(i)-yu(ku)* grow gradually
成 *seisei* creation, formation, generation
気 *seiki* animation, life, spirit, vitality
仲 *na(sanu)naka* no blood relationship
先 *o(i)saki* future career, remaining years
字引 *i(ki) jibiki* walking dictionary, living
如来 *i(ki) nyorai* living Buddha ⌊dictionary
地 *seichi* birthplace. *kiji* one's true colors; ground; body (of porcelain); cloth, suiting
地獄 *i(ki) jigoku* hell on earth, a living hell
合 *u(mare)-a(waseru)* be born at the same time ⌈conclusion
合点 *namagaten* premature judgment, hasty
年 *u(mare)doshi, seinen* year of birth; age. *shōnen* the years of one's life, age
年月日 *seinengappi* date of birth
死 *seishi, i(ki)shi(ni), shōshi, shōji* life or death, life and death ⌈ter
死問題 *seishi mondai* life-and-death mat-
死統計 *seishi tōkei* vital statistics
返 *i(ki)-kae(rasu)* revive, resuscitate; bring to life. *i(ki)-kae(ru)* revive, be resuscitated, come to life
返事 *nama henji* vague answer
返辞 *nama henji* vague answer

存 *i(ki)-naga(raeru)*＝生長 (see below–8). *seizon* existence, being, life, survival
存中 *seizonchū* during one's lifetime
存者 *seizonsha* survivor
存権 *seizonken* right to live
存競争 *seizon kyōsō* struggle for existence
7 身 *i(ki)mi, namami* living flesh, flesh and blood, the quick; raw meat, raw fish
抜 *ha(e)nu(ki)* native-born
肝 *i(ki)gimo* liver of a living animal
別 *i(ki)waka(re), seibetsu* lifelong separation
更 *o(i)-kawa(ru)* change as one grows older
花 *i(ke)bana* flower arrangement. *seika* flower arrangement; natural flower
良 *iki (no) i(i)* lively, fresh
来 *shōrai no, seirai no* natural, innate, inborn. *seirai* by nature, naturally, by birth
呑込 *namanomiko(mi)* incomplete understanding ⌈of knowledge
兵法 *namabyōhō* crude tactics; smattering
体 *seitai* living body
体学 *seitaigaku* somatology
体解剖 *seitai kaibō* vivisection
8 長 *i(ki)-naga(raeru)* live on, enjoy longevity; survive (a disaster); outlive (someone). *seichō* growth; increment
国 *shōkoku* one's native country or province
延 *i(ki)-no(biru)* live long, outlive (someone), survive (a disaster)
拡 *i(ki)-hiro(garu)* grow luxuriantly
限 *i(kiru) kagi(ri)* as long as life continues
育 *ha(e)-soda(tsu)* (flowers) spring up. *seiiku* growth, development; birth and breeding
直 *kisugu na* gentle and straightforward
易 *namayasa(shii)* easy, simple
若 *namawaka(i)* young, green ⌈ail
苦 *u(mi) (no) kuru(shimi)* birth pangs, trav-
茂 *o(i)-shi(geru)* grow luxuriantly
者 *shōja* living beings. *seisha* living person
味噌 *namamiso* uncooked bean paste
学者 *nama gakusha* dilettante, smatterer
学問 *nama gakumon* superficial knowledge
命 *seimei* life; soul
命保険 *seimei hoken* life insurance
命線 *seimeisen* lifeline
物 *i(ki)mono, seibutsu* living creature, life. *na(ri)mono* farm products. *namamono* uncooked food, raw fish, unbaked pastry
物地理学 *seibutsu chirigaku* biological ge-
物学 *seibutsugaku* biology ⌊ography
物物理学 *seibutsu butsurigaku* biophysics
物界 *seibutsukai* plants and animals, animate creation, life
9 面 *seimen* new field; first meeting
首 *nama kubi* freshly-severed head

保 *seiho* life insurance
垣 *i(ke)gaki* hedge
後 *seigo* after birth
枯 *namaga(re)* not quite dead (vegetation)
洲 *i(ke)su* (restaurant) fish tank
胆 *i(ki)gimo* liver of a living animal
変 *ha(e)-ka(waru)* grow up in place of previous vegetation; molt. *u(mare)-ka(waru)* be born again; be regenerated; transmigrate, be incarnated; start life anew. *u(mare)ka(wari)* new birth; rebirth, transmigration, incarnation, reincarnation
前 *seizen* during one's lifetime; lifetime
茹 *namayu(de)* half-boiled ⌈home
故郷 *u(mare) kokyō* birthplace; ancestral
神 *i(ki)gami* a god in human form, a living god ⌈living god
神様 *i(ki)gamisama* a god in human form, a
計 *seikei* livelihood, living
計費 *seikeihi* living costs
臭 *namagusa(i)* smelling of fish; bloody
臭坊主 *namagusa bōzu* corrupt or worldly priest ⌈and meat)
臭物 *namagusamono* raw things (like fish
活 *seikatsu* life, livelihood
活力 *seikatsuryoku* vitality, resourcefulness
活水準 *seikatsu suijun* standard of living
活史 *seikatsushi* life history (in biology)
活必需品 *seikatsu hitsujuhin* necessities
活困窮者 *seikatsu konkyūsha* needy person
活改善 *seikatsu kaizen* improvement of living conditions
活法 *seikatsuhō* way of life
活苦 *seikatsuku* hard life, economic distress
活物資 *seikatsu busshi* necessities
活科学 *seikatsu kagaku* domestic science
活給 *seikatsukyū* living wage, subsistence
活費 *seikatsuhi* living expenses ⌊pay
活賃金 *seikatsu chingin* living wage, subsistence pay
活戦線 *seikatsu sensen* battle of life
活様式 *seikatsu yōshiki* mode of living
活難 *seikatsunan* hard life, economic distress
10 馬 *i(ki)uma* living horse; shrewd fellow
起 *seiki* occurrence of phenomena
埋 *i(ki)u(me)* burying alive
娘 *kimusume* maiden, virgin, innocent girl
徒 *seito* student, pupil
捕 *i(ke)do(ru)* capture alive
酒 *kizake* pure saké
粋 *kissui* purity
紙 *kigami* unsized paper ⌈shame
恥 *i(ki) haji* living in dishonor, lifelong
家 *seika* the house of one's birth
害 *shōgai* suicide
素性 *uma(re)sujō* circumstances of birth
真面目 *kimajime* too serious; a person who is too serious; honesty, sincerity
残 *i(ki)-noko(ru)* survive, outlive. *i(ki)noko(ri)*, *seizon* survival
残者 *seizansha*, *i(ki)noko(ri)mono* survivor
殺 *seisatsu* life and death. *namagoro(shi) suru* half kill; keep in suspense; leave unfinished
殺与奪 *seisatsu-yodatsu* killing and letting live; giving and taking away
息 *seisoku suru* live, subsist; multiply
息子 *kimusuko* unsophisticated young man
11 魚 *namazakana, seigyo, nama uo* raw fish, fresh fish, live fish
麻 *kiasa* raw hemp
唾 *nama tsuba* sour spittle
得 *seitoku, shōtoku* nature; naturally; capturing alive. *shōtoku no* natural, inborn, inherent, congenital
涯 *shōgai* life, career, lifetime; for life
渋 *kishibu* puckery persimmon juice
酔 *namaei, namayo(i)* half-drunk
動 *seidō* being full of life
彩 *seisai* beautiful light, luster
菜 *namana* salad
乾 *namakawa(ki)* not fully dry
菓子 *namagashi* unbaked cakes ⌈man
菩薩 *i(ki) bosatsu* living Buddha; a great
理 *seiri* physiology
理休暇 *seiri kyūka* period between men-
理学 *seirigaku* physiology ⌊struations
理的 *seiriteki* physiological ⌈solution
理的食塩水 *seiriteki shokuensui* saline
理衛生 *seiri-eisei* physiology and hygiene
産 *seisan* production ⌈ductivity
産力 *seisanryoku* productive capacity, pro-
産手段 *seisan shudan* means of production
産地 *seisanchi* producing area
産年度 *seisan nendo* production year
産物 *seisambutsu* produce, product
産者 *seisansha* producer, maker
産高 *seisandaka* yield, production, output
産財 *seisanzai* producers' goods
産過剰 *seisan kajō* overproduction
産費 *seisanhi* production cost
産機関 *seisan kikan* means of production
産額 *seisangaku* amount of production
12 揚 *nama-a(ge)* fried tofu ⌈mild
温 *namanuru(i)* lukewarm; half-hearted;
焼 *namaya(ke), namaya(ki)* (food) not thoroly cooked. *namaya(ki)* poorly tempered sword
硬 *seikō* crudeness, immaturity
落 *u(mare)-o(chiru)* be born. *u(mi)-o(tosu)* give birth to (animals)

替 *ha(e)-kawa(ru)* grow up in place of. *hae-kawa(ri)* second dentition
煮 *namani(e)* half-cooked, rare; vague
覚 *namaobo(e)* smattering
証文 *i(ki)jōmon* living witness
殖 *seishoku* reproduction, procreation, generation
殖不能 *seishoku funō* impotence
殖器 *seishokki* reproductive organs
殖器崇拝 *seishokki sūhai* phallicism, phallic worship
13傷 *nama kizu* sore, unhealed wound
損 *u(mi)-sokona(u), u(mi)-soko(neru)* miscarry. *u(mare)sokona(i)* an unfortunate birth; a good-for-nothing
暖 *nama-atataka(i)* lukewarm
滅 *shōmetsu* birth and death; appearance and disappearance
猿 *kizaru* wild monkey
絹 *kiginu* raw silk cloth
腥 *namagusa(i)* smelling of fish; bloody
際 *ha(e)giwa* the hairline
新 *nama-atara(shii)* brand new
節 *namabushi, namaribushi* half-dried bonito
業 *seigyō, sugiwai, nariwai* occupation, calling, living, livelihood
意気 *nama-iki* conceit, impertinence
14聞 *namagi(ki)* smattering of knowledge
憎 *ainiku, ayaniku* unfortunately, unluckily; too bad; a pity
様 *o(i)zama* condition of growing plants
態 *seitai* mode of life, ecology
態学 *seitaigaku* ecology
15誕 *seitan* birth, nativity
餌 *i(ki)e, nama-e* live bait, raw bait
麩 *shōfu* wheat starch
蕃 *seiban* aborigines, wild tribesmen
霊 *i(ki)ryō* apparition of a living person. *seirei* life; people; the public
熟 *seijuku* ripeness, maturity
蕎麦 *kisoba* buckwheat noodles
還 *seikan* returning alive; scoring a run
還者 *seikansha* survivor
16獲 *seikaku* capturing alive
親 *u(mi) (no) oya* one's real parent; originator, creator
薑 *shōga* ginger
壁 *nama kabe* undried wall
薬 *i(ki)gusuri* the elixir of youth. *kigusuri* a natural drug
薬屋 *kigusuriya* drugstore, apothecary
17優 *o(i)-masa(ru)* grow older and more beautiful
簀 *i(ke)su* (restaurant) fish tank
鮮 *seisen na* fresh
鮮果物 *seisen kabutsu* perishable foods
18噛 *namaka(jiri)* superficial knowledge
類 *seirui* living creatures
顔 *i(ki)gao* the face of a living person
繭 *nama mayu* raw cocoon
贄 *i(ke)nie* (animal) sacrifice
醤油 *kijōyu* raw *shoyu*, raw soy
織物 *kiorimono* raw silk
20麺 *seimen* raw noodles
21蠟 *kirō* crude wax

—— 6 ——

産 産 See 3354.

—— 7 ——

甦 See 66.

甥 2992 / F1267 SEI. SŌ. *oi* nephew.
12御 *oigo* nephew (polite)

—— 9 ——

甦 See 甦 66.

RAD. 用 101

Mochi-iru to use. Nickname: Using.

A 用 2993 / F1267 YŌ business, work; function; errand; engagement; use, service; expenses; call of nature. *yō(zuru), mochi(iru)* use; adopt (a method); employ. *-yō* for, used for.
2人 *yōnin* steward, factotum
4方 *mochi(i)kata* directions, way to use
不用 *yōfuyō* needed or not; useful or not
心 *yōjin* care, caution, discretion
心深 *yōjimbuka(i)* careful, thoughtful, cautious, scrupulous, alert
心棒 *yōjimbō* cudgel; bodyguard, protector
水 *yōsui* city water; water for fire; irrigation water; cistern water
水池 *yōsuichi, yōsui ike* reservoir
水桶 *yōsui oke* water barrel
水路 *yōsuiro* flume; water system
水権 *yōsuiken* water rights

5弁 *yōben* errand, business
立 *yōda(teru)* lend, advance (money). *yōda(te)* accommodation (in business). *yō (ni) ta(tsu)* be useful
立金 *yōda(te)kin* a loan, an advance
6向 *yōmu(ki)* business, errand, commission
件 *yōken* business, matter, items
地 *yōchi* required land, reservation, lot, site
字 *yōji* the use of the characters
7言 *yōgen* declinable word
足 *yōta(shi)* performing an errand; taking care of nature's call
役 *yōeki* service
兵 *yōhei* tactics, troop manipulation
材 *yōzai* materials; lumber, timber
材林 *yōzairin* timber forest
8金 *yōkin* money wanted; extraordinary levy; public money
例 *yōrei* example, illustration
所 *mochi(i)dokoro* use
法 *yōhō* directions, how to use
命 *yōmei* command, order, request
事 *yōji* errand, business, appointment
具 *yōgu* tool, instrument; machinery; apparatus; utensils; appliances; (sporting) goods; (teaching) aids
具類 *yōgurui* furnishings
9度 *yōdo* expenses; supplies
途 *yōto* use, service
品 *yōhin* supplies
便 *yōben* defecation
便後 *yōbengo* after stool

10紙 *yōshi* blank form; stationery, writing paper
益権 *yōekiken* usufruct
11達 *yōtashi* transaction of business, running errands; purveyor
捨 *yōsha* forgiveness; hesitancy
済 *yōzu(mi)* business finished, affairs settled
船 *yōsen* chartered ship
務 *yōmu* business, cares, routine
務員 *yōmuin* clerks
12量 *yōryō* dosage, dose
筆 *yōhitsu* use of a brush
無 *yōna(shi) no* idle, leisurely, useless
13意 *yōi* preparation, arrangement
意周到 *yōi-shūtō* prudence, cautiousness, thoro preparation
14聞 *yōki(ki)* taking orders
箋 *yōsen* form, blank, stationery, writing pad
語 *yōgo* term, terminology, vocabulary, diction
語例 *yōgorei* examples of the use of words
語索引 *yōgo sakuin* (Bible) concordance
語解 *yōgokai* glossary
語癖 *yōgoheki* one's idiom
15談 *yōdan* business talk
器 *yōki* tool, instrument; chamber pot; using tools
器画 *yōkiga* mechanical drawing
18簞笥 *yōdansu* chest of drawers

2

甫 See 135.

RAD. 田 102

Ta rice paddy. At left: *ta hen*. Nickname: Rice Field.

甲 See 92.

申 See 93.

由 See 89.

A **田** 2994 / F1268 DEN *ta* rice field, paddy field.

3子 *tago* peasant, rustic
4井 *ta-i* rice-field well
五作 *tagosaku* peasant, rustic
夫 *dempu* peasant
夫野人 *dempu-yajin* rustic, boor
5打 *ta-u(chi)* rice-field tilling
6舟 *tabune* small flat-bottomed boat
虫 *tamushi* ringworm
地 *denchi, denji* land, farm, rice fields
毎月 *tagoto (no) tsuki* moon reflected in many paddy fields
7作 *tazuku(ri)* rice-field tilling
吾作 *tagosaku* peasant, rustic
8舎 *inaka* the country, the provinces, rural areas. *inaka(meku)* wear a rustic air
舎人 *inakajin, inakabito* a person from the country
舎大尽 *inaka daijin* provincial millionaire
舎生 *inaka-u(mare)* country-born
舎弁 *inakaben* provincialism
舎出 *inakade* from the country
舎回 *inakamawa(ri)* provincial tour
舎気質 *inaka katagi, inaka kishitsu* rusticity, provincialism
舎住 *inakazuma(i)* country life

舎侍 *inakazamurai* boorish samurai
舎育 *inakasoda(chi)* country-bred
舎者 *inakamono* a rustic
舎風 *inakafū* rustic manners, country style
舎臭 *inakakusa(i)* rustic, countrified
舎染 *inakajimi(ru)* wear a rustic air
舎家 *inakaya* rural cottage
9 面 *tazura* surface of the rice field
畑 *tahata, dembata, tahatake* fields and rice
草 *tagusa* rice-field weeds ⌊paddies
10 圃 *tambo* rice field
租 *denso* rice-field tax
家 *denka* rural cottage; the country
畠 *dembata, tahatake* fields and rice paddies
11 野 *den-ya* cultivated fields
紳 *denshin* country gentleman
12 植 *ta-ue* rice transplanting
植歌 *ta-ue uta* rice-planting song
13 鼠 *tanezumi* field rat ⌈tofu baked with *miso*
楽 *dengaku* ancient music and dancing;
園 *den-en* fields and gardens; rural districts
園都市 *den-en toshi* garden city; suburbs
園詩 *den-enshi* pastoral poem
園詩人 *den-en shijin* pastoral poet
16 鴫 *tashigi* snipe
17 螺 *tanishi* fresh-water snail

2

A 町 $\frac{2995}{F1272}$ CHŌ town; block; street; 2.45 acres; 119 yards. *machi* town; quarters; street.
2 人 *chōnin* merchant
人町 *chōnimmachi* the merchants' district
4 内 *chōnai* in the town; in the block; the neighborhood
中 *machijū* thruout the town, the whole town. *machinaka de* on the streets
5 立 *chōritsu* established by the town
外 *machihazu(re)* outskirts
民 *chōmin* townspeople ⌈ation
6 会 *chōkai* town council, town-block associ-
名 *chōmei* town name, block name, street
7 角 *machikado* street corner ⌊name
住 *machizuma(i)* town or city life
町 *machimachi* towns, cities
役場 *machi yakuba* town office
医 *machi-i* the local doctor
医者 *machi isha* practicing physician
村 *chōson* towns and villages
村会 *chōsonkai* town and village assemblies
村長 *chōsonchō* town and village mayors
村制 *chōsonsei* municipal organizations
8 長 *chōchō* town mayor
制 *chōsei* town organization
育 *machisoda(chi)* brought up in a town
並 *machina(mi)* row of houses along the street
歩 *chōbu* hectare (2.45 acres)
9 政 *chōsei* town government
10 家 *chōka* town house, tradesman's house
11 道場 *machi dōjō* small town temple; small
12 税 *chōzei* town tax ⌊martial-arts institute
筋 *machisuji* street
費 *chōhi* town expenses
13 続 *machitsuzu(ki)* continuation of the town
20 議 *chōgi* town councilman

A 男 $\frac{2996}{F1271}$ DAN baron; man, male. NAN counter for sons. *otoko, onoko* man, male; fellow; adult; manhood; male servant; paramour. *otoko(rashii)* manly, manful. *otoko(datera) ni* unmanly.
1 一匹 *otoko-ippiki* a full-grown man
3 工 *dankō* male worker
子 *danshi* man, male, boy, son. *o(no)ko, otoko (no) ko* boy, boy baby, son
子用 *danshiyō* for men
女 *danjo, nannyo* men and women, both sexes. *otoko-onna* hermaphrodite
女共学 *danjo kyōgaku* coeducation
女合唱 *danjo gasshō* mixed chorus
女同権 *danjo dōken* equality of the sexes
女組 *danjogumi* coeducational class
4 心 *otokogokoro* a man's heart
手 *otokode* man's hand; man's strength
木 *ogi* tenon ⌈characters
文字 *otoko moji* male handwriting; Chinese
5 生 *dansei* male student
立 *otokodate* one who champions the under-
囚 *danshū* male prisoner ⌊dog
世帯 *otokojotai* household of men
6 色 *nanshoku, danshoku, okama* sodomy
気 *otokogi* chivalry, manhood, gallantry. *otoko(k)ke* a male, a man
向 *otokomu(ki)* for men ⌈woman
好 *otokozu(ki)* men's favorite; amorous
同士 *otokodōshi* men companions
伊達 *otokodate*＝男立 (see above–5)
7 体 *nantai* a man's body
坂 *otokozaka* the steeper slope ⌈men
狂 *otokoguru(i)* wantonness, running after
系 *dankei* male line, father's side
声 *dansei* male voice
旱 *otoko hideri* dearth of men
児 *danji* boy, son
芸者 *otoko geisha* male entertainer
8 松 *otoko matsu* black (male) pine
泣 *otokona(ki)* unmanly weeping
波 *onami* advancing wave
物 *otokomono* men's wear
妾 *otoko mekake* paramour
所帯 *otokojotai* bachelor's home ⌈manliness
性 *dansei* male, male sex; masculinity,

5 玄 玉 王 瓜 瓦 甘 生 用 【田】3 疋 疒 癶 白 皮 皿 目 矛 矢 石 示 ネ 禸 禾 穴 立

性的 *danseiteki* manly
性美 *danseibi* masculine beauty
9持 *otokomo(chi)* for gentlemen
神 *ogami, o(no)kami* male god
前 *otokomae* man's looks; good bearing ⌈ing
10振 *otoko(p)pu(ri), otokobu(ri)* a man's bear-
殺 *otokokoro(shi), otokogoro(shi)* vampire,
帯 *otoko obi* man's belt ⌊unscrupulous flirt
根 *dankon, nankon* penis; phallus
根崇拝 *nankon sūhai* phallicism
冥加 *otoko myōga* blessing of being a man
冥利 *otoko myōri* the advantage of being a man ⌈champions the underdog
11達 *otokotachi* men. *otokodate* one who
娼 *danshō* sodomite, male prostitute
盛 *otokozaka(ri), osaka(ri)* prime of man-
12湯 *otokoyu* men's bath ⌊hood
勝 *otokomasa(ri)* spirited, strong-minded
衆 *otokoshū* manservant
装 *dansō* male attire
尊女卑 *danson-johi* subjection of women
13嫌 *otokogira(i)* man hater
滝 *odaki* the greater of two falls
節句 *Otoko (no) Sekku* Boys' Festival (May
14監 *dankan* male prisoners' ward ⌊Fifth)
16親 *otoko oya* father
17優 *dan-yū* actor
爵 *danshaku* baron
21鰥 *otoko yamome* widower

3

画 See 50.

畄 Nonstandard for **留** 3003.

4

畑 See 2757.

毘 2997/F1059 **毗** HI help, assist. [比]
7沙門 *Bishamon* a God of Wealth

界 2998/F1272 **堺** KAI circle, world, A boundary, limits. *sakai* (see under 境 1135.0).
11隈 *kaiwai* neighborhood; district
15標 *kaihyō* boundary marker

畏 2999/F1273 **畏** I. *oso(reru)* fear, be overawed, be apprehensive. *kashiko(mu)* fear. *kashiko(maru)* obey respectfully; sit respectfully. *kashiko(i)* august, majestic. *kashiko(kumo)* graciously.
4友 *iyū* honored friend
6多 *oso(re)ō(i)* gracious, august; awe-inspir-
8怖 *ifu* awe, fear, fright ⌊ing, awful
服 *ifuku suru* submit from fear
12敬 *ikei* reverence, awe, respect
17縮 *ishuku suru* wince, cower, recoil (from), be awestruck, shrink (from a difficulty)
21懼 *iku* reverence, awe, fear

胃 3000/F1537 I stomach; paunch, crop, craw. A [肉]
8炎 *ien* gastritis
10病 *ibyō* stomach trouble
部 *ibu* stomach region
弱 *ijaku* indigestion
11袋 *ibukuro* stomach; paunch, crop, craw
液 *ieki* gastric juice
液酸度 *ieki sando* gastric acidity
12痛 *itsū* stomach-ache
腑 *i(no)fu* stomach
散 *isan* stomach medicine
痙攣 *ikeiren* stomach cramps
13腸 *ichō* stomach and intestines
腸病 *ichōbyō* gastro-intestinal disorder
腸薬 *ichōyaku* stomach and bowel medicine
14酸 *isan* stomach acid
酸過多 *isankata* gastric hyperacidity
酸過多症 *isankatashō* gastric hyperacidity
15熱 *inetsu* gastric fever
潰瘍 *ikaiyō* stomach ulcer
16壁 *iheki* stomach lining
17癌 *igan* stomach cancer
19鏡 *ikyō* gastroscope
22嚢 *ibukuro* stomach

思 3001/F698 SHI. *omo(u)* think, believe, A judge, esteem; consider, realize; feel like; regard as; anticipate; imagine, suppose, guess; mistake for; recall; intend; desire; love, care for, yearn after; wonder; suspect. *omo(wareru)* seem, appear. *omo(waseru)* give the impression that. *omo(eba)* come to think about it. *omo(eraku)* it seems to me. *omo(i)* thought, idea, mind, heart, sense; feeling, emotion; affection; desire, wish; expectation; intention, will; pleasure; care, worry; experience. *omo(inashi)* fancy, imagination. *omo(wanu)* unexpected, inconceivable. *omo(washii)* satisfactory, desirable. *omo(wazu)* unintentionally, spontaneously, unconsciously. [心]
2人 *omo(i)bito* lover, sweetheart
入 *omo(i)-i(ru)* consider, ponder. *omo(i)i(re)* one's pleasure, heart's desire, meditation, reverie. *omo-i(re)*=*omo(i)i(re)*; specula-
3子 *omo(i)go* favorite child ⌊tion

及 *omo(i)-oyo(bu)* think up, remember, hit upon
上 *omo(i)-aga(ru)* be conceited
4止 *omo(i)-to(maru), omo(i)-todo(maru)* drop (the idea)
比 *omo(i)-kura(beru)* compare and consider
込 *omo(i)-ko(mu)* be impressed with (an idea); set one's heart on; imagine (something)
切 *omo(i)-ki(ru)* resign to fate; get over (a loss); give up, despair of; resolve. *omo(i)ki(ri)* resignation, determination, decision; vehemently, vigorously; terribly; to heart's content; with all one's might; thoroly, completely. *omo(i)ki(tta)* drastic, radical
5立 *omo(i)-ta(tsu)* plan, resolve. *omo(i)ta(chi)* resolve, intention, idea, plan, whim, impulse
巡 *omo(i)-megu(rasu), omo(i)-mawa(su)* recall, ponder over
付 *omo(i)-tsu(kaseru)* remind of, suggest
omo(i)-tsu(ku) hit upon, think up (ideas); *omo(i)tsu(ki)* plan, suggestion, casual idea
外 *omo(i)(no)hoka* unexpectedly, beyond expectations
召 *obo(shi)me(su), omōshime(su)=omo(u)* (see under 思 3001.0). *obo(shi)me(shi)* your opinion; your desire; token of gratitude; liking, fancy
弁 *shiben* discrimination, speculation
出 *omo(i)-da(su)* recall, remember. *omo(i)de* memories, recollections
出笑 *omo(i)-da(shi)-wara(u)* laugh at some recollection
出話 *omo(i)debanashi* reminiscences
6回 *omo(i)-megu(rasu), omo(i)-mawa(su)* recall, ponder over
返 *omo(i)-kae(su)* think over, reconsider
交 *omo(i)-ka(wasu)* love each other
合 *omo(i)-a(u)* love each other. *omo(i)-a(waseru)* consider together. *omo(i)a(i)* mutual love
当 *omo(i)-a(taru), omo(i)-a(teru)* occur to one, think of; suspect
存分 *omo(u)zombun* as one pleases
考 *shikō* thought, consideration, contemplation
考力 *shikōryoku* mental faculties
7迫 *omo(i)-sema(ru)* be driven to despair, be at one's wit's end
侘 *omo(i)-wa(biru)* feel lonely, be sick of
沈 *omo(i)-shizu(mu)* worry
乱 *omo(i)-mida(reru)* be distracted with the thought of
初 *omo(i)-so(meru)* fall in love with
余 *omo(i)-ama(ru)* be overcome with emotion
8固 *omo(i)-kata(meru)* resolve
迷 *omo(i)-mayo(u)* be unable to decide
知 *omo(i)-shi(ru)* perceive, realize; repent of. *omo(i)-shi(raseru)* teach (someone a lesson). *omo(wazu)-shi(razu)* unintentionally, unconsciously
念 *shinen* thought
直 *omo(i)-nao(su)* reconsider, change one's mind
定 *omo(i)-sada(meru)* resolve
者 *omo(i)mono* sweetheart
事 *omo(i)goto* one's desire, one's prayer
9通 *omo(i)dō(ri) ni* to one's satisfaction, as much as one likes
計 *omo(i)-haka(ru)* think up
思 *omo(i)omo(i) ni* as one pleases
春期 *shishunki* puberty
10起 *omo(i)-o(kosu)* remember, recall
悩 *omo(i)-naya(mu)* be depressed, be dejected, worry
振 *omo(wase)bu(ri)* coquetry; mystification
残 *omo(i)-noko(su)* leave with regret
浮 *omo(i)-u(kaberu)* recall, remember, hit upon, think up. *omo(i)-u(kabu)* occur to, remind of
料 *shiryō* consideration
索 *shisaku* speculation, thinking, meditation
索的 *shisakuteki* meditative, speculative
索家 *shisakuka* thinker, philosopher
案 *shian* thought, consideration, meditation; plan, resources
案投首 *shian-na(ge)kubi* tilting the head in deep thought
案沈 *shian (ni) shizu(mu)* be in deep thought
案余 *shian (ni) ama(ru)* be perplexed even after much pondering
案暮 *shian (ni) ku(reru)* be perplexed even after much pondering
11違 *omo(i)chiga(i)* misunderstanding
過 *omo(i)-su(gosu)* worry too much, be overanxious
惟 *shi-i* speculation, thinking
設 *omo(i)-mō(keru)* anticipate, think of beforehand, expect
寄 *omo(i)-yo(ru)* recall, remember. *omo(i)-(mo)yo(ranai)* unexpected, inconceivable
掛無 *omo(i)ga(ke)na(i)* unexpected
12遣 *omo(i)-ya(ru) vt* sympathize with, have consideration for. *omo(i)ya(ri)* sympathy, consideration, compassion
壺 *omo(u) tsubo* one's wishes or expectations
量 *shiryō* consideration
募 *omo(i)-tsuno(ru)* think more and more of
焦 *omo(i)-koga(reru)* pine for, be deeply in love
惑 *omo(i)-mado(u)* be unable to decide. *omowaku* thought, opinion; intention; expectation; ulterior aim; rumor
惑師 *omowakushi* speculator, plunger, operator
惑違 *omowakuchiga(i)* disappointment, miscalculation
惑買 *omowakuga(i)* speculative purchase

5 玄玉王瓜瓦甘生用【田】疋疒癶白皮皿目矛矢石示ネ内禾穴立

[13]煩 *omo(i)-wazura(u)* worry about, be concerned about
詰 *omo(i)-tsu(meru)* think hard, brood over
想 *shisō* thought, idea
想力 *shisōryoku* power of thought
想内容 *shisō naiyō* thought content
想犯 *shisōhan* dangerous-thought offense
想団体 *shisō dantai* radicalist association
想取締 *shisō torishima(ri)* thought control
想界 *shisōkai* world of thought, realm of ideas
想家 *shisōka* thinker
想問題 *shisō mondai* thought problem
想善導 *shisō zendō* guidance of public thought
想戦 *shisōsen* ideological warfare
想感情 *shisō-kanjō* thoughts and feelings
[14]様 *omo(u)sama, omo(u) yō ni* as one pleases
慕 *shibo* yearning, deep affection
暮 *omo(i)-ku(rasu)* live with one dominating thought
[15]潮 *shichō* trend of thought
澄 *omo(i)-su(masu)* meditate; lead a life of austerity
慮 *shiryo* discretion, thought, consideration
慮周密 *shiryo-shūmitsu ni* discreetly, prudently, judiciously, sensibly
慮深 *shiryobuka(ku)* discreetly, prudently judiciously, sensibly
[16]儘 *omo(u) mama, omo(i) (no) mama* as one pleases

5

畠 See 3102.

畢 See 3005.

畜 See 2920.

畝 See 311.

B **畔** 3002 / F1273 **畔** HAN. *aze, kuro* rice-paddy ridge, levee.

A **留** 3003 / F1274 F1278 **畱** RYŪ. RU. *to(me), todo(maru), to(meru), todo(meru), to(maru)* (see under 止 2429.0).
[3]山 *to(me)yama* mountain preserve
[5]処 *to(me)do* termination, end
[6]任 *ryūnin* remaining in office
守 *rusu* absence, being away from home; watching a house; neglecting (responsibilities)
守中 *rusuchū* during one's absence
守宅 *rusutaku* absent master's home
守居 *rusui* caretaker; watching a house
守師団 *rusu shidan* reserve division
守家族 *rusu kazoku* family of an internee
守隊 *rusutai* the force remaining behind
守番 *rusuban* caretaker; watching a house
[7]別 *ryūbetsu* farewell to those staying on
[8]金 *to(me)gane* clasp
学 *ryūgaku* studying abroad
学生 *ryūgakusei* overseas student
学者 *ryūgakusha* a person studying abroad
[9]保 *ryūho* reserving, withholding, saving, protection
[10]針 *to(me)bari* pin, safety pin; brooch; hairpin
[11]鳥 *ryūchō* nonmigratory bird
桶 *tomeoke* oval wooden bucket
[12]場 *tomeba* fish or forest preserve; usher's quarters
[13]意 *ryūi* attention, heed, consideration
置 *to(me)-o(ku)* lock up, detain, retain; leave till called for, quarantine. *ryūchi* detention, custody, retention
置郵便 *tomeoki yūbin* mail left till called for; general delivery
置場 *ryūchijō* house of detention; police cell; guardhouse
置電報 *tomeoki dempō* telegram to be called for
置権 *ryūchiken* lien
[15]鋲 *to(me)byō* thumbtack
[18]職 *ryūshoku* remaining in one's position

6

畱 See 3003.

畦 3004 / F1275 KEI. *aze* rice-paddy ridge. *une* ridge (in a field), furrow, rib or cord (in cloth).
[7]豆 *azemame* soy beans grown on rice-field ridges
[11]道 *azemichi* path between rice fields
[18]溝 *unemizo* furrow

畢 3005 / F1274 HITSU. *owa(ru), owa(ri)* (see under 終 3521.0).
[5]生 *hissei* lifelong
生作 *hissei (no) saku* one's masterpiece
生業 *hissei (no) gyō* lifework
[11]竟 *hikkyō* after all, in short, virtually

B **累** 3006 / F1447 RUI involvement, trouble; tie up; pile up; continually. [糸]
[4]日 *ruijitsu* many days
[5]代 *ruidai* successive generations; from generation to generation
加 *ruika* acceleration; accumulation
世 *ruisei*=*ruidai* 累代 (see above–5)
犯 *ruihan* repeated offense
犯者 *ruihansha* old offender
[6]次 *ruiji ni* successively, repeatedly
年 *ruinen* successive years, every year

年統計 *ruinen tōkei* annual statistics
7 卵危 *ruiran no ayau(ki)* imminent danger
9 計 *ruikei* total 「power (in math.)
乗 *ruijō* involution, raising to a higher
10 進 *ruishin* successive promotions; graduated
進税 *ruishinzei* graduated tax ⌊increase
進課税 *ruishin kazei* graduated tax
11 累 *ruirui(taru)* piled up; in heaps
砦 *ruisai* fort
14 増 *ruizō* gradual increase
算 *ruisan* total
16 積 *ruiseki* accumulation, pile, heap

A 略 3007/F1275 畧 RYAKU abbreviation, abridgment; omission; outline. *ryaku(su), ryaku(suru)* abridge, omit, shorten, abbreviate; capture, seize, plunder. *hobo* almost, nearly.
4 文 *ryakubun* abridged sentence
5 史 *ryakushi* brief history
6 式 *ryakushiki* informality
伝 *ryakuden* brief biography
号 *ryakugō* short address, abbreviated form
字 *ryakuji* simplified characters; abbrevia-
名 *ryakumei* initials; initialing ⌊tion
7 言 *ryakugen* brief statement, summary
図 *ryakuzu* outline map; rough plan
述 *ryakujutsu* brief account
体 *ryakutai* short form
8 取 *ryakushu* capture, occupation, plunder
服 *ryakufuku* ordinary dress, informal
画 *ryakuga* rough sketch ⌊attire; dishabille
9 則 *ryakusoku* regulations in brief
10 称 *ryakushō* abbreviation; abbreviated name
記 *ryakki* brief account, outline
11 章 *ryakushō* miniature decoration
12 帽 *ryakubō* ordinary cap 「ening sentences
筆 *ryakuhitsu* abbreviating characters; short-
装 *ryakusō*=*ryakufuku* 略服 (see above–8)
13 解 *ryakkai* brief explanation
意 *ryakui* the general meaning, the main reason 「biography
14 歴 *ryakureki* brief personal history, brief
綬 *ryakuju* miniature decoration
説 *ryakusetsu* brief explanation, outline
語 *ryakugo* abbreviation 「depredation
奪 *ryakudatsu* pillage, plunder, looting,
奪隊 *ryakudatsutai* raiding party
15 儀 *ryakugi* informality

A 異 3008/F1277 I uncommonness, strangeness. queerness; difference. *i na* strange, wonderful, curious. *koto(naru)* differ, vary; be unusual. *koto (ni) suru* differ, vary.
2 人 *ijin* foreigner; different person
人種 *ijinshu* alien race
3 才 *isai* genius, prodigy
口同音 *iku-dōon ni* with one accord, by common consent, unanimously
4 心 *ishin* treachery, intrigue 「strange tales
文 *ibun* variant (reading); strange report,
日 *ijitsu* another day; a day in the past; a day in the future
火 *kotobi* strange or unsacred fire
父 *ifu* different father
分子 *ibunshi* alien elements, outsider
5 母 *ibo* different mother 「strange book
本 *ihon* a different edition; another book; a
6 色 *ishoku* different color; novelty
名 *imyō, imei* another name, nickname,
存 *izon* objection ⌊alias
同 *idō* difference
同識別 *idō-shikibetsu* identification
邦 *ihō* foreign country
邦人 *ihōjin* foreigner, stranger, gentile
7 見 *iken* different opinion; objection
言 *igen* languages, tongues
図 *ito* sinister design, ulterior motive
状 *ijō* something wrong, accident, change, abnormality
形 *igyō na, ikei na* fantastic, grotesque
花受精 *ika-jusei* cross-pollinization
体 *itai* different shape or form; a non-standard character form
体同心 *itai-dōshin* perfect accord
8 例 *irei* exception; illness
姓 *isei* a different name
性 *isei* the opposite sex
物 *ibutsu* foreign substance, foreign body
宗 *ishū* different religion or sect
国 *ikoku, kotokuni* foreign country. *ikoku no*
国風 *ikokufū* foreign customs ⌊foreign
国情調 *ikoku-jōchō* exotic mood, foreign
国語 *ikokugo* foreign language ⌊sentiments
9 風 *ifū* unusual customs
俗 *izoku* strange custom
変 *ihen* accident, disaster
臭 *ishū* offensive smell
10 称 *ishō* another name, alias, pseudonym
郷 *ikyō* foreign country
書 *isho* rare book, strange book
11 域 *i-iki* foreign lands
動 *idō* change, shifting
彩 *isai* conspicuous color. *isai(aru)* conspicuous, brilliant, resplendent
教 *ikyō* heathenism, paganism, heresy
教主義 *ikyō shugi* paganism
教徒 *ikyōto* heathen, pagans, heretics
常 *ijō* anything unusual; abnormality
常人格 *ijō jinkaku* abnormal personality
常反応 *ijō-hannō* allergy

常感 *ijōkan* a strange feeling
12 朝 *ichō* a foreign court; foreign country
象 *ishō* strange phenomenon; vision
13 腹 *ifuku, kotohara* child of a different mother
数 *isū no* exceptional, unusual, phenomenal
義 *igi* different meaning
意 *i-i* different idea; ideas of rebellion
14 聞 *ibun* another story; a strange tale
境 *ikyō* foreign country
様 *iyō na* strange, quaint, outlandish
説 *isetsu* different opinion ⌈riety
種 *ishu* different kind, different species; va-
種繁殖 *ishu hanshoku* crossbreeding
端 *itan* heresy
端者 *itansha* heretic
端糾問 *itan kyūmon* inquisition
端排斥 *itan haiseki* anathema
15 論 *iron* different opinion; objection
質 *ishitsu* heterogeneity
18 類 *irui* varieties, different kinds
20 議 *igi* objection, protest
議無 *igina(shi)* no objection

7

番 See 4811.

畱 See 留 3003.

畫 See 画 50.

塁 3009/F443 壘 RUI fort, rampart, walls; B base (in baseball). [土]
4 手 *ruishu* baseman
5 打 *ruida* a base hit, a single
打数 *ruidasū* number of extra-base hits
15 摩 *rui (o) ma(su)* attack a fort; catch up with
審 *ruishin* umpire on bases ⌊(someone)
16 壁 *ruiheki* rampart, walls

畳 3010/F1281 疊 CHŌ. JŌ mat counter. B *tata(mu)* fold, fold up, furl, shut up, shut; wind up (affairs); do away with, kill; bear in mind. *tata(maru)* be folded (up). *tatami* mat, matting. *tata(mi)*- folding, collapsible.
2 入 *tata(mi)-i(reru)* fold up, fold in
3 上 *tata(mi)-a(geru)* fold up
小刀 *tatami kogatana* pocket knife
4 尺 *tatamijaku* folding rule ⌈in mind
込 *tata(mi)-ko(mu)* fold in; fold up; bear
水練 *tatami suiren* "swimming" on *tatami*; useless endeavor
5 用 *jōyō suru* use over again
目 *tata(mi)me* crease, fold. *tatamime* the mesh in mat facing
句 *jōku* repetition, burden, refrain
付 *tatamizu(ki)* covered with matting
叩 *tatamitata(ki)* mat beating
6 返 *tata(mi)-kae(su)* fold back
8 直 *tata(mi)-nao(su)* refold
表 *tatami omote* mat facing ⌈word
9 音 *jōon* repetition of the same sound in a
建具 *tatami-tategu* mats and fixtures
屋 *tatamiya* mat dealer, matmaker
屋台 *tata(mi)yatai* folding dancing stage
10 紙 *tatōgami, tata(mi)gami, tatō* paper handkerchief; kimono wrapping paper
針 *tatamibari* a *tatami* needle
11 掛 *tata(mi)-ka(keru)* press (someone), ply (with questions), follow up
梯子 *tata(mi)bashigo* folding ladder
12 替 *tatamiga(e)* refacing mats, renewing mats
13 寝台 *tata(mi) shindai* folding bed, camp cot
14 語 *jōgo* syllable repetition to indicate plurals, etc.
算 *tatamizan* fortunetelling by mat meshes
15 縁 *tatamiberi* mat border
18 職 *tatamishoku* mat maker

8

當 See 当 1359.

畫 See 画 50.

畷 3011/F1280 TETSU. TEI. SEI. *nawate* rice-field ridge path.

畸 3012/F1280 KI difference; strange; cripple.
7 形 *kikei* deformity, abnormality
形足 *kikeisoku* clubfoot
形児 *kikeiji* deformed child

10

畿 See 1497.

11

鴫 3013/F2142 (国字) *shigi* snipe. [鳥]

12

嬲 3014/F515 DŌ. JŌ. *nabu(ru)* sport with; ridicule; tease. [女]
8 物 *nabu(ri)mono* laughingstock
10 殺 *nabu(ri)goro(shi)* torturing

— 13 —

壘 3015/F443 See 塁 3009. [土]

— 14 —

疆 See 72.

嚋 3016/F1280 CHŪ before; companion; same kind.

— 17 —

疊 3017/F1281 See 畳 3010.

疋 RAD. 103

Hiki (counter for animals). At left 𤴔 *hiki hen.* Nickname: Animal Counter.

疋 3018/F1281 HITSU. *hiki* head (animal counter); roll of cloth.

— 6 —

蛋 3019/F1661 TAN barbarian; egg. [虫]

5 白 *tampaku* protein; albumen
白石 *tampakuseki* opal
白石映光 *tampakuseki eikō* opalescence
白光 *tampakukō* opalescence
白質 *tampakushitsu* protein; albumen

— 7 —

疏 3020/F1282 So estrangement; sparseness; neglect. (See note below.)

4 水 *sosui* drainage; canal
7 状 *sojō* written explanation
8 明 *somei* evidence for credibility
注 *sochū* notes and comments
9 通 *sotsū* drainage; mutual understanding
11 略 *soryaku na*=*somatsu na* 粗末 3473.5
12 註 *sochū* notes and comments

B 疎 3021/F1281 So rough; sparseness; estrangement. *uto*(*mu*), *uto*(*njiru*), *uto*(*nzuru*) neglect, shun, alienate. *maba*(*ra*) *na* sparse, thin (hair); scattered, sporadic, straggling (village). *oro*(*ka*) making light of; . . . to say nothing of . . . *oroso*(*ka*) *na* negligent, careless, *uto*(*i*) distant, estranged; disinterested, ignorant of. *uto*(*mashii*) disagreeable. (See note below.)

4 水 *sosui* drainage; canal
5 外 *sogai* estrangement, indifference, neglect
7 抜 *oronu*(*ku*) thin out (plants)
8 放 *sohō* carelessness, fault, oversight
明 *somei* evidence for credibility
林 *sorin* sparse woods
画 *soga* rough sketch
9 音 *so-in* estrangement, neglect, long silence
通 *sotsū* drainage; mutual understanding
相 *sosō* carelessness, fault, oversight
11 略 *soryaku na*=*somatsu na* 粗末 3473.5
野 *soya na* uncouth
密 *somitsu* sparseness and luxuriant growth
12 遠 *soen* estrangement, neglect (to write), long silence
疎 *uto-uto*(*shii*) estranged
隔 *sokaku* alienation, estrangement
開 *sokai* dispersal, evacuation, deployment
開先 *sokaisaki* reception area, place of refuge
開者 *sokaisha* evacuee
14 漏 *sorō* carelessness, negligence
雑 *sozatsu na* coarse, rough, crude

— 8 —

楚 3022/F992 So whip; cane. [木]

13 楚 *soso*(*taru*) graceful, neat

— 9 —

疑 See 755.

NOTE: Characters 3020 and 3021 are sometimes used interchangeably. It is therefore necessary to look under both for definitions and compounds.

RAD. 疒 104

Yamaidare trailing "sickness." Nickname: Sick.

2

疔 3023 / F1283 TEI. CHŌ carbuncle.

3

疚 3024 / F1284 KYŪ. *yama*(*shii*) ashamed, painful, having a guilty conscience, sickly.

疝 3025 / F1284 SEN colic, abdominal pain.
6 気 *senki* colic, abdominal pain
12 痛 *sentsū* colic, abdominal pain

4

疥 3026 / F1284 KAI. *hatake* scabby eruption, scabs.
22 癬 *kaisen* itch, scabies, mange

疣 3027 / F1284 YŪ. YU. *ibo* wart.
11 痔 *iboji* hemorrhoids
12 蛙 *ibogaeru* toad

B 疫 3028 / F1284 YAKU, EKI epidemic.
9 神 *ekijin* sickness-producing god
10 鬼 *ekiki* god of sickness
病 *ekibyō, yakubyō* pestilence, plague, epidemic
病神 *yakubyōgami* god of the plague
12 痢 *ekiri* children's dysentery
17 癘 *ekirei* pestilence, epidemic, plague

5

痊 Nonstandard for 痙 3052.

痀 3029 / F1285 = 痾 A chronic illness.

疸 3030 / F1285 TAN jaundice.

疽 3031 / F1285 So carbuncle.

疳 3032 / F1284 KAN children's diseases.
10 高 *kandaka*(*i*) shrill, high-pitched

疹 3033 / F1285 SHIN, CHIN measles; sickness.

痃 3034 / F1286 GEN cramps.
18 癖 *kempeki* stiff shoulders; massage

痀 3035 / F1286 KU crouch; hunchback.
16 瘻 *kuru* rickets
瘻病 *kurubyō* rickets

疱 3036 / F1284 HŌ smallpox; blister.
15 瘡 *hōsō* smallpox

疼 3037 / F1285 TŌ pain. *uzu*(*ku*) ache, pain; tingle; fester.
12 痛 *tōtsū* pain

痂 3038 / F1286 KA. KE. *kasa* scab. *ka*(*seru*) dry up, scab, slough.
5 皮 *kahi* scab

B 症 3039 / F1287 SHŌ illness; condition of a patient; nature of a disease, symptoms.
7 状 *shōjō* symptoms; condition of the illness
8 例 *shōrei* a case (a patient)
10 候 *shōkō* symptoms

B 疲 3040 / F1284 HI. *tsuka*(*reru*) get tired, grow weary. *tsuka*(*rakasu*), *tsuka*(*rasu*) tire (a horse), weary (one's mind), exhaust (one's energy).
4 切 *tsuka*(*re*)-*ki*(*ru*) be tired out
5 目 *tsuka*(*re*)*me* eyestrain
乍 *tsuka*(*re*)*naga*(*ra*) even tho tired
7 労 *hirō* fatigue
8 果 *tsuka*(*re*)-*ha*(*teru*) be tired out
10 衰 *tsuka*(*re*)-*otoro*(*eru*) languish
15 弊 *hihei* impoverishment, exhaustion
16 憊 *hihai* being tired out

B 疾 3041 / F1285 SHITSU illness, disease. *to*(*ku*) fast, swiftly; early. *to*(*kku*) *kara* since long ago. *to*(*u*) *ni*, *to*(*kku*) *ni* long ago; already. *to*(*u*) *kara* for a long time. *haya*(*i*) fast. *yama*(*shii*) (see under 疚 3024.0).
6 行 *shikkō suru* hasten, hurry
7 走 *shissō suru* scamper, dash along. *shissō* a sprint, a dash
8 呼 *shikko* shout, yell
苦 *shikku* affliction, distress, suffering
9 風 *shippū*, *hayate* squall, gale, hurricane, fresh breeze

風迅雷的 *shippū-jinraiteki ni* swiftly, with lightning speed

風雲 *hayategumo* hurricane clouds

10 病 *shippei* sickness

疾 *to(ku)to(ku)* in a great hurry

11 患 *shikkan* disease, ailment

強風 *shikkyōfū* gale

14 駆 *shikku suru* scamper, speed, dash along

A **病** 3042 F1286 **病** Byō. Hei. *ya(mu)* get sick, be sick, suffer from. *ya(meru)* be sick, be in ill health. *yamai* illness; bad habit; weakness; passion. *-ya(mi)* sufferer of (a disease). *ya(mi)-* diseased.

2 人 *byōnin* patient, invalid

3 上 *ya(mi)a(gari)* convalescence

4 犬 *byōken* sick dog

中 *byōchū* during an illness

夫 *byōfu* sick husband

5 付 *ya(mi)-tsu(ku)* get sick; be absorbed in; become confirmed in a habit. *ya(mi)tsu(ki)* becoming sick; infatuation; falling into a bad habit

6 因 *byōin* cause of the disease, etiology

死 *byōshi* natural death, death from illness

返 *ya(mi)kae(shi)* relapse

名 *byōmei* name of a disease

虫害 *byōchūgai* insect damage

気 *byōki* sickness, disease, ailment; fault; infirmity

気中 *byōkichū* during illness

気見舞 *byōki mima(i)* calling on the sick

7 足 *ya(mi)ashi* diseased foot

身 *byōshin* weak constitution, ill health

体 *byōtai* weak constitution, ill health

没 *byōbotsu*=病歿 (see below–8)

状 *byōjō* patient's condition

兵 *byōhei* sick soldier

児 *byōji* sick child

床 *byōshō* sickbed

床日誌 *byōshō nisshi* clinical report, nurse's report

床録 *byōshōroku* clinical record; nurse's report

8 性 *byōsei* nature of the disease

所 *byōsho* patient's location; the ailing part

歿 *byōbotsu* death from illness, natural death

牀 *byōshō* sickbed

舎 *byōsha* infirmary, hospital

苦 *byōku* suffering from illness

妻 *byōsai* sick wife

者 *byōsha* sick person

臥 *byōga suru* be sick in bed, be bedridden

臥中 *byōgachū* bedridden

毒 *byōdoku* virus, germ

毒保有者 *byōdoku hoyūsha* germ carrier

的 *byōteki* morbid, abnormal, unsound

的窃盗 *byōteki settō* kleptomaniac

的盗癖 *byōteki tōheki* kleptomania

9 後 *byōgo* convalescence; after an illness

変 *byōhen* pathological change

室 *byōshitu* sickroom, ward, sick bay, infirmary

院 *byōin* hospital, infirmary

院列車 *byōin ressha* hospital train

院車 *byōinsha* ambulance

院船 *byōinsen* hospital ship

院機 *byōinki* hospital plane

10 骨 *byōkotsu* weak constitution

症 *byōshō* nature of a disease

根 *byōkon* cause of the disease; root of an evil

衰 *byōsui* weakness from illness

害 *byōgai* health impairment from illness; crop damage due to disease

家 *byōka* patient's home

耄 *ya(mi)-hō(keru)* become emaciated

弱 *byōjaku* delicate constitution

原 *byōgen* cause of a disease

原体 *byōgentai* pathogenic agent

原菌 *byōgenkin* virus, germ

11 婦 *byōfu* sick wife

眼 *byōgan* sore eye

菌 *byōkin* bacteria

患 *byōkan, ya(mi)wazura(i)* sickness

巣 *byōsō* focus (of an infection)

理 *byōri* cause and extent of a disease

理学 *byōrigaku* pathology

理解剖学 *byōri-kaibōgaku* pathological anatomy

12 間 *byōkan* during illness

棟 *byōtō* ward

13 煩 *ya(mi)-wazura(u)* be sick

蓐 *byōjoku* sickbed

勢 *byōsei* progress of the disease

源 *byōgen* cause of a disease

源菌 *byōgenkin* germs, a virus

14 歴 *byōreki* patient's case history

態 *byōtai* patient's condition

15 褥 *byōjoku* sickbed

弊 *byōhei*=*heigai* 弊害 1551.10

18 癖 *byōheki* peculiarity, weakness, bad habit

軀 *byōku* ill health, sickly constitution

21 魔 *byōma* disease, demon of ill health

竈 *byōsō* focus of infection, disease center

— 6 —

痍 3043 F1288 I injury.

痒 3044 F1288 Yō. *kayu(garu)* itch. *kayu(i)*, *kai(i)* itchy.

痕 3045 F1288 Kon. *ato* mark; footprint.

18 跡 *konseki* traces, vestiges, evidences

跡器官 *konseki kikan* vestigial organ

痔 3046 F1288 Ji piles, hemorrhoids.
5 出血 *jishukketsu* bleeding of piles
10 疾 *jishitsu* hemorrhoids
核 *jikaku* hemorrhoids
16 瘻 *jirō* anal fistula, piles

疵 3047 F1285 Shi. *kizu* crack, flaw; scratch; speck; (fruit) bruise; fault; blemish, stain; weakness.
5 付 *kizutsu(ku)* get injured, be wounded; be damaged; be disgraced. *kizutsu(keru)* wound, injure; mar, damage; disgrace
8 咎 *kizutagame* inflamed wound
10 病 *kizuyami* illness from an injury
11 痕 *kizu ato* scar from a wound
13 瑕 *shika* defect, fault, weakness
跡 *kizu ato* scar from a wound
16 薬 *kizugusuri* salve, ointment

7

痾 3048 F1290 F1285 See 疴 3029.

B **痢** 3049 F1289 Ri diarrhea.
10 病 *ribyō* diarrhea

痣 3050 F1289 Shi. *aza* birthmark, mole.

痤 3051 F1289 Za. *enogo* swelling of the lymph glands.
15 瘡 *zasō* acne

痙 3052 F1288 Kei. *tsu(ru)* have a cramp.
23 攣 *keiren*, *hikitsuri* scar; cramp, spasm, twitch, convulsion

B **痘** 3053 F1288 Tō smallpox.
8 苗 *tōbyō* vaccine
9 面 *tōmen* pockmarked face
11 痕 *abata, tōkon* pockmark
痕面 *abatazura* pitted face
15 瘡 *tōsō* smallpox

B **痛** 3054 F1288 Tsū pain. *ita(mu)* feel a pain, hurt; be hurt, be damaged, be spoiled, be bruised, wear out, be worn out. *ita(meru)* (see under 傷 535.0). *ita(mi)* pain, ache. *ita(garu)* complain of pain. *ita(i)* painful, sore; trying. *ita(mashii)*, *ita(washii)* sad, pitiful, wretched, pathetic.
2 入 *ita(mi)-i(ru)* be grateful for
4 心 *tsūshin*=*shimpai* 心配 1645.10
手 *itade* serious wound; hard blow
切 *tsūsetsu ni* keenly, acutely
5 目 *ita(i)me* hard experience
付 *ita(me)-tsu(keru)* rebuke, reprove, scold severely
打 *tsūda* painful blow; grand-slam hit
7 言 *tsūgen* bitter criticism
快 *tsūkai* thrill, keen pleasure. *tsūkai na* extremely delightful, very gratifying; merciless; incisive
8 苦 *ita(mi)-kuru(shimu)* suffer. *tsūku* pain, pang, anguish
事 *itagoto* severe blow, pain
9 悔 *tsūkai* deep remorse, penitence
点 *tsūten* point of pain
恨 *tsūkon* great sorrow, bitterness
恨事 *tsūkonji* sad incident
10 烈 *tsūretsu na* severe, bitter, scathing
哭 *tsūkoku* lamentation
11 痒 *tsūyō* interest, concern; pain and tickling. *ita(shi)kayu(shi) no* delicate, ticklish (question)
惜 *tsūseki* great sorrow, deep regret, lamentation
責 *tsūseki suru* denounce vigorously
12 痛 *ita-ita(shii)* pitiful, pathetic
棒 *tsūbō* harsh criticism
飲 *tsūin* carousal
覚 *tsūkaku* sense of pain
13 嘆 *tsūtan* bitter grief, deep regret
感 *tsūkan suru* feel keenly; fully realize
15 歎 *tsūtan* bitter grief, deep regret
憤 *tsūfun* great indignation
論 *tsūron* vehement argument
罵 *tsūba* condemnation, denunciation
撃 *tsūgeki* hard blow, severe attack
20 癢 *tsūyō*=痛痒 (see above–11)

8

瘁 3055 F1290 Zui, Sui fatigue; take sick.

痼 3056 F1290 Ko chronic illness.
10 疾 *koshitsu* chronic disease

痲 3057 F1289 Ma measles; paralysis.
11 酔 *masui* anesthetic
13 痺 *mahi* paralysis, palsy, numbness, stupor
16 薬 *mayaku* anesthetic, narcotic

痳 3058 F1290 Rin gonorrhea.
8 毒 *rindoku* gonorrhea, clap
10 病 *rimbyō* gonorrhea, clap

10疾 *rinshitsu* gonorrhea, clap
11菌 *rinkin* gonococcus; gonorrhea, clap

痺 3059/F1290 **痹** Hi palsy. *shibi(reru)* become numb, be paralyzed.
16薬 *shibiregusuri* anesthetic
19鯰 *shibire namazu* electric catfish
22鰻 *shibire unagi* electric eel
23鱏 *shibire ei* electric ray

痰 3060/F1289 Dan, Tan sputum, phlegm.
4切飴 *tanki(ri) ame* cough syrup
6吐 *tanha(ki)* spittoon, cuspidor
9咳 *tanseki* mucous cough
11唾 *tantsuba* expectoration, spittle
12壺 *tantsubo* spittoon, cuspidor

B **痴** 3061/F1294 **癡** Chi foolish.
2人 *chijin* dunce, fool, idiot
7言 *shiregoto* foolish speaking
呆 *chihō* imbecility; dementia
呆症 *chihōshō* dementia
8者 *chisha, shiremono* fool; rascal
事 *shiregoto* foolish thing
11情 *chijō* blind love
12鈍 *chidon* stupidity, dullness
13漢 *chikan* an erotic person; a fool
愚 *chigu* stupidity, imbecility
話 *chiwa* lovers' talk
話言 *chiwagoto* love-talk vocabulary
話狂 *chiwaguru(i)* petting, dalliance
話喧嘩 *chiwa genka* lovers' quarrel
14態 *chitai* silliness

9

瘦 See 3069.

瘍 3062/F1291 Yō boil, carbuncle.

瘧 3063/F1292 Gyaku ague, intermittent fever. *okori* fever and ague.

瘋 3064/F1290 Fū insanity; headache.
24癲 *fūten* insanity

10

瘟 3065/F1291 On contagious disease.

瘢 3066/F1292 Han scar.
11痕 *hankon* scar, cicatrix

瘡 3067/F1291 Sō wound; boil. *kasa* syphilis.
6気 *kasake* symptoms of syphilis
8毒 *sōdoku* (old word for) syphilis
13蓋 *kasabuta* scab

瘤 3068/F1292 Ryū. *kobu* wen, lump, bump, swelling.
5付 *kobutsu(ki)* wen; nuisance; having a child along
8取 *kobuto(ri)* (story of the) removal of the wen
9胃 *kobui* rumen, paunch
10起 *ryūki* swelling like a boil

瘦 3069/F1292 Sō. Shū. Shu. *yase(ru)* get thin.
3女 *yase onna* thin woman
4犬 *yase inu* skinny dog
7男 *yase otoko* thin man
我慢 *yase gaman* enduring to the breaking point
身 *sōshin* slender body, thin body
身法 *sōshinhō* slenderizing
10衰 *ya(se)-otoro(eru)* (see 瘠衰 3070.10)
11細 *ya(se)-boso(ru)* get thin; become just skin and bones
脛 *yasezune* thin legs
18軀 *sōku* a lean figure
19羸 *sōrui* fatigue

瘠 3070/F1291 Seki. Jaku. *yase(ru)* get thin, lose weight; pine away; get sterile. *yase(gisu) no* slim, slender, thin. *yase(ppochi)* mere skeleton; rawboned.
3土 *yasetsuchi* barren soil
5世帯 *yasejotai* poor household, straitened circumstances
6地 *yasechi, sekichi* barren land, arid soil
7形 *yasegata* slender figure
身代 *yase shindai* scanty means
我慢 *yase gaman* strained endurance; feeble resistance
9面 *yaseomote* thin face
10馬 *yaseuma* scrawny horse
衰 *ya(se)-otoro(eru)* become emaciated, waste away; be blighted
11細 *ya(se)-hoso(ru)* get thin, lose weight
12腕 *yaseude* weak arm; feeble strength, poor ability
落 *ya(se)-o(chiru)* get thin, lose weight
16薬 *yasegusuri* reducing medicine

11

瘤 See 3068.

瘻 3071/F1292 Ru, Rō fistula.

瘭 3072 / F1292 Hyō a whitlow.
10疽 *hyōso* felon, whitlow

瘴 3073 / F1292 Shō miasma.
6気 *shōki*＝*jaki* 邪気 2849.6

瘰 3074 / F1292 Rui swollen neck glands.
21癧 *ruireki* scrofula

12

癘 3075 / F1294 Rei contagious disease; leprosy.

癌 3076 / F1293 Gan cancer; cancerous evil; stumbling block.
13腫 *ganshu* cancer, cancerous growth

廃 3077 / F1293 Hai chronic illness; getting crippled.
2人 *haijin* invalid, cripple; useless person; abandoned person
10疾 *haishitsu* disablement, deformity

療 3078 / F1293 B Ryō heal, cure.
8法 *ryōhō* medical treatment, remedy
治 *ryōji* medical treatment, remedy
15養 *ryōyō* recuperation, medical care
養中 *ryōyōchū* under medical care
養所 *ryōyōjo* sanitorium

癇 3079 / F1293 **癎** Kan hot temper, irritability, nervousness, sensitiveness.
7声 *kangoe* angry voice
9持 *kammo(chi)* hot-tempered person
10症 *kanshō* irritability, hot temper
18癖 *kampeki* hot temper, irritability
21癪 *kanshaku* passion, temper, irritability
癪玉 *kanshakudama* anger
癪持 *kanshakumo(chi)* hot-tempered person

13

癕 3080 / F1295 **癰** Yō carbuncle.

癒 3081 / F1290 Yu. *i(yasu)* heal, cure; quench (thirst); wreak (vengeance). *i(eru)*, *nao(ru)* recover, be healed, heal.
6合 *yugō* agglutination, adhesion, knitting
12着 *yuchaku suru* adhere, knit, unite, heal up. *yuchaku* adhesion
18難 *iegata(i)* hard to cure

癖 3082 / F1294 B Heki habit-ity, vice, trai mannerism. *-kuse ni* and y
4毛 *kusege* curly hair, kinky
5付 *kusezu(ku)* become a h strange reading tone; sn
8直 *kusenao(shi)* straightening
者 *kusemono*＝曲者 103.8
事 *kusegoto* characteristic habit

14

癡 3083 / F1294 See 痴 3061.

15

癢 3084 / F1294 Yō ichy. *kayu(i)*, *kai(i)* itching.

16

癧 3085 / F1295 Reki swollen neck glands.

癪 3086 / F1295 (国字) *shaku* spasms, convulsions, hysteria, sharp pain.
6虫 *shaku (no) mushi* feeling of intense anger
13触 *shaku (ni) sawa(ru)* irritate, exasperate
14種 *shaku (no) tane* reason for an outburst of anger

癩 3087 / F1295 Rai leprosy.
8者 *raisha* leprosy victim
10病 *raibyō*, *kattai* leprosy, Hansen's disease
病人 *raibyōnin* leper
11菌 *raikin* the germ of leprosy
13患者 *raikanja* lepers
17療養所 *rairyōyōsho* leprosarium

17

癬 3088 / F1295 Sen ringworm.

18

癰 3089 / F1295 See 癕 3080.

19

癲 3090 / F1295 Ten insanity.
7狂 *tenkyō* insanity
17癇 *tenkan* epilepsy; epileptic fit
癇持 *tenkammo(chi)* an epileptic

RAD. 癶 105

Hatsugashira (crown like that on *hatsu* "to depart"). Nickname: Dotted Tent.

4

癸 3091 / F1295 Ki J, 10th. *mizunoto* 10th calendar sign.

A **発** 3092 / F1296 = **發** Hotsu, Hatsu departure; discharge (of a gun). *has*(*suru*) discharge, fire; emit, emanate, radiate, give out; publish; utter, give vent to; give rise to; originate in, spring from, emanate from; start from; flow from; send out, dispatch, forward; leave, start, take off, announce; break out (a disease). *aba*(*ku*) unearth, disclose, divulge, reveal; open (a grave). *-hatsu* departure; round, shot; dated.

4 心 *hosshin* new intention; (Buddhist) religious awakening
火 *hakka* ignition, combustion; discharge, firing
火点 *hakkaten* combustion point
火演習 *hakka enshū* firing practice
5 句 *hokku*=*haiku* 俳句 485.5
刊 *hakkan* publication
令 *hatsurei* official announcement
布 *happu* proclamation; issuance; promulgation
生 *hassei* occurrence, outbreak; genesis; production, growth, development, rise
生学 *hasseigaku* genetics, embryology
6 向 *hakkō* departure
汗 *hakkan* perspiring
企 *hokki* promotion of a plan
会 *hakkai suru* open a meeting
会式 *hakkaishiki* opening ceremony
光 *hakkō* radiation, luminescence
光体 *hakkōtai* luminous stellar bodies
行 *hakkō* publication; flotation; issue
行人 *hakkōnin* publisher
行日 *hakkōbi* date of issue
行元 *hakkō moto* place of publication
行所 *hakkōsho* publishing house
行者 *hakkōsha* publisher
行高 *hakkōdaka* the amount of an issue
行部数 *hakkō busū* circulation (of a magazine)
行停止 *hakkō teishi* ceasing publication
7 見 *hakken* discovery, detection, revelation
赤 *hosseki* redness
走 *hassō* starting; first race
足 *hossoku, hassoku* starting, inauguration
車 *hassha* departure of a vehicle
狂 *hakkyō* madness, insanity
兌 *hatsuda* issue, publication
来 *hatsurai* beginnings, appearance
作 *hossa* fit, spasm, an attack of
作的 *hossateki* spasmodic, fitful
売 *hatsubai* sale
売部数 *hatsubai busū* circulation
条 *hatsujō, bane, zemmai* (metal) spring
条仕掛 *banejikake* spring mechanism, clockwork
条秤 *zemmaibakari* spring balances
言 *hatsugen* speaking, speech, proposal
言力 *hatsugenryoku* the authority behind a speech
言投票 *hatsugen tōhyō* voice vote
言者 *hatsugensha* speaker
言権 *hatsugenken* right to speak, a voice
声 *hassei* utterance, exclamation, speaking
声法 *hasseihō* vocalization, enunciation; elocution
声映画 *hassei eiga* sound picture
声帯 *hasseitai* vocal cords
声器 *hasseiki* vocal organs
声爆弾 *hassei bakudan* scream bomb
8 送 *hassō* sending, forwarding, shipping
明 *hatsumei* invention, contrivance; cleverness
泡 *happō* blister
注 *hatchū* ordering (goods)
効 *hakkō* coming into effect
芽 *hatsuga* germination, sprouting
券 *hakken* note issuing
表 *happyō* announcement, communiqué
明者 *hatsumeisha* inventor
明品 *hatsumeihin* invention, contrivance
明家 *hatsumeika* inventor
育 *hatsuiku* growth, development, progress
育不全 *hatsuiku fuzen na* abortive; underdeveloped
育時代 *hatsuiku jidai* formative years
育時期 *hatsuiku jiki* formative years
9 信 *hasshin* sending a letter or telegram
剌 *hatsuratsu* liveliness, spirit
音 *hatsuon* pronunciation, enunciation, articulation
音学 *hatsuongaku* phonetics
音符号 *hatsuon fugō* phonetic symbols
10 病 *hatsubyō* onset of a disease, stroke
疹 *hasshin, hosshin* eruption, rash
破 *happa* blasting
航 *hakkō* departure, sailing
振器 *hasshinki* oscillator
祥 *hasshō* ancestral origin; appearance of a good omen
祥地 *hasshōchi* cradle, birthplace

射 *hassha* discharge, firing; emanation, ra-
射管 *hasshakan* torpedo tube ⌊diation
案 *hatsuan* suggestion, proposition, motion
案者 *hatsuansha* proposer ⌈suggestion
起 *hokki* promotion (of a plan); proposition,
起人 *hokkinin* originator, promoter, sponsor
起者 *hokkisha* originator
砲 *happō* firing, discharge
砲事件 *happō jiken* a shooting affair
砲戦 *happōsen* shooting war
展 *hatten* expansion, extension, development, growth; dissipation
展性 *hattensei* possibilities for growth
展的 *hattenteki* expanding, growing
展家 *hattenka* a man about town; fast liver
展期 *hattenki* period of expansion
11 達 *hattatsu* growth, development, progress, advancement ⌈huming
掘 *hakkutsu* excavation; disinterring, ex-
現 *hatsugen* revelation, manifestation
著 *hatchaku* departure and arrival ⌈animals)
情 *hatsujō* sexual excitement, heat (in
情期 *hatsujōki* puberty; mating season
動 *hatsudō* motion, activity, exercise (of
動力 *hatsudōryoku* motive power ⌊power)
動的 *hatsudōteki* active
動機 *hatsudōki* motor, engine
動機船 *hatsudōkisen* motorboat, motor ship
12 揚 *hatsuyō* exaltation, promotion
揮 *hakki* exhibition, demonstration; real-
港 *hakkō* leaving port ⌊ization
程 *hattei* start of a journey
給 *hakkyū suru* issue (passports, etc.)
註 *hatchū* ordering (goods)
散 *hassan* exhalation; emanation; diffusion; radiation; evaporation; divergence
着 *hatchaku* departure and arrival
覚 *hakkaku* detection, disclosure
喪 *hatsumo* death announcement
13 源 *hatsugen* source of water, origins
煙 *hatsuen* fuming, emitting smoke
艇 *hattei* start of a boat race
意 *hatsui, hotsui* initiative, suggestion, original idea ⌈(of an idea)
想 *hassō* expression (in music); conception
禁 *hakkin, hatsukin* banned, sale prohibited
電 *hatsuden* generation of electricity; dispatch of a telegram
電子 *hatsudenshi* armature
電体 *hatsudentai* charged body
電所 *hatsudensho* powerhouse
電機 *hatsudenki* dynamo, generator
14 端 *hottan, hattan* origin, commencement
語 *hatsugo* speech, utterance; introductory word to a sentence such as "well"
駅 *hatsueki* starting station

酵 *hakkō* fermentation
酵素 *hakkōso* ferment, yeast, leaven
15 憤 *happun suru* be enraged, be inspired
熱 *hatsunetsu* attack of fever; generation of heat
輦 *hatsuren* imperial-carriage departure
16 奮 *happun suru* be enraged; be inspired
頭人 *hottōnin* ringleader, originator, pro-
20 議 *hatsugi* proposal, motion ⌊moter
21 露 *hatsuro* expression, manifestation, revelation

7

發 3093 F1296 See 発 3092.

A **登** 3094 F1296 Tō. To. *nobo(ru), nobo(ri)* (see under 上 798.0).
3 口 *nobo(ri)guchi* = 上口 798.3
山 *tozan* mountain climbing, mountain
山者 *tozansha* mountain climber ⌊ascent
山家 *tozanka* mountaineer, alpinist
山隊 *tozantai* mountain-climbing party
山期 *tozanki* mountain-climbing season
5 用 *tōyō* appointment; promotion
庁 *tōchō* attendance at the office
仙 *tōsen suru* die; become a deathless saint
6 行 *tōkō* hill climbing
7 坂 *nobo(ri)zaka* ascent, upgrade
8 板 *tōban suru* step into the pitcher's box
9 城 *tojō* attendance at the castle
院 *tōin* attendance at the diet
省 *tōshō* attendance at the ministry
10 高 *tokō suru* climb up, ascend
校 *tōkō* attending school
祚 *tōso* accession to the throne
記 *tōki* registry, registration
記所 *tōkisho* registration place
記料 *tōkiryō* registration fee
11 庸 *tōyō* appointment; promotion ⌈mountain
道 *nobo(ri)michi* uphill road, road up a
頂 *tochō, tōchō* ascent (of a mountain)
第 *tōdai suru* pass an exam
舷礼 *tōgenrei* salute from the deck
12 遐 *tōka* death of an emperor
極 *tōkyoku* accession, enthronement ⌈scene
場 *tōjō suru* enter the stage; appear on the
場人物 *tōjō jimbutsu* cast of a play
13 楼 *tōrō* going up a tower; visiting a brothel
載 *tōsai suru* register, record, enter
14 閣 *tōkaku* climbing a tower; entering the
16 壇 *tōdan* ascending the platform ⌊cabinet
龍門 *tōryūmon* the only gateway to eminence
録 *tōroku* registration, entry, record, enroll-
録済 *tōrokuzu(mi)* registered ⌊ment
録商標 *tōroku shōhyō* registered trademark

録簿 *tōrokubo* register
17臨 *tōrin suru* mount an eminence; ascend the throne
19簿 *tōbo* registration

攀 *tōhan suru* climb up, ascend
攀者 *tōhansha* climber
攀隊 *tōhantai* climbing party

RAD. 白 106

Shiroi white. Nickname: White.

A 白 3095 / F1298 HAKU, BYAKU white. *shiro(mu)*, *shira(mu)* grow light; turn gray, whiten; weaken. *shiro* white; innocence. *shiro(i)* white; fair (skin); gray (hair); blank (paper); spotless; innocent. *shiro(ppoi)* whitish. *shira* feigned ignorance. *serifu*=台詞 848.12. *shiro(meru) vt* whiten. *shira(keru)* become cheerless; become chilled; be spoiled (as a child). *shira-* white.

2十字 *hakujūji* white cross
人 *hakujin* white man, Caucasian
人種 *hakujinshu* white race
3土 *shiratsuchi* kaolin; mortar
下 *shiroshita* treacle, molasses
刃 *hakujin, shiraha* naked sword, drawn sword
小豆 *shiroazuki* small white bean
子 *shirako* milt, roe; albino. *shiro(k)ko* albino
子鳩 *shirakobato* turtledove
4文 *hakubun* old unpunctuated Chinese text
水 *shiromizu* white water left after washing rice
太 *shirata* sapwood
内障 *hakunaishō* white cataract
日 *hakujitsu* daytime, broad daylight
日夢 *hakujitsumu* daydream
木 *shiraki* plain wood, unfinished woodwork
木綿 *shiro momen* white cotton cloth
切 *shira(o)ki(ru)* pretend not to know
切符 *shirogippu* first-class ticket
5目 *shirome* whites of the eyes
生地 *shirokiji* white cloth; white ground
白 *shirojiro* pure white. *shirajira* dawning. *hakuhaku* very clear. *shirajira(shii)* barefaced (lie). *shirajira(shiku)* with feigned ignorance; under false premises
白明 *shirashira-a(ke)* dawn, daybreak
玉 *hakugyoku* white jade. *shiratama* white gem, pearl; rice-flour dumplings
玉粉 *shiratamako* rice flour
玉椿 *shiratama tsubaki* white camellia
6糸 *shira-ito* white thread
衣 *byakui, byakue, hakui* white robe
地 *shiroji* white cloth; white ground
地図 *hakuchizu* outline map, contour map
帆 *shiraho* white sail; boat with a white sail
光 *hakkō* white light, corona
百合 *shirayuri* Easter lily

灯油 *hakutōyu* kerosene
米 *hakumai* polished rice
米食 *hakumaishoku* white-rice diet
羽 *shiraha* white feather
羽矢立 *shiraha (no) ya (o) ta(teru)* choose a human sacrifice; select someone
血病 *hakketsubyō* leukemia
血球 *hakkekkyū* white corpuscles
色 *hakushoku* white
色人種 *hakushoku jinshu* white race
色金 *hakushokukin* white gold
7身 *shiromi* white of an egg; white meat; sap; sapwood
妙 *shirotae* white; white cloth
状 *hakujō* confession, acknowledgment
兎 *shiro-usagi* white rabbit
系露人 *Hakkei Rojin* White Russian
亜 *hakua* chalk, chalkstone
亜館 *Hakuakan* White House
兵 *hakuhei* naked sword, drawn sword
兵戦 *hakuheisen* hand-to-hand fight
8金 *hakkin* platinum
雨 *haku-u* shower
味 *shiromi* whiteness; white of an egg
波 *shiranami* white-capped waves; thief
泡 *shira-awa* white bubbles, foam
狐 *byakko, shirogitsune* white fox
夜 *hakuya* white (arctic) night, short night
苔 *hakutai* fur on the tongue
事 *shiregoto* foolish thing
拍子 *shirabyōshi* medieval female dancer
虎隊 *Byakkotai* the White Tiger Band
河夜船 *shirakawa-yofune* sound sleep
9面 *hakumen* unpainted face; pale face; fair skin; inexperience. *shirafu* sobriety, soberness
眉 *hakubi* prominence, excellence, best example, the pick of
洲 *shirasu* sand bar; court, the bar
虹 *shironiji* fog bow, white rainbow
星 *shiroboshi* white dot; victory mark
茶 *shiracha* straw color, light brown
昼 *hakuchū* daytime, broad daylight, midday
飛白 *shiro kasuri* white cloth with black splashed patterns
胡麻 *shirogoma* white seasame seed

5 玄 玉 王 瓜 瓦 甘 生 用 田 疋 疒 癶 【白】 皮 皿 目 矛 矢 石 示 ネ 内 禾 穴 立

砂 *hakusha, shirasuna, hakusa* white sand
砂青松 *hakusa-seishō* white sand and green pines; beautiful seashore scene
砂糖 *shirozatō* white sugar
10 馬 *hakuba, shiro-uma, shira-uma* white horse
骨 *hakkotsu* skeleton, bleached bones
扇 *hakusen* white fan
閃 *hakusen* white flash (on TV)
梅 *shira-ume* white plum blossoms; white-blossom plum tree
浜 *shirahama* white beach
酒 *shirozake* white saké
書 *hakusho* a white paper, a white book
陶土 *hakutōdo* kaolin
栗毛 *shirakurige* light-chestnut-colored horse
紙 *shirakami, hakushi* white paper; blank paper; flyleaf; clean slate
紙委任状 *hakushi ininjō* a blank power of attorney
粉 *oshiroi* face powder, face paint
粉下 *oshiroishita* powder base, face cream, beauty wash
粉気無 *oshiroike (no) na(i)* without make-up
粉刷毛 *oshiroibake* powder puff
粉臭 *oshiroikusa(i)* make-up overdone
粉焼 *oshiroiya(ke)* (cosmetic) powder burn
粉箱 *oshiroibako* face-powder box
11 魚 *shira-uo* whitebait
鳥 *hakuchō* swan
黒 *shiro-kuro* black and white; good and bad; right or wrong; guilty or innocent
描 *hakubyō* plain sketch
菜 *hakusai* Chinese cabbage; celery cabbage
菊 *shiragiku* white chrysanthemum
票 *hakuhyō* white (affirmative) vote; blank vote ; favorable vote
雪 *hakusetsu, shirayuki* (white) snow
粘土 *hakunendo* alumina, argil
鹿毛 *shirakage* light-fawn-colored horse
張提灯 *shiraha(ri)jōchin* white paper lantern
眼 *shirome, hakugan* the whites of the eyes
眼視 *hakuganshi suru* look coldly at, look askance at, frown upon
堊 *hakua* chalk; chalkstone; white wall
堊館 *Hakuakan* White House
12 歯 *shiraha* white teeth
晰 *hakuseki* white
湯 *sayu* plain hot water
焼 *shiraya(ki)* broiling fish unseasoned
斑 *shirafu, shirobuchi* white spot
絣 *shiro kasuri* white cloth with black splashed patterns
貂 *shiroten* ermine
皙 *hakuseki* white (race), white complexion
煮 *shirani* boiled salted fish
葦毛 *shiro ashige* gray horse
装束 *shiroshōzoku* white dress
無垢 *shiromuku* white silk kimono
葡萄酒 *hakubudōshu, shiro budōshu* white wine
雲 *haku-un, shirakumo* white clouds, fleecy clouds
雲母 *shiro ummo* muscovite, mica
13 鼠 *shironezumi* white rat
痴 *hakuchi* imbecility
蓮 *byakuren* white lotus
滝 *shirataki* a sheet-like waterfall
絹 *shiroginu* white silk
鉛 *hakuen* white lead
戦 *hakusen* hand-to-hand fight; barehanded fight
塗 *shironu(ri)* whitewashed, white-painted, white-plastered
詰草 *shirotsumekusa* white clover
鉢巻 *shirohachimaki* white headband
話 *hakuwa* colloquial Chinese
話文学 *hakuwa bungaku* colloquial Chinese literature
14 旗 *hakki, shirahata* white flag; flag of truce
樺 *shirakaba, shirakamba* white birch
磁 *hakuji* white chinaware
綾 *shira-aya* figured white silk
銀 *shirogane* silver
墨 *hakuboku* chalk
熊 *shirokuma, shiroguma* polar bear
綿布 *shiromempu* white cotton
銅 *hakudō* nickel
銅貨 *hakudōka* nickel coins
髪 *hakuhatsu, shiraga* white hair, gray hair
髪染 *shiragezo(me)* dyeing gray hair black
髪頭 *shiraga atama* gray head
15 線 *hakusen* white line, white tape
蝶 *shirochō* white butterfly
熱 *hakunetsu* white heat, incandescence; climax
熱化 *hakunetsuka suru* approach the climax
熱灯 *hakunetsutō* incandescent lamp
熱戦 *hakunetsusen* an exciting game
16 糖 *hakutō* white sugar
鞘 *shirasaya* a plain wood scabbard
髭 *shirahige* gray mustache
壁 *shirakabe. hakuheki* white wall, white-washed wall
頭翁 *hakutōō* white-haired old man
17 濠 *Hakugō* White Australia
鍵 *hakken* the white keys
檀 *byakudan* sandalwood, almug wood
檀油 *byakudan-yu* sandalwood oil
18 襟 *shiroeri* white collar
璧 *hakuheki* white gem; a treasure
19 癡 *hakuchi* imbecility
蟻 *shiroari* white ant, termite
20 蘭 *hakuran* white orchid
21 魔 *hakuma* white devil, the snow
蠟 *hakurō* white refined wax
露 *Hakuro* White Russia; white dew
23 鑞 *byakurō, shirome* pewter, solder
24 鷺 *shirasagi* snowy heron

— 1 —

百 See 33.

— 3 —

帛 3096/F613 HAKU cloth. [巾]

A **的** 3097/F1304 **的** TEKI. *mato* mark, target; object; the point. *-teki* adjective ending.
4 中 *tekichū suru* hit the mark, come true, guess right
5 外 *matohazu(re)* wide of the mark; out of focus
9 屋 *tekiya* racketeer, faker; stall-keeper
15 確 *tekkaku, tekikaku* precision, accuracy, infallibility

— 4 —

皆 See 2471.

皈 3098/F1306/F1041 See **帰** 1582.

B **泉** 3099/F1088 SEN. *izumi* spring, fountain (head), source. [水]
3 下 *senka* hades; the next world
4 水 *sensui* fountain, miniature lake
5 石 *senseki* ponds, streams, and rocks (in a garden)
9 亭 *sentei* garden-pond arbor
11 貨紙 *senkashi* reclaimed paper
13 殿 *izumi dono* ancient garden pavilion
源 *sengen* source of a stream
15 熱 *izumi netsu* a type of scarlet fever

A **皇** 3100/F1305 KŌ. Ō. *sumeragi, sumera* emperor.
3 土 *kōdo* the emperor's domain
女 *kōjo, ōjo* imperial princess
子 *ōji, kōshi* imperial prince
上 *kōjō* the emperor
4 化 *kōka* imperial authority
天 *kōten* heaven, providence
太子 *kōtaishi* crown prince
太后 *kōtaikō, kōtaigō* empress dowager, queen mother
太妃 *kōtaihi* an emperor's secondary wife who bears an heir
太弟 *kōtaitei* emperor's younger brother
太神宮 *Kōtai Jingū* the Ise Shrine
太孫 *kōtaison* emperor's eldest direct-line grandson
5 兄 *kōkei* the emperor's elder brother
礼砲 *kōreihō* imperial salute, 21 guns
6 妃 *kōhi* empress, queen
考 *kōkō* the late emperor
后 *kōgō* empress, queen
后陛下 *Kōgō Heika* Her Majesty the Empress
7 図 *kōto* the emperor's plan
位 *kōi* imperial throne
沢 *kōtaku* imperial favors
系 *kōkei* imperial line
弟 *kōtei* emperor's younger brother
君 *sumeragimi* (the Japanese) emperor
8 国 *kōkoku* the (Japanese) Empire
妹 *kōmai* the emperor's younger sister
姉 *kōshi* the emperor's elder sister
宗 *kōsō* emperor's ancestors
典 *kōten* Japanese classics
居 *kōkyo* Imperial Palace
居前広場 *Kōkyomae Hiroba* Palace Plaza
9 威 *kōi* imperial power or prestige
胤 *kōin* imperial descendant
城 *kōjō* imperial palace
祖 *kōso* founder of the Imperial Family, Emperor Jimmu; the Sun Goddess
軍 *kōgun* imperial army
室 *Kōshitsu* the Imperial Household, the reigning line
紀 *Kōki* Imperial Era
紀紀元 *Kōki Kigen* Imperial Era
帝 *kōtei* emperor
帝礼拝 *kōtei reihai* emperor worship
10 孫 *kōson* imperial grandchild, imperial descendant
祚 *kōso* imperial throne
陵 *kōryō* imperial mausoleum
都 *kōto* imperial capital
恩 *kōon* imperial favor
宮 *kōgū* imperial palace
宮警察 *Kōgū Keisatsu* Imperial Guards
11 道 *kōdō* the imperial way
運 *kōun* prosperity of the imperial throne
基 *kōki* foundation of the imperial rule
族 *kōzoku* member of the Imperial Family
族会議 *Kōzoku Kaigi* Imperial Family Council
族旗 *kōzokuki* imperial standard
12 統 *kōtō* imperial line
朝 *kōchō* imperial court; Japan
御国 *Sumeramikuni* Japan
13 継 *kōkei* emperor's successor
嗣 *kōshi* imperial heir, crown prince
漢薬 *kōkan-yaku* Chinese herb remedies
14 旗 *kōki* imperial standard
15 霊 *kōrei* spirits of the emperors
17 謨 *kōbo* imperial policy
18 闕 *Kōketsu* Imperial Palace
儲 *kōcho* heir apparent, crown prince

— 5 —

皋 3101/F1306 See **皐** 3104.

畠 3102 F1274 (国字) *hatake, hata* garden, field, farm, plantation. [田]
8 物 *hatamono* field crop

— 6 —

皎 3103 F1306 Kyō white; shining.
15 潔 *kyōketsu* purity, innocence, integrity, bravery

皐 3104 F1306 **臯** Kō swamp; shore.
4 月 *satsuki* lunar 5th month

— 7 —

皓 3105 F1306 Kō white, clear.
12 歯 *kōshi* white teeth

— 10 —

緜 3106 F1469 F1467 See **綿** 3566. [糸]

皚 3107 F1307 Gai white.
15 皚 *gaigai(taru)* snowy, silver white

魄 3108 F2125 Taku, Haku soul, spirit. [鬼]
2 力 *hakuryoku* force, intensity, appeal

RAD. 皮 107

Kegawa animal hide or *hi no kawa* (*kawa* "leather" or "skin" written with the character read *hi*) as distinguished from Rad. 177. Nickname: Skin

A **皮** 3109 F1308 Hi. *kawa* skin; hide; leather; fur, pelt; bark; peeling, husk, shell; film, cream.
3 工場 *kawa kōba* tannery
下 *hika no* subcutaneous
下注射 *hika chūsha* hypodermic injection
4 切 *kawaki(ri)* leather cutter; beginning; originator
5 付 *kawatsu(ki)* unskinned
6 衣 *kawagoromo, kawaginu* fur coat, leather coat
肉 *hiniku(ru)* be sarcastic. *hiniku* sarcasm, irony
肉屋 *hinikuya* cynic, a sarcastic person
肉家 *hinikuya* cynic, a sarcastic person
8 具 *kawagu* leather goods
9 革 *hikaku* hides, leather
屋 *kawaya* furrier, tanner
相 *hisō na* apparent, outward, surface, superficial
10 被 *kawakabu(ri)* leather headgear; wearing leather headgear
針 *kawabari* leather needle
剝 *kawaha(gi)* skinner. *kawamu(ki)* paring, peeling
11 笛 *kawabue* whistling with the lips
袋 *kawabukuro* leather bag, wineskin
12 殻 *hikaku* shell, crust
13 想 *hisō*＝皮相 (see above–9)
14 層 *hisō* cortex
製 *kawasei* made of leather
算用 *kawazan-yō, kawasan-yō* counting one's unhatched chickens
15 膚 *hifu* skin
膚炎 *hifuen* dermatitis
膚科 *hifuka* dermatology
膚科学 *hifukagaku* dermatology
膚骨 *hifu (to) hone* skin and bone
膚病 *hifubyō* skin disease
膚感覚 *hifu kankaku* sense of touch
22 癬 *hizen* itch, scabies, mange

— 9 —

皷 See 5415. [鼓]

頗 3110 F2059 Ha be prejudiced. *sukobu(ru)* exceedingly, extremely. [頁]

皸 3111 F1308 **皹** Kun. *hibi* skin cracks or roughness (due to cold or wind).

— 10 —

皺 3112 F1309 Shū. *shiwa* wrinkles, lines (on the face); creases, rumples, folds. *shiwa(darake)* wrinkled.
5 立 *shiwada(tsu)* wrinkle up
6 曲 *shūkyoku* a fold (in geology)
7 伸 *shiwano(bashi)* smoothing; recreation, amusement
8 苦茶 *shiwakucha* wrinkled, crumpled, withered
11 寄 *shiwayo(ru)* become wrinkled. *shiwayo(se)* shifting (the loss) to
13 腹 *shiwabara* wrinkled abdomen

RAD. 皿 108

Sara dish or *shitazara* bottom "dish." Nickname: Dish.

皿 3113 F1309 BEI. MYŌ. *sara* dish; a helping; a course.
[6]回 *saramawas(shi)* dish-spinning trick
[9]洗 *sara-ara(i)* dishwashing; dishwasher
[10]秤 *sarabakari* balances

— 3 —

盂 See 48.

— 4 —

盆 盆 See 594.

盃 See 杯 2206.

盈 3114 F1310 EI. *mi(chiru)*, *mi(tsuru)* (see under 満 2636.0).
[4]月 *eigetsu* waxing moon
[11]虚 *eikyo suru* wax and wane
[17]虧 *eiki*, *michikake* waxing and waning phases (of the moon)

— 5 —

益 益 See 597.

— 6 —

盒 See 496.

B 盗 3115 F1312 盜 TŌ thief. *nusu(mu)* steal, rob, pilfer.
[2]人 *nusubito, nusutto* thief
人根性 *nusubito konjō* thievish propensity
人猛猛 *nusubito-takedake(shii)* brazen (robber) ⌈thieving propensity
[4]心 *tōshin, nusu(mi)gokoro* impulse to steal,
[5]用 *tōyō* embezzlement; surreptitious use
犯 *tōhan* burglary, theft
去 *nusu(mi)-sa(ru)* run away with, kidnap
出 *nusu(mi)-da(su)* steal
[6]伐 *tōbatsu* secret felling (of trees)
汗 *tōkan, nease* night sweat
[7]見 *nusu(mi)-mi(ru)* steal a glance
足 *nusu(mi)ashi* walking stealthily
作 *tōsaku* plagiarism
[8]取 *nusu(mi)-to(ru)* steal
[9]食 *nusu(mi)gu(i)* stealing and eating
品 *tōhin* stolen article, stolen goods
[10]笑 *nusu(mi)wara(i)* laughing up one's sleeve
[11]視 *tōshin suru* peek unseen
[12]塁 *tōrui* stolen base
[13]賊 *tōzoku* thief, robber, burglar
電 *tōden* stealing electricity by wire tapping
載 *tōsai* plagiarism ⌈ping
[14]聞 *nusu(mi)gi(ki)* eavesdropping, wire tap-
読 *nusu(mi)yo(mi)* surreptitious reading
[17]聴 *tōchō* wire tapping; unlicensed radio
[18]癖 *tōheki* kleptomania ⌊listening
難 *tōnan* robbery, burglary, theft
難品 *tōnanhin* stolen goods
難保険 *tōnan hoken* theft insurance

B 盛 3116 F1311 盛 SHŌ. SEI. JŌ. *saka(ru)* prosper, flourish; copulate (animals). *mo(ru)* serve, fill; heap up; prescribe or give (medicine); poison; mark out, graduate. *mo(ri)* quantity; good measure, liberal serving. *saka(n) na* prosperous; successful (meeting); energetic; enthusiastic; popular; furious (attack); keen (competition); extensive, large. *saka(ri)* height, peak; prime, bloom; heat (in animals).
[3]土 *mo(ri)tsuchi* raising the ground level
大 *seidai na* prosperous, grand, magnificent, successful (meeting), enthusiastic (welcome) ⌈pile up, heap up
上 *mo(ri)-a(garu)* rise, swell. *mo(ri)-a(geru)*
[4]込 *mo(ri)-ko(mu)* incorporate in
切 *mo(ri)ki(ri)* single helping
[5]代 *seidai* prosperous age
[6]返 *mo(ri)-kae(su)* rally, recover
会 *seikai* successful meeting
年 *seinen* prime of life
名 *seimei* fame, reputation
[7]花 *mo(ri)bana* a vase of solid-packed flowers
沢山 *mo(ri)dakusan* many, a lot of, all kinds of; crowded (program)
[8]況 *seikyō* prosperity, success, boom
典 *seiten* grand ceremony
者 *shōja* prosperous person
事 *seiji* grand event; splendid enterprise
[9]砂 *mo(ri)zuna* a pile of sand
[10]時 *seiji* prime of life; prosperous age. *saka(ri)doki* prosperous time; crowded time; season or heat (in animals)
殺 *mo(ri)-koro(su)* kill by poisoning
夏 *seika* midsummer
衰 *seisui* rise and fall, ups and downs, vicissitudes; welfare

5 玄 玉 王 瓜 瓦 甘 生 用 田 疋 疒 癶 白 皮 7【皿】 目 矛 矢 石 示 ネ 内 禾 穴 立

宴 *seien* grand banquet 「enterprise
挙 *seikyo* an excellent plan; a prosperous
11運 *seiun* prosperity, good fortune 「ket
菓子 *mo(ri)gashi* cakes arranged in a bas-
12場 *saka(ri)ba* pleasure resort; busiest quarters (of a town), crowded place
粧 *seisō* heavy elegant make-up
装 *seisō* best clothes, beautiful attire, full regalia, full armor
14徳 *seitoku* illustrious virtues
15儀 *seigi* grand ceremony
潰 *mo(ri)-tsubu(su)* get a person drunk
蕎麦 *mo(ri)soba* buckwheat noodles served on a draining receptacle
18観 *seikan* grand spectacle

7

盜 3117/F1312 See 盗 3115.

盛 3118/F1311 See 盛 3116.

8

盞 See 1808.

A 盟 3119/F1313 MEI oath; alliance.
4友 *meiyū* staunch friend
5主 *meishu* leader, leading power (of an al-
兄 *meikei* an honored friend 」liance)
6休 *meikyū* student strike
邦 *meihō* ally
9約 *meiyaku* pledge, pact, alliance

9

盡 3120/F1313 See 尽 1380.

B 監 3121/F1313 監 KAN. *tsukasa* (see under 司 877.0).
6守 *kanshu* custody, surveillance
守人 *kanshunin* custodian, (forest) ranger
8房 *kambō* cell, ward 「sor, auditor
事 *kanji* inspector, superintendent, supervi-
9軍 *kangun* command of an army
査 *kansa* inspection; auditing; auditor
査役 *kansayaku* inspector, controller, audi-
10修 *kanshū* (editorial) supervision 」tor
11理下 *kanrika* under the supervision of
視 *kanshi* guarding, observation, inspection, supervision, surveillance
視所 *kanshisho* observation post, guard box, lookout 「caretaker
視者 *kanshisha* superintendent, watchman,
視班 *kanshihan* inspection team
視船 *kanshisen* police boat
視線 *kanshisen* picket line
13禁 *kankin* imprisonment
督 *kantoku* supervision, surveillance; jurisdiction; inspector, superintendent; direction; (film) producer; manager; bishop
督下 *kantokuka* under the jurisdiction of
督者 *kantokusha* overseer, superintendent, inspector
督官 *kantokukan* inspector, superintendent
督官庁 *kantoku kanchō* competent authorities
14獄 *kangoku* prison, jail, penitentiary, place of detention
製 *kansei* controlled manufacturing
察 *kansatsu* inspection; inspector
察官 *kansatsukan* police supervisor
20護 *kango* custody

10

盡 See 尽 1380.

B 盤 3122/F1314 BAN, HAN shallow bowl, platter, tray, tub; board; phonograph record.
5石 *banjaku* huge rock. *banseki* the *go* board and its checkers
台 *bandai* shallow fish tray
7陀 *handa* solder; pewter
9面 *bammen* face of a record or board
10秤 *sarabakari* balances
根 *bankon* coiled root; obstacle; hardship
根錯節 *bankon-sakusetsu* severe trials, hardships
15踞 *bankyo suru* lurk in the way; proudly occupy (territory)

11

盧 See 4114.

盥 3123/F1315 KAN. *tarai* tub, washbasin.
6回 *taraimawa(shi)* balancing a spinning wash tub; monopolizing power in a clique; working thru a profitable deal; holding at one police station after another

12

盪 3124/F1315 TŌ *toro(keru) vi* melt; be charmed, be captivated. *toro(kasu) vt* melt, fuse; charm, captivate.

— 14 —

[illegible] 3125/F-X See 塩 1125. [鹵]

— 19 —

鹽 3126/F2153 See 塩 1125. [鹵]

目 RAD. 109

Me eye. At left: *me hen*. Nickname: Eye.

A 目 3127/F1315 MOKU item, division, class; order (of plants or animals). *me* eye; look, gaze; notice, attention; viewpoint; discrimination, insight; experience; treatment; care, favor, pity; texture, weave; mesh; grain, square; sight, vision; tooth (of a saw); weight; momme (.1325 oz.); eye (of a needle). *moku(suru)* regard as. *me(boshii)* attractive, conspicuous, notable; valuable. *me(magurushii)* dizzy; bewildering; bustling. *ma* eye. *-me* ordinal ending, -st, -nd, -rd, -th; point; degree, extent.

2 八分 *mehachibu* a little below the eyes; most respectfully; a little less than full

3 下 *meshita* subordinate, junior, inferior. *mokka* now, at present

上 *me-ue* seniors, superiors

子勘定 *me(no)ko kanjō* measuring with the eye; mental arithmetic

子算 *me(no)kozan*=word above

4 方 *mekata* weight

止 *me (o) to(meru)* examine carefully

辺 *ma(no)ata(ri)* in one's presence, before one's eyes

切 *me(k)ki(ri)* considerably, noticeably

元 *memoto* the eyes

今 *mokkon* now, at present

分量 *mebunryō* eye measurement

引 *mehi(ki) suru, mebi(ki) suru* heighten the color

引袖引 *mehi(ki)-sodehi(ki)* calling attention by winking or sleeve pulling

5 立 *meda(tsu)* be conspicuous. *me (ni) ta(tsu)* be prominent. *meta(te)* setting (a saw)

処 *medo* aim, goal; outlook: eye (of a needle)

尻 *mejiri* the outside corner of the eye

打 *me-u(chi)* perforation

礼 *mokurei* nod, nodding

白押 *mejiro-o(shi)* jostling, milling

出度 *medeta(i)* happy, auspicious; stupid, half-witted. *(o)medeto(u) (gozaimasu)* congratulations. *medeta(ku)* happily, successfully, auspiciously

玉 *me (no) tama, medama* eyeball; scolding

玉焼 *medamaya(ki)* eggs sunny side up

付 *metsu(ki)* look, eye expression. *metsu(karu), me(kkaru)*=*mitsu(karu)* 見付 4284.5. *me(kkeru)*=*mitsu(keru)* 見付 4284.5. *metsu(ke)*=next word

付役 *metsu(ke)yaku* feudal overseer, public censor

付物 *metsu(ke)mono* a find, acquisition

6 色 *me (no) iro, me-iro* expression of the eyes, ⌊one's countenance

近 *mejika* nearness

印 *mejirushi* landmark, pylon, guide, mark

次 *mokuji* table of contents

安 *meyasu* standard, criterion; aim

当 *mea(te)* guide (as a star); aim. *ma(no)a(tari)* face to face, on the spot, in one's presence, with one's own eyes

早 *mebaya(i)* sharp-eyed, shrewd, easily awakened

先 *mesaki* before one's eyes, under one's nose; immediate future; foresight, acumen; appearance

7 見 *memi(e)* audience, interview; stage debut; service on-trial (of a servant)

角 *mekado* corner of the eye; a sharp look

庇 *mabisashi* visor; eyeshade

利 *meki(ki)* judging; judge, connoisseur, virtuoso. *me (ga) ki(ku)* have good judgment; be a good superintendent

余 *me(ni)ama(ru)* scandalous, intolerable

呉 *me (o) ku(reru)* examine carefully

医者 *me-isha* oculist

抜 *menu(ki) no* main, important

抜通 *menu(ki)dō(ri)* principal street

8 送 *mokusō suru* gaze after

明 *mea(ki)* one who can see, educated person. *mea(kashi)* detective, (police) spy

注 *me (o) soso(gu)* examine carefully

肥 *me (ga) koe(ru)* have good judgment

刺 *meza(shi)* dried sardines tied thru their ⌊eyes

毒 *me(no)doku* something tempting

的 *mokuteki* aim, purpose, intention

的地 *mokutekichi* destination

的物 *mokutekibutsu* objective

的格 *mokutekikaku* objective case

的税 *mokutekizei* special-purpose tax ⌈ment

的補語 *mokuteki hogo* objective comple-

5 玄玉王瓜瓦甘生用田疋疒癶白皮皿【目】0 矛矢石示ネ内禾穴立

9 面 *mezura* appearance, outward show
屎 *mekuso* eye wax, eye discharge
途 *mokuto* aim, goal
通 *medō(ri)* an audience (with); height of the eyes. *me (o) tō(su)* glance thru
垢 *meaka* eye mucus
指 *meza(su)* aim at; spot or eye (someone)
映 *mabayu(i)* glaring, dazzling, blinding
前 *me(no)mae* in one's presence, close at hand. *mokuzen* under one's nose, before one's eyes; immediate (gain). *mesaki*=目先 (see above-6)
星 *meboshi* objective
10 高 *me (ga) taka(i)* have good judgment
病 *meyami* eye trouble; person with eye trouble
眩 *mekurume(ku)* be dazzled. *me (ga) kura(mu)* be dizzy. *memai* dizziness
紛 *memaguru(shii)* dizzy, bewildering, dazzled, confused
脂 *meyani* eye wax, eye secretion
配 *mekuba(se) suru* wink significantly at. *mekuba(ri)* vigilance, surveillance
敏 *mezato(i), mebashiko(i)* quick-eyed, sharp-eyed
笑 *mokushō* laughing with the eyes
差 *meza(su)* aim at; spot (someone). *manaza(shi)* a glance, a look
11 違 *mechiga(i)* mistaken observation
張 *meba(ri) suru* paste paper over, seal up
掛 *mega(keru)* aim at
深 *mabuka ni, mebuka ni* down over the eyes
移 *me-utsu(ri)* distraction, difficulty in choosing
許 *memoto* the eyes
盛 *memo(ri)* scale, graduation
12 減 *mebe(ri)* weight loss
測 *mokusoku* measuring with the eye
覚 *meza(masu)* **vt** rouse, awaken. *meza(meru)* wake up; awake to (reality). *meza(me)* waking, awakening, conversion. *meza(mashii)* remarkable, conspicuous, brilliant. *meza(mashi)* eye-opener (a drink)
覚時計 *meza(mashi)dokei* alarm clock
13 溢 *mekobo(re)* overlooking, oversight. *mekobo(shi)* connivance, overlooking
隠 *mekaku(shi)* eye bandage; blinkers; a (board) screen
障 *mezawa(ri)* eyestore, disfigurement, unsightly object; unsightly area
馴 *mena(reru)* get used to seeing
新 *meatara(shii)* novel, original
蓋 *mabuta* eyelid
睫 *mokushō* eyes and eyebrows; something very close
睫間 *mokushō (no) aida ni* imminently
塗 *menu(ri)* sealing, plastering up
14 端 *mehashi* tact
語 *mokugo suru* wink at
算 *mokusan* anticipation, calculation
旗魚 *mekajiki* swordfish
鼻 *mehana* eyes and nose
鼻立 *mehanada(chi)* looks, features
腐 *mekusa(re)* bleary-eyed person (not alcoholic)
腐金 *mekusa(re)gane* pittance
15 標 *mokuhyō* sign, mark; target; objective; standard
潰 *metsubu(shi)* powder thrown to blind the eyes
縁 *mabuchi* eyelid
論 *mokuromi* plan, scheme; aim, intention; frame-up. *mokuro(mu)* plan, scheme, contemplate
敵 *me (no) kataki* enmity, hostility
撃 *mokugeki* observation
撃者 *mokugekisha* eyewitness
16 積 *mezumo(ri)* estimating by the eye
睹 *mokuto suru* see, observe, witness
醒 *meza(masu)*=目覚 (see above-12)
録 *mokuroku* contents, list, inventory, catalog
薬 *megusuri* eye medicine. *me (no) kusuri* a treat for sore eyes
17 瘉 *meshii* blindness; a blind man
糞 *mekuso* eye discharge
18 癖 *mekuse* twitching of the eye
顔 *megao, mekao* a look
19 鏡 *megane* glasses
20 懸 *me (ni) kake(ru)* show; help
22 籠 *mekago* openwork basket

— 2 —

助 See 719. [力]

— 3 —

直 See 775.

盲 See 297.

A **具** 3128 F208 **具** Gu tool; vessel; means; ingredients (in a dish); counter for armor, suits, sets of furniture. *gu(suru)* possess, have; be accompanied by. *sona(waru), sona(eru)* (see under 備 519.0). *tsubusa ni* minutely, fully. [八]
5 申 *gushin* reporting (to a superior)
6 合 *guai*=工合 1451.6
有 *guyū* preparedness. *guyū suru* have, possess, be endowed with
7 述 *gujutsu* speaking in detail
状 *gujō* full report. *gujō suru* tell the circumstances in detail
足 *gusoku* completeness; armor
足師 *gusokushi* armorer

体 *gutai* concreteness
体化 *gutaika* embodiment, materialization
体的 *gutaiteki* concrete, tangible, definite
体策 *gutaisaku* concrete plan
8 者 *gu(no)mono* companion, follower
10 陳 *guchin* formal statement
案 *guan* framing a plan; concrete plan
11 現 *gugen* incarnation, embodiment
現化 *gugenka* materialization, realization
眼 *gugan* discrimination
眼士 *gugan(no)shi* man of discernment
眼者 *gugansha* man of discernment
12 備 *gubi suru* have, possess, be endowed with
象 *gushō suru* embody, express concretely
象化 *gushōka suru* incorporate, materialize
象的 *gushōteki* concrete, material
14 徳 *gutoku* (Buddhist) merit

4

盾 See 215.

眉 See 219.

相 See 2241.

省 See 218.

看 See 222.

冒 See 冐 2117. [冂]

眄 3129 / F1321 BEN looking askance.

眇 3130 / F1321 BYŌ minuteness. *byō(taru)* little, tiny, insignificant. *sugame* squint, cross-eyes, walleyes.
9 眇 *byōbyō(taru)* trifling, slight

5

看 See 看 222.

眞 真 See 783.

眛 3131 / F1323 MAI dark.

B **眠** 3132 / F1324 MIN sleep. *nebu(ru)*, *nemu(ru)* sleep, die. *nemu(tagaru)* feel sleepy. *nemu(ri-kokeru)* sleep soundly. *nemu(i)*, *nebu(tai)*, *nemu(tai)*, *nemu(ge) ni* *nemu(tage) ni*, *nemu(sō) ni*, *nemu(tasō) ni* sleepy, drowsy, lethargic.
6 気 *nemuke* sleepiness, drowsiness
気覚 *nemukeza(mashi)* cure for drowsiness
9 草 *nemu(ri)gusa* mimosa, sensitive plant
10 病 *nemu(ri)byō* sleeping sickness
16 薬 *nemu(ri)gusuri* sleeping medicine; narcotics

眩 3133 / F1324 GEN faint. *gen(su)* get dizzy; dazzle. *kurume(ku)* go round and round; get dizzy *mabu(shii)* dazzling, glaring, blinding. *mabayu(i)* glaring, dazzling, blinding.
11 彩 *gensai* camouflage
12 惑 *genwaku suru vt* dazzle, daze, blind
然 *genzen* dizziness; dazzling
18 暈 *gen-un*, *memai* dizziness

6

眼 See 3132.

眶 3134 / F1325 KYŌ eyelid.

眥 3135 / F1324 **眦** SEI. SHI. SAI. *manajiri*, *mejiri* outside corner of the eye.

眴 3136 / F1325 SHUN. JUN. KEN. GEN. *mekuwa(su)*, *mekuwa(seru)* signal with the eyes.

眸 3137 / F1325 BŌ pupil (of the eye). *manazashi* a look (at someone). *hitomi* pupil of the eye.
8 子 *bōshi* pupil of the eye

眺 3138 / F1326 CHŌ. *naga(meru)* watch, look at, see; scrutinize. *naga(me)* view, scene.
11 望 *chōbō* prospect, view, outlook

眷 3139 / F1325 KEN look around, consider, regard affectionately.
10 恋 *kenren* attachment, love, yearning
11 族 *kenzoku* family, dependents, household
12 属 *kenzoku*=word above
13 愛 *ken-ai suru* love, be fond of
21 顧 *kenko* favor, patronage

A **眼** 3140 / F1326 GAN. GEN. *me* (see under 目 3127.0). *manako* eye.
2 力 *ganriki*, *ganryoku* insight, power of observation

3 下 *ganka* (a view) below one's eyes
4 辺 *ma(no)ata(ri)* in one's presence, before one's eyes
孔 *gankō* eye socket
中 *ganchū ni* in one's eyes; in one's view
中置 *ganchū (ni) o(kanai)* disregard, ignore
5 玉 *medama* eyeball
目 *gammoku* core, point, gist, essence, main object
6 気 *ganki* eye disease
光 *gankō* glint of the eye; discernment, insight
7 医者 *me-isha* oculist
8 底出血 *gantei shukketsu* eye hemorrhage
9 前 *ganzen* before one's eyes
界 *gankai* field or range of vision
科 *ganka* ophthalmology
科医 *ganka-i* ophthalmologist
10 病 *gambyō, meya(mi)* eye disease, person with sore eyes
疾 *ganshitsu* eye disease
差 *manaza(shi)* a look (at someone)
帯 *gantai* eye bandage
11 深 *mabuka ni* down over the eyes
球 *gankyū* eyeball. *medama, me (no) tama* eyeball; scolding
球銀行 *gankyū ginkō* eye bank
12 筋 *gankin* eye muscles
13 窠 *ganka* eye socket
勢 *gansei* expression of the eyes
14 窩 *ganwa, ganka* eye socket
精疲労 *gansei hirō* eyestrain
18 瞼 *ganken, mabuta* eyelid
19 識 *ganshiki* insight, discrimination, discernment
鏡 *gankyō, megane* spectacles, glasses
鏡屋 *meganeya* optician
鏡蛇 *megane hebi* cobra
鏡越 *meganego(shi) ni* over one's spectacles
鏡橋 *meganebashi* arched bridge

7

睍 Nonstandard for 睨 3148.

睇 3141 / F1327 TEI looking askance at.
11 視 *teishi suru* look askance at

8

睛 3142 / F1327 SEI. *hitomi* pupil of the eye.

睢 3143 / F1328 KI. SUI open the eyes wide.

睥 3144 / F1328 睤 HEI glare at.
13 睨 *heigei suru* glare at, scowl at, frown on, look askance at, leer at

睫 3145 / F1329 SHŌ. *matsuge* eyelashes.
4 毛 *matsuge* eyelashes; cilia

睦 3146 / F1328 BOKU. *mutsu(majii)* friendly, intimate, harmonious. *mutsu(mu), mutsu(bu)* get along well together.
4 月 *mutsuki* 1st lunar month
7 言 *mutsugoto* lovers' talk, words of friendship

督 3147 / F1328 B TOKU. *toku(suru)* command, lead, supervise; urge.
7 励 *tokurei* encouragement
9 促 *tokusoku suru* urge, dun, press (a person for action)
13 戦 *tokusen suru* urge on to victory
戦隊 *tokusentai* front-line disciplinary corps

睨 3148 / F1328 GEI. *nira(mi)* glaring at; authority, power. *nira(mu), nira(meru)* glare at, scowl at; keep an eye on; suspect (of a crime); estimate.
5 付 *nira(mi)-tsu(keru), ne(me)-tsu(keru)* glare at, scowl at
6 回 *ne(me)-mawa(su)* glare around
返 *nira(mi)-kae(su)* glare back
合 *nira(mi)-a(u)* glare at each other, be at odds. *nira(mi)-a(waseru)* take (something) for comparison

睡 3149 / F1327 B SUI. *nemu(ru), nebu(ru)* sleep, die. *nemu(garu)* feel sleepy. *nemu(gari), nemu(gariya)* sleepyhead.
6 気 *nemuke, suike* sleepiness, drowsiness
7 余 *suiyo* after awakening
10 眠 *suimin* sleep
眠中 *suiminchū* while sleeping
眠不足 *suimin fusoku* lack of sleep
眠剤 *suiminzai* sleeping drug, narcotic
眠時間 *suimin jikan* hours of sleep
13 蓮 *suiren* water lily
21 魔 *suima* sleepiness, drowsiness; sandman

9

睾 See 4211.

睿 See 叡 865.

10

瞋 3150 / F1329 瞋 SHIN. *ika(ru)* be angry, get excited, be offended.
10 恚 *shin-i* wrath, indignation

瞑 3151 / F1330 MEI sleep, dark. *mei(suru)* close (one's eyes); sleep in peace. *tsubu(ru)* close (one's eyes).

5 目 *meimoku suru* close one's eyes; die
13 想 *meisō* meditation, contemplation

11

瞟 3152 / F-X Hyō, Byō scrutinizing search.
5 目 *higarame* eyes out of line

瞞 3153 / F1330 Man, Mon deception; coaxing; imposition; obscuring.
11 著 *manchaku* imposture, deception
12 着 *manchaku* imposture, deception

瞠 3154 / F1330 Dō stare intently.
5 目 *dōmoku suru* stare in wonder
8 若 *dōjaku* amazement
12 然 *dōzen* eye-popping surprise

12

瞥 3155 / F1331 Betsu glance at.
7 見 *bekken* glance, glimpse

瞭 3156 / F1331 Ryō clear.
12 然 *ryōzen(taru)* obvious, clear, plain

瞳 3157 / F1331 **瞳** Dō. *hitomi* pupil of the eye.
4 孔 *dōkō* pupil of the eye

瞰 3158 / F1331 Kan look, see.
3 下 *kanka suru* overlook, command a bird's-eye view of
10 射 *kansha suru* fire down on
11 視 *kanshi* overlooking; bird's-eye view

B **瞬** 3159 / F1331 **瞬** Shun. *mabata(ku), majiro(gu)* wink, blink. *matata(ku)* wink, twinkle, flicker. *shibatata(ku), shibata(ku)* wink, blink. *mebata(ki), mabata(ki)* wink, blink. *matata(ki)* wink; twinkling (of stars).
8 刻 *shunkoku* moment, instant
10 時 *shunji* instant, moment, second, minute
息 *shunsoku* instant, moment, second
12 間 *shunkan* instant, moment, second. *matata(ku)ma ni, mabata(ku)ma ni* in the twinkling of an eye

13

瞽 See 5416.

瞼 3160 / F1332 Ken. *mabuta* eyelids.

14

矇 3161 / F1332 Mō blind.
9 昧 *mōmai* ignorance

15

矍 See 867.

19

矗 See 796.

矚 3162 / F1332 Ban. *misona(wasu)* see, witness, inspect.

21

矚 3163 / F1333 Shoku look intently.
5 目 *shokumoku* attention, observation

矛 RAD. 110

Hoko spear. At left: *hoko hen.* Nickname: Spear (cf. Rad. 62).

B **矛** 3164 / F1333 **鉾** Mu. Bō. *hoko* halbert; arms; festival car, float.
6 先 *hokosaki* the point of a sword; spearhead; the brunt (of an argument); the aim (of an attack)
9 盾 *mujun* contradiction
13 楯 *mujun* contradiction

4

矜 3165 / F1333 Kin, Kyō pride; respect.
9 持 *kyōji, kinji* dignity, pride

B **柔** 3166 / F964 Jū, Nyū weakness; gentleness; softness. *yawa(rageru), yawa(ragu)* (see under 和 3268.0). *yawa(rakai), yawa(rakana), yawa(i)* soft, tender, plastic; limp; gentle; mellow. *yawa(ra)* jujitsu. [木]
4 毛 *jūmō* soft hair
5 皮 *jūhi* tanned leather
6 肌 *yawahada* soft skin
8 物 *yawa(raka)mono* silks
和 *nyūwa* gentleness, meekness, mildness

9 柔 *yawayawa* softly, pliantly; gently, mildly; gradually
10 弱 *jūjaku, nyūjaku* weakness, effeminacy, enervation
11 魚 *ika* squid, cuttlefish
婉 *jūen na* gentle and graceful
術 *jūjutsu* jujitsu, jujutsu
道 *jūdō* jujitsu, jujutsu, judo
道家 *jūdōka* judo expert
軟 *jūnan na* soft, pliable, flexible, elastic
軟体操 *jūnan taisō* callisthenics
軟性 *jūnansei* pliability, softness, elasticity, suppleness
12 順 *jūjun* obedience, meekness, docility
靭 *jūjin* elasticity, flexibility
靭性 *jūjinsei* elasticity, flexibility
15 膚 *yawahada* soft skin
17 懦 *jūda* effeminacy

6

A 務 3167 F265 務 Mu. *tsuto(me), tsuto(meru)* (see under 勤 732.0). [力]

11 盛 *tsuto(me)zaka(ri)* a worker's prime

RAD. 矢 111

Ya arrow. At left: *ya hen.* Nickname: Arrow.

B 矢 3168 F1334 Shi. *ya* arrow.

4 文 *yabumi* letter tied to an arrow, a succession of letters
木 *ya(no)ki* arrowwood
5 玉 *yadama* arrows and bullets, missiles
立 *yata(te)* inkhorn; ink-and-pen case
6 竹 *yadake, yatake* arrow bamboo, arrow shaft
印 *yajirushi* a direction arrow
叫 *yasake(bi)* archers' cries, din of battle
先 *yasaki* arrowhead; the point; the moment
羽 *yabane* arrow feathers
羽根 *yabane* weather vane
7 来 *yarai* picket fence, palisade, stockade, barrier
8 表 *yaomote*=矢面 (see below–9)
長 *yatake ni* impetuously, courageously
長心 *yatakegokoro* courageous heart
9 面 *yaomote* thick of the fight; front line of archers; face of the enemy
音 *yaoto* hum of an arrow
柄 *yagara* arrow shaft
飛白 *yagasuri* arrow patterns
狭間 *yazama* loophole, crenel
矧 *yahagi* arrow making
矧師 *yahagishi* arrow maker
10 庭 *yaniwa* archery grounds. *yaniwa ni* suddenly, instantly
師 *yashi* arrow maker
根 *ya(no)ne* arrowhead
根石 *ya(no)ne ishi* flint arrowhead
11 頃 *yagoro* bowshot
張 *ya(p)pari, yahari* too, also, as well, likewise, like the rest, still, just the same, after all, nevertheless
12 場 *yaba* archery ground, archery gallery; house of ill fame
軸 *yajiku* arrow shaft
壺 *yatsubo* aim of an arrow
筒 *yazutsu* quiver
筈 *yahazu* notch of an arrow
筈模様 *yahazu moyō* herringbone pattern
13 傷 *yakizu* arrow wound
継早 *yatsu(gi)baya ni* rapidly, in quick succession
催促 *ya (no) saisoku* urgent demand
14 種 *yadane* remaining arrows (in the quiver)
18 衾 *yabusuma* shower of arrows
22 鱈 *yatara ni* indiscriminately, blindly, recklessly
鱈書 *yataraga(ki)* scribbling

3

A 知 3169 F1335 Chi knowledge, acquaintance, sense. *shi(ru)* know; understand; appreciate, recognize; realize; notice, sense, feel; remember; infer, gather; be concerned with. *shi(reru)* become known, be disclosed, be found out, turn out to be. *shi(rasu)* rule (a country). *shi(raseru)* inform, give notice. *shi(rase)* information, report, news; omen. *shi(reta)* obvious; negligible. -*(kamo)shi(renai)* maybe, perhaps, One can't tell. -*(ka)shi(ra)* I wonder if.... -*shi(razu)* unconsciously, unknowingly; free from (hot weather).

2 人 *chijin, shiryūdo, shi(ri)bito* acquaintance
力 *chiryoku* wisdom, intellectual power, mental capacity, intellect, mentality, brains
3 己 *chiki* acquaintance, appreciative friend
4 日 *chinichi* pro-Japanese
辺 *shi(ru)be* acquaintance, friend
切 *shi(re)ki(tta)* obvious
友 *chiyū* intimate acquaintance
5 召 *shi(roshi)me(su)* know; rule, reign
6 合 *shi(ri)-a(u)* know each other. *shiria(i)* an acquaintance

名 *chimei no* noted, well-known
行 *chigyō* fief, stipend, land tenure, daimyo's estate. *chikō* knowledge and action
行地 *chigyōchi* a fief
行取 *chigyōto(ri)* feudal vassal, daimyo
7見 *chiken* knowledge, information; view, opinion
抜 *shi(ri)-nu(ku)* know thoroly
8性 *chisei* intellect, intelligence, mentality
知 *shi(razu)-shi(razu)* unconsciously, unknowingly
育 *chi-iku* mental training
命 *chimei* age fifty; knowing life
者 *chisha* wise man, sage
事 *chiji* governor
的 *chiteki* mental, intellectual
的労働 *chiteki rōdō* brain work; intelligent service
9勇 *chiyū* wisdom and valor
10振 *shi(ranu) fu(ri)* feigned ignorance; indifference. *shi(tta) fu(ri)* pretending to know
恵 *chie*=智恵 2144.10
恵者 *chiesha* wise man
恵袋 *chiebukuro* brain trust, close advisers
恵歯 *chieba* wisdom tooth
恵輪 *chie (no) wa* puzzle ring
恵熱 *chie netsu* fever accompanying dentition
能 *chinō* intellect, intelligence, mental faculties
能犯 *chinōhan* the crimes of forgery, deception, etc.
能的 *chinōteki* intellectual
能係数 *chinō keisū* intelligence quotient, I.Q.
能商 *chinōshō* intelligence quotient, I.Q.
能検査 *chinō kensa* mental test
11遇 *chigū* favor, friendship, appreciation
略 *chiryaku* ingenuity, talents
悉 *chishitsu* complete knowledge of
過程知 *shi(ri)-su(giru) hodo shi(ru)* know full well
12歯 *chishi* wisdom tooth
渡 *shi(re)-wata(ru)* become widely known
覚 *chikaku* perception, sensation
覚力 *chikakuryoku* perceptibility, sensibility
覚神経 *chikaku shinkei* sensory nerves
14徳 *chitoku* knowledge and virtue; erudition and character
徳体 *chi-toku-tai* mental, spiritual, and physical
15慮 *chiryo* wise idea; planning ability
16謀 *chibō* ingenuity, resourcefulness
18顔 *shi(ri)gao* knowing look. *shi(ranu) kao, shi(ran) kao* unconcerned air, indifference
19識 *chishiki* knowledge, information, learning, attainments, understanding
識人 *chishikijin* a highbrow, an intellectual
識欲 *chishikiyoku* love of learning
識階級 *chishiki kaikyū* intelligentsia
識階層 *chishiki kaisō* intelligentsia
識慾 *chishikiyoku* love of learning

4

矧 3170 F1336 SHIN. *ha(gu)* feather (an arrow).

矩 3171 F1336 KU. *kane* ruler, carpenter's square.
4手 *kane(no)te* right angle
尺 *kanejaku*=曲尺 103.4
勾配 *kane kōbai* 45-degree slope
7折 *kaneo(ri)* bent into a right angle
形 *kukei* rectangle

7

䂓 See 規 4285. [見]

短 3172 F1336 A TAN shortness, brevity; fault, defect, demerit, weak point. *mijika(i)* short, brief.
2刀 *tantō* short sword, dagger
刀直入 *tantō-chokunyū* getting right into the subject; frankness
3小 *tanshō na* small, stunted
才 *tansai* little talent
4文 *tambun* short sentence; short composition
尺 *tanzaku*=短冊 (see below–5)
水路 *tansuiro* 25-meter swim
日 *tanjitsu* short days; a short time
日月 *tanjitsugetsu* short period of time
5打 *tanda* chopping (in baseball)
冊 *tanzaku, tanjaku* small vertical poem card
句 *tanku* short phrase
句集 *tankushū* phrase book
6衣 *tan-i* waistcoat, jacket
気 *tanki* quick temper, irritability, impatience
曲 *tankyoku* short musical piece
7見 *tanken* shortsightedness, narrow view
身 *tanshin* small stature
兵急 *tampeikyū na* impetuous; sudden
兵戦 *tampeisen* hand-to-hand fight
8所 *tansho* shortcoming, defect, fault
夜 *miji(ka)yo, tan-ya* short (summer) night
命 *tammei* short life
波 *tampa* short-wave (length)
波長 *tanhachō* short wave
9信 *tanshin* brief note, news brief
音 *tan-on* short sound
音階 *tan-onkai* minor scale
10針 *tanshin* hour hand
剣 *tanken* dagger; hour hand
時日 *tanjijitsu* short time
時間 *tanjikan* short time
11脚 *tankyaku* short leg
距離 *tankyori* short distance, short range; short-distance race, dash, sprint

距離競走 *tankyori kyōsō* short-distance race, dash, sprint
12 絡 *tanraku* short circuit
評 *tampyō* short criticism, brief review
軸 *tanjiku* minor axis
策 *tanzaku*＝短冊 (see above–5)
期 *tanki* short term, short time
期大学 *tanki daigaku* junior college
期間 *tankikan* short time
期戦 *tankisen* short war
期興行 *tanki kōgyō* play with a short run
期講習 *tanki kōshū* short course
13 路 *tanro* short circuit
靴 *tangutsu* low shoes
資 *tanshi* short-term loan, call loan
詩 *tanshi* short poem
詩形 *tanshikei* short-poem forms
艇 *tantei* boat
艇操練 *tantei sōren* lifeboat drill
艇競漕 *tantei kyōsō* boat race, regatta
14 銃 *tanjū* pistol, revolver
歌 *tanka* 31-syllable poem, tanka
髪 *tampatsu* short hair
15 慮 *tanryo* hot temper; shallowness; narrow-mindedness
編 *tampen* short story, short novel
調 *tanchō* minor key
篇 *tampen* short story, short novel
篇小説 *tampen shōsetsu* short story, short novel
篇集 *tampenshū* sketch book, collection of short stories or essays; short novel
17 縮 *tanshuku* shortening, curtailment, reduction, abridgment, abbreviation
縮形 *tanshukukei* shortened form
18 軀 *tanku* short stature
簡 *tankan* brevity, simplicity
20 籍 *tanzaku*＝短冊 (see above–5)

8

雉 3173/F2013 CHI. *kiji* pheasant. [隹]
3 子 *kiji, kigisu* pheasant

矮 3174/F1337 WAI, AI low; short.
2 人 *waijin* dwarf, manikin, pigmy
3 小 *waishō na* diminutive, pigmy, Lilliputian; stunted
8 林 *wairin* brushwood
9 屋 *waioku* humble cottage; my house
16 樹 *waiju* dwarf tree
18 軀 *waiku* small stature
19 鶏 *chabo* bantam; midget

12

P **矯** 3175/F1337 KYŌ. *ta(meru)* straighten; correct, reform, cure; control (one's feelings); pretend, falsify; aim.
5 正 *kyōsei* reform, correction, training
正院 *kyōsei-in* reform school
正保護 *kyōsei-hogo* correction and rehabilitation
正教育 *kyōsei kyōiku* corrective education
8 直 *ta(me)-nao(su)* set up again; correct, reform, cure
9 風 *kyōfū* moral reform
眇 *ta(metsu)-suga(metsu)* with scrutinizing eyes
15 弊 *kyōheki* reform of evil habits; correction of abuses
16 激 *kyōgeki na* radical, extreme, eccentric

RAD. 石 112

Ishi stone. At left: *ishi hen*. Nickname: Stone.

A **石** 3176/F1338 石 SEKI. SHAKU. *ishi* stone, pebble, rock; jewel; the go playing stones. *koku* 4.96 bushels; 10 cubic feet (of lumber).
3 女 *sekijo, umazume* barren woman
山 *ishiyama* quarry, stony mountain
川 *ishikawa* river with a stony bottom
工 *ishiku, sekkō* stonemason, stonecutter
弓 *ishiyumi* crossbow, catapult
小屋 *ishigoya* stone hut
4 文 *ishibumi* stone monument
火 *sekka* flint fire; flash
片 *sekihen* piece of stone, stone chip
化 *sekka* petrifaction
仏 *ishibotoke, sekibutsu* stone Buddha; stony-hearted person; taciturn person
引 *ishihi(ki)* hauling large stones
切 *ishiki(ri)* stonecutting, quarrying; stonecutter
切場 *ishikiri(ba)* quarry, stone pit
5 目 *ishime* crack in a rock; grain in stone
打 *ishiu(chi)* stoning
本 *ishizuri* rubbing of an inscription
6 臼 *ishi usu* stone mortar, stone mill
匠 *sekishō* stonemason
合戦 *ishi gassen* a fight with stones
灯籠 *ishidōrō* stone lantern
竹 *sekichiku* a pink
竹色 *sekichiku iro* pink color
地 *ishiji* stony ground
地蔵 *ishi Jizō* stone image of Jizo
灰 *ishibai, sekkai* lime
灰水 *sekkaisui* limewater

灰石 *sekkaiseki* limestone
灰泥 *sekkaidei* lime mortar
灰岩 *sekkaigan* limestone
灰窯 *ishibaigama* limekiln
7 床 *ishidoko* masonry river bed
投 *ishina(ge)* stone throwing; sling; catapult
花菜 *tengusa* agar-agar, Ceylon moss
材 *sekizai* stone, building stone
材商 *sekizaishō* stone merchant
8 門 *sekimon* stone gate
径 *ishimichi* stony road
刻 *sekkoku* stone carving; carved stone
斧 *sekifu, ishi ono* stone ax
突 *ishizu(ki)* the point of a sword scabbard; a cover for a spear handle
版 *sekiban* lithography; lithograph
版刷 *sekibanzu(ri)* lithography
英 *sekiei* quartz
英灯 *sekieitō* quartz light
英岩 *sekieigan* quartzite
油 *sekiyu* kerosene, petroleum
油王 *sekiyuō* oil king
油井戸 *sekiyu ido* oil well
油坑 *sekiyukō* oil well
油焜炉 *sekiyu konro* kerosene stove
油鉱床 *sekiyu kōshō* oil deposit
油資源 *sekiyu shigen* oil resources
油槽 *sekiyusō* oil tank
9 屋 *ishiya* stone merchant, stonemason
造 *ishizuku(ri), sekizō* masonry; made of stone
垢 *ishi aka* vegetation clinging to river-bot-
垣 *ishigaki* stone wall ⌊tom rocks
柱 *sekichū* stone pillar
神 *ishigami, shakujin* a stone that is worshipped, a stone god
段 *ishidan* stone step, stone steps
風呂 *ishiburo* stone bath
炭 *sekitan* coal; carboniferous
炭粉 *sekitanko* coal dust
炭船 *sekitansen* coal ship
炭液化 *sekitan ekika* coal liquefaction
炭産地 *sekitan sanchi* coal field
炭殻 *sekitangara* cinders
炭鉱業 *sekitan kōgyō* coal-mining industry
炭層 *sekitansō* coal bed, coal seam
炭酸 *sekitansan* carbolic acid, phenol
炭積込 *sekitan-tsu(mi)ko(mi)* loading coal
10 高 *kokudaka* crop, yield; stipend, salary;
原 *ishiwara* stony field ⌊amount of rice
屑 *ishi kuzu* stone chips, rubble
挽 *ishihiki* hauling large stones
剣 *sekken* stone sword ⌈character, a Joseph
部金吉 *ishibekinkichi* man of incorruptible
11 道 *ishimichi* stony road
婦 *sekifu* barren woman

組 *ishigu(mi)* arrangements of stones in a
船 *ishibune* stone-carrying boat ⌊garden
崖 *ishigake* cliff, stone wall
細工 *ishizaiku* masonry
脳油 *sekinōyu* crude oil
12 間 *ishi(no)ma* stone-floored room (in certain
塀 *ishibei* stone wall ⌊shrines)
塔 *sekitō*=*sekihi* 石碑 (see below–14)
弾 *ishihaji(ki)* marbles (the game)
棺 *sekkan, sekikan* sarcophagus, stone coffin
焼 *ishiya(ki)* roasting on hot stones
割 *ishiwa(ri)* breaking up stones
畳 *ishidatami* stone pavement, stone flooring; checkered pattern
筆 *sekihitsu* slate pencil
筍 *sekijun* stalagmite
13 塚 *ishizuka* pile of stones, cairn
塊 *sekkai, ishikoro, ishikure* stones, pebbles, piece of stone
槌 *ishizuchi* stone hammer; tamper
鉢 *ishibachi* stone bowl
窟 *sekkutsu* stone cave
楠花 *shakunage* rhododendron
14 像 *sekizō* stone image; stone statue
摺 *ishizuri* a rubbing of a carved inscription
榻 *ishizuri*=word above
碑 *sekihi* tombstone, stone slab, stone monu-
綿 *ishiwata, sekimen* asbestos ⌊ment
膏 *sekkō* gypsum, satin spar, alabaster, plaster of Paris
墨 *sekiboku* graphite, black lead
製 *ishisei* made of stone
榴 *zakuro* pomegranate
榴石 *sekiryūseki, zakuro ishi* garnet
15 盤 *sekiban* a slate
器 *sekki* stonework; stone implement
器時代 *sekki jidai* Stone Age
16 橋 *ishibashi, sekkyō* stone bridge
積 *ishizu(mi)* masonry
頭 *ishi atama* hard head, obstinate person
龍子 *tokage* lizard
19 蹴 *ishikeri* hopscotch
鏃 *sekizoku* flint arrowhead
21 蠟 *sekirō* paraffin
24 鹸 *sekken* soap
鹸石 *sekkenseki* soapstone
25 鼈 *hizaragai* a chiton, a coat-of-mail (a shell)

— 1 —

石 See 石 3176.

— 4 —

砌 $\frac{3177}{F1341}$ SAI. SEI. *migiri* time, occasion.

5 玄玉王瓜瓦甘生用田疋疒癶白皮皿目矛矢4【石】示ネ内禾穴立

砒 3178/F1341 HI arsenic.
10 素 *hiso* arsenic
14 酸 *hisan* arsenic acid

B **砕** 3179/F1346 **碎** SAI. *kuda(ku)* break, smash, crush; pulverize; tax (one's ingenuity); explain simply. *kuda(keru)* break, crumble, be crushed, go to pieces; become familiar. *kuda(keta)* broken, crushed; familiar, popular, friendly.
4 片 *saihen* fragment, splinter
5 石 *saiseki* broken stone, rubble; something worthless; crushing rock
氷 *saihyō* rubble ice, fragmentary ice
氷船 *saihyōsen* icebreaker
6 米 *kuda(ke)mai, kuda(ke)gome* broken rice
7 身 *saishin* extreme hardship
8 波 *kuda(ke)nami* breakers, surf
岩機 *saiganki* rock crusher
9 炭器 *saitanki* coal crusher
10 屑 *saisetsu* fragments, splinters, smashed up scrap materials
13 鉱 *saikō* ore crushing
鉱機 *saikōki* ore crusher
19 離 *kuda(ki)-hana(su)* break off from

A **研** 3180/F1344 **硏** KEN. *to(gu)* sharpen, grind, scour, hone, polish; wash (rice).
3 上 *to(gi)-a(geru)* sharpen up
4 水 *to(gi) mizu* whetstone water; water rice has been washed in
5 立 *to(gi)ta(te)* just sharpened
7 究 *kenkyū* study, research, investigation
究心 *kenkyūshin* inquiring mind
究生 *kenkyūsei* research student
究会 *kenkyūkai* research society
究所 *kenkyūjo, kenkyūsho* laboratory, research institute
究科 *kenkyūka* postgraduate course, seminar
究室 *kenkyūshitsu* laboratory, seminar room
究員 *kenkyūin* researcher
究家 *kenkyūka* researcher
8 歩 *kempo* a lady's graceful walk
学 *kengaku* study
物師 *togimonoshi* tool grinder; polisher of swords and mirrors
9 革 *to(gi)kawa* strop
屋 *togiya* polisher, grinder, sharpener
10 修 *kenshū* study and training
修所 *kenshūjo* training institute
15 摩 *kemma* grinding, polishing; studying
澄 *to(gi)-su(masu)* polish well; sharpen well
16 磨 *kemma* grinding, polishing; studying
磨機 *kemmaki* grinder, polisher
23 鑽 *kensan* study

B **砂** 3181/F1341 SA. SHA. *isago, suna* sand.
3 土 *sado, shado* sandy soil
子 *sunago* sand; paper speckled with gold or silver; gold dust; silver dust
山 *sunayama* sand hill, sand bank
上 *sajō* on the sand
5 丘 *sakyū, shakyū* sand dune, sand hill
丘林 *sakyūrin* forest on a sand dune
6 色 *suna iro* sand color
地 *sunaji* sandy soil
防 *sabō* erosion control
州 *sasu* sand bar, sandbank, reef
7 吹 *sunafu(ki)* sandblast
利 *jari, zari* gravel, ballast, pebbles
利土 *jarido* gravelly soil
利道 *jari michi* gravel road
8 岩 *sagan, shagan* sandstone
岸 *sagan* sandy river bank
金 *sakin, shakin* gold dust, alluvial gold, placer gold
金採集 *sakin saishū* placer mining
9 洲 *sasu* sand bar, sandbank, reef
型 *sunagata* (foundry) sandbox
風 *safū* sandstorm
風呂 *sunaburo* sand bath
10 原 *sunahara* desert, sandy plain
埃 *sunabokori* dust, dust storm
浜 *sunahama, sahin* sandy beach
留 *sunado(me)* sand-erosion barrier
蚤 *suna nomi* sand flea
時計 *sunadokei* sand clock, hourglass
11 遊 *suna-aso(bi)* playing in the sand
粒 *suna tsubu* grain of sand
12 場 *sunaba* sand pit
絵 *sunae* sand picture
13 漠 *sabaku* desert
煙 *suna kemuri* dust clouds
路 *suna michi* sandy road
鉄 *shatetsu, satetsu* iron sand, magnetic sand
14 塵 *sajin* dust storm
漉 *sunago(shi)* sand filtering
15 箱 *sunabako* sandbox; sander (on an engine)
16 嘴 *shashi, sashi* sand bar; sandspit
篩 *sunaburui* sand strainer
糖 *satō* sugar
糖大根 *satō daikon* sugar beet
糖黍 *sato kibi* sugar cane
糖煮 *satōni* preserving by boiling with sugar
糖楓 *satō kaede* sugar maple
糖漬 *satōzuke* food preserved in sugar; sweetmeats
20 礫 *sareki, shareki* gravel, pebbles
22 嚢 *sanō, shanō, sunabukuro* sandbag

—— 5 ——

砿 3182/F1968 See **鉱** 4843.

砧 3183 F1342 **碪** CHIN. *kinuta* fulling block.

砥 3184 F1341 SHI. *to* whetstone, grindstone.
[5]石 *to-ishi* whetstone, hone, grindstone
[9]革 *to(gi)kawa* strop
[10]粉 *tonoko* polishing powder

B **砲** 3185 F1342 **砲** Hō gun, cannon, battery; gunnery, ordnance, artillery. *tsutsu* gun.
[3]口 *hōkō* caliber, muzzle (of a gun)
工 *hōkō* artillery and engineers
丸 *hōgan* cannon ball
丸投 *hōganna(ge)* shot-put
[4]手 *hōshu* gunner
火 *hōka* gunfire, shellfire
[5]台 *hōdai* battery, fort
[6]列 *hōretsu* gun emplacement
[7]身 *hōshin* gun barrel
車 *hōsha* gun carriage
尾 *hōbi* breech (of gun or cannon)
床 *hōshō* gun platform
声 *hōsei* sound of firing, roar of a gun
兵 *hōhei* artillery; gunner
兵工廠 *hōhei kōshō* arsenal, armory
[8]金 *hōkin* gun metal
門 *hōmon* embrasure; battleship porthole; gun
卒 *hōsotsu* artilleryman
[10]座 *hōza* gun platform
[11]術 *hōjutsu* gunnery, artillery
[12]塔 *hōtō* turret, cupola
弾 *hōdan* projectile
塁 *hōrui* battery, fort
[13]戦 *hōsen* artillery duel
煙 *hōen* cannon smoke
煙弾雨 *hōen-dan-u* the smoke of guns and a hail of bullets
[14]銅 *hōdō* gun metal
[15]撃 *hōgeki* bombardment, cannonade
[20]艦 *hōkan* gunboat

A **破** 3186 F1343 HA. *ya(buru)* *vt* tear, rip, rend; break, crush, destroy; violate, transgress; defeat; baffle, frustrate. *yabu(ku)* *vt* tear, rip, rend. *yabu(reru)*, *yabu(keru)* *vi* be torn, tear, rip open; be broken, burst; rupture, collapse; be worn out; be defeated; be frustrated. *yabu(re)* rupture, breach, rent, tear, breakdown, collapse. *yabu(re-kabure)* desperation.
[3]口 *yabu(re)guchi* breach (in a wall)
[4]片 *hahen* fragment, splinter; scrap, broken piece
太鼓 *yabu(re)daiko* drum with a broken cover; human wreck
天荒 *hatenkō* unprecedented, record-breaking
天候 *hatenkō*=word above
[5]目 *yabu(re)me, ya(re)me* tear, rent, split, breach
出 *ya(buri)-de(ru)* bursting out (of water)
瓜 *haka* girls at 16; men at 64
瓜期 *hakaki* pubescence (in girls)
甲弾 *hakōdan* armor-piercing shell
甲爆弾 *hakō bakudan* armor-piercing bomb
[6]竹 *hachiku* splitting bamboo. *hachiku no ikio(i)* violent force
防法 *Habōhō* Subversion Prevention Law
[7]戒 *hakai* breaking the (Buddhist) commandments
却 *hakyaku* destruction, demolition
牢 *harō* jailbreak
邪顕正 *haja-kenshō* the destruction of wickedness and the establishment of righteousness
局 *hakyoku* catastrophe, cataclysm, collapse
局的 *hakyokuteki* catastrophic, cataclysmic
[8]門 *hamon* excommunication, expulsion
取 *yabu(ri)-to(ru)* conquer
物 *waremono* broken article; fragile article
[9]風 *hafu* gable
屋 *haoku* dilapidated house
垣 *yaregaki* broken fence or hedge
砕 *hasai* crushing, smashing, splintering
約 *hayaku* breach of contract
[10]倫 *harin* immorality
格 *hakaku* exception
浪 *harō* breakers, surf
[11]船 *hasen* shipwreck
産 *hasan* bankruptcy
産者 *hasansha* bankrupt person
[12]裂 *haretsu* explosion, bursting, rupture, eruption
落戸 *narazumono* shiftless person. *gorotsuki* bully, ruffian, desperado
[13]損 *hason* damage, breakage, breach
滅 *hametsu* ruin, destruction, collapse
毀 *haki* destruction; reversal (by a court)
棄 *haki* breaking (a treaty), revocation, annulment, downfall
傷風 *hashōfū* tetanus, lockjaw
廉恥 *harenchi* shamelessness, infamy
[14]摧 *hasai* crushing, smashing, splintering
獄 *hagoku* jailbreak
綻 *hatan* failure, ruin, bankruptcy (of business or character)
算 *hasan* checking, refiguring; doing over again
[15]談 *hadan* cancellation, annulment, rupture, breaking off, rejection
[16]壊 *hakai* destruction, demolition, collapse
壊力 *hakairyoku* destructive power
壊分子 *hakai bunshi* subversive elements
壊主義 *hakai shugi* vandalism
壊的 *hakaiteki* destructive
壊者 *hakaisha* destroyer, desolator

5 玄玉王瓜瓦甘生用田疋疒癶白皮皿目矛矢【石】示ネ禸禾穴立

壊消防 *hakai shōbō* wrecking
壊消防隊 *hakai shōbōtai* wrecking crew
17鍋 *ware nabe* cracked pot
18顔 *hagan* broad smile
顔一笑 *hagan-isshō* broad smile
19鏡 *hakyō* broken mirror; divorce
20鐘 *waregane* cracked bell
21魔弓 *hamayumi* exorcising bow (used in ridgepole-raising ceremony); toy bow and arrow

6

研 3187/F1344 See 研 3180.

硅 3188/F1344 See 珪 2937.

砦 3189/F1341 SAI. *toride* fort, stronghold, entrenchments.

7

硯 3190/F1346 KEN. *suzuri* inkstone.
5石 *suzuri ishi* inkstone
9海 *suzuri (no) umi* well of the inkstone
15箱 *suzuribako* inkstone case

硫 3191/F1345 B RYŪ sulphur.
6安 *ryūan* ammonium sulphate
11黄 *iō, yuō* sulphur, brimstone
黄泉 *iōsen* sulphur spring
黄華 *iōka* flowers of sulphur
14酸 *ryūsan* sulphuric acid
酸紙 *ryūsanshi* parchment paper

硝 3192/F1345 B 硝 SHŌ saltpeter.
8子 *garasu* glass, pane
子戸 *garasudo* glass door
子切 *garasuki(ri)* glass cutter
子糸 *garasu ito* spun glass
子板 *garasu ita* plate glass; pane
子屋 *garasuya* glass shop
子張 *garasuba(ri)* glazing
子商 *garasushō* glass shop
子窓 *garasu mado* glazed window
子細工 *garasuzaiku* glasswork
子棒 *garasubō* glass rod
子綿 *garasumen* glass wool
子管 *garasukan* glass tube
子器 *garasuki* glassware
子職工 *garasu shokkō* glass blower
4化 *shōka* nitrification
化綿 *shokamen* guncotton
13煙 *shōen* gunpowder smoke
14酸 *shōsan* nitric acid
酸銀 *shōsangin* silver nitrate
16薬 *shōyaku* gunpowder

硬 3193/F1345 B KŌ. *kata(i)* (see under 堅 1096.0).
3口蓋 *kōkōgai* hard palate
4木 *kōboku* hardwood
水 *kōsui* hard water
文学 *kōbungaku* solid reading
化 *kōka* hardening; vulcanization; sclerosis; stiffening
化病 *kōkabyō* sclerosis, hardening
化症 *kōkashō* sclerosis, hardening
5玉 *kōgyoku* jadeite
石鹼 *kōsekken* hard soap
6式 *kōshiki* hard, rigid
式飛行船 *kōshiki hikōsen* rigid dirigible
式庭球 *kōshiki teikyū* hardball tennis
8直 *kōchoku na* sturdy, stout, inflexible
性 *kōsei* hardness
性下疳 *kōsei gekan* hard (syphilitic) chancre
9派 *kōha* tough elements
度 *kōdo* hardness, solidity
度計 *kōdokei* hardness tester
10骨 *kōkotsu* hard bone; firmness, inflexibility, stubbornness
骨漢 *kōkotsukan* sturdy individual, man of will power
11球 *kōkyū* hard (tennis) ball
軟 *kōnan* (relative) hardness
貨 *kōka* metallic money, coin
教育 *kōkyōiku* Spartan discipline
12筆 *kōhitsu* hard writing instruments (pen and pencil)
14膏 *kōkō* ointment, salve
15質 *kōshitsu* hardness; firmness of disposition
質護謨 *kōshitsu gomu* hard rubber

8

碎 3194/F1346 See 砕 3179.

碑 3195/F1347 See 碑 3206.

碗 3196/F1347 WAN porcelain bowl, teacup.

碕 3197/F1347 KI. *saki* cape, spit, promontory.

碍 3198/F1353 礙 GE. GAI obstacle.
8子 *gaishi* insulator

碌 3199/F1346 ROKU. *roku na* satisfactory, proper, respectable, right, good,

worth mentioning; many, much; enough. *roku ni* well, properly, satisfactorily; sufficiently, enough.
[12]無 *roku(demo)na(i)* useless
[13]碌 *rokuroku*＝碌 *roku ni* (see under 碌 3199.0); to no purpose, in idleness

硼 3200 / F1346 **硼** Hō sound of stones struck together.
[9]砂 *hōsha* borax
[10]素 *hōso* boron
[14]酸 *hōsan* boric acid

碇 3201 / F1346 TEI. *ikari* anchor, grapnel.
[8]泊 *teihaku* anchorage, moorings
泊地 *teihakuchi* anchorage, moorings, berth
泊灯 *teihakutō* anchor light
泊所 *teihakujo* anchorage, moorings, berth
泊料 *teihakuryō* anchorage dues
泊船 *teihakusen* ship at anchor
泊港 *teihakukō* anchorage harbor
[13]置 *teichi* anchorage, moorings

碁 3202 / F1346 Go Japanese checkers.
B
[5]石 *go-ishi* a *go* stone, a checker
打 *go-u(chi)* a *go* player
布 *kifu suru* be scattered around
[6]会 *gokai* commercial *go*-playing parlor
会所 *gokaijo*＝word above
[9]客 *gokaku* a *go* player
[15]盤 *goban* checkerboard, *go* board
盤乗 *gobanno(ri)* standing on a checkerboard
盤割 *gobanwa(ri)* laid out like a checkerboard
盤縞 *gobanjima* checkered pattern
[19]羅星如 *kira-hoshi (no) goto(ku)* a galaxy of great men

9

碓 3203 / F1342 See **砧** 3183.

碬 3204 / F-X KA, KE tool grinder.

碣 3205 / F1347 KETSU round stone monument.

碑 3206 / F1347 HI monument, tombstone. *ishibumi* stone monument.
B
[4]文 *hibun* epitaph, inscription
[5]石 *hiseki*＝*sekihi* 石碑 3176.14
[8]帖 *hijō* a rubbing of a stone monument
[9]面 *himen* the face of a monument or its inscription
[14]誌 *hishi* epitaph, inscription
銘 *himei* epitaph, inscription

碩 3207 / F1348 SEKI large; great, eminent.
[8]学 *sekigaku* profound scholar
[14]徳 *sekitoku* man of great virtue
[16]儒 *sekiju* Confucian scholar; scholar

碧 3208 / F1347 HEKI blue; green.
[4]水 *hekisui* blue water
[5]玉 *hekigyoku* jasper
[8]空 *hekikū, aozora* azure sky
[11]眼 *hekigan* blue eyes
[15]潭 *hekitan* blue expanse (of water)

磁 3209 / F1349 **磁** JI magnetism; porcelain.
B
[2]力 *jiryoku* magnetism
[3]土 *jido* kaolin, clay for making chinaware
[4]化 *jika* magnetization
[5]北 *jihoku* magnetic north
石 *jishaku, jiseki* magnet, compass
石盤 *jishakuban* mariner's compass
[6]気 *jiki* magnetism
気学 *jikigaku* magnetics
気嵐 *jiki arashi* magnetic storm
[8]性 *jisei* magnetism
[9]界 *jikai* magnetic field
南極 *jinankyoku* south magnetic pole
[10]針 *jishin* magnetic needle
荷 *jika* magnetic charge
[12]場 *jijō, jiba* magnetic field
極 *jikyoku* magnetic pole
[13]鉄 *jitetsu* magnetic iron
鉄鉱 *jitekkō* loadstone, magnetite
[15]器 *jiki* porcelain

10

磁 3210 / F1349 See **磁** 3209.

磋 3211 / F1350 SA polish.

磑 3212 / F1350 GAI mortar, hand mill.

磊 3213 / F1350 RAI many stones.
[12]落 *rairaku* frankness, openheartedness

磐 3214 / F1350 HAN, BAN wall (in a mine). *iwa* rock, crag; reef.
[5]石 *banjaku* huge rock

磔 3215 / F1350 TAKU crucifixion; pulling limb from limb; exposing a corpse. *haritsuke* crucifixion.

⁶刑 *haritsuke* crucifixion
刑柱 *haritsukebashira* stake, cross
¹⁰殺 *takusatsu* crucifixion by lance thrusts

碾 3216 F1349 TEN, DEN mortar, hand mill. *hi(ku)* grind (grain).
⁶臼 *hikiusu* hand grinding mill
¹²割 *hi(ki)-wa(ru)* grind. *hikiwa(ri)* cracked or ground barley
割麦 *hikiwa(ri) mugi* cracked or ground barley
¹⁵磑 *atsu-usu* stone hand mill

A 確 3217 F1348 確 KAKU firm, tight, hard, solid. *tashi(kameru)* ascertain, confirm, verify. *kaku(taru)*, *tashi(ka)* sure, positive; accurate; reliable; sound, firm; clear, evident; genuine; able, competent; sober, sane; I think; if I remember right. *tashi(ka) ni* certainly, doubtless. *tashi(ka) niwa* for certain. *shika to* certainly, definitely, exactly, firmly, fully.
⁵立 *kakuritsu* establishment
乎 *kakko(taru)* firm, determined, indomitable
乎不抜 *kakko-fubatsu* invincible, indefatigable
乎不動 *kakko-fudō* invincible, indefatigable
⁶守 *kakushu suru* adhere to, cling to, be loyal to
⁷言 *kakugen* positive statement
⁸固 *kakko(taru)* sure, firm
実 *kakujitsu* certainty, authenticity, reliability
実性 *kakujitsusei* reliability, certainty, validity
定 *kakutei* decision, confirmation
定的 *kakuteiteki* definite
定期限 *kakutei kigen* definite period
⁹保 *kakuho suru* secure, ensure, assure, guarantee, maintain
信 *kakushin* conviction, confidence, assurance
約 *kakuyaku* definite promise
¹¹率 *kakuritsu* probability
執 *kakushitsu* discord, antagonism
¹²答 *kakutō* definite answer
然 *kakuzen(taru)* definite, positive
報 *kakuhō* definite news, authentic report
証 *kakushō* conclusive evidence, assurance, confirmation, corroboration
証的 *kakushōteki* corroborative
¹⁴聞 *kakubun suru* learn reliably
徴 *kakuchō* positive proof
認 *kakunin suru* verify, certify, confirm, validate
説 *kakusetsu* established theory
¹⁵論 *kakuron* sound reasoning, incontrovertible argument

11

磨 See 5393.

碻 3218 F-X 確 See 3217.

磚 3219 F1350 F1261 甎 SEN tile.
⁹茶 *dancha* (cheap) brick tea

12

B 礁 3220 F1352 SHŌ sunken rock.

磯 3221 F1351 KE. KI. *iso* seashore, beach.
⁴辺 *isobe* seashore, beach
⁶伝 *isozuta(i)* following the beach
⁸松 *isomatsu* seashore pines
波 *isonami* breakers
⁹臭 *isokusa(i)* smelling of the beach (fish and shells)
¹⁰浪 *isonami* breaker, surf
¹¹釣 *isozuri* beach fishing
¹³路 *isoji* beach road; vicinity of the beach
¹⁹蟹 *isogani* sand crab

13

磔 Nonstandard for 礫 3227.

B 礎 3222 F1352 So. *ishizue* foundation stone, cornerstone.
⁵石 *soseki* cornerstone, foundation stone, footstone
⁷材 *sozai* foundation materials

14

礙 3223 F1353 See 碍 3198.

礪 3224 F1353 REI whetstone; polish.

15

礦 3225 F1968 See 鉱 4843.

礬 3226 F1353 BAN alum.
³土 *hando, bando* alumina, aluminum oxide
⁴水 *dōsa* sizing, glaze

礫 3227 F1353 REKI *tsubute* small stones.
³土 *rekido* gravelly soil
⁸岩 *rekigan* conglomerate

RAD. 示 113

Shimesu to show. At left: 礻 or ネ (4 strokes) *shimesu hen*. Nickname: Showing.

A 示 3228 F1354 JI. SHI indication. *shime(su)* show, indicate, point out, give (an example), signify, display, express. *shime(shi)* (parental) discipline; revelation.

5 圧計 *shiatsukei* pressure gauge

6 合 *shime(shi)-a(u)* inform one another; show one another. *shime(shi)-a(waseru)*, *shime(shi)-a(wasu)* inform one another; plan together; plot together

9 威 *ji-i* demonstration (against something)

威的 *ji-iteki* demonstrative, threatening

威運動 *ji-i undō* demonstration (against

10 唆 *shisa* suggestion ⌊something)

11 達 *shitatsu* directions, instructions

現 *jigen* divine revelation; divine miracles (in Buddhism or Shinto)

教 *shikyō* instruction, information

15 談 *jidan* settlement out of court

1

A 礼 3229 F1368 礼 禮 RAI, REI salutation, salute, bow, courtesy, propriety, ceremony, thanks, appreciation, remuneration, return present. *uya* courtesy.

6 回 *reimawa(ri)* round of thank-you visits

式 *reishiki* etiquette, manners

7 状 *reijō* letter of thanks ⌈ward, fee

8 金 *reikin* honorarium, remuneration, re-

法 *reihō*=*reigi* 礼儀 (see below–15)

物 *reimotsu* present, gift

服 *reifuku* full dress, dress suit, ceremonial dress, evening dress, dress uniform, vestments

参 *reimai(ri)* thanksgiving visit to a shrine

奉公 *reibōkō* unremunerated post-apprenticeship service

典 *reiten* ceremony, ritual, rite, sacraments

典律 *reitenritsu* ceremonial law

拝 *reihai*, *raihai* worship; adoration; church

拝式 *reihaishiki* church services ⌊service

拝学 *reihaigaku* liturgics

拝者 *reihaisha* worshipper

拝堂 *reihaidō* chapel, church, tabernacle,

10 砲 *reihō* gun salute ⌊worship hall

11 遇 *reigū* cordial reception; honors, privi-

12 帽 *reibō* ceremonial hat, silk hat ⌊leges

装 *reisō* ceremonial dress, full dress

13 節 *reisetsu* courtesy, etiquette, propriety,

義 *reigi*=礼儀 (see below–15) ⌊manners

楽 *reigaku* etiquette and music

15 賛 *raisan*=礼讃 (see below–22)

儀 *reigi* courtesy, propriety, manners, de-

儀正 *reigitada(shii)* courteous ⌊corum

儀作法 *reigisahō* courtesy, propriety, manners, decorum

20 譲 *reijō* politeness, courtesy ⌈praise

22 讃 *raisan* worship, adoration, admiration,

3

祀 3230 F1355 SHI. *matsu(ru)* enshrine; worship

A 社 3231 F1354 社 SHA Shinto shrine; association; firm, company, office. *yashiro* Shinto shrine.

2 人 *shajin* shrine priests; villagers

4 中 *shachū* office staff; clique, troupe

友 *shayū* friend of the firm; colleague

内 *shanai* in the shrine; in the company

内電話 *shanai denwa* office telephone sys-

5 主 *shashu* the head of a company ⌊tem

司 *shashi* a Shinto priest

用 *shayō* for company business

用族 *shayōzoku* expense-account aristocrats

外 *shagai* outside the company

外船 *shagaisen* tramp steamer

6 号 *shagō* shrine category; company name

寺 *shaji* shrines and temples

宅 *shataku* company living quarters

名 *shamei* company name

団 *shadan* corporation, association

団法人 *shadan hōjin* corporate person

交 *shakō* society; social life

交性 *shakōsei* sociability

交的 *shakōteki* social, sociable

交服 *shakōfuku* party clothes, evening dress

交室 *shakōshitsu* social hall

交界 *shakōkai* society circles

交家 *shakōka* a social person

交場 *shakōjō* social hall

交場裏 *shakōjōri ni* in fashionable society

交喫茶 *shakō kissa* cabaret ⌈social (service)

会 *shakai* society, community, the world;

会人 *shakaijin* a member of society

会化 *shakaika* socialization

会不安 *shakai fuan* social unrest

会史 *shakaishi* social history ⌈mocracy

会民主主義 *shakai minshu shugi* social de-

会生活 *shakai seikatsu* social life, com-

会主義 *shakai shugi* socialism ⌊munity life

会主義者 *shakai shugisha* socialist

5 玄 玉 王 瓜 瓦 甘 生 用 田 疋 疒 癶 白 皮 皿 目 矛 矢 石 【示 ネ】[4] 内 禾 穴 立

会生態学 *shakai seitaigaku* ecology
会改良 *shakai kairyō* social reform
会状勢 *shakai jōsei* social conditions
会性 *shakaisei* social nature
会的 *shakaiteki* social
会学 *shakaigaku* sociology
会奉仕 *shakai hōshi* social service
会制度 *shakai seido* social system
会事情 *shakai jijō* social conditions
会事業 *shakai jigyō* social service, public-welfare work
会面 *shakaimen* society page, local news page
会相 *shakaisō* phase of life
会科 *shakaika* social studies
会科学 *shakai kagaku* social science
会革命 *shakai kakumei* social revolution
会連帯 *shakai rentai* social solidarity
会政策 *shakai seisaku* social policy
会保障 *shakai hoshō* social security
会党 *Shakaitō* Socialist Party
会部 *shakaibu* city editor's section
会部長 *shakai buchō* city editor
会悪 *shakaiaku* social crime
会教育 *shakai kyōiku* social education
会探訪 *shakai tambō* local-news reporter
会運動 *shakai undō* social movement; public campaign
会組織 *shakai soshiki* social structure
会問題 *shakai mondai* social problem
会福祉 *shakai fukushi* social welfare
会意識 *shakai ishiki* social consciousness
会層 *shakaisō* social strata
会鍋 *shakai nabe* charity kettle
会観 *shakaikan* one's view of society
[7]告 *shakoku* public announcement
[8]長 *shachō* firm president
命 *shamei* company orders
参 *shasan* visiting a shrine
[9]風 *shafū* company customs
則 *shasoku* company regulations
是 *shaze* company policy
[10]格 *shakaku* shrine rank
員 *sha-in* company personnel, clerk
家 *shake* hereditary family of Shinto priests
[11]運 *sha-un* company fortunes
船 *shasen* company boat
務 *shamu* shrine affairs
務所 *shamusho* shrine office
[12]葬 *shasō* company funeral
費 *shahi* company expenses
[13]殿 *shaden* main shrine building
業 *shagyō* company business
債 *shasai* company bonds
債発行 *shasai hakkō* bond issue
[14]旗 *shaki* company flag
説 *shasetsu* an editorial

領 *sharyō* shrine land
[15]稷 *shashoku* the sovereign family, the state
線 *shasen* private railway line
[16]頭 *shatō* shrine precincts

— 4 —

祉 3232 F1356 = **祉** B SHI happiness.
[13]福 *shifuku* happiness, prosperity, well-being

祇 3233 F1356 = GI national god, local god; peaceful; great.

祈 3234 F1356 = **祈** B KI. *ino(ru)* pray; wish. *ino(ri)* prayer, grace.
[6]合 *ino(ri)-a(u)* pray together
[7]求 *ino(ri)-moto(meru)* pray for
[8]雨 *kiu* praying for rain
念 *kinen* prayer
奉 *ino(ri)-tatematsu(ru)* pray (polite)
事 *negigoto* prayer
[10]殺 *ino(ri)-koro(su)* pray for someone's death
[14]誓 *kisei* vow, oath, pledge
[15]請 *kisei* praying (to Shinto or Buddhist deities)
[19]願 *kigan suru, ino(ri)-nega(u)* pray, implore prayer, supplication
願文 *kigambun* optative sentence
禱 *kitō* prayer; devotions; grace; exorcism
禱会 *kitōkai* prayer meeting
禱者 *kitōsha* suppliant
禱週 *kitōshū* week of prayer
禱師 *kitōshi* faith healer, medicine man, shaman
禱料 *kitōryō* gift in return for prayers
禱書 *kitōsho* prayer book
禱僧 *kitōsō* a praying priest

— 5 —

祢 3235 F1362 F1369 = See **禰** 3261.

祕 3236 F1357 = See **秘** 3281.

祚 3237 F1358 = SO imperial throne; happiness.

祗 3238 F1358 = SHI be respectful.

祟 3239 F1362 = SUI curse. *tata(ru)* bring evil upon, curse, haunt, torment.

祐 3240 F1356 = **祐** YŪ help.
[12]筆 *yūhitsu* private secretary

祠 3241 F1362 SHI small shrine; worship, deify; festival. *hokora* small shrine.

11堂 *shidō* mortuary temple

祓 3242 F1356 FUTSU. *hara(u)* purify, exorcise, drive out (spirits). *hara(i)* Shinto prayer; purification; exorcism.

11清 *hara(i)-kiyo(meru)* purify, exorcise

A 祖 3243 F1357 祖 So ancestor, founder, originator, pioneer.

4父 *sofu, ōji* grandfather
父母 *sofubo* grandparents
父祖母 *jiji-baba* grandparents; old people
6母 *sobo, baba, ōba, oba* grandmother
考 *sokō* deceased father and grandfather
先 *sosen* ancestors
先崇拝 *sosen sūhai* ancestor worship
7述 *sojutsu* exposition, propagation
述者 *sōjutsusha* expounder, exponent
8宗 *sosō* ancestors, ancestry
国 *sokoku* fatherland, native country
国愛 *sokokuai* love of one's motherland
9神 *soshin* ancestral gods
10師 *soshi* sect founder
13業 *sogyō* a business kept in the family for many generations
15廟 *sobyō* ancestral tomb

A 祝 3244 F1359 祝 SHUKU, SHŪ celebration, congratulations. *shuku(suru)* celebrate, congratulate, bless. *iwa(u)* congratulate, celebrate, commemorate. *iwa(i)* celebration, festival, congratulations.

4文 *shukubun* congratulatory address
日 *iwa(i)bi, shukujitsu* holiday, festival day, feast day
火 *iwa(i)bi* festival bonfire
7言 *shūgen, hogigoto* congratulations; celebration; wedding
言客 *shūgenkyaku* wedding guest
8杯 *shukuhai* congratulatory cup, a toast
物 *iwa(i)mono* congratulatory gift
典 *shukuten* celebration, festival
事 *iwa(i)goto* auspicious occasion, celebration
10砲 *shukuhō* artillery salute
宴 *shukuen* congratulatory banquet, feast
11祭 *shukusai* festivals, feasts
祭日 *shukusaijitsu* festivals, feasts
12勝 *shukushō* victory celebration
詞 *norito, shukushi* Shinto ritual prayer, congratulatory address
着 *shūchaku* felicitations
賀 *shukuga* celebration, congratulations
賀会 *shukugakai* congratulatory party
13福 *shukufuku* blessing; benediction
辞 *shukuji* congratulatory address
電 *shukuden* congratulatory telegram
意 *shukui* congratulations
14歌 *shukuka* festive song
15儀 *shūgi* congratulations; celebration; congratulatory gift; tip
19禱 *shukutō* benediction, blessing

A 神 3245 F1359 神 JIN, SHIN god, deity; mind, soul. *kami* God, god, Allah. *kami(sabita), kan(sabita)* venerable, hallowed. *kan-, kamu-* god.

2人 *kamibito* Shinto priest. *shinjin* god and man; man of god; Shinto priest
力 *shinryoku* divine power
4文 *shimmon* written vow to a god
木 *shimboku* sacred tree
火 *shinka* sacred fire
父 *shimpu* priest, father
化 *shinka* deification
少女 *kami otome* shrine maidens
仏 *shimbutsu, kami-hotoke* gods and Buddhas
仏基 *Shim-Butsu-Ki* Shinto, Buddhism, and Christianity
仏混淆 *Shim-Butsu konkō* Shinto-Buddhist amalgamation
5田 *kamita* shrine rice field
矢 *kamiya* the arrows of the gods
主 *kannushi* Shinto priest
占 *shinsen* divination
去 *kamisa(ru), kansa(ru)* decease of a noble
功皇后 *Jingū Kōgō* Empress Jingu
出鬼没 *shinshutsu-kibotsu* elusiveness
代 *jindai, shindai, kamiyo* age of the gods
代杉 *jindai sugi* lignitized cryptomeria
仙 *shinsen* wizard, Taoist hermit-wizard
仙境 *shinsenkyō* fairyland, unearthly place
6式 *shinshiki* Shinto rites
気 *shinki* energy, spirits; a feeling of veneration
曲 *Shinkyoku* (Dante's) Divine Comedy
托 *shintaku* an oracle
灯 *shintō* sacred lantern, festival lantern
州 *shinshū* divine land, land of the gods
色 *shinshoku* the heart and the countenance; attitude
色自若 *shinshoku-jijaku* perfect composure, presence of mind
7身 *kami(naranu) mi* not a god
佑 *shin-yū* providence, divine help
体 *shintai* god-body in a Shinto shrine
妙 *shimmyō na, shimbyō na* mysterious, marvelous; admirable; docile, tame, meek; faithful
技 *shingi* consummate skill
杉 *kami sugi* a sacred cryptomeria; ancient cryptomeria on shrine grounds

助 *shinjo* divine aid
兵 *shimpei* soldiers of the gods, soldiers protected by the gods
来 *shinrai* divine inspiration
社 *jinja, jinsha* Shinto shrine
社局 *Jinjakyoku* Shrine Bureau
社参拝問題 *Jinja Sampai Mondai* The Shrine Question
社神道 *Jinja Shintō* Shrine Shinto
8 国 *shinkoku, kamiguni* the land of the gods
性 *shinsei* divinity, divine nature, godliness
明 *shimmei* deity
命 *shimmei* divine command
参 *kamimai(ri)* visiting shrines
宝 *shimpō* sacred treasure
官 *shinkan* Shinto priest
苑 *shin-en* shrine garden
事 *shinji, jinji* Shinto ceremonies. *kamigoto* work of the gods; religious rites
知学 *shinchigaku* theosophy
武天皇祭 *Jimmu Tennō Sai* Emperor Jimmu's death anniversary
学 *shingaku* theology
学的 *shingakuteki* theological
学校 *shingakkō* theological seminary
9 威 *shin-i* power or majesty of the gods
速 *shinsoku* speed, promptness, quickness
垣 *kamigaki* Shinto shrine fence
神 *kōgō(shii)* divine, solemn, awe-inspiring. *kamigami* gods, idols
勅 *shinchoku* oracle
品 *shimpin* inspired work, masterpiece
泉 *shinsen* spring on shrine grounds
通力 *jintsūriki, shintsūriki* occult, supernatural, or divine power
信心 *kami-shinjin* (Shinto) piety
風 *kamikaze* providential wind; suicide plane. *shimpu* providential wind
風特攻隊員 *kamikaze tokkōtai-in* suicide pilot
降 *kamio(roshi)* spiritism, spiritualism, necromancy
降会 *kamio(roshi) (no) kai* séance
政 *shinsei* theocracy
政国 *shinseikoku* a theocracy
変 *shimpen* a tremendous change
変化 *shimpenka* a strange change
変不思儀 *shimpen-fushigi* marvel, miracle
前 *shinzen* at the shrine, before the god
前結婚 *shinzen kekkon* Shinto wedding
祇 *jingi* deities of heaven and earth
祇局 *Jingikyoku* Shrine Bureau
祇歌 *jingika* Shinto hymn
10 馬 *shimme* sacred horse
酒 *miki, shinshu* sacred wine, wine offering
託 *shintaku* divine message, oracle
剣 *shinken* divine sword, sacred sword
都 *shinto* holy town
宮 *jingū* Shinto shrine; Ise Shrines
恩 *shin-on* God's goodness
格 *shinkaku* Godhead, divinity, fatherhood of God
格化 *shinkakuka* deification
秘 *shimpi* mystery
秘小説 *shimpi shōsetsu* mystery novel
秘主義 *shimpi shugi* mysticism
秘的 *shimpiteki* mystic, mysterious, miraculous
秘派 *shimpiha* mystic school
秘家 *shimpika* a mystic
秘哲学 *shimpi tetsugaku* mystic philosophy, esoterics
秘説 *shimpisetsu* mysticism
秘境 *shimpikyō* land of mystery
秘劇 *shimpigeki* mystery drama
11 遊 *kamiaso(bi)* dancing before the gods
道 *Shintō, Kami (no) Michi, Kan(nagara) no Michi, Shindō* Shinto
域 *shin-iki* shrine precincts
術 *shinjutsu* a strange act
掛 *kamika(kete)* swearing by a god; positively
授 *shinju* divine gift
略 *shinryaku* a strange plan
寄 *kamiyo(se)* oracle of a god
異 *shin-i* miracle, marvel
符 *shimpu* talisman, amulet, charm
経 *shinkei* nerves
経中枢 *shinkei chūsū* nerve center
経系 *shinkeikei* nervous system
経学 *shinkeigaku* neurology
経病 *shinkeibyō* nervous disease
経症 *shinkeishō* nervous disease
経家 *shinkeika* nervous person
経衰弱 *shinkei suijaku* nervous exhaustion
経過敏 *shinkei-kabin* oversensitiveness
経痛 *shinkeitsū* neuralgia
経戦 *shinkeisen* war of nerves, psychological warfare
経節 *shinkeisetsu* ganglion
経質 *shinkeishitsu* nervousness, nervous temperament
12 棚 *kamidana* Shinto god shelf
童 *shindō* prodigy, child wonder
葬 *shinsō* Shinto funeral
智 *shinchi* divine wisdom
然 *kansa(bu), kamusa(bu)* majestic, impressive
無月 *kannazuki, kaminazuki, kamina(shi)-zuki* 10th lunar month (the month the gods are all away at the Izumo shrine)
13 詣 *kami mōde* shrine visitation
隠 *kamikaku(shi), kamigaku(shi)* hidden by the gods. *kamigaku(re)* hiding of the gods; hiding from everybody
意 *shin-i* divine will, divine decree, providence
感 *shinkan* inspiration, intuition
業 *kamiwaza* providence; act of God; superhuman feat

殿 *shinden* temple, shrine, sanctuary
殿男娼 *shinden danshō* male cult prostitute
殿娼婦 *shinden shōfu* cult prostitute
話 *shinwa* myth; mythology
話学 *shinwagaku* mythology
話劇 *shinwageki* mythological play
楽 *kagura* Shinto dance
楽堂 *kaguradō* Shinto dance pavilion
楽殿 *kaguraden* Shinto dance pavilion
楽獅子 *kagurajishi* festival lion masks
聖 *shinsei* divine nature; sacredness, sanctity, holiness; godliness; dignity. *shinsei na* sacred, divine
聖同盟 *Shinsei Dōmei* the Holy Alliance
聖冒瀆 *shinsei bōtoku* blasphemy
聖視 *shinseishi suru* regard as sacred
聖羅馬帝国 *Shinsei Rōma Teikoku* Holy Roman Empire
14 像 *shinzō* (rare) Shinto image; Shinto picture
僕 *shimboku* a (Christian) believer
徳 *shintoku* divine virtues
様 *kamisama* god; God
語 *kamigata(ri)* oracle of a god
魂 *shinkon* heart, soul
罰 *shimbatsu* divine punishment
嘗祭 *Kannamesai* Shinto Festival of New Rice (Oct. 17)
15 廟 *shimbyō* Shinto shrine
慮 *shinryo* divine will, divine decree, providence
調 *kamitsugi* an offering to the gods
箭 *kamiya* arrows of the gods
器 *jingi, shinki* the sacred treasures
権 *shinken* divine right
権政治 *shinken seiji* theocracy
霊 *shinrei* divine spirit
霊界 *shinreikai* spirit world
16 橋 *shinkyō* sacred bridge
頼 *kamidano(mi)* calling on a god in distress
薬 *shin-yaku* wonder drug
憑 *kamigaka(ri)* spirit possession
17 厳 *shingen na* solemn, grave, awe-inspiring
輿 *mikoshi, shin-yo* palanquin of a Shinto god
18 癒 *shin-yu* divine healing, faith healing
職 *shinshoku* Shinto priest
髄 *shinzui* true meaning, mystery
19 鏡 *shinkyō* divine mirror; the Mirror of the Three Imperial Treasures
韻 *shin-in* superb spirit
璽 *shinji* sacred jewels; emperor's seal
20 懸 *kamigaka(ri)*, *kangaka(ri)* spirit possession
饌 *shinsen* offering, oblation
21 籤 *mikuji* sacred lot, written oracle, divination
25 籬 *himorogi* offerings to the gods

6

票 See 4276.

祥 3246/F1362 **祥** B Jō, Shō happiness. *saga* good omen.
4 月 *shōtsuki* death month
12 雲 *jōun* auspicious clouds
無 *sagana(i)* bad, not good
13 瑞 *shōzui* good omen

祭 3247/F1363 A Sai. *matsu(ru)* offer prayers; celebrate; deify; enshrine; worship. *matsu(ri)* festival, feast. *-sai* festival.
3 上 *matsu(ri)-a(geru)* exalt (someone)
4 文 *saimon* Shinto funeral prayer; address to the gods
日 *saijitsu* national holiday, festival day, feast day
込 *matsu(ri)-ko(mu)* "kick upstairs"
5 礼 *sairei* festival, feast, rituals
主 *saishu* master of (religious) ceremonies; chief priestess of Ise
司 *saishi* priest
司長 *saishichō* high priest (of the Jews)
司長達 *saishichōtachi* chief priests (of the Jews)
司職 *saishishoku* priesthood
6 式 *saishiki* rites, ritual, ceremony
8 具 *saigu* equipment used in ceremonies
典 *saiten* festival, rite
事 *saiji* sacred rites, festival
祀 *saishi* Shinto ceremony, religious ceremony
祀料 *saishiryō* funeral expense grant
服 *saifuku* vestments
服室 *saifukushitsu* vestry
9 神 *saijin, saishin* the enshrined deity
政 *saisei* church and state, ceremonies and government
政一致 *saisei itchi* union of Religion and the State
10 酒 *saishu* (ancient) master of ceremonies; college president; education minister
12 場 *saijō* place of a ceremony
詞 *saishi* Shinto priest's address
13 殿 *saiden* shrine, sanctuary
15 儀 *saigi* festival
器 *saiki* ceremonial equipment
16 壇 *saidan* altar
18 騒 *matsu(ri)sawa(gi)* festivities, merrymaking

7

祷 Nonstandard for **禱** 3260.

視 3248/F1715 **視** A Shi regard as. *mi(ru)* see, look at; guard. *-shi suru* regard as, look upon as. *shi-* apparent (in astronomy). [見]
2 力 *shiryoku* eyesight, visual power
力検査 *shiryoku kensa* eye test
6 号通信 *shigō tsūshin* communication by visible signals
7 角 *shikaku* angle of vision; optic angle; viewpoint

8官 *shikan* the organ of sight 「spector

学 *shigaku* school inspection; school in-

学官 *shigakkan* government school inspec-

9度 *shido* visibility ⌊tor

点 *shiten* viewpoint

界 *shikai* range of vision, visibility

神経 *shishinkei* optic nerve

10差 *shisa* parallax

11野 *shiya* field of vision

運動 *shiundō* apparent motion

12程 *shitei* visibility, visual range

診 *shishin* examination of a patient by in-

覚 *shikaku* sense of sight, vision ⌊spection

14察 *shisatsu* inspection, observation

15線 *shisen* line of vision

17聴 *shichō* attention, interest; viewing TV

聴覚 *shichōkaku* visual and auditory senses, sight and hearing, audiovisual

聴覚教材 *shichōkaku kyōzai* audio-visual aids 「education

聴覚教育 *shichōkaku kyōiku* audio-visual

8

稟 3249 F1364 F1381 See **稟** 325.

禄 3250 F1364 = **祿** Roku fief, allowance, pension, grant; happiness.

9食 *roku (o) ha(mu)* receive salary (from a daimyo)

10高 *rokudaka*=*roku* (see under 禄 3250.0)

11盗人 *rokunusubito* drawer of salary tho performing little of importance

A **禁** 3251 F1364 Kin prohibition, ban, embargo; law. *kin(jiru), kin(zuru)* prohibit, ban, forbid, repress, restrain; abstain from.

8山 *tomeyama* mountain preserve

4方 *kimpō* secret formula

中 *kinchū* the Court, Imperial Palace, Im-

内 *kindai* palace ⌊perial Household

止 *kinshi* prohibition, ban, taboo, embargo

止令 *kinshirei* prohibition decree; injunction 「injunction

止命令 *kinshi meirei* prohibition decree,

5穴 *kinketsu* important parts of the body; important places

句 *kinku* tabooed word

圧 *kin-atsu* prohibition, suppression, ban

処 *kinsho*=禁所 (see below-8)

札 *kinsatsu* prohibition notice board 「tion

令 *kinrei* ban, embargo, interdict, prohibi-

6伐 *kimbatsu* prohibition of tree cutting

7足 *kinsoku* confinement

廷 *kintei* imperial court, imperial palace

戒 *kinkai* commandment

忌 *kinki* taboo, contraindication

8固 *kinko* imprisonment

所 *kinsho* place of confinement; a place of

法 *kimpō* prohibitory law ⌊no admittance

物 *kimmotsu* taboo, forbidden thing, injurious thing, something to avoid

苑 *kin-en* imperial garden 「law)

治産 *kinchisan, kinjisan* incompetency (in

治産者 *kinchisansha* a person adjudged incompetent

制 *kinsei* prohibition, ban, embargo

制品 *kinseihin* contraband articles

9城 *kinjō* palace

軍 *kingun* palace guard

10秘 *kimpi* palace secret; top secret

殺 *kinsatsu* imprisonment and execution

書 *kinsho* prohibited literature; proscribed book 「nence

酒 *kinshu* prohibition, temperance, absti-

酒令 *kinshurei* prohibition law

酒州 *kinshushū* prohibition state

酒会 *kinshukai* temperance society

酒国 *kinshukoku* a country prohibiting

酒法 *kinshuhō* prohibition law ⌊liquors

酒家 *kinshuka* total abstainer

酒党 *kinshutō* prohibition party

酒薬 *kinshuyaku* medicines to break alcohol

11鳥 *kinchō* protected birds ⌊habit

教 *kinkyō* prohibition of a religion

転載 *kintensai* reprinting forbidden, all rights reserved

断 *kindan* prohibition 「fruit

断木実 *kindan (no) ko(no)mi* the forbidden

欲 *kin-yoku* self-denial, asceticism; abstinence, continence, mortification

欲主義 *kin-yoku shugi* asceticism, stoicism

欲主義者 *kin-yoku shugisha* ascetics

猟 *kinryō* prohibition of hunting; No

猟区 *kinryōku* no-hunting area ⌊Hunting

猟地 *kinryōchi* no-hunting area

猟期 *kinryōki* closed hunting season

12遏 *kin-atsu* forcible prohibition

絶 *kinzetsu* prohibition

裡 *kinri* imperial court, imperial palace

13煙 *kin-en* prohibition of smoking; No Smoking

裏 *kinri* imperial court, imperial palace

裏様 *kinrisama* the (Japanese) emperor

14厭 *majinai, kin-en* spell, charm, enchantment

獄 *kingoku* imprisonment 「Fishing

漁 *kinryō, kingyo* prohibition of fishing; No

漁区 *kingyoku* no-fishing area

漁期 *kingyoki* out of season for fishing

15 衛 *kin-ei* imperial guards
慾 *kin-yoku* abstinence, self-denial, asceticism
慾主義 *kin-yoku shugi* asceticism, stoicism
16 錮 *kinko* imprisonment
輸 *kin-yu* embargo on shipments
輸品 *kin-yuhin* contraband
18 闕 *kinketsu* imperial palace

9

禎 3252/F1366 **禎** TEI happiness.

禊 3253/F1365 **禊** KEI. KATSU. *misogi* Shinto purification ceremony.
8 事 *keiji* Shinto purification

B **禍** 3254/F1366 **禍** KA calamity, misfortune. *maga, wazawai* calamity, misfortune, woe, evil, curse.
4 心 *kashin* treachery, malice
6 因 *ka-in* cause of trouble
7 言 *magagoto* unlucky words
乱 *karan* disturbances; disasters
災 *kasai* disaster, misfortune
8 幸 *magasachi* fortunes
事 *magagoto* evil, mishap, disaster
10 根 *kakon* root of evil
害 *kagai* evil, harm, mischief
11 患 *kakan* disaster, calamity, evil
13 福 *kafuku* weal or woe; ups and downs
16 機 *kaki* root of evil
18 難 *kanan* calamity, disaster, accident, misfortune

B **禅** 3255/F1367 **禪** ZEN silent meditation; Buddhist sect originating in the twelfth century.
5 尼 *zenni* Zen nun
6 寺 *zendera* Zen temple
7 杖 *zenjō* stick to keep Zen meditators awake
8 門 *zemmon* entering the Zen priesthood
房 *zembō* Zen temple; Zen priest's cell
味 *zemmi* Zen flavor, mysticism
林 *zenrin* Zen temple
宗 *zenshū* Zen sect
学 *zengaku* Zen doctrines
10 師 *zenji* high priest in a Zen sect
家 *zenka, zenke* Zen sect; Zen temple; Zen priest
11 堂 *zendō* Zen study temple
13 僧 *zensō* Zen priest
話 *zenwa* Zen talk
14 閣 *zenkaku* Zen temple
20 譲 *zenjō* abdication

A **福** 3256/F1366 **福** FUKU fortune, blessing, luck, wealth; food which has been offered to gods.
2 人 *fukujin* fortunate person
3 千年 *fukusennen* the millennium
4 引 *fukubiki* lottery
引券 *fukubikiken* lottery ticket
7 沢 *fukutaku* happiness and blessings
利 *fukuri* prosperity, welfare, well-being
助 *fukusuke* a large-headed male doll which brings good luck; a large-headed person
寿 *fukuju* prosperity and longevity
8 祉 *fukushi* prosperity, welfare, well-being
祉国家 *fukushi kokka* a welfare state
9 相 *fukusō* happy look, radiant face
神 *fukujin, fuku (no) kami* god of wealth, god of good fortune
神漬 *fukujinzuke* pickles preserved in soy
音 *fukuin* gospel, good news, glad tidings
音主義 *fukuin shugi no* evangelical
音的 *fukuinteki* evangelical
音書 *Fukuinsho* The Gospels
音書対観 *Fukuinsho taikan* a harmony of the Gospels
11 運 *fuku-un* happiness and good fortune
13 福 *fukubuku(shii)* radiant, genial
禄寿 *Fukurokuju* a god of wealth
14 徳 *fukutoku* good fortune, happiness and prosperity; good deeds and the resultant prosperity

10

禊 See **禊** 3253.

12

禪 3257/F1367 See **禅** 3255.

禦 3258/F1367 GYO. *fuse(gu)* (see under 防 4980.0).

13

禮 3259/F1368 See **礼** 3229.

14

禱 3260/F1369 **祷** TŌ. *ino(ru)* pray.

禰 3261/F1369 **祢** NE ancestral shrine.
8 宜 *negi* Shinto priest of lower rank

5 玄玉王瓜瓦甘生用田疋疒癶白皮皿目矛矢石示ネ【8 肉】禾穴立

RAD. 肉 114

Jū or *ashiato* footprint. Note that this is a 5-stroke radical and is so counted whenever it appears. Nickname: Footprint.

8

禽 See 528.

RAD. 禾 115

Nogi the katakana *no* plus *ki* "tree." At left: *nogi hen.* Nickname: 2-Branch Tree (cf. Rads. 75 and 127).

2

禿 3262 / F1370 TOKU. *ha(geru)* become bald; become bare. *chibi(ru)* wear out, waste away. *hage* baldness, bald person. *kaburo* baldhead. *kamuro* little girl employed in a brothel.

8 山 *hageyama* bare mountain
上 *hage-a(garu)* (hair) recedes
9 茶瓶 *hage chabin* baldheaded man
12 筆 *chibi fude, tokohitsu* worn-down writing brush
14 髪 *tokuhatsu* baldness
16 頭 *hageatama, tokutō* baldness, bald head; baldheaded person
頭病 *tokutōbyō* pathological baldness

B **秀** 3263 / F1370 SHŪ excellence; beauty. *hi-i-(deru), sugu(reru)* surpass, excel, tower above, rise to eminence.

3 才 *shūsai* genius, talent man, prodigy
5 句 *shūku* excellent *haiku* poem; wisecrack
7 吟 *shūgin* excellent poem
抜 *shūbatsu* excellence, pre-eminence
8 英 *shūei* excelling
9 眉 *shūbi* prominent eyebrows; beautiful eyebrows
美 *shūbi* superb beauty
10 逸 *shūitsu* supreme excellence; masterpiece
12 絶 *shūzetsu* supreme excellence
14 歌 *shūka* gems of poetry
19 麗 *shūrei na* graceful, beautiful

A **利** 3264 / F239 RI advantage, benefit, gain; interest; victory. *ri(suru)* benefit, do good, profit, gain. *ki(ku)* take effect, do (a person) good; work, operate; tell (on one's strength); be available (bus or phone). *ki(kasu)* use (one's head); exert (influence). *ki(keru)* be influential. *kiki* efficacy. [刀]

2 刀 *ritō* sharp sword
3 子 *rishi* interest
下 *risa(ge)* lowering the interest rate
上 *ria(ge)* raising the interest rate
刃 *rijin* sharp sword
口 *rikō* cleverness, wisdom, intelligence
口者 *rikōmono* clever person
己 *riko* selfishness
己心 *rikoshin* selfishness
己主義 *riko shugi* egoism, selfishness
己性 *rikosei* selfishness
己説 *rikosetsu* egoism
4 方 *rikata* profitableness
水 *risui* irrigation, water utilization
5 目 *kikime* effect, efficacy, impression
払 *ribar(ai)* interest payment
出 *ki(ki)-da(su)* begin to take effect
付 *ritsu(ki)* interest-bearing
付債券 *ritsuki saiken* coupon bond
巧 *rikō* skill and speed, cleverness
巧者 *rikōmono* clever person
札 *risatsu, rifuda* coupon, interest coupon
札付債券 *rifudazu(ki) saiken* coupon bond
他 *rita* altruism
他主義 *rita shugi* altruism
他的 *ritateki* altruistic
用 *riyō* use, utilization; improvement (of opportunities); making a tool of
用者 *riyōsha* user
用価値 *riyō kachi* usefulness, utility value
用厚生 *riyō kōsei* promotion of public welfare
6 回 *rimawa(ri)* interest, yield, profit
7 役 *kikiyaku* influential person
売 *riu(ri)* selling at a profit
男 *kiki otoko* man of ability
尿 *rinyō* urination
尿剤 *rinyōzai* diuretic
8 金 *rikin* interest, gain
所 *kikidokoro* effective points

者 *ki(ki)mono* influential person. *ki(ke)mono* able man, man of influence
9 食 *rigui* profit taking
便 *riben* convenience
点 *riten* advantage, point in favor
発 *rihatsu* cleverness, wisdom, intelligence
10 根 *rikon na* bright (child)
酒 *kikizake* wine tasting
害 *rigai* advantages and disadvantages, interests
害関係 *rigai kankei* interests
息 *risoku* interest
息算 *risokuzan* interest calculation
益 *rieki* profit, gain; benefit, advantage. *riyaku* the favor of a Buddha; answer to prayer; help
益代表国 *rieki daihyōkoku* a country representing the diplomatic interests of another
益交換 *rieki kōkan* reciprocity, reciprocal benefits
益金 *riekikin* amount of profit
益配当 *rieki haitō* distribution of profits; profit-sharing; dividend
11 達 *ritatsu* success in life
運 *riun* good fortune
欲 *riyoku* greed, covetousness
率 *riritsu* rate of interest
得 *ritoku* profit, benefit
得税 *ritokuzei* profits tax
12 殖 *rishoku* money-making
腕 *ki(ki)ude* the right arm, the whip hand
鈍 *ridon* sharp or blunt, bright or dull
13 福 *rifuku* public welfare, prosperity
15 潤 *rijun* profit
慾 *riyoku* greed, covetousness
器 *riki* sharp swords; good cutting knives; convenient machine; useful talents; a superior person
権 *riken* rights, concessions
権屋 *riken-ya* concession hunter, grafter
16 鞘 *rizaya, risaya* margin of profit
18 鎌 *tokama* sharp sickle

A **私** 3265 / F1371 SHI I; private affairs. *watakushi, watashi, washi* I, myself, private (affairs). *watakushi suru* think only of one's own gain. *hiso(ka) na* secret, private, stealthy, hushed.
2 人 *shijin* private individual
3 大 *shidai* private college
子 *shishi* illegitimate child
小説 *watakushi shōsetsu* novel concerning the author
4 心 *shishin* selfishness, private interest
方 *watakushikata* I; on my part
文書 *shibunsho* private document
5 用 *shiyō* personal use; private business, misappropriation, embezzlement
田 *shiden* private rice land
立 *shiritsu* private, nongovernment
立学校 *shiritsu gakkō* private school
生子 *shiseishi, shiseiji* illegitimate child
生児 *shiseiji*, illegitimate child
生活 *shiseikatsu* one's private life
6 行 *shikō* private conduct
印 *shi-in* personal seal
曲 *shikyoku* unfair dealings, irregularities, graft
刑 *shikei* lynching
交 *shikō* private relations
宅 *shitaku* private house
考 *shikō* personal opinion
自身 *watakushi jishin* myself
有 *shiyū* private ownership
有地 *shiyūchi* private land
有物 *shiyūbutsu* private property
有財産 *shiyū zaisan* private property
有権 *shiyūken* right of private property
7 見 *shiken* personal opinion
利 *shiri* self-interest, personal gain
邸 *shitei* private residence
兵 *shihei* private army
8 法 *shihō* private law
版 *shihan* private publication
物 *shibutsu* private property, personal effects
的 *shiteki* private, personal
事 *shiji, watakushigoto* personal affairs
学 *shigaku* private school; one's personal theory
学校 *shigakkō* private school
服 *shifuku* ordinary clothes; plain-clothes man
服刑事 *shifuku keiji* plain-clothes man
服肥 *shifuku (o) ko(yasu)* line one's own pockets
服警官 *shifuku keikan* plain-clothes man
9 通 *shitsū* illicit intercourse
信 *shishin* private message
恨 *shikon* personal grudge
室 *shishitsu* private room
怨 *shien* grudge, enmity
10 消 *shishō* embezzlement, misappropriation
流 *watakushiryū* one's personal method
称 *shishō* pretension, assumption (of a title)
記 *shiki* private record
財 *shizai* private means, private property
益 *shieki* self-interest, personal gain
案 *shian* one's personal plan
党 *shitō* faction, junta
恩 *shion* personal obligations
書 *shisho* private document, private letter
書函 *shishokan, shishobako* post-office box
書箱 *shishobako* post-office box
11 道 *shidō* private road, private path
達 *watakushitachi* we
情 *shijō* personal feelings, bias

淑 *shishuku suru* adore, look up to, pattern
設 *shisetsu* private ⌊after
欲 *shiyoku* self-interest, selfish desire
娼 *shishō* streetwalker, unlicensed prostitute
娼窟 *shishōkutsu* a brothel
12 訴 *shiso* civil suit
費 *shihi* private expense, one's own expense
報 *shihō* private message, private report
貿易 *shibōeki* private trade
営 *shiei* private operation
営事業 *shiei jigyō* private enterprise
13 腹 *shifuku* one's own pocket
話 *shiwa* whispered conversation
鉄 *shitetsu* private railway line
罪 *shizai* personal injury
意 *shi-i* selfishness; bias; one's own idea
14 選 *shisen* personal choice, personal appointment
語 *sasaya*(*ku*) whisper, murmur. *sasayakigoto, shigo* secret talk, whispering
説 *shisetsu* privately held theory
蔵 *shizō suru* possess
塾 *shijuku* private school
製 *shisei* privately manufactured
15 憤 *shifun* enmity, grudge
撰 *shisen* personal choice
権 *shiken* private rights
線 *shisen* private railway line
談 *shidan* private conversation
論 *shiron* private opinion
慾 *shiyoku* self-interest, selfish desire
鋳 *shichū* secret minting
鋳銭 *shichūsen* counterfeit coins
18 闘 *shitō* private strife
20 議 *shigi* personal view; private discussion;
23 讎 *shishū* personal enemy ⌊backbiting

3

季 3266 / F521 (A) KI season. *sue* end. [子]

3 子 *sueko, kishi* the last child
4 月 *rigetsu* December
父 *kifu* youngest uncle
5 末 *kimatsu* term end
世 *kisei* the last age; the last degenerate age
刊 *kikan* quarterly publication
刊誌 *kikanshi* quarterly magazine
9 後 *kioku*(*re*) late in the season
指 *kishi* little finger
春 *kishun* late spring
10 候 *kikō* season
候病 *kikōbyō* seasonal disease
11 違 *kichiga*(*i*) off-season
貨 *kika* late summer; 6th lunar month
12 報 *kihō* quarterly report or bulletin
13 節 *kisetsu* the seasons, the time of year
節的 *kisetsuteki* seasonal
節物 *kisetsumono* things in season
節風 *kisetsufū* seasonal wind, monsoon
14 語 *kigo* word referring to seasons (in poetry)
18 題 *kidai* seasonal theme (in poetry)

委 3267 / F498 (A) I. *i*(*suru*) entrust to, discard. *yuda*(*neru*) entrust to, devote (oneself) to. *maka*(*su*), *maka*(*seru*) entrust to, leave to. *kuwa*(*shii*) (see under 詳 4357.0). [女]

3 女 *obako* lass
5 付 *ifu* abandonment (of rights or property)
6 曲 *ikyoku* details, circumstances
任 *inin* trust, delegation, authorization, charge, commission, mandate
任状 *ininjō* power of attorney
任統治 *inin tōchi* mandate
任統治権 *inin tōchiken* mandate
10 託 *itaku* trust, consignment, commission
託加工 *itaku kakō* processing materials
託金 *itakukin* money in trust ⌊brought in
託販売 *itaku hambai* sale on consignment
員 *i-in* committeeman, committee, commission ⌈mittee
員付託 *i-in-futaku* referring to a committee
員会 *i-inkai* committee (meeting), board
員長 *i-inchō* chairman
11 細 *isai* details, particulars
細文 *isai fumi* details by letter
細面談 *isai mendan* details when I see you
13 棄 *iki* abandonment, desertion, relinquish- ⌊ment
15 嘱 *ishoku suru* entrust with
17 縮 *ishuku* withering; contraction; atrophy
20 譲 *ijō suru* transfer to

和 3268 / F350 **咊** (A) KA. WA sum; peace, harmony, reconciliation, unity. *wa*(*suru*) harmonize, be in harmony with; make peace, be reconciled; respond, echo. *yawa*(*ragu*) *vi* soften, be reconciled; lessen; calm down. *yawa*(*rageru*) *vt* soften, moderate, ease, alleviate, mitigate, relax; appease; dilute (wine); tone down (colors); comfort; pacify, quiet. *nago*(*mu*) *vi* be softened; get quiet. *nago*(*meru*) *vt* soften, quiet down. *na*(*gu*) get calm, die down. *nago*(*yakana*) mellow, matured, refined, genial. *nagi* lull, calm. [口]

2 人 *wajin* (an old word for) a Japanese
4 毛 *nikoge* (bird's) down
牛 *wagyū* Japanese cow
文 *wabun* Japanese, Japanese writing
文英訳 *wabun-eiyaku* Japanese-English translation
5 平 *wahei* peace

本 *wahon* Japanese book, book bound in Japanese style
6合 *wagō* harmony, unity, union
字 *waji* Japanese syllabaries; characters originating in Japan; Japanese literature
名 *wamyō, wamei* Japanese name
気 *waki* harmony, peacefulness ⌈harmony
気藹藹 *wakiaiai* maturity; refinement;
7声 *kasei, wasei* harmony (in music), concord
8協 *wakyō* harmony, concord
物 *aemono* vegetable side dish
服 *wafuku* Japanese clothes, kimono
尚 *oshō* chief priest of a temple
英 *wa-ei* Japanese-English
学 *wagaku* Japanese literature
9音 *waon* the rare *on* pronunciations originating in Japan
風 *wafū* light breeze; Japanese style
食 *washoku* Japanese food
独 *wa-doku* Japanese and German lan-
約 *wayaku* treaty of peace ⌊guages
姦 *wakan* fornication, adultery
室 *washitsu* Japanese-style room
臭 *washū* Japanese flavor, Japanism
衷 *wachū* harmony, concord
衷協同 *wachū kyōdō* harmonious co-opera-
洋 *wayō* Japanese and foreign ⌊tion
洋折衷 *wayō setchū* semi-European style
洋酒 *wayōshu* Japanese and Western liquors
10紙 *washi* Japanese paper
訓 *wakun* Japanese reading (of a character)
書 *washo*=*wahon* 和本 (see above–5)
11船 *wasen* Japanese-style ship
訳 *wayaku* Japanese translation
寇 *wakō* Japanese pirates
菓子 *wagashi* Japanese confectionery
12順 *wajun* normal weather; docile; quiet
硫 *waryū* vulcanization ⌊(person)
装 *wasō* Japanese dress; Japanese binding
裁 *wasai* Japanese sewing
琴 *wagon* Japanese harp, ancient koto
13睦 *waboku* reconciliation, conclusion of a peace treaty
解 *wakai* reconciliation; atonement; compromise. *wakai, wage* translation; rewriting Chinese (*kambun*) in mixed script
戦 *wasen* peace and war
楽 *wagaku* Japanese music. *waraku* peace and harmony ⌈Chinese
漢 *wa-kan* Japan and China; Japanese and
漢混淆文 *wa-kan konkōbun* (ancient) mixture of Japanese and Chinese writing
14語 *wago* pure Japanese words
歌 *waka* thirty-one-syllable poem, tanka
算 *wasan* Japanese mathematics; abacus
製 *wasei* Japanese manufacture ⌊calculation

魂漢才 *wakon-kansai* Japanese spirit and Chinese learning
15談 *wadan* a talk to settle differences
16親 *washin* harmony, amity, friendship
親条約 *washin jōyaku* treaty of friendship
親国 *washinkoku* friendly country
親協商 *washin kyōshō* treaty of friendship
20議 *wagi* peace negotiations, reconciliation
20蘭 *Oranda* Holland
蘭語 *Orandago* Dutch language
22讃 *wasan* (Buddhist) hymns of praise

4

香 See 5188. [香]

秕 3269 F1376 See **粃** 3466.

秔 3270 F1376 See **粳** 3478.

A **秒** 3271 F1376 Byō one-sixtieth of a minute (of time, latitude, degree, etc.).
9速 *byōsoku* speed per second
10針 *byōshin* second hand (of a watch)
時計 *byōdokei* stop watch
記時計 *byōkidokei* stop watch

A **科** 3272 F1375 Ka course, branch, department, faculty, school, college; arm (of defense); family (in biology). *ka-(suru), ka(su)* inflict (punishment), fine. *toga* fault, blame; charge, offense, sin, transgressions, trespasses. *shina* actions, deportment. *shigusa* acting, gestures.
2人 *toganin* criminal, offender
5白 *serifu, kahaku*=*serifu* 台詞 848.12
目 *kamoku* subdivision (in scientific classification)
6名 *kamei* family name (in biology)
7条 *kajō* laws; assortment, category
8長 *kachō* department head
学 *kagaku* science
学小説 *kagaku shōsetsu* science fiction
学用語 *kagaku yōgo* scientific term
学技術 *kagaku gijutsu* scientific technique
学的 *kagakuteki* scientific
学者 *kagakusha* scientist
学書 *kagakusho* scientific book
学戦 *kagakusen* scientific warfare
学語 *kagakugo* scientific term ⌈fault
9怠 *katai* inexcusable error, carelessness,
10料 *karyō* minor fine ⌈service examinations
挙 *kakyo* the (ancient) Chinese higher civil-
12程 *katei* circumstances; order; degree

5 玄 玉 王 瓜 瓦 甘 生 用 田 疋 疒 癶 白 皮 皿 目 矛 矢 石 示 ネ 内 4【禾】 穴 立

A **秋** 3273/F1373 SHŪ *aki* autumn. *aki*(*meku*), *aki*(*sabu*) feel like fall.
2 七草 *aki* (*no*) *nanakusa* fall flowers
刀魚 *samma* saury, skipper, mackerel, pike
3 口 *akiguchi* early fall
山 *akiyama* mountains in the fall
4 水 *shūsui* clear river water in autumn
日 *shūjitsu* autumn day
日和 *akibiyori* clear fall weather
分 *shūbun* fall equinox ⌈day, September 23)
分日 *Shūbun* (*no*) *Hi* the Fall Equinox (holi-
5 田 *akita* ripened rice fields, fall rice fields
立 *akita*(*tsu*) fall arrives
収 *akiosa*(*me*) fall crops ⌈fall colors
6 色 *shūshoku*, *aki* (*no*) *iro* autumn scenery,
気 *shūki* fall air ⌈crops
7 作 *akisaku* fall-sown crops; fall-harvested
冷 *shūrei* autumn chill, cool fall weather
声 *shūsei* sound of the autumn wind
8 雨 *shūu*, *akisame* autumn rain
波 *shūha* amorous glance, wink
郊 *shūkō* autumn fields
空 *akizora* autumn sky
季 *shūki* autumn
季皇霊祭 *Shūki Kōreisai* Shinto Festival of the Autumnal Equinox
9 風 *shūfū*, *aki kaze* autumn breeze
咲 *akisa*(*ki*) fall blooming
思 *shūshi* the lonely feeling of fall
草 *akigusa* fall flowers
10 蚕 *akiko*, *akigo*, *shūsan* fall silkworms
12 晴 *akiba*(*re*) clear fall weather
植 *akiue* fall planting
湿 *akijime*(*ri*) long fall rain
期 *shūki* autumn
買 *akiga*(*i*) buying up in the fall
落 *akio*(*chi*) poor rice crop
場 *akiba* autumn time
場所 *akibasho* fall wrestling tournament
13 蒔 *akimaki* fall sowing
16 曇 *akigumo*(*ri*) cloudy fall weather
霖 *akijime*(*ri*) long fall rain
17 闌 *akita*(*keru*) autumn ends
霜 *shūsō* autumn frost
霜烈日 *shūsō-retsujitsu* withering frost and scorching sun; severe punishment
18 穫 *shūkaku* fall crop
繭 *aki mayu* fall cocoon crop
19 霧 *akigiri* autumn mists
21 露 *shūro* autumn dew
23 黴雨 *akijime*(*ri*) long fall rain

5

秦 3274/F1377 SHIN Manchu dynasty. *hata* name given anciently to naturalized foreigners.

秤 3275/F1377 SHŌ. *hakari* balances, scales, steelyard.
12 量 *hyōryō* estimation, weighing

B **秩** 3276/F1377 CHITSU salary; order.
7 序 *chitsujo* order, system, discipline, regularity, method
序正 *chitsujo-tada*(*shii*) in good order

秣 3277/F1376 MATSU. *magusa* fodder, feed, hay.
4 切 *magusaki*(*ri*) hay cutter
11 桶 *magusa oke* manger

秧 3278/F1377 Ō. *sanae* rice seedlings.
8 取 *sanaeto*(*ru*) transplant rice
14 歌 *sanae uta* rice-planting song

B **租** 3279/F1376 So crop tax; borrowing.
9 界 *sokai* concession, settlement
10 借 *soshaku suru* lease
借地 *soshakuchi* leased territory, leasehold
借権 *soshakuken* lease, leasehold
12 税 *sozei* taxes, taxation

A **称** 3280/F1382 **稱** SHŌ name, title; fame; praise. *tona*(*eru*), *shō*(*suru*) name, entitle; claim, plead, pretend to be; praise, admire. *tona*(*eru*) (see under 唱 941.0). *tata*(*eru*) praise, admire.
6 号 *shōgō* title, degree ⌈prayer
名 *shōmyō* reciting the "Hail Amida"
8 呼 *shōko* appellation, name, title
9 美 *shōbi* praise, admiration
11 道 *shōdō* advocacy
12 揚 *shōyō* praise, admiration
15 賛 *shōsan* praise, admiration
22 讃 *shōsan* praise, admiration

B **秘** 3281/F1376/F1357 **祕** HI secret. *hi*(*meru*), *hi*(*suru*) conceal, keep a secret. *hisoka ni* secretly.
4 文 *himon* magic formula, incantation, curse, spell, charm
方 *hihō* secret formula, secret process
中 *hichū* in secret
仏 *hibutsu* a Buddhist idol kept hidden
5 史 *hishi* secret history
本 *hihon* treasured book, tabooed book
6 曲 *hikyoku* secret or esoteric music
伝 *hiden* secret, mystery, secret formula
8 法 *hihō* secret formula, secret process
宝 *hihō* treasure, treasured article

事 *hiji* secret; mystery; private affairs. *hi(me)goto* secret. *misokagoto* secret; clandestine relationship
9計 *hikei* secret plan, deep plot
封 *hifū* carefully sealing (a letter)
要 *hiyō* mystery, secret
10匿 *hitoku suru* hide, conceal
書 *hisho* private secretary
書官 *hishokan* private secretary
書室 *hishoshitsu* secretarial office
11術 *hijutsu* secret art; the mysteries
訣 *hiketsu* secret; the mysteries; the key to
密 *himitsu* secrecy, privacy, mystery, secret
密外交 *himitsu gaikō* secret diplomacy
密会 *himitsukai* secret meeting
密教 *himitsukyō* esoteric Buddhism
密探偵 *himitsu tantei* secret agent
密結社 *himitsu kessha* secret society
密話 *himitsubanashi* confidential talk
12結 *hiketsu* constipation
奥 *hiō* secrets, mysteries
策 *hissaku* a secret plan
13話 *hiwa* secret story; secret history
置 *hi(me)-o(ku)* hide
義 *higi* mystery
14語 *higo* secret words
蔵 *hizō* treasuring
16謀 *hibō* clandestine plan
録 *hiroku* confidential document, secret memoirs
薬 *hiyaku* nostrum, secret medicine
18蹟 *hiseki* (Catholic) sacraments
19願 *higan* unspoken prayer
25鑰 *hiyaku* secret, key

6

A 移 3282/F1378 I. *utsu(ru)* move, change, shift. pass into, drift; soak in; be infected, catch (a cold); catch fire, spread. *utsu(su)* move, transfer; pour into, divert (attention), give (a disease to someone). *utsu(rou)* change, shift, fade, decline.
2入 *inyū* import
5民 *imin* immigration; emigration; immigrant; emigrant; settler, colonist
出 *ishutsu suru* ship out; export
出入 *ishutsunyū* trade with parts of the prewar empire
6行 *ikō suru* veer to, shift to, switch over to. *utsu(ri)-yu(ku)* change, shift, come and go
気 *utsu(ri)gi* whim, frivolity, fickleness
安 *utsu(ri)ya(sui)* changeable, fickle; transient; infectious, contagious
7住 *ijū* migration; emigration; immigration; moving
住民 *ijūmin* emigrant; immigrant; settler; colonist
住者 *ijūsha* emigrant; immigrant
8送 *isō* transfer, transport, remove
9香 *utsu(ri)ga* lingering scent
乗 *ijō suru* transfer to
変 *utsu-(ri)-kawa(ru)* change, shift, come and go. *utsu(ri)kawa(ri)* change, transition.
10記 *iki* transfer of entry
11転 *iten* moving; transfer; demise
動 *idō* movement, transfer, migration, turnover, locomotion
動大使 *idō taishi* roving ambassador
動図書館 *idō toshokan* mobile library
動警察 *idō keisatsu* mobile police
12棲 *isei* migration (of birds)
植 *ishoku* transplanting; naturalization (of plants); (skin) grafting
絵 *utsushie* decalcomania, process of transferring pictures to china etc.
13牒 *ichō* notification to the authorities
14管 *ikan* transfer of control
15調 *ichō* transposition
駐 *ichū suru* move, transfer
20譲 *ijō suru* transfer, assignment
籍 *iseki* changing one's domiciliary registry

7

黍 See 5400. [黍]

稈 3283/F1379 KAN hollow jointed stem; straw.

稍 3284/F1380 SŌ. *yaya* a little, slightly, somewhat.
3久 *yayahisa(shiku)* for some time
12稍 *yaya* (see under 稍 3284.0)

A 程 3285/F1379 程 TEI degree; law; formula; distance. *hodo* limits, limit, extent, degree; moderation; social status; distance; time; amount. *-hodo* about, more or less, as, to the degree.
6近 *hodochika(i)* near
好 *hodoyo(ku)* properly, judiciously, moderately
合 *hodoa(i)* limit, limits
7良 *hodoyo(i)* good, favorable, proper; moderate, temperate; vague (answer)
9度 *teido* degree, extent, limit, level, standard. *hodohe(te)* after a while
11経 *hodohe(te)* after a while
12遠 *hodotō(karanu)* not too far
程 *hodohodo ni* properly, judiciously, temperately, moderately
無 *hodona(ku)* soon afterward

稀 3286/F1378 KI. KE. *ma(rena)* rare, phenomenal, few. *ki-* dilute (acid).

5 玄 玉 王 瓜 瓦 甘 生 用 田 疋 疒 癶 白 皮 皿 目 矛 矢 石 示 ネ 内 7【禾】 穴 立

3 土類元素 *kidorui genso* rare earth elements
4 元素 *kigenso* rare element
少 *kishō* scarcity
少物資 *kishō busshi* scarce materials
5 代 *kidai na, kitai na* uncommon, rare; remarkable, matchless; notorious
世 *kisei no* extraordinary, unique. *kisei* rare
6 有 *keu* rare, extraordinary
8 金属 *kikinzoku* rare metals
10 書 *kisho* rare book
11 釈 *kishaku* dilution
12 稀 *ma(re)ma(re)* very few; very strange
14 酸 *kisan* dilute acid
17 覯 *kikō* accidental meeting; infrequent meeting; something strange
覯本 *kikōbon* rare book
覯書 *kikōsho* rare book
19 薄 *kihaku na* thin, lean, rare, diluted, sparse, weak

A **税** 3287/F1379 **税** ZEI tax, duty.
4 込 *zeiko(mi)* (salary) before tax is taken out
引 *zeibi(ki)* after taxes
引給与 *zeibi(ki) kyūyo* take-home pay
5 目 *zeimoku* tariff items
収 *zeishū* tax revenue
6 吏 *zeiri* customs officer
吏長 *zeirichō* head tax collector
8 金 *zeikin* tax, duty
法 *zeihō* tax law, taxation scheme
制 *zeisei* tax system
表 *zeihyō* tariff
11 率 *zeiritsu* tax rates; tariff
務 *zeimu* tax business
務官吏 *zeimu kanri* tax collector, revenue officer
務署 *zeimusho* tax office
12 期 *zeiki* tax period
13 源 *zeigen* tax source
14 関 *zeikan* customs; customs house
関司 *zeikanshi* customs inspector
関吏 *zeikanri* customs inspector
関長 *zeikanchō* superintendent of customs
18 額 *zeigaku* tax amount

8

稟 See 325.

稔 3288/F1380 JIN, NIN, NEN harvest; ripen.

稠 3289/F1381 CHŪ density.
11 密 *chūmitsu na* dense, thick, crowded

稗 3290/F1380 HAI humble. *hie* deccan grass, a barnyard grass.
5 史 *haishi* legend, fiction, romance
10 益 *hieki* usefulness

稜 3291/F1381 RYŌ angle, edge, corner; power, majesty.
9 威 *ryōi, mi-itsu* imperial majesty
15 線 *ryōsen* mountain-ridge line
18 稜 *ryōryō(taru)* rugged

B **稚** 3292/F1380 CHI young. *itokena(i)* young (child).
3 子 *chishi* a little child; a seedling, a bud, a sprout
4 心 *chishin* a childish mind
6 気 *chiki* childishness
7 児 *chigo* baby, child; page; festive children
8 拙 *chisetsu na* unskillful, childish
拙美 *chisetsubi* beauty of artlessness
11 魚 *chigyo* young fish

9

穀 See 2461.

稱 3293/F1382 See **称** 3280.

B **稲** 3294/F1383 **稻** TŌ. *ine, ina-* rice plant.
3 子 *inago* locust
4 木 *inagi* rice-drying rack
刈 *inaka(ri)* rice reaping
5 田 *inada* rice field
6 舟 *inabune* boats that carry rice sheaves
扱 *ineko(ki), inako(ki)* threshing; threshing machine
光 *inabikari* lightning
7 作 *inasaku* rice crop; rice cultivation
8 苗 *tōbyō* rice seedlings
妻 *inazuma* lightning
9 架 *inakake, inaka, hasa* rice-drying rack
10 株 *inakabu, ine kabu* rice stubble
荷 *Inari* harvest god; fox god
荷鮨 *inarizushi* fried tofu stuffed with seasoned rice
11 掛 *ineka(ke)* rice-drying rack
粒 *inatsubu* a grain of rice
13 幹 *inagara* grain stems
15 穂 *inaho, inabo* heads of rice
熱 *imochi* rice blight
熱病 *imochibyō* rice blight
17 藁 *inawara* rice straw
18 叢 *inamura* stack of rice straw
20 懸 *inekake* rice-drying rack

A **種** 3295/F1381 SHU kind, class, variety; seed; species. *tane* seed, kernel; kind, species; quality, tone; material; breed;

topic; cause, source; trick; data; inside story; secret; leaven. *kusa* materials, origins.
2 入 *tane(irenu)* unleavened
3 下 *taneoro(shi)* sowing, seeding
子 *shushi* seed, pit, stone
子島 *tanegashima* matchlock gun, arquebus
4 牛 *tane ushi* bull
切 *tanegi(re)* exhaustion of seed; exhaustion of materials
5 皮 *shuhi* seed coat
目 *shumoku* item; lot; event (as a race)
付 *tanetsu(ke)* mating
本 *tanehon* source book; original; manual
仕掛 *tanejika(ke)* secret; secret device
6 牝 *tane mesu* a breeding mare
芋 *tane imo* seed potatoes
名 *shumei* species name
7 牡 *tane osu* a stud horse
別 *shubetsu* classification, assortment
芸 *shugei* planting trees and plants
卵 *tane tamago* nest egg
牡蠣 *tanegaki* seed oyster
8 明 *taneaka(shi)* exposure of a trick; exposing a secret
板 *tane-ita* negative
油 *taneabura* vegetable oil, rapeseed oil
取 *taneto(ri)* plants grown for seeds; seed raising; breeding; reporting, reporter
苗園 *shubyōen* nursery company
物 *tanemono* seeds; buckwheat noodle dish; shaved ice with fruit syrup
物屋 *tanemonoya* seed store
9 畑 *tanebatake* seed garden
籾 *tanemomi* seed rice
変 *tanegawa(ri)* half-brother; half-sister; variety (of plant)
10 馬 *tane uma, shuba* stud horse, stallion
紙 *tanegami* (silkworm) egg card
起原 *shu (no) kigen* origin of the species
畜 *shuchiku* breeding stock
畜農業 *shuchiku nōgyō* animal husbandry
11 違 *tanechiga(i)* half-brother, half-sister
掛 *tane (o) ka(keru)* breed
粒 *tanetsubu* kernel, a grain
族 *shuzoku* race, tribe, family, caste; genus, species
族的 *shuzokuteki* racial, tribal
12 属 *shuzoku* kind, genus, species
無 *tanena(shi)* seedless
痘 *shutō* vaccination, inoculation
痘料 *shutōryō* vaccination fee
痘証明書 *shutō shōmeisho* vaccination certificate
13 蒔 *tanemaki* sowing, seeding, planting
14 種 *shuju* variety. *kusagusa* various
種相 *shujusō* various phases
種雑多 *shuju-zatta* various kinds
種様様 *shuju-samazama* great variety
18 類 *shurui* kind, variety, class, species
類分 *shuruiwa(ke)* classification, assortment
類別 *shuruibetsu* classification, assortment

10

黎 See 2648. [黍]

黐 See 5402. [黍]

穀 See **穀** 2461.

稲 3296 F1383 See **稲** 3294.

稗 3297 F1383 See **稗** 3303.

稷 3298 F1382 Shoku. *kibi* millet.

稿 3299 F1383 **稾** Kō copy, manuscript, draft; straw.
B
5 本 *kōhon* manuscript
10 料 *kōryō* payment for a manuscript

穂 3300 F1386 **穗** Sui. *ho* ear, head (of grain); crest (of waves).
B
6 先 *hosaki* beard of grain; head of grain; spearhead
7 状 *suijō* a shape like a head of grain
8 波 *honami* waving grain
11 掛 *hoka(ke)* offering of heads of grain

稼 3301 F1383 Ka. *kase(gu)* work; earn money. *kasegi* work; income.
2 人 *kaseginin* breadwinner, hard worker
4 手 *kasegite*=word above
6 行 *kakō* operation (of a factory)
8 取 *kase(gi)-to(ru)* earn by working
10 高 *kasegidaka* earnings
11 動 *kadō* operation, actual work
18 穡 *kashoku* farming

11

穎 See 5127.

黐 See 5402. [黍]

穇 3302 F-X San. *hie* deccan grass, a barnyard grass.

穉 3303 F1384 F1383 **稚** Chi infancy.
6 気 *chiki* childishness

5 玄玉王瓜瓦甘生用田疋疒癶白皮皿目矛矢石示ネ内 11【禾】穴立

稽 3304 / F1383 KEI think, consider; quarrel.

5古 *keiko* practice, training, study, instruction
古所 *keikojo* practice room
古着 *keikogi* gym suit
9首 *keishu* bowing to the floor and worshiping
10留 *keiryū* stopping

B **穏** 3305 / F1386 **穩** ON. *oda(yaka)* calm, quiet, peace; moderation. *oda(yakanaranu)* disquieting, alarming, serious, threatening.

6当 *ontō na* proper, reasonable, just, right, moderate
8和 *onwa* moderation
和派 *onwaha* moderate party
和論者 *onwaronsha* a moderate
9便 *ombin na* gentle, quiet, peaceable; private, out of court
11健 *onken na* quiet, dependable, uniform
健派 *onkenha* moderate party

A **積** 3306 / F1384 SEKI product (in math.); acreage, contents, measurement. *tsu(mu) vt* pile up, stack, lay; load, ship, take on; accumulate, amass, save. *tsu(moru) vi* accumulate, be piled up, be amassed; lie on, be covered (with snow); amount to; estimate, calculate, measure. *tsu(mori)* intention, purpose; belief; motive; expectation; idea; estimate. *tsu(mi)* loading; shipment; capacity. *-zu(mi)* shipment, lading, burden, capacity.

2入 *tsu(mi)-i(reru)* ship, take on
3上 *tsu(mi)-a(geru)* pile up, accumulate
4方 *tsu(mi)kata* manner of loading
木 *tsu(mi)ki* toy blocks; piled timber
切 *tsu(mi)-ki(ru)* ship completely
込 *tsu(mi)-ko(mu)* load, take on, ship. *tsu(mi)ko(mi)* shipping, loading; shipment
込値段 *tsumiko(mi) nedan* price F.O.B.
分 *sekibun* integral calculus
分学 *sekibungaku* integral calculus
5石 *tsu(mi) ishi* pile of stones; cornerstone
立 *tsu(mi)-ta(teru)* save, reserve, amass. *tsu(mi)ta(te)* reserve funds
立金 *tsumitatekin* reserve fund
出 *tsu(mi)-da(su)* send, ship, forward. *tsu(mi)da(shi)* shipment, forwarding
出人 *tsu(mi)da(shi)nin* shipper
出費 *tsu(mi)da(shi)hi* shipping expenses
6返 *tsu(mi)-kae(su)* ship back
年 *sekinen* (many) years
7戻 *tsu(mi)-mo(dosu)* re-export, reship, send back
乱雲 *sekiran-un* cumulo-nimbus clouds
8金 *tsu(mi)gane, tsu(mi)kin* reserve funds, savings
取 *tsu(mi)-to(ru)* take on, load
肥 *tsu(mi)hi* compost, barnyard manure
直 *tsu(mi)-nao(su)* reload, pile over again
送 *sekisō, tsu(mi)oku(ri)* consignment, shipment. *tsu(mi)-oku(ru)* consign, ship
送品 *sekisōhin* consignment, shipment
9恨 *tsu(moru) urami* growing hatred, suppressed hatred
卸 *tsu(mi)oro(shi)* loading and unloading; unloading; cargo handling
重 *tsu(mi)-kasa(naru) vi* be piled up, accumulate. *tsu(mi)-kasa(neru) vt* pile up, accumulate
怨 *sekien* a succession of grudges
10残 *tsu(mi)-noko(su)* leave out of shipment. *tsu(mi)noko(ri), tsu(mi)noko(shi)* short shipment, goods left behind
財 *sekizai* building up wealth; accumulated wealth
荷 *tsu(mi)ni* load, freight, cargo, shipment
書 *tsu(mori)ga(ki)* written estimate
11違 *tsu(mori)chiga(i)* miscalculation
過 *tsu(mi)-su(giru)* overload. *tsu(mori)-su(giru)* overestimate, overvalue
悪 *sekiaku* accumulated wickedness, series of evil deeds
雪 *sekisetsu* drifted snow, deep snow, snowdrifts
12貯 *tsu(mi)-takuwa(eru)* store up
善 *sekizen* accumulation of good deeds
量 *sekiryō* carrying capacity, tonnage
雲 *sekiun* cumulus clouds
替 *tsu(mi)-ka(eru)* transship, reship. *tsu(mori)ga(e)* recalculation
極 *sekkyoku* the positive
極外交 *sekkyoku gaikō* positive foreign policy
極性 *sekkyokusei* positiveness
極的 *sekkyokuteki* positive, active, constructive, progressive
13置場 *tsu(mi)o(ki)ba* freight yard
載 *sekisai* lading, loading, carrying
載量 *sekisairyō* carrying capacity, load
載噸数 *sekisai tonsū* freight capacity
14読 *tsundo(ku)* pile up on the desk without reading
算 *sekisan* addition
15憤 *sekifun* grudge, resentment
弊 *sekihei* deep-seated evil
16積 *tsu(mori)-tsu(moru)* go on, pile up, accumulate

12

稺 See 3303.

黏 See **粘** 3472. [黍]

穂 3307 / F1386 See **穗** 3300.

— 13 —

馥 See 5189. [香]

穰 3308/F1387 穰 Jō good crops; prosperity.

B 穫 3309/F1387 KAKU harvest; reap. *to(ru)* to harvest.

穡 3310/F1386 SHOKU harvest.

穢 3311/F1386 AI, E. *kega(su)*, *kega(reru)*, *kega(re)* (see under 汚 2494.0).

6多 *eta* outcasts, the eta class
8苦 *musakuru(shii)* filthy, shabby, untidy

— 14 —

穩 3312/F1386 See 穏 3305.

— 17 —

穰 See 穰 3308.

— 18 —

黐 See 5402. [黍]

穴 RAD. 116

Ana kammuri "hole" crown. Variants: 穴, 宂. Nickname: Cave.

B 穴 3313/F1387 穴 宂 KETSU, *ana* hole, aperture, slit; gap, stop (of musical instrument); eyelet; cavity; socket; cave; den; hiding place; pit; fault, defect; deficit; grave; dark horse.

3子 *anago* sea eel, conger eel
8居 *kekkyo* cave dwelling
居人 *kekkyojin* cave dweller, cave man
明 *ana-a(ki)* perforated; drilled (pearls)
明真珠 *ana-a(ki) shinju* drilled pearls
10埋 *ana-u(me)* filling a hole; stopgap; covering a deficit
11痔 *anaji* anal fistula
道 *anamichi* tunnel, gallery
探 *anasaga(shi)* faultfinding
掘 *anaho(ri)* excavation, digging a hole; novice, bungler
釣 *anazu(ri)* sniggling for eels
12植 *ana-u(e)* dibbling
開工具 *ana-a(ke) kōgu* drill bit
開器 *ana-a(ke)ki* punch, stiletto
13隙 *ketsugeki* aperture, crevice
塞 *anafusa(gi)* stopgap; plugging a hole
14蔵 *anagura* cellar
熊 *anaguma* badger
練瓦 *ana renga* perforated brick
15播 *anamaki* dibbling
16縢 *anakaga(ri)* buttonhole sewing

— 2 —

A 究 3314/F1387 KYŪ. *kiwa(meru)* (see under 極 2305.0).

7局 *kyūkyoku* eventuality, extremity
8明 *kyūmei* investigation, inquiry
10理 *kyūri* study of natural laws
11竟 *kyūkyō* end, extremity. *kukyō na, kukkyō na* superb, best, ideal
12極 *kyūkyoku* eventuality, extremity, desperate situation

— 3 —

穹 3315/F1388 KYŪ sky.

13蒼 *kyūsō* blue vault of heaven
15窿 *kyūryū* the vault of heaven

B 突 3316/F1390 突 TOTSU protruding, thrusting. *tsu(ku)* thrust, pierce, spear, stab, prick; gore; lunge at; push, poke; strike (a bell); attack; strike (at the heart); brave (a storm); be pungent; strike against; (words) rush (to one's lips). *tsutsu(ku)* poke, pick at, peck, elbow. *tsun-*, *tsu(ki)-* prefix meaning *tsu(ku)*.

2入 *totsunyū suru* plunge into, rush in, cut in between. *tsu(ki)-i(ru)* rush into. *tsu(ki)-i(reru)* thrust into
3上 *tsu(ki)-a(geru)* push up; toss up; nauseate
上戸 *tsu(ki)a(ge)do* overhung door
4止 *tsu(ki)-to(meru)* make sure of
込 *tsu(ki)-ko(mu)*, *tsu(k)ko(mu)* thrust into, poke into; plunge into, dip; penetrate, pierce; ram in; close in on; give (one) a thrust
切 *tsu(ki)-ki(ru)* break thru, go right across
支 *tsukkai* prop, stay, support, brace
支棒 *tsukkaibō* prop, stay, support, brace

5 目 *tsukime* hitting the eye on some projection
付 *tsu(ki)-tsu(keru)* point (a gun at); put right under one's nose
出 *tsu(ki)-da(su), tsunda(su)* push out, stick out, stretch out, jut out. *tsu(ki)-de(ru)* project, stick out, jut, bulge out. *tsu(ki)-da(shi)* protrusion; start; newcomer; hors d'oeuvre. *tosshutsu* projection, protrusion, prominence
立 *tsu(t)ta(tsu)* stand, stand up straight. *tsu(ki)-ta(teru)* stab, thrust violently, set a stake. *tsu(ki)-ta(tsu) vi* stick in; rise sharply
立上 *tsu(t)ta(chi)-a(garu)* jump to one's feet
6 返 *tsu(ki)-kae(su)* thrust in return; refuse to accept
回 *tsutsu(ki)-mawa(su)* poke around
如 *totsujo, totsujo toshite* suddenly, unexpectedly
合 *tsu(ki)-a(u)* poke each other, thrust each other. *tsu(ki)-a(waseru), tsu(ki)-a(wasu)* confront (someone) with, bring face to face; compare with. *tsu(ki)a(i)* thrusting one another
当 *tsu(ki)-ata(ru)* collide; come to the end of a street. *tsu(ki)-a(teru)* dash against, run against. *tsu(ki)ata(ri)* collision; dead end of a street
先 *tossaki* tip (of something)
7 角 *tokkaku* convex angle
走 *tsu(p)pashi(ru)* run swiftly
戻 *tsu(ki)-modo(su)* give a thrust in return; thrust back; refuse to accept
抜 *tsu(ki)-nu(keru) vi* pierce thru, break thru. *tsu(ki)-nu(ku) vt* pierce, shoot thru, penetrate
8 放 *tsu(p)pana(su), tsu(ki)-hana(su)* throw off, forsake
明 *tsu(ki)-a(keru)* push open
刺 *tsu(ki)-sa(saru) vi* stick, pierce. *tsu(ki)-sa(su) vt* pierce, penetrate
突 *tsu(t)tsu(ku)* prompt (someone)
拍子無 *toppyōshi (mo) na(i)* out of tune; exorbitant
9 風 *toppū* squall, sudden gust
飛 *tsu(ki)-to(basu)* knock (a person) down; push away. *toppi na* wild, extraordinary, fantastic, risky, reckless, eccentric
通 *tsu(ki)-tō(ru) vi* pierce, penetrate, stick into. *tsu(ki)-tō(su) vt* pierce, penetrate
指 *tsu(ki)yubi* sprained finger
除 *tsu(ki)-no(keru)* push aside, elbow out
発 *toppatsu* burst, gust, outbreak
10 起 *tokki* protuberance, prominence, projection
進 *tosshin* rush, onrush, dash, charge
倒 *tsu(ki)-tao(su)* knock (a person) down
破 *toppa suru* break thru; overcome. *tsu(ki)-yabu(ru)* break thru, pierce, pass (an exam); exceed, go over (a goal)
殺 *tsu(ki)-koro(su)* stab to death; gore to death
11 張 *tsu(p)pa(ru)* stretch (an arm) against, plant (one's foot) on; insist on. *tsu(p)pa(ri)* prop, brace, support, bolster, strut, buttress, (door) bar
眼 *tsu(ki) me*=突目 (see above-5)
転 *tsu(k)koro(basu), tsu(ki)-koro(basu)* knock (a person) down
崩 *tsu(ki)-kuzu(su)* level, rout
掛 *tsu(ki)-ka(karu)* thrust at (with a knife)
掛草履 *tsukka(ke) zōri* slipper-type zori
貫 *tokkan* a charge (in war)
貫作業 *tokkan sagyō* rush work
12 遣 *tsu(ki)-ya(ru)* push away
堤 *tottei* pier, breakwater
棒 *tsu(ki)bō* goad
落 *tsu(ki)-o(tosu)* push off, thrust down. *tsu(ki)oto(shi)* sag (in the stock market)
然 *totsuzen* suddenly, unexpectedly
然変異 *totsuzen hen-i* mutation
13 傷 *tsu(ki) kizu* stab wound
詰 *tsu(ki)-tsu(meru)* investigate; think hard; brood over
14 端 *toppana, tottan* tip of a headland. *toppashi* extreme end
慳貪 *tsu(k)kendon na* sharp, blunt, harsh
15 撥 *tsu(p)pa(neru)* reject, spurn, refuse
撃 *totsugeki* charge, assault
撃兵 *totsugekihei* shock troops
撃隊 *totsugekitai* shock troops
撃路 *totsugekiro* a breach
16 錐 *tsu(ki)giri* awl
28 鑿 *tsu(ki)nomi* scraper (the tool)

空 3317 F1388 空 空 A **Kū** air, sky; emptiness; vanity, unreality; hollow; void. *su(ku), a(ku) vi* become empty, be less crowded. *a(keru) vt* empty. *a(ita)* open; empty, vacant. *a(ki)* gap, opening, aperture; space, blank, vacancy. *kara* emptiness, vacancy, hollowness, vacuum. *kara, kara(ppo)* empty. *muna(shii)* void, empty, vain; ineffective; lifeless. *sora* sky, heavens, air, weather, memory, absent-mindedness. *utsu(ro)* hollow, cavity, void; emptiness. *utsuke, ukke* emptiness; dumbness. *kū ni* vainly, ineffectively. *a(ki)-* empty, vacant, unoccupied, spare (hours). *sora-* pretended, sham, mock.
4 文 *kūbun* dead letter, scrap of paper
井 *kara-i* empty well
元気 *kara genki* mere bravado
手 *karate de, kūshu de* empty-handed; with bare fists. *karate* barehanded fighting
手形 *kara tegata* bad check; empty promise
中 *kūchū* air, sky, space. *kūchū no* aerial, air

中分解 *kūchū bunkai* disintegration of a plane in flight
中広告 *kūchū kōkoku* skywriting
中写真 *kūchū shashin* air photo; aerial photography
中征服 *kūchū seifuku* mastery of the air
中飛行 *kūchū hikō* aviation
中窒素 *kūchū chisso* atmospheric nitrogen
中魚雷 *kūchū gyorai* aerial torpedo
中偵察 *kūchū teisatsu* air reconnaissance
中戦 *kūchūsen* air battle; aerial warfare
中滑走 *kūchū kassō* gliding
中滑走機 *kūchū kassōki* glider, sailplane
中楼閣 *kūchū rōkaku* castle in the air; mirage
中線 *kūchūsen* antenna
中輸送 *kūchū yusō* air transportation
中優越 *kūchū yūetsu* air superiority
5 母 *kūbo* aircraft carrier
白 *kūhaku* blank space, vacuum, void
目 *sorame* misperception, mistake; pretending not to see; upward look
尻 *kara(k)ketsu na* penniless
世辞 *karaseji* flattery, empty compliments
6 耳 *soramimi* mishearing; feigned deafness
舟 *karabune, karafune* empty ship
色 *sora-iro* sky blue; weather
回 *karamawa(ri)* racing (of a propeller); skidding (of a car); profitless business activity; fruitless effort
死 *soraji(ni)* feigned death
似 *sorani* accidental resemblance
地 *akichi, kūchi* vacant lot, open space, room
合 *sora-a(i)* looks of the sky, weather
名 *kūmei* empty name; false reputation
返事 *sora henji* random answer
自慢 *karajiman* vain boast, braggadocio
気 *kūki* air, atmosphere
気力学 *kūki rikigaku* aerodynamics
気弁 *kūkiben* air valve
気伝染 *kūki densen* infection
気抜 *kūkinu(ki)* ventilator
気冷却 *kūki reikyaku* air cooling
気枕 *kūki makura* air pillow
気制動機 *kūki seidōki* air brake
気浴 *kūkiyoku* air bath
気袋 *kūkibukuro* air sac
気銃 *kūkijū* air gun
気療法 *kūki ryōhō* air cure
7 言 *kūgen* idle talk. *soragoto* falsehood, lie
谷 *kūkoku* lonely valley
身 *karami* light luggage
車 *karaguruma, kūsha* empty conveyance
位 *kūi* vacant post, post in name only
冷 *kūrei* air cooled
冷式 *kūreishiki* air-cooled
8 店 *akidana, aki mise* vacant store
房 *kūbō* vacant room
送 *kūsō* air transportation
所 *kūsho* space, open space, blank space
明 *kūmei* moon's reflection in clear water
泣 *sorana(ki)* crocodile tears
取引 *kara torihiki* bogus transaction
念仏 *kara nembutsu* formal Buddhist prayer; empty phrases, fruitless talk. *sora nembutsu* pretending to pray
空 *kūkū* vanity, nothing; absent-mindedness; lack of tenacity; evil passions. *sorazora(shii)* feigned, false, empty, obvious, transparent
空寂寂 *kūkū-jakujaku* absent-minded; null and void
空漠漠 *kūkū-bakubaku(taru)* vast and empty
9 音 *sorane* false cry, falsehood
屋 *akiya* vacant house
咳 *karazeki, karaseki* dry or hacking cough
恍 *soratobo(keru)* feign innocence; feign ignorance
洞 *kūdō* cave, hollow, cavity
軍 *kūgun* air force
室 *kūshitsu* vacant room
茶 *karacha* tea without cakes
勇気 *kara yūki* mere bravado
威張 *kara-ibari* bluff; mock dignity
相場 *kūsōba* speculation, fictitious transaction
要塞 *sora (no) yōsai* flying fortress
飛円盤 *sorato(bu) emban* flying saucer
海作戦 *kūkai sakusen* air-sea operations
風 *kara(k)kaze, karakaze* dry wind
風呂 *karaburo* steam bath, Turkish bath
前 *kūzen no* unprecedented, record-breaking
前絶後 *kūzen-zetsugo* unparalleled
10 馬 *kara uma* unloaded horse
席 *kūseki* vacant seats, vacancy
悦 *sora yoroko(bi)* premature joy
振 *karabu(ri)* missing a ball, strike
涙 *sora namida* crocodile tears
眠 *sora nemu(ri)* feigned sleep
砲 *kūhō* blank shot
紙 *kūshi* blank paper
恥 *sorahazu(kashii)* feeling strangely ashamed
冥 *kūmei* sky, empty sky, the heavens
家 *akiya* vacant house
笑 *sorawara(i)* forced laugh, feigned smile
荷 *karani* no load
恐 *sora-osoro(shii)* having vague fears
拳 *kūken* empty hand; one's own efforts
梅雨 *kara tsuyu* dry rainy season
部屋 *akibeya* vacant room
時間 *aki jikan* open period, spare time
11 虚 *kūkyo na* empty, vacant, hollow; inane
唾 *kara tsuba* spittle
堀 *karabori* dry moat
惚 *soratobo(keru)* feign innocence; feign ignorance
理 *kūri* abstract or impracticable theory

5 玄 玉 王 瓜 瓦 甘 生 用 田 疋 疒 癶 白 皮 皿 目 矛 矢 石 示 ネ 内 禾 [穴] 立

脛 *karahagi* bare shins
船 *kūsen, karabune* empty ship
転 *kūten, karamawa(ri)* racing (an engine)
釣 *karazu(ri)* fishing without bait
瓶 *akibin* empty bottle ⌈tent; fruitlessness
虚 *kūkyo* emptiness; hollow; without con-
虚感 *kūkyokan* feeling of emptiness
巣 *akisu* sneak thief, prowler
巣狙 *akisunera(i)* sneak thief, prowler
12 間 *akima* vacant room. *kūkan* space; room;
弾 *kūdan* blank shot ⌊air space
港 *kūkō* airfield, airport
疎 *kūso na* vain, groundless, futile
殻 *akigara* empty sea shell
寝 *sorane* feigned sleep
蒸 *karamushi* steaming, sultriness
覚 *sora obo(e)* memorization. *uro-obo(e)*
費 *kūhi* wastefulness ⌊faint memory
閑地 *kūkanchi* an open (unused) field ⌈tivity
景気 *karageiki* false boom; false show of ac-
13 漠 *kūbaku(taru)* vast, boundless; vague,
渓 *kūkei* dry valley; lonely valley ⌊dreamy
路 *kūro* air lane
隙 *kūgeki* vacant space, aperture, gap
際 *kūsai* the distant sky
夢 *sora yume* false dream
雷 *kūrai* aerial torpedo
電 *kūden* static ⌈tridge; falsehood
鉄砲 *karadeppō* empty gun; empty car-
艇隊 *kūteitai* airborne unit ⌈empty stomach
腹 *kūfuku, sukihara, suki(p)para* hunger,
腹時 *kūfukuji* the time when the stomach is
寝 *sorane* feigned sleep ⌊empty
寝入 *sorane-i(ri)* feigned sleep
想 *kūsō* day dream, air castle, fancy, imagination, vision
想的 *kūsōteki* visionary, Utopian
想家 *kūsōka* dreamer, idealist, visionary
想論 *kūsōron* idle theory, pipe dream
14 閨 *kūkei* deserted wife's chamber
嘔 *kara ezuki* nausea (without being able to vomit)
模様 *sora moyō* looks of the sky, weather
説 *kūsetsu* empty theorizing; baseless rumor
説法 *kara seppō* empty preaching (in Bud-
15 嘘 *kara uso* barefaced lie ⌊dhism)
穂 *utsubo, utsuo* quiver
談 *kūdan* gossip, idle talk
論 *kūron* abstract or impracticable theory
褒 *sorabo(me)* empty praise
箱 *karabako* empty box
16 嘯 *sora usobu(ku)* feign unconcern
濛 *kūmō* drizzly murkiness
錠 *karajō* worthless lock
頼 *soradano(mi)* vain hopes, hoping against
輪 *kūyu* air transportation ⌊hope
輪作業 *kūyu sagyō* airlift operation
輪部隊 *kūyu butai* airborne unit
17 壕 *kūgō, karabori* dry moat
鼾 *sora ibiki* sham snoring
18 臑 *karasune* bare shins
蝉 *utsusemi* cicada's discarded skin
騒 *kara sawa(gi)* much ado about nothing
19 罎 *akibin* empty bottle
爆 *kūbaku* bombing
21 籤 *karakuji* a blank (in lottery)
22 聾 *sora tsumbo* feigned deafness
襲 *kūshū* air raid
襲警戒 *kūshū keikai* air-raid precaution
襲警報 *kūshū keihō* air-raid alarm
23 罐 *akikan* empty can

4

穾 $\frac{3318}{F1390}$ See 宎 3316.

穽 $\frac{3319}{F1390}$ SEI sunken trap.

B **窃** $\frac{3320}{F1396}$ 竊 SETSU. *nusu(mu)* steal. *hiso(ka) na* secret, private, stealthy, hushed.

5 用 ***setsuyō suru*** use secretly
8 取 *sesshu* theft, stealing
11 盗 *settō* theft, larceny
盗罪 *settōzai* theft, larceny

5

容 See 1309. [宀]

窈 $\frac{3321}{F1391}$ YŌ quiet.

11 窕 *yōchō na* refined, attractive, charming; wide and quiet; deep and significant

窄 $\frac{3322}{F1391}$ SAKU narrow. *subo(mu), subo(maru)* narrow, get narrower. *subo(meru)* make narrower; shut (an umbrella); fold, furl; shrug; pucker up. *tsubo(mu), tsubo(maru) vi* shut, close, get narrower. *tsubo(meru) vt* shut, close; fold; make narrower; gather up (skirts); shrug; pucker up.

8 門 ***sema(ki)*** *mon* narrow gate

穿 $\frac{3323}{F1390}$ SEN. *ha(ku)* put on (the feet or legs). *uga(tsu)* dig, cut thru, pierce, drill, penetrate; put on, wear. *hoji-ku(ru), hoji(ru)* dig up; pick (ears or teeth); examine closely; worm out; pick at (a person). *uga(tta)* happy (expression), witty (remark).

4 孔 *senkō* perforation; punching; rupture
心地 *ha(ki)gokochi* comfortable on the feet
5 古 *ha(ki)furu(shi)* worn-out shoes
出 *hojiku(ri)-da(su)=hojiku(ru)* (see under 穿 3323.0)
7 初 *ha(ki)zo(me)* first wearing of footwear
8 刺 *senshi* puncturing a body cavity
9 屋 *hojiku(ri)ya* inquisitive person
10 索 *sensaku* search, inquiry, investigation
11 違 *ha(ki)-chiga(eru)* put on someone else's footwear; be mistaken. *hakichiga(e)* misunderstanding, misconception
掘 *senkutsu* excavation
捨 *ha(ki)-su(teru)* wear out (footwear)
12 替 *ha(ki)-ka(eru)* change socks or footwear
28 鑿 *sensaku* excavation, boring

6

窕 3324/F1392 Chō quiet.

窒 3325/F1391 Chitsu plug up, obstruct.
B
6 死 *chisshi* death from suffocation
10 息 *chissoku* suffocation, asphyxiation
素 *chisso* nitrogen
素肥料 *chisso hiryō* nitrogenous fertilizer

窓 3326/F1392 **窗** Sō window. *mado* window, windowpane.
B
3 口 *madoguchi* window
5 外 *sōgai* out of the window; outside the window
台 *madodai* window sill
付封筒 *madozu(ki) fūtō* window envelope
8 明 *mado aka(ri)* window light
枠 *mado waku* window frame or sash
9 前 *sōzen* in front of the window
11 掛 *madoka(ke)* window curtain
12 越 *madogo(shi) ni* over the window sill
割 *madowa(ri)* fenestration
硝子 *mado garasu* window pane
13 際 *madogiwa ni* at the window
飾 *sōshoku, mado kaza(ri)* window display

7

窗 3327/F1392 See **窓** 3326.

窘 3328/F1392 Kin. *tashina(meru)* rebuke, reprove.

窖 3329/F1392 Kō. Kyō. *anagura* cellar.
10 倉 *kōsō* cellar

8

窠 3330/F1392 Ka nest, hole. *su* (see under 巣 141.0).

窟 3331/F1392 Kutsu. *iwaya* cavern.

9

窬 3332/F1393 Yu dig (a hole); bore (a hole).

窩 3333/F1393 Ka, Wa cave; pouch.

窪 3334/F1393 A. *kubo(mu)* cave in, sink, become hollow. *kubo(mi)* hollow, cavity, dent, pit. *kubo* depression, hollow.
5 田 *kubota* a rice field in a low place
6 地 *kubochi* hollow, depression, low ground

10

窿 3335/F1395 Ryū vault (of the sky), dome.

窯 3336/F1394 Yō. *kama* kiln, oven, furnace, stove.
B
13 業 *yōgyō* ceramics, brickmaking, glassmaking, and cement manufacture
業美術 *yōgyō bijutsu* ceramic art
業家 *yōgyōka* ceramist

窮 3337/F1393 **竆** Kyū. *kyū(suru)* be destitute; suffer; be perplexed; be cornered. *kiwa(maru), kiwa(meru)* (see under 極 2305.0).
B
2 人 *kyūjin* poor people
3 乏 *kyūbō* poverty
5 冬 *kyūtō* end of winter; year end
民 *kyūmin* poor people
6 死 *kyūshi* dying of distress and poverty
地 *kyūchi* dilemma, predicament
7 困 *kyūkon* distress, pain, poverty
局 *kyūkyoku* eventuality, extremity
迫 *kyūhaku* financial difficulty, distress
状 *kyūjō* distress, sad plight
余 *kyūyo* desperation
余一策 *kyūyo (no) issaku* the last resort
8 屈 *kyūkutsu* narrowness; being cramped; formality, strictness; restraint, oppressiveness
追 *kyūtsui suru* drive into a corner; corner with questions
11 鳥 *kyūchō* a cornered bird
達 *kyūtatsu* poverty and fame
理 *kyūri* mastery of truth
訳 *kyūyaku* strained translation
12 極 *kyūkyoku* eventuality, extremity

策 *kyūsaku* last resort
無 *kiwama(ri)na(ku)* endless
[13]鼠 *kyūso* a cornered mouse
[14]境 *kyūkyō* dilemma, predicament, extremity

11

窶 3338/F1395 Rō. Ku. Ru. *yatsu(su)* (see under 俏 439.0). *yatsu(reru)* become emaciated, be worn out.

窺 3339/F1395 Ki. *ukaga(u)* watch for (a chance), lie in wait, spy on, reconnoiter; see, discover.
[7]見 *kiken suru* peek
[8]知 *kichi suru, ukaga(i)-shi(ru)* perceive, understand
[11]探 *ukaga(i)-sagu(ru)* spy out
[14]窬 *kiyu* maliciously looking for a break

13

竄 3340/F1395 Zan, San flee; hide; renew.
[2]入 *zannyū suru* take refuge in, enter by mistake
入者 *zannyūsha* refugee, fugitive
[6]伏 *zampuku* running off and hiding
[7]走 *zansō* fleeing

14

竆 See 窮 3337.

16

竈 3341/F1396 Sō. *kamado, kama* kitchen stove, furnace, oven; household. *hettsui* hearth; kitchen stove.
[4]元 *kamamoto* kitchen
[9]神 *kamagami* god of the hearth

18

竊 3342/F1396 See 窃 3320.

RAD. 立 117

Tatsu to stand. At left: 立 *tatsu hen.* Nickname: Standing.

A **立** 3343/F1396 Ryū, Ritsu standing. *ta(tsu)* stand, rise; rouse oneself; be built, be established; go up (smoke); burn out; depart; take flight; run high (waves); stick into; be worked out; be maintained; save (face); establish oneself, begin life; spread (rumors); shut (doors); be active; open (markets); be excited; come (seasons); makes (a total of thirty). *ta(teru)* stand something up, set up, raise; put up; set on edge; prick up (one's ears); build, erect; close (a door); establish; institute, enact; lay (plans); map out; set forth, lay down (a proposition); formulate; render (services), perform; look up to, respect; be loyal to; do justice to; circulate (rumors); have (an aim); establish (oneself), make (a success); support (oneself); make (an oath); sharpen, set (a saw); put up (a candidate); make (tea); save (face). *ta(taseru)* make stand, set upright, raise, lift up; rouse (to activity). *ta(chi)* start, departure; (a charcoal fire) burning out. *ta(tchi)* standing up (juvenile). *ta(te)* leading part; leading actor. *ta(chi-hadakaru)* stand in one's way, confront. *rittoru* liter. *-ta(teru)* up (as in stir up noise). *ta(chi)-* standing; emphatic prefix.
[2]入 *ta(chi)-i(ru)* enter, penetrate; interfere in, be inquisitive
入検査 *tachi-i(ri) kensa* spot inspection
入禁止 *Tachi-iri Kinshi* Keep Out
[3]上 *ta(chi)-a(garu)* stand up, rise, spring up, regain one's feet, stand erect. *ta(chi)-nobo(ru)* rise, ascend. *ta(chi)-a(gari)* starting; beginning
女形 *ta(te) oyama* leading female-role actor
小便 *ta(chi) shōben* urinating in the street
巾跳 *ta(chi) habatobi* standing broad jump
[4]日 *ta(chi)bi* anniversary of a death
木 *ta(chi)ki* standing tree, standing timber
止 *ta(chi)-do(maru)* stop, halt, stand still
毛 *ta(chi)ke, ta(chi)ge* crops yet to be harvested
込 *ta(chi)-ko(mu)* be crowded. *ta(te)-ko(meru)* shut (the doors of a room). *ta(chi)-ko(meru)* (smoke or fog) spreads all over
切 *ta(te)-ki(ru)* close up, shut up
太子 *rittaishi* investiture of the crown prince
方 *rippō* cube
方体 *rippōtai* a cube
方根 *rippōkon* cube root
方容積 *rippō yōseki* cubic capacity
[5]石 *ta(te)-ishi* stone signpost, milestone, standing stone

代 *ta(chi)ka(wari)* taking turns. *ta(chi)ka(watte)* in place of
付 *ta(te)tsu(ke)* the movement of doors; doing (something) continuously
札 *ta(te)fuda* notice board, signboard
礼 *ritsurei* deciding on ceremony; standing courtesies; rising courtesy; passing
去 *ta(chi)-sa(ru)* leave, depart ⌊courtesies
冬 *rittō* setting in of winter
出 *ta(chi)-ide(ru)* emphatic for *de(ru)* (see under 出 97.0)
正安国 *risshō-ankoku* establishment of national peace and security
6 至 *ta(chi)-ita(ru)* come to this pass
尽 *ta(chi)-tsuku(su)* continue standing
返 *ta(chi)-kae(ru)* return; recover (one's senses) ⌈against; head for
向 *ta(chi)-mu(kau)* face, confront; fight
地 *ritchi* location of industry
交 *ta(chi)-ma(jiru)* join
行 *ta(chi)-yu(ku)* maintain itself, last, stand, make itself pay; get along, make a living
行司 *ta(te) gyōji* the chief wrestling umpire
回 *ta(chi)-megu(ru)* walk around. *ta(te)-mawa(su)* surround with. *ta(chi)-mawa(ru)* move around; act, conduct oneself; maneuver; go to; haunt; enact (a fighting scene) ⌈out
回先 *ta(chi)mawa(ri) saki* a criminal's hang-
合 *ta(chi)-a(u)* attend, be present at, take part in, witness; be pitted against. *tachia(i)* presence, attendance; conference, session; witnessing ⌈debate
合演説 *tachiai enzetsu* competitive speech;
会 *tachia(i)* attendance, presence, witnessing ⌈observer
会人 *tachiainin* witness, teller (in voting),
会演説 *tachiai enzetsu* competitive speech;
7 言 *ritsugen* expression of opinion ⌊debate
戻 *ta(chi)-modo(ru)* return to, fall back on
坊 *ta(chim)bō* casual laborer; tramp, loafer;
坑 *ta(te)kō* mine shaft ⌊standing around
別 *ta(chi)-waka(reru)* part (company)
彷徨 *ta(chi)-samayo(u)* wander, roam
身 *risshin* success in life
身出世 *risshin-shusse* success in life
役 *ta(chi)yaku* leading role. *ta(te)yaku* leading actor ⌈onist; leading spirit
役者 *ta(te) yakusha* leading actor; protag-
売 *tachiu(ri)* street peddling; street peddler
売人 *tachiurinin* street peddler
志 *risshi* fixing one's aim and pressing on
志伝 *risshiden* success story ⌈standing
見 *ta(chi)mi* viewing from the gallery while
見客 *ta(chi)mikyaku* the gallery; standee
見席 *ta(chi)miseki* gallery, standing room

体 *rittai* solid, solid body
体交叉点 *rittai kōsaten* overhead pass
体図形 *rittai zukei* solid figure
体的 *rittaiteki* three-dimensional
体美 *rittaibi* beauty of sculpture; beauty of buildings
体映画 *rittai eiga* three-dimension movie
体幾何学 *rittai kikagaku* solid geometry
体戦 *rittaisen* three-dimensional warfare
8 国 *rikkoku* rebuilding a country ⌈ment
居 *ta(chi)-i* standing and sitting; deport-
迷 *ta(chi)-mayo(u)* (clouds) float along, drift
坪 *ta(te)tsubo, rittsubo* a cubic *ken*. 6×6×6 feet
所 *ta(chi)dokoro ni* immediately, in an instant, on the spur of the moment, in no time; impromptu
板 *ta(te)-ita* standing board
枠 *ta(te)waku* upright frame
泳 *tachioyo(gi)* treading water
物 *ta(te)mono* leading actor; protagonist
並 *ta(chi)-nara(bu)* stand in a row, line up;
命 *ritsumei* quietness of spirit ⌊be equal to
直 *ta(te)-nao(ru) vi* recover, rally, pick up. *ta(te)-nao(su) vt* recover, rally; make over; recover (one's energy); reorganize, reshuffle. *ta(chi)nao(shi)* rebuilding as before. *tachinao(ri)* recovery, restoration
歩 *ta(chi)aru(ki)* toddling, walking
往生 *ta(chi)ōjō suru* make a last stand; be stalled, be stranded; be nonplused; be at a standstill ⌈evacuate; take refuge
退 *ta(chi)-no(ku)* leave, depart, vacate,
退人 *ta(chi)no(ki)nin* one who quits the premises ⌈moval
退料 *ta(chi)no(ki)ryō* compensation for re-
法 *rippō* legislation, lawmaking
法上 *rippōjō no* legislative
法者 *rippōsha* lawgiver, lawmaker
法権 *rippōken* legislative power
法機関 *rippō kikan* legislative body
9 飛 *ta(chi)to(bi)* standing plunge
食 *tachigu(i), risshoku* eating while standing
通 *ta(chi)-dō(su)* stand all the way. *ta(te)-tō(su)* maintain to the last
後 *ta(chi)-oku(reru)* be slow in jumping into (the fray); make a belated start; be too late; allow (someone) to get a head start
枯 *ta(chi)ga(rashi), tachiga(re)* blight
派 *rippa na* fine, handsome, excellent, grand; imposing, commanding, honorable, respectable; commendable; noble; prominent; honest; legal, legitimate; sufficient, justifiable
秋 *risshū* setting in of fall ⌈system
前 *ta(te)mae* principle, policy, rule, basis,

姿 *ta(chi)sugata* standing pose, standing position
春 *risshun* setting in of spring
待月 *ta(chi)ma(chi)zuki* 17-day-old moon
看板 *ta(te)kamban* standing signboard
草臥 *ta(chi)-kutabi(reru)* get tired standing
10 席 *ta(chi)seki* standing room (at a performance)
疲 *ta(chi)-tsuka(reru)* be tired of standing
哨 *risshō* standing guard
悩 *ta(chi)-naya(mu)* hesitate, come to a standstill, be held up
消 *tachigi(e)* going out, dying out, flickering out
眩 *ta(chi)kura(mi), ta(chi)gura(mi)* dizziness
射 *rissha* firing from a standing position
夏 *rikka* the official first day of summer
党 *rittō* formation of a new party
帰 *ta(chi)-kae(ru)* return, go back to, come back to (the subject)
候補 *rikkōho* announcing one's candidacy
高跳 *ta(chi) takatobi* standing high jump
振舞 *ta(chi)burumai* farewell dinner. *ta(chi)furumai* deportment
烏帽子 *ta(te) eboshi* noble's high headgear
案 *ritsuan* plan, design, draft
案者 *ritsuansha* planner, designer, drafter
11 遅 *ta(chi)oku(re)* losing an opportunity
掛 *ta(chi)-ka(keru), ta(chi)-ka(karu)* begin to rise
添 *ta(chi)-so(u)* stand close
寄 *ta(chi)-yo(ru)* get near; call at, drop in, look (someone) up; stop over
脚 *rikkyaku suru* be based on
脚地 *rikkyakuchi* position, standpoint, viewpoint
脚点 *rikkyakuten*=word above
12 越 *ta(chi)-ko(eru)* surpass, be superior to; go
喰 *ta(chi)kui* eating while standing
場 *tachiba* standpoint, position, footing, station; attitude; situation; viewpoint; standing room. *ta(te)ba* stopping place, stage; cab stand; wholesaler
竦 *ta(chi)-suku(mu)* be petrified
勝 *ta(chi)-masa(ru)* excel, surpass, outrival
証 *risshō* proof, demonstration, substantiation
飲 *ta(chi)no(mi)* drinking while standing
葵 *ta(chi)aoi* hollyhock
番 *ta(chi)ban* watch, guarding; guard, sentry, picket
琴 *ta(te)goto* harp
替 *ta(te)-ka(eru)* advance money; pay for another; lend
替金 *tatekaekin* advance money
13 働 *ta(chi)-hatara(ku)* work, go about one's work
続 *ta(te)tsuzu(ke)* succession, continuation
腹 *rippuku* anger, indignation
話 *ta(chi)banashi* standing and chatting
詰 *ta(chi)-zu(me)* being kept standing

塞 *ta(chi)-fusa(garu)* stand in the way, block the way, confront, head off
罩 *ta(chi)-ko(meru)* hang over, envelop, shroud
14 腐 *ta(chi)gusa(re)* dilapidation
聞 *ta(chi)gi(ku)* overhear, eavesdrop. *tachigi(ki)* eavesdropping, overhearing
像 *ritsuzō* a standing image
構 *ta(chi)-kama(eru)* take an attitude; be ready for a fight
網 *ta(te)ami* dragnet, set net, seine
15 穂 *ta(chi)ho* standing grain
膝 *ta(te)hiza* drawn-up knee
論 *ritsuron* argument; argumentation
撃 *ta(chi)u(chi)* firing from a standing position
16 稽古 *ta(chi)geiko* rehearsal
錐 *rissui* a standing drill (the tool)
錐地 *rissui(no)chi* a small plot of ground
錐余地 *rissui (no) yochi* standing room
憲 *rikken* adopting a constitution
憲民主政体 *rikken minshu seitai* constitutional democracy
憲君主政体 *rikken kunshu seitai* constitutional monarchy
憲国 *rikkenkoku* a country with a constitution
憲的 *rikkenteki* constitutional
憲政体 *rikken seitai* constitutional form of government
憲政治 *rikken seiji* constitutional government
18 襟 *ta(chi)eri* stand-up collar
騒 *ta(chi)-sawa(gu)*=*sawagu* (see under 騒 5221.0)
19 願 *ritsugan* praying to a god
離 *ta(chi)-hana(reru)* be away from
瀬 *ta(tsu)se* standpoint, position
瀬無 *ta(tsu)se (ga) na(i)* be in a dilemma
22 籠 *ta(te)-komo(ru)* remain in seclusion; entrench oneself in a castle

2

辛 See 4646. [辛]

竍 3344 / F-X (国字) *dekarittoru* decaliter, 10 liters.

3

竏 3345 / F-X (国字) *kirorittoru* kiloliter, 1000 liters.

妾 3346 / F496 SHŌ *mekake, sobame* concubine. *warawa* I. [女]
5 出 *shōshutsu* illegitimate birth
6 宅 *shōtaku* concubine's house
13 腹 *shōfuku* illegitimate birth. *mekakebara* illegitimate child

4

音 See 5110. [音]

彦 3347/F665 彥 GEN. *hiko* (ancient) boy. [彡]

竕 3348/F-X (国字) *deshirittoru* deciliter.

竓 3349/F-X (国字) *miririttoru* milliliter.

— 5 —

竝 3350/F1398/F43 See 並 589.

P 竜 3351/F1398 竜 See 龍 5440. [竜]

站 3352/F1398 TAN stop, halt.

— 6 —

章 See 5112.

竟 竟 See 5111.

竡 3353/F-X (国字) *hekutorittoru* hectoliter, 100 liters.

A 産 3354/F1267 產 SAN childbirth; product; native (of a place); fortune, property. *san(suru) vi* and *vt* produce, yield, bring up, bear (a child); appear; be born; be brought up. *u(mu)* bear, give birth to, breed, spawn; produce, yield (interest). *u(mareru)* be born. *u(mi)* childbirth, bearing a child. [生]

3 土 *ubusuna* tutelary deity, guardian god
土神 *ubusunagami* tutelary deity, guardian god
4 月 *u(mi)zuki* last month of pregnancy
毛 *ubuge* downy, hairy; down, fluff, pin feathers
5 出 *sanshutsu* output, yield, production
出物 *sanshutsubutsu*＝*sambutsu* 産物 (see below–8)
出高 *sanshutsudaka* output, yield, production
6 米 *sambei* the rice production
衣 *san-i, ubugi* clothes for a new-born baby
地 *sanchi* producing area
気 *sanke, san(no)ke* labor pains
気付 *sankezu(ki)* premonition of labor pains
7 別 *sambetsu* industrial union
声 *ubugoe* baby's first cry
児 *sanji* newborn baby; the baby about to be born
児制限 *sanji seigen* birth control
卵 *sanran* egg-laying, spawning
卵期 *sanranki* breeding season, spawning season
8 物 *sambutsu* product, production, produce; result
具 *sangu* obstetrical supplies
金 *sankin* gold mining
金地 *sankinchi* gold-producing area
金地帯 *sankin chitai* gold field
金高 *sankindaka* gold output
金業 *sankingyō* gold mining industry
金熱 *sankin netsu* gold rush
9 屋 *ubuya* maternity room
後 *sango* after childbirth
院 *san-in* maternity hospital
室 *sanshitsu* maternity ward, delivery room
前 *sanzen* before delivery (of the baby)
前産後 *sanzen-sango* before and after childbirth
科 *sanka* obstetrics
科医 *sanka-i* obstetrician
科学 *sankagaku* obstetrics
科病院 *sanka byōin* maternity hospital
科婦人科 *sanka fujinka* obstetrics and gynecology
10 馬 *samba* horse breeding
破 *san (o) yabu(ru)* use up all one's property
11 婦 *sampu* woman in childbirth
婆 *samba* midwife
婆役 *sambayaku* sponsor
12 殖 *sanshoku* breeding, propagation
湯 *ubuyu* baby's first bath
落 *u(mi)-oto(su)* give birth to
13 傾 *san (o) katamu(keru)* use up all one's property
業 *sangyō* industry
業人 *sangyōjin* industrialist
業立国 *sangyō-rikkoku* national economy based on industry
業合理化 *sangyō gōrika* well-regulated industry
業住宅 *sangyō jūtaku* industrial worker's housing
業国 *sangyōkoku* industrial nation
業国営 *sangyō kokuei* nationalization of industry
業界 *sangyōkai* industrial world
業革命 *Sangyō Kakumei* the Industrial Revolution
業婦人 *sangyō fujin* industrial woman
業組合 *sangyō kumiai* industrial guild, industrial association
業転換 *sangyō tenkan* industrial conversion
15 褥 *sanjoku* confinement; labor bed
褥期 *sanjokuki* lying-in period
褥熱 *sanjoku netsu* puerperal fever
16 親 *u(mi) (no) oya* one's true parent
18 額 *sangaku* production, yield, output

— 7 —

竦 3355/F1399 SHŌ revere, fear. *suku(mu) vi* crouch, cower, lie quiet; be cramped; get wrinkled. *suku(meru) vt* duck (one's head); shrug (one's shoulders); make (someone) crouch.

12 然 *shōzen* horror; shuddering

5 玄 玉 王 爪 瓦 甘 生 用 田 疋 疒 癶 白 皮 皿 目 矛 矢 石 示 ネ 内 禾 穴 7【立】

竣 3356 F1399 SHUN end, finish.
3 工 *shunkō* completion
工式 *shunkōshiki* ceremony of completion
工期 *shunkōki* time of completion
5 功 *shunkō* completion
6 成 *shunsei* completion

A **童** 3357 F1399 **童** Dō child. *warawa, warabe* child.
8 女 *dōjo, dōnyo* girl, maiden, lass
子 *dōji* child, boy
4 心 *dōshin* child's mind, naïveté
5 幼 *dōyō* child, infant
7 児 *dōji* a child
8 画 *dōga* pictures drawn by a child; pictures for children
9 貞 *dōtei* chastity; (Catholic) nun
13 蒙 *dōmō* child
話 *dōwa* nursery tale, fairy tale, juvenile tale
話劇 *dōwageki* juvenile play
14 歌 *warabe uta* children's folk songs
16 謡 *dōyō* children's song, nursery rhyme
18 顔 *dōgan* boyish face

8

意 See 5113. [心]

靖 3358 F2038 **竫** SEI. *yasu(i)* peaceful. [青]

竪 3359 F1400 JU. *tate* length; height; warp.
5 穴 *tateana* pit, hole; mine shaft; site of ancient pit dwelling
7 坑 *tatekō* mine shaft
8 物 *tatemono* vertical scroll
10 框 *tategamachi* door frame
挽大鋸 *tatebiki ōnokogiri* pit saw
11 笛 *tatebue* clarinet
12 棺 *tatekan* upright coffin
琴 *tategoto* harp; lyre
14 樋 *tatedoi, tatetoyu* downspout
21 鰭 *tatebire* vertical fin
23 罐 *tategama* vertical boiler

9

竰 3360 F-X (国字) *senchirittoru* centiliter.

竭 3361 F1400 KETSU end, exhaust. *tsu(kusu)* (see under 尽 1380.0).
6 尽 *ketsujin* used up

颯 3362 F2074 SATSU. *sat(to)* suddenly, smoothly. [風]
11 爽 *sassō(taru)* gallant, dashing, stately
14 颯 *sassatsu(taru)* rustling; whistling; murmuring

B **端** 3363 F1400 TAN origin; end; point. *hashi, haji, ha* end, tip; edge, border, one side; corner; beginning; scrap of cloth. *hana* beginning, inception; end, edge, verge, point, extremity, cape. *hashita* fraction, odd sum, fragment, scrap. *hashitana(i)* uncouth, rude. *hata* side, edge. *tsuma* end. *hashi kara* one after another. *hashi(kure), hashi(kkure)* scrap, fag end, piece, bit. *-tan* tip, extremity.
3 女 *hashitame* maidservant
子 *tanshi* terminal (in electricity)
山 *hayama* foothill
4 切 *hashigi(re)* cloth scraps, odds and ends
午 *Tango* Boys' Festival (May 5)
5 正 *tansei* correct, just, orderly, proper
本 *hahon* odd volume
6 近 *hashijika ni* near the edge; just at the threshold
7 役 *hayaku* minor post; minor role
折 *hasho(ru), hashio(ru)* tuck up; abridge
坐 *tanza suru* sit erect
8 金 *hashitagane* small change; pittance
居 *hashi-i* being at the end of the house or on the veranda
物 *hamono* incomplete set; odds and ends
的 *tanteki na* direct, blunt, frank
武者 *hamusha* private, common soldier
9 乗 *hashinori* climbing on the end; just riding a bit
10 座 *tanza suru* sit erect
倪 *tangei* limit; from beginning to end; mountain tops and river banks; guess, conjecture
唄 *ha-uta* ditty, short popular song
書 *hagaki* postcard. *hashiga(ki)* preface, introduction; postscript
12 喰 *hashibami* clamp (in building)
無 *hashitana(i)* rude. *hashina(ku) mo* suddenly, unexpectedly, accidentally
然 *tanzen(taru)* correct, proper
13 艇 *tantei* boat
数 *hasū* fraction, odd sum
14 端 *hashibashi* parts, odds and ends
綱 *hazuna* halter
緒 *tansho, tancho* beginning, first step, clue
銭 *hasen* small change; pittance
境 *hazakai* between harvests, lean period
境期 *hazakaiki* between harvests, lean period
16 整 *tansei na* correct, just, orderly, proper
17 厳 *tangen na* solemn and serene
19 麗 *tanrei* grace, beauty

— 14 —

韻 See 5115. [音]

— 15 —

A 競 3364 F1401 竸 KYŌ. KEI. *kiso(u), kio(u)* emulate, compete with. *se(ru)* compete, vie, bid; sell at auction. *seri* auction. *-kura* race, bout, contest.

3 上 *se(ri)-a(geru)* auction off
4 手 *serite* bidder
5 市 *seri-ichi* auction house
6 肌 *kio(i)hada* gallantry
合 *se(ri)-a(u)* compete with, vie for. *araso-(i)-a(u)* contend with, quarrel. *kyōgō* concurrence, conflict, competition
争 *kyōsō* rivalry, contest, competition
争入札 *kyōsō nyūsatsu* sealed bidding
争心 *kyōsōshin* competitive or fighting spirit
争車 *kyōsōsha* racing car
争者 *kyōsōsha* contestant, competitor, rival
争価格 *kyōsō kakaku* competitive price
争相手 *kyōsō aite* competitor, rival
争場裡 *kyōsō jōri* area of competition
争試験 *kyōsō shiken* competitive examination
7 走 *kiso(i)-hashi(ru)* to race. *kyōsō* race
走者 *kyōsōsha* runner, racer
技 *kyōgi* contest, sporting event, tournament, race
技会 *kyōgikai* athletic meet, contest
技場 *kyōgijō* stadium
売 *seri-u(ri)* auction; auctioneer. *kyōbai* auction
売人 *kyōbainin* auctioneer
売台 *kyōbaidai* auction block
売場 *kyōbaijō* auction house, auction room
8 泳 *kyōei* swimming race
歩 *kyōho* walking race
9 映 *kyōei* competitive film exhibition
10 射 *kyōsha* shooting contest
馬 *keiba* horse race; horse racing
馬馬 *keiba uma* race horse
馬場 *keibajō* race track
馬騎手 *keiba kishu* jockey
11 掛 *kio(i)-ka(karu)* be determined to win
12 落 *se(ri)-o(tosu)* bid successfully, knock down. *kyōraku* auctioning, bidding
買人 *kyōbainin* bidder
13 艇 *keitei, kyōtei* boat race
業 *kyōgyō* business competition
14 漕 *kyōsō* regatta, boat race
演 *kyōen* recital contest
演会 *kyōenkai* recital contest
15 輪 *keirin* bicycle race
20 競 *kyōkyō* fear and caution

— 17 —

竸 3365 F1401 See 競 3364.

6-STROKE RADICALS

RAD. 竹 118

Take bamboo. Variant: ⺮ *take kammuri* "bamboo" crown. Nickname: Bamboo.

A 竹 3366 F1401 CHIKU bamboo. *take* bamboo; bamboo wind instrument.

2 刀 *chikutō, shinai* fencing stick
3 子 *take (no) ko* bamboo shoots
下駄 *takegeta* bamboo clogs
5 皮 *take(no)kawa* bamboo sheath
矢来 *take yarai* bamboo palisade
6 光 *takemitsu* bamboo sword; a blunt sword
7 材 *chikuzai* bamboo
8 林 *chikurin, takebayashi* bamboo grove
帛 *chikuhaku* history
9 屋 *takeya* bamboo dealer
垣 *takegaki* bamboo fence, bamboo hedge
柱 *takebashira* bamboo pole, bamboo post
竿 *takezao* bamboo pole
柄杓 *takebishaku* bamboo ladle
10 原 *takahara* bamboo grove
釘 *take kugi* bamboo peg
格子 *takegōshi* bamboo lattice
馬 *takeuma, chikuba* bamboo horse; stilts
馬友 *chikuba (no) tomo* a small child's playmate
11 梯子 *takebashigo* bamboo ladder
細工 *takezaiku* bamboo work. bamboo ware
12 筒 *takezutsu* bamboo pipe
13 楊子 *take yōji* bamboo-handled toothbrush
園生 *take (no) sono-o* bamboo garden; the Imperial Family
14 槍 *take yari* bamboo spear
箒 *takebōki* bamboo broom
製 *takesei* made of bamboo
15 縁 *take-en* bamboo-floored veranda
器 *chikki* bamboo ware
16 篦 *takebera* bamboo spatula. *shippei* tit for tat
篦返 *shippeigae(shi)* retaliation

6 【2竹】米糸缶网四羊羽老耂而耒耳聿肉月臣自至臼舌舛舟艮色艸艹虍虫血行衣衤西

17簀 *takesu* removable bamboo floor
18藪 *take yabu* bamboo grove
叢 *takamura* bamboo grove
22籠 *take kago* bamboo basket

2

竺 3367 / F1402 JIKU, CHIKU bamboo.

3

笈 3368 / F1403 KYŪ portable bookcase carried on the back.

9負 *kyū (o) o(u)* depart for an education

竿 3369 / F1403 KAN. *sao* pole, rod; beam (of scales); (well) sweep; neck (of a violin).

6竹 *saodake* bamboo pole
10秤 *saobakari* steelyard, beam balance
11掛 *saoka(ke)* fishpole holder
釣 *saozuri* pole fishing
16頭 *kantō* top of a pole

4

笋 3370 / F1403 F1409 See 筍 3390.

笊 3371 / F1403 SŌ. *zaru* bamboo basket.

笏 3372 / F1403 KOTSU. *shaku* mace, baton, scepter.

笄 3373 / F1403 笄 KEI. *kōgai* ornamental hairpin; metal rod attached to sword sheath; crossbar of an anchor; ancient comb.

B **笑** 3374 / F1403 SHŌ laughter. *wara(u)* laugh, smile; ridicule; be in full bloom. *e(mu)* smile, bloom; split, open, crack. *emi* smile. *wara(i)* laughing, smile; derision.

3上戸 *wara(i) jōgo* a merry drinker; one who is always laughing ⌈contemptible
4止 *shōshi na* laughable, ridiculous; pitiful;
止千万 *shōshi-semban* extremely funny
5出 *wara(i)-da(su)* burst out laughing
6気 *shōki* laughing gas, nitrous oxide
7声 *wara(i)goe, shōsei* laughter, laugh; laughing voice
8物 *wara(i)mono* object of ridicule
者 *wara(ware)mono* laughingstock
事 *wara(i)goto* laughing matter
9柄 *shōhei* laughingstock
草 *wara(i)gusa* laughingstock
10納 *shōnō* your acceptance; receiving
殺 *shōsatsu suru* laugh off; laugh to scorn
12絵 *wara(i)e* comic picture; pornographic
割 *e(mi)-wa(reru)* crack, split open ⌊picture
壺 *etsubo* smile of satisfaction
13話 *wara(i)banashi, shōwa* humorous story
14種 *wara(i)gusa, wara(i)dane* laughingstock
語 *shōgo* laughing and talking at the same
15劇 *shōgeki* farce (in dramatics) ⌊time
談 *shōdan* jolly talk
16覧 *shōran* your inspection ⌈look
18顔 *egao, wara(i)gao* smiling face, radiant

5

笨 3375 / F1405 HON coarse (not fine).

笴 3376 / F1406 KA arrow shaft.

笙 3377 / F1404 SHŌ a reed instrument.

笥 3378 / F1405 SU, SHI *ke* lunch box; food box; clothes chest.

笧 3379 / F-X SAKU. *shigara(mu), shigara(mi)* (see under 柵 2229.0).

笞 3380 / F1404 CHI whip; crime punishable by flogging. *shimoto* whip, scourge. *muchi* whip, rod.

6刑 *chikei* whipping, flogging; the lash
13罪 *chizai* crime punishable by flogging

笠 3381 / F1404 RYŪ. *kasa* bamboo hat; one's influence; lampshade; (chimney) hood.

3子 *kasago* rock cod, rockfish
4切 *kasa (ni) ki(ru)* brag
5石 *kasa-ishi* capstone
8松 *kasamatsu* umbrella-like pine

B **笛** 3382 / F1404 TEKI flute. *fue* flute, pipe, clarinet, whistle, fife, pitch pipe, bagpipe, piccolo.

4手 *tekishu* flutist
7吹 *fue-fu(ku)* play a flute. *fuefu(ki)* flute player, clarinetist ⌈whistle
声 *tekisei* sound of a flute, piping; (train)

B **符** 3383 / F1405 FU sign, mark, tally; charm, amulet.

2丁 *fuchō*＝符牒 (see below–13)
6合 *fugō* agreement, coincidence, correspondence, conformity
号 *fugō* mark, sign, symbol, code

9点 *futen* dot (in music)
13牒 *fuchō* sign, mark, token, symbol; code; secret (price) mark; password, countersign
節 *fusetsu* tally, check

笹 $\frac{3384}{F1406}$ (国字) *sasa* bamboo grass.
6舟 *sasabune* toy bamboo-leaf boat
10原 *sasawara* field of bamboo grass
12葉 *sasaba, sasa(p)pa* bamboo leaf
14飴 *sasa ame* glutinous rice jelly wrapped in bamboo-grass leaves
15縁 *sasaberi* lace, frill, edging
18藪 *sasayabu* bamboo-grass brush

A **第** $\frac{3385}{F1405}$ TEI, DAI residence. DAI- number (1, 2, 3, etc.).
1一 *dai-ichi ni* first, in the first place. *dai-ichi no* first, foremost, primary, initial, principal, chief. *dai-ichi* the first, the best, number one, the greatest (in his field)
一人者 *dai-ichininsha* an authority, tops
一人称 *dai-ichininshō* first person (in grammar)
一次 *dai-ichiji* first
一次世界大戦 *Dai Ichiji Sekai Taisen* the First World War
一印象 *dai-ichi inshō* first impression
一位 *dai-ichi-i* first rank
一声 *dai-issei* first talk (on returning from abroad)
一歩 *dai-ippo* first step, initial step
一担保 *dai-ichi tampo* first mortgage
一流 *dai-ichiryū no* first-rate, topnotch, foremost, gilt-edged
一党 *dai-ittō* dominant party
一着 *dai-itchaku* first arrival; first step (to take)
一義 *dai-ichigi* original meaning; first principal, essential point, first consideration
一種 *dai-isshu* first class (mail, etc.)
一線 *dai-issen* front line
一審 *dai-isshin* first trial, first instance
2二人称 *dai-nininshō* second person (in grammar)
二次 *dai-niji* second
二次世界大戦 *Dai Niji Sekai Taisen* the Second World War
二次的 *dai-nijiteki* secondary
二義 *dai-nigi* secondary meaning
3三人称 *dai-sanninshō* third person (in grammar)
三者 *dai-sansha* third party, disinterested person
三国 *dai-sankoku* third power
三国人 *dai-sangokujin* third-power national
三帝国 *Dai-san Teikoku* the Third Reich
三階級 *dai-san kaikyū* bourgeoisie, middle class
4内 *teinai* grounds, premises
六感 *dai-rokkan* the sixth sense
五列 *dai-goretsu* fifth column
五部隊 *dai-go butai* fifth column
5四階級 *dai-shi kaikyū* proletariat

6

筓 See 笄 3373.

筐 $\frac{3386}{F1409}$ KYŌ. *katami* bamboo basket.

筈 $\frac{3387}{F1408}$ KATSU. *hazu* notch of an arrow; something that ought to, must, or should be; something to be expected; be due to.

筌 $\frac{3388}{F1409}$ SEN fish trap. *uke, ue* weir, fish trap.

筑 $\frac{3389}{F1409}$ 筑 CHIKU an ancient musical instrument.
12紫 *Tsukushi* Kyushu

筍 $\frac{3390}{F1409}$ 笋 JUN. *takenoko* bamboo shoots.
5生活 *takenoko seikatsu* red-ink living, living by selling personal effects
7医者 *takenoko isha* quack doctor

筏 $\frac{3391}{F1409}$ BATSU. *ikada* raft.
3士 *ikadashi* raftsman
9乗 *ikadano(ri)* raftsman
10師 *ikadashi* raftsman

B **筒** $\frac{3392}{F1409}$ TŌ pipette, tube. *tsutsu* pipe, tube, case, gun barrel, sleeve, well curb.
3口 *tōko* tube end; nozzle
4井 *tsutsui* round well
6先 *tsutsusaki* pipe end, hose nozzle, gun muzzle; the fireman holding the nozzle
7抜 *tsutsunu(ke) ni* directly, clearly, just as told
形 *tsutsugata* cylindrical shape, barrel shape
10袖 *tsutsusode, tsutsuppo* tight sleeve, tight-sleeved dress

A **策** $\frac{3393}{F1410}$ SAKU plan, scheme, policy; step, means; whip. *saku(suru)* plan.
3士 *sakushi* schemer, tactician, man of resources
7応 *sakuō* co-operation, concert, collusion
11略 *sakuryaku* stratagem, scheme, plan, policy, frame-up
動 *sakudō* scheming, maneuvering, manipulation

6 [竹] 米糸缶网罒羊羽老耂而耒耳聿肉月臣自至臼舌舛舟艮色艸艹虍虫血行衣衤西

動家 *sakudōka* schemer, mischief-maker, a Machiavellian
13 戦 *sakusen* military or naval operations
源 *sakugen* base of operations
源地 *sakugenchi* base of operations
16 謀 *sakubō* artifice, stratagem, frame-up

A 答 3394 / F1409 Tō answer. *kota(eru)* answer; respond; solve. *kota(e)* answer; solution.

5 弁 *tōben* reply, explanation, defense
申 *tōshin* a report
申案 *tōshin-an* draft of a report
申書 *tōshinsho* findings, report, draft
礼 *tōrei* return salute, return courtesy
礼使節 *tōrei shisetsu* good-will envoy
礼砲 *tōreihō* return gun salute
6 返 *kota(e)-kae(su)* return an answer
10 砲 *tōhō* return salute
案 *tōan* examination paper
11 訪 *tōhō* return visit
13 辞 *tōji* formal reply, response
酬 *tōshū* answer
電 *tōden* reply telegram
17 謝 *tōsha* acknowledgment

B 筋 3395 / F1408 Kin muscle, sinew, tendon. *suji* muscle; sinew, tendon; vein; fiber; string; line; stripe, streak; plot, plan; reason, logic; circumstances; thread, sequence; quarters, sources, authorities; lineage, strain, stock, descent; grain, texture, *suji(darake)* sinewy; stringy.

2 力 *kinryoku* physical strength
3 子 *sujiko* salmon roe
5 目 *sujime* fold, crease; lineage, pedigree; = *sujimichi* 筋道 (see below–11)
6 向 *sujimu(kai), sujimu(kou)* diagonally opposite
交 *sujika(i)* diagonal, oblique; brace
合 *sujiai* reason
肉 *kinniku* muscles, sinews
肉労働 *kinniku rōdō* physical labor
8 金 *sujigane* metal reinforcement
10 骨 *kinkotsu, sujibone* sinews and bones
書 *sujiga(ki)* synopsis, outline; scenario, plot, story; plan, program, schedule
11 道 *sujimichi* reason, logic, thread, chain (of reasoning); method, system
違 *sujichiga(i)* cramp, sprain, absurdity; intersection. *sujikai* diagonal, oblique; brace
張 *sujiba(ru)* become stringy, become brawny; stand on ceremony
12 揉 *sujimomi* muscle massage
筋 *sujisuji* lines
14 膜 *kimmaku* the fascia

A 等 3396 / F1408 Tō class, grade, degree; and so forth; equality. *hito(shii)* equal, similar, alike, equivalent. *-nado* and so forth. *-ra* and others, and the like; a plural ending.

4 分 *tōbun* division into equal parts; equal parts
比 *tōhi* proportion
比級数 *tōhi kyūsū* geometrical progression, geometrical series
辺 *tōhen* equal sides
辺三角形 *tōhen sankakukei* equilateral triangle
5 外 *tōgai* inferior grades
圧線 *tōatsusen* isobar
6 式 *tōshiki* equality
号 *tōgō* the sign of addition
7 角 *tōkaku* equal angles
位 *tōi* rank, grade, class, scale
身 *tōshin* life-size
身像 *tōshinzō* life-size statue
8 並 *hitona(mi)* same, ordinary
雨線図 *tōusenzu* rainfall map
価 *tōka* equivalence, parity
価量 *tōkaryō* equivalent amount
9 級 *tōkyū* class, grade, order, rank, magnitude, rating, classification
10 値 *tōchi* equal value
高耕作 *tōkō kōsaku* contour plowing
高線 *tōkōsen* contour line
差 *tōsa* difference; equal difference
差中項 *tōsa chūkō* arithmetical mean
差級数 *tōsa kyūsū* arithmetical series, progression
11 閑 *naozari* negligence
距離 *tōkyori* equal distances; equidistance
脚三角形 *tōkyaku sankakukei* isosceles triangle
12 間 *tōkan* neglect, disregard
閑 *naozari, tōkan* neglect, disregard
量 *tōryō no* equivalent
等 *tōtō* etc., and so forth
温 *tōon* equal temperature
温線 *tōonsen* isotherm
15 輩 *tōhai* companions
質 *tōshitsu* homogeneity
16 親 *tōshin* degree of kinship

A 筆 3397 / F1406 Hitsu. *fude* writing brush, paintbrush; writing, drawing, painting; the pen; handwriting, penmanship; literary work.

2 入 *fude-i(re)* writing-brush holder. *fude (o) i(reru)* correct a document
力 *hitsuryoku* power of the pen
3 工 *hikkō* writing-brush maker
才 *hissai* literary talent
4 太 *fudebuto ni* in bold strokes, in a bold hand, in bold lettering
不精 *fudebushō* poor correspondent
5 生 *hissei* copyist, amanuensis

立 *fudeta(te)* writing-brush holder. *fude (ga) ta(tsu)* be clever and fast in writing
写 *hissha* copying
6舌 *hitsuzetsu* the pen and the tongue
先 *fudesaki* brush tip; handling the brush; writing. *(o)fudesaki* prophecy, oracle
名 *hitsumei* pen name, pseudonym
8使 *fudezuka(i)* penmanship; writing technique, stroke of the pen
法 *hippō* penmanship style; manner
者 *hissha* writer, author
忠実 *fudemame* ready writer, good correspondent
9洗 *hissen* brush-washing receptacle
研 *hikken* pen and ink; literary work
陣 *hitsujin* composing sentences, writing
架 *hikka* pen rack
10紙 *hisshi* pen and paper
致 *hitchi* stroke of the brush; style
耕 *hikkō suru* copy, stencil
耕料 *hikkōryō* copying fee
記 *hikki* taking notes; notes, copying
記者 *hikkisha* copyist
記帳 *hikkichō* notebook
記試験 *hikki shiken* written examination
12順 *hitsujun* stroke order
硯 *hikken* pen and ink; literary work
答 *hittō* written reply
13禍 *hikka* serious slip of the pen
触 *hisshoku* touch of the pen
誅 *hitchū* an attack in the press
跡 *hisseki* holograph; handwriting (specimen)
馴 *fudena(rashi)* writing exercise
戦 *hissen* the war of the pen
置 *fude (o) o(ku)* leave off writing
意 *hitsui* one's feeling when writing; writing style; the meaning
勢 *hissei* power of the pen; penmanship
14端 *hittan* brush or pen tip; stroke of the pen
算 *hissan* calculation
管 *hikkan* handle of a writing brush; a writing brush
罰 *hitsubatsu* an attack in the press
墨 *hitsuboku* pen and ink
墨紙 *hitsubokushi* pen, ink, and paper
15談 *hitsudan* conversation by writing
調 *hitchō* penmanship, calligraphy
鋒 *hippō* literary style
16録 *hitsuroku* recording
頭 *hittō* head of a brush; first in the list
頭書 *hittōsha* head of the house (in a government registry)
18蹟 *hisseki* holograph; handwriting (specimen)

7

⿱竹沄 Nonstandard for 簿 3448.

筩 3398/F1410 Tō bamboo tube.

筧 3399/F1410 KEN. *kakehi* water pipe, conduit, flume.

筵 3400/F1411 莚 EN mat, matting; feast, banquet, party, entertainment; seat. *mushiro* straw mat, matting.

筮 3401/F1411 ZEI divining; diviner's equipment.
2卜 *zeiboku* divining with divining rods
6竹 *zeichiku* divining rods

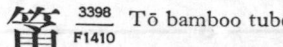

A 節 3402/F1415 節 節 SETSU season, period, occasion, time; verse, clause, paragraph, section, stanza; integrity, honor. *ses(suru)* be temperate, be moderate; control, restrain; save, be sparing. *fushi* joint, knuckle; knob, lump, knot; tune, melody; point (in a talk). *notto* knot, nautical mile.
2刀 *settō* sword given by the emperor to the commander-in-chief
4水 *sessui* water economy
介 *sekkai* untimely interference
分 *setsubun* last day of winter
5用 *setsuyō* frugality, economy
目 *fushime* knots in lumber
穴 *fushiana* knothole
立 *fushi(kure)da(tsu)* be knotty; be bony
句 *sekku* annual festival
付 *fushizu(ke)* setting to music
6米 *setsumai* rice economy
回 *fushimawa(shi)* melody, intonation
会 *sechie* court banquet
8供 *sekku* annual festival
制 *sessei* temperance, moderation, self-restraint
季 *sekki* year end
9食 *sesshoku* moderation in eating, spare diet
度 *setsudo* rule, standard; instructions; moderation
約 *setsuyaku* economy
奏 *sessō* rhythm
10倹 *sekken* economy, thrift
酒 *sesshu* temperance, sobriety; moderation in drinking
11婦 *seppu* virtuous wife
欲 *setsuyoku* curbing desires
12減 *setsugen* curtailment, economy, retrenchment
期 *sekki* time, chance
13煙 *setsuen* moderation in smoking
節 *fushibushi* joints; points (in a talk)
義 *setsugi* fidelity to principle, constancy; honor
電 *setsuden* economy of electricity
16操 *sessō* constancy, integrity, honor, chastity
18織 *fushio(ri)* pongee, coarse silk

6 【竹】 8 米糸缶网四羊羽老耂而耒耳聿肉月臣自至臼舌舛舟艮色艸艹虍虫血行衣衤西

8

筵 See 3400.

箳 3403 F1409 F1403 See 笄 3373.

箸 Nonstandard for 箸 3422.

箋 3404 F1412 戔 SEN paper; label; letter; composition.

箚 3405 F1413 劄 SATSU a retainer's written report to his lord.

箙 3406 F1413 FUKU. *ebira* quiver.

箕 3407 F1412 KI winnowing device. *mi* winnow, winnowing fan, winnowing fork.

箒 3408 F1412 SŌ. *hōki* broom.

箍 3409 F1412 KO. *taga* barrel hoop.

6回 *tagamawa(shi)* rolling a hoop

15緩 *taga (ga) yuru(mu)* weaken; lose interest (in a task)

箆 3410 F1419 篦 HEI. HAI. *hera* spatula. *no* arrow shaft; arrow-shaft bamboo.

12棒 *berabō na* absurd, unreasonable, exorbitant; awful, terrible

箔 3411 F1412 BAKU, HAKU foil, leaf, tinsel, gilt.

5打 *haku-u(chi)* goldbeater; the work of a goldbeater

9屋 *hakuya* goldbeater, gilder

箏 3412 F1412 SŌ a koto. *koto* (see under 琴 2949.0). *sōnokoto* a koto.

6曲 *sōkyoku* koto music

12琴 *sō (no) koto* a koto

箝 3413 F1413 KAN. KEN. *su(geru)* insert (in a tube or hole); fit into; attach (a clog thong).

3口 *kankō suru* muzzle, hush up, restrict liberty of speech. *kankō, kenkō* gagging, silencing

12替 *su(ge)-kae(ru)* change (buttons, clog cords, etc.)

B 箇 3414 F1411 KA, KO counters for things.

7条 *kajō* items; errors; articles

条書 *kajōgaki* itemization, items

8所 *kasho* place, spot, point, section, part, passage (in a book)

13数 *kosū* number of articles

14箇 *koko* one by one; individuals. *koko ni* individually, separately

箇別別 *koko-betsubetsu* each one separately

A 算 3415 F1413 SAN divining (block); calculation; number; abacus; plan; probability. *kazo(eru)*, *san(suru)* number, count, calculate.

2入 *sannyū* inclusion in the calculation

4木 *sangi* divining block; calculating device

5出 *sanshutsu* computation, calculation

用 *san-yō, sannyō* calculation, computation

用高 *san-yōdaka(i)* stingy, close (in figuring)

用数字 *san-yō sūji* the Arabic figures

7乱 *san(o)mida(su)* scatter in all directions

8法 *sampō* arithmetic

定 *santei* calculation, estimate, assessment, amount

9段 *sandan suru* try, contrive, manage

11術 *sanjutsu* arithmetic

術平均 *sanjutsu heikin* arithmetical mean

術級数 *sanjutsu kyūsū* arithmetical progression

術家 *sanjutsuka* arithmetician

12散 *san(o)chi(rasu)* scatter in all directions

筆 *sampitsu* writing and arithmetic

無 *sanna(shi)* countless

13数 *sansū* calculation, computation; arithmetic, mathematics

置 *san (o) o(ku)* divine, foretell; calculate

14暦 *sanreki* arithmetic and the calendar studies

15盤 *soroban* abacus; account

盤珠 *sorobandama* abacus beads; counting beads; account abacus

盤勘定 *soroban kanjō* calculation on the abacus

A 管 3416 F1414 KAN pipe, tube; (brush) holder; wind instrument. *kuda* pipe, tube; drunken talk.

3下 *kanka* jurisdiction, control

4区 *kanku* jurisdictional area; parish

内 *kannai* within the jurisdiction of

切器 *kanki(ri)ki* pipe cutter

5玉 *kudatama* ancient cylindrical jewels

外 *kangai* outside the jurisdiction

主 *kanshu* head priest

6守 *kanshu* custody and protection

7見 *kanken* narrow view; view; personal views

状 *kanjō* tubular

8長 *kanchō* superintendent priest (in shrines and temples)

制 *kansei* control

弦 *kangen* wind and string instruments; music

弦楽 *kangengaku* orchestra; orchestral music

弦楽器 *kangen gakki* wind and string instruments

[10]流 *kudanaga(shi)* shooting logs down a stream

財人 *kanzainin* trustee, custodian, administrator, receiver

[11]絃 *kangen* wind and string instruments; music

絃楽 *kangengaku* orchestra; orchestral music

絃楽器 *kangen gakki* wind and string instruments

理 *kanri* managing, administration, supervision, control

理人 *kanrinin* steward, manager, supervisor; executor, caretaker, trustee, steward

理下 *kanrika* under the supervision of

理図 *kanrizu* control chart

理法 *kanrihō* methods of administration, management

理者 *kanrisha*=*kanrinin* 管理人 (see above–11)

理費 *kanrihi* administrative expense

理貿易 *kanri bōeki* government-managed trade

理職 *kanrishoku* management

[12]掌 *kanshō* management, charge

[13]楽 *kangaku* the music of wind instruments

楽器 *kangakki* wind instruments

[14]領 *kanrei* governor-general

管 *kudakuda(shii)* tedious, verbose; detailed

[17]轄 *kankatsu* jurisdiction, control

轄官庁 *kankatsu kanchō* competent authorities

轄違 *kankatsuchiga(i)* lack of jurisdiction

轄権 *kankatsuken* jurisdiction

9

節 3417 F1415 節 See 節 3402.

篇 3418 F1418 HEN volume, book; chapter, section, part; compilation, editing.

箭 3419 F1414 SEN. *ya* arrow.

篁 3420 F1417 KŌ. *takamura* bamboo grove.

箴 3421 F1415 SHIN warning, counsel, precept; needle.

[7]言 *shingen* proverb, maxim, warning

箸 3422 F1415 DO. CHO. JAKU. CHAKU. *hashi* chopsticks.

[13]置 *hashio(ki)* chopstick holder

篆 3423 F1417 TEN seal-style characters.

[6]字 *tenji* seal character

[8]刻 *tenkoku* seal engraving

[10]書 *tensho* seal characters (ancient forms)

範 3424 F1417 B HAN example, model, pattern; limit.

[7]囲 *han-i* extent, scope, limits, sphere, range; purview

囲内 *han-inai* within the bounds

囲外 *han-igai* beyond the pale, beyond bounds

[8]例 *hanrei* example

[9]型 *hankei* (iron) mold

[19]疇 *hanchū* category

箱 3425 F1415 B SŌ. *hako* box, case, chest, bin, coffer, railway car.

[2]入 *hako-i(ri)* boxed

入娘 *hako-i(ri) musume* innocent maiden, well-protected daughter

[4]火鉢 *hako hibachi* boxed brazier

[5]代 *hakodai* charge for the box

[6]舟 *hakobune* an ark; (Noah's) ark

自動車 *hako jidōsha* sedan, limousine

[8]枕 *hako makura* box pillow

[9]屋 *hakoya* boxmaker

型 *hakogata* coupé, limousine, closed car

[10]庭 *hako niwa* miniature garden

師 *hakoshi* train thief

書 *hakoga(ki)* painter's or calligrapher's autograph on the box

馬車 *hako basha* closed carriage

根草 *hakonesō* maidenhair fern

[11]梯子 *hakobashigo* staircase-cupboard combination

[13]詰 *hakozume* boxed, cased

10

篋 3426 F1419 See 篋 3410.

簑 3427 F1420 F1628 See 蓑 4009.

篠 3428 F1418 See 篠 3440.

篭 Nonstandard for 籠 3458.

篥 3429 F1419 RIKI, RITSU, RICHI horn, flageolet.

簒 3430 F1419 簒 SAN rob.

[5]立 *sanritsu suru* usurp the throne

[12]弑 *sanshi* killing a ruler and usurping the throne

[14]奪 *sandatsu* usurpation

篳 3431 / F1420 HICHI, HITSU fence.
16 篥 *hichiriki* flageolet, Shinto flute

篝 3432 / F1418 Kō basket. *kagari*＝*kagaribi* 篝火 (see below–4).
4 火 *kagaribi* camp fire, fishing fire, beacon fire
11 船 *kagaribune* boats fishing with lights

篩 3433 / F1420 SHI. *furu(u)* sieve, sift, screen. *furui* sieve, sifter.
4 分 *furu(i)-wa(keru)* screen, sieve, sift out

篤 3434 / F1419 B TOKU. *atsu(i)* kind, cordial, fervent, affectionate; serious (illness). *toku to* deliberately, carefully, seriously.
6 行 *tokkō* good deeds, goodness
7 志 *tokushi* benevolence; zeal; volunteering
志家 *tokushika* volunteer, self-sacrificing person
8 実 *tokujitsu* sincerity, faithfulness
学 *tokugaku* love of learning
9 厚 *tokkō na* sincere, warmhearted
信 *tokushin* devotion
13 農 *tokunō* conscientious farmer

築 3435 / F1418 A CHIKU. *kizu(ku)* build, construct.
3 山 *tsukiyama* artificial miniature hill
上 *kizu(ki)-a(geru)* build up
5 立 *kizu(ki)-ta(teru)* build up
6 地 *tsukiji* reclaimed land. *tsukiji*, *tsuiji* a roofed mud wall
地塀 *tsukijibei* a roofed mud wall
8 直 *kizu(ki)-nao(su)* repair, rebuild
9 造 *chikuzō* building, construction
城 *chikujō* fortification; castle construction
12 堤 *chikutei* embankment, banking
港 *chikkō*, *chikukō* harbor construction
13 園 *chikuen* construction of a park or garden
14 増 *kizu(ki)-ma(su)* build on to
16 墻 *tsuiji* roofed mud wall

11

篹 3436 / F1419 See 簒 3430.

篳 See 3431.

簗 3437 / F-X *yana* weir, fish trap, fishpond.

簓 3438 / F1421 (国字) *sasara* bamboo whisk; broken end of a bamboo stalk.

簀 3439 / F1420 SAKU. *su* rough mat (of bamboo or reeds).
8 子 *sunoko* portable slatted floor piece

篠 篠 3440 / F1418 ZŌ. *shino* a small bamboo. *sasa* bamboo grass.
6 竹 *shinodake* small bamboo
虫 *sanada mushi* tapeworm
8 突雨 *shinotsu(ku) ame* driving rain, cloudburst
11 笛 *shinobue* bamboo flute

簇 3441 / F1420 ZOKU. *muraga(ru)* (see under 群 3667.0).
5 生 *zokusei suru* (plants) grow in clusters; (animals) live in herds or flocks
出 *zokushutsu suru* spring up like mushrooms

12

簧 3442 / F1423 Kō flute reed.

簞 3443 / F1421 TAN bamboo rice basket.
11 笥 *tansu* chest of drawers, dresser, buffet, cupboard
笥預金 *dansu yokin* hoarded cash

簡 簡 3444 / F1422 B KEN, KAN. brevity, simplicity. *fuda* (see under 札 2171.0).
5 札 *kansatsu* wooden tag
古 *kanko na* simple and antique
6 朴 *kamboku* simplicity
7 抜 *kambatsu* selection
8 明 *kammei* brevity, conciseness
法 *kanpō* simple method
易 *kan-i* simplicity, easiness
易化 *kan-ika* simplification
易住宅 *kan-i jūtaku* simple house, prefabricated house, Quonset hut
易保険 *kan-i hoken* post-office life insurance
易食堂 *kan-i shokudō* quick lunch
易旅館 *kan-i ryokan* cheap lodging house
易書簡 *kan-i shokan* letter card
易宿泊所 *kan-i shukuhakujo* cheap lodging house
易裁判所 *kan-i saibansho* police court
9 便 *kamben* simplicity; convenience; expediency
約 *kan-yaku* conciseness, brevity, simplification, abbreviation
勁 *kankei* strength in spite of small stature
要 *kan-yō na* brief and to the point
単 *kantan* brevity, simplicity
単服 *kantanfuku* women's light summer wear; utility dress
単着 *kantangi*＝word above
10 素 *kanso* simplicity

素化 *kansoka* simplification
11略 *kanryaku* simplicity; brevity, conciseness; informality
12短 *kantan* brevity, simplicity
14読 *kandoku* epistle, letter
15潔 *kanketsu* brevity, conciseness, simplicity
閲 *kan-etsu suru* investigate; choose
閲点呼 *kan-etsu tenko* (ancient) periodic roll call of veterans
16樸 *kamboku* simplicity
19牘 *kandoku* document, letter

13

簷 3445 F1423 En eaves.

簽 3446 F1424 Sen label; signature.

簸 3447 F1424 Ha. *hi(ru)* winnow, fan.

簿 3448 F1424 **簿** B Bo. Haku. *-bo* record book.
10記 *boki* bookkeeping

簾 3449 F1424 Ren a screen. *sudare, su* bamboo screen, rattan blind.
4戸 *sudo* reed door
11屏風 *sudare byōbu* bamboo folding screen

14

籍 3450 F1425 **籍** B Seki domiciliary register; membership.

簪 3451 F1423 Shin. *kanzashi* ornamental hairpin.

籃 3452 F1424 Ran basket.
11球 *rankyū* basket ball

籌 3453 F1425 Chū plan.
11略 *chūryaku*=*hakarigoto* (see under 謀 4414.0)

纂 3454 F1485 San editing, compiling. [糸]
7述 *sanjutsu suru* gather materials and write
10修 *sanshū* compiling, editing

15

籤 See **籤** 3459.

籔 3455 F1425 F1646 See **藪** 4088.

籐 3456 F1425 Tō rattan, cane.
11細工 *tōzaiku* rattan work
12椅子 *tōisu* cane chair, rattan chair
13蓆 *tōmushiro* rattan mat

16

籟 3457 F1426 Rai rustling of the wind.

籠 3458 F1426 Rō. *ko(mu)*, *ko(meru)* (see under 込 4660.0). *komo(ru)* seclude oneself, be confined in; be implied; be stuffy, be filled with (smoke). *kago* cage, coop; basket. *ko* basket, bamboo containers.
4手 *kote* fencing gloves, gauntlet; forearm
5目 *kagome* basket interstices; woven bamboo pattern
6耳 *kagomimi* poor memory
7抜 *kagonu(ke)* defrauding, swindling
8居 *rōkyo* confinement (indoors)
枕 *kago makura* basket pillow
9屋 *kagoya* basketmaker; basket shop
城 *rōjō* siege, confinement (indoors). *rōjō suru* be besieged
11球 *rōkyū* basketball
12絡 *rōraku suru* cajole, inveigle, entice

17

籤 3459 F1426 **籖** Sen *kuji* lottery, lot, raffle.
4中 *kujiata(ri)* winning in a lottery
引 *kujibi(ki)* drawing lots
5札 *kuji fuda* lottery ticket
8逃 *kujinoga(re)* elimination by lottery
10弱 *kujiyowa(i)* unlucky in lotteries
11運 *kujiun* one's luck in lottery
強 *kujizuyo(i)* lucky in lotteries

19

籬 3460 F1427 Ri. *magaki* rough-woven fence; bamboo hedge.

RAD. 米 119

Kome rice. At left: *kome hen*. Nickname: Rice.

A 米 3461/F1427 BEI. MAI *kome, yone* rice. *-Bei-* U.S.A. *bei-* rice. *mētoru* meter.

[2]人 *Beijin* an American
[4]仏 *Bei-Futsu* America and France
[5]代 *komedai* rice money
加 *Bei-Ka* America and Canada
本土 *Beihondo* Stateside, the States
[6]虫 *kome no mushi* rice weevil
州 *Beishū* the Americas
[7]麦 *beibaku* rice and barley; grain
作 *beisaku* rice culture, rice crop
杉 *beisugi* cedar
材 *beizai* American timber
兵 *beihei* U.S. soldier; U.S. sailor
系 *beikei* American (enterprise)
寿 *beiju* 88th birthday
利堅 *Meriken* American
利堅粉 *merikenko* wheat flour
[8]国 *Beikoku* U.S.A.
使 *beishi* an American envoy
価 *beika* the price of rice
所 *komedokoro* rice-producing area
松 *beimatsu* Oregon pine, Douglas fir
英 *Bei-Ei* America and England
英系 *Bei-Eikei* American and British (enterprises)
[9]屋 *komeya* rice merchant
栂 *beitsuga* hemlock, hemlock-spruce
独 *Bei-Doku* America and Germany
軍 *Beigun* U.S. armed forces
食 *beishoku* rice diet
食虫 *komeku(i)mushi* drone, idler
食鳥 *komeku(i)dori* bobolink
[10]俵 *komedawara* straw rice bag
粉 *komeko, kome(no)ko* rice flour
納 *beinō* payment of taxes in rice
紙 *beishi* American paper; the American press
倉 *komegura* rice granary
案 *beian* American proposal
華 *Bei-Ka* America and China
[11]粒 *kome tsubu, beiryū* a grain of rice
貨 *beika* American currency, U.S. dollar
商 *beishō* rice dealer
問屋 *komedonya* rice wholesaler
産 *beisan* rice production
産地 *kome (no) sanchi* rice-producing district
[12]飯 *beihan, kome (no) meshi* boiled rice
[13]塩 *beien* rice and salt; livelihood
搗 *kometsuki* polishing rice
資 *beishi* American capital
[14]綿 *beimen* American (raw) cotton
語 *Beigo* Americanism, American English, American
誌 *beishi* American magazine
穀 *beikoku* rice
[16]磨 *kometo(gi)* washing rice
噸 *beiton* short ton
[17]檜 *beihinoki* spruce
糠 *kome nuka* rice bran
[18]櫃 *komebitsu* rice bin; one's source of a living; breadwinner
騒動 *kome sōdō* rice riot
[19]蘇 *Bei-So* American and Soviet Russia
[20]艦 *beikan* American warship

2

料 3462/F-X (国字) *dekamētoru* decameter, 10 meters.

3

粁 3463/F1428 (国字) *kiromētoru* kilometer, 1000 meters.

籾 3464/F1428 籾 (国字) *momi* unhulled rice.

[12]殻 *momigara* chaff
[14]摺 *momizuri* hulling rice

4

粍 3465/F1429 (国字) *mirimētoru* millimeter, $\frac{1}{1000}$ meter.

粃 3466/F1428 秕 HI. *shiina* empty grain husk, immature ear of grain.

[9]政 *hisei* misgovernment

B 粋 3467/F1429 粹 SUI purity, essence, pith, cream, pick, elite, choice; elegance; fashion; taste; gracefulness; considerateness. SAI. *iki* chic, style.

[2]人 *suijin* refined man, romantic man, man about town
[7]狂 *suikyō* raving drunkenness
[8]事 *ikigoto* love intrigue, romance
[9]美 *suibi* exquisite beauty

A 料 3468/F869 RYŌ charge, rate, fee; allowance; materials; measuring. [斗]

[6]地 *ryōchi* preserve, estate
[8]金 *ryōkin* charge, rate, fee, fare
[9]亭 *ryōtei* restaurant
[10]紙 *ryōshi* paper, writing paper
[11]率 *ryōritsu* tariff, rates

理 *ryōri* cooking, cuisine; dish, food, fare; management, administration
理人 *ryōrinin* cook
理役 *ryōriyaku* chef
理店 *ryōriten* restaurant
理屋 *ryōriya* restaurant
理室 *ryōrishitsu* kitchen
理番 *ryōriban* cook
[12]飲 *ryōin* food and drink
[18]簡 *ryōken*=了簡 268.18

A **粉** 3469/F1428 **粉** Fun dust, powder. *ko, kona* flour, meal, powder. *deshimētoru*, decimeter, $\frac{1}{10}$ meter.
[5]末 *fummatsu* powder, dust
本 *fumpon* copy, reproduction
白粉 *kona oshiroi* face powder
石鹸 *kona sekken* powdered soap
[6]米 *kogome* broken rice
[7]状 *funjō* powder
[8]乳 *funnyū* powdered milk
味噌 *kona miso* powdered bean paste
[9]食 *funshoku* powdered food
屋 *konaya* flour mill, flour dealer
糾 *funkyū* disorder, entanglement, confusion
炭 *funtan* pulverized coal. *konazumi* pulverized charcoal
茶 *konacha* pulverized tea, powdered tea
砕 *funsai* pulverization, smashing, crushing
砕機 *funsaiki* crusher, pulverizer
[10]粉 *konagona* in very small pieces
骨 *funkotsu* earnestness, diligence
骨砕身 *funkotsu-saishin suru* do one's very best
骨細心 *funkotsu-saishin suru* do one's very best
[11]雪 *kona yuki* powdery snow
[13]飾 *funshoku* make-up, showy ornaments; embellishment
微塵 *kona mijin, komijin* smithereens, fragments
[14]塵 *funjin* flour and dust; inconsequential things; mundane things
[16]薬 *konagusuri, kogusuri* medicine powder
篩機 *konafuruiki* flour bolter
[17]黛 *funtai* cosmetics

5

粕 3470/F1429 Haku. *kasu* scrap, waste.
[6]取 *kasuto(ri)* low-grade liquor
取雑誌 *kasuto(ri) zasshi* cheap magazine
[14]漬 *kasuzuke* vegetables pickled in saké lees

B **粒** 3471/F1429 Ryū grain; drop. *tsubu* grain, drop; counter for tiny particles.
[3]子 *ryūshi* particle (of matter), corpuscle
[7]択 *tsubuyori* the pick of the lot
状 *ryūjō no* granular
形 *tsubugata* a tablet (in medicine)
[9]食 *ryūshoku* eating rice, rice diet
[11]粒 *ryūryū to* assiduously, painstakingly, strenuously. *tsubutsubu no* lumpy, granulated
粒辛苦 *ryūryū-shinku no* strenuous, painstaking, assiduous
[12]揃 *tsubuzoroi* uniformly good

B **粘** 3472/F1430 **黏** Nen. *neba(ru)* be sticky, be glutinous, be greasy; persevere. *ne(ru)* knead. *neba(ri)* stickiness, viscosity; tenacity, perseverance. *neba(i), neba(tta)* sticky.
[2]力 *nenryoku* tenacity; viscosity
[3]土 *nendo, nebatsuchi* clay, slime
[5]付 *nebatsu(ku)* be sticky, adhere to
[6]気 *neba(ri)ke, neba(rik)ke*=*neba(ri)* (see under 粘 3472.0)
[7]体 *nentai* waxy substance
[8]性 *nensei* viscosity
泥 *nendei* slime
[9]度 *nendo* viscosity
[11]強 *neba(ri)zuyo(i)* tenacious, persevering
粘 *nebaneba suru* sticky, syrupy, gummy
著 *neba(ri)-tsu(ku)* be sticky, adhere to
液 *nen-eki* mucus, phlegm; slime
液質 *nen-ekishitsu no* phlegmatic
[12]結 *nenketsu* coking, caking
着 *neba(ri)-tsu(ku)* be sticky, adhere to. *nenchaku* adhesion
着力 *nenchakuryoku* adhesive power, tenacity
[13]滑 *nenkatsu na* greasy and slippery
稠 *nenchū* stickiness
[14]膜 *nemmaku* mucous membrane
[15]質 *nenshitsu* viscosity

B **粗** 3473/F1429 So roughness, coarseness; not fine; neglect; carelessness. *ara(i), ara(ppoi)* coarse, rough, rugged; loose (fabric); large (meshes). *ara* defect, flaw, blemish. *ara-* rough, coarse, natural, sparse, crude.
[3]大 *sodai na* coarse, rough
[4]方 *arakata* mostly, almost, roughly
毛布 *somōfu* duffel blanket
[5]皮 *arakawa* raw hide, bark, husk
布 *sofu* coarse cloth, canvas, sackcloth. *aranuno* gunny, sacking, sackcloth
末 *somatsu na* crude, rough, plain, humble, shabby; careless, rude. *somatsu ni suru* waste
仕上 *arashiage* rough work, roughing
目 *zarame* coarse, brown crystallized sugar
目鉅 *arame yasuri* rasp
[6]衣 *so-i* coarse clothing, poor garb
朶 *soda* faggot, brushwood
[7]材 *sozai* raw materials

8 金 *aragane* ore
放 *sohō* carelessness, fault, oversight
板 *ara-ita* rough lumber
服 *sofuku* plain dress, poor clothing
肴 *sokō* simple food
忽 *sokotsu* carelessness, rashness, absent-mindedness; blunder, fault, error
忽者 *sokotsumono* careless person, absent-mindedness
9 食 *soshoku* coarse fare, plain food, poor diet
造 *sozō* crude manufacture; crude articles
拵 *aragoshira(e)* spadework, preliminary work
拭 *arabuki* rough wiping
研 *aratogi* rough grinding
品 *soshina, sohin* trifling gift; inferior goods
茶 *socha* coarse tea
相 *sosō* carelessness, oversight
相火 *sosōbi* accidental fire
10 起 *ara-oko(shi)* rough ground-breaking
酒 *soshu* cheap saké
砥 *arato* grindstone, coarse whetstone
莚 *aramushiro* loosely-woven mat
11 彫 *arabori* rough carving
探 *arasaga(shi)* faultfinding (see above-5)
略 *soryaku na, zonzai na*=*somatsu na* 粗末
野 *soya na* rustic, rude, vulgar
密 *somitsu* roughness and fineness
笨 *sohon* crudeness, roughness
菓 *soka* cakes, refreshments
悪 *soaku na* coarse, crude, inferior
悪品 *soakuhin* crude articles, inferior goods
12 遠 *soen*=疎遠 3021.12
隔 *sokaku* alienation, estrangement
飯 *sohan* plain meal
筋 *arasuji* outline, summary, synopsis
13 鉋 *araganna* jack plane
鉱 *sokō* unprocessed ore
塗 *aranu(ri)* first plaster coat, roughly plastered walls
14 漉 *aragoshi* rough filter; rough filtering
漏 *sorō* carelessness, negligence
銅 *sodō* unrefined copper
雑 *sozatsu na* coarse, rough, rude
製 *sosei* crude manufacture
製品 *soseihin* crude articles
製塩 *soseien* coarse salt
製糖 *soseitō* unrefined sugar
製濫造 *sosei-ranzō* mass production of poor articles
15 縫 *aranu(i)* basting, tacking
暴 *sobō na* wild, rude, violent, hard, fierce
16 積 *arazu(mori)* rough estimate
糖 *sotō* raw sugar
餐 *sosan* plain meal

— 6 —

粥 See 1574.

粟 See 4277.

粤 See 237.

粮 3474 / F1431 F1436 See **糧** 3490.

B **粧** 3475 / F1431 Shō *yosō(u)* adorn (one's person).

粨 3476 / F-X (国字) ***hekutomētoru*** hectometer, 100 meters.

— 7 —

粲 3477 / F1431 San bright.
12 然 *sanzen* brilliance; smiling with rows of white teeth showing

粳 3478 / F1376 **秔** Kō. *uruchi* ordinary rice.
12 黍 *urukibi* nonglutinous millet

— 8 —

粹 3479 / F1431 See **粋** 3467.

A **精** 3480 / F1432 **精** Shō. Sei spirit, ghost, fairy; energy, vitality; semen; white rice; details; excellence, purity; skill. *shira(geru)* refine, polish. *kuwa(shii)* (see under 詳 4357.0).
1 一 *sei-itsu* purity
一杯 *sei-ippai* with all one's might
2 入 *sei (o) i(reru)* work earnestly
力 *seiryoku* energy, vigor, vitality
力家 *seiryokka, seiryokuka* energetic person, go-getter
3 子 *seishi* sperm
4 分 *seibun* nourishment; energy, strength
5 巧 *seikō na* elaborate, exquisite, delicate
出 *seida(su)* exert oneself, be diligent, work hard
白 *seihaku* refining, polishing
白米 *seihakumai* polished rice
白所 *seihakusho* rice mill
白糖 *seihakutō* refined sugar
6 肉 *seiniku* fresh meat
虫 *seichū* spermatozoa
気 *seiki* energy, spirit; essence
米 *seimai* white rice
米所 *seimaisho* rice mill
7 麦 *seibaku* cleaning; cleaned wheat or barley
励 *seirei* diligence, industry
妙 *seimyō na* fine, exquisite; subtle
兵 *seihei, seibyō* picked troops

8 金 *seikin* refined gold
舎 *shōja* temple, monastery, convent
限根限 *seikagi(ri)-konkagi(ri)* with all one's might
油 *seiyu* refined oil
油所 *seiyujo* oil refinery
9 通 *seitsū suru* be versed in, be conversant with, be posted on
洗 *seisen* scouring
査 *seisa* careful investigation
度 *seido* accuracy
神 *seishin* mind, spirit, soul, heart; intention, motive; the spirit (of the thing)
神力 *seishinryoku* mental power
神文化 *seishim-bunka* moral culture
神分析 *seishim-bunseki* psychoanalysis
神分析学 *seishim-bunsekigaku* psychoanalysis
神分裂症 *seishim-bunretsushō* schizophrenia
神外科 *seishin-geka* psychosurgery
神生物学 *seishin-seibutsugaku* psychobiology
神生理学 *seishin-seirigaku* psychophysiology
神年齢 *seishin nenrei* mental age
神身体医学 *seishin-shintai igaku* psychosomatic medicine
神医学 *seishin igaku* psychiatry
神労働 *seishin rōdō* mental work
神状態 *seishin jōtai* mental condition
神的 *seishinteki* mental, spiritual
神的援助 *seishinteki enjo* moral support
神物理学 *seishin butsurigaku* psychophysics
神界 *seishinkai* mental world
神科 *seishinka* psychiatry
神科学 *seishin kagaku* mental science
神家 *seishinka* idealist
神病 *seishimbyō* insanity, mental disease
神病学 *seishimbyōgaku* psychiatry
神病学者 *seishimbyōgakusha* psychiatrist
神病院 *seishim-byōin* mental hospital, insane asylum
神病理学 *seishim-byōrigaku* psychopathology
神修養 *seishin shūyō* mental training
神異状 *seishin ijō* mental derangement
神感応 *seishin kannō* telepathy
神障害 *seishin shōgai* mental derangement
神衛生 *seishin eisei* mental therapy
神論 *seishinron* idealism
神論者 *seishinronja* idealist
神錯乱 *seishin sakuran* delirium
神薄弱 *seishin hakujaku* weak-mindedness
神薄弱児 *seishin-hakujakuji* retarded child
神療法 *seishin ryōhō* psychotherapy
神療養所 *seishin ryōyōjo* mental hospital
10 悍 *seikan na* intrepid, fierce
根 *seikon* energy, vitality
酒 *seishu* refined saké
粉 *seifun* fine powder
粋 *seisui* purity; unselfishness; clear weather
華 *seika* essence, ; brilliance
進 *shōjin* concentration, diligence, devotion; purification; abstinence
進日 *shōjimbi* day of abstinence from flesh food
進料理 *shōjin ryōri* vegetarian diet, vegetarian food
進揚 *shōjin-a(ge)* vegetable *tempura*, vegetables fried in deep fat
進落 *shōjin-o(chi)* first meat after fasting
11 液 *seieki* semen, sperm
粗 *seiso* fineness or coarseness
細 *seisai* minuteness, precision, accuracy
彩 *seisai* luster, brilliance; vividness
巣 *seisō* seminal glands
密 *seimitsu* precision, accuracy; minuteness
密工業 *seimitsu kōgyō* precision-machine industry
密科学 *seimitsu kagaku* exact sciences
密計器 *seimitsu keiki* precision gauge
密機械 *seimitsu kikai* precision instruments
密爆撃 *seimitsu bakugeki* precision bombing
12 勤 *seikin* diligence, good attendance
13 解 *seikai* detailed commentary
鉄 *seitetsu* refined iron
鉋 *shiage kanna* finishing plane
義 *seigi* exact meaning; detailed exposition
農 *seinō* industrious farmer
14 選 *seisen* careful selection
精 *seizei* to the utmost, as far as possible; at most; at best
読 *seidoku* careful reading, discriminate reading
銀 *seigin* refined silver
銅 *seidō* refined copper
管 *seikan* seminal duct
魂尽 *seikontsu(kiru)* lose all one's energy
選 *seisen* careful selection
選品 *seisenhin* select goods
練 *seiren* refining, smelting, tempering
練剤 *seirenzai* scouring agent
算 *seisan* exact calculation, accurate account; adjustment; settlement of accounts
算所 *seisanjo* fare-adjustment office
製 *seisei* careful manufacture; refining
製所 *seiseijo* refinery
製油 *seiseiyu* refined oil
製法 *seiseihō* refining process
製品 *seiseihin* refined article; finished goods
製糖 *seiseitō* refined sugar
15 撰 *seisen* careful preparation
確 *seikaku* accuracy, precision
鋭 *seiei na* very powerful; highly efficient (weapons). *seiei* picked (troops)
霊 *seirei* spirit, soul (of the deceased). *shōryō* spirits of the dead, spirit visitor
霊崇拝 *seirei sūhai* animism
霊崇拝者 *seirei sūhaisha* animist
霊説 *seirei setsu* animism

16緻 *seichi na* nice, fine, minute, subtle, delicate, exquisite, elaborate
糖 *seitō* sugar refining; refined sugar
糖所 *seitōjo* sugar refinery
錬 *seiren* refining, smelting
錬所 *seirenjo* refinery, smelter
18髄 *seizui*=*shinzui* 真髄 783.18
22嚢 *seinō* seminal vesicle

9

粍 3481/F1434 (国字) *senchimētoru* centimeter $\frac{1}{100}$ meter

粿 3482/F1434 Jū mix.
12飯 *katemeshi* rice mixed with whatever is available

糊 3483/F1434 Ko. Kotsu. *nori* paste, glue; starch; sizing.
2入 *nori-i(re)* paste container
3口 *kokō* bare existence, livelihood, living on others
5目 *norime* starching
付 *noritsu(ke)* starching; pasting
8板 *nori ita* paste-making board
刷毛 *noribake* paste brush
11張 *noriba(ri)* pasting, starching
12壺 *nori tsubo* paste pot
13塗 *koto suru* patch up, gloss over

10

糒 3484/F1434 Bi. Hai. *hoshi-i, hoshi-ii* dried boiled rice.

糖 = **糖** 3485/F1435 Tō sugar.
B
4化 *tōka* turning to sugar
分 *tōbun* sugar content
6衣 *tōi* sugar coating
衣錠 *tōijō* sugar-coated pill
7尿病 *tōnyōbyō* diabetes
8乳 *tōnyū* sweetened condensed milk
11菓 *tōka* sweets, candy
13楓 *tōfū* sugar maple
業 *tōgyō* sugar industry
14蜜 *tōmitsu* molasses
15質 *tōshitsu* sugariness, saccharinity
18類 *tōrui* sugars

11

糜 See 5395.

糝 3486/F1435 Shin, San rice grain.
10粉 *shinko* rice flour, rice-flour dough

糟 3487/F1435 Sō. *kasu* (see under 滓 2642.0).
8取 *kasuto(ri)* low-grade liquor
11粕 *sōhaku* lees, dregs, leavings
17糠 *sōkō* humble living
糠妻 *sōkō (no) tsuma* a wife married in poverty, a faithful companion

糠 3488/F1436 Kō. *nuka* rice bran.
4中 *kōchū* in rice bran
8雨 *nuka-ame* drizzle
油 *nuka abura* rice-bran oil
味噌 *nuka miso* salted rice-bran paste (for pickling)
味噌漬 *nukamisozuke* vegetables pickled in rice-bran paste
10悦 *nuka yoroko(bi)* premature rejoicing
12喜 *nuka yoroko(bi)* premature rejoicing
13働 *nukabatara(ki)* fruitless effort

糞 3489/F1435 Fun excrement. *kuso* feces, excrement, droppings.
2力 *kusojikara* brute force, great strength
3土 *fundo* loose dirt, black earth; dirt, filth
7尿 *funnyō* excreta, feces and urine
8味噌 *kuso miso* sweeping condemnation
9便 *fumben* excrement, night soil, stools
度胸 *kuso dokyō* foolhardiness, reckless bravery
10骨 *kusobone* needless exertion
勉強 *kuso benkyō* cramming
真面目 *kusomajime* absurd seriousness
12壺 *kuso tsubo* night-soil receptacle
落着 *kuso-ochitsu(ki) no* provokingly calm
13塚 *funzuka* dunghill
塊 *funkai* stools
溜 *kusodame* manure tank
詰 *funzuma(ri)*constipation

12

糧 3490/F1436 **粮** Ryō. Rō. *kate* food, provisions, bread.
B
9食 *ryōshoku* provisions, food, victuals, rations
10秣 *ryōmatsu* provisions and fodder
11道 *ryōdō* supply of provisions

14

糯 3491/F1436 Da. *mochigome* glutinous rice.
6米 *mochigome* glutinous rice

19

糶 See 3682.

糸 RAD. 120

Ito thread. At left: *ito hen.* Nickname: Long Thread (cf. Rad. 52).

A 糸 3492/F1437 絲 SHI thread; one ten-thousandth of a hair. *ito* thread, yarn; gut; string (of violin); (fish) line.
²入 *ito-i(ri)* cotton-silk mixture
³口 *itoguchi* thread end; beginning; clue
⁴切歯 *itoki(ri)ba* eyetooth, canine tooth
⁵瓜 *hechima* snake gourd
目 *itome* fine line; kite string; thread weight
⁶竹 *itotake, shichiku* musical instruments; music
⁷車 *itoguruma* spinning wheel
杉 *itosugi* cypress
状 *shijō no* thready
⁸雨 *itosame* fine rain
底 *itozoko* bottom rim line (of porcelain)
価 *shika* price of thread; price of raw silk
物 *itomono* haberdashery
取 *itoto(ri)* silk reeling, silk spinning
⁹屋 *itoya* thread and yarn shop; raw silk merchant
柳 *itoyanagi* weeping willow
巻 *itomaki* spool, bobbin, reel; beam (in weaving); turning peg
巻鱏 *itomaki ei* manta ray
¹⁰屑 *itokuzu* waste thread, ravelings
捌 *itosabaki* playing a stringed instrument
桜 *itozakura* drooping cherry
¹¹遊 *itoyū* shimmering of heated air
釣 *itozu(ri)* line fishing
毫 *shigō* infinitesimal quantity, a hair, a thread, a tiny bit
偏景気 *itohen keiki* textile boom
¹²硝子 *itogarasu* spun glass
¹³路 *itomichi* samisen training; fishline or thread guide
蒟蒻 *itogonnyaku* devil's-tongue vermicelli
¹⁵撚 *itoyori* twining
¹⁶鋸 *itonoko* scroll saw; jeweler's saw
¹⁹繰 *itoku(ri)* reeling, filature; spinner; reel
²⁰蘭 *itoran* thready orchid

1

系 See 195.

糺 3493/F1437 See 糾 3498.

2

糾 3494/F1437 See 糾 3498.

3

紆 3495/F1440 U crouch.
⁶曲 *ukyoku suru* meander
⁷余 *uyo* meandering; beating around the bush; abundant talent
余曲折 *uyo-kyokusetsu* meandering; complications; vicissitudes

A 級 3496/F1443 級 KYŪ grade, class, rank; steps; decapitated head.
⁴友 *kyūyū* classmate
⁵外 *kyūgai* offgrade; below par
⁷別 *kyūbetsu* grading
⁸長 *kyūchō* head of his class, monitor
¹³数 *kyūsū* series or progression (in math.)

A 紀 3497/F1438 KI account, narrative, history, annals, geological period.
⁴元 *kigen* era, epoch; imperial era; A.D.
元前 *kigenzen* B.C.
元後 *kigengo* A.D.
元節 *Kigensetsu* Empire Day (Feb. 11)
⁶伝体 *kidentai* biographical history
行 *kikō* travelogue
行文 *kikōbun* travelogue
⁸念 *kinen* commemoration, remembrance
⁹律 *kiritsu*＝規律 4285.9
要 *kiyō* memoirs, bulletin

B 糾 3498/F1437 糾 糺 糺 KYŪ. *tada(su)*(see under 質 4518.0). *azana(u)* twist (rope).
⁶合 *kyūgō suru* rally, muster
⁸明 *kyūmei* arraignment; searching examination
¹¹問 *kyūmon* cross-examination; arraignment
¹²弾 *kyūdan* impeachment, censure
¹³罪 *kyūzai* investigating a crime

A 約 3499/F1438 約 YAKU promise, vow; approximately; abridgment. *yaku(suru)* promise; economize. *tsuzu(maru)* shrink; be summarized. *tsuzu(meru)* condense, reduce, shorten, curtail, abridge; economize. *tsuzu(mari)* conclusion. *tsuzu(mayakana)* neat and small, modest, unpretentious; concise; frugal.
⁴手 *yakute* promissory note
文 *yakubun suru* summarize, condense
分 *yakubun* reduction of a fraction to lowest terms
⁷言 *yakugen* contraction; summary

束 *yakusoku* pledge, promise; appointment, date; contract, agreement, bargain, betrothal, convenant; condition; convention, rule; destiny

束手形 *yakusoku tegata* promissory note

束事 *yakusokugoto* promise, engagement, pledge

8 定 *yakujō* promise, agreement, contract

定書 *yakujōsho* written contract, agreement

定済 *yakujōsu(mi)* sold; promised; engaged

12 款 *yakkan* stipulation, agreement, article

14 説 *yakusetsu* summary

15 諾 *yakudaku suru* promise and be responsible for

B **紅** 3500/F1439 Gu. Ku. Kō red, crimson. *beni* red, crimson; rouge, lipstick. *kurenai* deep red, crimson. *momi* red silk cloth.

1 一点 *kōitten* one red flower in the foliage; sole woman in a men's party; a touch of color

4 毛 *kōmō* red hair

毛人 *kōmōjin* European, foreigner

5 生姜 *beni shōga* red pickled ginger

玉 *kōgyoku* ruby, carbuncle (gem)

玉髄 *kōgyokuzui, benigyokuzui* carnelian, sardius, sard

白 *kōhaku* red and white

白粉 *beni-oshiroi* rouge and powder

6 色 *kōshoku* red

血 *kōketsu* blood, red blood

灯 *kōtō* red light; red lantern

灯巷 *kōtō (no) chimata* red-light district

8 於 *kōo* maples

炎 *kōen* red blazes

宝玉 *kōhōgyoku* ruby

9 革 *benigawa* red leather

海 *Kōkai* Red Sea

茶 *kōcha* black tea

染 *benizo(me)* red cloth

10 唇 *kōshin* red lips

梅 *kōbai* red-blossom plum tree

涙 *kōrui* tears of blood; tears of a beautiful woman; dew on the flowers

粉 *beniko* powdered rouge. *kōfun* rouge and powder

脂 *kōshi* rouge

差指 *benisa(shi)yubi* ring finger, third finger

11 殻 *benigara* Indian red, red-ocher rouge, red oxide of iron

12 斑 *kōhan* red spots (on the skin)

裙 *kōkun* scarlet border; beautiful geisha

葉 *kōyō* fall colors. *momiji* maple; autumnal foliage; venison

葉狩 *momijiga(ri)* viewing autumn leaves

葉葉 *momijiba* scarlet maple leaves

13 楼 *kōrō* red-lacquered building; brothel

煙 *kōen* scarlet smoke

絹 *momi* red silk (cloth)

蓮 *guren* red lotus flower

蓮焔 *guren (no) honō* roaring flames

14 塵 *kōjin* clouds of dust; the dust of a busy city; this world's troubles

閨 *kōkei* bedroom of a beautiful woman

榴石 *kōryūseki* carbuncle (gem)

15 潮 *kōchō suru* blush, redden, be rosy; be flushed with drink; menstruate

熱 *kōnetsu* heating red hot

16 燄 *kōen* red blazes, solar prominences

縞瑪瑙 *beni shimamenō* sardonyx

17 鮭 *benizake* red salmon, sockeye

18 顔 *kōgan* rosy cheeks, ruddy face

28 鱒 *beni masu* red trout, blueback salmon, sockeye

4

紊 See 2071.

索 See 782.

級 3501/F1443 See 級 3496.

紘 3502/F1443 Kō large.

紗 3503/F1443 Sa. Sha gauze, gossamer.

紐 3504/F1441 Chū. Jū. *himo* string, cord, braid, lace, band, tape, strap, thong, ribbon; restrictions, conditions.

5 付 *himotsu(ki)* encumbrance, strings, conditions

7 状 *chūjō* string shape

9 革 *himokawa* strap, flat thong

10 帯 *jūtai, chūtai* band, bond, tie

13 解 *himoto(ku)* read, peruse

B **紡** 3505/F1445 Bō. *tsumu(gu)* spin, make yarn.

4 毛 *bōmō* carded wool

16 機 *bōki* spinning machine

錘 *bōsui, tsumu* spindle

17 績 *bōseki* spinning

績工 *bōsekikō* spinner

績工場 *bōseki kōjō* spinning mill

績業 *bōsekigyō* spinning industry

18 織 *bōshoku* spinning and weaving

織機 *bōshokuki* spinning and weaving machinery

B **紛** 3506/F1443 紛 Fun. *magi(reru), magu(reru)* be mistaken for, be confused with; go astray; be diverted from. *magi(rawasu), magi(rasu)* divert, distract; beguile; evade; conceal. *maga(u)* be mistaken for; become confused. *magi(rawashii)* misleading, ambiguous. *magi(remonai)* obvious, certain. *-magi(re) ni* in a fit of (anger); under the influence of (alcohol).

4 込 *magi(re)-ko(mu), magu(re)-ko(mu)* get lost with; disappear in (the crowd)
方無 *mago(u)katana(ki)* unmistakable, evi-
5 失 *funshitsu* loss ⌊dent, authentic
6 当 *ma-gu(re)ata(ri)* lucky hit
争 *funsō* dispute, quarrel, complications
7 乱 *funran* disorder, confusion, entanglement
8 易 *magi(re)yasu(i)* ambiguous, misleading
9 糾 *funkyū* complication, entanglement,
10 紛 *fumpun* confusedly, pell-mell ⌊confusion
12 然 *funzen* confusion, complications
13 飾 *funshoku*＝粉飾 3469.13
18 擾 *funjō* disorder, uproar, agitation, complications, trouble
20 議 *fungi* dissension, controversy, dispute

B **紋** 3507 / F1441 Mon crest; (textile) figures.

4 日 *mombi* holiday ⌈neyed, stereotyped
切形 *monki(ri)gata no* conventional, hack-
切型 *monki(ri)gata*＝word above
5 付 *montsu(ki)* crested kimono
6 羽二重 *mon habutae* figured habutae
7 形 *mongata* crest design
8 所 *mondokoro* crest
8 服 *mompuku* crested kimono
11 章 *monshō* crest; coat of arms
章学 *monshōgaku* heraldry
14 様 *mon-yō* crest pattern
15 標 *monjirushi* armorial bearings
17 縮緬 *mon chirimen* figured crepe
18 織 *mon-o(ri)* figured textiles

A **納** 3508 / F1441 **納** Nō. Tō. Na. *osa(meru)* obtain, reap; dedicate, consecrate; pay; supply; store; finish; collect; restore, replace; accept (a present); bury; gather; rally (troops); sheathe (the sword). *osa(maru)* be paid; be restored; stay (in the stomach); look composed; be contented; be satisfied; be settled. *osa(mari)* end, settlement, conclusion. *osa(me)* tax; the end.

2 入 *nōnyū* payment; delivery
入後 *nōnyūgo* after payment
4 戸 *nando* closet, back room, storeroom
戸色 *nando iro* sky blue, grayish blue
5 札 *nōsatsu* pilgrim's card (left at temples)
本 *nōhon* presentation copy; censor's copy
付 *nōfu* payment, delivery
付金 *nōfukin* contribution
6 返 *osa(mari)-kae(ru)* be satisfied with; be in one's element; be unmoved, be cool
会 *nōkai* the last meeting (of the period)
7 豆 *nattō* fermented soy beans
8 金 *nōkin* payment; money due; money paid
所 *nassho* tax office, temple office
杯 *nōhai* the last cup
受 *nōju* receipt, acceptance
采 *nōsai* betrothal gift
9 屋 *naya* shed, barn
品 *nōhin* delivery; delivered goods
10 家 *naya* shed, barn
骨 *nōkotsu* depositing the ashes (of the dead)
骨堂 *nōkotsudō* ossuary, crypt ⌈compliance
11 得 *nattoku* assent, agreement, consent,
涼 *nōryō* enjoying the cool of the evening
12 棺 *nōkan* placing in the coffin
期 *nōki* payment date, delivery date
税 *nōzei* tax payment
税者 *nōzeisha* taxpayer
税額 *nōzeigaku* amount of one's taxes

A **純** 3509 / F1442 Jun purity, innocence; net (profit). *jun na* pure, innocent, chaste, natural, genuine.

1 一 *jun-itsu* purity, genuineness, homogeneity, uniformity
4 心 *junshin* purity, sincerity
毛 *jummō* all-wool
化 *junka* purification
文学 *jumbungaku* pure literature
日本風 *jun-Nihonfū* pure Japanese style
分 *jumbun* fineness
分度 *jumbundo* fineness
5 白 *jumpaku* pure white
乎 *junko no* pure, sheer, unalloyed
正 *junsei na* pure, genuine
正科学 *junsei kagaku* pure science
6 朴 *jumboku* simplicity and honesty
血 *junketsu no* pure-bred, thorobred
血種 *junkesshu* pure breed
7 利 *junri* net profit
良 *junryō* pure, genuine
8 金 *junkin* pure gold, solid gold
忠 *junchū* unselfish loyalty
国産 *junkokusan* an all-Japanese product
所得 *jun shotoku* net income
9 度 *jundo* purity
美 *jumbi* unalloyed beauty
重量 *junjūryō* net weight
10 真 *junshin* purity, sincerity
粋 *junsui* purity, genuineness
粋主義 *junsui shugi* purism (in art)
益 *jun-eki* clear profit
益金 *jun-ekikin* clear profit
11 黒 *junkoku* jet black ⌈devotion
情 *junjō* pure heart; naïveté; self-sacrificing
理 *junri* pure reason, scientific principle

理論 *junriron* rationalism
12 然 *junzen(taru)* pure, sheer, veritable, absolute, perfect
13 損 *junson* complete loss
絹 *junken* pure silk
鉄 *juntetsu* malleable iron
14 種 *junshu* thorobred
綿 *jummen* all-cotton
銀 *jungin* pure silver, solid silver
15 潔 *junketsu* purity, integrity, innocence
潔教育 *junketsu kyōiku* sex-morality education

A **紙** 3510/F1443 SHI *kami* paper.

1 一重 *kami hitoe* tiny crack; something very thin; very slight difference
2 入 *kami-i(re)* purse, wallet
3 子 *kamiko* paper garment
上 *shijō de* on paper; by letter; in the newspaper or magazine
上投票 *shijō tōhyō* straw vote
4 片 *shihen* piece of paper
切 *kamiki(re)*, *kamigi(re)* piece of paper. *kamiki(ri)* paper knife; paper cutter
5 札 *kami fuda* tag, label
包 *kamizutsumi* paper package
芝居 *kami shibai* picture-story show
白粉 *kami oshiroi* face-powder paper
石盤 *kami sekiban* paper slate
石鹸 *kami sekken* soap paper
6 灯 *shitō* paper-enclosed light
7 折 *kamio(ri)* paper folding
花 *kamibana* paper flowers
8 函 *kamibako* carton
価 *shika* price of paper
表紙 *kamibyōshi* paper cover
9 面 *shimen* (newspaper) space; letter; newspaper
屋 *kamiya* paper store, paper mill
草 *kamigusa* papyrus
型 *shikei* stereotype
背 *shihai* back of the paper; (reading) between the lines
巻 *kamimaki* cigarette
巻煙草 *kamimaki tabako* cigarette
10 挾 *kamibasami* paper clip
紐 *kami himo* paper twine
差 *kamisashi* paper feeding (in printing)
屑 *kamikuzu* waste paper
屑拾 *kamikuzuhiro(i)* ragpicker
屑買 *kamikuzuka(i)* ragman
屑籠 *kamikuzu kago* wastebasket
11 魚 *shimi*, *shigyo* clothes moth, silverfish, bookworm
帳 *shichō* paper mosquito net
張 *kamiha(ri)* papering
捻 *koyori* twisted-paper string
袋 *kamibukuro*, *kambukuro* paper sack or bag
細工 *kamizaiku* making articles out of paper (by hand)
12 幅 *shifuku* paper width
絵 *kamie* picture drawn on paper
13 数 *shisū* number of pages
障子 *kami shōji*, *kami sōji* translucent paper door
鉄砲 *kamideppō* popgun
14 漉 *kamisu(ki)* papermaking
製 *kamisei* made of paper
鳶 *ikanobori*, *ika* (flying) kite
15 撚 *koyori* twisted-paper string
箱 *kamibako* carton
幣 *shihei* paper money
質 *shishitsu* quality of paper
器 *shiki* paper articles, paper container
16 縒 *koyori*, *kamiyori* twisted-paper string
18 雛 *kamibina* paper doll
19 縄 *kami nawa* paper string
24 鑢 *kami yasuri* sandpaper; emery paper

A **素** 3511/F1444 So principle; element. Su naked, uncovered, simple. *moto* (see under 元 275.0). *moto(yori)* from the beginning; of course.

2 人 *shirōto*, *shiroto* amateur; layman; novice; outsider; unskilled hand; decent woman
人女 *shirōto onna* a respectable (nonprofessional) woman
人下宿 *shirōto geshuku* lodging in a private home
人目 *shirōtome* untrained eye
人芝居 *shirōto shibai* amateur theatricals
人臭 *shirōtokusa(i)* amateurish, untrained
人劇 *shirōtogeki* amateur dramatics
4 手 *sude* empty hands, bare hands. *sude de* barehanded, unarmed, with naked fists
5 生 *sujō*=素性 (see below–8)
6 行 *sokō* conduct, behavior
因 *so-in* basic factor; predisposition
地 *sochi*, *soji* grain of wood; plain wood; foundation, groundwork
朴 *soboku* simplicity, artlessness
肌 *suhada* bare skin; stark naked
早 *subaya(i)* quick, agile
気無 *sokkena(i)* curt, blunt, brusque
7 見 *hiyaka(su)* only pretend to be buying
足 *suashi* bare feet
材 *sozai* raw materials; matter, material, subject matter
志 *soshi* original purpose
町人 *suchōnin* ordinary townsmen
8 姓 *sujō*=next word
性 *sujō* birth, parentage, lineage; identity, personal history
的 *suteki* grand, cute, fine, big, splendid, remarkable, superb
服 *sofuku* plain white clothes; mourning clothes
直 *sunao na* gentle, meek; obedient; tame; honest, frank
知顔 *soshi(ranu) kao* innocent look

⁹面 *shirafu* sobriety, soberness. *sumen* sober face, unmasked face ⌈"block" (head)
首 *sokubi, so(k)kubi* one's head, one's
通 *sudō(ri)* passing thru without stopping
透 *sudō(shi) no* transparent; plain glass (spectacles)
封 *sohō* rich family; rich man
封家 *sohōka* rich family; rich man
¹⁰振 *sobu(ri)* manner, behavior, attitude, bearing, look ⌈retainer
浪人 *surōnin* (derogatory word for) lordless
破抜 *suppanu(ku)* expose, disclose
¹¹描 *sobyō, suga(ki)* rough sketch
瓶 *sugame* unglazed pottery
祭 *sosai* cereal offering
乾 *subo(shi)* drying in the shade
粒子 *soryūshi* the tiniest particle of matter, elemental (subatomic) particles
¹²晴 *suba(rashii)* splendid, magnificent, glorious, excellent, superb, remarkable
焼 *suya(ki)* unglazed pottery
寒貧 *sukampin* poverty; pauper; beggar
¹³絹 *soken* coarse silk
裸 *suhadaka* nudity
跣 *suhadashi* going barefooted
数 *sosū* indivisible numbers
意 *so-i* original purpose
¹⁴語 *sugata(ri)* recital without samisen accompaniment
読 *sodoku* reading without getting the
¹⁵膚 *suhada* stark naked ⌊meaning
敵 *suteki*＝素的 (see above–8)
養 *soyō* elementary attainments
質 *soshitsu* temperament, character, nature; constitution; quality; predisposition
¹⁶懐 *sokai* cherished desire
樸 *soboku* simplicity, artlessness
餐 *sosan* a sinecure
¹⁸顔 *sugao* unpainted face; sober face
²⁰麺 *sōmen* vermicelli

5

累 See 3006.

紲 3512/F1449 SETSU. *kizuna* fetters, yoke, encumbrance.

紬 3513/F1447 CHŪ. *tsumugi* pongee.
⁶糸 *tsumugi ito* silk thread from waste cocoons

紮 3514/F1447 SATSU. *kara(geru)* tie up, pack up; tuck up.
⁸上 *kara(ge)-a(geru)* tie tightly, bind up
⁵付 *kara(ge)-tsu(keru)* tie tightly, bind up

絆 3515/F1452 HAN. *hoda(su)* tie. *kizuna* bonds, fetters; yoke; encumbrance; ties.
¹²創膏 *bansōkō* adhesive plaster
²¹纏 *hanten*＝半纏 132.21

紹 3516/F1449 B SHŌ inherit; help.
⁴介 *shōkai* introduction, presentation
介状 *shōkaijō* letter of introduction
介者 *shōkaisha* introducer ⌈one else
⁷述 *shōjutsu* a further explanation by some-

紺 3517/F1450 B KON dark blue, navy blue.
⁶地 *konji* dark blue ground (cloth)
⁸青 *konjō* Prussian blue, deep blue
⁹屋 *kon-ya, kōya* dyer
¹⁴碧 *kompeki* dark blue

紳 3518/F1449 B SHIN good belt; gentleman.
³士 *shinshi* gentleman
士的 *shinshiteki* gentlemanly
士服 *shinshifuku* suits for gentlemen
士協定 *shinshi kyōtei* gentlemen's agreement
士録 *shinshiroku* who's who, directory
¹¹商 *shinshō* merchant prince

絃 3519/F1451 GEN string, chord. *ito* string (on a violin); samisen music.
⁷声 *gensei* sound of the strings
¹³楽 *gengaku* string music
楽器 *gengakki* stringed instruments
¹⁴歌 *genka* singing accompanied by stringed instruments
管 *genkan* wind and stringed instruments
¹⁵線 *gensen* catgut

組 3520/F1451 A So. *kumi(suru)* (see under 与 6.0). *ku(mu)* braid, plait; construct; assemble; cross (legs); fold (arms); unite with, co-operate with; grapple with. *kumi* class, party, group; set; pack (of cards); suit; assortment; typesetting. *-gumi* group, gang; company.
²入 *ku(mi)-i(reru)* include, insert, enroll
³子 *ku(mi)ko* member of a squad (of firemen, etc.)
下 *kumishita* subordinates; privates
上 *ku(mi)-a(geru)* compose; build up. *ku(mi)-a(garu)* be composed (in printing); be framed (in construction)
⁴戸 *ku(mi)do* lattice door
方 *ku(mi)kata* way of constructing, etc.

6 竹米 5【糸】缶网四羊羽老耂而耒耳聿肉月臣自至臼舌舛舟艮色艸艹虍虫血行衣衤西

込 *ku(mi)-ko(mu)* cut in (in printing); insert, include
分 *kumiwa(ke)* sorting, separation into groups
5 付 *ku(mi)-tsu(ku)* grapple with, clinch, pounce on
打 *kumiu(chi)* grapple, scrimmage
立 *ku(mi)-ta(teru)* construct, erect, frame, assemble. *kumita(te)* construction, framework, organization, composition, assembly, erection
立工 *kumita(te)kō* assembler, fitter
立工場 *kumita(te) kōjō* assembly plant
立式 *kumitateshiki* prefabricated, collapsible, convertible (car)
立住宅 *kumita(te) jūtaku* prefabricated house, Quonset house
6 糸 *ku(mi)-ito* braid
成 *sosei* composition, formation, constitution
曲 *kumikyoku* suite, selection (in music)
伏 *ku(mi)-fu(seru)* get or hold (a person) down
会 *kumikai* class meeting, group meeting
合 *ku(mi)-a(u)* form a partnership; grapple with; be pitted against. *ku(mi)-a(wasu)*, *ku(mi)-a(waseru)* combine; intertwine; dovetail. *kumiai* association, league, fraternity, union, partnership, guild, trust, cartel, syndicate. *ku(mi)a(i)* grapple, scrimmage. *kumiawa(se)* combination; assortment; braid; matching, pairing; schedule
合工場 *kumiai kōjō* union shop
合主義 *kumiai shugi* unionism
合役員 *kumiai yakuin* union official
合法 *kumiawa(se)hō* matching test
合員 *kumiai-in* partner, union member
合教会 *Kumiai Kyōkai* Congregational Church
合教会制 *kumiai-kyōkaisei* congregationalism
合組織 *kumiai soshiki* union organization
合組織化 *kumiai soshikika* unionization
合組織者 *kumiai soshikisha* union organizer
合費 *kumiaihi* union dues
8 長 *kumichō* group leader, foreman
版 *ku(mi)han* typesetting, composition
物 *ku(mi)mono* plaiting, braiding, knitting
直 *ku(mi)-nao(su)* recompose; rebraid; reknit
9 重 *ku(mi)jū* tier of boxes
10 紐 *ku(mi)himo* braid
討 *kumiu(chi)* grappling; scrimmage
11 違 *ku(mi)-chiga(eru)* make a mistake in construction
掛 *ku(mi)ka(ke)* partly completed
12 換 *ku(mi)-ka(eru)* rearrange
替 *ku(mi)-ka(eru)* rearrange
14 閣 *sokaku* formation of a cabinet
15 敷 *ku(mi)-shi(ku)* get or hold (a person) down
16 頭 *kumigashira* group leader, foreman
18 織 *soshiki* organization, inauguration, composition, structure, set-up; anatomy, texture, tissue, organism; system
織立 *soshikida(tta)* systematic
織化 *soshikika* systematization, organization
織労働者 *soshiki rōdōsha* organized labor
織的 *soshikiteki* systematic, methodical
織学 *soshikigaku* histology
織神学 *soshiki shingaku* systematic theology
19 縄 *ku(mi)nawa* plaited rope

終 3521 F1450 終

A SHŪ end. *owa(ru)* vi end, terminate, adjourn, be over; die. *vt* end, finish, complete. *o(eru)* *vt* end, finish, complete. *owa(ri)* end, conclusion, expiration. *tsui ni* finally, after all.

2 了 *shūryō* end, termination, signing off, expiration, conclusion, completion
了後 *shūryōgo* after the termination of
3 夕 *shūseki* all night
4 日 *shūjitsu, hinemosu, himosugara, hisugara* all day
止 *shūshi* termination, cessation, stop
止符 *shūshifu* full stop, period, end
5 生 *shūsei* all thru life; a lifetime
世 *shūsei* all thru life, lifelong
刊 *shūkan* ceasing publication
刊号 *shūkangō* final issue
末 *shūmatsu* end, conclusion, termination, settlement, result
末時代 *shūmatsu jidai* last days
末論 *shūmatsuron* eschatology
末観 *shūmatsukan* eschatology
6 曲 *shūkyoku* the final musical number
年 *shūnen* the whole year; the whole life
列車 *shūressha* last train
7 車 *shūsha* the last streetcar for the day
尾 *shūbi* end
局 *shūkyoku* end, conclusion, finale
決 *shūketsu* settlement
身 *shūshin* the whole life
身刑 *shūshinkei* life sentence
身年金 *shūshin nenkin* life annuity
身会員 *shūshin kai-in* life membership
身官 *shūshinkan* life appointment; official appointed for life
身保険 *shūshin hoken* life insurance
身恩給 *shūshin onkyū* life pension
身禁錮 *shūshin kinko* life imprisonment
身懲役 *shūshin chōeki* life imprisonment
8 油 *shūyu* extreme unction
夜 *shūya, yomosugara* all night
始 *shūshi* beginning and end; from first to last; always
始一貫 *shūshi-ikkan shita* constant, consistent

9 点 *shūten* terminus
10 航 *shūkō* last voyage
宵 *shūshō* all night
息 *shūsoku* cessation, eradication
11 焉 *shūen* last moments, death
雪 *shūsetsu* the last snow
12 極 *shūkyoku* finality, extremity
結 *shūketsu* conclusion, termination
期 *shūki* expiration, termination
着駅 *shūchaku eki* terminal station
13 幕 *shūmaku* end, close, curtain; closing scene, closing drama
電 *shūden* the last streetcar for the day
電車 *shūdensha* the last streetcar for the day
業 *shūgyō* close of work, end of a school term
業式 *shūgyōshiki* closing ceremony
戦 *shūsen* end of the war, termination of hostilities
戦処理費 *shūsen shorihi* occupation expenses
戦直後 *shūsen chokugo* right after the war
戦後 *shūsengo* after the war
戦前後 *shūsen zengo* before and after the war
14 演 *shūen* end of a performance
熄 *shūsoku* cessation, eradication
端 *shūtan* terminus, terminal
駅 *shūeki* terminal station
15 審 *shūshin* final trial
盤 *shūban* nearing the end of the (chess or checker) game
盤戦 *shūbansen* the ending of a campaign
17 霜 *shūsō* the last frost
19 禱 *shūtō* closing prayer, benediction

A 細 3522 / F1448 SAI. *hoso(ru)* get thin; taper off. *hoso(meru)* make narrow. *hoso(i)* fine (line); thin (voice); slender; narrow (trousers); *koma(ka) na, koma(kai), koma(i)* small, fine; detailed; minor, trifling; elaborate, delicate; stingy, frugal; small (change). *koma(kashii)* very small. *koma(yakana)* warm, tender, close; minute; deep (color). *(ka)boso(i)* slender, slim, feeble, delicate. *sasa(yakana)* small. *isasa* small. *sazare-* small. *sasa-* small; a few.

3 小 *saishō* the finest, the minute, the infinitesimal. *sasayaka na* small; poor, humble
大 *saidai* great and small
大洩 *saidai-mo(rasazu)* absolutely everything
工 *saiku* work, craftsmanship, ware; artifice, device, tactics, trick
工人 *saikunin* craftsman, artisan, workman
工物 *saikumono* handiwork
4 心 *saishin* carefulness, discretion
手 *hosode no* thin, fine
毛 *saimō* cilia
片 *saihen* fragment, piece, splinter
孔 *saikō* small cavity; pore; small hole
切 *komagi(re)* small pieces of cloth; chopped meat. *komagi(ri)* chopped meat
分 *saibun suru* divide into small parts
5 目 *saimoku* details, specifications, items.
hosome narrow eyes; narrow openings
石 *sazare-ishi* pebble, gravel
末 *saimatsu* a trifle; powder
民 *saimin* the poor, paupers
民窟 *saiminkutsu* slums
6 糸 *hoso-ito* fine thread, fine-yarn count
行 *saikō* small acts
字 *saiji* small characters, small type
7 見 *saiken* close inspection
身 *hosomi* narrow blade
別 *saibetsu* itemization, subdivision
声 *hosogoe* weak voice
君 *saikun* wife; my wife
8 長 *hosonaga(i)* slender, lanky, linear, long and narrow
雨 *saiu* misty rain, drizzle
波 *sasanami, sazanami* ripples
事 *saiji* minor affair; trifle; details
9 面 *hoso-omote* slender face
革 *hosokawa* shoe welt
首 *hosokubi* slender neck
則 *saisoku* by-laws, detailed rules
胞 *saibō, saihō* cell
胞学 *saibōgaku* cytology
10 流 *sairyū* brook, rivulet
記 *saiki* minute description, full account
部 *saibu* details
書 *hosoga(ki), saisho* small writing, fine writing
帯 *hoso-obi* undersash, girdle
11 道 *hosomichi* path, narrow lane
粒 *sairyū* granule, infinitesimal grains
細 *komagoma* in pieces, in detail. *hosoboso(shita)* slender, delicate, scanty (living). *sasayaka na* small; poor, humble
密 *saimitsu* minuteness
雪 *sasameyuki* light snow
菌 *saikin* germ, microbe, bacteria, bacillus
菌学 *saikingaku* bacteriology, microbiology
菌戦 *saikinsen* germ warfare
菌爆弾 *saikim-bakudan* germ bomb
12 腕 *hoso-ude* thin arm; slender means; poor ability
評 *saihyō* detailed criticism
筆 *saihitsu* fine brush; writing fine
13 微 *saibi* minuteness
腰 *saiyō, hosogoshi* slender hips, slender waist
隙 *saigeki* slit
節 *saisetsu* minor details
14 塵 *saijin* dust in the atmosphere
説 *saisetsu* detailed explanation
15 瑾 *saikin* small defect
論 *sairon* full treatment, detailed explanation
16 濁 *sasanigo(ri)* somewhat muddy
緻 *saichi na* minute, detailed

[17]螺 *kisago, kishago* periwinkle
謹 *saikin* small defect

A **経** 3523/F1460 **經** KEI longitude; sutra; warp. KYŌ sutra. *he(ru)* pass, elapse; pass thru; experience. *ta(tsu)* pass, elapse, expire. *he(te)* thru, by way of, via. *tate* length; height; warp. *ta(teba)* (a few days) hence. *tate ito* warp (in weaving).

[3]上 *he-aga(ru)* rise to fame
口的 *keikōteki* oral (medication)
口感染 *keikō kansen* infection by the oral route
[4]文 *kyōmon* sutras
木 *kyōgi* thin sheets of wood
水 *keisui* menstruation
[5]由 *keiyu* via. *keiyu suru* go by way of
史 *keishi* ethics and history books
札 *kyōfuda* phylactery
外典 *Keigaiten* the Apocrypha
外聖書 *Keigai Seisho* the Apocrypha
世 *keisei* government, administration; statesmanship, statecraft
世家 *keiseika* statesman, administrator
[6]糸 *tate ito* warp
血 *keiketsu* menstrual flow
伝 *keiden* scriptures and commentary
[7]声 *kyōgoe* sutra-reading voice
[8]国 *keikoku* administration, government
帙 *kyōchitsu* sutra covers
函 *kyōkan* sutra box
学 *Keigaku* Confucianism
典 *kyōten, keiten* sacred books; sutras; the Bible; the canon; the Scriptures
典外 *keitengai* the Apochrypha
[9]度 *keido* longitude
廻 *he-megu(ru)* travel about, wander about
界 *keikai* boundary, border
[10]差 *keisa* longitudinal difference
書 *keisho* Chinese classics
師 *kyōji* paperhanger
師屋 *kyōjiya* paperhanger; philanderer
[11]過 *keika* progress, course, development; interim; lapse; expiration; transit (of a moon)
略 *keiryaku* governing (a country)
堂 *kyōdō* sutra library
帷子 *kyōkatabira* shroud, grave clothes
常 *keijō* ordinary, current (budget)
常費 *keijōhi* current expenditures
理 *keiri* management, accounting
理士 *keirishi* public accountant
理学 *keirigaku* accounting
理学校 *keiri gakkō* paymasters' school
済 *keizai* economy; economics; finance; thrift
済人 *keizaijin* financial expert
済力 *keizairyoku* economic strength
済上 *keizaijō* economically, financially
済状態 *keizai jōtai* financial condition
済的 *keizaiteki* financial; economic; economical
済学 *keizaigaku* economics; political economy
済面 *keizaimen* economic situation
済界 *keizaikai* financial circles
済封鎖 *keizai fūsa* economic blockade
済家 *keizaika* economist, thrifty person
済違犯 *keizai ihan* violation of commercial laws (price control, etc.)
済博 *Keizaihaku* Doctor of Economics
済圏 *keizaiken* international economic block
済戦 *keizaisen* economic war
済網 *keizaimō* unified economic area
済欄 *keizairan* financial column
[12]費 *keihi* expenses, cost, outlay
営 *keiei* construction; management, operation; development; project
営法 *keieihō* management
営学 *keieigaku* business management
営者 *keieisha* operator, management
営参加 *keiei sanka* management participation
営経済学 *keiei keizaigaku* business economics
営費 *keieihi* operating expenses
営権 *keieiken* rights of management
営難 *keieinan* financial difficulties
[13]路 *keiro* the road one has traveled; channel; circumstances
[14]綸 *keirin* government, administration, statesmanship
読 *kyōyo(mi)* reading sutras; Buddhist priest
歴 *keireki* personal history, career; pilgrimage
歴公報 *keireki kōhō* bulletin of candidates' careers
歴放送 *keireki hōsō* broadcast of candidates' careers
[15]線 *keisen* meridian
緯 *kei-i* longitude and latitude, position; warp and woof; particulars. *ikisatsu* complication, troubles. *tateyoko*＝縦横 3597.15
緯儀 *kei-igi* theodolite; altazimuth
[18]櫃 *kyōbitsu* large sutra box
験 *keiken* experience
験上 *keikenjō* from experience
験主義 *keiken shugi* empiricism
験死亡表 *keiken shibōhyō* mortality tables
験的 *keikenteki* experiential, empirical
験者 *keikensha* experienced person
験表 *keikenkyō* mortality tables
験学派 *keikengakuha* empiric school
験科学 *keiken kagaku* experimental science
験家 *keikenka* experienced person
験談 *keikendan* personal-experience narrative
験論 *keikenron* empiricism

綵 3524 / F1458 See 糸 3492.

絏 3525 / F1452 SETSU tie.

絖 3526 / F1455 KŌ. *nume* white satin.

絣 3527 / F1456 絣 HŌ. *kasuri* splashed pattern; cloth with a splashed pattern.

絮 3528 / F1457 JO cotton.

14説 *josetsu* detailed explanation

絓 3529 / F1453 KAI catch on something.

6糸 *shike ito, suga ito* raw silk thread

絢 3530 / F1456 KEN kimono design.

21爛 *kenran(taru)* dazzling, gorgeous, flowery, gaudy

絎 3531 / F1452 KŌ. *ku(keru)* to blindstitch.

15縫 *kukenu(i)* blind stitch

絨 3532 / F1457 JŪ wool cloth.

4毛 *jūmō* wool
12毯 *jūtan* rug, carpet
15緞 *jūtan* rug, carpet

B **絡** 3533 / F1456 RAKU. *kara(mu) vi* coil around, get twisted; stick to; pick a quarrel. *kara(meru) vt* twine around. *shigara(mu), kara(maru)* twist around; get caught in; be urged on by. *mato(u)* wear; wind around.

5付 *kara(mi)-tsu(ku)* twist about, entwine; cling to; be caught in
6合 *kara(mi)-a(u)* get or be intertwined, be in gear with
19繹 *rakueki* ceaseless traffic
19繰 *karaku(ri)* mechanism, contrivance, scheme, makeshift
繰人形 *karaku(ri) ningyō* marionette, puppet

B **紫** 3534 / F1446 SHI purple, violet. *murasaki* purple, violet; soy.

4水晶 *murasaki suishō, murasakizuishō* amethyst
5布 *murasaki nuno* (ancient) purple cloth
外線 *shigaisen* ultraviolet rays
石 *shiseki* an inkstone
石英 *shisekiei, murasaki sekiei* amethyst
7花地丁 *sumire* the violet
8金 *shikin* gold-copper alloy
11紺 *shikon* purplish blue
陽花 *ajisai* hydrangea
12斑病 *shihambyō* purpura
雲 *shiun* purple congratulatory clouds
雲英 *rengesō* a purple vetch
13煙 *shien* tobacco smoke; purple smoke; purple haze
電 *shiden* flashes of lightning
16壇 *shitan* red sandalwood, rosewood
19蘇 *shiso* beefsteak plant
蘇湯 *shisoyu* beefsteak-plant tea

B **絞** 3535 / F1456 KŌ. *shi(meru)* strangle, constrict, wring. *shibo(ru)* wring, squeeze, press, extract; milk; close tight; extort; scold. *shibo(ri)* dapple, white-spotted cloth; stop, diaphragm.

8上 *shibo(ri)-a(geru)* gather up (a curtain); squeeze (money) out of
5弁 *shibo(ri)ben* throttle valve
出 *shibo(ri)-da(su)* press out, squeeze out, drain out. *shibo(ri)da(shi)* (tooth-paste) tube
6刑 *kōkei* death by hanging
7扼 *kōyaku* strangulation
9染 *shibo(ri)zo(me)* a dyeing process where the designs are formed by tightly tying small places here and there
首 *kōshu* hanging, strangulation
首台 *kōshudai* gallows
首刑 *kōshukei* death by hanging
10殺 *kōsatsu* hanging, strangulation. *shi(me)-koro(su)* strangle to death
13罪 *kōzai* hanging (criminals)
15盤 *kōban* capstan

A **統** 3536 / F1457 TŌ relationship; lineage; beginning. *su(beru)* control, supervise, govern. *sube(te)* (see under 凡 654.0).

1一 *tōitsu* unity, unification, consolidation, uniformity, coherence; standardization; rule, dominance; concentration
一力 *tōitsuryoku* unifying power
一性 *tōitsusei* unity, uniformity
一的 *tōitsuteki* unified
一国 *tōitsukoku* a unified country
一戦線 *tōitsu sensen* united front
6合 *tōgō suru* integrate, combine, unify
合参謀本部 *Tōgō Sambō Hombu* Joint Chiefs of Staff
8治 *tōchi suru, tōji suru, su(be)-osa(meru)* reign over, rule
治者 *tōchisha, tōjisha* ruler, sovereign
治権 *tōchiken* sovereignty
制 *tōsei* control, regulation

制下 *tōseika* under the control of
制品 *tōseihin* controlled goods
9 括 *tōkatsu* generalization. *su(be)kuku(ru)* generalize
帥 *tōsui* high command
帥部 *tōsuibu* the high command
帥権 *tōsuiken* authority of the supreme command
計 *tōkei* statistics
計分析 *tōkei bunseki* statistical analysis
計年鑑 *tōkei nenkan* statistical yearbook
計的 *tōkeiteki* statistical
計学 *tōkeigaku* science of statistics
計表 *tōkeihyō* statistical table, returns
計家 *tōkeika* statistician
計報告 *tōkei hōkoku* statistical report
計調査 *tōkei chōsa* statistical research
11 率 *tōsotsu suru* command, lead
率者 *tōsotsusha* commander, leader
12 御 *tōgyo suru* rule, control, administer
覚 *tōkaku* apperception
14 領 *tōryō* chief, manager, dictator
監 *tōkan* supervision; commander; resident-general
17 轄 *tōkatsu* control
轄者 *tōkatsusha* the one in charge

A **絵** 3537 F1483 **繪** KAI. *e* picture, drawing, painting, sketch, illustration, cut, print.

2 入 *e-i(ri)* illustrated, pictorial
4 心 *egokoro* artistic taste
手本 *edehon* illustrated copybook
文字 *emoji* picture writing, hieroglyphics
双紙 *ezōshi* picture book
5 凧 *edako* picture kite
札 *efuda* picture card
本 *ehon* picture book
6 羽 *eba* figured haori coat
羽羽織 *eba haori* figured haori coat
羽織 *ebaori* figured haori coat
7 図 *ezu* drawing, illustration, diagram, plan, design, sketch, map, chart
図引 *ezuhi(ki)* drawing; one who draws
図面 *ezumen* plan, design
8 取 *edo(ru)* paint, color, trace
具 *e(no)gu* paints, colors, oils, pigments
事 *kaiji* picture, painting
刷毛 *ebake* artist's brush
空言 *esoragoto* fabrication, unreality
物語 *emonogatari* illustrated book
画 *kaiga* picture, painting, drawing
画界 *kaigakai* painting circles
9 柄 *egara* pattern, design
姿 *esugata* portrait, likeness, picture
看板 *ekamban* billboard
草紙 *ezōshi* picture book
巻 *emaki* picture scroll
巻物 *emakimono* picture scroll
10 師 *eshi* painter, artist
捜 *esaga(shi)* picture puzzle
書 *eka(ki)* painter, artist
馬 *e-uma, ema* votive picture (originally of a horse)
馬屋 *emaya* votive-picture dealer
馬堂 *emadō* votive-picture gallery
馬殿 *emaden* votive-picture hall
11 探 *esaga(shi)* picture puzzle
描 *eka(ki)* painter, artist; painting
12 詞 *ekotoba* words explaining a picture
筆 *efude* paintbrush
葉書 *ehagaki* picture postcard
13 絹 *eginu* silk canvas, drawing silk
解 *eto(ki)* explanation of a picture, illustration
話 *ebanashi* picture story
14 像 *ezō* portrait, likeness, picture
15 踏 *efu(mi), ebu(mi)* image trampling, trampling on the image of Christ
16 謎 *enazo* picture puzzle

A **給** 3538 F1456 KYŪ wage; gift; wage grade. *kyū(suru)* allow, grant, supply; favor. *tama(waru), tama(u), tamo(u)* deign to, grant, give, bestow on, honor with.

3 与 *kyūyo* grant, ration; compensation, allowance
与水準 *kyūyo suijun* wage level
与体系 *kyūyo taikei* wage system
与金 *kyūyokin* allowance, grant, dole
4 分 *kyūbun* salary
水 *kyūsui* water supply, water distribution
水自動車 *kyūsui jidōsha* water wagon
水車 *kyūsuisha* water wagon
水所 *kyūsuijo* water station
水栓 *kyūsuisen* hydrant, faucet
水塔 *kyūsuitō* water tower, tank
水量 *kyūsuiryō* amount of water supplied
水管 *kyūsuikan* water pipe
5 付 *kyūfu suru* present, pay, deliver, furnish
仕 *kyūji* office boy or girl, page, bellhop; waiter, waitress; table service
仕人 *kyūjinin* waiter, waitress
仕役 *kyūjiyaku* butler, cupbearer
6 血者 *kyūketsusha* blood donor
気管 *kyūkikan* air duct
7 助 *kyūjo* charity, alms
8 金 *kyūkin* wages
所 *kyūsho* granted land, territory
油 *kyūyu* supply of oil; refueling
油所 *kyūyusho* filling station
油船 *kyūyusen* tanker
9 食 *kyūshoku* providing with food, supplying (school) lunches
食施設 *kyūshoku shisetsu* cooking facilities
炭 *kyūtan* supply of coal
炭所 *kyūtanjo* coaling station
炭船 *kyūtansen* coal ship, collier

10料 *kyūryō* wages, salary, payroll
料日 *kyūryōbi* pay day
料支払簿 *kyūryō shiharaibo* pay roll
料生活者 *kyūryō seikatsusha* salary man
料取 *kyūryōto(ri)* salaried man
料袋 *kyūryōbukuro* pay envelope
12費 *kyūhi* scholarship, student support
費生 *kyūhisei* scholarship student
13源 *kyūgen* source of supply
電 *kyūden* supply of electricity
15養 *kyūyō* rations, provisions, allowance
養係 *kyūyōgakari* quartermaster

A **絶** 3539/F1453 **絕** ZETSU. *zes(suru)* be beyond (words). *ta(tsu)* sever, cut off; shut off, interrupt; abstain from; eradicate; suppress. *ta(eru)* become extinct, die out, discontinue, end, fail, peter out. *ta(yasu)* exterminate, eradicate, root out; run out of (stock); let (a fire) go out. *ta(ete)* (with neg.) never. *ta(ezaru)* unceasing, continual. *ta(ezu)* constantly, unceasingly; always.

2入 *ta(e)-i(ru)* expire, die
3大 *zetsudai na* tremendous, immense
4水 *zessui* abstaining from water
5句 *zekku suru* forget one's lines. *zekku* a style of Chinese poetry
世 *zessei* peerless, unrivaled, unequaled
6叫 *zekkyō* scream, exclamation
好 *zekkō no* splendid, grand, first-rate
好機 *zekkōki* best chance
交 *zekkō* breaking off friendship; breaking off diplomatic relations
交状 *zekkōjō* letter breaking off relations
7妙 *zetsumyō no* most admirable, exquisite, superb ⌈unconditional
対 *zettai no* absolute, positive, categorical,
対化 *zettaika suru* make absolute
対反対 *zettai hantai* positive opposition
対多数 *zettai tasū* absolute majority
対安静 *zettai ansei* complete rest
対的 *zettaiteki* absolute, positive, imperative
対性 *zettaisei* absoluteness ⌊tive
対者 *zettaisha* God; the Absolute ⌈ship
対所有権 *zettai shoyūken* absolute owner-
対服従 *zettai fukujū* absolute obedience
対音高 *zettai onkō* absolute pitch
対音感 *zettai onkan* absolute pitch
対過半数 *zettai kahansū* absolute majority
対量 *zettairyō* absolute minimum quantity (required) ⌈last extremity
対絶命 *zettai-zetsumei* desperate situation,
対温度 *zettai ondo* absolute temperature
対零度 *zettai reido* absolute zero
対禁酒 *zettai kinshu* total abstinence
対権 *zettaiken* absolute authoriy
対権力 *zettai kenryoku* absolute authority
対優位 *zettai yūi* absolute advantage
8佳 *zekka no* superb ⌈roads
所 *zessho* steepness and impassability of
命 *zetsumei* death
果 *ta(e)-ha(teru)* be extinguished, be exterminated, die out
東 *Zettō* Far East ⌊terminated, die out
版 *zeppan* out of print
版書 *zeppansho* a book that is out of print
9後 *zetsugo* no precedent involved
海 *zekkai* distant seas
品 *zeppin* rare article, masterpiece
美 *zetsubi* exquisiteness, matchless beauty
食 *zesshoku* fasting
食療法 *zesshoku ryōhō* fast treatment
10倫 *zetsurin* excellence, superiority
倒 *zettō suru* be convulsed with laughter
島 *zettō* lonely island
家 *zekke* extinct family
息 *zessoku suru* expire, die
11唱 *zesshō* fine poem; excellent song
頂 *zetchō* summit, peak, climax, acme,
望 *zetsubō* hopelessness, despair ⌊zenith
望的 *zetsubōteki* hopeless, desperate
12絶 *ta(e)da(e)* faint, almost exhausted
勝 *zesshō* fine scenery
景 *zekkei* superb view
筆 *zeppitsu* one's last literary work
無 *zetsumu* nothing, naught, nil
間 *ta(e)ma* interval, intermission, pause; break, gap
間無 *ta(e)mana(ku)* continually, unceasingly
13滅 *ta(e)-horo(bosu)* quench, put out. *zetsumetsu* eradication, extermination
15賛 *zessan* great praise
縁 *zetsuen* insulation; isolation; breaking off relations; dissociating oneself from
縁体 *zetsuentai* insulator, nonconductor
縁線 *zetsuensen* insulated wire
縁器 *zetsuenki* insulator
16壁 *zeppeki* precipice, cliff, bluff
22讃 *zessan* great praise

A **結** 3540/F1452 KETSU. *musu(bu)* tie, bind; tie a knot; make (contracts, treaties, and friendships); join; finish, wind up; unite with; organize. *musu(boreru)* = *motsu(reru)* 縺 3592.0. *yu(u)*, *i(u)* do up (the hair); make (a braided fence). *iwa(eru)*, *yuwa(eru)* bind, fasten, tie, tie up. *su(ku)* make (a net). *musu(bi)* knot; end, conclusion.

2了 *ketsuryō suru* end, terminate
3上 *yu(i)-a(geru)* do up (the hair)
4文 *ketsubun* epilogue, conclusion, complimentary closing
手 *sukite* net maker ⌊mentary closing

6 竹米 7[糸]缶网四羊羽老耂而耒耳聿肉月臣自至臼舌舛舟艮色艸艹虍虫血行衣ネ西

方 *yu(i)kata* hair style. *musu(bi)kata* hair style; way of tying
5目 *musu(bi)me, shiba(ri)me* knot
石 *kesseki* calculus, stones (in the biliary or urinary tracts) ⌈of a poem
句 *kekku* conclusion; after all; the last line
付 *musu(bi)-tsu(keru) vt* tie up, join together, link together. *musu(bi)-tsu(ku) vi* join with, ally with
氷 *keppyō* freezing; frost ⌈settlement, result
末 *ketsumatsu* end, conclusion, termination,
6成 *kessei* formation, organization
托 *kettaku* collusion, complicity, conspiracy
肌帯 *yuwada-obi* maternity belt
合 *ketsugō suru, musu(bi)-a(waseru)* tie together, unite, combine. *musu(bi)-a(u)* unite with, cleave to. *ketsugō* union, fusion, cohesion, joint, coupling, link
合体 *ketsugōtai* a united body
7尾 *ketsubi* end, conclusion
局 *kekkyoku* after all, in conclusion
社 *kessha* association, society
束 *kessoku* union, unity
8実 *ketsujitsu* fruit bearing; success
果 *kekka* consequences, result, effect
9姻 *ketsuin* becoming relatives
神 *Musu(bi) (no) Kami* Cupid
約 *ketsuyaku* making a promise
巻 *kekkan* the last volume (of a sutra)
10託 *kettaku* conspiracy, collusion, complicity
党 *kettō* formation of a party
納 *yuinō* engagement present
納金 *yuinōkin* engagement gift of money
核 *kekkaku* tubercule; tuberculosis
核菌 *kekkakukin* tuberculosis germ
核療養所 *kekkaku ryōyōjo* tuberculosis
11紮 *kessatsu* ligature ⌊sanitorium
婚 *kekkon* marriage
婚生活 *kekkon seikatsu* married life
婚行進曲 *kekkon kōshinkyoku* wedding
婚式 *kekkonshiki* wedding ⌊march
婚式場 *kekkon shikijō* wedding parlor
婚届 *kekkon todoke* marriage registration
婚披露 *kekkon hirō* wedding reception
婚相手 *kekkon (no) aite* person one is to marry ⌈agency
婚相談所 *kekkon sōdanjo* matrimonial
婚指環 *kekkon yubiwa* wedding ring
婚記念日 *kekkon kinembi* wedding anni-
婚期 *kekkonki* marriageable age ⌊versary
婚媒介人 *kekkon baikainin* matchmaker
婚媒介所 *kekkon baikaijo* matrimonial
婚詐欺 *kekkon sagi* fake marriage ⌊agency
婚観 *kekkonkan* ideas of marriage
12着 *ketchaku* conclusion, settlement ⌈shifts
番 *ketsuban* determining the order of work

集 *kesshū* concentration; regimentation; the editing of Gautama's works by his disciples
晶 *kesshō* crystal; crystallization
晶体 *kesshōtai* crystal
晶学 *kesshōgaku* crystallography
13滞 *kettai* the rest between heartbeats
腸 *ketchō* the colon
解 *ketsuge* settlement of accounts
節 *kessetsu* knot; tubercle; nodule
盟 *ketsumei* pledging
14語 *ketsugo* conclusion
髪 *keppatsu* hairdressing; hairdo
構 *kekkō* structure; architecture; set-up; quite sufficient; very well; fairly well. *kekkō na* splendid, excellent
構人 *kekkōjin* good-natured man, an honest
膜 *ketsumaku* conjunctiva ⌊man
膜炎 *ketsumakuen* conjuntivitis
15縁 *ketsuen* accepting Buddhism; forming
論 *ketsuron* conclusion ⌊karma relationships
審 *kesshin* conclusion of a hearing
17霜 *kessō* formation of frost
19願 *kechigan* expiration of a (Buddhist) vow
縄 *ketsujō* knotted cord
21露 *ketsuro* formation of dew
露点 *ketsuroten* dew point

7

經 3541 F1460 See **経** 3523.

絽 3542 F1459 Ro a silk gauze.
18織 *ro-o(ri)* gauze fabric
縮緬 *rochirimen* gauze crepe

絹 3543 F1459 Ken silk. *kinu* silk, silk thread.
A
5布 *kempu* silk, silk cloth
本 *kempon* silk used for art painting
6地 *kinuji* silk fabrics
糸 *kinu ito, kenshi* silk thread
糸紡績 *kenshi bōseki* silk reeling, silk spin-
8物 *kinumono* silk goods ⌊ning
10紡 *kembō* spun silk
11張 *kinuba(ri)* silk covered
紬 *kenchū* pongee
笠 *kinugasa* long-handled silk umbrella
12絵 *kinue* picture on silk
13業 *kengyō* silk industry
業者 *kengyōsha* silk dealer
14綾 *kinu aya* silk damask
綿 *kinu wata* silk floss
17縮 *kinuchiji(mi)* crinkled silk
18織物 *kinu orimono* silk goods

A 続 3544/F1486 續 ZOKU continuation, second and series. *tsuzu(ku) vi* continue; be contiguous. *tsuzu(keru) vt* continue. *tsuzu(ki)* continuation, succession; another installment, sequel; series; row. -*tsuzu(ki)* row; continuity; succession.

5 生 *zokusei* = *zokushutsu* 続出 (see below-5)
刊 *zokkan suru* continue publication
出 *zokushutsu* frequent occurrence, series of events
6 行 *zokkō suru* go on, continue, resume
会 *zokkai suru* resume, continue
合 *tsuzu(ki)a(i)* connection, relationship
8 物 *tsuzu(ki)mono* serial story
9 映 *zokuei* continued run of a film
柄 *tsuzu(ki)gara* family relationship
発 *zokuhatsu* = *zokushutsu* 続出 (see above-5)
発症 *zokuhatsushō* secondary disease
10 航 *zokkō suru* continue the voyage; hold the course
書 *tsuzu(ke)ga(ki)* cursive handwriting
12 開 *zokkai suru* resume, continue
飯 *sokui* rice paste
報 *zokuhō* further news
番号 *tsuzu(ki) bangō* serial number
13 続 *zokuzoku* successively, one after another
14 様 *tsuzu(ke)sama ni* successively, consecutively, in a row
演 *zokuen* continued run of a show
15 稿 *zokkō* remaining manuscripts (to be furnished)
審 *zokushin* re-examination, retrial
篇 *zokuhen* sequel, continuation, supplementary volume
20 騰 *zokutō* continued advance in prices

B 継 3545/F1485 繼 KEI. *tsu(gu)* succeed to, inherit; follow; patch; graft (trees); tell. *tsu(gi)* patch. *mama(shii)* fostered (child). *mama-* step- (child, etc.).

3 子 *mamako, keishi* stepchild
子虐 *mamako iji(me)* ill-treatment of a stepchild
4 手 *tsu(gi)te* joint, pipe coupling
木 *tsu(gi)ki* grafting, grafted tree
父 *mamachichi, keifu* stepfather
切 *tsu(gi)gi(re)* patch
夫 *keifu* second husband
5 母 *mamahaha, keibo* stepmother
目 *tsu(gi)me* joint, seam, suture
立 *tsu(gi)ta(te)* relay
兄弟 *mama kyōdai* half brothers from different mothers
6 合 *tsu(gi)-a(wasu), tsu(gi)-a(waseru)* join together, patch, splice, dovetail, glue together
当 *tsugia(te)* patchwork
7 走 *keisō* relay race
足 *tsu(gi)-ta(su)* add to, extend, piece. *tsu(gi)ta(shi)* adding to
述 *keijutsu suru* pass on the word
承 *keishō* succession, accession, inheritance
承者 *keishōsha* successor
8 泳 *keiei* relay swimming
物 *tsu(gi)mono* patch
受 *keiju* inheritance
妻 *keisai* second wife
9 室 *keishitsu* second wife
竿 *tsu(gi)zao* jointed fishing rod; jointed stem
10 紛 *mamako* undissolved powder lump
剝 *tsu(gi)ha(gi)* patching; patch
13 継 *tsu(gi)tsu(gi)* in turn, one after another
嗣 *keishi* successor, heir
電器 *keidenki* (electric) relay
続 *keizoku* continuation
続性 *keizokusei* continuity
続的 *keizokuteki* continuous, habitual
続飛行 *keizoku hikō* endurance flight
16 親 *mama-oya* stepparent

8

絣 See 絣 3527.

緍 3546/F1470 See 緡 3573.

綬 3547/F1463 JU cordon, ribbon (a decoration).

綮 3548/F1464 KEI a device or emblem on a flag or banner.

綰 3549/F1464 WAN. *waga(neru)* bend round, bend into a hoop.

綯 3550/F1464 TŌ. *na(u)* twist, twine, make (rope).

綻 3551/F1466 TAN. *hokoro(biru)* be rent, be ripped; unravel, run; begin to open; smile. *hokoro(basu), hokoro(baseru)* tear, rip; smile.

B 維 3552/F1464 I tie; rope.

9 持 *iji* upkeep, support, maintenance
13 新 *Ishin* 1868 Imperial Restoration

緋 3553/F1468 HI scarlet, cardinal.

6 衣草 *higoromosō* salvia
18 鯉 *higoi* red carp, golden carp

綽 3554/F1466 SHAKU loose; lenient.

6名 *adana* nickname ⌈liberate
14綽 *shakushaku(taru)* ample, leisurely, de-

綜 3555/F1462 Sō rule.

6合 *sōgō* synthesis, co-ordination, composite
合大学 *sōgō daigaku* university
合的 *sōgōteki*＝総合的 3567.6
9括 *sōkatsu*＝総括 3567.9

綸 3556/F1466 RIN thread; silk cloth.

3子 *rinzu* figured satin
6旨 *rinji* imperial order
7言 *ringen* emperor's word, imperial mandate

B 緒 3557/F1468 緖 SHO, CHO beginning, inception; end. *itoguchi* thread end; beginning; clue. *o* cord, strap, thong; clog cord; string.

7言 *chogen, shogen* forward, preface, intro-
12就 *sho(ni)tsu(ku)* be started ⌊duction
13戦 *shosen* beginning of hostilities
業 *shogyō* work undertaken
15締 *oji(me)* pouch drawstring
論 *choron, shoron* introduction, preface

綺 3558/F1466 KI figured cloth; beautiful.

14語 *kigo* flowery language
15談 *kidan* a strange story; an adventure story
19羅 *kira* fine clothes. *kira(biyakana)* gorgeous, gaudy, dazzling ⌈great men
羅星如 *kiraboshi (no) goto(ku)* a galaxy of
麗 *kirei na* beautiful, lovely; clean, neat. *kirei ni* completely; beautifully
麗好 *kireizu(ki)* love of cleanliness
麗事 *kireigoto* fine skill, simplicity
麗星 *kiraboshi* glittering stars

綾 3559/F1466 RYŌ. *aya* design, figured cloth, twill.

5布 *ayanuno* twill damask and brocade
6糸 *aya-ito* colored thread
地 *ayaji* figured cloth
8取 *ayato(ru)* tie across (the back). *ayato(ri)* string play (cat's-cradle, etc.)
13絹 *ayaginu* figured silk
15緞子 *ayadonsu* damask
16錦 *aya nishiki* twill damask and brocade
18織 *ayao(ri)* twill

B 緊 3560/F1468 KIN hard, solid; reliable; tight. *shi(maru) vi* be tightened. *shi(meru) vt* tighten.

3子兎 *shimeko (no) usagi* I've got it; All right,
4切 *kinsetsu na* urgent, pressing ⌊fine.
7迫 *kimpaku* tension, strain
束 *kinsoku* tying up firmly
9要 *kin-yō* important, momentous
急 *kinkyū* crisis, emergency; urgency, rush
11密 *kimmitsu* rigor; closeness; compactness
張 *kinchō* strain, tension, seriousness
張味 *kinchōmi* strain, tension, seriousness
14緊 *hishihishi*＝犇犇 2862.12
褌一番 *kinkon-ichiban suru* gird oneself for
16縛 *kimbaku suru* bind tightly ⌊an effort
17縮 *kinshuku* shrinkage, contraction, constriction; strict economy, retrenchment

B 綱 3561/F1464 KŌ class (in zoology). *tsuna* rope, cord, string, line, hawser, cable; morality.

4手 *tsunade* mooring rope, towing line
引 *tsunahi(ki)* tug-of-war; forward puller
5目 *kōmoku* gist, outline, main points
打 *tsuna-u(chi)* ropemaking; ropemaker
8具 *tsunagu* cordage, rigging, tackle
9要 *kōyō* outline, summary, essentials
紀 *kōki* ropes; law and order, administration, official discipline
紀粛正 *kōki shukusei* enforcement of official
11常 *kōjō* morals, morality ⌊discipline
梯子 *tsunabashigo* rope ladder
12渡 *tsunawata(ri)* tightrope walking, tightrope walker; danger. *tsunawata(shi)* rope ferry ⌈mary
14領 *kōryō* general plan; main points, sum-

綴 3562/F1465 TEI. TETSU. SETSU. *tsuzu(ru)* spell; compose, write; bind; patch. *to(jiru)* bind, file, sew up. *tsuzuri* spelling, orthography; binding, patching. *tsuzu(re)* rags, tatters. *to(ji)* binding, sewing.

4方 *tsuzu(ri)kata* composition, theme; spelling, how to spell. *tojikata* binding, how to bind ⌈*ko(mi)* file
込 *to(ji)-ko(mu)* file; interleave, insert. *toji-*
5目 *tojime* seam. *tsuzu(ri)me* joint, seam
付 *to(ji)-tsu(keru)* sew together
本 *tojihon* bound book
6糸 *toji-ito* binding thread, basting thread
合 *tsuzu(ri)-a(waseru)* sew together, patch; bind together, fasten, file
字 *setsuji, teiji, tsuzuriji* spelling, orthog-
8金 *tojigane* binding strip ⌊raphy
直 *to(ji)-nao(su)* rebind
10釘 *toji kugi* rivet
13蓋 *tojibuta* mended lid
16機械 *toji kikai* stitching machine

B 網 3563/F1465 MŌ net; network. *ami* net, netting.

3 子 *amiko* netter (one who handles the nets)
4 戸 *amido* screen door
引 *amihi(ki)* net puller; pulling in a net
元 *amimoto* head fisherman
5 石 *ami ishi* net weights
打 *amiu(chi)* net fishing
目 *amime, ami (no) me* net meshes
目版 *amimeban* halftone (plate)
代 *ajiro* wickerwork; wicker net
代笠 *ajirogasa* wicker hat
7 抄 *amisuki* netmaker, netmaking
状 *mōjō* net form
形 *amigata no* reticulated
杓子 *amijakushi* ladle, scoop, skimmer
8 版 *amihan* halftone (plate)
刺 *amisa(shi)* netmaking
10 針 *amibari* netting needle
11 麻 *amiso* net cord
船 *amibune* fishing boat (using nets)
袋 *amibukuro* (lady's) net bag
細工 *amizaiku* net maker; filigree work
12 棚 *amidana* baggage rack
14 膜 *mōmaku* retina
19 羅 *mōra suru* include, contain; collect

A 緑 3564 / F1462 綠 RYOKU, ROKU. *midori* green; verdure.

3 土 *ryokudo* a verdant area
4 化 *ryokka, ryokuka* tree planting, afforestation
内障 *ryokunaishō* glaucoma
5 石鹸 *ryokusekken* green soap, soft soap
玉 *ryokugyoku* emerald, beryl
玉石 *ryokugyokuseki* emerald, beryl
玉髄 *midori gyokuzui* chrysoprase
6 色 *midori iro* green. *ryokushoku* green, verdure
地 *ryokuchi* green stretch of land; oasis
地化 *ryokuchika* afforestation
地帯 *ryokuchitai* green belt
8 門 *ryokumon* arch of leaves or evergreens
雨 *ryoku-u* rain falling on fresh verdure
青 *rokushō* green rust, copper rust
林 *ryokurin* a green forest; a robber
肥 *ryokuhi* green-manure crop
岩 *ryokugan* greenstone
9 便 *ryokuben* child's green bowel movement
茶 *ryokucha* green tea, Japanese tea
草 *ryokusō* green grass
柱石 *ryokuchūseki* beryl
10 陰 *ryokuin* tree shade, shady nook
陰樹 *ryokuinju* shade tree
11 野 *ryokuya* green field
12 葉 *ryokuyō* green leaves
13 煙 *ryokuen* evening haze
16 樹 *ryokuju* green tree, foliage
19 藻 *ryokusō* green algae

A 練 3565 / F1472 練 REN. *ne(ru)* gloss, soften; train, drill; polish; refine. *ne(reru)* be docile, be teachable; become dependable. *ne(reta)* mellowed. *ne(ri)* kneading; glossing (silk).

6 糸 *ne(ri)-ito* glossed silk thread
回 *ne(ri)-mawa(ru)* parade, march
成 *rensei* training
7 兵 *rempei* military drill, parade
兵場 *rempeijō* parade ground
8 金 *renkin* refining, smelting, tempering
固 *ne(ri)-kata(meru)* harden by kneading
乳 *rennyū* condensed milk
歩 *ne(ri)-aru(ku)* parade, march
9 炭 *rentan* briquette
10 粉 *ne(ri)ko* dough
11 達 *rentatsu* skill, dexterity
習 *renshū* training, practice, rehearsal
習不足 *renshūbusoku* lack of training
習生 *renshūsei* student, trainee, apprentice
習用 *renshūyō* for training purposes
習曲 *renshūkyoku* étude, a study (in music)
習所 *renshūjo* training institute
習帳 *renshūchō* exercise book, workbook
12 塀 *ne(ri)bei* mud or plastered wall
13 絹 *ne(ri)ginu* glossed silk
鉄 *rentetsu, ne(ri) kurogane* wrought iron
14 獄 *rengoku* purgatory
16 磨 *remma* exercise, training, drilling
薬 *ne(ri)gusuri, ne(ri)yaku* ointment

A 綿 3566 / F1467 緜 MEN cotton; cotton thread; cotton cloth. *wata* cotton, cotton wool.

2 入 *wata-i(re)* padded clothes; cotton-quilted bedclothes
3 子 *watako* a cape (the wearing apparel)
4 火薬 *menkayaku* guncotton
天鵞絨 *membirōdo* cotton velvet, velveteen
毛 *watage* fluff, nap, fuzz, down, pile, fleece
毛布 *memmōfu* cotton blanket
5 打 *wata-u(chi)* cotton willowing
布 *mempu* cotton cloth
6 糸 *menshi* cotton thread or yarn
羊 *men-yō* sheep
衣 *men-i* cotton clothing; clothing of a cotton mixture
7 花 *menka* raw cotton
8 物 *memmono* cotton piece goods
服 *mempuku* cotton clothes
実 *menjitsu, wata(no)mi* cotton seed
実虫 *wata(no)mi mushi* bollworm
実油 *menjitsuyu, wata(no)mi abura* cotton-seed oil
9 屋 *wataya* cotton dealer
津見 *watatsumi* god of the sea
10 紡 *membō* cotton spinning
11 商 *watashō* cotton dealer

密 *memmitsu na* minute, detailed; careful,
12 雲 *watagumo* fleecy clouds ⌊meticulous
帽子 *watabōshi* bride's silk-floss veil
13 業 *mengyō* cotton industry
14 綿 *memmen(taru)* endless, continuous
製品 *menseihin* cotton goods
17 縮 *menchijimi* cotton crepe
18 織物 *men orimono* cotton goods
19 繰 *wataku(ri)* cotton ginning
繰工 *wataku(ri)kō* cotton ginner
繰機 *wataku(ri)ki* cotton gin
20 繻子 *menjusu* cotton satin, sateen

A **総** 3567 / F1478 **総總** Sō- whole, all, general, gross, total, full. *su(beru)* control, supervise. *fusa* tuft, tassel, fringe, lock (of hair); cluster, bunch, segment (of an orange). *sō(jite)* in general, as a rule. *sato(i)* clever, intelligent; keen, quick. *sube(te)* (see under 凡 654.0).

2 二階 *sōnikai* full two-story house
入歯 *sōi(re)ba* full set of false teeth
力 *sōryoku* full strength
力戦 *sōryokusen* total war
3 大将 *sōtaishō* commander-in-chief
4 予算 *sōyosan* complete budget
元締 *sōmotoji(me)* general manager
支出 *sōshishutsu* total expenditure
支配人 *sōshihainin* general manager ⌈wool
毛 *fusage* lock, tuft, tassel. *sōke, sōmō* all
毛立 *sōkeda(tsu)* shudder, have goose flesh, feel one's hair standing on end
5 立 *sōda(chi)* all standing up together
代 *sōdai* representative, delegate
出 *sōde* full force ⌈secretary
主事 *sōshuji* executive director, general
仕舞 *sōjimai* closing up, selling out
皮 *sōhi* full leather ⌈ing
皮製 *sōgawasei, sōkawasei* full-leather bind-
目 *sōmoku* catalog; table of contents
目録 *sōmokuroku* catalog; table of contents
収入 *sōshūnyū* total income
収益 *sōshūeki* gross earnings
司令官 *Sōshireikan* SCAP; Supreme Commander ⌈Headquarters
司令部 *Sōshireibu* SCAP, GHQ; General
本山 *sōhonzan* sectarian headquarters
本店 *sōhonten* head office ⌊temple
本部 *sōhombu* general headquarters
本家 *sōhonke* head family ⌈assembly, synod
6 会 *sōkai* general meeting, annual conference,
回診 *sōkaishin* the doctor's rounds (in a
同盟 *sōdōmei* federation ⌊hospital)
同盟罷業 *sōdōmei higyō* general strike
合 *sōgō* synthesis, co-ordination, composite
合大学 *sōgō daigaku* university
合写真 *sōgō shashin* composite photo
合的 *sōgōteki* over-all, all-around, collective, synthetic, composite, comprehensive
合計画 *sōgō keikaku* comprehensive plan
合雑誌 *sōgō zasshi* all-purpose magazine
合競技 *sōgō kyōgi* all-round games
7 見 *sōken* attending in a large party
身 *sōmi* the whole body ⌈ters
局 *sōkyoku* overseas (newspaper) headquar-
社 *sōsha* shrine enshrining several gods
花 *sōbana* tips to all
決算 *sōkessan* complete financial statements
攻撃 *sōkōgeki* general attack, general
投票数 *sōtōhyōsū* total votes cast ⌊offensive
体 *sōtai* all, the whole. *sōtai ni* on the whole, in general
体的 *sōtaiteki ni* generally ⌈general
8 長 *sōchō* (college) president; secretary-
和 *sōwa* total ⌈a character)
画 *sōkaku* complete number of strokes (in
退却 *sōtaikyaku* general retreat
所得 *sōshotoku* gross income
坪数 *sōtsubosū* total area in *tsubo* (see Weights and Measures)
9 帥 *sōsui* commander, leader
計 *sōkei* total
則 *sōsoku* general rules, general provisions
軍 *sōgun* the whole army
点 *sōten* total marks
重量 *sōjūryō* gross weight
革 *sōgawa* full-leather binding
革製 *sōgawasei* leather-bound ⌈commander
指揮 *sōshiki* supreme command; supreme
指揮官 *sōshikikan* supreme commander
括 *su(be)-kuku(ru)* generalize. *sōkatsu* synthesis, summarization, recapitulation
括的 *sōkatsuteki* all-inclusive, all-embracing, lump-sum, general
括保険 *sōkatsu hoken* blanket insurance
括運賃 *sōkatsu unchin* lump-sum freight
10 高 *sōdaka* total amount ⌈general terms
称 *sōshō* general term. *sōshō suru* speak in
書 *sōsho* series (of publications); library (of
益 *sōeki* gross profit ⌊literature)
益金 *sōekikin* gross profit
員 *sōin* full force, all hands, the entire staff
員集合 *sōin shūgō* muster ⌈criticism
11 捲 *sōmaku(ri)* general survey, sweeping
舐 *sōna(me)* sweeping victory
崩 *sōkuzure* general rout, collapse, stampede
菜 *sōzai* daily fare, plain food, ordinary side dish
勘定 *sōkanjō* full payment, final settlement
動員 *sōdōin* general mobilization
掛 *sōga(kari)* combined efforts

掛費 *sōga(kari)hi* total expenses
理 *sōri* president; leader; prime minister
理大臣 *sōri daijin* prime minister
理庁 *sōrichō* prime minister's office
理府 *sōrifu* prime minister's office
務 *sōmu* general affairs; manager
務局 *sōmukyoku* general-affairs department
務長官 *sōmu chōkan* director-general
務部長 *sōmu buchō* general manager
12 揚 *sōa(ge)* calling all geisha
統 *sōtō* leader, president, generalissimo
集 *sōshū* an anthology of prose and poetry by many writers
復習 *sōfukushū* complete final review. *sōzarai* rehearsal; complete final review
量 *sōryō* gross weight, gross volume
量噸 *sōryō ton* gross tonnage
裁 *sōsai* president, governor (of a bank)
裁職 *sōsaishoku* the presidency (of an organization)
13 数 *sōsū* total number
意 *sōi* consensus of opinion
勢 *sōzei* the whole army; all members
幹事 *sōkanji* general secretary
義歯 *sōgishi* full set of false teeth
辞職 *sōjishoku* resignation en masse
督 *sōtoku* governorship; governor; governor-general
督府 *sōtokufu* government-general
14 総 *fusafusa* tufty, fringy, bushy (tail), fleecy
説 *sōsetsu* introduction, general remarks
嘗 *sōna(me)* tasting everything; a sweeping victory
選挙 *sōsenkyo* general election
監 *sōkan* inspector general, commissioner, president
監督 *sōkantoku* general manager
領 *sōryō* ruling; heir, eldest son, eldest child, family head
領事 *sōryōji* consul-general
領事館 *sōryōjikan* consulate-general
領娘 *sōryō musume* eldest daughter
領息子 *sōryō musuko* eldest son and heir
15 締 *sōji(me)* total; general manager
論 *sōron* general remarks, introduction
調書 *sōchōsho* summarized statement
罷業 *sōhigyō* general strike
16 噸数 *sōtonsū* gross tonnage
17 轄 *sōkatsu* general control, general supervision
18 額 *sōgaku* total amount
19 蹶起 *sōkekki suru* arouse (people)
24 攬 *sōran* superintendence, control

9

緜 See 綿 3566.

緟 3568/F-X See 緟 3617.

練 3569/F1472 See 練 3565.

緖 3570/F1468 See 緒 3557.

緼 3571/F1474 See 縕 3591.

縅 3572/F1473 (国字) *odo(su)* (see under 威 1803.0).

緡 3573/F1470 BIN. KON. *sashi* paper string, straw string.

緬 3574/F1472 MEN fine thread.
6 羊 *men-yō* sheep

緻 3575/F1473 CHI fine (not coarse).
11 密 *chimitsu na* minute, fine, nice, elaborate, delicate, accurate, discriminating

縋 3576/F1473 TSUI. *suga(ru)* cling to, hang on to, lean on; depend on; appeal to.
5 付 *suga(ri)-tsu(ku)*=*sugaru* (see under 縋 3576.0)

緘 3577/F1469 KAN. *kan(suru)* shut, close, seal.
3 口 *kankō suru* keep silent
15 黙 *kammoku* silence, reticence

緞 3578/F1470 DON, TAN damask.
3 子 *donsu* damask
11 帳 *donchō* drop curtain; second-rate (actor)
帳役者 *donchō yakusha* barnstormer, second-rate actor

緯 3579/F1472 B I woof; horizontal. left and right; parallels of latitude; latitude. *nuki* woof.
6 糸 *nuki ito, yoko ito* woof
9 度 *ido* latitude
15 線 *isen* parallel of latitude

線 3580/F1469 A SEN line; track, route; wire.
4 分 *sembun* line segment
内球 *sennaikyū* fair ball
引 *sembi(ki)* ruling lines
引小切手 *sembi(ki) kogitte* crossed check
7 材 *senzai* wire rod, wire
形 *senkei* straight alignment

条 *senjō* streak, line
8画 *senga* line drawing, line engraving
9香 *senkō* incense stick
香花火 *senkō hanabi* firecracker
12間 *senkan* spaces (on a musical staff)
13路 *senro* railway track
路工手 *senro kōshu* railway section hand
路用地 *senro yōchi* railway right of way
路伝 *senrozuta(i)* along the tracks
15輪 *senrin* (electric) coil
審 *senshin* linesman (in a game)

B **締** 3581/F1470 **締** TEI. *shi(meru)* tie, tighten; wring, constrict, strangle; shut; total; control strictly; rebuke. *shi(maru)* be shut, be locked, be fastened; be tight, be firm; become sober, reform; be thrifty. *shi(mete)* total.

3上 *shi(me)-a(geru)* tie up
4込 *shi(me)-ko(mu)* shut in, lock in
切 *shi(me)-ki(ru)* close, close up, keep closed. *shimeki(ri)* closing, closing up; deadline; cutoff; cofferdam
太鼓 *shi(me)daiko* drum whose heads are tied on with tightening cords
5付 *shi(me)-tsu(keru)* bind, throttle; strangle, choke; press hard, compress; control
出 *shi(me)-da(su)* shut out, lock out ⌊strictly
7売 *shi(me)u(ri)* cornering the market and making large profits
8金 *shi(me)gane* clamp
具 *shi(me)gu* clamp, fastener
9屋 *shi(mari)ya* thrifty person; stingy person
括 *shi(me)-kuku(ru)* hold together, bind; supervise, control. *shi(me)kuku(ri)* supervision, control; completion
約 *teiyaku suru* make a treaty. *teiyaku* treaty, agreement
約国 *teiyakukoku* treaty powers, signatories
10高 *shi(me)daka* total
12結 *teiketsu suru* conclude, contract
13盟 *teimei* conclusion of a treaty
盟国 *teimeikoku* treaty powers, signatories

B **縫** 3582/F1475 **縫** HŌ. *nu(u)* sew, stitch, embroider. *nu(i)* sewing; embroidery.

3工 *hōkō* seamstress, tailor
上 *nu(i)a(ge)* tuck
4反 *nu(i)-kae(su)* sew over, remake
込 *nu(i)-ko(mu)* sew in, tuck
5目 *nu(i)me* seam, suture
付 *nu(i)-tsu(keru)* sew on ⌈seam
代 *nu(i)shiro* the margin left for a seam; a
包 *nu(i)guru(mi)* actors' clothing to imitate
6糸 *nui-ito* sewing thread ⌊animals
合 *nu(i)-a(waseru)* sew up, sew together. *hōgō* suturing, stitching
8取 *nu(i)to(ri)* embroidery, sewing
直 *nu(i)-nao(su)* sew over, remake
物 *nuimono* sewing, needlework
物台 *nuimono dai* sewing table
10紋 *nu(i)mon* embroidered crest
針 *nu(i)bari* sewing needle
12揚 *nu(i)a(ge)* tuck
14箔 *nu(i)haku* embroidery
模様 *nu(i)moyō* embroidered figures
18繕 *nu(i)-tsukuro(u)* patch; sew on a patch

A **編** 3583/F1471 **編** HEN compilation, editing; completed poem; a book; a part of a book. *a(mu)* knit, plait, braid, net, weave, twist, crochet; compile, edit, frame. *a(mi)-* braided, knitted.

2入 *hennyū* entry, incorporation, enlistment,
3上 *ami(age)* high lace shoes ⌊enrollment
上靴 *amia(ge)gutsu* high lace shoes
4戸 *a(mi)do* braided door
5目 *a(mi)me* knitting stitch ⌈work out
出 *a(mi)-da(su)* invent, devise, originate,
6成 *hensei* formation, organization, composi-
曲 *henkyoku* arrangement (in music) ⌊tion
次 *henji suru vt* line up ⌈twine, knit together
合 *a(mi)-a(wasu)*, *a(mi)-a(waseru)* inter-
年史 *hennenshi* annals, chronicle
年体 *hennentai* chronological order ⌈a book
7述 *henjutsu* gathering materials and writing
8物 *amimono* knitting, crocheting ⌈sition
制 *hensei* formation, organization, compo-
者 *hensha* editor, compiler
10修 *henshū* compilation, editing
針 *a(mi)bari* knitting needle, crochet hook
11組 *henso* combination; braid
隊 *hentai* formation (flight)
笠 *a(mi)gasa* braided hat
12棒 *a(mi)bō* knitting needle
集 *henshū* editing, compilation
集局 *henshūkyoku* editorial department
集長 *henshūchō* editor in chief
16輯 *henshū* editing, compilation
20纂 *hensan* compilation, editing

B **緩** 3584/F1471 **緩** KAN. *yuru(mu) vi* loosen, lessen; relax; be unguarded; be moderate. *yuru(meru) vt* loosen, unbend, unfasten; relax, ease, slacken; mitigate. *yuru(yakana)* loose; easy (grade); gentle, lenient, generous; slow (stream). *yukku(ri)* slowly, gently, leisurely. *yuru(i)* loose, slack; lenient, generous, slow.

3下剤 *kangezai* laxative
6曲球 *kankyokkyū* slow curve

行 *kankō* going slowly
行車 *kankōsha* local train
[8]歩 *kampo* slow walk ⌈pacification
和 *kanwa* relief; mitigation; alleviation;
和政策 *kanwa seisaku* appeasement policy
[9]怠 *kantai* neglect (of duty); rough manners; fault, error ⌈emergency, circumstances
急 *kankyū* high and low speed; tempo;
急車 *kankyūsha* caboose
[10]流 *kanryū* slow current
[11]球 *kankyū* slow ball
[12]焼 *kanshō* slow-burning
焼性 *kanshōsei* slow-burning
[13]傾斜 *kankeisha* gentle slope
[14]慢 *kamman* slow moving; inactivity
漫 *kamman* slow moving; inactivity
[15]緩 *yuruyuru* slowly, leisurely, gently
衝 *kanshō* mediation
衝地 *kanshōchi* neutral zone
衝地帯 *kanshō chitai* demilitarized zone
衝国 *kanshōkoku* buffer country
衝帯 *kanshōtai* neutral zone ⌈absorber
衝器 *kanshōki* buffer, bumper, shock

B **縁** 3585/F1470 **緣** EN relation, connection, affinity, ties, bond; blood relation; karma relation; fate, destiny; chance; marriage; acquaintance; marriage alliance; veranda, balcony. *fuchido(ru)* add a border. *enishi* relation, connection, affinity, ties, bond; blood relation; karma relation; fate, destiny; chance; marriage; acquaintance; marriage alliance. *fuchi* edge, verge, shore, side, brink, margin, brim, rim, flange, frill, frame, bank, fringe, border. *heri* edge, verge, brink, margin, border, fringe, rim, brim, hem, limb (of the sun). *yukari* acquaintance; relation; affinity. *yosuga* way, means.

[3]下 *en(no)shita ni* under the floor; out of sight, in the background
[4]日 *ennichi* a fair; temple festival
辺 *empen* connections, relatives, kith and kin
引 *embi(ki)* relation, connection, relative
切 *enki(ri)* separation, divorce, severing of
[5]石 *fuchi ishi* curb, curbstone ⌊connections
由 *en-yū* relationship
付 *enzu(ku)* get married. *enzu(keru)* give in
台 *endai* bench ⌊marriage
[6]先 *ensaki* edge of the veranda
[8]板 *en-ita* veranda flooring
取 *fuchito(ri), herito(ri)* bordering, hemming
定 *ensada(me)* marriage contract
者 *enja* relative
[9]柱 *embashira* veranda post
故 *enko* relation, connection, affinity
故者 *enkosha* relative ⌈portent
[10]起 *engi* history, origin, legend; omen; luck;
家 *enka* related family ⌈corridor
[11]側 *engawa* veranda, porch, balcony, open
組 *engumi* betrothal, wedding, marriage; alliance; adoption; fraternization, affilia- ⌊tion
[12]遠 *endōi* late marriage
結 *emmusu(bi)* marriage, marriage tie, love
無 *herina(shi)* unbordered ⌊knot
[13]続 *entsuzu(ki)* relationship, connection
飾 *fuchikaza(ri)* frill, edging, fringe
[14]端 *embana* edge
語 *engo* associated word ⌈bordering
[15]縫 *fuchinu(i)* hemming, hemstitching,
談 *endan* marriage proposal, offer of marriage, marriage engagement
[16]頭 *fuchigashira* pommel (of a sword)
[18]類 *enrui* connections, relatives

10

縣 See **県** 1362.

縫 3586/F1475 See **縫** 3582.

緻 3587/F1473 See **緻** 3575.

縒 3588/F1474 SHI. SA. *yo(ru)* vt twist.

縟 3589/F1474 JOKU decoration.

[5]礼 *jokurei* officialism, red tape

縉 3590/F1473 **縉** SHIN thin red cloth; high officer.

[9]神 *shinshin*=搢紳 1971.11

縕 3591/F1473 **縕** ON, UN old cotton.

[10]袍 *dotera* padded lounging kimono

縺 3592/F1478 REN. *motsu(reru)* tangle, knot, kink, get twisted; get complicated. *motsu(re)* tangle, entanglement, trouble, complication.

[4]毛 *motsu(re)ge* matted or tangled hair

B **縛** 3593/F1474 **縛** BAKU arrest, binding. *shiba(ru)* bind, tie, fasten, truss, fetter, restrain, chain; arrest, catch. *imashi(me)* binding, bonds.

[3]上 *shiba(ri)-a(geru)* tie up; truss up
[5]付 *shiba(ri)-tsu(keru)* tie up, fasten to
[9]首 *shiba(ri)kubi* beheading

縊 3594/F1473 I. *kubi*(*ru*) strangle (a person) to death. *kubi*(*reru*) strangle oneself, hang oneself.

6 死 *ishi, kubi*(*re*)*ji*(*ni*) death by strangling
刑 *ikei* death by strangling, hanging
10 殺 *kubi*(*ri*)-*koro*(*su*) strangle (a person) to death

縞 3595/F1474 Kō. *shima* stripe.

3 大理石 *shima dairiseki* Oriental alabaster
5 玉髄 *shima gyokuzui* chalcedony
8 物 *shimamono* striped cloth
9 柄 *shimagara* striped pattern
10 馬 *shima uma* zebra
11 蛇 *shima hebi* striped snake
13 鼠 *shima nezumi* squirrel
14 瑪瑙 *shima menō* onyx, wood agate, sardonyx
14 模様 *shima moyō* striped pattern
18 織 *shima-ori* woven in stripes
織物 *shima orimono* striped cloth

B **繁** 3596/F1479 **繁** Han frequency, complexity, trouble. *shige*(*ru*) grow thick, be overgrown, be luxuriant. *shige*(*ku*) thickly, densely; frequently. *shige*(*ri*), *shige*(*mi*) thicket, bush.

4 文 *hambun* extreme rhetorical flourishes
文縟礼 *hambun jokurei* red tape, officialism
6 忙 *hambō* pressure of business
多 *hanta* very numerous; many things to do
7 吹 *shibu*(*ki*) spray, splash
8 昌 *hanjō* prosperity, success
茂 *hammo* luxuriant growth
9 栄 *han-ei* prosperity
10 華 *hanka* prosperity, bustle
華街 *hankagai* a busy street
11 務 *hammu* exhausting work, an arduous task; pressure of business
盛 *hanjō, hansei* prosperity
12 閑 *hankan* rush and leisure
殖 *hanshoku suru* breed, propagate, increase, multiply
14 雑 *hanzatsu* complexity, intricacy, trouble
15 劇 *hangeki* pressure of business
16 凝 *shikori* muscle stiffness
18 簡 *hankan* simplicity and complexity

B **縦** 3597/F1476 **縱** Shō. Jū length, height. *hoshiimama* self-indulgent, wayward, selfish, arbitrary. *tate* length; height; warp. *yoshi* a hesitant OK; if, if by any chance. *tatoe, tatoi* if, even if, tho, altho.

4 引鋸 *tatebi*(*ki*) *nokogiri* ripsaw
6 糸 *tate ito* warp (in weaving)
列 *jūretsu* column, file, queue
7 走 *jūsō* following a mountain ridge
坑 *tatekō* mine shaft
坐標 *jūzahyō* ordinate (in math.)
8 波 *tatenami* longitudinal wave
9 陣 *jūjin* column (of soldiers)
10 射 *jūsha* raking fire
書 *tatega*(*ki*) vertical writing
座標 *tate zahyō* ordinate (in math.)
11 隊 *jūtai* column (of soldiers)
断 *jūdan* cutting vertically
貫 *jūkan suru* traverse from end to end
12 揺 *tateyu*(*re*) pitch (of a ship)
結 *tate musu*(*bi*) vertical knot
軸 *tatejiku* spindle
筋 *tatesuji* vertical line, longitudinal stripe
裂 *tateza*(*ki*) ripping lengthwise
14 様 *tatezama* lengthwise
15 線 *jūsen* vertical line
談 *jūdan* speaking out frankly
横 *tate-yoko, jūō* length and breadth; every direction; right and left; warp and woof. *jūō ni* vertically and horizontally
横無尽 *jūō-mujin* rush of business
横無礙 *jūō-muge* free, unrestricted
横談 *jūōdan* a talk on miscellaneous subjects
16 縞 *tatejima* vertical stripes; striped fabric
覧 *jūran* inspection; reading
覧御随意 *jūran gozui-i* admission free, open to the public
18 観 *jūkan* inspection; reading

— 11 —

縻 **縻** See 5394.

繁 3598/F1479 See **繁** 3596.

總 3599/F1478 See **総** 3567.

縱 3600/F1476 See **縦** 3597.

繍 Nonstandard for **繡** 3616.

繋 Nonstandard for **繫** 3618.

繆 3601/F1480 Byū error; wrap around.

A **績** 3602/F1479 Seki exploits; unreeling cocoons.

縲 3603 F1477 RUI tie.

12 絏 *ruisetsu* fetters, bonds

繃 3604 F1480 HŌ wrap.

10 帯 *hōtai* bandage, dressing
帯所 *hōtaijo* first-aid station

縷 3605 F1477 RU thread.

7 述 *rujutsu suru* tell in detail
10 骨 *rukotsu suru* work hard, take great pains
14 説 *rusetsu suru* tell in detail
17 縷 *ruru* minutely. *ruru(taru)* continuous

縹 3606 F1478 HYŌ. *hanada* light blue.

6 色 *hanada iro, hana iro* light blue
12 渺 *hyōbyō* haziness; vastness
16 緻 *kiryō* looks, features, personal beauty; ability, dignity
緻好 *kiryōyo(shi)* belle, a beauty. *kiryōgono(mi)* love of good looks
緻自慢 *kiryō jiman* proud of one's beauty

B **繊** 3607 F1487 **纖 纎** SEN fine, slender; thin kimono.

4 手 *senshu* slender hand; woman's work
毛 *semmō* cilia, fine hair
5 巧 *senkō* cleverness at fine work
7 条 *senjō* filament
9 指 *senshi* a woman's slender fingers
柔 *senjū na* graceful, lithe; limber
10 弱 *senjaku* weakness, frailty
11 細 *sensai na* fine, nice; delicate; subtle
14 維 *sen-i* fiber, textiles, strand
維工業 *sen-i kōgyō* textile industry
維学 *sen-igaku* (study of) textiles
維性 *sen-isei no* fibrous
維品 *sen-ihin* textiles
維根 *sen-ikon* fibrous roots
維素 *sen-iso* cellulose, fibrin
19 麗 *senrei na* splendid and beautiful

B **縮** 3608 F1476 SHUKU. *chiji(kamu), chiji(mu), chiji(komaru)* shrink, contract, shrivel, wrinkle. *chiji(masu), chiji(meru), chiji(komeru)* shorten, contract, shrink, reduce, boil down, simplify, abbreviate, abridge, condense, compress, crumple, wrinkle, withdraw. *chiji(keru), chiji(maru)* be shortened, be contracted, be reduced, be abridged; be abbreviated, shrink, shrivel, wrinkle. *chijiku(reru), chiji(kamaru)* curl up; squeeze into; shrink, shorten, contract, be abridged. *chiji(reru)* be wavy, curl; shrink; be corrugated, be wrinkled. *chiji(rakasu), chiji(rasu), chiji(raseru) vt* curl, crinkle, crimp. *chiji(mi)* crepe, shrunken cloth.

3 小 *shukushō* reduction, retrenchment, cut
上 *chiji(mi)-a(garu)* shrink up; quail, flinch, wince, cower
4 毛 *chiji(re)ge* curly, wavy, or fuzzy hair
尺 *shukushaku* reduced scale
少 *shukushō* reduction, retrenchment, cut
5 写 *shukusha* copying on a small scale; reduced copy
7 図 *shukuzu* reduced drawing, miniature copy; epitome
8 刷 *shukusatsu* small-type edition, pocket edition
刷版 *shukusatsuban* small-type edition, pocket edition
10 留 *chiji(mi)do(me)* shrinkproof
12 減 *shukugen suru* reduce
15 緬 *chirimen* crepe
緬皺 *chirimenjiwa* facial wrinkles
18 織 *chiji(mi)o(ri)* cotton crepe, preshrunk cloth

12

繭 See 4087.

繞 3609 F1482 JŌ. NYŌ. *megu(ru)* surround; return (seasons); *mawa(ru)* (see under 回 1028.0). *motō(ru)* wander around.

繚 3610 F1482 RYŌ put on; twist around.

7 乱 *ryōran* scattering far and wide

繙 3611 F1482 HAN. *himoto(ku)* read, peruse.

14 読 *handoku* perusal

B **繕** 3612 F1481 ZEN. *tsukuro(u)* repair, mend, darn; trim, tidy up, adjust.

5 立 *tsukuro(i)-ta(teru)* put up a good front
8 直 *tsukuro(i)-nao(su)* repair
13 飾 *tsukuro(i)-kaza(ru)* conceal (a mistake)

A **織** 3613 F1481 **織** SHOKU, SHIKI weaving. *o(ru)* weave. *o(ri)* fabric, weave.

3 女 *o(ri)me, shokujo* woman weaver
子 *o(ri)ko* weaver, textile worker
工 *shokkō* weaver
上 *o(ri)-a(geru)* be completely woven
4 手 *o(ri)te* weaver
文 *shokubun* an inwoven design; figured cloth
方 *o(ri)kata* the weave; how to weave
込 *o(ri)-ko(mu)* weave into
元 *o(ri)moto* weaver, textile manufacturing

5 目 *o(ri)me* texture
出 *o(ri)da(shi)* woven figures; selvage.
o(ri)-da(su) inweave designs
6 糸 *o(ri)-ito* strand; thread for weaving
色 *o(ri)-iro* natural-color cloth (undyed after weaving)
返 *o(ri)-kae(su)* reweave
成 *o(ri)-na(su)* weave (something); assemble
地 *o(ri)ji* texture
交 *o(ri)-maji(eru)* weave into
合 *o(ri)-a(waseru)* interweave, inweave
8 物 *orimono* cloth; textiles
物商 *orimonoshō* draper
物業 *orimonogyō* textile manufacturing
9 姫 *o(ri)hime* woman textile worker
10 紋 *o(ri)mon* crest woven into the cloth
14 模様 *o(ri) moyō* woven design
15 縫 *o(ri)nu(i), shokuhō* weaving and sewing
16 機 *shokki* weaving machine, loom

13

繪 3614 / F1483 See **絵** 3537.

繹 3615 / F1484 Eki pull out.

繍 3616 / F1482 Shū sew; figured cloth.
6 匠 *shūshō* embroiderer

繩 = **縄** 3617 / F1483 Jō. *nawa* rope, cord.
4 文 *jōmon* straw-rope pattern
手 *nawate* rope
5 目 *nawame* fetters, chains; arrest; knot
付 *nawatsu(ki)* prisoner in bonds
7 抜 *nawanu(ke)* slipping one's bonds
9 飛 *nawato(bi)* skipping rope
矩 *jōku* marking line and a square
10 帯 *nawa obi* rope belt
11 張 *nawaba(ri)* stretching a rope; cordon; sphere of influence, jurisdiction
規 *jōki* provisions, rules
梯子 *nawabashigo* rope ladder
13 暖簾 *nawa noren* rope curtain; tavern; cheap restaurant
14 墨 *jōboku* inked timber-marking string; standard
19 簾 *nawa sudare*=*nawa noren* 縄暖簾 (see above–13)

繋 3618 / F1483 Kei. *tsuna(gu)* tie, fasten, chain, hitch, tether; moor; keep on a leash; connect, join; sustain, preserve (life). *tsuna(garu)* be connected, be tied up, be fastened to; be related to, follow closely. *kaka(ru)* anchor, lie at anchor. *tsuna(gi)* connection, bond, tie; stopgap, substitute.
4 止 *tsuna(gi)-to(meru)*=*tsuna(gu)* (see under 繋 3618.0)
爪 *ka(ke)zume* plectrum
5 目 *tsuna(gi)me* joint
6 合 *tsuna(gi)-a(waseru)* connect, join
争 *keisō* dispute, contention
7 束 *keisoku* tying up in bundles; depriving of liberty
10 索 *keisaku* mooring ropes
留 *keiryū* mooring, anchorage
留気球 *keiryū kikyū* captive balloon
留船 *keiryūsen* moored ship
留塔 *keiryūtō* mooring mast
留場 *keiryūjō* moorings
11 累 *keirui* encumbrances dependents
船 *keisen* mooring (a ship)
船所 *keisenjo* moorings, berthage
船料 *keisenryō* mooring charge
12 属 *keizoku* relationship
場 *kaka(ri)ba* anchorage, berth, moorings, roadstead
13 辞 *keiji* copula
16 縛 *keibaku* tying up; destiny

B **繰** 3619 / F1484 Sō. *ku(ru)* reel (thread); wind; gin (cotton); spin; turn (pages); look up (a word, etc.); refer to; count (the days); open (shutters).
2 入 *ku(ri)-i(reru)* deposit, transfer (money)
入金 *kuri-irekin* transfer money, transfer balance, transfer fund
3 下 *ku(ri)-sa(geru)* move ahead (an appointment). *ku(ri)-oro(su)* gradually lower
上 *ku(ri)-a(geru)* advance (a date)
4 戸 *ku(ri)do* sliding door
込 *ku(ri)-ko(mu)* deposit, transfer; assign; march in; rush in; turn out
5 広 *ku(ri)-hiro(geru)* unroll; spread (a rug)
出 *ku(ri)-da(su)* pay out (rope); call out (troops); go forth; disburse
出梯子 *ku(ri)da(shi)bashigo* extension ladder
出鉛筆 *ku(ri)da(shi) empitsu* automatic pencil
6 返 *ku(ri)-kae(su)* do over, repeat, duplicate
合 *ku(ri)-a(wasu)* arrange things, manage
糸 *ku(ri)-ito* reeling thread; raw silk thread
糸工 *ku(ri)-itokō* silk reeler
7 言 *ku(ri)goto* tedious talk; repetition; complaint
戻 *ku(ri)-modo(su)* telescope (a fishing rod); repeat
形 *ku(ri)kata* molding
8 延 *ku(ri)-no(beru)* postpone, defer
取 *ku(ri)-to(ru)* reel off (thread)
11 寄 *ku(ri)-yo(seru)* pull toward one
12 替 *ku(ri)-ka(eru)* change, shift; appropriate
越 *ku(ri)-ko(su)* transfer, carry forward
越金 *kurikoshikin* balance forwarded
14 綿 *ku(ri)wata* ginned cotton
綿機械 *ku(ri)wata kikai* cotton gin

— 14 —

纂 See 3454.

辮 See 弁 844.

纘 3620 F1485 See 纉 3545.

繻 3621 F1485 SHU satin, fine silk.
8子 *shusu* satin
9珍 *shuchin* figured satin

— 15 —

續 3622 F1486 See 続 3544.

纖 3623 F1487 See 繊 3607.

纏 3624 F1487 See 纒 3627.

— 16 —

纜 3625 F1488 纜 RAN. *tomozuna* hawser.

— 17 —

纖 3626 F1487 See 繊 3607.

纒 3627 F1487 纏 TEN. *mato(u)* wear; wrap up, tie up. *mato(maru)*, *matsu(waru)* coil around; follow about; dangle after. *mato(meru)* settle, complete, agree upon, arrange; collect; put in order; unify, co-ordinate. *mato(maru)* be settled, be completed; be collected; be in order; be coherent; be united. *kuru(mu)* wrap up, tuck in. *kuru(meru)* (see under 包 176.0). *mato(matta)* round, large, definite, coherent. *mato(i)* fireman's standard.
8上 *mato(me)-a(geru)* sum up, unite
5付 *mato(i)-tsu(ku)*=*matsuwaru* (see under ⌊纒 3627.0)
7足 *tensoku* foot binding
役 *matomeyaku* mediator
9持 *matoimo(chi)* standard bearer
14綿 *temmen* involvement, entanglement
16頭 *tentō* celebration

— 18 —

纔 3628 F1487 SAN. ZAN. SAI. *wazuka* a little, a small quantity.
18繞 *tenjō suru* creep, twine around

— 21 —

纜 3629 F1488 See 纜 3625.

RAD. 缶 121

Mizugame water jar. At left: *hodogi hen* left-side "earthen jar." Nickname: Jar.

缶 Nonstandard for 罐 3634.
割 *hibiwa(re)* crack
裂 *karetsu* tearing; cracking

— 4 —

缺 3630 F1489 See 欠 2412.

— 11 —

罐 Nonstandard for 罐 3634.

罅 3631 F1490 KA. *hibi* crack, fissure, hole.
12焼 *hibiya(ki)* crackleware

— 14 —

罌 3632 F1490 Ō vase.
12粟 *keshi* poppy
粟種 *keshidane* poppy seed

— 16 —

罎 3633 F1491 See 壜 1156.

17

鑵 3634/F1491 **鑵** KAN can. *kama* steam boiler.

4 切 *kanki*(*ri*) can opener ⌈fining
13 詰 *kanzume* canning, canned goods; con-
詰工 *kanzumekō* canner, packer
詰工場 *kanzume kōjō* cannery
詰屋 *kanzumeya* cannery
詰業 *kanzumegyō* canning business

网 RAD. 122

Amigashira "net" crown. Variant: 罒 (5 strokes) *ami me* ("net" shaped like *me* "eye"), *megashira* "eye" crown, or *yoko me* sideways "eye" Nickname: Net.

3

罔 See 620.

5

罠 3635/F1492 BIN. MIN. *wana* trap, snare.

12 結 *wana musu*(*bi*) running knot

7

詈 3636/F1735 RI ridicule. [言]

A **買** 3637/F1795 BAI buying. *ka*(*u*) buy, invest in; incur; appreciate; call in (geisha). *ka*(*i*) buying. [貝]

2 入 *ka*(*i*)-*i*(*reru*) purchase, lay in
〆 *ka*(*i*)*shime* cornering the market
人 *kaite* buyer ⌈tone
人気 *ka*(*i*) *ninki* bullish sentiment, buying
3 上 *ka*(*i*)-*a*(*geru*) buy, buy up; bid up
上品 *kaiagehin* purchases
4 手 *kaite* buyer
方 *ka*(*i*)*kata* purchaser; way to buy
込 *ka*(*i*)-*ko*(*mu*) purchase, buy up
切 *ka*(*i*)-*ki*(*ru*) buy up, reserve, book, charter
5 立 *ka*(*i*)*ta*(*te*) *no* brand-new
付 *kaitsu*(*ke*) buying
収 *baishū* buying up, purchasing
主 *kainushi* buyer ⌈market)
占 *ka*(*i*)-*shi*(*meru*) buy up, corner (the
出 *ka*(*tte*)-*de*(*ru*) proceed without detailed instructions. *kaida*(*shi*) wholesale purchasing, laying in (supplies)
弁資本家 *baiben shihonka* a comprador
6 気 *ka*(*i*)*ki* bullish sentiment
地 *ka*(*i*)*chi* land buying; bought-up land
合 *ka*(*i*)*a*(*wase*) having (goods) on hand
7 足 *ka*(*i*)-*ta*(*su*) make additional purchases
戻 *ka*(*i*)-*modo*(*su*) buy back, redeem
初 *ka*(*i*)*zo*(*me*) first purchase of the new
求 *ka*(*i*)-*moto*(*meru*) purchase ⌊year
言葉 *ka*(*i*) *kotoba* a like answer to a cutting
8 価 *ka*(*i*)*ka* buying price ⌊remark
物 *kaimono* purchase; shopping; bargain
取 *ka*(*i*)-*to*(*ru*) buy, buy up
注文 *ka*(*i*)*chūmon* buying orders
受 *ka*(*i*)-*u*(*keru*) acquire by purchase
受人 *kaiu*(*ke*)*nin* buyer ⌈between meals
9 食 *ka*(*i*)*gui* buying and eating (sweets)
乗 *ka*(*i*)-*no*(*seru*) buy more; make more commitments ⌈bull market
相場 *ka*(*i*) *sōba* buying rate (of exchange);
為替 *ka*(*i*)*gawase* buying exchange
10 進 *ka*(*i*)*susu*(*mi*) active buying
値 *kaine* cost price
埋 *ka*(*i*)-*u*(*meru*) cover (a short sale)
時 *ka*(*i*)*doki* time to buy
被 *ka*(*i*)-*kabu*(*ru*) pay too much for; overestimate, overvalue
11 過 *ka*(*i*)-*su*(*giru*) overbuy
唱 *ka*(*i*)*tona*(*e*) bidding (on the stock market)
控 *ka*(*i*)-*hika*(*eru*) refrain from buying
掛 *ka*(*i*)*ka*(*ke*) buying on credit
掛金 *ka*(*i*)*ga*(*ke*)*kin* debt, accounts payable
12 集 *ka*(*i*)-*atsu*(*meru*) buy up
13 溜 *ka*(*i*)*da*(*meru*) hoard, buy up
置 *ka*(*i*)*o*(*ki*) hoarding
馴染 *ka*(*i*)*naji*(*mi*) being a regular customer
14 徳 *kaidoku* buying at a bargain
漁 *ka*(*i*)-*asa*(*ru*) buy up
煽 *ka*(*i*)-*ao*(*ru*) bid up, corner (the market)

8

罩 3638/F1492 TŌ fish basket kept in water.

罨 3639/F1492 AN cover.

8 法 *ampō* fomentation, compress, pack, poultice

蜀 3640/F1663 SHOKU Szechwan; green caterpillar. [虫]

12 葵 *tachiaoi* hollyhock
黍 *morokoshi* Indian millet; sorghum, kaoliang
黍紛 *morokoshiko* corn meal

罫 3641/F1493 KAI. KE, KEI ruled line.

4 引 *keibi(ki)* ruling; ruler; marking gauge; scriber
引紙 *keibi(ki)gami* ruled paper
10 紙 *keishi, keigami, kegami* lined paper
15 線 *keisen* ruled line

署 3642/F1494 **署** B SHO government office, (police) station. *sho(suru)* sign, write one's name. *tsukasa* (see under 司 877.0).

6 名 *shomei* signature, autograph
名国 *shomeikoku* signatory power
名捺印 *shomei-natsuin* signature and seal
8 長 *shochō* government office chief; police chief
10 員 *shoin* an official attached to an office

罪 3643/F1492 A ZAI. *tsumi* sin, crime, offense, guilt, blame, fault, misconduct. *tsumi suru* charge; sentence; punish.

2 人 *tsumibito* sinner. *zainin* criminal
6 名 *zaimei* the charge, name of the crime
7 作 *tsumitsuku(ri)* sinfulness; sinner
状 *zaijō* nature of an offense, charges
状書 *zaijōga(ki)* (criminal's) superscription
9 科 *zaika* crime; wickedness; punishment
11 過 *zaika* offense, sin, fault
得 *tsumi (o) e(ru)* become guilty
深 *tsumibukai* sinful, guilty
祭 *zaisai* sin offering
責 *zaiseki* liability of the accused; guilt, sin, wrongdoing
悪 *zaiaku* crime, sin, vice
悪感 *zaiakukan* sense of wrong, guilty conscience
12 証 *zaishō* proofs of guilt
13 滅 *tsumihorobo(shi)* amends, expiation, penance, conscience money
跡 *zaiseki* proofs of guilt
業 *zaigō* sin, iniquity, crime
障 *zaishō* sins, offenses
障消滅 *zaishō shōmetsu* expiation of one's sins
14 罰 *zaibatsu* crime, offense
15 質 *zaishitsu* nature of a crime

置 3644/F1493 A CHI. *o(ku)* *vt* place, put, set, deposit, lay; leave behind; keep, have, leave; establish; employ; appoint; post, station; pawn; skip (one day). *vi* be formed (dew). *o(keru)* go on (this way); keep (over night). *oi(tekibori), oi(tekebori)* leaving behind, giving the slip to. *-o(ki)* every other (day). *o(ki)-* standing, placed.

3 土産 *o(ki)miyage* souvenir, memento, parting present
4 文 *o(ki)bumi* a book left to posterity
方 *o(ki)kata* manner of placing
引 *okibi(ki)* taking someone's baggage and leaving an empty bag
手紙 *o(ki)tegami* letter left behind
戸棚 *o(ki)todana* chest of drawers
火燵 *o(ki)gotatsu* portable brazier
5 石 *o(ki)-ishi* garden landscape stone
旧 *o(ki)-furu(su)* leaving around to deteriorate
去 *okiza(ri)* deserting (someone)
6 行 *o(ite) yu(ku)* leave behind
返 *o(ki)-kae(ru)* replace
字 *o(ki)ji* characters skipped over in reading Chinese
7 床 *o(ki)doko* movable *tokonoma* alcove
忘 *o(ki)-wasu(reru)* mislay; leave behind, forget
来 *o(ite) ku(ru)* leave behind
8 迷 *o(ki)-mayo(u)* be at at loss as to where to put (something)
所 *o(ki)dokoro=okiba* 置場 (see below–12)
放 *o(kip)pana(shi), o(ki)hana(shi)* leaving things around
物 *okimono* ornament for display (in tokonoma), objet d'art
直 *o(ki)-nao(su)=o(ki)-ka(eru)* 置換 (see below–12)
炬燵 *o(ki)gotatsu* portable boxed brazier
9 屋 *o(ki)ya* geisha house; red-light district
10 酒 *chishu* opening a drinking party
時計 *o(ki)dokei* table clock
11 鳥 *o(ki)tori* decorative bird
道 *o(ki)michi* raised road
違 *o(ki)-chiga(eru)* misplace
据 *o(ki)-su(eru)* lay (a stone)
12 換 *o(ki)-ka(eru)* replace, rearrange, transpose, interchange. *chikan* substitution, replacement, displacement (in chemistry)
惑 *o(ki)-mado(wasu)* mislay
場 *o(ki)ba* storehouse, yard, place to put something
場所 *o(ki)basho*=word above
13 路 *o(ki)michi* raised road
15 潮 *o(ki)shio* a good chance to stop

9

署 3645/F1494 See **署** 3642.

罰 3646/F1493 **罸** B BATSU punishment, penalty. BACHI retribution, divine punishment. *bas(suru)* punish.

6 当 *bachia(tari)* the damned, the cursed
8 金 *bakkin* fine, penalty
杯 *bappai* penalty cup (that the loser has to drink)
9 則 *bassoku* penal regulations
点 *batten* demerit marks
10 俸 *bappō* docking of salary

10

罸 3647 / F1493 See 罰 3646.

罵 3648 / F1494 BA. *nonoshi(ru)* abuse, insult, speak ill of.

7言 *bagen*=*akkō* 悪口 62.3
声 *basei* boos, jeers
10倒 *batō* denunciation, abuse
12詈 *bari* abuse, reviling
詈雑言 *barizōgon* abusive language

B **罷** 3649 / F1494 HI. *ya(meru)*, *ya(mu)* (see under 止 2429.0). *maka(ru)* leave, withdraw, go. *ya(me)* end, discontinuance, stop.
3工 *hikō* strike, walkout
5市 *hishi* merchants' selling strike
出 *maka(ri)-de(ru)* present oneself; appear before; leave, withdraw
6成 *maka(ri)-na(ranu)* must not be; be not allowed
8免 *himen* dismissal
9通 *maka(ri)-tō(ru)* pass
為 *maka(ri)-na(ranu)* must not be; be not allowed
11患 *rikan* contraction of a disease
12越 *maka(ri)-ko(su)* visit, call on, go
間違 *maka(ri)-machiga(u)* make a mistake. *maka(ri)-machiga(ttemo)* at the worst. *maka(ri)-machiga(eba)* if worse comes to worst
13業 *higyō* strike, walkout

11

罹 3650 / F1495 RI. *kaka(ru)* catch, get, contract (illness).
7災 *risai* suffering (from a calamity), affliction
災民 *risaimin* victims, sufferers
災者 *risaisha* victims, sufferers
10病 *ribyō* contraction of a disease
11患 *rikan* contracting a disease

13

羃 3651 / F216 **冪** BEKI power (in math.); cover.

羂 3652 / F1495 KEN. *wana* trap, snare.

14

羆 3653 / F1496 HI. *higuma*, *shiguma* brown bear.

羅 3654 / F1495 RA silk gauze, thin silk.
6列 *raretsu* marshalling; an array. *raretsu suru* arrange; enumerate, itemize
宇 *rau*, *rao* bamboo pipestem
宇竹 *raudake* bamboo pipestem
宇替 *raoga(e)* bamboo pipestem seller
8典 *Raten* Latin
典語 *Ratengo* Latin
10紗 *rasha* woolen cloth
針 *rashin* compass needle
針儀 *rashingi* compass
針盤 *rashimban* compass
馬 *Rōma* Rome
馬加特力 *Rōma Katoriku* Roman Catholic
馬字 *Rōmaji* Roman letters, Roman alphabet
馬字綴 *rōmajitsuzu(ri)* romanization
馬教 *Rōmakyō* Roman Catholicism
馬数字 *Rōma sūji* Roman numerals
13漢 *rakan* arhat

19

羈 3655 / F1496 **覊 羇** KI reins; connection.
7束 *kisoku* suppression of freedom
10旅 *kiryo* travel
11絆 *kihan* restraint, yoke, shackles; ties, bonds

RAD. 羊 123

Hitsuji sheep. At left: 𦍌 *hitsuji hen*. At top ⺶. Nickname: Sheep.

B **羊** 3656 / F1497 YŌ. *hitsuji* sheep.
3小屋 *hitsujigoya* sheepfold
4水 *yōsui* amniotic fluid
毛 *yōmō* wool
5本 *yōhon* Western book
皮 *yōhi* sheepskin
皮紙 *yōhishi* parchment, sheepskin
皮綴 *yōhi toji* sheepskin binding
6肉 *yōniku* mutton
7角 *yōkaku* ram's horns
8舎 *yōsha* sheep shed
10脂 *yōshi* mutton tallow
12歯 *shida* fern
歯類 *yōshirui* ferns
13腸 *yōchō(taru)* meandering, zigzag, winding
飼 *hitsujika(i)* shepherd, shepherdess
群 *yōgun* flock of sleep
酪 *yōraku* sheep's milk
16頭 *yōtō* (going around in) sheep's clothing

頭狗肉 *yōtō-kuniku* **selling inferior goods under a famous name**
19 羹 *yōkan* **sweet bean jelly**
羹色 *yōkan iro* **a dull purplish color**

— 3 —

姜 3657 F499 Kyō. Kō. (Used in family and river names.) [女]

A **美** 3658 F1497 Bɪ beauty, grace, charm. *utsuku(shii)* beautiful, lovely, fine, good-looking; picturesque; sweet (voice); noble, pure.
2 人 *bijin* a beautiful woman
人比 *bijin-kura(be)* beauty contest
人投票 *bijin tōhyō* beauty contest
人画 *bijinga* picture of a beautiful woman
人草 *bijinsō* poppy
3 女 *bijo* beautiful woman
4 文 *bibun* ornate writing
化 *bika* beautification, idealization
少年 *bishōnen* handsome youth
爪術 *bisōjutsu* manicure, pedicure
以教会 *Mi-i Kyōkai* Methodist Church
5 玉 *bigyoku* gem, precious stone
田 *biden* good rice field
目 *bimoku* beautiful eyes
本 *bihon* beautifully bound book
6 色 *bishoku* beautiful color
衣 *bi-i* beautiful clothes
名 *bimei* good name, fame, high reputation
7 言 *bigen* honeyed words; maxim
妙 *bimyō* elegance, grace, exquisiteness
妓 *bigi* beautiful geisha
技 *bigi* brilliant performance, fine play
形 *bikei* beautiful form; beautiful woman
声 *bisei* beautiful voice
男 *binan, bidan* handsome man
男子 *binanshi, bidanshi* handsome man
男美女 *binan-bijo* beautiful men and women
8 味 *bimi* relish, good flavor, delicacy, rich dishes, deliciousness. *oi(shii)* delicious
服 *bifuku* fine clothes
的 *biteki* esthetic
育 *bi-iku* esthetic culture
果 *bika* good results
事 *migoto* splendid, beautiful. *biji* commendable act
学 *bigaku* esthetics
学的 *bigakuteki* esthetic
9 音 *bion* beautiful voice
風 *bifū* beautiful custom
俗 *bizoku* beautiful custom
姫 *biki* beautiful girl, beauty
点 *biten* good point, virtue, merit
美 *bibi(shii)* beautiful, splendid
食 *bishoku* dainty food; lavish diet
食主義 *bishoku shugi* epicureanism
食家 *bishokuka* gourmet
10 酒 *bishu, umazake* quality saké
称 *bishō* euphemism
挙 *bikyo* commendable act
容 *biyō* beautiful face
容体操 *biyō taisō* calisthenics
容的 *biyōteki* beautiful
容学校 *biyō gakkō* beauticians' school
容院 *biyōin* beauty parlor
容室 *biyōshitsu* beauty parlor
容師 *biyōshi* beautician
容術 *biyōjutsu* beauty culture
11 術 *bijutsu* art, fine arts
術工芸 *bijutsu kōgei* industrial art, arts and crafts, artistic handicrafts
術心 *bijutsushin* artistic sense
術史 *bijutsushi* history of art
術的 *bijutsuteki* artistic
術学校 *bijutsu gakkō* school of fine arts
術院 *bijutsuin* academy of art
術品 *bijutsuhin* work of art
術界 *bijutsukai* the world of art
術家 *bijutsuka* artist
術眼 *bijutsugan* artistic eye
術商 *bijutsushō* art dealer
術館 *bijutsukan* art gallery
12 粧 *bishō* beautiful attire; a beautiful make-up
景 *bikei* lovely view
装 *bisō* rich attire, fine dress
13 禄 *biroku* handsome stipend
感 *bikan* sense of beauty
意識 *bi-ishiki* art appreciation
辞 *biji* flowery language; clever writing
辞学 *bijigaku* rhetoric
14 徳 *bitoku* virtue, fine trait; good deed
貌 *bibō* good looks
髪 *bihatsu* beautiful hair
15 調 *bichō* harmony, melody
談 *bidan* praiseworthy anecdote, story
髯 *bizen* fine beard; fine mustache
質 *bishitsu* good quality, merit, fine traits
17 醜 *bishū* personal appearance, beauty or ugliness
18 観 *bikan* lovely view, beautiful sight
顔 *bigan* beautiful face
顔水 *bigansui* face lotion
顔術 *biganjutsu* facial treatment, the beautician's art
19 麗 *birei* beautiful; clean, pure

— 4 —

羔 3659 F1499 Kō. *kohitsuji* lamb.

恙 3660/F706 Yō. *tsutsuga* illness. *tsutsuga-(naku)* safely; in good health. [心]

羞 3661/F1500 Shū. *haji(ru)* feel ashamed.

10恥 *shūchi* shyness, bashfulness; dishonor, disgrace 「modesty
恥心 *shūchishin* sense of shame, shyness,

差 3662/F606 A Shi, Sa difference, variation; discrepancy; margin; balance; remainder (in subtraction). *sa(su)* **vt** raise (the hands); stretch out (the hands in dancing); put up (an umbrella); carry (on the shoulder); build (a hut); stretch (a rope); graft (trees); carry (in the belt); lift up; offer. **vi** (the sun) shines; appear on the surface. *sa(shi)* sharpened tube for testing rice in bags; ruler. *sa(shi) de* between two persons. *sa(shi)-* emphatic verbal prefix. *sa(shi)* ruler (for measuring); face to face; hindrance; sharing a load. [工]

2入 *sa(shi)-i(reru)* insert; send to a prisoner. *sashi-i(re)* insertion; something sent to a prisoner 「prisoner
入品 *sashi-irehin* something sent to a
3口 *sa(shi)guchi* suggestion from the outside
上 *sa(shi)-a(geru)* lift up, raise; give, present, offer; let (a person) have
上物 *sa(shi)a(ge)mono* gift
4止 *sa(shi)-to(meru)* prohibit, forbid, ban
込 *sa(shi)-ko(mu)* insert, thrust in; flow into; plug in; have a sharp pain. *sashiko(mi)* thrusting; insertion; socket; plug; cap; sharp pain
支 *sa(shi)-tsuka(eru)* be hindered, be interrupted, be prevented; be engaged; suffer inconvenience, have difficulty (in doing); be unable to; be hard up. *sa(shi)-tsuka(e)* hindrance, impediment, interference, interruption; previous engagement
支無 *sa(shi)tsuka(e)na(i)* OK, no trouble, no objection, justifiable, allowable
引 *sa(shi)-hi(ku)*, *sa(p)pi(ku)* deduct. *sashi-hi(ki)* deduction, subtraction; balance; ebb and flow, rise and fall; intermittence
引勘定 *sashihiki kanjō* account balance
5立 *sa(shi)-ta(teru)* send, forward, dispatch
付 *sa(shi)-tsu(keru)* point (a gun at); put right under one's nose
加 *sa(shi)-kuwa(eru)* add to 「sword)
古 *sa(shi)-furu(su)* wear out (a comb or a
出 *sa(shi)-da(su)*, *sa(shi)-ida(su)* present, submit, tender; send in (a card); produce (evidence); file (a petition); send, forward; reach out; extend; mail (a letter). *sa(shi)de(gamashii)* forward, intrusive, impertinent. *sa(shi)-de(ru)* push oneself forward. *sa(shi)-ide*, *sa(shi)de* impertinence
出人 *sashidashinin* sender; addresser
出口 *sa(shi)deguchi* uncalled-for remark
出者 *sa(shi)demono* intruder, meddler, busybody
6回 *sa(shi)-mawa(su)* send (a car) around
向 *sa(shi)-mu(keru)* send around; direct; turn (the light) toward; cover (with a gun). *sashimu(ki)* for the time being. *sashimuka(i)* face to face
仰 *sa(shi)-ao(gu)* respect, look up to
汐 *sa(shi)shio*, *sa(shi)jio* rising tide
合 *sa(shi)a(i)*=*sa(shi)tsuka(e)* 差支 (see above–4) and *sa(shi)sawa(ri)* 差障 (see below–13)
当 *sa(shi)ata(ri)* for the time being. *sa(shi)-ata(ru)* happen to meet; (the sun) shines
7足 *sa(shi)ashi* stealthy steps 「in
戻 *sa(shi)-modo(su)* send back, refer back
迫 *sa(shi)-sema(ru)* be imminent, be impending
伸 *sa(shi)-no(beru)* hold out (the hand), extend (the arm), reach out for; thrust (a javelin) 「differentiation
別 *sabetsu* discrimination, distinction,
別的 *sabetsuteki* discriminatory
別界 *sabetsukai* world of inequality 「ment
別待遇 *sabetsu taigū* discriminatory treat-
別関税 *sabetsu kanzei* differential tariff
8金 *sakin*, *sa(shi)kin* bargain money; covering money. *sa(shi)gane* carpenter's square; metal foot rule; tip; suggestion; inspiration; instigation
固 *sa(shi)-kata(meru)* shut; warn sternly
送 *sa(shi)-oku(ru)*=emphatic for *oku(ru)* (see under 送 4683.0)
担 *sa(shi)nina(i)* shouldering a load
枝 *sa(shi)eda* graft, slip, scion
油 *sa(shi)abura* lamp oil
知恵 *sa(shi)jie* suggestion, hint 「impound
押 *sa(shi)-osa(eru)* seize, attach, garnishee,
押品 *sashiosa(e)hin* seized goods
物屋 *sashimonoya* cabinetmaker
物師 *sashimonoshi* cabinetmaker
9廻 *sa(shi)-mawa(su)* send (a car) around
10俯 *sa(shi)-utsumu(ku)* look down, hang the head
挟 *sa(shi)-hasa(mu)* insert, put between; interrupt (a conversation); harbor, entertain
紙 *sa(shi)gami* summons, official order
益 *saeki* marginal profit

差 sa(shitsu)-sa(saretsu) exchanging saké cups ⌈agency, agent
配 sahai conduct of business; management;
配人 sahainin landlord's agent
11違 sa(shi)-chiga(eru) misplace. sa-i difference
控 sa(shi)-hika(eru) be temperate, use moderation; withhold, refrain from
添 sa(shi)-so(eru) present in addition to. sa(shi)zo(e) the shorter sword; assistant, auxiliary, second. sa(shi)zo(i) assistance, auxiliary, second
許 sa(shi)-yuru(su)=emphatic for yuru(su) (see under 許 4324.0)
寄 sa(shi)-yo(ru), sa(shi)-yo(seru)=emphatic for yo(ru), yo(seru) (see under 寄 1318.0)
異 sa-i difference, disparity
率税 saritsuzei graduated tax
掛 sa(shi)-ka(keru) hold (an umbrella) over (someone). sa(shi)-ka(karu) approach, come near, arrive, hang over, overhang; be urgent, be imminent; be on the point of; be covered; pass by. sa(shi)ka(ke) penthouse, lean-to
掛小屋 sa(shi)ka(ke)goya, sakka(ke)goya
12遣 saken suru dispatch ⌊penthouse, lean-to
渡 sa(shi)-wata(ru) cross in a boat. sa(shi)-wata(shi) diameter, caliber, distance across
隔 sa(shi)-heda(teru)=emphatic for heda-(teru) (see under 隔 5016.0)
覗 sa(shi)-nozo(ku)=nozo(ku) (see under 覗 4287.0) ⌈3094.0)
登 sa(shi)-nobo(ru)=nobo(ru) (see under 登
等 satō difference in rank, grade, or class
替 sa(shi)-ka(eru) replace, substitute, change
13詰 sa(shi)zu(me) for the time being
障 sa(shi)-sawa(ru) be obstructed, be hindered. sa(shi)sawa(ri) obstacle, hindrance; offense ⌈neglect, slight
置 sa(shi)-o(ku) leave, let alone; ignore,
15潮 sa(shi)shio, sa(shi)jio rising tide
16薬 sa(shi)gusuri eye drops; subcutaneous injection ⌈(see under 翳 3679.0)
17翳 sa(shi)-kaza(su)=emphatic for kaza(su)
18額 sagaku balance, difference, margin
19繰 sa(shi)-ku(ru) manage skillfully
響 sa(shi)-hibi(ku) affect, influence

5

羚 3663 F1500 REI antelope.

6羊 kamoshika, reiyō antelope

6

善 See 606. [口]

翔 3664 F1507 SHŌ. ka(keru) soar, fly. [羽]

3上 ka(ke)-nobo(ru) fly up, mount up
10破 shōha suru complete a flight

A**着** 3665 F1500 CHAKU arrival, finish (in a race); suit counter. ki(ru), chaku(suru) put on, wear. ki(seru) clothe, dress, put on; cover, plate, coat, gild; veneer; blame for, impute a crime to. ki(konasu) wear, dress. tsu(ku), chaku(suru) arrive at, reach, attain to. ki(se) dish cover. ki(gonashi) style of dress. ki(nikui) uncomfortable or awkward to wear. -ki wearing; clothes.

3工 chakkō starting construction
4手 chakushu start, commencement
火 chakka igniting
水 chakusui alighting on water
尺 kijaku suit measurement; dress length; kimono-length bolt ⌈underwear
込 ki-ko(mu) wear extra clothes. kigo(mi)
丈 kitake dress length
心 kigokoro the feeling of clothes
心地 kigokochi fit and feel (of clothes)
切 ki-ki(ru) wear to rags, wear out completely. ki(ta)ki(ri) wearing all one owns
切雀 ki(ta)ki(ri) suzume a person with only
5用 chakuyō suru wear, have on ⌊one kimono
目 chakumoku viewpoint, observation
旧 ki-furu(su)=着古 (see below–5)
付 kitsu(ke) dressing (someone); attire
古 kifuru(su), kiburu(su) wear out. kifuru(shi), kiburu(shi) old clothes
6衣 chakui dressing (oneself); one's clothes
任 chakunin arrival at one's post
色 chakushoku color, coloration, coloring; embellishment
色写真 chakushoku shashin color photograph
7車 chakusha train arrival
初 kiso(me) first wearing (of a suit)
良 kiyo(i) comfortable to wear
身着儘 ki(no)mi-ki(no)mama de (sleep) in one's clothes; without changing one's clothes; with only the clothes on one's back
8逃 kini(ge) running off wearing someone
物 kimono clothes, kimono ⌊else's clothes
服 chakufuku dressing (oneself); embezzlement, misappropriation
直 ki-nao(su) change clothes ⌈steady
実 chakujitsu na trustworthy, sober-minded,
9通 kidō(shi) wearing continuously
重 ki-kasa(neru) wear layers of clothes
発 chakuhatsu arrival and departure
草臥 ki-kutabi(reru) be worn out, wear out
信 chakushin arrival of mail

信局 *chakushinkyoku* destination post office
10 席 *chakuseki* taking a seat
座 *chakuza* taking a seat
倒 *kidao(re)* extravagance in dress
値 *chakune* C.I.F. (cost, insurance, and freight)
時 *kidoki* the proper time to wear (certain clothes)
流 *kinaga(shi)* not dressed up
破 *ki-yabu(ru)* wear out (clothes)
料 *kiryō* clothing materials
剣 *chakken, tsu(ke)ken* fixed bayonet
殺 *ki-koro(su)* wear out (clothes) without repairing
荷 *chakuni, chakka* goods arrived
帯 *chakutai* wearing a maternity belt
茣蓙 *kigoza* mat that is worn
陸 *chakuriku* landing, alighting
陸地 *chakurikuchi* landing zone
陸車輪 *chakuriku sharin* landing wheel
陸料 *chakurikuryō* (airplane) landing charges
陸場 *chakurikujō* landing field, airstrip
11 添 *ki-so(u)* put on extra clothing
船 *chakusen* ship arrival
道楽 *kidōraku* love of dress; lover of fine clothes
眼 *chakugan* viewpoint, observation
眼点 *chakuganten* point observed or aimed at; viewpoint
12 御 *chakugyo suru* (the emperor) takes his seat
換 *ki-ka(eru)* change clothes
港 *chakkō* arrival at port
脹 *ki-buku(reru)* be fat with extra winter clothes
筆 *chakuhitsu* beginning to write; manner of writing
着 *chakuchaku* steadily
弾距離 *chakudan kyori* range (of a gun)
替 *kiga(e)* changing clothes; change of clothes
替所 *kiga(e)jo* dressing room
13 腹 *chakufuku* embezzlement, misappropriation
際 *kigiwa* being about to wear; one's appearance in (certain clothes)
飾 *ki-kaza(ru)* dress up; wear fine clothes
馴 *ki-na(rasu)* get used to wearing
電 *chakuden* telegram received
意 *chakui* conception; caution
想 *chakusō* conception, idea
14 慣 *ki-na(rasu)* get used to wearing
駅 *chakueki* destination station
18 癖 *kiguse* dressing habits
類 *kirui* clothing
20 艦 *chakkan* deck landing
22 籠 *kigomi, kigome* underwear

7

羨 3666 F1502 SEN. *uraya(mu)* be envious, be jealous, covet. *uraya(mashii)* enviable.

11 望 *sembō* envy

A **群** 3667 F1500 **羣** GUN group, crowd, gang, herd, swarm, flock; common run. *mu(reru), mura(garu)* crowd, flock, swarm. *mu(re)* group, crowd, flock, herd, bevy, school, swarm; cluster (of stars); clump. *mura* crowd; swarming.

3 口 *gunkō* the words of many people
小 *gunshō* the small, the many, the vulgar
山 *gunzan* many mountains; mountain ranges
下 *gunka* many retainers
5 生 *gunsei* all animate creation; many people; gregariousness
立 *murada(tsu)* gather and stand together. *murada(chi)* standing in a group
民 *gummin* masses, populace, multitude
6 羊 *gun-yō* many sheep
臣 *gunshin* the whole body of officials
邦 *gumpō* many countries
7 体 *guntai* colony (in biology)
芳 *gumpō* many beautiful flowers
8 青 *gunjō* ultramarine, navy blue
居 *mure-i(ru)* crowding in, coming together. *gunkyo* gregariousness
牧 *gumboku* many local officials
盲 *gummō* blind populace; illiterates
9 俗 *gunzoku* many people, the public
神 *gunshin* many gods
10 起 *gunki* insurrection
島 *guntō* archipelago, group of islands
党 *guntō* many political parties; organizing a party
書 *gunsho* many books
11 遊 *gun-yū* many swimming together
盗 *guntō* gang of robbers
12 棲 *gunsei* gregariousness
雲 *murakumo* cloud masses
落 *gunraku* many communities; a cluster of plants
衆 *gunshū* crowd, multitude
雄 *gun-yū* rival chiefs
雄割拠 *gun-yū kakkyo* rivalry of local barons
集 *mu(re)-atsu(maru)* gather in large groups. *gunshū* crowd, multitude, group
集心理 *gunshū shinri* mob psychology, mass psychology
集心理学 *gunshū shinrigaku* mob psychology, mass psychology
14 像 *gunzō* sculptured group
疑 *gungi* many doubts; doubts of the people
聚 *gunshū* a herd, a flock
20 議 *gungi* multitudinous opinions

A **義** 3668 F1502 GI justice, righteousness, morality; humanity; integrity, honor, loyalty, chivalry, devotion; meaning, significance. *gi to suru* justify. *gi-* in-law; artificial.

2 人 *gijin* righteous man, noble-hearted man

3 士 *gishi* loyal retainer; righteous person; martyr
子 *gishi* adopted child
4 心 *gishin* chivalrous spirit, public spirit
手 *gishu* artificial arm; artificial hand
父 *gifu* father-in-law; foster father; stepfather
犬 *giken* faithful dog
化 *gika* (Catholic) justification
太夫 *gidayū* ballad-drama music
5 母 *gibo* mother-in-law, foster mother, stepmother
甲 *gikō* plectrum
民 *gimin* public-spirited man
兄 *gikei* elder brother-in-law
兄弟 *gikyōdai* brother-in-law, stepbrother, sworn brother
6 気 *giki* chivalrous spirit, chivalry, heroism
7 足 *gisoku* artificial leg
兵 *gihei* loyal soldier, volunteer corps
弟 *gitei* younger brother-in-law
8 金 *gikin* contribution
姉 *gishi* elder sister-in-law
枝 *gishi* grafting (plants)
肢 *gishi* artificial limb
者 *gisha* righteous person
和団 *Giwadan* the Boxers
妹 *gimai* younger sister-in-law
姉妹 *gishimai* sister-in-law
9 軍 *gigun* righteous army
俠 *gikyō* chivalry, generosity, heroism
俠心 *gikyōshin* chivalrous spirit, public spirit
勇 *giyū* heroism, loyalty and courage
勇団 *giyūdan* patriotic volunteer corps
勇兵 *giyūhei* volunteer soldier
勇軍 *giyūgun* volunteer corps
勇艦隊 *giyū kantai* volunteer fleet
10 徒 *gito* champions of righteousness
倉 *gisō* emergency grain storehouses
挙 *gikyo* worthy undertaking; heroic deed
烈 *giretsu* heroism, nobility of soul
捐 *gien* donation, contribution
捐金 *gienkin* donation, contribution
11 眼 *gigan* artificial eye
脚 *gikyaku* artificial leg
務 *gimu* duty, obligation, responsibility, liability
務心 *gimushin* sense of duty
務年限 *gimu nengen* obligatory term of service
務的 *gimuteki* obligatory, binding, compulsory
務者 *gimusha* debtor, responsible person
務教育 *gimu kyōiku* compulsory education
務観念 *gimu kannen* sense of duty
理 *giri* sense of duty, sense of honor, obligation, justice, courtesy, debt of gratitude
理人情 *giri-ninjō* justice and charity, duty and humanity
理不知 *girishirazu* ignorant of one's duty; a person ignorant of one's duty
理付合 *girizu(ki)a(i)* association based merely on duty
理尽 *girizu(ku) de* out of deference to; as a matter of duty
理合 *giria(i)* association based merely on duty
理知 *girishi(razu)* ungrateful person
理張 *giriba(ru)* be faithful to duty; be overzealous socially
理堅 *girigata(i)* loyal to duty
12 歯 *gishi* artificial tooth, false tooth
絶 *gizetsu suru* disown, break off relationship
援 *gien* contribution
援金 *gienkin* donation, contribution
13 解 *gikai* exposition, commentary
賊 *gizoku* chivalrous robber
戦 *gisen* holy war, crusade
14 僕 *giboku* faithful servant
旗 *giki* flag of loyalty, banner of righteousness
認 *ginin* (Christian) justification
塾 *gijuku* a private school
15 憤 *gifun* righteous indignation

9

羮 3669 F1503 F1504 **羹** Kō. *atsumono* hot soup.

羯 3670 F1503 F1504 KATSU, KETSU barbarian.

16 磨 *katsuma* karma

養 3671 F2083 A **養** Yō. *yashina(u)* bring up, rear; adopt, foster; support; promote (health); cultivate, develop. *yashina(i)* nutrition, nurture; rearing; sustenance; manure. [食]

3 女 *yōjo* adopted daughter; stepdaughter; daughter-in-law
子 *yashina(i)go* foster child. *yōshi* adopted son
子先 *yōshisaki* one's adopted home
子縁組 *yōshi engumi* adopting an heir
4 手 *yashina(i)te* supporter
分 *yōbun* nourishment, sustenance
毛剤 *yōmōzai* hair tonic
父 *yōfu* foster father
父母 *yōfubo* adopted parents
5 母 *yōbo* foster mother
兄 *yōkei* elder adopted brother
生 *yōjō* health care, hygiene; recuperation
生法 *yōjōhō* hygiene, sanitation, rules of health
生訓 *yōjōkun*＝word above
6 成 *yōsei* training, education
成所 *yōseijo* training school
成学校 *yōsei gakkō* training school
老 *yōrō* provision for the aged
老年金 *yōrō nenkin* endowment annuity, old-age pension
老金 *yōrōkin* old-age pension

老院 *yōrōin* old-folks home
老保険 *yōrō hoken* endowment insurance
老施設 *yōrō shisetsu* old folks' home
老資金 *yōrō shikin* old-age endowment
7兵 *yōhei* feeding soldiers
兎 *yōto* rabbit raising
兎場 *yōtojō* rabbit warren
8狐 *yōko* fox farming
育 *yōiku suru, yashina(i)-soda(teru)* bring up, rear; cultivate
育者 *yōikusha* guide, nurse, guardian
育院 *yōikuin* orphanage
育掛 *yōikugakari* guide, nurse, guardian
9祖父 *yōsofu* foster grandfather
祖母 *yōsobo* foster grandmother
10家 *yōka* adopted family
蚕 *yōsan* silkworm culture
蚕地 *yōsanchi* silk-raising district
蚕所 *yōsanjo* cocoonery
蚕室 *yōsanshitsu* silkworm nursery
蚕家 *yōsanka* silk raiser
蚕業 *yōsangyō* sericulture
蚕農家 *yōsan nōka* silk-raising farmer
11豚 *yōton* hog raising, hogs
豚者 *yōtonsha* hog raiser, swineherd
豚場 *yōtonjō* hog farm
豚業 *yōtongyō* hog-raising industry
魚 *yōgyo* fish farming, fish breeding
魚池 *yōgyochi* fishpond, breeding pond
魚家 *yōgyoka* fish farmer, fish breeder
魚場 *yōgyojō* fish farm; fish hatchery
魚槽 *yōgyosō* fish tank
12殖 *yōshoku* culture, raising, breeding
殖真珠 *yōshoku shinju* cultured pearl
13嗣子 *yōshishi* adopted heir
蜂 *yōhō* beekeeping
蜂所 *yōhōjo* apiary
蜂舎 *yōhōsha* beehive stand
蜂家 *yōhōka* beekeeper
蜂植物 *yōhō shokubutsu* plants for bees
蜂園 *yōhōen* bee farm
蜂箱 *yōhōbako* beehive
16親 *yōshin, yashina(i) oya* foster parents
樹園 *yōjuen* arboretum, tree nursery
19鶏 *yōkei* poultry
鶏家 *yōkeika* poultryman
鶏場 *yōkeijō* poultry farm
鶏業 *yōkeigyō* poultry farming
20護 *yōgo* protection, care
護学級 *yōgo gakkyū* retarded-children's class
護学校 *yōgo gakkō* school for handicapped children
護施設 *yōgo shisetsu* children's home
護教諭 *yōgo kyōyu* nurse-teacher

13

羹 3672/F1504 See 羹 3669.

15

羸 See 337.

RAD. 羽 124

Hane feather, wing. At top: *hane kammuri*. Variant: 羽. Nickname: Wing.

羽 3673/F1504 羽 B U. *ha* feather. *hane* feather, plumage, wing; blade, paddle, fan. *wa* bird counter.

2二重 *habutae* habutae silk
3子 *hago, hane* shuttlecock
子板 *hago-ita* battledore
子突 *hanetsu(ki)* battledore and shuttlecock
4毛 *umō* feathers, plumage, down
化 *uka* emergence (of insects); people sprouting wings and flying
太 *hata* grouper (a fish)
5目 *hame* panel, wainscoting; predicament, plight
目板 *hame-ita* wainscoting
6衣 *hagoromo* robe of feathers
交 *hagai* pinion, wings
団扇 *ha-uchiwa* feather fan
7抜 *hanu(ke)* molting
8突 *hanetsu(ki)* battledore and shuttlecock
9音 *haoto, hane oto* flapping sound, sound of birds on the wing
風 *hakaze* breeze caused by flapping wings
10振 *habu(ri)* plumage; influence, power
根突 *hanetsu(ki)* battledore and shuttlecock
13搏 *habata(ku)* flap, flutter. *habataki* flapping, fluttering
裏 *ha-ura* the underside of a bird's wings
蒲団 *hanebuton* down puff; quilt of down, feather bed
14箒 *habōki, hanebōki* feather brush
15撃 *ha-u(tsu), habata(ku)* flap wings
17翼 *uyoku* wings; assistance
18織 *haori* Japanese coat. *hao(ru)* put on, slip over
19蟻 *ha-ari, hane ari* winged ant

4

翁 翁 See 596.

翅 See 2040.

5

翌 3674/F1506 翌 Yoku *akuru* next, following.
B
4日 *yokujitsu* the next day
月 *yokugetsu* the next month
6年 *yokutoshi, yokunen* the next year
11翌日 *yokuyokujitsu* two days after
翌年 *yokuyokunen* year after next
12晩 *yokuban* the next evening, the next night
暁 *yokugyō* at dawn the next day
朝 *yokuchō, yokuasa* the next morning

習 3675/F1506 習 Shū. *nara(u)* learn, be
A taught, take lessons, practice. *nara(wasu)* have children study or practice. *nara(i)* habit, custom, usage; the way, the lot. *nara(washi)* custom, usage, tradition.
4込 *nara(i)-ko(mu)* master, be grounded in
6行 *nara(i)-okona(u)* learn to do, learn to
字 *shūji* penmanship, calligraphy └follow
合 *shūgō* reconciling or compromising views
7作 *shūsaku* a practice project
8性 *shūsei* habit, second nature
学 *shūgaku* learning, studying
9俗 *shūzoku* usage, convention
11得 *shūtoku* learning, acquirement
12覚 *nara(i)-obo(eru)* learn (a trade)
14練 *shūren* drill, training
慣 *shūkan* custom, habit, way, usage,
慣性 *shūkansei* tendency └practice
慣法 *shūkanhō* common law
15熟 *shūjuku* mastery, proficiency
18癖 *shūheki* habit

6

翕 See 514.

翔 See 3664.

8

翡 See 5083.

翠 3676/F1508 Sui. *midori* green, verdure.
5玉 *suigyoku* emerald; jade
6色 *suishoku* verdure, green
8雨 *suiu* rain falling on green leaves
13微 *suibi* blue mountains, mountain side
楊 *suiyō* willows in leaf
14緑玉 *suiryokugyoku* emerald
22巒 *suiran* green hills, verdant mountains

9

翦 See 剪 599.

翩 See 245.

翥 3677/F1508 Sho fly up.

翫 3678/F1509 Gan. *moteaso(bu)* (see under 玩 2925.0).
8味 *gammi suru* taste; enjoy; appreciate
15賞 *ganshō* appreciation, admiration

10

翰 See 794.

11

翳 3679/F1510 Ei. *kaza(su)* hold aloft; shade the eyes); stick (something) in the hair. *kasu(mu)* be purblind.
5目 *kasumime* blurred eyes

翼 3680/F1511 翼 Yoku wing; plane;
B flank. *tsubasa* wings.
7状 *yokujō* wing shape
10桁 *yokuketa* spar
12幅 *yokufuku* wingspread
14端 *yokutan* wing tip
15賛 *yokusan* support, approval, countenance
17翼 *yokuyoku na* careful, prudent

12

翹 See 1153.

翻 3681/F1511 飜 Hon. Han. *hirugae(ru)*
B *vi* turn over, wave, flutter. *hirugae(su) vt* change (one's mind); turn, reverse; wave, flutter; dodge. *kobo(reru), kobo(su)* (see under 零 5048.0). *hirugae(tte)* on second thought.
7弄 *honrō suru* toss (a ship) about; flirt with; make fun of
8刻 *honkoku, hankoku* reprint
10案 *hon-an* an adaptation
11訳 *hon-yaku* translation, version

訳官 *hon-yakkan* official translator
訳者 *hon-yakusha* translator
訳物 *hon-yakumono* a translation
訳家 *hon-yakuka* translator
訳書 *hon-yakusho* a translation
訳違 *hon-yakuchiga(i)* mistranslation
訳権 *hon-yakuken* translation rights
[12] 然 *honzen to, hanzen to* suddenly
筋斗 *tombogaeri, mondori* somersault, handspring, tumbling
[13] 意 *hon-i suru* change one's mind

— 14 —

耀 See 1375.

— 19 —

糶 3682/F1437 Chō. *seri* auction. [米]

[3] 下 *serisa(ge)* Dutch auction
[7] 売 *seriu(ri)* auction

RAD. 老 125

Rō or *oi* old. Variant: 耂 (4 strokes) *oi kammuri* or *oigashira*. Nickname: Old Man.

A 老 3683/F1512 Rō aging, old age, old men. *o(iru), oiba(mu)* grow old. *fu-keru)* grow old. *o(iraku)* old age. *o(i)* old age; old man. *o(i)-* old, aging.

[2] 人 *rōjin* old man; old folks
[3] 女 *rōjo* old woman; senior lady-in-waiting
子 *o(i)go* child of one's old age. *Rōshi* Lao-tse, founder of Taoism
大 *rōdai* aging
大国 *rōtaikoku, rōdaikoku* decadent nation
大家 *rōtaika* veteran authority
[4] 手 *rōshu* an old hand, past master, veteran, expert
木 *rōboku, o(i)ki* an old tree
父 *rōfu* one's aged father
込 *o(i)-ko(mu)* grow old, weaken with age
中 *rōjū* councilor of the shogun
公 *rōkō* (polite) old nobleman
友 *rōyū* an old friend
水夫 *rōsuifu* an old sailor
心 *o(i)gokoro* feeling old
心地 *o(i)gokochi* feeling old
少 *rōshō* old and young
少不定 *rōshō-fujō* uncertainty of life
夫 *rōfu* an old man; this old man (oneself)
夫婦 *rōfūfu* an old couple
[5] 母 *rōbo* an aged mother
生 *rōsei* an old man (referring to himself)
功 *rōkō na* veteran, experienced
巧 *rōkō na* veteran, experienced
幼 *rōyō* old people and children, young and old
台 *rōdai* (polite word in letters) an old person
兄 *rōkei* aging elder brother, respected aging friend
[6] 臣 *rōshin* senior retainer
行 *o(i)-yu(ku)* gradually grow old
成 *hine(ru)* grow old. *mase(ta)* precocious, forward, sophisticated. *rōsei* maturity, experience, precocity
死 *rōshi suru* die of old age
朽 *rōkyū* superannuation, decrepitude. *o(i)-ku(chiru)* grow old and useless
壮 *rōsō* young and old
吏 *rōri* an experienced official
先 *o(i)saki* an old person's remaining years
先生 *rōsensei* an old teacher
年 *rōnen* old age, declining years
年者 *rōnensha* old people
年期 *rōnenki* old age
[7] 身 *rōshin* aged body; an old person (polite)
体 *rōtai* old body, an aged person
妓 *rōgi* an old geisha
杉 *rōsan* an old cryptomeria
兵 *rōhei* an old soldier, veteran
来 *rōrai* since growing old
寿 *rōju* longevity, old age
[8] 松 *o(i)matsu, rōshō* an old pine tree
波 *o(i)nami* growing old and wrinkled
若 *rōjaku, rōnyaku* old and young
苦 *rōku* the troubles of old age
妻 *rōsai* aged wife
果 *o(i)-ha(teru)* weaken with age
者 *rōsha* an old person
[9] 後 *rōgo* old age, declining years
荘学 *Rōsōgaku* Taoism
[10] 馬 *rōba, o(i)uma* old horse
骨 *rōkotsu* old bones, old man
病 *oiyami, rōbyō* infirmities of age
師 *rōshi* an aged teacher; aged priest
酒 *rōshu* old wine
将 *rōshō* veteran general
衰 *o(i)-otoro(eru)* grow old and weak. *rōsui* senility, old-age infirmity
翁 *rōō* an old man
耄 *o(i)-bo(reru)* to age and weaken. *rōmō, o(i)bo(re)* second childhood; senile person; age and weakness

叟 *rōsō* an old man
弱 *rōjaku* old-age infirmity; old and young
11婦 *rōfu* an old woman; this old woman (oneself)
惚 *o(i)bore(ru)* to age and weaken. *o(i)bore* second childhood; senile person; age and weakness
悴 *rōsui* getting old and emaciated
盛 *o(i)-saka(ru)* be vigorous in old age
視眼 *rōshigan* farsightedness
眼 *rōgan* farsightedness
眼鏡 *rōgankyō* glasses for older people
婆 *rōba* an old woman
婆心 *rōbashin* grandmotherly concern, excessive solicitude
12雄 *rōyū* an old hero
爺 *oyaji, rōya* elderly man, old man
廃 *rōhai* superannuation
廃物 *rōhaibutsu* waste matter, waste products
13僧 *rōsō* an old priest
媼 *rōon* an old woman
歳 *rōsai* old age
楽 *oiraku* an old man's leisure
農 *rōnō* an old farmer
14僕 *rōboku* old manservant
境 *rōkyō* old age, declining years
緑 *o(i)midori* dark green
練 *rōren na* experienced, veteran, skilled
練家 *rōrenka* expert, veteran
15輩 *rōhai* the aged
熟 *rōjuku* mature skill, maturity, mellowness
舗 *rōho, shinise* long-established shop
16儒 *rōju* an old Confucian scholar; a great teacher
嬢 *rōjō* maiden lady
樹 *rōju* an old tree
獪 *rōkai na* crafty, astute, wily
17優 *rōyū* an old actor or actress
齢 *rōrei* old age
齢者 *rōreisha* old people
齢艦 *rōreikan* superannuated vessel
18軀 *rōku* old age; enfeebled body
顔 *rōgan* face of an old person
19識 *rōshiki* mature ideas
20艦 *rōkan* superannuated ship
21鶯 *o(i)uguisu, rōō* a nightingale still singing when spring is past

4方 *kanga(e)kata* way of thinking; point of view; solution
込 *kanga(e)-ko(mu)* be absorbed in thought, meditate
5付 *kanga(e)-tsu(ku)* recall, remember; invent
出 *kanga(e)-da(su)* think out, invent; recall, remember; begin to think
古 *kōko* study of antiquities
古学 *kōkogaku* archeology
古学者 *kōkogakusha* archeologist
6回 *kanga(e)-megu(rasu)* ponder, think out (a solution)
合 *kanga(e)-a(waseru)* think of together
当 *kanga(e)-a(taru)* occur to one; suspect
7妣 *kōhi* one's deceased parents
抜 *kanga(e)-nu(ku)* reflect, think over
究 *kōkyū* investigation, research
8味 *kanga(e)-aji(wau)* carefully think over
物 *kanga(e)mono* puzzle, problem
直 *kanga(e)-nao(su)* reconsider
事 *kanga(e)goto* something to think about; concern, preoccupation, worry
9計 *kanga(e)-haka(ru)* plan
訂 *kōtei* critical historical research
査 *kōsa* consideration; test; quiz
10案 *kōan suru* contrive, plan, originate. *kōan* idea, plan; project; scheme; device, gadget
11違 *kanga(e)chiga(i)* misconception, mistake
深 *kanga(e)buka(i)* thoughtful, prudent
12証 *kōshō* investigation, research
量 *kōryō* consideration
13試 *kōshi* examination
14慣 *kanga(e)-na(reru)* be accustomed to think
様 *kanga(e)yō* way of thinking, viewpoint
察 *kōsatsu* consideration, inquiry
15慮 *kōryo* careful thought, consideration, deliberation
課 *kōka* studying students' or personnel records (for placement purposes)
課表 *kōkahyō* business record; personnel record
18験 *kōken* investigation
19覈 *kōkaku* thinking and investigating

2

A **考** 3684 / F1515 Kō thought, consideration; research, treatise. *kanga(eru)* think, consider, believe, suspect; be of the opinion; intend; expect, hope, fear; judge, conclude; imagine, suppose; regard as; be discreet; ponder over; reconsider; be prepared for; invent. *kanga(e)* thought; idea; opinion; intention; discretion; consideration; deliberation; resolution, plan; expectation; imagination.

3

考 See 3684.

孝 See 773. [子]

4

A **者 者** 3685 / F1516 SHA person; thing. *mono* person, somebody. *-sha* agent, actor.

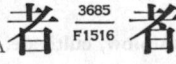

耄 3686 F1516 老 Bō, Mō senility.
[12]期 *bōki* age of senility
[13]碌 *mōroku* senility, second childhood

耆 3687 F1516 Ki, Shi senility.
[6]老 *kirō* old person in the fifties
那教 *Jainkyō* Jainism
[11]宿 *kishuku* veteran (educator), authority
[14]徳 *kitoku* an old man of character

5

者 3688 F1516 See 者 3685.

而 RAD. 126

Shikashite and then. Nickname: Rake.

而 3689 F1517 Ji. *shika(shite)* but, however. *shika(mo)* moreover, nevertheless. *sōshi(te)*, *soshi(te)* and.

3

B 耐 3690 F1518 Tai enduring. *ta(eru)* (see under 堪 1112.0).
[3]乏 *taibō* austerity, voluntary privation
乏生活 *taibō seikatsu* life of austerity, hard life
久 *taikyū* endurance, persistence, permanence, durability
久力 *taikyūryoku* durability, persistence, staying power, lasting quality
久性 *taikyūsei*＝word above
[4]水 *taisui* waterproof, watertight
切 *ta(e)-ki(reru)* be able to endure
火 *taika* fireproof
火材 *taikazai* fireproof material
火性 *taikasei* fire-resistant
火粘土 *taika nendo* fireproof clay
火煉瓦 *taika renga* firebrick
[7]忍 *ta(e)-shino(bu)* patiently endure. *tainin* patience, perseverance, fortitude
[11]貧生活 *taihin seikatsu* hard life
[12]湿 *taishitsu* moistureproof
寒 *taikan* coldproof
寒性 *taikansei* cold-resistant
寒装置 *taikan sōchi* winterizing
[14]酸 *taisan* acidproof, acid-resistant
[15]熱 *tainetsu* heat-resisting
震 *taishin* earthquake-proof
震力 *taishinryoku* strength to withstand earthquakes

耒 RAD. 127

Suki hen left-side "plow" or *rai-suki* (*rai* being the *on* both of *suki* "plow" and 來 or 耒 *kuru* "come"). Nickname: 3-Branch Tree (cf. Rads. 75 & 115).

耒 3691 F-X See 来 202.

4

耙 3692 F1519 Ha forked hoe.

耘 3693 F1519 Un. *kusagi(ru)* weed.

B 耗 3694 F1519 耗 Mō, Kō *he(ru)* decrease.
[10]高 *he(ri)daka* ullage, loss in weight
[12]廃 *kōhai* decline (in morality)

A 耕 3695 F1518 Kō. *tagaya(su)* plow, cultivate.
[3]土 *kōdo* rich soil, mold
土機 *kōdoki* farm tractor
[4]夫 *kōfu* farmer
[6]地 *kōchi* arable land; farm land
地整理 *kōchi seiri* resurvey of farm lands making certain adjustments
[7]作 *kōsaku* cultivation, farming
作地 *kōsakuchi* arable or cultivated land
作物 *kōsakubutsu* farm products
作者 *kōsakusha* tiller, farmer
作器械 *kōsaku kikai* farm implements
[8]牧 *kōboku* farming and dairying
[10]馬 *kōba* plow horse
耘 *kōun* farming, cultivation
耘機 *kōunki* farm tractor
[11]野 *kōya* arable land
運機 *kōunki* farm tractor

[18]農 *kōnō* farming; farmer
[14]種 *kōshu* (land) cultivation
種学 *kōshugaku* agronomy
[15]稼 *kōka* farming, agriculture
[18]織 *kōshoku* farming and weaving

9

耦 3696/F1519 Gū plowing; a pair.
[8]刺 *gūshi* killing each other

RAD. 耳 128

Mimi ear. At left: *mimi hen.* Enclosure: 耳. Nickname: Ear.

A 耳 3697/F1520 Ji ear. *mimi* ear; edge, border; loop; selvage; bread crusts.
[3]下腺 *jikasen* parotid gland
下腺炎 *jikasen-en* mumps
[4]孔 *jikō* ear orifice
元 *mimimoto de* around one's ears
[5]目 *jimoku* eye and ear; one's attention; informer
旧 *mimifuru(i)* stale, hackneyed
打 *mimiu(chi) suru* whisper in another's ear
[6]早 *mimibaya(i)* quick of hearing
朶 *mimitabu* ear lobe. *jida* ear lobe, ears
[8]門 *jimon* ear orifice
底 *jitei* ears
垂 *mimidare* ear discharge
学問 *mimi gakumon* learning by the ear, picked-up knowledge
[9]屎 *mimi kuso* ear wax
垢 *mimi aka* ear wax
科 *jika* otology
[10]疾 *jishitsu* ear diseases
[11]埵 *mimitabu* ear lobe
許 *mimimoto de* around one's ears
殼 *jikaku* auricle, external ear
寄 *mimiyo(ri) na* welcome, encouraging
[12]痛 *jitsū* earache 「*mi (ga) tō(i)* to be deaf
遠 *mimidō(i)* strange, uncommon; deaf. *mi-*
順 *jijun* intelligent and understanding heart; sixtieth year of age
[13]傾 *mimi (o) katamu(keru)* listen
掻 *mimikaki* ear pick
隠 *mimikaku(shi)* ear-covering hairdo
障 *mimizawa(ri) na* discordant, harsh
飾 *mimikaza(ri)* ear ornament
新 *mimiatara(shii)* new, novel
[14]鳴 *jimei, mimina(ri)* ringing in the ears
慣 *mimina(reru)* get used to hearing
漏 *jirō, mimidare* ear discharge, ear wax
語 *sasaya(ku)* whisper, murmur. *jigo* whisper
鼻 *jibi* ear and nose
鼻咽喉 *jibi-inkō* ear, nose, and throat
[16]盥 *mimidarai* tub with handles
[17]聾 *mimishii* deafness; a deaf person
擦 *mimikosuri* whispering
環 *mimiwa, jikan* earring

翼 *jiyoku* auricle, pinna
[19]鏡 *jikyō* ear speculum

2

耶 3698/F1521 Ya. Ja. *ya, ka* question mark.
[19]蘇 *Yaso* Jesus
蘇紀元 *Yaso Kigen* Christian Era
蘇紀元後 *Yaso Kigengo* After Christ, A.D.
蘇紀元前 *Yaso Kigenzen* Before Christ, B.C.
蘇教 *Yasokyō* Christianity

A 取 3699/F315 取 Shu. *to(ru)* take, hold, seize, catch, capture; fetch; receive, procure, obtain; adopt (a measure); engage (graduates); choose; order (foodstuffs); pick, pluck; make, produce; eat; set up (camp); charge; administer; transact; take (pains); make out (the meaning); remove; take off (one's hat); take out (spots); strike out (words); weed, catch (fish); deprive of; steal; capture (territory), annex; need, require; reserve (rooms); subscribe to; press (a point home); take (a (picture); possess. *to(reru)* can be held, can take; come off, come apart, be off, be removed; be relieved (of pain); be obtained, be produced; be caught; be earned; come out (well) (a photo); require (time); be interpreted as; can get; let (light) in; take (one's measure); can feel (the pulse); take (a pen and write). *to(tchimeru)* drive into a corner, take to task, take it out on. *to(ttoku)* =*to(tte)o(ku)* 取置 (see below–13). *to(tte)* to, for, in the case of; including. [又]
[2]入 *to(ri)-i(reru)* take in, gather in, harvest; accept, adopt, introduce (customs). *to(ri)-i(ru)* get into (someone's favor), win (another's heart), ingratiate oneself with. *to(ri)-i(re)* ingathering, taking in, harvest
入口 *tori-ireguchi* intake
入祭 *To(ri)-i(re) (no) Matsu(ri)* Harvest Festival
[3]下 *to(ri)-sa(geru)* withdraw, dismiss. *to(ri)-o(rosu)*=*o(rosu)* (see under 下 9.0)

竹米糸缶网四羊羽老耂而耒【耳】2聿肉月臣自至臼舌舛舟艮色艸艹虍虫血行衣ネ西 6

6 竹米糸缶网罒羊羽老耂而耒【2耳】聿肉月臣自至臼舌舛舟艮色艸卄虍虫血行衣ネ西

上 *to(ri)-a(geru)* take up, pick up; deal with; adopt, accept, listen to; dispossess, expropriate, confiscate, revoke; deliver (a baby) 「handle, knob, grip

4 手 *to(ri)te* receiver, recipient, taker. *to(t)te*

方 *to(ri)kata* way of taking (a photo)

止 *to(ri)-ya(meru)* stop, withdraw. *to(ri)-to(meru)*＝取留 (see below–10). *to(ri)-ya(me)* cancellation

切 *to(ri)ki(ri)* taking and not returning

分 *to(ri)-wa(keru)* divide, separate; distribute; assort. *to(ri)wa(ke)*, *to(ri)wa(kete)* especially, particularly. *toribun* share, portion 「付 2842.5

片付 *to(ri)-katazu(keru)*＝*katazu(keru)* 片

込 *to(ri)-ko(mu)* take in; introduce into; embezzle; be in confusion; get into favor with 「tions

込事 *toriko(mi)goto* confusion, complica-

込詐欺 *toriko(mi) sagi* confidence game

引 *torihiki* transactions, deal, business

引先 *torihikisaki* customer, client, business connection

引所 *torihikijo, torihikisho* stock exchange

引高 *torihikidaka* turnover, volume of

引員 *torihiki-in* broker ⌊business

引量 *torihikiryō* volume of business

引銀行 *torihiki ginkō* one's bankers

5 広 *to(ri)-hiro(geru)*, *to(ri)-hiro(meru)*＝取拡 (see below–8) 「replace

代 *to(tte) ka(waru)* supplant, supersede,

外 *to(ri)-hazu(su)* remove, take away; dismantle; demount 「molish, dismantle

払 *to(ri)-hara(u)* remove, take away, de-

去 *to(ri)-sa(ru)* take away, remove, leave out

出 *to(ri)-da(su)* take out; produce; pick out

仕切 *to(ri)-shiki(ru)* manage alone

立 *to(ri)-ta(teru)* collect; employ, appoint; promote; patronize; exact (taxes). *torita(te)* collection, levy; appointment, employment; promotion; patronage. *torita(te) no* fresh, freshly picked. *torita(tete)* particularly

立金 *toritatekin* collected money

付 *to(ri)-tsu(keru)* draw, cash; patronize; furnish, install; establish (regulations). *to(ri)-tsu(ku)* hold fast to, catch hold of; possess, obsess, haunt. *toritsu(ke)* run on a bank; drawing, cashing; installation, furnishing. *toritsu(ke) no* regular (tradesman). *toritsu(ki)* beginning; rudiments; foot (of a hill road); edge (of town). *to(t)tsu(ki)* the beginning; the first you come to; first impression

付工事 *toritsuke kōji* installation (of built-in furnishings

付品 *toritsu(ke)hin* fixtures, furnishings

付様 *to(tte) tsu(keta) yō na* artificial, affected, forced, unnatural

6 回 *to(ri)-mawa(su)* manage, treat

尽 *to(ri)-tsuku(su)* take all

成 *to(ri)na(shi)*, *to(ri)-na(su)*＝執成 1097.6

交 *to(ri)-ma(zeru)* mix, put together. *to(ri)-kawa(su)* exchange, interchange. *to(ri)-ma(zete)* all together, in all

合 *to(ri)-a(u)* take each other's (hand); scramble for; take notice of; have to deal with. *tori-a(waseru)* assort, arrange, group, combine, mix; match, garnish. *toria(i)* a scramble. *toriawa(se)* combination

返 *tori-kae(su)* get back, regain, retrieve, recover; recuperate; recall; undo; make good, make up for, redeem; withdraw. *to(tte) kae(su)* turn back, hurry back. *to(ri)kae(shi)* recovery, making up for, catching up

返付 *to(ri)kae(shi) (no) tsu(kanai)* irrevocable, irretrievable, irreparable

次 *to(ri)-tsu(gu)* act as agent; intermediate; transmit, convey. *toritsu(gi)* agency; agent; intermediation; relaying (a tele-

次店 *toritsugiten* agency ⌊gram).

次所 *toritsugijo* agency

次商 *toritsugishō* agency

扱 *to(ri)-atsuka(u)* treat; manage; handle, manipulate; conduct, transact; take charge of; accept (telegrams). *tori-atsuka(i)* treatment, dealing, service; handling, manipulation; transaction, management

扱人 *toriatsukainin* agent, person in charge

扱所 *toriatsukaijo* office, agency

扱法 *toriatsukaihō* method of handling

7 足 *to(runi)ta(ranai)* beneath notice, insignificant, trifling

囲 *to(ri)-kako(mu)* surround, crowd around

戻 *to(ri)-modo(su)* take back, regain, resume, recover, redeem, recapture

抑 *to(ri)-osa(eru)*＝取押 (see below–8)

材 *shuzai* choice of subject

決 *toriki(me)*＝取極 (see below–12)

糺 *to(ri)-tada(su)*＝取糾 (see below–9)

乱 *to(ri)-mida(su)* mess up, disturb; be

来 *to(tte) ku(ru)* fetch, go and get ⌊agitated

沙汰 *to(ri)zata, to(ri)sata* rumor, gossip, criticism, comment

8 固 *to(ri)-kata(meru)* defend, fortify 「miss

逃 *to(ri)-ni(gasu)* let escape, fail to catch,

所 *to(ri)dokoro*＝*torie* 取柄 (see below–9)

押 *to(ri)-osa(eru)* catch, seize, capture; quiet (a horse)

拡 *to(ri)-hiro(meru)*, *to(ri)-hiro(geru)* enlarge, extend; widen; spread (to air
拉 *to(ri)-hishi(gu)* defeat, crush ⌊something)
取 *to(ri)do(ri) no* various
舎 *shusha*＝取捨 (see below–11)
並 *to(ri)-nara(beru)* emphatic for *nara(beru)* (see under 並 589.0)
直 *to(rimo)nao(sazu)* namely, in other words. *to(ri)-nao(su)* recover, mend, change one's mind; get a firmer hold of; wrestle over again ⌈4685.3
逆上 *to(ri)-nobo(seru)*＝*nobo(seru)* 逆上
放題 *to(ri)hōdai* taking as much as you wish
9 持 *to(ri)-mo(tsu)* treat, entertain; mediate; recommend. *torimo(chi)* treatment, reception; mediation, recommendation
柄 *to(ri)e* worth, merit, redeeming future
糾 *to(ri)-tada(su)* ask, demand; investigate
計 *to(ri)-hakara(u)* manage, arrange, dispose of, settle, deal with
除 *to(ri)-no(keru)* remove, clear away, get rid of; make an exception of; lay aside, reserve. *to(ri)-nozo(ku)* remove, take
前 *to(ri)mae* share, portion ⌊away; set apart
急 *to(ri)-iso(gu)* hurry. *to(ri)iso(gi)* in haste
巻 *to(ri)-ma(ku)* surround, encircle, enclose. *torima(ki)* followers, adherents
巻連 *torima(ki) ren* followers, adherents
10 高 *to(re)daka* catch, yield
進 *to(ri)-susu(mu)* go on to the finals
捉 *to(t)tsuka(maeru)* catch, seize, arrest, capture. *to(t)tsuka(maru)* be caught, can catch
捌 *to(ri)-saba(ku)* manage; settle, judge, try
残 *to(ri)-noko(su)* leave behind
紛 *to(ri)-magi(reru)* be in confusion; be perplexed; be busily engaged
粉 *to(ri)ko* rice meal
殺 *to(ri)-koro(su)* curse (a person) to death, haunt to death ⌈(a life)
留 *to(ri)-to(meru)* ascertain, make sure; save
留無 *to(ri)to(me)na(i)*, *to(ri)to(meno)na(i)* rambling, incoherent, vague, absurd
消 *to(ri)-ke(su)* cancel, nullify, revoke, rescind, withdraw, retract, take back, repeal, quash, abrogate, annul, countermand, recall
消不能 *torike(shi)-funō* irrevocable
消記事 *torikeshi kiji* announcement for correction
消権 *torike(shi)ken* right to rescind
11 違 *to(ri)-chiga(eru)* mistake, take the wrong one; misunderstand
掛 *to(ri)-kaka(ru)*, *to(k)kaka(ru)* begin, set to work, proceed to business. *to(ri)-ka(keru)* begin to take

捨 *shusha* adoption or rejection, choice,
混 *to(ri)-ma(zeru)* mix ⌊option
舵 *to(ri)kaji* port; turning (a ship) to port
寄 *to(ri)-yo(seru)* send for, write for, procure, order, obtain ⌈(see below–13)
崩 *to(ri)-kuzu(su)*＝*to(ri)-kowa(su)* 敢毀
得 *to(ri)doku* gain, profit. *shutoku* acquisition, possession. *to(ri)e*＝取柄 (see
得権 *shutokuken* ownership ⌊above–9)
組 *to(ri)-ku(mu)* wrestle; be matched against, tackle. *torikumi* match, bout
組合 *to(k)ku(mi)-a(u)* grapple, tussle
12 遣 *to(ri)ya(ri)* exchange, give-and-take
揃 *to(ri)-soro(eru)*＝*soro(eru)* (see under 揃 1957.0)
極 *to(ri)-ki(meru)* arrange, agree upon, settle, make an appointment. *to(ri)ki(me)* arrangement, agreement, settlement
結 *to(ri)-musu(bu)* conclude; act as go-between; curry favor
散 *to(ri)-chi(rasu)* scatter around, clutter up
敢 *to(ri)a(ezu)* immediately; for the present; first of all ⌈4003.0)
落 *to(ri)-oto(su)*＝*o(tosu)* (see under 落
集 *to(ri)-atsu(meru)* gather, collect, assort
税人 *shuzeinin* tax collector, publican
越 *to(ri)-ko(su)* anticipate, do ahead of time
越苦労 *torikoshigurō*, *torikoshi kurō* unnecessary worry
替 *to(ri)-ka(eru)* exchange; barter; change, renew. *torika(e)*, *torika(ekko)* a swap, an
替品 *torikaehin* substitute ⌊exchange
13 損 *to(ri)-sokona(u)* fail to take, fail to get, miss ⌈brood over, pine for
詰 *to(ri)-tsu(meru)* corner; take to task;
毀 *to(ri)-kowa(su)*, *tori-kobo(tsu)* break down, demolish; tear down; dismantle
置 *to(tte) o(ku)* keep, hold, save, reserve, set aside
14 様 *to(ri)yō* way of taking; interpretation
静 *to(ri)-shizu(meru)* quiet (someone)
15 澄 *to(ri)-su(masu)* put on airs, put on company manners ⌈3576.0)
縋 *to(ri)-suga(ru)*＝*suga(ru)* (see under 縋
調 *to(ri)-shira(beru)* investigate, examine
締 *to(ri)-shima(ru)* manage, control, oversee. *torishima(ri)* control, management, regulation, discipline, supervision; good order; supervisor, superintendent, director, foreman
締役 *torishimariyaku* director ⌈lations
締規則 *torishima(ri) kisoku* control regu-
16 壊 *to(ri)-kowa(su)*＝取毀 (see above–13)
17 鍋 *to(ri)nabe* ladle
18 繕 *to(ri)-tsukuro(u)* mend, repair, patch; smooth over, temporize

[19]離 *to(ri)-hana(su)* detach, remove, drop, let go of
[20]競 *to(rik)kura* scramble
[21]纏 *to(ri)-mato(meru)*＝*mato(meru)* (see under 纏 3627.0)
[22]籠 *to(ri)-ko(meru)* confine, surround

4

耺 3700/F-X Nonstandard for 職 3718.

耾 3701/F-X Kō deafness.

耿 3702/F1521 Kō light.
[12]然 *kōzen* clearness, shining

耽 3703/F1521 TAN. *fuke(ru)* be addicted to; be absorbed in.
[9]美 *tambi* estheticism
美主義 *tambi shugi* estheticism
美的 *tambiteki* esthetic
美派 *tambiha* esthetic school
[13]溺 *tandeki* addiction, dissipation
溺生活 *tandeki seikatsu* riotous life
[14]読 *tandoku suru* read with avidity
読者 *tandokusha* inveterate reader

B **恥** 3704/F707/F1521 **耻** CHI. *haji* shame, dishonor, disgrace, humiliation, insult. *ha(jiru), ha(zuru)* feel ashamed. *ha(zubeki)* disgraceful, unbecoming. *ha(jirau)* feel shy, be coy, be bashful, blush. *ha(zukashigaru)* be shy, be bashful, be ashamed. *ha(zukashii)* bashful, ashamed, coy; disgraceful, shameful. *ha(zukashikaranu)* worthy, decent, honorable. [心]
[2]入 *ha(ji)-i(ru)* feel ashamed
[8]使 *ha(ji)-shi(meru)* put to shame, insult
知 *hajishi(razu)* shameless. *haji (o) shi(ru)* refrain from shameful acts
[10]骨 *chikotsu* pubic bone
晒 *hajisara(shi)* disgrace, shame
辱 *chijoku* disgrace, shame, insult
[11]雪 *haji (o) susu(gu)* restore face
[12]慌 *ha(ji)-awa(teru)* put to shame
[18]曝 *hajisara(shi)* shame, disgrace

5

聊 3705/F1522 RYŌ. *isasa(ka)* a little, slightly, somewhat. *isasaka no* scanty, trivial.

联 Nonstandard for 聯 3713.

聒 3706/F1522 KATSU noisy.
[3]子 *kasshi* polliwog, tadpole

7

聖 See 2960.

聘 3707/F1524 **聘** HEI. *hei(suru)* engage, invite, summon.
[5]用 *heiyō suru* engage, hire

8

聘 See 3707.

聞 See 4959.

聡 3708/F1526 **聰** SŌ. *sato(i)* wise; having a quick memory. *mimizato(i)* excellent hearing; quick understanding.
[8]明 *sōmei* wisdom, sagacity
[10]敏 *sōbin* sagacity, cleverness

聟 3709/F1525 See 婿 1239.

聳 Nonstandard for 聳 3715.

聢 3710/F1525 (国字) *shika to* certainly, definitely, exactly.

聚 3711/F1524 SHU. SHŪ. *atsu(maru)* assemble. *atsu(meru)* gather (people) together.
[12]落 *shuraku, shūraku* centers of population (towns and villages)
[17]斂 *shūren* gathering in; heavy taxation

11

聲 3712/F1527 See 声 1066.

聯 3713/F1526 REN.＝連 4702, q.v. for compounds.

聱 3714/F1527 Gō poor sentences.

聽 See 聡 3708.

聳 3715/F1528 SHŌ. *sobi(eru)* rise, soar, tower. *sobi(yakasu)* throw back (the shoulders and swagger along).

5 立 *sobi(e)-ta(tsu)* tower up. *shōritsu suru* rise
11 動 *shōdō* shock ⌊precipitously

B **聴** 3716/F1529 **聽** CHŌ careful inquiry. *ki(kanai)* headstrong, naughty. *ki(ku)* (see under 聞 4959.0).

2 力 *chōryoku* hearing ability
力計 *chōryokukei* audiometer
4 込 *ki(ki)-ko(mu), kikiko(mi)*＝聞込 4959.4
8 官 *chōkan* auditory organ
者 *chōsha* hearer, listener
取 *chōshu* listening, hearing, audition, radio reception
取者 *chōshusha* radio listener
取料 *chōshuryō* radio license fee
取書 *chōshusho* write-up of a criminal investigation
9 度 *chōdo* audibility
神経 *chōshinkei* auditory nerve
音 *chōon* hearing, sound detection, sound transmission ⌈listening instrument
音器 *chōonki* audiophone, hydrophone,
音機 *chōonki* sound detector (for approach of enemy planes)
10 従 *chōjū suru* follow advice
容 *chōyō* compliance, permission
11 許 *chōkyo* permission, approval
問会 *chōmonkai* public hearing
視 *chōshi* viewing and listening (to TV)
視覚 *chōshikaku* audio-visual ⌈aids
視覚教具 *chōshikaku kyōgu* audio-visual
12 衆 *chōshū* audience
集 *chōshū* audience
覚 *chōkaku* sense of hearing
診 *chōshin* stethoscopy
診器 *chōshinki* stethoscope
13 罪師 *chōzaishi* (Catholic) confessor
14 聞 *chōmon* audience, audition. *chōbun* hearing, listening
聞会 *chōmonkai* public hearing
15 器 *chōki* auditory organ
17 講 *chōkō* lecture attendance, auditing
講生 *chōkōsei* auditing student, listener
講券 *chōkōken* lecture admittance ticket
講者 *chōkōsha* a lecture audience

12

聶 3717/F1528 SHŌ whisper.

A **職** 3718/F1528 SHOKU employment, work, job, office. SHIKI occupation, handicraft. *tsukasa* (see under 司 877.0).

2 人 *shokunin* workman, mechanic, craftsman
人気質 *shokunin katagi, shokunin kishitsu* ⌊artisan spirit
3 工 *shokkō* factory worker
4 分 *shokubun* duties; vocation
6 印 *shokuin* a government seal
安 *shokuan* employment security office
名 *shokumei* occupation name; official title
7 別 *shokubetsu* class of service
8 長 *shokuchō* foreman, overseer
制 *shokusei* office organization; holy orders; ministry
9 級 *shokkyū* position, job grade
10 能 *shokunō* work efficiency
能給 *shokunōkyū* efficiency pay
員 *shokuin* staff, personnel, faculty; staff member, employee
員団 *shokuindan* a staff of assistants
員組合 *shokuin kumiai* employees' union
員録 *shokuinroku* list of government officials; army register, bluebook
11 域 *shokuiki* occupation, one's post
責 *shokuseki* official duties
階 *shokkai* position, job grade
階制 *shokkaisei* civil-service system
務 *shokumu* office, job, duties
務執行 *shokumu shikkō* performance of duties
務質問 *shokumu shitsumon* police check-up (on a criminal)
12 場 *shokuba* place of work, workshop
掌 *shokushō* duties, functions, office
13 群 *shokugun* occupational group
業 *shokugyō* occupation, business, trade, vocation, profession
業安定 *shokugyō antei* employment security
業安定所 *shokugyō anteijo, shokugyō anteisho* employment security office
業別 *shokugyōbetsu* by occupations
業性 *shokugyōsei* occupational
業軍人 *shokugyō gunjin* professional soldier
業病 *shokugyōbyō* occupational diseases
業婦人 *shokugyō fujin* career woman; employed woman
業紹介 *shokugyō shōkai* employment service
業紹介所 *shokugyō shōkaijo* employment agency
業教育 *shokugyō kyōiku* vocational education ⌈ball
業野球 *shokugyō yakyū* professional base-
業補導 *shokugyō hodō* vocational guidance
業適性 *shokugyō tekisei* vocational aptitudes
業斡旋所 *shokugyō assenjo* employment agency
14 歴 *shokureki* one's occupational history
種 *shokushu* occupation category
種別 *shokushubetsu* by occupations
15 権 *shokken* official authority
権上 *shokkenjō* by virtue of office, ex officio
19 蟻 *shokugi* worker ant

— 16 —

聾 See 5442.

聽 See 聴 3716.

聿 RAD. 129

Fude writing brush. At right: *fudezukuri*. Variant: 聿. Nickname: Brush.

— 4 —

A 書 3719 F923 SHO handwriting; letter, note; book. *sho(suru)* write. *ka(ku)* write, compose; draw, paint. *fumi* letter, note. [曰]

2 入 *ka(ki)-i(reru)* enter, write in, mortgage
入日 *kaki-i(re)bi* red-letter day, a day to look forward to
入時 *kaki-i(re)doki* best season (for profits)
3 及 *ka(ki)-oyo(bu)* be able to write (a certain amount) ⌈(*su*) write a new play
下 *ka(ki)-kuda(su)* write down. *ka(ki)-oro-*
上 *ka(ki)-a(geru)* finish writing; write out
4 手 *ka(ki)te* calligrapher, copyist; painter
方 *ka(ki)kata* manner of writing; penmanship, (prescribed) form
止 *ka(ki)-todo(meru)* record, chronicle. *ka(ki)-sa(su)* leave off writing, leave unfinished
込 *ka(ki)-ko(mu)* enter, write in; mortgage
中 *shochū* within the letter, the book, or the document
分 *ka(ki)-wa(keru)* classify and write up
5 目 *shomoku* catalog of books
立 *ka(ki)-ta(teru)* write up; feature; write against; enumerate
史 *shoshi* books; history of books; history of calligraphy ⌈*tsuke* note; bill
付 *ka(ki)-tsu(keru)* make a note of. *kaki-*
加 *ka(ki)-kuwa(eru)* add; add a postscript
写 *ka(ki)-utsu(su)* copy, transcribe. *shosha* copying
出 *ka(ki)-da(su)* begin to write; make an excerpt; make out a bill; present in writing. *ka(ki)da(shi)* opening paragraph;
冊 *shosatsu* books ⌊bill
生 *shosei* student; one studying while working in a teacher's home
生論 *shoseiron* impractical argument
6 尽 *ka(ki)-tsuku(su)* write exhaustively
式 *shoshiki* blank form ⌈(in writing)
伝 *ka(ki)-tsuta(eru)* hand down to posterity
交 *ka(ki)-ka(wasu)* exchange notes. *ka(ki)-ma(zeru)*＝書混 (see below–11)
名 *shomei* title of a book
7 見 *shoken* reading
足 *ka(ki)-ta(su)* add, write a postscript
体 *shotai* penmanship style; style of one's
改 *ka(ki)-arata(meru)* rewrite ⌊characters
役 *ka(ki)yaku* copyist, scribe
抜 *ka(ki)-nu(ku)* abstract, copy out, take an excerpt. *kakinu(ki)* quotation, excerpt
状 *shojō* letter
狂 *shokyō* bibliomania; bibliomaniac
乱 *ka(ki)-mida(su)* scribble, scrawl
初 *ka(ki)zo(me)* first writing of the new year
判 *ka(ki)han* written seal, monogram, signature
言葉 *ka(ki) kotoba* written language
8 店 *shoten* bookstore; publisher
房 *shobō* library; bookstore
送 *ka(ki)-oku(ru)* write a letter, send a letter
林 *shorin* bookstore
板 *ka(ki)-ita* writing tablet
法 *shohō* calligraphy, penmanship
取 *ka(ki)-to(ru)* take down, write from dictation. *kakito(ri)* dictation
画 *shoga* pictures and writings
並 *ka(ki)-nara(beru)* line up points in a
直 *ka(ki)-nao(su)* rewrite ⌊speech
表 *ka(ki)-ara(wasu)* write out, express,
具合 *ka(ki)guai* style of writing ⌊publish
物 *shomotsu* books. *ka(ki)mono* something written, papers ⌈lover
物道楽 *shomotsu dōraku* bibliomania; book-
9 面 *shomen* letter, document, contents
風 *shofū* style of calligraphy
信 *shoshin* letter, message, correspondence
洩 *ka(ki)-mo(rasu)* omit, leave out (words)
巻 *shokan* book
架 *shoka* bookshelf, bookcase
院 *sho-in* window writing alcove; drawing room; study; school; publishing house
院造 *sho-inzuku(ri)* palatial Momoyama residential architecture
10 庫 *shoko* book room, library
起 *ka(ki)oko(shi)* opening paragraph
振 *kakibu(ri)* style of writing
残 *ka(ki)-noko(su)* omit (something) in writing; leave a will behind; leave a history behind
流 *ka(ki)-naga(su)* write with ease
消 *ka(ki)-ke(su)* erase and rewrite

破 *ka(ki)-yabu(ru)* write and tear up
紋 *ka(ki)mon* hand-drawn family crest
家 *shoka* good penman, calligrapher
留 *ka(ki)-to(meru)* write down; make a note of; jot down. *kakitome* registered mail
留料 *kakitomeryō* registration fee
留郵便 *kakitome yūbin* registered mail
記 *ka(ki)-shiru(su)* write down, record. *shoki* clerk, secretary, scribe
記会計 *shoki-kaikei* secretary-treasurer
記長 *shokichō* chief clerk, chief secretary
記官 *shokikan* secretary
記官長 *shokikanchō* chief secretary
記補 *shokiho* assistant clerk
[11]道 *shodō* calligraphy
過 *ka(ki)su(gi)* writing too much
違 *ka(ki)-chiga(eru)* miswrite. *ka(ki)chiga(i)* clerical error, slip of the pen
添 *ka(ki)-so(eru)* add, write a postscript
淫 *sho-in* booklover, bookworm
渋 *ka(ki)-shibu(ru)* hesitate to write or sign
混 *ka(ki)-ma(zeru)* write a medley of ideas
経 *Shokyō* Shu Ching (a Chinese classic)
終 *ka(ki)-owa(ru)* finish writing
崩 *ka(ki)-kuzu(su)* write in slurred characters
著 *ka(ki)-arawa(su)* publish
斎 *shosai* study, library, den
[12]越 *ka(ki)-ko(su)* write and send hither
遣 *ka(ki)-ya(ru)* send a note
換 *ka(ki)-kae(ru)* = 書替 (see below–12). *kakika(e)* writing over again
棚 *shodana* bookshelf
絵 *ka(ki)e* original picture; hand-drawn picture
証 *shoshō* documentary evidence
割 *kakiwa(ri)* background, scenery (on a stage)
散 *ka(ki)-chi(rasu)* scribble, scrawl
落 *ka(ki)-oto(su)* omit, leave out (words)
集 *ka(ki)-atsu(meru)* compile, collect
替 *ka(ki)-ka(eru)* rewrite; renew (a bond); transfer, convey
評 *shohyō* book review
評家 *shohyōka* book reviewer
[13]損 *ka(ki)-sokona(u)*, *ka(ki)-son(jiru)* miswrite
続 *ka(ki)-tsuzu(keru)* continue to write
辞 *shoji* the words of a letter
肆 *shoshi* bookstore
置 *kakio(ki)* farewell note, will
賈 *shoko* bookseller
聖 *shosei* master calligrapher
賃 *ka(ki)chin* writing charge
載 *ka(ki)-no(seru)* publish, print; register, enroll, enter
[14]慣 *ka(ki)-na(reru)* get used to writing
様 *ka(ki)zama* manner of writing
漏 *ka(ki)-mo(rasu)* omit in writing, leave out
誤 *ka(ki)-aya(maru)* miswrite
算 *shosan* writing and arithmetic
誌学 *shoshigaku* bibliography
[16]翰 *shokan* letter, note, epistle
翰文 *shokambun* letter-writing style
翰箋 *shokansen* letter paper
[17]擲 *ka(ki)-nagu(ru)* dash off (articles)
[18]難 *ka(ki)niku(i)* difficult to write or draw
類 *shorui* documents, papers
類箱 *shoruibako* filing cabinet
簡 *shokan* letter, note, epistle
簡文 *shokambun* letter-writing style, epistolary style
簡紙 *shokanshi* stationery
簡集 *shokanshū* collected letters
簡箋 *shokansen* letter paper
[20]籍 *shoseki, shojaku* books, publication
籍商 *shosekishō* bookseller, bookstore
籍業 *shosekigyō* publishing business

5

晝 3720/F907 See 昼 53. [日]

6

粛 See 115.

畫 3721/F1276 See 画 50. [田]

7

肆 See 4939.

畫 3722/F1278 See 画 50. [田]

8

肅 See 粛 115.

肇 3723/F1531 See 肈 CHŌ beginning.
[8]国 *chōkoku* founding a nation

9

盡 See 尽 1380. [皿]

RAD. 肉 130

Niku flesh, meat. Variants: 肉 and 月 or 月 (4 strokes) *nikuzuki* ("flesh" written like character for *tsuki* "moon"). These variants may often belong to Rad. 74 but, except for "moon" itself, are treated herein as Rad. 130. Nickname: Meat.

A 肉 3724/F1532 肉 宍 NIKU flesh, muscles; meat; the flesh; seal pad, ink pad; thickness, succulence. *shishi* muscles; meat. (Today 宍 is only pronounced *shishi*.)

2 入 *nikui(re)* seal pad, stamp pad. *nikui(ri)* container for meat
3 叉 *nikusa, nikusashi* meat fork
4 片 *nikuhen* piece of meat; folds of flesh
牛 *nikugyū* beef cattle
太 *nikubuto* bold-faced (type)
切 *nikuki(re)* slice of meat ⌈er
切庖丁 *nikuki(ri)bōchō* butcher knife, carv-
5 付 *nikuzu(ku)* put on flesh. *nikuzu(ki)*, *nikutsu(ki)* one's build. *nikuzu(ke)* modeling (in clay, etc.)
汁 *nikujū, nikuju* meat juice, broth, soup
6 色 *niku iro, nikushoku* flesh color
団 *shishimura* a piece of flesh
池 *nikuchi* seal pad, stamp pad
刑 *nikukei* corporal punishment; the punishment of mutilating the body
交 *nikkō* sexual intercourse
7 迫 *nikuhaku*＝肉薄 (see below–16)
声 *nikusei* natural voice, lifelike tone
豆蔻 *nikuzuku* nutmeg ⌈blood relationship
身 *nikushin* the flesh, the body; kindred,
身間 *nikushinkan* among relatives
体 *nikutai* the flesh, the body
体小説 *nikutai shōsetsu* sexy fiction
体文学 *nikutai bungaku* sensual literature
体的 *nikutaiteki* corporal, concerning the
体美 *nikutaibi* physical beauty ⌊body
8 刺 *nikusashi* meat fork. *mame* a corn, blister
芽 *nikuga, nikuge* granulation (in medicine)
9 食 *nikushoku, nikujiki* meat diet
屋 *nikuya* butcher shop; butcher
冠 *nikkan* cockscomb, crest (of a bird)
界 *nikukai, nikkai* sensual world, physical
10 挽 *nikuhi(ki)* meat grinder ⌊world
桂 *nikkei* cinnamon, cassia bark
11 彫 *nikubori* relief (in sculpture)
情 *nikujō* carnal desire
眼 *nikugan* naked eye
欲 *nikuyoku* animal passions, lusts of the
12 弾 *nikudan* human bullet ⌊flesh
筆 *nikuhitsu* autograph, one's own handwriting; one's own painting
筆画 *nikuhitsuga* original painting
18 腫 *nikushu* sarcoma
感 *nikkan* animal passion, carnal desire,
感的 *nikukanteki* carnal ⌊sexual feeling
14 製品 *niku seihin* meat products ⌈the body
塊 *nikukai, nikkai* piece of flesh; the flesh,
15 縁 *nikuen* blood relative
慾 *nikuyoku*＝肉欲 (see above–11) ⌈of flesh
質 *nikushitsu* nature of the flesh; composed
16 親 *nikushin* kindred, blood relationship
薄 *nikuhaku suru* close in on, press hard, compete fiercely
17 鍋 *niku nabe* meat pot; a meat meal
18 類 *nikurui* meats
叢 *shishimura* a piece of flesh
19 襦袢 *niku juban* tights
20 饅頭 *niku manjū* meat bun

1

且 See 23. [一]

2

肋 3725/F1533 ROKU. *abara* rib.
4 木 *rokuboku* Swedish bars, wall bars (for calisthenics)
7 材 *rokuzai* framing timbers (as in a ship)
10 骨 *rokkotsu, abarabone* ribs
12 間 *rokkan* intercostal, between the ribs
14 膜 *rokumaku* pleura
膜炎 *rokumakuen* pleurisy

肌 3726/F1533 KI. *hada, hadae* skin, body; grain, texture; disposition.
6 色 *hada iro* flesh color
衣 *hadagi* underwear
合 *hada-a(i)* disposition
7 身 *hadami* the body
11 理 *kime* grain; texture
脱 *hadanu(gi)* bare to the waist
12 寒 *hadasamu(i), hadazamu(i)* chilly
着 *hadagi* underwear
13 触 *hadazawa(ri)* the touch, the feel
19 襦袢 *hada juban* underwear

A 有 3727/F930 YŪ possession. U being, existence. *yū(suru)* have, own, possess. *a(ru)* there is, have, exist; occur; be located, be contained in; (it) measures;

happen; be found; be held; consist of. *a(ramashi)* approximately, almost. *a(rayuru)*, *a(ritoarayuru)* all, every. *a(risōna)* probable. *a(rimoshinai)* imaginary, nonexistent. [月]

2 力 ***yūryoku na*** influential ⌈powerful man
力者 ***yūryokusha*** an influential person, a
力筋 ***yūryoku suji*** influential quarters
3 士 ***yūshi*** sympathy, interest
丈 ***a(rit)take, a(ri)take*** all there is
4 心 ***ushin*** thoughtful consideration
夫 ***yūfu*** married
夫姦 ***yūfukan*** adultery
孔材 ***yūkōzai*** porous wood
孔性 ***yūkōsei*** porosity, porousness
孔質 ***yūkōshitsu*** porosity, porousness
孔螺旋 ***yūkō rasen*** screw eye
5 功 ***yūkō*** efficient; meritorious
司 ***yūshi*** authorities, officials
用 ***yūyō na*** useful, available, serviceable. ***yūyō(sa)*** usefulness, helpfulness
用性 ***yūyōsei*** usefulness
史 ***yūshi*** historical
史以来 ***yūshi irai*** since the dawn of history
史前 ***yūshizen no*** prehistoric
史時代 ***yūshi jidai*** historic period
6 米 ***a(ri)mai*** rice on hand
合 ***a(ri)-a(u)*** happen to be, happen to have on hand. ***a(ri)a(wase)*** what's on hand
気音 ***yūkion*** an aspirate
色 ***yūshoku*** colored (race)
色人種 ***yūshoku jinshu*** colored race
色星 ***yūshokusei*** colored star
名 ***yūmei na*** famous; notorious; proverbial
名人 ***yūmeijin*** celebrity, man of distinction
名品 ***yūmeihin*** well-known
名税 ***yūmeizei*** penalty for greatness
名無実 ***yūmei-mujitsu*** nominal, titular
7 利 ***yūri na*** advantageous, profitable, better
余 ***a(ri)-ama(ru)*** be superfluous, be in excess. ***yūyo*** excess
位者 ***yūisha*** holder of court rank
形 ***yūkei*** material, concrete, visible
形無形 ***yūkei-mukei*** visible and invisible; material and spiritual
志 ***yūshi*** sympathy, interest; volunteer
志者 ***yūshisha*** sympathizer, supporter, vol-
体 ***a(ri)tei*** the plain truth ⌊unteer
体物 ***yūtaibutsu*** something material
体動産 ***yūtai dōsan*** tangible property
体資産 ***yūtai shisan*** tangible assets
声 ***yūsei*** voiced, vocal
声子音 ***yūsei shion, yūsei shi-in*** voiced con-
声音 ***yūseion*** voiced sound ⌊sonant
声音化 ***yūseionka*** vocalization
8 金 ***a(ri)gane*** ready cash
性 ***yūsei*** sexual; having sex
卦 ***uke*** period of luck
実 ***a(ri)(no)mi*** pear
妻 ***yūsai*** married
毒 ***yūdoku*** poisonous
事 ***yūji*** emergency, unusual event
耶無耶 ***uyamuya na*** noncommital
明 ***aria(ke)*** daybreak, dawn with the moon shining; all night long
明月 ***aria(ke)zuki*** the moon shining at dawn
刺鉄条網 ***yūshi tetsujōmō*** barbed-wire entanglements
刺鉄線 ***yūshi tessen*** barbed wire
価 ***yūka*** valuable, negotiable
価物 ***yūkabutsu*** valuables
価証券 ***yūka shōken*** valuable securities
限 ***a(ru)kagi(ri)*** as long as we have some. ***a(ran)kagi(ri)*** all, to the utmost. ***yūgen*** limited, finite. ***a(ri)kiri*** only that, only that much; as much as possible
限会社 ***yūgengaisha*** limited company, ltd.
限責任 ***yūgen sekinin*** limited liability
限責任会社 ***yūgen-sekiningaisha*** limited liability company, inc.
効 ***yūkō*** effectiveness, efficiency; validity;
効性 ***yūkōsei*** validity ⌊availability
効期限 ***yūkō kigen*** term of validity
効期間 ***yūkō kikan*** term of validity, available period ⌈propriate
効適切 ***yūkō-tekisetsu*** effective and ap-
効数字 ***yūkō sūji*** significant figures
9 神論 ***yūshinron*** deism, theism
為 ***ui*** vicissitudes of life; perpetual change in destiny caused by karma. ***yūi no*** capable, efficient, promising
為転変 ***ui-tempen*** vicissitudes of life
10 高 ***a(ri)daka*** amount on hand; goods on hand ⌈tive, edifying
益 ***yūeki na*** beneficial, profitable, instruc-
兼 ***a(ri)ka(nenai)*** possible, not impossible
能 ***yūnō na*** capable, efficient
租地 ***yūsochi*** taxable land
脊動物 ***yūseki dōbutsu*** vertebrate animal
畜農業 ***yūchiku nōgyō*** diversified farming
害 ***yūgai na*** harmful, noxious, destructive
害物 ***yūgaibutsu*** dangerous substances
料 ***yūryō*** toll; charge
料入場者 ***yūryō nyūjōsha*** paid admissions
料図書館 ***yūryō toshokan*** rental library
料道路 ***yūryō dōro*** toll road
料橋梁 ***yūryō kyōryō*** toll bridge
11 得 ***a(ri)u(beki)*** possible, probable, likely. ***a(ri)-u(ru)*** possible, probable, likely
情 ***ujō*** sentience, sentient being
理 ***yūri*** rational
望 ***yūbō*** good prospects
頂天 ***uchōten*** exaltation, rapture, ecstacy

袋動物 *yūtai dōbutsu* pouched animal
情 *yūjō no, ujō no* sentient, sensitive, animate
情物 *yūjōbutsu* sentient beings
終 *yūshū* a fine conclusion
終美 *yūshū (no) bi* perfection, crowning ⌊glory
産 *yūsan* having wealth; millionaire
産階級 *yūsan kaikyū* propertied class
12 勝 *a(ri)ga(chi)* common, frequent, incidental; apt to happen
衆 *yūshū* multitude, people
象無象 *uzō-muzō* riffraff, rabble
閑 *yūkan* leisure
閑階級 *yūkan kaikyū* the leisure class
給 *yūkyū* salaried
給休暇 *yūkyū kyūka* paid vacations
無 *umu, yūmu* existence; presence; yes or no. *a(ri)na(shi)* whether there is any or not
無相通 *umu-aitsū(zuru), umu-aitsū(jiru)* ⌈share, help mutually
税 *yūzei* taxable, dutiable
税地 *yūzeichi* taxable land
税品 *yūzeihin* dutiable goods
期 *yūki* a definite period
期刑 *yūkikei* penal servitude for a stated ⌈period
期懲役 *yūki chōeki* penal servitude with hard labor for a stated period
13 福 *yūfuku* prosperity, affluence
触 *a(ri)fu(reta)* ordinary, stereotyped
数 *yūsū no* prominent, distinguished; very ⌈few
煙炭 *yūentan* soft coal
感地震 *yūkan jishin* an earthquake which ⌈is felt
資格者 *yūshikakusha* eligible person, qual⌊ified person
蓋 *yūgai* covered
蓋車 *yūgaisha* covered wagon
蓋貨車 *yūgai kasha* box car
意 *yūi no* conscious, voluntary, intentional
意犯 *yūihan* deliberate offense; deliberate ⌊offender
意味 *yūimi na* significant
意義 *yūigi na* significant
罪 *yūzai* guilt, criminality
罪人 *yūzaijin* guilty person
罪判決 *yūzai hanketsu* conviction
罪者 *yūzaimono* guilty person
罪認定 *yūzai nintei* finding guilty
罪議決 *yūzai giketsu* verdict of conviction
14 徳 *yūtoku* virtuous, good. *utoku* virtuous person
様 *a(ri)sama, a(ri)yō* situation, circumstances; sight; the (naked) truth
髪 *uhatsu* unshorn (nun)
15 髯 *yūzen* bearded, male
勲者 *yūkunsha* the holder of a decoration
権 *yūken* one's rights; voting rights
権者 *yūkensha* qualified person; eligible voter; electorate; franchise holder; constituent body

線 *yūsen* wire (as opposed to wireless)
線電信 *yūsen denshin* wire telegraph
線電話 *yūsen denwa* wire telephone
16 儘 *a(rino)mama, a(ruga)mama* as it is, the simple truth
機 *yūki* organic
機化合物 *yūki kagōbutsu* organic com⌈pound
機化学 *yūki kagaku* organic chemistry
機体 *yūkitai* organism
機性 *yūkisei* organic
機物 *yūkibutsu* organic matter, organism
機的 *yūkiteki* organic
機肥料 *yūki hiryō* organic fertilizer
機酸 *yūkisan* an organic acid
機質 *yūkishitsu* organic matter
機質肥料 *yūkishitsu hiryō* organic fertilizer
17 償 *yūshō* compensation, consideration
鍵楽器 *yūken gakki* keyed musical instru⌊ment
爵 *yūshaku* titled
爵者 *yūshakusha* titled person, peer
18 職 *yūshoku*, employed; ancient court and military practices
職者 *yūshokusha* employed people
職家 *yūshokuka* person versed in ancient court and military practices
難 *a(ri)gata(garu)* be thankful. *a(ri)gata(i)* thankful, grateful, blessed. *a(ri)gato(u)* thank you
難味 *arigatami* value, virtue, blessing, dignity, sanctity (of)
難迷惑 *a(ri)gata-meiwaku* embarrassing ⌈favor
難涙 *a(ri)gata-namida* tears of gratitude
19 繋 *sasuga ni*＝流石 2576.5
識 *yūshiki* intellectual (person)
識者 *yūshikisha* intellectual person, learned ⌈man

3

肖 See 1360.

肛 3728 / F1533 Kō anus.

8 門 *kōmon* anus

肚 3729 / F1533 To *hara* (see under 腹 3800.0).

7 芸人 *haragei* composure, wisdom, and steady leadership in crises
13 裏 *tori* in the heart

肘 3730 / F1533 CHŪ. *hiji* elbow; arm (of something).

4 木 *hijiki* bracket
8 金 *hijigane* hook, hinge
枕 *hiji makura (o) suru* use the elbow for a ⌈pillow
突 *hijitsu(ki)* elbow rest

11 掛 *hijika(ke)* elbow rest; bay window
12 壺 *hijitsubo* socket hinge
13 鉄 *hijitetsu* rebuff
鉄砲 *hijideppō* rebuff

B **肝** 3731 / F1533 KAN liver. *kimo* liver; pluck, courage, nerve.

2 入 *kimo-i(ri)* assisting
3 小 *kimo (ga) chii(sai)* cowardly
4 文 *kammon* important passage (in a text)
太 *kimofuto(i)* courageous
心 *kanjin na* essential, important, fundamental
心要 *kanjin-kaname no* main, basic
5 玉 *kimo(t)tama, kimodama* courage, nerve
7 冷 *kimo (o) hi(yasu)* be startled
8 油 *kan-yu* liver oil, cod-liver oil
炎 *kan-en* hepatitis
9 要 *kan-yō* import; importance; necessity
胆 *kantan* liver and gall; innermost heart
胆相照 *kantan-aite(rasu)* become intimate
11 脳 *kannō* liver and brains
12 腎 *kanjin na* fundamental, important, essential
腎要 *kanjin-kaname no* main, basic
13 煎 *kimo-i(ri)* good offices, sponsorship, go-between, promoter, overseer
14 銘 *kammei* deep impression
魂 *kimodama, kimotama, kimo(t)tama, kimodamashii* courage, nerve
15 潰 *kimotsubu(shi)* terrific surprise
18 臓 *kanzō* liver
臓炎 *kanzōen* hepatitis

— 4 —

肩 肩 See 1820.

肯 See 2432.

育 See 296.

肺 See 3752.

肫 3732 / F15.5 JUN dried meat.

肭 3733 / F1535 TOTSU, JIKU new moon.

B **肪** 3734 / F1535 BŌ fat.

肴 3735 / F1536 KŌ. *sakana* fish.

肢 3736 / F1534 SHI limbs, arms and legs.

7 体 *shitai* limbs, members; body
体不自由児 *shitai fujiyūji* crippled child

朋 3737 / F932 朋 HŌ friend, companion. [月]

4 友 *hōyū* friend, companion
10 党 *hōtō* faction, clique
15 輩 *hōbai* comrade, friend, associate, fellow apprentice

肱 3738 / F1536 KŌ. *kaina* arm; ability, talent. *hiji* elbow; arm (of something).

4 木 *hijiki* (temple) bracketing
11 掛 *hijika(ke)* resting the elbows; armrest; bay window
掛窓 *hijika(ke) mado* bay window

股 3739 / F1534 KO thigh, crotch; yarn; strand; ply. *mata* crotch, thigh, groin. *momo* thigh; femur.

4 火 *matabi* sitting astride a brazier
引 *momohi(ki)* drawers
8 肱 *kokō* right-hand man
10 骨 *kokotsu* femur, thigh bone
座 *matagura* crotch, thigh, groin
旅 *matatabi* gambler's wandering life
14 関節 *kokansetsu* hip joint
17 擦 *matazu(re)* saddle sore, thigh sore

A **肥** 3740 / F1534 HI. *ko(eru)* get fat; get fertile. *ko(yasu)* fertilize, enrich; fatten; feather one's nest; pamper one's taste. *futo(ru)* get fat, gain, fill out. *koyashi* manure, fertilizer. *koe* night soil; manure.

3 土 *ko(e)tsuchi, hido* rich soil, loam, mold
大 *hidai* corpulence, hypertrophy
4 太 *ko(e)-futo(ru)* grow fat, be well fed
5 立 *hida(tsu)* grow up; get well. *hida(chi)* convalescence after childbirth, growth of an infant
代 *koedai* cost of manuring; cost of getting night soil carried away
6 肉 *hiniku* fat flesh
舟 *koebune* night-soil boats
地 *ko(e)chi* fertile soil
汲 *koyashiku(mi), koeku(mi),* carrying night soil; night-soil carrier
7 車 *koyashiguruma, koeguruma* night-soil cart
沃 *hiyoku* fertility
8 取 *koeto(ri)* emptying night-soil; night-soil man
育 *hi-iku* fattening cattle for slaughtering
担桶 *koe tago* night-soil bucket
9 厚 *hikō* thickening (of the skin, etc.)
柄杓 *koebishaku* night-soil dipper
10 馬 *hiba* a fat horse
料 *hiryō* fertilizer, compost, manure

[11]桶 *koe oke, koyashi oke* night-soil bucket
船 *koebune* fertilizer boat
[12]満 *himan suru* become obese
満症 *himanshō* illness due to obesity
[13]溜 *koeda(me)* night-soil vat

A 服 3741 / F932 服 FUKU dress, costume, clothes, garment, suit, uniform. *fuku(suru)* yield to, obey; abide by; be devoted to, acknowledge, admit; serve (in the army); discharge (duties). *matsuro(u)* obey. [月]

[5]用 *fukuyō suru* take (medicine, etc.), use internally; dress (oneself)
[6]地 *fukuji* cloth, suiting, dress materials
刑 *fukukei* servitude
[7]役 *fukueki* servitude, military service
忌 *fukuki* mourning
[8]制 *fukusei* dress regulations, costume
毒 *fukudoku* taking poison
毒自殺 *fukudoku jisatsu* suicide by poisoning
[9]屋 *fukuya* tailor, dressmaker
[10]従 *fukujū* obedience, submission
従心 *fukujūshin* obedience, submissive spirit
従的 *fukujūteki* obedient, submissive
[11]務 *fukumu* duties, public service
務年限 *fukumu nengen* tenure of office
務時間 *fukumu jikan* office hours
[12]属 *fukuzoku suru* become a retainer; yield allegiance to
量 *fukuryō* dose, dosage
装 *fukusō* dress, garments, costume, attire
装随意 *fukusō zui-i* dress optional, informal attire
喪 *fukumo* mourning
喪者 *fukumosha* mourners
[13]飾 *fukushoku* dress and its ornaments, attire, personal appearance
罪 *fukuzai* pleading guilty, confession of guilt, submission
[16]薬 *fukuyaku* taking medicine
[17]膺 *fukuyō suru* bear in mind, take to heart, treasure

5

俎 俎 See 441. [夊]

胤 See 217.

胃 See 3000.

冐 3742 / F212 See 冒 2117. [冂]

脉 3743 / F1542 See 脈 3764.

胝 3744 / F1538 CHI chap, crack, corn, callus.

胛 3745 / F1538 KŌ shoulder blade.

胙 3746 / F1538 SO. *himorogi* offerings to the gods.

冑 3747 / F1537 CHŪ lineage; helmet. *kabuto* helmet, headpiece. *yoroi* armor. *yoro(u)* arm oneself; put on the armor.

胚 3748 / F1538 HAI embryo.

[8]芽 *haiga* embryo bud, germ
芽米 *haigamai* rice with the germ remaining
[9]胎 *haitai suru* germinate; be pregnant with; originate in, result from

B 胞 3749 / F1538 胞 HŌ theca, sac, sheath, case; placenta.

[3]子 *hōshi* spore
[6]衣 *ena, hōi* placenta
[9]胎 *hōtai* placenta

B 胎 3750 / F1538 TAI womb, uterus.

[4]内 *tainai* interior of the womb. *tainai kara* from the mother's womb
[5]生 *taisei* gestation
生学 *taiseigaku* embryology, ontology
[7]位 *tai-i* presentation (in childbirth)
児 *taiji* fetus
児殺 *taijigoro(shi)* aborticide
[8]芽 *taiga* embryo
毒 *taidoku* congenital syphilis
[11]教 *taikyō* prenatal care; antenatal training
動 *taidō* quickening, fetal movement; (trouble) fomenting
動期 *taidōki* quickening time
[15]盤 *taiban* placenta, afterbirth

B 胆 3751 / F1553 膽 TAN gall bladder; courage. *i* gall bladder. *kimo* liver; pluck, nerve, courage.

[2]力 *tanryoku* courage, nerve, grit
[5]汁 *tanjū* bile, gall
汁質 *tanjūshitsu* bilious or choleric temperament
石 *tanseki* gallstones
石病 *tansekibyō* illness due to gallstones
石症 *tansekishō* illness due to gallstones
[9]勇 *tan-yū* fearlessness, pluck
[11]液 *tan-eki* bile, gall
略 *tanryaku* courage and resourcefulness
[12]結石 *tan kesseki* biliary calculus, gallstones
[14]管 *tankan* biliary ducts

20礬 *tamban* blue vitriol, copper sulfate
22嚢 *tannō* gall bladder
嚢炎 *tannōen* gall bladder inflammation

肺 3752/F1536 HAI lung.
B
5出血 *haishukketsu* lung hemorrhage
6血 *haiketsu* lung hemorrhage
尖 *haisen* lung apex
先 *haisen* lung apex
7肝 *haikan* lungs and liver; innermost heart
8門 *haimon* hilum of a lung
炎 *haien* pneumonia
9活量 *haikatsuryō* lung capacity
10病 *haibyō* pulmonary tuberculosis, consumption
部 *haibu* lungs
浸潤 *haishinjun* tuberculosis
11魚 *haigyo* lungfish
患 *haikan* pulmonary tuberculosis
12葉 *haiyō* lobe of the lung
結核 *hai kekkaku* pulmonary tuberculosis
腑 *haifu* lungs; (one's imnost) heart; important point
腑衝 *haifu* (*o*) *tsu*(*ku*) be deeply impressed
17癌 *haigan* lung cancer
18臓 *haizō* lungs
22嚢 *hainō* lung sac

胡 3753/F1539 U. Go. Ko barbarian, foreign.
5瓜 *kyūri* cucumber
7坐 *agura* sitting cross-legged
乱 *uron na* suspicious-looking
8国 *kokoku* (ancient) North China barbarian nations
9臭 *wakiga* abnormal underarm odor
10馬 *koba* northern barbarian's horse
桃 *kurumi* walnut; nut
桃割 *kurumiwa*(*ri*) nutcracker
11麻 *goma* sesame, sesame seed
麻油 *goma abura* sesame-seed oil
麻塩 *goma shio* salted parched sesame seed; gray hair
麻摺 *gomasu*(*ri*) apple polisher
麻蝿 *goma*(*no*)*hai* a crook
12散臭 *usankusa*(*i*) suspicious-looking
椒 *koshō* pepper
椒入 *koshōi*(*re*) pepper shaker
14歌 *koka* song of the North China barbarians
15蝶 *kochō* butterfly
22蘿蔔 *ninjin* carrot; ginseng

背 3754/F1537 HAI back, behind. *somu*(*ku*)
B act contrary to, go back on, disobey, defy, rebel against, turn one's back on. *somu*(*keru*) look away from, avert. *se* back, back side; stature, height; ridge. *sei* stature, height. *sobira*, *sena* back.
3丈 *setake, seitake* height, stature
4比 *seikura*(*be*) comparison of statures
反 *haihan*=*haichi* 背馳 (see below–13)
水陣 *haisui* (*no*) *jin* last stand
戸 *sedo* back door, back gate
戸口 *sedoguchi* back door, back gate
中 *senaka* back
中合 *senaka-a*(*wase*) back to back; discord, feud
5広 *sebiro* business suit
去 *somu*(*ki*)-*sa*(*ru*) go astray
付鋸 *sezu*(*ki*) *noko* backsaw
6向 *haikō* facing toward the back; obedience and disobedience. *se* (*o*) *mu*(*keru*) turn the back on; pretend not to see; not co-operate with
任 *hainin* breach of trust
汗 *haikan* humiliation; cold sweat (on the back)
7戻 *hairei suru* disobey, transgress; run counter to, be contrary to
伸 *seno*(*bi*) *suru* stretch oneself, stand on tiptoe
8板 *se-ita* slab (of a log)
泳 *haiei, seoyo*(*gi*) backstroke swimming
9面 *haimen* rear, back, reverse
信 *haishin* breach of faith, betrayal, apostasy
後 *haigo* back, rear; backing
約 *haiyaku* breach of promise, default
叛 *haihan* rebellion, revolt
恰好 *seikakkō* stature, height, size, build, shape of the back
革 *segawa* leatherback (book)
革綴 *segawa toji* half-leather binding
負 *seo*(*u*), *sho*(*u*) carry on the back, shoulder, be burdened with
負子 *sho*(*i*)*ko, seo*(*i*)*go* pack frame
負込 *sho*(*i*)*ko*(*mi*), *seo*(*i*)*ko*(*mi*) unsalable goods. *sho*(*i*)-*ko*(*mu*), *seo*(*i*)-*ko*(*mu*) carry on the back; be saddled with
負投 *sho*(*i*)*na*(*ge*), *seo*(*i*)*na*(*ge*) throwing over the shoulder; betrayal
負梯子 *sho*(*i*)*bashigo, seo*(*i*)*bashigo* pack frame
10骨 *sebone* backbone, spinal column, spine
高 *seitaka no* taller than average
進 *haishin* withdrawal, retreat
峰 *semine* (horse's) back
振 *seburu*(*i*) *suru* shake oneself
部 *haibu* back, posterior
恩 *haion* ingratitude
11理 *hairi* absurdity
教 *haikyō* apostasy
教国 *haikyōkoku* apostate country
教者 *haikyōsha* apostate
12開 *sebira*(*ki*) slicing a fish down the back
順 *sejun* order of height
景 *haikei* background; scenery, setting; backing, pull
筋 *sesuji* line of the backbone; seam down the back. *haikin* the muscles of the back

番号 *sebangō* number on a player's back
13 較 *seikura(be)* comparison of statures
馳 *haichi suru* contradict, be contrary to, interfere with
14 徳 *haitoku* immorality, corruption
15 震 *seburu(i) suru* shake oneself
19 離 *hairi* estrangement
21 鰭 *sebire* dorsal fin
22 嚢 *hainō* knapsack, pack

—— 6 ——

脅 See 727.

能 See 853.

脱 3755/F1540 Kō bladder.

胶 3756/F-X Nonstandard for 脇 3765.

B 朕 3757/F933 朕 CHIN imperial we. [月]

胼 3758/F1546 胼 HEN callus, corn.
9 胝 *tako* callus, corn

胯 3759/F1540 Kō. *mata* crotch.
4 火 *matabi* sitting astride a brazier
10 座 *matagura* crotch, thigh, groin

脆 3760/F1542 ZEI. *moro(i)* brittle, fragile; easy (to beat); sentimental, susceptible. *moro(ku)* easily.
8 性 *zeisei* brittleness; frailty ⌈flimsy, brittle
10 弱 *zeijaku na* fragile, frail, delicate, tender,

朔 3761/F933 SAKU conjunction (in astronomy). *tsuitachi* first day of the month. [月]
4 日 *tsuitachi* the first day of the month
5 北 *sakuhoku* north
9 風 *sakufū* north wind
11 雪 *sakusetsu* northern snows

B 朗 3762/F933 朗 Rō. *hogara(ka) na* clear, bright, serene; melodious; cheerful, sunny. [月]
7 吟 *rōgin suru* recite, sing
10 朗 *rōrō(taru)* sonorous, silvery (voice or
12 詠 *rōei* recitation ⌊moon)
報 *rōhō* good news
14 誦 *rōshō* recitation, reading aloud

読 *rōdoku* reading aloud
読演説 *rōdoku enzetsu* a speech that's read

脊 3763/F1543 SEKI. *se, sei* stature, height.
3 丈 *setake* height, stature
9 柱 *sekichū* spine, spinal column, backbone
10 骨 *sebone* backbone, spinal column, spine
峰 *semine* (horse's) back
索 *sekisaku* notochord
11 梁 *sekiryō* spine, spinal column
12 椎 *sekitsui* spinal column, spine; vertebra
椎骨 *sekitsuikotsu* vertibrae
椎動物 *sekitsui dōbutsu* vertebrates
18 髄 *sekizui* spinal cord

A 脈 3764/F1542 脈 脉 MYAKU vein (of ore); blood vessel; pulse; pulsation; hope.
5 打 *myaku-u(tsu)* (the heart) pounds
圧計 *myakuatsukei* sphygmomanometer
7 状 *myakujō* veinlike
8 所 *myakudokoro* place where the pulse is
拍 *myakuhaku* pulsation ⌊felt; vital point
10 脈 *myakumyaku* continuous
11 動 *myakudō* pulsating motion
12 絡 *myakuraku* context, logical connection
13 搏 *myakuhaku* pulsation. *myaku-u(tsu)* pul-
数 *myakusū* pulse rate ⌊sate
14 管 *myakkan* blood vessel; duct

脇 3765/F1542 Kyō. *waki* the other way; another place; side, armpit, flank; supporting role.
3 下 *waki (no) shita* armpit; armhole
5 目 *wakime* onlooker's eyes; looking aside
付 *wakizu(ke)* directional words on an envelope ⌈away
7 見 *wakimi suru* look aside, look off, look
役 *wakiyaku* supporting role
9 柱 *wakibashira* door post, door jamb
10 師 *wakishi* assistant actor
挟 *wakibusa(mu)* hold under the arm
差 *wakiza(shi)* short sword
息 *kyōsoku* armrest
11 道 *wakimichi* side road, branch road; di-
12 間 *wakima* side room ⌊gression
13 腹 *wakibara* side of the chest, flank

B 脂 3766/F1542 SHI fat; rouge. *abura* fat, grease, tallow, blubber, lard, suet. *abura(gitta)* greasy, oily; fleshy. *yani* resin, rosin, gum; nicotine, tar; earwax, eye discharge.
3 下 *yanisa(garu)* assume airs; be complacent; chuckle (to oneself)

4 太 *aburabuto(ri)* obesity
6 気 *aburake* greasiness, oiliness
汗 *abura ase* greasy sweat
7 身 *aburami* fat meat
尾 *aburao* fat tail (of sheep)
8 油 *shiyu* fatty oil
肪 *shibō* fat, grease, blubber, suet, lard
肪症 *shibōshō* adiposity
肪組織 *shibō soshiki* fatty tissue
肪過多 *shibō kata* obesity
肪過多症 *shibō katashō* obesity
肪腫 *shibōshu* fatty tumor, lipoma
肪酸 *shibōsan* fatty acids
肪質 *shibōshitsu* fats
9 染 *aburaji(miru)* become oily or oil-stained
10 粉 *shifun* cosmetics
11 菜 *aburana* rape, mustard plant
14 漲 *aburagi(tta)* obese, very fat
15 質 *shishitsu* fats

B **胴** 3767 / F1540 Dō torso, trunk (of a body); body armor; body (of a suit); drum (of a machine); barrel (of a horse); cylinder (of a drum); bulge (of a bucket); hull (of a ship); hub (of a wheel).

3 上 *dōa(ge)* tossing (a person); hoisting (a person to the shoulders)
4 中 *dōnaka* torso
6 回 *dōmawa(ri)* girth
7 体 *dōtai* body, torso, trunk; hull; fuselage
乱 *dōran* wallet, grip, collecting case
忘 *dōwasu(re)* memory slip, forgetting for the moment
声 *dōgoe* heavy voice, deep resonant voice
8 金 *dōgane* metal clasp
長 *dōnaga* long-torsoed
9 巻 *dōmaki* bellyband
枯病 *dōga(re)byō* blight
10 部 *dōbu* abdomen (in animals)
11 張声 *dōba(ri)goe* thick voice
欲 *dōyoku* avarice, greed; cruelty, inhumanity
欲者 *dōyokumono* greedy person
12 揚 *dōa(ge)* congratulatory tossing of a hero
脹 *dōbuku(re)* swollen abdomen
着 *dōgi* undergarment; vest, waistcoat
間声 *dōmagoe* thick voice; deep resonant voice
13 慄 *dōburu(i)* shivering, trembling
15 締 *dōji(me)* belt, waistband
震 *dōburu(i)* shivering, trembling
慾 *dōyoku* avarice, greed; cruelty; inhumanity
18 鎧 *dōyoroi* body armor

B **胸** 3768 / F1540 Kyō. *mune* chest, breast, bosom; heart, mind, feelings.

3 三寸 *mune-sanzun* heart, mind, feelings
4 毛 *munage* chest hair, breast down
水 *kyōsui* pleural effusion (the fluid in pleurisy)
中 *kyōchū* one's heart, mind, or intentions
元 *munamoto* breast; pit of the stomach
6 回 *munemawa(ri)* chest measurement
宇 *kyōu* heart
先 *munasaki* breast; pit of the stomach, solar plexus
当 *munea(te)* breastplate, bib, chest-protector
当錐 *munea(te)giri* breast drill
7 囲 *kyōi* chest measurement
8 底 *kyōtei, munazoko* innermost heart
板 *mana-ita* the breast
泳 *kyōei* breast stroke
苦 *munaguru(shii)* feeling heavy in the chest
9 前 *munasaki*＝胸先 (see above-6)
背 *kyōhai* chest and back; front and back
10 骨 *kyōkotsu* breastbone, sternum
座 *munagura* the breast
部 *kyōbu* chest, breast
郭 *kyōkaku* the chest wall
倉 *munagura* the breast
11 勘定 *munakanjō* mental arithmetic; expectation
12 痛 *kyōtsū* chest pain
間 *kyōkan* breast, chest
幅 *munehaba, munahaba* chest breadth
椎 *kyōtsui* thoracic vertebrae
焼 *muneya(ke), munayak(e)* heartburn, sour stomach
腔 *kyōkō, kyōkū* thorax, thoracic cavity
13 廓 *kyōkaku* chest, thorax
飾 *munekaza(ri)* brooch
裏 *kyōri* one's inmost heart, one's bosom
14 像 *kyōzō* bust
膜 *kyōmaku* pleura
膜炎 *kyōmakuen* pleurisy
算 *munazan* mental arithmetic; expectation
算用 *munazan-yō* mental arithmetic; expectation
16 墻 *kyōshō* breastwork, parapet
懐 *kyōkai* heart; in the heart; thoughts
壁 *kyōheki* chest walls; breastworks; parapet
17 糞悪 *munekuso (ga) waru(i)* feel grieved, feel disgusted
18 騒 *munasawa(gi)* uneasiness; (heart) flutter; emotional upset
襟 *kyōkin* heart, bosom
襟開 *kyōkin (o) hira(ite)* frankly

— 7 —

脣 See 4656.
脈 See 3764.
脩 See 497
望 See 2940. 【月】

朗 3769 F933 See 朗 3762. [月]

脰 3770 F1545 Tō nape of the neck

脛 3771 F1543 KEI. *hagi, sune* leg, shin.

3 巾 *habaki* leggings
6 当 *sunea(te)* leggings, shin guards
10 骨 *keikotsu* shinbone, tibia
18 噛 *sunekaji(ri)* hanger-on, sponger, one still dependent on his parents

B **豚** 3772 F1780 TON hog. *buta* pig, hog, swine. [豕]

3 小屋 *butagoya* hogpen; hovel, shack
4 毛 *tommō* hog bristle
犬 *tonken* hogs and dogs; foolish people
6 肉 *butaniku, tonniku* pork, hog meat
肉商 *tonnikushō* pork butcher
7 尾 *tombi* pigtail, queue
児 *tonji* my son (humble)
8 舎 *tonsha* pigsty
10 脂 *tonshi* lard
15 箱 *butabako* police detention jail

B **脚** 3773 F1543 KAKU, KYAKU leg, skid; undercarriage. *ashi* (see under 足 4546.0). *-kyaku* chair counter.

2 力 *kyakuryoku, kyakuriki* walking ability
3 下 *kyakka ni* at one's feet
4 元 *ashimoto*＝足下 4546.3
5 立 *kyatatsu* footstool; stepladder
付 *ashitsu(ki)* something with legs; sole of the foot
半 *kyahan* leggings, gaiters
本 *kyakuhon* play, drama, script
本家 *kyakuhonka* playwright, dramatist
本書 *kyakuhonka(ki)* script writer, playwright
6 光 *kyakkō* footlights
色 *kyakushoku* plot, dramatization; stage or screen version
色者 *kyakushokusha* dramatizer, adapter
気 *kakke* beriberi
気衝心 *kakke shōshin* beriberi heart disease
8 注 *kyakuchū* footnotes
並 *ashina(mi)* pace, step
9 首 *ashikubi* ankle
10 部 *kyakubu* leg
荷 *ashini* ballast
11 絆 *kyahan* leggings, gaiters
12 湯 *kyakutō* hot foot bath
註 *kyakuchū* footnotes
14 榻 *kyatatsu* footstool; stepladder
15 線美 *kyakusembi* beauty of leg lines
19 韻 *kyakuin* rhyme

B **脳** 3774 F1547 **腦** Nō brain; memory.

3 下垂体 *nōkasuitai* pituitary gland
4 天 *nōten* scalp, pate, crown of the head; head; brain
中 *nōchū* in one's head
5 出血 *nōshukketsu* apoplexy, cerebral hemorrhage
6 充血 *nōjūketsu* brain congestion
7 乱 *nōran* worry, anguish
8 炎 *nōen* brain inflammation, encephalitis
卒中 *nōsotchū* apoplexy
垂体 *nōsuitai* pituitary gland
味噌 *nōmiso* gray matter, brains
10 症 *nōshō* brain fever
振盪 *nōshintō* brain concussion
病 *nōbyō* brain fever; nervous disorder, neurosis; mental disease
病院 *nōbyōin* mental hospital, hospital for brain diseases
脊髄 *nōsekizui* brain and spinal cord
脊髄炎 *nōsekizuien* encephalomyelitis
脊髄膜炎 *nōsekizuimakuen* cerebro-spinal meningitis
11 貧血 *nōhinketsu* cerebral anemia
軟化症 *nōnankashō* softening of the brain
13 裏 *nōri* brain; mind; memory; in the mind; in the heart
溢血 *nōikketsu* apoplexy, cerebral hemorrhage
14 漏 *nōrō* softening of the brain
膜炎 *nōmakuen* meningitis
15 漿 *nōshō* gray matter, brains
震盪 *nōshintō* concussion of the brain
18 髄 *nōzui* brain
20 騒 *munasawa(gi)* trouble at heart

B **脱** 3775 F1544 **脫** DATSU removing. *das(suru)* vi escape from; get rid of; be omitted, be left out. *vt* take off (clothes); omit; rise above. *nu(gu)* take off (clothes), undress. *nu(geru)* come off, slip off, slip down. *nu(gasu), nu(gaseru)* strip off clothes, undress (someone). *nu(keru)* (see under 抜 1854.0). *to(reru)* (See under 取 3699.0).

2 刀 *dattō* drawing a sword; ceasing to carry a sword
力感 *datsuryokukan* feeling of exhaustion
4 文 *datsubun* missing passage (in a document)
水 *dassui* dehydration, desiccation, evaporation
化 *dakke suru* change plans
毛 *datsumō, nu(ke)ge* falling out of hair; depilation; shed feathers
毛剤 *datsumōzai* a depilatory
5 皮 *dappi* shedding, molting, emergence
出 *dasshutsu* escape, extrication; prolapse. *nu(ke)-da(su)* leave; escape
6 臼 *dakkyū* dislocation
色 *dasshoku* decoloration, bleaching

会 *dakkai* withdrawal (from an organization)
字 *datsuji* omitted character; omitted word
衣 *datsui* undressing
7衣所 *datsuijo* dressing room, bathhouse
肛 *dakkō* prolapse of the anus
却 *dakkyaku suru* get rid of, extricate oneself from, emerge from
兎 *datto* dashing away; tremendous speed
走 *dassō* escape, flight, desertion, abscondence
走軍 *dassōgun* an army in flight
8退 *dattai* secession, withdrawal
垂 *dassui* prolapse
法 *dappō* fleeing from the law
法行為 *dappō kōi* law evasion
9胎 *dattai* plagiarism
臭 *dasshū* deodorization
俗 *datsuzoku* becoming a hermit; separating oneself from the world
俗味 *datsuzokumi* unworldliness
俗的 *datsuzokuteki* unworldly, saintly
10疽 *dasso* gangrene
党 *dattō* withdrawal from a party
脂 *dasshi* fat removal; nonfat, skim (milk); flesh-reducing
脂粉乳 *dasshi funnyū* powdered skim milk
脂綿 *dasshimen* absorbent cotton
11捨 *nu(gi)-su(teru)* throw off (clothes), kick off (boots)
掛 *nu(gi)-ka(keru)* take off (garments) and hang up
船 *dassen* desertion from a ship
殼 *dakkaku* shedding, molting, casting off. *nu(ke)gara* cast-off skin
殼機 *dakkakuki* threshing machine
12帽 *datsubō* removing the headgear; hats off
税 *datsuzei* tax evasion
落 *datsuraku* molting, falling off; omission; defection, desertion, apostasy
営 *datsuei* desertion from barracks
13棄 *nu(gi)-su(teru)*=脱捨 (see above–11)
腸 *datchō* hernia, rupture
腸帯 *datchōtai* truss
14漏 *datsurō* omission
獄 *datsugoku* jail-breaking
誤 *datsugo* omissions and errors
監 *dakkan* jail-break
穀 *dakkoku* threshing
穀機 *dakkokuki* threshing machine
15稿 *dakkō* completion of writing
線 *dassen* derailment; deviation, aberration, digression
17糞 *dappun* evacuation (of bowels)
18藩 *dappan* (a samurai) leaving his lord and becoming a *rōnin* or lordless samurai
19離 *datsuri* severing (oneself) from, getting rid of
20艦 *dakkan* desertion from a warship
籍 *dasseki* omission from the register

—— 8 ——

腐 See 1532.

腁 See 胼 3758.

脐 Nonstandard for 臍 3829.

腔 3776 / F1547 Kō body cavity.

腊 3777 / F1546 Seki dried meat.
12葉 *sakuyō* pressed leaves

朞 3778 / F937 Ki one period. [月]
6年 *kinen* one year

腓 3779 / F1546 Hi. *fukurahagi, komura, kobura* calf (of the leg).
6返 *komuragae(ri)* leg cramps

脾 3780 / F1545 Hi spleen.
8炎 *hien* splenitis
13腹 *hibara* sides (of a person)
18臓 *hizō* spleen

腑 3781 / F1546 Fu viscera, bowels; mind; reason, understanding.
5甲斐無 *fugaina(i)* spiritless, cowardly; worthless
7抜 *funu(ke)* dunce, fool, idiot, imbecile, simpleton
12落 *fu (ni) o(chinai)* cannot fathom, cannot understand

B 脹 3782 / F1545 Chō. *fuku(ramu)* *vi* distend, bulge, fill out, swell, dilate, rise. *fuku(reru)* *vi* swell, fill out, get big, bulge, expand, dilate, distend, rise, be inflated. *fuku(ramasu)*, *fuku(rakasu)*, *fuku(raseru)* *vt* dilate, expand, distend, swell, blow up, puff out, inflate, pump up, raise (bread). *fuku(yokana)* plump, fat, well-rounded.
9面 *fuku(ret)tsura no* sulky, sullen
10粉 *fuku(rashi)ko* baking powder
13腫 *chōshu* swelling

腋 3783 / F1546 Eki. *waki* armpit, side.
3下 *ekika* armpit
4毛 *wakige, ekimō* underarm hair

8明 *wakia*(*ke*) side kimono slits. *wakia*(*ki*) placket (in a skirt)
9臭 *wakiga, ekishū* abnormal underarm odor
14窩 *ekika* armpit

腎 3784/F1546 JIN kidney.

5石 *jinseki* kidney stone
8炎 *jin-en* nephritis
18臓 *jinzō* kidney
臓炎 *jinzōen* Bright's disease, nephritis
臓病 *jinzōbyō* kidney disease
臓結石 *jinzō kesseki* kidney stones

A **期** 3785/F937 **期** KI, GO time, date, period, term; an age; season; session; a stage; opportunity. *ki*(*suru*) expect, anticipate, hope for, rely on; appoint (a day). *go*(*suru*) wait expectantly for. *ki*(*sezu*) *shite* unexpectedly, accidentally. [月]

4日 *kijitsu, kinichi* date; time limit
月 *kigetsu* the appointed month; one full month
5末 *kimatsu* term end
6米 *kimai* rice for future delivery
年 *kinen* one year
成 *kisei* realization (of a plan) ⌈plan
成同盟 *kisei dōmei* uniting to carry out a
先 *kisaki* future stocks, forward merchandising ⌈merchandising
先物 *kisakimono* future stocks, forward
8限 *kigen* term, period, time limit
限経過 *kigen keika* overdue
限満了 *kigen manryō* expiration of a term
9首 *kishu* beginning of a period
待 *kitai* expectation, hope, anticipation, contemplation
待外 *kitaihazu*(*re*) disappointment
11望 *kibō* expectant waiting
12間 *kikan* term, period
間中 *kikanchū* during the period
間外 *kikangai* between sessions
間満了 *kikam-manryō* maturity, expiration
13節 *kisetsu*, season, opportunity

B **腕** 3786/F1547 **捥** WAN arm. *ude* arm; ability, talent. *kaina* arm.

2力 *wanryoku* muscular strength, brute force,
力沙汰 *wanryokuzata* fist fighting ⌊brawn
4比 *udekura*(*be*) trial of strength, trial of skill
木 *udegi* bracket, crosspiece, roof truss, arm-
木信号 *udegi shingō* semaphore ⌊rest
5白 *wampaku* naughtiness, mischief
仕事 *udeshigoto* manual labor
立 *udeda*(*te*) *suru* fight, resort to force
立伏 *udeta*(*te*)*fu*(*se*) lie down on one's arms ⌈forcible, strong-arm
6尽 *udezu*(*ku*) *de* by main force. *udezu*(*ku*) *no*
扱 *udeko*(*ki*) man of ability ⌈own strength
先 *udesaki* the hand. *udesaki de* by one's
次第 *ude-shidai de* according to one's ability
7利 *udeki*(*ki*) man of ability
角力 *udezumō* hand wrestling
8金 *udegane* outrigger; bracket, bracketing
押 *udeo*(*shi*) hand wrestling
限 *udekagi*(*ri*) with all one's might
9首 *udekubi* wrist
前 *udemae* ability, skill, capacity
相撲 *udezumō* hand wrestling
10骨 *udebone* arm bone, wristbone; strength
時計 *udedokei* wrist watch
11捲 *udemaku*(*ri*) *suru* roll up one's arms, bare one's arm
組 *udegu*(*mi*) folding one's arms
章 *wanshō* armband, arm badge, chevron,
12揃 *udezoro*(*i*) a line-up of experts ⌊stripes
無 *udena*(*shi*) armless person; weak person; unskilled person
13試 *udedame*(*shi*) trial of strength
飾 *udekaza*(*ri*) bracelet
節 *udebushi, ude*(*p*)*pushi* arm joint, muscular strength ⌈cular
節強 *ude*(*p*)*pushi* (*no*) *tsuyo*(*i*) strong, mus-
14関節 *wankansetsu* wrist joint
15輪 *udewa* bracelet
20競 *udekura*(*be*) trial of strength, trial of skill

A **勝** 3787/F265 **勝** SHŌ victory; beauty spot. *ka*(*tsu*) win; prevail, predominate, surpass. *masa*(*ru*) excel, surpass, outrival. *sugu*(*reru*) excel, surpass; have advantages over; be excellent. *ka*(*chi*) victory, success. *-ga*(*chi*) be apt to, be prone to, be liable to, tend to; predominating. [力]

4手 *katte* kitchen; condition, circumstances; one's own convenience; wilfulness, selfishness
手口 *katteguchi* back door, service door
手向 *kattemu*(*ki*) kitchen affairs; one's financial circumstances
手次第 *katte-shidai* having one's own way
手気儘 *katte-kimama* selfishness. *katte*(*gamashii*) selfish
手道具 *katte dōgu* kitchen utensils
5目 *ka*(*chi*)*me* chances of winning
6色 *ka*(*chi*)*-iro* signs of victory
因 *shōin* cause of victory
気 *ka*(*chi*)*ki* determination to win ⌈victor
向 *ka*(*chi*)*muka*(*i*) the defeated treating the

地 *shōchi* scenic spot
守 *ka(chi)mamo(ri)* victory charm
7車 *shōsha* winning car
投手 *ka(chi) tōshu* winning pitcher
抜 *ka(chi)-nu(ku)* win one game after another
抜戦 *ka(chi)nu(ki)sen* tournament
利 *shōri* victory
利者 *shōrisha* winner, victor, conqueror
利投手 *shōri tōshu* winning pitcher
8逃 *ka(chi)ni(ge)* running away with a game
味 *ka(chi)mi* chances of winning
放 *ka(chi)-hana(su)* win by a big score. *ka(chip)pana(shi)* string of victories
取 *ka(chi)-to(ru)* gain a victory
者 *shōsha* winner, victor, conqueror
9通 *ka(chi)-tō(su), ka(chi)-dō(su)* win straight victories
乗 *ka(chi) (ni) no(ru)* win straight victories
軍 *shōgun* military victory; victorious army. *ka(chi) ikusa* victory
星 *ka(chi)boshi* winning mark
負 *shōbu* victory or defeat; game, bout. *ka(chi)ma(ke)* victory or defeat
負事 *shōbugoto* game of skill; gambling
負師 *shōbushi* gambler; chess or *go* player
負無 *shōbuna(shi)* a tie (in games)
10馬 *ka(chi) uma* winning horse
残 *ka(chi)-noko(ru)* make the finals
栗 *ka(chi)guri* dried chestnut
11得 *ka(chi)-u(ru), ka(chi)-e(ru)* achieve, win, earn, gain
敗 *shōhai* victory or defeat; the issue (of a battle)
率 *shōritsu* chances of victory
12越 *ka(chi)ko(shi)* more wins than losses
訴 *shōso* winning a lawsuit
景 *shōkei* beautiful view, scenic spot
報 *shōhō* news of victory
13鼓 *ka(chi)tsuzumi* drums of victory
続 *ka(chi)tsuzu(ke)* series of victories
誇 *ka(chi)-hoko(ru)* triumph, be elated with success
14算 *shōsan* chances of victory
16鬨 *ka(chi)doki* shout of victory; victory song
21籤 *ka(chi) kuji* winning ticket

A **朝** 3788 / F935 **朝** CHŌ dynasty; reign, regime; period, epoch; the court. *asa* morning, forenoon. *ashita* morn, morning. *chō(suru)* proceed to the palace; empty into (the sea). [月]

3夕 *asayū, chōseki* day and night, morning and evening; always; daily. *asa(na)-yū(na)* morning and evening
三暮四 *chōsan-boshi* six of one and half a dozen of the other
4方 *asagata* toward morning; during the morning
込 *asago(me)* a morning raid
月夜 *asazukuyo* the moon shining toward morning
日 *asahi* morning sun, rising sun
日影 *asahi kage* morning sunshine
5立 *asada(chi)* early-morning departure
刊 *chōkan* morning paper
礼 *chōrei* morning meeting, morning exercises
市 *asa ichi* morning market
出 *asade* morning attendance, morning duty
未来 *asamadaki* before daybreak
令暮改 *chōrei-bokai* the issuance of an order in the morning and its repeal in the evening; lack of principle
6臣 *chōshin* courtier; the court. *ason* a high-ranking noble
衣 *chōi* court dress
凪 *asa nagi* morning calm (at sea)
早 *asa haya(ku)* early in the morning
7見 *chōken* imperial audience
廷 *chōtei* imperial court
来 *chōrai* since morning
改暮変 *chōkai-bohen* the issuance of an order in the morning and its repeal in the evening; lack of principle
8雨 *asa ame* morning rain
拝 *chōhai* morning worship; congratulations to the emperor
明 *asa-a(ke)* daybreak, dawn
和 *asanagi* morning calm (at sea)
服 *chōfuku* court dress
命 *chōmei* imperial command, government order
参 *asamai(ri)* morning visit to a shrine or temple
典 *chōten* court ceremony
東風 *asakochi* east wind in the morning
9威 *chōi* imperial authority
政 *chōsei* imperial government
星 *asaboshi* morning star
風 *asa kaze* morning breeze
風呂 *asaburo* morning bath
食 *chōshoku* breakfast
食後 *chōshokugo* after breakfast
10起 *asao(ki)* early rising
酒 *asazake* a morning saké drink
陰 *asakage* morning shade; shady places in the morning
朗 *asaborake* dawn, daybreak
家 *choka* imperial court
貢 *chōkō suru* bring tribute
恩 *chōon* favor of a ruler
帰 *asagae(ri)* returning after an overnight stay
11鳥 *asadori* early rooster
涼 *asasuzu, asasuzu(mi)* morning coolness
船 *asabune* boat setting out in the morning
野 *chōya* government and people; the whole nation
陽 *chōyō, asahi* morning sun
12間 *asama, asa(no)ma* during the morning
開 *asa-a(ke)* dawn, daybreak
晴 *asaba(re)* clear morning
晩 *asaban* morning and evening; always

湿 *asajime(ri)* morning dampness
湯 *asayu* morning bath
焼 *asaya(ke)* sunrise colors
朝 *asa(na)-asa(na)* morning after morning
寒 *asasamu* morning coolness
雲 *asagumo* morning clouds
賀 *chōga* congratulating the emperor
飯 *asahan, asameshi* breakfast
飯前 *asameshimae* before breakfast; something so simple it can be done before breakfast
13 腹 *asabara, asa(p)para* morning empty feeling; something very easy
意 *chōi* the opinion of the imperial court
寝 *asane* morning sleep, late rising
寝坊 *asa nebō* late rising; late riser
14 駆 *asaga(ke)* attack in the morning; departure in the morning
暮 *chōbo* morning and evening
髪 *asagami* hair still uncombed
15 儀 *chōgi* court ceremonies
権 *chōken* imperial authority
潮 *asa shio* morning tide
課 *chōka* (Catholic) matins
餉 *asage* breakfast
影 *asa kage* morning shadows; morning reflections; morning sunshine
敵 *chōteki* traitor, rebel, enemy of the emperor
16 憲 *chōken* constitution
曇 *asagumo(ri)* cloudy morning
餐 *chōsan* breakfast
稽古 *asageiko* morning exercise
17 霞 *asagasumi* morning mist
鮮 *Chōsen* Korea
鮮人参 *Chōsen ninjin* gingseng
鮮民主主義人民共和国 *Chōsen Minshu Shugi Jimmin Kyōwakoku* (North) Korean Democratic People's Republic
18 顔 *asagao* morning glory
19 禱 *chōtō* (Catholic) matins
霧 *asagiri* morning fog
20 議 *chōgi* imperial court conference
懸 *asagake* attack in the morning, departure in the morning
21 露 *chōro, asa tsuyu* morning dew
24 靄 *asa moya* morning mist

— 9 —

腴 See 3804.

腦 3789 F1547 See 脳 3774.

腭 3790 F1548 腭 See 齶 5437.

腟 3791 F1547 膣 CHITSU vagina.

腱 3792 F1548 KEN tendon.

腮 3793 F1548 F2063 顋 SAI. *ago* jaw.

腥 3794 F1547 SEI. *namagusa(i)* bloody, smelling of fish, smelling raw.
8 物 *namagusamono* raw things (like fish and meat)

腿 3795 F1550 TAI. *momo* thigh, femur.
6 肉 *momoniku* round steak; ham

腺 3796 F1549 SEN gland.
10 病質 *sembyōshitsu* weak constitution
15 熱 *sennetsu* glandular fever

腫 3797 F1548 SHU tumor, swelling. *ha(reru)* swell, become swollen. *ha(rebottai)* beginning to swell. *ha(rasu)* inflame, cause to swell. *ha(re)* swelling, dropsy.
3 上 *ha(re)-a(garu)* swell up
大症 *shudaishō* bunion
8 物 *shumotsu, haremono* tumor, abscess, boil, swelling
12 脹 *shuchō* swelling, puffiness, protuberance
14 瘍 *shuyō* tumor, neoplasm
瘍学 *shuyōgaku* oncology
15 瘤 *shuryū* tumor

A 腸 3798 F1549 腸 CHŌ intestines, bowels, entrails; digestive system in lower animals. *harawata* intestines, bowels, entrails, viscera; the heart. *wata* entrails.
4 中 *chōchū ni* in the intestines
8 炎 *chōen* enteritis, inflammation of the intestines
9 胃 *chōi* stomach and intestines
10 部 *chōbu* intestinal region
11 閉塞 *chōheisoku* intestinal obstruction
12 満 *chōman* abdominal dropsy
結核 *chōkekkaku* intestinal tuberculosis
13 詰 *chōzume* sausage
15 線 *chōsen* catgut
潰瘍 *chōkaiyō* intestinal ulcer
16 壁 *chōheki* intestinal wall

B 腰 3799 F1548 腰 YŌ. *koshi* hips, loins, waist, pelvic region; small of the back; haunch; lower-panel wainscoting (lower wall only); stem (of a wine glass).
3 下 *koshi(o)oro(su)* sit down

巾着 *koshiginchaku* belt purse; one's shadow; a henchman ⌈family; the hips

4 元 *koshimoto* woman working for a noble

5 付 *koshitsu*(*ki*) gait; posture

布 *koshi nuno* loincloth ⌈worker

弁 *koshiben* petty official, low-salaried

弁当 *koshi bentō* lunch tied to the belt; lunch-carrying workmen. *koshi-bentō de* carrying a lunch

6 肉 *koshi niku* loin, sirloin

回 *koshimawa*(*ri*) hip measure

当 *koshia*(*te*) bustle

羽目 *koshihame* panel, wainscoting

7 囲 *yōi* the hip measurement

抜 *koshinu*(*ke*) cowardice; coward; cripple. *koshi* (*ga*) *nu*(*keru*) be very much sur-

低 *koshi* (*ga*) *hiku*(*i*) humble ⌊prised

折 *koshio*(*re*) poor poem, doggerel; stooped over (old people). *koshi* (*o*) *o*(*ru*) bow; surrender; interrupt (someone)

8 板 *koshi ita* panels; wainscoting (lower wall only)

物 *koshi* (*no*) *mono* sword worn at the side

9 砕 *koshikuda*(*ke*) weakening, hips giving way (and falling) ⌈nel waistband

巻 *koshima*(*ki*) underskirt; loincloth, flan-

10 骨 *koshibone*, *chōkotsu* hipbone; perseverence

高 *koshidaka* high wainscoting; long-stemmed goblet. *koshi* (*ga*) *taka*(*i*) proud

部 *yōbu* pelvic region, hips, loins, waist

帯 *koshi obi* waistband; narrow obi used to hold the tucked-up kimono in place

弱 *koshiyowa* lack of persistence. *koshi* (*ga*) *yowa*(*i*) weak, vacillating

11 張 *koshiba*(*ri*) papering or wainscoting lower part of a wall

強 *koshi* (*ga*) *tsuyo*(*i*) firm (character); strong (paste); stiff (paper)

掛 *koshika*(*keru*) sit down, *koshikake* seat, chair, bench, stool, pew, bleachers; steppingstone to something higher

掛仕事 *koshikake shigoto* temporary work

12 痛 *yōtsū*, *koshi-ita* lumbago, pain in the hip, pain in the back

間 *yōkan* the hips

揚 *koshia*(*ge*) tuck at the waist

椎 *yōtsui* lumbar vertebrae

湯 *koshiyu* hip bath, sitz bath

18 髄麻酔 *yōzai masui* spinal anesthesia

19 縄 *koshinawa* waist cord (for tying prisoners)

B **腹** 3800 F1549 FUKU. (*o*)*naka* belly, stomach. *hara* abdomen, belly, bowels, stomach; heart, mind; intention; courage, spirit, pluck; anger; womb; thickest or widest part.

1 一杯 *hara-ippai* full stomach; to one's

3 子 *harako* fish eggs ⌊heart's content

下 *harakuda*(*ri*) diarrhea. *harakuda*(*shi*) diarrhea; laxative

工合 *haraguai* condition of the bowels

4 心 *fukushin* trusted friend; trusted retainer

水 *fukusui* abdominal dropsy

中 *fukuchū* in the abdomen; in the heart

切 *haraki*(*ri*) suicide by disembowelment

5 圧 *fukuatsu* muscular abdominal pressure

打 *hara-u*(*chi*) bellyflop

立 *harada*(*tsu*) get angry, take offense. *harada*(*tashii*) irritating, exasperating

立紛 *harada*(*chi*)-*magi*(*re*) beside oneself with anger

6 臣 *fukushin* trusted retainer, trusted friend

虫 *hara* (*no*) *mushi* intestinal worms; heart, intention; courage

汚 *haragitana*(*i*) low-minded

合 *hara-a*(*wase*) facing each other

当 *hara-a*(*te*) chest and stomach armor; belly band

式 *fukushiki no* abdominal ⌈ing

式呼吸 *fukushiki kokyū* abdominal breath-

7 芸人 *haragei no hito* a man of strong personality

8 具合 *haraguai* condition of the bowels

9 持 *haramo*(*chi*) slow digestion; feeling of

拵 *haragoshira*(*e*) eating ⌊fullness

巻 *haramaki* waistband

背 *fukuhai* front and back; close relative

10 這 *harabai*, *hara*(*m*)*bai* lying on the stomach. *haraba*(*u*) crawl

部 *fukubu* abdomen, belly

案 *fukuan* plan, scheme, idea ⌈saddle girth

帯 *haraobi*, *fukutai* health band, bellyband;

消化 *haragonashi* digestion ⌈schemer

11 黒 *haraguro*(*i*) evilhearted, crafty. *haraguro*

違 *harachiga*(*i*) born of a different mother

掛 *haraga*(*ke*) workman's backless pocketed vest

探 *hara* (*o*) *sagu*(*ru*) probe another's feelings

据 *hara* (*o*) *su*(*eru*) make a decision ⌈tolerate

据兼 *hara* (*ni*) *su*(*e*)-*ka*(*neru*) be unable to

12 痛 *fukutsū*, *hara-ita*, *hara ita*(*mi*) stomachache, colic, abdominal pain

減 *hara* (*ga*) *he*(*ru*) be hungry

腔 *fukkō*, *fukukō*, *fukukū* abdominal or peritoneal cavity ⌈sion; tell everything

割 *hara* (*o*) *wa*(*ru*) make an abdominal inci-

筋 *hara suji*, *fukukin* abdominal muscles

13 鼓 *haratsuzumi* drum of the belly

塞 *harafusa*(*gi*) staying one's hunger

話術 *fukuwajutsu* ventriloquy

14膜 *fukumaku* peritoneum
膜炎 *fukumakuen* peritonitis
蔵 *fukuzō* keeping things to oneself
蔵無 *fukuzōna(ku)* freely, frankly, plainly
15稿 *fukkō* plan, scheme, idea
16壁 *fukuheki* abdominal wall
18癒 *hara-ise* retaliation. *hara (ga) i(reru)* be satisfied with one's revenge
穢 *haragitana(i)* base-minded
臓無 *fukuzōna(ku)* frankly, freely, plainly
21鰭 *harabire* ventral fin

10

膏 See 5250.

膀 膀 See 髈 5437.

膊 3801 / F1550 HAKU arm.

膌 3802 / F-X SEKI become emaciated.

B 膜 3803 / F1551 MAKU membrane.

膄 3804 / F1550 SHŪ, SHU become emaciated.

膈 3805 / F1550 KAKU area between the chest and the abdomen.
14膜 *kakumaku* the diaphragm

膃 3806 / F1550 OTSU fat, corpulent.
8肭臍 *ottosei* fur seal

膂 3807 / F1550 RYO backbone.
2力 *ryoryoku* muscular strength

膀 3808 / F1550 BŌ bladder.
10胱 *bōkō* urinary bladder
胱結石 *bōkō kesseki* bladder stones

11

膚 See 4113.

膣 3809 / F1552 See 腟 3791.

膓 3810 / F1551 F1549 See 腸 3798.

膕 3811 / F-X KAKU. KOKU. KYOKU. *hikagami* hollow of the knee.

膵 3812 / F1553 (国字) SUI pancreas.
11液 *suieki* pancreatic juice
18臓 *suizō* pancreas

膠 3813 / F1552 KŌ. *nikawa* glue. *nibe* fish glue, isinglass.
4水 *kōsui* sizing
化 *kōka suru* gelatinize
11接 *kōsetsu* sticking
12着 *kōchaku* agglutination; stalemate
着剤 *kōchakuzai* glue, binder
14漆 *kōshitsu* glue and lacquer; great intimacy
15質 *kōshitsu no* gluey, gelatinous, colloidal
22嚢 *kōnō* capsule

膝 3814 / F1551 SHITSU. *hiza* knee; lap.
8下 *shikka* paternal home; at the knees. *hizamoto*=膝元 (see below–4)
小僧 *hizakozō* kneecap
4元 *hizamoto* with one's parents; with one's lord close by; ruler's capital city
反射 *shitsuhansha* knee jerk
5正 *hiza (o) tada(su)* sit (on floor) correctly
6行 *shikkō* going on one's knees
交 *hiza (o) maji(eru)* have a frank talk ⌈seats)
8送 *hizaoku(ri)* moving closer together (in
枕 *hizamakura* using someone's lap for a
突 *hizatsu(ki)* small knee mat ⌊pillow
拍子 *hizabyōshi* beating time on one's knee
10株 *hizakabu* kneecap
栗毛 *hizakurige* a hike
11掛 *hizaka(ke)* lap robe ⌈crossed legs
組 *hizagu(mu)* cross the knees. *hizagu(mi)*
崩 *hiza (o) kuzu(su)* relax one's squatting position ⌈tions
13詰談話 *hizazu(me) danwa* direct negotia-
蓋骨 *shitsugaikotsu* kneecap
蓋腱反射 *shitsugaiken hansha* knee jerk
14関節 *shitsukansetsu* knee joint
16頭 *hizagashira* kneecap
19繰 *hizagu(ri)* sitting closer

12

膰 3815 / F1552 HAN. *himorogi* offerings to the gods.

縢 3816 / F1475 TŌ. DŌ. *kaga(ru)* cross-stitch; hemstitch; sew up; darn. 【糸】

膳 3817 / F1552 ZEN small low table; tray.

[4]夫 *kashiwade* butler
[5]立 *zenda(te)* setting the table; preparations, program, scheme
[10]部 *zembu* tray of food

膨 3818/F1552 Bō get fat; get thick, swell. *fuku(reru)* swell. B
[3]大 *bōdai* swelling, expansion
[10]粉 *fukura(shi)ko* baking powder
隆 *bōryū suru* swell up
[11]張 *bōchō*=膨脹 (see below–12)
[12]満 *bōman suru* be inflated「growth, increase
脹 *bōchō* swelling; inflation; expansion,

13

膺 See 1542.

膽 3819/F1553 See 胆 3751.

臂 3820/F1554 Hɪ. *hiji* elbow; arm (of something).

膾 3821/F1554 Kᴀɪ. *namasu* fish salad, raw fish and vegetables.
[8]炙 *kaisha* a household word; universal praise

臀 3822/F1554 臋 Dᴇɴ. *shiri* (see under 尻 1379.0).
[6]肉 *denniku* rump flesh (of animals)
[7]位 *den-i* breech presentation (obstetrics)
[10]部 *dembu* buttocks, hips, haunch

朦 3823/F937 Mō dim, obscure. [月]
[6]気 *mōki* fog, mist, vapor
[17]朦 *mōmō(taru)* gloomy; depressed
[20]朧 *mōrō(taru)* dim, hazy, vague, obscure

謄 3824/F1760 謄 Tō copy. [言] B
[5]本 *tōhon* certified copy, transcript, duplicate; domiciliary registration copy
写 *tōsha* copy, reproduction; mimeographing「chine
写版 *tōshaban* mimeograph, copying ma-
写版刷 *tōshabanzu(ri)* mimeographed copy
写料 *tōsharyō* copying fee
写機 *tōshaki* mimeograph, copying ma-
[12]貴 *tōki* rise in prices ⌊chine

臆 3825/F1554 Oᴋᴜ timidity; breast, heart, mind. *oku(suru)* fear, hesitate, be nervous, be cowardly, be timid.
[7]見 *okken* one's own idea, my guess
[9]面 *okumen* shy face
[10]病 *okubyō* cowardice, timidity
病者 *okubyōmono* coward
病風 *okubyō kaze* panic, loss of nerve
病神 *okubyōgami* god of cowardice
[11]断 *okudan* guess, hypothesis, supposition
[12]測 *okusoku* guess, speculation, supposition
[14]説 *okusetsu* conjecture, hypothesis

膿 3826/F1554 Nō pus, discharge. *u(mu)* form pus, fester, suppurate. *umi* pus, discharge.
[5]汁 *nōjū, umishiru* pus, discharge
[6]血 *umichi* blood and pus, bloody pus
[8]毒症 *nōdokushō* blood poisoning
[10]疱 *nōhō* pustule
痂疹 *nōkashin* impetigo
[13]腫 *nōshū* abscess
[14]漏 *nōrō* pyorrhea
瘍 *nōyō* boil, abscess
瘍歯 *nōyōshi* abscessed tooth
[15]潰 *nōkai* suppuration, ulceration

14

臑 3827/F1555 Dō. *sune* leg, shin.
[6]当 *sunea(te)* leggings, shin guards
[18]噛 *sunekaji(ri)* hanger-on, sponger

臟 3828/F1556 =臓 Zō viscera, bowels. B
[8]物 *zōmotsu, harawata* entrails, giblets
[12]腑 *zōfu* intestines, entrails「bowels
[15]器 *zōki* intestines, internal organs, viscera,

臍 3829/F1555 Sᴇɪ. Zᴀɪ. *heso, hozo* navel.
[3]下 *seika* lower abdomen
下丹田 *seika-tanden* pit of the stomach
[6]曲 *heso (o) ma(garu)* get cross. *hesomaga(ri)* perverse person
[10]帯 *saitai, seitai* umbilical cord
[14]緒 *heso(no)o* umbilical cord
[19]繰 *hesoku(ri)* secret savings, pin money
繰金 *hesoku(ri)gane* secret savings; pin money

15

臘 3830/F1555 Rō 12th lunar month.

鵬 3831/F2145 Hō phoenix, huge mythical bird. *ōtori* fabulous bird. [鳥]
[12]程 *hōtei* a great distance
[17]翼 *hōyoku* phoenix wings; airplane wings; airplanes

6 竹米糸缶网皿羊羽老耂而耒耳聿【肉月】臣自至臼舌舛舟艮色艸艹虍虫血行衣衤西

16

— 16 —

臙 3832 F1555 EN rouge.
10脂 *enji* rouge; lipstick; a dark-red pigment;
脂色 *enji iro* deep red ⌊cochineal

朧 3833 F938 Rō. *oboro* haziness, dreaminess, gloom. [月]
4月 *oborozuki* hazy moon
月夜 *oborozukiyo* misty moonlit night
6気 *oboroge na* indistinct, misty, dreamy
8夜 *oboroyo* misty moonlit night
昆布 *oboro kombu* sliced tangle
20朧 *oboro-oboro* haziness, dreaminess

B騰 3834 F2103 騰 Tō rising; price rise. *a(gari)* advancing, going up. [馬]
5写 *tōsha* copy, reproduction, mimeographing
本 *tōhon*＝謄本 3824.5
8奔 *tōhon* running and jumping; jumping of prices
9降 *tōkō* rising and falling (prices)
12落 *tōraku* fluctuations
貴 *tōki* rise (in prices)
13勢 *tōsei* rising trend in prices

— 17 —

臟 3835 F1556 See 臓 3828.

— 19 —

臠 3836 F1556 REN. *misona(wasu)* see, witness, inspect.

RAD. 臣 131

Shin or *kerai* retainer, minister, subject. This is always counted as 6 strokes even tho it often seems to have 7. The reason is that such a form is not a true variant but an alternate way of writing a parent radical that has traditionally always been counted as 6 strokes. Nickname: Minister (of State).

A臣 3837 F1556 SHIN *omi* retainer, subject.
3子 *shinshi* retainer
下 *shinka* subject, retainer, vassal
5民 *shimmin* subject, national
8服 *shimpuku suru* obey, follow
事 *shinji* allegiance, retainer's service
10従 *shinjū* serving as a retainer; retainer
11庶 *shinsho* retainers and the people
道 *shindō* practice of loyalty
12属 *shinzoku* vassalage, subjection
13節 *shinsetsu* a retainer's integrity
14僚 *shinryō* officials in service
僕 *shimboku* retainer, servant, retinue
16隷 *shinrei* retainer
20籍 *shinseki* status of a subject
籍降下 *shinseki kōka* (royalty) becoming subjects ⌈ing a commoner
籍降嫁 *shinseki kōka* (a princess) marry-

— 2 —

臤 3838 F-X KAN, KEN hard; wise.

臥 3839 F1557 卧 GA. *fu(su)*, *ga(su)* bend down, bow down, lie prostrate. *fu(seru)* lie down, retire, go to bed.
7床 *gashō* confined to bed. *fushido* a bed
8所 *fushido* bed, cot, place to sleep
10病 *gabyō* bedridden
11雪 *neyuki* lingering snow
13煙 *gaen* ancient fireman
16薪嘗胆 *gashin-shōtan* perseverance and determination ⌈in obscurity
龍 *garyū* a reclining dragon; a great man
龍点睛 *garyū tensei* finishing touch

— 11 —

A臨 3840 F1557 RIN. *nozo(mu)* face, front on, border on; meet; be confronted by; be on the verge of; attend, assist at; deal with; rule over; command a view of; deign to; visit, call on; come upon; come up to.
4月 *ringetsu* last month of pregnancy
5写 *rinsha* copying
6行 *rinkō* proceeding to a place
休 *rinkyū* special holiday
地 *rinchi no* on-the-spot, field
在 *rinzai* presence
7床 *rinshō* clinical
床医学 *rinshō igaku* clinical medicine
床的 *rinshōteki* clinical
床家 *rinshōka* clinician

床訊問 *rinshō jimmon* clinical examination
床像 *rinshōzō* clinical picture, clinical findings
床講義 *rinshō kōgi* clinical lecture, clinic, bedside instruction
[8]幸 *rinkō* imperial visit
[9]界 *rinkai* limit; critical (temperature)
海 *rinkai* marine, seaside
海実験所 *rinkai jikkenjo* marine laboratory
[10]席 *rinseki* presence, attendance, those present
書 *rinsho* copying characters from a model book
時 *rinji* temporary, special, extraordinary
時利得税 *rinji-ritokuzei* excess-profits tax
時国会 *rinji kokkai* special session of congress
時費 *rinjihi* emergency expenses
[11]終 *rinjū* dying hour, deathbed, one's last hour
船 *rinsen* ship visit, ship search
船権 *rinsenken* right to search a ship
[12]場 *rinjō* visit, presence, attendance
御 *ringyo* imperial visit
検 *rinken* inspection visit, raid, domiciliary search
港列車 *rinkō ressha* train to the port
港線 *rinkōsen* railway line to the port
[13]戦 *rinsen* going to the battlefield
[16]機 *rinki ni* extemporaneously, impromptu
機応変 *rinki-ōhen* adaptation to circumstances

RAD. 自 132

Mizukara oneself. Nickname: Dotted Eye (cf. Rad. 109).

A 自 3841 F1558 SHI, JI oneself. *mizuka(ra)* oneself, personally. *onozuka(ra)*, *ino(zuto)* naturally, of itself.
[2]力 *jiryoku* self-reliance, one's own efforts, self-help. *jiriki* (Buddhist) salvation by works
力本願 *jiriki hongan* salvation by works; continence, self-control, self-denial
力更生 *jiryoku-kōsei* attaining success by overcoming difficulties
[3]大 *jidai* boasting
刃 *jijin* suicide
己 *jiko* oneself, ego. *jiko-* self-, auto-
己中心 *jiko-chūshin no* selfish, self-centered
己反省 *jiko-hansei* introspection
己本位 *jiko-hon-i* egotism, selfishness
己主義 *jiko-shugi* egoism, selfishness
己弁護 *jiko-bengo* self-justification
己批判 *jiko-hihan* self-criticism
己実現 *jiko-jitsugen* self-realization, self-expression
己表現 *jiko-hyōgen* self-expression
己保存 *jiko-hozon* self-preservation
己宣伝 *jiko-senden* self-advertisement
己発展 *jiko-hatten* self-aggrandizement
己流 *jikoryū* one's own style; *jikoryū no* self-styled, self-taught
己訓練 *jiko-kunren* self-discipline
己紹介 *jiko-shōkai* self-introduction
己満足 *jiko-manzoku* self-satisfaction
己欺瞞 *jiko-giman* self-deception
己暗示 *jiko-anji* autosuggestion
己催眠 *jiko-saimin* autohypnosis
己解剖 *jiko-kaibō* self-analysis
己感情 *jiko-kanjō* emotional result of one's own estimate of himself
己嫌悪 *jiko-ken-o* self-abhorrence
己犠牲 *jiko-gisei* self-sacrifice
己犠牲的 *jiko-giseiteki* self-sacrificing
[4]火 *jika* a fire starting in one's home
今 *jikon* hereafter
分 *jibun* self, oneself. *jibun no* one's own, personal
分天狗 *jibun-tengu* self-conceited man
分自身 *jibun-jishin* oneself (emphatic)
分持 *jibummo(chi)* paying one's own way, providing for oneself
分勝手 *jibun-katte* selfishness, egoism
[5]生 *jisei* spontaneous generation, wild or natural growth
用 *jiyō* for personal use
白 *jihaku* confession, acknowledgment
他 *jita* oneself and others; transitive and intransitive
弁 *jiben* paying one's own expenses
失 *jishitsu* absent-mindedness; stupor, daze; unconsciousness; apathy
立 *jiritsu* independence, self-reliance, self-support
立経済 *jiritsu keizai* economic independence
主 *jishu* independence, autonomy
主化 *jishuka suru* make independent
主的 *jishuteki* independent, autonomous
主番組 *jishu bangumi* sustaining program (sponsorless)
主権 *jishuken* independence, autonomy
由 *jiyū* independence, freedom, liberty; liberal; voluntary
由人 *jiyūjin* freemen
由民 *jiyūmin* free people, freemen
由平等 *jiyū-byōdō* freedom and equality before the law
由市場 *jiyū shijō* free market
由主義 *jiyū shugi* liberalism
由自在 *jiyū-jizai na* free, unrestricted

6 竹米糸缶网四羊羽老而耒耳聿肉月臣【自】至臼舌舛舟艮色艸卄虍虫血行衣ネ西

由行動 *jiyū kōdō* free hand, independent action
由形 *jiyūgata* free style
由労働者 *jiyū rōdōsha* casual laborer
由画 *jiyūga* freehand drawing
由国 *jiyūkoku* independent nation
由国家 *jiyū kokka* the free nations
由放任 *jiyū hōnin* noninterference, laissez faire
由型 *jiyūgata* free style (swimming)
由研究 *jiyū kenkyū* independent investigation
由神学 *jiyū shingaku* liberal theology
由思想 *jiyū shisō* liberal thought
由思想家 *jiyū shisōka* freethinkers
由党 *jiyūtō* liberal party
由都市 *jiyū toshi* free city
由航行権 *jiyū kōkōken* freedom of the seas
由恋愛 *jiyū ren-ai* free love
由訳 *jiyūyaku* free translation
由販売 *jiyū hambai* unrestricted trade
由教育 *jiyū kyōiku* liberal education
由経済 *jiyū keizai* free economy
由船舶 *jiyū sempaku* neutral ship
由港 *jiyūkō* free port
由勝手 *jiyū katte* wilfulness
由貿易 *jiyū bōeki* free trade
由渡航 *jiyū tokō* unrestricted ship passage
由結婚 *jiyū kekkon* common-law marriage
由裁量 *jiyū sairyō* latitude, discretion
由廃業 *jiyū haigyō* prostitute's self-emancipation
由営業 *jiyū eigyō* nonrestricted business
由詩 *jiyūshi* free verse
由意志 *jiyū ishi* free will; spontaneity
由解放 *jiyū kaihō* setting free
由選択 *jiyū sentaku* free choice
由権 *jiyūken* civil liberties
由輪 *jiyūrin* free wheel
由諸国 *jiyū shokoku* the free nations
由憲法 *jiyū kempō* flexible constitution
由競争 *jiyū kyōsō* open competition
6 尽 *jijin* suicide
伝 *jiden* autobiography
任 *jinin* pretension, bragging
刎 *jifun suru* decapitate oneself
存 *jison* self-existence
宅 *jitaku* one's home, private residence
宅教授 *jitaku kyōju* tutoring in the home
在 *jizai ni* freely, at will
在書架 *jizai shoka* expandable bookcase
在梯子 *jizaibashigo* extension ladder
在鉤 *jizai kagi* pot hanger
在継手 *jizai tsu(gi)te* universal joint
在錐 *jizaisui* expanding bit
在鍵 *jizai kagi* a suspended pot hook
7 足 *jisoku* self-sufficiency, satisfaction with what one possesses
身 *jishin* self, oneself, itself, yourself. *jishin de* by oneself, in person, personally
序 *jijo* author's preface
戒 *jikai* self-discipline
体 *jitai* one's own body, oneself, itself; originally
決 *jiketsu* self-determination; resignation; suicide
沈 *jichin suru* scuttle one's own boat
利 *jiri* self-interest, personal gain
判 *jihan* one's own decision, one's own judgment
助 *jijo* self-help, self-reliance
邸 *jitei* one's residence
余 *jiyo* the others, the rest
来 *jirai* since
花受粉 *jika-jufun* self-pollination
作 *jisaku* one's own work
作農 *jisakunō* owner farmer
作農民 *jisaku nōmin* owner farmers
我 *jiga* self, the ego
我主義 *jigashugi* egotism, egoism
我自讃 *jiga-jisan* self-praise
我実現 *jiga jitsugen* self-realization
8 供 *jikyō* confession
侍 *jiji* self-reliance
明 *jimei* self-evidence
注 *jichū* annotating one's own writings; such annotations
炊 *jisui* cooking for oneself
知 *jichi* knowing oneself
若 *jijaku* composure, calmness
制力 *jiseiryoku* power of self-control
制心 *jiseishin* self-control
国 *jikoku* one's own country. *jikoku no* native, domestic
国民 *jikokumin* one's countrymen
国語 *jikokugo* one's mother tongue
画 *jiga* picture painted by oneself
画自賛 *jiga-jisan* praising one's own picture
画像 *jigazō* self-portrait
画賛 *jigasan* praising one's own picture
画讃 *jigasan* praising one's own picture
治 *jichi* self-government
治会 *jichikai* student council
治体 *jichitai* self-governing body
治的 *jichiteki* automous, self-governing
治制 *jichisei* self-governing system
治植民地 *jichi shokuminchi* dominion, self-governing colony, crown colony
治領 *jichiryō* self-governing dominion
治権 *jichiken* autonomy
9 首 *jishu* surrender (to police)
派 *jiha* one's own party
活 *jikatsu* self-support
科 *jika* one's own sins
剄 *jikei suru* decaptitate oneself
剃 *jizo(ri) suru* shave oneself
卑 *jihi* debasing oneself
前 *jimae de* at one's own expense. *jimae no* independent (geisha)

省 *jisei* self-examination
浄作用 *jijō-sayō* self-purification
信 *jishin* self-confidence
信満満 *jishim-mamman* great self-confidence
叙 *jijo* writing one's story
叙伝 *jijoden* autobiography
乗 *jijō suru* square (a number)
乗根 *jijōkon* square root
重 *jijū* dead weight. *jichō* self-respect, self-love, prudence, circumspection; care of the body
重心 *jichōshin* (proper) pride
負 *jifu* bragging about one's ability; conceit
負心 *jifushin* conceit
律 *jiritsu* autonomy, self-control, self-determination
律性 *jiritsusei* autonomy
律神経 *jiritsu shinkei* autonomic nerves
発 *jihatsu* spontaneousness
発性 *jihatsusei* spontaneousness
発的 *jihatsuteki* spontaneous, voluntary, free-will
10 修 *jishū* self-study
称 *jishō* self-styled, would-be; first person
害 *jigai* suicide
党 *jitō* one's own party
差 *jisa* deviation
書 *jisho* one's own writing, autograph
記 *jiki* writing personally; self-registering
記晴雨計 *jiki seiukei* recording barometer
記寒暖計 *jiki kandankei* recording thermometer
殺 *jisatsu* suicide
殺未遂 *jisatsu-misui* attempted suicide
殺未遂者 *jisatsu-misuisha* attempted suicide (the person)
殺的 *jisatsuteki* suicidal
殺者 *jisatsusha* a suicide (the person)
家 *jika* one's own home; one's self
家中毒 *jika-chūdoku* autointoxication
家用 *jikayō* private use
家用車 *jikayōsha* private automobile
家広告 *jika-kōkoku* self-advertisement, publicity stunt
家本位 *jika-hon-i* egotism, selfishness
家伝染 *jika-densen* autoinfection
家受精 *jika-jusei* self-reproduction
家保存 *jiko-hozon* self-preservation
家保険 *jika-hoken* self-insurance
家製 *jikasei no* home-brewed
家撞着 *jika-dōchaku* self-contradiction
11 得 *jitoku* self-satisfaction; self-acquirement; apprehension, understanding
晦 *jikai* hiding oneself and one's talents
著 *jicho* one's own publication
粛 *jishuku* self-control, self-discipline
堕落 *jidaraku* depravity
問 *jimon suru* question oneself
問自答 *jimon-jitō* soliloquy, monologue, answering one's own question
惚 *unubo(reru)* be conceited, flatter oneself
惚者 *unubo(re)mono* conceited person
転 *jiten* rotation
転車 *jitensha* bicycle
習 *jishū* studying by oneself
習自学 *jishū-jigaku* studying by oneself
責 *jiseki* self-condemnation
責点 *jisekiten* earned run
動 *jidō* automatic action
動人形 *jidōningyō* automaton, robot
動小銃 *jidō shōjū* automatic rifle
動火器 *jidō kaki* automatic firearms
動収穫機 *jidō shūkakuki* threshing machine
動自転車 *jidōjitensha* motorcycle
動式 *jidōshiki no* automatic
動式電話機 *jidōshiki denwaki* dial phone
動車 *jidōsha* automobile
動車王 *jidōshaō* automobile king
動車屋 *jidōshaya* garage, auto repair shop
動車速度計 *jidōsha sokudokei* speedometer
動車庫 *jidōshako* garage
動車部隊 *jidōsha butai* motorized unit
動車隊 *jidōshatai* automobile corps
動車強盗 *jidōsha gōtō* automobile thief
動車税 *jidōshazei* automobile tax
動車路 *jidōsharo* driveway, auto road
動車置場 *jidōsha okiba* motor pool
動車駐車場 *jidōsha chūshajō* parking place
動的 *jidōteki* automatic
動計 *jidōkei* meter
動連結機 *jidō renketsuki* automatic coupler
動計算器 *jidō keisanki* taximeter
動消火器 *jidō shōkaki* automatic sprinkler system
動販売食堂 *jidō hambai shokudō* automat
動販売器 *jidō hambaiki* automatic vending machine
動階段 *jidō kaidan* escalator
動扉 *jidō tobira* automatic doors
動詞 *jidōshi* intransitive verb
動艇 *jidōtei* motorboat
動電話 *jidō denwa* public telephone
動橇 *jidō sori* motor sledge
動操縦装置 *jidō sōjū sōchi* automatic pilot
12 廃 *jihai* (prostitute's) voluntary emancipation
評 *jihyō* self-criticism
訴 *jiso* surrender (to police)
証 *jishō* one's own evidence
敬 *jikei* self-respect
筆 *jihitsu* one's own handwriting
営 *jiei* self-management
裁 *jisai* suicide
給 *jikyū* self-support
給自足 *jikyū-jisoku* self-support, self-sufficiency
尊 *jison* self-respect; self-esteem, conceit
尊心 *jisonshin* self-respect; self-esteem, conceit
覚 *jikaku* consciousness; self-consciousness; insight; realization
覚的 *jikakuteki* subjective (symptoms)

覚症 *jikakushō* subjective symptoms, patient's complaints
覚症状 *jikaku shōjō* subjective symptoms, patient's complaints
費 *jihi* one's own expense
費出版 *jihi shuppan* publication at one's own expense ⌈(sponsorless)
費番組 *jihi bangumi* sustaining program
然 *shizen, jinen* nature. *shizen no* natural; unaffected; spontaneous, automatic
然人 *shizennin* natural person
然力 *shizenryoku* natural agencies
然木 *shizemboku* naturally grown trees
然生 *jinensei* wild growth
然本然 *shizen-honnen no* natural
然主義 *shizen shugi* naturalism
然色 *shizenshoku* natural color
然死 *shizenshi* natural death
然林 *shizenrin* natural forest, virgin forest
然物 *shizembutsu* natural objects
然的 *shizenteki* natural
然法 *shizenhō* natural law, law of nature
然法則 *shizen hōsoku* natural law
然界 *shizenkai* natural world ⌈nature
然美 *shizembi* natural beauty; beauty of
然発火 *shizen hakka* spontaneous combustion ⌈tion; spontaneity
然発生 *shizen hassei* spontaneous genera-
然科学 *shizen kagaku* natural science
然秩序 *shizen chitsujo* natural order
然教 *shizenkyō* nature worship
然描写 *shizembyōsha* description of nature
然崇拝 *shizen sūhai* nature worship
然淘汰 *shizen tōta* natural selection
然現象 *shizen genshō* natural phenomena
然数 *shizen (no) sū* fate
然増加 *shizen zōka* unearned increment
然増収 *shizen zōshū* natural increase, accre-
然権 *shizenken* natural rights ⌊tion
然論 *shizenron* naturalism
然燃焼 *shizen nenshō* spontaneous combus-
然薯 *jinenjo* a wild mountain potato ⌊tion
然療法 *shizen ryōhō* nature cure; physiotherapy
然観 *shizenkan* view of nature
13 適 *jiteki* easy and comfortable living
働 *jidō* automatic action
滅 *jimetsu* natural decay; self-ruin, suicide, self-destruction
腹 *jibara* one's own pocketbook
愛 *jiai* self-love, selfishness, egoism, self-
署 *jisho* autograph, signature ⌊regard
意識 *ji-ishiki* self-consciousness
業自得 *jigō-jitoku* reaping what one sows
棄 *jiki yake* despair; desperation
棄八 *yake(noyam)pachi* desperate person
棄酒 *yakezake* drowning one's cares in saké
棄飲 *yakeno(mi)* drinking to forget one's troubles ⌈despair
棄腹 *yakebara, yake(p)para* desperation,
棄糞 *yakekuso* desperation; despair
14 選 *jisen* personal choice
像 *jizō* self-bust (sculpture)
説 *jisetsu* one's own view
認 *jinin* admission
製 *jisei* one's own making
堕落 *jidaraku* personal untidiness
慢 *jiman* pride, boasting
慢臭 *jimankusa(i)* boastful
慢話 *jimambanashi* boastful talk
慢顔 *jimangao* boastful look
15 嘲 *jichō* self-scorn
慰 *ji-i* self-consolation; self-abuse
賛 *jisan* self-praise
暴 *jibō* neglecting or injuring one's body
暴自棄 *jibōjiki* despair, desperation
暴酒 *yakezake* drowning one's cares in saké
衛 *jiei* self defense; bodyguard
衛長 *jieichō* captain of the guard
衛隊 *jieitai* Self-defense Force
衛権 *jieiken* right of self-defense
16 儘 *jimama*=*wagamama* 我儘 200.16
彊 *jikyō* strenuous efforts
燃 *jinen* spontaneous combustion
縛 *jibaku* being circumscribed by one's own words and actions
薦 *jisen* recommending oneself
壊 *jikai* disintegration
壊作用 *jikai sayō* disintegration
18 瀆 *jitoku* masturbation
瀆行為 *jitoku kōi* masturbation
19 縄自縛 *jijō-jibaku* caught in one's own trap
爆 *jibaku* suicide explosion
爆機 *jibakuki* suicide bomber
警 *jikei* self-warning, vigilance
警団 *jikeidan* vigilance committee
22 讃 *jisan* praising oneself

3

B 臭 $\frac{3842}{\text{F1562}}$ 臭 SHŪ odor, savor, fragrance. *kusa(i)* ill-smelling; suspicious-looking. *nio(i)* (see under 匂 742.0). *-kusa(i)* smelling; smacking of; looking (suspicious).

6 名 *shūmei* shameful reputation
気 *shūki* offensive odor, stench
気止 *shūkido(me)* deodorizer
8 味 *kusami, shūmi* offensive odor; savor, flavor, smack; group, faction
物 *kusa(i) mono* scandal
10 素 *shūso* bromine

素酸 *shūsosan* bromic acid
13 跡 *shūseki* scent, trail
14 聞 *shūbun* scandal, ill-fame

— 4 —

臬 3843 F1562 See 臭 3842.

息 3844 F710 A Soku son; interest (on money). *iki* breath, respiration. *iki(mu)* =*riki(mu)* (see under 力 715.0.) *iki(ru)* be hot with anger. *iko(u)* rest, relax, repose. [心]
3 女 *sokujo* daughter
子 *musuko* son, boy, young man
4 切 *ikigi(re)* breathlessness
5 付 *ikitsu(ku)* have a respite. *iki (mo) tsu(kasezu)* without giving any respite. *iki (mo) tsu(kazu) ni* holding one's breath
出 *ikida(shi)* air vent; bunghole
6 休 *ikiyasu(me)* breathing spell
7 吹 *ibu(ki)* breath
抜 *ikinu(ki)* ventilator; breathing space; diversion. *iki-nuku* live thru, survive
杖 *ikizue* (palanquin bearer's) resting staff
災 *sokusai*=*buji* 無事 2773.8
男 *sokunan* son
8 苦 *ikiguru(shii)* stuffy, suffocating
9 臭 *ikikusa(i)* having offensive breath
巻 *ikima(ku)* fume, be enraged
急 *ikise(ku)* breathe hard
急切 *ikise(ki)-ki(ru)* gasp, pant 「life
10 根 *ikine* breathing; breath; voice. *iki(no)ne*
11 張 *ikiba(ru)*=*riki(mu)* 力 715.0
12 遣 *ikizuka(i)* breathing
絶 *ikita(eru)* die
絶絶 *ikita(e)da(e)* on the verge of death
13 継 *ikitsu(gi)* breathing spell
詰 *ikizu(maru)* be choked, be stifled
15 衝 *ikizu(ku)* heave a sigh
22 籠 *ikigomo(ru)* breathe with difficulty

RAD. 至 133

Itaru to arrive. Nickname: Arriving.

至 3845 F1562 A Shi. *ita(ru)* go, proceed, come; arrive, reach, attain; result in, lead to. *ita(ri)* the utmost, the height of, climax; on account of. *ita(ru made)* to, until. *ita(ranai)* imperfect, incompetent, careless. *ita(tte)* very, exceedingly. *ita(tte) wa* as for, as to.
3 大 *shidai no* vast, enormous; remarkable; important
才 *shisai* rare talents; a man of rare talents
上 *shijō* supremacy
上命令 *shijō meirei* a supreme (inviolable) command; the categorical imperative
上権 *shijōken* supremacy, sovereignty
4 心 *shishin* sincerity
仁 *shijin* great sympathy
公 *shikō* supreme fairness
公至平 *shikō-shihei* very just
6 尽 *ita(reri)-tsu(kuseri)* complete, thoro
当 *shitō* proper, reasonable, fair
近 *shikin* very very near
近弾 *shikindan* near miss
7 言 *shigen* wise saying
妙 *shimyō na* very strange
材 *shizai*=*shisai* 至才 (see above–3)
芸 *shigei* top artistic skill
孝 *shikō* supreme filial piety
8 所 *ita(ru) tokoro* everywhere
幸 *shikō* supreme happiness
宝 *shihō* the greatest treasure
9 便 *shiben* very convenient
点 *shiten* solstice, equinoctial point
要 *shiyō* essence; vital importance
急 *shikyū* urgent
急便 *shikyūbin* express mail
急報 *shikyūhō* urgent telegram, urgent call
10 純 *shijun* purity, sincerity
高 *shikō* supremacy, sublimity
高者 *Shikōsha* the Most High, God
11 情 *shijō* sincerity; natural feelings
理 *shiri* a well-understood truth
軟風 *shinampū* light breeze
12 極 *shigoku* very, quite, exceedingly
尊 *Shison* the Throne, the Emperor
善 *shizen* supreme good
軽風 *shikeifū* light breeze
13 福 *shifuku* beatitude, supreme bliss, highest good 「true heart
誠 *shisei* sincerity, faith, devotion; one's
愚 *shigu* height of folly; biggest fool
楽 *shiraku* supreme happiness. *shigaku* excellent music
聖 *shisei* highest virtue 「Mosaic sanctuary)
聖所 *Shiseijo* the Most Holy Place (in
14 徳 *shitoku* highest virtue
15 論 *shiron* a very reasonable argument
18 難 *shinan* extreme difficulty
難事 *shinanji* a most difficult problem

2

到 $\frac{3846}{F241}$ Tō. *ita(ru)* (see under 至 3845.0). [刂] B

[7]来 *tōrai* arrival, advent, visitation
来物 *tōraimono* something sent as a gift
[8]底 *tōtei* after all, in the long run; (with neg.) (cannot) possibly, (none) at all, impossible; absolutely
[11]著 *tōchaku* arrival
達 *tōtatsu* arrival
達地 *tōtatsuchi* destination
達局 *tōtatsukyoku* office of destination
達点 *tōtatsuten* destination
達港 *tōtatsukō* port of destination
[12]着 *tōchaku* arrival
着早早 *tōchaku sōsō* immediately upon arrival
着地点 *tōchaku chiten* destination; objective (of an army)
着港 *tōchakukō* port of arrival
着駅 *tōchaku eki* arrival station
[16]頭 *tōtō* at last, finally, after all

4

致 $\frac{3847}{F1564}$ Chi. *ita(su)* do; send, forward; cause, incur; render (assistance); exert (oneself); engage, call in (a doctor). B

[4]方 *ita(shi)kata* way, method, means, help, course, resource
方無 *ita(shi)katana(ku)* unavoidably
[5]仕 *chishi suru* resign
[6]死 *chishi no* fatal, deadly, lethal, mortal
[7]身 *chishin* sacrificing one's life for one's lord
[8]知 *chichi* great wisdom
命的 *chimeiteki* fatal, deadly, lethal, mortal
命傷 *chimeishō* fatal injury
[14]様 *ita(shi)yō*=*ita(shi)kata* 致方 (see above -4)

8

臺 See **台** 848.

鵄 $\frac{3848}{F2143}$ See **鴟** 5347. [鳥]

RAD. 臼 134

Usu mortar. Nickname: Mortar.

臼 $\frac{3849}{F1565}$ Kyū. *usu* mortar, hand mill.

[5]石 *usu-ishi* millstone, stone mortar, stone mill, burstone
[10]挽 *usuhi(ki)* milling; miller
砲 *kyūhō* mortar
[12]歯 *kyūshi, usuba* molar
[14]歌 *usu-uta* rice-pounders' song

2

臾 See 106.

兒 $\frac{3850}{F189}$ See **児** 572. [儿]

3

舁 $\frac{3851}{F1565}$ **舁** Yo. *ka(ku), ka(ki)-a(geru)* bear, carry (a palanquin).

[2]入 *ka(ki)-i(reru)* carry in
[3]上 *ka(ki)-a(geru)* shoulder (a palanquin).
ka(ki)-nobo(ru) carry up, bring up
[7]戻 *ka(ki)-modo(ru), ka(ki)-modo(su)* carry back

5

舂 $\frac{3852}{F1565}$ Shō. *usutsu(ku)* pound (in a mortar); sink, set (the sun).

7

與 See **与** 6.

舅 $\frac{3853}{F1566}$ Kyū. *shūto* father-in-law.

[8]姑 *kyūko* parents-in-law

9

興 See 615.

11

舊 See **旧** 94.

擧 $\frac{3854}{F1567}$ **擧** See **挙** 1902.

RAD. 舌 135

Shita tongue. At left: *shita hen*. Nickname: Tongue.

A 舌 $\frac{3855}{F1571}$ ZETSU. *shita* tongue; reed; clapper. *shita*(*tarui*) lisping.

3 口 *zekkō* tongue and mouth; lips; way of speaking
上 *shita-ue* words
4 不足 *shitatarazu* lisping; one who lisps, tongue-tied person
5 代 *zetsudai, shitadai* notice, announcement
打 *shita-u*(*chi*) smacking one's lips; clicking the tongue; hissing; saying "tut-tut"
圧子 *zetsuatsushi* tongue depressor
6 先 *shitasaki* tongue tip
先三寸 *shitasaki-sanzun* eloquence
7 足 *shitata*(*razu*) lisp; lisper
車 *shitaguruma* chattering steadily
状 *zetsujō* tongue shape
利 *shitaki*(*ki*) taster
8 長 *shitanaga* boaster
苔 *zettai* fur on the tongue
9 音 *zetsuon* lingual sound
巻 *shita* (*o*) *ma*(*ku*) be astonished
10 舐 *shitana*(*mezuri*) licking the lips, licking one's chops
11 強 *shitagowa*(*i*) unable to speak distinctly
13 鼓 *shitatsuzumi* smacking one's lips (when eating)
触 *shitazawa*(*ri*) taste
戦 *zessen* a war of words
禍 *zekka* an unfortunate slip of the tongue
禍事件 *zekka jiken* incriminating utterance
14 端 *zettan* tip of the tongue
15 鋒 *zeppō* tongue
16 縺 *shitamotsu*(*re*) lisp; lisper
頭 *zettō* tip of the tongue
17 癌 *zetsugan* tongue cancer

1

B 乱 $\frac{3856}{F66}$ 亂 亂 RAN, RON riot, rebellion, war, disorder. *mida*(*re*) disorder, disturbance, agitation. *mida*(*su*), *mida*(*ru*) put in disorder; disturb, agitate; corrupt; derange (the mind). *mida*(*reru*) be out of order, be confused; be disturbed, be disorganized; be demoralized, be lax; be disheveled. *mida*(*ri*) *ni* (see under 妄 288.0). *mida*(*rigamashii*) morally corrupt. [乙]

2 丁 *ranchō* mixed up pages (in a book)
入 *rannyū* intrusion, raid. *rannyū suru* intrude, break into
入者 *rannyūsha* intruder, trespasser
3 山 *ranzan* a jumble of high and low mountains
4 心 *ranshin* insanity, derangement
文 *rambun* careless writing (in composition)
反射 *ranhansha* diffused reflection
5 用 *ran-yō* misuse, abuse, misappropriation
立 *ranritsu* flood (of candidates)
打 *randa* pommeling, random blows
世 *ransei* troublous times
民 *rammin* insurgents, rioters, mob
6 臣 *ranshin* traitorous vassal, traitor
行 *rangyō* profligacy, debauchery, misconduct
伐 *rambatsu* indiscriminate deforestation
7 足 *mida*(*re*) *ashi* out of step
売 *rambai* underselling, panicky selling
8 国 *rangoku* a disturbed country, strife-torn country
刺 *ranshi* scarification
拍子 *rambyōshi* out of tune
杭 *rangui* (defense) palisade; fence
杭歯 *ranguiba* irregular teeth
9 飛 *mida*(*ri*)-*to*(*bu*) (rumors) spread wildly, run wild
造 *ranzō* overproduction; careless manufacture
後 *rango* after the rebellion
軍 *rangun* mixed fight, rough-and-tumble
発 *rampatsu* random or reckless firing
10 倫 *ranrin* immorality, immoral conduct
流 *ranryū* turbulent flow
酒 *ranshu* drunken frenzy; vicious drinker
脈 *rammyaku* confusion, disorder, chaos
射 *ransha* random firing, wild shot
書 *mida*(*re*)*ga*(*ki*) careless composition (of an article)
11 麻 *ramma* confusion, chaos, anarchy
視 *ranshi* astigmatism, distorted vision
酔 *ransui* dead drunk
12 筆 *rampitsu* bad writing, scribbling
雲 *ran-un* nimbus clouds, rain clouds, torn clouds
費 *rampi* waste, extravagance
13 賊 *ranzoku* gangsters, rebels
戦 *ransen* free-for-all fight, melee
痴気 *ranchiki* quarreling, carousing, disorderliness
痴気騒 *ranchiki sawa*(*gi*) uproarious festivity
14 雑 *ranzatsu* disorder, confusion
髪 *mida*(*re*)*gami*, *mida*(*shi*)*gami*, *rampatsu* unkempt hair
舞 *rambu* boisterous dance
読 *randoku* indiscriminate reading
読家 *randokuka* indiscriminate reader
15 箱 *mida*(*re*)*bako* box for kimono and accessories
撃 *rangeki* confused fighting, melee
調 *ranchō* discord; ragtime; confusion, irregularity; market fluctuation
調子 *ranchōshi* discord; ragtime; confusion, irregularity; market fluctuation

暴 *rambō* violence, rudeness, rowdyism, carelessness, lawlessness, recklessness
暴者 *rambōmono* rowdy, vandal, rascal
16獲 *rankaku* indiscriminate fishing or hunting
18闘 *rantō* free-for-all fight, melee
19離 *ranri* dispersion
22籠 *mida(re)kago* clothes basket (in a bathhouse)

—— 2 ——

舍 See 舎 423.

刮 3857/F241 Katsu. *koso(geru)* scrape off. [刀]

—— 4 ——

舐 3858/F1572 碭 Shi. *nebu(ru)*, *na(meru)* (see under 嘗 1369.0). *name(zuru)* lick one's lips.

—— 5 ——

甜 3859/F1263 甛 Ten sweet. [甘]
5瓜 *makuwa uri* muskmelon
11菜 *tensai, satō daikon* sugar beet
菜糖 *tensaitō* beet sugar

—— 7 ——

A 辞 3860/F1855 辭 Ji word, term, expression; sentence; an address. *ji(suru)* resign, leave, decline. *ya(meru)* resign. *ina(mu)* refuse, decline; deny. [辛]
5令 *jirei* written appointment, government order; commission; wording
去 *jikyo suru* leave, quit, retire
世 *jisei* passing away; last words; deathbed poem
6色 *jishoku* words and looks
任 *jinin* resignation
7別 *jibetsu* saying farewell
8退 *jitai* refusal, declining
林 *jirin* dictionary
典 *jiten* dictionary
表 *jihyō* written resignation
9柄 *jihei* excuse; pretense
10書 *jisho* dictionary, glossary
11章 *jishō* a composition, an article
13彙 *ji-i* letter of resignation
意 *ji-i* intention to resign
15儀 *jigi* bow, greeting; refusal, declining; hesitation
18職 *jishoku* resignation
職願 *jishoku nega(i)* letter of resignation
20譲 *jijō suru* give way to another

—— 8 ——

碭 3861/F1572 See 舐 3858.

—— 9 ——

舗 See 舖 552.

—— 10 ——

舘 舘 See 館 5174.

RAD. 舛 136

Mai ashi dancing "legs" (i.e., the lower element in *mau* "to dance") or *masu* (i.e., the right-hand element in the character for *masu* "a measure"). As commonly printed and written, this rather rare element actually has 7 strokes, but it is traditionally a 6-stroke radical and is so counted herein. Nickname: Dancing.

—— 8 ——

B 舞 3862/F1573 Bu. *ma(u)* dance; flutter about, flit; circle, wheel. *mai* dancing; dance.
3子 *maiko* dancing girl
下 *ma(i)-sa(garu)* come down dancing
上 *ma(i)-a(garu)* soar, fly high, be whirled up
4手 *ma(i)te* dancer
込 *ma(i)-ko(mu)* come in dancing; drop in on, visit; befall; (snow) blows in
5台 *butai* stage
台中継 *butai chūkei* stage-to-radio hookup
台生活 *butai seikatsu* stage career
台芸術 *butai geijutsu* theatrical art
台効果 *butai kōka* stage effect
台面 *butai men* scene
台負 *butaima(ke)* stage fright
台度胸 *butai dokyō* stage nerve
台開 *butaibira(ki)* opening of a new theater
台装置 *butai sōchi* stage setting
台裏 *butai ura* behind the scene
台劇 *butaigeki* stage drama
台稽古 *butaigeiko* dress rehearsal
台顔 *butaigao* face with a heavy make-up
6衣 *ma(i)ginu* dancing costume
曲 *bukyoku* musical dance, music and dancing

7戻 *ma(i)-modo(ru)* find one's way back, re-
妓 *ma(i)ko, bugi* dancing girl ⌊turn
狂 *ma(i)-kuru(u)* dance wildly, dance in a
9姫 *maihime* dancing girl ⌊frenzy
10扇 *maiōgi* dancer's fan
納 *ma(i)-osa(meru)* end the dance
容 *buyō* dancing form
11掛 *ma(i)-ka(keru)* flutter over
13楽 *bugaku* Court dance and Court music
14踊 *ma(i)-odo(ru)* dance. *buyō* dancing;
踊劇 *buyōgeki* dance drama ⌊dance
15踏 *butō* dancing
踏曲 *butōkyoku* dance music
踏会 *butōkai* ball, dance
踏狂 *butōkyō* dance craze
踏者 *butōsha* dancer
踏病 *butōbyō* St. Vitus' dance, chorea
踏場 *butōjō* dance hall

RAD. 舟 137

Fune hen left-side "ship." Variant: 舟. Nickname: Ship.

舟 3863 / F1574 **舟** SHŪ boat. *fune* (see under 船 3873.0). ⌈ger
B
2人 *funabito, shūjin* a seaman, a ship passen-
3子 *shūshi*=*shūjin* 舟人 (see word above)
6行 *shūkō* navigation; going by ship
7足 *funa-ashi* draft; speed (of a ship)
車 *shūsha* boats and vehicles; transportation
9軍 *shūgun* (ancient) navy ⌊facilities
10師 *shūshi* (ancient) navy
航 *shūkō* voyage
11運 *shūun* ship transportation, freighting by
遊 *funa-aso(bi), shūyū* boating ⌊ship
脚 *funa-ashi* draft of a ship; speed of a ship
12筏 *shūbatsu* boats and rafts; boat
13艇 *shūtei* boat, craft
路 *shūro, funaji* ship's course
14瑞 *funabata* gunwale
歌 *funa-uta* sailor's song, boat song
16橋 *shūkyō* pontoon bridge

3

舡 3864 / F1574 KŌ boat.
11魚 *takobune, funedako* paper nautilus

4

般 3865 / F1575 HAN carry; all.
B
8若 *hannya* wisdom personified; demoness
若湯 *hannyatō* saké

舫 3866 / F1575 HŌ, BŌ. *moya(u)* moor, berth, tie up (a boat). *moya(i)* moorings.
11船 *moyaibune* moored boat, berthed vessel
12結 *moyai musu(bi)* bowline knot

航 3867 / F1574 KŌ navigation; cross over. *kō(suru)* sail, cruise, navigate; fly.
A
6行 *kōkō* navigation, cruise
8送 *kōsō suru* send by ship or plane
空 *kōkū* aviation, flight, air navigation
空力学 *kōkū rikigaku* aerodynamics
空士 *kōkūshi* aviator
空写真 *kōkū shashin* air photograph
空母艦 *kōkū bokan* aircraft carrier
空灯台 *kōkū tōdai* aerial lighthouse
空会社 *kōkugaisha* aviation company
空自衛隊 *kōkū jieitai* Air Self-defense
空服 *kōkūfuku* aviator's uniform ⌊Force
空学 *kōkūgaku* aeronautics
空学校 *kōkū gakkō* aviation school
空事業 *kōkū jigyō* air transportation busi-
空便 *kōkūbin* airmail ⌊ness
空病 *kōkūbyō* air sickness
空家 *kōkūka* aviator
空時代 *kōkū jidai* air age
空郵便 *kōkū yūbin* airmail
空部 *kōkūbu* air force
空部隊 *kōkū butai* air force
空書簡 *kōkū shokan* air letter
空術 *kōkūjutsu* aviation, aeronautics
空船 *kōkūsen* airship, dirigible, blimp
空隊 *kōkūtai* air force
空基地 *kōkū kichi* air bases
空貨物 *kōkū kamotsu* air freight
空港 *kōkūkō* airport, airfield
空路 *kōkūro* air route, air lane
空機 *kōkūki* airplane, aircraft
空輸送 *kōkū yusō* air transportation
9海 *kōkai* voyage, ocean navigation
海士 *kōkaishi* mate, navigating officer
海日誌 *kōkai nisshi* ship's log
海者 *kōkaisha* navigator, mariner, seaman
海時 *kōkaiji* ship's time
海術 *kōkaijutsu* navigation, seamanship
海証明書 *kōkai shōmeisho* navicert
海暦 *kōkaireki* nautical almanac ⌈way
11船 *kōsen* ocean-going vessel; vessel under
12程 *kōtei* ship's run; voyage; lap, leg

6 竹米糸缶网四羊羽老耂而耒耳聿肉月臣自至臼舌舛【舟】4 艮色艸艹虍虫血行衣衤西

13跡 *kōseki* wake of a ship
続力 *kōzokuryoku* cruising range; flying range
続距離 *kōzoku kyori* cruising range
路 *kōro* sea route, steamer lane, service
路標識 *kōro hyōshiki* navigation aids, lighthouse

5

舸 3868/F1575 KA large boat.

舳 3869/F1575 JIKU. *he, hesaki* bow, prow.
6先 *hesaki* bow, prow
22艫 *jikuro* stem to stern, fore and aft

B **船** 3870/F1575 HAKU ship.
5用 *hakuyō* marine
用機関 *hakuyō kikan* marine engine
7来 *hakurai* importation; imported goods
来品 *hakuraihin* imported goods
来種 *hakuraishu* foreign varieties
13載 *hakusai* ocean transportation; importation; imported goods

舵 3871/F1575 F962 **柁** DA rudder. *kaji* rudder, helm, wheel.
3子 *kajiko* helmsman
4手 *dashu* helmsman, coxswain
8取 *kajito(ri)* steering; helmsman; coxswain; guidance, leadership; leader
9柄 *kajizuka* tiller
15輪 *darin* steering wheel, helm
16機 *daki* helm, steering gear, rudder

舷 3872/F1575 GEN gunwale. *funabei, funabata* ship's side, gunwale.
6灯 *gentō* running light, side light
8門 *gemmon* gangway (to a ship)
11梯 *gentei* gangway, gangway ladder
舷 *gengen* gunwale to gunwale
窓 *gensō* porthole
側 *gensoku* ship's side, broadside
側上縁 *gensoku uwabuchi* gunwale
15縁 *gen-en* gunwale
16墻 *genshō* ship's bulwarks
頭 *gentō* gunwale, ship's side
17牆 *genshō* ship's bulwarks

A **船** 3873/F1576 **船 船** SEN ship. *fune* boat, ship, vessel, steamer, liner, barge; shipping; tank, trough, cistern, vat. *-sen* ship, vessel.
2人 *funabito* seaman; passenger
3子 *funako* boatman
大工 *funadaiku* ship carpenter
小屋 *funagoya* boathouse
4方 *funakata* boatman
中 *senchū* ship's interior
内 *sennai* on the ship
夫 *sempu* seaman
火事 *funakaji* ship fire
5尻 *funajiri* stern
主 *funanushi, senshu* shipowner
台 *sendai* ways, shipbuilding slip
出 *funade* ship's departure
外 *sengai* overboard
外機 *sengaiki* outboard motor
6匠 *senshō* ship carpenter
団 *sendan* fleet of vessels
曳 *funahi(ki)* towing
灯 *sentō* ship's lamp
号 *sengō* ship name
守 *funamori* boat watcher
成金 *funanarikin* shipping magnate
7貝 *funegai* ark shell
足 *funa-ashi* draft; speed (of a ship)
医 *sen-i* ship doctor
尾 *sembi* ship's stern
体 *sentai* hull, ship
材 *senzai* ship timber
形 *funagata* boat-shaped
位推算 *sen-i suisan* dead reckoning
位推算法 *sen-i suisanhō* dead reckoning
8長 *senchō* ship's captain
底 *funazoko, sentei* ship's bottom; bilge
房 *sembō* ship's cabin
価 *senka* cost of a ship
板 *funa-ita* ship timber
泊 *funadoma(ri)* anchorage; anchoring, calling
具 *funagu, sengu* ship tackle, rigging
具商 *sengushō* ship chandler
9首 *senshu, miyoshi* bow, prow
便 *funabin, sembin, funadayo(ri)* shipping service
卸 *funaoro(shi)* ship launching
乗 *funano(ri)* sailor, seaman, mariner; traveling by ship
軍 *funa-ikusa* sea battle
客 *senkyaku, senkaku* ship passenger
室 *senshitsu* stateroom, cabin
型 *senkei* boat shape; model of a boat
幽霊 *funayūrei* siren, spirit of the sea
10骨 *senkotsu* ship's ribs
唄 *funa-uta* sailor's song; boat-rowing song
旅 *funatabi* voyage
倉 *sensō* hold (of a ship), hatch
員 *sen-in* crew, ship's company, sailors
荷 *funani* ship's cargo, freight
荷証券 *funani shōken* bill of lading
11淦 *funa-aka* bilge water
脚 *funa-ashi, senkyaku* draft; speed (of a ship)

酔 *funayo(i)* seasickness
隊 *sentai* fleet of ships
宿 *funayado* shipping agent
窓 *funamado, sensō* porthole, cabin window
渠 *senkyo* dock
梯子 *funabashigo* gangplank
道具 *funadōgu* ship's tackle, rigging
問屋 *funadonya, funadoiya* shipping agent
遊 *funa-aso(bi)* boat ride, boating
遊山 *funayusan* boat ride, excursion
側 *sensoku* ship's side
側渡 *sensoku-wata(shi)* free alongside
著 *funatsuki* harbor, wharf, anchorage
著場 *funatsukiba* harbor, wharf, anchorage
舶 *sempaku* ship, vessel, bottoms
舶法 *sempakuhō* shipping law
舶業 *sempakugyō* shipping business
12 場 *funaba* harbor, wharf, anchorage
幅 *sempuku* ship's beam
渡 *funawata(shi)* ferry; delivery from ship; free on board, F.O.B.
喰虫 *funakuimushi* shipworm
着 *funatsu(ki)* wharf, anchorage
着場 *funatsukiba* harbor, wharf, anchorage
13 溜 *funadama(ri)* coastal anchorage
腹 *sempuku* shipping, bottoms, cargo space
蛸 *funedako* paper nautilus
路 *funaji, funamichi, senro* course, channel; sea route; voyage; wake
跡 *funa-ato* wake (of a ship)
賃 *funachin* boat fare; freight rates; charterage
14 端 *funabata* ship's side, gunwale
綱 *funatsuna* ship's tackle
歌 *funa-uta* sailor's song, boat-rowing song
蔵 *funagura* boathouse
15 縁 *funaberi* ship's side, gunwale
影 *sen-ei* sign of a ship
霊 *funadama* ship's guardian deity
16 橋 *funabashi, senkyō* floating bridge, pontoon bridge
積 *funazu(mi)* shipment, shipping, loading, lading
艙 *sensō* hold (of a ship), hatch
頭 *sendō* boatman, seaman, mariner
17 檣 *senshō* mast
齢 *senrei* ship's age
19 瀬 *funase* coastal anchorage
繰 *funagu(ri), funaku(ri)* shipping schedule
繋 *funagaka(ri)* anchorage; anchoring, calling
20 艦 *senkan* ships
籍 *senseki* ship's registry
籍港 *sensekikō* ship's port of registry

7

艀 3874 / F1576 Fu. *hashike* sampan, lighter, barge.
11 船 *hashikebune* sampan, lighter, barge

艇 B 3875 / F1576 Tei small boat.
7 身 *teishin* boat length
体 *teitai* hull
8 長 *teichō* coxswain; submarine captain
9 首 *teishu* bow (of a boat)
10 員 *tei-in* boat crew
庫 *teiko* boathouse
庫番 *teikoban* boathouse keeper
11 舳 *teijiku* stern
11 隊 *teitai* flotilla

9

艘 See 3876.

10

艘 3876 / F1577 Shō. Shū. Sō ship counter.

艙 3877 / F1577 Sō hold (of a ship).
8 口 *sōkō* hatch, hatchway

12

艟 3878 / F1577 Dō fighting ship.
19 艨 *dōmō* warship

艨 3879 / F1577 Mō.
18 艟 *mōdō* warship

13

艤 = **様** 3880 / F1577 Gi landing a boat.
6 舟 *gishū* ship's outfit, rigging, preparation for sailing
12 装 *gisō* ship's outfit, rigging
装品 *gisōhin* ship fittings

14

艦 = **艦** B 3881 / F1577 Kan warship.
3 上 *kanjō* aboard a warship
上機 *kanjōki* carrier-based plane
6 列 *kanretsu* column of warships
7 尾 *kambi* stern (of a warship)
体 *kantai* warship's hull
8 長 *kanchō* captain of a warship
底 *kantei* warship's bottom
9 首 *kanshu* bow of a warship
型 *kankei* warship type
10 砲 *kampō* ship's guns
砲射撃 *kampō shageki* warship bombardment
11 側 *kansoku ni* alongside a warship

6 竹米糸缶网四羊羽老耂而耒耳聿肉月臣自至臼舌舛【舟】艮色艸艹虍虫血行衣衤西

15 隊 *kantai* squadron, fleet
船 *kansen* ships and warships
船使用時 *kansen shiyōji* ship's time
12 幅 *kampuku* the beam of a warship
13 艇 *kantei* naval vessels
載 *kansai* carried on board a warship
載機 *kansaiki* carrier-based plane
14 旗 *kanki* warship's ensign
種 *kanshu* warship class
16 橋 *kankyō* bridge of a warship
17 齢 *kanrei* age or life of a warship

15

艪 3882/F1578/F1021 See 櫓 2397.

16

艫 3883/F1578 Ro bow, prow; stern. *tomo* stern.
14 綱 *tomozuna* hawser

RAD. 艮 138

Nezukuri (the right-hand side of *ne* "root"). Variant: 艮 (5 strokes).
Nickname: Good (as in 良 *yoi* good).

艮 3884/F1578 Gon, Kon stopping. *ushitora* northeast.

1

良 3885/F1578 良良良 Ryō good, fine. *i(i)*, A *yo(i)* good, good-natured; pleasing; precious; noble; lovely, beautiful, fine; lucky; efficacious; right; suitable; justifiable; appropriate, satisfactory; better; all right; unnecessary; no objection; intimate, friendly; easy; well; desirous. *yo(ku) suru* be skilled in. *yo(sa)* goodness, virtue, merit. *yo(shi)* good, all right, well, so.
2 人 *i(i) hito* good person, good-natured person; sweetheart; a certain person. *ryōjin* good person; husband. *otto* husband
3 工 *ryōkō* good workman, skilled artisan
才 *ryōsai* excellent talent
4 心 *ryōshin* conscience
方 *ryōhō* good method; good prescription
日 *ryōjitsu* lucky day, auspicious day
月 *ryōgetsu* a beautiful moon; 10th lunar month
友 *ryōyū* good friend, good company
5 田 *ryōden* fertile rice field
主 *ryōshu* good master; good ruler
民 *ryōmin* good citizens
6 匠 *ryōshō* good carpenter; good workman
好 *ryōkō na* good, favorable, satisfactory
年 *i(i) toshi* good mature age
吏 *ryōri* good official, talented official
7 辰 *ryōshin* good day, good opportunity
医 *ryōi* good doctor
図 *ryōto* good plan
材 *ryōzai* good timber. *ryōsai* excellent talent
否 *ryōhi* good or bad; quality
兵 *ryōhei* good soldier; picked army
良 *yo(ku)yo(ku)* very carefully, exceedingly, heartily
8 性 *ryōsei* benign (tumor)
法 *ryōhō* good method, excellent plan
知 *ryōchi* intuition
夜 *ryōya* moonlight night
果 *ryōka* good results
妻 *ryōsai* good wife
妻賢母 *ryōsai-kembo* good wife and wise mother
9 俗 *ryōzoku* good customs
相 *ryōsō* wise and good cabinet minister
計 *ryōkei* good plan, clever scheme
政 *ryōsei* good government
品 *ryōhin* superior article
風 *ryōfū* good custom
風美俗 *ryōfū-bizoku* good customs
10 馬 *ryōba* fine horse
師 *ryōshi* good teacher
将 *ryōshō* good general
剤 *ryōzai* an effective medicine
家 *ryōka* good family
案 *ryōan* good idea
書 *ryōsho* good book
能 *ryōnō* natural ability
11 過 *yosu(giru)* be too good
習 *ryōshū* good customs
貨 *ryōka* good money
12 港 *ryōkō* good harbor
筆 *ryōhits* good writing brush; good article; good book; good writer
策 *ryōsaku* good plan, good policy
13 賈 *ryōko* virtuous merchant
農 *ryōnō* good farmer
14 種 *ryōshu* thorobred, good breed
導体 *ryōdōtai* good conductor
15 縁 *ryōen* happy (marital) match
質 *ryōshitsu* good quality

器 *ryōki* a good receptacle; excellent talent
16薬 *ryōyaku* good medicine
19識 *ryōshiki* good sense

2

B 即 3886/F300 = 卽卽 SOKU namely; as is. *soku(suru)* conform to, agree with; be adapted to; be based on. *sunawa(chi)* namely, viz. *tsu(ku)* ascend (a throne); take root; begin work; be settled (questions). [卩]

4今 *sokkon* this moment
日 *sokujitsu* the same day
日速達 *sokujitsu sokutatsu* special delivery ⌊the same day
5功 *sokkō* immediate effect
6行 *sokkō* prompt execution
死 *sokushi* instant death
死者 *sokushisha* persons instantly killed
7応 *sokuō* adaptation, compliance, conformity
応性 *sokuōsei* relevance ⌈sion
位 *sokui* enthronement, coronation, acces-
吟 *sokugin suru* improvise (poems or songs)
妙 *sokumyō* tact
売 *sokubai* sale on the spot ⌈the throne
位 *sokui* enthronement. *sokui suru* ascend
位式 *sokuishiki* enthronement ceremony
決 *sokketsu* prompt decision, snap judgment
決処分 *sokketsu shobun* summary convic-
決裁判 *sokketsu saiban* summary trial ⌊tion
8金 *sokkin, sokukin* spot cash, down payment
刻 *sokkoku* instantly, immediately
効 *sokkō* immediate effect
夜 *sokuya* the same night
事 *sokuji* the matters at hand
10座 *sokuza* prompt; impromptu
納 *sokunō* prompt payment
席 *sokuseki* extemporaneous, offhand, ad-
席料理 *sokuseki ryōri* quick lunch ⌊lib
時 *sokuji* promptly, immediately
時払 *sokujibarai* immediate payment
時渡 *sokujiwata(shi)* spot delivery
11達 *sokutatsu* special delivery
断 *sokudan* prompt decision, snap judgment
12答 *sokutō* prompt answer
買 *sokubai* buying on the spot
14製 *sokusei* making on the spot
15諾 *sokudaku* ready consent
16興 *sokkyō* improvisation, impromptu
興詩 *sokkyōshi* impromptu poem
18題 *sokudai* an impromptu composition; a school task to be done on the spot

5

B 既 3887/F885 = 旣旣 KI. *sude ni, sunde ni* previously; already, long ago; on the point of; actually. *sude ni shite* meanwhile. [无]

5刊 *kikan* already published
刊号 *kikangō* back numbers
6存 *kison* existing ⌈established
成 *kisei* existing, accomplished, completed,
成作家 *kisei sakka* established writer
成事実 *kisei jijitsu* accomplished fact
成宗教 *kisei shūkyō* the old established
成品 *kiseihin* finished articles ⌊religions
成訳 *kiseiyaku* existing translations
7決 *kiketsu* settled, decided; convicted
決因 *kiketsushū* convict, convicted person
8定 *kitei* fixed, prearranged ⌈3887.0)
事 *sunde (no) koto ni*=*sude ni* (see under 既
知 *kichi* (already) known, well-known
知数 *kichisū* known quantity
往 *kiō* the past
往症 *kiōshō* patient's history
往歴 *kiōreki* patient's history
10記 *kiki no* the above-mentioned
耕地 *kikōchi* land under cultivation
11遂 *kisui* consummated, perpetrated
済 *kisai* already paid up
習 *kishū* already learned
望 *kibō* 16th night of a lunar month
婚 *kikon* already married
婚者 *kikonsha* married person
得 *kitoku* already acquired
得権 *kitokuken* vested interests
設 *kisetsu* already constructed, established, existing
設線 *kisetsusen* lines in operation
12報 *kihō* previous report
13電 *kiden* previous message
14製 *kisei* ready-made
製服 *kiseifuku* ready-made clothing
製品 *kiseihin* manufactured goods, ready-made goods

11

艱 3888/F1579 KAN difficult. *naya(mu)* be distressed.

8苦 *kanku* privation, suffering
18難 *kannan* privations, hardships, trouble
難辛苦 *kannan-shinku* privations, hardships, trouble

RAD. 色 139

Iro color. Nickname: Color.

A 色 3889/F1580 SHOKU, SHIKI color. *iro* color, tint, tinge; complexion; countenance, look; sensual pleasure; sweetheart; charms; fall colors; embellishment; slight concession; kind. *iro(meku)* color, be tinged, liven, become active, be stirred; begin to waver (in battle). *iro(zuku)* color, color up. *iro(ppoi)*, *iro(mekashii)* amorous, fascinating, seductive. *iro(nna)* various.

3 女 *iro onna* concubine
4 文 *irobumi* love letter
止 *irodo(me)* color fixing
分 *irowa(ke)* coloring; classification; colored
分地図 *irowa(ke) chizu* colored map
5 白 *irojiro* light complexion; white
目 *irome* amorous glance
代 *shikidai*＝式台 1556.5
付 *irozu(ku)* color, color up; (leaves) redden. *irotsu(ke)* coloring, painting
収差 *iro shūsa* chromatic aberration
写真 *irojashin* color photo
仕掛 *irojika(ke)* feigned love
6 糸 *iro ito* colored thread
色 *iro-iro na* various
尽 *irozu(kume)* dressing colorfully
好 *irogono(mi)* sensuality, lust
灯 *shikitō* colored lamp
合 *iroa(i)* coloring, tint, shade, tone. *iroa(wase)* color matching
気 *iroke* coloring, shade, tone; coquetry; passion; romance; inclination, interest
気付 *irokezu(ku)* arrive at puberty
気違 *iro kichiga(i)* sex mania
7 里 *irozato* red-light district
抜 *ironu(ki)* decoloration
沢 *shikitaku* complexion; luster, polish
狂 *iroguru(i)*, *iro kichigai* sex mania
町 *iromachi* red-light district
良 *iroyo(i)* favorable (answer)
即是空 *shikisoku-zeku* the vanity of all things (a Buddhist concept)
男 *iro otoko* paramour, lady-killer
男役 *iro-otokoyaku* handsome male actor
8 刷 *irozu(ri)* color print; color printing
物 *iromono* colored fabrics
取 *irodo(ru)* color, paint, make up. *irodori* coloring, coloration; color scheme; make-up
盲 *shikimō* color blindness
直 *ironao(shi)* changing wedding garments for ordinary clothes; redyeing
金巾 *iroganakin* colored shirtings
事 *irogoto* love affair; love scene
事師 *irogotoshi* philanderer, lady-killer
9 革 *irogawa* dyed leather
香 *iroka* color and scent; loveliness, charm
変 *irogawa(ri)* discoloration; queer color, different kind
染 *irozo(me)* dyeing; dyed
度測定 *shikido sokutei* colorimetry
10 消 *iroke(shi)* achromatism. *iroke(shina)* unromantic, prosaic
紙 *irogami* colored paper. *shikishi* square drawing paper
恋 *irokoi* love, sentiment
差 *iroza(shi)* coloring, tone, shade
素 *shikiso* coloring matter, pigment
弱 *shikijaku* slight color blindness
配合 *iro (no) haigō* color scheme
11 黒 *iroguro* dark complexion
道 *shikidō* sexual passion
欲 *shikiyoku* sexual passion, lust
彩 *shikisai* color, coloration, hue, tint
盛 *irozaka(ri)* sweet sixteen; female maturity
眼鏡 *iro megane* colored glasses; prejudiced view
情 *shikijō* sexual passion, lust
情狂 *shikijōkyō* sex mania
12 揚 *iroa(ge)* redyeing
絵 *iroe* colored picture
覚 *shikikaku* color sense
硝子 *iro garasu* colored glass
13 絹 *iroginu* colored silk
話 *irobanashi* love story; love talk
感 *shikikan* color vision
鉛筆 *iro empitsu* crayon, colored pencil
14 摺 *irozuri* color printing
褪 *iroza(meru)* fade. *irozame* fading of colors
様様 *irosamazama no* multicolored
15 敵 *irogataki* love rival
慾 *shikiyoku* sexual passion, lust
調 *shikichō* color tone
調和 *iro (no) chōwa* color harmony
19 艶 *iro tsuya* complexion; luster, polish
21 魔 *shikima* masher, libertine, lady-killer

13

艶 3890/F1581 ＝艷 豔 EN luster, glaze, polish; charm. *tsuya(meku)* be glossy, be charming, be colorful. *nama(meku)* be charming, be colorful, be of excellent quality, be beautiful. *tsuya(yakana)* glossy and beautiful. *nama(mekashii)* charming, captivating. *tsuya* gloss, luster, glaze, polish, brightness; charm,

romance, love. *tsuya(ppoi)* romantic, spicy, amorous. *ade(yakana)* charming, fascinating.
4文 *embun* love letter
5出 *tsuyada(shi)* burnishing, glazing, polishing, mercerizing, calendering
布巾 *tsuyabukin* polishing cloth
6色 *enshoku* bright countenance
7言 *engen* love talk
8物 *tsuyamono* love story
事 *tsuyagoto* love affair, romance
9拭 *tsuyabu(ki) suru* rub and polish
美 *embi* beauty, charm
姿 *adesugata* charming figure
10紙 *tsuyagami* glossy paper
殺 *ensatsu*＝*nōsatsu* 悩殺 1698.10
書 *ensho* love letter
消 *tsuyake(shi)* frosted (glass)
消硝子 *tsuyake(shi) garasu* frosted glass
13福 *empuku* good fortune in love; beau, gallant
話 *enwa, tsuyabanashi* love story, romance
14聞 *embun* love affair, love rumor
種 *tsuyadane* love affair, love rumor
歌師 *enkashi* street troubadour
16薬 *tsuyagusuri* a chemical for adding luster
19艶 *tsuyatsuya shita* glossy, bright, slick
麗 *enrei* beauty, charm

18

豔 3891 / F1581 See 艶 3890.

RAD. 艸 140

Kusa grass. At top: 艹 (4 strokes) or 艹 (3 strokes) *kusa kammuri* or *sōkō* "grass" crown. These variants are here always counted as 3 strokes. Do not confuse with 廾 Rad. 55, which has longer verticals. Nickname: Grass.

2

艾 3892 / F1582 KAI. *mogusa* moxa. *yomogi* (see under 蓬 4023.0)

B **芝** 3893 / F1584 SHI. *shiba* lawn, sod, turf.
4刈機 *shibaka(ri)ki* lawn mower
5生 *shibafu, shibau* lawn, turf, grass plot
6地 *shibachi* grass plot, lawn
8居 *shibai* play, drama, show
居小屋 *shibaigoya* playhouse, theater
居気 *shibaigi* striving for effect; dramatic behavior
居染 *shibaiji(miru)* be stage-minded
9草 *shibakusa* lawn, sod, turf

3

共 See 581. [八]

芒 3894 / F1583 BŌ beard (of grains). *nogi, noge* beard (of grains). *susuki* Japanese pampas grass.

芍 3895 / F1583 SHAKU peony.
16薬 *shakuyaku* peony

B **芋** 3896 / F1583 U. *imo* potato.
6虫 *imomushi* a green caterpillar
8茎 *zuiki* taro stem
11掘 *imoho(ri)* digging sweet potatoes
12焼酎 *imojōchū* sweet-potato liquor
14種 *imodane* seed potatoes
蔓 *imozuru* sweet-potato vines

4

芻 See 226.

芽 3897 / F1589 See 芽 3920.

苅 3898 / F-X KAI cutting (grass).

芹 3899 / F1589 KIN. *seri* parsley.

苣 3900 / F1592 KYO torch.

芬 3901 / F1585 FUN perfume.
7芬 *fumpun(taru)* fragrant
19蘭 *Fuinrando* Finland

芟 3902 / F1584 SEN. SAN. *ka(ru)* cut, clip, trim, harvest, mow.
9除 *senjo suru, sanjo suru* cut away

6 竹米糸缶网四羊羽老耂而耒耳聿肉月臣自至臼舌舛舟艮色[艸4艹]虍虫血行衣ネ西

芭 3903 F1585 Ba banana.
15蕉 *bashō* banana plant
蕉布 *bashōfu* abaca cloth

芦 蘆 3904 F1647 Ro. *ashi, yoshi* reed, rush.
11笛 *yoshibue* reed flute
16薈 *rokai* aloes

芯 3905 F1585 Shin wick.
4切 *shinki(ri)* snuffers
6地 *shinji* padding
8取皿 *shinto(ri)zara* snuffer tray

芥 3906 F1584 Kai. Ke. *karashi* mustard. *karashina* mustard (plant), rape. *gomi, akuta* dust, trash, rubbish.
8子 *karashi* mustard. *keshi* poppy
子人形 *keshi ningyō* miniature doll
子泥 *kaishidei, karashidei* mustard plaster
子油 *karashiyu* mustard oil
子粒 *keshitsubu* poppy seed; something tiny
子菜 *karashina* mustard (plant), rape
子漬 *karashizuke* mustard pickles
子種 *karashidane* mustard seed. *keshidane* poppy seed
子雛 *keshibina* tiny doll
8取 *gomito(ri)* dustpan; garbage man
9屋 *gomiya* garbage man
10浚 *gomisarai* garbage man ⌈heap
11捨場 *gomisu(te)ba* garbage dump, refuse
13溜 *gomitame* garbage dump, refuse heap
15箱 *gomibako* garbage box

B **芳** 3907 F1588 Hō fragrance. *kōba(shii), kamba(shii)* fragrant; balmy; favorable. *kamba(shikunai)* poor, unfavorable; disgraceful. *hō-* a prefix of respect.
3山 *Hōzan* Mt. Yoshino ⌈intentions
4心 *hōshin* your good wishes, your kind
5札 *hōsatsu* your honorable letter
6気 *hōki* a fragrant scent
年 *hōnen* the years of youth
名 *hōmei* good name, your name; praise
名録 *hōmeiroku* visitors' register, list of
7辰 *hōshin* auspicious day ⌊acquaintances
声 *hōsei* high fame
志 *hōshi* your kindness
8味 *hōmi* a good taste
枝 *hōshi* a fragrant branch of flowers
郊 *hōkō* a field of fragrant flowers; suburbs
命 *hōmei* your orders ⌊in spring
9香 *hōkō* perfume, fragrance
眉 *hōbi* eyebrows of a beautiful woman
信 *hōshin* your kind letter
紀 *hōki* age (of a young lady)
草 *hōsō* fragrant grass
契 *hōkei* your promise
春 *hōshun* the fragrance of spring flowers
10書 *hōsho* your kind letter
華 *hōka* the fragrance of flowers
恩 *hōon* people's kindnesses
烈 *hōretsu na* rich, aromatic (wine)
11情 *hōjō* your good wishes, your kindness
液 *hōeki* delicious-smelling soup
12景 *hōkei* the flower-decked spring landscape ⌈flowers
13園 *hōen* a park fragrant with beautiful
意 *hōi* a suggestion of spring; your desire
14墨 *hōboku* scented ink; your esteemed letter
15慮 *hōryo* your mind
醇 *hōjun na* well-mellowed (saké)
16翰 *hōkan* your fine letter
18馥 *hōfuku* spreading of sweet perfume
顔 *hōgan* your beautiful face
20醸 *hōjō* saké with an enticing aroma

A **芸 藝** 3908 F1644 Gei art, craft; artistic accomplishment; performance, acting; trick, stunt, feat.
2人 *geinin* player, performer, entertainer,
3子 *geiko* geisha ⌊actor
才 *geisai* artistic talent
4文 *geibun* art and literature ⌈ance
6当 *geitō* an art, trick, feat, stunt, perform-
名 *geimei* stage name, screen name
7妓 *geigi* geisha
8林 *geirin* art and literary circles
苑 *geien* art and literary circles
事 *geigoto* accomplishments ⌈er
者 *geisha* geisha girl, singing girl, entertain-
者屋 *geishaya* geisha house ⌈sha
者買 *geishaka(i)* buying the favors of a gei-
9風 *geifū* acting; technique (in music, etc.)
10能 *geinō* public entertainment; accomplishments, attainments
能人 *geinōjin* star, entertainer
能科 *geinōka* art course ⌈arts
能祭 *geinōsai* festival of the entertaining
11道 *geidō* art, accomplishments
術 *geijutsu* art, the arts
術肌 *geijutsuhada* artistic nature
術的 *geijutsuteki* artistic
術院 *Geijutsuin* Academy of Art
術家 *geijutsuka* artist
術祭 *geijutsusai* arts festival
12無 *geina(shi)* uncultured person
無猿 *geina(shi)zaru* uncultured person
13園 *geien* art and literary circles
18題 *geidai* title of a play

A **花** 3909 F1586 **花** KE. KA flower. *hana* flower, blossom; cherry blossoms; essence, spirit, pride; pearl; youth; best days; beautiful woman; flower arrangement; floral playing cards. *hana-(yakana)* gay, showy, brilliant, gorgeous. *hanaya(gu)* become brilliant.

2 入 *hana-i(re)* flower vase ⌈arts
4 月 *kagetsu* flowers and the moon; poetic
木 *kaboku* flowers and trees; flowering trees. *hana (no) ki* flowering tree
片 *kahen* petal
王 *kaō* king of flowers, peony
文字 *hana moji* capital letter
毛氈 *hana mōsen* figured carpet
火 *hanabi* fireworks, firecrackers
火線香 *hanabi senkō* joss-stick fireworks; mere fireworks (nothing to worry about)
5 生 *hana-i(ke)* flower vase
立 *hanata(te)* flower vase
甲 *kakō* aged sixty
代 *hanadai* price of the flowers; geisha fee
札 *hanafuda* floral playing cards
永 *hanagōri* flowers frozen in ice
市 *hana ichi* flower market
台 *kadai* stand for a vase
弁 *hanabira, kaben* petal
兄 *kakei* the plum tree
田色 *hanada iro* light blue
卉 *kaki* flowering plant
卉園芸 *kaki engei* floriculture
6 色 *hana iro* light blue
匠 *kashō* landscape gardener
尽 *hanazu(kushi)* flower enumeration; many-flowered design
合 *hana-a(wase)* floral playing cards
会 *kakai* flower-arrangement meeting
守 *hanamori* flower guard (against theft)
自動車 *hana jidōsha* flower-decked auto- ⌊mobile
7 作 *hanazukuri* floriculture; florist
形 *hanagata* floral pattern; flourish; ornament; star actor; a popular person
売 *hana-u(ri)* flower seller
花 *hanabana(shii)* brilliant, magnificent, ⌊spectacular
束 *hanataba* bouquet
吹雪 *hana fubuki* falling cherry blossoms
見 *hanami* flower viewing
見酒 *hanamizake* viewing cherry blossoms and drinking saké
言 *kagen* untruth; flowery words
言葉 *hana kotoba* the language of flowers
8 押 *kaō* signature (not a stamp) ⌈interior
実 *kajitsu* flowers and fruit; exterior and
季 *kaki* flowering season
9 面 *kamen* a beautiful face
香 *kakō* the fragrance of flowers
信 *kashin* tidings of flowers
咲 *hanasa(kaseru)* cause to bloom. *hanasa-* ⌊*(ku)* bloom
垣 *hanagaki* a flowering hedge
持 *hana (o) mo(tasu)* humbly crediting another with one's exploits
活 *hana-ike* flower vase
畑 *hanabatake* flower bed, flower garden
神 *kashin* flower goddess; spirit of a flower
冠 *kakan* corolla (of a flower); garland, ⌊wreath
品 *kahin* the value of flowers
客 *kakaku* flower-viewing guests; customers
紅葉 *hana-momiji* flowers and maples; fine spring and autumn leaves
相撲 *hanazumō* amateur wrestling
屋 *hanaya* flower store
屋敷 *hana yashiki* flower garden
柳 *karyū* blossoms and willows; geisha; prostitutes; red-light district
柳界 *karyūkai* geisha quarters; red-light ⌊district
柳病 *karyūbyō* venereal disease
10 圃 *kaho* flower garden
唇 *kashin* petals; lips; flower-like lips
候 *kakō* the flowering season
時 *hanadoki* the flowering season; the ⌊cherry season
紋 *kamon* flower design
陰 *hana kage* shadow of flowers; shadow of flowering trees
宴 *kaen, hana(no)en* flower-viewing party
容 *kayō* beautiful looks
莚 *hana mushiro* figured mat
茣蓙 *hana goza* flowered mat
粉 *kafun* pollen
粉症 *kafunshō* hay fever
11 道 *kadō* flower arrangement. *hana michi* passage thru the audience to the stage
野 *hanano* field of flowers
瓶 *kabin, hanagame* vase
笠 *hanagasa* flower-decked hat
梨 *karin* Chinese quince
盛 *hanazaka(ri)* flowers in full bloom
祭 *hana matsuri* Buddha's birthday festival (April 8)
紺青 *hana konjō* royal blue, cobalt blue
崗岩 *kakōgan* granite
菱草 *hanabishisō* California poppy
菖蒲 *hana shōbu, hana ayame* iris, blue flag
鳥 *kachō* flowers and birds
鳥風月 *kachōfūgetsu* beauties of nature; ⌊elegant pursuits
12 婿 *hanamuko* bridegroom
街 *kagai* red-light district
結 *hanamusu(bi)* rosette
詞 *hana kotoba* the language of flowers
軸 *kajiku* flower stalk
期 *kaki* the flowering season
傘 *hanagasa* painted paper umbrella
筐 *hanagatami* flower basket

6 竹米糸缶网四羊羽老耂而耒耳聿肉月臣自至臼舌舛舟艮色[艸 5 艹]虍虫血行衣衤西

筏 *hana ikada* blossoms floating down a stream
筒 *hanazutsu* flower tube
葵 *hana-aoi* hollyhock
葉 *kayō* floral leaf
椰菜 *hanayasai* cauliflower
13園 *hanazono, kaen* flower garden
蜂 *hanabachi* bumblebee
鉢 *hanabachi* flowerpot
飾 *hana kaza(ri)* floral decoration
電車 *hana densha* floral streetcar
嫁 *hanayome* bride
嫁料 *hanayomeryō* marriage present (from the groom)
嫁御 *hanayomego* bride
嫁御寮 *hanayome goryō* bride
14魁 *oiran* prostitute, courtesan
暦 *hanagoyomi* a calendar with information about flowers
摘 *hanatsu(mi)* flower picking
綵 *hanazuna* festoons; festoonery
蜜 *kamitsu* nectar
聟 *hanamuko* bridegroom
模様 *hana moyō* floral design
15輪 *hanawa* wreath
鋏 *hanabasami* pruning shears
影 *kaei* reflection of flowers
器 *kaki* flower vase
16壇 *kadan* flower bed, flower garden
樹 *kaju* flowering tree
曇 *hanagumo(ri)* hazy weather in spring
17環 *hanawa* wreath
18顔 *kagan* a beautiful face
19櫚 *karin* Chinese quince
譜 *kafu* flower album
20簪 *hana kanzashi* floral hairpin
22鰹 *hanagatsuo* dried bonito shavings
籠 *hanakago* flower basket

5

昔 See 2108. [日]

苒 3910 / F1590 ZEN flourishing, luxuriant.

苺 3911 / F1595 BAI. *ichigo* strawberry.

B **茎** 3912 / F1606 **莖** KEI, KYŌ *kuki* stem, stalk.

苴 3913 / F1595 SO. *tsuto* (see under 苞 3917.0).

茄 3914 / F1596 KA eggplant.
3子 *nasu, nasubi* eggplant

B **茂** 3915 / F1596 MO. *shige(ru)* grow thick, be overgrown, be luxuriant.
6合 *shige(ri)-a(u)* grow luxuriantly
8林 *morin* a luxuriant forest

苑 3916 / F1590 EN garden, farm, yard. *sono* park, garden.
6地 *enchi* park

苞 3917 / F1591 HŌ (corn) husk, bract. *tsuto* straw wrapper; souvenir gift.
8苴 *tsuto* straw wrapper, souvenir gift. *hōsho, hōso* straw wrapper; gift; bribe. *aramaki* gift of fish wrapped in bamboo leaves, etc.

苟 3918 / F1591 KŌ *iyashiku(mo)* any, at all, in the least, even in the slightest degree.
5且 *kōsho* neglecting, slighting. *karisome* neglecting, slighting; trifling; temporary
6安 *kōan* procrastination, momentary ease

苧 3919 / F1594 CHO. *o* hemp, flax; hemp thread. *karamushi* ramie.
11麻 *karamushi, choma* ramie, China grass
12殻 *ogara* hemp reed, hemp stalk

A **芽** 3920 / F1589 **芽** GA. *me* sprout, spear, germ. *megu(mu)* bud, sprout.
5生 *mebae* bud, sprout, seedling. *meba(eru)* sprout, bud
出度 *medeta(i)* congratulatory, auspicious
9胞 *gahō* spore
11接 *metsu(gi)* bud grafting, inlay graft

苔 3921 / F1590 TAI moss. *koke* moss; lichen; incrustation; fur (on the tongue). *kokera* moss.
5生 *kokemu(su)* the moss grows or spreads
13筵 *kokemushiro* moss-covered ground
20蘚 *taisen* moss, lichen

苫 3922 / F1594 SEN. *toma* rush matting.
6舟 *tomabune* rush-thatched boat
9屋 *tomaya* a hut roofed and walled with rushes
11船 *tomasen* rush-roofed boat
12葺 *tomabuki* rush thatch

B **苗** 3923 / F1590 BYŌ. MYŌ. *nae* seedling, sapling, shoot.
4木 *naegi* sapling, seedling
5代 *nawashiro, naeshiro* rice-seedling bed
代田 *naeshiroda, nawashiroda* rice-seedling bed
6字 *myōji* surname

[7]床 *naedoko* seedbed, nursery
売 *naeu(ri)* seedling seller
[10]圃 *byōho* seedbed, nursery ⌈tain tribes
[11]族 *byōzoku* relatives; south China moun-

茅 3924 F1596 Bō. *kaya, chigaya, chi* miscanthus reed.
[8]舎 *bōsha* thatched cottage, hovel, my humble cottage ⌈ble cottage
[9]屋 *bōoku* thatched cottage, hovel, my hum-
[11]船 *kayabune* miscanthus-carrying boat (often set afire in the midst of an enemy fleet) ⌈(a roof-thatch reed)
[12]場 *kayaba* hayfield; field of miscanthus
葺 *kayabuki* miscanthus-thatched
萱 *chigaya* a kind of grass
[14]蜩 *higurashi* clear-toned cicada

苛 3925 F1591 KA. *iji(meru), saina(mu)* torment, scold, chastise
[3]小 *kashō* too fine
[5]立 *irada(teru)* irritate, exasperate. *irada(tsu)* be irritated, be exasperated
令 *karei* harsh orders
[8]法 *kahō* severe laws
刻 *kakoku* severity, cruelty
苛 *ira-ira suru* get nervous, be irritated,
性 *kasei* caustic ⌊fret
性石灰 *kasei sekkai* quicklime
性曹達 *kasei sōda* caustic soda, sodium
[9]虐 *kagyaku* cruel treatment ⌊hydroxide
政 *kasei* tyranny, despotism
重 *kajū no* burdensome, excessive
[10]烈 *karetsu na* severe, stern
[11]責 *kashaku* torture, maltreatment
[12]税 *kazei* heavy taxation
[14]酷 *kakoku* rigor, severity, cruelty
[17]厳 *kagen* severe cruelty
斂 *karen* oppression (by taxation, etc.)
斂誅求 *karen-chūkyū* exaction, extortion

若 3926 F1592 B JAKU. NYA. *mo(shi), mo(shimo)* if. *moshi(kashitara), moshi(ka) suru to* perhaps, possibly. *mo(shikuwa)* or, otherwise. *mo(shiya)* by any chance, perchance. *waka-, waka(i)* young, juvenile, youthful; younger, junior; immature, inexperienced; low number. *waka(yagu)* grow young again, look young. *shi(ku)* be equal to, compare with.
[2]人 *wakōdo, waka(i) hito* young person, young man ⌈number of
[3]干 *jakkan, sokobaku, sokubaku* some, a
[4]手 *wakate* young man; young official
木 *wakagi* sapling, young tree ⌈Year's Day
水 *wakamizu* first water drawn on New
夫婦 *wakafūfu* young couple
[5]布 *wakame* an edible seaweed
旦那 *wakadanna* young master, young gentleman
白髪 *wakajiraga, wakashiraga,* prematurely
[6]竹 *wakatake* young bamboo ⌊gray hair
死 *wakaji(ni)* premature death
気 *wakage, wakagi* youthful vigor
返 *wakaga(eru)* grow young again
向 *wakamuki* suitable for the young
年 *jakunen* youth
年者 *jakunemmono* youngster
年寄 *wakadoshiyo(ri)* a young person with old characteristics
[7]作 *wakazuku(ri)* make-up to look younger
役 *wakayaku* role for a young actor
禿 *wakahage* premature baldness
君 *wakagimi* young lord
[8]松 *wakamatsu* young pine tree; New Year's pine-tree decorations
枝 *wakaeda* shoot, young branch
命 *jakumei* young life
芽 *wakame* young buds, sprouts, shoots
苗 *wakanae* young plants
若 *wakawaka(shii)* youthful, young
者 *wakamono, waka(i) mono* young person; young manservant; young apprentice, young man, lad, youth ⌈contingency
事 *mo(shimono)koto* accident, emergency,
武者 *wakamusha* young warrior
[9]造 *wakazō* youngster, stripling
冠 *jakkan* aged twenty; youth ⌈grass
草 *wakagusa, wakakusa* tender grass, young
後家 *wakagoke* young widow
[10]宮 *wakamiya* young prince; newly-built shrine; subshrine to a son of a main deity
党 *wakatō* young servant, attendant
[11]菜 *wakana* young greens, herbs ⌈life
盛 *wakazaka(ri)* bloom of youth, prime of
紳士 *wakashinshi* young gentleman
[12]湯 *wakayu* first water boiled on New Year's
葉 *wakaba* new leaves, fresh verdure ⌊Day
衆 *wakashū, waka(i)shū* = *wakamono* 若者 (see above–8)
紫 *wakamurasaki* light purple
[13]殿 *wakatono* young lord
隠居 *waka-inkyo* man who retired early
[14]様 *wakasama* young lord, young master
緑 *wakamidori* new foliage
[15]輩 *jakuhai* young people; novice
[19]鶏 *wakadori* pullet

英 3927 F1594 A EI England, Britain; gifted person; wit. *-Ei, Ei-* English.
[2]人 *Eijin* Englishman
[3]寸 *eisun* English inch

才 *eisai* brilliant intellect, talent, genius
下院 *Eika-in* British House of Commons
4 斤 *eikin* pound
尺 *eishaku* English foot
文 *Eibun* English, English composition
文法 *Eibumpō* English grammar
文学 *Eibungaku* English literature
文典 *Eibunten* English grammar
文和訳 *Eibun Wayaku* English-to-Japanese translation
5 主 *eishu* wise ruler
本国 *Ei-hongoku* England
6 米 *Ei-Bei* England and America
気 *eiki* excellent talent
名 *eimei* fame, glory, reputation
会話 *Ei-kaiwa* English conversation
字 *Eiji* English letter
字新聞 *Eiji shimbun* English-language newspaper
7 里 *eiri* English mile
図 *eito* excellent plan
系 *Eikei* British (enterprise)
声 *eisei* fame, glory, reputation
8 法 *Eihō* English law
知 *eichi* wisdom, intelligence; intellect
和 *Ei-Wa* English-Japanese
京 *Eikyō* London, the British capital
武 *eibu* distinguished bravery
果 *eika* decisiveness
明 *eimei na* clever, intelligent, clear-sighted
明果断 *eimei-kadan no* wise and decisive
学 *Eigaku* study of English
学者 *Eigakusha* English scholar
国 *Eikoku* England, Great Britain, United Kingdom
国人 *Eikokujin* Britisher, Englishman
国風 *Eikokufū* Briticism
9 風 *eifū* eminent virtues
俊 *eishun* genius, prodigy, talented person
軍 *Eigun* British army
発 *eihatsu* great wisdom
姿 *eishi* noble figure
10 書 *Eisho* English book, English literature
哲 *eitetsu* genius, prodigy, talented person
11 偉 *ei-i* outstanding fame
略 *eiryaku* excellent talent
船 *Eisen* English ship
訳 *Eiyaku* English translation
断 *eidan* prompt decision, resolution, drastic steps
貨 *Eika* English currency, sterling; English goods
12 傑 *eiketsu* an outstanding person
尋 *eibiro* English fathom
雄 *eiyū* hero
雄的 *eiyūteki* heroic
雄崇拝 *eiyū sūhai* hero worship
13 詩 *Eishi* English poem, English poetry
聖 *eisei* natural wisdom
誉 *eiyo* fame, great praise
資 *eishi* brilliant qualities, fine character. *Eishi* British capital (money)
14 語 *Eigo* the English language
領 *Eiryō* British possession, dominion, or territory
魂 *eikon* departed spirit
15 邁 *eimai* wise and brave, great, talented
15 霊 *eirei* spirits of the war dead; great men
16 噸 *eiton* British ton, long ton
19 蘭 *Ei-Ran* England and Holland
蘭銀行 *Eiran Ginkō* Bank of England
20 艦 *Eikan* British battleship
21 露 *Ei-Ro* England and Russia

A **苦** 3928 F1592 Ku suffering, trial, worry, trouble, hardship, difficulty, toil. *kuru(shimu), kuru(shigaru)* suffer; groan; be troubled, be worried, be perplexed; strive, try hard. *kuru(shimeru)* torment; harass, worry; persecute, inflict pain. *niga(mu), niga(ru)* feel bitter; scowl. *ku ni suru* worry. *kuru(shii)* painful; distressing, embarrassing, difficult, bitter; straitened; farfetched; stiff (climb). *niga(i)* bitter; hard, trying. *kuru(shimi)* pain, agony, torment, trouble, distress; mortification.

2 力 *kūrii* coolie
3 口 *nigaguchi* gossip, criticism
土 *kudo, ku(no)do* this painful world; magnesia. *nigatsuchi* poor soil
4 心 *kushin* pains, trouble, anxiety; hard work, diligence
手 *nigate* weak point; ugly customer, tough antagonist
切 *niga(ri)-ki(ru)* look blue, look disgusted
5 汁 *kujū* bitterness of life; a hard time. *nigari* brine
艾 *nigayomogi* wormwood
6 肉 *kuniku* countermeasure at personal sacrifice
虫 *nigamushi* bitterness
行 *kugyō* penance, austerities, mortification
行者 *kugyōsha* ascetics, flagellants
7 言 *kugen* frank advice, exhortation
走 *niga(mi)bashi(ru)* have a manly bearing
吟 *kugin suru* compose laboriously
役 *kueki* hard labor, drudgery; penal servitude
労 *kurō* hardships, difficulties, trials; toil; anxiety
労人 *kurōnin* worldly-wise man
労性 *kurōshō* worry habit
8 使 *kushi* abuse, exploitation, overworking
杯 *kuhai* bitter cup, ordeal
況 *kukyō*＝苦境 (see below–14)
苦 *niganiga(shii)* unpleasant, disgusting, loathsome, shameful, scandalous
味 *kumi, nigami* bitter taste
味走 *nigamibashi(tta)* sternly handsome
学 *kugaku* studying under adversity
学生 *kugakusei* self-supporting student
9 海 *kukai* this world of suffering

界 *kukai, kugai* the world of suffering; life of prostitution
思 *kushi*=*kushin* 苦心 (see above–4)
茗 *kumei* strong tea
衷 *kuchū* distress
10悩 *kunō* distress, suffering. *kuru(shimi)-naya(mu)* be in distress
紛 *kuru(shi)magi(re)ni* out of desperation, driven by distress, under pressure
笑 *kushō, nigawara(i)* bitter smile, forced smile
11渋 *kujū* bitter and puckery; drenched; sentences hard to understand
菜 *nigana* bitter herbs
患 *kugen* agony
情 *kujō* complaint, objections, troubles
情処理 *kujō shori* settling grievances
12痛 *kutsū* pain, suffering, agony
悶 *kumon* agony, anguish
寒 *kukan* suffering from cold; coldest season; 13th lunar month
無 *ku(mo)na(ku)* easily, without trouble
13塩 *nigari, nigashio* brine
戦 *kusen* hard fighting; tight game
節 *kusetsu* fidelity in adversity
楽 *kuraku* pleasure and pain
楚 *kuso* hardships, troubles, distress
14境 *kukyō* hard circumstances, trouble, predicament, crisis
15慮 *kuryō*=*kushin* 苦心 (see above–4)
熱 *kunetsu* oppressive heat
16諫 *kukan* frank exhortation
18闘 *kutō suru* fight hard; struggle (for a living)
難 *kunan* suffering, hardship; passion (of Christ)
難者 *kunansha* sufferer

6

巻 See 1465. [巳]

前 See 595. [刂]

茲 兹 See **玆** 2919. [玄]

荆 荊 荊 See 689.

茗 3929/F1597 Myō, Mei tea.

10荷 *myōga* ginger

茨 3930/F1598 Shi. *ibara* thorn, brier.

茵 3931/F1599 In. *shitone* cushion; mattress.

茜 3932/F1598 Sen. *akane* madder, red dye, madder red, Turkey red.

荏 3933/F1603 Jin bean.

8苒 *jinzen to* procrastinatingly

茘 3934/F1598 = **荔** Rei scallion, a small onion.

8枝 *reishi* litchi (nut)

茸 3935/F1600 Jō. *take* mushroom.

9狩 *takega(ri)* mushroom gathering

茫 3936/F1598 Bō wide, extensive.

9洋 *bōyō(taru)* limitless, boundless
茫 *bōbō(taru)* vague, vast, extensive
12然 *bōzen* absent-mindedly, in a daze
然自失 *bōzen-jishitsu* abstraction, stupefaction, entrancement
13漠 *bōbaku* vague, vast, extensive

茹 3937/F1601 Jo. *yu(deru), u(deru) vt* boil, seethe. *yu(daru), u(daru) vi* boil, seethe. *yu(de)* boiled.

3上 *yu(de)-a(geru)* finish boiling
5汁 *yudejiru* broth
玉子 *yude tamago, ude tamago* boiled egg
7卵 *yude tamago, ude tamago* boiled egg
13溢 *yu(de)-kobo(su)* scald, parboil

B **荘** 3938/F1605 = **莊** Sō villa, inn. Shō villa, cottage, feudal manor.

3大 *sōdai*=壮大 2837.3
9屋 *shōya* village headman
重 *sōchō* solemnity, gravity, impressiveness
13園 *shōen, sōen* manor
17厳 *sōgon*=壮厳 2837.17
19麗 *sōrei* splendor, grandeur

A **草** 3939/F1601 Sō. *kusa* grass; grass hand (writing); weeds; herbs, plants; pasture. *sō(suru)* write, draft. *kusa-(ikire)* hot and humid feeling when walking thru tall summer grass

3子 *sōshi* storybook; copybook
4火 *kusabi* grass fire
分 *kusawa(ke)* going thru deep grass; founding a village; village founder; pioneer
双紙 *kusazōshi* picture book
刈 *kusaka(ri)* grass cutting, mowing
刈鎌 *kusaka(ri)gama* sickle

木 *sōmoku, kusaki* vegetation, trees and plants
木灰 *sōmokubai* ash from burnt vegetation
木靡 *kusaki (mo) nabi(ku)* everyone obeys
5 生 *kusafu* grassy field
田 *kusata* weedy rice field; a growing rice field
市 *kusa ichi* a special one-night market selling altar equipment for the Buddhist Obon Festival
本 *sōhon* herbs; draft, manuscript
6 色 *kusa iro* dark green, emerald green
衣 *kusagoromo* grass clothes
地 *sōchi* steppes. *kusachi* meadow, grassland
仮名 *sōgana* hiragana, the cursive syllabary
7 村 *kusamura* remote country
花 *sōka, kusabana* flowering plant
8 枕 *kusamakura* traveling
取 *kusato(ri)* weeding; weeding tool; weeder
臥 *kutabi(reru)* be tired, be exhausted. *kusabushi* lying on the grass; sleeping in the field
苺 *kusa ichigo* wild strawberry
毟 *kusamushi(ri)* weeding
9 食 *sōshoku no* herbivorous
屋 *kusaya, sōoku* thatched hut, straw hut
昧 *sōmai* primitive state
枯 *kusaga(re)* dying of the grass; the fall
草 *sōsō* brevity; rudeness; hurry; the closing words of a letter
紅葉 *kusa momiji* fall colored grasses
相撲 *kusazumō* local wrestling match
10 原 *sōgen* prairie, grassy plain, steppe. *kusawara, kusahara* meadow, grass plot
紙 *sōshi* copybook; storybook
陰 *kusakage* shadow of the grass
案 *sōan* draft (of a law or manuscript)
書 *sōsho* cursive script, grass hand
莽 *sōmō* grassy field; the bush; the populace
莚 *kusa mushiro* grass rug; grassy field
根 *sōkon* grass roots
根木皮 *zōkombokuhi* roots and bark; Chinese medicinal materials. *sōkommokuhi* medicinal plants
11 庵 *kusa (no) irori, kusa (no) io, sōan* hut, hermitage, thatched cottage
深 *kusabuka(i)* grassy; backwoods; remote
堂 *sōdō* thatched cottage; my humble abode
笛 *kusabue* reed whistle
萌 *kusamoe* sprouting of the grass in spring
野 *kusano* grassy field. *sōya* citizenry; lower strata (of people)
野球 *kusa yakyū* grass-lot baseball
12 間 *sōkan* in the grass; deep rural area
場 *kusaba* grass plot, meadow, pasture, turf
葺 *kusabuki* grass thatch
創 *sōsō* inauguration, beginning, origination
創期 *sōsōki* early period
葉 *kusa (no) ha* blade of grass
葉蔭 *kusaba (no) kage de* under the sod, in the grave
13 播 *kusaka(ki)* hoe, rake
隠 *kusagaku(re)* hiding in the grass; retired to the country
飼 *kusaka(i)* raising cattle on grass
蓬蓬 *kusabōbō* rank weed growth
14 箒 *kusabōki* broom
15 稿 *sōkō* lecture notes, outline, draft, manuscript
履 *zōri* sandals, zori
履掛 *zoriga(ke) de* wearing zori
鞋 *waraji* straw sandals
鞋虫 *waraji mushi* sow bug
鞋銭 *warajisen* trip money
16 薙剣 *Kusanagi (no) Tsurugi* the Sacred Sword (one of the Three Imperial Treasures)
17 藁 *kusawara* grass and straw, fodder
18 鎌 *kusagama* sickle
叢 *kusamura* (see under 叢 144.0)
19 廬 *sōro* thatched hut, humble abode
20 競馬 *kusa keiba* local horse race
21 露 *kusa tsuyu, sōro* dewdrops on the grass; fleeting things

A **茶** 3940 / F1599 **茶** SA, CHA tea; tea plant; tea leaves; light brown. *cha(gakatta)* brownish. *cha (ni) suru* make fun of. *cha(ppoi)* brownish, light brown.
2 人 *chajin, sajin* tea-ceremony expert
入 *cha-i(re)* tea canister
3 巾 *chakin* tea cloth
4 化 *chaka(su)* laugh away, make fun of
5 代 *chadai* charge for tea; tip
礼 *sarei* tea ceremony
台 *chadai* teacup saucer
出 *chada(shi)* teapot
目 *chame(ru)* play pranks. *chame* playfulness, mischief; urchin; brown eyes
目気 *chameki* mischief, playfulness
6 臼 *cha usu* hand tea-grinding mill
色 *cha-iro* light brown, tawny
気 *chaki* playfulness, mischievousness; unworldliness
托 *chataku* teacup holder
汲 *chakumi* serving tea
会 *chakai, cha(no)e* tea party, tea ceremony
7 杓 *chashaku* tea ladle
利 *chaki(ki)* tea tasting; tea taster
呑 *chanomi* teacup; tea lover; tea drinking
坊主 *chabōzu* tea server (to a shogun)
8 店 *cha mise* teahouse
房 *chabō* refreshment parlor
所 *chadokoro* tea-growing area
9 柱 *chabashira* tiny tea stalk (in a cup of tea)
畑 *chabatake* tea plantation

亭 *satei* tea pavilion, tea room
盆 *chabon* tea tray
室 *chashitsu* tea arbor; tea cottage; tearoom
茶 *chacha* interruption
柄杓 *chabishaku* tea dipper
屋 *chaya* teahouse; tea dealer
屋酒 *chayazake* saké drunk at a teahouse
10 席 *chaseki* tea arbor, tea cottage; tea-ceremony seat
釜 *chagama* teakettle
11 渋 *chashibu* tea incrustation
断 *chada(chi)* abstinence from tea
商 *chashō* tea merchant
匙 *chasaji* teaspoon
道 *chadō, sadō* tea cult
道具 *chadōgu* tea-service set
瓶 *chabin* tea urn, teapot
瓶頭 *chabin atama* bald head
菓 *chaka, saka* tea and cakes, light refreshments
菓子 *chagashi* teacakes
12 間 *cha(no)ma* family living room
粥 *chagayu* tea gruel
棚 *chadana* tea-service shelf
湯 *cha(no)yu* tea ceremony; tea cult
殻 *chagara* tea grounds
壺 *chatsubo* tea canister
筌 *chasen* tea whisk
筒 *chazutsu* tea container
椀 *chawan* teacup; rice bowl
椀蒸 *chawammu(shi)* ＝茶碗蒸 (see below–13)
飯 *chameshi* rice boiled in tea, oil, or saké
飯事 *sahanji* everyday occurrence
番 *chaban* tea-ceremony assistants; burlesque, low comedy
番狂言 *chaban kyōgen* burlesque, low comedy
番劇 *chabangeki* burlesque, low comedy
飲 *chano(mi)* teacup; tea lover; tea drinking
飲友達 *chano(mi) tomodachi* crony, pal
飲茶碗 *chano(mi)jawan* teacup
飲話 *chano(mi)banashi* gossip
13 園 *chaen, saen* tea plantation
滓 *cha kasu* tea grounds
腹 *chafuku* the bowels after heavy tea drinking; drinking tea to satisfy hunger
業 *chagyō* tea industry
碗 *chawan* rice bowl; teacup
碗蒸 *chawammu(shi)* steamed custard of vegetables, egg, and meat
話 *chabanashi, chawa, sawa* tea-table talk, gossip
話会 *chawakai, sawakai* tea party
14 摘 *chatsumi* tea picking; tea picker
漉 *chako(shi)* tea strainer
漬 *chazuke* simple meal; rice and tea mixed
箒 *chabōki* feather brush used in the tea ceremony
褐色 *chakasshoku* yellowish brown
15 碾 *cha usu* tea-grinding hand mill
請 *cha-u(ke)* teacakes
寮 *charyō* tea-ceremony cottage; tea-ceremony room
箱 *chabako* tea chest, tea caddy
舗 *chaho* tea store
器 *chaki* tea-serving equipment
16 濁 *cha (o) nigo(su)* cover up one's mistakes
18 簞笥 *chadansu* tea cupboard
23 罐 *chakan* tea canister

荒 3941 / F1603 B Kō. *ara(i)* rough, rude, wild, harsh, violent, gruff, fierce. *ara(ppoi)* rough, rude, violent, wild. *sabi(reru)*, *a(reru)* be ruined, become stormy; tear around; get chapped. *a(rabiru)*, *a(raburu)* get rough, be insolent. *susa(bu)*, *susa(mu)* get desolate, go wild; decline; get rough. *a(rasu)* lay waste. *a(rarageru)* raise voice in anger. *a(rekure)* daredevil, rowdy, a tough. *are* storm, stormy weather; chapping, roughness. *arara(ka) ni* violently, roughly. *ara-* wild, rough, fierce, wild; drastic. *-ara(shi)* robbery, robber.

3 土 *kōdo* barren land
山 *arayama* steep mountain
亡 *kōbō* dissipation
4 日 *a(re)bi, kōjitsu* stormy day
木 *araki* logs in bark
毛 *arage* bristle
牛 *ara-ushi* untamed ox
凶 *kōkyō* famine; poor crops
天 *kōten* stormy weather
5 田 *kōden, a(re)ta, arata* uncultivated rice field
石 *ara-ishi* rough stone
立 *arada(tsu)* be excited, be exasperated, be agitated. *arada(teru)* aggravate, exasperate
外 *kōgai* outside the country, foreign
民 *kōmin* people suffering from famine
仕事 *arashigoto* rough work, hard work; ＝*arakase(gi)* 荒稼 (see below–15)
目 *arame* large net meshes; net with large meshes
目鉅 *arame yasuri* rasp
布 *aranuno* sackcloth
布衣 *aranuno (no) koromo* sackcloth
6 行 *a(re)-yu(ku)* gradually get rough. *aragyō* religious austerities, asceticism
回 *a(re)-mawa(ru)*, *ara(shi)-mawa(ru)* rampage, tear around, break into
地 *arachi* waste land, wilderness, desert
肌 *arahada* rough skin
年 *kōnen* year of bad crops
夷 *ara-ebisu* barbarians
7 作 *arazuku(ri)* spadework, preliminary arrangements
狂 *a(re)-kuru(u)* get stormy, rage; get angry
肝 *aragimo* liver; pluck, courage
8 波 *aranami* stormy seas, raging waves

6 竹米糸缶网四羊羽老耂而耒耳聿肉月臣自至臼舌舛舟艮色【艸6 艹】虍虫血行衣衤西

育 *arasoda(chi)* careless upbringing; a spoiled child
果 *a(re)-ha(teru)* be dilapidated, be ruined, lie waste, be desolate
者 *ara(kure)mono* a ruffian
事 *aragoto* ruffian's part (in a play)
性人 *a(re)shō (no) hito* person whose skin chaps easily
武者 *aramusha* daredevil, rowdy, a tough
放題 *a(re)hōdai* left to go to ruin
物 *aramono* kitchenware, sundries
物屋 *aramonoya* kitchenware store
9 屋 *kōoku* dilapidated house
造 *arazuku(ri)* =荒作 (see above–7)
垣 *aragaki* shrine fence
海 *ara-umi* rough sea
畑 *arahata* a field left uncultivated
研 *aratogi* rough grinding
神 *aragami* fierce deity. *kōjin* kitchen god
胆 *aragimo* courage, nerve
削 *arakezu(ri)* roughing, rough planing, rough hewing, rough turning
怠 *kōtai* laziness and pleasure-seeking
荒 *a(re)-sabi(reru)* become desolate. *ara-ara(shii)* rough, wild, violent, rude, harsh, gruff, fierce
巻 *aramaki* fresh slightly-salted salmon; a gift of fish wrapped in bamboo leaves
10 馬 *ara-uma, a(re)uma* untamed horse, restive horse
原 *kōgen* wilderness, desert
涼 *kōryō(taru)* bleak
陬 *kōsū* deep rural areas
都 *kōto* destroyed city
唐 *kōtō* absurdity, nonsense
唐言 *kōtō(no)gen* nonsense, wild talk
唐無稽 *kōtō-mukei* absurdity, nonsense
11 涼 *kōryō(taru)* desolate, dreary
淫 *kōin* sexual indulgence
球 *a(re)dama* poor pitching
酔 *kōsui* dead drunk
野 *arano, a(re)no, kōya* wilds, wilderness, desert
菰 *aragomo* coarse straw mat
12 廃 *a(re)-suta(reru)* become desolate, be dilapidated. *kōhai* desolation, ruin, dilapidation
廃地 *kōhaichi* waste land, devastated area
13 働 *arabatara(ki)* rough work, hard work
塚 *a(re)zuka* heap, bare mound
損 *kōson* dilapidation, ruin
滅 *a(rashi)-horo(bosu)* ravage, devastate
跡 *a(re)ato* ruins, desolation
歳 *kōsai* year of bad crops
蒔 *aramaki* sowing untilled soil
14 寥 *kōryō na* desolate and lonely
模様 *a(re)moyō* threatening sky
15 瘠 *kōseki no* waste and worn-out (land)
潮 *arashio* stormy tide
稼 *arakase(gi)* robbery, burglary; a big haul; heavy manual labor
誕 *kōtan* nonsense
蕪 *kōbu* wilderness, desolation
蕪地 *kōbuchi* deserted and desolate place
16 壁 *arakabe* rough plaster coat
17 磯 *ara-iso, ariso* a reefy coast, a windswept seashore
療治 *araryōji* drastic treatment; murder
19 繩 *aranawa* rough straw rope
23 鷲 *arawashi* fierce eagle; air ace

7

莽 See 3971.

恭 See 1680. [心]

莖 3942 F1606 See 茎 3912.

莊 3943 F1605 See 荘 3938.

莩 3944 F1607 HYŌ very thin.

莓 3945 F1606 BAI, MAI wild strawberry.

莨 3946 F1607 RŌ. *tabako* tobacco.
2 入 *tabako-i(re)* cigarette case
9 屋 *tabakoya* cigar store
盆 *tabako bon* tobacco tray
14 銭 *tabakosen* pocket money

莟 3947 F1606 GAN. *tsubomi* bud.

莚 3948 F1606 F1411 See 筵 3400.

茣 3949 F-X Go mat, matting.
13 蓙 *goza* mat, matting

莞 3950 F1606 KAN reed used for *tatami* covers.
14 爾 *kanji toshite* with a smile

荼 3951 F1605 TA, ZU, TO, DA, a weed.
9 毘 *dabi* cremation

荻 3952 F1605 TEKI. *ogi* reed.
10 原 *ogihara* reedy field

莢 3953 F1606 KYŌ. *saya* pod, hull, husk, shell, boll, case.
13 隠元 *saya ingen* kidney bean
15 豌豆 *saya endō* garden pea, field pea

莫 3954 F1607 BAKU. BO. *naka(re)* must not, do not, be not.
3 大 *bakudai na* vast, immense, enormous
大小 *meriyasu* knitted goods
6 年 *bonen* one's later years
8 夜 *boya* night, evening
逆 *bakugyaku* firm friendship
逆友 *bakugyaku (no) tomo* an intimate friend
13 義道 *mogidō na* cruel, brutal, heartless

B **華** 3955 F1610 GE. KA flower; petal; shining, luster; appearance; ostentation. *hanaya(gu)* become brilliant. *hana* flower. *hana(yakana)* gay, showy, brilliant, gorgeous. *-ka*-China.
4 中 *Kachū* Central China
氏 *kashi* Fahrenheit
氏寒暖計 *kashi kandankei* Fahrenheit thermometer
5 甲 *kakō* aged sixty-one
北 *Kahoku* North China
6 名 *kamei* fame, good reputation
字紙 *Kajishi* Chinese newspaper
7 言 *kagen* flowery words
押 *kaō* signature
8 京 *kakei* the flowery capital; the beautiful capital
実 *kajitsu* flowers and fruit; appearance; content
表 *kahyō* monument at a cemetery entrance; a torii
9 南 *Kanan* South China
客 *kakyaku, kakaku* special guests
美 *kabi* pomp, splendor; gaudiness, colorfulness
冑 *kachū* aristocracy, nobility
10 容 *kayō* a beautiful face
華 *hanabana(shii)* brilliant, magnificent, spectacular
11 道 *kadō* flower arrangement
族 *kazoku* noble, peer
12 奢 *kasha* luxury, pomp, extravagance. *kasha na* delicate, slender; fragile
落 *karaku* capital; Kyoto
14 僑 *Kakyō* overseas Chinese merchants
墨 *kaboku* your beautiful letter
16 翰 *kakan* your publication
17 厳 *Kegon* Buddhist sect originating in the eighth century
燭 *kashoku* bright light
燭典 *kashoku (no) ten* wedding ceremony
18 顔 *kagan* a beautiful face
19 麗 *karei* splendor, magnificence

A **荷** 3956 F1604 KA shoulder-pole load. *nina(u)* carry, bear (a burden), shoulder (a gun). *ni* load, baggage, freight, cargo; burden.
3 下 *nioro(shi)* unloading, discharge. *ni (ga) o(riru)* be freed from responsibility
4 厄介 *niyakkai* encumbrance
5 札 *nifuda* tag, label
主 *ninushi* shipper
6 扱 *niatsuka(i)* freight handling
印 *nijirushi* mark on the baggage
7 車 *niguruma* cart, wagon
作 *nizuku(ri)* packing, baling, crating
抜 *ninu(ki)* pilferage
足 *niashi* sale; ballast; lading. *nita(ri)* barge, lighter
足船 *nita(ri)bune* barge, lighter
役 *niyaku* handling cargo
役人夫 *niyaku nimpu* longshoreman
8 物 *nimotsu* baggage; load
凭 *nimota(reru)* to oversupply, overstock
送 *nioku(ri)* consignment
送人 *nioku(ri)nin* sender
担 *katan* support; conspiracy, complicity. *nikatsu(gi)* carrying; laden
担者 *katansha* participants, supporters; conspirators
受 *niu(ke)* receipt of goods
受入 *niu(ke)nin* consignee
9 拵 *nigoshira(e)* packing, crating
持 *nimo(chi)* porter, carrier
卸 *nioro(shi)* unloading, discharge
重 *kajū* load
姿 *nisugata* type of packing
負 *nio(i)* shouldering a load
造 *nizuku(ri)* packing, baling, crating
造人 *nizuku(ri)nin* packer
造費 *nizuku(ri)hi* packing charges
10 捌 *nisaba(ki)* sale, disposal of goods
馬 *niuma* pack horse
馬車 *nibasha* wagon, dray, cart
11 脚 *niashi* sale; ballast; lading
船 *nibune* freighter; lighter
動 *niugo(ki)* movement of goods
12 渡 *niwata(shi)* delivery
勝 *ni (ga) ka(tsu)* the responsibilities are too heavy
葉 *kayō* lotus leaves
揚 *nia(ge)* unloading, landing
揚人足 *nia(ge) ninsoku* longshoreman
揚料 *nia(ge)ryō* landing charges
揚船 *nia(ge)sen* lighter, barge
揚場 *nia(ge)ba* landing place
13 解 *nihodo(ki)* unpacking
嵩 *nigasa* bulk. *nigasa(mi)* overstocked, glutted
電 *kaden* electric charge
14 駄 *nida* horseload, pack
15 鞍 *nigura* pack saddle
16 積 *nizu(mi)* loading
薄 *niusu* shortage of goods

8

莚 See 筵 3400.

剪 See 599. [刀]

菴 3957 F1612 F638 See 庵 1521.

菔 3958 F1609 F1631 See 蔔 4031.

菁 3959 F1608 菁 SEI turnip.

萊 3960 F1613 RAI goosefoot, pigweed.

菆 3961 F1608 SHU arrow.

萄 3962 F1612 DŌ, TŌ grape vine, wild grape.

萍 3963 F1613 HEI, HYŌ *ukikusa* floating plants.

菟 3964 F1609 TO, TSU dodder (plant).

萃 3965 F1612 SUI, ZUI, SAI gather, collect, assemble.

菰 3966 F1611 KO. *komo* a reed used for matting.

萁 3967 F1612 KI. *mamegara* bean stocks and pods.

菠 3968 F1609 HA spinach.
16 薐草 *hōrensō* spinach

菖 3969 F1609 SHŌ iris.
13 蒲 *ayame* Japanese iris. *shōbu* iris, flag
蒲湯 *shōbuyu* bath water with iris leaves

菲 3970 F1611 HI thin; inferior.
3 才 *hisai* lack of ability, incompetence

莽 3971 F1607 莽 BŌ, MŌ grass, grassy field.
10 莽 *bōbō to*＝蓬蓬 4023.13

菫 3972 F1610 KIN. *sumire* the violet.
5 外線 *kingaisen* ultraviolet; black light
11 菜 *sumire* the violet

萎 3973 F1613 I. *na(eru)* wither, droop, weaken; be paralyzed, be lame. *shibo(mu), shio(reru), shina(biru)* droop, wither, wilt, fade; be downcast.
17 縮 *ishuku* withering, contraction, atrophy
19 靡 *ibi* decline, decay, drooping

菎 3974 F1608 菎 KON a kind of fragrant herb.
11 麻 *hima, tōgoma* castor-oil plant; castor beans
麻子 *himashi* castor bean
麻子油 *himashiyu* castor oil

菅 3975 F1608 KAN. *suge* sedge.
10 原 *sugawara* field of sedge
莚 *sugamushiro* sedge mat
11 笠 *sugegasa* sedge hat
12 畳 *sugadatami* sedge mat

菌 3976 F1608 B KIN fungus, germ, bacteria.
8 毒 *kindoku* mushroom poison
9 保有者 *kin-hoyūsha* germ carrier
18 類 *kinrui* fungi
類学 *kinruigaku* study of fungi

菱 3977 F1611 RYŌ. *hishi* water chestnut; diamond (shape).
7 形 *ryōkei, hishigata* rhombus shape, diamond shape
13 鉄鉱 *ryōtekkō* loadstone
14 模様 *hishi moyō* diamond design
15 餅 *hishi mochi* colored rice cakes for the Girls' Doll Festival

菩 3978 F1609 BO kind of grass; sacred tree.
12 提 *bodai* Buddhahood; supreme enlightenment; repose; salvation
提心 *bodaishin* aspiration for Buddhahood; devout disposition
提寺 *bodaiji* one's family's temple
提所 *bodaisho* one's family's temple
提樹 *bodaiju* bo tree; lime tree; linden tree
16 薩 *bosatsu* bodhisattva; Buddhist saint

萌 3979 F1613 萠 HŌ. BŌ. *moe(ru)* sprout, bud. *moya(su)* to malt, cause to sprout artificially. *kiza(su)* show signs or symptoms of. *moya(shi)* malt; artificially sprouted beans or grains. *kiza(shi)* signs, omen, symptoms; germination.

[4]木 *moegi* sprouts; tree coming into leaf
[5]立 *moe-ta(tsu)* sprout, bud
出 *moe-de(ru)* sprout, bud
[7]豆 *moya(shi)mame* sprouting beans
[8]芽 *hōga* germination; germ, sprout
[11]黄色 *moegi iro* light green

B 菓 3980 F1609 KA cakes; fruit.
[3]子 *kashi* confectionery, pastry, candy
子皿 *kashizara* cake plate
子折 *kashio(ri)* cake box
子屋 *kashiya* confectionery
子重 *kashijū* small tier of cake boxes
子料 *kashiryō* cake money; cake-money tip
子鉢 *kashibachi* cookie jar
子箱 *kashibako* box of sweets
子器 *kashiki* cake-serving bowl

B 菊 3981 F1608 KIKU chrysanthemum.
[2]人形 *kiku ningyō* a doll made of a shaped growing chrysanthemum
[4]月 *kikuzuki* 9th lunar month
日和 *kikubiyori* fine fall chrysanthemum weather
[6]芋 *kiku imo* Jerusalem artichoke
[7]見 *kikumi* chrysanthemum viewing
作 *kikuzuku(ri)* chrysanthemum growing; chrysanthemum grower
判 *kikuban* small octavo
花 *kikka* chrysanthemum
[9]炭 *kikuzumi* chrysanthemum charcoal
[11]細工 *kikuzaiku* skillful chrysanthemum culture
[18]節句 *Kiku (no) Sekku* Chrysanthemum Festival

A 菜 3982 F1609 菜 SAI side dish; greens; vegetables. *na* greens; vegetables; the rape or mustard plant.
[2]刀 *nagatana* kitchen knife
[4]切庖丁 *na(k)ki(ri)bōchō* kitchen knife
[7]花 *na (no) hana* mustard flowers, rape blossoms
[9]食 *saishoku* vegetarian diet; plain food
食主義 *saishoku shugi* vegetarianism
食主義者 *saishoku shugisha* a vegetarian
食動物 *saishoku dōbutsu* herbivorous animal
[10]根 *saikon* vegetable roots
[12]葉 *na(p)pa* greens
葉服 *na(p)pafuku* overalls
[13]園 *saien* vegetable garden
[14]漬 *nazuke* pickled vegetables
種 *natane* rapeseed
種油 *natane abura* rape-seed oil
[15]箸 *saibashi* chopsticks for serving vegetables

A 著 3983 F1619 著 CHO literary work. CHAKU arrival, finish (in a race); suit counter. *tsu(ku)* arrive at, reach (an aim). *ki(ru)* put on, don, wear. *ki(seru)* (see under 着 3665.0). *ara(wasu)* write, publish. *ichijiru(shii)* remarkable, phenomenal.
[3]大 *chodai na* exceptionally large
[4]手 *chakushu* start, commencement
[5]用 *chakuyō suru* put on, wear
目 *chakumoku* viewpoint, observation
[6]色 *chakushoku*=着色 3665.6
任 *chakunin* arrival at one's post
名 *chomei* eminence, celebrity, fame
[7]述 *chojutsu* literary work
述家 *chojutsuka* a writer
述業 *chojutsugyō* literary profession
作 *chosaku* literary work, book; authorship
作物 *chosakubutsu* literary work, book
作者 *chosakusha* author, writer
作家 *chosakuka* author, writer
作権 *chosakuken* copyright
[8]明 *chomei na* clear, plain, obvious, conspicuous
服 *chakufuku*=着服 3665.8
実 *chakujitsu na* trustworthy, soberminded, steady
者 *chosha* author, writer
[9]信 *chakushin* arrival of mail
変 *chohen* a big change
発 *chakuhatsu* arrival and departure
[10]座 *chakuza* taking a seat
席 *chakuseki* taking a seat
陸 *chakuriku* alighting, landing
荷 *chakka, chakuni* arrival of goods
書 *chosho* literary work, book
書目録 *chosho mokuroku* bibliography
[11]眼 *chakugan* viewpoint, observation
船 *chakusen* ship arrival
著 *chakuchaku* steadily
患 *chokan* serious illness
[12]筆 *chakuhitsu* beginning to write; manner of writing
弾 *chakudan* a shell hitting the target
弾距離 *chakudan kyori* range of a gun
[13]電 *chakuden* telegram received
意 *chakui* conception; caution
想 *chakusō* conception, idea

9

萬 3984 F1614 See 万 7.

著 3985 F1619 See 著 3983.

董 3986 F1621 TŌ correct.

萼 3987/F1616 蕚蕚 GAKU calyx, cup.

韮 3988/F2052 韭 KYŪ. *nira* leek. [韭]

萱 3989/F1616 KEN. *kaya* miscanthus reed.
12葺 *kayabuki* the common miscanthus thatch

葵 3990/F1622 KI. *aoi* hollyhock.

惹 3991/F725 JAKU attract, captivate. [心]
10起 *jakki suru* bring about, cause, provoke (discussion)

萩 3992/F1614 SHŪ. *hagi* bush clover.
10原 *hagiwara* reedy field

葱 3993/F1622 SŌ. *negi* stone leek, Welsh onion, long onion.
7坊主 *negi bōzu* flowering onion head

葭 3994/F1622 KA. *yoshi, ashi* reed.
17簀 *yoshizu* reed screen

葺 3995/F1623 SHŪ. *ashi* reed, rush. *fu(ku)* to thatch, cover, shingle, tile.
4刈 *ashika(ri)* cutting reeds; the cutter
5石 *fuki-ishi* slate
8板 *fuki-ita* shingles
12替 *fu(ki)-ka(eru)* rethatch, reroof, retile

B 募 3996/F267 BO. *tsuno(ru)* gather (contributions); campaign (for students); float (a loan); enlist (troops); grow violent. [力]
7兵 *bohei* recruiting, enlistment, drafting
8金 *bokin* fund raising
金運動 *bokin undō* fund-raising campaign
金趣意書 *bokin shuisho* subscription prospectus
12集 *boshū* recruiting; invitation, collection; enrollment; solicitation; flotation
18債 *bosai* loan flotation

葛 3997/F1620 KATSU. *tsuzura* arrowroot, a strong-fiber vine. *kuzu* arrowroot; arrowroot starch.
5布 *kuzufu* grass cloth
6衣 *katsui* thin coarse hemp kimono
7折 *tsuzura-o(ri)* winding path
折道 *tsuzura-o(ri) michi* winding path
10粉 *kuzuko* arrowroot starch or flour
15餅 *kuzu mochi* arrowroot-flour cake
18藤 *kattō* complications, dissension
22籠 *tsuzura* suitcase, wicker basket, trunk

葦 3998/F1621 I. *ashi, yoshi* reed, bulrush.
4戸 *yoshido* (sliding) reed door
毛 *ashige* a grey horse, a dappled gray
火 *ashibi* torchlight of reeds
5生 *ashifu* reedy area
6舟 *ashibune* reed boat
9垣 *ashigaki* reed fence
11船 *ashibune* reed-carrying boat; boat used for harvesting reeds
笛 *ashibue* reed flute
17簀 *yoshizu* reed screen

葡 3999/F1621 BU, HO wild grape.
11萄 *budō* grapes, grapevine
萄状菌 *budōjōkin* staphylococcus
萄畑 *budōbatake* vineyard
萄酒 *budōshu* wine
萄液 *budōeki* grape juice
萄園 *budōzono, budōen* vineyard
萄酸 *budōsan* racemic acid
萄糖 *budōtō* grape sugar, dextrose, glucose

B 葬 4000/F1621 SŌ. *hōmu(ru)* bury; shelve. *tomura(u), tomura(i)* (see under 弔 80.0).
5礼 *sōrei* funeral service
主 *sōshu* chief mourner
6式 *sōshiki* funeral ceremony
列 *sōretsu* funeral procession
8具 *sōgu* funeral accessories
具師 *sōgushi* undertaker
送 *sōsō* attendance at a funeral
送曲 *sōsōkyoku* funeral march
送行進曲 *sōsō kōshinkyoku* funeral march
送歌 *sōsōka* funeral dirge
11祭 *sōsai* funerals and festivals
14歌 *sōka* dirge, elegy
15儀 *sōgi* funeral service
儀社 *sōgisha* undertaker
儀屋 *sōgiya* undertaker
儀場 *sōgijō* funeral parlor

A 葉 4001/F1618 YŌ leaf; plane; lobe; counter for flat things. *ha, ha(ppa)* leaf, foliage, needle, blade, spear, frond.
4月 *hazuki* 8th lunar month
5広 *habiro* broadness of leaves
末 *hazue* leaf tip
7状 *hajō* leaflike
牡丹 *habotan* cabbage

[8]物 *hamono* leafy plants and trees
並 *hana(mi)* leaf arrangement
芽 *yōga* leaf bud
[9]風 *hakaze* the wind passing thru the leaves
柄 *yōhei* leaf stem
茶 *hacha* leaf tea
巻 *hamaki* cigar
[10]振 *habu(ri)* leaf arrangement
桜 *hazakura* cherry foliage
脈 *hamyaku* leaf vein
陰 *hakage ni* under the leaves
書 *hagaki* postcard
[12]越 *hago(shi)* (seen) thru the leaves
[13]鉄 *yōtetsu* sheet iron
隠 *hagaku(reru)* hide in the trees
裏 *ha-ura* lower side of a leaf
[14]酸 *yōsan* folic acid
[15]縁 *yōen* margin of a leaf
緑素 *yōryokuso* chlorophyll

B **蒸** 4002/F1625 Jō. Shō. *mu(su)* steam, heat up (with steam); be close, be sultry; foment, poultice. *mu(reru)* be stuffy, get musty; moulder, heat. *mu(rasu)* steam, cook by steam. *fu(kasu)* steam. *fu(keru)* be steamed, be boiled. *mu(shi)*- steamed (dish).

[5]立 *mu(shi)ta(te) no* just steamed
[6]返 *mu(shi)-kae(su)* reheat, steam over; repeat, bring up again
気 *jōki* steam, vapor; steamship
気力 *jōkiryoku* steam power
気孔 *jōkikō* volcanic vent
気汽罐 *jōki kikan* steam boiler
気室 *jōkishitsu* steam chamber
気風呂 *jōkiburo* steam bath
気釜 *jōkigama* steam boiler
気船 *jōkisen* steamship
気管 *jōkikan* steampipe
気機関 *jōki kikan* steam engine
気機関車 *jōki kikansha* steam locomotive
[8]物 *mu(shi)mono* steamed food
[9]風呂 *mu(shi)buro* Turkish bath
発 *jōhatsu* evaporation, volatilization
発熱 *jōhatsu netsu* heat of evaporation
発器 *jōhatsuki* evaporator
[10]釜 *mu(shi)gama* steam kettle
留 *jōryū* distillation
留水 *jōryūsui* distilled water
留酒 *jōryūshu* distilled liquor
留器 *jōryūki* a still
[11]菓子 *mu(shi)gashi* steamed cake
[12]飯 *mu(shi)meshi* reheated rice
散 *jōsan* evaporation, volatilization
暑 *mu(shi)atsu(i)* sultry, sweltering
蒸 *mu(shi)mu(shi) suru* be sultry, be close
焼 *mushiya(ki)* baking in covered casseroles
焼器 *mushiyakiki* oven
[13]溜 *jōryū* distillation
溜水 *jōryūsui* distilled water
溜器 *jōryūki* a still
[14]腐 *mu(re)gusa(re)* dry rot
[15]熱 *ikire* stuffiness, sultriness
[17]鍋 *mu(shi)nabe* casserole
[19]餾 *jōryū* distillation
[22]籠 *seiro, seirō* steamer, basket for steaming rice

A **落** 4003/F1616 Raku. *o(chiru)* fall, drop, come down, go down; drip; collapse, cave in; sink; fail (in exams); be missing; come off, come out; flee; lose popularity; abate; flow into; be inferior; fall unconscious; fade; be captured, be carried away by. *o(tosu)* drop, let fall; throw down; throw (a shadow); miss (a ball), fumble; lose; capture; omit; degrade; depreciate, detract from; decrease; make worse; drive away, exorcise; leave behind; knock down (an article); cause abortion; entrap; end (a story) with a punch; remove (stains). *o(chibureru)* be ruined, sink into poverty. *o(chi)* error, fault, slip; point (of a joke); outcome. *o(toshi)* trap; false bottom; ash-pan; chute; brazier. -*o(chi)* off, less, minus; flight. *o(chi)*- lower, low; fallen (fruit); defeated.

[2]人 *ochūdo, ochibito, ochiudo* refugee; deserter; fugitive
入 *o(chi)-i(ru)* (see under 陥 4990.0)
丁 *rakuchō* missing pages
[3]口 *o(chi)guchi* beginning of the fall of leaves; spout; mouth (of a river); brink (of a waterfall); successful bidder, lottery winner
子 *o(toshi)go*=*rakuin* 落胤 (see below–9)
下 *rakka* falling, descent
下傘 *rakkasan* parachute
下傘兵 *rakkasanhei* paratrooper
[4]戸 *o(toshi)do* trap door
手 *rakushu* receiving
文 *o(toshi)bumi* letter purposely dropped or left behind
方 *o(chi)gata* weakening, falling
日 *rakujitsu* setting sun
月 *rakugetsu* setting moon
水 *o(toshi)mizu* letting water out of a rice field; such water
毛 *o(chi)ge* falling hair
込 *o(chi)-ko(mu)* fall in; sink, subside; decline (of prices); come in
[5]目 *o(chi)me* declining fortune, adversity
穴 *o(toshi)ana* pitfall, trap
付 *o(chi)tsu(ki)* serenity, calmness, stability
主 *o(toshi)nushi* loser (of something)

6 竹米糸缶网四羊羽老耂而耒耳聿肉月臣自至臼舌舛舟艮色【艸9 艹】虍虫血行衣ネ西

失 *o(chi)-u(seru)* flee, escape, abscond

札 *rakusatsu* successful bid. *o(chi)fuda* prize-winning ticket

札人 *rakusatsunin* successful bidder

札値 *rakusatsune* contract price

6 行 *o(chi)-yu(ku)* flee

合 *o(chi)-a(u)* meet, come upon, rendezvous. *o(chi)a(i)* meeting; confluence

字 *rakuji* omitted character

成 *rakusei* completion of construction

成式 *rakuseishiki* building-completion ceremony

伍 *rakugo* straggling, dropping out; losing out (in the struggle for existence)

伍者 *rakugosha* straggler

7 足 *o(chi)ashi* flight; time of fleeing; receding of water

車 *rakusha suru* fall off a racing vehicle

体 *rakutai* falling body

卵 *o(toshi)tamago* poached eggs

花 *rakka* falling of blossoms; scattered blossoms

花生 *rakkasei* peanuts

花狼藉 *rakka-rōzeki suru* fall off, pass away, scatter

8 延 *o(chi)-no(biru)* make good one's escape

物 *o(toshi)mono* lost article

命 *rakumei* death

英 *rakuei*＝*rakka* 落花 (see above 7)

武者 *ochimusha* fugitive warrior

9 首 *rakushu* lampoon, satirical poem

胤 *rakuin, o(toshi)dane* illegitimate child

城 *rakujō* fall of a castle

後 *rakugo* straggling, dropping out; losing out in the struggle for existence

胆 *rakutan* discouragement

重 *o(chi)-kasa(naru)* fall upon; fall in a heap

度 *o(chi)do* fault, error, slip, lapse, oversight; blame, guilt

度無 *o(chi)dona(ku)* blamelessly

星 *rakusei* falling star, meteor

星雨 *rakuseiu* meteoric shower

10 馬 *rakuba* a fall from a horse. *rakuba suru* fall from a horse, be thrown from a horse

涙 *rakurui suru* shed tears

紙 *o(toshi)gami* toilet paper

差 *rakusa* water level, head, fall

書 *rakuga(ki)* scribbling in public places. *rakusho* anonymous critical broadsides

莫 *rakubaku(taru)* dreary, desolate, lonesome

栗 *o(chi)guri* fallen chestnut

11 魚 *o(chi)uo* dead fish

掛 *o(chi)-ka(karu)* fall upon; begin to fall

球 *rakkyū* missing a ball; muffed ball

脱 *rakudatsu* omission

陽 *rakuyō* setting sun; Loyang (in China)

欸 *rakkan* writer's or artist's signature

第 *rakudai* failure in an examination

第生 *rakudaisei* student who failed

第点 *rakudaiten* failing mark

12 款 *rakkan* writer's or artist's signature

掌 *rakushō* receiving

筆 *rakuhitsu* beginning to write

落 *o(chi)o(chi)* quietly, peacefully, comfortably

無 *o(chi)na(ku)* without exception, thoroly

着 *o(chi)-tsu(keru)* calm (oneself). *o(chi)-tsu(ku)* calm down; settle down; keep cool; subside (pain;) be steady; harmonize with. *ochitsu(ki)* calmness, serenity; stability. *rakuchaku* settlement, end, conclusion

着払 *o(chi)-tsu(ki)-hara(u)* be perfectly calm

着先 *ochitsu(ki)saki* place where one stays

着所 *ochitsu(ki)dokoro* happy dwelling, haven of rest

葉 *o(chi)ba* fallen leaves. *rakuyō* fall of leaves; fallen leaves

葉松 *karamatsu, rakuyōshō* larch

葉樹 *rakuyōju* deciduous tree

葉籠 *o(chi)ba kago* stray notes

13 暉 *rakki* setting sun

話 *o(toshi)banashi* funny story, pointed story

飾 *rakushoku* taking the tonsure

雷 *rakurai suru* be struck by lightning

零 *o(chi)kobo(re)* what's left; things scattered around

勢 *o(chi)zei* fleeing army. *rakusei* declining market

照 *rakushō* setting sun

14 髪 *rakuhatsu* tonsure. *o(chi)gami* falling hair

選 *rakusen* election defeat; rejection

選者 *rakusensha* unsuccessful candidate

語 *rakugo* humorous story

語家 *rakugoka* storyteller; comedian

15 潮 *rakuchō, o(chi)shiro* low tide, ebb tide

魄 *ochibure(ru)* be ruined, be reduced to poverty, fall low. *ochibure* stricken with adversity. *rakuhaku* straitened circumstances

縁 *o(chi)en* low veranda

盤 *rakuban* cave-in

磐 *rakuban* cave-in

穂 *o(chi)bo* gleanings

穂拾 *o(chi)bo-hiro(i)* gleaning; gleaner

16 鮎 *o(chi)ayu* sweetfish descending rivers for spawning

17 藉 *rakuseki* ransom (of a prostitute)

18 羂 *o(toshi)wana* pit trap

20 籍 *rakuseki* no registration (in the census register); buying a geisha her contractual freedom

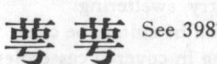

10

蒸 See 4002.

蕚 萼 See 3987.

慈 See 612. [心]

煎 See 611. [火]

蓮 4004 F1629 See 蓮 4731.

蓏 4005 F1628 RA fruit growing on low plants.

蒴 4006 F1625 SAKU (seed) capsule.

蒻 4007 F1625 NYAKU. JAKU a kind of water plant.

蓙 4008 F-X (国字) ZA. *goza* mat, matting.

蓑 4009 F1628 簑 SA. *mino* straw raincoat.

蒜 4010 F1624 SAN. *ninniku* garlic.

蒡 4011 F1624 BŌ, HŌ burdock.

蓚 4012 F-X SHŪ (used only in compounds).

14 酸 *shūsan* oxalic acid

蒿 4013 F1626 KŌ mugwort.

7 苣 *chisha, chisa* lettuce

蓆 4014 F1627 SEKI. *mushiro* straw mat, matting.

5 包 *mushirozutsu(mi)* mat-wrapped bundle

蓐 4015 F1628 JOKU bed.

13 傷 *jokushō* bedsores
15 瘡 *jokusō* bedsores

蒟 4016 F1624 KU devil's tongue (plant).

13 蒻 *konnyaku* devil's tongue
蒻版 *konnyakuban* hectograph

蔭 4017 F1632 IN. *kage* shade; backing, (your) assistance.

5 乍 *kagenaga(ra)* secretly
7 言 *kagegoto* malicious gossip
位 *in-i* hereditary court rank

蒔 4018 F1623 SHI. JI. *ma(ku)* sow (seed).

5 付 *ma(ki)tsu(ke)* sowing, seeding
12 絵 *makie* gold or silver lacquer work
22 蘿 *inondo* dill

蓋 4019 F1627 GAI cover. *futa* cover, lid, flap, hood. *keda(shi)* probably; after all; in the long run.

7 車 *gaisha* covered wagon
8 明 *futa-a(ke)* opening, commencement
物 *futamono* covered dish
12 然 *gaizen* probable
然性 *gaizensei* probability
然的 *gaizenteki* probable

蒙 4020 F1623 MŌ ignorance; darkness. *kōmu(ru)* get, receive, be subjected to, sustain (damage), suffer (loss). *kōmu(rasu)* cause (damage); inflict on; subject to.

5 古 *Mōko* Mongolia
古人 *Mōkojin* a Mongol, a Mongolian
古襲来 *Mōko Shūrai* Mongolian Invasion
9 昧 *mōmai* ignorance
14 塵 *mōjin suru* flee from the palace (the emperor)

蒲 4021 F1624 FU. BO. HO. BU. *gama* flag, cattail, bulrush. *kaba* bulrush.

4 公英 *tampopo* dandelion
6 色 *kaba iro* reddish yellow
団 *futon* bedding; mattress; pallet
団蒸 *futommu(shi)* wrapping up (someone) in a quilt
9 柳質 *horyū (no) shitsu* delicate health
14 鉾 *kamaboko* boiled fish paste
鉾小屋 *kamabokogoya* a beggar's hut

蒐 4022 F1623 SHŪ gather.

10 荷 *shūka* collection of cargo
12 集 *shūshū* collection, accumulation
集品 *shūshūhin* collectors' items
集美術品 *shūshū bijutsuhin* art collection
集家 *shūshūka* collector
集欲 *shūshūyoku* collecting craze
集癖 *shūshūheki* collecting habit
16 輯 *shūshū* collection, gathering up, accumulation

蓬 4023 F1628 HŌ. *yomogi* sagebrush, wormwood, mugwort; an edible weed.

5 生 *yomogifu, yomogiu* waste land, area overgrown with weeds
11 莱 *hōrai* isle of eternal youth; fairyland; Elysian fields; eternal-youth ornament
莱米 *hōraimai* Formosan rice

萊豆 *hōrai mame* sugar-coated beans
18 蓬 *bōbō to* thickly; untrimmed, shaggy; bursting (into flames)
14 髪 *hōhatsu* unkempt hair
16 頭 *hōtō* tousled hair

B **蓄** 4024/F1627 CHIKU. *takuwa(e), takuwa(eru)* (see under 貯 4502.0).
2 力 *chikuryoku* accumulating power
5 生腹 *chikushōbara* multiple (human) births
8 妾 *chikushō* keeping a concubine
9 音器 *chikuonki* phonograph
音機 *chikuonki* phonograph
10 財 *chikuzai* amassing of wealth
13 電 *chikuden* charging with electricity
電池 *chikudenchi* storage battery
電器 *chikudenki* electric condenser
16 積 *chikuseki* accumulation, amassing
17 膿症 *chikunōshō* sinusitis

蒼 4025/F1625 SŌ. *ao* blue, pale.
4 天 *sōten* blue sky
5 生 *sōsei* the people, the masses
白 *aojiro(i), sōhaku na* pale, pallid, livid
8 穹 *sōkyū* blue sky
空 *sōkū* blue sky
氓 *sōbō* the people
9 海 *sōkai* blue sea
茫 *sōbō na* dusky, shadowy
10 浪 *sōrō* blue waves
11 黄 *sōkō* bustle, fluster
12 惶 *sōkō* bustle, hurry
然 *sōzen(taru)* blue; dim; gloomy, somber
13 鉛 *sōen* bismuth
14 褪 *aoza(meru)* get pale

B **幕** 4026/F620 BAKU, MAKU curtain; bunting; an act (in a play); end; first rank (in wrestling); a matter, a case. *tobari* curtain. [巾]
8 下 *bakka* shogun; shogun's staff; vassal, feudatory, follower. *makushita* second-class Japanese wrestler
4 切 *makugi(re)* fall of the curtain
内 *maku-uchi, maku(no)uchi* first-class wrestler. *maku(no)uchi* a Japanese lunch
5 末 *bakumatsu* latter days of the Tokugawas
6 臣 *bakushin* shogun's vassal
合 *makua(i)* interval between acts
吏 *bakuri* shogunate official
7 兵 *bakuhei* shogunate soldiers
8 府 *bakufu* shogunate
舎 *bakusha* barracks; camp
命 *bakumei* shogunate orders
9 屋 *makuya* tent, tabernacle
政 *bakusei* shogunate government
軍 *bakugun* shogunate army
10 将 *bakushō* shogunate general
12 間 *makuai* interval between acts
開 *makuaki* opening of a play; beginning
無 *makuna(shi)* always
13 電 *makuden* sheet lightning
14 閣 *bakkaku* shogunate cabinet
僚 *bakuryō* staff; staff officer; brain trust; brain truster; adviser

A **墓** 4027/F437 BO. *haka* grave, tomb. [土]
5 石 *boseki, haka ishi* tombstone
穴 *boketsu* grave hole
6 地 *bochi* cemetery
守 *hakamori* grave keeper
8 所 *bosho, hakadokoro, hakasho* cemetery
参 *bosan, hakamai(ri)* visit to a grave
表 *bohyō* grave marker, epitaph
9 前 *bozen* before the grave
10 原 *hakawara* cemetery
畔 *bohan de* at the grave
11 掘 *hakaho(ri)* grave-digging; gravedigger
12 場 *hakaba* cemetery
14 銘 *bomei* epitaph
碑 *bohi* tombstone
碑銘 *bohimei* epitaph
誌 *boshi* epitaph
誌銘 *boshimei* epitaph
15 標 *bohyō* grave marker, tombstone
20 籍 *boseki* cemetery register

B **夢** 4028/F455 MU. *yume* dream; vision; illusion, delusion; reverie. [夕]
4 幻 *mugen* dreams, visions. *yume-maboroshi* dreams and visions; something visionary
心 *yumegokoro* trance, ecstasy
心地 *yumegokochi* trance, ecstasy
中 *muchū* unconscious; ecstasy; absorption; abstraction
中歩行 *muchū hokō* walking in one's sleep
5 占 *yume urana(i)* fortunetelling by a dream
6 死 *mushi suru* die without accomplishing anything
合 *yumea(wase)* interpretation of dreams
7 判断 *yume handan* interpretation of dreams
見 *yumemi(ru)* dream, fancy. *yumemi* a dream
見者 *yumemi(ru)mono* dreamer
8 枕 *yume makura ni* in a dream
物語 *yume monogatari* story of a dream; fantastic story
11 現 *yumeutsutsu* trance, ecstasy; dream and reality
遊 *muyū* walking in one's sleep
遊病 *muyūbyō* sleepwalking
12 寐 *mubi* awake or asleep

13 解 *yumeto(ki)* interpretation of a dream
路 *yumeji* traveling in a dream; Land of Nod
想 *musō* dream, vision, reverie
想家 *musōka* dreamer
14 語 *yumegata(ri)* = *yume monogatari* 夢物語 (see above–8)
21 魔 *muma* a fearful disturbing dream

11

蕁 4029 / F-X 蕁 See 4052.

蔲 4030 / F1630 蔻 Kō, Ku nutmeg.

蔔 4031 / F1631 / F1609 菔 Fuku giant radish, daikon.

蔘 4032 / F-X Shin luxurious growth of grass.

蔟 4033 / F1632 Zoku gather together.

蔗 4034 / F1631 Sha, Sho sugar cane.

摹 4035 / F827 Bo. *mo(suru)* imitate. [手]

蔣 4036 / F1632 Shō a reed.
9 政権 *Shōseiken* Chiang (Kai Shek) regime

蔦 4037 / F1632 Chō. *tsuta* ivy.
12 葛 *tsutakazura* vines, creepers

蔑 4038 / F1630 Betsu. *naigashiro (ni) suru* ignore, despise, neglect, ridicule. *nami(suru)* set at naught, ridicule. *sagesu(mu)*, *sageshi(mu)* despise, ridicule.
11 視 *besshi* contempt, derision; slight

蔓 4039 / F1631 Man. *habiko(ru)* spread, sprawl; overgrow; thrive; be rampant, become powerful. *tsuru* vine, tendril, runner; influence, connections, medium, good offices.
8 延 *habiko(ru)*, *man-en suru* spread, diffuse, prevail, be widespread, gain headway
苔桃 *tsurukokemomo* cranberry
9 草 *tsurukusa* creeper, climber, vine

B **慕** 4040 / F738 Bo. *shita(u)* yearn for, love dearly, adore, follow. *shita(washii)* dear, beloved, fond of. [小]
4 心 *boshin* yearning (for someone)
7 求 *shita(i)-moto(meru)* desire, long for
11 情 *bojō* longing, affection
12 喘 *shita(i)-ae(gu)* long for
喜 *shita(i)-yoroko(bu)* hold dear
12 焦 *shita(i)-koga(reru)* yearn for

B **暮** 4041 / F914 Bo. *kura(su)* live, make a living; spend (one's time). *ku(reru)* get dark; (the sun) sets; (the season) ends; (time) passes; be overwhelmed. *kura(shi)* living, livelihood; circumstances. *ku(re)* sunset, nightfall; year-end; end. [日]
4 方 *ku(rashi)kata* manner of living. *ku(re)-gata*, *kure(tsu)kata* nightfall
5 払 *ku(re)bara(i)* paying at the year end; year-end payment
6 色 *boshoku* twilight scene
行 *ku(re)-yu(ku)* get dark
向 *ku(rashi)mu(ki)* circumstances, livelihood
合 *ku(re)a(i)* about sunset
年 *bonen* one's later years
8 雨 *bo-u* an evening shower
夜 *boya* evening, night
果 *ku(re)-ha(teru)* get completely dark
9 秋 *boshū* late fall
春 *boshun* late spring
10 紛 *ku(re)magi(re)* being benighted
11 移 *ku(re)-utsu(ru)* get dark
雪 *bosetsu* evening snowfall
12 渡 *ku(re)-wata(ru)* the whole landscape darkens
景 *bokei* twilight, evening scene
雲 *boun* evening clouds
13 塞 *ku(re)-fusaga(ru)* get completely dark
愁 *boshū* the loneliness of evening
14 様 *ku(rashi)yō* manner of living
暮 *ku(re)gu(re)* nightfall

A **蔵** 4042 / F1643 藏 Sō. Zō. *kura* (see under 倉 486.0). *zō(suru)* hide; accumulate; have, own, keep, cherish. *osa(meru)* (see under 納 3508.0). -*zō* possession.
2 人 *kurando* imperial-archives keeper
入 *kura-i(re)* warehousing
4 方 *kurakata* the one in charge of a storehouse
元 *kuramoto* warehouse superintendent
5 払 *kurabara(i)* clearance (sale)
出 *kurada(shi)* releasing (goods) from a storehouse
本 *zōhon* one's library
6 米 *kuramai* stored rice
7 作 *kurazukur(i)* storehouse style (architecture)
8 版 *zōhan* copyrighted by
9 持 *kuramo(chi)* warehouse owner; warehousing
相 *zōshō*, *zōso* finance minister
屋敷 *kura yashiki* daimyo's city storehouse
10 匿 *zōtoku suru vt* and *vi* hide

浚 *kurazara(e)* clearance sale
書 *zōsho* one's library, book collection
書狂 *zōshokyō* bibliomania; bibliomaniac
書家 *zōshoka* book collector, large library owner
11 移 *kura-utsu(shi)* transporting to another storehouse
船 *kurabune* ship used for storage
12 開 *kurabira(ki)* first opening of the storehouse in the new year
番 *kuraban* warehouse watchman
13 置 *zōchi, kura-o(ki)* storing

12

蒭 See 剪 599.[羽]

蕚 4043 F1616 蕚 See 萼 3987.

蕑 4044 F1634 KAN. *fujibakama* agueweed (a fall flower)

蕊 4045 F1634 蕋蘂蘃 ZUI. *shibe* pistil; stamen.

甍 4046 F1261 BŌ. MYŌ. *iraka* roof tile; tiled roof. [瓦]

蕈 4047 F1634 蕈 JIN. *kinoko* mushroom; toadstool; fungus. *take* mushroom.
9 狩 *kinokoga(ri)* hunting mushrooms

蕉 4048 F1634 SHŌ banana.
9 風 *shōfū* correct style in a haiku (like Bashō's)

蔬 4049 F1632 SO greens, vegetables.
11 菜 *sosai* vegetables, greens

蔽 4050 F1633 HEI. *ō(i), ō(u)* (see under 覆 4279.0).
13 隠 *ō(i)-kaku(su)* cover; conceal

蕨 4051 F1635 KETSU. *warabi* bracken, fernbrake.
9 狩 *warabiga(ri)* bracken gathering

蕁 4052 F1633 蕁 JIN a kind of grass.
11 麻 *irakusa* nettle
麻疹 *jimmashin* hives, rash

蕪 4053 F1636 BU. *kabu, kabura* turnip.
11 菁 *kabura* turnip
13 辞 *buji* my humble remarks
14 雑 *buzatsu na* unpolished, crude

蕎 4054 F1634 KYŌ buckwheat.
7 麦 *soba* buckwheat; buckwheat noodles
麦屋 *sobaya* buckwheat-noodle shop
麦粉 *sobako* buckwheat flour
麦殻 *sobagara* buckwheat chaff

蕩 4055 F1635 TŌ. *toro(kasu), toro(keru)* (see under 盪 3124.0).
3 子 *tōshi* prodigal son; profligate
4 心 *tōshin* debauchery, dissipation
6 尽 *tōjin* squandering
7 児 *tōji* debauchee, libertine
15 蕩 *tōtō(taru)* vast, rushing (water)

蕃 4056 F1633 BAN, HAN grow luxuriously.
2 人 *banjin* aboriginal
6 地 *banchi* barbaric region
夷 *ban-i* barbarians, savages
7 社 *bansha* aborigines' village
8 国 *bankoku* backward country; foreign country
11 族 *banzoku* savage tribe
12 椒 *tōgarashi* red pepper
殖 *hanshoku*=繁殖 3596.12
14 語 *bango* aboriginal language

13

蕚蕚 See 4043.

薯 See 4080.

薇 4057 F1638 BI an edible fern.

薈 4058 F1639 KAI luxuriant vegetation.

薤 4059 F1640 KAI. *rakkyō* scallion, shallot, a small onion.

薑 4060 F1639 KYŌ. *hajikami* ginger.

薊 4061 F1639 KEI. *azami* thistle.

蕷 4062 F1637 YO. *imo* potato.

蕾 4063 F1637 RAI. *tsubo(mu)* bear buds. *tsubomi* bud.

薨 4064 / F1640 Kō. *kō(jiru), kō(zuru)* die.
5去 *kōkyo* death, demise

蟇 4065 / F1673 **蟆** BA. MA. *hiki* toad. [虫]
12蛙 *hikigaeru* toad

薩 4066 / F1641 SATSU Buddha.
15摩守 *satsuma (no) kami* one who steals a ride
摩焼 *satsumayaki* Satsuma ware
摩薯 *satsuma imo* sweet potato

B **薦** 4067 / F1640 SEN. *susu(me), susu(meru)* (see under 勧 736.0). *komo* mat.
5包 *komozutsu(mi)* wrapping in matting; mat-wrapped bundle
7抜 *sembatsu* recommendation; promoting (someone)
10骨 *senkotsu* the sacrum
被 *komokaburi* mat-wrapped saké cask
挙 *senkyo* recommendation

蕭 4068 / F1636 SHŌ a weed, mugwort; lonely; silent, calm.
7条 *shōjō(taru)* bleak, desolate, lonely
12然 *shōzen(taru)* bleak, desolate, lonely
16蕭 *shōshō(taru)* bleak, desolate

B **薪** 4069 / F1640 **薪** SHIN. *maki* firewood. *takigi* firewood, kindling, fuel.
4木 *shimboku* firewood
水 *shinsui* fuel and water; cooking; salary; board
7材 *shinzai* branches for firewood
9屋 *makiya, takigiya* firewood dealer
炭 *shintan* wood and charcoal, fuel
炭商 *shintanshō* fuel business
12割 *takigiwa(ri), makiwa(ri)* chopping wood; ax, hatchet

燕 4070 / F1202 EN *tsubame, tsubakura, tsubakuro* the swallow. [火]
7麦 *karasu mugi, embaku* oats
尾服 *embifuku* swallow-tailed coat
11雀 *enjaku* small birds
巣 *enzu* swallow's nest; edible bird's-nest

薔 4071 / F1639 SHOKU, SHŌ a kind of grass.
16薇 *bara, shōbi, ibara* rose, rosebush
薇水晶 *bara suishō* rose quartz
薇石英 *shōbi sekiei* rose quartz
薇色 *bara iro* rose color, rose pink
薇園 *baraen* rose garden

薙 4072 / F1639 TEI. *na(gu)* mow down (the enemy).
2刀 *naginata* halberd
5立 *na(gi)-ta(teru)* mow down right and left
6伏 *na(gi)-fu(seru)* cut down
10倒 *na(gi)-tao(su)* mow down (the enemy)
射 *chisha* strafing; heavy gunfire
14髪 *chihatsu, teihatsu* tonsure, cutting off the hair

B **薫** 4073 / F1641 **薰** KUN. *kun(zuru)* send forth fragrance, be scented, impregnate with. *kao(ru)* smell, be fragrant. *kuyu(rasu)* smoke (tobacco); burn (incense). *kao(ri)* (see under 香 5188.0).
4化 *kunka* influencing people by one's virtue
8物 *takimono* incense
育 *kun-iku* moral education
9風 *kumpū* balmy breeze
香 *kunkō* incense, fragrance
染 *kunsen* being under good influence
10陶 *kuntō* education, training, instruction, discipline
13煙 *kun-en* fragrant smoke
14製 *kunsei* smoking (fish or pork)

A **薬** 4074 / F1644 **藥** YAKU medicine. *kusuri* medicine; glaze, enamel; chemical; gunpowder; benefit.
2九層倍 *kusuri-kusōbai* the high cost of medicine
4方 *yakuhō* prescription, formula
5玉 *kusudama* decorative rosette
代 *kusuridai, yakudai* medical fee, doctor's fee, charge for medicine
礼 *yakurei* medical charge
用 *yakuyō* medicinal use
用石鹸 *yakuyō sekken* medicated soap
石 *yakuseki* medical treatment
石効無 *yakuseki kō na(ku)* in spite of all medical treatment
包 *yakuhō* gun cartridge; a wrapped dose of medicine
包紙 *yakuhōshi* a paper wrapping for a dose of medicine
7売 *kusuriu(ri)* medicine salesman
局 *yakkyoku* dispensary, medical office, pharmacy
局方 *yakkyokuhō* pharmacopoeia
8店 *yakuten* drugstore
価 *yakuka, yakka* medical charge
味 *yakumi* spices, flavor, seasoning; the taste of a medicine
効 *yakkō* medicinal value, remedial result
物 *yakubutsu* medicines, drugs, materia medica
物学 *yakubutsugaku* pharmacology, materia medica
物学者 *yakubutsu gakusha* pharmacologist
物療法 *yakubutsu ryōhō* medication, medicinal therapy
学 *yakugaku* pharmocology
学士 *Yakugakushi* Bachelor of Pharmacology

学者 *yakugakusha* pharmacologist
学博士 *Yakugaku Hakushi* Doctor of Pharmacology
9 屋 *kusuriya* drug store
指 *kusuri yubi* third finger, ring finger
研 *yagen* druggist's mortar
品 *yakuhin* medicines, drugs, chemicals
室 *yakushitsu* dispensary, pharmacy; powder chamber
草 *yakusō* medicinal plants
草学 *yakusōgaku* medicinal botany
草園 *yakusōen* a garden of medicinal plants
10 師 *yakushi* the Buddha of healing
酒 *yakushu* saké containing medicine
莢 *yakkyō* cartridge, cartridge case
剤 *yakuzai* medicine, drugs, compounded medicines
剤学 *yakuzaigaku* pharmacology
剤師 *yakuzaishi* pharmacist
11 液 *yakueki* liquid medicine
瓶 *kusuri bin, yakubin* vial, medicine bottle
袋 *yakutai* small paper containers for dispensing medicine
理的 *yakuriteki* pharmacological
12 湯 *kusuriyu, yakutō* medicated bath
筒 *yakutō* cartridge
13 園 *yakuen* medicinal-herb garden
14 種 *yakushu* drugs, pharmacopoeia, materia medica
種商 *yakushushō* druggist
15 餌 *yakuji* medicine; medicine and food
箱 *kusuribako* medicine chest
舗 *yakuho* drug store
22 嚢 *yakunō* medicine bag; cartridge bag
籠 *yakurō* medicine chest
籠中物 *yakurōchū (no) mono* a puppet, a tool (in someone's hand)
23 罐 *yakan* teakettle
25 鑵 *yakan* teakettle
鑵頭 *yakan atama* bald head

B 薄 4075 F1637 **薄** HAKU. *usu(i)* thin, weak (tea), light, pale, faint, scanty, ungenerous. *usu(meru)* dilute, weaken. *usu(ragu), usu(rogu), usu(reru)* thin, thin out, fade, grow pale, be toned down, get dim, cool (emotions), abate, lessen, decline. *usu(ppera) na* thin; shallow-minded, superficial, frivolous. *-usu, usu-* thin, weak, scanty, slightly, light (color).

3 刃 *usuba* thin blade; vegetable knife
才 *hakusai* mediocre ability
4 手 *usude* slight wound, minor injury; a thin article
日 *usubi* soft beams of sunlight
片 *hakuhen* thin leaf, thin layer; splinter, potsherd
切 *usugir(i)* slicing thin
化粧 *usugeshō* light make-up
5 白 *usushiro(i)* off-white
皮 *hakuhi* thin leather. *usukawa* thin skin, film, thin layer, membrane; scum
目 *usume* rather light, comparatively thin; half-closed eyes
収 *hakushū* a small income
氷 *hakuhyō, usugōri* thin ice; danger
6 色 *usu-iro* light color, pale color
行 *hakkō* careless behavior
衣 *usugoromo, haku-i* thin garment; shabby garment
地 *usuji* thin cloth; thin metal
汚 *usugitana(i)* filthy, dirty, bedraggled
光 *hakkō* pale light, faint light
肉彫 *usunikubo(ri)* low relief, bas-relief
気味悪 *usukimi (no) waru(i), usukimiwaru(i)* weird, uncanny, eerie, unearthly; ominous
7 赤 *usuaka(i)* light red
利 *hakuri* small profits, narrow margin, low interest
利多売 *hakuri-tabai* small profits and large sales
志 *hakushi* weakness of mind; weakness of purpose; small token of gratitude
志弱行 *hakushi-jakkō* weak purpose and indecision
8 明 *hakumei, usuaka(ri)* twilight, dawn. *usuakaru(i)* dim; gloomy, somber
物 *usumono* thin silk, flimsy dress
盲 *usumekura* gravel-blindness
命 *hakumei* evil fate, misfortune
幸 *hakkō* misfortune, bad luck
板 *hakuhan, usu-ita* thin plate, sheet
板硝子 *usu-ita garasu* sheet glass
9 柿 *usugaki* light persimmon color
紅 *usubeni, usukurenai* light crimson; light rouge
茶 *usucha* weak tea
茶色 *usucha iro* light brown, buff
10 俸 *hakuhō* low salary
倖 *hakkō* misfortune, bad luck
桜 *usuzakura* slightly tinted cherry blossoms
紙 *usugami* thin paper, tissue paper
紗 *hakusha* delicate gauze, gossamer
笑 *usue(mu)* smile, laugh a little. *usuwara(i)* faint smile
弱 *hakujaku* flimsiness, weakness; feebleness, infirmity
桃色 *usumomo-iro* peach-blossom pink
馬鹿 *usubaka* fool, simpleton, sluggard, half-wit
荷 *hakka* mint, peppermint
荷水 *hakkasui* peppermint solution
荷油 *hakayu* peppermint oil
荷脳 *hakkanō* menthol crystals
荷糖 *hakkatō* peppermint
11 黒 *usuguro(i)* dark, dusky, dingy
遇 *hakugū* cold reception
運 *haku-un* evil fate, misfortune
情 *hakujō* poor sense of duty; unkindness; coldheartedness; cruelty
商 *usuakina(i)* light trading

雪 *usuyuki* light snow; sugar-coated cookie
野呂 *usunoro* stupidity
12 給 *hakkyū* meager salary
鈍 *usunoro* simpleton, sluggard, half-wit
寒 *usu*(*ra*)*samu*(*i*) chilly
着 *usugi* thin clothing, scanty clothes
葉 *usuyō* thin paper, tracing paper
雲 *usugumo* thin clouds, fleecy clouds
紫 *usumurasaki* light purple, orchid
痘痕 *usuabata* light pockmarks
13 塩 *usujio* slightly salted
暗 *usugura*(*i*) dim; gloomy, somber. *usukura*(*gari*) dim light, gloom, dusk
絹 *usuginu* thin silk, sheer silk
14 層 *hakusō* thin layer, seam (in geology)
徳 *hakutoku* easy virtue
緑 *usumidori* light green
綿 *usuwata* light cotton padding
暮 *hakubo* nightfall, dusk, twilight
墨 *usuzumi* thin India ink
15 縁 *usuberi* bordered matting, thin matting
16 曇 *usugumo*(*ri*) slightly cloudy
薄 *usu-usu* thinly, slightly, vaguely, a little
髭 *usuhige* thin beard
鋼板 *usukōban* sheet steel
17 謝 *hakusha* small token of gratitude
霞 *usugasumi* light haze
18 織 *usuo*(*ri*) gauze
藤色 *usufuji iro* lilac color
19 霧 *usugiri* thin mist

14

舊 4076 / F1569 See 旧 94. [臼]

薰 4077 / F1641 See 薫 4073.

藏 4078 / F1643 See 蔵 4042.

薹 4079 / F1641 TAI. *tō* seed pod.

薯 4080 / F1641 SHO. *imo* potato.

藉 4081 / F1642 SHA, SEKI rug; borrow; lend; make excuses; spread out.
3 口 *shakō* pretense

藍 4082 / F1642 RAN. *ai* indigo (blue); indigo plant.
5 玉 *rangyoku* aquamarine (a gem). *aidama* indigo ball
6 色 *ai iro, ranshoku* dark blue
13 鼠 *ainezumi* bluish gray
16 靛 *ranjō* indigo

藁 4083 / F1642 KŌ. *wara* straw.
2 人形 *wara ningyō* straw effigy
4 火 *warabi* straw fire
5 半紙 *warabanshi* a low-grade paper
打機 *wara-u*(*chi*)*ki* straw-softening machine
6 灰 *warabai* straw ashes
8 沓 *waragutsu* straw shoes
苞 *warazuto* straw wrapper
9 屋根 *wara yane* straw roof
草履 *wara zōri* straw sandals
10 紙 *waragami* rice paper
家 *waraya* straw-thatched house
11 細工 *warazaiku* straw work
12 葺 *warabuki* straw thatch
13 靴 *waragutsu* straw shoes
筵 *wara mushiro* straw mat; straw matting
蓆 *wara mushiro* straw mat; straw matting
蒲団 *warabuton* straw mattress, straw pallet
19 縄 *wara nawa* straw rope

15

藷 See 4093.

藝 4084 / F1644 See 芸 3908.

藥 4085 / F1644 See 薬 4074.

藕 4086 / F1643 GŪ carpet; lend; borrow.
7 花 *gūke* lotus

繭 4087 / F1484 繭 KEN. *mayu* cocoon. [糸]
B
6 糸 *kenshi* cocoon and silk thread
8 価 *mayuka* the price of cocoons
11 紬 *kenchū* pongee

藪 4088 / F1646 籔 SŌ. *yabu* thicket, bush, underbrush, grove.
2 入 *yabu-i*(*ri*) servants' day, apprentices' holiday
7 医 *yabui* quack doctor
医者 *yabu isha* quack doctor
11 蛇 *yabuhebi* boomerang, hornet's nest, stirring up unnecessary trouble
13 睨 *yabunira*(*mi*) squint, cross-eye; wrong view

藩 4089 / F1645 HAN feudal clan; enclosure.
B
3 士 *hanshi* retainer
4 内 *hannai* within the fief
5 札 *hansatsu* a daimyo's paper money
主 *hanshu* feudal lord, daimyo

竹米糸缶网四羊羽老耂而耒耳聿肉月臣自至臼舌舛舟艮色【艸】
15【艹】虍虫血行衣ネ西

6老 *hanrō* head retainer
7邸 *hantei* daimyo's estate; daimyo's Edo estate
兵 *hampei* a daimyo's soldiers
8治 *hanchi* government of a fief
学 *hangaku* school for samurai children
9侯 *hankō* daimyo
政 *hansei* clan government
10校 *hankō* clan schools
恩 *han-on* the favor of a daimyo
11屏 *hampei* bulwark, pillar
12営 *han-ei* operated by the clan
14閥 *hambatsu* clanship, clannism
境 *hankyō* boundary of a fief
16儒 *hanju* a daimyo's scholar
20籍 *hanseki* fief

藤 4090/F1644 **藤** Tō. *fuji* wisteria.

4氏 *Tōshi* Fujiwara family
6色 *fuji iro* light purple, lilac, mauve, lavender
7花 *tōka* wisteria blossoms
8波 *fujinami* waves of wisteria flowers
10浪 *fujinami* waves of wisteria flowers
12棚 *fujidana* wisteria trellis
壺 *fujitsubo* barnacle
紫 *fuji murasaki* dark lilac, smalt, powder blue

16

蘂 See **蕊** 4045.

蘭 4091/F1649 **蘭** Ran orchid; Dutch.

2人 *Ranjin* Dutch people
4方 *Rampō* Dutch medicine
方医学 *Rampō igaku* Dutch medicine
6印 *Ran-in* Netherlands East Indies
7医 *Ran-i* Dutch physician
8学 *Rangaku* study of the Dutch language
14語 *Rango* the Dutch language
領東印度諸島 *Ranryō Higashi Indo Shotō* Netherlands East Indies

蘆 4092/F1647 See **芦** 3904.

藷 4093/F1646 Sho. *imo* potato.

藹 4094/F1646 Ai flourishing; be luxuriant; harmonize. *rō(taketa)* graceful, noble, refined.

19藹 *aiai to* harmoniously, peacefully

蘊 4095/F1648 Un pile up.

12奥 *un-ō, unnō* abstruse principles, esoteric doctrines, mysteries
13蓄 *unchiku* erudition, learning

藺 4096/F1646 Rin. *i* a rush (used for *tatami* covers).

9草 *igusa* a rush (used for *tatami* covers)
10莚 *imushiro* rush mat

蘇 4097/F1647 **蘓** So. Su. *yomigae(ru)* be resurrected, be revived, be resuscitated, be rehabilitated. *yomigae(ri)* resurrection; reviving, resuscitation; rehabilitation. *-So, So-* Soviet Union.

5生 *sosei* revival, resuscitation; resurrection
9連 *Soren* Union of Soviet Socialist Republics
連邦 *Sorempō* Soviet Union
連圏 *Sorenken* Soviet spere of influence
12満 *So-Man* Soviet and Manchuria

藻 4098/F1646 Sō. *mo* duckweed, seaweed.

7抜 *monu(ke)* cast-off skin
10屑 *mokuzu* seaweeds
13塩 *moshio* salt from burning seaweed
塩草 *moshiogusa* seaweed used in making salt; anthology
18類 *morui* seaweeds

17

蘖 4099/F1648 Getsu. *hikobae* sprout, offshoot, shoot.

蘞 4100/F1649 Ren a kind of weed.

7辛 *egara(i), egara(ppoi)* acrid, pungent

蘚 4101/F1649 Sen moss.

8苔学 *sentaigaku* bryology, the study of mosses
18類 *senrui* moss, lichen

驀 4102/F2104 Baku going straight forward; crossing over. [馬]

6地 *masshigura* straight
10進 *bakushin* dash, rush
12然 *bakuzen to* dashingly

蘭 4103/F1649 See **蘭** 4091.

19

蘿 4104/F1650 Ra ivy.

虍 RAD. 141

Tora kammuri or *toragashira* "tiger" top—really an enclosure. Nickname: Tiger.

2

虎 4105/F1651 虎 Ko. *tora* tiger, drunkard.
3口 *kokō* very dangerous place; tiger's den
子 *omaru* bedpan, pot. *tora (no) ko* tiger cub; one's treasure; one's savings
4刈 *toraga(ri)* close-cropped (head)
5穴 *koketsu* tiger's den; dangerous place
9狩 *toraga(ri)* tiger hunt
巻 *tora(no)maki* pony, answer book; trade secrets; the trump card; the authority; the open sesame
10挟 *torabasami* rattrap, steel trap
狼 *korō* tiger and wolf; wild beast; cruel man, brute
11視 *koshi suru* glare at
視眈眈 *koshi-tantan* on the alert; gloatingly; with vigilant hostility
12斑 *torafu, torabuchi* tiger's stripes
16嘯 *koshō* tiger's roar; hero's exploits
22鬚 *torahige* bristly beard

3

B 虐 4106/F1652 虐 Gyaku. *shieta(geru)*, *shiita(geru)* oppress, tyrannize.
3刃 *gyakujin* a cruel killing
6使 *gyakushi* driving hard, immoderation, abuse; exploitation
9待 *gyakutai* maltreatment, abuse, cruelty
政 *gyakusei* tyranny, despotism, oppressive government
10悩 *shieta(ge)-naya(masu)* oppress and afflict
殺 *gyakusatsu* massacre, butchery, carnage
11遇 *gyakugū* maltreatment, abuse, cruelty

4

虔 4107/F1652 Ken respect; be just.

5

處 4108/F1653 See 処 1162.

B 虚 4109/F1654 虚 Kyo, Ko emptiness; unpreparedness; crack, fissure; unguarded position; untruth. *muna(shiku) suru* make empty. *uro* cavity, hollow, hole. *ukke* emptiness. *muna(shii)* (see under 空 3317.0).
3士 *kyoshi* careless critic; samurai in name only
4文 *kyobun* worthless argument; mere surface decoration
日 *kyojitsu* day of leisure
心 *kyoshin* disinterestedness, lack of prejudice
心坦懐 *kyoshin tankai* frankness
5礼 *kyorei* formalities, empty forms
6伝 *kyoden* false rumor, false reputation
妄 *kyomō, kyobō* falsehood, something unsubstantiated; delusion, superstition
名 *kyomei* notoriety, false reputation, publicity
仮 *koke* dunce, idiot
仮威 *kokeodo(shi)* empty threat, bluff, imposing display
7言 *kyogen* falsehood
位 *kyo-i* titular post; vacant post
声 *kyosei* threatening voice
労 *kyorō* emaciation
8実 *kyojitsu* truth and falsehood; preparedness and unpreparedness; the situation
空 *kokū* empty space, empty sky
空摑 *kokū (o) tsuka(mu)* struggle for breath
9威 *kyo-i* empty boasting
乗 *kyo (ni) jō(jiru)* take advantage of someone's negligence
室 *kyoshitsu* an empty house
栄 *kyoei* vanity, vainglory
栄心 *kyoeishin* vanity, vainglory
10病 *kyobyō* feigned illness
耗 *kyomō* deterioration; disappearance; emaciation
弱 *kyojaku* feebleness, weakness; imbecility
弱児童 *kyojaku jidō* feeble children
弱者 *kyojakusha* feeble person
11虚実実 *kyokyo-jitsujitsu* clever competition; clever fighting
偽 *kyogi* falsehood, fiction, fallacy
偽申告 *kyogi shinkoku* perjury
脱 *kyodatsu* prostration, collapse
脱状態 *kyodatsu jōtai* despondency
12報 *kyohō* false alarm
無 *kyomu* nothingness
無主義 *kyomu shugi* nihilism
無党 *kyomutō* nihilists
無僧 *komusō* flute-playing Zen mendicant priests, mendicant flute player
13辞 *kyoji* a lie, falsehood
飾 *kyoshoku* ostentation, show, affectation
数 *kyosū* imaginary number
勢 *kyosei* bluff
勢張 *kyosei (o) ha(ru)* boast without reason
14聞 *kyobun* false rumor; false reputation
像 *kyozō* virtual image, ghost image (in optics)
構 *kyokō* fabrication, falsehood

6 竹米糸缶网四羊羽老耂而耒耳聿肉月臣自至臼舌舛舟艮色艸艹【虍5】虫血行衣衤西

説 *kyosetsu* false report; false theory
静 *kyosei* a calm and carefree heart
15 線 *kyosen* dotted line
談 *kyodan* baseless talk, rumor; false theory; Taoist talk; idle talk
誕 *kyotan* falsehood, fiction, fallacy
論 *kyoron* false argument
器 *kyoki* something in name only; nominal position
16 懐 *kyokai* a carefree heart

6

虛 See 虚 4109.

7

號 See 号 882.

B 虞 4110 / F1656 虞 Gu. *osore* fear; anxiety; concern; uneasiness.
9 美人草 *gubijinsō* field poppy, red poppy

B 虜 4111 / F1655 虜 Ryo captive; barbarian; low epithet for the enemy. *toriko* captive, victim, slave.
5 囚 *ryoshū* captive, prisoner
16 獲 *ryokaku* captive; capturing alive; capturing and killing

8

號 See 号 882.

9

B 慮 4112 / F741 Ryo thought, concern, agreement. *omombaka(ru), omompaka(ru)* consider, deliberate, fear. *omombaka(ri), omompaka(ri)* thought, consideration, prudence; fears, apprehension, strategy. [心]
5 外 *ryogai* emergency; unexpectedness; impoliteness

B 膚 4113 / F1551 Fu. *hada, hadae* skin, body; grain, texture; disposition. [肉]
6 色 *hada iro* flesh color
7 見 *fuken* superficial views
身 *hadami* the body
身離 *hadami-hana(sazu)* (purse and other articles) always carried on one's person
9 浅 *fusen* superficiality
11 脱 *hadanu(gi)* bare to the waist
12 焼 *hadaya(ki)* casehardening
寒 *hadasamu(i), hadazamu(i)* chilly
着 *hadagi* underwear
13 触 *hadazawa(ri)* the touch, the feel
19 襦袢 *hada juban* underwear

10

盧 4114 / F1315 Ro hut. [皿]

11

虧 See 252.

RAD. 虫 142

Mushi insect. At left: *mushi hen*. Nickname: Bug.

A 虫 4115 / F1657 / F1674 蟲 Chū *mushi* worm, vermin, bug, insect; temper; nervousness, peevishness; bad company.
3 干 *mushibos(hi)* airing (clothes and books)
下 *mushikuda(shi)* worm medicine
6 気 *mushike* bowel complaint, nervous weakness, trouble with worms
7 良 *mushi(no)i(i), mushi (ga)su(kanai)* selfish; arbitrary
売 *mushi-u(ri)* insect dealer
声 *chūsei* the humming of insects
8 送 *mushioku(ri)* torch procession to drive away insects
知 *mushi (ga) shi(rasu)* have a premonition
供養 *mushi kuyō* Buddhist memorial service for the bugs killed by the farmers plowing their fields
垂 *chūsui* the appendix
垂切除術 *chūsui setsujojutsu* appendectomy
垂炎 *chūsuien* appendicitis
9 食 *mushiba(mu)* be wormy. *mushiku(i)* worm-eaten spot
除 *mushiyo(ke)* insect powder, charm against insects
封 *mushifū(ji)* exorcism
10 害 *chūgai* insect pests, insect damage, blight
11 唾 *mushizu* sour eructation
眼鏡 *mushimegane* magnifying glass
12 歯 *mushiba* decayed tooth
喰 *mushikui* worm-eaten spot
媒花 *chūbaika* flower fertilized by insects
13 腹 *mushibara* worm pains
14 様垂 *chūyōsui* vermiform appendix
様突起 *chūyō tokki* the appendix
様突起炎 *chūyō tokkien* appendicitis

16薬 *mushigusuri* worm medicine
17螻 *mushikera* worm, insect; someone beneath one's notice
18類 *chūrui* worms and insects
22籠 *mushikago* insect case

2

虱 4116 F1669 蝨 SHITSU. *shirami* lice, vermin.
15潰 *shiramitsubu(shi) ni* one by one, individually

3

虻 4117 F1669 䖟 蝱 Bō. *abu* horsefly, gadfly.

虹 4118 F1657 Kō. *niji* rainbow.
11彩 *kōsai* iris (of the eye)
23鱒 *niji masu* rainbow trout

4

蚕 See 57.

蚜 See 蚜 4127.

蚪 4119 F1659 To tadpole.

蚓 4120 F1659 In earthworm.

蚋 4121 F1666 蜹 ZEI. NEI. ZETSU. NECHI. *buyu, buyo, butto* gnat, sand fly.
3子 *buyu* gnat, sand fly

蚤 4122 F1659 Sō. *nomi* flea.
8取 *nomito(ri)* flea catching; flea powder
取粉 *nomito(ri)ko* flea powder
取眼 *nomito(ri) manako* keen eyes

蚊 4123 F1658 蚉 BUN. *ka* mosquito.
B
8取線香 *katori senkō* mosquito incense
9屋 *kaya* mosquito net ⌈longlegs
姥 *ga(no)uba, kagambo, gagambo* daddy
柱 *kabashira* column of flying mosquitoes
除 *kayo(ke)* mosquito smudge; mosquito ⌊net
10針 *kabari* fishing fly, fly hook
11帳 *kaya, kachō* mosquito net
帳地 *kayaji* mosquito netting
12遣 *kayari* mosquito smudge
遣火 *kayaribi* mosquito smudge
遣線香 *kayari senkō* mosquito incense
13鉤 *kabari* fishing fly, fly hook
15幮 *kaya* mosquito net ⌈quitoes
18燻 *kafusu(be), ka-ibu(shi)* smoking out mos-

5

蛋 See 3019.

蛍 Nonstandard for 螢 4176.

蛉 4124 F1661 REI dragonfly; moon moth

蛅 4125 F1660 SEN larva of moth; grub.
18蟖 *kemushi* caterpillar

蚰 4126 F1660 Yū millipede.
13蜒 *gejigeji* millipede; wretch

蚜 4127 F1659 蚜 KA plant louse, aphis.
6虫 *aburamushi* plant louse, aphis

蛆 4128 F1660 So. *uji* worm, grub, maggot, larva.
6虫 *ujimushi*=*uji* (see under 蛆 4128.0)

蚯 4129 F1660 Kyū earthworm.
10蚓 *mimizu* earthworm
蚓書 *mimizuga(ki)* scrawl
蚓腫 *mimizubare* welt, inflamed scratch

蛇 4130 F1661 JA, DA (large) snake, serpent; hard drinker. *hebi, kuchinawa* snake.
3口 *jaguchi* faucet, hydrant; drain
5皮 *hebikawa* snakeskin
目 *ja(no)me* bull's-eye; umbrella with a bull's-eye design ⌈eye design
目傘 *ja(no)megasa* umbrella with a bull's-
6行 *dakō suru* crawl meanderingly. *dakō* meandering
7足 *dasoku* superfluity, redundancy, padding
身 *jashin* snakelike body
体 *jatai no* serpentine
状運動 *dajō undō* serpentine motion
8使 *hebitsuka(i)* snake charmer
毒 *jadoku* snake poison, venom
10紋石 *jamonseki* serpentine (a gem)
13腹 *jabara* bellows; cornice
14管 *jakan* hose
19蠍視 *dakatsushi suru* detest, hate like poison

22籠 *jakago* gabion, rock-filled bamboo embankment basket

6

蛮 See 322.

蛛 4131 F1662 CHU spider.

蛭 4132 F1662 SHITSU. *hiru* leech.

蛞 4133 F1662 KATSU a kind of slug.
15蝓 *namekuji* slug, dew snail

蛔 4134 F1661 KAI intestinal worms.
6虫 *kaichū* round intestinal worm

蛟 4135 F1662 KŌ dragon.
16龍 *kōryō* rain dragon; hidden genius

蛤 4136 F1662 KŌ. *hamaguri* clam.
17鍋 *hamanabe, hamagurinabe* clam chowder

蛙 4137 F1661 A. *kaeru, kawazu* frog.
7足 *kaeruashi* frog kick (in swimming)
8泳 *kaeruoyo(gi)* breast stroke
9飛 *kawazuto(bi)* leapfrog, island hopping
11釣 *kaerutsuri* frog fishing
13跳 *kaerutobi* leapfrog

7

蜃 See 4657.

蜀 See 3640.

蛸 4138 F1666 See 蚋 4121.

蜒 4139 F1665 EN meandering, serpentine.

蜓 4140 F1665 TEI millipede; lizard.

蜊 4141 F1664 RI a kind of bivalve.

蜍 4142 F1665 SHO toad.

蜋 4143 F1665 蜋 RŌ mantis.

蜆 4144 F1664 KEN. *shijimi* a fresh-water clam.
5汁 *shijimijiru* fresh-water-clam soup
7貝 *shijimigai* a fresh-water clam

蛻 4145 F1663 ZEI. *monu(keru)* (insects) molt; excel. *monuke* cast-off skin.

蜉 4146 F1664 FU kind of ant; May fly.
15蝣 *fuyū* May fly; something ephemeral

蛾 4147 F1663 GI. GA moth.
9眉 *gabi* arched eyebrows; a beauty

蛹 4148 F1663 YŌ *sanagi* chrysalis, pupa.
6虫 *yōchū* chrysalis, pupa

蛸 4149 F1663 SŌ. SHŌ. *tako* octopus, devilfish; pile driver; dirt tamper.
2入道 *takonyūdō* octopus; bald-headed man; ram
7坊主 *tako bōzu* octopus; bald-headed man
10配当 *tako haitō* bogus dividend (from fictitious profits)
11船 *takobune* paper nautilus
12壺 *takotsubo* octopus trap; foxhole

蜂 4150 F1664 HŌ. *hachi* bee, wasp, hornet.
8房 *hōbō* honeycomb; beehive; apiary
10起 *hōki* insurrection; disturbance
11鳥 *hachidori* hummingbird
雀 *hachisuzume* hummingbird
巣 *hachi (no) su* beehive, honeycomb
13腰 *hōyō* slender waist
14蜜 *hachimitsu* honey
窩 *hōka* beehive
21蠟 *hachirō* beeswax, bee glue

8

蜒 See 4139.

蝕 See 5165.

蜚 See 5084.

蜜 See 1336.

蜩 4151 / F1666 Chō *higurashi* clear-toned cicada.

蜴 4152 / F1666 Eki lizard.

蜱 4153 / F-X *dani* tick, mite.

蜿 4154 / F1667 En meandering.
13 蜒 *en-en(taru)* meandering, serpentine

蜥 4155 / F1666 Shaku, Seki a lizard.
14 蜴 *tokage* lizard

蜷 4156 / F1666 Ken. *nina* a small spiral edible river shell.
7 局 *toguro* coil, spiral

蜻 4157 / F1667 Sei dragonfly.
11 蛉 *tombo* dragonfly
蛉返 *tombogae(ri)* somersault; looping the loop
蛉釣 *tombotsu(ri)* dragonfly catching; dragonfly catcher
13 蜓 *tombo* dragonfly

蜘 4158 / F1665 Chi spider.
12 蛛 *kumo* spider
蛛手 *kumode* crossing of many streets; confusion of mind. *kumode ni* crosswise; in various directions
蛛巣 *kumo(no)su* spiderweb
蛛蟹 *kumogani* spider crab

9

蜱 See 4153.

蝱 See 虻 4117.

蝨 4159 / F1669 See 虱 4116.

螂 4160 / F1670 See 蜋 4143.

蝉 Nonstandard for 蟬 4190.

蝿 Nonstandard for 蠅 4194.

蝓 4161 / F1667 Yu slug, snail.

蝣 4162 / F1668 Yū May fly.

蝠 4163 / F1668 Fuku bat.

蝎 4164 / F1667 蠍 Katsu. *sasori* scorpion.

蝮 4165 / F1669 Fuku. *mamushi* viper, adder, asp.

蝌 4166 / F1667 Ka tadpole.
10 蚪 *otamajakushi, kato* tadpole

蝟 4167 / F1668 I. *harinezumi* hedgehog.
12 集 *ishū suru* swarm, throng, flock together

蝙 4168 / F1668 Hen bat.
15 蝠 *kōmori* bat; umbrella, parasol
蝠傘 *kōmorigasa* umbrella, parasol

蝗 4169 / F1668 Kō. *inago, batta* locust.
6 虫 *inago* grasshopper
10 害 *kōgai* locust damage

蝸 4170 / F1669 Ka snail.
4 牛 *katatsumuri, katatsuburi, dedemushi, dendemmushi, kagyū* snail
牛殻 *kagyūkaku* snail shell
19 廬 *karo* little house; my humble home

蝶 4171 / F1669 Chō butterfly.
7 貝 *chōgai* pearl oyster, mother-of-pearl
形 *chōgata* butterfly-shaped
12 結 *chōmusu(bi)* bowknot
番 *chōtsugai* hinge, hinge joint
15 蝶 *chōchō* butterfly
17 鮫 *chōzame* sturgeon
18 類 *chōrui* butterflies

蝦 4172 / F1668 Ka. Ge. *ebi* lobster, shrimp, prawn.
6 夷 *Ezo* Ainu; Hokkaido. *Emishi, Emisu* Ainu
夷地 *Ezochi* Hokkaido
夷松 *Ezo matsu* spruce, silver fir
13 腰 *ebigoshi* bent with age
16 錠 *ebijō* podlock
蟇 *gama* toad, bullfrog
蟇口 *gamaguchi* purse
蟇足 *gama ashi* breast stroke
19 蟹 *ebigani* crawfish, crayfish

10

融 See 5274.

蟆 4173/F1673 See 蟇 4065.
3子 *buyo* gnat, sand fly

螕 4174/F1670 Hei. *dani* tick, mite.

螟 4175/F1670 Mei an injurious parasite.
6虫 *meichū* rice borer, pearl moth

螢 4176/F1671 Kei. *hotaru* firefly.
4火 *keika* light of a firefly. *hotarubi* the light of a firefly; small banked fire (charcoal)
5石 *keiseki, hotaru ishi* fluorspar, fluorite
6光 *keikō* fluorescence. *hotaru (no) hikari* light of a firefly
光灯 *keikōtō* fluorescent light
光体 *keikōtai* fluorescent body
光板 *keikōban* fluorescent screen or plate
光物質 *keikō busshitsu* fluorescent body
光染料 *keikō senryō* fluorescent dyes
光透視法 *keikōtōshihō* fluoroscopy
光塗料 *keikō toryō* fluorescent paint
9狩 *hotaruga(ri)* firefly catching
11雪 *keisetsu* diligent study
雪功 *keisetsu (no) kō* the fruit of diligent study
雪時代 *keisetsu jidai* school days

11

螽 See 1165.

螳 4177/F1671 See 蟷 4193.

螯 4178/F1671 Gō. *hasami* claws, pincers.

蟒 4179/F1673 蠎 Bō. Mō. *uwabami* anaconda; boa constrictor; python.

螫 4180/F1671 Seki. *sa(su)*, (bee's) sting.
13傷 *sashikizu* a bite (injury)

蟀 4181/F1672 Shutsu cricket; grasshopper.
7谷 *komekami* temple (of the head)

蟋 4182/F1673 Shitsu cricket; grasshopper.
17蟀 *kōrogi* cricket
18蟖 *kirigirisu* grasshopper, katydid

蟄 4183/F1672 Chitsu. *chis(suru)* hibernation of insects.
6伏 *chippuku* hibernation; concealment
8居 *chikkyo suru* be cooped up, stay indoors. *chikkyo* house arrest

螺 4184/F1672 Ra. *nishi* a small edible spiral river shell.
3子 *neji, rashi* screw, faucet, (watch) spring
7状 *rajō* screw shape, spiral
11階 *rakai* winding staircase
旋 *neji* screw; faucet; (watch) spring. *rasen* screw; spiral; spiral spring
旋切 *nejiki(ri)* threader; thread cutting
旋回 *nejimawa(shi)* screwdriver, wrench
旋状 *rasenjō* screw shape, spiral
旋形 *rasenkei* screw shape, spiral
旋降下 *rasen kōka* spiral dive
旋銃 *rasenjū* rifle
13鈿 *raden* mother-of-pearl

12

蟲 4185/F1674 See 虫 4115.

蠎 4186/F1676 See 蟒 4179.

蟖 4187/F1673 Shi larva of a moth; grasshopper.

蟯 4188/F1674 Gyō an intestinal worm.
6虫 *gyōchū* pinworm, threadworm

蟠 4189/F1673 Han. Ban. *wadakama(ru)* be coiled up; stretch out tortuously; lurk, be harbored. *wadakama(ri)* vexations, cares; ill feeling; reserve.
15踞 *bankyo suru* possess and dominate a wide area

蟬 4190/F1674 Sen. *semi* cicada, locust.
7吟 *sengin* cry of the cicada
声 *semigoe* voice like a cricket
10時雨 *semi shigure* an outburst of cricket chirping
11脱 *sendatsu* a cicada's shell; leaving this world; a shell only
13蛻 *senzei* a cicada's shell; leaving this world

6 竹米糸缶网罒羊羽老耂而耒耳聿肉月臣自至臼舌舛舟艮色艸卝虍【虫】20 血行衣衤西

13

蠍 4191 F-X See 蝎 4164.

蟾 4192 F1675 SEN toad.
13 蜍 *hikigaeru* toad

蟷 4193 F1671 = 螳 Tō mantis.
13 蜋 *kamakiri, tōrō* praying mantis

蠅 4194 F1675 Yō. *hae, hai* fly.
5 叩 *haitataki* fly swatter
打 *haeu(chi)* fly swatter
6 取 *haeto(ri), haito(ri)* flycatcher
取草 *haito(ri)gusa* Venus's flytrap
取粉 *haito(ri)ko* fly powder
取紙 *haito(ri)gami* flypaper

蟹 4195 F1675 = 蠏 KAI. *kani* crab.
3 工船 *kanikōsen* crab-canning ship
4 文字 *kani monji, kani moji* horizontal writing, Western writing
6 行 *kaikō* walking sideways
行文字 *kaikō monji, kaikō moji* horizontal writing, Western writing
8 股 *ganimata* bowlegged
23 罐 *kanikan* canned crab

蟻 4196 F1675 GI. *ari* ant.
6 地獄 *arijigoku* ant lion
7 町 *ari(no)machi* slum
9 軍 *gigun* ant army
巻 *arimaki* ant cow
10 差 *ariza(shi)* dovetail joint
12 塔 *ari(no)tō* anthill
集 *gishū suru* swarm, crowd together, flock together
13 塚 *arizuka* anthill
継 *aritsu(gi)* dovetail joint
14 酸 *gisan* formic acid

14

蠕 419, F1676 ZEN crawling (of a worm), squirming, moving.
11 動 *zendō suru* creep, worm along. *zendō* peristaltic movement
動運動 *zendō undō* peristaltic movement

15

蠣 4198 F1677 REI oyster.

蠢 4199 F1677 SHUN. *ugo(meku)* wriggle, squirm. *ugo(mekasu)* be elated with success.
11 動 *shundō* wriggling, squirming; despicable acts

蠟 4200 F1677 Rō wax.
2 人形 *rō ningyō* wax figure
4 引 *rōbi(ki)* waxing
5 石 *rōseki* alabaster, pencil stone
付 *rōzu(ke)* soldering
付鏝 *rōzu(ke) kote* soldering iron
10 紙 *rōgami* wax paper
11 細工 *rōzaiku* waxwork
12 着剤 *rōzu(ke)zai* soldering flux
14 様 *rōyō no* waxy, waxen
製 *rōsei* waxen, wax
17 燭 *rōsoku* candle

16

蠧 See 1158.

17

蠱 4201 F1678 Ko a destructive rice worm; lead astray.
12 惑 *kowaku* fascination, enchantment, glamor; delusion, seduction
惑的 *kowakuteki* fascinating, alluring

18

蠹 4202 F1679 See 蠧 1158.

蠵 4203 F1678 KEI, KI a kind of turtle.
11 亀 *taimai* hawksbill turtle; tortoise shell

19

蠻 4204 F1679 See 蛮 322.

20

蠶 蠺 See 蚕 57.

RAD. 血 143

Chi blood. At left: 血 *chi hen*. Nickname: Dotted Dish (cf. Rad. 108).

A 血 4205/F1680 KETSU blood. *chi* blood, consanguinity. *chi(bamu)* become bloody. *chi(darake)* bloody, bloodstained.

2 刀 *chigatana* bloodstained blade
4 文 *chibumi* document written in blood
止 *chido(me)* styptic
友病 *ketsuyūbyō* bleeders' affliction, hemophilia
5 石 *kesseki* bloodstone
巡 *chi (no) megu(ri)* circulation of the blood
玉髄 *ketsugyokuzui* bloodstone
圧 *ketsuatsu* blood pressure
圧計 *ketsuatsukei* sphygmomanometer
6 肉 *ketsuniku* flesh and blood
行 *kekkō* circulation of the blood
印 *ketsuin* blood seal
汗 *kekkan* bloody sweat. *chi(to)ase* industry and patience
合 *chia(i)* fish meat of bloody color
色 *kesshoku* complexion
色素 *kesshikiso* hemoglobin
汐 *chishio* blood
汐海 *chishio (no) umi* pool of blood
気 *kekki* youthful vigor, hot blood. *chi(no)ke* blood
気多 *chi(no)ke (no) ō(i)* ruddy, full-blooded, hotheaded
気無 *chi(no)ke (no) na(i)* pale, white as a sheet
気盛 *kekkizaka(ri) no* vigorous, sanguine
7 豆 *chimame* blood blister
走 *chibashi(ru)* become bloodshot
尿 *ketsunyō* blood in the urine
沈 *ketchin* precipitation of blood
判 *keppan* seal of blood
判書 *keppansho* petition sealed in blood
8 雨 *chi(no)ame* bloodshed
迷 *chimayo(u)* lose control of oneself, run wild, be out of one's head
性 *kessei no* bloody
性便 *kesseiben* bloody stools
9 胤 *ketsuin* lineage, descendants
便 *ketsuben* bloody stools
相 *kessō* expression, looks
染 *chizo(me) no* bloodstained
10 振 *chibu(rui)* shaking off the blood; puerperal vertigo
涙 *chi (no) namida, ketsurui* tears of blood; bitter tears
脈 *ketsumyaku* blood vessel; blood relationship
書 *kessho* writing in blood
栓 *kessen* thrombus
栓症 *kessenshō* thrombosis
11 痕 *kekkon* bloodstain
道 *chi (no) michi* (women's) dizziness; hysterics; brain congestion
清 *kessei* blood serum, lymph
眼 *chimanako* bloodshot eye; earnest searching
祭 *chimatsu(ri)* blood offering, offering to the war god
達磨 *chidaruma* covered with blood
族 *ketsuzoku* blood relative
族結婚 *ketsuzoku kekkon* consanguineous marriage, intermarriage
球 *kekkyū* corpuscle
球計算 *kekkyū keisan* blood count
液 *ketsueki* blood
液欠乏 *ketsueki ketsubō* anemia
液型 *ketsuekigata* blood type
液病 *ketsuekibyō* a blood disorder
液移送 *ketsueki isō* blood transfusion
液検査 *ketsueki kensa* blood test
液循環 *ketsueki junkan* blood circulation
液像 *ketsuekizō* differential blood count
液銀行 *ketsueki ginkō* blood bank
液輸送 *ketsueki yusō* blood transfusion
12 斑 *keppan* blood spot
税 *ketsuzei* blood tax, heavy taxation; conscription
統 *kettō* lineage, pedigree, family line
筋 *chisuji* blood relationship, lineage, stock, strain
13 痰 *kettan* bloody phlegm
塊 *kekkai* bloot clot, clotted blood
煙 *chi kemuri* spray of blood
続 *chitsuzu(ki)* continuous lineage
腥 *chinamagusa(i)* bloody
路 *ketsuro* a way out, the way thru, a way of escape
戦 *kessen* bloody battle
塗 *chinu(ru)* smear with blood. *chimami(re)*, *chimidoro* bloodstained
盟 *ketsumei* blood pledge
盟団 *ketsumeidan* blood brotherhood, daredevil party
14 管 *kekkan* blood vessel
瑪瑙 *ketsumenō* bloodstone
15 潮 *chishio* the blood
糊 *chinori* slimy blood
縁 *ketsuen* blood relative; blood relationship
漿 *kesshō* blood plasma, serum
16 糖 *kettō* blood sugar
17 膿 *chi umi* bloody pus

2

衂 See 衄 4208.

衄 4206/F300 SHUTSU, JUTSU have mercy on. [卩]

— 3 —

衂 4207/F-X See 衄 4208.

— 4 —

衄 4208/F1681 = 衂 衂 衂 𧗼

JIKU nosebleed.
[6] 血 *hanaji, jinketsu* nosebleed

— 6 —

衉 4209/F1682 KAKU vomit.

A 衆 4210/F1681 SHU, SHŪ great numbers, multitude, populace; companions.
[2] 人 *shūjin* many people; the public
[3] 口一致 *shūkō-itchi shite* by common consent, unanimously
[4] 心 *shūshin* public feeling, the feeling of many
[5] 生 *shujō* mankind, human beings; all living beings
目 *shūmoku* public attention
[6] 多 *shūta* great numbers
[7] 芳 *shūhō* all kinds of flowers; many fragrant flowers
[8] 知 *shūchi* the wisdom of all
苦 *shūku* much distress; the hardships of people
参両院 *Shūsan-ryōin* both Houses of the Diet
[9] 院 *Shūin* House of Representatives
怨 *shūen* public hatred, public grievance
怒 *shūdo* the wrath of many
[10] 座 *shūza* large meetinghouse
徒 *shuto, shūto* many priests. *shuto* priests studying in a large temple; priest soldiers
辱 *shūjoku* being humiliated before many
[11] 庶 *shūsho* common people, populace, masses
遇 *shūgu* ignorant crowd, mob, unthinking masses
望 *shūbō* the hope of many people; popular sentiment
[12] 評 *shūhyō* popular opinion
智 *shūchi* the wisdom of many
[13] 意 *shūi* the ideas of the people
愚 *shūgu* many fools
[14] 説 *shūsetsu* many theories
寡 *shūka* odds, disparity in numbers
[15] 慮 *shūryo* the ideas of many
論 *shūron* the argument of many
敵 *shūteki* numerous enemies
[20] 議 *shūgi* deliberation, public discussion
議一決 *shūgi-ikketsu suru* decide in council
議所 *shūgisho* council
議院 *Shūgi-in* Lower House
議院議長 *Shūgi-in Gichō* Speaker of the House Lower House
議院議員 *Shūgi-in gi-in* member of the

— 8 —

睾 4211/F1329 KŌ testicles. [目]
[3] 丸 *kōgan* testicles

— 14 —

𧗼 4212/F-X See 衄 4208.

行 RAD. 144

Yukigamae or *gyōgamae* "going" enclosure. With the exception of the radical character itself, shown below, all characters historically belonging to this radical are herein treated under Rad. 60. Nickname: Going.

A 行 4213/F1682 AN. KŌ party, suite; journey; expedition; line, row. GYŌ line, row; religious austerities. *i(ku), yu(ku)* go; run (water). *gyō(suru)* act, conduct oneself. *i(keru)* can go; can drink; can speak (a language); good. *oko(nau)* do, act, conduct oneself; carry out; perform, conduct (school); exercise (control); hold (a ceremony). *okona(wareru)* be practiced; become operative; take place; prevail, obtain; come into use; continue. *ya(ru)* (see under 遣 4732.0). *yu(ki), i(ki)* going; travel. *i(ttakiri)* gone for good. *yu(kikkiri)* gone for good. *oko(nai)* act, action, deed, conduct, behavior, religious austerities. *kudari* column of print; sentence. *-yuki* bound for.
[2] 人 *kōjin* passerby, pedestrian
[4] 手 *yukute* destination, route, objective
止 *yu(ki)do(mari), i(ki)do(mari)* no passage, dead end, blind alley
水 *gyōzui* tub bath
火 *anka* bed warmer, foot warmer
文 *kōbun* writing; style; diction; literature
文流麗 *kōbun-ryūrei* clever and speedy writing
方 *yu(ki)gata* the direction one is to go. *yu(ki)kata* way of doing. *yukue* whereabouts

方不明 *yukue-fumei* missing; unaccounted for ⌈homeless
方定 *yukue-sada(menu)* aimless, wandering,
5 巡 *yu(ki)-megu(ru), i(ki)-megu(ru)* go around
付 *i(ki)isu(ke), yu(ki)tsu(ke) no* habitual, regular, favorite
末 *yu(ku)sue* one's future, fate
司 *gyōji* wrestling referee ⌈lain pan
平 *yukihira* casserole, white glazed porce-
平鍋 *yukihira nabe* casserole, white glazed porcelain pan
6 行 *yu(ku)yu(ku)* on the way; go on and on. *yu(ku)yu(ku) wa* in the future, some day
回 *yu(ki)-megu(ru)* go around
返 *yu(ki)-kae(ru)* make a round trip. *i(ki)-kae(ri)* round trip
次 *yu(ki)shina, i(ki)shina* on the way
列 *gyōretsu* procession, parade, queue
灯 *andon* paper-enclosed oil light
交 *yu(ki)-ka(u)* come and go. *yu(ki)kō, yu(ki)ka(i)* coming and going; street traffic; swing (of a pendulum); social intercourse ⌈with
合 *yu(ki)-a(u)* meet, come across, fall in
会 *i(ki)-a(u)* meet on the way
当 *yu(ki)-a(taru), i(ki)-a(taru)*, come up against, be struck by. *yu(ki)a(tari-battari)* haphazard, happy-go-lucky ⌈of years
年 *gyōnen* age at death. *kōnen* age, number
先 *yu(ku)saki, yu(ki)saki, i(ki)saki, i(ku)saki* destination, whereabouts, address. *yu(ku)saki* one's future, fate
先先 *yu(ku) sakisaki de* wherever one goes
在 *anzai*=next word
在所 *anzaisho* emperor's temporary headquarters
成 *yu(ki)na(ri)* leaving things to chance. *i(ki)nari* suddenly, abruptly
成三宝 *yu(ki)na(ri)-sambō* careless fellow
成放題 *i(ki)na(ri)-hōdai, yu(ki)na(ri)-hōdai* letting things slide; careless and slovenly
7 戻 *yu(ki)modo(ri)* round trip; divorced wife
体 *gyōtai* appearance; cursive characters
状 *gyōjō* behavior, conduct, deportment, manners
別 *yu(ki)-waka(reru)* go separate ways
住坐臥 *gyōjū-zaga* daily life; walking, stopping, sitting and lying down
李 *kōri* wicker telescope trunk; baggage; travel preparations ⌈trunks
李詰 *kōrizume* packing in wicker telescope
8 金 *kōkin* bank funds
届 *yu(ki)-todo(ku)* be scrupulous, be attentive, be careful, be prudent, be thoro, be hospitable
迷 *yu(ki)-mayo(u)* miss one's way
使 *kōshi suru* use; exercise (rights); put in circulation
所 *yu(ki)dokoro* destination; whereabouts
幸 *gyōkō, miyuki* journey, visit, or attendance of the emperor
者 *gyōja* devotee, ascetic, pilgrim
事 *gyōji* event, function, observance
9 連 *yu(ki)-tsu(reru)* accompany
通 *yu(ki)-kayo(u), i(ki)-kayo(u)* come and go
客 *kōkaku* passer-by, pedestrian, traveler
星 *kōsei* planet
草 *gyōsō* cursive and grass hand
春 *yu(ku) haru* departing spring
軍 *kōgun* march, marching
軍命令 *kōgun meirei* marching orders
軍路 *kōgunro* line of march, route
為 *kōi* act, deed, conduct, transaction, practices. *yu(ki)na(ri)* leaving things to chance
為三宝 *yu(ki)na(ri)-sambō* careless fellow
為者 *kōisha* actor, transactor, offender
政 *gyōsei* administration
政下 *gyōseika* under the jurisdiction of
政学 *gyōseigaku* political science
政部 *gyōseibu* the adminstration
政権 *gyōseiken* administrative authority
10 逸 *yu(ki)-hagu(reru)* go astray, get lost
逢 *i(ki)-a(u)* meet on the way
倒 *ikidao(re), yukidao(re)* falling ill on the road; falling dead on the road
悩 *yu(ki)-naya(mu)* be deadlocked, be in
旅 *kōryo* travel; traveler ⌊difficulty
員 *kōin* bank clerk
宮 *angū* emperor's temporary palace
書 *gyōsho* semicursive writing
進 *kōshin* advance; march; parade
進曲 *kōshinkyoku* (musical) march
11 過 *i(ki)-su(giru), yu(ki)-su(giru)* go too far, go to extremes, go beyond. *yukisu(gi)* going too far; going to extremes; overdoing
違 *yu(ki)-chiga(eru)* mistake one's direction. *yu(ki)chiga(i), i(ki)chiga(i)* crossing; missing each other; misunderstanding, disagreement; error
務 *kōmu* bank business ⌈or a crown prince
啓 *gyōkei* visit or attendance of an empress
掛 *yu(ki)ga(ke), i(ki)ga(ke)* on the way. *yu(ki)-ga(kari) de* by force of circumstances ⌈stances
掛上 *yu(ki)ga(kari)jō* by force of circum-
脚 *angya* pilgrimage; (a priest's) walking
脚僧 *angyasō* itinerant priest ⌊tour; tour
商 *gyōshō* peddling, itinerant trade; peddler
商人 *gyōshōnin* peddler, commercial traveler

動 *kōdō* action, conduct, movements, operations
動力 *kōdōryoku* ability to act
動半径 *kōdō hankei* cruising radius; sphere of activity
動主義 *kōdō shugi* behaviorism
動隊 *kōdōtai* action group
動開始 *kōdō kaishi* deployment
動開始日 *kōdō kaishibi* D-day
動開始時間 *kōdō kaishi jikan* zero hour
動様式 *kodō yōshiki* behavior pattern
動態型 *kōdō taikei* behavior pattern
動範囲 *kōdō han-i* sphere of action
[12] 場 *yu(ki)ba* place to go, resort, destination
渡 *yu(ki)-wata(ru), i(ki)-wata(ru)* extend; prevail; spread; penetrate; reach
程 *kōtei* distance; journey; march; itinerary; stroke (of a piston)
着 *i(ki)-tsu(ku), yu(ki)-tsu(ku)* arrive at, reach
惑 *yu(ki)-mayo(u)* miss one's way
装 *kōsō* traveling attire
雲 *kōun* moving clouds
雲流水 *kōun-ryūsui* moving clouds and running water; taking life easy
間 *gyōkan* between the lines
間注 *gyōkanchū* interlinear notes
[13] 殿 *anden* emperor's temporary abode
続 *yu(ki)-tsuzu(keru)* continue to frequent
詰 *yu(ki)-zu(maru), i(ki)-zu(maru), yu(ki)-tsu(maru)* be deadlocked, come to a standstill, be reduced to the last extremity, go to the wall; be tongue-tied
跡 *gyōseki* conduct, behavior
路 *kōro* path, road, course, career
路病者 *kōro byōsha* person taken ill on the road
楽 *kōraku* picnic, excursion; having a good time
楽地 *kōrakuchi* pleasure resort
楽客 *kōrakukyaku* excursionists
[14] 摺 *yukizuri*＝行摩 (see below–15)
暮 *yu(ki)kureta* belated, benighted
[15] 摩 *yukizuri* passing closely; time of passing; on the way; temporary action
儀 *gyōgi* behavior, manners, deportment
澄 *okona(i)-su(masu)* follow Buddhist teachings; put on airs; pose (as someone)
賞 *kōshō* conferring of rewards
[22] 嚢 *kōnō* knapsack; mail bag; wallet

RAD. 衣 145

Koromo clothes. At left: 衤 (5 strokes), *koromo hen*. Nickname: Clothing.

A **衣** 4214 / F1689 E, I garment. *koromo* clothes, robe; dressing; frosting; coating. *kinu* clothing, kimono.
[4] 手 *koromode* sleeve
[5] 生活 *iseikatsu* clothing habits
[8] 服 *ifuku* clothes, clothing
服室 *ifukushitsu* wardrobe (room)
[9] 香 *ikō* perfume on the clothing
架 *ika* clothes rack
食 *ishoku* food and clothes, livelihood
食住 *ishokujū* food, clothing, and shelter; necessities of life
冠 *ikan* kimono and (ancient) head dress
冠束帯 *ikan-sokutai* full traditional ceremonial court dress; Shinto priest's garb
[10] 桁 *ikō* clothes rack
料 *iryō* clothing
帯 *itai* clothes and obi; full court dress
紋 *emon* dress, clothes, drapery (of a statue)
紋掛 *emonka(ke)* coat hanger
[11] 魚 *shimi* clothes moth, silverfish, bookworm
[12] 替 *koromoga(e)* seasonal change of clothes
装 *ishō* clothes, wardrobe, costume
[13] 鉢 *ihatsu, ehatsu* assuming the mantle of
[14] 摺 *kinuzure* rustling (of clothes)
裳 *ishō* clothes, costume, wardrobe
裳方 *ishōkata* theatrical dresser
裳屋 *ishōya* costumer
裳持 *ishōmo(chi)* woman with a large wardrobe
裳部屋 *ishōbeya* wardrobe
裳道楽 *ishō-dōraku* extravagant in dress
[15] 摩 *kinuzure* rustling of clothes
[18] 類 *irui* clothing
[22] 嚢 *kakushi* pocket

— 2 —

表 See 108.

A **初** 4215 / F236 SHO beginning; first. *haji(meru), haji(maru)* (see under 始 1208.0). *haji(mete)* (for) the first time; not until. *hatsu* beginning, first, new. *haji(me)* beginning, origin. *-haji(me)* including, and, as well as. *-so(meru)* begin to. *ui-* first (time), beginning. *hatsu-* new, the first (snow), maiden (voyage). *-some* begin to.... 【刀】
[1] 一見 *sho-ikken* first sight, first glance
一念 *sho-ichinen* original intention, first desire
[2] 七日 *shonanuka* seventh day since death

3口 *shokuchi* beginning, start
子 *hatsugo* first child
4手 *shote* beginning, start
天辺 *shoteppen* topmost, first and foremost
公演 *shokōen* premiere
心 *shoshin* original aim, original intention; inexperience
心者 *shoshinsha* beginner
日 *hatsuhi* New Year's Day sunrise. *shonichi* first day, opening day, first performance. *shojitsu* first day; dawn
日出 *hatsuhi(no)de* New Year's Day sunrise
中 *shotchū* all the time, constantly, always
中終 *shotchū* all the time, constantly, always
5句 *shoku* first line (of a poem)
犯 *shohan* first offense; first offender
冬 *shotō* beginning of winter; 10th lunar month
氷 *hatsugōri* the first ice
出 *shoshutsu* first appearance
生 *hatsunari* first fruit of the season
生児 *shoseiji* newborn infant
代 *shodai* the first generation; the founder
代教会 *Shodai Kyōkai* the Early Church
6老 *shorō* age forty
耳 *hatsumimi* something heard for the first time
旬 *shojun* first ten days of the month
回 *shokai* first time; first inning
号 *shogō* first number (of a magazine, etc.)
任 *shonin* first appointment
任給 *shoninkyū* initial salary
年 *shonen* first year, early years
年兵 *shonenhei* new conscript, raw recruit
年級 *shonenkyū* beginners' class
7初 *uiui(shii)* innocent, artless, unsophisticated
更 *shokō* the first of five night watches, 8-10 p.m.
志 *shoshi* original aim, original intention
売 *hatsu-u(ri)* first sale of the new year
花 *hatsuhana* the first flowers; the first cherry blossoms
対面 *shotaimen* first meeting, first interview
見 *shoken* seeing for the first time
見参 *uikenzan* first interview
8刷 *hatsuzu(ri)* first printing; first printing of the new year
版 *shohan* first edition
物 *hatsumono* season's first product
夜 *shoya* first watch of the night; bridal night
歩 *shoho* first steps, elements, primer
空 *hatsusora* first springlike sky; first sky suggesting the new season
学 *shogaku* beginning to study; such a person
学者 *shogakusha* beginning student
学書 *shogakusho* primer, elementary book
9音 *hatsune* first song (of a bird)
速 *shosoku* initial velocity, muzzle velocity
便 *hatsudayo(ri)* first letter of the new year
秋 *hatsuaki, shoshū* early fall
級 *shokyū* beginners' class
陣 *uijin* one's first battle, baptism of fire
段 *shodan* lowest grade
茸 *hatsutake* a kind of mushroom
春 *hatsuharu, shoshun* early spring
信者 *shoshinja* new believer
紅葉 *hatsumomijiba, hatsumomiji* first colored maple leaves
発 *shohatsu* first, initial, incipient
発病 *shohatsubyō* incipient disease
10値 *hatsune* first price
孫 *uimago, hatsumago* first grandchild
校 *shokō* first proof
夏 *shoka, hatsunatsu* early summer
恋 *hatsukoi* first love; puppy love
荷 *hatsuni* first load of the new year
時雨 *hatsushigure* first winter rain
航海 *hatsukōkai* maiden voyage
11頃 *hajimegoro* near the beginning
婚 *shokon* first marriage
経 *shokei* first menstruation
終 *haji(me)-owa(ri)* beginning and end, particulars, circumstances
雪 *hatsuyuki* the first snow
教会 *Shokyōkai* the Early Church
産 *hatsuzan, uizan, shozan* first childbirth
産婦 *shosampu* primipara, a woman having her first child
12雁 *hatsukari* first wild goose
給 *shokyū* initial salary
期 *shoki* early days, early years, early stage, beginning
筆 *shohitsu, shofude* first writing
診 *shoshin* first medical examination
診料 *shoshinryō* first medical examination fee
等 *shotō* elementary
等科 *shotōka* elementary course, beginners' class
等教育 *shotō kyōiku* elementary education
13詣 *hatsumōde* first shrine or temple visit in the new year
戦 *shosen* beginning of hostilities
幕 *shomaku* curtain raiser
夢 *hatsuyume* first dream of the new year
14演 *shoen* first performance
舞台 *hatsubutai* stage debut
15幟 *hatsunobori* first Boys' Festival streamer
潮 *shochō* first menstruation
穂 *hatsuho* first harvest, first fruits, first grains
縁 *shoen* first marriage
審 *shoshin* first trial
審裁判所 *shoshin saibansho* court of first instance
16頭 *shotō* early, elementary; at first
興行 *hatsukōgyō* first performance
17臨 *Shorin* First Advent (of Christ)
霜 *hatsushimo* the first frost
18雛 *hatsubina* a girl's first Doll Festival
顔合 *hatsukao-a(wase)* first meeting

3

衷 See 110.

表 See 108.

4

袁 See 1082.

衾 See 317.

衾 See 465.

衰 衰 See 312.

衷 See 衷 110.

袂 4216 F1694 BEI. *tamoto* sleeve; bag of the sleeve; foot (of a hill); edge; approach.

衿 4217 F1693 KIN. *eri* neck, neckband, collar, lapel. (See under 襟 4267 for compounds.)

衽 4218 F1693 袵 JIN. *kokubi* neck of a garment. *okumi* gusset, gore.

5

袠 See 315.

衾 See 317.

袍 4219 F1694 HŌ coat.

袒 4220 F1694 TAN baring the shoulder; strip to the waist.

袢 4221 F1695 HAN summer kimono, short clothing.

袈 4222 F1694 KE a coarse camlet.

13裟 *kesa* Buddhist priest's stole, sacred shoulder scarf

裟掛 *kesaga(ke)* hanging diagonally from the shoulder; a diagonal sword-cut from the shoulder

裟斬 *kesagi(ri)* cutting (a man) diagonally from the shoulder

B 袋 4223 F1694 TEI. TAI bag; bag counter. *fukuro* bag, sack, pouch. (*o*)-*fukuro* mama.

2入 *fukuro-i(ri)* pouched, sacked
3小路 *fukurokōji* blind alley
4戸棚 *fukurotodana* book shelves
5叩 *fukurodataki* sound thrashing, beating
6耳 *fukuromimi* retentive memory; a person with a good memory
地 *fukurochi* land cut off from access to a road
7町 *fukuromachi* blind alley
8物 *fukuromono* bags and pouches
11道 *fukuromichi* blind road
張 *fukurohar(i)* paper bagmaking
13鼠 *fukuro (no) nezumi* trapped mouse; tight box, fine fix
15縫 *fukuronu(i)* double sewing

袖 4224 F1694 SHŪ. *sode* sleeve; sleeve pocket; wing (of a building); extension (of a table). *sode ni suru* jilt, cold shoulder (someone).

3口 *sodeguchi* cuff, sleeve band
下 *sode(no)shita* bribe
乞 *sodego(u)* beg. *sodego(i)* beggar; begging
丈 *sode take* sleeve length
4手 *shūshu* putting one's hands in one's sleeves; detestation of work
手傍観 *shūshu-bōkan* passively looking on
9垣 *sodegake* low fence; fence flanking a gate
珍 *shūchin* pocket (edition)
珍本 *shūchimbon* pocket-size book; manual
10振 *sodebu(ru)* wave the sleeve (in sad parting or in dancing)
時雨 *sode shigure* weeping
11章 *sodeshō* (soldier's) stripes
12無 *sodena(shi)* sleeveless coat
13裏 *sode ura* sleeve lining

B 被 4225 F1695 HI receiving. *kabu(ru) vi* and *vt* wear, put on; take (the blame); pour on; be covered with; ship (a wave); have (labor pains); be accidentally exposed (a film). *kabu(seru)* cover with; put on; pour on, play (a stream of water) on; fix (blame) on; shift (responsibility) on. *kabu(saru)* get covered; overlap; hang over. *ō(u)* cover, veil; hang over; brood over; conceal; overlap; shelter; screen; disguise; wrap, envelop; obscure; shade; overshadow. *hi-* recipient or victim of (an action). *kōmu(ru)* get, receive, sustain (an injury), be subjected to (criticism). *kazu(ku)* put on, wear. *kazu(keru)* blame. *ō(i)* (see under 覆 4279.0).

8 下 *kudasa(reru)* give, send (polite)
下物 *kudasaremono* something received (polite)
4 引者 *hikaremono* criminal under arrest
支払人 *hishiharainin* payee
5 圧迫 *hiappaku* oppressed
写体 *hishatai* the one being photographed
用者 *hiyōsha* employee
6 衣 *kazuki, katsugi* lady's veil
7 抑留者 *hiyokuryūsha* internee
災 *hisai* suffering (from a calamity); affliction
災者 *hisaisha* victim, sufferer
告 *hikoku* defendant
告人 *hikokunin* defendant
告席 *hikokuseki* tribunal, the bar, the dock
8 金 *kabu(se)kin* rolled gold, filled gold
物 *kabu(ri)mono* headgear, headdress. *ki(se)mono* clothes
使者 *tsukawaremono* employee
治者 *hichisha* the governed
拘束者 *hikōsokusha* the restrained
服 *hifuku* clothing
服庫 *hifukuko* clothing depot
服廠 *hifukushō* clothing depot
9 造物 *hizōbutsu* creation, creatures
後見者 *hikōkensha* ward, protégé
保険物 *hihokembutsu* insured property
保険者 *hihokensha* insured person
保護国 *hihogokoku* dependency, protector-
保護者 *hihogosha* ward, protégé ⌊ate
10 病 *hibyō* contraction of a disease
害 *higai* damage, harm, casualties, injury
害地 *higaichi* stricken area
害妄想 *higai mōsō* persecution complex
害者 *higaisha* victim, injured party, sufferer
害高 *higaidaka* amount of damage
11 斬損 *kirarezon* no redress if cut by a samurai
推薦者 *hisuisensha* nominee
12 弾 *hidan* being bombed
13 傭者 *hiyōsha* employee
裏書人 *hiuragakinin* indorsee
14 疑者 *higisha* a suspect ⌈election
選挙人 *hisenkyonin* person eligible for
選挙資格 *hisenkyo shikaku* qualification for election
選挙権 *hisenkyoken* eligibility for election
18 覆 *hifuku* covering, mantle, insulation
贈与者 *hizōyosha* donee
19 爆 *hibaku* being bombed
爆地 *hibakuchi* bombed area
爆者 *hibakusha* bombing victims

6

裁 See 788.

祗 4226 / F1696 See 衽 4218.

袱 4227 / F1696 FUKU a wrapper made of cloth.
10 紗 *fukusa* silk wrapper (for gifts); tea-ceremony dishcloth

裃 4228 / F1697 (国字) *kamishimo* old ceremonial garb; samurai garb

袴 4229 / F1696 KO. *hakama* men's formal divided skirt, women's pleated skirt.

袷 4230 / F1696 KŌ. KYŌ. *awase* lined; lined kimono.

裄 4231 / F1697 (国字) *yuki* sleeve length.
3 丈 *yukitake* sleeve and dress length

袿 4232 / F1696 KEI. *uchiki* an ancient ordinary kimono.
11 袴 *keiko* lady's court robe

裂 4233 / F1697 B RETSU. *sa(ku) vt* split, rend, tear, burst, rip, crack. *sa(keru) vi* split, rend, tear, burst, rip, crack.
5 目 *sa(ke)me* rent, tear, crack, fissure, split, slit, cleft, rip, rift
8 帛 *reppaku* a woman's wail
10 殺 *sa(ki)-koro(su)* tear to death
11 痔 *sa(ke)ji, ki(re)ji* anal fistula
12 開 *rekkai suru* burst open
13 傷 *resshō* lacerated wound
溝 *rekkō* tooth grooves ⌈thing) away from
19 離 *sa(ki)-hana(su)* rend from, tear (some-

装 4234 / F1700 B 裝 SŌ. SHŌ. *yosō(u)* dress; spruce up; pretend, disguise; profess. *yosō(i)* array, dress, equipment.
2 丁 *sōtei* binding, format
5 本 *sōhon* binding, format
甲 *sōkō* armor, armor plate
甲自動車 *sōkō jidōsha* armored car
甲車 *sōkōsha* armored car
甲艦 *sōkōkan* armored warship
7 束 *sōzoku, shōzoku* costume (of ancient nobles); personal appearance; clothing; interior decoration; landscaping; household furniture
身具 *sōshingu* personal ornaments
8 具 *sōgu* equipment; harness; trappings; furnishings, fittings
10 釘 *sōtei* binding, format

12 備 *sōbi* equipment, outfit, rigging
幀 *sōtei* binding, format
弾 *sōdan suru* load (a gun)
着 *sōchaku suru* equip, fit, install, lay, lay
13 塡 *sōten* gun charge ⌊down, place
置 *sōchi* equipment, installation, plant, apparatus, device ⌈ration, adornment
飾 *sōshoku* ornament, ornamentation, deco-
飾用 *sōshokuyō* for decoration
飾法 *sōshokuhō* ornamentation, decoration
飾的 *sōshokuteki* ornamental, decorative
飾画 *sōshokuga* decorative painting
飾具 *sōshokugu* jewelry
飾音 *sōshokuon* grace note
飾品 *sōshokuhin* ornaments, decorations, upholstery; trinkets, trimmings
16 薬 *sōyaku* charging with gunpowder
蹄 *sōtei* shoeing (a horse)
蹄師 *sōteishi* horseshoer

7

袴 See 4229.

裡 4235 F1698 See 裏 327.

装 4236 F1700 See 装 4234.

裟 4237 F1700 Sa surplice (Buddhist).

裘 4238 F1698 Kyū leather clothing.

裔 4239 F1698 Ei descendant; border.

裙 4240 F1698 Kun hem (of a garment); underwear.

B 裕 4241 F1698 Yū. *yutaka* abundant, rich, fruitful, fertile.
7 余 *yūyo*=猶予 2897.4
12 然 *yūzen*=*yūyū* 悠悠 1701.11
13 福 *yūfuku* prosperity, affluence

A 補 4242 F1699 Ho assistant, learner. *ogina(u)* supply, make good, make up (losses), stop (a gap), offset, piece out; compensate for; supplement. *ho(suru)* appoint, select. *-ho* assistant.
2 力 *horyoku suru* intensify ⌈shortage
4 欠 *hoketsu* filling a vacancy; making up a
欠募集 *hoketsu-boshū suru* inviting (students) to fill vacancies
欠選手 *hoketsu senshu* substitute player
欠選挙 *hoketsu senkyo* by-election, special election
5 正 *hosei* revision; correction; compensation (in machines); supplementary (budget)
6 血 *hoketsu* replenishing a patient's blood
回 *hokai* extra innings ⌊supply
任 *honin suru* appoint to office; take up one's duties ⌈replacement
充 *hojū* supplement, complement, draft,
充兵 *hojūhei* reservist, recruit
充隊 *hojūtai* draft, reserves
7 角 *hokaku* supplementary angle
完税 *hokanzei* surtax
足 *hosoku* replenishment, complement, amendment ⌈er
足合 *hosoku(shi)a(u)* complement each oth-
足語 *hosokugo* complement (in grammar)
佐 *hosa* assistance; assistant; counselor
佐人 *hosanin* assistant
佐役 *hosayaku* adviser
助 *hojo* assistance; subsidy; supplement; auxiliary ⌈bounty
助金 *hojokin* subsidy, grant, appropriation,
助貨幣 *hojo kahei* subsidiary coin
8 注 *hochū* supplementary note
肥 *hohi* supplementary fertilizer
乳 *honyū* lactation, suckling
9 則 *hosoku* supplementary rules
10 修 *hoshū* repair, mending; correction
記 *hoki suru* add more to an article
殺 *hosatsu* an assist (in baseball)
11 強 *hokyō suru* strengthen the weak places
習 *hoshū* supplementary study materials
祭 *hosai* (Catholic) deacon
12 遺 *ho-i* supplement, appendix
註 *hochū* supplementary note
筆 *hohitsu suru* add to (in writing); finish writing
給 *hokyū* supply, replenishment
給金 *hokyūkin* subsidy, bonus
13 塡 *hoten suru* fill, supply (a deficiency), make up (a loss)
14 綴 *hotei suru* replenish
語 *hogo* complement (in grammar)
箋 *hosen* tag, slip, label
導 *hodō* guidance
16 薬 *ogina(i)gusuri* tonic, restorative
整 *hosei* manipulation
17 講 *hokō* supplementary lecture
翼 *hoyoku* assistance; assistant; counselor
聴器 *hochōki* hearing aid ⌈tion
償 *hoshō* indemnity, compensation, repara-
償金 *hoshōkin* indemnity, compensation ⌊money
18 闕 *hoketsu* filling a vacancy
職 *hosoku* appointment to a position

8

裹 See 328.

裳 See 1370.

褐 4243 F-X Nonstandard for **褐** 4254.

裨 4244 F-X HI help.

10益 *hieki* profit, benefit, good

裲 4245 F1701 RYŌ ancient robe.

18襠 *uchikake* long outer robe

褄 4246 F1702 (国字) *tsuma* skirt.

8取 *tsumado(ru)* tuck up a skirt

裾 4247 F1702 KYO. *suso* cuff (of trousers); hem (of a skirt); foot (of a mountain).

3山 *susoyama* foothills
4分 *susowa(ke)* distribution of a gift; sharing
6回 *susomawa(shi)* hem line
8物 *susomono* lower-grade wares
9持 *susomo(chi)* train bearer
11野 *susono* foot (of a mountain)
13裏 *suso-ura* hem
14綿 *susowata* cotton skirt padding; kimono with padded skirts
模様 *suso moyō* skirt design

B **裸** 4248 F1701 RA. *hadaka* naked body, nude; uncovered, only partially clothed, undressed; without investing; leafless; unpreparedness (for a wedding); unsaddled; denuded, bare.

1一貫 *hadaka ikkan* starting from scratch; bankrupt
8女 *rajo* nude woman
山 *hadaka yama* bare mountain; deforested mountain
4文 *hadakabumi* folded letter sent without an envelope
火 *hadakabi* open fire
5出 *rashutsu* exposure, denudation
6虫 *hadaka mushi* caterpillar
7足 *hadashi* bare feet
身 *rashin* nakedness; bareness
麦 *hadaka mugi* a species of rye
形 *rakei* naked; uncovered
体 *ratai* naked body, nakedness, nudity
体主義 *ratai shugi* nudism
体画 *rataiga* nude picture
8岩 *hadaka iwa* bare rock
10馬 *hadaka uma* barebacked horse
11婦 *rafu* nude woman
眼 *ragan* the naked eye
商売 *hadaka shōbai* wrestling; boxing
14像 *razō* nude statue
15線 *hadakasen, rasen* bare wire

A **製** 4249 F1702 SEI. *sei(suru)* make, manufacture. *-sei* make, manufacture.

5出 *seishutsu* production
氷 *seihyō* ice manufacture
氷所 *seihyōjo* ice plant
本 *seihon* bookbinding
本屋 *seihon-ya* bookbinder
本業 *seihongyō* bookbinding business
6式 *seishiki* style
糸 *seishi* silk-thread manufacture
糸工場 *seishi kōjō* silk mill
糸学 *seishigaku* filature science
糸業 *seishigyō* silk industry
7図 *seizu* drafting; cartography, mapmaking; drawing
図家 *seizuka* cartographer
作 *seisaku* manufacture, production
作所 *seisakujo* factory, workshop, plant
作者 *seisakusha* manufacturer, maker; producer
材 *seizai* sawing, lumbering
材工 *seizaikō* sawyer
材所 *seizaisho* sawmill
材業 *seizaigyō* lumber industry
材機 *seizaiki* sawmill machinery
8法 *seihō* method of manufacture, process, recipe
表 *seihyō* tabulation
油 *seiyu* oil refining
油所 *seiyujo* oil factory; oil refinery
油業 *seiyugyō* oil industry
版 *seihan* platemaking (printing)
版所 *seihanjo* platemaker's shop
版者 *seihansha* platemaker
版屋 *seihan-ya* platemaker's shop
9品 *seihin* manufactured goods, products
炭 *seitan* charcoal manufacture
茶 *seicha* tea processing
茶業 *seichagyō* tea-processing industry
革 *seikaku* tanning
革所 *seikakujo* tannery
革業 *seikakugyō* tanning industry
造 *seizō* manufacture, production, making
造人 *seizōnin* maker
造元 *seizōmoto* manufacturer
造所 *seizōjo* factory, workshop
造法 *seizōhō* process of manufacture
造者 *seizōsha* maker
造品 *seizōhin* manufactured goods
造場 *seizōjō* factory, mill, workshop
造業 *seizōgyō* manufacturing industry
造権 *seizōken* manufacturing rights

10釘機 *seichōki* nail-making machine
粉 *seifun* milling flour
粉所 *seifunjo* flour mill
粉機 *seifunki* flour grinder
陶 *seitō* porcelain manufacturing
陶術 *seitōjutsu* ceramics
陶業 *seitōgyō* porcelain industry
紙 *seishi* paper manufacture
紙工場 *seishi kōjō* paper mill
紙会社 *seishigaisha* paper mill
紙場 *seishijō* paper mill
紙業 *seishigyō* paper-manufacturing industry
11麻 *seima* flax or jute or hemp spinning
産 *seisan* production
菓 *seika* confectionery
菓業 *seikagyō* confectionery business
12帽 *seibō* hat manufacture
帽業 *seibōgyō* hat industry
絨 *seijū* wool weaving
絨所 *seijūjo* woolen mills
13塩 *seien* salt manufacture
塩業 *seiengyō* salt industry
鉄 *seitetsu* iron manufacture
鉄所 *seitetsujo* iron works
鉄業 *seitetsugyō* iron industry
靴 *seika* shoemaking
靴工 *seikakō* shoemaker
靴業 *seikagyō* shoemaking industry
14銑 *seisen* pig-iron manufacture
16錬 *seiren* refining, smelting
錬所 *seirenjo* refinery, smelter
糖 *seitō* sugar manufacture
糖会社 *seitōgaisha* sugar company
糖所 *seitōjo* sugar refinery
糖業 *seitōgyō* sugar industry
鋼 *seikō* steel manufacturing
鋼法 *seikōhō* steelmaking process
鋼所 *seikōjo* steel works
鋼業 *seikōgyō* steel industry
薬 *seiyaku* medicine manufacture; manufactured medicine
薬化学 *seiyaku kagaku* pharmaceutical chemistry
薬会社 *seiyakugaisha* pharmaceutical company
薬業 *seiyakugyō* pharmaceutical industry
20艦 *seikan* naval construction
麵 *seimen* noodle manufacture
麵機 *seimenki* noodle-making machine
25罐 *seikan* can manufacturing; boiler manufacturing

9

褒 See 331.

裸 4250 / F1704 Ho. Hō diaper.

褌 4251 / F1703 Kon. *fundoshi* loincloth.

褊 4252 / F1703 Hen narrow, small.
9狭 *henkyō* narrow-mindedness

褪 4253 / F1704 Ton. Tai *a(seru)*, *sa(meru)* fade, discolor.
6色 *taishoku* fading; faded color
9紅色 *taikōshoku* light pink

褐 4254 / F1703 Katsu woolen kimono.
4夫 *kappu* cloth made from waste fibers
6色 *kasshoku* brown. *kachi-iro* dark blue
色人種 *kasshoku jinshu* brown race, Malay race
9炭 *kattan* brown coal, lignite

A **複** 4255 / F1702 Fuku double, compound, composite, multiple. *futatabi*, *mata* again.
4文 *fukubun* compound sentence
火山 *fukukazan* compound volcano
5仕合 *fukushiai* doubles (in tennis)
母音 *fukubo-in* diphthong
写 *fukusha* copying, duplication; duplicate, copy, facsimile
写写真 *fukusha shashin* photostat
本 *fukuhon* duplicate, copy
本位制 *fukuhon-isei* bimetallism
6式 *fukushiki* double-entry (bookkeeping)
式学級 *fukushiki gakkyū* multiple-grade classroom
合 *fukugō* composite, complex, compound
合名詞 *fukugō meishi* compound noun
合動詞 *fukugō dōshi* compound verb
合詞 *fukugōshi* compound word
合語 *fukugōgo* compound word
7利 *fukuri* compound interest
8刻 *fukkoku* reproducing book plates
屈折 *fukukussetsu* double refraction
9星 *fukusei* multiple star
10座機 *fukuzaki* two-seater plane
11眼 *fukugan* compound eye (of an insect)
視 *fukushi* double vision
習 *fukushū* review
12葉 *fukuyō* biplane; compound leaf
13滑車 *fukukassha* compound pulley
数 *fukusū* plural
数型 *fukusūkei* plural form
14製 *fukusei* reproduction, duplication, reprinting
複線 *fukufukusen* four-track railway

6 竹米糸缶网罒羊羽老耂而耒耳聿肉月臣自至臼舌舛舟艮色艸艹虍虫血行[衣衤9]西

6 竹米糸缶网四羊羽老耂而耒耳聿肉月臣自至臼舌舛舟艮色艸艹虍虫血行【衣衤】[10]西

雑 *fukuzatsu* complexity, complication, intricacy; maze, labyrinth
雑化 *fukuzatsuka* complication
雑骨折 *fukuzatsu kossetsu* compound fracture
15縁 *fukuen* conjugal reconciliation
線 *fukusen* double track

10

⿰衤拳 Nonstandard for 襷 4272.

褞 4256/F1704 Un, On robe.

褥 4257/F1704 Joku. *shitone* cushion, mattress, bedding.
11婦 *jokufu* a woman resting after childbirth

褫 4258/F1704 Chi rob.
14奪 *chidatsu suru* deprive, degrade, strip

11

褻 See 334.

襃 See 褒 331.

褸 4259/F1705 Ro, Ru rags.

襀 4260/F1705 Seki. *hida* pleat, fold, tuck, crease.

襁 4261/F1705 ⿰衤强 Kyō diaper.
14褓 *kyōhō, (o)mutsu, oshime, mutsuki* diaper, swaddling clothes

褶 4262/F1705 Shū pleats.
6曲 *shūkyoku* a fold (in geology)

12

⿰衤强 4263/F1705 See 襁 4261.

13

襖 4264/F1706 Ō. *fusuma* opaque sliding paper door.
13障子 *fusuma shōji* opaque sliding paper door

襞 4265/F1707 Heki. *hida* pleat, fold, tuck, crease.

襠 4266/F1707 Tō. *machi* gusset, gore, etc. (in sewing).

襟 4267/F1707 Kin. *eri* neck, neckband, collar, lapel.
4止 *eridome* brooch, breast pin
元 *erimoto* front of neck
6当 *eria(te)* cloth to protect the back of the collar
7足 *eriashi* border of the hair in back
9首 *erikubi* nape of the neck
度 *kindo* magnanimity, generosity
巻 *erimaki* muffler, scarf, neckpiece
10留 *erido(me)* brooch, breast pin
11章 *erishō* badge
13飾 *erikaza(ri)* necktie, cravat, bow
裏 *eri ura*=*eria(te)* 襟当 (see above–6)
14髪 *erigami* back hair
16懐 *kinkai* the heart; thought; magnanimity

14

襦 4268/F1707 Ju. *shitagi* underwear.
10袢 *juban* underwear

襤 4269/F1707 Ran rags.
16褸 *boro, ranru, tsuzure* rag, scrap; tattered clothes; fault, defect; shabbiness
褸糞 *borokuso* trash, a word of disparagement

16

襲 See 5443.

襯 4270/F1708 Shin underwear.
6衣 *shin-i, shatsu* underwear

17

襴 4271/F1708 Ran a kind of cloth.

襷 4272/F1708 (国字) *tasuki* cord for holding up sleeves.
11掛 *tasukiga(ke)* holding up sleeves with a cord

RAD. 西 146

Nishi west. Variants: 覀, 襾. Nickname: West.

A 西 4273 F1709 SEI, SAI *nishi* west.

[2]人 *seijin* a Westerner
力東侵 *seiryoku-tōshin* inroads of the Western Powers in the Far East
[3]土 *seido* western lands
山 *seizan* western hills ⌈Japan
下 *saika suru* start for Kansai or western
上 *saijō suru* going to Kyoto from the east
[4]日 *nishibi* westering sun
天 *seiten* western sky
方 *seihō* west, western, westward; the West. *Saihō* Western Paradise
方浄土 *Saihō Jōdo* Western Paradise
方教会 *Seihō Kyōkai* the Western Church
方極楽 *Saihō Gokuraku* Western Paradise
[5]史 *seishi* Occidental history
北 *seihoku, nishikita* northwest
瓜 *suika* watermelon
瓜糖 *suikatō* watermelon sugar
半 *seihan* western half
半球 *nishi hankyū* Western Hemisphere
[6]行 *seikō* westbound
向 *nishimu(ki)* facing west
[8]門 *seimon* west gate
明 *nishi aka(ri)* twilight
郊 *seikō* western suburbs
京 *Saikyō* Kyoto, the Western Capital
学 *Seigaku* Western learning
東 *nishi-higashi* east and west; direction
国 *saikoku* the western countries; western Japan ⌈three-temple pilgrimage
国巡礼 *saikoku junrei* west Japan thirty-
岸 *seigan* west coast; west bank
岸沿 *seiganzo(i) ni* along the western coast; along the western seashore ⌈Occident
欧 *Seiō* Western Europe; the West, the
欧人 *Seiōjin* Westerner, European
欧化 *Seiōka* Europeanization
欧的 *Seiōteki* Western (style) ⌈facing west
[9]面 *seimen* west face, west side; the west;
風 *nishi kaze, seifū* west wind; autumn wind; zephyr ⌈sea; the Kyushu seas
海 *seikai* the western sea. *saikai* the western
独 *Sei-Doku* West Germany
紀 *Seiki* A.D.
軍 *seigun* the western army
南 *seinan, nishiminami* southwest
南役 *Seinan (no) Eki* Satsuma Rebellion
洋 *Seiyō* the West, the Occident; the western ocean
洋人 *Seiyōjin* Westerner, European
洋大根 *Seiyō daikon* radish ⌈zation
洋化 *Seiyōka* Westernization, Europeani-
洋気触 *Seiyō kabure* influence of the Occi-
洋杉 *Seiyō sugi* cedar ⌊dent
洋李 *Seiyō sumomo* prune, plum
洋画 *Seiyōga* Occidental painting
洋風 *Seiyōfū* Western style
洋造 *Seiyōzuku(ri)* Western-style building
洋紀元 *Seiyō kigen* Christian Era
洋南瓜 *Seiyō kabocha* pumpkin
洋独活 *Seiyō udo* asparagus
洋思想 *Seiyō shisō* Western ideas
洋流 *Seiyōryū* Western ways
洋料理 *Seiyō ryōri* Western cooking
洋菓子 *Seiyōgashi* Western confectionery
洋間 *Seiyōma* Western-style room
洋館 *Seiyōkan* Western-style building
[10]進 *seishin suru* proceed west
航 *seikō* sailing west, westbound
哲 *seitetsu* Western philosophy; Western philosopher
部 *seibu* the west, western part
部物 *seibumono* a Western (film)
部前線 *Seibu Zensen* the Western Front
部劇 *seibugeki* a Western (film)
[11]遊 *saiyū, seiyū* visiting the west; visiting the Occident ⌈China
域 *sei-iki* India and lands to the west of
側 *nishigawa* west side, west bank; the Western Powers. *seisoku* west side, west
経 *seikei* west longitude ⌊bank
教 *seikyō* Western religion, Christianity
寄 *nishiyo(ri)* westerly
[14]漸 *seizen* westward advance
端 *seitan* western extremity
暦 *Seireki* Christian Era, A.D.
暦紀元 *Seireki Kigen* Christian Era, A.D.
[16]諺 *seigen* Occidental proverb

3

A 要 4274 F1710 要 Yō main point, essence; aim; secret; need. *yō(suru), i(ru)* require, need; waylay, ambush. *yō(suru) ni* in the last analysis, in short. *i(ranu)* unwanted, useless, unnecessary. *kaname* pivot; the main point; the key (to).

[2]人 *yōjin* leading personage, important man
[4]心 *yōjin* care, caution, discretion
[5]用 *yōyō* important matter; necessity; use
目 *yōmoku* principal items

6 竹米糸缶网罒羊羽老耂而耒耳聿肉月臣自至臼舌舛舟艮色艸艹虍虫血行衣衤【西】4

石 *kaname ishi* keystone
処 *yōsho* the important points; the gist
6 因 *yōin* primary factor, main cause, prerequisite
式 *yōshiki* formality
件 *yōken* requisite, important matter; qualification; essentials
地 *yōchi* strategic point, important place
旨 *yōshi* gist, point, essentials; argument; summary; fundamental principles
7 図 *yōzu* rough sketch, sketch map
求 *yōkyū* request, demand, requirement
8 枢 *yōsū* importance
具 *yōgu* necessary tools
注意 *yōchūi* requiring (medical) care
所 *yōsho* important position, strategic point
所要所 *yōsho-yōsho* important places
9 約 *yōyaku* summary, digest
点 *yōten* gist, essentials, substance
10 部 *yōbu* essential part
員 *yōin* necessary personnel
害 *yōgai* fort, stronghold
素 *yōso* element, essential, requisite, constituent
11 略 *yōryaku* choosing the important sections and omitting the rest; digest of an article; gist, summary
務 *yōmu* important business
訣 *yōketsu* secret, key
望 *yōbō suru* cry for, demand, long for
望書 *yōbōsho* written request
12 項 *yōkō* gist, synopsis, important point
港 *yōkō* important port
13 義 *yōgi* essentials, essence, digest
路 *yōro* important road, main artery; responsible position; the authorities
路者 *yōrosha* the authorities
塞 *yōsai* fort, stronghold, fortification
塞地帯 *yōsai chitai* fortified zone
塞戦 *yōsaisen* siege warfare
14 綱 *yōkō* outline, summary; general idea; general plan, prospectus
語 *yōgo* the important words; the summary
説 *yōsetsu* outline, general statement
領 *yōryō* the point, gist, essentials, outline, summary
領良 *yōryōyo(ku)* pointedly, sensibly, practically
15 衝 *yōshō* important place
談 *yōdan* important talks
請 *yōsei* demand, request, requirement
撃 *yōgeki* ambush attack
16 諦 *yōtei* secret (of success)
覧 *yōran* survey, summary, outline; handbook, directory, catalog
17 償 *yōshō* claim for damages
18 職 *yōshoku* responsible post

4

栗 4275 / F968 RITSU. *kuri* chestnut. [木]

4 毛 *kurige* chestnut color; bay horse, sorrel
5 石 *kuri ishi* chestnut-size stone, pebble
6 色 *kuri iro* chestnut color
名月 *kuri meigetsu* hunters' moon
羊羹 *kuri yōkan* chestnut bean-jelly
11 毬 *iga* burr
12 飯 *kuri meshi* chestnut rice
13 鼠 *risu* squirrel
17 餡 *kurian* chestnut bean jam
20 饅頭 *kuri manjū* chestnut-jam steamed dumpling

5

A **票** 4276 / F1363 HYŌ label; ballot; ticket; sign. [示]

5 札 *hyōsatsu* name plate, doorplate
7 決 *hyōketsu* vote, voting
13 数 *hyōsū* number of votes

6

粟 4277 / F1430 ZOKU. *awa* millet. [米]

5 立 *awada(tsu)* have goose flesh (from cold or horror)
9 畑 *awabata* millet field
11 粒 *awatsubu, zokuryū* millet grain
12 粥 *awagayu* millet gruel
15 穂 *awabo* heads of millet
餅 *awamochi* millet *mochi*, millet rice-cake

7

賈 4278 / F1798 Ko buy; tradesman. [貝]

12

B **覆** 4279 / F1712 **覆** FUKU. FU. *kutsuga(eru)* overturn, capsize; fall; be ruined. *kutsuga(esu)* overturn, capsize; overthrow; undermine; frustrate; veto; disprove (a theory). *ō(u)* (see under 被 4225.0). *ō(i)* cover, covering; shade; mantle, coat; hood, bonnet; casing; awning.

4 水 *fukusui* spilt water
7 没 *fukubotsu suru* capsize and sink; suffer a serious defeat or a serious reverse in family fortunes
8 刻 *fukkoku* reproducing a book from identical plates
9 奏 *fukusō suru* reinvestigate and report
面 *fukumen* mask, veil, disguise
面子 *fukumenshi* anonymous writer
10 書 *fukusho* an answer by letter
11 啓 *fukukei* my answer (a letter salutation)
13 滅 *fukumetsu* overthrow, destruction

[14]墜 *fukutsui* leaning and falling; the destruction of a family
蔵 *fukuzō* keeping things to oneself
蔵無 *fukuzōna(ku)*=腹蔵無 3800.14
[15]輪 *fukurin* ornamental border
審 *fukushin* retrial
[19]轍 *fukutetsu* ruts of an overturned carriage; the mistakes of our predecessors

13

覈 4280 F1713 KAKU investigate.

覇 4281 F1713 F2033 霸 HA supremacy, leadership, domination, hegemony; supreme ruler; champion.

[6]気 *haki* ambition
[8]府 *hafu* shogunate
者 *hasha* supreme ruler; champion
[11]道 *hadō* military rule
道政策 *hadō seisaku* plans for world conquest
[13]業 *hagyō* exploits; domination
[15]権 *haken* domination, supremacy, leadership

17

覉 4282 F1713 See 羈 3655.

19

覊 4283 F1713 F1476 See 羈 3655.

7-STROKE RADICALS

RAD. 見 147

Miru to see. Nickname: Seeing.

A 見 4284 F1713 KEN, GEN hopes, chances; idea, opinion. *mi(ru)* see, look at, witness, observe; regard as; sight-see; look thru; examine; consult (a lexicon); tell (one's fortune); estimate; care for; try, test. *mi(eru)* see; be seen, be visible, be in sight; look like; seem, appear; come, show up; be found. *mi(seru)* show, let see, display; make look like, pretend. *mami(eru)* see, be presented to, have an audience with. *mi(sebirakasu)* display, flaunt, parade. *mi(seshime)* object lesson, warning, example. *mi(ttomonai)* indecent, unbecoming, scandalous; unsightly. ugly. *mi(e)* ostentation. *mi(tekure)* appearance.
[2]入 *mi-i(ru)* gaze intently at, scrutinize; curse; (devils) possess (people)
[3]上 *mi-a(geru)* look up at; admire, respect
下 *mi-kuda(su)* command a view of; look down on, despise. *mi-o(rosu)* overlook, command a view of. *mi-sa(geru)* look down over; look down on
下果 *mi-sa(ge)-ha(teru)* looking despisingly down on. *misa(ge)ha(teta)* mean, contemptible
[4]手 *mite* onlooker
方 *mikata* viewpoint, way of looking
比 *mi-kura(beru)* compare with the eye
込 *mi-ko(mu)* expect, anticipate; estimate; trust; mark (as a victim). *miko(mi)* hope, prospects, possibility, forecast, expectation
込違 *miko(mi)chiga(i)* miscalculation
切 *mi-ki(ru)* see all; abandon; sell at a bargain
切品 *mikirihin* clearance goods
分 *miwa(keru)* distinguish, recognize; judge; identify. *miwa(ke)* distinction; discrimination, judgment; identification, recognition
分難 *miwa(ke)gata(i)* indistinguishable, unrecognizable
[5]立 *mi-ta(teru)* diagnose; choose; compare to; form an opinion. *mida(te)* appearance. *mita(te)* diagnosis; choice; opinion;
処 *midokoro* merit, promise
巡 *mi-megu(ru)* inspect, make the rounds
外 *mi-hazu(su)* miss seeing. *mi-so(reru)* fail to recognize
収 *miosa(me)* farewell look
台 *kendai* rack for holding a book
失 *mi-ushina(u)* lose sight of, miss
左右 *gen (o) sayū ni suru* answer equivocally
付 *mitsu(karu)* be found; be found out, be discovered. *mitsu(keru)* find; find out; discover, locate; catch sight of; notice, recognize; hunt for, get used to seeing, be familiar to. *mitsuke* approach (to a castle gate)
付出 *mitsu(ke)-da(su)* search out, hunt up
出 *mi-ida(su)* discover, detect, select, find out. *mida(shi)* heading, caption, subtitle, index
出語 *mida(shi)go* index word

本 *mihon* sample, pattern, specimen, copy, model, example
本市 *mihon ichi* industrial fair
世 *mise* store, shop, booth, office
世物 *misemono* show, exhibition, circus
世開 *misebira(ki)* opening a new store
目 *mi(ru)me* the sight; power of observation. *mi(ta)me ni* to look at. *mime* looks, features, face, form
目好 *mimeyo(i)* good-looking
目形 *mimekatachi* looks, features, face, form
目良 *mimeyo(i)* good-looking
目姿 *mimesugata* form, figure, appearance
目麗 *mime-uruwa(shii)* beautiful (woman)
6 回 *mi-mawa(ru)* patrol, inspect. *mimawa(ri)* patrol, round of inspection; patrolman, inspector, floorwalker
尽 *mi-tsu(kusu)* see all
向 *mi-mu(ku)* look around, look toward (us)
印 *ken-in* ordinary seal
地 *kenchi* standpoint, viewpoint
交 *mi-ka(wasu)* exchange glances
守 *mi-mamo(ru)* watch over
劣 *mioto(ri)* unfavorable comparison
合 *mi-a(u)* exchange glances; counterbalance. *mi-a(waseru)* exchange glances; postpone. *mia(i)* marriage interview
合結婚 *miai kekkon* marriage after just one interview
当 *mi-ata(ru)* be found. *kentō* aim, mark; estimate, guess; direction; approximation
当違 *kentōchiga(i)* wrong guess, miscalculation
返 *mi-kae(ru)* look back or over the shoulder. *mi-kae(su)* look back, stare back at; triumph over. *mikae(shi)* inside the cover
返物資 *mikaeri busshi* collateral goods
返品 *mikae(ri)hin* returned goods
7 見 *mi(ru)mi(ru)* in an instant. *mi(su)mi(su)* before one's very eyes. *mi(ru)mi(ru) uchi ni* while looking
辛 *mizura(i)* unbearable to look at; ugly, unattractive
坊 *mi(e)bō* vain person, a fop
抜 *mi-nu(ku)* see thru
初 *mi-so(meru)* see for the first time, fall in love at first sight
附 *mitsuke* approach (to a castle gate)
兵 *gempei* soldiers at hand
忘 *mi-wasu(reru)* forget, fail to recognize
良 *mi(ttomo)i(i)* respectable, dignified
8 金 *mi(se)gane* show money
届 *mi-todo(keru)* ascertain, verify
逃 *mi-noga(su)* miss, overlook, let pass, wink at, leave at large
送 *mi-oku(ru)* see off, bid farewell; follow with one's eyes; escort (home); care for till death; let pass; wait and see

始 *mihaji(me)* seeing for the first time
所 *midokoro* merit, promise. *mi(ta) tokoro* to all appearances
放 *mi-sa(ku)* look afar. *mi-hana(su)* forsake, abandon. *mi-hana(su)*＝見離 (see below–19)
限 *mi-kagi(ru)* forsake, desert, abandon, despair of
直 *mi-nao(su)* look again; take a turn for the better; think better of
参 *kenzan suru* see, meet
定 *mi-sada(meru)* ascertain, make sure of
易 *miyasu(i)* easy to see; obvious, clear; easy to read (a thermometer)
受 *mi-u(keru)* see, come across, judge by appearances
苦 *miguru(shii)* disgraceful; unsightly; indecent; clumsy
咎 *mi-toga(meru)* question, challenge; find fault with
学 *kengaku* study and observation
者 *kensha* sight-seer
果 *mi-ha(teru)* see thru to the finish; be seen to the last
事 *migoto* beautiful, splendid
知 *kenchi suru, mi-shi(ru)* know by inspection, knowing by sight. *mishi(ri)* an acquaintance. *mi-shi(ranu), mi(zu)-shi(razu) no* strange, unknown
知越 *mishi(ri)go(shi)* well acquainted
取 *mi-to(ru)* see and know, notice, discern, recognize; see and copy. *mi(te) to(ru)* realize, understand
取図 *mitorizu* rough sketch, sketch map
物 *mimono* sight, spectacle, attraction. *kembutsu* sight-seeing. *mi(se)mono* show, circus
物人 *kembutsunin* sight-seer, visitor, spectator
物席 *kembutsuseki* seats at a game or theater
物衆 *kembutsushū* theater audience; crowd at a game
9 透 *mi(e)-su(ku)* be transparent. *mi-su(kasu)* see thru. *mitō(su)*＝next word
通 *mi-tō(su)* get an unobstructed view; see thru. *mitō(shi)* perspective, unobstructed view; outlook, forecast
映 *mibae* outward appearance
神 *kenshin* vision of God; actually perceiving a god
計 *mi-haka(ru), mi-haka(rau)* choose freely; time (a visit)
変 *mi-ka(eru)* prefer; forsake for some other (person or thing)
栄 *mie* appearance; show, display
栄坊 *miebō* fop, coxcomb, vain person
栄張 *mie(o)ha(ru)* show off, be vainglorious. *mie(p)pari* personal display
10 逸 *mi-so(reru)* miss seeing. *mi-hagu(reru)* miss, lose sight of
振 *mi(nu)fu(ri) (o) suru* pretend not to see

残 *mi-noko(su)* leave unseen
破 *mi-yabu(ru)* see thru
料 *kenryō* admission fee
納 *miosa(me)* farewell look
紛 *mi-mago(u)* err in observing
殺 *migoro(shi)* letting (someone) die before one's eyes without helping
兼 *mi-ka(neru)* be unable to look on with indifference; can't stand to see
真似 *mimane* seeing and copying
11 違 *mi-chiga(eru)* mistake, cannot recognize. *michiga(i)*, *michiga(e)* misperception, mistake 「逃 (see above–8)
過 *mi-su(gosu)*, *mi-su(gusu)* = *mi-noga(su)* 見
做 *mina(su)* regard as, consider, presume
頃 *migoro* the time to see
得 *mie* pose, posture, gesture. *mi(eru)* (see under 見 4284.0) 「gaze in rapture
惚 *mi-to(reru)*, *mi-ho(reru)* be charmed by,
据 *mi-su(eru)* stare at, gaze at
捨 *mi-su(teru)* forsake, desert, abandon, leave desolate
悪 *miniku(i)* hard to see, indistinct; illegible
掛 *mi-ka(keru)* see, meet; perceive, notice. *mika(ke)* appearance; apparent
掛通 *mika(ke)dō(ri)* true to appearances
掛倒 *mika(ke)dao(shi)* mere show, deceptive appearances
習 *mi-nara(u)* receive training; learn by observation; follow an example. *minarai* apprenticeship; apprentice, learner
習工 *minaraikō* apprentice
習士官 *minarai shikan* cadet
習生 *minaraisei* trainee
張 *miha(ru)* watch, stand guard, picket; strain (one's eyes). *miha(ri)* guard, lookout, picket; floorwalker
張人 *miha(ri)bito*, *miha(ri)nin* watchman
張台 *miha(ri)dai* watchtower 「watchtower
張所 *miha(ri)sho* lookout, crow's nest,
張番 *mihariban* guard, picket; floorwalker
12 開 *mi-hira(ku)* open (the eyes) wide. *mihira(ki)* a double page picture or chart
遣 *mi-ya(ru)* look at, glance at
遁 *mi-noga(su)* = 見逃 (see above–8)
場 *miba* looks, appearance. *mi(se)ba* highlight (of a play)
晴 *miha(rasu)* command a view of. *miha(rashi)* view, outlook, visibility
極 *mi-kiwa(meru)* see thru, discern, probe, make sure of 「scene)
渡 *mi-wata(su)* look out over, survey (the
落 *mi-o(tosu)* miss seeing, overlook, lose
番 *kemban* geisha exchange ⌊sight of
装 *minari* attire, personal appearance
覚 *mi-obo(eru)* remember, recognize

間 *mi(ru) ma ni* before one's very eyes
間違 *mi-machiga(eru)* mistake, cannot recognize
越 *mi-ko(su)* anticipate, foresee; look across
越松 *miko(shi) (no) matsu* overhanging pine
13 損 *mi-sokona(u)* misjudge, mistake, miss seeing. *mi-son(zuru)*, *mi-son(jiru)* make a mistake in observation
解 *kenkai* opinion, view
詰 *mi-tsu(meru)* gaze at, stare at, behold
較 *mi-kura(beru)* compare with the eye
隠 *mi(e)gaku(re)* appearing and disappearing; visible and invisible
飽 *mi-a(kiru)* be tired of looking at
馴 *mi-na(reru)* get used to seeing, be familiar to
置 *mi(te) o(ku)* count on (an hour)
14 聞 *kemmon*, *kembun*, *miki(ki)* information; experience, observation
境 *misakai* distinction, discrimination
慣 *mi-na(reru)* get used to seeing; be familiar to (me)
様 *miyō* viewpoint, way of looking
誤 *mi-aya(maru)* err in observing, mistake a signal
舞 *mima(u)* inquire about a sick person. *mima(i)* inquiry, expression of sympathy
舞人 *mima(i)nin* sympathizer, visitor
舞状 *mima(i)jō* letter of sympathy
舞金 *mima(i)kin* money present to a sick person
舞品 *mimaihin* present to a sick person
舞客 *mima(i)kyaku* hospital visitors
15 澄 *mi-su(masu)* observe carefully; make sure
蕩 *mi-to(reru)* be charmed by, gaze in rapture 「able
影無 *mi(ru)kage(mo)na(i)* wretched, miser-
16 縊 *mi-kubi(ru)* belittle, underrate
積 *mitsu(moru)* estimate at, value at, assess (damage). *mitsumo(ri)* estimate, quo-
積書 *mitsumorisho* written estimate ⌊tation
17 優 *mimasa(ri) suru* look better, compare favorably
18 繕 *mi-tsukuro(u)* choose freely; time (a
顕 *mi-ara(wasu)* reveal ⌊visit)
19 離 *mi-hana(su)* desert, abandon, give up (hope) 「dignity, self-respect
識 *kenshiki* views, discernment, knowledge;
識振 *kenshikibu(ru)* pretend to know it all
識張 *kenshikiba(ru)* pretend to know it all
21 露 *mi-ara(wasu)* detect, expose, see thru
22 霽 *mi-haru(kasu)* see over a broad area

4

視 視 See 3248.

7

A **規** 4285/F1714 **規** Ki standard; measure.

5 正 *kisei* regulation, control
6 那 *kina* quinine, cinchona
8 制 *kisei* regulation, control
定 *kitei* bylaws, provisions, regulations
9 律 *kiritsu suru* govern (a program). *kiritsu* regulations; order; discipline; system; regularity
矩 *kiku* compasses and ruler; standard, criterion, rule
約 *kiyaku* agreement, pact, rules, code, bylaws, articles
則 *kisoku* regulation, rule
則立 *kisokuda(tsu)* be perfectly arranged
則尽 *kisokuzu(kume)* bound by rules
則的 *kisokuteki* regular, systematic, orderly
則書 *kisokusho* prospectus, (school) catalog, regulations
則動詞 *kisoku dōshi* regular verb
10 格 *kikaku* standard, norm, gauge, rule
格化 *kikakuka* standardization, normalization; prefabrication; reorientation
格品 *kikakuhin* standardized goods
12 程 *kitei* bylaws, provisions, regulations
13 準 *kijun* standard, basis
準化 *kijunka* normalization
14 模 *kibo* scale, scope, plan, structure
15 範 *kihan* standard, norm, criterion

5

規 See **規** 4285.

覘 4286/F1716 Ten. *nozo(ku)* (see under 覗 4287.0).

覗 4287/F1716 Shi. *nozo(ku)* peep, peek; come in sight.

4 込 *nozo(ki)-ko(mu)* look into, peer into, peep in
5 穴 *nozoki ana* peep hole, sky hole

A **覚** 4288/F1719 **覺** Kaku. *obo(eru)* remember, memorize; learn, perceive; feel, experience, know; expect. *sato(ru)* (see under 悟 1700.0). *sa(masu)* *vt* awake, wake up. *sa(meru)* *vi* awake; be disillusioned; sober up. *obo(ezu)* involuntarily, unwittingly, instinctively. *obo(shii)* looking like a, apparently a (foreigner). *obo(e)* feeling; learning; memory, recollection; esteem; memo.

7 束無 *obotsukana(i)* uncertain, dubious, uneasy, precarious (living), unsteady, unreliable, well-nigh hopeless
8 知 *kakuchi* perception
知主義 *kakuchi shugi* gnosticism
10 書 *oboegaki* memo, note; memorial, protocol; book of remembrance
悟 *kakugo* resolution, readiness, expectation, resignation; perception (of truth)
悟前 *kakugo (no) mae* resignation to whatever may happen
11 違 *obo(e)chiga(i)* misunderstanding; memory slip
頃 *obo(shii) koro* about that time
帳 *obo(e)chō* memorandum, notebook
13 際 *sa(me)giwa* on the verge of awakening
16 醒 *kakusei* awakening, disillusionment
醒剤 *kakuseizai* stimulant
19 識 *kakushiki suru* know and understand

7

覡 4289/F1716 Geki. *kannagi* medium, diviner.

9

覩 4290/F1716 To see.

覦 4291/F1716 Yu coveting high rank.

B **覧** 4292/F1719 **覽** Ran. *mi(ru)* see.

12 勝 *ranshō* beholding a marvelous view

A **親** 4293/F1717 **親** Shin intimacy; parents; relative. *oya* parent; dealer (in card games); banker (in gambling). *chika(i)*, *shita(shii)* intimate, familiar, friendly. *shita(shimu)* be intimate with; have a liking for; take habitually. *shita(shimi)* intimacy, familiarity, friendship. *mizukara* oneself, personally. *shin-* pro- (American).

3 子 *oyako* parent and child; bowl of rice topped with chicken and eggs. *shinshi* parent and child
子丼 *oyako domburi* bowl of rice topped with chicken and eggs
4 心 *oyagokoro* parental love, parent's heart
方 *oyakata* boss, foreman
日 *shin-Nichi* pro-Japanese
木 *oyagi* the host plant of a graft
父 *shimpu* father. *oyaji* (in familiar talk) governor, judge, father
犬 *oya inu* mother dog
仏 *shin-Futsu* pro-French
仁 *oyaji*=親父 (see above–4)
元 *oyamoto ni* at home, with one's parents
友 *shin-yū* close friend, chum, pal
文字 *oya moji* capital letter
不孝 *oyafukō* lack of filial piety
王 *shinnō* imperial prince

王家 *shinnōke* imperial prince's family
切 *shinsetsu* kindness
切気 *shinsetsugi* kindliness, friendship
分 *oyabun* boss, chief, head
分子分 *oyabun-kobun* leaders and followers
5 母 *shimbo* one's true mother
玉 *oyadama* boss, chief, leader
石 *oya ishi* cornerstone
旧 *shinkyū* relatives and old friends
代代 *oyadaidai no* ancestral
旦那 *oya danna* the old master
兄弟 *oya-kyōdai* parents, brothers, and sisters; nearest relatives
6 米 *shim-Bei* pro-American
好 *shinkō* intimacy, friendship
交 *shinkō* friendship, intimacy
合 *shita(mi)-a(u)* be familiar with
団体 *oya dantai* parent organization
会社 *oyagaisha, oya kaisha* parent company; holding corporation; assembly plant
近 *shinkin* familiarity; personal attendants
近性 *shinkinsei* familiarity
近感 *shinkinkan* feeling of familiarity
任 *shinnin* personal imperial appointment
任式 *shinninshiki* imperial investiture ceremony ⌈pointed by the emperor
任官 *shinninkan* official personally ap-
7 身 *shimmi* relative. *shimmei no* kind, cordial,
里 *oyazato* home town ⌊sincere
兵 *shimpei* bodyguard, imperial bodyguard
告 *shinkoku* personal statement; personal
孝行 *oya-kōkō* filial piety ⌊accusation
8 征 *shinsei* emperor's personal campaign
披 *shimpi* confidential, personal, private
拝 *shimpai* worship (by the emperor)
泣 *oyana(kase)* disappointment to parents
和 *shinwa* friendship, fellowship, fraternity
英 *shin-Ei* pro-English
炙 *shinsha* close contact
知 *oyashi(razu)* wisdom tooth; dangerous place; everyone for himself; a child who does not know his parents ⌈affinity
和力 *shinwaryoku* chemical attraction,
9 風 *oyakaze* parental authority
厚 *shinkō* intimacy; kindness
指 *oyayubi* thumb; the boss
昵 *shinjitsu* familiarity
柱 *oyabashira* central pillar
独 *shin-Doku* pro-German
神 *oyagami* clan god, ancestral god
政 *shinsei* direct imperial rule
思 *oyaomo(i)* filial affection
重代 *oyajūdai* successive generations
10 骨 *oyabone* outer rib of a fan
株 *oyakabu* original stock ⌈matricide
殺 *oyagoro(shi), oyakoro(shi)* parricide,
書 *shinsho* autographed letter
馬鹿 *oyabaka* parental overindulgence
展 *shinten* confidential, personal (letter)
展書 *shintensho* confidential letter
11 鳥 *oyadori* parent bird, mother bird
掛 *oyaga(kari)* dependence on father
猫 *oya neko* mother cat
船 *oyabune* depot ship; large Chinese junk
許 *oyamoto* parental roof; parents; home; banker for gamblers
密 *shimmitsu* intimacy, close friendship
祭 *shinsai* Shinto rites conducted by the emperor
教会 *oya kyōkai* mother church
戚 *shinseki* relative
戚関係 *shinseki kankei* kinship
族 *shinzoku* relatives
族会議 *shinzoku kaigi* family council
族結婚 *shinzoku kekkon* consanguinous marriage, intermarriage
族閥 *shinzokubatsu* nepotism
12 御 *oyago* (your) parents
椀 *oyawan* large rice bowl
疎 *shinso* degree of intimacy ⌈parents
勝 *oyamasa(ri)* a child surpassing his
爺 *oyaji*＝親父 (see above 4)
等 *shintō* degree of kinship
筆 *shimpitsu* one's own writing
裁 *shinsai* imperial decision
証券 *oya shōken* master (insurance) policy
無 *oyana(shi)* orphaned
無子 *oyana(shi)go* orphan
善 *shinzen* friendship, amity, good will
善日 *shinzembi* good-neighbor day
善条約 *shinzen jōyaku* treaty of amity
善使節 *shinzen shisetsu* good-will envoy
善飛行 *shinzen hikō* good-will flight
善関係 *shinzen kankei* friendly relations
13 馴 *shitashi(mi)-na(reru)* become friends
愛 *shin-ai* affection, love
署 *shinsho* personal signature
電 *shinden* ruler's telegram
睦 *shimboku* friendship, reunion
睦会 *shimbokkai, shimbokukai* social gather-
14 銀行 *oya ginkō* parent bank ⌊ing
15 閲 *shin-etsu* personal inspection ⌈sibility
権 *shinken* parental authority and respon-
縁 *shin-en* relative
鋭 *shin-ei* imperial guards
衛兵 *shin-eihei* bodyguard
衛隊 *shin-eitai* bodyguard troops ⌈parents
17 優 *oyamasa(ri)* a child surpassing his
臨 *shinrin* imperial visit, personal presence
鍵 *oya kagi* master key
18 藩 *shimpan* daimyos related to the Toku-
類 *shinrui* relative ⌊gawa shoguns

類付合 *shinruizu(ki)a(i)* association among relatives; intimate association
[19]蘇 *shin-So* pro-Soviet
[20]譲 *oyayuzu(ri)* inheritance from a parent
[21]露 *shin-Ro* pro-Russian

10

覯 4294 F1718 Kō happening to meet.

覬 4295 F1718 Ki coveting high rank.
[16]覦 *kiyu suru* have designs on

11

A 観＝觀 4296 F1720 Kan look, appearance; spectacle; condition; view, outlook. *kan(zuru)* view, contemplate. *mi(ru)* (see under 見 4284.0).
[4]月 *kangetsu* moon viewing
天喜地 *kanten kichi* ecstasy
[5]世音 *Kanzeon* Goddess of Mercy
世音菩薩 *Kanzeon Bosatsu* Goddess of Mercy
[6]光 *kankō* sight-seeing
光団 *kankōdan* tourist party
光客 *kankōkyaku* tourist, sight-seer
光船 *kankōsen* excursion ship
[7]花植物 *kanka shokubutsu* flowering plant
兵 *kampei* show of force
兵式 *kampeishiki* military review, parade
[8]取 *kanshu suru*＝看取 222.8
者 *kansha* sight-seer
念 *kannen* meditation; idea; intention; sense (of duty); resignation to, preparation; conviction
念主義 *kannen shugi* idealism
念的 *kannenteki* ideal, ideological
念連合 *kannen rengō* association of ideas
念論 *kannenron* idealism, ideology
念闘争 *kannen tōsō* ideological warfare
[9]点 *kanten* viewpoint, angle of vision
相学 *kansōgaku* phrenology
相術 *kansōjutsu* phrenology
客 *kankaku, kankyaku* visitors, spectators, audience
客層 *kankakusō, kankyakusō* the audience level
音 *Kannon* Goddess of Mercy
音堂 *Kannondō* a temple to the Goddess of Mercy
音菩薩 *Kannon Bosatsu* Goddess of Mercy
音開 *kannombira(ki)* folding doors
[10]梅 *kambai* viewing plum blossoms
桜 *kan-ō* viewing the cherries
桜会 *kan-ōkai* cherry-blossom party
[11]菊 *kangiku* chrysanthemum viewing
望 *kambō* observation
[12]衆 *kanshū* audience, spectators
象 *kanshō* meteorological observation
葉植物 *kan-yō shokubutsu* foliage plant
測 *kansoku* observation, survey; thinking, opinion
測気球 *kansoku kikyū* observation balloon
測所 *kansokujo* observatory; observation post
[13]楓 *kampū* viewing maple leaves
想 *kansō* contemplation, observation
照 *kanshō* contemplation; (esthetic) intuition
楽境 *kanrakukyō* pleasure resort
戦 *kansen suru* witness a battle or a game
戦武官 *kansembukan* military observer
[14]察 *kansatsu* observation, survey, investigation, supervision; view
察力 *kansatsuryoku* power of observation
察者 *kansatsusha* observer
察眼 *kansatsugan* an observing eye
[15]劇 *kangeki* theatergoing
潮 *kanchō* watching the tide
賞 *kanshō* admiration, enjoyment
賞植物 *kanshō shokubutsu* ornamental plants
[16]覧 *kanran* inspection, viewing
覧券 *kanranken* admission ticket
覧者 *kanransha* spectator, visitor
覧席 *kanranseki* seats, grandstand
覧料 *kanranryō* admission fee
覧税 *kanranzei* entertainment tax
[20]艦式 *kankanshiki* naval review

13

覺 4297 F1719 See 覚 4288.

14

覽＝覧 4298 F1719 See 覧 4292.

15

覿 4299 F1720 Teki meet, see.
[9]面 *tekimen no* immediate, instantaneous, swift

17

觀 4300 F1720 See 観 4296.

RAD. 角 148

Tsuno horn. At left: *tsuno hen*. Nickname: Horn.

A 角 4301/F1721 KAKU angle; corner; square; squared timber; target. *kado* corner; angle; edge; angularity; harshness. *kaku na* square, four-cornered. *tsuno* horn, antlers; feeler, tentacle. *tsuno(gumu)* sprout. *sumi* corner, nook.
2 力 *sumō* wrestling; wrestler
3 叉 *tsunomata* points on antlers
4 刈 *kakuga(ri)* square-cut hair
5 皿 *kakuzara* square plate
石 *kakuishi* square stone
立 *tsunoda(teru)*, *kadoda(teru)* be sharp, be pointed; be rough; sound harsh, *kado (ga) ta(tsu)* sound harsh
目立 *tsunomeda(teru)*=word above
6 字 *kakuji* square characters
行灯 *kakuandon* square paper lantern
7 角 *kadokado ni* on every corner. *kadokado-(shii)* angularity, stiffness, harshness
材 *kakuzai* squared timber, lumber
形 *kakugata* square shape
8 店 *kado mise* corner store
取 *kado (ga) to(reru)* be tactful 「wrangling
突 *tsunotsu(ki)* bullfight; brushing by;
突合 *tsunotsu(ki)a(i)* bickering, wrangling
9 革 *kadogawa* corner leather (on a book)
度 *kakudo* angle
通 *kakutsū* an expert on wrestling
逐 *kakuchiku suru* compete with, vie with
柱 *kakuchū* square pillar, prism (in math.). *kakubashira* square pillar
盆 *kakubon* square tray
背革 *kadosegawa* three-quarter binding
速度 *kaku sokudo* angular velocity
屋敷 *kado yashiki* corner house
砂糖 *kakuzato* cube sugar
10 帯 *kaku obi* a man's stiff obi
素 *kakuso* keratin
袖 *kaku sode* square bag sleeves; civilian clothes; plain-clothes man
袖巡査 *kaku-sode junsa* plain-clothes man
11 張 *kakuba(ru)* be angular; become formal
距 *kakkyo* angular distance
瓶 *kakubin* square bottle
笛 *tsunobue* bugle, trumpet, horn
細工 *tsunozaiku* horn work
視差 *kaku shisa* angular parallax
12 帽 *kakubō* square college cap
鉔 *kaku yasuri* square file
13 隠 *tsunokaku(shi)* bride's wedding hood
14 膜 *kakumaku* cornea
膜炎 *kakumakuen* inflammation of the cornea
15 質 *kakushitsu* keratin, horniness
質物 *kakushitsubutsu* horny (keratin) material
16 樽 *tsunodaru* two-handled keg
鋼 *kakkō* square bar steel
錐 *kakusui* pyramid
17 壔 *kakutō* prism
18 襟 *kakueri* square neck (in a garment)

4

斛 4302/F869 KOKU a measure, 10 *to* (see Weights and Measures). [斗]

5

觚 4303/F1722 KO cup; piece of wood used before paper for writing letters.

6

觜 4304/F1722 See 嘴 1000.

B 触 4305/F1725 = 觸 SHOKU touching. *fu(reru)* touch, feel, hit, strike, graze; announce, proclaim, mention, refer to; conflict with, be contrary to. *sawa(ru)* touch, feel. *fu(re)* touch, contact; official notice. *sawa(ri)* touch, feel; point (of a story); good mixer.
4 手 *shokushu* feeler, tentacle
込 *fu(re)-ko(mu)* announce, pretend to be, pass off for, pose as 「wrestling)
太鼓 *fu(re)daiko* drum beating (to announce
5 目 *shokumoku* seeing
示 *fu(re)-shime(su)* proclaim, announce
出 *fu(re)da(shi)* announcement, advertisement; introduction
6 回 *fu(re)-mawa(su)*, *fu(re)-mawa(ru)* spread (a rumor), noise abroad, broadcast
合 *fu(re)-a(u)* touch, come in contact with
7 角 *shokkaku* feeler, antenna, tentacle
吻 *shokufun* proboscis
8 知 *shokuchi suru* feel, perceive by touching
官 *shokkan* the organ of touch
9 発 *shokuhatsu* contact detonation
発水雷 *shokuhatsu suirai* contact mine
10 書 *fu(re)ga(ki)* circularized official announcement
11 接 *shokusetsu* touching
12 媒 *shokubai* catalyst 「(see above–6)
渡 *fu(re)wata(su)*=*fu(re)-mawa(ru)* 触回

診 *shokushin* palpation, manipulation, manual examination
覚 *shokkaku* sense of touch
13 感 *shokkan* touch sensation

A **解** 4306 / F1723 **觧** GE, KAI explanation, notes; key; excuse; understanding. *kai(suru)* understand, comprehend, interpret. *to(ku)* untie, undo, loosen, unpack; unravel, disentangle; unsew; dismantle; solve, answer; dispel; cancel; absolve; release; dismiss (a person); explain. *to(ku), to(kasu)* comb out. *to(keru)* get loose, come untied; relent; be solved, be dispelled; be relieved (of a job). *hodo(ku)* *vi* and *vt* undo, untie, unpack, unfasten, loosen, unlace; unravel; get untied. *hogu(reru), hodo(keru)* get loose, get untied. *hogu(su), hogo(su)* untie, unfasten, loosen, fray, unknit, untwist, unravel, disentangle. *hogo(reru)* get loose, get untied; fray, get disentangled. *hotsu(reru)* fray, ravel, stray, become loose. *waka(ru)* (see under 分 578.0). *ge(senai)* (it) passes understanding.

5 付 *to(ki)-tsu(keru)* comb; persuade
氷 *kaihyō* thaw; thawing
6 団 *kaidan* disbanding
式 *kaishiki* solution, key
任 *kainin* dismissal, release
合 *to(ke)-a(u)* be melted together, be reconciled. *to(ke)a(i)* compromise
7 体 *kaitai* dismantling, dissolution, liquidation; autopsy
決 *kaiketsu* solution, settlement
8 明 *to(ki)-a(kasu), kaimei suru* explain, elucidate
法 *kaihō* (key to) a solution
版 *kaihan* type distribution
物 *to(ki)mono* old clothes to be ripped apart
官 *gekan* dismissing an official
毒剤 *gedokuzai* antidote
析 *kaiseki* analysis
析幾何学 *kaiseki kikagaku* analytical geometry
放 *to(ki)-hana(tsu), kaihō suru* release, deliver, liberate, emancipate
放的 *kaihōteki* open-minded, frank
放感 *kaihōkan* the feeling of freedom upon release
9 約 *kaiyaku* cancellation of a contract
除 *kaijo* cancellation, rescinding; release; exoneration
10 悟 *kaigo* enlightenment
消 *kaishō* dissolution, liquidation; cancellation; settlement
党 *kaitō* dissolution of a party
帰 *to(ki)-kae(su)* let go free, release (prisoners)
剖 *kaibō* dissection; autopsy; analysis
剖学 *kaibōgaku* anatomy
剖室 *kaibōshitsu* dissecting room
11 停 *kaitei* removing a ban, releasing from suspension
捨 *to(ki)-su(teru)* break the bonds
脱 *gedatsu* (Buddhist) salvation, emancipation, deliverance
釈 *kaishaku* explanation, interpretation
隊 *kaitai* demobilization
12 雇 *kaiko* discharge, dismissal
散 *kaisan* dispersion, disbanding, dissolution, dismissal
答 *kaitō* answer, solution
13 傭 *kaiyō* dismissal, discharge
解 *to(ki)-hogo(su), to(ki)-hodo(ku)* *vt* unravel; rip apart
義 *kaigi* explanation
禁 *kaikin* lifting a ban or embargo
14 読 *kaidoku* deciphering, decoding
語 *kaigo* understanding a word
髪 *hotsu(re)gami* uncombed hair, stray hair
説 *kaisetsu* explanation, commentary
説者 *kaisetsusha* commentator, expounder
説欄 *kaisetsuran* commentator's column
15 熱 *genetsu* alleviation of fever
熱剤 *genetsuzai* antipyretic
16 薬 *geyaku* antidote
18 職 *kaishoku* discharge, dismissal
題 *kaidai* synopsis, review of a subject
27 纜 *kairan* sailing, leaving

11

觴 4307 / F1725 SHŌ cup.

13

觸 4308 / F1725 See **触** 4305.

RAD. 言 149

Kotoba word. At left: *gomben* left-side "speaking." Nickname: Speaking.

A 言 4309 F1726 GEN, GON word; phrase; speech; statement. *yu(u), i(u)* say, tell, talk, speak, declare; call, term, name. *kotoba* word, term; phrase; language; a language; dialect; statement. *i(i-konasu)* express correctly. *i(i-sobireru)* fail to tell, miss a chance of telling. *i(waba)* so to speak, in a sense. *(to) i(eba)* speaking of. *(towa) i(u) monono, (towa)i(e)* but, still, however. *i(ikonashi)* an expression. *i(wambakari)* as much as to say. *i(wazumogana)* better left unsaid. *-koto* word.

[2]入 *i(i)-i(reru)* propose, suggest ⌈reference
[3]及 *i(i)-oyo(bu)* refer to, mention. *genkyū*
上 *gonjō suru* relate, inform, report (to a higher person) ⌈ing
丸 *i(i)-maru(meru)* skillfully deceive in talk-
下 *genka ni, gonka ni* promptly, readily
下手 *i(i)beta* poor speaker
[4]止 *i(i)-ya(meru)* finish speaking
込 *i(i)-ko(meru)* propose, make an overture
中 *i(i)-a(teru)* guess right
切 *i(i)-ki(ru)* declare, say definitely; tell all
分 *i(i)bun* one's say, one's point; objection, complaint; excuse, explanation; case
文 *gembun* words and sentences
文一致 *gembun itchi* unification of the written and spoken languages
方 *i(i)kata* way of saying
方無 *i(wan)katana(shi)* inexpressible, indescribable
[5]立 *i(i)-ta(teru)* state, maintain, allege
句 *genku* words, phrases
広 *i(i)-hiro(meru)* proclaim, noise abroad
旧 *i(i)furu(su)* say the same thing all the time. *i(i)furu(shita)* hackneyed, stale
外 *gengai no* unexpressed, implied, implicit
古 *i(i)furu(shita)* hackneyed, stale
去 *i(i)-sa(ru)* leave a message and depart
乍 *-i(i)naga(ra)* even so, granting that
出 *i(i)-da(su), i(i)-ida(su)* start talking; break the ice, speak out; propose
甲斐 *i(i)gai no aru* worth mentioning
付 *i(i)-tsu(karu)* have orders (to do). *i(i)-tsu(karu)* order (to do). *kotozu(karu)* be entrusted with; be asked to send word. *kotozu(ke)* message. *kotozu(keru)* entrust with (a message). *i(i)tsu(ke)* order, instructions
付口 *i(i)tsu(ke)guchi* talebearing
[6]色 *genshoku* words and facial expression
回 *i(i)-mawa(su)* express (well). *iimawa(shi)* an expression; phraseology
尽 *i(i)-tsu(kusu)* tell all, exhaust (a subject)
返 *i(i)kae(su)* talk back to
伝 *i(i)-tsuta(eru)* hand down, circulate, inform. *iitsuta(e)* tradition, legend. *kotozuta(e), kotozu(te)* declaration, hearsay
伏 *i(i)-fu(seru)* argue down, confute
交 *i(i)-kawa(su)* pledge one's love; talk together ⌈arrange beforehand
合 *i(i)-a(u)* quarrel, argue. *i(i)-a(waseru)*
当 *i(i)-a(teru)* guess right
争 *i(i)-araso(u)* quarrel, dispute
迄無 *i(u)made(mo)na(i)* a matter of course; it goes without saying
行 *genkō* speech and conduct, profession and practice
行録 *genkōroku* memoirs ⌈to all
成 *i(i)na(ri)* being submissive, saying yes
成次第 *i(i)na(ri) shidai*=next entry
成放題 *i(i)na(ri) hōdai* submissive to everyone ⌈inexpressible, indescribable
[7]言 *gengen* every word. *i(u) (ni) i(warenu)*
足 *i(i)-ta(su)* say something further
改 *i(i)-arata(meru)* correct oneself
抜 *i(i)-nu(keru)* give an evasive answer, excuse oneself, explain away, quibble. *iinu(ke)* evasion, excuse, prevarication
乱 *i(i)-mida(reru)* confuse, refute; interrupt (a conversation); talk confusedly
含 *i(i)-fuku(meru)* instruct, inculcate
来 *i(i)ki(tari)* legend, tradition
[8]延 *i(i)-no(basu)* postpone with excuses
逆 *i(i)-sakara(u)* speak against
逃 *i(i)noga(re)* evasion, excuse, prevarication
送 *i(i)-oku(ru)* send word
退 *i(i)-no(keru)* argue away, refute
拡 *i(i)-hiro(meru)* proclaim, noise abroad
明 *i(i)-a(kasu)* talk the whole night thru. *gemmei* declaration, announcement, statement ⌈sert
放 *i(i)-hana(tsu), i(i)-hana(su)* declare, as-
知 *i(i)shi(renu)* unspeakable, inexpressible
並 *i(i)-nara(beru)* line up points in a speech
直 *i(i)-nao(su)* restate, correct
歩 *i(i)-aru(ku)* spread tales
表 *i(i)-ara(wasu)* declare, express
事 *i(i)goto*=*i(i)gusa* 言草 (see below–9)
[9]廻 *i(i)-mawa(su)* express (well)
通 *(i)i-tō(su)* persist in saying
連 *i(i)-tsura(neru)* enumerate, line up

拵 *i(i)-koshira(eru)* make up a story
洩 *i(i)-mo(rasu)* disclose; leave unsaid
祝 *kotoho(gu)* congratulate
前 *i(i)mae* excuse, pretense
草 *i(i)gusa* one's remarks; topic of conversation; excuse, pretext; complaint
負 *i(i)-ma(keru)* lose out in an argument.
10 値 *i(i)ne* seller's price ⌊*i(i)-ma(kasu)* refute
悩 *i(i)-naya(mu)* hesitate to say
振 *i(i)bu(ri)*, *i(ip)pu(ri)* manner of speaking
残 *i(i)-noko(su)* leave word; leave unsaid. *i(i)noko(ri)* something left unsaid
消 *i(i)-ke(su)* deny, retract
破 *i(i)-yabu(ru)* refute
紛 *i(i)-magi(rasu)*, *i(i)-magi(rawasu)* prevaricate, quibble. *i(i)-hagura(su)* deceive (someone) in talking ⌈to say
兼 *i(i)-ka(neru)* hesitate to say, be unable
容 *gen-yō* words and facial expression
差 *i(i)-sa(su)* check oneself in speaking, stop short
挙 *kotoa(ge) suru* speak; criticize
11 黒 *i(i)-kuro(meru)*, *i(i)-kuru(meru)* quibble
違 *i(i)-chiga(eru)*, misstate, make a slip. *iichiga(i)* misstatement
過 *i(i)-su(giru)*, *i(i)-su(gosu)* overstate, say too much. *i(i)-ayama(tsu)* misstate, make a slip ⌈fact; offer excuses; describe
做 *i(i)-na(su)* state something dubious as a
張 *i(i)-ha(ru)* insist on, maintain
掛 *i(i)-ka(keru)* speak to; start talking; accuse. *i(i)ga(kari)* false accusation; pretext; commitment
捲 *i(i)-ma(kuru)* argue down, confute
捨 *i(i)-su(teru)* make a parting remark
淀 *i(i)-yodo(mu)* hesitate in saying
渋 *i(i)-shibu(ru)* hesitate to say, falter
終 *i(i)-owa(ru)* finish talking ⌈justification
訳 *i(i)wake* apology, excuse, explanation,
訛 *i(i)nama(ri)* corrupt form. *i(i)-nama(ru)*
動 *gendō* speech and conduct ⌊be corrupted
悪 *i(i)niku(i)* awkward to say
寄 *i(i)-yo(ru)* court, woo; approach defiantly. *kotoyo(su)* spread rumors; pass on a message
習 *i(i)-nara(wasu)* be handed down; have a habit of saying. *i(i)nara(washi)* tradition, legend; usage
責 *genseki* responsibility for a statement
12 遣 *i(i)-tsuka(wasu)*, *i(i)-ya(ru)* send a message
開 *i(i)-hira(ku)* justify, explain, vindicate
換 *i(i)-ka(eru)* say in other words
渡 *i(i)-wata(su)* sentence, condemn; order, instruct, announce ⌈argument
竦 *i(i)-suku(meru)* down someone in an

散 *i(i)-chi(rasu)* spread (a report)
募 *i(i)-tsuno(ru)* argue vehemently ⌈tion
落 *i(i)-o(tosu)* leave unsaid, neglect to men-
葉 *koto(no)ha* words; a tanka poem. *kotoba* words ⌈tongue
葉尻 *kotobajiri* end of a word; slip of the
葉付 *kotobatsu(ki)* way of speaking
葉返 *kotoba (o) kae(su)* answer, refute
葉尽 *kotoba (o) tsu(kusu)* explain carefully
葉余 *kotoba (ni) ama(ru)* inexpressible
葉使 *kotobazuka(i)* speech, diction
葉違 *kotobataga(i)* quarreling; breaking a promise; slip of the tongue ⌈port
葉添 *kotobazo(e)* advice, good offices, sup-
葉遣 *kotobazuka(i)* speech, diction
葉数 *kotobakazu* words, speech
葉濁 *kotoba (o) nigo(su)* speak ambiguously
13 損 *i(i)-sokona(u)*, *i(i)-son(jiru)* make a slip; fail to tell, misstate
継 *i(i)-tsu(gu)* transmit, inform (someone)
続 *i(i)-tsuzu(keru)* continue to say
辞 *genji* words, speech, language, expression
触 *i(i)-fu(rasu)* spread a report or rumor
詰 *i(i)-tsu(meru)* argue down ⌈tell
詫 *i(i)-wa(biru)* fail to tell, miss a chance to
馴 *i(i)-na(reru)* be accustomed to say
置 *i(i)-o(ku)* leave a message
14 腐 *i(i)-kusa(su)* speak evil of
聞 *i(i)-ki(kasu)*, *i(i)-ki(kaseru)* tell (a person to do something), instruct; persuade, admonish
漏 *i(i)-mo(rasu)* disclose; leave unsaid
種 *i(i)gusa* one's remarks
説 *gensetsu* remark, opinion, statement
誤 *i(i)-ayama(ru)* misstate, make a slip
貌 *gembō* words and facial expression
暮 *i(i)-ku(rasu)* pass the time talking
様 *i(i)yō*, *i(i)zama* way of saying ⌈pressible
様無 *i(i)yō (no) na(i)* indescribable, inex-
語 *gengo*, *gongo* language, speech, words. *i(wazu)-kata(rasu)* tacitly, by implication
語不随 *gengo fuzui* speech impediment
語同断＝言語道断 (see below–14)
語形態学 *gengo keitaigaku* morphology
語学 *gengogaku* philology; linguistics
語学者 *gengogakusha* linguist, philologist
語道断 *gongo-dōdan* unmentionable, outrageous, unpardonable
語障害 *gengo shōgai* speech impediment
15 談 *gendan* conversation, talk
諍 *i(i)isakai* verbal quarrel
霊 *kotodama* soul or power of language
慰 *i(i)-nagusa(meru)* console
質 *genshitsu*, *genchi* pledge, commitment, promise
論 *genron* speech, discussion

論自由 *genron no jiyū* freedom of speech
論界 *genronkai* the press
18繕 *i(i)-tsukuro(u)* gloss over
難 *i(i)gata(i)* difficult to say, unmentionable, inexpressible
顕 *ii-arawa(su)* declare, express
21囃 *i(i)-haya(su)* praise; spread (a report)
22籠 *i(i)-ko(meru)* argue down, confute

2

B **訂** 4310 / F1727 TEI correct; decide.
5正 *teisei* correction; revision

訃 4311 / F1728 FU obituary, report of a death.
7告 *fukoku* obituary, report of a death
9音 *fuin, fuon* report of a death
12報 *fuhō* report of a death, obituary

A **計** 4312 / F1728 KEI plan, scheme, trick; total; meter, gauge. *haka(ru)* measure, gauge, weigh; fathom, sound; compute, estimate. *haka(ru)* (see under 謀 4414.0); measure. *haka(rau)* manage, arrange, dispose of, see about, talk over.
3上 *keijō suru* add up, appropriate
6吏 *keiri* treasurer
7売 *haka(ri)-u(ri)* selling by measure
8直 *haka(ri)-nao(su)* reweigh, remeasure
歩器 *keihoki* pedometer
画 *keikaku* plan, scheme, project; intention
画的 *keikakuteki* planned, intentional, premeditated
画者 *keikakusha* planner, promoter
画案 *keikakuan* plan, blueprint, schedule
画経済 *keikaku keizai* planned economy
画線 *keikakusen* projected (railway) line
10料 *keiryō* estimating
時 *keiji* timing (in races)
時員 *keiji-in* timers (at a race)
11略 *keiryaku* plan, trick, stratagem
理士 *keirishi* public accountant
12策 *keisaku* plan, stratagem
量 *keiryō* measuring, weighing, computation, measurement
量器 *keiryōki* meter, gauge, scale
13数 *keisū* calculation, computation
14算 *keisan* computation, calculation
算日 *keisambi* settlement day
算尺 *keisanjaku* slide rule
算学 *keisangaku* (science of) accounting
算式 *keisanshiki* formula
算係 *keisangakari* accountant
算書 *keisansho* statement (of account)
算器 *keisanki* calculator, computer
算簿 *keisambo* account book
15慮 *keiryo* planning
器 *keiki* meter, gauge

3

訌 4313 / F1729 KŌ get confused.
6争 *kōsō* confused fighting

訊 4314 / F1729 JIN request; question, investigate. *ki(ku), tazu(neru)* ask, inquire.
6返 *tazu(ne)-kae(su)* question again ⌈inquest
11問 *jimmon* cross examination, interrogation,

B **託** 4315 / F1730 TAKU requesting, entrusting with. *taku(suru)* entrust with, charge with; pretend; hint. *kotozu(karu)* be requested. *kako(tsu), kakotsu(keru), kotozu(keru)* pretend; plead; make excuses. *kako(chi)* complaining, grumbling.
3子所 *takujisho* day nursery; nursery school
7言 *kagoto, takugen, kakotsukegoto* excuse, pretext, plea
児所 *takujisho* day nursery; nursery school
8送 *takusō suru* consign, send by (someone), check (baggage)
9宣 *takusen* (Buddhist or Shinto) oracle

A **討** 4316 / F1729 TŌ. *u(tsu)* attack, defeat, destroy, conquer.
2入 *u(chi)-i(ru)* break into, raid
4手 *u(chi)te, u(t)te* attacking party, punitive force, pursuers; shooter, murderer
6死 *uchijini* death in battle
伐 *tōbatsu* subjugation, suppression
伐軍 *tōbatsugun* punitive force
伐隊 *tōbatsutai* punitive force
伐戦 *tōbatsusen* punitive expedition
7究 *tōkyū* study, research, investigation
8取 *u(chi)-to(ru)*＝打取 1829.8
果 *u(chi)-hata(su)* slay
9洩 *u(chi)-mo(rasu)* let escape, faii to kill
10匪 *tōhi* bandit suppression
13滅 *u(chi)-horo(bosu)* destroy
幕 *tōbaku suru* attack the shogunate
14漏 *u(chi)-mo(rasu)* let escape, fail to kill
15論 *tōron* debate, discussion, contention, argumentation
論会 *tōronkai* forum, debate; debating society
論終結 *tōron shūketsu* closure of debate
20議 *tōgi* debate, discussion
議事項 *tōgi jikō* agenda items
議案 *tōgian* subject for debate
議場 *tōgijō* forum

7 見 角 3【言】谷 豆 豕 豕 豸 貝 赤 走 足 身 車 辛 辰 辵 辶 邑 阝 酉 釆 里

A **訓** 4317/F1729 KIN, KUN Japanese reading (of a character); explanation of a character; lesson; regulation; rule. *oshi(eru)* instruct. *yo(mu)* read. *kun(zuru)* read; read in the *kun*.

4 化 *kunka* instruction
5 示 *kunji* instruction
令 *kunrei* directive, instructions
7 言 *kungen* instruction, precept
戒 *kunkai* admonition, warning
状 *kunjō* letter of instruction
告 *kunkoku* instruction
8 育 *kun-iku* education, discipline
9 点 *kunten* punctuation marks
10 陶 *kuntō*＝薫陶 4073.10 ⌈characters
11 釈 *kunshaku* explaining the meaning of
12 詁 *kunko* exegesis, interpretation of old
詁学 *kunkogaku* exegetics ⌊words
13 辞 *kunji* address to students
解 *kunkai* explanation of terms; interpretation of a passage
話 *kunwa* fable, moral tale ⌈character
義 *kungi* the reading and meaning of a
蒙 *kummō* enlightenment, instruction
電 *kunden* telegraphic instructions
14 読 *kundoku, kun-yo(mi)* reading characters with Japanese sounds
誨 *kunkai suru* instruct, enlighten
誡 *kunkai* admonition, warning
導 *kundō* training ⌈pline, schooling
練 *kunren* training, practice, drill, disci-
練所 *kunrenjo* training institute
16 諭 *kun-yu* admonition, exhortation

A **記** 4318/F1731 KI account, narrative, history, annals; remembering; writing; the Kojiki. *ki(suru)* write down, record, describe; remember. *shiru(su)* write down; inscribe; mention, give an account of. *shirushi* record.

2 入 *kinyū* entry (in a record)
6 伝 *kiden* history and biography
号 *kigō* mark, sign, symbol
名 *kimei* signature
名投票 *kimei tōhyō* signed ballot
名株 *kimei kabu* registered stock
名株券 *kimei kabuken* registered stock
名帳 *kimeichō* register
7 述 *kijutsu* description, account
8 法 *kihō* notation
帖 *kichō*＝記帳 (see below–11)
帖係 *kichōgakari* bookkeeper
者 *kisha* journalist, reporter ⌈tion
者団 *kishadan* press group, press associa-
者会見 *kisha kaiken* news conferences, press interview
者席 *kishaseki* press box, press table
事 *kiji* description, statement, news item, article
事文 *kijibun* descriptive composition
事広告 *kiji kōkoku* article-type advertise-
事体 *kijitai* factual style (of article) ⌊ment
念 *kinen* remembrance, commemoration
念日 *kinembi* memorial day, anniversary
念切手 *kinen kitte* commemorative stamp
念会 *kinenkai* commemorative meeting, memorial service ⌈zine)
念号 *kinengō* memorial number (of a maga-
念物 *kinembutsu* souvenir, keepsake, monu-
念品 *kinenhin* souvenir, memento ⌊ment
念章 *kinenshō* commemorative medal
念祭 *kinensai* anniversary
念碑 *kinenhi* monument
念樹 *kinenju* memorial tree
念館 *kinenkan* memorial hall
9 紀 *Kiki* the Kojiki and Nihonshoki
11 章 *kishō* medal, badge, insignia
帳 *kichō* registry; entry, posting, bookkeeping; signature
帳所 *kichōsho* place where visitors sign
帳係 *kichōgakari* bookkeeper
13 載 *kisai* statement, publication; entry
数法 *kisūhō* numerical notation
14 聞 *kibun* dictated record
誦 *kishō* memorizing
銘 *kimei* inscription, engraving
16 憶 *kioku* memory, remembrance, recollec-
憶力 *kiokuryoku* memory ⌊tion
憶術 *kiokujutsu* mnemonics
憶喪失 *kioku sōshitsu* loss of memory, amnesia ⌈ry, amnesia
憶喪失症 *kioku sōshitsushō* loss of memo-
録 *kiroku* record, document, archives, minutes, proceedings, chronicle
録文学 *kiroku bungaku* documentary literature
録的 *kirokuteki* record-making
録係 *kirokugakari* recorder, one in charge of records
録映画 *kiroku eiga* documentary film
録破 *kirokuyabu(ri)* record-breaking; extraordinary
録漏 *kirokumo(re)* omitted from the record

— 4 —

訝＝**訝** 4319/F1731 GA. GE. *ibuka(ru)* doubt, be suspicious of, wonder. *ibuka(shii)*＝*ayashii* (see under 怪 1665.0).

B **訟**＝**訟** 4320/F1731 SHŌ accuse.

訥 4321 / F1732 TOTSU stutter.

5弁 *totsuben* slow of speech, defective speech
7言 *totsugen* slow of speech, defective speech

訣 4322 / F1732 KETSU separation; part; secret.

7別 *ketsubetsu* separation, farewell
10宴 *ketsuen* parting spree
12飲 *ketsuin* parting cup
13辞 *ketsuji* farewell words

訛 4323 / F1731 F1766 **譌** KA. *nama(ru)* speak with an accent; be corrupted. *ayama(ri)* mistake. *nama(ri)* dialect, brogue, accent.

6伝 *kaden* false report, misinformation
7言 *kagen* dialect, brogue
声 *damigoe* hoarse voice, thick voice
9音 *kaon* provincialism, brogue
10称 *kashō* a corruption (in speech)
14語 *kago* dialect, brogue

A **許** 4324 / F1733 KYO. KO. *yuru(su)* permit, approve; authorize; acknowledge; confide in; forgive, pardon; release, acquit; overlook. *moto* (parental) roof, a person's house. *-bakari* approximately; only, merely, alone; degree; almost, practically; absorbed in; continue doing; just now; be about to do; be ready for; have no alternative; now or never.

5可 *kyoka* permission, approval, license, permit, authorization, admission
可申請 *kyoka shinsei* license application
可制 *kyokasei* license system
可料 *kyokaryō* license fee
可書 *kyokasho* written permission
可証 *kyokashō* permit, license
7否 *kyohi* permission, sanction
10容 *kyoyō* permission, approval; pardon
11婚 *iinazuke* fiancé, fiancée
13嫁 *iinazuke* fiancée
15諾 *kyodaku* consent, approval, permit

A **設** 4325 / F1732 SETSU. *mō(keru)* prepare, provide; establish, found, set up, organize; enact, lay down (rules); get (a child).

5立 *setsuritsu suru* establish, found, organize, promote, incorporate
立者 *setsuritsusha* founder, organizer
8定 *settei* establishment, creation
9計 *sekkei* plan, design
計図 *sekkeizu* plan, draft, blueprint
計者 *sekkeisha* planner, designer
11問 *setsumon* question
12備 *setsubi* equipment, fixtures, installations, arrangements, accommodations, convenience, facilities
営 *setsuei* construction, arrangements
13置 *setchi suru* establish, found

B **訪** 4326 / F1732 HŌ. *otozu(reru)* visit, call on. *tazu(neru)* call on, visit, look up. *tobura(u)*, *to(u)* call on, visit, offer sympathy.

4日 *hō-Nichi* visiting Japan
中 *hō-Chū* visiting Communist China
6米 *hō-Bei* visiting America
9客 *hōkyaku, hōkaku* visitor
11問 *hōmon* visit, interview, call
問先 *hōmonsaki* place visited
問者 *hōmonsha* caller, visitor
問客 *hōmonkyaku* caller, visitor
問飛行 *hōmon hikō* good-will flight
問記者 *hōmon kisha* interviewer
問着 *hōmongi* visiting dress
問談 *hōmondan* interview

A **訳** 4327 / F1769 **譯** YAKU translation. EKI. *yaku(su)*, *yaku(suru)* translate. *wake* meaning, sense; reason, cause; circumstances, the case; understanding (between them). *yaku* translation, version; interpretation.

2了 *yakuryō suru* finish translating
4文 *yakubun* translation, version, rendering
方 *yaku(shi)kata* how to translate; method of translation
5出 *yakushutsu* translation
本 *yakuhon* translated book
6合 *wakea(i)* meaning; reason; circumstances
7述 *yakujutsu suru* translate and explain. *yakujutsu* translation
述者 *yakujutsusha* translator
8注 *yakuchū* translation with notes
知 *wakeshi(razu)* a boor; one who doesn't understand anything. *wakeshi(ri)* one who understands
者 *yakusha* translator
9柄 *wakegara*=*wake* (see under 訳 4327.0)
10書 *yakusho* a translation, a version, translated book
11違 *yaku(shi)chiga(i)* mistranslation
12無 *wakena(i)*, *wake(no)na(i)* easy, simple
13解 *yakkai* annotated translation, paraphrase
詩 *yakushi* translated poem
14語 *yakugo* word used in translation, an equivalent
読 *yakudoku* reading a manuscript and giving explanations
18難 *yaku(shi)niku(i)* difficult to translate

5

訔 See 3636.

訶 4328/F1734 KA scold.

詁 4329/F1734 KO chatter.

詛 4330/F1737 SO. *noro(u)* curse.

8呪 *noroi* curse

訝 4331/F1731 See 訝 4319.

詑 4332/F1735 I. TA deceive, delude. *wa(biru)* apologize. *wa(bi)* apology

詔 4333/F1736 B SHŌ imperial edict. *mikotonori* imperial edict, decree.

5令 *shōrei* imperial edict
9勅 *shōchoku* imperial proclamation
10書 *shōsho* imperial edict

註 4334/F1734 CHŪ notes, comment. *chū(suru)* comment on; annotate.

4文 *chūmon* an order
10記 *chūki suru* make entries; write down
11釈 *chūshaku* notes, comment, exegesis
釈本 *chūshakubon* commentary
釈者 *chūshakusha* commentator, annotator
釈書 *chūshakusho* a commentary
12疏 *chūso*=next word
13解 *chūkai* notes, comment; commentary

詞 4335/F1737 A SHI words; poetry. *kotoba* words.

8宗 *shisō* great scholar, literary man
10致 *shichi* the import of words
書 *kotobaga(ki)* notes; foreword
華 *shika* beautiful phraseology
11章 *shishō* poetry and prose
19藻 *shisō* figure of speech, rhetorical flourishes; prose and poetry

詠 4336/F1737 咏 詠 B EI poem; song; singing; composing. *yo(mu)* recite, chant. *ei(suru)* write poems; recite poems.

2入 *yo(mi)-i(reru)* mention (in a poem)
5史 *eishi* epic, historical poem
出 *eishutsu* writing poetry or songs
7吟 *eigin* reciting poetry
8物 *eibutsu* a nature poem
9草 *eisō* draft of a poem
10進 *eishin* presentation of a poem (to the Court)
13嘆 *eitan* exclamation, admiration
14誦 *eishō* reciting poetry
歌 *eika* composition of a poem or song; poem; song; Buddhist pilgrim's song
15歎 *eitan* exclamation, admiration

詐 4337/F1735 B SA. *itsuwa(ru)* (see under 偽 510.0).

8取 *sashu* fraud, swindle
10病 *sabyō* feigned illness
称 *sashō* misrepresentation, false statement. impersonation
害 *sagai* prejudice (in law)
11偽 *sagi* lie, falsehood
術 *sajutsu* deceptive means
略 *saryaku* fraud, swindle
12欺 *sagi* fraud, swindling
欺投票 *sagi tōhyō* fraudulent voting
欺師 *sagishi* swindler, impostor, crook
16謀 *sabō* fraud, swindle

診 4338/F1734 B SHIN seeing; diagnosing. *mi(ru)* diagnose, examine.

11断 *shindan* diagnosis
断書 *shindansho* medical certificate
14察 *shinsatsu* medical examination
察日 *shinsatsubi* consultation day
察台 *shinsatsudai* examining table
察券 *shinsatsuken* consultation ticket
察室 *shinsatsushitsu* doctor's examining room
察料 *shinsatsuryō* medical fee, doctor bill
察時間 *shinsatsu jikan* consultation hours
察無料 *shinsatsu muryō* free consultation
17療 *shinryō* examination and treatment
療中 *Shinryōchū* The Doctor is in.
療所 *shinryōjo* clinic, medical office
療時間 *shinryō jikan* consultation hours

評 4339/F1736 評 A HYŌ criticism, comment. *hyō(suru)* criticize, comment on.

6伝 *hyōden* critical biography
7言 *hyōgen* critical remark
決 *hyōketsu* decision, verdict
判 *hyōban* fame, reputation, popularity; sensation; rumor
判物 *hyōbammono* well-known or popular person
8注 *hyōchū* commentary
定 *hyōjō* conference, consultation. *hyōtei* rating, evaluation
者 *hyōsha* critic, reviewer
価 *hyōka* appraisal, valuation, assessment; appreciation
価額 *hyōkakaku* estimated value
9点 *hyōten* examination marks
11釈 *hyōshaku* annotation, commentary
12註 *hyōchū* commentary

14語 *hyōgo* critical remark; mark; epithet
15論 *hyōron* criticism, review, comment, editorial
論界 *hyōronkai* the commentators' circle
論家 *hyōronka* critic, commentator, reviewer
20議 *hyōgi* consultation, discussion, conference, deliberation
議会 *hyōgikai* council, conference
議所 *hyōgijo* conference room, forum
議員 *hyōgi-in* councillor; trustee; board of trustees
議員会 *hyōgi-inkai* council, conference, board meeting

B **訴** 4340/F1733 So. *utta(eru)* sue; complain of (pain); appeal to; have recourse to. *utta(e)* lawsuit, complaint, accusation, charge, indictment; appeal, petition.
2人 *sonin* accuser, one who sues
5出 *utta(e)-de(ru)* lodge a complaint
6因 *so-in* cause of action, charge, count
件 *soken* a case (at law)
7状 *sojō* petition, written complaint
8追 *sotsui* legal action, proceedings; prosecution, impeachment; charges
事 *utta(e)goto* a case, legal suit
10陳 *sochin suru* sue
11訟 *soshō* lawsuit, litigation
訟人 *soshōnin* plaintiff
訟手続 *soshō tetsuzuki* legal proceedings
訟代理人 *soshō dairinin* counsel, attorney
訟当事者 *soshō tōjisha* litigant
訟法 *soshōhō* legal procedure (code)
訟事件 *soshō jiken* case, lawsuit
訟依頼人 *soshō irainin* client
訟費用 *soshō hiyō* costs (of a lawsuit)
訟関係人 *soshō kankeinin* litigant
15権 *soken* right to sue
19願 *sogan* appeal, petition
願人 *sogannin* appellant, petitioner

A **証** 4341/F1766 **證** Shō proof, evidence; certificate. *shō(suru)* prove, guarantee. *akashi suru* witness. *akashi* proof, evidence, vindication, witnessing.
2人 *akashibito, shōnin* witness
人台 *shōnindai* witness stand
人席 *shōninseki* witness chair
4文 *shōmon* deed, bond, promissory note
5左 *shōsa* proof, evidence, testimony
6印 *shōin* document seal
会 *akashikai* testimony meeting
7言 *shōgen* testimony, evidence
8明 *shōmei* proof, evidence; testimony, witness; certification
明書 *shōmeisho* certificate
明済 *shōmeizu(mi)* already proved
券 *shōken* securities, bonds, deed, certificate
券会社 *shōkengaisha* securities company
券取引所 *shōken torihikijo* securities exchange
券業 *shōkengyō* security business
拠 *shōko* proof, evidence, testimony
拠人 *shōkonin* witness
拠立 *shōkoda(teru)* prove, substantiate, corroborate
拠物 *shōkobutsu* material evidence
拠物件 *shōko bukken* material evidence
10紙 *shōshi* sticker, tourist stamp, inspection stamp
書 *shōsho* bond, deed, certificate
11票 *shōhyō* voucher
13跡 *shōseki* evidence, traces, vestiges
14認状 *shōninjō* (church-worker's license)
16憑 *shōhyō* evidence, proof, testimony

6

諛 4342/F1754 See 諛 4399.

詠 4343/F1737 See 詠 4336.

誨 Nonstandard for 誨 4363.

詢 4344/F1738 Jun consult with.

詫 4345/F1740 Ta. *wa(biru)* apologize, make an excuse. *wabi* apology, excuse, intercession.
2入 *wa(bi)-i(ru)* humbly apologize
7言 *wabigoto* apology
状 *wabijō* written apology

詣 4346/F1738 Kei. *kei(suru)* visit a temple or shrine. *mai(ru), mō(deru)*=*mai(ru)* (see under 参 850.0). *mō(de), mai(ri)* temple or shrine visit.

詬 4347/F1740 Kō ridicule, put to shame. *nonoshi(ru)* revile.
10辱 *kōjoku* disgrace, insult

誂 4348/F1743 Chō. *atsura(eru)* order.
6向 *atsura(e)mu(ki)* suitable, satisfactory, ideal
8物 *atsura(e)mono* goods ordered

B **該** 4349/F1741 **該** Gai the said.
6地 *gaichi* the said area
当 *gaitō* pertinence, relevance
当者 *gaitōsha* the person concerned or qualified
10案 *gaian* the said proposal
12博 *gaihaku na* profound, extensive (knowledge)

誄 4350 / F1743 Rui condolence message.
[4]文 *ruibun* funeral address
[12]詞 *ruishi* message of sympathy
[13]詩 *ruishi* elegy
[14]歌 *ruika* dirge

誅 4351 / F1743 Chū death penalty; punishment. *chū(suru)* punish with death.
[6]伐 *chūbatsu* punitive expedition
[7]求 *chūkyū suru* extort, squeeze, exact tribute
[15]戮 *chūriku* death punishment

A **誠** 4352 / F1746 **誠** Sei. *imashi(meru)* admonish, warn; prohibit. *makoto* sincerity, honesty, fidelity; truth. *makoto no* true, genuine, actual. *makoto ni* really; extremely. *makoto(shiyakana)* plausible.
[4]心 *seishin* sincerity
心誠意 *seishin-sei-i* sincerity, wholehearted devotion; sincerely, devotedly
[8]直 *seichoku* honest and sincere
実 *seijitsu* sincerity, honesty, truthfulness, faithfulness
忠 *seichū* true loyalty
[9]信 *seishin* sincerity
[10]恐 *seikyō* fear and reverence
烈 *seiretsu* sincerity and purity
[11]情 *seijō* sincerity, a true heart
[13]意 *sei-i* sincerity, good faith

B **誉** 4353 / F1771 **譽** Yo. *home(ru)* praise. *homa(re)* honor, glory.
[5]立 *ho(me)-ta(teru)* praise, praise profusely
[7]言葉 *homekotoba* words of praise
[8]者 *homemono* someone praised by all
奉 *ho(me)-matsu(ru)* praise (God)
[10]高 *homa(re)taka(i)* renowned
称 *ho(me)-soya(su)* praise profusely
[11]望 *yobō* fame
[14]歌 *ho(me)-uta(u)* praise (God)
[21]囃 *ho(me)-haya(su)* praise profusely

B **誇** 4354 / F1744 Ko. *hoko(ru)* boast of, be proud of. *hoko(rakasu)* take a boastful attitude. *hoko(rashii)* proud. *hoko(rashigeni)* proudly, triumphantly. *hoko(ri)* pride.
[3]大 *kodai* exaggeration, hyperbole, bombast
大妄想狂 *kodai mōsōkyō* megalomania
[5]示 *koshi, koji* ostentation, display
[6]色 *koshoku* a proud countenance
[10]高 *hoko(ri)taka(i)* proud, lordly. *hoko(ri)-taka(buru)* be boastful, be proud
称 *koshō* exaggeration, boasting
[11]張 *kochō* exaggeration
張法 *kochōhō* hyperbole
張的 *kochōteki* exaggerated, bombastic
[18]顔 *hoko(ri)gao* triumphant look

詭 4355 / F1740 Ki lie; deceive.
[5]弁 *kiben* sophism, sophistry; chicanery; paradox; play on words
弁学派 *Kiben Gakuha* the Sophists
弁家 *kibenka* sophist; quibbler
[9]計 *kikei* trick, wiles
[11]道 *kidō* deceptive methods, questionable means
偽 *kigi* deception
術 *kijutsu* trickery
[12]策 *kisaku* trick, stratagem
[16]謀 *kibō* ruse, trick

詮 4356 / F1741 Sen discussion; selection; methods called for; result, effect. *sen(zuru)* think over; discuss. *kai* effect, result, use.
[4]方 *senkata* resources, means, way
方無 *senkatana(ku)* unavoidably, helplessly
[10]索 *sensaku* search, inquiry, investigation
索好 *sensakuzu(ki)* inquisitive, prying, curious
[11]術 *sensube* proper methods
[12]無 *senna(i)* useless
[16]衡 *senkō* selection, choice; evaluation
[20]議 *sengi* discussion, investigation, inquiry, examination
議立 *sengida(te)* inquiry, thoro investigation
[28]鑿 *sensaku* excavation, boring

B **詳** 4357 / F1742 Shō. *tsumabira(kana)*, *kuwa(shii)* full, detailed, minute, accurate; versed in, well-informed on.
[6]伝 *shōden* detailed biography
[7]言 *shōgen* detailed explanation
述 *shōjutsu* detailed explanation
[10]記 *shōki* minute description, full account
[11]略 *shōryaku* details and rough outlines
細 *shōsai* details, particulars
密 *shōmitsu na* detailed
[12]註 *shōchū* copious notes
報 *shōhō* particulars, full report
[13]解 *shōkai* detailed explanation
[14]説 *shōsetsu* detailed explanation
察 *shōsatsu* careful observation
[15]論 *shōron* full treatment, detailed explanation
[16]録 *shōroku* detailed record
覧 *shōran* looking over in detail

A **話** 4358 / F1741 Wa. *hana(su)* talk, speak, converse; tell; explain. *hana(seru)* sensible, intelligent, agreeable. *hanashi tsuide ni* in the course of the conversation.

hanashi talk, chat, conversation; story; rumor; news; consultation, negotiations; facts, reasons.

8口 *hana(shi)kuchi* opening up a conversation; way of speaking; one's real meaning

下手 *hanashibeta* poor talker

上手 *hanashijōzu* good conversationalist

4手 *hana(shi)te* speaker

方 *hana(shi)kata* way of speaking

込 *hana(shi)-ko(mu)* have a long talk with

5半分 *hanashi-hambun* statements that must be discounted 50%

甲斐 *hana(shi)gai* effect of a speech

6好 *hana(shi)zu(ki) na* talkative, gossipy

合 *hana(shi)-a(u)* discuss, talk over, consult with. *hanashia(i)* consultation; agreement

7材 *wazai* material for a talk

声 *hana(shi)goe* a voice, a whisper

言葉 *hana(shi)kotoba* speech, spoken language

8法 *wahō* parlance; narration

実入 *hanashi (ni) mi (ga) i(ru)* put one's whole self into a talk

9柄 *wahei* topic of conversation

相手 *hanashi aite* adviser, someone to talk to

10振 *hana(shi)buri* manner of speaking

家 *hana(shi)ka* storyteller

11術 *wajutsu* storyteller's art

掛 *hana(shi)-ka(keru)* accost, speak to

12替 *hanashika(watte)* not to change the subject but...

13嫌 *hana(shi)gira(i)* taciturn, reticent

14種 *hanashi (no) tane* topic of conversation

語 *wago* conversational language

16頭 *watō* topic of conversation

18題 *wadai* topic of conversation

B **詰** 4359 F1741 KITSU. *tsu(mu)* be pressed in, be packed, become close; be checkmated. *tsu(meru) vt* stuff, fill, pack, plug; place closely; write closely; sit closely; shorten; curtail; checkmate; keep doing; hold (one's breath). *vi* attend (office). *tsu(maru)* be stopped up, be blocked; be full, be stuffed; be shortened, contract; be hard up; be held up, be deadlocked. *naji(ru)* reprove, rebuke, blame. *tsu(me)* stuffing, packing, stopper; end, foot of, edge; checkmate; appointment to. *tsu(maranai)* trifling, insignificant, small, of no account, worthless, trashy, foolish, despicable, uninteresting, cheerless, monotonous. *tsu(mari)* after all, eventually; in short, to sum up; in other words. *-zu(me)* packed in, bottled in; boxed in; kept (standing); on duty at.

4手 *tsu(me)te* packer

木 *tsu(me)ki* wooden plug

込 *tsu(me)-ko(mu)* stuff, pack, jam into; crowd into; tamp

切 *tsu(me)-ki(ru)* be in constant attendance (as a valet); be always on the job

5石 *tsu(me) ishi* foundation stone

6伏 *tsu(me)-fu(seru)* explain and secure compliance

合 *tsu(me)-a(waseru)* assort, pack an assortment. *tsumeawa(se)* assortment (of cakes). *tsumia(i)* working at the same place; coworker; arguing

8屈 *kikkutsu* crouching; difficulty in explaining characters or writing

所 *tsumesho* office; guard room; crew room; side room. *tsu(maru) tokoro* after all

物 *tsu(me)mono* stuffing, dressing (a fowl), filling, packing, padding, plugging

11問 *kitsumon* grilling, cross-examination

掛 *tsu(me)-ka(keru)* crowd into, throng around

寄 *tsu(me)-yo(ru)*, *tsu(me)-yo(seru)* draw near, approach, edge in, press upon

責 *kisseki* reproof, censure

12番 *tsu(me)ban* one's turn for duty

替 *tsu(me)-ka(eru)* repack, refill, rebottle

朝 *kitchō* tomorrow morning

13腹 *tsu(me)bara* forced suicide, forced disembowelment; forced resignation

14綿 *tsu(me)wata* padding, filler; sanitary pad

18襟 *tsu(me)-eri* stand-up collar; close-buttoned collar

A **詩** 4360 F1739 SHI poem, poetry.

2人 *shijin* poet; minstrel

3才 *shisai* poetic genius

4心 *shishin* poetic sentiment

文 *shibun* prose and poetry, literature

友 *shiyū* poetical friend

5句 *shiku* verse, stanza

史 *shishi* an epic poem

仙 *shisen* great poet

6会 *shikai* poetry meeting

7作 *shisaku suru* write poetry

体 *shitai* poetic form

吟 *shigin* reciting Chinese poems

抄 *shishō* selection of poems

材 *shizai* material for poetry

形 *shikei* poetic form; poetic rhythm

8味 *shimi* poetic sentiment

的 *shiteki* poetical, poetic

宗 *shisō* great poet

学 *shigaku* study of poetry

的情緒 *shiteki jōcho* poetic mood

9律 *shiritsu* poetic rhythm

思 *shishi* poetic sentiment; poetic talent

草 *shisō* first draft of a poem

巻 *shikan* an anthology of poetry
10 格 *shikaku* laws of poetry; poetic quality
家 *shika* poet
11 情 *shijō* poetic sentiment, poetic interest
眼 *shigan* poetic understanding
経 *Shikyō* Book of Songs. *Shi King* (a Chinese classic)
12 詞 *shishi* poetic diction
集 *shishū* anthology of poetry
13 話 *shiwa* a talk on poetry
意 *shi-i* meaning of a poem
想 *shisō* thought of a poem
聖 *shisei* great poet
14 選 *shisen* anthology of poems
境 *shikyō* a poetic location
歌 *shika, shiika* Chinese and Japanese poetry
魂 *shikon* poetic sentiment, poetic interest
15 趣 *shishu* poetic beauty, poetic sentiment
劇 *shigeki* dramatic poem
稿 *shikō* draft of a poem
論 *shiron* essay on poetry
篇 *Shihen* Psalms, Psalter
篇記者 *Shihen Kisha* the Psalmist
16 壇 *shidan* poetry circles
興 *shikyō* poetic inspiration
18 題 *shidai* title of a poem; material for a poem
19 藻 *shisō* poetic language, poetic skill; poem; prose composition

A **試** 4361/F1738 SHI testing. *kokoro(miru)* try, attempt. *tame(su)* attempt, try, experiment, test, sample. *kokoro(mi)* trial, test, attempt, experiment; ordeal, temptation.
5 用 *shiyō* trial
写 *shisha* preview, private showing
6 行錯誤 *shikō-sakugo* trial and error
合 *shiai* contest, match, game, bout, tournament, joust
合場 *shiaijō* ball park, football field, court, ring
7 作 *shisaku* trial manufacture, first production, trial production
売 *shibai* commercial adventure
8 刷 *shisatsu* proof printing
金 *shikin* assaying
金石 *shikinseki* touchstone; test, test case
9 食 *shishoku* sampling food
乗 *shijō* trial ride
10 剤 *shizai* reagent
案 *shian* draft, tentative plan
射 *shisha* test firing
射弾 *shishadan* trial shot
11 問 *shimon* question, interview, test, quiz, examination
斬 *tame(shi)gi(ri)* trying out a new sword (on corpses or prisoners)
毫 *shigō* first writing of the year
球式 *shikyū shiki* the first ball; opening of the first ball game
運転 *shiunten* trial run, test run
掘 *shikutsu* prospecting
掘者 *shikutsusha* prospector
掘権 *shikutsuken* mining claim
12 植 *shishoku* experimental planting
焼 *tame(shi)ya(ki)* photographic proof
補 *shiho* probationer, beginner
飲 *shi-in suru* sample (drinks)
筆 *shihitsu* first writing of the new year
検官 *shikenkan* inspector
13 煉 *shiren* test, trial, probation, ordeal
14 演 *shien* rehearsal, preview
練 *shiren* test, trial, probation, ordeal
算 *shisan* preliminary calculation; auditing accounts
算表 *shisanhyō* trial balance
15 論 *shiron* preliminary essay, sketch
16 錬 *shiren* test, trial, probation, ordeal
薬 *shiyaku* reagent; a test
17 聴 *shichō* audition
18 験 *shiken* examination; experiment; test, trial; demonstration
験工場 *shiken kōjō* pilot plant
験台 *shikendai* test case, guinea pig, test
験地獄 *shiken jigoku* the hell of (entrance) examinations
験所 *shikensho* laboratory, experimental station
験的 *shikenteki* experimental; tentative
験官 *shikenkan* examiner
験紙 *shikenshi* litmus paper
験勉強 *shikem-benkyō* cramming for examinations
験済 *shikenzu(mi)* tried, proved
験問題 *shikem-mondai* examination questions
験場 *shikenjō* examination hall; laboratory; experimental station
験管 *shikenkan* test tube

— 7 —

誕 See 誕 4386.

誠 4362/F1746 See 誠 4352.

誨 4363/F1748 KAI instruct.
16 諭 *kaiyu* enlightenment

誡 4364/F1747 KAI commandment, admonition. *imashi(meru)* admonish, caution, reprove. *imashime* admonition, rebuke.
7 告 *kaikoku* warning, caution

誣 4365/F1747 FU. BU. *shii(ru)* slander, accuse falsely.

⁷言 *bugen, fugen, shiigoto* calumny, slander, false charge
告 *bukoku, fukoku* slander, false charge

誌 4366/F1744 B Shi records; document; magazine. *shirushi, shiru(su)* (see under 記 4318.0). *-shi* magazine.
³上 *shijō* in a magazine
⁴友 *shiyū* fellow subscriber
⁵代 *shidai* price of a magazine
⁹面 *shimen* a page of a magazine

誑 4367/F1744 Kyō. *tara(kasu), tabura(kasu)* ＝*dama(su)* (see under 騙 5223.0). *tabaka(ru)* cheat; impose on. *ta(rasu)* coax, cajole; deceive.
⁴込 *ta(rashi)-ko(mu)* coax, cajole; deceive
¹²詐 *kyōsa* deception

誦 4368/F1747 Shō. Ju. *shō(suru)* recite, chant.
¹⁰記 *shōki* reciting from memory
¹¹経 *zukyō, jukyō* reading the sutras
習 *shōshū suru* learn by memorizing
¹²詠 *shōei* reciting poetry

誓 4369/F1744 B Sei. *chika(u)* swear, pledge, vow. *chika(i)* oath, pledge, vow. *chika(tte)* positively, surely.
⁴文 *seibun, seimon* written oath
文立 *seimonda(te)* making a vow; delivering a written vow
文払 *seimombara(i)* bargain sale
⁷言 *seigon, seigen* oath, vow, pledge, affirmation
⁹約 *seiyaku* a written vow
約者 *seiyakusha* party to a covenant
約書 *seiyakusho* written pledge, covenant
¹⁰紙 *seishi* written pledge
¹²詞 *seishi* oath, pledge
¹³盟 *seimei* a vow
¹⁹願 *seigan* oath, pledge, vow
願者 *seigansha* one who makes a vow

認 4370/F1744 A 認 Nin. *mito(meru)* witness; sight; discern, authorize, recognize; appreciate; approve of; judge, conclude; believe; regard as. *shitata(meru)* write, draw up; eat. *mito(me)* approval; private seal.
⁵用 *nin-yō*＝認容 (see below–10)
可 *ninka* approval, license, permission
可状 *ninkajō* permit, license
可書 *ninkasho* permit, license, charter
可証 *ninkashō* permit, license, charter
⁶印 *mito(me)in, nin-in* personal seal, signet
合 *mito(me)-a(u)* see another's viewpoint
⁷否 *nimpi* approval or disapproval
⁸知 *ninchi* recognition, acknowledgment
定 *nintei* authorization, recognition, acknowledgment, presumption, permission; identification
¹⁰容 *nin-yō* admission, tolerance, acknowledgement
¹¹許 *ninkyo* consent, recognition
¹²証 *ninshō* approval, validation, confirmation, certification
¹⁵諾 *nindaku* assent, admission, approval
¹⁹識 *ninshiki* recognition, understanding, knowledge
識不足 *ninshiki fusoku* lack of understanding
識票 *ninshikihyō* identification

誘 4371/F1745 B Yū. *saso(u)* invite, ask; call for; provoke, cause; bring (tears); allure, tempt, seduce. *izana(u)* invite; lead, tempt. *obi(ku)* decoy, entice, lure.
²入 *obi(ki)-i(reru)* decoy, entice, lure into
⁴水 *saso(i) mizu* pump priming
込 *saso(i)-ko(mu)* entice into ; attract, allure
引 *yūin suru* entice, invite, beguile, induce,
⁵出 *obi(ki)-ida(su), obi(ki)-da(su), saso(i)-da(su), yūshutsu suru* decoy, entice, lure away
⁶因 *yūin* immediate cause; incentive, motive
虫灯 *yūchūtō* luring lamp
⁸拐 *yūkai* kidnapping, abduction
拐者 *yūkaisha* kidnapper, abductor
拐罪 *yūkaizai* the crime of kidnapping
⁹発 *yūhatsu suru* cause, induce, lead up to, give advice to
¹⁰起 *yūki suru* give rise to, lead to, cause
致 *yūchi suru* lure, entice, invite, bring about
殺 *yūsatsu suru* seduce and kill
益 *yūeki suru* lead and help
¹¹掖 *yūeki suru* lead, guide, help, instruct
寄 *obi(ki)-yo(seru)* lure toward
¹²惑 *yūwaku* temptation, seduction
惑物 *yūwakubutsu* temptation, seduction
惑者 *yūwakusha* tempter, seducer
¹³蛾灯 *yūgatō* luring lamp
¹⁴導 *yūdō* induction, incitement, inducement, encouragement
導兵器 *yūdō heiki* guided missiles
導訊問 *yūdō jimmon* leading question
導弾 *yūdōdan* guided missile
導爆弾 *yūdō bakudan* guided missile

誤 4372/F1747 A 誤 Go. *ayama(ru) vi* and *vt* err, be mistaken; do wrong; mislead. *ayama(ri)* mistake, error. *ayama(tte)* by mistake, accidentally.
⁵用 *goyō* misapplication, misuse, abuse
写 *gosha* scribal error, error in copying
⁶伝 *goden* misinformation, incorrect report

字 *goji* wrong character, wrong word, misprint
7判 *gohan* mistrial, miscarriage of justice, misjudgment
8送 *gosō suru* missend
9信 *goshin* mistaken belief
10称 *goshō* misnomer
記 *goki* clerical error, misentry, error in writing
配 *gohai* misdelivery (of letters)
殺 *gosatsu suru* kill by mistake; kill the wrong person
差 *gosa* error, aberration
11脱 *godatsu* mistakes and omissions
訳 *goyaku* mistranslation
12植 *goshoku* typographical error, erratum, misprint
診 *goshin* wrong diagnosis
報 *gohō* misinformation, incorrect report
13解 *gokai* misunderstanding, misconception, delusion
電 *goden* incorrect telegram
載 *gosai*=*goki* 誤記 (see above–10)
14聞 *gobun* misunderstanding, false report, misinformation
綴 *gosetsu* misspelling
認 *gonin* misunderstanding, misconception, mistake
読 *godoku* misreading
説 *gosetsu* mistaken theory
算 *gosan* miscalculation
15審 *goshin* wrong refereeing
18謬 *gobyū* error, fallacy, mistake
21魔化 *gomaka(su)* cheat, deceive, camouflage, hoodwink, prevaricate; gloss over, cover up; tamper with, doctor up; patch up; quibble; embezzle

A **説** 4373/F1748 ZEI. ETSU. SETSU opinion, view, assertion; comment; theory; rumor, report; version. *to(ku)* explain, expound, advocate, preach, teach, persuade.

3及 *to(ki)-oyo(bu)* mention, refer to
4分 *to(ki)-wa(keru)* explain
5付 *to(ki)-tsu(keru)* talk into, persuade, prevail upon
去 *to(ki)-sa(ru)* completely explain
出 *to(ki)-ida(su)* begin to speak; begin to explain
6伏 *to(ki)-fu(seru)*, *to(ki)-fu(su)* confute, argue down, convince; prevail on, persuade to do. *seppuku* persuading, persuasion, convincing
7述 *setsujutsu* explanation, exposition
8法 *seppō* (Buddhist) sermon
服 *seppuku* persuading, convincing
明 *setsumei suru*, *to(ki)-aka(su)* explain, interpret, illustrate, solve (a riddle). *setsumei*, *tokiaka(shi)* explanation, interpretation, description
明文 *setsumeibun* accompanying explanation
明図 *setsumeizu* explanatory diagram
明的 *setsumeiteki* explanatory
明者 *setsumeisha* expositor; exponent
明書 *setsumeisho* explanatory note
10起 *to(ki)-o(kosu)* begin to explain
破 *to(ki)-yabu(ru)* confute. *seppa* refutation
11問 *setsumon* investigation of a question; a proposition, a problem
掛 *yo(mi)-ka(keru)* begin to read; stop reading
経 *sekkyō* (Buddhist) sermon
得 *settoku* persuasion
得力 *settokuryoku* persuasive power
得代表 *settoku daihyō* a representative who explains a proposition
教 *to(ki)-oshi(eru)* propound, preach. *sekkyō* sermon; preaching; admonition; scolding
教所 *sekkyōjo* preaching place
教学 *sekkyōgaku* homiletics, sermonology
教者 *sekkyōja*, *sekkyōsha* preacher
教師 *sekkyōshi* preacher
教壇 *sekkyōdan* pulpit
12落 *to(ki)-o(tosu)* talk into, win over
13勧 *to(ki)-susu(meru)* persuade, urge, exhort
話 *setsuwa* story, narrative
話的 *setsuwateki* narrative (form)
14聞 *to(ki)-ki(kasu)* explain, instruct, reason with
16諭 *setsuyu suru*, *to(ki)-sato(su)* convince, persuade; reprove

A **語** 4374/F1745 Go word, speech, language, term. GYO. *kata(ru)* talk, tell, narrate, recite. *kata(rau)* talk, chat; pledge one's troth; invite, entice; win; conspire with. *kata(rai)* talk, chat; lovers' vow. *kata(ri)* narrative (in the noh); reciter. *-go* (technical) term.

4手 *kata(ri)te* speaker, narrator, reciter
5句 *goku* words, phrases
出 *kata(ri)-da(su)* utter, speak out
6気 *goki* tone of voice, manner of speaking
伝 *kata(ri)-tsuta(eru)* pass on (traditions)
次 *goji ni* while on the subject
合 *kata(ri)-a(u)* talk together
7尾 *gobi* word ending, the inflected end of a word
尾変化 *gobi henka* inflection of words
述 *kata(ri)-no(beru)* proclaim, tell
形 *gokei* word form
告 *kata(ri)-tsu(geru)* tell
呂 *goro* the sound, euphony
呂合 *goroa(wase)* rhyming game
8明 *kata(ri)-aka(su)* talk all night
法 *gohō* diction, phraseology, grammar, syntax
物 *kata(ri)mono* narrative; theme of a folk song
学 *gogaku* language study; linguistics
学者 *gogakusha* linguist
9草 *kata(ri)gusa* topic, story
10根 *gokon* stem, root of a word
格 *gokaku* grammar

脈 *gomyaku* interrelationship of words
部 *kataribe* family of professional narrators
原 *gogen* derivation, etymology
原学 *gogengaku* etymology
11掛 *kata(ri)-ka(keru)* address, speak to
族 *gozoku* a family of languages
釈 *goshaku* explanation of words
13源 *gogen* derivation, etymology
継 *kata(ri)-tsu(gu)* transmit, hand down
数 *gosū* number of words
群 *gogun* a family of languages
彙 *go-i* vocabulary, glossary
義 *gogi* meaning of a word
意 *go-i* meaning of a word
勢 *gosei* stress, emphasis, tone, accent; the power of words; manner of speaking
感 *gokan* the impression of words
幹 *gokan* stem, root of a word
路 *goro* the sound, euphony
路合 *goroa(wase)* parody ⌈form, tell
14聞 *kata(ri)-ki(kaseru)*, *kata(ri)-ki(kasu)* in-
15調 *gochō* accent, tone, rhythm
弊 *gohei* unhappy expression, faulty expression, misleading statement, misunder-
16頭 *gotō* first part of a word ⌊standing
録 *goroku* analects, book of aphorisms
18類 *gorui* parts of speech

A **読** 4375/F1771 **讀** Tō, Toku, Doku reading. *yo(mu)* read, peruse; understand, read (one's heart), guess, divine. *yo(meru)* can read; be legible, be readable; read well; be decipherable; understand, perceive, see thru. *yo(mi-konasu)* read thoroly. *yo(mi)* reading; Japanese rendering of a Chinese character. *yo(mide)* worthwhile reading.

2入 *yo(mi)-i(ru)* read earnestly, be absorbed in reading. *yo(mi)-i(reru)* mention (in a
了 *dokuryō suru* finish reading ⌊poem)
人 *yomibito* author of a poem
人知 *yo(mi)bitoshi(razu)* writer of the poem unknown
3下 *yo(mi)-kuda(su)* read thru, peruse
上 *yo(mi)-a(geru)* read aloud, read off, read out (the names)
4手 *yo(mi)te* reader; composer of a poem
方 *yo(mi)kata* way of reading; lesson; pro-
止 *yo(mi)sa(shi)* half-read ⌊nunciation
切 *yo(mi)-ki(ru)* read thru, finish reading
心術 *tokushinjutsu* mind reading, mental telepathy
心術師 *tokushinjutsushi* mind reader
5本 *tokuhon* reader. *yomihon* reader, story-
6尽 *yo(mi)-tsuku(su)* read everything ⌊book
返 *yo(mi)-kae(su)* reread
会 *dokkai* reading (of a bill) ⌈and compare
合 *yo(mi)-a(waseru)*, *yo(mi)-a(wasu)* read
8物 *yomimono* reading matter, a reading
取 *yo(mi)-to(ru)* read (someone's) mind,
直 *yo(mi)-nao(su)* reread ⌊guess, divine
易 *yo(mi)yasu(i)* easy to read; legible
者 *dokusha* reader, subscriber
者層 *dokushasō* class of readers
9通 *yo(mi)-tō(su)* read thru
点 *tōten* comma
後 *dokugo* after reading
後感 *dokugokan* impression of a book
10流 *yo(mi)-naga(su)* read fluently; read without thinking
破 *dokuha suru*, *yo(mi)-yabu(ru)* read thru
耽 *yo(mi)-fuke(ru)* be absorbed in reading
唇 *dokushin* lip reading
唇術 *dokushinjutsu* lip reading
書 *yo(mi)ka(ki)* reading and writing. *dokusho*, *tokusho* reading a book
書人 *dokushojin* a reader of books, a scholar; the intelligentsia
書力 *dokushoryoku* reading ability ⌈time
書三昧 *dokusho-zammai* only reading all the
書会 *dokushokai* reading circle, reading
書狂 *dokushokyō* a bookworm ⌊club
書室 *dokushoshitsu* reading room
書界 *dokushokai* reading public
書家 *dokushoka* well-read person
11過 *dokka suru* skim over, miss, overlook
違 *yom(i)chiga(i)* misreading
頃 *yo(mi)goro no* readable, fit to read
終 *yo(mi)-owa(ru)*, *yo(mi)-o(eru)* *vt* finish reading
経 *dokyō*, *dokkyō* chanting Buddhist sutras
12落 *yo(mi)-o(tosu)* overlook in reading
13溜 *yo(mi)-to(meru)* read and retain
解 *dokukai* reading and explaining a book
話術 *dokuwajutsu* lip reading
14聞 *yo(mi)-ki(kasu)* read to, read for. *yomiki(ki)* reading and listening
慣 *yo(mi)-na(reru)* get used to reading
誤 *yo(mi)-aya(maru)* misread, mispronounce
18癖 *yo(mi)kuse* peculiar pronunciation
難 *yo(mi)niku(i)* hard to read; illegible

— **8** —

諛 See 4399.

諚 4376/F1754 (国字) Jō command.

諏 4377/F1753 Shu, Su, Sō consult.

諍 4378 / F1753 Sō remonstrate. *isaka(u)*, *ara-so(u)* quarrel, dispute.

誼 4379 / F1750 Gi friendship, intimacy, good will. *yoshi(mi)* friendship, intimacy, good will.

諄 4380 / F1751 Jun. *hichikudo(i)* tedious.

15諄 *junjun to* earnestly, patiently, repeatedly

諂 4381 / F1751 Ten. *hetsura(u)* flatter, curry favor.

16諛 *ten-yu* flattery

B **謁** 4382 / F1760 = **謁** Etsu audience (with a ruler). *es(suru)* have an audience with.

7見 *ekken* an audience (with someone)

見室 *ekkenshitsu* audience chamber

B **諾** 4383 / F1759 Daku assent, consent, agreement. *daku(suru)* agree to. *ubena(u)* agree to; follow.

7否 *dakuhi* definite answer, yes or no, ac-

15諾 *dakudaku* yes yes ⌊ceptance or refusal

誰 4384 / F1749 Sui. *tare*, *dare* who. *dare(ka)* someone, somebody. *dare mo*, *dare(shimo)* everyone; (neg.) no one.

1一人 *dare hitori mo* (neg.) no one

4方 *donata* who

7何 *suika suru* challenge, question

8彼 *darekare*, *tarekare* this or that person; many people; anyone. *dare(mo)-kare-(mo)* everyone

彼無 *darekarena(shi)* everybody

9某 *taresore*, *taregashi* Mr. So-and-so

誹 4385 / F1749 Hi ridicule, slander.

13毀 *hiki* slander, calumny, libel

毀罪 *hikizai* defamation, libel

16諧 *haikai* 17-syllable poem; a humorous

17謗 *hibō* slander; abuse ⌊*haiku* poem

20議 *higi* abusive argument

B **誕** 4386 / F1745 = **誕** Tan be born; deceive; lie; be arbitrary.

5生 *tanjō* birth, nativity

生日 *tanjōbi* birthday

生石 *tanjōseki* birthstone

生祝 *tanjō iwa(i)* birthday party; birthday

7辰 *tanshin* birthday ⌊gift

諒 4387 / F1753 Ryō fact, reality. *ryō (to) suru* understand; appreciate; excuse.

7承 *ryōshō* acknowledgment

10陰 *ryōan*＝諒闇 (see below-17)

13解 *ryōkai* understanding, comprehension

14察 *ryōsatsu* understanding, sympathy, consideration ⌈or)

17闇 *ryōan* national mourning (for an emper-

A **談** 4388 / F1751 = **譚** Dan conversation, talk. *dan(jiru)*, *dan(zuru)* discuss, talk (with or about); negotiate with.

4片 *dampen* short talk, occasional talk

込 *dan(ji)-ko(mu)* protest against

6合 *dan(ji)-a(u)* negotiate with, consult together. *dangō* consultation, conference

合尽 *dangōzu(ku)* (not a verb) mutual agreement ⌈discussion

7判 *dampan* negotiation, conference, parley,

余 *dan-yo* after speaking; while speaking

10笑 *danshō* friendly chat

13義 *dangi* lecture, lesson, sermon (Buddhist)

話 *danwa* conversation, talk, chat, speaking

話体 *danwatai* conversational style

話管 *danwakan* speaking tube

15論 *danron* discussion, argument, discourse

論風発 *danron-fūhatsu* eloquence; ready controversialist

20議 *dangi*＝談義 (see above-13)

A **課** 4389 / F1749 Ka lesson; section, department; allotment, division. *ka(suru)*, *ka(su)* levy, assess; assign (a task); charge with.

5目 *kamoku* subject, course, curriculum;

外 *kagai* extracurricular ⌊items

外活動 *kagai katsudō* extracurricular activities ⌈lecture

外講義 *kagai kōgi* university extension

7役 *kaeki* taxes; conscripted labor

8長 *kachō* section head

10員 *ka-in* section staff

11率 *karitsu* tax rate

12程 *katei* course, curriculum, routine ⌈levy

税 *kazei* taxation, assessment, tax, duty,

税所得 *kazei shotoku* taxable income

税品 *kazeihin* taxable or dutiable article

税率 *kazeiritsu* tax rate

13業 *kagyō* schoolwork, lessons

14徴金 *kachōkin* charges ⌈work

18題 *kadai* subject, theme, problem, home-

B **請** 4390 / F1752 = **請** Shin. Shō. Jō. Sei requesting, inviting. *shō(jiru)*, *shō(zuru)* invite, usher in. *ko(u)* ask, request; invite; pray for; beg, solicit. *u(keru)* (see under 受 2826.0).

2人 *u(ke)nin* guarantor, bondsman

入 *shō(ji)-i(reru)* usher in, ask in
5出 *u(ke)-da(su)*＝受出 2826.5
6托 *seitaku* solicitation, entreaty
合 *u(ke)-a(u)* undertake; promise, guarantee. *u(ke)a(i)* guarantee, assurance
7判 *u(ke)han* surety seal
売 *u(ke)ū(ri)* retailing
求 *ko(i)-moto(meru)* ask for, beg. *seikyū* demand, claim, application
求人 *seikyūnin* claimant, applicant
求者 *seikyūsha* claimant, applicant
求書 *seikyūsho* application, written claim
8取 *u(ke)-to(ru)* receive, accept; believe, understand. *uketori* receipt, acknowledgment
歩 *ko(i)-aru(ku)* go around begging
受 *ko(i)-u(keru)* ask and receive
9待 *shōdai* invitation
負 *u(ke)-o(u)* contract for, undertake. *ukeoi* contract
負人 *ukeoinin* contractor
負入札 *ukeoi nyūsatsu* contract bid
負工 *ukeoikō* pieceworker
負仕事 *ukeoi shigoto* job work, piecework, contract work
負契約 *ukeoi keiyaku* contract
負師 *ukeoishi* contractor
負値段 *ukeoi nedan* contract price
負業 *ukeoigyō* contracting business
負賃金 *ukeoi chingin* piecework pay
10託 *seitaku* request, secret request
訓 *seikun* request for instructions
書 *u(ke)ga(ki), u(ke)sho* written acknowledgment; letter of acceptance; receipt
11宿 *u(ke)yado* servants' registry
13暇 *seika* requesting a vacation; a vacation
19願 *seigan* petition
願者 *seigansha* petitioner
願書 *seigansho* (written) petition

A **論** 4391/F1753 Ron argument; discourse. *agetsura(u), ron(jiru), ron(zuru)* discuss, argue, comment on, deal with, consider.

3及 *ronkyū suru* touch on, refer to, enter into
4文 *rombun* dissertation, thesis, article, paper, treatise, essay
5立 *ron(ji)-ta(teru)* argue eloquently
外 *rongai* beside the point, irrelevant
弁 *romben* argument
功 *ronkō* decision on service merits
功行賞 *ronkō kōshō* distribution of awards
6尽 *ron(ji)-tsu(kusu)* discuss thoroly
合 *ron(ji)-a(u)* discuss together, argue with
旨 *ronshi* point of an argument
考 *ronkō* a study
争 *ronsō* dispute, controversy, argument
争点 *ronsōten* point of dispute
7述 *ronjutsu* statement, enunciation
決 *ronketsu* conclusion, decision
判 *rompan* argument, disputation
究 *ronkyū suru* discuss thoroly
告 *ronkoku* stating one's belief; prosecution; prosecutor's address
8拠 *ronkyo* basis of an argument, data
法 *rompō* argument, reasoning, logic
者 *ronsha* disputant; advocate; the present writer
9陣 *ronjin* argument
点 *ronten* point at issue, disputed point
客 *ronkaku* disputant, controversialist
10破 *rompa suru* refute, argue against. *rompa* rebuttal
11断 *rondan* verdict, conclusion
理 *ronri* logic
理上 *ronrijō* logically (speaking)
理的 *ronriteki* logical
理学 *ronrigaku* logic
理学上 *ronrigakujō* logically (speaking)
12結 *ronketsu* conclusion of an argument
評 *rompyō* criticism, review, comment
証 *ronshō* proof, demonstration
策 *ronsaku* an article on current problems
13詰 *ron(ji)-na(jiru), ronkitsu suru* argue and criticise. *ron(ji)-tsu(meru)* drive an argument home
戦 *ronsen* verbal battle, argument
罪 *ronzai suru* prosecute
意 *ron-i* point of an argument
14語 *Rongo* Confucian Analects
説 *ronsetsu* discourse, dissertation; editorial
駁 *rombaku suru* refute, argue against
15調 *ronchō* tone of the argument
談 *rondan* arguing
鋒 *rompō* force of an argument, logic
敵 *ronteki* opponent (in debate), adversary
16壇 *rondan* world of criticism; lecture platform
18難 *ronnan* denunciation, criticism, censure
題 *rondai* subject, theme, topic for debate
叢 *ronsō* collection of treatises
20議 *rongi* discussion, controversy, argument

A **調** 4392/F1750 **調** Chō tune, tone, meter; key (in music); style of writing; tax in kind. *chō(zuru)* investigate, scrutinize; provide, prepare; make; curse, exorcise; ridicule. *shira(beru)* test, examine, investigate, survey, check up; inspect, overhaul; search for; look up (a word); refer to (a book); interrogate; correct (papers); play (on an instrument). *totono(eru)* prepare, arrange; fill (orders); supply; raise (money); put in order, tidy up, adjust (clothes); regulate; settle; purchase. *totono(u)* be prepared, be arranged, be in order, be adjusted,

be well regulated; be settled. *mitsugi* tribute.
shira(be) melody, tune; notes.
8 上 *shira(be)-a(geru)* investigate thoroly
子 *chōshi* tune, tone, key, note, pitch; time, rhythm; accent; vein; manner, style; condition, state (of health); trend
子付 *chōshizu(ku)* relax; warm up to; be elated by; be gay-spirited ⌈of tune
子外 *chōshihazu(re)* discord, false note, out
子物 *chōshimono* matter of chance; person easily elated
子者 *chōshimono* person easily elated
6 糸 *shira(be)ito* belt lacing
伏 *chōbuku* curse, exorcism
号 *chōgō* key signature (in music)
色 *chōshoku* mixing colors; toning (in
色板 *chōshokuban* palette ⌊movies)
印 *chōin* signature, signing, sealing
印式 *chōinshiki* ceremony of signing
印国 *chōinkoku* signatory powers
合 *chōgō* mixing, compound
合物 *chōgōbutsu* mixture, compound, concoction
合剤 *chōgōzai*=word above
8 法 *chōhō* convenience, usefulness. *chōhō(garu)* find useful, think highly of
物 *shira(be)mono* research; matter for investigation
和 *chōwa* harmony, accord, agreement; symphony; symmetry; conformity
直 *shira(be)-nao(su)* reinvestigate, re-ex-
定 *chōtei* settlement ⌊amine
味 *chōmi* seasoning, flavoring
味料 *chōmiryō* condiments, seasoning, relishes, dressing
9 革 *shira(be)gawa* belt, band, belting
速機 *chōsokuki* governor, speed regulator
度 *chōdo*=next word ⌈sils, supplies
度品 *chōdohin* furniture, appliances, uten-
律 *chōritsu* tuning
律師 *chōritsushi* piano tuner
査 *chōsa* investigation, examination, inquiry, survey, research
査委員 *chōsa-i-in* examiner, investigator
10 進 *chōshin* preparation
貢 *chōkō* tribute ⌈randum, record
書 *chōsho* protocol, preliminary memo-
帯 *chōtai* belt, belting
剤 *chōzai* compounding medicines
剤師 *chōzaishi* druggist
馬 *chōba* horsebreaking, horse training
馬師 *chōbashi* horse trainer
馬場 *chōbajō* riding ground
11 達 *chōtatsu, chōdatsu* supply, procurement,
略 *chōryaku* plan ⌊provision
教 *chōkyō* breaking or training (animals)
停 *chōtei* arbitration, conciliation, mediation, intercession, intervention
停裁判 *chōtei saiban* court arbitration
理 *chōri* cooking
理人 *chōrinin* cook
理台 *chōridai* kitchen table
理法 *chōrihō* cookery; recipe
理場 *chōriba* kitchen
13 節 *chōsetsu* regulation, adjustment, control, modulation, governing, tempering,
14 練 *chōren* military drill ⌊tuning, tuning in
製 *chōsei* manufacture, preparation
髪 *chōhatsu* barbering
髪室 *chōhatsushitsu* barber shop
16 整 *chōsei* regulation, adjustment, governing, control, co-ordination, correction, modulation, tuning

諸 4393 / F1758 **諸** A SHO- many, several, various, all. *moro-* every; many; two; together.

2 人 *shonin, shojin, morobito* all people,
入費 *shonyūhi* sundry expenses ⌊everyone
3 士 *shoshi* many people
子 *shoshi* you; sage, master
刃 *moroha no* double-edged
4 氏 *shoshi* all of you
王 *shoō* all the kings, many kings
仏 *shobutsu* all Buddhas
天 *shoten* the heavens
公 *shokō* government officials; gentlemen
手 *morote* with both hands
手当 *shoteate* sundry allowances
方 *shohō* every direction, all sides, every-
方面 *shohōmen* all directions ⌊where
5 白 *morohaku* quality saké
処 *shosho* many places
兄 *shokei* dear friends
司 *shoshi* many officials
本 *shohon* many kinds of books
外国 *shogaikoku* many foreign countries
民族 *shominzoku* many nations or races
6 色 *shoshiki* commodities
式 *shoshiki* commodities
肌 *morohada* stripped to the waist
州 *shoshū* all the provinces
寺 *shoji* various temples, all temples
共 *morotomo ni* altogether, together
行 *shogyō* all worldly things; all phenomena
行無常 *shogyō-mujō* the vanity of all things (a Buddhist concept)
7 声 *morogoe ni* with one voice, in unison
芸 *shogei* arts, accomplishments
君 *shokun* gentlemen, ladies and gentlemen, my friends, you ⌈Stop Here
車通行止 *Shosha Tsūkōdome* All Vehicles

8味 *moromi* unrefined saké or soy
姉 *shoshi* all you women
所 *shosho* here and there
宗 *shoshū* all sects; various sects
物価 *shobukka* the prices of commodities
事 *shoji* various matters, everything
事万端 *shoji-bantan* everything
事倹約 *shoji ken-yaku* all-around economy
国 *shokoku* all countries, various countries; all provinces
国民 *shokokumin* all the nations, all peoples
国家 *shokokka* all nations
国語 *shokokugo* all languages
9侯 *shokō* the princes, the daimyos
相 *shosō* various aspects, all phases
派 *shoha* the minor parties (in a legislature)
神 *shoshin* all the gods; many gods
政 *shosei* all phases of government
点 *shoten* all points
彦 *shogen* many fine people; you (polite)
星 *shosei* leaders, celebrities
10将 *shoshō* the commanders
般 *shohan no* various, several, all, every
島 *shotō* group of islands, archipelago
家 *shoka* many houses; many people in the area; many schools of thought; many scholars
都市 *shotoshi* all cities
11道 *shodō* arts, accomplishments
掛 *shoka(kari)*, *shoga(kari)* expenses, charges, costs
経費 *shokeihi* costs, expenses
問題 *shomondai* all questions, various questions
13聖徒日 *Shoseitobi* All Saints Day
14種 *shoshu* various kinds; all kinds
説 *shosetsu* various views, various theories
雑費 *shozappi* miscellaneous expenses
15膝 *morohiza* both knees
諸 *moromoro no* all, all kinds of, various
賢 *shoken* ladies and gentlemen
権利 *shokenri* all rights
膚 *morohada* stripped to the waist
膚脱 *morohadanu(gu)* bare both shoulders; exert supreme effort
18藩 *shohan* the clans

9

謁 4394 F1760 See 謁 4382.

諸 4395 F1758 See 諸 4393.

謔 4396 F1761 謔 GYAKU sport with.

諱 4397 F1757 KI. *imina* posthumous name; real name.

諡 4398 F1755 SHI. *okurina* posthumous name.
6号 *shigō* posthumous name

諛 4399 F1754 諛 YU. *hetsura(u)* flatter.
7言 *yugen* flattery

諠 4400 F1755 KEN forget; noisy.
17譁 *kenka* quarrel, dispute

諤 4401 F1755 GAKU speaking the truth.
16諤 *gakugaku no* outspoken

謂 4402 F1760 I. *iwa(re)* reason; origin; a history; oral tradition. *u(i)* meaning. *yu(u)*, *i(u)* (see under 言 4309.0).
6因縁 *i(ware)-innen*=*iwa(re)* (see under 謂 4402.0)

諺 4403 F1759 GEN. *kotowaza* maxim, proverb.
4文 *ommon, ommun, gemmon, gembun* Korean script
13解 *genkai* colloquial explanation

諮 4404 F1757 B SHI. *haka(ru)* consult with.
11問 *shimon* question, inquiry
13詢 *shijun* question, inquiry

謎 4405 F1761 MEI. *nazo* riddle, puzzle, enigma; hint, tip.
11掛 *nazoka(ke)* asking riddles
13解 *nazoto(ki)* riddle solving
16謎 *nazonazo*=*nazo* (see under 謎 4405.0)

諳 4406 F1757 AN. *sora(njiru)*, *sora(nzuru)* memorize; recite from memory.
10記 *anki* memorization
記力 *ankiryoku* memory, retentive power
14誦 *anshō* recitation, memorization

諦 4407 F1755 諦 TEI. TAI. *aki(rameru)* abandon, give up, resign to, be reconciled to.
8念 *teinen* a heart that understands truth
11視 *teishi suru* stare, watch carefully
18観 *teikan* clear vision; resignation (to)

諫 4408 F1756 KAN. *isa(meru)* remonstrate with, admonish, dissuade.
4止 *kanshi* dissuasion
6死 *kanshi suru* remonstrate at the risk of one's life
争 *kansō* outspoken remonstrance
7言 *kangen* remonstrance; admonition

諜 4409/F1755 Chō. *chō(zuru)* spy out, reconnoiter.
6合 *shime(shi)-a(waseru)* arrange previously; conspire with
8者 *chōja* spy
12報 *chōhō* intelligence, secret information
報網 *chōhōmō* intelligence network

B **謡** 4410/F1763 **謠** Yō. *uta(u)* chant. *utai* chanting of the noh; noh singer.
5本 *utaibon* text of a noh drama
6曲 *yōkyoku* noh chant
7初 *uta(i)zo(me)* first singing of the *utai* in the new year
8物 *utaimono* an *utai* poem for recitation

B **諭** 4411/F1756 **諭** Yu. *sato(su)* admonish, charge, remonstrate with, counsel, persuade, warn; make known to. *sato(shi)* advice, reproof, admonition; oracle.
5示 *yushi* instructions, message, admonition
6旨 *yushi* explanation, reasoning
7告 *yukoku* counsel, instruction, warning
11達 *yutatsu* official instructions, notice

諷 4412/F1758 Fū. Fu. *fū(suru)* hint, suggest, insinuate; satirize, lampoon.
7言 *fūgen* allusion, hint, insinuation, sarcasm, innuendo
8刺 *fūshi* sarcasm, innuendo, irony
刺文 *fūshibun* satirical prose
刺画 *fūshiga* cartoon
16諫 *fūkan* exhortation by insinuation
諭 *fūyu* hint, insinuation; allegory
諭法 *fūyuhō* allegory

諧 4413/F1756 Kai harmony, order, suitability.
9音 *kaion* melody, harmony
15調 *kaichō* melody, harmony, unity
16謔 *odoke, kaigyaku* joke
謔口 *odokeguchi* joke, jest
謔芝居 *odoke shibai* comedy, burlesque
謔者 *odokemono* joker, humorist
謔話 *odokebana(shi)* funny story

B **謀** 4414/F1759 Bō. Mu. *haka(ru)* plan, devise, scheme; counsel with; have in mind; aim at; deceive, impose on. *tabaka(ru)* cheat, impose on. *hakarigoto* plan, scheme, policy, stratagem, plot, trick.
3士 *bōshi* planner
4反 *muhon* rebellion, insurrection, treason
5主 *bōshu* chief plotter
6臣 *bōshin* strategist, tactician
7判 *bōhan* forged seal
9計 *bōkei* plot, plan, scheme, stratagem, ruse
叛 *muhon, bōhan* rebellion, insurrection, treason
叛人 *muhonnin* conspirator, rebel
叛心 *muhonshin* spirit of revolt
叛気 *muhongi* spirit of revolt
10殺 *bōsatsu* premeditated murder
書 *bōsho* forged document
11略 *bōryaku* strategy, scheme, plot
20議 *bōgi* consultation; conspiracy

10

謄 See 3824.

謗 See 4401.

謠 4415/F1763 See **謡** 4410.

譁 4416/F1765 See **嘩** 964.

謚 4417/F1762 Eki laughing.

謨 4418/F1764 Bo plan, deliberate.

謐 4419/F1761 Hitsu quiet, peaceful.

諡 See 4398.

謟 4420/F1763 Tō. *utaga(u)* doubt.
11晦 *tōkai suru* maintain incognito, disappear

謗 4421/F1761 Bō. *soshi(ru)* slander, revile, disparage, censure, criticize.
6合 *soshi(ri)-a(u)* slander each other
20議 *bōgi* slander, abuse, criticism

B **謙** 4422/F1761 **謙** Ken. *herikuda(ru)* humble oneself, condescend, be modest.
7抑 *ken-yoku* humbling oneself
8退 *kentai* humility
10称 *kenshō* humble expression
11虚 *kenkyo* modesty, humility
13辞 *kenji* humble words
遜 *kenson* humility, modesty
遜家 *kensonka* modest person
14徳 *kentoku* humility, modesty
20譲 *kenjō* modesty, humility

A **謝** 4423/F1763 Sha. *sha(suru)* thank; apologize; decline, refuse; take one's leave. *ayama(ru)* apologize; be floored. *ayama(ri)* apology, excuse.

5 礼 *sharei* thanks; remuneration, honorarium
6 肉祭 *shanikusai* fiesta, carnival
7 状 *shajō* letter of thanks; letter of apology
8 金 *shakin* monetary gift of thanks
10 恩 *shaon* repaying a kindness, expression of gratitude
恩会 *shaonkai* a party to show gratitude
12 絶 *shazetsu suru* refuse, decline (to see)
13 辞 *shagi* address of thanks; apology
電 *shaden* telegram of thanks
意 *sha-i* gratitude, thanks; apology
罪 *shazai* apology
罪状 *shazaijō* written apology
15 儀 *shagi* pastor's salary

B **謹** 4424/F1765 **謹** Kin. *tsutsushi(mu), tsutsushi(mi)* (see under 慎 1742.0). *tsutsushi(nde)* respectfully, reverently, humbly.

5 白 *kimpaku* Sincerely yours
写 *kinsha* respectfully copied
7 言 *kingen* Sincerely yours
告 *kinkoku suru* respectfully inform
承 *kinshō suru* listen respectfully
8 直 *kinchoku* conscientiousness
9 勅 *kinchoku* deep reverence
奏 *kinsō* reverent report to the emperor
10 書 *kinshō* respectively written
11 啓 *kinkei* Dear Sirs, Gentlemen
12 賀新年 *Kinga Shinnen* Happy New Year
13 慎 *kinshin* penitence; discipline; domiciliary confinement
話 *kinwa* respectful remarks
飭 *kinchoku* deep reverence
14 選 *kinsen* reverent choice
製 *kinsei* carefully produced by
15 撰 *kinsen* reverent writing
17 厳 *kingen na* stern, serious, solemn, austere
聴 *kinchō suru* listen attentively

A **講** 4425/F1762 **講** Kō club, association; lecture. *kō(jiru), kō(zuru)* read aloud; lecture on; read with; study; practice; conceive, devise.

4 中 *kōchū* religious association (of non-Christians)
7 社 *kōsha* religious association (of non-Christians)
究 *kōkyū* research, investigation
8 学 *kōgaku* research, pursuit of study
武 *kōbu* military training
和 *kōwa suru* make peace with
和全権 *kōwa zenken* peace delegate
和会議 *kōwa kaigi* peace conference
和条約 *kōwa jōyaku* peace treaty
和使 *kōwashi* peace emissary
和使節 *kōwa shisetsu* peace mission
和談判 *kōwa dampan* peace negotiations
10 席 *kōseki* lecture hall
座 *kōza* lectureship; correspondence course of study
師 *kōshi* speaker, lecturer, instructor
書 *kōsho* interpretation of a book
11 堂 *kōdō* lecture hall, auditorium
釈 *kōshaku* lecture, storytelling
釈師 *kōshakushi* professional storyteller
習 *kōshū* short training course
習会 *kōshūkai* short training course, institute, training school
習所 *kōshūjo* training school
12 評 *kōhyō* criticism, review
13 話 *kōwa* lecture, address, talk
筵 *kōen* lecture, address
解 *kōkai* discourse, expository sermon
解説教 *kōkai sekkyō* discourse, expository sermon
義 *kōgi* lecture, exposition
義録 *kōgiroku* correspondence course; text of lectures
14 説 *kōsetsu* exposition, explanation
読 *kōdoku suru* read and explain
読者 *kōdokusha* one who reads and explains
演 *kōen* lecture, address
演会 *kōenkai* lecture meeting; series of lectures
演者 *kōensha* lecturer, speaker
15 談 *kōdan* storytelling; narrative
談師 *kōdanshi* professional storyteller
16 壇 *kōdan* lecture platform, rostrum, pulpit
壇討論会 *kōdan tōronkai* panel discussion

11

謹 4426/F1765 See **謹** 4424.

謾 4427/F1765 Man despise, deceive.

謦 4428/F1763 Kei coughing, clearing the throat.

9 咳 *keigai* pleasure of meeting
10 欬 *keigai* pleasure of meeting

謳 4429/F1764 Ō. *uta(u)* extol; declare, state expressly. *uta(wareru)* be famous, be notorious.

12 揚 *uta(i)-a(geru)* energetically propagandize
14 歌 *ōka* glorification, eulogy, applause; song of praise

謫 4430/F1764 **謫** Taku crime; criticism; blame; dismissal; exile.

8 居 *takkyo* exile, seclusion, confinement

所 *takusho* place of exile
10流 *takuryū* banishment, exile

謬 4431 / F1764 BYŪ. *ayamari* mistake.
6伝 *byūden* false report, false rumor
7見 *byūken* wrong view, mistaken notion, false idea, misconception, misunderstanding
「report
14説 *byūsetsu* fallacy, mistaken opinion, false
15論 *byūron* fallacy, fallacious argument

12

譚 4432 / F1768 See 談 4388.

證 4433 / F1766 See 証 4341.

譌 4434 / F1766 F1731 See 訛 4323.

譎 4435 / F1766 KETSU. *itsuwa(ru)* (see under 偽 510.0).
12詐 *kissa, kessa* falsehood

譏 4436 / F1766 KI. *soshi(ru)* (see under 謗 4421.0).
6合 *soshi(ri)-a(u)* slander each other
15誹 *kihi* slander, abuse

B **譜** 4437 / F1768 **譜** FU music, note, staff, score; album, record, table; genealogy.
5代 *fudai* successive generations; hereditary Tokugawa daimyo
代大名 *fudai daimyō* hereditary Tokugawa
8表 *fuhyō* staff (in music) ⌊daimyo
11第 *fudai* successive generations

A **識** 4438 / F1767 **識** SHIKI know, discriminate, write.
2力 *shikiryoku*＝next word
7見 *shikken* knowledge, judgment, discernment, vision, intelligence
別 *shikibetsu* discrimination, discernment, identification
「intelligentsia
8者 *shikisha* intelligent people, thinkers,
9度 *shikido* intelligence and magnanimity
12量 *shikiryō* personal appearance, features
16閾 *shiki-iki* threshold of consciousness

B **警** 4439 / F1768 KEI. *imashi(meru), imashime* (see under 戒 1801.0).
5句 *keiku* aphorism, witticism
巡 *keijun* patrol
「the wall
世 *keisei* warning to the public; writing on
世家 *keiseika* seer, prophet
6吏 *keiri* police officer
防 *keibō* preserving order
「unit
防団 *keibōdan* civilian guards, air-defense
7抜 *keibatsu* something extraordinary
告 *keiku* warning, advice
戒 *keikai* warning, admonition; vigilance
戒色 *keikaishoku* warning color
戒網 *keikaimō* police cordon
戒管制 *keikai kansei* air defense dim-out
戒線 *keikaisen* police cordon
戒警報 *keikai keihō* air-raid warning
8固 *keigo*＝警護 (see below–20)
官 *keikan* police officer
官隊 *keikantai* police force, posse
9急 *keikyū* alarm, emergency
乗警察 *keijō keisatsu* railway police
10悟 *keigo na* clever and quick to understand
砲 *keihō* warning gun
部 *keibu* police inspector
11務 *keimu* police affairs
笛 *keiteki* horn, alarm whistle, foghorn
視 *keishi* police superintendent
視庁 *Keishichō* Metropolitan Police Head-
12棒 *keibō* policeman's club ⌊quarters
報 *keihō* warning, alarm
報器 *keihōki* warning bell or siren
報機 *keihōki* warning bell or siren
備 *keibi* defense, guard, policing
備兵 *keibihei* guard
備隊 *keibitai* garrison, guards; squad of
備艦 *keibikan* guard ship ⌊patrolmen
14語 *keigo* words of admonition
察 *keisatsu* police (force); police station
察犬 *keisatsuken* police dog, bloodhound
察手帳 *keisatsu techō* police blotter
察分署 *keisatsu bunsho* police substation
察庁 *Keisatsuchō* National Police Agency
察犯 *keisatsuhan* police offense
察医 *keisatsu-i* police doctor
察長 *keisatsuchō* chief of police
察官 *keisatsukan* police officer
察国家 *keisatsu kokka* police state
察隊 *keisatsutai* police force, constabulary
察群 *keisatsugun* police force
察署 *keisatsusho* police station
察署長 *keisatsushochō* chief of police
察権 *keisatsuken* police power
15衛 *keiei* guard, patrol, escort
標 *keihyō* danger sign
16醒 *keisei suru* warn, awake, arouse
18蹕 *keihitsu* heralding, clearing the road
20鐘 *keishō* fire bell, alarm bell
護 *keigo* guard, escort, convoy, patrol
護者 *keigosha* watcher, watchman
22邏 *keira* patrolman

13

譜 4440/F1768 See 譜 4437.

譽 4441/F1771 See 誉 4353.

譯 4442/F1769 See 訳 4327.

譴 4443/F1770 KEN scold. *seme(ru)* reproach.
11責 *kenseki* rebuke, reprimand, censure

譫 4444/F1769 Tō, SEN delirious talk.
6妄 *semmō* delirium
7言 *uwakoto, uwagoto* foolish talk; delirious utterances
14語 *uwagoto* talking in a delirium

譬 4445/F1769 HI. *tato(eru)* compare, illustrate, speak figuratively. *tatoe, tatoi* parable, illustration, figure of speech.
12喩 *hiyu*＝比喩 2470.12
13話 *tatoebanashi* parable, fable, allegory

B **讓** 4446/F1775 **譲** Jō. *yuzu(ru)* turn over, hand over, transfer, convey, assign, deed, bequeath, give away, give up; sell, dispose of; yield to; be inferior to; defer, postpone.
3与 *jōyo* cession, transfer; concession
6合 *yuzu(ri)-a(u)* compromise, concede
7位 *jōi* abdication
状 *yuzurijō* deed, grant, assignment
8歩 *jōho* concession, conciliation, compromise, condescension
受 *yuzu(ri)-u(keru)* inherit, receive, take over, obtain by transfer
12渡 *yuzu(ri)-wata(su)* turn over, hand over, convey, cede. *jōto* transfer, conveyance, delivery, grant
渡人 *jōtonin, yuzuriwata(shi)nin* grantor, transferor
渡証書 *yuzuriwata(shi) shōshō, jōto shōsho* deed of conveyance, assignment

A **護** 4447/F1771 Go. *mamo(ru)* (see under 守 1282.0).
7身 *goshin* self-protection, self-defense, self-preservation
身仏 *goshimbutsu* personal guardian Buddha
身法 *goshinhō* methods of self-defense
身術 *goshinjutsu* art of self-defense
8法 *gohō* defense of the constitution; defense of a religion
8国 *gokoku* defense of the fatherland
国神社 *gokoku jinja* shrine of the war dead
送 *gosō* convoy, escort
送車 *gosōsha* patrol wagon or car
送船 *gosōsen* convoying vessel
岸 *gogan* sea wall; river dike
岸工事 *gogan kōji* riparian works, embankment, levee
岸基礎 *gogan kiso* riprap
9持 *goji* defense, protection, maintenance, retention; prayer
11符 *gofu* charm, amulet, talisman
15摩 *goma* offering incense and praying
摩灰 *goma(no)hai* highway robber
衛 *goei* guard, convoy, escort
衛巡査 *goei junsa* police escort, police guard
衛兵 *goeihei* military escort, guard, bodyguard
衛者 *goeisha* guard
衛艦 *goeikan* escort ship
16憲 *goken* safeguarding the constitution
17謨 *gomu* rubber

A **議** 4448/F1770 GI consultation, deliberation, debate; consideration, proposal, suggestion. *gi(suru)* discuss, deliberate on, consider.
2了 *giryō suru* close a debate, finish deliberation
3士 *gishi* counselor
6会 *gikai* deliberative assembly
会政治 *gikai seiji* parliamentary government
7判 *gihan* deliberation and decision
決 *giketsu* decision, resolution
決権 *giketsuken* voting right
決機関 *giketsu kikan* legislative assembly
8長 *gichō* chairman, speaker, president (of the senate)
官 *gikan* counselor, judge
定 *gitei, gijō* agreement
定書 *giteisho, gijōsho* protocol; written agreement
事 *giji* proceedings
事日程 *giji nittei* agenda
事目録 *giji mokuroku* agenda
事妨害 *giji bōgai* filibuster, obstructive tactics
事堂 *gijidō* assembly hall, capitol, diet building
事項目 *giji kōmoku* agenda
事録 *gijiroku* minutes, proceedings, report, journal
9院 *gi-in* the House, the Diet Chamber
院制度 *gi-in seido* parliamentary system
院政治 *gi-in seiji* parliamentary government
10席 *giseki* parliamentary seat, the floor
案 *gian* bill, measure
員 *gi-in* member of an assembly
員総会 *gi-in sōkai* party caucus
12場 *gijō* assembly hall, chamber, the House, the floor
15論 *giron* argument, discussion, controversy, debate

7 見角[言]谷豆豕豸貝赤走足身車辛辰釆⻌邑阝酉釆里 (14 beside 言)

論好 *gironzu(ki) na* argumentative
論家 *gironka* argumentative person, good debater
18 題 *gidai* topic for discussion, agenda

—— 14 ——

讁 4449 / F1772 See **謫** 4430.

—— 15 ——

變 See **変** 306.

讀 4450 / F1771 See **読** 4375.

讃 4451 / F1775 See **讚** 4457.

—— 16 ——

變 See **変** 306.

讐 4452 / F1774 See **讎** 5041.

讌 4453 / F1773 EN. *utage* party, banquet.
12 飲 *en-in* drinking bout

—— 17 ——

讓 4454 / F1775 See **譲** 4446.

讖 4455 / F1775 SHIN foretelling, presage, omen.

讒 4456 / F1774 ZAN defamation.
2 人 *zannin* slanderer
3 口 *zankō* false charge, slander, defamation
6 奸 *zankan* wicked slanderer
7 言 *zangen* false charge, slander, defamation
8 者 *zansha* slanderer
9 奏 *zansō* slandering the emperor
12 間 *zankan* separating people by slandering
訴 *zanso* false charge, slander, defamation
17 謗 *zambō* libel, slander, defamation

—— 19 ——

讚 4457 / F1775 **讃** SAN praise; title or brief inscription on a picture.
6 仰 *sankō* praise
9 美 *sambi* praise, adoration
美歌 *sambika* hymn
13 嘆 *santan* praise, admiration
辞 *sanji* eulogy, compliment
14 歌 *sanka* praise, admiration
15 歎 *santan* praise, admiration

RAD. 谷 150

Tani valley. At left: *tani hen*. Nickname: Valley.

A **谷** 4458 / F1776 KOKU. *tani* valley, dale, ravine; trough (of a wave); trough (in atmospheric pressure). *-ya* valley.
3 口 *taniguchi* mouth of a valley
川 *tanigawa* valley stream, mountain stream
4 水 *tanimizu* valley water, rill
6 地 *yachi* low damp area, swamp
7 谷 *tanidani* valleys
8 底 *tanizoko, tanisoko* bottom of a ravine; valley bottom
9 風 *tanikaze* valley wind
11 道 *tanimichi* pass, defile, notch
12 渡 *taniwata(ri)* flying over the valleys (birds); trees spanning a valley with with their branches
間 *tanima, taniai* ravine, chasm, dell, valley
間百合 *tanima (no) yuri* lily of the valley
間姫百合 *tanima (no) hime yuri* lily of the valley

—— 2 ——

郤 4459 / F300 See **却** 808. [卩]

—— 4 ——

谺 4460 / F1776 See **谺** 4462.

A **欲** 4461 / F1027 **慾** YOKU covetousness; greed, passion, desire, craving, appetite. *hos(suru)* desire, want. *ho(shigaru)* desire, want, covet. *ho(shii)* desire, want. [欠]
4 心 *yokushin* selfishness, acquisitiveness
5 目 *yokume* partial view; partiality; sanguine hope
7 求 *yokkyū* desire, craving, aspiration
8 念 *yokunen* desire, wish, appetite, passions
9 相 *yokusō* acquisitiveness

界 *yokukai* this greedy world
11 張 *yokuba(ru)* be greedy, be covetous. *yokuba(ri)* greed, covetousness
得 *yokutoku* self-interest, selfishness. *yokutoku(zuku) no* selfish, mercenary
情 *yokujō* desire, craving, passion
深 *yokufuka* greed, covetousness. *yokufuka(i)* greedy; covetous
望 *yokubō* desire, craving; wants; ambition

— 5 —

谺 4462/F1776 **谺** KA. *kodama* spirit of a tree; echo.

— 10 —

豁 4463/F1777 KATSU empty, wide.
11 達 *kattatsu* magnanimity, generosity
12 然 *katsuzen to* all of a sudden; extensively
17 闊 *kattatsu* magnanimity, generosity

谿 4464/F1776 KEI valley. *tani* valley.
7 谷 *keikoku* valley, ravine, canyon
10 流 *keiryū* mountain stream
16 壑 *keigaku* deep valley

RAD. 豆 151

Mame bean. At left: 豆 *mame hen.* Nickname: Bean.

B **豆** 4465/F1777 TŌ. ZU. *mame* beans, peas, pulse. *mame-* miniature, midget, pocket (battleship), small.
2 人形 *mame ningyō* miniature doll
5 本 *mame hon* miniature book
台風 *mame taifū* small typhoon
6 名月 *mame meigetsu* moon of 13th day of 9th lunar month
自動車 *mame jidōsha* midget auto
8 油 *mame abura* soybean oil
炒 *mame-i(ri)* parched beans
乳 *tōnyū* soybean milk
9 柿 *mamegaki* small persimmon
炭 *mametan* oval briquets
11 粒 *mame tsubu* separate beans
萌 *mame moya(shi)* bean sprouts
12 絞 *mameshibo(ri)* polka-dot pattern
13 幹 *mamegara* beanstalks and pods
戦車 *mame sensha* midget tank
鉄砲 *mamedeppō* popgun, bean shooter
電球 *mame denkyū* miniature light bulb
14 腐 *tōfu* bean curd, tofu
15 撒 *mamema(ki)* bean-scattering ceremony
17 糟 *mamekasu* beancake

— 3 —

豈 See 1420.

— 6 —

A **豊** 4466/F1778 **豐** HŌ. *yuta(kana)* abundant; rich; fruitful. *toyo-* excellent, rich.
4 凶 *hōkyō* rich or poor harvest, nature of the harvest
水 *hōsui* abundance of water
水期 *hōsuiki* high-water season, rainy season
6 年 *hōnen* fruitful year
年万作 *hōnen-mansaku*=next entry
年満作 *hōnen-mansaku* a good year and bumper crops
7 作 *hōsaku* abundant harvest
沃 *hōyoku* fertility
9 栄昇 *toyosakanobo(ru)* rise in brilliance (the sun)
12 満 *hōman* stout, corpulent
富 *hōfu* abundance, wealth
葦原 *Toyoashihara* (ancient) Japan
14 漁 *hōryō, hōgyo* big catch (of fish)
旗雲 *toyohatagumo* pretty bank of clouds
15 潤 *hōjun* rich and prosperous; luxurious (fruit)
熟 *hōjuku* abundant harvest. *hōjuku suru* ripen
16 頰 *hōkyō* plump cheeks
18 穣 *hōjō* abundant harvest; excellent crop
19 艶 *hōen* voluptuous beauty
21 饒 *hōjō* fertility

— 8 —

豌 4467/F1778 EN pea.
7 豆 *endō* peas
豆豆 *endō mame* peas

豎 4468/F1778 JU vertical; child.
3 子 *jushi* child, lad, youngster; stripling, greenhorn
6 吏 *juri* subordinate official

— 9 —

A **頭** 4469/F2060 TŌ head, counter for cattle. ZU head. *atama* head; brain, mind, intellect; leader; top; head (of boil); idea; hair; idea, point of view, consideration. *kashira* head; hair; leader, chief. *kōbe, kaburi, kabu, tsumuri* head. *atama kara* from the beginning; (not) at all. *atama(dekkachi)* top-heaviness. *atama(gonashi) ni* unsparingly, categorically. *-gashira* the very moment; the beginning. [頁]

3 大 *tōdai no* big-headed, top-heavy
巾 *zukin* hood, turban
上 *zujō* overhead
4 分 *kashirabun* leader, chief
文字 *kashira moji* capital letter; initials; first word
5 目 *tōmoku* chief, head, leader
石 *kashira ishi* cornerstone
付 *kashiratsu(ki)* fish cooked whole
打 *zu-u(chi), atama-u(chi)* hit the top
6 刎 *atamaha(ne)* kickback, squeeze (stocks)
字 *kashiraji* capital letter; initials; first word
7 角 *tōkaku* top of the head
囲 *tōi* head measurement
位 *tōi* cephalic presentation (obstetrics)
陀袋 *zudabukuro* wallet, (pilgrim's) scrip, beggar's bag
8 金 *atamakin* down payment, key money
注 *tōchū* notes at the top of the page
取 *tōdori* (private bank) president; manager
9 首 *tōshu* boss, head, chief
垢 *fuke* dandruff
重 *zuomo(i)* dull, top-heavy market. *zuomo* a thick head; impoliteness
10 骨 *tōkotsu* skill
振 *kashira (o) fu(ru)* shake the head (negatively)
株 *atamakabu* leader, executives
部 *tōbu, zubu* the head
書 *tōsho* superscription; the above-mentioned. *kashiraga(ki)* top notes; heading
11 脳 *zunō* head, brain
脳労働者 *zunō rōdōsha* brainworker
脳明晰 *zunō-meiseki na* clearheaded
12 註 *tōchū* notes at the top of the page
割 *atamawa(ri)* sharing, per capita
寒足熱 *zukan-sokunetsu* keeping the head cool and the feet warm
痛 *zutsū, tōtsū* headache; worry
痛持 *zutsūmo(chi)* chronic headache sufferer
13 数 *atamakazu, tōsū* number of persons, numerical strength
蓋 *tōgai* skull, cranium
蓋骨 *zugaikotsu* skull, cranium
14 領 *tōryō* chief, manager, dictator
髪 *tōhatsu* hair, head of hair
19 韻 *tōin* alliteration

— 11 —

豐 4470/F1778 See 豊 4466.

— 21 —

豔 See 艶 3890.

RAD. 豕 152

Buta or *inoko* pig. At left: *inoko hen.* Variant: 豕 (6 strokes). Nickname: Pig.

豕 4471/F1779 SHI. *inoko* hog.

— 4 —

豚 See 3772.

— 6 —

A 象 4472/F1780 象 SHŌ image; shape; sign (of the times). ZŌ elephant. *katado(ru)* pattern after, imitate; symbolize.

5 皮病 *zōhibyō* elephantiasis
牙 *zōge* ivory
牙細工 *zōgezaiku* ivory work
牙塔 *zōge (no) tō* ivory tower
牙質 *zōgeshitsu* dentine
6 虫 *zōmushi* weevil
7 形 *shōkei* copying the form (of something); hieroglyphics; a type of characters resembling pictures (e.g. 馬, 魚, and 鳥)
形文字 *shōkei monji, shōkei moji* hieroglyphics, Chinese characters
11 眼 *zōgan* inlay, damascene work
12 嵌 *zōgan* inlay, damascene work
14 鼻虫 *zōhanamushi* weevil
徵 *shōchō suru* symbolize, foreshadow. *shōchō* symbol, emblem
徵主義 *shōchō shugi* symbolism
徵的 *shōchōteki* symbolic
徵詩 *shōchōshi* symbolic poetry

— 7 —

豪 See 329.

豨 4473 F1781 豬 Kɪ large hog.
[9]勇 *kiyū* fierce courage

— 10 —

豫 4474 F1783 See 予 271.

RAD. 豸 153

Mujina badger or *ashinakimushi* reptiles. At left: *mujina hen.*
Nickname: Clawed Dog (cf. Rads. 87 & 94).

— 3 —

豹 4475 F1784 Hyō leopard, panther.
[9]変 *hyōhen* sudden change

豺 4476 F1784 Sᴀɪ jackal.
[10]狼 *sairō* jackals and wolves; cruel person; wicked person

— 4 —

貅 4477 F1784 See 貅 4481.

豼 4478 F1786 貔 Hɪ a heraldic beast symbolizing bravery.
[13]貅 *hikyū* brave warrior

— 5 —

貂 4479 F1784 Chō. *ten* marten, sable.

— 6 —

貉 4480 F1785 狢 Kᴀᴋᴜ. *mujina* badger.

貅 4481 F1785 貅 Kyū a heraldic beast symbolizing bravery.

— 7 —

貍 4482 F1785 F1228 See 狸 2887.

貌 4483 F1785 Bō form, appearance; countenance.

— 10 —

貘 4484 F1786 See 獏 2902.

貔 4485 F1786 See 豼 4478.

RAD. 貝 154

Kai shell or *ko gai* small "shell" (to distinguish it from Rad. 181). At left: *kai hen.*
Nickname: Small Shell.

A 貝 4486 F1786 Bᴀɪ shellfish. *kai* shell; shellfish.
[9]拾 *kaihiro(i)* shell gathering
柱 *kaibashira* shell ligament
[11]細工 *kaizaiku* shellwork
[12]焼 *kaiya(ki)* baking in the shell
殼 *kaigara* sea shell
殼石灰 *kaigara sekkai* shell lime
殼追放 *kaigara tsuihō* ostracism
殼骨 *kaigarabone* shoulder blade
殼細工 *kaigarazaiku* shellwork
[13]塚 *kaizuka* shell mound, kitchen midden
[18]類 *kairui* shellfish
類学 *kairuigaku* conchology

— 2 —

貞 See 803.

A 則 4487 F245 Sᴏᴋᴜ. *norito(ru), notto(ru)* follow (precedent), be based on, go by; live up to; model after; be in accordance with. *nori* law, rule; model, doctrine. *sunawa(chi)* whereupon, accordingly. [刀]

A 負 4488 F1787 負 Fu negative, minus; minus sign. *ma(keru)* be defeated; get the worst of it; be overcome with; yield to; be inferior to; lower the price; be poisoned with lacquer. *ma(kasu)* overcome, outrival, defeat. *ma(karu)* reduce the price. *ma(kesaseru)* knock the price down. *o(u)* bear, carry on the back; owe; assume, bear (a responsibility); be accused of; sustain (an injury). *o(wasu)*, *o(waseru)* make carry, burden with, entrust with, charge with, blame. *o(mbu)*, *o(buu)* carry on the back. *o(busaru)* ride on the back; rely on, be dependent on. *ma(ke)* defeat. *(o)ma(ke)* a small discount; a little extra thrown in; exaggeration, embellishment. *(o)ma(ke) ni* in addition, besides.

4 心 *ma(keji)kokoro* working to keep ahead of others
方 *ma(ke)kata* extent of a defeat
切 *o(i)-ki(ru)* be able to bear
5 目 *oime* debt
6 色 *ma(ke)-iro* signs of defeat
気 *ma(ken)ki* unyielding spirit, competitive spirit
号 *fugō* minus sign
劣 *ma(kezu)-oto(razu)* equally strong; neck and neck
7 投手 *ma(ke) tōshu* losing pitcher
8 退 *ma(ke)-shirizo(ku)* defeat and leave
担 *futan* encumbrance, burden, load, responsibility, obligation, liability
物 *o(i)mono* burden, debt
9 革 *o(i)kawa* shoulder carrying strap
軍 *ma(ke) ikusa* defeat, losing battle
10 馬 *ma(ke) uma* losing horse
紐 *obuihimo* cloth cord tying the baby to the mother's back. *o(i)himo* cloth cord for carrying things on the back
荷 *fuka* burden, load (electricity)
根性 *ma(keji)konjō* working to keep ahead of others
11 運 *o(i)-hako(bu)* carry burdens
惜 *ma(ke)o(shimi)* unwillingness to admit defeat
12 越 *ma(ke)ko(shi)* more losses than wins
量 *furyō* minus quantity, negative quantity
13 債 *fusai* debt, liabilities, loan
嫌 *ma(ke)gira(i)* unyielding, unbending. *ma(kezu)gira(i)* having a will to win
数 *fusū* negative number
傷 *fushō* injury, wound, bruise, cut
傷兵 *fushōhei* wounded soldier
傷者 *fushōsha* wounded or injured person
14 魂 *ma(keji)damashii* unyielding spirit; working to keep ahead of others

3

貢 See 1458.

貶 4489 / F1794 HEN. *hen(suru)* degrade, demote, belittle. *kena(su)* disparage, despise, denounce. *otoshi(meru)* look down on.

7 言 *otoshi(me)goto* insult
14 様 *otoshi(me)zama* insulting way
18 謫 *hentaku suru* degrade, demote, debase

A 財 4490 / F1788 ZAI, SAI money, wealth, assets; property; commodities.

2 力 *zairyoku* financial ability, competence; resources, assets; solvency
5 布 *saifu* purse
6 団 *zaidan* foundation, financial group, consortium, syndicate, endowment
団法人 *zaidan hōjin* incorporated foundation; juridical person
8 物 *zaibutsu, zaimotsu* property, goods
宝 *zaihō* wealth, treasure, valuables
9 界 *zaikai* financial world, money market
界人 *zaikaijin* financier, businessman
政 *zaisei* public financial affairs; economy
政学 *zaiseigaku* the science of finance
政学者 *zaiseigakusha* teacher of finance
政的 *zaiseiteki* financial
政的負債 *zaiseiteki fusai* financial obligations
政的援助 *zaiseiteki enjo* financial support
政家 *zaiseika* financier
11 欲 *zaiyoku* greed for wealth
貨 *zaika* commodities, property, wealth
務 *zaimu* financial affairs
務官 *zaimukan* finance secretary
務顧問 *zaimu komon* financial adviser
産 *zaisan* property, estate, fortune, assets
産没収 *zaisan bosshū* confiscation of property
産家 *zaisanka* wealthy person
産税 *zaisanzei* property tax, capital tax
産管理 *zaisan kanri* property management
産権 *zaisanken* property rights
13 源 *zaigen* source of funds, resources, finances
14 閥 *zaibatsu* financial clique, giant family trust
22 嚢 *zainō* purse, moneybag, riches

4

貶 See 4489.

貪 See 505.

貧 貧 See 600.

貫 See 2469.

B 販 4491 / F1791 販 HAN sell, trade.

7 売 *hambai* sale, selling
売人 *hambainin* seller, agent
売元 *hambaimoto* selling agency
売店 *hambaiten* shop, store
売所 *hambaisho* shop, store
売価格 *hambai kakaku* selling price
売係 *hambaigakari* salesman
売品 *hambaihin* articles for sale
売員 *hambai-in* salesman
売術 *hambaijutsu* salesmanship
売組合 *hambai kumiai* marketing co-operative
売税 *hambaizei* sales tax
売戦 *hambaisen* sales war
売網 *hambaimō* sales network
13 路 *hanro* market, outlet

A **責** 4492 / F1792 SEKI. SHAKU. *se*(*meru*) condemn, blame, censure, criticize, take to task; torture, persecute; urge, tease (to do something). *se*(*me*) responsibility, liability, blame, guilt, censure; torture, torment.
4 手綱 *se*(*me*)*tazuna* gag rein
5 立 *se*(*me*)-*ta*(*teru*) persecute, torture severely; urge
付 *se*(*me*)-*tsu*(*keru*) vehemently criticize
6 任 *sekinin* responsibility, liability
任者 *sekininsha* person responsible
任感 *sekininkan* sense of responsibility
8 具 *se*(*me*)*gu* instruments of torture
苦 *semeku* torture, torment, cruelty
苛 *se*(*me*)-*saina*(*mu*) ill-treat, torment, torture, molest, persecute
11 問 *se*(*me*)-*do*(*u*) question critically; question by third-degree
務 *sekimu* duty, obligation
道具 *semedōgu* instruments of torture
12 惑 *se*(*me*)-*mado*(*wasu*) criticize violently and confuse
13 塞 *se*(*me*)-*fusa*(*gi*) fulfillment of one's responsibility

A **貨** 4493 / F1790 **貨** KA freight; goods, property.
7 車 *kasha* freight car; van
車渡 *kashawata*(*shi*) F.O.B., free on board
8 物 *kamotsu, kabutsu* freight, cargo, goods
物列車 *kamotsu ressha* freight train
物自動車 *kamotsu jidōsha* truck
物車 *kamotsusha* freight car
物取扱 *kamotsu toriatsukai* forwarding, transportation
物係 *kamotsugakari* freight clerk
物陸揚 *kamotsu rikua*(*ge*) cargo unloading
物船 *kamotsusen* freighter
物置場 *kamotsu okiba* freight yard
物駅 *kamotsu eki* freight depot
物廠 *kamotsushō* freight depot
9 客車 *kakyakusha* freight and passenger train
客船 *kakakusen, kakyakusen* cargo and passenger ship
10 財 *kazai* wealth, worldly goods
12 殖 *kashoku* money-making
15 幣 *kahei* money, currency, coin, coinage
幣学 *kaheigaku* numismatics

A **敗** 4494 / F855 HAI defeat, reversal. *yabu*(*ru*) *vt* defeat. *yabu*(*reru*) *vi* be defeated. [文]
3 亡 *haibō* defeat, reversal, rout
5 北 *haiboku* defeat, reversal, rout
6 色 *haishoku* omens of defeat
因 *hai-in* cause of defeat
死 *haishi suru* be defeated and killed
兆 *haichō* sign of defeat; signs of failure
血症 *haiketsushō* blood poisoning
7 走 *haisō* rout, flight
兵 *haihei* routed troops
8 退 *haitai* defeat, retreat
者 *haisha* the defeated
9 屋 *haioku* dilapidated cottage
軍 *haigun* defeated army
10 将 *haishō* defeated general
衄 *haijiku* defeat in war
残 *haizan* survival after defeat; decline; ruin. *haizan no* defeated, vanquished
残兵 *haizanhei* troop remnants, deserting troops
12 訴 *haiso* lost case; losing a case
報 *haihō* news of defeat
13 滅 *haimetsu* crushing defeat
戦 *haisen* defeat, a lost battle
戦投手 *haisen tōshu* losing pitcher
15 敵 *haiteki* vanquished enemy

— 5 —

買 See 3637.

貳 See 弐 32.

賁 4495 / F1796 FUN decorate; ornament.

貽 4496 / F1796 I. leave behind; gift.
7 貝 *igai* mussel (shell)

A **費** 4497 / F1795 HI expenses, cost. *tsuiya*(*su*) spend, consume, waste. *tsui*(*eru*) become less; be wasted. *tsuie* expenses.
5 用 *hiyō* expense, cost
目 *himoku* expense item
9 途 *hito* expense item
10 消 *hishō* embezzlement, misappropriation

貼 4498 / F1796 Chō counter for medicine packages. *ha(ru)* stick, paste, affix, post, paper, apply (tile, etc.).
5用 *chōyō* pasting, affixing
付 *ha(ri)-tsu(keru)* stick on, paste up, affix (stamps). *chōfu suru* affix, stick, attach, apply, paste
札 *ha(ri)fuda* placard, bill, poster; tag
出 *ha(ri)-da(su)* put up a notice. *harida(shi)* bill, poster, notice
10紙 *ha(ri)gami* sticker, bill, tag, label
紙厳禁 *Harigami Genkin* Post No Bills

A **貿** 4499 / F1796 Bō exchange.
8易 *bōeki* trade, commerce
易会社 *bōekigaisha* trading firm
易風 *bōekifū* trade wind
易品 *bōekihin* articles of commerce
易船 *bōekisen* trading vessel
易商 *bōekishō* trader, importer, exporter
易商人 *bōeki shōnin* trader
易場 *bōekijō* foreign market
易港 *bōekikō* trading port, commercial port
易業 *bōekigyō* trading business

貰 4500 / F1793 Sei. *mora(u)* get, have, obtain, receive, accept; get (him) to do (it). *morai* tip, gratuity; geisha's call from another entertainment. *(o)morai* beggar.
3子 *moraigo* adoption, adopted child
4手 *moraite* recipient, receiver
方 *mora(i)kata* manner of receiving
水 *morai mizu* water from a neighbor
火 *moraibi* a neighbor's fire that spreads to one's home
8泣 *mora(i)na(ki)* weeping in sympathy
物 *moraimono* present, gift
乳 *morai chichi* milk from another breast
受 *mora(i)-u(keru)* receive (something)
10涙 *morai namida* tears of sympathy

A **賀** 4501 / F1796 Ga congratulations, felicitations, compliments, joy of the occasion. *ga(suru)* celebrate, congratulate, compliment, approve of.
5正 *gashō* New Year's congratulations, ⌊Happy New Year
7状 *gajō* greeting card
寿 *gaju* congratulations on a long life
8表 *gahyō* congratulatory card to a high personage
9客 *gakaku* well-wisher, congratulator
10席 *gaseki* seat of honor
宴 *gaen* banquet
書 *gasho* congratulatory letter
12詞 *gashi* greetings, congratulations
13辞 *gaji* congratulations, felicitations
筵 *gaen* congratulatory banquet
意 *ga-i* congratulatory feeling

A **貯** 4502 / F1793 Cho. *takuwa(eru)* store, lay in stock, save, keep, wear (a mustache). *ta(meru)* (see under 溜 2658.0). *takuwa(e)* store, hoard, savings.
4木池 *chobokuchi* mill pond
木場 *chomokujō* log-storage place
水 *chosui* storage of water
水池 *chosuichi* reservoir
水塔 *chosuitō* water tower
水量 *chosuiryō* amount of stored water
水槽 *chosuisō* water tank
6米 *chomai* storing rice; stored rice
8金 *chokin* savings, deposit
金通帳 *chokin tsūchō* bank book
金箱 *chokimbako* savings box, bank
9炭 *chotan* storing coal; stored coal
炭所 *chotanjo* coal-storage place
13溜 *choryū* accumulation (of body fluids)
蓄 *chochiku* savings
蓄心 *chochikushin* thriftiness
蓄預金 *chochiku yokin* savings deposit
14蔵 *chozō* storage, preservation
蔵米 *chozōmai* stored rice 「depot
蔵所 *chozōsho* storage place, repository,
蔵物 *chozōbutsu* stock, supplies
蔵者 *chozōsha* hoarder
蔵品 *chozōhin* stock, supplies
蔵室 *chozōshitsu* storeroom, stock room
蔵庫 *chozōko* storehouse

A **貸** 4503 / F1795 Tai. *ka(su)* lend; hire out, rent, lease; give credit to. *ka(shi)* loan, lending; bill, account, debt; hire, renting; for rent, for hire.
3下 *ka(shi)-sa(geru)* lend; lease. *ka(shi)sa(ge)* government loan or lease
与 *kashi-ata(eru)* let out, lease, lend. *taiyo* loan, lending
4手 *ka(shi)te* creditor, lender; landlord
方 *kashikata* creditor; how to lend; credit ⌊side
元 *ka(shi)moto* banker; boss gambler
切 *kashi-ki(ru)* reserve, book. *kashiki(ri)* reserved; reservation
切扱 *kashiki(ri) azuka(i)* carload consign- ⌊ment
切車 *kashiki(ri)sha* reserved car
5主 *kashinushi* lender, creditor; landlord
布団 *ka(shi)buton* bedding for rent
付 *kashi-tsu(keru)* lend, advance. *kashitsu(ke)* lending
付金 *kashitsukekin* loan, advance
本 *kashihon* book for lending
本屋 *kashihon-ya* rental library

出 *ka(shi)-da(su)* lend. *kashida(shi)* loan, lending; advance; credit
出図書館 *kashida(shi) toshokan* lending library
出金 *kashidashikin* a loan
6 舟 *ka(shi)bune* boat for rent
地 *ka(shi)chi* lot or land for rent
衣裳 *ka(shi) ishō* clothes or costumes for rent
自動車 *ka(shi) jidōsha* hired car, taxi
7 売 *ka(shi)u(ri)* sale on credit
8 店 *ka(shi)dana, ka(shi) mise* store for rent
物 *ka(shi)mono* things for rent
金 *kashikin* loan
金庫 *ka(shi) kinko* safety deposit box
金業 *kashikingyō* moneylender
9 室 *kashishitsu* room for rent
10 席 *kashiseki* hall for rent, room for rent
借 *taishaku* loan, debit and credit, lending and borrowing. *ka(shi)ka(ri)* loan; lending and borrowing
料 *ka(shi)ryō* rent, hire; loan charge
馬車 *ka(shi)basha* carriage for hire
部屋 *ka(shi)beya* room for rent
座敷 *ka(shi) zashiki* room for rent; house of ill-fame
倒 *kashidao(re)* bad debts
倒金 *kashidao(re)kin* bad debts
家 *ka(shi)-ie, kashiya* house for rent
家札 *kashiya fuda* for-rent sign
家普請 *kashiyabushin* flimsy structure
11 渋 *ka(shi)-shibu(ru)* be unwilling to lend
12 越 *kashiko(shi)* overdraft; outstanding account
間 *kashima* room for rent
証文 *ka(shi) shōmon* promissory note
費 *taihi* loan; scholarship
費生 *taihisei* scholarship student
13 賃 *ka(shi)chin* rent, hire
14 厩 *ka(shi) umaya* livery stable

A **貴** 4504 / F1793 KI. *tōto(bu), tatto(bu), tōto(mu), tatto(mu)* value, prize, esteem; respect, honor, revere. *tōto(i), tatto(i)* valuable, precious; noble, exalted, venerable. *ki-* your.

2 人 *kijin* noble, nobleman, man of rank, dignitary; the nobility
3 女 *kijo, anata* lady, you (feminine)
下 *kika* you
4 方 *anata, anta, kihō* you
公 *kikō* you
公子 *kikōshi* young noble
5 石 *kiseki* gem, precious stone
札 *kisatsu* your letter
台 *kidai* you
兄 *kikei* you
6 臣 *kishin* high-ranking retainer, your retainer
地 *kichi* your place, there
邦 *kihō* your country
号 *kigō* honorary title; rank of nobility; scholastic degree
宅 *kitaku* your home
7 状 *kijō* your letter
社 *kisha* your company
男 *kidan, anata* you (masculine)
君 *kikun* you (classical and masculine)
8 所 *kisho* your place
命 *kimei* your orders
官 *kikan* you (an official)
金属 *kikinzoku* precious metals
国 *kikoku* your country
国語 *kikokugo* your language
9 相 *kisō* noble features
重 *kichō na* precious, priceless
重品 *kichōhin* valuables; treasure
10 紙 *kishi* your magazine, your newspaper; your letter
家 *kika* your home
書 *kisho* your letter
息 *kisoku* your son
11 紳 *kishin* men of rank
著 *kicho* the book you wrote
婦人 *kifujin* lady. *kifujin(rashii)* ladylike
族 *kizoku* nobility
族的 *kizokuteki* aristocratic
族院 *kizokuin* House of Peers, Upper House, House of Lords
族政治 *kizoku seiji* aristocracy
12 答 *kitō* your answer
報 *kihō* your report
13 殿 *kiden* you (at present a term of ridicule)
僧 *kisō* you (a ranking priest)
酬 *kishū* reply to your letter
意 *ki-i* your will, your opinion, your pleasure
14 様 *kisama* you
15 慮 *kiryo* your idea
賤 *kisen* high and low, rich and poor
賓 *kihin* a noble visitor
賓室 *kihinshitsu* distinguished visitors' reception room
賓席 *kihinseki* distinguished visitors' gallery
16 覧 *kiran* your observation (of something)
翰 *kikan* your letter
橄欖石 *kikanranseki* chrysolite
18 顕 *kiken* men of distinction, dignitaries
簡 *kikan* your letter

—— 6 ——

貿 See 4499.

貫 See 4278.

賎 4505 / F-X See **賤** 4515.

賂 4506/F1797 Ro. *mainai* bribe.

B**賄** 4507/F1797 Wai. Kai. *makana(u)* board; supply; finance. *makana(i)* board, meals; catering, feeding.
13 賂 *wairo* bribe, bribery

B**賊** 4508/F1798 **賊** Zoku rebel; traitor; robber. *zoku(suru)* injure, kill.
3 子 *zokushi* traitor, rebel, conspirator
4 心 *zokushin* planning to steal; defiant spirit, determination to inflict damage
6 臣 *zokushin* traitor, rebel, conspirator
名 *zokumei* name of a rebel
7 兵 *zokuhei* insurgents, rebels
9 虐 *zokugyaku* damage and ill-treatment
軍 *zokugun* insurgents, rebel army
10 徒 *zokuto* rebels, traitors
将 *zokushō* insurgent army leader
党 *zokutō* rebels, traitors
11 船 *zokusen* pirate ship
14 魁 *zokkai* rebel leader

A**賃** 4509/F1797 Chin hire, rent, wages, fare, freight, charge, fee.
8 上 *chin-a(ge)* wage increase
5 仕事 *chin shigoto* piecework
7 労働 *chinrōdō* working for wages
8 金 *chingin* wages, pay. *chinkin* wages; fare; (freight) rates
金支払日 *chingin shiharaibi* payday
金労働者 *chingin rōdōsha* those working for wages
金制 *chinginsei* wage system
金表 *chinginhyō* wage table
金指数 *chingin shisū* wage index
金率 *chinginritsu* wage scale
金統制 *chingin tōsei* wage control
10 借 *chinshaku, chinga(ri)* hiring, renting, leasing, hire
借人 *chinshakunin* lessee, leaseholder
借地 *chinshakuchi* leased land
借料 *chinshakuryō* rent
12 貸 *chintai, chingashi* lease, hire
貸人 *chintainin* lessor
貸借 *chintaishaku* leasing, chartering
貸料 *chintairyō* rent
14 銀 *chingin* wages, pay
銭 *chinsen* wages
15 稼 *chinkase(gi)* working for wages
餅 *chimmochi* commercial rice cake

A**資** 4510/F1797 Shi resources, capital, funds; materials; data; quality, disposition; help. *shi(suru)* be conducive to, contribute to, assist.
2 力 *shiryoku* means, resources, funds
5 本 *shihon* capital; fund
本力 *shihonryoku* amount of capital
本化 *shihonka* capitalization
本主 *shihon nushi* capitalist, financier
本主義 *shihon shugi* capitalism
本金 *shihonkin* capital, capital stock
本財 *shihonzai* capital goods
本家 *shihonka* capitalist, financier
7 材 *shizai* materials, supplies
8 性 *shisei* nature, disposition
金 *shikin* fund, capital
金化 *shikinka* capitalization, converting (goods) into money
金源 *shikingen* source of funds
10 料 *shiryō* materials, data
財 *shizai* property, means, assets
格 *shikaku* qualifications, requirements, capabilities
格審査 *shikaku shinsa* screening, qualifying examination
11 産 *shisan* property, means, assets
産家 *shisanka* man of wealth
産凍結 *shisan tōketsu* freezing of assets
13 源 *shigen* resources
15 質 *shishitsu* nature, disposition

7

賓 See **賓** 1339.

賍 Nonstandard for **贓** 4532.

賑 4511/F1799 Shin. *nigi(wau)* flourish, be bustling. *nigi(wai)* prosperity, bustle, crowd. *nigi(washii)*, *nigi(yakana)* lively, gay, cheerful; bustling, populous; noisy; prosperous.
9 恤 *shinjutsu* relief, charity, alms
恤金 *shinjutsukin* relief fund, alms
14 賑 *niginigi(shii)* prosperous; merry

8

賭 See 4519.

賓 See 1339.

賞 See 1372.

賣 賣 See **売** 1067.

B **賠** = **賠** 4512 F1800 BAI indemnify.

17償 *baishō* reparation, indemnity, compensation

17償金 *baishōkin* indemnity, reparations, damages

B **賦** 4513 F1802 FU ode, prose poem, poetical prose; tribute, exacted service; installment. *fu(suru)* compose, write; allot.

3与 *fuyo suru* give

5払 *bubara(i), fubara(i)* installment plan

7役 *fueki* forced labor; exacted service

8金 *fukin* installment

性 *fusei* heredity

10租 *fuso* tribute, tax

12税 *fuzei* taxation

13詩 *fushi* writing poetry

15課 *fuka* tax, levy, assessment

B **賜** 4514 F1800 SHI. *tama(waru), tamo(u), tama(u)* (see under 給 3538.0). *tamamono* gift, boon; results.

8金 *shikin* government money award

杯 *shihai* trophy from the imperial family

10宴 *shien* court banquet

書 *shisho* a book gift from the emperor

13暇 *shika* furlough, leave of absence

15謁 *shietsu* an audience with the emperor

16諡 *shishi* posthumous name conferred by the emperor

餐 *shisan* court banquet

21饌 *shisen* lunch in imperial company

賤 4515 F1802 **賎** SEN. *iya(shimu)* despise. *iya(shii)* (see under 卑 221.0). *shizu* low-rank person; poverty.

3女 *shizu(no)me* woman of humble birth

5民 *semmin* the lowly, the poor, the outcasts, serfs, peasants

民層 *semminsō* the poor class; the outcasts

6劣 *senretsu* meanness, foul play

7坊 *iya(shim)bō* greedy person

役 *sen-eki* menial service

男 *shizu(no)o* man of humble birth

8金属 *senkinzoku* base metals

10家 *shizu(ga)ya* humble cottage, hovel

13業 *sengyō* mean occupation; shameful calling

業婦 *sengyōfu* prostitute

A **賛** 4516 F1806 **贊** SAN praise; title or brief inscription on a picture; agreement. *san(su)* assist, agree with, support; praise.

6同 *sandō* approval, endorsement

仰 *sankō* praise

成 *sansei* approval, agreement, support, favor

成者 *sanseisha* approver, supporter, patron

7助 *sanjo* support, backing, approval

否 *sampi* approval or disapproval, yes and no, for and against

9美 *sambi* praise, adoration

美歌 *sambika* hymn

12評 *sampyō* favorable criticism

13嘆 *santan* praise, admiration

辞 *sanji* eulogy, compliment

意 *san-i* approval

14歌 *sanka* praise, admiration

B **賢** 4517 F1801 KEN wisdom, cleverness. *kashiko(i)* wise, intelligent. *saka(shirana)* pert, impertinent. *saka(shii)* clever, bright, intelligent, wise.

2人 *kenjin* wise man

3女 *kenjo* wise woman

才 *kensai* man of ability

4夫人 *kempujin* wise lady

5母 *kembo* wise mother

主 *kenshu* wise lord

兄 *kenkei* elder brother (referring to a friend)

6臣 *kenshin* wise retainer

7否 *kempi* wisdom and its lack

良 *kenryō* wisdom and virtue, the wise and virtuous

弟 *kentei* your young son

8所 *Kashikodokoro* Palace Sanctuary

明 *kemmei* wisdom, intelligence, advisability, prudence

郎 *kenrō* your son

妻 *kensai* intelligent housewife

者 *kenja* wise man

9相 *kenshō* wise premier; wise minister; wise councilor

10息 *kensoku* your son

哲 *kentetsu* wise man

能 *kennō* wisdom and talent; a wise and talented person

11婦 *kempu* wise woman

12策 *kensaku* wise policy

13愚 *kengu* wisdom or folly; wisdom; the wise and the foolish

聖 *kensei* wise men and saints

14察 *kensatsu* your discernment, judgment, understanding, or sympathy

15慮 *kenryo* wise consideration

A **質** 4518 F1803 SHITSU substance, matter, quality, temperament. SHICHI hostage, pawn, pledge, hock. *tada(su)* ask, demand, question; investigate, ascertain, verify. *tachi* nature (of a person); quality.

2入 *shichi-i(re)* pawning

5札 *shichifuda* pawn ticket

6地 *shichichi* pawning land; pawned land

朴 *shitsuboku* simplicity

7材 *shichizai* pawned article

8店 *shichiten* pawnshop

物 *shichimono, shichimotsu* pawned article

的 *shitsuteki* qualitative
受 *shichiu(ke)* redeeming a pawned article
券 *shichiken* pawn ticket
実 *shitsujitsu* plainness, simplicity
実剛健 *shitsujitsu-gōken* frugal and courageous
9 屋 *shichiya* pawnshop
草 *shichigusa* article for pawning
10 流 *shichinaga(re)* unredeemed pawn
素 *shisso* simplicity, modesty, frugality
11 商 *shichishō* pawnshop
問 *shitsumon* question; interrogation
問者 *shitsumonsha* questioner, interrogator
問書 *shitsumonsho* written inquiry; questionnaire
問戦 *shitsumonsen* interpellation war (in parliamentary assemblies)
問演説 *shitsumon enzetsu* interpellation speech
問欄 *shitsumon ran* question column
12 量 *shitsuryō* mass (in physics)
13 置 *shichio(ki)* pawning
14 種 *shichigusa* article for pawning
疑 *shitsugi* question, inquiry
疑応答 *shitsugi-ōtō* questions and answers
16 樸 *shitsuboku* simplicity

9

頼 頼 See 5129.

賭 4519 / F1804 To gambling. *to(suru)* wager, bet; risk, stake, hazard. *ka(keru)* wager, place a bet. *kake* a bet, wager, gambling.
4 手 *kakete* one who bets
元 *kakemoto* bookmaker
8 金 *kakekin* stakes, bet
物 *kakemono, tobutsu* wager, bet, stake
事 *kakegoto* wager, gambling
9 屋 *kakeya* bookmaker
10 馬 *kakeuma* race horse; horse race
12 場 *toba* gambling place
博 *tobaku* gambling
博犯 *tobakuhan* gambling (crime)
博場 *tobakujo* gambling house
13 碁 *kakego* playing game of *go* for stakes

10

賽 See 1344.

賻 4520 / F1804 Fu condolence gift.

賺 = 賺 4521 / F1804 Tan. Ren. *suka(su)* coax, humor, persuade.

購 = 購 4522 / F1805 B Kō. *agana(u)* buy.
2 入 *kōnyū* purchase, buying
入者 *kōnyūsha* purchaser
入通帳 *kōnyū tsūchō* consumer's purchasing book, ration book
7 求 *kōkyū* purchase
10 書 *kōsho* purchasing books; purchased books
12 買 *kōbai* purchasing
買力 *kōbairyoku* purchasing power
買心 *kōbaishin* customer's interest
買者 *kōbaisha* buyer
買部 *kōbaibu* shopping service
買組合 *kōbai kumiai* co-operative society
14 読 *kōdoku* subscription
読者 *kōdokusha* subscriber
読料 *kōdokuryō* subscription charge

11

贓 贓 See 4529.

贄 4523 / F1805 Shi gift; offering. *nie* sacrifice, offering; gift.

贅 4524 / F1805 Zei luxury, extravagance; wen; uselessness.
6 肉 *zeiniku* superfluous flesh, fat, excrescence; proud flesh
尽 *zei (o) tsu(kusu)* live luxuriously
7 言 *zeigen* redundant words
沢 *zeitaku* luxury, extravagance
沢屋 *zeitakuya* luxury-loving person
沢品 *zeitakuhin* article of luxury
沢税 *zeitakuzei* luxury tax
8 物 *zeibutsu* a luxury, something superfluous
14 語 *zeigo* redundant words

贈 = 贈 4525 / F1806 B Zō, Sō presenting (something). *oku(ru)* send, give to, award to, confer on.
3 与 *zōyo* donation, presentation
与者 *zōyosha* donor
与物 *zōyobutsu* gift, present
与財産 *zōyo zaisan* donated property
与税 *zōyozei* gift tax
5 本 *zōhon* book gift, complimentary copy
収賄 *zōshūwai* corruption, bribery
6 号 *zōgō* posthumous name
7 位 *zōi suru* confer a posthumous rank
呈 *zōtei* presentation
呈本 *zōteihon* presentation copy, gift book
呈式 *zōteishiki* presentation ceremony
呈者 *zōteisha* giver, donor
呈品 *zōteihin* present, gift
呈株 *zōtei kabu* bonus stock
8 物 *oku(ri)mono* present, gift

10 進 *zōshin* presentation
12 答 *zōtō* exchange of presents
答用 *zōtōyō* for gifts
答品 *zōtōhin* present, gift
13 賄 *zōwai* bribery, corruption, graft
賄罪 *zōwaizai* bribery crime
16 謚 *zōshi* posthumous title

— 12 —

贋 4526 / F1808 See 贗 840.

贈 4527 / F1806 See 贈 4525.

贊 4528 / F1806 See 贊 4516.

— 13 —

贏 See 337.

— 14 —

贓 4529 / F1807 = 贜 贓 Zō bribery.
8 物 *zōbutsu* stolen goods
9 品 *zōhin* stolen goods

贔 4530 / F1807 Hɪ strength, power.
9 負 *hiiki* = next word
10 屓 *hiiki* patronage, partiality, favoritism
屓目 *hiikime* viewing favorably

— 15 —

贗 4531 / F1808 See 贗 840.

贖 4532 / F1807 Sʜᴏᴋᴜ. *agana(u)* redeem, ransom, purchase, expiate. *agana(i)* redemption, atonement.
5 代 *agana(i)shiro* ransom
主 *agana(i)nushi* redeemer
出 *agana(i)-da(su)* rescue, redeem
9 宥 *shokuyū* (Catholic) indulgence, pardon
13 罪 *shokuzai* atonement, redemption, expiation
罪金 *shokuzaikin* ransom
罪所 *shokuzaisho* mercy seat (in the sanctuary)

— 17 —

贜 4533 / F-X See 贓 4529.

RAD. 赤 155

Aka red. Nickname: Red.

A **赤** 4534 / F1808 Sᴇᴋɪ. Sʜᴀᴋᴜ. *aka, aka(i)* red, crimson, scarlet. *aka* Communist, Red. *aka(bamu)* redden, color up, blush. *aka(ramu)* become red. *aka(rameru), aka(meru), aka(mu)* blush, redden. *aka(chan)* baby. *aka-* complete, entirely.
2 十字 *sekijūji* red cross; Red Cross
十字社 *Sekijūjisha* Red Cross Society
3 土 *akatsuchi, sekido* red clay, red loam
子 *akago* baby. *sekishi* baby; subjects
小豆 *azuki* small red bean
大根 *aka daikon* red radish; lip communist
4 心 *sekishin* sincerity, true heart
手 *sekishu* bare hand, bare fists
日 *sekijitsu* burning sun
化 *sekika, sekka* communization
切符 *akagippu* third-class ticket
毛 *akage* red hair
毛布 *akagetto* red blanket; a rustic
5 玉 *akadama* red ball; wind signal; amber; the red ball (in billiards); a red gem; amber
瓦 *akagawara* red tile
目 *akame* bloodshot eyes. *akambei* turning the eyelids inside out, making faces at someone
札 *akafuda* goods sold; clearance goods
本 *akahon* dime novel
他人 *aka (no) tanin* strangers
広場 *Aka(i) Hiroba* the Red Square
外線 *sekigaisen* infrared rays
6 色 *sekishoku, aka iro* red color; Communism
地 *akaji* red cloth; red ground
肌 *akahada* plucked (chicken) skin; abraded skin; nakedness; bareness
字 *akaji* red figures, deficit
合羽 *akagappa* red oil-paper raincoat
血球 *sekkekkyū* red corpuscle
7 貝 *akagai* ark shell, bloody clam
赤 *aka-aka to* brightly
身 *akami* heartwood; lean meat
坊 *aka(m)bō, aka(m)bo* baby
沈検査 *sekichin kensa* blood sedimentation test
8 門 *akamon* red gate; Tokyo University
松 *aka matsu* red pine

茄子 *akanasu* tomato, love apple
9 面 *sekimen* a blush, shamefacedness. *akatsura* red face
軍 *Sekigun* Red Army
信号 *aka shingō* red light, red danger signal
砂糖 *akazatō* brown sugar
茶 *akacha(keru)* turn reddish. *akacha* russet, reddish brown
茶色 *akacha iro* russet, reddish brown
10 馬 *aka uma* red horse
鬼 *aka oni* red devil; merciless debt collector
恥 *akahaji* public disgrace, open shame
剝 *akamu(ke)* skin abrasion
11 黒 *akaguro(i)* dark red
道 *sekidō* equator
脚 *sekkyaku no* barefooted
貧 *sekihin* extreme poverty
雪 *sekisetsu* red snow (due to mountain moss)
12 痢 *sekiri* dysentery
帽 *akabō* redcap
蛙 *akagaeru* reddish frog
飯 *akameshi, sekihan* rice and red-bean dish
紫 *aka murasaki* purplish red
13 禍 *sekka* Red Peril
誠 *sekisei* sincerity
靴 *akagutsu* brown shoes
電車 *aka densha* red-lamp car, last streetcar
新聞 *aka shimbun* yellow journal
裸 *akahadaka* stark naked. *sekira* stark naked; open, frank
裸裸 *sekirara* nakedness, nudity; frankness
14 旗 *sekki* red flag; the Taira flag; danger flag; revolution flag. *aka hata* red flag; the Red Flag
墨 *akazumi* vermilion stick, red ink
熊 *akaguma* brown bear
褐色 *sekkasshoku* reddish brown
瑪瑙 *aka menō* sardius
銅 *shakudō* gold-copper alloy
銅色 *shakudō iro* brown color
15 膚 *akahada*＝赤肌 above (see above–6)
嘘 *aka uso* barefaced lie
衛軍 *Sekieigun* the Red Army

樫 *akagashi* red oak, live oak
潮 *aka shio* reddish-brown tide
蕪 *akakabu* red turnip
熱 *sekinetsu* red heat
線区域 *akasen kuiki* red-light district
16 燐 *sekirin* red phosphorus
髭 *aka hige* red beard
縞瑪瑙 *aka-shima menō* sardonyx
18 顔 *aka(ra)gao* ruddy face
19 鯛 *akadai* red bream
21 魔 *sekima* Red menace
鰯 *aka-iwashi* dried salted sardines
露 *Sekiro* Red Russia

— 4 —

赧 4535 / F1809 TAN get red.

B **赦** 4536 / F1809 SHA forgiveness. *yuru(su)* (see under 許 4324.0).
5 令 *sharei* amnesty order
7 状 *shajō* an official letter pardoning a criminal
8 免 *shamen* pardon, amnesty, absolution, clemency
免券 *shamenken* (Catholic) indulgence
13 罪 *shazai* pardon, amnesty, absolution

— 7 —

赫 4537 / F1809 KAKU. *kat(to)* suddenly. *kagaya(kasu)* (see under 輝 1371.0).
7 灼 *kakushaku(taru)* brilliant, glorious, bright, blazing, glittering
9 怒 *kakudo* fury, burst of temper
14 赫 *kakukaku, kakkaku(taru)* bright, brilliant, distinguished

— 9 —

赭 4538 / F1810 SHA red.
3 土 *shado* red soil
9 面 *shamen, akatsura* ruddy face
18 顔 *shagan* ruddy face

RAD. 走 156

Hashiru to run. Variant: 走 *sōnyō* "running" enclosure. Nickname: Running.

A **走** 4539 / F1810 Sō. *hashi(ru)* run, rush, flee; turn to, become; go to excess. *hashi(rakasu), hashi(raseru)* make (someone or something) run. *hashi(ri)* first of the season; first supplies.
3 下 *hashi(ri)-o(riru)* run down
上 *hashi(ri)-a(garu)* run up
4 込 *hashi(ri)-ko(mu)* run into (a house)
5 去 *hashi(ri)-sa(ru)* run away
出 *hashi(ri)-de(ru)* pull out (of a station); run toward; run out of (a house)
6 回 *hashi(ri)-mawa(ru)* run around
7 抜 *hashi(ri)-nu(keru)* run thru. *hashi(ri)-nu(ku)* outrun; run thru till the end

8使 *hashi(ri)zuka(i)* errand boy, messenger
法 *sōhō* running form
狗 *sōku* hunting dog; tool, cat's-paw
卒 *sōsotsu* footman, courier
者 *sōsha* (base) runner, (track) runner
9査 *sōsa* scanning (in TV)
10破 *sōha suru* run thru
書 *hashi(ri)ga(ki)* cursive writing, scrawl, hasty writing
帰 *hashi(ri)-kae(ru)* run back, run home
馬灯 *sōmatō, sōbatō* revolving lantern; ever-changing panorama
高跳 *hashi(ri) takatobi* running high jump
11道 *hashi(ri) michi* runway
過 *hashi(ri)-su(giru)* run past
寄 *hashi(ri)-yo(ru)* come running, run up to
12越 *hashi(ri)-ko(su)* outrun, outdistance
幅跳 *hashi(ri) habatobi* running broad jump
程 *sōtei* a drive, a run (in a conveyance)
程計 *sōteikei* taximeter
塁 *sōrui* base running
塁者 *sōruisha* base runner
13路 *sōro* race track, course; escapee's trail
14読 *hashi(ri)yo(mi)* reading hurriedly

2

B **赴** 4540/F1811 Fu. *omomu(ku)* proceed to; get, become, tend toward.
6任 *funin suru* proceed to a new appointment. *funin* (new) appointment
任地 *funinchi* place of appointment
12援 *fuen suru* come to the rescue, reinforce, help

3

A **起** 4541/F1811 **起** Ki. *o(kiru)* get up, rise, awake; occur; (a fire) is kindled. *oko(su)* raise up, set up, pick up (someone); open, begin; promote, organize; generate; get sick; awaken; establish; plow; kindle (a fire). *oko(ru)* happen; break out; originate in; rise, flourish, spring up; be produced; have an attack of. *ta(tsu)*, *ta(taseru)* (see under 立 3343.0). *oko(ri)* origin, source, beginning; cause.
3工 *kikō* breaking ground
工式 *kikōshiki* ground-breaking ceremony
上 *ta(chi)-a(garu), o(ki)-a(garu)* get up, rise
上小法師 *o(ki)a(gari)-koboshi* tumbler, self-righting toy
4毛 *kimō* nap raising
5用 *kiyō* appointment, employment
句 *kiku* opening line of a Chinese poem
出 *o(ki)-de(ru)* get up, rise up
立 *oko(ri)-ta(tsu)* rise up. *o(ki)-ta(tsu)* rise, get up. *kiritsu* rising, standing
立投票 *kiritsu tōhyō* standing vote
6因 *ki-in suru* originate in; be attributable to
返 *o(ki)-kae(ru)* turn over in bed; get up; sit up
伏 *kifuku* ups and downs, undulations; relief (map). *o(ki)fu(shi)* getting around; rising and lying down; morning and evening, daily life
死 *kishi* saving from the jaws of death
死回生 *kishi kaisei* revival, resuscitation; entering great happiness
7床 *kishō* getting up, rising
抜 *o(ki)nu(ke) ni* on arising
承転結 *kishō-tenketsu* rules for composing Chinese poetry
8明 *o(ki)-a(kasu)* stay up all night
臥 *kiga suru* live, dwell. *kiga* daily life
直 *o(ki)-nao(ru)* sit up
居 *kikyo* state of health; daily life. *tachi-i* one's movement
居振舞 *tachi-i furumai* deportment, manners
9首 *kishu* beginning
点 *kiten* starting point; terminus; home port
重機 *kijūki* crane, derrick
重機船 *kijūkisen* floating crane
草 *kisō* drafting
草者 *kisōsha* draftsman, drafter
10原 *kigen* origin, beginning
座 *kiza suru* sit up in bed
起 *o(ki)o(ki)* just out of bed
案 *kian suru* draft, draw up
11掛 *o(ki)ga(ke)* just after getting up
動 *kidō* starting
動機 *kidōki* starter, starting motor
12結 *kiketsu* beginning and end
筆 *kihitsu* beginning to write
番 *o(ki)ban* night watch
訴 *kiso* prosecution, indictment, accusation, litigation
訴状 *kisojō* written indictment
訴猶予 *kiso yūyo* stay of prosecution
13債 *kisai* bond issue, loan flotation
源 *kigen* origin, beginning
準 *kijun* starting point
業 *kigyō* starting a business, promotion of an enterprise
電 *kiden* generation of electricity
電力 *kidenryoku* electromotive force
14端 *tachiha* chance to stand; chance to leave
誓 *kisei* vow, pledge, pact
磁力 *kijiryoku* magnetomotive force
算 *kisan* starting point in reckoning
算日 *kisambi* beginning date
15稿 *kikō* drafting an article
請 *kishō* written vow, pledge (in Buddhism or Shinto)
請文 *kishōmon* personal contract
19爆 *kibaku* priming (in explosives)
爆剤 *kibakuzai* detonator, percussion cap
爆薬 *kibakugaku* detonator, percussion cap

5

越 4542 / F1813 B Otsu. Etsu. *ko(su)* cross; pass; spend; tide over; outrun; exceed; surpass; move; go; come. *ko(eru)* cross; go beyond; exceed; clear (an obstacle); overstep (authority). *ko(ezaru)* not more than (two months). *(o)ko(shi)* coming. *-go(shi)* over, across, long-standing, beyond.

5 冬 *ettō* passing the winter
6 次 *etsuji* cutting across a normal process
年 *etsunen suru, otsunen suru* ring out the old year; tide over the year end; pass the winter, hibernate
年生 *etsunensei* biennial (plant)
9 度 *etsudo* exceeding. *ochido* error
11 階 *ekkai* skipping up thru court ranks irregularly
14 獄 *etsugoku* jailbreak
境 *ekkyō* border transgression
境事件 *ekkyō jiken* border incident
15 権 *ekken no* unauthorized. *ekken, okken* arrogation, abuse of confidence, going beyond one's authority

超 4543 / F1812 B Chō- super-, ultra-. *ko(eru)* (see under 越 4542.0).

2 人 *chōjin* superman
人的 *chōjinteki* superhuman
人間的 *chōningenteki* superhuman
3 凡 *chōbon* extraordinary, unusual
大型 *chōōgata* supersize
大型爆弾 *chōōgata bakudan* blockbuster
6 自然 *chōshizen* supernaturalness
自然力 *chōshizenryoku* supernatural power
7 克 *chōkoku suru* conquer, overcome, tide over, surmount
8 弩級艦 *chōdokyūkan* superdreadnaught
国家主義 *chōkokka shugi* ultranationalism
国家的 *chōkokkateki* ultranationalistic
9 俗 *chōzoku* unworldliness
重戦車 *chōjū sensha* super tank, mammoth tank
音 *chōon* supersonic
音波 *chōompa* supersonic waves
音速 *chōonsoku* supersonic speed
10 悟 *chōgo* superior wisdom
党派 *chōtōha* bipartisanship
高 *chōkō* ultrahigh
高速度 *chōkōsokudo* super high speed
高速道路 *chōkōsoku dōro* freeway, super highway
特作 *chōtokusaku* super film, feature
特作品 *chōtokusakuhin* super film, feature
特急 *chōtokkyū* super express
11 脱 *chōdatsu suru* transcend, stand aloof, rise above
現実主義 *chōgenjitsu shugi* surrealism
現実派 *chōgenjitsuha* surrealists
過 *chōka* excess. *chōka suru* exceed
過勤務 *chōka kimmu* overtime work
過額 *chōkagaku* excess, surplus, overflow
12 越 *chōetsu suru* be superior, excel, surpass, stand above, stand aloof. *chōetsu* superiority, excellence, pre-eminence, transcendency
超 *chōchō-* super-, ultra-
短波 *chōtampa* ultrashort wave, ultrahigh frequency
満員 *chōman-in* packed with people
然 *chōzen(taru)* transcendental, standing aloof, with a detached air
然内閣 *chōzen naikaku* supraparty government
絶 *chōzetsu* transcendence; superiority, excellence
絶性 *chōzetsusei* transcendence
絶論 *chōzetsuron* transcendentalism
13 感覚的 *chōkankakuteki* beyond the reach of the senses
18 顕微鏡 *chōkembikyō* ultramicroscope

6

越 See 4542.

8

趣 4544 / F1814 B Shu. *omomu(ku)* proceed to; become; tend toward. *omomuki* import, meaning, contents, tenor, gist; tone, touch, sentiment, charm; aspect, appearance.

6 向 *shukō* plan, idea, device, plot
好 *shukō* plan, idea, device, plot
旨 *shushi*=*shui* 趣意 (see below–13)
8 味 *shumi* taste, charm; zest, interest
13 意 *shui* opinion, idea; meaning, gist, tenor; aim, motive, purpose
意書 *shuisho* prospectus

10

趨 4545 / F1814 Sū, Shu run; go; quick; tend towards.

6 向 *sūkō* trend, tendency
8 拝 *sūhai* going out to meet (an important person)
13 勢 *sūsei* trend, tendency

RAD. 足 157

Ashi leg, foot. At left: ⻊ *ashi hen*. Nickname: Foot.

A 足 4546 / F1815 Soku foot; leg; counter for pairs of footwear. *ashi* foot; leg; paw; flipper, tentacles, arms; walk, step, pace, speed; footing; draft (of a ship); foot (of a mountain); trace; deficit, shortage. *ashi*, (*o*)*ashi* money. *ta*(*ru*), *ta*(*riru*) be sufficient, suffice; serve, answer, will do (for something); be worth, deserve; be satisfied; qualify. *ta*(*su*) add to, add up; make up for; make good; supply, supplement. *ta*(*rinai*), *ta*(*ranai*), *ta*(*ranu*), *ta*(*razu*) be insufficient, lack; be missing; be unworthy, be not worth it; be beneath notice; dull, stupid. *ta*(*rinasa*) insufficiency, shortcomings. *ta*(*shi*) complement, supplement; making up; supply; help. -*soku* pair (a counter).

3 下 *ashimoto* gait, pace, step. *ashimoto ni*, *sokka ni* at one's feet. *sokka* you (familiar and polite)
4 止 *ashido*(*me*) confinement; inducement to stay
元 *ashimoto*＝足下 (see above–3)
手 *ashite* hands and feet
手纏 *ashitemato*(*i*) encumbrance, hindrance, impediment
5 付 *ashitsu*(*ki*) gait; legged (utensil)
代 *ashidai* traveling expenses
台 *ashidai* step, stool, footstool; stepping-stone; springboard
6 早 *ashibaya* quick, swift-footed
7 序 *ashitsuide ni* while on one's feet
利 *Ashikaga* Era (1392–1573)
形 *ashigata* footprint
芸 *ashigei* foot tricks
労 *sokurō* trouble of going somewhere
8 長 *ashinaga* long-legged person
固 *ashigata*(*me*) walking practice
取 *ashido*(*ri*) gait, manner of swimming or walking; trace, track (of an offender); trend (of prices)
並 *ashina*(*mi*) pace, step
炙 *ashiabu*(*ri*) foot warmer
拍子 *ashibyōshi* beating time with feet
忠実 *ashimame na* faithful (in work)
9 音 *ashioto* sound of footsteps
首 *ashikubi* ankle
拭 *ashifu*(*ki*) foot towel, foot wiper
拵 *ashigoshi*(*rae*) footgear
枷 *ashigase*, *ashikase* fetters, shackles, irons, hobbles
洗 *ashiara*(*i*) tub; foot washing
前 *ta*(*shi*)*mae*＝*tashi* (see under 足 4546.0)
型 *ashigata* shoe last
10 高 *ashidaka* long-legged
捌 *ashisaba*(*ki*) footwork (in sports)
浴 *sokuyoku* foot bath
部 *sokubu* the foot
釜 *ashigama* kettle with legs
弱 *ashiyowa* poor walker
真似 *ashi mane* gesturing with the feet
11 掛 *ashiga*(*kari*) scaffolding; foothold; clue. *ashika*(*ke*) footing, foothold; pedal, footboard; step; going on (about so many years)
許 *ashimoto*＝足下 (see above–3)
萎 *ashina*(*e*) lame person
袋 *tabi* foot gloves, Japanese socks, tabi
袋屋 *tabiya* dealer in tabi
袋跣足 *tabihadashi* in stocking (tabi) feet
12 痛 *sokutsū* footsore, pain in the foot
場 *ashiba* scaffold; footing, foothold; situation
湯 *ashiyu* foot bath
勝 *ta*(*razu*)*ga*(*chi*) unable to make ends meet
軽 *ashigaru* footman, foot soldier; lowest samurai
13 鼎 *ashiganae* 3-legged kettle
搔 *aga*(*ku*) paw, struggle, wriggle, flounder
溜 *ashidamari* stand, foothold, footing; stopping place; center of activity
継 *ashitsu*(*gi*) footstool
腰 *ashikoshi* legs and loins
触 *ashiza*(*wari*) the feel to the foot
跡 *ashiato*, *sokuseki* footprint
障 *ashiza*(*wari*) in the way when walking
馴 *ashina*(*rashi*) walking practice
裏 *ashiura*, *ashi*(*no*)*ura*, *ana-ura* sole of the foot
業 *ashiwaza* footwork (in judo); foot tricks
14 摺 *ashizu*(*ri*) stamping or scraping the feet
駄 *ashida* high clogs
算 *tashizan* addition
15 踏 *ashibu*(*mi*), *ashifu*(*mi*) stepping, stamping; step; stalemate, marking time; treadle machine
16 縺 *ashimotsu*(*re*) faltering walk
頸 *ashikubi* ankle
盥 *ashidarai* foot tub
繁 *ashi-shige*(*ku*) frequently
18 癖 *ashikuse* gait
19 蹴 *ashige* kicking
20 競 *ashikura*(*be*) foot race
21 纏 *ashimato*(*i*) impediment, encumbrance, hindrance

4

趾 4547 / F1816 Shi footprint; feet. *ato* remains.

距 4548 F1818 Kyo *heda(taru)* be distant. B
10骨 *kyokotsu* anklebone
19離 *kyori* distance, range, interval; gap
離測定器 *kyori sokuteiki* range finder

5

趺 4549 F1817 Tetsu stumble.

跚 4550 F1817 **跚** San stagger, reel, stumble.

跑 4551 F1817 Hō. *daku* trotting, trot.

跛 4552 F1818 Ha. Hi. Bi. *bikko, chimba* lameness, lame person; an odd (shoe), one of a pair. *chimba na* odd (pair), odd (shoe).
6行 *hakō* limping; lack of coordination

跋 4553 F1816 **跋** Hatsu, Batsu epilogue, book postscript.
4文 *batsubun* epilogue, book postscript
11扈 *bakko* rampancy, prevalence, domination
渉 *basshō* traveling, hiking

6

跟 4554 F1818 Kon heel.

跫 4555 F1819 Kyō sound of footsteps.
9音 *kyōon, ashioto* footsteps

跣 4556 F1818 Sen barefooted.
7足 *hadashi* bare feet

跨 4557 F1818 Ko. Ka. *mataga(ru)* be, sit, or stand astride; extend over; be laid across. *mata(gu)* straddle, bestride.
15線橋 *kosenkyō* overpass

践 4558 F1821 **踐** Sen. *fu(mu)* (see 踏 4571.0). B
10祚 *senso* accession to the throne
祚式 *sensoshiki* accession ceremony

跪 4559 F1818 Ki. *hizamazu(ku)* kneel.
6伏 *kifuku suru* kneel and lie down
7坐 *kiza suru* kneel down
8拝 *kihai suru* kneel and worship. *kihai* genuflection

跡 4560 F1818 Seki. *ato* mark, print, impression; trace, track, trail; wake; marks, traces, evidence; scar; ruins, precedent. B
4片付 *atokatazu(ke)* cleaning up, putting things in order
切 *togi(reru)* stop, cease
切跡切 *togi(re)-togi(re) ni* (working) spasmodically
5白波 *atoshiranami* complete disappearance
目 *atome* heir, successor
目相続 *atome sōzoku* heirship
7役 *atoyaku* successor
形 *atokata* traces, marks, vestiges, evidence
形無 *atokatana(i)* no traces
8取 *atoto(ri)* heir, successor
始末 *atoshimatsu* settlement, liquidation, clearing up
12絶 *toda(eru)* stop, cease
13継 *atotsu(gi)* heir, successor

路 4561 F1819 Ro road, route, path. *-ji* route, road; distance. *michi* (see under 道 4724.0). A
2人 *rojin* passers-by
3上 *rojō* on the road; road
4辺 *rohen* roadside
5用 *royō* traveling expenses
6次 *roji* road, route; on the way
地 *roji* alley, lane, garden path
7床 *roshō* roadbed
9面 *romen* road surface
面電車 *romen densha* streetcar
12程 *rotei* distance, mileage
費 *rohi* traveling expenses
傍 *robō* roadside, wayside
傍人 *robō (no) hito* a passer-by; one with whom one has no connections
傍伝道 *robō dendō* street evangelism
傍演説 *robō enzetsu* wayside speech
傍演説者 *robō enzetsusha* street preacher
14銀 *rogin* traveling expenses
15標 *rohyō* road sign
線 *rosen* route, way
盤 *roban* roadbed
16頭 *rotō* wayside, roadside

跳 4562 F1820 Chō. *ha(neru)* leap, spring up, hop; jerk, prance, buck; bound; spatter, splash; snap, crack, sputter; close, be over. *odo(ru)* (see under 踊 4565.0). *to(bu)* jump, leap, spring, bound, vault, hop. *ha(ne)* splashes (of mud). B
3上 *ha(ne)-a(garu)* jump up, spring up
下 *tobio(ri)* jumping off a (moving vehicle)
下自殺 *tobio(ri) jisatsu* suicide by leaping off (a height)
4手 *to(bi)te* jumper (sport)

反 *ha(ne)-kae(ru) vi* rebound, recoil, bounce, spring back. *ha(ne)-kae(su) vt* kick back, throw off

込台 *tobiko(mi)dai* diving board

5台 *to(bi)dai* vaulting horse ⌈spring out

出 *ha(ne)-da(su), ha(ne)-de(ru), to(bi)-de(ru),*

6回 *odo(ri)-mawa(ru), ha(ne)-mawa(ru), to(bi)-mawa(ru)* jump around, cut capers, romp, gambol

返 *ha(ne)-kae(su)* bounce back

8退 *ha(ne)-no(ku), to(bi)-no(ku)* jump back

板 *ha(ne)-ita, to(bi)-ita,* springboard

9飛 *ha(ne)-to(bu)* = *ha(neru)* (see under 跳 4562.0)

10起 *ha(ne)-o(kiru)* jump up, spring up

11梁 *chōryō* rampancy, domination

12越 *to(bi)-ko(eru)* jump over, fly over, fly

弾 *chōdan* ricocheting bullet ⌊across

開橋 *chōkaikyō* balanced drawbridge

13蜋 *chōryō* rampancy, domination

16橋 *ha(ne)bashi* drawbridge

20競 *to(bi)kura, to(bi)kura(be)* jumping match

21躍 *ha(ne)-odo(ru)* prance around. *chōyaku suru* jump, leap, skip, bounce, spring

躍板 *chōyakuban* springboard, diving board

7

踉 $\frac{4563}{F1820}$ Rō, Ryō stagger, falter.

跼 $\frac{4564}{F1820}$ Kyoku. *kogo(mu), kuguma(ru)* bow, stoop, bend over, crouch.

17蹐 *kyokuseki suru* crouch, stoop; sneak around

B **踊** $\frac{4565}{F1821}$ Yō. *odo(ru)* dance; leap, skip; throb (the heart); act as a cat's-paw; double (the interest on a debt). *odo(ri)* dance; dancing; step.

3子 *odo(ri)ko* dancer, dancing girl

6字 *odo(ri)ji* sign of repetition of characters or *kana*

7抜 *odo(ri)-nu(ku)* dance thru (the night)

12場 *odo(ri)ba* dance hall; stair landing

15戯 *odo(ri)-tawamu(reru)* dance around

8

踐 $\frac{4566}{F1821}$ See **践** 4558.

踞 $\frac{4567}{F1822}$ Kyo crouch, cower.

踠 $\frac{4568}{F1822}$ En. *moga(ku)* writhe, struggle, squirm, wriggle; be impatient for.

踪 $\frac{4569}{F1823}$ **蹤** Sō, Shō remains (of something); clue, footprint.

13跡 *sōseki* one's whereabouts

踝 $\frac{4570}{F1822}$ Ka. *kurubushi* ankle; anklebone.

10骨 *kakotsu* anklebone

B **踏** $\frac{4571}{F1821}$ **蹈** Tō. *fu(mu)* step on, trample on, stamp on; carry thru, practice; appraise; set foot on; evade payment. *fu(maeru)* step on, stand on.

2入 *fu(mi)-i(reru), fu(mi)-i(ru)* walk in on, step in, tread upon

4止 *fu(mi)-todo(maru)* stand one's ground, hold one's own; stay in office. *fu(mi)-todo(meru)* bring oneself to a stop

込 *fu(mi)-ko(mu), fu(n)go(mu)* step into; break into, raid

分 *fu(mi)-wa(keru)* push one's way thru

反返 *fu(n)zo(ri)-ka(eru)* lean back, fall backward; assume a haughty attitude

切 *fu(mi)-ki(ru)* cross; push off (in jumping). *fungi(ru)* proceed with decision. *fumikiri* railway crossing

切番 *fumikiriban* railway-crossing gateman

5石 *fu(mi)ishi* steppingstone

立 *fu(mi)-ta(teru)* to injure the foot by stepping on something sharp

付 *fu(mi)-tsu(keru), fu(n)zu(keru)* step on and scatter, tread on, trample; spurn, despise, slight ⌈springboard

台 *fu(mi)dai* footstool, step, steppingstone,

外 *fu(mi)-hazu(su)* miss one's footing, make a false step ⌈tread upon

出 *fu(mi)-da(su)* step forward, advance,

6臼 *fu(mi)usu* mortar worked by treading

7車 *fu(mi)guruma* treadmill

均 *fu(mi)-na(rasu)* level by treading

抜 *fu(mi)-nu(ku)* to injure the foot by stepping on something sharp ⌈down (snow)

8固 *fu(mi)-kata(meru)* stamp down, pack

退 *fu(mi)-no(ku)* liquidate (stocks)

迷 *fu(mi)-mayo(u)* lose the way, go astray

所 *fu(mi)dokoro* footing, place to step. *fu(mae)dokoro* footing; standpoint

拉 *fu(mi)-shida(ku)* step on and break, crush underfoot ⌈ning board

板 *fu(mi)-ita* footboard, pedal, treadle, run-

9砕 *fu(mi)-kuda(ku)* crush, trample to pieces

段 *fu(mi)dan* step, stair, carriage step, footboard

査 *tōsa* survey, exploration, investigation

荒 *fu(mi)-ara(su)* trample down, ravage, devastate

10進 *fu(mi)-susu(mu)* tread upon
倒 *fu(mi)-tao(su)* evade payment; trample over, kick down
従 *fu(mi)-shitaga(u)* follow in one's footsteps
消 *fu(mi)-ke(su)* stamp out (a fire)
破 *fu(mi)-yabu(ru)* walk across; travel on foot. *tōha suru* crush underfoot; travel on foot
殺 *fu(mi)-koro(su)* trample to death
11違 *fu(mi)-chiga(eru)* dislocate, turn, twist, put out of joint
張 *fu(m)ba(ru)* stretch (the legs); straddle; hold out, persist in; exert oneself
涸 *fu(mi)-ka(rasu)* dry up by treading
貫 *fu(mi)-nu(ku)*＝踏抜 (see above–7)
12越 *fu(mi)-ko(eru), fu(mi)-ko(su)* step over, step across
堪 *fu(mi)-kota(eru)* hold one's own, hold one's ground
場 *fu(mi)ba* footing, place to step
幅 *fu(mi)haba* (stair) tread
換 *fu(mi)-ka(eru)* change step, shift from one foot to another
渡 *fu(mi)-wata(ru)* cross over
絵 *fu(mi)e* crucifix plaque for trampling test
絞 *fu(mi)-shibo(ru)* tread out (the wine)
割 *fu(mi)-wa(ru)* step on and break
13砕 *fu(mi)-kuda(ku)* crush, trample to pieces
継 *fu(mi)tsu(gi)* footstool
跡 *fu(mi)ato* footprint
毀 *fu(mi)-kowa(su)* trample to pieces, crush
14鳴 *fu(mi)-na(rasu)* stamp noisily
15潰 *fu(mi)-tsubu(su)* crush under foot
締 *fu(mi)-shi(mesu)* step firmly, step cautiously
17藁 *fu(mi)wara* litter
19鞴 *tatara* foot bellows
韛 *tatara* foot bellows
22襲 *tōshū suru* follow, follow suit
26躙 *fu(mi)-niji(ru)* trample down

9

蹂 4572 / F1824 Jū step on.
26躙 *jūrin* trampling, overrunning, devastation; infringement, violation

踵 4573 / F1823 Shō. *kakato, kubisu, kibisu, kagato* heel.
6返 *kubisu (o) kae(su)* return, go back
10骨 *shōkotsu* heel bone
11接 *kubisu (o) ses(suru)* follow one after another

蹄 4574 / F1824 Tei. *hizume* hoof.
7状 *teijō* horseshoe shape
形 *teikei* U shape, horseshoe shape
形磁石 *teikei jishaku* horseshoe magnet
13鉄 *teitetsu* horseshoe
鉄工 *teitetsukō* horseshoer
鉄形 *teitetsukei* horseshoe shape
鉄術 *teitetsujutsu* horseshoeing

10

蹇 See 1343.

蹕 See 4581.

蹈 4575 / F1824 See 踏 4571.

蹊 4576 / F1825 Kei path.

蹐 4577 / F1825 Seki stealthy footsteps.

蹉 4578 / F1825 Sa stumble.
12跌 *satetsu* stumbling, failure, setback, reverses, deadlock

蹌 4579 / F1825 Sō move; run; stagger.
13踉 *yorobo(u)* totter along. *yoroyoro to, yoboyobo to, sōrō to* unsteadily, totteringly
17蹌 *sōsō* moving; dancing; staggering

11

躇 See 4585.

蹤 4580 / F1827 See 踪 4569.

蹙 See 蹙 254.

蹕 4581 / F1826 Hitsu one who precedes a king in a procession.

蹟 4582 / F1826 Seki, Shaku remains (of something), footprint, traces.

蹠 4583 / F1826 Seki. *ashiura, ashi(no)ura, anaura* sole of the foot.

蹣 4584 / F1826 Man staggering, tottering.
12跚 *yoro(keru), yorome(ku), yorobo(u)* stagger, totter along, reel, falter. *mansan(taru)* reeling, staggering. *yoroyoro to* totteringly

12

躇 4585 F1829 Cho hesitate.

蹼 4586 F1828 Boku. *mizukaki* webfoot, web.

蹶 4587 F1828 **蹷 蹙** Ketsu stumble; overturn.
10起 *kekki suru* jump to one's feet, stand up against
12然 *ketsuzen to* resolutely; with a spring

蹲 4588 F1827 Son. Shun. *uzukuma(ru)* crouch, squat down, cower. *tsukuba(u)* crouch, squat. *tsukuba(i)* wash basin in the garden.
8居 *sonkyo* crouching
15踞 *sonkyo* crouching

蹴 4589 F1827 Shuku. Shū. *ke(ru)* kick.
3上 *ke-aga(ru)* jump up. *ke-a(geru)* kick up
4爪 *kezume* spur, cockspur ⌊*kea(ge)* step riser
込 *ke-ko(mu)* kick in
5立 *ke-ta(teru)* kick up
出 *ke-da(su)*, *ke(ri)-da(su)* start kicking; kick ⌊off
6返 *ke-kae(su)* kick back
合 *ke-a(u)*, *ke(ri)-a(u)* kick each other. *kea(i)* cockfight
8放 *ke-hana(su)* kick open, kick off ⌈down
9飛 *ke-to(basu)* kick off; kick down; turn
10起 *kekki suru* rise, spring to one's feet
倒 *ke-tao(su)*, *ke(ri)-tao(su)* kick down, kick over
破 *ke-yabu(ru)*, *ke(ri)-yabu(ru)* kick open
殺 *ke-koro(su)*, *ke(ri)-koro(su)* kick to death
11毬 *kemari* (ancient) football
違 *ke-chi(gaeru)* dislocate by kicking. *kechiga(i)* stumble; blunder, failure
転 *ke-koro(basu)* kick down
球 *shūkyū* football
球界 *shūkyūkai* world of football
球場 *shūkyūjō* football field
12散 *ke-chi(rasu)* kick around, rout
落 *ke-oto(su)* kick down; kick overboard
22躓 *ke-tsumazu(ku)* stumble over, trip, fail, bog down

13

躅 4590 F1828 **躑** Choku, Taku tap with the feet; ruins.

躄 4591 F1828 **躃** Heki. *iza(ru)* crawl along. *izari*, *ashinae* a cripple.

躁 4592 F1828 Sō noisy.
7狂 *sōkyō* frenzy, raving madness, wild excitement
9急 *sōkyū* quick temper, impatience
10病 *sōbyō* mania
26鬱病 *sōutsubyō* depressive insanity

14

躊 4593 F1829 Chū hesitate.
19躇 *chūcho* hesitation, vacillation, indecision. *tamera(u)* hesitate, waver

躑 4594 F1829 Teki *shaga(mu)* squat, crouch, sit on the heels.
20躅 *tsutsuji* azalea

B **躍** 4595 F1829 **躍** Yaku. *odo(ru)* (see under 踊 4565.0).
3上 *odo(ri)-a(geru)* jump up, dance for joy
4込 *odo(ri)-ko(mu)* jump into
6気 *yakki*＝躍起 (see below–10)
如 *yakujo(taru)* vivid, graphic, lifelike, true
字 *odo(ri)-ji* sign of repetition ⌊to nature
10起 *yakki* excitement; jumping up and down; desperation; enthusiasm, zeal
進 *yakushin* rush, dash; onslaught; prancing, dancing ahead ⌈swoop down on
11掛 *odo(ri)-ka(karu)* spring upon, jump,
動 *yakudō suru* move lively
12越 *odo(ri)-ko(su)*, *odo(ri)-ko(eru)* jump over
20懸 *odo(ri)-ka(karu)*＝躍掛 (see above–11)

15

躓 4596 F1830 Chi. *tsumazu(ku)* stumble, trip; falter, be balked.
10倒 *tsumazu(ki)-tao(reru)* stumble and fall

16

躙 4597 F1830 See **躪** 4599.

18

躡 4598 F1830 Jō step on.

19

躪 4599 F1830 **躙** Rin. *niji(ru)* edge forward; trample down.
11寄 *niji(ri)-yo(ru)* edge up to

21

躅 4600 F1831 See **躅** 4590.

RAD. 身 158

Mi body. At left: *mi hen.* Nickname: Body.

A 身 4601 F1831 SHIN. *mi, karada* body; person; the quick; one's station in life; self; heart, soul, mind; ability; flesh, meat; life; blade; container; garment width. *mi(jirogu)* stir (oneself) slightly. *mi(gonashi)* deportment.

3 巾 *mihaba* width of a garment
丈 *mitake, mi (no) take* height, stature
上 *shinjō* merit; body; one's fortune, one's history; estate; social position. *mi(no)ue* one's fortune, one's future, one's lot; one's history. *shinshō* one's fortune, one's history; one's property; social position
上判断 *mi(no)ue handan* telling a person's fortune ⌈ing
上持 *shinshōmo(chi)* rich man; housekeep-
上相談 *mi(no)ue sōdan* consultation about personal affairs
上話 *mi(no)uebanashi* life story
4 心 *shinshin* body and mind
方 *mikata* friend, ally, supporter
欠 *mika(ki)* dried herring
辺 *shimpen* one's person ⌈camp
中 *shinchū* in the body; in the bosom; in the
内 *miuchi* one's whole body; relatives; friends, followers
支度 *mijitaku* dress, outfit (for a trip)
毛 *mi(no)ke* body hair
毛立 *mi(no)keda(tsu)* (hair) stands on end (because of fear or the cold)
元 *mimoto* one's birth, identity, history, career; character
元保証 *mimoto hoshō* personal references
元保証人 *mimoto hoshōnin* surety
分 *mibun* status, social position, identity, birth, circumstances
分不相応 *mibun-fusōō* beyond one's means
分制 *mibunsei* caste, social stratification
分相応 *mibun sōō* within one's means
分違 *mibunchiga(i)* difference in social standing ⌈document
分証明書 *mibun shōmeisho* identification
5 包 *miguru(mi)* one's belongings
仕度 *mijitaku* preparation
仕舞 *mijimai* clothes; outfit (for a trip)
代 *shindai* property, estate, wealth. *migawa(ri)* vicarious substitute. *mi(no)shiro* ransom money
代金 *mi(no)shirokin, migawa(ri)kin* ransom
代限 *shindaikagi(ri)* bankruptcy ⌊money
6 近 *miji(ka)ni* near oneself

任 *mimaka(se)* doing as one pleases
共 *midomo* I (familiar)
回 *mi-mawa(ru)* make rounds, inspect, patrol. *mi-mawa(su)* look around, survey. *mi(no)mawa(ri)* personal belogings
回品 *mi(no)mawa(ri)hin, mimawa(ri)hin* personal belongings
7 投 *mina(ge)* drowning oneself; drowned person. *mi (o) na(geru)* drown oneself
抜 *minu(ke)* severing connections
形 *minari* (a person's) appearance
売 *miu(ri)* selling oneself for a term of ser-
体 *shintai, karada* the body ⌊vice
体付 *karadatsu(ki)* build, figure
体的 *shintaiteki* physical
体粉 *karada (o) ko ni suru* work hard ⌈lazy
体惜 *karada (o) o(shimu)* spare oneself, be
体検査 *shintai kensa* physical examination; searching a person
体障害者 *shintai shōgaisha* the physically handicapped, cripple
体髪膚 *shintai-happu* body, hair, and skin; the whole body ⌈height
8 長 *mitake, shinchō, mi (no) take* stature,
固 *migatame* personal preparation
性 *mijō* (a person's) nature; rank; behavior
知 *mishi(razu)* self-conceit
舎 *moya* main building of a noble's home
命 *shimmei* the body and life; life
受 *miu(ke)* buying a geisha; redeeming a
空 *misora* the body; one's fortune ⌊geisha
9 首 *shinshu* head and body
屋 *moya* main building of a noble's home
後 *shingo* after one's death
拵 *migoshira(e)* outfit (for a trip); make-up
柄 *migara* one's person
重 *miomo* pregnancy
持 *mimo(chi)* conduct, morals; pregnancy
持女 *mimo(chi) onna* pregnant woman
10 振 *miburu(i)* shivering, shuddering. *miburi(ri)* gesture
粉 *mi (o) ko ni suru* work assiduously
窄 *misubora(shii)* shabby, poor, miserable
11 廊 *shinrō* nave
過 *misu(gi)* living, livelihood
動 *miugo(ki)* moving around
寄 *miyo(ri)* a relative
許 *mimoto*＝身元 (see above–4)
許引受人 *mimoto hikiukenin* guarantor,
12 悶 *mimoda(eru)* writhe in pain ⌊surety
幅 *mihaba* width of a garment

軽 *migaru na* light, agile
替 *miga(wari)*＝身代 (see above–5)
勝手 *migatte* selfishness, egotism
程 *mi(no)hodo* social standing ⌈one's place
程知 *mi(no)hodo shi(razu)* not knowing
13嗜 *midashina(mi)* care of personal appearance, grooming ⌈stand on guard
14構 *migama(eru), migama(e) suru* stand ready,
銭 *mizeni* one's pocket money
15締 *miji(mari)* preparation; behavior
請 *miu(ke)* ransom, redemption
褒 *mibo(me)* praising oneself; pride
罷 *mi-maka(ru)* die, pass away
震 *miburu(i)* shivering, trembling, shudder-
16儘 *mimama* freedom ⌊ing
18繕 *mizukuro(i) suru* dress up
21贔屓 *mibiiki* nepotism, clannishness
22籠 *migomo(ru)* conceive, become pregnant; hide

— 3 —

躬 $\frac{4602}{F1832}$ = **躳** Kyū body; self.
6行 *kyūkō suru* practice, exemplify, take the initiative

B **射** $\frac{4603}{F561}$ Sha archery; shooting. *i(ru)* shoot. *sa(su)* shine into, shine upon. [寸]
3干玉 *nubatama* pitch-black ⌈win (a girl)
4止 *i-to(meru)* shoot (an animal) to death;
込 *sa(shi)-ko(mu)* shine into. *i-ko(mu)* hit the mark
手 *ite, shashu* archer, bowman, shooter
手船 *itebune* archer's boat (in a battle)
5出 *ida(su)* shoot. *shashutsu suru* emit, project, shoot out, catapult, radiate, be
6尽 *i-tsuku(su)* shoot all arrows ⌊radiant
返 *i-kae(su)* shoot back, reflect
合 *i-a(u)* exchange shooting
当 *i-a(teru)* hit the target, shoot
7角 *shakaku* angle of fire
抜 *inu(ku)* shoot thru ⌈moneymaking
利 *shari* commercialism, love of gain.
利心 *sharishin* mercenary spirit
8法 *shahō* archery
取 *i-to(ru)* shoot (something)
的 *shateki* target practice
的場 *shatekijō* rifle range
幸 *shakō* speculative spirit
幸心 *shakōshin* speculative spirit
9通 *i-tō(su)* shoot thru
垜 *shada* firing mound (in target practice)
界 *shakai* field of fire
10倒 *i-tao(su)* shoot down, kill by a shot
流 *i-na(gasu)* miss the mark
殺 *i-koro(su), shasatsu suru* shoot to death
倖 *shakō* speculative spirit
倖心 *shakōshin* mercenary spirit
11掛 *i-ka(keru)* attack with arrows
貫 *i-nu(ku)* shoot thru
距離 *shakyori* rifle range ⌈ery ground
12場 *shajō* firing range; target practice; arch-
程 *shatei* rifle range ⌈take cover
竦 *i-suku(meru)* shoot and make the enemy
割 *i-wa(ru)* shoot and split with an arrow
散 *i-chi(rasu)* scatter the enemy (in a volley
落 *i-oto(su)* shoot down ⌊of arrows)
13損 *i-sokona(u), i-son(zuru), i-son(jiru)* miss
14精 *shasei* ejaculation, emission ⌊the mark
15影 *shaei* projection (in math.) ⌈ship
撃 *shageki* shooting; gunshot; marksman-
撃場 *shagekijō* target range, rifle range

— 4 —

躯 Nonstandard for **軀** 4606.

— 5 —

躰 See **体** 405.

— 7 —

躳 $\frac{4604}{F1832}$ See **躬** 4602.

— 9 —

躾 $\frac{4605}{F1832}$ (国字) *shitsu(keru)* discipline, train, bring up. *shitsuke* discipline, training, upbringing.
4方 *shitsukekata* way of training

— 11 —

軀 $\frac{4606}{F1832}$ Ku body. *mukuro, karada* body; corpse; tree with a rotten heart.
13幹 *kukan* torso; the body proper (without head and appendages)

— 17 —

軈 $\frac{4607}{F1833}$ (国字) *yaga(te)* soon after, soon, presently; almost, all but; no more than; after all.

RAD. 車 159

Kuruma vehicle. At left: *kuruma hen*. Nickname: Car.

A **車** 4608 F1833 SHA vehicle; a vehicle load. *kuruma* wheel; vehicle, carriage, wagon; cart, wheelbarrow; gocart; jinricksha; van, automobile.

2 力 *shariki* cart coolie; cart
3 上 *shajō* on the train, in the car
大工 *kuruma daiku* wheelwright
4 戸 *kurumado* wheeled sliding door
止 *kurumado(me)* wheel block; railway buffer stop; Closed to Vehicles
内 *shanai* inside the car
引 *kurumahi(ki)* jinricksha man
夫 *shafu* jinricksha man
井戸 *kuruma ido* well provided with pulley and rope
中 *shachū* in a vehicle
中談 *shachūdan* train interview
5 代 *kurumadai*＝*kurumachin* 車賃 (see below–13)
外 *shagai* outside the car
台 *shadai* chassis
付椅子 *kurumatsu(ki) isu* chair on casters
6 地 *shachi* capstan, windlass
両 *sharyō* vehicles, rolling stock
7 体 *shatai* chassis, car body
8 券 *shaken* bicycle-race ticket
9 屋 *kurumaya* jinricksha man; jinricksha station; wheelwright
室 *shashitsu* (train) compartment
10 座 *kurumaza* sitting in a circle
庫 *shako* carbarn, garage
馬 *shaba* horses and vehicles
馬代 *shabadai* traveling expenses
馬道 *shabadō* road for vehicles and horses
11 道 *shadō* roadway, driveway
寄 *kurumayo(se)* entrance way for vehicles
窓 *shasō* car window
12 軸 *shajiku* axle
裂 *kurumaza(ki)* tearing a body apart with the legs tied to separate carts
掌 *shashō* conductor
掌区 *shashōku* conductor's station
13 賃 *kurumachin* fare, hire; cartage charge; tip
14 塵 *shajin* dust raised by vehicles
15 輪 *sharin* wheel
駕 *shaga* imperial carriage
輛 *sharyō* heavy vehicles; rolling stock
輛連結 *sharyō renketsu* car coupling
19 轍 *shatetsu* rut

1

軋 4609 F1834 ATSU. *kishi(ru)*, *kishime(ku)* squeak, grate, creak, clash with. *kishi(mu)* squeak, grate, creak.

22 轢 *atsureki* friction, discord, strife

2

軍 See 628.

B **軌**＝**軌** 4610 F1834 KI wheel track; railway; orbit; rut; rule; model; road; way of doing.

1 一 *ki (o) itsu ni suru* act in the same way (as someone)
7 条 *kijō* rails
11 道 *kidō* railway, tramway; orbit; beaten track
12 間 *kikan* railwav-track gauge
13 跡 *kiseki* wagon tracks
15 範 *kihan* model, standard, pattern

3

B **軒** 4611 F1837 KEN house counter. *noki* eaves.

3 下 *nokishita* under the eaves
6 灯 *kentō* eaves lantern, door light
合 *nokia(i)* chinks in the eaves; the eaves; the sky seen beyond the eaves
先 *nokisaki* edge of the eaves; house frontage
7 別 *kembetsu* house to house
8 並 *nokinara(bi)*, *nokina(mi)* row of houses
9 昂 *kenkō* climbing high; high spirits, full of energy
10 高 *kenkō* high spirits
12 提灯 *nokijōchin* eaves lantern
13 軽 *kenchi* difference, inequality
数 *kensū* number of houses
14 樋 *nokidoi* eaves gutter
端 *nokibata*, *nokiba* edge of the eaves
16 頭 *kentō* edge of the eaves
18 檻 *kenkan* railing

4

軛 4612 F1838 YAKU. *kubiki* yoke.

斬 4613 F872 ZAN beheading. *ki(ru)* kill; cut. *-kiri* murder. [斤]

5 処 *zan (ni) sho(suru)* behead
6 死 *kiriji(ni)* fighting to death (with swords)
合 *kiria(i)* crossing swords, fighting with swords
奸 *zankan* slaying the wicked
奸状 *zankanjō* assassin's written vindication
8 苛 *ki(ri)-saina(mu)* hack to pieces
9 首 *zanshu* decapitation. *ki(ri)kubi* decapitation; a severed head

首刑 *zanshukei* execution
10 殺 *zansatsu suru* slay, kill
11 得 *ki(ri)doku*=切得 667.11
据 *ki(ri)-su(eru)*=切据 667.11
掛 *ki(ri)-ka(karu)* stab at, attack (with a sword)
笥 *ki(ri)-saina(mu)* hack to pieces
12 割 *ki(ri)-sa(ku), ki(ri)-wa(ru)* cut up
13 新 *zanshin* novelty, originality, newness
罪 *zanzai* sword execution, beheading
14 嘖 *ki(ri)-saina(mu)* hack to pieces
髪 *zampatsu* cutting off the topknot

軟 4614 / F1838 B NAN. *yawaraka(i)* soft.

3 口蓋 *nankōgai* soft palate
4 木 *namboku* soft lumber, softwood
毛 *nammō* pubescence; downy hair
化 *nanka* softening, mollification; weakening (of a market)
文学 *nambungaku* light literature
水 *nansui* soft water
水剤 *nansuizai* water softener
5 打 *nanda* a bunt (in baseball)
6 式飛行船 *nanshiki hikōsen* nonrigid airship
式庭球 *nanshiki teikyū* softball tennis
式野球 *nanshiki yakyū* softball
7 体動物 *nantai dōbutsu* mollusc
8 泥 *nandei* sludge, mud, ooze
性下疳 *nansei gekan* soft chancre
9 風 *nampū* gentle breeze, zephyr
便 *namben* loose bowel movement
派 *nampa* moderate party
炭 *nantan* soft coal
10 骨 *nankotsu* cartilage, gristle
弱 *nanjaku* weakness, effeminacy
11 球 *nankyū* softball
13 絹 *nanken* glossed silk
鉄 *nantetsu* malleable iron, wrought iron
禁 *nankin* internment; house arrest
14 膏 *nankō* soft ointment
15 論 *nanron* weak argument

転 4615 / F1849 **轉** A TEN turn, remove, change. *ten(jiru), ten(zuru)* vt and vi revolve, rotate, turn around; turn, shift; alter, change; move, be transferred. *koro(bu), maro(bu)* fall down, tumble. *koro(geru), koro(garu)* roll over, tumble; lie down (on the lawn); be convulsed (with laughter). *koro(gasu), koro(basu), maro(basu), maro(bakasu)* knock down, roll over. *utata* more and more, increasingly; somehow; indeed.

2 入 *tennyū* transfer into, moving into. *maro(bi)-i(ru)* roll into
入学 *tennyūgaku* transferring from another school
入者 *tennyūsha* members received
4 込 *koro(ge)-ko(mu), koro(gari)-ko(mu)* roll into, come one's way, devolve on, fall heir to
化 *tenka suru* change, be transformed
切支丹 *koro(bi) Kirishitan* Christians who gave in to persecution
5 用 *ten-yō suru* divert, convert
写 *tensha suru* transfer, transcribe, copy
去 *koro(gashi)-sa(ru)* roll away
出 *tenshutsu* transfer, moving out; transfer (of a ration record or church membership)
出先 *tenshutsusaki* new address
出届 *tenshutsu todoke* notification of moving
出者 *tenshutsusha* person transferred
出証明 *tenshutsu shōmei* moving certificate
6 回 *koro(bi)-mawa(ru)* wallow, welter, tumble about. *koro(ge)-mawa(ru)* tumble about; writhe. *tenkai* revolution, rotation
成 *tensei* changing form
任 *tennin* change of post
宅 *tentaku suru* move, change one's address
向 *tenkō* turn, conversion, about-face
向点 *tenkōten* turning point
会 *tenkai* transfer of church membership
会状 *tenkaijō* (church) letter of transfer
地 *tenchi* change of air, change of climate
地療養 *tenchi ryōyō* changing climate for one's health
地療養所 *tenchi-ryōyōjo* convalescent rest home
7 身 *tenshin* changing one's status or occupation
位 *ten-i* transposition, dislocation, displacement
住 *tenjū* changing one's residence
把 *tempa* a handle
売 *tembai* resale
車台 *tenshadai* turntable
8 居 *tenkyo* moving, changing quarters
送 *tensō suru* transmit; refer back (to a committee); translate (a cable); forward (mail)
注 *tenchū* a type of characters which now also represent concepts related to the original (e.g. 金 "money" as well as the original "metal")
官 *tenkan suru* be transferred to another office
免 *temmen* transferring and dismissal
学 *tengaku* changing schools
炉 *tenro* revolving furnace, converter
炉鋼 *tenrokō* converter steel, Bessemer steel
9 音 *ten-on* euphonic change
科 *tenka suru* change one's course
封 *tempō* changing fiefs
変 *tempen* mutation, change, vicissitude
室 *tenshitsu* changing rooms
10 進 *tenshin suru* shift (army) field positions

借 *tenshaku* sublease
倒 *koro(bi)-tao(reru)* fall down. *tentō suru* turn over, turn upside down, fall down violently; invert; reverse
校 *tenkō* changing schools
記 *tenki* posting (in bookkeeping)
帰 *tenki* turning point
11得 *tentoku* subsequent purchase
移 *ten-i* change, transition
訛 *tenka* corruption (of a word)
転 *tenten suru* pass from hand to hand, change hands often; go rolling along; roam around
宿 *tenshuku suru* change lodgings
婆 *(o)temba* tomboy, flapper
12属 *tenzoku suru* be transferred
結 *tenketsu* development and conclusion
補 *tempo* transfer, shuffling
勤 *tenkin suru* be transferred to another
期 *tenki* crisis (in sickness) ⌊office
落 *maro(bashi)-o(tosu)*, *koro(bashi)-o(tosu)* roll (something) down (a hill). *tenraku suru*, *koro(ge)-o(chiru)* fall off, tumble
貸 *tentai* sublease ⌊down
貸借 *tentaishaku* sublease
換 *tenkan suru* convert; divert, distract; reconvert; switch; transpose
換期 *tenkanki* turning point
換器 *tenkanki* commutator
13嫁 *tenka* blame another for one's mistake
禍 *tenka* changing calamity into happiness
戦 *tensen suru* take part in various battles, fight here and there
寝 *koro(bi)ne*, *utatane* nap, doze. *gorone* sleeping with the clothes on
置 *tenchi suru* transpose, displace, dislocate
義 *tengi* figurative meaning
意 *ten-i* figurative meaning
業 *tengyō suru* change one's employment
載 *tensai* reproduction, reprinting in another
路手 *tenroshu* switchman ⌊publication
路機 *tenroki* railway switch
14漕 *tensō* water transportation
15調 *tenchō* changing the key in the midst of a musical piece
輪羅針儀 *tenrin rashingi* gyrocompass
16機 *tenki* turning point
18覆 *tempuku*＝顛覆 5140.18
職 *tenshoku* change of post; change of occupation ⌈changed his work
職者 *tenshokusha* newcomer, one who has
19鏡儀 *tenkyōgi* transit
轍 *tentetsu* shunting, switching
轍手 *tentetsushu* switchman, pointsman
轍器 *tentetsuki* (railway) switch
轍機 *tentetsuki* railway switch

20籍 *tenseki* transfer of domicile, church membership, or school enrollment
21鐶 *tenkan* swivel

5

軻 4616 / F1839 KA difficult progress (as of wheels); Mencius' given name.

軫 4617 / F1838 SHIN be sad; revolve.
8念 *shinnen* imperial solicitude
15憂 *shin-yū* deep grief, worry

軼 4618 / F1839 ITSU pass along; rut.
8事 *itsuji* unknown fact
10書 *issho* a lost book

B **軸** 4619 / F1839 JIKU axis; axle; spindle; shaft; pivot; stem, stalk; (pen) holder; scroll picture.
4木 *jikugi* splint; matchstick; scroll rod
7承 *jiku-uke* bearings (in machines)
8物 *jikumono* scroll picture
受 *jiku-u(ke)* bearing
11距 *jikukyo* wheelbase

A **軽** 4620 / F1842 **輕** KEI. *karu(i)*, *karo(i)* light; trifling, unimportant; simple, easy; plain or light (meal); undignified. *karon(jiru)*, *karo(nzuru)* slight, make light of; neglect; belittle; underrate; pay no attention to. *karu(ku) suru* lighten, relieve. *karu(yakana)* light, easy. *kei-* light.
3口 *karukuchi*, *karuguchi* joke; talkativeness
子 *karuko* coolie, porter
小 *keishō na* slight, trifling
工業 *keikōgyō* light industry
4少 *keishō na* trifling, slight
文学 *keibungaku* light literature
5目 *karume* light weight. *karumi ni* rather
石 *karu-ishi* pumice stone ⌊lightly
打 *keida* light blow; pat; light hit
犯罪 *keihanzai* minor offense
巡 *keijun* light cruiser
巡洋艦 *keijun-yōkan* light cruiser
6舟 *keishū* fast light boat, skiff
衣 *kei-i* simple clothing, light clothing
合金 *keigōkin* light alloy
気球 *keikikyū* dirigible balloon
自動車 *keijidōsha* a light car
7妙 *keimyō na* facile, clever, witty
快 *keikai* nimbleness; lightheartedness; convalescence
兵 *keihei* light-armed soldier
作業 *keisagyō* light work

労働 *keirōdō* light work
8 雨 *keiu* light rain
侮 *keibu* contempt, scorn
油 *keiyu* light fuel oil
物 *karumono* lightweight silks
卒 *keisotsu* rashness, haste
易 *kei-i* easy, light, simple
忽 *keikotsu* carelessness, indiscretion
金属 *keikinzoku* light metals
佻 *keichō* frivolity, thoughtlessness
佻浮華 *keichō-fuka*=*fuka* 浮華 2575.10
佻浮薄 *keichō-fuhaku* irresponsibility; frivolity
9 風 *keifū* light breeze
食 *keishoku* light meal
度 *keido* slight degree
科 *keika* minor offense, light punishment
重 *keijū, keichō* relative importance; relative seriousness; relative weight
音楽 *keiongaku* light music
飛行機 *keihikōki* light plane
便 *keiben* convenience, simplicity
便食堂 *keiben shokudō* snack bar
便鉄道 *keiben tetsudō* narrow-gauge railway
10 病 *keibyō* slight illness
捷 *keishō* agility
浮 *keifu* frivolity, fickleness
砲 *keihō* light gun
荷 *karuni* light load, ballast
航空機 *keikōkūki* lighter-than-air aircraft
症 *keishō* minor illness
症例 *keishōrei* light cases (of illness)
挙 *keikyo* carelessness; rash undertaking
挙妄動 *keikyo-mōdō* rash behavior
挙盲動 *keikyo-mōdō* rash behavior
11 視 *keishi suru* despise, slight, ignore, neglect
粧 *keishō* light make-up
舸 *keika* a light fast boat
率 *karohazumi, karuhazumi, keisotsu* rashness, hastiness
12 減 *keigen* reduction, alleviation, commutation
焼 *karuya(ki)* wafer
軽 *karugaru(shii)* indiscreet, thoughtless, careless; frivolous. *karugaru to* easily. *keikei ni* carelessly, rashly
寒 *keikan* slightly cold spell; chilly feeling
装 *keisō* lightweight equipment; lightweight dress
喜劇 *keikigeki* light comedy
飲食店 *kei-inshokuten* light lunch
量 *keiryō* light weight
量拳闘選手 *keiryō kentō senshu* lightweight boxer
量選手 *keiryō senshu* lightweight-class athlete
13 傷 *keishō* minor injury
微 *keibi na* insignificant, minor, slight, light (illness)
罪 *keizai* minor offense
裘 *keikyū* light fur robe
戦車 *keisensha* light tank
禁錮 *keikinko* minor imprisonment
業 *karuwaza* acrobatics; risky undertaking
業師 *karuwazashi* acrobat, tumbler
14 罰 *keibatsu* light punishment
蔑 *keibetsu* contempt, slight, scorn
演劇 *keiengeki* light theatricals
歌劇 *keikageki* light opera
15 輩 *keihai* underling, small fry
16 薄 *keihaku* insincerity; untruthfulness; frivolity; inconstancy; flattery
機 *keiki* light machine gun
機関銃 *keikikanjū* light machine gun
18 騎兵 *keikihei* light cavalry
19 羅 *keira* gossamer, silk gauze
爆 *keibaku* light bomber
爆撃機 *keibakugekiki* light bomber
20 躁 *keisō na* thoughtless, rash, flighty

6

載 See 789.

輀 4621 F1840 F1852 See 轜 4642.

輌 Nonstandard for 輛 4628.

輊 4622 F1841 CHI low.

較 4623 F1840 B 較 KAKU. KŌ. *kura(beru)* (see under 比 2470.0).
12 量 *kōryō, kyōryō* comparison, guessing

7

輕 4624 F1842 See 軽 4620.

輓 4625 F1841 BAN pull.
6 近 *bankin* recent times

輔 4626 F1841 HO helping; helper. *tasu(keru)* help.
7 佐 *hosa* assistance; assistant; counselor
12 弼 *hohitsu* assistance, counsel
14 導 *hodō* guidance
17 翼 *hoyoku* assistance

8

輝 See 1371.

輩 See 5086.

7 見角言谷豆豕豸貝赤走足身【車】辛辰釆⻌邑阝酉釆里

軺 4627 / F1844 F1851 See 轗 4641.

輛 4628 / F1845 Ryō counter for heavy vehicles and railway cars.

輦 4629 / F1845 Ren palanquin; carriage of a noble.

[8]下 *renka* imperial capital
[17]轂 *renkoku* imperial carriage

A **輪** 4630 / F1845 Rin ring, circle; wheel; corolla; wheel counter. *wa* circle, ring, link, wheel, hoop, loop.

[4]止 *wado(me)* wheel block; railway buffer └stop
切 *wagi(ri)* round slices
[6]回 *wamawa(shi)* hoop rolling
死 *rinshi suru* run over and kill
伐 *rimbatsu* lumbering area by area (in a permanent forest)
灯 *rintō* a light on a Buddhist altar
[7]作 *rinsaku* crop rotation
投 *wana(ge)* quoits
抜 *wanu(ke)* jumping thru a hoop
状 *rinjō* ring shape
形 *wanari, wagata, rinkei* circle, ring, ring shape
[9]廻 *rinne* transmigration
乗 *wano(ri)* riding in a circle
姦 *rinkan suru* rape by turns
[10]郭 *rinkaku*＝輪廓 (see below–13)
索 *wanawa* lasso
差 *wasa* loop
[11]違 *wachiga(i)* two interlaced circles
唱 *rinshō* a round (in music)
袈裟 *wagesa* simple circular priest's scarf
転 *rinten* rotation
転機 *rintenki* cylinder press; mimeograph
[12]軸 *rinjiku* wheel and axle
番 *rimban* turn, rotation; executive committee chairman (of a Buddhist sect)
番制 *rimbansei* rotation system, job rotation
[13]禍 *rinka* traffic accident
廓 *rinkaku* outlines, contours, profile, skyline; sketch, outline
廓地図 *rinkaku chizu* outline map
[14]読 *rindoku* reading by turns
蔵 *rinzō* prayer wheel
舞 *rimbu* round dance
[15]縁 *wabuchi* rim of a wheel
[17]講 *rinkō* several people taking turns reading and explaining (a book)

— 9 —

輳 4631 / F1846 Sō gather.

輯 4632 / F1846 Shū gather, collect, compile.

[16]録 *shūroku* compilation, editing

輻 4633 / F1847 Fuku *ya* spoke (of a wheel).

[10]射 *fukusha* radiation (of heat, light, etc.)
射線 *fukushasen* rays of radiation
射熱 *fukusha netsu*, reflected heat, radiant └heat
[12]湊 *fukusō* convergence
[16]輳 *fukusō* convergence

A **輸** 4634 / F1847 **輸** Yu send, transport. *yu(suru)* be inferior to.

[2]入 *yunyū* imports; importation; introduc- └tion
入国 *yunyūkoku* importing nation
入品 *yunyūhin* imports
入港 *yunyūkō* an importing port ┌balance
入超過 *yunyū chōka* unfavorable trade
入額 *yunyūgaku* amount of imports
[5]出 *yushutsu* exports; exportation
出入 *yushutsunyū* exporting and importing
出入品 *yushutsunyūhin* exports and imports
出入差 *yushutsunyū (no) sa* balance of trade
出国 *yushutsukoku* exporting nation
出品 *yushutsuhin* exports, goods for export
出許可 *yushutsu kyoka* export license
出港 *yushutsukō* an exporting port
出税 *yushutsuzei* export tax
出割当 *yushutsu waria(te)* export quota
出超過 *yushutsu chōka* favorable balance of └trade
出業 *yushutsugyō* export business
出禁止 *yushutsu kinshi* export embargo
出額 *yushutsugaku* amount of exports
[6]血 *yuketsu* blood transfusion
[7]尿管 *yunyōkan* ureter
卵管 *yurankan* oviduct, fallopian tube
[8]卒 *yusotsu* transport soldier
乳管 *yunyūkan* milk duct
送 *yusō* transportation
送列車 *yusō ressha* transport train
送船 *yusōsen* transport ship
送路 *yusōro* trucking road
送機 *yusōki* transport plane
送難 *yusōnan* transportation difficulties
[9]胆管 *yutankan* bile duct
[11]移出入 *yuishutsunyū* exporting and import- └ing
[14]精管 *yuseikan* spermaduct
[20]贏 *yuei, shūei* gain or loss; victory or defeat

— 10 —

轂 See 2465.

輿 See 616.

轅 4635 F1849 EN. *nagae* shaft.

B 轄 4636 F1848 轄 KATSU. *kusabi* wedge.

輾 4637 F1847 TEN. DEN. *kishi(ru)* squeak, creak, grate.
11 転 *tenten suru* roll
転反側 *tenten-hansoku suru* toss around in bed

11

轉 4638 F1849 See 転 4615.

轆 4639 F1849 ROKU pulley. *koro* roller.
23 轤 *rokuro* pulley; lathe; windlass; potter's wheel
轤首 *rokurokubi, rokurokkubi* long-necked monster

12

轍 4640 F1851 TETSU rut, wheel track. *wadachi* rut, wheel track.
3 叉 *tessa* (railway) frog 「one's predecessor
15 踏 *tetsu (o) fu(mu)* follow the footsteps of

13

轗 4641 F1851 轞 KAN difficulty, misfortune.
12 軻 *kanka* separation from the world

14

轜 4642 F1852 輀 JI hearse.
7 車 *jisha* hearse

轟 4643 F1852 GŌ. *todoro(ku)* roar, thunder, boom, resound, ring; become well-known; throb.
7 沈 *gōchin* instant sinking
9 音 *gōon* deafening roar, loud report
12 渡 *todoro(ki)-wata(ru)* roar, boom, thunder
然 *gōzen(taru)* roaring, deafening, thunderous
21 轟 *todo(ro)todo(ro) to* with a rumbling sound. *gōgō to* thunderously, with a rumble

15

轡 See 1022.

轢 4644 F1852 REKI. *hi(ku)* run over (people). *kishi(ru)* creak, squeak, grate.
6 死 *rekishi suru* be run over and killed
8 逃 *hi(ki)ni(ge)* hit-and-run 「car)
10 倒 *hi(ki)-tao(su)* run down (someone with a
殺 *rekisatsu suru, hi(ki)-koro(su)* run over and kill 「ing a body
11 断 *rekidan* (a train) running over and sever-

16

轤 4645 F1852 RO pulley, capstan.

RAD. 辛 160

Karai bitter. Variant: 𨐋. Nickname: Bitter.

B 辛 4646 F1852 辛 SHIN H, 8th. *kara(i)* hot, acrid, sharp; salty; bitter, trying; harsh, severe. *kara(kumo), karō(jite)* barely. *tsura(i)* painful, trying, bitter, cruel. *kanoto* 8th calendar sign.
3 口 *karakuchi* salty tooth; dry (saké); bitterness, acrimony
5 目 *kara(i)me, tsura(i)me* hard time, bitter experience. *karame* saltiness
6 気 *shinki* ill-feeling, unhappiness
気臭 *shinkikusa(i)* feeling depressed, having the blues
7 辛 *karagara* barely, with difficulty
労 *shinrō* hardship, toil, trouble 「ance
8 抱 *shimbō* patience, perseverance, endur-
苦 *shinku* hardship, toil, trouble
味 *karami* salty, hot, or sharp taste
味噌 *karamiso* salty *miso* (bean paste)
10 党 *karatō* drinker
12 勝 *shinshō* narrow victory
煮 *karani* cooking with a generous amount of salt
14 辣 *shinratsu na* bitter, sharp, acrimonious
酸 *shinsan* hardships, privations
17 螺 *nishi* whelk (a shell)

5

幸 See 786.

— 6 —

辟 See 241.

辞 See 3860.

— 7 —

辣 4647/F1854 RATSU bitter.

[12]腕 *ratsuwan* shrewdness, sharpness, acumen, great tact

— 9 —

辨 4648/F1854 See 弁 846.

— 12 —

辦 4649/F1259 See 弁 845.［瓜］

辭 4650/F1855 See 辞 3860.

— 13 —

辮 4651/F1484 See 弁 844.［糸］

— 14 —

辯 4652/F1856 See 弁 847.

RAD. 辰 161

Tatsu dragon or, commonly, *shin no tatsu* (the character for "dragon" that is also read *shin*, as distinguished from Rad. 212). As enclosure: 㞢. Nickname: Small Dragon.

辰 4653/F1857 SHIN. *tatsu* 7–9 a.m.; 5th zodiac sign; dragon.

[9]砂 *shinsha* cinnabar

— 3 —

辱 4654/F360 唇 SHIN. *kuchibiru* lip.［口］

[9]音 *shin-on* labial sound

[12]歯輔車 *shinshi-hosha* interdependence

辱 4655/F1857 B JOKU. *hazuka(shimeru)* humiliate, put to shame, disgrace, insult; rape, assault. *katajikena(i)* thankful, indebted. *haji* (see under 恥 3704.0).

[8]知 *jokuchi* acquaintance

命 *jokumei* grateful orders

[10]涙 *katajike namida* tears of gratitude

— 4 —

脣 4656/F1543 脣 SHIN. *kuchibiru* lip.［肉］

— 6 —

蜃 4657/F1664 蜃 SHIN clam.［虫］

[6]気楼 *shinkirō* mirage

農 4658/F1857 A NŌ agriculture; farmers

[8]山村 *nōsanson* agricultural and mountain villages

山漁村 *nōsangyoson* agricultural and fishing villages

工 *nōkō* agriculture and industry

工商 *nōkōshō* agriculture-industry-commerce; farmers-artisans-merchants

工業 *nōkōgyō* agriculture and industry

[4]父 *nōfu* husbandman

夫 *nōfu* farmer, farmhand

水産 *nōsuisan* agricultural and marine products

[5]奴 *nōdo* serf

民 *nōmin* peasants, farmers

本主義 *nōhon shugi* building a nation on an agricultural economy

[6]会 *nōka* agricultural association

地 *nōchi* farmland

地改革 *nōchi kaikaku* agrarian reform

[7]兵 *nōhei* agrarian soldiers

作 *nōsaku* land cultivation

作物 *nōsakubutsu* crops, farm produce

村 *nōson* farm village, rural community, agricultural district

村伝道 *nōson dendō* rural evangelism

芸 *nōgei* agricultural technology

芸化学 *nōgei kagaku* agricultural chemistry

[8]協 *nōkyō* agricultural co-operative

法 *nōhō* agricultural law; farming methods

牧 *nōboku* general farming (crops and animals)

具 *nōgu* farm implements

事 *nōji* agriculture

事試験所 *nōji shikenjo* agricultural experiment station

学 *nōgaku* agriculture

学校 *nōgakkō* agricultural school

学書 *nōgakusho* agricultural books

林 *nōrin* agriculture and forestry

林大臣 *Nōrin Daijin* Agriculture and Forestry Minister
林学校 *nōrin gakkō* agriculture and forestry school
林省 *Nōrinshō* Ministry of Agriculture and Forestry
9相 *Nōshō* Agriculture and Forestry Minister
科 *nōka* agriculture department; agricultural course
科大学 *nōka daigaku* agricultural college
政 *nōsei* agricultural administration
政学 *nōseigaku* agricultural economics
10時 *nōji* the farmers' busy season
家 *nōka* farmhouse; farmers
耕 *nōkō* farming; farm labor
耕用水 *nōkō yōsui* irrigation water
11道 *nōdō* agricultural road
婦 *nōfu* farmerette
務 *nōmu* agricultural affairs
産 *nōsan* agricultural products
産物 *nōsambutsu* agricultural products
12場 *nōjō* farm, ranch, plantation
期 *nōki* farming season
閑 *nōkan* farmers' slack season
閑期 *nōkanki* farmers' slack season
13園 *nōen* farm, plantation
業 *nōgyō* agriculture
業大学 *nōgyō daigaku* agricultural college
業国 *nōgyōkoku* agricultural nation
業協同組合 *nōgyō kyōdō kumiai* agricultural co-operative
業組合 *nōgyō kumiai* agricultural association
16機具 *nōkigu* farm equipment
薬品 *nōyakuhin* agricultural chemicals
繁 *nōhan* farmers' busy season
繁休暇 *nōhan kyūka* school vacation during the busy farming season
繁期 *nōhanki* the farmers' busy season
17鍛冶 *nōkaji* a farm blacksmith

RAD. 辵 162

Always used as an enclosure in the modified form ⻌ (2 strokes) or ⻍ (3 strokes) *shinnyū* "advancing" enclosure (like that of *shin, susumu* "to advance").
Nickname: Road (as in 道 *michi* road).

1

辷 4659 F1858 (国字) *sube(ru)* (see under 滑 2663.0).

2

B 込 4660 F1858 込 (国字). *ko(mu)* be crowded; requiring (a lot of work). *ko(meru)* include; load (a gun); concentrate on; devote oneself to. *-ko(mu)* (get) into, (slip) into, (fall) into. *ko(mi)* mixture; a line of plants. *-ko(mi) de* in bulk; included.
2入 *ko(mi)-i(ru)* be complicated
3上 *ko(mi)-a(geru)* feel nauseated, feel like vomiting; be filled (with anger)
5矢 *ko(me)ya, ko(mi)ya* ramrod
6合 *ko(mi)-a(u)* be crowded, be jammed. *ko(mi)a(i)* a crowd
8物 *ko(me)mono, ko(mi)mono* stuffing
直 *ko(me)-nao(su)* reload

A 辺 4661 F1902 邊 Hen side; boundary, border; beach; region, district, rural areas; vicinity; approximation. *ata(ri), hoto(ri), he* vicinity. *-be* vicinity.
3土 *hendo* remote region
5民 *hemmin* people in the deep rural areas
6地 *henchi* remote place
防 *hembō* frontier defenses
9要 *hen-yō* frontier fort
10陲 *hensui* remote place
陬 *hensū* deep rural areas
11涯 *hengai* limit, end, extremity
12幅 *hempuku* personal appearance
13鄙 *hempi na* remote, secluded
塞 *hensai* frontier fort
14境 *henkyō* frontier, remote region
境精神 *henkyō seishin* frontier spirit
19疆 *henkyō* frontier, remote region

辻 4662 F1859 (国字) *tsuji* crossroad, street crossing, street corners; streets; roadside.
5辻 *tsujitsuji ni* at every street corner
占 *tsujiura* omen, divining papers, fortune-telling slips of paper
6自動車 *tsuji jidōsha* taxi
7車 *tsujiguruma* jinricksha for hire
8店 *tsuji mise* corner store
9待 *tsujima(chi)* waiting to be hired
便所 *tsuji benjo* public lavatory
10馬車 *tsuji basha* cab
11斬 *tsujigi(ri)* street murder
堂 *tsujidō* wayside shrine
商人 *tsuji shōnin* street vendor

7 見角言谷豆豕豸豸貝赤走足身車辛辰【辵⻌2】邑阝酉釆里

7 見角言谷豆豕豸貝赤走足身車辛辰【辵 3辶】邑阝酉釆里

強盗 *tsuji gōtō* highway robbery, holdup
12番 *tsujiban* guard, watchman
番人 *tsujibannin* guard, watchman
13褄 *tsujitsuma* consistency, coherence, reasonableness
14説法 *tsuji seppō* street preaching
15談義 *tsuji dangi* street lecture; wayside storyteller
17講釈 *tsuji gōshaku* wayside storyteller

3

迄 4663/F1859 KITSU. *made* to, till, until, up to; as far as; to the extent of; limited to. *made ni* by, before, not later than.

B **迅** 4664/F1859 迅 JIN *haya(i)* fast.
9速 *jinsoku* swiftness, promptness
13雷 *jinrai* thunderclap; suddenness

辿 4665/F1859 TEN. *tado(ru)* follow (a road), pursue (a course), follow up.
10書 *tado(ri)ga(ki)* poor handwriting
12着 *tado(ri)-tsu(ku)* grope along to, struggle on to
14読 *tado(ri)yo(mi)* reading with difficulty

迂 4666/F1859 迃 U roundabout way.
6回 *ukai* detour, roundabout way
曲 *ukyoku suru* meander
12遠 *uen na* roundabout; devious; circumlocutory
13路 *uro* detour, roundabout way
愚 *ugu* stupidity, silliness
17闊 *ukatsu* carelessness, stupidity
濶 *ukatsu* carelessness, stupidity

B **巡** 4667/F601 巡 JUN going around; circumference. *megu(ru)* go around. *megu(ri)* girth, circumference; tour, round, pilgrimage; flow, circulation; menstruation. *megu(rasu)* surround, make (someone) go around. *(o)mawa(ri)san* policeman. [巛]
5礼 *junrei* pilgrimage; pilgrim
礼者 *junreisha* pilgrim
6行 *junkō* patrol, beat, round, tour
合 *megu(ri)-a(u)* meet by chance, come across
回 *junkai* tour, round, patrol
回文庫 *junkai bunko* traveling library
回図書館 *junkai toshokan* traveling library
回裁判 *junkai saiban* circuit court
回路 *junkairo* circuit
回講演 *junkai kōen* lecture tour
回講演者 *junkai kōensha* circuit rider, traveling lecturer
7囲 *megu(ri)-kako(mu)* encircle
8拝 *jumpai* circuit pilgrimage
幸 *junkō* imperial tour
歩 *megu(ri)-aru(ku)* walk around, travel around
9廻 *junkai* tour, round, patrol
洋 *jun-yō* cruise; cruising
洋艦 *jun-yōkan* (navy) cruiser
査 *junsa* police, patrolman
査駐在所 *junsa chūzaisho* police substation
10航 *junkō* cruise; cruising
航船 *junkōsen* cruiser
航艦 *junkōkan* cruiser
11遊 *jun-yū* tour
視 *junshi* inspection tour
視人 *junshinin* patrolman; floorwalker
12検 *junken* tour of inspection
13業 *jungyō* provincial tour
14歴 *junreki* tour, trip
察 *junsatsu* patrol, inspection round; visitation
15閲 *jun-etsu* tour of inspection
16錫 *junshaku* (Buddhist) teaching tour
覧 *junran* tour, sightseeing
19警 *junkei* patrolman
22邏 *junra* patrol, round, beat
邏船 *junrasen* patrol boat, revenue cutter

4

迃 See 迂 4666.

迚 4668/F1862 (国字) *totemo* some way or other; very.

B **迎** 4669/F1860 迎 GEI. *muka(eru)* meet, greet, welcome; invite, engage. *muka(e)* meeting; person sent to meet.
2入 *muka(e)-i(reru)* usher in, welcome
4水 *muka(e) mizu* priming
火 *muka(e)bi* fire to welcome returning souls
5打 *muka(e)-u(tsu)* await and attack an approaching enemy
6合 *geigō* flattery, ingratiation
7角 *muka(e)kaku* angle of attack
車 *muka(e)guruma* vehicle sent to meet someone
8送 *geisō* meeting and seeing off
9春 *geishun* welcoming the new year
10酒 *muka(e)zake* drinking again (the next day)
11接 *geisetsu* meeting and entertaining
13聘 *geihei* meeting and entertaining
15撃 *geigeki* ambush attack
賓 *geihin* welcoming guests
賓館 *geihinkan* reception hall

A **返** 4670/F1861 返 HEN answer. *kae(ru)* go back; return to former employer; (colors) fade. *kae(su) vt* return, give back; repay; put back; overturn; requite (favors); take vengeance; turn around; answer; regurgitate. *kae(shi)* return gift; (money) change; return poem; answer; change of scene. *(o)kae(shi)* return; reply.

2 刀 *kae(su) katana de* (killing) with the return blow of the sword
3 上 *henjō suru* send back, return, resign (a rank)
5 付 *hempu suru* give back, return
礼 *henrei* return gift
本 *hempon* books and magazines returned
6 返 *kae(su)gae(su)* repeatedly. *kae(su)gae(su) mo* really, certainly
7 戻 *henrei suru* give back, return
却 *henkyaku* return, repayment
花 *kae(ri)bana* unseasonable flower
8 金 *henkin* repayment
送 *hensō suru* send back, return
忠 *kae(ri)chū* treachery, betrayal
事 *henji* reply
9 咲 *kae(ri)za(ku)* bloom a second time. *kae(ri)za(ki)* second bloom; a comeback (in business)
盃 *hempai suru* offer the cup in return
点 *kae(ri)ten* marks indicating the Japanese order of reading Chinese (*kambun*)
品 *hempin* returned goods
信 *henshin* reply
信料 *henshinryō* return postage
10 納 *hennō* return, restoration
討 *kae(ri)u(chi)* killing a would-be avenger
書 *hensho* reply
11 済 *hensai* payment, refunding, redemption, repayment
12 答 *hentō* reply
着 *kae(ri)-tsu(ku)* get back, return
報 *hempō* requital, retaliation, retort
13 辞 *henji* reply
電 *henden* reply telegram
照 *henshō* evening glow
14 歌 *henka, kae(shi) uta* poem in reply
15 還 *henkan* return, restoration, repayment

A 近 4671/F1860 近 **KIN**. *chika(i)* early, immediate; near, short (road), close by; akin to; nearby, bordering on, verge of, tantamount to; intimate, friendly. *chika(zuku) vi* approach, get acquainted with, associate with. *chika(zukeru) vt* allow to approach, associate with. *chika(zuki)* acquaintance, friendship. *chika(ku)* before long; nearby, neighborhood, vicinity; approximately. *chika(shii)* intimate, friendly.

4 火 *kinka, chikabi* nearby fire
辺 *kimpen* neighborhood, vicinity
日 *kinjitsu* soon, in a few days
日点 *kinjitsuten* perihelion
5 目 *chikame* nearsightedness; short sightedness
処 *kinjo* neighborhood, vicinity
付 *chikazu(ki)* acquaintance, friendship
刊 *kinkan* recent issue; forthcoming book
古 *kinko* early modern age
民 *kimmin* nearby peoples
世 *kinsei* recent times
世史 *kinseishi* modern history
代 *kindai* modern times
代人 *kindaijin* modern person, a modern
代化 *kindaika* modernization
代文学 *kindai bungaku* modern literature
代史 *kindaishi* modern history
代主義 *kindai shugi* modernism
代主義者 *kindai shugisha* modernist
代的 *kindaiteki* modern
代味 *kindaimi* modernity
代国家 *kindai kokka* a modern nation
代思想 *kindai shisō* modern thought, modernism
代戦 *kindaisen* modern warfare
代劇 *kindaigeki* modern drama
6 臣 *kinshin* trusted vassal, personal attendant
回 *chikamawa(ri)* neighborhood, vicinity; short cut
因 *kin-in* immediate cause
近 *chikajika, kinkin* nearness; before long, at an early date
年 *kinnen* in recent years
在 *kinzai* neighboring villages, suburban districts
地点 *kinchiten* perigee
似 *kinji* approximation; very similar
似値 *kinjichi* approximate decimal fraction
7 体 *kintai* recent style
作 *kinsaku* recent literary work
村 *kinson* neighboring villages
状 *kinjō* one's daily life; recent events; present situation
来 *kinrai* recently
8 国 *kingoku* neighboring countries or districts
侍 *kinji* attendant, suite
況 *kinkyō* recent condition
郊 *kinkō* suburbs
東 *Kintō* Near East
事 *kinji* recent events
所 *kinjo* neighborhood, vicinity
所回 *kinjomawa(ri)* formal neighborhood calls
所合壁 *kinjo gappeki* immediate neighborhood
所迷惑 *kinjo meiwaku* neighborhood nuisance
所泣 *kinjo-na(kase)* troubling the neighbors
所騒 *kinjosawa(gase)* neighborhood disturbance
9 姻 *kin-in* near relative
県 *kinken* neighboring prefectures
海 *kinkai* coastal waters, adjacent seas
海物 *kinkaimono* inshore fish
海航路 *kinkai kōro* coastwise service

海魚 *kinkaigyo* inshore fish
海漁業 *kinkai gyogyō* coastwise fisheries
10 時 *kinji* recently
郷 *kingō* neighboring districts, countryside
家 *kinka* neighboring house
11 道 *chikamichi* short cut
頃 *chikagoro* recently, nowadays
情 *kinjō*＝近状 (see above–7)
接 *kinsetsu* neighboring, adjacent
寄 *chikayo(ru)* approach. *chikayo(seru)* allow to approach, associate with
習 *kinjū* daimyo's personal retainer
著 *kincho* recent work
距離 *kinkyori* short distance, close range
視 *kinshi* nearsightedness, shortsightedness
視眼 *kinshigan* nearsightedness, shortsightedness
眼 *chikame, kingan* nearsighted, shortsighted
眼的 *kinganteki* nearsighted
眼者 *kingansha* nearsighted person
眼鏡 *kingankyō* glasses for the nearsighted
12 間 *chikama* neighborhood, vicinity
傍 *kimbō* vicinity, neighborhood, environs
詠 *kin-ei* recent poems
着 *kinchaku* recent arrival
13 路 *chikamichi* short cut
数 *kinsū* approximate number
電 *kinden* recent cable, wire just received
業 *kingyō* recent (literary) work
14 隣 *kinrin* neighborhood, vicinity
15 影 *kin-ei* recent portrait
畿 *Kinki*＝the following term
畿地方 *Kinki chihō* the Osaka-Kyoto area, the prefectures of Hyogo, Kyoto, Osaka, Mie, Nara, Shiga, and Wakayama
衛 *konoe* imperial guards; bodyguards
衛兵 *konoehei* imperial guards; bodyguards
衛隊 *konoetai* imperial guards; bodyguards
16 親 *kinshin* near relative
親者 *kinshinsha, kinshinja* near relative
親相姦 *kinshin sōkan* incest
親結婚 *kinshin kekkon* consanguineous marriage

— 5 —

迎 See 4669.

迭 4672 / F1863 **迭** B TETSU alternation.
5 立 *tetsuritsu suru* alternate

迦 4673 / F1862 KA, KE (used phonetically).

迠 4674 / F1862 SHŌ. *made* (see under 迄 4663.0.)

述 4675 / F1863 **述** A JUTSU state, speak, relate. *nobe(ru)* state, speak, recite, relate, mention.
7 作 *jussaku* writing a book, literary work
10 部 *jutsubu* predicate
14 語 *jutsugo* predicate
16 懐 *jukkai* recollections, reminiscences

迫 4676 / F1863 **迫** B HAKU. *se(maru)* press for, urge, force, spur on; approach; gain on, close in on; be on the verge of; be imminent. *se(ru)* urge on.
2 力 *hakuryoku* force; intensity; appeal
3 上 *se(ri)-a(geru)* push up
5 出 *se(ri)-da(su)* push out, come up thru a trap door
9 促 *sema(ri)-unaga(su)* urge and press on
持 *serimo(chi)* arch
持台 *serimo(chi)dai* abutment
10 真 *hakushin*＝next word
真性 *hakushinsei* truthfulness to life, verisimilitude
害 *hakugai* oppression, persecution
害者 *hakugaisha* persecutor
12 間 *hazama*＝狭間 2882.12
15 撃 *hakugeki suru* attack at close quarters
撃砲 *hakugekihō* mortar, mine thrower

— 6 —

迴 4677 / F1863 KAI go around.

逅 4678 / F1868 KŌ meet.

迹 4679 / F1864 SEKI. SHAKU. *ato* (see under 跡 4560.0).

迸 4680 / F1864 / F1876 **迸** HŌ. *hotobashi(ru), tobashi(ru)* gush out, spurt, spout, splash, spray. *tabashi(ru)*＝手走 1827.7. *tobatchi(ri)* splash, spray; involvement.

迷 4681 / F1863 **迷** A MEI. *mayo(u)* be perplexed, be in doubt, hesitate, vacillate, go astray, err; be tempted; be infatuated; be misguided. *mayo(wakasu), mayo(wasu)* perplex; mislead, deceive; tempt; seduce; charm, infatuate. *samayo(u)* wander around, stray, loiter. *mayo(i)* perplexity; doubt; ignorance; illusion, delusion, infatuation, skepticism.
2 入 *mayo(i)-i(ru)* wander into
3 子 *maigo, mayo(i)go* lost child
子札 *maigo fuda* child's identification tag
4 込 *mayo(i)-ko(mu)* go astray, lose one's way
5 去 *mayo(i)-sa(ru)* wander away

出 *mayo(i)-de(ru)* go astray. *mayo(i)-da(su)* lead astray, cause to wander
6 妄 *meimō* illusion, fallacy, delusion
7 言 *yomaigoto* grumbling, muttering, non- ⌊sense
9 信 *meishin* superstition
信家 *meishinka* superstitious person
10 宮 *meikyū* maze, labyrinth; mystery
11 彩 *meisai* camouflage
12 惑 *meiwaku* trouble, annoyance
惑気 *meiwakuge na* bothersome
13 路 *meiro* maze, labyrinth, blind alley
夢 *meimu* illusion, fallacy, delusion
想 *meisō* fallacy
15 論 *meiron* fallacy, absurd opinion ⌈away
19 離 *samayo(i)-hana(reru)* stray away, wander

B **逃** $\frac{4682}{F1867}$ **逃** Tō. *ni(geru)* flee, run away, escape; shirk, evade, back out. *noga(su), ni(gasu)* let go, set free, let escape, miss (a chance). *noga(reru)* escape, avoid, evade, shirk.
2 了 *ni(ge)-ō(seru)* escape safely
3 口 *ni(ge)guchi* way of escape, loophole
口上 *ni(ge) kōjō* excuse, evasion, quibbling
亡 *tōbō* flight, escape, abscondence, desertion
亡者 *tōbōsha* absconder, deserter, escapee
4 水 *ni(ge)mizu* mirage of water
込 *ni(ge)-ko(mu)* run into, seek shelter
支度 *ni(ge)jitaku* preparation for flight
5 打 *ni(ge) (o) u(tsu)* flee from responsibility
去 *ni(ge)-sa(ru)* flee away
失 *ni(ge)-u(seru)* flee, run away, disappear
出 *ni(ge)-da(su), noga(re)-de(ru)* flee, run away
6 回 *ni(ge)-mawa(ru)* run around trying to ⌊escape
返 *ni(ge)-kae(ru)* flee home
7 足 *ni(ge)ashi* flight; preparation to flee
町 *noga(reru) machi, noga(re) (no) machi* city of refuge ⌈bling
言葉 *ni(ge)kotoba* excuse, evasion, quibbling
走 *ni(ge)-hashi(ru)* flee, run away. *tōsō* flight, desertion, escape
走者 *tōsōsha* fugitive, deserter
8 延 *ni(ge)-no(biru)* escape safely
迷 *ni(ge)-mayo(u)* flee hither and yon
易 *ni(ge)yasu(i)* evanescent
9 途 *ni(ge)michi* way of escape, loophole
後 *ni(ge)-oku(reru)* fail to escape
10 残 *noga(re)-noko(ru)* escape capture
帰 *ni(ge)-kae(ru)* run back, return safely, flee home ⌈difficulty)
11 道 *ni(ge)michi* way of escape; way out (of a
張 *ni(ge) (o) ha(ru)* flee from responsibility
眼 *ni(ge) manako* eyes bent on fleeing
12 場 *ni(ge)ba* place of refuge; means of escape; exit. *noga(re)ba* refuge, shelter, asylum ⌈routed. *tōsan* flight
散 *ni(ge)-chi(ru)* disperse, scatter; be
落 *ni(ge)-o(chiru)* escape safely
惑 *ni(ge)-mado(u)* flee hither and yon
13 損 *ni(ge)-sokona(u)* fail to escape ⌈attitude
腰 *ni(ge)goshi* preparation to flee; evasive
路 *ni(ge)michi* way of escape, loophole
隠 *ni(ge)-kaku(reru) vi* hide
15 避 *tōhi* escape, evasion, flight
18 竄 *tōzan suru* flee

A **送** $\frac{4683}{F1867}$ **送** Sō sending. *oku(ru)* send, ship; transmit; remit; see off; see home, escort; spend (one's time), live (a life); add *okurigana* (*kana* showing inflection). ⌈spirits
4 火 *oku(ri)bi* bonfire speeding home the
込 *oku(ri)-ko(mu)* see (someone) home; usher in. *oku(ri)ko(mi)* feeding (a machine)
5 付 *sōfu* sending, forwarding, remitting
主 *oku(ri)nushi* sender
出 *oku(ri)-da(su)* forward, send out; see (a person) out, send away
本 *sōhon* delivery of books
本料 *sōhonryō* book delivery charge
6 返 *oku(ri)-kae(su)* send back, repatriate
先 *oku(ri)saki* forwarding address, consignee
仮名 *oku(ri)gana* suffixed *kana* showing
気管 *sōkikan* air pipe, air duct ⌊inflection
迎 *sōgei, oku(ri)muka(e)* seeing (someone) off and meeting upon return
迎者 *sōgeisha* people seeing (someone) off and meeting upon return
7 状 *oku(ri)jō* invoice
兵 *sōhei* dispatch of troops
呈 *sōtei* presentation
言葉 *oku(ri)kotoba* cue, catchword
別 *sōbetsu* farewell, send-off
別会 *sōbetsukai* farewell party
8 届 *oku(ri)-todo(keru)* see (a person) home;
油管 *sōyukan* oil pipeline ⌊usher in
受信機 *sōjushinki* transceiver
金 *sōkin* remittance; remitting
金人 *sōkinnin* remitter
金先 *sōkinsaki* person to whom remitted
金額 *sōkingaku* amount remitted
9 風 *sōfū* air blast, forced draft, ventilation
風機 *sōfūki* air blower, ventilator
信 *sōshin* transmission of a message
信局 *sōshinkyoku* transmitting station
信機 *sōshinki* transmitter
10 狼 *oku(ri)ōkami* a following wolf; a man who persists in following a woman
料 *sōryō* postage, shipping cost

致 sōchi sending, dispatch, commitment
荷 sōka consignment, forwarding, delivery
11 達 sōtatsu delivery, dispatch
球 sōkyū handball; throwing a ball; missing a ball (by catchers)
12 検 sōken sending to the prosecutor
葬 sōsō funeral
13 賃 oku(ri)chin shipping charges
電 sōden transmission of electricity
電線 sōdensen power line
話 sōwa transmission (of a telephone message)
話口 sōwaguchi telephone mouthpiece
話料 sōwaryō (telephone) charges
話器 sōwaki transmitter
話機 sōwaki transmitter
15 還 sōkan repatriation
還者 sōkansha a repatriate
20 籍 sōseki transfer of domicile

A 退 4684 F1866 退 TAI. shirizo(ku). shisa(ru), shiza(ru), susa(ru), shirizo(ku) retreat, recede, withdraw; retire, resign. shirizo(keru) repel, drive away, expel; depose; keep away; reject, turn down. no(ku) get out of the way; go away. no(keru), do(keru) get rid of, remove; finish; omit, exclude. hi(ku) retreat, withdraw, retire; subside, abate, ebb. do(ku) get out of the way, move aside.

3 下 taige suru retire from the imperial presence
4 化 taika degeneration, retrogression, depravation, atrophy
引 no(p)piki(naranu) unavoidable, inevitable, imperative
5 庁 taichō leaving the office
去 taikyo evacuation, withdrawal, removal, exodus, departure
出 taishutsu leaving, withdrawal
出時間 taishutsu jikan closing hour
6 色 taishoku fading; faded color
行 taikō regression (in psychoanalysis)
任 tainin retirement from office
会 taikai withdrawal from membership
7 身 taishin dropping out of government work
廷 taitei leaving the court
却 taikyaku retreat, withdrawal
位 tai-i abdication
位説 tai-isetsu proposed abdication
社 taisha retirement from a firm; leaving the office
社時間 taisha jikan closing time
役 taieki retirement from military service
役後 taiekigo after retirement from military service
役軍人 taieki gunjin war veteran
役艦 taiekikan decomissioned warship
8 治 taiji subjugation; extermination; crusade (against); control
京 taikyō leaving the capital; leaving Tokyo
官 taikan retirement from office
歩 taiho suru retrograde, degenerate; deteriorate
学 taigaku dropping out of school
屈 taikutsu tedium, boredom
屈凌 taikutsushino(gi) killing time
9 院 tai-in leaving the hospital
陣 taijin decampment, retirement
軍 taigun retreat, withdrawal
紅色 taikōshoku pink color
10 席 taiseki suru leave one's seat; withdraw, retire
修 taishū spiritual retreat
時 hikedoki closing time
校 taikō expulsion from school; leaving school
耕 taikō retirement in the country
11 敗 taihai defeat
転 taiten distraction. taiten(naku) diligently
12 場 taijō suru leave, walk out, exit, withdraw
結 gyaku musu(bi) granny knot
散 taisan suru disperse, break up (a crowd)
廃 taihai=頽廃 5130.12
廃的 taihaiteki corrupt
13 路 tairo path of retreat
勢 taisei downward tendency, decline, decay
隠 tai-in retirement
隠料 tai-inryō retiring allowance
14 蔵 taizō hoarding
蔵者 taizōsha hoarder
蔵物資 taizō busshi hoarded goods
15 避 taihi taking refuge, evacuation
潮 taichō ebb tide, low tide
17 嬰 taiei conservatism; retrogression
嬰的 taieiteki conservative, negative, passive, destructive
18 職 taishoku retirement (from office)
職手当 taishoku teate retiring allowance, severance pay
職年限 taishoku nengen age limit
職年齢 taishoku nenrei retiring age
職金 taishokukin quitting allowance
職者 taishokusha retired employee
職資金 taishoku shikin retirement allowance
職積立金 taishoku tsumetatekin retirement fund
20 譲 taijō modesty, humility

A 逆 4685 F1868 逆 GYAKU, GEKI reverse, inverse, opposite, unnatural; wicked; traitorous. saka(rau) oppose, act contrary to; offend. gyaku ni conversely, inversely, contrariwise, on the other hand, vice versa. saka(sa), saka(sama), saka(shima) reverse, inversion, upside down.
3 子 sakago breech presentation (in obstetrics)
下 gyakka, gyakuka nose dive

上 *nobo(seru)* be dizzy, be feverish, get excited, be enthusiastic over. *gyakujō, nobose* rush of blood to the head, dizziness, madness, distraction
叉 *sakamata* killer whale
4 心 *gyakushin* treachery, perfidy, treason
手 *gyakute* foul trick, dirty trick. *sakate ni* with point downward, (holding) upside ⌊down
日 *gyakubi* evil day (for fishermen)
水 *gyakusui* water diverted to check a flood
卍 *sakasa manji* reversed swastika, Western swastika (see 卐 12.0)
比 *gyakuhi* inverse ratio
比例 *gyaku hirei* inverse proportion
5 用 *gyakuyō* reverse use, perversion ⌈grain
目 *sakame* interlocked grain; against the
立 *sakada(teru) vt* stand on end (hair), bristle up, ruffle up (feathers). *sakada(tsu) vi* stand on end, stand up, bristle up, oppose. *saka(rai)-ta(tsu)* rise against. *sakada(chi)* handstand, standing on one's head ⌈insurgent
6 臣 *gyakushin* rebellious retainer, traitor,
行 *gyakkō, gyakukō* retrogression, backward movement; countermarch
争 *saka(rai)-araso(u)* rebel against
名 *gyakumyō* posthumous (Buddhist) name
光 *gyakkō* backlighting (in photography)
光線 *gyakkōsen*=above word
7 戻 *gyakumodo(ri)* retrogression, reversal, relapse, reverting to, going back to
乱 *gyakuran* rebellion, insurrection
児 *sakago* breech presentation (in obstetrics)
作用 *gyaku sayō* reaction, adverse effect
攻撃 *gyaku kōgeki* counterattack
8 送 *gyakusō* sending back
追 *saka-o(i)* turning to chase one's pursuers
波 *sakanami* choppy sea, head sea
事 *saka(sama)goto* wrong order
宣伝 *gyaku senden* counterpropaganda
効果 *gyakkōka, gyakukōka* reverse effect
性石鹼 *gyakusei sekken* antiseptic soap
9 風 *gyakufū* adverse wind, head wind
恨 *saka-ura(mi)* returned hate
剃 *sakazori* shaving against the "grain"
変 *gyakuhen* adverse change
巻 *sakama(ku)* roll, surge, boil, rage
飛込 *sakato(bi)ko(mi)* headlong plunge
10 進 *gyakushin* backward movement
徒 *gyakuto* rebel, traitor, insurgent
旅 *gekiryo* inn; entertaining travelers
流 *gyakuryū* countercurrent, adverse tide; regurgitation (of blood)
浪 *sakanami* head sea, choppy sea
討 *saka-u(chi)* counterattack
剝 *sakamu(ke)* hangnail
11 運 *gyaku-un* reverse of fortune
捲 *sakama(ku)* roll, surge, boil, rage
理 *gyakuri* paradox
転 *gyakuten* (sudden) change, reversal, retrogression; loop; reverse
産 *gyakuzan* breech presentation
淘汰 *gyaku tōta* reverse selection (in the evolutionary theory) ⌈a corpse)
屛風 *sakasa byōbu* inverted screen (beside
捩 *sakane(ji)* twisting contrariwise; retort; turning the tables on ⌈return
捩食 *sakane(ji) (o) ku(wasu)* criticize in
12 結 *gyaku musu(bi)* granny knot
落 *saka-o(toshi)* descending a steep cliff; dropping (something) straight down; steep cliff; storming a castle from the rear; headlong fall; downhill rush
富士 *sakasa Fuji* inverted reflection of Mt.
貸与 *gyaku taiyō* reverse lend-lease ⌊Fuji
13 睫 *sakasa matsuge, sakamatsuge* turned-in eyelashes
賊 *gyakuzoku* rebel, traitor, insurgent
数 *gyakusū* reciprocal number
夢 *sakayume* vain dream
意 *gyakui* treachery, perfidy, treason
14 境 *gyakkyō* reverses, adversity, unfavorable circumstances
漕 *gyakusō* backing (with an oar)
睹 *gyakuto* a conjecture
語 *sakasa kotoba* word of opposite meaning
算 *gyakusan* counting backwards
説 *gyakusetsu* paradox
説的 *gyakusetsuteki* paradoxical
15 撫 *sakana(de)* rubbing against the grain
潮 *gyakuchō, sakashio* head tide, reverse tide, adverse current, weather tide, cross tide
縁 *gyakuen* irony of fate
撃 *gyakugeki* counterattack
磔 *sakaharitsuke, sakabaritsuke* crucifixion upside down
磔刑 *gyaku haritsuke* crucified upside down
16 賭 *gyakuto suru* foresee, predict, conjecture
輸入 *gyaku yunyū* reimportation
輸出 *gyaku yushutsu* re-exportation
22 襲 *gyakushū* counterattack, sortie
23 鱗 *gekirin* imperial wrath

A 追 $\frac{4686}{F1864}$ 追 TSUI. *o(u)* drive away; chase; drive (cattle); follow, pursue (pleasure). *o(tte)* later on, soon after. *o(kkake)* meanwhile, presently. *o(i)-* follow-up. *-o(i)* herder.
2 入 *o(i)-i(reru)* chase in
3 及 *tsuikyū suru* gain on; overtake, carry out; solve (a crime)
4 手 *otte, o(i)te* tail wind; pursuer

込 *o(i)-ko(mu)* corner, drive into; run on (a certain page—in printing); strike inward (a disease)
弔 *tsuichō* mourning
分 *oiwake* forked road, parting of the ways; pack-horse driver's song
分節 *oiwakebushi* pack-horse driver's song
5 白 *tsuihaku* postscript
目 *o(i)me* always losing battles
立 *o(i)-ta(teru), o(t)ta(teru)* hurry off, urge on, drive away, evict
申 *tsuishin* postcript; additional application
付 *o(i)-tsu(ku), o(t)tsu(ku)* overtake
打 *o(i)u(chi)*=追撃 (see below–15)
払 *o(p)para(u), o(i)-hara(u)* drive away, rout. *o(i)bara(i)* later payment
出 *o(i)-da(su)* expel, put out, eject, dismiss
加 *tsuika* addition, appendix, supplement
加予算 *tsuika yosan* additional budget, supplementary estimates
6 行 *o(i)-yu(ku)* pursue. *tsuikō* following suit; pursuit
回 *o(i)-mawa(su)* chase around; follow about; order around. *oimawa(shi)* chasing around; factory handy man
返 *o(i)-kae(su), o(k)kae(su)* repeal, repulse, send away, turn back
伏 *o(i)-fu(seru)* drive into a corner
羽子 *o(i)hago* playing battledore and shuttlecock
羽根 *o(i)bane* playing battledore and shuttlecock
而 *otte* soon, afterwards
而書 *ottega(ki)* postscript
7 走 *o(i)-hashi(rasu)* chase away. *tsuisō* pursuit
尾 *tsuibi* pursuit
迫 *o(i)-sema(ru)* overtake
伸 *tsuishin* postscript
抜 *o(i)-nu(ku)*=*o(i)-ko(su)* 追越 (see below–12)
利 *tsuiri* seeking only profit
完 *tsuikan suru* complete subsequently
究 *tsuikyū* investigation, inquiry
求 *o(i)-moto(meru), tsuikyū suru* pursue; follow up, seek for
求者 *tsuikyūsha* pursuer
8 金 *o(i)gane* throwing good money after bad
退 *o(i)-no(keru), o(i)-shirizo(keru)* chase (the enemy) back
追 *o(i)o(i) ni* gradually; in due time
送 *tsuisō suru* send promptly afterwards
使 *o(i)-tsuka(u)* work (someone) hard
炊 *o(i)da(ki)* additional boiling (of rice)
肥 *tsuihi, o(i)goe* supplementary fertilizer
突 *tsuitotsu* rear-end collision, bump
注文 *o(i)-chūmon* repeat order
取込 *o(t)to(ri)-ko(mu)* pursue and surround
放 *o(i)-hana(tsu)* chase away. *tsuihō* exile, banishment, excommunication, deportation; purge
放人 *tsuihōnin* an exile
放令 *tsuihōrei* purge directive
放令該当者 *tsuihōrei gaitōsha* persons affected by a purge
放者 *tsuihōsha* purgee
放解除 *tsuihō kaijo* depurging
放解除者 *tsuihō kaijosha* depurgee
9 颪 *o(i)kaze, o(i)te* tail wind
悔 *tsuikai* repentance
10 修 *tsuishu* requiem mass, memorial service
従 *tsuijū suru* follow; imitate; be servile to. *tsuishō* flattery
捕 *tsuiho suru, tsuibu suru, o(i)-tora(eru)* pursue and capture, hunt down
納 *tsuinō* supplementary payment
記 *tsuiki* postscript
随 *tsuizui suru* follow in the wake of
剝 *o(i)hagi* highway robber
書 *o(tte)ga(ki)* postscript
起訴 *tsuikiso* supplementary indictment
討 *tsuitō, o(i)u(chi)* subjugation, chastisement
討軍 *tsuitōgun* punitive force
11 惜 *tsuiseki* mourning
掛 *o(i)-ka(keru), o(k)ka(keru)* chase, run after
捲 *o(i)-maku(ru)* drive away, rout
崩 *o(i)-kuzu(su)* pursue and crush
悼 *tsuitō* mourning; memorial (address)
悼会 *tsuitōkai* memorial services
悼歌 *tsuitōka* dirge
12 越 *o(i)-ko(su)* pass (a car), outdistance, outsail, outstrip
遣 *o(i)-ya(ru)* drive away
訴 *tsuiso* supplementary suit
散 *o(i)-chi(rasu)* disperse, scatter, drive away, rout
落 *o(i)-oto(su)* chase away; capture (a castle); pillage
善 *tsuizen* Buddhist memorial service
善供養 *tsuizen-kuyō*=preceding word
13 福 *tsuifuku* requiem mass; memorial service
腹 *o(i)bara, tsuifuku* suicide to follow one's dead master
詰 *o(i)-tsu(meru)* corner, drive to the wall, run down, track down
想 *tsuisō* recollection, reminiscence
試験 *tsui shiken* supplementary exam
頌 *tsuishō suru* confer posthumous honors
跡 *tsuiseki* pursuit
跡者 *tsuisekisha* pursuer
跡機 *tsuisekiki* pursuit plane
14 増 *tsuizō* addition, supplement
様 *sakasama* upside down; end for end; (something) incorrect
認 *tsuinin* ratification, confirmation
銭 *o(i)sen* throwing good money after bad
罰 *tsuibatsu* additional punishment
慕 *tsuibo suru* cherish the memory of, yearn for
徴 *tsuichō* additional collection, supplementary charge
徴金 *tsuichōkin* additional collection, supplementary charge
徴税 *tsuichōzei* supplementary tax

15 縋 *o*(*i*)-*suga*(*ru*) close in on, tread on the heels of
踪 *tsuishō suru* shadow (someone); recollect
撃 *tsuigeki, o*(*i*)*u*(*chi*) pursuit, attack
撃戦 *tsuigekisen* running fight, pursuit battle
撃機 *tsuigekiki* pursuit plane
16 懐 *tsuikai* recollection, reminiscence
憶 *tsuioku* recollection, reminiscence
録 *tsuiroku* supplement, postscript, addendum
18 贈 *tsuizō* posthumous conferment of court rank
蹤 *tuishō suru* pursue; recollect
21 儺 *tsuina* exorcism
22 籠 *o*(*i*)-*ko*(*meru*) confine in house arrest
25 躡 *tsuijō* pursuit

7

逋 4687 / F1869 Ho flee.

逞 4688 / F1873 Tei. *takuma*(*shii*) sturdy, brawny, stalwart, masculine; resolute, bold. *takuma*(*shiku*) vigorously, powerfully. *takuma*(*shū*) *suru* give free play to; stretch one's imagination; rage; be rampant; increase in violence.

逍 4689 / F1869 Shō saunter, loaf.
13 遙 *shōyō* ramble, saunter, walk

逡 4690 / F1874 Shun fall back, go back.
5 巡 *shunjun* hesitation, vacillation, indecision

逝 4691 / F1873 Sei. *yu*(*ku*) die, pass away.
5 去 *seikyo* death
9 春 *yu*(*ku*) *haru* departing spring

逕 4692 / F1870 Kei path.
10 庭 *keitei* difference, discrepancy
13 路 *keiro* course, channel, route

逗 4693 / F1870 Tō stop.
10 留 *tōryū* stay, sojourn
留客 *tōryūkyaku* guest, visitor, sojourner

逢 4694 / F1874 Hō. *a*(*u*), *a*(*waseru*) (see under 会 381.0).
4 引 *aibi*(*ki*) date, rendezvous, clandestine courting
6 曳 *aibiki* lovers' secret meeting, a date
12 着 *hōchaku suru* face, encounter
19 瀬 *ōse* meeting, tryst, date

B **逓** 4695 / F1890 **遞** Tei in turn; sending (parcels) in feudal times.
5 加 *teika* successive increase, acceleration
6 伝 *teiden* relaying a message; the post horse; the post rider
6 次 *teiji* in order, successively
8 送 *teisō* forwarding
9 信 *teishin* communications
信省 *Teishinshō* (prewar) Communications Ministry
12 減 *teigen* successive diminution
14 増 *teizō* gradual increase

B **逐** 4696 / F1869 **逐** Chiku. *o*(*u*) (see under 追 4686.0). *to*(*geru*) accomplish, attain; commit (suicide).
1 一 *chikuichi* one by one, in detail, minutely
4 日 *chikujitsu* daily, day after day
6 次 *chikuji* one by one, point by point, in order, in succession, successively, gradually
年 *chikunen* annually, year by year
字的 *chikujiteki* literal, word for word
7 条 *chikujō* section by section, point by point
11 鹿 *chikuroku* competition (in elections)
鹿戦 *chikurokusen* election campaign
13 電 *chikuden* flight, abscondence
14 語的 *chikugoteki* literal, word for word
語訳 *chikugoyaku* literal translation

B **途** 4697 / F1870 **途** To, Zu way, road. *michi* (see under 道 4724.0).
3 上 *tojō* on the way; on the road
4 切 *togi*(*reru*) break, pause, be interrupted
切途切 *togi*(*re*)-*togi*(*re*) interruption
方 *tohō* way, destination, direction, reason
方無 *tohō*(*mo*)*na*(*i*) extraordinary, absurd, preposterous, exorbitant, ludicrous
方暮 *tohō* (*ni*) *ku*(*reru*) be at one's wit's end
中 *tochū* on the way, enroute
中下車 *tochū gessha* stopover
中計時 *tochū keiji* lap time (in races)
6 次 *toji* on the way
12 絶 *toda*(*eru*) cease, stop, end. *tozetsu* suspension, interruption
14 端 *totan ni* in the act of, just as
19 轍無 *totetsu*(*mo*)*na*(*i*) wild, absurd, exorbitant

這 4698 / F1871 Sha. *ha*(*u*) crawl, creep; grovel; trail (vines).
2 入 *hai*(*ru*) enter, break into; join; enroll; contain, hold; accommodate; have (an income of)
入口 *hairiguchi* entrance
入込 *hai*(*ri*)-*ko*(*mu*) get into, come in
3 下 *ha*(*i*)-*o*(*riru*) crawl down
上 *ha*(*i*)-*a*(*garu*) crawl up, climb up
4 込 *ha*(*i*)-*ko*(*mu*) crawl into
5 出 *ha*(*i*)-*de*(*ru*), *ha*(*i*)-*da*(*su*) crawl out

6回 *ha*(*i*)-*mawa*(*ru*) crawl about
8松 *haimatsu* creeping pine
物 *ha*(*u*)*mono* creeping things
歩 *ha*(*i*)-*aru*(*ku*) crawl along
10般 *shahan no* such, of this kind
這 *ha*(*i*)*ha*(*i*) creeping, crawling. *hōhō* confusedly; proceeding with difficulty; perplexity
這体 *hōhō*(*no*)*tei* hurriedly, precipitately
12渡 *ha*(*i*)-*wata*(*ru*) crawl across; walk a short distance
登 *ha*(*i*)-*nobo*(*ru*) crawl up, climb up
21纏 *ha*(*i*)-*matsuwa*(*ru*) crawl up and cling to

透 4699 / F1869 **透** B Tō. *tō*(*ru*) permeate, penetrate. *su*(*ku*) be transparent; be seen thru; be thin; leave a gap. *su*(*kasu*) leave a space; thin (trees); make transparent; look thru. *su*(*kashi*) watermark; openwork; transparent. *su*(*ki*) (see under 隙 5017.0). *su*(*kasazu*) at once, right away. *tō*(*su*) let (light) thru, penetrate.

5目 *sukime* crevice, gap, space
写 *tōsha, su*(*ki*)*utsu*(*shi*) tracing, copy
写紙 *tōshashi* tracing paper
7見 *su*(*ki*)*mi* stealing a glance; casting a furtive glance
8明 *tōmei* transparency
明体 *tōmeitai* a transparent medium
明度 *tōmeido* transparency, clearness
9通 *su*(*ki*)-*tō*(*ru*) be transparent
11彫 *su*(*kashi*)*bori* openwork
過 *tōka*=next word
過性 *tōkasei* permeability
視 *tōshi* seeing thru; clairvoyance
視力 *tōshiryoku* penetration; psychic powers
視図 *tōshizu* cutaway view
視者 *tōshisha* clairvoyance
視画 *tōshiga* perspective drawing
視画法 *tōshigahō* perspective
12間 *su*(*ki*)*ma* crevice, gap, opening, space
絵 *su*(*kashi*)*e* transparency (pictures)
14察 *tōsatsu* insight, discernment
模様 *su*(*kashi*) *moyō* designs in a transparent medium
15徹 *su*(*ki*)-*tō*(*ru*) be transparent, be clear, be seen thru. *tōtetsu suru* penetrate, pierce, permeate; be transparent; prevail; penetrating; coherent. *tōtetsu*(*shita*) transparent, clear; pure.

速 4700 / F1873 **速** A Soku. *haya*(*i*), *sumi*(*yakana*) speedy, prompt, swift. *haya*(*meru*) (see under 早 2100.0).

2力 *sokuryoku* speed, velocity, rate
5写 *sokusha* quick copying; snapshot
6成 *sokusei* quick training, short course instruction
成科 *sokuseika* short course, intensive course
7決 *sokketsu* quick decision, snap judgment
8刻 *sokkoku* instantly, immediately
歩 *haya-ashi, sokuho* quick march, quick time, fast walking, trot
効 *sokkō* immediate effect
効薬 *sokkōyaku* quick remedy
9度 *sokudo* speed, velocity, pace, rate; tempo (in music), time
度計 *sokudokei* speedometer
10座 *sokuza* prompt, impromptu
進 *sokushin*=促進 444.10
時 *sokuji* promptly, immediately
射 *sokusha* quick firing, quick fire
射砲 *sokushahō* rapid-firing gun
記 *sokki* shorthand
記者 *sokkisha* shorthand writer
記術 *sokkijutsu* shorthand, stenography
記録 *sokkiroku* shorthand notes
11球 *sokkyū* fast ball
断 *sokudan* prompt decision; hasty conclusion, snap judgment
達 *sokutatsu* special delivery
達郵便 *sokutatsu yūbin* special delivery
12答 *sokutō* prompt answer
報 *sokuhō* urgent message
報板 *sokuhōban* a newspaper bulletin board
13戦即決 *sokusen-sokketsu* blitz warfare
14読 *sokudoku* rapid reading
算 *sokusan* rapid calculation

造 4701 / F1874 **造** A Zō. *tsuku*(*ru*) (see under 作 407.0). *tsuku*(*ri*) make, structure, construction; physique, build; workmanship; (a woman's) make-up; cultivation; a mounting. -*zuku*(*ri*) made of; work; architectural style.

2上 *tsuku*(*ri*)-*a*(*geru*) build up; complete
4方 *tsuku*(*ri*)*kata*=作方 407.4
反 *zōhan* revolution
仏 *zōbutsu* making (Buddhist) images
5付 *tsuku*(*ri*)-*tsu*(*keru*) fix, fasten firmly. *tsuku*(*ri*)*tsu*(*ke*) fixture, built-in furnishings
主 *tsuku*(*ri*)*nushi* creator, maker; the Creator
出 *tsuku*(*ri*)-*da*(*su*) make, manufacture, raise (crops)
本 *zōhon* bookbinding
石税 *zōkokuzei* brewage tax
6血 *zōketsu* blood making
成 *tsuku*(*ri*)-*na*(*su*) create
返 *tsuku*(*ri*)-*kae*(*su*) make over again
合 *tsuku*(*ri*)-*a*(*waseru*) make two (things) and join (them) together; make a duplicate

寺 *zōji* temple building
7言 *zōgen, tsuku(ri)goto* fabrication, lie, false report ⌈voice
声 *tsuku(ri)goe* unnatural voice; imitating
花 *tsuku(ri)bana, zōka* artificial flower
形 *zōkei* modeling, molding ⌈plastic arts
形美術 *zōkei bijutsu* sculpture and the
兵 *zōhei* ordnance, arms manufacture
兵廠 *zōheishō* arms factory, arsenal, armory
作 *zōsaku* making; house fixtures; facial features. *zōsa* trouble, difficulty
作付 *zōsakutsu(ki)* furnished (house) with
作無 *zōsana(i)* easy, simple ⌊fixtures
8直 *tsuku(ri)-nao(su)* remake, rebuild
事 *tsuku(ri)goto* falsehood, fabrication
林 *zōrin* forestation; reforestation
林法 *zōrinhō* forest management, forestry
林学 *zōringaku* the science of forestry
物 *zōbutsu* God's creation, heaven and earth
物主 *Zōbutsushu* Creator, Maker, God
物者 *Zōbutsusha* Creator, Maker, God
9型 *zōkei* modeling, molding
10修 *zōshū suru* construct
笑 *tsuku(ri)wara(i)* a forced laugh
酒 *zōshu* saké brewing
酒屋 *zōshuya* saké brewer
11船 *zōsen* shipbuilding
船所 *zōsenjo* shipyards
船界 *zōsenkai* shipbuilding world
船業 *zōsengyō* shipbuilding industry
12営 *zōei* building, construction
営地 *zōeichi* building site
営物 *zōeibutsu* buildings
営費 *zōeihi* building expenses
13詣 *zōkei* scholarship, erudition
話 *tsuku(ri)banashi* fabrication
意 *zōi* inventiveness; planning
園 *zōen* landscape gardening
園術 *zōenjutsu* landscape gardening
14鼻 *zōbi* nasal plastic surgery
語 *zōgo* coined word
15幣 *zōhei* minting, coinage
幣局 *zōheikyoku* the mint
16機 *zōki* engine building
20艦 *zōkan* naval construction

A 連 4702 F1875 連 Ren ream; set; party, company, gang, clique; series counter. *tsura(naru)* range, be connected with, join; stand in a row; attend; join one's people (in death). *tsura(neru)* put in a row, join. *tsu(reru)* take (someone) along. *tsu(re)* companion. *(ni) tsu(rete)* in proportion to; accompanied by; to the accompaniment of.
3山 *renzan* mountain range
下 *tsu(re)-ku(daru)* lead down, bring down
上 *tsu(re)-no(boru)* bring up out of
子 *tsure(k)ko, tsu(re)ko* child brought by a second wife or husband. *renji* lattice
子窓 *renji mado* lattice window ⌊work
4日 *renjitsu* day after day, every day
木 *rengi* pestle
中 *renchū, renjū* party, company, clique
5用 *ren-yō* continuous use
句 *renku* couplet
打 *renda* succession of hits (in baseball)
去 *tsu(re)-sa(ru)* lead away
出 *tsu(re)-da(su)* lead (someone) out, bring out; entice, abduct
立 *tsu(re)da(tsu)* accompany. *renritsu* alliance, coalition, union ⌈equation
立方程式 *renritsu hōteishiki* simultaneous
立内閣 *renritsu naikaku* coalition cabinet
6行 *tsu(re)-yu(ku)* take (someone) along. *renkō suru* walk a suspect to the police
休 *renkyū* consecutive holidays
年 *rennen* every year; many years
名 *remmei* joint signature ⌈ball)
安打 *ren-anda* succession of hits (in base-
邦 *rempō* federated states, union, commonwealth, federal state; federation
邦政府 *Rempō Seifu* Federal Government
邦準備銀行 *Rempō Jumbi Ginkō* Federal Reserve Bank
合 *tsu(re)-a(u)* keep company with, get married. *rengō* union, combination, federation, alliance. *tsurea(i)* spouse, mate
合国 *rengōkoku* allied nations, allies
合軍 *rengōgun* allied armies
合責任 *rengō sekinin* joint responsibility
合艦隊 *rengō kantai* combined squadron
7戻 *tsu(re)-modo(su)* take back, bring back, lead back
作 *rensaku* joint authorship; repeated cultivation of the same field ⌈the same seat
坐 *renza* implication, complicity; sitting in
判 *rempan, remban* joint signature, joint seal
判状 *rempanjō, rembanjō* jointly sealed compact ⌈portant personage
8枝 *renshi* (polite for) the brother of an im-
夜 *ren-ya* night after night, nightly
呼 *renko* repeated calls
呼音 *renko-on* repetition of a syllable
9係 *renkei* connection, liaison, contact
枷 *karazao, renka* flail
星 *rensei* binary star
奏 *rensō* instrumental number
袂 *rembei* en masse, all together, in a body
袂辞職 *rembei jishoku* mass resignation
発 *rempatsu* occurring continually; running
発銃 *rempatsujū* magazine rifle ⌊fire, volley

10 座 *renza* implication, complicity; sitting in the same seat
借 *renshaku* joint debt
峰 *rempō* series of peaks, range
珠 *renju* five-in-a-row game
破 *rempa* a succession of victories (in games)
記 *renki suru* list, catalog
帰 *tsu(re)-kae(ru)* bring (someone) back
帯 *rentai* joint responsibility, solidarity
帯責任 *rentai sekinin* joint liability
帯責務 *rentai sekimu* joint liability
11 接 *rensetsu* combination, connection
添 *tsu(re)-so(u)* be married to
敗 *rempai* successive defeats
動 *rendō* gearing, linkage, drive
累 *renrui* implication, involvement, complicity
理松 *renri (no) matsu* pines with entwined branches
隊 *rentai* regiment
隊長 *rentaichō* regimental commander
隊旗 *rentaiki* regimental colors
12 弾 *tsu(re)bi(ki)* accompaniment; accompanist. *rendan* two-piano number
勝 *renshō* series of victories
衆 *tsu(re)shu* one's companion, one's party
絡 *renraku* connection, contact, liaison, communication
絡船 *renrakusen* ferryboat, connecting steamer
結 *renketsu* coupling, connection, joint; combination
結器 *renketsuki* coupling
結機 *renketsuki* coupling
13 携 *renkei* co-operation, collaboration, association
続 *renzoku* continuation, succession, sequence, series
署 *rensho* joint signature
想 *rensō* association of ideas
盟 *remmei* league, federation, union
載 *rensai suru* publish serially
戦 *rensen* series of battles; every battle
戦連敗 *rensen-rempai* succession of defeats
戦連勝 *rensen-renshō* succession of victories
14 関 *renkan* connection, relation, association
綿 *remmen(taru)* consecutive, continuous
語 *rengo* compound word, phrase
歌 *renga* linked *haiku* poems
銀 *Rengin* Federal Reserve Bank
銀券 *renginken* Federal Reserve Bank notes
16 濁 *rendaku* a euphonic change of an unvoiced to a voiced sound
17 環 *renkan* chain link
18 類 *renrui* same kind; accomplice
顔 *tsu(renai) kao* an unsympathetic countenance
鎖 *rensa* chain, series, links
鎖反応 *rensa hannō* chain reaction
鎖店 *rensaten* chain store
鎖劇 *rensageki* combination of moving pictures and vaudeville
19 禱 *rentō* litany
覇 *rempa* successive championships
繫 *renkei* connection, liaison, contact

通 4703 / F1871 A **通** TSU. TŌ. TSŪ pass; expert. *tsū(zuru), tsū(jiru)* pass, run; be opened (to traffic); prevail, pervade, transmit (elecrricity); be well versed in; be understood; become intimate with; communicate secretly with; send in (one's card). *tō(ru)* walk along, pass by; pass thru; pass (exams); be known as; be admissible; come in; be understood; reach; draw (on a pipe); drain (as a sink); be consistent. *tō(su)* let (someone) pass; pass (something) thru; make way for; let in, admit; usher in; cut thru; pierce; permeate, penetrate; carry one's point; persist in; look over (a book); keep on doing, continue; pose as; pass (a law); order (a meal). *kayo(u)* commute; attend (school); ply between; frequent (a place); go (for treatments); circulate; breathe; be charged with. *kayo(wasu), kayo(waseru)* send (to school); charge (with electricity); circulate. *tsū(garu)* make a show of knowledge. *tō(risugari)* on the way. *tsū(jite)* thru, via; thruout, all over; total, together with; in collusion with. *tō(shite)* thru, thru the medium of, thru the good offices of; for (five days). *tō(shi)* consecutive (pages). *tō(tte)* via, by way of. *tsū(ji)* bowel evacuation, stool; effect. *tō(ri)* road, street, thorofare; street traffic; drainage; penetration (of a voice); kind; suite, set (of furniture); way, manner; reputation, favor; understanding; like, the same. *kayo(i)* daily attendance; living out; plying; a line, a run; bankbook; chit book. *tō(shi) de* straight thru, without stopping. *(o)tō(shi) suru* usher in. *tō(shi)* hors d'œuvre. *tō(shi)-* thru (bill of lading). *-tsū* thoro knowledge of, authority on, expert judge, connoisseur; knowledge of the world; occult powers; part, copy; counter for cables, letters, or copies. *-dō(ri)* street; in accordance with; according to; just as, as. *-dō(shi)* all thru (the night); all the time.

1 一片 *tō(ri)-ippen no*=next word
一遍 *tō(ri)-ippen no* casual, passing, perfunctory, formal
2 人 *tsūjin* man about town; a well-informed person; brothel visitor; a romantic man
力 *tsūriki* supernatural power, occult power
4 分 *tsūbun* reduction of fractions to common denominator
切符 *tō(shi) kippu, tō(shi)gippu* thru ticket
5 矢 *tō(shi)ya* long-distance archery
弁 *tsūben* interpreter, interpreting

用 *tsūyō* common use, circulation, currency
用口 *tsūyōguchi* service entrance, side door
用門 *tsūyōmon* service entrance, side door
用期間 *tsūyō kikan* period of (a ticket's) validity
6好 *tsūkō* friendship; amity, friendly relations
交 *tsūkō* diplomatic relations
合 *tsū(ji)-a(waseru), tsū(ji)-a(u)* plot together. *tō(ri)-a(waseru)* happen to come along
名 *tō(ri)na* one's popular name; house name
気 *tsūki* ventilation, draft, airing
気孔 *tsūkikō* vent
有 *tsūyū no* common properties
有性 *tsūyūsei* common trait, common properties
行 *tō(ri)-yu(ku)* pass by. *tsūkō* passing, passage, transit, traffic
行人 *tsūkōnin* passer-by, pedestrian, wayfarer
行止 *Tsūkōdo(me)* No Thorofare, road blocked
行区分 *tsūkō kubun* traffic lane
行券 *tsūkōken* a pass, safe-conduct, toll-road ticket
行料 *tsūkōryō* passage money, toll
行税 *tsūkōzei* transit duty, traveling tax
行権 *tsūkōken* right-of-way
7見 *tsūken* general view, perusal
坊 *tō(sem)bō suru* bar the way, head off; interrupt (by making a human chain)
抜 *tō(ri)-nu(keru)* pass thru
狂言 *tō(shi) kyōgen* presentation of a whole play
言 *tsūgen* popular saying
言葉 *tō(ri) kotoba* catchword; thieves' slang, group jargon; a common phrase
告 *tsūkoku* notification, announcement
告書 *tsūkokusho* written notice
告済 *tsūkokuzu(mi)* notified
8雨 *tō(ri)ame* passing shower
例 *tsūrei* usually, customarily
性 *tsūsei* common quality; common gender
法 *tsūhō* universal law
念 *tsūnen* common sense, generally accepted idea
宝 *tsūhō* coin, currency
券 *tsūken* ticket, pass
者 *tō(ri)mono* well-known person, popular figure, man about town
事 *tsūji* interpreter; (Dutch) interpreter
夜 *tsuya* deathwatch, wake. *tsūya* all night
夜僧 *tsuyasō* priest engaged for a deathwatch
学 *tsūgaku* attending school
学生 *tsūgakusei* day student
知 *tsūchi* notification, information
知洩 *tsūchimo(re)* uninformed of
知書 *tsūchisho* notice
知簿 *tsūchibo* school report card
9計 *tsūkei* total
則 *tsūsoku* general rules
院中 *tsūinchū* coming for treatments
相場 *tō(ri) sōba* market price; accepted custom
風 *tsūfū* ventilation, airing, draft
風筒 *tsūfūtō* ventilator
風器 *tsūfūki* ventilator, aerator
俗 *tsūzoku* popularity, conventionality
俗小説 *tsūzoku shōsetsu* popular fiction
俗文 *tsūzokubun* popular writing
俗化 *tsūzokuka* popularization
俗体 *tsūzokutai* colloquial style
俗的 *tsūzokuteki* popular
俗語 *tsūzokugo* colloquialism
信 *tsūshin* correspondence, communication, intelligence, information, news, dispatch, report
信士 *tsūshinshi* telegraph operator
信文 *tsūshimbun* written communication
信伝道 *tsūshin dendō* newspaper evangelism
信社 *tsūshinsha* news agency
信妨害 *tsūshin bōgai* communications jamming
信学校 *tsūshin gakkō* correspondence school
信施設 *tsūshin shisetsu* communications system
信紙 *tsūshinshi* correspondence card
信員 *tsūshin-in* correspondent, reporter
信隊 *tsūshintai* signal corps
信販売 *tsūshin hambai* mail-order business; mail-order sale
信教育 *tsūshin kyōiku* education by correspondence
信教授 *tsūshin kyōju* instruction by correspondence
信筒 *tsūshintō* message tube
信費 *tsūshinhi* postage
信路 *tsūshinro* news channel
信網 *tsūshimmō* news-gathering facilities
信線 *tsūshinsen* lines of communication
信機関 *tsūshin kikan* communication facilities
信講座 *tsūshin kōza* correspondence course
信簿 *tsūshimbo* report card
信欄 *tsūshinran* correspondence column
10称 *tsūshō* popular name, alias
航 *tsūkō suru* navigate, sail, ply
11廊 *tsūrō* passageway, corridor
違 *tō(ri)-chiga(u)* go past (a person)
道 *tō(ri)michi* passage, path, route; one's way; (cattle) runway
達 *tsūtatsu, tsūdatsu* communication, notification; proficiency, mastery, skill
帳 *kayo(i)chō, tsūchō* bankbook; chit book
掛 *tō(ri)-ga(karu), tō(ri)-ka(karu)* happen to come along. *tō(ri)ga(kari) ni* as one passes on the way. *tō(ri)ga(ke)* passing on the way
患 *tsūkan* common evil, universal trouble
過 *tō(ri)-su(giru), tsūka suru* to pass, pass thru. *tsūka* passage, transit
過駅 *tsūka eki* nonstop station

運 *tsūun* express, transportation, forwarding
運機関 *tsūun kikan* transportation facilities
産相 *Tsūsanshō* Minister of International Trade and Industry
産省 *Tsūsanshō* Ministry of International Trade and Industry
貨 *tsūka* currency
貨収縮 *tsūka shūshuku* (money) deflation
貨膨脹 *tsūka bōchō* (money) inflation
訳 *tsūyaku* interpreting; interpreter
訳生 *tsūyakusei* student interpreter
訳官 *tsūyakukan* official interpreter
訳者 *tsūyakusha* interpreter
商 *tsūshō* commerce, trade
商条約 *tsūshō jōyaku* commercial treaty
商航海条約 *tsūshō kōkai jōyaku* treaty of commerce and navigation
商産業省 *Tsūshō-sangyōshō* Ministry of International Trade and Industry
常 *tsūjō* normally, generally, ordinarily; regular (meeting)
常日 *tsūjōbi* ordinary day, week day, work day
常礼服 *tsūjō reifuku* dress suit
常会員 *tsūjō kai-in* ordinary member
常服 *tsūjōfuku* everyday clothes, business suit
常国会 *tsūjō kokkai* ordinary Diet session
常郵便物 *tsūjō yūbimbutsu* ordinary mail matter
常総会 *tsūjō sōkai* ordinary general meeting
12越 *tō(ri)-ko(su)* go beyond; pass thru; be more than
暁 *tsūgyō* all night; thoro knowledge
詞 *tsūshi* (ancient) interpreter
勤 *tsūkin, kayo(i)zuto(me)* living away from one's work
款 *tsūkan* treachery
筋 *tō(ri)suji* route, course, road
報 *tsūhō* report, bulletin, news
番号 *tō(shi)bangō* serial number
13辞 *tsūji* interpreter, Dutch interpreter
解 *tsūkai* a commentary
詰 *kayo(i)zu(me)* frequent visiting. *kayo(i)-tsu(meru)* visit frequently
路 *tō(ri)michi, kayo(i)michi, kayo(i)ji* route, path. *tsūro* passageway, path, thorofare, entranceway, aisle, catwalk
義 *tsūgi* general principle; common interpretation
電 *tsūden* circular telegram
牒 *tsūchō* notification
牒者 *tsūchōsha* spy, secret agent
話 *tsūwa* phone call
話口 *tsūwaguchi* mouthpiece
話室 *tsūwashitsu* phone booth
話料 *tsūwaryō* phone-call charge
話量 *tsūwaryō* telephone traffic
話管 *tsūwakan* speaking tube
14関 *tsūkan* customs clearance

説 *tsūsetsu* common opinion
読 *tsūdoku suru* read thru
語 *tsūgo* cant phrase, lingo
算 *tsūsan* totaling
15論 *tsūron* outline, introduction (to literature)
弊 *tsūhei* common evil
16謀 *tsūbō suru* conspire with, work in concert
薬 *tsū(ji)gusuri* a laxative
覧 *tsūran* general view, perusal
稽古 *kayo(i)geiko* taking lessons
18観 *tsūkan* general view
21魔 *tō(ri)ma* phantom

8

迸 4704/F1876 See 迸 4680.

遁 Nonstandard for 遁 4719.

逵 4705/F1878 Ki broad road.
13路 *kiro* highway

逮 4706/F1876 逮 Tai chase.
B
8夜 *taiya* death anniversary
10捕 *taiho* arrest, capture
捕令 *taihorei* arrest warrant
捕状 *taihojō* arrest warrant
捕者 *taihosha* captor
捕命令 *taiho meirei* arrest warrant

週 4707/F1877 週 Shū week.
A
4日 *shūjitsu* week day
5刊 *shūkan* weekly publication
刊新聞 *shūkan shimbun* weekly newspaper
刊誌 *shūkanshi* weekly publication
末 *shūmatsu* week end
末中 *shūmatsujū* over the week end
末旅行 *shūmatsu ryokō* week-end trip
6休 *shūkyū* weekly holiday
7忌 *shūki* death anniversary
12間 *shūkan* week
給 *shūkyū* weekly pay
評 *shūhyō* weekly review
番 *shūban* weekly duty
報 *shūhō* weekly bulletin, weekly paper
期 *shūki* period, cycle
期的 *shūkiteki* periodic

逸 4708/F1878 逸 Itsu idleness, leisure.
B
is(suru) miss (a chance); let escape; deviate from. *so(reru)* miss the mark, deviate from, diverge, glance off, go

astray; be off (the tune). *so(raseru)*, *so(rasu)* look away, evade, elude, parry. *hagu(reru)* go astray, become separated from. *haya(ru)* be hasty, be rash.

4 文 *itsubun* unknown writings, lost writings; excellent writings
5 矢 *so(re)ya* stray arrow
出 *isshutsu* escape; excelling, prominence
民 *itsumin* retired person, hermit
6 早 *ichihaya(ku)* promptly
7 走 *issō suru* escape, scud, scamper away
足 *issoku* a fast runner; excellence
材 *itsuzai* outstanding talent
8 居 *ikkyō suru* living a lazy life
物 *itsubutsu* excellent person, superb article. *ichimotsu* excellent animal
事 *itsuji* anecdote; unknown fact
9 速 *ichihaya(ku)* promptly
品 *ippin* superb article
10 書 *issho* a lost book
11 球 *ikkyū* muffed ball
脱 *itsudatsu* deviation, omission
12 弾 *so(re)dama* stray bullet
散 *issan ni* at top speed
13 話 *itsuwa* anecdote
楽 *itsuraku* pleasure
14 聞 *itsubun* something unheard of

A **進** 4709/F1877 **進** SHIN advancing. *shin(zuru)*, *shin(jiru)*, *shin(zeru)* give, present. *susu(mu)* *vi* advance, proceed, progress; be promoted; be in an advanced stage; (watches) gain; feel like (doing). *susu(meru)* *vt* move forward; set (watches) ahead; promote, elevate; stimulate; speed up; present.

2 入 *shinnyū suru*, *susu(mi)-i(ru)* go on into, penetrate, enter
3 上 *susu(mi)-nobo(ru)* go up to. *shinjō suru* give, offer, present
4 化 *shinka* evolution; progress
化論 *shinkaron* theory of evolution
化論者 *shinkaronja* evolutionist
水 *shinsui* launching (a ship)
水台 *shinsuidai* launching ways
水式 *shinsuishiki* launching ceremony
5 出 *susu(mi)-de(ru)* step forward. *susu(mi)-da(su)* bring forward. *shinshutsu* advance, march, inroad, push; expansion
6 行 *shinkō suru*, *susu(mi)-yu(ku)* go forward, advance
行係 *shinkōgakari* steering committee, person directing proceedings
7 言 *shingen* advice, memorial, proposal
攻 *shinkō* attack, drive
来 *susu(mi)-ku(ru)* advance toward
呈 *shintei* presentation
呈本 *shinteihon* complimentary copy
呈者 *shinteisha* presenter
8 物 *shimmotsu* present, gift
取 *shinshu* enterprise
退 *shintai* advance or retreat; movement; course of action; conduct; attitude; resigning or carrying on
退伺 *shintai ukaga(i)* informal resignation (leaving the decision to superiors)
学 *shingaku* entrance to a higher school
学適性検査 *shingaku tekisei kensa* aptitude test, achievement test
歩 *shimpo* advance, progress
歩主義 *shimpo shugi* progressivism
歩派 *shimpoha* progressives
歩党 *shimpotō* progressive party
9 度 *shindo* progress
級 *shinkyū* (school) promotion
発 *shimpatsu suru* march off, start
軍 *shingun* a march, an advance
軍中 *shingunchū* on the march
10 捗 *shinchoku* progress, advance
航 *shinkō suru* proceed, sail ahead
展 *shinten* development, progress
展振 *shintembu(ri)* nature of developments
貢 *shinkō* paying tribute
貢国 *shinkōkoku* tributary nation
貢船 *shinkōsen* tribute-bearing ships; ships trading with the Mings
11 運 *shin-un* progress, advancement
略 *shinryaku suru* advance and capture
寄 *susu(mi)-yo(ru)* approach
12 塁 *shinrui suru* advance a base
13 適 *shinteki* aptitude test, achievement test
路 *shinro* course, way, route
14 境 *shinkyō* progress, improvement
15 撃 *shingeki* assault, charge, attack, advance
駐 *shinchū* occupation, stationing
駐兵 *shinchūhei* occupation soldier
駐軍 *shinchūgun* occupation army
17 講 *shinkō* lecturing to the emperor

9

遥 Nonstandard for **遙** 4729.

逬 4710/F-X Nonstandard for **迸** 4744.

遏 4711/F1885 ATSU stop; suppress.

遐 4712/F1885 KA distant.

遑 4713/F1886 KAN. *itoma* leisure.

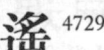

7 見角言谷豆豕豖豸貝赤走足身車辛辰 9【辵辶】邑阝酉釆里

逭 4714 / F1881 TEI. *sasuga ni*=流石 2576.5.

B **遇** 4715 / F1881 **遇** GŪ. GU. *gū(suru)* treat, entertain, receive, deal with. *ashira(u)* receive, entertain; deal with, treat, manage, manipulate. *a(u)* meet, interview.

4 不遇 *gūfugū* happiness and sorrows

B **遂** 4716 / F1880 **遂** SUI. *to(geru)* accomplish, attain, commit (suicide). *tsui ni* finally, after all.

6 行 *suikō* accomplishment, execution, prosecution (of a war)

逼 4717 / F1880 FUKU. HITSU. *sema(ru)* (see under 迫 4676.0).

13 塞 *hissoku* poverty-stricken and slipping into obscurity; house arrest

7 迫 *hippaku* (money) stringency

B **遍** 4718 / F1884 **遍** HEN times. *amane(ku)* widely, generally, everywhere.

6 在 *henzai* omnipresence, ubiquity

12 幅 *hempuku* personal appearance

13 路 *henro* pilgrim

14 歴 *henreki* travels, pilgrimage

遁 4719 / F1880 **遯** TON. *noga(reru)* (see under 逃 4682.0).

2 入 *tonnyū suru* flee to a safe place

5 世 *tonsei* seclusion from the world, escape from life

世主義 *tonsei shugi* monasticism, asceticism

世者 *tonseisha* hermit, recluse

7 走 *tonsō* flight

8 退 *noga(re)-shirizo(ku)* flee back

13 辞 *tonji* excuse, evasion, prevarication

18 竄 *tonzan* flight

B **違** 4720 / F1889 **違** I. *chiga(u)* differ, vary; disagree with; be mistaken; cross or pass (someone); No (negation). *chiga(eru)* change, alter, vary, disguise; make a mistake; break (a promise); sprain, dislocate; cross (two sticks). *taga(u)* differ from, vary; violate, break, transgress. *taga(eru)* break (a promise or a law), violate. *chiga(i)* difference, divergence, disparity, discrepancy. *chiga(inai)* I am sure.

4 反 *ihan* violation, infringement, breach (of contract)

5 犯 *ihan* violation, transgression

失 *ishitsu* mistake

6 式 *ishiki* informality; breach of etiquette

8 例 *irei* unconventionality

法 *ihō* unlawfulness; foul (play)

法性 *ihōsei* illegality

9 勅 *ichoku* disobeying an imperial decree

背 *ihai* violation, transgression

約 *iyaku* breach of contract, default

約金 *iyakukin* breach of contract penalty

12 棚 *chiga(i)dana* staggered shelves

14 算 *isan* miscalculation

16 憲 *iken* unconstitutionality

19 警罪 *ikeizai* police offense, petty crime

A **達** 4721 / F1888 **達** TATSU. *tas(suru)* reach, arrive at, attain; amount to; become expert, be versed in; accomplish; notify. *tat(te)* forcibly, unreasonably. *tas(shinai)* fall short of; be uncompleted. *tas(shi)* government notice. *-tachi* plural ending.

2 人 *tatsujin* expert, master, master mind, great character, philosopher

3 士 *tasshi* expert, master

4 文 *tatsubun* clear composition

5 示 *tasshi* government notice

弁 *tatsuben* eloquence, fluency

6 成 *tassei* achievement, accomplishment

7 見 *takken*=卓見 802.7

8 者 *tassha na* healthy, strong; skillful; free (in a language)

10 書 *tas(shi)ga(ki)* government notification

11 眼 *tatsugan* farsightedness, insight

12 筆 *tappitsu* facile pen, skillful hand; speedy writing

13 意 *tatsu-i* intelligibility, perspicuity

15 摩 *Daruma*=達磨 (see below–16)

16 頼喇嘛 *Darai Rama* Dalai Lama

磨 *Daruma* Dharma (an Indian priest, the founder of Zen Buddhism in China); tumbler (toy)

磨船 *darumabune, darumasen* lighter, barge

18 観 *takkan* farsighted view; philosophic view

19 識 *tasshiki* great insight, farsightedness

B **遅** 4722 / F1894 **遲 遅** CHI. *oku(reru), oku(rasu), oku(raseru)* (see under 後 1610.0). *oso(nawaru)* be late. *oso(i)* late; slow. *oso(kutomo)* at the latest. *oso-* slow, late.

4 日 *chijitsu* long spring days

5 生 *oso-uma(re)* born after April 1 (school entrance date)

6 成 *osona(ri)* late crop

早 *oso(kare)-haya(kare)* sooner or later

7 足 *osoashi* slow speed

8 延 *chien* delay, retardation, procrastination

参 *chisan* lateness, tardiness

知恵 *osojie* retarded development of understanding

刻 *chikoku* tardiness, lateness

刻届 *chikoku todoke* excuse for tardiness

刻者 *chikokusha* latecomer
9 速 *chisoku* speed; progress
咲 *osoza(ki)* late blooming; late flower
発 *chihatsu* delayed start, delayed action
発爆弾 *chihatsu bakudan* time bomb
10 桜 *osozakura* late-blooming cherries
脈 *chimyaku* slow pulse
配 *chihai* delay in rationing
11 遅 *chichi* slow, lagging
過 *oso-su(giru)* be too late
12 鈍 *chidon* dullness, stupidity
着 *chichaku* late arrival
智慧 *osojie*＝遅知恵 (see above–8)
13 滞 *chitai* delay, procrastination, arrearage
蒔 *osoma(ki)* late planting. *osoma(ki) ni* late, too late
14 疑 *chigi* hesitation, vacillation, indecision

A **過** 4723 / F1884 **過** KA error; excess. *su(giru)* pass, go past; elapse; exceed. *su(gosu)* pass, spend; tide over; go thru; live, (eat) too much. *yo(giru)* pass by, cross, go across. *ayama(tsu)* err. *ayama(chi)* fault, error, indiscretion. *ayama(tte)* by mistake, accidentally. *su(ginai)* nothing more than, merely. *-su(giru)* over-, too; to a fault, in excess. *-su(gi)* past, after; over; too; excessive.

3 大 *kadai na* excessive; unreasonable; too large
大評価 *kadai hyōka* overvaluation
小 *kashō* too small
小評価 *kashō hyōka* undervaluation
4 日 *kajitsu* recently, the other day
分 *kabun na* excessive; unmerited; generous
不及 *kafukyū* excess or deficiency
不足 *kafusoku* excess or deficiency
少 *kashō* too few
少生産 *kashō seisan* underproduction
5 半 *kahan* the greater part
半数 *kahansū* majority, plurality, greater part
去 *su(gi)-sa(ru)* pass. *kako* the past; previous life; previous existence; past tense
去完了 *kako kanryō* past perfect tense
去帳 *kakochō* death registry (in a temple)
失 *kashitsu* error, blunder; accident; negligence
失者 *kashitsusha* party at fault
失致死罪 *kashitsu chishizai* accidental homicide
6 行 *su(gi)-yu(ku)* pass, go past
当 *katō na* excessive, undeserved, unreasonable, exorbitant
多 *kata* excess, superabundance
年度 *kanendo* past financial year
7 言 *kagen, kagon* exaggeration; saying too much
労 *karō* overwork, strain
9 食 *kashoku* overeating
信 *kashin suru* trust too much; overestimate (ability); be overconfident
怠 *katai* negligence, carelessness, mistake
美 *kabi* exceedingly beautiful
負荷 *kafuka* overload (in electricity)
重 *kajū* overweight
重労働 *kajū rōdō* overwork
度 *kado* excess
度緊張 *kado-kinchō* hypertension
10 振 *kabu(ri)* overdraft
称 *kashō* undeserved praise
料 *karyō* correctional fine
納 *kanō suru* overpay
員 *ka-in* supernumerary
般 *kahan* some time ago, recently
般来 *kahanrai* for some time
敏 *kabin* nervousness, oversensitiveness
敏症 *kabinshō* hypersensitiveness
11 剰 *kajō* excess, surplus
剰人口 *kajō jinkō* surplus population
剰生産 *kajō seisan* overproduction
12 程 *katei* process, course
勤 *kakin* overwork
給器 *kakyūki* supercharger
越 *Sugikoshi* the Passover
越節 *Sugikoshi Setsu, Sugikoshi no Iwai, Sugikoshi no Matsuri* the Passover
渡 *kato* crossing; ferry; changing from the old (to the new)
渡時代 *kato jidai* transition period
渡期 *katoki* transition period
14 誤 *kago* mistake; fault
酷 *kakoku* rigor, severity, cruelty
酸化 *kasanka* peroxide
酸化水素 *kasanka suiso* hydrogen peroxide
15 褒 *kahō* overpraise
賞 *kashō* undeserved praise
熱 *kanetsu* superheating
16 激 *kageki na* extreme, radical
激主義 *kageki shugi* extremism, radicalism
激派 *kagekiha* extremists, radical party

A **道** 4724 / F1886 **道** DŌ district, province, prefecture; road. *michi* road, path, lane, way, street, highway, route; journey; distance; course, way, means; duty, morality, moral doctrine; teachings; specialty; an art; reason, justice. *michi(naranu)* improper, illicit. *michi(sugara)* on the way.

4 心 *dōshin* moral sense; piety, faith
中 *dōchū* during the journey
中記 *dōchūki* trip record
中駕籠 *dōchū kago* sedan chair
化 *dōke(ru)* jest, clown. *dōke* clowning, antics, tomfoolery, pleasantry

化芝居 *dōke shibai* farce, low comedy
化役 *dōkeyaku* a clown, fool, mimic
5庁 *Dōchō* Hokkaido Government Office
民 *Dōmin* the people of Hokkaido
6行 *michiyu(ki)* going down the road; eloping; Japanese traveling garb
次 *michisugara* on the way
7床 *dōshō* roadbed
均 *michinara(shi)* road leveling; bulldozer
8念 *dōnen* moral sense; piety, faith
者 *dōsha, dōja* pilgrim
学 *dōgaku* Confucianism; Taoism; moral philosophy
学者 *dōgakusha* moralist
学家 *dōgakuka* Confucian scholar; moralist
具 *dōgu* tool, instrument, implement, utensil, appliance; furniture; (stage) scenery; instrumentality, means, vehicle; steppingstone
具方 *dōgukata* scene shifter, stage carpenter
具立 *dōguda(te)* tool layout; preparatory work; preliminary arrangements; one's features
具作 *dōguzuku(ri)* toolmaker
具屋 *dōguya* secondhand furniture dealer
具造 *dōguzuku(ri)* toolmaker
具部屋 *dōgubeya* toolroom; property room
具箱 *dōgubako* toolbox
9途 *dōto*=*michi* (see under 道 4724.0)
連 *michizu(re)* traveling companion
俗 *dōzoku* priests and laity
草 *michikusa* roadside grass; playing along the way
祖神 *dōsojin* traveler's guardian deity
10師 *dōshi* moralist; Taoist
破 *dōha* declaration
家 *Dōka* Taoist scholar
案内 *michi-annai* guidance; guide; signpost
11道 *michimichi* on the way, while walking
教 *Dōkyō* Taoism
断 *dōdan* unreasonable, absurd
理 *dōri* reason, right, truth. *kotowari* reason
理詰 *dōrizu(me)* persuasion, reasoning
12場 *dōjō* gymnasium, arena; Buddhist seminary
順 *michijun* route, itinerary
程 *dōtei, michinori* distance; journey; process
筋 *michisuji* path, way, route, itinerary; reason
普請 *michi bushin* road repair
13話 *dōwa* moral discourse, parable
路 *dōro* road, way, street, route, highway, thorofare
義 *dōgi* morality, moral principles
義心 *dōgishin* moral sense, moral scruples
楽 *dōraku* dissipation, prodigality, hobby
楽者 *dōrakumono* a profligate, a libertine
楽息子 *dōraku musuko* prodigal son
14端 *michibata* roadside
歌 *dōka* didactic poem

導 *michishirube* road marker
徳 *dōtoku* morals, morality, virtue
徳上 *dōtokujō* morally, from a moral standpoint
徳心 *dōtokushin* moral sense
徳主義 *dōtoku shugi* moralism, moralizing
徳的 *dōtokuteki* moral, ethical
徳学 *dōtokugaku* moral philosophy
徳律 *dōtokuritsu* moral law
徳家 *dōtokuka* man of virtue
徳教育 *dōtoku kyōiku* moral education
徳劇 *dōtokugeki* morality play
15標 *michi shirube, michijirushi, dōhyō* road marker, milestone

A **運** 4725 F1883 **運** UN destiny, fate, lot, fortune, luck. *hako(bu)* carry, transport; progress, advance. *megu(ru), megu(rasu)* (see under 回 1028.0). *hako(bi)* carrying; arrangements, managing, paving the way; progress; stage; step, pace.

8上 *hako(bi)-nobo(ru), hako(bi)-a(geru)* carry up, bring up
4込 *hako(bi)-ko(mu)* carry in, bring in
不運 *unfu-un* luck
5用 *un-yō suru* make use of, employ (capital), enforce (laws); invest, put in practice
去 *hako(bi)-sa(ru)* carry away, carry off
出 *hako(bi)-da(su)* carry out
6行 *unkō* motion, movement, revolution. *unkō suru* ply between, run
気 *unki* fate, fortune
休 *unkyū* service suspended (trains, etc.)
任 *ummaka(se)* trusting to luck
7良 *un-yo(ku)* fortunately, luckily
否天賦 *umpu-tempu* trusting to chance
8性 *unsei* determining one's fate by the sexagenary cycle
河 *unga* canal, waterway
命 *ummei* destiny, fate
命付 *ummeizu(keru)* condemn
命論 *ummeiron* fatalism
命論者 *ummeironsha* fatalist
送 *unsō* shipping, transportation, forwarding
送会社 *unsōgaisha* transportation company
送状 *unsōjō* invoice, waybill
送店 *unsōten* forwarding agency, express company
送屋 *unsōya* forwarding agency, express company
送保険 *unsō hoken* transportation insurance
送料 *unsōryō* transportation charge
送船 *unsōsen* transport ship, freighter
送費 *unsōhi* transportation expense
送業 *unsōgyō* transportation business
送業者 *unsōgyōsha* expressman, forwarding agent
9指 *unshi* fingering (in music)
炭船 *untansen* coal vessel, collier
炭機 *untanki* coal conveyor

[10]座 *unza* a meeting of poets to write and criticize *haiku* poems
航 *unkō suru* operate (ships or aircraft)
針 *unshin* handling the needle
帰 *hako(bi)-kae(ru)* carry back
[11]転 *unten* operation; motion; running, working; driving (a car) ⌈motorman
転士 *untenshi* mate, officer (on a ship);
転手 *untenshu* motorman, engineer, chauffeur, operator (of a machine)
転中 *untenchū* in motion, running
転台 *untendai* motorman's platform, driver's cab ⌈route
転系統 *unten keitō* transportation system,
転資本 *unten shihon* operating fund, working capital
転資金 *unten shikin* working capital, operating fund, campaign fund
動 *undō* motion, movement; exercise; sports, games; campaign; agitation; lobbying
動用具 *undō yōgu* sporting goods
動失調 *undō shitchō* lack of muscular coordination; locomotor ataxia
動会 *undōkai* athletic meet
動服 *undōfuku* sports clothes, uniform
動具 *undōgu* sporting goods
動屋 *undōya* campaigner (for a candidate)
動界 *undōkai* sporting circles
動神経 *undō shinkei* motor nerves
動施設 *undō shisetsu* sports equipment
動員 *undōin* campaigner
動記者 *undō kisha* sports writer
動記事 *undō kiji* sports news
動家 *undōka* sportsman, athlete
動家的 *undōkateki* sportsmanlike ⌈ship
動家的精神 *undōkateki seishin* sportsman-
動場 *undōjō* playing field
動帽 *undōbō* sports cap
動量 *undōryō* momentum
動着 *undōgi* athletic suit
動費 *undōhi* campaign fund
動靴 *undōgutsu* sports shoes
動障碍 *undō shōgai* motor disturbance
動選手 *undō senshu* athlete, sportsman
動精神 *undō seishin* sportsmanship
動熱 *undō netsu* love of sports
動器官 *undō kikan* organ of locomotion
動器具 *undō kigu* sporting goods
動療法 *undō ryōhō* exercise cure
動競技 *undō kyōgi* athletic sports
動欄 *undōran* sporting columns ⌈the brush
[12]筆 *umpitsu* strokes of the brush, handling
営 *un-ei* operation, management, administration ⌈chance
[13]試 *undame(shi) suru* try one's luck, take a
勢 *unsei* fate, fortune
賃 *unchin* shipping charges ⌈freight, C.I.F.
賃込 *unchinko(mi) de* cost including
搬 *umpan* transportation, transfer
搬人 *umpannin* porter, carrier
搬夫 *umpanfu* porter, carrier
搬車 *umpansha* cart, wagon, truck, lorry
搬費 *umpanhi* transportation charges
搬器 *umpanki* carts
[14]漕 *unsō* shipping, marine transportation
算 *unzan* mathematical operation, calcula- ⌊tion
[16]輸 *un-yu* transportation
輸会社 *un-yugaisha* transportation company
輸省 *Un-yushō* Transportation Ministry
輸業 *un-yugyō* transportation business

A **遊** 4726/F1881 **遊** YŪ. YU. *aso(bu)* play; enjoy oneself; visit; take a holiday; be out of use, be unemployed, be idle; study under; go on a spree. *aso(baseru)*, *aso(basu)* amuse, entertain; let play; be pleased to. *aso(bi)* play, game, sport, amusement, recreation, fun, outing; play (of a wheel); gambling; dissipation; dull business; idle time; light (literature). *susa(bi)* amusement, recreation.

[2]人 *aso(bi)nin* gambler; a jobless person
[3]士 *yūshi* playboy
子 *yūshi* wanderer, traveler, capital
山 *yusan* excursion, outing, picnic
弋 *yūyoku* cruise
女 *aso(bi)me, yūjo* harlot, prostitute
女町 *yūjo machi* red-light district
女屋 *yūjoya* brothel
[4]心 *aso(bi)gokoro, yūshin* a desire to play or have a good time ⌈person
手 *aso(bi)te* man of pleasure, fast-living
友達 *aso(bi)tomodachi* playmate, companion
[5]失 *yūshitsu* shortstop error ⌊in play
民 *yūmin* idle people, idlers; the unemployed; unemployment
半分 *aso(bi)hambun* half in fun
仕事 *aso(bi) shigoto* pastime, diversion, avocation ⌈olution
[6]行 *yūkō* tour, wandering, movement, rev-
好 *aso(bi)zu(ki)* pleasure seeker
仲間 *aso(bi)nakama* playmate, companion
休 *yūkyū* idle, unused ⌊(in amusement)
休施設 *yūkyū shisetsu* idle facilities
休資本 *yūkyū shihon* idle capital
[7]車 *aso(bi)guruma* idle pulley
里 *yūri* red-light district
技 *yūgi* commercially licensed games (like mahjong) ⌈questionable habits
冶 *yūya* playboy, classy dresser; person of

冶郎 *yūyarō* a profligate, a libertine
芸 *yūgei* the polite accomplishments
芸人 *yūgeinin* actors, singers
芸師 *yūgeishi* entertainer
8金 *yūkin, aso(bi)gane* idle money
底 *yūtei* breechblock (of a gun)
明 *aso(bi)-a(kasu)* play all night
直 *yūchoku* a short liner that is caught (in baseball)
歩 *yūho* walk, stroll, ramble
学 *yūgaku* traveling to study
事 *aso(bi)goto, susa(bi)goto* game, pastime, diversion
泳 *yūei* swimming
泳術 *yūeijutsu* getting along in the world
牧 *yūboku* nomadism
牧民 *yūbokumin* nomads
9食 *yūshoku suru* live in idleness
匍 *yūho* grounder to short stop
侠 *yūkyō* chivalrous man; gangster
軍 *yūgun* reserve corps, flying column
客 *yūkyaku* playboy; tourist; frequenter of brothels
星 *yūsei* planet
相手 *aso(bi)aite* playmate, companion (in amusement)
10郭 *yūkaku* red-light district
宴 *yūen* banquet
時間 *aso(bi)jikan* recess, playtime
11道具 *aso(bi)dōgu* plaything, toy
船 *yūsen* yacht, pleasure boat
船宿 *yūsen yado* riverside teahouse
動気球 *yūdō kikyū* dirigible balloon
動隊 *yūdōtai* mobile corps
猟 *yūryō* hunting
猟地 *yūryōchi* game preserve
猟会 *yūryōkai* hunting party
猟服 *yūryōfuku* hunting suit
猟免状 *yūryō menjō* hunting license
猟家 *yūryōka* hunter
猟期 *yūryōki* hunting season
12場 *aso(bi)ba* playground
惰 *yūda* laziness, indolence
13廓 *yūkaku* red-light district
楽 *yūraku* amusement, pleasure, recreation
資 *yūshi* idle capital
園 *yūen* amusement park, recreation area
園地 *yūenchi* amusement park, recreation area, playground
14歴 *yūreki* tour, pleasure trip
暮 *aso(bi)-ku(rasu)* idle time away
説 *yūzei* electioneering tour, oratorical campaign, agitation tour; campaign speech
説員 *yūzei-in* stump speaker
説旅行 *yūzei ryokō* speaking tour, junket
15標 *yūhyō* vernier
標尺 *yūhyōshaku* vernier scale
撃 *yūgeki* raid; shortstop
撃手 *yūgekishu* shortstop
戯 *aso(bi)-tawamu(reru)* play, frolic. *yūgi* games, sport, play, entertainment, amusement, pastime
戯的 *yūgiteki* playful, sportive
戯場 *yūgijō* playground
蕩 *yūtō* dissipation, profligacy
蕩文学 *yūtō bungaku* pornographic literature
蕩児 *yūtōji* dissipated person
16覧 *yūran* excursion, sightseeing
覧地 *yūranchi* tourist point, pleasure resort
覧客 *yūrankyaku* tourists, sight-seers
覧船 *yūransen* excursion boat
興 *yūkyō* pleasure-seeking, amusement, spree
興者 *yūkyōsha* carouser, reveler
興街 *yūkyōgai* amusement center; red-light district
興税 *yūkyōzei* entertainment tax
興費 *yūkyōhi* amusement expenses, price of a spree
18癖 *aso(bi)guse* habit of idlenss
19離 *yūri* separation, isolation

10

遡 4727 F1892 See **溯** 2653.

遞 4728 F1890 See **逓** 4695.

遙 4729 F1890 Yō. *haru(ka)ni* far off, in the distance; a long time ago; by far. *haru(keshi)* distant.
8拝 *yōhai* worshipping from afar
13遙 *harubaru* from afar, all the way, far out over (the sea)

遜 4730 F1890 Son. *herikuda(ru)* (see under 謙 4422.0).
6色 *sonshoku* inferiority
18辞 *sonji* modest speech
20譲 *sonjō* humility, modesty

蓮 4731 F1629 **蓮** Ren. *hasu, hachisu* lotus.
6池 *hasu ike* lotus pond
12葉 *hasuha, hasu(p)pa* lotus leaf. *hassuha na, hasu(p)pa na* wanton, loose, coquettish
葉女 *hasuha onna, hasu(p)pa onna* hussy, flapper
葉者 *hasuhamono, hasup(p)amono* hussy, flapper
葉娘 *hasuha musume, hasu(p)pa musume* hussy, flapper
10根 *renkon* lotus root
華 *renge* lotus, lotus flower
華草 *rengesō* a purple vetch

遣 4732 F1892 **遣** B Ken. *tsuka(wasu)* send, dispatch; give, donate, bestow on; do for (someone). *ya(ru)* give, let have, bestow on, present; send; do, perform, undertake; do for; act; study; row; operate; hold (a meeting), give (a dinner); eat, drink, smoke; find solace in. *yoko(su)* send, forward, deliver. *ya(ri-konasu)* manage a difficult task. *tsuka(u)* (see under 使 432.0).

3口 *yarikuchi* procedure, policy, way of doing
上 *ya(ri)-a(geru)* finish; wind up
4戸 *yarido* sliding door
手 *yarite* man of ability, tactician, former
水 *ya(ri)mizu* water conduit; stream coursed thru a garden
込 *ya(ri)-ko(meru)* snub, refute, corner
方 *ya(ri)kata* way of doing, method, manner of doing, means, arrangement, management
方無 *yarukatana(i)* inexpressible (feeling)
切 *ya(ri)-ki(renai)* cannot stand, cannot go on, cannot make ends meet, be intolerable
5外 *kengai* sent abroad
出 *ya(ri)-da(su)* begin, embark on, take up
付 *ya(ri)-tsu(keru)*, *ya(t)tsu(keru)* be accustomed to do; always be giving; defeat
付仕事 *yatsu(ke) shigoto* hurried work
6米 *kembei* sent to America
尽 *ya(ri)-tsuku(su)* do all in one's power
返 *ya(ri)-kae(su)* try again, make over; refute, answer back
合 *ya(ri)-a(u)* do (something) against each other, quarrel, argue
7抜 *ya(ri)-nu(ku)* carry thru, do thoroly, complete, accomplish
8放 *ya(rip)pana(shi)*, *ya(ri)bana(shi)* leave in disorder, leave half done; carelessness, negligence
取 *ya(ri)to(ri) suru* give and take, reciprocate, exchange
直 *ya(ri)-nao(su)* do over, remake, resume, begin again
9通 *ya(ri)-tō(su)* carry out, complete, accomplish
10時 *ya(ri)doki* proper time to do, convenient time, opportunity; marriageable age
兼 *ya(ri)-ka(neru)* dare not do, hesitate to do
唐使 *kentōshi* envoy to Tang China
11違 *ya(ri)-chiga(eru)*=*ya(ri)-sokona(u)* 遣損 (see below–13)
過 *ya(ri)-su(giru)* overdo, carry too far, drink too much, give too much. *ya(ri)-su(gosu)* let a person go past
遂 *ya(ri)-to(geru)* accomplish, fulfill, finish
掛 *ya(ri)-ka(keru)* begin to do, proceed to make. *ya(ri)ka(ke)* leaving (work) half done
12場 *yariba* disposal; use; place (to put a thing)
替 *ya(ri)-kae(ru)* do over again, start over
13損 *ya(ri)-sokona(u)* bungle, mismanage, spoil, make a mistake, be unsuccessful
14端 *yariha* the method to be followed; the time to deliver; the opportunity
18難 *ya(ri)niku(i)* hard to do
19瀬無 *yarusena(i)*, *yaruse (ga) na(i)* uneasy, cheerless, dreary, grief-stricken, wretched
繰 *ya(ri)-ku(ru)* proceed in spite of shortages. *ya(ri)ku(ri)* tiding over, makeshift, manipulation to settle a problem
繰算段 *yariku(ri) sandan* hurrying around

遠 4733 F1890 **遠** A En. On. *tō(i)* far, distant, remote; hard (of hearing). *tō(ku)* far away, in the distance. *tō(zakaru) vi* become more distant, recede; die away; keep away, stand aloof, be estranged. *tō(zakeru) vt* keep away, keep at a distance, shun, abstain from; alienate. *tō(karazu)*, *tō(karazu) shite* soon, in the near future. *tō-* far, distant.

2人 *enjin* a man from a faraway land
3大 *endai na* far-reaching, grand, lofty
山 *enzan*, *tōyama* distant mountain
干潟 *tōhigata* broad lagoon left by a receding tide
4方 *empō* great distance, long way; distant place. *tōchi* distant place
4火 *tōbi* building a fire at a distance
心力 *enshinryoku* centrifugal force
日点 *ennichiten*, *enjitsuten* aphelion
5目 *tōme* distant view, farsightedness
矢 *tōya* long-distance arrow; long-distance archery
由 *en-yū* remote cause
去 *tōza(karu)* recede into the distance
出 *tōde* going afar; changing a geisha registry to another city
6耳 *tōmimi* sharp ear
回 *tōmawa(ri)* roundabout way, detour. *tōmawa(shi)* roundabout expression
因 *en-in* remote, underlying, or predisposing cause
地 *enchi* distant place, remote place
交近攻 *enkō-kinkō* befriending distant states and antagonizing those near
近 *enkin* distance, far and near, perspective. *ochikochi* here and there
近法 *enkinhō* law of perspective
近調節 *enkin chōsetsu* (eye) accommodation
7走 *to(p)pashi(ri)* long-distance flight
足 *ensoku* trip, hike, picnic, excursion, outing
吠 *tōboe* howling
攻 *tōze(me)* attacking from afar and besieging
声 *tōgoe* distant howl (of a dog)
来 *enrai* foreign visitor, visitor from afar
見 *tōmi* watchtower; distant view, background. *enken* looking into the distance; distant view
見櫓 *tōmi yagura* watchtower

[8]国 *engoku, ongoku* distant land
退 *tōno(keru)* keep (someone) at a distance. *tōno(ku)* stay at a distance; recede, fade ⌊away
泳 *en-ei* long-distance swim
歩 *tōaru(ki)* long walk
昔 *tō (no) mukashi* long ages ago
征 *ensei* expedition, invasion, campaign; a tour (by a team of performers)
征軍 *enseigun* invaders, expeditionary force; visiting team
征隊 *enseitai* invaders, expeditionary force; ⌈visiting team
[9]音 *tōne* distant sound
廻 *tōmawa(ri)* circuitous route. *tōmawa(shi)* roundabout expression
浅 *tōasa* a wide shallow beach; a shoal
祖 *enso, tōtsu oya* forefathers, remote ances- ⌊tors
乗 *tōno(ri)* a long ride
巻 *tōma(ki)* surrounding at a distance
海 *enkai* deep sea, ocean
海魚 *enkaigyo* deep-sea fish
洋 *en-yō* ocean, deep sea
洋航海 *en-yō kōkai* ocean navigation
洋漁業 *en-yō gyogyō* deep-sea fishing
[10]馬 *emba* long ride on a horse
流 *onru* exile. 孫 *enson* distant relative
陬 *ensū* far country
島 *entō, tōjima* a distant island. *entō* exile ⌊to an island
[11]戚 *enseki* distant relative
道 *endō* a long walk; a roundabout way
略 *enryaku* farsighted policy or program
野 *tōno* a distant field
望 *embō* vista, distant view, perspective
距離 *enkyori* long distance, great distance, ⌊long-range
眼 *engan* farsightedness
眼鏡 *tōmegane* (old word for) telescope
視 *enshi* farsightedness
視画 *enshiga* perspective
視眼 *enshigan* farsightedness
[12]遠 *tōdō(shii)* distant
遐 *enka* distance ⌈background
景 *enkei* distant view, vista, perspective,
隔 *enkaku* distant, remote, isolated
隔操縦 *enkaku sōjū* remote control
[13]路 *enro, tōmichi* long road, long journey; roundabout way, detour, long distance
裔 *en-ei* remote descendant
雷 *enrai* distant thunder
[14]鳴 *tōna(ri)* distant peals (of thunder); distant roar (of the sea)
境 *enkyō* distant borders
[15]縁 *tōen* distant relative
慮 *enryo* reserve, modesty, deference, restraint, discretion, hesitation; forethought, prudence
慮深 *enryobuka(i)* reserved, backward, bashful, shy, modest
慮勝 *enryoga(chi)* modest, reserved, diffident
慮無 *enryona(ku)* unreservedly, frankly
[16]謀 *embō* forethought, foresight
[18]竄 *enzan* exile

11

遲 4734/F1894 遲 See 遅 4722.

遷 See 遷 4743.

遯 4735/F1894/F1880 See 遁 4719.

遭 4736/F1894 遭 Sō. *a(u), a(waseru)* (see under 会 381.0).
B
[11]遇 *sōgū* an encounter, meeting someone
遇戦 *sōgūsen* encounter, battle action ⌈tress
[18]難 *sōnan* disaster, accident, shipwreck, dis-
難者 *sōnansha* victim, sufferer, survivor
難信号 *sōnan shingō* distress signal, SOS

遮 4737/F1894 Sha. *saegi(ru)* interrupt, obstruct, intercept.
[2]二無二 *shanimuni* recklessly, furiously, desperately, forcibly
[6]光 *shakō suru* shade, darken, cut off the light
[11]断 *shadan* interception, isolation
断器 *shadanki* circuit breaker; railway crossing gate
断機 *shadanki*=preceding word
[15]蔽 *shahei* cover, shelter
蔽物 *shaheibutsu* cover, shelter

適 4738/F1893 適 Teki suitable. *teki(suru)* fit, suit, agree with, be adapted to, be qualified for. *kana(u)* suit, be capable of; measure up to expectations; match, rival, keep up with; stand (the work); bear (the heat). *kana(eru)* grant, hear, answer. *tama no* occasional, rare. *tamasaka* occasionally. *tamatama* casually, unexpectedly; few.
A
[4]中 *tekichū suru* hit the mark, guess right, come right ⌈quate, timely
切 *tekisetsu na* pertinent, appropriate, ade-
不適 *teki-futeki* fitness, aptitude, propriety
[5]用 *tekiyō suru* apply ⌈mal
正 *tekisei na* proper, right, reasonable, nor-
[6]地 *tekichi* suitable site ⌈tion
合 *tekigō* conformity, compatibility, adapta-
当 *tekitō na* suitable, proper, right; adequate; competent, qualified; reasonable,
任 *tekinin* suitability, competence ⌊timely

任者 *tekininsha* well-qualified person
任証 *tekininshō* efficiency certificate
7役 *tekiyaku* suitable post
否 *tekihi* propriety, fitness, aptitude
材 *tekizai, tekisai* the right man
材適所 *tekizai-tekisho* the right man in the right place ⌈ment, conformity
応 *tekiō* adaptation, accommodation, adjust-
応性 *tekiōsei* adaptability, flexibility
応症 *tekiōshō* diseases for which there is a specific medicine
8例 *tekirei* good example, typical instance
所 *tekisho* proper place
法 *tekihō* legality, lawfulness
宜 *tekigi* suitableness
性 *tekisei* adaptability
性検査 *tekisei kensa* aptitude test, qualifying examination
者 *tekisha* suitable person
者生存 *tekisha seizon* survival of the fittest
9度 *tekido ni* moderately, in moderation,
10従 *tekijū suru* follow ⌊temperately
帰 *tekki suru* lead to, follow
時 *tekiji* timely, at any time, at all times
時打 *tekijida* a timely hit
時安打 *tekiji anda*, timely hit
格 *tekikaku, tekkaku* competency, fitness
格性 *tekikakusei* fitness
格者 *tekikakusha* qualified person
11訳 *tekiyaku* exact translation
12温 *tekion* correct temperature ⌈ment
評 *tekihyō* just criticism; appropriate com-
量 *tekiryō* proper quantity, proper dose
策 *tekisaku* appropriate countermeasures
13業 *tekigyō* the right vocation
16薬 *tekiyaku* specific remedy
17齢 *tekirei* marriageable age; conscription
齢期 *tekireiki* marriageable age ⌊age
18職 *tekishoku* an appropriate occupation (for a certain person)

12

遅 4739/F1894 **遲** See **遅** 4722.

邁 4740/F1900 MAI go; excel.
10進 *maishin suru* push on, press on

遼 4741/F1899 RYŌ distant.
8東半島 *Ryōtō Hantō* Liaotung Peninsula
12遠 *ryōen na* distant, remote

B **遵** 4742/F1896 **遵** JUN follow, obey; learn.
6行 *junkō* obedience
守 *junshu suru* obey, observe
守者 *junshusha* observers (of a law)
8奉 *jumpō suru* obey, observe
法 *jumpō na* law-abiding
法精神 *jumpō seishin* law-abiding spirit

B **遷** 4743/F1895 **遷** SEN. *utsu(ru), utsu(su)* (see under 移 3282.0).
4化 *senge* demise of a dignitary
8幸 *senkō suru* (the emperor) moves away (from the capital)
延 *sen-en* delay, procrastination, postpone-
延策 *sen-ensaku* delaying tactics ⌊ment
10座 *senza* transfer of a shrine
都 *sento* moving the capital
宮 *sengū* transferring the god-body to a
11移 *sen-i* transition, change ⌊new shrine
12御 *sengyo* moving (of the emperor or the *shintai* of a shrine)
15避 *utsu(ri)-sa(keru)* move away from

A **選** 4744/F1896 **選** SEN selection, choice. *yo(ru), era(bu), e(ru), era(mu)* choose, select; cull out; elect; prefer; decide on. *sugu(ru)* choose, select, cull out.
3士 *senshi* select samurai
4分 *yo(ri)-wa(keru), e(ri)-wa(keru), era(bi)-wa(keru), e(ri)-wa(katsu)* set apart, sort out, sift, cull, separate, pick out
手 *senshu* athlete, player
手団 *senshudan* team, squad
手控場 *senshu hikaejō* players' dugout
手権 *senshuken* championship title
5出 *e(ri)-da(su), era(bi)-da(su)* select, pick out, cull out. *senshutsu* election
民 *semmin* chosen people, the elect
外 *sengai* left out, not chosen
外佳作 *sengai kasaku* honorable mention
6任 *sennin suru* select, appoint, assign; nominate; elect ⌈ness, overnicety in choice
好 *yo(ri)gono(mi), e(ri)gono(mi)* fastidious-
当 *era(bi)-a(teru)* make a happy choice
考 *senkō* selection, evaluation (of people)
7別 *era(bi)-waka(tsu)* set apart. *sembetsu* selection, separation, concentration (in mining)
良 *senryō* the people's choice; diet member
択 *sentaku* selection, choice, option, selectivity
択権 *sentakuken* right of choice, option
抜 *e(ri)-nu(ku)* choose, select, pick out, sort out. *sembatsu* selection, choice ⌈tion
抜試験 *sembatsu shiken* selective examina-
8取 *era(bi)-to(ru), e(ri)-to(ru), yo(ri)-to(ru), yo(ri)do(ru)* pick out, select, choose

直 *era(bi)-nao(su)* re-elect
定 *era(bi)-sada(meru)* appoint. *sentei* selection, choice
者 *senja* judge, selector
9 除 *e(ri)-no(keru)* sort out, weed out
炭 *sentan* coal screening
科 *senka* special course
科生 *senkasei* special student
10 屑 *e(ri)kuzu, yo(ri)kuzu* waste, trash, refuse
都 *sento* transfer of the capital
挙 *senkyo* election
挙人 *senkyonin* elector, voter; electorate
挙干渉 *senkyo kanshō* government election intervention
挙日 *senkyobi* election day
挙区 *senkyoku* election district, precinct, constituency
挙民 *senkyomin* electorate
挙立会人 *senkyo tachiainin* election witness
挙母体 *senkyo botai* electorate; electoral college
挙法 *senkyohō* election law
挙侯 *senkyokō* elector (of Saxony)
挙違反 *senkyo ihan* election irregularity
挙運動 *senkyo undō* election campaign
挙場 *senkyojō* the polls, election booth
挙期日 *senkyo kijitsu* election day
挙戦 *senkyosen* election campaign
挙演説 *senkyo enzetsu* campaign speech
挙権 *senkyoken* suffrage, franchise, right to vote
11 捨 *e(ri)-su(teru)* in choosing leave the bad behind
球眼 *senkyūgan* batting eye
12 集 *senshū* selection, anthology
13 嫌 *erigira(i)* choosing only what suits the fancy
滓 *yo(rik)kasu, e(ri)kasu* remnants, refuse
鉱 *senkō* concentration of ore
14 歌 *senka* selected poem; selection of poems
管 *senkan* election administration
16 衡 *senkō* selection, evaluation
録 *senroku suru* select, gather materials, and write

A 遺 4745 / F1897 遺

I. YUI. *noko(su)* leave behind; bequeath; save, reserve.

3 子 *ishi* posthumous child
4 文 *ibun* literary remains
5 功 *ikō* works following the deceased
令 *irei* dying orders
失 *ishitsu* loss
失物 *ishitsubutsu* lost article
失品 *ishitsuhin* lost article
6 臣 *ishin* surviving retainer
存 *ison* extant, still existing
伝 *iden* heredity
伝子 *idenshi* gene
伝因子 *iden-inshi* gene
伝法 *idenhō* law of heredity
伝学 *idengaku* genetics
伝病 *idembyō* hereditary disease
7 図 *ito* posthumous plan, person's last wishes
尿 *inyō* bed-wetting
作 *isaku* posthumous works
体 *itai* corpse, remains
址 *ishi* (historic) ruins
利 *iri* unexploited source of wealth
志 *ishi* dying wish
芳 *ihō* memory or autograph of the deceased
児 *iji* orphan
言 *yuigon, igen, igon* will, testament, last request
言状 *yuigonjō* will, testament
言者 *yuigonsha* testator
言書 *yuigonsho* will, testament
8 孤 *iko* orphan
法 *ihō* a law established by a deceased ruler
物 *yuimotsu* keepsake; inheritance, bequest. *ibutsu* relic, (old) remains, memento
制 *isei* institutions bequeathed from the past
命 *imei* will, dying instructions
事 *iji* reminiscences, memories
9 風 *ifū* tradition, hereditary custom
香 *ikō* a lingering odor reminding one of the giver (of clothes, etc.)
俗 *izoku* ancient customs which survive
恨 *ikon* grudge, ill-will, enmity
品 *ihin* articles of the deceased
臭 *ishū* scent (in hunting)
草 *isō* posthumous works
10 骨 *ikotsu* remains, ashes of the deceased
訓 *ikun, yuikun* dying instructions
財 *izai* inheritance, bequest, heritage
書 *isho* posthumous work; note left by the dead
烈 *iretsu* distinguished deeds of the departed
家族 *ikazoku* bereaved family
留 *iryū suru* bequeath
留品 *iryūhin* lost articles
11 族 *izoku* bereaved family
脱 *idatsu* omission
著 *icho* posthumous work
産 *isan* inheritance, bequest, heritage
産相続 *isan sōzoku* succession to property
産相続人 *isan sōzokunin* heir
産管理人 *isan kanrinin* administrator of an estate
12 詠 *iei* posthumous song or poem; one by an ancient composer
詔 *ishō* the last will of an emperor
13 跡 *iseki, yuiseki* (historic) ruins, remains, relics
棄 *iki* abandonment, desertion
愛 *iai* bequest, relic of the dead
業 *igyō* work left at death
腹 *ifuku* posthumous child
腹子 *ifuku (no) ko* posthumous child
14 像 *izō* afterimage
徳 *itoku* benefit from ancestors' virtue
漏 *irō* omission, negligence, oversight

精 *isei* nocturnal emission
誡 *ikai, yuikai* dying instructions
算 *isan* miscalculation
髪 *ihatsu* hair of the deceased
墨 *iboku* autograph of the deceased
15稿 *ikō* posthumous manuscript
賢 *iken* able men left out of office
16骸 *igai, yuigai* remains, corpse, (dead) body
薫 *ikun* lingering fragrance
憾 *ikan na* regrettable, unsatisfactory
憾乍 *ikannaga(ra)* regrettably
18贈 *izō, isō* bequest, legacy
蹟 *iseki* (historic) ruins
類 *irui* surviving animals; party remnants

13

遽 4746 / F1899 KYO fear; quick; be agitated. *awa(teru)* be hurried, be confused. *awatada(shii)* busy, bustling, hurried, confused. *niwaka(ni)* suddenly.

邂 4747 / F1900 KAI meet unexpectedly.
9逅 *kaikō* chance meeting

邀 4748 / F1900 YŌ go to meet; call.
15撃 *yōgeki suru, muka(e)-u(tsu)* ambush, assault, execute a surprise attack

B **避** 4749 / F1900 避 HI. *yo(keru), sa(keru)* avoid, avert, ward off, keep aloof from, stay away from; evade, shirk, shun.
7妊 *hinin* contraception
妊法 *hininhō* contraceptive method
8所 *sa(ke)dokoro* refuge, stronghold
泊所 *hihakusho* harborage
10病院 *hibyōin* isolation hospital
12寒 *hikan* wintering, hibernation
寒地 *hikanchi* winter resort
暑 *hisho* summering; going to a summer resort
暑地 *hishochi* summer resort
暑客 *hishokyaku* summer residents
13雷針 *hiraishin* lightning rod
雷器 *hiraiki* lightning arrester
18難 *hinan* shelter, refuge, evacuation
難民 *hinammin* refugees
難所 *hinanjo* shelter structures
難者 *hinansha* refugees
難場 *hinanjō* shelter area

B **還** 4750 / F1900 還 KAN. GEN. *kae(ru), kae(su)* (see under 帰 1582.0).
4元 *kangen* restoration; reduction (chem.)
元牛乳 *kangen gyūnyū* mixed powdered milk
元米 *kangemmai* requisitioned rice returned to the farmer
5付 *kampu* return, restitution, restoration
収 *kanshū suru* take back from
6任 *gennin* return of an official to his former post
7却 *kankyaku suru* send (something) back
8幸 *kankō* return of the emperor
9俗 *genzoku* quitting the priesthood, return to secular life
10流 *kanryū* a return, flowing back, convection, return current
納 *kannō* repayment
都 *kanto* return of the government
11啓 *kankei* return of the empress or crown prince
12御 *kangyo* return of members of the Imperial Family
14暦 *kanreki* one's 61st birthday
魂 *kankon* resurrection of the dead

14

邇 4751 / F1901 JI approach; near.

邃 4752 / F1901 SUI deep in the interior; profound.

15

邊 4753 / F1902 See 辺 4661.

邌 4754 / F-X REI. RAI. *ne(ru)* walk slowly, parade.

19

邏 4755 / F1903 RA go around; conceal.
8卒 *rasotsu* patrolman, policeman

RAD. 邑 163

Ōzato large village (in contradistinction to Rads. 166 & 170). Except for the radical character itself, always used at the right in the modified form ⻏ (2 strokes) *ōzatozukuri*. Nickname: Right Village.

邑 4756 / F1903 Yū village, rural community, town; dominion.

— 4 —

邪 See 邪 2849.

那 4757 / F1904 Na what?
[4]辺 *nahen ni* where, whither

B **邦** 4758 / F1904 邦 Hō country. *kuni* country.
[2]人 *hōjin* fellow countryman; a Japanese
[3]土 *hōdo* country, realm
[4]文 *hōbun* Japanese language
[6]字 *hōji* Japanese characters
字新聞 *hōji shimbun* a Japanese-language newspaper
[8]国 *hōkoku* country, nation
画 *hōga* a Japanese movie or painting
[10]家 *hōka* one's country
[11]域 *hōiki* political boundaries
訳 *hōyaku* translation into Japanese
貨 *hōka* Japanese money or goods; yen
[13]楽 *hōgaku* Japanese music
[14]語 *hōgo* vernacular; Japanese language

— 5 —

邪 See 2849.

B **邸** 4759 / F1906 Tei *yashiki* mansion, residence.
[4]中 *teichū* in the mansion
内 *teinai* grounds, premises
[6]宅 *teitaku* mansion, residence
[8]門 *teimon* mansion gate

— 6 —

郁 4760 / F1906 Iku cultural progress; perfume.

B **郊** 4761 / F1907 Kō suburbs; rural area.
[5]外 *kōgai* suburbs, outskirts
[11]野 *kōya* suburban fields

B **郎** 4762 / F1908 郎 Rō man; husband; counter for sons.
[3]女 *iratsume* (familiar word for an ancient) young lady
[7]君 *rōkun* young nobleman, young lord
[10]従 *rōjū* a samurai's retainer
党 *rōtō, rōdō* retainers, vassals
[12]等 *rōdō* retainers, vassals

— 7 —

郎 4763 / F1908 See 郎 4762.

A **郡** 4764 / F1908 Gun *kōri* county, district.
[6]会 *gunkai* county assembly
[7]役所 *gunyakusho* county office
[8]長 *gunchō* head county official
制 *gunsei* county system
[9]県 *gunken* counties and prefectures
県制度 *gunken seido* prefectural system
[10]部 *gumbu* rural districts; counties

— 8 —

B **郭** 4765 / F1909 Kaku enclosure; quarters. *kuruwa* enclosure, fortification; quarters; red-light district.
[3]大 *kakudai* large and wide. *kakudai suru* enlarge
[4]内 *kakunai* within the enclosure
中 *kakuchū* within the enclosure
公 *kakkō* cuckoo
公鳥 *kakkōdori* cuckoo
[5]外 *kakugai* outside the enclosure
[11]清 *kakusei suru* purify

B **郷** 4766 / F1911 郷 Kyō, village, native place. Gō country, district, village.
[2]人 *kyōjin* villagers; townmate
[3]士 *gōshi* a country samurai
土 *kyōdo* one's birthplace, one's old home
土文学 *kyōdo bungaku* local literature
土色 *kyōdoshoku* local color
土芸術 *kyōdo geijutsu* rural crafts
土愛 *kyōdoai* local patriotism
土閥 *kyōdobatsu* group of clansmen
土誌 *kyōdoshi* local history
[5]民 *gōmin* rural folk
[7]邑 *kyōyū* village, hamlet
里 *kyōri* one's old home, native place
村 *gōson* villages

社 *gōsha* village shrine, district shrine
8国 *kyōkoku* native land
学 *kyōgaku* village school
9信 *kyōshin* message from home
俗 *kyōzoku* village customs
保 *kyōhō* villages
軍 *gōgun* ex-soldier, reservist, veteran
思 *kyōshi* thoughts of home
10党 *kyōtō* one's fellow villagers; one's village
党心 *kyōtōshin* provincialism
13愁 *kyōshū* nostalgia, homesickness
14関 *kyōkan* the gate of one's home town; home town, birthplace
塾 *kyōjuku* teaching in a rural environment
15閭 *kyōryo* village gate; the village; one's home town
15談 *kyōdan* rural talk, rural speech

A 部 4767/F1909 部 Bu department, bureau, section; faculty; division, class, category; part, portion, region; copy, volume, set. Be the large ancient family.

3下 *buka* subordinate, follower; under one's command ⌈ment, the staff
4内 *bunai* circles; the service; the depart-
分 *bubun* part, portion, section. *buwa(ke)* classification
分食 *bubunshoku* partial eclipse
分品 *bubunhin* parts, accessories
分蝕 *bubunshoku* partial eclipse
5民 *bemin* members of the large ancient
外 *bugai* outside the service ⌊family
外秘 *bugaihi* restricted to the service
6会 *bukai* sectional meeting
7局 *bukyoku* department, bureau
位 *bui* part (of the body), region ⌈or section
8長 *buchō* head of a division, department,
門 *bumon* class, group, department, section, category; branch, line, field; genus, or-
所 *busho* one's post of duty ⌊der, type
9面 *bumen* field, aspect, phase, side
首 *bushu* radical (of a character)
厚 *buatsu na, buatsu(i)* thick, bulky, massive
品 *buhin* parts, accessories
屋 *heya* room, apartment
屋中 *heyajū* thruout the room
屋代 *heyadai* room rent
屋住 *heyazu(mi)* homeless hanger-on; an heir who has not yet taken over
屋着 *heyagi* house dress
10将 *bushō* a general
員 *buin* staff; staff member, member
11族 *buzoku* tribe
隊 *butai* unit, corps, squad, detachment
隊長 *butaichō* commanding officer
12属 *buzoku* attached to an office
落 *buraku* community, settlement, village
13数 *busū* number of copies, circulation
署 *busho* one's post of duty ⌈order, division
18類 *burui* class, heading, group, category,
類分 *buruiwa(ke)* classification, grouping

B 郵 4768/F1909 Yū stagecoach stop; mail.

8券 *yūken* postage stamp
送 *yūsō* mailing
送料 *yūsōryō* postage
送差止 *yūsō sashitome* postal ban
送費 *yūsōhi* postage expense
送無料 *yūsō muryō* postage-free
送禁止 *yūsō kinshi* postal ban
9政 *yūsei* postal system
政省 *Yūseishō* Ministry of Postal Services
便 *yūbin* mail ⌈der
便小為替 *yūbin kogawase* small money or-
便切手 *yūbin kitte* postage stamp
便年金 *yūbin nenkin* post office annuity
便行嚢 *yūbin kōnō* mailbag
便車 *yūbinsha* mail car
便局 *yūbinkyoku* post office
便私書函 *yūbin shishokan* post office box
便物 *yūbimbutsu* mail matter
便函 *yūbimbako* mailbox
便受 *yūbin-u(ke)* mailbox
便注文 *yūbin chūmon* mail order
便屋 *yūbin-ya* postman
便為替 *yūbingawase, yūbin kawase* postal
便料 *yūbinryō* postage ⌊money order
便馬車 *yūbimbasha* mail coach ⌈man
便配達 *yūbin haitatsu* mail delivery, post-
便振替貯金 *yūbin furikae chokin* postal
便船 *yūbinsen* mail boat ⌊transfer account
便袋 *yūbimbukuro* mailbag
便落 *yūbin-oto(shi)* mail chute
便貯金 *yūbin chokin* postal savings
便葉書 *yūbin hagaki* postcard
便集配人 *yūbin shūhainin* postman
便電信為替 *yūbin denshingawase* postal telegraphic money order
便箱 *yūbimbako* mailbox
10書 *yūsho* a letter sent by mail
11船 *yūsen* mail steamer
袋 *yūtai* mailbag
12税 *yūzei* postage; rate of postage
税不足 *yūzei busoku* postage due
15趣家 *yūshuka* philatelist

A 都 4769/F1910 都 To, Tsu *miyako* capital, metropolis.

2人 *miyakobito, tojin* town or city people

7 見角言谷豆豕豸貝赤走足身車辛辰釆辶【邑阝8】酉釆里

7 見角言谷豆豕豸貝赤走足身車辛辰釆辶【邑 9 阝】酉釆里

人士 *tojinshi* townspeople, a metropolitan, citizens of the capital
³下 *toka* thruout the capital, in the metropolis
大路 *miyako ōji* main thorofare of the metropolis
⁴心 *toshin* heart of the city
内 *tonai* within the capital
⁵立 *toritsu* metropolitan, municipal
庁 *Tochō* Tokyo Government Office
民 *Tomin* Tokyo citizens
民税 *tominzei* residents' tax
市 *toshi* cities; towns and cities
市生活 *toshi seikatsu* city life
市伝道 *toshi dendō* city evangelism
市対抗 *toshi taikō* intercity match
市計画 *toshi keikaku* town planning
⁶合 *tsugō* circumstances, conditions, reasons; convenience; opportunity, occasion; arrangement, management; accommodation; in all
合上 *tsugōjō* for convenience' sake, in view of circumstances
合良 *tsugōyo(ku)* fortunately, successfully, satisfactorily
会 *Tokai* Tokyo Assembly. *tokai* city, town
会人 *tokaijin* townsmen, city residents
会生活 *tokai seikatsu* city life
会地 *tokaichi* urban areas
会風 *tokaifū* urban manners, urbanity
会発達 *tokai hattatsu* urbanization
⁷住居 *miyakozumai* city life
⁸門 *tomon* city gates; the capital
府 *tofu* cities and towns
制 *tosei* metropolitan government
育 *miyakosoda(chi)* town-bred
長官 *To chōkan* Tokyo governor
知事 *To chiji* Tokyo governor
⁹度 *tsudo* each time, whenever, as often as
俗 *tozoku* metropolitan customs
城 *tojō* castle town
¹¹鳥 *miyakodori* sea gull
道府県 *to-dō-fu-ken* urban and rural prefectures
¹²落 *miyako-o(chi)* leaving or fleeing from the capital
営 *Toei* operated by Tokyo
¹³雅 *toga* elegance, refinement
詣 *miyakomō(de)* going to the capital
路 *miyakoji* road to the capital; roads in the capital
鄙 *tohi* town and country
²⁰議会 *To Gikai* Tokyo Assembly

9

都 4770 F1910 See 都 4769.

10

鄕 4771 F1911 See 郷 4766.

11

鄙 4772 F1913 Hɪ lowliness; countryside. *hina* countryside. *hina(biru)* be countrified.

²人 *hinabito, hijin* a rustic
⁶劣 *hiretsu* meanness, foul play
⁷見 *hiken* my humble opinion
言 *higen* slang expression
⁸陋 *hirō* low rank; wickedness, vulgarity
⁹俗 *hizoku na* rustic, countrified; low-class
¹²猥 *hiwai* indecency, obscenity
¹⁴語 *higo* slang
歌 *hinata uta* pastoral song

12

鄰 4773 F1914 See 隣 5023.

鄭 4774 F1914 Tᴇɪ an ancient Chinese province.

⁹重 *teichō* courtesy

16

嚮 See 1013. [口]

酉 RAD. 164

Tori bird or *hiyomi no tori* ("the bird of the zodiac," as distinguished from the common bird of Rad. 196). At left: *tori hen.* In combinations this element connotes liquid and hence in any position is generally called *sakezukuri* (i.e., the right-hand element of the character for saké). Nickname: Saké.

酉 4775/F1916 Yū. *tori* 5–7 p.m., 10th zodiac sign; bird; west.
5 市 *tori (no) ichi* year-end fair

— 2 —

酋 酋 See 593.

酊 4776/F1916 Tei intoxication.

— 3 —

酒 See 2573.

酎 4777/F1917 Chū saké.

P **酌** 4778/F1916 **酌** Shaku serving saké; the server. *ku(mu)* (see under 汲 2492.0).
6 交 *ku(mi)-ka(wasu)* rearrange
11 婦 *shakufu* waitress, barmaid
12 量 *shakuryō* consideration, pardon, extenuation

A **配** 4779/F1916 **配** Hai distribute; spouse; exile; rationing. *hai(suru)* allot; arrange; match (a couple); exile; subordinate. *kuba(ru)* distribute; serve (food); allocate; keep (your eyes) on. *ashira(u)* arrange, decorate; garnish; accompany (a singer).
3 下 *haika* subordinates, followers, adherents
4 水 *haisui* water supply; water distribution
分 *haibun* distribution, apportionment
5 付 *haifu* distribution, apportionment
布 *haifu* distribution, apportionment
本 *haihon* book distribution
6 色 *haishoku* color scheme
列 *hairetsu* arrangement, grouping, disposition
合 *haigō* composition, combination, distribution, arrangement, harmony, match, (color) scheme; mixture
当 *haitō* dividend, share, quota, allotment
当金 *haitōkin* share, dividend
7 車 *haisha* car allocation
役 *haiyaku* cast (of a play)
8 所 *haisho* place of exile
物 *kuba(ri)mono* things to distribute; gifts
祀 *haishi suru* enshrine; dedicate a shrine
9 陣 *haijin* camp layout
炭 *haitan* coal distribution
10 流 *hairyū, hairu* exile, banishment
剤 *haizai* compounding a prescription; correct handling (of a question)
11 船 *haisen* ship allocation
偶 *haigū* combination; spouse; marriage
偶者 *haigūsha* spouse, consort
達 *haitatsu* delivery, distribution; delivery man
達人 *haitatsunin* delivery man, postman, milkman
達先 *haitatsusaki* destination, receiver
達料 *haitatsuryō* delivery charge
達違 *haitatsuchiga(i)* misdelivery
12 属 *haizoku* attached to, assigned to
備 *haibi* arrangement, disposition, stationing
給 *haikyū* distribution, rationing
給米 *haikyūmai* rationed rice
給所 *haikyūjo* distribution point
給物 *haikyūmono* rationed goods, a ration
給品 *haikyūhin* rationed goods
給量 *haikyūryō* a ration
13 置 *haichi* arrangement, disposition (of troops)
意 *hai-i* concern, anxiety, worry
電 *haiden* distribution of electricity
電会社 *haiden gaisha* power company
電所 *haidensho* power station
電線 *haidensen* service wire
電盤 *haidemban* switchboard
14 管 *haikan* plumbing, piping
15 慮 *hairyo* consideration, solicitation, care, concern, anxiety, trouble
線 *haisen* (electric) wiring
16 餐 *haisan suru* distribute the elements (in the Christian Communion Service)
膳 *haizen suru* set the table
膳室 *haizenshitsu* serving room
18 謫 *haitaku* exile

— 4 —

酖 4780/F1919 Tan addicted to. Chin poison.
13 溺 *tandeki* addiction, dissipation

B **酔** 4781/F1923 **醉** Sui. *yo(u)* get drunk; feel sick; be poisoned;

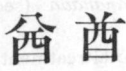

be elated, be spellbound. *yo(pparau)* get drunk. *yo(i), ei* intoxication. *yo(idore)* drunkard.

2 人 *suijin* a drunk
4 心地 *yo(i)gokochi, eigokochi* a gloriously drunk feeling
5 払 *yoppara(i)* drunkard
生夢死 *suisei-mushi* dreaming one's life away
7 言 *eigoto* words of a drunkard
狂 *yo(i)-kuru(u)* be raving drunk. *suikyō* raving drunkenness
余 *suiyo* drunken
8 泣 *eina(ki)* crying while drunk
臥 *yo(i)-fu(su), ei-fu(su)* sleep off a drunk
歩 *suiho* staggering gait, grogginess
事 *eigoto* actions of a drunkard
10 倒 *yo(i)-tao(re), eidao(re)* falling down drunk
酒 *suishu* drunkenness
紛 *yo(i)magire, eimagire* hopelessly drunk
11 眼 *suigan* bleary eyes with drink
眼朦朧 *suigammōrō(taru)* (eyes) dimmed
13 痴 *yo(i)-shi(reru)* be befuddled. *eikurui, eigurui* crazed with drink
漢 *suikan* drunkard
14 態 *suitai* intoxication, drunkenness
15 潰 *yo(i)-tsubu(reru)* be dead drunk. *yo(i)-tsu(busu)* make someone dead drunk
16 醒 *yoiza(me), eiza(me), yoizama(shi)* sobering up
18 顔 *suigan* face of a drunkard

5

酣 4782 / F1920 Kan. *takenawa* height of, full swing, thick of.

酢 B 4783 / F1920 Saku. So. *su* vinegar. *su(i), su(ppai)* sour, acid, tart.
8 物 *su(no)mono* vinegared dish
14 漬 *suzuke* pickling
酸 *sakusan* acetic acid

6

酩 4784 / F1920 Mei sweet saké.
9 酊 *meitei* drunkenness

酬 B 4785 / F1921 Shū. *mukui* reward; retribution.
10 恩祭 *shūonsai* peace offering

酪 B 4786 / F1921 Raku whey; broth; fruit juice.
8 制品 *rakuseihin* dairy products
13 農 *rakunō* dairy farming
農家 *rakunōka* dairy farmer
農場 *rakunōjō* dairy farm
14 酸 *rakusan* butyric acid

7

酵 B 4787 / F1921 Kō fermentation. *moto* materials for making saké.
5 母 *kōbo* yeast, leaven
母菌 *kōbokin* yeast fungus
10 素 *kōso* enzyme, ferment
素学 *kōsogaku* enzymology

酷 B 4788 / F1921 酷 Koku severity, cruelty. *hido(i), mugo(i)* cruel, harsh, merciless, atrocious; unjust, unfair; severe, intense, bitter, serious, terrible, outrageous, unreasonable. *hanahada* (see under 甚 111.0).
5 目 *hido(i)me* rough handling, maltreatment
6 似 *kokuji* close resemblance
刑 *kokkei* severe punishment
吏 *kokuri* exacting official
8 使 *kokushi* hard-driving, abuse, exploitation
10 烈 *kokuretsu no* severe, intense, rigorous
11 遇 *kokugū* maltreatment
12 税 *kokuzei* severe taxes
寒 *kokkan* intense cold; depth of winter
暑 *kokusho* intense heat
評 *kokuhyō* severe criticism
評家 *kokuhyōka* bitter critic
15 熱 *kokunetsu* intense heat
16 薄 *kokuhaku* brutality, atrocity

酸 A 4789 / F1922 San acid; bitterness. *su(i), su(ppai)* sour, acid, tart.
4 化 *sanka* oxidation
化物 *sankabutsu* oxide
化窒素 *sanka chisso* nitrous oxide, laughing gas
8 味 *su(i)mi, sammi* acidity, sourness
性 *sansei* acidity
性反応 *sansei hannō* acid reaction
性症 *sanseishō* acidosis
9 度 *sando* acidity
10 素 *sanso* oxygen
素吸入 *sansō kyūnyū* oxygen inhalation
素補給装置 *sanso hokyū sōchi* oxygen equipment
11 基 *sanki* acid radical (in chemistry)
敗 *sampai* acidification
敗乳 *sampainyū* sour milk
14 鼻 *sambi* extreme pain; deep sorrow
15 漿提灯 *hōzukijōchin* small round red lantern
18 類 *sanrui* acids

8

醉 4790 / F1923 See 酔 4781.

醋 4791 / F1924 Saku. *su* vinegar.
14 酸 *sakusan* acetic acid

酴 4792 F1923 RAN. *awa(su)*, *sawa(su)* remove astringency; bleach in water.
[9]柿 *sawa(shi)gaki* persimmons with astringency removed

醇 4793 F1923 JUN pure saké; purity; affection.
[4]化 *junka suru* refine, purify, chasten, sublimate; be refined, be chastened
[5]正 *junsei* pure, genuine
乎 *junko no* pure, sheer, unalloyed
[6]朴 *jumboku* simplicity and honesty
[8]味 *jummi* a pure, rich taste
[9]厚 *junkō no* kindhearted, courteous
風 *jumpū* good custom
風美俗 *jumpū bizoku* good customs
[15]醇 *junjun to* in a kindly manner

9

醗 Nonstandard for 醱 4802.

醐 4794 F1924 GO a kind of cream obtained from boiling butter.

醍 4795 F1924 DAI whey; good Buddhist teaching.
[16]醐味 *daigomi* sweet taste; zest for life; Buddha's excellent teachings

醒 4796 F1924 SEI. *sa(meru) vi* awake; be disillusioned; sober up. *sa(masu) vt* wake up, awake.
[18]際 *sa(me)giwa ni* on the verge of awakening

10

醞 4797 F1925 UN fermentation.
[20]釀 *unjō suru vt* ferment, brew

B 醜 4798 F1925 SHŪ ugliness; uncleanness; shame. *miniku(i)* bad-looking, ugly; unsightly; indecent, disgraceful.
[3]女 *shūjo*, *shikome* homely woman, plain-looking woman
[6]行 *shūkō* disgraceful conduct, scandal, immoral relations
交 *shūkō* immoral relations, intimacy
名 *shūmei* scandal, ill fame. *shikona* true name; nickname; wrestler's name
[7]状 *shūjō* disgraceful state of affairs
声 *shūsei* embarrassing rumor, scandal
男 *buotoko*, *shiko-o* ugly-looking man
[9]美 *shūbi* beauty or ugliness, personal appearance
[11]婦 *shūfu* homely woman
悪 *shūaku* unsightliness, ugliness, meanness, offensiveness
[13]業 *shūgyō* shameful calling, prostitution
業婦 *shūgyōfu* prostitute
[14]聞 *shūbun* scandal, ill fame
態 *shūtai* shameful conduct; ugly scene
関係 *shūkankei* immoral relations, intimacy
[18]類 *shūrui* "black sheep"; corrupt element

11

醫 4799 F1926 See 医 763.

醪 4800 F1926 RŌ. *moromi* unrefined saké or soy.

醬 4801 F1926 SHŌ. *hishio* a kind of *miso*.
[8]油 *shōyu* soy

12

醱 4802 F1927 HATSU fermentation, brewing.
[14]酵 *hakkō* fermentation
酵物 *hakkōbutsu* products of fermentation

13

醵 4803 F1927 KYO contribution for a feast.
[5]出 *kyoshutsu* donation, contribution
[8]金 *kyokin* raising money

B 醸 4804 F1928 釀 JŌ. *kamo(su)* brew; cause, give rise to.
[5]母 *jōbo* yeast, leaven
出 *kamo(shi)-da(su)* cause, bring about
[6]成 *jōsei suru* brew; foment, breed, cause, create
[9]造 *jōzō* brewing, distilling
造人 *jōzōnin* brewer, distiller
造所 *jōzōsho* brewery
造学 *jōzōgaku* science of brewing
造酒 *jōzōshu* brewage
造家 *jōzōka* brewer, distiller
造業 *jōzōgyō* brewing industry

14

醺 4805 F1927 KUN hunger.

17

釀 4806 F1928 See 醸 4804.

18

釁 See 714.

RAD. 釆 165

Nogome (i.e., the katakana *no* plus Rad. 119 *kome* "rice"). At left: *nogome hen*. Nickname: Topped Rice.

釆 4807/F1928 Nonstandard for 采 2825.

4

悉 4808/F712 SHITSU. *tsu(kusu)* (see under 尽 1380.0). *kotogoto(ku)* all, entirely, altogether, completely. *tsubusa ni* minutely, fully. [心]

9 皆 *shikkai* entirely, without exception

A **釈** 4809/F1929 **釋** SHAKU, SEKI explanation. *to(ku)* explain.

7 言 *shakugen* excuse
8 放 *shakuhō* release, liberation, acquittal
明 *shakumei* explanation; vindication
典 *shakuten* Buddhist literature
迦 *Shaka* Gautama, Sakyamuni ⌈Buddha
迦牟尼 *Shakamuni* Sakyamuni, Gautama,
迦如来 *Shaka Nyorai* Sakyamuni
迦象 *Shakazō* an image of Gautama
11 教 *Shakkyō* Buddhism
12 尊 *Shakuson* Buddha, Gautama
奠 *shakuten, sekiten* a festival to Confucius and his disciples
然 *shakuzen toshite* with sudden awakening, well satisfied with (an explanation)
18 義 *shakugi* commentary, exposition
義学 *shakugigaku* exegesis

5

釉 4810/F1929 YŪ glaze, enamel.

16 薬 *uwagusuri* glaze, enamel

A **番** 4811/F1275 BAN watch, guard; duty; number; order; size, game, round, turn, bout. *ban(suru)* keep watch, guard. *tsuga(u)* pair, mate, join, copulate. *tsuga(eru)* mate, pair; notch (an arrow); exchange (promises). *tsugai* pair, couple, brace (of ducks); joint. [田]

2 人 *bannin* watchman, guard; caretaker, ⌊janitor
3 小屋 *bangoya* watcher's hut
4 手 *bante* (thread) count (size)
犬 *banken* watchdog
5 目 *tsugaime* joint, hinge
代 *bangawa(ri)* shift, relief, alternation
付 *banzuke* graded list; program
台 *bandai* watcher's seat
外 *bangai* outside; extra
外物 *bangaimono* oversize item
6 地 *banchi* number
号 *bangō* number
号付 *bangōtsuke* numbering
7 狂 *bankuru(wase)* program change; upset; ⌊surprise
兵 *bampei* sentry, guard, sentinel
8 所 *bansho* guard box
卒 *bansotsu* sentinel, sentry
9 茶 *bancha* coarse tea
11 組 *bangumi* program
12 傘 *bangasa* coarse oilpaper umbrella
16 頭 *bantō* clerk, secretary, attendant; steward, manager

13

釋 4812/F1929 See 釈 4809.

RAD. 里 166

Sato village or *ri* two and a half miles. At left: 里 *sato hen*. Nickname: Village.

A **里** 4813/F1930 RI village; a Japanese league, 2.44 miles. *sato* village, hamlet, the country; parents' home.

2 人 *rijin, satobito* villagers, countryfolk
3 子 *satogo* child put out to nurse, foster child
4 心 *satogokoro* homesickness, nostalgia
方 *satokata* wife's home, wife's folks; childhood home of an adopted son
中 *satonaka* rural town
6 芋 *sato-imo* taro
7 扶持 *satobuchi* child-fostering expenses
言 *rigen* slang, dialect
言葉 *sato kotoba* courtesan's language; rural dialect
9 俗 *rizoku* local customs
神楽 *sato kagura* local shrine pantomime; village dramatic performance
10 帰 *satogae(ri)* bride's first visit to her old ⌊home
12 程 *ritei* mileage; distance
程標 *riteihyō* posts marking distances in *ri*

13数 *risū* mileage, distance
15標 *rihyō* milestone
16謡 *riyō* ballad, folk song, popular song
親 *sato oya* foster parent

2

重 See 224.

4

A野 4814/F1933 YA field, plain; the Opposition; civilian life; rustic. *no* field, plain. *ya-*, *no-* wild.

2人 *yajin* a rustic; a boor; common people
3山 *noyama* hills and fields
川 *nogawa* stream flowing thru a field
下 *ya* (*ni*) *kuda*(*ru*) resign from government ⌊service
4火 *nobi* brush fire, prairie fire
牛 *no-ushi*, *yagyū* wild ox, bison, buffalo,
犬 *yaken* stray dog
中 *nonaka no*, *nonaka ni* in the field
天 *noten* open air
分 *nowaki* wintry blast
太 *nobuto*(*i*) audacious, impudent
夫 *yafu* rural man
手 *yashu* fielder
手選択 *yashu sentaku* fielder's choice
辺 *nobe* fields
辺送 *nobeoku*(*ri*) funeral ⌈matory
辺煙 *nobe* (*no*) *kemuri* the smoke of a cre-
心 *yashin* ambition, aspiration, sinister design, intrigue, treachery
心家 *yashinka* an ambitious person
心満満 *yashimmamman na* very ambitious
5立 *noda*(*chi*), *noda*(*te*) (nobles) resting in the field. *noda*(*te*) an outside bath
史 *yashi* an unauthorized history
末 *nozue* edge of the field, corner of the
生 *yasei* wildness; wild ⌊field
生果物 *yasei kudamono* wild fruit
生動物 *yasei dōbutsu* wild animals
生植物 *yasei shokubutsu* wild plants
外 *yagai* the fields, the open air, outdoors;
外劇 *yagaigeki* outdoor drama ⌊suburbs
外撮影 *yagai satsuei* location (in filming)
外撮影中 *yagai satsueichū* on location
6羊 *yagi* goat
色 *yashoku* views of fields
伏 *nobushi*=*yamabushi* 山伏 1407.6
寺 *nodera* temple in a field
守 *nomori* a field watch
合 *yagō* illicit cohabitation
合夫婦 *yagō fūfu* common-law couple
7沢 *nozawa* swampy fields
兎 *no-usagi* wild rabbit, hare
良 *nora* the fields; laziness
良犬 *nora inu* stray dog
良仕事 *nora shigoto* farm work, field work
良猫 *nora neko* stray cat
良着 *noragi* farm field smock
8郎 *yarō* fellow, guy, rogue
育 *nosoda*(*chi*) wild
武士 *nobushi* wandering samurai, free lance
性 *yasei* wild nature, uncouthness
性児 *yaseiji* wild boy
性的 *yaseiteki* wild, rough, mean, rude
性味 *yaseimi* roughness, wildness, rusticity
放 *nobana*(*shi*) pasturing; pasture; leaving things to themselves
放図 *nohōzu na* haphazard, wild, proud
放途 *nohōzu na* haphazard, wild, proud
放埒 *nohōratsu* unbridled license
9面 *nozura* the field
陣 *nojin* bivouac
卑 *yahi na* rude, coarse, vulgar
荒 *noara*(*shi*) theft or damage of crops
草 *yasō* wild grass, wild plants. *nogusa* grass in a field
10馬 *no-uma* wild horse ⌈prairie
原 *nohara* plain, field, moor, wilderness,
師 *yashi* showman; quack, charlatan
晒 *nozara*(*shi*) *no* weatherworn
致 *yachi*=*yashu* 野趣 (see below–15)
党 *yatō* opposition party
叟 *yasō* elderly rural man ⌈nightfall
帰 *noragae*(*ri*) returning from the fields at
倒 *nota*(*reru*) fall by the wayside
倒死 *notareji*(*ni*) dying of exposure
砲 *yahō* field gun; field artillery
砲兵 *yahōhei* field artilleryman; field artil-
11鳥 *yachō* wild fowl, wild bird ⌊lery
遊 *noaso*(*bi*) picnic, outing
道 *nomichi* road across a field
帳 *yachō*, *nochō* field notes; (surveyor's) field notebook
情 *yajō* rural feeling, rural sentiment
猫 *nora neko* stray cat
宿 *nojuku* camping out
菊 *nogiku* wild camomile
望 *yabō*=*yashin* 野心 (see above–4)
菜 *yasai* vegetables
菜物 *yasaimono* vegetables
菜畑 *yasaibatake* vegetable garden
球 *yakyū* baseball
球気違 *yakyū kichiga*(*i*) baseball fan
球狂 *yakyūkyō* baseball fan
球界 *yakyūkai* baseball world
球連盟 *yakyū remmei* baseball league
球場 *yakyūjō* baseball park
球試合 *yakyū shiai* baseball game
球選手 *yakyū senshu* baseball player
球熱 *yakyū netsu* baseball fever

12焼 *noya(ki)* winter burning of the fields
猪 *yacho* wild boar ⌈views
景 *yakei* view of open fields; landscape
葡萄 *nobudō* wild grapes
蛮 *yaban* heathenism, barbarism
蛮人 *yabanjin* barbarian, savage
蛮国 *yabankoku* uncivilized country
営 *yaei* camping, camp, bivouac
営地 *yaeichi* camping ground
営者 *yaeisha* camper
13鼠 *nonezumi* field mouse
僧 *yasō* rural priest
猿 *yaen* wild monkey
路 *nomichi, noji* road across a field
飼 *noga(i)* pasturing, turning (animals) loose in a field. *noga(i) no* wild
鄙 *yahi na* vulgar, coarse, ill-mannered
禽 *yakin* wild fowl, wild bird
戦 *yasen* open warfare, field operations
戦病院 *yasembyōin* field hospital
14選 *yasen* fielder's choice
蜜 *nomitsu* wild honey
暮 *yabo na* rustic, unrefined; stupid, unfeeling; stale; conventional ⌈above)
暮天 *yaboten na*=*yabo na* 野暮 (see word
15趣 *yashu* rural beauty, rural air, rusticity
16積 *nozu(mi)* piling up (supplies) outside
薔薇 *nobara, no-ibara* a wild rose
獣 *yajū* wild animal, wild game
獣狩 *yajūga(ri)* wild animal hunt
18斃死 *notareji(ni)* dying of exposure
19鶏 *yakei* pheasant
26驢馬 *noroba* wild donkey

5

量 See 2141.

釐 See 2062.

8-STROKE RADICALS

RAD. 金 167

Kane metal, money, gold. At left: 釒 *kane hen.* Nickname: Metal.

A 金 4815 / F1935 Kon. Kin gold; money; Friday. *kane* money, metal; *kana-* metal.

1一封 *kin-ippū* a wrapped gift of money
2入 *kane-i(re)* purse, wallet; till
力 *kinryoku* the power of wealth
3口 *kinguchi, kinkuchi, kinkō* gold-tipped
子 *kinsu* money, funds
山 *kanayama* metal mine. *kinzan* gold mine; mountain fortress ⌈work
工 *kinkō* goldsmith; metalworker; metal-
巾 *kanakin* shirtings, calico, unbleached
才覚 *kane saikaku* raising money ⌊muslin
4円 *kin-en* money
仏 *kanabutsu, kanabotoke* metal Buddha;
元 *kanemoto* financial backer ⌊cold person
水引 *kimmizuhiki* golden paper cord
文字 *kimmoji* gilt letters
火箸 *kanahibashi* iron tongs
比羅 *Kompira* the seafarer's god
欠 *kinketsu* money stringency
欠病 *kinketsubyō* sick from shortage of
切 *kinki(ri)* castration ⌊money
切声 *kanaki(ri)goe* shrill voice, scream
5玉 *kingyoku* jewels, gold and gems. *kintama* gold ball; testicles
瓦 *kanagawara* copper roof tiles
穴 *kinketsu* capitalist, financial backer
句 *kinku* beautiful phrase; beautiful saying
打 *kinchō* sword oath
札 *kinsatsu* golden label
主 *kinshu* financier, capitalist, backer
台 *kindai* gold mounting
氷 *kanakōri* something very cold ⌈money
包 *kanezutsu(mi)* moneybag, bundle of
生木 *kane (no) na(ru) ki* the goose that lays
目 *kaneme* monetary value ⌊the golden egg
目品 *kaneme no shina* valuable goods
本位 *kinhon-i* gold standard
本位制 *kinhon-isei* gold standard ⌈lidity
石 *kinseki* metal and rock; monument; so-
石文 *kinsekibun* stone monument inscription
石交 *kinseki no majiwa(ri)* close friendship
石学 *kinsekigaku* study of stone monument inscriptions
6臼 *kana-usu* metal (perfumery) mortar
衣 *kin-i* beautiful clothes
匠 *kinshō* worker in gold and silver
回 *kanemawa(ri)* money circulation; financial condition ⌈any cost
尽 *kanezu(ku) de* by the power of money, at

印 *kin-in* gold seal
地 *kinji* ground strewn with gold dust
合金 *kin gōkin* gold alloy
米糖 *kompeitō* confetti
灯籠 *kanadōrō* metal lantern
糸 *kinshi* gold thread, spun gold
糸入 *kinshi-i(ri)* interwoven gold thread
気 *kanake* metallic taste; money
気違 *kane kichiga(i)* miser
字 *kinji* gold letters ⌈work
字塔 *kinjitō* a pyramid; a monumental
光 *kimpika* golden luster; that which glitters. *kimpika no* glittering, sparkling
光物 *kimpikamono* tinsel, trinkets
色 *kinshoku, kin-iro, konjiki* golden color
色夜叉 *konjiki yasha* usurer, miser
色堂 *konjikidō* the golden pavilion in a temple
7 見 *kanemi* testing money; money tester
言 *kingen* maxim, golden rule, aphorism
位 *kin-i* fineness of gold
作 *kinzuku(ri)* made of gold
吹 *kanefu(ki)* assaying
坑 *kinkō* gold mine
利 *kinri* interest rate, bank rate
判 *kanaban* metal stamp, metal seal
声 *kinsei* sound emitted by metal objects
売 *kane-u(ri)* gold-dust dealer
串 *kanagushi* iron skewer
杓子 *kanajakushi* metal ladle, dipper
沙汰 *kanezata* a money problem
8 使 *kanezuka(i)* way of spending
味 *kana-aji* quality of iron; sharpness of edged tools ⌈of metal
性 *kinshō* fineness of gold. *kaneshō* quality
所 *kanedokoro* source of funds, metal-
杯 *kimpai* gold cup ⌊mining area
泥 *kondei, kindei* gold dust; gold paint
波 *kimpa* golden waves
的 *kinteki* bull's-eye; object to long for
肥 *kimpi* commercial fertilizer
帛 *kimpaku* gold and cloth; return gift
具 *kanagu* metal fittings or fixtures
券 *kinken* gold certificate
事 *kanegoto* a matter of money
門海峡 *Kimmon Kaikyō* Golden Gate
枝 *Kinshi* the Imperial Family
枝玉葉 *Kinshi Gyokuyō* the Imperial
物 *kanamono* hardware ⌊Family
物屋 *kanamonoya* hardware store
9 風 *kimpū* autumn breeze ⌈money
食 *kaneku(i)* spendthrift; taking a lot of
屎 *kanakuso* slag, dross ⌈in gold
建 *kinda(te), kinta(te)* gold basis, quotations
廻 *kanemawa(ri)* money circulation; financial condition

造 *kanazuku(ri)* metalworker; metalworking
持 *kanemochi* wealthy man
柑 *kinkan* kumquat
冠 *kinkan* a gold crown (on a tooth)
品 *kimpin* money and valuables
星 *Kinsei* Venus. *kimboshi* splendid victory
臭 *kanakusa(i)* smelling of metal
茶 *kincha* reddish brown
型 *kanegata* metal pattern
巻 *kanema(ki)* metal hoop
相学 *kinsōgaku* metallography ⌈slogan
看板 *kin kamban* gilt signboard; a catchy
毘羅 *Kompira* the seafarer's god
科玉条 *kinkagyokujō* one's watchword; a consuming principle; an excellent law
単本位 *kintan hon-i* gold standard
砂 *kinsha* gold dust ⌈lacquer
砂子 *kin sunago* gold dust, gold-sprinkled
為替 *kinkawase* gold exchange
為替本位制 *kinkawase hon-isei* gold exchange standard
城 *kinjō* an impregnable castle
城湯池 *kinjō-tōchi* an impregnable castle
城鉄壁 *kinjō-teppeki* an impregnable castle
10 高 *kindaka* amount of money ⌈filings
屑 *kanakuzu* scrap metal, scrap iron, metal
扇 *kinsen* gilt fan
借 *kanakar(i)* borrowing money; debt
砧 *kanatoko* anvil
粉 *kimpun, kinko* gold dust
納 *kinnō* cash payment
紛 *kimmaga(i)* imitation gold
紗 *kinsha* high-class kimono cloth
紙 *kingami, kinshi* gold paper, gilt paper
脈 *kimmyaku* gold vein
被 *kinki(se) no* gold-plated
針 *kinshin* needle; golden needle
員 *kin-in* money, cash
容 *kin-yō* image of Buddha
財布 *kane saifu* moneybag
時計 *kindokei* gold watch
庫 *kinko, kanegura* safe, vault; cashbox; depository; treasure house; financier
庫破 *kinkoyabu(ri), kanegurayabu(ri)* safe-
釘 *kanakugi* iron nail ⌊breaking
釘流 *kanakugiryū* scrawl
剛 *kongō* diamond; great strength; strong man; emery powder
剛力 *kongōriki* Herculean strength
剛心 *kongōshin* earnest faith
剛不壊 *kongō-fue* adamant
剛石 *kongōseki* diamond
剛杖 *kongōzue* pilgrim staff
剛砂紙 *kongōshashi* emery powder, corun-
11 側 *kingawa no* gold-cased ⌊dum
帳 *kinchō* gold-decorated doors

張 *kimba(ri)* rolled gold, gold-plated, gold-filled
掘 *kaneho(ri)* miner
梃 *kanateko* crowbar
渋 *kanashibu* rusty water
絆 *kanahodashi* fetters, shackles, irons, hobbles
堂 *kondō* main temple structure
章 *kinshō* beautiful writing (literature)
袋 *kanabukuro* moneybag
商人 *kane akindo* gold-dust dealer
婚式 *kinkonshiki* golden wedding
産地 *kinsanchi* gold field
偏景気 *kanehen keiki* metal-industry boom
屏 *kimbyō* a screen coated with gold
屏風 *kimbyōbu* a screen coated with gold
細工 *kinzaiku* goldwork, gold ware, gold mounting
細工人 *kinzaikunin* goldsmith
魚 *kingyo* goldfish
魚屋 *kingyoya* goldfish seller
魚草 *kingyosō* snapdragon
魚鉢 *kingyobachi* goldfish bowl
貨 *kinka* gold coin
貨本位 *kinka hon-i* gold standard
貨国 *kinkakoku* gold-standard country
貨制 *kinkasei* gold-coinage system
貨幣 *kinkahei* gold coin
12 歯 *kimba* gold tooth
遣 *kanezuka(i)* way of spending
椀 *kanawan, kanamari* metal bowl
焼 *kanaya(ki), kaneya(ki)* branding
創 *kinsō* sword cut
策 *kinsaku suru* raise money, get a loan. *kinsaku* means of raising money
筋 *kinsuji* gold stripes
着 *kinki(se) no* gold-plated
無垢 *kimmuku* pure gold
満家 *kimmanka* man of wealth, millionaire
象眼 *kin zōgan* inlaying with gold, gold inlay
棒 *kanabō*＝鉄棒 4844.12
棒引 *kanabōhi(ki)* night watchman; gossiper
牌 *kimpai* gold medal
牌受領者 *kimpai juryōsha* gold medalist
壺 *kanatsubo* metal jar
壺眼 *kanatsubo manako* eyes glaring with infuriation
貸 *kaneka(shi)* moneylender; moneylending
貸業 *kaneka(shi)gyō* moneylending business
属 *kinzoku* metal
属工業 *kinzoku kōgyō* metalworking industry
属性 *kinzokusei* metal. *kinzokusei no* metallic
属細工 *kinzokuzaiku* metal working; metalwork
属貨幣 *kinzoku kahei* metallic currency
属製 *kinzokusei* made of metal
属製品 *kinzoku seihin* hardware
13 鼓 *kinko* drum and cymbals
塊 *kinkai* nugget, gold bullion, gold bar
搔 *kanaga(ki)* farmer's hoeing fork
滓 *kanakasu, kanakuso* slag, dross
詰 *kanezuma(ri), kinzuma(ri)* shortage of money
鉄 *kintetsu* metal; firmness
蓮花 *kinrenge* nasturtium
盞花 *kinsenka* marigold
準備 *kin jumbi* gold reserves
蒔絵 *kimmakie* gold lacquer work
解禁 *kin kaikin* lifting the gold embargo
殿 *kinden* golden palace, luxurious palace
殿玉楼 *kinden gyokurō* palace, mansion
槌 *kanazuchi* hammer, sledge
槌頭 *kanazuchi atama* hardhead; stubborn person
鉱 *kinkō* gold ore
鉱脈 *kinkōmyaku* gold vein
14 閣 *kinkaku* golden building; beautiful building
網 *kana-ami* wire netting, screen
酸 *kinsan* auric acid
銅 *kondō* gilt bronze
穀 *kinkoku* money and grain
箍 *kanataga* metal hoop
罰 *kanebachi* the results of foolish spending
蔵 *kanegura* treasure house; financier, backer
蔓 *kanezuru* source of money, a "gold mine"
髪 *kimpatsu* fair hair; blonde; golden hair, auburn hair
製 *kinsei* made of gold
鳳花 *kimpōge* buttercup
管楽器 *kinkan gakki* brass musical instrument
緑玉 *kinryokugyoku* chrysoberyl
緑石 *kinryokuseki* chrysoberyl
銀 *kingin* gold and silver; money
銀複本位制 *kingin fukuhon-isei* bimetallism
箔 *kimpaku* gold leaf, gold foil
箔屋 *kimpakuya* goldbeater
銭 *kinsen* money, cash. *kinsen no* pecuniary
銭出納係 *kinsen suitōgakari* cashier, teller, treasurer
銭出納簿 *kinsen suitōbo* cashbook
銭尽 *kinsenzu(ku) de* by the power of money
銭花 *kinsenka* marigold
銭貸付 *kinsen kashitsu(ke)* moneylending
銭登録器 *kinsen tōrokuki* cash register
15 衡 *kinkō* troy weight
線 *kinsen* gold lines
談 *kindan* conference about money; request for a loan
賦 *kanekuba(ri)* passing out money
鋤 *kanasuki* iron plow
鋏 *kanabasami* metal shears
敷 *kanashiki* anvil
箱 *kanebako* cashbox, money chest; capitalist, backer; resources; breadwinner
箸 *kanahashi, kanabashi* iron tongs
幣 *kimpei* gold coin; gold-colored Shinto offerings
質 *kinshitsu* fineness of gold

器 *kinki* golden furniture, golden vessel
縁 *kimbuchi* gold rims, gilt frame, gilt edges; gold-rimmed (glasses)
縁眼鏡 *kimbuchi megane* gold-rimmed glasses
輪 *kanawa* hoop, ring, or band of metal; dog collar
輪際 *konrinzai* never, by no means
権 *kinken* almighty dollar, financial influence
権政治 *kinken seiji* plutocracy
権貴族 *kinken kizoku* the wealthy
16縛 *kanashiba(ri)* binding hand and foot
錆 *kanasabi* rust
鋸 *kane nokogiri* hacksaw
親 *kane oya* financier, capitalist, backer
箆 *kanabera* trowel
盥 *kanadarai* metal basin, washbowl
甌 *kinnō* gold vase
甌無欠 *kinnō-muketsu* perfect, flawless, ideal
輸出 *kin yushutsu* export of gold
輸出禁止 *kin-yushutsu kinshi* gold embargo
輸出解禁 *kin-yushutsu kaikin* lifting the gold embargo
融 *kin-yū* money (market), credit situation, money circulation; financial
融市場 *kin-yū shijō* money market
融団 *kin-yūdan* syndicate
融界 *kin-yūkai* financial circles
融政策 *kin-yū seisaku* financial policy
融恐慌 *kin-yū kyōkō* financial panic
融梗塞 *kin-yū kōsoku* tight money
融組織 *kin-yū soshiki* banking system
融筋 *kin-yū suji* financial interests
融統制 *kin-yū tōsei* monetary control
融業 *kin-yūgyō* financial operations, banking business
融資本 *kin-yū shihon* financial capital
融機関 *kin-yū kikan* banking facilities
17糟 *kanakasu* metal dross
鎚 *kanazuchi* hammer, sledge
鍼 *kinshin* needle; golden needle
鍍金 *kimmekki* gilding, gold plating
環 *kinkan* gold ring
環食 *kinkanshoku* annular solar eclipse
環蝕 *kinkanshoku* annular solar eclipse
18闕 *kinketsu* palace
櫃 *kanebitsu*=*kanebako* 金箱 (see above-15)
鎖 *kingusari* gold chain
額 *kingaku* amount of money
儲 *kanemōke* money-making
儲主義 *kanemōke shugi* the almighty-dollar principle
曜 *Kin-yō* Friday
曜日 *Kin-yōbi* Friday
19繰 *kanegu(ri), kaneku(ri)* financing
鯱 *kin (no) shachihoko* golden dolphin
離 *kanebana(re)* spending money freely
鶏 *kinkei* golden pheasant
蘭 *kinran* intimate friendship
20鐘 *kinshō* gold bell
簪 *kin kanzashi, kinsan* gold hairpin
22襴 *kinran* gold brocade
聾 *kanatsumbo* stone-deaf
轡 *kanagutsuwa* horse's bit; hush money
嚢 *kinnō* purse, moneybag
23鑞 *kinrō* solder

2

釜 釡 See 2834.

釘 4816 / F1941 TEI. CHŌ. *kugi* nail, spike, tack; rivet; peg.
5目 *kugime* location of the nail
付 *kugitsu(ke)* nailing; pegging; standing transfixed
打 *kugi (o) u(tsu)* pound in a nail; renew a promise
打機 *kugiu(chi)ki* riveting machine
7応 *kugigota(e)* holding strength of a nail; staying power; effectiveness
抜 *kuginu(ki)* pinchers, nail-puller, claw hammer
12裂 *kugiza(ki)* tearing clothes on a nail
13隠 *kugikaku(shi)* decorative cover for a nail head
15締 *kugiji(me)* nailing shut

B **針** 4817 / F1941 SHIN needle. *hari* needle, pin; staple; fishhook; stinger; spine (of a fish); thorn; stitch; (watch) hand; (phonograph) needle; (hypodermic) needle; sting; molehill; acupuncture. *(o)hari* needlework, sewing; seamstress.
3女 *harime* seamstress
山 *hariyama* pincushion
小棒大 *shinshō-bōdai* exaggeration, hyperbole
4毛 *harige* bristle
孔 *shinkō* pinhole
孔写真機 *shinkō shashinki* pinhole camera
5目 *harime* seam
仕事 *hari shigoto* needlework, sewing
6耳 *hari (no) mimi* the eye of a needle
尖 *harisaki* needle point
7状 *harijō no* needle-shaped, pointed
8刺 *harisa(shi)* pincushion
灸 *shinkyū* acupuncture and moxibustion
金 *harigane* wire
金綴 *hariganetoji* stapler
10師 *harishi* needlemaker; acupuncture practitioner
11術 *shinjutsu* acupuncture
12葉 *shin-yō* evergreen needles
葉樹 *shin-yōju* coniferous tree, needle-leaf tree
13路 *shinro* direction, compass bearing
15箱 *haribako* needlecase, sewing box

3

釧 4818 / F1942 SEN bracelet.

鈕 4819 / F1942 KŌ. *botan* button.

P **釣** 4820 / F1941 **釣** CHŌ. *tsu*(*ru*) angle, fish, catch; decoy, allure, ensnare. *tsu*(*reru*) be caught; have a cramp. *tsu*(*ri*) change (for a dollar); (rod) fishing.

3 下 *tsu*(*ri*)-*sa*(*geru*) suspend from
上 *tsu*(*ri*)-*a*(*geru*) pull in (a fish); raise (one's eyes); boost (prices). *tsu*(*ri*)-*a*(*garu*) be hung up, be lifted up, turn up
4 戸 *tsurido* overhead door
手 *tsurite* angler; mosquito-net hanger
込 *tsu*(*ri*)-*ko*(*mu*) decoy into, lure, ensnare, tempt, attract
天井 *tsuri tenjō* suspended ceiling
太鼓 *tsuridaiko* suspended drum
5 目 *tsurime* slant eyes
台 *tsuridai* stretcher, litter
出 *tsu*(*ri*)-*da*(*su*) pull out (a fish); decoy, lure
6 糸 *tsuri ito* fishing line
合 *tsu*(*ri*)-*a*(*u*) match, suit, balance, be in harmony, be in proportion. *tsuriai* balance, equilibrium, proportion, symmetry, harmony, match
仲間 *tsuri nakama* fishing companion
灯籠 *tsuridōrō* hanging lantern
7 床 *tsuridoko* hammock
花 *tsuribana* flowers in a hanging vase
花活 *tsuribana-i*(*ke*) hanging vase
花瓶 *tsuri kabin* hanging vase
8 具 *tsurigu* fishing tackle
9 革 *tsurikawa* bus straps, streetcar straps
竿 *tsurizao* fishing rod
10 師 *tsurishi* angler
針 *tsuribari* fishhook
11 堀 *tsuribori* fishpond
船 *tsuribune* fishing boat; boat-shaped vase
梯子 *tsuribashigo* rope ladder
道具 *tsuri dōgu* fishing tackle
魚 *tsuriuo* game fish. *chōgyo* angling, fishing
魚法 *chōgyohō* angling, fishing
瓶 *tsurube* well bucket
瓶打 *tsurube-u*(*chi*) volley, firing in succession
瓶落 *tsurube-oto*(*shi*) dropping straight down
12 場 *tsuriba* fishing place
棚 *tsuridana* hanging shelf
提灯 *tsurijōchin* hanging lantern
13 殿 *tsuridono* (ancient) pond pavilion
14 銭 *tsurisen* change (for a dollar)
漁具 *tsuri gyogu* fishing tackle
16 橋 *tsuribashi* suspension bridge
髭 *tsurihige* upturned mustache
20 鐘 *tsurigane* hanging bell; temple bell
22 籠 *tsuri kago* fisherman's basket; hanging basket

4

鈎 4821 / F1943 See **鉤** 4841.

鈩 4822 / F1968 **鑪** RO hearth, fireplace; furnace.

鈞 4823 / F1944 KIN equal; important point; thirty *kin.*

鈕 4824 / F1943 CHŪ. *botan* button.

鈑 4825 / F-X HAN. *itagane* sheet metal.

鈀 4826 / F1942 HAKU. *kanagaki* farmer's hoeing fork.

鈔 4827 / F1943 SHŌ selection, summary; one-tenth of a shaku (勺). *shō*(*su*) copy; copy out.

鈇 4828 / F1943 FU axe.

13 鉞 *fuetsu* ax; battle-ax

欽 4829 / F1028 KIN respect, revere; long for. [欠]

6 仰 *kingyō suru* revere and honor
8 定 *kintei* authorized, appointed
定訳聖書 *Kinteiyaku Seisho* Authorized Version; King James Version
定詩人 *kintei shijin* poet laureate
定憲法 *kintei kempō* constitution granted by the emperor
14 慕 *kimbo suru* revere and long for

B **鈍** 4830 / F1943 DON dullness, slowness, foolishness. *nibu*(*ru*) become dull, weaken. *nibu*(*rasu*), *nibu*(*raseru*) dull, blunt, take the edge off, weaken. *nama*(*ru*) get dull. *nama*(*kura*) blunt sword, lazy fellow. *noro*(*i*) slow, dilatory, dull; flirtatious. *nibu*(*i*) dull, slow; blunt (tool); dim (light); thick (voice). *noro* dullness.

2 刀 *dontō, namakuragatana* blunt sword
3 才 *donsai* dullness, stupidity
6 色 *nibu-iro, nibi-iro* dark gray
行 *donkō* ordinary train
百姓 *dombyakushō* dumb farmer

7角 *donkaku* obtuse angle
8物 *dombutsu* dunce, blockhead. *namakura-mono* dull sword
9重 *donjū* dull-witted, stolid, phlegmatic
臭 *norokusa(i)*, *donkusa(i)* slow, leisurely, sluggish
10根 *donkon* dull, foolish, incapable
11麻 *domma* dullness
12痛 *dontsū* dull pain
間 *noroma* stupidity
鈍 *noronoro* slowly, leisurely, sluggishly
13感 *donkan* stolidity, thickheadedness
15調 *donchō* dull (market)
器 *donki* dull weapon, blunt sword

5

鈸 4831/F1944 HACHI, HATSU, BACHI cymbals.

鉉 4832/F1945 GEN. *tsuru* handle.

鉈 4833/F1945 SHA. *nata* hatchet.

鈿 4834/F1944 DEN. *kanzashi* ornamental hair-pin.

鉞 4835/F1946 ETSU. *masakari* battle-ax, broad-ax.

鉗 4836/F1945 KEN. KAN. *tsugu(mu)* shut (one's mouth).
3子 *kanshi* forceps

鈴 B 4837/F1944 REI, RIN bell, hand bell, buzzer. *suzu* bell.
5生 *suzuna(ri)* abundance of fruit (on a tree)
19蘭 *suzuran* lily-of-the-valley
蘭灯 *suzurantō* an arch of lights

鉋 4838/F1945 HŌ, BYŌ. *kanna* carpenter's plane.
10屑 *kannakuzu* shavings
11掛 *kannaka(ke)* planing
15盤 *kannaban* planer

鉦 4839/F1947 SEI, SHŌ gong. *kane* bell, gong, chimes, carillon.
5叩 *kanetata(ki)* rod used in ringing a bell; a man who goes around ringing a bell while reciting sutras and begging
13鼓 *shōko* bell and drum

鉢 4840/F1946 HATSU, HACHI bowl, rice tub, pot; crown, brainpan.
4木 *hachi (no) ki* potted tree
6合 *hachia(wase)* bumping of heads, collision
8物 *hachimono* food served in bowls; potted plant
9巻 *hachimaki* (towel) headband, hatband, frontlet
12植 *hachiu(e)* potted plant

鉤 4841/F1946 **鈎** KŌ. *kagi* hook, barb, gaff; brackets (in punctuation).
2十字 *kagi jūji* swastika
4手 *kagi(no)te* right angle; bend; bend in the road; kleptomaniac
6虫 *kōchū* hookworm
7状 *kōjō* hook-shaped
10針 *kagibari* hook, crochet hook
12裂 *kagiza(ki)* tear, rent (in one's clothes)
14鼻 *kagibana* hooked nose
15餌 *kōji* hook and bait
19縄 *kagi nawa* hooked rope

鉛 B 4842/F1945 **鉛 鈆** EN. *namari* lead (metal).
8山 *enzan* lead mine, lead deposits
工 *enkō* plumber
4中毒 *enchūdoku* lead poisoning
5白 *empaku* white lead
6色 *namari iro*, *enshoku* lead color
8版 *emban* stereotype
直 *enchoku* perpendicular, plumb
毒 *endoku* lead poisoning
10華 *enka* former word for face paint
12筆 *empitsu* lead pencil
測線 *ensokusen* sounding line
13塊 *enkai* lead ingot
鉱 *enkō* lead mine
14管 *enkan* lead pipe
16錘 *ensui* plumb bob, plummet

鉱 A 4843/F1968 **鑛 礦 砿** KŌ ore.
3工業 *kōkōgyō* mining and manufacturing
山 *kōzan*, *kanayama* mine
山王 *kōzan-ō* mining king
山技師 *kōzan gishi* mining engineer
山学 *kōzangaku* mining engineering
山師 *kōzanshi* mine operator
山業 *kōzangyō* mining industry
4水 *kōsui* mineral water
夫 *kōfu* miner
区 *kōku* mining area, diggings
区税 *kōkuzei* mine-lot tax
5石 *kōseki* ore, mineral, (radio) crystal
石受信機 *kōseki jushinki* crystal (radio) set
7床 *kōshō* ore deposits
坑 *kōkō* mine, shaft, pit
8油 *kōyu* kerosene, mineral oil
毒 *kōdoku* mine pollution; copper poisoning
物 *kōbutsu* minerals, inorganic substances

物油 *kōbutsuyu* mineral oil
物学 *kōbutsugaku* mineralogy
物質 *kōbutsushitsu* mineral matter
9 泉 *kōsen* mineral springs
10 脈 *kōmyaku* vein of ore
員 *kōin* miners
11 産 *kōsan* mineral product
産地 *kōsanchi* district rich in minerals
産物 *kōsambutsu* mineral products
13 滓 *kōsai* slag, dross
業 *kōgyō* mining industry
業地 *kōgyōchi* mining area
業家 *kōgyōka* mine operator
業税 *kōgyōzei* mining tax
業権 *kōgyōken* mining rights
14 層 *kōsō* ore bed
21 蠟 *kōrō* mineral wax
蠟油 *kōrōyu* paraffin oil

A **鉄** 4844/F1965 **鐵** TETSU iron, steel; reddish black, iron blue. *kurogane* iron.

2 人 *tetsujin* a very robust man
十字勲章 *Tetsujūji Kunshō* the Iron Cross
刀 *tettō* steel sword
刀木 *tagayasan, tettōboku* ironwood
3 山 *tetsuzan* iron mountain
叉 *kanamata* forked iron poker
工 *tekkō* ironworker, blacksmith
工場 *tekkōjō* ironworks
4 心 *tesshin* iron core; firm will
片 *teppen* piece of iron
尺 *kanezashi*=*kanejaku* 曲尺 103.4
分 *tetsubun* iron content
牛 *tetsugyū* army tank
牛部隊 *tetsugyū butai* tank corps
火 *tekka* red-hot iron; ordeal; gunfire; swords and guns; brave heart
火場 *tekkaba* gambling room; battlefield
火箸 *kanahibashi* iron tongs
5 甲 *tekkō* iron armor; iron helmet
石 *tesseki* iron and steel. *tesseki no* adamantine, firm
石心 *tessekishin* adamantine will
6 色 *tetsu iro* reddish black, iron blue
血 *tekketsu* blood and iron; war preparations; military strength
衣 *tetsui* armor
合金 *tetsugōkin* ferroalloy
舟 *tesshū* steel boat, steel pontoon
舟橋 *tesshūkyō* pontoon bridge
7 床 *kanatoko* anvil
坑 *tekkō* iron mine
材 *tetsuzai* iron or steel material
条網 *tetsujōmō* barbed-wire entanglement
8 門 *tetsumon* iron gate
味 *kaneaji* quality of iron
板 *teppan, tetsu ita, tetsuban* steel plate, sheet of iron
沓 *kanagutsu* horseshoe
灸 *tekkyū* roasting grill
9 柵 *tessaku* iron railing, iron fence
炮 *teppō*=鉄砲 (see below–10)
肺 *tetsuhai, tetsu (no) hai* iron lung
則 *tessoku* ironclad rule
軌 *tekki* iron rail
面皮 *tetsumempi* impudence, audacity
10 屑 *tetsu kuzu* scrap iron
扇 *tessen* iron-ribbed fan
挺 *kanateko* crowbar
粉 *teppun* iron filings
剤 *tetsuzai* iron pills (medicine)
索 *tessaku* cable, cableway (for hauling)
案 *tetsuan* irrevocable decision
格子 *tetsugōshi* iron-barred window, iron grating
拳 *tekken* clenched fist
拳制裁 *tekken-seisai* the law of the clenched fist
骨 *tekkotsu* steel frame
骨木船 *tekkotsu mokusen* steel-framed wooden ship
骨構造 *tekkotsu kōzō* steel-frame construction
砲 *teppō* gun, firearms; bath fire-pipe
砲玉 *teppōdama* bullet; lost messenger
砲打 *teppō-u(chi)* shooting
砲傷 *teppō kizu* bullet wound
砲腹 *teppōbara* suicide by shooting in the abdomen
砲鍛冶 *teppō kaji* gunsmith
11 桶 *tettō* steel vat
渋 *kanashibu* rusty water
脚 *tekkyaku* iron legs
船 *tessen* steel ship; ironclad
瓶 *tetsubin* iron teakettle
窓 *tessō* steel-barred window; prison bars; prison
兜 *tetsu kabuto* steel helmet
道 *tetsudō* railway, railroad
道工手 *tetsudō kōshu* railway trackman
道工学 *tetsudō kōgaku* railway engineering
道公安官 *tetsudō kōankan* railway police
道用地 *tetsudō yōchi* railway land
道自殺 *tetsudō jisatsu* railway suicide
道往生 *tetsudō ōjō* railway suicide
道便 *tetsudōbin* railway express
道馬車 *tetsudō basha* horsecar
道電化 *tetsudō denka* railway electrification
道網 *tetsudōmō* railway network
道敷設権 *tetsudō fusetsuken* railway right-of-way
道線路 *tetsudō senro* railroad track; right-of-way
12 扉 *teppi* iron door
塔 *tettō* steel tower
帽 *tetsubō* steel helmet
弾 *tetsudan* iron ball, shot
棍 *tekkon* iron club
湯 *tettō* molten iron
傘 *tessan* steel dome, steel-roofed stadium
筋 *tekkin* ferro-(concrete), iron bar

筆 *teppitsu* stylus, stencil pen, steel pen; engraving tool; powerful pen
腕投手 *tetsuwan tōshu* cannon-ball pitcher
棒 *kanabō, tetsubō* iron rod, metal rod, bar; crowbar; iron club; horizontal bar
棒曳 *kanabōhiki* night watchman; a gossip
13路 *tetsuro* railroad
鉢 *teppachi, teppatsu* priest's iron begging bowl
槌 *tettsui* iron hammer; large hammer; hammer (in sports)
槌投 *tettsuina(ge)* hammer throw
鉱 *tekkō* iron ore
鉱泉 *tekkōsen, tetsu kōsen* ferruginous springs
14銭 *tessen* iron coin
管 *tekkan* iron pipe
製 *tessei* made of iron or steel
褐色 *tekkasshoku* iron gray
15線 *tessen* steel wire
敷 *kanashi(ki)* anvil
箸 *kanabashi* iron tongs
質 *tesshitsu no* ferrous
器 *tekki* ironware, hardware; grill, gridiron; iron tool
器時代 *Tekki Jidai* Iron Age
漿 *kane, tesshō* tooth blackening
漿染 *kanezo(me)* blackening the teeth
漿黒 *kaneguro* blackening the teeth
16橋 *tekkyō* steel bridge
蹄 *tettei* horseshoe
錆 *tetsu sabi* iron rust; rust color
壁 *teppeki* iron wall; impregnable fortress
鋼 *tekkō* iron and steel
鋼業 *tekkōgyō* iron-and-steel industry
17環 *tekkan* steel cordon; iron ring. *tetsuwa* iron quoits
鍋 *tetsu nabe, kananabe* iron or copper kettle
鎚 *kanazuchi* hammer
18鎖 *tessa* iron chain
鞭 *kanabuchi, kanamuchi* metal whip
騎 *tekki* armored cavalry; brave cavalry
20艦 *tekkan* an ironclad warship

6

銜 See 1632.

鉞 See 4835.

鉾 4845 / F1947 F1333 See 矛 3164.

鉒 4846 / F1953 鋲 Bō sword point.

銚 4847 / F1950 Chō saké bottle.
3子 *chōshi* saké dipper; saké bottle

銓 4848 / F1949 Sen measure; scales; weigh.
7考 *senkō* careful selection; careful analysis (of abilities)
16衡 *senkō*=preceding word

銛 4849 / F1950 Sen. *mori* harpoon, gaff.
12筒 *morizutsu* harpoon gun

B 銑 4850 / F1949 Sen. *zuku* pig iron.
13鉄 *sentetsu, zukutetsu* pig iron
16鋼 *senkō* pig iron

A 銭 4851 / F1955 錢 戋 Sen one-hundredth of a yen; coin. *zeni* money.
2入 *zeni-i(re)* purse; till
7形 *zenigata* shape of a coin; paper money offered to a god
8金 *zenikane* money
放 *zenibana(re)* spending money freely
取 *zenito(ri)* profiting; expensiveness
9型 *zenigata* coin casting
11貨 *senka* coins
12湯 *sentō* bathhouse, public bath
無 *zenina(shi)* penniless
14穀 *senkoku* money and grain
15箱 *zenibako* cashbox, till, money box
18儲 *zenimō(ke)* money-making
19離 *zenibana(re)* spending money freely

B 銘 4852 / F1950 Mei inscription, signature (of an artisan); precept, motto. *mei(jiru), mei(zuru)* engrave, impress upon.
2刀 *meitō* a sword inscribed by the maker
4文 *meimon* maker's inscription
5仙 *meisen* a silk cloth
打 *meiu(tsu)* sign, name, announce
7肝 *meikan* permanently remembering
8刻 *meikoku suru* engrave; impress upon
9柄 *meigara* brand, name, description
茶 *meicha* refined tea
10記 *meiki suru* impress upon
酒 *meishu* superior saké
酒屋 *meishuya* saloon; brothel
14旗 *meiki* funeral banner (carrying name of the deceased)
銘 *meimei ni* apiece, to each
銘伝 *meimeiden* lives, biographies

A 銅 4853 / F1948 Dō copper. *aka, akagane* copper.
3山 *dōzan* copper mine
6色 *dōshoku* copper-colored
7坑 *dōkō* copper mine

8 板 *dōban* sheet copper
版 *dōban* copperplate
9 臭 *dōshū* corruption, mercenary spirit
11 貨 *dōka* copper coin
細工 *dōzaiku* copper work
細工人 *dōzaikunin* coppersmith
12 牌 *dōhai* bronze medal
壺 *dōko* copper boiler
13 塊 *dōkai* copper ingot
鉱 *dōkō* copper ore
14 像 *dōzō* bronze statue, bronze image
銭 *dōsen* copper coins
製 *dōsei* made of copper
15 線 *dōsen* copper wire, copper wiring
盤 *dōban* bronze basin
器 *dōki* bronze or copper utensil, copperware
器時代 *dōki jidai* Bronze Age
19 鏡 *dōkyō* bronze mirror
21 鐸 *dōtaku* bronze bell
27 鑼 *dora* gong, tomtom
鑼声 *doragoe* gruff voice

B **銃** 4854 / F1948 Jū gun, arms. *tsutsu* gun.

3 口 *jūkō, tsutsuguchi* gun muzzle
士 *jūshi* musketeer
工 *jūkō* gunsmith, armorer
丸 *jūgan* bullet
4 火 *jūka* gunfire
6 刑 *jūkei* execution by a firing squad
7 身 *jūshin* gun barrel
尾 *jūbi* breech of a small gun
床 *jūshō* gun stock
把 *jūha* grip of a gun
声 *jūsei* a shot, gun report
9 後 *jūgo* home front
架 *jūga* gun rest, gun mount
前哨 *jūzenshō* arms sentry
10 砲 *jūhō* firearms
殺 *jūsatsu* shooting to death, execution by shooting
剣 *jūken* bayonet, side arms
剣道 *jūkendō* bayonet fencing
剣術 *jūkenjutsu* bayonet practice
11 眼 *jūgan* loophole
猟 *jūryō* hunting
猟会 *jūryōkai* hunting party
猟法 *jūryōhō* game laws
猟服 *jūryōfuku* hunting coat
猟免状 *jūryō menjō* hunting license
猟家 *jūryōka* hunter, sportsman
猟税 *jūryōzei* hunting tax
猟期 *jūryōki* hunting season
猟禁止期 *jūryō kinshiki* closed hunting season
12 弾 *jūdan* bullet
創 *jūsō* bullet wound
13 傷 *jūshō* gunshot wound
14 槍 *jūsō* bayonet
槍突撃 *jūsō totsugeki* bayonet charge
15 撃 *jūgeki* rifle shooting
器 *jūki* small arms

A **銀** 4855 / F1947 Gin silver. *shirogane* silver. *gin(bura)* a stroll along the Ginza.

2 入 *gin-i(ri)* decorating with silver or silver thread
3 山 *ginzan* silver mine
5 台 *gindai* silver building; beautiful building; a silver ground of an industrial-art piece
世界 *gin sekai* silvery world, vast snowy scene
本位 *gin hon-i* silver standard
本位制 *gin hon-isei* silver standard
6 糸 *ginshi* silver thread, silver cord
色 *gin-iro, ginshoku* silver color, silvery
字 *ginji* silver letters
光 *ginkō* silvery light
地 *ginji* silvery ground
地金 *gin jigane* silver bullion
行 *ginkō* bank
行手形 *ginkō tegata* bank draft
行団 *ginkōdan* banking syndicate
行券 *ginkōken* bank note
行取引 *ginkō torihiki* bank account; banking transactions
行界 *ginkōkai* banking circles
行荒 *ginkō-a(rashi)* bank robbery; bank robber
行為替 *ginkō kawase* bank draft
行員 *ginkōin* bank clerk, bank staff
行家 *ginkōka* banker
7 作 *ginzuku(ri)* made of silver
位 *gin-i* silver quality
坑 *ginkō* silver mine
芦 *shirogane yoshi* pampas grass
杏 *ginnan* gingko nut. *ichō* gingko tree, maidenhair tree
杏返 *ichōgae(shi)* butterfly coiffure
8 性 *ginshō* quality of silver
杯 *gimpai* silver cup
波 *gimpa* silvery waves
河 *Ginga* Milky Way
泥 *gindei* silver paint
狐 *gingitsune* silver fox
券 *ginken* silver certificate
板写真 *gimban shashin* daguerreotype
9 盃 *gimpai* silver cup
茶色 *gincha iro* silver gray
単本位 *gintan hon-i* silver standard
砂 *ginsha* silver dust
砂子 *gin sunago* silver dust
10 座 *ginza* silver mint; the Ginza
扇 *ginsen* silver fan
流 *ginnaga(shi)* silvering; a dandy; an impostor
粉 *gimpun* powdered silver
紙 *gingami* silver paper

脈 *gimmyaku* vein of silver ore
被 *ginki(se)* silvering, silver plating
11側 *gingawa* silver (watch) case
液 *gin-eki* silver bath
瓶 *gimbin* silver vase, silver teapot
笛 *ginteki* flageolet
婚式 *ginkonshiki* silver wedding
屏 *gimbyō* screen coated with silver
屏風 *gimbyōbu* screen coated with silver
細工 *ginzaiku* silverwork
細工師 *ginzaikushi* silversmith
貨 *ginka* silver coin
貨幣 *ginkahei* silver coin
12牌 *gimpai* silver medal
筋 *ginsuji* silver line
着 *ginki(se)* silvering, silver plating
無垢 *gimmuku* pure silver
13鼠 *ginnezumi, ginnezu* silver gray
漢 *Ginkan* Milky Way
鉱 *ginkō* silver ore, silver mine
鈴 *ginrei* silver bell
幕 *gimmaku* silver screen
塊 *ginkai* silver ingot, silver bullion, bar silver
塊色 *ginkaishoku* silver gray
14閣 *ginkaku* silver building; beautiful building
箔 *gimpaku* silver foil
髪 *gimpatsu* silver hair
製 *ginsei* made of silver
製品 *ginseihin* silverware, silver utensil
15縁 *gimbuchi* silver rim
線 *ginsen* silver line
髯 *ginsen* beautiful white beard
幣 *gimpei* silver coin; silver-colored Shinto offerings
盤 *gimban* skating rink; ice surface; large silver platter
器 *ginki* silver utensils
輪 *ginrin* silver ring
輪部隊 *ginrimbutai* bicycle unit
16磨 *gimmiga(ki)* silver polish
17燭 *ginshoku* silvery light from a candlestick
環 *ginwa* silver ring
翼 *gin-yoku* silvery wings
21蠟 *ginrō* silver solder
22襴 *ginran* silver brocade

7

鋪 See 舗 552.

鋜 4856 / F-X SAKU. ZAKU. *kanahodashi* fetters, shackles.

銹 4857 / F1951 鏽 SHŪ. SHU. *sabi* rust, tarnish.

鋏 4858 / F1952 KYŌ. *hasami* scissors; punch. *yattoko* pinchers, pliers.

錺 4859 / F1958 (国字) *kazari* metal jewelry.
18職 *kazarishoku* jeweler

鋒 4860 / F1952 HŌ dagger, sword's point. *hoko* halberd; arms; festival car, float.
6先 *hokosaki*＝矛先 3164.6
14鋩 *hōbō* sword's point, sharp disposition

銷 4861 / F1951 SHŌ erase. *sa(su)* shut (the door).
7沈 *shōchin* dejection, depression
却 *shōkyaku*＝消却 2574.7
10夏 *shōka* summering, going away for the summer

鋲 4862 / F1953 (国字) *byō* rivet, tack, thumbtack, hobnail.
5打 *byō-u(chi)* riveting
10釘法 *byōteihō* riveting
15締 *byōji(me)* riveting

鋤 4863 / F1953 JO. *su(ku)* spade up; plow. *suki* spade for cultivation, plow.
4込 *su(ki)-ko(mu)* plow in
6返 *su(ki)-kae(su)* turn over (soil), plow
10起 *su(ki)-oko(su)* turn over (soil), plow
12焼 *sukiyaki* Japanese beef meal, sukiyaki
17鍬 *suki-kuwa* plows and hoes, farm tools
19簾 *joren* small hand scoop

B 鋭 4864 / F1950 銳 EI sharpness; edge; (sharp) weapon; picked men (soldiers), the pick. *surudo(i)* pointed, sharp; violent, scathing; keen (sense); sharp (ear); penetrating (eye); shrewd.
6気 *eiki* courage, ardor, high spirits
7角 *eikaku* acute angle
利 *eiri* sharpness, keenness
兵 *eihei* picked troops
9音 *eion* shrill sound
10師 *eishi* efficient army corps
10敏 *eibin* sharpness, keenness, sensitiveness; mental acumen
12傑 *eiketsu* hero, great man, mastermind
13意 *ei-i* eagerly, earnestly
感 *eikan* sensitiveness
15鋒 *eihō* brunt of an attack or argument

B 鋳 4865 / F1967 鑄 SHU. SHŪ, CHŪ casting. *i(ru)* cast, mint, coin.
3工 *chūkō* caster, cast-iron worker
4込 *i-ko(mu)* cast in a mold
8金 *chūkin* casting
物 *imono* cast metal; casting
直 *i-nao(su)* recast, recoin
9型 *igata* mold; pig bed; matrix; die
造 *chūzō* casting, founding; minting, coining

造所 *chūzōsho* mint; foundry; type foundry
11 貨 *chūka* minting; coinage; coin
掛 *i-ka(keru)* tinker with, mend
掛屋 *ika(ke)ya* tinner
13 塊 *chūkai* ingot
鉄 *itetsu, chūtetsu, igane* cast iron, iron casting
14 像 *chūzō* molten image
15 潰 *i-tsubu(su)* melt down
16 鋼 *chūkō* steel casting; cast steel
鋼所 *chūkōjo* steel mill
鋼塊 *chūkōkai* ingot steel

8

錢 4866 F1955 See **銭** 4851.

錮 4867 F1957 Ko to tie.

錣 4868 F1956 TETSU. *shikoro* armor neck-plates.

鋺 4869 F1953 EN. *kanamari* metal bowl.

錻 4870 F-X Bu tin plate.
2 力 *buriki* tin plate

錚 4871 F1955 Sō gong.
16 錚 *sōsō(taru)* prominent, outstanding

B **錘** 4872 F1955 SUI. *omori* weight, plumb bob, sinker, sounding lead. *tsumu* spindle.
7 状 *suijō* spindle-shaped
9 重 *suijū* plumb bob

錫 4873 F1957 SEKI, SHAKU copper; gold-copper alloy. *suzu* tin.
7 杖 *shakujō* priest's staff
14 製 *suzusei* (made of) tin
製品 *suzu seihin* tinware

B **錠** 4874 F1955 CHŌ. TEI. Jō lock, padlock, latch; pill; close up; counter for pills.
9 前 *jōmae* lock
前直 *jōmaenao(shi)* locksmith
前屋 *jōmaeya* locksmith
10 剤 *jōzai* pill, lozenge, tablet

錐 4875 F1954 SUI pyramid; cone; gimlet. *kiri* auger, drill, awl, gimlet.
5 穴 *kiri ana* gimlet hole; bull's-eye
7 体 *suitai* conical form
形 *suikei* pyramidal
12 揉 *kirimo(mi)* drilling, boring; tailspin

錨 4876 F1958 BYŌ. MYŌ. *ikari* anchor, grapnel.
6 地 *byōchi* anchorage
8 泊 *byōhaku* anchorage, anchoring
12 結 *ikari musu(bi)* fisherman's bend
18 鎖 *byōsa* chain cable

錆 4877 F1954 SHŌ. *sabi(ru)* get rusty, rust; mature and die (fish). *sabi* rust, tarnish.
2 刀 *sabigatana* rusty sword
4 止 *sabido(me)* rust preventive
5 付 *sabi-tsu(ku)* rust together
6 色 *sabi iro* rust color, reddish brown
16 鮎 *sabi ayu* mature trout

鋸 4878 F1953 KYO. *nokogiri, noko* saw.
10 屑 *nokokuzu* sawdust
12 歯 *nokogiriba, kyoshi* saw tooth; indentation
歯車 *noko haguruma* ratchet wheel
歯状 *kyoshijō* indentation, saw-tooth formation
17 鮫 *nokogirizame* saw shark
23 鱏 *nokogiriei* sawfish

A **録** 4879 F1954 **錄** ROKU. *shiru(su), roku-(suru)* record.
8 画 *rokuga* television recording
事 *rokuji* recorder, secretary
9 音 *rokuon* sound recording, transcription
音板 *rokuomban* record, transcription
音放送 *rokuon hōsō* broadcast of a transcription
音盤 *rokuomban* recording disk
音器 *rokuonki* recorder
音機 *rokuonki* recorder

B **錯** 4880 F1957 SAKU mix; be in disorder. *ma-(jiru), ma(zeru)* (see under 混 2604.0).
7 角 *sakkaku* alternate angles
乱 *sakuran* confusion, distraction, derangement
12 覚 *sakkaku* optical illusion; hallucination
14 綜 *sakusō* complication, intricacy
誤 *sakugo* mistake
雑 *sakuzatsu* complication, intricacy
18 簡 *sakkan* paragraphs or pages out of order

B **錬** 4881 F1958 **鍊** REN. *ne(ru)* refine (metals); drill, train; polish (sentences). *ne(ri)* tempering.
6 成 *rensei* training, drilling
8 金 *ne(ri)gane* tempered steel
金術 *renkinjutsu* alchemy
11 達 *rentatsu* skill, dexterity
清 *ne(ri)-kiyo(meru)* test and purify

13 鉄 *rentetsu, ne(ri) kurogane* wrought iron
16 鋼 *renkō* wrought steel

錦 4882 / F1956 KIN. *nishiki* brocade; fine dress; honors.
6 地 *kinchi* your place
11 眼鏡 *nishiki megane* kaleidoscope
12 絵 *nishikie* woodblock color print
14 旗 *kinki* gold-brocade flag; imperial standard
19 繡 *kinshū* embroidered brocade; rich autumnal tints
鶏 *kinkei* golden pheasant
22 嚢 *kinnō* brocade bag

鋼 4883 / F1954 B Kō steel. *hagane* steel.
4 心 *kōshin* steel core
片 *kōhen* steel billet, steel slab
5 玉石 *kōgyokuseki* corundum
6 色 *hagane iro* steel blue
7 材 *kōzai* rolled steel; steel materials
8 板 *kōhan, kōban* steel sheet, steel plate
10 索 *kōsaku* wire rope or cable
12 筆 *kōhitsu* ruling pen
13 塊 *kōkai* steel ingot
鉄 *kōtetsu* steel
鉄車 *kōtetsusha* steel (railway) car
鉄板 *kōtetsuban* steel plate
鉄管 *kōtetsukan* steel tubing
鉄製 *kōtetsusei* made of steel
鉄線 *kōtetsusen* steel wire
14 管 *kōkan* steel tubing
製 *kōsei* steel manufacture; steel products
15 線 *kōsen* steel wire

9

鍊 4884 / F1958 See 錬 4881.

鍮 4885 / F1959 CHŪ brass.

鎹 4486 / F1962 (国字) *kasugai* clamp.

鎚 4887 / F1961 TSUI. *tsuchi* hammer, mallet.

鍾 4888 / F1960 SHŌ gather, collect.
13 愛 *shōai* deep affection

鍍 4889 / F1958 To plating, gilding.
8 金 *mekki, tokin* gilt; gilding, plating; gold plating; gold-filled
14 銀 *togin* silvering

鍔 4890 / F1958 鍔 GAKU. *tsuba* sword guard; supporting brim of a kettle.
7 迫合 *tsubazeria(i)* close fighting
20 競合 *tsubazeria(i)* close fighting

鍬 4891 / F1959 SHŌ. *kuwa* hoe with long blade set at an acute angle.
2 入 *kuwa-i(re)* first (ceremonial) plowing of the new year
6 先 *kuwasaki* metal blade of the hoe

鍋 4892 / F1958 KA. *nabe* pan, pot, kettle.
8 金 *nabegane* cast iron
底景気 *nabezoko keiki* economic depression
12 焼 *nabeya(ki)* scalloped
13 蓋 *nabebuta* kettle lid
14 墨 *nabezumi* kettle soot

鍼 4893 / F1960 SHIN needle. *hari* needle.
7 灸 *shinkyū* acupuncture and moxibustion
医 *shin-i* acupuncture doctor
医者 *hari-isha* needle doctor, acupuncture practitioner
8 治 *shinji* acupuncture
11 術 *shinjutsu* acupuncture

鍵 4894 / F1960 KEN (piano) key. *kagi* key.
4 孔 *kagi ana* keyhole
5 穴 *kagi ana* keyhole
11 袋 *kagibukuro* key bag
13 楽器 *kengakki* keyed musical instrument
15 盤 *kemban* keyboard
17 環 *kagiwa* key ring
25 鑰 *ken-yaku* key, solution

鍛 4895 / F1959 B TAN. *kita(eru)* forge, temper; drill, train, discipline, practice.
3 上 *kita(e)-a(geru)* temper thoroly; train well
工 *tankō* metalworker
工所 *tankōjo, tankōsho* foundry
7 冶 *tan-ya* forging. *kaji* blacksmith
冶工 *kajikō* metalworker, blacksmith
冶屋 *kajiya* blacksmith
8 金 *tankin* wrought gold
9 造 *tanzō* forging
11 接 *tansetsu* welding
13 鉄 *tantetsu* tempering iron; wrought iron, malleable iron
16 鋼 *tankō* forged steel
錬 *tanren* temper, forging; hardening; discipline, training

10

鎗 4896 / F1961 Sō. *yari* spear, lance, javelin.

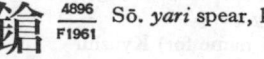

8
10【金】長門阜阝隶隹雨青非

鎬 4897/F1962 Kō. *shinogi* sword-blade ridges.
9削 *shinogi (o) kezu(ru)* fight desperately

鎍 4898/F-X Saku wire; (watch) spring.
7条 *sakujō* cable, steel rope
条鉄道 *sakujō tetsudō* cable railway

鏈 4899/F1963 Ren. *kusari* chain; irons; connection. *kusa(ru)* *vt* and *vi* connect.
11帷子 *kusari katabira* coat of mail
19縄 *kusari nawa* chain cable

鎧 4900/F1961 Gai. *yoro(u)* put on the armor; arm oneself. *yoroi* suit of armor.
4戸 *yoroido* Venetian blinds
8板 *yoroi ita* louver boards
武者 *yoroi musha* armed warrior
10袖一触 *gaishū-isshoku* easy victory
11窓 *yoroi mado* louver window
12装 *gaisō* sheathing, armoring

B 鎖 4901/F1961 鏁 Sa. *kusari* chain; irons; connection. *to(zasu)* (see under 閉 4945.0).
4止 *kusarido(me)* sprocket
7状 *sajō* chainlike
8国 *sakoku* national isolation, exclusion of foreigners
10骨 *sakotsu* clavicle, collarbone
12港 *sakō* closing the ports
歯車 *kusari haguruma* sprocket wheel

鎌 4902/F1960 鎌 Ren. *kama* sickle, scythe; trick.
2入 *kama-i(re)* harvesting
4止 *kamado(me)* cutting grass and trees prohibited
切 *kamaki(ri)* praying mantis
7足 *kama ashi* legs bowed in; sitting (on floor) with heels spread apart
9首 *kamakubi* gooseneck
10倉 *Kamakura* Era (1185–1333)
差 *kamasa(shi)* sickle sheath
11脚 *kama ashi*＝鎌足 (see above-7)
14槍 *kamayari* forked spear

B 鎮 4903/F1962 鎭 Chin ancient peace-preservation centers. *shizu(maru)*, *shizu(meru)* (see under 静 5077.0). *shizu(me)* pillar (of society).
4止 *chinshi suru* allay pain
火 *chinka suru* be extinguished, be brought under control
5圧 *chin-atsu* suppression, subjugation
台 *chindai* army camp
6西 *Chinzei* (old name for) Kyushu
守 *chinju* local Shinto deity, tutelary god
守府 *chinjufu* navy yard, naval station, admiralty port
8定 *chintei suru* suppress, repress, subdue, pacify
10座 *chinza suru* be enshrined
12痛 *chintsū* relieving pain
痛剤 *chintsūzai* painkiller, sedative
痛薬 *chintsūyaku* painkiller, sedative
14静 *chinsei* calm, quiet, tranquillity; appeasement, pacification
静剤 *chinseizai* sedative, tranquilizer
静期間 *chinsei kikan* cooling-off period
魂 *chinkon* repose of souls
魂曲 *chinkonkyoku* requiem
魂祭 *chinkonsai* Shinto service for the repose of the dead
15撫 *chimbu* pacification, placating
20護 *chingo suru* pacify and preserve a country

鎔 4904/F1961 熔 Yō. *to(keru)* *vi* fuse, melt. *to(kasu)* *vt* fuse, melt, smelt.
4化 *yōka* melting
8和 *yōwa* fusion
岩 *yōgan* lava
岩流 *yōganryū* lava flow
9点 *yōten* melting point
10剤 *yōzai* flux (in metallurgy)
11接 *yōsetsu* welding
接工 *yōsetsukō* welder
接剤 *yōsetsuzai* welding flux
接管 *yōsetsukan* welded pipe
接機 *yōsetsuki* welding machine
13滓 *yōshi* slag
鉱炉 *yōkōro* blast furnace
解 *yōkai* melting, fusing
解性 *yōkaisei* fusibility
鉄 *yōtetsu* ingot iron, ingot steel
鉄場 *yōtetsuba* forge
16融 *yōyū* fusion, melting, smelting, flux
融点 *yōyūten* melting point

11

鏖 See 5379.

鏁 4905/F1962 See 鎖 4901.

鏑 4906/F1963 鏑 Teki. *kabura* arrowhead.

鏨 4907/F1964 San. *tagane* cold chisel, graver.

鏃 4908/F1962 Soku. Zoku. *yajiri* arrowhead; barb of an arrow.

鏘 4909/F1963 Sō the tinkling of jade or metal pendants
12然 *sōzen* clink, metallic sound

鏤 4910/F1964 Ru. *chiriba(meru)*, inlay, set, mount.
10骨 *rukotsu no* painstaking

鏝 4911/F1963 Man. *kote* laundry iron; curling iron; soldering iron; trowel.
8板 *kote-ita* ironing board

A 鏡 4912/F1964 鏡 Kyō. *kagami* mirror; speculum; barrelhead. (*o*)*kagami* round rice-cake offering.
4戸 *kagamido* paneled door
5玉 *kyōgyoku* objective lens
立 *kagamida(te)* mirror stand
台 *kyōdai* dresser, mirror stand
8板 *kagami ita* panels
9面 *kyōmen* surface of a mirror
11掛 *kagamika(ke)* mirror stand
12開 *kagamibira(ki)* cutting the New Year's rice cakes
13裏 *kyōri ni* in the mirror
15餅 *kagami mochi* round glutenous-rice cakes (often used as offerings)

12

鐙 4913/F1965 Tō. *abumi* stirrup.

鐫 4914/F1965 Sen. *ho(ru)* (see under 彫 236.0).

鐃 4915/F1964 Dō. Nyō gong.
13鉢 *nyōhachi* cymbals

鐚 4916/F1965 Wa. *bita* coin of smallest value.
14銭 *bitasen* coin of smallest value

B 鐘 4917/F1965 鐘 Shō. Shu. *kane* bell, gong, chimes, carillon.
7状 *shōjō* bell-shaped
声 *shōsei* the sound of a bell
8乳石 *shōnyūseki* stalactite
乳洞 *shōnyūdō* stalactite cave
13鼓 *shōko* bell and drum
楼 *shōrō, shurō* belfry, bell tower
14銅 *shōdō* bell metal
銘 *shōmei* a bell inscription
15樓 *shōrō* belfry, bell tower
鋳 *kane-i* bell casting
撞 *kanetsu(ki)* bell ringer; bell ringing
撞堂 *kanetsukidō* bell tower, belfry

13

鏽 4918/F1964/F1951 See 銹 4857.

鐵 4919/F1965 See 鉄 4844.

鐸 4920/F1967 Taku large hand bell.

鑓 4921/F1968 (国字) *yari* spear, lance, javelin.

鐶 4922/F1967 Kan metal ring; link; drawer handle. *tamaki* circle, ring.

14

鑄 4923/F1967 See 鋳 4865.

B 鑑 4924/F1967 鑑 鑒 Kan. *kanga(miru)* take warning from, learn a lesson from. *kagami* mirror, pattern, example. *kanga(mite)* in view of, learning a lesson from.
5札 *kansatsu* license, permit
7別 *kambetsu* discrimination, judgment
8定 *kantei* judgment, expert opinion, legal advice, appraisal, criticism
定人 *kanteinin* appraiser; connoisseur; expert witness
定者 *kanteisha* = word above
定家 *kanteika* = *kanteinin* 鑑定人 (see above–8)
定料 *kanteiryō* legal fee, expert's fee
定書 *kanteisho* expert's report
9査 *kansa* inspection; inspector
15賞 *kanshō* appreciation
賞力 *kanshōryoku* power of appreciation, an eye for (something)
賞眼 *kanshōgan* an eye for; an artist's eye
19識 *kanshiki* judgment, discernment, discrimination, appreciation
識力 *kanshikiryoku* discernment
識家 *kanshikika* connoisseur, appraiser, discerner
識眼 *kanshikigan* discerning eye

15

鑛 4925/F1968 See 鉱 4843.

鑣 4926/F1968 Hyō. *kutsuwa* (horse's) bit.

鑢 4927/F1968 Ro. Ryo. *yasuri* file, rasp.

8
15[金]長門阜阝隶隹雨青非

鑠 4928/F1968 SHAKU. *toro*(*kasu*) (see under 盪 3124.0).

鑞 4929/F1968 RŌ solder.
5付 *rōzu*(*ke*) soldering

鑚 4930/F1969 鑽 SAN. *ki*(*ru*) make a fire by rubbing sticks together.
4孔機 *sankōki* boring machine
5出 *ki*(*ri*)-*da*(*su*) rub sticks to make a fire

16

鑪 4931/F1968 See 鈩 4822.

17

鑵 4932/F1969 See 罐 3634.

鑰 4933/F1969 YAKU lock.

鑲 4934/F1969 JŌ fit into.
12嵌 *jōkan* dental inlay

18

鑲 See 4934.

19

鑽 4935/F1969 See 鑚 4930.

鑼 4936/F1969 RA gong.

20

鑿 4937/F1970 SAKU. *nomi* chisel.
4井 *sakusei* well drilling
孔機 *sakkōki* mortising machine
8岩機 *sakugaki* rock drill

RAD. 長 168

Nagai long. At left: 镸 (7 strokes) *nagai hen*. Nickname: Long.

長 4938/F1970 長 A CHŌ head, chief, headman, commander, director, manager; merit, forte, advantage; superiority; length. *chō*(*jiru*), *chō*(*zuru*) grow up; be one's senior; excel in. *naga*(*raeru*) live long, live on. *naga*(*meru*) lengthen, prolong. *ta*(*keru*) excel in, be proficient in; grow older. *naga*(*i*) long, lengthy. *naga*(*ki*) length, long period. *naga*(*ku*) long, a long time, eternally. *naga*(*sa*) length. *naga*(*tarashii*) lengthy, long and boring. *osa* chief, head. *naga*(*no*) long, eternal. *tokoshi*(*e*) *ni* forever. *naga*(*raku*) long, a long time. *chō-* long; deep.
2刀 *naginata* halberd. *chōtō* long sword
3女 *chōjo* eldest daughter
子 *chōshi* eldest son; first child
弓 *chōkyū* longbow
久 *chōkyū* permanence, endurance; eternity, perpetuity
上 *chōjō* a senior, one's elder, a superior
口説 *chōkōzetsu* long talk, long lecture
大 *chōdai na* tall and stout
大息 *chōtaisoku* deep sigh
4月 *nagatsuki* 9th lunar month
引 *nagabi*(*kaseru*) prolong, drag out. *nagabi*(*ku*) be prolonged, drag out
日月 *chōjitsugetsu* long period of time
方形 *chōhōkei* rectangle, oblong
水路 *chōsuiro* 50-meter course
火鉢 *nagahibachi* oblong brazier
文 *chōbun* long letter, long document
文句 *nagamonku* lengthy speech
円 *chōen* ellipse, oval
円形 *chōenkei* ellipse, oval
5生 *chōsei*, *naga-i*(*ki*) long life, longevity
目 *nagame ni* lengthily, a little longer
石 *chōseki* feldspar
尻 *nagajiri* long visit, overstaying
幼 *chōyō* young and old
打 *chōda* extra-base hit, long drive
汀 *chōtei* long beach
兄 *chōkei* eldest brother
広告 *chōkōzetsu* eloquence; long-windedness
6舌 *chōzetsu* eloquence
虫 *nagamushi* snake
江 *chōkō* long river; Yangtse Kiang
芋 *naga-imo* yam
老 *chōrō* an elder, a senior, a superior; priest, presbyter
老教会 *Chōrō Kyōkai* Presbyterian Church

年 *naganen* a long time, many years
年月 *chōnengetsu* a long period of time
7 足 *chōsoku* rapid strides, leaps and bounds
身 *chōshin* great stature
男 *chōnan* eldest son
寿 *chōju* longevity, long life
8 長 *naganaga(shii)* long-drawn-out. *naganaga to* very long, at great length; tediously
雨 *naga-ame* a long rain
居 *naga-i* a long visit, overstaying
追 *naga-oi* a long pursuit
押 *nageshi* horizontal timbers in a house frame
所 *chōsho* one's forte, strong point; advantages
枕 *nagamakura* bed bolster
泣 *nagana(ki) suru* weep long
夜 *chōya* a long night
命 *chōmei* a long life, longevity
官 *chōkan* magistrate, chief, governor, president, secretary, administrator, director
者 *chōja* millionaire, rich person. *chōsha* one's superior, one's senior
事 *naga(i) koto* for a long time
波 *chōha* a long wave
波長 *chōhachō* long wave length
物 *chōbutsu* useless thing, white elephant
物語 *nagamonogatari* tedious speech
9 屋 *nagaya* tenement building, long apartment house
途 *chōto, nagamichi* a long way, a great distance
城 *chōjō* a long castle; the Great Wall of China; a great national leader
恨 *chōkon* long-standing hatred
持 *nagamo(chi)* oblong chest; durability, endurance
柄 *nagae* a long handle; spear
客 *nagakyaku* a guest who stays long
洋袴 *nagazubon* long trousers
音 *chōon* a long sound, a long vowel, long tone, dash
音階 *chōonkai* major scale; gamut
音符 *chōompu* macron, long-vowel mark
10 座 *chōza* a long stay (in someone's home)
逝 *chōsei suru* die, pass away
唄 *naga-uta* song accompanied by the samisen
旅 *nagatabi* a long trip
袖 *nagasode, chōshū* long-sleeved kimono or its wearer; courtiers
針 *chōshin* the long hand, the minute hand
剣 *chōken* a long sword; the minute hand
家 *nagaya*＝長屋 (see above-9)
脇差 *nagawakizashi* a long sword; professional gambler
時日 *chōjijitsu* a long period of time
時間 *chōjikan* a long time; long-playing
射程 *chōshatei* a long range
射程砲 *chōshateihō* long-range artillery
11 蛇 *chōda* a long snake; a long line, a long queue; a hero
符 *chōfu* dash (in telegraphy)
距離 *chōkyori* a long distance, a long range
距離電話 *chōkyori denwa* long-distance telephone
12 閑 *nodo(kana), nodo(yakana)* tranquil, mild, peaceful, balmy. *nodo(kesa)* tranquillity, serenity, calmness
堤 *chōtei* a long dike
湯 *nagayu* staying in the bath a long time
程 *chōtei* a great distance
軸 *chōjiku* major axis
葱 *naganegi* long onions
椅子 *naga-isu* couch, settee
須鯨 *nagasu kujira* razorback whale
短 *chōtan* length; long and short, merits and demerits. *naga(shi)-mijika(shi)* either too long or too short
短打 *chōtanda* long and short hits
期 *chōki* a long period
期予報 *chōki yohō* long-range forecasting
期戦 *chōkisen* prolonged war
13 煩 *nagawazura(i)* a long illness
話 *nagabanashi* a long talk, tedious talk
路 *nagamichi* a long road
靴 *nagagutsu* boots; high shoes, boots. *chōka* high shoes
寝 *nagane* a long sleep
嘆 *chōtan* a deep sigh
嘆息 *chōtansoku* a deep sigh
14 旗 *chōki* pennant
駆 *chōku suru* ride a long distance; pursue the enemy a long distance
歌 *chōka, naga-uta* a long epic poem
髪 *chōhatsu* long hair
髪賊 *Chōhatsuzoku* Taiping Rebellion
15 編 *chōhen* a long story; a long poem; a long film
調 *chōchō* major key
談 *chōdan* a long talk
談議 *nagadangi* tedious discourse, a long talk
歎 *chōtan* a deep sigh
歎息 *chōtansoku* a deep sigh
篇 *chōhen* a long story; a long poem; a long film
篇小説 *chōhen shōsetsu* a long fiction story
16 噸 *chōton* a long ton
17 講 *chōkō* a long talk, a long lecture
講説 *chōkōzetsu* a long talk, a long lecture
18 軀 *chōku* tall stature
鞭 *chōben* a long whip
19 襦袢 *nagajuban* long underwear
22 鬚鯨 *nagasu kujira* fin whale, common finback whale

6

肆 4939/F1531 Shi four. [聿]

RAD. 門 169

Mon or *kado* gate. As enclosure: *mongamae* or *kadogamae*. Nickname: Gate.

A 門 4940 F1972 MON gate, gateway; private school; class; counter for cannon. *kado* gate, door.

2 人 *monjin* disciple, pupil
3 口 *kadoguchi* gateway, entrance, front door
上 *monjō* above the gate
乞食 *kado kojiki* beggar at the gate
下 *monka* vicinity of the gate; disciple, pupil; discipleship
下生 *monkasei* disciple, pupil
4 火 *kadobi* funeral bonfire (at the gate), Lantern Festival fire
辺 *kadobe* gate, door; vicinity
内 *monnai* within the gate
戸 *monko* door; entrance; pedigree, lineage
戸張 *monko (o) ha(ru)* build a house; open an institute
戸開放主義 *monko-kaihō shugi* open-door policy
5 生 *monsei* pupil, disciple
田 *kadoda* rice field at the gates
付 *kadozu(ke)* strolling singer, street musician
札 *monsatsu, kado fuda* name plate
出 *kadode, kado-ide* departure, setting out, start
外 *mongai* outside the gate; outside one's specialty; another matter
外漢 *mongaikan* outsider, layman, someone outside the field
6 迎 *kadomuka(e)* standing at the gate waiting for a visitor
地 *monchi* pedigree, lineage
灯 *montō* gate light
守 *kadomori* gatekeeper
先 *kadosaki* front of a house; entrance; the door
毎 *kadogoto ni* at every gate, from door to door
行灯 *kado andon* advertising lantern
百姓 *kadobyakushō* gate attendant who farms nearby
7 弟 *montei* pupil, disciple
8 送 *kado-oku(ri)* seeing (someone) off at the gate
松 *kadomatsu* New Year's pine-and-bamboo decorations
臥 *kadobu(shi)* beggar lying at the gate
限 *mongen* closing time
並 *kadona(mi)* row of houses. *kadona(mi) ni* at every door, from door to door. *kadonara(bi)* row of houses; neighbors. *kadonara(be)* houses whose ridges are continuous
9 屋 *kadoya* gatehouse
柱 *monchū, mombashira* gatepost
院 *mon-in* the mother of an emperor who is not herself an empress
前 *monzen* before the gate
前市 *monzen-ichi* a gate crowded with callers
前払 *monzembara(i)* turning people away at the gate
前町 *monzemmachi* a temple town, a shrine town
前雀羅 *monzen-jakura* deserted, lonely
10 徒 *monto* believer, adherent; student
脇 *kado waki ni* at the gate
11 違 *kadochiga(i), kadochiga(e), kadotaga(i), kadotaga(e)* barking up the wrong tree; the wrong house or man; irrelevant; wrong
涼 *kadosuzu(mi)* cooling off at the gate
12 歯 *monshi* front teeth, incisors
扉 *mompi* leaves of a gate
開 *kadobira(ki)* opening a store
番 *momban* doorkeeper
13 詰 *kadozu(me)* threshold; house entrance
跡 *monzeki* priest prince; temple whose head is a prince; Honganji Temple
14 閥 *mombatsu* pedigree, lineage
構 *mongama(e), kadogama(e)* gate style; *mongama(e) no* with a stately gate. *mongama(e)* the radical 門
15 衛 *mon-ei* guard, porter, gatekeeper
標 *mompyō* name plate
16 謡 *kado utai* beggar singing at the gates
19 櫓 *kado yagura* gate watchtower
22 鑑 *monkan* gate pass

1

閂 4941 F1974 SAN. SEN. *kannuki* gate bar, gate bolt.

2

閃 4942 F1974 SEN. *hirame(kasu)* brandish, flash; display. *hirame(ku)* flash, flicker; flutter, wave.

6 光 *senkō* flash, glint
光写真 *senkō shashin* flashlight photography
光灯 *senkōtō* flashlight; photoflash, flash bulb
光電球 *senkō denkyū* flash bulb
光器 *senkōki* flash outfit
10 閃 *sensen(taru)* flashing, bright, glistening
12 渡 *hirame(ki)-wata(ru)* flash across, flash continually
15 輝 *senki* flash, glint

3

閊 4943 F1974 (国字) *tsuka(eru)* (see under 支 2039.0).

A 問 4944 F365 MON question, problem, subject, discussion. *to(u)* ask, question, inquire; accuse. *to*(*i*) question, inquiry. -*to*(*wazu*) without distinction, regardless of, irrespective. [口]

6 返 *to*(*i*)-*kae*(*su*) ask again

合 *to*(*i*)-*a*(*waseru*), *to*(*i*)-*a*(*wasu*) inquire of

9 屋 *ton-ya*, *toiya* wholesaler, forwarding agent

屋業 *ton-yagyō* wholesale business

11 掛 *to*(*i*)-*ka*(*keru*) inquire of; begin to ask

責 *monseki* reproof, censure

12 尋 *to*(*i*)-*tazu*(*neru*)=*tazu*(*neru*) (see under 尋 1585.0) and *to*(*u*) (see under 問 4944.0)

答 *mondō* questions and answers; catechism; discussion; dispute

13 詰 *to*(*i*)-*tsu*(*meru*) press for an answer, cross-examine

罪 *monzai* accusation, indictment

14 語 *to*(*wazu*)*gata*(*ri*) voluntary remark, unasked-for remark

15 質 *to*(*i*)-*tada*(*su*) inquire of, question

18 題 *mondai* problem, question, issue, case, matter; discussion; trouble

題化 *mondaika suru* become an issue

題外 *mondaigai* beside the question

題点 *mondaiten* the point at issue

B 閉 4945/F1974 HEI. *to*(*jiru*), *shi*(*meru*) shut, close. *to*(*zasu*) shut, close, lock, fasten; plunge (in grief).

3 口 *heikō suru* be dumbfounded, be stumped, be silent

4 込 *to*(*ji*)-*ko*(*meru*) lock up, shut in, confine, *ta*(*te*)-*ko*(*meru*) shut up (the house)

止機 *heishiki* circuit breaker; railway crossing gate

5 出 *shi*(*me*)-*da*(*su*) shut out, lock out

6 会 *heikai* adjournment, closing

7 尿 *heinyō* retention of urine

廷 *heitei* court adjournment

8 門 *heimon* closing the gate; house imprisonment

居 *heikyo suru* stay indoors

店 *heiten* closing the shop; going out of business

9 院 *hei-in* adjournment of congress

10 校 *heikō* closing a school

息 *heisoku suru* bate one's breath; be cowed into silence

12 場 *heijō* closing a place

13 塞 *to*(*ji*)-*fusa*(*geru*), close up, cover over. *heisoku* blockade

幕 *heimaku* falling of the curtain

業 *heigyō* closing shop or office

電路 *heidenro* closed circuit

16 館 *heikan suru* close the doors (of a hall)

18 鎖 *heisa* closing, closure, lockout

22 籠 *to*(*ji*)-*komo*(*ru*) confine oneself, remain indoors

—— 4 ——

閏 4946/F1976 閠 JUN intercalation; intercalary month; illegitimate throne. *urū* intercalation.

4 日 *junjitsu* leap day

月 *urūzuki*, *jungetsu* intercalary month

6 年 *urūdoshi*, *junnen* leap year; intercalary year

悶 4947/F717 MON. *moda*(*eru*) be in agony, be worried. [心]

6 死 *monshi* agonizing death

8 苦 *moda*(*e*)-*kuru*(*shimu*) writhe in pain

11 著 *monchaku* trouble; dispute

12 悶 *mommon*(*taru*) discontented

絶 *monzetsu suru* faint; fall in convulsions

着 *monchaku* trouble; dispute

B 閑 4948/F1977 KAN leisure.

2 人 *himajin*, *kanjin* man of leisure

3 子鳥 *kankodori* cuckoo

4 月 *kangetsu* farmers' quiet months

中 *kanchū* leisure time

文字 *kammoji*, *kammonji* idle word; leisurely writing

日 *kanjitsu* holiday

日月 *kanjitsugetsu* long period of leisure

5 田 *kanden* fallow rice field

古鳥 *kankodori* cuckoo

6 地 *kanchi* secluded place; retirement; easy post

宅 *kantaku* quiet home

7 言 *kangen* useless words

住 *kanjū* quiet home

吟 *kangin* leisurely reciting of poems

却 *kankyaku* negligence, oversight

8 居 *kankyo* leisurely life; quiet retreat

所 *kansho* quiet place. *kanjo* lavatory

官 *kankan* a post requiring little work

歩 *kampo* leisurely walk

事 *kanji* idleness

事業 *kanjigyō* work in leisure hours

9 客 *kankaku* person of leisure

10 庭 *kantei* quiet garden

11 寂 *kanjaku* quiet; tranquillity

窓 *kansō* a quiet window

12 閑 *himahima ni*, at one's leisure. *kankan* quiet, leisure, rolling quietly along (in a vehicle)

疎 *kanso na* quiet and isolated

散 *kansan* leisure; quiet; inactivity

雲 *kan-un* lazily floating clouds

13 暇 *kanka* leisure

雅 *kanga* refinement; quietude

話 *kanwa* quiet talk; gossip

14 語 *kango* idle talk

静 *kansei* quietness, tranquillity

15 談 *kandan* quiet conversation, idle talk

18 職 *kanshoku* an easy job; a leisurely task

A 間 4949/F1977 閒 KAN interval; space; between; among; discord; favorable opportunity. KEN six feet. *machiai* interval; between; medium; crossbred. *aida, awai* space, interval, gap; between, among; midway; on the way; distance; time, period; relationship. *ma* space, room; interval; pause; rest (in music); time; a while; leisure; luck; timing, harmony. *ma(monaku)* soon.

1 一髪 *kan-ippatsu* a hair's breadth

3 口 *maguchi* frontage, width

子 *ai(no)ko* Eurasian, mulatto; crossbreed, ⌊hybrid

4 手 *ai(no)te*=合手 383.4

欠 *kanketsu* intermittence; intermittent

尺 *mashaku* measurement; accounting

中 *-aidajū* during ⌈unwanted children

引 *mabi(ki)* thinning out (plants); killing

切 *magi(ri)* tacking (in sailing). *magi(ru)* tack; divide, partition

5 田 *kanden* fallow rice field

代 *madai* room rent

仕切 *majiki(ri)* partition, division

6 色 *kanshoku* intermediary colors

近 *majika* nearness, proximity. *majika(i)* near at hand

伐 *kambatsu* periodic thinning (of a forest)

合 *ma(ni)a(u)* be in time for; serve the purpose; can do without. *ma(ni)a(waseru)* make (something) do; get (something) ready. *ma(ni)a(wase)* makeshift, expedient. *ma-a(i)* interval ⌈rows

7 作 *kansaku* intercrop, crop planted between

判 *aiban* medium size (in printing)

男 *ma-otoko* adultery; adulterer

投詞 *kantōshi* interjection

抜 *ma(ga)nu(keru)* be stupid; be funny; be out of harmony. *manu(ke)* disharmony; stupidity; simpleton, moron. *manu(kesa)* stupidity

抜面 *manu(ke)zura* dumb look ⌈ing (face)

8 延 *mano(binoshita)* slow, dull, vacant-look-

性 *kansei no* asexual; having some characteristics of both parents

取 *mado(ri)* plan of the house, room

服 *aifuku* spring or fall wear ⌊arrangement

者 *kanja* spy

9 食 *kanshoku, aidagu(i)* eating between meals

柄 *aidagara* relation; relationship

怠 *madaru(i)*, *madaru(kkoi)* slow, dull,

竿 *kenzao* measuring rod ⌊tedious

奏曲 *kansōkyoku* interlude

点線 *kantensen* boundary line of crosses and dots on a map

10 紙 *aigami* sheets inserted to prevent smudg-

借 *maga(ri)* renting a room ⌊ing

借人 *magarinin* roomer

11 違 *machiga(u)*, *machiga(eru)* *vt* mistake. *machiga(tta)* wrong, mistaken. *machiga(e)*, *machiga(i)* mistake; fault, failure; indiscretion; dispute

道 *kandō* secret path, side road, short cut

脳 *kannō* interbrain ⌈conscious

悪 *ma(ga)waru(i)* be embarrassed, feel self-

断 *kandan* interruptions; intervals

断無 *kandanna(ki)* incessant, continuous

接 *kansetsu* indirect

接伝染 *kansetsu densen* indirect infection

接税 *kansetsuzei* indirect tax

接費 *kansetsuhi* overhead cost

接照明 *kansetsu shōmei* indirect lighting

接話法 *kansetsu wahō* indirect quotation

接選挙 *kanketsu senkyo* indirect election (e.g., via electors)

12 間 *mama* occasionally, frequently

遠 *madō ni* at long intervals

税 *kanzei* indirect tax

隔 *kankaku* space

着 *aigi* spring or fall wear

無 *ma(mo)na(ku)* soon, in a moment

然 *kanzen* subject to criticism

貸 *maga(shi)* renting a room

13 隙 *kangeki* gap, aperture, opening, space, interstice, crevice. *ma(gana)-suki(gana)* always, constantly ⌈at the eleventh hour

際 *magiwa ni* just before, on the verge of,

数 *kensū* number of *ken* in length. *makazu* number of rooms

歇 *kanketsu* intermittence; intermittent

歇泉 *kanketsusen* geyser; intermittent hot-water service (at hot springs)

歇温泉 *kanketsu onsen* geyser

歇熱 *kanketsu netsu* intermittent fever, ague

14 髪入 *kanhatsu (o) i(rezu)* in the twinkling

15 緩 *manuru(i)* slow, sluggish ⌊of an eye

16 積 *kenzumo(ri)* measuring land

諜 *kanchō* spy, secret agent

A 開 4950/F1975 KAI opening. *hira(ku)* open, unfold, unroll, uncover, unpack, untie, unseal; establish; clear (land); pioneer; clear the way; convene; enlighten (a country); bloom; differ, have a margin; widen (the space between). *hira(keru)* become civilized, become modernized; become sensible; be opened to traffic; feel relief; be open; grow, develop (a town). *a(keru)*, *a(ku)* (see under 明 2110.0). *a(karu)* *vi* open. *a(ita)* open; empty, vacant. *hira(keta)* open, clear, commodious; civilized, modernized; sociable. *hira(ki)* opening; cupboard; difference; margin; aperture; breaking up (of a meeting).

3 口 *kaikō* opening a speech

山 *kaizan, kaisan* (sect) founder; pioneer
4戸 *hira(ki)do* hinged door
方 *kaihō* extraction of roots (in math.)
化 *kaika* civilization, enlightenment
5田 *kaiden* making paddy fields
立 *kairyū, kairitsu* extraction of the cube
広 *a(ke)-hiro(geru)* open wide ⌊root
庁 *kaichō* opening a government office
札 *kaisatsu* opening of bids
平 *kaihei* extraction of the square root
市 *kaishi* opening a city (to commerce)
6地 *kaichi* opened-up land
帆 *kaihan suru* set sail
会 *kaikai* opening a meeting
会日 *kaikaibi* opening day
会中 *kaikaichū* during the session
会辞 *kaikai(no)ji* opening address
7局 *kaikyoku* opening a new telephone exchange or a new post office
廷 *kaitei* court session; trial
作 *kaisaku* opening up land and planting
坑 *kaikō* opening a mine
花 *kaika* flowering, blossoming
8門 *kaimon* opening of the gate
国 *kaikoku* founding of a country; opening of a country
店 *kaiten* opening of a new shop
始 *kaishi* commencement, inauguration
披 *kaihi suru* open (a letter)
明 *kaimei* civilization, enlightenment
函 *kaikan* emptying a mailbox
直 *hira(ki)-nao(ru)* become defiant, become serious; turn upon ⌈up land
拓 *kaitaku* clearing, reclamation, opening
拓者 *kaitakusha* cultivator; settler, colonist, pioneer
放 *kaihō suru, hira(ki)-hana(tsu)* open, throw open; leave open. *a(ke)-hana(su)* throw open, open wide. *a(kep)pana(shi) no* frank, openhearted; leaving (a door) wide open
放的 *kaihōteki* frank, candid, openhearted
放性結核 *kaihōsei kekkaku* active tuberculosis
放無用 *Kaihō muyō* Keep the Door Closed.
9通 *kaitsū* opening to traffic
城 *kaijō* capitulation (of a fort)
祖 *kaiso* (sect) founder; apostle (to the . . .); originator, author, inventor
院 *kai-in* opening congress; hospital open-
陣 *kaijin* breaking camp ⌊ing
削 *kaisaku* cutting thru (a road); digging a canal; clearing (land, for farming)
封 *kaifū suru* break the seal, open. *hira(ki)-fū, kaifū* unsealed letter ⌈lightenment
発 *kaihatsu* colonization; development; en-
巻 *kaikan* opening a book and reading; first part of a book
10進 *kaishin* (military) developments
悟 *kaigo* enlightenment, wisdom
陳 *kaichin suru* express (opinions). *kaichin*
校 *kaikō* opening a school ⌊statement
校式 *kaikōshiki* school opening ceremony
11運 *kaiun* better fortune
帳 *kaichō* exhibiting a Buddhist image; opening a gambling game
設 *kaisetsu* establishment, inauguration, opening; installation (of telephones)
窓 *hira(ki) mado* casement window
基 *kaiki* laying a foundation; founding;
渠 *kaikyo* open ditch ⌊founder
船渠 *kaisenkyo* tidal basin
眼 *kaigen, kaigan* enlightenment, spiritual awakening; opening the eyes (investing a new image with sacred qualities)
眼式 *kaigenshiki* ceremony of opening the eyes (of an image)
票 *kaihyō* counting the ballots
票所 *kaihyōjo* ballot-counting place
閉 *kaihei* opening and shutting; (electrical) make and break. *a(ke)ta(te)* opening and shutting
閉器 *kaiheiki* a make-and-break switch
閉機 *kaiheiki* circuit breaker; railway-
閉橋 *kaiheikyō* drawbridge ⌊crossing gate
12扉 *kaihi suru* open the door
場 *kaijō* opening
期 *kaiki* session (of congress)
港 *kaikō* opening a port; open port
港場 *kaikōjō* treaty port, open port
13催 *kaisai* holding (a meeting)
催中 *kaisaichū* in session
催地 *kaisaichi* site (of an exhibition)
路 *kairō* open circuit
幕 *kaimaku* rising of the curtain
障子 *hira(ki) shōji* casement translucent
電路 *kaidenro* open circuit ⌊doors
戦 *kaisen* outbreak of war
戦後 *kaisengo* after the opening of hostilities ⌈tilities
戦前 *kaisenzen* before the opening of hos-
業 *kaigyō* opening a business or a practice
業医 *kaigyōi* doctor in private practice
業届 *kaigyō todo(ke)* report of the opening of a business ⌈lecture
14演 *kaien* opening of a play; opening of a
綱 *hira(ki)zuna* ripcord
16橋 *kaikyō suru* open a new bridge
館 *kaikan* opening of a new hall
墾 *kaikon* cultivating new land
墾可能地 *kaikon-kanōchi* arable land
墾地 *kaikonchi* cultivated land

17講 *kaikō* opening of a lecture course
豁 *kaikatsu na* open (land); magnanimous
18襟 *kaikin* open-collared (shirt)
21闢 *kaibyaku* beginnings, creation, founding (of an empire)
28鑿 *kaisaku* clearing (land, for farming); cutting thru (a road); digging (a canal)

5

鬧 4951 F1979 F2120 鬧 Dō noisy.

閘 4952 F1979 Kō water gate, lock.
8門 *kōmon* lock gate (for ships)

6

閤 4953 F1980 Kō small side gate.

B 閥 4954 F1980 Batsu lineage, pedigree; clique; faction, clan, combine.
11族 *batsuzoku* clan, clique

鬨 4955 F1980 Kō. *toki* war cry.
7声 *toki (no) koe* war cry

閨 4956 F1980 Kei. *neya* bedroom.
4中 *keichū* bedroom; family life; harem
7秀 *keishū* accomplished woman
8門 *keimon* bedroom, family life
房 *keibō* bedroom; family life; harem
9室 *keishitsu* bedroom; harem; wife
怨 *keien* the ill-feeling of a divorcee; a woman's ill feeling
14閥 *keibatsu* nepotism

B 閣 4957 F1979 Kaku tower, tall building, palace; cabinet (of a government).
3下 *Kakka* Your Excellency
4内 *kakunai* within the cabinet
5外 *kakugai* outside the cabinet
令 *kakurei* cabinet order
10員 *kakuin* cabinet member
12筆 *kakuhitsu suru* conclude writing
14僚 *kakuryō* cabinet members
20議 *kakugi* cabinet meeting

A 関 4958 F1985 關 Kan barrier, gateway. *kan(suru)* related to, be connected with, concern, affect, involve, pertain to. *kaka(waru)* (see under 係 449.0). (*ni*) *kan(shite)* concerning. *kaka(wari)* relation, connection. *seki* barrier, checking station.

2八州 *Kanhasshū* the Eight Provinces of Kantō
3山 *seki (no) yama* one's utmost. *kanzan* the mountains around one's home; the mountains around a border station
与 *kan-yo* participation
ケ原 *Sekigahara* a decisive battle, a Waterloo
4木 *kangi* gate bar
心 *kanshin* concern, interest, regard
心事 *kanshinji* a matter of serious concern
5白 *kampaku* (ancient) chief adviser to the emperor; a domineering husband
市 *kanshi* border market town
6守 *sekimori* barrier keeper
8門 *kammon* barrier, gateway; Shimonoseki-Moji
所 *sekisho* barrier, checking station
知 *kanchi* concern
取 *sekitori* champion *sumō* wrestler
9連 *kanren* connection, relation, association
連事項 *kanren jikō* related matters
連質問 *kanren shitsumon* related question
係 *kankei* relation, connection, concern, participation; influence, effect; illicit relations. *kankei(naku)* regardless of
係代名詞 *kankei daimeishi* relative pronoun
係会社 *kankei gaisha* affiliated company
係当局 *kankei tōkyoku* the authorities concerned
係形容詞 *kankei keiyōshi* relative adjective
係者 *kankeisha* participant; interested party, the person concerned
係官庁 *kankei kanchō* authorities concerned
係副詞 *kankei fukushi* relative adverb
係湿度 *kankei shitsudo* relative humidity
10釜 *Kampu* Shimonoseki-Fusan
12税 *kanzei* customs, duty, tariff
税率 *kanzeiritsu* customs tariff
税障壁 *kanzei shōheki* tariff wall, customs barrier
13塞 *kansai* border fortification
節 *kansetsu* joint
節炎 *kansetsuen* arthritis
16頭 *kantō* turning point; parting of the ways; place of execution
17聯 *kanren*=関連 (see above-9)
25鑰 *kan-yaku* bolt and key; key (to the solution); clue (to the mystery)

A 聞 4959 F1525 Bun. Mon. *ki(ku)* hear, listen to; learn of; inquire; follow advice. *ki(kasu)*, *ki(kaseru)* inform; secure acquiescence; read to, play for, sing to; give the tune. *ki(koeru)* hear, be heard; sound, ring, seem; be well known; be reasonable. *ki(kareru)* be overheard; be tolerable; be fairly good. *ki(kitagaru)* be inquisitive, be curious. *ki(koenai)* be unreasonable, be cruel. *ki*(*koe*) reputation, fame, notoriety, publicity. *ki*(*koegashi*) *ni* within hearing; wanting to be heard. [耳]

2 入 *ki*(*ki*)-*i*(*reru*) comply with, grant (a request), accept (a resignation), assent to. *ki*(*ki*)-*i*(*ru*) listen attentively

3 及 *ki*(*ki*)-*oyo*(*bu*) learn of, hear about. *ki*(*ki*)-*oyo*(*bi*) hearsay

下手 *ki*(*ki*)*beta na hito* a poor listener

上手 *ki*(*ki*)*jōzu na hito* a good listener

4 手 *ki*(*ki*)*te* listener, audience

方 *ki*(*ki*)*kata* way of listening

込 *ki*(*ki*)-*ko*(*mu*) be informed of. *kikiko*(*mi*) tip, hearsay, information

切 *ki*(*ki*)-*ki*(*ru*) learn from hearing just once

分 *ki*(*ki*)-*wa*(*keru*) be reasonable, understand. *ki*(*ki*)*wa*(*ke*) reasonableness; listening to reason

分無 *ki*(*ki*)*wa*(*ke*)*na*(*i*) helpless, innocent, naïve ⌈hearing

5 旧 *ki*(*ki*)-*fu*(*ru*), *ki*(*ki*)-*furu*(*su*) get tired of

付 *ki*(*ki*)-*tsu*(*keru*) hear (the sound of); learn of, overhear, get wind of

外 *ki*(*ki*)-*hazu*(*su*) miss hearing ⌈drink

召 *ki*(*koshi*)-*me*(*su*) hear, learn of; take a

古 *ki*(*ki*)*furu*(*shita*) timeworn, hackneyed

出 *ki*(*ki*)-*da*(*su*), *ki*(*ki*)-*ida*(*su*) find out, hear

巧者 *ki*(*ki*)*gōsha* a good listener

6 尽 *ki*(*ki*)-*tsuku*(*su*) hear all about

気 *ki*(*kanu*) *ki* determination to win

返 *ki*(*ki*)-*kae*(*su*) be told again, inquire again ⌈*kikitsuta*(*e*) hearsay

伝 *ki*(*ki*)-*tsuta*(*eru*) hear at second hand.

交 *ki*(*ki*)-*ka*(*wasu*) hear here and there, hear among ourselves ⌈*a*(*wase*) inquiry

合 *ki*(*ki*)-*a*(*waseru*) inquire about. *ki*(*ki*)-

耳 *ki*(*ki*)*mimi* attentive ears

耳立 *ki*(*ki*)*mimi* (*o*) *ta*(*teru*) listen carefully

7 見 *ki*(*ki*)-*mi*(*ru*) hear and see

辛 *ki*(*ki*)*zura*(*i*) hard to hear ⌈complaints

役 *ki*(*ki*)*yaku* official who hears people's

糺 *ki*(*ki*)-*tada*(*su*) ascertain, verify

忘 *ki*(*ki*)-*wasu*(*reru*) forget what one hears; forget to inquire about (something)

忌 *ki*(*ki*)*i*(*mi*) mourning for distant relatives

8 届 *ki*(*ki*)-*todo*(*keru*) grant (a request); hear; accept (a resignation), accede to, comply with; acknowledge

始 *ki*(*ki*)-*haji*(*meru*) begin to hear. *ki*(*ki*)-*haji*(*me*) something heard for the first time ⌈listen for

所 *ki*(*ki*)*dokoro*, *ki*(*ki*)*doko* essential point to

物 *ki*(*ki*)*mono* news, highlights ⌈informed of

知 *bunchi suru*, *ki*(*ki*)-*shi*(*ru*) hear of, be

直 *ki*(*ki*)-*nao*(*su*) inquire again ⌈hears

定 *ki*(*ki*)-*sada*(*meru*) check on what one

苦 *ki*(*ki*)*guru*(*shii*) offensive to the ear, hard to grasp the meaning of; scandalous, objectionable ⌈rebuke

咎 *ki*(*ki*)-*toga*(*meru*) challenge (a speaker);

学 *ki*(*ki*)*gaku* learn by being with someone

事 *ki*(*ki*)*goto* something worth listening to

取 *ki*(*ki*)-*to*(*ru*) catch, follow, understand. *ki*(*ki*)*to*(*ri*) hearing, audition

取難 *ki*(*ki*)*to*(*ri*)*gata*(*i*) hard to understand

9 通 *ki*(*ki*)-*tō*(*su*) listen clear thru

洩 *ki*(*ki*)-*mo*(*rasu*) miss hearing. *ki*(*ki*)-*mo*(*re*) something one missed hearing

栄 *ki*(*ki*)*ba*(*e*) *no aru* worth listening to

10 従 *ki*(*ki*)-*shitaga*(*u*) hearken unto

挿 *ki*(*ki*)-*hasa*(*mu*) listen and retain

残 *ki*(*ki*)-*noko*(*su*) fail to hear

流 *ki*(*ki*)-*naga*(*su*) pay no attention to

酒 *ki*(*ki*)*zake* tasting wine

納 *kikiosa*(*me*) the last time we heard (him)

差 *ki*(*ki*)-*sa*(*su*) listen only halfway thru

書 *kikiga*(*ki*) verbatim notes

留 *ki*(*ki*)-*todo*(*meru*) listen carefully ⌈ing

11 過 *ki*(*ki*)-*sugo*(*su*) listen without remember-

違 *ki*(*ki*)-*chiga*(*eru*), *ki*(*ki*)-*chiga*(*u*) mishear, be misinformed. *ki*(*ki*)*chiga*(*i*), *ki*(*ki*)*chiga*(*e*), *kikitaga*(*i*), *kikitaga*(*e*) hearing incorrectly

達 *buntatsu* fame, reputation

惚 *ki*(*ki*)-*ho*(*reru*) listen with rapt interest

捨 *ki*(*ki*)-*su*(*teru*) ignore, overlook ⌈hear

悪 *ki*(*ki*)*niku*(*i*) awkward to ask; hard to

12 遁 *ki*(*ki*)-*ni*(*geru*) listen and run off without paying the lecture fee

渡 *ki*(*koe*)-*wata*(*ru*) be noised abroad. *ki*(*ki*)-*wata*(*su*), *ki*(*ki*)-*wata*(*ru*) keep hearing, hear continually

善 *ki*(*ki*)*yo*(*i*) good to hear

落 *ki*(*ki*)-*o*(*tosu*) miss hearing ⌈hears

惑 *ki*(*ki*)-*mado*(*u*) be perplexed by what one

覚 *ki*(*ki*)-*obo*(*eru*) learn by ear

13 損 *ki*(*ki*)-*sokona*(*u*) mishear. *ki*(*ki*)*zon* hearing about something to one's disadvantage ⌈hears

煩 *ki*(*ki*)-*wazura*(*u*) be pained by what one

継 *ki*(*ki*)-*tsu*(*gu*) keep on listening; hear from a line of informants

隠 *ki*(*ki*)-*kaku*(*su*) pretend not to listen

飽 *ki*(*ki*)-*a*(*kiru*) be tired of, get tired of

馴 *ki*(*ki*)-*na*(*reru*) get used to hearing

置 *ki*(*ki*)-*o*(*ku*) hear, keep in mind

業 *ki*(*ki*)*waza* the business of listening

寝入 *ki*(*ki*)*ne-i*(*ri*) listening and falling

14 徳 *ki*(*ki*)*doku* worthwhile hearing ⌊asleep

慣 *ki*(*ki*)-*na*(*reru*) get used to hearing

漏 *ki*(*ki*)-*mo*(*rasu*) miss hearing. *ki*(*ki*)-*mo*(*re*) something one missed hearing

[15]澄 *ki(ki)-su(masu)* listen attentively
蕩 *ki(ki)-to(reru)* be completely taken up by what one hears
[16]積 *ki(ki)-tsumo(ru)* listen clear thru
質 *ki(ki)-tada(su)* ascertain, verify
[18]噛 *ki(ki)-kaji(ru)* have a smattering of knowledge
[21]囃 *ki(ki)-haya(su)* hear and praise

7

閭 4960/F1981 Ryo rural area.

B 閲 4961/F1981 閱 Etsu inspection, revision. *es(suru)* review, revise. *kemi(suru)* read, look over; examine; pass. elapse.
[7]兵 *eppei* parade, review, inspection of troops
兵式 *eppeishiki* troop review
[14]歴 *etsureki* career, personal history
読 *etsudoku* reading, perusal
[16]覧 *etsuran* perusal, inspection, reading
覧者 *etsuransha* reader, visitor
覧室 *etsuranshitsu* reading room

8

閾 4962/F1982 Iki threshold.

閹 4963/F1982 En eunuch.
[2]人 *enjin* eunuch

閼 4964/F1982 閼 A obstruct, conceal; (used phonetically).
[7]伽 *aka* Buddhist water offering
伽桶 *aka oke* Buddhist water-offering receptacle

閻 閻 4965/F1982 En town.
[21]魔 *Emma* King of Hades
魔帳 *emmachō* teacher's black list

9

闊 4966/F1983 See 濶 2721.

闋 4967/F1983 Ketsu rest.

闌 4968/F1983 Ran. *ta(keru)* rise high, be well up; be well along, be well advanced. *takenawa* height of; full swing; the thick of.
[3]干 *rankan* railing, balustrade

闇 4969/F1982 An. *kura(garu)* get dark, get gloomy. *yami* darkness; grief, gloom; disorder, black market. *kura(i)* (see under 暗 2154.0).
[5]打 *yamiu(chi)* assassination, foul murder
仕合 *yamijiai* fighting in the dark; fighting an unknown assailant
市 *yami ichi* black market
市場 *yami ichiba* black market
[6]合 *angō* coincidence
行為 *yami kōi* illegal act, black-market dealings
[7]売 *yamiu(ri)* black-market selling
売買 *yami baibai* black-market dealing
[8]夜 *yamiyo, an-ya* dark night
取引 *yami torihiki* black-market dealings, undercover dealings
価格 *yami kakaku* black-market price
物資 *yami busshi* black-market goods
金融 *yami kin-yū* illegal lending
[9]屋 *yamiya* black marketeer
相場 *yami sōba* black-market price
[10]値 *yamine* black-market price
冥 *ammei* darkness
弱 *anjaku* weak-mindedness
[11]黒 *ankoku* darkness
商人 *yami shōnin* black marketeer
[12]買 *yamiga(i)* black-market purchasing
雲 *yamikumo ni* thoughtlessly, haphazardly, at random
[13]路 *yamiji* dark road
[17]闇 *yamiyami* suddenly, without one's knowledge; easily. *an-an* darkness; stillness in the depths

10

闔 4970/F1984 Kō doors.
[8]国 *kōkoku* the whole country

闖 4971/F1985 Chin inquire about.
[2]入 *chinnyū* intrusion, trespassing, raiding
入者 *chinnyūsha* intruder, trespasser, raider

闕 4972/F1984 Ketsu imperial palace. *ka(keru)* (see under 欠 2412.0).
[3]下 *kekka* emperor; palace gate
[4]文 *ketsubun* missing part (of a manuscript)
[5]本 *keppon* missing volume
[6]如 *ketsujo* lack, deficiency, privation
字 *ketsuji*＝欠字 2412.6
[8]所 *kessho* confiscation of an estate
官 *kekkan* vacant post
[10]席 *kesseki* absence, default
員 *ketsu-in* vacancy, vacant position, opening

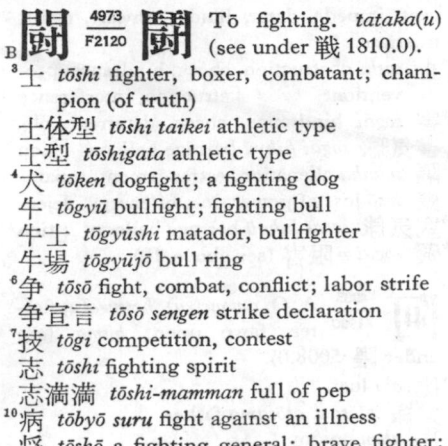

B 鬪 4973/F2120 鬭 Tō fighting. *tataka(u)* (see under 戦 1810.0).

[3]士 *tōshi* fighter, boxer, combatant; champion (of truth)
士体型 *tōshi taikei* athletic type
士型 *tōshigata* athletic type
[4]犬 *tōken* dogfight; a fighting dog
牛 *tōgyū* bullfight; fighting bull
牛士 *tōgyūshi* matador, bullfighter
牛場 *tōgyūjō* bull ring
[6]争 *tōsō* fight, combat, conflict; labor strife
争宣言 *tōsō sengen* strike declaration
[7]技 *tōgi* competition, contest
志 *tōshi* fighting spirit
志満満 *tōshi-mamman* full of pep
[10]病 *tōbyō suru* fight against an illness
将 *tōshō* a fighting general; brave fighter; champion of a principle
[11]魚 *tōgyo* fighting fish
[14]歌 *tōka* poetry contest
魂 *tōkon* fighting spirit
[19]鶏 *tōkei* cockfight; cockfighting; fighting cock

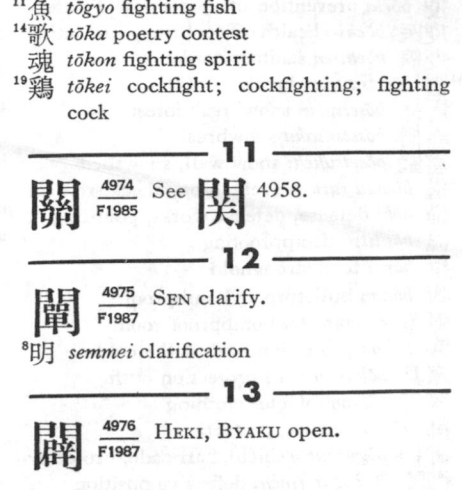

— 11 —

鬮 4974/F1985 See 閧 4958.

— 12 —

闡 4975/F1987 Sen clarify.

[8]明 *semmei* clarification

— 13 —

闢 4976/F1987 Heki, Byaku open.

RAD. 阜 170

Kozato small village (i.e., in contradistinction to Rads. 163 & 166). Except for the radical character itself, it is always used at the left in the modified form 阝 (2 strokes) *kozato-hen*. Nickname: Left Village.

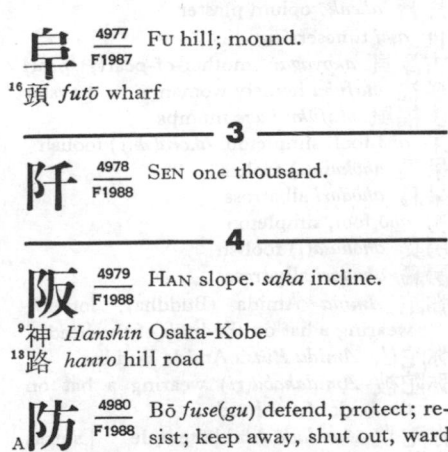

阜 4977/F1987 Fu hill; mound.

[16]頭 *futō* wharf

— 3 —

阡 4978/F1988 Sen one thousand.

— 4 —

阪 4979/F1988 Han slope. *saka* incline.

[9]神 *Hanshin* Osaka-Kobe
[13]路 *hanro* hill road

A 防 4980/F1988 Bō *fuse(gu)* defend, protect; resist; keep away, shut out, ward off; prevent.

[2]人 *sakimori* ancient military guards
[4]手 *fuse(gi)te* defender
止 *bōshi* prevention
水 *bōsui* waterproof, watertight; holding back flood waters
水布 *bōsuifu* waterproof cloth, oilskin, tarpaulin
水剤 *bōsuizai* waterproofing material
水帽 *bōsuibō* tarpaulin
水着 *bōsuigi* raincoat
水隔室 *bōsui kakushitsu* watertight compartment
火 *bōka* fire prevention, fire fighting, fireproof
火戸 *bōkado* fire door
火金庫 *bōka kinko* fireproof safe
火栓 *bōkasen* fire hydrant
火剤 *bōkazai* fireproof stuff
火樹 *bokaju* firebreak planting
火壁 *bōkaheki* fire wall
[5]圧 *bōatsu* prevention
犯 *bōhan* crime prevention
氷 *bōhyō* deicing
[6]守 *bōshu* defense; defensive
虫剤 *bōchūzai* insecticide
共 *bōkyō* anti-Communist
共協定 *Bōkyō Kyōtei* Anti-Comintern Pact
[7]材 *bōzai* protecting boom; bar (to a harbor entrance)
[8]波堤 *bōhatei* breakwater
毒 *bōdoku* gasproof
毒面 *bōdokumen* gas mask
空 *bōkū* air defense
空対策 *bōkū taisaku* air-raid precautions
空壕 *bōkūgō* air-raid shelter
空警報 *bōkū keihō* air-raid alarm
[9]音 *bōon* soundproof; soundproofing
音装置 *bōon sōchi* soundproofing
風 *bōfū* wind protection
風林 *bōfūrin* windbreak
砂林 *bōsarin* trees holding drifting sand
砂堤 *bōsatei* sand dike
臭 *bōshū* deodorization
臭剤 *bōshūzai* deodorant, deodorizer

8 金長門【阜 5阝】隶隹雨青非

疫 *bōeki* prevention of epidemics, disinfection, quarantine
疫医 *bōeki-i* health officer
疫線 *bōekisen* sanitary cordon
11雪 *bōsetsu* snowbreak
雪林 *bōsetsurin* snowbreak forest
雪柵 *bōsetsusaku* snowbreak
雪壁 *bōsetsuheki* snow wall, snowshed
12遏 *bōatsu suru* prevent, stop, check, repress
備 *bōbi* defense, defense works, guarding
湿 *bōshitsu* dampproofing
塁 *bōrui* fort, stronghold
弾 *bōdan* bulletproof; bombproof
弾室 *bōdanshitsu* bombproof room
寒 *bōkan* protection against the cold
寒具 *bōkangu* cold-protection outfit
寒着 *bōkangi* winter clothing
御 *bōgyo* defense, protection
御物 *bōgyobutsu* shield, barricade, protector
御陣地 *bōgyo jinchi* defensive position
御線 *bōgyosen* defense line
13楯 *bōjun* gun shield
戦 *bōsen* defensive war
塞 *bōsai* roadblock, barricade
14塵 *bōjin* dustproof
腐 *bōfu* preservation; embalmment; antisepsis
腐的 *bōfuteki* antiseptic, aseptic
腐剤 *bōfuzai* antiseptic; preservative
15蝕剤 *bōshokuzai* anticorrosive
潮門 *bōchōmon* tide gate
潮林 *bōchōrin* forest controlling tidewater
衛 *bōei* defense, protection
衛庁 *Bōeichō* Defense Agency
衛隊 *bōeitai* defense corps, defense force
16諜 *bōchō* antiespionage, counterintelligence
壁 *bōheki* barrier, bulwark, wall of defense
17禦 *bōgyo* defense, protection
禦物 *bōgyobutsu* shield, barricade, protector
禦陣地 *bōgyo jinchi* defensive position
禦戦 *bōgyosen* defensive war
禦線 *bōgyosen* defense line
20護 *bōgo* protection, custody
護団 *bōgodan* air-raid defense corps

5

阼 4981 F1989 So eastern steps; throne.

陀 4982 F1991 Ta, Da steep.

附 B 4983 F1991 Fu. (See under 付 363 for compounds). *tsu(ku)*, *tsu(keru)*, *tsu(ketari)* (see under 付 363.0).

阻 B 4984 F1989 So separate from; prevent, stop. *haba(mu)* obstruct, prevent, impede, deter, hinder, thwart, resist, frustrate.
4止 *soshi* obstruction, check, hindrance, prevention
10害 *sogai* hindrance, check, deterrent, obstruction, interference
害気球 *sogai kikyū* barrage balloon
12隔 *sokaku* alienation, estrangement, separation
喪 *sosō* loss of power, loss of energy, dejection
13塞気球 *sosai kikyū* barrage balloon
19礙 *sogai*＝阻害 (see above-10)

阿 4985 F1990 A. O. *omone(ru)*, *hetsura(u)* flatter, fawn upon. *kuma* (see under 隈 5008.0).
4比 *abi* loon
父様 *otōsan, otōsama* father
片 *ahen* opium
片中毒 *ahen chūdoku* opium poisoning
片吸飲 *ahen kyūin* opium smoking
片吸飲者 *ahen kyūinsha* opium smoker
片売買 *ahembaibai* opium traffic
片酒 *ahenshu* opium wine
片剤 *ahenzai* opiate
片常用 *ahen jōyō* opium habit
片窟 *ahenkutsu* opium den
片戦争 *Ahen Sensō* Opium War
片膏 *ahenkō* opium plaster
5世 *asei* timeserving
古屋貝 *akoyagai* mother-of-pearl; pearl oyster
6多福 *otafuku* homely woman
多福風 *otafuku kaze* mumps
7呆 *ahō* fool, simpleton. *ahora(shii)* foolish
呆臭 *ahōkusa(i)* foolish
呆鳥 *ahōdori* albatross
8房 *ahō* fool, simpleton
房臭 *ahōkusa(i)* foolish
房鳥 *ahōdori* albatross
弥陀 *Amida* Amida (Buddha); lottery; wearing a hat on the back of the head
弥陀仏 *Amida Butsu* Amida Buddha
弥陀被 *Amidakabu(ri)* wearing a hat on the back of the head
弥陀堂 *Amidadō* Amida temple
弥陀経 *Amidakyō* one of the Pure Land sutras
9娜 *ada* charm, flirtation. *ada(ppoi)* flirtatious, bewitching
娜者 *adamono* bewitching woman
11亀 *okame* homely woman, fat-woman's mask
婆擦 *abazure* wickedness; wicked woman
13媽 *ama* amah, nurse
14漕 *akogi* frequency; insatiableness; cruelty
鼻叫喚 *abikyōkan* two of Buddhism's hells
15諛 *ayu* flattery, adulation
16諛 *ayu* flattery
19羅漢 *arakan* arhat
蘭陀 *Oranda* Holland

— 6 —

陋 4986/F1992 RŌ narrowness; meanness, humbleness.
6宅 *rōtaku* squalid home; my home
劣 *rōretsu* baseness, meanness
7見 *rōken* narrow view; my humble opinion
8居 *rōkyo* hovel
拙 *rōsetsu na* vulgar, low-class
9風 *rōfū* evil custom, abuse
屋 *rōoku* squalid hut, hovel; my humble cottage
巷 *rōkō* narrow alley; slums
11習 *rōshū* evil custom, abuse
12策 *rōsaku* poor plan

A **限** 4987/F1993 GEN. *kagi(ru)* limit, restrict, confine. *kagi(ri)* limit(s); as far as possible, as much as possible, to the best of (one's ability). *(ni) kagi(tte)* of all (days, persons, etc.); alone. *-kagi(ri)* insofar as; this time only. *-kiri* (June) delivery.
5外 *gengai* outside the limits
外発行 *gengai hakkō* excess (currency) issue
7局 *genkyoku* limiting
8限 *girigiri* extreme limit
定 *gentei* limitation, qualification, definition, determination
定版 *genteiban* limited edition
9界 *genkai* boundary, limit, limits, bounds
度 *gendo* limit, limits, limitation
度内 *gendonai* within the limits
11産 *gensan* production limit
12無 *kagi(ri)na(i)* eternal, unlimited, endless. *kagi(ri)na(ku)* without end, exceedingly

— 7 —

A **陛** 4988/F1994 HEI *kizahashi* steps (of the throne).
3下 *Heika* His Majesty or Her

陞 4989/F1994 SHŌ go up, climb, rise.
9叙 *shōjo* promotion, advancement
10進 *shōshin* promotion, advancement

B **陥** 4990/F2000 **陷** KAN. *ochi-i(ru)* fall into, get into, slide into, lapse into; cave in, sink; fall (a fort). *otoshi-i(reru)* ensnare, tempt.
2入 *kannyū suru* subside, collapse, cave in
7没 *kambotsu* a cave-in; subsidence
9穽 *kansei* trap, pitfall
12落 *kanraku* fall, sinking, a cave-in; surrender; giving in

A **院** 4991/F1994 IN mansion; temple; palace; hospital; school; institution; congress; ex-emperor.
4内 *innai* inside congress; within the institution
内幹事 *innai kanji* whip, floor leader
内総務 *innai sōmu* floor leader, chief whip
5庁 *inchō, in(no)chō* retired emperor's office
主 *inshu* head priest of a temple; owner of a hospital
本 *impon* drama; playbook
外 *ingai* outside congress; nonparliamentary; outside the institution
外団 *ingaidan* lobbying group
外者 *ingaisha* lobbyist; persons outside congress
8長 *inchō* head of a hospital, court, or school
9政 *insei* government by cloistered emperors
宣 *inzen* decree of a cloistered emperor
11務 *immu* the business of the institution
20議 *in-gi* decision of congress

B **陣** 4992/F1995 JIN battle array, ranks; camp; position. *jin(suru)* set up (an army) camp.
4中 *jinchū ni* in the field, in camp
太鼓 *jindaiko* war drum
5立 *jinda(te)* battle array
払 *jimbara(i)* breaking up camp and withdrawing
6伍 *jingo* the ranks of the army
列 *jinretsu* arrangement of the camp; encampment
羽織 *jimbaori* coat worn over the armor; coat of arms
地 *jinchi* encampment; position
地戦 *jinchisen* position or stabilized warfare
7没 *jimbotsu* death in action
形 *jinkei* battle array
8門 *jimmon* camp gate
所 *jinsho* encampment
歿 *jimbotsu* death in action
法 *jimpō* battle array
取 *jindo(ru)* encamp, take up a position. *jindo(ri)* battle array; playing war
9風 *jimpū* squall, gust
屋 *jin-ya* encampment
後 *jingo* the rear of the army
10容 *jin-yō* battle array
11笠 *jingasa* (ancient) soldier's helmet; rank and file (of a party)
12痛 *jintsū* labor pains
備 *jinzona(e)* setting up camp
営 *jin-ei* camp; barracks
替 *jinga(e)* moving camp
13幕 *jimmaku* camp enclosure
16頭 *jintō* the head of an army; the field of battle
頭指揮 *jintō shiki* a commander personally leading his army into battle

A **除** 4993/F1995 JI. JO division (in math.). *jo(suru)* divide (in math.); exclude. *nozo(ku)* remove, abolish, cancel; exclude, except. *no(keru)* (see under 退 4684.0). *no-*

zo(*ite*), *nozo*(*ite wa*) except, exclusive of.
-*yoke* protection, shelter, charm.
4毛剤 *jomōzai* depilatory
5斥 *joseki suru* exclude, expel, reject
去 *nozo*(*ki*)-*sa*(*ru*) remove, take away. *jokyo* removal, exclusion
外 *jogai* exclusion, exception
外例 *jogairei* exceptional case
6行 *jokō* going slowly
号 *jogō* sign of division
名 *jomei* disfellowshipping, expulsion, dropping a name, excommunication ⌈mum
虫菊 *jochūgiku* the vermifuge chrysanthe-
7役 *joeki* exemption from military service
8法 *johō* division (in math.)
物 *no*(*ke*)*mono* outcast
服 *jofuku* going out of mourning
者 *no*(*ke*)*mono* outcast
夜 *joya* New Year's Eve
夜祭 *Joyasai* Shinto New Year's Eve ceremony ⌈bells
夜鐘 *joya* (*no*) *kane* New Year's midnight
9除 *jojo ni*, *sorosoro* gradually, steadily,
草 *josō* weeding ⌊slowly
草器 *josōki* weeder
11隊 *jotai* military discharge
隊兵 *jotaihei* discharged soldier
雪 *josetsu* snow removal ⌈plow
雪機関車 *josetsu kikansha* railway snow-
13幕式 *jomakushiki* unveiling (ceremony)
14酵 *jokō ni* unleavened
酵祭 *jokōsai* feast of unleavened bread
17霜 *josō* defrosting, deicing
20籍 *joseki suru* remove a name, expel, denationalize; decommission (warships)

B **降** 4994/F1992 Kō going down; surrender. *fu*(*ru*) fall, drop, come down (rain, etc.). *kuda*(*su*), *o*(*riru*), *o*(*rosu*) (see under 下 9.0). *kuda*(*ru*) surrender. *kuda*(*su*), *fu*(*rasu*) make it rain. *kuda*(*tte*) on down; as for me (humble).
2人 *kōjin* prisoner of war ⌈station)
3口 *o*(*ri*)*kuchi*, *o*(*ri*)*guchi* way out (of a
下 *kōka* fall, descent; losing altitude; outpouring; (plane) landing; (atmospheric) depression
下部隊 *kōka butai* parachute troops
4止 *fu*(*ri*)-*ya*(*mu*) stop raining or snowing
込 *fu*(*ri*)-*ko*(*mu*) rain in on; shut people in
水 *kōsui* precipitation ⌊by raining
水量 *kōsuiryō* precipitation
5出 *fu*(*ri*)-*da*(*su*) begin to rain or snow
6而 *kudatte* as for me (humble)
灰 *kōkai* falling ash
伏 *kōfuku* surrender, submission
伏文書 *kōfuku bunsho* instrument of surrender ⌈render
伏宣言 *kōfuku sengen* instrument of sur-
伏旗 *kōfukuki* white surrender flag
7車 *kōsha* alighting
車口 *kōshaguchi* way out, station exit
8明 *fu*(*ri*)-*a*(*kasu*) rain all night
注 *fu*(*ri*)-*soso*(*gu*) rain on (something)
服 *kōfuku* surrender, submission
参 *kōsan* surrender; giving in; being non-
雨 *kōu* rain, rainfall ⌊plussed
雨日 *kōujitsu* rainy day
雨図 *kōuzu* rain chart, rain map
雨期 *kōuki* rainy season
雨量 *kōuryō* amount of precipitation
9通 *fu*(*ri*)-*dō*(*su*) rain continuously
神術 *kōshinjutsu* spiritism, spiritualism, necromancy
10将 *kōshō* surrendered commander
11掛 *fu*(*ri*)-*ka*(*karu*) fall on; befall, happen to; hang over, overhang; impend
雪 *kōsetsu* snow; a snowfall
12勝 *fu*(*ri*)*ga*(*chi*) *na* rainy, wet
等 *kōtō* demotion
落 *fu*(*ri*)-*o*(*chiru*) to rain, to fall
着装置 *kōchaku sōchi* landing gear ⌈moner
13嫁 *kōka* marriage of a princess to a com-
続 *fu*(*ri*)-*tsuzu*(*ku*) rain or snow continu-
雹 *kōhyō* hailstorm ⌊ously
14旗 *kōki* lowering the flag; white surrender
15誕 *kōtan* birth, nativity ⌊flag
誕祭 *kōtansai* birthday celebration; Christ-
16壇 *kōdan suru* leave the rostrum ⌊mas
頻 *fu*(*ri*)-*shiki*(*ru*) rain or snow incessantly
17濡 *fu*(*ri*)-*sobo*(*tsu*) get soaked in a rain
臨 *kōrin* advent, descent
霜 *kōsō* a frost
18職 *kōshoku* demotion ⌈from above
20懸 *fu*(*ri*)-*ka*(*karu*) fall down (on something)
22籠 *fu*(*ri*)-*ko*(*merareru*) be kept in by rain

8

陥 4995/F2000 See 陷 4990.

陲 4996/F1998 Sui boundary.

陬 4997/F1996 Sū corner.
12遠 *sūen* deep rural area

B **陵** 4998/F1998 Ryō *misasagi* imperial tomb.
10辱 *ryōjoku* insult; outrage, rape
11域 *ryōiki* imperial tomb precincts

13墓 *ryōbo* imperial tomb
15駕 *ryōga suru* excel, surpass, outdo

B 隆 4999/F2002 隆 Ryū high; noble; prosperity.
6肉 *ryūniku* hunch; hump (as on camels)
8昌 *ryūshō* energy, vitality; prosperity
10起 *ryūki* protuberance, bulging, upheaval, elevation 「brawny
隆 *ryūryū(taru)* prosperous, thriving;
11運 *ryūun* prosperity, good fortune
盛 *ryūsei* prosperity
12替 *ryūtai, ryūtei* prosperity and decline
14鼻術 *ryūbijutsu* nasal plastic surgery
16興 *ryūkō* continued prosperity

A 険 5000/F2007 險 嶮 Ken inaccessible place, impregnable pass, strategic position; steep place; sharp (eyes); sinister (look). *kewa(shii)* steep;
7坂 *kenhan* steep hill ⌊severe, angry.
阻 *kenso* steepness; precipice
呑 *kennon na* dangerous, unsafe, unsteady
8固 *kengo* strong defenses
岨 *kenso* steepness; precipice
所 *kensho* steep place
9恃 *ken (o) tano(mu)* rely on strong fortifica-
相 *kensō* uncanny look ⌊tions
要 *ken-yō no* strategic
10峻 *kenshun* steepness, precipice
11悪 *ken-aku na* dangerous; inclement; serious, gloomy
12隘 *ken-ai* steep and narrow place
13路 *kenro* steep path
塞 *kensai* fort built on a precipice
18難 *kennan* steep, dangerous place; danger

B 陳 5001/F1998 Chin. *no(beru), chin(zuru), chin(jiru)* state, relate, explain. *hineku(reru)* get warped, become distorted. *hine* old grain; old goods; precocity.
5皮 *chimpi* dried orange peel
弁 *chimben* explanation, defense, justification
6列 *chinretsu* exhibition, display, show
列会 *chinretsukai* exhibition
列窓 *chinretsu mado* show window, store
列棚 *chinretsudana* showcase ⌊window
列館 *chinretsukan* museum
7述 *chinjutsu* statement, declaration
述書 *chinjutsusho* statement, declaration
10套 *chintō=chimpu* 陳腐 (see below–14)
11情 *chinjō* petition, appeal
情書 *chinjōsho* petition, memorial
14腐 *chimpu na* trite, commonplace, worn out, old-fashioned, out-of-date, stereotyped
17謝 *chinsha* apology

B 陪 5002/F1996 陪 Bai follow, accompany, attend on.
6臣 *baishin* samurai's retainer
8侍 *baiji* attendance on the nobility
9音 *baion* overtone; harmonics
食 *baishoku* dining with a superior
乗 *baijō* riding with a superior
10従 *baijū suru* wait upon, accompany
席 *baiseki* sitting with a superior
席判事 *baiseki hanji* associate judge
15賓 *baihin* accompanying guest
審 *baishin* jury
審公判 *baishin kōhan* trial by jury
審制度 *baishin seido* jury system
審室 *baishinshitsu* jury room
審員 *baishin-in* jury, juror
18観 *baikan suru* view with one's superior
観者 *baikansha* visitor's guests

B 陶 5003/F1999 Tō. *sue* porcelain, pottery.
3土 *tōdo* potter's clay, porcelain clay
工 *tōkō* potter, ceramist
5瓦 *tōga* porcelain tile
7芸 *tōgei* ceramic art
冶 *tōya* training, education; culture
冶性 *tōyasei* docility
8画 *tōga* pictures on porcelain
11酔 *tōsui* intoxication; fascination; rapture
12棺 *tōkan* earthenware coffin
然 *tōzen* gloriously drunk
13業 *tōgyō* porcelain industry
14像 *tōzō* figurine
管 *tōkan* earthenware pipe
碧玉 *tōhekigyoku* porcelain jasper
磁器 *tōjiki* porcelain, pottery
磁器製造法 *tōjiki seizōhō* ceramics
製 *tōsei* ceramic, earthen
製品 *tōseihin* ceramics, earthenware
15器 *tōki* porcelain, pottery
器工 *tōkikō* potter
器師 *tōkishi* potter
器商 *tōkishō* dish store
器製造所 *tōki seizōjo* pottery works
器製造術 *tōki seizōjutsu* ceramics
窯 *tōyō* ceramic kiln

B 随 5004/F2006 隨 Zui. *manimani* at the mercy of (the waves). *mama* (see under 儘 558.0). *-naga(ra)* (see under 乍 172.0). *shitaga(u)* (see 従 1613).
1一 *zui-ichi=dai ichi* 第一 3385.1
4分 *zuibun* very, extremely; tolerably; cruel, terrible; many
5処 *zuisho ni* everywhere, anywhere, here and there

8 金長門【阜阝】8 隶隹雨青非

6行 *zuikō* attendant, follower. *zuikō suru* attend on, accompany, follow
行者 *zuikōsha* attendants, suite
行員 *zuikōin* attendants, suite
7身 *zuijin* attendant; attending (on someone)
伴 *zuihan suru* attend on, accompany
伴者 *zuihansha* attendant, follower, suite, ⌊retinue
8所 *zuisho* everywhere
9神 *kannagara* as of old
神道 *Kannagara (no) Michi* Shinto
10時 *zuiji* any time, at all times; whenever required
員 *zui-in* attendants, suite ⌈fiddle to
従 *zuijū suru* follow the lead of, play second
従者 *zuijūsha* henchman, satellite, follower
12順 *zuijun* faithfully following (one's master)
喜 *zuiki* adoration, idolization
筆 *zuihitsu* essays, miscellaneous writings
13想 *zuisō* occasional thoughts
想録 *zuisōroku* stray notes; essays
感 *zuikan* random thoughts
感録 *zuikanroku* stray notes
意 *zui-i* voluntary, optional. *manimani* at ⌊the mercy of
意科 *zui-ika* elective course
意科目 *zui-i kamoku* elective course
意筋 *zui-ikin* voluntary muscles
意選択 *zui-i sentaku* free choice

A **陸** 5005/F2000 ROKU. RIKU *oka, kuga* land.

3上 *rikujō* on shore, land (events)
上生活 *rikujō seikatsu* life ashore
上自衛隊 *Rikujō Jieitai* Ground Self-Defense Force
上班 *rikujōhan* ground crew
上部隊 *rikujō butai* a land force
上動物 *rikujō dōbutsu* land animal
上勤務 *rikujō kimmu* shore duty
上機 *rikujōki* land-based plane
5生 *rikusei* terrestrial life
田 *okada* vegetable field
6行 *rikkō* going by land
地 *rikuchi* land
7兵 *rikuhei* land forces
8物 *okamono* land products
岸 *rikugan* shore; land
9風 *rikufū* land breeze
相 *Rikushō* War Minister
屋根 *rokuyane* flat roof
海 *rikukai* land and sea ⌈the 3 services
海空 *rikukaikū, rikkaikū* land, sea, and air;
海軍 *rikukaigun, rikkaigun* army and navy
海軍人 *rikkaigunjin* military and naval men
軍 *rikugun* army
軍大臣 *Rikugun Daijin* War Minister
軍大学校 *Rikugun Daigakkō* War College
軍士官学校 *Rikugun Shikan Gakkō* Military Academy
軍用地 *rikugun yōchi* army reservation
軍省 *Rikugunshō* War Department
11運 *riku-un* land transportation
釣 *okazuri* fishing from the shore
産 *rikusan* land products
軟風 *rikunampū* land breeze
12揚 *rikua(ge)* landing, unloading
棚 *rikubō, rikuhō, rikudana* continental shelf
棲 *rikusei* land (animal), terrestrial
蒸汽 *okajōki* steam train
13続 *rikuzoku to* continuously, successively
路 *rikuro, kugaji* land route
戦 *rikusen* land battle, land warfare
戦法規 *rikusen hōki* articles of war
戦隊 *rikusentai* landing forces
14境 *rikuzakai* land frontier
稲 *rikutō, okabo* upland rice, dry-land rice
16橋 *rikkyō* overpass; viaduct; land bridge
19離 *rikuri* dazzling
霧 *rikumu* land fog
蟹 *rikugani* land crab

B **陰** 5006/F1996 ON. AN. IN the yin principle; negative; melancholy; north side of a mountain; sex organs; secret; shadow; south side of a river; negative electrode; earth; bottom; back; inactivity; nighttime; moon. *kage(ru)* darken; cloud up; be obscured. *kage* shade; back; (your) assistance. *(o)kage* indebtedness, favor, help, patronage, support. *hisoka ni, in ni* secretly.

3口 *kageguchi* malicious gossip
干 *kagebo(shi)* drying in the shade
4文 *imbun, immon* the lettering of an engrav-
日向 *kage-hinata* light and shade ⌊ing
5弁慶 *kage benkei* a lion at home but a weak-
6気 *inki* gloom, melancholy ⌊ling elsewhere
気臭 *inkikusa(i)* gloomy
7言 *kagegoto* malicious gossip
坊 *ombō* cremator
声 *kage (no) koe* mystery voice; backstage
忍 *innin* patience, endurance ⌊voices
8門 *immon* vagina
雨 *in-u* dark and rainy
府 *impu, yomi* hades, realm of the dead
板 *imban* a negative
画 *inga* a negative
茎 *inkei* penis
事 *inji* secret
性 *insei* dormant; negative
性反応 *insei hanno* negative reaction (in a patient)
9風 *impū* cold wind, north wind
10唄 *kage uta* song behind the scenes

険 *inken na* tricky, wily, treacherous
陰 *in-in* gloomy and lonely
部 *imbu* pubic region
11 惨 *insan* sadness and gloom
悪 *in-aku* lurking evil, hidden evil
乾 *kagebo(shi)* drying in the shade
陽 *in-yō, on-yō* cosmic dual forces, positive and negative principles, active and passive, male and female, shade and light, sun and moon
陽道 *on-yōdō* divination
陽師 *on-yōji* diviner, fortuneteller
12 晴 *insei* unsettled weather, fine weather and cloudy weather
湿 *inshitsu* the dampness of shady places
雲 *in-un* dark or threatening clouds
然 *inzen* hidden power
極 *inkyoku* negative pole
極線 *inkyokusen* cathode rays
13 路 *kagemichi* shady road
電子 *indenshi* negatron
電気 *indenki* negative electricity
14 暦 *inreki* lunar calendar
徳 *intoku* secret charity
語 *ingo* secret language
歌 *kage uta* song behind the scenes
15 影 *in-ei* shadow; shading; gloom
蔽 *impei* covering up
16 膳 *kagezen* a tray for the absent one
謀 *imbō* plot, intrigue, conspiracy
謀者 *imbōsha* conspirator, intriguer
謀家 *imbōka* schemer
17 翳 *in-ei* shadow; shading; gloom
22 嚢 *innō* scrotum, testicles
26 鬱 *in-utsu* gloom, melancholy

9

隆 5007/F2002 See **隆** 4999.

隈 5008/F2003 Wai. *kuma* corner, nook, recess; indentation, bend, turn; shade, shading; make-up. *kuma(naku)* everywhere; universally.
8 取 *kumado(ru)* tint, shade; make up (the face); *kumadori* shading; make-up
11 隈 *kumaguma* nooks, corners
12 無 *kumana(ku)* completely

隅 5009/F2002 Gū corner. *sumi, sumi(kko)* corner, nook.
4 木 *sumigi* hip rafter
切 *sumiki(ri)* beveled, octagonal
5 石 *sumi ishi* cornerstone
11 隅 *sumizumi* every nook and corner
12 棟 *sumimune* hip of a roof

A **隊** 5010/F2003 **隊** Tai party, company, corps, squad, crew, band, posse, force, unit.
5 付 *taizu(ki), taitsu(ki)* field, regimental
6 伍 *taigo* the ranks, a line, procession
次 *taiji* order, battle formation
列 *tairetsu* ranks, file, procession
名 *taimei* unit designation
7 形 *taikei* battle formation, disposition of troops
8 長 *taichō* captain, leader, commander
10 員 *tai-in* members of the group
11 商 *taishō* caravan
商宿 *taishōjuku* caravansary
13 勢 *taisei* (flight formation)
14 旗 *taiki* flag of a unit

A **階** 5011/F2003 Kai stair, staircase; round; step; grade; story, floor; counter for stories (in a building). *kizahashi, kidahashi* stairway; ladder; order.
8 下 *kaika* lower floor, downstairs; under the stairway
上 *kaijō* upper floor; the head of the stairs
7 位 *kai-i* court rank, rank of officials
9 前 *kaizen* before the stairs; at the garden
段 *kaidan, kizahashi* steps, stairway
段席 *kaidan seki* rows of ascending seats
段教室 *kaidan kyōshitsu* lecture theater
級 *kaikyū* class, estate, caste, rank, grade
級差 *kaikyūsa* class distinction
級意識 *kaikyū-ishiki* class conciousness
級闘争 *kaikyū tōsō* class struggles
11 梯 *kaitei* step, stairs, ladder; threshold, steppingstone; guide, manual, primer
14 層 *kaisō* classes of people

A **陽** 5012/F2001 Yō yang principle, positive; male; heaven; daytime; sun; top; movement; facing the sun; sunshine; south face of a mountain; north side of a river; pride; positive electrode. *arawa ni* (see under 露 5069.0). *yō ni* openly, publicly.
3 子 *yōshi* proton
5 皮 *yō(no)kawa, yōhi* foreskin
6 気 *yōki* season, weather; vivacity, cheerfulness, gaiety
光 *yōkō* sunshine, sunlight; the sun
当 *hiata(ri)* sunny place; exposure to the sun
8 画 *yōga* positive photographic print
炎 *yōen, kagerō, kageroi* simmering of the air
性 *yōsei no* positive, plus
性反応 *yōsei hannō* positive reaction
物 *yōbutsu* phallus; penis
物崇拝 *yōbutsu sūhai* phallicism
9 春 *yōshun* spring, springtime
10 核 *yōkaku* positive nucleus
差 *hizashi* sunlight, sun's height

11 転 *yōten* positive (TB) test
動作戦 *yōdō sakusen* feint operation
12 極 *yōkyoku* anode, positive pole
報 *yōhō* open reward; rewarding openly
13 溜 *hidama(ri)* sunny place; exposure to the sun
電気 *yōdenki* positive electricity
電荷 *yōdenka* positive charge
14 暦 *yōreki* solar calendar; Julian calendar

10

隙 5013/F2005 See **隙** 5017.

隘 5014/F2004 AI narrow; obstruct.
18 路 *airo* defile, narrow path

隕 5015/F2004 IN fall.
5 石 *inseki* meteorite
9 星 *insei* meteor, falling star
13 鉄 *intetsu* meteoric iron

B **隔** 5016/F2004 **隔** KAKU every other, alternate; distance. *heda(teru)* separate, interpose; screen, shield; estrange. *hedata(ru)* be distant from, be separated from, become estranged. *heda(tari)* distance; interval; gap; gulf, difference, disparity; distance; coolness. *heda(te)* partition; interval; barrier; distinction; discrimination; reserve, coolness.
4 心 *kakushin*=*kakui* 隔意 (see below–13)
日 *kakujitsu* alternate days
月 *kakugetsu* alternate months
5 世 *kakusei* distant age; a different world
世遺伝 *kakusei iden* atavism
6 地 *kakuchi* distant place
年 *kakunen* alternate years
8 板 *kakuhan* partition; bulkhead
10 週 *kakushū* biweekly
12 晩 *kakuban* alternate evenings
絶 *kakuzetsu* isolation, separation, blockade
番 *kakuban* alternation. *kakuban ni* in turn, alternately
13 歳 *kakusai* every other year
意 *kakui* reserve, estrangement, alienation
靴掻痒 *kakka-sōyō* irritation, impatience
16 壁 *kakuheki* partition; bulkhead; septum
19 離 *kakuri* isolation, separation

11

隙 5017/F2005 **隙** GEKI crevice, fissure, chink; discord; opportunity. *su(kasu)* (see under 透 4699.0). *hima* time; leisure; poor business; leave of absence; dismissal; divorce; opening. *suki* time; leisure; gap, crack; room, space; chance; unpreparedness, unguarded moment
2 人 *himajin* man of leisure
7 見 *sukimi* peeping, peeking
8 取 *himado(ru)* take time, be delayed
12 間 *sukima* crevice, gap, opening, space
間風 *sukimakaze* draft
13 飽 *hima (ni) a(kasete)* no matter how long it takes

A **際** 5018/F2005 SAI time, occasion; when. *kiwa* side, edge, verge. *sai(suru)* meet, encounter. *kiwa(doi)* dangerous; adventurous; delicate; indecent. *(ni) sai(shite)* at that time.
5 立 *kiwada(tsu)* be prominent, be conspicuous
払 *kiwabara(i)* paying when due
6 会 *saikai suru* meet, face, confront
8 物 *kiwamono* seasonal goods
限 *saigen* limits, end, bounds
11 涯 *saigai* extremity

B **障** 5019/F2005 **障** SHŌ. *sawa(ru)* hinder, interfere with; affect; hurt, harm. *sawa(ri)* hindrance, interference; harm, bad aftereffects; menses.
3 子 *shōji* translucent sliding paper door
子紙 *shōjigami* translucent door paper
10 害 *shōgai* obstacle, hindrance, difficulty, handicap; hurdles
害物 *shōgaibutsu* obstacle, obstruction
害物競走 *shōgaibutsu kyōsō* obstacle race; steeplechase; hurdle race; slalom
害競走 *shōgai kyōsō* obstacle race; steeplechace; hurdle race; slalom
13 碍 *shōgai, shōge*=*shōgai* 障害 (see above–10)
16 壁 *shōheki* enclosing wall, barrier
19 礙 *shōgai, shōge*=*shōgai* 障害 (see above–10)

B **隠** 5020/F2007 **隱** IN. ON. *kaku(su)* hide, conceal, cover, veil, cloak, disguise. *kaku(reru)* hide, disappear; pass away; be anonymous; lurk. *komo(ru)* (see under 籠 3458.0). *kaku(renaki)* well-known, open (secret).
3 士 *inshi* hermit, recluse
女 *kaku(shi) onna* concubine
子 *kaku(shi)go* illegitimate child
亡 *ombō* cremator
4 戸 *kaku(shi)do* hidden door, trap door
文 *kaku(shi)bumi* anonymous letter
元 *ingen* kidney bean
元豆 *ingem-mame* kidney bean
5 田 *onden, kaku(shi)da* unregistered rice field
立 *kaku(shi)da(te)* secrecy
句 *inku* enigma
処 *kaku(re)ga* hiding place

世 *insei* retirement, seclusion
目付 *kaku(shi) metsuke* (ancient) spy
6宅 *intaku* a retreat (of one retired)
7見 *inken* appearance and disappearance
坊 *kaku(rem)bō* hide-and-seek. *ombō* cemetery guard; crematory worker
抜 *kaku(shi)-nu(ku)* hide out successfully
男 *kaku(shi) otoko* paramour
芸 *kaku(shi)gei* stunt, trick; an accomplishment unknown to others
忍 *innin* patience, endurance
君子 *inkunshi* hermit
言葉 *kaku(shi) kotoba* secret language, secret jargon
8居 *inkyo* retirement; retired person; old person
所 *kaku(shi)dokoro* hiding place; nakedness; private parts
岩 *kaku(re) iwa* sunken rock, reef
果者 *kaku(shi)-ō(seru)* succeed in hiding
者 *inja* hermit, recluse
事 *kaku(shi)goto, inji* secret
退 *intai* retirement, seclusion
退生活 *intai seikatsu* secluded life
退所 *intaisho* place of seclusion
退蔵物資 *intaizō busshi* hoarded goods
9食 *kaku(shi)gu(i)* eating on the sly
室 *inshitsu* living in retirement
10匿 *intoku* concealment
逸 *in-itsu* retirement, seclusion
栖 *insei* secluded life
釘 *kaku(shi) kugi* concealed nail
剣 *onken* concealed sword
家 *kaku(re)ga* retreat, refuge
11道 *kaku(re) michi* secret passage
遊 *kaku(re) aso(bi)* clandestine visit to a red-light district
設 *kaku(shi)-mō(keru)* spread a net for
密 *ommitsu, immitsu* privacy, secrecy; detective; spy, secret agent
12遁 *inton* retirement, seclusion
喩 *in-yu* metaphor
棲 *insei* secluded life
然 *inzen toshite* in reality, actually; in secret
場 *kaku(re)ba* refuge, hiding place
場所 *kaku(shi) basho* cache, place to hide (something). *kaku(re) basho* refuge, hiding place
13微 *imbi* obscurity, abstruseness, mystery
滅 *immetsu* destruction, suppression
蓑 *kaku(re) mino* a magic coat that can make wearer invisible
14徳 *intoku* secret charity
語 *ingo* secret language; password
15縫 *kaku(shi)nu(i)* concealed sewing
蔽 *impei* concealment, suppression, hiding
16謀 *imbō* plot, intrigue, conspiracy
躾 *kaku(shi) shitsuke* concealed basting
18顕 *inken* appearance and disappearance
顕砲 *inkenhō* disappearing gun
顕墨 *inkemboku* invisible ink

12

隋 5021/F2006 See **随** 5004.

隧 5022/F2006 Sui fall; go around.

11道 *suidō, tonneru* tunnel; fielding error

隣 5023/F2006/F1914 B **鄰** Rin neighboring. *tona(ru)* adjoin. *tonari* next-door neighbor; adjoining.

2人 *rinjin, tonaribito* neighbor
人愛 *rinjin-ai* love of one's fellow men
4比 *rimpi* nearness; neighborhood; neighboring
5付合 *tonarizu(ki)a(i)* neighborliness
6地 *rinchi* adjoining land
好 *rinkō* neighborhood friendship; friendly relations with neighboring countries
邦 *rimpō* neighboring country
交 *rinkō*=隣好 (see above–6)
合 *tona(ri)-a(u)* adjoin, be next to. *tona(ri)-a(i), tona(ri)a(wase)* adjoining
近所 *tonari-kinjo* neighborhood
同士 *tonaridōshi* next door to each other
同志 *tonaridōshi* next door to each other
7村 *tonari mura, rinson* neighboring village
8国 *ringoku, tonariguni* neighboring country
9室 *rinshitsu* the next room
県 *rinken* neighboring prefectures
保 *rimpo* neighborhood
保事業 *rimpo jigyō* welfare work, social service
保館 *rimpokan* settlement house
10席 *rinseki* the next seat
郷 *ringō* neighboring village
家 *rinka* neighboring house
座敷 *tonari zashiki* the next room
11接 *rinsetsu(shita)* adjacent, adjoining, neighboring; related
組 *tonarigumi* neighborhood association
13続 *tonaritsuzu(ki)* being neighbors

13

險 5024/F2007 See **険** 5000.

14

隱 5025/F2007 See **隠** 5020.

RAD. 隶 171

Reizukuri (i.e., the right-hand element of the character for *rei* "servant, slave"). Nickname: Slave.

8

B 隷 5026/F2009 隸 REI servant; criminal; prisoner; follower.

10従 *reijū* slavery
書 *reisho* ancient squared character
12属 *reizoku* subordination, dependency
属民 *reizokumin* an oppressed people
属国 *reizokukoku* dependency, subordination

9

隸 5027/F2009 See 隷 5026.

RAD. 隹 172

Furutori old "bird" (i.e., the less complicated "bird," as distinguished from the "long-tailed" bird of Rad. 196). Nickname: Old Bird.

2

B 隻 5028/F2010 SEKI counter for ships, fish, birds, arrows, etc., and one of a pair.

4手 *sekishu* one arm, one hand
7言 *sekigen* just a word
11眼 *sekigan* one eye; an eye (for pictures, etc.)
脚 *sekkyaku* one leg
12腕 *sekiwan* one arm
14語 *sekigo* just a word
15影 *sekiei* a single shadow, a trace, a sign
18騎 *sekiki* a lone rider; a lone cavalryman

3

雀 See 233.

4

雁 See 830.

雇 See 1826.

雅 See 雅 2850.

B 焦 5029/F1191 SHŌ. *ko*(*geru*) *vi* burn, scorch, singe, char. *ko*(*gasu*) *vt* burn, scorch, char, singe; pine for. *koga*(*reru*) pine for, yearn for; be deeply in love with; be scorched. *ase*(*ru*) be in a hurry, be hasty, be impatient, be overzealous. *ji*(*reru*) be irritated. *ji*(*rasu*) irritate. *ji*(*rettagaru*) be impatient. *ko*(*gashi*) parched-barley flour. *ji*(*rettai*) irritating, provoking; impatient, vexed. [灬]

3土 *shōdo* burnt ground; scorched earth
土戦術 *shōdo senjutsu* scorched-earth strategy
4心 *shōshin* impatience, worry, excitement
5付 *ko*(*ge*)-*tsu*(*ku*) get charred, get burnt
6死 *koga*(*re*)*jini suru* die of love for
9眉 *shōbi* emergency, urgency, imminence
点 *shōten* focus
臭 *kogekusa*(*i*), *kinakusa*(*i*) smelling burnt
茶 *kogecha* dark brown
茶色 *kogecha iro* dark brown
15慮 *shōryo* impatience, worry
熱 *shōnetsu* scorching heat; scorching
熱地獄 *shōnetsu jigoku* burning hell
17燥 *shōsō* impatience, irritation, uneasiness
20躁 *shōsō* = word above

B 雄 5030/F2011 YŪ male; hero; great leader; superiority, excellence. *osu*, *on*-, *o*- male.

8大 *yūdai na* grand, majestic, sublime
才 *yūsai* talents
4心 *yūshin*, *ogokoro* manly spirit, ambition, aspiration, gallant spirit
牛 *o-ushi* bull, steer
5弁 *yūben* oratory, eloquence
6羊 *ohitsuji* ram
叫 *otake*(*bi*), *osake*(*bi*) war cry; courageous shout; roar of an animal
壮 *yūsō* bravery, heroism
名 *yūmei* fame, great renown
7図 *yūto* ambitious undertaking
材 *yūzai* outstanding talent
志 *yūshi* high aspiration, ambition

花 *obana* male flower
8 性 *yūsei* male characteristics; manliness
松 *omatsu* black pine, seaside pine, male
武 *yūbu* bravery ⌊pine
9 風 *yūfū* strong breeze
飛 *yūhi* flying jump; great achievement
途 *yūto* a courageous departure
勁 *yūkei na* pithy, vigorous (style)
姿 *yūshi* gallant figure
10 馬 *o-uma* stallion
峰 *yūhō* high majestic mountain
将 *yūshō* a great general
11 鳥 *ondori* cock, rooster
偉 *yūi no* imposing, grand, magnificent
健 *yūken na* vigorous, virile, sturdy
強 *yūkyō* very strong character
猛 *yūmō* daring, bravery, valor
略 *yūryaku* big plans
断 *yūdan* a manly decision
12 傑 *yūketsu* something outstanding
渾 *yūkon na* magnificent, sublime; vigorous, virile, sturdy, bold
雄 *o-o(shii)* manly, brave, heroic
筆 *yūhitsu* powerful writing
13 滝 *odaki* the greater of two waterfalls
蜂 *obachi* drone (bee)
獅子 *ojishi* male lion
14 魂 *yūkon* brave soul; fine manliness
15 編 *yūhen* a masterpiece
篇 *yūhen* a masterpiece
蕊 *oshibe, yūzui* stamen
16 鴨 *ogamo* drake
17 螺旋 *oneji* male screw
18 藩 *yūhan* large fief
26 驢馬 *oroba* male donkey

A **集** 5031/F2013 SHŪ collection, gathering. *atsu(maru)*, *tsudo(u)* meet, assemble, congregate; swarm, flock or gather together; be collected, be gathered together; converge. *atsu(meru)* gather, collect; focus (something on). *atsu(mari)*, *tsudo(i)* assembly, meeting; collection; gathering.
3 大成 *shūtaisei* compilation
4 中 *shūchū* concentration, convergence, centralization, integration ⌈ball)
中打 *shūchūda* a succession of hits (in base-
中攻撃 *shūchū kōgeki* concentrated attack
中排除 *shūchū haijo* deconcentration
5 出 *atsu(me)-da(su)* gather out
札係 *shūsatsugakari* ticket collector
6 成 *shūsei* collection, compilation ⌈tion
合 *shūgō* gathering, meeting, group; collec-
合名詞 *shūgō meishi* collective noun
合的 *shūgōteki* collective
会 *shūkai* meeting, assembly
会所 *shūkaijo* meeting place, assembly hall
会室 *shūkaishitsu* assembly hall, meeting room
会場 *shūkaijō* meeting place, assembly hall
団 *shūdan* group, body, mass, crowd, host
団心理 *shūdan shinri* mass psychology
団安全保障 *shūdan anzen hoshō* collective
団的 *shūdanteki* collective ⌊security
団軍 *shūdangun* group army
団保険 *shūdan hoken* group insurance
団家屋 *shūdan kaoku* group of houses
団部隊 *shūdambutai* troops in mass formation
団討論 *shūdan tōron* group discussion
団移民 *shūdan imin* mass immigration
団強盗 *shūdan gōtō* gang of robbers
団結婚 *shūdan kekkon* group marriage
団疎開 *shūdan sokai* mass evacuation
団農業 *shūdan nōgyō* collective farming
団意識 *shūdan ishiki* group consciousness
7 来 *tsudo(i)-ku(ru)* come together, assemble
8 注 *shūchū* variorum edition; directing atten-
金 *shūkin* collecting money ⌊tion to
金人 *shūkinnin* money collector
9 約 *shūyaku suru* intensify
約的 *shūyakuteki* intensive
計 *shūkei* total
計表 *shūkeihyō* tabulation
10 書 *shūsho* series (of publications); library (of literature)
荷 *shūka* collection of freight
配 *shūhai* collection and delivery
配人 *shūhainin* postman
11 貨 *shūka* collection of freight
魚灯 *shūgyotō* fish-luring light
12 註 *shūchū* variorum edition
落 *shūraku* centers of population, towns and villages ⌈sembling
結 *shūketsu* concentration, collection, as-
結所 *shūketsusho* concentration center
散 *shūsan* collection and distribution
散地 *shūsanchi* collection and distributing
13 塊 *shūkai* mass, cluster ⌊center
14 蔵 *shūzō* garnering; collecting
15 権 *shūken* centralization of power
16 録 *shūroku* compilation, editing
積 *shūseki* accumulation, pile
積地 *shūsekichi* storage place
20 議 *shūgi* deliberative meeting

5

雅 See 2850.

雃 See 3173.

8 金長門阜阝隶【隹】雨青非 5

雍 See 324.

6

雎 See 2435.

A **雑** 5032/F2016 **雜** Zō. ZATSU miscellany; miscellaneous. *ma(zeru), ma(zaru), ma(jiru)* (see under 混 2604.0). *maji(eru)* mix; converse with; cross (swords). *zatsu na* rough, coarse, rude; miscellaneous.

2 人 *zōnin* low-class people
3 巾 *zōkin* mop, scrubbing cloth
巾掛 *zōkinga(ke)* scrubbing
4 文 *zatsubun* literary miscellany
支出 *zatsu shishutsu* miscellaneous expenditures
手当 *zatsu teate* miscellaneous allowances
木 *zōki, zōboku, zatsuboku* miscellaneous trees
木林 *zōkibayashi, zōbokurin* grove of miscellaneous trees
5 用 *zatsuyō* miscellaneous business. *zōyō* miscellaneous business, miscellaneous expenses
収入 *zatsu shūnyū, zasshūnyū* miscellaneous income
6 色 *zasshoku* various colors
気 *majirike* mixture, impurity
返 *ma(ze)-kae(su)*＝混返 2604.6
曲 *zakkyoku* popular song, musical medley
件 *zakken* miscellaneous affairs
多 *zatta na* miscellaneous, various
交 *zakkō* crossing (in biology)
交受精 *zakkō jusei* cross-fertilization
7 言 *zōgon*＝*akkō* 悪口 62.3
作 *zōsaku* interior finishing (of a house)
兵 *zappei, zappyō, zōhyō* ordinary soldiers, rank and file
芸 *zatsugei* miscellaneous accomplishments
役 *zatsueki* odd jobs, sundry services
役夫 *zatsuekifu* handy man
役服 *zatsuekifuku* fatigues
役婦 *zatsuekifu* charwoman
8 炊 *zōsui* medley soup; hodgepodge
物 *zatsubutsu* sundries; impurities, mixture. *maza(ri)mono* mixture, impurities. *zōmotsu* inferior goods; entrails
卒 *zassotsu* rank and file, soldiers
念 *zatsunen, zōnen* worldly thoughts
沓 *zattō* congestion, traffic jam, throng
具 *zatsugu* various tools
学 *zatsugaku* wide knowledge
事 *zatsuji* miscellaneous affairs
居 *zakkyo suru* live together (in the same room, area, or country)
居地 *zakkyochi* mixed-residence quarter
9 音 *zatsuon* noise, static, jamming; (heart) murmur
食 *zasshoku no* omnivorous
則 *zassoku* miscellaneous rules
軍 *zatsugun* disorganized army
品 *zappin* sundries, odds and ends
草 *zassō* weeds
10 株 *zatsu kabu, zakkabu* miscellaneous stocks; minor stocks
書 *zassho* miscellaneous books; book on miscellaneous subjects
記 *zakki* miscellaneous notes
記帳 *zakkichō* notebook; exercise book
11 婚 *zakkon* racial intermarriage
務 *zatsumu* miscellaneous business
勘定 *zatsu kanjō* miscellaneous accounts
魚 *zako, jako* small fish; various kinds of small fish
魚寝 *zakone suru* sleep together in a group
貨 *zakka* sundries, notions; general cargo; miscellaneous goods
貨店 *zakkaten* emporium, variety store
貨商 *zakkashō* general store
12 税 *zatsuzei* miscellaneous taxes
詠 *zatsuei* miscellaneous poems
筆 *zappitsu* miscellaneous writings
然 *zatsuzen to* promiscuously, in confusion
煮 *zōni* glutinous rice cakes boiled with vegetables
費 *zappi* miscellaneous expenses
報 *zappō* miscellaneous news
13 話 *zatsuwa* chitchat, gossip
感 *zakkan* miscellaneous impressions
楽 *zatsugaku* miscellaneous popular music
業 *zatsugyō* miscellaneous work, miscellaneous enterprises
損益 *zasson-eki* petty gains and losses
14 種 *zasshu* mixed breed, hybrid, mongrel; various kinds
説 *zassetsu* various theories
駁 *zappaku na* confused, incoherent, desultory, hazy
歌 *zōka* miscellaneous poems
誌 *zasshi* magazine, periodical
誌記者 *zasshi kisha* magazine writer
穀 *zakkoku* minor grains
穀商 *zakkokushō* grain merchant
15 鬧 *zattō* congestion, traffic jam, throng
踏 *zattō* congestion, traffic jam, throng
篇 *zappen* miscellaneous writing
輩 *zappai* rank and file; nonentity
談 *zatsudan* chitchat, gossip
談会 *zatsudankai* talkfest
16 録 *zatsuroku* miscellaneous notes
18 観 *zakkan* miscellaneous impressions
題 *zatsudai* miscellaneous subjects
20 纂 *zassan* miscellaneous collection
22 嚢 *zatsunō* duffel bag

— 8 —

雞 Nonstandard for 鶏 5359.

雕 5033/F2015 Chō carving.

— 9 —

雖 5034/F2015 Sui. *iedo(mo)* tho, altho, however.

— 10 —

離 See 5040.

雙 See 双 859.

雜 5035/F2016 See 雑 5032.

雞 5036/F2018 See 鶏 5359.

雛 5037/F2016 Sū. *hina* chick, squab, duckling; doll. *hiyoko* chick; stripling.
2 人形 *hina ningyō* festival dolls
7 形 *hinagata* pattern, model, sample, specimen, form, copy, miniature
9 型 *hinagata*=word above
11 鳥 *hinadori* chick, young bird
遊 *hina-aso(bi)* playing with dolls; playing before the doll tiers
菊 *hinagiku* daisy
祭 *Hinamatsu(ri)* Girls' March Doll Festival
13 僧 *hinasō* boy priest
節句 *Hina (no) Sekku* Girls' March Doll Festival
16 壇 *hinadan* doll stand; musicians' platform; state ministers' gallery (on the doll stands)

難 5038/F2021 難 Nan trouble, difficulty; A accident, disaster; defect; criticism. *kata(i)* difficult; impossible. *mutsuka(shii), muzuka(shii)* hard, difficult; delicate; troublesome; doubtful; hopeless; stern; sullen; hard to please; serious; technical. *nan(zuru)* criticize. *haba(mu)* (see under 阻 4984.0). *nan(naku)* easily, successfully. *-niku(i)* difficult, awkward. *-gata(i)* difficult (to do). *-ka(neru)* cannot; hesitate to; be impatient.
4 中難事 *nanchū (no) nanji* the hardest thing to do
5 句 *nanku* difficult phrase or passage
民 *nammin* needy people, sufferers; displaced persons, refugees
6 色 *nanshoku* hesitation; disapproval
件 *nanken* difficult problem, delicate matter
地 *nanchi* predicament, trouble
字 *nanji* a difficult character
行 *nangyō* penance, austerities
行苦行 *nangyō-kugyō* penance, austerities
行道 *nangyōdō* the way of hardships, salvation by works
7 局 *nankyoku* difficult situation, crisis
攻不落 *nankō-furaku* impregnability
8 所 *nansho, nanjo* steep, difficult, or dangerous places
治 *nanji, nanchi* incurable; rebellious; difficult
物 *nambutsu* hard customer
易 *nan-i* relative difficulty; difficulty and ease
事 *nanji* difficult matter; hardship
波 *nampa* shipwreck
波船 *nampasen* shipwreck
9 風 *nampū* adverse wind
点 *nanten* difficult point
10 病 *nambyō* serious illness
症 *nanshō* serious illness
航 *nankō* stormy voyage; rough flight; rough sledding
訓 *nankun* difficult reading of characters
破 *nampa* shipwreck
破船 *nampasen* shipwreck
11 渋 *nanjū* suffering, distress, hardship
球 *nankyū* a batted ball hard to catch
船 *nansen* shipwreck
産 *nanzan* difficult delivery (in childbirth)
問 *nammon* difficult question
問題 *nammondai* difficult problem
12 場 *nanjō, namba* predicament, difficulty; dangerous path, rough place
無 *nanna(ku)* easily
13 解 *nankai na* hard to understand; unintelligible; illegible
詰 *nankitsu* blame, censure
路 *nanro* difficult road
戦 *nansen* hard fight; hard fighting
義 *nangi* hardship; trouble
14 関 *nankan* strong barrier, obstacle, difficulty
境 *nankyō* difficult situation
語 *nango* difficult word
読 *nandoku* difficult reading
15 儀 *nangi* hardship, trouble
17 聴 *nanchō* hard of hearing
18 癖 *nankuse* fault, bad habit
題 *nandai* difficult topic; hard question; unreasonable charge; unreasonable demand

— 11 —

難 5039/F2021 See 難 5038.

8 金 長 門 阜 阝 隶 11 【隹】 雨 青 非

B 離 5040 F2019 RI separation. *hana(reru), saka-(ru) vi* and *vt* separate, part from; come off, become disjoined; digress; get free; become estranged; be (3 miles) away; be separated (by 3 years); leave, quit, depart from. *hana(su) vt* separate, disconnect, sever; detach; keep apart; alienate; isolate; let go, release, set free. *hana(re)* detached (building).

3 山 *rizan* a mountain off by itself; leaving a temple
4 日 *rinichi* departure from Japan
水 *risui* taking off from water
反 *rihan* estrangement, alienation, desertion, revolt
5 去 *hana(re)-sa(ru)* leave, depart from; drift away
6 任 *rinin* leaving one's position
合 *rigō* meeting and parting
7 床 *rishō suru* get up, leave the sickbed
村 *rison* rural exodus
別 *ribetsu* divorce; dissolution of adoption
8 迷 *hana(re)-mayo(u)* wander away; err from
退 *hana(re)-shirizo(ku)* turn back from
京 *rikyō* leaving the capital
岸 *rigan* setting sail
苦 *riku* agony of separation
乳 *rinyū* weaning
乳食 *rinyūshoku* a baby's weaning meal
9 洲 *risu* floating, refloating
叛 *rihan*＝離反 (see above–4)
10 郷 *rikyō* leaving one's home town
島 *hana(re)jima, ritō* outlying island
宮 *rikyū* detached palace
家 *hana(re)ya* detached building, solitary house
宴 *rien* farewell drinking party
党 *ritō* withdrawal from a party
座敷 *hana(re) zashiki* detached room
陸 *ririku* take-off; pulling out from the shore
陸場 *ririkujō* airstrip
11 脱 *ridatsu* secession; separation; abolition; giving up (one's membership)
船 *risen* leaving a ship
婚 *rikon* divorce
婚届 *rikon todoke* notice of divorce
婚訴訟 *rikon soshō* divorce suit
12 隔 *rikaku* isolation, separation
散 *risan* dispersion, scattering, breakup
塁 *rirui* leading off from the base
着 *richaku* taking off and landing
間 *rikan* estrangement, separation, rupture
間策 *rikansaku* alienation maneuver
13 殿 *hana(re)dono* separate house
路 *riro* deviation (in navigation)
愁 *rishū* the pain of parting
業 *hana(re)waza* stunt, feat
14 魂病 *rikombyō* somnambulism
15 縁 *rien* divorce; separation of an adopted son
縁状 *rienjō* divorce papers
17 礁 *rishō suru* refloat, get off the reef
18 難 *hana(re)gata(i)* inseparable
職 *rishoku* quitting one's job, loss of employment
職手当 *rishoku teate* quitting allowance
職者 *rishokusha* the unemployed
職票 *rishokuhyō* separation notice
19 離 *hana(re)bana(re)* scattered, dispersed, separated, disconnected
20 艦 *rikan* taking off from a carrier
籍 *riseki* removal of a name from a registry

15

讎 5041 F1774 讐 SHŪ enemy. *ada* enemy; revenge. [言]

雨 RAD. 173

Ame rain. At top: ⻗ or 雨 *ame kammuri*. Nickname: Rain.

A 雨 5042 F2022 U. *ame* rain, rainfall. *ama-* rain.

3 上 *ameaga(ri), ama-aga(ri)* after the rain
乞 *amagoi* praying for rain
下駄 *amageta* rain clogs
4 戸 *amado* shutter, storm door
止 *amaya(mi)* stopping of rain, lull in the rain
水 *amamizu, usui* rain water
中 *uchū* in the rain
支度 *amajitaku* preparation for rain
天 *uten* rainy weather
天順延 *uten-jun-en* in case of rain postponed to the next good day
5 氷 *uhyō* silver frost, glaze
外套 *amagaitō* raincoat
6 衣 *ui* raincoat
気 *amake* threatening to rain, signs of rain
合 *ama-a(i)* between showers
合羽 *amagappa* raincoat, oilcoat
7 足 *ame ashi, ama-ashi* a passing shower
囲 *amago(i)* rain shelter
余 *uyo* after the rain
声 *usei* the sound of rain

承 *ama-u(ke)* water table, gutter
8 押 *ama-osa(e)* flashing (in building)
注 *uchū suru* shower (arrows) upon
夜 *amayo* rainy evening, rainy night
具 *amagu* rain gear
季 *uki* rainy season
空 *amazora* threatening sky
垂 *amadare* raindrops, eavesdrops
垂石 *amadare ishi* dripstone, weather molding
9 音 *ama-oto* sound of falling rain ⌈wind
風 *ame-kaze* rain and wind. *amakaze* rainy
飛 *uhi* coming down like rain (bullets)
食 *ushoku* rainwash
後 *ugo* after a rain ⌈cover
除 *amayo(ke)* shelter from the rain, shed,
降 *amefu(ri)* rainfall; rain; rainy weather
染 *amaji(mi)* rain stain
10 師 *ushi* rain god
11 粒 *amatsubu* raindrop
脚 *ama-ashi, ame ashi* a passing shower
宿 *amayado(ri)* taking shelter from the rain
笠 *amagasa* rain hat
雫 *amashizuku* raindrop
12 間 *ama-ai* between showers
湿 *amajime(ri)* wet from rain
疏 *amaha(ke)* rain-water drainage
勝 *amega(chi)* rainy period
蛙 *amagaeru* tree frog
期 *uki* rainy season
傘 *amagasa* umbrella
着 *amagi* raincoat
落 *amao(chi)* gutter for eavesdrops
集 *ushū* crowds gathering; men of talent
雲 *amagumo* rain cloud ⌊gathering
裂 *uretsu* rain gully
量 *uryō* rain, rainfall
量計 *uryōkei* rain gauge
13 催 *amamoyo(i), amemoyo(i)* sign of rain
続 *amatsuzu(ki), ametsuzu(ki)* long rain, rainy spell
隠 *amagaku(re)* taking shelter from the rain. *amagomo(ri)* rainbound
靴 *amagutsu* overshoes
意 *ui* threat of rain ⌈doors
障子 *amashōji* translucent oiled-paper
14 樋 *amadoi* eaves trough
漏 *amamo(ri)* roof leak
滴 *uteki* raindrop
模様 *amamoyō, ame moyō* signs of rain
15 避 *amayo(ke)* taking shelter from the rain
16 曇 *amagumo(ri)* overcast weather
18 曝 *amazara(shi)* exposure to rain, weather-
覆 *amaōi* tarpaulin, rain cover ⌊beaten
21 露 *uro* rain and dew
22 籠 *amagomo(ri)* rainbound

3

雫 **5043** **F2024** DA. DAN. *shizuku* drop, trickle, dripping.

雪 雪 **5044** **F2023** A SETSU. *yuki* snow, snowfall. *susu(gu), soso(gu)* rinse, wash, pour on.

2 人形 *yuki ningyō* snowman
3 山 *yuki yama, setsuzan* snowy mountain; mountain of snow
下 *yuki oro(shi)* snowy wind
女 *yuki onna* snow fairy
女郎 *yuki jorō* snow fairy
上 *setsujō* on the snow
上車 *setsujōsha* snow tractor ⌈guard
4 止 *yukido(me)* snowshed, snow guard, roof
水 *yuki mizu* slush, thawing snow; snow
片 *seppen* snowflake ⌊water
中 *setchū* in the snow; in a snowstorm
仏 *yukibotoke* snow Buddha
月花 *setsugekka* snow, moon, and flowers
日和 *yukibiyori* signs of snow
5 玉 *yukidama* snowball
田 *setsuden* eternal snow fields
白 *seppaku* snow-white. *yukijiro* refined
目 *yukime* snow blindness ⌊sugar
氷 *seppyō* snow ice
6 気 *yukige* threat of snow
肌 *yuki (no) hada* smooth skin, fair skin
交 *yukima(jiri)* fall and winter weather; mixture of rain and snow
合戦 *yuki gassen* snowball fight
7 囲 *yukigako(i)* snowshed
庇 *seppi* overhanging snow
折 *yukio(re)* a snowbreak; bent by snow
投 *yukina(ge)* throwing snowballs
見 *yukimi* snow viewing
見灯籠 *yukimidōrō* large-topped three-legged stone lantern
見酒 *yukimizake* drinking saké at a snow
花 *sekka* snowflakes ⌊scene
花石膏 *sekka-sekkō* alabaster
花菜 *kirazu* tofu refuse
8 国 *yukiguni* snowy country
明 *yukiaka(ri)* snow light
泥 *setsudei* slush
夜 *yukiyo* snowy night
盲 *setsumō, yuki mekura* snow blindness
沓 *yukigutsu* snowshoes, snow boots
空 *yukizora* snowy sky, leaden sky
9 後 *setsugo* after the snowfall
洞 *bombori* hand lamp; lampstand
除 *yukiyo(ke)* snow guard, snowshed, roof guards (to prevent snow sliding off)
降 *yukifu(ri)* snowfall

10 原 *setsugen* snow field, frozen waste
峰 *seppō* snowy peak
消 *yukige* thaw, melting snow
冤 *setsuen* vindication, exoneration
害 *setsugai* snow damage
留 *yukidama(ri)* snowdrift, snowbank
辱 *setsujoku* vindication of honor, making up for a loss, revenge
辱戦 *setsujokusen* return match; a fight for vindication
11 道 *yukimichi* snowy road
遊 *yuki aso(bi)* playing with snow
袴 *yukibakama* snow trousers
転 *yukikoro(gashi), yukimaro(bashi)* rolling a snowball
崩 *nada(reru)* incline toward, give way and fall. *nadare, yuki nadare* snowslide, snow avalanche
達磨 *yuki daruma* snowman
眼鏡 *yuki megane* snow glasses
12 間 *yukima* interval between snowfalls; in the snow
堤 *settei* a snow embankment (to prevent further slides)
晴 *yukiba(re)* clearing after a snowfall
焼 *yukiya(ke)* snow tan
颪 *yuki oro(shi)* snowy wind
嵐 *yuki arashi* snowstorm, blizzard
雲 *yukigumo* snow cloud
景 *sekkei* snowscape
景色 *yukigeshiki* snow scene
13 催 *yuki moyo(i)* threatening to snow
掻 *yukikaki* snow shoveling, snow removal; snow shovel, snow scraper; snowplow
渓 *sekkei* perpetually snowy valley
解 *yukige, yukido(ke)* thaw, melting snow
路 *yukiji, yuki michi* snowy road
靴 *yukigutsu* snowshoes, snow boots
隠 *setchin, setsuin* lavatory, toilet
隠大工 *setchin daiku* a clumsy carpenter
隠詰 *setchinzu(me) ni suru* argue (someone) into a corner
14 駄 *setta* leather-soled sandals
雑 *yukimaji(ri)* (rain) mixed with snow
模様 *yuki moyō* snowflake pattern; threatening to snow
15 線 *sessen* snow line
踏 *setta* leather-soled sandals
輪 *yukiwa* ski disk
16 頽 *yuki nadare* snowslide, avalanche
曇 *yukigumo(ri)* threatening to snow
17 嶺 *setsurei* snow-capped peak
20 礫 *yuki tsubute* snowball

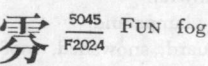

4

雰 5045 F2024 **Fun** fog.

7 囲気 *fun-iki* atmosphere, environment, surroundings

A **雲** 5046 F2024 **Un.** *kumo* cloud.

3 山 *unzan* cloud-covered mountains
上 *unjō* above the clouds. *kumo (no) ue* above the clouds; the heavens; the palace
上人 *unjōbito, kumo(no)uebito* nobles
4 水 *unsui* itinerant priest; clouds and water
切 *kumogi(re)* rift in the clouds
丹 *uni* sea urchin
井 *kumoi* sky; palace, court circles
5 外 *ungai* above the clouds; the depths of the sky
母 *ummo, umbo, kirara* isinglass, mica
母引 *kirabi(ki)* mica sheet
母片岩 *ummo hengan* mica schist
6 行 *kumoyu(ki)* cloud movements; situation, turn of events; progress; signs
合 *kumoa(i)* the look of the sky
7 足 *kumo-ashi* cloud movements; overhanging clouds
状 *unjō* nebulous, cloudlike
助 *kumosuke* palanquin bearer, coolie, wandering robber
助根性 *kumosuke-konjō* one who enriches himself at the expense of others
形 *kumogata, unkei* cloud formations
形定規 *kumogata jōgi* draftsman's curve
8 突 *kumotsu(ku)* towering
表 *umpyō* above the clouds
泥差 *undei (no) sa* a wide difference
居 *kumoi* a cloudy place; distant place; sky; palace; court circles
居遙 *kumoi-haruka ni* very far away
9 海 *unkai* sea of clouds; sea of clouds meeting the great ocean
級 *unkyū* cloud types
客 *unkaku* a noble
10 高 *unkō* height of clouds
根 *unkon* place where clouds form; the mountains
脂 *fuke* dandruff
峯 *kumo (no) mine* cloud bank, cumulus-cloud columns
11 鳥 *kumo-tori* clouds and birds; birds flying in the sky
梯 *untei* scaling ladder
脚 *unkyaku* cloud movements; overhanging clouds
雀 *hibari* skylark
12 間 *kumoma* rift between clouds
桟 *unsan* a high bridge
量 *unryō* degree of cloudiness
散 *unsan* scattering like clouds
散霧消 *unsam-mushō* vanishing like clouds and mist
集 *unshū suru* swarm, throng, gather in crowds
集霧散 *unshū-musan* people gathering and quickly dispersing
13 煙 *un-en* clouds and smoke; a landscape; a beautiful picture
路 *kumoji* cloud ways (of the birds)
隠 *kumogaku(re)* demise, passing; disappearance

際 *unsai* edge of the clouds; distant sky
15 影 *un-ei* cloud shape ⌈showers
16 霓 *ungei* clouds and a rainbow; sign of
17 霞 *unka* clouds and haze. *kumo-kasumi* clouds and fog; disappearance, fleeing
翳 *un-ei* cloud shade ⌈tains) soar high
聳 *kumo (ni) sobie(ru)* (buildings or moun-
19 簾 *kumo sudare* cloud screen (over the
霧 *ummu* clouds and fog ⌊moon)
20 壌 *unjō* clouds and earth; heaven and earth; great contrast

5

雹 5047/F2028 HAKU. HOKU. *hyō* hail.

10 害 *hyōgai* hail damage

B 零 5048/F2026 REI zero, nothing, cipher; fall. *kobo(reru) vi* spill, overflow, be scattered. *kobo(su) vt* spill; grumble over.

3 下 *reika* below zero, subzero
7 余 *reiyo* residue, remnant
位 *rei-i* zero
位線 *rei-isen* zero line
8 幸 *kobo(re)zaiwa(i)* a godsend, a windfall
9 度 *reido* zero, freezing point
砕 *reisai* a tiny bit
点 *reiten* zero; freezing point; zero grade
10 時 *reiji* twelve o'clock; noon; midnight
11 敗 *reihai* a shutout (in a game); losing out (in love)
細 *reisai na* petty, small, infinitesimal
細農 *reisainō* poor peasant
12 落 *ochibu(reru)*＝落魄 4003.15. *reiraku* ruin, downfall, reduced circumstances,
13 戦 *reisen* zero fighter ⌊withering

B 雷 5049/F2027 RAI *ikazuchi* thunder. *kaminari* thunder; thunderbolt.

4 文 *raimon* zigzag
火 *raika* lightning; fire caused by lightning
公 *raikō* the god of thunder
6 同 *raidō* blindly following the crowd
光 *raikō* lightning
名 *raimei* renown, fame; your famous name
7 声 *raisei* noise of thunder
8 雨 *raiu* thunderstorm
9 神 *raijin* the god of thunder
除 *raiyo(ke)* lightning rod
10 師 *raishi* the god of thunder
11 動 *raidō* rumble of thunder; roaring
雪 *raisetsu* snow thunderstorm
12 雲 *raiun* thunderhead
13 電 *raiden* thunder and lightning, thunder-
14 鳴 *raimei* thunder ⌊bolt
酸 *raisan* fulminic acid
管 *raikan* percussion cap, detonator
15 避 *kaminari-yo(ke)* lightning rod
霆 *raitei* thunder
撃 *raigeki* torpedo attack
撃機 *raigekiki* torpedo-carrying plane
16 親爺 *kaminari oyaji* snarling old man

A 電 5050/F2028 DEN electricity. *inazuma* lightning.

2 力 *denryoku* electric power
力学 *denryokugaku* electrodynamics
3 工 *denkō* electrician
工長 *denkōchō* head electrician
子 *denshi* electron
子工学 *denshi kōgaku* electronics
子学 *denshigaku* electronics ⌈scope
子顕微鏡 *denshi kembikyō* electron micro-
4 文 *dembun* telegram, telegraphic message
化 *denka* electrification
火 *denka* electric spark
火距離 *denka kyori* sparking distance
火間隙 *denka kangeki* spark gap
5 圧 *den-atsu* voltage
6 池 *denchi* electric battery
休日 *denkyūbi* no-electricity day
光 *denkō* electric light; lightning
光石火 *denkō-sekka* an instant, a flash
光形 *denkōkei* zigzag
灯 *dentō* electric light
灯会社 *dentōgaisha* electric-light company
灯料 *dentōryō* electric-light charges
灯料金 *dentō ryōkin* electric-light charges
灯線 *dentōsen* lamp cord
気 *denki* electricity; electric light
気力学 *denki rikigaku* electrodynamics
気工 *denkikō* electrician
気工学 *denki kōgaku* electrical engineering
気分析 *denki bunseki* electroanalysis
気分解 *denki bunkai* electrolysis; electroanalysis
気写字機 *denki shajiki* teletype
気広告 *denki kōkoku* electric sign
気灯 *denkitō* electric light
気死刑 *denki shikei* electrocution
気会社 *denkigaisha* electric company
気技師 *denki gishi* electrical engineer
気店 *denkiten* electric shop
気板 *denkiban* electrotype
気炉 *denkiro* electric furnace; electric oven
気学 *denkigaku* science of electricity
気抵抗 *denki teikō* electrical resistance
気始動機 *denki shidōki* electric starter
気炬燵 *denkigotatsu* electric foot warmer
気係 *denkigakari* electrician
気剃刀 *denki kamisori* electric razor
気通信 *denki tsūshin* telecommunication

8 金 長 門 阜 阝 隶 隹 6【雨】 青 非

気浴 *denkiyoku* electric bath
気料 *denkiryō* charge for electricity
気料金 *denki ryōkin* charge for electricity
気時計 *denkidokei* electric clock
気量 *denkiryō* amount of electricity
気椅子 *denki isu* electric chair
気蒲団 *denkibuton* electric blanket
気照明 *denki shōmei* electric lighting
気暖房 *denki dambō* electric heating
気暖房法 *denki dambōhō* electric heating
気銅 *denkidō* electrolytic copper
気磁石 *denki jishaku* electromagnet
気熔接 *denki yōsetsu* electric welding
気器具 *denki kigu* electrical appliances
気鋼 *denkikō* electric steel
気鍍金 *denki mekki* electroplating, galvanizing
気療法 *denki ryōhō* electrotherapy
気竈 *denki kamado* electric range
気鰻 *denki unagi* electric eel
7位 *den-i* electric potential
車 *densha* electric car, streetcar, tramcar, electric train
車通 *denshadō(ri)* streetcar line
車賃 *denshachin* carfare
8弧 *denko* electric arc
命 *demmei* telegraphic instructions
送 *densō* electrical facsimile transmission
送写真 *densō shashin* phototelegraph
波 *dempa* electric wave, radio wave
波妨害 *dempa bōgai* jamming
波波長 *dempa hachō* wave length
波計 *dempakei* wave meter
波料 *demparyō* air-time charge
波探知機 *dempa tanchiki* radar
9柱 *denchū* telephone pole
信 *denshin* telegraph, telegram, wire, cable, cablegram
信印字機 *denshin injiki* teletype
信柱 *denshimbashira* telegraph pole
信為替 *denshingawase* telegraphic transfer
信料 *denshinryō* telegram charge
信術 *denshinjutsu* telegraphy
信線 *denshinsen* telegraph line
信機 *denshinki* telegraph instrument
10原 *dengen* source of electricity
閃 *densen* electric lightning flash
荷 *denka* electric charge
訓令 *denkunrei* telegraphic instructions
流 *denryū* electric current
流計 *denryūkei* galvanometer, ammeter
流転換器 *denryū tenkanki* commutator
11探 *dentan* radar
液 *den-eki* electrolyte
球 *denkyū* electric-light bulb
瓶 *dembin* battery jar
動力 *dendōryoku* electromotive power
動機 *dendōki* electric motor
12場 *denjō* electric field
極 *denkyoku* electrode, pole, terminal
量 *denryō* amount of electricity
報 *dempō* telegram
報用紙 *dempō yōshi* telegram blank
報為替 *dempōgawase* telegraphic transfer
報料 *dempōryō* telegram charge
報略号 *dempō ryakugō* telegraphic address
報暗号帳 *dempō angōchō* telegraphic code
報頼信紙 *dempō raishinshi* telegram blank
13源 *dengen* source of electricity
路 *denro* electric circuit
鉄 *dentetsu* electric railway
鈴 *denrei* electric bell
飾 *denshoku* illumination; electric decorations
蓄 *denchiku* electric phonograph
解 *denkai* electrolysis
解液 *denkai eki* electrolyte
解質 *denkaishitsu* electrolyte
話 *denwa* telephone
話口 *denwaguchi* mouthpiece; telephone
話加入者 *denwa kanyūsha* telephone subscriber
話交換手 *denwa kōkanshu* telephone operator
話交換局 *denwa kōkankyoku* telephone central, telephone exchange
話料 *denwaryō* telephone charges
話帳 *denwachō* telephone directory
話術 *denwajutsu* telephony
話管 *denwakan* speaking tube, mouthpiece
話機 *denwaki* telephone instrument
14髪 *dempatsu* permanent wave
磁石 *denjishaku* electromagnet
磁気 *denjiki* electromagnetism
磁波 *denjiha* electromagnetic waves
磁鉄 *denjitetsu* electromagnet
15鋳 *denchū* electrotyping
撃 *dengeki* electric shock
撃作戦 *dengeki sakusen* blitzkrieg
熱 *dennetsu* electric heat
熱器 *dennetsuki* electric heater
線 *densen* electric wire, electric line, telegraph wire, telephone wire, electric cord, cable
線布設 *densen fusetsu* cable laying
線病 *densembyō* runner, run (in a stocking)
16機 *denki* electrical machinery and appliances
機子 *denkishi* armature
17鍵 *denken* telegraph key
19離 *denri* electrolysis, ionization
27纜 *denran* electric cable

6

霊 5051 / F-X Nonstandard for 霊 5056.

A 需 5052 / F2028 JU request; need.

5 用 *juyō* consumption (of goods)
9 品 *juhin* supplies
要 *juyō* demand (for commodities); requirements
要者 *juyōsha* user
要供給 *juyō-kyōkyū* supply and demand
要家 *juyōka* user
12 給 *jukyū* supply and demand

7

霈 See 5059.

霆 5053 / F2029 TEI lightning; thunder.

霄 5054 / F2029 SHŌ sky.

20 壌 *shōjō* heaven and earth

B **震** 5055 / F2029 SHIN. *furu(eru)*, *furu(u)* shake, tremble, quiver, shiver, shudder; vibrate. *furu(i)*, *furu(e)* shivering, shaking, trembling, shuddering.

3 上 *furu(e)-a(garu)* tremble, shiver; be frightened, be intimidated
4 天 *shinten* heaven-shaking; very energetic; tremendous (voice)
天動地 *shinten-dōchi* stunning heaven and earth
5 付 *furu(i)-tsu(ku)* grapple with
央 *shin-ō* earthquake center
6 死 *shinshi* death by lightning
7 声 *furu(e)goe*, *furu(i)goe* trembling voice
災 *shinsai* earthquake disaster
災地 *shinsaichi* earthquake disaster area
9 度 *shindo* earthquake magnitude
10 害 *shingai* earthquake damage
恐 *furu(e)-oso(reru)* shudder, quake with fear
11 動 *furu(i)-ugo(ku)* quake, tremble, shake, reel, rock. *shindō* tremor, shock, concussion, vibration
12 幅 *shimpuku* earthquake amplitude
13 慄 *shinritsu* shuddering in fear
戦 *furu(e)-onono(ku)*, *furu(e)-wanana(ku)* fear and tremble, shudder
源 *shingen* earthquake center; center of a disturbance
源地 *shingenchi* earthquake center; center of a disturbance
15 蕩 *shintō* concussion, shock, impact
16 撼 *shinkan* terror, alarm, fright
駭 *shingai* terror, alarm, fright
17 盪 *shintō* concussion, shock, impact
22 顫 *shinsen* tremor
顫麻痺 *shinsen mahi* paralysis agitans

B **霊** 5056 / F2035 **靈** REI soul, spirit; Holy Spirit. RYŌ spirits who possess men. *tamashii*, *tama* soul, spirit.

3 山 *reizan* sacred mountain
4 木 *reiboku* sacred tree; famous tree
水 *reisui* miracle-working water
化 *reika* spiritualization
5 生 *reisei* spiritual life
石 *reiseki* a sacred rock
代 *reidai*, *tamashiro* visible symbol of the soul
6 肉 *reiniku* soul and body
気 *reiki* an atmosphere (feeling) of mystery
地 *reichi* hallowed ground, sacred place
安室 *reianshitsu* morgue
交 *reikō* communion, spiritual fellowship
交術 *reikōjutsu* spiritualism, spirit communication
7 位 *rei-i* Buddhist mortuary tablet
妙 *reimyō na* wonderful, marvelous, miraculous
8 雨 *reiu* a good rain
性 *reisei* divine nature, divinity, spirituality
物 *reimotsu* worker of miracles
的 *reiteki* spiritual
宝 *reihō* precious treasure
長 *reichō* a leader with miraculous powers; an outstanding leader; mankind
長類 *reichōrui* primates, man
9 屋 *tamaya* mausoleum, ancestral shrine, tomb
迹 *reiseki*＝霊跡 (see below–13)
前 *reizen* before a god; before the spirit of the deceased
界 *reikai* spiritual world; psychic world
泉 *reisen* fountain or hot springs with magical powers
草 *reisō* sacred herb
柩 *reikyū* coffin, casket
柩車 *reikyūsha* hearse
10 峰 *reihō* sacred mountain; beautiful mountain
祠 *reishi* shrine
11 鳥 *reichō* sacred bird
域 *rei-iki* hallowed ground, sacred place
液 *reieki* an elixir
動 *reidō* psychic activity
堂 *reidō* shrine or temple
異 *rei-i* miracle, wonder
12 場 *reijō* hallowed ground, sacred place
筆 *reihitsu* refined style
雲 *reiun* a strange high cloud
媒 *reibai* spirit medium
媒術 *reibaijutsu* spiritualism
智 *reichi* intellect, wisdom
智学 *reichigaku* theopathy
13 園 *reien* cemetery park
殿 *reiden* mausoleum, shrine
瑞 *reizui* miraculous sign
跡 *reiseki* the aftermath of a miracle; the site of a miracle

夢 *reimu* divine revelation, inspired dream, prophetic vision
感 *reikan* inspiration; sacred intuition
14境 *reikyō* hallowed ground, sacred place
歌 *reika* spiritual (song)
魂 *reikon* soul, spirit
魂不滅 *reikon-fumetsu* immortality of the soul
15廟 *reibyō* mausoleum, shrine
16薬 *reiyaku* panacea, wonder medicine
18蹟 *reiseki*=霊跡 (see above-13)
験 *reigen, reiken* miracle, miraculous virtue
顕 *reiken*=word above

8

霓 5057 / F2030 GEI rainbow.

霑 5058 / F2030 **沾** TEN moisten, water, soak. *uruo(u)* be moistened, be wet; profit by, be benefited. *uruo(su)* wet, moisten, irrigate, dip; profit, enrich, make prosperous.

霈 5059 / F2030 HAI. *hisame* big rain; long rainy spell.

霙 5060 / F2031 EI. *mizore* sleet, rain-and-snow mixture.

霏 5061 / F2030 HI falling rain or snow.
16霏 *hihi toshite* (falling) thick and fast

霖 5062 / F2031 RIN long rainy spell.
8雨 *rin-u* long rainy spell

9

霞 5063 / F2031 KA. *kasu(mu)* be hazy; grow dim (eyes), be blurred. *kasumi* haze, mist; dimness of sight.
9草 *kasumisō* babies'-breath (a flower)
13隠 *kasumigaku(re)* behind or in the mist
14関 *Kasumigaseki* Foreign Ministry (Japan)

B **霜** 5064 / F2031 Sō. *shimo* frost.
4月 *shimotsuki* 11th lunar month
7囲 *shimogako(i)* chilblains; frostbite
8夜 *shimoyo* frosty night
9風 *shimo kaze* a cold frosty wind
柱 *shimobashira* frost columns, ice needles
除 *shimoyo(ke)* frost protection
降 *shimofu(ri)* frosting; gray, salt-and-pepper color
枯 *shimoga(reru)* be killed by the frost. *shimoga(re) no* wintry, bleak, frost-nipped
枯時 *shimoga(re)doki* winter, dead season, slack season
10害 *sōgai* frost damage
11雪 *sōsetsu* frost and snow; white hair or beard; purity of heart
12焼 *shimoya(ke)* chilblains; frostbite
割 *shimowa(re)* splitting of trees from freezing
13解 *shimodo(ke)* thaw, thawing

11

B **霧** 5065 / F2032 MU. *kiri* mist, fog, spray. *ki(ru)* get foggy, get cloudy.
4中信号 *muchū shingō* fog signal
5氷 *muhyō* fog freezing on vegetation; frost flowers
7吹 *kirifu(ki)* atomizer, sprayer, vaporizer
吹器 *kirifu(ki)ki* atomizer, sprayer, vaporizer
8雨 *kiriame, kirisame* drizzle
9海 *mukai* foggy sea
虹 *kiri niji* fogbow, white rainbow
除 *kiriyo(ke)* eaves, entrance eaves
信号所 *kiri shingōjo* fog-signal station
10島 *kirishima* wild honeysuckle
11笛 *muteki* fog horn
12渡 *kiriwata(ru)* fog covers all
散 *musan suru* dissipate, be dispelled
集 *mushū* great crowds gathering like fog
量計 *muryōkei* fog gauge
13暖簾 *kiri noren* sign curtain
20鐘 *mushō* fog bell

12

霰 5066 / F2032 SEN. SAN. *arare* hail, hailstones; small cubes.
12弾 *sandan* buckshot, slugs

13

霸 5067 / F2033 See **覇** 4281.

霹 5068 / F2034 HEKI thunder.
24靂 *hekireki* thunder, thunderclap

B **露** 5069 / F2032 RO dew; Russia. *tsuyu* dew, dewdrops; tears; mortality, flimsiness; (with neg.) not a bit. *ara(wa) ni* openly, publicly; frankly, clearly. *tsuyu, tsuyu (hodo mo)* (not) in the least, (not) a particle. *tsuyu(keshi)* dampness. *-Ro-* Russia.
2人 *Rojin* a Russian
4支 *Ro-Shi* Russia and China
天 *roten* open air
天掘 *rotembo(ri)* strip mining
天街 *rotengai* district of open-air shops
5玉 *tsuyutama* dewdrops
払 *tsuyuhara(i)* herald, pioneer
台 *rodai* outside balcony

出 *roshutsu* exposure; disclosure; outcrop; (photographic) exposure
出工事 *roshutsu kōji* openwork
出計 *roshutsukei* light meter
6地 *roji* farming fields
西亜 *Roshiya* Russia
光 *rokō* exposure (in photography)
光計 *rokōkei* exposure meter
7見 *roken* discovery, detection
里 *Rori* Russian verst (.6629 mile)
助 *Rosuke* a Russian (derogative)
呈 *rotei* exposure, disclosure
8国 *Rokoku* Russia
命 *romei* transient life
店 *roten* roadside stand
店商人 *roten shōnin* stall vendor
9帝 *Rotei* Czar
軍 *Rogun* the Russian army
点 *roten* dew point
10骨 *rokotsu na* plain, frank, undisguised; conspicuous, acute; lewd
座 *roza* sitting out in the open
都 *Roto* Russian capital (city)
11探 *Rotan* Czarist spy
清 *Ro-Shin* Russia and China
聊 *tsuyu-isasa(ka) mo* (not) in the least
悪 *roaku* boasting of one's wickedness
宿 *roshuku* sleeping out in the open
貨 *Roka* Russian money
12満 *Ro-Man* Russia and Manchuria
営 *roei* bivouac, camping out
14暦 *Roreki* Julian calendar
層 *rosō* outcrop
滴 *roteki* dewdrop
語 *Rogo* the Russian language
領 *Roryō* Russian territory
疑 *tsuyu-utaga(wazu)* not a shadow of a doubt
16頭 *rotō* outcrop; uncovered head
17礁 *roshō* a rock protruding above the surface of the sea
霜 *tsuyujimo* frozen dew
18顕 *roken* discovery, detection
20艦 *Rokan* Russian warship

14

霽 5070 F2034 SEI. *ha(reru)*, *ha(rasu)* (see under 晴 2143.0).

15

靆 5071 F2035 TAI.

16

靈 5072 F2035 See 霊 5056.

靂 5073 F2034 REKI violent thunder or lightning.

靄 5074 F2034 AI. *moya* mist, haze, fog.

17

靉 5075 F2036 AI.

23靆 *tanabi(ku)* (clouds) trail, hang over. *aitai(taru)* trailing (clouds)

RAD. 青 174

Aoi blue. Variant: 靑. Nickname: Blue.

A 青 5076 F2036 靑 SEI. SHŌ. *ao* blue, green; green light. *ao(mu)* turn green. *ao(bamu)* turn greenish, be tinged with green. *ao(i)* blue, green; pale; unripe, green, inexperienced. *ao-* unripe; new; immature; novice; blue, green.
2二才 *aonisai* green youth, stripling
3土 *aoni* blue earth, blue-black earth
女 *seijo* the goddess of frost and snow; frost
山 *aoyama*, *seizan* blue mountain, green hills. *seizan* cemetery
大将 *aodaishō* common harmless snake
4木 *aoki* green tree; gold-leaf plant
丹 *aoni* blue earth, blue-black earth
少年 *seishōnen* youth, younger generation
水無月 *aominazuki* 6th lunar month
天 *seiten* blue sky
天井 *aotenjō* blue sky
天白日 *seiten-hakujitsu* clear weather; clearing of one's reputation
天白日旗 *seiten-hakujitsuki* Nationalist China flag
天霹靂 *seiten-hekireki* a bolt from the blue, a bombshell
5玉 *seigyoku* sapphire; jacinth
白 *aojiro(i)* pale, pallid; bluish white
目 *aome* blue eyes
史 *seishi* history, annals
写真 *aojashin*, *aoshashin* blueprint
田 *aota*, *aoda* green rice fields
田刈 *aotaga(ri)* a green crop
田売 *aota-u(ri)* selling unharvested rice

田売買 *aota baibai* dealing in unharvested rice
田買 *aotaga(i)* buying unharvested rice
6 米 *aomai* green rice
色 *seishoku* blue
虫 *aomushi* green caterpillar, grub
地 *aoji* blue material, blue cloth
光 *aobikari* phosphorescent light, green
竹 *aodake* green bamboo ⌊light
竹色 *aodake iro* bluish green
年 *seinen* youth, young people
年子女 *seinen shijo* young men and women
年団 *seinendan* young men's association
年会 *seinenkai* young people's society; young men's association
年男女 *seinen danjo* young men and
年期 *seinenki* adolescence ⌊women
7 豆 *aomame* green beans
貝 *aogai* mother-of-pearl
8 青 *aoao(shita)*, *aoao(toshita)* verdant, fresh
松 *seishō* a green pine ⌊and green
波 *aonami* blue waves
空 *aozora, seikū* blue sky
苔 *aogoke* green moss
果 *seika* vegetables and fruit
金石 *seikinseki* lapis lazuli
宝玉 *seihōgyoku* sapphire
物 *aomono* greens, vegetables
物市 *aomono ichi* vegetable market
物市場 *aomono ichiba* vegetable market
物屋 *aomonoya* vegetable store, vegetable
9 柳 *aoyagi, aoyanagi* green willow tree ⌊man
臭 *aokusa(i)* smelling grassy or unripe; inexperienced, unskilled
茶 *aocha* bluish brown
草 *aokusa* green grass
信号 *aoshingō* a green light
枯病 *aoga(re)byō* wilting disease
春 *seishun* springtime of life, youth. *seishun no* youthful, adolescent
春期 *seishunki* puberty, adolescence
海 *aoumi* blue sea
海苔 *aonori* green edible seaweed
海原 *ao-unabara* blue expanse of water
海亀 *aoumigame* large green turtle
10 馬 *aouma* gray horse
梅 *aoume* unripe plum
砥 *aoto* blue whetstone
書 *seisho* a "blue book" (goverment report)
書生 *aoshosei* young inexperienced student
息 *ao-iki* an anxious sigh
息吐息 *ao-iki-to-iki* pitiful dejection
11 黒 *aoguro(i)* pale and dark
眼 *seigan* aiming at the eye (with a sword)
菜 *aona* greens
票 *aohyō* blue vote, opposing vote
瓷 *seiji* celadon porcelain
12 蛙 *aogaeru* tree frog, green frog
嵐 *aoarashi, seiran* wind blowing thru new
畳 *aodatami* new mat, green mat ⌊verdure
筋 *aosuji* blue vein
葉 *aoba* foliage, greenery, green leaves
雲 *seiun* blue sky; high rank. *aokumo* white clouds in a blue sky ⌈to succeed
雲志 *seiun (no) kokorozashi* determination
13 楼 *seirō* brothel ⌈last streetcar
電車 *aodensha* green-lamp car, next to the
14 旗 *aohata* blue flag; safety flag
磁 *seiji* celadon porcelain
緑 *aomidori* dark green
褪 *aoza(meru)* turn pale, turn white
鼻汁 *ao(p)pana, aobana* green nasal mucus
酸 *seisan* hydrocyanic acid, prussic acid
酸塩 *seisan-en* cyanide
銅 *seidō, karakane* bronze
銅工 *seidōkō* worker in bronze
銅貨 *seidōka* bronze coin
銅製 *aodōsei* made of bronze
銅器 *seidōki* bronze ware
銅器時代 *seidōki jidai* Bronze Age
15 銹 *aosabi* green rust; patina
豌豆 *aoendō* green peas
16 膨 *aobuku(re)* dropsical swelling
瓢箪 *aobyōtan* green gourd; pale-faced
17 藍 *seiran* indigo blue ⌊weakling
19 蠅 *aobae, aobai* blowfly
簾 *aosudare* green bamboo screen
23 黴 *aokabi* green mold; penicillium
24 鷺 *aosagi* blue heron

5

靖 See 3358.

6

A 静 $\frac{5077}{F2039}$ 靜 Jō, Sei quiet, peace, inactivity. *shizu(maru)* *vi* get quiet, calm down, grow still; subside, die down; be suppressed. *shizu(meru)* *vt* calm, pacify; soothe, alleviate; appease; suppress, quell. *shizu(kana)* quiet, still, silent; calm, placid; serene, peaceful; soft (rain); gentle (voice); graceful; slow (walk); deserted. *shizu(kesa)*, *shizu(kasa)* stillness, silence, hush; calm, serenity.

2 力学 *seirikigaku* statics
4 心 *shizugokoro* relaxed spirit
止 *seishi* stillness, repose, standing still
水 *seisui* still water, stagnant water
水力学 *seisui rikigaku* hydrostatics
6 返 *shizu(mari)-kae(ru)* become perfectly quiet, be as still as death

7坐 *seiza* sitting quietly; meditation
8的 *seiteki* static
夜 *seiya* quiet night
物 *seibutsu* object at rest; still life
物画 *seibutsuga* still-life picture
9思 *seishi* meditation, contemplation
10座 *seiza* sitting quietly, meditation
修 *seishū* spiritual retreat
脈 *jōmyaku* vein
脈血 *jōmyakuketsu* venous blood
脈炎 *jōmyakuen* phlebitis
脈注射 *jōmyaku chūsha* intravenous injection
11粛 *seishuku* silence, quiet
寂 *seijaku* silence, quiet, hush
寂主義 *seijaku shugi* quietism
13電気 *seidenki* static electricity
電気学 *seidenkigaku* electrostatics
電学 *seidengaku* electrostatics
電誘導 *seiden yūdō* electrostatic induction
14静 *shizushizu to* calmly, quietly
態 *seitai no* static, stationary
15養 *seiyō* rest, recuperation, convalescence
養中 *seiyōchū* resting, recuperating
16穏 *seion* calm, tranquillity
17聴 *seichō* quietly listening; attention
謐 *seihitsu* peace, tranquillity
18観 *seikan* serene contemplation; watchful waiting

8

靛 5078/F2039 TEN a blue plant dye.

靜 5079/F2039 See **静** 5077.

RAD. 非 175

Arazu not. Nickname: Negative.

A **非** 5080/F2040 HI mistake; misdeed; injustice; wrong; non-, un-, anti-. *ara(zu)* not, not so, not to be. *ara(zaru)* other than. *ara(zareba)* unless, except. *hi (to) suru* condemn, denounce, disapprove.

2力 *hiriki* disability, incompetence
人 *hinin* beggar; outcast; criminal
人道 *hijindō* inhumanity
人情 *hininjō* heartlessness
人間的 *hiningenteki* inhuman
3凡 *hibon na* extraordinary, unusual
才 *hisai* lack of ability, incompetence
4日 *hi-Nichi* un-Japanese
文明 *hibummei na* uncivilized
公式 *hikōshiki* informal, unofficial, exhibition (game)
公開 *hikōkai* closed (meeting)
友誼的 *hiyūgiteki* unfriendly
友誼的行為 *hiyūgiteki kōi* unfriendly act
5礼 *hirei* impoliteness
民主的 *himinshuteki* undemocratic
生産的 *hiseisanteki* nonproductive, unproductive
立憲 *hirikken* unconstitutional
立憲的 *hirikkenteki* unconstitutional
打所無 *hi(no)u(chi)dokorona(ku)* nothing to criticize
打算的 *hidasanteki* unselfish, disinterested
正統派 *hiseitōha* heterodoxy
正統説 *hiseitōsetsu* heterodoxy
6米 *hi-Bei* un-American
行 *hikō* misdemeanor, evil deed, immoral act
合法 *higōhō* illegal; out of order
合法的 *higōhōteki* illegal
合理的 *higōriteki* unreasonable, irrational
7役 *hiyaku, hieki* retirement
妥協的 *hidakyōteki* uncompromising
芸術的 *higeijutsuteki* inartistic
社交的 *hishakōteki* unsociable, retiring
社会的 *hishakaiteki* antisocial
売同盟 *hibai dōmei* sellers' strike
売品 *hibaihin* articles not for sale
8命 *himei* untimely death
金属 *hikinzoku* nonmetal
学術的 *higakujutsuteki* unscientific
定期船 *hiteikisen* tramp steamer
法 *hihō* unlawfulness, lawlessness
法人 *hihōjin* unincorporated person
実用品 *hijitsuyōhin* unnecessary things
実際的 *hijissaiteki* impractical, unpractical
武装 *hibusō* demilitarization
武装地帯 *hibusō chitai* demilitarized zone
国民 *hikokumin* unpatriotic person, traitor
国家的 *hikokkateki* unpatriotic
国教徒 *hikokkyōto* nonconformists, dissenters
9道 *hido(i)* (see 酷 under 4788.0)
急品 *hikyūhin* a nonessential
政治的 *hiseijiteki* nonpolitical
科学的 *hikagakuteki* unscientific
軍人 *higunjin* civilian
軍事化 *higunjika* demilitarization
軍事的 *higunjiteki* nonmilitary, civilian
10能率的 *hinōritsuteki* inefficient
党派的 *hitōhateki* nonpartisan
党員 *hitōin* a nonmember (of a party)

11違 *hi-i* lawlessness, unlawfulness
運 *hiun* bad luck; misfortune
情 *hijō* inanimate nature
理 *hiri* unreasonableness, absurdity
望 *hibō* ulterior motive, evil design
紳士的 *hishinshiteki* ungentlemanly
組合員 *hikumiai-in* nonunionist, nonmember ⌈ness, unfairness
道 *hidō* tyranny, cruelty, injustice, lawless-
道徳的 *hidōtokuteki* immoral
現実的 *higenjitsuteki* unreal, impracticable
現業員 *higengyōin* office worker
常 *hijō* emergency, unforseen occurrence, calamity. *hijō na* remarkable, unusual. *hijō ni* exceedingly, extremely, remarkably, unusually
常口 *hijōguchi* emergency exit
常手段 *hijō shudan* emergency measures
常用 *hijōyō* (for) emergency use
常米 *hijōmai* emergency rice
常灯 *hijōtō* emergency light
常号音 *hijō gōon* alarm call
常事態 *hijō jitai* state of emergency
常時 *hijōji* crisis, emergency
常勤 *hijōkin* part-time work
常報知 *hijō hōchi* alarm; emergency report
常電話 *hijō denwa* emergency phone call
常線 *hijōsen* cordon
常識 *hijōshiki* lack of common sense, absurdity, thoughtlessness
12番 *hiban* off duty, off guard
統制 *hitōsei* uncontrolled (goods)
買同盟 *hibai dōmei* boycott
営利的 *hieiriteki* nonprofit
13毀 *hiki* slander, calumny, libel
愛国的 *hiaikokuteki* disloyal, unpatriotic
鉄金属 *hitetsu kinzoku* nonferrous metals
聖書的 *hi-seishoteki* un-Biblical
業死 *higōshi* untimely death
業最後 *higō (no) saigo* untimely death
戦 *hisen* war renunciation
戦災 *hisensai* undamaged by the war
戦論 *hisenron* pacifism
戦闘員 *hisentōin* noncombatant
14認 *hinin*＝否認 40.14
15霊的 *hireiteki* unspiritual
課税 *hikazei* tax exemption
衛生的 *hieiseiteki* unsanitary, unhealthful, unwholesome
論理的 *hironriteki* irrational, illogical
16機密 *hikimitsu* nonsecret
18職 *hishoku* retired
難 *hinan* criticism, denunciation
難攻撃 *hinan-kōgeki suru* castigate
難者 *hinansha* critic, accuser ⌈argument
20議 *higi suru* criticize, blame. *higi* abusive

4

斐 5081/F867 Hɪ beautiful; patterned. [文]

悲 5082/F715 Hɪ. *kana(shimu)*, *kana(shigaru)* grieve, be sad, deplore, mourn for, regret. *kana(shimi)* sorrow, grief. *kana(shige) na* sad, sorrowful, plaintive. *kana(shii)* sad, pathetic, plaintive. [心]

A

6曲 *hikyoku* plaintive melody
壮 *hisō na* pathetic, tragic ⌈song
壮慷慨 *hisō-kōgai* angrily singing a tragic
8泣 *kana(shimi)-na(ku)* mourn and weep.
況 *hikyō* distress, adversity ⌊*hikyū* wailing
歩 *kana(shimi)-aru(ku)* go around mourning
9風 *hifū* a sighing wind; a late-fall wind; the tragedy of life
哀 *hiai* sorrow, grief, misery, pathos
10涙 *hirui* tears of sadness
恋 *hiren* disappointed love
11運 *hiun* bad luck, misfortune, sad fate
惨 *hisan* misery, wretchedness
望 *hibō* wicked ambition
12痛 *hitsū* bitterness, pathos
報 *hihō* sad news, news of a death
喜 *hiki* joy and sorrow
喜劇 *hikigeki* tragicomedy
13傷 *hishō* misery, wretchedness
嘆 *kana(shimi)-nage(ku)* weep and wail.
愴 *hisō* pathetic, sad ⌊*hitan* grief, sorrow
話 *hiwa* sad story
愁 *hishū* pathos, sorrow
業 *higō* misfortune
14鳴 *himei* shriek, scream
境 *hikyō* adversity, distress
酸 *hisan* misery, wretchedness
歌 *hika* elegy, dirge
15憤 *hifun* indignation, resentment
調 *hichō* plaintive note, mournful melody,
歎 *hitan* grief, sorrow ⌊touch of sadness
劇 *higeki* tragedy, tragic drama
劇的 *higekiteki* tragic
18観 *hikan* pessimism, disappointment
観主義 *hikan shugi* pessimism
観主義者 *hikan shugisha* pessimist
観的 *hikanteki* pessimistic
観説 *hikan setsu* pessimism
観論 *hikanron* pessimism
観論者 *hikanronsha* pessimist
19願 *higan* Buddhist prayer for mankind

6

翡 5083/F1508 Hɪ a kind of kingfisher. [羽]

⌈*kawasemi* kingfisher
14翠 *hisui* jade, chrysoprase; kingfisher.

蜚 5084 / F1665 HI cockroach. [虫]

14 語 *higo* rumor, gossip

— 7 —

靠 5085 / F2041 Kō. *mota(reru)* (see under 凭 659.0).

11 掛 *mota(re)-ka(karu)*=凭掛 659. 11

B 輩 5086 / F1845 HAI fellow, people, companion; line. *tomogara, yakara* fellows, men, set. [車]

3 下 *haika* followers, adherents

5 出 *haishutsu suru* (men of talent) appear successively; come crowding on

靡 See 靡 5397.

9-STROKE RADICALS

RAD. 面 176

Men face. Nickname: Face.

A 面 5087 / F2041 MEN face. features; mask; face guard; surface; plane; side, facet; aspect, phase, corner (of a board); page. *men(suru)* face, border, front on. *omo, omote* face, honor, reputation. *tsura* face, surface.

3 子 *mentsu* face, honor

5 立 *omoda(chi), omoda(te)* looks, countenance, features

付 *tsuratsu(ki)* expression, look

皮 *mempi* countenance

皮厚 *tsura (no) kawa (no) atsu(i)* brazen-faced, impudent, shameless

目 *memmoku, memboku* face, honor, dignity; credit; appearance, aspect

目一新 *memboku isshin suru* take on a completely new appearance

目玉 *membokudama* face, honor, dignity

目無 *membokuna(i)* ashamed

白 *omoshiro(garu)* amuse oneself, be amused. *omoshiro(garaseru)* amuse, entertain. *omoshiro(i)* interesting; entertaining; delightful, amusing, comical, queer, promising; favorable

白半分 *omoshiro-hambun ni* half in fun, jokingly

白可笑 *omoshiro-okashi(i)* amusing, funny

白尽 *omoshirozu(ku) de* for the fun of it

白味 *omoshiromi* interest, fun, enjoyment

6 色 *menshoku* complexion, countenance, expression

伏 *omobu(se)* ashamed, confused, crestfallen

汚 *tsuragoyo(shi)* disgrace, dishonor, shame

当 *tsura-a(te)* mean words, innuendo

争 *mensō* pointing out people's failures before others

会 *menkai* interview, meeting

会人 *menkainin* visitor, caller

会日 *menkaibi* visitors' day

7 疔 *menchō* face carbuncle

体 *mentei* face, looks, features

妖 *men-yō na* strange, mysterious

忘 *omowasu(re)* failing to recognize

8 長 *omonaga na* long-faced, oval-faced

9 面 *memmen* each one, all; every direction

食 *menku(rau)* be confused, be bewildered, be embarrassed. *menku(i)* emphasizing looks in choosing a mate

持 *omomo(chi)* countenance, look, features

映 *omoha(yui)*=*hazuka(shii)* (see under 恥 3704.0)

相 *mensō* countenance, features, looks

変 *omogawa(ri)* change in one's looks

前 *menzen* presence; before one's eyes

10 部 *membu* face, facial region

容 *men-yō* countenance, looks, features

差 *omoza(shi)* features

倒 *mendō* trouble, difficulty, complications; care, attention. *mendō na, mendō(i)* troublesome, complicated

倒臭 *mendōkusa(i)* troublesome, tiresome

従 *menjū* obeying only when watched

従腹背 *menjū-fukuhai* passive resistance

11 晤 *mengo* interview, meeting

舵 *omokaji* starboard; turning to starboard

責 *menseki* personal reproof

接 *mensetsu* interview

接試問 *mensetsu shimon* oral examination

12 喰 *menkura(u)*=面食 (see above-9)

訴 *menso* direct appeal

無 *omona(shi)* be ashamed

13 腫 *omoba(ru)* the face swells

詰 *menkitsu* personal reproof

隠 *omogaku(shi)* covering the face. *omogaku(re)* hiding the face
照 *omode(ru)* (the face) shines; blush
14 憎 *tsuraniku(i)* disgusting, detestable
構 *tsuragama(e)* expression, look
語 *mengo*=*mendan* 面談 (see below–15)
貌 *membō* looks, features, countenance
魂 *tsuradamashii* countenance, facial expression
15 瘡 *omokusa* facial acne
談 *mendan* personal conversation, interview, talk
謁 *men-etsu* audience (with the emperor)
輪 *omowa* looks, features, face
影 *omokage* visage, face; trace, shadow; memory
罵 *memba suru* abuse (someone) to his face
16 積 *menseki* area
皰 *nikibi* pimple, acne
窶 *omoyatsu(re)* careworn look
壁 *mempeki* meditation facing a wall
19 識 *menshiki* acquaintance

— 14 —

靨 See 73.

RAD. 革 177

Tsukuri kawa tanned hide or *kaku no kawa* (*kawa* "leather" written with the character read *kaku* as distinguished from Rad. 107). At left: *kawa hen.* Nickname: Shoe Leather (as in 靴 *kutsu* shoe).

A **革** 5088/F2043 KAKU tanned leather. *arata(maru)* become serious (illness). *kawa* (see under 皮 3109.0).
2 刀 *kawagatana* leather knife
3 工場 *kawa kōba* tannery
4 文庫 *kawa bunko* leather case
5 正 *kakusei* reform
6 色 *kawa iro* greenish blue
8 沓 *kawagutsu* leather shoes
具 *kawagu* leather goods
表紙 *kawabyōshi* leather binding
命 *kakumei* revolution
命児 *kakumeiji* revolutionist
命的 *kakumeiteki* revolutionary, radical
命軍 *kakumeigun* revolutionary army
命家 *kakumeika* revolutionist
命旗 *kakumeiki* revolutionists' flag
命歌 *kakumeika* revolutionary song
9 草履 *kawazōri* leather sandals
10 砥 *kawato* razor strop
紐 *kawahimo* strap; thong; lash; leash
帯 *kawa obi* leather belt
11 張 *kawaba(ri) no* leather-covered
細工 *kawazaiku* leathercraft
13 靴 *kawagutsu* leather shoes or boots
新 *kakushin* reform, innovation
新的 *kakushinteki* reformatory
新派 *kakushinha* reformists; reformer
14 綴 *kawatoji* leather binding
緒 *kawao* sword strap; clog thong
鞄 *kawa kaban* leather bag, suitcase, briefcase
製 *kawasei* made of leather
15 質 *kakushitsu* coriaceous, leathery
16 鞘 *kawazaya* leather sheath, holster
18 鞣 *kawaname(shi)* tanning; tanner
職人 *kawa shokunin* leatherworker
22 嚢 *kawabukuro* leather bag

— 2 —

勒 5089/F263 ROKU halter and bit. *roku(suru)* carve, engrave; lead; control. [力]

— 3 —

靫 5090/F2044 SAI. SA. SATSU. *utsubo, utsuo* quiver.

靭 5091/F2044 = **靱** JIN. soft, pliable. NIN. *utsubo, utsuo* quiver.
8 性 *jinsei* tenacity
10 帯 *jintai* ligament

— 4 —

靴 5092/F2044 KA shoes. *kutsu* shoes; boots.
3 工 *kutsukō* shoemaker
下 *kutsushita* socks, stockings
下止 *kutsushitado(me)* garters
下留 *kutsushitado(me)* garters
下編機 *kutsushita a(mi)ki* hosiery knitting machine
5 皮 *kutsugawa* shoe leather
8 底 *kutsuzoko* shoe sole
直 *kutsunao(shi)* shoe repair; cobbler
刷毛 *kutsubake* shoebrush
9 音 *kutsu oto* sound of someone walking
屋 *kutsuya* shoemaker, shoe store
拭 *kutsufu(ki), kutsunugu(i)* doormat
型 *kutsugata* shoe last; shoe stretcher
10 師 *kutsushi* shoemaker

紐 *kutsuhimo* shoelaces
釘 *kutsu kugi* shoe peg, shoe nail
11脱 *kutsunu(gi)* bootjack
13傷 *kashō* shoe sore
14摺 *kutsuzuri* doorsill
箆 *kutsubera* shoehorn
墨 *kutsuzumi* shoe polish; bootblack
15摩 *kutsuzure* shoe sore
縫 *kutsunu(i)* sewing shoes
16磨 *kutsumigaki* shoe polish; bootblack
17擦 *kutsuzure* shoe sore

5

鞆 5093/F2045 (国字) *tomo* archer's arm protector.

鞅 5094/F2045 Ō connection.

12掌 *ōshō suru* be busy with

鞄 5095/F2045 HAKU. HŌ. BYŌ. *kaban* suitcase, brief case, bag.

9持 *kabammo(chi)* private secretary

6

鞋 5096/F2045 AI straw sandals. *waraji* straw sandals.

鞏 5097/F2046 KYŌ hard.

8固 *kyōko* firmness, stability, security, strength

鞍 5098/F2046 AN *kura* saddle.

3下 *kurashita* saddlecloth; sirloin; saddle (of mutton)
5尻 *kurajiri* back of the saddle
8坪 *kura tsubo* seat of a saddle
9屋 *kuraya* saddler
10部 *ambu* col, saddle (between mountains)
12替 *kuraga(e)* changing quarters (by geisha or prostitutes); changing jobs
13数 *kura kazu* number of times one has ridden (horses)
15敷 *kurashi(ki)* saddlecloth
17擦 *kurazure* saddle sores
22嚢 *annō* saddlebag

7

鞘 5099/F2046 SHŌ. *saya* (sword) sheath, case, cap; margin, difference, brokerage; spread; (bean) shells.

6当 *saya-a(te)* courtship rivalry
8取 *sayato(ri)* brokerage

8

鞜 5100/F2046 TŌ. *kutsu* shoes, boots.

鞠 5101/F2047 KIKU. KYŪ. *mari* ball.

8育 *kikuiku* bringing up, nurture
10訊 *kikujin* investigation; questioning, interrogation
躬 *kikkyū* bowing respectfully
躬如 *kikkyūjo toshite* reverently, humbly, respectfully

9

鞫 5102/F2047 KIKU investigate a crime.

10訊 *kikujin*＝鞠訊 5101.10
11問 *kikumon* interrogation (of suspects)

鞣 5103/F2047 JŪ tanned leather. NYU. *name(su)* tan (hides). *nameshigawa* tanned leather.

5皮 *jūhi*, *name(shi)gawa* tanned leather
皮業 *jūhigyō* tannery
9屋 *name(shi)ya* tanner; tannery

鞭 5104/F2048 BEN whip, rod. *muchi* whip, rod. *muchiu(tsu)*＝鞭打 (see below–5).

5打 *muchiu(tsu)* whip, flog; urge on, encourage
打苦行者 *Muchiu(chi) Kugyōsha* Flagellants
7声 *bensei* the crack of a whip
15撻 *bentatsu* urging, spurring on; whipping

10

鞴 5105/F2048 HI. BI. *fuigo*, *fuigō* bellows.

11

鞺 5106/F2049 TŌ sound of drums.

20鞳 *tōtō* drumming; rumbling, roaring

RAD. 韋 178

Nameshigawa tanned leather. This rare radical actually has 10 strokes, but it is traditionally a 9-stroke element and is so counted herein. Nickname: Different (as in 違 *chigau* differ).

8

韓 5107/F2050 KAN *Kara* Korea.

2 人 *Kanjin, Karabito* ancient word for a Korean
6 衣 *Kara koromo* ancient Korean clothes
8 国 *Kankoku, Karakuni* Korea
9 竿 *karasao* flail
14 語 *Kara kotoba* ancient Korean words; a foreign language
15 鋤 *karasuki* plow
18 櫃 *karabitsu* Korean chest

10

韜 5108/F2051 TŌ bag; wrapping.

11 晦 *tōkai suru* hide (talents, etc.)
略 *tōryaku* strategy, tactics

RAD. 韭 179

Nira leek. Nickname: Leek.

韭 5109/F2052 See 韮 3988.

3

韮 See 3988.

RAD. 音 180

Oto sound. Variant: 音. At left: *oto hen*. Nickname: Noisy.

A **音** 5110/F2052 音 ON sound; noise; pronunciation. IN sound, tone. *oto* sound, noise, roar; fame. *ne* sound, tone, note, voice, chirping.

2 力 *onryoku* strength of the voice
3 上 *ne(o)a(geru)* be tired out
叉 *onsa* tuning fork
4 引 *ombi(ki)* dictionary arranged by the syllabary
太 *nebuto* voice huskiness
6 色 *ne-iro, onshoku* tone color, tone quality
曲 *ongyoku, onkyoku* songs accompanied by the samisen; musical performance
字 *onji* phonetic symbol; syllabary
名 *ommei* names of musical notes
吐 *onto* speaking voice
吐朗朗 *onto-rōrō to* sonorously
7 沙汰 *otosata* news, letter
声 *onsei, onjō* voice
声言語 *onsei gengo* the spoken language
声学 *onseigaku* phonetics
8 波 *ompa* sound wave
物 *immotsu* friendship gift
画 *onga* sound movies
9 速 *onsoku* speed of sound
便 *ombin* euphony, euphonic change
信 *onshin, inshin, otozure* correspondence, message, news, tidings
律 *onritsu* meter, rhythm
度 *ondo* musical interval, step
度取 *ondoto(ri)* chorus leader; leading spirit, leader
10 栓 *onsen* organ stop
訓 *onkun* Chinese and Japanese pronunciations of characters
容 *on-yō* voice and countenance; visage
部記号 *ombu kigō* clef (in music)
11 域 *on-iki* voice range
訳 *on-yaku* transliteration
階 *onkai* musical scale
符 *ompu* note, score, notation;
12 揚 *ne(o)a(geru)* be tired out
程 *ontei* musical interval, step
量 *onryō* voice volume
18 痴 *onchi* tone deafness, no ear for music
溝 *onkō* sound track

節 *onsetsu* syllable
勢 *onsei* vocal stress
感 *onkan* sense of sound
楽 *ongaku* music
楽会 *ongakkai, ongakukai* concert, musicale
楽学校 *ongaku gakkō* music school
楽家 *ongakka, ongakuka* musician
楽隊 *ongakutai* orchestra, band
楽堂 *ongakudō* concert hall
14読 *ondoku* reading aloud. *on-yo(mi)* the *on* or Chinese reading of a character or a compound
管 *onkan* organ pipe
15締 *neji(me)* tune
調 *onchō* tune, tone, rhythm, melody, harmony, euphony
盤 *omban* phonograph record
質 *onshitsu* tone quality
標文字 *ompyō monji, ompyō moji* phonetic symbols
16頭 *ondo* workmen's songs, marching songs
19譜 *ompu* music, notes, notation
韻 *on-in* vocal sound
韻学 *on-ingaku* phonetics
韻論 *on-inron* phonetics
響 *onkyō* sound, noise, echo
響学 *onkyōgaku* acoustics
響爆弾 *onkyō bakudan* scream bomb

2

竟 5111/F1398 竟 KYŌ. *owa(ru), owa(ri)* (see under 終 3521.0). *tsui ni* finally, after all. [立]

A 章 5112/F1398 章 SHŌ chapter; composition; poem; badge, mark, sign; design. [立]
5句 *shōku* passage, chapter and verse
11魚 *tako* octopus
13数 *shōsū* number of chapters
節 *shōsetsu* chapter and verse

4

A 意 5113/F728 意 I mind, heart; care; liking, taste; inclination, will, intention; thought, idea; desire. [心]
2力 *iryoku* will, will power
4中 *ichū* intention
中人 *ichū (no) hito* lovers
5外 *igai na* unexpected, surprising
6匠 *ishō* design, idea
向 *ikō* intention, idea, inclination
地 *iji* temper; disposition; will power; obstinacy
地汚 *ijikitana(i)* greedy, gluttonous
地張 *ijiba(ru)* persist in, be obstinate. *iji(p)pa(ri)* obstinacy; obstinate person
地悪 *ijiwaru(i)* ill-tempered; unfortunate
地穢 *ijikitana(i)* greedy, gluttonous
気 *iki* spirit, heart; disposition
気込 *ikigo(mu)* be enthusiastic about
気地 *ikuji, ikiji* self-respect, honor, pride
気投合 *iki-tōgō* sympathy, mutual understanding
気阻喪 *iki-sosō* depression, dejection
気沮喪 *iki-sosō* depression, dejection
気消沈 *iki-shōchin* depression, dejection
気軒昂 *iki-kenkō* high spirits, high morale
気盛 *ikisaka(n)* high spirits
気筋 *ikisuji* flirting
気揚揚 *iki-yōyō(taru)* triumphant, exultant
気銷沈 *iki-shōchin* depression, dejection
気衝天 *iki-shōten* high spirits, high morale
7図 *ito* intention, aim
見 *iken* opinion, idea, suggestion; remonstrance, admonition
見書 *ikensho* written opinion
志 *ishi* will, mind, volition
志力 *ishiryoku* will power
志薄弱 *ishi-hakujaku* weak will, lacking a purpose
志薄弱者 *ishi-hakujakusha* weak-willed person
8表 *ihyō* surprise, something unexpected
味 *imi* meaning, significance
味合 *imia(i)* meaning, reason
味深長 *imi-shinchō ni* significantly
味深重 *imi-shinchō na* significant, pregnant with meaning
味論 *imiron* semantics
9恨 *ikon* grudge, ill-will, enmity
相 *isō* thoughts
思 *ishi* intention, purpose, mind
思表示 *ishi-hyōji* declaration of intention
思能力 *ishi-nōryoku* mental capacity
10馬心猿 *iba-shin-en* uncontrollable passions
11訳 *iyaku* free translation
欲 *iyoku* volition, will
13想外 *isōgai no* unexpected, unsuspected
義 *igi* meaning, significance
義深 *igibuka(i)* full of meaning; of great value
15趣 *ishu* grudge, malice, spite; thoughts; intention
趣返 *ishugae(shi)* revenge
趣斬 *ishugi(ri)* killing (someone) because of a grudge
18嚮 *ikō* intention, idea, inclination
19識 *ishiki* consciousness
識的 *ishikiteki ni* consciously

10

B 響 5114/F2054 響 響 KYŌ. *hibi(ku)* sound, resound, reverberate, echo, ring, vibrate; grate on; affect, find an echo in; become known. *hibi(ki)* sound, noise, peal, boom, crash, explosion; echo, reverberation; influence, effect; vibration, shock.
7応 *kyōō* hurrying to ally oneself with (someone)

[11]動 *doyo(mu), doyo(meku), toyo(mu)* be very noisy; resound; stir up (enthusiasm)
[12]渡 *hibi(ki)-wata(ru)* resound thruout

B 韻 5115/F2053 韻 IN rhyme; elegance; tone.
[4]文 *imbun* poetry, verse
[6]字 *inji* rhyming words
[8]学 *ingaku* prosody, versification
事 *inji* artistic pursuits
[9]律 *inritsu* rhythm
[11]脚 *inkyaku* metrical foot
[12]無 *in (no) na(i)* blank (verse)
[14]語 *ingo* rhyming words

— 12 —

響 5116/F2054 響 See 響 5114.

頁 RAD. 181

Ōgai big "shell (to distinguish it from Rad. 154), *ichi no kai* (i.e., the character *ichi* "one" plus *kai* shell, or *peiji* "page."). Nickname: Big Shell.

頁 5117/F2054 KETSU. *peiji* page, leaf.
[8]岩 *ketsugan* shale

— 2 —

頃 See 754.

B 頂 5118/F2054 CHŌ. *itadaki* head; top of the head; top, summit, peak; spire. *itada(ku)* (see under 戴 795.0). *unaji* nape of the neck.
[3]上 *chōjō* top, summit, crest, peak, apex; climax, acme
[7]角 *chōkaku* vertical angle
[8]垂 *unada(reru)* drop one's head
門一針 *chōmon (no) isshin* admonition concerning one's shortcomings
[9]度 *chōdo* exactly, just right
点 *chōten* apex, vertex, peak, climax, acme, top, height
[10]華 *chōka* finial
[17]戴 *chōdai suru* accept, receive; take, eat, enjoy. *chōdai* please, be good enough to
戴物 *chōdaimono* a gift received

— 3 —

項 See 1459.

須 See 1592.

順 See 1450.

— 4 —

B 頒 5119/F2058 HAN. *waka(tsu)* (see under 分 578.0).
[3]与 *waka(chi)-ata(eru)* make available to
[5]白 *hampaku* grayish hair
布 *hampu* distribution, circulation, dissemination
[6]行 *hankō* distribution, wide dissemination

頌 5120/F2057 JU. SHŌ eulogy. *shō(suru)* extol, praise.
[9]栄 *shōei* doxology; the Gloria
[12]詞 *shōshi* eulogy, compliment
[13]詩 *shōshi* poem of praise
[14]徳 *shōtoku* eulogy
徳碑 *shōtokuhi* monument to some one's honor
[14]歌 *shōka* anthem, carol, hymn of praise
歌隊 *shōkatai* choir

頓 5121/F2058 TON. *tomi ni, niwaka ni* suddenly, in a hurry, immediately. *ton to* entirely; (neg.) not in the least.
[3]才 *tonsai* ready wit, tact
[6]死 *tonshi* sudden death
[7]狂 *tonkyō na* flurried, hysteric, wild; discordant
[8]知 *tonchi* ready wit, tact
服 *tompuku* dose
服薬 *tompukuyaku* dose (of medicine)
[9]首 *tonshu* kowtow, very low bow; your humble servant
珍漢 *tonshinkan* absurdity, contradiction
[10]馬 *tomma* dunce, simpleton. *tomma na* silly
挫 *tonza* setback, rebuff, standstill, impasse, deadlock
[12]着 *tonjaku, tonchaku* care, heed, concern, anxiety
智 *tonchi* ready wit, tact
[13]痴気 *tonchiki* dunce, simpleton

頑 5122/F2057 GAN stubborn; foolish. *gan(to shite)* firmly, stubbornly, resolutely. *kataku(na) na* obstinate, stubborn.
[3]丈 *ganjō na* solid, firm, stout
[8]固 *ganko* obstinacy, stubbornness, persistence, bigotry

迷 *gammei* obstinacy, perversity, bigotry
物 *gambutsu* hardheaded person
陋 *ganrō* stubbornness and meanness
9是無 *ganzena(i)* helpless, innocent, naïve
10冥 *gammei* bigotry, obstinacy
11健 *ganken* robust health
張 *gamba(ru)* persist in, insist on, be inflexible
強 *gankyō* obstinacy, persistence
強派 *gankyōha* die-hards
13愚 *gangu* stupid and obstinate
22癬 *gansen, tamushi* ringworm

A **預** 5123 F2057 Yo. *azu(keru)* *vt* place in custody, deposit, leave with, entrust with, commit to, give. *azu(karu)* *vi* take charge of; receive on deposit; undertake to do; call off (as a tie); refrain from; receive, enjoy. *azu(kari)* depositing; custody. *azu(ke)* entrusting to, committing to. (*o*)*azu(ke)* not carrying out a promise; making a dog wait for a command to eat.
2人 *azu(kari)nin* one placed in charge of a thing. *azu(ke)nin*, depositor
入 *azu(ke)-i(reru)* make a deposit
3子 *azu(kari)go* foster child
5主 *azu(kari)nushi* possessor. *azu(ke)nushi* depositor
7言 *yogen* prophecy
言者 *yogensha* prophet
8物 *azu(ke)mono* checked article, article left in charge of someone. *azu(kari)mono* a thing on deposit; consignment
金 *yokin* deposit, bank account, credit. *azu(ke)kin* key money
金主 *yokinnushi* depositor
金者 *yokinsha* depositor
金通帳 *yokin tsūchō* bankbook
金票 *yokinhyō* deposit slip
10託 *yotaku suru* deposit
託金 *yotakukin* deposit
11票 *azu(kari)hyō* claim check
12貯金 *yochokin* deposit, bank account
証 *azu(kari)shō* baggage check; warehouse receipt; deposit certificate
証券 *azu(kari) shōken* warehouse receipt, deposit certificate
証書 *azu(kari) shōshō* baggage check; warehouse receipt, deposit certificate

5

頗 See 3110.

頚 Nonstandard for **頸** 5132.

A **領** 5124 F2059 Ryō dominion, territory, possession, fief; suit (of armor). *ryō(suru)* govern, reign, be in possession of.
3土 *ryōdo* territory, dominion, possession
土保全 *ryōdo hozen* territorial integrity
土拡張 *ryōdo kakuchō* territorial expansion
4水 *ryōsui* territorial waters
内 *ryōnai* domains, territory
分 *ryōbun* territory, dominion, possession; domain, sphere, field
5外 *ryōgai* outside the territory
民 *ryōmin* population of a fief
主 *ryōshu* lord of a fief, daimyo
主権 *ryōshuken* feudal lord's authority
収 *ryōshū* receipt, voucher
収者 *ryōshūsha* receiver, recipient
収書 *ryōshūsho* receipt, voucher
収証 *ryōshūshō* receipt, voucher 「fief
6地 *ryōchi* territory, dominion, possession;
会 *ryōkai* understanding, comprehension
有 *ryōyū* possession
7邑 *ryōyū* one's land
承 *ryōshō* acknowledgment
8国 *ryōkoku* the national domain
空 *ryōkū* territorial air
事 *ryōji* consul
事団 *ryōjidan* consular corps
事裁判 *ryōji saiban* consular jurisdiction
事裁判所 *ryōji saibansho* consular court
事裁判権 *ryōji saibanken* consular jurisdic-
事館 *ryōjikan* consulate 」tion
9首 *erikubi* nape of the neck
海 *ryōkai* territorial waters
10袖 *ryōshū* leader, chief, boss
11域 *ryōiki* territory, dominion, possession, domain, sphere
13解 *ryōkai suru* understanding, comprehension
置 *ryōchi suru* take over documents and material evidence

6

頬 Nonstandard for **頰** 5131.

7

頭 See 4469.

頷 5125 F2062 Gan. *unazu(ku)* nod, nod approval.

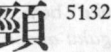

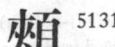

頤 5126 F2060 **頥** I. *otogai* chin. *ago* jaw.
8使 *ishi suru* have a person under one's absolute control

穎 5127/F1385 **穎** Ei heads of grain; point (of an instrument); cleverness. [禾]

8才 *eisai*＝英才 3927.3
10悟 *eigo* intelligent, shrewd
11脱 *eidatsu suru* gain recognition

頻 5128/F2063 Hin. *shiki(ru)* *vi* repeat, occur repeatedly. *shiki(ri) ni* repeatedly, incessantly, insistently, intently.

5出 *hinshutsu* frequent appearance
6回 *hinkai* frequent
9発 *himpatsu* frequent occurrence, frequency
度 *hindo* frequency
度数 *hindosū* frequency
13数 *hinsū* frequency
16頻 *himpin to, shikushiku to* frequently
繁 *himpan* frequency

B**頼** 5129/F1804 **賴** Rai. *tano(mu)* ask, request, entreat, appeal; entrust to, commission; employ, call in; depend on, have recourse to, trust in. *tayo(ru)* rely on, have recourse to. *tano(moshii)* reliable, trustworthy; hopeful. *tayo(rinai)* forlorn, helpless; vague; unreliable. *tano(mō)* hello there. [貝]

2入 *tano(mi)-i(ru)* earnestly request
4込 *tano(mi)-ko(mu)* earnestly request
少 *tano(mi)sukuna(i)* not too reliable; hopeless, helpless, forlorn
5母 *tanomo(shii)* reliable, trustworthy; hopeful
8所 *tayo(ri)dokoro* one's resort, dependence
信紙 *raishinshi* telegram blank
14綱 *tano(mi) (no) tsuna* last resort, only hope

頽 5130/F2062 Tai. *kuzu(reru)* decline; crack up (a baseball pitcher); decay; fester. *kuzu(oreru)* be discouraged. *nada(reru)* slope, descend, slide down. *nada(re)* avalanche; snowslide; slope, sloping; surging (crowd).

4込 *nada(re)-ko(mu)* rush into, crowd
10唐 *taitō* decadence, decline
11運 *taiun* declining fortune
12落 *nada(re)-o(chiru)* slide down
廃 *taihai* deterioration, degeneration, laxness, corruption, decadence, ruin
廃的 *taihaiteki* corrupt
13勢 *taisei* downward tendency, decline, decay
17齢 *tairei* declining years

頰 5131/F2062 Kyō. *hō, ho-o, hoho* cheek.

4辺 *ho(p)peta* cheek
6当 *hōa(te)* (helmet) visor; (fencing) mask
7杖突 *hōzue (o) tsu(ku)* rest the chin on one's hands
9紅 *hōbeni* rouge
冠 *hōkabu(ri)* tying a cloth around the cheeks; affecting ignorance
10骨 *hōbone, kyōkotsu* cheekbone
被 *hōkabu(ri)* tying a cloth around the cheeks; affecting ignorance
11張 *hōba(ru)* take (food); take a big mouthful
14摺 *hōzuri* pressing cheeks together
15髯 *hōhige* sideburns

頸 5132/F2062 Kei. *kubi* neck, head.

3丈 *kubidake* height to the neck. *kubi(t)take* complete devotion
4木 *kubiki* yoke
5玉 *kubitama*＝首玉 5186.5
9巻 *kubima(ki)* muffler, comforter
10骨 *keikotsu* neckbone
部 *keibu* neck (region)
11桶 *kubi oke* box for a severed head
動脈 *keidōmyaku* carotid artery
12椎 *keitsui* cervical vertebrae
筋 *kubisuji* nape of the neck
13際 *kubigiwa* the neck
飾 *kubikaza(ri)* necklace
14綱 *kubizuna* neck tether
静脈 *keijōmyaku* jugular vein
15輪 *kubiwa* necklace; collar
19縄 *kubinawa* neck tether

8

頻 Nonstandard for **頻** 5128.

顆 5133/F2063 Ka a grain (of rice, etc.); small round object; clod of earth.

11粒 *karyū* granule

9

題 See 2164.

顋 5134/F2063 See **腮** 3793.

顎 5135/F2064 **顎** Gaku jaw. *ago* jaw, chin. *agito* gill.

10骨 *agobone, gakkotsu* jawbone
紐 *agohimo* chin strap
22鬚 *agohige* beard

A**額** 5136/F2064 Gaku tablet, plaque, framed picture; sum, quantity, amount, volume; denomination. *hitai* forehead, brow. *nuka(zuku)* bow, kowtow, prostrate oneself.

6行灯 *gaku andon* horizontal paper lantern

[8]突 *nukazu(ku)* bow, kowtow, prostrate oneself
[9]面 *gakumen* face value; par; denomination; mere outlook
[10]帯鏡 *gakutaikyō* doctor's head mirror
[13]殿 *gakuden* votive-picture hall
際 *hitaigiwa* margin of the hair
裏 *gaku ura* back of a framed picture or motto
[15]縁 *gakubuchi* picture frame

B 顕 5137/F2068 顯 KEN. *ara(wareru)*, *ara(wasu)* (see under 現 2943.0).

[5]示 *kenji suru* show, unfold, unveil, uncover
[6]在 *kenzai suru* reveal
[7]位 *ken-i* high office, high rank
花植物 *kenka shokubutsu* flowering plant
[8]官 *kenkan* dignitary, high official
[9]界 *genkai* this world
要 *ken-yō* prominence, importance
栄 *ken-ei* attaining fame
[11]現 *kengen* manifestation
著 *kencho na* remarkable, striking, obvious
[12]揚 *ken-yō suru* extol, exalt
然 *kenzen(taru)* obvious, clear, conspicuous
貴 *kenki* position of honor
[13]微鏡 *kembikyō* microscope
微鏡写真 *kembikyō shashin* microphotograph
[14]彰 *kenshō suru* manifest, display, exalt, honor
[15]賞 *kenshō* public rewarding
[17]爵 *kenshaku* high rank of nobility
[18]職 *kenshoku* important post

A 類 5138/F2066 類 RUI kind, variety, class, genus; description; parallel case, an equal. *rui(suru)* be similar to, be akin to. *tagu(eru)* compare with. *tagui* kind, sort, class; match, equal. *-rui* resembling.

[2]人猿 *ruijin-en* anthropoid ape, orangutan
[4]比 *ruihi* analogy; parallel; equal
火 *ruika* spreading fire
化 *ruika suru* assimilate, incorporate
[5]句 *ruiku* synonymous expression; similar *haiku* poems
[6]同 *ruidō* similarity; same kind
名 *ruimei* generic name
似 *ruiji* resemblance, analogy, kinship
似点 *ruijiten* points of similarity
似品 *ruijihin* an imitation
似療法 *ruijiryōhō* homeopathy
[7]伴 *ruihan* same kind; companion; accomplice
別 *ruibetsu* classification
[8]例 *ruirei* similar example; analogy
[9]型 *ruikei* similar type
[10]症 *ruishō* similar diseases, similar cases
書 *ruisho* similar books
[11]推 *ruisui* analogy
[12]焼 *ruishō* spreading fire
[14]語 *ruigo* synonym
[15]縁 *ruien* affinity, family relationship
[18]題 *ruidai* similar question
[20]纂 *ruisan* classified collection in book form

A 顔 5139/F2064 顏 GAN. *kambase* face, countenance. *kao* face, countenance, expression; honor, prestige.

[5]立 *kaoda(chi)* facial features. *kao (ga) ta(tsu)* save face
付 *kaotsu(ki)* countenance, looks, features
出 *kaoda(shi) suru* visit, put in an appearance
[6]色 *kao iro*, *ganshoku* complexion, countenance, expression, color
向 *kaomu(ke)* facing the public
合 *kaoa(wase)* meeting, presentation, being matched against or paired with
先 *kaosaki* face, countenance; facial protrusions (nose or cheeks); right in front
気色 *kaokeshiki* looks, countenance
[7]作 *kaozuku(ri)* make-up
役 *kaoyaku* leader, boss
利 *kao (ga) ki(ku)* be influential
売 *kao (o) u(ru)*, *kao (ga) u(reru)* become famous
見 *kaomi(se)* meeting for the first time
見世 *kaomise* debut, first stage appearance
見知 *kaomishi(ri)* one whose face one recognizes
[9]持 *kaomo(chi)* looks, countenance
変 *kaogawa(ri)* changing one's looks
負 *kaoma(ke) suru* be outshone, be made to blush
造作 *kao (no) zōsa* countenance
面 *gammen* the face
面角 *gammenkaku* facial angle
[10]振 *kaobu(re)* personnel, line-up
料 *ganryō* cosmetics
容 *kaokatachi*, *kambase* looks, features, countenance
[11]違 *kaochiga(i)* changed looks
寄 *kaoyo(se)* meeting, presentation; being matched against or paired with
[12]揃 *kaozoro(i)* galaxy of notables; all present
貸 *kao (o) ka(su)* come and assist
[13]触 *kaobure* personnel, line-up
[14]貌 *kaokatachi*, *gambō* features, looks, personal appearance
[15]潰 *kao (ga) tsubu(reru)* lose face
[18]癖 *kaoguse* facial habits
[19]繫 *kaotsuna(gi)* getting acquainted

10

願 See 255.

顎 See 5135.

類 See 5138.

顛 5140/F2066 = 顚 TEN overturn; summit; origin.
5末 *temmatsu* circumstances, facts, details
8沛 *tempai* stumbling and falling; moment of time
10倒 *tentō suru* fall down violently, upset, overturn, tumble; invert, reverse
12落 *tenraku suru* stumble and fall; become suddenly poor
18覆 *tempuku suru* overthrow, overturn; subvert; upset, capsize

12

顧 5141/F2067 = 顧 顧 Ko. *kaeri(miru)* look back; turn B around, look back upon, review; examine onself; take notice of.
5用 *kaeri(mi)-mochi(iru)* to favor
9眄 *koben* looking around
客 *kokyaku, kokaku* customer, patron, client
11視 *koshi suru* glance back, turn around
望 *kobō suru* look around; hesitate
問 *komon* adviser, consultant
問弁護士 *komon bengoshi* legal adviser
問団 *komondan* advisory group, brain trust
問医 *komon-i* consulting physician
問官 *komonkan* councilor
15慮 *koryo* concern, solicitude

顥 5142/F2067 Kō clarity.

13

顫 5143/F2068 SEN. *furu(eru), furu(u)* tremble, shudder.

14

顯 5144/F2068 See 顕 5137.

顬 5145/F2068 JU temple (of the head).

15

纇 See 2437.

16

顱 See 259.

17

顴 5146/F2069 KEN cheekbone.
10骨 *kankotsu* cheekbone

18

顳 5147/F2069 SHŌ temple (of the head).
23顬 *komekami* temple (of the head)

RAD. 風 182

Kaze wind. Variant: 風 *fū-nyō* "wind" enclosure. Nickname: Wind (cf. Rad. 16).

風 5148/F2069 FU, FŪ wind; air, look, appear-A ance, bearing, mien, deportment; manners, custom; trend, tone, tendency; way, fashion, manner; style, type; disposition, turn of mind; kind; vein; state, condition. *kaze* wind, storm, breeze, draught, current of air; a cold. *furi* form; condition; deportment; pretense; discipline; custom. *kaza-* wind.
2入 *kaza-i(re)* airing, ventilation
力 *fūryoku* wind force
3口 *kazaguchi* air intake
子 *kaze (no) ko* open-air creatures; children
下 *kazashimo, kazashita* leeward
上 *kazakami* windward
上置 *kazakami ni o(kenu)* cannot associate with
土 *fūdo* climate, topography, natural fea- ⌊ture
土病 *fūdobyō* endemic disease
土記 *fudoki* topography, description of natural features
土馴化 *fūdo junka* acclimatization 「nature
4月 *fūgetsu* wind and moon; beauties of
引 *kazehi(ki)* catching cold
切 *kazeki(ri)* leading edge of a wing; car radiator ornament. *kaze (o) ki(ru)* strut along 「form
丰 *fūbō* appearance, attire; visage; beautiful
心地 *kazegokochi* signs of wind; a slight
水 *fūsui* wind and flowing water ⌊cold
水害 *fūsuigai* storm and flood damage
化 *fūka* weathering; efflorescence; influence of a ruler on the governed
化作用 *fūka sayō* weathering

5 穴 *kaza-ana* air hole, ventilator
立 *kazedat(su)* get windy, begin to blow hard
圧 *fūatsu* wind pressure, air pressure; leeway, driftage
6 色 *fūshoku* scenery, landscape, view. *kaze iro* the wind blowing thru the flowers and branches
気 *kazake* slight cold; signs of wind. *kazake, kazek(k)e* slight cold. *fūki* climate; customs and climate; the spirit of the people; a slight cold; palsy
向 *fūkō, kazemu(ki), kazamu(ki)* wind direction; situation; tendency
光 *fūkō* scenery, natural beauty
当 *kaza-a(tari), kazea(tari)* force of the wind; fierce criticism; oppression
7 足 *kaza-ashi* wind velocity
車 *fūsha* windmill. *kazaguruma* windmill; ⌊pinwheel
伯 *fūhaku* wind god
位 *fūi* wind direction ⌈posture, attitude
体 *fūtei, fūtai* appearance, looks, dress,
抜 *kazanu(ki), kazenu(ki)* airhole, ventilation
折 *kaza-o(re)* broken by the wind
邪 *fūja, kaze* a cold
声 *fūsei* the sound of wind; rumor, false alarm. *kazegoe* huskiness from a cold
災 *fūsai* storm damage
吹回 *kaze (no) fu(ki)mawa(shi)* wind direction; devolopments
見 *kazami* weather vane
見舞 *kaze mimai* inquiry after a storm
来 *fūrai* the coming of the wind; showing up from nowhere; ill at ease; useless; no place of abode
来人 *fūraijin* a person showing up from nowhere; wanderer; an unsettled person; a worthless person ⌈tramp
来坊 *fūraibō* wanderer, vagabond, waif,
来者 *fūraimono* wanderer, vagabond, waif, ⌊tramp
呂 *furo* bath; bathtub
呂代 *furodai* bath charge
呂屋 *furoya* bathhouse, public bath
呂釜 *furogama* bath heater, bath boiler
呂桶 *furo-oke* bathtub
呂場 *furoba* bathroom
呂番 *furoban* one who lights the bath
呂銭 *furosen* bath charge
呂敷 *furoshiki* wrapping cloth, kerchief
8 雨 *fūu* wind and rain, rainstorm
味 *fūmi* taste, flavor ⌈blowing away
押 *kaza-osa(e)* stones to keep things from
波 *fūha* wind and waves, storm, rough seas;
炉 *fūro* wind furnace ⌊discord, quarrel
和 *kazanagi* a calm
刺 *fūshi* sarcasm, innuendo, irony ⌈tains
炎 *fūen* foehn, warm wind from the moun-
采 *fūsai* appearance, mien, bearing
物 *fūbutsu* natural objects, nature, scenery, landscape; scenes and manners
物詩 *fūbutsushi* nature poem
9 面 *kaza-omote* wind direction
音 *kaze-oto* sound of the wind
食 *fūshoku* weathering, wind erosion
通 *kazetō(shi), kazatō(shi), kazetō(ri)* ven-
便 *kaze (no) tayo(ri)* rumor ⌊tilation
待 *kazama(chi), kazema(chi)* waiting for a
洞 *fūdō* wind tunnel ⌊favorable wind
神 *kaze(no) kami* wind god; demon of colds. *fūshin* wind god; character
紀 *fūki* discipline, public morals
級 *fūkyū* wind classification
除 *kazayo(ke)* windbreak, windshield
変 *fūgawa(ri)* eccentricity, peculiarity
発 *fūhatsu* sudden gust; voluble speech
姿 *fūshi* appearance, looks, mien
速 *fūsoku* wind velocity
速計 *fūsokukei* anemometer
前 *fūzen* the place the wind strikes
前灯 *fūzen (no) tomoshibi* flickering light; dangerous situation; verge of death
信 *fūshin* news; wind direction
信子 *fūshinshi* hyacinth
信子石 *fūshinshiseki* zircon
信旗 *fūshinki* weather vane
信器 *fūshinki* weather vane
俗 *fūzoku* manners, customs, morals
俗画 *fūzokuga* paintings depicting customs
俗営業 *fūzoku eigyō* business affecting public morals ⌈lic morals
俗壊乱 *fūzoku kairan* offense against pub-
10 疹 *fūshin* German measles ⌈ance, style
格 *fūkaku* character, personality, appear-
浪 *fūrō* wind and waves, heavy seas
流 *fūryū* taste, elegance, refinement
陰 *kazakage* wind shelter
害 *fūgai* storm damage
馬 *fūba* indifference, apathy
馬牛 *fūbagyū* indifference, apathy; something of no concern; widely separated
致 *fūchi* taste, elegance; scenic beauty
致地区 *fūchi chiku* scenic zone
致林 *fūchirin* ornamental forest
11 鳥 *fūchō* bird of paradise
情 *fuzei* appearance, air; taste; elegance; entertainment, hospitality
眼 *fūgan* gonorrheal ophthalmia
脚 *kaza-ashi* wind velocity
船 *fūsen* balloon
彩 *fūsai* taste, elegance, refinement
教 *fūkyō* public morals
窓 *kazamado* ventilator, small vent
笛 *fūteki, kazabue* bagpipe

習 *fūshū* manners, customs, usage
雪 *fūsetsu* snowstorm, blizzard
袋 *fūtai* weight of packing, tare; exterior; outward appearance 「spell
12 間 *kazama, kazema* lull in the wind; windy
評 *fūhyō* rumor 「wind
落 *kaza-o(chi)* fruit blown down by the
琴 *fūkin* organ; hand organ; accordion
媒 *fūbai* wind fertilization
媒花 *fūbaika* wind-pollinated flower
景 *fūkei* landscape, scenery, view
景画 *fūkeiga* landscape painting
雲 *kazagumo* wind clouds. *fūun* wind and clouds; state of affairs
雲児 *fūunji* a lucky adventurer
13 雅 *fūga* taste, elegance, refinement; literature, poetry
路 *kazamichi* wind lane; draught
鈴 *fūrin* wind bell
隠 *kazagaku(re)* protected from the wind; taking shelter from the wind
14 聞 *fūbun, kaze (no) ki(koe)* report, rumor
塵 *fūjin* dust; worldly affairs
説 *fūsetsu* rumor, report, hearsay
貌 *fūbō* looks, features, appearance
態 *fūtai* attitude
模様 *kaze-moyō, kazamoyō* wind direction; signs of a wind; looks of a windy sky
15 趣 *fūshu*=*omomuki* (see under 趣 4544.0)
儀 *fūgi* manners, customs, habits, morality,
標 *kazejirushi* weather vane 「demeanor
潮 *fūchō* lee tide; current (of the times), fashion, trend
蝕 *fūshoku* weathering, wind erosion
16 薫 *kazekao(ru)* fragrant breezes blow
薬 *kazagusuri, kazegusuri* medicine for cold
諭 *fūyu* hint, insinuation; allegory
諭法 *fūyuhō* allegory
17 濤 *fūtō* wind and waves, storm
霜 *fūsō* wind and frost; hardships
18 鎮 *fūchin* decorative hanging-scroll weight
19 靡 *fūbi suru* overwhelm, conquer, dominate, sway
韻 *fūin* grace, taste
22 籟 *fūrai* rustle of leaves

3

凬 See 65.

5

颯 See 3362.

颱 5149/F2075 TAI typhoon.
9 風 *taifū* typhoon
風眼 *taifūgan* eye of a typhoon

7

颶 See 5150.

8

颶 5150/F2075 **颶** GU storm.
9 風 *gufū* tornado, hurricane, typhoon

11

飄 5151/F2075 HYŌ wavy. *hiruga(eru), hiruga(esu)* (see under 翻 3681.0). *tsumuji* whirlwind.
5 乎 *hyō to* aimlessly; unexpectedly
10 逸 *hyōitsu na* buoyant, detached, aloof
12 然 *hyōzen to* aimlessly; unexpectedly
20 飄 *hyōhyō toshite* buoyantly; roaming

飛 RAD. 183

Tobu to fly. Nickname: Flying

A **飛** 5152/F2076 HI. *to(bu)* fly; skip (pages). *to(basu)* fly (a kite); let fly; blow away; scatter; splash; drive fast; skip over, omit; issue, send out. *ton(da)* surprising, extraordinary, shocking, terrible, tremendous, strange, serious. *to(ndemonai)* absurd; unexpected; fantastic; strange, extraordinary.
2 入 *to(bi)-i(ru)* jump into; dive in; fly into; thrust oneself into. *tobi-i(ri)* outside competitor, volunteer speaker; patches of color (in shrubbery)
入勝手 *tobi-i(ri) katte* free-for-all, open to all
3 下 *to(bi)-o(riru)* jump down. *to(bi)-sa(garu)* jump down. *to(bi)o(ri)* jumping off a moving vehicle
上 *to(bi)-a(garu)* fly up, jump up. *to(bi)a(gari)* an upstart; a rash person
4 火 *to(bi)hi* flying sparks; leaping flames; repercussions
切 *tobiki(ri)* top quality, beyond comparison; a flying shot (at a bird)

込 *to(bi)-ko(mu)* jump into; dive in; fly into; thrust oneself into
込台 *tobikomidai* diving board
込自殺 *tobiko(mi) jisatsu* railroad suicide
込様 *to(bi)ko(mi)zama ni* just as one jumps
5 白 *kasuri* (see 絣 under 3527.0) ⌊in
立 *to(bi)-ta(tsu)* jump to one's feet; fly away
付 *to(bi)-tsu(ku)* fly at, leap at, snatch at,
札 *hisatsu* urgent letter ⌊spring on
去 *to(bi)-sa(ru)* flee away, scatter
出 *to(bi)-da(su)* fly away; rush out; project, protrude; appear. *to(bi)-de(ru)* protrude, project, stand out of
石 *to(bi)-ishi* steppingstones ⌈pingstones
石伝 *to(bi)ishizuta(i)* following the step-
石作戦 *to(bi)-ishi sakusen* island-hopping operations ⌈invasion
石攻撃 *to(bi)-ishi kōgeki* island-hopping
6 回 *to(bi)-mawa(ru)* fly around; gambol, romp; hustle around
地 *to(bi)chi* isolated land
交 *to(bi)-ka(u)* fly about, flit about
行 *hikō* flight, flying, aviation
行士 *hikōshi* aviator
行甲板 *hikō kampan* flight deck
行免状 *hikō menjō* pilot's license
行服 *hikōfuku* flying suit
行学 *hikōgaku* aeronautics
行学校 *hikō gakkō* flying school
行速度 *hikō sokudo* air speed
行家 *hikōka* aviator, pilot
行郵便 *hikō yūbin* airmail
行時間 *hikō jikan* flying time
行術 *hikōjutsu* aeronautics, aviation
行船 *hikōsen* airship, dirigible
行隊 *hikōtai* flying corps, air force
行基地 *hikō kichi* air base
行場 *hikōjō* airfield, airport
行帽 *hikōbō* flying helmet
行艇 *hikōtei* flying boat, hydroplane
行機 *hikōki* airplane, aircraft
行翼 *hikōyoku* a flying wing
7 言 *higen* groundless rumor
走 *to(bi)-hashi(ru)* leap for joy
来 *hirai suru* come flying; come by air. *to-(bi)-kita(ru)* come flying, come running, come in a hurry
8 退 *to(bi)-no(ku)* jump back, jump aside
板 *to(bi)-ita* springboard
歩 *to(bi)-aru(ku)* gad about; run around
沫 *himatsu* splash, spray
沫伝染 *himatsu densen* droplet-spread infection
9 飛 *to(bi)to(bi) no* desultory, sporadic
降 *to(bi)o(ri)* jumping off a moving vehicle
乗 *to(bi)-no(ru)* jump on (a horse); jump on a moving vehicle
泉 *hisen* rapids, cataract, waterfall
10 起 *to(bi)-o(kiru)* jump out of bed; start up, spring to one's feet
11 魚 *to(bi)uo* flying fish ⌈(593–710)
鳥 *hichō* flying bird. *Asuka* Asuka Era
違 *to(bi)-chiga(u)* fly around
掛 *to(bi)-ka(karu)* pounce on, turn upon
球 *kikyū* fly ball ⌈another
移 *to(bi)-utsu(ru)* jump from one thing to
脚 *hikyaku* runner, courier; (ancient) post-
雪 *hisetsu* blowing snow ⌊man
道具 *to(bi)dōgu* missile, firearms
12 越 *to(bi)-ko(su)* jump over, fly cross. *to(bi)-*
弾 *hidan* flying bullet ⌊*ko(shi)* leapfrog
揚 *hiyō* flying; flight
渡 *to(bi)-wata(ru)* come tearing along; be spread all over, fly across
翔 *hishō* flight, flying, soaring
散 *hisan suru, to(bi)-chi(ru)* scatter, disperse
雲 *hiun* fleeting cloud
報 *hihō* urgent message
13 跳 *to(bi)-hane(ru)* jump up; fly away
節 *hisetsu* gambrel, hock (of a horse)
電 *hiden* urgent telegram
14 語 *higo* rumor, gossip
読 *to(bi)yo(mi)* skimming thru (a book),
15 蝗 *batta* grasshopper ⌊reading desultorily
16 龍 *hiryū* flying dragon; enlightened emperor
燕 *hien* flying swallow
燕草 *hiensō* larkspur, delphinium
17 檄 *higeki* urgent manifesto
翼 *to(bu) tsubasa* flying wing
18 瀑 *hibaku* waterfall
19 縄 *to(bi)nawa* jumping rope
離 *to(bi)-hana(reru)* fly apart; tower above; out of the ordinary
簷 *hien* high roof; upturned eaves
20 礫 *tsubute* stone throwing; a thrown stone
21 躍 *hiyaku* leap; activity; rapid progress; flight (of imagination); maneuvers
躍的 *hiyakuteki* rapid

— 12 —

飜 5153 F2078 See 翻 3681.

9
面革韋韭音頁風【飛】12 食首香

RAD. 食 184

Shoku food. Variant: 食. At left: 飠 or 食 (8 strokes) *shoku hen*. Nickname: Food.

A 食 5154 F2078 食 倉 SHI, JIKI food. SHOKU food, provisions; eating, meal; appetite. *ta(beru)*, *shoku(suru)* eat. *ku(u)* eat; subsist on; support oneself; consume; get (a scolding); encroach; bite at, gnaw at; (shoes) pinch; be cheated. *ku(rau)* eat, drink; receive (a blow). *ku(rawasu)* feed; strike (someone). *ha(mu)* eat, feed on, graze on, live on, prey on, receive (an allowance). *ku(i-chigiru)* eat off, bite off. *ku(enai)* inedible; hard to get along; cunning, crafty. *ku(eru)* edible; can get along. *shoku(pan)* bread.

2 入 *ku(i)-i(ru)* eat into; encroach upon
匕 *shokuhi* spoon
人種 *shokujinshu* cannibals
3 下 *ku(i)-sa(garu)* hang on to; hold on to convictions)
上 *ku(i)-a(geru)* eat all
4 手 *ku(i)te* eater; glutton
方 *ta(be)kata, ku(i)kata* manner of eating; how to eat, table manners
止 *ku(i)-to(meru)* restrain, resist, prevent. *ku(i)sa(shi)* food remnants. *ku(i)sa(shi) no* half-eaten
込 *ku(i)-ko(mu)* eat into, eat up; bore into; cut into; be deep-seated; erode, corrode; drain (funds). *kura(i)-ko(mu)* go to jail; shoulder a debt or other load; be deceived; abandon oneself to vice; fall heir to (trouble). *ku(i)ko(mi)* thrust; intrusion; deficit
切 *ku(i)-ki(ru)* gnaw off, bite off; eat up
分 *ku(i)-wa(keru)* eat and taste carefully. *ku(i)bun* board bill. *shokubun* phase of an eclipse
中 *shokuata(ri)* food poisoning, food disagreement
中毒 *shoku chūdoku* food poisoning
5 代 *ku(i)shiro* board bill
付 *ta(be)-tsu(keru)* get used to eating. *ku(i)-tsu(ku)* bite at, fasten one's teeth on, snap at, nibble at; hold on to. *kura(i)-tsu(ku)* bite
外 *ku(i)-hazu(su)* miss a meal; lose a job
台 *shokudai* dining table
出 *ha(mi)-da(su), ha(mi)-de(ru)* protrude, project, jut out, bulge out, be forced out, be pressed out, be crowded out. *ku(i)de* size of a serving. *kuide (ga aru)* have plenty of food
生活 *shoku seikatsu* eating habits, dietary life
用 *shokuyō no* edible, used for food
用牛 *shokuyō ushi* beef cattle
用供 *shokuyō ni kyō(suru)* use for food
用油 *shokuyō abura* cooking oil, edible oil
用品 *shokuyōhin* foodstuffs, groceries
用蛙 *shokuyōgaeru* edible frog
用植物 *shokuyō shokubutsu* food plants
6 虫 *shokuchū* insect eating
回 *ku(i)-mawa(ru)* go around eating
尽 *ku(i)-tsu(kusu)* eat up, consume. *shokujin* maximum obscuration (in an eclipse)
気 *ku(i)ki, ku(i)ke* appetite
休 *shokuyasu(mi)* rest after meals
汚 *ta(be)-yogo(su)* making a mess at the table
合 *ku(i)-a(waseru)* eat two things together; dovetail. *ku(i)-a(u)* bite each other; engage (gears); fit together exactly. *ku(i)a(i)* fighting, biting each other
当 *shokua(tari)* upset stomach
肉 *shokuniku* meat eating
肉類 *shokunikurui* carnivorous animals
7 言 *shokugen* eating one's words; breaking one's word; falsifying
足 *ku(i)-ta(rinai)* have not eaten enough; be unsatisfied; be dissatisfied with (someone)
坊 *ku(ishim)bō* gourmand; gluttony
初 *ta(be)zo(me), ku(i)zo(me)* weaning ceremony
余 *ta(be)-ama(su), ku(i)-ama(su)* leave meals unfinished. *ta(be)ama(ri)* leftover food. *ku(i)ama(ri), ku(i)ama(shi)* food remnants
扶持 *ku(i)buchi* board expense
8 延 *ku(i)-no(basu)* save on provisions; conserve (materials)
逃 *ku(i)ni(ge)* run off without paying for food
取 *ku(i)-to(ru)* pick and eat
券 *shokken* meal ticket
放題 *ku(i)hōdai, ta(be)hōdai* overeating
物 *ta(be)mono, ku(i)mono* food, provisions; victim, prey. *ku(u)mono* food, feed. *shokumotsu* food, provisions; diet; feed. *ku(wase)mono* imitation, counterfeit, fraud; impostor, hypocrite, crook (a person)
物中毒 *shokumotsu chūdoku* food poisoning
卓 *shokutaku* dining table
卓用 *shokutakuyō* for table use
卓塩 *shokutakuen* table salt
事 *shokuji* meal, diet, board
事中 *shokujichū* while eating, during a meal
事時 *shokujidoki* mealtime
9 食 *ku(uya)-ku(wazu) de* penniless
通 *shokutsū* connoisseur of food

後 *shokugo* after eating; after a meal
持 *ku(i)-mo(tsu)* hold between the teeth
相 *shokusō* eclipse phase
紅 *shoku beni* food coloring
封 *shokuhō* feudal estate
前 *shokuzen* before meals
客 *shokkaku* a dependent
荒 *ku(i)-a(rasu)* devour; eat a little of everything; work at this and that
甚 *shokujin* maximum obscuration (in an
指 *shokushi* forefinger, index finger ⌊eclipse)
指動 *shokushi (ga) ugo(ku)* have a desire to secure (something) ⌈table
前 *shokuzen* before the meal, at the dinner
前服用 *shokuzen fukuyō* to be taken before
思 *shokushi* appetite ⌊meals
思不振 *shokushi fushin* loss of appetite
品 *shokuhin* foodstuffs, groceries
品工業 *shokuhin kōgyō* food industry
品中毒 *shokuhin chūdoku* food poisoning
品化学 *shokuhin kagaku* food chemistry
品加工 *shokuhin kakō* food processing
品店 *shokuhinten* grocery
品衛生 *shokuhin eisei* food sanitation
10 逸 *ku(i)-hagu(reru)* miss a meal; lose a job
倒 *ku(i)-tao(su)* sponge on. *ku(i)dao(re)* wasting one's money on food
時 *ta(be)doki* season for (certain foods)
残 *ta(be)-noko(su), ku(i)-noko(su)* leave half-eaten. *ta(be)noko(shi)* leftover food
破 *ku(i)-yabu(ru)* bite and tear up
紛 *ku(i)-magira(wasu)* eat and forget one's troubles
殺 *ku(i)-koro(su)* kill and eat; bite to death
兼 *ta(be)-ka(neru), ku(i)-ka(neru)* have more than one can eat; cannot make a living
料 *shokuryō* food; main article of diet. *kuiryō* food, board
料品 *shokuryōhin* foodstuffs, groceries
料品店 *shokuryōhinten* grocery
料品商 *shokuryōhinshō* grocery business
11 過 *ku(i)-su(giru)* overeat
違 *ku(i)-chiga(u)* cross, interlock; run counter to, clash with; go amiss
頃 *ta(be)goro, ku(i)goro* time to eat; season for; done to a turn; period of big appetite
得 *ku(i)doku* a windfall for one's stomach
掛 *ku(i)-ka(keru), ku(i)-ka(karu)* begin to eat. *ku(tte)-ka(karu)* defy, challenge, flare up at, go after. *tabekake, kuika(ke)* food remnants. *kuika(ke) no* half-eaten
盛 *ta(be)zaka(ri)* growing period. *ku(i)zaka(ri)*=*ku(i)goro* 食頃 (see above-11)
堂 *shokudō* dining hall, mess hall
堂車 *shokudōsha* dining car
習 *ta(be)-nara(u)* get used to eating
習慣 *shokushūkan* dietary habits
道 *shokudō* alimentary canal, esophagus
道楽 *ku(i)dōraku* epicureanism; gourmet
道癌 *shokudō gan* cancer of the esophagus
欲 *shokuyoku* appetite
欲欠乏 *shokuyoku-ketsubō* lack of appetite
欲不振 *shokuyoku-fushin* poor appetite
12 間 *shokkan* between meals
飲 *ku(i)no(mi)* eating and drinking
散 *ku(i)-chi(rasu)* eat a bit of everything
裂 *ku(i)-sa(ku)* bite and tear up
費 *shokuhi* food expense, board charge
13 傷 *shokushō* food poisoning; food disagreement; surfeiting
嫌 *ku(wazu)gira(i), ta(bezu)gira(i)* disliking without tasting; prejudice, antipathy
溜 *ku(i)da(me)* storing food in the stomach
滅 *ku(i)-horo(bosu)* devour
滞 *shokutai* indigestion
滓 *ta(be)kasu* leavings of food
続 *ku(i)-tsuzu(keru)* continue to eat; continue to make a living
詰 *ku(i)-tsu(meru)* fail, go broke, lose one's job, be in penury
飽 *ku(i)-a(kiru)* be surfeited; have plenty. *ta(be)-a(kiru)* eat to the full
馴 *ku(i)-na(reru)* be used to eating
置 *ku(i)o(ki)* storing food in the stomach
意地 *ku(i)-iji* gluttony ⌈person out of work
詰者 *ku(i)tsu(me)mono* a tramp, a failure, a
塩 *shokuen* table salt, sodium chloride
塩水 *shokuensui* normal salt solution
14 厭 *ku(i)-a(kiru)* be fed up, have plenty
様 *ta(be)yō*=*ta(be)kata* 食方 (see above-4)
緊 *ku(i)-shiba(ru)* clench (teeth); compress (lips)
15 縛 *ku(i)-shiba(ru)* grit one's teeth; staying
慾 *shokuyoku* appetite ⌊by (a job)
器 *shokki* tableware, dinner set
養生 *shokuyōjō* taking nourishment; diet therapy. *ku(i)yōjō* dietary care
潰 *ku(i)-tsubu(su)* sponge on. *ku(i)tsubu(shi)* parasite, hanger-on
潰者 *ku(i)tsubu(shi)mono* parasite, hanger-
餌 *shokuji* food; feed ⌊on
餌性 *shokujisei* dietary, dietetic
餌療法 *shokuji ryōhō* diet therapy
16 膳 *shokuzen* dining table
18 嚙 *ku(i)-kaji(ru)* gnaw, nibble; have a smattering of knowledge
糧 *shokuryō* food, provisions, rations
糧事情 *shokuryō jijō* food situation
糧品 *shokuryōhin* foodstuffs, groceries
19 蟻獣 *arikui* anteater
20 競 *ta(bek)kura* eating contest
22 籠 *jikirō* lunch box; nest of boxes

2

B **飢** 5155/F2079 **飢** KI. *u(eru)* be hungry, starve.

5民 *kimin* starving people
6色 *kishoku* starved look
死 *ueji(ni)* starving to death
9食 *kishoku* a hungry look
10疲 *u(e)-tsuka(reru)* be famished
11渇 *kikatsu* hunger and thirst, starvation
12寒 *kikan* hunger and cold
15餓 *kiga* hunger, starvation, famine
餓同盟 *kiga dōmei* hunger strike
餓輸出 *kiga yushutsu* exporting at the expense of home consumers
20饉 *kikin* famine

4

飩 5156/F2080 DON, TON Japanese noodles.

飭 5157/F2080 CHOKU arrange.

A **飯** 5158/F2081 **飯 飰** HAN cooked rice; food; meal. *meshi* cooked rice; meal; food, livelihood. *mamma, mama* cooked rice (a child's word). *ii* cooked grains.

5台 *handai* dining table
6米 *hammai* food; farmer's rice for his own consumption; rice for food (not for saké)
8炊 *meshita(ki)* cooking rice
事 *mamagoto* (children) playing house
9屋 *meshiya* eating house
前 *meshimae* before a meal; having not yet eaten
茶碗 *meshi chawan* rice bowl
10時 *meshidoki* mealtime
11粒 *meshitsubu* a grain of boiled rice
盒 *hangō* mess tin, canteen
盛 *meshimo(ri)* maidservant at an inn
12場 *hamba* workman's temporary quarters
焚 *meshita(ki)* cooking rice
18櫃 *meshibitsu* cooked-rice tub; boiled-rice box

A **飲** 5159/F2080 **飮** IN drinking; feast. *no(mu)* drink, taste, take; swallow, devour; smoke; conceal (a weapon); accept (an idea); despise. *no(meru)* can drink; be good to drink; drinkable. *non(dakureru)* be dead drunk. *no(mikko)* drinking contest.

8口 *no(mi)guchi* tap, faucet, spigot, bunghole. *no(mi)kuchi* taste, flavor
干 *no(mi)-ho(su)* drink up, drain (the cup)
下 *no(mi)-kuda(su)* swallow, gulp down
4込 *no(mi)-ko(mu)* swallow, gulp down; understand
手 *no(mi)te* heavy drinker
止 *no(mi)-sa(su)* stop drinking; stop smoking
水 *no(mi)mizu* drinking water
友達 *no(mi) tomodachi* drinking companion
5代 *no(mi)shiro* drink money
用 *in-yō* drinking
用水 *in-yōsui* drinking water
用噴水 *in-yō funsui* drinking fountain
6回 *no(mi)-mawa(ru)* drink at a round of places. *no(mi)-mawa(su)* pass the cup around
尽 *no(mi)-tsu(kusu)* drink up; devour
仲間 *no(mi) nakama* drinking companion
7抜 *no(mi)nu(ke)* drunkard
助 *no(mi)suke* tippler, drunkard
良 *no(mi)yo(i)* good to drink
8逃 *no(mi)ni(ge)* leaving drinks unpaid for
明 *no(mi)-a(kasu)* drink all night
物 *nomimono* beverage, drinks
直 *no(mi)-nao(su)* drink again
9屋 *no(mi)ya* tavern, grogshop
食 *no(mi)ku(i), inshoku* food and drink, eating and drinking
食店 *inshokuten* restaurant
食物 *inshokubutsu* food and drink
10倒 *no(mi)-tao(su)* leave drinks unpaid for
残 *no(mi)noko(ri)* dregs, leftover drinks
酒 *inshu* drinking saké
酒家 *inshuka* habitual drinker
料 *no(mi)ryō* drink money; drink reserved for oneself. *inryō* a drink, beverage
料水 *inryōsui* drinking water
11過 *no(mi)-su(giru)* drink too much
掛 *no(mi)ka(ke)* (a cup) half-drunk; half-smoked (cigar)
13続 *no(mi)-tsuzu(keru)* keep on drinking
14歌 *no(meya)uta(e)* merrymaking
15潰 *no(mi)-tsubu(reru)* be dead drunk. *no(mi)-tsubu(su)* make (someone) drunk; drink up (a fortune)
16薬 *no(mi)gusuri* an internal medicine
18癖 *no(mi)kuse* drinking habit
騒 *no(mi)sawa(gi)* revelry
20競 *no(mi)kura(be)* drinking contest

5

飴 5160/F2081 I. *ame* rice jelly, candy.

5玉 *amedama* taffies, toffies
6色 *ame-iro* light brown, amber
7売 *ameu(ri)* candy vendor, candy store
9屋 *ameya* candy vendor, candy store
12棒 *amembō* stick of candy

B **飾** 5161/F2082 **飾** SHOKU. *kaza(ru)* ornament, decorate, adorn, embellish; exhibit; be ostentatious; white-

wash. *kaza(ri)* adornment, decoration, ornament.
2人形 *kaza(ri) ningyō* decorative doll; figurehead
5立 *kaza(ri)-ta(teru)* adorn, dress up; play up. *kaza(ri)ta(te)* ornamentation, decoration
付 *kaza(ri)-tsu(keru)* decorate, arrange
6気 *kaza(ri)ke* showing off, affectation
7言 *shokugen* ornate writing
8板 *kaza(ri)ita* plaque
物 *kaza(ri)mono* ornament, decoration; figurehead
9屋 *kaza(ri)ya* jewelry worker
11窓 *kaza(ri) mado* show window
12棚 *kaza(ri)dana* display shelves
15縁 *kaza(ri)buchi* molding
18職 *kaza(ri)shoku* precious-metal worker

B 飽 5162/F2082 飽 Hō. *a(kiru)*, *a(ku)* get tired of, lose interest in, have enough. *a(kasu)* *vt* satiate, surfeit; bore, tire, weary. *a(kumademo)* to the utmost, to the bitter end, persistently, strictly. *a(kunaki)* insatiable, rapacious. *a(kanu)* untiring, reluctant, unwilling, inseparable. *aki(ppoi)* fickle; soon tired of (something).
6迄 *a(ku)made* to the bitter end, tenaciously, persistently, strictly, exceedingly
安 *a(ki)yasu(i)* fickle, soon tired of
気味 *a(ki)gimi* weariness, being tired of
7足 *a(ki)-ta(ranai)* be unsatisfying, be not content with. *a(ki)-ta(raseru)* eat to the full. *a(ki)-ta(riru)* be satisfied
8性 *a(ki)shō* fickleness, flightiness
果 *a(ki)-ha(teru)* be tired of
和 *hōwa* saturation
和空気 *hōwa kūki* saturated air
和点 *hōwaten* saturation point
9食 *hōshoku* satiety; gluttony
食暖衣 *hōshoku-dan-i* well fed and well clad
12満 *hōman* satiety
18飽 *a(ki)a(ki) suru* be tired of, be bored with

B 飼 5163/F2082 飼 Shi raising (animals). *ka(u)* raise, keep, feed.
4手 *ka(i)te* (dog) owner
犬 *ka(i) inu* pet dog
5付 *ka(i)tsu(ke)* feeding
主 *ka(i)nushi* (dog) owner; shepherd
7兎 *ka(i) usagi* tame rabbit
8育 *shi-iku suru* breed, raise, rear, keep
育者 *shi-ikusha* breeder, fancier, raiser
9草 *ka(i)kusa* hay
10料 *shiryō* fodder, feed
殺 *ka(i)goro(shi)* caring for till death
畜 *shichiku* cattle raising
11鳥 *ka(i)dori* poultry
桶 *ka(i)oke* manger
猫 *ka(i)neko* pet cat
12葉 *ka(i)ba* fodder
葉桶 *ka(i)ba oke* feed tub, manger
13馴 *ka(i)-na(rasu)* tame, domesticate
15養 *shiyō* breeding, raising, keeping
17藁 *ka(i)wara* fodder straw

6

養 See 3671.

餞 Nonstandard for 餞 5173.

餉 5164/F2062 Shō provisions; a meal; boiled rice. *karei*, *kareii* dried boiled rice.

蝕 5165/F1667 Shoku eclipse, occultation; be defective. *mushiba(mu)* be wormy. [虫] eclipse)
9甚 *shokujin* maximum obscuration (in an

餅 5166/F2087 餅 Hei. *mochi*, *mochi-i* rice cake.
6肌 *mochihada* soft white skin
9屋 *mochiya* rice-cake dealer
13搗 *mochitsu(ki)* making rice cake
14網 *mochiami* rice-cake net
15膚 *mochihada* soft white skin

餌 5167/F2084 Ji food. *e*, *eba*, *esa* feed, food; bait, prey; tempting profit.
5付 *ezu(ku)* (birds) begin to eat
9食 *eba(mu)* feed. *ejiki* food, bait, prey, victim
10料 *jiryō* feed, fodder, storage
差 *esa(shi)* birdcatching; birdcatcher
11袋 *ebukuro* crop, craw, gizzard
12壺 *etsubo* bird-feeding receptacle
13飼 *ega(i)* feeding and raising animals. *eko(u)* hunt and eat; feed and raise animals

7

餘 5168/F2085 See 余 408.

餒 5169/F2084 Dai hunger; spoil.

餐 5170/F2084 San eat; drink; swallow.

B 餓 5171/F2084 餓 Ga. *u(eru)*, *katsu(eru)* be hungry, starve, thirst. *himo(jii)* hungry.

⁶死 *gashi, ueji(ni), katsu(e)ji(ni)* death from starvation
死者 *gashisha* people who starved to death
¹⁰殺 *katsu(e)-koro(su)* starve (someone) to death
莩 *gahyō* person who has starved to death
鬼 *gaki* hungry ghost; urchin, brat, mischievous child
鬼道 *gakidō* (Buddhist) hell of hungry spirits

8

餅 5172 F2087 See 餅 5166.

餞 5173 F2087 SEN. *hanamuke* farewell gift.
⁷別 *sembetsu* farewell gift

A 館 5174 F2087 餅 館 舘 舘
KAN mansion, large building, hall. *tachi* mansion; small castle; government housing. *tate* mansion, palace, fort. *yakata* mansion; temporary residence.
⁴内 *kannai* in the building
⁸長 *kanchō* superintendent of a building
¹⁰員 *kan-in* personnel (of a public building)

餡 5175 F2087 餡 AN bean jam.
³子 *anko* bean jam
¹¹掛 *anka(ke)* food topped with bean jam
¹⁵餅 *ammochi* rice cake stuffed with bean jam

9

餬 5176 F2088 Ko rice broth.
³口 *kokō*=糊口 3483.3

10

饗 Nonstandard for 饗 5184.

餾 5177 F2088 RYŪ steaming (rice).

饂 5178 F2089 (国字) *udon* Japanese noodles.
¹³飩 *udon* Japanese noodles
飩粉 *udonko* wheat flour
飩粉病 *udonkobyō* mildew

11

饉 5179 F2089 KIN hunger.

饅 5180 F2089 MAN bean-jam dumpling.
¹⁶頭 *manjū* steamed rice-flour dumpling with bean-jam center
頭笠 *manjūgasa* round wicker hat

12

饌 5181 F2089 SEN food; offering.

饐 5182 F2089 I. EI. *su(eru)* go bad, turn sour.

饒 5183 F2090 JŌ. NYŌ. *yutaka* abundant, rich, fruitful.
⁶舌 *jōzetsu, nyōzetsu* talkativeness
舌家 *jōzetsuka* chatterbox

饗 5184 F2090 KYŌ banquet. *kyō(suru)* banquet, treat.
⁷応 *kyōō* treat, feast, banquet
¹⁰宴 *kyōen* banquet, dinner
¹³筵 *kyōen* seats at a banquet

饑 5185 F2089 KI. *u(eru)* be hungry, starve, thirst. *himo(jii), hidaru(i)* hungry.
⁶色 *kishoku* starved look
死 *uejini* death from starvation
¹¹渇 *kikatsu* hunger and thirst, starvation
¹²寒 *kikan* hunger and cold
¹⁵餓 *kiga* hunger, starvation
²⁰饉 *kikin* famine

14

饜 饜 See 841.

RAD. 首 185

Kubi neck. Nickname: Neck.

A 首 5186/F2091 SHU head; neck; beginning, the first; poem and song counter. *kubi* neck, head. *kōbe* the head. *kubi ni suru* dismiss (someone). *kubi ni naru* be dismissed.

3 丈 *kubidake, kubi(t)take* up to the neck, complete devotion

4 引 *kubi(p)pi(ki)* tug of war using necks; constantly using reference books

切 *kubiki(ri)* decapitation, execution; dismissal

5 玉 *kubitama, kubi(t)tama* ancient necklace; neck bell (for animals); the neck; collar

功 *shukō* outstanding achievement

犯 *shuhan* principal offense

出 *kadode* departure 「a crooked neck

6 曲 *kubimaga(ri)* crooked neck; person with

吊 *kubitsu(ri)* hanging oneself

合点 *kubigatten* nodding assent

7 足 *shusoku* head and feet; the whole body

位 *shui* first place, head position

陀羅 *sudara* sutra

尾 *shubi* issue, course (of events), arrangements, result; beginning and end; head and tail; attitude; rendezvous

尾良 *shubiyo(ku)* successfully, smoothly

8 長 *shuchō* leader, chief, head. *kubi (o) naga(ku) suru* wait expectantly

固 *kubikata(me)* half nelson

府 *shufu* capital

肯 *shukō* assent, consent

実検 *kubi jikken* inspection of a severed head; identification of a suspect 「head

実験 *kubi jikken* checking on the severed

9 飛 *kubi (ga) to(bu)* be beheaded

途 *kadode, shuto* departure

相 *shushō* prime minister 「brance, ties

枷 *kubikase, kubikashi* pillory; encum-

狩 *kubiga(ri)* headhunting

級 *shukyū* decapitated head

巻 *kubimaki* (neck) muffler

10 座 *shuza* seat of honor. *kubi(no)za* seat for

席 *shuseki*＝主席 285.10 ⌊decapitation

振 *kubifu(ri)* gooseneck. *kubi (o) fu(ru)* shake the head in disagreement

根 *kubine(kko), kubi(no)ne* neck

将 *shushō* commander-in-chief

班 *shuhan* head position; prime minister

都 *shuto* capital

11 捻 *kubi (o) hine(ru)* disagree

桶 *kubi oke* box for a severed head 「missal

斬 *kubikiri* decapitation, execution; dis-

釣 *kubitsuri* hanging oneself

章 *shushō* the beginning of a book

唱 *shushō* advocacy, promotion

唱者 *shushōsha* advocate, proponent

脳 *shunō* head, brains, leading spirit

脳者 *shunōsha* leader, head

脳部 *shunōbu* brain trust, leaders

12 班 *shuhan* head, chief, premier

筋 *kubisuji* nape of the neck

無 *kubina(shi)* headless

13 鼠 *shuso* sitting on the fence, vacillating

飾 *kubikaza(ri)* necklace

14 魁 *shukai* leader, ringleader

領 *shuryō* head, chief, boss, leader

導 *shudō* main leadership

15 輪 *kubiwa* necklace, collar

16 縊 *kubikuku(ri)* hanging oneself

謀 *shubō* planning; plotting; main planner,

謀者 *shubōsha* ringleader ⌊ringleader

18 題 *shudai* the first paragraph

8

馘 5187/F2092 KAKU, KYOKU behead; dismiss.

9 首 *kakushu suru* behead; dismiss

RAD. 香 186

Nioi odor or *kaori* fragrance. Nickname: Perfume.

B 香 5188/F2092 KŌ incense, fragrance. *ka* smell, scent, odor; aroma, perfume, fragrance, flavor. *kao(ru)* smell, be fragrant. *kōbo(shi), kamba(shii)* fragrant; balmy; favorable. *kao(ri)* fragrance, perfume, aroma, odor, scent, smell. *nioi* (see under 匂 742.0).

4 木 *kōboku* aromatic tree, scented wood

水 *kōsui* perfume

6 気 *kōki* fragrance, aroma, perfume

合 *kōgō* incense container. *kōa(wase)* incense-smelling game

7 花 *kōge* (Buddhist) flowers and incense

辛料 *kōshinryō* spices, seasoning
8油 *kōyu* pomade, balm, perfumed oil
炉 *kōro* censer
物 *kō(no)mono* pickled vegetables
味 *kōmi* flavor
味料 *kōmiryō* spices, seasoning
具 *kōgu* perfumes, perfumery, (nonreligious) incense set ⌈quack, charlatan
具師 *kōgushi* perfumer. *yashi* showman,
典 *kōden* condolence gift ⌈dolence gift
典返 *kōdengae(shi)* return present for a con-
9香 *kōkō* pickles, pickled vegetables
柏 *kōhaku* cedars of Lebanon, Himalaya
草 *kōsō* aromatic grasses ⌊cedar
10料 *kōryō* spices; perfumes; condolence gift
脂 *kōshi* hair oil
案 *kōan* incense table
華 *kōge* (Buddhist) flowers and incense
華院 *kōge-in* family temple
11魚 *kōgyo* fresh-water trout, sweet smelt
道 *kōdō* incense-smelling game
液 *kōeki* balsam, balm
盒 *kōgō* incense container
12壺 *kōgo* perfume receptacle
奠 *kōden* condolence gift
奠返 *kōdengae(shi)* return present for a con- ⌊dolence gift
13煙 *kōen* incense smoke
腺 *kōsen* scent gland
蒲 *gama* flag, cattail, bulrush
14聞 *kōgi(ki)* perfume smelling
膏 *kōkō* balm, balsam
15箱 *kōbako* incense box
16壇 *kōdan* altar of incense
22嚢 *kōbukuro* incense bag

9

馥 5189 F2093 FUKU perfume, fragrance.
8郁 *fukuiku(taru)* fragrant; balmy

11

馨 5190 F2093 KEI. *kao(ru)* be fragrant. *kamba(shii)*, *kōba(shii)* fragrant; balmy; favorable.

10-STROKE RADICALS

RAD. 馬 187

Uma horse. At left: *uma hen.* Nickname: Horse.

A馬 5191 F2093 ME, BA, MA horse. *uma* horse; horseflesh; stepladder.
2丁 *batei* groom, footman, stableman
力 *bariki* horsepower; energy; cart, wagon
刀貝 *mategai* jackknife clam, razor clam
3子 *mago* pack-horse driver
上 *bajō* horseback, mounted
小屋 *umagoya* horse barn
4手 *mete* right hand, right side
方 *umakata* pack-horse driver, wagon driver
匹 *bahitsu* horses
引 *umahi(ki)* pack-horse driver, wagon ⌊driver
5皮 *bahi, umagawa* horsehide
市 *uma ichi* horse market
6肉 *baniku* horse meat
返 *umagae(shi)* the place on the mountain where the horses return
印 *umajirushi* (ancient) commander's standard
耳東風 *bajitōfū* utter indifference
7足 *uma (no) ashi* human horse; poor actor
身 *bashin* horse length
車 *basha* carriage, coach; cart, wagon
車鉄道 *basha tetsudō* horse tramway
尾毛 *basu* horsehair
尾藻 *hondawara* a kind of seaweed
8追 *umao(i)* horse driver
肥 *umagoyashi* horse manure
学 *bagaku* hippology
券 *baken* pari-mutuel ticket
券税 *bakenzei* pari-mutuel tax
具 *bagu* harness, saddlery
具屋 *baguya* saddler; saddlery
具師 *bagushi* saddler; saddlery
9面 *umazura* horse's face; long face
革 *bakaku* horsehide
食 *bashoku* eating like a horse
首 *bashu* a horse's head
屋 *umaya* stable, barn ⌈horse user
持 *umamo(chi)* horse owner; horse renter;
虻 *uma-abu* horsefly
政 *basei* legislation and administration of equestrian affairs ⌈astraddle
乗 *umano(ri)* horse riding; horseman;
草 *magusa* hay, fodder, feed
10骨 *uma(no)hone* person of doubtful origin, a nondescript
耕 *bakō* cultivating with a horse

陸 *yasude* millipede
栗 *umaguri* horse chestnut
11術 *bajutsu* horsemanship
脚 *bakyaku* horse's legs; true character. *uma (no) ashi* human horse; poor actor
脚露 *bakyaku (o) arawa(su)* reveal a secret
鹿 *baka* dunce, fool; folly, farce, nonsense; benumbed; dull. *baka(geta)* foolish. *baka ni* extremely. *baka(rashii)* foolish, ridiculous
鹿力 *bakajikara* brute force, great strength
鹿丁寧 *baka-teinei* excessively polite
鹿正直 *baka-shōjiki* simple honesty, foolishly honest, credulity ⌈stupidity
鹿加減 *baka(sa)-kagen* the extent of one's
鹿安 *bakayasu(i)* ridiculously cheap
鹿見 *baka (o) mi(ru)* meet an unfortunate experience
鹿声 *bakagoe* wild yell ⌈fool
鹿呼 *bakayo(bawari)*, calling (someone) a
鹿者 *bakamono* fool ⌈stupid look
鹿面 *bakazura* foolish face, vacant look,
鹿臭 *bakakusa(i)* foolish, absurd
鹿高 *bakadaka(i)* ridiculously high
鹿値 *bakane* ridiculous price
鹿笑 *bakawara(i)* horselaugh
鹿馬鹿 *bakabaka(shii)* silly, absurd
鹿遊 *baka-aso(bi)* spree, riotous pleasure
鹿野郎 *baka-yarō* fool, simpleton, idiot
鹿強情 *baka-gōjō* pigheadedness, irrational obstinacy
鹿揃 *bakazoroi* a lot of foolishness
鹿景気 *bakageiki* market boom
鹿話 *bakabanashi* idle talk, silly talk
鹿慇懃 *baka-ingin* excessive politeness
鹿騒 *baka-sawa(gi)* spree, uproarious gaiety
鹿囃子 *bakabayashi* festival music; Japa-
12喰 *bakurō* horse trader ⌊nese jazz band
場 *baba* riding ground, racecourse
13賊 *bazoku* mounted bandits
跳 *umatobi* leapfrog
飼 *umaka(i)* raising horses
鈴薯 *bareisho, jaga-imo* Irish potato
14銜 *hami* horse's bit
15槽 *umabune, mabune* manger
16橇 *basori* horse sleigh
頭 *batō* a horse's head; on a horse
蹄 *batei* horse's hoof
蹄石 *bateiseki* obsidian
蹄形 *bateigata* horseshoe shape
蹄磁石 *batei jishaku* horseshoe magnet
17鍬 *manga, maguwa* harrow, rake
齢 *barei* one's age (humble), insignificant
糞 *bafun, maguso* horse manure ⌊years
糞紙 *bafunshi* strawboard, millboard
18糧 *baryō* fodder

顔 *umagao* extremely long face
19櫛 *umagushi* currycomb
蠅 *umabae* horsefly
20籍 *baseki* horse registration

2

馭 5192/F2095 Gyo driving (a horse).

8法 *gyohō* horsemanship
者 *gyosha* driver, coachman, bus driver

3

馱 5193/F2095 See **馱** 5198.

馴 5194/F2096 Jun. *na(reru)* get used to, become experienced; be tamed; get too familiar, mature. *na(rasu)* tame, charm (snakes); train, exercise, drill; habituate, accustom to. *nara(u)* experience; become a habit. *na(re)* practice, habit, skill, experience. *na(rekko)* being used to.

4化 *junka suru* acclimate
6合 *na(re)-a(u)* conspire with, be intimate. *narea(i)* collusion, conspiracy; illicit intercourse
7初 *nareso(me)* beginning of a romance
良 *junryō* docile and good
8育 *jun-iku* taming, domesticating
9染 *na(re)-so(meru)* become intimate. *naji(mu)* become familiar with. *najimi* intimacy; friend ⌈way for
10致 *junchi suru* tame, domesticate; pave the
11鹿 *junroku, tonakai, nareshika* reindeer
13馴 *na(re)na(reshii)* familiar, too free, unceremonious
15養 *jun-yō suru* tame, domesticate

馳 5195/F2096 Chi. *ha(seru)* run, gallop; sail; drive (a wagon); win (fame); dispatch.

3下 *ha(se)-kuda(ru)* run downhill; run out of the metropolis
6回 *ha(se)-mawa(ru)* run around, jump about, gallop around
向 *ha(se)-muka(u)* ride off in a hurry
7走 *chisō* treat, banquet, entertainment, feast, dinner; hospitality, good things to eat
8参 *ha(se)-san(zuru)* hurry to
11掛 *ha(se)-ka(keru), ha(se)-ka(karu)* gallop
12越 *ha(se)-ko(eru)* jump over (on a horse); ride past ⌈(the enemy)
散 *ha(se)-chi(rasu)* ride into and disperse
着 *ha(se)-tsu(keru)* come riding at top speed
集 *ha(se)-atsu(maru)* run or ride together to, flock to, rally around

14駆 *chiku suru* ride fast, run around, play an active part
15還 *hase-kae(ru)* return running

— 4 —

馿 5196/F2097/F2107 See **驢** 5233.

駁 5197/F2096 HAKU, BAKU refutation, contradiction. *buchi* spots, specks, patches.
14説 *bakusetsu* refutation
15論 *bakuron* refutation, rebuttal
撃 *bakugeki* refutation, contradiction, attack

駄 5198/F2095 **馱** TA, DA horse load; pack horse; sending by horses.
4文 *dabun* poor piece of writing
5目 *dame* useless; impossible; ruined; unsuccessful, hopeless; must not
句 *daku(ru)* write doggerel. *daku* doggerel, poor poem
弁 *dabe(ru)* jabber, chatter, chat with. *daben* foolish talk
7作 *dasaku* poor piece of writing
8物 *damono* low-grade goods, trash
法螺 *dabora* bragging, fish story
9洒落 *dajare* poor joke
10馬 *daba* draft horse, pack horse; poor horse
荷 *dani* horse load
11菓子 *dagashi* cheap sweets
13賃 *dachin* carriage or horse charge; reward, tip
14駄 *dada* fretfulness, disobedience
駄子 *dada(k)ko* stubborn child, spoiled child
駄児 *dada(k)ko* stubborn child, spoiled child

A **駅** 5199/F2107 **驛** EKI. post town; stage; station.
4手 *ekishu* station hand, baggageman
止 *ekido(me)* station delivery
夫 *ekifu* railway porter, railway employee
5弁 *ekiben* station lunch
6名 *ekimei* station name
伝 *ekiden* stagecoach, post horse
伝競走 *ekiden kyōsō* cross-country race
8長 *ekichō* stationmaster
舎 *ekisha* station building
9逓 *ekitei* postal service
前 *ekimae* in front of the station
10員 *eki-in* station employee, station staff
馬 *ekima, ekiba* post horse
馬車 *ekibasha* stagecoach
12渡 *ekiwata(shi)* station delivery
程 *ekitei* distance between stations
13路 *ekiro, umayaji* post road
勢 *ekisei* traffic volume
16頭 *ekitō* station

B **駆** 5200/F2104 **驅** KU. *ka(keru)* run, gallop; advance. *ka(ru)* drive (a car); spur on, prompt, actuate, inspire, sway, impel. *ka(rareru)* be carried away by, be actuated by. *ka(kezuru)* run around, bustle around. *ka(kekko), ka(kekkura), ka(kekura)* foot race.
2入 *ka(ke)-i(ru)* gallop in on a horse
3下 *ka(ke)-o(riru), ka(ke)-kuda(ru)* run downhill
上 *ka(ke)-a(garu)* run up, dash up
4比 *ka(ke)kura(be)* foot race
込 *ka(ke)-ko(mu)* dash into, seek refuge in, run into
引 *ka(ke)hi(ki)* bargaining, maneuvering; advancing and retreating; dickering
5立 *ka(ke)-ta(tsu)* run, gallop; chase (the enemy). *ka(ri)-ta(teru)* drive, round up; spur on, stir up, chase away
巡 *ka(ke)-megu(ru)* run around, bustle around
付 *ka(ke)-tsu(keru)* hurry to (the place)
出 *ka(ke)-da(su)* run out, start running. *ka(ri)-da(su)* chase away. *kakeda(shi)* beginner; amateur
6回 *ka(ke)-mawa(ru), ka(kezuri)-mawa(ru)* bustle about, run around
合 *ka(ke)-a(wasu)* fight on horseback
虫 *kuchū* deworming
虫剤 *kuchūzai* insecticide, vermicide
虫薬 *kuchūyaku* insecticide, vermicide
7足 *ka(ke)ashi* running fast, double time
抜 *ka(ke)-nu(keru)* run thru (a gate)
8使 *kushi suru* order around; use freely
並 *ka(ke)-nara(bu)* gallop abreast
9通 *ka(ke)-tō(ru)* run thru. *ka(ke)dō(shi)* riding thru, riding on without resting
降 *ka(ke)-o(riru)* come running down
逐 *kuchiku* expulsion, extermination
逐艦 *kuchikukan* destroyer
除 *kujo* extermination, destruction
除剤 *kujozai* insecticide, expellent
10悩 *ka(ke)-naya(masu)* ride into the midst of the enemy and disconcert him
破 *ka(ke)-yabu(ru)* break up with a cavalry charge
11寄 *ka(ke)-yo(ru)* ride up (on horseback). *ka(ke)-yo(seru)* come running up
動 *kudō* driving (force)
動装置 *kudō sōchi* running gear
12越 *ka(ke)-ko(su)* run all the way; outdistance
場 *ka(ke)ba* riding grounds
散 *ka(ke)-chi(rasu)* scatter a crowd (on horseback)
落 *kakeo(chi)* defeat and flight; disappearance without a trace; elopement
集 *ka(ri)-atsu(meru)* mobilize, round up
13馳 *kuchi suru* drive swiftly; bustle around
塞 *ka(ke)-fusa(garu)* ride up and block the way
15潜艇 *kusentei* subchaser
23黴 *kubai* antisyphilis

徽法 *kubaihō* venereal disease prevention law
徽薬 *kubaiyaku* antisyphilitic medicine

5

駟 5201 F2098 SHI four horses; four-horse carriage.

駛 5202 F2098 SHI. *ha(seru)* run fast.

駘 5203 F2098 TAI stupid.
15蕩 *taitō(taru)* calm, serene, mild, genial

駝 5204 F2098 DA hunchback; (an animal) load.
11鳥 *dachō* ostrich

駑 5205 F2097 DO slow horse; a foolish fellow.
10馬 *doba* worn-out horse
12鈍 *dodon* dumb and lazy

駒 5206 F2097 KU. *koma* horse; colt, pony; chessman; frame (of a film); bridge (of a violin).
3下駄 *komageta* low clogs
11鳥 *komadori* robin

駕 5207 F2098 KA, GA vehicle. *kago* palanquin, litter. *ga(suru)* hitch up an animal.
22籠 *kago* palanquin, litter
籠屋 *kagoya* palanquin carriers
籠舁 *kagoka(ki)* palanquin bearer
籠脇 *kagowaki* palanquin bearer; the side of the palanquin

駈 5208 F2097 KU. *ka(keru)* run, gallop; advance. *ka(ru)* drive, urge on; prompt; inspire.
4手 *ka(ke)te* runner
引 *ka(ke)hi(ki)* bargaining; maneuvering
5出 *ka(ke)da(shi)* start; novice
6回 *ka(ke)-mawa(ru)* run around, ride around; hurry about; campaign
7足 *ka(ke)ashi* running fast, double quick
抜 *ka(ke)-nu(ku)* run all the way, outdistance
12登 *ka(ke)-nobo(ru)* run up
落 *kakeo(chi)* elopement; running away

駐 5209 F2097 駐 CHŪ. *todo(maru)* stop; reside in. *chū-* resident in.
B 4支 *chū-Shi* resident in China
日 *chū-Nichi* resident in Japan
仏 *chū-Futsu* resident in France
屯 *chūton* stationing (troops), occupation
6米 *chū-Bei* resident in America
在 *chūzai* residence, stay
在所 *chūzaisho* police substation
7兵 *chūhei* stationing troops; garrison
車 *chūsha* parking
車場 *chūshajō* parking area
8英 *chū-Ei* resident in England
9独 *chū-Doku* resident in Germany
軍 *chūgun* stationing an army
10留 *chūryū* retention, stationing (of troops)
留軍 *chūryūgun* army of occupation
11劄 *chūsatsu* ambassador's residence abroad
12営 *chūei* encampment
14箚 *chūsatsu* resident at
15輦 *chūren* stopping of the imperial carriage
19蘇 *chū-So* resident in Soviet Russia

6

駮 5210 F2099 HAKU. *buchi* spots, specks, patches.

駢 5211 F2101 騈 HEN two-horse carriage.
21儷体 *benreitai* euphemism; ornate style

駱 5212 F2099 RAKU white horse.
15駝 *rakuda* camel

駭 5213 F2099 GAI. *odoro(ku)* be surprised; be frightened.
12然 *gaizen to* in surprise, in alarm

7

駸 5214 F2100 SHIN speed; horses running.
17駸 *shinshin to* rapidly, with rapid strides

駻 5215 F2100 KAN rage, run wild.
10馬 *kamba* unruly horse, bronco

駿 5216 F2100 SHUN a good horse; speed; a fast person.
3才 *shunsai* talented person, genius, prodigy
7足 *shunsoku* swift horse; talented person
10馬 *shumme, shumba* swift horse
逸 *shun-itsu* swift horse

8

騐 5217 F2102 F2106 See 験 5220.

騈 5218 F2101 See 駢 5211.

10

8【馬】骨高髟門鬯鬲鬼

騏 5219 / F2102 Ki fast horse.
23 麟 *kirin* fabulous mythical horse; talent

A **験** 5220 / F2106 **驗 騐** Ken effect; testing. Gen beneficial effect (of austerities). *tame(su)*, *ken(suru)* test, attempt. *shirushi* sign, indication, omen.
11 問 *kemmon suru* investigate and question
14 算 *kenzan* verification of accounts, checking figures

B **騒** 5221 / F2103 **騷** Sō. *sawa(gu)* make a noise, be boisterous, shout, clamor; raise an uproar; be excited, be agitated; bustle around; make a fuss about; make merry, go on a spree. *sawa(gaseru)* disturb, trouble, agitate, excite, create a sensation. *sawa(gareru)* be made much of. *zawame(ku)*, *zawatsu(ku)* be noisy, be boisterous. *zome(ku)*, *some(ku)* be noisy. *sawa(gashii)* noisy, boisterous; tumultuous, troubled, agitated. *sawa(gi)* noise, uproar; turmoil, trouble, agitation; fuss, ado; affair; dispute; excitement; sensation; merrymaking, spree.
2 人 *sōjin* literary man, poet
5 立 *sawa(gi)-ta(tsu)* be agitated, be stirred up. *sawa(gi)-ta(teru)* make an uproar, make a fuss, make an outcry, raise an alarm
5 出 *sawa(gi)-da(su)* begin to riot, start tearing around
7 乱 *sōran* commotion, riot
声 *sawa(gi)goe* tumult, outcry
9 音 *sōon* noise, cacophony
11 動 *sōdō* disturbance, strife, riot, rebellion
12 然 *sōzen(taru)* noisy, confused, uproarious
18 騒 *sōzō(shii)*, *zawazawa(toshita)* noisy, boisterous, turbulent
擾 *sōjō* disturbance, commotion, riot
擾罪 *sōjōzai* crime of sedition

B **騎** 5222 / F2101 Ki riding on horses; counter for horsemen
3 士 *kishi* horseman, equestrian, knight
士道 *kishidō* knighthood, chivalry
4 手 *kishu* rider, horseman, jockey
6 行 *kikō* horseback riding
7 兵 *kihei* cavalry; cavalryman, horseman
兵隊 *kiheitai* cavalry
8 虎 *kiko* riding on a tiger
虎勢 *kiko (no) ikio(i) de* by force of circumstances
9 乗 *kijō no* mounted, on horseback
10 従 *kijū* following on a horse; the following rider
射 *kisha* equestrian archery
砲兵 *kihōhei* horse artillery
馬 *kiba* riding on a horse; the rider
馬巡査 *kiba junsa* mounted police
馬武者 *kiba musha* mounted samurai
馬戦 *kibasen* cavalry battle
14 銃 *kijū* carbine

9

騙 5223 / F2102 Hen. *dama(su)* deceive, cheat, defraud; bewitch; delude; soothe, calm. *dama(kasu)*, *tabura(kasu)* deceive, cheat, defraud; bewitch; delude. *kata(ru)* swindle, defraud; assume (another's name). *kata(ri)* fraud, swindle; impostor, swindler.
4 込 *dama(shi)-ko(mu)* deceive, cheat, defraud, take in
6 合 *damashia(i)* cheating each other
8 取 *henshu* swindling, defrauding
取者 *henshusha* swindler
10 討 *dama(shi)u(chi)* surprise attack, foul play

10

驀 See 4102.

騰 See 3834.

騷 5224 / F2103 See **騒** 5221.

11

驅 5225 / F2104 See **駆** 5200.

騾 5226 / F2104 Ra mule.
10 馬 *raba* mule

12

驍 5227 / F2105 Gyō strong; good horse.
6 名 *gyōmei* military fame, fame for bravery
8 武 *gyōbu* strong and brave
9 勇 *gyōyū* bravery, valor
10 将 *gyōshō* valiant general, veteran general; a leader

驕 5228 / F2105 Kyō. *ogo(ru)* be proud or haughty. *ogo(ri)* pride, haughtiness.
6 気 *kyōki* pride
7 兵 *kyōhei* triumphant soldier; boastful soldier
児 *kyōji* spoiled child
10 恣 *kyōshi* being proud and self-willed
振舞 *ogo(ri)-furuma(u)* carry on proudly
12 奢 *kyōsha* luxury, extravagance
13 傲 *kyōgō* pride, arrogance
肆 *kyōshi* being proud and self-willed

[14]慢 *kyōman* pride, arrogance
[15]横 *kyōō* pride and stubbornness

驚 5229/F2106 Kyō. Kei. *odoro(ku)* be surprised; be frightened, be taken aback; be appalled; be amazed. *odoro(kasu)* surprise; frighten; create a stir. *odoro(kubeki)* amazing, surprising, wonderful. B

[2]入 *odoro(ki)-i(ru)* be filled with amazement
[4]天動地 *kyōten-dōchi* world-shaking, astounding, tremendous
[7]呆 *odoro(ki)-aki(reru)* be appalled
[8]怪 *odoro(ki)-aya(shimu)* marvel
怖 *kyōfu* fear and surprise
[10]倒 *kyōtō* astonishment
破 *suwa(ya)*, *suwa* exclamation of sudden surprise
[11]異 *kyōi* wonder, miracle
異的 *kyōiteki* wonderful, phenomenal
[12]慌 *odoro(ki)-awa(teru)* be surprised and excited
愕 *keigaku*, *kyōgaku* surprise, fright, shock
程 *odoro(ku) hodo* surprisingly, wonderfully
喜 *kyōki* pleasant surprise
[13]嘆 *kyōtan* wonder, admiration
[16]駭 *odoro(ki)-sawa(gu)* be surprised and excited. *kyōgai* surprise, fright.
[18]騒 *odoro(ki)-sawa(gu)* be surprised and excited

13

驛 5230/F2107 See 駅 5199.

驗 5231/F2106 See 験 5220.

14

驟 5232/F2107 Shū run; suddenly.

[8]雨 *shūu* (sudden) shower
[12]然 *shūzen toshite* suddenly

16

驢 5233/F2107 驴 Ro donkey.

[10]馬 *roba* donkey

驥 5234/F2107 Ki fast horse; talent.

[7]足 *kisoku* full ability

17

驩 5235/F2108 Kan greetings, courtesies.

骨 RAD. 188

Hone bone. At left: *hone hen*. Nickname: Bone.

骨 5236/F2108 Kotsu bone; remains; knack. *hone* bone; skeleton; frame; rib (of an umbrella); grit, backbone; effort, pains. B

[3]子 *kosshi* bones; marrow; essentials, gist
上 *kotsua(ge)* gathering the ashes (of the deceased)
[4]片 *koppen* pieces of bone
化 *kokka* ossification
太 *honebuto na* large-boned
[6]肉 *kotsuniku* one's own flesh and blood; flesh and blood
灰 *kotsubai* bone ashes
休 *honeyasu(mi)*, *honeyasu(me)* relaxation, recreation
[7]身 *honemi* flesh and bones; marrow
折 *honeo(ru)* take pains, exert oneself. *kossetsu* broken bone, bone fracture. *honeo(ri)* pains, exertion. *hone (ga) o(reru)* be difficult
折損 *honeo(ri)zon* wasted effort
抜 *honenu(ki) no* boned; mutilated; watered down
抜外交 *honenu(ki) gaikō* spineless diplomacy
[8]法 *koppō* frame, a person's build; good manners; nice technique
肥 *koppi* bone fertilizer
[9]拾 *kotsuhiro(i)*=*kotsua(ge)* 骨揚 (see below-12)
柄 *kotsugara* build, physique, personal appearance
炭 *kottan* bone charcoal
相 *kossō* physique, features
相学 *kossōgaku* phrenology
[10]格 *kokkaku* physique, build, frame
粉 *koppun* bone meal, bone dust
[11]張 *honeba(ru)* get thin. *honeba(tta)* bony, thin
惜 *honeo(shimi)* sparing oneself, laziness
接 *honetsu(gi)* bone setting; bone setter
組 *honegu(mi)* skeleton; framework
瓶 *kotsugame* cinerary urn
頂 *kotchō* height (of foolishness); Number 1
軟化症 *kotsu nankashō* softening of the bones
[12]揚 *kotsua(ge)* gathering the ashes (of the deceased)
牌 *karuta* playing cards. *koppai* bone chessman

結核 *kotsu kekkaku* tuberculosis of the bones
壺 *kotsu tsubo* mortuary urn
無 *honena*(*shi*) rickets; spineless person; an invertebrate
董 *kottō* curios, antiques
董品 *kottōhin* curios, antiques
13 節 *kossetsu, honebushi* joint. *hone*(*p*)*pushi* joint; strong character, spirit
幹 *kokkan* physique, build, frame
14 関節 *kokkansetsu* bone joint
膜 *kotsumaku* the periosteum
膜炎 *kotsuen* periostitis
15 箱 *kotsubako* cinerary box; box for cinerary urn
盤 *kotsuban* pelvis, pelvic bone
質 *kosshitsu* bony tissue
16 骼 *kokkaku* physique, build, frame
17 癌 *kotsugan* bone cancer
18 甕 *honegame* cinerary urn
髄 *kotsuzui* marrow; true spirit
髄炎 *kotsuzuien* osteomyelitis

— 4 —

骰 5237/F2109 Tō. *sai* dice, bones.
8 子 *saikoro, sai* dice
子入 *saikoro-i*(*re*) dice box

— 5 —

骶 5238/F2110 Tei backbone; hips.

— 6 —

骼 5239/F2110 Kaku bleached bones.

骸 5240/F2110 Gai bone, body. *mukuro* body; corpse.
9 炭 *gaitan* coke
10 骨 *gaikotsu* skeleton
骨乞 *gaikotsu* (*o*) (*ko*(*u*)) request to resign

— 8 —

髀 5241/F2110 Hi thigh.
6 肉嘆 *hiniku* (*no*) *tan* determination to act in face of frustration

髄 5242/F2111 B **髓** Zui marrow, pith.
6 虫 *zuichū* rice borer, pearl moth

— 11 —

髏 5243/F2111 Ro skull.

— 12 —

髓 5244/F2111 See **髄** 5242.

— 13 —

體 5245/F2111 See **体** 405.

髑 5246/F2111 Doku skull.
21 髏 *dokuro, sharekōbe, sharikōbe, sarekōbe* skull, cranium

RAD. 高 189

Takai high. Variant: 髙 (11 strokes). Nickname: High.

髙 5247/F2116 See **高** 5248.

A **高** 5248/F2112/F2116 **髙** Kō high. *taka*(*i*) high, tall, lofty, raised, elevated, eminent; exalted, noble; loud, stentorian; expensive; widely known. *taka* quantity, volume, amount, sum; rise (in prices); high; fief. *taka*(*maru*) rise; swell; be elevated, be promoted; increase. *taka*(*meru*) raise, lift, promote, elevate; improve, enhance; ennoble; heighten; boost. *kō*(*jiru*), *kō*(*zuru*) increase; be proud. *taka*(*buru*) be proud, be arrogant; be high. *taka*(*mi*) height, eminence. *taka*(*raka ni*) loudly. (*o*)*taka*(*ku*) proudly (in a bad sense). *taka*(*ga*) only, merely, at best, after all.
2 人 *kōnin, kōjin* person of high rank; person of noble character
3 士 *kōshi* high-minded person
大 *kōdai na* grand, sublime, excellent; large and tall
工 *kōkō* higher technical school
上 *taka-a*(*gari*) expensive; occupying a place of honor (at a banquet)
下 *kōge* rise and fall, fluctuations; rank, grade, quality
下駄 *takageta* high clogs, high *geta*
山 *kōzan* high mountain, lofty peak
山病 *kōzambyō* mountain sickness

山動物 *kōzan dōbutsu* alpine fauna
山植物 *kōzan shokubutsu* alpine flora
4木 *takagi, kōboku* tall tree, large tree
止 *taka(ku) to(maru)* be proud
天原 *Takamagahara, Takama(no)hara* the heavens, the abode of the gods
水準 *kōsuijun* high level
手 *takate* upper arm. *kōshu* outstanding skill; highly skilled person
手小手 *takate-kote* tying (someone's) hands behind his back
5処 *takami* high place
札 *kōsatsu* placard; bulletin board; highest bid
丘 *kōkyū* high hill
台 *kōdai* tall building, tall tower. *takadai* eminence, high ground, hill
目 *takame no* high (baseball)
目内角球 *takame naikakkyū* high inside
目外角球 *takame gaikakkyū* high outside
圧 *kōatsu* high tension, high voltage; highhandedness
圧的 *kōatsuteki* highhanded, overbearing, arbitrary
圧電気 *kōatsu denki* high-tension electricity
圧電流 *kōatsu denryū* high current of electricity
圧電線 *kōatsu densen* high-tension line
圧線 *kōatsusen* high-tension line
圧竈 *kōatsugama* high-pressure kiln; pressure cooker
6行 *kōkō* an outstanding deed
次 *kōji* the higher powers (of a number); high standards
地 *kōchi* high ground, plateau, heights
名 *kōmyō* renown, fame; your name. *kōmei* fame, good reputation
血圧 *kōketsuatsu* high blood pressure
気圧 *kōkiatsu* high atmospheric pressure, anticyclone
気圧病 *kōkiatsubyō* the bends
年 *kōnen* old people; old age
年者 *kōnensha* elderly person
7見 *kōken* your opinion; excellent idea
言 *kōgen* boastful speech; excellent speech
庇 *kōhi* the shadow of a high tree or building; your favor
吠 *takabo(e)* loud barking
吟 *kōgin* reciting a poem; your poem
坏 *takatsuki* (ancient) serving table
妙 *kōmyō* very skillful
批 *kōhi* your esteemed criticism
材 *kōzai* outstanding talent; talented man; a large, splendid physique
弟 *kōtei* best student; senior disciple
志 *kōshi* noble spirit
声 *kōsei, kōjō* loud voice, high voice, loud talking
寿 *kōju* advanced age
角 *kōkaku* high angle, vertical angle, altitude
角砲 *kōkakuhō* high-angle gun, antiaircraft gun
低 *kōtei, takahiku* unevenness, undulations; fluctuations; modulation; height; pitch
低差 *kōteisa* difference in altitude
位 *kōi* honors, high rank
位高官 *kōi-kōkan* dignitaries
足 *kōsoku* the outstanding disciple, best student. *taka-ashi* stilts
足駄 *taka-ashida* high clogs, high *geta*
足蟹 *taka-ashigani* giant spider crab
利 *kōri* high interest
利金 *kōrikin* high-interest money
利貸 *kōriga(shi)* usury; usurer
8所 *kōsho* elevation, height; altitude; long view (of things). *taka(ki) tokoro* high places (in ancient Palestinian paganism)
明 *kōmei na* noble and well-versed
杯 *takatsuki* small one-legged table
枕 *takamakura* high pillow. *takamakura de* peacefully (sleeping)
炉 *kōro* blast furnace
知 *taka (ga) shi(reru)* be insignificant
臥 *kōga suru* live in proud seclusion (from the world)
岳 *kōgaku* high mountain
直 *takane* high prices
官 *kōkan* high office; high official, dignitary
尚 *kōshō na* high, noble, refined, advanced
空 *kōkū* high altitude
学年 *kōgakunen* upper grades in school
周波 *kōshūha* high frequency
物価 *kōbukka* high prices
性能 *kōseinō* high (explosives); high efficiency; high fidelity
価 *kōka* high price
価品 *kōkahin* valuables, costly article
9風 *kōfū* noble mien; noble character
屋 *kōoku, taka(ki)ya* tall house; your house
度 *kōdo* altitude, height; high degree; high power; intense; advanced (stage)
度計 *kōdokei* altimeter
括 *taka (o) kuku(ru)* belittle, disparage
相 *kōsō* noble looks
卑 *kōhi* high and low, noble and base
専 *kōsen* (prewar) college
飛 *takato(bi)* high jump; dancing and jumping; abscondence. *takato(bi)* flying high; skipping the country
飛車 *takabisha na* highhanded
音 *takane, kōon* high tone; high key; loud sound
音部記号 *kōombu kigō* treble clef
砂 *Takasago* Formosa
砂族 *Takasagozoku* Formosan natives
点 *kōten* high score
点者 *kōtensha* persons with the highest scores or votes
架 *kōka* elevated (line)
架鉄道 *kōka tetsudō* elevated railway
祖 *kōso* founder of a dynasty or a sect
祖父 *kōsofu* great-great-grandfather
祖母 *kōsobo* great-great-grandmother

速 *kōsoku* high speed, high gear ⌈chanics
速力学 *kōsoku rikigaku* high-speed me-
速度 *kōsokudo* high speed ⌈motion movies
速度撮影 *kōsokudo satsuei* taking slow-
速度鋼 *kōsokudokō* high-speed steel
速道路 *kōsoku dōro* expressway
級 *kōkyū* high rank, seniority; high grade, high class
級車 *kōkyūsha* high-class automobile
級社員 *kōkyū sha-in* senior clerk
級店 *kōkyūten* fashionable store
級品 *kōkyūhin* high-grade goods
級船員 *kōkyū sen-in* ship's officers
10 原 *kōgen* tableland, plateau
座 *kōza* platform; dais; stage; upper seat
這 *takabai* crawling on hands and knees
逸 *kōitsu* excellence
値 *takane* high price
峰 *kōhō* lofty peak
峻 *kōshun na* high, steep
根 *takane* lofty peak
浪 *takanami* high waves ⌈teaching
訓 *kōkun* excellent teaching; your excellent
配 *kōhai* your good offices, your trouble
家 *kōke* noble samurai family; shogunate liaison official
笑 *takawara(i)* loud laughter
書 *kōsho* your letter
恩 *kōon* a great blessing
陵土 *kōryōdo* kaolin, porcelain clay
島田 *takashimada* a coiffure for unmarried
射砲 *kōshahō* antiaircraft gun ⌊girls
浮彫 *taka-u(ki)bo(ri)* high relief
校 *kōkō* senior high school
校生 *kōkōsei* senior-high-school student
高 *takadaka* very high; at most, at best. *takadaka to* aloft, very high; loudly
高指 *takatakayubi* middle finger
高度飛行 *kōkōdo hikō* stratospheric flight
11 匐 *takabai* crawling on hands and knees
唱 *kōshō suru* sing loudly; advocate, urge,
情 *kōjō* nobility of soul ⌊stress
距 *kōkyo* altitude
率 *kōritsu* high rate
商 *kōshō* higher commercial school
堂 *kōdō* beautiful tall building; your beauti-
著 *kōcho* your (literary) work ⌊ful home
粱 *kōryō, kaoryan, kōryan* kaoliang, Indian millet, sorghum ⌈high hopes
望 *takanozo(mi)* viewing from the heights;
脚蟹 *taka-ashigani* giant spider crab
張提灯 *takaha(ri) chōchin* paper lantern on
野豆腐 *kōyadōfu* frozen tofu ⌊a pole
野槙 *kōyamaki* umbrella pine
教 *kōkyō*=*kōkun* 高訓 (see above-10)
教会 *Kōkyōkai* the High Church

12 遠 *kōen na* high and distant; high, lofty, noble; hard to understand
塀 *takabei* high wall
揚 *kōyō suru* enhance, exalt, promote
温 *kōon* high temperature
禄 *kōroku* high salary
給 *kōkyū* high salary
評 *kōhyō* your esteemed opinion; criticism
貴 *kōki* nobility ⌊by famous people
裁 *kōsai* higher court ⌈highest
順位 *kōjun-i ni* in order beginning with the
御位 *takamikurai* emperor's throne
御座 *takamikura* the throne
等 *kōtō* high class, high grade
等小学校 *kōtō shōgakkō* (prewar) higher elementary school ⌈school
等女学校 *kōtō jogakkō* (prewar) girls' high
等弁務官 *kōtō bemmukan* high commis-
等批評 *kōtō hihyō* higher criticism ⌊sioner
等官 *kōtōkan* higher official
等法院 *kōtō hōin* higher court
等学校 *kōtō gakkō* senior high school
等科 *kōtōka* advanced course
等飛行 *kōtō hikō* stunt flying
等飛行術 *kōtō hikōjutsu* stunt flying
等遊民 *kōtō yūmin* idle rich
等教育 *kōtō kyōiku* higher education
等動物 *kōtō dōbutsu* higher animals
等裁判所 *kōtō saibansho* higher court
等普通教育 *kōtō futsū kyōiku* liberal education
等数学 *kōtō sūgaku* higher mathematics
等試験 *kōtō shiken* higher civil service examination
等警察 *kōtō keisatsu* secret police
13 厦 *kōka* tall building
殿 *takadono* stately mansion
僧 *kōsō* high priest, prelate; virtuous priest
楼 *kōrō* tall building, skyscraper
雅 *kōga na* refined, elegant; chaste
腰 *takagoshi* pride
話 *takabanashi* loud talk
節 *kōsetsu* noble character, lofty virtues
義 *kōgi* high morality; kindness, favor; noble act ⌈when surfeited
楊枝 *takayōji* leisurely using a toothpick
蒔絵 *takamakie* raised lacquer work
障害 *kōshōgai* high hurdles
障礙 *kōshōgai* high hurdles
14 閣 *kōkaku* high tower
聞 *kōbun* your attention to my speech
鳴 *takana(ru)* ring loud, clang; throb, be thrilled (with hope)
徳 *kōtoku* eminent virtue
慢 *kōman* pride, insolence, arrogance. *kōman(chiki) na* haughty, arrogant

説 *kōsetsu* valuable opinion; your views
歌 *kōka* loud singing
察 *kōsatsu* your idea ⌈strata; tall (building)
層 *kōsō* high altitude, upper (atmospheric)
層気流 *kōsō kiryū* upper air current
層気象学 *kōsō kishōgaku* aerology
層飛行 *kōsō hikō* high-altitude flying
層建築 *kōsō kenchiku* skyscraper
層建築物 *kōsō kenchikubutsu* skyscraper
層雲 *kōsōun* alto-stratus clouds
15 趣 *kōshu* noble otherworldly interests
邁 *kōmai na* high, lofty, noble
嘱 *kōshoku* your request
潔 *kōketsu* purity, nobility
論 *kōron* exalted view; your opnion
談 *kōdan* lofty discourse; your discourse
誼 *kōgi* your kindness
熱 *kōnetsu* high fever
緯度 *kōido* high or cold latitudes
潮 *kōchō*, *takashio* spring tide, flood tide. *kōchō* high tide; climax, acme
潮時 *kōchōji* time of high tide
調 *kōchō suru* emphasize, urge
調子 *takachōshi* high pitch; high stock-market tone ⌈world
踏 *kōtō* living a holy life aloof from the
踏主義 *kōtō shugi* transcendentalism
踏的 *kōtōteki* transcendent; high-toned; highbrowed
16 館 *kōkan* lofty structure; your home
覧 *kōran* your perusal
積雲 *kōsekiun* alto-cumulus clouds
17 燥 *kōsō na* elevated, high and dry
聴 *kōchō* your kind attention
鼾 *taka-ibiki* loud snore
齢 *kōrei* advanced age
齢者 *kōreisha* very old person
嶺 *takane* lofty peak
嶺花 *takane (no) hana* flowers on inaccessible heights; unattainable object
翼 *kōyoku* high wing
翼機 *kōyokuki* high-wing plane
18 額 *kōgaku* high price, expensiveness
19 識 *kōshiki* exalted views
瀬 *takase* shallows
瀬舟 *takasebune* flatboat, river boat
麗 *Kōrai, Koma* an ancient Korean kingdom
麗鶯 *kōrai uguisu* oriole
20 欄 *kōran* railing, balcony
騰 *kōtō* sudden price jump

— 4 —

敲 5249/F860 **敲** Kō. *tata(ku)* (see under 叩 876.0). [攴]

膏 5250/F1550 Kō paste, ointment, plaster. *abura* fat, grease, tallow, lard, suet, blubber. [肉]

6 血 *kōketsu* sweat and blood
8 油 *kōyu* lamp oil
16 薬 *kōyaku* salve, ointment, plaster
薬張 *kōyakuba(ri)* patchwork, makeshift
壌 *kōjō* fertile soil

— 5 —

稾 5251/F1383 See **稿** 3299. [禾]

RAD. 髟 190

Kami hair. At top: *kamigashira* or *kami kammuri*. Nickname: Long Hair (cf. Rad. 59).

— 3 —

髢 5252/F2117 Tei. Seki. *kamoji* false hair, wig.

— 4 —

髳 5253/F2117 See **髯** 5259.

髣 5254/F2117 Hō dimly.

15 髴 *hōfutsu suru* closely resemble

B **髪** 5255/F2118 **髮** Hatsu. *kami* the hair.

3 上 *kamia(ge)* doing up the hair
4 毛 *kami (no) ke* the hair
化粧 *kami keshō* dolling up the hair
切 *kamiki(ri)* haircutting
切虫 *kamiki(ri) mushi* long-horned beetle
5 付 *kamitsu(ki)* hairdo
7 床 *kamidoko* barbershop
形 *kamikatachi* hairdo
8 油 *kami abura* hair oil, pomade
9 型 *kamigata* hairdo
洗 *kamiara(i)* washing the hair
洗粉 *kamiara(i)ko* shampoo powder
10 容 *kamikatachi* hairdo
12 揚 *kan-a(ge)* doing up the hair

筋 *kamisuji* comb lines; a hair
結 *kamiyu(i)* combing the hair; hairdressing; hairdresser
結床 *kamiyu(i)doko* (Edo) barbershop
13際 *kamigiwa* the hairline
飾 *kamikaza(ri)* hair ornament
14綱 *kamizuna* hair rope
15膚 *happu* hair and skin; body
16頭 *kamigashira* head of hair
18癖 *kamikuse* hair twist, kink

5

髮 5256/F2118 See 髪 5255.

髴 5257/F2118 See 彿 1601.

髱 5258/F2118 Hō. *tabo* topknot; bun, coiled hair knot.

髯 5259/F2117 髥 ZEN. *hige* beard; mustache; hairspring.
9茫茫 *hige-bōbō* bushy-bearded

6

髷 5260/F2118 KYOKU. *mage* topknot.

髻 5261/F2118 KEI. KITSU. *tabusa* a samurai hairdo. *motodori* topknot.

髭 5262/F2117 SHI. *hige* beard; mustache; hairspring. *hige (zemmai)* hairspring.
8口 *higeguchi* bearded mouth; a man's mouth
7男 *hige otoko* heavily bearded man
9面 *higezura* unshaven face, hairy face
剃 *higesori* shaving

11

鬘 5263/F2119 BAN. MAN. *katsura* wig, false hair.

12

鬣 See 鬣 5265.

鬚 5264/F2119 SHU. *hige* beard; mustache; hairspring.
8武者 *higemusha* heavily bearded man
15髯 *shuzen* mustache and beard

14

鬣 5265/F2120 鬣 RYŌ. *tategami* mane.

鬢 5266/F2119 BIN side locks, sideburns.
5付 *bintsu(ke)* hair cosmetic
付油 *bintsu(ke) abura* hair cosmetic
8長 *binnaga* albacore (a fish)

15

鬣 5267/F2120 See 鬣 5265.

RAD. 鬥 191

Tō or *tatakai* fighting. As enclosure: *tōgamae* or *tatakaigamae*.
Nickname: Broken Gate (cf. Rad. 169).

5

鬧 5268/F2120 See 閙 4951.

6

鬨 5269/F2120 KŌ. GŌ. GU. fight. *toki* war cry.
7声 *toki (no) koe* war cry

8

鬩 5270/F2120 KEKI. KAKU. GEKI. *seme(gu)* quarrel.
17牆 *gekishō* internal strife

10

鬪 5271/F2120 See 闘 4973.

14

鬭 See 闘 4973.

— 17 —

鬮 5272 F2121 See 鬮 5273.

— 18 —

鬮 5273 F2121 Kyū. *kuji* lottery, lot, raffle.

RAD. 鬯 192

Kaorigusa fragrant herbs. Nickname: Herb.

— 19 —

鬱 See 欝 2410.

RAD. 鬲 193

Ashi kamae tripod. Nickname: Tripod.

— 6 —

融 5274 F1670 B Yū. *to(keru) vi, to(kasu) vt* dissolve, melt. [虫]

4込 *to(ke)-ko(mu)* melt into, merge into
化 *yūka suru* soften, dissolve
6合 *yūgō* fusion, union
会 *yūkai* melting together; naturally understanding
8和 *yūwa* melting; softening; conciliation; soothing
9点 *yūten* melting point
通 *yūzū* accommodation, financing, loan; circulation; transfer; elasticity, adaptability, versatility
通手形 *yūzū tegata* negotiable paper
通念仏 *Yūzūnembutsu* Buddhist sect originating in the 12th century
10剤 *yūzai* flux
11雪 *yūsetsu* thaw, melting snow
12然 *yūzen toshita* quiet, calm, leisurely
13解 *yūkai* fusing, melting, dissolving
資 *yūshi* financing
15熱 *yūnetsu* heat of fusion

— 12 —

鬻 5275 F2123 Juku. *hisa(gu)* sell, deal in.

RAD. 鬼 194

Oni devil. Variant: 鬼 *kinyō* "devil" enclosure. Nickname: Devil.

鬼 5276 F2123 B Ki devil, demon; spirits of the dead. *oni* devil, demon, ghost; spirits of the dead; fiend; creditor; the one who is "it" (in games). *oni-* sharp, relentless, crack (detective), tough, extremely competent. *oni(gokko)* tag games.

3女 *kijo* demoness; witch
才 *kisai* genius, wizard, prodigy
子 *onigo* child born with teeth; a child not resembling his parents; a fierce child; tag games
子母神 *kishimojin, kishibojin* goddess of children
4心 *onigokoro* wicked heart
火 *onibi* will-o'-the-wisp, ignis fatuus
5瓦 *onigawara* ridge-end tile; gargoyle
6虫 *oni mushi* stag beetle
気 *kiki* weirdness, ghastliness
百合 *oniyuri* tiger lily
8門 *kimon* unlucky quarter (northeast); anathema; defect, weakness; undesirable person
板 *oni-ita* wooden ridge-end ornament
物 *kibutsu* ghost, goblin
事 *onigoto* tag games
武者 *oni-musha* intrepid warrior, daredevil
9面 *kimen* devil mask; bluff
神 *kishin, kijin, onigami,* terrible god, fierce god; departed spirit; demon, ghost, monster, goblin
界 *kikai* realm of the demons; realm of the dead

10殺 *onikoro(shi)* strong-minded person; strong person; strength; cheap drink of high alcoholic content
畜 *kichiku* a devil
哭 *kikoku* wail of a ghost
11遊 *oniaso(bi)* tag games
婆 *onibaba* witch, hag
鹿毛 *onikage* unbroken horse
12歯 *oniba* protruding tooth
16録 *kiroku* hell's record book
19簿 *kibo* death register
20籍 *kiseki* record of the dead

4

魁 5277/F2124 KAI. *sakigake* charging ahead of others.
11偉 *kai-i na* brawny, muscular, impressive

魂 5278/F2124 B KON. *tamashii, tama* soul, spirit.
6気 *konki* soul
迎 *tamamuka(e)* welcoming the spirits of the dead
8送 *tama-oku(ri)* sending off the spirits of the dead
9胆 *kontan* soul; plot, intrigue
10消 *tamage(ru)* be startled, be astonished
11祭 *tama matsu(ri)* memorial service for the dead
15魄 *kompaku* soul, spirit

5

魄 See 3108.

魃 5279/F2124 HATSU drought; god of drought.

魅 5280/F2125 B MI. *mi(suru)* charm, fascinate, bewitch, enchant. *baka(su)* bewitch, confuse, enchant, delude.
2力 *miryoku* charm, glamor, appeal
了 *miryō suru* charm, fascinate
12惑 *miwaku* fascination, enchantment, charm
惑的 *miwakuteki* charming, fascinating, seductive

11

魔 魔 See 5398.

14

魘 See 258.

11-STROKE RADICALS

RAD. 魚 195

Sakana or *uo* fish. At left: *uo hen.* Nickname: Fish.

魚 5281/F2126 A GYO *uo, sakana* fish.
4切 *uogi(re)* sold out of fish
介 *gyokai* marine products, sea food
5目 *iome, io(no)me, uo(no)me* corn (on the foot)
市 *uo-ichi* fish market
市場 *uo-ichiba* fish market
6肉 *gyoniku* fish meat
扠 *gyosa* fish spear, gaff, harpoon
灯 *gyotō* fishing lights
7見 *uomi* fish lookout (the person, place, or act)
貝 *gyokai* marine products, sea food
形 *gyokei* fishlike, fish-shaped
売 *sakana-u(ri)* fish peddler
卵 *gyoran* fish eggs, spawn, roe
串 *uogushi* fish skewer
8虎 *kawasemi* kingfisher
板 *gyoban* fish-shaped temple gong
油 *gyoyu* fish oil
狗 *kawasemi* kingfisher
肥 *gyohi* fish fertilizer
毒 *gyodoku* poison in fish
河岸 *uogashi* riverside fish market
9食 *gyoshoku* fish eating
屋 *sakanaya* fish shop, fish peddler
臭 *gyoshū* fish smell; smell of rotten fish
10粉 *gyofun* fish meal
脂 *gyoshi* fish fat
座目 *uonome* foot corn
11鳥 *gyochō* birds and fishes
道 *gyodō* fish paths in the sea; fish ladder, fishway
族 *gyozoku* the fishes
粕 *uokasu* fish cake
釣 *uotsuri* fishing
問屋 *uodon-ya* fish wholesaler
眼写真 *gyogan shashin* fish-eye (180-degree) photo
梯 *gyotei* fish ladder, fishway
梯子 *uobashigo* fish ladder
12棚 *uodana* fish shop; fish shelves
13塩 *gyoen* fish and salt; fish-and-salt business

鉤 *uokagi* fish gaff, fishhook
肆 *gyoshi* fish shop
群 *gyogun* school of fish
腹 *gyofuku* the entrails of fish
腹葬 *gyofuku (ni) hōmu(rareru)* drown
雷 *gyorai* torpedo
雷艇 *gyoraitei* torpedo boat
14 精 *gyosei* milt
網 *gyomō* fishing net
15 膠 *uo nikawa* fish glue
餌 *gyoji* fish bait
18 類 *gyorui* the fishes
類学 *gyoruigaku* ichthyology
19 繋 *uotsuna(gi)* lined up like fish on a skewer
20 籃 *gyoran* fish basket
22 鰾 *gyohyō* fish bladder
23 鱗 *gyorin* fish scales

4

魳 5282 / F2128 SHI. *kamasu* barracuda.

魯 5283 / F2127 RO foolish; Russia
8 国 *Rokoku* Russia
12 鈍 *rodon* foolishness, stupidity
20 艦 *Rokan* Russian battleship

5

鮑 5284 / F2128 HŌ. *awabi* abalone, ear shell.

鮃 5285 / F2128 HEI. *hirame* flatfish, flounder.

鮓 5286 / F2129 SA. *sushi* vinagered rice balls with fish or vegetables.

鮒 5287 / F2129 HO, FU. *funa* carp.

鮎 5288 / F2128 DEN. NEN. *ayu* fresh-water trout, sweet smelt.
8 並 *ainame* rock trout

6

鮞 5289 / F2129 JI *hararago* roe, milt, fish eggs.

鮪 5290 / F2129 KI. YŪ. *maguro, shibi* tuna, tunny.

鮭 5291 / F2129 KAI. KEI. *sake, shake* salmon.

鮠 5292 / F2129 KAI. GE. *hae, haya* dace (of the carp family).

鮨 5293 / F2129 SHI. KI. *sushi* seasoned rice mixed with fish or vegetables.
9 屋 *sushiya* sushi shop
13 詰 *sushizume* packed audience

鮫 5294 / F2129 KŌ. *same* shark.
5 皮 *samegawa* sharkskin
6 肌 *samehada* goose flesh (due to cold, etc.)
15 膚 *samehada*=preceding word
25 鑢 *same yasuri* sharkskin rasp

B **鮮** 5295 / F2129 SEN. Korea. *azaya(ka) na* vivid, clear, brilliant, fresh, graceful, splendid, beautiful.
4 少 *senshō* few, a little
6 肉 *senniku* fresh meat
血 *senketsu* lifeblood; flowing blood
7 花 *senka* beautiful bright flowers
赤色 *sensekishoku* bright red
8 味 *semmi* freshness
明 *semmei* clearness, distinctness
9 度 *sendo* (degree of) freshness
紅 *senkō* scarlet
美 *sembi* bright and beautiful
11 魚 *sengyō* fresh fish
12 満 *Semman* Korea and Manchuria
15 鋭度 *sen-eido* clarity, clearness
19 麗 *senrei na* gorgeous, vivid

7

鯒 5296 / F2131 (国字) *kochi* flathead (a fish).

鮹 5297 / F2130 SHŌ. *tako* octopus, devilfish.

鯁 5298 / F2130 KŌ fishbones.
10 骨 *kōkotsu*=硬骨 3193.10

鯉 5299 / F2130 RI. *koi* carp.
3 口 *koiguchi* mouth of a sword sheath
15 幟 *koinobori* carp streamer

8

鯰 5300 / F2132 (国字) *namazu* fresh-water catfish.

鯖 5301 / F2131 SEI. *saba* mackerel.
14 読 *saba (o) yo(mu)* cheat in counting

鯡 5302 / F2131 HI. *nishin* herring.

鰯 5303 F2131 EKI. *surume* a cuttlefish.

鯔 5304 F2131 SHI. *bora* mullet.

鯛 5305 F2131 CHŌ. *tai* sea bream, red snapper.
12 飯 *taimeshi* rice and minced sea bream

鯱 5306 F2132 (国字) *shachihoko* fabulous dolphin-like fish. *shachi* killer whale.
5 立 *shachihokoda(chi)* standing on one's head; exerting extreme effort
11 張 *shachikoba(ru)*, *shachihokoba(ru)* be stiff and formal

鯨 5307 F2132 GEI. *kujira* whale.
B
4 尺 *kujirajaku* long foot (14.91 inches) (a cloth measure)
6 肉 *geiniku* whale meat
8 油 *geiyu* whale oil
波 *geiha* raging waves; tidal wave; shout of victory. *toki* war cry
10 浪 *geirō* huge waves
脂 *geishi* blubber
差 *kujirazashi*＝鯨尺 *kujirajaku* (see above –4)
11 脳油 *geinōyu* sperm oil
12 飲 *gei-in suru* drink hard, drink like a fish
13 幕 *kujiramaku* black and white bunting curtain
17 糞 *geifun* ambergris
19 臘 *geirō* whale tallow

—— 9 ——

鰕 5308 F2133 KA *ebi* shrimp, prawn, lobster.

鰊 5309 F2133 REN. *nishin* herring.

鯷 5310 F2132 TEI. *hishiko* anchovy.

鰍 5311 F2133 SHŪ. SHU. *kajika* bullhead.

鰂 5312 F2132 SEKI. SHIKI. SHAKU. SHOKU *tanago* surf perch.

鰈 5313 F2133 CHŌ. *karei* sole, flatfish, flounder.
17 鮫 *chōzame* sturgeon

鰌 5314 F2133 SHU. SHŪ. *dojō* loach.
16 髭 *dojō hige* thin mustache

鰓 5315 F2133 SAI. *era* gills, gill slits.
4 孔 *era ana*, *saikō* gill slits

鰒 5317 F2133 F2136 FUKU. *awabi* abalone.

鰐 5317 F2133 F2136 ＝鰐 鱷 GAKU. *wani* crocodile, alligator.
3 口 *waniguchi* wide mouth; alligator; a temple gong
5 皮 *wanigawa*, *wanikawa* alligator skin
7 足 *waniashi* bowlegs
11 魚 *gakugyo* crocodile, alligator
17 鮫 *wanizame* shark

—— 10 ——

鰐 鰐 See 5317.

鰯 5318 F2134 (国字) *iwashi* sardine.

鰮 5319 F2134 ON. *iwashi* sardine.

鰤 5320 F2133 SHI. *buri* yellowtail (a fish).

鰥 5321 F2133 鰥 KAN. *yamome*, *yamo-o* widower, unmarried man.
4 夫 *yamo-o* widower
14 寡孤独 *kanka-kodoku* loneliness

鰭 5322 F2134 KI. GI. *hire* fin.
7 足 *hireashi* flipper

—— 11 ——

鰾 5323 F2134 HYŌ. *fue*, *ukibukuro* fish bladder, air bladder.

鰺 5324 F2134 SŌ. *aji* horse mackerel.

鱆 5325 F-X SHŌ. *tako* octopus, devilfish.

鰻 5326 F2134 MAN. *unagi* eel.
3 上 *unaginobo(ri)* rapid promotion
5 丼 *unagi domburi*, *unadon* rice-and-eel dish
9 屋 *unagiya* eel shop

鰹 5327 F2134 KEN. *katsuo* bonito, skipjack.

4木 *katsuogi* cigar-shaped cross logs on shrine ridgepole
13節 *katsuobushi, katsubushi* dried bonito
節削 *katsuobushikezu(ri)* dried bonito shavings

鱈 5328 F2135 (国字) Setsu. *tara* codfish.
3子 *tarako* cod roe
12場蟹 *tarabagani* king crab
13腹 *tarafuku* to heart's content

12

鱉 5329 F2135 F2169 See 鼈 5413.

鱏 5330 F2135 Jin. *ei*, ray, skate.

鱓 5331 F2135 Sen. Zen. *utsubo* moray eel.

鱒 5332 F2135 Son. Zon. Sen. Zan. *masu* salmon trout.

鱘 5333 F2135 Jin sturgeon.
11魚 *chōzame* sturgeon
17鮫 *chōzame* sturgeon

鱗 5334 F2135 Rin. *uroko, koke, kokera* (fish) scales.
7状 *rinjō* scaly
形 *urokogata* imbricate pattern. *urokogata no* imbricate, scalelike
9界 *rinkai* fish, the finny tribe
11族 *rinzoku* fish, the finny tribe
14模様 *uroko moyō* imbricate pattern

13

鱞 See 鰥 5321.

鱮 5335 F2136 Shō. *tanago* minnow, shiner.

鱧 5336 F2136 Rei. *hamo* conger eel, sea eel.

15

鱶 5337 F2136 Shō. *fuka* shark.

16

鱷 5338 F2136 See 鰐 5317.

鱸 5339 F2137 Ro. *suzuki* sea bass.

RAD. 鳥 196

Tori bird. Nickname: Bird.

鳥 5340 F2137 A Chō bird. *tori* bird; chicken; fowl.
2人 *chōjin* birdman, aviator
3小屋 *torigoya* aviary; henhouse
4毛 *torige* feathers, down
5目 *torime* night blindness. *chōmoku* an ancient coin; money
打 *toriuchi* fowling, shooting; cap
打帽 *toriu(chi)bō* cap
打帽子 *toriuchi bōshi* cap
6肉 *chōniku, toriniku* poultry meat
肌 *torihada* goose flesh (due to cold, etc.)
羽絵 *tobae* comic picture, cartoon
7貝 *torigai* cockle (shell)
声 *chōsei, torigoe* bird's cry, birdcall
8居 *torii* Shinto gateway
追 *torio(i)* scaring birds; wandering minstrel
9屋 *toriya* poultryman, bird fancier. *toya* hen coop, roost; actors' rest room
威 *toriodo(shi)* scarecrow
冠 *tosaka* cockscomb, crest (of a bird)
竿 *torizao* limed fowling rod
10差 *torisa(shi)* birdcatcher
11寄 *toriyo(se)* birdcall
笛 *toribue* birdcall
12媒 *chōbai* decoy
渡 *chotto* a short time; just a minute
飯 *torimeshi* chicken and rice
葬 *chōsō* Parsee burial (in the tower of silence)
13跡 *chōseki* bird tracks; writing
14滸 *oko(gamashii)* presumptuous, impertinent; ridiculous
網 *tori ami* fowler's net
語 *chōgo* bird chatter, bird songs
銃 *chōjū* fowling piece
15膚 *torihada* goose flesh
餌 *torie* birdseed, bird food
影 *torikage* shadow of a bird
16獣 *chōjū, tori-kedamono* birds and animals

17鍋 *torinabe* chicken cooked in a pan; shallow cooking pan
瞰図 *chōkanzu* bird's-eye view
糞 *chōfun* droppings, guano
糞石 *chōfunseki* guano deposit
18観図 *chōkanzu* bird's-eye view
類 *chōrui* the birds, fowls
類図鑑 *chōrui zukan* bird book
類学 *chōruigaku* ornithology
22籠 *torikago* bird cage
23黐 *torimochi* birdlime

2

鳧 5341 / F2137 Fu. *keri* wild duck; end, settlement; suffix.

鳩 5342 / 2138 Kyū. *hato* dove, pigeon.

8小屋 *hatogoya* pigeon house
5目 *hatome* eyelet
6羽色 *hatoba iro* bluish gray
7麦 *hatomugi* pearl barley
尾 *kyūbi, mizo-ochi, mizuochi* solar plexus, pit of the stomach
8舎 *kyūsha* pigeon house
9首 *kyūshu suru* go into a huddle
信 *kyūshin* carrier-pigeon communication
便 *hatobin* carrier-pigeon mail. *hatobin de* by carrier pigeon
10胸 *hatomune* pigeon breast, deformed protruding chest

3

鳴 See 983.

鳳 See 662.

鳶 See 1559.

鴎 Nonstandard for 鷗 5367.

島 5343 / F597 / F592 嶋 See 島 230. [山]

4

鴈 See 雁 830.

5

鴉 See 2851.

鴨 See 121.

鴫 See 3013.

鴬 Nonstandard for 鶯 5364.

鴒 5344 / F2141 Rei the wagtail.

鴦 5345 / F2142 Ō female mandarin duck.

鴛 5346 / F2141 En male mandarin duck.

16鴦 *oshidori, oshi* mandarin duck

鴟 5347 / F2141 鵄 鴲 Shi. *tobi* kite.

7尾 *shibi* ornamental ridge-end tile

6

鴻 See 2722.

鴲 5348 / F2142 See 鴟 5347.

鴿 5349 / F2143 Kō. *hato, dobato* dove, temple pigeon.

鴇 5350 / F2143 Bō. *toki* crested ibis.

6色 *toki iro* yellowish pink

7

鵑 5351 / F2144 Ken the cuckoo.

鵠 5352 / F2144 Koku swan.

鵞 5353 / F2144 鵝 Ga goose.

11鳥 *gachō* goose

鵜 5354 / F2144 Tei. *u* cormorant.

5目鷹目 *u(no)me-taka(no)me de* with sharp eyes
6舟 *ubune* cormorant-fishing boat
匠 *ushō* cormorant fisherman
8使 *uzuka(i)* cormorant fishing
12飲 *uno(mi)* swallowing whole
18飼 *uka(i)* cormorant fishing

8

鵬 See 3831.

鵡 5355 F2145 Bu, Mu the cockatoo.

鵲 5356 F2145 Shaku. *kasasagi* magpie.

鵼 5357 F2146 鵺 Kō. *nue* fabulous night bird; grotesque monster.

鶉 5358 F2146 Jun. *uzura* quail.
6衣 *uzuragoromo* patched clothes
7豆 *uzura mame* mottled kidney beans

鶏 5359 F2149 F2018 B 鷄 雞 Kei. *niwatori* chicken.
6肉 *keiniku* chicken (meat)
肋 *keiroku* fowl's breastbone; weakness; worthlessness
7声 *keisei* cockcrowing
卵 *keiran* hen egg
卵大 *keirandai* the size of a hen's egg
8林 *Keirin* Korea
舎 *keisha* poultry house
9冠 *keikan, tosaka* cockscomb
姦 *keikan* sodomy
11唱 *keishō* cockcrowing
眼 *keigan* foot corn
豚 *keiton* chickens and hogs; domestic animals
13群 *keigun* flock of chickens
14鳴 *keimei* cockcrowing
16頭 *keitō* cockscomb
17糞 *keifun* chicken manure

9

鶩 5360 F2147 Boku. Bu. *ahiru* domestic duck.

10

鷄 5361 F2149 See 鶏 5359.

鶸 5362 F2148 Jaku. *hiwa* light yellowish green.

鶺 5363 F2148 Seki wagtail.
16鴒 *sekirei* wagtail

鶯 5364 F2147 Ō. *uguisu* nightingale, bush warbler.
6色 *uguisu iro* greenish brown
9垣 *uguisugaki* brushwood fence
茶 *uguisu cha* greenish brown
11張 *uguisuba(ri)* singing floor boards

鶴 5365 F2147 Kaku. *tsuru* crane, stork.
9首 *kakushu suru* stretch out the neck
11亀 *tsurukame* crane and tortoise; congratulations
亀鶴亀 *tsurukame-tsurukame* That must not be.
14髪 *kakuhatsu* gray hair
16嘴 *tsuruhashi, tsurubashi* pick, pickax, mattock
頸 *tsurukubi* long-necked gourd; long-necked person; long-necked bottle

11

鷚 5366 F-X Ryū. Ru. Bō. Hyū. Mu. Kyū. Gu. Ryō. *hibari* skylark. (Listed as an example of the many *on* that have accompanied some characters from China. As a rule, however, this dictionary includes only *on* in current use.)

鷗 5367 F2149 Ō. *kamome* sea gull.

12

鷲 5368 F2150 Shū. Ju. *washi* eagle.
14鼻 *washibana* aquiline nose, Roman nose
摑 *washizuka(mi)* clutch, grab

13

鷹 See 1544.

鷺 5369 F2151 Ro. *sagi* heron.

17

鸛 5370 F2152 Kan. *kōnotori* Japanese stork.

鸚 5371 F2151 Ō parrot.
10哥 *inko* parakeet
19鵡 *ōmu* parrot
鵡返 *ōmugae(shi)* parrot-like repetition
鵡貝 *ōmugai* chambered nautilus

RAD. 鹵 197

Shio salt. Nickname: Salt.

鹵 5372 F2152 Ro natural salt; salty soil; shield; plunder; poor, barren.
16獲 *rokaku suru* capture, plunder
獲物 *rokakubutsu* booty, trophy, spoils
獲品 *rokakuhin* booty, trophy, spoils
19簿 *robo* imperial procession

— 8 —

塩 See 塩 1125.

鹸 Nonstandard for 鹼 5374.

— 9 —

鹹 5373 F2153 KAN. *kara(i)* salty.
4水 *kansui* brackish water, sea water, salt water
水沼沢 *kansui shōtaku* salt marsh
水魚 *kansuigyo* salt-water fish
水湖 *kansuiko* salt lake
6気 *shioke* saltiness
7沢 *kantaku* salt marsh
8味 *kammi* saltiness
11魚 *kangyo* salted fish
菜 *kansai* vegetables pickled in salt
12湖 *kanko* salt lake, lagoon

— 13 —

鹽 See 塩 1125.

鹼 5374 F2153 KEN saltiness; lye; salt.
4化 *kenka* saponification

RAD. 鹿 198

Shika deer. At left: *shika hen*. As enclosure: 鹿. Nickname: Deer.

鹿 5375 F2154 ROKU. *shika* deer.
3子 *ka(no)ko* fawn; dapples, white spots
子斑 *ka(no)ko madara no* spotted like a deer
4毛 *kage* fawn-colored horse
爪 *shikatsume(rashii)* formal; solemn, serious
5皮 *shikagawa* deerskin
逐 *shika (o) o(u)* run for office
10島立 *kashimada(chi)* departure on a journey
11砦 *rokusai* abatis; entanglement

— 3 —

塵 5376 F435 CHIN. JIN dust. *chiri, gomi* dust, trash, rubbish. *chiri(bamu)* be covered with dust. [土]
4心 *jinshin* one contaminated with worldly interests
中 *jinchū ni* in the dust; in the world
5外 *jingai ni* aloof from the world
払 *chirihara(i), chirihata(ki)* duster
世 *chiri (no) yo, jinsei* this contaminating world
6灰 *jinkai* dust and ashes
7劫 *jingō* forever
芥 *chiri akuta, jinkai* rubbish, garbage
8取 *chiritor(i)* dustpan
事 *jinji* earthly things affairs
9垢 *jinkō, chiriaka* rubbish, dust, worldly
除 *chiriyo(ke)* dust cloth; dust coat, duster
界 *jinkai* this mundane life
点劫 *jintengō* forever
10埃 *jin-ai, chiri-hokori* dust, dirt; this drab world
紙 *chirigami* coarse toilet paper
12葉 *chiri(p)pa* dust, a tiny bit
13塚 *chirizuka* dust heap, dump
溜 *chirida(me)* dust box, garbage can, ash can
煙 *chiri kemuri, jin-en* cloud of dust
14境 *jinkyō* this mundane life
15箱 *gomibako* garbage box
19霧 *jimmu* dust haze

— 8 —

麓 5377 F2155 ROKU. *fumoto* foot of a mountain.

麑 5378 F2155 GEI. *kojika* fawn, young deer.

鏖 5379 F1963 Ō. *minagoro(shi)* massacre, annihilation. [金]
10殺 *ōsatsu* massacre, annihilation, extermination

麒 5380/F2155 KI giraffe.
²³麟 *kirin* giraffe
麟児 *kirinji* infant prodigy

B 麗 5381/F2155 REI. RAI. *urara(ka)na* beautiful, bright and clear, fine, serene. *uruwa(shii)* beautiful, lovely, graceful
²人 *reijin* beauty, belle
⁴日 *reijitsu* beautiful day
⁵句 *reiku* beautiful phrase
⁶色 *reishoku* beautiful views; beautiful countenance
⁸服 *reifuku* beautiful clothes
⁹姿 *reishi* beautiful figure
¹⁰容 *reiyō* beautiful figure
¹²筆 *reihitsu* beautifully written poetry; the writing brush (ornate)
¹³雅 *reiga* beauty and nobility
辞 *reiji* beautiful words
¹⁵質 *reishitsu* beauty, charms
¹⁸顔 *reigan* beautiful face
¹⁹麗 *reirei to, reirei(shiku)* ostentatiously, pretentiously

10

麝 5382/F2156 JA musk deer.
⁹香 *jakō* musk
香水 *jakōsui* musk water, musk scent
香鹿 *jakōjika* musk deer
香猫 *jakō neko* musk cat
香鼠 *jakō nezumi* muskrat
香豌豆 *jakō endō* sweet peas

12

麟 5383/F2156 RIN giraffe.

22

麤 5384/F2156 So rough.

RAD. 麥 199

Mugi wheat. Variant: 麦 (7 strokes). Variant: 夌 *bakunyō* "wheat" enclosure. Nickname: Wheat.

A 麦 5385/F2157 麥 BAKU. *mugi* wheat, barley, oats, rye.
⁴刈 *mugika(ri)* wheat harvest
⁵田 *mugita* a rice field used for growing wheat
打 *mugiu(chi)* wheat threshing
⁶扱 *mugiko(ki)* wheat threshing
⁷作 *mugisaku* wheat raising
束 *mugitaba* sheaf of wheat, stacked wheat
⁸芽 *bakuga* malt
芽糖 *bakugatō* maltose, malt sugar
⁹畑 *mugibatake, mugibata* wheat field; barley field
秋 *mugiaki, mugi (no) aki, bakushū* wheat harvest
茶 *mugicha* parched-barley tea
¹⁰酒 *bakushu, biiru* beer
粉 *mugiko* (wheat) flour
¹¹笛 *mugibue* wheat-straw whistle
粒腫 *bakuryūshu* sty (on the eyelid)
¹²湯 *mugiyu* parched-barley tea
飯 *mugimeshi, bakuhan* boiled barley and rice
焦 *mugikoga(shi)* parched-barley flour
稈 *bakkan, mugiwara* wheat straw
稈細工 *mugiwarazaiku* straw work
稈帽子 *mugiwara bōshi* straw hat
¹³搗 *mugitsu(ki)* polishing wheat
蒔 *mugimaki* wheat planting
¹⁵踏 *mugifu(mi)* treading wheat plants
¹⁷藁 *mugiwara* wheat straw
藁帽子 *mugiwara bōshi* straw hat

4

麪 See 麵 5389.

麩 5386/F2157 FU light wheat-gluten bread. *fusuma* wheat bran, mash.
¹⁵質 *fushitsu* gluten

5

麭 5387/F2158 Hō sticky rice ball.

8

麴 5388/F2158 KIKU. *kōji* malt, leaven, yeast.
¹¹菌 *kōjikin* yeast plant, yeast cell
²³黴 *kōji kabi* yeast plant, yeast cell

9

麵 5389/F2158/F2157 麵 麪 MEN noodles; wheat flour.
¹²棒 *membō* rolling pin
¹⁶麭 *pan* bread
¹⁸類 *menrui* noodles

麻 RAD. 200

Asa hemp. Variant: 麻 and 𢆯 *asa kammuri*, used as an enclosure.
Nickname: Hemp.

麻 5390/F2158 **麻** B Ma. *asa* flax, hemp, ramie, jute, linen.

5 布 *mafu, asa nuno* hemp cloth, linen
6 糸 *asa ito* linen thread, hemp yarn
衣 *asagoromo, asaginu, ma-i* linen robe
10 屑 *asakuzu* oakum, tow
疹 *hashika, mashin* measles
11 雀 *mājan* mahjong
雀屋 *mājan-ya* mahjong parlor
酔 *masui* anesthesia
酔剤 *masuizai* anesthetic; narcotic
酔薬 *masuiyaku* anesthetic; narcotic
13 痺 *mahi* paralysis, palsy, numbness, stupor, anesthesia
睡 *masui* anesthesia
幹 *ogara* hemp reed, hemp stalk
裏 *asa-ura* hemp-soled sandals
裏草履 *asa-ura zōri* hemp-soled sandals
14 綱 *asazuna* hemp rope
16 薬 *mayaku* anesthetic; narcotic
薬常用 *mayaku jōyō* narcotic addiction
18 織 *asao(ri)* hemp cloth
19 縄 *asa nawa* hemp rope

4

麾 5391/F2159 Ki. *sashimane(ku)* beckon to; command, take command.

3 下 *kika* under one's command
7 兵 *kihei* soldiers under one's command

摩 5392/F825 **摩** B Ma. *ma(suru)* rub; rub off; polish; grind; graze; scrape; be equal to; be about to reach. *sa(su-ru)* pat, stroke. *su(ru), su(reru)* (see under 擦 2025.0). [手]

4 込 *su(ri)-ko(mu)* rub in
切 *su(ri)-ki(ru)* *vt* wear out; spend all. *su-(ri)-ki(reru)* *vi* wear out
天楼 *matenrō* skyscraper
5 付 *su(ri)-tsu(keru)* scratch (a match); (dogs) nose (people)
7 利支天 *Marishiten* Buddhist god of war
9 枯 *su(ri)-ka(rashi)* serious abrasion, wearing out (of clothes)
11 寄 *su(ri)-yo(ru)* draw near, snuggle up to
12 替 *su(ri)-ka(eru)* secretly substitute
13 滅 *mametsu*=磨滅 5393.13
17 擦 *masatsu* rubbing, chafing; friction; discord
擦音 *masatsuon* fricative sound

5

磨 5393/F1351 **磨** Ma. *miga(ku)* polish, scour; shine (shoes); brush (teeth); improve (skill), cultivate (character), train (the mind). *su(ru)* rub, chafe, file; lose. *su(reru)* *vi* (see under 擦 2025.0). *to(gu)* (see under 研 3180.0). [石]

4 込 *su(ri)-ko(mu)* grind and mix
切 *su(ri)-ki(ru)* cut by rubbing; spend all (one's money)
5 石 *togi-ishi* whetstone, grindstone
汁 *togishiru* the water in which rice has been washed
出 *su(ri)-da(su)* polish
6 合 *su(ri)-a(waseru)* fit by rubbing together
9 砂 *miga(ki)zuna* polishing sand
砕 *su(ri)-kuda(ku)* rub to pieces
研紙 *makenshi* emery paper
10 消 *su(ri)-ke(su)* erase, efface
粉 *miga(ki)ko* polishing powder
紙 *miga(ki)gami* emery paper
耗 *mamō* abrasion, wear
11 崩 *su(ri)-kuzu(su)* rub to pieces
12 揉 *sut(ta)mon(da) suru* be confused
減 *su(ri)-he(rasu)* wear away, rub down, abrade
13 損 *mason* wear and tear
滅 *mametsu* wear and tear; defacement; crushing (a nerve) lose (a fortune)
15 潰 *su(ri)-tsubu(su)* pulverize; mash; deface;

6

縻 5394/F-X **縻** Bi. Mi rope. [糸]

糜 5395/F1435 Bi be inflamed. [米]

21 爛 *biran* inflammation, erosion of skin or mucous membranes
爛性 *biransei* irritating, poisonous (gas)

7

麿 5396/F2159 **麿** (国字) *maro* I; you

8

靡 5397/F2041 **靡** Hi. Bi. *nabi(ku)* flutter, wave; bow to, yield to, obey, be swayed by. *nabi(kasu)* seduce; win over; conquer. [非]

10

B 魔 5398 F2125 魔 MA demon, devil, evil spirit. [鬼]

²力 *maryoku* magical power, charm
³女 *majo* witch, sorceress
⁴手 *mashu* evil influence
王 *maō* the devil
⁸性 *mashō* devilishness
物 *mamono* goblin, apparition
法 *mahō* magic, sorcery, witchcraft
法使 *mahōtsuka(i)* magician, sorcerer
法的 *mahōteki* magic (adjective)
法罎 *mahōbin* thermos bottle
⁹凮 *makaze* a storm caused by the devil; an evil wind
神 *mashin, majin* devil, evil spirit
除 *mayo(ke)* charm against evil spirits, talisman, amulet
界 *makai* world of spirits, infernal regions, hell
¹¹道 *madō* heresy; evil ways
球 *makyū* curve (in baseball)
術 *majutsu* magic, sorcery, witchcraft, augury
術師 *majutsushi* magician, conjurer
¹²街 *magai*=*makutsu* 魂窟 (see below–13)
訶不思議 *maka-fushigi* profound mystery
¹³睡 *masui* anesthesia
窟 *makutsu* den (of thieves); brothel, red-light district
¹⁴境 *makyō* haunts of wicked men
¹⁵魅 *mami* a deceiving spirit

12-STROKE RADICALS

RAD. 黄 201

Kiiroi yellow. Variant: 黃 (11 strokes) Nickname: Yellow.

A 黄 5399 F2159 黃 KŌ. Ō. *ki* yellow. *ki(bamu)* turn yellow. *ki(bami)* yellow tint.

³土 *ōdo* yellow ocher. *kōdo*, the earth; yellow soil, loess; hades
口 *kōkō* a baby chick; a young and inexperienced person
口児 *kōkōji* immature youth
⁴水 *kimizu* bile, gall
水仙 *kisuisen* jonquil
水晶 *kizuishō* citrine, yellow quartz
⁵瓜 *kyūri* cucumber
玉 *ōgyoku, kōgyoku* topaz
玉石 *ōgyokuseki, kōgyokuseki* topaz
白 *kōhaku* yellow and white; gold and silver; bribery, corruption
白色 *kōhakushoku* pale yellow
⁶色 *ki-iro, kiiro(i), kōshoku, ōshoku* yellow
色人種 *ōshoku jinshu* yellow race
色声 *kiiro(i) koe* shrill voice
⁷身 *kimi* yolk of an egg
吻 *kōfun* young and inexperienced person
花 *kōga, kōka* chrysanthemum
⁸味 *kimi(gakatta)* yellowish, cream-colored
昏 *kōkon, tasogare* dusk, twilight
表紙 *kibyōshi* dime novel
金 *kogane*, gold. *ōgon* gold; gold pieces; money
金万能 *ōgon bannō* the almighty dollar
金世界 *ōgon sekai* Utopia
金色 *ōgonshoku* gold color
金国 *ōgonkoku* an El Dorado
金律 *ōgonritsu* golden rule
金時代 *ōgon jidai* the golden age
金術 *ōgonjutsu* alchemy
金率 *ōgonritsu* golden mean
金崇拝 *ōgon sūhai* mammon worship
⁹海 *Kōkai* Yellow Sea
変米 *ōhemmai* spoiled rice
枯茶 *kigaracha* bluish yellow
泉 *kōsen* underground spring. *kōsen, yomi,* hades, realm of the dead
泉国 *yomi (no) kuni* hades, realm of the dead
¹⁰疸 *ōdan* jaundice
班 *ōhan* yellow spot
粉 *kinako* soybean flour
¹¹鳥 *ōchō* nightingale
麻 *tsunaso, kōma,* jute
梢 *kōshō* a sprig of yellow buds
菊 *kigiku* yellow chrysanthemum
雀 *kōjaku* sparrow
菖蒲 *kishōbu* yellow iris
道 *ōdo, kōdō* ecliptic
道十二宮 *kōdō jūnikyū* twelve signs of the zodiac
道色 *kōdōshoku* brassy yellow
道光 *kōdōkō* zodiacal light
道吉日 *ōdō kichinichi, kōdō kichinichi* lucky day
道面 *kōdōmen* plane of the ecliptic

道帯 *kōdōtai* zodiac
12 葉 *kōyō* fall colors
13 楊 *tsuge* boxwood, box tree
禍 *Kōka* Yellow Peril
鉛 *ōen* chrome yellow
鉄鉱 *ōtekkō* iron pyrites, fool's gold
14 塵 *kōjin* dust (in the air); this dusty world
碧玉 *kōhekigyoku* yellow jasper, beryl
緑色 *ōryokushoku* yellow green, pea green
褐色 *ōkasshoku* yellowish brown
銅 *kōdō, ōdō* brass
銅鉱 *ōdōkō, kōdōkō* copper pyrites, fool's gold
15 熟 *kōjuku* ripening and turning yellow
熱 *ōnetsu* yellow fever
熱病 *ōnetsubyō, kōnetsubyō* yellow fever
16 燐 *ōrin* yellow phosphorus, white phosphorus
頷蛇 *aodaishō* common harmless snake
21 蠟 *ōrō* beeswax

RAD. 黍 202

Kibi millet. Nickname: Millet.

黍 5400/F2161 SHO. *kibi* millet.
6 団子 *kibi dango* millet dumplings

— 3 —

黎 See 2648.

— 5 —

黏 5401/F2162 See 粘 3472.

— 11 —

黐 5402/F2162 CHI. *mochi* birdlime.
9 竿 *mochizao* lime stick (to catch insects)

RAD. 黑 203

Kuroi black. Variant: 黒 (11 strokes). Nickname: Black (cf. Rad. 95).

A **黒** 5403/F2162 **黑** KOKU. *kuro* black; dark. *kuro(zumu), kuro(zuku)* blacken, darken. *kuro(bamu), kuro(maru) vi* blacken, become black. *kuro(meru) vt* blacken; talk wrong into right. *kuro(raka)* blackness, deep black. *kuro(ku) suru vt* blacken. *kuro(i)* black; dark, swarthy, browned; dirty. *kuro(ppoi)* dark, blackish.
2 人 *Kokujin* Negro. *kurōto*=玄人 2918.2
人霊歌 *Kokujin reika* a Negro spiritual
3 土 *kokudo, kurotsuchi* black soil
子 *kokushi* face mole; mite. *kurogo* prompter, stagehand. *hokuro* dark mole; beauty spot
山 *kuroyama* a large crowd
巾 *kurogo* prompter, stagehand
丸 *kuromaru*=*kuroboshi* 黒星 (see below–9)
4 木 *kuroki* unbarked lumber
円 *kuromaru*=*kuroboshi* 黒星 (see below–9)
内障 *kokunaishō* black cataract
水引 *kuromizuhiki* black-and-white string
水熱 *kokusuinetsu* blackwater fever
5 白 *kokuhaku, kokubyaku, kuro-shiro* black and white; right and wrong
目 *kurome* black iris, black eyes
奴 *kokudo, kurombō, kurombo* Negro; dark-skinned person; smut; prompter, stagehand
6 米 *kurogome* unpolished rice
肉 *kuroniku* black sealing ink; black stamp pad
血 *kurochi* venous blood
地 *kuroji* black ground, black cloth
字 *kuroji* black figures
光 *kurobika(ri)* black luster
死病 *kokushibyō* bubonic plague, black death
色 *kokushoku* black
色人種 *kokushoku jinshu* black race
衣 *kokui, kokue* black clothes
衣宰相 *kokui (no) saishō* Buddhist priest who is a government minister
7 豆 *kuromame* black soy bean
麦 *kuromugi* rye
坊 *kuro(m)bō*=*kokudo* 黒奴 (see above–5)
8 枠 *kurowaku* black (mourning) borders
松 *kuromatsu* black pine
服 *kurofuku* black suit, mourning clothes
苺 *kuro-ichigo* blackberry
表 *kokuhyō* black list

金 *kurogane* iron
金剛石 *kuro kongōseki* black diamond, carbon, carbonado
板 *kokuban* blackboard
板拭 *kokubanfu(ki)* blackboard eraser
9海 *Kokkai* Black Sea
点 *kokuten* black spot, dark spot; sunspot
炭 *kokutan* bituminous coal
星 *kuroboshi* black spot, black dot; bull's-eye; failure
茶 *kurocha* deep brown
砂糖 *kurozatō* unrefined sugar
風 *kokufū* sky-darkening dust storm
風白雨 *kokufū-haku-u* sudden shower in a dust storm
10酒 *kuroki* black saké
苺 *kuro-ichigo* blackberry
紋付 *kuromontsu(ki)* black crested haori
11黒 *kuroguro* deep black
船 *kurofune* the black ships (of the foreigners)
蛇 *kurohebi* blacksnake
眼鏡 *kuromegane* dark glasses
12痣 *kuroaza* black mole
焼 *kuroya(ki)*, *kuroya(ke)* charring; something charred
斑 *kurobuchi*, *kurofu* black spots
焦 *kuroko(ge)* something burnt black
装束 *kuroshōzoku* black clothes
猩猩 *kuroshōjō* chimpanzee
雲 *koku-un*, *kurokumo* dark clouds, black clouds
雲母 *kuro ummo* biotite, black or green mica
13煙 *kokuen*, *kurokemuri* black smoke
鉛 *kokuen* black lead, graphite
鉄 *kurogane* iron
幕 *kuromaku* black curtain; wirepuller
塗 *kuronu(ri)* blackening; blackened thing; *kuronu(ri) no* black-lacquered, black-colored
14漆 *kokushitsu* black lacquer
緑 *kuromidori* blackish green
髪 *kurokami*, *kokuhatsu* black hair
熊 *kuroguma*, *kurokuma* black bear
褐色 *kokkasshoku* blackish brown
15潮 *Kuroshio* Japan Current
穂 *kurobo*, *kuroho* smut
線 *kokusen* black line
縁 *kurobuchi* black rim, black edge
影 *kokuei* silhouette, dark shadow
銹病 *kurosabibyō* black rust
16頭巾 *kurozukin* black hood
17檀 *kokutan* ebony, blackwood
鍵 *kokken* the black keys
18曜石 *kokuyōseki* obsidian
曜岩 *kokuyōgan* obsidian
19蟻 *kuroari* black ant, carpenter ant
20繻子 *kurojusu* black satin
23黴 *kurokabi* bread mold

3

墨 5404 / F439 **墨** B Boku. *sumi* India ink, Chinese ink; ink stick; inked marking string; ink (of a squid). [土]
5付 *sumitsu(ke)* blackening the face. *sumitsu(ki)* handwriting, autograph; black (not red) seal
汁 *bokujū* India ink
6糸 *sumi ito* inked marking string
色 *sumi iro* India-ink color
池 *bokuchi* inkstone well, inkhorn
刑 *bokukei* punishment by tattooing
守 *bokushu* strict adherence
8画 *bokuga* India-ink drawing
9客 *bokkaku*, *bokkyaku* artist; writer
染 *sumizo(me)* dying black; dyed black; dark ink
染衣 *sumizo(me)goromo*, *sumizo(me) no koromo* black robe of a priest
10消 *sumike(shi)* blotting out characters with ink
書 *sumiga(ki)* inking the outlines of a picture. *bokusho* writing in India ink
11魚 *ika* squid, cuttlefish
痕 *bokkon* ink marks; handwriting
描 *sumiga(ki)* inking the outlines of a picture
12堤 *Bokutei* banks of the Sumida river
絵 *sumie* India-ink drawing, black-and-white drawing
11壷 *sumitsubo* ink bottle; carpenter's inking device
19縄 *suminawa* inked marking string

4

默 5405 / F2163 **默** See 2796.

5

點 5406 / F2164 See **点** 804.

黜 5407 / F2164 Chutsu draw back.

黛 5408 / F2164 Tai blackened eyebrows; blue black. *mayuzumi* blackened eyebrows.
8青 *taisei* blackish blue

6

黠 5409 / F2165 Katsu crafty.

8

黨 See **党** 1363.

黥 5410 / F2165 Kei, Gei tattooing. *irezumi* tattooing.

—— 9 ——

黯 5411 F2166 AN black; dark.
12然 *anzen(taru)* tearful, doleful

—— 11 ——

黴 See 1643.

黹 RAD. 204

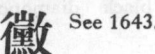

Nuu to embroider, sew. Nickname: Sewing.

13-STROKE RADICALS

黽 RAD. 205

Aogaeru tree frog. Nickname: Frog.

黽 5412 F2168 BŌ, BIN, BEN green frog; industry.
10勉 *bimben* industry, diligence

—— 12 ——

鼈 5413 F2169 鱉 BETSU. *suppon* snapping turtle, mud turtle.
5甲 *bekkō* tortoise shell
甲色 *bekkō iro* amber color
23鱉 *suppon* fresh-water soft-shell turtle

鼎 RAD. 206

Kanae kettle. This is actually a 12-stroke radical but is placed here in its traditional place among the 13-stroke radicals. Nickname: Kettle.

鼎 5414 F2169 鼑 TEI. *kanae* three-legged kettle.
5立 *teiritsu* triangular position; three-cornered (contest)
立戦 *teiritsusen* three-cornered contest
7坐 *teiza suru* sit in a triangle
15談 *teidan* three-man talk, tripartite talk
談会 *teidankai* three-man talk, tripartite talk

14-STROKE RADICALS

鼓 RAD. 207

Tsuzumi hand-drum. Variant: 皷 (14 strokes). Nickname: Drum.

B鼓 5415 F2170 皷 KO *tsuzumi* drum. *ko(su)* beat; rouse, muster (courage). *tsuzumi* hand drum.
4手 *koshu* drummer
手長 *koshuchō* drum major
7吹 *kosui* inspiration; advocacy; encouragement
吹者 *kosuisha* advocate, propagator
9室 *koshitsu* eardrum
11動 *kodō* beat, palpitation, pulsation, throbbing
笛隊 *kotekitai* drum-and-fife band
14舞 *kobu* inspiration, stimulation, encouragement
舞激励 *kobu-gekirei* encouragement

13腸 *kochō* flatulence, bloating
腹 *kofuku suru* be happy and contented
14膜 *komaku* eardrum
15楼 *korō* drum tower (at a temple)

— 5 —

瞽 5416 / F1332 Ko blind person. [目]
8者 *kosha* blind person

RAD. 鼠 208

Nezumi rat. As enclosure: 鼠. Nickname: Rat.

鼠 5417 / F2172 So. *nezumi, nezu* rat, mouse; dark gray.
2入 *nezumi-i(razu)* a ratproof cupboard
6色 *nezumi iro* dark gray, slate
8取 *nezumitor(i)* rat poison; mousetrap
9疫 *soeki* plague, pest
咬症 *sokōshō* ratbite disease
海豚 *nezumi iruka* porpoise
11族 *sozoku* rodents
盗 *sotō* pilfering
12落 *nezumioto(shi)* rattrap
13賊 *sozoku* petty thief, pilferer; sneak thief
嫁入 *nezumi (no) yome-i(ri)* a light shower
14算 *nezumizan* multiplying like rats
15輩 *sohai* small fry, unimportant people
17蹊 *sokei* the groin
蹊部 *sokeibu* the groin

— 5 —

鼬 5418 / F2172 鼬 Yū. *itachi* weasel; skunk; mink; ermine.

— 9 —

鼹 5419 / F2173 See 鼴 5420.

— 10 —

鼴 5420 / F2173 鼴 En mole.
13鼠 *mogura* mole (the rodent)

RAD. 鼻 209

Hana nose. Variant: 鼻. Nickname: Nose.

A鼻 5421 / F2173 鼻 Bi nasal. *hana* nose; snout, muzzle. *hana(p-pashi)* bridge of the nose.
3口 *bikō* nose and mouth; nostrils; muzzle (of a dog)
下 *bika* under the nose
下長 *bikachō* amorous man; henpecked husband
4木 *hanagi* nose hitch (for cattle)
毛 *hanage* nostril hairs
水 *hanamizu* nasal discharge
内 *binai* in the nose
孔 *bikō* nostrils
元 *hanamoto* root of the nose
5白 *hanashiro(mu)* feel let down; feel ashamed
汁 *hanashiru* nasal discharge
出血 *bishukketsu* nosebleed
6血 *hanaji* nosebleed
向 *hanamu(ke)* smelling (something); farewell present
汗 *hana ase* nose sweat
先 *hanasaki* tip of the nose. *hanasaki ni* under one's nose; imminent
7折 *hana (o) o(ru)* to humble (a person)
声 *hanagoe, bisei* nasal voice
8明 *hana (o) aka(su)* take advantage of another's misfortune
炎 *bien* nasal inflammation
呼吸 *bikokyū* nasal respiration
突 *hanatsu(ki)* meeting head on
突合 *hanatsu(ki)a(i)* quarreling. *hana (o) tsu(ki)-a(wasu)* be closely crowded together
9面 *hanazura* muzzle, snout
革 *hanagawa* toe cover for clogs
音 *bion* a nasal sound
屎 *hana kuso* nasal discharge
拭 *hanafu(ki)* handkerchief
持 *hanamo(chinaranu)* intolerable, disgusting
柱 *hana(p)pashira, hanabashira* septum, bridge of the nose
祖 *biso* founder, originator, introducer
茸 *biji, hanatake* nasal polyps, adenoids
風 *hana kaze* head cold

風邪 *hana kaze* head cold
10骨 *bikotsu* nasal bone
疾 *bishitsu* diseases of the nose
唄 *hana-uta* humming, crooning
根 *bikon* root of the nose
紙 *hanagami* handkerchief paper
高 *hanataka* high nose; person with a high nose; pride. *hana ga taka(i)* proud. *hana (o) taka(ku) suru* be proud
高高 *hanatakadaka* proudly, triumphantly
息 *bisoku, hana-iki* nasal breathing; a person's pleasure
息荒 *hana-iki (ga) ara(i)* imperious, proud
11張 *hana(p)pa(ri)* overconfidence
許 *hanamoto* root of the nose
梁 *biryō* bridge of the nose
眼鏡 *hana megane* pince-nez glasses
12腔 *bikō, bikū* nasal cavity
筋 *hanasuji* bridge of the nose
13詰 *hanazuma(ri)* nose being clogged up
14摘 *hanatsuma(mi)* uncouth person, bore
端 *bitan* nose tip
緒 *hanao* clog thong
綱 *hanazuna* halter
歌 *hana-uta* humming, crooning
歌交 *hana-utamaji(ri)* humming unconcernedly
15衝 *hanatsu(ki)* meeting head on
潰 *hanatsubu(re)* flat nose; flat-nosed person
輪 *hanawa* nose ring
16薬 *hanagusuri* bribe, hush money
髭 *hanahige* mustache
17麼 *hanazura* halter
糞 *hana kuso* nasal discharge
19鏡 *hana kagami, bikyō* nasal speculum

3

鼾 5422/F2173 KAN. *ibiki* snoring.
7声 *kansei* snoring
11酔 *kansui* snoring

RAD. 齊 210

Sai or *hitoshii* alike. Variant: 斉 (8 strokes). Nickname: Mr. Saito (i.e., the first character of this common surname).

P 斉 5423/F2174 齊 SEI. *hito(shii)* equal, similar. *totono(eru)* (see under 調 4392.0).
1一 *sei-itsu* equality; good order
6列 *seiretsu* array, line-up, parade
10射 *seisha* volley, fusillade
11唱 *seishō suru* sing in unison
12備 *seibi*=整備 2436.12
4日 *saijitsu* fast day. *i(mi)bi*=忌日 1463.4
5主 *saishu*=祭主 3247.5
7戒 *saikai* purification
8服 *saifuku* priestly vestments
9垣 *igaki, i(mi)gaki* shrine fence
10部 *Imbe, Imibe* ancient (Shinto) priestly family
宮 *saigū* the (ancient) imperial princesses serving at the Ise shrine
11祭 *itsu(ki)-matsu(ru)* deify and worship
12場 *saijō* place of ceremony, place of a funeral service

2

B 剤 5424/F255 劑 ZAI medicine, drug, dose. [刂]

3

B 斎 5425/F2175 齋 斋 SAI, SEI Buddhist food; room. *imi* religious purification. *itsu(ku)* worship, enshrine. *i(mu)* avoid, refrain from, shun. *toki* meals exchanged by parishioners and priests. *hito(shii)* equal, similar, like, equivalent.

7

齎 5426/F2175 齎 SEI. *mota(rasu)* bring, take; bring about.

9

齏 5427/F2175 齏 SEI. *a(eru)* dress vegetables (as in salad).
8物 *aemono* vegetable side dish

15-STROKE RADICALS

RAD. 齒 211

Ha tooth. Variant: 歯 (12 strokes). Nickname: Tooth.

A 歯 5428/F2176 齒 SHI tooth; age. *ha* tooth, cog, dent.
2入 *ha-i(re)* repairing clogs
4止 *hado(me)* brake
切 *hagi(ri)* gnashing the teeth; cutting cogs. *hagi(re)* the feel when biting; manner of enunciation
切良 *hagi(re) (no) yo(i)* crisp, stacatto
5石 *shiseki* hard tooth tartar, calculus deposit
立 *ha (ga) ta(tanai)* hard to chew; unable to compete with
牙 *shiga* teeth; teeth and tusks
牙状 *shigajō* dentation
牙疾患 *shiga shikkan* dental disease
牙掛 *shiga (ni) ka(kenai)* no argument necessary
牙萠出 *shiga hōshutsu* dentition, teething
牙矯正術 *shiga kyōseijutsu* orthodontia
6肉 *haniku, shiniku* gums, tooth ridge
向 *hamu(kau)*＝刃向 152.6
朶 *hida* fern
列 *shiretsu* row of teeth
列矯正 *shiretsu kyōsei* orthodontia
7車 *haguruma* cogwheel, gear
応 *hagota(e)* hard to chew; tough; crisp
状 *shijō* dentation; tooth shape
形 *hagata* tooth mark, impression of the teeth
医者 *ha-isha* dentist
8固 *hagata(me)* tooth-hardening meal; New Year's feast
軋 *hagishi(ri)* involuntary nocturnal tooth grinding
並 *hanara(bi), hana(mi)* row of teeth; set of teeth; dentition
芽 *shiga* tooth germ
茎 *haguki* gum, tooth ridge
9面 *shimen* surface of a tooth
音 *shion* sibilant
食 *ha (o) ku(i-shibaru)* bear up in tragedy; stand pain well; hold one's temper
垢 *shikō* tooth tartar
冠 *shikan* crown of a tooth
軌条 *shikijō* cograil
神経 *shishinkei* dental nerve
科 *shika* dentistry
科大学 *shika daigaku* dental college
科医 *shika-i* dentist
科医学 *shika igaku* dentistry
科医院 *shika i-in* dentist's office
科医師 *shika-ishi* dentist
科医術 *shika-ijutsu* dentistry
科病院 *shika byōin* dental hospital
10根 *shikon, ha(no)ne* root of a tooth; fang
浮 *ha (ga) u(ku)* teeth get loose; to tire of someone's bragging
11黒 *(o)haguro* tooth blackening
痒 *hagayu(i)* impatient, tantalized, chagrined, vexed
脱 *hanu(ke)* falling out of teeth; a person with missing teeth. *hanu(ke) no* toothless
12痛 *ha-ita, shitsū* toothache
15質 *shishitsu* quality of teeth
槽 *shisō* tooth socket, alveolar bone
槽膿漏 *shisō nōrō* pyorrhea
16磨 *hamiga(ki)* dentifrice
磨粉 *hamigakiko* tooth powder
磨楊子 *hamigaki yōji* toothbrush
18噛 *haga(mi)* gnashing of teeth
髄 *shizui* pulp of a tooth, the nerve
21齦 *shigin* the gums
齦炎 *shigin-en* gingivitis

5

齣 5429/F2177 SHAKU a paragraph, a section; frame, scene.

齝 5430/F-X *nire(gamu), nige(kamu)* chew the cud.

B 齢 5431/F2177 齡 REI. *yowai* age.

齟 5432/F2176 So. uneven; bite; disagree.
22齬 *sogo* inconsistency, discord, conflict, discrepancy, contradiction; failure, frustration

6

齦 5433/F2177 GIN. KON. *haguki* gums.

齧 5434/F2177 GETSU. *kaji(ru)* gnaw, nibble, bite at, munch, crunch; have a smattering of.

5付 *kaji(ri)-tsu(ku)* bite into, stick to
12散 *kaji(ri)-chi(rasu)* gnaw at and scatter around; start a lot of things without finishing any

7

齬 5435 F2177 Go irregular teeth; discord.

齪 5436 F2177 SAKU, SOKU grating the teeth; fretful.

9

齶 5437 F1548 腭 GAKU. *ago* jaw.

齷 5438 F2178 AKU grating the teeth; fretful.
22齪 *akuseku suru* worry about; be busy about. *akuseku* fussily, busily, sedulously

齲 5439 F2177 KU, U *mushiba* decayed tooth; cavity.
12歯 *ushi, mushiba* decayed tooth; cavity
15蝕 *ushoku* tooth decay

10

齶 See 5437.

16-STROKE RADICALS

RAD. 龍 212

Tatsu dragon. Variants: 竜 or 竜 (10 strokes). Nickname: Big Dragon (cf. Rad. 161).

P 竜 5440 F2178 龍竜 RYŪ, RYŌ dragon; imperial. *tatsu* dragon.
3口 *tatsu(no)kuchi* dragon-head gargoyle; spout of a gutter
4王 *ryūō* dragon god, dragon king
5田姫 *tatsutahime* goddess of autumn
6舌蘭 *ryūzetsuran* century plant
7車 *ryūsha* imperial carriage
8虎 *ryūko, ryōko* dragon and tiger; hero; clever writing; good writer
9神 *ryūjin* dragon god, dragon king
胆 *rindō* gentian, bellflower
巻 *tatsuma(ki)* waterspout
10骨 *ryūkotsu* keel
宮 *ryūgū* sea god's dragon palace
涎香 *ryūzenkō* ambergris
12落子 *tatsu (no) oto(shi)go* sea horse
15蝦 *Ise ebi* spiny lobster
16頭 *ryūzu* watch stem
頭蛇尾 *ryūtō-dabi* fast start and slow finish; ending in an anticlimax
18顔 *ryōgan, ryūgan* imperial countenance
駕 *ryōga* imperial carriage
20攘虎搏 *ryūjō-kohaku* fierce fighting

3

壟 5441 F444 壠 RŌ mound; grave; rice-field division dikes. *oka* hill. [土]
11断 *rōdan suru* monopolize

6

龕 See 568.

聾 5442 F1530 RŌ deafness. *rō(suru)* deafen. *tsumbo, mimishii* deafness; deaf person. [耳]
8者 *rōsha* deaf person
学校 *rōgakkō* deaf school
11啞 *rōa* deaf-mute, deaf and dumb
啞学校 *rōa gakkō* deaf and dumb school
12桟敷 *tsumbo sajiki* upper gallery, blind seat

B 襲 5443 F1708 SHŪ attack. *oso(u)* attack, advance on; succeed to; call unexpectedly. *kasa(ne)* (see under 重 224.0). [衣]
5用 *shūyō suru* adopt, follow
6名 *shūmei* succession to another's professional name
7攻 *oso(i)-se(meru)* array against
来 *shūrai* invasion, raid, attack; visitation (of a calamity)
11掛 *oso(i)-ka(karu)* rush on, attack, swoop down on
15撃 *shūgeki* attack, charge, raid
17爵 *shūshaku* succession to the peerage

32

龖 5444 F-X DŌ. TŌ. dragons moving.

RAD. 龜 213

Kame turtle. Variant: 亀 (11 strokes). Nickname: Turtle.

亀 5445/F2180 龜 龜 KI. KIN. *kame* turtle, tortoise.

2 卜 *kiboku, kameura* tortoise-shell divination
3 子 *kame* (*no*) *ko* young tortoise
4 手 *kame(no)te* barnacle
5 甲 *kikō, kikkō, kame* (*no*) *kō* tortoise shell
12 裂 *kiretsu* crack, crevice, fissure, chap
22 鑑 *kikan* pattern, model, example

17-STROKE RADICALS

RAD. 龠 214

Fue flute. Nickname: Flute.

龠 5446/F2180 YAKU flute.

APPENDIX 1. HOW TO FIND A CHARACTER

Some three centuries ago the Chinese evolved the system of classifying their characters according to 214 basic elements or radicals. This system is still used today in Chinese and Japanese character dictionaries and, with certain improvements, is followed in the present dictionary also. This, then, brings us to the first of several steps to be followed in finding a character:

1. Determine the radical of the character (see Appendix 3), count the strokes of the radical, and find the radical number on the chart inside the front covers.

2. Spin the pages of the dictionary till you come to that radical number in the upper, outer corners of the pages.

Another method, replacing the foregoing two steps (this short cut is recommended only for those familiar enough with the radicals to realize immediately that, for example, the common 3-stroke grass radical is actually a variant of the 6-stroke grass radical—No. 140—and is to be looked for under the larger stroke-count): Having determined the radical and without worrying about its number, spin immediately to the place where all the radicals of the same stroke-count appear in the marginal radical strings, the stroke-count being shown by the large numeral at the head of each string. (*In case of a variant radical, use the stroke-count of its parent radical.*) Now find your radical in the radical string and spin the pages slowly one way or the other till the brackets moving up and down the string reach your radical.

3. Count the number of strokes in the non-radical part of the character and then, as a guide to the eye, place your thumb near the proper radical in the radical string and slowly spin the pages one way or the other till the tiny numeral opposite your radical reaches your stroke-count.

4. Glance thru the main-character entries nearby to find the one you want; it will be somewhere in those pages with the proper non-radical stroke-count as indicated either by the tiny marginal numeral or the large numerals in the column-wide dividers. Within any given stroke-count section, the main character entries are arranged with cross-reference and rarer characters first, followed by the more familiar characters in the ascending order of the number of compounds listed under each.

APPENDIX 2. HOW TO FIND A COMPOUND

1. Find the first character of the compound by the procedure described in the preceding appendix.

2. Count the total number of strokes in the 2nd character and then glance down the series of tiny numerals immediately to the left of the list of compounds till you find the proper 2nd-character stroke-count.

3. Look for the 2nd character of your compound among those with this stroke-count. Note that in listing each compound its 1st character has been omitted, since it is the same as the character shown in the main entry above it. Also note that the character-repetition sign has not been used; since the 1st character is omitted in listing compounds, in such cases it was felt better to repeat the full character.

4. If there are many compounds listed under the same 2nd-character stroke-count, time can be saved by keeping in mind that, within such a grouping, the compounds have been arranged in the following order: (a) 2-character compounds, (b) 3-character compounds, (c) 4-character compounds, and (d) "families" of compounds, i.e., a group of compounds whose 2nd characters, as well as the 1st, are identical.

5. If you cannot find your compound, possible reasons and remedies are: (a) You may have miscounted the strokes of the 2nd character. So look for it up and down the adjacent stroke-count groups. (b) The 2nd character of your compound may be in a variant form that differs in shape, and probably in stroke-count as well, from the standard form used in the compounds of this dictionary. For example, it may be a Tōyō Kanji given in its older form, while in our lists of compounds all Tōyō Kanji appear only in their newer forms. Or again, it may be a non-Tōyō Kanji in which, according to the unauthorized usage of some printers, one element has been simplified by analogy with the same element in a Tōyō Kanji, while in our lists non-Tōyō Kanji usually appear only in their original forms. To have included such variants in our lists would have led to endless duplication of entries. But we do give the important variants in our main-character entries. Hence the surest remedy, which is unfortunately also the most time consuming, is to look up the 2nd character of your compound in the main-character entries, there ascertain its standard form, and then look for such standard form in your list of compounds. But we recommend first trying two possible short cuts: (1) Check quickly through the same stroke-count group and the immediately adjacent groups for a character that looks almost the same as the one you are looking for. This method will usually work when the variation is slight. (2) Look up your character in the chart inside the back cover and find its new form. This method will work in those many cases when you have encountered the older form of a Tōyō Kanji. That chart will prove invaluable, particularly when reading prewar publications. (c) The word may be one of the less frequently used ones which do not appear in this dictionary. So either look for it in one of the large Japanese character dictionaries (the F numbers provide ready reference to Fuzambō's dictionary) or determine its probable reading by looking up the individual characters of which it is composed and then consult a Japanese-English romanized dictionary like Kenkyūsha's. (d) In the case of a compound of 3 or more characters, it may be a "compound compound." So try, for example in the case of 4 characters, looking for separate compound forms of the first 2 and the last 2.

APPENDIX 3. HOW TO DETERMINE THE RADICAL OF A CHARACTER—A NEW AND SPEEDIER WAY

THE RADICAL PRIORITY SYSTEM. Those who are familiar with character dictionaries know how difficult it often is to decide which is the traditional radical of a character. This is due to the fact that nearly every character, excepting only about five, contains from two to seven or eight radicals. The character 截, for example, contains the following seven elements, each of which happens to be a radical (the radical numbers are shown in parentheses): 一(1), 丨(2), 丶(3), 丿(4), 十(24), 戈(62), 隹(172). So it is anybody's guess as to which of these is the traditional radical under which this character would be listed. The process of deciding under which radical to search is far too often a time-wasting and discouraging trial-and-error process. Even the substantial contributions Rose-Innes made toward standardization in his valuable character dictionary went only part way.

We believe we have solved the problem by arbitrarily arranging each character under the first radical encountered by dropping down THE TWELVE STEPS ***of the Radical Priority System given below.***

By arranging the characters in this way, 88 percent of them fall in their traditional places anyway. And this without any guesswork! Cross-reference entries for the other 12 percent of the characters, those that fall under non-traditional radicals, make it easy to locate a character by either the former traditional but slow system or the new and speedy Radical Priority System.

We have also made many "kindness" cross-reference entries to take care of those cases when the user who is not yet entirely familiar with the Radical Priority System might look for a character under the wrong radical.

The new and speedier Radical Priority System is the essense of simplicity. Its main rule will save hours of time: *Always take a* LEFT *radical in preference to a right when both sides of a character are radicals; always take a* TOP *in preference to a bottom when both top and bottom are radicals.* This rule alone takes care of 75 percent of the characters. But the Radical Priority System, with its 12 steps as described below, has taken care of *all* situations, making the choice of a character unmistakable in all cases.

THE 12 STEPS. Here, then, is how to choose the radical automatically and, after a little practice, almost instantaneously by using the 12 steps. Drop down the steps and stop at the first question that can be answered in the affirmative. (The numerals given below in parentheses show the numbers of the radicals.)

N.B. In Steps 1 thru 11, if there are two radicals in the same designated position, always take the one with the GREATER *stroke-count.*

STEP 1. ALL? *Is* ALL *the character a radical?* For a complete listing, see Appendix 13. Here are a few examples:

土(32), 方(70), 生(100), 米(119), 辛(160), 高(189), 鼻(209).

STEP 2. LONE? *Does it have only one* LONE *radical?* There are only five such characters in common use:

乃(丿4), 〆(丶3), 及(丿4), 久(丿4), 了(亅6).

STEP 3. ENCLOSURE? *Does it have a completely exterior* ENCLOSURE *radical?* The test is whether the radical actually encloses 2 or more sides; if it protrudes into the rest of the character (as 戈 in the character 截) or merely sits on one side (as 戈 in 枝), it is not an enclosure. Thus the element 勹, which is Rad. 20 and usually an enclosure radical, is not the radical in 包 as it does not completely enclose two sides, and this character falls under Step 8 below to give Rad. 4 丿.

Examples of characters containing all the radicals that *enclose two sides* (the radicals and their numbers being shown in parentheses):

巴(乚5), 勿(勹20), 原(厂27), 処(夂34), 局(尸44), 度(广53), 廻(廴54),

式(弋56), 成(戈62), 肩(戸63), 翅(支65), 死(歹78), 毬(毛82), 気(气84),

爬(爪87), 瓸(瓦98), 病(疒104), 取(耳128), 虎(虍141), 起(走156), 唇(辰161),

速(辶162), 颱(風182), 魁(鬼194), 麞(鹿198), 麪(麦199), 摩(麻200), 鼴(鼠208)

Examples of all the radicals that *enclose three sides:*

同(冂13), 凶(凵17), 医(匸22), 問(門169), 斎(斉210), 齋(齊210)

Example of the one radical that *encloses four sides:* 国(囗31)

3. Determining the Radical

STEP 4. LEFT? *Is there a clearly defined* LEFT *radical?* By "clearly defined" we mean a radical that completely dominates the left side, i.e., one that is unobstructed both above and below, such as 十 in 協. It follows that in the character 截, for example, neither 十 nor 隹 can be chosen as a left radical. Note also that the radical may touch the rest of the character but may not protrude into it. Hence 丨 (2) is the left radical not only of 旧 but also of 帥, 師, 曲, 由, 甲, 曳, 申, 暢, and 鴨. Similarly, ノ (4) is the left radical of 斥, 后, 励, 眉, 彫, 劂, 劇, 壓, 勵, 厳, 願, 殷, and 殿, as well as being the left radical of 胤 and 頤. Other examples:

杉—both left and right are radicals; take the left, 木 (75).

和—again both left and right are radicals, and in this case the right is the traditional radical; but we still take the left, 禾 (115).

彫—both left and right are radicals; take the left ノ (4) even tho it touches the rest of the character.

STEP 5. RIGHT? *Is there a clearly defined* RIGHT *radical?* Again it may touch but not protrude into the rest. Hence 丨 (2) is the right radical of 幽. Other examples:

頂—left not a radical; take the right, 頁 (181).

欧—left not a radical; take the right, 欠 (76). Note that we ignore any slight interference with the left by a left-tapering stroke.

STEP 6. TOP? *Is there a clear* TOP *radical?* Examples:

空—take the top, 穴 (116). Note that we take this in place of 宀 (40) because of our rule always to take the more complex of two similarly placed radicals in Steps 1 thru 11.

安—take 宀 (40). Do not take 女 (38) as it is at the bottom.

男—take 田 (102). Do not take 力 (19) as it is at the bottom.

套—take 大 (37).

分—take 八 (12). Note that Rad. 12 has three forms 八, 𠆢, and ソ, the last being a kind of inverted 八 which appears in many of the Tōyō Kanji. Thus this Rad. 12 is the radical of 公, 酓, 酋, and 前 but not of 巻, for here it is cut in two by the vertically protruding element.

善—take ソ (12), not 羊 as it protrudes into the bottom part of the character.

啻—take 二 (7).

Note that many top radicals are closed canopies like 冖, 大, 宀, 夂, or 穴.

STEP 7. BOTTOM? *Is there a clear* BOTTOM *radical?* Note that this may or not be resting under a canopy. Examples:

嗇—top not a radical; take the bottom, 一 (1).

急—top not a radical; take the bottom, 心 (61).

学—top not a radical; take the bottom, 子 (39).

嚮—top not a radical; take 口 (30) at the bottom under the canopy.

梵—top not a radical; take 丶 (3) at the bottom under the canopy.

釁—top not a radical; take 刀 (18) at the bottom under the canopy.

朶—top not a radical; take the bottom, 木 (75).

N.B. The foregoing seven steps will determine the radical for about 97 percent of all characters. For the remaining 3 percent we turn next to the four corners of an imaginary square around each character, designating these with four conventional compass directions. Corner radicals must be unobstructed in their two outer directions to qualify. The size of the corner space they occupy is immaterial. It may be large or small. To illustrate, 丶 (3) is the NORTHEAST corner radical of 戔 and 虫 is the SOUTHWEST corner radical of 虱.

STEP 8. NW? *Is there a radical in the* NORTHWEST *corner?* Examples:

報—Going down our table of twelve steps, we find this is neither ALL, LONE, ENCLOSURE, LEFT, RIGHT, TOP, nor BOTTOM. So we start around the corner clockwise beginning in the NORTHWEST, and there sits 土 (32). This is our radical. There is also 十 (24) in that same corner; but remember, in Steps 1 thru 11 we take the more complex of two possible radicals.

截—the character referred to on page 1002 as having 7 possible radicals. The traditional one is 戈 (62), and you will of course find the character so listed in this dictionary with a cross reference. But it will be much quicker to go unerringly to the main entry for the character by the Radical Priority System, which quickly gives 十 (24) in the NW corner. Note that it could not be the enclosure radical 戈 (62) because this protrudes into the rest of the character; nor, for the same season, could it be the NW 土 (32).

One will soon be able to go thru this process of picking the radical much more quickly that it takes to say it!

STEP 9. NE? *Is there a radical in the* NORTHEAST *corner?* Example: 求—There is nothing in the NW, so we quickly move on and find 丶 (3) in the NE.

STEP 10. SE? *Is there a radical in the* SOUTHEAST *corner?* Example: 君—Here again we find that 口 (30) is the radical in the SE corner. Note that this is not the case of a lone radical because we also have radicals ノ (4), 一 (1), 尸 (44), and ⺕ (58).

STEP 11. SW? *Is there a radical in the* SOUTHWEST *corner?* Example: 虱—For a moment we might think this is a case of an enclosure, but by consulting either the chart inside the front cover or, better still, the list of enclosure radicals in Appendix 13, we soon discover the enclosing element is not a radical and are left with the SW radical, 虫 (142). Note again that a corner radical may occupy any amount of space as long as it has two free sides.

STEP 12. HIGH? In those rare cases where you have not yet encountered a radical, you have a case of crossed radicals or, rarely, of radicals in unusual positions, and one of these three rules will apply:

(a) In nearly all cases, *choose the radical that protrudes the highest or, if there is no high protruding radical, the highest in the character*. This rule gives the twelfth and final key word—HIGH. Examples:

事—Here we quickly see that it is a case of crossed radicals, in which case we choose the one that protrudes the *highest*, 亅 (6).

民—Here there is no high protruding radical, so we simply take the *highest,* which is 一 (1). Were it not for that little back flip at the SW corner, a flip that often is tied to the vertical line above it, we could have chosen 丨 (2) as the left radical. As a matter of fact, this perplexing character is also listed under 丨 (2) as well as under 一 (1) and the traditional radical 氏 (83).

与—Similarly we take the *highest* radical, a short 一(1). We do not take the radical 二 (7) for the reason explained in (b) below.

4. More About Radicals

叏—While both 又 (29) and 丶 (3) are radicals, we take 又 because it is the highest.

夫—crossed radicals again, take the highest 丿 (4).

(b) *In case two radicals are equally high, take the simpler,* which is usually one of one stroke. Examples:

丹—Take 丿 (4) rather than 冂 (13) since they are equally high and 4 is the *simpler*.

冊—Take 丨 (2) rather than 冂 (13) for the same season.

(c) *In case two radicals are both equally high and equally simple, take the one to the left*. Examples:

井—Take the left, 丿 (4), in preference to the right, 丨 (2).
井—Take the left, 丿 (4), in preference to the right, 丨 (2).
必—Take the left, 丶 (3), in preference to the right, 丿 (4).

APPENDIX 4. MORE ABOUT RADICALS

MISCELLANEOUS EXAMPLES OF RADICALS. The following table, arranged by the Twelve Steps of the Radical Priority System, shows how easy it now is to choose the radicals of characters, even in those cases which have been so perplexing heretofore. In each case we show: (a) the character and its entry number, (b) the traditional radical and its number, and (c) the radical and its number according to our Radical Priority System.

STEP 1. ALL

木	2170	→ 木	75	→ 木	75
高	5248	→ 高	189	→ 高	189
黒	5403	→ 黒	203	→ 黒	203
欠	2412	→ 欠	76	→ 欠	76

STEP 2. LONE

〆	126	→ 丿	4	→ 丶	3
乃	145	→ 丿	4	→ 丿	4
及	154	→ 又	29	→ 丿	4
了	268	→ 亅	6	→ 亅	6
久	153	→ 丿	4	→ 丿	4

STEP 3. ENCLOSURE

旬	747	→ 日	72	→ 勹	20
唐	1516	→ 口	30	→ 广	53
聞	4959	→ 耳	128	→ 門	169
巡	4667	→ 巛	47	→ 辶	162
同	619	→ 口	30	→ 冂	13
威	1803	→ 女	38	→ 戈	62
反	817	→ 又	29	→ 厂	27
鏖	5379	→ 金	167	→ 鹿	198

STEP 4. LEFT

利	3264	→ 刂	18	→ 禾	115
初	4215	→ 刀	19	→ 衤	145
脩	497	→ 月	130	→ 亻	9
徽	1643	→ 黑	203	→ 彳	60
謄	3824	→ 言	149	→ 月	130
順	1450	→ 頁	181	→ 川	47
瓣	4649	→ 瓜	97	→ 辛	160
和	3268	→ 口	30	→ 禾	115
酒	2573	→ 酉	164	→ 氵	85
由	89	→ 田	102	→ 丨	2
欲	4461	→ 欠	67	→ 谷	150
鳴	983	→ 鳥	196	→ 口	30
相	2241	→ 目	109	→ 木	75
后	181	→ 口	30	→ 丿	4
師	113	→ 巾	50	→ 丨	2
眉	219	→ 目	109	→ 丿	4

STEP 5. RIGHT

穀	2461	→ 禾	115	→ 殳	79
頂	5118	→ 頁	181	→ 頁	181
欧	2413	→ 欠	76	→ 欠	76

STEP 6. TOP

纂	3454	→ 糸	120	→ 竹	118
幸	1073	→ 干	51	→ 土	32
差	3662	→ 工	48	→ 羊	123
嘗	1369	→ 口	30	→ ⺍	42
前	595	→ 刂	18	→ 丷	12
委	3267	→ 女	38	→ 禾	115
喜	1115	→ 口	30	→ 士	32
垂	211	→ 土	32	→ 丿	4
夜	298	→ 夕	36	→ 亠	8
并	580	→ 廾	55	→ 丷	12
啻	279	→ 口	30	→ 二	7
受	2826	→ 又	29	→ 爫	87
番	4811	→ 田	102	→ 釆	165

STEP 7. BOTTOM

釁	714	→ 酉	164	→ 刀	18
黎	2648	→ 黍	202	→ 氺	85
默	2796	→ 黒	203	→ 灬	86

啇 67 → 口 30 → 一 1
興 615 → 臼 134 → 八 12
聖 2960 → 耳 128 → 王 96
準 791 → 氵 85 → 十 24

STEP 8. NORTHWEST

半 132 → 十 24 → 丶 3
失 178 → 大 37 → ノ 4
牛 167 → 十 24 → ノ 4
朱 184 → 木 75 → ノ 4
呡 292 → 氏 83 → 亠 8
剋 776 → 刂 18 → 十 24
叢 144 → 又 29 → 丶 3
我 200 → 戈 62 → ノ 4
武 51 → 止 77 → 一 1

果 107 → 木 75 → 丨 2

STEP 9. NORTHEAST

求 137 → 氺 85 → 丶 3
鳶 1559 → 鳥 196 → 弋 56
承 197 → 手 64 → ノ 4

STEP 10. SOUTHEAST

友 858 → 又 29 → 又 29
君 899 → 口 30 → 口 30
粛 115 → 聿 129 → 丨 2
肅 118 → 聿 129 → 丨 2

STEP 11. SOUTHWEST

虱 4116 → 虫 142 → 虫 142

弱 650 → 弓 57 → 冫 15
末 177 → 木 75 → ノ 4
来 202 → 人 9 → ノ 4

STEP 12. HIGH

夫 164 → 大 37 → ノ 4
事 272 → 亅 6 → 亅 6
井 165 → 二 7 → ノ 4
丼 171 → 丶 3 → ノ 4
吏 183 → 口 30 → ノ 4
夾 192 → 大 37 → ノ 4
寿 194 → 士 33 → ノ 4
与 6 → 臼 134 → 一 1
叉 856 → 又 29 → 又 29

NOTES ON THE 1-STROKE RADICALS. The 1-stroke radicals play a larger part and are used more under the Radical Priority System than under the traditional system. That is, more characters are now listed under them than under the old system. Hence a few additional examples and notes concerning them are in order.

Radical 1, 一 一

1. It occurs as a clear TOP radical under Step 6: 丁, 三, 下, 万, 互, 五, 夭, 不, 吾, 夏, 否.
2. It occurs as a clear BOTTOM radical under Step 7: 丑, 坐, 昼, 啇. *N.B.* In choosing 一 (1) as the bottom radical in the last example, it is important to note that the lower left-hand corner of the element 口 is not continuous.
3. It occurs as a clear NORTHWEST radical under Step 8, this radical being the first encountered in the 12 steps: 武, 弍.

Radical 2, 丨 ı

1. It occurs as a clear LEFT radical under Step 4: 旧, 曲, 由, 甲, 曳, 暢, 鴨, 内. *N.B.* (a) Remember that there is no objection if a LEFT radical touches the rest of the character just as long as it does not protrude into it. (b) In all but the first and last examples, it is important to note that the lower left-hand corner is not a continuous stroke.
2. It occurs in its short form as a LEFT radical under Step 4: 中, 史, 串. *N.B.* In the following characters this Rad. 2 is the radical whether you take it as a LEFT, or whether, missing that, you go on and choose it as a HIGH protruding radical: 中, 串, 申.
3. It occurs as a RIGHT radical under Step 5: 州. *N.B.* Note that the small tittle on the left is not a radical: it is neither 丶 (3) nor ノ (4).
4. It occurs as a NORTHWEST radical in its short form in 央 under Step 8.
5. It occurs as a SOUTHEAST radical under Step 10: 肅.
6. It occurs as the HIGHEST of crossed radicals under step 12: 甚.

4. More About Radicals

Radical 3 、

N.B. This is always a short stroke and is written downward from the upper left.

1. It occurs as a LONE radical under Step 2: 〆.
2. It occurs as a TOP radical under Step 6: 永.
3. It occurs as a BOTTOM radical under Step 7: 梵.
4. It occurs as a NORTHWEST radical under Step 8: 半, 氷, 業, 単, 叢.
5. It occurs as a NORTHEAST radical under Step 9: 戋, 求, 甫, 尠, 尤.

Radical 4, ㇀ 一 ノ 一

1. It occurs as a LONE radical under Step 2: 乃, 及.
2. It occurs as a LEFT radical under Step 4: 般, 后, 殿, 斥, 励, 盾, 彫, 咫, 眉.
N.B. The elements 尸 and 冂 are not enclosure radicals here.
3. It occurs as a TOP radical under Step 6: 奥, 重, 丘, 兵, 看, 乗, 烏, 島, 梟, 喬, 兜, 卑.
4. It occurs as a NORTHWEST radical under Step 8: 失, 卵, 我, 炙, 雀, 勉, 孵, 餤.
5. It occurs as a NORTHEAST radical under Step 9: 承.
6. It occurs as a SOUTHWEST radical under Step 11: 東, 來, 束, 来, 未, 末.
N.B. The long mark in the southeast corners of these characters is not a radical. It is neither 、(3) nor ノ (4).
7. It occurs as a HIGH radical under Step 12: 夫, メ, 爽, 奉, 寿, 夷, 吏.
N.B. 寸 is not a corner radical in 寿 as it is cut by another element.

Radical 5, 乙 乚 ⺃

1. It is ALL a radical under Step 1: 乙.
2. It is an ENCLOSURE radical under Step 3: 巳. Here it encloses two sides.
3. It is a RIGHT radical under Step 5: 乳.
4. It is a HIGH radical under Step 12 七.

Radical 6, 亅

1. It is a LONE radical under Step 2: 了. *N.B.* This is really a one-stroke character but we cut it to get a radical.
2. It is a BOTTOM radical under Step 7: 予. *N.B.* We ignore the interference of the little hook in the horizontal member. Note also that this is not a character with a LONE radical as the little Radical 3 (、) is also found here.
3. It is HIGH radical under Step 12: 事.

IMPORTANT RADICALS. Here are the 67 radicals that you will most often encounter. They are classified by stroke-count and arranged by their numbers. It will definitely be worth your while to memorize their numbers and the recommended "nicknames" which accompany them. Note that only the parent form of each radical is shown here; consult the chart inside the front cover for important variant forms.

ONE STROKE

一 1—one
丨 2—rod
、 3—dot
ノ 4—*kana no*

TWO STROKE

亠 8—lid
人 9—man
八 12—eight
刀 18—sword
力 19—strong
十 24—cross
厂 27—cliff

THREE STROKE

口 30—mouth
囗 31—box
土 32—earth
女 38—woman
宀 40—*kana u*
小 42—little
尸 44—flag
山 46—mountain
巾 50—cloth
广 53—dotted cliff
弓 57—bow

彳 60—going man

FOUR STROKES

心 61—heart
手 64—hand
支 66—folding chair
日 72—sun
木 75—tree
水 85—water
火 86—fire
牛 93—cow
犬 94—dog

FIVE STROKES

玉 96—jewel
田 102—rice field
疒 104—sick
皿 108—dish
目 109—eye
石 112—stone
示 113—showing
禾 115—2-branch tree
立 117—standing

SIX STROKES

竹 118—bamboo
米 119—rice
糸 120—thread
耳 128—ear
肉 130—meat
舟 137—ship
艸 140—grass
虫 142—bug
衣 145—clothing

SEVEN STROKES

見 147—seeing
言 149—speaking
貝 154—small shell
足 157—foot
車 159—car
辵 162—road
邑 163—right village

EIGHT STROKES

金 167—metal
門 169—gate
阜 170—left village
隹 172—old bird
雨 173—rain

NINE STROKES

頁 181—big shell
食 184—food

TEN STROKES

馬 187—horse

ELEVEN STROKES

魚 195—fish
鳥 196—bird

WARNINGS ON UNUSUAL RADICALS. It is well, occasionally, to look over the Step-1 table of the last appendix in the book to refresh your memory as to which current characters are their own radicals.

It will also be well to reread the "Notes on the 1-Stroke Radicals" beginning on page 1007, as they play a larger part now than under the traditional system.

Remember that 彑 is a variety of 彐 (Rad. 58).

Note the distinct difference between Rads. 71 and 92 as shown on the chart inside the front cover.

Note that 内 (114) is a 5-stroke, not a 4-stroke, radical and is always counted as 5 wherever it appears in any character.

Remember that 豕 is a 6-stroke variant of the 7-stroke 豕 (152).

Glance over the chart inside the front cover beginning with Rad. 187 and note the many radicals in the 10- to 17-stroke categories. You will encounter them more or less frequently.

Let us repeat that it is very important to be able to recognize a radical when you see one, even tho you may not be able to recall its name nor its number.

When you are not sure whether an element of a character is a radical or not, consult the chart inside the front cover or the tables in the last appendix.

Remember that 牙 is a 5-stroke variant of the 4-stroke 牙 (92) and that it is encountered more often than the parent.

Remember that 无 is a 5-stroke variant of the 4-stroke 无 (71) and that it is also encountered more often than the parent.

Note that the vertical members of radical 艹 (140) are short. The following characters have similar top elements but the vertical strokes are longer. While they have cross references under 140, as well as under 55, their main entries will be under their bottom elements: 共, 昔, 恭.

LOST RADICALS. In the recent simplification of characters by the Japanese Government, some have actually lost their traditional radicals, making them most difficult to find in ordinary dictionaries. The Radical Priority System of choosing the radical of a character automatically takes care of these cases as well.

The following table gives a representative list of characters that have lost their radicals together with our simple solution of the problem presented. Each entry shows, first, the original form of the character followed by its traditional radical (now lost) and radical number; and then, following an arrow, are given the present simplified form of the character, the number under which it is entered in this dictionary, the radical and radical number under which we classify it, and the applicable step of the Radical Priority System by means of which the radical is determined.

來	人 (9)	→	来 (202)	ノ (4)	Step 11.	SW
兩	入 (11)	→	両 (34)	一 (1)	Step 6.	TOP
單	口 (30)	→	単 (141)	丶 (3)	Step 8.	NW
嚴	口 (30)	→	厳 (253)	ノ (4)	Step 4.	LEFT
壽	士 (32)	→	寿 (194)	ノ (4)	Step 12.	HIGH
會	日 (72)	→	会 (381)	人 (9)	Step 6.	TOP
營	火 (86)	→	営 (963)	口 (30)	Step 7.	BOTTOM
爲	爫 (87)	→	為 (138)	丶 (3)	Step 8.	NW
當	田 (102)	→	当 (1359)	小 (42)	Step 6.	TOP
盡	皿 (108)	→	尽 (1380)	尸 (44)	Step 3.	ENCLOSURE
縣	糸 (120)	→	県 (1362)	小 (42)	Step 7.	BOTTOM
聲	耳 (128)	→	声 (1066)	士 (32)	Step 6.	TOP
舊	臼 (134)	→	旧 (94)	丨 (2)	Step 4.	LEFT
處	虍 (141)	→	処 (1162)	夂 (34)	Step 3.	ENCLOSURE
豫	豕 (152)	→	予 (271)	亅 (6)	Step 7.	BOTTOM
醫	酉 (164)	→	医 (763)	匚 (22)	Step 3.	ENCLOSURE
貳	貝 (154)	→	弐 (32)	一 (1)	Step 8.	NW

APPENDIX 5. HOW TO COUNT STROKES

Nothing will so much speed up your dictionary work as skill and accuracy in counting strokes, whether of whole characters, radicals, or non-radical elements. Therefore every effort has been made in this dictionary to make this process free of guesswork. In this connection, some knowledge of how to write characters is needed; such a study is outside the scope of this dictionary, but an excellent treatment can be found in *A Guide to Reading and Writing Japanese* edited by Florence Sakade (Tuttle, 1959).

ACCURACY. The general rule is: No matter how a line may twist and turn nor how complex its printed form, if it is written without lifting your pencil, count it as a single stroke. Examples:

2 strokes: 乃, 辶, 阝, 之.
3 strokes: 及, 与, 辶, 弓.

Exceptions to this rule are as follows:

1. The character 了, tho generally written with 1 stroke, is divided so as to get a radical (亅, 6). But it is counted as 1 stroke when a part of other characters.
2. Similarly, 之 is divided to get a radical (亠, 8), but is written and counted as 2 strokes when a part of other characters.

STROKE DETAILS TO BE IGNORED. Because of variations in type fonts and other practical considerations the following details are ignored in counting strokes:

1. *Ignore* the little flip at the bottom of the element 𠄌 as found in such characters as the following, thus giving them the stroke-counts shown in parentheses; in handwritten characters, such a little flip is a mere continuation of the vertical member above it and even in printed form it seldom touches or cuts thru the next element to the right: 良(7), 卯(5), 留(10), 以(4), 似(6), 民(5), and especially in characters traditionally belonging to the 6-stoke radical 衣, such as 衾(10), 袈(11), 袋(11), and 裂(12). It also follows logically not to count the similarly situated flip in such characters as 表(8), 喪(12), or 畏(9). *However,* we do count a similar stroke in the following three pairs of characters as the said stroke either cuts thru or takes a firm grip on the next element to the right: 䜴 or 叫(6); 収 or 收(7); and 糾 or 糾(9).

2. *Ignore* the little protrusion in the elements 勹 and 彑 in such characters as the following, counting these as 1 and 2 strokes respectively, especially so since in some type fonts the protrusion is scarcely visible: 考(6), 顎(18), 互(4), and 禄(12). *However,* we do count the protrusion in the character 号 as this is a new Tōyō Kanji and almost invariably appears with this strong protrusion, making this a 6-stroke character.

3. *Ignore* the downward protrusion of 口 as found in characters like the following in some fonts: 啼, 嗚, 啞. We still consider the left member the radical, i.e., 口 (30). The element 丰 is counted as three strokes, as in 韋 (Rad. 178).

4. *Ignore* any interference with another member of a character (usually a left radical) by a left-tapering stroke as such vary in length. These usually involve the radical 口 and examples follow: 吸, 呎, 吹, 呱, 唆, 喫, 喀, 毎, 史. This latter is an example of a character with such a left-tapering stroke whose interference with the left radical 亅 (2) is ignored. (It will be noted that this radical is a part of the element *kuchi* 口, which is also a radical but not in this case as it is cut by other strokes.

5. *Ignore* the slight left interference with a left radical of an *ichi* (一) stroke at the bottom of such characters as 岨, 阻, 組, and 粗.

6. *Ignore* any interference of any slightly hooked stroke like the horizontal element in the character 予, where we take 亅 (6) as the radical, or the hooked left 弓 element in the character 弱, where we take 冫 (15) as the southwest radical.

7. Remember that the lower left corners in such characters as 断, 臣, 巨, etc., are continuing strokes, and hence *ignore* any protrusion there when counting strokes.

COUNTING STROKES OF PARENT RADICALS AND THEIR VARIANTS.

1. The stroke-count of a *parent radical* is always that shown in the chart inside the front cover. Thus the following radicals whose stroke-count, at least in the printed form, appears to differ from that historically assigned to them are always given the stroke-count indicated in the following examples: 廴(3), 厶(2), 内(5), 舛(6), 韋(9). Thus when the element 厶 appears in the character 宏 it is counted as 2 and not 3 strokes, making this character one of 7 strokes, not 8.

2. *Radical variants*, however, always carry their natural stroke-count wherever they appear. Thus the parent radical 水 is always a 4-stroke element but it has the following variants which carry the indicated stroke-counts: 氵(3), 氺(5). Similarly:

Rad. 92, a parent radical of 4 strokes (牙), has a 5-stroke variant in 牙.
Rad. 64, a parent radical of 4 strokes (手), has a 3-stroke variant in 扌.
Rad. 61, a parent radical of 4 strokes (心), has a 3-stroke variant in 忄.
Rad. 125, a parent radical of 6 strokes (老), has a 4-stroke variant in 耂.
Rad. 152, a parent radical of 7 strokes (豕), has a 6-stroke variant in 豖.

Rad. 140, a parent radical of 6 strokes (艸) has a 3-stroke variant in ⺾ and a 4-stroke variant in ++. The latter, however, is always counted as 3 strokes as it is often impossible to detect the space betweet the two crosses.

APPENDIX 6. HINTS FOR SPEED

Much has been done in the arrangement of this dictionary to speed up the process of finding a character. But much will also depend upon the user, and here a little effort will pay great dividends. When one is reading a Japanese book or magazine, speed in looking up a new word is of the essence if the chain of thought is not to be interrupted. Several suggestions to this end:

The Radical Priority System, as explained in Appendix 3, speeds up the decision as to which radical to look under to find your character. In a nutshell, the system may be crystallized around the TWELVE KEY WORDS of the twelve steps followed in picking the radical, as follows:

Steps 1 to 3:	ALL—LONE—ENCLOSURE.
Steps 4 to 7:	LEFT—RIGHT—TOP—BOTTOM.
Steps 8 to 11:	NW—NE—SE—SW.
Step 12:	HIGH.

Each person will probably gradually develop his own way of remembering these important key words, but here is a little jingle that may be of help:

> ALL the LONE ENCLOSURES have been LEFT RIGHT here,
> Floating on TOP of a BOTTOMless mere.
> But box the compass clockwise round,
> With west for best when north's been found,
> And they'll finally end on HIGH dry ground.

The process of deciding on the radical will quickly become automatic. Follow these 12 steps in making your decision and you will be surprised at your speed.

Spinning the pages of this book, which has been made strong and flexible for this very purpose, will often get you to your character almost immediately. Many of you will soon have memorized many radicals numbers and you will spin quickly to the correct radical area. Some of you will prefer to spin to the proper radical string and locate your radical there. Having located your radical in its proper string, you will now spin again, and perhaps more slowly, until the heavy brackets scurrying up and down the strings crawl around your radical. Spinning further and a bit more slowly, you will see the tiny numeral beside the radical change to the stroke-count of the non-radical part of your character and your compound will not be far away. For you have now arrived at the proper stroke-count group, wherein the characters are arranged in the ascending order of the number of their compounds.

Quick stroke-counting is important in the speeding-up process. You will soon learn the stroke-counts of the commoner radicals as you will be using them frequently, and you should also make an effort to memorize the stroke-counts of other elements which, tho not radicals, reoccur frequently. Then make a habit of counting the strokes by mentally adding up the number of strokes of their larger components. For example, in 截 you should not laboriously count the strokes one by one but as follows: 2(十)+4(戈)+8(隹)=14

A good magnifying glass is most helpful in counting strokes, especially when reading type that is small or not clear.

All *cross references are in the Arabic notation* and refer to the serial numbers of the 5446 numbered character entries. These character numbers also appear conveniently at the lower outer corners of the pages, a contribution to speed.

Whenever you are not sure whether an element of a character is a radical or not, consult *the chart inside the front cover* or the last appendix.

By all means familiarize yourself with the 214 historic radicals as given inside the front cover so that you can always recognize a radical when you see one. And if you wish to quadruple your speed in dictionary work, memorize their numbers. Missionaries in China used to do this as a matter of course during their first year of language study. A few brave souls in Japan have also done so. Why not be among the brave? You should at least memorize the 67 more important radicals as given on pages 1008–9.

APPENDIX 7. THE *KANA* SYSTEMS

There are two syllabaries in Japan, called *kana*. One of these is the *katakana*, or the squared form, and the other the *hiragana*, or the cursive. They are arranged in two ways, one the A-I-U-E-O, or systematic, arrangement and the other the I-RO-HA arrangement, which forms a poem on the Buddhist theme of the transitoriness of life. This latter arrangement is still occasionally used in indexes, outlines, and the like, much as the alphabet is used in the West; but it is rapidly giving way to the easily remembered A-I-U-E-O arrangement.

The use of *katakana* is largely limited to domestic telegrams, foreign names, and foreign words that have entered the Japanese language. *Hiragana,* however, are widely used, particularly as *okurigana* to indicate the inflexions of verbs and certain words, the stems of which are written in characters. With the limitation of the use of the characters, many words are now written in *hiragana*. Formerly, and to some extent today, *hiragana* have been used along the side of the text to indicate the pronunciation of the characters. When used in this way they are called *furigana*.

THE HIRAGANA A-I-U-E-O ARRANGEMENT

あ *a*	か *ka*	さ *sa*	た *ta*	な *na*	は *ha*	ま *ma*	や *ya*	ら *ra*	わ *wa*	
い *i*	き *ki*	し *shi*	ち *chi*	に *ni*	ひ *hi*	み *mi*	[1] い *(y)i*	り *ri*	[2] ゐ *(w)i*	
う *u*	く *ku*	す *su*	つ *tsu*	ぬ *nu*	ふ *fu*	む *mu*	ゆ *yu*	る *ru*	う *(w)u*	
え *e*	け *ke*	せ *se*	て *te*	ね *ne*	へ *he*	め *me*	[1] え *(y)e*	れ *re*	[2] ゑ *(w)e*	
お *o*	こ *ko*	そ *so*	と *to*	の *no*	ほ *ho*	も *mo*	よ *yo*	ろ *ro*	[3] を *(w)o*	ん *n*

[1] Pronounced as a simple vowel. A repetition of the corresponding *kana* in the first column.

[2] Pronounced as a simple vowel. Not used in approved postwar orthography, having been replaced by the corresponding *kana* in the first column.

[3] Pronounced as a simple vowel. In approved orthography, now used only for the particle *o*.

7. The *Kana* Systems

THE KATAKANA A-I-U-E-O ARRANGEMENT

ア *a*	カ *ka*	サ *sa*	タ *ta*	ナ *na*	ハ *ha*	マ *ma*	ヤ *ya*	ラ *ra*	ワ *wa*	
イ *i*	キ *ki*	シ *shi*	チ *chi*	ニ *ni*	ヒ *hi*	ミ *mi*	[1] イ *(y)i*	リ *ri*	[2] ヰ *(w)i*	
ウ *u*	ク *ku*	ス *su*	ツ *tsu*	ヌ *nu*	フ *fu*	ム *mu*	ユ *yu*	ル *ru*	[1] ウ *(w)u*	
エ *e*	ケ *ke*	セ *se*	テ *te*	ネ *ne*	ヘ *he*	メ *me*	[1] エ *(y)e*	レ *re*	[2] ヱ *(w)e*	
オ *o*	コ *ko*	ソ *so*	ト *to*	ノ *no*	ホ *ho*	モ *mo*	ヨ *yo*	ロ *ro*	[3] ヲ *(w)o*	ン *n*

[1, 2, 3] See footnotes on preceding page.

THE I-RO-HA ARRANGEMENT

The Poem	*Romanization*	*Kana Represented*
色は匂へど	Iro wa nioedo	I-ro ha ni-ho-he-to
散りぬるを	Chirinuru o	Chi-ri-nu-ru (w)o
我世誰ぞ	Waga yo tare zo	Wa-ka yo ta-re so
常ならむ	Tsune naran	Tsu-ne na-ra-mu
有為の奥山	Ui no okuyama	U-(w)i no o-ku-ya-ma
今日越えて	Kyō koete	Ke-fu ko-e-te
浅き夢みじ	Asaki yume miji	A-sa-ki yu-me mi-shi
酔もせず	Ei mo sezu.	(W)e-hi mo se-su.

A roughly literal paraphrase might run: "Colors are fragrant, but they fade away. In this world of ours none lasts forever. Today cross the high mountain of life's illusions [i.e., rise above this physical world], and there will be no more shallow dreaming, no more drunkenness [i.e., there will be no more uneasiness, no more temptations]."

SOUND CHANGES. The sounds of the basic *kana* given above, as well as of the *kana* combinations treated hereafter, may be changed in any one of three ways or in a combination of these ways. (Note that, although all the examples below are given in *hiragana*, the same remarks apply to *katakana* unless otherwise indicated.) The three ways are:

1) By lengthening the vowels. This is done in *hiragana* by adding the appropriate vowel *kana* to sounds ending in *a, i, e,* or *u.* In the case of sounds ending in *o,* usually the *kana u* is added but in some few cases it is the *kana o* that is added. For example, か *ka* becomes かあ *kā;* き *ki,* きい *kii;* く *ku,* くう *kū;* ね *ne,* ねえ *nē;* and と *to,* とう *tō* or とお *tō*. In *katakana* the lengthening of a vowel is indicated by a dash-like symbol in place of the additional *kana.* For example, カ *ka* becomes カー *kā*, etc.

2) By inserting つ *tsu* before a *kana* beginning with *k, s, t,* or *p,* thereby doubling that consonant. For example. また *mata* becomes まった *matta.*

3) By adding two kinds of diacritical marks to certain of the *kana* to produced voiced sounds (called *nigori* in Japanese) as follows:

が ga	ざ za	だ da	ば ba	ぱ pa
ぎ gi	じ ji	ぢ ji	び bi	ぴ pi
ぐ gu	ず zu	づ zu	ぶ bu	ぷ pu
げ ge	ぜ ze	で de	べ be	ぺ pe
ご go	ぞ zo	ど do	ぼ bo	ぽ po

***KANA* COMBINATIONS**. Certain *kana* clusters represent given combinations of sounds. The combinations approved today are as follows (note that the preceding sound-change rules also apply here):

きゃ *kya*	しゃ *sha*	ちゃ *cha*	ひゃ *hya*	みゃ *mya*	りゃ *rya*
きゅ *kyu*	しゅ *shu*	ちゅ *chu*	ひゅ *hyu*	みゅ *myu*	りゅ *ryu*
きょ *kyo*	しょ *sho*	ちょ *cho*	ひょ *hyo*	みょ *myo*	りょ *ryo*

In addition to the approved *kana* combinations given above, there are certain historical combinations which were used in the pre-war literature. Though no longer approved, they are still occasionally encountered. Following is a list of such historical *kana* combinations, in the A-I-U-E-O arrangement and likewise subject to the sound-change rules; also included are a few single *kana* which had special pronunciations in certain words instead of the standard pronunciations shown in parentheses:

あう	*ō*	こふ	*kō*	ちふ	*chū*	はふ	*hō*
あふ	*ō*	さふ	*sō*	づふ	*zū*	ひ	*i (hi)*
いふ	*yū (iu)*	しう	*shū*	てう	*chō*	ひう	*hyū*
おふ	*ō*	しふ	*shū*	てふ	*chō*	ふ	*u, o (fu)*
かう	*kō*	すふ	*sū*	なう	*nō*	へ	*e (he)*
かふ	*kō*	せう	*shō*	なふ	*nō*	へう	*hyō*
きう	*kyū*	せふ	*shō*	にふ	*nyū*	ほ	*o (ho)*
きふ	*kyū*	そふ	*sō*	ぬふ	*nū*	ほふ	*hō*
くふ	*kū*	たう	*tō*	ねう	*nyō*	まう	*mō*
けう	*kyō*	たふ	*tō*	のふ	*nō*	まふ	*mō*
けふ	*kyō*	ちう	*chū*	はう	*hō*	む	*n (mu)*

めう	*myō*	らう	*rō*	れう	*ryō*	ゑ	*e*
もふ	*mō*	らふ	*rō*	れふ	*ryō*	ゑふ	*yō*
やう	*yō*	りう	*ryū*	ろふ	*rō*	をう	*ō*
ゆふ	*yū*	りふ	*ryū*	わう	*ō*	をふ	*ō*
よふ	*yō*	るふ	*rū*	ゐ	*i*		

APPENDIX 8. HISTORICAL TABLES

CHINESE DYNASTIES AND PERIODS. Listed here are the more important of the Chinese dynasties and historic periods. The principal sources used for compiling this table were Edwin O. Reischauer's *Chronological Chart of Far Eastern History* (Harvard Press, 1947), René Grousset's *Chinese Art and Culture* (Orion Press, New York, 1959), and R. H. Mathews' *Chinese-English Dictionary* (Harvard Press, 1950). There is often some question as to exactly when a given dynasty began or ended; in such case the *circa* abbreviation has been prefixed to the date, while the question mark indicates rough conjecture. Japanese readings are given in italics following the Chinese characters.

Hsia	夏	*Ka*	?1989 to ?1523 B.C.
Shang or Yin	商, 殷	*Shō* or *In*	?1523 to ?1028
Anyang	安陽	*An-yō*	?1350 to ?1122
Western Chou	西周	*Seishū*	?1122 to 770
Eastern Chou	東周	*Tōshū*	770 to *c.* 256
Spring and Autumn Annals	春秋	*Shunjū*	722 to 481
Warring States	戦国	*Sengoku*	*c.* 403 to 221
Ch'in	秦	*Shin*	*c.* 221 to 206
Early, Former, or Western Han	前漢	*Zenkan*	206 B.C. to *c.* A.D. 8
Later or Eastern Han	後漢	*Gokan*	A.D. 25 to 220
Three Kingdoms	三国	*Sangoku*	*c.* 220 to *c.* 280
Six Dynasties	六代	*Rikudai*	*c.* 222 to 589
Northern and Southern Dynasties	南北朝	*Nambokuchō*	*c.* 317 to *c.* 589
Sui	隋	*Zui*	*c.* 581 to 618
T'ang	唐	*Tō*	618 to *c.* 907
Northern Sung	北宋	*Hokusō*	960 to 1126
Southern Sung	南宋	*Nansō*	*c.* 1127 to 1279
Yüan (Mongol)	元	*Gen*	*c.* 1280 to 1368
Ming	明	*Min*	1368 to *c.* 1644
Ch'ing (Manchu)	清	*Shin*	*c.* 1644 to 1912
Republic	民国	*Minkoku*	Since 1912

PERIODS OF JAPANESE HISTORY AND ART. There is often little agreement as to the exact nomenclature for and the years covered by the various periods of Japanese history and art. As a rough guide, the chart presented here has been prepared from the following sources:

(1) G.B. Sansom: *Japan: A Short Cultural History*. Appleton-Century-Crofts, New York, 1943, p. xviii. This list gives the classification of art periods adopted by the Art Research Institute of Tokyo.

(2) Edwin O. Reischauer: *Chronological Chart of Far Eastern History*. Harvard Press, Cambridge, 1947. This is a chart of political rather than art periods.

(3) Chronological chart of art periods published by the Japanese Art Dealers' Association, Tokyo, 1958.

(4) Andrew N. Nelson: *The Origin, History, and Present Status of the Temples of Japan*. Unpublished doctorate thesis, University of Washington, Seattle, 1938.

(5) Suwa Tokutarō: *Nihonshi no Yōryō* (Outline of Japanese History). Ōbunsha, Tokyo, 1957.

The numerals in parentheses in the chart refer to the foregoing sources.

Jōmon 縄文
(3) To 200 B.C.
(5) To A.D. 8

Yayoi 彌生
(3) 200 B.C. to A.D. 250
(5) 8-300

Kofun (Tumulus) 古墳
(3) 250-552

Clan or Pre-Asuka
飛鳥前
(2) To 252
(4) Same

Yamato 大和
(5) 300-710

Asuka or Suiko
飛鳥, 推古
(1) 552-646
(3) 552-645
(4) Same

Borrowing from China
(2) 552-866

Early Nara or Hakuhō
奈良前期, 白鳳
(1) 646-710
(3) 645-710
(4) Same

Nara, Late Nara, or Tempyō
奈良後期, 天平
(1) 710-794
(2) 710-784
(3) 710-794
(4) Same
(5) Same

Early Heian or Kōnin
平安前期, 弘仁
(1) 794-897
(2) 794-866
(3) 794-898
(4) Same
(5) Same

Late Heian or Fujiwara
平安後期, 藤原
(2) 866-1160
(3) 897-1185
(4) 898-1185
(5) Same

Main Fujiwara
藤原前期
(1) 897-1086

Late Fujiwara
藤原後期
(1) 1086-1185

Taira 平
(2) 1160-1185

Kamakura or Minamoto
鎌倉, 源
(2) 1185-1333
(3) 1185-1392
(4) 1185-1333
(5) Same

Early Kamakura
鎌倉前期
(1) 1185-1249

Late Kamakura
鎌倉後期
(1) 1249-1382

Yoshino or Nambokuchō (Northern and Southern Courts)
吉野, 南北朝
(2) 1336-1392
(3) Same
(4) Same
(5) Same

Ashikaga or Muromachi
足利, 室町
(1) 1392-1568
(2) 1336-1568
(3) 1473-1568
(4) 1392-1573
(5) 1333-1573

Sengoku (Warring Countries) 戦国
(5) 1482-1558

Momoyama or Azuchi-Momoyama
桃山, 安土桃山
(1) 1568-1615
(2) 1568-1600
(3) Same
(4) 1573-1615
(5) 1573-1603

Tokugawa or Edo
徳川, 江戸
(1) 1615-1867
(2) 1600-1867
(3) 1600-1868
(4) 1615-1867
(5) 1603-1868

Modern 現代
1868 to date

JAPANESE SHOGUNATES. Here again there is often reason for choosing different dates. In this case we follow Tōkyōdō's *Sekai Jimmei Jiten: Tōyō Hen* (1952, p. 922), which consistently begins each period with the formal nomination of its first shogun and ends it with the abdication or death of its last shogun. Note that the first three entries are usually known collectively as the Kamakura

Shogunate; during much of this period the shoguns themselves had no real power, being ruled in turn by the Hōjō regents from 1205 to 1333.

Minamoto (Kamakura)	源 (鎌倉)	1192-1219
Fujiwara (Kamakura)	藤原 (鎌倉)	1226-1252
Imperial Princes (Kamakura)	(鎌倉)	1252-1333
Ashikaga (Muromachi)	足利 (室町)	1338-1573
Tokugawa (Edo)	徳川 (江戸)	1603-1867

JAPANESE EMPERORS AND ERA NAMES. The following list of the Japanese sovereigns, together with era names (*nengō*), begins with the legendary first emperor, Jimmu. Much of the early chronology before the introduction of writing is legendary rather than historical. Japanese textbooks now usually begin such a list with Emperor Kimmei (reigned 539-571). But legends often play an equal role with history in a nation's literature, and it has been thought well to give the full traditional list.

The list is based on three sources. Nippon Hōsō Kyōkai's *Songō to Nengō no Yobikata* (1953), being based on studies with the Imperial Household, has been taken as the final authority for the reading of all names and for the era dates. Reign dates have been taken from Tōkyōdō's *Sekai Jimmei Jiten: Tōyō Hen* (1952, pp. 919–22) and Shinchōsha's *Shukuyaku Nippon Bungaku Daijiten* (1955, appendix pp. 1–92).

Asterisks indicate empresses. The system of era names was not adopted until the time of the 36th emperor, and there is some confusion regarding the first few eras. Reign dates show: (1) the year of actual accession to the throne if known and, in parentheses, of formal coronation, but the latter date is not repeated when it is the same as the former; and (2) the year in which the reign ended, whether by death or abdication. An era date shows the first year of the era. Era names are indented beneath the names of the respective emperors.

1. 神武 Jimmu, (660)–585 B.C.
2. 綏靖 Suizei, 581–549
3. 安寧 Annei, 549–511
4. 懿徳 Itoku, 510–477
5. 孝昭 Kōshō, 475–393
6. 孝安 Kōan, 392–291
7. 孝霊 Kōrei, 290–215
8. 孝元 Kōgen, 214–158
9. 開化 Kaika, 158–98
10. 崇神 Sujin, (97)–30
11. 垂仁 Suinin, (29 B.C.)–A.D. 70
12. 景行 Keikō, (71)–130
13. 成務 Seimu, (131)–190
14. 仲哀 Chūai, (192)–200
    神功皇后 Jingū Kōgō (Regent), 201–269
15. 応神 Ōjin, (270)–310
16. 仁徳 Nintoku, (313)–399
17. 履中 Richū, (400)–405
18. 反正 Hanzei, (406)–410
19. 允恭 Ingyō, (412)–453
20. 安康 Ankō, 453–456
21. 雄略 Yūryaku, 456–479
22. 清寧 Seinei, (480)–484
23. 顕宗 Kenzō, (485)–487
24. 仁賢 Ninken, (488)–498
25. 武烈 Buretsu, 498–506
26. 継体 Keitai, (507)–531
27. 安閑 Ankan, 531–535
28. 宣化 Senka, 535–539
29. 欽明 Kimmei, 539–571
30. 敏達 Bidatsu, (572)–585
31. 用明 Yōmei, 585–587
32. 崇峻 Sushun, 587–592
33. 推古 *Suiko, 592–628
34. 舒明 Jomei, (629)–641
35. 皇極 *Kōgyoku, (642)–645
36. 孝徳 Kōtoku, 645–654
    大化 Taika 645
    白雉 Hakuchi 650
37. 斉明 *Saimei, (655)–661
38. 天智 Tenji, (662)–671
39. 弘文 Kōbun, 671–672
    白鳳 Hakuhō 672
40. 天武 Temmu, (673)–686
    朱鳥 Shuchō 686
41. 持統 *Jitō, (690)–697
42. 文武 Mommu, 697–707
    大宝 Taihō 701
    慶雲 Keiun 704

43.	元明	*Gemmei, 707–715	
	和銅	Wadō	708
44.	元正	*Genshō, 715–724	
	霊亀	Reiki	715
	養老	Yōrō	717
45.	聖武	Shōmu, 724–749	
	神亀	Jinki	724
	天平	Tempyō	729
46.	孝謙	*Kōken, 749–758	
	天平感宝	Tempyō-kampō	749
	天平勝宝	Tempyō-shōhō	749
	天平宝字	Tempyō-hōji	757
47.	淳仁	Junnin, 758–764	
48.	称徳	*Shōtoku, 764–770	
	天平神護	Tempyō-jingo	765
	神護景雲	Jingo-keiun	767
49.	光仁	Kōnin, 770–781	
	宝亀	Hōki	770
50.	桓武	Kammu, 781–806	
	天応	Ten-ō	781
	延暦	Enryaku	782
51.	平城	Heizei, 806–809	
	大同	Daidō	806
52.	嵯峨	Saga, 809–823	
	弘仁	Kōnin	810
53.	淳和	Junna, 823–833	
	天長	Tenchō	824
54.	仁明	Nimmyō, 833–850	
	承和	Shōwa	834
	嘉祥	Kajō	848
55.	文徳	Montoku, 850–858	
	仁寿	Ninju	851
	斉衡	Saikō	854
	天安	Tennan	857
56.	清和	Seiwa, 858–876	
	貞観	Jōgan	859
57.	陽成	Yōzei, 876(877)–884	
	元慶	Genkei	877
58.	光孝	Kōkō, 884–887	
	仁和	Ninna	885
59.	宇多	Uda, 887–897	
	寛平	Kampyō	889
60.	醍醐	Daigo, 897–930	
	昌泰	Shōtai	898
	延喜	Engi	901
	延長	Enchō	923
61.	朱雀	Suzaku, 930–946	
	承平	Shōhei	931
	天慶	Tengyō	938
62.	村上	Murakami, 946–967	
	天暦	Tenryaku	947
	天徳	Tentoku	957
	応和	Ōwa	961
	康保	Kōhō	964
63.	冷泉	Reizei, 967–969	
	安和	Anna	968
64.	円融	En-yū, 969–984	
	天禄	Tenroku	970
	天延	Ten-en	973
	貞元	Jōgen	976
	天元	Tengen	978
	永観	Eikan	983
65.	花山	Kazan, 984–986	
	寛和	Kanna	985
66.	一条	Ichijō, 986–1011	
	永延	Ei-en	987
	永祚	Eiso	989
	正暦	Shōryaku	990
	長徳	Chōtoku	995
	長保	Chōhō	999
	寛弘	Kankō	1004
67.	三条	Sanjō, 1011–1016	
	長和	Chōwa	1012
68.	後一条	Go-ichijō, 1016–1036	
	寛仁	Kannin	1017
	治安	Jian	1021
	万寿	Manju	1024
	長元	Chōgen	1028
69.	後朱雀	Gosuzaku, 1036–1045	
	長暦	Chōryaku	1037
	長久	Chōkyū	1040
	寛徳	Kantoku	1044
70.	後冷泉	Goreizei, 1045–1068	
	永承	Eishō	1046
	天喜	Tengi	1053
	康平	Kōhei	1058
	治暦	Jiryaku	1065
71.	後三条	Gosanjō, 1068–1072	
	延久	Enkyū	1069
72.	白河	Shirakawa, 1072–1086	
	承保	Jōhō	1074
	承暦	Shōryaku	1077
	永保	Eihō	1081
	応徳	Ōtoku	1084
73.	堀河	Horikawa, 1086–1107	
	寛治	Kanji	1087
	嘉保	Kahō	1094
	永長	Eichō	1096
	承徳	Jōtoku	1097
	康和	Kōwa	1099
	長治	Chōji	1104
	嘉承	Kajō	1106
74.	鳥羽	Toba, 1107–1123	
	天仁	Tennin	1108
	天永	Ten-ei	1110
	永久	Eikyū	1113
	元永	Gen-ei	1118
	保安	Hōan	1120
75.	崇徳	Sutoku, 1123–1141	
	天治	Tenji	1124

大治 Daiji 1126
天承 Tenshō 1131
長承 Chōshō 1132
保延 Hōen 1135

76. 近衛 Konoe, 1141–1155
永治 Eiji 1141
康治 Kōji 1142
天養 Ten-yō 1144
久安 Kyūan 1145
仁平 Nimpei 1151
久寿 Kyūju 1154

77. 後白河 Goshirakawa, 1155–1158
保元 Hōgen 1156

78. 二条 Nijō, 1158–1165
平治 Heiji 1159
永暦 Eiryaku 1160
応保 Ōhō 1161
長寛 Chōkan 1163

79. 六条 Rokujō, 1165–1168
永万 Eiman 1165
仁安 Ninnan 1166

80. 高倉 Takakura, 1168–1180
嘉応 Kaō 1169
承安 Shōan 1171
安元 Angen 1175
治承 Jishō 1177

81. 安徳 Antoku, 1180–1183
養和 Yōwa 1181
寿永 Juei 1182

82. 後鳥羽 Gotoba, 1183 (1184)–1198
元暦 Genryaku 1184
文治 Bunji 1185
建久 Kenkyū 1190

83. 土御門 Tsuchimikado, 1198–1210
正治 Shōji 1199
建仁 Kennin 1201
元久 Genkyū 1204
建永 Ken-ei 1206
承元 Jōgen 1207

84. 順徳 Juntoku, 1210–1221
建暦 Kenryaku 1211
建保 Kempō 1213
承久 Jōkyū 1219

85. 仲恭 Chūkyō, 1221

86. 後堀河 Gohorikawa, 1221–1232
貞応 Jōō 1222
元仁 Gennin 1224
嘉禄 Karoku 1225
安貞 Antei 1227
寛喜 Kanki 1229

87. 四条 Shijō, 1232–1242
貞永 Jōei 1232
天福 Tempuku 1233
文暦 Bunryaku 1234
嘉禎 Katei 1235
暦仁 Ryakunin 1238
延応 En-ō 1239
仁治 Ninji 1240

88. 後嵯峨 Gosaga, 1242–1246
寛元 Kangen 1243

89. 後深草 Gofukakusa, 1246–1259
宝治 Hōji 1247
建長 Kenchō 1249
康元 Kōgen 1256
正嘉 Shōka 1257

90. 亀山 Kameyama, 1259–1274
正元 Shōgen 1259
文応 Bun-ō 1260
弘長 Kōchō 1261
文永 Bun-ei 1264

91. 後宇多 Go-uda, 1274–1287
建治 Kenji 1275
弘安 Kōan 1278

92. 伏見 Fushimi, (1288)–1298
正応 Shōō 1288
永仁 Einin 1293

93. 後伏見 Gofushimi, 1298–1301
正安 Shōan 1299

94. 後二条 Gonijō, 1301–1308
乾元 Kengen 1302
嘉元 Kagen 1303
徳治 Tokuji 1306

95. 花園 Hanazono, 1308–1318
延慶 Enkyō 1308
応長 Ōchō 1311
正和 Shōwa 1312
文保 Bumpō 1317

96. 後醍醐 Godaigo, 1318–1339
元応 Gen-ō 1319
元亨 Genkō 1321
正中 Shōchū 1324
嘉暦 Karyaku 1326
元徳 Gentoku 1329
元弘 Genkō 1331
建武 Kemmu 1334
延元 Engen 1336

97. 後村上 Gomurakami, 1339 (coronation?)–1368
興国 Kōkoku 1340
正平 Shōhei 1346

98. 長慶 Chōkei, 1368 (coronation?)–1383
建徳 Kentoku 1370
文中 Bunchū 1372
天授 Tenju 1375
弘和 Kōwa 1381

99. 後亀山 Gokameyama, 1383–1392
元中 Genchū 1384
明徳 Meitoku 1390

100. 後小松 Gokomatsu, 1392–1412

应永 Ōei 1394
101. 称光 Shōkō, 1412 (1414)–1428
正長 Shōchō 1428
102. 後花園 Gohanazono, (1429)–1464
永享 Eikyō 1429
嘉吉 Kakitsu 1441
文安 Bunnan 1444
宝徳 Hōtoku 1449
享徳 Kyōtoku 1452
康正 Kōshō 1455
長禄 Chōroku 1457
寛正 Kanshō 1460
103. 後土御門 Gotsuchimikado, (1465)–1500
文正 Bunshō 1466
応仁 Ōnin 1467
文明 Bummei 1469
長享 Chōkyō 1487
延徳 Entoku 1489
明応 Meiō 1492
104. 後柏原 Gokashiwabara, 1500 (1521)–1526
文亀 Bunki 1501
永正 Eishō 1504
大永 Daiei 1521
105. 後奈良 Gonara, 1526 (1536)–1557
享禄 Kyōroku 1528
天文 Temmon 1532
弘治 Kōji 1555
106. 正親町 Ōgimachi, 1557 (1560)–1586
永禄 Eiroku 1558
元亀 Genki 1570
天正 Tenshō 1573
107. 後陽成 Goyōzei, 1586–1611
文禄 Bunroku 1592
慶長 Keichō 1596
108. 後水尾 Gomizuno-o, 1611–1629
元和 Genna 1615
寛永 Kan-ei 1624
109. 明正 *Meishō, (1630)–1643
110. 後光明 Gokōmyō, 1643–1654
正保 Shōhō 1644
慶安 Keian 1648
承応 Jōō 1652
明暦 Meireki 1655
111. 後西 Gosai, (1656)–1663
万治 Manji 1658
寛文 Kambun 1661
112. 霊元 Reigen, 1663–1687
延宝 Empō 1673
天和 Tenna 1681
貞享 Jōkyō 1684
113. 東山 Higashiyama, 1687–1709
元禄 Genroku 1688
宝永 Hōei 1704
114. 中御門 Nakamikado, (1710)–1735
正徳 Shōtoku 1711
享保 Kyōhō 1716
115. 桜町 Sakuramachi, 1735–1747
元文 Gembun 1736
寛保 Kampō 1741
延享 Enkyō 1744
116. 桃園 Momozono, 1747–1762
寛延 Kan-en 1748
宝暦 Hōreki 1751
117. 後桜町 Gosakuramachi, (1763)–1770
明和 Meiwa 1764
118. 後桃園 Gomomozono, (1771)–1779
安永 An-ei 1772
119. 光格 Kōkaku, (1780)–1817
天明 Temmei 1781
寛政 Kansei 1789
享和 Kyōwa 1801
文化 Bunka 1804
120. 仁孝 Ninkō, 1817–1846
文政 Bunsei 1818
天保 Tempō 1830
弘化 Kōka 1844
121. 孝明 Kōmei, (1847)–1866
嘉永 Kaei 1848
安政 Ansei 1854
万延 Man-en 1860
文久 Bunkyū 1861
元治 Genji 1864
慶応 Keiō 1865
122. 明治 Meiji, 1866 (1868)–1912
明治 Meiji 1868
123. 大正 Taishō, 1912 (1915)–1926
大正 Taishō 1912
124. 今上陛下 The Present Emperor, 1926 (1928)–
昭和 Shōwa 1926

THE BRIEF NORTHERN DYNASTY

1. 光厳 Kōgon, 1332–1333
正慶 Shōkei 1332
2. 光明 Kōmyō, (1337)–1348
暦応 Ryakuō 1338
康永 Kōei 1342
貞和 Jōwa 1345
3. 崇光 Sukō, (1349)–1351
観応 Kan-ō 1350
4. 後光厳 Gokōgon, (1353)–1371
文和 Bunna 1352
延文 Embun 1356
康安 Kōan 1361
貞治 Jōji 1362
応安 Ōan 1368

5. 後円融 Goen-yū, (1374)–1382
- 永和 Eiwa 1375
- 康暦 Kōryaku 1379
- 永徳 Eitoku 1381

6. 後小松 Gokomatsu, 1382–1392 (becoming 100th in main line)
- 至徳 Shitoku 1384
- 嘉慶 Kakei 1387
- 康応 Kōō 1389
- 明徳 Meitoku 1390

APPENDIX 9. JAPANESE GEOGRAPHICAL NAMES

ANCIENT KUNI AND MODERN PREFECTURES

THE ANCIENT KUNI (国)	THE MODERN PREFECTURES (KEN 県)
(東北) THE TŌHOKU AREA	
陸奥 Mutsu	青森 Aomori
羽後 Ugo	秋田 Akita
陸中 Rikuchū	岩手 Iwate
陸前 Rikuzen	宮城 Miyagi
羽前 Uzen	山形 Yamagata
岩代 Iwashiro	福島 Fukushima
磐城 Iwaki	
(関東) THE KANTŌ AREA	
常陸 Hitachi	茨城 Ibaraki
下野 Shimotsuke	栃木 Tochigi
上野 Kōzuke	群馬 Gumma
武蔵 Musashi	埼玉 Saitama
	東京都 Tōkyō To
相模 Sagami	神奈川 Kanagawa
下総 Shimōsa	千葉 Chiba
上総 Kazusa	
安房 Awa	
(中部) THE CHŪBU AREA	
越後 Echigo	新潟 Niigata
佐渡 Sado	
越中 Etchū	富山 Toyama
加賀 Kaga	石川 Ishikawa
能登 Noto	
越前 Echizen	福井 Fukui
若狭 Wakasa	
駿河 Suruga	静岡 Shizuoka
伊豆 Izu	
甲斐 Kai	山梨 Yamanashi
信濃 Shinano	長野 Nagano
三河 Mikawa	愛知 Aichi
尾張 Owari	
美濃 Mino	岐阜 Gifu
飛驒 Hida	
(近畿) THE KINKI AREA (ŌSAKA-KYŌTO)	
近江 Ōmi	滋賀 Shiga
山城 Yamashiro	京都府 Kyōto Fu
丹波 Tamba	
丹後 Tango	
和泉 Izumi	大阪府 Ōsaka Fu
河内 Kawachi	
大和 Yamato	奈良 Nara
紀伊 Kii	和歌山 Wakayama
伊勢 Ise	三重 Mie
伊賀 Iga	
但馬 Tajima	兵庫 Hyōgo
丹波 Tamba	
摂津 Settsu	
播磨 Harima	
淡路 Awaji	
(中国) CHŪGOKU AREA	
備前 Bizen	岡山 Okayama
備中 Bitchū	
美作 Mimasaka	
備後 Bingo	広島 Hiroshima
安芸 Aki	
長門 Nagato	山口 Yamaguchi
周防 Suō	
因幡 Inaba	鳥取 Tottori
伯耆 Hōki	
出雲 Izumo	島根 Shimane
石見 Iwami	
隠岐 Oki	
(四国) SHIKOKU	
讃岐 Sanuki	香川 Kagawa
伊予 Iyo	愛媛 Ehime
阿波 Awa	徳島 Tokushima
土佐 Tosa	高知 Kōchi
(九州) KYŪSHŪ	
筑前 Chikuzen	福岡 Fukuoka
豊前 Buzen	
豊後 Bungo	大分 Ōita
日向 Hyūga	宮崎 Miyazaki
筑後 Chikugo	佐賀 Saga
肥前 Hizen	長崎 Nagasaki
壱岐 Iki	(the island)
対馬 Tsushima	(the island)
肥後 Higo	熊本 Kumamoto
薩摩 Satsuma	鹿児島 Kagoshima
大隅 Ōsumi	
(琉球) RYŪKYŪ	
琉球 Ryūkyū	沖縄 Okinawa

9. Japanese Geography

CITIES OF OVER 100,000 (as of 1960). Listed from north to south.

PREFECTURES	CITIES
北海道 Hokkaidō	札幌 Sapporo
	旭川 Asahikawa
	小樽 Otaru
	函館 Hakodate
	室蘭 Muroran
	釧路 Kushiro
	夕張 Yūbari
青森 Aomori	青森 Aomori
	弘前 Hirosaki
	八戸 Hachinoe
岩手 Iwate	盛岡 Morioka
宮城 Miyagi	仙台 Sendai
秋田 Akita	秋田 Akita
山形 Yamagata	山形 Yamagata
福島 Fukushima	福島 Fukushima
茨城 Ibaraki	水戸 Mito
	日立 Hitachi
栃木 Tochigi	宇都宮 Utsunomiya
	足利 Ashikaga
群馬 Gumma	前橋 Maebashi
	高崎 Takasaki
	桐生 Kiryū
埼玉 Saitama	川越 Kawagoe
	浦和 Urawa
	川口 Kawaguchi
	大宮 Ōmiya
千葉 Chiba	千葉 Chiba
	市川 Ichikawa
	船橋 Funabashi
東京都 Tōkyō To	八王子 Hachiōji
神奈川 Kanagawa	横浜 Yokohama
	横須賀 Yokosuka
	川崎 Kawasaki
	藤沢 Fujisawa
	小田原 Odawara
新潟 Niigata	新潟 Niigata
	長岡 Nagaoka
富山 Toyama	富山 Toyama
	高岡 Takaoka
石川 Ishikawa	金沢 Kanazawa
福井 Fukui	福井 Fukui
山梨 Yamanashi	甲府 Kōfu
長野 Nagano	長野 Nagano
	松本 Matsumoto
岐阜 Gifu	岐阜 Gifu
静岡 Shizuoka	静岡 Shizuoka
	浜松 Hamamatsu
	沼津 Numazu
	清水 Shimizu
愛知 Aichi	名古屋 Nagoya
	豊橋 Toyohashi
	岡崎 Okazaki

	一宮 Ichinomiya
三重 Mie	津 Tsu
	四日市 Yokka-ichi
	松阪 Matsuzaka
滋賀 Shiga	大津 Ōtsu
京都府 Kyōto Fu	京都 Kyōto
	舞鶴 Maizuru
大阪府 Ōsaka Fu	大阪 Ōsaka
	堺 Sakai
	岸和田 Kishiwada
	豊中 Toyonaka
	布施 Fuse
	茨木 Ibaraki
兵庫 Hyōgo	神戸 Kōbe
	姫路 Himeji
	尼崎 Amagasaki
	明石 Akashi
	西宮 Nishinomiya
奈良 Nara	奈良 Nara
和歌山 Wakayama	和歌山 Wakayama
鳥取 Tottori	鳥取 Tottori
島根 Shimane	松江 Matsue
岡山 Okayama	岡山 Okayama
	倉敷 Kurashiki
広島 Hiroshima	広島 Hiroshima
	呉 Kure
	福山 Fukuyama
山口 Yamaguchi	下関 Shimonoseki
	宇部 Ube
徳島 Tokushima	徳島 Tokushima
香川 Kagawa	高松 Takamatsu
愛媛 Ehime	松山 Matsuyama
	新居浜 Niihama
高知 Kōchi	高知 Kōchi
福岡 Fukuoka	福岡 Fukuoka
	八幡 Yawata
	久留米 Kurume
	大牟田 Ōmuta
	門司 Moji
	小倉 Kokura
	田川 Tagawa
佐賀 Saga	佐賀 Saga
長崎 Nagasaki	長崎 Nagasaki
	佐世保 Sasebo
熊本 Kumamoto	熊本 Kumamoto
大分 Ōita	大分 Ōita
	別府 Beppu
宮崎 Miyazaki	宮崎 Miyazaki
	延岡 Nobeoka
鹿児島 Kagoshima	鹿児島 Kagoshima

9. Japanese Geography

MISCELLANEOUS JAPANESE NAMES

Bays

Ise Wan	伊勢湾	Ise Bay including Nagoya Harbor
Ōsaka Wan	大阪湾	Osaka Bay including the Kobe and Osaka harbors
Tōkyō Wan	東京湾	Tokyo Bay including the Yokohama and Tokyo harbors

Islands

Amami Ōshima	奄美大島	South of Kagoshima
Awaji Shima	淡路島	West side of Osaka Bay
Chishima Rettō	千島列島	The Kurile Islands
Hachijōjima	八丈島	South of Tokyo Bay
Hokkaidō	北海道	
Honshū	本州	
Iki (no) Shima	壱岐島	Between Kyushu and Korea
Karafuto	樺太	Sakhalin
Kunashiritō	国後島	Off the east coast of Hokkaido
Kyūshū	九州	
Ogasawara Shotō	小笠原諸島	The Bonin Islands
Ryūkyū Rettō	琉球列島	The Ryukyu Islands
Oki (no) Shima	隠岐島	In the Japan Sea
Ōshima	大島	Off Tokyo Bay
Sado(ga)shima	佐渡島	In the Japan Sea
Shikoku	四国	
Shōdo Shima	小豆島	In the Inland Sea
Tanegashima	種子島	South of Kagoshima
Tsushima	対馬	Between Kyushu and Korea

Rivers

Arakawa	荒川	Flows into Tokyo Bay at Tokyo
Edogawa	江戸川	Flows into Tokyo Bay at Ichikawa
Fujigawa	富士川	At the foot of Mt. Fuji
Ishikarigawa	石狩川	Hokkaido
Kisogawa	木曾川	Flows into Ise Bay at Nagoya
Kitakamigawa	北上川	Tohoku
Kumagawa	球磨川	Kyushu
Mogamigawa	最上川	Tohoku
Nagaragawa	長良川	Famed for the cormorant fishing at Gifu
Ōigawa	大井川	Between Mt. Fuji and Nagoya
Sagamigawa	相模川	Near Odawara
Sumidagawa	隅田川	Flows thru Tokyo into Tokyo Bay
Tamagawa	多摩川	Flows into Tokyo Bay
Tenryūgawa	天龍川	Between Mt. Fuji and Nagoya
Tonegawa	利根川	Flows into the Pacific at Choshi in Chiba Ken
Yodogawa	淀川	Flows through Osaka

Seas

Higashi Shinakai	東支那海	East China Sea
Nihonkai	日本海	Japan Sea
Minami Shinakai	南支那海	South China Sea
Kōkai	黄海	Yellow Sea

Straits

Kammon Kaikyō	関門海峡	Between Shimonoseki and Moji
Mamiya Kaikyō	間宮海峡	Between Hokkaido and Sakhalin

Naruto Kaikyō	鳴門海峡	The entrance to Osaka Bay
Sōya Kaikyō	宗谷海峡	Between Hokkaido and Sakhalin
Tsugaru Kaikyō	津軽海峡	Between Honshu and Hokkaido
Tsushima Kaikyō	対馬海峡	Between Iki and Tsushima island

Mountains

Asama Yama	浅間山	Mt. Asama near Karuizawa
Asozan	阿蘇山	Kyushu
Bandaisan	磐梯山	Tohoku near Aizu-Wakamatsu
Daisen	大山	Tottori Ken
Daisetsuzan	大雪山	Hokkaido
Fujisan	富士山	Mt. Fuji
Hakusan	白山	Northwest of Nagoya
Hakone Yama	箱根山	South of Tokyo
Hieizan	比叡山	Near Kyoto
Kōyasan	高野山	Near Kyoto
Tateyama	立山	In the Japan Alps
Unzendake	雲仙岳	Near Nagasaki
Yari(ga)take	槍岳	In the Japan Alps

APPENDIX 10. FOREIGN GEOGRAPHICAL NAMES

For Chinese and Korean place names the Japanese have customarily used the original Chinese characters with Japanese *on* readings as given in the two immediately following lists, but there is a growing tendency to indicate the current Chinese or Korean pronunciations in *katakana*. In the case of Western names, for which the characters in the third list were formerly used, the present tendency is to transcribe them phonetically in *katakana*, but the older literature is, of course, always with us.

Altho when used today the characters of the names in all three lists would be subject to the Tōyō Kanji rules, they are given here in their older forms since, particularly in the case of the third list, they are more likely to be encountered in the older literature. Those names in the third list that are the most commonly used today are indicated with asterisks. Note also that the rare characters in these lists will not be found in the body of this dictionary.

See Kenkyūsha's 1954 edition of the *New Japanese-English Dictionary* (pp. 2086–91) for additional foreign geographical terms.

CHINESE PLACES

NAME	JAPANESE PRONUNCIATION	CHARACTERS
Amoy	Amoi	厦門
Amur River	Kokuryūkō	黑龍江
Anhwei	Anki	安徽
Antung	Antō	安東
Canton	Kanton	廣東
Central China	Kachū	華中
Chahar	Chaharu	察哈爾
Changsha	Chōsha	長沙
Cheefoo	Chiifu	芝罘
Chekiang	Sekkō	浙江
China	Chūgoku	中國
China—Taiwan	Chūka Minkoku	中華民國
China—People's Republic	Chūka Jimmin Kyōwakoku	中華人民共和國

Dairen	Dairen	大連
Foochow	Fukushū	福州
Fukien	Fukken	福建
Great Wall of China	Banri(no)chōjō	萬里長城
Hainan Island	Kainantō	海南島
Han River	Kansui	漢水
Hangchow	Kōshū	杭州
Hankow	Kankō	漢口
Honan	Kanan	河南
Hong Kong	Honkon	香港
Hunan	Konan	湖南
Ichang	Gishō	宜昌
Jehol	Nekka	熱河
Kalgan	Chōkakō	張家口
Kansu	Kanshuku	甘肅
Keelung	Kiirun	基隆
Kowloon	Kūron	九龍
Kunming	Kommei	昆明
Kwangsi	Kanshii	廣西
Kwangtung	Kanton	廣東
Kwantung	Kantō	關東
Kweichow	Kishū	貴州
Lhasa	Rassa	拉薩
Liaotung Peninsula	Ryōtō Hantō	遼東半島
Macao	Makao	澳門
Manchuli	Manchuri	滿洲里
Manchuria	Manshū	滿洲
Marco Polo Bridge	Rokōkyō	蘆溝橋
Mukden	Hōten	奉天
Nanchang	Nanshō	南昌
Nanking	Nankin	南京
Nanning	Nannei	南寧
Ningpo	Neiha	寧波
North China	Kahoku	華北
Pearl River	Shukō	珠江
Peiping	Peipin, Hokuhei	北平
Peking	Pekin	北京
Pescadores	Hōkoshotō	澎湖諸島
Port Arthur	Ryojun	旅順
Pukow	Hokō	浦口
Shanghai	Shanhai	上海
Shansi	Sansei	山西
Shantung	Santō	山東
Shensi	Sensei	陝西
Sian	Seian	西安
Sikang	Seikō	西康
Sinkiang	Shinkyō	新疆
Soochow	Soshū	蘇州
Soochow Creek	Soshūga	蘇州河
South China	Kanan	華南
Suiyan	Suien	綏遠
Sungari River	Shōkakō	松花江
Swatow	Suwatō	汕頭
Szechwan	Shisen	四川
Taichung	Taichū	臺中

Tainan	Tainan	臺南
Taipei	Taihoku	臺北
Taiwan	Taiwan	臺灣
Taku	Tākū	大沽
Tibet	Chibetto	西藏
Tientsin	Tenshin	天津
Tsinan	Sainan	濟南
Tsingtao	Chintō, Seitō	青島
Weihaiwei	Ikaiei	威海衛
Woosung	Ūsun, Goshō	呉淞
Yangtze River	Yōsukō	揚子江
Yunnan	Unnan	雲南
Yellow River	Kōga	黃河

KOREAN PLACES

NAME	JAPANESE PRONUNCIATION	CHARACTERS
Andong	Antō	安東
Cheju Island	Saishūtō	濟州島
Chinnampo	Chinnampo	鎮南浦
Han River	Kankō	漢江
Inchon	Jinsen	仁川
Kaesong	Kaijō	開城
Kimpo	Kimpo	金浦
Korea	Chōsen	朝鮮
Korea—North	Hokusen	北鮮
	Chōsen Minshu-shugi Jimmin Kyōwakoku	朝鮮民主主義人民共和國
Korea—South	Nansen	南鮮
	Daikamminkoku (Kankoku)	大韓民國 (韓國)
Kum River	Kinkō	錦江
Panmunjom	Hammonten	板門店
Pusan	Fuzan	釜山
Pyongyang	Heijō	平壤
Seoul	Keijō	京城
Taegu	Taikyū	大邱
Wonsan	Genzan	元山
Yalu River	Ōryokkō	鴨綠江

MISCELLANEOUS FOREIGN PLACES

NAME	JAPANESE PRONUNCIATION	CHARACTERS
Africa	Afurika	阿弗利加
America	Amerika	亞米利加
The Americas	Beishū	米洲
Annam	Annan	安南
Antarctic Ocean	Nampyōyō	南氷洋*
Arabia	Arabiya	亞剌比亞
Arctic Ocean	Hoppyōyō	北氷洋*
Argentina	Aruzenchin	亞爾然丁
Asia	Ajia	亞細亞
Asia Minor	Shōajia	小亞細亞
Atlantic Ocean	Taiseiyō	大西洋*
Australia	{Osutoraria	濠太剌利
	{Gōshū	濠洲*

10. Foreign Geography

Austria	Ōsutoria	墺太利
Belgium	Berugii	白耳義
Berlin	Berurin	伯林
Black Sea	Kokkai	黑海*
California	{Karifuorunia	
	Kashū	加州
Canada	Kanada	加奈陀
Cape of Good Hope	Kibōhō	喜望峰*
Central America	{Chūō Amerika	中央亞米利加
	Chūbei	中米*
Chicago	Shikago	市俄古
Coral Sea	Sangokai	珊瑚海*
Dead Sea	Shikai	死海*
Denmark	Demmāku	丁抹
East Indies	Higashi Indo Shotō	東印度諸島
Egypt	Ejiputo	埃及
England	{Eikoku	英國*
	Ingurando	英蘭
English Channel	Ei-Futsu Kaikyō	英佛海峽*
Europe	{Yōroppa	歐羅巴
	Ōshū	歐洲*
Far East	Kyokutō	極東*
France	Furansu	佛蘭西
French Indo-China	Futsuin	佛印
Germany	Doitsu	獨逸
Golden Gate	Kimmon Kaikyō	金門海峽*
Great Britain	{Igirisu	英吉利
	Eikoku	英國*
Greece	Girisha	希臘
Greenland	Gurinrando, Ryokutō	綠島
Hanoi	Hanoi	河内
Hawaii	Hawai	布哇
Holland	Oranda	和蘭陀
Hungary	Hangarii	洪牙利, 匈牙利
Iceland	Aisurando	氷洲
India	Indo	印度
Indian Ocean	Indoyō	印度洋
Indo-China	Indo-Shina	印度支那
Ireland	Airurando, Airan	愛蘭
Italy	{Itarii	伊太利
	Itaria	伊太利亞
Java	Jawa	瓜哇
Kurile Current	Oyashio	親潮*
London	Rondon	倫敦
Los Angeles	Rafu, Rosuanzeresu	羅府
Malaya	Marai	馬來
Mediterranean Sea	Chichūkai	地中海*
Mexico	Mekishiko	墨西哥
Middle East	Chūtō	中東*
Mongolia	Mōko	蒙古*
Near East	Kintō	近東*
Newfoundland	Nyūfuaundorando	新發見島
New York	Nyūyōku	紐育
New Zealand	Nyūjiirando	新西蘭
North America	Hokubei	北米*

Pacific Ocean	Taiheiyō	太平洋*
Paris	Parii	巴里
Philadelphia	Fuiraderufuia	費拉府，費府
Philippines	{Fuirippin	比律賓
	{Hitō	比島
Poland	Porando	波蘭
Portugal	Porutogaru	葡萄牙
Prussia	Purosha	普魯西
Persia	Perusha	波斯
Red Sea	Kōkai	紅海*
Rome	Rōma	羅馬
Russia	{Roshia	露西亜
	{Rokoku	露國，魯國
Saigon	Saigon	西貢
San Francisco	{San Furanshisuko	
	{Sōkō	桑港
Siberia	Shiberia	西伯利亜
Singapore	Shingapōru	星港，新嘉坡
South America	{Minami Amerika	南亜米利加
	{Nambei	南米
Spain	Supein	西班牙
Sweden	Suēden	瑞典
Switzerland	Suisu	瑞西
Thailand, Siam	Tai, Taikoku	泰，泰國
Tibet	Chibetto	西藏
Turkey	Toruko	土耳古
Union of Soviet Socialist Republics	Sorempō, Soren	蘇連邦，蘇連
United Kingdom	Eikoku	英國*
United States	Beikoku	米國*
Vietnam	Betonamu, Etsunan	越南
Washington	Washinton, Kafu	華聖頓，華府
West Indies	Nishi Indo Shotō	西印度諸島
White Russia	Haku Roshia	白露西亜
Vienna, Wien	Uinna, Uiin	維也納

APPENDIX 11. WEIGHTS AND MEASURES

The metric system is now official in Japan but of course the older units will remain in the literature.

LINEAR MEASURE

1 *rin* (厘)		= .012 inch	= .303 millimeter
10 *rin*	= 1 *bu*	= .12 inch	= 3.03 millimeters
10 *bu* (分)	= 1 *sun*	= 1.2 inches	= 3.03 centimeters
10 *sun* (寸)	= 1 *shaku*	= .994 foot	= 30.3 centimeters
6 *shaku* (尺)	= 1 *ken*	= 1.99 yards	= 1.82 meters
6 *shaku*	= 1 *hiro* (尋)	= .994 fathom	= 1.82 meters
10 *shaku*	= 1 *jo* (丈)	= 3.31 yards	= 3.03 meters
60 *ken* (間)	= 1 *chō*	= 119. yards	= 109. meters
36 *cho* (町 or 丁)	= 1 *ri* (里)	= 2.44 miles	= 3.93 kilometers
1 *kairi* (海里)		= 1. knot	= 1852. meters

SQUARE MEASURE

1 square *ken* (坪)	=1 *tsubo*	=3.95 sq. yds.	=3.31 sq. meters
1 square *ken*	=1 *bu*	=3.95 sq. yds.	=3.31 sq. meters
30 *bu* (歩)	=1 *se*	=119. sq. yds.	=99.3 sq. meters
10 *se* (畝)	=1 *tan*	=.245 acres	=993. sq. meters
10 *tan* (段 or 反)	=1 *chō* (町)	=2.45 acres	=.992 hectares
10 *tan*	=1 *chōbu* (町歩)	=2.45 acres	=.992 hectares

CAPACITY

1 *shaku* (勺)		=.0384 pint (U.S.)	=.018 liter
10 *shaku*	=1 *gō*	= .384 pint (U.S.)	= .18 liter
10 *gō* (合)	=1 *shō*	= 1.92 quarts (U.S.)	= 1.8 liters
10 *shō* (升)	=1 *to*	= 4.8 gallons (U.S.)	= 18. liters
10 *to* (斗)	=1 *koku* (石)	= 44.8 gallons (U.S.)	=180. liters

WEIGHTS

1 *momme* (匁)		=.1325 oz.	=3.75 grams
100 *momme*	=*hyakume* (百目)	=13.25 oz.	=375. grams
160 *momme*	=1 *kin* (斤)	=1.32 lb.	= .6 kilogram
1000 *momme*	=1 *kan* (貫 or 〆) or 1 *kamme* (貫目)	=8.72 lb.	=3.75 kilograms
100 *kin* (斤)	=1 *bikoru* (擔 or 担)	=132. lb. (1 picul)	= 60. kilograms

METRIC SYSTEM

粍 millimeter	瓱 milligram	竓 milliliter
糎 centimeter	甅 centigram	竰 centiliter
粉 decimeter	瓰 decigram	竕 deciliter
米 meter	瓦 gram	立 liter
籵 decameter	瓧 decagram	竍 decaliter
粨 hectometer	瓸 hectogram	竡 hectoliter
粁 kilometer	瓩 kilogram	竏 kiloliter

APPENDIX 12. TŌYŌ KANJI LISTS

For convenience, particularly when studying characters, we have gathered into this appendix a complete listing of all the Tōyō Kanji as established by the Japanese Government, arranging them under four headings: essential characters, general use characters, recommended substitutions, and additions for proper names. Also shown, for purpose of speedy reference, is the number under which each character has been listed in the body of this dictionary.

881 ESSENTIAL CHARACTERS. These have been marked with a small capital A in the body of this dictionary and are here arranged according to the elementary-school grades in which they are taught; within each grade the characters are arranged in the order of their appearance in this dictionary.

GRADE ONE—46 CHARACTERS

一	三	下	五	正	中	本	九	七	二
1	**8**	**9**	**15**	**27**	**81**	**96**	**146**	**261**	**273**
六	人	先	八	十	上	口	右	四	土
283	**339**	**571**	**577**	**768**	**798**	**868**	**878**	**1025**	**1050**

大 1171	女 1185	子 1264	小 1355	山 1407	川 1447	左 1455	手 1827	日 2097	月 2169
木 2170	森 2301	水 2482	火 2743	生 2991	田 2994	白 3095	目 3127	石 3176	耳 3697
花 3909	赤 4534	足 4546	金 4815	雨 5042	青 5076				

GRADE TWO—105 CHARACTERS

天 16	百 33	夏 58	出 97	半 132	千 156	少 166	年 188	来 202	東 213
元 275	京 295	夜 298	今 352	休 380	会 381	合 383	作 407	何 409	入 574
分 578	前 595	円 617	切 667	力 715	北 751	古 770	南 778	友 858	国 1037
地 1056	声 1066	冬 1161	夕 1167	外 1168	多 1169	名 1170	学 1271	字 1281	家 1311
光 1358	工 1451	心 1645	戸 1817	文 2064	方 2082	早 2100	明 2110	春 2122	時 2126
村 2191	林 2210	校 2260	歩 2433	母 2466	毛 2473	気 2480	池 2489	汽 2507	海 2553
父 2832	牛 2852	犬 2868	王 2922	玉 2923	用 2993	町 2995	男 2996	思 3001	知 3169
秋 3273	空 3317	立 3343	竹 3366	米 3461	糸 3492	紙 3510	組 3520	考 3684	書 3719
朝 3788	色 3889	草 3939	虫 4115	行 4213	西 4273	見 4284	話 4358	読 4375	谷 4458
走 4539	車 4608	道 4724	長 4938	門 4940	間 4949	雪 5044	雲 5046	音 5110	風 5148
馬 5191	高 5248	鳥 5340	麦 5385	黒 5403					

GRADE THREE—187 CHARACTERS

万 7	平 26	両 34	画 50	昼 53	悪 62	由 89	申 93	世 95	向 101
表 108	午 162	乗 223	重 224	勉 228	島 230	才 270	事 272	市 284	主 285
交 290	化 350	仕 362	全 384	住 404	体 405	使 432	公 579	弟 584	同 619
次 638	弱 650	刀 665	助 719	動 730	点 804	原 825	台 848	兄 875	号 882
君 899	品 923	鳴 983	回 1028	図 1034	園 1047	去 1051	寺 1054	坂 1061	売 1067
場 1113	太 1172	妹 1204	始 1208	安 1283	実 1297	室 1300	客 1302	寒 1322	当 1359

県 1362	局 1384	屋 1392	岸 1413	岩 1414	炭 1418	広 1499	店 1509	度 1511	庫 1512
引 1562	強 1571	帰 1582	形 1589	役 1598	待 1609	後 1610	急 1667	感 1731	所 1821
投 1856	持 1903	指 1904	教 2052	数 2057	新 2080	旅 2088	昭 2114	星 2121	暑 2138
晴 2143	暗 2154	曜 2162	板 2213	柱 2236	根 2261	楽 2324	様 2341	橋 2378	歌 2422
止 2429	死 2439	毎 2467	決 2509	波 2529	注 2531	活 2552	流 2576	深 2606	温 2634
畑 2757	受 2826	物 2857	球 2941	理 2942	界 2998	病 3042	発 3092	皮 3109	研 3180
礼 3229	社 3231	神 3245	和 3268	科 3272	究 3314	第 3385	答 3394	算 3415	級 3496
終 3521	細 3522	絵 3537	買 3637	美 3658	着 3665	者 3685	取 3699	肉 3724	期 3785
勝 3787	自 3841	船 3873	苦 3928	茶 3940	荷 3956	葉 4001	落 4003	親 4293	角 4301
計 4312	記 4318	語 4374	頭 4469	貝 4486	負 4488	起 4541	身 4601	返 4670	近 4671
送 4683	追 4686	通 4703	週 4707	進 4709	運 4725	遊 4726	遠 4733	都 4769	配 4779
番 4811	里 4813	野 4814	鉄 4844	銀 4855	開 4950	聞 4959	集 5031	電 5050	面 5087
意 5113	顔 5139	食 5154	首 5186	駅 5199	魚 5281	黄 5399			

GRADE FOUR—205 CHARACTERS

丁 2	不 17	民 25	内 82	史 91	州 99	印 102	曲 103	必 129	氷 131
業 143	夫 164	包 176	末 177	失 178	争 186	刷 210	願 255	予 271	卒 294
育 296	変 306	商 321	以 348	他 361	付 363	代 364	位 401	命 430	係 449
便 450	信 454	借 490	停 507	働 532	共 581	写 626	冷 642	別 674	加 716
努 717	労 720	勇 726	勢 735	医 763	協 774	直 775	真 783	反 817	歴 835
司 877	告 900	味 913	員 928	唱 941	器 994	囲 1032	固 1036	幸 1073	喜 1115
塩 1125	士 1160	姉 1207	孫 1273	守 1282	官 1295	定 1296	害 1306	案 1308	宮 1310
察 1334	堂 1365	順 1450	改 1464	帳 1478	府 1507	底 1508	席 1513	庭 1514	建 1549

式 1556	徒 1614	成 1799	戦 1810	打 1829	拾 1901	挙 1902	散 2056	対 2067	放 2084
族 2090	旗 2093	昨 2119	景 2142	最 2146	題 2164	材 2189	相 2241	械 2264	植 2303
極 2305	横 2361	機 2379	整 2436	列 2438	残 2445	泳 2520	治 2528	油 2534	法 2535
洋 2550	酒 2573	消 2574	清 2605	湖 2628	港 2630	湯 2633	然 2770	焼 2772	照 2785
熱 2797	燈 2800	愛 2829	望 2940	登 3094	的 3097	具 3128	短 3172	祭 3247	福 3256
利 3264	季 3266	委 3267	秒 3271	種 3295	積 3306	産 3354	童 3357	競 3364	等 3396
節 3402	料 3468	粉 3469	結 3540	続 3544	緑 3564	練 3565	線 3580	置 3644	差 3662
習 3675	老 3683	有 3727	服 3741	脈 3764	臣 3837	息 3844	航 3867	良 3885	芸 3908
芽 3920	英 3927	菜 3982	薬 4074	血 4205	衣 4214	初 4215	覚 4288	観 4296	言 4309
詩 4360	試 4361	談 4388	調 4392	貨 4493	費 4497	路 4561	転 4615	軽 4620	輪 4630
農 4658	速 4700	連 4702	達 4721	選 4744	郡 4764	部 4767	録 4879	鏡 4912	問 4944
関 4958	院 4991	陸 5005	隊 5010	階 5011	陽 5012	静 5077	悲 5082	章 5112	類 5138
飛 5152	飲 5159	館 5174	鼻 5421	歯 5428					

GRADE FIVE—194 CHARACTERS

武 51	蚕 57	央 86	果 107	師 113	永 130	求 137	単 139	久 153	承 197
兵 201	省 218	仏 351	令 360	件 368	任 374	似 376	伝 379	仮 382	低 406
余 408	価 422	舎 423	念 424	例 428	保 455	俵 467	候 481	倍 483	倉 486
個 489	修 491	側 509	健 512	備 519	像 540	億 551	典 588	貧 600	興 615
周 622	軍 628	副 699	句 745	区 757	博 787	準 791	圧 818	厚 824	弁 845–7
参 850	能 853	収 860	因 1026	団 1027	在 1055	志 1064	均 1065	型 1077	報 1114
増 1137	各 1163	婦 1237	完 1288	容 1309	宿 1317	寄 1318	導 1354	常 1364	賞 1372
居 1387	功 1454	布 1468	希 1470	帯 1474	序 1502	応 1504	康 1518	張 1570	往 1605

術 1621	復 1627	衛 1639	快 1654	性 1666	恩 1684	情 1714	想 1728	慣 1756	技 1853
折 1855	接 1951	支 2039	政 2045	救 2051	敵 2060	易 2107	量 2141	査 2235	栄 2239
格 2259	標 2359	欠 2412	殺 2454	毒 2468	比 2470	氏 2478	河 2530	浅 2549	浴 2568
液 2599	測 2632	満 2636	漢 2662	漁 2684	演 2685	無 2773	燃 2808	牧 2856	特 2860
独 2884	現 2943	胃 3000	留 3003	務 3167	破 3186	確 3217	示 3228	祖 3243	祝 3244
移 3282	筆 3397	管 3416	築 3435	精 3480	紀 3497	約 3499	素 3511	経 3523	統 3536
給 3538	綿 3566	総 3567	編 3583	績 3602	織 3613	群 3667	義 3668	養 3671	肥 3740
腸 3798	辞 3860	製 4249	要 4274	票 4276	規 4285	解 4306	許 4324	設 4325	説 4373
課 4389	謝 4423	講 4425	識 4438	護 4447	議 4448	象 4472	則 4487	責 4492	敗 4494
貿 4499	賀 4501	貯 4502	貸 4503	賛 4516	質 4518	輸 4634	辺 4661	迷 4681	造 4701
過 4723	適 4738	酸 4789	鉱 4843	銭 4851	銅 4853	防 4980	限 4987	際 5018	雑 5032
非 5080	領 5124	飯 5158	験 5220						

GRADE SIX—144 CHARACTERS

可 24	弐 32	再 35	否 40	旧 94	未 179	后 181	系 195	我 200	厳 253
率 319	就 323	仁 349	供 431	俗 453	児 572	益 597	兼 598	善 606	尊 607
判 673	券 678	制 683	創 702	効 722	勤 732	勧 736	疑 755	孝 773	幹 790
営 963	壱 1059	基 1098	境 1135	処 1162	条 1164	奮 1184	妻 1206	存 1267	宗 1294
宣 1301	富 1321	憲 1342	専 1350	党 1363	届 1385	展 1396	属 1400	災 1448	己 1462
刊 1493	延 1547	律 1608	従 1613	得 1622	徳 1633	忠 1653	態 1743	拡 1876	招 1882
拝 1884	授 1946	採 1947	推 1950	提 1967	損 1979	故 2044	敬 2055	断 2078	是 2120
暴 2157	株 2257	検 2304	構 2343	権 2360	歓 2425	穀 2461	派 2547	済 2597	混 2604
減 2637	潔 2698	状 2839	版 2843	犯 2869	聖 2960	略 3007	異 3008	皇 3100	盟 3119

眼 3140	視 3248	禁 3251	私 3265	称 3280	程 3285	税 3287	策 3393	納 3508	純 3509
絶 3539	絹 3543	罪 3643	耕 3695	職 3718	臨 3840	至 3845	舌 3855	著 3983	墓 4027
蔵 4042	衆 4210	補 4242	複 4255	討 4316	訓 4317	訳 4327	詞 4335	評 4339	証 4341
誠 4352	認 4370	誤 4372	論 4391	諸 4393	欲 4461	豊 4466	財 4490	貴 4504	賃 4509
資 4510	述 4675	退 4684	逆 4685	遺 4745	釈 4809	陛 4988	除 4993	険 5000	難 5038
需 5052	革 5088	預 5123	額 5136						

969 GENERAL-USE CHARACTERS. These are the rest of the 1,850 Tōyō Kanji, which have been marked with a small capital B in the body of this dictionary. They are arranged here in the order of their appearance in this dictionary.

与 6	互 14	丙 22	且 23	更 42	亜 43	憂 70	璽 71	弔 80	冊 88
甲 92	帥 109	衷 110	幽 112	剛 114	粛 115	喪 117	為 138	巣 141	乏 150
丈 151	刃 152	及 154	丸 155	匁 159	升 160	丹 163	井 165	丘 174	斥 175
吏 183	朱 184	劣 185	危 187	励 193	寿 194	束 196	卵 199	岳 208	垂 211
奉 212	盾 215	卑 221	看 222	尉 231	彫 236	奥 240	殿 242	戯 246	劇 247
乙 260	乳 266	了 268	亡 281	充 289	忘 291	享 293	盲 297	哀 304	帝 305
畝 311	衰 312	恋 313	蛮 322	棄 326	裏 327	豪 329	介 347	伐 370	企 373
仰 375	伏 377	仲 378	佐 392	但 394	伺 395	伴 396	伯 397	含 402	伸 403
侮 421	併 425	依 426	侍 427	佳 429	侯 443	促 444	俊 448	侵 452	倣 466
倫 474	倹 479	俳 485	倒 487	値 488	偉 506	偶 508	偽 510	偏 511	傑 517
傍 520	債 531	催 533	傾 534	傷 535	僧 536	僚 545	舗 552	儀 554	儒 561
償 563	優 564	免 573	呉 583	並 589	盆 594	翁 596	普 605	慈 612	冗 625
冠 627	兆 637	准 648	凍 649	凝 652	凡 654	凶 663	刈 666	召 668	刑 670
刻 681	刺 682	削 690	剖 693	剣 696	剰 698	割 703	劾 721	勅 725	脅 727

勘 729	勺 740	旬 747	旨 752	匹 756	巨 758	匠 761	匿 764	克 772	栽 781
索 782	乾 784	裁 788	載 789	占 799	卓 802	貞 803	却 808	卸 812	灰 820
厘 823	暦 833	怠 851	又 855	双 859	叔 861	叙 862	桑 864	叫 881	吐 883
吸 885	呈 895	吟 898	吹 901	呼 914	咲 922	唆 925	哲 931	啓 940	唯 942
喚 958	喫 961	嗣 969	嘆 974	嘱 989	噴 995	嚇 1008	囚 1024	困 1033	圏 1045
吉 1053	坊 1062	坑 1063	坪 1072	城 1078	埋 1084	域 1085	培 1091	堕 1092	堅 1096
執 1097	堤 1108	塔 1109	堪 1112	塑 1121	塊 1122	塗 1124	墜 1132	墳 1141	墾 1142
壇 1146	壊 1147	壁 1148	奔 1175	奇 1176	契 1177	奏 1178	奨 1181	奪 1183	奴 1186
妃 1188	如 1189	好 1191	妨 1196	妊 1197	妙 1199	姓 1203	姻 1214	姿 1215	姫 1216
娠 1220	娘 1225	娯 1226	婆 1234	婚 1236	婿 1239	媒 1241	嫁 1249	嫡 1253	嬢 1257
孔 1265	孤 1270	宅 1279	宇 1280	宜 1290	宙 1291	宝 1293	宰 1303	宴 1304	寂 1315
密 1316	寛 1325	寝 1326	寧 1335	寡 1337	賓 1339	寮 1340	審 1341	寸 1348	封 1349
肖 1360	掌 1366	輝 1371	尺 1377	尼 1378	尽 1380	尿 1382	尾 1383	屈 1386	層 1402
履 1404	岐 1410	峠 1416	峡 1417	峰 1423	崇 1429	崩 1430	巧 1453	攻 1457	貢 1458
項 1459	忌 1463	巻 1466	帆 1469	帽 1483	幅 1484	幣 1490	干 1492	幻 1494	幼 1495
幾 1496	庁 1498	床 1503	座 1515	唐 1516	廊 1519	庸 1520	庶 1522	廃 1526	廉 1530
腐 1532	慶 1539	廷 1546	弊 1551	弓 1560	弧 1567	弦 1568	弾 1575	尋 1585	彩 1590
彰 1593	影 1594	径 1602	征 1603	彼 1604	徐 1612	循 1625	街 1626	御 1628	微 1631
徴 1634	徹 1637	衝 1638	衡 1641	忙 1647	忍 1648	怖 1662	怒 1664	怪 1665	恨 1677
恭 1680	恵 1681	悔 1682	恒 1683	恐 1685	悦 1696	患 1697	悩 1698	悟 1700	悼 1706
惑 1710	惜 1712	惨 1713	慌 1725	愉 1726	惰 1727	愁 1729	愚 1730	慨 1741	慎 1742
慢 1755	憎 1757	慰 1758	憩 1765	憤 1773	憾 1778	憶 1780	懇 1781	懐 1782	懲 1785

懸 1790	戒 1801	威 1803	房 1819	肩 1820	扇 1823	雇 1826	払 1828	扱 1836	択 1845
拒 1847	批 1848	抄 1849	扶 1850	抑 1851	抗 1852	抜 1854	拠 1871	拍 1872	拓 1873
抽 1877	抵 1878	担 1879	拙 1880	拘 1881	抱 1883	押 1885	拷 1895	括 1896	捜 1917
捕 1919	振 1920	措 1930	掲 1934	描 1936	控 1941	掘 1943	捨 1944	掃 1945	排 1948
探 1949	掛 1952	揮 1960	援 1961	握 1963	換 1964	揺 1965	揚 1966	搬 1973	搾 1975
摂 1976	携 1977	撃 1986	摘 1987	撲 1993	撤 1999	撮 2001	擁 2013	操 2015	擦 2025
擬 2026	敏 2047	敢 2054	敷 2059	斗 2073	斜 2074	斤 2076	施 2085	旋 2091	昔 2108
昇 2109	冒 2117	映 2118	晶 2137	暁 2139	替 2140	晩 2145	暇 2152	暖 2153	暫 2156
曇 2160	札 2171	机 2174	朽 2175	析 2194	枚 2202	杯 2206	枢 2208	枝 2211	松 2212
柳 2233	柄 2234	架 2237	枯 2238	染 2240	核 2254	桃 2255	桜 2256	梅 2258	棋 2294
棺 2298	棒 2302	楼 2322	概 2344	模 2345	樹 2377	欄 2401	欧 2413	款 2818	欺 2419
肯 2432	歳 2434	雌 2435	殊 2443	殉 2444	殖 2448	殴 2451	段 2452	貫 2469	皆 2471
江 2491	汗 2493	汚 2494	沢 2503	沖 2505	没 2506	沈 2508	況 2516	沼 2521	泌 2522
沸 2524	沿 2525	泰 2526	泊 2527	泣 2532	津 2543	浄 2548	洗 2551	浜 2567	涙 2569
浪 2570	浦 2571	浸 2572	浮 2575	渉 2591	淑 2592	渇 2596	涼 2598	渋 2600	添 2601
淡 2602	滋 2626	湾 2627	湿 2631	渡 2635	滝 2655	源 2656	溶 2659	滅 2660	滞 2661
滑 2663	滴 2674	漂 2678	漆 2679	漸 2680	漏 2682	漫 2683	澄 2699	潤 2700	潮 2702
潜 2703	濁 2710	濃 2711	激 2712	濫 2724	瀬 2735	炉 2750	炎 2751	炊 2752	烈 2761
煮 2771	煩 2782	煙 2784	勲 2794	熟 2795	黙 2796	燥 2810	爆 2818	妥 2823	爵 2830
壮 2837	将 2840	片 2842	邪 2849	雅 2850	牲 2858	犠 2865	狂 2872	狭 2882	狩 2883
猟 2894	猛 2895	猶 2897	献 2901	獄 2906	獣 2909	獲 2912	玄 2918	畜 2920	珍 2933
班 2935	珠 2936	琴 2949	環 2970	甘 2988	某 2989	畔 3002	累 3006	塁 3009	畳 3010

疎	疫	症	疲	疾	痢	痘	痛	痴	療
3021	3028	3039	3040	3041	3049	3053	3054	3061	3078
癖	泉	盗	盛	監	盤	眠	督	睡	瞬
3082	3099	3115	3116	3121	3122	3132	3147	3149	3159
矛	柔	矢	砕	砂	砲	硫	硝	硬	碁
3164	3166	3168	3179	3181	3185	3191	3192	3193	3202
碑	磁	礁	礎	祉	祈	祥	禍	禅	秀
3206	3209	3220	3222	3232	3234	3246	3254	3255	3263
秩	租	秘	稚	稲	稿	穂	穏	穫	穴
3276	3279	3281	3292	3294	3299	3300	3305	3309	3313
突	窃	窒	窓	窯	窮	端	笑	笛	符
3316	3320	3325	3326	3336	3337	3363	3374	3382	3383
筒	筋	箇	範	箱	篤	簡	簿	籍	粋
3392	3395	3414	3424	3425	3434	3444	3448	3450	3467
粒	粘	粗	粧	糖	糧	糾	紅	紡	紛
3471	3472	3473	3475	3485	3490	3498	3500	3505	3506
紋	紹	紺	紳	絡	紫	絞	継	維	緒
3507	3516	3517	3518	3533	3534	3535	3545	3552	3557
緊	綱	網	緯	締	縫	緩	縁	縛	繁
3560	3561	3563	3579	3581	3582	3584	3585	3593	3596
縦	繊	縮	繕	繰	署	罰	罷	羊	羽
3597	3607	3608	3612	3619	3642	3646	3649	3656	3673
翌	翼	翻	耐	耗	恥	聴	肝	肪	胞
3674	3680	3681	3690	3694	3704	3716	3731	3734	3749
胎	胆	肺	背	朕	朗	脂	胴	胸	豚
3750	3751	3752	3754	3757	3762	3766	3767	3768	3772
脚	脳	脱	脹	腕	腰	腹	膜	膨	謄
3773	3774	3775	3782	3786	3799	3800	3803	3818	3824
臓	騰	臭	到	致	乱	舞	舟	般	舶
3828	3834	3842	3846	3847	3856	3862	3863	3865	3870
艇	艦	即	既	芝	芋	芳	茎	茂	苗
3875	3881	3886	3887	3893	3896	3907	3912	3915	3923
若	荘	荒	華	菌	菓	菊	募	葬	蒸
3926	3938	3941	3955	3976	3980	3981	3996	4000	4002
蓄	幕	夢	慕	暮	薦	薪	薫	薄	藻
4024	4026	4028	4040	4041	4067	4069	4073	4075	4087
藩	虐	虚	虞	虜	慮	膚	蚊	袋	被
4089	4106	4109	4110	4111	4112	4113	4123	4223	4225
裂	装	裕	裸	覆	覧	触	訂	託	訟
4233	4234	4241	4248	4279	4292	4305	4310	4315	4320
訪	詔	詠	詐	診	訴	該	誉	誇	詳
4326	4333	4336	4337	4338	4340	4349	4353	4354	4357
詰	誌	誓	誘	謁	諾	誕	請	諮	謡
4359	4366	4369	4371	4382	4383	4386	4390	4404	4410

諭 4411	謀 4414	謙 4422	謹 4424	譜 4437	警 4439	譲 4446	豆 4465	販 4491	賄 4507
賊 4508	賠 4512	賦 4513	賜 4514	賢 4517	購 4522	贈 4525	赦 4536	赴 4540	越 4542
超 4543	趣 4544	距 4548	践 4558	跡 4560	跳 4562	踊 4565	踏 4571	躍 4595	射 4603
軌 4610	軒 4611	軟 4614	軸 4619	較 4623	轄 4636	辛 4646	辱 4655	込 4660	迅 4664
巡 4667	迎 4669	迭 4672	迫 4676	逃 4682	逓 4695	逐 4696	途 4697	透 4699	逮 4706
逸 4708	遇 4715	遂 4716	遍 4718	違 4720	遅 4722	遣 4732	遭 4736	遵 4742	遷 4743
避 4749	還 4750	邦 4758	邸 4759	郊 4761	郎 4762	郭 4765	郷 4766	郵 4768	酔 4781
酢 4783	酬 4785	酪 4786	酵 4787	酷 4788	醜 4798	醸 4804	針 4817	鈍 4830	鈴 4837
鉛 4842	銑 4850	銘 4852	銃 4854	鋭 4864	鋳 4865	錘 4872	錠 4874	錯 4880	錬 4881
鋼 4883	鍛 4895	鎖 4901	鎮 4903	鐘 4917	鑑 4924	閉 4945	閑 4948	閥 4954	閣 4957
閲 4961	闘 4973	附 4983	阻 4984	陥 4990	陣 4992	降 4994	陵 4998	隆 4999	陳 5001
陪 5002	陶 5003	随 5004	陰 5006	隔 5016	障 5019	隠 5020	隣 5023	隷 5026	隻 5028
焦 5029	雄 5030	離 5040	零 5048	雷 5049	震 5055	霊 5056	霜 5064	霧 5065	露 5069
輩 5086	響 5114	韻 5115	項 5118	頒 5119	頼 5129	顕 5137	顧 5141	飢 5155	飾 5161
飽 5162	飼 5163	餓 5171	香 5188	駆 5200	駐 5209	騒 5221	騎 5222	驚 5229	骨 5236
髄 5242	髪 5255	融 5274	鬼 5276	魂 5278	魅 5280	鮮 5295	鯨 5307	鶏 5359	麗 5381
麻 5390	摩 5392	魔 5398	墨 5404	鼓 5415	剤 5424	斎 5425	齢 5431	襲 5443	

28 RECOMMENDED SUBSTITUTIONS. These have been adopted by the Japanese press after a careful study of character frequencies and are quite generally accepted. In order to keep the number of characters at 1,850, it has also been recommended that 28 of the present Tōyō Kanji be dropped. In the body of this dictionary the 28 new characters have been marked with a small capital P (for Press). In addition to these 28 changes, the press also recommends and uses the abbreviated character 灯 (2745) rather than its full Tōyō Kanji form 燈 (2800).

ADDED				DROPPED			
亭 303	俸 480	偵 502	僕 544	且 23	璽 71	丹 163	但 394
厄 816	堀 1095	壌 1143	宵 1307	劾 721	又 855	嚇 1008	堪 1112
尚 1361	戻 1818	披 1874	挑 1898	奴 1186	寡 1337	唐 1516	悦 1696
据 1935	朴 2176	杉 2190	桟 2252	濫 2724	煩 2782	爵 2830	箇 3414
殻 2456	汁 2485	泥 2533	洪 2544	罷 3649	朕 3757	脹 3782	虞 4110
渓 2581	涯 2584	渦 2629	矯 3175	謁 4382	迅 4664	逓 4695	遵 4742
酌 4778	釣 4820	斉 5423	竜 5440	錬 4881	附 4983	隷 5026	頒 5119

92 ADDITIONS FOR PROPER NAMES. The following characters, in addition to the 1,850 Tōyō Kanji, have been approved by the Goverment for use in proper names.

丑 13	丞 21	亙 31	吾 37	晋 55	爾 69	也 75	甚 111	暢 119	乃 145
胤 217	之 280	亦 286	亥 287	享 293	亮 302	仙 359	伊 372	匡 760	哉 777
卯 806	只 874	呂 891	圭 1052	嘉 1136	奈 1174	宏 1286	寅 1314	尚 1361	巌 1442
巳 1460	庄 1500	弘 1563	弥 1565	須 1592	悌 1690	惣 1708	敦 2053	欣 2077	昌 2105
晃 2123	智 2144	杉 2190	桐 2249	桂 2253	楠 2317	橘 2368	毅 2463	浩 2563	淳 2590
熊 2791	猪 2889	玲 2928	琢 2946	瑞 2959	睦 3146	磯 3221	祐 3240	禄 3250	禎 3252
稔 3288	穣 3308	彦 3347	靖 3358	綾 3559	聡 3708	肇 3723	朋 3737	艶 3890	蔦 4037
藤 4090	蘭 4091	虎 4105	蝶 4171	輔 4626	辰 4653	郁 4760	酉 4775	欽 4829	錦 4882
鎌 4902	馨 5190	駒 5206	鯉 5299	鯛 5305	鶴 5365	鹿 5375	磨 5393	麿 5396	斉 5423
龍 5440	亀 5445								

APPENDIX 13. THE RADICALS CLASSIFIED BY POSITION

The charts which follow are arranged in the same order as the 12 Steps of the Radical Priority System (see Appendix 3). They have been placed here at the end of the book for ready reference. Thus, whenever you wonder whether a certain element of a character is a radical, you can turn here, to the step showing the position in which the element is found, for a speedy answer. Such an answer, of course, can likewise be obtained from the radical chart inside the front cover, but the positional arrangement used here may often be found more convenient.

In the case of the corner elements (Steps 8 to 11) and of crossed radicals (Step 12), only a few representative examples are given since you will already have encountered your radical in 97 percent of the characters before reaching these last steps. For the remaining 3 percent, consult the chart inside the front cover to determine whether a given element can be a radical.

The make-up of the charts is similar to that of the radical chart inside the front cover (see explanation on page 1) except where noted otherwise. Note, however, that variants that differ in stroke-count from their parent radicals have been entered—in brackets—only under the actual stroke-count, not being repeated after their parent radicals.

STEP 1. ALL

The Characters Which Are Also Radicals

1	一 1	乙 5	**2**	二 7	人 9	入 11	八 12	刀 18	力 19	匕 21	十 24
卜 25	厶 28	又 29	**3**	口 30	土 32	士 33	夕 36	大 37	女 38	子 39	寸 41
小 42	尸 44	山 46	川 47	工 48	己 49	已 49	巳 49	巾 50	干 51	廾 55	弋 56
弓 57	彳 60	**4**	心 61	戸 63	戶 63	手 64	文 67	斗 68	斤 69	方 70	日 72
曰 73	月 74	木 75	欠 76	止 77	毌 80	比 81	毛 82	氏 83	水 85	火 86	爪 87
父 88	片 91	牙 92	牛 93	犬 94	王 [96]	**5**	母 [80]	牙 [92]	玄 95	玉 96	瓜 97
瓦 98	甘 99	生 100	用 101	田 102	疋 103	白 106	皮 107	皿 108	目 109	矛 110	矢 111
石 112	示 113	穴 116	立 117	**6**	竹 118	米 119	糸 120	缶 121	羊 123	羽 124	羽 124

老 125	而 126	耒 127	耳 128	肉 130	臣 131	自 132	至 133	臼 134	舌 135	舟 137	色 139
虫 142	血 143	行 144	衣 145	西 146	**7**	臣 [131]	見 147	角 148	言 149	谷 150	豆 151
豕 152	貝 154	赤 155	走 156	足 157	身 158	車 159	辛 160	辛 160	辰 161	邑 163	酉 164
釆 165	里 166	麦 [199]	**8**	金 167	長 168	門 169	阜 170	雨 173	雨 173	青 174	青 174
非 175	斉 [210]	**9**	面 176	革 177	韭 179	音 180	音 180	頁 181	風 182	飛 183	食 184
食 184	首 185	香 186	**10**	馬 187	骨 188	高 189	鬼 194	竜 [212]	竜 [212]	**11/17**	魚 195
鳥 196	鹵 197	鹿 198	麥 199	麻 200	麻 200	黄 [201]	黒 [203]	亀 [213]	黃 201	黍 202	黑 203
歯 [211]	鼎 206	鼓 207	鼠 208	皷 [207]	鼻 209	鼻 209	齊 210	齒 211	龍 212	龜 213	龠 214

STEP 2. LONE

The Common Characters Having But One Radical

(each followed by its rad. & rad. no.)

〆→丶 3	久→丿 4	乃→丿 4	及→丿 4	了→亅 6

STEP 3. ENCLOSURE

The Radicals Found as Enclosures

1	乚 5	**2**	冂 13	冂 13	冂 13	冂 13	几 16	几 16	凵 17	勹 20	匚 22
匸 22	厂 27	辶 [162]	**3**	囗 31	夂 34	尸 44	广 53	廴 54	弋 56	辶 [162]	

4	戈 62	戸 63	戶 63	攴 65	歹 78	毛 82	气 84	爪 87	5	瓦 98	疒 104
6	耳 128	虍 141	7	走 156	辰 161	8	門 169	斉 [210]		9	風 182
10	鬥 191	鬼 194		11	鹿 198	麦 199	麻 200		13/14	鼠 208	齊 210

STEP 4. LEFT
The Radicals Found at the Left

1	丨 2	丨 2	丿 4	2	亻 9	冫 15	力 19	十 24	又 29	㐅 29	阝 [170]
3	口 30	土 32	夕 36	女 38	子 39	山 46	川 47	工 48	己 49	巾 50	干 51
幺 52	弓 57	彡 59	彳 60	忄 [61]	扌 [64]	氵 [85]	丬 [90]	犭 [94]			
4	戸 63	戶 63	手 64	文 67	斤 69	方 70	旡 71	日 72	木 75	止 77	歹 78
火 86	爻 89	爿 90	片 91	牙 92	牛 93	王 [96]	礻 [113]	月 [130]	月 [130]		
5	旡 [71]	牙 [92]	玄 95	瓦 98	甘 99	生 100	田 102	疋 103	白 106	皮 107	目 109
矛 110	矢 111	石 112	示 113	禾 115	立 117	艮 [138]	衤 [145]	6	米 119	糸 120	缶 121
羊 123	羽 124	羽 124	而 126	耒 127	耒 127	耳 128	臣 131	至 133	舌 135	舟 137	虫 142
血 143	7	臣 [131]	角 148	言 149	谷 150	豆 151	豕 152	豸 153	貝 154	赤 155	足 157
身 158	車 159	辛 160	酉 164	釆 165	里 166	長 [168]	8	金 167	隹 172	青 174	青 174
食 [184]	斉 [210]	9	面 176	革 177	韋 178	音 180	音 180	首 185	香 186		

10	韋 [178]	馬 187	骨 188	鬲 193	**11**	魚 195	鳥 196	鹵 197	鹿 198	麥 199	黃 [201]
黑 [203]	**12/17**		黃 201	黍 202	黑 203	齒 [211]	鼠 208	鼻 209	齊 210	齒 211	龍 212

STEP 5. RIGHT
The Radicals Found at the Right

1	丨 2	丨 2	乚 5	**2**	人 9	儿 16	刀 18	刂 18	力 19	匕 21	十 24
卜 25	卩 26	又 29	阝 [163]	**3**	口 30	子 39	寸 41	彡 59	**4**	戈 62	支 65
攴 66	攵 66	斗 68	斤 69	欠 76	殳 79	比 81	毛 82	犬 94	月 [130]	月 [130]	
5	旡 [71]	瓜 97	瓦 98	甘 99	皮 107	目 109	立 117	**6**	羊 123	羽 124	羽 124
耳 128	聿 129	艮 138	色 139	虫 142	**7**	見 147	角 148	谷 150	豕 152	辛 160	辛 160
酉 164	里 166	**8**	隶 171	隹 172	青 174	靑 174	**9**	韋 178	頁 181	風 182	飛 183
10	韋 [178]	鬼 194		**11**	鳥 196		**12**	齒 [211]		**15**	齒 211

STEP 6. TOP
The Radicals Found at the Top

1	一 1	一 1	丶 3	丿 4	ノ 4	**2**	二 7	亠 8	亠 8	八 9	入 11
八 12	八 12	丷 12	冖 14	刀 18	力 19	匕 21	十 24	卜 25	厶 28	又 29	

3	口 30	土 32	士 32	夂 34	夕 36	大 37	女 38	子 39	宀 40	小 42	⺌ 42
山 46	巛 47	工 48	己 49	彐 58	⺕ 58	⺕ 58	彑 58	廾 [140]	**4**	戈 62	攵 66
文 67	日 72	日 72	木 75	止 77	毋 80	比 81	氏 83	水 85	火 86	爫 87	爪 87
父 88	牛 93	王 [96]	艹 [140]	**5**	玄 95	甘 99	田 102	癶 105	白 106	目 109	矛 110
石 112	禾 115	穴 116	穴 116	穴 116	立 117	罒 [122]	**6**	竹 118	米 119	羊 123	羽 124
羽 124	老 125	而 126	耳 128	聿 129	自 132	臼 134	虫 142	血 143	衣 145	西 146	襾 146
7	貝 154	車 159	辰 161	釆 165		**8**	隹 172	雨 173	非 175	斉 [210]	
9	音 180	音 180	**10**	馬 187	高 189	髟 190	**11**	魚 195	鳥 196	鹿 198	麻 200
麻 200	黑 [203]			**12**	黑 203		**13/16**		鼓 207	齊 210	龍 212

STEP 7. BOTTOM

The Radicals Found at the Bottom

1	一 1	丶 3		**2**	二 7	儿 10	八 12	冫 15	几 16	刀 18	力 19
十 24	巳 26	厶 28	又 29	又 29		**3**	口 30	土 32	夂 34	夂 34	夕 36
大 37	女 38	子 39	寸 41	小 42	山 46	工 48	己 49	巾 50	干 51	廾 55	弓 57
彐 58	彡 59		**4**	心 61	㣺 61	手 64	斤 69	方 70	日 72	日 72	木 75
止 77	毋 80	比 81	毛 82	水 85	灬 86	灬 86	牛 93	犬 94	王 [96]	玉 [96]	月 [130]

5	母 [80]	氺 [85]	玉 96	瓦 98	甘 99	用 101	田 102	疋 103	白 106	皿 108	目 109
矢 111	石 112	示 113	禾 115		**6**	米 119	糸 120	缶 121	羊 123	羽 124	羽 124
而 126	耳 128	聿 129	肉 130	至 133	臼 134	舌 135	舛 136	艮 138	虫 142	衣 145	豕 [152]
7	舛 [136]	見 147	角 148	言 149	豆 151	豕 152	貝 154	足 157	車 159	辛 160	辛 160
辰 161	酉 164	里 166		**8**	金 167	隹 172	非 175		**9**	面 176	革 177
韭 179	音 180	音 180	風 182	食 184	食 184	香 186		**10**	馬 187	鬲 193	鬼 194
11	魚 195	鳥 196	鹿 198		**12**	黃 201	黑 203		**16**	龍 212	

STEPS 8 to 11

Some Characters Having Corner Radicals
(each followed by its rad. and rad. no.)

STEP 8 NORTHWEST		武→一 1	争→ノ 4	裁→十 24	能→ム 28
	疑→ヒ 21	名→夕 36	叢→、 3	執→土 32	聽→一 1
STEP 9 NORTHEAST		求→、 3	呉→口 30	耀→羽 124	弑→弋 56
STEP 10 SOUTHEAST		肅→丨 2	在→土 32	蝨→虫 142	灰→火 86
		肴→月 130	君→口 30	希→巾 50	
STEP 11 SOUTHWEST		未→ノ 4	弱→冫 15	東→ノ 4	末→ノ 4
		司→口 30	棘→ノ 4	虱→虫 142	

STEP 12. HIGH

Some Characters Having Crossed Radicals

(each followed by its rad. and rad. no.)

事→亅 6	世→丨 2	井→丿 4	丈→丿 4	卌→丨 2	本→丨 2
册→丿 4	九→丿 4	丰→丨 2	夫→丿 4	弗→丿 4	弔→丨 2
表→丨 2	丹→丿 4	壱→丨 2	衷→丨 2	尹→丿 4	卉→丨 2
甚→丨 2	丸→丿 4	冊→丨 2	喪→丨 2	刃→丿 4	嚢→丨 2

APPENDIX 14. THE ON-KUN INDEX

This ON-kun index will greatly assist in making the *Modern Reader's Japanese-English Character Dictionary* a *Modern Writer's Japanese-English Character Dictionary* also.

It is a Romanized listing of all the ONs, or Chinese pronunciations, and all the *kun*s, or Japanese pronunciations, of all the individual characters in the book in one alphabetical order.

Thus, in writing Japanese, when one fails to clearly recall a character, a simple reference to this index will give the needed information.

You will notice that there are often several characters listed for many ONs but usually one or two for the *kun*s.

The order of each entry is as follows: The On (in capitals) or the *kun* (in italics), followed by their various characters and their numbers. In this index the *okurigana* part of a word is not placed in parentheses, as this is shown under the character concerned, in the body of the book.

In this index, as in the body of the dictionary, prefixes, suffixes, verbs, and phrases, even though they may contain Ons, are printed in italics along with the *kun*s for simplicity's sake.

—B—

— D —

eru 得 1622
択 1845
獲 2912
選 4744
esa 餌 5167
esuru 会 381
essuru 謁 4382
閲 4961
etagaru 得 1622
etari 得 1622
ete 得 1622
ETSU 粵 237
咽 920
悦 1696
曰 2168
説 4373
謁 4382
越 4542
鉞 4835
閲 4961

— F —

FU 不 17
巫 38
甫 135
夫 164
孵 244
仆 343
付 363
俘 442
俯 484
傅 515
普 605
埠 1089
婦 1237
富 1321
布 1468
府 1507
腐 1532
怖 1662
扶 1850
拊 1863
敷 2059
桴 2270
楓 2315
浮 2575
父 2832
斧 2833
釜 2834
符 3383
腑 3781
艀 3874
蒲 4021
膚 4113
蜉 4146
覆 4279
訃 4311
誣 4365
諷 4412
譜 4437
負 4488
賦 4513
賻 4520
赴 4540
鈇 4828
阜 4977
附 4983
風 5148
鮒 5287
鳧 5341
麩 5386
fu 二 273
歩 2433
斑 2950
-fu 生 2991
FŪ 夫 164
富 1321
封 1349
楓 2315
瘋 3064
諷 4412
風 5148
fū 二 273
fuchi 淵 2625
潭 2692
縁 3585
fuchidoru 縁 3585
fuda 札 2171
簡 3444
fude 筆 3397
fue 笛 3382
鰾 5323
fueru 増 1137
殖 2448
fugo 畚 852
fuigo 鞴 5105
fuigō 鞴 5105
fuiito 呎 890
fuji 藤 4090
fujibakama 蘭 4044
fūjiru 封 1349
fuka 鱶 5337
fukai 深 2606
fukamaru 深 2606
fukameru 深 2606
fukami 深 2606
fukasu 更 42
吹 901
深 2606
蒸 4002
fukeru 更 42
化 350
深 2606
老 3683
耽 3703
蒸 4002
FUKU 伏 377
副 699
匐 749
幅 1484
復 1627
福 3256
箙 3406
服 3741
腹 3800
蔔 4031
蝠 4163
蝮 4165
袱 4227
複 4255
覆 4279
輻 4633
逼 4717
馥 5189
鰒 5316
fuku 吹 901
噴 995
拭 1897
葺 3995
fukumaseru 含 402
fukumasu 含 402
fukumeru 含 402
fukumi 含 402
fukumu 含 402
fukurahagi 腓 3779
fukurakasu 脹 3782
fukuramasu 脹 3782
fukuramu 脹 3782
fukuraseru 脹 3782
fukureru 脹 3782
膨 3818
fukuro 嚢 124
袋 4223
fukurō 梟 235
fukusuru 伏 377
復 1627
服 3741
腹 3800
fukuyokana 脹 3782
fumaeru 踏 4571
fumi 文 2064
書 3719
fumoto 麓 5377
fumu 履 1404
践 4558
踏 4571
FUN 分 578
忿 587
刎 669
吻 892
噴 995
墳 1141
奮 1184
憤 1773
扮 1844
濆 2691
焚 2769
粉 3469
糞 3489
紛 3506
芬 3901
賁 4495
雰 5045
funa 鮒 5287
funabata 舷 3872
funabei 舷 3872
fundoshi 褌 4251
fune 舟 3863
船 3873
funsuru 扮 1844
furareru 振 1920
furasu 降 4994
fure 振 1920
触 4305
fureru 振 1920
狂 2872
触 4305
furi 振 1920
風 5148
furu 古 770
振 1920
降 4994
furu- 旧 94
古 770
furubiru 古 770
furubokeru 古 770
furue 震 5055
furueru 震 5055
顫 5143
furui 旧 94
古 770
故 2044
篩 3433
震 5055
furuku 古 770
furumekashii 古 770
furutta 振 1920
furutte 奮 1184
furuu 奮 1184
振 1920
揮 1960
篩 3433

— G —

— H —

I

—— J ——

— K —

MAN	万	7
	卐	12
	卍	79
	幔	1486
	慢	1755
	懣	1783
	曼	2132
	満	2636
	漫	2683
	瞞	3153
	蔓	4039
	謾	4427
	蹣	4584
	鏝	4911
	饅	5180
	鬘	5263
	鰻	5326
man-	満	2636
mana-	愛	2829
manabi	学	1271
manabu	学	1271
mana-ita	俎	441
manajiri	眥	3135
manako	眼	3140
manazashi	眸	3137
maneki	招	1882
maneku	招	1882
manimani	随	5004
manji	卐	12
	卍	79
manugareru	免	573
manukareru	免	573
mare na	希	1470
	稀	3286
mari	毬	2474
	鞠	5101
maro	麿	5396
marobakasu	転	4615
marobasu	転	4615
marobu	転	4615
maroyaka na	円	617
maru	丸	155
	円	617
maru de	丸	155
marui	丸	155
	円	617
marukkoi	丸	155
marumeru	丸	155
masa	柾	2228
masakari	鉞	4835
masaki	柾	2228
masame	柾	2228
masani	正	27
	当	1359
	応	1504
	方	2082
	将	2840
masaru	優	564
	増	1137
	勝	3787
masashiku	正	27
mashi	増	1137
mashi na	増	1137
mashira	猿	2905
mashite	況	2516
masu	升	160
	益	597
	増	1137
	枡	2207
	鱒	5332
masuru	摩	5392
mata	亦	286
	俣	437
	又	855
	叉	856
	復	1627
	股	3739
	胯	3759
	複	4255
matagaru	跨	4557
matagu	跨	4557
matamoya	又	855
mataseru	待	1609
mata shitemo	又	855
matataki	瞬	3159
matataku	瞬	3159
mato	的	3097
matoi	纏	3627
matomaru	纏	3627
matomatta	纏	3627
matomeru	纏	3627
matou	絡	3533
	纏	3627
MATSU	末	177
	抹	1870
	沫	2515
	秣	3277
matsu	俟	438
	待	1609
	松	2212
-matsu	末	177
matsuge	睫	3145
matsuri	祭	3247
matsurigoto	政	2045
matsurou	服	3741
matsuru	奉	212
	祀	3230
	祭	3247
matsuwaru	纏	3627
matta	待	1609
mattaki	全	384
mattaku	全	384
	完	1288
mattōsuru	全	384
	完	1288
mau	舞	3862
mawarasu	回	1028
mawari	周	622
	回	1028
-mawari	回	1028
mawari-kudoi	回	1028
mawaru	回	1028
	廻	1548
	繞	3609
mawashi	回	1028
mawasu	回	1028
	廻	1548
mayoi	迷	4681
mayou	迷	4681
mayo-wakasu	迷	4681
mayowasu	迷	4681
mayu	眉	219
	繭	4087
mayumi	檀	2386
mayuzumi	黛	5408
mazaru	混	2604
	雑	5032
mazeru	交	290
	混	2604
	錯	4880
	雑	5032
mazu	先	571
mazui	拙	1880
mazushii	貧	600
ME	瑪	2963
	馬	5191
me	匁	159
	目	3127
	眼	3140
	芽	3920
me-	女	1185
	奴	1186
	雌	2435
	牝	2853
-me	目	3127
meawaseru	娶	1230
meboshii	目	3127
mederu	賞	1372
	愛	2829
mebataki	瞬	3159
megumi	恵	1681
megumu	恤	1676
	恵	1681
	芽	3920
megurasu	回	1028
	巡	4667
	運	4725
meguri	廻	1548
	巡	4667
meguru	回	1028
	廻	1548
	繞	3609
	巡	4667
	運	4725
MEI	命	430
	冥	630
	鳴	983
	名	1170
	明	2110
	暝	2155
	溟	2640
	盟	3119
	瞑	3151
	茗	3929
	螟	4175
	謎	4405
	迷	4681
	酩	4784
	銘	4852
mei	姪	1212
-mei	名	1170
meijiru	命	430
	銘	4852
meisuru	瞑	3151
meizuru	命	430
	銘	4852
mejiri	眥	3135
mekake	妾	3346
mekura	盲	297
mekuru	捲	1933
mekuwa-seru	眴	3136
mekuwasu	眴	3136
memagurushii	目	3127
MEN	免	573
	棉	2295
	綿	3566
	緬	3574
	面	5087
	麵	5389
men	牝	2853
men-	雌	2435
menjiru	免	573
mensuru	面	5087
menzuru	免	573
meri	滅	2660
	減	2637
meru	減	2637
meshi	召	668

黙 2796
目 3127
momareru 揉 1962
mome 揉 1962
momeru 揉 1962
momi 樅 2353
籾 3464
紅 3500
momme 匁 159
momo 百 33
桃 2255
股 3739
腿 3795
momu 揉 1962
MON 捫 1922
文 2064
瞞 3153
紋 3507
門 4940
問 4944
悶 4947
聞 4959
-mon 文 2064
mō ni 猛 2895
mono 物 2857
者 3685
monogusai 懶 1789
mono no 物 2857
monosuru 物 2857
monoui 懶 1789
monuke 蛻 4145
monukeru 蛻 4145
moppara 専 1350
morai 貰 4500
morasu 洩 2540
漏 2682
morau 貰 4500
moreru 洩 2540
漏 2682
mori 守 1282
杜 2188
森 2301
漏 2682
盛 3116
銛 4849
moro- 諸 4393
moroi 脆 3760
moroku 脆 3760
moromi 醪 4800
moru 守 1282
洩 2540
漏 2682
盛 3116
moshi 若 3926
moshika-shitara 若 3926
moshika-suru to 若 3926
moshikuwa 若 3926
moshimo 若 3926
moshiya 若 3926
mosu 燃 2808
mōsu 申 93
mosuru 摸 1974
模 2345
摹 4035
motageru 擡 2021
motanai 持 1903
motanu 持 1903
motarasu 齎 5426
motareru 凭 659
靠 5085
motaseru 持 1903
moteasobu 挵 1908
弄 2924
玩 2925
翫 3678
moteru 持 1903
moto 下 9
本 96
元 275
基 1098
素 3511
許 4324
酵 4787
motodori 髻 5261
motoi 基 1098
motomeru 求 137
索 782
motoru 悖 1699
戻 1818
motōru 回 1028
繞 3609
motoyori 元 275
固 1036
素 3511
motozuku 基 1098
MOTSU 没 2506
物 2857
motsu 持 1903
motsure 縺 3592
motsureru 縺 3592
motte 以 348
mottomo 尤 128
最 2146
mottomo-rashii 尤 128
moya 靄 5074
moyai 舫 3866
moyashi 萌 3979
moyasu 燃 2808
萌 3979
moyau 舫 3866
moyōshi 催 533
moyōsu 催 533
moyuru 燃 2808
MU 武 51
亡 281
牟 849
無 2773
矛 3164
務 3167
夢 4028
謀 4414
霧 5065
鵡 5355
鷚 5366
mu 六 283
mube 宜 1290
muchi 笞 3380
鞭 5104
muchiutsu 鞭 5104
muda 徒 1614
mugi 麦 5385
mugoi 惨 1713
酷 4788
mugotara-shii 惨 1713
mujina 貉 4480
mukae 迎 4669
mukaeru 迎 4669
mukai 向 101
mukashi 昔 2108
mukatsuku 嘔 982
噦 1009
mukau 向 101
muke 向 101
mukeru 向 101
剝 695
mukete 向 101
muki 向 101
muko 婿 1239
mukō 向 101
muku 向 101
剝 695
mukuge 毳 2476
mukui 報 1114
酬 4785
mukuiru 報 1114
mukureru 剝 695
mukuro 軀 4606
骸 5240
munashii 空 3317
虚 4109
munashiku suru 虚 4109
mune 旨 752
宗 1294
munc 棟 2299
胸 3768
mu ni suru 無 2773
mura 村 2191
斑 2950
mura- 叢 144
muragaru 叢 144
簇 3441
群 3667
murasaki 紫 3534
murasu 蒸 4002
mure 群 3667
mureru 群 3667
蒸 4002
muro 室 1300
musaboru 貪 505
musebu 咽 920
噎 990
museppoi 咽 920
museru 咽 920
噎 990
mushi 虫 4115
mushi- 蒸 4002
mushiba 齲 5439
mushibamu 蝕 5165
mushiro 寧 1335
席 1513
筵 3400
蓆 4014
mushiru 毟 207
挘 1891
musu 蒸 4002
musubi 結 3540
musuboreru 結 3540
musubu 掬 1937
結 3540
musume 娘 1225
mutsu 六 283
mutsubu 睦 3146
mutsukaru 憤 1773
mutsukashii 難 5038
mutsumajii 睦 3146
mutsumu 睦 3146
muttsu 六 283
muzukashii 六 283
難 5038
MYAKU 脈 3764
MYŌ 命 430
冥 630
名 1170
妙 1199
明 2110
苗 3923
茗 3929
蘉 4046
錨 4876

nashi 梨 2275
無 2773
nashi de 亡 281
無 2773
nashi ni 亡 281
無 2773
nasu 為 138
成 1799
済 2597
生 2991
-nasu 做 495
nasuru 擦 2025
nata 鉈 4833
NATSU 捺 1929
natsu 夏 58
natsukashi-garu 懐 1782
natsukashii 懐 1782
natsukashi-mi 懐 1782
natsukashi-mu 懐 1782
natsukeru 懐 1782
natsukkoi 懐 1782
natsuku 懐 1782
natsume 棗 116
nau 綯 3550
naute no 名 1170
nawa 縄 3617
nawate 畷 3011
nayamashii 悩 1698
nayamasu 悩 1698
nayami 悩 1698
nayamu 悩 1698
艱 3888
nayoyaka-na 嫋 1247
nazo 謎 4405
nazoraeru 准 648
準 791
擬 2026
nazukeru 名 1170
nazumu 泥 2533
滞 2661
NE 禰 3261
ne 値 488
直 775
子 1264
寝 1326
峰 1423
嶺 1440
根 2261
音 5110
nebai 粘 3472
nebari 粘 3472
nebaru 粘 3472
nebatta 粘 3472
neburu 眠 3132
睡 3149
舐 3858
nebutai 眠 3132
NECHI 蚋 4121
negai 願 255
negau 願 255
negawashii 願 255
negawa-kuwa 願 255
negi 葱 3993
negirau 労 720
犒 2864
negura 塒 1117
NEI 佞 400
嚀 1007
寧 1335
柄 2199
濘 2717
獰 2913
蚋 4121
nejikeru 拗 1869
nejikureru 拗 1869
nejire 捩 1942
nejireru 拗 1869
捻 1940
捩 1942
nejiri 捩 1942
nejiru 拗 1869
捻 1940
捩 1942
nekaseru 寝 1326
nekasu 寝 1326
nekkara 根 2261
neko 猫 2893
nekosoge 根 2261
nekosogi 根 2261
nemugari 睡 3149
nemugariya 睡 3149
nemugaru 睡 3149
nemugeni 眠 3132
nemui 眠 3132
nemuri-kokeru 眠 3132
nemuru 眠 3132
睡 3149
nemusō ni 眠 3132
nemutagaru 眠 3132
nemutage ni 眠 3132
nemutai 眠 3132
nemutasō ni 眠 3132
NEN 年 188
念 424
拈 1866
捻 1940
撚 1997
然 2770
燃 2808
稔 3288
粘 3472
鮎 5288
nengoro na 懇 1781
nenjiru 念 424
nenzuru 念 424
nerai 狙 2877
nerau 狙 2877
nereru 練 3565
nereta 練 3565
neri 煉 2783
練 3565
錬 4881
neru 寐 1319
寝 1326
捏 1905
煉 2783
粘 3472
練 3565
邌 4754
錬 4881
nēsan 姉 1207
neseru 寝 1326
neshina ni 寝 1326
nesoberu 寝 1326
nesobireru 寝 1326
nessuru 熱 2797
netamashii 妬 1205
netami 妬 1205
嫉 1248
netamu 妬 1205
嫉 1248
NETSU 捏 1905
涅 2564
熱 2797
neya 閨 4956
nēya 姉 1207
nezu 鼠 5417
nezumi 鼠 5417
nezu ni 寝 1326
NI 弐 32
爾 69
二 273
児 572
尼 1378
ni 丹 163
煮 2771
荷 3956
-ni 似 376
ni atari 方 2082
nibe 膠 3813
nibui 鈍 4830
niburaseru 鈍 4830
niburasu 鈍 4830
niburu 鈍 4830
NICHI 日 2097
-Nichi- 日 2097
nie 牲 2858
贄 4523
nieru 煮 2771
nigai 苦 3928
nigamu 苦 3928
nigaru 苦 3928
nigasu 逃 4682
nigekamu 齝 5430
nigeru 逃 4682
nigirasu 握 1963
nigiri 握 1963
nigiru 握 1963
nigiwai 賑 4511
nigiwashii 賑 4511
nigiwau 賑 4511
nigiyakana 賑 4511
nigorasu 濁 2710
nigori 濁 2710
nigoru 濁 2710
nigosu 濁 2710
nii- 新 2080
niisan 兄 875
niji 虹 4118
nijimu 滲 2677
nijiru 躙 4599
nijū 廿 1550
ni junjite 准 648
準 791
ni kagitte 限 4987
ni kanshite 関 4958
nikawa 膠 3813
NIKU 肉 3724
nikugaru 憎 1757
nikui 悪 62
憎 1757
-nikui 悪 62
難 5038
nikumu 悪 62
憎 1757
nikurashi-geni 憎 1757
nikurashii 憎 1757
nikushimi 悪 62
憎 1757
ni menjite 免 573
NIN 刃 152
人 339
仁 349
任 374
妊 1197
忍 1648
壬 2921

稔 3288
認 4370
靭 5091
-nin 人 339
nina 蜷 4156
ninau 担 1879
荷 3956
ninjiru 任 374
ninniku 蒜 4010
ninzuru 任 374
nioi 匂 742
臭 3842
香 5188
ni oite 於 2083
ni ōjite 応 1504
ni okeru 於 2083
niou 匂 742
niowaseru 匂 742
niowasu 匂 742
nira 韮 3988
nirameru 睨 3148
nirami 睨 3148
niramu 睨 3148
nire 楡 2309
niregamu 齝 5430
niru 烹 309
似 376
煮 2771
ni saishite 際 5018
nise 偽 510
贋 840
擬 2026
niseru 似 376
贋 840
擬 2026
nishi 螺 4184
西 4273
nishiki 錦 4882
nishin 鯡 5302
鰊 5309
ni suru 為 138
ni taisuru 対 2067
NITSU 日 2097
ni tsuite 就 323
付 363
nitsukawa-shii 似 376
ni tsuki 付 363
ni tsurete 連 4702
niwa 庭 1514
niwaka 俄 447
遽 4746
頓 5121
niwatori 鶏 5359
ni yori 依 426
NŌ 嚢 124
能 853
悩 1698
曩 2167
濃 2711
瑙 2952
納 3508
脳 3774
膿 3826
農 4658
no 乃 145
篦 3410
野 4814
no- 野 4814
nobasu 伸 403
延 1547
nobe 延 1547
noberu 伸 403
宣 1301
延 1547
述 4675
陳 5001
nobi 伸 403
延 1547
nobiru 伸 403
延 1547
nobiyakana 伸 403
nobori 上 798
幟 1488
昇 2109
登 3094
noboru 上 798
昇 2109
登 3094
noboseru 上 798
nobosu 上 798
nochi 後 1610
nodo 咽 920
喉 960
nogareru 逃 4682
遁 4719
nogasu 逃 4682
noge 芒 3894
nogi 芒 3894
nokeru 退 4684
除 4993
noki 軒 4611
nokkaru 乗 223
noko 鋸 4878
nokogiri 鋸 4878
nokorazu 残 2445
nokori 残 2445
nokoru 残 2445
nokosu 残 2445
遺 4745
noku 退 4684
nomeru 飲 5159
nomi 蚤 4122
鑿 4937
nomikko 飲 5159
nomu 呑 39
飲 5159
nondaku-reru 飲 5159
nonoshiru 罵 3648
詬 4347
nori 乗 223
典 588
法 2535
糊 3483
則 4487
nori-konasu 乗 223
noritoru 則 4487
noro 鈍 4830
noroi 呪 912
鈍 4830
norou 呪 912
詛 4330
noru 乗 223
載 789
宣 1301
noseru 乗 223
載 789
noshi 伸 403
熨 2793
nosu 伸 403
熨 2793
notamau 宣 1301
曰 2168
notto 節 3402
nottoru 則 4487
nozoite 除 4993
nozoku 覘 4286
覗 4287
除 4993
nozomashii 望 2940
nozomi 望 2940
nozomu 望 2940
臨 3840
NU 奴 1186
怒 1664
nue 鵼 5357
nugaseru 脱 3775
nugasu 脱 3775
nugeru 脱 3775
nugu 脱 3775
nuguu 拭 1897
nui 縫 3582
nuka 糠 3488
nukaranu 抜 1854
nukari 抜 1854
nukaru 抜 1854
濘 2717
nukasu 抜 1854
nukazuku 額 5136
nukeru 抜 1854
脱 3775
nuki 抜 1854
貫 2469
緯 3579
nukinderu 抜 1854
抽 1877
擢 2022
nuku 抜 1854
抽 1877
擢 2022
nukui 温 2634
nukumaru 温 2634
nukumeru 温 2634
nukumi 温 2634
nukumori 温 2634
nukumoru 温 2634
nukutoi 温 2634
numa 沼 2521
nume 絖 3526
numerakasu 滑 2663
numeri 滑 2663
numeru 滑 2663
nuno 布 1468
nurasu 濡 2723
nureru 濡 2723
nuri 塗 1124
nuru 塗 1124
nusa 幣 1490
nushi 主 285
nusumu 盗 3115
窃 3320
nuu 縫 3582
NYA 若 3926
NYAKU 蒻 4007
NYO 女 1185
如 1189
NYŌ 女 1185
尿 1382
繞 3609
鐃 4915
饒 5183
NYU 鞣 5103
NYŪ 乳 266
入 574
柔 3166

— O —

O 悪 62
烏 229
嗚 968
於 2083
汚 2494

逐 4696
ōu 掩 1932
蔽 4050
被 4225
覆 4279
owari 畢 3005
終 3521
竟 5111
owaru 畢 3005
終 3521
竟 5111
owaseru 負 4488
owasu 在 1055
負 4488
oya 親 4293
ōyake 公 579
oyatsu 八 577
oyobi 及 154
oyobosu 及 154
oyobu 及 154
oyogi 泳 2520
oyogu 泳 2520
游 2620
oyoso 凡 654
ōyoso 凡 654
ōyumi 弩 1566
ōzappana 大 1171
ōzuru 応 1504

— P —

pai 牌 2845
peiji 頁 5117

— R —

RA 喇 957
拉 1867
羅 3654
蓏 4005
蘿 4104
螺 4184
裸 4248
邏 4755
鑼 4936
騾 5226
-ra 等 3396
RACHI 埒 1083
捋 1907
rachiga aku 埒 1083
RAI 来 202
儡 562
懶 1789
擂 2014
瀬 2735
癩 3087
磊 3213
礼 3229
籟 3457
萊 3960
蕾 4063
邂 4754
雷 5049
頼 5129
麗 5381
rai- 来 202
-rai 来 202
rakkyō 薤 4059
RAKU 擽 2028
楽 2324
洛 2541
烙 2760
珞 2934
絡 3533
落 4003
酪 4786
駱 5212
raku na 楽 2324
RAN 卵 199
婪 1228
嵐 1431
巒 1445
攬 2038
欖 2399
欄 2401
欒 2407
濫 2724
瀾 2737
燗 2806
爛 2820
籃 3452
纜 3625
乱 3856
藍 4082
蘭 4091
襤 4269
襴 4271
覧 4292
醂 4792
闌 4968
rassuru 拉 1867
RATSU 刺 688
喇 957
埒 1083
拉 1867
捋 1907
辣 4647
REI 励 193
令 360
伶 388
例 428
儷 566
冷 642
厲 831
囹 1035
嶺 1440
怜 1658
戻 1818
捩 1942
黎 2648
犁 2863
玲 2928
癘 3075
礪 3224
礼 3229
羚 3663
茘 3934
蛉 4124
蠣 4198
邂 4754
鈴 4837
隷 5026
零 5048
霊 5056
鱧 5336
鴒 5344
麗 5381
齢 5431
reisuru 令 360
REKI 暦 833
歴 835
擽 2028
櫟 2395
瀝 2733
癧 3085
礫 3227
轢 4644
靂 5073
rekki to shita 歴 835
REN 恋 313
廉 1530
憐 1772
攣 2035
斂 2061
漣 2641
煉 2783
簾 3449
練 3565
縺 3592
聯 3713
臠 3836
蘞 4100
賺 4521
輦 4629
連 4702
蓮 4731
錬 4881
鏈 4899
鎌 4902
鰊 5309
ressuru 列 2438
RETSU 劣 185
冽 643
埒 1083
捩 1942
列 2438
洌 2536
烈 2761
裂 4233
RI 吏 183
裏 327
俐 433
俚 446
哩 927
履 1404
釐 2062
李 2179
梨 2275
浬 2557
漓 2668
犁 2863
狸 2887
理 2942
璃 2967
痢 3049
利 3264
籬 3460
詈 3636
罹 3650
蜊 4141
里 4813
離 5040
鯉 5299
RICHI 律 1608
篥 3429
RIKI 力 715
篥 3429
-riki 力 715
rikimu 力 715
RIKU 六 283
戮 1813
陸 5005
RIN 稟 325
倫 474
凛 651
厘 823
廩 1540
悋 1692
吝 2066
林 2210
淪 2587
淋 2595
燐 2807

— S —

汐 2488
潮 2702
shioreru 萎 3973
shiori 栞 2243
shioru 撓 1994
shira 白 3095
shira- 白 3095
shirabe 調 4392
shiraberu 調 4392
shirageru 精 3480
shirakeru 白 3095
shirami 虱 4116
shiramu 白 3095
shirase 報 1114
知 3169
shiraseru 知 3169
shirasu 知 3169
-shirazu 知 3169
shireru 知 3169
shireta 知 3169
shiri 尻 1379
臀 3822
shiringu 志 1064
shirizokeru 斥 175
退 4684
shirizoku 斥 175
退 4684
shiro 代 364
城 1078
白 3095
shirogane 銀 4855
shiroi 白 3095
shiromeru 白 3095
shiromu 白 3095
shiroppoi 白 3095
shiru 汁 2485
知 3169
shirube 導 1354
shirushi 印 102
徴 1634
標 2359
記 4318
誌 4366
験 5220
shirusu 記 4318
誌 4366
録 4879
shisaru 退 4684
shishi 猪 2889
獅 2904
肉 3724
shissuru 失 178
執 1097
shisuru 死 2439
資 4510
-shi suru 視 3248
shita 下 9
舌 3855
shitagaeru 従 1613
shitagau 従 1613
shitagatte 従 1613
shitagi 襦 4268
shitami 湑 2616
shitashii 親 4293
shitashimi 親 4293
shitashimu 親 4293
shitataka ni 健 512
shitatameru 認 4370
shitatari 滴 2674
shitataru 滴 2674
shitatarui 舌 3855
shitau 慕 4040
shitawashii 慕 4040
shito 尿 1382
shitone 茵 3931
褥 4257
shitoru 湿 2631
shitoyaka-na 淑 2592
SHITSU 失 178
叱 873
執 1097
嫉 1248
室 1300
桎 2245
櫛 2398
湿 2631
漆 2679
瑟 2953
疾 3041
膝 3814
虱 4116
蛭 4132
蟋 4182
質 4518
悉 4808
shitsuke 躾 4605
shitsukeru 躾 4605
shiwa 皺 3112
shiwabuki 咳 921
shiwabuku 咳 921
shiwa-darake 皺 3112
shiwa-gareru 嗄 971
shiwai 吝 2066
shiwaru 撓 1994
shizaru 退 4684
shizu 賤 4515
shizukana 静 5077
shizukasa 静 5077
shizukesa 静 5077
shizuku 滴 2674
雫 5043
shizumaru 鎮 4903
静 5077
shizume 沈 2508
鎮 4903
shizumeru 沈 2508
鎮 4903
静 5077
shizumu 沈 2508
SHO 且 23
処 1162
嶼 1438
庶 1522
所 1821
抒 1841
暑 2138
曙 2163
杵 2201
櫧 2400
湑 2616
渚 2617
緒 3557
署 3642
翥 3677
書 3719
蔗 4034
薯 4080
藷 4093
蜍 4142
初 4215
鱮 5335
黍 5400
sho- 諸 4393
-sho 所 1821
SHŌ 丞 21
正 27
升 160
井 165
少 166
承 197
省 218
商 321
俏 439
倢 461
倘 468
倡 478
傷 535
償 563
召 668
剿 704
勦 734
匠 761
上 798
咲 922
哨 930
唱 941
噌 984
嘯 999
囁 1018
声 1066
墻 1144
奨 1181
姓 1203
娼 1235
宵 1307
小 1355
肖 1360
尚 1361
常 1364
掌 1366
嘗 1369
裳 1370
賞 1372
峭 1421
庄 1500
床 1503
廂 1525
廠 1536
彰 1593
従 1613
徜 1618
衝 1638
性 1666
悚 1689
悄 1695
慫 1749
慴 1752
憧 1767
憔 1768
抄 1849
拯 1864
招 1882
捷 1938
摺 1984
政 2045
昌 2105
昇 2109
昭 2114
星 2121
晶 2137
松 2212
相 2241
梢 2276
椒 2286
樅 2353
樟 2358
橡 2366
樵 2370
檣 2387
沼 2521
消 2574

側 509
仄 815
喞 950
嗾 977
塞 1324
惻 1722
戚 1804
捉 1909
数 2057
測 2632
熄 2788
燭 2811
息 3844
即 3886
則 4487
足 4546
速 4700
鏃 4908
齪 5436
-soku 足 4546
sokusuru 即 3886
soma 杣 2186
somaru 染 2240
some 染 2240
-some 初 4215
someku 騒 5221
someru 染 2240
-someru 初 4215
somosomo 抑 1851
somu 染 2240
somukeru 背 3754
somuku 叛 220
背 3754
SON 巽 601
尊 607
噀 986
噂 991
存 1267
孫 1273
忖 1646
拵 1893
損 1979
村 2191
樽 2375
洒 2545
蹲 4588
遜 4730
鱒 5332
sonae 備 519
sonaeru 供 431
備 519
具 3128
sonawaru 備 519
具 3128
sonemi 嫉 1248
sonemu 嫉 1248
-sonji 損 1979
sonjiru 損 1979
-sonjiru 損 1979
sono 其 590
園 1047
苑 3916
sōnokoto 箏 3412
sonsuru 存 1267
損 1979
sonzuru 損 1979
sora 空 3317
sora- 空 3317
soranjiru 諳 4406
soranzuru 諳 4406
soraseru 反 817
逸 4708
sorasu 反 817
逸 4708
sore 夫 164
其 590
soregashi 某 2989
soreru 逸 4708
sori 反 817
橇 2373
sōrō 候 481
soroeru 揃 1957
soroi 揃 1957
-soroi 揃 1957
sorotte 揃 1957
sorou 揃 1957
soru 剃 691
反 817
soshiru 謗 4421
譏 4436
soshite 然 2770
而 3689
sōshite 然 2770
而 3689
sosogu 注 2531
濯 2718
灌 2739
雪 5044
sosonokasu 唆 925
sossuru 卒 294
sōsuru 奏 1178
草 3939
soto 外 1168
SOTSU 帥 109
卒 294
率 319
倅 366
sotsu 帥 109
sou 副 699
沿 2525
添 2601
soyogu 戦 1810
sozoro 漫 2683
SU 甦 66
州 99
寿 194
主 285
娵 1231
子 1264
守 1282
須 1592
数 2057
洲 2539
笥 3378
素 3511
蘇 4097
諏 4377
su 巣 141
栖 2248
窠 3330
簀 3439
簾 3449
酢 4783
醋 4791
SŪ 芻 226
崇 1429
嵩 1433
数 2057
枢 2208
趨 4545
陬 4997
雛 5037
sū- 数 2057
sube 術 1621
subekaraku 須 1592
subekkoi 滑 2663
suberakana 滑 2663
suberasu 滑 2663
suberi 滑 2663
suberu 滑 2663
統 3536
総 3567
辷 4659
subete 凡 654
渾 2624
統 3536
総 3567
subomaru 窄 3322
subomeru 窄 3322
subomu 窄 3322
sudare 簾 3449
sude ni 已 1461
既 3887
sue 末 177
季 3266
陶 5003
sue ni 末 177
sueru 据 1935
饐 5182
sugame 眇 3130
sugaru 縋 3576
sugata 姿 1215
suge 菅 3975
sugeru 箝 3413
sugi 杉 2190
-sugi 過 4723
suginai 過 4723
sugiru 過 4723
-sugiru 過 4723
sugoi 凄 647
sugomu 凄 647
sugosu 過 4723
sugu 直 775
sugu na 直 775
sugureru 傑 517
優 564
秀 3263
勝 3787
suguru 選 4744
SUI 出 97
帥 109
垂 211
衰 312
吹 901
彗 1584
悴 1704
推 1950
揣 1958
水 2482
炊 2752
燧 2805
瘁 3055
睢 3143
睡 3149
祟 3239
穂 3300
粋 3467
翠 3676
膵 3812
萃 3965
誰 4384
遂 4716
邃 4752
酔 4781
錘 4872
錐 4875
陲 4996
隧 5022
雖 5034
sui 酢 4783
酸 4789
suitarashii 好 1191
suji 筋 3395
sujidarake 筋 3395

— T —

取 3699
tōru 徹 1637
透 4699
通 4703
toshi 年 188
歳 2434
tōshi 通 4703
tōshi- 通 4703
tōshide 通 4703
tōshite 通 4703
tōsu 徹 1637
透 4699
通 4703
tosuru 賭 4519
tōsuru 党 1363
totchimeru 取 3699
totemo 迚 4668
tōtobu 尊 607
貴 4504
tōtoi 尊 607
貴 4504
tōtomu 尊 607
貴 4504
totonoeru 整 2436
調 4392
斉 5423
totonou 整 2436
調 4392
TOTSU 凸 90
吶 894
咄 909
柮 2215
突 3316
肭 3733
訥 4321
totsugu 嫁 1249
totte 取 3699
tōtte 通 4703
tottoku 取 3699
tou 訪 4326
問 4944
tou kara 疾 3041
tou ni 疾 3041
towa 永 130
常 1364
towaie 言 4309
towa iumonono 言 4309
-towazu 問 4944
toya 塒 1117
toyo- 豊 4466
tōzakaru 遠 4733
tōzakeru 遠 4733
tozasu 鎖 4901
閉 4945
tōzuru 投 1856
TSU 偸 504
菟 3964
通 4703
都 4769
tsu 津 2543
TSŪ 痛 3054
通 4703
-tsū 通 4703
tsuba 唾 938
鍔 4890
tsubaki 唾 938
椿 2319
tsubakura 燕 4070
tsubakuro 燕 4070
tsubame 燕 4070
tsubasa 翼 3680
tsubo 坪 1072
壺 1093
歩 2433
tsubomaru 窄 3322
tsubomeru 窄 3322
tsubomi 莟 3947
蕾 4063
tsubomu 窄 3322
蕾 4063
tsubone 局 1384
tsubu 粒 3471
tsubura na 円 617
tsubureru 潰 2701
tsuburu 瞑 3151
tsubusa ni 備 519
具 3128
悉 4808
tsubusu 潰 2701
tsubute 礫 3227
tsubuyaku 呟 903
tsuchi 土 1050
椎 2296
槌 2308
鎚 4887
tsuchikau 培 1091
tsuchinoe 戊 1795
tsuchinoto 己 1462
tsudoi 集 5031
tsudou 集 5031
tsue 仗 357
杖 2183
tsuga 栂 2227
tsugaeru 番 4811
tsugai 番 4811
tsūgaru 通 4703
tsugau 番 4811
tsuge 告 900
tsugeru 告 900
tsugi 次 638
継 3545
tsugomori 晦 2135
tsugu 亜 43
次 638
嗣 969
接 1951
注 2531
継 3545
tsugumu 噤 1004
鉗 4836
tsugunau 償 563
TSUI 墜 1132
椎 2296
槌 2308
縋 3576
追 4686
鎚 4887
tsui 対 2067
tsuibamu 啄 935
tsuide 次 638
序 1502
尋 1585
tsuide ni 序 1502
tsuie 弊 1551
費 4497
tsuieru 潰 2701
費 4497
tsui ni 終 3521
遂 4716
竟 5111
tsuitachi 朔 3761
tsuite wa 就 323
tsuiyasu 費 4497
tsuji 辻 4662
tsūji 通 4703
tsūjiru 通 4703
tsūjite 通 4703
tsuka 束 196
塚 1120
柄 2234
欛 2409
tsukaeru 事 272
仕 362
使 432
支 2039
閊 4943
tsukai 使 432
tsukai-konasu 使 432
tsukai suru 使 432
tsuka-maeru 捉 1909
捕 1919
摑 1985
tsukamaru 捉 1909
捕 1919
摑 1985
tsukama-seru 摑 1985
tsukama-tsuru 仕 362
tsukami 摑 1985
tsukamu 摑 1985
攫 2036
tsukaneru 束 196
tsukara-kasu 疲 3040
tsukarasu 疲 3040
tsukareru 憑 1769
疲 3040
tsukaru 浸 2572
漬 2676
tsukasa 省 218
司 877
台 848
坊 1062
官 1295
寮 1340
府 1507
監 3121
署 3642
職 3718
tsukasa-doru 司 877
掌 1366
tsukau 使 432
遣 4732
tsukawasu 使 432
遣 4732
tsuke 付 363
tsuke- 付 363
-tsuke 付 363
tsukeru 付 363
漬 2676
附 4983
tsuketari 付 363
附 4983
tsuki 付 363
坏 1063
月 2169
槻 2352
tsuki- 突 3316
-tsuki 付 363
tsukimashi-te wa 就 323
tsukiru 尽 1380
tsuku 就 323
付 363
点 804
吐 883
衝 1638
憑 1769
搗 1978

— U —

ANDREW NATHANIEL NELSON *was born at Great Falls, Montana, in 1893. He received his B.A. from Walla Walla College and his Ph.D. from the University of Washington, where he majored in Far Eastern studies and education. As a Seventh-day Adventist missionary to the Orient from 1918 to 1961, he was prominent in the fields of education and language training.*

At various times he served as Dean of Emmanuel Missionary College, Berrien Springs, Michigan; President of Philippine Union College, Manila; President of the Oriental Home Study Institute, Shanghai; President of Japan Missionary College, Chiba Ken, Japan; and founder of Mountain View College, Philippines. During World War II he compiled two technical Japanese-English dictionaries for the Department of the Army. After the war he served for a time on General MacArthur's staff as the Director of the Religions Research Section, and he also became well known to many Japanese for his work as prison chaplain to Japanese prisoners of war held in the New Bilibid Prison in the Philippines.

In the midst of these many activities he found time to devote a lifetime to the study of the Japanese language and the fundamentals of Chinese. Retiring from his missionary vocation early in 1961, he made a leisurely voyage around the world before taking up his present post as Professor of Education at La Sierra College, La Sierra, California.

NOTE CONCERNING CHART INSIDE BACK COVER. The chart lists those Tōyō Kanji which show more or less significant changes between their older and newer forms. The arrangement is by the total stroke-count of the older-form characters. In each case the older form is given first, followed by the newer form and the number under which the character is treated in this dictionary. In the interest of space, some characters have been omitted when the changes are very slight and do not involve a change in stroke-count.

As explained in Appendix 2, this chart will be of considerable use when attempting to locate a compound whose second character is in a variant form that differs in shape, and probably stroke-count, from the standard Tōyō Kanji form used in the compounds of this dictionary.

SIGNIFICANTLY CHANGED TŌYŌ KANJI

3 Strokes

刃 → 刄 (152)

4 Strokes

及 → 及 (154)

6 Strokes

决 → 決 (2509)
收 → 収 (860)
灰 → 灰 (820)

7 Strokes

延 → 延 (1547)
佛 → 仏 (351)
扱 → 扱 (1836)
沒 → 没 (2506)
壯 → 壮 (2837)
糺 → 糾 (3498)
兔 → 免 (573)
免 → 免 (573)
每 → 毎 (2467)

8 Strokes

屆 → 届 (1385)
戾 → 戻 (1818)
拂 → 払 (1828)
拔 → 抜 (1854)
拒 → 拒 (1847)
狀 → 状 (2839)
社 → 社 (3231)
亞 → 亜 (43)
兩 → 両 (34)
卑 → 卑 (221)
爭 → 争 (186)

兒 → 児 (572)
冐 → 冒 (2117)
來 → 来 (202)

9 Strokes

侮 → 侮 (421)
恆 → 恒 (1683)
祈 → 祈 (3234)
祉 → 祉 (3232)
卽 → 即 (3886)
突 → 突 (3316)
勉 → 勉 (228)
勉 → 勉 (228)
毒 → 毒 (2468)

10 Strokes

氣 → 気 (2480)
倂 → 併 (425)
凉 → 涼 (2598)
姬 → 姫 (1216)
峽 → 峡 (1417)
徑 → 径 (1602)
涉 → 渉 (2591)
海 → 海 (2553)
狹 → 狭 (2882)
祕 → 秘 (3281)
祖 → 祖 (3243)
祝 → 祝 (3244)
神 → 神 (3245)
竝 → 並 (589)
缺 → 欠 (2412)
乘 → 乗 (223)
益 → 益 (597)
兼 → 兼 (598)

莖 → 茎 (3912)

11 Strokes

麥 → 麦 (5385)
麻 → 麻 (5390)
區 → 区 (757)
國 → 国 (1037)
處 → 処 (1162)
假 → 仮 (382)
條 → 条 (1164)
從 → 従 (1613)
晚 → 晩 (2145)
梅 → 梅 (2258)
淨 → 浄 (2548)
淺 → 浅 (2549)
將 → 将 (2840)
祥 → 祥 (3246)
敍 → 叙 (862)
敘 → 叙 (862)
敏 → 敏 (2047)
敕 → 勅 (725)
欵 → 款 (2418)
殺 → 殺 (2454)
參 → 参 (850)
巢 → 巣 (141)
產 → 産 (3354)
晝 → 昼 (53)
帶 → 帯 (1474)

12 Strokes

圍 → 囲 (1032)
貳 → 弐 (32)
閒 → 間 (4949)
帽 → 帽 (1483)
帽 → 帽 (1483)
帽 → 帽 (1483)
强 → 強 (1571)
惱 → 悩 (1698)
慌 → 慌 (1725)
揭 → 掲 (1934)
棧 → 桟 (2252)
殘 → 残 (2445)
渴 → 渇 (2596)
雅 → 雅 (2850)
剩 → 剰 (698)
旣 → 既 (3887)
殼 → 殻 (2456)
鄕 → 郷 (4766)
壹 → 壱 (1059)
爲 → 為 (138)
發 → 発 (3092)
萬 → 万 (7)
勞 → 労 (720)
單 → 単 (139)

13 Strokes

圓 → 円 (617)
遞 → 逓 (4695)
傳 → 伝 (379)
微 → 微 (1631)
愼 → 慎 (1742)
搖 → 揺 (1965)
搜 → 捜 (1917)
溫 → 温 (2634)
溪 → 渓 (2581)
碎 → 砕 (3179)
碑 → 碑 (3206)
經 → 経 (3523)
腦 → 脳 (3774)
勤 → 勤 (732)
款 → 款 (2418)
奧 → 奥 (240)

會 → 会 (381)
當 → 当 (1359)
暑 → 暑 (2138)
與 → 与 (6)
煮 → 煮 (2771)
號 → 号 (882)
肅 → 粛 (115)

14 Strokes

齊 → 斉 (5423)
圖 → 図 (1034)
團 → 団 (1027)
像 → 像 (540)
僞 → 偽 (510)
僧 → 僧 (536)
嘆 → 嘆 (974)
慘 → 惨 (1713)
構 → 構 (2343)
滿 → 満 (2636)
漢 → 漢 (2662)
禍 → 禍 (3254)
福 → 福 (3256)
稱 → 称 (3280)
粹 → 粋 (3467)
綠 → 緑 (3564)
隨 → 随 (5004)
亂 → 乱 (3856)
對 → 対 (2067)
鄰 → 隣 (5023)
壽 → 寿 (194)
臺 → 台 (848)
寢 → 寝 (1326)
實 → 実 (1297)
寬 → 寛 (1325)
盡 → 尽 (1380)
墮 → 堕 (1092)
獎 → 奨 (1181)
榮 → 栄 (2239)

SEE PAGE 1109 FOR EXPLANATORY NOTE